Peterson's Vocational and Technical Schools East

9th Edition

PETERSON'S

A **nelnet** COMPANY

About Peterson's

To succeed on your lifelong educational journey, you will need accurate, dependable, and practical tools and resources. That is why Peterson's is everywhere education happens. Because whenever and however you need education content delivered, you can rely on Peterson's to provide the information, know-how, and guidance to help you reach your goals. Tools to match the right students with the right school. It's here. Personalized resources and expert guidance. It's here. Comprehensive and dependable education content—delivered whenever and however you need it. It's all here.

For more information, contact Peterson's, 2000 Lenox Drive, Lawrenceville, NJ 08648; 800-338-3282; or find us on the World Wide Web at www.petersons.com/about.

© 2009 Peterson's, a Nelnet company

Previous editions © 1994, 1996, 1998, 2000, 2001, 2003, 2006, 2008

Stephen Clemente, President; Bernadette Webster, Director of Publishing; Mark D. Snider, Editor; John Wells, Research Project Manager; Tim Nelson, Programmer; Ray Golaszewski, Manufacturing Manager; Linda M. Williams, Composition Manager

Peterson's makes every reasonable effort to obtain accurate, complete, and timely data from reliable sources. Nevertheless, Peterson's and the third-party data suppliers make no representation or warranty, either expressed or implied, as to the accuracy, timeliness, or completeness of the data or the results to be obtained from using the data, including, but not limited to, its quality, performance, merchantability, or fitness for a particular purpose, non-infringement or otherwise.

Neither Peterson's nor the third-party data suppliers warrant, guarantee, or make any representations that the results from using the data will be successful or will satisfy users' requirements. The entire risk to the results and performance is assumed by the user.

ISBN-13: 978-0-7689-2809-9
ISBN-10: 0-7689-2809-5

Printed in the United States of America

10 9 8 7 6 5 4 3 2 1   11 10 09

Ninth Edition

By producing this book on recycled paper (40% post-consumer waste) 103 trees were saved.

Contents

A Note from the Peterson's Editors

If you're thinking of attending a vocational-technical school, you have probably decided to enter a specific trade, occupation, or profession and found that it requires you to have certain entry-level skills or training. With so many schools to choose from, you may be wondering how you will find the right one. Or maybe you're undecided on a career and are looking for guidance as to which career or occupation is right for you. And if you're a working adult thinking of going back to school, there is even more to consider. *Peterson's Vocational and Technical Schools East* has the information you need to make the right decisions.

The **Choosing a Vo-Tech Program** section contains insightful articles on preparing for a career—how careers, income, and education relate; which are the fastest-growing occupations; and much more. There is valuable advice about apprenticeships and financial aid and tips on how to manage being an adult student. In this section you also will find descriptions of various career areas and lists of occupations within each one. Included are six of the most popular areas, as well as new and emerging occupations you may not have considered. Finally, the "How to Use This Guide" article provides explanations of each element in the school profiles, the criteria used to select the programs in the book, and our data collection procedures.

The **Profiles of Vo-Tech Schools** section contains detailed profiles of more than 2,600 vocational-technical schools and programs located east of the Mississippi River. Each profile contains comprehensive information about the school, including a list of the vo-tech programs offered and the name and phone number of the person to contact.

The **Appendixes** contain two listings. The first lists the State Offices of Apprenticeship Contacts. The second listing contains the accrediting organizations that are recognized by the Council for Higher Education Accreditation (CHEA) of the U.S. Department of Education.

The **Indexes** make it easy to locate a school by program and state or alphabetically.

Peterson's publishes a full line of resources to help gather all the information you need to make informed career and education decisions. Peterson's publications can be found at your local bookstore or library; you can access us online at **www.petersons.com.**

We welcome any comments or suggestions you may have about this publication and invite you to complete our online survey at **www.petersons.com/booksurvey.** Or, you can fill out the printed survey at the back of the book, tear it out, and mail it to us at:

Publishing Department
Peterson's, a Nelnet company
2000 Lenox Drive
Lawrenceville, NJ 08648

Your feedback will help us make your educational dreams possible.

The editors at Peterson's wish you the best of luck in your search for the perfect vo-tech school for you!

Choosing a Vo-Tech Program

The Expanding Role of America's Career Colleges

Nicholas Glakas
Former President, Career College Association

Editor's Note: Career colleges are privately owned and operated schools and colleges that provide postsecondary (after high school) technical and vocational training. Most of the institutions represented in this publication are career colleges, but publicly supported two-year and four-year colleges and private nonprofit institutions also are represented. Mr. Glakas's comments about the advantages of a vocational or technical education apply whether you are considering a career college or another kind of vocational and technical career training institution.

Most of us have been told all of our lives, "If you don't go to college, you'll never get a good job." Many of us have been conditioned to equate a traditional four-year college degree with a guarantee of professional success. This is not necessarily the case.

Most employers look upon a person with a college degree as a person with persistence and stamina. With a degree as a credential, the newly graduated enter the workforce with a reasonably proven ability to learn but often without a marketable skill. To overcome that pitfall, many college graduates attend career colleges to expand their experience and learn skills that will get them a job. In fact, on many career college campuses, more than 40 percent of the students already have their baccalaureate degrees.

Recent statistics indicate that nearly 65 percent of the workforce in this country is made up of skilled laborers. Only 20 percent of that same workforce are considered professionals. These figures show that the majority of this nation's new jobs in the next decade will require strong technical skills—the exact type of skills taught in this country's career colleges.

If you lack the time and financial resources to spend four years in a traditional college or university, a career college is an excellent alternative. Whether this choice is made directly after high school or after spending a few years in the workforce, successful completion of the program is not likely to be affected.

In good economic times or bad, you will always have a distinct advantage if you have a skill and can be immediately productive while continuing to learn and improve. If you are technologically savvy, work collaboratively, and find creative solutions to difficult problems, you will always be in demand. Less than half of the students who start at a traditional college ever obtain their degree. One half or two thirds of a degree is of little value; all the time and financial resources invested help to produce no dividend because they do not develop marketable skills.

Like most of us, you will spend more of your waking hours in the workplace than anywhere else. If you don't like what you are doing—the financial, emotional, and spiritual rewards will not be there—it is likely that you will be unhappy and not do well. As you begin to decide on how to prepare for your future, consider the following guidelines:

- Identify what interests you, and consider careers that relate to these interests
- Seek the counsel of individuals working in the jobs in which you are interested
- Try to combine school and real-world work experience during your training
- Understand that skills are transferable, and your initial job choice may prepare you for other opportunities

Career colleges offer scores of opportunities to learn the technical skills required by many of today's top jobs. This is especially true in the areas of computer and information technology, health care, and hospitality (culinary arts, travel and tourism, and hotel and motel management). Career colleges range in size from those with a handful of students to universities with enrollments in the thousands. They are located in every state in the nation and share one common objective—to prepare students for a successful career in the world of work through a focused, intensive curriculum. America's career colleges are privately owned and operated for-profit companies. Instead of using tax support to operate, career colleges pay taxes. Because career colleges are businesses, they must be responsive to the needs of the workforce and of their communities, or they will cease to exist.

When choosing an institution of higher education, consider the following:

- What percentage of the students who begin programs actually graduate?
- Of those who graduate, how many get jobs in their chosen career, and how long does it take to be hired?
- Is there full-service placement assistance available at the school?

Today's jobs demand skills that are ever changing. In the future, this demand will be even greater. The education system necessary to provide you with the skills you need exists. It is made up of this country's career and technical colleges.

How Career, Income, and Education Relate

The relationship between education and work—the more you invest in your education, the more you will earn—has been repeated so often that it has almost lost its meaning. Here are the most recent figures from the U.S. Census Bureau:

Level of Education Attained	Average Annual Income
Bachelor's Degree	$58,613
Associate Degree	39,506
High School Graduate	31,283
Not a High School Graduate	21,056

Source: U.S. Census Bureau, *Current Population Survey, 2009 Annual Social and Economic Supplement.*

Reliable data on the incomes of vocational-technical school graduates are not available, but there are other data that might provide some clues as to what these might be. A study of two-year college graduates showed that associate degree earners who took vocational programs had higher incomes than graduates from nonvocational programs. This difference in incomes expanded from 16 percent greater within five years after graduation to 37 percent greater within nine years after graduation. Approximately 59 percent of two-year college graduates in 1992 earned degrees in vocational programs.

Fastest-Growing Occupations Require Vocational Training

The table on the next page shows the latest projections from the Bureau of Labor Statistics of the fastest-growing occupations in the ten years from 2006 to 2016. Programs for many of these occupations are offered by schools that are represented in this book.

College Is Not For Everybody

Forty years ago, most young people went directly to work after high school. Today, most young people first go to school for more training. The above figures on income and education demonstrate why this is a good idea. They also demonstrate that earning a bachelor's degree is a better option than going to vocational-technical school, but we know that college is not for everybody.

Life events often can interfere with plans to attend college. Responsibilities to a family may materialize that make it impossible to delay earning an income for four years. One may have to work and go to school. In this situation, as demonstrated below, career training that is measured in months instead of years can be the best choice.

Also, let's be real. College demands certain conventions, behaviors, and attitudes that do not fit every kind of person. Some people need a lot of physical activity to feel satisfied, while others just are not academically attuned. Whether the reasons are rooted in personality or upbringing, for these individuals, the intellectual path of college life is dry, cold, and unsatisfying; day after day of sitting, reading, memorizing, and analyzing is pure agony. Years of strict time management and postponed rewards are more than they can stand. On the other hand, the clear structure and demands of a worker in a real career might be an appealing and satisfying alternative to the vague, indefinite life of a student who lacks career direction.

Certainly, the college world has made great attempts to be more inclusive. It is no longer a world of kids under the age of 23, but at their heart, from their standardized tests through to their campus social life, most colleges are defined by the standards and norms of the majority culture, which remains largely younger than age 23. Adults who have lived in the "real world," although aware of the rewards that are promised by spending a few years in college, may not want to go through the years of self-denial, isolation, and cultural displacement that a college experience seems to entail.

FASTEST-GROWING OCCUPATIONS, 2006–2016

The 10 fastest-growing occupations, 2006–2016
[Numbers in thousands of jobs]

Occupation	Employment 2006	Employment 2016	Change Number	Change Percent
Network systems and data communications analyst	262	402	140	53.4
Personal and home care aides	767	1,156	389	50.6
Home health aides	787	1,171	384	48.7
Computer software engineers, applications	507	733	226	44.6
Veterinary technogists and technicians	71	100	29	41.0
Personal financial advisors	176	248	72	41.0
Makeup artists, theatrical and performance	2	3	1	39.8
Medical assistants	417	565	148	35.4
Veterinarians	62	84	22	35.0
Substance abuse and behavioral disorder counselors	83	112	29	34.3

Source: U.S. Department of Labor Statistics, Occupational Employment Projections 2006 to 2016.

Vocational-Technical Students Achieve Their Goals

A truly positive aspect of vocational-technical education is that most students who enter it are likely to complete their educational goals. Fifty-five percent of all students working toward an educational certificate (the category defining vo-tech students) complete their educational program. By contrast, only 24 percent of all students working toward an associate degree complete their degree work, while 54 percent of all students working toward a bachelor's degree complete their degree work. As the following chart demonstrates, these differences become even more dramatic when factors such as delaying one's education for more than a year after high school, studying part-time, or working while studying are considered.

For most students, vocational-technical education programs offer a truer chance of achievement than other alternative paths of education. The range of possible careers provides the satisfaction of a fulfilling work life with exceptional compensation. Vocational-technical education can be a lifesaver for the men and women who choose to refrain from or postpone going to a two- or four-year college.

POSTSECONDARY STUDENTS WHO ATTAINED THEIR INITIAL DEGREE OBJECTIVE

	Vocational-Technical (Certificate) Programs	Associate Degree Programs	Bachelor's Degree Programs
Enrollment More Than a Year After High School	54%	14%	50%
Part-Time Student	41%	18%	13%
Also Worked 1–20 Hours per Week	75%	42%	51%
Also Worked More Than 20 Hours per Week	47%	28%	40%

Source: U.S. Department of Education, National Center for Education Statistics.

Student Financial Aid: Paying for Your College Education

Heidi B. Granger
Director of Financial Aid
College of the Desert, Palm Desert, CA

The decision to attend a vocational-technical college is an extremely important one. The specialized education and training will provide you with the necessary tools and knowledge to be successful in the career of your choice. You will have the opportunity to grow in many areas. You will learn the skills needed to prosper, and your abilities will be developed to their greatest potential.

Education is an investment in your future. Before you choose your career, it is necessary to consider how much time, money, and commitment you have to prepare yourself for a career. Remember, your career goals should be reasonable and realistic in terms of your ability, interests, and values. All students are encouraged to think about the amount of educational debt that might be necessary to achieve one's educational goals and objectives. In addition, students should also look at the effect that student loan indebtedness can have on one's future lifestyle. Choosing the right career and paying for college takes planning, forethought, dedication, and commitment.

This article is designed to assist you with your college plans and to familiarize you with the various kinds of financial aid programs available to help you meet the costs of attending a vocational institution. Understanding the policies and procedures necessary to obtain financial assistance is essential. Although the process may seem confusing and complicated, the purpose of financial aid is to assist students with their educational expenses so that financial barriers do not prevent them from achieving their educational goals.

What Is Financial Aid?

Financial aid is the assistance available to help students pay for the costs of attending a vocational-technical institution. Financial aid is provided by federal, state, institutional, or private sources and may consist of grants, loans, work study, or scholarships. Qualified students may be offered combinations of the various types of aid or aid from a single source. Each year, billions of dollars are given or lent to students, and about half of all college students receive some sort of financial aid.

Most financial aid is awarded based on an individual's financial need, college costs, and the availability of funds. This aid is provided to students because neither they nor their families have all of the resources needed to pay for a college education. This kind of aid is referred to as need-based aid.

Merit-based aid is awarded to students who may or may not have financial need. Students are given assistance because they have a special skill or ability, display a particular talent, have a certain grade point average, or are enrolled in a specific program.

Types and Sources of Financial Aid

There are several types of financial aid offered to help pay for educational expenses: grants, loans, student employment (work), and scholarships. Grants and scholarships are "gifts" and do not have to be repaid. Loans are borrowed money that must be paid back over a period of time, usually after the student leaves school. Student employment is normally part-time work arranged for a student during the school year.

7

WHAT ARE THE ELIGIBILITY REQUIREMENTS?

In general, to be considered eligible for federal financial aid, you must:

❏ Be a United States citizen or eligible noncitizen

❏ Be enrolled or accepted for enrollment in an accredited institution

❏ Be making satisfactory academic progress in your course of study

❏ Not be in default on any loan or owe a refund or repayment on any previous financial aid received at any institution attended

❏ Be registered with the Selective Service, if you are required to do so

Wages received by the student are used for specific college expenses.

The primary source of aid for students attending a vocational institution of higher education is from the federal government. The federal government offers both grant and loan financial aid programs. Another source of aid is state assistance. Many states across the country provide some aid for students attending colleges in their own home states. Most state aid programs are grants, although there are a few states that offer special loan and work-study programs. Other sources of aid that award money to students come from private foundations such as corporations, civic associations, unions, fraternal organizations, and religious groups. Most of these awards are not based solely on need, although the amount of the award may vary depending on your financial need. In addition, many companies offer tuition reimbursement to their employees and/or their employees' dependents. The personnel department at either your or your parent's place of employment can tell you whether or not the company offers this benefit and who may be eligible. Lastly, there are some colleges that offer awards from their own funds or from money received from various organizations. This type of aid is often referred to as "institutional aid." Although most vocational institu-

tions have little or no institutional aid available, the student should still be sure to ask the college about this type of assistance.

Grants

Federal Pell Grant—Funded by the federal government, this need-based grant is available for undergraduate students who have financial need. Award amounts vary according to an eligibility index. The maximum award amount based on congressional appropriations for the 2009–10 award year is $5350.

> **Note:** The actual amount of a student's Federal Pell Grant depends upon several factors in addition to eligibility. These include the calculated expected family contribution (EFC), your cost of attendance, your enrollment status (full-time, half-time, etc.), the length of your period of enrollment, the college's definition of the academic year for your program of study, and the structure and length of your program of study.

Federal Supplemental Educational Opportunity Grant (FSEOG)—Funded by the federal government, this need-based grant is available for undergraduate students who have exceptional financial need. Although the maximum award per year can be $4000, few vocational schools have an abundance of FSEOG funds, and therefore the average award is usually around $760 as of 2008.

Loans

Federal Perkins Loan—The Federal Perkins Loan is awarded on the basis of demonstrated financial need. The interest rate is 5 percent, and the first payment is due nine months after you leave school or drop below half-time status. The maximum award is $4000 for undergraduate students but, like the FSEOG funds, most vocational schools have limited Perkins funding and will award what they can to the neediest students.

Subsidized Federal Stafford Student Loans—Subsidized Federal Stafford Student Loans are for students who demonstrate financial need. FFEL Stafford Loans are made to students through lending institutions such as banks and credit unions. Direct Stafford Loans are made to students by the Department of Education. Not every college participates in the Direct Loan Program. The interest rate for undergraduate Direct and Stafford Loans first disbursed between July 1, 2009, and June 30, 2010, is 5.6 percent. This rate became fixed on July 1, 2006 (for loans with a first disbursement on or after that date). The fixed interest rate will drop on new loans each year until it reaches

3.4 percent for loans first disbursed between July 1, 2011, and June 30, 2012. After that the interest rate reverts to 6.8 percent. All lenders offer the same rate for the Stafford Loan, although some give discounts for on-time and electronic payments. Stafford Loans have loan fees of 1.5 percent, which are deducted from the disbursement check. These fees consist of a 0.5 percent origination fee and a 1 percent default fee, which was previously called a "guarantee fee." The origination fee will be phased out entirely on July 1, 2010. Loan repayment begins six months after you leave school or drop below half-time status. The government pays the interest while you are in school and during the six-month grace period. Both FFEL and Direct Stafford Loans have a basic ten-year repayment period. The borrower may select from a variety of repayment plans, some of which will lengthen the repayment period, and thus increase the amount of interest paid.

Unsubsidized Federal Stafford Loans—Unsubsidized Federal Stafford Loans are for students who do not demonstrate financial need. Students may borrow within the same loan limits and at the same interest rates as the subsidized Stafford Loan program. The interest rate is 6.8 percent, which became fixed on July 1, 2006. A 1.5 percent fee is deducted and interest payments begin immediately. Students may defer payments while enrolled at least part-time at school, but most lenders allow students to defer payments while in school, but interest continues to accrue and is added to the principle balance. Regular payments begin six months after the student either leaves school or drops below half-time status.

Borrowers of additional unsubsidized loan amounts must meet the federal definition of independent or have exceptional circumstances as documented by the financial aid office.

Note: The loan amounts for which you are eligible may be prorated if your program's length is less than thirty weeks.

Federal PLUS Loans—The Federal PLUS Loan program enables parents of dependent students to obtain loans to pay for their child's educational costs. The interest rate for the FFELP PLUS loan is now fixed at 8.5 percent; the interest rate for a Direct PLUS Loan is fixed at 7.9 percent. Parents may borrow up to the cost of attendance minus any other financial aid received by the student.

FINANCIAL AID ELIGIBILITY FORMULA:

Cost of Attendance

– Expected Family Contribution (student and parents)

= Financial Need (Financial Aid Eligibility)

Primary responsibility for financing a college education must be assumed by the student and often by the student's parents. Students and their families are expected to make a maximum effort to pay for college expenses. Financial assistance should be viewed as supplementary to the efforts of the family. Financial aid is available to assist students with educational costs, and students should be aware that financial aid usually does not cover 100 percent of educational expenses.

Work

Federal Work-Study Program—The Federal Work-Study Program provides jobs for students with financial aid eligibility. It gives students a chance to earn money to help pay for educational expenses while providing valuable work experience. All eligible students are also afforded the opportunity to perform community service work. Many vocational schools offer the Federal Work-Study Program, but the number of jobs available tend to be limited.

Understanding the Cost of Attendance

Every college establishes an estimate of what it will cost each student to attend the school. There are usually several types of budgets: one for students living on campus (if a school has dormitories), one for students living off campus, and one for students living with their parents. The expenses included in the cost of attendance are tuition and fees, books and supplies, room and board (includes food, rent, and utilities), personal expenses, and transportation. The total educational expenses or budgets are referred to as the student's cost of attendance.

Determining Financial Aid Eligibility and Financial Need

Eligibility for financial aid is determined by subtracting the amount you and your parents can contribute from the cost of attendance (the "budget" as explained in the previous section). An assessment of your family's ability to contribute toward educational expenses is made based on the information you provide when applying for financial aid. Income, assets, family size, and number of family members in college are some of the factors considered in this calculation. This assessment, referred to as need analysis, determines your financial need, which is defined as the difference between the total cost of attendance and what you are expected to pay. The need analysis uses a formula mandated by legislation. It determines the ability, not the willingness, of the student and parents to finance the cost of attendance. Everyone who applies is treated equally under this analysis. The end result of the need analysis is your expected family contribution and represents the amount your family should be able to contribute toward the cost of attendance. The cost of attendance will vary at each college, but the amount your family is expected to contribute should stay the same. Financial need will vary between colleges because of each school's different costs of attendance.

Determining the Student's Status: Independent or Dependent?

Remember that both students and parents are expected to help pay for college costs. This means that you, the student, will be expected to contribute to your educational expenses.

If you are considered dependent by federal definition, then your parents' income and assets, as well as yours, will be counted toward the family contribution. If you are considered independent of your parents, only your income (and that of your spouse, if you are married) will count in the need analysis formula.

To be considered independent for financial aid, you must meet one of the following criteria:

- Be at least 24 years old.
- Be a veteran of the U.S. armed forces.
- Be married.
- Be an orphan or ward of the court.
- Have legal dependents other than a spouse.
- Be a graduate professional student.

If you can document extraordinary circumstances that might indicate independent status, you will need to show this information to the financial aid administrator at the college you will be attending.

Only the financial aid administrator has the authority to make exceptions to the requirements listed above.

Applying for Financial Aid

To apply for financial aid, it is essential that you properly complete the necessary forms so that your individual financial need can be evaluated. It is important to read all application materials and instructions very carefully. The application process can be a bit long and confusing, so remember to take one step at a time. If you run into any problems or have specific questions, contact the financial aid office at the college you will be attending. The financial aid office will be happy to provide you with guidance and assistance.

Most vocational schools use just one financial aid application called the Free Application for Federal Student Aid (FAFSA). This form is a four-page application available at your college's financial aid office, local high school guidance offices, and state education department offices. Students can apply for federal student aid via the Internet by using FAFSA on the Web. FAFSA on the Web can be accessed at www.fafsa.ed.gov. The process is self-paced and interactive, with step-by-step guidance. Depending on the availability of information about your income and financial situation, the process can take as little as 20 minutes to complete. The FAFSA that students will use to apply for aid for each school year becomes available in the December prior to the year in which aid is needed. However, do *not* fill out the form until after January 1 of the year you will require aid.

> **Note:** You want to complete the FAFSA as soon as possible after January 1, 2010. Although you may apply for aid at any time during the year, many state agencies have early cut-off dates for state aid funding.

To complete this application, you will need to gather specific family information and financial records, such as tax forms, if they are available. If they are not, use estimates. You can make corrections later. Be sure to answer all questions. Omitted information may delay the processing of your application. Be sure that you and your parents (if needed) have signed the form and that you keep a copy of the form for your records. The FAFSA processing center will calculate your expected family contribution and will distribute the information back to the college.

About two to four weeks after you submit your completed FAFSA, you will receive a Student Aid Report (SAR) that shows the information you reported and your calculated EFC. If you need to make any corrections, you may do so at this time. The college may also have this same information in an ISIR (Institutional Student Information Record) or electronic Student Aid Report (ESAR).

If you are chosen for verification by the school, you may be asked to submit documentation that will verify the information you reported on the FAFSA. Once the financial aid office is satisfied that all of the information is correct, the college can then determine your financial need and provide you with a financial aid offer for funding your education. If you are eligible to receive aid, most schools will either mail you an award letter or will ask you to come into the financial aid office to discuss your financial aid eligibility.

Note: Financial aid is not renewed automatically; you must apply each year. Often, if you are in a program that lasts longer than one year, a renewal application will automatically be mailed to you by the federal processor.

Student Loans and Debt Management

More than ever before, loans have become an important part of financial assistance. The majority of students find that they must borrow money to finance their education. If you accept a loan, you are incurring a financial obligation. You will have to repay the loan in full, along with any interest and additional fees (collection, legal, etc.). Since you will be making loan payments to satisfy the loan obligation, carefully consider the burden your loan amount will impose on you after you leave school. Defaulting on a student loan can jeopardize your entire future by harming your credit history. Borrow intelligently.

Your Rights and Responsibilities as a Financial Aid Recipient

As a student consumer, you have a right to:
- be informed of the correct procedures for applying for aid, cost of attendance, types of aid available, how financial need is determined, criteria for awarding aid, how satisfactory academic progress is determined, and what you need to do to continue receiving aid.
- be informed of the type and amount of assistance you will receive, how much of your need has been met, and how and when you will be paid.
- appeal any decision of the financial aid office if you feel you have been treated unfairly with regard to your application.
- view the contents in your financial aid file, in accordance with the Family Educational Rights and Privacy Act.
- know the conditions of any loan you accept.

It is your responsibility to:

- complete all application materials truthfully and accurately and comply with deadline dates.
- review all materials sent to you and read and understand all documents. Be sure to keep copies of all forms you sign.
- know and comply with the rules governing the aid you receive.
- provide additional documentation and/or new information requested by the financial aid office.
- maintain satisfactory academic progress.
- keep your local and permanent addresses current with all pertinent school offices.
- use financial aid only for expenses related to the college.

Remember that your dreams can come true when you act to turn them into realities. Financial aid is the means by which you can achieve your dream of obtaining an education and pursuing your career. Use it wisely and you will succeed.

Apprenticeships: Valuable Training for Higher-Paying Jobs

Kenneth Edwards
Former Director of Technical Services, International Brotherhood of Electrical Workers

To remain competitive, America needs highly skilled workers. One of the best possible ways to obtain the skills that will lead to a career in a high-paying occupation is through a formal apprenticeship program.

Apprenticeship provides structured on-the-job training under the supervision of a qualified craftsperson, technician, or professional. This training is supplemented by related classroom instruction conducted either by the sponsor or by an educational institution.

The advantages of apprenticeships are numerous. First and foremost, an apprenticeship leads to a lasting lifetime skill. As a highly trained worker, you can take your skill anywhere. The more creative, exciting, and challenging jobs are put in the hands of the fully skilled worker, the all-around person who knows his or her trade inside and out.

Skilled workers advance much more quickly than those who are semiskilled or whose skills are not broad enough to equip them to assume additional responsibilities. Those who complete an apprenticeship have also acquired the skills and judgment necessary to go into business for themselves, if they choose.

About Apprenticeships

Although there are more than 20,000 occupations listed in the *Dictionary of Occupational Titles,* the Employment and Training Administration's Office of Apprenticeship and state apprenticeship registration agencies consider only 1,000 of these "apprenticeable." To be apprenticeable, an occupation must be commonly practiced in industry and must lend itself to sequential learning experiences accompanied by a program of related instruction.

Currently, approximately 468,000 apprentices are being trained by 28,000 programs registered with either the Office of Apprenticeship or with state apprenticeship registration agencies.

How Apprenticeships Are Regulated

Registration of an apprenticeship program with the Office of Apprenticeship or with a state apprenticeship registration agency is purely voluntary. Having such status is significant, however, a "registered apprenticeship" must meet certain minimum standards of training established by federal regulations. Registration thus serves as an official stamp of approval.

This does not mean, however, that nonregistered apprenticeships are not quality programs. Quite a number of major corporations have outstanding apprenticeship programs that have never been registered. If you want to inquire about the validity of a certain apprenticeship, you should contact a state apprenticeship registration agency or a regional office of the Office of Apprenticeship; addresses of state offices are listed in an appendix in this book.

National guideline standards are in place for many recognized occupations. These standards are established in each field by a nationally recognized association of employers or by a recognized labor organization and an employer association. For example, the International Brotherhood of Electrical Workers and the National Electrical Contractors Association have established national guideline standards for training apprentices in the electrical construction industry. National guideline standards ensure uniformity of training across the country, so an apprentice can seek employment anywhere in the United States and have his or her training accepted without questions.

In general, apprenticeship is legally recognized only if it is recorded in a written contract or agreement called an "indenture," in which the employer promises to teach the worker the processes of his or her trade in return for services rendered to the employer. Standards of a registered apprenticeship program are defined in Title 29, Code of Federal Regulations (CFR) Parts 29 and 30. A total of twenty-two standards identified in Title 29 CFR Part 29 must be incorporated into an apprenticeship program before it can be registered with the Office of Apprenticeship or a state-recognized registration agency. Standards include such provisions as the term/length of apprenticeship, a progressive wage scale, the ratio of apprentices to journey worker, credit for prior experience, safety on the job, and related classroom instruction.

What to Do If You're Interested in an Apprenticeship

A person seeking an apprenticeship fills out what amounts to an application for employment. These applications may be available year-round or at certain times during the year. Because an apprentice must be trained in an area where work actually exists and

where a certain pay scale is guaranteed upon completion of the program, waits for application acceptance may be quite lengthy in areas of low employment. Such a standard works to the advantage of the potential apprentice; certainly no one would want to encourage you to spend one to six years of your life learning an occupation where no work exists or where the wage is the same as, or a little above, that of the common laborer.

Federal regulations prohibit anyone younger than age 16 from being considered as an apprentice. Some programs require that the individual receive a high school degree or complete certain course work. Other requirements could include passing certain validated aptitude tests or proof of physical ability to perform the essential functions of the occupation.

Program sponsors register different procedures with the registration agency. An example of a selection procedure is an interview process. The apprentice is rated during the oral interview process based on responses directly related to determining the ability to perform in the apprenticeable occupation. Apprentices are then placed based on rank.

For More Information

If you're considering an apprenticeship, the best sources of assistance and information are vocational or career counselors, local one-stop career centers, field offices of state apprenticeship agencies, and regional offices of the Office of Apprenticeship.

Placement Rate Data

Philip Roush
Former Commissioner for the Indiana Commission on Proprietary Education

When you undertake the complex task of selecting the "right" vocational-technical school, you must collect as much information as possible about each school you are considering. One major piece of information you should obtain is the placement rate data, which is available from most, if not all, vocational-technical schools. This information indicates how effective the school's academic programs are in meeting the needs of today's employers. Because you want the skills you acquire at the school you choose to lead to a great job, this data will be very important as you decide which school to attend.

The school's placement rates may be obtained in several ways. Most schools will provide this data as an integral part of their prospective student-orientation program. If not, ask for it. Be cautious about considering a school that does not make its placement rates readily available.

All fifty states, the District of Columbia, and Puerto Rico have laws requiring state authorization, approval, or registration to offer educational programs to the general public. Ask the school's administration which state agency provides the required legal authority to operate its educational program; you may be able to obtain placement information from that state agency. If you are considering an occupation that requires a state license, such as a cosmetologist, barber, or medical assistant, you should also inquire about the percent of graduates who have passed or failed required licensing examinations.

Keep in mind that, while placement rate data reflects the success rate of the school's graduates, this is not the only criterion you should use in your school-selection process. Placement services are an integral part of most schools' education programs. You should remember, however, that no school can guarantee you a job upon graduation. A high placement rate simply indicates that a large number of the school's graduates are employed—as determined by a calculation method selected by the school. Currently, since there is not a nationally prescribed method of computing placement rates, placement rate data may include three categories of graduates: graduates placed in the specific vocation for which they were trained, graduates placed in a vocation related to their training, or graduates employed prior to their enrollment. It is very important to identify the method the school used to calculate its placement rates.

As you contact schools during your search, it is also important that you obtain the names and addresses of any graduates employed in your vocational interest and the names of their employers. Although placement rate data will provide you with a statistical basis from which to begin, alumni and employer comments about the school and opinions about the quality of its vocational programs will also be integral to your decision-making process.

Returning to School: Advice for Adult Students

Sandra Cook, Ph.D.

Executive Director of Enrollment Services, San Diego State University

Many adults think for a long time about returning to school without taking any action. One purpose of this article is to help the "thinkers" finally make some decisions by examining what is keeping them from action. Another purpose is to describe not only some of the difficulties and obstacles that adult students may face when returning to school, but also to explore tactics for coping with them.

If you have been thinking about going back to school and feel as though you are the only person your age contemplating this, you should know that approximately 8 million adult students are currently enrolled in higher education institutions. This number represents 46 percent of total higher education enrollments. The majority of adult students are enrolled at two-year colleges.

There are many reasons why adult students choose to return to school. Studies have shown that the three most important criteria that adult students consider when choosing a school are location, cost, and availability of the major or program desired. Most two-year colleges are public institutions that serve a geographic district, making them readily accessible to the community. Costs at most two-year colleges are far less than at other types of higher education institutions. If you are interested in a vocational or technical program, two-year colleges excel in providing this type of training.

Uncertainty, Choice, and Support

There are three different "stages" in the process of adults returning to school. The first stage is uncertainty. Do I really want to go back to school? What will my friends or family think? Can I compete with those 18-year-old whiz kids? Am I too old? The second stage is choice. Once you make the decision to return, you must choose where you will attend. There are many criteria to use in making this decision. The third stage

is support. You have just added another role to your already-too-busy life. There are, however, strategies that will help you accomplish your goals—perhaps not without struggle, but with grace and humor nonetheless. Let's look at each of these stages.

Uncertainty

Why are you thinking about returning to school? Is it to:
- fulfill a dream that had to be delayed?
- become more educationally well-rounded?

These reasons focus on *personal growth*.

If you are returning to school to:
- meet people and make friends;
- attain and enjoy higher social status and prestige among friends, relatives, and associates;
- understand/study a cultural heritage; or
- have a medium in which to exchange ideas,

you are interested in *social and cultural opportunities*.

If you are like most adult students, you want to:
- qualify for a new occupation;
- enter or reenter the job market;
- increase earnings potential; or
- qualify for a more challenging position in the same field of work,

you are seeking *career growth*.

Understanding the reasons why you want to go back to school is an important step in setting your educational goals and will help you to establish some criteria for selecting a college. However, don't delay your decision because you have not been able to clearly define your motives. Many times, these aren't clear until you have already begun the process, and they may change as you move through your college experience.

Assuming you agree that additional education will benefit you, what is it that prevents you from returning to school? You may have a litany of excuses running through your mind:

- I don't have time.
- I can't afford it.
- I'm too old to learn.
- My friends will think I'm crazy.
- The teachers will be younger than I.
- My family can't survive without me to take care of them every minute.
- I'll be x years old when I finish.
- I'm afraid.
- I don't know what to expect.

And that is just what these are—excuses. You can make school, like anything else in your life, a priority or not. If you really want to return, you can. The more you understand your motivation for returning to school and the more you understand what excuses are keeping you from taking action, the easier your task will be.

If you think you don't have time: The best way to decide how attending class and studying can fit into your schedule is to keep track of what you do with your time each day for several weeks. Completing a standard time-management grid (each day is plotted out by the half hour) is helpful for visualizing how your time is spent. For each 3-credit-hour class you take, you will need to find 3 hours for class, plus 6 to 9 hours for reading-studying-library time. This study time should be spaced evenly throughout the week, not loaded up on one day. It is not possible to learn or retain the material that way. When you examine your grid, see where there are activities that could be replaced with school and study time. You may decide to give up your bowling league or some time in front of the TV. Try not to give up sleeping, and don't cut out every moment of free time. Here are some suggestions that have come from adults who have returned to school:

- Enroll in a time-management workshop. It helps you rethink how you use your time.
- Don't think you have to take more than one course at a time. You may eventually want to work up to taking more, but consider starting with one. (It is more than you are taking now!)
- If you have a family, start assigning to them those household chores that you usually do—and don't redo what they do.
- Use your lunch hour or commuting time for reading.

If you think you cannot afford it: As mentioned earlier, two-year colleges are extremely affordable. If you cannot afford the tuition, look into the various financial aid options. Most federal and state funds are available to full- and part-time students. Loans are also available. While many people prefer not to accumulate a debt for school, these same people will think nothing of taking out a loan to buy a car. After five or six years, which is the better investment? Adult students who work should look into whether their company has a tuition-reimbursement policy. There are also private scholarships, available through foundations, service organizations, and clubs, that are focused on adult learners. Your public library and a college financial aid adviser are two excellent sources for reference materials regarding financial aid.

If you think you are too old to learn: This is pure myth. A number of studies have shown that adult learners perform as well as or better than traditional-age students.

If you are afraid your friends will think you're crazy: Who cares? Maybe they will, maybe they won't. They may admire your courage and even be just a little jealous of your ambition (although they'll never tell you that). Follow your dreams, not theirs.

If you are concerned because the teachers or students will be younger than you: Don't be. The age differences that may be apparent in other settings evaporate in the classroom. If anything, an adult in the classroom strikes fear into the hearts of some 18-year-olds. Adult students have been known to be more prepared, ask better questions, be truly motivated, and be there to learn!

If you think your family members will have a difficult time surviving while you are in school: If you have done everything for them up to now, they might struggle. Consider this an opportunity to help them become independent and self-sufficient. Your family members can only make you feel guilty if you let them. You are not abandoning them; you are becoming an educational role model. When you are happy and working toward your goals, everyone benefits. Admittedly, it sometimes takes time for family members to realize this. For single parents, there are schools that offer support groups, child care, and cooperative babysitting.

If you're appalled at the thought of being X years old when you graduate in Y years: How old will you be in Y years if you *don't* go back to school?

If you are afraid or don't know what to expect: These are natural feelings when one encounters any new situation. Adult students find that their fears usually dissipate once they begin classes. Fear of trying is usually the biggest roadblock to the reentry process.

No doubt you have dreamed up a few more reasons for not deciding to return to school. Keep in mind that what you are doing is making up excuses, and you are using these excuses to release you from the obligation to make a decision about your life. The thought of returning to college can be scary. Anytime you venture into unknown territory, you take a risk, but taking risks is a necessary component of personal and professional growth. It is your life, and you alone are responsible for making the decisions that determine its course. Education is an investment in your future.

Choice

Once you have decided to go back to school, your next task is to decide where to go. If your educational goals are well defined (e.g., you want to pursue a degree to change careers), then your task is a bit easier.

Most students who attend a public two-year college choose the community college in the district in which they live. This is generally the closest and least expensive option if the school offers the programs you want. If you are planning to begin your education at a two-year college and then transfer to a four-year school, there are distinct advantages to choosing your four-year school early. Many community and four-year colleges have "articulation" agreements that designate what credits from the two-year school will transfer to the four-year college, and how they can be transferred. Some four-year institutions accept an associate degree as equivalent to the freshman and sophomore years, regardless of the courses you have taken. Some four-year schools accept two-year college work only on a course-by-course basis. If you can identify which school you will transfer to, you can know in advance exactly how your two-year credits will apply and prevent an unexpected loss of credit or time.

Each institution of higher education is distinctive. Your goal in choosing a school is to come up with the best student-institution fit—matching your needs with the offerings and characteristics of the school. The first step is to determine what criteria are most important to you in attaining your educational goals. Location, cost, and program availability are the three main factors that influence an adult student's college choice. In considering location, don't forget that some colleges have conveniently located branch campuses. In considering cost, remember to explore your financial aid options before ruling out an institution because of its tuition. Program availability should

include not only the area in which you are interested, but also whether or not classes in that area are available when you can take them.

Here are some additional considerations beyond location, cost, and programs:

- Does the school have a commitment to adult students and offer appropriate services, such as child care, tutoring, and advising?
- Are classes offered at times when you can take them?
- Is the faculty sensitive to the needs of adult learners?

Once you determine which criteria are vital in your choice of an institution, you can begin to narrow your choices. There are myriad ways for you to locate the information you desire. Many urban newspapers publish a "School Guide" several times a year in which colleges and universities advertise to an adult student market. In addition, schools themselves publish catalogs, class schedules, and promotional materials that contain much of the information you need, and they are yours for the asking. Many colleges sponsor information sessions and open houses that allow you to visit the campus and ask questions. An appointment with an adviser is a good way to assess the fit between you and the institution. Be sure to bring your questions with you to your interview.

Support

Once you have made the decision to return to school and have chosen the institution that best meets your needs, take some additional steps to ensure your success during your crucial first semester. Take advantage of institutional support and build some social support systems of your own. Here are some ways to do that:

- Plan to participate in orientation programs. These serve the threefold purpose of providing you with a great deal of important information, familiarizing you with the school and its facilities, and giving you the opportunity to meet and begin networking with other students.
- Build new support networks by joining an adult student organization, making a point of meeting other adult students through workshops, or actively seeking out a "study buddy" in each class—that invaluable friend who shares and understands your experience.
- Incorporate your new status as student into your family life. Doing your homework with your

children at a designated homework time is a valuable family activity and reinforces the importance of education.

- Make sure you take a reasonable course load in your first semester. It is far better to have some extra time on your hands and to succeed magnificently than to spend the entire semester on the brink of a breakdown. Also, whenever possible, try to focus your first courses not only on requirements, but also on areas of personal interest.

- Seek out faculty members, advisers, and student affairs personnel who are there to help you during difficult times—let them assist you as often as necessary.

After completing your first semester, you will probably look back in wonder why you feared returning to school. Certainly, it's not without its occasional exasperations. But keeping things in perspective and maintaining your sense of humor will make the difference between merely coping and succeeding brilliantly.

Careers in Business

When it comes to work environments, people's tastes generally fall into three categories. There are those who enjoy structure, working at a desk, and dressing in suits; those who appreciate some routine but want a certain amount of freedom in their schedule and appearance; and those who prefer to work in a workshop or outdoors. If you fall into the first category, you may find a career in business well-suited to your personality.

The good news is that you don't need Ivy League connections or an M.B.A. to land a good job in the business arena. In fact, many vocational school programs will teach you the ins and outs of the white-collar world and prepare you to be, for example, an administrative assistant, accounting technician, real-estate agent, or paralegal.

Now that most offices are computerized, administrative assistants—who used to be called secretaries—have much larger roles than ever before. They perform a wide range of administrative and clerical jobs that keep an organization running smoothly, including scheduling appointments, organizing and maintaining files, filling out forms, and operating office equipment such as personal computers, fax machines, scanners, and photocopiers.

Accounting technicians, who are perhaps more "behind the scenes" but very important for a business's success, keep track of a company's finances using computers, calculators, and ledger books. Accounting technicians may also prepare financial reports and handle bank deposits. With computerization, accounting work is faster and more efficient. Those who are well trained on the latest equipment stand a good chance of finding great jobs.

Another important business occupation is that of the paralegal, who assists lawyers in legal research. Paralegals help prepare cases by searching for information in law books, public records, computer databases, and various documents. They may also work on wills, inheritances, and income tax returns. Some paralegals write drafts of important documents, including contracts, mortgages, and separation agreements.

Many businesspeople dream of being their own boss one day, and in the field of real estate, they have a good chance of achieving that goal. Real estate agents that have a thorough knowledge of the housing market in their community, including information about neighborhoods, zoning, and tax laws, work with buyers and sellers of homes.

With the variety of business professions available to vocational school graduates, you're sure to find a career that suits you.

Business Professions

Accounting

Accounting technical services

Administrative and secretarial services

Administrative assistant/secretarial science

Advertising

Agricultural and food products processing operations and management

Agricultural business/agribusiness operations

Agricultural business and management

Agricultural business and production

Apparel and accessories marketing operations

Auctioneering

Aviation and airway science

Aviation management

Banking and financial support services

Broadcast journalism

Business administration and management

Business and personal services marketing operations

Business communications

Business management and administrative services

Business marketing and marketing management

Business services marketing operations

Business systems networking and telecommunications

Buying operations

Child-care services management

Communications

Computer and information sciences

Court reporting

Distribution operations

Enterprise management and operation

Entrepreneurship

Executive assistant/secretarial services

Farm and ranch management

Fashion merchandising

Finance

Financial management and services

Financial services marketing operations

Fire services administration

Floristry marketing operations

Food and beverage/restaurant operations management

Food products retailing and wholesaling operations

Food sales operations

Franchise operation

General office/clerical and typing services

Home and office products marketing operations

Home products marketing operations

Hospitality/administration management

Hospitality and recreation marketing operations

Hospitality services management

Hotel/motel and restaurant management

Hotel/motel services marketing operations

Human resources management

Information processing/data entry services

Institutional food service and administration

Insurance and risk management

Insurance marketing operations

Journalism

Journalism and mass communication

Labor/personnel relations and studies

Legal administrative assistant/secretarial services

Library assistance

Logistics and materials management

Marketing management and research

Marketing operations/marketing and distribution

Medical administrative assistant/secretarial services

Natural resource management and protective services

Nonprofit and public management

Office management and supervision

Operations management and supervision

Paralegal/legal assistance

Parks, recreation, and leisure facilities management

Personal services marketing operations

Purchasing, procurement, and contracts management

Radio and television broadcasting

Real estate

Reception

Recreation products/services marketing operations

Retailing and wholesaling operations and skills

Retailing operations

Sales operations

Security and loss prevention services

Taxation

Tourism and travel services marketing operations

Tourism promotion operations

Travel services marketing operations

Travel-tourism management

Vehicle and petroleum products marketing operations

Vehicle parts and accessories marketing operations

Wildlife and wildlands management

Careers in Health Care

Do you enjoy watching TV shows and movies about hospitals and doctors? Do you feel a thrill when you see an ambulance race down the street with its lights flashing? Do you like helping family members or friends when they are sick or injured? If so, you can find a fulfilling career in the rapidly growing health-care industry—without the time and expense involved in attending medical school.

Many vocational school programs, ranging from licensed practical nurse training to emergency medical technical preparation, are currently available to guide those interested in health care.

Licensed practical nurses (LPNs) care for sick, injured, recovering, and disabled people under the guidance of physicians and registered nurses. Most LPNs work at the patient's bedside, checking blood pressure, pulse, and respiration. They may also give injections and change bandages. Their responsibilities may include bathing, dressing, and feeding patients and helping to keep them comfortable.

The responsibilities of medical assistants are closely tied to the routine of a doctor's office. While duties vary from office to office, medical assistants generally perform a combination of clerical and clinical duties. Clerical duties might include answering telephones, keeping patient files, filling out insurance forms, and scheduling appointments, while clinical tasks could involve collecting and preparing laboratory specimens, instructing patients about medication, taking EKGs, and removing stitches.

Dental assistants, like medical assistants, perform a variety of clinical, office, and laboratory duties. They work beside the dentist at the patient's chair, preparing trays with dental tools, assisting the dentist, and instructing patients in brushing and flossing. They may also make impressions of teeth and take and develop X-rays. Dental assistants often schedule appointments, keep records, receive payments from patients, and order supplies.

Emergency medical technicians (EMTs) work with sick and injured people before they reach a doctor's office or hospital. Their job is to treat the problem immediately—whether it's a wound, a heart attack, or poisoning—and then transport the patient to the proper place as quickly as possible. EMTs generally work in teams of 2 to assess and treat the illness or injury. They are also trained to perform a variety of emergency procedures, including restoring breathing, controlling bleeding, and assisting in childbirth.

As the population increases and the average lifespan lengthens, jobs in health care will be interesting and plentiful for those with the right preparation. Employment opportunities in these professions are expected to increase much more quickly through the year 2016 than the average compared to other professions.

Health-Care Professions

Acupuncture and Oriental medicine

Alcohol/drug abuse counseling

Athletic training and sports medicine

Blood bank technical services

Cardiovascular technology

Child care and guidance work and management

Child-care service/assistance

Community health liaison

Cytotechnology

Dental assistance

Dental hygiene

Dental laboratory technical services

Dental services

Dietetics/human nutritional services

Diagnostic medical sonography

Elder-care provider/companion services

Electrocardiograph technology

Electroencephalograph technology

Emergency medical technical services

Environmental health

Health aide services

Health and medical administrative services

Health and medical assistance

Health and medical diagnostic and treatment services

Health and medical laboratory technologies

Health and physical education/fitness

Health physics/radiologic health

Health professions and related sciences

Health unit coordination/ward clerk

Health unit management/ward supervision

Hematology technology

Home health aide services

Hypnotherapy

Medical assistance

Medical dietician

Medical laboratory assistance

Medical laboratory technical services

Medical office management

Medical radiologic technology

Medical records administration

Medical records technical services

Medical transcription

Mental health services

Naturopathic medicine

Nuclear medical technology

Nurse assistance/aide

Nursing

Nursing (RN training)

Occupational health and industrial hygiene

Occupational therapy assistance

Ophthalmic medical assistance

Ophthalmic medical technical services

Ophthalmic/optometric laboratory technology

Ophthalmic/optometric services

Optical technical services/assistance

Opticianry/dispense opticianry

Orthotics/prosthetics

Parks, recreation, leisure, and fitness studies

Pharmacy technical services/assistance

Physical therapy

Physical therapy assistance

Physician assistance

Practical nursing (LPN training)

Psychiatric/mental health services technical services

Recreational therapy

Rehabilitation/therapeutic services

Respiratory therapy technology

Surgical/operating room technical services

Vocational rehabilitation counseling

Careers in Technology

It's hard to go a single day without noticing the huge role technology plays in our daily lives. Even something as familiar as the mail demonstrates the impact of technology: Bills are computed on lightning-fast machines, letters are written with word-processing programs, mailing lists are kept on huge electronic databases, and barcode readers help scan and sort mail. If you're interested in how computers streamline any of these or a million other processes, you can excel in a technology-related career.

People interested in learning how electronic systems work might consider jobs as data-processing technicians—people who install, maintain, and repair computers. They also keep records of repairs and order parts. Data-processing technicians often work for computer manufacturers, but they also find employment with businesses that maintain large computer systems, such as banks, insurance firms, and public utility companies.

Electronics engineering technicians need to be familiar with technical machines other than computers, because they help design, build, install, maintain, and repair electronic equipment such as radios, tele-visions, control devices, and sonar, radar, and navigational equipment, as well as computers. Electronics engineering technicians often rely on high-tech measuring and diagnostic devices to get the job done. Employment opportunities in this field are expected to rise more quickly than the average for many other professions through the year 2016.

People who are more interested in the "brains" of the machine than in the "muscle" may want to consider a career in computer programming. Computer programmers write step-by-step instructions that direct computers to process information in a series of logical steps. Programmers work in all types of businesses, from hospitals to schools, since just about every line of work relies on computer power these days.

Whether you're interested in the miniature silicon chips inside computers or the larger parts that make technical equipment function correctly, a vocational school program could help prepare you for a career in one of the most exciting, fastest-growing fields.

Technology Professions

Aeronautical and aerospace engineering technology

Air traffic control

Architectural engineering technology

Automotive engineering technology

Aviation science

Aviation systems and avionics maintenance technology

Biological technology

Biomedical engineering-related technology

Business computer facilities operation

Business computer programming

Business information and data processing services

Chemical technology

Civil engineering

Civil engineering/civil technology

Communications technology

Computer and information sciences

Computer engineering technology

Computer maintenance technology

Computer typography and composition equipment operation

Construction/building technology

Data processing technology

Careers in Technology

Desktop publishing equipment operation

Educational/instructional media technology

Electrical and electronic engineering-related technologies

Electrical, electronic, and communications engineering technology

Electromechanical instrumentation and maintenance technologies

Electromechanical technology

Energy management and systems technology

Engineering-related technologies

Environmental and pollution control technologies

Forensic technical services

Forest harvesting and production technology

Forest products technology

Heating, air conditioning, and refrigeration technology

Hydraulic technology

Industrial production technologies

Industrial/manufacturing technology

Laser and optical technology

Management information systems and business data processing

Mechanical engineering/mechanical technology

Mechanical engineering-related technologies

Metallurgical technology

Mining technology

Nuclear and industrial radiologic technologies

Nuclear/nuclear power technology

Occupational safety and health technology

Petroleum technology

Photographic technology

Physical science technologies

Plastics technology

Quality control and safety technology

Quality control technology

Radio and television broadcasting technology

Robotics technology

Science technologies

Solar technology

Surveying

Water quality and wastewater treatment technology

Careers in the Trade

For some people, a day's work doesn't count for much if it doesn't involve getting their hands dirty or breaking a sweat. To these achievers, work means a lot more than wearing a suit and shuffling papers at a desk. If you're a get-down-to-the-nitty-gritty kind of person, you might consider a career in auto mechanics, electrical work, carpentry, or law enforcement. Many vocational school programs are available to give you the information and training you need to break into these and other related fields.

Auto mechanics, also called automotive service technicians, repair and service automobiles and light trucks. Mechanics must have in-depth knowledge about how vehicles work to be able to identify what caused a car or truck to break down and to perform routine tasks that keep automobiles running smoothly.

Those who are fascinated by wires and connections might consider a career as an electrician. Although the main responsibility of an electrician is to install and maintain electrical systems, specific systems can range from climate control to communications. Some electricians specialize in preventive maintenance; they routinely inspect equipment, searching for problems before systems break down.

Within the building trade, the most plentiful positions are for carpenters—people who cut, shape, and assemble wood to construct buildings or create other products such as cabinets and doors. Carpenters work on construction sites, inside buildings, in factories, and in woodworking shops. The majority of those employed as carpenters work for contractors who build, remodel, or repair buildings and other structures.

If you're interested in challenging, physical work outside of a traditional office environment, you might find that a trade career will satisfy these needs.

Trade Professions

Agricultural animal husbandry and production management

Agricultural mechanization

Agricultural power machinery operation

Agricultural production work and management

Agricultural supplies and related services

Agricultural supplies retailing and wholesaling

Agriculture/agricultural sciences

Air transportation services

Animal training

Aquaculture operations and production management

Architectural drafting

Auto/automotive body repair

Auto/automotive mechanical/technical services

Building/property maintenance and management

Business machine repair

Cabinet making and millworking

Carpentry

Civil/structural drafting

Clothing, apparel, and textile work and management

Commercial garment and apparel services

Commercial photography

Communication systems installation and repair

Computer installation and repair

Conservation and renewable natural resources

Construction and building finishing and management

Construction/building inspecting

Construction equipment operating

Construction trades

Crop production operations and management

Custodial, housekeeping, and home services and management

Careers in the Trade

Custodial services/caretaking

Custom tailoring

Diesel engine mechanical and repair services

Dietitian assistance

Diving (professional)

Drafting

Dry cleaning and laundering (commercial)

Electrical and electronics equipment installation and repair

Electrical and power transmission installation

Electrical/electronics drafting

Electrician

Equestrian/equine studies, horse management, and training

Fire protection

Fire protection and safety technology

Fire science/firefighting

Fishing technology/commercial fishing

Food catering

Forest production and processing

Forestry

Furniture design and craft

Graphic and printing equipment operation

Greenhouse operations and management

Gunsmithing

Heating, air conditioning, and refrigeration mechanical and repair services

Heavy equipment maintenance and repair

Home furnishings and equipment installation and consultation

Horseshoeing

Horticulture services operations and management

Industrial design

Industrial electronics installation and repair

Industrial equipment maintenance and repair

Industrial machinery maintenance and repair

Instrument calibration and repair

Landscaping operations and management

Leather working and upholstering

Line work

Lithography and platemaking

Locksmithing and safe repair

Logging/timber harvesting

Machine shop assistance

Machinist/machine technology

Major appliance installation and repair

Marine maintenance and ship repair

Masonry and tile setting

Mechanical and repair services

Mechanical drafting

Mechanical typesetting and composing

Mechanical and repair services

Motorcycle mechanical and repair services

Musical instrument repair

Nursery operations and management

Ornamental horticulture operations and management

Painting and wall covering

Plumbing and pipe fitting

Precision metal working

Precision production trades

Printing press operation

Sheet metal working

Shoe, boot, and leather repair

Small engine mechanical and repair services

Stationary energy sources installation and operation

Tool- and die-making/technology

Transportation and materials moving

Truck, bus, and other commercial vehicle operation

Vehicle and equipment operation

Vehicle and mobile equipment mechanical and repair services

Watch, clock, and jewelry repair

Water transportation services

Welding

Window treatment making and installation

Woodworking

Careers in Visual and Performing Arts

If you feel the need to express yourself on canvas or on a stage, or you enjoy making your own clothes or jewelry, taking photographs, singing, dancing, or doodling, chances are that a career in visual and performing arts is for you.

There are numerous careers where you can use your creativity and self-expression as a service to others. For example, some visual artists use computer techniques to create art to meet clients' needs, whether for packaging and promotional displays, company logos and stationery, or newspaper or magazine ads.

In addition to the programs listed here, you may want to consult *Peterson's College Guide for Performing Arts Majors* or *Peterson's College Guide for Visual Arts Majors*.

Visual and Performing Arts Professions

Acting and directing

Ceramic arts and ceramics

Crafts, folk art, and artisanry

Design and applied arts

Design and visual communications

Dramatic/theater arts and stagecraft

Drawing

Fashion and fabric consultation

Fashion design and illustration

Fashion modeling

Film/video and photographic arts

Film-video making/cinematography and production

Fine arts and art studies

Fine/studio arts

Graphic design, commercial art, and illustration

Interior design

Intermedia

Metal and jewelry arts

Music

Music—piano and organ performance

Music—voice and choral/opera performance

Painting

Photography

Printmaking

Technical theater/theater design and stagecraft

Careers in Personal Services

It's hard for some people to believe they can earn a living doing something they enjoy, particularly when it involves helping or serving others in a calm environment. Are you one of those people who cuts your friends' hair for free? Would you enjoy using your artistic talent to enhance the looks of other people through cosmetics? If so, many vocational school programs can help you turn these interests into a steady paycheck.

Barbers and hairstylists shampoo and cut hair, shave and cut beards and mustaches, give facial massages and hair and scalp treatments, and recommend and sell grooming products. Cosmetologists—who may also be called beauty operators, hairdressers, and beauticians—perform many similar duties: They care for their clients' skin and nails by giving massages and facials, shaping eyebrows, and offering makeup advice.

If you have the talent and the patience necessary to figure out what others need and want, consider checking out vocational programs for personal service careers, which are fun—and profitable.

Personal Services Professions

Barbering/hairstyling

Cosmetic services

Cosmetology

Electrolysis technician services

Executive housekeeping

Funeral services and mortuary science

Homemaker's aide services

Make-up artistry

Massage services

Careers in Other Fields

A number of career areas do not fall neatly into any of the six major categories already covered. These careers include criminal justice and law enforcement, teacher education, language instruction, culinary arts, fashion modeling, and bartending.

Police officers are charged with protecting the lives and property of citizens, and their days are filled with work aimed at preventing crime. Officers may work in investigation, at police departments, in traffic control, or for crime prevention. The majority of police officers, detectives, and special agents are employed by local city governments.

Bartenders prepare alcoholic drinks for restaurant, bar, and cocktail lounge patrons and need to know exact recipes for a multitude of drinks. Busy workers in this profession take drink orders, mix and serve the drinks, and collect money; they may also wash and dry glasses behind the bar and be responsible for keeping the bar area clean and well-stocked.

If you are interested in an unconventional work schedule and enjoy interacting with people, consider enrolling in programs in these areas.

Other Professions

Adult and continuing teacher education

Agriculture/agricultural sciences

Animal sciences

Baking/pastry chef training

Bartending/mixology

Card dealing

Corrections/correctional administration

Criminal justice and corrections

Criminal justice/law enforcement administration

Culinary arts/chef training

Custodial, housekeeping, and home services work and management

Education

Elementary teacher education

Flight attending

Foreign language interpretation and translation

Gaming and sports officiating services

Home economics

Kitchen personnel/cook and assistant training

Law enforcement/police science

Marine science/merchant marine official

Meatcutting

Pet grooming

Pre-elementary/early childhood/ kindergarten teacher education

Protective services

Public administration and services

Sign language interpretation

Social work

Special education

Teacher assistance

Veterinarian assistant/animal health technician services

Vocational home economics

Waiter/waitress and dining room management

New and Emerging Careers

As the job market continues to expand and redefine itself, several new employment opportunities have become available. Emerging occupations can be characterized as new occupations created by changes in technology, society, markets, or regulations. Emerging occupations may also describe existing occupations that have been substantially modified by the same changes and are increasing in employment opportunities. The following are a few of the new and emerging occupations identified by the U.S. Department of Labor, Bureau of Labor Statistics.

Now with the emerging employment trend of "going green," many new and exciting careers have emerged in regards to the environment and environmental protection. Environmental engineers, environmental compliance managers, regulatory compliance managers, and environmental scientists and technicians work together to ensure compliance with environmental regulations and company policy. Environmental compliance managers direct the work of scientists, technicians and hazardous materials removal workers and field technicians. The work may involve the disposal of hazardous materials, monitoring emissions of pollutants, or protecting the safety of employees on the job. Environmental engineers and scientists may also work on environmental impact statements or environmental assessments. Some may work as contractors advising clients on how to ensure compliance with environmental law and regulations. These environmental professionals were mostly reported in industries that must adhere to environmental regulations, such as the paper and allied products; fabricated metal products; industrial machinery and equipment; electric, gas, and sanitary services; construction; wholesale trade; business services; health services; and engineering and management services industries.

Consumer credit counselors provide advice on personal finance, such as budgeting, money management, mortgages, and financial planning, especially to those with money management or credit problems. They may help negotiate with creditors to arrange a debt repayment plan to help clients avoid personal bankruptcy. They may conduct public education workshops and seminars on personal finance subjects. They are employed in the nonprofit social services industry.

Convention managers, meeting planners, conference planners, and convention coordinators convention planning personnel serve as liaisons between their own organization and various outside vendors that provide goods and services for a convention. Convention managers coordinate activities of convention center/hotel/banquet personnel to make arrangements for group meetings and conventions. Convention managers were most prominent in the membership organizations industry. They were also reported in the following industries: business services; educational services; printing and publishing; social services; health services; transportation services; wholesale trade; depository institutions; insurance carriers; and hotels, rooming houses, camps, and other lodging industries.

Continued technological advances in computer hardware, software, printers, and related equipment now allow firms to do more document production in-house and on demand. Doing the work this way is faster than sending it to an outside vendor. Desktop publishing specialists and desktop publishing operators use advanced computer graphics and word processing computer systems to produce documents such as reports, proposals, benefit books, advertisements, brochures, and flyers. Firms in the finance, insurance and real estate, and wholesale trade industries, among others, reported desktop publishing occupations.

Nonprofit organizations are the primary employers of volunteer coordinators. Volunteer coordinators and volunteer directors work to recruit, train, schedule, and organize volunteers in the educational services, local government, health services, residential care, membership organizations, and social services industries.

Web masters, web site technicians, and web site coordinators write the computer code necessary to publish or update text and images on Web sites. They also design and maintain Web sites. As more organizations project a presence on the Internet, more Web workers are being reported. Establishments in the printing and publishing, wholesale trade, retail trade, business services, and membership organizations industries have reported employment of Internet publishing personnel.

More specialized fields will continue to emerge, making the job market even more attractive to students of vocational and technical schools.

How to Use This Guide

Profiles of Vo-Tech Schools

Institution Name: The heading for each institution gives the name of the school or institution, the street address, the Web address (if available), the chief officer to contact for admissions information, and the admissions phone number.

General Information: This section lists key facts and figures about the institution, including institution type, when it was founded, the type of accreditation it has, the total enrollment of students in its vo-tech programs as of the official fall reporting date, and the application fee.

Program(s) Offered: Programs that a school offers are listed, followed by their individual program enrollment or their length and cost. The Integrated Postsecondary Education Data System (IPEPS) collects and collates data in two different ways depending on whether a school is a degree-granting institute or if it grants certificates. Therefore, the type of data presented may differ from program to program.

Student Services: This section details support services, ranging from career counseling to child day care, that are offered to program participants.

Appendixes

The Appendixes contain two listings. The first lists the State Offices of Apprenticeship Contacts. The second listing contains the accrediting organizations that are recognized by the Council for Higher Education Accreditation (CHEA) of the U.S. Department of Education. Recognition by CHEA affirms that the standards and processes of the accrediting organization are consistent with the academic quality, improvement, and accountability expectations that CHEA has established. The organizations are listed alphabetically by their region or by their field of specialization and include contact information, should you wish to check on a particular program's accreditation.

Indexes

The Career Training Programs index allows you to search by a given career area to see which schools offer training programs in your field of interest. Career areas are listed alphabetically. Within each career area, institution names are broken down by state to facilitate your search. The location of each school appears after the school name.

If you can't find the career area you're looking for, refer to the "Careers in..." articles. Career areas found in the index are listed at the end of each of the articles. Be sure to look at all the lists to make sure you're not forgetting any career opportunities you hadn't thought of previously.

The Alphabetical Listing of Vo-Tech Schools index of institutions can help you find a particular school by name.

Data Collection Procedures

Information for schools was obtained from IPEDS (The Integrated Postsecondary Education Data System) 2007–08 data file. All usable information received in time for publication has been included. The omission of a particular item from a profile means either that it is not applicable to that particular school or not available or usable. Because of the system of checks performed on the data collected by Peterson's, we believe that the information presented in this guide is accurate. Nonetheless, errors and omissions are possible in a data collection endeavor of this scope. Also, facts and figures are subject to change. Therefore, students should check at the time of application with the specific institution to verify all pertinent information.

Criteria for Inclusion in This Book

Peterson's Vocational and Technical Schools East profiles more than 2,600 U.S. institutions of higher education that offer postsecondary awards, certificates, or diplomas requiring less than two years of study. Institutions that are included meet the qualifications of having been in operation for at least two years and must be accredited by a national, regional, state, or specialized accrediting body.

The programs included are defined as instructional and designed to prepare individuals with entry-level skills and training required for employment in a specific trade, occupation, or profession.

This definition of vocational and technical schools includes private colleges (also called career colleges), public colleges, and regional technical training centers. For information on schools offering associate degree programs in the career areas listed in this book, refer to *Peterson's Two-Year Colleges*.

Profiles of Vo-Tech Schools

ALABAMA

Alabama Southern Community College

PO Box 2000, Monroeville, AL 36461
http://www.ascc.edu/

CONTACT John A. Johnson, President
Telephone: 251-575-3156 Ext. 8252

GENERAL INFORMATION Public Institution. Founded 1965. **Accreditation:** Regional (SACS/CC). **Total program enrollment:** 853.

PROGRAM(S) OFFERED
• Administrative Assistant and Secretarial Science, General *1 student enrolled* • Cosmetology/Cosmetologist, General *9 students enrolled* • Industrial Technology/Technician • Licensed Practical/Vocational Nurse Training (LPN, LVN, Cert, Dipl, AAS) *28 students enrolled* • Tool and Die Technology/Technician *9 students enrolled* • Welding Technology/Welder *8 students enrolled*

STUDENT SERVICES Academic or career counseling, employment services for current students, placement services for program completers, remedial services.

Alabama State College of Barber Styling

9480 Parkway East, Birmingham, AL 35215

CONTACT Donald S. Mathews, Owner Director
Telephone: 205-836-2404

GENERAL INFORMATION Private Institution. **Total program enrollment:** 4.

PROGRAM(S) OFFERED
• Barbering/Barber *1500 hrs./$4931*

Bevill State Community College

PO Box 800, Sumiton, AL 35148
http://www.bscc.edu/

CONTACT Neal Morrison, President
Telephone: 205-648-3271 Ext. 5400

GENERAL INFORMATION Public Institution. Founded 1969. **Accreditation:** Regional (SACS/CC); medical laboratory technology (NAACLS). **Total program enrollment:** 2183.

PROGRAM(S) OFFERED
• Administrative Assistant and Secretarial Science, General *2 students enrolled* • Autobody/Collision and Repair Technology/Technician *11 students enrolled* • Automobile/Automotive Mechanics Technology/Technician • Barbering/Barber *11 students enrolled* • Child Care and Support Services Management • Computer and Information Sciences, General • Cosmetology and Related Personal Grooming Arts, Other • Cosmetology/Cosmetologist, General • Diesel Mechanics Technology/Technician *6 students enrolled* • Drafting and Design Technology/Technician, General *1 student enrolled* • Electrician • Emergency Medical Technology/Technician (EMT Paramedic) *15 students enrolled* • Heating, Air Conditioning and Refrigeration Technology/Technician (ACH/ACR/ACHR/HRAC/HVAC/AC Technology) • Industrial Electronics Technology/Technician • Legal Assistant/Paralegal • Licensed Practical/Vocational Nurse Training (LPN, LVN, Cert, Dipl, AAS) *71 students enrolled* • Nurse/Nursing Assistant/Aide and Patient Care Assistant • Surgical Technology/Technologist *16 students enrolled* • Tool and Die Technology/Technician • Truck and Bus Driver/Commercial Vehicle Operation *95 students enrolled* • Welding Technology/Welder *17 students enrolled*

STUDENT SERVICES Academic or career counseling, daycare for children of students, employment services for current students, placement services for program completers, remedial services.

Bishop State Community College

351 North Broad Street, Mobile, AL 36603-5898
http://www.bscc.cc.al.us/

CONTACT James Lowe, President
Telephone: 251-405-7000

GENERAL INFORMATION Public Institution. Founded 1965. **Accreditation:** Regional (SACS/CC); funeral service (ABFSE); health information technology (AHIMA); physical therapy assisting (APTA). **Total program enrollment:** 1314.

PROGRAM(S) OFFERED
• Accounting Technology/Technician and Bookkeeping • Administrative Assistant and Secretarial Science, General • Apparel and Textile Manufacture *4 students enrolled* • Autobody/Collision and Repair Technology/Technician *2 students enrolled* • Barbering/Barber *8 students enrolled* • Carpentry/Carpenter *1 student enrolled* • Child Care and Support Services Management *4 students enrolled* • Cosmetology/Cosmetologist, General *21 students enrolled* • Diesel Mechanics Technology/Technician *1 student enrolled* • Drafting and Design Technology/Technician, General • Electrical, Electronic and Communications Engineering Technology/Technician • Electrician *6 students enrolled* • Foodservice Systems Administration/Management *1 student enrolled* • Graphic Communications, Other • Health Information/Medical Records Technology/Technician • Heating, Air Conditioning and Refrigeration Technology/Technician (ACH/ACR/ACHR/HRAC/HVAC/AC Technology) *8 students enrolled* • Instrumentation Technology/Technician • Licensed Practical/Vocational Nurse Training (LPN, LVN, Cert, Dipl, AAS) *16 students enrolled* • Mason/Masonry *2 students enrolled* • Medical Transcription/Transcriptionist *2 students enrolled* • Plumbing Technology/Plumber *4 students enrolled* • Tool and Die Technology/Technician *3 students enrolled* • Truck and Bus Driver/Commercial Vehicle Operation *55 students enrolled* • Watchmaking and Jewelrymaking *8 students enrolled* • Welding Technology/Welder *6 students enrolled*

STUDENT SERVICES Academic or career counseling, daycare for children of students, remedial services.

Calhoun Community College

PO Box 2216, Decatur, AL 35609-2216
http://www.calhoun.edu/

CONTACT Dr. Marilyn C. Beck, President
Telephone: 256-306-2500

GENERAL INFORMATION Public Institution. Founded 1965. **Accreditation:** Regional (SACS/CC); dental assisting (ADA); practical nursing (NLN). **Total program enrollment:** 4263.

PROGRAM(S) OFFERED
• Allied Health Diagnostic, Intervention, and Treatment Professions, Other • Applied Horticulture/Horticultural Operations, General *16 students enrolled* • Autobody/Collision and Repair Technology/Technician *11 students enrolled* • Automobile/Automotive Mechanics Technology/Technician *10 students enrolled* • Barbering/Barber *1 student enrolled* • Business Administration and Management, General • Carpentry/Carpenter *2 students enrolled* • Child Care and Support Services Management *1 student enrolled* • Computer and Information Sciences, General *1 student enrolled* • Cosmetology and Related Personal Grooming Arts, Other • Cosmetology/Cosmetologist, General • Criminal Justice/Police Science • Dental Assisting/Assistant *7 students enrolled* • Drafting and Design Technology/Technician, General *25 students enrolled* • Electrical, Electronic and Communications Engineering Technology/Technician • Electrician • Emergency Medical Technology/Technician (EMT Paramedic) • Fire Services Administration *1 student enrolled* • Heating, Air Conditioning and Refrigeration Technology/Technician (ACH/ACR/ACHR/HRAC/HVAC/AC Technology) *1 student enrolled* • Licensed Practical/Vocational Nurse Training (LPN, LVN, Cert, Dipl, AAS) *37 students enrolled* • Mason/Masonry *8 students enrolled* • Massage Therapy/Therapeutic Massage *8 students enrolled* • Medical Radiologic Technology/Science—Radiation Therapist • Music History, Literature, and Theory *1 student enrolled* • Nail Technician/Specialist and Manicurist *1 student enrolled* • Nurse/Nursing Assistant/Aide and Patient Care Assistant • Quality Control and Safety Technologies/Technicians, Other • Science Technologies/Technicians, Other • Surgical Technology/Technologist *13 students enrolled* • Tool and Die Technology/Technician • Truck and Bus Driver/Commercial Vehicle Operation • Upholstery/Upholsterer *15 students enrolled* • Welding Technology/Welder *9 students enrolled*

STUDENT SERVICES Academic or career counseling, employment services for current students, placement services for program completers, remedial services.

Capps College

914 North McKenzie Street, Foley, AL 36535
http://medcareers.net/

CONTACT Allison Schmaeling, Corporate Director of Education
Telephone: 251-650-0800

GENERAL INFORMATION Private Institution. Founded 1996. **Total program enrollment:** 179. **Application fee:** $25.

PROGRAM(S) OFFERED
• **Medical Office Assistant/Specialist** *1060 hrs./$10,548* • **Medical/Clinical Assistant** *1060 hrs./$11,128* • **Pharmacy Technician/Assistant** *1020 hrs./ $10,548*

STUDENT SERVICES Academic or career counseling, employment services for current students, placement services for program completers.

Capps College

3590 Pleasant Valley Road, Mobile, AL 36609
http://medcareers.net/

CONTACT Allison Schmaeling, Corporate Director of Education
Telephone: 251-650-0800

GENERAL INFORMATION Private Institution. Founded 1984. **Total program enrollment:** 417. **Application fee:** $25.

PROGRAM(S) OFFERED
• **Cosmetology/Cosmetologist, General** *1500 hrs./$13,980* • **Dental Assisting/ Assistant** *1060 hrs./$10,392* • **Massage Therapy/Therapeutic Massage** *1060 hrs./$10,548* • **Medical Office Assistant/Specialist** *1060 hrs./$10,548* • **Medical/Clinical Assistant** *1060 hrs./$11,128* • **Pharmacy Technician/ Assistant** *1020 hrs./$13,185*

STUDENT SERVICES Academic or career counseling, employment services for current students, placement services for program completers.

Central Alabama Community College

PO Box 699, Alexander City, AL 35011-0699
http://www.cacc.cc.al.us/

CONTACT Stephen Franks, President
Telephone: 256-234-6346

GENERAL INFORMATION Public Institution. Founded 1965. **Accreditation:** Regional (SACS/CC). **Total program enrollment:** 1319.

PROGRAM(S) OFFERED
• **Administrative Assistant and Secretarial Science, General** *2 students enrolled* • **Automobile/Automotive Mechanics Technology/Technician** • **Business and Personal/Financial Services Marketing Operations** • **Business/Commerce, General** • **Cabinetmaking and Millwork/Millwright** • **Child Care and Support Services Management** • **Computer and Information Sciences, General** • **Cosmetology/Cosmetologist, General** *2 students enrolled* • **Criminal Justice/ Police Science** • **Drafting and Design Technology/Technician, General** • **Emergency Medical Technology/Technician (EMT Paramedic)** • **Environmental Control Technologies/Technicians, Other** • **Fire Services Administration** • **General Office Occupations and Clerical Services** *2 students enrolled* • **Heating, Air Conditioning, Ventilation and Refrigeration Maintenance Technology/Technician (HAC, HACR, HVAC, HVACR)** *2 students enrolled* • **Industrial Electronics Technology/Technician** *1 student enrolled* • **Licensed Practical/Vocational Nurse Training (LPN, LVN, Cert, Dipl, AAS)** *34 students enrolled* • **Machine Shop Technology/Assistant** *2 students enrolled* • **Manufacturing Technology/Technician** *2 students enrolled* • **Precision Metal Working, Other** *1 student enrolled* • **Welding Technology/Welder**

STUDENT SERVICES Academic or career counseling, remedial services.

Chattahoochee Valley Community College

2602 College Drive, Phenix City, AL 36869-7928
http://www.cv.edu/

CONTACT Dr. Laurel Blackwell, President
Telephone: 334-291-4900

GENERAL INFORMATION Public Institution. Founded 1974. **Accreditation:** Regional (SACS/CC). **Total program enrollment:** 874.

PROGRAM(S) OFFERED
• **Administrative Assistant and Secretarial Science, General** • **Child Care and Support Services Management** • **Criminal Justice/Police Science** • **Design and Visual Communications, General** *1 student enrolled* • **Emergency Medical Technology/Technician (EMT Paramedic)** *1 student enrolled* • **Fire Services Administration** *1 student enrolled* • **Licensed Practical/Vocational Nurse Training (LPN, LVN, Cert, Dipl, AAS)** *24 students enrolled* • **Medical/Clinical Assistant**

STUDENT SERVICES Academic or career counseling, remedial services.

Enterprise-Ozark Community College

PO Box 1300, Enterprise, AL 36331-1300
http://www.eocc.edu/

CONTACT Nancy Chandler, EdD, Interim President
Telephone: 334-347-2623

GENERAL INFORMATION Public Institution. Founded 1965. **Accreditation:** Regional (SACS/CC). **Total program enrollment:** 1375.

PROGRAM(S) OFFERED
• **Administrative Assistant and Secretarial Science, General** • **Aircraft Powerplant Technology/Technician** *31 students enrolled* • **Airframe Mechanics and Aircraft Maintenance Technology/Technician** *205 students enrolled* • **Avionics Maintenance Technology/Technician** • **Business Administration and Management, General** *4 students enrolled* • **Cartography** • **Child Care and Support Services Management** *6 students enrolled* • **Computer Technology/Computer Systems Technology** *3 students enrolled* • **Computer and Information Sciences, General** *1 student enrolled* • **Criminal Justice/Police Science** *1 student enrolled* • **Emergency Medical Technology/Technician (EMT Paramedic)** • **Health Information/Medical Records Technology/Technician** *2 students enrolled* • **Legal Assistant/Paralegal**

STUDENT SERVICES Academic or career counseling, daycare for children of students, employment services for current students, placement services for program completers, remedial services.

Gadsden State Community College

PO Box 227, Gadsden, AL 35902-0227
http://www.gadsdenstate.edu/

CONTACT Valerie Richardson, Acting President
Telephone: 256-549-8200

GENERAL INFORMATION Public Institution. Founded 1965. **Accreditation:** Regional (SACS/CC); emergency medical services (JRCEMTP); medical laboratory technology (NAACLS); radiologic technology: radiography (JRCERT). **Total program enrollment:** 3354.

PROGRAM(S) OFFERED
• **Accounting Technology/Technician and Bookkeeping** • **Administrative Assistant and Secretarial Science, General** *3 students enrolled* • **Aquaculture** *3 students enrolled* • **Autobody/Collision and Repair Technology/Technician** *4 students enrolled* • **Automobile/Automotive Mechanics Technology/Technician** *7 students enrolled* • **Carpentry/Carpenter** *19 students enrolled* • **Child Care and Support Services Management** • **Civil Engineering Technology/Technician** • **Computer and Information Sciences, General** • **Cosmetology/Cosmetologist, General** *17 students enrolled* • **Court Reporting/Court Reporter** *5 students enrolled* • **Diesel Mechanics Technology/Technician** *20 students enrolled* • **Drafting and Design Technology/Technician, General** *1 student enrolled* • **Electrical, Electronic and Communications Engineering Technology/Technician** • **Emergency Medical Technology/Technician (EMT Paramedic)** • **Furniture Design and Manufacturing** *8 students enrolled* • **General Office Occupations and Clerical Services** • **Heating, Air Conditioning and Refrigeration Technology/Technician (ACH/ACR/ACHR/HRAC/HVAC/AC Technology)**

• **Industrial Mechanics and Maintenance Technology** *15 students enrolled*
• **Licensed Practical/Vocational Nurse Training (LPN, LVN, Cert, Dipl, AAS)** *69 students enrolled* • **Mason/Masonry** • **Massage Therapy/Therapeutic Massage** *30 students enrolled* • **Nurse/Nursing Assistant/Aide and Patient Care Assistant** *5 students enrolled* • **Surgical Technology/Technologist** *18 students enrolled* • **Tool and Die Technology/Technician** *11 students enrolled* • **Welding Technology/Welder** *4 students enrolled*

STUDENT SERVICES Academic or career counseling, daycare for children of students, employment services for current students, placement services for program completers, remedial services.

George Corley Wallace State Community College

PO Box 2530, Selma, AL 36702-2530
http://www.wccs.edu/

CONTACT Dr. James M. Mitchell, President
Telephone: 334-876-9227

GENERAL INFORMATION Public Institution. Founded 1966. **Accreditation:** Regional (SACS/CC); practical nursing (NLN). **Total program enrollment:** 1118.

PROGRAM(S) OFFERED

• **Administrative Assistant and Secretarial Science, General** *21 students enrolled* • **Autobody/Collision and Repair Technology/Technician** *1 student enrolled* • **Computer and Information Sciences, General** • **Cosmetology and Related Personal Grooming Arts, Other** • **Cosmetology/Cosmetologist, General** *22 students enrolled* • **Criminal Justice/Police Science** • **Drafting and Design Technology/Technician, General** *6 students enrolled* • **Electrician** *9 students enrolled* • **Licensed Practical/Vocational Nurse Training (LPN, LVN, Cert, Dipl, AAS)** *14 students enrolled* • **Mason/Masonry** *15 students enrolled* • **Nurse/Nursing Assistant/Aide and Patient Care Assistant** *23 students enrolled* • **Welding Technology/Welder** *17 students enrolled*

STUDENT SERVICES Academic or career counseling, employment services for current students, placement services for program completers, remedial services.

George C. Wallace Community College

1141 Wallace Drive, Dothan, AL 36303-9234
http://www.wallace.edu/

CONTACT Linda C. Young, President
Telephone: 334-983-3521

GENERAL INFORMATION Public Institution. Founded 1949. **Accreditation:** Regional (SACS/CC); emergency medical services (JRCEMTP); medical assisting (AAMAE); physical therapy assisting (APTA); radiologic technology: radiography (JRCERT). **Total program enrollment:** 2123.

PROGRAM(S) OFFERED

• **Administrative Assistant and Secretarial Science, General** • **Aircraft Powerplant Technology/Technician** • **Airframe Mechanics and Aircraft Maintenance Technology/Technician** • **Autobody/Collision and Repair Technology/Technician** *1 student enrolled* • **Automotive Engineering Technology/Technician** • **Cabinetmaking and Millwork/Millwright** *14 students enrolled* • **Child Care and Support Services Management** *2 students enrolled* • **Computer and Information Sciences, General** • **Cosmetology/Cosmetologist, General** • **Drafting and Design Technology/Technician, General** *4 students enrolled* • **Electrician** *9 students enrolled* • **Emergency Medical Technology/Technician (EMT Paramedic)** *17 students enrolled* • **Heating, Air Conditioning and Refrigeration Technology/Technician (ACH/ACR/ACHR/HRAC/HVAC/AC Technology)** *8 students enrolled* • **Industrial Electronics Technology/Technician** • **Industrial Mechanics and Maintenance Technology** • **Licensed Practical/Vocational Nurse Training (LPN, LVN, Cert, Dipl, AAS)** *55 students enrolled* • **Mason/Masonry** • **Medical/Clinical Assistant** *8 students enrolled* • **Opticianry/Ophthalmic Dispensing Optician** • **Plumbing Technology/Plumber** *9 students enrolled* • **Respiratory Care Therapy/Therapist** • **Small Engine Mechanics and Repair Technology/Technician** *28 students enrolled* • **Tool and Die Technology/Technician** • **Welding Technology/Welder** *5 students enrolled*

STUDENT SERVICES Academic or career counseling, employment services for current students, placement services for program completers, remedial services.

H. Councill Trenholm State Technical College

1225 Air Base Boulevard, Montgomery, AL 36116-2699
http://www.trenholmtech.cc.al.us/

CONTACT Mr. Samuel Munnerlyn, President
Telephone: 334-420-4200

GENERAL INFORMATION Public Institution. Founded 1962. **Accreditation:** State accredited or approved. **Total program enrollment:** 759.

PROGRAM(S) OFFERED

• **Accounting Technology/Technician and Bookkeeping** • **Administrative Assistant and Secretarial Science, General** • **Apparel and Textile Manufacture** • **Autobody/Collision and Repair Technology/Technician** *1 student enrolled* • **Automotive Engineering Technology/Technician** *1 student enrolled* • **Building/Construction Finishing, Management, and Inspection, Other** *2 students enrolled* • **Cabinetmaking and Millwork/Millwright** *1 student enrolled* • **Carpentry/Carpenter** • **Child Care and Support Services Management** • **Computer and Information Sciences, General** • **Cosmetology and Related Personal Grooming Arts, Other** • **Cosmetology/Cosmetologist, General** *59 students enrolled* • **Culinary Arts/Chef Training** • **Dental Assisting/Assistant** • **Diesel Mechanics Technology/Technician** *2 students enrolled* • **Drafting and Design Technology/Technician, General** • **Electrician** *2 students enrolled* • **Emergency Medical Technology/Technician (EMT Paramedic)** *54 students enrolled* • **Graphic Communications, Other** *2 students enrolled* • **Heating, Air Conditioning and Refrigeration Technology/Technician (ACH/ACR/ACHR/HRAC/HVAC/AC Technology)** • **Home Furnishings and Equipment Installers** *2 students enrolled* • **Industrial Electronics Technology/Technician** • **Industrial Mechanics and Maintenance Technology** *7 students enrolled* • **Licensed Practical/Vocational Nurse Training (LPN, LVN, Cert, Dipl, AAS)** *19 students enrolled* • **Machine Tool Technology/Machinist** • **Massage Therapy/Therapeutic Massage** *12 students enrolled* • **Medical/Clinical Assistant** *2 students enrolled* • **Nurse/Nursing Assistant/Aide and Patient Care Assistant** *6 students enrolled* • **Ornamental Horticulture** • **Radio and Television Broadcasting Technology/Technician** *12 students enrolled* • **Tool and Die Technology/Technician** • **Truck and Bus Driver/Commercial Vehicle Operation** *71 students enrolled* • **Welding Technology/Welder** *20 students enrolled*

STUDENT SERVICES Academic or career counseling, employment services for current students, placement services for program completers, remedial services.

Herzing College

280 West Valley Avenue, Birmingham, AL 35209
http://www.herzing.edu/birmingham/

CONTACT Donald E. Lewis, President
Telephone: 205-916-2800

GENERAL INFORMATION Private Institution. Founded 1965. **Accreditation:** State accredited or approved. **Total program enrollment:** 163.

PROGRAM(S) OFFERED

• **Medical Insurance Specialist/Medical Biller** *2 students enrolled* • **Medical/Clinical Assistant** *17 students enrolled* • **Nursing, Other** *44 students enrolled*

STUDENT SERVICES Academic or career counseling, employment services for current students, placement services for program completers.

Huntsville Bible College

904 Oakwood Avenue, Huntsville, AL 35811-1632
http://www.hbc1.edu

CONTACT John L. Clay, President
Telephone: 256-539-0834

GENERAL INFORMATION Private Institution. **Total program enrollment:** 7. **Application fee:** $10.

PROGRAM(S) OFFERED

• **Bible/Biblical Studies** *6 students enrolled*

James H. Faulkner State Community College

1900 Highway 31 South, Bay Minette, AL 36507
http://www.faulknerstate.edu/

CONTACT Gary Branch, President
Telephone: 251-580-2100

GENERAL INFORMATION Public Institution. Founded 1965. **Accreditation:** Regional (SACS/CC); dental assisting (ADA); surgical technology (ARCST). **Total program enrollment:** 2221.

PROGRAM(S) OFFERED
• Child Care and Support Services Management • Commercial and Advertising Art *4 students enrolled* • Computer Technology/Computer Systems Technology • Computer and Information Sciences, General *2 students enrolled* • Dental Assisting/Assistant *19 students enrolled* • Emergency Medical Technology/Technician (EMT Paramedic) • Environmental Control Technologies/Technicians, Other • Hospitality Administration/Management, General • Landscaping and Groundskeeping *1 student enrolled* • Licensed Practical/Vocational Nurse Training (LPN, LVN, Cert, Dipl, AAS) *5 students enrolled* • Mechanic and Repair Technologies/Technicians, Other • Parks, Recreation and Leisure Facilities Management *1 student enrolled* • Real Estate • Surgical Technology/Technologist

STUDENT SERVICES Academic or career counseling, employment services for current students, placement services for program completers, remedial services.

Jefferson Davis Community College

PO Box 958, Brewton, AL 36427-0958
http://www.jdcc.edu/

CONTACT Dr. Susan McBride, President
Telephone: 251-867-4832

GENERAL INFORMATION Public Institution. Founded 1965. **Accreditation:** Regional (SACS/CC). **Total program enrollment:** 609.

PROGRAM(S) OFFERED
• Accounting Technology/Technician and Bookkeeping *10 students enrolled* • Administrative Assistant and Secretarial Science, General • Applied Horticulture/Horticultural Operations, General • Autobody/Collision and Repair Technology/Technician *10 students enrolled* • Automobile/Automotive Mechanics Technology/Technician *8 students enrolled* • Barbering/Barber *14 students enrolled* • Business and Personal/Financial Services Marketing Operations • Business/Commerce, General • Cabinetmaking and Millwork/Millwright *6 students enrolled* • Carpentry/Carpenter • Chemical Technology/Technician • Construction/Heavy Equipment/Earthmoving Equipment Operation • Drafting and Design Technology/Technician, General • Electrical/Electronics Equipment Installation and Repair, General • Electrician • Emergency Medical Technology/Technician (EMT Paramedic) • Fine Arts and Art Studies, Other • Fire Services Administration • Foodservice Systems Administration/Management *7 students enrolled* • Gunsmithing/Gunsmith • Heating, Air Conditioning and Refrigeration Technology/Technician (ACH/ACR/ACHR/HRAC/HVAC/AC Technology) *4 students enrolled* • Home Health Aide/Home Attendant • Locksmithing and Safe Repair • Mason/Masonry *20 students enrolled* • Non-Profit/Public/Organizational Management • Nurse/Nursing Assistant/Aide and Patient Care Assistant • Real Estate • Shoe, Boot and Leather Repair • Small Engine Mechanics and Repair Technology/Technician *11 students enrolled* • Upholstery/Upholsterer *3 students enrolled* • Welding Technology/Welder *17 students enrolled*

STUDENT SERVICES Academic or career counseling, employment services for current students, placement services for program completers, remedial services.

Jefferson State Community College

2601 Carson Road, Birmingham, AL 35215-3098
http://www.jeffstateonline.com/

CONTACT Judy Merritt, President
Telephone: 205-853-1200

GENERAL INFORMATION Public Institution. Founded 1965. **Accreditation:** Regional (SACS/CC); funeral service (ABFSE); medical laboratory

technology (NAACLS); physical therapy assisting (APTA); radiologic technology: radiography (JRCERT). **Total program enrollment:** 3209.

PROGRAM(S) OFFERED
• Accounting Technology/Technician and Bookkeeping *7 students enrolled* • Administrative Assistant and Secretarial Science, General *29 students enrolled* • Agricultural Business and Management, General *5 students enrolled* • Banking and Financial Support Services *5 students enrolled* • Business/Commerce, General *24 students enrolled* • Child Care and Support Services Management *16 students enrolled* • Computer and Information Sciences, General *25 students enrolled* • Construction Engineering Technology/Technician *8 students enrolled* • Criminal Justice/Police Science *9 students enrolled* • Emergency Medical Technology/Technician (EMT Paramedic) • Engineering Technology, General *14 students enrolled* • Fire Services Administration *7 students enrolled* • Funeral Service and Mortuary Science, General *23 students enrolled* • Hospitality Administration/Management, General *6 students enrolled* • Licensed Practical/Vocational Nurse Training (LPN, LVN, Cert, Dipl, AAS) *10 students enrolled* • Manufacturing Technology/Technician • Radio and Television Broadcasting Technology/Technician *4 students enrolled*

STUDENT SERVICES Academic or career counseling, employment services for current students, placement services for program completers, remedial services.

J. F. Drake State Technical College

3421 Meridian Street North, Huntsville, AL 35811-1584
http://www.drakestate.edu/

CONTACT Helen T. McAlpine, President
Telephone: 256-539-8161

GENERAL INFORMATION Public Institution. Founded 1961. **Accreditation:** State accredited or approved. **Total program enrollment:** 485.

PROGRAM(S) OFFERED
• Accounting Technology/Technician and Bookkeeping *5 students enrolled* • Administrative Assistant and Secretarial Science, General • Automobile/Automotive Mechanics Technology/Technician • Barbering/Barber *4 students enrolled* • Computer and Information Sciences, General *4 students enrolled* • Cosmetology/Cosmetologist, General *12 students enrolled* • Drafting and Design Technology/Technician, General *1 student enrolled* • Electrician • Graphic Communications, Other *1 student enrolled* • Heating, Air Conditioning, Ventilation and Refrigeration Maintenance Technology/Technician (HAC, HACR, HVAC, HVACR) • Industrial Electronics Technology/Technician *15 students enrolled* • Industrial Mechanics and Maintenance Technology *7 students enrolled* • Licensed Practical/Vocational Nurse Training (LPN, LVN, Cert, Dipl, AAS) *41 students enrolled* • Nurse/Nursing Assistant/Aide and Patient Care Assistant • Tool and Die Technology/Technician • Welding Technology/Welder *2 students enrolled*

STUDENT SERVICES Academic or career counseling, employment services for current students, placement services for program completers, remedial services.

Lawson State Community College

3060 Wilson Road, SW, Birmingham, AL 35221-1798
http://www.lawsonstate.edu/

CONTACT Perry W. Ward, President
Telephone: 205-925-2515

GENERAL INFORMATION Public Institution. Founded 1949. **Accreditation:** Regional (SACS/CC). **Total program enrollment:** 1908.

PROGRAM(S) OFFERED
• Accounting Technology/Technician and Bookkeeping • Administrative Assistant and Secretarial Science, General *8 students enrolled* • Apparel and Textile Manufacture • Autobody/Collision and Repair Technology/Technician *21 students enrolled* • Automobile/Automotive Mechanics Technology/Technician *3 students enrolled* • Barbering/Barber *12 students enrolled* • Building/Construction Finishing, Management, and Inspection, Other *4 students enrolled* • Business/Commerce, General *8 students enrolled* • Cabinetmaking and Millwork/Millwright • Carpentry/Carpenter *2 students enrolled* • Cartography *4 students enrolled* • Child Care and Support Services Management *9 students enrolled* • Commercial and Advertising Art *1 student enrolled* • Computer and Information Sciences, General • Cosmetology/Cosmetologist, General • Dental Assisting/Assistant *11 students enrolled*

• Diesel Mechanics Technology/Technician 2 *students enrolled* • Drafting and Design Technology/Technician, General 3 *students enrolled* • Electrical, Electronic and Communications Engineering Technology/Technician • Electrician 13 *students enrolled* • Emergency Medical Technology/Technician (EMT Paramedic) 3 *students enrolled* • Fashion Merchandising • Fire Services Administration 1 *student enrolled* • Foodservice Systems Administration/Management 9 *students enrolled* • Graphic and Printing Equipment Operator, General Production 2 *students enrolled* • Heating, Air Conditioning and Refrigeration Technology/Technician (ACH/ACR/ACHR/HRAC/HVAC/AC Technology) 5 *students enrolled* • Industrial Electronics Technology/Technician • Industrial Mechanics and Maintenance Technology 7 *students enrolled* • Licensed Practical/Vocational Nurse Training (LPN, LVN, Cert, Dipl, AAS) 35 *students enrolled* • Mason/Masonry 2 *students enrolled* • Ornamental Horticulture • Plumbing Technology/Plumber 9 *students enrolled* • Radio and Television Broadcasting Technology/Technician 4 *students enrolled* • Welding Technology/Welder 6 *students enrolled*

STUDENT SERVICES Academic or career counseling, employment services for current students, placement services for program completers, remedial services.

Lurleen B. Wallace Community College

PO Box 1418, Andalusia, AL 36420-1418
http://www.lbwcc.edu/

CONTACT Mr. L. Wayne Bennett, Acting President
Telephone: 334-222-6591

GENERAL INFORMATION Public Institution. Founded 1969. **Accreditation:** Regional (SACS/CC); emergency medical services (JRCEMTP). **Total program enrollment:** 962.

PROGRAM(S) OFFERED
• Accounting Technology/Technician and Bookkeeping • Administrative Assistant and Secretarial Science, General 12 *students enrolled* • Automobile/Automotive Mechanics Technology/Technician • Child Care and Support Services Management 1 *student enrolled* • Computer and Information Sciences, General • Cosmetology/Cosmetologist, General 20 *students enrolled* • Diesel Mechanics Technology/Technician 4 *students enrolled* • Drafting and Design Technology/Technician, General 1 *student enrolled* • Emergency Medical Technology/Technician (EMT Paramedic) 1 *student enrolled* • Forestry Technology/Technician • Heating, Air Conditioning and Refrigeration Technology/Technician (ACH/ACR/HRAC/HVAC/AC Technology) • Industrial Electronics Technology/Technician • Licensed Practical/Vocational Nurse Training (LPN, LVN, Cert, Dipl, AAS) 44 *students enrolled* • Massage Therapy/Therapeutic Massage 12 *students enrolled* • Surgical Technology/Technologist 4 *students enrolled* • Upholstery/Upholsterer 12 *students enrolled* • Welding Technology/Welder

STUDENT SERVICES Academic or career counseling, daycare for children of students, employment services for current students, placement services for program completers, remedial services.

Mimi's Beauty Academy of Cosmetology

2115 Johnathan Drive, Huntsville, AL 35810
http://www.mimisbeautyacademy.info

CONTACT Sabrina Jenkins, CEO
Telephone: 256-859-1572

GENERAL INFORMATION Private Institution. **Total program enrollment:** 23. **Application fee:** $50.

PROGRAM(S) OFFERED
• Cosmetology, Barber/Styling, and Nail Instructor 650 *hrs./*$2645 • Cosmetology/Cosmetologist, General 1500 *hrs./*$9250 • Nail Technician/Specialist and Manicurist 750 *hrs./*$2745

STUDENT SERVICES Academic or career counseling, employment services for current students.

Northeast Alabama Community College

PO Box 159, Rainsville, AL 35986-0159
http://www.nacc.edu/

CONTACT J. David Campbell, President
Telephone: 205-638-4418 Ext. 234

GENERAL INFORMATION Public Institution. Founded 1963. **Accreditation:** Regional (SACS/CC); emergency medical services (JRCEMTP). **Total program enrollment:** 1422.

PROGRAM(S) OFFERED
• Child Care and Support Services Management 9 *students enrolled* • Cosmetology/Cosmetologist, General 7 *students enrolled* • Drafting and Design Technology/Technician, General 7 *students enrolled* • Emergency Medical Technology/Technician (EMT Paramedic) 20 *students enrolled* • Industrial Electronics Technology/Technician 19 *students enrolled* • Licensed Practical/Vocational Nurse Training (LPN, LVN, Cert, Dipl, AAS) 22 *students enrolled* • Medical/Clinical Assistant 20 *students enrolled*

STUDENT SERVICES Academic or career counseling, employment services for current students, placement services for program completers, remedial services.

Northwest-Shoals Community College

PO Box 2545, Muscle Shoals, AL 35662
http://www.nwscc.edu/

CONTACT Humphrey Lee, President
Telephone: 256-331-5200

GENERAL INFORMATION Public Institution. Founded 1963. **Accreditation:** Regional (SACS/CC). **Total program enrollment:** 2077.

PROGRAM(S) OFFERED
• Accounting Technology/Technician and Bookkeeping 3 *students enrolled* • Administrative Assistant and Secretarial Science, General 2 *students enrolled* • Autobody/Collision and Repair Technology/Technician 3 *students enrolled* • Automobile/Automotive Mechanics Technology/Technician 3 *students enrolled* • Business Administration and Management, General 1 *student enrolled* • Cabinetmaking and Millwork/Millwright 10 *students enrolled* • Carpentry/Carpenter 12 *students enrolled* • Chemical Technology/Technician 1 *student enrolled* • Child Care and Support Services Management 5 *students enrolled* • Computer and Information Sciences, General 8 *students enrolled* • Cosmetology and Related Personal Grooming Arts, Other 1 *student enrolled* • Cosmetology/Cosmetologist, General 10 *students enrolled* • Drafting and Design Technology/Technician, General 6 *students enrolled* • Electrician 5 *students enrolled* • Emergency Medical Technology/Technician (EMT Paramedic) 2 *students enrolled* • Energy Management and Systems Technology/Technician • Environmental Engineering Technology/Environmental Technology • Fire Services Administration 1 *student enrolled* • Heating, Air Conditioning and Refrigeration Technology/Technician (ACH/ACR/ACHR/HRAC/HVAC/AC Technology) 4 *students enrolled* • Industrial Radiologic Technology/Technician • Licensed Practical/Vocational Nurse Training (LPN, LVN, Cert, Dipl, AAS) 20 *students enrolled* • Machine Shop Technology/Assistant 2 *students enrolled* • Water Quality and Wastewater Treatment Management and Recycling Technology/Technician 1 *student enrolled* • Welding Technology/Welder 13 *students enrolled*

STUDENT SERVICES Academic or career counseling, daycare for children of students, employment services for current students, placement services for program completers, remedial services.

Prince Institute of Professional Studies

7735 Atlanta Highway, Montgomery, AL 36117-4231
http://www.princeinstitute.edu/

CONTACT Patricia L. Hill, Director
Telephone: 334-271-1670

GENERAL INFORMATION Private Institution. Founded 1976. **Accreditation:** State accredited or approved. **Total program enrollment:** 76. **Application fee:** $100.

Prince Institute of Professional Studies (continued)
PROGRAM(S) OFFERED
• **Legal Support Services, Other**

STUDENT SERVICES Academic or career counseling, placement services for program completers.

Reid State Technical College

PO Box 588, Evergreen, AL 36401-0588
http://www.rstc.edu/

CONTACT Dr. Douglas M. Littles, President
Telephone: 251-578-1313

GENERAL INFORMATION Public Institution. Founded 1966. **Accreditation:** State accredited or approved. **Total program enrollment:** 345.

PROGRAM(S) OFFERED
• **Administrative Assistant and Secretarial Science, General** • **Autobody/Collision and Repair Technology/Technician** 1 *student enrolled* • **Carpentry/Carpenter** 1 *student enrolled* • **Child Care and Support Services Management** 10 *students enrolled* • **Computer and Information Sciences, General** • **Cosmetology and Related Personal Grooming Arts, Other** • **Cosmetology/Cosmetologist, General** • **Industrial Electronics Technology/Technician** • **Licensed Practical/Vocational Nurse Training (LPN, LVN, Cert, Dipl, AAS)** 35 *students enrolled* • **Nurse/Nursing Assistant/Aide and Patient Care Assistant** 22 *students enrolled* • **Truck and Bus Driver/Commercial Vehicle Operation** 17 *students enrolled* • **Welding Technology/Welder** 3 *students enrolled*

STUDENT SERVICES Academic or career counseling, placement services for program completers, remedial services.

Remington College–Mobile Campus

828 Downtowner Loop West, Mobile, AL 36609-5404
http://www.remingtoncollege.edu/

CONTACT Stephen M. Backman, Campus President
Telephone: 251-343-8200

GENERAL INFORMATION Private Institution. **Accreditation:** State accredited or approved. **Total program enrollment:** 540. **Application fee:** $50.

PROGRAM(S) OFFERED
• **Medical Insurance Coding Specialist/Coder** 59 *students enrolled* • **Medical/Clinical Assistant** 97 *students enrolled* • **Pharmacy Technician/Assistant** 36 *students enrolled*

STUDENT SERVICES Academic or career counseling, employment services for current students, placement services for program completers.

Samford University

800 Lakeshore Drive, Birmingham, AL 35229
http://www.samford.edu/

CONTACT Andrew Westmoreland, President
Telephone: 205-726-2011

GENERAL INFORMATION Private Institution. Founded 1841. **Accreditation:** Regional (SACS/CC); athletic training (JRCAT); home economics (AAFCS); interior design: professional (CIDA); music (NASM). **Total program enrollment:** 3985. **Application fee:** $35.

PROGRAM(S) OFFERED
• **Legal Assistant/Paralegal** 12 *students enrolled*

STUDENT SERVICES Academic or career counseling, employment services for current students, placement services for program completers.

Shelton State Community College

9500 Old Greensboro Road, Tuscaloosa, AL 35405-8522
http://www.sheltonstate.edu/

CONTACT Dr. Mark A. Heinrich, President
Telephone: 205-391-2347

GENERAL INFORMATION Public Institution. Founded 1979. **Accreditation:** Regional (SACS/CC). **Total program enrollment:** 3390.

PROGRAM(S) OFFERED
• **Administrative Assistant and Secretarial Science, General** 6 *students enrolled* • **Adult Development and Aging** • **Autobody/Collision and Repair Technology/Technician** 8 *students enrolled* • **Automobile/Automotive Mechanics Technology/Technician** 2 *students enrolled* • **Barbering/Barber** • **Carpentry/Carpenter** 4 *students enrolled* • **Child Care and Support Services Management** • **Commercial and Advertising Art** 3 *students enrolled* • **Computer and Information Sciences, General** • **Construction/Heavy Equipment/Earthmoving Equipment Operation** 6 *students enrolled* • **Cosmetology and Related Personal Grooming Arts, Other** 1 *student enrolled* • **Cosmetology/Cosmetologist, General** • **Diesel Mechanics Technology/Technician** 1 *student enrolled* • **Drafting and Design Technology/Technician, General** • **Electrician** 1 *student enrolled* • **Emergency Medical Technology/Technician (EMT Paramedic)** • **Fire Services Administration** • **Foodservice Systems Administration/Management** • **Health and Physical Education/Fitness, Other** 9 *students enrolled* • **Heating, Air Conditioning and Refrigeration Technology/Technician (ACH/ACR/ACHR/HRAC/HVAC/AC Technology)** 1 *student enrolled* • **Industrial Electronics Technology/Technician** • **Industrial Mechanics and Maintenance Technology** • **Legal Assistant/Paralegal** 1 *student enrolled* • **Licensed Practical/Vocational Nurse Training (LPN, LVN, Cert, Dipl, AAS)** 59 *students enrolled* • **Nail Technician/Specialist and Manicurist** • **Nurse/Nursing Assistant/Aide and Patient Care Assistant** • **Precision Metal Working, Other** 1 *student enrolled* • **Tool and Die Technology/Technician** • **Welding Technology/Welder** 1 *student enrolled*

STUDENT SERVICES Academic or career counseling, employment services for current students, placement services for program completers, remedial services.

Snead State Community College

220 N Walnut Street, PO Box 734, Boaz, AL 35957-0734
http://www.snead.edu/

CONTACT Dr. Robert J. Exley, President
Telephone: 256-593-5120

GENERAL INFORMATION Public Institution. Founded 1898. **Accreditation:** Regional (SACS/CC). **Total program enrollment:** 1169.

PROGRAM(S) OFFERED
• **Accounting Technology/Technician and Bookkeeping** 3 *students enrolled* • **Administrative Assistant and Secretarial Science, General** • **Child Care and Support Services Management** 3 *students enrolled* • **Cosmetology/Cosmetologist, General** • **Licensed Practical/Vocational Nurse Training (LPN, LVN, Cert, Dipl, AAS)** 10 *students enrolled* • **Medical Transcription/Transcriptionist** 6 *students enrolled*

STUDENT SERVICES Academic or career counseling, employment services for current students, placement services for program completers, remedial services.

Southeastern Bible College

2545 Valleydale Road, Birmingham, AL 35244-2083
http://www.sebc.edu/

CONTACT Dr. Don Hawkins, President
Telephone: 205-970-9200

GENERAL INFORMATION Private Institution. Founded 1935. **Accreditation:** State accredited or approved. **Total program enrollment:** 162. **Application fee:** $30.

PROGRAM(S) OFFERED
• **Bible/Biblical Studies** 1 *student enrolled*

STUDENT SERVICES Academic or career counseling, employment services for current students, remedial services.

Southeastern School of Cosmetology

26b Phillips Drive, Midfield, AL 35228
http://www.southeasternschoolofcosmetology.com/

CONTACT Tracy Cunningham, Chief Administrative Officer
Telephone: 205-323-1011

GENERAL INFORMATION Private Institution. **Total program enrollment:** 93. **Application fee:** $25.

PROGRAM(S) OFFERED
• **Cosmetology/Cosmetologist, General** *1500 hrs./$7000*

STUDENT SERVICES Academic or career counseling, placement services for program completers.

Southern Union State Community College

PO Box 1000, Roberts Street, Wadley, AL 36276
http://www.suscc.cc.al.us/

CONTACT Amelia Pearson, Interim President
Telephone: 256-395-2211

GENERAL INFORMATION Public Institution. Founded 1922. **Accreditation:** Regional (SACS/CC); emergency medical services (JRCEMTP); radiologic technology: radiography (JRCERT). **Total program enrollment:** 3202.

PROGRAM(S) OFFERED
• **Administrative Assistant and Secretarial Science, General** *1 student enrolled* • **Autobody/Collision and Repair Technology/Technician** *2 students enrolled* • **Automobile/Automotive Mechanics Technology/Technician** *1 student enrolled* • **Business/Commerce, General** *2 students enrolled* • **Cabinetmaking and Millwork/Millwright** • **Child Care and Support Services Management** *1 student enrolled* • **Computer and Information Sciences, General** *1 student enrolled* • **Cosmetology/Cosmetologist, General** *22 students enrolled* • **Drafting and Design Technology/Technician, General** *7 students enrolled* • **Emergency Medical Technology/Technician (EMT Paramedic)** *2 students enrolled* • **Fire Services Administration** • **Heating, Air Conditioning, Ventilation and Refrigeration Maintenance Technology/Technician (HAC, HACR, HVAC, HVACR)** *8 students enrolled* • **Home Health Aide/Home Attendant** • **Industrial Electronics Technology/Technician** *8 students enrolled* • **Industrial Mechanics and Maintenance Technology** *6 students enrolled* • **Licensed Practical/Vocational Nurse Training (LPN, LVN, Cert, Dipl, AAS)** *17 students enrolled* • **Machine Shop Technology/Assistant** *2 students enrolled* • **Massage Therapy/Therapeutic Massage** *16 students enrolled* • **Medical Radiologic Technology/Science—Radiation Therapist** • **Medical Transcription/Transcriptionist** • **Surgical Technology/Technologist** *18 students enrolled* • **Upholstery/Upholsterer** • **Welding Technology/Welder** *15 students enrolled*

STUDENT SERVICES Academic or career counseling, employment services for current students, placement services for program completers, remedial services.

Spring Hill College

4000 Dauphin Street, Mobile, AL 36608-1791
http://www.shc.edu/

CONTACT Gregory F. Lucey, SJ, President
Telephone: 251-380-4000

GENERAL INFORMATION Private Institution. Founded 1830. **Accreditation:** Regional (SACS/CC). **Total program enrollment:** 1185. **Application fee:** $25.

PROGRAM(S) OFFERED
• **Computer and Information Sciences, General** • **Theology/Theological Studies** *1 student enrolled*

STUDENT SERVICES Academic or career counseling, employment services for current students, placement services for program completers.

United States Sports Academy

One Academy Drive, Daphne, AL 36526-7055
http://www.ussa.edu/

CONTACT Dr. Thomas P. Rosandich, President/CEO
Telephone: 251-626-3303

GENERAL INFORMATION Private Institution. Founded 1972. **Accreditation:** Regional (SACS/CC). **Total program enrollment:** 148. **Application fee:** $50.

STUDENT SERVICES Academic or career counseling.

The University of Alabama at Birmingham

1530 3rd Avenue South, Birmingham, AL 35294
http://www.uab.edu/

CONTACT Carol Z. Garrison, President
Telephone: 205-934-4011

GENERAL INFORMATION Public Institution. Founded 1969. **Accreditation:** Regional (SACS/CC); art and design (NASAD); cytotechnology (ASC); dietetics: postbaccalaureate internship (ADtA/CAADE); emergency medical services (JRCEMTP); engineering-related programs (ABET/RAC); health information administration (AHIMA); medical technology (NAACLS); music (NASM); nuclear medicine technology (JRCNMT); radiologic technology: radiation therapy technology (JRCERT). **Total program enrollment:** 11097. **Application fee:** $30.

PROGRAM(S) OFFERED
• **Dental Assisting/Assistant** *21 students enrolled*

STUDENT SERVICES Academic or career counseling, employment services for current students, placement services for program completers, remedial services.

University of Alabama System

401 Queen City Avenue, Tuscaloosa, AL 35401-1569

CONTACT Malcolm Portera, Chancellor
Telephone: 205-348-9731

GENERAL INFORMATION Public Institution.

University of South Alabama

307 University Boulevard, Mobile, AL 36688-0002
http://www.southalabama.edu/

CONTACT V. Gordon Moulton, President
Telephone: 251-460-6101

GENERAL INFORMATION Public Institution. Founded 1963. **Accreditation:** Regional (SACS/CC); art and design (NASAD); audiology (ASHA); computer science (ABET/CSAC); emergency medical services (JRCEMTP); medical technology (NAACLS); music (NASM); speech-language pathology (ASHA). **Total program enrollment:** 10398. **Application fee:** $35.

PROGRAM(S) OFFERED
• **Emergency Medical Technology/Technician (EMT Paramedic)** *35 students enrolled*

STUDENT SERVICES Academic or career counseling, employment services for current students, placement services for program completers, remedial services.

Virginia College at Birmingham

65 Bagby Drive, Birmingham, AL 35209
http://www.vc.edu/

CONTACT Mr. Mike Largent, President
Telephone: 205-802-1200

GENERAL INFORMATION Private Institution. Founded 1989. **Accreditation:** State accredited or approved. **Total program enrollment:** 3142. **Application fee:** $100.

PROGRAM(S) OFFERED
• **Accounting** 5 *students enrolled* • **Administrative Assistant and Secretarial Science, General** 8 *students enrolled* • **Athletic Training/Trainer** 5 *students enrolled* • **Computer Systems Networking and Telecommunications** • **Cooking and Related Culinary Arts, General** 37 *students enrolled* • **Medical Insurance Specialist/Medical Biller** 1 *student enrolled* • **Medical Office Assistant/Specialist** 36 *students enrolled* • **Pharmacy Technician/Assistant** 18 *students enrolled*

STUDENT SERVICES Academic or career counseling, employment services for current students, placement services for program completers, remedial services.

Virginia College at Huntsville

2800-A Bob Wallace Avenue, Huntsville, AL 35805
http://www.vc.edu/

CONTACT James D. Foster, President
Telephone: 256-533-7387

GENERAL INFORMATION Private Institution. Founded 1989. **Accreditation:** State accredited or approved. **Total program enrollment:** 511. **Application fee:** $100.

PROGRAM(S) OFFERED
• **Accounting Technology/Technician and Bookkeeping** 2 *students enrolled* • **Administrative Assistant and Secretarial Science, General** 8 *students enrolled* • **Computer Systems Networking and Telecommunications** 1 *student enrolled* • **Cosmetology/Cosmetologist, General** 62 *students enrolled* • **Medical Insurance Coding Specialist/Coder** 17 *students enrolled* • **Medical/Clinical Assistant** 32 *students enrolled* • **Pharmacy Technician/Assistant** 11 *students enrolled*

STUDENT SERVICES Employment services for current students, placement services for program completers, remedial services.

Virginia College at Mobile

5901 Airport Boulevard, Mobile, AL 36608-3156
http://www.vc.edu/

CONTACT Eric Berrios, President
Telephone: 251-343-7227

GENERAL INFORMATION Private Institution. **Total program enrollment:** 608. **Application fee:** $100.

PROGRAM(S) OFFERED
• **Accounting and Related Services, Other** 1 *student enrolled* • **Administrative Assistant and Secretarial Science, General** 8 *students enrolled* • **Criminal Justice/Law Enforcement Administration** • **Human Resources Management/Personnel Administration, General** • **Legal Assistant/Paralegal** • **Medical Insurance Coding Specialist/Coder** 8 *students enrolled* • **Medical/Clinical Assistant** 11 *students enrolled* • **Pharmacy Technician/Assistant** 11 *students enrolled* • **Surgical Technology/Technologist** 5 *students enrolled*

STUDENT SERVICES Academic or career counseling, employment services for current students, placement services for program completers, remedial services.

Wallace State Community College

PO Box 2000, 801 Main Street, Hanceville, AL 35077-2000
http://www.wallacestate.edu/

CONTACT Vicki Hawsey, President
Telephone: 256-352-8000

GENERAL INFORMATION Public Institution. Founded 1966. **Accreditation:** Regional (SACS/CC); dental assisting (ADA); dental hygiene (ADA); diagnostic medical sonography (JRCEDMS); emergency medical services (JRCEMTP); health information technology (AHIMA); medical assisting (AAMAE); medical laboratory technology (NAACLS); physical therapy assisting (APTA); radiologic technology: radiography (JRCERT). **Total program enrollment:** 3144.

PROGRAM(S) OFFERED
• **Agricultural Production Operations, General** 3 *students enrolled* • **Allied Health Diagnostic, Intervention, and Treatment Professions, Other** 22 *students enrolled* • **Autobody/Collision and Repair Technology/Technician** 8 *students enrolled* • **Automobile/Automotive Mechanics Technology/Technician** 9 *students enrolled* • **Child Care and Support Services Management** 2 *students enrolled* • **Cosmetology/Cosmetologist, General** 16 *students enrolled* • **Dental Assisting/Assistant** 9 *students enrolled* • **Diesel Mechanics Technology/Technician** 5 *students enrolled* • **Drafting and Design Technology/Technician, General** 1 *student enrolled* • **Emergency Medical Technology/Technician (EMT Paramedic)** 56 *students enrolled* • **Foodservice Systems Administration/Management** 6 *students enrolled* • **Health Information/Medical Records Technology/Technician** 5 *students enrolled* • **Heating, Air Conditioning, Ventilation and Refrigeration Maintenance Technology/Technician (HAC, HACR, HVAC, HVACR)** 7 *students enrolled* • **Industrial Electronics Technology/Technician** 1 *student enrolled* • **Licensed Practical/Vocational Nurse Training (LPN, LVN, Cert, Dipl, AAS)** 30 *students enrolled* • **Manufacturing Technology/Technician** 1 *student enrolled* • **Medical Transcription/Transcriptionist** 21 *students enrolled* • **Pharmacy Technician/Assistant** 4 *students enrolled* • **Precision Metal Working, Other** 9 *students enrolled* • **Tool and Die Technology/Technician** 5 *students enrolled* • **Upholstery/Upholsterer** 3 *students enrolled* • **Welding Technology/Welder** 10 *students enrolled*

STUDENT SERVICES Academic or career counseling, employment services for current students, placement services for program completers, remedial services.

CONNECTICUT

Academy Di Capelli—School of Cosmetology

950 Yale Avenue, Unit 20, Wallingford, CT 06492
http://www.academydicapelli.com

CONTACT Bradford Kelley, Director of Academic Affairs
Telephone: 203-294-9496 Ext. 0

GENERAL INFORMATION Private Institution. **Total program enrollment:** 61. **Application fee:** $100.

PROGRAM(S) OFFERED
• **Aesthetician/Esthetician and Skin Care Specialist** 300 *hrs./*$3800
• **Cosmetology, Barber/Styling, and Nail Instructor** 1500 *hrs./*$15,500
• **Cosmetology/Cosmetologist, General** 27 *students enrolled*

STUDENT SERVICES Academic or career counseling, employment services for current students, placement services for program completers.

Albert School

63 Pennsylvania Avenue, Niantic, CT 06357-3224
http://www.thealbertschool.com/

CONTACT Stuart L. Arnheim, President/CEO
Telephone: 860-739-2466

GENERAL INFORMATION Private Institution. **Total program enrollment:** 69. **Application fee:** $50.

PROGRAM(S) OFFERED
• **Aesthetician/Esthetician and Skin Care Specialist** *600 hrs./$6785*
• **Cosmetology/Cosmetologist, General** *1500 hrs./$17,700*

STUDENT SERVICES Academic or career counseling, employment services for current students, placement services for program completers.

Albertus Magnus College

700 Prospect Street, New Haven, CT 06511-1189
http://www.albertus.edu/

CONTACT Julia McNamara, President
Telephone: 203-773-8550

GENERAL INFORMATION Private Institution. Founded 1925. **Accreditation:** Regional (NEASC/NEASCCIHE). **Total program enrollment:** 1861. **Application fee:** $35.

PROGRAM(S) OFFERED
• **Business/Managerial Economics** *3 students enrolled* • **Management Information Systems, General** *1 student enrolled*

STUDENT SERVICES Academic or career counseling, placement services for program completers, remedial services.

Asnuntuck Community College

170 Elm Street, Enfield, CT 06082-3800
http://www.acc.commnet.edu/

CONTACT Martha McLeod, President
Telephone: 860-253-3000

GENERAL INFORMATION Public Institution. Founded 1972. **Accreditation:** Regional (NEASC/NEASCCIHE). **Total program enrollment:** 642. **Application fee:** $20.

PROGRAM(S) OFFERED
• **Accounting Technology/Technician and Bookkeeping** *7 students enrolled* • **Administrative Assistant and Secretarial Science, General** *6 students enrolled* • **Business, Management, Marketing, and Related Support Services, Other** *30 students enrolled* • **Child Care and Support Services Management** *6 students enrolled* • **Commercial and Advertising Art** *1 student enrolled* • **Corrections and Criminal Justice, Other** • **Criminal Justice/Police Science** • **Engineering Technology, General** *110 students enrolled* • **Health Services/Allied Health/Health Sciences, General** *1 student enrolled* • **Industrial Technology/Technician** • **Management Information Systems, General** *5 students enrolled* • **Psychiatric/Mental Health Services Technician** *4 students enrolled* • **Radio and Television Broadcasting Technology/Technician**

STUDENT SERVICES Academic or career counseling, daycare for children of students, employment services for current students, placement services for program completers, remedial services.

Baran Institute of Technology

611 Day Hill Road, Windsor, CT 06095
http://www.baraninstitute.com/

CONTACT Executive Director
Telephone: 860-627-4300

GENERAL INFORMATION Private Institution. **Total program enrollment:** 1073.

PROGRAM(S) OFFERED
• **Autobody/Collision and Repair Technology/Technician** *79 hrs./$25,000*
• **Automobile/Automotive Mechanics Technology/Technician** *88 hrs./$26,476*
• **Diesel Mechanics Technology/Technician** *86 hrs./$27,100* • **Electrical/Electronics Equipment Installation and Repair, General** *38 students enrolled*
• **Electrician** *78 hrs./$24,900* • **Heating, Air Conditioning, Ventilation and Refrigeration Maintenance Technology/Technician (HAC, HACR, HVAC, HVACR)** *106 hrs./$24,300* • **Motorcycle Maintenance and Repair Technology/Technician** *36 students enrolled* • **Truck and Bus Driver/Commercial Vehicle Operation** *56 students enrolled* • **Welding Technology/Welder** *68 hrs./$24,600*

STUDENT SERVICES Employment services for current students, placement services for program completers, remedial services.

Branford Academy of Hair & Cosmetology

4 Brushy Plains Road, Suite 115, Branford, CT 06405

CONTACT Diana Leonardi-Discher, Head of School
Telephone: 203-315-2985

GENERAL INFORMATION Private Institution. **Total program enrollment:** 27. **Application fee:** $150.

PROGRAM(S) OFFERED
• **Cosmetology/Cosmetologist, General** *1500 hrs./$19,900*

STUDENT SERVICES Academic or career counseling, placement services for program completers.

Branford Hall Career Institute–Branford Campus

9 Business Park Drive, Branford, CT 06405
http://www.branfordhall.com/

CONTACT Joe Chadwick, School Director
Telephone: 800-959-7599

GENERAL INFORMATION Private Institution. Founded 1965. **Total program enrollment:** 327. **Application fee:** $75.

PROGRAM(S) OFFERED
• **Computer Systems Networking and Telecommunications** *3 students enrolled*
• **Legal Assistant/Paralegal** *47 hrs./$14,240* • **Massage Therapy/Therapeutic Massage** *52 hrs./$14,290* • **Medical Insurance Specialist/Medical Biller** *48 hrs./$14,240* • **Medical/Clinical Assistant** *46 hrs./$15,090*

STUDENT SERVICES Academic or career counseling, placement services for program completers.

Branford Hall Career Institute–Southington Campus

35 North Main Street, Southington, CT 06459
http://www.branfordhall.com/

CONTACT Frank Bonilla, School Director
Telephone: 800-959-7599

GENERAL INFORMATION Private Institution. **Total program enrollment:** 289. **Application fee:** $75.

PROGRAM(S) OFFERED
• **Computer Systems Networking and Telecommunications** *34 students enrolled*
• **Legal Assistant/Paralegal** *47 hrs./$14,240* • **Massage Therapy/Therapeutic Massage** *52 hrs./$15,240* • **Medical Insurance Specialist/Medical Biller** *48 hrs./$14,240* • **Medical/Clinical Assistant** *46 hrs./$15,090*

STUDENT SERVICES Academic or career counseling, placement services for program completers.

Branford Hall Career Institute–Windsor Campus

995 Day Hill Road, Windsor, CT 06095
http://www.branfordhall.com/

CONTACT Jim Troisi, School Director
Telephone: 800-959-7599

GENERAL INFORMATION Private Institution. **Total program enrollment:** 283. **Application fee:** $75.

PROGRAM(S) OFFERED
● **Computer Technology/Computer Systems Technology** *33 students enrolled* ● **Legal Assistant/Paralegal** *47 hrs./$14,240* ● **Massage Therapy/Therapeutic Massage** *52 hrs./$14,290* ● **Medical Insurance Specialist/Medical Biller** *48 hrs./$14,240* ● **Medical/Clinical Assistant** *44 hrs./$15,090*

STUDENT SERVICES Academic or career counseling, placement services for program completers.

Briarwood College

2279 Mount Vernon Road, Southington, CT 06489-1057
http://www.briarwood.edu/

CONTACT Lynn Brooks, President
Telephone: 860-628-4751

GENERAL INFORMATION Private Institution. Founded 1966. **Accreditation:** Regional (NEASC/CVTCI); dental assisting (ADA); funeral service (ABFSE); health information technology (AHIMA); medical assisting (AAMAE). **Total program enrollment:** 450. **Application fee:** $25.

PROGRAM(S) OFFERED
● **Child Care and Support Services Management** ● **Dental Assisting/Assistant** *6 students enrolled* ● **Executive Assistant/Executive Secretary** ● **Health Information/Medical Records Technology/Technician** *2 students enrolled* ● **Legal Administrative Assistant/Secretary** *1 student enrolled* ● **Medical Administrative/Executive Assistant and Medical Secretary** ● **Medical Transcription/Transcriptionist** ● **Medical/Clinical Assistant** *1 student enrolled* ● **Nuclear Medical Technology/Technologist** ● **Pharmacy Technician/Assistant**

STUDENT SERVICES Academic or career counseling, employment services for current students, placement services for program completers, remedial services.

Bridgeport Hospital School of Nursing

200 Mill Hill Avenue, Bridgeport, CT 06610
http://www.bhson.com/

CONTACT Hope Juckel Regan, Vice President
Telephone: 203-384-3205

GENERAL INFORMATION Private Institution. **Total program enrollment:** 114. **Application fee:** $25.

PROGRAM(S) OFFERED
● **Nursing—Registered Nurse Training (RN, ASN, BSN, MSN)** *105 students enrolled* ● **Surgical Technology/Technologist** *7 students enrolled*

STUDENT SERVICES Academic or career counseling, daycare for children of students, employment services for current students, placement services for program completers, remedial services.

Brio Academy of Cosmetology–East Hartford

1000 Main Street, East Hartford, CT 06108
http://www.brioacademy.com/

CONTACT Stuart L. Arnheim, President/CEO
Telephone: 860-528-7178 Ext. 100

GENERAL INFORMATION Private Institution. Founded 1923. **Total program enrollment:** 72. **Application fee:** $50.

PROGRAM(S) OFFERED
● **Aesthetician/Esthetician and Skin Care Specialist** *600 hrs./$6785* ● **Cosmetology/Cosmetologist, General** *1500 hrs./$17,850*

STUDENT SERVICES Academic or career counseling, employment services for current students, placement services for program completers.

Brio Academy of Cosmetology–Fairfield

675 Kings Highway East, Fairfield, CT 06825
http://www.brioacademy.com/

CONTACT Stuart L. Arnheim, President/CEO
Telephone: 203-331-0852 Ext. 100

GENERAL INFORMATION Private Institution. **Total program enrollment:** 112. **Application fee:** $50.

PROGRAM(S) OFFERED
● **Aesthetician/Esthetician and Skin Care Specialist** *600 hrs./$6785* ● **Cosmetology/Cosmetologist, General** *1500 hrs./$17,700*

STUDENT SERVICES Academic or career counseling, employment services for current students, placement services for program completers.

Brio Academy of Cosmetology–Meriden

1231 East Main Street, Meriden, CT 06450
http://brioacademy.com/

CONTACT Stuart L. Arnheim, President
Telephone: 203-237-6683 Ext. 13

GENERAL INFORMATION Private Institution. Founded 1975. **Total program enrollment:** 41. **Application fee:** $50.

PROGRAM(S) OFFERED
● **Aesthetician/Esthetician and Skin Care Specialist** *600 hrs./$6785* ● **Cosmetology/Cosmetologist, General** *1500 hrs./$17,850*

STUDENT SERVICES Academic or career counseling, employment services for current students, placement services for program completers.

Brio Academy of Cosmetology–New Haven

514 Orchard Street, New Haven, CT 06511
http://www.brioacademy.com/

CONTACT Stuart Arnheim, President
Telephone: 203-287-1500

GENERAL INFORMATION Private Institution. **Total program enrollment:** 53. **Application fee:** $50.

PROGRAM(S) OFFERED
● **Aesthetician/Esthetician and Skin Care Specialist** *600 hrs./$6785* ● **Cosmetology/Cosmetologist, General** *1500 hrs./$17,850*

STUDENT SERVICES Academic or career counseling, employment services for current students, placement services for program completers.

Brio Academy of Cosmetology–Torrington

33 East Main Street, Torrington, CT 06790
http://www.brioacademy.edu

CONTACT Stuart L. Arnheim, President/CEO
Telephone: 860-482-0189

GENERAL INFORMATION Private Institution. **Total program enrollment:** 25. **Application fee:** $50.

PROGRAM(S) OFFERED
● **Aesthetician/Esthetician and Skin Care Specialist** *600 hrs./$6785* ● **Cosmetology/Cosmetologist, General** *1500 hrs./$17,850*

STUDENT SERVICES Academic or career counseling, employment services for current students, placement services for program completers.

Brio Academy of Cosmetology–Willimantic

1320 Main Street Tyler Square, Willimantic, CT 06626
http://www.brioacademy.edu

CONTACT Stuart L. Arnheim, President/CEO
Telephone: 860-423-6339

GENERAL INFORMATION Private Institution. **Total program enrollment:** 38. **Application fee:** $50.

PROGRAM(S) OFFERED
• **Aesthetician/Esthetician and Skin Care Specialist** 600 hrs./$6785
• **Cosmetology/Cosmetologist, General** 1500 hrs./$17,700

STUDENT SERVICES Academic or career counseling, employment services for current students, placement services for program completers.

Butler Business School

2710 North Avenue, Bridgeport, CT 06604

CONTACT Carol Paradise, President
Telephone: 203-333-3601

GENERAL INFORMATION Private Institution. **Total program enrollment:** 255. **Application fee:** $100.

PROGRAM(S) OFFERED
• **Administrative Assistant and Secretarial Science, General** • **Hospitality Administration/Management, General** 54 hrs./$19,300 • **Management Information Systems and Services, Other** 54 hrs./$19,300 • **Management Information Systems, General** 48 hrs./$19,200 • **Medical Administrative/Executive Assistant and Medical Secretary** 36 hrs./$16,300 • **Medical/Clinical Assistant** 54 hrs./$19,300

STUDENT SERVICES Academic or career counseling, employment services for current students, placement services for program completers, remedial services.

Capital Community College

950 Main Street, Hartford, CT 06103
http://www.ccc.commnet.edu/

CONTACT Calvin E. Woodland, President
Telephone: 860-906-5000

GENERAL INFORMATION Public Institution. Founded 1946. **Accreditation:** Regional (NEASC/NEASCCIHE); emergency medical services (JRCEMTP); medical assisting (AAMAE); physical therapy assisting (APTA); radiologic technology: radiography (JRCERT). **Total program enrollment:** 1078. **Application fee:** $20.

PROGRAM(S) OFFERED
• **Accounting Technology/Technician and Bookkeeping** 3 students enrolled • **Administrative Assistant and Secretarial Science, General** • **Allied Health and Medical Assisting Services, Other** • **Business, Management, Marketing, and Related Support Services, Other** • **Child Care and Support Services Management** 3 students enrolled • **Communication, Journalism and Related Programs, Other** 1 student enrolled • **Computer Engineering Technology/Technician** • **Computer Programming, Specific Applications** 1 student enrolled • **Computer and Information Sciences and Support Services, Other** 3 students enrolled • **Computer and Information Sciences, Other** • **Criminal Justice/Police Science** • **Emergency Medical Technology/Technician (EMT Paramedic)** 21 students enrolled • **Engineering Technology, General** • **Fine/Studio Arts, General** • **Fire Services Administration** • **Industrial Production Technologies/Technicians, Other** • **Labor Studies** • **Management Information Systems, General** • **Mechanical Engineering/Mechanical Technology/Technician** • **Medical Radiologic Technology/Science—Radiation Therapist** • **Medical/Clinical Assistant** 1 student enrolled • **Nursing—Registered Nurse Training (RN, ASN, BSN, MSN)** 1 student enrolled • **Printmaking** • **Psychiatric/Mental Health Services Technician** • **Social Work** 8 students enrolled

STUDENT SERVICES Academic or career counseling, daycare for children of students, employment services for current students, placement services for program completers, remedial services.

Central Connecticut State University

1615 Stanley Street, New Britain, CT 06050-4010
http://www.ccsu.edu/

CONTACT John W. Miller, President
Telephone: 860-832-3200

GENERAL INFORMATION Public Institution. Founded 1849. **Accreditation:** Regional (NEASC/NEASCCIHE); athletic training (JRCAT); computer science (ABET/CSAC); engineering technology (ABET/TAC); music (NASM). **Total program enrollment:** 8291. **Application fee:** $50.

PROGRAM(S) OFFERED
• **American/United States Studies/Civilization**

STUDENT SERVICES Academic or career counseling, daycare for children of students, employment services for current students, placement services for program completers, remedial services.

Charter Oak State College

55 Paul Manafort Drive, New Britain, CT 06053-2142
http://www.charteroak.edu/

CONTACT Ed Klonoski, President
Telephone: 860-832-3800

GENERAL INFORMATION Public Institution. Founded 1973. **Accreditation:** Regional (NEASC/NEASCCIHE). **Total program enrollment:** 131. **Application fee:** $75.

STUDENT SERVICES Academic or career counseling.

Connecticut Center for Massage Therapy–Groton

1154 Poquonnock Road, Groton, CT 06340
http://ccmt.com/

CONTACT Steohen Lazarus, Chief Executive Officer
Telephone: 877-295-2268

GENERAL INFORMATION Private Institution. **Application fee:** $25.

PROGRAM(S) OFFERED
• **Massage Therapy/Therapeutic Massage** 72 students enrolled

STUDENT SERVICES Academic or career counseling, placement services for program completers, remedial services.

Connecticut Center for Massage Therapy–Newington

75 Kitts Lane, Newington, CT 06111
http://www.ccmt.com/

CONTACT Stephen Lazarus, Chief Executive Officer
Telephone: 877-282-2268

GENERAL INFORMATION Private Institution. Founded 1980. **Total program enrollment:** 69. **Application fee:** $25.

PROGRAM(S) OFFERED
• **Massage Therapy/Therapeutic Massage** 42 students enrolled

STUDENT SERVICES Academic or career counseling, placement services for program completers, remedial services.

Connecticut Center for Massage Therapy–Westport

25 Sylvan Road, S, Westport, CT 06880
http://www.ccmt.com/

CONTACT Stephen Lazarus, Chief Executive Officer
Telephone: 877-292-2268

GENERAL INFORMATION Private Institution. **Total program enrollment:** 61. **Application fee:** $25.

PROGRAM(S) OFFERED
• **Massage Therapy/Therapeutic Massage** *93 students enrolled*

STUDENT SERVICES Academic or career counseling, placement services for program completers, remedial services.

Connecticut Culinary Institute–Hartford

85 Sigourney Street, Hartford, CT 06105
http://www.ctculinary.edu/

CONTACT Louis Giannelli, Executive Director
Telephone: 860-895-6100

GENERAL INFORMATION Private Institution. Founded 1987. **Total program enrollment:** 418.

PROGRAM(S) OFFERED
• **Baking and Pastry Arts/Baker/Pastry Chef** *42 hrs./$27,100* • **Culinary Arts/Chef Training** *59 hrs./$35,375*

STUDENT SERVICES Employment services for current students, placement services for program completers, remedial services.

Connecticut Culinary Institute–Suffield

1760 Mapleton Avenue, Suffield, CT 06078
http://www.ctculinary.com/

CONTACT Paul Montalto, Executive Director
Telephone: 860-668-3500

GENERAL INFORMATION Private Institution. **Total program enrollment:** 139.

PROGRAM(S) OFFERED
• **Baking and Pastry Arts/Baker/Pastry Chef** *42 hrs./$27,100* • **Culinary Arts/Chef Training** *59 hrs./$35,375*

STUDENT SERVICES Employment services for current students, placement services for program completers, remedial services.

Connecticut Institute of Hair Design

1681 Meriden Road, Wolcott, CT 06716

CONTACT Laurie A. Czarzasty, President
Telephone: 203-879-4247

GENERAL INFORMATION Private Institution. **Total program enrollment:** 19. **Application fee:** $25.

PROGRAM(S) OFFERED
• **Barbering/Barber** *1500 hrs./$13,775*

STUDENT SERVICES Academic or career counseling, employment services for current students, placement services for program completers.

Connecticut School of Electronics

221 West Main Street, Branford, CT 06405
http://www.ctschoolofelectronics.com/

CONTACT Brian Malanson, Executive Director
Telephone: 203-315-1060

GENERAL INFORMATION Private Institution. **Total program enrollment:** 385. **Application fee:** $50.

PROGRAM(S) OFFERED
• **Allied Health and Medical Assisting Services, Other** *23 students enrolled* • **Architectural Drafting and Architectural CAD/CADD** *16 students enrolled* • **Automobile/Automotive Mechanics Technology/Technician** *21 students enrolled* • **Computer Technology/Computer Systems Technology** • **Dental Assisting/Assistant** • **Drafting/Design Engineering Technologies/Technicians, Other** • **Electrical/Electronics Equipment Installation and Repair, General** *57 students enrolled* • **Heating, Air Conditioning, Ventilation and Refrigeration Maintenance Technology/Technician (HAC, HACR, HVAC, HVACR)** *49 students enrolled*

STUDENT SERVICES Academic or career counseling, employment services for current students, placement services for program completers.

Connecticut Training Centers

763 Burnside Avenue, East Hartford, CT 06108
http://www.cttraining.org/

CONTACT William Mangini, Executive Director
Telephone: 860-291-9898 Ext. 101

GENERAL INFORMATION Private Institution. **Total program enrollment:** 181. **Application fee:** $25.

PROGRAM(S) OFFERED
• **Nurse/Nursing Assistant/Aide and Patient Care Assistant** *24 hrs./$7700*

STUDENT SERVICES Academic or career counseling, employment services for current students, placement services for program completers.

Fox Institute of Business

765 Asylum Avenue, Hartford, CT 06105
http://foxinstitute.com/

CONTACT Christopher Coutts, President
Telephone: 860-947-2299

GENERAL INFORMATION Private Institution. Founded 1924. **Total program enrollment:** 373. **Application fee:** $25.

PROGRAM(S) OFFERED
• **Computer Installation and Repair Technology/Technician** *36 hrs./$12,995* • **Computer and Information Sciences and Support Services, Other** *20 students enrolled* • **Diagnostic Medical Sonography/Sonographer and Ultrasound Technician** *60 hrs./$28,500* • **Legal Administrative Assistant/Secretary** *35 hrs./$12,995* • **Massage Therapy/Therapeutic Massage** *40 hrs./$12,995* • **Medical Insurance Specialist/Medical Biller** *40 hrs./$15,995* • **Medical/Clinical Assistant** *44 hrs./$15,995*

STUDENT SERVICES Academic or career counseling, placement services for program completers.

Gateway Community College

60 Sargent Drive, New Haven, CT 06511-5918
http://www.gwcc.commnet.edu/

CONTACT Dorsey L. Kendrick, President
Telephone: 203-285-2000

GENERAL INFORMATION Public Institution. Founded 1992. **Accreditation:** Regional (NEASC/NEASCCIHE); engineering technology (ABET/TAC); nuclear medicine technology (JRCNMT); radiologic technology:

radiation therapy technology (JRCERT); radiologic technology: radiography (JRCERT). **Total program enrollment: 2351. Application fee:** $20.

PROGRAM(S) OFFERED
• **Administrative Assistant and Secretarial Science, General** 7 *students enrolled* • **Allied Health Diagnostic, Intervention, and Treatment Professions, Other** 3 *students enrolled* • **Allied Health and Medical Assisting Services, Other** • **Automotive Engineering Technology/Technician** 4 *students enrolled* • **Business, Management, Marketing, and Related Support Services, Other** 5 *students enrolled* • **Child Care and Support Services Management** 3 *students enrolled* • **Computer Engineering Technology/Technician** 4 *students enrolled* • **Computer Installation and Repair Technology/Technician** 11 *students enrolled* • **Criminal Justice/Police Science** • **Diagnostic Medical Sonography/Sonographer and Ultrasound Technician** • **Dietitian Assistant** 2 *students enrolled* • **Engineering Technology, General** 3 *students enrolled* • **Fashion Merchandising** • **Foodservice Systems Administration/Management** 5 *students enrolled* • **Graphic and Printing Equipment Operator, General Production** • **Hotel/Motel Administration/Management** 1 *student enrolled* • **Industrial Production Technologies/Technicians, Other** • **Information Science/Studies** 1 *student enrolled* • **Management Information Systems, General** 2 *students enrolled* • **Mechanical Drafting and Mechanical Drafting CAD/CADD** 1 *student enrolled* • **Natural Resources Management and Policy** • **Nuclear Medical Technology/Technologist** • **Psychiatric/Mental Health Services Technician** 6 *students enrolled* • **Sales, Distribution and Marketing Operations, General** 1 *student enrolled* • **Special Education and Teaching, General** 3 *students enrolled* • **Substance Abuse/Addiction Counseling** 29 *students enrolled* • **Therapeutic Recreation/Recreational Therapy** 6 *students enrolled* • **Web Page, Digital/Multimedia and Information Resources Design**

STUDENT SERVICES Academic or career counseling, daycare for children of students, employment services for current students, placement services for program completers, remedial services.

Goodwin College

745 Burnside Avenue, East Hartford, CT 06108
http://www.goodwin.edu/

CONTACT Mark Scheinberg, President
Telephone: 860-528-4111

GENERAL INFORMATION Private Institution. Founded 1999. **Accreditation:** Regional (NEASC/CVTCI); medical assisting (AAMAE); state accredited or approved. **Total program enrollment: 324. Application fee:** $50.

PROGRAM(S) OFFERED
• **Accounting** • **Allied Health and Medical Assisting Services, Other** • **Business Administration and Management, General** • **Business/Commerce, General** 1 *student enrolled* • **Child Care Provider/Assistant** 9 *students enrolled* • **Computer Engineering, General** • **Computer Programming/Programmer, General** • **Computer and Information Sciences, General** • **Criminal Justice/Police Science** • **Customer Service Support/Call Center/Teleservice Operation** 8 *students enrolled* • **Emergency Medical Technology/Technician (EMT Paramedic)** 5 *students enrolled* • **Entrepreneurship/Entrepreneurial Studies** 9 *students enrolled* • **Histologic Technician** • **Human Services, General** 1 *student enrolled* • **Medical Insurance Coding Specialist/Coder** 6 *students enrolled* • **Medical Office Assistant/Specialist** 2 *students enrolled* • **Medical/Clinical Assistant** 1 *student enrolled* • **Nurse/Nursing Assistant/Aide and Patient Care Assistant** • **Phlebotomy/Phlebotomist** 13 *students enrolled* • **Teacher Assistant/Aide** • **Youth Services/Administration**

STUDENT SERVICES Academic or career counseling, employment services for current students, placement services for program completers, remedial services.

Housatonic Community College

900 Lafayette Boulevard, Bridgeport, CT 06604-4704
http://www.hctc.commnet.edu/

CONTACT Anita Gliniecki, President
Telephone: 203-332-5000

GENERAL INFORMATION Public Institution. Founded 1965. **Accreditation:** Regional (NEASC/NEASCCIHE); medical laboratory technology

(NAACLS); physical therapy assisting (APTA). **Total program enrollment: 1878. Application fee:** $20.

PROGRAM(S) OFFERED
• **Accounting Technology/Technician and Bookkeeping** 1 *student enrolled* • **Administrative Assistant and Secretarial Science, General** 4 *students enrolled* • **Allied Health and Medical Assisting Services, Other** • **Child Care and Support Services Management** 7 *students enrolled* • **Commercial and Advertising Art** 1 *student enrolled* • **Criminal Justice/Police Science** 7 *students enrolled* • **Engineering Technology, General** • **Management Information Systems, General** 18 *students enrolled* • **Psychiatric/Mental Health Services Technician** 13 *students enrolled*

STUDENT SERVICES Academic or career counseling, daycare for children of students, employment services for current students, remedial services.

Industrial Management Training Institute

233 Mill Street, Waterbury, CT 06706
http://imtiusa.com/

CONTACT Marcel Veronneau, President
Telephone: 203-753-7910

GENERAL INFORMATION Private Institution. **Total program enrollment: 185. Application fee:** $50.

PROGRAM(S) OFFERED
• **Electrical/Electronics Equipment Installation and Repair, General** 51 *students enrolled* • **Electrician** 738 hrs./$13,800 • **Heating, Air Conditioning and Refrigeration Technology/Technician (ACH/ACR/ACHR/HRAC/HVAC/AC Technology)** 738 hrs./$12,700 • **Heating, Air Conditioning, Ventilation and Refrigeration Maintenance Technology/Technician (HAC, HACR, HVAC, HVACR)** 14 *students enrolled* • **Pipefitting/Pipefitter and Sprinkler Fitter** 18 *students enrolled* • **Plumbing Technology/Plumber** 658 hrs./$12,370

STUDENT SERVICES Employment services for current students, placement services for program completers.

International College of Hospitality Management

1760 Mapleton Avenue, Suffield, CT 06078
http://www.ichm.edu/

CONTACT Tad Graham Handley, President
Telephone: 860-668-3515

GENERAL INFORMATION Private Institution. Founded 1992. **Accreditation:** Regional (NEASC/CVTCI). **Total program enrollment: 80. Application fee:** $40.

PROGRAM(S) OFFERED
• **Hotel/Motel Administration/Management** 7 *students enrolled*

STUDENT SERVICES Academic or career counseling, employment services for current students, placement services for program completers, remedial services.

The Leon Institute of Hair Design

111 Wall Street, Bridgeport, CT 06604

CONTACT Patrick Vitale, Jr., Director
Telephone: 203-335-0364

GENERAL INFORMATION Private Institution. Founded 1934. **Total program enrollment: 28.**

PROGRAM(S) OFFERED
• **Barbering/Barber** 1500 hrs./$8600 • **Cosmetology, Barber/Styling, and Nail Instructor** 20 *students enrolled*

STUDENT SERVICES Placement services for program completers.

Lincoln Technical Institute

106 Sebethe Drive, Cromwell, CT 06416
http://www.lincolntech.com/c_cromwell_ct.php

CONTACT Craig Avery, Regional Executive Director
Telephone: 860-613-3350

GENERAL INFORMATION Private Institution. **Total program enrollment:** 98. **Application fee:** $50.

PROGRAM(S) OFFERED
• Culinary Arts/Chef Training *1590 hrs./$25,650*

STUDENT SERVICES Academic or career counseling, employment services for current students, placement services for program completers.

Lincoln Technical Institute

109 Sanford Street, Hamden, CT 06514
http://www.lincolntech.com/c_hamden_ct.php

CONTACT Craig Avery, Regional Executive Director
Telephone: 203-287-7300

GENERAL INFORMATION Private Institution. **Total program enrollment:** 319. **Application fee:** $50.

PROGRAM(S) OFFERED
• Electrical and Power Transmission Installation/Installer, General *52 students enrolled* • Electrician *60 hrs./$20,063* • Licensed Practical/Vocational Nurse Training (LPN, LVN, Cert, Dipl, AAS) *68 hrs./$30,041* • Medical/Clinical Assistant *55 hrs./$14,675*

STUDENT SERVICES Academic or career counseling, employment services for current students, placement services for program completers.

Lincoln Technical Institute

200 John Downey Drive, New Britain, CT 06051-0651
http://www.lincolntech.com/c_new_britain_ct.php

CONTACT Craig Avery, Regional Executive Director
Telephone: 860-225-8641

GENERAL INFORMATION Private Institution. Founded 1940. **Total program enrollment:** 709. **Application fee:** $50.

PROGRAM(S) OFFERED
• Automobile/Automotive Mechanics Technology/Technician *19 students enrolled* • Electrical and Power Transmission Installers, Other *57 students enrolled* • Electrician *53 hrs./$16,845* • Heating, Air Conditioning, Ventilation and Refrigeration Maintenance Technology/Technician (HAC, HACR, HVAC, HVACR) *49 hrs./$16,845* • Licensed Practical/Vocational Nurse Training (LPN, LVN, Cert, Dipl, AAS) *68 hrs./$30,041* • Medical/Clinical Assistant *39 students enrolled*

STUDENT SERVICES Academic or career counseling, employment services for current students, placement services for program completers.

Lincoln Technical Institute

8 Progress Drive, Shelton, CT 06848
http://www.lincolntech.com/c_shelton_ct.php

CONTACT Craig Avery, Regional Executive Director
Telephone: 860-225-8641

GENERAL INFORMATION Private Institution. **Total program enrollment:** 695. **Application fee:** $50.

PROGRAM(S) OFFERED
• Culinary Arts/Chef Training *63 hrs./$23,496* • Electrical and Power Transmission Installers, Other *82 students enrolled* • Electrician *53 hrs./$16,845* • Licensed Practical/Vocational Nurse Training (LPN, LVN, Cert, Dipl, AAS) *68 hrs./$30,041* • Medical/Clinical Assistant *56 hrs./$14,675*

STUDENT SERVICES Academic or career counseling, employment services for current students, placement services for program completers.

Manchester Community College

PO Box 1046, Manchester, CT 06045-1046
http://www.mcc.commnet.edu/

CONTACT Gena Glickman, President
Telephone: 860-512-3000

GENERAL INFORMATION Public Institution. Founded 1963. **Accreditation:** Regional (NEASC/NEASCCIHE); medical laboratory technology (NAACLS); physical therapy assisting (APTA); surgical technology (ARCST). **Total program enrollment:** 3227. **Application fee:** $20.

PROGRAM(S) OFFERED
• Accounting Technology/Technician and Bookkeeping *4 students enrolled* • Administrative Assistant and Secretarial Science, General *11 students enrolled* • Allied Health and Medical Assisting Services, Other *1 student enrolled* • Baking and Pastry Arts/Baker/Pastry Chef *17 students enrolled* • Business, Management, Marketing, and Related Support Services, Other *7 students enrolled* • Child Care Provider/Assistant *9 students enrolled* • Commercial and Advertising Art • Community Organization and Advocacy *2 students enrolled* • Computer Programming/Programmer, General *4 students enrolled* • Computer Technology/Computer Systems Technology • Computer and Information Sciences, General • Criminal Justice/Police Science *50 students enrolled* • Engineering Technology, General • Foodservice Systems Administration/Management *17 students enrolled* • General Merchandising, Sales, and Related Marketing Operations, Other • Information Science/Studies • Legal Assistant/Paralegal *5 students enrolled* • Management Information Systems, General • Mechanical Drafting and Mechanical Drafting CAD/CADD *7 students enrolled* • Mental and Social Health Services and Allied Professions, Other • Psychiatric/Mental Health Services Technician • Radio and Television *1 student enrolled* • Real Estate • Receptionist • Substance Abuse/Addiction Counseling • Therapeutic Recreation/Recreational Therapy *6 students enrolled*

STUDENT SERVICES Academic or career counseling, employment services for current students, placement services for program completers, remedial services.

Middlesex Community College

100 Training Hill Road, Middletown, CT 06457-4889
http://www.mxcc.commnet.edu/

CONTACT Wilfredo Nieves, President
Telephone: 860-343-5701

GENERAL INFORMATION Public Institution. Founded 1966. **Accreditation:** Regional (NEASC/NEASCCIHE); ophthalmic dispensing (COA); radiologic technology: radiography (JRCERT). **Total program enrollment:** 1017. **Application fee:** $20.

PROGRAM(S) OFFERED
• Accounting Technology/Technician and Bookkeeping *1 student enrolled* • Administrative Assistant and Secretarial Science, General *3 students enrolled* • Allied Health and Medical Assisting Services, Other • Business, Management, Marketing, and Related Support Services, Other *2 students enrolled* • Child Care and Support Services Management *1 student enrolled* • Criminal Justice/Police Science • Educational/Instructional Media Design *1 student enrolled* • Engineering Technology, General • Environmental Science • General Merchandising, Sales, and Related Marketing Operations, Other • Management Information Systems, General • Psychiatric/Mental Health Services Technician • Radio and Television Broadcasting Technology/Technician • Therapeutic Recreation/Recreational Therapy *7 students enrolled*

STUDENT SERVICES Academic or career counseling, daycare for children of students, employment services for current students, placement services for program completers, remedial services.

Naugatuck Valley Community College

750 Chase Parkway, Waterbury, CT 06708-3000
http://www.nvcc.commnet.edu/

CONTACT Daisy Cocco De Filippis, President
Telephone: 203-575-8040

GENERAL INFORMATION Public Institution. Founded 1992. **Accreditation:** Regional (NEASC/NEASCCIHE); engineering technology (ABET/

TAC); physical therapy assisting (APTA); radiologic technology: radiography (JRCERT). **Total program enrollment: 2564. Application fee:** $20.

PROGRAM(S) OFFERED
● **Accounting Technology/Technician and Bookkeeping** *3 students enrolled* ● **Administrative Assistant and Secretarial Science, General** ● **Aeronautics/ Aviation/Aerospace Science and Technology, General** ● **Allied Health and Medical Assisting Services, Other** ● **Architectural Drafting and Architectural CAD/CADD** ● **Art/Art Studies, General** *9 students enrolled* ● **Automobile/ Automotive Mechanics Technology/Technician** *1 student enrolled* ● **Banking and Financial Support Services** ● **Business, Management, Marketing, and Related Support Services, Other** *5 students enrolled* ● **Child Care and Support Services Management** *1 student enrolled* ● **Communications Technologies/Technicians and Support Services, Other** *1 student enrolled* ● **Computer Engineering Technology/Technician** *7 students enrolled* ● **Computer Programming, Specific Applications** ● **Computer and Information Sciences, General** ● **Criminal Justice/Police Science** ● **Engineering Technologies/Technicians, Other** *3 students enrolled* ● **Engineering Technology, General** ● **Engineering-Related Technologies, Other** ● **Environmental Engineering Technology/Environmental Technology** ● **Fine/Studio Arts, General** *2 students enrolled* ● **Foodservice Systems Administration/Management** *3 students enrolled* ● **General Merchandising, Sales, and Related Marketing Operations, Other** ● **Horticultural Science** *11 students enrolled* ● **Legal Assistant/Paralegal** *8 students enrolled* ● **Manufacturing Technology/Technician** ● **Mechanical Drafting and Mechanical Drafting CAD/CADD** *1 student enrolled* ● **Operations Management and Supervision** ● **Physical Education Teaching and Coaching** ● **Plastics Engineering Technology/Technician** ● **Psychiatric/Mental Health Services Technician** *2 students enrolled* ● **Quality Control Technology/ Technician**

STUDENT SERVICES Academic or career counseling, daycare for children of students, employment services for current students, placement services for program completers, remedial services.

New England Tractor Trailer Training of Connecticut

32 Field Road, Somers, CT 06071
http://www.nettts.com/

CONTACT Mark Greenberg, President
Telephone: 800-243-3544

GENERAL INFORMATION Private Institution. **Total program enrollment:** 226.

PROGRAM(S) OFFERED
● **Truck and Bus Driver/Commercial Vehicle Operation** *40 hrs./$2295*

STUDENT SERVICES Placement services for program completers.

Northhaven Academy

352 State Street, North Haven, CT 06473
http://www.northhavenacademy.com/

CONTACT Laura Landino, School Director
Telephone: 203-985-0222 Ext. 10

GENERAL INFORMATION Private Institution. **Total program enrollment:** 219. **Application fee:** $100.

PROGRAM(S) OFFERED
● **Cosmetology/Cosmetologist, General** *1500 hrs./$20,942*

STUDENT SERVICES Academic or career counseling, employment services for current students, placement services for program completers, remedial services.

Northwestern Connecticut Community College

Park Place East, Winsted, CT 06098-1798
http://www.nwctc.commnet.edu/

CONTACT Barbara Douglass, President
Telephone: 860-738-6300

GENERAL INFORMATION Public Institution. Founded 1965. **Accreditation:** Regional (NEASC/NEASCCIHE); medical assisting (AAMAE); physical therapy assisting (APTA). **Total program enrollment:** 570. **Application fee:** $20.

PROGRAM(S) OFFERED
● **Administrative Assistant and Secretarial Science, General** ● **Allied Health and Medical Assisting Services, Other** ● **Art/Art Studies, General** *6 students enrolled* ● **Business, Management, Marketing, and Related Support Services, Other** *1 student enrolled* ● **Child Care and Support Services Management** *2 students enrolled* ● **Commercial and Advertising Art** *5 students enrolled* ● **Computer Programming, Specific Applications** ● **Computer Technology/ Computer Systems Technology** ● **Computer and Information Sciences, Other** *2 students enrolled* ● **Educational/Instructional Media Design** ● **Electrical and Electronic Engineering Technologies/Technicians, Other** ● **Engineering Technology, General** ● **Mechanical Drafting and Mechanical Drafting CAD/ CADD** ● **Medical/Clinical Assistant** *15 students enrolled* ● **Psychiatric/Mental Health Services Technician** ● **Sign Language Interpretation and Translation** ● **Sport and Fitness Administration/Management** *1 student enrolled* ● **Therapeutic Recreation/Recreational Therapy** *6 students enrolled*

STUDENT SERVICES Academic or career counseling, daycare for children of students, employment services for current students, placement services for program completers, remedial services.

Norwalk Community College

188 Richards Avenue, Norwalk, CT 06854-1655
http://www.ncc.commnet.edu/

CONTACT David Levinson, President
Telephone: 203-857-7060

GENERAL INFORMATION Public Institution. Founded 1961. **Accreditation:** Regional (NEASC/NEASCCIHE). **Total program enrollment:** 2389. **Application fee:** $20.

PROGRAM(S) OFFERED
● **Accounting Technology/Technician and Bookkeeping** *2 students enrolled* ● **Administrative Assistant and Secretarial Science, General** *4 students enrolled* ● **Archeology** *2 students enrolled* ● **Architectural Engineering Technology/Technician** ● **Child Care and Support Services Management** *13 students enrolled* ● **Child Development** *8 students enrolled* ● **Commercial and Advertising Art** ● **Computer Programming/Programmer, General** *1 student enrolled* ● **Computer and Information Sciences and Support Services, Other** ● **Culinary Arts and Related Services, Other** *8 students enrolled* ● **Data Entry/ Microcomputer Applications, General** ● **Emergency Medical Technology/ Technician (EMT Paramedic)** *2 students enrolled* ● **Information Science/Studies** ● **Legal Administrative Assistant/Secretary** ● **Legal Assistant/Paralegal** *10 students enrolled* ● **Management Information Systems, General** *10 students enrolled* ● **Medical Office Management/Administration** *17 students enrolled* ● **Parks, Recreation and Leisure Studies** *3 students enrolled* ● **Psychiatric/ Mental Health Services Technician** *2 students enrolled*

STUDENT SERVICES Academic or career counseling, daycare for children of students, employment services for current students, placement services for program completers, remedial services.

Paier College of Art, Inc.

20 Gorham Avenue, Hamden, CT 06514-3902
http://www.paiercollegeofart.edu/

CONTACT Jonathan E. Paier, President
Telephone: 203-287-3031

GENERAL INFORMATION Private Institution. Founded 1946. **Accreditation:** State accredited or approved. **Total program enrollment:** 163. **Application fee:** $25.

PROGRAM(S) OFFERED
● **Commercial and Advertising Art** *1 student enrolled* ● **Painting**

STUDENT SERVICES Academic or career counseling, employment services for current students, placement services for program completers.

Paul Mitchell the School—Danbury

109 South Street, Danbury, CT 06810-8039
http://www.paulmitchelltheschool.com/

CONTACT Michael Galvin, President
Telephone: 203-744-0900

GENERAL INFORMATION Private Institution. Founded 1960. **Total program enrollment:** 96. **Application fee:** $100.

PROGRAM(S) OFFERED
• Cosmetology/Cosmetologist, General *1500 hrs./$14,900*

Porter and Chester Institute

670 Lordship Boulevard, Stratford, CT 06497

CONTACT Raymond R. Clark, President
Telephone: 203-375-4463

GENERAL INFORMATION Private Institution. **Total program enrollment:** 2491. **Application fee:** $50.

PROGRAM(S) OFFERED
• Architectural Drafting and Architectural CAD/CADD *95 students enrolled* • Automobile/Automotive Mechanics Technology/Technician *198 students enrolled* • Computer Technology/Computer Systems Technology *38 students enrolled* • Dental Assisting/Assistant *54 students enrolled* • Electrical/Electronics Maintenance and Repair Technology, Other *3 students enrolled* • Electrician *226 students enrolled* • Heating, Air Conditioning, Ventilation and Refrigeration Maintenance Technology/Technician (HAC, HACR, HVAC, HVACR) *248 students enrolled* • Licensed Practical/Vocational Nurse Training (LPN, LVN, Cert, Dipl, AAS) • Mechanical Drafting and Mechanical Drafting CAD/CADD • Medical/Clinical Assistant *206 students enrolled*

STUDENT SERVICES Academic or career counseling, employment services for current students, placement services for program completers.

Post University

800 Country Club Road, Waterbury, CT 06723-2540
http://www.post.edu/

CONTACT Kenneth Zirkle, President
Telephone: 800-345-2562

GENERAL INFORMATION Private Institution. Founded 1890. **Accreditation:** Regional (NEASC/NEASCCIHE). **Total program enrollment:** 1095. **Application fee:** $40.

PROGRAM(S) OFFERED
• Child Care Provider/Assistant • Child Care and Support Services Management • Equestrian/Equine Studies • Finance, General • Human Development, Family Studies, and Related Services, Other • Human Resources Management/Personnel Administration, General • International Business/Trade/Commerce • Legal Assistant/Paralegal • Legal Support Services, Other • Management Information Systems, General

STUDENT SERVICES Academic or career counseling, employment services for current students, placement services for program completers, remedial services.

Quinebaug Valley Community College

742 Upper Maple Street, Danielson, CT 06239-1440
http://www.qvcc.commnet.edu/

CONTACT Dianne Williams, President
Telephone: 860-774-1130

GENERAL INFORMATION Public Institution. Founded 1971. **Accreditation:** Regional (NEASC/NEASCCIHE); medical assisting (AAMAE). **Total program enrollment:** 715. **Application fee:** $20.

PROGRAM(S) OFFERED
• Accounting Technology/Technician and Bookkeeping *1 student enrolled* • Administrative Assistant and Secretarial Science, General *9 students enrolled* • Allied Health and Medical Assisting Services, Other • Art/Art Studies, General • Business, Management, Marketing, and Related Support Services, Other *3 students enrolled* • Child Care and Support Services Management *3 students enrolled* • Computer Systems Networking and Telecommunications *5 students enrolled* • Data Processing and Data Processing Technology/Technician *5 students enrolled* • Engineering Technology, General • Health Information/Medical Records Technology/Technician *8 students enrolled* • Medical/Clinical Assistant *20 students enrolled* • Plastics Engineering Technology/Technician • Psychiatric/Mental Health Services Technician *1 student enrolled*

STUDENT SERVICES Academic or career counseling, daycare for children of students, employment services for current students, remedial services.

Renasci Academy of Hair

Station House Square, 2505 Main Street, Stratford, CT 06497
http://www.renasciacademy.com/

CONTACT Jeanne Iacono, Director
Telephone: 203-878-4900

GENERAL INFORMATION Private Institution. Founded 1959. **Total program enrollment:** 12. **Application fee:** $25.

PROGRAM(S) OFFERED
• Cosmetology/Cosmetologist, General *1500 hrs./$13,875*

STUDENT SERVICES Academic or career counseling, employment services for current students, placement services for program completers, remedial services.

Ridley-Lowell Business and Technical Institute

470 Bank Street, New London, CT 06320
http://www.ridley.edu/

CONTACT Terry Weymouth, President
Telephone: 860-443-7441

GENERAL INFORMATION Private Institution. Founded 1887. **Total program enrollment:** 176. **Application fee:** $100.

PROGRAM(S) OFFERED
• Accounting Technology/Technician and Bookkeeping • Accounting and Related Services, Other *6 students enrolled* • Accounting *67 hrs./$12,500* • Administrative Assistant and Secretarial Science, General *60 hrs./$12,500* • Business/Office Automation/Technology/Data Entry *3 students enrolled* • Computer Systems Networking and Telecommunications *71 hrs./$12,500* • Massage Therapy/Therapeutic Massage *87 hrs./$14,425* • Medical Insurance Coding Specialist/Coder *14 students enrolled* • Medical Insurance Specialist/Medical Biller *71 hrs./$12,570* • Medical/Clinical Assistant *80 hrs./$17,727*

STUDENT SERVICES Placement services for program completers.

Sacred Heart University

5151 Park Avenue, Fairfield, CT 06825-1000
http://www.sacredheart.edu/

CONTACT Anthony J. Cernera, President
Telephone: 203-371-7999

GENERAL INFORMATION Private Institution. Founded 1963. **Accreditation:** Regional (NEASC/NEASCCIHE); athletic training (JRCAT). **Total program enrollment:** 4059. **Application fee:** $50.

PROGRAM(S) OFFERED
• Legal Assistant/Paralegal

STUDENT SERVICES Academic or career counseling, employment services for current students, placement services for program completers, remedial services.

Saint Joseph College

1678 Asylum Avenue, West Hartford, CT 06117-2700
http://www.sjc.edu/

CONTACT Dr. Pamela Trotman Reid, President
Telephone: 860-232-4571

GENERAL INFORMATION Private Institution. Founded 1932. **Accreditation:** Regional (NEASC/NEASCCIHE); dietetics: undergraduate, post-baccalaureate internship (ADtA/CAADE); home economics (AAFCS). **Total program enrollment:** 983. **Application fee:** $50.

PROGRAM(S) OFFERED
• Education, Other

STUDENT SERVICES Academic or career counseling, employment services for current students, placement services for program completers.

St. Vincent's College

2800 Main Street, Bridgeport, CT 06606-4292
http://www.stvincentscollege.edu/

CONTACT Dr. Martha Shouldis, President
Telephone: 203-576-5235

GENERAL INFORMATION Private Institution (Affiliated with Roman Catholic Church). Founded 1991. **Accreditation:** Regional (NEASC/NEASCCIHE); medical assisting (AAMAE). **Total program enrollment:** 49. **Application fee:** $50.

PROGRAM(S) OFFERED
• Medical Office Assistant/Specialist *14 students enrolled*

STUDENT SERVICES Academic or career counseling, employment services for current students, placement services for program completers, remedial services.

Stone Academy

403 Main Street, East Hartford, CT 06118
http://www.stoneacademy.com/

CONTACT Mark Scheinberg, Owner
Telephone: 860-569-0618

GENERAL INFORMATION Private Institution. **Total program enrollment:** 73. **Application fee:** $25.

PROGRAM(S) OFFERED
• Licensed Practical/Vocational Nurse Training (LPN, LVN, Cert, Dipl, AAS) *61 hrs./$25,200*

STUDENT SERVICES Academic or career counseling, placement services for program completers, remedial services.

Stone Academy

1315 Dixwell Avenue, Hamden, CT 06514
http://www.stoneacademy.com/

CONTACT Robin Treybal, School Director
Telephone: 203-288-7474

GENERAL INFORMATION Private Institution. **Total program enrollment:** 281. **Application fee:** $25.

PROGRAM(S) OFFERED
• Administrative Assistant and Secretarial Science, General *3 students enrolled* • Licensed Practical/Vocational Nurse Training (LPN, LVN, Cert, Dipl, AAS) *61 hrs./$25,200* • Medical Administrative/Executive Assistant and Medical Secretary *56 hrs./$15,600* • Medical Office Assistant/Specialist *39 hrs./$10,500* • Medical/Clinical Assistant *43 students enrolled* • Nurse/Nursing Assistant/Aide and Patient Care Assistant *24 hrs./$7400* • Office Management and Supervision *35 hrs./$10,800*

STUDENT SERVICES Academic or career counseling, placement services for program completers.

Stone Academy

101 Pierpont Road, Waterbury, CT 06705
http://www.stoneacademy.com/

CONTACT Mark Scheinberg, President
Telephone: 203-756-5500

GENERAL INFORMATION Private Institution. **Total program enrollment:** 283. **Application fee:** $25.

PROGRAM(S) OFFERED
• Administrative Assistant and Secretarial Science, General *48 hrs./$10,800* • Medical Administrative/Executive Assistant and Medical Secretary *52 hrs./$10,500* • Medical/Clinical Assistant *48 hrs./$16,600* • Nurse/Nursing Assistant/Aide and Patient Care Assistant *24 hrs./$7500*

STUDENT SERVICES Academic or career counseling, placement services for program completers.

Three Rivers Community College

574 New London Turnpike, Norwich, CT 06360
http://www.trcc.commnet.edu/

CONTACT Grace S. Jones, President
Telephone: 860-886-0177

GENERAL INFORMATION Public Institution. Founded 1963. **Accreditation:** Regional (NEASC/NEASCCIHE); engineering technology (ABET/TAC). **Total program enrollment:** 1423. **Application fee:** $20.

PROGRAM(S) OFFERED
• Accounting Technology/Technician and Bookkeeping • Administrative Assistant and Secretarial Science, General • Advertising • Allied Health and Medical Assisting Services, Other • Architectural Drafting and Architectural CAD/CADD *2 students enrolled* • Business, Management, Marketing, and Related Support Services, Other • CAD/CADD Drafting and/or Design Technology/Technician *4 students enrolled* • Child Care and Support Services Management *1 student enrolled* • Commercial and Advertising Art *2 students enrolled* • Computer Engineering Technology/Technician *2 students enrolled* • Construction Management *2 students enrolled* • Criminal Justice/Police Science *1 student enrolled* • Engineering Technology, General *1 student enrolled* • Environmental Engineering Technology/Environmental Technology *2 students enrolled* • General Merchandising, Sales, and Related Marketing Operations, Other *2 students enrolled* • General Office Occupations and Clerical Services *2 students enrolled* • Hospitality Administration/Management, General • Hotel/Motel Administration/Management *1 student enrolled* • Library Assistant/Technician *8 students enrolled* • Psychiatric/Mental Health Services Technician • Public Administration and Social Service Professions, Other • Technical Theatre/Theatre Design and Technology • Tourism Promotion Operations • Tourism and Travel Services Management

STUDENT SERVICES Academic or career counseling, daycare for children of students, employment services for current students, placement services for program completers, remedial services.

Tunxis Community College

271 Scott Swamp Road, Farmington, CT 06032-3026
http://www.tunxis.commnet.edu/

CONTACT Cathryn L. Addy, President
Telephone: 860-255-3500

GENERAL INFORMATION Public Institution. Founded 1969. **Accreditation:** Regional (NEASC/NEASCCIHE); dental assisting (ADA); dental

Tunxis Community College (continued)

hygiene (ADA); physical therapy assisting (APTA). **Total program enrollment:** 1840. **Application fee:** $20.

PROGRAM(S) OFFERED

• **Accounting Technology/Technician and Bookkeeping** *13 students enrolled* • **Administrative Assistant and Secretarial Science, General** *27 students enrolled* • **Business, Management, Marketing, and Related Support Services, Other** *8 students enrolled* • **Child Care and Support Services Management** *13 students enrolled* • **Commercial and Advertising Art** *5 students enrolled* • **Communication Studies/Speech Communication and Rhetoric** *2 students enrolled* • **Criminal Justice/Police Science** • **Dental Assisting/Assistant** *3 students enrolled* • **Engineering Technology, General** *3 students enrolled* • **General Merchandising, Sales, and Related Marketing Operations, Other** *2 students enrolled* • **Management Information Systems, General** *7 students enrolled* • **Marketing/Marketing Management, General** *5 students enrolled* • **Psychiatric/Mental Health Services Technician** *15 students enrolled* • **Visual and Performing Arts, Other** *1 student enrolled*

STUDENT SERVICES Academic or career counseling, daycare for children of students, employment services for current students, remedial services.

University of Bridgeport

126 Park Avenue, Bridgeport, CT 06604
http://www.bridgeport.edu/

CONTACT Neil Albert Salonen, President
Telephone: 203-576-4000

GENERAL INFORMATION Private Institution. Founded 1927. **Accreditation:** Regional (NEASC/NEASCCIHE); art and design (NASAD); dental hygiene (ADA). **Total program enrollment:** 3216. **Application fee:** $25.

PROGRAM(S) OFFERED

• **Business Administration and Management, General** *4 students enrolled*

STUDENT SERVICES Academic or career counseling, employment services for current students, placement services for program completers, remedial services.

University of Hartford

200 Bloomfield Avenue, West Hartford, CT 06117-1599
http://www.hartford.edu/

CONTACT Walter Harrison, President
Telephone: 860-768-4100

GENERAL INFORMATION Private Institution. Founded 1877. **Accreditation:** Regional (NEASC/NEASCCIHE); art and design (NASAD); dance (NASD); engineering technology (ABET/TAC); medical technology (NAACLS); music (NASM); radiologic technology: radiography (JRCERT). **Total program enrollment:** 5421. **Application fee:** $30.

PROGRAM(S) OFFERED

• **Legal Assistant/Paralegal** *17 students enrolled* • **Sociology**

STUDENT SERVICES Academic or career counseling, employment services for current students, placement services for program completers, remedial services.

University of New Haven

300 Boston Post Road, West Haven, CT 06516-1916
http://www.newhaven.edu/

CONTACT Steven H. Kaplan, President
Telephone: 203-932-7000

GENERAL INFORMATION Private Institution. Founded 1920. **Accreditation:** Regional (NEASC/NEASCCIHE); computer science (ABET/CSAC); dental hygiene (ADA). **Total program enrollment:** 4047. **Application fee:** $25.

PROGRAM(S) OFFERED

• **Computer Programming/Programmer, General** • **Corrections and Criminal Justice, Other** *9 students enrolled* • **Criminal Justice/Police Science** *20 students enrolled* • **Culinary Arts and Related Services, Other** • **Fire Protection and Safety Technology/Technician** *1 student enrolled* • **Fire Protection, Other** *3 students enrolled* • **Forensic Science and Technology** *13 students enrolled* • **Hospitality Administration/Management, General** • **Journalism** • **Legal Assistant/Paralegal** *11 students enrolled* • **Logistics and Materials Management** • **Mass Communication/Media Studies** • **Occupational Health and Industrial Hygiene** • **Occupational Safety and Health Technology/Technician** • **Political Science and Government, Other** • **Security and Loss Prevention Services** • **Tourism and Travel Services Management**

STUDENT SERVICES Academic or career counseling, employment services for current students, placement services for program completers, remedial services.

DELAWARE

Academy of Massage and Bodywork

1218 Pulaski Highway, Suite 324, Bear, DE 19701
http://www.massage-academy.com

CONTACT Gheorghe N. Nastase, President/Director
Telephone: 302-392-6768

GENERAL INFORMATION Private Institution. **Total program enrollment:** 36. **Application fee:** $25.

PROGRAM(S) OFFERED

• **Aesthetician/Esthetician and Skin Care Specialist** *300 hrs./$3075* • **Massage Therapy/Therapeutic Massage** *330 hrs./$3275*

STUDENT SERVICES Placement services for program completers.

Dawn Training Centre

3700 Lancaster Pike, Wilmington, DE 19805
http://www.dawntrainingcentre.edu/

CONTACT Hollis Anglin, President
Telephone: 302-633-9075

GENERAL INFORMATION Private Institution. **Total program enrollment:** 134. **Application fee:** $25.

PROGRAM(S) OFFERED

• **Aesthetician/Esthetician and Skin Care Specialist** *36 hrs./$10,495* • **Dental Assisting/Assistant** *36 hrs./$11,495* • **Health and Medical Administrative Services, Other** *52 students enrolled* • **Legal Assistant/Paralegal** *15 students enrolled* • **Massage Therapy/Therapeutic Massage** *36 hrs./$9295* • **Medical Insurance Specialist/Medical Biller** *36 hrs./$9995* • **Medical Transcription/Transcriptionist** *4 students enrolled* • **Medical/Clinical Assistant** *36 hrs./$11,570* • **Nurse/Nursing Assistant/Aide and Patient Care Assistant** *72 students enrolled* • **Pharmacy Technician/Assistant** *36 hrs./$9995*

STUDENT SERVICES Academic or career counseling, employment services for current students, placement services for program completers.

Deep Muscle Therapy School

5341 Limestone Road, Wilmington, DE 19808
http://www.dmtsmassage.com/

CONTACT Barbara Uniatowski, School Director
Telephone: 302-478-8890

GENERAL INFORMATION Private Institution. **Total program enrollment:** 378. **Application fee:** $30.

PROGRAM(S) OFFERED
• Health Information/Medical Records Technology/Technician *900 hrs./ $11,930* • Massage Therapy/Therapeutic Massage *900 hrs./$13,236* • Medical/Clinical Assistant *900 hrs./$11,930*

STUDENT SERVICES Academic or career counseling, placement services for program completers.

Delaware College of Art and Design

600 North Market Street, Wilmington, DE 19801
http://www.dcad.edu/

CONTACT James P. Lecky, Director
Telephone: 302-622-8000

GENERAL INFORMATION Private Institution. Founded 1997. **Accreditation:** Regional (MSA/CIHE). **Total program enrollment:** 204. **Application fee:** $25.

PROGRAM(S) OFFERED
• Graphic Design *3 students enrolled* • Interior Design *8 students enrolled* • Photography • Web Page, Digital/Multimedia and Information Resources Design

STUDENT SERVICES Academic or career counseling, employment services for current students, remedial services.

Delaware Learning Institute of Cosmetology

32448 Royal Boulevard, Suite A, Dagsboro, DE 19939
delawarecosmetology.com

CONTACT John H. Cook, School Director
Telephone: 302-732-6704

GENERAL INFORMATION Private Institution. **Total program enrollment:** 48. **Application fee:** $100.

PROGRAM(S) OFFERED
• Aesthetician/Esthetician and Skin Care Specialist *600 hrs./$7500* • Cosmetology, Barber/Styling, and Nail Instructor *250 hrs./$2100* • Cosmetology/Cosmetologist, General *1500 hrs./$14,100* • Massage Therapy/ Therapeutic Massage *600 hrs./$7500* • Nail Technician/Specialist and Manicurist *300 hrs./$3750*

STUDENT SERVICES Academic or career counseling, employment services for current students, placement services for program completers, remedial services.

Delaware Technical & Community College, Jack F. Owens Campus

PO Box 610, Georgetown, DE 19947
http://www.dtcc.edu/

CONTACT Ileana Smith, Vice President
Telephone: 302-856-5400

GENERAL INFORMATION Public Institution. Founded 1967. **Accreditation:** Regional (MSA/CIHE); medical laboratory technology (NAACLS); physical therapy assisting (APTA); radiologic technology: radiography (JRCERT). **Total program enrollment:** 1956. **Application fee:** $10.

PROGRAM(S) OFFERED
• Accounting Technology/Technician and Bookkeeping *23 students enrolled* • Administrative Assistant and Secretarial Science, General • Agricultural Production Operations, General • Agriculture, Agriculture Operations and Related Sciences, Other • Allied Health and Medical Assisting Services, Other • Applied Horticulture/Horticultural Operations, General • Architectural Engineering Technology/Technician • Automobile/Automotive Mechanics Technology/Technician *29 students enrolled* • Automotive Engineering Technology/Technician • Biology Technician/Biotechnology Laboratory Technician • Business Administration and Management, General • Business Operations Support and Secretarial Services, Other • Business/Commerce, General *42 students enrolled* • Business/Office Automation/Technology/Data Entry *10*

students enrolled • CAD/CADD Drafting and/or Design Technology/Technician • Child Development • Computer Programming/Programmer, General • Computer Software Technology/Technician • Computer Technology/Computer Systems Technology *4 students enrolled* • Computer and Information Sciences, General • Construction Engineering Technology/Technician • Drafting/Design Engineering Technologies/Technicians, Other • Early Childhood Education and Teaching • Education, Other • Educational Administration and Supervision, Other *1 student enrolled* • Electrical and Electronic Engineering Technologies/ Technicians, Other • Electrical, Electronic and Communications Engineering Technology/Technician *22 students enrolled* • Engineering Technologies/ Technicians, Other • Heating, Air Conditioning and Refrigeration Technology/ Technician (ACH/ACR/ACHR/HRAC/HVAC/AC Technology) • Heating, Air Conditioning, Ventilation and Refrigeration Maintenance Technology/ Technician (HAC, HACR, HVAC, HVACR) *24 students enrolled* • Human Services, General *28 students enrolled* • Landscaping and Groundskeeping *1 student enrolled* • Legal Administrative Assistant/Secretary *7 students enrolled* • Licensed Practical/Vocational Nurse Training (LPN, LVN, Cert, Dipl, AAS) *102 students enrolled* • Marketing/Marketing Management, General *7 students enrolled* • Medical Transcription/Transcriptionist • Medical/Clinical Assistant *1 student enrolled* • Mental and Social Health Services and Allied Professions, Other • Nurse/Nursing Assistant/Aide and Patient Care Assistant • Nursing— Registered Nurse Training (RN, ASN, BSN, MSN) • Office Management and Supervision *1 student enrolled* • Poultry Science • Psychiatric/Mental Health Services Technician • Survey Technology/Surveying • Teacher Education and Professional Development, Specific Levels and Methods, Other *118 students enrolled* • Truck and Bus Driver/Commercial Vehicle Operation *13 students enrolled* • Turf and Turfgrass Management • Vehicle Maintenance and Repair Technologies, Other *45 students enrolled*

STUDENT SERVICES Academic or career counseling, daycare for children of students, employment services for current students, placement services for program completers, remedial services.

Delaware Technical & Community College, Stanton/Wilmington Campus

400 Stanton-Christiana Road, Newark, DE 19713
http://www.dtcc.edu/

CONTACT Lawrence Miller, Vice President
Telephone: 302-454-3900

GENERAL INFORMATION Public Institution. Founded 1968. **Accreditation:** Regional (MSA/CIHE); dental hygiene (ADA); diagnostic medical sonography (JRCEDMS); engineering technology (ABET/TAC); histologic technology (NAACLS); medical assisting (AAMAE); nuclear medicine technology (JRCNMT); physical therapy assisting (APTA); radiologic technology: radiography (JRCERT). **Total program enrollment:** 2941. **Application fee:** $10.

PROGRAM(S) OFFERED
• Accounting Technology/Technician and Bookkeeping *1 student enrolled* • Accounting • Administrative Assistant and Secretarial Science, General • American Sign Language (ASL) *7 students enrolled* • American Sign Language, Other • Automobile/Automotive Mechanics Technology/Technician • Biology Technician/Biotechnology Laboratory Technician • Business Administration and Management, General • Business/Commerce, General • Child Development • Computer Engineering Technology/Technician • Computer Programming/Programmer, General • Construction Trades, General • Diagnostic Medical Sonography/Sonographer and Ultrasound Technician • Drafting/Design Engineering Technologies/Technicians, Other • Early Childhood Education and Teaching • Education, Other • Electrical and Electronic Engineering Technologies/Technicians, Other *1 student enrolled* • Electrical, Electronic and Communications Engineering Technology/ Technician • Elementary Education and Teaching • Emergency Medical Technology/Technician (EMT Paramedic) • Fire Protection and Safety Technology/Technician • Health Professions and Related Clinical Sciences, Other • Histologic Technology/Histotechnologist • Hotel/Motel Administration/ Management • Human Services, General • Industrial Production Technologies/Technicians, Other • Laser and Optical Technology/Technician *1 student enrolled* • Manufacturing Technology/Technician • Marketing/Marketing Management, General • Mathematics and Statistics, Other • Mathematics, General • Mechanical Engineering Related Technologies/Technicians, Other • Mechanical Engineering/Mechanical Technology/Technician • Medical Insurance Coding Specialist/Coder *4 students enrolled* • Medical Transcription/ Transcriptionist • Medical/Clinical Assistant • Mental and Social Health Services and Allied Professions, Other • Nurse/Nursing Assistant/Aide and Patient Care Assistant *17 students enrolled* • Occupational Safety and Health Technology/Technician • Office Management and Supervision *1 student*

Delaware Technical & Community College, Stanton/Wilmington Campus
(continued)

enrolled • Physical Science Technologies/Technicians, Other • Radiologic Technology/Science—Radiographer • Restaurant, Culinary, and Catering Management/Manager • Science Technologies/Technicians, Other *1 student enrolled* • Sign Language Interpretation and Translation • Substance Abuse/Addiction Counseling • Teacher Education and Professional Development, Specific Levels and Methods, Other *81 students enrolled* • Turf and Turfgrass Management

STUDENT SERVICES Academic or career counseling, daycare for children of students, employment services for current students, placement services for program completers, remedial services.

Delaware Technical & Community College System

PO Box 897, Dover, DE 19903-0897

CONTACT Orlando George, President
Telephone: 302-739-3737

GENERAL INFORMATION Public Institution.

Delaware Technical & Community College, Terry Campus

100 Campus Drive, Dover, DE 19904-1383
http://www.dtcc.edu/terry/

CONTACT Daniel Simpson, Vice President
Telephone: 302-857-1000

GENERAL INFORMATION Public Institution. Founded 1972. **Accreditation:** Regional (MSA/CIHE); emergency medical services (JRCEMTP). **Total program enrollment:** 1390. **Application fee:** $10.

PROGRAM(S) OFFERED
• Accounting Technology/Technician and Bookkeeping • Accounting • Administrative Assistant and Secretarial Science, General • Allied Health and Medical Assisting Services, Other • Business Administration and Management, General • Business/Commerce, General *1 student enrolled* • Business/Office Automation/Technology/Data Entry • Computer Engineering Technology/Technician • Computer Hardware Technology/Technician *2 students enrolled* • Computer Software Technology/Technician • Computer Systems Networking and Telecommunications • Computer Technology/Computer Systems Technology *2 students enrolled* • Construction Management • Criminal Justice/Law Enforcement Administration • Early Childhood Education and Teaching • Education, Other • Educational Administration and Supervision, Other *5 students enrolled* • Electrical, Electronic and Communications Engineering Technology/Technician *1 student enrolled* • Emergency Care Attendant (EMT Ambulance) *4 students enrolled* • Emergency Medical Technology/Technician (EMT Paramedic) • Human Services, General • Licensed Practical/Vocational Nurse Training (LPN, LVN, Cert, Dipl, AAS) *80 students enrolled* • Marketing/Marketing Management, General • Medical Insurance Coding Specialist/Coder • Nurse/Nursing Assistant/Aide and Patient Care Assistant *2 students enrolled* • Nursing—Registered Nurse Training (RN, ASN, BSN, MSN) • Office Management and Supervision • Substance Abuse/Addiction Counseling *2 students enrolled* • Teacher Education and Professional Development, Specific Levels and Methods, Other *85 students enrolled*

STUDENT SERVICES Academic or career counseling, daycare for children of students, employment services for current students, placement services for program completers, remedial services.

Schilling-Douglas School of Hair Design

70 Amstel Avenue, Newark, DE 19711
http://schillingdouglas.com/

CONTACT Victor A. David, Director
Telephone: 302-737-5100 Ext. 101

GENERAL INFORMATION Private Institution. Founded 1977. **Total program enrollment:** 87.

PROGRAM(S) OFFERED
• Cosmetology, Barber/Styling, and Nail Instructor *250 hrs./$6200* • Cosmetology/Cosmetologist, General *400 hrs./$2100* • Nail Technician/Specialist and Manicurist *125 hrs./$1100*

STUDENT SERVICES Academic or career counseling, employment services for current students, placement services for program completers.

Star Technical Institute

Blue Hen Corporate Center, 655 S. Bay Road, Suite 5G2, Dover, DE 19901
http://starinstitute.com/

CONTACT Jamie Kavelak, Director
Telephone: 302-736-6111

GENERAL INFORMATION Private Institution. **Total program enrollment:** 141. **Application fee:** $25.

PROGRAM(S) OFFERED
• Computer and Information Sciences and Support Services, Other *900 hrs./$13,426* • Medical Administrative/Executive Assistant and Medical Secretary *750 hrs./$10,270* • Medical Insurance Specialist/Medical Biller *800 hrs./$10,667* • Medical/Health Management and Clinical Assistant/Specialist *750 hrs./$10,621* • Pharmacy Technician/Assistant *4 students enrolled* • Surgical Technology/Technologist *950 hrs./$14,764*

STUDENT SERVICES Placement services for program completers.

Wesley College

120 North State Street, Dover, DE 19901-3875
http://www.wesley.edu/

CONTACT William N. Johnston, President
Telephone: 302-736-2300

GENERAL INFORMATION Private Institution. Founded 1873. **Accreditation:** Regional (MSA/CIHE). **Total program enrollment:** 1961. **Application fee:** $25.

PROGRAM(S) OFFERED
• Legal Assistant/Paralegal • Religion/Religious Studies

STUDENT SERVICES Academic or career counseling, employment services for current students, placement services for program completers, remedial services.

Widener University–Delaware Campus

4601 Concord Pike, Wilmington, DE 19803
http://www.widener.edu/

CONTACT James T. Harris, III, President
Telephone: 302-477-2100

GENERAL INFORMATION Private Institution. **Total program enrollment:** 983. **Application fee:** $30.

STUDENT SERVICES Academic or career counseling, employment services for current students, placement services for program completers, remedial services.

DISTRICT OF COLUMBIA —

American University

4400 Massachusetts Avenue, NW, Washington, DC 20016-8001
http://www.american.edu/

CONTACT Cornelius M. Kerwin, President
Telephone: 202-885-1000

GENERAL INFORMATION Private Institution. Founded 1893. **Accreditation:** Regional (MSA/CIHE); journalism and mass communications (ACEJMC); music (NASM). **Total program enrollment:** 8950. **Application fee:** $60.

PROGRAM(S) OFFERED
• **American/United States Studies/Civilization** 6 *students enrolled* • **Applied Mathematics** • **International Economics** • **Language Interpretation and Translation** 21 *students enrolled* • **Near and Middle Eastern Studies** 1 *student enrolled* • **Political Science and Government, General** 34 *students enrolled* • **Political Science and Government, Other** 3 *students enrolled* • **Teaching English as a Second or Foreign Language/ESL Language Instructor**

STUDENT SERVICES Academic or career counseling, daycare for children of students, employment services for current students.

Bennett Beauty Institute

680 Rhode Island Avenue NE, Suite J, Washington, DC 20002
http://www.bennettcareerinstitute.com/

CONTACT Chet A. Bennett, CEO
Telephone: 202-526-1400

GENERAL INFORMATION Private Institution. **Total program enrollment:** 91. **Application fee:** $25.

PROGRAM(S) OFFERED
• **Barbering/Barber** 1500 *hrs./$9550* • **Cosmetology, Barber/Styling, and Nail Instructor** 1000 *hrs./$5550* • **Cosmetology/Cosmetologist, General** 1500 *hrs./$12,000* • **Salon/Beauty Salon Management/Manager** 600 *hrs./$3750*

STUDENT SERVICES Daycare for children of students, placement services for program completers.

Career Blazers Learning Center

1025 Connecticut Avenue, NW, Suite 209, Washington, DC 20036
http://www.careerblazers.com

CONTACT Moses Rabi, Director
Telephone: 202-467-4223 Ext. 100

GENERAL INFORMATION Private Institution. Founded 1990. **Total program enrollment:** 307.

PROGRAM(S) OFFERED
• **Computer Technology/Computer Systems Technology** 22 *students enrolled* • **Data Entry/Microcomputer Applications, General** 148 *students enrolled* • **Medical Insurance Specialist/Medical Biller** 44 *students enrolled* • **Teaching English as a Second or Foreign Language/ESL Language Instructor** 2 *students enrolled*

STUDENT SERVICES Academic or career counseling, employment services for current students, placement services for program completers.

Corcoran College of Art and Design

500 17th Street NW, Washington, DC 20006-4804
http://www.corcoran.edu/

CONTACT Kirk Pillow, Dean
Telephone: 202-639-1800

GENERAL INFORMATION Private Institution. Founded 1890. **Accreditation:** Regional (MSA/CIHE); art and design (NASAD). **Total program enrollment:** 389. **Application fee:** $45.

PROGRAM(S) OFFERED
• **Animation, Interactive Technology, Video Graphics and Special Effects** • **Drawing** 2 *students enrolled* • **Graphic Design** 7 *students enrolled* • **Illustration** 1 *student enrolled* • **Interior Design** • **Metal and Jewelry Arts** • **Prepress/Desktop Publishing and Digital Imaging Design** 2 *students enrolled* • **Printmaking** • **Sculpture** • **Web Page, Digital/Multimedia and Information Resources Design** 3 *students enrolled*

STUDENT SERVICES Academic or career counseling, employment services for current students.

Dudley Beauty College

2031 Rhode Island Avenue, NE, Washington, DC 20018-2834

CONTACT Alfred Dudley, School Director
Telephone: 202-269-3666

GENERAL INFORMATION Private Institution. **Total program enrollment:** 40. **Application fee:** $10.

PROGRAM(S) OFFERED
• **Cosmetology, Barber/Styling, and Nail Instructor** 1000 *hrs./$4750* • **Cosmetology/Cosmetologist, General** 1500 *hrs./$11,490* • **Nail Technician/Specialist and Manicurist** 350 *hrs./$2025* • **Salon/Beauty Salon Management/Manager** 500 *hrs./$2375*

STUDENT SERVICES Academic or career counseling, placement services for program completers.

Georgetown University

37th and O Streets, NW, Washington, DC 20057
http://www.georgetown.edu/

CONTACT John J. Degioia, President
Telephone: 202-687-0100

GENERAL INFORMATION Private Institution. Founded 1789. **Accreditation:** Regional (MSA/CIHE). **Total program enrollment:** 13072. **Application fee:** $65.

PROGRAM(S) OFFERED
• **Ophthalmic Technician/Technologist**

STUDENT SERVICES Academic or career counseling, employment services for current students, placement services for program completers.

The George Washington University

2121 Eye Street, NW, Washington, DC 20052
http://www.gwu.edu/

CONTACT Steven Knapp, President
Telephone: 202-994-1000

GENERAL INFORMATION Private Institution. Founded 1821. **Accreditation:** Regional (MSA/CIHE); athletic training (JRCAT); computer science (ABET/CSAC); counseling (ACA); diagnostic medical sonography (JRCEDMS); interior design: professional (CIDA); medical technology (NAACLS); music (NASM); speech-language pathology (ASHA). **Total program enrollment:** 15798. **Application fee:** $65.

The George Washington University (continued)

PROGRAM(S) OFFERED
• **Clinical/Medical Laboratory Technician** *302 students enrolled* • **Criminal Justice/Police Science** *35 students enrolled* • **Diagnostic Medical Sonography/ Sonographer and Ultrasound Technician** *2 students enrolled*

STUDENT SERVICES Academic or career counseling, employment services for current students, placement services for program completers.

National Conservatory of Dramatic Arts

1556 Wisconsin Avenue, NW, Washington, DC 20007-2758
http://www.theconservatory.org/

CONTACT Raymond G. Ficca, President
Telephone: 202-333-2202

GENERAL INFORMATION Private Institution. Founded 1975. **Total program enrollment:** 31. **Application fee:** $30.

PROGRAM(S) OFFERED
• **Dramatic/Theatre Arts and Stagecraft, Other** *8 students enrolled*

STUDENT SERVICES Academic or career counseling, placement services for program completers.

Potomac College

4000 Chesapeake Street, NW, Washington, DC 20016
http://www.potomac.edu/

CONTACT Florence Tate, President
Telephone: 202-686-0876

GENERAL INFORMATION Private Institution. Founded 1991. **Accreditation:** Regional (MSA/CIHE); state accredited or approved. **Total program enrollment:** 233. **Application fee:** $15.

PROGRAM(S) OFFERED
• **Business Administration and Management, General** *13 students enrolled*
• **Computer and Information Systems Security**

STUDENT SERVICES Academic or career counseling.

Sanz School

1511 K Street, N.W., Suite 210, Washington, DC 20005
http://sanz.edu/

CONTACT Burl Dicken, Executive Director
Telephone: 202-872-4700

GENERAL INFORMATION Private Institution. **Total program enrollment:** 899. **Application fee:** $50.

PROGRAM(S) OFFERED
• **English Language and Literature, General** *720 hrs./$5454* • **Health Information/Medical Records Technology/Technician** *1410 hrs./$24,200* • **Medical Insurance Specialist/Medical Biller** *740 hrs./$12,100* • **Medical Office Assistant/Specialist** *875 hrs./$12,100* • **Medical Office Management/ Administration** *45 students enrolled* • **Medical/Clinical Assistant** *720 hrs./ $12,100*

STUDENT SERVICES Academic or career counseling, placement services for program completers.

Strayer University

1025 15th Street, NW, Washington, DC 20005-2603
http://www.strayer.edu/

CONTACT Sondra Stallard, President
Telephone: 202-408-2400

GENERAL INFORMATION Private Institution. Founded 1892. **Accreditation:** Regional (MSA/CIHE). **Total program enrollment:** 8119. **Application fee:** $50.

PROGRAM(S) OFFERED
• **Accounting** *6 students enrolled* • **Business Administration and Management, General** *17 students enrolled* • **Information Science/Studies** *14 students enrolled* • **Purchasing, Procurement/Acquisitions and Contracts Management** *2 students enrolled*

STUDENT SERVICES Academic or career counseling, employment services for current students, remedial services.

Technical Learning Centers

1001 Connecticut Avenue NW, Suite 435, Washington, DC 20036-5540
http://www.tlc-corp.com/

CONTACT Mark Toufanian, School Director
Telephone: 202-223-3500

GENERAL INFORMATION Private Institution. **Total program enrollment:** 82. **Application fee:** $25.

PROGRAM(S) OFFERED
• **Allied Health and Medical Assisting Services, Other** *29 hrs./$12,231* • **Computer Software and Media Applications, Other** *30 hrs./$11,831* • **Computer and Information Sciences, General** *54 students enrolled*

STUDENT SERVICES Employment services for current students, placement services for program completers.

University of the District of Columbia

4200 Connecticut Avenue, NW, Washington, DC 20008-1175
http://www.udc.edu/

CONTACT Dr. Allen L. Sessoms, President
Telephone: 202-274-5000

GENERAL INFORMATION Public Institution. Founded 1976. **Accreditation:** Regional (MSA/CIHE); computer science (ABET/CSAC); engineering technology (ABET/TAC); funeral service (ABFSE); radiologic technology: radiography (JRCERT); speech-language pathology (ASHA). **Total program enrollment:** 2743. **Application fee:** $75.

STUDENT SERVICES Academic or career counseling, daycare for children of students, employment services for current students, placement services for program completers, remedial services.

FLORIDA

Academy for Practical Nursing & Health Occupations

5154 Okeechobee Boulevard, Suite 201, West Palm Beach, FL 33417
http://www.apnho.com/

CONTACT Lois M. Gackenheimer, Executive Director
Telephone: 561-683-1400

GENERAL INFORMATION Private Institution. **Total program enrollment:** 480.

PROGRAM(S) OFFERED
• **Licensed Practical/Vocational Nurse Training (LPN, LVN, Cert, Dipl, AAS)** *1518 hrs./$17,990* • **Nurse/Nursing Assistant/Aide and Patient Care Assistant** *603 hrs./$5789* • **Physical Therapist Assistant** *603 hrs./$5789*

STUDENT SERVICES Academic or career counseling, employment services for current students, placement services for program completers, remedial services.

Academy of Career Training

3501 W. Vine Street, Suite 111, Kissimmee, FL 34741
academyofcareertraining.com

CONTACT Elizabeth Petrusa, President
Telephone: 407-943-8777

GENERAL INFORMATION Private Institution. **Total program enrollment:** 93. **Application fee:** $100.

PROGRAM(S) OFFERED
• **Aesthetician/Esthetician and Skin Care Specialist** *300 hrs./$2500*
• **Barbering/Barber** *1200 hrs./$7850* • **Cosmetology/Cosmetologist, General** *1200 hrs./$8395* • **Massage Therapy/Therapeutic Massage** *500 hrs./$3200*
• **Nail Technician/Specialist and Manicurist** *240 hrs./$1150*

STUDENT SERVICES Placement services for program completers.

Academy of Cosmetology

85 Richland Avenue, Merritt Island, FL 32953
http://floridacosmetologyschools.com/

CONTACT Jacquilyn Eusanio, President
Telephone: 321-452-8490

GENERAL INFORMATION Private Institution. Founded 1968. **Total program enrollment:** 75.

PROGRAM(S) OFFERED
• **Cosmetology and Related Personal Grooming Arts, Other** *600 hrs./$4490*
• **Cosmetology, Barber/Styling, and Nail Instructor** *600 hrs./$4490*
• **Cosmetology/Cosmetologist, General** *1200 hrs./$9800* • **Facial Treatment Specialist/Facialist** *260 hrs./$2300* • **Massage Therapy/Therapeutic Massage** *600 hrs./$4700* • **Nail Technician/Specialist and Manicurist** *240 hrs./$1990*
• **Teacher Education and Professional Development, Specific Subject Areas, Other**

STUDENT SERVICES Placement services for program completers.

Academy of Cosmetology

4711 Babcock Street NE, Suite 26, Palm Bay, FL 32905
http://floridacosmetologyschools.com/

CONTACT Jacquilyn Eusanio, President
Telephone: 321-951-0595

GENERAL INFORMATION Private Institution. **Total program enrollment:** 45.

PROGRAM(S) OFFERED
• **Cosmetology and Related Personal Grooming Arts, Other** *600 hrs./$4490*
• **Cosmetology/Cosmetologist, General** *1200 hrs./$9800* • **Facial Treatment Specialist/Facialist** *260 hrs./$2300* • **Massage Therapy/Therapeutic Massage** *600 hrs./$4700* • **Nail Technician/Specialist and Manicurist** *240 hrs./$1990*

STUDENT SERVICES Placement services for program completers.

Academy of Healing Arts, Massage, and Facial Skin Care

3141 South Military Trail, Lake Worth, FL 33463-2113
http://www.ahamassage.org/

CONTACT Angela Artemik, Co-Owner
Telephone: 561-965-5550

GENERAL INFORMATION Private Institution. Founded 1983. **Total program enrollment:** 78. **Application fee:** $75.

PROGRAM(S) OFFERED
• **Aesthetician/Esthetician and Skin Care Specialist** *9 students enrolled*
• **Cosmetology/Cosmetologist, General** *1200 hrs./$9700* • **Facial Treatment Specialist/Facialist** *300 hrs./$3550* • **Massage Therapy/Therapeutic Massage** *624 hrs./$7900* • **Nail Technician/Specialist and Manicurist** *240 hrs./$1150*
• **Personal and Culinary Services, Other** *900 hrs./$10,975*

STUDENT SERVICES Academic or career counseling, placement services for program completers.

Academy of Professional Careers

114 S. Sermoran Boulevard, Suite 1, Winter Park, FL 32792

CONTACT Frank Capostagno, President
Telephone: 407-673-8477

GENERAL INFORMATION Private Institution. **Total program enrollment:** 100. **Application fee:** $50.

PROGRAM(S) OFFERED
• **Aesthetician/Esthetician and Skin Care Specialist** *600 hrs./$3960*
• **Barbering/Barber** *1200 hrs./$5832* • **Cosmetology and Related Personal Grooming Arts, Other** *1200 hrs./$6408* • **Cosmetology, Barber/Styling, and Nail Instructor** *600 hrs./$3000* • **Cosmetology/Cosmetologist, General** *39 students enrolled* • **Massage Therapy/Therapeutic Massage** *600 hrs./$5100*
• **Nail Technician/Specialist and Manicurist** *240 hrs./$1152*

STUDENT SERVICES Placement services for program completers, remedial services.

Acupuncture and Massage College

10506 North Kendall Drive, Miami, FL 33176
http://www.amcollege.edu/

CONTACT Richard Browne, President
Telephone: 305-595-9500

GENERAL INFORMATION Private Institution. Founded 1983. **Accreditation:** Acupuncture and Oriental Medicine (ACAOM). **Total program enrollment:** 103. **Application fee:** $50.

PROGRAM(S) OFFERED
• **Massage Therapy/Therapeutic Massage** *42 students enrolled*

STUDENT SERVICES Academic or career counseling.

Advanced Technical Centers

42 NW 27th Avenue, Suite 421, Miami, FL 33125-5124
http://www.advancedtechnicalcenters.com/

CONTACT Jose L. Cela, President
Telephone: 305-871-2820 Ext. 113

GENERAL INFORMATION Private Institution. **Total program enrollment:** 27.

PROGRAM(S) OFFERED
• **Business/Office Automation/Technology/Data Entry** *600 hrs./$3250* • **Computer Systems Networking and Telecommunications** • **Customer Service Support/Call Center/Teleservice Operation** *150 hrs./$770* • **Data Entry/ Microcomputer Applications, Other** *600 hrs./$3500* • **Tourism and Travel Services Marketing Operations** *300 hrs./$2255*

STUDENT SERVICES Academic or career counseling, employment services for current students, placement services for program completers, remedial services.

Advance Science Institute

3750 W. 12 Avenue, Hialeah, FL 33012

CONTACT Pablo J. Perez, School Director
Telephone: 305-827-5452

GENERAL INFORMATION Private Institution. **Total program enrollment:** 48.

PROGRAM(S) OFFERED
• **Biomedical/Medical Engineering** *2 students enrolled* • **Medical Office Assistant/Specialist** *1020 hrs./$12,970* • **Medical Radiologic Technology/ Science—Radiation Therapist** *59 students enrolled* • **Radiation Protection/ Health Physics Technician** *930 hrs./$12,660*

STUDENT SERVICES Employment services for current students, placement services for program completers.

American Advanced Technicians Institute

6801 W. 20th Street, Hialeah, FL 33014
http://www.aationline.com/

CONTACT Nayibe Marino, School Director
Telephone: 305-362-5519

GENERAL INFORMATION Private Institution. **Total program enrollment:** 90. **Application fee:** $100.

PROGRAM(S) OFFERED
• **Automobile/Automotive Mechanics Technology/Technician** *300 hrs./$3258* • **Mechanics and Repairers, General** *620 hrs./$8650*

STUDENT SERVICES Employment services for current students, placement services for program completers.

American Institute

416 E. Atlantic Boulevard, Pompano Beach, FL 33060

CONTACT Linda Portillo, Corporate Business Office Mana
Telephone: 954-781-2468 Ext. 204

GENERAL INFORMATION Private Institution. **Total program enrollment:** 249.

PROGRAM(S) OFFERED
• **Cosmetology/Cosmetologist, General** *1200 hrs./$12,100* • **Massage Therapy/ Therapeutic Massage** *54 hrs./$12,000*

STUDENT SERVICES Academic or career counseling, placement services for program completers.

American Institute of Beauty

13244 66th Street North, Largo, FL 33773
http://www.aibschool.com/

CONTACT Michael Halmon, Director
Telephone: 727-532-2125

GENERAL INFORMATION Private Institution. **Total program enrollment:** 29. **Application fee:** $50.

PROGRAM(S) OFFERED
• **Barbering/Barber** *1200 hrs./$13,995* • **Cosmetology/Cosmetologist, General** *23 students enrolled* • **Hair Styling/Stylist and Hair Design** *1200 hrs./$12,450*

STUDENT SERVICES Academic or career counseling, placement services for program completers.

Americare School of Nursing

7275 Estapona Circle, Fern Park, FL 32730
http://americareschoolofnursing.com/

CONTACT Justin Berkowitz, Executive Director
Telephone: 407-673-7406

GENERAL INFORMATION Private Institution. **Total program enrollment:** 348. **Application fee:** $50.

PROGRAM(S) OFFERED
• **Allied Health and Medical Assisting Services, Other** *10 students enrolled* • **Dental Assisting/Assistant** *63 hrs./$11,500* • **Licensed Practical/Vocational Nurse Training (LPN, LVN, Cert, Dipl, AAS)** *87 hrs./$17,125* • **Medical Insurance Coding Specialist/Coder** *38 students enrolled* • **Medical/Clinical Assistant** *108 hrs./$13,400* • **Nurse/Nursing Assistant/Aide and Patient Care Assistant** *35 hrs./$6000* • **Pharmacy Technician/Assistant** *8 students enrolled* • **Radiologic Technology/Science—Radiographer** *1 student enrolled* • **Surgical Technology/ Technologist** *90 hrs./$22,350*

STUDENT SERVICES Employment services for current students, placement services for program completers.

Americare School of Nursing

5335 66th Street North, St. Petersburg, FL 32730
http://www.americareschools.com

CONTACT Justin Berkowitz, Executive Director
Telephone: 407-673-7406

GENERAL INFORMATION Private Institution. **Total program enrollment:** 98. **Application fee:** $50.

PROGRAM(S) OFFERED
• **Allied Health and Medical Assisting Services, Other** *15 students enrolled* • **Dental Assisting/Assistant** *63 hrs./$11,500* • **Medical Insurance Coding Specialist/Coder** *85 hrs./$10,550* • **Medical/Clinical Assistant** *108 hrs./ $13,400* • **Nurse/Nursing Assistant/Aide and Patient Care Assistant** *35 hrs./ $6000* • **Surgical Technology/Technologist** *83 hrs./$13,800*

STUDENT SERVICES Employment services for current students, placement services for program completers.

Angley College

230 N. Woodland Boulevard, Suite 310, Deland, FL 32720
http://www.angley.edu/

CONTACT Joseph T. Angley, Owner
Telephone: 386-740-1215

GENERAL INFORMATION Private Institution. **Total program enrollment:** 206. **Application fee:** $25.

PROGRAM(S) OFFERED
• Dental Assisting/Assistant • Massage Therapy/Therapeutic Massage *1 student enrolled* • Medical/Clinical Assistant *1 student enrolled* • Nurse/Nursing Assistant/Aide and Patient Care Assistant • Phlebotomy/Phlebotomist *2 students enrolled*

STUDENT SERVICES Academic or career counseling, placement services for program completers.

Ari Ben Aviator

3800 St. Lucie Boulevard, Fort Pierce, FL 34946
http://www.aribenaviator.com/

CONTACT Michael Cohen, President
Telephone: 772-466-4822

GENERAL INFORMATION Private Institution. **Total program enrollment:** 57.

PROGRAM(S) OFFERED
• Airline/Commercial/Professional Pilot and Flight Crew *285 hrs./$35,690*

STUDENT SERVICES Academic or career counseling, placement services for program completers.

The Art Institute of Fort Lauderdale

1799 Southeast 17th Street Causeway, Fort Lauderdale, FL 33316-3000
http://www.artinstitutes.edu/fortlauderdale/

CONTACT Charles J. Nagele, President
Telephone: 954-463-3000 Ext. 2122

GENERAL INFORMATION Private Institution. Founded 1968. **Accreditation:** State accredited or approved. **Total program enrollment:** 1642. **Application fee:** $50.

PROGRAM(S) OFFERED
• Commercial Photography *13 students enrolled* • Commercial and Advertising Art *25 students enrolled* • Culinary Arts/Chef Training *52 students enrolled*

STUDENT SERVICES Academic or career counseling, employment services for current students, placement services for program completers, remedial services.

Artistic Nails and Beauty Academy

4951-A Adamo Drive, Tampa, FL 33605
http://www.artisticbeautyschool.com/

CONTACT Robert Rosenburg, Director
Telephone: 813-654-4529

GENERAL INFORMATION Private Institution. **Total program enrollment:** 53. **Application fee:** $50.

PROGRAM(S) OFFERED
• Aesthetician/Esthetician and Skin Care Specialist *300 hrs./$4320* • Barbering/Barber *1200 hrs./$13,835* • Cosmetology and Related Personal Grooming Arts, Other *42 students enrolled* • Cosmetology/Cosmetologist, General *1200 hrs./$13,285* • Facial Treatment Specialist/Facialist *600 hrs./$8294* • Nail Technician/Specialist and Manicurist *300 hrs./$1575*

STUDENT SERVICES Academic or career counseling, employment services for current students, placement services for program completers.

ASM Beauty World Academy

2510 North 60th Avenue, Hollywood, FL 33021

CONTACT Sal Milazzo, Secretary Treasure
Telephone: 954-321-8411

GENERAL INFORMATION Private Institution. Founded 1986. **Application fee:** $100.

PROGRAM(S) OFFERED
• Aesthetician/Esthetician and Skin Care Specialist *260 hrs./$1382* • Cosmetology and Related Personal Grooming Arts, Other *15 students enrolled* • Cosmetology, Barber/Styling, and Nail Instructor *600 hrs./$5276* • Cosmetology/Cosmetologist, General *1200 hrs.* • Nail Technician/Specialist and Manicurist *240 hrs./$782*

STUDENT SERVICES Academic or career counseling, employment services for current students, placement services for program completers, remedial services.

ATI Career Training Center

2880 NW 62nd Street, Fort Lauderdale, FL 33309-9731
http://www.aticareertraining.com/

CONTACT Kim Stone, Executive Director
Telephone: 954-973-4760

GENERAL INFORMATION Private Institution. **Accreditation:** State accredited or approved. **Total program enrollment:** 423. **Application fee:** $100.

PROGRAM(S) OFFERED
• Allied Health and Medical Assisting Services, Other *680 hrs./$13,700* • Computer Systems Networking and Telecommunications *1200 hrs./$21,300* • Health and Medical Administrative Services, Other *720 hrs./$10,400* • Health and Physical Education/Fitness, Other *880 hrs./$16,780* • Industrial Electronics Technology/Technician *1440 hrs./$25,340*

STUDENT SERVICES Employment services for current students, placement services for program completers, remedial services.

ATI Career Training Center

1 NE 19th Street, Miami, FL 33132
http://www.aticareertraining.com/

CONTACT Maribel Cintron, Executive Director
Telephone: 305-591-3060

GENERAL INFORMATION Private Institution. **Accreditation:** State accredited or approved. **Total program enrollment:** 432. **Application fee:** $100.

PROGRAM(S) OFFERED
• Automotive Engineering Technology/Technician *111 students enrolled* • Clinical Laboratory Science/Medical Technology/Technologist *6 students enrolled* • Engineering Technologies/Technicians, Other *13 students enrolled* • Heating, Air Conditioning and Refrigeration Technology/Technician (ACH/ACR/ACHR/HRAC/HVAC/AC Technology) *41 students enrolled* • Medical Administrative/Executive Assistant and Medical Secretary *2 students enrolled*

STUDENT SERVICES Academic or career counseling, employment services for current students, placement services for program completers, remedial services.

ATI Career Training Center

3501 NW 9th Avenue, Oakland Park, FL 33309-9612
http://www.aticareertraining.edu/

CONTACT Kertney Thompson, Executive Director
Telephone: 954-563-5899

GENERAL INFORMATION Private Institution. **Accreditation:** State accredited or approved. **Total program enrollment:** 772. **Application fee:** $100.

PROGRAM(S) OFFERED
• Automobile/Automotive Mechanics Technology/Technician *99 hrs./$26,800* • Business/Commerce, General *70 hrs./$16,180* • Heating, Air Conditioning

ATI Career Training Center (continued)

and Refrigeration Technology/Technician (ACH/ACR/ACHR/HRAC/HVAC/AC Technology) *61 students enrolled* • **Heating, Air Conditioning, Ventilation and Refrigeration Maintenance Technology/Technician (HAC, HACR, HVAC, HVACR)** *93 hrs./$22,400* • **Industrial Electronics Technology/Technician** *54 hrs./$13,900*

STUDENT SERVICES Academic or career counseling, employment services for current students, placement services for program completers, remedial services.

Atlantic Vocational-Technical Center

4700 Coconut Creek Parkway, Coconut Creek, FL 33063
http://www.atlantictechcenter.com/

CONTACT Robert B. Crawford, Center Director
Telephone: 754-321-5100

GENERAL INFORMATION Public Institution. Founded 1973. **Total program enrollment:** 1092.

PROGRAM(S) OFFERED
• **Accounting** *900 hrs./$1945* • **Administrative Assistant and Secretarial Science, General** *10 students enrolled* • **Architectural Drafting and Architectural CAD/CADD** *2 students enrolled* • **Autobody/Collision and Repair Technology/Technician** *11 students enrolled* • **Automobile/Automotive Mechanics Technology/Technician** *1800 hrs./$4570* • **Computer Installation and Repair Technology/Technician** *1650 hrs./$3955* • **Computer Programming, Specific Applications** *2 students enrolled* • **Computer Science** *2 students enrolled* • **Cosmetology and Related Personal Grooming Arts, Other** *23 students enrolled* • **Cosmetology/Cosmetologist, General** *30 students enrolled* • **Culinary Arts/Chef Training** *19 students enrolled* • **Dental Assisting/Assistant** • **Digital Communication and Media/Multimedia** *4 students enrolled* • **Electrician** *1200 hrs./$2880* • **Electrocardiograph Technology/Technician** *11 students enrolled* • **Health Services/Allied Health/Health Sciences, General** *10 students enrolled* • **Health Unit Coordinator/Ward Clerk** *10 students enrolled* • **Heating, Air Conditioning, Ventilation and Refrigeration Maintenance Technology/Technician (HAC, HACR, HVAC, HVACR)** *1350 hrs./$3630* • **Legal Support Services, Other** *2 students enrolled* • **Licensed Practical/Vocational Nurse Training (LPN, LVN, Cert, Dipl, AAS)** *1350 hrs./$3854* • **Machine Tool Technology/Machinist** *3 students enrolled* • **Massage Therapy/Therapeutic Massage** *19 students enrolled* • **Medical Administrative/Executive Assistant and Medical Secretary** *2 students enrolled* • **Medical Insurance Coding Specialist/Coder** *11 students enrolled* • **Nursing, Other** *13 students enrolled* • **Pharmacy Technician/Assistant** *5 students enrolled* • **Phlebotomy/Phlebotomist** *11 students enrolled* • **Renal/Dialysis Technologist/Technician** *7 students enrolled* • **System, Networking, and LAN/WAN Management/Manager** *1 student enrolled* • **Web Page, Digital/Multimedia and Information Resources Design** *11 students enrolled* • **Welding Technology/Welder** *4 students enrolled*

STUDENT SERVICES Academic or career counseling, placement services for program completers, remedial services.

Audio Recording Technology Institute

4525 Vineland Road, Suite 201b, Orlando, FL 32811-7231
http://www.audiocareer.com/

CONTACT Steve Pietrofesa, President
Telephone: 402-423-2784 Ext. 117

GENERAL INFORMATION Private Institution. **Total program enrollment:** 43. **Application fee:** $75.

PROGRAM(S) OFFERED
• **Recording Arts Technology/Technician** *640 hrs./$19,075*

STUDENT SERVICES Placement services for program completers.

Aveda Institute–Saint Petersburg

235 3rd Street South, Saint Petersburg, FL 33701

GENERAL INFORMATION Private Institution. **Total program enrollment:** 115. **Application fee:** $50.

PROGRAM(S) OFFERED
• **Cosmetology/Cosmetologist, General** *1244 hrs./$13,400* • **Massage Therapy/Therapeutic Massage** *1072 hrs./$13,000*

STUDENT SERVICES Academic or career counseling, placement services for program completers.

Aveda Institute–Tallahassee

2020 W. Pensacola Street, Tallahassee, FL 32304

GENERAL INFORMATION Private Institution. **Total program enrollment:** 104. **Application fee:** $50.

PROGRAM(S) OFFERED
• **Cosmetology/Cosmetologist, General** *1244 hrs./$11,400*

STUDENT SERVICES Academic or career counseling, placement services for program completers.

The Beauty Institute

2215 N. Military Trail, West Palm Beach, FL 33409
http://www.thebeautyinstitute.edu/

CONTACT Debra Edwards, President
Telephone: 561-688-0225

GENERAL INFORMATION Private Institution. **Total program enrollment:** 24.

PROGRAM(S) OFFERED
• **Aesthetician/Esthetician and Skin Care Specialist** *260 hrs./$1645* • **Barbering/Barber** *1200 hrs./$8600* • **Cosmetology and Related Personal Grooming Arts, Other** *500 hrs./$2665* • **Cosmetology/Cosmetologist, General** *1200 hrs./$9198* • **Nail Technician/Specialist and Manicurist** *240 hrs./$1120*

STUDENT SERVICES Placement services for program completers.

Beauty Schools of America

1060 W. 49th Street, Hialeah, FL 33012-3322
http://www.beautyschoolsofamerica.com/

CONTACT John W. Rebstock, President/CEO
Telephone: 305-362-9003

GENERAL INFORMATION Private Institution. **Total program enrollment:** 499.

PROGRAM(S) OFFERED
• **Aesthetician/Esthetician and Skin Care Specialist** *900 hrs./$10,539* • **Barbering/Barber** *1200 hrs./$12,868* • **Cosmetology/Cosmetologist, General** *1200 hrs./$14,405* • **Make-Up Artist/Specialist** *300 hrs./$3337* • **Massage Therapy/Therapeutic Massage** *625 hrs./$8166* • **Nail Technician/Specialist and Manicurist** *240 hrs./$1283*

STUDENT SERVICES Academic or career counseling, employment services for current students, placement services for program completers, remedial services.

Beauty Schools of America

1176 SW 67th Avenue, Miami, FL 33144
http://www.beautyschoolsofamerica.com/

CONTACT John W. Rebstock, President/CEO
Telephone: 305-267-6604

GENERAL INFORMATION Private Institution. **Total program enrollment:** 467.

PROGRAM(S) OFFERED

• **Aesthetician/Esthetician and Skin Care Specialist** *900 hrs./$10,539*
• **Barbering/Barber** *1200 hrs./$12,868* • **Cosmetology/Cosmetologist, General** *1200 hrs./$14,405* • **Make-Up Artist/Specialist** *300 hrs./$3337* • **Nail Technician/Specialist and Manicurist** *240 hrs./$1283*

STUDENT SERVICES Academic or career counseling, employment services for current students, placement services for program completers, remedial services.

Beauty Schools of America

1813 NE 163rd Street, North Miami Beach, FL 33162
http://www.thebeautyschoolsofamerica.com

CONTACT John W. Rebstock, President/CEO
Telephone: 305-947-0832

GENERAL INFORMATION Private Institution. **Total program enrollment:** 249.

PROGRAM(S) OFFERED

• **Cosmetology/Cosmetologist, General** *1200 hrs./$14,405*

STUDENT SERVICES Academic or career counseling, employment services for current students, placement services for program completers, remedial services.

Benes International School of Beauty

7127 US Highway 19, New Port Richey, FL 34652
http://www.isbschool.com/

CONTACT Patrick Bene, Director
Telephone: 727-848-8415

GENERAL INFORMATION Private Institution. Founded 1976. **Total program enrollment:** 230. **Application fee:** $50.

PROGRAM(S) OFFERED

• **Aesthetician/Esthetician and Skin Care Specialist** *360 hrs./$5600*
• **Barbering/Barber** *1200 hrs./$12,200* • **Cosmetology and Related Personal Grooming Arts, Other** *600 hrs./$8360* • **Cosmetology/Cosmetologist, General** *1200 hrs./$12,450* • **Massage Therapy/Therapeutic Massage** *600 hrs./$9200*
• **Nail Technician/Specialist and Manicurist** *360 hrs./$4340*

STUDENT SERVICES Academic or career counseling, placement services for program completers, remedial services.

Bradenton Beauty Academy

3928C Manatee Avenue, W, Bradenton, FL 34205
http://www.beauty-academy.us/

CONTACT A. Patricia Galdamez, CEO
Telephone: 941-761-4400

GENERAL INFORMATION Private Institution. Founded 1954. **Total program enrollment:** 167.

PROGRAM(S) OFFERED

• **Aesthetician/Esthetician and Skin Care Specialist** *310 hrs./$2845*
• **Barbering/Barber** *1200 hrs./$10,200* • **Cosmetology and Related Personal Grooming Arts, Other** *610 hrs./$4025* • **Cosmetology, Barber/Styling, and Nail Instructor** *600 hrs./$5400* • **Cosmetology/Cosmetologist, General** *1500 hrs./$13,209* • **Nail Technician/Specialist and Manicurist** *300 hrs./$2100*

STUDENT SERVICES Academic or career counseling, placement services for program completers.

Bradford Union Area Vocational Technical Center

609 North Orange Street, Starke, FL 32091
http://www.bradfordvotech.com/

CONTACT Randy Starling, Director
Telephone: 904-966-6764

GENERAL INFORMATION Private Institution. **Total program enrollment:** 104.

PROGRAM(S) OFFERED

• **Accounting** • **Administrative Assistant and Secretarial Science, General** *1050 hrs./$2247* • **Child Care Provider/Assistant** *13 students enrolled*
• **Computer Installation and Repair Technology/Technician** *1650 hrs./$3436*
• **Computer and Information Sciences, General** *1 student enrolled*
• **Cosmetology/Cosmetologist, General** *1200 hrs./$3221* • **Diesel Mechanics Technology/Technician** *1680 hrs./$3497* • **Health Professions and Related Clinical Sciences, Other** *9 students enrolled* • **Licensed Practical/Vocational Nurse Training (LPN, LVN, Cert, Dipl, AAS)** *19 students enrolled* • **Nursing, Other** *1350 hrs./$3799* • **Truck and Bus Driver/Commercial Vehicle Operation** *320 hrs./$653* • **Welding Technology/Welder**

STUDENT SERVICES Academic or career counseling, employment services for current students, placement services for program completers, remedial services.

Brevard Community College

1519 Clearlake Road, Cocoa, FL 32922-6597
http://www.brevardcc.edu/

CONTACT James A. Drake, District President
Telephone: 321-632-1111

GENERAL INFORMATION Public Institution. Founded 1960. **Accreditation:** Regional (SACS/CC); dental assisting (ADA); dental hygiene (ADA); emergency medical services (JRCEMTP); medical laboratory technology (NAACLS); radiologic technology: radiography (JRCERT). **Total program enrollment:** 6125. **Application fee:** $30.

PROGRAM(S) OFFERED

• **Accounting Technology/Technician and Bookkeeping** *5 students enrolled* • **Accounting and Related Services, Other** *2 students enrolled* • **Administrative Assistant and Secretarial Science, General** • **Architectural Engineering Technology/Technician** *16 students enrolled* • **Blood Bank Technology Specialist** *31 students enrolled* • **Business, Management, Marketing, and Related Support Services, Other** *2 students enrolled* • **Chemical Technology/Technician** *1 student enrolled* • **Child Care Provider/Assistant** *5 students enrolled*
• **Cinematography and Film/Video Production** *21 students enrolled* • **Commercial and Advertising Art** *14 students enrolled* • **Computer Systems Analysis/Analyst** *4 students enrolled* • **Computer Technology/Computer Systems Technology** *12 students enrolled* • **Computer/Information Technology Services Administration and Management, Other** *1 student enrolled* • **Corrections** *105 students enrolled* • **Cosmetology/Cosmetologist, General** *33 students enrolled* • **Criminal Justice/Police Science** *78 students enrolled* • **Dental Assisting/Assistant** *32 students enrolled* • **Drafting and Design Technology/Technician, General** *25 students enrolled* • **Electrical and Electronic Engineering Technologies/Technicians, Other** • **Electrical/Electronics Maintenance and Repair Technology, Other** *1 student enrolled* • **Electromechanical Technology/Electromechanical Engineering Technology** *25 students enrolled* • **Emergency Medical Technology/Technician (EMT Paramedic)** *78 students enrolled* • **Entrepreneurship/Entrepreneurial Studies** *11 students enrolled* • **Executive Assistant/Executive Secretary** *14 students enrolled* • **Facial Treatment Specialist/Facialist** *19 students enrolled* • **Fire Science/Firefighting** *127 students enrolled* • **Foodservice Systems Administration/Management** *8 students enrolled* • **Health Information/Medical Records Technology/Technician** *11 students enrolled* • **Heating, Air Conditioning, Ventilation and Refrigeration Maintenance Technology/Technician (HAC, HACR, HVAC, HVACR)** *2 students enrolled* • **Licensed Practical/Vocational Nurse Training (LPN, LVN, Cert, Dipl, AAS)** *22 students enrolled* • **Management Information Systems and Services, Other** • **Management Information Systems, General** *2 students enrolled*
• **Marketing/Marketing Management, General** *7 students enrolled* • **Medical Administrative/Executive Assistant and Medical Secretary** *6 students enrolled*
• **Medical/Clinical Assistant** *28 students enrolled* • **Nursing, Other** • **Surgical**

Brevard Community College (continued)

Technology/Technologist 9 *students enrolled* ● **Teacher Education and Professional Development, Specific Levels and Methods, Other** 6 *students enrolled* ● **Welding Technology/Welder** 2 *students enrolled*

STUDENT SERVICES Academic or career counseling, daycare for children of students, employment services for current students, placement services for program completers, remedial services.

Broward Community College

225 East Las Olas Boulevard, Fort Lauderdale, FL 33301-2298
http://www.broward.edu/

CONTACT J. David Armstrong, Jr., President
Telephone: 954-201-7400

GENERAL INFORMATION Public Institution. Founded 1960. **Accreditation:** Regional (SACS/CC); dental assisting (ADA); dental hygiene (ADA); diagnostic medical sonography (JRCEDMS); emergency medical services (JRCEMTP); health information technology (AHIMA); music (NASM); nuclear medicine technology (JRCNMT); physical therapy assisting (APTA); respiratory therapy technology (CoARC). **Total program enrollment:** 11540. **Application fee:** $35.

PROGRAM(S) OFFERED
● **Accounting and Related Services, Other** 32 *students enrolled* ● **Aircraft Powerplant Technology/Technician** 20 *students enrolled* ● **Airframe Mechanics and Aircraft Maintenance Technology/Technician** 23 *students enrolled* ● **Architectural Engineering Technology/Technician** ● **Biomedical Technology/Technician** ● **Business Administration and Management, General** 18 *students enrolled* ● **Business, Management, Marketing, and Related Support Services, Other** 1 *student enrolled* ● **Cinematography and Film/Video Production** 16 *students enrolled* ● **Commercial and Advertising Art** 17 *students enrolled* ● **Computer Programming, Specific Applications** ● **Computer Systems Analysis/Analyst** 2 *students enrolled* ● **Computer/Information Technology Services Administration and Management, Other** 10 *students enrolled* ● **Corrections** 21 *students enrolled* ● **Criminal Justice/Police Science** 263 *students enrolled* ● **Dental Assisting/Assistant** 23 *students enrolled* ● **Diagnostic Medical Sonography/Sonographer and Ultrasound Technician** ● **Emergency Medical Technology/Technician (EMT Paramedic)** 207 *students enrolled* ● **Entrepreneurship/Entrepreneurial Studies** 40 *students enrolled* ● **Executive Assistant/Executive Secretary** 11 *students enrolled* ● **Hospital and Health Care Facilities Administration/Management** ● **Hotel/Motel Administration/Management** 1 *student enrolled* ● **Management Information Systems and Services, Other** 1 *student enrolled* ● **Marketing/Marketing Management, General** 3 *students enrolled* ● **Massage Therapy/Therapeutic Massage** 16 *students enrolled* ● **Medical Administrative/Executive Assistant and Medical Secretary** ● **Medical Radiologic Technology/Science—Radiation Therapist** 7 *students enrolled* ● **Medical/Clinical Assistant** 13 *students enrolled* ● **Nuclear Medical Technology/Technologist** 12 *students enrolled* ● **Nursing—Registered Nurse Training (RN, ASN, BSN, MSN)** 79 *students enrolled* ● **Office Management and Supervision** ● **Restaurant/Food Services Management** 15 *students enrolled* ● **Security and Protective Services, Other** 41 *students enrolled*

STUDENT SERVICES Academic or career counseling, daycare for children of students, employment services for current students, placement services for program completers, remedial services.

Brown Mackie College–Miami

1501 Biscayne Boulevard, Miami, FL 33132
http://www.brownmackie.edu/Miami/

CONTACT Julia Denniston, President
Telephone: 305-341-6600

GENERAL INFORMATION Private Institution. **Total program enrollment:** 716.

PROGRAM(S) OFFERED
● **Medical/Clinical Assistant** 13 *students enrolled*

STUDENT SERVICES Academic or career counseling, employment services for current students, placement services for program completers, remedial services.

Cambridge Institute of Allied Health

1912 Boothe Circle, Suite 200, Longwood, FL 32750

CONTACT Karen A. Tolley, Owner
Telephone: 407-265-8383

GENERAL INFORMATION Private Institution. **Total program enrollment:** 156. **Application fee:** $100.

PROGRAM(S) OFFERED
● **Health Services/Allied Health/Health Sciences, General** 15 *students enrolled* ● **Medical/Clinical Assistant** 900 *hrs./*$10,201 ● **Nurse/Nursing Assistant/Aide and Patient Care Assistant** 720 *hrs./*$9403 ● **Radiologic Technology/Science—Radiographer** 660 *hrs./*$9970

STUDENT SERVICES Academic or career counseling, placement services for program completers.

Career Institute of Florida

701 94th Avenue N., Suite 100, Saint Petersburg, FL 33702
http://www.cif.edu/

CONTACT Jane Mercer, President & CEO
Telephone: 727-576-9597

GENERAL INFORMATION Private Institution. **Total program enrollment:** 109.

PROGRAM(S) OFFERED
● **Information Technology** 960 *hrs./*$9950 ● **Medical Insurance Coding Specialist/Coder** 1004 *hrs./*$12,350 ● **Medical Office Assistant/Specialist** 1080 *hrs./*$12,500 ● **Medical Office Management/Administration** 1050 *hrs./*$11,950 ● **Medical Transcription/Transcriptionist** 900 *hrs./*$12,350 ● **System Administration/Administrator** 400 *hrs./*$8450

STUDENT SERVICES Placement services for program completers.

Central Florida College

1500 663 North, Saint Petersburg, FL 33710

CONTACT Duncan Anderson, CEO
Telephone: 727-531-5900

GENERAL INFORMATION Private Institution. **Total program enrollment:** 69. **Application fee:** $50.

PROGRAM(S) OFFERED
● **Allied Health and Medical Assisting Services, Other** 54 *hrs./*$13,745 ● **Cosmetology/Cosmetologist, General** 60 *hrs./*$15,145 ● **Facial Treatment Specialist/Facialist** 51 *hrs./*$9945 ● **Health and Medical Administrative Services, Other** 10 *students enrolled* ● **Medical Insurance Specialist/Medical Biller** 54 *hrs./*$13,745 ● **Medical/Clinical Assistant** 7 *students enrolled*

STUDENT SERVICES Placement services for program completers.

Central Florida College

1573 West Fairbanks Avenue, Suite 100, Winter Park, FL 32789
http://www.centralfloridacollege.edu/

CONTACT David Ray, Campus Director
Telephone: 407-843-3984

GENERAL INFORMATION Private Institution. Founded 1984. **Accreditation:** State accredited or approved. **Total program enrollment:** 374. **Application fee:** $50.

PROGRAM(S) OFFERED
● **Aesthetician/Esthetician and Skin Care Specialist** 51 *hrs./*$9945 ● **Allied Health and Medical Assisting Services, Other** 100 *hrs./*$21,345 ● **Facial Treatment Specialist/Facialist** 24 *students enrolled* ● **Health Information/Medical Records Technology/Technician** 102 *hrs./*$21,245 ● **Medical Insurance Specialist/Medical Biller** 101 *hrs./*$26,035 ● **Medical Office Assistant/**

Specialist *100 hrs./$21,345* • **Medical/Clinical Assistant** *30 students enrolled* • **Nurse/Nursing Assistant/Aide and Patient Care Assistant** *22 students enrolled* • **Pharmacy Technician/Assistant** *100 hrs./$20,245*

STUDENT SERVICES Academic or career counseling, placement services for program completers.

Central Florida Community College

PO Box 1388, Ocala, FL 34478-1388
http://www.cf.edu/

CONTACT Charles R. Dassance, President
Telephone: 352-873-5800

GENERAL INFORMATION Public Institution. Founded 1957. **Accreditation:** Regional (SACS/CC); emergency medical services (JRCEMTP); physical therapy assisting (APTA). **Total program enrollment:** 2953. **Application fee:** $20.

PROGRAM(S) OFFERED
• **Accounting and Related Services, Other** *2 students enrolled* • **Autobody/Collision and Repair Technology/Technician** *3 students enrolled* • **Barbering/Barber** *7 students enrolled* • **Business Administration and Management, General** *1 student enrolled* • **Business, Management, Marketing, and Related Support Services, Other** *2 students enrolled* • **Child Care Provider/Assistant** • **Community Health Services/Liaison/Counseling** • **Computer Systems Analysis/Analyst** *2 students enrolled* • **Corrections** *150 students enrolled* • **Cosmetology/Cosmetologist, General** *49 students enrolled* • **Criminal Justice/Police Science** *31 students enrolled* • **Dental Assisting/Assistant** *7 students enrolled* • **Emergency Medical Technology/Technician (EMT Paramedic)** *73 students enrolled* • **Entrepreneurship/Entrepreneurial Studies** *5 students enrolled* • **Equestrian/Equine Studies** *2 students enrolled* • **Executive Assistant/Executive Secretary** *7 students enrolled* • **Health Information/Medical Records Technology/Technician** *12 students enrolled* • **Heating, Air Conditioning, Ventilation and Refrigeration Maintenance Technology/Technician (HAC, HACR, HVAC, HVACR)** *7 students enrolled* • **Landscaping and Groundskeeping** • **Licensed Practical/Vocational Nurse Training (LPN, LVN, Cert, Dipl, AAS)** *18 students enrolled* • **Plant Nursery Operations and Management** • **Restaurant/Food Services Management** *1 student enrolled* • **Surgical Technology/Technologist** *10 students enrolled* • **Truck and Bus Driver/Commercial Vehicle Operation** *84 students enrolled* • **Welding Technology/Welder**

STUDENT SERVICES Academic or career counseling, daycare for children of students, employment services for current students, placement services for program completers, remedial services.

Central Florida Institute

60522 US Highway 19 North, Suite 200, Palm Harbor, FL 34684
http://www.cfinstitute.com/

CONTACT Olivia T. Fields, School Director
Telephone: 727-786-4707 Ext. 250

GENERAL INFORMATION Private Institution. Founded 1997. **Accreditation:** Surgical technology (ARCST); state accredited or approved. **Total program enrollment:** 655. **Application fee:** $50.

PROGRAM(S) OFFERED
• **Cardiovascular Technology/Technologist** *1755 hrs./$16,259* • **Dental Assisting/Assistant** *980 hrs./$11,259* • **Diagnostic Medical Sonography/Sonographer and Ultrasound Technician** *18 students enrolled* • **Electroneurodiagnostic/Electroencephalographic Technology/Technologist** • **Medical/Clinical Assistant** *1130 hrs./$11,259* • **Surgical Technology/Technologist** *1500 hrs./$16,259*

STUDENT SERVICES Academic or career counseling, employment services for current students, placement services for program completers.

Charlotte Vocational-Technical Center

18300 Toledo Blade Boulevard, Port Charlotte, FL 33948-3399
http://charlottetechcenter.ccps.k12.fl.us/

CONTACT Barbara Witte, Center Director
Telephone: 941-255-7500

GENERAL INFORMATION Public Institution. Founded 1980. **Total program enrollment:** 449.

PROGRAM(S) OFFERED
• **Accounting** *8 students enrolled* • **Administrative Assistant and Secretarial Science, General** *5 students enrolled* • **Child Care Provider/Assistant** *13 students enrolled* • **Computer/Information Technology Services Administration and Management, Other** *7 students enrolled* • **Cosmetology and Related Personal Grooming Arts, Other** *1 student enrolled* • **Cosmetology/Cosmetologist, General** *20 students enrolled* • **Culinary Arts and Related Services, Other** *7 students enrolled* • **Dental Assisting/Assistant** *23 students enrolled* • **Electrical, Electronic and Communications Engineering Technology/Technician** *16 students enrolled* • **Licensed Practical/Vocational Nurse Training (LPN, LVN, Cert, Dipl, AAS)** *54 students enrolled* • **Medical Administrative/Executive Assistant and Medical Secretary** *13 students enrolled* • **Nurse/Nursing Assistant/Aide and Patient Care Assistant** *150 students enrolled*

STUDENT SERVICES Academic or career counseling, daycare for children of students, employment services for current students, placement services for program completers, remedial services.

Chipola College

3094 Indian Circle, Marianna, FL 32446-3065
http://www.chipola.edu/

CONTACT Dr. Gene Prough, President
Telephone: 850-526-2761

GENERAL INFORMATION Public Institution. Founded 1947. **Accreditation:** Regional (SACS/CC). **Total program enrollment:** 1129. **Application fee:** $20.

PROGRAM(S) OFFERED
• **Child Care Provider/Assistant** • **Computer Installation and Repair Technology/Technician** *3 students enrolled* • **Corrections** *136 students enrolled* • **Cosmetology/Cosmetologist, General** *12 students enrolled* • **Criminal Justice/Police Science** *30 students enrolled* • **Emergency Medical Technology/Technician (EMT Paramedic)** *27 students enrolled* • **Fire Science/Firefighting** *58 students enrolled* • **Mason/Masonry** • **Nurse/Nursing Assistant/Aide and Patient Care Assistant** *16 students enrolled* • **Survey Technology/Surveying** • **Welding Technology/Welder**

STUDENT SERVICES Academic or career counseling, placement services for program completers, remedial services.

City College

2400 Southwest 13th Street, Gainesville, FL 32608
http://www.citycollege.edu/

CONTACT Cliff Phillips, Executive Director
Telephone: 352-335-4000

GENERAL INFORMATION Private Institution. Founded 1986. **Accreditation:** State accredited or approved. **Total program enrollment:** 278. **Application fee:** $25.

PROGRAM(S) OFFERED
• **Phlebotomy/Phlebotomist** *2 students enrolled*

STUDENT SERVICES Academic or career counseling, employment services for current students, placement services for program completers, remedial services.

College of Business and Technology

8991 SW 107th Avenue, Suite 200, Miami, FL 33176
http://www.cbt.edu/

CONTACT Fernando N. Llerena, President
Telephone: 305-273-4499 Ext. 1100

GENERAL INFORMATION Private Institution. Founded 1988. **Accreditation:** State accredited or approved. **Total program enrollment: 57. Application fee:** $100.

PROGRAM(S) OFFERED
• **Administrative Assistant and Secretarial Science, General** *5 students enrolled* • **Business Administration and Management, General** • **Computer Technology/Computer Systems Technology** • **Electrical/Electronics Maintenance and Repair Technology, Other** • **Heating, Air Conditioning and Refrigeration Technology/Technician (ACH/ACR/ACHR/HRAC/HVAC/AC Technology)** • **Medical Insurance Coding Specialist/Coder** *8 students enrolled* • **Medical/Clinical Assistant** • **Nursing, Other** • **Phlebotomy/Phlebotomist** • **Web Page, Digital/Multimedia and Information Resources Design** *1 student enrolled*

STUDENT SERVICES Academic or career counseling, placement services for program completers, remedial services.

College of Business and Technology–Flagler Campus

8230 W. Flagler Street, Miami, FL 33144
http://www.cbt.edu/

CONTACT Luis Llerena, School Director
Telephone: 305-273-4499 Ext. 2200

GENERAL INFORMATION Private Institution. **Total program enrollment:** 142. **Application fee:** $100.

PROGRAM(S) OFFERED
• **Administrative Assistant and Secretarial Science, General** • **Business Administration and Management, General** *2 students enrolled* • **Computer Technology/Computer Systems Technology** *3 students enrolled* • **Electrical/Electronics Maintenance and Repair Technology, Other** • **Heating, Air Conditioning and Refrigeration Technology/Technician (ACH/ACR/ACHR/HRAC/HVAC/AC Technology)** *132 students enrolled* • **Medical Insurance Coding Specialist/Coder** *7 students enrolled* • **Medical/Clinical Assistant** • **Nursing, Other** • **Phlebotomy/Phlebotomist** • **Web Page, Digital/Multimedia and Information Resources Design**

STUDENT SERVICES Academic or career counseling, placement services for program completers, remedial services.

College of Business and Technology–Hialeah Campus

935 West 49 Street, # 203, Hialeah, FL 33012
http://www.cbt.edu/

CONTACT Fernando N. Llerena, President
Telephone: 305-273-4499 Ext. 300

GENERAL INFORMATION Private Institution. **Total program enrollment:** 128. **Application fee:** $100.

PROGRAM(S) OFFERED
• **Administrative Assistant and Secretarial Science, General** *12 students enrolled* • **Business Administration and Management, General** *4 students enrolled* • **Computer Technology/Computer Systems Technology** • **Heating, Air Conditioning and Refrigeration Technology/Technician (ACH/ACR/ACHR/HRAC/HVAC/AC Technology)** *123 students enrolled* • **Medical Insurance Coding Specialist/Coder** • **Medical/Clinical Assistant** • **Nursing, Other** • **Phlebotomy/Phlebotomist** • **Web Page, Digital/Multimedia and Information Resources Design**

STUDENT SERVICES Academic or career counseling, placement services for program completers, remedial services.

Commercial Diving Academy

8137 N. Main Street, Jacksonville, FL 32208
http://commercialdivingacademy.com/

CONTACT David Weisman, Director
Telephone: 904-766-7736

GENERAL INFORMATION Private Institution. **Total program enrollment:** 217. **Application fee:** $25.

PROGRAM(S) OFFERED
• **Diver, Professional and Instructor** *221 students enrolled* • **Emergency Medical Technology/Technician (EMT Paramedic)** *59 students enrolled* • **Marine Transportation, Other** *28 students enrolled* • **Welding Technology/Welder** *2 students enrolled*

STUDENT SERVICES Academic or career counseling, employment services for current students, placement services for program completers.

Comp-Med Vocational Careers Corporation

2900 W. 12th Avenue, 3rd Floor, Hialeah, FL 33012-4861
http://compumedschool.com/

CONTACT Mayra Rodriquez, President
Telephone: 305-888-9200

GENERAL INFORMATION Private Institution. **Total program enrollment:** 728. **Application fee:** $100.

PROGRAM(S) OFFERED
• **Allied Health Diagnostic, Intervention, and Treatment Professions, Other** *180 hrs./$800* • **Computer and Information Sciences, General** *720 hrs./$5600* • **Dental Assisting/Assistant** *720 hrs./$5600* • **Health Professions and Related Clinical Sciences, Other** *11 students enrolled* • **Medical/Clinical Assistant** *840 hrs./$5850* • **Nursing, Other** *600 hrs./$4200* • **Teaching English as a Second or Foreign Language/ESL Language Instructor** *720 hrs./$5600*

STUDENT SERVICES Academic or career counseling, employment services for current students, placement services for program completers.

Concorde Career Institute

1960 Arlington Expressway, Suite 120, Jacksonville, FL 32211-7429
http://www.concorde.edu/

CONTACT Michael Beaty, Campus President
Telephone: 904-725-0525

GENERAL INFORMATION Private Institution. Founded 1968. **Total program enrollment:** 654.

PROGRAM(S) OFFERED
• **Dental Assisting/Assistant** *720 hrs./$11,843* • **Health Aide** *480 hrs./$7668* • **Health Information/Medical Records Administration/Administrator** *720 hrs./$11,318* • **Health and Medical Administrative Services, Other** *65 students enrolled* • **Home Health Aide/Home Attendant** *39 students enrolled* • **Licensed Practical/Vocational Nurse Training (LPN, LVN, Cert, Dipl, AAS)** *1220 hrs./$21,055* • **Massage Therapy/Therapeutic Massage** *17 students enrolled* • **Medical/Clinical Assistant** *810 hrs./$12,660* • **Surgical Technology/Technologist** *1220 hrs./$20,285*

STUDENT SERVICES Academic or career counseling, employment services for current students, placement services for program completers, remedial services.

Concorde Career Institute

4000 North Street Road 7, Lauderdale Lake, FL 33319
http://www.concorde.edu/

CONTACT Tim Vogley, Campus President
Telephone: 954-731-8880

GENERAL INFORMATION Private Institution. **Total program enrollment:** 393.

PROGRAM(S) OFFERED
• **Dental Assisting/Assistant** *720 hrs./$12,333* • **Health Information/Medical Records Administration/Administrator** *720 hrs./$12,333* • **Health and Medical Administrative Services, Other** *49 students enrolled* • **Medical/Clinical Assistant** *720 hrs./$12,967* • **Nurse/Nursing Assistant/Aide and Patient Care Assistant** *480 hrs./$7870* • **Pharmacy Technician/Assistant** *800 hrs./$11,007* • **Surgical Technology/Technologist** *1220 hrs./$21,783*

STUDENT SERVICES Academic or career counseling, employment services for current students, placement services for program completers, remedial services.

Concorde Career Institute

4202 West Spruce Street, Tampa, FL 33607-4127
http://www.concorde.edu/

CONTACT Donna Hallam, Campus President
Telephone: 813-874-0094

GENERAL INFORMATION Private Institution. Founded 1978. **Total program enrollment:** 575.

PROGRAM(S) OFFERED
• **Allied Health and Medical Assisting Services, Other** *480 hrs./$7818* • **Dental Assisting/Assistant** *720 hrs./$11,913* • **Health Information/Medical Records Administration/Administrator** *720 hrs./$11,913* • **Health Unit Coordinator/Ward Clerk** *14 students enrolled* • **Health and Medical Administrative Services, Other** *51 students enrolled* • **Medical/Clinical Assistant** *720 hrs./ $12,590* • **Pharmacy Technician/Assistant** *800 hrs./$10,390* • **Surgical Technology/Technologist** *1220 hrs./$19,788*

STUDENT SERVICES Academic or career counseling, employment services for current students, placement services for program completers, remedial services.

Coral Ridge Nurses Assistant Training School

2740 E. Oakland Park Boulevard, Ft. Lauderdale, FL 33306

CONTACT Ethylene Maise, Director
Telephone: 954-714-0061

GENERAL INFORMATION Private Institution. **Total program enrollment:** 31. **Application fee:** $50.

PROGRAM(S) OFFERED
• **Child Care Provider/Assistant** *500 hrs./$5550* • **Clinical/Medical Social Work** • **Health Information/Medical Records Technology/Technician** • **Health Unit Coordinator/Ward Clerk** *720 hrs./$6050* • **Licensed Practical/Vocational Nurse Training (LPN, LVN, Cert, Dipl, AAS)** *1350 hrs./$18,750* • **Medical Insurance Specialist/Medical Biller** *720 hrs./$6050* • **Nurse/Nursing Assistant/Aide and Patient Care Assistant** *720 hrs./$6050* • **Pharmacy Technician/Assistant** *720 hrs./$6050*

STUDENT SERVICES Academic or career counseling, placement services for program completers, remedial services.

Cortiva Institute—Humanities Center

4045 Park Boulevard, Pinellas Park, FL 33781
http://www.cortiva.com/locations/tampa/

CONTACT Greg Fears, President
Telephone: 727-541-5200

GENERAL INFORMATION Private Institution. **Total program enrollment:** 75. **Application fee:** $100.

PROGRAM(S) OFFERED
• **Massage Therapy/Therapeutic Massage** *750 hrs./$11,195*

STUDENT SERVICES Academic or career counseling, placement services for program completers, remedial services.

Dade Medical College

2750 West 68th Street, # 202, Hialeah, FL 33016
dademedicalcollege.com

CONTACT Fabian Fernandez, Executive Corporate Director
Telephone: 786-363-3340

GENERAL INFORMATION Private Institution. **Total program enrollment:** 317. **Application fee:** $100.

PROGRAM(S) OFFERED
• **Diagnostic Medical Sonography/Sonographer and Ultrasound Technician** *102 hrs./$30,050* • **Massage Therapy/Therapeutic Massage** *59 hrs./$12,050* • **Medical/Clinical Assistant** *72 hrs./$14,050* • **Radiologic Technology/ Science—Radiographer** *130 hrs./$32,000*

STUDENT SERVICES Placement services for program completers.

Dade Medical Institute

3401 NW 7th Street, Miami, FL 33125
http://www.dademedicalinstitute.com/

CONTACT Ernesto Perez
Telephone: 305-644-1171

GENERAL INFORMATION Private Institution. **Total program enrollment:** 374. **Application fee:** $100.

PROGRAM(S) OFFERED
• **Diagnostic Medical Sonography/Sonographer and Ultrasound Technician** *102 hrs./$30,050* • **Massage Therapy/Therapeutic Massage** *59 hrs./$12,050* • **Medical/Clinical Assistant** *72 hrs./$14,050* • **Radiologic Technology/ Science—Radiographer** *130 hrs./$32,100*

STUDENT SERVICES Placement services for program completers.

David G. Erwin Technical Center

2010 East Hillsborough Avenue, Tampa, FL 33610-8299
http://erwin.edu/

CONTACT James Rich, Principal
Telephone: 813-231-1800

GENERAL INFORMATION Public Institution. **Total program enrollment:** 726. **Application fee:** $10.

PROGRAM(S) OFFERED
• **Automotive Engineering Technology/Technician** *32 students enrolled* • **Barbering/Barber** • **Building/Property Maintenance and Management** *7 students enrolled* • **Business/Commerce, General** *114 students enrolled* • **Carpentry/Carpenter** *16 students enrolled* • **Clinical/Medical Laboratory Technician** *13 students enrolled* • **Cosmetology/Cosmetologist, General** *36 students enrolled* • **Culinary Arts and Related Services, Other** *14 students enrolled* • **Dental Assisting/Assistant** *29 students enrolled* • **Drafting and Design Technology/Technician, General** *44 students enrolled* • **Electrical/Electronics Equipment Installation and Repair, General** *33 students enrolled* • **Electrician** *22 students enrolled* • **Electrocardiograph Technology/Technician** *38 students enrolled* • **Health and Medical Administrative Services, Other** *90 students enrolled* • **Heating, Air Conditioning and Refrigeration Technology/Technician (ACH/ACR/ACHR/HRAC/HVAC/AC Technology)** *50 students enrolled* • **Interior Design** *16 students enrolled* • **Licensed Practical/Vocational Nurse Training (LPN, LVN, Cert, Dipl, AAS)** *316 students enrolled* • **Massage Therapy/ Therapeutic Massage** *32 students enrolled* • **Medical/Clinical Assistant** *39 students enrolled* • **Plumbing Technology/Plumber** *11 students enrolled* • **Special Products Marketing Operations** *7 students enrolled* • **Surgical Technology/ Technologist** *58 students enrolled* • **Welding Technology/Welder** *13 students enrolled*

STUDENT SERVICES Academic or career counseling, employment services for current students, placement services for program completers, remedial services.

Daytona College

469 South Nova Road, Ormond Beach, FL 32174-8445
http://www.daytonainstituteofmassagetherapy.net/

CONTACT Roger Bradley, CEO
Telephone: 386-267-0565

GENERAL INFORMATION Private Institution. **Total program enrollment:** 56. **Application fee:** $100.

PROGRAM(S) OFFERED
• **Aesthetician/Esthetician and Skin Care Specialist** *51 hrs./$9590* • **Facial Treatment Specialist/Facialist** *6 students enrolled* • **Massage Therapy/ Therapeutic Massage** *130 hrs./$16,895*

STUDENT SERVICES Placement services for program completers.

Daytona State College

1200 W. International Speedway Boulevard, Daytona Beach, FL 32114
http://www.daytonastate.edu/

CONTACT D. Kent Sharples, President
Telephone: 386-506-3000

GENERAL INFORMATION Public Institution. Founded 1958. **Accreditation:** Regional (SACS/CC); dental assisting (ADA); dental hygiene (ADA); emergency medical services (JRCEMTP); health information technology (AHIMA); physical therapy assisting (APTA). **Total program enrollment:** 3650.

PROGRAM(S) OFFERED
• **Accounting and Related Services, Other** *5 students enrolled* • **Architectural Engineering Technology/Technician** *3 students enrolled* • **Autobody/Collision and Repair Technology/Technician** *5 students enrolled* • **Building/Property Maintenance and Management** • **Computer Installation and Repair Technology/Technician** *1 student enrolled* • **Computer Systems Analysis/Analyst** *11 students enrolled* • **Computer Technology/Computer Systems Technology** *3 students enrolled* • **Computer/Information Technology Services Administration and Management, Other** *26 students enrolled* • **Corrections** *37 students enrolled* • **Cosmetology/Cosmetologist, General** *80 students enrolled* • **Criminal Justice/ Police Science** *95 students enrolled* • **Dental Assisting/Assistant** *7 students enrolled* • **Drafting and Design Technology/Technician, General** *12 students enrolled* • **Electrical, Electronic and Communications Engineering Technology/ Technician** *7 students enrolled* • **Emergency Medical Technology/Technician (EMT Paramedic)** *189 students enrolled* • **Entrepreneurship/Entrepreneurial Studies** *4 students enrolled* • **Executive Assistant/Executive Secretary** *29 students enrolled* • **Fire Science/Firefighting** *100 students enrolled* • **Health Information/Medical Records Technology/Technician** *9 students enrolled* • **Heating, Air Conditioning, Ventilation and Refrigeration Maintenance Technology/ Technician (HAC, HACR, HVAC, HVACR)** *15 students enrolled* • **Licensed Practical/Vocational Nurse Training (LPN, LVN, Cert, Dipl, AAS)** *84 students enrolled* • **Management Information Systems and Services, Other** *4 students enrolled* • **Management Information Systems, General** *5 students enrolled* • **Massage Therapy/Therapeutic Massage** *28 students enrolled* • **Medical/ Clinical Assistant** *13 students enrolled* • **Nail Technician/Specialist and Manicurist** • **Nursing, Other** *125 students enrolled* • **Photographic and Film/ Video Technology/Technician and Assistant** • **Surgical Technology/ Technologist** *13 students enrolled* • **Welding Technology/Welder** *4 students enrolled*

STUDENT SERVICES Academic or career counseling, daycare for children of students, employment services for current students, placement services for program completers, remedial services.

Edison State College

PO Box 60210, Fort Myers, FL 33906-6210
http://www.edison.edu/

CONTACT Kenneth Walker, District President
Telephone: 239-489-9300

GENERAL INFORMATION Public Institution. Founded 1962. **Accreditation:** Regional (SACS/CC); cardiovascular technology (JRCECT); dental assisting (ADA); dental hygiene (ADA); emergency medical services (JRCEMTP); radiologic technology: radiography (JRCERT). **Total program enrollment:** 4570. **Application fee:** $30.

PROGRAM(S) OFFERED
• **Accounting and Related Services, Other** • **Computer/Information Technology Services Administration and Management, Other** *3 students enrolled* • **Dental Assisting/Assistant** *4 students enrolled* • **Emergency Medical Technology/ Technician (EMT Paramedic)** *177 students enrolled* • **Entrepreneurship/ Entrepreneurial Studies** *1 student enrolled* • **Management Information Systems, General**

STUDENT SERVICES Academic or career counseling, daycare for children of students, employment services for current students, placement services for program completers, remedial services.

Edutech Centers

18850 US Highway 19 North, Building 5, Clearwater, FL 33764
http://www.edutechctr.com/

CONTACT David Knobel, CEO
Telephone: 727-724-1037

GENERAL INFORMATION Private Institution. **Total program enrollment:** 749. **Application fee:** $100.

PROGRAM(S) OFFERED
• **Aesthetician/Esthetician and Skin Care Specialist** *120 students enrolled* • **Massage Therapy/Therapeutic Massage** *100 students enrolled* • **Medical Insurance Coding Specialist/Coder** *97 students enrolled* • **Medical/Clinical Assistant** *89 students enrolled* • **System, Networking, and LAN/WAN Management/Manager** *1 student enrolled*

STUDENT SERVICES Academic or career counseling, employment services for current students, placement services for program completers.

Everest Institute

1040 Bayview Drive, Fort Lauderdale, FL 33304
http://www.everest.edu/

CONTACT Calvin E. Lawrence, President
Telephone: 954-630-0066

GENERAL INFORMATION Private Institution. Founded 2003. **Accreditation:** State accredited or approved. **Total program enrollment:** 131.

PROGRAM(S) OFFERED
• **Allied Health and Medical Assisting Services, Other** *720 hrs./$11,770* • **Massage Therapy/Therapeutic Massage** *110 students enrolled* • **Medical Insurance Coding Specialist/Coder** *720 hrs./$13,705* • **Medical/Clinical Assistant** *720 hrs./$13,475* • **Pharmacy Technician/Assistant** *720 hrs./$12,265*

STUDENT SERVICES Placement services for program completers.

Everest Institute

530 W. 49th Street, Hialeah, FL 33012
http://www.everest.edu/

CONTACT Patricia Bisciotti, School President
Telephone: 305-558-9500

GENERAL INFORMATION Private Institution. Founded 1977. **Accreditation:** Surgical technology (ARCST); state accredited or approved. **Total program enrollment:** 1182.

PROGRAM(S) OFFERED
• **Business Administration and Management, General** *96 hrs./$33,600* • **Cardiovascular Technology/Technologist** *94 students enrolled* • **Criminal Justice/Law Enforcement Administration** *96 hrs./$33,600* • **Diagnostic Medical Sonography/Sonographer and Ultrasound Technician** *6 students enrolled* • **Massage Therapy/Therapeutic Massage** *58 students enrolled* • **Medical Insurance Coding Specialist/Coder** *720 hrs./$11,605* • **Medical/Clinical Assistant** *47 hrs./$14,725* • **Pharmacy Technician/Assistant** *720 hrs./$12,265* • **Surgical Technology/Technologist** *47 hrs./$23,100*

STUDENT SERVICES Placement services for program completers.

Everest Institute

111 Northwest 183rd Street, Second Floor, Miami, FL 33169
http://www.everest.edu/

CONTACT Mario Miro, College President
Telephone: 305-949-9500

GENERAL INFORMATION Private Institution. Founded 1977. **Accreditation:** State accredited or approved. **Total program enrollment:** 1052.

PROGRAM(S) OFFERED
● **Business Administration and Management, General** *96 hrs./$33,600* ● **Criminal Justice/Law Enforcement Administration** *96 hrs./$33,600* ● **Massage Therapy/Therapeutic Massage** *80 students enrolled* ● **Medical Insurance Coding Specialist/Coder** *47 hrs./$11,605* ● **Medical/Clinical Assistant** *47 hrs./$13,475* ● **Nurse/Nursing Assistant/Aide and Patient Care Assistant** *51 hrs./$11,770* ● **Pharmacy Technician/Assistant** *47 hrs./$12,265*

STUDENT SERVICES Placement services for program completers.

Everest Institute

9020 SW 137th Avenue, Miami, FL 33186
http://www.everest.edu/

CONTACT Darrell Rhoten, School President
Telephone: 305-893-0005

GENERAL INFORMATION Private Institution. Founded 1977. **Accreditation:** Surgical technology (ARCST); state accredited or approved. **Total program enrollment:** 222.

PROGRAM(S) OFFERED
● **Cardiovascular Technology/Technologist** *9 students enrolled* ● **Criminal Justice/Law Enforcement Administration** *96 hrs./$33,600* ● **Massage Therapy/Therapeutic Massage** *720 hrs./$12,295* ● **Medical Insurance Coding Specialist/Coder** *720 hrs./$11,605* ● **Medical/Clinical Assistant** *47 hrs./$13,475* ● **Pharmacy Technician/Assistant** *47 hrs./$12,265* ● **Surgical Technology/Technologist** *77 hrs./$23,100*

STUDENT SERVICES Placement services for program completers.

Everest University

2471 McMullen Booth Road, Clearwater, FL 33759
http://www.everest.edu/

CONTACT John Buck, President
Telephone: 727-725-2688

GENERAL INFORMATION Private Institution. Founded 1890. **Accreditation:** Medical assisting (AAMAE); state accredited or approved. **Total program enrollment:** 719. **Application fee:** $25.

PROGRAM(S) OFFERED
● **Massage Therapy/Therapeutic Massage** *82 students enrolled* ● **Pharmacy Technician/Assistant** *14 students enrolled*

STUDENT SERVICES Academic or career counseling, employment services for current students, placement services for program completers.

Everest University

8226 Phillips Highway, Jacksonville, FL 32256
http://www.everest.edu/

CONTACT Dr. Jerry Causey, President
Telephone: 904-731-4949

GENERAL INFORMATION Private Institution. Founded 2000. **Accreditation:** State accredited or approved. **Total program enrollment:** 290.

PROGRAM(S) OFFERED
● **Medical Insurance Specialist/Medical Biller** *167 students enrolled*

STUDENT SERVICES Academic or career counseling, employment services for current students, placement services for program completers, remedial services.

Everest University

995 East Memorial Boulevard, Suite 110, Lakeland, FL 33801
http://www.everest.edu/

CONTACT Silvina Lamoureux, President
Telephone: 863-686-1444

GENERAL INFORMATION Private Institution. Founded 1890. **Accreditation:** Medical assisting (AAMAE); state accredited or approved. **Total program enrollment:** 717. **Application fee:** $25.

PROGRAM(S) OFFERED
● **Massage Therapy/Therapeutic Massage** *76 students enrolled* ● **Medical/Clinical Assistant** ● **Pharmacy Technician/Assistant** *22 students enrolled*

STUDENT SERVICES Academic or career counseling, employment services for current students, placement services for program completers.

Everest University

2401 North Harbor City Boulevard, Melbourne, FL 32935-6657
http://www.everest.edu/

CONTACT Mark W. Judge, President
Telephone: 321-253-2929 Ext. 161

GENERAL INFORMATION Private Institution. Founded 1953. **Accreditation:** Medical assisting (AAMAE); state accredited or approved. **Total program enrollment:** 119.

STUDENT SERVICES Academic or career counseling, employment services for current students, placement services for program completers.

Everest University

805 Wells Road, Orange Park, FL 32073
http://www.everest.edu/

CONTACT Bruce Jones, President
Telephone: 904-264-9122

GENERAL INFORMATION Private Institution. Founded 2003. **Accreditation:** State accredited or approved. **Total program enrollment:** 218.

PROGRAM(S) OFFERED
● **Massage Therapy/Therapeutic Massage** *69 students enrolled* ● **Medical/Clinical Assistant**

STUDENT SERVICES Academic or career counseling, employment services for current students, placement services for program completers, remedial services.

Everest University

5421 Diplomat Circle, Orlando, FL 32810-5674
http://www.everest.edu/

CONTACT Ouida B. Kirby, President
Telephone: 407-628-5870 Ext. 104

GENERAL INFORMATION Private Institution. Founded 1953. **Accreditation:** State accredited or approved. **Total program enrollment:** 1239.

Everest University (continued)

PROGRAM(S) OFFERED
• **Massage Therapy/Therapeutic Massage** 93 *students enrolled* • **Medical/Clinical Assistant**

STUDENT SERVICES Academic or career counseling, employment services for current students, placement services for program completers.

Everest University

9200 South Park Center Loop, Orlando, FL 32819
http://www.everest.edu/

CONTACT Peter Neigler, Regional Vice President, Acting Campus President
Telephone: 407-851-2525

GENERAL INFORMATION Private Institution. Founded 1987. **Accreditation:** Medical assisting (AAMAE); state accredited or approved. **Total program enrollment:** 2910.

PROGRAM(S) OFFERED
• **Massage Therapy/Therapeutic Massage** 110 *students enrolled*

STUDENT SERVICES Academic or career counseling, employment services for current students, placement services for program completers, remedial services.

Everest University

225 North Federal Highway, Pompano Beach, FL 33062
http://www.everest.edu/

CONTACT Dr. Ilia Martin, Campus President
Telephone: 954-783-7339

GENERAL INFORMATION Private Institution. Founded 1940. **Accreditation:** State accredited or approved. **Total program enrollment:** 318. **Application fee:** $35.

PROGRAM(S) OFFERED
• **Massage Therapy/Therapeutic Massage** 4 *students enrolled* • **Medical Insurance Coding Specialist/Coder** 5 *students enrolled* • **Medical/Clinical Assistant** • **Pharmacy Technician/Assistant**

STUDENT SERVICES Academic or career counseling, employment services for current students, placement services for program completers, remedial services.

Everest University

3319 West Hillsborough Avenue, Tampa, FL 33614-5899
http://www.everest.edu/

CONTACT Mike Barlow, President
Telephone: 813-879-6000 Ext. 176

GENERAL INFORMATION Private Institution. Founded 1890. **Accreditation:** Medical assisting (AAMAE); state accredited or approved. **Total program enrollment:** 874.

PROGRAM(S) OFFERED
• **Massage Therapy/Therapeutic Massage** 77 *students enrolled*

STUDENT SERVICES Academic or career counseling, employment services for current students, placement services for program completers.

Everest University

3924 Coconut Palm Drive, Tampa, FL 33619
http://www.everest.edu/

CONTACT David Splitstone, President
Telephone: 813-621-0041

GENERAL INFORMATION Private Institution. Founded 1890. **Accreditation:** Medical assisting (AAMAE); state accredited or approved. **Total program enrollment:** 1716.

PROGRAM(S) OFFERED
• **Massage Therapy/Therapeutic Massage** 54 *students enrolled*

STUDENT SERVICES Academic or career counseling, employment services for current students, placement services for program completers.

Fashion Focus Hair Academy

2184 Gulf Gate Drive, Sarasota, FL 34231
http://www.fashionfocusacad.com/

CONTACT Byron Weintraub, Chief Executive Officer
Telephone: 941-921-4877

GENERAL INFORMATION Private Institution. Founded 1988. **Total program enrollment:** 36.

PROGRAM(S) OFFERED
• **Aesthetician/Esthetician and Skin Care Specialist** 260 *hrs./$3700* • **Cosmetology/Cosmetologist, General** 1500 *hrs./$11,725* • **Facial Treatment Specialist/Facialist** 23 *students enrolled* • **Nail Technician/Specialist and Manicurist** 240 *hrs./$1900*

STUDENT SERVICES Placement services for program completers.

FastTrain of Clearwater

29399 US Highway 19 North, Suite 104, Clearwater, FL 33761
http://www.fasttrain.com

CONTACT Alex Amor, President/CEO
Telephone: 727-507-7999

GENERAL INFORMATION Private Institution. **Total program enrollment:** 11. **Application fee:** $50.

PROGRAM(S) OFFERED
• **Computer Installation and Repair Technology/Technician** 3 *students enrolled* • **Computer and Information Systems Security** 2 *students enrolled* • **Management Information Systems, General** 1 *student enrolled* • **Medical Insurance Coding Specialist/Coder** • **Medical/Clinical Assistant**

STUDENT SERVICES Academic or career counseling, employment services for current students, placement services for program completers.

FastTrain of Ft. Lauderdale

1620 W. Oakland Park Boulevard, 2nd Floor, Ft. Lauderdale, FL 33311
http://www.fasttrain.com

CONTACT Alex Amor, President
Telephone: 954-730-8711

GENERAL INFORMATION Private Institution. **Total program enrollment:** 46. **Application fee:** $50.

PROGRAM(S) OFFERED
• **Computer Installation and Repair Technology/Technician** 28 *students enrolled* • **Computer and Information Systems Security** 1 *student enrolled* • **Management Information Systems, General** • **Medical Insurance Coding Specialist/Coder** 6 *students enrolled* • **Medical/Clinical Assistant**

STUDENT SERVICES Academic or career counseling, employment services for current students, placement services for program completers.

FastTrain of Jacksonville

10748 Deerwood Park Boulevard, Suite 150, Jacksonville, FL 32256
http://www.fasttrain.com

CONTACT Alex Amor, President/CEO
Telephone: 904-265-3278

GENERAL INFORMATION Private Institution. **Total program enrollment:** 67. **Application fee:** $50.

PROGRAM(S) OFFERED
• **Computer Installation and Repair Technology/Technician** *14 students enrolled* • **Computer and Information Systems Security** *1 student enrolled* • **Management Information Systems, General** *4 students enrolled* • **Medical Insurance Coding Specialist/Coder** • **Medical/Clinical Assistant**

STUDENT SERVICES Academic or career counseling, employment services for current students, placement services for program completers.

FastTrain of Kendall

10701 SW 104th Street, Miami, FL 33176
http://www.fasttrain.com

CONTACT Alex Amor, President
Telephone: 305-412-3232

GENERAL INFORMATION Private Institution. **Total program enrollment:** 64. **Application fee:** $50.

PROGRAM(S) OFFERED
• **Computer Installation and Repair Technology/Technician** *10 students enrolled* • **Computer and Information Systems Security** *2 students enrolled* • **Management Information Systems, General** *1 student enrolled* • **Medical Insurance Coding Specialist/Coder** *1 student enrolled* • **Medical/Clinical Assistant**

STUDENT SERVICES Academic or career counseling, employment services for current students, placement services for program completers.

FastTrain of Miami

5555 W. Flagler Street, Miami, FL 33134
http://www.fasttrain.com

CONTACT Alex Amor, President/CEO
Telephone: 305-266-2800

GENERAL INFORMATION Private Institution. **Total program enrollment:** 52. **Application fee:** $50.

PROGRAM(S) OFFERED
• **Computer Installation and Repair Technology/Technician** *26 students enrolled* • **Computer and Information Systems Security** *7 students enrolled* • **Management Information Systems, General** *3 students enrolled* • **Medical Insurance Coding Specialist/Coder** • **Medical/Clinical Assistant**

STUDENT SERVICES Academic or career counseling, employment services for current students, placement services for program completers.

FastTrain of Pembroke Pines

2000 NW 150th Avenue, Suite 1102, Pembroke Pines, FL 33028
http://www.fasttrain.com

CONTACT Alex Amor, President
Telephone: 954-392-7080

GENERAL INFORMATION Private Institution. **Total program enrollment:** 40. **Application fee:** $50.

PROGRAM(S) OFFERED
• **Computer Installation and Repair Technology/Technician** *14 students enrolled* • **Computer and Information Systems Security** *5 students enrolled* • **Management Information Systems, General** *1 student enrolled* • **Medical Insurance Coding Specialist/Coder** *3 students enrolled* • **Medical/Clinical Assistant**

STUDENT SERVICES Academic or career counseling, employment services for current students, placement services for program completers.

FastTrain of Tampa

4350 W. Cypress Street, Suite 100, Tampa, FL 33607
http://www.fasttrain.com

CONTACT Alex Amor, President
Telephone: 813-874-0660

GENERAL INFORMATION Private Institution. **Total program enrollment:** 55. **Application fee:** $50.

PROGRAM(S) OFFERED
• **Computer Installation and Repair Technology/Technician** *6 students enrolled* • **Computer and Information Systems Security** *3 students enrolled* • **Management Information Systems, General** *8 students enrolled* • **Medical Insurance Coding Specialist/Coder** *2 students enrolled* • **Medical/Clinical Assistant**

STUDENT SERVICES Academic or career counseling, employment services for current students, placement services for program completers.

First Coast Technical Institute

2980 Collins Avenue, St. Augustine, FL 32095-1919
http://www.fcti.org/

CONTACT Christine Cothron, President
Telephone: 904-824-4401

GENERAL INFORMATION Public Institution. Founded 1969. **Total program enrollment:** 552. **Application fee:** $20.

PROGRAM(S) OFFERED
• **Administrative Assistant and Secretarial Science, General** *10 students enrolled* • **Applied Horticulture/Horticultural Business Services, Other** *1 student enrolled* • **Automobile/Automotive Mechanics Technology/Technician** *25 students enrolled* • **Carpentry/Carpenter** *2 students enrolled* • **Child Care Provider/Assistant** *58 students enrolled* • **Commercial and Advertising Art** *1 student enrolled* • **Cosmetology/Cosmetologist, General** *1200 hrs./$3300* • **Culinary Arts/Chef Training** *1500 hrs./$6400* • **Dental Assisting/Assistant** *6 students enrolled* • **Emergency Medical Technology/Technician (EMT Paramedic)** *1144 hrs./$3463* • **Fire Science/Firefighting** *269 students enrolled* • **Fire Services Administration** *28 students enrolled* • **Graphic and Printing Equipment Operator, General Production** *5 students enrolled* • **Health Aides/Attendants/Orderlies, Other** *65 students enrolled* • **Heating, Air Conditioning, Ventilation and Refrigeration Maintenance Technology/Technician (HAC, HACR, HVAC, HVACR)** *33 students enrolled* • **Landscaping and Groundskeeping** *3 students enrolled* • **Licensed Practical/Vocational Nurse Training (LPN, LVN, Cert, Dipl, AAS)** *1350 hrs./$3850* • **Massage Therapy/Therapeutic Massage** *750 hrs./$3800* • **Medical Administrative/Executive Assistant and Medical Secretary** *27 students enrolled* • **Medical/Clinical Assistant** *73 students enrolled* • **Nurse/Nursing Assistant/Aide and Patient Care Assistant** *115 students enrolled* • **Plant Nursery Operations and Management** *2 students enrolled* • **Turf and Turfgrass Management** *2 students enrolled* • **Welding Technology/Welder** *1170 hrs./$3200*

STUDENT SERVICES Academic or career counseling, daycare for children of students, employment services for current students, placement services for program completers, remedial services.

Florida Academy of Health & Beauty

2300 NW 9th Avenue, Wilton Manor, FL 33311

CONTACT Thomas Thompson, Chief Administrator
Telephone: 954-563-9098

GENERAL INFORMATION Private Institution. **Total program enrollment:** 19.

PROGRAM(S) OFFERED
• **Barbering/Barber** *1200 hrs./$5950* • **Cosmetology and Related Personal Grooming Arts, Other** *600 hrs./$3650* • **Cosmetology, Barber/Styling, and Nail Instructor** *18 students enrolled* • **Cosmetology/Cosmetologist, General** *1200 hrs./$6800*

STUDENT SERVICES Academic or career counseling, employment services for current students, placement services for program completers.

Florida Barber Academy

3269 North Federal Highway, Pompano Beach, FL 33064

CONTACT Jackie Lombardi, Director
Telephone: 954-781-6066

GENERAL INFORMATION Private Institution. **Total program enrollment:** 139. **Application fee:** $100.

PROGRAM(S) OFFERED
● **Barbering/Barber** *1200 hrs./$8300*

STUDENT SERVICES Academic or career counseling, placement services for program completers.

Florida Career College

1321 Southwest 107 Avenue, Suite 201B, Miami, FL 33174
http://www.careercollege.edu/

CONTACT David Knobel, CEO
Telephone: 305-553-6065

GENERAL INFORMATION Private Institution. Founded 1982. **Accreditation:** State accredited or approved. **Total program enrollment:** 2948. **Application fee:** $100.

PROGRAM(S) OFFERED
● **Allied Health and Medical Assisting Services, Other** *571 students enrolled* ● **Computer Engineering, General** *56 students enrolled* ● **Computer Hardware Technology/Technician** *224 students enrolled* ● **Data Entry/Microcomputer Applications, General** *73 students enrolled* ● **Massage Therapy/Therapeutic Massage** *19 students enrolled* ● **Medical Insurance Coding Specialist/Coder** *400 students enrolled* ● **Web Page, Digital/Multimedia and Information Resources Design** *27 students enrolled*

STUDENT SERVICES Academic or career counseling, employment services for current students, placement services for program completers.

Florida Career Institute

4222 South Florida Avenue, Lakeland, FL 33813
http://www.floridacareerinstitute.edu/

CONTACT Duncan Anderson, President and CEO
Telephone: 863-646-1400

GENERAL INFORMATION Private Institution. Founded 1984. **Total program enrollment:** 64. **Application fee:** $100.

PROGRAM(S) OFFERED
● **Administrative Assistant and Secretarial Science, General** *2 students enrolled* ● **Computer Engineering Technology/Technician** *3 students enrolled* ● **Electrical, Electronic and Communications Engineering Technology/Technician** *5 students enrolled* ● **Emergency Medical Technology/Technician (EMT Paramedic)** ● **Massage Therapy/Therapeutic Massage** *16 students enrolled* ● **Medical Insurance Coding Specialist/Coder** *13 students enrolled* ● **Medical/Clinical Assistant** *50 students enrolled*

STUDENT SERVICES Academic or career counseling, employment services for current students, placement services for program completers.

Florida Christian College

1011 Bill Beck Boulevard, Kissimmee, FL 34744-5301
http://www.fcc.edu/

CONTACT Harold Armstrong, President
Telephone: 407-847-8966

GENERAL INFORMATION Private Institution (Affiliated with Christian Churches and Churches of Christ). Founded 1976. **Accreditation:** Regional (SACS/CC); state accredited or approved. **Total program enrollment:** 171. **Application fee:** $35.

STUDENT SERVICES Academic or career counseling, employment services for current students, remedial services.

Florida College of Natural Health

616 67th Street Circle East, Bradenton, FL 34208
http://www.fcnh.com/

CONTACT Stephen Lazarus, Chief Operations Officer
Telephone: 941-744-1244

GENERAL INFORMATION Private Institution. Founded 1998. **Accreditation:** State accredited or approved. **Total program enrollment:** 277.

PROGRAM(S) OFFERED
● **Aesthetician/Esthetician and Skin Care Specialist** *15 hrs./$4700* ● **Massage Therapy/Therapeutic Massage** *71 hrs./$20,845*

STUDENT SERVICES Academic or career counseling, employment services for current students, placement services for program completers.

Florida College of Natural Health

2600 Lake Lucien Drive, Suite 140, Maitland, FL 32751
http://www.fcnh.com/

CONTACT Stephen Lazarus, Chief Operations Officer
Telephone: 407-261-0319

GENERAL INFORMATION Private Institution. Founded 1995. **Accreditation:** State accredited or approved. **Total program enrollment:** 508.

PROGRAM(S) OFFERED
● **Aesthetician/Esthetician and Skin Care Specialist** *15 hrs./$4700* ● **Massage Therapy/Therapeutic Massage** *71 hrs./$20,845*

STUDENT SERVICES Academic or career counseling, employment services for current students, placement services for program completers.

Florida College of Natural Health

7925 Northwest 12th Street, Suite 201, Miami, FL 33126
http://www.fcnh.com/

CONTACT Stephen Lazarus, Chief Operations Officer
Telephone: 305-597-9599

GENERAL INFORMATION Private Institution. Founded 1993. **Accreditation:** State accredited or approved. **Total program enrollment:** 321.

PROGRAM(S) OFFERED
● **Aesthetician/Esthetician and Skin Care Specialist** *15 hrs./$4700* ● **Massage Therapy/Therapeutic Massage** *71 hrs./$20,845*

STUDENT SERVICES Academic or career counseling, employment services for current students, placement services for program completers.

Florida College of Natural Health

2001 West Sample Road, Suite 100, Pompano Beach, FL 33064
http://www.fcnh.com/

CONTACT Stephen Lazarus, Chief Operations Officer
Telephone: 954-975-6400

GENERAL INFORMATION Private Institution. Founded 1986. **Accreditation:** State accredited or approved. **Total program enrollment:** 406.

PROGRAM(S) OFFERED
● **Aesthetician/Esthetician and Skin Care Specialist** *15 hrs./$4700* ● **Massage Therapy/Therapeutic Massage** *71 hrs./$20,854*

STUDENT SERVICES Academic or career counseling, employment services for current students, placement services for program completers.

Florida Community College at Jacksonville

501 West State Street, Jacksonville, FL 32202-4030
http://www.fccj.edu/

CONTACT Steven R. Wallace, College President
Telephone: 904-632-3000

GENERAL INFORMATION Public Institution. Founded 1963. **Accreditation:** Regional (SACS/CC); dental hygiene (ADA); emergency medical services (JRCEMTP); funeral service (ABFSE); health information technology (AHIMA); histologic technology (NAACLS); medical laboratory technology (NAACLS); physical therapy assisting (APTA). **Total program enrollment:** 8080. **Application fee:** $15.

PROGRAM(S) OFFERED
- **Accounting Technology/Technician and Bookkeeping** *64 students enrolled* • **Aircraft Powerplant Technology/Technician** *28 students enrolled* • **Airframe Mechanics and Aircraft Maintenance Technology/Technician** *34 students enrolled* • **Architectural Engineering Technology/Technician** *5 students enrolled* • **Autobody/Collision and Repair Technology/Technician** *12 students enrolled* • **Barbering/Barber** *2 students enrolled* • **Business Administration and Management, General** *61 students enrolled* • **Business and Personal/Financial Services Marketing Operations** *1286 students enrolled* • **Business, Management, Marketing, and Related Support Services, Other** *3 students enrolled* • **Carpentry/Carpenter** • **Child Care Provider/Assistant** *271 students enrolled* • **Child Care and Support Services Management** *64 students enrolled* • **Cinematography and Film/Video Production** *7 students enrolled* • **Commercial and Advertising Art** *16 students enrolled* • **Computer Installation and Repair Technology/Technician** *3 students enrolled* • **Computer Programming, Specific Applications** *2 students enrolled* • **Computer Systems Analysis/Analyst** *26 students enrolled* • **Computer Technology/Computer Systems Technology** *70 students enrolled* • **Computer/Information Technology Services Administration and Management, Other** *24 students enrolled* • **Corrections** *11 students enrolled* • **Cosmetology/Cosmetologist, General** *29 students enrolled* • **Criminal Justice/Police Science** *159 students enrolled* • **Dental Assisting/Assistant** *18 students enrolled* • **Diesel Mechanics Technology/Technician** *2 students enrolled* • **Dietitian Assistant** *1 student enrolled* • **Drafting and Design Technology/Technician, General** *19 students enrolled* • **Electrical, Electronic and Communications Engineering Technology/Technician** • **Electrician** *7 students enrolled* • **Emergency Medical Technology/Technician (EMT Paramedic)** *58 students enrolled* • **Entrepreneurship/Entrepreneurial Studies** *21 students enrolled* • **Environmental Control Technologies/Technicians, Other** *1 student enrolled* • **Executive Assistant/Executive Secretary** *15 students enrolled* • **Facial Treatment Specialist/Facialist** *25 students enrolled* • **Finance, General** *8 students enrolled* • **Fire Science/Firefighting** *58 students enrolled* • **Foodservice Systems Administration/Management** • **Health Information/Medical Records Technology/Technician** *16 students enrolled* • **Heating, Air Conditioning and Refrigeration Technology/Technician (ACH/ACR/ACHR/HRAC/HVAC/AC Technology)** *9 students enrolled* • **Heating, Air Conditioning, Ventilation and Refrigeration Maintenance Technology/Technician (HAC, HACR, HVAC, HVACR)** *7 students enrolled* • **Hotel/Motel Administration/Management** • **Licensed Practical/Vocational Nurse Training (LPN, LVN, Cert, Dipl, AAS)** *101 students enrolled* • **Management Information Systems and Services, Other** *14 students enrolled* • **Management Information Systems, General** • **Massage Therapy/Therapeutic Massage** *20 students enrolled* • **Medical Administrative/Executive Assistant and Medical Secretary** • **Medical Radiologic Technology/Science—Radiation Therapist** *9 students enrolled* • **Medical/Clinical Assistant** *13 students enrolled* • **Nail Technician/Specialist and Manicurist** • **Nursing—Registered Nurse Training (RN, ASN, BSN, MSN)** • **Nursing, Other** • **Office Management and Supervision** *5 students enrolled* • **Pharmacy Technician/Assistant** *8 students enrolled* • **Plumbing Technology/Plumber** • **Real Estate** *157 students enrolled* • **Restaurant/Food Services Management** • **Security and Loss Prevention Services** • **Security and Protective Services, Other** *2 students enrolled* • **Surgical Technology/Technologist** *18 students enrolled* • **Truck and Bus Driver/Commercial Vehicle Operation** *34 students enrolled* • **Vehicle and Vehicle Parts and Accessories Marketing Operations** *1 student enrolled* • **Visual and Performing Arts, Other** *2 students enrolled* • **Welding Technology/Welder** *1 student enrolled*

STUDENT SERVICES Academic or career counseling, daycare for children of students, employment services for current students, placement services for program completers, remedial services.

Florida Education Center

1299-B NW 40th Avenue, Lauderhill, FL 33313
http://www.khec.com/

CONTACT Patrick Comstock, Executive Director
Telephone: 954-797-6140

GENERAL INFORMATION Private Institution. **Total program enrollment:** 402.

PROGRAM(S) OFFERED
- **Computer Technology/Computer Systems Technology** *54 hrs./$13,120* • **Dental Assisting/Assistant** *53 hrs./$13,410* • **Medical Office Assistant/Specialist** *51 hrs./$12,980* • **Medical/Clinical Assistant** *46 hrs./$13,716* • **Pharmacy Technician/Assistant** *52 hrs./$11,260*

STUDENT SERVICES Academic or career counseling, employment services for current students, placement services for program completers.

Florida Education Institute

5818 SW. 8th Street, Miami, FL 33144

CONTACT Ramon Valenti, President
Telephone: 305-263-9990

GENERAL INFORMATION Private Institution. **Total program enrollment:** 296. **Application fee:** $30.

PROGRAM(S) OFFERED
- **Business Administration and Management, General** *36 hrs./$12,500* • **Massage Therapy/Therapeutic Massage** *36 hrs./$13,500* • **Medical Insurance Coding Specialist/Coder** *36 hrs./$13,500* • **Medical/Clinical Assistant** *36 hrs./$13,500* • **Nurse/Nursing Assistant/Aide and Patient Care Assistant** *36 hrs./$7950* • **Pharmacy Technician/Assistant** *49 hrs./$13,100* • **Teaching English as a Second or Foreign Language/ESL Language Instructor**

STUDENT SERVICES Academic or career counseling, placement services for program completers.

Florida Hospital College of Health Sciences

800 Lake Estelle Drive, Orlando, FL 32803
http://www.fhchs.edu/

CONTACT David E. Greenlaw, President
Telephone: 407-303-7742

GENERAL INFORMATION Private Institution. Founded 1913. **Accreditation:** Regional (SACS/CC); diagnostic medical sonography (JRCEDMS); nuclear medicine technology (JRCNMT); radiologic technology: radiography (JRCERT). **Total program enrollment:** 725. **Application fee:** $20.

PROGRAM(S) OFFERED
- **Diagnostic Medical Sonography/Sonographer and Ultrasound Technician** *1 student enrolled* • **Nuclear Medical Technology/Technologist** *8 students enrolled* • **Radiologic Technology/Science—Radiographer** *14 students enrolled*

STUDENT SERVICES Academic or career counseling, employment services for current students, remedial services.

Florida Institute of Animal Arts

3776 Howell Branch Road, Winter Park, FL 32792
http://fifi-inc.com/

CONTACT Laura Neary, CEO
Telephone: 407-657-5033

GENERAL INFORMATION Private Institution. **Total program enrollment:** 224. **Application fee:** $50.

Florida Institute of Animal Arts (continued)

PROGRAM(S) OFFERED
● **Dog/Pet/Animal Grooming** *300 hrs./$3450* ● **Veterinary/Animal Health Technology/Technician and Veterinary Assistant** *600 hrs./$6900*

STUDENT SERVICES Placement services for program completers.

Florida Keys Community College

5901 College Road, Key West, FL 33040-4397
http://www.fkcc.edu/

CONTACT Jill Landesberg-Boyle, President
Telephone: 305-296-9081

GENERAL INFORMATION Public Institution. Founded 1965. **Accreditation:** Regional (SACS/CC). **Total program enrollment:** 345. **Application fee:** $30.

PROGRAM(S) OFFERED
● **Corrections** *21 students enrolled* ● **Criminal Justice/Police Science** *20 students enrolled* ● **Emergency Medical Technology/Technician (EMT Paramedic)** *39 students enrolled* ● **Entrepreneurship/Entrepreneurial Studies** ● **Management Information Systems, General** *11 students enrolled* ● **Mechanical Engineering Related Technologies/Technicians, Other** ● **Psychiatric/Mental Health Services Technician** *1 student enrolled*

STUDENT SERVICES Academic or career counseling, employment services for current students, remedial services.

Florida National College

4425 West 20th Avenue, Hialeah, FL 33012
http://www.fnc.edu/

CONTACT Jose Regueiro, President
Telephone: 305-821-3333

GENERAL INFORMATION Private Institution. Founded 1982. **Accreditation:** Regional (WASC/ACSCU). **Total program enrollment:** 1661.

PROGRAM(S) OFFERED
● **Computer Software and Media Applications, Other** *38 students enrolled* ● **Computer Systems Networking and Telecommunications** ● **Data Entry/Microcomputer Applications, General** *5 students enrolled* ● **Dental Assisting/Assistant** *65 students enrolled* ● **Dental Laboratory Technology/Technician** *20 students enrolled* ● **Dental Services and Allied Professions, Other** *9 students enrolled* ● **Health and Medical Administrative Services, Other** *7 students enrolled* ● **Legal Professions and Studies, Other** ● **Licensed Practical/Vocational Nurse Training (LPN, LVN, Cert, Dipl, AAS)** *56 students enrolled* ● **Medical Administrative/Executive Assistant and Medical Secretary** *1 student enrolled* ● **Medical Radiologic Technology/Science—Radiation Therapist** ● **Medical/Clinical Assistant** *6 students enrolled* ● **Nurse/Nursing Assistant/Aide and Patient Care Assistant** *7 students enrolled* ● **Teaching English or French as a Second or Foreign Language, Other** *551 students enrolled*

STUDENT SERVICES Employment services for current students, placement services for program completers, remedial services.

Florida School of Massage

6421 SW 13th Street, Gainesville, FL 32608-5419
http://www.massageonline.com

CONTACT Paul Davenport, President
Telephone: 352-378-7891

GENERAL INFORMATION Private Institution. Founded 1973. **Total program enrollment:** 109. **Application fee:** $100.

PROGRAM(S) OFFERED
● **Massage Therapy/Therapeutic Massage** *665 hrs./$8200*

STUDENT SERVICES Academic or career counseling.

Florida Technical College

8711 Lone Star Road, Jacksonville, FL 32211
http://www.flatech.edu/

CONTACT Don Slayter, Executive Director
Telephone: 904-724-2229

GENERAL INFORMATION Private Institution. Founded 1982. **Accreditation:** State accredited or approved. **Total program enrollment:** 176. **Application fee:** $25.

PROGRAM(S) OFFERED
● **Business Administration and Management, General** *98 hrs./$26,207* ● **CAD/CADD Drafting and/or Design Technology/Technician** *6 students enrolled* ● **Computer Programming/Programmer, General** ● **Computer Systems Networking and Telecommunications** *90 hrs./$22,125* ● **Drafting and Design Technology/Technician, General** *41 hrs./$12,225* ● **Medical/Clinical Assistant** *93 hrs./$28,753*

STUDENT SERVICES Academic or career counseling, employment services for current students, placement services for program completers, remedial services.

Florida Technical College

12689 Challenger Parkway, Orlando, FL 32826
http://www.flatech.edu/

CONTACT Gabe Garces, Executive Director
Telephone: 407-447-7300

GENERAL INFORMATION Private Institution. Founded 1982. **Accreditation:** State accredited or approved. **Total program enrollment:** 1459. **Application fee:** $25.

PROGRAM(S) OFFERED
● **Business Administration and Management, General** *98 hrs./$26,207* ● **Computer Programming/Programmer, General** ● **Computer Systems Networking and Telecommunications** *90 hrs./$22,125* ● **Criminal Justice/Law Enforcement Administration** *98 hrs./$22,025* ● **Drafting and Design Technology/Technician, General** *90 hrs./$26,207* ● **Medical Insurance Specialist/Medical Biller** *49 hrs./$11,125* ● **Medical/Clinical Assistant** *55 hrs./$14,475*

STUDENT SERVICES Academic or career counseling, employment services for current students, placement services for program completers, remedial services.

Fort Pierce Beauty Academy

3028 South US 1, Fort Pierce, FL 34982

CONTACT Michael Prevette, Director
Telephone: 772-464-4885

GENERAL INFORMATION Private Institution. Founded 1972. **Total program enrollment:** 23.

PROGRAM(S) OFFERED
● **Barbering/Barber** *1200 hrs./$6050* ● **Cosmetology/Cosmetologist, General** *1200 hrs./$6550*

Full Sail University

3300 University Boulevard, Winter Park, FL 32792-7437
http://www.fullsail.edu/

CONTACT Edward E. Haddock, Jr., CEO/Co-Chairman
Telephone: 407-679-0100

GENERAL INFORMATION Private Institution. Founded 1979. **Accreditation:** State accredited or approved. **Total program enrollment:** 6979.

STUDENT SERVICES Academic or career counseling, placement services for program completers.

Galen Health Institute–Tampa Bay

9549 Koger Boulevard, Suite 100, St. Petersburg, FL 33702
http://www.galened.com/

CONTACT Sharon A. Roberts, Institute Director
Telephone: 727-577-1497

GENERAL INFORMATION Private Institution. **Total program enrollment:** 455. **Application fee:** $100.

PROGRAM(S) OFFERED
• Licensed Practical/Vocational Nurse Training (LPN, LVN, Cert, Dipl, AAS) *1440 hrs./$16,545* • Nursing—Registered Nurse Training (RN, ASN, BSN, MSN) *76 hrs./$19,505*

STUDENT SERVICES Academic or career counseling, placement services for program completers.

Galiano Career Academy

1140 East Altamonte Drive, Suite 1020, Altamonte Sprints, FL 32701
http://galiano.edu/

CONTACT Michael Galiano, President/CEO
Telephone: 407-331-3900 Ext. 1209

GENERAL INFORMATION Private Institution. **Total program enrollment:** 477.

PROGRAM(S) OFFERED
• Administrative Assistant and Secretarial Science, General *6 students enrolled* • Hospitality Administration/Management, Other *9 students enrolled* • Medical Administrative/Executive Assistant and Medical Secretary *1050 hrs./$18,470* • Medical Office Assistant/Specialist *10 students enrolled* • Medical Office Computer Specialist/Assistant *57 hrs./$16,000* • Medical Office Management/ Administration *18 students enrolled* • Medical/Clinical Assistant *65 hrs./ $18,130* • Office Management and Supervision • Pharmacy Technician/ Assistant *67 hrs./$17,180* • Tourism and Travel Services Management *1050 hrs./$18,470* • Tourism and Travel Services Marketing Operations *59 hrs./ $16,000*

STUDENT SERVICES Academic or career counseling, employment services for current students, placement services for program completers, remedial services.

George Stone Area Vocational-Technical Center

2400 Longleaf Drive, Pensacola, FL 32526-8922
http://www.georgestonecenter.com/

CONTACT Daniel Busse, Principal
Telephone: 850-941-6200 Ext. 2103

GENERAL INFORMATION Public Institution. **Total program enrollment:** 477.

PROGRAM(S) OFFERED
• Accounting *2 students enrolled* • Administrative Assistant and Secretarial Science, General *1150 hrs./$2404* • Architectural Drafting and Architectural CAD/CADD *2 students enrolled* • Autobody/Collision and Repair Technology/ Technician *1 student enrolled* • Automobile/Automotive Mechanics Technology/ Technician *1 student enrolled* • Cabinetmaking and Millwork/Millwright • Carpentry/Carpenter *1200 hrs./$2508* • Computer Systems Networking and Telecommunications • Computer and Information Sciences and Support Services, Other *4 students enrolled* • Corrections *33 students enrolled* • Cosmetology/Cosmetologist, General *1200 hrs./$2508* • Criminal Justice/ Law Enforcement Administration *770 hrs./$2206* • Criminal Justice/Police Science *38 students enrolled* • Culinary Arts/Chef Training • Electrician *9 students enrolled* • Heating, Air Conditioning, Ventilation and Refrigeration Maintenance Technology/Technician (HAC, HACR, HVAC, HVACR) *1350 hrs./ $2822* • Landscaping and Groundskeeping *1 student enrolled* • Marine Maintenance/Fitter and Ship Repair Technology/Technician *9 students enrolled* • Medical Administrative/Executive Assistant and Medical Secretary *3 students enrolled* • Nurse/Nursing Assistant/Aide and Patient Care Assistant *24*

students enrolled • Small Engine Mechanics and Repair Technology/Technician *1 student enrolled* • Web Page, Digital/Multimedia and Information Resources Design *3 students enrolled* • Welding Technology/Welder *1170 hrs./$2445*

STUDENT SERVICES Academic or career counseling, employment services for current students, placement services for program completers, remedial services.

George T. Baker Aviation School

3275 NW 42nd Avenue, Miami, FL 33142
http://bakeraviation.dadeschools.net/

CONTACT Sean Gallagan, Principal
Telephone: 305-871-3143 Ext. 2312

GENERAL INFORMATION Public Institution. Founded 1937. **Total program enrollment:** 235. **Application fee:** $15.

PROGRAM(S) OFFERED
• Aircraft Powerplant Technology/Technician *30 students enrolled* • Airframe Mechanics and Aircraft Maintenance Technology/Technician *38 students enrolled* • Industrial Electronics Technology/Technician

STUDENT SERVICES Academic or career counseling, employment services for current students, placement services for program completers, remedial services.

Gulf Coast College

3910 US Highway 301 North, Suite 200, Tampa, FL 33619-1259
http://gulfcoastcollege.com/

CONTACT Tracey Schoonmaker, Executive Director
Telephone: 813-620-1446

GENERAL INFORMATION Private Institution. Founded 1978. **Accreditation:** State accredited or approved. **Total program enrollment:** 155. **Application fee:** $50.

PROGRAM(S) OFFERED
• Aesthetician/Esthetician and Skin Care Specialist *10 students enrolled* • Medical/Clinical Assistant *2 students enrolled* • Nursing, Other *36 students enrolled*

STUDENT SERVICES Employment services for current students, placement services for program completers, remedial services.

Gulf Coast Community College

5230 West Highway 98, Panama City, FL 32401-1058
http://www.gulfcoast.edu/

CONTACT A. James Kerley, President
Telephone: 850-769-1551

GENERAL INFORMATION Public Institution. Founded 1957. **Accreditation:** Regional (SACS/CC); dental assisting (ADA); dental hygiene (ADA); emergency medical services (JRCEMTP); physical therapy assisting (APTA); radiologic technology: radiography (JRCERT). **Total program enrollment:** 2297.

PROGRAM(S) OFFERED
• Accounting and Related Services, Other *2 students enrolled* • Child Care Provider/Assistant *23 students enrolled* • Cinematography and Film/Video Production • Corrections *214 students enrolled* • Criminal Justice/Police Science *38 students enrolled* • Dental Assisting/Assistant *14 students enrolled* • Diagnostic Medical Sonography/Sonographer and Ultrasound Technician *1 student enrolled* • Drafting and Design Technology/Technician, General • Emergency Medical Technology/Technician (EMT Paramedic) *39 students enrolled* • Executive Assistant/Executive Secretary *1 student enrolled* • Fire Science/Firefighting *39 students enrolled* • Forensic Science and Technology *1 student enrolled* • Licensed Practical/Vocational Nurse Training (LPN, LVN, Cert, Dipl, AAS) *25 students enrolled* • Management Information Systems,

Gulf Coast Community College (continued)

General *2 students enrolled* • **Plumbing Technology/Plumber** • **Surgical Technology/Technologist** *16 students enrolled* • **Truck and Bus Driver/Commercial Vehicle Operation**

STUDENT SERVICES Academic or career counseling, employment services for current students, placement services for program completers, remedial services.

Health Opportunity Technical Center

18441 NW 2nd Avenue, Suite 300, Miami Gardens, FL 33169
http://www.hotc.edu

CONTACT Joyce Byrd-Strozier, President
Telephone: 305-249-2275

GENERAL INFORMATION Private Institution. **Total program enrollment:** 148. **Application fee:** $10.

PROGRAM(S) OFFERED
• **Electrocardiograph Technology/Technician** *465 hrs./$4250* • **Emergency Care Attendant (EMT Ambulance)** *300 hrs./$2900* • **Licensed Practical/Vocational Nurse Training (LPN, LVN, Cert, Dipl, AAS)** *1350 hrs./$22,250* • **Nurse/Nursing Assistant/Aide and Patient Care Assistant** *165 hrs./$750* • **Pharmacy Technician/Assistant** *1202 hrs./$9750* • **Phlebotomy/Phlebotomist** *180 hrs./$1500* • **Renal/Dialysis Technologist/Technician**

STUDENT SERVICES Placement services for program completers.

Henry W. Brewster Technical Center

2222 North Tampa Street, Tampa, FL 33602
http://www.brewster.edu/

CONTACT Michael D. Donohue, Principal
Telephone: 813-276-5448

GENERAL INFORMATION Public Institution. Founded 1925. **Total program enrollment:** 273. **Application fee:** $10.

PROGRAM(S) OFFERED
• **Administrative Assistant and Secretarial Science, General** *10 students enrolled* • **Automobile/Automotive Mechanics Technology/Technician** *1800 hrs./$6418* • **Child Care Provider/Assistant** *24 students enrolled* • **Civil Engineering Technology/Technician** • **Computer Technology/Computer Systems Technology** *1650 hrs./$3382* • **Early Childhood Education and Teaching** *600 hrs./$1320* • **Health Aide** *600 hrs./$1301* • **Health Aides/Attendants/Orderlies, Other** *36 students enrolled* • **Health Unit Coordinator/Ward Clerk** • **Hotel/Motel Administration/Management** *91 students enrolled* • **Industrial Mechanics and Maintenance Technology** *40 students enrolled* • **Legal Administrative Assistant/Secretary** *7 students enrolled* • **Licensed Practical/Vocational Nurse Training (LPN, LVN, Cert, Dipl, AAS)** *1350 hrs./$2871* • **Medical Administrative/Executive Assistant and Medical Secretary** *17 students enrolled* • **Pharmacy Technician/Assistant** *1050 hrs./$2225* • **Psychiatric/Mental Health Services Technician** *15 students enrolled*

STUDENT SERVICES Academic or career counseling, employment services for current students, placement services for program completers, remedial services.

Heritage Institute

6811 Palisades Park Court, Fort Myers, FL 33912
http://heritage-education.com/

CONTACT Eva Hutson, School Director
Telephone: 239-936-5822

GENERAL INFORMATION Private Institution. **Total program enrollment:** 819.

PROGRAM(S) OFFERED
• **Aesthetician/Esthetician and Skin Care Specialist** *94 hrs./$18,836* • **Allied Health and Medical Assisting Services, Other** *94 hrs./$22,850* • **Health and Physical Education/Fitness, Other** *94 hrs./$20,917* • **Massage Therapy/Therapeutic Massage** *102 hrs./$20,827* • **Pharmacy Technician/Assistant** *54 hrs./$12,053*

STUDENT SERVICES Academic or career counseling, employment services for current students, placement services for program completers.

Heritage Institute

4130 Salisbury Road, Suite 1100, Jacksonville, FL 32216
http://www.heritage-education.com/

CONTACT Sonnie Willingham, Director
Telephone: 904-332-0910

GENERAL INFORMATION Private Institution. **Total program enrollment:** 390.

PROGRAM(S) OFFERED
• **Aesthetician/Esthetician and Skin Care Specialist** *94 hrs./$19,836* • **Allied Health and Medical Assisting Services, Other** *94 hrs./$22,850* • **Massage Therapy/Therapeutic Massage** *102 hrs./$19,853* • **Pharmacy Technician/Assistant** *54 hrs./$12,053*

STUDENT SERVICES Academic or career counseling, employment services for current students, placement services for program completers.

Herzing College

1595 South Semoran Boulevard, Suite 1501, Winter Park, FL 32792-5509
http://www.herzing.edu/

CONTACT Heather Antonacci, Campus President
Telephone: 407-478-0500

GENERAL INFORMATION Private Institution. Founded 1989. **Accreditation:** State accredited or approved. **Total program enrollment:** 79.

PROGRAM(S) OFFERED
• **Massage Therapy/Therapeutic Massage** *4 students enrolled* • **Medical Insurance Coding Specialist/Coder** *3 students enrolled* • **Medical/Health Management and Clinical Assistant/Specialist** • **System, Networking, and LAN/WAN Management/Manager**

STUDENT SERVICES Academic or career counseling, employment services for current students, placement services for program completers, remedial services.

High-Tech Institute

3710 Maguire Boulevard, Orlando, FL 32803
http://www.high-techinstitute.com/

CONTACT Ron Usiewicz, Campus President
Telephone: 407-893-7400

GENERAL INFORMATION Private Institution. Founded 1998. **Accreditation:** State accredited or approved. **Total program enrollment:** 667. **Application fee:** $50.

PROGRAM(S) OFFERED
• **Dental Assisting/Assistant** *746 hrs./$11,340* • **Massage Therapy/Therapeutic Massage** *820 hrs./$13,083* • **Medical Insurance Specialist/Medical Biller** *14 students enrolled* • **Medical Radiologic Technology/Science—Radiation Therapist** *810 hrs./$13,550* • **Medical/Clinical Assistant** *746 hrs./$11,361* • **Pharmacy Technician/Assistant** *720 hrs./$11,237* • **Surgical Technology/Technologist** *1160 hrs./$22,681*

STUDENT SERVICES Placement services for program completers.

Hillsborough Community College

PO Box 31127, Tampa, FL 33631-3127
http://www.hccfl.edu/

CONTACT Dr. Gwendolyn W. Stephenson, President
Telephone: 813-253-7000

GENERAL INFORMATION Public Institution. Founded 1968. **Accreditation:** Regional (SACS/CC); dental assisting (ADA); dental hygiene (ADA); diagnostic medical sonography (JRCEDMS); emergency medical services (JRCEMTP); nuclear medicine technology (JRCNMT); ophthalmic dispensing (COA); radiologic technology: radiation therapy technology (JRCERT); radiologic technology: radiography (JRCERT). **Total program enrollment:** 8629. **Application fee:** $20.

PROGRAM(S) OFFERED
• **Accounting and Related Services, Other** • **Aquaculture** • **Architectural Engineering Technology/Technician** 5 *students enrolled* • **Autobody/Collision and Repair Technology/Technician** 16 *students enrolled* • **Business Administration and Management, General** 50 *students enrolled* • **Child Care Provider/Assistant** 8 *students enrolled* • **Cinematography and Film/Video Production** • **Community Health Services/Liaison/Counseling** 1 *student enrolled* • **Computer Programming, Specific Applications** 1 *student enrolled* • **Computer Systems Analysis/Analyst** 5 *students enrolled* • **Computer Technology/Computer Systems Technology** 15 *students enrolled* • **Computer/Information Technology Services Administration and Management, Other** 1 *student enrolled* • **Corrections** 69 *students enrolled* • **Criminal Justice/Police Science** 84 *students enrolled* • **Dental Assisting/Assistant** 7 *students enrolled* • **Drafting and Design Technology/Technician, General** 14 *students enrolled* • **Electrical, Electronic and Communications Engineering Technology/Technician** • **Emergency Medical Technology/Technician (EMT Paramedic)** 201 *students enrolled* • **Entrepreneurship/Entrepreneurial Studies** 5 *students enrolled* • **Executive Assistant/Executive Secretary** 6 *students enrolled* • **Fire Science/Firefighting** 209 *students enrolled* • **Forensic Science and Technology** 8 *students enrolled* • **Health Information/Medical Records Technology/Technician** 15 *students enrolled* • **Legal Assistant/Paralegal** 7 *students enrolled* • **Management Information Systems and Services, Other** • **Management Information Systems, General** • **Medical Radiologic Technology/Science—Radiation Therapist** 3 *students enrolled* • **Nursing—Registered Nurse Training (RN, ASN, BSN, MSN)** • **Opticianry/Ophthalmic Dispensing Optician** 2 *students enrolled* • **Restaurant/Food Services Management** • **Security and Loss Prevention Services** 110 *students enrolled*

STUDENT SERVICES Academic or career counseling, daycare for children of students, employment services for current students, placement services for program completers, remedial services.

Hi-Tech School of Cosmetology

1303 SW 107 Avenue, Miami, FL 33174
http://www.hitechtheschool.com

CONTACT Patricia Herrera, Financial Aid Director
Telephone: 305-487-9997

GENERAL INFORMATION Private Institution. **Total program enrollment:** 35.

PROGRAM(S) OFFERED
• **Aesthetician/Esthetician and Skin Care Specialist** 300 *hrs./$3075*
• **Cosmetology/Cosmetologist, General** 1200 *hrs./$14,000*

STUDENT SERVICES Academic or career counseling, employment services for current students, placement services for program completers, remedial services.

Hobe Sound Bible College

PO Box 1065, Hobe Sound, FL 33475-1065
http://www.hsbc.edu/

CONTACT P. Daniel Stetler, President
Telephone: 772-546-5534

GENERAL INFORMATION Private Institution. Founded 1960. **Accreditation:** State accredited or approved. **Total program enrollment:** 99. **Application fee:** $25.

PROGRAM(S) OFFERED
• Bible/Biblical Studies

Indian River State College

3209 Virginia Avenue, Fort Pierce, FL 34981-5596
http://www.ircc.edu/

CONTACT Dr. Edwin R. Massey, President
Telephone: 772-462-4772

GENERAL INFORMATION Public Institution. Founded 1960. **Accreditation:** Regional (SACS/CC); dental assisting (ADA); dental hygiene (ADA); dental laboratory technology (ADA); emergency medical services (JRCEMTP); health information technology (AHIMA); medical assisting (AAMAE); medical laboratory technology (NAACLS); physical therapy assisting (APTA); radiologic technology: radiography (JRCERT). **Total program enrollment:** 5394.

PROGRAM(S) OFFERED
• **Accounting and Related Services, Other** 7 *students enrolled* • **Aquaculture** 3 *students enrolled* • **Autobody/Collision and Repair Technology/Technician** • **Barbering/Barber** 1 *student enrolled* • **Blood Bank Technology Specialist** • **Carpentry/Carpenter** 3 *students enrolled* • **Child Care Provider/Assistant** • **Corrections** 160 *students enrolled* • **Cosmetology/Cosmetologist, General** 35 *students enrolled* • **Criminal Justice/Police Science** 87 *students enrolled* • **Dental Assisting/Assistant** 18 *students enrolled* • **Dietitian Assistant** • **Electrical, Electronic and Communications Engineering Technology/Technician** 46 *students enrolled* • **Emergency Medical Technology/Technician (EMT Paramedic)** 149 *students enrolled* • **Entrepreneurship/Entrepreneurial Studies** 127 *students enrolled* • **Executive Assistant/Executive Secretary** 4 *students enrolled* • **Facial Treatment Specialist/Facialist** 45 *students enrolled* • **Fire Science/Firefighting** 78 *students enrolled* • **General Merchandising, Sales, and Related Marketing Operations, Other** • **Health Information/Medical Records Technology/Technician** 1 *student enrolled* • **Health and Medical Administrative Services, Other** • **Heating, Air Conditioning and Refrigeration Technology/Technician (ACH/ACR/ACHR/HRAC/HVAC/AC Technology)** 1 *student enrolled* • **Heating, Air Conditioning, Ventilation and Refrigeration Maintenance Technology/Technician (HAC, HACR, HVAC, HVACR)** 8 *students enrolled* • **Housing and Human Environments, Other** 38 *students enrolled* • **Human Development and Family Studies, General** • **Landscaping and Groundskeeping** 1 *student enrolled* • **Licensed Practical/Vocational Nurse Training (LPN, LVN, Cert, Dipl, AAS)** 56 *students enrolled* • **Management Information Systems, General** 1 *student enrolled* • **Marketing/Marketing Management, General** 8 *students enrolled* • **Medical Administrative/Executive Assistant and Medical Secretary** 2 *students enrolled* • **Medical Radiologic Technology/Science—Radiation Therapist** • **Medical/Clinical Assistant** 10 *students enrolled* • **Nail Technician/Specialist and Manicurist** 45 *students enrolled* • **Nuclear Medical Technology/Technologist** 8 *students enrolled* • **Nursing—Registered Nurse Training (RN, ASN, MSN)** 3 *students enrolled* • **Nursing, Other** • **Office Management and Supervision** 11 *students enrolled* • **Pharmacy Technician/Assistant** 4 *students enrolled* • **Physical Therapist Assistant** 10 *students enrolled* • **Plant Protection and Integrated Pest Management** 4 *students enrolled* • **Public Administration** 1 *student enrolled* • **Respiratory Care Therapy/Therapist** • **Security and Loss Prevention Services** 175 *students enrolled* • **Small Engine Mechanics and Repair Technology/Technician** • **Surgical Technology/Technologist** 11 *students enrolled* • **Truck and Bus Driver/Commercial Vehicle Operation** 96 *students enrolled* • **Welding Technology/Welder**

STUDENT SERVICES Academic or career counseling, daycare for children of students, employment services for current students, placement services for program completers, remedial services.

International Academy

2550 S. Ridgewood Avenue, South Daytona, FL 32119
http://www.intl-academy.com/

CONTACT M. Varol, Administrator
Telephone: 386-767-4600 Ext. 226

GENERAL INFORMATION Private Institution. **Total program enrollment:** 119.

PROGRAM(S) OFFERED
• **Aesthetician/Esthetician and Skin Care Specialist** 600 *hrs./$7800*
• **Cosmetology/Cosmetologist, General** 1200 *hrs./$17,425* • **Facial Treatment**

International Academy (continued)

Specialist/Facialist *310 hrs./$5270* • **Massage Therapy/Therapeutic Massage** *600 hrs./$7200* • **Nail Technician/Specialist and Manicurist** *240 hrs./$2600*

STUDENT SERVICES Academic or career counseling, employment services for current students, placement services for program completers, remedial services.

International Training Careers

7360 SW 24th Street, Suite 121-B, Miami, FL 33155

CONTACT Robert Teich, President
Telephone: 305-263-9696

GENERAL INFORMATION Private Institution. **Total program enrollment:** 277. **Application fee:** $100.

PROGRAM(S) OFFERED
• **Nurse/Nursing Assistant/Aide and Patient Care Assistant** *720 hrs./$12,315*

STUDENT SERVICES Academic or career counseling, employment services for current students, placement services for program completers, remedial services.

Jacksonville Beauty Institute

5045 Soutel Drive, Suite 80, Jacksonville, FL 32208
http://www.jacksonvillebeautyinstitute.com/

CONTACT Misty Craig, Director
Telephone: 904-768-9001

GENERAL INFORMATION Private Institution. **Total program enrollment:** 61. **Application fee:** $100.

PROGRAM(S) OFFERED
• **Cosmetology/Cosmetologist, General** *1200 hrs./$12,090*

STUDENT SERVICES Placement services for program completers.

James Lorenzo Walker Vocational-Technical Center

3702 Estey Avenue, Naples, FL 34104-4498
http://www.lwit.edu/

CONTACT Jeanette Johnson, Principal
Telephone: 239-377-0900

GENERAL INFORMATION Public Institution. Founded 1974. **Total program enrollment:** 526. **Application fee:** $30.

PROGRAM(S) OFFERED
• **Accounting Technology/Technician and Bookkeeping** *11 students enrolled* • **Administrative Assistant and Secretarial Science, General** • **Aircraft Powerplant Technology/Technician** *1400 hrs./$3356* • **Airframe Mechanics and Aircraft Maintenance Technology/Technician** *1400 hrs./$3356* • **Architecture and Related Services, Other** *3 students enrolled* • **Automobile/Automotive Mechanics Technology/Technician** *1800 hrs./$2687* • **Child Care Provider/Assistant** *14 students enrolled* • **Computer Engineering Technology/Technician** *14 students enrolled* • **Computer Technology/Computer Systems Technology** *1650 hrs./$3603* • **Construction Trades, Other** • **Cosmetology and Related Personal Grooming Arts, Other** *31 students enrolled* • **Cosmetology/Cosmetologist, General** *21 students enrolled* • **Criminal Justice/Police Science** *22 students enrolled* • **Culinary Arts/Chef Training** *1500 hrs./$3702* • **Dental Assisting/Assistant** *3 students enrolled* • **Facial Treatment Specialist/Facialist** *19 students enrolled* • **Fire Science/Firefighting** *62 students enrolled* • **Legal Administrative Assistant/Secretary** *2 students enrolled* • **Licensed Practical/Vocational Nurse Training (LPN, LVN, Cert, Dipl, AAS)** *1350 hrs./$3223* • **Management Information Systems and Services, Other** • **Mason/Masonry** • **Massage Therapy/Therapeutic Massage** *12 students enrolled* • **Mechanic and Repair Technologies/Technicians, Other** *5 students enrolled* • **Medical Administrative/Executive Assistant and Medical Secretary** *3 students enrolled*

• **Medical/Clinical Assistant** *7 students enrolled* • **Nurse/Nursing Assistant/Aide and Patient Care Assistant** *136 students enrolled* • **Phlebotomy/Phlebotomist** *4 students enrolled* • **Surgical Technology/Technologist** *15 students enrolled*

STUDENT SERVICES Academic or career counseling, daycare for children of students, employment services for current students, placement services for program completers, remedial services.

Jones College

5353 Arlington Expressway, Jacksonville, FL 32211
http://www.jones.edu/

CONTACT Dorothy D. Jones, CEO/President
Telephone: 904-743-1122

GENERAL INFORMATION Private Institution. Founded 1918. **Accreditation:** State accredited or approved. **Total program enrollment:** 223.

PROGRAM(S) OFFERED
• **Administrative Assistant and Secretarial Science, General** *2 students enrolled* • **Medical Insurance Coding Specialist/Coder** *4 students enrolled* • **Medical/Clinical Assistant** *4 students enrolled*

STUDENT SERVICES Academic or career counseling, employment services for current students, placement services for program completers, remedial services.

Keiser Career College–Greenacres

6812 Forest Hill Boulevard, Suite D-1, Greenacres, FL 33413
http://www.keisercareer.edu/kcc2005/ga_campus.htm

CONTACT Carole Fuller, President
Telephone: 561-433-2330

GENERAL INFORMATION Private Institution. **Total program enrollment:** 846. **Application fee:** $50.

PROGRAM(S) OFFERED
• **Aesthetician/Esthetician and Skin Care Specialist** *21 students enrolled* • **Emergency Medical Technology/Technician (EMT Paramedic)** *38 students enrolled* • **Licensed Practical/Vocational Nurse Training (LPN, LVN, Cert, Dipl, AAS)** *44 students enrolled* • **Massage Therapy/Therapeutic Massage** *409 students enrolled* • **Medical Insurance Coding Specialist/Coder** *60 students enrolled* • **Medical/Clinical Assistant** *53 students enrolled* • **Pharmacy Technician/Assistant** *16 students enrolled*

STUDENT SERVICES Academic or career counseling, employment services for current students, placement services for program completers, remedial services.

Key College

225 East Dania Beach Boulevard, Dania, FL 33004
http://www.keycollege.edu/

CONTACT Ronald Dooley, President/Director
Telephone: 954-923-4440

GENERAL INFORMATION Private Institution. Founded 1881. **Accreditation:** State accredited or approved. **Total program enrollment:** 80. **Application fee:** $35.

STUDENT SERVICES Academic or career counseling, employment services for current students, placement services for program completers.

La Belle Beauty Academy

2960 SW 8th Street, Miami, FL 33135
http://www.beautyacademy.com/

CONTACT Humberto L. Balboa, CEO
Telephone: 305-649-2800

GENERAL INFORMATION Private Institution. Founded 1954. **Total program enrollment:** 23. **Application fee:** $100.

PROGRAM(S) OFFERED
• **Cosmetology and Related Personal Grooming Arts, Other** 4 *students enrolled* • **Cosmetology, Barber/Styling, and Nail Instructor** 600 *hrs./*$2938
• **Cosmetology/Cosmetologist, General** 1230 *hrs./*$10,033 • **Facial Treatment Specialist/Facialist** 300 *hrs./*$1350 • **Make-Up Artist/Specialist** 900 *hrs./*$5571
• **Nail Technician/Specialist and Manicurist** 240 *hrs./*$750

STUDENT SERVICES Academic or career counseling, placement services for program completers, remedial services.

La Belle Beauty School

750-D West 49th Street, Hialeah, FL 33012
http://www.beautyacademy.com/

CONTACT Linda Balboa, Chief Administrative Officer
Telephone: 305-558-0562

GENERAL INFORMATION Private Institution. **Total program enrollment:** 66. **Application fee:** $100.

PROGRAM(S) OFFERED
• **Cosmetology and Related Personal Grooming Arts, Other** • **Cosmetology, Barber/Styling, and Nail Instructor** 600 *hrs./*$2938 • **Cosmetology/ Cosmetologist, General** 1230 *hrs./*$10,033 • **Facial Treatment Specialist/ Facialist** 300 *hrs./*$1350 • **Make-Up Artist/Specialist** 900 *hrs./*$5571 • **Nail Technician/Specialist and Manicurist** 240 *hrs./*$750

STUDENT SERVICES Academic or career counseling, placement services for program completers, remedial services.

Lake City Community College

149 SE College Place, Lake City, FL 32025
http://www.lakecitycc.edu/

CONTACT Charles W. Hall, President
Telephone: 386-752-1822

GENERAL INFORMATION Public Institution. Founded 1962. **Accreditation:** Regional (SACS/CC); emergency medical services (JRCEMTP); medical laboratory technology (NAACLS); physical therapy assisting (APTA). **Total program enrollment:** 1013. **Application fee:** $15.

PROGRAM(S) OFFERED
• **Accounting and Related Services, Other** 2 *students enrolled* • **Agricultural Mechanization, Other** 23 *students enrolled* • **Blood Bank Technology Specialist** 20 *students enrolled* • **Commercial and Advertising Art** 5 *students enrolled* • **Corrections** 195 *students enrolled* • **Cosmetology/Cosmetologist, General** 26 *students enrolled* • **Criminal Justice/Police Science** 44 *students enrolled* • **Emergency Medical Technology/Technician (EMT Paramedic)** 34 *students enrolled* • **Entrepreneurship/Entrepreneurial Studies** 1 *student enrolled* • **Executive Assistant/Executive Secretary** 1 *student enrolled* • **Facial Treatment Specialist/Facialist** 2 *students enrolled* • **Forest Management/Forest Resources Management** 8 *students enrolled* • **General Merchandising, Sales, and Related Marketing Operations, Other** • **Health Information/Medical Records Technology/Technician** 13 *students enrolled* • **Heating, Air Conditioning, Ventilation and Refrigeration Maintenance Technology/Technician (HAC, HACR, HVAC, HVACR)** • **Licensed Practical/Vocational Nurse Training (LPN, LVN, Cert, Dipl, AAS)** 30 *students enrolled* • **Management Information Systems and Services, Other** • **Nail Technician/Specialist and Manicurist** 5 *students enrolled* • **Nursing, Other** 17 *students enrolled* • **Pharmacy Technician/Assistant** 5 *students enrolled* • **Plant Protection and Integrated Pest Management** 2 *students enrolled* • **Truck and Bus Driver/Commercial Vehicle Operation** 42 *students enrolled* • **Water Quality and Wastewater Treatment Management and Recycling Technology/Technician**

STUDENT SERVICES Academic or career counseling, employment services for current students, placement services for program completers, remedial services.

Lake-Sumter Community College

9501 US Highway 441, Leesburg, FL 34788-8751
http://www.lscc.edu/

CONTACT Dr. Charles R. Mojock, President
Telephone: 352-787-3747

GENERAL INFORMATION Public Institution. Founded 1962. **Accreditation:** Regional (SACS/CC); health information technology (AHIMA). **Total program enrollment:** 1384. **Application fee:** $25.

PROGRAM(S) OFFERED
• **Accounting and Related Services, Other** 1 *student enrolled* • **Computer Systems Analysis/Analyst** 1 *student enrolled* • **Electrical, Electronic and Communications Engineering Technology/Technician** 8 *students enrolled* • **Entrepreneurship/Entrepreneurial Studies** 1 *student enrolled* • **Executive Assistant/Executive Secretary** 1 *student enrolled* • **Health Information/Medical Records Technology/Technician** 8 *students enrolled* • **Management Information Systems, General**

STUDENT SERVICES Academic or career counseling, employment services for current students, placement services for program completers, remedial services.

Lake Technical Center

2001 Kurt Street, Eustis, FL 32726
http://www.laketech.org/

CONTACT Terry Miller, Director
Telephone: 352-589-2250 Ext. 0

GENERAL INFORMATION Public Institution. **Total program enrollment:** 423.

PROGRAM(S) OFFERED
• **Accounting** 5 *students enrolled* • **Administrative Assistant and Secretarial Science** 7 *students enrolled* • **Allied Health and Medical Assisting Services, Other** • **Architectural Drafting and Architectural CAD/CADD** 4 *students enrolled* • **Autobody/Collision and Repair Technology/Technician** 1400 *hrs./*$3038 • **Child Care Provider/Assistant** • **Commercial and Advertising Art** 1 *student enrolled* • **Computer Installation and Repair Technology/Technician** 1 *student enrolled* • **Computer Programming, Specific Applications** 4 *students enrolled* • **Corrections and Criminal Justice, Other** 16 *students enrolled* • **Corrections** 55 *students enrolled* • **Cosmetology/Cosmetologist, General** 1200 *hrs./*$2574 • **Criminal Justice/Law Enforcement Administration** 770 *hrs./*$1992 • **Criminal Justice/Police Science** 53 *students enrolled* • **Culinary Arts/Chef Training** 10 *students enrolled* • **Emergency Medical Technology/Technician (EMT Paramedic)** 250 *hrs./*$633 • **Facial Treatment Specialist/Facialist** 13 *students enrolled* • **Fire Science/Firefighting** 450 *hrs./*$1464 • **Legal Administrative Assistant/Secretary** 7 *students enrolled* • **Licensed Practical/Vocational Nurse Training (LPN, LVN, Cert, Dipl, AAS)** 1350 *hrs./*$3463 • **Massage Therapy/Therapeutic Massage** 11 *students enrolled* • **Mechanic and Repair Technologies/Technicians, Other** 3 *students enrolled* • **Mechanical Drafting and Mechanical Drafting CAD/CADD** • **Medium/Heavy Vehicle and Truck Technology/Technician** 2 *students enrolled* • **Nail Technician/Specialist and Manicurist** 11 *students enrolled* • **Nurse/Nursing Assistant/Aide and Patient Care Assistant** 107 *students enrolled* • **Welding Technology/Welder** 7 *students enrolled*

STUDENT SERVICES Academic or career counseling, placement services for program completers, remedial services.

Lee County High Tech Center North

360 Santa Barbara Boulevard North, Cape Coral, FL 33993,
http://www.hightechnorth.com/

CONTACT Michael A. Schiffer, Director
Telephone: 239-574-4440

GENERAL INFORMATION Public Institution. **Total program enrollment:** 300. **Application fee:** $15.

PROGRAM(S) OFFERED
• **Accounting** 2 *students enrolled* • **Administrative Assistant and Secretarial Science, General** • **Banking and Financial Support Services** • **Business Administration and Management, General** 7 *students enrolled* • **Commercial**

Lee County High Tech Center North (continued)

and Advertising Art *2 students enrolled* ● **Computer Installation and Repair Technology/Technician** *1650 hrs./$3711* ● **Computer Systems Networking and Telecommunications** *1 student enrolled* ● **Culinary Arts/Chef Training** *3 students enrolled* ● **Digital Communication and Media/Multimedia** *1 student enrolled* ● **Drafting/Design Engineering Technologies/Technicians, Other** *1 student enrolled* ● **Electrical/Electronics Equipment Installation and Repair, General** *1400 hrs./$3176* ● **Facial Treatment Specialist/Facialist** *15 students enrolled* ● **General Office Occupations and Clerical Services** ● **Health and Medical Administrative Services, Other** *1000 hrs./$2340* ● **Legal Administrative Assistant/Secretary** ● **Licensed Practical/Vocational Nurse Training (LPN, LVN, Cert, Dipl, AAS)** *1350 hrs./$4182* ● **Management Information Systems, General** *1 student enrolled* ● **Medical Administrative/Executive Assistant and Medical Secretary** ● **Medical/Clinical Assistant** ● **Nail Technician/Specialist and Manicurist** *18 students enrolled* ● **Nursing, Other** ● **Surgical Technology/Technologist** *1330 hrs./$3146* ● **Web Page, Digital/Multimedia and Information Resources Design** *1050 hrs./$2367*

STUDENT SERVICES Academic or career counseling, employment services for current students, remedial services.

Lee County Vocational High Tech Center–Central

3800 Michigan Avenue, Fort Myers, FL 33916
http://www.hightechcentral.org/

CONTACT Robert R. Durham, Director
Telephone: 239-334-4544

GENERAL INFORMATION Public Institution. Founded 1967. **Total program enrollment:** 510. **Application fee:** $15.

PROGRAM(S) OFFERED

● **Accounting** *14 students enrolled* ● **Administrative Assistant and Secretarial Science, General** *14 students enrolled* ● **Autobody/Collision and Repair Technology/Technician** *1400 hrs./$3206* ● **Automobile/Automotive Mechanics Technology/Technician** *1800 hrs./$4254* ● **Business Administration and Management, General** *8 students enrolled* ● **Carpentry/Carpenter** *5 students enrolled* ● **Child Care Provider/Assistant** *8 students enrolled* ● **Computer and Information Sciences and Support Services, Other** *9 students enrolled* ● **Cosmetology/Cosmetologist, General** *1200 hrs./$2583* ● **Culinary Arts and Related Services, Other** *10 students enrolled* ● **Electrical/Electronics Maintenance and Repair Technology, Other** *3 students enrolled* ● **Electrician** *1200 hrs./$3069* ● **Heating, Air Conditioning, Ventilation and Refrigeration Maintenance Technology/Technician (HAC, HACR, HVAC, HVACR)** *5 students enrolled* ● **Licensed Practical/Vocational Nurse Training (LPN, LVN, Cert, Dipl, AAS)** *1350 hrs./$3713* ● **Marine Maintenance/Fitter and Ship Repair Technology/Technician** *9 students enrolled* ● **Massage Therapy/Therapeutic Massage** *12 students enrolled* ● **Nurse/Nursing Assistant/Aide and Patient Care Assistant** *120 hrs./$257* ● **Phlebotomy/Phlebotomist** *4 students enrolled* ● **Plumbing Technology/Plumber** *7 students enrolled* ● **Small Engine Mechanics and Repair Technology/Technician** *8 students enrolled* ● **Web Page, Digital/Multimedia and Information Resources Design** *9 students enrolled* ● **Web/Multimedia Management and Webmaster** *3 students enrolled* ● **Welding Technology/Welder** *7 students enrolled*

STUDENT SERVICES Academic or career counseling, daycare for children of students, employment services for current students, placement services for program completers, remedial services.

Lincoln College of Technology

2410 Metro Centre Boulevard, West Palm Beach, FL 33407
http://www.lincolnedu.com/

CONTACT Charles Halliday, President
Telephone: 561-842-8324

GENERAL INFORMATION Private Institution. Founded 1983. **Accreditation:** Medical assisting (AAMAE); state accredited or approved. **Total program enrollment:** 1426. **Application fee:** $25.

PROGRAM(S) OFFERED

● **Architectural Drafting and Architectural CAD/CADD** *2 students enrolled* ● **Automobile/Automotive Mechanics Technology/Technician** *46 students enrolled* ● **Baking and Pastry Arts/Baker/Pastry Chef** *21 students enrolled* ● **Computer Systems Networking and Telecommunications** *2 students enrolled*

● **Cosmetology/Cosmetologist, General** *49 students enrolled* ● **Culinary Arts/Chef Training** *41 students enrolled* ● **Dental Assisting/Assistant** *58 students enrolled* ● **Health and Physical Education/Fitness, Other** *1 student enrolled* ● **Heating, Air Conditioning, Ventilation and Refrigeration Maintenance Technology/Technician (HAC, HACR, HVAC, HVACR)** *35 students enrolled* ● **Medical Insurance Coding Specialist/Coder** *4 students enrolled* ● **Medical/Clinical Assistant** *26 students enrolled*

STUDENT SERVICES Academic or career counseling, employment services for current students, placement services for program completers, remedial services.

Lindsey Hopkins Technical Education Center

750 NW 20th Street, Miami, FL 33127
http://lindsey.dadeschools.net/

CONTACT Rosa Borgen, Principal
Telephone: 305-324-6070 Ext. 7005

GENERAL INFORMATION Public Institution. Founded 1942. **Total program enrollment:** 565.

PROGRAM(S) OFFERED

● **Automobile/Automotive Mechanics Technology/Technician** *1800 hrs./$4050* ● **Commercial and Advertising Art** ● **Computer Technology/Computer Systems Technology** ● **Cosmetology, Barber/Styling, and Nail Instructor** *5 students enrolled* ● **Cosmetology/Cosmetologist, General** *1200 hrs./$3150* ● **Culinary Arts and Related Services, Other** *5 students enrolled* ● **Dental Assisting/Assistant** *5 students enrolled* ● **Dietetics and Clinical Nutrition Services, Other** *4 students enrolled* ● **Early Childhood Education and Teaching** *11 students enrolled* ● **Electrical and Power Transmission Installation/Installer, General** *3 students enrolled* ● **Electrical, Electronic and Communications Engineering Technology/Technician** ● **Electrician** *1200 hrs./$3150* ● **Facial Treatment Specialist/Facialist** *3 students enrolled* ● **Fashion/Apparel Design** ● **Food Preparation/Professional Cooking/Kitchen Assistant** *1500 hrs./$3900* ● **Health Aides/Attendants/Orderlies, Other** *4 students enrolled* ● **Heating, Air Conditioning, Ventilation and Refrigeration Maintenance Technology/Technician (HAC, HACR, HVAC, HVACR)** ● **Home Health Aide/Home Attendant** *26 students enrolled* ● **Licensed Practical/Vocational Nurse Training (LPN, LVN, Cert, Dipl, AAS)** *1350 hrs./$3302* ● **Mason/Masonry** *1 student enrolled* ● **Medical Insurance Specialist/Medical Biller** ● **Nail Technician/Specialist and Manicurist** *19 students enrolled* ● **Nurse/Nursing Assistant/Aide and Patient Care Assistant** *30 students enrolled* ● **Phlebotomy/Phlebotomist** *22 students enrolled* ● **Surgical Technology/Technologist** *1330 hrs./$3525*

STUDENT SERVICES Academic or career counseling, daycare for children of students, employment services for current students, placement services for program completers, remedial services.

Lively Technical Center

500 North Appleyard Drive, Tallahassee, FL 32304
http://www.livelytech.com/

CONTACT Woody Hildebrandt, Principal
Telephone: 850-487-7555

GENERAL INFORMATION Private Institution. **Total program enrollment:** 468.

PROGRAM(S) OFFERED

● **Accounting** *6 students enrolled* ● **Architectural Drafting and Architectural CAD/CADD** ● **Automobile/Automotive Mechanics Technology/Technician** *1800 hrs./$3000* ● **Barbering/Barber** *3 students enrolled* ● **Carpentry/Carpenter** ● **Child Care and Support Services Management** ● **Commercial Photography** *1 student enrolled* ● **Commercial and Advertising Art** ● **Computer Programming, Specific Applications** ● **Computer Systems Analysis/Analyst** *7 students enrolled* ● **Computer Systems Networking and Telecommunications** *2 students enrolled* ● **Cosmetology/Cosmetologist, General** *1200 hrs./$3000* ● **Electrical, Electronic and Communications Engineering Technology/Technician** *3 students enrolled* ● **Electrician** *9 students enrolled* ● **Electrocardiograph Technology/Technician** *1 student enrolled* ● **Foods, Nutrition, and Related Services, Other** *4 students enrolled* ● **Heating, Air Conditioning, Ventilation and Refrigeration Maintenance Technology/Technician (HAC, HACR, HVAC, HVACR)** *1350 hrs./$3000* ● **Legal Administrative Assistant/Secretary** *1 student enrolled* ● **Licensed Practical/Vocational Nurse Training (LPN, LVN, Cert, Dipl, AAS)** *1350 hrs./$4499* ● **Machine Shop Technology/Assistant** ● **Medical Administrative/Executive Assistant and Medical Secretary** *2 students enrolled* ● **Medical**

Transcription/Transcriptionist • Medical/Clinical Assistant *1300 hrs./$3000* • Nail Technician/Specialist and Manicurist • Nurse/Nursing Assistant/Aide and Patient Care Assistant *18 students enrolled* • Office Management and Supervision • Phlebotomy/Phlebotomist *12 students enrolled* • Radio and Television • Real Estate • Web Page, Digital/Multimedia and Information Resources Design *5 students enrolled* • Welding Technology/Welder *1170 hrs./$3000*

STUDENT SERVICES Academic or career counseling, daycare for children of students, employment services for current students, placement services for program completers, remedial services.

Loraine's Academy.

1012 58th Street, North, Tyrone Garden Center, St. Petersburg, FL 33710
http://www.lorainesacademy.edu/

CONTACT Nancy B. Fordham, Administrator
Telephone: 727-347-4247 Ext. 105

GENERAL INFORMATION Private Institution. Founded 1966. **Total program enrollment: 123.**

PROGRAM(S) OFFERED
• Cosmetology/Cosmetologist, General *1200 hrs./$13,045* • Facial Treatment Specialist/Facialist *300 hrs./$3900* • Massage Therapy/Therapeutic Massage *600 hrs./$7455* • Nail Technician/Specialist and Manicurist *11 students enrolled* • Special Education and Teaching, General *600 hrs./$4550*

STUDENT SERVICES Academic or career counseling, employment services for current students, placement services for program completers, remedial services.

Management Resources Institute

4343 W. Flagler Street, Suite 203, Miami, FL 33134

GENERAL INFORMATION Private Institution. **Total program enrollment: 64.**

PROGRAM(S) OFFERED
• Computer and Information Sciences and Support Services, Other • Customer Service Support/Call Center/Teleservice Operation *41 hrs./$5775* • Data Entry/Microcomputer Applications, General *1 student enrolled* • General Office Occupations and Clerical Services *27 hrs./$3825* • Medical Insurance Coding Specialist/Coder *50 hrs./$11,473* • Nursing, Other *83 hrs./$10,660* • Office Management and Supervision • Organizational Behavior Studies • Teacher Education and Professional Development, Specific Levels and Methods, Other *39 hrs./$6140* • Teacher Education and Professional Development, Specific Subject Areas, Other *83 hrs./$11,710* • Teaching English as a Second or Foreign Language/ESL Language Instructor

STUDENT SERVICES Academic or career counseling, employment services for current students, placement services for program completers, remedial services.

Manatee Technical Institute

5603 34th Street, West, Bradenton, FL 34210
http://www.manateetechnicalinstitute.org/

CONTACT Mary Cantrell, Director
Telephone: 941-751-7900

GENERAL INFORMATION Public Institution. Founded 1964. **Total program enrollment: 711. Application fee: $30.**

PROGRAM(S) OFFERED
• Accounting *11 students enrolled* • Administrative Assistant and Secretarial Science, General *8 students enrolled* • Allied Health and Medical Assisting Services, Other • Appliance Installation and Repair Technology/Technician *3 students enrolled* • Automobile/Automotive Mechanics Technology/Technician *1800 hrs./$4166* • Barbering/Barber *3 students enrolled* • Carpentry/Carpenter • Child Care and Support Services Management *26 students enrolled* • Communication and Media Studies, Other • Computer Systems Networking and Telecommunications • Computer Technology/Computer Systems Technology

• Construction Trades, General • Cosmetology/Cosmetologist, General *1200 hrs./$3244* • Criminal Justice/Law Enforcement Administration *34 students enrolled* • Culinary Arts/Chef Training *1500 hrs./$3370* • Dental Assisting/Assistant *16 students enrolled* • Early Childhood Education and Teaching *3 students enrolled* • Electrical and Electronic Engineering Technologies/Technicians, Other *11 students enrolled* • Electrical and Power Transmission Installation/Installer, General • Electrical, Electronic and Communications Engineering Technology/Technician *2 students enrolled* • Electrician *6 students enrolled* • Emergency Care Attendant (EMT Ambulance) *250 hrs./$855* • Emergency Medical Technology/Technician (EMT Paramedic) *33 students enrolled* • Facial Treatment Specialist/Facialist *16 students enrolled* • Fire Science/Firefighting *46 students enrolled* • Heating, Air Conditioning, Ventilation and Refrigeration Maintenance Technology/Technician (HAC, HACR, HVAC, HVACR) *8 students enrolled* • Industrial Mechanics and Maintenance Technology • Industrial Technology/Technician • Licensed Practical/Vocational Nurse Training (LPN, LVN, Cert, Dipl, AAS) *1350 hrs./$3429* • Machine Shop Technology/Assistant • Marine Maintenance/Fitter and Ship Repair Technology/Technician • Mason/Masonry *4 students enrolled* • Massage Therapy/Therapeutic Massage *21 students enrolled* • Medical Administrative/Executive Assistant and Medical Secretary *4 students enrolled* • Medical Insurance Coding Specialist/Coder • Medical Office Computer Specialist/Assistant *2 students enrolled* • Medium/Heavy Vehicle and Truck Technology/Technician • Nail Technician/Specialist and Manicurist *11 students enrolled* • Nurse/Nursing Assistant/Aide and Patient Care Assistant *117 students enrolled* • Nursing, Other • Ophthalmic and Optometric Support Services and Allied Professions, Other • Plant Nursery Operations and Management • Plumbing Technology/Plumber *1 student enrolled* • Precision Metal Working, Other • Psychiatric/Mental Health Nurse/Nursing • Radio and Television Broadcasting Technology/Technician • Renal/Dialysis Technologist/Technician *8 students enrolled* • Robotics Technology/Technician • Surgical Technology/Technologist • Tourism and Travel Services Marketing Operations *4 students enrolled* • Web Page, Digital/Multimedia and Information Resources Design *5 students enrolled* • Welding Technology/Welder *1170 hrs./$2480* • Woodworking, Other

STUDENT SERVICES Academic or career counseling, daycare for children of students, employment services for current students, placement services for program completers, remedial services.

Manhattan Beauty School

4315 South Manhattan Avenue, Tampa, FL 33611

CONTACT Robert E. Valdez, Chief Executive Director
Telephone: 813-258-0505

GENERAL INFORMATION Private Institution. Founded 1960. **Total program enrollment: 588. Application fee: $100.**

PROGRAM(S) OFFERED
• Aesthetician/Esthetician and Skin Care Specialist *260 hrs./$3000* • Cosmetology and Related Personal Grooming Arts, Other *600 hrs./$4100* • Cosmetology/Cosmetologist, General *1200 hrs./$12,800* • Nail Technician/Specialist and Manicurist *240 hrs./$1100*

STUDENT SERVICES Academic or career counseling, employment services for current students, placement services for program completers, remedial services.

Marion County Community Technical and Adult Education Center

1014 SW 7th Road, Ocala, FL 34474
http://www.mcctae.com/

CONTACT Deborah Jenkins, Director
Telephone: 352-671-7200

GENERAL INFORMATION Public Institution. **Total program enrollment: 491. Application fee: $10.**

PROGRAM(S) OFFERED
• Administrative Assistant and Secretarial Science, General *7 students enrolled* • Allied Health and Medical Assisting Services, Other *1300 hrs./$2900* • Clinical/Medical Laboratory Technician *10 students enrolled* • Cooking and Related Culinary Arts, General *5 students enrolled* • Cosmetology/Cosmetologist, General *1200 hrs./$2680* • Fire Science/Firefighting *308 students enrolled* • Massage Therapy/Therapeutic Massage *750 hrs./$1843* • Medical Insurance Specialist/Medical Biller *14 students enrolled* • Medical Radiologic Technology/Science—Radiation Therapist *2700 hrs./$6620*

Marion County Community Technical and Adult Education Center (continued)
- **Nurse/Nursing Assistant/Aide and Patient Care Assistant** *165 hrs./$535*
- **Phlebotomy/Phlebotomist** *165 hrs./$635* ● **Veterinary/Animal Health Technology/Technician and Veterinary Assistant** *12 students enrolled* ● **Welding Technology/Welder** *3 students enrolled*

STUDENT SERVICES Academic or career counseling, daycare for children of students, remedial services.

McFatter Technical Center

6500 Nova Drive, Davie, FL 33317
http://www.mcfattertech.com/

CONTACT Mark Thomas, Director
Telephone: 754-321-5700

GENERAL INFORMATION Public Institution. Founded 1985. **Total program enrollment:** 893.

PROGRAM(S) OFFERED
- **Allied Health and Medical Assisting Services, Other** *15 students enrolled*
- **Architectural Drafting and Architectural CAD/CADD** *6 students enrolled*
- **Automobile/Automotive Mechanics Technology/Technician** *12 students enrolled* ● **Commercial Photography** *1 student enrolled* ● **Computer Programming/Programmer, General** *6 students enrolled* ● **Culinary Arts and Related Services, Other** *14 students enrolled* ● **Dental Laboratory Technology/Technician** *13 students enrolled* ● **Digital Communication and Media/Multimedia** *6 students enrolled* ● **Emergency Medical Technology/Technician (EMT Paramedic)** *74 students enrolled* ● **Fire Science/Firefighting** *159 students enrolled* ● **Graphic and Printing Equipment Operator, General Production** *10 students enrolled* ● **Heavy/Industrial Equipment Maintenance Technologies, Other** *9 students enrolled* ● **Marine Maintenance/Fitter and Ship Repair Technology/Technician** *25 students enrolled* ● **Mechanical Drafting and Mechanical Drafting CAD/CADD** *1 student enrolled* ● **Nurse/Nursing Assistant/Aide and Patient Care Assistant** *148 students enrolled* ● **Optometric Technician/Assistant** *7 students enrolled* ● **Pharmacy Technician/Assistant** *9 students enrolled* ● **Radio and Television Broadcasting Technology/Technician** *7 students enrolled* ● **Truck and Bus Driver/Commercial Vehicle Operation** *324 students enrolled* ● **Welding Technology/Welder** *4 students enrolled*

STUDENT SERVICES Academic or career counseling, employment services for current students, placement services for program completers, remedial services.

Medical Career Institute of South Florida

1750 45th Street, West Palm Beach, FL 33460
http://www.MCISF.com/

CONTACT Doug McVay, President
Telephone: 561-296-0824

GENERAL INFORMATION Private Institution. **Total program enrollment:** 227. **Application fee:** $50.

PROGRAM(S) OFFERED
- **Health Information/Medical Records Administration/Administrator** *900 hrs./$12,500* ● **Massage Therapy/Therapeutic Massage** *609 hrs./$9200* ● **Medical/Clinical Assistant** *920 hrs./$12,500*

STUDENT SERVICES Academic or career counseling, employment services for current students, placement services for program completers, remedial services.

MedVance Institute

170 JFK Drive, Atlantis, FL 33462
http://www.medvance.edu/

CONTACT John Hopkins, CEO
Telephone: 561-304-3466

GENERAL INFORMATION Private Institution. Founded 1970. **Accreditation:** State accredited or approved. **Total program enrollment:** 659. **Application fee:** $25.

PROGRAM(S) OFFERED
- **Health Information/Medical Records Technology/Technician** *67 hrs./$14,995* ● **Licensed Practical/Vocational Nurse Training (LPN, LVN, Cert, Dipl, AAS)** *24 students enrolled* ● **Massage Therapy/Therapeutic Massage** *47 hrs./$11,750* ● **Medical Radiologic Technology/Science—Radiation Therapist** *130 hrs./$35,500* ● **Medical/Clinical Assistant** *49 hrs./$12,995* ● **Nurse/Nursing Assistant/Aide and Patient Care Assistant** *4 students enrolled* ● **Nursing, Other** *82 hrs./$25,995* ● **Pharmacy Technician/Assistant** ● **Surgical Technology/Technologist** *98 hrs./$23,100*

STUDENT SERVICES Employment services for current students, placement services for program completers.

MedVance Institute

4101 Northwest 3rd Court, Suite 9, Fort Lauderdale, FL 33317-2857
http://www.medvance.edu/

CONTACT John Hopkins, CEO
Telephone: 954-587-7100

GENERAL INFORMATION Private Institution. **Total program enrollment:** 628. **Application fee:** $25.

PROGRAM(S) OFFERED
- **Health Information/Medical Records Technology/Technician** *67 hrs./$14,995* ● **Health Professions and Related Clinical Sciences, Other** ● **Massage Therapy/Therapeutic Massage** *47 hrs./$11,750* ● **Medical Radiologic Technology/Science—Radiation Therapist** *130 hrs./$35,500* ● **Medical/Clinical Assistant** *49 hrs./$12,995* ● **Nurse/Nursing Assistant/Aide and Patient Care Assistant** *18 students enrolled* ● **Pharmacy Technician/Assistant** *49 hrs./$10,500* ● **Surgical Technology/Technologist** *98 hrs./$23,100*

STUDENT SERVICES Employment services for current students, placement services for program completers.

MedVance Institute

9035 Sunset Drive, Suite 200, Miami, FL 33173
http://www.medvance.edu/

CONTACT John Hopkins, CEO
Telephone: 305-596-5553

GENERAL INFORMATION Private Institution. **Total program enrollment:** 314. **Application fee:** $25.

PROGRAM(S) OFFERED
- **Health Information/Medical Records Technology/Technician** *67 hrs./$14,995* ● **Licensed Practical/Vocational Nurse Training (LPN, LVN, Cert, Dipl, AAS)** *40 students enrolled* ● **Medical Radiologic Technology/Science—Radiation Therapist** *130 hrs./$35,500* ● **Medical/Clinical Assistant** *49 hrs./$12,995* ● **Nursing, Other** *82 hrs./$25,995*

STUDENT SERVICES Employment services for current students, placement services for program completers.

MedVance Institute

851 SE Johnson Avenue, Stuart, FL 34994
http://www.medvance.edu/

CONTACT John Hopkins, CEO
Telephone: 772-221-9799

GENERAL INFORMATION Private Institution. **Total program enrollment:** 353. **Application fee:** $25.

PROGRAM(S) OFFERED
- **Health Information/Medical Records Technology/Technician** *67 hrs./$14,995* ● **Licensed Practical/Vocational Nurse Training (LPN, LVN, Cert, Dipl, AAS)** *32 students enrolled* ● **Massage Therapy/Therapeutic Massage** *47 hrs./$11,750* ● **Medical Administrative/Executive Assistant and Medical Secretary** *49 hrs./$10,995* ● **Medical/Clinical Assistant** *49 hrs./$12,995* ● **Nurse/Nursing Assistant/Aide and Patient Care Assistant** ● **Nursing, Other** *82 hrs./$25,995*

STUDENT SERVICES Employment services for current students, placement services for program completers.

Mercy Hospital School of Practical Nursing

3663 South Miami Avenue, Miami, FL 33133
http://mercymiami.org/

CONTACT Elizabeth Hernandez, Director & Finacial Aid Officer
Telephone: 305-285-2777 Ext. 3251

GENERAL INFORMATION Private Institution. **Total program enrollment:** 127. **Application fee:** $50.

PROGRAM(S) OFFERED
• **Licensed Practical/Vocational Nurse Training (LPN, LVN, Cert, Dipl, AAS)** *1439 hrs./$6970*

STUDENT SERVICES Academic or career counseling, employment services for current students, placement services for program completers, remedial services.

Miami Dade College

300 Northeast Second Avenue, Miami, FL 33132-2296
http://www.mdc.edu/

CONTACT Eduardo J. Padron, College President
Telephone: 305-237-8888

GENERAL INFORMATION Public Institution. Founded 1960. **Accreditation:** Regional (SACS/CC); dental hygiene (ADA); diagnostic medical sonography (JRCEDMS); emergency medical services (JRCEMTP); funeral service (ABFSE); health information technology (AHIMA); medical laboratory technology (NAACLS); ophthalmic dispensing (COA); physical therapy assisting (APTA); radiologic technology: radiation therapy technology (JRCERT); radiologic technology: radiography (JRCERT); respiratory therapy technology (CoARC). **Total program enrollment:** 21768. **Application fee:** $20.

PROGRAM(S) OFFERED
• **Accounting Technology/Technician and Bookkeeping** *20 students enrolled* • **Accounting and Related Services, Other** *18 students enrolled* • **Architectural Engineering Technology/Technician** *29 students enrolled* • **Aviation/Airway Management and Operations** *84 students enrolled* • **Banking and Financial Support Services** *17 students enrolled* • **Biology Technician/Biotechnology Laboratory Technician** • **Blood Bank Technology Specialist** *71 students enrolled* • **Business Administration and Management, General** *208 students enrolled* • **Business, Management, Marketing, and Related Support Services, Other** *2 students enrolled* • **Commercial and Advertising Art** *1 student enrolled* • **Computer Programming, Specific Applications** *4 students enrolled* • **Computer Systems Analysis/Analyst** *4 students enrolled* • **Computer Technology/Computer Systems Technology** *106 students enrolled* • **Computer/Information Technology Services Administration and Management, Other** • **Corrections** *315 students enrolled* • **Criminal Justice/Police Science** *108 students enrolled* • **Drafting and Design Technology/Technician, General** *257 students enrolled* • **Education/Teaching of Individuals with Hearing Impairments, Including Deafness** *11 students enrolled* • **Emergency Medical Technology/Technician (EMT Paramedic)** *144 students enrolled* • **Entrepreneurship/Entrepreneurial Studies** *12 students enrolled* • **Executive Assistant/Executive Secretary** *31 students enrolled* • **Finance, General** *1 student enrolled* • **Fire Science/Firefighting** *79 students enrolled* • **Health Information/Medical Records Technology/Technician** *31 students enrolled* • **Hotel/Motel Administration/Management** • **International Marketing** • **Legal Administrative Assistant/Secretary** *2 students enrolled* • **Licensed Practical/Vocational Nurse Training (LPN, LVN, Cert, Dipl, AAS)** *39 students enrolled* • **Management Information Systems and Services, Other** *1 student enrolled* • **Management Information Systems, General** *1 student enrolled* • **Marketing/Marketing Management, General** *10 students enrolled* • **Massage Therapy/Therapeutic Massage** *46 students enrolled* • **Medical/Clinical Assistant** *14 students enrolled* • **Nuclear Medical Technology/Technologist** *2 students enrolled* • **Office Management and Supervision** *2 students enrolled* • **Pharmacy Technician/Assistant** *12 students enrolled* • **Psychiatric/Mental Health Services Technician** *5 students enrolled* • **Radio and Television Broadcasting Technology/Technician** • **Real Estate** *8 students enrolled* • **Restaurant/Food Services Management** • **Security and Loss Prevention Services** *34 students enrolled* • **Security and Protective Services, Other** *9 students enrolled* • **Tourism and Travel Services Marketing Operations**

STUDENT SERVICES Academic or career counseling, employment services for current students, placement services for program completers, remedial services.

Miami-Dade County Public Schools

1450 NE Second Avenue, Miami, FL 33132
http://www2.dadeschools.net/index.htm

CONTACT Chely Rajoy-Tarpin, Principal
Telephone: 305-445-7731

GENERAL INFORMATION Public Institution. **Total program enrollment:** 43. **Application fee:** $15.

PROGRAM(S) OFFERED
• **Accounting Technology/Technician and Bookkeeping** *900 hrs./$1898* • **Child Care Provider/Assistant** *1 student enrolled* • **Computer Graphics** *1 student enrolled* • **Cosmetology/Cosmetologist, General** *1200 hrs./$2444* • **Data Entry/Microcomputer Applications, General** *900 hrs./$2563* • **Facial Treatment Specialist/Facialist** *260 hrs./$545* • **Nail Technician/Specialist and Manicurist** *240 hrs./$505* • **System, Networking, and LAN/WAN Management/Manager** *1050 hrs./$2211* • **Web Page, Digital/Multimedia and Information Resources Design** *1 student enrolled* • **Web/Multimedia Management and Webmaster**

STUDENT SERVICES Academic or career counseling, daycare for children of students, employment services for current students, placement services for program completers, remedial services.

Miami Lakes Technical Education Center

5780 NW 158th Street, Miami, FL 33169
http://mlec.dadeschools.net/

CONTACT James V. Parker, Principal
Telephone: 305-557-1100

GENERAL INFORMATION Private Institution. **Total program enrollment:** 965. **Application fee:** $15.

PROGRAM(S) OFFERED
• **Accounting Technology/Technician and Bookkeeping** • **Administrative Assistant and Secretarial Science, General** • **Appliance Installation and Repair Technology/Technician** • **Architectural Drafting and Architectural CAD/CADD** • **Autobody/Collision and Repair Technology/Technician** • **Automobile/Automotive Mechanics Technology/Technician** *2250 hrs./$4914* • **Child Care Provider/Assistant** • **Child Care and Support Services Management** • **Computer Installation and Repair Technology/Technician** *1400 hrs./$4095* • **Computer Programming/Programmer, General** • **Construction Trades, Other** • **Cosmetology/Cosmetologist, General** *1200 hrs./$3456* • **Culinary Arts/Chef Training** *4 students enrolled* • **Diesel Mechanics Technology/Technician** *3 students enrolled* • **E-Commerce/Electronic Commerce** • **Electrical and Electronic Engineering Technologies/Technicians, Other** • **Graphic Design** • **Heating, Air Conditioning and Refrigeration Technology/Technician (ACH/ACR/ACHR/HRAC/HVAC/AC Technology)** *1350 hrs./$3496* • **Heavy Equipment Maintenance Technology/Technician** *2 students enrolled* • **Licensed Practical/Vocational Nurse Training (LPN, LVN, Cert, Dipl, AAS)** *1350 hrs./$2519* • **Marine Maintenance/Fitter and Ship Repair Technology/Technician** • **Medical/Clinical Assistant** *1300 hrs./$3276* • **Nurse/Nursing Assistant/Aide and Patient Care Assistant** *2 students enrolled* • **Radio and Television Broadcasting Technology/Technician** • **Truck and Bus Driver/Commercial Vehicle Operation** *186 students enrolled*

STUDENT SERVICES Academic or career counseling, daycare for children of students, employment services for current students, placement services for program completers, remedial services.

Mid-Florida Tech

2900 West Oak Ridge Road, Orlando, FL 32809
http://www.mft.ocps.net/

CONTACT Joseph A. McCoy, Senior Director
Telephone: 407-251-6047 Ext. 0

GENERAL INFORMATION Private Institution. **Total program enrollment:** 1758. **Application fee:** $25.

PROGRAM(S) OFFERED
• **Autobody/Colfision and Repair Technology/Technician** *46 students enrolled* • **Automobile/Automotive Mechanics Technology/Technician** *1620 hrs./$3722* • **Carpentry/Carpenter** • **Commercial Photography** *15 students enrolled* • **Computer Installation and Repair Technology/Technician** *20 students enrolled*

Mid-Florida Tech (continued)

• **Construction Trades, Other** *104 students enrolled* • **Construction/Heavy Equipment/Earthmoving Equipment Operation** *6 students enrolled* • **Culinary Arts/Chef Training** *1500 hrs./$3870* • **Data Processing and Data Processing Technology/Technician** *1 student enrolled* • **Diesel Mechanics Technology/Technician** *1680 hrs./$3713* • **Digital Communication and Media/Multimedia** *12 students enrolled* • **Electrical, Electronic and Communications Engineering Technology/Technician** *11 students enrolled* • **Electrician** *94 students enrolled* • **Emergency Medical Technology/Technician (EMT Paramedic)** *266 hrs./$559* • **Fire Science/Firefighting** *450 hrs./$3040* • **Fire Services Administration** *28 students enrolled* • **Glazier** *4 students enrolled* • **Heating, Air Conditioning, Ventilation and Refrigeration Maintenance Technology/Technician (HAC, HACR, HVAC, HVACR)** *39 students enrolled* • **Hospitality Administration/Management, Other** *41 students enrolled* • **Machine Shop Technology/Assistant** *12 students enrolled* • **Mason/Masonry** *7 students enrolled* • **Painting/Painter and Wall Coverer** *25 students enrolled* • **Pipefitting/Pipefitter and Sprinkler Fitter** *5 students enrolled* • **Plumbing Technology/Plumber** *9 students enrolled* • **Precision Metal Working, Other** *19 students enrolled* • **Real Estate** • **Security and Loss Prevention Services** *40 hrs./$168* • **Tourism and Travel Services Marketing Operations** *1 student enrolled* • **Truck and Bus Driver/Commercial Vehicle Operation** *96 students enrolled* • **Vehicle and Vehicle Parts and Accessories Marketing Operations** *42 students enrolled* • **Welding Technology/Welder** *29 students enrolled*

STUDENT SERVICES Academic or career counseling, employment services for current students, placement services for program completers, remedial services.

Motorcycle and Marine Mechanics Institute–Division of Universal Technical Institute

9751 Delegates Drive, Orlando, FL 32837-9835
http://www.uticorp.com/

CONTACT Dianne Ely, Campus President
Telephone: 407-240-2422

GENERAL INFORMATION Private Institution. Founded 1977. **Total program enrollment:** 3114.

PROGRAM(S) OFFERED
• **Automobile/Automotive Mechanics Technology/Technician** *66 hrs./$32,850*
• **Mechanic and Repair Technologies/Technicians, Other** *60 hrs./$25,300*
• **Motorcycle Maintenance and Repair Technology/Technician** *48 hrs./$17,900*

STUDENT SERVICES Academic or career counseling, employment services for current students, placement services for program completers.

National Aviation Academy

5770 Roosevelt Boulevard, Suite 105, Clearwater, FL 34620
http://www.naa.edu/

CONTACT Michael Wisniewski, President
Telephone: 727-531-2080 Ext. 10

GENERAL INFORMATION Private Institution. Founded 1970. **Total program enrollment:** 355.

PROGRAM(S) OFFERED
• **Airframe Mechanics and Aircraft Maintenance Technology/Technician** *3000 hrs./$39,750* • **Avionics Maintenance Technology/Technician** *1000 hrs./$13,500*

STUDENT SERVICES Academic or career counseling, employment services for current students, placement services for program completers.

New Concept Massage and Beauty School

2022 SW 1st Street, Miami, FL 33135

CONTACT Maria Vazquez, President
Telephone: 305-642-3020

GENERAL INFORMATION Private Institution. **Total program enrollment:** 38. **Application fee:** $50.

PROGRAM(S) OFFERED
• **Aesthetician/Esthetician and Skin Care Specialist** *325 hrs./$2179*
• **Cosmetology and Related Personal Grooming Arts, Other** *4 students enrolled*
• **Cosmetology/Cosmetologist, General** *1200 hrs./$8239* • **Massage Therapy/Therapeutic Massage** *24 hrs./$6983* • **Nail Technician/Specialist and Manicurist** *240 hrs./$1250* • **Personal and Culinary Services, Other** *10 students enrolled*

STUDENT SERVICES Academic or career counseling, placement services for program completers.

New Professions Technical Institute

4100 West Flagler Street, Suite A1, Miami, FL 33134
http://www.npti.com/

CONTACT Jose Vazquez, Vice President
Telephone: 305-461-2223

GENERAL INFORMATION Private Institution. **Total program enrollment:** 323. **Application fee:** $50.

PROGRAM(S) OFFERED
• **Computer and Information Sciences, General** *550 hrs./$8100* • **Computer/Information Technology Services Administration and Management, Other** *25 students enrolled* • **Health Information/Medical Records Administration/Administrator** *550 hrs./$8100* • **International Business/Trade/Commerce** *550 hrs./$8100* • **Medical Office Assistant/Specialist** *840 hrs./$10,440* • **Medical Office Management/Administration** *33 students enrolled* • **Teaching English as a Second or Foreign Language/ESL Language Instructor** *720 hrs./$4716* • **Transportation and Materials Moving, Other** *13 students enrolled*

STUDENT SERVICES Academic or career counseling, employment services for current students, placement services for program completers.

North Florida Community College

1000 Turner Davis Drive, Madison, FL 32340-1602
http://www.nfcc.edu/

CONTACT John Grosskopf, Interim President
Telephone: 904-973-2288

GENERAL INFORMATION Public Institution. Founded 1958. **Accreditation:** Regional (SACS/CC). **Total program enrollment:** 474. **Application fee:** $30.

PROGRAM(S) OFFERED
• **Child Care Provider/Assistant** *5 students enrolled* • **Corrections** *20 students enrolled* • **Criminal Justice/Police Science** *27 students enrolled* • **Emergency Medical Technology/Technician (EMT Paramedic)** *23 students enrolled* • **Executive Assistant/Executive Secretary** *1 student enrolled* • **Legal Administrative Assistant/Secretary** • **Licensed Practical/Vocational Nurse Training (LPN, LVN, Cert, Dipl, AAS)** *20 students enrolled* • **Nursing, Other** *23 students enrolled* • **Office Management and Supervision** • **Security and Loss Prevention Services** *7 students enrolled*

STUDENT SERVICES Academic or career counseling, employment services for current students, placement services for program completers, remedial services.

North Florida Cosmetology Institute

2424 Allen Road, Tallahassee, FL 32312
http://www.cosmetologyinst.com/

CONTACT Anita Coppedge, Owner/President
Telephone: 850-878-5269

GENERAL INFORMATION Private Institution. **Total program enrollment:** 50.

PROGRAM(S) OFFERED
• Aesthetician/Esthetician and Skin Care Specialist *260 hrs./$2035*
• Barbering/Barber *1200 hrs./$7450* • Cosmetology and Related Personal Grooming Arts, Other *600 hrs./$4500* • Cosmetology/Cosmetologist, General *1500 hrs./$11,025* • Nail Technician/Specialist and Manicurist *240 hrs./$1890*
• Permanent Cosmetics/Makeup and Tattooing *7 students enrolled*

STUDENT SERVICES Academic or career counseling.

North Florida Institute

2186 Park Avenue, Orange Park, FL 32073-5524

CONTACT Wyman Dickey, Campus Director
Telephone: 904-269-7086

GENERAL INFORMATION Private Institution. **Total program enrollment:** 356. **Application fee:** $67.

PROGRAM(S) OFFERED
• Aesthetician/Esthetician and Skin Care Specialist *51 hrs./$9945* • Criminal Justice/Safety Studies *118 hrs./$24,145* • Health and Medical Administrative Services, Other *100 hrs./$21,245* • Medical/Clinical Assistant *53 hrs./$13,945*
• Nursing, Other *20 students enrolled* • Pharmacy Technician/Assistant • Surgical Technology/Technologist *101 hrs./$26,945*

STUDENT SERVICES Placement services for program completers.

North Florida Institute–Jacksonville

5995-3 University Boulevard West, Jacksonville, FL 32216

CONTACT Roger Buck, Regional Director of Operations
Telephone: 904-443-6300

GENERAL INFORMATION Private Institution. **Total program enrollment:** 307. **Application fee:** $50.

PROGRAM(S) OFFERED
• Barbering/Barber *1200 hrs./$13,842* • Cosmetology/Cosmetologist, General *525 hrs./$7345* • Facial Treatment Specialist/Facialist *300 hrs./$4000* • Hair Styling/Stylist and Hair Design *1500 hrs./$17,295* • Nail Technician/Specialist and Manicurist *240 hrs./$3595*

STUDENT SERVICES Placement services for program completers.

Northwest Florida State College

100 College Boulevard, Niceville, FL 32578-1295
http://www.nwfstatecollege.edu/

CONTACT James R. Richburg, President
Telephone: 850-678-5111

GENERAL INFORMATION Public Institution. Founded 1963. **Accreditation:** Regional (SACS/CC); dental assisting (ADA). **Total program enrollment:** 2636.

PROGRAM(S) OFFERED
• Accounting Technology/Technician and Bookkeeping • Accounting and Related Services, Other *2 students enrolled* • Architectural Engineering Technology/Technician *3 students enrolled* • Child Care Provider/Assistant *61 students enrolled* • Cinematography and Film/Video Production *73 students enrolled* • Commercial and Advertising Art *61 students enrolled* • Computer Programming, Specific Applications *4 students enrolled* • Computer Systems Analysis/Analyst • Computer Technology/Computer Systems Technology *2 students enrolled* • Computer/Information Technology Services Administration and Management, Other *2 students enrolled* • Corrections *33 students enrolled*
• Criminal Justice/Police Science *90 students enrolled* • Dental Assisting/Assistant *9 students enrolled* • Drafting and Design Technology/Technician, General *18 students enrolled* • Emergency Medical Technology/Technician (EMT Paramedic) *60 students enrolled* • Entrepreneurship/Entrepreneurial Studies *3 students enrolled* • Executive Assistant/Executive Secretary *5 students enrolled* • General Merchandising, Sales, and Related Marketing Operations, Other • Health Information/Medical Records Technology/Technician *18 students enrolled* • Management Information Systems, General • Marketing/Marketing Management, General *1 student enrolled* • Music, Other *3 students*

enrolled • Occupational Safety and Health Technology/Technician • Office Management and Supervision • Public Administration • Surgical Technology/Technologist *8 students enrolled*

STUDENT SERVICES Academic or career counseling, daycare for children of students, employment services for current students, placement services for program completers, remedial services.

Nouvelle Institute

3271 Northwest 7th Street, Suite 106, Miami, FL 33125

CONTACT Gerardo Vallejo, Executive Director
Telephone: 305-643-3360

GENERAL INFORMATION Private Institution. **Total program enrollment:** 128. **Application fee:** $25.

PROGRAM(S) OFFERED
• Cosmetology and Related Personal Grooming Arts, Other *4 students enrolled*
• Cosmetology/Cosmetologist, General *20 hrs./$4481*

STUDENT SERVICES Academic or career counseling, employment services for current students, placement services for program completers.

Okaloosa Applied Technology Center

1976 Lewis Turner Boulevard, Ft. Walton Beach, FL 32547
http://www.okaloosa.k12.fl.us/oatc/

CONTACT Al Gardner, Principal
Telephone: 850-833-3500

GENERAL INFORMATION Private Institution. **Total program enrollment:** 242.

PROGRAM(S) OFFERED
• Administrative Assistant and Secretarial Science, General *5 students enrolled*
• Agricultural/Farm Supplies Retailing and Wholesaling *3 students enrolled*
• Animal Sciences, Other *3 students enrolled* • Automobile/Automotive Mechanics Technology/Technician *1800 hrs./$4141* • Carpentry/Carpenter *1200 hrs./$1913* • Computer Installation and Repair Technology/Technician
• Cosmetology/Cosmetologist, General *21 students enrolled* • Electrical, Electronic and Communications Engineering Technology/Technician *1400 hrs./$1913* • Electrical/Electronics Equipment Installation and Repair, General
• Electrician • Facial Treatment Specialist/Facialist • Heating, Air Conditioning, Ventilation and Refrigeration Maintenance Technology/Technician (HAC, HACR, HVAC, HVACR) *1350 hrs./$1913* • Legal Administrative Assistant/Secretary • Licensed Practical/Vocational Nurse Training (LPN, LVN, Cert, Dipl, AAS) *1350 hrs./$2903* • Marine Maintenance/Fitter and Ship Repair Technology/Technician *1350 hrs./$1913* • Medical Administrative/Executive Assistant and Medical Secretary *5 students enrolled* • Nail Technician/Specialist and Manicurist • Plumbing Technology/Plumber *1 student enrolled*
• Welding Technology/Welder

STUDENT SERVICES Academic or career counseling, placement services for program completers, remedial services.

Orlando Culinary Academy

8511 Commodity Circle, Suite 100, Orlando, FL 32819
http://www.orlandoculinary.com/

CONTACT Joe Hardiman, President
Telephone: 407-888-4000 Ext. 8780

GENERAL INFORMATION Private Institution. Founded 2002. **Accreditation:** State accredited or approved. **Total program enrollment:** 982. **Application fee:** $50.

PROGRAM(S) OFFERED
• Baking and Pastry Arts/Baker/Pastry Chef *96 hrs./$33,500* • Culinary Arts/Chef Training *38 hrs./$15,800* • Hospitality Administration/Management, General *90 hrs./$33,500*

STUDENT SERVICES Academic or career counseling, employment services for current students, placement services for program completers.

Orlando Technical Center

301 West Amelia Street, Orlando, FL 32801
http://www.orlandotech.ocps.net/

CONTACT F. Lynne Voltaggio, Senior Director
Telephone: 407-317-3431

GENERAL INFORMATION Public Institution. Founded 1981. **Total program enrollment:** 400. **Application fee:** $25.

PROGRAM(S) OFFERED
● **Accounting Technology/Technician and Bookkeeping** 24 *students enrolled* ● **Administrative Assistant and Secretarial Science, General** 8 *students enrolled* ● **Animation, Interactive Technology, Video Graphics and Special Effects** 1050 *hrs./$2296* ● **Apparel and Textiles, Other** 23 *students enrolled* ● **Child Care Provider/Assistant** 600 *hrs./$1264* ● **Child Care and Support Services Management** 45 *hrs./$95* ● **Clinical/Medical Laboratory Assistant** 28 *students enrolled* ● **Dental Assisting/Assistant** 22 *students enrolled* ● **Digital Communication and Media/Multimedia** 12 *students enrolled* ● **Health Unit Coordinator/Ward Clerk** 620 *hrs./$1245* ● **Home Health Aide/Home Attendant** 18 *students enrolled* ● **Institutional Food Workers** 9 *students enrolled* ● **Licensed Practical/Vocational Nurse Training (LPN, LVN, Cert, Dipl, AAS)** 53 *students enrolled* ● **Management Information Systems and Services, Other** 1 *student enrolled* ● **Medical Administrative/Executive Assistant and Medical Secretary** 7 *students enrolled* ● **Medical Radiologic Technology/Science—Radiation Therapist** 15 *students enrolled* ● **Nurse/Nursing Assistant/Aide and Patient Care Assistant** 600 *hrs./$1202* ● **Nursing, Other** 1350 *hrs./$3933* ● **Radio and Television Broadcasting Technology/Technician** 17 *students enrolled* ● **Real Estate** ● **Surgical Technology/Technologist** 12 *students enrolled* ● **Web Page, Digital/Multimedia and Information Resources Design**

STUDENT SERVICES Academic or career counseling, employment services for current students, placement services for program completers, remedial services.

Palm Beach Academy of Health & Beauty

1220-A 10th Street, Lake Park, FL 33403
http://www.pbacademy.net

CONTACT David L. Creef, Executive Director
Telephone: 561-845-1400

GENERAL INFORMATION Private Institution. **Total program enrollment:** 135. **Application fee:** $100.

PROGRAM(S) OFFERED
● **Cosmetology/Cosmetologist, General** 1200 *hrs./$11,965* ● **Facial Treatment Specialist/Facialist** 320 *hrs./$3600* ● **Massage Therapy/Therapeutic Massage** 25 *hrs./$5000*

STUDENT SERVICES Employment services for current students, placement services for program completers.

Palm Beach Community College

4200 Congress Avenue, Lake Worth, FL 33461-4796
http://www.pbcc.edu/

CONTACT Dennis P. Gallon, President
Telephone: 561-967-7222

GENERAL INFORMATION Public Institution. Founded 1933. **Accreditation:** Regional (SACS/CC); dental assisting (ADA); dental hygiene (ADA); emergency medical services (JRCEMTP); radiologic technology: radiography (JRCERT). **Total program enrollment:** 9308. **Application fee:** $20.

PROGRAM(S) OFFERED
● **Accounting Technology/Technician and Bookkeeping** 3 *students enrolled* ● **Accounting and Related Services, Other** 1 *student enrolled* ● **Architectural Engineering Technology/Technician** 2 *students enrolled* ● **Autobody/Collision and Repair Technology/Technician** 9 *students enrolled* ● **Banking and Financial Support Services** ● **Business Administration and Management, General** 1 *student enrolled* ● **Business and Personal/Financial Services Marketing Operations** 140 *students enrolled* ● **Child Care Provider/Assistant** 63 *students enrolled* ● **Child Care and Support Services Management** ● **Cinematography and Film/Video Production** 6 *students enrolled* ● **Commercial and Advertising Art** 3

students enrolled ● **Communication, Journalism and Related Programs, Other** ● **Computer Programming, Specific Applications** 1 *student enrolled* ● **Computer Technology/Computer Systems Technology** 6 *students enrolled* ● **Computer/Information Technology Services Administration and Management, Other** 11 *students enrolled* ● **Construction Engineering Technology/Technician** 8 *students enrolled* ● **Corrections** 44 *students enrolled* ● **Cosmetology/Cosmetologist, General** 41 *students enrolled* ● **Criminal Justice/Police Science** 83 *students enrolled* ● **Dental Assisting/Assistant** 13 *students enrolled* ● **Diagnostic Medical Sonography/Sonographer and Ultrasound Technician** 13 *students enrolled* ● **Diesel Mechanics Technology/Technician** 5 *students enrolled* ● **Electrical, Electronic and Communications Engineering Technology/Technician** ● **Electrician** ● **Emergency Medical Technology/Technician (EMT Paramedic)** 65 *students enrolled* ● **Entrepreneurship/Entrepreneurial Studies** 8 *students enrolled* ● **Executive Assistant/Executive Secretary** 11 *students enrolled* ● **Facial Treatment Specialist/Facialist** 56 *students enrolled* ● **Fire Protection and Safety Technology/Technician** 1 *student enrolled* ● **Fire Protection, Other** ● **Fire Science/Firefighting** 107 *students enrolled* ● **Fire Services Administration** 4 *students enrolled* ● **Forensic Science and Technology** 29 *students enrolled* ● **Health Information/Medical Records Technology/Technician** 7 *students enrolled* ● **Heating, Air Conditioning, Ventilation and Refrigeration Maintenance Technology/Technician (HAC, HACR, HVAC, HVACR)** 5 *students enrolled* ● **Landscaping and Groundskeeping** 20 *students enrolled* ● **Licensed Practical/Vocational Nurse Training (LPN, LVN, Cert, Dipl, AAS)** 29 *students enrolled* ● **Machine Shop Technology/Assistant** 4 *students enrolled* ● **Management Information Systems and Services, Other** 1 *student enrolled* ● **Management Information Systems, General** ● **Marketing/Marketing Management, General** ● **Massage Therapy/Therapeutic Massage** 24 *students enrolled* ● **Medical Administrative/Executive Assistant and Medical Secretary** ● **Medical Radiologic Technology/Science—Radiation Therapist** 1 *student enrolled* ● **Medical/Clinical Assistant** 3 *students enrolled* ● **Nail Technician/Specialist and Manicurist** 11 *students enrolled* ● **Nursing—Registered Nurse Training (RN, ASN, BSN, MSN)** ● **Nursing, Other** ● **Office Management and Supervision** 1 *student enrolled* ● **Psychiatric/Mental Health Services Technician** 6 *students enrolled* ● **Public Administration** ● **Real Estate** 64 *students enrolled* ● **Small Engine Mechanics and Repair Technology/Technician** ● **Surgical Technology/Technologist** 9 *students enrolled* ● **Teacher Education and Professional Development, Specific Levels and Methods, Other** 3 *students enrolled* ● **Truck and Bus Driver/Commercial Vehicle Operation** 31 *students enrolled* ● **Welding Technology/Welder** 4 *students enrolled*

STUDENT SERVICES Academic or career counseling, daycare for children of students, employment services for current students, placement services for program completers, remedial services.

Pasco-Hernando Community College

10230 Ridge Road, New Port Richey, FL 34654-5199
http://www.phcc.edu/

CONTACT Katherine M. Johnson, EdD, President
Telephone: 727-847-2727

GENERAL INFORMATION Public Institution. Founded 1972. **Accreditation:** Regional (SACS/CC); dental hygiene (ADA); emergency medical services (JRCEMTP). **Total program enrollment:** 3398. **Application fee:** $25.

PROGRAM(S) OFFERED
● **Blood Bank Technology Specialist** 52 *students enrolled* ● **Business Administration and Management, General** 46 *students enrolled* ● **Computer Programming, Specific Applications** 11 *students enrolled* ● **Computer/Information Technology Services Administration and Management, Other** 3 *students enrolled* ● **Corrections** 79 *students enrolled* ● **Cosmetology/Cosmetologist, General** ● **Criminal Justice/Police Science** 81 *students enrolled* ● **Dental Assisting/Assistant** 13 *students enrolled* ● **Drafting and Design Technology/Technician, General** 16 *students enrolled* ● **Emergency Medical Technology/Technician (EMT Paramedic)** 76 *students enrolled* ● **Entrepreneurship/Entrepreneurial Studies** 16 *students enrolled* ● **Executive Assistant/Executive Secretary** 31 *students enrolled* ● **Health Information/Medical Records Technology/Technician** 20 *students enrolled* ● **Health Unit Coordinator/Ward Clerk** 2 *students enrolled* ● **Licensed Practical/Vocational Nurse Training (LPN, LVN, Cert, Dipl, AAS)** 88 *students enrolled* ● **Management Information Systems and Services, Other** 4 *students enrolled* ● **Management Information Systems, General** 1 *student enrolled* ● **Marketing/Marketing Management, General** 6 *students enrolled* ● **Medical Administrative/Executive Assistant and Medical Secretary** 10 *students enrolled* ● **Nurse/Nursing Assistant/Aide and Patient Care Assistant** 40 *students enrolled*

• **Psychiatric/Mental Health Services Technician** 5 *students enrolled* • **Welding Technology/Welder** 3 *students enrolled*

STUDENT SERVICES Academic or career counseling, daycare for children of students, employment services for current students, placement services for program completers, remedial services.

Paul Mitchell the School—Orlando

1271 Semoran Boulevard, Suite 131, Casselberry, FL 32707
http://www.paulmitchelltheschool.com/

CONTACT Giulio Veglio, Owner
Telephone: 801-302-8801 Ext. 1021

GENERAL INFORMATION Private Institution. **Total program enrollment:** 196. **Application fee:** $75.

PROGRAM(S) OFFERED
• **Aesthetician/Esthetician and Skin Care Specialist** 450 *hrs./$5825*
• **Cosmetology/Cosmetologist, General** 1200 *hrs./$16,250*

STUDENT SERVICES Academic or career counseling, employment services for current students, placement services for program completers, remedial services.

Paul Mitchell the School—Tampa

14210 N. Nebraska Avenue, Tampa, FL 33613

CONTACT Giulio Veglio, Owner
Telephone: 801-302-8801 Ext. 1021

GENERAL INFORMATION Private Institution. **Total program enrollment:** 111. **Application fee:** $75.

PROGRAM(S) OFFERED
• **Cosmetology/Cosmetologist, General** 1200 *hrs./$13,925*

STUDENT SERVICES Academic or career counseling, placement services for program completers, remedial services.

Pensacola Junior College

1000 College Boulevard, Pensacola, FL 32504-8998
http://www.pjc.edu/

CONTACT Dr. Ed Meadows, President
Telephone: 850-484-1000

GENERAL INFORMATION Public Institution. Founded 1948. **Accreditation:** Regional (SACS/CC); dental assisting (ADA); dental hygiene (ADA); emergency medical services (JRCEMTP); health information technology (AHIMA); physical therapy assisting (APTA); radiologic technology: radiography (JRCERT). **Total program enrollment:** 4443. **Application fee:** $30.

PROGRAM(S) OFFERED
• **Accounting and Related Services, Other** 9 *students enrolled* • **Architectural Engineering Technology/Technician** 8 *students enrolled* • **Barbering/Barber** 7 *students enrolled* • **Blood Bank Technology Specialist** 43 *students enrolled* • **Carpentry/Carpenter** 2 *students enrolled* • **Child Care Provider/Assistant** 39 *students enrolled* • **Construction Engineering Technology/Technician** 7 *students enrolled* • **Cosmetology/Cosmetologist, General** 57 *students enrolled* • **Dental Assisting/Assistant** 10 *students enrolled* • **Drafting and Design Technology/Technician, General** 8 *students enrolled* • **Electrical, Electronic and Communications Engineering Technology/Technician** 6 *students enrolled* • **Electrician** 4 *students enrolled* • **Emergency Medical Technology/Technician (EMT Paramedic)** 42 *students enrolled* • **Executive Assistant/Executive Secretary** 4 *students enrolled* • **Facial Treatment Specialist/Facialist** 32 *students enrolled* • **Fire Science/Firefighting** 28 *students enrolled* • **Health Information/Medical Records Technology/Technician** 15 *students enrolled* • **Health Unit Coordinator/Ward Clerk** 8 *students enrolled* • **Heating, Air Conditioning, Ventilation and Refrigeration Maintenance Technology/Technician (HAC, HACR, HVAC, HVACR)** • **Landscaping and Groundskeeping** 2 *students enrolled* • **Licensed Practical/Vocational Nurse Training (LPN, LVN, Cert, Dipl, AAS)** 17 *students enrolled* • **Management Information Systems and Services, Other** 4 *students*

enrolled • **Management Information Systems, General** 1 *student enrolled* • **Massage Therapy/Therapeutic Massage** 15 *students enrolled* • **Mechanical Engineering/Mechanical Technology/Technician** 1 *student enrolled* • **Medical/Clinical Assistant** 9 *students enrolled* • **Nail Technician/Specialist and Manicurist** 17 *students enrolled* • **Nursing, Other** • **Plumbing Technology/Plumber** • **Surgical Technology/Technologist** 15 *students enrolled*

STUDENT SERVICES Academic or career counseling, daycare for children of students, employment services for current students, placement services for program completers, remedial services.

Pensacola School of Massage Therapy & Health Careers

2409 Creighton Road, Pensacola, FL 32504
http://www.psmthc.com

CONTACT Billy L. Clark, President
Telephone: 850-474-1330

GENERAL INFORMATION Private Institution. **Total program enrollment:** 46. **Application fee:** $50.

PROGRAM(S) OFFERED
• **Health and Medical Administrative Services, Other** 720 *hrs./$3995* • **Massage Therapy/Therapeutic Massage** 640 *hrs./$6868* • **Medical/Clinical Assistant** 816 *hrs./$3995*

STUDENT SERVICES Placement services for program completers.

Pinellas Technical Education Center–Clearwater

6100 154th Avenue N, Clearwater, FL 33760-2140
http://www.myptec.org/

CONTACT Mr. Mark Ericksen, Site Director
Telephone: 727-538-7167 Ext. 2106

GENERAL INFORMATION Public Institution. **Total program enrollment:** 918. **Application fee:** $15.

PROGRAM(S) OFFERED
• **Accounting** 9 *students enrolled* • **Automobile/Automotive Mechanics Technology/Technician** 1800 *hrs./$3852* • **Building/Property Maintenance and Management** 4 *students enrolled* • **Cabinetmaking and Millwork/Millwright** 4 *students enrolled* • **Commercial and Advertising Art** 3 *students enrolled* • **Computer Installation and Repair Technology/Technician** 6 *students enrolled* • **Computer Technology/Computer Systems Technology** 1650 *hrs./$3531* • **Cosmetology/Cosmetologist, General** 13 *students enrolled* • **Culinary Arts/Chef Training** 7 *students enrolled* • **Data Processing and Data Processing Technology/Technician** 8 *students enrolled* • **Diesel Mechanics Technology/Technician** 6 *students enrolled* • **E-Commerce/Electronic Commerce** 11 *students enrolled* • **Electrical, Electronic and Communications Engineering Technology/Technician** 4 *students enrolled* • **Electrician** 14 *students enrolled* • **Heating, Air Conditioning, Ventilation and Refrigeration Maintenance Technology/Technician (HAC, HACR, HVAC, HVACR)** 12 *students enrolled* • **Industrial Mechanics and Maintenance Technology** 1 *student enrolled* • **Licensed Practical/Vocational Nurse Training (LPN, LVN, Cert, Dipl, AAS)** 1350 *hrs./$4358* • **Machine Tool Technology/Machinist** 6 *students enrolled* • **Marine Maintenance/Fitter and Ship Repair Technology/Technician** 5 *students enrolled* • **Telecommunications Technology/Technician** 28 *students enrolled* • **Truck and Bus Driver/Commercial Vehicle Operation** 40 *hrs./$86* • **Web Page, Digital/Multimedia and Information Resources Design** 1050 *hrs./$2247* • **Welding Technology/Welder** 1170 *hrs./$2504*

STUDENT SERVICES Academic or career counseling, employment services for current students, placement services for program completers, remedial services.

Pinellas Technical Education Center–St. Petersburg

901 34th Street, St. Petersburg, FL 33711-2298
http://myptec.org/

CONTACT Dr. Peter Berry, Director
Telephone: 727-893-2500

GENERAL INFORMATION Public Institution. Founded 1967. **Total program enrollment:** 1140. **Application fee:** $15.

PROGRAM(S) OFFERED
● **Architectural Drafting and Architectural CAD/CADD** *3 students enrolled* ● **Autobody/Collision and Repair Technology/Technician** *8 students enrolled* ● **Building/Construction Finishing, Management, and Inspection, Other** *6 students enrolled* ● **Child Care Provider/Assistant** *600 hrs./$1284* ● **Dental Assisting/Assistant** *8 students enrolled* ● **Electrician** *32 students enrolled* ● **Electromechanical and Instrumentation and Maintenance Technologies/Technicians, Other** *25 students enrolled* ● **Family and Consumer Sciences/Human Sciences Business Services, Other** *9 students enrolled* ● **Family and Consumer Sciences/Human Sciences, General** *109 students enrolled* ● **Fire Science/Firefighting** *13 students enrolled* ● **Heating, Air Conditioning, Ventilation and Refrigeration Maintenance Technology/Technician (HAC, HACR, HVAC, HVACR)** *1350 hrs./$2889* ● **Industrial Mechanics and Maintenance Technology** ● **Licensed Practical/Vocational Nurse Training (LPN, LVN, Cert, Dipl, AAS)** *1350 hrs./$4729* ● **Mason/Masonry** *3 students enrolled* ● **Medical/Clinical Assistant** *1300 hrs./$2782* ● **Metal and Jewelry Arts** *1 student enrolled* ● **Nurse/Nursing Assistant/Aide and Patient Care Assistant** *290 hrs./$621* ● **Pharmacy Technician/Assistant** *8 students enrolled* ● **Photography** *3 students enrolled* ● **Pipefitting/Pipefitter and Sprinkler Fitter** *13 students enrolled* ● **Plant Nursery Operations and Management** *19 students enrolled* ● **Plumbing Technology/Plumber** *5 students enrolled* ● **Radio and Television Broadcasting Technology/Technician** *1 student enrolled* ● **Surgical Technology/Technologist** *1330 hrs./$2846* ● **Truck and Bus Driver/Commercial Vehicle Operation** *38 students enrolled*

STUDENT SERVICES Academic or career counseling, employment services for current students, placement services for program completers, remedial services.

Polk Community College

999 Avenue H, NE, Winter Haven, FL 33881-4299
http://www.polk.edu/

CONTACT Eileen Holden, President
Telephone: 863-297-1000

GENERAL INFORMATION Public Institution. Founded 1964. **Accreditation:** Regional (SACS/CC); emergency medical services (JRCEMTP); health information technology (AHIMA); physical therapy assisting (APTA); radiologic technology: radiography (JRCERT). **Total program enrollment:** 2791. **Application fee:** $20.

PROGRAM(S) OFFERED
● **Computer Systems Analysis/Analyst** ● **Computer Technology/Computer Systems Technology** *3 students enrolled* ● **Corrections** *71 students enrolled* ● **Criminal Justice/Police Science** *1 student enrolled* ● **Emergency Medical Technology/Technician (EMT Paramedic)** *107 students enrolled* ● **Executive Assistant/Executive Secretary** *3 students enrolled* ● **Health Information/Medical Records Technology/Technician** *31 students enrolled* ● **Management Information Systems, General** *2 students enrolled*

STUDENT SERVICES Academic or career counseling, employment services for current students, placement services for program completers, remedial services.

Polytechnic Institute of America

6359 Edgewater Drive, Orlando, FL 32810
http://www.polytechnic.edu/

CONTACT Deborah Harrison
Telephone: 407-275-9696

GENERAL INFORMATION Private Institution. **Total program enrollment:** 74. **Application fee:** $25.

PROGRAM(S) OFFERED
● **Computer Systems Networking and Telecommunications** *36 hrs./$11,880* ● **Legal Assistant/Paralegal** *90 hrs./$27,000* ● **Massage Therapy/Therapeutic Massage** *100 hrs./$30,000* ● **Medical/Clinical Assistant** *99 hrs./$31,754* ● **Nursing, Other** *72 hrs./$28,800*

STUDENT SERVICES Academic or career counseling, employment services for current students, placement services for program completers.

Praxis Institute

2100 Coral Way, Suite 100, Miami, FL 33145
http://the-praxisinstitute.com/

CONTACT Miguel Alfie, President
Telephone: 305-642-4104

GENERAL INFORMATION Private Institution. **Total program enrollment:** 296. **Application fee:** $100.

PROGRAM(S) OFFERED
● **Cosmetology and Related Personal Grooming Arts, Other** *900 hrs./$7200* ● **Cosmetology/Cosmetologist, General** *600 hrs./$7000* ● **Massage Therapy/Therapeutic Massage** *600 hrs./$9000*

STUDENT SERVICES Academic or career counseling, placement services for program completers.

Professional Training Centers

13250-52 SW 8th Street, Miami, FL 33184
http://www.ptcmatt.com/

CONTACT Marc Mattia, CEO
Telephone: 305-220-4120

GENERAL INFORMATION Private Institution. **Total program enrollment:** 434.

PROGRAM(S) OFFERED
● **Diagnostic Medical Sonography/Sonographer and Ultrasound Technician** *128 hrs./$24,775* ● **Medical Insurance Coding Specialist/Coder** *73 hrs./$11,250* ● **Medical/Clinical Assistant** *62 hrs./$11,250* ● **Pharmacy Technician/Assistant** *66 hrs./$11,250* ● **Radiologic Technology/Science—Radiographer** *2192 hrs./$28,200*

STUDENT SERVICES Academic or career counseling, employment services for current students, placement services for program completers, remedial services.

Radford M. Locklin Technical Center

5330 Berryhill Road, Milton, FL 32570
http://www.santarosa.k12.fl.us/ltc/

CONTACT Charles A. Etheredge, Principal
Telephone: 850-983-5700

GENERAL INFORMATION Public Institution. Founded 1982. **Total program enrollment:** 161. **Application fee:** $2.

PROGRAM(S) OFFERED
● **Accounting** ● **Administrative Assistant and Secretarial Science, General** ● **Building/Home/Construction Inspection/Inspector** ● **Carpentry/Carpenter** ● **Child Care Provider/Assistant** *14 students enrolled* ● **Computer Systems Networking and Telecommunications** ● **Computer Technology/Computer Systems Technology** *1 student enrolled* ● **Cooking and Related Culinary Arts, General** *2 students enrolled* ● **Electrician** *2 students enrolled* ● **Heating, Air Conditioning, Ventilation and Refrigeration Maintenance Technology/Technician (HAC, HACR, HVAC, HVACR)** *9 students enrolled* ● **Mason/Masonry** *8 students enrolled* ● **Medical Administrative/Executive Assistant and Medical**

Secretary *6 students enrolled* • **Nurse/Nursing Assistant/Aide and Patient Care Assistant** *10 students enrolled* • **Plumbing Technology/Plumber** • **Web Page, Digital/Multimedia and Information Resources Design** • **Welding Technology/ Welder** *4 students enrolled*

STUDENT SERVICES Academic or career counseling, daycare for children of students, employment services for current students, placement services for program completers, remedial services.

Rasmussen College Fort Myers

9160 Forum Corporate Parkway, Suite 100, Fort Myers, FL 33905-7805
http://www.rasmussen.edu

CONTACT Eric Whitehouse, Campus Director
Telephone: 239-477-2100

GENERAL INFORMATION Private Institution. **Total program enrollment:** 87. **Application fee:** $20.

PROGRAM(S) OFFERED
• **Legal Assistant/Paralegal** • **Medical Insurance Coding Specialist/Coder** • **Medical/Clinical Assistant**

STUDENT SERVICES Academic or career counseling, employment services for current students, placement services for program completers, remedial services.

Rasmussen College Ocala

2221 Southwest 19th Avenue Road, Ocala, FL 34471
http://www.rasmussen.edu/

CONTACT Pete Beasley, Campus Director
Telephone: 352-629-1941

GENERAL INFORMATION Private Institution. Founded 1984. **Accreditation:** State accredited or approved. **Total program enrollment:** 610. **Application fee:** $20.

PROGRAM(S) OFFERED
• **Accounting** • **Medical Insurance Coding Specialist/Coder** *1 student enrolled* • **Medical/Clinical Assistant** *3 students enrolled*

STUDENT SERVICES Academic or career counseling, employment services for current students, placement services for program completers, remedial services.

Rasmussen College Pasco County

2127 Grand Boulevard, Holiday, FL 34690
http://www.rasmussen.edu/

CONTACT Claire Walker, Campus Director
Telephone: 727-942-0069

GENERAL INFORMATION Private Institution. **Accreditation:** State accredited or approved. **Total program enrollment:** 188. **Application fee:** $20.

PROGRAM(S) OFFERED
• **Accounting** • **Licensed Practical/Vocational Nurse Training (LPN, LVN, Cert, Dipl, AAS)** *33 students enrolled* • **Medical/Clinical Assistant** *7 students enrolled*

STUDENT SERVICES Academic or career counseling, employment services for current students, placement services for program completers, remedial services.

Remington College–Largo Campus

8550 Ulmerton Road, Largo, FL 33771
http://www.remingtoncollege.edu/

CONTACT Michael Seltzer, Campus Vice President
Telephone: 727-532-1999

GENERAL INFORMATION Private Institution. **Accreditation:** State accredited or approved. **Total program enrollment:** 168. **Application fee:** $50.

PROGRAM(S) OFFERED
• **Medical Insurance Coding Specialist/Coder** *20 students enrolled* • **Medical/Clinical Assistant** *73 students enrolled* • **Pharmacy Technician/Assistant** *8 students enrolled*

STUDENT SERVICES Academic or career counseling, employment services for current students, placement services for program completers.

Remington College–Tampa Campus

2410 East Busch Boulevard, Tampa, FL 33612-8410
http://www.remingtoncollege.edu/

CONTACT Rosalie Lampone, Campus President
Telephone: 813-935-5700

GENERAL INFORMATION Private Institution. Founded 1948. **Accreditation:** State accredited or approved. **Total program enrollment:** 314. **Application fee:** $50.

PROGRAM(S) OFFERED
• **Electrical, Electronic and Communications Engineering Technology/Technician** • **Medical Insurance Coding Specialist/Coder** *22 students enrolled* • **Medical/Clinical Assistant** *70 students enrolled* • **Pharmacy Technician/Assistant** *9 students enrolled*

STUDENT SERVICES Academic or career counseling, employment services for current students, placement services for program completers.

Ridge Technical Center

7700 State Road 544, Winter Haven, FL 33881
http://www.polk-fl.net/ridge/

CONTACT Lisa B. Harden, Director
Telephone: 863-419-3060

GENERAL INFORMATION Private Institution. **Total program enrollment:** 506. **Application fee:** $20.

PROGRAM(S) OFFERED
• **Accounting** *6 students enrolled* • **Administrative Assistant and Secretarial Science, General** *1 student enrolled* • **Carpentry/Carpenter** *3 students enrolled* • **Computer Systems Networking and Telecommunications** *1 student enrolled* • **Cosmetology/Cosmetologist, General** *22 students enrolled* • **Customer Service Support/Call Center/Teleservice Operation** *1 student enrolled* • **Diesel Mechanics Technology/Technician** *8 students enrolled* • **Electrician** *8 students enrolled* • **Facial Treatment Specialist/Facialist** *15 students enrolled* • **Fire Science/Firefighting** *74 students enrolled* • **Food Service, Waiter/Waitress, and Dining Room Management/Manager** *3 students enrolled* • **Ground Transportation, Other** *22 students enrolled* • **Heating, Air Conditioning, Ventilation and Refrigeration Maintenance Technology/Technician (HAC, HACR, HVAC, HVACR)** *8 students enrolled* • **Licensed Practical/Vocational Nurse Training (LPN, LVN, Cert, Dipl, AAS)** *29 students enrolled* • **Massage Therapy/Therapeutic Massage** *16 students enrolled* • **Medical Administrative/Executive Assistant and Medical Secretary** • **Nail Technician/Specialist and Manicurist** *5 students enrolled* • **Nurse/Nursing Assistant/Aide and Patient Care Assistant** *40 students enrolled* • **Nursing, Other** *12 students enrolled* • **Pharmacy Technician/Assistant** *3 students enrolled* • **Teacher Assistant/Aide** • **Truck and Bus Driver/Commercial Vehicle Operation** *62 students enrolled* • **Welding Technology/Welder** *2 students enrolled*

STUDENT SERVICES Academic or career counseling, employment services for current students, placement services for program completers, remedial services.

Riverside Hairstyling Academy

3530 Beach Boulevard, Jacksonville, FL 32207

CONTACT Howard Troutman, CEO
Telephone: 904-398-0502

GENERAL INFORMATION Private Institution. **Total program enrollment:** 25. **Application fee:** $50.

PROGRAM(S) OFFERED
● **Cosmetology/Cosmetologist, General** *1200 hrs./$11,850*

STUDENT SERVICES Academic or career counseling, placement services for program completers.

Robert Morgan Vocational-Technical Center

18180 SW 122nd Avenue, Miami, FL 33177
http://rmec.dadeschools.net/

CONTACT Greg Zawyer, Principal
Telephone: 305-253-9920

GENERAL INFORMATION Public Institution. Founded 1978. **Total program enrollment:** 406. **Application fee:** $15.

PROGRAM(S) OFFERED
● **Accounting** *5 students enrolled* ● **Administrative Assistant and Secretarial Science, General** *4 students enrolled* ● **Aesthetician/Esthetician and Skin Care Specialist** *17 students enrolled* ● **Allied Health and Medical Assisting Services, Other** *5 students enrolled* ● **Appliance Installation and Repair Technology/Technician** *2 students enrolled* ● **Architectural Drafting and Architectural CAD/CADD** *2 students enrolled* ● **Autobody/Collision and Repair Technology/Technician** *8 students enrolled* ● **Automobile/Automotive Mechanics Technology/Technician** *10 students enrolled* ● **Computer Installation and Repair Technology/Technician** *1 student enrolled* ● **Cooking and Related Culinary Arts, General** *15 students enrolled* ● **Cosmetology/Cosmetologist, General** *13 students enrolled* ● **Dental Assisting/Assistant** *15 students enrolled* ● **Diesel Mechanics Technology/Technician** *12 students enrolled* ● **Early Childhood Education and Teaching** *5 students enrolled* ● **Graphic Design** *2 students enrolled* ● **Heating, Air Conditioning and Refrigeration Technology/Technician (ACH/ACR/ACHR/HRAC/HVAC/AC Technology)** *13 students enrolled* ● **Industrial Electronics Technology/Technician** *2 students enrolled* ● **Licensed Practical/Vocational Nurse Training (LPN, LVN, Cert, Dipl, AAS)** *46 students enrolled* ● **Nail Technician/Specialist and Manicurist** *15 students enrolled* ● **Nurse/Nursing Assistant/Aide and Patient Care Assistant** *2 students enrolled* ● **Vehicle Maintenance and Repair Technologies, Other** *14 students enrolled* ● **Web Page, Digital/Multimedia and Information Resources Design** *1 student enrolled* ● **Welding Technology/Welder** *5 students enrolled*

STUDENT SERVICES Academic or career counseling, daycare for children of students, placement services for program completers, remedial services.

Saber

3990 W. Flagler Street, Suite 103, Miami, FL 33134

CONTACT Josefina B. Habif, Chief Executive Officer
Telephone: 305-443-7601

GENERAL INFORMATION Private Institution. **Total program enrollment:** 208. **Application fee:** $50.

PROGRAM(S) OFFERED
● **Adult Health Nurse/Nursing** *65 students enrolled* ● **Computer Technology/Computer Systems Technology** *620 hrs./$3550* ● **Computer and Information Sciences and Support Services, Other** ● **Medical Insurance Specialist/Medical Biller** ● **Nurse/Nursing Assistant/Aide and Patient Care Assistant** ● **Nursing—Registered Nurse Training (RN, ASN, BSN, MSN)** *9 students enrolled* ● **Nursing, Other** *280 hrs./$3040* ● **Pre-Nursing Studies** ● **Teaching English as a Second or Foreign Language/ESL Language Instructor** *880 hrs./$9290*

STUDENT SERVICES Placement services for program completers.

St. Johns River Community College

5001 Saint Johns Avenue, Palatka, FL 32177-3897
http://www.sjrcc.cc.fl.us/

CONTACT Dr. Robert L. McLendon, Jr., President
Telephone: 386-312-4200

GENERAL INFORMATION Public Institution. Founded 1958. **Accreditation:** Regional (SACS/CC). **Total program enrollment:** 2163. **Application fee:** $30.

PROGRAM(S) OFFERED
● **Accounting Technology/Technician and Bookkeeping** ● **Accounting and Related Services, Other** *2 students enrolled* ● **Architectural Engineering Technology/Technician** *1 student enrolled* ● **Blood Bank Technology Specialist** *30 students enrolled* ● **Business Administration and Management, General** *17 students enrolled* ● **Chemical Technology/Technician** *1 student enrolled* ● **Child Care Provider/Assistant** ● **Computer Programming, Specific Applications** ● **Computer Technology/Computer Systems Technology** *2 students enrolled* ● **Computer/Information Technology Services Administration and Management, Other** ● **Corrections** *19 students enrolled* ● **Criminal Justice/Police Science** *78 students enrolled* ● **Entrepreneurship/Entrepreneurial Studies** *6 students enrolled* ● **Executive Assistant/Executive Secretary** *5 students enrolled* ● **Health Information/Medical Records Technology/Technician** ● **Hospital and Health Care Facilities Administration/Management** ● **Management Information Systems and Services, Other** *3 students enrolled* ● **Management Information Systems, General** *1 student enrolled* ● **Marketing/Marketing Management, General** ● **Nurse/Nursing Assistant/Aide and Patient Care Assistant** *31 students enrolled* ● **Nursing, Other** ● **Security and Protective Services, Other**

STUDENT SERVICES Academic or career counseling, employment services for current students, remedial services.

St. Petersburg College

PO Box 13489, St. Petersburg, FL 33733-3489
http://www.spjc.edu/

CONTACT Dr. Carl Kuttler, Jr., President
Telephone: 727-341-4772

GENERAL INFORMATION Public Institution. Founded 1927. **Accreditation:** Regional (SACS/CC); dental hygiene (ADA); emergency medical services (JRCEMTP); funeral service (ABFSE); health information technology (AHIMA); medical laboratory technology (NAACLS); physical therapy assisting (APTA). **Total program enrollment:** 8669. **Application fee:** $35.

PROGRAM(S) OFFERED
● **Accounting Technology/Technician and Bookkeeping** *19 students enrolled* ● **Accounting and Related Services, Other** *2 students enrolled* ● **Architectural Engineering Technology/Technician** *11 students enrolled* ● **Business Administration and Management, General** *2 students enrolled* ● **Cinematography and Film/Video Production** *15 students enrolled* ● **Commercial and Advertising Art** *6 students enrolled* ● **Computer Programming, Specific Applications** *1 student enrolled* ● **Computer Systems Analysis/Analyst** *13 students enrolled* ● **Computer Technology/Computer Systems Technology** *9 students enrolled* ● **Computer/Information Technology Services Administration and Management, Other** *1 student enrolled* ● **Corrections** *49 students enrolled* ● **Criminal Justice/Police Science** *75 students enrolled* ● **Drafting and Design Technology/Technician, General** *5 students enrolled* ● **Electrical, Electronic and Communications Engineering Technology/Technician** *5 students enrolled* ● **Emergency Medical Technology/Technician (EMT Paramedic)** *98 students enrolled* ● **Entrepreneurship/Entrepreneurial Studies** *20 students enrolled* ● **Executive Assistant/Executive Secretary** *4 students enrolled* ● **Fire Science/Firefighting** *44 students enrolled* ● **Forensic Science and Technology** *48 students enrolled* ● **Health Information/Medical Records Technology/Technician** *6 students enrolled* ● **Hospital and Health Care Facilities Administration/Management** *6 students enrolled* ● **Hotel/Motel Administration/Management** *3 students enrolled* ● **Industrial Production Technologies/Technicians, Other** *6 students enrolled* ● **Management Information Systems and Services, Other** *1 student enrolled* ● **Management Information Systems, General** *18 students enrolled* ● **Nursing—Registered Nurse Training (RN, ASN, BSN, MSN)** *12 students enrolled* ● **Opticianry/Ophthalmic Dispensing Optician** *2 students enrolled* ● **Plumbing Technology/Plumber** *5 students enrolled* ● **Psychiatric/Mental Health Services Technician** *9 students enrolled* ● **Public Administration** *12 students enrolled* ● **Quality Control Technology/Technician** *56 students enrolled* ● **Restaurant/Food**

Services Management *4 students enrolled* • **Veterinary/Animal Health Technology/Technician and Veterinary Assistant** *2 students enrolled*

STUDENT SERVICES Academic or career counseling, employment services for current students, placement services for program completers, remedial services.

St. Petersburg Theological Seminary

10830 Navajo Drive, St. Petersburg, FL 33708
http://www.sptseminary.edu/

CONTACT John Guedes, CEO
Telephone: 727-399-0276

GENERAL INFORMATION Private Institution. Founded 1983. **Accreditation:** State accredited or approved. **Total program enrollment:** 4. **Application fee:** $50.

STUDENT SERVICES Academic or career counseling.

St. Thomas University

16401 Northwest 37th Avenue, Miami Gardens, FL 33054-6459
http://www.stu.edu/

CONTACT President
Telephone: 305-625-6000

GENERAL INFORMATION Private Institution. Founded 1961. **Accreditation:** Regional (SACS/CC). **Total program enrollment:** 1933. **Application fee:** $40.

PROGRAM(S) OFFERED
• **Criminal Justice/Safety Studies** *4 students enrolled* • **Religion/Religious Studies** • **Security and Protective Services, Other** *4 students enrolled*

STUDENT SERVICES Academic or career counseling, employment services for current students, placement services for program completers, remedial services.

Sanford-Brown Institute

1201 West Cypress Creek Road, Fort Lauderdale, FL 33309
http://www.sbftlauderdale.com/

CONTACT Michael Labelle, Campus President
Telephone: 954-308-7400

GENERAL INFORMATION Private Institution. **Total program enrollment:** 786. **Application fee:** $25.

PROGRAM(S) OFFERED
• **Dental Assisting/Assistant** *900 hrs./$13,900* • **Diagnostic Medical Sonography/Sonographer and Ultrasound Technician** *1905 hrs./$38,000* • **Massage Therapy/Therapeutic Massage** *37 students enrolled* • **Medical Insurance Coding Specialist/Coder** *900 hrs./$13,900* • **Medical/Clinical Assistant** *900 hrs./$13,900* • **Pharmacy Technician/Assistant** *900 hrs./$11,900* • **Surgical Technology/Technologist** *1200 hrs./$22,900*

STUDENT SERVICES Academic or career counseling, employment services for current students, placement services for program completers.

Sanford-Brown Institute

10255 Fortune Parkway, Suite 501, Jacksonville, FL 32256
http://www.sbjacksonville.com/

CONTACT Scott Nelowet, Campus President
Telephone: 904-363-6221

GENERAL INFORMATION Private Institution. Founded 1992. **Accreditation:** State accredited or approved. **Total program enrollment:** 695. **Application fee:** $25.

PROGRAM(S) OFFERED
• **Diagnostic Medical Sonography/Sonographer and Ultrasound Technician** *77 hrs./$35,100* • **Massage Therapy/Therapeutic Massage** *58 hrs./$10,150* • **Medical Insurance Coding Specialist/Coder** *71 hrs./$13,250* • **Medical Insurance Specialist/Medical Biller** *33 students enrolled* • **Medical/Clinical Assistant** *67 hrs./$13,250* • **Pharmacy Technician/Assistant** *64 hrs./$13,250* • **Surgical Technology/Technologist** *69 hrs./$19,000*

STUDENT SERVICES Academic or career counseling, employment services for current students, placement services for program completers.

Sanford-Brown Institute

5701 East Hillsborough Avenue, Tampa, FL 33610
http://www.sbtampa.com/

CONTACT Steeve Dumerve, President
Telephone: 813-621-0072

GENERAL INFORMATION Private Institution. **Accreditation:** State accredited or approved. **Total program enrollment:** 868. **Application fee:** $25.

PROGRAM(S) OFFERED
• **Allied Health and Medical Assisting Services, Other** *157 students enrolled* • **Cardiovascular Technology/Technologist** *80 hrs./$35,150* • **Dental Assisting/Assistant** *82 hrs./$13,275* • **Diagnostic Medical Sonography/Sonographer and Ultrasound Technician** *77 hrs./$35,150* • **Massage Therapy/Therapeutic Massage** *58 hrs./$11,025* • **Medical Insurance Coding Specialist/Coder** *71 hrs./$13,275* • **Medical/Clinical Assistant** *67 hrs./$13,275* • **Pharmacy Technician/Assistant** *1 student enrolled* • **Surgical Technology/Technologist** *13 students enrolled*

STUDENT SERVICES Employment services for current students, placement services for program completers.

Santa Fe Community College

3000 Northwest 83rd Street, Gainesville, FL 32606-6200
http://www.sfcc.edu/

CONTACT Jackson N. Sasser, President
Telephone: 352-395-5000

GENERAL INFORMATION Public Institution. Founded 1966. **Accreditation:** Regional (SACS/CC); dental assisting (ADA); dental hygiene (ADA); emergency medical services (JRCEMTP); health information technology (AHIMA); nuclear medicine technology (JRCNMT); radiologic technology: radiography (JRCERT). **Total program enrollment:** 6743.

PROGRAM(S) OFFERED
• **Accounting and Related Services, Other** *1 student enrolled* • **Business Administration and Management, General** *27 students enrolled* • **Child Care Provider/Assistant** *5 students enrolled* • **Commercial and Advertising Art** *4 students enrolled* • **Computer Systems Analysis/Analyst** *24 students enrolled* • **Computer Technology/Computer Systems Technology** *20 students enrolled* • **Computer/Information Technology Services Administration and Management, Other** • **Corrections** *20 students enrolled* • **Criminal Justice/Police Science** *54 students enrolled* • **Dental Assisting/Assistant** *22 students enrolled* • **Diagnostic Medical Sonography/Sonographer and Ultrasound Technician** *11 students enrolled* • **Emergency Medical Technology/Technician (EMT Paramedic)** *74 students enrolled* • **Entrepreneurship/Entrepreneurial Studies** *11 students enrolled* • **Executive Assistant/Executive Secretary** *17 students enrolled* • **Forensic Science and Technology** • **Health Information/Medical Records Technology/Technician** *22 students enrolled* • **Heating, Air Conditioning, Ventilation and Refrigeration Maintenance Technology/Technician (HAC, HACR, HVAC, HVACR)** *11 students enrolled* • **Licensed Practical/Vocational Nurse Training (LPN, LVN, Cert, Dipl, AAS)** *27 students enrolled* • **Nursing, Other** *54 students enrolled* • **Surgical Technology/Technologist** *16 students enrolled* • **Welding Technology/Welder** *5 students enrolled*

STUDENT SERVICES Academic or career counseling, daycare for children of students, employment services for current students, placement services for program completers, remedial services.

Sarasota County Technical Institute

4748 Beneva Road, Sarasota, FL 34235
http://www.sarasotatech.org/

CONTACT Todd Bowden, Director
Telephone: 941-924-1365

GENERAL INFORMATION Public Institution. Founded 1967. **Total program enrollment:** 455. **Application fee:** $35.

PROGRAM(S) OFFERED
● **Accounting Technology/Technician and Bookkeeping** *14 students enrolled* ● **Accounting** *900 hrs./$2223* ● **Administrative Assistant and Secretarial Science, General** *2 students enrolled* ● **Autobody/Collision and Repair Technology/Technician** *1 student enrolled* ● **Child Care and Support Services Management** *14 students enrolled* ● **Computer Installation and Repair Technology/Technician** *3 students enrolled* ● **Computer and Information Sciences and Support Services, Other** *7 students enrolled* ● **Corrections** *21 students enrolled* ● **Cosmetology and Related Personal Grooming Arts, Other** *3 students enrolled* ● **Cosmetology/Cosmetologist, General** *1200 hrs./$3828* ● **Criminal Justice/Law Enforcement Administration** *11 students enrolled* ● **Criminal Justice/Police Science** *457 hrs./$1596* ● **Culinary Arts/Chef Training** *10 students enrolled* ● **Customer Service Support/Call Center/Teleservice Operation** *4 students enrolled* ● **Dietitian Assistant** *5 students enrolled* ● **Early Childhood Education and Teaching** *600 hrs./$1569* ● **Emergency Medical Technology/Technician (EMT Paramedic)** *250 hrs./$907* ● **Fire Science/Firefighting** *37 students enrolled* ● **Legal Administrative Assistant/Secretary** *5 students enrolled* ● **Licensed Practical/Vocational Nurse Training (LPN, LVN, Cert, Dipl, AAS)** *1350 hrs./$3655* ● **Marine Maintenance/Fitter and Ship Repair Technology/Technician** *3 students enrolled* ● **Medical Administrative/Executive Assistant and Medical Secretary** *9 students enrolled* ● **Medical Insurance Specialist/Medical Biller** *6 students enrolled* ● **Nail Technician/Specialist and Manicurist** *4 students enrolled* ● **Nurse/Nursing Assistant/Aide and Patient Care Assistant** *27 students enrolled* ● **Phlebotomy/Phlebotomist** *11 students enrolled* ● **Prepress/Desktop Publishing and Digital Imaging Design** *9 students enrolled* ● **Surgical Technology/Technologist** *31 students enrolled* ● **Web Page, Digital/Multimedia and Information Resources Design** *6 students enrolled*

STUDENT SERVICES Academic or career counseling, employment services for current students, placement services for program completers, remedial services.

Sarasota School of Massage

1970 Main Street, Sarasota, FL 34236
http://www.sarasotamassageschool.com/

CONTACT Joe Lubow, Director
Telephone: 941-957-0577

GENERAL INFORMATION Private Institution. **Total program enrollment:** 37. **Application fee:** $100.

PROGRAM(S) OFFERED
● **Massage Therapy/Therapeutic Massage** *730 hrs./$10,875*

STUDENT SERVICES Academic or career counseling, placement services for program completers.

School of Health Careers

3190 N. State Road 7, Lauderdale Lakes, FL 33319
http://www.schoolofhealth.edu/

CONTACT Mrs. Stefanie Fiacos, Registrar
Telephone: 954-777-0083

GENERAL INFORMATION Private Institution. **Total program enrollment:** 142. **Application fee:** $25.

PROGRAM(S) OFFERED
● **Dental Assisting/Assistant** *57 hrs./$15,970* ● **Diagnostic Medical Sonography/Sonographer and Ultrasound Technician** *93 hrs./$28,500* ● **Medical Insurance Coding Specialist/Coder** *22 students enrolled* ● **Medical Office Management/Administration** *62 hrs./$15,970* ● **Medical/Clinical Assistant** *59 hrs./$16,070*

STUDENT SERVICES Academic or career counseling, employment services for current students, placement services for program completers, remedial services.

Seminole Community College

100 Weldon Boulevard, Sanford, FL 32773-6199
http://www.scc-fl.edu/

CONTACT E. Ann McGee, President
Telephone: 407-708-4722

GENERAL INFORMATION Public Institution. Founded 1966. **Accreditation:** Regional (SACS/CC); emergency medical services (JRCEMTP); physical therapy assisting (APTA). **Total program enrollment:** 5835.

PROGRAM(S) OFFERED
● **Accounting Technology/Technician and Bookkeeping** *51 students enrolled* ● **Accounting and Related Services, Other** *9 students enrolled* ● **Blood Bank Technology Specialist** ● **Business Administration and Management, General** *4 students enrolled* ● **Child Care Provider/Assistant** *22 students enrolled* ● **Child Care and Support Services Management** ● **Commercial and Advertising Art** *6 students enrolled* ● **Computer Systems Analysis/Analyst** ● **Computer Technology/Computer Systems Technology** *19 students enrolled* ● **Construction Engineering Technology/Technician** *3 students enrolled* ● **Criminal Justice/Police Science** *98 students enrolled* ● **Drafting and Design Technology/Technician, General** *23 students enrolled* ● **Electrical, Electronic and Communications Engineering Technology/Technician** ● **Emergency Medical Technology/Technician (EMT Paramedic)** *261 students enrolled* ● **Entrepreneurship/Entrepreneurial Studies** *4 students enrolled* ● **Executive Assistant/Executive Secretary** *36 students enrolled* ● **Fire Science/Firefighting** *93 students enrolled* ● **Health Information/Medical Records Technology/Technician** *16 students enrolled* ● **Heating, Air Conditioning, Ventilation and Refrigeration Maintenance Technology/Technician (HAC, HACR, HVAC, HVACR)** *7 students enrolled* ● **Home Health Aide/Home Attendant** ● **Licensed Practical/Vocational Nurse Training (LPN, LVN, Cert, Dipl, AAS)** *32 students enrolled* ● **Management Information Systems, General** *1 student enrolled* ● **Medical/Clinical Assistant** *10 students enrolled* ● **Nurse/Nursing Assistant/Aide and Patient Care Assistant** ● **Nursing, Other** *27 students enrolled* ● **Security and Loss Prevention Services** ● **Selling Skills and Sales Operations**

STUDENT SERVICES Academic or career counseling, employment services for current students, placement services for program completers, remedial services.

Shear Excellence International Hair Academy

7243 N. Nebraska Avenue, Tampa, FL 33604

CONTACT Rosita Donaldson, President
Telephone: 813-232-4368

GENERAL INFORMATION Private Institution. **Total program enrollment:** 38. **Application fee:** $50.

PROGRAM(S) OFFERED
● **Barbering/Barber** *1000 hrs./$8600* ● **Cosmetology, Barber/Styling, and Nail Instructor** *1200 hrs./$10,895* ● **Nail Technician/Specialist and Manicurist**

STUDENT SERVICES Academic or career counseling, employment services for current students, placement services for program completers.

Sheridan Vocational-Technical Center

5400 Sheridan Street, Hollywood, FL 33021
http://www.sheridantechnical.com/

CONTACT Dr. Robert Boegli, Director
Telephone: 754-321-5400 Ext. 2053

GENERAL INFORMATION Public Institution. Founded 1967. **Total program enrollment:** 1282.

PROGRAM(S) OFFERED
● **Accounting Technology/Technician and Bookkeeping** *6 students enrolled* ● **Administrative Assistant and Secretarial Science, General** *7 students enrolled* ● **Allied Health and Medical Assisting Services, Other** ● **Architectural Drafting and Architectural CAD/CADD** *7 students enrolled* ● **Autobody/Collision and Repair Technology/Technician** *10 students enrolled* ● **Automobile/Automotive Mechanics Technology/Technician** *2250 hrs./$5733* ● **Barbering/Barber** *5 students enrolled* ● **Business, Management, Marketing, and Related Support Services, Other** *6 students enrolled* ● **Business/Commerce, General**

• Civil Drafting and Civil Engineering CAD/CADD • Clinical/Medical Laboratory Technician *14 students enrolled* • Communications Technology/Technician • Computer Installation and Repair Technology/Technician *6 students enrolled* • Computer Science *1 student enrolled* • Computer Systems Networking and Telecommunications *7 students enrolled* • Cosmetology and Related Personal Grooming Arts, Other *85 students enrolled* • Cosmetology, Barber/Styling, and Nail Instructor *47 students enrolled* • Cosmetology/Cosmetologist, General *1200 hrs./$3000* • Court Reporting/Court Reporter *2850 hrs./$6768* • Culinary Arts/Chef Training *9 students enrolled* • Digital Communication and Media/Multimedia *1 student enrolled* • Drafting/Design Engineering Technologies/Technicians, Other • Early Childhood Education and Teaching *77 students enrolled* • Electrical, Electronic and Communications Engineering Technology/Technician • Electrical/Electronics Drafting and Electrical/Electronics CAD/CADD *1 student enrolled* • Health Unit Coordinator/Ward Clerk *15 students enrolled* • Health and Medical Administrative Services, Other *13 students enrolled* • Heating, Air Conditioning and Refrigeration Technology/Technician (ACH/ACR/ACHR/HRAC/HVAC/AC Technology) *1350 hrs./$3630* • Heating, Air Conditioning, Ventilation and Refrigeration Maintenance Technology/Technician (HAC, HACR, HVAC, HVACR) *23 students enrolled* • Industrial Electronics Technology/Technician • Legal Administrative Assistant/Secretary *2 students enrolled* • Licensed Practical/Vocational Nurse Training (LPN, LVN, Cert, Dipl, AAS) *1350 hrs./$3360* • Marketing/Marketing Management, General • Massage Therapy/Therapeutic Massage *29 students enrolled* • Mechanical Drafting and Mechanical Drafting CAD/CADD • Medical Administrative/Executive Assistant and Medical Secretary *1 student enrolled* • Medical Insurance Specialist/Medical Biller *25 students enrolled* • Medical Transcription/Transcriptionist *13 students enrolled* • Nursing, Other *13 students enrolled* • Prepress/Desktop Publishing and Digital Imaging Design *1 student enrolled* • Real Estate *142 students enrolled* • Surgical Technology/Technologist *22 students enrolled* • Teacher Assistant/Aide *11 students enrolled* • Web Page, Digital/Multimedia and Information Resources Design *10 students enrolled*

STUDENT SERVICES Academic or career counseling, daycare for children of students, placement services for program completers, remedial services.

Southeastern School of Neuromuscular & Massage Therapy–Jacksonville

9424 Baymeadows Road, Suite 200, Jacksonville, FL 32256
http://www.southeasternmassageschools.com/

CONTACT Shaun Humphry, Vice President
Telephone: 904-448-9499

GENERAL INFORMATION Private Institution. **Total program enrollment:** 58. **Application fee:** $100.

PROGRAM(S) OFFERED
• Massage Therapy/Therapeutic Massage *25 hrs./$10,356*

STUDENT SERVICES Academic or career counseling, employment services for current students, placement services for program completers, remedial services.

Southern Technical Institute

3592 Aloma Avenue, #2, Winter Park, FL 32792
http://www.stiorlando.com/

CONTACT Neil R. Euluano, President
Telephone: 407-438-6000

GENERAL INFORMATION Private Institution. **Total program enrollment:** 409. **Application fee:** $25.

PROGRAM(S) OFFERED
• Administrative Assistant and Secretarial Science, General • Allied Health and Medical Assisting Services, Other *44 hrs./$14,100* • Business Administration and Management, General *104 hrs./$28,200* • Computer Engineering, General • Computer and Information Sciences and Support Services, Other • Electrical/Electronics Maintenance and Repair Technology, Other *90 hrs./$28,200* • Heating, Air Conditioning, Ventilation and Refrigeration Maintenance Technology/Technician (HAC, HACR, HVAC, HVACR) *44 hrs./$14,100* • Industrial Electronics Technology/Technician

STUDENT SERVICES Academic or career counseling, employment services for current students, placement services for program completers.

South Florida Community College

600 West College Drive, Avon Park, FL 33825-9356
http://www.sfcc.cc.fl.us/

CONTACT Dr. Norman L. Stephens, Jr., President
Telephone: 863-453-6661

GENERAL INFORMATION Public Institution. Founded 1965. **Accreditation:** Regional (SACS/CC); dental assisting (ADA); dental hygiene (ADA). **Total program enrollment:** 1087.

PROGRAM(S) OFFERED
• Accounting and Related Services, Other • Autobody/Collision and Repair Technology/Technician *6 students enrolled* • Building/Property Maintenance and Management • Carpentry/Carpenter • Computer Installation and Repair Technology/Technician *2 students enrolled* • Computer/Information Technology Services Administration and Management, Other *6 students enrolled* • Corrections *96 students enrolled* • Cosmetology/Cosmetologist, General *11 students enrolled* • Criminal Justice/Police Science *47 students enrolled* • Dental Assisting/Assistant *6 students enrolled* • Electrical, Electronic and Communications Engineering Technology/Technician *1 student enrolled* • Emergency Medical Technology/Technician (EMT Paramedic) *10 students enrolled* • Entrepreneurship/Entrepreneurial Studies *2 students enrolled* • Executive Assistant/Executive Secretary *1 student enrolled* • Foodservice Systems Administration/Management *5 students enrolled* • Heating, Air Conditioning, Ventilation and Refrigeration Maintenance Technology/Technician (HAC, HACR, HVAC, HVACR) *7 students enrolled* • Housing and Human Environments, Other • Landscaping and Groundskeeping • Licensed Practical/Vocational Nurse Training (LPN, LVN, Cert, Dipl, AAS) *33 students enrolled* • Lineworker *6 students enrolled* • Management Information Systems, General • Medical Administrative/Executive Assistant and Medical Secretary *2 students enrolled* • Nurse/Nursing Assistant/Aide and Patient Care Assistant • Nursing, Other *3 students enrolled* • Office Management and Supervision *1 student enrolled* • Truck and Bus Driver/Commercial Vehicle Operation *12 students enrolled*

STUDENT SERVICES Academic or career counseling, employment services for current students, placement services for program completers, remedial services.

South Florida Institute of Technology

2141 SW 1st Street, Suite 104, Miami, FL 33135

CONTACT Silvio Incer, CEO
Telephone: 305-649-2050

GENERAL INFORMATION Private Institution. **Total program enrollment:** 565. **Application fee:** $100.

PROGRAM(S) OFFERED
• Computer Graphics *24 hrs./$5271* • Data Entry/Microcomputer Applications, Other *24 hrs./$5271* • Electrical/Electronics Equipment Installation and Repair, General *24 hrs./$5451* • Heating, Air Conditioning and Refrigeration Technology/Technician (ACH/ACR/ACHR/HRAC/HVAC/AC Technology) *24 hrs./$5451* • Medical/Clinical Assistant *31 hrs./$6579* • Plumbing Technology/Plumber *36 hrs./$8446*

STUDENT SERVICES Academic or career counseling, placement services for program completers.

Southwest Florida College

1685 Medical Lane, Fort Myers, FL 33907
http://www.swfc.edu/

CONTACT Gregory H. Jones, President
Telephone: 239-939-4766

GENERAL INFORMATION Private Institution. Founded 1940. **Accreditation:** State accredited or approved. **Total program enrollment:** 1477. **Application fee:** $25.

PROGRAM(S) OFFERED
• Computer Engineering Technology/Technician *2 students enrolled* • Health Information/Medical Records Administration/Administrator *31 students enrolled* • Massage Therapy/Therapeutic Massage *13 students enrolled* • Medical/Clinical Assistant *6 students enrolled*

STUDENT SERVICES Academic or career counseling, employment services for current students, placement services for program completers, remedial services.

State College of Florida Manatee-Sarasota

5840 26th Street West, PO Box 1849, Bradenton, FL 34206-7046
http://www.scf.edu/

CONTACT Lars Hafner, President
Telephone: 941-752-5000

GENERAL INFORMATION Public Institution. Founded 1957. **Accreditation:** Regional (SACS/CC); dental hygiene (ADA); physical therapy assisting (APTA); radiologic technology: radiography (JRCERT). **Total program enrollment:** 5084. **Application fee:** $40.

PROGRAM(S) OFFERED
• **Accounting and Related Services, Other** • **Child Care Provider/Assistant** *1 student enrolled* • **Computer Programming, Specific Applications** *1 student enrolled* • **Entrepreneurship/Entrepreneurial Studies** *1 student enrolled* • **Executive Assistant/Executive Secretary** • **Fire Protection and Safety Technology/Technician** *2 students enrolled* • **Legal Assistant/Paralegal** *4 students enrolled* • **Management Information Systems, General** • **Marketing/Marketing Management, General**

STUDENT SERVICES Academic or career counseling, employment services for current students, placement services for program completers, remedial services.

Sunstate Academy of Hair Design

18453 US 19 North, Clearwater, FL 34624-2702
http://www.sunstate.edu/

CONTACT Tom Timothy, Director of Education
Telephone: 727-538-3827

GENERAL INFORMATION Private Institution. **Total program enrollment:** 178. **Application fee:** $15.

PROGRAM(S) OFFERED
• **Cosmetology, Barber/Styling, and Nail Instructor** *1500 hrs./$16,490* • **Cosmetology/Cosmetologist, General** *1200 hrs./$14,265* • **Massage Therapy/Therapeutic Massage** *600 hrs./$7015* • **Nail Technician/Specialist and Manicurist** *240 hrs./$2315*

STUDENT SERVICES Placement services for program completers.

Sunstate Academy of Hair Design

2418 Colonial Boulevard, Fort Myers, FL 33907-1491
http://www.sunstate.edu/

CONTACT Deborah Rodriguez, Campus Director
Telephone: 239-278-1311

GENERAL INFORMATION Private Institution. Founded 1988. **Total program enrollment:** 226. **Application fee:** $15.

PROGRAM(S) OFFERED
• **Barbering/Barber** • **Cosmetology and Related Personal Grooming Arts, Other** *1500 hrs./$14,225* • **Cosmetology, Barber/Styling, and Nail Instructor** • **Cosmetology/Cosmetologist, General** *1200 hrs./$12,450* • **Nail Technician/Specialist and Manicurist** *240 hrs./$2320*

STUDENT SERVICES Academic or career counseling, employment services for current students, placement services for program completers.

Sunstate Academy of Hair Design

4424 Bee Ridge Road, Sarasota, FL 34233-2502
http://www.sunstate.edu/

CONTACT Tammy Mairs, Financial Aid Advisor
Telephone: 941-377-4880

GENERAL INFORMATION Private Institution. Founded 1982. **Total program enrollment:** 223. **Application fee:** $50.

PROGRAM(S) OFFERED
• **Aesthetician/Esthetician and Skin Care Specialist** *30 hrs./$7200* • **Allied Health and Medical Assisting Services, Other** *36 hrs./$8640* • **Barbering/Barber** *2 students enrolled* • **Cosmetology and Related Personal Grooming Arts, Other** *10 students enrolled* • **Cosmetology/Cosmetologist, General** *60 hrs./$14,805* • **Health Services/Allied Health/Health Sciences, General** *36 hrs./$8640* • **Massage Therapy/Therapeutic Massage** *30 hrs./$7200* • **Medical Office Management/Administration** *36 hrs./$8640* • **Nail Technician/Specialist and Manicurist** *10 students enrolled*

STUDENT SERVICES Employment services for current students, placement services for program completers.

Superior Career Institute

3714 W. Oakland Park Boulevard, Lauderdale Lakes, FL 33311

CONTACT Christian de Vera, Financial Aid Director
Telephone: 954-741-0088

GENERAL INFORMATION Private Institution. **Total program enrollment:** 221. **Application fee:** $65.

PROGRAM(S) OFFERED
• **Barbering/Barber** • **Cosmetology/Cosmetologist, General** *1200 hrs./$9740* • **Dental Assisting/Assistant** *901 hrs./$10,500* • **Facial Treatment Specialist/Facialist** *11 students enrolled* • **Health Information/Medical Records Technology/Technician** *901 hrs./$10,500* • **Home Health Aide/Home Attendant** • **Massage Therapy/Therapeutic Massage** *700 hrs./$6945* • **Medical Insurance Coding Specialist/Coder** • **Medical/Clinical Assistant** *903 hrs./$10,500* • **Nail Technician/Specialist and Manicurist** *605 hrs./$5600* • **Nurse/Nursing Assistant/Aide and Patient Care Assistant** • **Permanent Cosmetics/Makeup and Tattooing** • **Phlebotomy/Phlebotomist**

STUDENT SERVICES Academic or career counseling, placement services for program completers.

Suwannee-Hamilton Area Vocational, Technical, and Adult Education Center

415 SW Pinewood Drive, Live Oak, FL 32060
http://www.suwannee.k12.fl.us/shtc/

CONTACT Dianne Westcott, Principal
Telephone: 386-364-2750

GENERAL INFORMATION Public Institution. Founded 1967. **Total program enrollment:** 89. **Application fee:** $50.

PROGRAM(S) OFFERED
• **Autobody/Collision and Repair Technology/Technician** *1625 hrs./$3307* • **Automobile/Automotive Mechanics Technology/Technician** *1225 hrs./$2680* • **Blood Bank Technology Specialist** • **Child Care Provider/Assistant** *600 hrs./$1349* • **Child Care and Support Services Management** • **Construction Engineering Technology/Technician** • **Cosmetology/Cosmetologist, General** *4 students enrolled* • **Culinary Arts/Chef Training** • **Licensed Practical/Vocational Nurse Training (LPN, LVN, Cert, Dipl, AAS)** *1350 hrs./$3291* • **Mason/Masonry** • **Medical Administrative/Executive Assistant and Medical Secretary** *1050 hrs./$2335* • **Medical Radiologic Technology/Science—Radiation Therapist** • **Nurse/Nursing Assistant/Aide and Patient Care Assistant** *600 hrs./$2240* • **Office Management and Supervision**

STUDENT SERVICES Academic or career counseling, employment services for current students, placement services for program completers, remedial services.

Tallahassee Community College

444 Appleyard Drive, Tallahassee, FL 32304-2895
http://www.tcc.fl.edu/

CONTACT William D. Law, Jr., President
Telephone: 850-201-6200

GENERAL INFORMATION Public Institution. Founded 1966. **Accreditation:** Regional (SACS/CC); dental assisting (ADA); dental hygiene (ADA); emergency medical services (JRCEMTP). **Total program enrollment:** 7168.

PROGRAM(S) OFFERED
• **Communication, Journalism and Related Programs, Other** • **Corrections** *109 students enrolled* • **Criminal Justice/Police Science** *91 students enrolled* • **Dental**

Assisting/Assistant *11 students enrolled* • **Diagnostic Medical Sonography/ Sonographer and Ultrasound Technician** • **Emergency Medical Technology/ Technician (EMT Paramedic)** *11 students enrolled* • **Entrepreneurship/ Entrepreneurial Studies** *8 students enrolled* • **Executive Assistant/Executive Secretary** • **Fire Science/Firefighting** *46 students enrolled* • **Forensic Science and Technology** *2 students enrolled* • **Health Information/Medical Records Technology/Technician** • **Management Information Systems and Services, Other** *1 student enrolled* • **Management Information Systems, General** *8 students enrolled* • **Mason/Masonry**

STUDENT SERVICES Academic or career counseling, daycare for children of students, employment services for current students, placement services for program completers, remedial services.

Taylor College

5190 SE 125th Street, Belleview, FL 34420

CONTACT Diana Brumm, President
Telephone: 352-245-4119

GENERAL INFORMATION Private Institution. **Total program enrollment:** 54. **Application fee:** $50.

PROGRAM(S) OFFERED
• **Home Health Aide/Home Attendant** *90 hrs./$345* • **Nurse/Nursing Assistant/ Aide and Patient Care Assistant** *120 hrs./$390* • **Nursing, Other** *1369 hrs./ $9013*

STUDENT SERVICES Academic or career counseling, placement services for program completers, remedial services.

Taylor Technical Institute

3233 Highway 19 South, Perry, FL 32347
http://www.taylortech.org/

CONTACT Ken Olsen, Director
Telephone: 850-838-2545

GENERAL INFORMATION Public Institution. Founded 1967. **Total program enrollment:** 148. **Application fee:** $5.

PROGRAM(S) OFFERED
• **Automobile/Automotive Mechanics Technology/Technician** • **Business Operations Support and Secretarial Services, Other** *9 students enrolled* • **Carpentry/ Carpenter** *2 students enrolled* • **Computer Engineering Technology/Technician** • **Cosmetology and Related Personal Grooming Arts, Other** • **Cosmetology/ Cosmetologist, General** *11 students enrolled* • **Emergency Medical Technology/ Technician (EMT Paramedic)** *14 students enrolled* • **Industrial Mechanics and Maintenance Technology** *6 students enrolled* • **Information Technology** • **Nurse/ Nursing Assistant/Aide and Patient Care Assistant** *14 students enrolled* • **Precision Metal Working, Other** • **Welding Technology/Welder** *7 students enrolled*

STUDENT SERVICES Academic or career counseling, employment services for current students, placement services for program completers, remedial services.

Technical Career Institute

4299 NW 36th Street, Suite 300, Miami Springs, FL 33166
http://www.technicalcareerinstitute.edu/

CONTACT Denyse Antunes, School Director
Telephone: 305-261-5511

GENERAL INFORMATION Private Institution. **Total program enrollment:** 800. **Application fee:** $100.

PROGRAM(S) OFFERED
• **Accounting Technology/Technician and Bookkeeping** *10 students enrolled* • **Accounting** *16 students enrolled* • **Blood Bank Technology Specialist** *30 students enrolled* • **Business Administration and Management, General** *21 students enrolled* • **Business/Office Automation/Technology/Data Entry** *35 students enrolled* • **Computer Installation and Repair Technology/Technician** *52*

students enrolled • **Massage Therapy/Therapeutic Massage** *19 students enrolled* • **Medical Office Management/Administration** *76 students enrolled* • **Medical/ Clinical Assistant** *226 students enrolled* • **Pharmacy Technician/Assistant** *41 students enrolled*

STUDENT SERVICES Academic or career counseling, employment services for current students, placement services for program completers.

Tom P. Haney Technical Center

3016 Highway 77, Panama City, FL 32405
http://www.bay.k12.fl.us/

CONTACT Sandra D. Davis, Director
Telephone: 850-747-5500

GENERAL INFORMATION Public Institution. Founded 1965. **Total program enrollment:** 242. **Application fee:** $15.

PROGRAM(S) OFFERED
• **Accounting Technology/Technician and Bookkeeping** *3 students enrolled* • **Administrative Assistant and Secretarial Science, General** *3 students enrolled* • **Architectural Drafting and Architectural CAD/CADD** *4 students enrolled* • **Autobody/Collision and Repair Technology/Technician** *3 students enrolled* • **Automobile/Automotive Mechanics Technology/Technician** *8 students enrolled* • **Business Administration and Management, General** *2 students enrolled* • **Cabinetmaking and Millwork/Millwright** *1 student enrolled* • **Carpentry/Carpenter** *2 students enrolled* • **Child Care and Support Services Management** *13 students enrolled* • **Civil Drafting and Civil Engineering CAD/ CADD** • **Computer Installation and Repair Technology/Technician** • **Cosmetology/Cosmetologist, General** *1200 hrs./$2868* • **Design and Visual Communications, General** *5 students enrolled* • **Early Childhood Education and Teaching** *11 students enrolled* • **Electrical, Electronic and Communications Engineering Technology/Technician** *1 student enrolled* • **Electrician** *4 students enrolled* • **Heating, Air Conditioning and Refrigeration Technology/Technician (ACH/ACR/ACHR/HRAC/HVAC/AC Technology)** *1350 hrs./$3227* • **Legal Administrative Assistant/Secretary** *4 students enrolled* • **Licensed Practical/ Vocational Nurse Training (LPN, LVN, Cert, Dipl, AAS)** *1350 hrs./$4298* • **Marine Maintenance/Fitter and Ship Repair Technology/Technician** • **Massage Therapy/Therapeutic Massage** *750 hrs./$1793* • **Mechanical Drafting and Mechanical Drafting CAD/CADD** *4 students enrolled* • **Medical Administrative/ Executive Assistant and Medical Secretary** *1050 hrs./$2510* • **Nurse/Nursing Assistant/Aide and Patient Care Assistant** *6 students enrolled* • **Welding Technology/Welder** *1170 hrs./$2796*

STUDENT SERVICES Academic or career counseling, daycare for children of students, employment services for current students, placement services for program completers, remedial services.

Total International Career Institute

3060 W. 12th Avenue, Hialeah, FL 33012-4836

CONTACT Julio Torrecilla, President
Telephone: 305-681-6622

GENERAL INFORMATION Private Institution. **Total program enrollment:** 11. **Application fee:** $50.

PROGRAM(S) OFFERED
• **Computer Technology/Computer Systems Technology** *25 students enrolled*

STUDENT SERVICES Academic or career counseling, employment services for current students, placement services for program completers.

Traviss Technical Center

3225 Winter Lake Road, Lakeland, FL 33813
http://www.travisstech.org/

CONTACT Kenneth Lloyd, Director
Telephone: 863-499-2700

GENERAL INFORMATION Public Institution. Founded 1964. **Total program enrollment:** 464. **Application fee:** $30.

Traviss Technical Center (continued)

PROGRAM(S) OFFERED
• **Accounting** *7 students enrolled* • **Administrative Assistant and Secretarial Science, General** *9 students enrolled* • **Autobody/Collision and Repair Technology/Technician** *10 students enrolled* • **Automobile/Automotive Mechanics Technology/Technician** *15 students enrolled* • **Building/Property Maintenance and Management** *1 student enrolled* • **Computer Systems Networking and Telecommunications** *17 students enrolled* • **Cosmetology and Related Personal Grooming Arts, Other** *37 students enrolled* • **Cosmetology/Cosmetologist, General** *30 students enrolled* • **Culinary Arts and Related Services, Other** *1 student enrolled* • **Dental Assisting/Assistant** *15 students enrolled* • **Diesel Mechanics Technology/Technician** *10 students enrolled* • **Electrician** *15 students enrolled* • **Health Unit Coordinator/Ward Clerk** *14 students enrolled* • **Heating, Air Conditioning, Ventilation and Refrigeration Maintenance Technology/Technician (HAC, HACR, HVAC, HVACR)** *17 students enrolled* • **Legal Administrative Assistant/Secretary** *6 students enrolled* • **Licensed Practical/Vocational Nurse Training (LPN, LVN, Cert, Dipl, AAS)** *99 students enrolled* • **Massage Therapy/Therapeutic Massage** *12 students enrolled* • **Mechanical Drafting and Mechanical Drafting CAD/CADD** *2 students enrolled* • **Medical Administrative/Executive Assistant and Medical Secretary** *21 students enrolled* • **Nurse/Nursing Assistant/Aide and Patient Care Assistant** *96 students enrolled* • **Optometric Technician/Assistant** • **Phlebotomy/Phlebotomist** • **Surgical Technology/Technologist** *8 students enrolled* • **Teacher Education and Professional Development, Specific Levels and Methods, Other** *2 students enrolled* • **Welding Technology/Welder** *15 students enrolled*

STUDENT SERVICES Academic or career counseling, daycare for children of students, employment services for current students, placement services for program completers, remedial services.

Trendsetters School of Beauty & Barbering

5337 Lenox Avenue, Jacksonville, FL 32205

CONTACT Barbara Collier, Administrator
Telephone: 904-781-1587

GENERAL INFORMATION Private Institution. **Total program enrollment:** 26. **Application fee:** $50.

PROGRAM(S) OFFERED
• **Barbering/Barber** *1200 hrs./$10,410* • **Cosmetology, Barber/Styling, and Nail Instructor** *21 students enrolled* • **Cosmetology/Cosmetologist, General** *1200 hrs./$9810*

STUDENT SERVICES Placement services for program completers.

Trinity College of Florida

2430 Welbilt Boulevard, New Port Richey, FL 34655
http://www.trinitycollege.edu/

CONTACT Mark T. O'Farrell, President
Telephone: 727-376-6911

GENERAL INFORMATION Private Institution. Founded 1932. **Accreditation:** State accredited or approved. **Total program enrollment:** 157. **Application fee:** $25.

PROGRAM(S) OFFERED
• **Bible/Biblical Studies** *1 student enrolled*

STUDENT SERVICES Academic or career counseling, remedial services.

Tulsa Welding School

3500 Southside Boulevard, Jacksonville, FL 32216
http://www.tulsaweldingschool.com/

CONTACT Wayne Gordin, School Director
Telephone: 877-935-3529

GENERAL INFORMATION Private Institution. **Total program enrollment:** 516.

PROGRAM(S) OFFERED
• **Welding Technology/Welder** *405 hrs./$7815*

STUDENT SERVICES Academic or career counseling, employment services for current students, placement services for program completers.

Ultimate Medical Academy

1218 Court Street, Suite C, Clearwater, FL 33756
http://studymedical.com/

CONTACT Steve Kemler, Chief Executive Officer
Telephone: 727-298-8685

GENERAL INFORMATION Private Institution. **Total program enrollment:** 630.

PROGRAM(S) OFFERED
• **Aesthetician/Esthetician and Skin Care Specialist** *720 hrs./$11,900* • **Clinical/Medical Laboratory Assistant** *720 hrs./$9262* • **Health Aides/Attendants/Orderlies, Other** *720 hrs./$11,900* • **Medical Insurance Coding Specialist/Coder** *720 hrs./$10,850* • **Nurse/Nursing Assistant/Aide and Patient Care Assistant** *5 students enrolled* • **Phlebotomy/Phlebotomist** *200 hrs./$1006* • **Radiologic Technology/Science—Radiographer** *720 hrs./$15,300*

STUDENT SERVICES Academic or career counseling, employment services for current students, placement services for program completers.

Ultimate Medical Academy–Tampa

9309 N. Florida Avenue, Suite 100, Tampa, FL 33612
http://www.studymedical.com

CONTACT William D. Polmear, Campus Director
Telephone: 813-386-6350

GENERAL INFORMATION Private Institution. **Total program enrollment:** 884.

PROGRAM(S) OFFERED
• **Clinical/Medical Laboratory Assistant** *31 hrs./$9262* • **Health Aides/Attendants/Orderlies, Other** *33 hrs./$11,900* • **Health Professions and Related Clinical Sciences, Other** *36 hrs./$11,900* • **Medical Insurance Coding Specialist/Coder** *37 hrs./$10,850* • **Nurse/Nursing Assistant/Aide and Patient Care Assistant** *25 students enrolled* • **Phlebotomy/Phlebotomist** *200 hrs./$1006* • **Radiologic Technology/Science—Radiographer** *29 hrs./$13,924*

STUDENT SERVICES Academic or career counseling, employment services for current students, placement services for program completers.

Universal Massage and Beauty Institute

10720 W. Flagler School, Suite 21, Sweetwater, FL 33174
http://www.universalbeautyschool.com/

CONTACT Iris Garcia, School Director and CEO
Telephone: 305-485-7700

GENERAL INFORMATION Private Institution. **Total program enrollment:** 102. **Application fee:** $100.

PROGRAM(S) OFFERED
• **Aesthetician/Esthetician and Skin Care Specialist** *600 hrs./$5500* • **Barbering/Barber** *1200 hrs./$10,500* • **Cosmetology and Related Personal Grooming Arts, Other** *37 students enrolled* • **Cosmetology/Cosmetologist, General** *1200 hrs./$11,000* • **Facial Treatment Specialist/Facialist** *300 hrs./$2200* • **Massage Therapy/Therapeutic Massage** *750 hrs./$5500* • **Nail Technician/Specialist and Manicurist** *240 hrs./$700* • **Trade and Industrial Teacher Education** *3 students enrolled*

STUDENT SERVICES Academic or career counseling, employment services for current students, placement services for program completers, remedial services.

University of Florida

Gainesville, FL 32611
http://www.ufl.edu/

CONTACT Dr. James Bernard Machen, President
Telephone: 352-392-3261

GENERAL INFORMATION Public Institution. Founded 1853. **Accreditation:** Regional (SACS/CC); art and design (NASAD); athletic training (JRCAT); audiology (ASHA); counseling (ACA); dietetics: post-baccalaureate internship (ADtA/CAADE); engineering-related programs (ABET/RAC); forestry (SAF); home economics (AAFCS); interior design: professional (CIDA); journalism and mass communications (ACEJMC); music (NASM); recreation and parks (NRPA); speech-language pathology (ASHA); theater (NAST). **Total program enroll-ment:** 44776. **Application fee:** $30.

STUDENT SERVICES Academic or career counseling, daycare for children of students, employment services for current students, placement services for program completers.

University of Miami

University of Miami Branch, Coral Gables, FL 33124
http://www.miami.edu/

CONTACT Dr. Donna E. Shalala, President
Telephone: 305-284-2211

GENERAL INFORMATION Private Institution. Founded 1925. **Accredita-tion:** Regional (SACS/CC); journalism and mass communications (ACE-JMC); music (NASM). **Total program enrollment:** 14088. **Application fee:** $55.

STUDENT SERVICES Academic or career counseling, daycare for children of students, employment services for current students, placement services for program completers, remedial services.

University of Phoenix–Central Florida Campus

2290 Lucien Way, Suite 400, Maitland, FL 32751-7057
http://www.phoenix.edu/

CONTACT William Pepicello, PhD, President
Telephone: 407-667-0555

GENERAL INFORMATION Private Institution. Founded 1996. **Accredita-tion:** Regional (NCA). **Total program enrollment:** 1637.

STUDENT SERVICES Academic or career counseling, remedial services.

University of Phoenix–North Florida Campus

4500 Salisbury Road, Jacksonville, FL 32216-0959
http://www.phoenix.edu/

CONTACT William Pepicello, PhD, President
Telephone: 904-636-6645

GENERAL INFORMATION Private Institution. Founded 1976. **Accredita-tion:** Regional (NCA). **Total program enrollment:** 1356.

STUDENT SERVICES Academic or career counseling, remedial services.

University of Phoenix–South Florida Campus

600 North Pine Island Road, Fort Lauderdale, FL 33309
http://www.phoenix.edu/

CONTACT William Pepicello, PhD, President
Telephone: 954-382-5303

GENERAL INFORMATION Private Institution. **Accreditation:** Regional (NCA). **Total program enrollment:** 2560.

STUDENT SERVICES Academic or career counseling, remedial services.

University of Phoenix–West Florida Campus

12802 Tampa Oaks Boulevard, Suite 200, Temple Terrace, FL 33637
http://www.phoenix.edu/

CONTACT William Pepicello, PhD, President
Telephone: 813-626-7911

GENERAL INFORMATION Private Institution. **Accreditation:** Regional (NCA). **Total program enrollment:** 983.

PROGRAM(S) OFFERED
● **Business Administration and Management, General** 1 *student enrolled*

STUDENT SERVICES Academic or career counseling, remedial services.

Valencia Community College

PO Box 3028, Orlando, FL 32802-3028
http://www.valencia.cc.fl.us/

CONTACT Sanford C. Shugart, PhD, President
Telephone: 407-299-2187

GENERAL INFORMATION Public Institution. Founded 1967. **Accreditation:** Regional (SACS/CC); dental hygiene (ADA); diagnostic medical sonog-raphy (JRCEDMS); emergency medical services (JRCEMTP); radiologic technology: radiography (JRCERT). **Total program enrollment:** 15814. **Application fee:** $35.

PROGRAM(S) OFFERED
● **Accounting and Related Services, Other** 10 *students enrolled* ● **Architectural Engineering Technology/Technician** 66 *students enrolled* ● **Baking and Pastry Arts/Baker/Pastry Chef** 9 *students enrolled* ● **Business Administration and Man-agement, General** 752 *students enrolled* ● **Cinematography and Film/Video Production** 67 *students enrolled* ● **Commercial and Advertising Art** 88 *students enrolled* ● **Computer Programming, Specific Applications** 58 *students enrolled* ● **Computer Systems Analysis/Analyst** 74 *students enrolled* ● **Computer Technology/Computer Systems Technology** 174 *students enrolled* ● **Computer/ Information Technology Services Administration and Management, Other** 28 *students enrolled* ● **Construction Engineering Technology/Technician** 46 *students enrolled* ● **Corrections** 150 *students enrolled* ● **Criminal Justice/Police Science** 177 *students enrolled* ● **Culinary Arts/Chef Training** 20 *students enrolled* ● **Draft-ing and Design Technology/Technician, General** 74 *students enrolled* ● **Electri-cal, Electronic and Communications Engineering Technology/Technician** 60 *students enrolled* ● **Emergency Medical Technology/Technician (EMT Paramedic)** 240 *students enrolled* ● **Entrepreneurship/Entrepreneurial Studies** 146 *students enrolled* ● **Executive Assistant/Executive Secretary** 132 *students enrolled* ● **Health Information/Medical Records Technology/Technician** 20 *students enrolled* ● **Hotel/Motel Administration/Management** 68 *students enrolled* ● **Landscaping and Groundskeeping** 8 *students enrolled* ● **Management Information Systems, General** 1 *student enrolled* ● **Medical Radiologic Technology/Science—Radiation Therapist** ● **Music, Other** 19 *students enrolled* ● **Respiratory Care Therapy/Therapist** ● **Restaurant/Food Services Man-agement** 30 *students enrolled* ● **Visual and Performing Arts, Other** 37 *students enrolled*

STUDENT SERVICES Academic or career counseling, employment services for current students, placement services for program completers, remedial services.

Virginia College at Pensacola

19 West Garden Street, Pensacola, FL 32501
http://www.vc.edu/

CONTACT Sara Lawhorne, President
Telephone: 850-436-8444 Ext. 2302

GENERAL INFORMATION Private Institution. Founded 1992. **Total program enrollment:** 264. **Application fee:** $100.

PROGRAM(S) OFFERED
• **Accounting and Related Services, Other** • **Criminal Justice/Law Enforcement Administration** 4 *students enrolled* • **Human Resources Management/Personnel Administration, General** • **Legal Assistant/Paralegal** • **Licensed Practical/Vocational Nurse Training (LPN, LVN, Cert, Dipl, AAS)** 15 *students enrolled* • **Medical Insurance Coding Specialist/Coder** 11 *students enrolled* • **Medical/Clinical Assistant** 20 *students enrolled* • **Pharmacy Technician/Assistant** 1 *student enrolled* • **Surgical Technology/Technologist** 1 *student enrolled*

STUDENT SERVICES Academic or career counseling, employment services for current students, placement services for program completers, remedial services.

Warner University

13895 US Highway 27, Lake Wales, FL 33859
http://www.warner.edu/

CONTACT Gregory V. Hall, President
Telephone: 863-638-1426

GENERAL INFORMATION Private Institution (Affiliated with Church of God). Founded 1968. **Accreditation:** Regional (SACS/CC). **Total program enrollment:** 1004. **Application fee:** $20.

PROGRAM(S) OFFERED
• **Theology/Theological Studies**

STUDENT SERVICES Academic or career counseling, remedial services.

Washington-Holmes Technical Center

757 Hoyt Street, Chipley, FL 32428
http://www.firn.edu/schools/washington/whtech/

CONTACT Tommy Smith, Director
Telephone: 850-638-1180

GENERAL INFORMATION Private Institution. **Total program enrollment:** 156.

PROGRAM(S) OFFERED
• **Administrative Assistant and Secretarial Science, General** 1050 *hrs./*$2426 • **Architectural Drafting and Architectural CAD/CADD** 1900 *hrs./*$4389 • **Autobody/Collision and Repair Technology/Technician** 6 *students enrolled* • **Carpentry/Carpenter** 13 *students enrolled* • **Computer Engineering Technology/Technician** 16 *students enrolled* • **Computer Programming, Specific Applications** 4 *students enrolled* • **Computer Systems Networking and Telecommunications** 9 *students enrolled* • **Construction/Heavy Equipment/Earthmoving Equipment Operation** 33 *students enrolled* • **Corrections and Criminal Justice, Other** • **Corrections** 142 *students enrolled* • **Cosmetology/Cosmetologist, General** 1200 *hrs./*$2772 • **Culinary Arts and Related Services, Other** 26 *students enrolled* • **Electrician** 9 *students enrolled* • **Fire Science/Firefighting** 30 *students enrolled* • **Heating, Air Conditioning, Ventilation and Refrigeration Maintenance Technology/Technician (HAC, HACR, HVAC, HVACR)** 6 *students enrolled* • **Heavy Equipment Maintenance Technology/Technician** 6 *students enrolled* • **Home Furnishings and Equipment Installers** 6 *students enrolled* • **Landscaping and Groundskeeping** 2 *students enrolled* • **Licensed Practical/Vocational Nurse Training (LPN, LVN, Cert, Dipl, AAS)** 1350 *hrs./*$3143 • **Make-Up Artist/Specialist** • **Nurse/Nursing Assistant/Aide and Patient Care Assistant** 600 *hrs./*$1410 • **Plant Nursery Operations and Management** 5 *students enrolled* • **Real Estate** 12 *students enrolled* • **Sales, Distribution and Marketing Operations, General** 13 *students enrolled* • **Transportation and Materials Moving, Other** • **Truck and Bus Driver/Commercial Vehicle Operation** 320 *hrs./*$2000 • **Turf and Turfgrass Management** 1 *student enrolled* • **Welding Technology/Welder** 32 *students enrolled*

STUDENT SERVICES Academic or career counseling, employment services for current students, placement services for program completers, remedial services.

Westside Tech

955 E. Story Road, Winter Garden, FL 34787
http://www.westside.ocps.net/

CONTACT Adelina Brann, Senior Director
Telephone: 407-905-2018

GENERAL INFORMATION Public Institution. **Total program enrollment:** 584. **Application fee:** $25.

PROGRAM(S) OFFERED
• **Administrative Assistant and Secretarial Science, General** 11 *students enrolled* • **Aesthetician/Esthetician and Skin Care Specialist** 260 *hrs./*$696 • **Allied Health and Medical Assisting Services, Other** 1300 *hrs./*$2780 • **Building/Property Maintenance and Management** 8 *students enrolled* • **Commercial and Advertising Art** • **Computer Technology/Computer Systems Technology** 1 *student enrolled* • **Cosmetology/Cosmetologist, General** 1200 *hrs./*$3514 • **Electrician** 62 *students enrolled* • **Heating, Air Conditioning, Ventilation and Refrigeration Maintenance Technology/Technician (HAC, HACR, HVAC, HVACR)** 1350 *hrs./*$2935 • **Institutional Food Workers** 1500 *hrs./*$3200 • **Massage Therapy/Therapeutic Massage** 750 *hrs./*$1880 • **Medical Administrative/Executive Assistant and Medical Secretary** 16 *students enrolled* • **Nail Technician/Specialist and Manicurist** 19 *students enrolled* • **Pharmacy Technician/Assistant** 29 *students enrolled* • **Special Products Marketing Operations** 3 *students enrolled* • **System Administration/Administrator** • **Veterinary/Animal Health Technology/Technician and Veterinary Assistant** 22 *students enrolled* • **Welding Technology/Welder** 21 *students enrolled*

STUDENT SERVICES Academic or career counseling, employment services for current students, placement services for program completers, remedial services.

Winter Park Tech

901 Webster Avenue, Winter Park, FL 32789
http://www.wpt.ocps.net/

CONTACT Diane Culpepper, Senior Director
Telephone: 407-622-2900

GENERAL INFORMATION Public Institution. Founded 1974. **Total program enrollment:** 292. **Application fee:** $25.

PROGRAM(S) OFFERED
• **Accounting and Related Services, Other** 9 *students enrolled* • **Administrative Assistant and Secretarial Science, General** 5 *students enrolled* • **Communications Technologies/Technicians and Support Services, Other** 5 *students enrolled* • **Computer Programming, Other** 1 *student enrolled* • **Computer Technology/Computer Systems Technology** 1650 *hrs./*$3540 • **Electrocardiograph Technology/Technician** 12 *students enrolled* • **Facial Treatment Specialist/Facialist** 21 *students enrolled* • **Home Furnishings and Equipment Installers** 7 *students enrolled* • **Interior Design** 11 *students enrolled* • **Legal Administrative Assistant/Secretary** 3 *students enrolled* • **Medical Administrative/Executive Assistant and Medical Secretary** 13 *students enrolled* • **Medical Insurance Coding Specialist/Coder** 1000 *hrs./*$2150 • **Medical Transcription/Transcriptionist** 8 *students enrolled* • **Medical/Clinical Assistant** 1300 *hrs./*$3612 • **Nail Technician/Specialist and Manicurist** 5 *students enrolled* • **Nurse/Nursing Assistant/Aide and Patient Care Assistant** 600 *hrs./*$1285 • **Pharmacy Technician/Assistant** 1050 *hrs./*$2557 • **Phlebotomy/Phlebotomist** 51 *students enrolled* • **Prepress/Desktop Publishing and Digital Imaging Design** 13 *students enrolled* • **Renal/Dialysis Technologist/Technician** 28 *students enrolled* • **System Administration/Administrator** 2 *students enrolled* • **Watchmaking and Jewelrymaking** 5 *students enrolled* • **Web Page, Digital/Multimedia and Information Resources Design** 1050 *hrs./*$2255

STUDENT SERVICES Academic or career counseling, employment services for current students, placement services for program completers, remedial services.

Withlacoochee Technical Institute

1201 West Main Street, Inverness, FL 32650

http://www.wtionline.cc/

CONTACT Denise Willis, Director
Telephone: 352-726-2430

GENERAL INFORMATION Public Institution. **Total program enrollment:** 243.

PROGRAM(S) OFFERED
• **Administrative Assistant and Secretarial Science, General** 16 *students enrolled* • **Autobody/Collision and Repair Technology/Technician** 12 *students enrolled* • **Automobile/Automotive Mechanics Technology/Technician** 8 *students enrolled* • **Carpentry/Carpenter** 3 *students enrolled* • **Computer Technology/Computer Systems Technology** 16 *students enrolled* • **Corrections and Criminal Justice, Other** 552 *hrs./$1821* • **Corrections** 73 *students enrolled* • **Cosmetology/Cosmetologist, General** 1200 *hrs./$2473* • **Criminal Justice/Law Enforcement Administration** 770 *hrs./$1873* • **Criminal Justice/Police Science** 16 *students enrolled* • **Culinary Arts/Chef Training** 14 *students enrolled* • **Early Childhood Education and Teaching** 7 *students enrolled* • **Electrician** 18 *students enrolled* • **Heating, Air Conditioning and Refrigeration Technology/Technician (ACH/ACR/ACHR/HRAC/HVAC/AC Technology)** 17 *students enrolled* • **Licensed Practical/Vocational Nurse Training (LPN, LVN, Cert, Dipl, AAS)** 1350 *hrs./$2839* • **Marine Maintenance/Fitter and Ship Repair Technology/Technician** 14 *students enrolled* • **Massage Therapy/Therapeutic Massage** 18 *students enrolled* • **Medical Administrative/Executive Assistant and Medical Secretary** 21 *students enrolled* • **Nail Technician/Specialist and Manicurist** 240 *hrs./$504* • **Nurse/Nursing Assistant/Aide and Patient Care Assistant** 290 *hrs./$605* • **Welding Technology/Welder** 16 *students enrolled*

STUDENT SERVICES Academic or career counseling, daycare for children of students, employment services for current students, placement services for program completers, remedial services.

Wyotech–Daytona

3042 West International Speedway Boulevard, Daytona Beach, FL 32124

http://www.wyotech.edu/campus/daytona

CONTACT Roland Palot, President
Telephone: 386-255-0295 Ext. 308

GENERAL INFORMATION Private Institution. Founded 1972. **Total program enrollment:** 286. **Application fee:** $100.

PROGRAM(S) OFFERED
• **Marine Maintenance/Fitter and Ship Repair Technology/Technician** 1000 *hrs./$16,830* • **Motorcycle Maintenance and Repair Technology/Technician** 1000 *hrs./$16,830*

STUDENT SERVICES Placement services for program completers.

GEORGIA ————————

Abraham Baldwin Agricultural College

2802 Moore Highway, Tifton, GA 31793

http://www.abac.edu/

CONTACT David C. Bridges, President
Telephone: 229-391-5001

GENERAL INFORMATION Public Institution. Founded 1933. **Accreditation:** Regional (SACS/CC). **Total program enrollment:** 2577. **Application fee:** $20.

PROGRAM(S) OFFERED
• **Animal/Livestock Husbandry and Production** 4 *students enrolled* • **Education, General** 4 *students enrolled* • **Marketing/Marketing Management, General** 1 *student enrolled*

STUDENT SERVICES Academic or career counseling, employment services for current students, placement services for program completers, remedial services.

Academy of Somatic Healing Arts

1924 Cliff Valley Way, NE, Atlanta, GA 30329

CONTACT Sandy Templeton, Administrative Director
Telephone: 770-368-2661

GENERAL INFORMATION Private Institution. Founded 1991. **Total program enrollment:** 140. **Application fee:** $50.

PROGRAM(S) OFFERED
• **Massage Therapy/Therapeutic Massage** 840 *hrs./$10,430*

STUDENT SERVICES Placement services for program completers.

Advanced Career Training

1 Corporate Square, Suite 110, Atlanta, GA 30329

http://www.actglobal.com/

CONTACT Fardad Fateri, Chief Executive Officer
Telephone: 404-321-2929

GENERAL INFORMATION Private Institution. Founded 1975. **Total program enrollment:** 1417. **Application fee:** $100.

PROGRAM(S) OFFERED
• **Administrative Assistant and Secretarial Science, General** 55 *students enrolled* • **Business/Office Automation/Technology/Data Entry** 36 *hrs./$13,640* • **Computer Engineering Technology/Technician** 20 *students enrolled* • **Computer Technology/Computer Systems Technology** 36 *hrs./$13,640* • **Dental Assisting/Assistant** 36 *hrs./$13,640* • **Massage Therapy/Therapeutic Massage** 36 *hrs./$13,640* • **Medical Insurance Specialist/Medical Biller** 36 *hrs./$13,640* • **Medical/Clinical Assistant** 36 *hrs./$13,640*

STUDENT SERVICES Academic or career counseling, employment services for current students, placement services for program completers.

Albany Technical College

1704 South Slappey Boulevard, Albany, GA 31701-3514

http://www.albanytech.edu/

CONTACT Anthony O. Parker, President
Telephone: 229-430-3500

GENERAL INFORMATION Public Institution. Founded 1961. **Accreditation:** Regional (SACS/CC); dental assisting (ADA); radiologic technology: radiography (JRCERT); state accredited or approved. **Total program enrollment:** 1728. **Application fee:** $15.

PROGRAM(S) OFFERED
• **Accounting Technology/Technician and Bookkeeping** 28 *students enrolled* • **Administrative Assistant and Secretarial Science, General** 26 *students enrolled* • **Adult Development and Aging** 3 *students enrolled* • **Applied Horticulture/Horticultural Operations, General** 3 *students enrolled* • **Autobody/Collision and Repair Technology/Technician** 39 *students enrolled* • **Automobile/Automotive Mechanics Technology/Technician** 60 *students enrolled* • **Carpentry/Carpenter** 19 *students enrolled* • **Child Care Provider/Assistant** 11 *students enrolled* • **Child Care and Support Services Management** 7 *students enrolled* • **Commercial and Advertising Art** 1 *student enrolled* • **Computer Installation and Repair Technology/Technician** 12 *students enrolled* • **Computer Systems Networking and Telecommunications** 9 *students enrolled* • **Cosmetology/Cosmetologist, General** 44 *students enrolled* • **Criminal Justice/Safety Studies** 59 *students enrolled* • **Customer Service Support/Call Center/Teleservice Operation** 31 *students enrolled* • **Data Entry/Microcomputer Applications, General** 5 *students enrolled* • **Data Processing and Data Processing Technology/Technician** 6 *students enrolled* • **Dental Assisting/Assistant** 22

Albany Technical College (continued)

students enrolled • **Drafting and Design Technology/Technician, General** 4 *students enrolled* • **Early Childhood Education and Teaching** 62 *students enrolled* • **Electrical/Electronics Equipment Installation and Repair, General** 9 *students enrolled* • **Electrician** 7 *students enrolled* • **Emergency Medical Technology/ Technician (EMT Paramedic)** 14 *students enrolled* • **Entrepreneurship/ Entrepreneurial Studies** 9 *students enrolled* • **Fire Science/Firefighting** 57 *students enrolled* • **Floriculture/Floristry Operations and Management** 4 *students enrolled* • **Food Preparation/Professional Cooking/Kitchen Assistant** 4 *students enrolled* • **Graphic and Printing Equipment Operator, General Production** 2 *students enrolled* • **Heating, Air Conditioning, Ventilation and Refrigeration Maintenance Technology/Technician (HAC, HACR, HVAC, HVACR)** 32 *students enrolled* • **Heavy Equipment Maintenance Technology/Technician** 29 *students enrolled* • **Hospitality Administration/Management, General** 5 *students enrolled* • **Industrial Mechanics and Maintenance Technology** 47 *students enrolled* • **Landscaping and Groundskeeping** 7 *students enrolled* • **Logistics and Materials Management** 47 *students enrolled* • **Medical Insurance Coding Specialist/ Coder** 11 *students enrolled* • **Medical Transcription/Transcriptionist** 2 *students enrolled* • **Medical/Clinical Assistant** 9 *students enrolled* • **Nurse/Nursing Assistant/Aide and Patient Care Assistant** 17 *students enrolled* • **Operations Management and Supervision** 50 *students enrolled* • **Pharmacy Technician/ Assistant** 14 *students enrolled* • **Plant Nursery Operations and Management** 11 *students enrolled* • **Sales, Distribution and Marketing Operations, General** 20 *students enrolled* • **Security and Loss Prevention Services** 8 *students enrolled* • **Surgical Technology/Technologist** 20 *students enrolled* • **Truck and Bus Driver/Commercial Vehicle Operation** 95 *students enrolled* • **Web Page, Digital/Multimedia and Information Resources Design** 2 *students enrolled* • **Welding Technology/Welder** 183 *students enrolled*

STUDENT SERVICES Academic or career counseling, daycare for children of students, employment services for current students, placement services for program completers, remedial services.

Altamaha Technical College

1777 West Cherry Street, Jesup, GA 31545
http://www.altamahatech.edu/

CONTACT Lorette M. Hoover, President
Telephone: 912-427-5800

GENERAL INFORMATION Public Institution. **Accreditation:** State accredited or approved. **Total program enrollment:** 340. **Application fee:** $15.

PROGRAM(S) OFFERED
• **Accounting Technology/Technician and Bookkeeping** 7 *students enrolled* • **Administrative Assistant and Secretarial Science, General** 12 *students enrolled* • **Automobile/Automotive Mechanics Technology/Technician** 4 *students enrolled* • **Civil Engineering Technology/Technician** 4 *students enrolled* • **Computer and Information Systems Security** 1 *student enrolled* • **Cosmetology/Cosmetologist, General** 21 *students enrolled* • **Criminal Justice/ Safety Studies** 4 *students enrolled* • **Customer Service Support/Call Center/ Teleservice Operation** 20 *students enrolled* • **Data Entry/Microcomputer Applications, General** 58 *students enrolled* • **Early Childhood Education and Teaching** 5 *students enrolled* • **Electrical/Electronics Equipment Installation and Repair, General** 4 *students enrolled* • **Electrician** 49 *students enrolled* • **Emergency Medical Technology/Technician (EMT Paramedic)** 6 *students enrolled* • **Food Preparation/Professional Cooking/Kitchen Assistant** 2 *students enrolled* • **Heating, Air Conditioning, Ventilation and Refrigeration Maintenance Technology/Technician (HAC, HACR, HVAC, HVACR)** 22 *students enrolled* • **Heavy Equipment Maintenance Technology/Technician** 8 *students enrolled* • **Industrial Mechanics and Maintenance Technology** 2 *students enrolled* • **Instrumentation Technology/Technician** 1 *student enrolled* • **Machine Shop Technology/Assistant** 4 *students enrolled* • **Mason/Masonry** 1 *student enrolled* • **Medical Insurance Coding Specialist/Coder** 18 *students enrolled* • **Medical Transcription/Transcriptionist** 1 *student enrolled* • **Nurse/Nursing Assistant/Aide and Patient Care Assistant** 66 *students enrolled* • **Plumbing Technology/Plumber** 1 *student enrolled* • **Sales, Distribution and Marketing Operations, General** 2 *students enrolled* • **Small Business Administration/ Management** 5 *students enrolled* • **Truck and Bus Driver/Commercial Vehicle Operation** 79 *students enrolled* • **Welding Technology/Welder** 12 *students enrolled* • **Wood Science and Wood Products/Pulp and Paper Technology** 2 *students enrolled*

STUDENT SERVICES Academic or career counseling, employment services for current students, placement services for program completers, remedial services.

American Professional Institute

1990 Riverside Drive, Macon, GA 31211

CONTACT Gaylinda Lippmann-Cuff, CEO-President
Telephone: 478-314-4444

GENERAL INFORMATION Private Institution. **Total program enrollment:** 1013. **Application fee:** $25.

PROGRAM(S) OFFERED
• **Cosmetology and Related Personal Grooming Arts, Other** 5 *students enrolled* • **Cosmetology/Cosmetologist, General** 16 *students enrolled* • **Massage Therapy/Therapeutic Massage** 24 *students enrolled* • **Medical Insurance Coding Specialist/Coder** 57 *students enrolled* • **Medical/Clinical Assistant** 78 *students enrolled* • **Pharmacy Technician/Assistant** 13 *students enrolled* • **Surgical Technology/Technologist** 3 *students enrolled*

STUDENT SERVICES Employment services for current students, placement services for program completers.

Appalachian Technical College

100 Campus Drive, Jasper, GA 30143
http://www.appalachiantech.edu/

CONTACT Sanford Chandler, President
Telephone: 706-253-4500

GENERAL INFORMATION Public Institution. Founded 1965. **Accreditation:** State accredited or approved. **Total program enrollment:** 433. **Application fee:** $15.

PROGRAM(S) OFFERED
• **Accounting Technology/Technician and Bookkeeping** 64 *students enrolled* • **Administrative Assistant and Secretarial Science, General** 15 *students enrolled* • **Aesthetician/Esthetician and Skin Care Specialist** 5 *students enrolled* • **Autobody/Collision and Repair Technology/Technician** 2 *students enrolled* • **Automobile/Automotive Mechanics Technology/Technician** 8 *students enrolled* • **CAD/CADD Drafting and/or Design Technology/Technician** 5 *students enrolled* • **Computer Installation and Repair Technology/Technician** 4 *students enrolled* • **Cosmetology/Cosmetologist, General** 13 *students enrolled* • **Criminal Justice/ Safety Studies** 9 *students enrolled* • **Data Entry/Microcomputer Applications, General** 13 *students enrolled* • **Drafting and Design Technology/Technician, General** 2 *students enrolled* • **Early Childhood Education and Teaching** 26 *students enrolled* • **Electrical/Electronics Equipment Installation and Repair, General** 2 *students enrolled* • **Emergency Medical Technology/Technician (EMT Paramedic)** 11 *students enrolled* • **Interior Design** 7 *students enrolled* • **Legal Assistant/Paralegal** 2 *students enrolled* • **Machine Shop Technology/Assistant** 2 *students enrolled* • **Medical Office Assistant/Specialist** 2 *students enrolled* • **Medical/Clinical Assistant** 10 *students enrolled* • **Nurse/Nursing Assistant/ Aide and Patient Care Assistant** 2 *students enrolled* • **Operations Management and Supervision** 3 *students enrolled* • **Phlebotomy/Phlebotomist** 17 *students enrolled* • **Small Business Administration/Management** 2 *students enrolled* • **Welding Technology/Welder** 5 *students enrolled*

STUDENT SERVICES Academic or career counseling, employment services for current students, placement services for program completers, remedial services.

Armstrong Atlantic State University

11935 Abercorn Street, Savannah, GA 31419-1997
http://www.armstrong.edu/

CONTACT Thomas Z. Jones, President
Telephone: 912-344-2806

GENERAL INFORMATION Public Institution. Founded 1935. **Accreditation:** Regional (SACS/CC); computer science (ABET/CSAC); dental hygiene (ADA); medical technology (NAACLS); music (NASM); public health: community health education (CEPH); radiologic technology: radiation therapy technology (JRCERT); radiologic technology: radiography (JRCERT). **Total program enrollment:** 4408. **Application fee:** $25.

PROGRAM(S) OFFERED
• Criminal Justice/Police Science *12 students enrolled*

STUDENT SERVICES Academic or career counseling, employment services for current students, remedial services.

The Art Institute of Atlanta

6600 Peachtree Dunwoody Road, 100 Embassy Row, Atlanta, GA 30328
http://www.artinstitutes.edu/atlanta

CONTACT Janet S. Day, President
Telephone: 770-394-8300

GENERAL INFORMATION Private Institution. Founded 1949. **Accreditation:** Regional (SACS/CC); interior design: professional (CIDA). **Total program enrollment:** 2908. **Application fee:** $50.

PROGRAM(S) OFFERED
• Advertising *2 students enrolled* • Culinary Arts/Chef Training *20 students enrolled* • Graphic Design *2 students enrolled* • Interior Design *3 students enrolled* • Photography *4 students enrolled*

STUDENT SERVICES Academic or career counseling, employment services for current students, placement services for program completers, remedial services.

Athens Technical College

800 US Highway 29 North, Athens, GA 30601-1500
http://www.athenstech.edu/

CONTACT Flora W. Tydings, President
Telephone: 706-355-5000

GENERAL INFORMATION Public Institution. Founded 1958. **Accreditation:** Regional (SACS/CC); dental assisting (ADA); dental hygiene (ADA); physical therapy assisting (APTA); radiologic technology: radiography (JRCERT). **Total program enrollment:** 1612. **Application fee:** $20.

PROGRAM(S) OFFERED
• Accounting Technology/Technician and Bookkeeping *22 students enrolled* • Administrative Assistant and Secretarial Science, General *6 students enrolled* • Autobody/Collision and Repair Technology/Technician *53 students enrolled* • Automobile/Automotive Mechanics Technology/Technician *58 students enrolled* • CAD/CADD Drafting and/or Design Technology/Technician *1 student enrolled* • Chemical Technology/Technician *2 students enrolled* • Child Care and Support Services Management *11 students enrolled* • Computer Programming, Specific Applications *7 students enrolled* • Computer and Information Systems Security *8 students enrolled* • Cosmetology/Cosmetologist, General *60 students enrolled* • Criminal Justice/Safety Studies *5 students enrolled* • Dental Assisting/Assistant *7 students enrolled* • Drafting and Design Technology/Technician, General *7 students enrolled* • Early Childhood Education and Teaching *14 students enrolled* • Electrical/Electronics Equipment Installation and Repair, General *6 students enrolled* • Electrician *10 students enrolled* • Emergency Medical Technology/Technician (EMT Paramedic) *54 students enrolled* • Food Preparation/Professional Cooking/Kitchen Assistant *7 students enrolled* • Heating, Air Conditioning, Ventilation and Refrigeration Maintenance Technology/Technician (HAC, HACR, HVAC, HVACR) *16 students enrolled* • Home Health Aide/Home Attendant *4 students enrolled* • Hospitality Administration/Management, General *4 students enrolled* • Industrial Mechanics and Maintenance Technology *11 students enrolled* • Machine Shop Technology/Assistant *5 students enrolled* • Medical/Clinical Assistant *31 students enrolled* • Nail Technician/Specialist and Manicurist • Nurse/Nursing Assistant/Aide and Patient Care Assistant *111 students enrolled* • Operations Management and Supervision *2 students enrolled* • Phlebotomy/Phlebotomist *42 students enrolled* • Sales, Distribution and Marketing Operations, General *5 students enrolled* • Small Business Administration/Management *4 students enrolled* • Surgical Technology/Technologist *7 students enrolled* • Technical and Business Writing *1 student enrolled* • Truck and Bus Driver/Commercial Vehicle Operation *51 students enrolled* • Web Page, Digital/Multimedia and Information Resources Design *14 students enrolled*

STUDENT SERVICES Academic or career counseling, employment services for current students, placement services for program completers, remedial services.

Atlanta Institute of Music

5985 Financial Drive, Suite 200, Norcross, GA 30071
http://www.aim-music.com/

CONTACT Harvey Denite Driscoll, President/CEO
Telephone: 770-242-7717

GENERAL INFORMATION Private Institution. **Total program enrollment:** 76. **Application fee:** $100.

PROGRAM(S) OFFERED
• Music Performance, General *900 hrs./$16,838* • Music, General *41 students enrolled*

STUDENT SERVICES Academic or career counseling, employment services for current students, placement services for program completers, remedial services.

Atlanta School of Massage

2300 Peachford Road, Suite 3200, Atlanta, GA 30338-5820
http://www.atlantaschoolofmassage.com/

CONTACT Leticia Allen, Owner
Telephone: 770-454-7167

GENERAL INFORMATION Private Institution. Founded 1980. **Total program enrollment:** 145. **Application fee:** $100.

PROGRAM(S) OFFERED
• Aesthetician/Esthetician and Skin Care Specialist *1000 hrs./$13,999* • Massage Therapy/Therapeutic Massage *45 hrs./$13,999*

Atlanta Technical College

1560 Metropolitan Parkway, Atlanta, GA 30310
http://www.atlantatech.org/

CONTACT Alvetta Thomas, EdD, President
Telephone: 404-225-4601

GENERAL INFORMATION Public Institution. Founded 1945. **Accreditation:** Dental assisting (ADA); dental laboratory technology (ADA); state accredited or approved. **Total program enrollment:** 1635. **Application fee:** $20.

PROGRAM(S) OFFERED
• Accounting Technology/Technician and Bookkeeping *28 students enrolled* • Administrative Assistant and Secretarial Science, General *7 students enrolled* • Architectural Drafting and Architectural CAD/CADD *4 students enrolled* • Autobody/Collision and Repair Technology/Technician *40 students enrolled* • Automobile/Automotive Mechanics Technology/Technician *153 students enrolled* • Barbering/Barber *2 students enrolled* • CAD/CADD Drafting and/or Design Technology/Technician *3 students enrolled* • Carpentry/Carpenter *35 students enrolled* • Child Care and Support Services Management *23 students enrolled* • Commercial and Advertising Art *5 students enrolled* • Computer Installation and Repair Technology/Technician • Computer Systems Networking and Telecommunications *7 students enrolled* • Cosmetology/Cosmetologist, General *88 students enrolled* • Data Entry/Microcomputer Applications, General *7 students enrolled* • Data Modeling/Warehousing and Database Administration *1 student enrolled* • Dental Assisting/Assistant *17 students enrolled* • Diesel Mechanics Technology/Technician *13 students enrolled* • Drafting and Design Technology/Technician, General *2 students enrolled* • Early Childhood Education and Teaching *23 students enrolled* • Electrician *34 students enrolled* • Emergency Medical Technology/Technician (EMT Paramedic) *35 students enrolled* • Fire Science/Firefighting *8 students enrolled* • Food Preparation/Professional Cooking/Kitchen Assistant *49 students enrolled* • General Office Occupations and Clerical Services *14 students enrolled* • Health Information/Medical Records Technology/Technician • Heating, Air Conditioning, Ventilation and Refrigeration Maintenance Technology/Technician (HAC, HACR, HVAC, HVACR) *69 students enrolled* • Legal Assistant/Paralegal *20 students enrolled* • Logistics and Materials Management *10 students enrolled* • Medical Insurance Coding Specialist/Coder *5 students enrolled* • Medical Insurance Specialist/Medical Biller • Medical Transcription/Transcriptionist *2 students enrolled* • Medical/Clinical Assistant *26 students enrolled* • Medium/Heavy Vehicle and Truck Technology/Technician *16 students enrolled* • Nurse/Nursing Assistant/Aide and Patient Care Assistant *90 students enrolled* • Pharmacy Technician/Assistant *4*

Atlanta Technical College (continued)

students enrolled • **Phlebotomy/Phlebotomist** 15 students enrolled • **Plumbing Technology/Plumber** 24 students enrolled • **Renal/Dialysis Technologist/ Technician** 11 students enrolled • **Sales, Distribution and Marketing Operations, General** 4 students enrolled • **Small Business Administration/ Management** 12 students enrolled • **Welding Technology/Welder** 2 students enrolled • **Word Processing** 6 students enrolled

STUDENT SERVICES Academic or career counseling, daycare for children of students, employment services for current students, placement services for program completers, remedial services.

Augusta School of Massage

608 Ponder Place Drive, Evans, GA 30809
http://www.augustamassage.com/

CONTACT Leigh Ann Keels, Director
Telephone: 706-863-4799

GENERAL INFORMATION Private Institution. **Total program enrollment:** 43. **Application fee:** $25.

PROGRAM(S) OFFERED
• **Massage Therapy/Therapeutic Massage** 600 hrs./$6500

Augusta Technical College

3200 Augusta Tech Drive, Augusta, GA 30906
http://www.augustatech.edu/

CONTACT Terry Elam, President
Telephone: 706-771-4000

GENERAL INFORMATION Public Institution. Founded 1961. **Accreditation:** Regional (SACS/CC); cardiovascular technology (JRCECT); dental assisting (ADA); engineering technology (ABET/TAC); surgical technology (ARCST). **Total program enrollment:** 2262. **Application fee:** $15.

PROGRAM(S) OFFERED
• **Accounting Technology/Technician and Bookkeeping** 20 students enrolled • **Administrative Assistant and Secretarial Science, General** 76 students enrolled • **Applied Horticulture/Horticultural Operations, General** 9 students enrolled • **Automobile/Automotive Mechanics Technology/Technician** 42 students enrolled • **Barbering/Barber** 5 students enrolled • **CAD/CADD Drafting and/or Design Technology/Technician** 9 students enrolled • **Chemical Technology/Technician** 9 students enrolled • **Civil Engineering Technology/ Technician** 3 students enrolled • **Computer Installation and Repair Technology/ Technician** 8 students enrolled • **Computer Systems Networking and Telecommunications** 125 students enrolled • **Cosmetology/Cosmetologist, General** 52 students enrolled • **Criminal Justice/Safety Studies** 4 students enrolled • **Customer Service Support/Call Center/Teleservice Operation** 1 student enrolled • **Data Entry/Microcomputer Applications, General** 18 students enrolled • **Dental Assisting/Assistant** 24 students enrolled • **Early Childhood Education and Teaching** 4 students enrolled • **Electrician** 77 students enrolled • **Emergency Medical Technology/Technician (EMT Paramedic)** 56 students enrolled • **Fire Science/Firefighting** 12 students enrolled • **Food Preparation/Professional Cooking/Kitchen Assistant** 5 students enrolled • **General Office Occupations and Clerical Services** 21 students enrolled • **Graphic and Printing Equipment Operator, General Production** 3 students enrolled • **Heating, Air Conditioning, Ventilation and Refrigeration Maintenance Technology/Technician (HAC, HACR, HVAC, HVACR)** 24 students enrolled • **Industrial Mechanics and Maintenance Technology** 7 students enrolled • **Landscaping and Groundskeeping** 9 students enrolled • **Legal Administrative Assistant/Secretary** 2 students enrolled • **Machine Shop Technology/Assistant** 6 students enrolled • **Medical Insurance Coding Specialist/Coder** 41 students enrolled • **Medical Transcription/Transcriptionist** 9 students enrolled • **Medical/Clinical Assistant** 49 students enrolled • **Nail Technician/Specialist and Manicurist** 5 students enrolled • **Nurse/Nursing Assistant/Aide and Patient Care Assistant** 297 students enrolled • **Operations Management and Supervision** 29 students enrolled • **Pharmacy Technician/Assistant** 6 students enrolled • **Radio and Television Broadcasting Technology/Technician** 3 students enrolled • **Sales, Distribution and Marketing Operations, General** 8 students enrolled • **Surgical Technology/Technologist** 19 students enrolled • **Turf and Turfgrass Management** 3 students enrolled • **Web Page, Digital/Multimedia and Information Resources Design** 4 students enrolled • **Welding Technology/Welder** 80 students enrolled

STUDENT SERVICES Academic or career counseling, employment services for current students, placement services for program completers, remedial services.

Bainbridge College

2500 East Shotwell Street, Bainbridge, GA 39819
http://www.bainbridge.edu/

CONTACT Thomas A. Wilkerson, President
Telephone: 866-825-1715

GENERAL INFORMATION Public Institution. Founded 1972. **Accreditation:** Regional (SACS/CC). **Total program enrollment:** 1236.

PROGRAM(S) OFFERED
• **Accounting Technology/Technician and Bookkeeping** 2 students enrolled • **Administrative Assistant and Secretarial Science, General** 12 students enrolled • **Business Administration, Management and Operations, Other** 50 students enrolled • **Business/Office Automation/Technology/Data Entry** 2 students enrolled • **Child Care and Support Services Management** 3 students enrolled • **Computer Installation and Repair Technology/Technician** 13 students enrolled • **Criminal Justice/Safety Studies** 1 student enrolled • **Customer Service Support/Call Center/Teleservice Operation** 34 students enrolled • **Data Processing and Data Processing Technology/Technician** 2 students enrolled • **Drafting and Design Technology/Technician, General** 4 students enrolled • **Electrician** 4 students enrolled • **Emergency Medical Technology/Technician (EMT Paramedic)** 2 students enrolled • **Forestry Technology/Technician** 1 student enrolled • **Industrial Mechanics and Maintenance Technology** 1 student enrolled • **Licensed Practical/Vocational Nurse Training (LPN, LVN, Cert, Dipl, AAS)** 33 students enrolled • **Marketing/Marketing Management, General** 5 students enrolled • **Medical Administrative/Executive Assistant and Medical Secretary** 19 students enrolled • **Medical/Clinical Assistant** 4 students enrolled • **Nurse/Nursing Assistant/Aide and Patient Care Assistant** 90 students enrolled • **Phlebotomy/Phlebotomist** 14 students enrolled • **Security System Installation, Repair, and Inspection Technology/Technician** 17 students enrolled • **Small Business Administration/Management** 13 students enrolled • **Technical Theatre/ Theatre Design and Technology** 1 student enrolled • **Truck and Bus Driver/ Commercial Vehicle Operation** 59 students enrolled • **Welding Technology/ Welder** 8 students enrolled

STUDENT SERVICES Academic or career counseling, employment services for current students, placement services for program completers, remedial services.

Bauder College

384 Northyards Boulevard NW, Suites 190 and 400, Atlanta, GA 30313
http://www.bauder.edu/

CONTACT Reginald Morton, President
Telephone: 404-237-7573

GENERAL INFORMATION Private Institution. Founded 1964. **Accreditation:** Regional (SACS/CC). **Total program enrollment:** 981.

PROGRAM(S) OFFERED
• **Allied Health and Medical Assisting Services, Other** 106 hrs./$25,996 • **Business Administration and Management, General** 99 hrs./$29,596 • **Criminal Justice/Safety Studies** 122 hrs./$56,680 • **Fashion Merchandising** 94 hrs./$30,096 • **Fashion/Apparel Design** 103 hrs./$35,396

STUDENT SERVICES Academic or career counseling, employment services for current students, placement services for program completers, remedial services.

Beauty College of America

1171 Main Street, Forest Park, GA 30297
http://www.beautycl.com/

CONTACT Joy M. Carey, Chief Executive Officer/Owner
Telephone: 404-361-4098

GENERAL INFORMATION Private Institution. Founded 1965. **Total program enrollment:** 73.

PROGRAM(S) OFFERED
• **Cosmetology, Barber/Styling, and Nail Instructor** 751 hrs./$3500 • **Cosmetology/Cosmetologist, General** 1500 hrs./$7875 • **Hair Styling/Stylist and Hair Design** 1325 hrs./$6087 • **Nail Technician/Specialist and Manicurist** 525 hrs./$1175

STUDENT SERVICES Academic or career counseling, employment services for current students, placement services for program completers, remedial services.

Beulah Heights University

892 Berne Street, SE, PO Box 18145, Atlanta, GA 30316
http://www.beulah.org/

CONTACT Benson M. Karanja, President
Telephone: 404-627-2681

GENERAL INFORMATION Private Institution. Founded 1918. **Accreditation:** State accredited or approved. **Total program enrollment:** 420. **Application fee:** $30.

STUDENT SERVICES Academic or career counseling, remedial services.

Brown College of Court Reporting and Medical Transcription

1740 Peachtree Street, Atlanta, GA 30309
http://www.browncollege.com/

CONTACT Shirley Sotona, Director of Education
Telephone: 404-876-1227

GENERAL INFORMATION Private Institution. Founded 1972. **Total program enrollment:** 66. **Application fee:** $75.

PROGRAM(S) OFFERED
• Business/Office Automation/Technology/Data Entry 5 students enrolled
• Health Information/Medical Records Technology/Technician • Medical Transcription/Transcriptionist 4 students enrolled

STUDENT SERVICES Academic or career counseling, employment services for current students, placement services for program completers.

Brown Mackie College–Atlanta

6600 Peachtree Dunwoody Road NE, 600 Embassy Row, Atlanta, GA 30328
http://www.brownmackie.edu/Atlanta/

CONTACT Robert Campbell, President
Telephone: 770-510-2310

GENERAL INFORMATION Private Institution. **Accreditation:** State accredited or approved. **Total program enrollment:** 665.

PROGRAM(S) OFFERED
• Accounting Technology/Technician and Bookkeeping • Allied Health and Medical Assisting Services, Other • Business/Commerce, General • Criminal Justice/Law Enforcement Administration • Legal Assistant/Paralegal 4 students enrolled

STUDENT SERVICES Academic or career counseling, employment services for current students, placement services for program completers, remedial services.

Central Georgia Technical College

3300 Macon Tech Drive, Macon, GA 31206-3628
http://www.centralgatech.edu/

CONTACT Dr. Ronald Natale, President
Telephone: 478-757-3400

GENERAL INFORMATION Public Institution. Founded 1966. **Accreditation:** Regional (SACS/CC); dental hygiene (ADA); medical laboratory technology (NAACLS); state accredited or approved. **Total program enrollment:** 2722. **Application fee:** $15.

PROGRAM(S) OFFERED
• Accounting Technology/Technician and Bookkeeping 13 students enrolled
• Administrative Assistant and Secretarial Science, General 19 students enrolled • Aesthetician/Esthetician and Skin Care Specialist 15 students enrolled • Airframe Mechanics and Aircraft Maintenance Technology/Technician 58 students enrolled • Animation, Interactive Technology, Video Graphics and Special Effects 2 students enrolled • Autobody/Collision and

Repair Technology/Technician 6 students enrolled • Automobile/Automotive Mechanics Technology/Technician 18 students enrolled • Barbering/Barber 1 student enrolled • Cabinetmaking and Millwork/Millwright 3 students enrolled • Carpentry/Carpenter 3 students enrolled • Child Care Provider/Assistant 11 students enrolled • Child Care and Support Services Management 16 students enrolled • Computer Installation and Repair Technology/Technician 37 students enrolled • Computer Systems Networking and Telecommunications 67 students enrolled • Construction Management 1 student enrolled • Cosmetology, Barber/Styling, and Nail Instructor 2 students enrolled • Cosmetology/Cosmetologist, General • Criminal Justice/Police Science 4 students enrolled • Criminal Justice/Safety Studies 14 students enrolled • Customer Service Support/Call Center/Teleservice Operation 2 students enrolled • Data Entry/Microcomputer Applications, General 15 students enrolled • Drafting and Design Technology/Technician, General 2 students enrolled • Early Childhood Education and Teaching 18 students enrolled • Electrical/Electronics Equipment Installation and Repair, General 8 students enrolled • Electrical/Electronics Maintenance and Repair Technology, Other 1 student enrolled • Electrician 20 students enrolled • Electroneurodiagnostic/Electroencephalographic Technology/Technologist 24 students enrolled • Emergency Medical Technology/Technician (EMT Paramedic) 19 students enrolled • Entrepreneurship/Entrepreneurial Studies 3 students enrolled • Food Preparation/Professional Cooking/Kitchen Assistant 11 students enrolled • Heating, Air Conditioning, Ventilation and Refrigeration Maintenance Technology/Technician (HAC, HACR, HVAC, HVACR) 107 students enrolled • Home Health Aide/Home Attendant 18 students enrolled • Hospitality Administration/Management, General 2 students enrolled • Industrial Mechanics and Maintenance Technology 68 students enrolled • Instrumentation Technology/Technician 6 students enrolled • Insurance 3 students enrolled • Legal Administrative Assistant/Secretary 2 students enrolled • Logistics and Materials Management 8 students enrolled • Marine Maintenance/Fitter and Ship Repair Technology/Technician 6 students enrolled • Mason/Masonry 1 student enrolled • Medical Insurance Coding Specialist/Coder 58 students enrolled • Medical Reception/Receptionist 57 students enrolled • Medical Transcription/Transcriptionist 15 students enrolled • Medical/Clinical Assistant 76 students enrolled • Medical/Health Management and Clinical Assistant/Specialist 40 students enrolled • Nail Technician/Specialist and Manicurist 3 students enrolled • Nurse/Nursing Assistant/Aide and Patient Care Assistant 98 students enrolled • Operations Management and Supervision 8 students enrolled • Pharmacy Technician/Assistant 4 students enrolled • Phlebotomy/Phlebotomist 22 students enrolled • Plumbing Technology/Plumber 6 students enrolled • Radiologic Technology/Science—Radiographer 24 students enrolled • Renal/Dialysis Technologist/Technician 29 students enrolled • Sales, Distribution and Marketing Operations, General 1 student enrolled • Surgical Technology/Technologist 7 students enrolled • Web Page, Digital/Multimedia and Information Resources Design 1 student enrolled • Welding Technology/Welder 2 students enrolled

STUDENT SERVICES Academic or career counseling, placement services for program completers, remedial services.

Chattahoochee Technical College

980 South Cobb Drive, Marietta, GA 30060
http://www.chattcollege.com/

CONTACT Kary Porter, President
Telephone: 770-528-4545

GENERAL INFORMATION Public Institution. Founded 1961. **Accreditation:** Regional (SACS/CC); engineering technology (ABET/TAC). **Total program enrollment:** 2602. **Application fee:** $15.

PROGRAM(S) OFFERED
• Accounting Technology/Technician and Bookkeeping 125 students enrolled • Administrative Assistant and Secretarial Science, General 26 students enrolled • Applied Horticulture/Horticultural Operations, General 1 student enrolled • Architectural Drafting and Architectural CAD/CADD 28 students enrolled • Automobile/Automotive Mechanics Technology/Technician 224 students enrolled • Carpentry/Carpenter 10 students enrolled • Child Care Provider/Assistant 29 students enrolled • Child Care and Support Services Management 8 students enrolled • Computer Installation and Repair Technology/Technician 2 students enrolled • Computer Programming, Specific Applications 3 students enrolled • Computer Systems Networking and Telecommunications 19 students enrolled • Computer and Information Systems Security 1 student enrolled • Cosmetology/Cosmetologist, General 35 students enrolled • Criminal Justice/Safety Studies 26 students enrolled • Customer Service Support/Call Center/Teleservice Operation 3 students enrolled • Data Entry/Microcomputer Applications, General 39 students enrolled • Drafting and Design Technology/Technician, General 47 students enrolled • Early Childhood Education and Teaching 22 students enrolled • Electrician 34 students enrolled • Emergency Medical Technology/Technician (EMT Paramedic) 2 students enrolled • Food Preparation/Professional Cooking/Kitchen Assistant 66 students enrolled • Heating, Air Conditioning, Ventilation and Refrigeration

Chattahoochee Technical College (continued)

Maintenance Technology/Technician (HAC, HACR, HVAC, HVACR) *56 students enrolled* • Landscaping and Groundskeeping *3 students enrolled* • Mechanical Drafting and Mechanical Drafting CAD/CADD *38 students enrolled* • Medical/Clinical Assistant *14 students enrolled* • Motorcycle Maintenance and Repair Technology/Technician *106 students enrolled* • Nurse/Nursing Assistant/Aide and Patient Care Assistant *2 students enrolled* • Operations Management and Supervision *54 students enrolled* • Radio and Television Broadcasting Technology/Technician *46 students enrolled* • Sales, Distribution and Marketing Operations, General *5 students enrolled* • Small Business Administration/Management *77 students enrolled* • Surgical Technology/Technologist *13 students enrolled* • Web Page, Digital/Multimedia and Information Resources Design *2 students enrolled*

STUDENT SERVICES Academic or career counseling, daycare for children of students, employment services for current students, placement services for program completers, remedial services.

Clayton State University

5900 North Lee Street, Morrow, GA 30260-0285
http://www.clayton.edu/

CONTACT Dr. Thomas Harden, President
Telephone: 678-466-4000

GENERAL INFORMATION Public Institution. Founded 1969. **Accreditation:** Regional (SACS/CC); dental hygiene (ADA). **Total program enrollment:** 3397. **Application fee:** $40.

PROGRAM(S) OFFERED
• Computer Systems Networking and Telecommunications *6 students enrolled*
• Drafting and Design Technology/Technician, General *2 students enrolled*
• General Office Occupations and Clerical Services *5 students enrolled* • Legal Assistant/Paralegal *22 students enrolled* • Medical/Clinical Assistant *10 students enrolled* • Sales, Distribution and Marketing Operations, General *2 students enrolled*

STUDENT SERVICES Academic or career counseling, employment services for current students, placement services for program completers, remedial services.

Cobb Beauty College

3096 Cherokee Street, Kennesaw, GA 30144-2828
http://www.cobbbeautycollege.com/

CONTACT Larry Little, President
Telephone: 770-424-6915

GENERAL INFORMATION Private Institution. Founded 1980. **Total program enrollment:** 35. **Application fee:** $100.

PROGRAM(S) OFFERED
• Cosmetology, Barber/Styling, and Nail Instructor *1500 hrs./$8800*
• Cosmetology/Cosmetologist, General *1500 hrs./$11,750*

STUDENT SERVICES Academic or career counseling, employment services for current students, placement services for program completers.

College of Coastal Georgia

3700 Altama Avenue, Brunswick, GA 31520
http://www.ccga.edu/home.html

CONTACT Dr. Valerie Hepburn, Interim President
Telephone: 912-279-5701

GENERAL INFORMATION Public Institution. Founded 1961. **Accreditation:** Regional (SACS/CC); medical laboratory technology (NAACLS); radiologic technology: radiography (JRCERT). **Total program enrollment:** 1061. **Application fee:** $20.

PROGRAM(S) OFFERED
• Administrative Assistant and Secretarial Science, General *7 students enrolled*
• Autobody/Collision and Repair Technology/Technician *1 student enrolled*
• Automobile/Automotive Mechanics Technology/Technician *4 students enrolled*
• Banking and Financial Support Services *3 students enrolled* • Business Administration and Management, General *4 students enrolled* • Criminal Justice/Police Science *12 students enrolled* • Culinary Arts/Chef Training *7 students enrolled* • Drafting and Design Technology/Technician, General *2 students enrolled* • Emergency Medical Technology/Technician (EMT Paramedic) *2 students enrolled* • Heating, Air Conditioning, Ventilation and Refrigeration Maintenance Technology/Technician (HAC, HACR, HVAC, HVACR) *5 students enrolled* • Industrial Mechanics and Maintenance Technology *1 student enrolled* • Information Technology *5 students enrolled* • Instrumentation Technology/Technician *2 students enrolled* • Licensed Practical/Vocational Nurse Training (LPN, LVN, Cert, Dipl, AAS) *24 students enrolled* • Machine Shop Technology/Assistant *1 student enrolled* • Nurse/Nursing Assistant/Aide and Patient Care Assistant *21 students enrolled* • Surgical Technology/Technologist *8 students enrolled* • Welding Technology/Welder *1 student enrolled*

STUDENT SERVICES Academic or career counseling, employment services for current students, placement services for program completers, remedial services.

Columbus State University

4225 University Avenue, Columbus, GA 31907-5645
http://www.colstate.edu/

CONTACT Tim Mescon, President
Telephone: 706-568-2001

GENERAL INFORMATION Public Institution. Founded 1958. **Accreditation:** Regional (SACS/CC); art and design (NASAD); counseling (ACA); music (NASM); theater (NAST). **Total program enrollment:** 5105. **Application fee:** $25.

PROGRAM(S) OFFERED
• African Studies *1 student enrolled* • Criminal Justice/Safety Studies *92 students enrolled*

STUDENT SERVICES Academic or career counseling, employment services for current students, placement services for program completers, remedial services.

Columbus Technical College

928 Manchester Expressway, Columbus, GA 31904-6572
http://www.columbustech.edu/

CONTACT J. Robert Jones, President
Telephone: 706-649-1800

GENERAL INFORMATION Public Institution. Founded 1961. **Accreditation:** Regional (SACS/CC); dental hygiene (ADA); surgical technology (ARCST). **Total program enrollment:** 1572. **Application fee:** $25.

PROGRAM(S) OFFERED
• Accounting Technology/Technician and Bookkeeping *2 students enrolled*
• Administrative Assistant and Secretarial Science, General *1 student enrolled*
• Appliance Installation and Repair Technology/Technician *7 students enrolled*
• Applied Horticulture/Horticultural Operations, General *4 students enrolled*
• Autobody/Collision and Repair Technology/Technician *3 students enrolled*
• Automobile/Automotive Mechanics Technology/Technician *3 students enrolled*
• Banking and Financial Support Services *10 students enrolled* • Cabinetmaking and Millwork/Millwright *2 students enrolled* • Carpentry/Carpenter *4 students enrolled* • Child Care Provider/Assistant *5 students enrolled* • Computer Installation and Repair Technology/Technician *9 students enrolled* • Computer Systems Networking and Telecommunications *10 students enrolled*
• Cosmetology/Cosmetologist, General *30 students enrolled* • Customer Service Support/Call Center/Teleservice Operation *35 students enrolled* • Dental Assisting/Assistant *25 students enrolled* • Drafting and Design Technology/Technician, General *3 students enrolled* • Early Childhood Education and Teaching *7 students enrolled* • General Office Occupations and Clerical Services *13 students enrolled* • Heating, Air Conditioning, Ventilation and Refrigeration Maintenance Technology/Technician (HAC, HACR, HVAC, HVACR) *11 students enrolled* • Hospitality Administration/Management, General *21 students enrolled* • Industrial Mechanics and Maintenance Technol-

ogy 35 students enrolled • **Insurance** 177 students enrolled • **Landscaping and Groundskeeping** 7 students enrolled • **Logistics and Materials Management** 12 students enrolled • **Machine Shop Technology/Assistant** 2 students enrolled • **Medical Insurance Coding Specialist/Coder** 28 students enrolled • **Medical Office Assistant/Specialist** 28 students enrolled • **Medical Reception/ Receptionist** 18 students enrolled • **Medical/Clinical Assistant** 17 students enrolled • **Nurse/Nursing Assistant/Aide and Patient Care Assistant** 36 students enrolled • **Operations Management and Supervision** 5 students enrolled • **Pharmacy Technician/Assistant** 8 students enrolled • **Phlebotomy/ Phlebotomist** 13 students enrolled • **Surgical Technology/Technologist** 15 students enrolled • **Web Page, Digital/Multimedia and Information Resources Design** 5 students enrolled • **Welding Technology/Welder** 12 students enrolled

STUDENT SERVICES Academic or career counseling, employment services for current students, placement services for program completers, remedial services.

Coosa Valley Technical College

One Maurice Culberson Drive, Rome, GA 30161
http://www.coosavalleytech.edu/

CONTACT F. Craig McDaniel, EdD, President
Telephone: 706-295-6963

GENERAL INFORMATION Public Institution. Founded 1962. **Accreditation:** State accredited or approved. **Total program enrollment:** 1351. **Application fee:** $15.

PROGRAM(S) OFFERED
• **Accounting Technology/Technician and Bookkeeping** 87 students enrolled • **Administrative Assistant and Secretarial Science, General** 27 students enrolled • **Applied Horticulture/Horticultural Operations, General** 1 student enrolled • **Architectural Drafting and Architectural CAD/CADD** 3 students enrolled • **Autobody/Collision and Repair Technology/Technician** 19 students enrolled • **Automobile/Automotive Mechanics Technology/Technician** 85 students enrolled • **CAD/CADD Drafting and/or Design Technology/Technician** 2 students enrolled • **Cabinetmaking and Millwork/Millwright** 5 students enrolled • **Carpentry/Carpenter** 2 students enrolled • **Child Care Provider/Assistant** 13 students enrolled • **Child Care and Support Services Management** 3 students enrolled • **Civil Engineering Technology/Technician** 12 students enrolled • **Computer Installation and Repair Technology/Technician** 4 students enrolled • **Computer Programming, Specific Applications** 1 student enrolled • **Computer Systems Networking and Telecommunications** 11 students enrolled • **Construction Management** 13 students enrolled • **Cosmetology/Cosmetologist, General** 42 students enrolled • **Criminal Justice/Safety Studies** 18 students enrolled • **Customer Service Support/Call Center/Teleservice Operation** 45 students enrolled • **Data Entry/Microcomputer Applications, General** 54 students enrolled • **Data Processing and Data Processing Technology/Technician** 4 students enrolled • **Dental Assisting/Assistant** 14 students enrolled • **Drafting and Design Technology/Technician, General** 4 students enrolled • **Early Childhood Education and Teaching** 8 students enrolled • **Electrician** 6 students enrolled • **Emergency Medical Technology/Technician (EMT Paramedic)** 7 students enrolled • **Entrepreneurship/Entrepreneurial Studies** 6 students enrolled • **Fire Science/Firefighting** 52 students enrolled • **General Office Occupations and Clerical Services** 26 students enrolled • **Heating, Air Conditioning, Ventilation and Refrigeration Maintenance Technology/Technician (HAC, HACR, HVAC, HVACR)** 7 students enrolled • **Industrial Mechanics and Maintenance Technology** 2 students enrolled • **Machine Shop Technology/Assistant** 3 students enrolled • **Manufacturing Technology/Technician** 2 students enrolled • **Massage Therapy/ Therapeutic Massage** 7 students enrolled • **Mechanical Drafting and Mechanical Drafting CAD/CADD** 1 student enrolled • **Medical Insurance Coding Specialist/Coder** 17 students enrolled • **Medical Reception/Receptionist** 12 students enrolled • **Medical Transcription/Transcriptionist** 27 students enrolled • **Medical/Clinical Assistant** 31 students enrolled • **Nuclear Medical Technology/Technologist** 12 students enrolled • **Nurse/Nursing Assistant/Aide and Patient Care Assistant** 9 students enrolled • **Operations Management and Supervision** 15 students enrolled • **Phlebotomy/Phlebotomist** 22 students enrolled • **Radiologic Technology/Science—Radiographer** 8 students enrolled • **Sales, Distribution and Marketing Operations, General** 2 students enrolled • **Selling Skills and Sales Operations** 3 students enrolled • **Small Business Administration/Management** 2 students enrolled • **Surgical Technology/ Technologist** 15 students enrolled • **Truck and Bus Driver/Commercial Vehicle Operation** 33 students enrolled • **Web Page, Digital/Multimedia and Information Resources Design** 3 students enrolled • **Welding Technology/Welder** 5 students enrolled

STUDENT SERVICES Academic or career counseling, employment services for current students, placement services for program completers, remedial services.

Dalton State College

213 North College Drive, Dalton, GA 30720-3797
http://www.daltonstate.edu/

CONTACT John O. Schwenn, President
Telephone: 706-272-4436

GENERAL INFORMATION Public Institution. Founded 1963. **Accreditation:** Regional (SACS/CC); medical assisting (AAMAE); medical laboratory technology (NAACLS). **Total program enrollment:** 2705. **Application fee:** $30.

PROGRAM(S) OFFERED
• **Automobile/Automotive Mechanics Technology/Technician** 6 students enrolled • **Business Operations Support and Secretarial Services, Other** 8 students enrolled • **Business/Office Automation/Technology/Data Entry** 3 students enrolled • **Child Care and Support Services Management** 3 students enrolled • **Computer Engineering Technology/Technician** 4 students enrolled • **Drafting and Design Technology/Technician, General** 2 students enrolled • **Electrical/ Electronics Equipment Installation and Repair, General** 10 students enrolled • **General Office Occupations and Clerical Services** 4 students enrolled • **Licensed Practical/Vocational Nurse Training (LPN, LVN, Cert, Dipl, AAS)** 35 students enrolled • **Medical Radiologic Technology/Science—Radiation Therapist** 1 student enrolled • **Medical/Clinical Assistant** 20 students enrolled • **Small Business Administration/Management** 12 students enrolled • **Welding Technology/Welder** 2 students enrolled

STUDENT SERVICES Academic or career counseling, employment services for current students, placement services for program completers, remedial services.

Darton College

2400 Gillionville Road, Albany, GA 31707-3098
http://www.darton.edu/

CONTACT Peter J. Sireno, President
Telephone: 229-317-6000

GENERAL INFORMATION Public Institution. Founded 1965. **Accreditation:** Regional (SACS/CC); dental hygiene (ADA); health information technology (AHIMA); histologic technology (NAACLS); medical laboratory technology (NAACLS); physical therapy assisting (APTA). **Total program enrollment:** 2277. **Application fee:** $20.

PROGRAM(S) OFFERED
• **Accounting Technology/Technician and Bookkeeping** 1 student enrolled • **Administrative Assistant and Secretarial Science, General** 3 students enrolled • **Art/Art Studies, General** 1 student enrolled • **Business/Commerce, General** 1 student enrolled • **Counselor Education/School Counseling and Guidance Services** 1 student enrolled • **Emergency Medical Technology/Technician (EMT Paramedic)** 7 students enrolled • **Health Information/Medical Records Technology/Technician** 6 students enrolled • **Histologic Technician** 17 students enrolled • **Legal Assistant/Paralegal** 2 students enrolled • **Management Information Systems, General** 2 students enrolled • **Marketing, Other** 2 students enrolled • **Marketing/Marketing Management, General** 2 students enrolled • **Phlebotomy/Phlebotomist** 4 students enrolled • **Religious/Sacred Music** 1 student enrolled • **Respiratory Care Therapy/Therapist** 5 students enrolled • **Social Work** 5 students enrolled

STUDENT SERVICES Academic or career counseling, employment services for current students, remedial services.

DeKalb Technical College

495 North Indian Creek Drive, Clarkston, GA 30021-2397
http://www.dekalbtech.edu/

CONTACT Robin Hoffman, President
Telephone: 404-297-9522 Ext. 1127

GENERAL INFORMATION Public Institution. Founded 1961. **Accreditation:** Regional (SACS/CC); engineering technology (ABET/TAC); medical laboratory technology (NAACLS); ophthalmic dispensing (COA). **Total program enrollment:** 1551. **Application fee:** $20.

DeKalb Technical College *(continued)*

PROGRAM(S) OFFERED
- Accounting Technology/Technician and Bookkeeping 57 *students enrolled* • Administrative Assistant and Secretarial Science, General 10 *students enrolled* • Architectural Drafting and Architectural CAD/CADD 2 *students enrolled* • Automobile/Automotive Mechanics Technology/Technician 164 *students enrolled* • Banking and Financial Support Services 22 *students enrolled* • Carpentry/Carpenter 12 *students enrolled* • Child Care Provider/Assistant 2 *students enrolled* • Child Care and Support Services Management 11 *students enrolled* • Communications Systems Installation and Repair Technology 16 *students enrolled* • Computer Engineering Technology/Technician 17 *students enrolled* • Computer Installation and Repair Technology/Technician 5 *students enrolled* • Computer Programming, Specific Applications 1 *student enrolled* • Computer Systems Networking and Telecommunications 33 *students enrolled* • Computer and Information Systems Security 4 *students enrolled* • Cosmetology/Cosmetologist, General 50 *students enrolled* • Criminal Justice/Police Science 8 *students enrolled* • Criminal Justice/Safety Studies 3 *students enrolled* • Customer Service Support/Call Center/Teleservice Operation 32 *students enrolled* • Data Entry/Microcomputer Applications, General 29 *students enrolled* • Drafting and Design Technology/Technician, General 13 *students enrolled* • Early Childhood Education and Teaching 13 *students enrolled* • Electrical/Electronics Equipment Installation and Repair, General 21 *students enrolled* • Emergency Medical Technology/Technician (EMT Paramedic) 3 *students enrolled* • Graphic and Printing Equipment Operator, General Production 23 *students enrolled* • Heating, Air Conditioning, Ventilation and Refrigeration Maintenance Technology/Technician (HAC, HACR, HVAC, HVACR) 37 *students enrolled* • Hospitality Administration/Management, General 4 *students enrolled* • Human Resources Management/Personnel Administration, General 13 *students enrolled* • Industrial Mechanics and Maintenance Technology 24 *students enrolled* • Legal Administrative Assistant/Secretary 10 *students enrolled* • Legal Assistant/Paralegal 11 *students enrolled* • Lineworker 49 *students enrolled* • Machine Shop Technology/Assistant 3 *students enrolled* • Mechanical Drafting and Mechanical Drafting CAD/CADD 4 *students enrolled* • Medical/Clinical Assistant 6 *students enrolled* • Motorcycle Maintenance and Repair Technology/Technician 15 *students enrolled* • Nurse/Nursing Assistant/Aide and Patient Care Assistant 62 *students enrolled* • Operations Management and Supervision 28 *students enrolled* • Opticianry/Ophthalmic Dispensing Optician 31 *students enrolled* • Phlebotomy/Phlebotomist 18 *students enrolled* • Prepress/Desktop Publishing and Digital Imaging Design 7 *students enrolled* • Sales, Distribution and Marketing Operations, General 1 *student enrolled* • Small Business Administration/Management 3 *students enrolled* • Surgical Technology/Technologist 9 *students enrolled* • Truck and Bus Driver/Commercial Vehicle Operation 122 *students enrolled* • Welding Technology/Welder 30 *students enrolled* • Wood Science and Wood Products/Pulp and Paper Technology 4 *students enrolled*

STUDENT SERVICES Academic or career counseling, employment services for current students, placement services for program completers, remedial services.

East Central Technical College

667 Perry House Road, Fitzgerald, GA 31750
http://www.eastcentraltech.edu/

CONTACT E. J. Harris, President
Telephone: 229-468-2000

GENERAL INFORMATION Public Institution. Founded 1968. **Accreditation:** State accredited or approved. **Total program enrollment:** 643. **Application fee:** $15.

PROGRAM(S) OFFERED
- Accounting Technology/Technician and Bookkeeping 3 *students enrolled* • Administrative Assistant and Secretarial Science, General 31 *students enrolled* • Automobile/Automotive Mechanics Technology/Technician 2 *students enrolled* • Building/Property Maintenance and Management • Cartography • Communications Systems Installation and Repair Technology 49 *students enrolled* • Computer Programming, Specific Applications • Computer Programming/Programmer, General 2 *students enrolled* • Computer Systems Networking and Telecommunications 4 *students enrolled* • Computer and Information Systems Security • Cosmetology/Cosmetologist, General 11 *students enrolled* • Criminal Justice/Police Science • Criminal Justice/Safety Studies 15 *students enrolled* • Data Entry/Microcomputer Applications, General 29 *students enrolled* • Early Childhood Education and Teaching 10 *students enrolled* • Electrician 25 *students enrolled* • Heating, Air Conditioning, Ventilation and Refrigeration Maintenance Technology/Technician (HAC, HACR, HVAC, HVACR) 10 *students enrolled* • Home Health Aide/Home Attendant 6 *students enrolled* • Industrial Mechanics and Maintenance Technology 5 *students enrolled* • Medical Reception/Receptionist 1 *student enrolled* • Medical/Clinical Assistant 7 *students enrolled* • Nail Technician/Specialist and Manicur-

ist 6 *students enrolled* • Nurse/Nursing Assistant/Aide and Patient Care Assistant 63 *students enrolled* • Pharmacy Technician/Assistant 7 *students enrolled* • Phlebotomy/Phlebotomist 26 *students enrolled* • Sales, Distribution and Marketing Operations, General 1 *student enrolled* • Truck and Bus Driver/Commercial Vehicle Operation 77 *students enrolled* • Web Page, Digital/Multimedia and Information Resources Design 2 *students enrolled* • Welding Technology/Welder 20 *students enrolled*

STUDENT SERVICES Academic or career counseling, daycare for children of students, employment services for current students, placement services for program completers, remedial services.

East Georgia College

131 College Circle, Swainsboro, GA 30401-2699
http://www.ega.edu/

CONTACT Dr. John B. Black, President
Telephone: 478-289-2000

GENERAL INFORMATION Public Institution. Founded 1973. **Accreditation:** Regional (SACS/CC). **Total program enrollment:** 2000. **Application fee:** $20.

STUDENT SERVICES Academic or career counseling, employment services for current students, placement services for program completers, remedial services.

Empire Beauty School–Dunwoody

4719 Ashford-Dunwoody Road, Suite 205, Dunwoody, GA 30338
http://www.empire.edu/

CONTACT Michael Bouman, President
Telephone: 570-429-4321 Ext. 2414

GENERAL INFORMATION Private Institution. **Total program enrollment:** 98. **Application fee:** $100.

PROGRAM(S) OFFERED
- Cosmetology/Cosmetologist, General 1530 *hrs./$18,845*

STUDENT SERVICES Placement services for program completers.

Empire Beauty School–Kennesaw

425 Ernest Barrett Parkway, Suite H-2, Kennesaw, GA 30144
http://www.empire.edu/

CONTACT Michael Bouman, President
Telephone: 800-223-3271

GENERAL INFORMATION Private Institution. **Total program enrollment:** 90. **Application fee:** $100.

PROGRAM(S) OFFERED
- Cosmetology, Barber/Styling, and Nail Instructor 750 *hrs./$8625*
- Cosmetology/Cosmetologist, General 1530 *hrs./$19,845* • Technical Teacher Education 5 *students enrolled*

STUDENT SERVICES Placement services for program completers.

Empire Beauty School–Lawrenceville

1455 Pleasant Hill Road, Suite 105, Lawrenceville, GA 30044
http://www.empire.edu/

CONTACT Michael Bouman, President
Telephone: 800-223-3271

GENERAL INFORMATION Private Institution. **Total program enrollment:** 88. **Application fee:** $100.

PROGRAM(S) OFFERED
• Cosmetology/Cosmetologist, General *1530 hrs./$18,845* • Technical Teacher Education *5 students enrolled*

STUDENT SERVICES Placement services for program completers.

The Esani Institute

1003 Mansell Road, Roswell, GA 30076

CONTACT Arlene Lyons, CEO
Telephone: 678-795-0999

GENERAL INFORMATION Private Institution. Total program enrollment: 127. Application fee: $50.

PROGRAM(S) OFFERED
• Aesthetician/Esthetician and Skin Care Specialist *1000 hrs./$8950*
• Cosmetology, Barber/Styling, and Nail Instructor *1500 hrs./$18,450*
• Cosmetology/Cosmetologist, General

STUDENT SERVICES Academic or career counseling, placement services for program completers.

The Esani Institution

4971 Courtney Drive, Forest Park, GA 30050
http://www.arnold-padricks.com/

CONTACT Arlene Lyons, Owner
Telephone: 404-361-5641

GENERAL INFORMATION Private Institution. Founded 1965. Total program enrollment: 98. Application fee: $50.

PROGRAM(S) OFFERED
• Cosmetology, Barber/Styling, and Nail Instructor *750 hrs./$5965*
• Cosmetology/Cosmetologist, General *1500 hrs./$12,900*

Everest Institute

1706 Northeast Expressway, Atlanta, GA 30329
http://www.everest.edu/

CONTACT Tira Harney Clay, President
Telephone: 404-327-8787 Ext. 137

GENERAL INFORMATION Private Institution. Founded 1977. Accreditation: State accredited or approved. Total program enrollment: 682.

PROGRAM(S) OFFERED
• Massage Therapy/Therapeutic Massage *740 hrs./$13,750* • Medical Insurance Coding Specialist/Coder *720 hrs./$12,575* • Medical Office Management/Administration *720 hrs./$12,575* • Medical/Clinical Assistant *720 hrs./$14,620* • Renal/Dialysis Technologist/Technician *720 hrs./$13,668* • Respiratory Therapy Technician/Assistant *1670 hrs./$13,500*

STUDENT SERVICES Academic or career counseling, employment services for current students, placement services for program completers.

Everest Institute

6431 Tara Boulevard, Jonesboro, GA 30236-1214
http://www.everest.edu/

CONTACT Bryan Gulebian, School President
Telephone: 770-603-0000

GENERAL INFORMATION Private Institution. Total program enrollment: 1255.

PROGRAM(S) OFFERED
• Dental Assisting/Assistant *48 students enrolled* • Massage Therapy/Therapeutic Massage *780 hrs./$14,790* • Medical Administrative/Executive Assistant and Medical Secretary *720 hrs./$13,526* • Medical Insurance

Specialist/Medical Biller *720 hrs./$13,526* • Medical/Clinical Assistant *720 hrs./$14,641* • Nurse/Nursing Assistant/Aide and Patient Care Assistant *720 hrs./$13,249* • Pharmacy Technician/Assistant *720 hrs./$12,656*

STUDENT SERVICES Employment services for current students, placement services for program completers.

Everest Institute

1600 Terrell Mill Road, Suite D, Marietta, GA 30067
http://www.everest.edu/

CONTACT Liana Lusson, President
Telephone: 770-303-7997

GENERAL INFORMATION Private Institution. Total program enrollment: 701.

PROGRAM(S) OFFERED
• Allied Health and Medical Assisting Services, Other *47 hrs./$13,526*
• Health and Medical Administrative Services, Other *47 hrs./$13,526* • Massage Therapy/Therapeutic Massage *50 hrs./$14,790* • Medical Office Assistant/Specialist *81 students enrolled* • Medical/Clinical Assistant *168 students enrolled* • Surgical Technology/Technologist *1200 hrs./$28,794*

STUDENT SERVICES Academic or career counseling, employment services for current students, placement services for program completers.

Everest Institute

1750 Beaver Ruin Road, Norcross, GA 30093
http://www.everest.edu/

CONTACT Larry Veeneman, President
Telephone: 770-921-1085

GENERAL INFORMATION Private Institution. Total program enrollment: 386.

PROGRAM(S) OFFERED
• Dental Assisting/Assistant *720 hrs./$13,714* • Massage Therapy/Therapeutic Massage *55 hrs./$14,790* • Medical Insurance Coding Specialist/Coder *720 hrs./$13,526* • Medical Office Assistant/Specialist *720 hrs./$13,526* • Medical/Clinical Assistant *47 hrs./$14,517*

STUDENT SERVICES Academic or career counseling, employment services for current students, placement services for program completers, remedial services.

Fayette Beauty Academy

386 N. Glynn Street, Fayetteville, GA 30214
http://www.fayettebeautyacademy.com/

CONTACT Barbara Heaton, Owner
Telephone: 770-461-4669

GENERAL INFORMATION Private Institution. Total program enrollment: 38. Application fee: $100.

PROGRAM(S) OFFERED
• Cosmetology/Cosmetologist, General *1500 hrs./$8000*

STUDENT SERVICES Placement services for program completers.

Flint River Technical College

1533 US highway 19 South, Thomaston, GA 30286
http://www.flintrivertech.edu/

CONTACT Kathy S. Love, President
Telephone: 706-646-6148

GENERAL INFORMATION Public Institution. Founded 1961. Accreditation: State accredited or approved. Total program enrollment: 492. Application fee: $15.

Flint River Technical College (continued)

PROGRAM(S) OFFERED
● Accounting Technology/Technician and Bookkeeping *1 student enrolled* ● Administrative Assistant and Secretarial Science, General *30 students enrolled* ● Aesthetician/Esthetician and Skin Care Specialist *2 students enrolled* ● Automobile/Automotive Mechanics Technology/Technician *26 students enrolled* ● Banking and Financial Support Services *3 students enrolled* ● Barbering/Barber *1 student enrolled* ● Carpentry/Carpenter *11 students enrolled* ● Child Care Provider/Assistant *14 students enrolled* ● Child Care and Support Services Management *10 students enrolled* ● Civil Engineering Technology/Technician *2 students enrolled* ● Computer Systems Networking and Telecommunications *6 students enrolled* ● Cosmetology/Cosmetologist, General *17 students enrolled* ● Criminal Justice/Safety Studies *5 students enrolled* ● Customer Service Support/Call Center/Teleservice Operation *12 students enrolled* ● Data Entry/Microcomputer Applications, General *22 students enrolled* ● Early Childhood Education and Teaching *17 students enrolled* ● Electrical/Electronics Equipment Installation and Repair, General *6 students enrolled* ● Electrician *1 student enrolled* ● Graphic and Printing Equipment Operator, General Production *1 student enrolled* ● Heating, Air Conditioning, Ventilation and Refrigeration Maintenance Technology/Technician (HAC, HACR, HVAC, HVACR) *8 students enrolled* ● Industrial Mechanics and Maintenance Technology *1 student enrolled* ● Lineworker *10 students enrolled* ● Machine Shop Technology/Assistant *1 student enrolled* ● Medical Insurance Coding Specialist/Coder *4 students enrolled* ● Medical Reception/Receptionist *1 student enrolled* ● Medical Transcription/Transcriptionist *2 students enrolled* ● Medical/Clinical Assistant *30 students enrolled* ● Nail Technician/Specialist and Manicurist *4 students enrolled* ● Nurse/Nursing Assistant/Aide and Patient Care Assistant *142 students enrolled* ● Operations Management and Supervision *4 students enrolled* ● Phlebotomy/Phlebotomist *6 students enrolled* ● Surgical Technology/Technologist *5 students enrolled* ● Truck and Bus Driver/Commercial Vehicle Operation *105 students enrolled* ● Web Page, Digital/Multimedia and Information Resources Design *1 student enrolled* ● Welding Technology/Welder *26 students enrolled*

STUDENT SERVICES Academic or career counseling, daycare for children of students, employment services for current students, placement services for program completers, remedial services.

Gainesville State College

PO Box 1358, Gainesville, GA 30503-1358
http://www.gc.peachnet.edu/

CONTACT Martha T. Nesbitt, President
Telephone: 678-717-3639

GENERAL INFORMATION Public Institution. Founded 1964. **Accreditation:** Regional (SACS/CC); dental assisting (ADA). **Total program enrollment:** 5438. **Application fee:** $25.

PROGRAM(S) OFFERED
● Geography *9 students enrolled* ● Health and Physical Education/Fitness, Other *2 students enrolled* ● Legal Assistant/Paralegal *15 students enrolled*

STUDENT SERVICES Academic or career counseling, employment services for current students, placement services for program completers, remedial services.

Georgia Career Institute

1820 Highway 20, Suite 200, Conyers, GA 30208
http://gci.edu/

CONTACT Cory Erks, Financial Aid Director
Telephone: 770-922-7653

GENERAL INFORMATION Private Institution. Founded 1975. **Total program enrollment:** 1165.

PROGRAM(S) OFFERED
● Aesthetician/Esthetician and Skin Care Specialist *1000 hrs./$9700* ● Cosmetology, Barber/Styling, and Nail Instructor *750 hrs./$3750* ● Cosmetology/Cosmetologist, General *1500 hrs./$14,500* ● Massage Therapy/Therapeutic Massage *900 hrs./$11,250* ● Nail Technician/Specialist and Manicurist *620 hrs./$5700*

STUDENT SERVICES Academic or career counseling, employment services for current students, placement services for program completers.

Georgia Highlands College

3175 Cedartown Highway, SE, PO Box 1864, Rome, GA 30162-1864
http://www.highlands.edu/

CONTACT Randy Pierce, President
Telephone: 800-332-2406

GENERAL INFORMATION Public Institution. Founded 1970. **Accreditation:** Regional (SACS/CC); dental hygiene (ADA). **Total program enrollment:** 2653. **Application fee:** $20.

STUDENT SERVICES Academic or career counseling, employment services for current students, remedial services.

Georgia Institute of Cosmetology

3341 Lexington Road, Athens, GA 30605
http://gicschool.com/

CONTACT Fiesal Elkabbani, President
Telephone: 706-549-6400 Ext. 25

GENERAL INFORMATION Private Institution. Founded 1991. **Total program enrollment:** 100. **Application fee:** $100.

PROGRAM(S) OFFERED
● Cosmetology/Cosmetologist, General *1500 hrs./$17,420*

STUDENT SERVICES Placement services for program completers.

Georgia Perimeter College

3251 Panthersville Road, Decatur, GA 30034-3897
http://www.gpc.edu/

CONTACT Anthony S. Tricoli, President
Telephone: 678-891-2300

GENERAL INFORMATION Public Institution. Founded 1964. **Accreditation:** Regional (SACS/CC); dental hygiene (ADA). **Total program enrollment:** 9828. **Application fee:** $20.

PROGRAM(S) OFFERED
● Sign Language Interpretation and Translation *4 students enrolled*

STUDENT SERVICES Academic or career counseling, employment services for current students, placement services for program completers, remedial services.

Georgia Southwestern State University

800 Georgia Southwestern State University Drive, Americus, GA 31709-4693
http://www.gsw.edu/

CONTACT Kendall Blanchard, President
Telephone: 229-928-1279

GENERAL INFORMATION Public Institution. Founded 1906. **Accreditation:** Regional (SACS/CC). **Total program enrollment:** 1988. **Application fee:** $25.

PROGRAM(S) OFFERED
● Social Sciences, Other *1 student enrolled* ● Web Page, Digital/Multimedia and Information Resources Design *1 student enrolled* ● Women's Studies *1 student enrolled*

STUDENT SERVICES Academic or career counseling, employment services for current students, placement services for program completers, remedial services.

Georgia State University

PO Box 3965, Atlanta, GA 30303-3083
http://www.gsu.edu/

CONTACT Mark P. Becker, President
Telephone: 404-413-2000

GENERAL INFORMATION Public Institution. Founded 1913. **Accreditation:** Regional (SACS/CC); art and design (NASAD); counseling (ACA); dietetics: postbaccalaureate internship (ADtA/CAADE); music (NASM); speech-language pathology (ASHA). **Total program enrollment:** 20039. **Application fee:** $50.

STUDENT SERVICES Academic or career counseling, daycare for children of students, employment services for current students, placement services for program completers, remedial services.

Grady Health System

80 Butler Street, SE, PO Box 26095, Atlanta, GA 30335-3801
http://www.gradyhealthsystem.org/

CONTACT Michael A. Young, President & Chief Executive Officer
Telephone: 404-616-3505

GENERAL INFORMATION Public Institution. Founded 1940. **Total program enrollment:** 83. **Application fee:** $35.

PROGRAM(S) OFFERED
• Allied Health Diagnostic, Intervention, and Treatment Professions, Other 10 *students enrolled* • Diagnostic Medical Sonography/Sonographer and Ultrasound Technician 7 *students enrolled*

STUDENT SERVICES Academic or career counseling, employment services for current students, placement services for program completers.

Griffin Technical College

501 Varsity Road, Griffin, GA 30223
http://www.griffintech.edu/

CONTACT Dr. Robert H. Arnold, President
Telephone: 770-228-7348

GENERAL INFORMATION Public Institution. Founded 1965. **Accreditation:** Regional (SACS/CC); surgical technology (ARCST); state accredited or approved. **Total program enrollment:** 1884. **Application fee:** $15.

PROGRAM(S) OFFERED
• Accounting Technology/Technician and Bookkeeping 11 *students enrolled* • Administrative Assistant and Secretarial Science, General 18 *students enrolled* • Aesthetician/Esthetician and Skin Care Specialist • Applied Horticulture/Horticultural Operations, General 4 *students enrolled* • Autobody/Collision and Repair Technology/Technician 1 *student enrolled* • Automobile/Automotive Mechanics Technology/Technician 152 *students enrolled* • CAD/CADD Drafting and/or Design Technology/Technician 2 *students enrolled* • Cabinetmaking and Millwork/Millwright 2 *students enrolled* • Carpentry/Carpenter 30 *students enrolled* • Child Care Provider/Assistant 2 *students enrolled* • Child Care and Support Services Management • Communications Systems Installation and Repair Technology 7 *students enrolled* • Computer Installation and Repair Technology/Technician 14 *students enrolled* • Computer Systems Networking and Telecommunications 5 *students enrolled* • Construction Management 2 *students enrolled* • Cosmetology/Cosmetologist, General 48 *students enrolled* • Criminal Justice/Safety Studies 15 *students enrolled* • Data Entry/Microcomputer Applications, General 9 *students enrolled* • Data Processing and Data Processing Technology/Technician 4 *students enrolled* • Dental Assisting/Assistant 14 *students enrolled* • Early Childhood Education and Teaching 14 *students enrolled* • Electrician 19 *students enrolled* • Electrocardiograph Technology/Technician 9 *students enrolled* • Electroneurodiagnostic/Electroencephalographic Technology/Technologist 14 *students enrolled* • Emergency Medical Technology/Technician (EMT Paramedic) 4 *students enrolled* • Entrepreneurship/Entrepreneurial Studies 19 *students enrolled* • Fire Science/Firefighting 13 *students enrolled* • Graphic and Printing Equipment Operator, General Production 6 *students enrolled* • Heating, Air Conditioning, Ventilation and Refrigeration Maintenance Technology/Technician (HAC, HACR, HVAC, HVACR) 19 *students enrolled* • Home Health Aide/Home Attendant 2 *students enrolled* • Human Resources Management/

Personnel Administration, General 17 *students enrolled* • Industrial Mechanics and Maintenance Technology 9 *students enrolled* • Landscaping and Groundskeeping 2 *students enrolled* • Machine Shop Technology/Assistant 5 *students enrolled* • Medical Insurance Coding Specialist/Coder 14 *students enrolled* • Medical Insurance Specialist/Medical Biller 11 *students enrolled* • Medical Transcription/Transcriptionist 5 *students enrolled* • Medical/Clinical Assistant 36 *students enrolled* • Nail Technician/Specialist and Manicurist 8 *students enrolled* • Nurse/Nursing Assistant/Aide and Patient Care Assistant 93 *students enrolled* • Operations Management and Supervision 1 *student enrolled* • Pharmacy Technician/Assistant 12 *students enrolled* • Phlebotomy/Phlebotomist 31 *students enrolled* • Renal/Dialysis Technologist/Technician 11 *students enrolled* • Small Engine Mechanics and Repair Technology/Technician 13 *students enrolled* • Surgical Technology/Technologist 23 *students enrolled* • Truck and Bus Driver/Commercial Vehicle Operation 207 *students enrolled* • Welding Technology/Welder 3 *students enrolled*

STUDENT SERVICES Academic or career counseling, employment services for current students, placement services for program completers, remedial services.

Gwinnett College

4230 Highway 29, Suite 11, Lilburn, GA 30047
http://www.gwinnettcollege.edu/

CONTACT Michael Davis, President
Telephone: 770-381-7200

GENERAL INFORMATION Private Institution. Founded 1976. **Total program enrollment:** 254.

PROGRAM(S) OFFERED
• Accounting 6 *students enrolled* • Administrative Assistant and Secretarial Science, General 1 *student enrolled* • Business Administration and Management, General 2 *students enrolled* • Data Entry/Microcomputer Applications, General • Legal Administrative Assistant/Secretary • Legal Assistant/Paralegal • Massage Therapy/Therapeutic Massage 13 *students enrolled* • Medical Office Assistant/Specialist 5 *students enrolled* • Medical/Clinical Assistant 7 *students enrolled*

STUDENT SERVICES Academic or career counseling, employment services for current students, placement services for program completers.

Gwinnett Technical College

5150 Sugarloaf Parkway, PO Box 1505, Lawrenceville, GA 30046-1505
http://www.gwinnetttech.edu/

CONTACT Sharon Bartels, President
Telephone: 770-962-7580

GENERAL INFORMATION Public Institution. Founded 1984. **Accreditation:** Regional (SACS/CC); dental assisting (ADA); physical therapy assisting (APTA); radiologic technology: radiography (JRCERT). **Total program enrollment:** 2498. **Application fee:** $20.

PROGRAM(S) OFFERED
• Accounting Technology/Technician and Bookkeeping 14 *students enrolled* • Administrative Assistant and Secretarial Science, General 4 *students enrolled* • Animation, Interactive Technology, Video Graphics and Special Effects 3 *students enrolled* • Apparel and Accessories Marketing Operations 5 *students enrolled* • Applied Horticulture/Horticultural Operations, General 2 *students enrolled* • Automobile/Automotive Mechanics Technology/Technician 179 *students enrolled* • Banking and Financial Support Services 10 *students enrolled* • Biology Technician/Biotechnology Laboratory Technician 20 *students enrolled* • Building/Home/Construction Inspection/Inspector 18 *students enrolled* • CAD/CADD Drafting and/or Design Technology/Technician 49 *students enrolled* • Cabinetmaking and Millwork/Millwright 1 *student enrolled* • Carpentry/Carpenter 52 *students enrolled* • Child Care Provider/Assistant 1 *student enrolled* • Commercial Photography 6 *students enrolled* • Computer Installation and Repair Technology/Technician 153 *students enrolled* • Computer Programming, Specific Applications 20 *students enrolled* • Computer Systems Networking and Telecommunications 100 *students enrolled* • Computer and Information Systems Security 18 *students enrolled* • Construction Management 53 *students enrolled* • Cosmetology/Cosmetologist, General 11 *students enrolled* • Data Processing and Data Processing Technology/Technician 14 *students enrolled* • Dental Assisting/Assistant 41 *students enrolled* • Dental Laboratory Technology/Technician 10 *students*

Gwinnett Technical College (continued)

enrolled • **Drafting and Design Technology/Technician, General** *2 students enrolled* • **Early Childhood Education and Teaching** *4 students enrolled* • **Emergency Medical Technology/Technician (EMT Paramedic)** *151 students enrolled* • **Entrepreneurship/Entrepreneurial Studies** *26 students enrolled* • **Floriculture/Floristry Operations and Management** *2 students enrolled* • **Food Preparation/Professional Cooking/Kitchen Assistant** *21 students enrolled* • **General Office Occupations and Clerical Services** *24 students enrolled* • **Greenhouse Operations and Management** *2 students enrolled* • **Heating, Air Conditioning, Ventilation and Refrigeration Maintenance Technology/Technician (HAC, HACR, HVAC, HVACR)** *112 students enrolled* • **Heavy Equipment Maintenance Technology/Technician** *8 students enrolled* • **Hospitality Administration/Management, General** *44 students enrolled* • **Human Resources Management/Personnel Administration, General** *40 students enrolled* • **Interior Design** *7 students enrolled* • **Landscaping and Groundskeeping** *8 students enrolled* • **Machine Shop Technology/Assistant** *25 students enrolled* • **Medical Office Assistant/Specialist** *21 students enrolled* • **Medical Reception/Receptionist** *47 students enrolled* • **Medical Transcription/Transcriptionist** *8 students enrolled* • **Medical/Clinical Assistant** *20 students enrolled* • **Nurse/Nursing Assistant/Aide and Patient Care Assistant** *189 students enrolled* • **Operations Management and Supervision** *53 students enrolled* • **Parks, Recreation and Leisure Facilities Management** *6 students enrolled* • **Plant Nursery Operations and Management** *1 student enrolled* • **Radiologic Technology/Science—Radiographer** *6 students enrolled* • **Restaurant/Food Services Management** *7 students enrolled* • **Retailing and Retail Operations** *3 students enrolled* • **Sales, Distribution and Marketing Operations, General** *13 students enrolled* • **Selling Skills and Sales Operations** *26 students enrolled* • **Small Business Administration/Management** *7 students enrolled* • **Sport and Fitness Administration/Management** *4 students enrolled* • **Surgical Technology/Technologist** *19 students enrolled* • **Technical and Business Writing** *4 students enrolled* • **Tourism and Travel Services Management** *6 students enrolled* • **Veterinary/Animal Health Technology/Technician and Veterinary Assistant** *15 students enrolled* • **Web Page, Digital/Multimedia and Information Resources Design** *16 students enrolled* • **Welding Technology/Welder** *52 students enrolled*

STUDENT SERVICES Academic or career counseling, daycare for children of students, employment services for current students, placement services for program completers, remedial services.

Heart of Georgia Technical College

560 Pinehill Road, Dublin, GA 31021
http://www.heartofgatech.edu/

CONTACT Randall Peters, President
Telephone: 478-275-6589

GENERAL INFORMATION Public Institution. Founded 1984. **Accreditation:** Regional (SACS/CC); state accredited or approved. **Total program enrollment:** 595. **Application fee:** $15.

PROGRAM(S) OFFERED
• **Accounting Technology/Technician and Bookkeeping** *8 students enrolled* • **Administrative Assistant and Secretarial Science, General** *22 students enrolled* • **Applied Horticulture/Horticultural Operations, General** *5 students enrolled* • **Autobody/Collision and Repair Technology/Technician** *3 students enrolled* • **Automobile/Automotive Mechanics Technology/Technician** *10 students enrolled* • **Business Administration, Management and Operations, Other** *2 students enrolled* • **CAD/CADD Drafting and/or Design Technology/Technician** *2 students enrolled* • **Carpentry/Carpenter** *7 students enrolled* • **Child Care Provider/Assistant** *1 student enrolled* • **Child Care and Support Services Management** *1 student enrolled* • **Communications Systems Installation and Repair Technology** *2 students enrolled* • **Computer Installation and Repair Technology/Technician** *22 students enrolled* • **Computer Systems Networking and Telecommunications** *5 students enrolled* • **Criminal Justice/Safety Studies** *43 students enrolled* • **Customer Service Support/Call Center/Teleservice Operation** *16 students enrolled* • **Data Entry/Microcomputer Applications, General** *4 students enrolled* • **Early Childhood Education and Teaching** *10 students enrolled* • **Electrical/Electronics Equipment Installation and Repair, General** *25 students enrolled* • **Electrician** *6 students enrolled* • **Food Preparation/Professional Cooking/Kitchen Assistant** *9 students enrolled* • **Health Information/Medical Records Technology/Technician** *2 students enrolled* • **Heating, Air Conditioning, Ventilation and Refrigeration Maintenance Technology/Technician (HAC, HACR, HVAC, HVACR)** *5 students enrolled* • **Industrial Mechanics and Maintenance Technology** *8 students enrolled* • **Machine Shop Technology/Assistant** *1 student enrolled* • **Medical Insurance Coding Specialist/Coder** *8 students enrolled* • **Medical/Clinical Assistant** *12 students enrolled* • **Medium/Heavy Vehicle and Truck Technology/Technician** *11 students enrolled* • **Nurse/Nursing Assistant/Aide and Patient**

Care Assistant *63 students enrolled* • **Pharmacy Technician/Assistant** *9 students enrolled* • **Teacher Assistant/Aide** *2 students enrolled* • **Truck and Bus Driver/Commercial Vehicle Operation** *98 students enrolled* • **Welding Technology/Welder** *8 students enrolled*

STUDENT SERVICES Academic or career counseling, daycare for children of students, employment services for current students, placement services for program completers, remedial services.

Herzing College

3355 Lenox Road, Suite 100, Atlanta, GA 30326
http://www.herzing.edu/atlanta/

CONTACT Frank Webster, Campus President
Telephone: 404-816-4533 Ext. 116

GENERAL INFORMATION Private Institution. Founded 1949. **Accreditation:** State accredited or approved. **Total program enrollment:** 227.

PROGRAM(S) OFFERED
• **Medical Insurance Coding Specialist/Coder**

STUDENT SERVICES Academic or career counseling, employment services for current students, placement services for program completers, remedial services.

Hi-Tech Institute – Atlanta

1090 Northchase Parkway, Suite 150, Marietta, GA 30067

CONTACT Melissa Gray, Executive Assistant
Telephone: 678-279-7000

GENERAL INFORMATION Private Institution. Founded 2001. **Total program enrollment:** 212. **Application fee:** $50.

PROGRAM(S) OFFERED
• **Computer and Information Systems Security** *1620 hrs./$28,333* • **Massage Therapy/Therapeutic Massage** *8 students enrolled* • **Medical Insurance Specialist/Medical Biller** *720 hrs./$10,831* • **Medical/Clinical Assistant** *746 hrs./$10,536* • **Pharmacy Technician/Assistant** *5 students enrolled* • **Surgical Technology/Technologist** *1160 hrs./$22,446*

STUDENT SERVICES Placement services for program completers.

Interactive College of Technology

5303 New Peachtree Road, Chamblee, GA 30341
http://www.ict-ils.edu/

CONTACT Elmer R. Smith, President
Telephone: 770-216-2960

GENERAL INFORMATION Private Institution. **Accreditation:** State accredited or approved. **Total program enrollment:** 284. **Application fee:** $50.

PROGRAM(S) OFFERED
• **Accounting Technology/Technician and Bookkeeping** *6 students enrolled* • **Administrative Assistant and Secretarial Science, General** • **Computer and Information Sciences and Support Services, Other** *11 students enrolled* • **Computer and Information Sciences, General** *9 students enrolled* • **Heating, Air Conditioning and Refrigeration Technology/Technician (ACH/ACR/ACHR/HRAC/HVAC/AC Technology)** *91 students enrolled* • **Management Information Systems and Services, Other**

STUDENT SERVICES Academic or career counseling, employment services for current students, placement services for program completers, remedial services.

Interactive College of Technology

4814 Old National Highway, College Park, GA 30337
http://www.ict-ils.edu/

CONTACT Elmer R. Smith, President
Telephone: 770-960-1298

GENERAL INFORMATION Private Institution. **Total program enrollment:** 49. **Application fee:** $50.

PROGRAM(S) OFFERED
• **Accounting and Related Services, Other** *2 students enrolled* • **Administrative Assistant and Secretarial Science, General** *1 student enrolled* • **Computer Programming/Programmer, General** • **Computer and Information Sciences, General** *11 students enrolled*

STUDENT SERVICES Academic or career counseling, employment services for current students, placement services for program completers, remedial services.

Interactive College of Technology

2323-c Browns Bridge Road, Gainesville, GA 30504
http://www.ict-ils.edu/

CONTACT Elmer R. Smith, President
Telephone: 678-450-0550

GENERAL INFORMATION Private Institution. **Total program enrollment:** 38. **Application fee:** $50.

PROGRAM(S) OFFERED
• **Accounting Technology/Technician and Bookkeeping** • **Administrative Assistant and Secretarial Science, General** • **Computer Programming/Programmer, General** • **Computer and Information Sciences, General** *5 students enrolled*

STUDENT SERVICES Academic or career counseling, employment services for current students, placement services for program completers, remedial services.

International City Beauty College

1859 Watson Boulevard, Warner Robins, GA 31093

CONTACT Elfriede Goble, President
Telephone: 478-923-0915

GENERAL INFORMATION Private Institution. **Total program enrollment:** 34.

PROGRAM(S) OFFERED
• **Cosmetology and Related Personal Grooming Arts, Other** • **Cosmetology/Cosmetologist, General** *1500 hrs./$7631*

STUDENT SERVICES Academic or career counseling, employment services for current students, placement services for program completers.

International School of Skin and Nailcare

5600 Roswell Road, NE, Atlanta, GA 30342
http://www.skin-nails.com/

CONTACT Alan Shinall, Owner Director
Telephone: 404-843-1005 Ext. 106

GENERAL INFORMATION Private Institution. Founded 1985. **Total program enrollment:** 314. **Application fee:** $100.

PROGRAM(S) OFFERED
• **Aesthetician/Esthetician and Skin Care Specialist** *1000 hrs./$8695* • **Cosmetology, Barber/Styling, and Nail Instructor** *300 hrs./$2000* • **Facial Treatment Specialist/Facialist** • **Massage Therapy/Therapeutic Massage** *675 hrs./$5995* • **Nail Technician/Specialist and Manicurist** *600 hrs./$2900*

STUDENT SERVICES Academic or career counseling, employment services for current students, placement services for program completers.

Iverson Business School

6685 Peachtree Industrial, Atlanta, GA 30360
http://www.iversonschool.edu

CONTACT Alex Mithani, President and CEO
Telephone: 770-446-1333

GENERAL INFORMATION Private Institution. **Total program enrollment:** 214. **Application fee:** $100.

PROGRAM(S) OFFERED
• **Administrative Assistant and Secretarial Science, General** • **Computer Systems Networking and Telecommunications** • **General Office Occupations and Clerical Services** *3 students enrolled* • **Legal Assistant/Paralegal** *7 students enrolled* • **Medical Insurance Coding Specialist/Coder** *16 students enrolled* • **Medical Transcription/Transcriptionist** • **Medical/Clinical Assistant** *4 students enrolled* • **Pharmacy Technician/Assistant** • **Surgical Technology/Technologist** *7 students enrolled*

STUDENT SERVICES Placement services for program completers.

Javelin Technical Training Center

4501 Circle 75 Parkway, Suite C-3180, Atlanta, GA 30339
http://www.javelintraining.com/

CONTACT Robyn Taylor, Chief Executive Officer
Telephone: 770-859-9779

GENERAL INFORMATION Private Institution. **Total program enrollment:** 953.

PROGRAM(S) OFFERED
• **Computer Programming, Vendor/Product Certification** *480 hrs./$8895* • **Computer and Information Sciences and Support Services, Other** *520 hrs./$10,895* • **General Office Occupations and Clerical Services** *500 hrs./$10,295* • **Medical Insurance Coding Specialist/Coder** *720 hrs./$15,995* • **Medical Office Assistant/Specialist** *720 hrs./$17,995*

STUDENT SERVICES Academic or career counseling, employment services for current students, placement services for program completers.

Lanier Technical College

2990 Landrum Education Drive, PO Box 58, Oakwood, GA 30566
http://www.laniertech.edu/

CONTACT Dr. Michael D. Moye, President
Telephone: 770-531-6300

GENERAL INFORMATION Public Institution. Founded 1964. **Accreditation:** Dental assisting (ADA); dental hygiene (ADA); medical laboratory technology (NAACLS); state accredited or approved. **Total program enrollment:** 1109. **Application fee:** $15.

PROGRAM(S) OFFERED
• **Accounting Technology/Technician and Bookkeeping** *7 students enrolled* • **Administrative Assistant and Secretarial Science, General** *35 students enrolled* • **Aesthetician/Esthetician and Skin Care Specialist** *10 students enrolled* • **Architectural Drafting and Architectural CAD/CADD** *10 students enrolled* • **Autobody/Collision and Repair Technology/Technician** *3 students enrolled* • **Automobile/Automotive Mechanics Technology/Technician** *25 students enrolled* • **Banking and Financial Support Services** *3 students enrolled* • **CAD/CADD Drafting and/or Design Technology/Technician** *6 students enrolled* • **Child Care Provider/Assistant** *11 students enrolled* • **Child Care and Support Services Management** *2 students enrolled* • **Communications Systems Installation and Repair Technology** *1 student enrolled* • **Computer Installation and Repair Technology/Technician** *8 students enrolled* • **Computer Systems Networking and Telecommunications** *29 students enrolled* • **Cosmetology/Cosmetologist, General** *51 students enrolled* • **Criminal Justice/Safety Studies** *8 students enrolled* • **Data Entry/Microcomputer Applications, General** *24 students enrolled* • **Data Processing and Data Processing Technology/Technician** *7 students enrolled* • **Dental Assisting/Assistant** *5 students enrolled* • **Drafting and Design Technology/Technician, General** *16 students enrolled* • **Early Childhood Education and Teaching** *2 students enrolled* • **Electrical/Electronics Equipment Installation and Repair, General** *1 student enrolled* • **Electrician** *2 students enrolled* • **Emergency Medical Technology/Technician (EMT Paramedic)** *92 students enrolled* • **Entrepreneurship/Entrepreneurial Studies** *3 students enrolled* • **Fire Science/Firefighting** *18 students enrolled*

Lanier Technical College (continued)

• **Forestry Technology/Technician** • **General Office Occupations and Clerical Services** *4 students enrolled* • **Graphic and Printing Equipment Operator, General Production** *12 students enrolled* • **Heating, Air Conditioning, Ventilation and Refrigeration Maintenance Technology/Technician (HAC, HACR, HVAC, HVACR)** *8 students enrolled* • **Industrial Mechanics and Maintenance Technology** *20 students enrolled* • **Interior Design** *5 students enrolled* • **Landscaping and Groundskeeping** *1 student enrolled* • **Machine Shop Technology/Assistant** *3 students enrolled* • **Medical Administrative/Executive Assistant and Medical Secretary** *15 students enrolled* • **Medical Insurance Coding Specialist/Coder** *9 students enrolled* • **Medical Office Assistant/Specialist** • **Medical Reception/Receptionist** *33 students enrolled* • **Medical Transcription/Transcriptionist** *11 students enrolled* • **Medical/Clinical Assistant** *88 students enrolled* • **Nurse/Nursing Assistant/Aide and Patient Care Assistant** *41 students enrolled* • **Operations Management and Supervision** *4 students enrolled* • **Pharmacy Technician/Assistant** *8 students enrolled* • **Phlebotomy/Phlebotomist** *24 students enrolled* • **Plumbing Technology/Plumber** *2 students enrolled* • **Prepress/Desktop Publishing and Digital Imaging Design** *2 students enrolled* • **Sales, Distribution and Marketing Operations, General** *3 students enrolled* • **Small Business Administration/Management** *11 students enrolled* • **Surgical Technology/Technologist** *24 students enrolled* • **Turf and Turfgrass Management** • **Web Page, Digital/Multimedia and Information Resources Design** *2 students enrolled* • **Welding Technology/Welder** *30 students enrolled*

STUDENT SERVICES Academic or career counseling, employment services for current students, placement services for program completers, remedial services.

Laurus Technical Institute

1150 Lake Hearn Drive, Suite 260, Atlanta, GA 30342
http://www.eticareers.com/

CONTACT Walter Hess, President
Telephone: 404-303-2929

GENERAL INFORMATION Private Institution. Founded 1985. **Total program enrollment:** 174. **Application fee:** $25.

PROGRAM(S) OFFERED
• **Heating, Air Conditioning, Ventilation and Refrigeration Maintenance Technology/Technician (HAC, HACR, HVAC, HVACR)** *720 hrs./$14,750* • **Medical Insurance Specialist/Medical Biller** *720 hrs./$14,550* • **Medical Office Assistant/Specialist** *720 hrs./$14,550* • **Medical Reception/Receptionist** *720 hrs./$14,550*

STUDENT SERVICES Academic or career counseling, employment services for current students, placement services for program completers.

Le Cordon Bleu College of Culinary Arts, Atlanta

1957 Lakeside Parkway, Tucker, GA 30084
http://www.atlantaculinary.com/

CONTACT Peter Lee, President
Telephone: 770-938-4711

GENERAL INFORMATION Private Institution. **Total program enrollment:** 962. **Application fee:** $50.

PROGRAM(S) OFFERED
• **Baking and Pastry Arts/Baker/Pastry Chef** *51 hrs./$18,525* • **Culinary Arts/Chef Training** *100 hrs./$39,500*

STUDENT SERVICES Academic or career counseling, employment services for current students, placement services for program completers.

Macon State College

100 College Station Drive, Macon, GA 31206
http://www.maconstate.edu/

CONTACT David A. Bell, President
Telephone: 478-471-2700

GENERAL INFORMATION Public Institution. Founded 1968. **Accreditation:** Regional (SACS/CC); health information technology (AHIMA). **Total program enrollment:** 3157. **Application fee:** $20.

PROGRAM(S) OFFERED
• **Business Administration and Management, General** *2 students enrolled*
• **Business/Commerce, General** *17 students enrolled* • **Computer and Informa-**

tion Sciences and Support Services, Other *14 students enrolled* • **Criminal Justice/Police Science** *1 student enrolled* • **Operations Management and Supervision** *9 students enrolled* • **Teacher Assistant/Aide** *10 students enrolled*

STUDENT SERVICES Academic or career counseling, employment services for current students, placement services for program completers, remedial services.

Medical College of Georgia

1120 15th Street, Augusta, GA 30912
http://www.mcg.edu/

CONTACT Daniel W. Rahn, President
Telephone: 706-721-0211

GENERAL INFORMATION Public Institution. Founded 1828. **Accreditation:** Regional (SACS/CC); dental hygiene (ADA); diagnostic medical sonography (JRCEDMS); health information administration (AHIMA); medical technology (NAACLS); nuclear medicine technology (JRCNMT); radiologic technology: radiation therapy technology (JRCERT); radiologic technology: radiography (JRCERT). **Total program enrollment:** 2237. **Application fee:** $30.

PROGRAM(S) OFFERED
• **Health Information/Medical Records Administration/Administrator** *9 students enrolled* • **Nuclear Medical Technology/Technologist** *3 students enrolled*

STUDENT SERVICES Academic or career counseling, daycare for children of students, employment services for current students, placement services for program completers.

Medix School

2108 Cobb Parkway SE, Smyrna, GA 30080
http://medixschool.edu/

CONTACT William Armour, School Director
Telephone: 770-980-0002

GENERAL INFORMATION Private Institution. Founded 1968. **Total program enrollment:** 685. **Application fee:** $50.

PROGRAM(S) OFFERED
• **Dental Assisting/Assistant** *1035 hrs./$11,702* • **Emergency Medical Technology/Technician (EMT Paramedic)** *1020 hrs./$6165* • **Health Professions and Related Clinical Sciences, Other** *76 students enrolled* • **Heating, Air Conditioning and Refrigeration Technology/Technician (ACH/ACR/ACHR/HRAC/HVAC/AC Technology)** *1000 hrs./$12,567* • **Medical Office Management/Administration** *1035 hrs./$12,812* • **Medical/Clinical Assistant** *1035 hrs./$10,765* • **Nurse/Nursing Assistant/Aide and Patient Care Assistant** *75 students enrolled* • **Pharmacy Technician/Assistant** *46 students enrolled*

STUDENT SERVICES Academic or career counseling, employment services for current students, placement services for program completers, remedial services.

Michael's School of Beauty

630 North Avenue, Suite J, Macon, GA 31211
http://michaelsschoolofbeauty.com/

CONTACT Barry Broadnax, Director
Telephone: 706-342-9673

GENERAL INFORMATION Private Institution. **Total program enrollment:** 70. **Application fee:** $100.

PROGRAM(S) OFFERED
• **Cosmetology, Barber/Styling, and Nail Instructor** *750 hrs./$7600*
• **Cosmetology/Cosmetologist, General** *1500 hrs./$10,000*

STUDENT SERVICES Placement services for program completers.

Middle Georgia College

1100 Second Street, SE, Cochran, GA 31014-1599
http://www.mgc.edu/

CONTACT Dr. W. Michael Stoy, President
Telephone: 478-934-6221

GENERAL INFORMATION Public Institution. Founded 1884. **Accreditation:** Regional (SACS/CC). **Total program enrollment:** 2416. **Application fee:** $20.

PROGRAM(S) OFFERED
● **Aeronautics/Aviation/Aerospace Science and Technology, General** 1 student enrolled ● **Aircraft Powerplant Technology/Technician** 25 students enrolled ● **Airframe Mechanics and Aircraft Maintenance Technology/Technician** 50 students enrolled ● **Avionics Maintenance Technology/Technician** 12 students enrolled ● **Survey Technology/Surveying** 16 students enrolled

STUDENT SERVICES Academic or career counseling, employment services for current students, placement services for program completers, remedial services.

Middle Georgia Technical College

80 Cohen Walker Drive, Warner Robbins, GA 31088
http://www.middlegatech.edu/

CONTACT Ivan H. Allen, President
Telephone: 478-988-6800

GENERAL INFORMATION Public Institution. Founded 1973. **Accreditation:** Regional (SACS/CC); dental assisting (ADA); dental hygiene (ADA); state accredited or approved. **Total program enrollment:** 1395. **Application fee:** $15.

PROGRAM(S) OFFERED
● **Accounting Technology/Technician and Bookkeeping** 7 students enrolled ● **Administrative Assistant and Secretarial Science, General** 27 students enrolled ● **Airframe Mechanics and Aircraft Maintenance Technology/Technician** 46 students enrolled ● **Architectural Drafting and Architectural CAD/CADD** 7 students enrolled ● **Automobile/Automotive Mechanics Technology/Technician** 50 students enrolled ● **Banking and Financial Support Services** 3 students enrolled ● **Barbering/Barber** 2 students enrolled ● **CAD/CADD Drafting and/or Design Technology/Technician** 3 students enrolled ● **Child Care Provider/Assistant** 1 student enrolled ● **Computer Installation and Repair Technology/Technician** 27 students enrolled ● **Computer Programming, Specific Applications** 3 students enrolled ● **Computer Systems Networking and Telecommunications** 9 students enrolled ● **Cosmetology, Barber/Styling, and Nail Instructor** 2 students enrolled ● **Cosmetology/Cosmetologist, General** 35 students enrolled ● **Criminal Justice/Safety Studies** ● **Customer Service Support/Call Center/Teleservice Operation** 1071 students enrolled ● **Data Modeling/Warehousing and Database Administration** 2 students enrolled ● **Data Processing and Data Processing Technology/Technician** 15 students enrolled ● **Dental Assisting/Assistant** 9 students enrolled ● **Drafting and Design Technology/Technician, General** 5 students enrolled ● **Early Childhood Education and Teaching** 22 students enrolled ● **Electrical/Electronics Equipment Installation and Repair, General** 5 students enrolled ● **Entrepreneurship/Entrepreneurial Studies** 1 student enrolled ● **Food Preparation/Professional Cooking/Kitchen Assistant** 8 students enrolled ● **General Office Occupations and Clerical Services** 12 students enrolled ● **Heating, Air Conditioning, Ventilation and Refrigeration Maintenance Technology/Technician (HAC, HACR, HVAC, HVACR)** 40 students enrolled ● **Industrial Mechanics and Maintenance Technology** 14 students enrolled ● **Legal Assistant/Paralegal** 10 students enrolled ● **Machine Shop Technology/Assistant** 4 students enrolled ● **Mechanical Drafting and Mechanical Drafting CAD/CADD** 4 students enrolled ● **Medical Insurance Specialist/Medical Biller** 32 students enrolled ● **Medical Office Assistant/Specialist** 24 students enrolled ● **Medical Transcription/Transcriptionist** 4 students enrolled ● **Medical/Clinical Assistant** 3 students enrolled ● **Nuclear Medical Technology/Technologist** 7 students enrolled ● **Nurse/Nursing Assistant/Aide and Patient Care Assistant** 1 student enrolled ● **Plumbing Technology/Plumber** 40 students enrolled ● **Sales, Distribution and Marketing Operations, General** 3 students enrolled ● **Small Business Administration/Management** 2 students enrolled ● **Surgical Technology/Technologist** 1 student enrolled ● **Truck and Bus Driver/Commercial Vehicle Operation** 105 students enrolled ● **Web Page, Digital/Multimedia and Information Resources Design** 1 student enrolled ● **Welding Technology/Welder** 5 students enrolled

STUDENT SERVICES Academic or career counseling, employment services for current students, placement services for program completers, remedial services.

Moultrie Technical College

800 Veterans Parkway North, Moultrie, GA 31788
http://www.moultrietech.edu/

CONTACT Dr. Tina Anderson, President
Telephone: 229-891-7000

GENERAL INFORMATION Public Institution. Founded 1964. **Accreditation:** State accredited or approved. **Total program enrollment:** 1054. **Application fee:** $15.

PROGRAM(S) OFFERED
● **Accounting Technology/Technician and Bookkeeping** 55 students enrolled ● **Administrative Assistant and Secretarial Science, General** 44 students enrolled ● **Aesthetician/Esthetician and Skin Care Specialist** 5 students enrolled ● **Agricultural Business Technology** 1 student enrolled ● **Applied Horticulture/Horticultural Operations, General** 3 students enrolled ● **Autobody/Collision and Repair Technology/Technician** 11 students enrolled ● **Automobile/Automotive Mechanics Technology/Technician** 55 students enrolled ● **Banking and Financial Support Services** 21 students enrolled ● **CAD/CADD Drafting and/or Design Technology/Technician** 4 students enrolled ● **Cabinetmaking and Millwork/Millwright** 1 student enrolled ● **Carpentry/Carpenter** 17 students enrolled ● **Child Care Provider/Assistant** 10 students enrolled ● **Civil Engineering Technology/Technician** 1 student enrolled ● **Communications Systems Installation and Repair Technology** 30 students enrolled ● **Computer Installation and Repair Technology/Technician** 18 students enrolled ● **Cosmetology/Cosmetologist, General** 45 students enrolled ● **Criminal Justice/Safety Studies** 15 students enrolled ● **Data Entry/Microcomputer Applications, General** 12 students enrolled ● **Drafting and Design Technology/Technician, General** 5 students enrolled ● **Early Childhood Education and Teaching** 28 students enrolled ● **Electrical/Electronics Equipment Installation and Repair, General** 1 student enrolled ● **Electrician** 33 students enrolled ● **Emergency Medical Technology/Technician (EMT Paramedic)** 10 students enrolled ● **Entrepreneurship/Entrepreneurial Studies** 4 students enrolled ● **Fire Science/Firefighting** 31 students enrolled ● **Floriculture/Floristry Operations and Management** 15 students enrolled ● **General Office Occupations and Clerical Services** 42 students enrolled ● **Heating, Air Conditioning, Ventilation and Refrigeration Maintenance Technology/Technician (HAC, HACR, HVAC, HVACR)** 3 students enrolled ● **Industrial Mechanics and Maintenance Technology** 7 students enrolled ● **Interior Design** 4 students enrolled ● **Landscaping and Groundskeeping** 27 students enrolled ● **Massage Therapy/Therapeutic Massage** 4 students enrolled ● **Medical Insurance Coding Specialist/Coder** 21 students enrolled ● **Medical Reception/Receptionist** 25 students enrolled ● **Medical Transcription/Transcriptionist** 17 students enrolled ● **Medical/Clinical Assistant** 16 students enrolled ● **Nail Technician/Specialist and Manicurist** 1 student enrolled ● **Nurse/Nursing Assistant/Aide and Patient Care Assistant** 40 students enrolled ● **Operations Management and Supervision** 3 students enrolled ● **Plant Nursery Operations and Management** 2 students enrolled ● **Plumbing Technology/Plumber** 4 students enrolled ● **Sales, Distribution and Marketing Operations, General** 8 students enrolled ● **Small Business Administration/Management** 5 students enrolled ● **Surgical Technology/Technologist** 4 students enrolled ● **Truck and Bus Driver/Commercial Vehicle Operation** 80 students enrolled ● **Turf and Turfgrass Management** 2 students enrolled ● **Web Page, Digital/Multimedia and Information Resources Design** 4 students enrolled ● **Welding Technology/Welder** 3 students enrolled ● **Word Processing** 34 students enrolled

STUDENT SERVICES Academic or career counseling, employment services for current students, placement services for program completers, remedial services.

New Horizons Computer Learning Centers

211 Perimeter Center Parkway, Suite 200, Atlanta, GA 30346
http://www.nhgeorgia.com/LocalWeb/content/
Locations.aspx?TemplateId=587&GroupId=398

CONTACT Dee Austin, Academic Dean
Telephone: 770-226-0056

GENERAL INFORMATION Private Institution. **Total program enrollment:** 393. **Application fee:** $100.

PROGRAM(S) OFFERED
● **Computer Systems Networking and Telecommunications** 10 students enrolled ● **Criminal Justice/Safety Studies** 78 hrs./$18,125 ● **Electrical/Electronics Maintenance and Repair Technology, Other** 52 hrs./$17,589 ● **Industrial Electronics Technology/Technician** 70 hrs./$21,099 ● **Massage Therapy/Therapeutic Massage** 38 hrs./$12,360 ● **Medical Insurance Coding Specialist/Coder** 2 students enrolled ● **Medical/Clinical Assistant** 46 hrs./$14,314

STUDENT SERVICES Placement services for program completers.

North Georgia Technical College

1500 Georgia Highway 197, North, PO Box 65, Clarkesville, GA 30523
http://www.northgatech.edu/

CONTACT Steve Dougherty, President
Telephone: 706-754-7700

GENERAL INFORMATION Public Institution. Founded 1943. **Accreditation:** Medical laboratory technology (NAACLS); state accredited or approved. **Total program enrollment:** 1229. **Application fee:** $15.

PROGRAM(S) OFFERED

● Accounting Technology/Technician and Bookkeeping 4 *students enrolled* ● Administrative Assistant and Secretarial Science, General 11 *students enrolled* ● Aesthetician/Esthetician and Skin Care Specialist 3 *students enrolled* ● Applied Horticulture/Horticultural Operations, General 6 *students enrolled* ● Autobody/Collision and Repair Technology/Technician 10 *students enrolled* ● Automobile/Automotive Mechanics Technology/Technician 39 *students enrolled* ● Baking and Pastry Arts/Baker/Pastry Chef 2 *students enrolled* ● Business Administration, Management and Operations, Other 7 *students enrolled* ● Commercial Photography 1 *student enrolled* ● Computer Installation and Repair Technology/Technician 2 *students enrolled* ● Computer Systems Networking and Telecommunications 2 *students enrolled* ● Cosmetology/Cosmetologist, General 51 *students enrolled* ● Criminal Justice/Safety Studies 11 *students enrolled* ● Customer Service Support/Call Center/Teleservice Operation 5 *students enrolled* ● Data Entry/Microcomputer Applications, General 28 *students enrolled* ● Early Childhood Education and Teaching 1 *student enrolled* ● Electrician 8 *students enrolled* ● Emergency Medical Technology/Technician (EMT Paramedic) 30 *students enrolled* ● Entrepreneurship/Entrepreneurial Studies 3 *students enrolled* ● Fire Science/Firefighting 6 *students enrolled* ● Heating, Air Conditioning, Ventilation and Refrigeration Maintenance Technology/Technician (HAC, HACR, HVAC, HVACR) 35 *students enrolled* ● Heavy Equipment Maintenance Technology/Technician 13 *students enrolled* ● Industrial Mechanics and Maintenance Technology 11 *students enrolled* ● Lineworker 69 *students enrolled* ● Machine Shop Technology/Assistant 7 *students enrolled* ● Marine Maintenance/Fitter and Ship Repair Technology/Technician 6 *students enrolled* ● Massage Therapy/Therapeutic Massage 26 *students enrolled* ● Medical Insurance Coding Specialist/Coder 16 *students enrolled* ● Medical Office Assistant/Specialist 5 *students enrolled* ● Medical Reception/Receptionist 12 *students enrolled* ● Medical/Clinical Assistant 24 *students enrolled* ● Motorcycle Maintenance and Repair Technology/Technician 3 *students enrolled* ● Nail Technician/Specialist and Manicurist 5 *students enrolled* ● Nurse/Nursing Assistant/Aide and Patient Care Assistant 33 *students enrolled* ● Operations Management and Supervision 8 *students enrolled* ● Pharmacy Technician/Assistant 10 *students enrolled* ● Tool and Die Technology/Technician 4 *students enrolled* ● Truck and Bus Driver/Commercial Vehicle Operation 54 *students enrolled* ● Turf and Turfgrass Management 6 *students enrolled* ● Water Quality and Wastewater Treatment Management and Recycling Technology/Technician 3 *students enrolled* ● Web Page, Digital/Multimedia and Information Resources Design 2 *students enrolled* ● Welding Technology/Welder 15 *students enrolled*

STUDENT SERVICES Academic or career counseling, employment services for current students, placement services for program completers, remedial services.

North Metro Technical College

5198 Ross Road, Acworth, GA 30102
http://www.northmetrotech.edu/

CONTACT Ron Newcomb, Acting President
Telephone: 770-975-4000

GENERAL INFORMATION Public Institution. Founded 1989. **Accreditation:** State accredited or approved. **Total program enrollment:** 1159. **Application fee:** $15.

PROGRAM(S) OFFERED

● Accounting Technology/Technician and Bookkeeping 28 *students enrolled* ● Administrative Assistant and Secretarial Science, General 9 *students enrolled* ● Animation, Interactive Technology, Video Graphics and Special Effects 1 *student enrolled* ● Applied Horticulture/Horticultural Operations, General 14 *students enrolled* ● Automobile/Automotive Mechanics Technology/Technician 54 *students enrolled* ● Child Care Provider/Assistant 8 *students enrolled* ● Commercial and Advertising Art 9 *students enrolled* ● Communications Systems Installation and Repair Technology 8 *students enrolled* ● Computer Installation and Repair Technology/Technician 7 *students enrolled* ● Computer Systems Networking and Telecommunications 1 *student enrolled*

● Cosmetology/Cosmetologist, General 27 *students enrolled* ● Data Entry/Microcomputer Applications, General 4 *students enrolled* ● Early Childhood Education and Teaching 6 *students enrolled* ● Electrical/Electronics Equipment Installation and Repair, General 1 *student enrolled* ● Emergency Medical Technology/Technician (EMT Paramedic) 16 *students enrolled* ● Industrial Mechanics and Maintenance Technology 4 *students enrolled* ● Landscaping and Groundskeeping 34 *students enrolled* ● Medical Insurance Coding Specialist/Coder 17 *students enrolled* ● Medical Reception/Receptionist 10 *students enrolled* ● Medical Transcription/Transcriptionist 12 *students enrolled* ● Medical/Clinical Assistant 35 *students enrolled* ● Nurse/Nursing Assistant/Aide and Patient Care Assistant 100 *students enrolled* ● Operations Management and Supervision 4 *students enrolled* ● Parks, Recreation and Leisure Studies ● Phlebotomy/Phlebotomist 27 *students enrolled* ● Plant Nursery Operations and Management ● Sales, Distribution and Marketing Operations, General 3 *students enrolled* ● Small Business Administration/Management 5 *students enrolled* ● Technical and Business Writing 1 *student enrolled* ● Truck and Bus Driver/Commercial Vehicle Operation 71 *students enrolled* ● Web Page, Digital/Multimedia and Information Resources Design 2 *students enrolled*

STUDENT SERVICES Academic or career counseling, employment services for current students, placement services for program completers, remedial services.

Northwestern Technical College

PO Box 569, 265 Bicentennial Trail, Rock Spring, GA 30739
http://www.northwesterntech.edu/

CONTACT Mr. Ray King, Interim President
Telephone: 706-764-3510

GENERAL INFORMATION Public Institution. Founded 1966. **Accreditation:** Regional (SACS/CC); medical assisting (AAMAE); surgical technology (ARCST); state accredited or approved. **Total program enrollment:** 1116. **Application fee:** $15.

PROGRAM(S) OFFERED

● Accounting Technology/Technician and Bookkeeping 25 *students enrolled* ● Administrative Assistant and Secretarial Science, General 14 *students enrolled* ● Architectural Drafting and Architectural CAD/CADD 9 *students enrolled* ● Automobile/Automotive Mechanics Technology/Technician 77 *students enrolled* ● CAD/CADD Drafting and/or Design Technology/Technician 12 *students enrolled* ● Child Care Provider/Assistant 77 *students enrolled* ● Computer Installation and Repair Technology/Technician 19 *students enrolled* ● Computer Systems Networking and Telecommunications 10 *students enrolled* ● Computer and Information Systems Security ● Cosmetology/Cosmetologist, General 23 *students enrolled* ● Criminal Justice/Police Science 6 *students enrolled* ● Criminal Justice/Safety Studies 18 *students enrolled* ● Data Entry/Microcomputer Applications, General 13 *students enrolled* ● Data Processing and Data Processing Technology/Technician 5 *students enrolled* ● Drafting and Design Technology/Technician, General 4 *students enrolled* ● Early Childhood Education and Teaching 27 *students enrolled* ● Electrical/Electronics Equipment Installation and Repair, General 9 *students enrolled* ● General Office Occupations and Clerical Services 21 *students enrolled* ● Heating, Air Conditioning, Ventilation and Refrigeration Maintenance Technology/Technician (HAC, HACR, HVAC, HVACR) 13 *students enrolled* ● Human Resources Management/Personnel Administration, General 20 *students enrolled* ● Industrial Mechanics and Maintenance Technology 25 *students enrolled* ● Machine Shop Technology/Assistant 23 *students enrolled* ● Medical Insurance Coding Specialist/Coder 25 *students enrolled* ● Medical Reception/Receptionist 16 *students enrolled* ● Medical Transcription/Transcriptionist 25 *students enrolled* ● Medical/Clinical Assistant 10 *students enrolled* ● Nail Technician/Specialist and Manicurist 9 *students enrolled* ● Nurse/Nursing Assistant/Aide and Patient Care Assistant 66 *students enrolled* ● Operations Management and Supervision 59 *students enrolled* ● Pharmacy Technician/Assistant 8 *students enrolled* ● Phlebotomy/Phlebotomist 12 *students enrolled* ● Social Work, Other 1 *student enrolled* ● Surgical Technology/Technologist 4 *students enrolled* ● Technical and Business Writing 11 *students enrolled* ● Truck and Bus Driver/Commercial Vehicle Operation 128 *students enrolled* ● Web Page, Digital/Multimedia and Information Resources Design 1 *student enrolled* ● Welding Technology/Welder 17 *students enrolled* ● Word Processing 14 *students enrolled*

STUDENT SERVICES Academic or career counseling, employment services for current students, placement services for program completers, remedial services.

Ogeechee Technical College

One Joe Kennedy Boulevard, Statesboro, GA 30458
http://www.ogeecheetech.edu/

CONTACT Dr. Dawn Cartee, President
Telephone: 912-681-5500

GENERAL INFORMATION Public Institution. Founded 1989. **Accreditation:** Dental assisting (ADA); funeral service (ABFSE); ophthalmic dispensing (COA); state accredited or approved. **Total program enrollment:** 953. **Application fee:** $15.

PROGRAM(S) OFFERED

● **Accounting Technology/Technician and Bookkeeping** 10 students enrolled ● **Administrative Assistant and Secretarial Science, General** 24 students enrolled ● **Aesthetician/Esthetician and Skin Care Specialist** 4 students enrolled ● **Agribusiness/Agricultural Business Operations** 1 student enrolled ● **Agricultural Mechanization, General** 5 students enrolled ● **Applied Horticulture/Horticultural Operations, General** 4 students enrolled ● **Architectural Drafting and Architectural CAD/CADD** 3 students enrolled ● **Automobile/Automotive Mechanics Technology/Technician** 18 students enrolled ● **Carpentry/Carpenter** 1 student enrolled ● **Child Care Provider/Assistant** 1 student enrolled ● **Child Care and Support Services Management** 5 students enrolled ● **Computer Installation and Repair Technology/Technician** 17 students enrolled ● **Computer Systems Networking and Telecommunications** 19 students enrolled ● **Cosmetology/Cosmetologist, General** 44 students enrolled ● **Criminal Justice/Police Science** 10 students enrolled ● **Data Entry/Microcomputer Applications, General** 4 students enrolled ● **Dental Assisting/Assistant** 6 students enrolled ● **Drafting and Design Technology/Technician, General** 2 students enrolled ● **Early Childhood Education and Teaching** 16 students enrolled ● **Electrician** 16 students enrolled ● **Emergency Medical Technology/Technician (EMT Paramedic)** 7 students enrolled ● **Food Preparation/Professional Cooking/Kitchen Assistant** 4 students enrolled ● **General Office Occupations and Clerical Services** 7 students enrolled ● **Health Information/Medical Records Technology/Technician** 6 students enrolled ● **Heating, Air Conditioning, Ventilation and Refrigeration Maintenance Technology/Technician (HAC, HACR, HVAC, HVACR)** 8 students enrolled ● **Hospitality Administration/Management, General** 2 students enrolled ● **Human Resources Management/Personnel Administration, General** 2 students enrolled ● **Industrial Mechanics and Maintenance Technology** 3 students enrolled ● **Logistics and Materials Management** 11 students enrolled ● **Medical Insurance Coding Specialist/Coder** 9 students enrolled ● **Medical Reception/Receptionist** 31 students enrolled ● **Medical/Clinical Assistant** 24 students enrolled ● **Medical/Health Management and Clinical Assistant/Specialist** 55 students enrolled ● **Nurse/Nursing Assistant/Aide and Patient Care Assistant** 73 students enrolled ● **Opticianry/Ophthalmic Dispensing Optician** 5 students enrolled ● **Pharmacy Technician/Assistant** 13 students enrolled ● **Phlebotomy/Phlebotomist** 10 students enrolled ● **Radiologic Technology/Science—Radiographer** 4 students enrolled ● **Sales, Distribution and Marketing Operations, General** 2 students enrolled ● **Small Business Administration/Management** 2 students enrolled ● **Surgical Technology/Technologist** 4 students enrolled ● **Truck and Bus Driver/Commercial Vehicle Operation** 60 students enrolled ● **Turf and Turfgrass Management** 4 students enrolled ● **Welding Technology/Welder** 12 students enrolled ● **Wildlife and Wildlands Science and Management** 2 students enrolled

STUDENT SERVICES Academic or career counseling, daycare for children of students, employment services for current students, placement services for program completers, remedial services.

Okefenokee Technical College

1701 Carswell Avenue, Waycross, GA 31503
http://www.okefenokeetech.edu/

CONTACT Gail Thaxton, President
Telephone: 912-287-6584

GENERAL INFORMATION Public Institution. **Accreditation:** Medical laboratory technology (NAACLS); state accredited or approved. **Total program enrollment:** 473. **Application fee:** $20.

PROGRAM(S) OFFERED

● **Accounting Technology/Technician and Bookkeeping** 15 students enrolled ● **Administrative Assistant and Secretarial Science, General** 10 students enrolled ● **Adult Development and Aging** 2 students enrolled ● **Applied Horticulture/Horticultural Operations, General** 7 students enrolled ● **Autobody/Collision and Repair Technology/Technician** 1 student enrolled ● **Automobile/Automotive Mechanics Technology/Technician** 5 students enrolled ● **Building/Property Maintenance and Management** 2 students enrolled ● **Computer Instal-**

lation and Repair Technology/Technician 15 students enrolled ● **Computer Systems Networking and Telecommunications** 19 students enrolled ● **Cosmetology/Cosmetologist, General** 27 students enrolled ● **Criminal Justice/Safety Studies** 1 student enrolled ● **Customer Service Support/Call Center/Teleservice Operation** 30 students enrolled ● **Data Entry/Microcomputer Applications, General** 11 students enrolled ● **Drafting and Design Technology/Technician, General** 3 students enrolled ● **Early Childhood Education and Teaching** 10 students enrolled ● **Electrical/Electronics Equipment Installation and Repair, General** 10 students enrolled ● **Electrician** 1 student enrolled ● **Emergency Medical Technology/Technician (EMT Paramedic)** 23 students enrolled ● **Food Preparation/Professional Cooking/Kitchen Assistant** 17 students enrolled ● **Forestry Technology/Technician** 5 students enrolled ● **General Office Occupations and Clerical Services** 10 students enrolled ● **Heating, Air Conditioning, Ventilation and Refrigeration Maintenance Technology/Technician (HAC, HACR, HVAC, HVACR)** 16 students enrolled ● **Heavy Equipment Maintenance Technology/Technician** 25 students enrolled ● **Industrial Mechanics and Maintenance Technology** 3 students enrolled ● **Landscaping and Groundskeeping** 2 students enrolled ● **Lineworker** 64 students enrolled ● **Medical Transcription/Transcriptionist** 1 student enrolled ● **Medical/Clinical Assistant** 9 students enrolled ● **Medical/Health Management and Clinical Assistant/Specialist** 19 students enrolled ● **Nurse/Nursing Assistant/Aide and Patient Care Assistant** 28 students enrolled ● **Phlebotomy/Phlebotomist** 6 students enrolled ● **Sales, Distribution and Marketing Operations, General** 3 students enrolled ● **Surgical Technology/Technologist** 10 students enrolled ● **Survey Technology/Surveying** 3 students enrolled ● **Truck and Bus Driver/Commercial Vehicle Operation** 49 students enrolled ● **Web Page, Digital/Multimedia and Information Resources Design** 1 student enrolled ● **Welding Technology/Welder** 11 students enrolled

STUDENT SERVICES Academic or career counseling, daycare for children of students, employment services for current students, placement services for program completers, remedial services.

Omnitech Institute

4319 Covington Highway, Suite 204, Decatur, GA 30035
http://www.omnitechinc.com/

CONTACT Charlton C. Lester, President
Telephone: 404-284-8121 Ext. 229

GENERAL INFORMATION Private Institution. **Total program enrollment:** 109. **Application fee:** $30.

PROGRAM(S) OFFERED

● **Computer Engineering Technology/Technician** 24 hrs./$15,999 ● **Computer Engineering, General** 20 students enrolled ● **Computer Programming/Programmer, General** ● **Computer and Information Sciences and Support Services, Other** 16 students enrolled ● **Computer and Information Sciences, General** 28 students enrolled ● **Health Information/Medical Records Administration/Administrator** 24 hrs./$14,999 ● **Medical Insurance Coding Specialist/Coder** 24 hrs./$8999 ● **Music, General** 24 hrs./$14,999 ● **Music, Other** 41 students enrolled ● **System, Networking, and LAN/WAN Management/Manager**

STUDENT SERVICES Academic or career counseling, employment services for current students, placement services for program completers.

Powder Springs Beauty College

4114 Austell-Powder Springs Road, Powder Springs, GA 30127

CONTACT Janet Tedford, CEO
Telephone: 770-439-9432

GENERAL INFORMATION Private Institution. **Total program enrollment:** 22. **Application fee:** $100.

PROGRAM(S) OFFERED

● **Cosmetology/Cosmetologist, General** 1500 hrs./$6987

STUDENT SERVICES Employment services for current students, placement services for program completers.

Pro Way Hair School

6254 Memorial Drive, Suite M, Stone Mountain, GA 30083
http://www.prowayhairschool.com/

CONTACT Francis M. Sullivan, President
Telephone: 404-299-5156

GENERAL INFORMATION Private Institution. Founded 1940. **Total program enrollment:** 44.

PROGRAM(S) OFFERED
• **Barbering/Barber** *1500 hrs./$13,695* • **Cosmetology/Cosmetologist, General** *1500 hrs./$13,695*

STUDENT SERVICES Placement services for program completers.

Rising Spirit Institute of Natural Health

4330 Georgetown Square, Suite 500, Atlanta, GA 30338
http://www.risingspirit.edu/

CONTACT Michael Davis, President
Telephone: 770-457-2021

GENERAL INFORMATION Private Institution. **Total program enrollment:** 69. **Application fee:** $100.

PROGRAM(S) OFFERED
• **Massage Therapy/Therapeutic Massage** *65 hrs./$11,900* • **Medical Office Management/Administration** *54 hrs./$9416* • **Medical/Clinical Assistant** *60 hrs./$10,472*

STUDENT SERVICES Placement services for program completers.

Rivertown School of Beauty

3750 Woodruff Road, Columbus, GA 31904
http://rivertownschoolofbeauty.com/

CONTACT Winston Dahl, President
Telephone: 706-653-6561

GENERAL INFORMATION Private Institution. Founded 1992. **Total program enrollment:** 177. **Application fee:** $100.

PROGRAM(S) OFFERED
• **Aesthetician/Esthetician and Skin Care Specialist** *1000 hrs./$9570* • **Barbering/Barber** *1500 hrs./$9570* • **Cosmetology and Related Personal Grooming Arts, Other** *25 students enrolled* • **Cosmetology, Barber/Styling, and Nail Instructor** *250 hrs./$2425* • **Cosmetology/Cosmetologist, General** *1500 hrs./$9995* • **Nail Technician/Specialist and Manicurist** *600 hrs./$5375*

STUDENT SERVICES Academic or career counseling, placement services for program completers.

Roffler Moler Hairstyling College

1311 Roswell Road, Marietta, GA 30062
http://www.roffler.net/

CONTACT Dale Sheffield, Director
Telephone: 770-565-3285

GENERAL INFORMATION Private Institution. Founded 1988. **Total program enrollment:** 107.

PROGRAM(S) OFFERED
• **Barbering/Barber** *1500 hrs./$8200* • **Cosmetology and Related Personal Grooming Arts, Other** *5 students enrolled* • **Cosmetology, Barber/Styling, and Nail Instructor** *750 hrs./$3800* • **Cosmetology/Cosmetologist, General** *1500 hrs./$7400*

STUDENT SERVICES Academic or career counseling, placement services for program completers.

Sandersville Technical College

1189 Deepstep Road, Sandersville, GA 31082
http://www.sandersvilletech.edu/

CONTACT Lloyd Horadan, President
Telephone: 478-553-2050 Ext. 2066

GENERAL INFORMATION Public Institution. **Accreditation:** State accredited or approved. **Total program enrollment:** 233. **Application fee:** $15.

PROGRAM(S) OFFERED
• **Accounting Technology/Technician and Bookkeeping** *10 students enrolled* • **Administrative Assistant and Secretarial Science, General** *7 students enrolled* • **Animation, Interactive Technology, Video Graphics and Special Effects** • **Carpentry/Carpenter** *8 students enrolled* • **Child Care Provider/Assistant** *19 students enrolled* • **Child Care and Support Services Management** *5 students enrolled* • **Computer Installation and Repair Technology/Technician** *16 students enrolled* • **Computer Systems Networking and Telecommunications** *1 student enrolled* • **Cosmetology/Cosmetologist, General** *13 students enrolled* • **Data Processing and Data Processing Technology/Technician** *42 students enrolled* • **Early Childhood Education and Teaching** *9 students enrolled* • **Electrician** *23 students enrolled* • **General Office Occupations and Clerical Services** *9 students enrolled* • **Industrial Mechanics and Maintenance Technology** *43 students enrolled* • **Logistics and Materials Management** *3 students enrolled* • **Medical/Clinical Assistant** *5 students enrolled* • **Nurse/Nursing Assistant/Aide and Patient Care Assistant** *29 students enrolled* • **Plumbing Technology/Plumber** *11 students enrolled* • **Truck and Bus Driver/Commercial Vehicle Operation** *173 students enrolled* • **Web Page, Digital/Multimedia and Information Resources Design** *32 students enrolled* • **Welding Technology/Welder** *93 students enrolled*

STUDENT SERVICES Academic or career counseling, employment services for current students, placement services for program completers, remedial services.

Sanford-Brown Institute

1140 Hammond Drive, Suite A-1150, Atlanta, GA 30328
http://www.sb-atlanta.com/

CONTACT Danielle Millman, President
Telephone: 770-576-4498

GENERAL INFORMATION Private Institution. **Total program enrollment:** 1378. **Application fee:** $25.

PROGRAM(S) OFFERED
• **Cardiovascular Technology/Technologist** *76 hrs./$34,600* • **Diagnostic Medical Sonography/Sonographer and Ultrasound Technician** *74 hrs./$34,600* • **Massage Therapy/Therapeutic Massage** *70 hrs./$16,000* • **Medical Insurance Coding Specialist/Coder** *45 hrs./$12,500* • **Medical/Clinical Assistant** *41 hrs./$13,230*

STUDENT SERVICES Academic or career counseling, placement services for program completers.

Savannah College of Art and Design

342 Bull Street, PO Box 3146, Savannah, GA 31402-3146
http://www.scad.edu/

CONTACT Paula S. Wallace, President
Telephone: 912-525-5000

GENERAL INFORMATION Private Institution. Founded 1978. **Accreditation:** Regional (SACS/CC). **Total program enrollment:** 8676. **Application fee:** $50.

PROGRAM(S) OFFERED
• **Graphic Design**

STUDENT SERVICES Academic or career counseling, employment services for current students, placement services for program completers.

Savannah River College

2528 Center West Parkway, Augusta, GA 30909
http://www.savannahrivercollege.edu/

CONTACT Darryl Kerr, President
Telephone: 706-738-5046

GENERAL INFORMATION Private Institution. Founded 1983. **Total program enrollment: 163. Application fee: $50.**

PROGRAM(S) OFFERED
• **Accounting Technology/Technician and Bookkeeping** 2 *students enrolled* • **Administrative Assistant and Secretarial Science, General** 3 *students enrolled* • **Business/Commerce, General** 1 *student enrolled* • **Computer and Information Sciences, General** • **Medical Administrative/Executive Assistant and Medical Secretary** 2 *students enrolled* • **Medical Insurance Coding Specialist/Coder** 25 *students enrolled* • **Medical/Clinical Assistant** 21 *students enrolled* • **Nurse/Nursing Assistant/Aide and Patient Care Assistant** 14 *students enrolled*

STUDENT SERVICES Academic or career counseling, employment services for current students, placement services for program completers.

Savannah School of Massage Therapy

6413 Waters Avenue, Savannah, GA 31406
http://www.ssomt.com

CONTACT Christopher J. Masters, Educational Director
Telephone: 912-355-3011

GENERAL INFORMATION Private Institution. **Application fee: $100.**

PROGRAM(S) OFFERED
• **Massage Therapy/Therapeutic Massage** 600 *hrs.*

STUDENT SERVICES Academic or career counseling, placement services for program completers.

Savannah Technical College

5717 White Bluff Road, Savannah, GA 31405
http://www.savannahtech.edu/

CONTACT Mr. Terry Elam, Interim President
Telephone: 912-443-5700

GENERAL INFORMATION Public Institution. Founded 1929. **Accreditation:** Regional (SACS/CC); dental assisting (ADA); engineering technology (ABET/TAC). **Total program enrollment: 2016. Application fee: $15.**

PROGRAM(S) OFFERED
• **Accounting Technology/Technician and Bookkeeping** 7 *students enrolled* • **Administrative Assistant and Secretarial Science, General** 6 *students enrolled* • **Aircraft Powerplant Technology/Technician** 26 *students enrolled* • **Airframe Mechanics and Aircraft Maintenance Technology/Technician** 39 *students enrolled* • **Autobody/Collision and Repair Technology/Technician** 8 *students enrolled* • **Automobile/Automotive Mechanics Technology/Technician** 19 *students enrolled* • **CAD/CADD Drafting and/or Design Technology/Technician** 16 *students enrolled* • **Cabinetmaking and Millwork/Millwright** 17 *students enrolled* • **Carpentry/Carpenter** 59 *students enrolled* • **Child Care Provider/Assistant** 4 *students enrolled* • **Computer Installation and Repair Technology/Technician** 6 *students enrolled* • **Computer Systems Networking and Telecommunications** 3 *students enrolled* • **Cosmetology/Cosmetologist, General** 26 *students enrolled* • **Criminal Justice/Safety Studies** 1 *student enrolled* • **Data Processing and Data Processing Technology/Technician** 1 *student enrolled* • **Dental Assisting/Assistant** 19 *students enrolled* • **Drafting and Design Technology/Technician, General** 3 *students enrolled* • **Early Childhood Education and Teaching** 5 *students enrolled* • **Electrician** 50 *students enrolled* • **Emergency Medical Technology/Technician (EMT Paramedic)** 19 *students enrolled* • **Food Preparation/Professional Cooking/Kitchen Assistant** 27 *students enrolled* • **Heating, Air Conditioning, Ventilation and Refrigeration Maintenance Technology/Technician (HAC, HACR, HVAC, HVACR)** 151 *students enrolled* • **Hospitality Administration/Management, General** 4 *students enrolled* • **Industrial Mechanics and Maintenance Technology** 38 *students enrolled* • **Logistics and Materials Management** 17 *students enrolled* • **Machine Shop Technology/Assistant** 2 *students enrolled* • **Medical Insurance Specialist/Medical Biller** 34 *students enrolled* • **Medical Office Assistant/Specialist** 36 *students enrolled* • **Medical Transcription/Transcriptionist** 16 *students enrolled*

• **Medical/Clinical Assistant** 13 *students enrolled* • **Nurse/Nursing Assistant/Aide and Patient Care Assistant** 138 *students enrolled* • **Operations Management and Supervision** • **Phlebotomy/Phlebotomist** 43 *students enrolled* • **Psychiatric/Mental Health Services Technician** 2 *students enrolled* • **Sales, Distribution and Marketing Operations, General** • **Surgical Technology/Technologist** 1 *student enrolled* • **Technical and Business Writing** 4 *students enrolled* • **Truck and Bus Driver/Commercial Vehicle Operation** 160 *students enrolled* • **Web Page, Digital/Multimedia and Information Resources Design** 1 *student enrolled* • **Welding Technology/Welder** 91 *students enrolled*

STUDENT SERVICES Academic or career counseling, employment services for current students, placement services for program completers, remedial services.

Southeastern Beauty School

3448 N. Lumpkin Road, Columbus, GA 31903
http://www.sebeautyschool.com/

CONTACT James W. Dunson, President
Telephone: 706-687-1054

GENERAL INFORMATION Private Institution. **Total program enrollment: 67.**

PROGRAM(S) OFFERED
• **Cosmetology, Barber/Styling, and Nail Instructor** 750 *hrs./$4875* • **Cosmetology/Cosmetologist, General** 1500 *hrs./$10,350*

STUDENT SERVICES Academic or career counseling, placement services for program completers, remedial services.

Southeastern Beauty School

PO Box 12483, Columbus, GA 31917-2483
http://www.sebeautyschool.com/

CONTACT James W. Dunson, President
Telephone: 706-561-5616

GENERAL INFORMATION Private Institution. Founded 1958. **Total program enrollment: 41.**

PROGRAM(S) OFFERED
• **Barbering/Barber** 1500 *hrs./$10,350* • **Cosmetology, Barber/Styling, and Nail Instructor** 750 *hrs./$4875* • **Cosmetology/Cosmetologist, General** 1500 *hrs./$9750*

STUDENT SERVICES Academic or career counseling, placement services for program completers, remedial services.

Southeastern Technical College

3001 East First Street, Vidalia, GA 30474
http://www.southeasterntech.edu/

CONTACT Cathryn T. Mitchell, President
Telephone: 912-538-3100

GENERAL INFORMATION Public Institution. Founded 1989. **Accreditation:** State accredited or approved. **Total program enrollment: 484. Application fee: $15.**

PROGRAM(S) OFFERED
• **Accounting Technology/Technician and Bookkeeping** 5 *students enrolled* • **Administrative Assistant and Secretarial Science, General** 10 *students enrolled* • **Commercial and Advertising Art** 2 *students enrolled* • **Communications Systems Installation and Repair Technology** 4 *students enrolled* • **Computer Installation and Repair Technology/Technician** 4 *students enrolled* • **Cosmetology/Cosmetologist, General** 20 *students enrolled* • **Criminal Justice/Safety Studies** 5 *students enrolled* • **Data Entry/Microcomputer Applications, General** 1 *student enrolled* • **Early Childhood Education and Teaching** 1 *student enrolled* • **Electrical/Electronics Equipment Installation and Repair, General** 2 *students enrolled* • **Electrician** 1 *student enrolled* • **Emergency Medical Technology/Technician (EMT Paramedic)** 8 *students enrolled* • **General Office Occupations and Clerical Services** 1 *student enrolled* • **Heating, Air Conditioning, Ventilation and Refrigeration Maintenance Technology/Technician (HAC,**

Southeastern Technical College (continued)

HACR, HVAC, HVACR) *1 student enrolled* ● **Medical/Clinical Assistant** *6 students enrolled* ● **Medical/Health Management and Clinical Assistant/Specialist** *14 students enrolled* ● **Nurse/Nursing Assistant/Aide and Patient Care Assistant** *65 students enrolled* ● **Operations Management and Supervision** *6 students enrolled* ● **Pharmacy Technician/Assistant** *1 student enrolled* ● **Sales, Distribution and Marketing Operations, General** *1 student enrolled* ● **Surgical Technology/Technologist** *5 students enrolled* ● **Truck and Bus Driver/Commercial Vehicle Operation** *38 students enrolled* ● **Web Page, Digital/Multimedia and Information Resources Design** *1 student enrolled* ● **Welding Technology/Welder** *23 students enrolled*

STUDENT SERVICES Academic or career counseling, employment services for current students, placement services for program completers, remedial services.

Southern Polytechnic State University

1100 South Marietta Parkway, Marietta, GA 30060-2896
http://www.spsu.edu/

CONTACT Lisa A. Rossbacher, President
Telephone: 678-915-7778

GENERAL INFORMATION Public Institution. Founded 1948. **Accreditation:** Regional (SACS/CC); engineering technology (ABET/TAC). **Total program enrollment:** 3225. **Application fee:** $20.

PROGRAM(S) OFFERED
● **Construction Management** *1 student enrolled* ● **Industrial Production Technologies/Technicians, Other** *1 student enrolled* ● **Quality Control and Safety Technologies/Technicians, Other** *1 student enrolled* ● **Survey Technology/Surveying** *6 students enrolled*

STUDENT SERVICES Academic or career counseling, employment services for current students, placement services for program completers.

South Georgia College

100 West College Park Drive, Douglas, GA 31533-5098
http://www.sgc.edu/

CONTACT Dr. Virginia Carson, President
Telephone: 912-260-4200

GENERAL INFORMATION Public Institution. Founded 1906. **Accreditation:** Regional (SACS/CC). **Total program enrollment:** 1333. **Application fee:** $20.

PROGRAM(S) OFFERED
● **Business Administration and Management, General** *1 student enrolled* ● **Teacher Assistant/Aide**

STUDENT SERVICES Academic or career counseling, remedial services.

South Georgia Technical College

900 South Georgia Tech Parkway, Americus, GA 31709
http://www.southgatech.edu/

CONTACT Sparky Reeves, President
Telephone: 229-931-2394

GENERAL INFORMATION Public Institution. Founded 1948. **Accreditation:** State accredited or approved. **Total program enrollment:** 1137. **Application fee:** $20.

PROGRAM(S) OFFERED
● **Accounting Technology/Technician and Bookkeeping** *27 students enrolled* ● **Administrative Assistant and Secretarial Science, General** *15 students enrolled* ● **Airframe Mechanics and Aircraft Maintenance Technology/Technician** *15 students enrolled* ● **Applied Horticulture/Horticultural Operations, General** *6 students enrolled* ● **Autobody/Collision and Repair Technology/Technician** *1 student enrolled* ● **Automobile/Automotive Mechanics Technology/Technician** *34 students enrolled* ● **Avionics Maintenance Technology/Technician** *1 student enrolled* ● **CAD/CADD Drafting and/or Design Technology/Technician** *2 students enrolled* ● **Carpentry/Carpenter** *2 students enrolled* ● **Communications**

Systems Installation and Repair Technology *8 students enrolled* ● **Computer Installation and Repair Technology/Technician** *6 students enrolled* ● **Computer Programming/Programmer, General** *2 students enrolled* ● **Computer Systems Networking and Telecommunications** *6 students enrolled* ● **Cosmetology/Cosmetologist, General** *21 students enrolled* ● **Criminal Justice/Safety Studies** *32 students enrolled* ● **Data Entry/Microcomputer Applications, General** *8 students enrolled* ● **Data Processing and Data Processing Technology/Technician** *6 students enrolled* ● **Drafting and Design Technology/Technician, General** *1 student enrolled* ● **E-Commerce/Electronic Commerce** ● **Early Childhood Education and Teaching** *35 students enrolled* ● **Electrical/Electronics Equipment Installation and Repair, General** *34 students enrolled* ● **Electrician** *14 students enrolled* ● **Food Preparation/Professional Cooking/Kitchen Assistant** *21 students enrolled* ● **Heating, Air Conditioning, Ventilation and Refrigeration Maintenance Technology/Technician (HAC, HACR, HVAC, HVACR)** *18 students enrolled* ● **Industrial Mechanics and Maintenance Technology** *3 students enrolled* ● **Landscaping and Groundskeeping** *6 students enrolled* ● **Lineworker** *62 students enrolled* ● **Machine Shop Technology/Assistant** *21 students enrolled* ● **Medical Insurance Coding Specialist/Coder** *1 student enrolled* ● **Medical Office Assistant/Specialist** *31 students enrolled* ● **Medical/Clinical Assistant** *29 students enrolled* ● **Nail Technician/Specialist and Manicurist** *3 students enrolled* ● **Nurse/Nursing Assistant/Aide and Patient Care Assistant** *17 students enrolled* ● **Operations Management and Supervision** *10 students enrolled* ● **Plant Nursery Operations and Management** *2 students enrolled* ● **Plumbing Technology/Plumber** ● **Sales, Distribution and Marketing Operations, General** *9 students enrolled* ● **Small Business Administration/Management** *8 students enrolled* ● **Truck and Bus Driver/Commercial Vehicle Operation** *82 students enrolled* ● **Turf and Turfgrass Management** *3 students enrolled* ● **Welding Technology/Welder** *114 students enrolled* ● **Word Processing** *6 students enrolled*

STUDENT SERVICES Academic or career counseling, employment services for current students, placement services for program completers, remedial services.

Southwest Georgia Technical College

15689 US 19 North, Thomasville, GA 31792
http://www.southwestgatech.edu/

CONTACT Dr. Glenn Deibert, President
Telephone: 229-225-4096

GENERAL INFORMATION Public Institution. Founded 1963. **Accreditation:** Regional (SACS/CC); medical laboratory technology (NAACLS); physical therapy assisting (APTA); state accredited or approved. **Total program enrollment:** 507. **Application fee:** $20.

PROGRAM(S) OFFERED
● **Accounting Technology/Technician and Bookkeeping** *11 students enrolled* ● **Administrative Assistant and Secretarial Science, General** *13 students enrolled* ● **Adult Development and Aging** *5 students enrolled* ● **Architectural Drafting and Architectural CAD/CADD** *1 student enrolled* ● **Automobile/Automotive Mechanics Technology/Technician** *16 students enrolled* ● **Business Administration, Management and Operations, Other** *6 students enrolled* ● **CAD/CADD Drafting and/or Design Technology/Technician** *4 students enrolled* ● **Computer Installation and Repair Technology/Technician** *3 students enrolled* ● **Computer Systems Networking and Telecommunications** *18 students enrolled* ● **Cosmetology/Cosmetologist, General** *41 students enrolled* ● **Criminal Justice/Safety Studies** *16 students enrolled* ● **Customer Service Support/Call Center/Teleservice Operation** *18 students enrolled* ● **Drafting and Design Technology/Technician, General** *8 students enrolled* ● **Early Childhood Education and Teaching** *26 students enrolled* ● **Educational/Instructional Media Design** *17 students enrolled* ● **Electrical/Electronics Equipment Installation and Repair, General** *2 students enrolled* ● **Electrician** *13 students enrolled* ● **Emergency Medical Technology/Technician (EMT Paramedic)** *8 students enrolled* ● **General Office Occupations and Clerical Services** *12 students enrolled* ● **Health Unit Coordinator/Ward Clerk** *1 student enrolled* ● **Heating, Air Conditioning, Ventilation and Refrigeration Maintenance Technology/Technician (HAC, HACR, HVAC, HVACR)** *2 students enrolled* ● **Machine Shop Technology/Assistant** *2 students enrolled* ● **Medical Insurance Coding Specialist/Coder** *13 students enrolled* ● **Medical Transcription/Transcriptionist** *4 students enrolled* ● **Nurse/Nursing Assistant/Aide and Patient Care Assistant** *128 students enrolled* ● **Operations Management and Supervision** *3 students enrolled* ● **Pharmacy Technician/Assistant** *4 students enrolled* ● **Phlebotomy/Phlebotomist** *30 students enrolled* ● **Small Engine Mechanics and Repair Technology/Technician** *1 student enrolled* ● **Surgical Technology/Technologist** *9 students enrolled* ● **Web Page, Digital/Multimedia and Information Resources Design** *1 student enrolled* ● **Welding Technology/Welder** *86 students enrolled*

STUDENT SERVICES Academic or career counseling, employment services for current students, placement services for program completers, remedial services.

Swainsboro Technical College

346 Kite Road, Swainsboro, GA 30401
http://www.swainsborotech.edu/

CONTACT William Larry Calhoun, President
Telephone: 478-289-2200

GENERAL INFORMATION Public Institution. Founded 1963. **Accreditation:** State accredited or approved. **Total program enrollment:** 256. **Application fee:** $15.

PROGRAM(S) OFFERED
• Accounting Technology/Technician and Bookkeeping 14 *students enrolled* • Administrative Assistant and Secretarial Science, General 11 *students enrolled* • Automobile/Automotive Mechanics Technology/Technician 6 *students enrolled* • CAD/CADD Drafting and/or Design Technology/Technician 3 *students enrolled* • Child Care Provider/Assistant 15 *students enrolled* • Civil Engineering Technology/Technician • Computer Installation and Repair Technology/Technician 16 *students enrolled* • Computer Systems Networking and Telecommunications 13 *students enrolled* • Cosmetology/Cosmetologist, General 17 *students enrolled* • Criminal Justice/Safety Studies 7 *students enrolled* • Data Entry/Microcomputer Applications, General 1 *student enrolled* • Data Processing and Data Processing Technology/Technician 4 *students enrolled* • Dental Assisting/Assistant 4 *students enrolled* • Drafting and Design Technology/Technician, General 3 *students enrolled* • Early Childhood Education and Teaching 3 *students enrolled* • Electrical, Electronic and Communications Engineering Technology/Technician 1 *student enrolled* • Electrician 24 *students enrolled* • Emergency Medical Technology/Technician (EMT Paramedic) 8 *students enrolled* • Forestry Technology/Technician 8 *students enrolled* • Heating, Air Conditioning, Ventilation and Refrigeration Maintenance Technology/Technician (HAC, HACR, HVAC, HVACR) 10 *students enrolled* • Medical Office Assistant/Specialist 25 *students enrolled* • Medical/Clinical Assistant 20 *students enrolled* • Nurse/Nursing Assistant/Aide and Patient Care Assistant 26 *students enrolled* • Phlebotomy/Phlebotomist 27 *students enrolled* • Welding Technology/Welder 32 *students enrolled* • Wildlife and Wildlands Science and Management 1 *student enrolled* • Word Processing 13 *students enrolled*

STUDENT SERVICES Academic or career counseling, daycare for children of students, employment services for current students, placement services for program completers, remedial services.

Toccoa Falls College

325 Chapel Drive, Toccoa Falls, GA 30598
http://www.tfc.edu/

CONTACT Dr. Wayne Gardner, President
Telephone: 706-886-6831

GENERAL INFORMATION Private Institution. Founded 1907. **Accreditation:** Regional (SACS/CC); music (NASM); state accredited or approved. **Total program enrollment:** 824. **Application fee:** $25.

PROGRAM(S) OFFERED
• Pre-Theology/Pre-Ministerial Studies

STUDENT SERVICES Academic or career counseling, employment services for current students, placement services for program completers.

Valdosta Technical College

4089 Val Tech Road, Valdosta, GA 31602
http://www.valdostatech.edu/

CONTACT F. D. Toth, Interim President
Telephone: 229-333-2100

GENERAL INFORMATION Public Institution. Founded 1963. **Accreditation:** Dental assisting (ADA); dental hygiene (ADA); medical laboratory technology (NAACLS); radiologic technology: radiography (JRCERT); state accredited or approved. **Total program enrollment:** 1027. **Application fee:** $15.

PROGRAM(S) OFFERED
• Accounting Technology/Technician and Bookkeeping 18 *students enrolled* • Administrative Assistant and Secretarial Science, General 17 *students enrolled* • Aesthetician/Esthetician and Skin Care Specialist 5 *students enrolled*

• Applied Horticulture/Horticultural Operations, General 3 *students enrolled* • Autobody/Collision and Repair Technology/Technician 3 *students enrolled* • Automobile/Automotive Mechanics Technology/Technician 17 *students enrolled* • Banking and Financial Support Services 2 *students enrolled* • CAD/CADD Drafting and/or Design Technology/Technician 1 *student enrolled* • Child Care Provider/Assistant 1 *student enrolled* • Child Care and Support Services Management 2 *students enrolled* • Communications Systems Installation and Repair Technology 20 *students enrolled* • Cosmetology/Cosmetologist, General • Criminal Justice/Safety Studies 7 *students enrolled* • Customer Service Support/Call Center/Teleservice Operation 28 *students enrolled* • Data Entry/Microcomputer Applications, General 9 *students enrolled* • Data Processing and Data Processing Technology/Technician 1 *student enrolled* • Dental Assisting/Assistant 8 *students enrolled* • Drafting and Design Technology/Technician, General 2 *students enrolled* • Early Childhood Education and Teaching 3 *students enrolled* • Electrician 9 *students enrolled* • Emergency Medical Technology/Technician (EMT Paramedic) 6 *students enrolled* • Fire Science/Firefighting 1 *student enrolled* • Food Preparation/Professional Cooking/Kitchen Assistant 1 *student enrolled* • Graphic and Printing Equipment Operator, General Production 3 *students enrolled* • Heating, Air Conditioning, Ventilation and Refrigeration Maintenance Technology/Technician (HAC, HACR, HVAC, HVACR) 6 *students enrolled* • Human Resources Management/Personnel Administration, General 10 *students enrolled* • Industrial Mechanics and Maintenance Technology 1 *student enrolled* • Landscaping and Groundskeeping 2 *students enrolled* • Machine Shop Technology/Assistant 1 *student enrolled* • Medical Insurance Coding Specialist/Coder 19 *students enrolled* • Medical Transcription/Transcriptionist 13 *students enrolled* • Medical/Clinical Assistant 16 *students enrolled* • Nail Technician/Specialist and Manicurist 2 *students enrolled* • Nurse/Nursing Assistant/Aide and Patient Care Assistant 11 *students enrolled* • Operations Management and Supervision 17 *students enrolled* • Opticianry/Ophthalmic Dispensing Optician 30 *students enrolled* • Pharmacy Technician/Assistant 8 *students enrolled* • Phlebotomy/Phlebotomist 7 *students enrolled* • Prepress/Desktop Publishing and Digital Imaging Design 3 *students enrolled* • Sales, Distribution and Marketing Operations, General 9 *students enrolled* • Surgical Technology/Technologist 12 *students enrolled* • Truck and Bus Driver/Commercial Vehicle Operation 74 *students enrolled* • Web Page, Digital/Multimedia and Information Resources Design 1 *student enrolled* • Welding Technology/Welder 6 *students enrolled*

STUDENT SERVICES Academic or career counseling, employment services for current students, placement services for program completers, remedial services.

Vogue Beauty School

3655 Macland Road, Suite 109, Hiram, GA 30141-0426

CONTACT Betty Henry, Director/Vice President
Telephone: 770-943-6811

GENERAL INFORMATION Private Institution. **Total program enrollment:** 100. **Application fee:** $100.

PROGRAM(S) OFFERED
• Cosmetology, Barber/Styling, and Nail Instructor 900 *hrs./$6595* • Cosmetology/Cosmetologist, General 1500 *hrs./$12,800* • Nail Technician/Specialist and Manicurist

STUDENT SERVICES Placement services for program completers.

Waycross College

2001 South Georgia Parkway, Waycross, GA 31503-9248
http://www.waycross.edu/

CONTACT Dr. David A. Palmer, President
Telephone: 912-449-7600

GENERAL INFORMATION Public Institution. Founded 1976. **Accreditation:** Regional (SACS/CC). **Total program enrollment:** 446. **Application fee:** $20.

STUDENT SERVICES Academic or career counseling, employment services for current students, remedial services.

West Central Technical College

176 Murphy Campus Boulevard, Waco, GA 30182
http://www.westcentraltech.edu/

CONTACT Dr. Skip Sullivan, President
Telephone: 770-537-6000

GENERAL INFORMATION Public Institution. Founded 1968. **Accreditation:** Regional (SACS/CC); dental hygiene (ADA); medical laboratory technology (NAACLS); state accredited or approved. **Total program enrollment:** 1250. **Application fee:** $25.

PROGRAM(S) OFFERED
• **Accounting Technology/Technician and Bookkeeping** 45 *students enrolled* • **Administrative Assistant and Secretarial Science, General** 20 *students enrolled* • **Architectural Drafting and Architectural CAD/CADD** 6 *students enrolled* • **Automobile/Automotive Mechanics Technology/Technician** 58 *students enrolled* • **Barbering/Barber** • **CAD/CADD Drafting and/or Design Technology/Technician** 7 *students enrolled* • **Child Care Provider/Assistant** 1 *student enrolled* • **Computer Installation and Repair Technology/Technician** 29 *students enrolled* • **Cosmetology/Cosmetologist, General** 50 *students enrolled* • **Criminal Justice/Safety Studies** 39 *students enrolled* • **Data Entry/Microcomputer Applications, General** 58 *students enrolled* • **Data Processing and Data Processing Technology/Technician** 23 *students enrolled* • **Dental Assisting/Assistant** 68 *students enrolled* • **Early Childhood Education and Teaching** 14 *students enrolled* • **Electrician** 2 *students enrolled* • **Emergency Medical Technology/Technician (EMT Paramedic)** 51 *students enrolled* • **Food Preparation/Professional Cooking/Kitchen Assistant** 38 *students enrolled* • **General Office Occupations and Clerical Services** 14 *students enrolled* • **Heating, Air Conditioning, Ventilation and Refrigeration Maintenance Technology/Technician (HAC, HACR, HVAC, HVACR)** 52 *students enrolled* • **Heavy Equipment Maintenance Technology/Technician** 12 *students enrolled* • **Machine Shop Technology/Assistant** 8 *students enrolled* • **Medical Insurance Specialist/Medical Biller** 43 *students enrolled* • **Medical Office Assistant/Specialist** 16 *students enrolled* • **Medical Reception/Receptionist** 13 *students enrolled* • **Medical Transcription/Transcriptionist** 26 *students enrolled* • **Medical/Clinical Assistant** 20 *students enrolled* • **Nurse/Nursing Assistant/Aide and Patient Care Assistant** 113 *students enrolled* • **Phlebotomy/Phlebotomist** 33 *students enrolled* • **Sales, Distribution and Marketing Operations, General** 1 *student enrolled* • **Small Business Administration/Management** 10 *students enrolled* • **Surgical Technology/Technologist** 7 *students enrolled* • **Truck and Bus Driver/Commercial Vehicle Operation** 124 *students enrolled* • **Web Page, Digital/Multimedia and Information Resources Design** 1 *student enrolled* • **Welding Technology/Welder** 98 *students enrolled*

STUDENT SERVICES Academic or career counseling, employment services for current students, placement services for program completers, remedial services.

West Georgia Technical College

One College Circle, LaGrange, GA 30240
http://www.westgatech.edu/

CONTACT Mr. Perrin Alford, Acting President
Telephone: 706-845-4323

GENERAL INFORMATION Public Institution. Founded 1966. **Accreditation:** State accredited or approved. **Total program enrollment:** 728. **Application fee:** $15.

PROGRAM(S) OFFERED
• **Accounting Technology/Technician and Bookkeeping** 42 *students enrolled* • **Administrative Assistant and Secretarial Science, General** 16 *students enrolled* • **Aesthetician/Esthetician and Skin Care Specialist** • **Animation, Interactive Technology, Video Graphics and Special Effects** 34 *students enrolled* • **Architectural Drafting and Architectural CAD/CADD** 1 *student enrolled* • **Athletic Training/Trainer** 3 *students enrolled* • **Automobile/Automotive Mechanics Technology/Technician** 28 *students enrolled* • **Barbering/Barber** 3 *students enrolled* • **CAD/CADD Drafting and/or Design Technology/Technician** 1 *student enrolled* • **Child Care Provider/Assistant** 1 *student enrolled* • **Computer Installation and Repair Technology/Technician** 11 *students enrolled* • **Computer Systems Networking and Telecommunications** 6 *students enrolled* • **Cosmetology/Cosmetologist, General** 23 *students enrolled* • **Criminal Justice/Safety Studies** 5 *students enrolled* • **Customer Service Support/Call Center/Teleservice Operation** 8 *students enrolled* • **Data Entry/Microcomputer Applications, General** 54 *students enrolled* • **Drafting and Design Technology/Technician, General** 2 *students enrolled* • **Early Childhood Education and Teaching** 12 *students enrolled* • **Electrical/Electronics Equipment Installation and Repair, General** 1 *student enrolled* • **Fire Science/Firefighting** 47 *students*

enrolled • **Food Preparation/Professional Cooking/Kitchen Assistant** 9 *students enrolled* • **General Office Occupations and Clerical Services** 1 *student enrolled* • **Graphic and Printing Equipment Operator, General Production** 11 *students enrolled* • **Heating, Air Conditioning, Ventilation and Refrigeration Maintenance Technology/Technician (HAC, HACR, HVAC, HVACR)** 19 *students enrolled* • **Industrial Mechanics and Maintenance Technology** 1 *student enrolled* • **Information Technology** 2 *students enrolled* • **Landscaping and Groundskeeping** 19 *students enrolled* • **Lineworker** 26 *students enrolled* • **Machine Shop Technology/Assistant** 11 *students enrolled* • **Manufacturing Technology/Technician** 22 *students enrolled* • **Medical Insurance Coding Specialist/Coder** 17 *students enrolled* • **Medical Reception/Receptionist** 11 *students enrolled* • **Medical Transcription/Transcriptionist** 16 *students enrolled* • **Medical/Clinical Assistant** 5 *students enrolled* • **Nurse/Nursing Assistant/Aide and Patient Care Assistant** 72 *students enrolled* • **Operations Management and Supervision** 1 *student enrolled* • **Phlebotomy/Phlebotomist** 12 *students enrolled* • **Radiologic Technology/Science—Radiographer** 6 *students enrolled* • **Truck and Bus Driver/Commercial Vehicle Operation** 192 *students enrolled* • **Welding Technology/Welder** 5 *students enrolled*

STUDENT SERVICES Academic or career counseling, daycare for children of students, employment services for current students, placement services for program completers, remedial services.

ILLINOIS

Alvareitas College of Cosmetology

5400 West Main, Belleville, IL 62226

CONTACT Alvareita Giles, President
Telephone: 618-257-9193

GENERAL INFORMATION Private Institution. **Total program enrollment:** 19. **Application fee:** $50.

PROGRAM(S) OFFERED
• **Cosmetology, Barber/Styling, and Nail Instructor** 1000 *hrs./$3300* • **Hair Styling/Stylist and Hair Design** 1540 *hrs./$11,500*

STUDENT SERVICES Academic or career counseling.

Alvareita's College of Cosmetology

333 South Kansas Street, Edwardsville, IL 62025

CONTACT Alvreita Giles, President
Telephone: 618-656-2593

GENERAL INFORMATION Private Institution. Founded 1965. **Total program enrollment:** 29. **Application fee:** $50.

PROGRAM(S) OFFERED
• **Cosmetology, Barber/Styling, and Nail Instructor** 1000 *hrs./$3300* • **Hair Styling/Stylist and Hair Design** 1540 *hrs./$11,500*

STUDENT SERVICES Academic or career counseling.

Alvareita's College of Cosmetology

5711 Godfrey Road, Godfrey, IL 62035

CONTACT Alvareita Giles, President
Telephone: 618-466-9723

GENERAL INFORMATION Private Institution. Founded 1984. **Total program enrollment:** 35. **Application fee:** $50.

PROGRAM(S) OFFERED
• **Cosmetology, Barber/Styling, and Nail Instructor** 1000 *hrs./$4000* • **Hair Styling/Stylist and Hair Design** 1540 *hrs./$11,450* • **Massage Therapy/Therapeutic Massage** 720 *hrs./$5500*

STUDENT SERVICES Academic or career counseling.

American Career College

7000 W. Cermak Road, Berwyn, IL 60402

CONTACT Patricia Caraballo, President
Telephone: 708-795-1500

GENERAL INFORMATION Private Institution. **Total program enrollment:** 35.

PROGRAM(S) OFFERED
• **Cosmetology, Barber/Styling, and Nail Instructor** *500 hrs./$2500*
• **Cosmetology/Cosmetologist, General** *1500 hrs./$10,800* • **Nail Technician/ Specialist and Manicurist** *350 hrs./$2400*

STUDENT SERVICES Academic or career counseling, placement services for program completers, remedial services.

Beck Area Career Center–Red Bud

6137 Beck Road, Red Bud, IL 62278
http://www.schools.lth5.k12.il.us/beck/

CONTACT Dian Albert, Director
Telephone: 618-473-2222

GENERAL INFORMATION Public Institution. Founded 1972. **Total program enrollment:** 98.

PROGRAM(S) OFFERED
• **Licensed Practical/Vocational Nurse Training (LPN, LVN, Cert, Dipl, AAS)** *1463 hrs./$10,962* • **Nurse/Nursing Assistant/Aide and Patient Care Assistant** *138 hrs./$550*

STUDENT SERVICES Academic or career counseling, placement services for program completers, remedial services.

Bell Mar Beauty College

5717 West Cermak, Cicero, IL 60804

CONTACT Vincent Guarna, President
Telephone: 708-863-6644

GENERAL INFORMATION Private Institution.

PROGRAM(S) OFFERED
• **Cosmetology, Barber/Styling, and Nail Instructor** *1500 hrs./$8801*
• **Cosmetology/Cosmetologist, General** *250 hrs./$1000*

STUDENT SERVICES Academic or career counseling, placement services for program completers, remedial services.

BIR Training Center

3601 West Devon, Suite 210, Chicago, IL 60659
http://www.birtraining.com/

CONTACT Irene Zakon, CEO
Telephone: 773-866-0111

GENERAL INFORMATION Private Institution. **Total program enrollment:** 693. **Application fee:** $80.

PROGRAM(S) OFFERED
• **Accounting and Related Services, Other** *22 hrs./$5480* • **English Language and Literature, General** *35 hrs./$5680* • **Finance and Financial Management Services, Other** • **Health Information/Medical Records Technology/Technician** *23 hrs./$6790* • **Mechanical Engineering Related Technologies/Technicians, Other** *23 hrs./$8280* • **Medical Office Assistant/Specialist** *31 hrs./$9035* • **Medical Office Computer Specialist/Assistant** *36 students enrolled*

STUDENT SERVICES Academic or career counseling, placement services for program completers, remedial services.

Black Hawk College

6600 34th Avenue, Moline, IL 61265-5899
http://www.bhc.edu/

CONTACT Dr. R. Gene Gardner, Interim President
Telephone: 309-796-5000

GENERAL INFORMATION Public Institution. Founded 1946. **Accreditation:** Regional (NCA); physical therapy assisting (APTA). **Total program enrollment:** 2622.

PROGRAM(S) OFFERED
• **Accounting Technology/Technician and Bookkeeping** *3 students enrolled* • **Agricultural Mechanization, General** *3 students enrolled* • **Animal/Livestock Husbandry and Production** *17 students enrolled* • **Automobile/Automotive Mechanics Technology/Technician** *5 students enrolled* • **CAD/CADD Drafting and/or Design Technology/Technician** *2 students enrolled* • **Child Care Provider/ Assistant** *5 students enrolled* • **Computer Systems Networking and Telecommunications** *3 students enrolled* • **Criminal Justice/Police Science** *1 student enrolled* • **Electromechanical Technology/Electromechanical Engineering Technology** *4 students enrolled* • **Emergency Medical Technology/Technician (EMT Paramedic)** *1 student enrolled* • **Legal Administrative Assistant/Secretary** *1 student enrolled* • **Licensed Practical/Vocational Nurse Training (LPN, LVN, Cert, Dipl, AAS)** *41 students enrolled* • **Machine Tool Technology/Machinist** *1 student enrolled* • **Manufacturing Technology/Technician** *8 students enrolled* • **Massage Therapy/Therapeutic Massage** *13 students enrolled* • **Medical Insurance Coding Specialist/Coder** *13 students enrolled* • **Medical Insurance Specialist/Medical Biller** *6 students enrolled* • **Medical Transcription/ Transcriptionist** *9 students enrolled* • **Retailing and Retail Operations** *2 students enrolled* • **Welding Technology/Welder** *4 students enrolled*

STUDENT SERVICES Academic or career counseling, employment services for current students, placement services for program completers, remedial services.

Brown Mackie College–Moline

1527 47th Avenue, Moline, IL 61265-7062
http://www.brownmackie.edu/Moline/

CONTACT Kareem Odukale, Campus President
Telephone: 309-762-2100

GENERAL INFORMATION Private Institution. **Total program enrollment:** 165.

PROGRAM(S) OFFERED
• **Accounting** *4 students enrolled* • **Business Administration and Management, General** *16 students enrolled* • **Computer Software Technology/Technician** *4 students enrolled* • **Legal Assistant/Paralegal** *11 students enrolled* • **Medical Office Management/Administration** *13 students enrolled* • **Medical/Clinical Assistant** *47 students enrolled*

STUDENT SERVICES Academic or career counseling, employment services for current students, placement services for program completers, remedial services.

Cain's Barber College

365 East 51st Street, Chicago, IL 60615-3510
http://www.cainbarber1.org/

CONTACT Jessica Pearson-Cain, President/CEO
Telephone: 773-536-4441

GENERAL INFORMATION Private Institution. Founded 1985. **Total program enrollment:** 129. **Application fee:** $100.

PROGRAM(S) OFFERED
• **Barbering/Barber** *1500 hrs./$8985* • **Cosmetology, Barber/Styling, and Nail Instructor** *2 students enrolled*

STUDENT SERVICES Placement services for program completers.

CALC Institute of Technology

235-A E. Center Drive, Alton, IL 62002
http://www.calc4it.com/

CONTACT Fred Albrecht, Director
Telephone: 618-474-0616

GENERAL INFORMATION Private Institution.

PROGRAM(S) OFFERED
• Computer Systems Networking and Telecommunications *550 hrs./$7800* • Medical Office Assistant/Specialist *580 hrs./$7872* • Medical/Clinical Assistant *900 hrs.* • System, Networking, and LAN/WAN Management/Manager *850 hrs./$12,000*

STUDENT SERVICES Placement services for program completers.

Cameo Beauty Academy

9714 South Cicero Avenue, Oak Lawn, IL 60453
http://www.cameobeautyacademy.com/

CONTACT Herman A. Harrison, President
Telephone: 708-636-4660

GENERAL INFORMATION Private Institution. Founded 1960. **Total program enrollment:** 75.

PROGRAM(S) OFFERED
• Cosmetology, Barber/Styling, and Nail Instructor *5 students enrolled* • Cosmetology/Cosmetologist, General *1500 hrs./$17,300* • Trade and Industrial Teacher Education *1000 hrs./$10,700*

STUDENT SERVICES Academic or career counseling, placement services for program completers.

Cannella School of Hair Design

12840 South Western Avenue, Blue Island, IL 60406
http://djosephcannella@aol.com/

CONTACT Joseph Cannella, President
Telephone: 708-388-4949

GENERAL INFORMATION Private Institution. **Total program enrollment:** 18.

PROGRAM(S) OFFERED
• Cosmetology/Cosmetologist, General *1500 hrs./$12,990* • Teacher Education and Professional Development, Specific Subject Areas, Other *1000 hrs./$5750*

STUDENT SERVICES Academic or career counseling, placement services for program completers.

Cannella School of Hair Design

4217 West North Avenue, Chicago, IL 60639
http://djosephcannella@aol.com/

CONTACT Joseph Cannella, Owner
Telephone: 773-278-4477

GENERAL INFORMATION Private Institution. **Total program enrollment:** 8.

PROGRAM(S) OFFERED
• Cosmetology/Cosmetologist, General *1500 hrs./$10,900* • Teacher Education and Professional Development, Specific Subject Areas, Other *1000 hrs./$5750*

STUDENT SERVICES Academic or career counseling, placement services for program completers.

Cannella School of Hair Design

4269 South Archer Avenue, Chicago, IL 60632
http://djosephcannella@aol.com/

CONTACT Joseph Cannella, President
Telephone: 773-890-0412

GENERAL INFORMATION Private Institution. **Total program enrollment:** 23.

PROGRAM(S) OFFERED
• Cosmetology/Cosmetologist, General *1500 hrs./$10,900* • Teacher Education and Professional Development, Specific Subject Areas, Other *1000 hrs./$5750*

STUDENT SERVICES Academic or career counseling, placement services for program completers.

Cannella School of Hair Design

9012 South Commercial, Chicago, IL 60617
http://djosephcannella@aol.com/

CONTACT Joseph Cannella, Owner
Telephone: 773-221-4700

GENERAL INFORMATION Private Institution. **Total program enrollment:** 15.

PROGRAM(S) OFFERED
• Cosmetology/Cosmetologist, General *1500 hrs./$12,990* • Teacher Education and Professional Development, Specific Subject Areas, Other *1000 hrs./$5750*

STUDENT SERVICES Academic or career counseling, placement services for program completers.

Cannella School of Hair Design

113-117 West Chicago Street, Elgin, IL 60120
http://djosephcannella@aol.com/

CONTACT Joseph Cannella, Owner
Telephone: 708-742-6611

GENERAL INFORMATION Private Institution. **Total program enrollment:** 7.

PROGRAM(S) OFFERED
• Cosmetology/Cosmetologist, General *1500 hrs./$12,990* • Teacher Education and Professional Development, Specific Subject Areas, Other *1000 hrs./$5750*

STUDENT SERVICES Academic or career counseling, placement services for program completers.

Cannella School of Hair Design

191 North York Road, Elmhurst, IL 60126
http://djosephcannella@aol.com/

CONTACT Joseph Cannella, Owner
Telephone: 708-833-6118

GENERAL INFORMATION Private Institution. **Total program enrollment:** 13.

PROGRAM(S) OFFERED
• Cosmetology/Cosmetologist, General *1500 hrs./$10,900* • Teacher Education and Professional Development, Specific Subject Areas, Other *1000 hrs./$5750*

STUDENT SERVICES Academic or career counseling, placement services for program completers.

Capital Area School of Practical Nursing

2201 Toronto Road, Springfield, IL 62707

CONTACT Karen Riddell, Office Manager/Administrative Assistant
Telephone: 217-585-2160

GENERAL INFORMATION Public Institution. Founded 1958. **Total program enrollment: 65. Application fee:** $70.

PROGRAM(S) OFFERED
• Licensed Practical/Vocational Nurse Training (LPN, LVN, Cert, Dipl, AAS) 1330 hrs./$7688

STUDENT SERVICES Academic or career counseling.

Capri Garfield Ridge School of Beauty Culture

6301 South Washtenaw, Chicago, IL 60629
http://www.capribeautyschool.com/

CONTACT Frederick Seil, President
Telephone: 773-778-0882 Ext. 225

GENERAL INFORMATION Private Institution. Founded 1966. **Total program enrollment: 96. Application fee:** $100.

PROGRAM(S) OFFERED
• Cosmetology, Barber/Styling, and Nail Instructor 1000 hrs./$8100
• Cosmetology/Cosmetologist, General 1500 hrs./$15,700

STUDENT SERVICES Academic or career counseling, placement services for program completers.

Capri Oak Forest School of Beauty Culture

15815 South Robroy Drive, Oak Forest, IL 60452
http://www.capribeautycollege.com/

CONTACT Frederick C. Seil, President
Telephone: 708-687-3020

GENERAL INFORMATION Private Institution. Founded 1978. **Total program enrollment: 110. Application fee:** $100.

PROGRAM(S) OFFERED
• Cosmetology, Barber/Styling, and Nail Instructor 1000 hrs./$9714
• Cosmetology/Cosmetologist, General 1500 hrs./$17,750

STUDENT SERVICES Academic or career counseling, employment services for current students, placement services for program completers.

Carl Sandburg College

2400 Tom L. Wilson Boulevard, Galesburg, IL 61401-9576
http://www.sandburg.edu/

CONTACT Thomas A. Schmidt, President
Telephone: 309-344-2518

GENERAL INFORMATION Public Institution. Founded 1967. **Accreditation:** Regional (NCA); dental hygiene (ADA); funeral service (ABFSE); radiologic technology: radiography (JRCERT). **Total program enrollment:** 1178.

PROGRAM(S) OFFERED
• Accounting 4 students enrolled • Administrative Assistant and Secretarial Science, General 5 students enrolled • Automobile/Automotive Mechanics Technology/Technician 2 students enrolled • Business Administration and Management, General 1 student enrolled • Cosmetology, Barber/Styling, and Nail Instructor 1 student enrolled • Cosmetology/Cosmetologist, General 13 students enrolled • Criminal Justice/Police Science 1 student enrolled • Diagnostic Medical Sonography/Sonographer and Ultrasound Technician 7 students enrolled • Diesel Mechanics Technology/Technician 1 student enrolled • Licensed Practical/Vocational Nurse Training (LPN, LVN, Cert, Dipl, AAS) 66 students enrolled • Massage Therapy/Therapeutic Massage 6 students

enrolled • Medical Administrative/Executive Assistant and Medical Secretary 11 students enrolled • Medical/Clinical Assistant 10 students enrolled • Nuclear Medical Technology/Technologist 3 students enrolled • Radiologic Technology/Science—Radiographer 5 students enrolled • Social Work 3 students enrolled • Welding Technology/Welder 2 students enrolled

STUDENT SERVICES Academic or career counseling, daycare for children of students, employment services for current students, placement services for program completers, remedial services.

Center for Employment Training–Chicago

3301 West Arthington, Suite 101, Chicago, IL 60624

CONTACT Marie Pickett, Director
Telephone: 408-287-7924

GENERAL INFORMATION Private Institution. **Total program enrollment:** 400.

PROGRAM(S) OFFERED
• Administrative Assistant and Secretarial Science, General • Building/Property Maintenance and Management 630 hrs./$7083 • Medical/Clinical Assistant 900 hrs./$8864

STUDENT SERVICES Academic or career counseling, employment services for current students, placement services for program completers, remedial services.

Christian Life College

400 East Gregory Street, Mount Prospect, IL 60056
http://www.christianlifecollege.edu/

CONTACT Harry Schmidt, President
Telephone: 847-259-1840

GENERAL INFORMATION Private Institution. Founded 1950. **Accreditation:** State accredited or approved. **Total program enrollment: 36. Application fee:** $35.

STUDENT SERVICES Academic or career counseling, employment services for current students, placement services for program completers, remedial services.

City Colleges of Chicago, Harold Washington College

30 East Lake Street, Chicago, IL 60601-2449
http://hwashington.ccc.edu/

CONTACT John R. Wozniak, President
Telephone: 312-553-5600

GENERAL INFORMATION Public Institution. Founded 1962. **Accreditation:** Regional (NCA). **Total program enrollment:** 4173.

PROGRAM(S) OFFERED
• Accounting 3 students enrolled • Animation, Interactive Technology, Video Graphics and Special Effects 4 students enrolled • Architectural Drafting and Architectural CAD/CADD 1 student enrolled • Business Administration and Management, General 2 students enrolled • Child Care Provider/Assistant 8 students enrolled • Criminal Justice/Safety Studies 1 student enrolled • Foodservice Systems Administration/Management 1027 students enrolled • Information Science/Studies 2 students enrolled • Marketing/Marketing Management, General 3 students enrolled • Music, General 1 student enrolled • Nurse/Nursing Assistant/Aide and Patient Care Assistant 61 students enrolled • Social Work 3 students enrolled • Substance Abuse/Addiction Counseling 13 students enrolled • Truck and Bus Driver/Commercial Vehicle Operation 3183 students enrolled

STUDENT SERVICES Academic or career counseling, employment services for current students, placement services for program completers, remedial services.

City Colleges of Chicago, Harry S. Truman College

1145 West Wilson Avenue, Chicago, IL 60640-5616
http://www.trumancollege.cc/

CONTACT Lynn Walker, President
Telephone: 773-907-4700

GENERAL INFORMATION Public Institution. Founded 1956. **Accreditation:** Regional (NCA). **Total program enrollment:** 2569.

PROGRAM(S) OFFERED
• **Accounting** 3 *students enrolled* • **Appliance Installation and Repair Technology/Technician** 4 *students enrolled* • **Automobile/Automotive Mechanics Technology/Technician** 13 *students enrolled* • **Business Administration and Management, General** 1 *student enrolled* • **Child Care Provider/Assistant** 20 *students enrolled* • **Computer Systems Networking and Telecommunications** 1 *student enrolled* • **Cosmetology/Cosmetologist, General** 39 *students enrolled* • **Information Science/Studies** 11 *students enrolled* • **Mechanical Drafting and Mechanical Drafting CAD/CADD** 2 *students enrolled* • **Pharmacy Technician/Assistant** 48 *students enrolled* • **Phlebotomy/Phlebotomist** 11 *students enrolled* • **Web Page, Digital/Multimedia and Information Resources Design** 2 *students enrolled*

STUDENT SERVICES Academic or career counseling, daycare for children of students, employment services for current students, placement services for program completers, remedial services.

City Colleges of Chicago, Kennedy-King College

6800 South Wentworth Avenue, Chicago, IL 60621-3733
http://kennedyking.ccc.edu/

CONTACT Clyde El-Amin, President
Telephone: 773-602-5000

GENERAL INFORMATION Public Institution. Founded 1935. **Accreditation:** Regional (NCA); dental hygiene (ADA). **Total program enrollment:** 3090.

PROGRAM(S) OFFERED
• **Animation, Interactive Technology, Video Graphics and Special Effects** 1 *student enrolled* • **Autobody/Collision and Repair Technology/Technician** 4 *students enrolled* • **Automobile/Automotive Mechanics Technology/Technician** 9 *students enrolled* • **Baking and Pastry Arts/Baker/Pastry Chef** 24 *students enrolled* • **Building/Home/Construction Inspection/Inspector** 4 *students enrolled* • **Carpentry/Carpenter** 61 *students enrolled* • **Child Care Provider/Assistant** 16 *students enrolled* • **Criminal Justice/Safety Studies** 14 *students enrolled* • **Culinary Arts/Chef Training** 35 *students enrolled* • **Graphic Communications, General** 1 *student enrolled* • **Heating, Air Conditioning, Ventilation and Refrigeration Maintenance Technology/Technician (HAC, HACR, HVAC, HVACR)** 1 *student enrolled* • **Information Science/Studies** 2 *students enrolled* • **Lineworker** 30 *students enrolled* • **Mason/Masonry** 44 *students enrolled* • **Medical Insurance Coding Specialist/Coder** 5 *students enrolled* • **Mental Health Counseling/Counselor** 1 *student enrolled* • **Nurse/Nursing Assistant/Aide and Patient Care Assistant** 8 *students enrolled* • **Painting/Painter and Wall Coverer** 9 *students enrolled* • **Phlebotomy/Phlebotomist** 11 *students enrolled* • **Platemaker/Imager** 1 *student enrolled* • **Substance Abuse/Addiction Counseling** 28 *students enrolled* • **Web Page, Digital/Multimedia and Information Resources Design** 1 *student enrolled* • **Welding Technology/Welder** 11 *students enrolled*

STUDENT SERVICES Academic or career counseling, daycare for children of students, employment services for current students, placement services for program completers, remedial services.

City Colleges of Chicago, Malcolm X College

1900 West Van Buren Street, Chicago, IL 60612-3145
http://malcolmx.ccc.edu/

CONTACT Ghingo Brooks, President
Telephone: 312-850-7000

GENERAL INFORMATION Public Institution. Founded 1911. **Accreditation:** Regional (NCA); funeral service (ABFSE); radiologic technology: radiography (JRCERT); surgical technology (ARCST). **Total program enrollment:** 2584.

PROGRAM(S) OFFERED
• **Child Care Provider/Assistant** 14 *students enrolled* • **Emergency Care Attendant (EMT Ambulance)** 128 *students enrolled* • **Nurse/Nursing Assistant/Aide and Patient Care Assistant** 126 *students enrolled* • **Pharmacy Technician/Assistant** 14 *students enrolled* • **Phlebotomy/Phlebotomist** 6 *students enrolled* • **Renal/Dialysis Technologist/Technician** 8 *students enrolled* • **Surgical Technology/Technologist** 9 *students enrolled*

STUDENT SERVICES Academic or career counseling, daycare for children of students, employment services for current students, placement services for program completers, remedial services.

City Colleges of Chicago, Olive-Harvey College

10001 South Woodlawn Avenue, Chicago, IL 60628-1645
http://oliveharvey.ccc.edu/

CONTACT Dr. Valerie Roberson, President
Telephone: 773-291-6100

GENERAL INFORMATION Public Institution. Founded 1970. **Accreditation:** Regional (NCA). **Total program enrollment:** 1758.

PROGRAM(S) OFFERED
• **Accounting** 1 *student enrolled* • **Child Care Provider/Assistant** 29 *students enrolled* • **Criminal Justice/Safety Studies** 2 *students enrolled* • **Emergency Medical Technology/Technician (EMT Paramedic)** 30 *students enrolled* • **Ground Transportation, Other** 31 *students enrolled* • **Information Science/Studies** 1 *student enrolled* • **Marketing/Marketing Management, General** 1 *student enrolled* • **Medical Insurance Coding Specialist/Coder** 8 *students enrolled* • **Nurse/Nursing Assistant/Aide and Patient Care Assistant** 22 *students enrolled* • **Pharmacy Technician/Assistant** 6 *students enrolled* • **Phlebotomy/Phlebotomist** 6 *students enrolled*

STUDENT SERVICES Academic or career counseling, daycare for children of students, employment services for current students, placement services for program completers, remedial services.

City Colleges of Chicago, Richard J. Daley College

7500 South Pulaski Road, Chicago, IL 60652-1242
http://daley.ccc.edu/

CONTACT Dr. Sylvia Ramos, President
Telephone: 773-838-7500

GENERAL INFORMATION Public Institution. Founded 1960. **Accreditation:** Regional (NCA). **Total program enrollment:** 3507.

PROGRAM(S) OFFERED
• **Accounting** 7 *students enrolled* • **Business Administration and Management, General** 5 *students enrolled* • **Business/Office Automation/Technology/Data Entry** 1 *student enrolled* • **Child Care Provider/Assistant** 23 *students enrolled* • **Computer Installation and Repair Technology/Technician** 12 *students enrolled* • **Computer Systems Networking and Telecommunications** 2 *students enrolled* • **Criminal Justice/Police Science** 1 *student enrolled* • **Criminal Justice/Safety Studies** 4 *students enrolled* • **Emergency Medical Technology/Technician (EMT Paramedic)** 1 *student enrolled* • **Industrial Mechanics and Maintenance Technology** 12 *students enrolled* • **Information Science/Studies** 20 *students enrolled* • **Machine Tool Technology/Machinist** 4 *students enrolled* • **Marketing/Marketing Management, General** 44 *students enrolled* • **Medical Insurance Coding Specialist/Coder** 29 *students enrolled* • **Medical Staff Services**

Technology/Technician 2 *students enrolled* • **Nurse/Nursing Assistant/Aide and Patient Care Assistant** 95 *students enrolled* • **Pharmacy Technician/Assistant** 26 *students enrolled* • **Phlebotomy/Phlebotomist** 28 *students enrolled* • **Real Estate** 1 *student enrolled* • **Security and Loss Prevention Services** 2 *students enrolled*

STUDENT SERVICES Academic or career counseling, daycare for children of students, employment services for current students, placement services for program completers, remedial services.

City Colleges of Chicago System

226 West Jackson Boulevard, Chicago, IL 60606-6998
http://www.ccc.edu

CONTACT Dr. Wayne Watson, Chancellor
Telephone: 312-553-2500

GENERAL INFORMATION Public Institution.

City Colleges of Chicago, Wilbur Wright College

4300 North Narragansett Avenue, Chicago, IL 60634-1591
http://wright.ccc.edu/

CONTACT Charles Guengerich, President
Telephone: 773-777-7900

GENERAL INFORMATION Public Institution. Founded 1934. **Accreditation:** Regional (NCA); radiologic technology: radiography (JRCERT). **Total program enrollment:** 3547.

PROGRAM(S) OFFERED

• **Accounting** 3 *students enrolled* • **Architectural Drafting and Architectural CAD/CADD** 11 *students enrolled* • **Business Administration and Management, General** 2 *students enrolled* • **Business/Office Automation/Technology/Data Entry** 5 *students enrolled* • **Computer Installation and Repair Technology/Technician** 2 *students enrolled* • **Criminal Justice/Safety Studies** 2 *students enrolled* • **Criminalistics and Criminal Science** 1 *student enrolled* • **Dental Assisting/Assistant** 6 *students enrolled* • **Emergency Medical Technology/Technician (EMT Paramedic)** 56 *students enrolled* • **Energy Management and Systems Technology/Technician** 10 *students enrolled* • **Environmental Engineering Technology/Environmental Technology** 2 *students enrolled* • **Hospital and Health Care Facilities Administration/Management** 1 *student enrolled* • **Industrial Mechanics and Maintenance Technology** 11 *students enrolled* • **Information Science/Studies** 3 *students enrolled* • **Library Assistant/Technician** 1 *student enrolled* • **Licensed Practical/Vocational Nurse Training (LPN, LVN, Cert, Dipl, AAS)** 40 *students enrolled* • **Marketing/Marketing Management, General** 4 *students enrolled* • **Mechanical Drafting and Mechanical Drafting CAD/CADD** 6 *students enrolled* • **Medical Insurance Coding Specialist/Coder** 8 *students enrolled* • **Nurse/Nursing Assistant/Aide and Patient Care Assistant** 98 *students enrolled* • **Pharmacy Technician/Assistant** 3 *students enrolled* • **Phlebotomy/Phlebotomist** 49 *students enrolled* • **Psychiatric/Mental Health Services Technician** 17 *students enrolled* • **Substance Abuse/Addiction Counseling** 6 *students enrolled*

STUDENT SERVICES Academic or career counseling, employment services for current students, placement services for program completers, remedial services.

College of DuPage

425 Fawell Boulevard, Glen Ellyn, IL 60137-6599
http://www.cod.edu/

CONTACT Dr. Robert Breuder, President
Telephone: 630-942-2800

GENERAL INFORMATION Public Institution. Founded 1967. **Accreditation:** Regional (NCA); dental hygiene (ADA); health information technology (AHIMA); physical therapy assisting (APTA); radiologic technology: radiography (JRCERT); respiratory therapy technology (CoARC). **Total program enrollment:** 9882. **Application fee:** $10.

PROGRAM(S) OFFERED

• **Accounting Technology/Technician and Bookkeeping** 14 *students enrolled* • **Administrative Assistant and Secretarial Science, General** 50 *students enrolled* • **Applied Horticulture/Horticultural Operations, General** 5 *students enrolled* • **Architectural Drafting and Architectural CAD/CADD** 2 *students enrolled* • **Automobile/Automotive Mechanics Technology/Technician** 23 *students enrolled* • **Baking and Pastry Arts/Baker/Pastry Chef** 2 *students enrolled* • **Building/Property Maintenance and Management** 4 *students enrolled* • **Business Administration and Management, General** 65 *students enrolled* • **Child Care Provider/Assistant** 2 *students enrolled* • **Child Care and Support Services Management** 7 *students enrolled* • **Commercial Photography** 10 *students enrolled* • **Commercial and Advertising Art** 47 *students enrolled* • **Computer Installation and Repair Technology/Technician** 127 *students enrolled* • **Computer Programming, Specific Applications** 12 *students enrolled* • **Computer Technology/Computer Systems Technology** 2 *students enrolled* • **Criminal Justice/Police Science** 12 *students enrolled* • **Culinary Arts/Chef Training** 8 *students enrolled* • **Data Entry/Microcomputer Applications, General** 1 *student enrolled* • **Diagnostic Medical Sonography/Sonographer and Ultrasound Technician** 8 *students enrolled* • **Electrocardiograph Technology/Technician** 1 *student enrolled* • **Emergency Medical Technology/Technician (EMT Paramedic)** 212 *students enrolled* • **Entrepreneurship/Entrepreneurial Studies** 2 *students enrolled* • **Fashion Merchandising** 4 *students enrolled* • **Fashion and Fabric Consultant** 12 *students enrolled* • **Fire Protection and Safety Technology/Technician** 4 *students enrolled* • **Heating, Air Conditioning, Ventilation and Refrigeration Maintenance Technology/Technician (HAC, HACR, HVAC, HVACR)** 20 *students enrolled* • **Home Health Aide/Home Attendant** 27 *students enrolled* • **Hospital and Health Care Facilities Administration/Management** 9 *students enrolled* • **Hotel/Motel Administration/Management** 3 *students enrolled* • **Illustration** 1 *student enrolled* • **Interior Design** 40 *students enrolled* • **Landscaping and Groundskeeping** 7 *students enrolled* • **Library Assistant/Technician** 21 *students enrolled* • **Massage Therapy/Therapeutic Massage** 9 *students enrolled* • **Medical Insurance Coding Specialist/Coder** 12 *students enrolled* • **Medical Radiologic Technology/Science—Radiation Therapist** 15 *students enrolled* • **Medical Transcription/Transcriptionist** 76 *students enrolled* • **Nuclear Medical Technology/Technologist** 17 *students enrolled* • **Nurse/Nursing Assistant/Aide and Patient Care Assistant** 184 *students enrolled* • **Ornamental Horticulture** 2 *students enrolled* • **Pharmacy Technician/Assistant** 65 *students enrolled* • **Photographic and Film/Video Technology/Technician and Assistant** 5 *students enrolled* • **Plant Nursery Operations and Management** 3 *students enrolled* • **Plastics Engineering Technology/Technician** 1 *student enrolled* • **Platemaker/Imager** 1 *student enrolled* • **Prepress/Desktop Publishing and Digital Imaging Design** 8 *students enrolled* • **Restaurant, Culinary, and Catering Management/Manager** 3 *students enrolled* • **Robotics Technology/Technician** 1 *student enrolled* • **Sales, Distribution and Marketing Operations, General** 8 *students enrolled* • **Selling Skills and Sales Operations** 14 *students enrolled* • **Social Work** 5 *students enrolled* • **Substance Abuse/Addiction Counseling** 2 *students enrolled* • **Surgical Technology/Technologist** 23 *students enrolled* • **Technical and Business Writing** 1 *student enrolled* • **Tourism and Travel Services Marketing Operations** 32 *students enrolled* • **Web Page, Digital/Multimedia and Information Resources Design** 4 *students enrolled* • **Welding Technology/Welder** 1 *student enrolled*

STUDENT SERVICES Academic or career counseling, daycare for children of students, employment services for current students, remedial services.

College of Lake County

19351 West Washington Street, Grayslake, IL 60030-1198
http://www.clcillinois.edu/

CONTACT James Rock, Interim President
Telephone: 847-543-2000

GENERAL INFORMATION Public Institution. Founded 1967. **Accreditation:** Regional (NCA); dental hygiene (ADA); health information technology (AHIMA); radiologic technology: radiography (JRCERT). **Total program enrollment:** 5206.

PROGRAM(S) OFFERED

• **Accounting Technology/Technician and Bookkeeping** 2 *students enrolled* • **Accounting** 5 *students enrolled* • **Administrative Assistant and Secretarial Science, General** 49 *students enrolled* • **Architectural Drafting and Architectural CAD/CADD** 1 *student enrolled* • **Autobody/Collision and Repair Technology/Technician** 1 *student enrolled* • **Automobile/Automotive Mechanics Technology/Technician** 6 *students enrolled* • **Business/Office Automation/Technology/Data Entry** 39 *students enrolled* • **CAD/CADD Drafting and/or Design Technology/Technician** 5 *students enrolled* • **Child Care Provider/Assistant** 5 *students enrolled* • **Computer Installation and Repair Technology/Technician** 14 *students enrolled* • **Computer Programming, Specific Applications** 1 *student enrolled* • **Computer Systems Networking and Telecommunications** 6 *students enrolled* • **Computer and Information Systems Security** 4 *students enrolled* • **Construc-**

College of Lake County (continued)

tion Engineering Technology/Technician 1 *student enrolled* • **Criminal Justice/Police Science** 3 *students enrolled* • **Culinary Arts/Chef Training** 7 *students enrolled* • **Diagnostic Medical Sonography/Sonographer and Ultrasound Technician** 12 *students enrolled* • **Early Childhood Education and Teaching** 3 *students enrolled* • **Electrical, Electronic and Communications Engineering Technology/Technician** 1 *student enrolled* • **Emergency Medical Technology/Technician (EMT Paramedic)** 7 *students enrolled* • **Food Service, Waiter/Waitress, and Dining Room Management/Manager** 3 *students enrolled* • **Forestry Technology/Technician** 4 *students enrolled* • **Heating, Air Conditioning, Ventilation and Refrigeration Maintenance Technology/Technician (HAC, HACR, HVAC, HVACR)** 193 *students enrolled* • **Industrial Mechanics and Maintenance Technology** 2 *students enrolled* • **Landscaping and Groundskeeping** 3 *students enrolled* • **Legal Assistant/Paralegal** 53 *students enrolled* • **Library Assistant/Technician** 2 *students enrolled* • **Machine Tool Technology/Machinist** 2 *students enrolled* • **Manufacturing Technology/Technician** 2 *students enrolled* • **Medical Administrative/Executive Assistant and Medical Secretary** 1 *student enrolled* • **Medical Insurance Coding Specialist/Coder** 11 *students enrolled* • **Medical Insurance Specialist/Medical Biller** 27 *students enrolled* • **Medical Transcription/Transcriptionist** 5 *students enrolled* • **Medical/Clinical Assistant** 1 *student enrolled* • **Nurse/Nursing Assistant/Aide and Patient Care Assistant** 152 *students enrolled* • **Office Management and Supervision** 6 *students enrolled* • **Phlebotomy/Phlebotomist** 71 *students enrolled* • **Securities Services Administration/Management** 3 *students enrolled* • **Selling Skills and Sales Operations** 5 *students enrolled* • **Small Business Administration/Management** 7 *students enrolled* • **Social Work** 2 *students enrolled* • **Substance Abuse/Addiction Counseling** 1 *student enrolled* • **Surgical Technology/Technologist** 8 *students enrolled* • **System Administration/Administrator** 1 *student enrolled* • **Teacher Assistant/Aide** 8 *students enrolled* • **Teaching English as a Second or Foreign Language/ESL Language Instructor** 3 *students enrolled* • **Technical and Business Writing** 4 *students enrolled* • **Web Page, Digital/Multimedia and Information Resources Design** 4 *students enrolled* • **Welding Technology/Welder** 4 *students enrolled*

STUDENT SERVICES Academic or career counseling, daycare for children of students, employment services for current students, placement services for program completers, remedial services.

The College of Office Technology

1520 West Division Street, Chicago, IL 60622
http://www.cotedu.com/

CONTACT Pedro Galva, President
Telephone: 773-278-0042

GENERAL INFORMATION Private Institution. **Accreditation:** State accredited or approved. **Total program enrollment:** 365. **Application fee:** $50.

PROGRAM(S) OFFERED
• **Computer Systems Networking and Telecommunications** • **Data Entry/Microcomputer Applications, General** 55 *hrs./$10,533* • **Data Entry/Microcomputer Applications, Other** 75 *students enrolled* • **Data Processing and Data Processing Technology/Technician** 36 *hrs./$9763* • **Medical Office Assistant/Specialist** 45 *hrs./$10,368* • **Medical/Clinical Assistant** 70 *hrs./$10,995* • **Nurse/Nursing Assistant/Aide and Patient Care Assistant** 42 *hrs./$10,368* • **Phlebotomy/Phlebotomist** 46 *students enrolled*

STUDENT SERVICES Academic or career counseling, employment services for current students, placement services for program completers, remedial services.

Columbia College Chicago

600 South Michigan Avenue, Chicago, IL 60605-1996
http://www.colum.edu/

CONTACT Warrick Carter, President
Telephone: 312-663-1600

GENERAL INFORMATION Private Institution. Founded 1890. **Accreditation:** Regional (NCA). **Total program enrollment:** 10933. **Application fee:** $35.

PROGRAM(S) OFFERED
• **Arts Management** 1 *student enrolled* • **Cinematography and Film/Video Production** 5 *students enrolled* • **Fashion/Apparel Design** 1 *student enrolled* • **Graphic Design** 3 *students enrolled* • **Industrial Design** 1 *student enrolled*

• **Journalism** 1 *student enrolled* • **Marketing/Marketing Management, General** 1 *student enrolled* • **Photography** • **Radio and Television** 3 *students enrolled* • **Recording Arts Technology/Technician** 2 *students enrolled* • **Web Page, Digital/Multimedia and Information Resources Design** 1 *student enrolled*

STUDENT SERVICES Academic or career counseling, employment services for current students, placement services for program completers, remedial services.

Computer Systems Institute

8930 Gross Point Road, Skokie, IL 60077

CONTACT Julia Lowder, Executive Vice President
Telephone: 847-967-5030

GENERAL INFORMATION Private Institution. **Total program enrollment:** 266. **Application fee:** $35.

PROGRAM(S) OFFERED
• **Business/Office Automation/Technology/Data Entry** 36 *hrs./$10,950* • **Medical Insurance Specialist/Medical Biller** 36 *hrs./$11,700* • **Medical Office Management/Administration** 12 *students enrolled* • **System, Networking, and LAN/WAN Management/Manager** 36 *hrs./$10,950*

STUDENT SERVICES Academic or career counseling, placement services for program completers.

Concept College of Cosmetology

2500 Georgetown Road, Danville, IL 61832
http://conceptcollege.com/

CONTACT Janet Trosper, President
Telephone: 217-442-9329

GENERAL INFORMATION Private Institution. **Total program enrollment:** 48. **Application fee:** $25.

PROGRAM(S) OFFERED
• **Cosmetology, Barber/Styling, and Nail Instructor** 1000 *hrs./$3800* • **Cosmetology/Cosmetologist, General** 1500 *hrs./$11,200* • **Teacher Education and Professional Development, Specific Subject Areas, Other**

STUDENT SERVICES Academic or career counseling.

Concept College of Cosmetology

129 North Race Street, Urbana, IL 61802
http://conceptcollege.com/

CONTACT Janet Trosper, President
Telephone: 217-344-7550

GENERAL INFORMATION Private Institution. **Total program enrollment:** 42. **Application fee:** $25.

PROGRAM(S) OFFERED
• **Cosmetology, Barber/Styling, and Nail Instructor** 1000 *hrs./$3800* • **Cosmetology/Cosmetologist, General** 1500 *hrs./$11,200* • **Teacher Education and Professional Development, Specific Subject Areas, Other** 1 *student enrolled*

STUDENT SERVICES Academic or career counseling.

The Cooking and Hospitality Institute of Chicago

361 West Chestnut, Chicago, IL 60610-3050
http://www.chicnet.org/

CONTACT Lloyd Kirsch, President
Telephone: 312-944-0882

GENERAL INFORMATION Private Institution. Founded 1983. **Accreditation:** Regional (NCA); state accredited or approved. **Total program enrollment:** 1004. **Application fee:** $100.

PROGRAM(S) OFFERED
• Culinary Arts/Chef Training 76 students enrolled

STUDENT SERVICES Academic or career counseling, employment services for current students, placement services for program completers, remedial services.

Cortiva Institute—Chicago School of Massage Therapy

17 N. State Street, Suite 500, Chicago, IL 60602
http://www.cortiva.com/locations/csmt/

CONTACT Paul Myer, President
Telephone: 312-753-7900

GENERAL INFORMATION Private Institution. **Application fee:** $100.

PROGRAM(S) OFFERED
• Massage Therapy/Therapeutic Massage 750 hrs./$13,315

STUDENT SERVICES Academic or career counseling, placement services for program completers.

Coyne American Institute Incorporated

1235 West Fullerton Avenue, Chicago, IL 60614
http://www.coyneamerican.edu/

CONTACT Russell T. Freeman, President
Telephone: 773-577-8100

GENERAL INFORMATION Private Institution. **Total program enrollment:** 785. **Application fee:** $25.

PROGRAM(S) OFFERED
• Allied Health and Medical Assisting Services, Other 101 hrs./$18,507
• Communications Systems Installation and Repair Technology 103 hrs./$19,077 • Electrician 58 hrs./$10,764 • Heating, Air Conditioning, Ventilation and Refrigeration Maintenance Technology/Technician (HAC, HACR, HVAC, HVACR) 99 hrs./$18,433 • Medical Administrative/Executive Assistant and Medical Secretary 17 students enrolled • Medical Insurance Specialist/Medical Biller 21 students enrolled • Medical/Clinical Assistant 22 students enrolled • Pharmacy Technician/Assistant

STUDENT SERVICES Academic or career counseling, employment services for current students, placement services for program completers.

CSI The Cosmetology and Spa Institute

4320 West Elm Street, Suite 9, McHenry, IL 60050
http://csicl.com/

CONTACT Inaet Halimi, President
Telephone: 815-455-5900 Ext. 12

GENERAL INFORMATION Private Institution. Founded 1998. **Total program enrollment:** 129. **Application fee:** $100.

PROGRAM(S) OFFERED
• Cosmetology, Barber/Styling, and Nail Instructor 1000 hrs./$10,000
• Cosmetology/Cosmetologist, General 1500 hrs./$17,500 • Facial Treatment Specialist/Facialist 21 students enrolled

STUDENT SERVICES Academic or career counseling, employment services for current students.

Danville Area Community College

2000 East Main Street, Danville, IL 61832-5199
http://www.dacc.cc.il.us/

CONTACT Alice Jacobs, President
Telephone: 217-443-3222

GENERAL INFORMATION Public Institution. Founded 1946. **Accreditation:** Regional (NCA). **Total program enrollment:** 1178.

PROGRAM(S) OFFERED
• Accounting Technology/Technician and Bookkeeping 1 student enrolled
• Administrative Assistant and Secretarial Science, General 1 student enrolled
• Agricultural Mechanics and Equipment/Machine Technology 13 students enrolled • Business Administration and Management, General 5 students enrolled • Computer Programming/Programmer, General 1 student enrolled
• Construction Engineering Technology/Technician 6 students enrolled
• Culinary Arts/Chef Training 6 students enrolled • E-Commerce/Electronic Commerce 1 student enrolled • Heating, Air Conditioning, Ventilation and Refrigeration Maintenance Technology/Technician (HAC, HACR, HVAC, HVACR) 7 students enrolled • Machine Tool Technology/Machinist 3 students enrolled • Medical Administrative/Executive Assistant and Medical Secretary 3 students enrolled • Nurse/Nursing Assistant/Aide and Patient Care Assistant 135 students enrolled • Office Management and Supervision 9 students enrolled • Selling Skills and Sales Operations 2 students enrolled • Truck and Bus Driver/Commercial Vehicle Operation 29 students enrolled • Welding Technology/Welder 3 students enrolled

STUDENT SERVICES Academic or career counseling, daycare for children of students, employment services for current students, placement services for program completers, remedial services.

DePaul University

1 East Jackson Boulevard, Chicago, IL 60604-2287
http://www.depaul.edu/

CONTACT Dennis H. Holtschneider, President
Telephone: 312-362-8000

GENERAL INFORMATION Private Institution. Founded 1898. **Accreditation:** Regional (NCA); music (NASM). **Total program enrollment:** 17850. **Application fee:** $40.

PROGRAM(S) OFFERED
• Cartography • Music Teacher Education 9 students enrolled

STUDENT SERVICES Academic or career counseling, employment services for current students, placement services for program completers, remedial services.

Dominican University

7900 West Division Street, River Forest, IL 60305-1099
http://www.dom.edu/

CONTACT Dr. Donna M. Carroll, President
Telephone: 708-366-2490

GENERAL INFORMATION Private Institution. Founded 1901. **Accreditation:** Regional (NCA); library and information science (ALA). **Total program enrollment:** 2022. **Application fee:** $25.

Dominican University (continued)

PROGRAM(S) OFFERED
• Computer Science • Dietetics/Dietitians • Information Science/Studies
• Pastoral Studies/Counseling

STUDENT SERVICES Academic or career counseling, daycare for children of students, employment services for current students, placement services for program completers, remedial services.

East-West University

816 South Michigan Avenue, Chicago, IL 60605-2103
http://www.eastwest.edu/

CONTACT M. Wasi Khan, Chancellor
Telephone: 312-939-0111 Ext. 1800

GENERAL INFORMATION Private Institution. Founded 1978. **Accreditation:** Regional (NCA). **Total program enrollment:** 1141. **Application fee:** $40.

PROGRAM(S) OFFERED
• Accounting • Business Administration and Management, General *21 students enrolled* • Computer and Information Sciences, General *5 students enrolled* • Digital Communication and Media/Multimedia • Electrical, Electronic and Communications Engineering Technology/Technician *6 students enrolled* • Medical Insurance Specialist/Medical Biller *8 students enrolled* • Nurse/Nursing Assistant/Aide and Patient Care Assistant *30 students enrolled*

STUDENT SERVICES Academic or career counseling, employment services for current students, remedial services.

Educators of Beauty

122 Wright Street, La Salle, IL 61301
http://www.educatorsofbeauty.com/

CONTACT Diane Chamberlain, Director
Telephone: 815-223-7326

GENERAL INFORMATION Private Institution. Founded 1969. **Total program enrollment:** 57. **Application fee:** $100.

PROGRAM(S) OFFERED
• Cosmetology, Barber/Styling, and Nail Instructor *625 hrs./$4475*
• Cosmetology/Cosmetologist, General *1500 hrs./$14,775* • Nail Technician/Specialist and Manicurist *350 hrs./$3100*

STUDENT SERVICES Academic or career counseling, employment services for current students, placement services for program completers.

Educators of Beauty

128 South Fifth Street, Rockford, IL 61104
http://www.educatorsofbeauty.com/

CONTACT Rhonda Renner Loos, Owner
Telephone: 815-969-7030

GENERAL INFORMATION Private Institution. **Total program enrollment:** 81. **Application fee:** $100.

PROGRAM(S) OFFERED
• Cosmetology, Barber/Styling, and Nail Instructor *625 hrs./$4475*
• Cosmetology/Cosmetologist, General *1500 hrs./$14,675* • Nail Technician/Specialist and Manicurist *350 hrs./$3100*

STUDENT SERVICES Academic or career counseling, employment services for current students, placement services for program completers.

Educators of Beauty

211 East Third Street, Sterling, IL 61081
http://www.educatorsofbeauty.com/

CONTACT Rhonda Renner Reese, Owner
Telephone: 815-625-0247

GENERAL INFORMATION Private Institution. Founded 1946. **Total program enrollment:** 69. **Application fee:** $100.

PROGRAM(S) OFFERED
• Cosmetology, Barber/Styling, and Nail Instructor *650 hrs./$4475*
• Cosmetology/Cosmetologist, General *1500 hrs./$14,675* • Nail Technician/Specialist and Manicurist *350 hrs./$3100*

STUDENT SERVICES Academic or career counseling, employment services for current students, placement services for program completers.

Elgin Community College

1700 Spartan Drive, Elgin, IL 60123-7193
http://www.elgin.edu/

CONTACT David Sam, President
Telephone: 847-697-1000

GENERAL INFORMATION Public Institution. Founded 1949. **Accreditation:** Regional (NCA); dental assisting (ADA); medical laboratory technology (NAACLS). **Total program enrollment:** 3624.

PROGRAM(S) OFFERED
• Accounting and Business/Management *1 student enrolled* • Administrative Assistant and Secretarial Science, General *4 students enrolled* • Automobile/Automotive Mechanics Technology/Technician *145 students enrolled* • Baking and Pastry Arts/Baker/Pastry Chef *18 students enrolled* • Business/Office Automation/Technology/Data Entry *4 students enrolled* • CAD/CADD Drafting and/or Design Technology/Technician *20 students enrolled* • Child Care Provider/Assistant *54 students enrolled* • Clinical/Medical Laboratory Technician *2 students enrolled* • Computer Installation and Repair Technology/Technician *1 student enrolled* • Corrections and Criminal Justice, Other *21 students enrolled* • Culinary Arts/Chef Training *19 students enrolled* • Dental Assisting/Assistant *33 students enrolled* • Emergency Medical Technology/Technician (EMT Paramedic) *70 students enrolled* • Entrepreneurship/Entrepreneurial Studies *1 student enrolled* • Executive Assistant/Executive Secretary *1 student enrolled* • Fire Science/Firefighting *35 students enrolled* • Food Preparation/Professional Cooking/Kitchen Assistant *58 students enrolled* • General Office Occupations and Clerical Services *5 students enrolled* • Heating, Air Conditioning, Ventilation and Refrigeration Maintenance Technology/Technician (HAC, HACR, HVAC, HVACR) *82 students enrolled* • Hospitality Administration/Management, General *12 students enrolled* • Hotel/Motel Administration/Management *1 student enrolled* • Industrial Mechanics and Maintenance Technology *10 students enrolled* • Kinesiology and Exercise Science *7 students enrolled* • Legal Assistant/Paralegal *18 students enrolled* • Licensed Practical/Vocational Nurse Training (LPN, LVN, Cert, Dipl, AAS) *90 students enrolled* • Machine Tool Technology/Machinist *2 students enrolled* • Manufacturing Technology/Technician *2 students enrolled* • Marketing/Marketing Management, General *1 student enrolled* • Nurse/Nursing Assistant/Aide and Patient Care Assistant *79 students enrolled* • Office Management and Supervision *7 students enrolled* • Phlebotomy/Phlebotomist *17 students enrolled* • Plastics Engineering Technology/Technician *1 student enrolled* • Prepress/Desktop Publishing and Digital Imaging Design *3 students enrolled* • Psychiatric/Mental Health Services Technician *1 student enrolled* • Restaurant, Culinary, and Catering Management/Manager *3 students enrolled* • Retailing and Retail Operations *1 student enrolled* • Small Business Administration/Management *3 students enrolled* • Social Work *2 students enrolled* • Substance Abuse/Addiction Counseling *5 students enrolled* • Surgical Technology/Technologist *12 students enrolled* • Tool and Die Technology/Technician *2 students enrolled* • Truck and Bus Driver/Commercial Vehicle Operation *49 students enrolled* • Web Page, Digital/Multimedia and Information Resources Design *2 students enrolled* • Welding Technology/Welder *31 students enrolled* • Word Processing *2 students enrolled*

STUDENT SERVICES Academic or career counseling, daycare for children of students, employment services for current students, placement services for program completers, remedial services.

Empire Beauty School–Arlington Heights

264 West Rand Road, Arlington Heights, IL 60004
http://www.empire.edu

CONTACT Michael Bouman, President
Telephone: 847-394-8359

GENERAL INFORMATION Private Institution. **Total program enrollment:** 141. **Application fee:** $100.

PROGRAM(S) OFFERED
• **Cosmetology, Barber/Styling, and Nail Instructor** *1000 hrs./$6900*
• **Cosmetology/Cosmetologist, General** *1530 hrs./$18,845* • **Nail Technician/Specialist and Manicurist** *1 student enrolled*

STUDENT SERVICES Placement services for program completers.

Empire Beauty School–Hanover Park

1166 West Lake Street, Hanover Park, IL 60133-5421
http://www.empire.edu/

CONTACT Michael Bouman, President
Telephone: 800-223-3271

GENERAL INFORMATION Private Institution. **Total program enrollment:** 68. **Application fee:** $100.

PROGRAM(S) OFFERED
• **Cosmetology/Cosmetologist, General** *1530 hrs./$18,845* • **Nail Technician/Specialist and Manicurist**

STUDENT SERVICES Placement services for program completers.

Empire Beauty School–Lisle

2709 Maple Avenue, Lisle, IL 60532
http://www.empire.edu

CONTACT Michael Bouman, President
Telephone: 570-429-4321 Ext. 2414

GENERAL INFORMATION Private Institution. **Total program enrollment:** 52. **Application fee:** $100.

PROGRAM(S) OFFERED
• **Cosmetology, Barber/Styling, and Nail Instructor** *1530 hrs./$18,845*
• **Cosmetology/Cosmetologist, General** *17 students enrolled* • **Nail Technician/Specialist and Manicurist**

STUDENT SERVICES Placement services for program completers.

Environmental Technical Institute

1101 West Thorndale Avenue, Itasca, IL 60143-1334
http://eticampus.com/

CONTACT Camille M. Tortorello, Administration Director
Telephone: 630-285-9100

GENERAL INFORMATION Private Institution. Founded 1985. **Total program enrollment:** 98. **Application fee:** $75.

PROGRAM(S) OFFERED
• **Heating, Air Conditioning and Refrigeration Technology/Technician (ACH/ACR/ACHR/HRAC/HVAC/AC Technology)** *906 hrs./$12,517* • **Heating, Air Conditioning, Ventilation and Refrigeration Maintenance Technology/Technician (HAC, HACR, HVAC, HVACR)** *616 hrs./$9845*

STUDENT SERVICES Employment services for current students, placement services for program completers.

Environmental Technical Institute–Blue Island Campus

13010 South Division Street, Blue Island, IL 60406-2606
http://eticampus.com/

CONTACT Camille M. Tortorello, Administration Director
Telephone: 630-285-9100

GENERAL INFORMATION Private Institution. Founded 1985. **Total program enrollment:** 125. **Application fee:** $75.

PROGRAM(S) OFFERED
• **Heating, Air Conditioning and Refrigeration Technology/Technician (ACH/ACR/ACHR/HRAC/HVAC/AC Technology)** *906 hrs./$12,517* • **Heating, Air Conditioning, Ventilation and Refrigeration Maintenance Technology/Technician (HAC, HACR, HVAC, HVACR)** *616 hrs./$9845*

STUDENT SERVICES Employment services for current students, placement services for program completers.

European Massage Therapy School

8707 Skokie Boulevard, Suite 106, Skokie, IL 60077
http://www.school-for-massage.com/

CONTACT Arkady Khazin, Director
Telephone: 847-673-7595

GENERAL INFORMATION Private Institution. **Application fee:** $100.

PROGRAM(S) OFFERED
• **Massage Therapy/Therapeutic Massage** *110 students enrolled*

STUDENT SERVICES Academic or career counseling, employment services for current students, placement services for program completers.

Everest College

6880 Frontgate Road, Suite 400, Burr Ridge, IL 60527
http://www.everest.edu/

CONTACT Mark Sullivan, President
Telephone: 630-920-1102

GENERAL INFORMATION Private Institution. **Total program enrollment:** 527.

PROGRAM(S) OFFERED
• **Dental Assisting/Assistant** *720 hrs./$13,414* • **Massage Therapy/Therapeutic Massage** *720 hrs./$13,414* • **Medical Administrative/Executive Assistant and Medical Secretary** *720 hrs./$13,362* • **Medical Insurance Coding Specialist/Coder** *720 hrs./$13,414* • **Medical Office Assistant/Specialist** *258 students enrolled* • **Medical/Clinical Assistant** *720 hrs./$14,507*

STUDENT SERVICES Academic or career counseling, employment services for current students, placement services for program completers.

Everest College

247 South State Street, Suite 400, Chicago, IL 60604
http://www.everest.edu/

CONTACT Jeff Jarmes, President
Telephone: 312-913-1616

GENERAL INFORMATION Private Institution. **Total program enrollment:** 1745.

PROGRAM(S) OFFERED
• **Dental Assisting/Assistant** *720 hrs./$12,913* • **Massage Therapy/Therapeutic Massage** *750 hrs./$13,290* • **Medical Insurance Specialist/Medical Biller** *720 hrs./$12,735* • **Medical Office Assistant/Specialist** *165 students enrolled* • **Medical Office Management/Administration** *720 hrs./$13,290* • **Medical/Clinical Assistant** *720 hrs./$14,403* • **Pharmacy Technician/Assistant** *720 hrs./$12,913*

STUDENT SERVICES Academic or career counseling, placement services for program completers.

Everest College

11560 South Kedzie Avenue, Merrionette Park, IL 60803
http://www.everest.edu/

CONTACT Deann Fitzgerald, President
Telephone: 708-239-0055

GENERAL INFORMATION Private Institution. **Total program enrollment:** 358.

PROGRAM(S) OFFERED
• **Allied Health and Medical Assisting Services, Other** *720 hrs./$14,403* • **Massage Therapy/Therapeutic Massage** *750 hrs./$13,274* • **Medical Insurance Coding Specialist/Coder** *720 hrs./$13,274* • **Medical Office Assistant/Specialist** *237 students enrolled* • **Pharmacy Technician/Assistant** *720 hrs./ $12,913*

STUDENT SERVICES Employment services for current students, placement services for program completers.

Everest College

150 South Lincolnway, Suite 100, North Aurora, IL 60542
http://www.everest.edu/

CONTACT Robert Van Elsen, Campus President
Telephone: 630-896-2140

GENERAL INFORMATION Private Institution. **Total program enrollment:** 80.

PROGRAM(S) OFFERED
• **Accounting and Related Services, Other** *720 hrs./$11,797* • **Massage Therapy/Therapeutic Massage** *76 students enrolled* • **Medical Administrative/Executive Assistant and Medical Secretary** *720 hrs./$13,211* • **Medical Insurance Coding Specialist/Coder** *720 hrs./$13,251* • **Medical/Clinical Assistant** *720 hrs./$14,295*

STUDENT SERVICES Academic or career counseling, employment services for current students, placement services for program completers, remedial services.

Everest College

9811 Woods Drive, Suite 200, Skokie, IL 60077
http://www.everest.edu/

CONTACT Jeanette Prickett, School President
Telephone: 847-470-0277

GENERAL INFORMATION Private Institution. **Total program enrollment:** 896.

PROGRAM(S) OFFERED
• **Accounting and Related Services, Other** *720 hrs./$11,797* • **Health Information/Medical Records Administration/Administrator** *720 hrs./$13,251* • **Massage Therapy/Therapeutic Massage** *750 hrs./$13,236* • **Medical Administrative/Executive Assistant and Medical Secretary** *720 hrs./$13,104* • **Medical Insurance Specialist/Medical Biller** *36 students enrolled* • **Medical/Clinical Assistant** *720 hrs./$14,215* • **Pharmacy Technician/Assistant** *720 hrs./ $12,913*

STUDENT SERVICES Academic or career counseling, employment services for current students, placement services for program completers.

First Institute of Travel

790 McHenry Avenue, Crystal Lake, IL 60014
http://www.firstinstitute.com/

CONTACT Ron Beier, President
Telephone: 815-459-3500

GENERAL INFORMATION Private Institution. Founded 1982. **Total program enrollment:** 153. **Application fee:** $100.

PROGRAM(S) OFFERED
• **Allied Health and Medical Assisting Services, Other** *36 hrs./$13,050* • **Massage Therapy/Therapeutic Massage** *33 hrs./$11,815* • **Medical Office Assistant/Specialist** *24 hrs./$8620*

STUDENT SERVICES Employment services for current students, placement services for program completers.

Fox College

6640 South Cicero, Bedford Park, IL 60638
http://www.foxcollege.edu/

CONTACT Carey Cranston, President
Telephone: 708-636-7700

GENERAL INFORMATION Private Institution. Founded 1932. **Accreditation:** State accredited or approved. **Total program enrollment:** 345. **Application fee:** $50.

PROGRAM(S) OFFERED
• **Accounting Technology/Technician and Bookkeeping** • **Administrative Assistant and Secretarial Science, General** *9 students enrolled* • **Allied Health and Medical Assisting Services, Other** *5 students enrolled*

STUDENT SERVICES Academic or career counseling, employment services for current students, placement services for program completers.

Gem City College

PO Box 179, Quincy, IL 62301
http://www.gemcitycollege.com/

CONTACT Russell H. Hagenah, President
Telephone: 217-222-0391

GENERAL INFORMATION Private Institution. Founded 1870. **Accreditation:** State accredited or approved. **Total program enrollment:** 60. **Application fee:** $50.

PROGRAM(S) OFFERED
• **Business/Office Automation/Technology/Data Entry** • **Cosmetology/Cosmetologist, General** *50 hrs./$7200* • **Watchmaking and Jewelrymaking** *21 hrs./$7200*

STUDENT SERVICES Academic or career counseling, placement services for program completers.

Hairmasters Institute of Cosmetology

506 South McClun Street, Bloomington, IL 61701

CONTACT Julie A. Fritzsche, Chief Executive Officer
Telephone: 309-828-1884

GENERAL INFORMATION Private Institution. **Total program enrollment:** 99. **Application fee:** $50.

PROGRAM(S) OFFERED
• **Cosmetology, Barber/Styling, and Nail Instructor** *500 hrs./$4000* • **Cosmetology/Cosmetologist, General** *1500 hrs./$13,500*

STUDENT SERVICES Academic or career counseling, employment services for current students, placement services for program completers.

Hair Professional Career College

1734 Sycamore Road, De Kalb, IL 60115
http://www.hairpros.edu/

CONTACT Wanda Zachary, President
Telephone: 815-756-3596

GENERAL INFORMATION Private Institution. Founded 1983. **Total program enrollment:** 39. **Application fee:** $100.

PROGRAM(S) OFFERED
• **Aesthetician/Esthetician and Skin Care Specialist** *750 hrs./$9800*
• **Cosmetology, Barber/Styling, and Nail Instructor** *1000 hrs./$8100*
• **Cosmetology/Cosmetologist, General** *1500 hrs./$17,400* • **Nail Technician/Specialist and Manicurist**

STUDENT SERVICES Academic or career counseling, placement services for program completers.

Hair Professionals Academy of Cosmetology

440 Airport Road, Suite C, Elgin, IL 60123

CONTACT Carol Westphal, President
Telephone: 847-836-5900

GENERAL INFORMATION Private Institution. **Total program enrollment:** 110.

PROGRAM(S) OFFERED
• **Aesthetician/Esthetician and Skin Care Specialist** *750 hrs./$9800*
• **Cosmetology, Barber/Styling, and Nail Instructor** *500 hrs./$5100*
• **Cosmetology/Cosmetologist, General** *250 hrs./$2832* • **Nail Technician/Specialist and Manicurist**

STUDENT SERVICES Academic or career counseling, employment services for current students, placement services for program completers.

Hair Professionals Academy of Cosmetology

1145 East Butterfield Road, Wheaton, IL 60187

CONTACT Carol Westphal, President
Telephone: 630-653-6630

GENERAL INFORMATION Private Institution. **Total program enrollment:** 25.

PROGRAM(S) OFFERED
• **Aesthetician/Esthetician and Skin Care Specialist** *750 hrs./$9800*
• **Cosmetology, Barber/Styling, and Nail Instructor** *1000 hrs./$10,000*
• **Cosmetology/Cosmetologist, General** *250 hrs./$2833*

STUDENT SERVICES Academic or career counseling, employment services for current students, placement services for program completers.

Hair Professionals Career College

10321 S. Roberts Road, Palos Hills, IL 60485
http://www.hairpros.edu/

CONTACT Wanda S. Zachary, President
Telephone: 708-430-1755

GENERAL INFORMATION Private Institution. **Total program enrollment:** 73. **Application fee:** $100.

PROGRAM(S) OFFERED
• **Aesthetician/Esthetician and Skin Care Specialist** *750 hrs./$9800*
• **Cosmetology, Barber/Styling, and Nail Instructor** *1000 hrs./$8100*
• **Cosmetology/Cosmetologist, General** *1500 hrs./$17,400* • **Nail Technician/Specialist and Manicurist** *350 hrs./$2550* • **Teacher Education and Professional Development, Specific Subject Areas, Other** *2 students enrolled*

STUDENT SERVICES Academic or career counseling, placement services for program completers.

Hair Professionals School of Cosmetology

5460 Route 34, Box 40, Oswego, IL 60543
http://www.hairpros.edu/

CONTACT Wanda Zachary, Secretary-Treasurer
Telephone: 630-554-2266

GENERAL INFORMATION Private Institution. Founded 1979. **Total program enrollment:** 36. **Application fee:** $100.

PROGRAM(S) OFFERED
• **Cosmetology, Barber/Styling, and Nail Instructor** *1000 hrs./$8100*
• **Cosmetology/Cosmetologist, General** *1500 hrs./$17,400* • **Teacher Education and Professional Development, Specific Subject Areas, Other** *4 students enrolled*

STUDENT SERVICES Academic or career counseling, placement services for program completers.

Harper College

1200 West Algonquin Road, Palatine, IL 60067-7398
http://www.harpercollege.edu/

CONTACT Dr. John Pickelman, Interim President
Telephone: 847-925-6000

GENERAL INFORMATION Public Institution. Founded 1965. **Accreditation:** Regional (NCA); dental hygiene (ADA); medical assisting (AAMAE); music (NASM). **Total program enrollment:** 6753. **Application fee:** $25.

PROGRAM(S) OFFERED
• **Accounting Technology/Technician and Bookkeeping** *68 students enrolled*
• **Accounting** *4 students enrolled* • **Applied Horticulture/Horticultural Operations, General** *13 students enrolled* • **Architectural Drafting and Architectural CAD/CADD** *23 students enrolled* • **Baking and Pastry Arts/Baker/Pastry Chef** *5 students enrolled* • **Banking and Financial Support Services** *5 students enrolled* • **Building/Home/Construction Inspection/Inspector** *3 students enrolled* • **Building/Property Maintenance and Management** *6 students enrolled* • **Business Administration and Management, General** *122 students enrolled* • **Child Care Provider/Assistant** *69 students enrolled* • **Computer Programming/Programmer, General** *5 students enrolled* • **Computer Systems Networking and Telecommunications** *10 students enrolled* • **Computer and Information Systems Security** *1 student enrolled* • **Criminal Justice/Police Science** *4 students enrolled* • **Culinary Arts/Chef Training** *6 students enrolled* • **Dietetic Technician (DTR)** *11 students enrolled* • **Electrical/Electronics Equipment Installation and Repair, General** *25 students enrolled* • **Emergency Care Attendant (EMT Ambulance)** *1 student enrolled* • **Emergency Medical Technology/Technician (EMT Paramedic)** *1 student enrolled* • **Fashion and Fabric Consultant** *21 students enrolled* • **Floriculture/Floristry Operations and Management** *4 students enrolled* • **Food Service, Waiter/Waitress, and Dining Room Management/Manager** *7 students enrolled* • **Forestry Technology/Technician** *7 students enrolled* • **General Office Occupations and Clerical Services** *2 students enrolled* • **Graphic and Printing Equipment Operator, General Production** *1 student enrolled* • **Heating, Air Conditioning, Ventilation and Refrigeration Maintenance Technology/Technician (HAC, HACR, HVAC, HVACR)** *65 students enrolled* • **Hotel/Motel Administration/Management** *4 students enrolled* • **Human Resources Management/Personnel Administration, General** *4 students enrolled* • **Industrial Electronics Technology/Technician** *26 students enrolled* • **Information Science/Studies** *22 students enrolled* • **International Business/Trade/Commerce** *1 student enrolled* • **Landscaping and Groundskeeping** *1 student enrolled* • **Legal Administrative Assistant/Secretary** *1 student enrolled* • **Legal Assistant/Paralegal** *70 students enrolled* • **Licensed Practical/Vocational Nurse Training (LPN, LVN, Cert, Dipl, AAS)** *25 students enrolled* • **Medical Administrative/Executive Assistant and Medical Secretary** *4 students enrolled* • **Medical Insurance Coding Specialist/Coder** *16 students enrolled* • **Medical Transcription/Transcriptionist** *4 students enrolled* • **Medical/Clinical Assistant** *23 students enrolled* • **Nurse/Nursing Assistant/Aide and Patient Care Assistant** *190 students enrolled* • **Parts, Warehousing, and Inventory Management Operations** *18 students enrolled* • **Phlebotomy/Phlebotomist** *20 students enrolled* • **Plant Nursery Operations and Management** *1 student enrolled* • **Purchasing, Procurement/Acquisitions and Contracts Management** *14 students enrolled* • **Retailing and Retail Operations** *5 students enrolled* • **Sales, Distribution and Marketing Operations, General** *8 students enrolled* • **Selling Skills and Sales Operations** *23 students enrolled* • **Sign Language Interpretation and Translation** *9 students enrolled* • **System, Networking, and LAN/WAN Management/Manager** *2 students enrolled* • **Turf and Turfgrass Management** *8 students enrolled* • **Web Page, Digital/Multimedia and Information Resources Design** *3 students enrolled* • **Welding Technology/Welder** *10 students enrolled*

STUDENT SERVICES Academic or career counseling, daycare for children of students, employment services for current students, remedial services.

Harrington College of Design

200 West Madison Street, Chicago, IL 60606
http://www.interiordesign.edu/

CONTACT Erik Parks, President
Telephone: 312-939-4975

GENERAL INFORMATION Private Institution. Founded 1931. **Accreditation:** Art and design (NASAD); interior design: professional (CIDA). **Total program enrollment:** 540. **Application fee:** $60.

PROGRAM(S) OFFERED
• **Interior Design** *1 student enrolled*

STUDENT SERVICES Academic or career counseling, employment services for current students, placement services for program completers.

Heartland Community College

1500 West Raab Road, Normal, IL 61761
http://www.heartland.edu/

CONTACT Jonathan Astroth, President
Telephone: 309-268-8000

GENERAL INFORMATION Public Institution. Founded 1990. **Accreditation:** Regional (NCA). **Total program enrollment:** 2273.

PROGRAM(S) OFFERED
• **Accounting** *4 students enrolled* • **Administrative Assistant and Secretarial Science, General** *1 student enrolled* • **Business/Office Automation/Technology/Data Entry** *4 students enrolled* • **CAD/CADD Drafting and/or Design Technology/Technician** *1 student enrolled* • **Child Care Provider/Assistant** *10 students enrolled* • **Computer Technology/Computer Systems Technology** *10 students enrolled* • **Corrections** *4 students enrolled* • **Drafting and Design Technology/Technician, General** *2 students enrolled* • **Electrical, Electronic and Communications Engineering Technology/Technician** *3 students enrolled* • **Heating, Air Conditioning, Ventilation and Refrigeration Maintenance Technology/Technician (HAC, HACR, HVAC, HVACR)** *1 student enrolled* • **Licensed Practical/Vocational Nurse Training (LPN, LVN, Cert, Dipl, AAS)** *22 students enrolled* • **Manufacturing Technology/Technician** *5 students enrolled* • **Nurse/Nursing Assistant/Aide and Patient Care Assistant** *107 students enrolled* • **System Administration/Administrator** *1 student enrolled* • **Welding Technology/Welder** *1 student enrolled*

STUDENT SERVICES Academic or career counseling, daycare for children of students, employment services for current students, placement services for program completers, remedial services.

Hebrew Theological College

7135 North Carpenter Road, Skokie, IL 60077-3263
http://www.htc.edu/

CONTACT Rabbi Dr. Jerold Isenberg, Chancellor
Telephone: 847-982-2500

GENERAL INFORMATION Private Institution. Founded 1922. **Accreditation:** Regional (NCA). **Total program enrollment:** 530. **Application fee:** $75.

PROGRAM(S) OFFERED
• **Data Entry/Microcomputer Applications, General** • **Teacher Education and Professional Development, Specific Subject Areas, Other** *1 student enrolled*

STUDENT SERVICES Academic or career counseling, placement services for program completers.

Highland Community College

2998 West Pearl City Road, Freeport, IL 61032-9341
http://www.highland.edu/

CONTACT Joe M. Kanosky, President
Telephone: 815-235-6121

GENERAL INFORMATION Public Institution. Founded 1962. **Accreditation:** Regional (NCA). **Total program enrollment:** 1111.

PROGRAM(S) OFFERED
• **Accounting Technology/Technician and Bookkeeping** *8 students enrolled* • **Accounting** *3 students enrolled* • **Autobody/Collision and Repair Technology/Technician** *1 student enrolled* • **Child Care Provider/Assistant** *2 students enrolled* • **Computer Installation and Repair Technology/Technician** *3 students enrolled* • **Cosmetology/Cosmetologist, General** *10 students enrolled* • **General Office Occupations and Clerical Services** *2 students enrolled* • **Graphic Design** *1 student enrolled* • **Industrial Mechanics and Maintenance Technology** *1 student enrolled* • **Industrial Technology/Technician** *1 student enrolled* • **Licensed Practical/Vocational Nurse Training (LPN, LVN, Cert, Dipl, AAS)** *16 students enrolled* • **Manufacturing Technology/Technician** *6 students enrolled* • **Medical Insurance Coding Specialist/Coder** *2 students enrolled* • **Medical Transcription/Transcriptionist** *2 students enrolled* • **Nail Technician/Specialist and Manicurist** *2 students enrolled* • **Welding Technology/Welder** *2 students enrolled*

STUDENT SERVICES Academic or career counseling, daycare for children of students, employment services for current students, placement services for program completers, remedial services.

Illinois Center for Broadcasting

200 West 22nd Street, Suite 202, Lombard, IL 60148
http://www.beonair.com/

CONTACT Robert Mills, President
Telephone: 630-916-1700 Ext. 104

GENERAL INFORMATION Private Institution. **Total program enrollment:** 219. **Application fee:** $125.

PROGRAM(S) OFFERED
• **Radio and Television** *36 hrs./$14,889*

STUDENT SERVICES Academic or career counseling, employment services for current students, placement services for program completers, remedial services.

Illinois Central College

One College Drive, East Peoria, IL 61635-0001
http://www.icc.edu/

CONTACT Dr. John S. Erwin, President
Telephone: 309-694-5422

GENERAL INFORMATION Public Institution. Founded 1967. **Accreditation:** Regional (NCA); dental hygiene (ADA); medical laboratory technology (NAACLS); music (NASM); physical therapy assisting (APTA); radiologic technology: radiography (JRCERT); respiratory therapy technology (CoARC). **Total program enrollment:** 4798.

PROGRAM(S) OFFERED
• **Accounting Technology/Technician and Bookkeeping** *6 students enrolled* • **Administrative Assistant and Secretarial Science, General** *3 students enrolled* • **Applied Horticulture/Horticultural Operations, General** *27 students enrolled* • **Architectural Drafting and Architectural CAD/CADD** *1 student enrolled* • **Automobile/Automotive Mechanics Technology/Technician** *8 students enrolled* • **Banking and Financial Support Services** *4 students enrolled* • **Business Administration and Management, General** *39 students enrolled* • **Business/Office Automation/Technology/Data Entry** *20 students enrolled* • **Child Care Provider/Assistant** *5 students enrolled* • **Computer Systems Networking and Telecommunications** *24 students enrolled* • **Construction Trades, General** *15 students enrolled* • **Culinary Arts/Chef Training** *1 student enrolled* • **Data Entry/Microcomputer Applications, General** *1 student enrolled* • **E-Commerce/Electronic Commerce** *4 students enrolled* • **Electrical, Electronic and Communications Engineering Technology/Technician** *4 students enrolled* • **Emergency Care Attendant (EMT Ambulance)** *7 students enrolled* • **Food Service, Waiter/Waitress, and Dining Room Management/Manager** *17*

students enrolled • **Forensic Science and Technology** *3 students enrolled*
• **General Office Occupations and Clerical Services** *7 students enrolled*
• **Geography, Other** *5 students enrolled* • **Heating, Air Conditioning, Ventilation and Refrigeration Maintenance Technology/Technician (HAC, HACR, HVAC, HVACR)** *31 students enrolled* • **Housing and Human Environments, Other** *14 students enrolled* • **Industrial Mechanics and Maintenance Technology** *1 student enrolled* • **Legal Assistant/Paralegal** *9 students enrolled* • **Licensed Practical/Vocational Nurse Training (LPN, LVN, Cert, Dipl, AAS)** *25 students enrolled* • **Logistics and Materials Management** *7 students enrolled* • **Massage Therapy/Therapeutic Massage** *22 students enrolled* • **Medical Insurance Coding Specialist/Coder** *9 students enrolled* • **Medical Office Assistant/Specialist** *17 students enrolled* • **Medical Transcription/Transcriptionist** *3 students enrolled* • **Nurse/Nursing Assistant/Aide and Patient Care Assistant** *139 students enrolled* • **Phlebotomy/Phlebotomist** *17 students enrolled* • **Prepress/Desktop Publishing and Digital Imaging Design** *1 student enrolled* • **Psychiatric/Mental Health Services Technician** *2 students enrolled* • **Security and Loss Prevention Services** *3 students enrolled* • **Sign Language Interpretation and Translation** *1 student enrolled* • **Small Business Administration/Management** *3 students enrolled* • **Substance Abuse/Addiction Counseling** *6 students enrolled* • **Surgical Technology/Technologist** *11 students enrolled* • **Tourism and Travel Services Management** *1 student enrolled* • **Web Page, Digital/Multimedia and Information Resources Design** *6 students enrolled* • **Welding Technology/Welder** *11 students enrolled*

STUDENT SERVICES Academic or career counseling, daycare for children of students, employment services for current students, placement services for program completers, remedial services.

Illinois Eastern Community Colleges, Frontier Community College

Frontier Drive, Fairfield, IL 62837-2601
http://www.iecc.edu/fcc/

CONTACT Terry Bruce, Chief Executive Officer
Telephone: 618-393-2982

GENERAL INFORMATION Public Institution. Founded 1976. **Accreditation:** Regional (NCA). **Total program enrollment:** 303. **Application fee:** $10.

PROGRAM(S) OFFERED
• **Administrative Assistant and Secretarial Science, General** *1 student enrolled* • **Automobile/Automotive Mechanics Technology/Technician** *4 students enrolled* • **Electrical and Power Transmission Installation/Installer, General** *18 students enrolled* • **Emergency Care Attendant (EMT Ambulance)** *30 students enrolled* • **Fire Science/Firefighting** *1 student enrolled* • **Nurse/Nursing Assistant/Aide and Patient Care Assistant** *92 students enrolled* • **Psychiatric/Mental Health Services Technician** *6 students enrolled* • **Quality Control Technology/Technician** *13 students enrolled* • **Teacher Assistant/Aide** *1 student enrolled* • **Truck and Bus Driver/Commercial Vehicle Operation** *2 students enrolled*

STUDENT SERVICES Academic or career counseling, employment services for current students, placement services for program completers, remedial services.

Illinois Eastern Community Colleges, Lincoln Trail College

11220 State Highway 1, Robinson, IL 62454
http://www.iecc.edu/ltc/

CONTACT Terry Bruce, Chief Executive Officer
Telephone: 618-393-2982

GENERAL INFORMATION Public Institution. Founded 1969. **Accreditation:** Regional (NCA). **Total program enrollment:** 504. **Application fee:** $10.

PROGRAM(S) OFFERED
• **Administrative Assistant and Secretarial Science, General** *1 student enrolled* • **Applied Horticulture/Horticultural Operations, General** *6 students enrolled* • **Business Administration and Management, General** *20 students enrolled* • **Business/Office Automation/Technology/Data Entry** *15 students enrolled* • **Communications Systems Installation and Repair Technology** *20 students enrolled* • **Computer Installation and Repair Technology/Technician** *2 students enrolled* • **Food Service, Waiter/Waitress, and Dining Room Management/Manager** *16 students enrolled* • **Housing and Human Environments, Other** *72 students enrolled* • **Medical Transcription/Transcriptionist** *1 student enrolled* • **Medical/Clinical Assistant** *12 students enrolled* • **Nurse/Nursing Assistant/**

Aide and Patient Care Assistant *71 students enrolled* • **Pharmacy Technician/Assistant** *9 students enrolled* • **Restaurant, Culinary, and Catering Management/Manager** *1 student enrolled* • **System, Networking, and LAN/WAN Management/Manager** *1 student enrolled*

STUDENT SERVICES Academic or career counseling, employment services for current students, placement services for program completers, remedial services.

Illinois Eastern Community Colleges, Olney Central College

305 North West Street, Olney, IL 62450
http://www.iecc.edu/occ/

CONTACT Terry Bruce, Chief Executive Officer
Telephone: 618-393-2982

GENERAL INFORMATION Public Institution. Founded 1962. **Accreditation:** Regional (NCA); radiologic technology: radiography (JRCERT). **Total program enrollment:** 745. **Application fee:** $10.

PROGRAM(S) OFFERED
• **Automobile/Automotive Mechanics Technology/Technician** *2 students enrolled* • **Cosmetology/Cosmetologist, General** *10 students enrolled* • **Emergency Care Attendant (EMT Ambulance)** *2 students enrolled* • **Heating, Air Conditioning, Ventilation and Refrigeration Maintenance Technology/Technician (HAC, HACR, HVAC, HVACR)** *10 students enrolled* • **Industrial Mechanics and Maintenance Technology** *4 students enrolled* • **Licensed Practical/Vocational Nurse Training (LPN, LVN, Cert, Dipl, AAS)** *111 students enrolled* • **Massage Therapy/Therapeutic Massage** *6 students enrolled* • **Medical Transcription/Transcriptionist** *14 students enrolled* • **Nurse/Nursing Assistant/Aide and Patient Care Assistant** *102 students enrolled* • **Phlebotomy/Phlebotomist** *23 students enrolled* • **Web Page, Digital/Multimedia and Information Resources Design** *1 student enrolled* • **Welding Technology/Welder** *15 students enrolled*

STUDENT SERVICES Academic or career counseling, daycare for children of students, employment services for current students, placement services for program completers, remedial services.

Illinois Eastern Community Colleges, Wabash Valley College

2200 College Drive, Mount Carmel, IL 62863-2657
http://www.iecc.edu/wvc/

CONTACT Terry Bruce, Chief Executive Officer
Telephone: 618-393-2982

GENERAL INFORMATION Public Institution. Founded 1960. **Accreditation:** Regional (NCA). **Total program enrollment:** 665. **Application fee:** $10.

PROGRAM(S) OFFERED
• **Administrative Assistant and Secretarial Science, General** *1 student enrolled* • **Agricultural Business Technology** *3 students enrolled* • **Emergency Care Attendant (EMT Ambulance)** *1 student enrolled* • **Industrial Technology/Technician** *1 student enrolled* • **Machine Shop Technology/Assistant** *1 student enrolled* • **Mining Technology/Technician** *3 students enrolled* • **Nurse/Nursing Assistant/Aide and Patient Care Assistant** *54 students enrolled* • **Selling Skills and Sales Operations** *6 students enrolled* • **Truck and Bus Driver/Commercial Vehicle Operation** *9 students enrolled* • **Turf and Turfgrass Management** *4 students enrolled* • **Web Page, Digital/Multimedia and Information Resources Design** *1 student enrolled*

STUDENT SERVICES Academic or career counseling, daycare for children of students, employment services for current students, placement services for program completers, remedial services.

Illinois Eastern Community College System

Olney, IL 62450-2298

CONTACT Terry Bruce, Chief Executive Officer
Telephone: 618-393-2982

GENERAL INFORMATION Public Institution.

The Illinois Institute of Art–Chicago

350 North Orleans, Chicago, IL 60654
http://www.artinstitutes.edu/chicago

CONTACT John Jenkins, President
Telephone: 312-280-3500

GENERAL INFORMATION Private Institution. Founded 1916. **Accreditation:** Interior design: professional (CIDA); state accredited or approved. **Total program enrollment:** 1938. **Application fee:** $50.

PROGRAM(S) OFFERED
● **Baking and Pastry Arts/Baker/Pastry Chef** 20 students enrolled ● **Food Preparation/Professional Cooking/Kitchen Assistant** 7 students enrolled

STUDENT SERVICES Academic or career counseling, employment services for current students, placement services for program completers, remedial services.

The Illinois Institute of Art–Schaumburg

1000 Plaza Drive, Schaumburg, IL 60173
http://www.artinstitutes.edu/schaumburg

CONTACT David Ray, President
Telephone: 847-619-3450

GENERAL INFORMATION Private Institution. **Accreditation:** Interior design: professional (CIDA); state accredited or approved. **Total program enrollment:** 961. **Application fee:** $50.

PROGRAM(S) OFFERED
● **Graphic Design** 4 students enrolled ● **Interior Design** 3 students enrolled ● **Web Page, Digital/Multimedia and Information Resources Design** 5 students enrolled

STUDENT SERVICES Academic or career counseling, employment services for current students, placement services for program completers, remedial services.

Illinois School of Health Careers

220 South State Street, #600, Chicago, IL 60604
http://www.ishc.edu/

CONTACT Steve Strong, Executive Director
Telephone: 312-913-1230

GENERAL INFORMATION Private Institution. Founded 1990. **Total program enrollment:** 869. **Application fee:** $100.

PROGRAM(S) OFFERED
● **Allied Health and Medical Assisting Services, Other** 59 hrs./$14,400 ● **Dental Assisting/Assistant** 59 hrs./$13,000 ● **Medical/Clinical Assistant** 241 students enrolled

STUDENT SERVICES Academic or career counseling, employment services for current students, placement services for program completers, remedial services.

Illinois School of Health Careers–O'Hare Campus

8750 W. Bryn Mawr, Suite 300, Chicago, IL 60631
http://www.ishc.edu/

CONTACT Geralyn M. Randich, Executive Director
Telephone: 773-458-1111

GENERAL INFORMATION Private Institution. **Total program enrollment:** 276. **Application fee:** $100.

PROGRAM(S) OFFERED
● **Dental Assisting/Assistant** 880 hrs./$13,000 ● **Medical/Clinical Assistant** 880 hrs./$14,400

STUDENT SERVICES Academic or career counseling, employment services for current students, placement services for program completers, remedial services.

Illinois Valley Community College

815 North Orlando Smith Avenue, Oglesby, IL 61348-9692
http://www.ivcc.edu/

CONTACT Dr. Jerry Corcoran, President
Telephone: 815-224-2720

GENERAL INFORMATION Public Institution. Founded 1924. **Accreditation:** Regional (NCA); dental assisting (ADA). **Total program enrollment:** 1775.

PROGRAM(S) OFFERED
● **Accounting Technology/Technician and Bookkeeping** 4 students enrolled ● **Applied Horticulture/Horticultural Operations, General** 20 students enrolled ● **Architectural Drafting and Architectural CAD/CADD** 5 students enrolled ● **Automobile/Automotive Mechanics Technology/Technician** 7 students enrolled ● **Business/Office Automation/Technology/Data Entry** 3 students enrolled ● **CAD/CADD Drafting and/or Design Technology/Technician** 6 students enrolled ● **Child Care Provider/Assistant** 1 student enrolled ● **Computer Systems Networking and Telecommunications** 6 students enrolled ● **Computer Technology/Computer Systems Technology** 32 students enrolled ● **Criminal Justice/Police Science** 3 students enrolled ● **Dental Assisting/Assistant** 7 students enrolled ● **Electrician** 6 students enrolled ● **Food Service, Waiter/Waitress, and Dining Room Management/Manager** 15 students enrolled ● **Forensic Science and Technology** 4 students enrolled ● **General Office Occupations and Clerical Services** 7 students enrolled ● **Graphic Design** 3 students enrolled ● **Heating, Air Conditioning, Ventilation and Refrigeration Maintenance Technology/Technician (HAC, HACR, HVAC, HVACR)** 11 students enrolled ● **Housing and Human Environments, Other** 25 students enrolled ● **Industrial Mechanics and Maintenance Technology** 2 students enrolled ● **Licensed Practical/Vocational Nurse Training (LPN, LVN, Cert, Dipl, AAS)** 38 students enrolled ● **Machine Tool Technology/Machinist** 1 student enrolled ● **Manufacturing Technology/Technician** 1 student enrolled ● **Massage Therapy/Therapeutic Massage** 2 students enrolled ● **Nurse/Nursing Assistant/Aide and Patient Care Assistant** 213 students enrolled ● **Parts, Warehousing, and Inventory Management Operations** 7 students enrolled ● **Phlebotomy/Phlebotomist** 10 students enrolled ● **Selling Skills and Sales Operations** 1 student enrolled ● **Social Work** 2 students enrolled ● **Substance Abuse/Addiction Counseling** 2 students enrolled ● **Truck and Bus Driver/Commercial Vehicle Operation** 45 students enrolled ● **Welding Technology/Welder** 69 students enrolled

STUDENT SERVICES Academic or career counseling, daycare for children of students, employment services for current students, placement services for program completers, remedial services.

John A. Logan College

700 Logan College Road, Carterville, IL 62918-9900
http://www.jalc.edu/

CONTACT Robert Mees, President
Telephone: 618-985-3741

GENERAL INFORMATION Public Institution. Founded 1967. **Accreditation:** Regional (NCA); dental assisting (ADA); dental hygiene (ADA); health information technology (AHIMA); medical laboratory technology (NAACLS). **Total program enrollment:** 2418.

PROGRAM(S) OFFERED
● **Accounting Technology/Technician and Bookkeeping** 3 students enrolled ● **Administrative Assistant and Secretarial Science, General** 16 students enrolled ● **Autobody/Collision and Repair Technology/Technician** 34 students enrolled ● **Automobile/Automotive Mechanics Technology/Technician** 1 student enrolled ● **Business/Commerce, General** 3 students enrolled ● **Business/Office Automation/Technology/Data Entry** 10 students enrolled ● **CAD/CADD Drafting and/or Design Technology/Technician** 2 students enrolled ● **Child Care Provider/Assistant** 1 student enrolled ● **Computer Engineering Technology/Technician** 8 students enrolled ● **Cosmetology/Cosmetologist, General** 35 students enrolled ● **Criminal Justice/Police Science** 22 students enrolled ● **Dental Assisting/**

Assistant *16 students enrolled* • **Diagnostic Medical Sonography/Sonographer and Ultrasound Technician** *1 student enrolled* • **Electrical, Electronic and Communications Engineering Technology/Technician** *13 students enrolled* • **General Office Occupations and Clerical Services** *9 students enrolled* • **Heating, Air Conditioning, Ventilation and Refrigeration Maintenance Technology/Technician (HAC, HACR, HVAC, HVACR)** *2 students enrolled* • **Industrial Electronics Technology/Technician** *1 student enrolled* • **Information Science/Studies** *2 students enrolled* • **Legal Administrative Assistant/Secretary** *6 students enrolled* • **Licensed Practical/Vocational Nurse Training (LPN, LVN, Cert, Dipl, AAS)** *86 students enrolled* • **Machine Shop Technology/Assistant** *9 students enrolled* • **Massage Therapy/Therapeutic Massage** *10 students enrolled* • **Medical Administrative/Executive Assistant and Medical Secretary** *14 students enrolled* • **Medical Transcription/Transcriptionist** *8 students enrolled* • **Medical/Clinical Assistant** *9 students enrolled* • **Nurse/Nursing Assistant/Aide and Patient Care Assistant** *144 students enrolled* • **Retailing and Retail Operations** *1 student enrolled* • **Sign Language Interpretation and Translation** *7 students enrolled* • **Surgical Technology/Technologist** *3 students enrolled* • **Tool and Die Technology/Technician** *4 students enrolled* • **Welding Technology/Welder** *9 students enrolled*

STUDENT SERVICES Academic or career counseling, daycare for children of students, employment services for current students, placement services for program completers, remedial services.

John Wood Community College

1301 South 48th Street, Quincy, IL 62305-8736
http://www.jwcc.edu/

CONTACT Thomas D. Klincar, DA, President
Telephone: 217-224-6500

GENERAL INFORMATION Public Institution. Founded 1974. **Accreditation:** Regional (NCA). **Total program enrollment:** 1216.

PROGRAM(S) OFFERED
• **Accounting** *1 student enrolled* • **Administrative Assistant and Secretarial Science, General** *5 students enrolled* • **Animal/Livestock Husbandry and Production** *4 students enrolled* • **Applied Horticulture/Horticultural Operations, General** *2 students enrolled* • **Business Administration and Management, General** *4 students enrolled* • **Culinary Arts/Chef Training** *3 students enrolled* • **Electrician** *3 students enrolled* • **Licensed Practical/Vocational Nurse Training (LPN, LVN, Cert, Dipl, AAS)** *18 students enrolled* • **Medical Office Management/Administration** *1 student enrolled* • **Nurse/Nursing Assistant/Aide and Patient Care Assistant** *90 students enrolled* • **Selling Skills and Sales Operations** *1 student enrolled* • **Surgical Technology/Technologist** *7 students enrolled* • **Truck and Bus Driver/Commercial Vehicle Operation** *57 students enrolled*

STUDENT SERVICES Academic or career counseling, employment services for current students, remedial services.

Joliet Junior College

1215 Houbolt Road, Joliet, IL 60431-8938
http://www.jjc.edu/

CONTACT Dr. Eugenia Proulx, President
Telephone: 815-729-9020

GENERAL INFORMATION Public Institution. Founded 1901. **Accreditation:** Regional (NCA); music (NASM). **Total program enrollment:** 6054.

PROGRAM(S) OFFERED
• **Accounting** *2 students enrolled* • **Automobile/Automotive Mechanics Technology/Technician** *10 students enrolled* • **Child Care Provider/Assistant** *7 students enrolled* • **Computer Installation and Repair Technology/Technician** *3 students enrolled* • **Computer Systems Networking and Telecommunications** *1 student enrolled* • **Construction Trades, General** *13 students enrolled* • **Construction/Heavy Equipment/Earthmoving Equipment Operation** *2 students enrolled* • **Cosmetology/Cosmetologist, General** *1 student enrolled* • **Criminal Justice/Police Science** *3 students enrolled* • **Data Processing and Data Processing Technology/Technician** *4 students enrolled* • **Electrician** *5 students enrolled* • **Electrocardiograph Technology/Technician** *1 student enrolled* • **Entrepreneurship/Entrepreneurial Studies** *2 students enrolled* • **Finance, General** *3 students enrolled* • **Fire Science/Firefighting** *2 students enrolled* • **Fire Services Administration** *1 student enrolled* • **Floriculture/Floristry Operations and Management** *3 students enrolled* • **Food Preparation/Professional Cooking/Kitchen Assistant** *3 students enrolled* • **Heating, Air Conditioning, Ventilation and Refrigeration Maintenance Technology/Technician (HAC, HACR, HVAC,**

HVACR) *3 students enrolled* • **Heavy Equipment Maintenance Technology/Technician** *2 students enrolled* • **Hospitality Administration/Management, General** *2 students enrolled* • **Human Resources Management/Personnel Administration, General** *5 students enrolled* • **Industrial Electronics Technology/Technician** *21 students enrolled* • **Instrumentation Technology/Technician** *4 students enrolled* • **Library Assistant/Technician** *3 students enrolled* • **Licensed Practical/Vocational Nurse Training (LPN, LVN, Cert, Dipl, AAS)** *143 students enrolled* • **Manufacturing Technology/Technician** *9 students enrolled* • **Mechanical Engineering/Mechanical Technology/Technician** *3 students enrolled* • **Medical Insurance Coding Specialist/Coder** *11 students enrolled* • **Medical Transcription/Transcriptionist** *4 students enrolled* • **Nurse/Nursing Assistant/Aide and Patient Care Assistant** *3 students enrolled* • **Operations Management and Supervision** *8 students enrolled* • **Phlebotomy/Phlebotomist** *5 students enrolled* • **Plant Nursery Operations and Management** *2 students enrolled* • **Prepress/Desktop Publishing and Digital Imaging Design** *1 student enrolled* • **Word Processing** *3 students enrolled*

STUDENT SERVICES Academic or career counseling, daycare for children of students, employment services for current students, placement services for program completers, remedial services.

Kankakee Community College

PO Box 888, Kankakee, IL 60901-0888
http://www.kcc.cc.il.us/

CONTACT G. Weber, President
Telephone: 815-802-8500

GENERAL INFORMATION Public Institution. Founded 1966. **Accreditation:** Regional (NCA); medical laboratory technology (NAACLS). **Total program enrollment:** 1537.

PROGRAM(S) OFFERED
• **Accounting Technology/Technician and Bookkeeping** *3 students enrolled* • **Architectural Drafting and Architectural CAD/CADD** *2 students enrolled* • **Automobile/Automotive Mechanics Technology/Technician** *2 students enrolled* • **Business Administration and Management, General** *2 students enrolled* • **Business/Office Automation/Technology/Data Entry** *2 students enrolled* • **CAD/CADD Drafting and/or Design Technology/Technician** *3 students enrolled* • **Child Care Provider/Assistant** *2 students enrolled* • **Computer Installation and Repair Technology/Technician** *1 student enrolled* • **Construction Engineering Technology/Technician** *3 students enrolled* • **Criminal Justice/Police Science** *3 students enrolled* • **Data Entry/Microcomputer Applications, General** *1 student enrolled* • **Drafting and Design Technology/Technician, General** *4 students enrolled* • **Emergency Care Attendant (EMT Ambulance)** *1 student enrolled* • **Heating, Air Conditioning, Ventilation and Refrigeration Maintenance Technology/Technician (HAC, HACR, HVAC, HVACR)** *7 students enrolled* • **Industrial Electronics Technology/Technician** *14 students enrolled* • **Industrial Mechanics and Maintenance Technology** *2 students enrolled* • **Legal Assistant/Paralegal** *4 students enrolled* • **Licensed Practical/Vocational Nurse Training (LPN, LVN, Cert, Dipl, AAS)** *45 students enrolled* • **Mechanical Drafting and Mechanical Drafting CAD/CADD** *1 student enrolled* • **Medical Insurance Coding Specialist/Coder** *19 students enrolled* • **Medical Office Assistant/Specialist** *5 students enrolled* • **Nurse/Nursing Assistant/Aide and Patient Care Assistant** *39 students enrolled* • **Teacher Assistant/Aide** *1 student enrolled* • **Welding Technology/Welder** *5 students enrolled*

STUDENT SERVICES Academic or career counseling, daycare for children of students, employment services for current students, placement services for program completers, remedial services.

Kaskaskia College

27210 College Road, Centralia, IL 62801-7878
http://www.kaskaskia.edu/

CONTACT Dr. James Underwood, President
Telephone: 618-545-3000

GENERAL INFORMATION Public Institution. Founded 1966. **Accreditation:** Regional (NCA); dental assisting (ADA); physical therapy assisting (APTA); radiologic technology: radiography (JRCERT); respiratory therapy technology (CoARC). **Total program enrollment:** 1922.

PROGRAM(S) OFFERED
• **Accounting and Business/Management** *1 student enrolled* • **Accounting** *4 students enrolled* • **Administrative Assistant and Secretarial Science, General** *1 student enrolled* • **Architectural Drafting and Architectural CAD/CADD** *1*

Kaskaskia College (continued)

student enrolled • **Autobody/Collision and Repair Technology/Technician** 3 students enrolled • **Automobile/Automotive Mechanics Technology/Technician** 1 student enrolled • **Business/Office Automation/Technology/Data Entry** 3 students enrolled • **CAD/CADD Drafting and/or Design Technology/Technician** 12 students enrolled • **Carpentry/Carpenter** 2 students enrolled • **Computer Systems Networking and Telecommunications** 10 students enrolled • **Construction Trades, General** 17 students enrolled • **Cosmetology/Cosmetologist, General** 20 students enrolled • **Criminal Justice/Law Enforcement Administration** 7 students enrolled • **Culinary Arts/Chef Training** 5 students enrolled • **Dental Assisting/Assistant** 20 students enrolled • **Diagnostic Medical Sonography/Sonographer and Ultrasound Technician** 10 students enrolled • **Electrical, Electronic and Communications Engineering Technology/Technician** 15 students enrolled • **Electrical/Electronics Drafting and Electrical/Electronics CAD/CADD** 19 students enrolled • **Entrepreneurship/Entrepreneurial Studies** 1 student enrolled • **Food Preparation/Professional Cooking/Kitchen Assistant** 3 students enrolled • **Food Service, Waiter/Waitress, and Dining Room Management/Manager** 8 students enrolled • **General Office Occupations and Clerical Services** 3 students enrolled • **Graphic and Printing Equipment Operator, General Production** 4 students enrolled • **Heating, Air Conditioning, Ventilation and Refrigeration Maintenance Technology/Technician (HAC, HACR, HVAC, HVACR)** 18 students enrolled • **Housing and Human Environments, Other** 3 students enrolled • **Industrial Mechanics and Maintenance Technology** 3 students enrolled • **Instrumentation Technology/Technician** 1 student enrolled • **Legal Administrative Assistant/Secretary** 1 student enrolled • **Licensed Practical/Vocational Nurse Training (LPN, LVN, Cert, Dipl, AAS)** 43 students enrolled • **Massage Therapy/Therapeutic Massage** 7 students enrolled • **Mechanical Drafting and Mechanical Drafting CAD/CADD** 12 students enrolled • **Medical Administrative/Executive Assistant and Medical Secretary** 7 students enrolled • **Medical Transcription/Transcriptionist** 5 students enrolled • **Nurse/Nursing Assistant/Aide and Patient Care Assistant** 213 students enrolled • **Office Management and Supervision** 3 students enrolled • **Retailing and Retail Operations** 2 students enrolled • **System Administration/Administrator** 4 students enrolled • **Truck and Bus Driver/Commercial Vehicle Operation** 15 students enrolled • **Welding Technology/Welder** 2 students enrolled

STUDENT SERVICES Academic or career counseling, daycare for children of students, employment services for current students, placement services for program completers, remedial services.

Kendall College

900 North Branch Street, Chicago, IL 60622
http://www.kendall.edu/

CONTACT Nivine Megahed, President
Telephone: 312-752-2000

GENERAL INFORMATION Private Institution. Founded 1934. **Accreditation:** Regional (NCA). **Total program enrollment:** 1222. **Application fee:** $50.

PROGRAM(S) OFFERED
• **Business/Commerce, General** • **Culinary Arts/Chef Training** 66 students enrolled

STUDENT SERVICES Academic or career counseling, employment services for current students, placement services for program completers, remedial services.

Kishwaukee College

21193 Malta Road, Malta, IL 60150-9699
http://www.kishwaukeecollege.edu/

CONTACT Tom Choice, President
Telephone: 815-825-2086

GENERAL INFORMATION Public Institution. Founded 1967. **Accreditation:** Regional (NCA); radiologic technology: radiography (JRCERT). **Total program enrollment:** 2031.

PROGRAM(S) OFFERED
• **Administrative Assistant and Secretarial Science, General** 6 students enrolled • **Agricultural Power Machinery Operation** 28 students enrolled • **Airline/Commercial/Professional Pilot and Flight Crew** 1 student enrolled • **Autobody/Collision and Repair Technology/Technician** 5 students enrolled • **Automobile/Automotive Mechanics Technology/Technician** 3 students enrolled • **CAD/CADD**

Drafting and/or Design Technology/Technician 1 student enrolled • **Carpentry/Carpenter** 2 students enrolled • **Computer Installation and Repair Technology/Technician** 3 students enrolled • **Computer Systems Networking and Telecommunications** 1 student enrolled • **Electrical, Electronic and Communications Engineering Technology/Technician** 2 students enrolled • **Electrician** 3 students enrolled • **Emergency Care Attendant (EMT Ambulance)** 39 students enrolled • **Floriculture/Floristry Operations and Management** 1 student enrolled • **General Office Occupations and Clerical Services** 2 students enrolled • **Greenhouse Operations and Management** 1 student enrolled • **Licensed Practical/Vocational Nurse Training (LPN, LVN, Cert, Dipl, AAS)** 13 students enrolled • **Massage Therapy/Therapeutic Massage** 22 students enrolled • **Mechanical Drafting and Mechanical Drafting CAD/CADD** 1 student enrolled • **Medical Insurance Coding Specialist/Coder** 15 students enrolled • **Medical Transcription/Transcriptionist** 3 students enrolled • **Nurse/Nursing Assistant/Aide and Patient Care Assistant** 165 students enrolled • **Welding Technology/Welder** 1 student enrolled

STUDENT SERVICES Academic or career counseling, daycare for children of students, employment services for current students, placement services for program completers, remedial services.

La' James College of Hairstyling

485 42nd Avenue, East Moline, IL 61244
http://www.lajames.net/

CONTACT Cynthia Becher, President
Telephone: 309-755-1313

GENERAL INFORMATION Private Institution. Founded 1986. **Total program enrollment:** 25. **Application fee:** $50.

PROGRAM(S) OFFERED
• **Aesthetician/Esthetician and Skin Care Specialist** 600 hrs./$8860 • **Cosmetology, Barber/Styling, and Nail Instructor** 1000 hrs./$7565 • **Cosmetology/Cosmetologist, General** 1500 hrs./$18,365 • **Massage Therapy/Therapeutic Massage** 625 hrs./$8860 • **Nail Technician/Specialist and Manicurist** 350 hrs./$3925

STUDENT SERVICES Academic or career counseling, employment services for current students, placement services for program completers.

Lake Land College

5001 Lake Land Boulevard, Mattoon, IL 61938-9366
http://www.lakelandcollege.edu/

CONTACT Scott Lensink, President
Telephone: 217-234-5253

GENERAL INFORMATION Public Institution. Founded 1966. **Accreditation:** Regional (NCA); dental hygiene (ADA); physical therapy assisting (APTA); practical nursing (NLN). **Total program enrollment:** 3009.

PROGRAM(S) OFFERED
• **Accounting** 4 students enrolled • **Administrative Assistant and Secretarial Science, General** 27 students enrolled • **Agricultural Business and Management, General** 1 student enrolled • **Agricultural Power Machinery Operation** 1 student enrolled • **Animal Training** 19 students enrolled • **Applied Horticulture/Horticultural Operations, General** 48 students enrolled • **Autobody/Collision and Repair Technology/Technician** 28 students enrolled • **Automobile/Automotive Mechanics Technology/Technician** 106 students enrolled • **Building/Property Maintenance and Management** 4 students enrolled • **Business Administration and Management, General** 18 students enrolled • **Business/Office Automation/Technology/Data Entry** 142 students enrolled • **CAD/CADD Drafting and/or Design Technology/Technician** 8 students enrolled • **Child Care Provider/Assistant** 1 student enrolled • **Communications Systems Installation and Repair Technology** 3 students enrolled • **Computer Technology/Computer Systems Technology** 1 student enrolled • **Construction Trades, General** 97 students enrolled • **Cosmetology, Barber/Styling, and Nail Instructor** 1 student enrolled • **Cosmetology/Cosmetologist, General** 48 students enrolled • **Crop Production** 2 students enrolled • **Dog/Pet/Animal Grooming** 10 students enrolled • **Entrepreneurship/Entrepreneurial Studies** 2 students enrolled • **Food Service, Waiter/Waitress, and Dining Room Management/Manager** 47 students enrolled • **General Office Occupations and Clerical Services** 6 students enrolled • **Graphic and Printing Equipment Operator, General Production** 14 students enrolled • **Heating, Air Conditioning, Ventilation and Refrigeration Maintenance Technology/Technician (HAC, HACR, HVAC, HVACR)** 31 students enrolled • **Housing and Human Environments, Other** 126 students enrolled

• **Information Science/Studies** *4 students enrolled* • **Licensed Practical/Vocational Nurse Training (LPN, LVN, Cert, Dipl, AAS)** *28 students enrolled* • **Massage Therapy/Therapeutic Massage** *10 students enrolled* • **Medical Transcription/Transcriptionist** *7 students enrolled* • **Nail Technician/Specialist and Manicurist** *7 students enrolled* • **Parts, Warehousing, and Inventory Management Operations** *5 students enrolled* • **Prepress/Desktop Publishing and Digital Imaging Design** *1 student enrolled* • **Radio and Television** *4 students enrolled* • **Selling Skills and Sales Operations** *5 students enrolled*

STUDENT SERVICES Academic or career counseling, daycare for children of students, employment services for current students, placement services for program completers, remedial services.

Lakeview College of Nursing

903 North Logan Avenue, Danville, IL 61832
http://www.lakeviewcol.edu/

CONTACT Dick Shockey, CEO
Telephone: 217-443-5238

GENERAL INFORMATION Private Institution. Founded 1987. **Accreditation:** Regional (NCA). **Total program enrollment:** 226. **Application fee:** $100.

STUDENT SERVICES Academic or career counseling, remedial services.

Lewis and Clark Community College

5800 Godfrey Road, Godfrey, IL 62035-2466
http://www.lc.edu/

CONTACT Dale T. Chapman, President
Telephone: 618-468-3411

GENERAL INFORMATION Public Institution. Founded 1970. **Accreditation:** Regional (NCA); dental assisting (ADA); dental hygiene (ADA). **Total program enrollment:** 2813.

PROGRAM(S) OFFERED
• **Accounting Technology/Technician and Bookkeeping** *3 students enrolled* • **Accounting** *2 students enrolled* • **Administrative Assistant and Secretarial Science, General** *153 students enrolled* • **Automobile/Automotive Mechanics Technology/Technician** *9 students enrolled* • **Banking and Financial Support Services** *11 students enrolled* • **Business Administration and Management, General** *6 students enrolled* • **Business/Office Automation/Technology/Data Entry** *56 students enrolled* • **CAD/CADD Drafting and/or Design Technology/Technician** *5 students enrolled* • **Child Care Provider/Assistant** *1 student enrolled* • **Computer Installation and Repair Technology/Technician** *41 students enrolled* • **Computer Programming, Specific Applications** *6 students enrolled* • **Computer Systems Networking and Telecommunications** *26 students enrolled* • **Criminal Justice/Police Science** *19 students enrolled* • **Dental Assisting/Assistant** *25 students enrolled* • **Electrician** *43 students enrolled* • **Emergency Medical Technology/Technician (EMT Paramedic)** *8 students enrolled* • **Fire Science/Firefighting** *30 students enrolled* • **Fire Services Administration** *7 students enrolled* • **General Office Occupations and Clerical Services** *2 students enrolled* • **Graphic Design** *7 students enrolled* • **Human Resources Management/Personnel Administration, General** *13 students enrolled* • **Legal Administrative Assistant/Secretary** *2 students enrolled* • **Legal Assistant/Paralegal** *12 students enrolled* • **Library Assistant/Technician** *2 students enrolled* • **Machine Tool Technology/Machinist** *11 students enrolled* • **Massage Therapy/Therapeutic Massage** *9 students enrolled* • **Medical Insurance Specialist/Medical Biller** *11 students enrolled* • **Medical Transcription/Transcriptionist** *2 students enrolled* • **Nurse/Nursing Assistant/Aide and Patient Care Assistant** *162 students enrolled* • **Prepress/Desktop Publishing and Digital Imaging Design** *10 students enrolled* • **Radio and Television** *6 students enrolled* • **Selling Skills and Sales Operations** *15 students enrolled* • **System Administration/Administrator** *11 students enrolled* • **Web Page, Digital/Multimedia and Information Resources Design** *8 students enrolled* • **Welding Technology/Welder** *71 students enrolled*

STUDENT SERVICES Academic or career counseling, daycare for children of students, employment services for current students, placement services for program completers, remedial services.

Lewis University

One University Parkway, Romeoville, IL 60446
http://www.lewisu.edu/

CONTACT Brother James Gaffney, FSC, President
Telephone: 815-838-0500

GENERAL INFORMATION Private Institution (Affiliated with Roman Catholic Church). Founded 1932. **Accreditation:** Regional (NCA). **Total program enrollment:** 3219. **Application fee:** $40.

PROGRAM(S) OFFERED
• **Airframe Mechanics and Aircraft Maintenance Technology/Technician**

STUDENT SERVICES Academic or career counseling, employment services for current students, placement services for program completers, remedial services.

Lincoln Christian College

100 Campus View Drive, Lincoln, IL 62656-2167
http://www.lccs.edu/

CONTACT Keith Ray, President
Telephone: 217-732-3168

GENERAL INFORMATION Private Institution (Affiliated with Christian Churches and Churches of Christ). Founded 1944. **Accreditation:** Regional (NCA); state accredited or approved. **Total program enrollment:** 700. **Application fee:** $20.

PROGRAM(S) OFFERED
• **Bible/Biblical Studies** *3 students enrolled*

STUDENT SERVICES Academic or career counseling, employment services for current students, placement services for program completers, remedial services.

Lincoln College

300 Keokuk Street, Lincoln, IL 62656-1699
http://www.lincolncollege.edu/

CONTACT John Hutchinson, President
Telephone: 217-732-3155 Ext. 242

GENERAL INFORMATION Private Institution. Founded 1865. **Accreditation:** Regional (NCA). **Total program enrollment:** 983. **Application fee:** $25.

PROGRAM(S) OFFERED
• **Cosmetology/Cosmetologist, General** *31 students enrolled* • **Medical Administrative/Executive Assistant and Medical Secretary** • **Office Management and Supervision** • **Tourism and Travel Services Marketing Operations**

STUDENT SERVICES Academic or career counseling, employment services for current students, remedial services.

Lincoln Land Community College

5250 Shepherd Road, PO Box 19256, Springfield, IL 62794-9256
http://www.llcc.edu/

CONTACT Dr. Charlotte Warren, President
Telephone: 217-786-2200

GENERAL INFORMATION Public Institution. Founded 1967. **Accreditation:** Regional (NCA); radiologic technology: radiography (JRCERT). **Total program enrollment:** 2921.

PROGRAM(S) OFFERED
• **Architectural Drafting and Architectural CAD/CADD** *2 students enrolled*
• **Autobody/Collision and Repair Technology/Technician** *21 students enrolled*
• **Automobile/Automotive Mechanics Technology/Technician** *6 students enrolled*

Lincoln Land Community College (continued)

• **Baking and Pastry Arts/Baker/Pastry Chef** *5 students enrolled* • **Building/Property Maintenance and Management** *2 students enrolled* • **Business Administration and Management, General** *5 students enrolled* • **Business/Office Automation/Technology/Data Entry** *10 students enrolled* • **CAD/CADD Drafting and/or Design Technology/Technician** *3 students enrolled* • **Computer Engineering Technology/Technician** *4 students enrolled* • **Computer Programming/Programmer, General** *2 students enrolled* • **Computer Technology/Computer Systems Technology** *2 students enrolled* • **Criminal Justice/Police Science** *2 students enrolled* • **Dietitian Assistant** *1 student enrolled* • **Electrical, Electronic and Communications Engineering Technology/Technician** *3 students enrolled* • **Emergency Care Attendant (EMT Ambulance)** *59 students enrolled* • **Emergency Medical Technology/Technician (EMT Paramedic)** *23 students enrolled* • **Fire Protection and Safety Technology/Technician** *8 students enrolled* • **Fire Science/Firefighting** *72 students enrolled* • **Fire Services Administration** *15 students enrolled* • **General Office Occupations and Clerical Services** *7 students enrolled* • **Heating, Air Conditioning, Ventilation and Refrigeration Maintenance Technology/Technician (HAC, HACR, HVAC, HVACR)** *12 students enrolled* • **Hotel/Motel Administration/Management** *2 students enrolled* • **Industrial Electronics Technology/Technician** *10 students enrolled* • **Landscaping and Groundskeeping** *5 students enrolled* • **Legal Administrative Assistant/Secretary** *2 students enrolled* • **Licensed Practical/Vocational Nurse Training (LPN, LVN, Cert, Dipl, AAS)** *21 students enrolled* • **Medical Administrative/Executive Assistant and Medical Secretary** *3 students enrolled* • **Medical Insurance Coding Specialist/Coder** *2 students enrolled* • **Medical Transcription/Transcriptionist** *10 students enrolled* • **Nurse/Nursing Assistant/Aide and Patient Care Assistant** *323 students enrolled* • **Restaurant, Culinary, and Catering Management/Manager** *4 students enrolled* • **Security and Loss Prevention Services** *146 students enrolled* • **System Administration/Administrator** *3 students enrolled* • **Truck and Bus Driver/Commercial Vehicle Operation** *154 students enrolled* • **Web Page, Digital/Multimedia and Information Resources Design** *1 student enrolled* • **Welding Technology/Welder** *9 students enrolled* • **Word Processing** *4 students enrolled*

STUDENT SERVICES Academic or career counseling, daycare for children of students, employment services for current students, placement services for program completers, remedial services.

Lincoln Technical Institute

7320 West Agatite Avenue, Norridge, IL 60656-9975
http://www.lincolnedu.com/

CONTACT Helen Carver, President
Telephone: 203-582-8200

GENERAL INFORMATION Private Institution. Founded 1946. **Total program enrollment:** 1292. **Application fee:** $150.

PROGRAM(S) OFFERED
• **Automobile/Automotive Mechanics Technology/Technician** *30 hrs./$10,767* • **Construction Trades, Other** *52 hrs./$18,304* • **Health Services/Allied Health/Health Sciences, General** *40 hrs./$14,210* • **Medical/Clinical Assistant** *270 students enrolled*

STUDENT SERVICES Academic or career counseling, employment services for current students, placement services for program completers, remedial services.

Loyola University Chicago

1032 West Sheridan Road, Chicago, IL 60660
http://www.luc.edu/

CONTACT Michael J. Garanzini, SJ, President
Telephone: 312-915-6000

GENERAL INFORMATION Private Institution. Founded 1870. **Accreditation:** Regional (NCA); dietetics: postbaccalaureate internship (ADtA/CAADE); theater (NAST). **Total program enrollment:** 13561. **Application fee:** $25.

STUDENT SERVICES Academic or career counseling, employment services for current students, placement services for program completers, remedial services.

MacCormac College

506 South Wabash Avenue, Chicago, IL 60605-1667
http://www.maccormac.edu/

CONTACT Dr. Leo Loughead, President
Telephone: 312-922-1884 Ext. 401

GENERAL INFORMATION Private Institution. Founded 1904. **Accreditation:** Regional (NCA). **Total program enrollment:** 99. **Application fee:** $20.

PROGRAM(S) OFFERED
• **Business Administration and Management, General** • **Business/Office Automation/Technology/Data Entry** • **Information Science/Studies** • **International Business/Trade/Commerce** • **Legal Administrative Assistant/Secretary** • **Legal Assistant/Paralegal** • **Legal Support Services, Other** • **Medical Transcription/Transcriptionist** • **Tourism and Travel Services Marketing Operations**

STUDENT SERVICES Academic or career counseling, employment services for current students, placement services for program completers.

MacDaniel's Beauty School

5228 North Clark Street, Chicago, IL 60640

CONTACT Steven Papageorge, Director
Telephone: 773-561-2376

GENERAL INFORMATION Private Institution. Founded 1965. **Total program enrollment:** 37. **Application fee:** $100.

PROGRAM(S) OFFERED
• **Cosmetology, Barber/Styling, and Nail Instructor** *1000 hrs./$7600* • **Cosmetology/Cosmetologist, General** *1500 hrs./$11,750* • **Nail Technician/Specialist and Manicurist** *350 hrs./$2750*

STUDENT SERVICES Academic or career counseling, employment services for current students, placement services for program completers.

McHenry County College

8900 US Highway 14, Crystal Lake, IL 60012-2761
http://www.mchenry.edu/

CONTACT Walter Packard, President
Telephone: 815-455-3700

GENERAL INFORMATION Public Institution. Founded 1967. **Accreditation:** Regional (NCA). **Total program enrollment:** 2283. **Application fee:** $15.

PROGRAM(S) OFFERED
• **Accounting Technology/Technician and Bookkeeping** *1 student enrolled* • **Accounting** *1 student enrolled* • **Administrative Assistant and Secretarial Science, General** *5 students enrolled* • **Animation, Interactive Technology, Video Graphics and Special Effects** *4 students enrolled* • **Applied Horticulture/Horticultural Operations, General** *4 students enrolled* • **Automobile/Automotive Mechanics Technology/Technician** *10 students enrolled* • **Building/Home/Construction Inspection/Inspector** *11 students enrolled* • **Business Administration and Management, General** *53 students enrolled* • **Business/Office Automation/Technology/Data Entry** *5 students enrolled* • **CAD/CADD Drafting and/or Design Technology/Technician** *5 students enrolled* • **Child Care Provider/Assistant** *1 student enrolled* • **Computer Systems Networking and Telecommunications** *1 student enrolled* • **Computer Technology/Computer Systems Technology** *2 students enrolled* • **Emergency Care Attendant (EMT Ambulance)** *14 students enrolled* • **Fire Science/Firefighting** *56 students enrolled* • **Fire Services Administration** *1 student enrolled* • **Floriculture/Floristry Operations and Management** *4 students enrolled* • **Greenhouse Operations and Management** *2 students enrolled* • **Health and Physical Education, General** *14 students enrolled* • **International Business/Trade/Commerce** *1 student enrolled* • **Landscaping and Groundskeeping** *3 students enrolled* • **Mechanical Engineering/Mechanical Technology/Technician** *1 student enrolled* • **Medical Office Assistant/Specialist** *9 students enrolled* • **Nurse/Nursing Assistant/Aide and Patient Care Assistant** *175 students enrolled* • **Operations Management and Supervision** *2 students enrolled* • **Selling Skills and Sales Operations** *7 students enrolled*

STUDENT SERVICES Academic or career counseling, daycare for children of students, employment services for current students, placement services for program completers, remedial services.

Midstate College

411 West Northmoor Road, Peoria, IL 61614
http://www.midstate.edu/

CONTACT R. Dale Bunch, President
Telephone: 309-692-4092

GENERAL INFORMATION Private Institution. Founded 1888. **Accreditation:** Regional (NCA); medical assisting (AAMAE). **Total program enrollment:** 292. **Application fee:** $25.

PROGRAM(S) OFFERED
• Computer Software and Media Applications, Other • Computer Systems Networking and Telecommunications • General Office Occupations and Clerical Services 7 *students enrolled* • Medical Insurance Coding Specialist/Coder 16 *students enrolled* • Medical Transcription/Transcriptionist 3 *students enrolled* • Web Page, Digital/Multimedia and Information Resources Design

STUDENT SERVICES Academic or career counseling, employment services for current students, placement services for program completers.

Midwest Institute of Massage Therapy

4715 W. Main Street, Belleville, IL 62223

CONTACT Vinomani Gaddam, President
Telephone: 618-239-6468 Ext. 0

GENERAL INFORMATION Private Institution. **Total program enrollment:** 30. **Application fee:** $100.

PROGRAM(S) OFFERED
• Massage Therapy/Therapeutic Massage 700 hrs./$5660

STUDENT SERVICES Academic or career counseling, placement services for program completers.

Midwest Technical Institute

405 N. Limit Street., Lincoln, IL 62656-0506
http://midwesttechnicalinstitute.edu/

CONTACT Kathy Steinberg, President
Telephone: 217-527-8324

GENERAL INFORMATION Private Institution. **Total program enrollment:** 635. **Application fee:** $100.

PROGRAM(S) OFFERED
• Dental Assisting/Assistant 32 hrs./$9600 • Heating, Air Conditioning, Ventilation and Refrigeration Maintenance Technology/Technician (HAC, HACR, HVAC, HVACR) 30 hrs./$9315 • Massage Therapy/Therapeutic Massage 39 hrs./$9550 • Medical Insurance Coding Specialist/Coder 38 hrs./$9260 • Medical/Clinical Assistant 34 hrs./$9550 • Nurse/Nursing Assistant/Aide and Patient Care Assistant 36 *students enrolled* • Pharmacy Technician/Assistant 11 *students enrolled* • Welding Technology/Welder 30 hrs./$10,400

STUDENT SERVICES Academic or career counseling, employment services for current students, placement services for program completers.

Moraine Valley Community College

9000 W. College Parkway, Palos Hills, IL 60465
http://www.morainevalley.edu/

CONTACT Dr. Vernon O. Crawley, President
Telephone: 708-974-4300

GENERAL INFORMATION Public Institution. Founded 1967. **Accreditation:** Regional (NCA); health information technology (AHIMA); radiologic technology: radiography (JRCERT). **Total program enrollment:** 7368.

PROGRAM(S) OFFERED
• Accounting Technology/Technician and Bookkeeping 9 *students enrolled* • Administrative Assistant and Secretarial Science, General 12 *students enrolled* • Animation, Interactive Technology, Video Graphics and Special Effects 4 *students enrolled* • Automobile/Automotive Mechanics Technology/

Technician 9 *students enrolled* • Business/Commerce, General 18 *students enrolled* • Business/Office Automation/Technology/Data Entry 15 *students enrolled* • CAD/CADD Drafting and/or Design Technology/Technician 9 *students enrolled* • Computer Engineering Technology/Technician 5 *students enrolled* • Computer Programming, Specific Applications 4 *students enrolled* • Computer Systems Networking and Telecommunications 7 *students enrolled* • Computer and Information Systems Security 6 *students enrolled* • E-Commerce/Electronic Commerce 3 *students enrolled* • Electrical, Electronic and Communications Engineering Technology/Technician 2 *students enrolled* • Emergency Medical Technology/Technician (EMT Paramedic) 1 *student enrolled* • Executive Assistant/Executive Secretary 3 *students enrolled* • Heating, Air Conditioning, Ventilation and Refrigeration Maintenance Technology/Technician (HAC, HACR, HVAC, HVACR) 5 *students enrolled* • Hospitality Administration/Management, General 9 *students enrolled* • Human Resources Management/Personnel Administration, General 1 *student enrolled* • Kinesiology and Exercise Science 6 *students enrolled* • Legal Administrative Assistant/Secretary 3 *students enrolled* • Massage Therapy/Therapeutic Massage 25 *students enrolled* • Mechanical Drafting and Mechanical Drafting CAD/CADD 3 *students enrolled* • Medical Insurance Coding Specialist/Coder 59 *students enrolled* • Medical Transcription/Transcriptionist 10 *students enrolled* • Medical/Clinical Assistant 12 *students enrolled* • Phlebotomy/Phlebotomist 92 *students enrolled* • Psychiatric/Mental Health Services Technician 2 *students enrolled* • Respiratory Care Therapy/Therapist 14 *students enrolled* • Restaurant, Culinary, and Catering Management/Manager 3 *students enrolled* • Security and Loss Prevention Services 1 *student enrolled* • Substance Abuse/Addiction Counseling 2 *students enrolled* • System Administration/Administrator 4 *students enrolled* • System, Networking, and LAN/WAN Management/Manager 4 *students enrolled* • Teacher Assistant/Aide 5 *students enrolled* • Tourism and Travel Services Management 11 *students enrolled* • Web Page, Digital/Multimedia and Information Resources Design 4 *students enrolled* • Welding Technology/Welder 26 *students enrolled*

STUDENT SERVICES Academic or career counseling, daycare for children of students, employment services for current students, placement services for program completers, remedial services.

Morton College

3801 South Central Avenue, Cicero, IL 60804-4398
http://www.morton.edu/

CONTACT Leslie Navarro, President
Telephone: 708-656-8000

GENERAL INFORMATION Public Institution. Founded 1924. **Accreditation:** Regional (NCA); physical therapy assisting (APTA). **Total program enrollment:** 1332. **Application fee:** $10.

PROGRAM(S) OFFERED
• Administrative Assistant and Secretarial Science, General 5 *students enrolled* • Automobile/Automotive Mechanics Technology/Technician 1 *student enrolled* • Business/Office Automation/Technology/Data Entry 10 *students enrolled* • CAD/CADD Drafting and/or Design Technology/Technician 2 *students enrolled* • Child Care Provider/Assistant 37 *students enrolled* • Computer Installation and Repair Technology/Technician 2 *students enrolled* • Computer Programming, Vendor/Product Certification 24 *students enrolled* • Computer Programming/Programmer, General 1 *student enrolled* • Computer Systems Networking and Telecommunications 1 *student enrolled* • Computer Technology/Computer Systems Technology 1 *student enrolled* • General Office Occupations and Clerical Services 3 *students enrolled* • Health Information/Medical Records Technology/Technician 8 *students enrolled* • Heating, Air Conditioning, Ventilation and Refrigeration Maintenance Technology/Technician (HAC, HACR, HVAC, HVACR) 7 *students enrolled* • Licensed Practical/Vocational Nurse Training (LPN, LVN, Cert, Dipl, AAS) 41 *students enrolled* • Massage Therapy/Therapeutic Massage 13 *students enrolled* • Mechanical Drafting and Mechanical Drafting CAD/CADD 1 *student enrolled* • Nurse/Nursing Assistant/Aide and Patient Care Assistant 56 *students enrolled*

STUDENT SERVICES Academic or career counseling, daycare for children of students, employment services for current students, placement services for program completers, remedial services.

Mr. John's School of Cosmetology

1745 East Eldorado Street, Decatur, IL 62521
http://www.mrjohns.com/

CONTACT John W. Stubblefield, President
Telephone: 217-423-8173

GENERAL INFORMATION Private Institution. Founded 1967. **Total program enrollment:** 76. **Application fee:** $100.

PROGRAM(S) OFFERED
• **Aesthetician/Esthetician and Skin Care Specialist** *750 hrs./$6095*
• **Cosmetology and Related Personal Grooming Arts, Other** • **Cosmetology, Barber/Styling, and Nail Instructor** *1000 hrs./$5870* • **Cosmetology/Cosmetologist, General** *1900 hrs./$11,595* • **Make-Up Artist/Specialist** *4 students enrolled* • **Nail Technician/Specialist and Manicurist** *400 hrs./$2770*

STUDENT SERVICES Academic or career counseling, employment services for current students, placement services for program completers.

Mr. John's School of Cosmetology & Nails

1429 S. Main Street, Suite F, Jacksonville, IL 62650
http://mrjohns.com/

CONTACT John W. Stubblefield, President
Telephone: 217-243-1744

GENERAL INFORMATION Private Institution. **Total program enrollment:** 27. **Application fee:** $100.

PROGRAM(S) OFFERED
• **Cosmetology and Related Personal Grooming Arts, Other** *6 students enrolled* • **Cosmetology, Barber/Styling, and Nail Instructor** *1000 hrs./$5870* • **Cosmetology/Cosmetologist, General** *1700 hrs./$13,350* • **Nail Technician/Specialist and Manicurist** *400 hrs./$2745*

STUDENT SERVICES Academic or career counseling, employment services for current students, placement services for program completers.

Ms. Robert's Academy of Beauty Culture–Villa Park

17 East Park Boulevard, Villa Park, IL 60181

CONTACT Phil Sparagna, President
Telephone: 630-941-3880

GENERAL INFORMATION Private Institution. **Total program enrollment:** 55. **Application fee:** $100.

PROGRAM(S) OFFERED
• **Aesthetician/Esthetician and Skin Care Specialist** *750 hrs./$8150*
• **Cosmetology and Related Personal Grooming Arts, Other** *87 students enrolled* • **Cosmetology/Cosmetologist, General** *1500 hrs./$11,000*

STUDENT SERVICES Academic or career counseling, placement services for program completers.

National-Louis University

122 South Michigan Avenue, Chicago, IL 60603
http://www.nl.edu/

CONTACT Richard Pappas, President
Telephone: 800-443-5522

GENERAL INFORMATION Private Institution. Founded 1886. **Accreditation:** Regional (NCA); radiologic technology: radiation therapy technology (JRCERT). **Total program enrollment:** 2287. **Application fee:** $40.

STUDENT SERVICES Academic or career counseling, employment services for current students, placement services for program completers, remedial services.

National University of Health Sciences

200 East Roosevelt Road, Lombard, IL 60148-4583
http://www.nuhs.edu/

CONTACT James F. Winterstein, President
Telephone: 630-629-2000

GENERAL INFORMATION Private Institution. Founded 1906. **Accreditation:** Regional (NCA). **Total program enrollment:** 499. **Application fee:** $55.

PROGRAM(S) OFFERED
• **Chiropractic Assistant/Technician** *6 students enrolled* • **Massage Therapy/Therapeutic Massage** *69 students enrolled*
STUDENT SERVICES Academic or career counseling, employment services for current students, remedial services.

Niles School of Cosmetology

8057 North Milwaukee Avenue, Niles, IL 60714
http://nilesschoolofcosmetology.com/

CONTACT Filippo Livolsi, President
Telephone: 847-965-8061

GENERAL INFORMATION Private Institution. Founded 1975. **Total program enrollment:** 30. **Application fee:** $100.

PROGRAM(S) OFFERED
• **Cosmetology, Barber/Styling, and Nail Instructor** *1000 hrs./$4175*
• **Cosmetology/Cosmetologist, General** *1500 hrs./$9000* • **Education, Other** *53 students enrolled*

STUDENT SERVICES Placement services for program completers.

Northwestern Business College–Southwestern Campus

7725 South Harlem Avenue, Bridgeview, IL 60645
http://www.northwesternbc.edu/

CONTACT Lawrence Schumacher, President
Telephone: 888-205-2283

GENERAL INFORMATION Private Institution. **Total program enrollment:** 331. **Application fee:** $25.

PROGRAM(S) OFFERED
• **Accounting Technology/Technician and Bookkeeping** • **Administrative Assistant and Secretarial Science, General** • **Business Administration and Management, General** *3 students enrolled* • **Computer and Information Sciences and Support Services, Other** *7 students enrolled* • **Electroneurodiagnostic/Electroencephalographic Technology/Technologist** *31 students enrolled* • **Health Information/Medical Records Technology/Technician** *8 students enrolled* • **Hospitality Administration/Management, General** • **Legal Assistant/Paralegal** *18 students enrolled* • **Massage Therapy/Therapeutic Massage** *16 students enrolled* • **Medical Insurance Coding Specialist/Coder** *7 students enrolled* • **Medical/Clinical Assistant** • **Pharmacy Technician/Assistant** *16 students enrolled* • **Phlebotomy/Phlebotomist** *20 students enrolled* • **Real Estate** • **Tourism and Travel Services Management**

STUDENT SERVICES Academic or career counseling, employment services for current students, placement services for program completers, remedial services.

Northwestern College

4839 North Milwaukee Avenue, Chicago, IL 60630
http://www.northwesterncollege.edu/

CONTACT Lawrence Schumacher, President
Telephone: 773-777-4220

GENERAL INFORMATION Private Institution. Founded 1902. **Accreditation:** Regional (NCA); health information technology (AHIMA); medical assisting (AAMAE). **Total program enrollment:** 354. **Application fee:** $25.

PROGRAM(S) OFFERED
• **Accounting Technology/Technician and Bookkeeping** • **Business Administration and Management, General** *1 student enrolled* • **Computer Programming,**

Specific Applications • Computer and Information Sciences and Support Services, Other *2 students enrolled* • Electroneurodiagnostic/ Electroencephalographic Technology/Technologist *10 students enrolled* • Health Information/Medical Records Technology/Technician *3 students enrolled* • Hospitality Administration/Management, General • Legal Assistant/ Paralegal *6 students enrolled* • Management Information Systems, General • Massage Therapy/Therapeutic Massage *5 students enrolled* • Medical/Clinical Assistant *3 students enrolled* • Pharmacy Technician/Assistant *4 students enrolled* • Phlebotomy/Phlebotomist *3 students enrolled* • Real Estate

STUDENT SERVICES Academic or career counseling, employment services for current students, placement services for program completers, remedial services.

Northwestern University

Evanston, IL 60208
http://www.northwestern.edu/

CONTACT Henry S. Bienen, President
Telephone: 312-491-3741

GENERAL INFORMATION Private Institution. Founded 1851. **Accreditation:** Regional (NCA); audiology (ASHA); journalism and mass communications (ACEJMC); music (NASM); speech-language pathology (ASHA); theater (NAST). **Total program enrollment:** 16134. **Application fee:** $65.

PROGRAM(S) OFFERED
• Accounting Technology/Technician and Bookkeeping • Business Administration, Management and Operations, Other • Business/Commerce, General • Communication and Media Studies, Other • Computer and Information Sciences and Support Services, Other • Finance, General *9 students enrolled* • Health/Medical Preparatory Programs, Other *6 students enrolled*

STUDENT SERVICES Academic or career counseling, employment services for current students, placement services for program completers.

Oakton Community College

1600 East Golf Road, Des Plaines, IL 60016-1268
http://www.oakton.edu/

CONTACT Margaret B. Lee, President
Telephone: 847-635-1600

GENERAL INFORMATION Public Institution. Founded 1969. **Accreditation:** Regional (NCA); health information technology (AHIMA); medical laboratory technology (NAACLS); physical therapy assisting (APTA). **Total program enrollment:** 3444. **Application fee:** $25.

PROGRAM(S) OFFERED
• Accounting Technology/Technician and Bookkeeping *2 students enrolled* • Architectural Drafting and Architectural CAD/CADD *3 students enrolled* • Automobile/Automotive Mechanics Technology/Technician *1 student enrolled* • Banking and Financial Support Services *2 students enrolled* • Business Administration and Management, General *2 students enrolled* • CAD/CADD Drafting and/or Design Technology/Technician *5 students enrolled* • Child Care Provider/Assistant *41 students enrolled* • Commercial Photography *4 students enrolled* • Computer Programming, Vendor/Product Certification *2 students enrolled* • Computer Software Technology/Technician *1 student enrolled* • Computer Systems Networking and Telecommunications *9 students enrolled* • Computer Technology/Computer Systems Technology *2 students enrolled* • Construction Management *4 students enrolled* • Criminal Justice/Police Science *5 students enrolled* • Data Modeling/Warehousing and Database Administration *1 student enrolled* • Data Processing and Data Processing Technology/Technician *1 student enrolled* • Emergency Medical Technology/Technician (EMT Paramedic) *6 students enrolled* • Executive Assistant/Executive Secretary *2 students enrolled* • Fire Science/Firefighting *1 student enrolled* • Heating, Air Conditioning, Ventilation and Refrigeration Maintenance Technology/Technician (HAC, HACR, HVAC, HVACR) *20 students enrolled* • Human Resources Management/Personnel Administration, General *7 students enrolled* • Information Science/Studies *13 students enrolled* • International Marketing *1 student enrolled* • Investments and Securities *1 student enrolled* • Manufacturing Technology/Technician *8 students enrolled* • Mechanical Engineering/Mechanical Technology/Technician *3 students enrolled* • Medical Insurance Coding Specialist/Coder *12 students enrolled* • Medical Insurance Specialist/Medical Biller *18 students enrolled* • Medical Office Assistant/

Specialist *1 student enrolled* • Medical Transcription/Transcriptionist *2 students enrolled* • Nurse/Nursing Assistant/Aide and Patient Care Assistant *141 students enrolled* • Nursing—Registered Nurse Training (RN, ASN, BSN, MSN) *5 students enrolled* • Operations Management and Supervision *1 student enrolled* • Perioperative/Operating Room and Surgical Nurse/Nursing *10 students enrolled* • Pharmacy Technician/Assistant *98 students enrolled* • Phlebotomy/Phlebotomist *12 students enrolled* • Public Administration *1 student enrolled* • Purchasing, Procurement/Acquisitions and Contracts Management *1 student enrolled* • Real Estate *1 student enrolled* • Sales, Distribution and Marketing Operations, General *1 student enrolled* • Substance Abuse/Addiction Counseling *4 students enrolled* • System Administration/Administrator *3 students enrolled* • Web Page, Digital/Multimedia and Information Resources Design *2 students enrolled* • Web/Multimedia Management and Webmaster *2 students enrolled*

STUDENT SERVICES Academic or career counseling, daycare for children of students, employment services for current students, placement services for program completers, remedial services.

Oehrlein School of Cosmetology

100 Meadow Avenue, East Peoria, IL 61611

CONTACT Sandra L. Gay, President
Telephone: 309-699-1561

GENERAL INFORMATION Private Institution. Founded 1972. **Total program enrollment:** 74. **Application fee:** $100.

PROGRAM(S) OFFERED
• Cosmetology/Cosmetologist, General *1500 hrs./$11,670*

STUDENT SERVICES Academic or career counseling, placement services for program completers.

Olivet Nazarene University

One University Avenue, Bourbonnais, IL 60914-2271
http://www.olivet.edu/

CONTACT John C. Bowling, President
Telephone: 815-939-5011

GENERAL INFORMATION Private Institution (Affiliated with Church of the Nazarene). Founded 1907. **Accreditation:** Regional (NCA); home economics (AAFCS); music (NASM). **Total program enrollment:** 2667. **Application fee:** $25.

STUDENT SERVICES Academic or career counseling, employment services for current students, placement services for program completers, remedial services.

Pacific College of Oriental Medicine-Chicago

3646 North Broadway, 2nd Floor, Chicago, IL 60613
http://www.pacificcollege.edu/

CONTACT Ruth A. Levy, Chief Operating Officer
Telephone: 773-477-4822

GENERAL INFORMATION Private Institution. Founded 2000. **Accreditation:** Acupuncture and Oriental Medicine (ACAOM). **Total program enrollment:** 152. **Application fee:** $50.

PROGRAM(S) OFFERED
• Massage Therapy/Therapeutic Massage *6 students enrolled*

STUDENT SERVICES Academic or career counseling, remedial services.

Parkland College

2400 West Bradley Avenue, Champaign, IL 61821-1899
http://www.parkland.edu/

CONTACT Tom Ramage, President
Telephone: 217-351-2200

GENERAL INFORMATION Public Institution. Founded 1967. **Accreditation:** Regional (NCA); dental hygiene (ADA); practical nursing (NLN);

Parkland College (continued)

radiologic technology: radiography (JRCERT); surgical technology (ARCST). **Total program enrollment: 4410.**

PROGRAM(S) OFFERED

• **Accounting** *5 students enrolled* • **Administrative Assistant and Secretarial Science, General** *1 student enrolled* • **Agricultural Power Machinery Operation** *1 student enrolled* • **Autobody/Collision and Repair Technology/Technician** *23 students enrolled* • **Automobile/Automotive Mechanics Technology/Technician** *14 students enrolled* • **Building/Property Maintenance and Management** *2 students enrolled* • **Business/Office Automation/Technology/Data Entry** *1 student enrolled* • **CAD/CADD Drafting and/or Design Technology/Technician** *1 student enrolled* • **Carpentry/Carpenter** *4 students enrolled* • **Child Care Provider/Assistant** *2 students enrolled* • **Computer Graphics** *3 students enrolled* • **Computer Programming, Specific Applications** *1 student enrolled* • **Computer Programming/Programmer, General** *3 students enrolled* • **Computer Systems Networking and Telecommunications** *7 students enrolled* • **Construction Trades, General** *6 students enrolled* • **Data Modeling/Warehousing and Database Administration** *1 student enrolled* • **Emergency Care Attendant (EMT Ambulance)** *9 students enrolled* • **Emergency Medical Technology/Technician (EMT Paramedic)** *8 students enrolled* • **Entrepreneurship/Entrepreneurial Studies** *2 students enrolled* • **Floriculture/Floristry Operations and Management** *1 student enrolled* • **Glazier** *1 student enrolled* • **Heating, Air Conditioning, Ventilation and Refrigeration Maintenance Technology/Technician (HAC, HACR, HVAC, HVACR)** *4 students enrolled* • **Horse Husbandry/Equine Science and Management** *2 students enrolled* • **Hotel/Motel Administration/Management** *1 student enrolled* • **Industrial Electronics Technology/Technician** *4 students enrolled* • **International Business/Trade/Commerce** *1 student enrolled* • **Licensed Practical/Vocational Nurse Training (LPN, LVN, Cert, Dipl, AAS)** *18 students enrolled* • **Massage Therapy/Therapeutic Massage** *26 students enrolled* • **Medical Transcription/Transcriptionist** *1 student enrolled* • **Medical/Clinical Assistant** *17 students enrolled* • **Nurse/Nursing Assistant/Aide and Patient Care Assistant** *41 students enrolled* • **System Administration/Administrator** *1 student enrolled* • **Teaching English as a Second or Foreign Language/ESL Language Instructor** *6 students enrolled* • **Truck and Bus Driver/Commercial Vehicle Operation** *5 students enrolled* • **Web Page, Digital/Multimedia and Information Resources Design** *3 students enrolled* • **Web/Multimedia Management and Webmaster** *1 student enrolled*

STUDENT SERVICES Academic or career counseling, daycare for children of students, employment services for current students, placement services for program completers, remedial services.

Pivot Point Beauty School

1791 West Howard Street, Chicago, IL 60626
http://www.pivot-point.com/

CONTACT Janice Douglas, Director, Student Affairs
Telephone: 800-886-0500 Ext. 7351

GENERAL INFORMATION Private Institution. **Total program enrollment: 188. Application fee: $150.**

PROGRAM(S) OFFERED

• **Aesthetician/Esthetician and Skin Care Specialist** *750 hrs./$10,929* • **Cosmetology/Cosmetologist, General** *1500 hrs./$18,759* • **Teacher Education and Professional Development, Specific Subject Areas, Other** *500 hrs./$8349*

STUDENT SERVICES Academic or career counseling, placement services for program completers.

Pivot Point Beauty School

3901 West Irving Park, Chicago, IL 60618
http://www.pivot-point.com/

CONTACT Janice Douglas, Student Services Director
Telephone: 773-463-3121

GENERAL INFORMATION Private Institution. **Total program enrollment: 115. Application fee: $150.**

PROGRAM(S) OFFERED

• **Aesthetician/Esthetician and Skin Care Specialist** *750 hrs./$10,062* • **Cosmetology/Cosmetologist, General** *1500 hrs./$18,759* • **Nail Technician/Specialist and Manicurist**

STUDENT SERVICES Academic or career counseling, placement services for program completers.

Pivot Point International Cosmetology Research Center

525 Busse Road, Elk Grove Villiage, IL 60007-2116
http://www.pivot-point.com/

CONTACT Janice Douglas, Student Services Director
Telephone: 847-985-5900

GENERAL INFORMATION Private Institution. Founded 1988. **Total program enrollment: 217. Application fee: $150.**

PROGRAM(S) OFFERED

• **Aesthetician/Esthetician and Skin Care Specialist** *750 hrs./$10,929* • **Cosmetology/Cosmetologist, General** *150 hrs./$18,759*

STUDENT SERVICES Academic or career counseling, placement services for program completers.

Prairie State College

202 South Halsted Street, Chicago Heights, IL 60411-8226
http://www.prairiestate.edu/

CONTACT Eric Radtke, President
Telephone: 708-709-3500

GENERAL INFORMATION Public Institution. Founded 1958. **Accreditation:** Regional (NCA); dental hygiene (ADA). **Total program enrollment: 1908.**

PROGRAM(S) OFFERED

• **Accounting Technology/Technician and Bookkeeping** *2 students enrolled* • **Administrative Assistant and Secretarial Science, General** *5 students enrolled* • **Automobile/Automotive Mechanics Technology/Technician** *10 students enrolled* • **CAD/CADD Drafting and/or Design Technology/Technician** *2 students enrolled* • **Cabinetmaking and Millwork/Millwright** *4 students enrolled* • **Child Care Provider/Assistant** *21 students enrolled* • **Commercial Photography** *1 student enrolled* • **Computer Installation and Repair Technology/Technician** *2 students enrolled* • **Computer Systems Networking and Telecommunications** *7 students enrolled* • **Criminal Justice/Police Science** *1 student enrolled* • **Data Processing and Data Processing Technology/Technician** *2 students enrolled* • **E-Commerce/Electronic Commerce** *1 student enrolled* • **Electrician** *9 students enrolled* • **Emergency Care Attendant (EMT Ambulance)** *62 students enrolled* • **Emergency Medical Technology/Technician (EMT Paramedic)** *71 students enrolled* • **Fire Science/Firefighting** *38 students enrolled* • **Health and Physical Education, General** *8 students enrolled* • **Heating, Air Conditioning, Ventilation and Refrigeration Maintenance Technology/Technician (HAC, HACR, HVAC, HVACR)** *15 students enrolled* • **Industrial Mechanics and Maintenance Technology** *12 students enrolled* • **Kinesiology and Exercise Science** *7 students enrolled* • **Machine Tool Technology/Machinist** *4 students enrolled* • **Nurse/Nursing Assistant/Aide and Patient Care Assistant** *255 students enrolled* • **Operations Management and Supervision** *1 student enrolled* • **Prepress/Desktop Publishing and Digital Imaging Design** *3 students enrolled* • **Surgical Technology/Technologist** *15 students enrolled* • **Teacher Assistant/Aide** *2 students enrolled* • **Tool and Die Technology/Technician** *2 students enrolled* • **Web Page, Digital/Multimedia and Information Resources Design** *4 students enrolled* • **Web/Multimedia Management and Webmaster** *2 students enrolled* • **Welding Technology/Welder** *1 student enrolled*

STUDENT SERVICES Academic or career counseling, daycare for children of students, employment services for current students, placement services for program completers, remedial services.

Professionals Choice Hair Design Academy

2719 West Jefferson Street, Joliet, IL 60435
http://www.pchairdesign.com/

CONTACT John Thompson, President
Telephone: 815-741-8224

GENERAL INFORMATION Private Institution. Founded 1983. **Total program enrollment: 15. Application fee: $100.**

PROGRAM(S) OFFERED
- **Cosmetology and Related Personal Grooming Arts, Other** *1500 hrs./$14,550*
- **Cosmetology, Barber/Styling, and Nail Instructor** *1000 hrs./$9070*
- **Cosmetology/Cosmetologist, General** *38 students enrolled*

STUDENT SERVICES Academic or career counseling, employment services for current students, placement services for program completers.

Pyramid Career Institute

3057 N. Lincoln Avenue, Chicago, IL 60657-4207
http://www.pyramid-pci.com/

CONTACT Dr. Marianne King, Chief Administration Officer, Executive Director
Telephone: 773-975-9898

GENERAL INFORMATION Private Institution. **Total program enrollment:** 7. **Application fee:** $100.

PROGRAM(S) OFFERED
- **Business Operations Support and Secretarial Services, Other** *360 hrs./$3300* • **Business/Office Automation/Technology/Data Entry** *360 hrs./$3300*
- **Tourism and Travel Services Marketing Operations**

STUDENT SERVICES Academic or career counseling, employment services for current students, placement services for program completers, remedial services.

Quincy University

1800 College Avenue, Quincy, IL 62301-2699
http://www.quincy.edu/

CONTACT Robert Gervasi, PhD, President
Telephone: 217-228-5432

GENERAL INFORMATION Private Institution. Founded 1860. **Accreditation:** Regional (NCA); music (NASM). **Total program enrollment:** 1141. **Application fee:** $25.

PROGRAM(S) OFFERED
- **Business Administration and Management, General**

STUDENT SERVICES Academic or career counseling, employment services for current students, placement services for program completers, remedial services.

Rasmussen College Aurora

2363 Sequoia Drive, Aurora, IL 60506
http://www.rasmussen.edu/

CONTACT Bob Ernst, Campus Director
Telephone: 630-888-3500

GENERAL INFORMATION Private Institution. **Total program enrollment:** 41. **Application fee:** $60.

PROGRAM(S) OFFERED
- **Massage Therapy/Therapeutic Massage** • **Medical Insurance Coding Specialist/Coder** • **Medical Transcription/Transcriptionist**

STUDENT SERVICES Academic or career counseling, employment services for current students, placement services for program completers, remedial services.

Rasmussen College Rockford, Illinois

6000 East State Street, Fourth Floor, Rockford, IL 61108-2513
http://www.rasmussen.edu/

CONTACT Scott Vukoder, Campus Director
Telephone: 815-316-4800

GENERAL INFORMATION Private Institution. **Total program enrollment:** 540. **Application fee:** $60.

PROGRAM(S) OFFERED
- **Massage Therapy/Therapeutic Massage** • **Medical Insurance Coding Specialist/Coder** *1 student enrolled* • **Medical Transcription/Transcriptionist**

STUDENT SERVICES Academic or career counseling, employment services for current students, placement services for program completers, remedial services.

Regency Beauty Institute

4374 East New York Street, Aurora, IL 60504
http://www.regencybeauty.com/

CONTACT J. Hayes Batson, President
Telephone: 630-723-5051

GENERAL INFORMATION Private Institution. **Total program enrollment:** 89. **Application fee:** $100.

PROGRAM(S) OFFERED
- **Cosmetology/Cosmetologist, General** *1500 hrs./$16,011*

STUDENT SERVICES Academic or career counseling, placement services for program completers.

Regency Beauty Institute

517 Town Center Boulevard, Champaign, IL 61822
http://www.regencybeauty.com/

CONTACT J. Hayes Batson, President CEO
Telephone: 800-787-6456

GENERAL INFORMATION Private Institution. **Total program enrollment:** 93. **Application fee:** $100.

PROGRAM(S) OFFERED
- **Cosmetology/Cosmetologist, General** *1500 hrs./$16,011*

STUDENT SERVICES Academic or career counseling, placement services for program completers.

Regency Beauty Institute

7411 South Cass Avenue, Darien, IL 60561
http://www.regencybeauty.com/

CONTACT J. Hayes Batson, President
Telephone: 630-824-4022

GENERAL INFORMATION Private Institution. **Total program enrollment:** 70. **Application fee:** $100.

PROGRAM(S) OFFERED
- **Cosmetology/Cosmetologist, General** *1500 hrs./$16,011*

STUDENT SERVICES Academic or career counseling, placement services for program completers.

Regency Beauty Institute

10850 Lincoln Trail, Fairview Heights, IL 62208
http://www.regencybeauty.com/

CONTACT J. Hayes Batson, President CEO
Telephone: 800-787-6456

GENERAL INFORMATION Private Institution. **Total program enrollment:** 103. **Application fee:** $100.

PROGRAM(S) OFFERED
• **Cosmetology/Cosmetologist, General** *1500 hrs./$16,011*

STUDENT SERVICES Academic or career counseling, placement services for program completers.

Regency Beauty Institute

2601 West Lake Avenue, Peoria, IL 61602
http://www.regencybeauty.com/

CONTACT J. Hayes Batson, President CEO
Telephone: 800-787-6456

GENERAL INFORMATION Private Institution. **Total program enrollment:** 73. **Application fee:** $100.

PROGRAM(S) OFFERED
• **Cosmetology/Cosmetologist, General** *1500 hrs./$16,011*

STUDENT SERVICES Academic or career counseling, placement services for program completers.

Regency Beauty Institute–Elgin

609 S. Randall Road, Elgin, IL 60123

CONTACT J. Hayes Batson
Telephone: 224-856-4045

GENERAL INFORMATION Private Institution. **Application fee:** $100.

PROGRAM(S) OFFERED
• **Cosmetology/Cosmetologist, General** *1500 hrs./$16,011*

STUDENT SERVICES Academic or career counseling, placement services for program completers.

Regency Beauty Institute–Joliet

2904 Colorado Avenue, Joliet, IL 60431

GENERAL INFORMATION Private Institution. **Total program enrollment:** 90. **Application fee:** $100.

PROGRAM(S) OFFERED
• **Cosmetology/Cosmetologist, General** *1500 hrs./$16,011*

STUDENT SERVICES Academic or career counseling, placement services for program completers.

Regency Beauty Institute–Rockford

657 Highgrove Place, Rockford, IL 61108

GENERAL INFORMATION Private Institution. **Total program enrollment:** 106. **Application fee:** $100.

PROGRAM(S) OFFERED
• **Cosmetology/Cosmetologist, General** *1500 hrs./$16,011*

STUDENT SERVICES Academic or career counseling, placement services for program completers.

Rend Lake College

468 North Ken Gray Parkway, Ina, IL 62846-9801
http://www.rlc.edu/

CONTACT Mark S. Kern, President
Telephone: 618-437-5321

GENERAL INFORMATION Public Institution. Founded 1967. **Accreditation:** Regional (NCA); health information technology (AHIMA); medical laboratory technology (NAACLS). **Total program enrollment:** 1795.

PROGRAM(S) OFFERED
• **Agricultural Mechanization, General** *4 students enrolled* • **Applied Horticulture/Horticultural Operations, General** *6 students enrolled* • **Architectural Drafting and Architectural CAD/CADD** *8 students enrolled* • **Automobile/Automotive Mechanics Technology/Technician** *26 students enrolled* • **Business/Office Automation/Technology/Data Entry** *12 students enrolled* • **CAD/CADD Drafting and/or Design Technology/Technician** *7 students enrolled* • **Child Care Provider/Assistant** *23 students enrolled* • **Computer Engineering Technology/Technician** *12 students enrolled* • **Computer Systems Networking and Telecommunications** *11 students enrolled* • **Construction Trades, General** *33 students enrolled* • **Cosmetology, Barber/Styling, and Nail Instructor** *3 students enrolled* • **Cosmetology/Cosmetologist, General** *24 students enrolled* • **Criminal Justice/Police Science** *2 students enrolled* • **Culinary Arts/Chef Training** *6 students enrolled* • **Diesel Mechanics Technology/Technician** *4 students enrolled* • **Electrical, Electronic and Communications Engineering Technology/Technician** *2 students enrolled* • **Food Service, Waiter/Waitress, and Dining Room Management/Manager** *23 students enrolled* • **Graphic Design** *4 students enrolled* • **Housing and Human Environments, Other** *17 students enrolled* • **Industrial Mechanics and Maintenance Technology** *2 students enrolled* • **Licensed Practical/Vocational Nurse Training (LPN, LVN, Cert, Dipl, AAS)** *6 students enrolled* • **Massage Therapy/Therapeutic Massage** *14 students enrolled* • **Medical Transcription/Transcriptionist** *6 students enrolled* • **Nursing—Registered Nurse Training (RN, ASN, BSN, MSN)** *47 students enrolled* • **Surgical Technology/Technologist** *2 students enrolled* • **Turf and Turfgrass Management** *1 student enrolled* • **Welding Technology/Welder** *28 students enrolled*

STUDENT SERVICES Academic or career counseling, daycare for children of students, employment services for current students, placement services for program completers, remedial services.

Richland Community College

One College Park, Decatur, IL 62521-8513
http://www.richland.edu/

CONTACT Dr. Gayle Saunders, President
Telephone: 217-875-7200

GENERAL INFORMATION Public Institution. Founded 1971. **Accreditation:** Regional (NCA); surgical technology (ARCST). **Total program enrollment:** 1049.

PROGRAM(S) OFFERED
• **Accounting Technology/Technician and Bookkeeping** *2 students enrolled* • **Administrative Assistant and Secretarial Science, General** *8 students enrolled* • **Applied Horticulture/Horticultural Operations, General** *28 students enrolled* • **Automobile/Automotive Mechanics Technology/Technician** *4 students enrolled* • **Business Administration and Management, General** *37 students enrolled* • **Business/Office Automation/Technology/Data Entry** *12 students enrolled* • **Child Care Provider/Assistant** *9 students enrolled* • **Computer Programming, Vendor/Product Certification** *1 student enrolled* • **Computer Systems Networking and Telecommunications** *1 student enrolled* • **Construction Trades, General** *30 students enrolled* • **Corrections** *1 student enrolled* • **Criminal Justice/Police Science** *4 students enrolled* • **Electrical and Power Transmission Installation/Installer, General** *10 students enrolled* • **Emergency Medical Technology/Technician (EMT Paramedic)** *1 student enrolled* • **Family Systems** *4 students enrolled* • **Fire Science/Firefighting** *5 students enrolled* • **Fire Services Administration** *5 students enrolled* • **Food Service, Waiter/Waitress, and Dining Room Management/Manager** *26 students enrolled* • **Graphic Design** *2 students enrolled* • **Greenhouse Operations and Management** *1 student enrolled* • **Heating, Air Conditioning, Ventilation and Refrigeration Maintenance Technology/Technician (HAC, HACR, HVAC, HVACR)** *4 students enrolled* • **Housing and Human Environments, Other** *120 students enrolled* • **Industrial Electronics Technology/Technician** *2 students enrolled* • **Industrial Mechanics and Maintenance Technology** *2 students enrolled* • **Instrumentation Technology/Technician** *1 student enrolled* • **Legal Administrative Assistant/Secretary** *1 student enrolled* • **Licensed Practical/Vocational Nurse Training (LPN, LVN, Cert, Dipl, AAS)** *7 students enrolled* • **Lineworker** *1 student enrolled*

• **Manufacturing Technology/Technician** *3 students enrolled* • **Marketing/ Marketing Management, General** *1 student enrolled* • **Mechanical Drafting and Mechanical Drafting CAD/CADD** *8 students enrolled* • **Medical Insurance Coding Specialist/Coder** *3 students enrolled* • **Medical Office Assistant/Specialist** *2 students enrolled* • **Medical Transcription/Transcriptionist** *5 students enrolled* • **Pharmacy Technician/Assistant** *7 students enrolled* • **Prepress/Desktop Publishing and Digital Imaging Design** *1 student enrolled* • **Surgical Technology/Technologist** *6 students enrolled* • **System Administration/ Administrator** *1 student enrolled* • **Turf and Turfgrass Management** *1 student enrolled* • **Web Page, Digital/Multimedia and Information Resources Design** *1 student enrolled*

STUDENT SERVICES Academic or career counseling, daycare for children of students, employment services for current students, placement services for program completers, remedial services.

Robert Morris University

401 South State Street, Chicago, IL 60605
http://www.robertmorris.edu/

CONTACT Michael P. Viollt, President
Telephone: 312-935-6800

GENERAL INFORMATION Private Institution. Founded 1913. **Accreditation:** Regional (NCA); medical assisting (AAMAE). **Total program enrollment:** 4030. **Application fee:** $30.

PROGRAM(S) OFFERED
• **Accounting Technology/Technician and Bookkeeping** *43 students enrolled* • **Administrative Assistant and Secretarial Science, General** • **Business Administration and Management, General** *379 students enrolled* • **Commercial and Advertising Art** *95 students enrolled* • **Computer Systems Networking and Telecommunications** *105 students enrolled* • **Drafting and Design Technology/Technician, General** *22 students enrolled* • **Interior Design** • **Intermedia/Multimedia** • **Legal Administrative Assistant/Secretary** • **Legal Assistant/Paralegal** *88 students enrolled* • **Management Information Systems, General** • **Medical/Clinical Assistant** *222 students enrolled*

STUDENT SERVICES Academic or career counseling, employment services for current students, placement services for program completers.

Rockford Business College

730 North Church Street, Rockford, IL 61103
http://www.rbcsuccess.com/

CONTACT Steve W. Gibson, President
Telephone: 815-965-8616

GENERAL INFORMATION Private Institution. Founded 1862. **Accreditation:** Medical assisting (AAMAE); state accredited or approved. **Total program enrollment:** 254. **Application fee:** $150.

PROGRAM(S) OFFERED
• **Administrative Assistant and Secretarial Science, General** • **Business Administration and Management, General** • **Computer Software and Media Applications, Other** • **Computer and Information Sciences and Support Services, Other** • **Legal Administrative Assistant/Secretary** • **Massage Therapy/Therapeutic Massage** *18 students enrolled* • **Medical Transcription/Transcriptionist** • **Medical/Clinical Assistant** • **Nurse/Nursing Assistant/Aide and Patient Care Assistant** *40 students enrolled* • **Pharmacy Technician/Assistant** • **Web Page, Digital/Multimedia and Information Resources Design** *1 student enrolled*

STUDENT SERVICES Academic or career counseling, employment services for current students, placement services for program completers.

Rock Valley College

3301 North Mulford Road, Rockford, IL 61114-5699
http://www.rockvalleycollege.edu/

CONTACT Jack Becherer, President
Telephone: 815-921-7821

GENERAL INFORMATION Public Institution. Founded 1964. **Accreditation:** Regional (NCA); dental hygiene (ADA). **Total program enrollment:** 3569.

PROGRAM(S) OFFERED
• **Accounting Technology/Technician and Bookkeeping** *7 students enrolled* • **Administrative Assistant and Secretarial Science, General** *1 student enrolled*

• **Airframe Mechanics and Aircraft Maintenance Technology/Technician** *9 students enrolled* • **Architectural Drafting and Architectural CAD/CADD** *1 student enrolled* • **Automobile/Automotive Mechanics Technology/Technician** *46 students enrolled* • **Business/Commerce, General** *1 student enrolled* • **Business/ Office Automation/Technology/Data Entry** *4 students enrolled* • **Child Care Provider/Assistant** *1 student enrolled* • **Computer Programming, Specific Applications** *2 students enrolled* • **Computer Systems Networking and Telecommunications** *10 students enrolled* • **Construction Management** *4 students enrolled* • **Construction Trades, General** *16 students enrolled* • **Fire Protection and Safety Technology/Technician** *5 students enrolled* • **Fire Science/ Firefighting** *5 students enrolled* • **Fire Services Administration** *2 students enrolled* • **Graphic and Printing Equipment Operator, General Production** *1 student enrolled* • **Industrial Technology/Technician** *1 student enrolled* • **Licensed Practical/Vocational Nurse Training (LPN, LVN, Cert, Dipl, AAS)** *36 students enrolled* • **Medical Insurance Coding Specialist/Coder** *4 students enrolled* • **Medical Transcription/Transcriptionist** *4 students enrolled* • **Nurse/ Nursing Assistant/Aide and Patient Care Assistant** *421 students enrolled* • **Radio and Television** *2 students enrolled* • **Selling Skills and Sales Operations** *1 student enrolled* • **Substance Abuse/Addiction Counseling** *8 students enrolled* • **Surgical Technology/Technologist** *4 students enrolled*

STUDENT SERVICES Academic or career counseling, employment services for current students, placement services for program completers, remedial services.

Roosevelt University

430 South Michigan Avenue, Chicago, IL 60605-1394
http://www.roosevelt.edu/

CONTACT Charles R. Middleton, President
Telephone: 312-341-3500

GENERAL INFORMATION Private Institution. Founded 1945. **Accreditation:** Regional (NCA); counseling (ACA); music (NASM). **Total program enrollment:** 3891. **Application fee:** $25.

PROGRAM(S) OFFERED
• **Accounting and Related Services, Other** *3 students enrolled* • **Geography** *2 students enrolled* • **Health/Health Care Administration/Management** *1 student enrolled* • **Hospitality Administration/Management, General** *19 students enrolled* • **Human Resources Development** *82 students enrolled* • **Mental and Social Health Services and Allied Professions, Other** *9 students enrolled* • **Music Pedagogy** *1 student enrolled* • **Non-Profit/Public/Organizational Management** *4 students enrolled* • **Organizational Behavior Studies** *23 students enrolled* • **Real Estate** *1 student enrolled* • **Women's Studies** *2 students enrolled*

STUDENT SERVICES Academic or career counseling, employment services for current students, placement services for program completers, remedial services.

Rosel School of Cosmetology

2444 West Devon Avenue, Chicago, IL 60659

CONTACT Rosel Baek, Owner Director
Telephone: 773-508-5600

GENERAL INFORMATION Private Institution. Founded 1989. **Total program enrollment:** 81. **Application fee:** $100.

PROGRAM(S) OFFERED
• **Aesthetician/Esthetician and Skin Care Specialist** *750 hrs./$7100* • **Cosmetology and Related Personal Grooming Arts, Other** *250 hrs./$800* • **Cosmetology, Barber/Styling, and Nail Instructor** *500 hrs./$2300* • **Cosmetology/Cosmetologist, General** *1500 hrs./$8700* • **Nail Technician/ Specialist and Manicurist** *350 hrs./$1300*

STUDENT SERVICES Academic or career counseling, employment services for current students, placement services for program completers.

St. Augustine College

1333-1345 West Argyle, Chicago, IL 60640-3501
http://www.staugustinecollege.edu/

CONTACT Mr. Andrew C. Sund, President
Telephone: 773-878-8756

GENERAL INFORMATION Private Institution. Founded 1980. **Accreditation:** Regional (NCA); respiratory therapy technology (CoARC). **Total program enrollment:** 1018.

PROGRAM(S) OFFERED
• **Accounting Technology/Technician and Bookkeeping** *3 students enrolled* • **Administrative Assistant and Secretarial Science, General** *1 student enrolled* • **Computer and Information Sciences, General** *3 students enrolled* • **Cooking and Related Culinary Arts, General** *48 students enrolled* • **Early Childhood Education and Teaching** *51 students enrolled* • **Substance Abuse/Addiction Counseling** *3 students enrolled*

STUDENT SERVICES Academic or career counseling, daycare for children of students, placement services for program completers, remedial services.

St. Johns Hospital School of Clinical Lab Science

800 E. Carpenter, Springfield, IL 62769
http://www.st-johns.org/

CONTACT Gilma Roncancio-Weemer, Coordinator
Telephone: 217-757-6788

GENERAL INFORMATION Private Institution. **Total program enrollment:** 5. **Application fee:** $15.

PROGRAM(S) OFFERED
• **Clinical Laboratory Science/Medical Technology/Technologist** *5 students enrolled*

STUDENT SERVICES Academic or career counseling.

Saint Xavier University

3700 West 103rd Street, Chicago, IL 60655-3105
http://www.sxu.edu/

CONTACT Judith A. Dwyer, President
Telephone: 773-298-3000

GENERAL INFORMATION Private Institution. Founded 1847. **Accreditation:** Regional (NCA); music (NASM); speech-language pathology (ASHA). **Total program enrollment:** 2910. **Application fee:** $25.

PROGRAM(S) OFFERED
• **Accounting** • **Business/Commerce, General** • **Corrections and Criminal Justice, Other** • **Psychiatric/Mental Health Nurse/Nursing**

STUDENT SERVICES Academic or career counseling, employment services for current students, placement services for program completers, remedial services.

Sanford-Brown College

1101 Eastport Plaza Drive, Collinsville, IL 62234
http://www.sanford-brown.edu/

CONTACT Athena Seidel, Campus President
Telephone: 618-344-5600

GENERAL INFORMATION Private Institution. **Total program enrollment:** 398. **Application fee:** $100.

PROGRAM(S) OFFERED
• **Accounting and Business/Management** *92 hrs./$22,381* • **Business Administration and Management, General** *73 hrs./$17,804* • **Massage Therapy/Therapeutic Massage** *71 hrs./$17,328* • **Medical Insurance Coding Specialist/Coder** *70 hrs./$16,321* • **Medical/Clinical Assistant** *68 hrs./$18,539* • **Office Management and Supervision** *6 students enrolled*

STUDENT SERVICES Academic or career counseling, employment services for current students, placement services for program completers.

Sauk Valley Community College

173 Illinois Route 2, Dixon, IL 61021
http://www.svcc.edu/

CONTACT Dr. George Mihel, President
Telephone: 815-288-5511

GENERAL INFORMATION Public Institution. Founded 1965. **Accreditation:** Regional (NCA); radiologic technology: radiography (JRCERT). **Total program enrollment:** 1092.

PROGRAM(S) OFFERED
• **Accounting** *11 students enrolled* • **Business Administration and Management, General** *9 students enrolled* • **Business/Office Automation/Technology/Data Entry** *8 students enrolled* • **CAD/CADD Drafting and/or Design Technology/Technician** *3 students enrolled* • **Child Care Provider/Assistant** *13 students enrolled* • **Communications Systems Installation and Repair Technology** *2 students enrolled* • **Computer Installation and Repair Technology/Technician** *1 student enrolled* • **Computer Programming/Programmer, General** *4 students enrolled* • **Computer Systems Networking and Telecommunications** *10 students enrolled* • **Design and Visual Communications, General** *10 students enrolled* • **Drafting and Design Technology/Technician, General** *2 students enrolled* • **Emergency Care Attendant (EMT Ambulance)** *71 students enrolled* • **Emergency Medical Technology/Technician (EMT Paramedic)** *3 students enrolled* • **General Office Occupations and Clerical Services** *10 students enrolled* • **Heating, Air Conditioning, Ventilation and Refrigeration Maintenance Technology/Technician (HAC, HACR, HVAC, HVACR)** *17 students enrolled* • **Industrial Electronics Technology/Technician** *5 students enrolled* • **Licensed Practical/Vocational Nurse Training (LPN, LVN, Cert, Dipl, AAS)** *15 students enrolled* • **Machine Tool Technology/Machinist** *1 student enrolled* • **Management Information Systems, General** *1 student enrolled* • **Medical Administrative/Executive Assistant and Medical Secretary** *4 students enrolled* • **Nurse/Nursing Assistant/Aide and Patient Care Assistant** *101 students enrolled* • **Office Management and Supervision** *8 students enrolled* • **Prepress/Desktop Publishing and Digital Imaging Design** *1 student enrolled* • **Selling Skills and Sales Operations** *4 students enrolled* • **Social Work** *1 student enrolled* • **System Administration/Administrator** *11 students enrolled* • **Truck and Bus Driver/Commercial Vehicle Operation** *18 students enrolled* • **Welding Technology/Welder** *91 students enrolled* • **Word Processing** *1 student enrolled*

STUDENT SERVICES Academic or career counseling, employment services for current students, placement services for program completers, remedial services.

Shawnee Community College

8364 Shawnee College Road, Ullin, IL 62992-2206
http://www.shawneecc.edu/

CONTACT Larry E. Peterson, President
Telephone: 618-634-3200

GENERAL INFORMATION Public Institution. Founded 1967. **Accreditation:** Regional (NCA); health information technology (AHIMA); medical laboratory technology (NAACLS). **Total program enrollment:** 944.

PROGRAM(S) OFFERED
• **Automobile/Automotive Mechanics Technology/Technician** *1 student enrolled* • **Cosmetology/Cosmetologist, General** *8 students enrolled* • **Criminal Justice/Police Science** *2 students enrolled* • **Early Childhood Education and Teaching** *2 students enrolled* • **Information Science/Studies** *1 student enrolled* • **Licensed Practical/Vocational Nurse Training (LPN, LVN, Cert, Dipl, AAS)** *31 students enrolled* • **Massage Therapy/Therapeutic Massage** *4 students enrolled* • **Medical Administrative/Executive Assistant and Medical Secretary** *2 students enrolled* • **Medical Insurance Coding Specialist/Coder** *3 students enrolled* • **Medical Transcription/Transcriptionist** *1 student enrolled* • **Nurse/Nursing Assistant/Aide and Patient Care Assistant** *115 students enrolled* • **Psychiatric/Mental Health Services Technician** *1 student enrolled* • **Substance Abuse/Addiction Counsel-**

ing *2 students enrolled* ● **Surgical Technology/Technologist** *3 students enrolled* ● **Truck and Bus Driver/Commercial Vehicle Operation** *26 students enrolled* ● **Welding Technology/Welder** *1 student enrolled*

STUDENT SERVICES Academic or career counseling, daycare for children of students, employment services for current students, placement services for program completers, remedial services.

SOLEX Medical Academy

350 E. Dundee Road, Suite 207, Wheeling, IL 60090
massage.solex.edu/

CONTACT Leon E. Linton, Executive Director
Telephone: 847-229-9595 Ext. 103

GENERAL INFORMATION Private Institution. **Total program enrollment: 11. Application fee:** $150.

PROGRAM(S) OFFERED
● **Massage Therapy/Therapeutic Massage** *600 hrs./$7450*

STUDENT SERVICES Placement services for program completers.

Soma Institute–The National School of Clinical Massage Therapy

14 E. Jackson Boulevard, Suite 1300, Chicago, IL 60604-2232
http://www.soma.edu/

CONTACT Joan Hannant, President
Telephone: 312-939-2723

GENERAL INFORMATION Private Institution.

PROGRAM(S) OFFERED
● **Massage Therapy/Therapeutic Massage** *300 hrs./$5150*

STUDENT SERVICES Academic or career counseling, placement services for program completers, remedial services.

Southeastern Illinois College

3575 College Road, Harrisburg, IL 62946-4925
http://www.sic.edu/

CONTACT Dana Keating, Interim President
Telephone: 618-252-5400

GENERAL INFORMATION Public Institution. Founded 1960. **Accreditation:** Regional (NCA); health information technology (AHIMA); medical laboratory technology (NAACLS). **Total program enrollment:** 1105.

PROGRAM(S) OFFERED
● **Accounting Technology/Technician and Bookkeeping** *6 students enrolled* ● **Applied Horticulture/Horticultural Operations, General** *5 students enrolled* ● **Autobody/Collision and Repair Technology/Technician** *2 students enrolled* ● **Automobile/Automotive Mechanics Technology/Technician** *35 students enrolled* ● **Business Administration and Management, General** *4 students enrolled* ● **Business/Office Automation/Technology/Data Entry** *9 students enrolled* ● **CAD/CADD Drafting and/or Design Technology/Technician** *3 students enrolled* ● **Carpentry/Carpenter** *3 students enrolled* ● **Child Care Provider/Assistant** *1 student enrolled* ● **Construction Trades, General** *16 students enrolled* ● **Corrections** *1 student enrolled* ● **Cosmetology/Cosmetologist, General** *25 students enrolled* ● **Criminal Justice/Police Science** *1 student enrolled* ● **Diesel Mechanics Technology/Technician** *3 students enrolled* ● **Food Service, Waiter/Waitress, and Dining Room Management/Manager** *8 students enrolled* ● **General Office Occupations and Clerical Services** *6 students enrolled* ● **Health Professions and Related Clinical Sciences, Other** *1 student enrolled* ● **Housing and Human Environments, Other** *35 students enrolled* ● **Licensed Practical/Vocational Nurse Training (LPN, LVN, Cert, Dipl, AAS)** *44 students enrolled* ● **Massage Therapy/Therapeutic Massage** *10 students enrolled* ● **Medical Insurance Coding Specialist/Coder** *13 students enrolled* ● **Medical Transcription/Transcriptionist** *13 students enrolled* ● **Prepress/Desktop Publishing and Digital Imaging Design** *1 student enrolled* ● **Psychiatric/Mental Health Services Technician** *3 students*

enrolled ● **Substance Abuse/Addiction Counseling** *3 students enrolled* ● **Surgical Technology/Technologist** *3 students enrolled* ● **Teacher Assistant/Aide** *1 student enrolled* ● **Welding Technology/Welder** *3 students enrolled*

STUDENT SERVICES Academic or career counseling, daycare for children of students, placement services for program completers, remedial services.

South Suburban College

15800 South State Street, South Holland, IL 60473-1270
http://www.southsuburbancollege.edu/

CONTACT George Dammer, President
Telephone: 708-596-2000

GENERAL INFORMATION Public Institution. Founded 1927. **Accreditation:** Regional (NCA); music (NASM); practical nursing (NLN); radiologic technology: radiography (JRCERT). **Total program enrollment:** 2175.

PROGRAM(S) OFFERED
● **Accounting Technology/Technician and Bookkeeping** *2 students enrolled* ● **Accounting and Business/Management** *2 students enrolled* ● **Administrative Assistant and Secretarial Science, General** *1 student enrolled* ● **Biomedical Technology/Technician** *1 student enrolled* ● **CAD/CADD Drafting and/or Design Technology/Technician** *1 student enrolled* ● **Child Care Provider/Assistant** *52 students enrolled* ● **Computer Programming/Programmer, General** *1 student enrolled* ● **Computer Systems Networking and Telecommunications** *5 students enrolled* ● **Construction Management** *1 student enrolled* ● **Construction Trades, General** *18 students enrolled* ● **Court Reporting/Court Reporter** *4 students enrolled* ● **Criminal Justice/Police Science** *13 students enrolled* ● **Diagnostic Medical Sonography/Sonographer and Ultrasound Technician** *10 students enrolled* ● **Electrical, Electronic and Communications Engineering Technology/Technician** *2 students enrolled* ● **Emergency Care Attendant (EMT Ambulance)** *71 students enrolled* ● **Emergency Medical Technology/Technician (EMT Paramedic)** *82 students enrolled* ● **Entrepreneurship/Entrepreneurial Studies** *4 students enrolled* ● **Executive Assistant/Executive Secretary** *2 students enrolled* ● **Kinesiology and Exercise Science** *8 students enrolled* ● **Legal Assistant/Paralegal** *1 student enrolled* ● **Licensed Practical/Vocational Nurse Training (LPN, LVN, Cert, Dipl, AAS)** *17 students enrolled* ● **Massage Therapy/Therapeutic Massage** *16 students enrolled* ● **Medical Insurance Coding Specialist/Coder** *1 student enrolled* ● **Medical Radiologic Technology/Science—Radiation Therapist** *10 students enrolled* ● **Medical/Clinical Assistant** *8 students enrolled* ● **Nurse/Nursing Assistant/Aide and Patient Care Assistant** *239 students enrolled* ● **Office Management and Supervision** *23 students enrolled* ● **Pharmacy Technician/Assistant** *5 students enrolled* ● **Phlebotomy/Phlebotomist** *15 students enrolled* ● **Sign Language Interpretation and Translation** *1 student enrolled* ● **Small Business Administration/Management** *4 students enrolled* ● **Social Work** *1 student enrolled* ● **Substance Abuse/Addiction Counseling** *1 student enrolled* ● **Teacher Assistant/Aide** *7 students enrolled*

STUDENT SERVICES Academic or career counseling, daycare for children of students, employment services for current students, placement services for program completers, remedial services.

Southwestern Illinois College

2500 Carlyle Road, Belleville, IL 62221-5899
http://www.southwestern.cc.il.us/

CONTACT Georgia Costello, President
Telephone: 618-235-2700

GENERAL INFORMATION Public Institution. Founded 1946. **Accreditation:** Regional (NCA); health information technology (AHIMA); medical assisting (AAMAE); medical laboratory technology (NAACLS); physical therapy assisting (APTA); radiologic technology: radiography (JRCERT); respiratory therapy technology (CoARC). **Total program enrollment:** 5358.

PROGRAM(S) OFFERED
● **Administrative Assistant and Secretarial Science, General** *11 students enrolled* ● **Airline/Commercial/Professional Pilot and Flight Crew** *1 student enrolled* ● **Applied Horticulture/Horticultural Operations, General** *12 students enrolled* ● **Autobody/Collision and Repair Technology/Technician** *38 students enrolled* ● **Business Administration and Management, General** *37 students enrolled* ● **Business/Office Automation/Technology/Data Entry** *2 students enrolled* ● **Carpentry/Carpenter** *58 students enrolled* ● **Child Care Provider/Assistant** *32 students enrolled* ● **Computer Installation and Repair Technology/Technician** *1*

Southwestern Illinois College (continued)

student enrolled • **Computer Programming, Specific Applications** 49 *students enrolled* • **Computer Systems Networking and Telecommunications** 77 *students enrolled* • **Concrete Finishing/Concrete Finisher** 7 *students enrolled* • **Construction Trades, General** 7 *students enrolled* • **Criminal Justice/Law Enforcement Administration** 51 *students enrolled* • **Criminal Justice/Police Science** 36 *students enrolled* • **Culinary Arts/Chef Training** 21 *students enrolled* • **Electrical, Electronic and Communications Engineering Technology/Technician** 13 *students enrolled* • **Electrician** 36 *students enrolled* • **Fire Science/Firefighting** 152 *students enrolled* • **Fire Services Administration** 29 *students enrolled* • **Floriculture/Floristry Operations and Management** 1 *student enrolled* • **Food Preparation/Professional Cooking/Kitchen Assistant** 7 *students enrolled* • **Health Unit Coordinator/Ward Clerk** 67 *students enrolled* • **Heating, Air Conditioning, Ventilation and Refrigeration Maintenance Technology/Technician (HAC, HACR, HVAC, HVACR)** 55 *students enrolled* • **Industrial Electronics Technology/Technician** 3 *students enrolled* • **Machine Tool Technology/Machinist** 9 *students enrolled* • **Mason/Masonry** 1 *student enrolled* • **Massage Therapy/Therapeutic Massage** 25 *students enrolled* • **Mechanical Drafting and Mechanical Drafting CAD/CADD** 7 *students enrolled* • **Medical Insurance Coding Specialist/Coder** 15 *students enrolled* • **Medical Transcription/Transcriptionist** 1 *student enrolled* • **Medical/Clinical Assistant** 31 *students enrolled* • **Music, General** 5 *students enrolled* • **Nurse/Nursing Assistant/Aide and Patient Care Assistant** 270 *students enrolled* • **Painting/Painter and Wall Coverer** 3 *students enrolled* • **Parts, Warehousing, and Inventory Management Operations** 32 *students enrolled* • **Phlebotomy/Phlebotomist** 19 *students enrolled* • **Prepress/Desktop Publishing and Digital Imaging Design** 8 *students enrolled* • **Restaurant/Food Services Management** 6 *students enrolled* • **Sales, Distribution and Marketing Operations, General** 8 *students enrolled* • **Security and Loss Prevention Services** 1 *student enrolled* • **Sheet Metal Technology/Sheetworking** 7 *students enrolled* • **Sign Language Interpretation and Translation** 22 *students enrolled* • **Social Work** 1 *student enrolled* • **Web Page, Digital/Multimedia and Information Resources Design** 25 *students enrolled* • **Welding Technology/Welder** 228 *students enrolled*

STUDENT SERVICES Academic or career counseling, daycare for children of students, employment services for current students, placement services for program completers, remedial services.

Spanish Coalition for Jobs, Inc.

2011 West Pershing Road, Chicago, IL 60609
http://www.scj-usa.org/

CONTACT Mary Gonzalez Koenig, President
Telephone: 773-247-0707 Ext. 200

GENERAL INFORMATION Private Institution. Founded 1972. **Total program enrollment:** 121.

PROGRAM(S) OFFERED
• **Administrative Assistant and Secretarial Science, General** 36 *hrs./$4600* • **Customer Service Management** 44 *hrs./$4800* • **Medical/Clinical Assistant** 63 *hrs./$9038*

STUDENT SERVICES Academic or career counseling, employment services for current students, placement services for program completers, remedial services.

Sparks College

131 South Morgan Street, Shelbyville, IL 62565
http://www.sparkscollege.org/

CONTACT Judith A. Lehman, Director
Telephone: 217-774-5112

GENERAL INFORMATION Private Institution. Founded 1908. **Total program enrollment:** 20. **Application fee:** $50.

PROGRAM(S) OFFERED
• **Accounting and Related Services, Other** • **Accounting** 2 *students enrolled* • **Administrative Assistant and Secretarial Science, General** • **Business/Office Automation/Technology/Data Entry** 1 *student enrolled* • **Court Reporting/Court Reporter** 3 *students enrolled* • **Legal Administrative Assistant/Secretary** 2 *students enrolled* • **Medical Administrative/Executive Assistant and Medical Secretary** • **Medical Transcription/Transcriptionist** 3 *students enrolled*

STUDENT SERVICES Academic or career counseling, placement services for program completers.

Spoon River College

23235 North County 22, Canton, IL 61520-9801
http://www.spoonrivercollege.net/

CONTACT Dr. Robert Ritschel, President
Telephone: 309-647-4645

GENERAL INFORMATION Public Institution. Founded 1959. **Accreditation:** Regional (NCA). **Total program enrollment:** 890.

PROGRAM(S) OFFERED
• **Administrative Assistant and Secretarial Science, General** 3 *students enrolled* • **Applied Horticulture/Horticultural Operations, General** 5 *students enrolled* • **Automobile/Automotive Mechanics Technology/Technician** 7 *students enrolled* • **Business Administration and Management, General** 2 *students enrolled* • **Business/Office Automation/Technology/Data Entry** 2 *students enrolled* • **Computer Installation and Repair Technology/Technician** 2 *students enrolled* • **Computer Systems Networking and Telecommunications** 3 *students enrolled* • **Computer and Information Systems Security** 1 *student enrolled* • **Construction Trades, General** 4 *students enrolled* • **Electrical, Electronic and Communications Engineering Technology/Technician** 8 *students enrolled* • **Food Preparation/Professional Cooking/Kitchen Assistant** 14 *students enrolled* • **Graphic Design** 3 *students enrolled* • **Health Information/Medical Records Technology/Technician** 1 *student enrolled* • **Industrial Electronics Technology/Technician** 5 *students enrolled* • **Licensed Practical/Vocational Nurse Training (LPN, LVN, Cert, Dipl, AAS)** 18 *students enrolled* • **Medical Insurance Coding Specialist/Coder** 8 *students enrolled* • **Truck and Bus Driver/Commercial Vehicle Operation** 26 *students enrolled* • **Web Page, Digital/Multimedia and Information Resources Design** 1 *student enrolled* • **Welding Technology/Welder** 1 *student enrolled*

STUDENT SERVICES Academic or career counseling, daycare for children of students, employment services for current students, placement services for program completers, remedial services.

Taylor Business Institute

318 West Adams, Chicago, IL 60007
http://www.tbiil.edu/

CONTACT Janice C. Parker, President
Telephone: 312-658-5100

GENERAL INFORMATION Private Institution. Founded 1964. **Accreditation:** State accredited or approved. **Total program enrollment:** 318. **Application fee:** $25.

PROGRAM(S) OFFERED
• **Accounting** • **Criminal Justice/Law Enforcement Administration** • **Electrical, Electronic and Communications Engineering Technology/Technician** • **Medical Insurance Specialist/Medical Biller** • **Teaching English as a Second or Foreign Language/ESL Language Instructor**

STUDENT SERVICES Academic or career counseling, employment services for current students, placement services for program completers, remedial services.

Trend Setter's College of Cosmetology

665 West Broadway, Bradley, IL 60915
http://www.trendsetterscollege.com/

CONTACT Lori Clark, CEO
Telephone: 815-932-5049

GENERAL INFORMATION Private Institution. Founded 1986. **Total program enrollment:** 44. **Application fee:** $100.

PROGRAM(S) OFFERED
• **Aesthetician/Esthetician and Skin Care Specialist** 750 *hrs./$9850* • **Cosmetology, Barber/Styling, and Nail Instructor** 1000 *hrs./$7500* • **Cosmetology/Cosmetologist, General** 1500 *hrs./$17,900* • **Nail Technician/Specialist and Manicurist** 350 *hrs./$3206*

STUDENT SERVICES Academic or career counseling, placement services for program completers.

Tri-County Beauty Academy

219 North State Street, Litchfield, IL 62056

CONTACT Diane Riemann, Owner
Telephone: 217-324-9062

GENERAL INFORMATION Private Institution. Founded 1971. **Total program enrollment:** 25.

PROGRAM(S) OFFERED
• **Cosmetology, Barber/Styling, and Nail Instructor** *1000 hrs./$5650*
• **Cosmetology/Cosmetologist, General** *1500 hrs./$9825*

Trinity College of Nursing and Health Sciences

2122-25th Avenue, Rock Island, IL 61201
http://www.trinitycollegeqc.edu/

CONTACT Leanne Hullett, Dean
Telephone: 309-779-7700

GENERAL INFORMATION Private Institution. Founded 1994. **Accreditation:** Regional (NCA). **Total program enrollment:** 139. **Application fee:** $50.

PROGRAM(S) OFFERED
• **Emergency Medical Technology/Technician (EMT Paramedic)** *11 students enrolled* • **Surgical Technology/Technologist** *6 students enrolled*

STUDENT SERVICES Academic or career counseling, daycare for children of students, employment services for current students, placement services for program completers, remedial services.

Triton College

2000 5th Avenue, River Grove, IL 60171-1995
http://www.triton.cc.il.us/

CONTACT Dr. Patricia Granados, President
Telephone: 708-456-0300

GENERAL INFORMATION Public Institution. Founded 1964. **Accreditation:** Regional (NCA); diagnostic medical sonography (JRCEDMS); nuclear medicine technology (JRCNMT); ophthalmic medical technology (JCAHPO); practical nursing (NLN); radiologic technology: radiography (JRCERT). **Total program enrollment:** 4379. **Application fee:** $10.

PROGRAM(S) OFFERED
• **Accounting Technology/Technician and Bookkeeping** *10 students enrolled* • **Administrative Assistant and Secretarial Science, General** *7 students enrolled* • **Applied Horticulture/Horticultural Operations, General** *2 students enrolled* • **Architectural Drafting and Architectural CAD/CADD** *2 students enrolled* • **Automobile/Automotive Mechanics Technology/Technician** *1 student enrolled* • **Baking and Pastry Arts/Baker/Pastry Chef** *4 students enrolled* • **Business Administration and Management, General** *2 students enrolled* • **CAD/CADD Drafting and/or Design Technology/Technician** *1 student enrolled* • **Child Care Provider/Assistant** *5 students enrolled* • **Computer Installation and Repair Technology/Technician** *1 student enrolled* • **Computer Technology/Computer Systems Technology** *7 students enrolled* • **Construction Management** *2 students enrolled* • **Criminal Justice/Law Enforcement Administration** *5 students enrolled* • **Culinary Arts/Chef Training** *1 student enrolled* • **Data Modeling/Warehousing and Database Administration** *1 student enrolled* • **Design and Visual Communications, General** *1 student enrolled* • **Diagnostic Medical Sonography/Sonographer and Ultrasound Technician** *7 students enrolled* • **Electrician** *1 student enrolled* • **Emergency Medical Technology/Technician (EMT Paramedic)** *12 students enrolled* • **Fashion Merchandising** *1 student enrolled* • **Fire Science/Firefighting** *1 student enrolled* • **Health Information/Medical Records Technology/Technician** *3 students enrolled* • **Heating, Air Conditioning, Ventilation and Refrigeration Maintenance Technology/Technician (HAC, HACR, HVAC, HVACR)** *22 students enrolled* • **Hotel/Motel Administration/Management** *1 student enrolled* • **Human Resources Management/Personnel Administration, General** *4 students enrolled* • **Interior Design** *2 students enrolled* • **Kinesiology and Exercise Science** *1 student enrolled* • **Landscaping and Groundskeeping** *3 students enrolled* • **Licensed Practical/Vocational Nurse Training (LPN, LVN, Cert, Dipl, AAS)** *21 students enrolled* • **Mechanic and Repair Technologies/Technicians, Other** *10 students enrolled* • **Nurse/Nursing Assistant/Aide and**

Patient Care Assistant *172 students enrolled* • **Platemaker/Imager** *1 student enrolled* • **Security and Loss Prevention Services** *1 student enrolled* • **Substance Abuse/Addiction Counseling** *3 students enrolled* • **Surgical Technology/Technologist** *14 students enrolled* • **System Administration/Administrator** *4 students enrolled* • **Teacher Assistant/Aide** *2 students enrolled* • **Web Page, Digital/Multimedia and Information Resources Design** *2 students enrolled* • **Welding Technology/Welder** *1 student enrolled*

STUDENT SERVICES Academic or career counseling, daycare for children of students, employment services for current students, placement services for program completers, remedial services.

Universal Technical Institute

601 Regency Drive, Glendale Heights, IL 60139-2208
http://www.uticorp.com/

CONTACT Pat Kellen, Campus President
Telephone: 630-529-2662

GENERAL INFORMATION Private Institution. Founded 1965. **Total program enrollment:** 1613.

PROGRAM(S) OFFERED
• **Automobile/Automotive Mechanics Technology/Technician** *97 hrs./$32,050*
• **Diesel Mechanics Technology/Technician** *157 students enrolled*

University of Phoenix–Chicago Campus

1500 McConner Parkway, Suite 700, Schaumburg, IL 60173-4399
http://www.phoenix.edu/

CONTACT William Pepicello, PhD, President
Telephone: 847-413-1922

GENERAL INFORMATION Private Institution. Founded 2002. **Accreditation:** Regional (NCA). **Total program enrollment:** 1223.

STUDENT SERVICES Academic or career counseling, remedial services.

University of Spa & Cosmetology Arts

300 West Carpenter Street, Springfield, IL 62702
http://www.uscart.com/

CONTACT Lynne Lowder, Director of Admissions & Financial Aid
Telephone: 217-753-8990

GENERAL INFORMATION Private Institution. Founded 1978. **Total program enrollment:** 143. **Application fee:** $50.

PROGRAM(S) OFFERED
• **Aesthetician/Esthetician and Skin Care Specialist** *25 hrs./$6680*
• **Cosmetology/Cosmetologist, General** *50 hrs./$11,200* • **Massage Therapy/Therapeutic Massage** *600 hrs./$8000* • **Nail Technician/Specialist and Manicurist** *350 hrs./$2625* • **Teacher Education and Professional Development, Specific Subject Areas, Other** *1000 hrs./$2245*

STUDENT SERVICES Academic or career counseling, employment services for current students, placement services for program completers.

The Vanderschmidt School

4825 N. Scott Street, Suite 76, Schiller Park, IL 60176

CONTACT Alan Stutts, Executive Director
Telephone: 773-380-6800

GENERAL INFORMATION Private Institution. Founded 1950. **Total program enrollment:** 734. **Application fee:** $25.

The Vanderschmidt School (continued)

PROGRAM(S) OFFERED
• **Medical Office Assistant/Specialist** *53 students enrolled* • **Medical Staff Services Technology/Technician**

STUDENT SERVICES Academic or career counseling, employment services for current students, placement services for program completers, remedial services.

Vatterott College

501 North 3rd Street, Quincy, IL 62301
http://www.vatterott-college.edu/

CONTACT Leslie Fischer, Director
Telephone: 800-438-5621

GENERAL INFORMATION Private Institution. Founded 1969. **Total program enrollment:** 345.

PROGRAM(S) OFFERED
• **CAD/CADD Drafting and/or Design Technology/Technician** *16 students enrolled* • **Cosmetology/Cosmetologist, General** *7 students enrolled* • **Data Processing and Data Processing Technology/Technician** • **Electrician** *25 students enrolled* • **Heating, Air Conditioning, Ventilation and Refrigeration Maintenance Technology/Technician (HAC, HACR, HVAC, HVACR)** *18 students enrolled* • **Information Technology** *31 students enrolled* • **Medical Office Assistant/Specialist** *30 students enrolled*

STUDENT SERVICES Academic or career counseling, employment services for current students, placement services for program completers.

Vee's School of Beauty Culture

2701 State Street, East St. Louis, IL 62205

CONTACT Versie Ruffin, President
Telephone: 618-274-1751

GENERAL INFORMATION Private Institution. **Total program enrollment:** 33. **Application fee:** $100.

PROGRAM(S) OFFERED
• **Salon/Beauty Salon Management/Manager** *21 students enrolled*

STUDENT SERVICES Academic or career counseling, placement services for program completers.

Waubonsee Community College

Route 47 at Waubonsee Drive, Sugar Grove, IL 60554-9799
http://www.waubonsee.edu/

CONTACT Christine J. Sobek, President
Telephone: 630-466-7900 Ext. 2938

GENERAL INFORMATION Public Institution. Founded 1966. **Accreditation:** Regional (NCA). **Total program enrollment:** 3432.

PROGRAM(S) OFFERED
• **Accounting Technology/Technician and Bookkeeping** *4 students enrolled* • **Accounting** *1 student enrolled* • **Animation, Interactive Technology, Video Graphics and Special Effects** *2 students enrolled* • **Autobody/Collision and Repair Technology/Technician** *9 students enrolled* • **Building/Property Maintenance and Management** *1 student enrolled* • **Business Administration and Management, General** *2 students enrolled* • **Child Care Provider/Assistant** *1 student enrolled* • **Commercial Photography** *5 students enrolled* • **Computer Technology/Computer Systems Technology** *2 students enrolled* • **Criminal Justice/Police Science** *1 student enrolled* • **Data Entry/Microcomputer Applications, General** *1 student enrolled* • **Electrical, Electronic and Communications Engineering Technology/Technician** *4 students enrolled* • **Electrician** *16 students enrolled* • **Emergency Care Attendant (EMT Ambulance)** *91 students enrolled* • **Executive Assistant/Executive Secretary** *1 student enrolled* • **Fire Science/Firefighting** *1 student enrolled* • **Fire Services Administration** *1 student enrolled* • **General Office Occupations and Clerical Services** *1 student enrolled* • **Graphic Design** *2 students enrolled* • **Heating, Air Conditioning, Ventilation and Refrigeration Maintenance Technology/Technician (HAC, HACR, HVAC, HVACR)** *7 students*

enrolled • **Hydraulics and Fluid Power Technology/Technician** *1 student enrolled* • **Industrial Mechanics and Maintenance Technology** *3 students enrolled* • **Kinesiology and Exercise Science** *1 student enrolled* • **Logistics and Materials Management** *1 student enrolled* • **Massage Therapy/Therapeutic Massage** *15 students enrolled* • **Medical Administrative/Executive Assistant and Medical Secretary** *4 students enrolled* • **Medical Transcription/Transcriptionist** *2 students enrolled* • **Medical/Clinical Assistant** *5 students enrolled* • **Nurse/Nursing Assistant/Aide and Patient Care Assistant** *234 students enrolled* • **Phlebotomy/Phlebotomist** *38 students enrolled* • **Radio and Television Broadcasting Technology/Technician** *8 students enrolled* • **Real Estate** *81 students enrolled* • **Security and Loss Prevention Services** *1 student enrolled* • **Sign Language Interpretation and Translation** *5 students enrolled* • **Substance Abuse/Addiction Counseling** *3 students enrolled* • **Surgical Technology/Technologist** *3 students enrolled* • **Survey Technology/Surveying** *1 student enrolled* • **System Administration/Administrator** *1 student enrolled* • **Tourism and Travel Services Management** *3 students enrolled* • **Web Page, Digital/Multimedia and Information Resources Design** *2 students enrolled* • **Welding Technology/Welder** *1 student enrolled* • **Word Processing** *1 student enrolled*

STUDENT SERVICES Academic or career counseling, daycare for children of students, employment services for current students, placement services for program completers, remedial services.

Westwood College–Chicago River Oaks

80 River Oaks Drive, Suite D-49, Calumet City, IL 60409
http://www.westwood.edu/

CONTACT Bruce McKenzie, Executive Director
Telephone: 708-832-9760

GENERAL INFORMATION Private Institution. **Accreditation:** State accredited or approved. **Total program enrollment:** 538. **Application fee:** $25.

PROGRAM(S) OFFERED
• **Medical Insurance Coding Specialist/Coder** *11 students enrolled* • **Medical Staff Services Technology/Technician** *96 students enrolled*

STUDENT SERVICES Academic or career counseling, employment services for current students, placement services for program completers, remedial services.

Worsham College of Mortuary Science

495 Northgate Parkway, Wheeling, IL 60090-2646
http://www.worshamcollege.com/

CONTACT Stephanie J. Kann, President
Telephone: 847-808-8444

GENERAL INFORMATION Private Institution. Founded 1911. **Accreditation:** Funeral service (ABFSE). **Total program enrollment:** 91. **Application fee:** $30.

PROGRAM(S) OFFERED
• **Funeral Service and Mortuary Science, General** *39 students enrolled*

STUDENT SERVICES Academic or career counseling, employment services for current students, placement services for program completers.

Zarem/Golde ORT Technical Institute

3050 West Touhy Avenue, Chicago, IL 60645
http://www.zg-ort.org/

CONTACT Arthur A. Eldar, Director
Telephone: 847-324-5588 Ext. 18

GENERAL INFORMATION Private Institution. Founded 1991. **Total program enrollment:** 313. **Application fee:** $100.

PROGRAM(S) OFFERED
• **Accounting Technology/Technician and Bookkeeping** *32 hrs./$7200* • **Accounting** *32 students enrolled* • **CAD/CADD Drafting and/or Design Technology/Technician** *35 hrs./$7500* • **Computer Systems Networking and Telecommunications** *33 hrs./$7200* • **Drafting and Design Technology/Technician,**

General *16 students enrolled* • **English Language and Literature**, **General** *720 hrs./$4500* • **Executive Assistant/Executive Secretary** • **Medical/Clinical Assistant** *33 hrs./$7400* • **Prepress/Desktop Publishing and Digital Imaging Design** *36 hrs./$7200*

STUDENT SERVICES Academic or career counseling, employment services for current students, placement services for program completers, remedial services.

INDIANA ————————

A Cut Above Beauty College

3810 East Southport Road, Indianapolis, IN 46237

CONTACT Michael Bouman, President/COO
Telephone: 570-429-4321 Ext. 2414

GENERAL INFORMATION Private Institution. Founded 1981. **Total program enrollment:** 108. **Application fee:** $100.

PROGRAM(S) OFFERED
• **Aesthetician/Esthetician and Skin Care Specialist** *700 hrs./$6797*
• **Cosmetology/Cosmetologist**, **General** *1500 hrs./$13,250* • **Nail Technician/Specialist and Manicurist** *450 hrs./$3250*

STUDENT SERVICES Academic or career counseling, placement services for program completers.

Alexandria School of Scientific Therapeutics

809 South Harrison Street, PO Box 287, Alexandria, IN 46001
http://www.assti.com/

CONTACT Herbert L. Hobbs, Administrator
Telephone: 765-724-9152

GENERAL INFORMATION Private Institution. Founded 1982. **Total program enrollment:** 56. **Application fee:** $100.

PROGRAM(S) OFFERED
• **Massage Therapy/Therapeutic Massage** *672 hrs./$7750*

Ancilla College

Union Road, PO Box 1, Donaldson, IN 46513
http://www.ancilla.edu/

CONTACT Dr. Ronald May, President
Telephone: 574-936-8898

GENERAL INFORMATION Private Institution. Founded 1937. **Accreditation:** Regional (NCA). **Total program enrollment:** 362.

PROGRAM(S) OFFERED
• **Business Administration and Management**, **General** • **Business Operations Support and Secretarial Services**, **Other** • **Business/Commerce**, **General** • **Early Childhood Education and Teaching**

STUDENT SERVICES Academic or career counseling, remedial services.

Apex School of Beauty Culture

333 Jackson Street, Anderson, IN 46016

CONTACT Beverly Shrake, President
Telephone: 765-642-7560

GENERAL INFORMATION Private Institution. **Total program enrollment:** 16.

PROGRAM(S) OFFERED
• **Cosmetology/Cosmetologist**, **General** *1500 hrs./$8000*

The Art Institute of Indianapolis

3500 Depauw Boulevard, Indianapolis, IN 46268
http://www.artinstitutes.edu/indianapolis/

CONTACT Madeleine Slutsky, President, The Art Institute of Indianapolis
Telephone: 317-613-4800

GENERAL INFORMATION Private Institution. **Total program enrollment:** 389. **Application fee:** $50.

PROGRAM(S) OFFERED
• **Baking and Pastry Arts/Baker/Pastry Chef** • **Graphic Design** *5 students enrolled* • **Interior Design** *17 students enrolled*

STUDENT SERVICES Academic or career counseling, employment services for current students, placement services for program completers, remedial services.

Aviation Institute of Maintenance–Indianapolis

7251 West McCarty Street, Indianapolis, IN 46241
http://www.aviationmaintenance.edu/

CONTACT Carlos Irizarry, School Director
Telephone: 317-243-4519

GENERAL INFORMATION Private Institution. Founded 1992. **Accreditation:** State accredited or approved. **Total program enrollment:** 156. **Application fee:** $25.

PROGRAM(S) OFFERED
• **Airframe Mechanics and Aircraft Maintenance Technology/Technician** *130 hrs./$33,720* • **Avionics Maintenance Technology/Technician** *32 hrs./$5760*

STUDENT SERVICES Academic or career counseling, employment services for current students, placement services for program completers.

Brown Mackie College–Fort Wayne

3000 East Coliseum Boulevard, Fort Wayne, IN 46805
http://www.brownmackie.edu/fortwayne

CONTACT Jim Bishop, Campus President
Telephone: 260-484-4400

GENERAL INFORMATION Private Institution. **Accreditation:** State accredited or approved. **Total program enrollment:** 212.

PROGRAM(S) OFFERED
• **Accounting** *1 student enrolled* • **Business/Commerce**, **General** *1 student enrolled* • **Computer and Information Sciences and Support Services**, **Other** • **Corrections and Criminal Justice**, **Other** • **Legal Assistant/Paralegal** *2 students enrolled* • **Medical Insurance Coding Specialist/Coder** *40 students enrolled* • **Medical/Clinical Assistant** *13 students enrolled* • **Nurse/Nursing Assistant/Aide and Patient Care Assistant** *246 students enrolled*

STUDENT SERVICES Academic or career counseling, employment services for current students, placement services for program completers, remedial services.

Brown Mackie College–Indianapolis

1200 North Meridian Street, Suite 100, Indianapolis, IN 46204
http://www.brownmackie.edu/Indianapolis/

CONTACT Todd Matthews, President
Telephone: 866-255-0279

GENERAL INFORMATION Private Institution. **Total program enrollment:** 402.

PROGRAM(S) OFFERED
• Business/Office Automation/Technology/Data Entry • Medical/Clinical Assistant

STUDENT SERVICES Academic or career counseling, placement services for program completers, remedial services.

Brown Mackie College–Merrillville

1000 East 80th Place, Suite 101N, Merrillville, IN 46410
http://www.brownmackie.edu/Merrillville

CONTACT Sheryl Elston, Campus Director/President
Telephone: 219-769-3321 Ext. 2211

GENERAL INFORMATION Private Institution. Founded 1890. **Accreditation:** State accredited or approved. **Total program enrollment:** 775.

PROGRAM(S) OFFERED
• Accounting *1 student enrolled* • Business Administration and Management, General • Computer Software Technology/Technician *1 student enrolled* • Corrections and Criminal Justice, Other • Legal Assistant/Paralegal *5 students enrolled* • Medical/Clinical Assistant *9 students enrolled* • Nursing, Other *219 students enrolled*

STUDENT SERVICES Academic or career counseling, employment services for current students, placement services for program completers, remedial services.

Brown Mackie College–Michigan City

325 East US Highway 20, Michigan City, IN 46360
http://www.brownmackie.edu/MichiganCity

CONTACT Eric Rudie, Campus President
Telephone: 219-877-3100

GENERAL INFORMATION Private Institution. **Accreditation:** State accredited or approved. **Total program enrollment:** 378.

PROGRAM(S) OFFERED
• Accounting • Business/Commerce, General • Computer and Information Sciences and Support Services, Other *1 student enrolled* • Corrections and Criminal Justice, Other *1 student enrolled* • Legal Assistant/Paralegal *1 student enrolled* • Medical/Clinical Assistant *1 student enrolled*

STUDENT SERVICES Academic or career counseling, employment services for current students, placement services for program completers, remedial services.

Brown Mackie College–South Bend

1030 East Jefferson Boulevard, South Bend, IN 46617-3123
http://www.brownmackie.edu/SouthBend

CONTACT Connie Adelman, Campus President
Telephone: 574-237-0774

GENERAL INFORMATION Private Institution. Founded 1882. **Accreditation:** Medical assisting (AAMAE); physical therapy assisting (APTA); state accredited or approved. **Total program enrollment:** 823.

PROGRAM(S) OFFERED
• Business/Commerce, General *1 student enrolled* • Computer and Information Sciences and Support Services, Other • Corrections and Criminal Justice, Other • Electrical/Electronics Equipment Installation and Repair, General • Legal Assistant/Paralegal • Medical/Clinical Assistant *5 students enrolled* • Nursing, Other *108 students enrolled*

STUDENT SERVICES Academic or career counseling, employment services for current students, placement services for program completers, remedial services.

Calumet College of Saint Joseph

2400 New York Avenue, Whiting, IN 46394-2195
http://www.ccsj.edu/

CONTACT Dennis Rittenmeyer, President
Telephone: 219-473-7770

GENERAL INFORMATION Private Institution. Founded 1951. **Accreditation:** Regional (NCA). **Total program enrollment:** 520.

PROGRAM(S) OFFERED
• Accounting • Business Administration and Management, General • Criminal Justice/Law Enforcement Administration • Legal Assistant/Paralegal • Religion/Religious Studies, Other

STUDENT SERVICES Academic or career counseling, daycare for children of students, employment services for current students, placement services for program completers, remedial services.

College of Court Reporting

111 West Tenth Street, Suite 111, Hobart, IN 46342
http://www.ccredu.com/

CONTACT Jeff Moody, President
Telephone: 219-942-1459

GENERAL INFORMATION Private Institution. **Accreditation:** State accredited or approved. **Total program enrollment:** 100. **Application fee:** $50.

PROGRAM(S) OFFERED
• Administrative Assistant and Secretarial Science, General

STUDENT SERVICES Academic or career counseling, employment services for current students, placement services for program completers, remedial services.

Creative Hairstyling Academy

2549 Highway Avenue, Highland, IN 46322
http://creativehair.com/

CONTACT Deborah A. Marias, President
Telephone: 219-838-2004 Ext. 304

GENERAL INFORMATION Private Institution. Founded 1969. **Total program enrollment:** 63. **Application fee:** $50.

PROGRAM(S) OFFERED
• Aesthetician/Esthetician and Skin Care Specialist *750 hrs./$10,000* • Cosmetology, Barber/Styling, and Nail Instructor *1000 hrs./$4000* • Hair Styling/Stylist and Hair Design *1500 hrs./$8908* • Nail Technician/Specialist and Manicurist *450 hrs./$2595*

STUDENT SERVICES Academic or career counseling, placement services for program completers.

Crossroads Bible College

601 North Shortridge Road, Indianapolis, IN 46219
http://www.crossroads.edu/

CONTACT A. Charles Ware, President
Telephone: 317-352-8736 Ext. 234

GENERAL INFORMATION Private Institution. Founded 1980. **Accreditation:** State accredited or approved. **Total program enrollment:** 76. **Application fee:** $10.

PROGRAM(S) OFFERED
● **Religious Education** *1 student enrolled*

STUDENT SERVICES Academic or career counseling, employment services for current students, placement services for program completers, remedial services.

David Demuth Institute of Cosmetology

2 SW Fifth Street, Richmond, IN 47374
http://www.ddiccareer.com/

CONTACT David Michael Demuth, Owner/Administrator
Telephone: 765-935-7964 Ext. 10

GENERAL INFORMATION Private Institution. **Total program enrollment:** 16. **Application fee:** $100.

PROGRAM(S) OFFERED
● **Cosmetology, Barber/Styling, and Nail Instructor** *1000 hrs./$4250*
● **Cosmetology/Cosmetologist, General** *1500 hrs./$9200* ● **Nail Technician/Specialist and Manicurist** *450 hrs./$3450*

Don Roberts Beauty School

1354 West Lincoln Way, Valparaiso, IN 46385

CONTACT Lisa Collins, Office Manager
Telephone: 219-462-5189

GENERAL INFORMATION Private Institution. Founded 1961. **Total program enrollment:** 26. **Application fee:** $50.

PROGRAM(S) OFFERED
● **Cosmetology, Barber/Styling, and Nail Instructor** *1000 hrs./$7000*
● **Cosmetology/Cosmetologist, General** *1500 hrs./$9595* ● **Nail Technician/Specialist and Manicurist** *450 hrs./$3550*

STUDENT SERVICES Academic or career counseling, placement services for program completers.

Don Roberts School of Hair Design

7975 Calumet Avenue, Munster, IN 46321

CONTACT Janet Stemmer, Owner
Telephone: 219-864-1600

GENERAL INFORMATION Private Institution. **Total program enrollment:** 32. **Application fee:** $50.

PROGRAM(S) OFFERED
● **Aesthetician/Esthetician and Skin Care Specialist** *900 hrs./$11,750*
● **Cosmetology, Barber/Styling, and Nail Instructor** *1000 hrs./$8950*
● **Cosmetology/Cosmetologist, General** *1500 hrs./$11,425* ● **Facial Treatment Specialist/Facialist** *7 students enrolled* ● **Nail Technician/Specialist and Manicurist** *600 hrs./$6550*

STUDENT SERVICES Academic or career counseling, employment services for current students, placement services for program completers.

Everest College

Merrillville Corporate Lakes, 707 E. 80th Place, Suite 200, Merrillville, IN 46410
http://www.everest.edu/

CONTACT Sean Quinn, Regional Vice President
Telephone: 219-756-6811

GENERAL INFORMATION Private Institution. **Total program enrollment:** 928.

PROGRAM(S) OFFERED
● **Allied Health and Medical Assisting Services, Other** *71 students enrolled*
● **Dental Assisting/Assistant** *47 hrs./$13,326* ● **Licensed Practical/Vocational Nurse Training (LPN, LVN, Cert, Dipl, AAS)** *76 students enrolled* ● **Massage Therapy/Therapeutic Massage** *55 hrs./$13,200* ● **Medical Insurance Coding Specialist/Coder** *47 hrs./$12,873* ● **Medical Reception/Receptionist** *47 hrs./$12,873* ● **Medical/Clinical Assistant** *47 hrs./$13,823* ● **Nurse/Nursing Assistant/Aide and Patient Care Assistant** *86 hrs./$26,651* ● **Surgical Technology/Technologist** *55 students enrolled*

STUDENT SERVICES Academic or career counseling, employment services for current students, placement services for program completers.

Goshen College

1700 South Main Street, Goshen, IN 46526-4794
http://www.goshen.edu/

CONTACT James E. Brenneman, President
Telephone: 574-535-7000

GENERAL INFORMATION Private Institution. Founded 1894. **Accreditation:** Regional (NCA). **Total program enrollment:** 862. **Application fee:** $25.

PROGRAM(S) OFFERED
● **Business Administration and Management, General** ● **Computer Systems Analysis/Analyst** ● **Teaching English as a Second or Foreign Language/ESL Language Instructor**

STUDENT SERVICES Academic or career counseling, daycare for children of students, employment services for current students, placement services for program completers, remedial services.

Hair Arts Academy

933 North Walnut Street, Bloomington, IN 47404

CONTACT Michael V. Porter, General Manager
Telephone: 812-339-1117

GENERAL INFORMATION Private Institution. Founded 1984. **Total program enrollment:** 35.

PROGRAM(S) OFFERED
● **Cosmetology and Related Personal Grooming Arts, Other** ● **Cosmetology/Cosmetologist, General** *1500 hrs./$10,555* ● **Make-Up Artist/Specialist**

STUDENT SERVICES Academic or career counseling, employment services for current students, placement services for program completers, remedial services.

Hair Fashions by Kaye Beauty College

6316 East 82nd Street, Indianapolis, IN 46250

CONTACT Kaye Maxwell, Owner
Telephone: 317-576-8000

GENERAL INFORMATION Private Institution. Founded 1978. **Total program enrollment:** 144. **Application fee:** $100.

Hair Fashions by Kaye Beauty College (continued)

PROGRAM(S) OFFERED
• **Barbering/Barber** *1500 hrs./$13,600* • **Cosmetology and Related Personal Grooming Arts, Other** *600 hrs./$5440* • **Cosmetology/Cosmetologist, General** *1500 hrs./$15,390* • **Make-Up Artist/Specialist** *1000 hrs./$6020*

Hair Fashions by Kaye Beauty College

1111 South 10th Street, Noblesville, IN 46060

CONTACT Kaye Maxwell, Owner
Telephone: 317-773-6189

GENERAL INFORMATION Private Institution. Founded 1974. **Total program enrollment:** 73. **Application fee:** $100.

PROGRAM(S) OFFERED
• **Aesthetician/Esthetician and Skin Care Specialist** *700 hrs./$7550*
• **Cosmetology and Related Personal Grooming Arts, Other** *2 students enrolled*
• **Cosmetology, Barber/Styling, and Nail Instructor** *1000 hrs./$3750*
• **Cosmetology/Cosmetologist, General** *1500 hrs./$14,390* • **Make-Up Artist/Specialist** *22 students enrolled*

STUDENT SERVICES Academic or career counseling, employment services for current students, placement services for program completers.

Harrison College

140 East 53rd Street, Anderson, IN 46013
http://www.harrison.edu/

CONTACT Kenneth J. Konesco, President
Telephone: 765-644-7514

GENERAL INFORMATION Private Institution. Founded 1902. **Accreditation:** State accredited or approved. **Total program enrollment:** 149. **Application fee:** $50.

PROGRAM(S) OFFERED
• **Accounting** • **Administrative Assistant and Secretarial Science, General** *1 student enrolled* • **Medical Insurance Coding Specialist/Coder** • **Medical Office Assistant/Specialist** *6 students enrolled*

STUDENT SERVICES Academic or career counseling, employment services for current students, placement services for program completers, remedial services.

Harrison College

2222 Poshard Drive, Columbus, IN 47203-1843
http://www.harrison.edu/

CONTACT Kenneth J. Konesco, President
Telephone: 812-379-9000

GENERAL INFORMATION Private Institution. **Accreditation:** State accredited or approved. **Total program enrollment:** 133. **Application fee:** $50.

STUDENT SERVICES Academic or career counseling, employment services for current students, placement services for program completers, remedial services.

Harrison College

4601 Theatre Drive, Evansville, IN 47715-4601
http://www.harrison.edu/

CONTACT Kenneth J. Konesco, President
Telephone: 812-476-6000

GENERAL INFORMATION Private Institution. **Accreditation:** Medical assisting (AAMAE); state accredited or approved. **Total program enrollment:** 145. **Application fee:** $50.

STUDENT SERVICES Academic or career counseling, employment services for current students, placement services for program completers, remedial services.

Harrison College

6413 North Clinton Street, Fort Wayne, IN 46825
http://www.harrison.edu/

CONTACT Kenneth J. Konesco, President
Telephone: 260-471-7667

GENERAL INFORMATION Private Institution. **Accreditation:** State accredited or approved. **Total program enrollment:** 281. **Application fee:** $50.

PROGRAM(S) OFFERED
• **Accounting** *2 students enrolled* • **Administrative Assistant and Secretarial Science, General** *1 student enrolled* • **General Office Occupations and Clerical Services** • **Medical Insurance Coding Specialist/Coder** • **Medical Office Assistant/Specialist** *6 students enrolled*

STUDENT SERVICES Academic or career counseling, employment services for current students, placement services for program completers, remedial services.

Harrison College

550 East Washington Street, Indianapolis, IN 46204
http://www.harrison.edu/

CONTACT Kenneth J. Konesco, President
Telephone: 317-264-5656

GENERAL INFORMATION Private Institution. Founded 1902. **Accreditation:** State accredited or approved. **Total program enrollment:** 1220. **Application fee:** $50.

PROGRAM(S) OFFERED
• **Accounting** *1 student enrolled* • **Computer Technology/Computer Systems Technology** *1 student enrolled* • **Medical Office Assistant/Specialist** *3 students enrolled* • **Medical Transcription/Transcriptionist** *5 students enrolled*

STUDENT SERVICES Academic or career counseling, employment services for current students, placement services for program completers, remedial services.

Harrison College

6300 Technology Center Drive, Indianapolis, IN 46278
http://www.harrison.edu/

CONTACT Kenneth J. Konesco, President
Telephone: 317-873-6500

GENERAL INFORMATION Private Institution. **Total program enrollment:** 222. **Application fee:** $50.

PROGRAM(S) OFFERED
• **Medical Office Assistant/Specialist**

STUDENT SERVICES Academic or career counseling, employment services for current students, placement services for program completers, remedial services.

Harrison College

8150 Brookville Road, Indianapolis, IN 46239
http://www.harrison.edu/

CONTACT Kenneth J. Konesco, President
Telephone: 317-375-8000

GENERAL INFORMATION Private Institution. **Accreditation:** State accredited or approved. **Total program enrollment:** 407. **Application fee:** $50.

PROGRAM(S) OFFERED
• **Massage Therapy/Therapeutic Massage** 9 *students enrolled* • **Medical Insurance Coding Specialist/Coder** 16 *students enrolled* • **Medical Office Assistant/Specialist** 12 *students enrolled*

STUDENT SERVICES Academic or career counseling, employment services for current students, placement services for program completers, remedial services.

Harrison College

4705 Meijer Court, Lafayette, IN 47905
http://www.harrison.edu/

CONTACT Kenneth J. Konesco, President
Telephone: 765-447-9550

GENERAL INFORMATION Private Institution. **Accreditation:** State accredited or approved. **Total program enrollment:** 196. **Application fee:** $50.

PROGRAM(S) OFFERED
• **Accounting** 1 *student enrolled* • **Administrative Assistant and Secretarial Science, General** • **Medical Office Assistant/Specialist** 4 *students enrolled*

STUDENT SERVICES Academic or career counseling, employment services for current students, placement services for program completers, remedial services.

Harrison College

411 West Riggin Road, Muncie, IN 47303
http://www.harrison.edu/

CONTACT Kenneth J. Konesco, President
Telephone: 765-288-8681

GENERAL INFORMATION Private Institution. **Accreditation:** State accredited or approved. **Total program enrollment:** 199. **Application fee:** $50.

PROGRAM(S) OFFERED
• **Accounting** • **Administrative Assistant and Secretarial Science, General** • **Computer Systems Networking and Telecommunications** • **Computer Technology/Computer Systems Technology** • **Medical Insurance Coding Specialist/Coder** • **Medical Office Assistant/Specialist** 5 *students enrolled*

STUDENT SERVICES Academic or career counseling, employment services for current students, placement services for program completers, remedial services.

Harrison College

1378 South State Road 46, Terre Haute, IN 47803
http://www.harrison.edu/

CONTACT Kenneth J. Konesco, President
Telephone: 812-877-2100

GENERAL INFORMATION Private Institution. Founded 1902. **Accreditation:** State accredited or approved. **Total program enrollment:** 204. **Application fee:** $50.

PROGRAM(S) OFFERED
• **Accounting** • **Administrative Assistant and Secretarial Science, General** • **Medical Office Assistant/Specialist** 2 *students enrolled*

STUDENT SERVICES Academic or career counseling, employment services for current students, placement services for program completers, remedial services.

Honors Beauty College, Inc.

1315 East 86th, Indianapolis, IN 46240
http://www.honorsbeautycollege.com

GENERAL INFORMATION Private Institution. Founded 1992. **Total program enrollment:** 99. **Application fee:** $50.

PROGRAM(S) OFFERED
• **Aesthetician/Esthetician and Skin Care Specialist** 800 *hrs./$8900* • **Cosmetology, Barber/Styling, and Nail Instructor** 1000 *hrs./$7100* • **Cosmetology/Cosmetologist, General** 1500 *hrs./$12,350* • **Nail Technician/Specialist and Manicurist** 500 *hrs./$3600*

Ideal Beauty Academy

1401 Youngstown Drive, Jeffersonville, IN 47130-4215
idealbeautyacademy.net

CONTACT Imnmy Moberly, Director/President
Telephone: 812-282-1371

GENERAL INFORMATION Private Institution. **Total program enrollment:** 41. **Application fee:** $100.

PROGRAM(S) OFFERED
• **Aesthetician/Esthetician and Skin Care Specialist** 700 *hrs./$7200* • **Cosmetology/Cosmetologist, General** 1500 *hrs./$13,392* • **Nail Technician/Specialist and Manicurist**

STUDENT SERVICES Academic or career counseling, placement services for program completers.

Indiana Business College–Elkhart

56075 Parkway Avenue, Elkhart, IN 46516
http://www.ibcschools.edu

CONTACT Mr. Justin Elliott, Associate Dean
Telephone: 574-522-0397

GENERAL INFORMATION Private Institution. **Total program enrollment:** 134. **Application fee:** $50.

PROGRAM(S) OFFERED
• **Accounting** • **Administrative Assistant and Secretarial Science, General** • **Medical Office Assistant/Specialist**

STUDENT SERVICES Academic or career counseling, employment services for current students, placement services for program completers, remedial services.

Indiana State University

210 North Seventh Street, Terre Haute, IN 47809-1401
http://www.indstate.edu/

CONTACT Daniel J. Bradley, President
Telephone: 812-237-6311

GENERAL INFORMATION Public Institution. Founded 1865. **Accreditation:** Regional (NCA); art and design (NASAD); athletic training (JRCAT); home economics (AAFCS); music (NASM); recreation and parks (NRPA); speech-language pathology (ASHA). **Total program enrollment:** 7936. **Application fee:** $25.

PROGRAM(S) OFFERED
• **Foreign Languages, Literatures, and Linguistics, Other** • **Geography** • **Jazz/Jazz Studies** • **Teaching English as a Second or Foreign Language/ESL Language Instructor**

STUDENT SERVICES Academic or career counseling, daycare for children of students, employment services for current students, placement services for program completers.

Indiana Tech

1600 East Washington Boulevard, Fort Wayne, IN 46803-1297
http://www.indianatech.edu

CONTACT Dr. Arthur E. Snyder, President
Telephone: 800-937-2448

GENERAL INFORMATION Private Institution. Founded 1930. **Accreditation:** Regional (NCA). **Total program enrollment:** 2158. **Application fee:** $25.

STUDENT SERVICES Academic or career counseling, employment services for current students, placement services for program completers, remedial services.

Indiana University Bloomington

107 South Indiana Avenue, Bloomington, IN 47405-7000
http://www.iub.edu/

CONTACT Michael McRobbie, President
Telephone: 812-855-4848

GENERAL INFORMATION Public Institution. Founded 1820. **Accreditation:** Regional (NCA); art and design (NASAD); athletic training (JRCAT); audiology (ASHA); counseling (ACA); interior design: professional (CIDA); journalism and mass communications (ACEJMC); library and information science (ALA); music (NASM); ophthalmic dispensing (COA); optometric technology (AOA); public health: community health education (CEPH); recreation and parks (NRPA); speech-language pathology (ASHA); theater (NAST). **Total program enrollment:** 35742. **Application fee:** $50.

PROGRAM(S) OFFERED
• **Business/Commerce, General** 113 *students enrolled* • **Labor Studies** 1 *student enrolled* • **Occupational Safety and Health Technology/Technician** 5 *students enrolled*

STUDENT SERVICES Academic or career counseling, daycare for children of students, employment services for current students, placement services for program completers, remedial services.

Indiana University East

2325 Chester Boulevard, Richmond, IN 47374-1289
http://www.iue.edu/

CONTACT Nasser H. Paydar, Chancellor
Telephone: 765-973-8200

GENERAL INFORMATION Public Institution. Founded 1971. **Accreditation:** Regional (NCA). **Total program enrollment:** 1372. **Application fee:** $25.

STUDENT SERVICES Academic or career counseling, daycare for children of students, employment services for current students, remedial services.

Indiana University Kokomo

PO Box 9003, Kokomo, IN 46904-9003
http://www.iuk.edu/

CONTACT Stuart M. Green, Interim Chancellor
Telephone: 765-453-2000

GENERAL INFORMATION Public Institution. Founded 1945. **Accreditation:** Regional (NCA). **Total program enrollment:** 1349. **Application fee:** $30.

PROGRAM(S) OFFERED
• **Labor Studies** 2 *students enrolled*

STUDENT SERVICES Academic or career counseling, daycare for children of students, employment services for current students, placement services for program completers, remedial services.

Indiana University Northwest

3400 Broadway, Gary, IN 46408-1197
http://www.iun.edu/

CONTACT Bruce Bergland, Chancellor
Telephone: 219-980-6500

GENERAL INFORMATION Public Institution. Founded 1959. **Accreditation:** Regional (NCA); dental assisting (ADA); dental hygiene (ADA); health information technology (AHIMA); medical laboratory technology (NAACLS); radiologic technology: radiation therapy technology (JRCERT); radiologic technology: radiography (JRCERT). **Total program enrollment:** 2727. **Application fee:** $25.

PROGRAM(S) OFFERED
• **Dental Assisting/Assistant** 17 *students enrolled* • **Labor Studies** 2 *students enrolled*

STUDENT SERVICES Academic or career counseling, daycare for children of students, employment services for current students, placement services for program completers, remedial services.

Indiana University–Purdue University Fort Wayne

2101 East Coliseum Boulevard, Fort Wayne, IN 46805-1499
http://www.ipfw.edu/

CONTACT Michael A. Wartell, Chancellor
Telephone: 260-481-6100

GENERAL INFORMATION Public Institution. Founded 1917. **Accreditation:** Regional (NCA); dental assisting (ADA); dental hygiene (ADA); dental laboratory technology (ADA); engineering technology (ABET/TAC); health information technology (AHIMA); music (NASM). **Total program enrollment:** 7672. **Application fee:** $30.

PROGRAM(S) OFFERED
• **Anthropology** 2 *students enrolled* • **Business/Commerce, General** 10 *students enrolled* • **Computer and Information Sciences, General** 2 *students enrolled* • **Dental Assisting/Assistant** 23 *students enrolled* • **Electrical, Electronic and Communications Engineering Technology/Technician** 4 *students enrolled* • **Labor and Industrial Relations** 1 *student enrolled* • **Operations Management and Supervision** 1 *student enrolled* • **Political Science and Government, General** 11 *students enrolled* • **Public Administration** 4 *students enrolled* • **Quality Control Technology/Technician** 3 *students enrolled*

STUDENT SERVICES Academic or career counseling, daycare for children of students, employment services for current students, placement services for program completers, remedial services.

Indiana University–Purdue University Indianapolis

355 North Lansing, Indianapolis, IN 46202-2896
http://www.iupui.edu/

CONTACT Charles R. Bantz, Chancellor
Telephone: 317-274-5555

GENERAL INFORMATION Public Institution. Founded 1969. **Accreditation:** Regional (NCA); art and design (NASAD); cytotechnology (ASC); dental assisting (ADA); dental hygiene (ADA); dietetics: post-baccalaureate internship (ADtA/CAADE); engineering technology (ABET/TAC); health information administration (AHIMA); health information technology (AHIMA); histologic technology (NAACLS); medical technology (NAACLS); nuclear medicine technology (JRC-NMT); radiologic technology: radiation therapy technology (JRCERT); radiologic technology: radiography (JRCERT). **Total program enrollment:** 18857. **Application fee:** $50.

PROGRAM(S) OFFERED
● **Business/Commerce, General** *28 students enrolled* ● **Computer and Information Sciences and Support Services, Other** *7 students enrolled* ● **Computer and Information Sciences, General** *39 students enrolled* ● **Dental Assisting/Assistant** *34 students enrolled* ● **Histologic Technician** *52 students enrolled* ● **Hospitality Administration/Management, Other** *7 students enrolled* ● **Operations Management and Supervision** *70 students enrolled*

STUDENT SERVICES Academic or career counseling, daycare for children of students, employment services for current students, placement services for program completers, remedial services.

Indiana University South Bend

1700 Mishawaka Avenue, PO Box 7111, South Bend, IN 46634-7111
http://www.iusb.edu/

CONTACT Una Mae Reck, Chancellor
Telephone: 574-520-4872

GENERAL INFORMATION Public Institution. Founded 1922. **Accreditation:** Regional (NCA); dental assisting (ADA); dental hygiene (ADA); radiologic technology: radiography (JRCERT). **Total program enrollment:** 4106. **Application fee:** $47.

PROGRAM(S) OFFERED
● **Dental Assisting/Assistant** *18 students enrolled*

STUDENT SERVICES Academic or career counseling, daycare for children of students, employment services for current students, placement services for program completers, remedial services.

Indiana University Southeast

4201 Grant Line Road, New Albany, IN 47150-6405
http://www.ius.edu/

CONTACT Sandra Patterson-Randles, Chancellor
Telephone: 812-941-2000

GENERAL INFORMATION Public Institution. Founded 1941. **Accreditation:** Regional (NCA). **Total program enrollment:** 3570. **Application fee:** $30.

STUDENT SERVICES Academic or career counseling, daycare for children of students, employment services for current students, placement services for program completers, remedial services.

International Business College

5699 Coventry Lane, Fort Wayne, IN 46804
http://www.ibcfortwayne.edu/

CONTACT Jim Zillman, President
Telephone: 260-459-4500

GENERAL INFORMATION Private Institution. Founded 1889. **Accreditation:** Medical assisting (AAMAE); state accredited or approved. **Total program enrollment:** 571. **Application fee:** $50.

PROGRAM(S) OFFERED
● **Accounting Technology/Technician and Bookkeeping** *5 students enrolled* ● **Administrative Assistant and Secretarial Science, General** *5 students enrolled* ● **Commercial and Advertising Art** *14 students enrolled* ● **Computer and Information Sciences, General** *1 student enrolled* ● **Legal Administrative Assistant/Secretary** ● **Medical Office Management/Administration** *4 students enrolled* ● **Medical/Clinical Assistant** *18 students enrolled* ● **Retailing and Retail Operations** ● **Tourism Promotion Operations** *3 students enrolled*

STUDENT SERVICES Academic or career counseling, employment services for current students, placement services for program completers.

International Business College

7205 Shadeland Station, Indianapolis, IN 46256
http://www.ibcindianapolis.edu/

CONTACT Kathy Chiudioni, Director
Telephone: 317-813-2300

GENERAL INFORMATION Private Institution. Founded 1889. **Accreditation:** State accredited or approved. **Total program enrollment:** 406. **Application fee:** $50.

PROGRAM(S) OFFERED
● **Accounting** *3 students enrolled* ● **Administrative Assistant and Secretarial Science, General** *2 students enrolled* ● **Commercial and Advertising Art** *2 students enrolled* ● **Computer and Information Sciences, General** *1 student enrolled* ● **Legal Administrative Assistant/Secretary** *1 student enrolled* ● **Medical/Clinical Assistant** *34 students enrolled* ● **Tourism and Travel Services Management** *5 students enrolled*

STUDENT SERVICES Academic or career counseling, placement services for program completers.

Ivy Tech Community College–Bloomington

3116 Canterbury Court, Bloomington, IN 47404
http://www.ivytech.edu/

CONTACT John Whikehart, Chancellor
Telephone: 812-332-1559

GENERAL INFORMATION Public Institution. Founded 2001. **Accreditation:** Regional (NCA). **Total program enrollment:** 2871.

PROGRAM(S) OFFERED
● **Accounting Technology/Technician and Bookkeeping** *23 students enrolled* ● **Accounting and Related Services, Other** *11 students enrolled* ● **Business Administration and Management, General** *32 students enrolled* ● **Computer Programming, Other** *8 students enrolled* ● **Computer/Information Technology Services Administration and Management, Other** *9 students enrolled* ● **Early Childhood Education and Teaching** *5 students enrolled* ● **Executive Assistant/Executive Secretary** *28 students enrolled* ● **Heating, Air Conditioning, Ventilation and Refrigeration Maintenance Technology/Technician (HAC, HACR, HVAC, HVACR)** *16 students enrolled* ● **Industrial Production Technologies/Technicians, Other** *27 students enrolled* ● **Licensed Practical/Vocational Nurse Training (LPN, LVN, Cert, Dipl, AAS)** *41 students enrolled* ● **System Administration/Administrator** *7 students enrolled* ● **System, Networking, and LAN/WAN Management/Manager** *6 students enrolled* ● **Web/Multimedia Management and Webmaster** *2 students enrolled*

STUDENT SERVICES Academic or career counseling, employment services for current students, placement services for program completers, remedial services.

Ivy Tech Community College–Central Indiana

50 W. Fall Creek Parkway North Drive, Indianapolis, IN 46208
http://www.ivytech.edu/

CONTACT Hank Dunn, Chancellor
Telephone: 317-921-4800

GENERAL INFORMATION Public Institution. Founded 1963. **Accreditation:** Regional (NCA); medical assisting (AAMAE); practical nursing (NLN); radiologic technology: radiography (JRCERT); surgical technology (ARCST). **Total program enrollment:** 5974.

PROGRAM(S) OFFERED
● **Accounting Technology/Technician and Bookkeeping** *3 students enrolled* ● **Automobile/Automotive Mechanics Technology/Technician** *6 students enrolled* ● **Drafting and Design Technology/Technician, General** *5 students enrolled* ● **Executive Assistant/Executive Secretary** *3 students enrolled* ● **Industrial Production Technologies/Technicians, Other** *19 students enrolled* ● **Licensed Practical/Vocational Nurse Training (LPN, LVN, Cert, Dipl, AAS)** *74 students enrolled* ● **Medical/Clinical Assistant** *30 students enrolled*

STUDENT SERVICES Academic or career counseling, employment services for current students, placement services for program completers, remedial services.

Ivy Tech Community College–Columbus

4475 Central Avenue, Columbus, IN 47203-1868
http://www.ivytech.edu/

CONTACT John Hogan, Chancellor
Telephone: 812-372-9925

GENERAL INFORMATION Public Institution. Founded 1963. **Accreditation:** Regional (NCA); dental assisting (ADA); medical assisting (AAMAE); surgical technology (ARCST). **Total program enrollment: 1444.**

PROGRAM(S) OFFERED
• **Accounting Technology/Technician and Bookkeeping** 5 *students enrolled* • **Business Administration and Management, General** 3 *students enrolled* • **Computer and Information Sciences, General** 1 *student enrolled* • **Dental Assisting/Assistant** 8 *students enrolled* • **Early Childhood Education and Teaching** 2 *students enrolled* • **Executive Assistant/Executive Secretary** 6 *students enrolled* • **Industrial Production Technologies/Technicians, Other** 8 *students enrolled* • **Licensed Practical/Vocational Nurse Training (LPN, LVN, Cert, Dipl, AAS)** 42 *students enrolled* • **Medical/Clinical Assistant** 8 *students enrolled*

STUDENT SERVICES Academic or career counseling, employment services for current students, placement services for program completers, remedial services.

Ivy Tech Community College–East Central

4301 South Cowan Road, PO Box 3100, Muncie, IN 47302-9448
http://www.ivytech.edu/

CONTACT Gail Chesterfield, Chancellor
Telephone: 765-289-2291

GENERAL INFORMATION Public Institution. Founded 1968. **Accreditation:** Regional (NCA); medical assisting (AAMAE); physical therapy assisting (APTA); surgical technology (ARCST). **Total program enrollment: 3454.**

PROGRAM(S) OFFERED
• **Accounting Technology/Technician and Bookkeeping** 6 *students enrolled* • **Automobile/Automotive Mechanics Technology/Technician** 5 *students enrolled* • **Business Administration and Management, General** 14 *students enrolled* • **Computer and Information Sciences, General** 15 *students enrolled* • **Construction Trades, Other** 8 *students enrolled* • **Dental Assisting/Assistant** 18 *students enrolled* • **Early Childhood Education and Teaching** 3 *students enrolled* • **Electrician** 1 *student enrolled* • **Executive Assistant/Executive Secretary** 7 *students enrolled* • **Industrial Production Technologies/Technicians, Other** 10 *students enrolled* • **Information Technology** 1 *student enrolled* • **Licensed Practical/Vocational Nurse Training (LPN, LVN, Cert, Dipl, AAS)** 65 *students enrolled* • **Medical/Clinical Assistant** 43 *students enrolled* • **Psychiatric/Mental Health Services Technician** 8 *students enrolled*

STUDENT SERVICES Academic or career counseling, employment services for current students, placement services for program completers, remedial services.

Ivy Tech Community College–Kokomo

1815 East Morgan St, PO Box 1373, Kokomo, IN 46903-1373
http://www.ivytech.edu/

CONTACT Steve Daily, Chancellor
Telephone: 765-459-0561

GENERAL INFORMATION Public Institution. Founded 1968. **Accreditation:** Regional (NCA); medical assisting (AAMAE). **Total program enrollment: 1570.**

PROGRAM(S) OFFERED
• **Accounting Technology/Technician and Bookkeeping** 7 *students enrolled* • **Automobile/Automotive Mechanics Technology/Technician** 5 *students enrolled* • **Business Administration and Management, General** 2 *students enrolled* • **Computer and Information Sciences, General** 5 *students enrolled* • **Construction Trades, Other** 8 *students enrolled* • **Dental Assisting/Assistant** 16 *students enrolled* • **Early Childhood Education and Teaching** 8 *students enrolled* • **Executive Assistant/Executive Secretary** 6 *students enrolled* • **Industrial Production Technologies/Technicians, Other** 3 *students enrolled* • **Information Technology**

3 *students enrolled* • **Licensed Practical/Vocational Nurse Training (LPN, LVN, Cert, Dipl, AAS)** 47 *students enrolled* • **Medical/Clinical Assistant** 12 *students enrolled* • **Occupational Safety and Health Technology/Technician**

STUDENT SERVICES Academic or career counseling, employment services for current students, placement services for program completers, remedial services.

Ivy Tech Community College–Lafayette

3101 South Creasy Lane, Lafayette, IN 47905-5266
http://www.ivytech.edu/

CONTACT Dr. David Bathe, Chancellor
Telephone: 765-269-5000

GENERAL INFORMATION Public Institution. Founded 1968. **Accreditation:** Regional (NCA); dental assisting (ADA); medical assisting (AAMAE); surgical technology (ARCST). **Total program enrollment: 3129.**

PROGRAM(S) OFFERED
• **Accounting Technology/Technician and Bookkeeping** 1 *student enrolled* • **Automobile/Automotive Mechanics Technology/Technician** 16 *students enrolled* • **Computer Programming, Other** 4 *students enrolled* • **Computer/Information Technology Services Administration and Management, Other** 7 *students enrolled* • **Dental Assisting/Assistant** 23 *students enrolled* • **Drafting and Design Technology/Technician, General** 14 *students enrolled* • **Electrician** 1 *student enrolled* • **Executive Assistant/Executive Secretary** 23 *students enrolled* • **Heating, Air Conditioning, Ventilation and Refrigeration Maintenance Technology/Technician (HAC, HACR, HVAC, HVACR)** 7 *students enrolled* • **Industrial Production Technologies/Technicians, Other** 14 *students enrolled* • **Licensed Practical/Vocational Nurse Training (LPN, LVN, Cert, Dipl, AAS)** 48 *students enrolled* • **Medical/Clinical Assistant** 47 *students enrolled* • **System Administration/Administrator** 1 *student enrolled* • **System, Networking, and LAN/WAN Management/Manager** 28 *students enrolled* • **Web/Multimedia Management and Webmaster** 2 *students enrolled*

STUDENT SERVICES Academic or career counseling, employment services for current students, placement services for program completers, remedial services.

Ivy Tech Community College–North Central

220 Dean Johnson Boulevard, South Bend, IN 46601
http://www.ivytech.edu/

CONTACT Virginia Calvin, Chancellor
Telephone: 574-289-7001

GENERAL INFORMATION Public Institution. Founded 1968. **Accreditation:** Regional (NCA); medical assisting (AAMAE); medical laboratory technology (NAACLS). **Total program enrollment: 2029.**

PROGRAM(S) OFFERED
• **Accounting Technology/Technician and Bookkeeping** 9 *students enrolled* • **Accounting and Related Services, Other** 6 *students enrolled* • **Automobile/Automotive Mechanics Technology/Technician** 17 *students enrolled* • **Business Administration and Management, General** 15 *students enrolled* • **Computer and Information Sciences, General** 2 *students enrolled* • **Computer/Information Technology Services Administration and Management, Other** 1 *student enrolled* • **Drafting and Design Technology/Technician, General** 3 *students enrolled* • **Early Childhood Education and Teaching** 1 *student enrolled* • **Executive Assistant/Executive Secretary** 1 *student enrolled* • **Industrial Production Technologies/Technicians, Other** 8 *students enrolled* • **Licensed Practical/Vocational Nurse Training (LPN, LVN, Cert, Dipl, AAS)** 73 *students enrolled* • **Machine Tool Technology/Machinist** 1 *student enrolled* • **Mason/Masonry** 1 *student enrolled* • **Medical/Clinical Assistant** 36 *students enrolled* • **Psychiatric/Mental Health Services Technician** 11 *students enrolled* • **System, Networking, and LAN/WAN Management/Manager** 2 *students enrolled*

STUDENT SERVICES Academic or career counseling, employment services for current students, placement services for program completers, remedial services.

Ivy Tech Community College–Northeast

3800 North Anthony Boulevard, Fort Wayne, IN 46805-1430
http://www.ivytech.edu/

CONTACT Mark Keen, Chancellor
Telephone: 260-482-9171

GENERAL INFORMATION Public Institution. Founded 1969. **Accreditation:** Regional (NCA); medical assisting (AAMAE). **Total program enrollment:** 3270.

PROGRAM(S) OFFERED
● **Accounting Technology/Technician and Bookkeeping** *10 students enrolled* ● **Accounting and Related Services, Other** *11 students enrolled* ● **Automobile/Automotive Mechanics Technology/Technician** *9 students enrolled* ● **Business Administration and Management, General** *56 students enrolled* ● **Computer and Information Sciences, General** *5 students enrolled* ● **Construction Trades, Other** *16 students enrolled* ● **Drafting and Design Technology/Technician, General** *8 students enrolled* ● **Early Childhood Education and Teaching** *3 students enrolled* ● **Electrician** *8 students enrolled* ● **Executive Assistant/Executive Secretary** *16 students enrolled* ● **Hospitality Administration/Management, Other** *10 students enrolled* ● **Industrial Production Technologies/Technicians, Other** *40 students enrolled* ● **Information Technology** *2 students enrolled* ● **Ironworking/Ironworker** *5 students enrolled* ● **Licensed Practical/Vocational Nurse Training (LPN, LVN, Cert, Dipl, AAS)** *88 students enrolled* ● **Mason/Masonry** *2 students enrolled* ● **Massage Therapy/Therapeutic Massage** *21 students enrolled* ● **Medical/Clinical Assistant** *61 students enrolled* ● **Pipefitting/Pipefitter and Sprinkler Fitter** *10 students enrolled* ● **Telecommunications Technology/Technician** *2 students enrolled* ● **Tool and Die Technology/Technician** *1 student enrolled* ● **Woodworking, Other** *1 student enrolled*

STUDENT SERVICES Academic or career counseling, employment services for current students, placement services for program completers, remedial services.

Ivy Tech Community College–Northwest

1440 East 35th Avenue, Gary, IN 46409-1499
http://www.ivytech.edu/

CONTACT J. Guadalupe Valtierra, Chancellor
Telephone: 219-981-1111

GENERAL INFORMATION Public Institution. Founded 1963. **Accreditation:** Regional (NCA); medical assisting (AAMAE); physical therapy assisting (APTA); surgical technology (ARCST). **Total program enrollment:** 2329.

PROGRAM(S) OFFERED
● **Accounting Technology/Technician and Bookkeeping** *7 students enrolled* ● **Automobile/Automotive Mechanics Technology/Technician** *3 students enrolled* ● **Business Administration and Management, General** *28 students enrolled* ● **Computer and Information Sciences, General** *2 students enrolled* ● **Construction Trades, Other** *3 students enrolled* ● **Drafting and Design Technology/Technician, General** *4 students enrolled* ● **Early Childhood Education and Teaching** *2 students enrolled* ● **Electrician** *5 students enrolled* ● **Hospitality Administration/Management, Other** *2 students enrolled* ● **Industrial Production Technologies/Technicians, Other** *9 students enrolled* ● **Licensed Practical/Vocational Nurse Training (LPN, LVN, Cert, Dipl, AAS)** *87 students enrolled* ● **Medical/Clinical Assistant** *1 student enrolled*

STUDENT SERVICES Academic or career counseling, employment services for current students, placement services for program completers, remedial services.

Ivy Tech Community College–Southeast

590 Ivy Tech Drive, PO Box 209, Madison, IN 47250-1883
http://www.ivytech.edu/

CONTACT James Helms, Chancellor
Telephone: 812-265-2580

GENERAL INFORMATION Public Institution. Founded 1963. **Accreditation:** Regional (NCA). **Total program enrollment:** 984.

PROGRAM(S) OFFERED
● **Accounting Technology/Technician and Bookkeeping** *3 students enrolled* ● **Business Administration and Management, General** *4 students enrolled* ● **Executive Assistant/Executive Secretary** *1 student enrolled* ● **Industrial Production Technologies/Technicians, Other** *1 student enrolled* ● **Licensed Practical/Vocational Nurse Training (LPN, LVN, Cert, Dipl, AAS)** *42 students enrolled* ● **Medical/Clinical Assistant** *24 students enrolled* ● **Psychiatric/Mental Health Services Technician** *2 students enrolled*

STUDENT SERVICES Academic or career counseling, employment services for current students, placement services for program completers, remedial services.

Ivy Tech Community College–Southern Indiana

8204 Highway 311, Sellersburg, IN 47172-1829
http://www.ivytech.edu/

CONTACT Rita Shourds, Chancellor
Telephone: 812-246-3301

GENERAL INFORMATION Public Institution. Founded 1968. **Accreditation:** Regional (NCA); medical assisting (AAMAE). **Total program enrollment:** 1455.

PROGRAM(S) OFFERED
● **Accounting Technology/Technician and Bookkeeping** *12 students enrolled* ● **Automobile/Automotive Mechanics Technology/Technician** *5 students enrolled* ● **Business Administration and Management, General** *4 students enrolled* ● **Drafting and Design Technology/Technician, General** *20 students enrolled* ● **Early Childhood Education and Teaching** *11 students enrolled* ● **Industrial Production Technologies/Technicians, Other** *33 students enrolled* ● **Licensed Practical/Vocational Nurse Training (LPN, LVN, Cert, Dipl, AAS)** *49 students enrolled* ● **Medical/Clinical Assistant** *34 students enrolled* ● **Psychiatric/Mental Health Services Technician** *4 students enrolled* ● **System, Networking, and LAN/WAN Management/Manager** *8 students enrolled*

STUDENT SERVICES Academic or career counseling, employment services for current students, placement services for program completers, remedial services.

Ivy Tech Community College–Southwest

3501 First Avenue, Evansville, IN 47710-3398
http://www.ivytech.edu/

CONTACT Daniel L. Schenk, Chancellor
Telephone: 812-426-2865

GENERAL INFORMATION Public Institution. Founded 1963. **Accreditation:** Regional (NCA); emergency medical services (JRCEMTP); medical assisting (AAMAE); surgical technology (ARCST). **Total program enrollment:** 2066.

PROGRAM(S) OFFERED
● **Accounting Technology/Technician and Bookkeeping** *2 students enrolled* ● **Accounting and Related Services, Other** *2 students enrolled* ● **Automobile/Automotive Mechanics Technology/Technician** *23 students enrolled* ● **Business Administration and Management, General** *5 students enrolled* ● **Early Childhood Education and Teaching** *15 students enrolled* ● **Executive Assistant/Executive Secretary** *17 students enrolled* ● **Industrial Production Technologies/Technicians, Other** *26 students enrolled* ● **Licensed Practical/Vocational Nurse Training (LPN, LVN, Cert, Dipl, AAS)** *32 students enrolled* ● **Mason/Masonry** *2 students enrolled* ● **Medical/Clinical Assistant** *22 students enrolled* ● **Painting/Painter and Wall Coverer** *1 student enrolled*

STUDENT SERVICES Academic or career counseling, employment services for current students, placement services for program completers, remedial services.

Ivy Tech Community College System

1 West 26th Street, 1, Indianapolis, IN 46208-4777
http://www.ivytech.edu/

CONTACT Thomas J. Snyder, President
Telephone: 317-921-4800

GENERAL INFORMATION Public Institution.

Ivy Tech Community College–Wabash Valley

7999 US Highway 41, South, Terre Haute, IN 47802
http://www.ivytech.edu/

CONTACT Jeff Pittman, Chancellor
Telephone: 812-299-1121

GENERAL INFORMATION Public Institution. Founded 1966. **Accreditation:** Regional (NCA); medical assisting (AAMAE); medical laboratory technology (NAACLS); radiologic technology: radiography (JRCERT); surgical technology (ARCST). **Total program enrollment:** 2421.

PROGRAM(S) OFFERED
● **Accounting Technology/Technician and Bookkeeping** 3 *students enrolled* ● **Automobile/Automotive Mechanics Technology/Technician** 5 *students enrolled* ● **Early Childhood Education and Teaching** 2 *students enrolled* ● **Executive Assistant/Executive Secretary** 4 *students enrolled* ● **Industrial Production Technologies/Technicians, Other** 5 *students enrolled* ● **Licensed Practical/Vocational Nurse Training (LPN, LVN, Cert, Dipl, AAS)** 62 *students enrolled* ● **Mason/Masonry** 1 *student enrolled* ● **Medical/Clinical Assistant** 47 *students enrolled*

STUDENT SERVICES Academic or career counseling, daycare for children of students, employment services for current students, placement services for program completers, remedial services.

Ivy Tech Community College–Whitewater

2325 Chester Boulevard, Richmond, IN 47374-1220
http://www.ivytech.edu/

CONTACT James Steck, Chancellor
Telephone: 765-966-2656

GENERAL INFORMATION Public Institution. Founded 1963. **Accreditation:** Regional (NCA); medical assisting (AAMAE). **Total program enrollment:** 974.

PROGRAM(S) OFFERED
● **Accounting Technology/Technician and Bookkeeping** 7 *students enrolled* ● **Accounting and Related Services, Other** 6 *students enrolled* ● **Automobile/Automotive Mechanics Technology/Technician** 1 *student enrolled* ● **Computer and Information Sciences, General** 6 *students enrolled* ● **Construction Trades, Other** 3 *students enrolled* ● **Executive Assistant/Executive Secretary** 13 *students enrolled* ● **Information Technology** 1 *student enrolled* ● **Licensed Practical/Vocational Nurse Training (LPN, LVN, Cert, Dipl, AAS)** 5 *students enrolled* ● **Medical/Clinical Assistant** 51 *students enrolled* ● **System Administration/Administrator** 1 *student enrolled* ● **Web/Multimedia Management and Webmaster** 1 *student enrolled*

STUDENT SERVICES Academic or career counseling, daycare for children of students, employment services for current students, placement services for program completers, remedial services.

J. Everett Light Career Center

1901 East 86 Street, Indianapolis, IN 46240
http://www.jelcc.com/

CONTACT James D. Mervilde, EdD, Superintendent
Telephone: 317-259-5265

GENERAL INFORMATION Public Institution. Founded 1972. **Total program enrollment:** 58. **Application fee:** $100.

PROGRAM(S) OFFERED
● **Licensed Practical/Vocational Nurse Training (LPN, LVN, Cert, Dipl, AAS)** 49 *students enrolled*

STUDENT SERVICES Academic or career counseling, daycare for children of students, employment services for current students, placement services for program completers, remedial services.

J. Michael Harrold Beauty Academy

2232 Wabash Avenue, Terre Haute, IN 47807
http://harroldbeautyacademy.com/

CONTACT Patty A. Harrold, President
Telephone: 812-232-8334

GENERAL INFORMATION Private Institution. **Total program enrollment:** 51. **Application fee:** $40.

PROGRAM(S) OFFERED
● **Cosmetology and Related Personal Grooming Arts, Other** ● **Cosmetology/Cosmetologist, General** 1500 *hrs./$10,460*

STUDENT SERVICES Academic or career counseling, placement services for program completers.

Kaplan College–Hammond Campus

7833 Indianapolis Boulevard, Hammond, IN 46324
http://www.kc-hammond.com

CONTACT Linda Yednak, Executive Director
Telephone: 219-844-0100

GENERAL INFORMATION Private Institution. Founded 1962. **Accreditation:** State accredited or approved. **Total program enrollment:** 273.

PROGRAM(S) OFFERED
● **Data Processing and Data Processing Technology/Technician** 13 *students enrolled* ● **Medical Administrative/Executive Assistant and Medical Secretary** 20 *students enrolled* ● **Medical/Clinical Assistant** 72 *students enrolled*

STUDENT SERVICES Academic or career counseling, employment services for current students, placement services for program completers.

Kaplan College–Merrillville Campus

3803 East Lincoln Highway, Merrillville, IN 46410
http://www.kc-merrillville.com

CONTACT Chris Artim, Executive Director
Telephone: 219-947-8400

GENERAL INFORMATION Private Institution. Founded 1968. **Accreditation:** State accredited or approved. **Total program enrollment:** 289.

PROGRAM(S) OFFERED
● **Accounting** ● **Clinical/Medical Laboratory Assistant** ● **Computer Systems Networking and Telecommunications** ● **Data Processing and Data Processing Technology/Technician** 10 *students enrolled* ● **Massage Therapy/Therapeutic Massage** 20 *students enrolled* ● **Medical Insurance Specialist/Medical Biller** 21 *students enrolled* ● **Medical/Clinical Assistant** 58 *students enrolled* ● **Web Page, Digital/Multimedia and Information Resources Design**

STUDENT SERVICES Academic or career counseling, employment services for current students, placement services for program completers.

Kaplan College–Northwest Indianapolis Campus

7302 Woodland Drive, Indianapolis, IN 46278
http://www.kc-indy.com

CONTACT Barri Shirk, Executive Director
Telephone: 317-299-6001

GENERAL INFORMATION Private Institution. **Accreditation:** Dental assisting (ADA); state accredited or approved. **Total program enrollment:** 1107. **Application fee:** $20.

PROGRAM(S) OFFERED
• **Business Administration, Management and Operations, Other** • **Dental Assisting/Assistant** *1580 hrs./$24,430* • **Massage Therapy/Therapeutic Massage** *720 hrs./$13,790* • **Medical Administrative/Executive Assistant and Medical Secretary** *740 hrs./$13,480* • **Medical/Clinical Assistant** *800 hrs./ $14,560*

STUDENT SERVICES Academic or career counseling, employment services for current students, placement services for program completers.

Knox Beauty College

320 East Culver Road, Knox, IN 46534

CONTACT Loretta Rowe, Chief Executive Officer
Telephone: 574-772-5500

GENERAL INFORMATION Private Institution. Founded 1981. **Total program enrollment:** 22.

PROGRAM(S) OFFERED
• **Cosmetology, Barber/Styling, and Nail Instructor** *1000 hrs./$2660*
• **Cosmetology/Cosmetologist, General** *1500 hrs./$4730*

STUDENT SERVICES Placement services for program completers.

Lafayette Beauty Academy

833 Ferry Street, Lafayette, IN 47901-1149
http://lafayettebeautyacademy.com/

CONTACT Kim Briles, Chief Executive
Telephone: 765-742-0068

GENERAL INFORMATION Private Institution. Founded 1965. **Total program enrollment:** 41. **Application fee:** $100.

PROGRAM(S) OFFERED
• **Aesthetician/Esthetician and Skin Care Specialist** *700 hrs./$5715*
• **Cosmetology, Barber/Styling, and Nail Instructor** *1000 hrs./$3190*
• **Cosmetology/Cosmetologist, General** *1500 hrs./$6995* • **Electrolysis/ Electrology and Electrolysis Technician** *300 hrs./$5715* • **Nail Technician/ Specialist and Manicurist** *450 hrs./$5715*

Lincoln Technical Institute

7225 Winton Drive, Indianapolis, IN 46268
http://www.lincolnedu.com/

CONTACT Mary Jo Greco, President
Telephone: 317-632-5553

GENERAL INFORMATION Private Institution. Founded 1946. **Accreditation:** State accredited or approved. **Total program enrollment:** 1492.

PROGRAM(S) OFFERED
• **Autobody/Collision and Repair Technology/Technician** *1560 hrs./$25,360*
• **Automobile/Automotive Mechanics Technology/Technician** *1920 hrs./$27,370*
• **Diesel Mechanics Technology/Technician** *1920 hrs./$27,370* • **Electrical/ Electronics Equipment Installation and Repair, General** *207 students enrolled*
• **Electrical/Electronics Maintenance and Repair Technology, Other** *1080 hrs./ $17,650*

STUDENT SERVICES Academic or career counseling, employment services for current students, placement services for program completers, remedial services.

Marion Community Schools Tucker Area Vocational Tech Center

107 South Pennsylvania Avenue, Marion, IN 46952
http://www.mcslink.net/

CONTACT Jeffrey A. Hendrix, EdD, Superintendent
Telephone: 765-664-9091

GENERAL INFORMATION Private Institution. **Total program enrollment:** 74.

PROGRAM(S) OFFERED
• **Licensed Practical/Vocational Nurse Training (LPN, LVN, Cert, Dipl, AAS)** *1472 hrs./$7350*

STUDENT SERVICES Remedial services.

Masters of Cosmetology College

1732 Bluffton Road, Fort Wayne, IN 46809
http://www.mastersofcosmetology.com/

CONTACT Kaydean Blackman, President
Telephone: 260-747-6667

GENERAL INFORMATION Private Institution. Founded 1981. **Total program enrollment:** 97.

PROGRAM(S) OFFERED
• **Aesthetician/Esthetician and Skin Care Specialist** *900 hrs./$10,200*
• **Cosmetology and Related Personal Grooming Arts, Other** *45 students enrolled* • **Cosmetology, Barber/Styling, and Nail Instructor** *1000 hrs./$3000*
• **Cosmetology/Cosmetologist, General** *1800 hrs./$14,080* • **Nail Technician/ Specialist and Manicurist** *450 hrs./$2400*

MedTech College

6612 East 75th Street, Suite 300, Indianapolis, IN 46250-2865
http://www.medtechcollege.com/

CONTACT Joseph H. Davis, President/CEO
Telephone: 317-845-0100

GENERAL INFORMATION Private Institution. **Total program enrollment:** 462. **Application fee:** $50.

PROGRAM(S) OFFERED
• **Massage Therapy/Therapeutic Massage** *41 students enrolled* • **Medical Insurance Coding Specialist/Coder** *32 students enrolled* • **Medical/Clinical Assistant** *18 students enrolled*

STUDENT SERVICES Academic or career counseling, employment services for current students, placement services for program completers.

Merrillville Beauty College

48 West 67th Place, Merrillville, IN 46410
http://merrillvillebeautycollege.com/

CONTACT Cyril C. Kennedy, President
Telephone: 219-769-2232

GENERAL INFORMATION Private Institution. **Total program enrollment:** 24. **Application fee:** $25.

PROGRAM(S) OFFERED
• **Barbering/Barber** *1500 hrs./$9650* • **Cosmetology, Barber/Styling, and Nail Instructor** *1000 hrs./$4150* • **Cosmetology/Cosmetologist, General** *1500 hrs./ $9710* • **Nail Technician/Specialist and Manicurist** *600 hrs./$2450*

STUDENT SERVICES Academic or career counseling, placement services for program completers.

Moler Hairstyling College

4391 W. 5th Avenue, Gary, IN 46406

GENERAL INFORMATION Private Institution. **Total program enrollment:** 17.

PROGRAM(S) OFFERED
• **Barbering/Barber** *1500 hrs./$9895* • **Cosmetology/Cosmetologist, General** *1500 hrs./$10,645*

Ottawa University–Jeffersonville

287 Quarter Master Court, Jeffersonville, IN 47130
http://www.ottawa.edu/

CONTACT Lonnie Cooper, Campus Executive Officer
Telephone: 812-280-7271

GENERAL INFORMATION Private Institution (Affiliated with American Baptist Churches in the U.S.A.). **Total program enrollment:** 1. **Application fee:** $50.

STUDENT SERVICES Academic or career counseling.

PJ's College of Cosmetology

1414 Blackiston Mill Road, Clarksville, IN 47129
http://gotopjs.com/

CONTACT Judith Stewart, President
Telephone: 317-846-8999 Ext. 320

GENERAL INFORMATION Private Institution. **Total program enrollment:** 66.

PROGRAM(S) OFFERED
• **Cosmetology and Related Personal Grooming Arts, Other** *450 hrs./$6095*
• **Cosmetology, Barber/Styling, and Nail Instructor** *1000 hrs./$10,088*
• **Cosmetology/Cosmetologist, General** *700 hrs./$9358* • **Nail Technician/ Specialist and Manicurist** *2 students enrolled*

STUDENT SERVICES Academic or career counseling, employment services for current students, placement services for program completers.

PJ's College of Cosmetology

115 North Ninth Street, Richmond, IN 47374
http://gotopjs.com/

CONTACT Judith Stewart, President/Owner
Telephone: 317-846-8999 Ext. 320

GENERAL INFORMATION Private Institution. **Total program enrollment:** 20.

PROGRAM(S) OFFERED
• **Cosmetology, Barber/Styling, and Nail Instructor** *1000 hrs./$10,088*
• **Cosmetology/Cosmetologist, General** *450 hrs./$6095* • **Nail Technician/ Specialist and Manicurist**

STUDENT SERVICES Academic or career counseling, employment services for current students, placement services for program completers.

Purdue University

West Lafayette, IN 47907
http://www.purdue.edu/

CONTACT France A. Cordova, President
Telephone: 765-494-4600

GENERAL INFORMATION Public Institution. Founded 1869. **Accreditation:** Regional (NCA); athletic training (JRCAT); audiology (ASHA); counseling (ACA); engineering technology (ABET/TAC); engineering-related programs (ABET/RAC); forestry (SAF); home economics (AAFCS); interior design: professional (CIDA); speech-language pathology (ASHA); theater (NAST). **Total program enrollment:** 36761. **Application fee:** $30.

PROGRAM(S) OFFERED
• **Accounting** *14 students enrolled* • **Architectural Engineering Technology/ Technician** *2 students enrolled* • **Business Administration and Management, General** *100 students enrolled* • **Electrical, Electronic and Communications Engineering Technology/Technician** *1 student enrolled* • **Operations Management and Supervision** *39 students enrolled*

STUDENT SERVICES Academic or career counseling, daycare for children of students, employment services for current students, placement services for program completers.

Purdue University Calumet

2200 169th Street, Hammond, IN 46323-2094
http://www.calumet.purdue.edu/

CONTACT Howard Cohen, Chancellor
Telephone: 219-989-2400

GENERAL INFORMATION Public Institution. Founded 1951. **Accreditation:** Regional (NCA); engineering technology (ABET/TAC). **Total program enrollment:** 5736.

PROGRAM(S) OFFERED
• **Architectural Engineering Technology/Technician** *2 students enrolled* • **Child Care and Support Services Management** *1 student enrolled* • **Civil Engineering Technology/Technician** *1 student enrolled* • **Computer and Information Sciences and Support Services, Other** *1 student enrolled* • **Electrical, Electronic and Communications Engineering Technology/Technician** *5 students enrolled* • **Hospitality Administration/Management, Other** *2 students enrolled* • **Hotel/ Motel Administration/Management** *1 student enrolled* • **Industrial Technology/ Technician** *14 students enrolled* • **Mechanical Drafting and Mechanical Drafting CAD/CADD** *9 students enrolled* • **Nursing—Registered Nurse Training (RN, ASN, BSN, MSN)** *3 students enrolled* • **Operations Management and Supervision** *21 students enrolled* • **Robotics Technology/Technician** *10 students enrolled*

STUDENT SERVICES Academic or career counseling, daycare for children of students, employment services for current students, placement services for program completers, remedial services.

Purdue University North Central

1401 South US Highway 421, Westville, IN 46391-9542
http://www.pnc.edu/

CONTACT Dr. James B. Dworkin, Chancellor
Telephone: 219-785-5200

GENERAL INFORMATION Public Institution. Founded 1967. **Accreditation:** Regional (NCA); engineering technology (ABET/TAC). **Total program enrollment:** 2596.

PROGRAM(S) OFFERED
• **Communication Studies/Speech Communication and Rhetoric** *1 student enrolled* • **Management Information Systems and Services, Other** *27 students enrolled* • **Operations Management and Supervision** *56 students enrolled* • **Quality Control Technology/Technician** *1 student enrolled*

STUDENT SERVICES Academic or career counseling, daycare for children of students, employment services for current students, placement services for program completers, remedial services.

Ravenscroft Beauty College

6110 Stellhorn Road, Fort Wayne, IN 46815

CONTACT Sid McQueary, Executive Director
Telephone: 260-486-8868

GENERAL INFORMATION Private Institution. **Total program enrollment:** 137. **Application fee:** $100.

PROGRAM(S) OFFERED
• Aesthetician/Esthetician and Skin Care Specialist *700 hrs./$7300*
• Barbering/Barber *1500 hrs./$8925* • Cosmetology/Cosmetologist, General *1500 hrs./$10,350* • Education, Other *1000 hrs./$3750* • Nail Technician/Specialist and Manicurist *600 hrs./$3300*

STUDENT SERVICES Academic or career counseling, placement services for program completers.

Regency Beauty Institute

8811 Hardegan Street, Indianapolis, IN 46227
http://www.regencybeauty.com/

CONTACT J. Hayes Batson, President CEO
Telephone: 800-787-6456

GENERAL INFORMATION Private Institution. **Total program enrollment:** 90. **Application fee:** $100.

PROGRAM(S) OFFERED
• Cosmetology/Cosmetologist, General *1500 hrs./$16,011*

STUDENT SERVICES Academic or career counseling, placement services for program completers.

Regency Beauty Institute–Indianapolis

8252 Rockville Road, Indianapolis, IN 46214

GENERAL INFORMATION Private Institution. **Total program enrollment:** 55. **Application fee:** $100.

PROGRAM(S) OFFERED
• Cosmetology/Cosmetologist, General *1500 hrs./$16,011*

STUDENT SERVICES Academic or career counseling, placement services for program completers.

Roger's Academy of Hair Design, Inc.

2903 Mount Vernon Avenue, Evansville, IN 47712
http://rogershairacademy.com/

CONTACT Mary Hayden, Director
Telephone: 812-429-0110 Ext. 2

GENERAL INFORMATION Private Institution. Founded 1982. **Total program enrollment:** 124. **Application fee:** $100.

PROGRAM(S) OFFERED
• Cosmetology/Cosmetologist, General *1500 hrs./$10,000*

STUDENT SERVICES Academic or career counseling, employment services for current students, placement services for program completers.

Ruade's School of Beauty Culture

5317 Coldwater Road, Ft. Wayne, IN 46825-5444

CONTACT C. L. Craft, CEO
Telephone: 260-483-2466

GENERAL INFORMATION Private Institution. **Total program enrollment:** 115. **Application fee:** $100.

PROGRAM(S) OFFERED
• Cosmetology, Barber/Styling, and Nail Instructor *1000 hrs./$8385*
• Cosmetology/Cosmetologist, General *1500 hrs./$10,849* • Nail Technician/Specialist and Manicurist *450 hrs./$2400*

Rudae's School of Beauty Culture

208 West Jefferson Street, Kokomo, IN 46901-4516

CONTACT C. L. Craft, CEO
Telephone: 800-466-9744

GENERAL INFORMATION Private Institution. **Total program enrollment:** 56. **Application fee:** $100.

PROGRAM(S) OFFERED
• Aesthetician/Esthetician and Skin Care Specialist *900 hrs./$6903*
• Cosmetology, Barber/Styling, and Nail Instructor *1000 hrs./$8385*
• Cosmetology/Cosmetologist, General *1500 hrs./$10,849* • Nail Technician/Specialist and Manicurist *450 hrs./$2400*

Saint Joseph's College

U.S. Highway 231, PO Box 890, Rensselaer, IN 47978
http://www.saintjoe.edu/

CONTACT Ernest Mills, President
Telephone: 219-866-6000

GENERAL INFORMATION Private Institution. Founded 1889. **Accreditation:** Regional (NCA). **Total program enrollment:** 1017. **Application fee:** $25.

PROGRAM(S) OFFERED
• Pastoral Studies/Counseling *1 student enrolled* • Religious/Sacred Music

STUDENT SERVICES Academic or career counseling, employment services for current students, placement services for program completers, remedial services.

Success Schools LLC

8101 Polo Club Drive, Merrillville, IN 46410
http://www.successbarberschool.com

CONTACT Nancy Barsic, President
Telephone: 219-736-9999

GENERAL INFORMATION Private Institution. **Total program enrollment:** 86. **Application fee:** $100.

PROGRAM(S) OFFERED
• Barbering/Barber *1500 hrs./$12,000* • Cosmetology, Barber/Styling, and Nail Instructor *1000 hrs./$7500*

STUDENT SERVICES Academic or career counseling, employment services for current students, placement services for program completers.

TechSkills—Indianapolis

8555 North River Road, Suite 160, Indianapolis, IN 46240

CONTACT Jennifer Walters
Telephone: 317-251-4600

GENERAL INFORMATION Private Institution.

PROGRAM(S) OFFERED
• Accounting Technology/Technician and Bookkeeping • Business Administration and Management, General *2 students enrolled* • Business/Office Automation/Technology/Data Entry *1 student enrolled* • Computer Engineering, General • Computer Programming, Vendor/Product Certification • Computer Software Engineering • Computer Systems Networking and Telecommunications *60 hrs./$1425* • Computer and Information Sciences and Support Services, Other *150 hrs./$1890* • Computer and Information Systems Security • Computer/Information Technology Services Administration and Management, Other *19 students enrolled* • Data Modeling/Warehousing and Database Administration • Health Information/Medical Records Administration/Administrator *5 students enrolled* • Information Technology *360 hrs.* • Medical Insurance Coding Specialist/Coder *9 students enrolled* • Medical Insurance Specialist/Medical Biller • Medical Office Management/Administration *360 hrs./$4700* • Medical Transcription/Transcriptionist *2 students enrolled* • Pharmacy Technician/Assistant • System Administration/

TechSkills—Indianapolis (continued)

Administrator *555 hrs./$7850* ● **System, Networking, and LAN/WAN Management/Manager** *90 hrs./$1430* ● **Web Page, Digital/Multimedia and Information Resources Design** *2 students enrolled*

STUDENT SERVICES Academic or career counseling, placement services for program completers.

University of Phoenix–Northwest Indiana

359 East 81st Avenue, Merrillville, IN 46410
http://www.phoenix.edu/

CONTACT William Pepicello, PhD, President
Telephone: 219-794-1500

GENERAL INFORMATION Private Institution.

STUDENT SERVICES Academic or career counseling, remedial services.

University of Saint Francis

2701 Spring Street, Fort Wayne, IN 46808-3994
http://www.sf.edu/

CONTACT M. Elise Kriss, President
Telephone: 219-434-3100

GENERAL INFORMATION Private Institution. Founded 1890. **Accreditation:** Regional (NCA); physical therapy assisting (APTA); radiologic technology: radiography (JRCERT); surgical technology (ARCST). **Total program enrollment:** 1577. **Application fee:** $20.

STUDENT SERVICES Academic or career counseling, employment services for current students, placement services for program completers, remedial services.

University of Southern Indiana

8600 University Boulevard, Evansville, IN 47712-3590
http://www.usi.edu/

CONTACT H. Ray Hoops, President
Telephone: 812-464-8600

GENERAL INFORMATION Public Institution. Founded 1965. **Accreditation:** Regional (NCA); dental assisting (ADA); dental hygiene (ADA); engineering technology (ABET/TAC); radiologic technology: radiography (JRCERT). **Total program enrollment:** 7830. **Application fee:** $25.

PROGRAM(S) OFFERED
● **Dental Assisting/Assistant** *19 students enrolled*

STUDENT SERVICES Academic or career counseling, daycare for children of students, employment services for current students, placement services for program completers, remedial services.

Valparaiso University

1700 Chapel Drive, Valparaiso, IN 46383
http://www.valpo.edu/

CONTACT Mark A. Heckler, President
Telephone: 219-464-5000

GENERAL INFORMATION Private Institution (Affiliated with Lutheran Church). Founded 1859. **Accreditation:** Regional (NCA); music (NASM). **Total program enrollment:** 3547. **Application fee:** $30.

STUDENT SERVICES Academic or career counseling, employment services for current students, placement services for program completers, remedial services.

Vincennes Beauty College

12 South Second Street, Vincennes, IN 47591

CONTACT Pam Garrison, Administrator
Telephone: 812-882-1086

GENERAL INFORMATION Private Institution. Founded 1963. **Total program enrollment:** 53.

PROGRAM(S) OFFERED
● **Cosmetology, Barber/Styling, and Nail Instructor** *1000 hrs./$5650*
● **Cosmetology/Cosmetologist, General** *1500 hrs./$9425*

STUDENT SERVICES Academic or career counseling, placement services for program completers.

Vincennes University

1002 North First Street, Vincennes, IN 47591-5202
http://www.vinu.edu/

CONTACT Dr. Richard Helton, President
Telephone: 812-888-8888

GENERAL INFORMATION Public Institution. Founded 1801. **Accreditation:** Regional (NCA); art and design (NASAD); funeral service (ABFSE); health information technology (AHIMA); physical therapy assisting (APTA); practical nursing (NLN); surgical technology (ARCST); theater (NAST). **Total program enrollment:** 5314. **Application fee:** $20.

PROGRAM(S) OFFERED
● **Accounting and Business/Management** *7 students enrolled* ● **Agricultural Business and Management, General** *9 students enrolled* ● **Autobody/Collision and Repair Technology/Technician** ● **Avionics Maintenance Technology/Technician** ● **Banking and Financial Support Services** ● **Building/Property Maintenance and Management** *1 student enrolled* ● **Business Administration and Management, General** *1 student enrolled* ● **Business/Office Automation/Technology/Data Entry** *1 student enrolled* ● **Child Care Provider/Assistant** ● **Computer Systems Networking and Telecommunications** *1 student enrolled* ● **Computer and Information Sciences and Support Services, Other** ● **Computer and Information Sciences, General** ● **Construction Trades, General** ● **Criminal Justice/Police Science** ● **Culinary Arts/Chef Training** *4 students enrolled* ● **Dance, Other** ● **Data Processing and Data Processing Technology/Technician** ● **Dental Hygiene/Hygienist** ● **Electrical, Electronic and Communications Engineering Technology/Technician** ● **Emergency Medical Technology/Technician (EMT Paramedic)** *2 students enrolled* ● **Entrepreneurship/Entrepreneurial Studies** *1 student enrolled* ● **Fire Science/Firefighting** ● **Food Preparation/Professional Cooking/Kitchen Assistant** *1 student enrolled* ● **Furniture Design and Manufacturing** ● **General Merchandising, Sales, and Related Marketing Operations, Other** *1 student enrolled* ● **General Office Occupations and Clerical Services** ● **Health Information/Medical Records Technology/Technician** ● **Human Resources Management/Personnel Administration, General** *3 students enrolled* ● **Human Services, General** *2 students enrolled* ● **Licensed Practical/Vocational Nurse Training (LPN, LVN, Cert, Dipl, AAS)** ● **Massage Therapy/Therapeutic Massage** *14 students enrolled* ● **Medical Insurance Coding Specialist/Coder** *6 students enrolled* ● **Medical Office Assistant/Specialist** ● **Medical Transcription/Transcriptionist** ● **Pharmacy Technician/Assistant** *13 students enrolled* ● **Precision Metal Working, Other** ● **Recording Arts Technology/Technician** *1 student enrolled* ● **Substance Abuse/Addiction Counseling** *2 students enrolled* ● **Surgical Technology/Technologist** *1 student enrolled* ● **Truck and Bus Driver/Commercial Vehicle Operation** *31 students enrolled* ● **Web Page, Digital/Multimedia and Information Resources Design** *4 students enrolled* ● **Welding Technology/Welder** *16 students enrolled*

STUDENT SERVICES Academic or career counseling, employment services for current students, placement services for program completers, remedial services.

West Michigan College of Barbering and Beauty

3026 Lovers Lane, Kalamazoo, IN 49001-3702

CONTACT Linnea M. Barden, Owner
Telephone: 269-381-4424

GENERAL INFORMATION Private Institution. **Total program enrollment:** 39. **Application fee:** $100.

PROGRAM(S) OFFERED
• **Barbering/Barber** *2000 hrs./$9360* • **Cosmetology, Barber/Styling, and Nail Instructor** *1000 hrs./$1800* • **Cosmetology/Cosmetologist, General** *400 hrs./ $1100*

STUDENT SERVICES Academic or career counseling, placement services for program completers, remedial services.

KENTUCKY

Ashland Community and Technical College

1400 College Drive, Ashland, KY 41101-3683
http://www.ashland.kctcs.edu/

CONTACT Dr. Gregory D. Adkins, President/CEO
Telephone: 606-326-2000

GENERAL INFORMATION Public Institution. Founded 1937. **Accreditation:** Regional (SACS/CC); respiratory therapy technology (CoARC); surgical technology (ARCST); state accredited or approved. **Total program enrollment:** 1808.

PROGRAM(S) OFFERED
• **Automobile/Automotive Mechanics Technology/Technician** *8 students enrolled* • **Business Administration and Management, General** *14 students enrolled* • **Carpentry/Carpenter** *12 students enrolled* • **Child Care Provider/Assistant** *42 students enrolled* • **Computer and Information Sciences, General** *9 students enrolled* • **Cosmetology/Cosmetologist, General** *11 students enrolled* • **Culinary Arts/Chef Training** *15 students enrolled* • **Diesel Mechanics Technology/ Technician** *36 students enrolled* • **Drafting and Design Technology/Technician, General** *9 students enrolled* • **Electrician** *127 students enrolled* • **Executive Assistant/Executive Secretary** *116 students enrolled* • **Heating, Air Conditioning, Ventilation and Refrigeration Maintenance Technology/Technician (HAC, HACR, HVAC, HVACR)** *16 students enrolled* • **Industrial Mechanics and Maintenance Technology** *29 students enrolled* • **Licensed Practical/Vocational Nurse Training (LPN, LVN, Cert, Dipl, AAS)** *6 students enrolled* • **Machine Shop Technology/Assistant** *17 students enrolled* • **Pharmacy Technician/ Assistant** *1 student enrolled* • **Surgical Technology/Technologist** *2 students enrolled* • **Welding Technology/Welder** *142 students enrolled*

STUDENT SERVICES Academic or career counseling, daycare for children of students, employment services for current students, placement services for program completers, remedial services.

ATA Career Education

10180 Linn Station Road, Suite A200, Louisville, KY 40223
http://www.atai.com/

CONTACT Donald A. Jones
Telephone: 502-371-8330 Ext. 363

GENERAL INFORMATION Private Institution. **Total program enrollment:** 320. **Application fee:** $25.

PROGRAM(S) OFFERED
• **Clinical/Medical Laboratory Science and Allied Professions, Other** • **Dental Assisting/Assistant** *52 students enrolled* • **Medical Insurance Coding Specialist/ Coder** *128 students enrolled* • **Medical Reception/Receptionist** *49 students enrolled* • **Nursing, Other** • **System Administration/Administrator** *14 students enrolled*

STUDENT SERVICES Academic or career counseling, employment services for current students, placement services for program completers, remedial services.

Barrett and Company School of Hair Design

973 Kimberly Square, Nicholasville, KY 40356

CONTACT Jamie B. Lovern, Director
Telephone: 859-885-9136

GENERAL INFORMATION Private Institution. Founded 1984. **Total program enrollment:** 87.

PROGRAM(S) OFFERED
• **Cosmetology and Related Personal Grooming Arts, Other** *1000 hrs./$6600* • **Cosmetology, Barber/Styling, and Nail Instructor** • **Cosmetology/ Cosmetologist, General** *1800 hrs./$9535* • **Nail Technician/Specialist and Manicurist** *600 hrs./$3600*

STUDENT SERVICES Academic or career counseling.

Beckfield College

16 Spiral Drive, Florence, KY 41042
http://www.beckfield.edu/

CONTACT Dr. Ronald A. Swanson, President
Telephone: 859-371-9393

GENERAL INFORMATION Private Institution. Founded 1984. **Accreditation:** State accredited or approved. **Total program enrollment:** 441. **Application fee:** $20.

PROGRAM(S) OFFERED
• **Legal Assistant/Paralegal** *3 students enrolled* • **Medical Office Assistant/ Specialist** *13 students enrolled*

STUDENT SERVICES Academic or career counseling, employment services for current students, placement services for program completers, remedial services.

Bellefonte Academy of Beauty

420 Belfont Street, Russell, KY 41169

CONTACT William C. Stull, Jr., School Director/Owner
Telephone: 606-833-5446

GENERAL INFORMATION Private Institution. **Total program enrollment:** 111.

PROGRAM(S) OFFERED
• **Cosmetology, Barber/Styling, and Nail Instructor** *1000 hrs./$6600* • **Cosmetology/Cosmetologist, General** *1800 hrs./$12,300* • **Nail Technician/ Specialist and Manicurist** *600 hrs./$3900*

STUDENT SERVICES Academic or career counseling, placement services for program completers.

Big Sandy Community and Technical College

One Bert T. Combs Drive, Prestonsburg, KY 41653-1815
http://www.bigsandy.kctcs.edu/

CONTACT Dr. George D. Edwards, President/CEO
Telephone: 606-886-3863 Ext. 0

GENERAL INFORMATION Public Institution. Founded 1964. **Accreditation:** Regional (SACS/CC); dental hygiene (ADA); state accredited or approved. **Total program enrollment:** 1929.

PROGRAM(S) OFFERED

• Autobody/Collision and Repair Technology/Technician *5 students enrolled* • Automobile/Automotive Mechanics Technology/Technician *49 students enrolled* • Business Administration and Management, General *63 students enrolled* • Carpentry/Carpenter *6 students enrolled* • Communications Technology/Technician *1 student enrolled* • Computer and Information Sciences, General *19 students enrolled* • Cosmetology/Cosmetologist, General *2 students enrolled* • Diesel Mechanics Technology/Technician *59 students enrolled* • Drafting and Design Technology/Technician, General *7 students enrolled* • Electrician *10 students enrolled* • Engineering Technology, General *35 students enrolled* • Executive Assistant/Executive Secretary *9 students enrolled* • Heating, Air Conditioning, Ventilation and Refrigeration Maintenance Technology/Technician (HAC, HACR, HVAC, HVACR) *4 students enrolled* • Industrial Mechanics and Maintenance Technology *18 students enrolled* • Licensed Practical/Vocational Nurse Training (LPN, LVN, Cert, Dipl, AAS) *32 students enrolled* • Mason/Masonry *2 students enrolled* • Medical Administrative/Executive Assistant and Medical Secretary *84 students enrolled* • Respiratory Care Therapy/Therapist *19 students enrolled* • Survey Technology/Surveying *9 students enrolled* • Welding Technology/Welder *2 students enrolled*

STUDENT SERVICES Academic or career counseling, remedial services.

Bluegrass Community and Technical College

470 Cooper Drive, Lexington, KY 40506-0235
http://www.bluegrass.kctcs.edu/

CONTACT Dr. Augusta Julian, President/CEO
Telephone: 859-246-2400

GENERAL INFORMATION Public Institution. Founded 1965. **Accreditation:** Regional (SACS/CC); dental hygiene (ADA); dental laboratory technology (ADA). **Total program enrollment:** 5892.

PROGRAM(S) OFFERED

• Aesthetician/Esthetician and Skin Care Specialist *15 students enrolled* • Applied Horticulture/Horticultural Operations, General *14 students enrolled* • Autobody/Collision and Repair Technology/Technician *28 students enrolled* • Automobile/Automotive Mechanics Technology/Technician *66 students enrolled* • Carpentry/Carpenter *138 students enrolled* • Cartography *7 students enrolled* • Child Care Provider/Assistant *13 students enrolled* • Cinematography and Film/Video Production *24 students enrolled* • Clinical/Medical Laboratory Technician *14 students enrolled* • Computer and Information Sciences, General *48 students enrolled* • Cosmetology/Cosmetologist, General *6 students enrolled* • Data Processing and Data Processing Technology/Technician *5 students enrolled* • Dental Hygiene/Hygienist *18 students enrolled* • Dental Laboratory Technology/Technician *10 students enrolled* • Drafting and Design Technology/Technician, General *6 students enrolled* • Electrician *217 students enrolled* • Engineering Technology, General *209 students enrolled* • Environmental Engineering Technology/Environmental Technology *3 students enrolled* • Equestrian/Equine Studies *8 students enrolled* • Executive Assistant/Executive Secretary *55 students enrolled* • Fire Science/Firefighting *3 students enrolled* • Heating, Air Conditioning, Ventilation and Refrigeration Maintenance Technology/Technician (HAC, HACR, HVAC, HVACR) *5 students enrolled* • Industrial Mechanics and Maintenance Technology *33 students enrolled* • Licensed Practical/Vocational Nurse Training (LPN, LVN, Cert, Dipl, AAS) *175 students enrolled* • Machine Shop Technology/Assistant *62 students enrolled* • Mason/Masonry *38 students enrolled* • Medical Administrative/Executive Assistant and Medical Secretary *29 students enrolled* • Medical/Clinical Assistant *36 students enrolled* • Respiratory Care Therapy/Therapist *5 students enrolled* • Securities Services Administration/Management *7 students enrolled* • Surgical Technology/Technologist *20 students enrolled* • Teacher Assistant/Aide *2 students enrolled* • Welding Technology/Welder *3 students enrolled*

STUDENT SERVICES Academic or career counseling, employment services for current students, placement services for program completers, remedial services.

Bowling Green Technical College

1845 Loop Drive, Bowling Green, KY 42101
http://www.bowlinggreen.kctcs.edu/

CONTACT Dr. Nathan L. Hodges, CEO/President
Telephone: 270-901-1000

GENERAL INFORMATION Public Institution. Founded 1938. **Accreditation:** Respiratory therapy technology (CoARC); state accredited or approved. **Total program enrollment:** 909.

PROGRAM(S) OFFERED

• Autobody/Collision and Repair Technology/Technician *27 students enrolled* • Automobile/Automotive Mechanics Technology/Technician *46 students enrolled* • Communications Technology/Technician *1 student enrolled* • Computer Technology/Computer Systems Technology *3 students enrolled* • Computer and Information Sciences, General *93 students enrolled* • Culinary Arts/Chef Training *17 students enrolled* • Diagnostic Medical Sonography/Sonographer and Ultrasound Technician *7 students enrolled* • Drafting and Design Technology/Technician, General *7 students enrolled* • Electrician *7 students enrolled* • Electromechanical and Instrumentation and Maintenance Technologies/Technicians, Other *9 students enrolled* • Engineering Technology, General *222 students enrolled* • Executive Assistant/Executive Secretary *146 students enrolled* • Health Unit Coordinator/Ward Clerk *9 students enrolled* • Heating, Air Conditioning, Ventilation and Refrigeration Maintenance Technology/Technician (HAC, HACR, HVAC, HVACR) *5 students enrolled* • Industrial Mechanics and Maintenance Technology *18 students enrolled* • Licensed Practical/Vocational Nurse Training (LPN, LVN, Cert, Dipl, AAS) *46 students enrolled* • Machine Shop Technology/Assistant *12 students enrolled* • Medical Administrative/Executive Assistant and Medical Secretary *83 students enrolled* • Respiratory Care Therapy/Therapist *2 students enrolled* • Surgical Technology/Technologist *13 students enrolled* • Welding Technology/Welder *41 students enrolled*

STUDENT SERVICES Academic or career counseling, placement services for program completers, remedial services.

Brighton Center's Center for Employment Training

601 Washington Street, Suite 140, Newport, KY 41071

CONTACT Robert Brewster, Executive Director
Telephone: 859-491-8303 Ext. 2200

GENERAL INFORMATION Private Institution. **Total program enrollment:** 76.

PROGRAM(S) OFFERED

• Business Operations Support and Secretarial Services, Other *1020 hrs./$8107* • Medical/Clinical Assistant *1070 hrs./$8507*

STUDENT SERVICES Academic or career counseling, employment services for current students, placement services for program completers, remedial services.

Brown Mackie College–Hopkinsville

4001 Ft. Cambell Boulevard, Hopkinsville, KY 42240
http://www.brownmackie.edu/Hopkinsville/

CONTACT Lesley Wilbert, Registrar
Telephone: 270-886-1302

GENERAL INFORMATION Private Institution. **Accreditation:** State accredited or approved. **Total program enrollment:** 268.

PROGRAM(S) OFFERED

• Accounting *1 student enrolled* • Business Administration and Management, General • Computer Programming/Programmer, General • Computer Software and Media Applications, Other • Criminal Justice/Law Enforcement Administration *2 students enrolled* • Legal Assistant/Paralegal *2 students enrolled* • Medical Insurance Coding Specialist/Coder *20 students enrolled* • Medical/Clinical Assistant *26 students enrolled*

STUDENT SERVICES Academic or career counseling, employment services for current students, placement services for program completers, remedial services.

Brown Mackie College–Louisville

3605 Fern Valley Road, Louisville, KY 40219
http://www.brownmackie.edu/Louisville/

CONTACT Elyane Harney, President
Telephone: 502-968-7191

GENERAL INFORMATION Private Institution. Founded 1972. **Accreditation:** State accredited or approved. **Total program enrollment:** 906.

PROGRAM(S) OFFERED
• Computer Systems Networking and Telecommunications • Electrical, Electronics and Communications Engineering • Medical/Clinical Assistant

STUDENT SERVICES Academic or career counseling, employment services for current students, placement services for program completers, remedial services.

Brown Mackie College–Northern Kentucky

309 Buttermilk Pike, Fort Mitchell, KY 41017-2191
http://www.brownmackie.edu/NorthernKentucky/

CONTACT Rick Lemmel, President
Telephone: 859-341-5627

GENERAL INFORMATION Private Institution. Founded 1927. **Accreditation:** State accredited or approved. **Total program enrollment:** 352.

PROGRAM(S) OFFERED
• Health Services/Allied Health/Health Sciences, General *1 student enrolled*
• Nursing, Other *58 students enrolled*

STUDENT SERVICES Academic or career counseling, employment services for current students, placement services for program completers, remedial services.

Campbellsville University

1 University Drive, Campbellsville, KY 42718-2799
http://www.campbellsville.edu/

CONTACT Michael V. Carter, President
Telephone: 270-789-5000 Ext. 5000

GENERAL INFORMATION Private Institution (Affiliated with Kentucky Baptist Convention). Founded 1906. **Accreditation:** Regional (SACS/CC); music (NASM). **Total program enrollment:** 1581. **Application fee:** $20.

STUDENT SERVICES Academic or career counseling, employment services for current students, placement services for program completers, remedial services.

Clear Creek Baptist Bible College

300 Clear Creek Road, Pineville, KY 40977-9754
http://www.ccbbc.edu/

CONTACT Donald S. Fox, President
Telephone: 606-337-3196

GENERAL INFORMATION Private Institution. Founded 1926. **Accreditation:** Regional (SACS/CC); state accredited or approved. **Total program enrollment:** 116. **Application fee:** $40.

PROGRAM(S) OFFERED
• Theology/Theological Studies

STUDENT SERVICES Academic or career counseling, daycare for children of students, employment services for current students, placement services for program completers, remedial services.

Collins School of Cosmetology

111 West Chester Avenue, Middlesboro, KY 40965

CONTACT Reta Mc Daniel, Owner
Telephone: 606-248-3602

GENERAL INFORMATION Private Institution. **Total program enrollment:** 26. **Application fee:** $100.

PROGRAM(S) OFFERED
• Aesthetician/Esthetician and Skin Care Specialist • Cosmetology, Barber/Styling, and Nail Instructor • Cosmetology/Cosmetologist, General *1800 hrs./$8700* • Nail Technician/Specialist and Manicurist *600 hrs./$2800*

Daymar College

4400 Breckenridge Lane, Suite 415, Louisville, KY 40218
http://www.daymarcollege.edu/

CONTACT Mark A. Gabis, President
Telephone: 502-495-1040

GENERAL INFORMATION Private Institution. Founded 2001. **Accreditation:** State accredited or approved. **Total program enrollment:** 422.

PROGRAM(S) OFFERED
• Business/Office Automation/Technology/Data Entry • Computer and Information Sciences, General • Graphic Design • Health Information/Medical Records Technology/Technician • Medical Insurance Coding Specialist/Coder *7 students enrolled* • Medical Office Assistant/Specialist *4 students enrolled* • Medical Transcription/Transcriptionist *3 students enrolled*

STUDENT SERVICES Academic or career counseling, employment services for current students, placement services for program completers, remedial services.

Daymar College

76 Carothers Road, Newport, KY 41071
http://www.daymarcollege.edu/

CONTACT Mark A. Gabis, President
Telephone: 859-291-0800

GENERAL INFORMATION Private Institution. **Total program enrollment:** 76.

PROGRAM(S) OFFERED
• Medical Insurance Coding Specialist/Coder • Medical Office Assistant/Specialist *3 students enrolled*

STUDENT SERVICES Academic or career counseling, employment services for current students, placement services for program completers.

Daymar College

3361 Buckland Square, Owensboro, KY 42301
http://www.daymarcollege.edu/

CONTACT Mark A. Gabis, President
Telephone: 270-926-4040

GENERAL INFORMATION Private Institution. Founded 1963. **Accreditation:** State accredited or approved. **Total program enrollment:** 247.

PROGRAM(S) OFFERED
• Medical Insurance Specialist/Medical Biller • Medical Office Assistant/Specialist *5 students enrolled* • Office Management and Supervision

STUDENT SERVICES Academic or career counseling, employment services for current students, placement services for program completers.

Daymar College

509 South 30th Street, Paducah, KY 42001
http://www.daymarcollege.edu/

CONTACT Mark A. Gabis, President
Telephone: 270-444-9676 Ext. 203

GENERAL INFORMATION Private Institution. **Total program enrollment:** 104. **Application fee:** $75.

PROGRAM(S) OFFERED
● **Medical/Clinical Assistant**

STUDENT SERVICES Academic or career counseling, employment services for current students, placement services for program completers.

Daymar College

509 South 30th Street, PO Box 8252, Paducah, KY 42001
http://www.daymarcollege.edu/college/paducah

CONTACT Mark Gabis, President
Telephone: 270-444-9676

GENERAL INFORMATION Private Institution. Founded 1964. **Accreditation:** State accredited or approved. **Total program enrollment:** 137.

PROGRAM(S) OFFERED
● **Business Administration and Management, General** ● **Business/Office Automation/Technology/Data Entry** *88 hrs./$26,335* ● **Computer Engineering Technology/Technician** ● **Electrical and Electronic Engineering Technologies/Technicians, Other** ● **Electrical, Electronic and Communications Engineering Technology/Technician** *96 hrs./$15,354* ● **General Office Occupations and Clerical Services** ● **Medical Insurance Specialist/Medical Biller** *88 hrs./$26,335* ● **Pharmacy Technician/Assistant** *88 hrs./$26,335* ● **Real Estate**

STUDENT SERVICES Academic or career counseling, employment services for current students, placement services for program completers.

Donta School of Beauty Culture

515 West Oak Street, Louisville, KY 40203
http://www.beautyschooldirectory.com/

CONTACT Dale Jones, Owner
Telephone: 801-302-8801 Ext. 1021

GENERAL INFORMATION Private Institution. **Total program enrollment:** 84. **Application fee:** $100.

PROGRAM(S) OFFERED
● **Cosmetology/Cosmetologist, General** *1800 hrs./$14,800*

STUDENT SERVICES Academic or career counseling, employment services for current students, placement services for program completers.

Draughons Junior College

2421 Fitzgerald Industrial Drive, Bowling Green, KY 42101
http://www.draughons.edu/

CONTACT Melva Hale, Director
Telephone: 270-843-6750

GENERAL INFORMATION Private Institution. Founded 1989. **Accreditation:** State accredited or approved. **Total program enrollment:** 300.

PROGRAM(S) OFFERED
● **Accounting** *1 student enrolled* ● **Cardiovascular Technology/Technologist** *8 students enrolled* ● **Computer Science** ● **E-Commerce/Electronic Commerce** ● **Health Information/Medical Records Technology/Technician** *3 students enrolled* ● **Medical/Clinical Assistant** *10 students enrolled*

STUDENT SERVICES Academic or career counseling, employment services for current students, placement services for program completers, remedial services.

Eastern Kentucky University

521 Lancaster Avenue, Richmond, KY 40475-3102
http://www.eku.edu/

CONTACT Doug Whitlock, President
Telephone: 859-622-1000

GENERAL INFORMATION Public Institution. Founded 1906. **Accreditation:** Regional (SACS/CC); athletic training (JRCAT); computer science (ABET/CSAC); counseling (ACA); cytotechnology (ASC); dietetics: postbaccalaureate internship (ADtA/CAADE); emergency medical services (JRCEMTP); health information administration (AHIMA); health information technology (AHIMA); home economics (AAFCS); medical assisting (AAMAE); medical laboratory technology (NAACLS); medical technology (NAACLS); music (NASM); recreation and parks (NRPA); speech-language pathology (ASHA). **Total program enrollment:** 11761. **Application fee:** $30.

PROGRAM(S) OFFERED
● **Real Estate**

STUDENT SERVICES Academic or career counseling, employment services for current students, placement services for program completers, remedial services.

Elizabethtown Community and Technical College

620 College Street Road, Elizabethtown, KY 42701
http://www.elizabethtown.kctcs.edu/

CONTACT Dr. Thelma White, CEO/President
Telephone: 270-769-2371

GENERAL INFORMATION Public Institution. Founded 1966. **Accreditation:** State accredited or approved. **Total program enrollment:** 2675.

PROGRAM(S) OFFERED
● **Automobile/Automotive Mechanics Technology/Technician** *5 students enrolled* ● **Business Administration and Management, General** *199 students enrolled* ● **Carpentry/Carpenter** *25 students enrolled* ● **Child Care Provider/Assistant** *104 students enrolled* ● **Computer and Information Sciences, General** *82 students enrolled* ● **Culinary Arts/Chef Training** *3 students enrolled* ● **Diesel Mechanics Technology/Technician** *99 students enrolled* ● **Drafting and Design Technology/Technician, General** *20 students enrolled* ● **Electrician** *174 students enrolled* ● **Emergency Medical Technology/Technician (EMT Paramedic)** *38 students enrolled* ● **Engineering Technology, General** *69 students enrolled* ● **Executive Assistant/Executive Secretary** *157 students enrolled* ● **Fire Science/Firefighting** *11 students enrolled* ● **Industrial Mechanics and Maintenance Technology** *18 students enrolled* ● **Licensed Practical/Vocational Nurse Training (LPN, LVN, Cert, Dipl, AAS)** *263 students enrolled* ● **Machine Shop Technology/Assistant** *21 students enrolled* ● **Medical Administrative/Executive Assistant and Medical Secretary** *100 students enrolled* ● **Plumbing Technology/Plumber** *33 students enrolled* ● **Quality Control Technology/Technician** *11 students enrolled* ● **Social Work** *12 students enrolled* ● **Welding Technology/Welder** *82 students enrolled*

STUDENT SERVICES Academic or career counseling, remedial services.

Employment Solutions

1165 Centre Parkway, Suite 120, Lexington, KY 40517
http://www.employmentsolutionsinc.org/

CONTACT Rick Christman, CEO
Telephone: 859-272-5225

GENERAL INFORMATION Private Institution. **Total program enrollment:** 214.

PROGRAM(S) OFFERED
● **Building/Property Maintenance and Management** *9 students enrolled* ● **Cooking and Related Culinary Arts, General** *29 hrs./$6500* ● **General Office Occupations and Clerical Services** *28 hrs./$6700* ● **Mason/Masonry** *36 hrs./$6500*

STUDENT SERVICES Academic or career counseling, daycare for children of students, placement services for program completers, remedial services.

Ezell's Beauty School

504 Maple Street, Murray, KY 42071

CONTACT Brenda J. Brown, Owner, Administrator
Telephone: 270-753-4723

GENERAL INFORMATION Private Institution. **Total program enrollment:** 37. **Application fee:** $100.

PROGRAM(S) OFFERED
● **Cosmetology, Barber/Styling, and Nail Instructor** *1000 hrs./$5500* ● **Cosmetology/Cosmetologist, General** *1800 hrs./$10,050* ● **Nail Technician/Specialist and Manicurist** *600 hrs./$6500*

STUDENT SERVICES Academic or career counseling.

Galen Health Institutes

612 South 4th Street, Suite 400, Louisville, KY 40202
http://www.galened.com/

CONTACT Mark Vogt, President
Telephone: 502-410-6200

GENERAL INFORMATION Private Institution. Founded 1990. **Total program enrollment:** 883. **Application fee:** $100.

PROGRAM(S) OFFERED
● **Licensed Practical/Vocational Nurse Training (LPN, LVN, Cert, Dipl, AAS)** *1440 hrs./$16,420* ● **Nursing—Registered Nurse Training (RN, ASN, BSN, MSN)** *80 hrs./$20,935*

STUDENT SERVICES Academic or career counseling, placement services for program completers.

Gateway Community and Technical College

1025 Amsterdam Road, Covington, KY 41011
http://www.gateway.kctcs.edu/

CONTACT Dr. G. Edward Hughes, President
Telephone: 859-441-4500

GENERAL INFORMATION Public Institution. Founded 1961. **Accreditation:** State accredited or approved. **Total program enrollment:** 1158.

PROGRAM(S) OFFERED
● **Allied Health Diagnostic, Intervention, and Treatment Professions, Other** *3 students enrolled* ● **Autobody/Collision and Repair Technology/Technician** *6 students enrolled* ● **Automobile/Automotive Mechanics Technology/Technician** *17 students enrolled* ● **Business Administration and Management, General** *56 students enrolled* ● **Carpentry/Carpenter** *1 student enrolled* ● **Child Care Provider/Assistant** *38 students enrolled* ● **Communications Technology/Technician** *1 student enrolled* ● **Computer and Information Sciences, General** *17 students enrolled* ● **Cosmetology/Cosmetologist, General** *11 students enrolled* ● **Electrician** *5 students enrolled* ● **Executive Assistant/Executive Secretary** *3 students enrolled* ● **Health Information/Medical Records Technology/Technician** *1 student enrolled* ● **Health Unit Coordinator/Ward Clerk** *18 students enrolled* ● **Heating, Air Conditioning, Ventilation and Refrigeration Maintenance Technology/Technician (HAC, HACR, HVAC, HVACR)** *3 students enrolled* ● **Industrial Mechanics and Maintenance Technology** *9 students enrolled* ● **Licensed Practical/Vocational Nurse Training (LPN, LVN, Cert, Dipl, AAS)** *221 students enrolled* ● **Machine Shop Technology/Assistant** *6 students enrolled* ● **Medical Administrative/Executive Assistant and Medical Secretary** *1 student enrolled* ● **Medical/Clinical Assistant** *2 students enrolled*

STUDENT SERVICES Academic or career counseling, employment services for current students, placement services for program completers, remedial services.

The Hair Design School

7285 Turfway Road, Florence, KY 41042
http://hairdesignschool.com/

CONTACT Michael Bouman, President/COO
Telephone: 502-491-0077

GENERAL INFORMATION Private Institution. Founded 1972. **Total program enrollment:** 98. **Application fee:** $100.

PROGRAM(S) OFFERED
● **Aesthetician/Esthetician and Skin Care Specialist** ● **Cosmetology, Barber/Styling, and Nail Instructor** ● **Cosmetology/Cosmetologist, General** *1800 hrs./$12,230* ● **Nail Technician/Specialist and Manicurist** *9 students enrolled*

STUDENT SERVICES Academic or career counseling, placement services for program completers.

The Hair Design School

1049 Bardstown Road, Louisville, KY 40204
http://hairdesignschool.com/

CONTACT Michael Bouman, President/COO
Telephone: 502-491-0077

GENERAL INFORMATION Private Institution. Founded 1987. **Total program enrollment:** 85. **Application fee:** $100.

PROGRAM(S) OFFERED
● **Cosmetology, Barber/Styling, and Nail Instructor** *1 student enrolled* ● **Cosmetology/Cosmetologist, General** *1800 hrs./$12,230* ● **Nail Technician/Specialist and Manicurist** *600 hrs./$2898*

STUDENT SERVICES Academic or career counseling, placement services for program completers.

The Hair Design School

151 Chenoweth Lane, Louisville, KY 40207
http://hairdesignschool.com/

CONTACT Michael Bouman, President/COO
Telephone: 502-491-0077

GENERAL INFORMATION Private Institution. Founded 1965. **Total program enrollment:** 90. **Application fee:** $100.

PROGRAM(S) OFFERED
● **Aesthetician/Esthetician and Skin Care Specialist** ● **Cosmetology, Barber/Styling, and Nail Instructor** ● **Cosmetology/Cosmetologist, General** *1800 hrs./$12,230* ● **Nail Technician/Specialist and Manicurist**

STUDENT SERVICES Academic or career counseling, placement services for program completers.

The Hair Design School

3968 Park Drive, Louisville, KY 40216
http://hairdesignschool.com/

CONTACT Michael Bouman, President/COO
Telephone: 502-491-0077

GENERAL INFORMATION Private Institution. Founded 1972. **Total program enrollment:** 93. **Application fee:** $100.

PROGRAM(S) OFFERED
● **Cosmetology, Barber/Styling, and Nail Instructor** *2 students enrolled* ● **Cosmetology/Cosmetologist, General** *1800 hrs./$12,230* ● **Nail Technician/Specialist and Manicurist**

STUDENT SERVICES Academic or career counseling, placement services for program completers.

The Hair Design School

4160 Bardstown Road, Louisville, KY 40218
http://hairdesignschool.com/

CONTACT Michael Bouman, President/COO
Telephone: 502-499-0070

GENERAL INFORMATION Private Institution. Founded 1972. **Total program enrollment:** 170. **Application fee:** $100.

PROGRAM(S) OFFERED
• **Aesthetician/Esthetician and Skin Care Specialist** *1000 hrs./$6600* • **Cosmetology, Barber/Styling, and Nail Instructor** *2 students enrolled* • **Cosmetology/Cosmetologist, General** *1800 hrs./$12,230* • **Nail Technician/Specialist and Manicurist** *600 hrs./$2898*

STUDENT SERVICES Academic or career counseling, placement services for program completers.

The Hair Design School

640 Knox Boulevard, Radcliff, KY 40160
http://hairdesignschool.com/

CONTACT Michael Bouman, President/COO
Telephone: 270-765-3374

GENERAL INFORMATION Private Institution. **Total program enrollment:** 127. **Application fee:** $100.

PROGRAM(S) OFFERED
• **Aesthetician/Esthetician and Skin Care Specialist** *1000 hrs./$6600* • **Cosmetology, Barber/Styling, and Nail Instructor** • **Cosmetology/Cosmetologist, General** *1800 hrs./$12,230* • **Nail Technician/Specialist and Manicurist** *5 students enrolled*

STUDENT SERVICES Academic or career counseling, placement services for program completers.

Hazard Community and Technical College

1 Community College Drive, Hazard, KY 41701-2403
http://www.hazard.kctcs.edu/

CONTACT Dr. Allen F. Goben, President/CEO
Telephone: 606-436-5721 Ext. 73503

GENERAL INFORMATION Public Institution. Founded 1968. **Accreditation:** Regional (SACS/CC); medical laboratory technology (NAACLS); physical therapy assisting (APTA); radiologic technology: radiography (JRCERT). **Total program enrollment:** 1466.

PROGRAM(S) OFFERED
• **Autobody/Collision and Repair Technology/Technician** *17 students enrolled* • **Automobile/Automotive Mechanics Technology/Technician** *40 students enrolled* • **Business Administration and Management, General** *70 students enrolled* • **Carpentry/Carpenter** *27 students enrolled* • **Child Care Provider/Assistant** *38 students enrolled* • **Computer and Information Sciences, General** *6 students enrolled* • **Construction/Heavy Equipment/Earthmoving Equipment Operation** *9 students enrolled* • **Cosmetology/Cosmetologist, General** *11 students enrolled* • **Crafts/Craft Design, Folk Art and Artisanry** *1 student enrolled* • **Diesel Mechanics Technology/Technician** *76 students enrolled* • **Drafting and Design Technology/Technician, General** *50 students enrolled* • **Electrician** *35 students enrolled* • **Executive Assistant/Executive Secretary** *1 student enrolled* • **Fire Science/Firefighting** *2 students enrolled* • **Heating, Air Conditioning, Ventilation and Refrigeration Maintenance Technology/Technician (HAC, HACR, HVAC, HVACR)** *5 students enrolled* • **Industrial Mechanics and Maintenance Technology** *2 students enrolled* • **Licensed Practical/Vocational Nurse Training (LPN, LVN, Cert, Dipl, AAS)** *119 students enrolled* • **Medical Administrative/Executive Assistant and Medical Secretary** *11 students enrolled* • **Survey Technology/Surveying** *25 students enrolled* • **Welding Technology/Welder** *15 students enrolled*

STUDENT SERVICES Academic or career counseling, employment services for current students, remedial services.

Head's West Kentucky Beauty School

Briarwood Shopping Center, Madisonville, KY 42431

CONTACT Pat Wilson, Chief Administrator
Telephone: 270-825-3019

GENERAL INFORMATION Private Institution. Founded 1986. **Total program enrollment:** 22.

PROGRAM(S) OFFERED
• **Cosmetology, Barber/Styling, and Nail Instructor** *1000 hrs./$2800* • **Cosmetology/Cosmetologist, General** *1800 hrs./$9400* • **Nail Technician/Specialist and Manicurist** *600 hrs./$2550* • **Trade and Industrial Teacher Education**

Henderson Community College

2660 South Green Street, Henderson, KY 42420-4623
http://www.henderson.kctcs.edu/

CONTACT Dr. Patrick Lake, President
Telephone: 270-827-1867

GENERAL INFORMATION Public Institution. Founded 1963. **Accreditation:** Regional (SACS/CC); dental hygiene (ADA); medical laboratory technology (NAACLS). **Total program enrollment:** 647.

PROGRAM(S) OFFERED
• **Agricultural Production Operations, General** *4 students enrolled* • **Child Care Provider/Assistant** *1 student enrolled* • **Clinical/Medical Laboratory Technician** *18 students enrolled* • **Computer and Information Sciences, General** *12 students enrolled* • **Engineering Technology, General** *36 students enrolled* • **Industrial Mechanics and Maintenance Technology** *6 students enrolled* • **Medical/Clinical Assistant** *24 students enrolled*

STUDENT SERVICES Academic or career counseling, daycare for children of students, employment services for current students, placement services for program completers, remedial services.

Hopkinsville Community College

PO Box 2100, Hopkinsville, KY 42241-2100
http://www.hopcc.kctcs.edu/

CONTACT Dr. James E. Selbe, President
Telephone: 270-707-3700

GENERAL INFORMATION Public Institution. Founded 1965. **Accreditation:** Regional (SACS/CC). **Total program enrollment:** 1517.

PROGRAM(S) OFFERED
• **Agricultural Production Operations, General** *4 students enrolled* • **Business Administration and Management, General** *72 students enrolled* • **Child Care Provider/Assistant** *96 students enrolled* • **Computer and Information Sciences, General** *14 students enrolled* • **Drafting and Design Technology/Technician, General** *30 students enrolled* • **Electrician** *2 students enrolled* • **Engineering Technology, General** *34 students enrolled* • **Executive Assistant/Executive Secretary** *96 students enrolled* • **Industrial Mechanics and Maintenance Technology** *9 students enrolled* • **Licensed Practical/Vocational Nurse Training (LPN, LVN, Cert, Dipl, AAS)** *20 students enrolled* • **Machine Shop Technology/Assistant** *19 students enrolled*

STUDENT SERVICES Academic or career counseling, employment services for current students, placement services for program completers, remedial services.

Interactive Learning Systems

11 Spiral Drive, Suite 8, Florence, KY 41042
http://www.ict-ils.edu/

CONTACT Elmer R. Smith, President
Telephone: 859-282-8989

GENERAL INFORMATION Private Institution. Founded 1980. **Total program enrollment:** 53. **Application fee:** $50.

PROGRAM(S) OFFERED

• Accounting and Related Services, Other *1 student enrolled* • Administrative Assistant and Secretarial Science, General • Computer Programming/Programmer, General • Computer and Information Sciences, General *10 students enrolled* • Medical Insurance Coding Specialist/Coder *6 students enrolled*

STUDENT SERVICES Academic or career counseling, employment services for current students, placement services for program completers, remedial services.

J & M Academy of Cosmetology

110A Brighton Park Boulevard, Frankfort, KY 40601

CONTACT V. Michelle Whitaker, Director
Telephone: 502-695-9006

GENERAL INFORMATION Private Institution. Founded 1997. **Total program enrollment:** 14. **Application fee:** $100.

PROGRAM(S) OFFERED

• Cosmetology, Barber/Styling, and Nail Instructor *1000 hrs./$3300* • Cosmetology/Cosmetologist, General *1800 hrs./$8920* • Nail Technician/Specialist and Manicurist *600 hrs./$3000*

Jefferson Community and Technical College

109 East Broadway, Louisville, KY 40202-2005
http://www.jctc.kctcs.edu/

CONTACT Dr. Anthony Newberry, President and CEO
Telephone: 502-213-4000

GENERAL INFORMATION Public Institution. Founded 1968. **Accreditation:** Regional (SACS/CC); physical therapy assisting (APTA). **Total program enrollment:** 5128.

PROGRAM(S) OFFERED

• Accounting Technology/Technician and Bookkeeping *95 students enrolled* • Aircraft Powerplant Technology/Technician *30 students enrolled* • Applied Horticulture/Horticultural Operations, General *83 students enrolled* • Autobody/Collision and Repair Technology/Technician *13 students enrolled* • Automobile/Automotive Mechanics Technology/Technician *299 students enrolled* • Business Administration and Management, General *96 students enrolled* • Cabinetmaking and Millwork/Millwright *1 student enrolled* • Carpentry/Carpenter *170 students enrolled* • Child Care Provider/Assistant *213 students enrolled* • Clinical/Medical Laboratory Technician *2 students enrolled* • Communications Technology/Technician *12 students enrolled* • Computer and Information Sciences, General *55 students enrolled* • Cosmetology/Cosmetologist, General *9 students enrolled* • Culinary Arts/Chef Training *30 students enrolled* • Electrician *95 students enrolled* • Electromechanical Technology/Electromechanical Engineering Technology *5 students enrolled* • Emergency Medical Technology/Technician (EMT Paramedic) *4 students enrolled* • Engineering Technology, General *80 students enrolled* • Executive Assistant/Executive Secretary *109 students enrolled* • Health Unit Coordinator/Ward Clerk *22 students enrolled* • Heating, Air Conditioning, Ventilation and Refrigeration Maintenance Technology/Technician (HAC, HACR, HVAC, HVACR) *34 students enrolled* • Industrial Mechanics and Maintenance Technology *6 students enrolled* • Licensed Practical/Vocational Nurse Training (LPN, LVN, Cert, Dipl, AAS) *273 students enrolled* • Machine Shop Technology/Assistant *35 students enrolled* • Mason/Masonry *30 students enrolled* • Medical/Clinical Assistant *22 students enrolled* • Plumbing Technology/Plumber *35 students enrolled* • Radiologic Technology/Science—Radiographer *1 student enrolled* • Real Estate *25 students enrolled* • Respiratory Care Therapy/Therapist *1 student enrolled* • Small Engine Mechanics and Repair Technology/Technician *63 students enrolled* • Surgical Technology/Technologist *10 students enrolled* • Teacher Assistant/Aide *1 student enrolled* • Upholstery/Upholsterer *46 students enrolled* • Welding Technology/Welder *88 students enrolled*

STUDENT SERVICES Academic or career counseling, daycare for children of students, employment services for current students, placement services for program completers, remedial services.

Jenny Lea Academy of Cosmetology

114 North Cumberland Avenue, Harlan, KY 40831

CONTACT Virginia Lewis, President
Telephone: 606-573-4276

GENERAL INFORMATION Private Institution. Founded 1980. **Total program enrollment:** 14. **Application fee:** $100.

PROGRAM(S) OFFERED

• Cosmetology, Barber/Styling, and Nail Instructor *1000 hrs./$4450* • Cosmetology/Cosmetologist, General *1800 hrs./$9350* • Nail Technician/Specialist and Manicurist *600 hrs./$4050*

Jenny Lea Academy of Cosmetology

74 Parkway Plaza Loop, Whitesburg, KY 41858

CONTACT Virginia Lewis, President
Telephone: 606-573-4276

GENERAL INFORMATION Private Institution. Founded 1984. **Total program enrollment:** 13. **Application fee:** $100.

PROGRAM(S) OFFERED

• Cosmetology, Barber/Styling, and Nail Instructor *1000 hrs./$4450* • Cosmetology/Cosmetologist, General *1800 hrs./$9350*

Kaufman's Beauty School

701 East High Street, Lexington, KY 40502
http://kaufmaneducation.com/

CONTACT Leslie Foster, Owner
Telephone: 859-266-5531

GENERAL INFORMATION Private Institution. Founded 1959. **Total program enrollment:** 109.

PROGRAM(S) OFFERED

• Cosmetology, Barber/Styling, and Nail Instructor *1000 hrs./$5990* • Cosmetology/Cosmetologist, General *1800 hrs./$12,190* • Nail Technician/Specialist and Manicurist

STUDENT SERVICES Placement services for program completers.

Kentucky Community and Technical College System

300 North Main Street, Versailles, KY 40383
http://www.state.ky.us/agencies/kctcs/

CONTACT Dr. Michael B. McCall, President
Telephone: 859-256-3100

GENERAL INFORMATION Public Institution.

Lexington Beauty College

90 Southport Drive, Lexington, KY 40503
http://lexingtonbeautycollege.com/

CONTACT Ann Halloran, President
Telephone: 859-252-7647

GENERAL INFORMATION Private Institution. Founded 1967. **Total program enrollment:** 24.

Lexington Beauty College (continued)

PROGRAM(S) OFFERED
● **Aesthetician/Esthetician and Skin Care Specialist** *1000 hrs./$7600*
● **Cosmetology, Barber/Styling, and Nail Instructor** *1000 hrs./$8000*
● **Cosmetology/Cosmetologist, General** *1800 hrs./$9913* ● **Nail Technician/Specialist and Manicurist** *600 hrs./$3695*

STUDENT SERVICES Academic or career counseling, employment services for current students, placement services for program completers.

Lexington Healing Arts Academy

272 Southland Drive, Lexington, KY 40503
http://www.lexingtonhealingarts.com

CONTACT Bill Booker, Executive Director
Telephone: 859-252-5656

GENERAL INFORMATION Private Institution. **Application fee:** $50.

PROGRAM(S) OFFERED
● **Massage Therapy/Therapeutic Massage** *650 hrs.* ● **Yoga Teacher Training/Yoga Therapy** *200 hrs./$2500*

STUDENT SERVICES Academic or career counseling, placement services for program completers, remedial services.

Madisonville Community College

2000 College Drive, Madisonville, KY 42431-9185
http://www.madcc.kctcs.edu/

CONTACT Dr. Judith Rhoads, President
Telephone: 270-821-2250

GENERAL INFORMATION Public Institution. Founded 1968. **Accreditation:** Regional (SACS/CC); physical therapy assisting (APTA). **Total program enrollment:** 1690.

PROGRAM(S) OFFERED
● **Business Administration and Management, General** *22 students enrolled* ● **Carpentry/Carpenter** *41 students enrolled* ● **Child Care Provider/Assistant** *32 students enrolled* ● **Clinical/Medical Laboratory Technician** *20 students enrolled* ● **Computer and Information Sciences, General** *2 students enrolled* ● **Electrician** *1 student enrolled* ● **Engineering Technology, General** *1 student enrolled* ● **Heating, Air Conditioning, Ventilation and Refrigeration Maintenance Technology/Technician (HAC, HACR, HVAC, HVACR)** *15 students enrolled* ● **Industrial Mechanics and Maintenance Technology** *9 students enrolled* ● **Licensed Practical/Vocational Nurse Training (LPN, LVN, Cert, Dipl, AAS)** *234 students enrolled* ● **Machine Shop Technology/Assistant** *6 students enrolled* ● **Mason/Masonry** *28 students enrolled* ● **Medical Administrative/Executive Assistant and Medical Secretary** *41 students enrolled* ● **Medical Radiologic Technology/Science—Radiation Therapist** *2 students enrolled* ● **Mining Technology/Technician** *10 students enrolled* ● **Surgical Technology/Technologist** *23 students enrolled* ● **Welding Technology/Welder** *14 students enrolled*

STUDENT SERVICES Academic or career counseling, employment services for current students, placement services for program completers, remedial services.

Maysville Community and Technical College

1755 US 68, Maysville, KY 41056
http://www.maycc.kctcs.net/

CONTACT Dr. Edward Story, President
Telephone: 606-759-7141 Ext. 0

GENERAL INFORMATION Public Institution. Founded 1967. **Accreditation:** Regional (SACS/CC); respiratory therapy technology (CoARC). **Total program enrollment:** 1332.

PROGRAM(S) OFFERED
● **Applied Horticulture/Horticultural Operations, General** *5 students enrolled* ● **Automobile/Automotive Mechanics Technology/Technician** *57 students enrolled* ● **Business Administration and Management, General** *138 students enrolled* ● **Carpentry/Carpenter** *46 students enrolled* ● **Child Care Provider/**

Assistant *16 students enrolled* ● **Computer and Information Sciences, General** *18 students enrolled* ● **Diesel Mechanics Technology/Technician** *13 students enrolled* ● **Electrician** *33 students enrolled* ● **Electromechanical Technology/Electromechanical Engineering Technology** *1 student enrolled* ● **Energy Management and Systems Technology/Technician** *5 students enrolled* ● **Engineering Technology, General** *58 students enrolled* ● **Executive Assistant/Executive Secretary** *58 students enrolled* ● **Heating, Air Conditioning, Ventilation and Refrigeration Maintenance Technology/Technician (HAC, HACR, HVAC, HVACR)** *15 students enrolled* ● **Industrial Mechanics and Maintenance Technology** *3 students enrolled* ● **Licensed Practical/Vocational Nurse Training (LPN, LVN, Cert, Dipl, AAS)** *157 students enrolled* ● **Machine Shop Technology/Assistant** *3 students enrolled* ● **Mason/Masonry** *5 students enrolled* ● **Medical Administrative/Executive Assistant and Medical Secretary** *10 students enrolled* ● **Medical/Clinical Assistant** *38 students enrolled* ● **Nurse/Nursing Assistant/Aide and Patient Care Assistant** *6 students enrolled* ● **Plumbing Technology/Plumber** *73 students enrolled* ● **Real Estate** *1 student enrolled* ● **Small Engine Mechanics and Repair Technology/Technician** *38 students enrolled* ● **Surgical Technology/Technologist** *6 students enrolled* ● **Welding Technology/Welder** *72 students enrolled*

STUDENT SERVICES Academic or career counseling, employment services for current students, placement services for program completers, remedial services.

Murray State University

113 Sparks Hall, Murray, KY 42071
http://www.murraystate.edu/

CONTACT Randy J. Dunn, President
Telephone: 270-809-3011

GENERAL INFORMATION Public Institution. Founded 1922. **Accreditation:** Regional (SACS/CC); art and design (NASAD); counseling (ACA); dietetics: postbaccalaureate internship (ADtA/CAADE); engineering technology (ABET/TAC); engineering-related programs (ABET/RAC); home economics (AAFCS); journalism and mass communications (ACEJMC); music (NASM); speech-language pathology (ASHA). **Total program enrollment:** 7493. **Application fee:** $30.

STUDENT SERVICES Academic or career counseling, employment services for current students, placement services for program completers, remedial services.

National College

2376 Sir Barton Way, Lexington, KY 40509
http://www.national-college.edu/

CONTACT Frank Longaker, President
Telephone: 859-253-0621

GENERAL INFORMATION Private Institution. Founded 1947. **Accreditation:** Medical assisting (AAMAE); state accredited or approved. **Total program enrollment:** 1607. **Application fee:** $30.

PROGRAM(S) OFFERED
● **Accounting Technology/Technician and Bookkeeping** ● **Business Administration and Management, General** *1 student enrolled* ● **Business/Commerce, General** *12 students enrolled* ● **Computer and Information Sciences and Support Services, Other** *9 students enrolled* ● **Executive Assistant/Executive Secretary** *6 students enrolled* ● **Health and Medical Administrative Services, Other** *90 students enrolled* ● **Information Technology** ● **Medical Office Assistant/Specialist** *1 student enrolled* ● **Medical Transcription/Transcriptionist** *12 students enrolled* ● **Pharmacy Technician/Assistant** *60 students enrolled* ● **Phlebotomy/Phlebotomist** *6 students enrolled* ● **Radio and Television Broadcasting Technology/Technician**

STUDENT SERVICES Academic or career counseling, employment services for current students, placement services for program completers, remedial services.

Northern Kentucky University

Louie B Nunn Drive, Highland Heights, KY 41099
http://www.nku.edu/

CONTACT James C. Votruba, President
Telephone: 859-572-5100

GENERAL INFORMATION Public Institution. Founded 1968. **Accreditation:** Regional (SACS/CC); engineering technology (ABET/TAC); music (NASM); radiologic technology: radiography (JRCERT). **Total program enrollment:** 10047. **Application fee:** $40.

STUDENT SERVICES Academic or career counseling, daycare for children of students, employment services for current students, placement services for program completers, remedial services.

Nu-Tek Academy of Beauty

Maysville Road, Mount Sterling, KY 40391

CONTACT Rebecca H. Taylor, CEO
Telephone: 859-498-4460

GENERAL INFORMATION Private Institution. Founded 1973. **Total program enrollment:** 30. **Application fee:** $200.

PROGRAM(S) OFFERED
● Cosmetology, Barber/Styling, and Nail Instructor *1000 hrs./$3200*
● Cosmetology/Cosmetologist, General *1800 hrs./$9500* ● Nail Technician/Specialist and Manicurist *600 hrs./$5700*

STUDENT SERVICES Academic or career counseling, placement services for program completers.

Owensboro Community and Technical College

4800 New Hartford Road, Owensboro, KY 42303-1899
http://www.octc.kctcs.edu/

CONTACT Dr. Paula Gastenveld, President
Telephone: 270-686-4400

GENERAL INFORMATION Public Institution. Founded 1986. **Accreditation:** Regional (SACS/CC); radiologic technology: radiography (JRCERT); state accredited or approved. **Total program enrollment:** 1775.

PROGRAM(S) OFFERED
● Agricultural Production Operations, General *1 student enrolled* ● Autobody/Collision and Repair Technology/Technician *12 students enrolled* ● Automobile/Automotive Mechanics Technology/Technician *61 students enrolled* ● Business Administration and Management, General *17 students enrolled* ● Carpentry/Carpenter *20 students enrolled* ● Child Care Provider/Assistant *62 students enrolled* ● Computer and Information Sciences, General *20 students enrolled* ● Cosmetology/Cosmetologist, General *6 students enrolled* ● Culinary Arts/Chef Training *8 students enrolled* ● Diesel Mechanics Technology/Technician *22 students enrolled* ● Drafting and Design Technology/Technician, General *2 students enrolled* ● Electrician *19 students enrolled* ● Emergency Medical Technology/Technician (EMT Paramedic) *24 students enrolled* ● Engineering Technology, General *34 students enrolled* ● Executive Assistant/Executive Secretary *16 students enrolled* ● Heating, Air Conditioning, Ventilation and Refrigeration Maintenance Technology/Technician (HAC, HACR, HVAC, HVACR) *19 students enrolled* ● Industrial Mechanics and Maintenance Technology *58 students enrolled* ● Licensed Practical/Vocational Nurse Training (LPN, LVN, Cert, Dipl, AAS) *32 students enrolled* ● Machine Shop Technology/Assistant *21 students enrolled* ● Medical Administrative/Executive Assistant and Medical Secretary *31 students enrolled* ● Surgical Technology/Technologist *10 students enrolled* ● Welding Technology/Welder *36 students enrolled*

STUDENT SERVICES Academic or career counseling, daycare for children of students, employment services for current students, placement services for program completers, remedial services.

Pat Wilson's Beauty College

326 North Main, Henderson, KY 42420

CONTACT Pat Wilson, Director
Telephone: 270-826-5195

GENERAL INFORMATION Private Institution. Founded 1975. **Total program enrollment:** 42.

PROGRAM(S) OFFERED
● Cosmetology and Related Personal Grooming Arts, Other ● Cosmetology, Barber/Styling, and Nail Instructor *1000 hrs./$2800* ● Cosmetology/Cosmetologist, General *1800 hrs./$9400* ● Nail Technician/Specialist and Manicurist *600 hrs./$2050* ● Technical Teacher Education

STUDENT SERVICES Academic or career counseling, employment services for current students, placement services for program completers.

PJ's College of Cosmetology

1901 Russelville Road, Suite 10, Bowling Green, KY 42101
http://gotopjs.com/

CONTACT Judith Stewart, President/Owner
Telephone: 317-846-8999 Ext. 320

GENERAL INFORMATION Private Institution. **Total program enrollment:** 263.

PROGRAM(S) OFFERED
● Cosmetology and Related Personal Grooming Arts, Other *600 hrs./$8070* ● Cosmetology, Barber/Styling, and Nail Instructor *1000 hrs./$10,088* ● Cosmetology/Cosmetologist, General *1500 hrs./$14,870* ● Nail Technician/Specialist and Manicurist *450 hrs./$6095*

STUDENT SERVICES Academic or career counseling, employment services for current students, placement services for program completers.

PJ's College of Cosmetology

124 South Public Square, Glasgow, KY 42141
http://gotopjs.com/

CONTACT Judith Stewart, Owner/President
Telephone: 317-846-8999 Ext. 320

GENERAL INFORMATION Private Institution. **Total program enrollment:** 64.

PROGRAM(S) OFFERED
● Cosmetology and Related Personal Grooming Arts, Other *600 hrs./$8070* ● Cosmetology, Barber/Styling, and Nail Instructor *1000 hrs./$10,088* ● Cosmetology/Cosmetologist, General *1800 hrs./$15,400* ● Hair Styling/Stylist and Hair Design ● Nail Technician/Specialist and Manicurist *1 student enrolled*

STUDENT SERVICES Academic or career counseling, employment services for current students, placement services for program completers.

Regency School of Hair Design

567 North Lake Drive, Prestonburg, KY 41653

CONTACT Edith Dotson, Co-Owner
Telephone: 606-886-6457

GENERAL INFORMATION Private Institution. **Total program enrollment:** 35. **Application fee:** $100.

PROGRAM(S) OFFERED
● Cosmetology, Barber/Styling, and Nail Instructor *1000 hrs./$3600* ● Cosmetology/Cosmetologist, General *1800 hrs./$9362* ● Nail Technician/Specialist and Manicurist *3 students enrolled*

St. Catharine College

2735 Bardstown Road, St. Catharine, KY 40061-9499
http://www.sccky.edu/

CONTACT William D. Huston, President
Telephone: 859-336-5082

GENERAL INFORMATION Private Institution. Founded 1931. **Accreditation:** Regional (SACS/CC). **Total program enrollment:** 524. **Application fee:** $15.

PROGRAM(S) OFFERED
• **Child Care Provider/Assistant** • **Computer and Information Sciences, General** • **Pharmacy Technician/Assistant** *2 students enrolled*

STUDENT SERVICES Academic or career counseling, daycare for children of students, employment services for current students, placement services for program completers, remedial services.

Somerset Community College

808 Monticello Street, Somerset, KY 42501-2973
http://www.somerset.kctcs.edu/

CONTACT Dr. Jo Marshall, President & CEO
Telephone: 877-629-9722

GENERAL INFORMATION Public Institution. Founded 1965. **Accreditation:** Regional (SACS/CC); medical laboratory technology (NAACLS); physical therapy assisting (APTA); state accredited or approved. **Total program enrollment:** 3162.

PROGRAM(S) OFFERED
• **Accounting Technology/Technician and Bookkeeping** *1 student enrolled* • **Aircraft Powerplant Technology/Technician** *37 students enrolled* • **Autobody/Collision and Repair Technology/Technician** *5 students enrolled* • **Automobile/Automotive Mechanics Technology/Technician** *64 students enrolled* • **Business Administration and Management, General** *1 student enrolled* • **Carpentry/Carpenter** *33 students enrolled* • **Child Care Provider/Assistant** *19 students enrolled* • **Clinical/Medical Laboratory Technician** *55 students enrolled* • **Communications Technology/Technician** *11 students enrolled* • **Cosmetology/Cosmetologist, General** *2 students enrolled* • **Diesel Mechanics Technology/Technician** *117 students enrolled* • **Drafting and Design Technology/Technician, General** *24 students enrolled* • **Electrician** *20 students enrolled* • **Engineering Technology, General** *26 students enrolled* • **Executive Assistant/Executive Secretary** *23 students enrolled* • **Heating, Air Conditioning, Ventilation and Refrigeration Maintenance Technology/Technician (HAC, HACR, HVAC, HVACR)** *8 students enrolled* • **Industrial Electronics Technology/Technician** *14 students enrolled* • **Industrial Mechanics and Maintenance Technology** *37 students enrolled* • **Licensed Practical/Vocational Nurse Training (LPN, LVN, Cert, Dipl, AAS)** *127 students enrolled* • **Machine Shop Technology/Assistant** *34 students enrolled* • **Medical Administrative/Executive Assistant and Medical Secretary** *120 students enrolled* • **Medical/Clinical Assistant** *11 students enrolled* • **Welding Technology/Welder** *38 students enrolled*

STUDENT SERVICES Academic or career counseling, employment services for current students, placement services for program completers, remedial services.

Southeast Kentucky Community and Technical College

700 College Road, Cumberland, KY 40823-1099
http://www.soucc.kctcs.net/

CONTACT Dr. W. Bruce Ayers, President & CEO
Telephone: 606-589-2145

GENERAL INFORMATION Public Institution. Founded 1960. **Accreditation:** Regional (SACS/CC); medical laboratory technology (NAACLS); physical therapy assisting (APTA). **Total program enrollment:** 1676.

PROGRAM(S) OFFERED
• **Autobody/Collision and Repair Technology/Technician** *8 students enrolled* • **Automobile/Automotive Mechanics Technology/Technician** *19 students enrolled* • **Business Administration and Management, General** *21 students*

enrolled • **Carpentry/Carpenter** *25 students enrolled* • **Clinical/Medical Laboratory Technician** *10 students enrolled* • **Computer and Information Sciences, General** *7 students enrolled* • **Construction/Heavy Equipment/Earthmoving Equipment Operation** *17 students enrolled* • **Diesel Mechanics Technology/Technician** *49 students enrolled* • **Drafting and Design Technology/Technician, General** *1 student enrolled* • **Electrician** *31 students enrolled* • **Engineering Technology, General** *8 students enrolled* • **Executive Assistant/Executive Secretary** *44 students enrolled* • **Heating, Air Conditioning, Ventilation and Refrigeration Maintenance Technology/Technician (HAC, HACR, HVAC, HVACR)** *22 students enrolled* • **Licensed Practical/Vocational Nurse Training (LPN, LVN, Cert, Dipl, AAS)** *34 students enrolled* • **Machine Shop Technology/Assistant** *2 students enrolled* • **Medical Radiologic Technology/Science—Radiation Therapist** *11 students enrolled* • **Medical/Clinical Assistant** *5 students enrolled* • **Mining Technology/Technician** *1 student enrolled* • **Surgical Technology/Technologist** *14 students enrolled* • **Welding Technology/Welder** *54 students enrolled*

STUDENT SERVICES Academic or career counseling, employment services for current students, placement services for program completers, remedial services.

Southeast School of Cosmetology

19 Manchester Square, Manchester, KY 40962

CONTACT Betty S. Roberts, President
Telephone: 606-598-7901

GENERAL INFORMATION Private Institution. **Total program enrollment:** 51.

PROGRAM(S) OFFERED
• **Cosmetology, Barber/Styling, and Nail Instructor** *1000 hrs./$3390* • **Cosmetology/Cosmetologist, General** *1800 hrs./$8500*

STUDENT SERVICES Academic or career counseling.

Southwestern College of Business

8095 Connector Drive, Florence, KY 41042
http://www.swcollege.net/

CONTACT Tina M. Barnes, Executive Director
Telephone: 859-282-9999

GENERAL INFORMATION Private Institution. Founded 1978. **Accreditation:** State accredited or approved. **Total program enrollment:** 171. **Application fee:** $20.

PROGRAM(S) OFFERED
• **Blood Bank Technology Specialist** *24 students enrolled* • **Health and Medical Administrative Services, Other** *14 students enrolled* • **Information Science/Studies** • **Massage Therapy/Therapeutic Massage** *53 students enrolled* • **Medical/Clinical Assistant** *52 students enrolled*

STUDENT SERVICES Academic or career counseling, placement services for program completers.

Spalding University

851 South Fourth Street, Louisville, KY 40203-2188
http://www.spalding.edu/

CONTACT Jo Ann Rooney, President
Telephone: 502-585-9911

GENERAL INFORMATION Private Institution (Affiliated with Roman Catholic Church). Founded 1814. **Accreditation:** Regional (SACS/CC). **Total program enrollment:** 1086. **Application fee:** $20.

PROGRAM(S) OFFERED
• **Nursing—Registered Nurse Training (RN, ASN, BSN, MSN)** • **Pastoral Studies/Counseling** • **Teaching English as a Second or Foreign Language/ESL Language Instructor**

STUDENT SERVICES Academic or career counseling, employment services for current students, remedial services.

Spencerian College

4627 Dixie Highway, Louisville, KY 40216
http://www.spencerian.edu/

CONTACT Jan Gordon, Executive Director
Telephone: 502-447-1000

GENERAL INFORMATION Private Institution. Founded 1892. **Accreditation:** State accredited or approved. **Total program enrollment:** 834. **Application fee:** $100.

PROGRAM(S) OFFERED
• **Accounting Technology/Technician and Bookkeeping** 2 *students enrolled* • **Blood Bank Technology Specialist** 29 *students enrolled* • **Business, Management, Marketing, and Related Support Services, Other** 1 *student enrolled* • **Business/Office Automation/Technology/Data Entry** 2 *students enrolled* • **Clinical/Medical Laboratory Assistant** 36 *students enrolled* • **Executive Assistant/Executive Secretary** 1 *student enrolled* • **Health Information/Medical Records Technology/Technician** 14 *students enrolled* • **Health Unit Coordinator/Ward Clerk** 4 *students enrolled* • **Licensed Practical/Vocational Nurse Training (LPN, LVN, Cert, Dipl, AAS)** 146 *students enrolled* • **Massage Therapy/Therapeutic Massage** 21 *students enrolled* • **Medical Administrative/Executive Assistant and Medical Secretary** 4 *students enrolled* • **Medical Radiologic Technology/Science—Radiation Therapist** 53 *students enrolled* • **Medical Transcription/Transcriptionist** 8 *students enrolled* • **Medical/Clinical Assistant** 14 *students enrolled* • **Surgical Technology/Technologist** 27 *students enrolled*

STUDENT SERVICES Academic or career counseling, employment services for current students, placement services for program completers, remedial services.

Spencerian College–Lexington

2355 Harrodsburg Road, Lexington, KY 40504
http://www.spencerian.edu/

CONTACT Glen Sullivan, President
Telephone: 859-223-9608

GENERAL INFORMATION Private Institution. Founded 1997. **Accreditation:** State accredited or approved. **Total program enrollment:** 410. **Application fee:** $100.

PROGRAM(S) OFFERED
• **Allied Health and Medical Assisting Services, Other** • **Clinical/Medical Laboratory Technician** • **Computer Installation and Repair Technology/Technician** 1 *student enrolled* • **Drafting and Design Technology/Technician, General** 10 *students enrolled* • **Massage Therapy/Therapeutic Massage** 42 *students enrolled* • **Medical Insurance Coding Specialist/Coder** 9 *students enrolled* • **Medical Transcription/Transcriptionist** • **Medical/Clinical Assistant** 16 *students enrolled* • **Phlebotomy/Phlebotomist** 26 *students enrolled* • **Radiologic Technology/Science—Radiographer** 34 *students enrolled*

STUDENT SERVICES Academic or career counseling, placement services for program completers.

Sullivan College of Technology and Design

3901 Atkinson Square Drive, Louisville, KY 40218-4528
http://www.louisvilletech.com/

CONTACT David Winkler, Executive Director
Telephone: 502-456-6509

GENERAL INFORMATION Private Institution. Founded 1961. **Accreditation:** State accredited or approved. **Total program enrollment:** 404. **Application fee:** $100.

PROGRAM(S) OFFERED
• **Drafting and Design Technology/Technician, General** 26 *students enrolled* • **Interior Design** 44 *students enrolled*

STUDENT SERVICES Academic or career counseling, placement services for program completers, remedial services.

Sullivan University

3101 Bardstown Road, Louisville, KY 40205
http://www.sullivan.edu/

CONTACT G. Stephen Coppock, Executive Vice President
Telephone: 502-456-6504

GENERAL INFORMATION Private Institution. Founded 1864. **Accreditation:** Regional (SACS/CC); medical assisting (AAMAE). **Total program enrollment:** 1715. **Application fee:** $100.

PROGRAM(S) OFFERED
• **Baking and Pastry Arts/Baker/Pastry Chef** 13 *students enrolled* • **Business Administration and Management, General** 45 *students enrolled* • **Child Care Provider/Assistant** 11 *students enrolled* • **Computer and Information Sciences and Support Services, Other** 31 *students enrolled* • **Culinary Arts/Chef Training** 4 *students enrolled* • **Executive Assistant/Executive Secretary** 1 *student enrolled* • **Legal Professions and Studies, Other** • **Medical Office Management/Administration** 2 *students enrolled* • **Tourism and Travel Services Marketing Operations**

STUDENT SERVICES Academic or career counseling, employment services for current students, placement services for program completers.

Thomas More College

333 Thomas More Parkway, Crestview Hills, KY 41017-3495
http://www.thomasmore.edu/

CONTACT Sr. Margaret A. Stallmeyer, CDP, President
Telephone: 859-341-5800

GENERAL INFORMATION Private Institution. Founded 1921. **Accreditation:** Regional (SACS/CC). **Total program enrollment:** 1418. **Application fee:** $25.

PROGRAM(S) OFFERED
• **Accounting** • **Religion/Religious Studies** 1 *student enrolled*

STUDENT SERVICES Academic or career counseling, employment services for current students, placement services for program completers, remedial services.

Trend Setter's Academy

7283 Dixie Highway, Louisville, KY 40258

CONTACT Franci Buckler, Financial Aid Director
Telephone: 502-937-6816

GENERAL INFORMATION Private Institution. Founded 1974. **Total program enrollment:** 63. **Application fee:** $100.

PROGRAM(S) OFFERED
• **Cosmetology, Barber/Styling, and Nail Instructor** 1000 *hrs./$6100* • **Cosmetology/Cosmetologist, General** 1800 *hrs./$10,800* • **Nail Technician/Specialist and Manicurist** 600 *hrs./$3700*

STUDENT SERVICES Placement services for program completers.

Trend Setter's Academy of Beauty Culture

622B Westport Road, Elizabethtown, KY 40601

CONTACT Deborah Livers, Financial Aid Director
Telephone: 270-765-5243

GENERAL INFORMATION Private Institution. Founded 1984. **Total program enrollment:** 37. **Application fee:** $100.

PROGRAM(S) OFFERED
• **Cosmetology, Barber/Styling, and Nail Instructor** 1000 *hrs./$6100* • **Cosmetology/Cosmetologist, General** 1800 *hrs./$10,800* • **Nail Technician/Specialist and Manicurist** 600 *hrs./$3700*

STUDENT SERVICES Placement services for program completers.

University of Louisville

2301 South Third Street, Louisville, KY 40292-0001
http://www.louisville.edu/

CONTACT James R. Ramsey, President
Telephone: 502-852-5555

GENERAL INFORMATION Public Institution. Founded 1798. **Accreditation:** Regional (SACS/CC); audiology (ASHA); computer science (ABET/CSAC); dental hygiene (ADA); interior design: professional (CIDA); music (NASM); radiologic technology: radiography (JRCERT); speech-language pathology (ASHA). **Total program enrollment:** 15250. **Application fee:** $40.

PROGRAM(S) OFFERED
• **Criminal Justice/Law Enforcement Administration** 31 *students enrolled*

STUDENT SERVICES Academic or career counseling, employment services for current students, placement services for program completers, remedial services.

Western Kentucky University

1906 College Heights Boulevard, Bowling Green, KY 42101
http://www.wku.edu/

CONTACT Gary A. Ransdell, President
Telephone: 270-745-0111

GENERAL INFORMATION Public Institution. Founded 1906. **Accreditation:** Regional (SACS/CC); art and design (NASAD); computer science (ABET/CSAC); dental hygiene (ADA); engineering technology (ABET/TAC); health information technology (AHIMA); home economics (AAFCS); journalism and mass communications (ACEJMC); music (NASM); recreation and parks (NRPA); speech-language pathology (ASHA). **Total program enrollment:** 14328. **Application fee:** $40.

PROGRAM(S) OFFERED
• **Accounting** 3 *students enrolled* • **Canadian Studies** 1 *student enrolled* • **Cartography** 20 *students enrolled* • **Financial Planning and Services** 27 *students enrolled* • **Public Relations/Image Management** 1 *student enrolled*

STUDENT SERVICES Academic or career counseling, daycare for children of students, employment services for current students, placement services for program completers, remedial services.

West Kentucky Community and Technical College

4810 Alben Barkley Drive, PO Box 7380, Paducah, KY 42002-7380
http://www.westkentucky.kctcs.edu/

CONTACT Dr. Barbara Veazey, President/CEO
Telephone: 270-554-9200 Ext. 0

GENERAL INFORMATION Public Institution. Founded 1932. **Accreditation:** Regional (SACS/CC); dental assisting (ADA); physical therapy assisting (APTA); state accredited or approved. **Total program enrollment:** 2126.

PROGRAM(S) OFFERED
• **Accounting Technology/Technician and Bookkeeping** 25 *students enrolled* • **Aesthetician/Esthetician and Skin Care Specialist** 8 *students enrolled* • **Applied Horticulture/Horticultural Operations, General** 59 *students enrolled* • **Autobody/Collision and Repair Technology/Technician** 6 *students enrolled* • **Barbering/Barber** 5 *students enrolled* • **Business Administration and Management, General** 5 *students enrolled* • **Carpentry/Carpenter** 103 *students enrolled* • **Child Care Provider/Assistant** 17 *students enrolled* • **Clinical/Medical Laboratory Technician** 25 *students enrolled* • **Communications Technology/Technician** 37 *students enrolled* • **Computer and Information Sciences, General** 18 *students enrolled* • **Cosmetology/Cosmetologist, General** 8 *students enrolled* • **Culinary Arts/Chef Training** 29 *students enrolled* • **Dental Hygiene/Hygienist** 11 *students enrolled* • **Diesel Mechanics Technology/Technician** 72 *students enrolled* • **Drafting and Design Technology/Technician, General** 6 *students enrolled* • **Electrician** 143 *students enrolled* • **Emergency Medical Technology/Technician (EMT Paramedic)** 43 *students enrolled* • **Engineering Technology,**

General 5 *students enrolled* • **Executive Assistant/Executive Secretary** 226 *students enrolled* • **Fire Science/Firefighting** 2 *students enrolled* • **Health/Medical Physics** 1 *student enrolled* • **Heating, Air Conditioning, Ventilation and Refrigeration Maintenance Technology/Technician (HAC, HACR, HVAC, HVACR)** 32 *students enrolled* • **Industrial Mechanics and Maintenance Technology** 10 *students enrolled* • **Licensed Practical/Vocational Nurse Training (LPN, LVN, Cert, Dipl, AAS)** 373 *students enrolled* • **Machine Shop Technology/Assistant** 17 *students enrolled* • **Medical Radiologic Technology/Science—Radiation Therapist** 2 *students enrolled* • **Medical/Clinical Assistant** 24 *students enrolled* • **Nurse/Nursing Assistant/Aide and Patient Care Assistant** 23 *students enrolled* • **Pharmacy Technician/Assistant** 5 *students enrolled* • **Surgical Technology/Technologist** 6 *students enrolled* • **Truck and Bus Driver/Commercial Vehicle Operation** 28 *students enrolled* • **Welding Technology/Welder** 131 *students enrolled*

STUDENT SERVICES Academic or career counseling, employment services for current students, placement services for program completers, remedial services.

MAINE

Andover College

265 Western Avenue, South Portland, ME 04106
http://www.andovercollege.edu/

CONTACT Dr. Christopher Quinn, President
Telephone: 207-774-6126

GENERAL INFORMATION Private Institution. Founded 1966. **Accreditation:** Regional (NEASC/CVTCI). **Total program enrollment:** 666. **Application fee:** $20.

PROGRAM(S) OFFERED
• **Accounting** 14 *students enrolled* • **Administrative Assistant and Secretarial Science, General** 1 *student enrolled* • **Child Care and Support Services Management** 4 *students enrolled* • **Legal Assistant/Paralegal** 14 *students enrolled* • **Management Information Systems, General** • **Medical/Clinical Assistant** • **Tourism and Travel Services Management** 12 *students enrolled*

STUDENT SERVICES Academic or career counseling, employment services for current students, placement services for program completers, remedial services.

Beal College

629 Main Street, Bangor, ME 04401-6896
http://www.bealcollege.edu/

CONTACT Allen T. Stehle, President
Telephone: 207-947-4591

GENERAL INFORMATION Private Institution. Founded 1891. **Accreditation:** Medical assisting (AAMAE); state accredited or approved. **Total program enrollment:** 272. **Application fee:** $25.

PROGRAM(S) OFFERED
• **Administrative Assistant and Secretarial Science, General** 1 *student enrolled* • **Business/Commerce, General** 1 *student enrolled* • **Criminal Justice/Law Enforcement Administration** 73 *hrs./$13,665* • **Early Childhood Education and Teaching** 72 *hrs./$13,155* • **Health Information/Medical Records Technology/Technician** 14 *students enrolled* • **Human Services, General** 72 *hrs./$13,165* • **Medical Administrative/Executive Assistant and Medical Secretary** 72 *hrs./$13,340* • **Medical Insurance Coding Specialist/Coder** 39 *hrs./$6760* • **Medical Transcription/Transcriptionist** 10 *students enrolled* • **Medical/Clinical Assistant** 72 *hrs./$16,310*

STUDENT SERVICES Academic or career counseling, employment services for current students, placement services for program completers, remedial services.

Central Maine Community College

1250 Turner Street, Auburn, ME 04210-6498
http://www.cmcc.edu/

CONTACT Scott E. Knapp, President
Telephone: 207-755-5100

GENERAL INFORMATION Public Institution. Founded 1964. **Accreditation:** Regional (NEASC/NEASCCIHE); engineering technology (ABET/TAC); engineering-related programs (ABET/RAC); medical laboratory technology (NAACLS). **Total program enrollment: 1160. Application fee:** $20.

PROGRAM(S) OFFERED
• Administrative Assistant and Secretarial Science, General • Business Administration and Management, General • Child Development • Construction Engineering Technology/Technician • Culinary Arts/Chef Training *11 students enrolled* • Electromechanical Technology/Electromechanical Engineering Technology *2 students enrolled* • Graphic and Printing Equipment Operator, General Production • Licensed Practical/Vocational Nurse Training (LPN, LVN, Cert, Dipl, AAS) *12 students enrolled* • Machine Tool Technology/Machinist • Mechanical Engineering/Mechanical Technology/Technician • Medical Insurance Coding Specialist/Coder *8 students enrolled* • Medical Transcription/Transcriptionist *9 students enrolled* • Occupational Safety and Health Technology/Technician *1 student enrolled* • Teacher Assistant/Aide

STUDENT SERVICES Academic or career counseling, remedial services.

Eastern Maine Community College

354 Hogan Road, Bangor, ME 04401-4206
http://www.emcc.edu/

CONTACT Joyce B. Hedlund, President
Telephone: 207-974-4600

GENERAL INFORMATION Public Institution. Founded 1966. **Accreditation:** Regional (NEASC/CVTCI); radiologic technology: radiography (JRCERT). **Total program enrollment: 1099. Application fee:** $20.

PROGRAM(S) OFFERED
• Administrative Assistant and Secretarial Science, General *1 student enrolled* • Automobile/Automotive Mechanics Technology/Technician *5 students enrolled* • CAD/CADD Drafting and/or Design Technology/Technician *1 student enrolled* • Computer Installation and Repair Technology/Technician *2 students enrolled* • Construction Engineering Technology/Technician *2 students enrolled* • Culinary Arts/Chef Training *8 students enrolled* • Early Childhood Education and Teaching • Electrician *14 students enrolled* • Emergency Medical Technology/Technician (EMT Paramedic) *1 student enrolled* • Health Information/Medical Records Administration/Administrator *10 students enrolled* • Welding Technology/Welder

STUDENT SERVICES Academic or career counseling, daycare for children of students, employment services for current students, placement services for program completers, remedial services.

Husson University

One College Circle, Bangor, ME 04401-2999
http://www.husson.edu/

CONTACT William H. Beardsley, President
Telephone: 207-941-7000

GENERAL INFORMATION Private Institution. Founded 1898. **Accreditation:** Regional (NEASC/NEASCCIHE). **Total program enrollment: 1885. Application fee:** $25.

PROGRAM(S) OFFERED
• Legal Assistant/Paralegal • Marine Maintenance/Fitter and Ship Repair Technology/Technician

STUDENT SERVICES Academic or career counseling, employment services for current students, placement services for program completers, remedial services.

Intercoast Career Institute

207 Gannett Drive, South Portland, ME 04106
http://www.intercoastcolleges.com

CONTACT Sheila Swanson, Vice President, Student Financial Services
Telephone: 207-822-9802

GENERAL INFORMATION Private Institution. **Total program enrollment: 147. Application fee:** $75.

PROGRAM(S) OFFERED
• Massage Therapy/Therapeutic Massage *26 hrs./$14,465* • Medical Administrative/Executive Assistant and Medical Secretary *19 students enrolled* • Medical/Clinical Assistant *30 hrs./$15,750* • Nurse/Nursing Assistant/Aide and Patient Care Assistant *51 hrs./$25,850* • Pharmacy Technician/Assistant *27 hrs./$14,685* • Substance Abuse/Addiction Counseling *30 hrs./$16,300*

STUDENT SERVICES Academic or career counseling, employment services for current students, placement services for program completers.

Kennebec Valley Community College

92 Western Avenue, Fairfield, ME 04937-1367
http://www.kvcc.me.edu/

CONTACT Barbara Woodlee, President
Telephone: 207-453-5000

GENERAL INFORMATION Public Institution. Founded 1970. **Accreditation:** Regional (NEASC/NEASCCIHE); health information technology (AHIMA); physical therapy assisting (APTA); practical nursing (NLN). **Total program enrollment: 620. Application fee:** $20.

PROGRAM(S) OFFERED
• Drafting and Design Technology/Technician, General *4 students enrolled* • Electrician *3 students enrolled* • Emergency Medical Technology/Technician (EMT Paramedic) *25 students enrolled* • Executive Assistant/Executive Secretary • Forestry Technology/Technician • Health Information/Medical Records Technology/Technician *1 student enrolled* • Health Services/Allied Health/Health Sciences, General *5 students enrolled* • Licensed Practical/Vocational Nurse Training (LPN, LVN, Cert, Dipl, AAS) • Lineworker *24 students enrolled* • Machine Tool Technology/Machinist *1 student enrolled* • Management Information Systems, General • Massage Therapy/Therapeutic Massage *5 students enrolled* • Medical Administrative/Executive Assistant and Medical Secretary • Mental and Social Health Services and Allied Professions, Other • Psychiatric/Mental Health Services Technician

STUDENT SERVICES Academic or career counseling, daycare for children of students, employment services for current students, placement services for program completers, remedial services.

Landing School of Boat Building and Design

PO Box 1490, Kennebunkport, ME 04046-1490
http://www.landingschool.edu/

CONTACT Barry R. Acker, President
Telephone: 207-985-7976

GENERAL INFORMATION Private Institution. Founded 1978. **Total program enrollment: 70.**

PROGRAM(S) OFFERED
• Materials Engineering *6 students enrolled* • Naval Architecture and Marine Engineering *16 students enrolled* • Vehicle Maintenance and Repair Technologies, Other *22 students enrolled* • Woodworking, Other *26 students enrolled*

STUDENT SERVICES Academic or career counseling, placement services for program completers.

Mr. Bernard's School of Hair Fashion

711 Lisbon Street, PO Box 1163, Lewiston, ME 04243-1163
http://www.bernardschoolhairfashion.com/

CONTACT Andrew A. Fournier, President
Telephone: 207-783-7765

GENERAL INFORMATION Private Institution. Founded 1959. **Total program enrollment:** 80.

PROGRAM(S) OFFERED
- **Cosmetology, Barber/Styling, and Nail Instructor** *1000 hrs./$6650*
- **Cosmetology/Cosmetologist, General** *1500 hrs./$12,961*

STUDENT SERVICES Academic or career counseling, employment services for current students, placement services for program completers, remedial services.

Northern Maine Community College

33 Edgemont Drive, Presque Isle, ME 04769-2016
http://www.nmcc.edu/

CONTACT Timothy D. Crowley, President
Telephone: 207-768-2700

GENERAL INFORMATION Public Institution. Founded 1963. **Accreditation:** Regional (NEASC/NEASCCIHE). **Total program enrollment:** 589. **Application fee:** $20.

PROGRAM(S) OFFERED
- **Autobody/Collision and Repair Technology/Technician** *1 student enrolled*
- **Automobile/Automotive Mechanics Technology/Technician** *3 students enrolled*
- **Carpentry/Carpenter** *2 students enrolled* • **Child Development** *2 students enrolled* • **Computer Installation and Repair Technology/Technician** *1 student enrolled* • **Drafting and Design Technology/Technician, General** *1 student enrolled* • **Electrician** *3 students enrolled* • **Emergency Medical Technology/Technician (EMT Paramedic)** • **General Office Occupations and Clerical Services** • **Heating, Air Conditioning, Ventilation and Refrigeration Maintenance Technology/Technician (HAC, HACR, HVAC, HVACR)** *4 students enrolled* • **Machine Tool Technology/Machinist** *2 students enrolled* • **Medical Insurance Coding Specialist/Coder** *3 students enrolled* • **Pipefitting/Pipefitter and Sprinkler Fitter** *5 students enrolled* • **Sheet Metal Technology/Sheetworking** *15 students enrolled* • **Vehicle Maintenance and Repair Technologies, Other** *3 students enrolled*

STUDENT SERVICES Academic or career counseling, employment services for current students, placement services for program completers, remedial services.

Pierre's School of Beauty Culture

319 Marginal Way, Portland, ME 04101
http://www.pierresschool.com/

CONTACT Michael Bouman, President/COO
Telephone: 207-774-9413

GENERAL INFORMATION Private Institution. Founded 1958. **Total program enrollment:** 242. **Application fee:** $100.

PROGRAM(S) OFFERED
- **Aesthetician/Esthetician and Skin Care Specialist** *13 students enrolled*
- **Cosmetology, Barber/Styling, and Nail Instructor** *6 students enrolled*
- **Cosmetology/Cosmetologist, General** *1500 hrs./$14,300* • **Massage Therapy/Therapeutic Massage** *600 hrs./$7400*

STUDENT SERVICES Academic or career counseling, employment services for current students, placement services for program completers.

Saint Joseph's College of Maine

278 Whites Bridge Road, Standish, ME 04084-5263
http://www.sjcme.edu/

CONTACT Joseph Lee, President
Telephone: 207-892-6766

GENERAL INFORMATION Private Institution (Affiliated with Roman Catholic Church). Founded 1912. **Accreditation:** Regional (NEASC/NEASCCIHE). **Total program enrollment:** 1164. **Application fee:** $50.

PROGRAM(S) OFFERED
- **Christian Studies** *1 student enrolled* • **Criminal Justice/Safety Studies** *1 student enrolled* • **Health/Health Care Administration/Management** *7 students enrolled* • **Marketing/Marketing Management, General** *1 student enrolled*

STUDENT SERVICES Academic or career counseling, employment services for current students, placement services for program completers.

Seacoast Career Schools

One Eagle Drive, Suite 1, Sanford, ME 04073
http://www.seacoastcareerschools.com/

CONTACT David Palmer, School Director
Telephone: 207-490-0509

GENERAL INFORMATION Private Institution. **Total program enrollment:** 217. **Application fee:** $150.

PROGRAM(S) OFFERED
- **Health/Health Care Administration/Management** *40 hrs./$11,920* • **Massage Therapy/Therapeutic Massage** *44 hrs./$11,920* • **Medical/Clinical Assistant** *40 hrs./$13,120*

STUDENT SERVICES Academic or career counseling, placement services for program completers.

Southern Maine Community College

2 Fort Road, South Portland, ME 04106
http://www.smccme.edu/

CONTACT James O. Ortiz, President
Telephone: 207-741-5500

GENERAL INFORMATION Public Institution. Founded 1946. **Accreditation:** Regional (NEASC/NEASCCIHE); radiologic technology: radiation therapy technology (JRCERT); radiologic technology: radiography (JRCERT). **Total program enrollment:** 2702. **Application fee:** $20.

PROGRAM(S) OFFERED
- **Business Administration and Management, General** *4 students enrolled*
- **Construction/Heavy Equipment/Earthmoving Equipment Operation** *1 student enrolled* • **Dietetics and Clinical Nutrition Services, Other** *1 student enrolled* • **Fire Science/Firefighting** *1 student enrolled* • **Heating, Air Conditioning and Refrigeration Technology/Technician (ACH/ACR/ACHR/HRAC/HVAC/AC Technology)** *5 students enrolled* • **Machine Tool Technology/Machinist** • **Mason/Masonry** *1 student enrolled* • **Medical/Clinical Assistant** • **Mental and Social Health Services and Allied Professions, Other** *2 students enrolled* • **Plumbing Technology/Plumber** *7 students enrolled* • **Welding Technology/Welder** *4 students enrolled*

STUDENT SERVICES Academic or career counseling, daycare for children of students, employment services for current students, placement services for program completers, remedial services.

Spa Tech Institute–Portland

1041 Brighton Avenue, Portland, ME 04102
http://www.spatech.edu/

CONTACT Kris Stecker, Director
Telephone: 207-772-2591

GENERAL INFORMATION Private Institution. Founded 1976. **Total program enrollment:** 115. **Application fee:** $50.

PROGRAM(S) OFFERED
- **Cosmetology/Cosmetologist, General** *1500 hrs./$14,250*

STUDENT SERVICES Academic or career counseling, placement services for program completers.

Spa Tech Institute–Westbrook

100 Larrabee Road, Westbrook, ME 04092
http://www.spatech.edu/

CONTACT Kris Stecker, Director of Operations
Telephone: 207-591-4141

GENERAL INFORMATION Private Institution. **Total program enrollment:** 96. **Application fee:** $50.

PROGRAM(S) OFFERED
• **Aesthetician/Esthetician and Skin Care Specialist** *600 hrs./$10,250* • **Massage Therapy/Therapeutic Massage** *600 hrs./$12,750* • **Polarity Therapy** *660 hrs./$13,695*

STUDENT SERVICES Academic or career counseling, placement services for program completers.

University of Maine at Augusta

46 University Drive, Augusta, ME 04330-9410
http://www.uma.maine.edu/

CONTACT Allyson Handley, President
Telephone: 207-621-3000

GENERAL INFORMATION Public Institution. Founded 1965. **Accreditation:** Regional (NEASC/NEASCCIHE); dental assisting (ADA); dental hygiene (ADA); medical laboratory technology (NAACLS). **Total program enrollment:** 1550. **Application fee:** $40.

PROGRAM(S) OFFERED
• **Dental Assisting/Assistant** *12 students enrolled*

STUDENT SERVICES Academic or career counseling, employment services for current students, remedial services.

University of Maine System

107 Maine Avenue, Bangor, ME 04401-4330
http://www.maine.edu/

CONTACT Richard Pattenaude, Chancellor
Telephone: 207-973-3200

GENERAL INFORMATION Public Institution.

Washington County Community College

One College Drive, Calais, ME 04619
http://www.wccc.me.edu/

CONTACT William Cassidy, President
Telephone: 207-454-1000

GENERAL INFORMATION Public Institution. Founded 1969. **Accreditation:** Regional (NEASC/CVTCI). **Total program enrollment:** 235. **Application fee:** $20.

PROGRAM(S) OFFERED
• **Automobile/Automotive Mechanics Technology/Technician** *8 students enrolled* • **Child Development** • **Computer Installation and Repair Technology/Technician** • **Construction/Heavy Equipment/Earthmoving Equipment Operation** *12 students enrolled* • **Culinary Arts and Related Services, Other** • **Diesel Mechanics Technology/Technician** *6 students enrolled* • **Electrician** *10 students enrolled* • **Entrepreneurship/Entrepreneurial Studies** *4 students enrolled* • **Health Professions and Related Clinical Sciences, Other** • **Heating, Air Conditioning, Ventilation and Refrigeration Maintenance Technology/Technician (HAC, HACR, HVAC, HVACR)** • **Heavy Equipment Maintenance Technology/Technician** *3 students enrolled* • **Management Information Systems and Services, Other** • **Marine Maintenance/Fitter and Ship Repair Technology/Technician** *2 students enrolled* • **Mechanic and Repair Technologies/Technicians, Other** *4 students enrolled* • **Medical Administrative/Executive Assistant and Medical Secretary** *16 students enrolled* • **Parks, Recreation and**

Leisure Studies • **Plumbing Technology/Plumber** *10 students enrolled* • **Restaurant, Culinary, and Catering Management/Manager** *2 students enrolled* • **Teacher Assistant/Aide** *1 student enrolled* • **Welding Technology/Welder** *11 students enrolled*

STUDENT SERVICES Academic or career counseling, daycare for children of students, employment services for current students, placement services for program completers, remedial services.

York County Community College

112 College Drive, Wells, ME 04090
http://www.yccc.edu/

CONTACT Dr. Charlie Lyons, President
Telephone: 207-646-9282

GENERAL INFORMATION Public Institution. Founded 1994. **Accreditation:** Regional (NEASC/CVTCI). **Total program enrollment:** 368. **Application fee:** $20.

PROGRAM(S) OFFERED
• **CAD/CADD Drafting and/or Design Technology/Technician** • **Child Development** • **Construction Trades, Other** • **Culinary Arts/Chef Training** *1 student enrolled*

STUDENT SERVICES Academic or career counseling, employment services for current students, placement services for program completers, remedial services.

MARYLAND

Aaron's Academy of Beauty

340 Post Office Road, Waldorf, MD 20602

CONTACT Jack Church, Owner
Telephone: 301-645-3681

GENERAL INFORMATION Private Institution. Founded 1969. **Total program enrollment:** 58. **Application fee:** $100.

PROGRAM(S) OFFERED
• **Cosmetology/Cosmetologist, General** *1500 hrs./$13,900* • **Nail Technician/Specialist and Manicurist** *100 hrs./$2300*

STUDENT SERVICES Academic or career counseling, employment services for current students, placement services for program completers.

Aesthetics Institute of Cosmetology

15958C Shady Grove Road, Gaithersburg, MD 20877

CONTACT Laila Hamdan, Director
Telephone: 301-330-9252

GENERAL INFORMATION Private Institution. **Total program enrollment:** 12. **Application fee:** $100.

PROGRAM(S) OFFERED
• **Aesthetician/Esthetician and Skin Care Specialist** *600 hrs./$7200* • **Cosmetology/Cosmetologist, General** *1500 hrs./$11,100* • **Make-Up Artist/Specialist** • **Nail Technician/Specialist and Manicurist** *250 hrs./$2500* • **Permanent Cosmetics/Makeup and Tattooing** *40 hrs./$1000*

STUDENT SERVICES Academic or career counseling, employment services for current students.

Allegany College of Maryland

12401 Willowbrook Road, SE, Cumberland, MD 21502-2596
http://www.allegany.edu/

CONTACT Bruce Exstrom, President
Telephone: 301-784-5000

GENERAL INFORMATION Public Institution. Founded 1961. **Accreditation:** Regional (MSA/CIHE); dental hygiene (ADA); medical laboratory technology (NAACLS); physical therapy assisting (APTA); radiologic technology: radiography (JRCERT). **Total program enrollment:** 2077.

PROGRAM(S) OFFERED
• **Accounting Technology/Technician and Bookkeeping** 6 *students enrolled* • **Administrative Assistant and Secretarial Science, General** 5 *students enrolled* • **Automobile/Automotive Mechanics Technology/Technician** 10 *students enrolled* • **Business Administration and Management, General** 3 *students enrolled* • **Clinical/Medical Laboratory Science and Allied Professions, Other** • **Computer Technology/Computer Systems Technology** 5 *students enrolled* • **Construction Trades, Other** 1 *student enrolled* • **Criminal Justice/Police Science** 3 *students enrolled* • **Forestry Technology/Technician** • **Health Information/Medical Records Technology/Technician** 25 *students enrolled* • **Health Professions and Related Clinical Sciences, Other** 40 *students enrolled* • **Home Health Aide/Home Attendant** • **Hospitality Administration/Management, General** • **Licensed Practical/Vocational Nurse Training (LPN, LVN, Cert, Dipl, AAS)** 6 *students enrolled* • **Management Information Systems, General** 1 *student enrolled* • **Nurse/Nursing Assistant/Aide and Patient Care Assistant** 24 *students enrolled* • **Occupational Safety and Health Technology/Technician** • **Pharmacy Technician/Assistant** 11 *students enrolled* • **Receptionist** • **Tourism and Travel Services Management** 1 *student enrolled*

STUDENT SERVICES Academic or career counseling, daycare for children of students, employment services for current students, placement services for program completers, remedial services.

All-State Career School

2200 Broening Highway, Suite 160, Baltimore, MD 21224
http://www.allstatecareer.com/

CONTACT William Bowker, School Director
Telephone: 410-631-1818 Ext. 426

GENERAL INFORMATION Private Institution. Founded 1967. **Total program enrollment:** 673.

PROGRAM(S) OFFERED
• **Allied Health and Medical Assisting Services, Other** 760 *hrs./$12,130* • **Dental Assisting/Assistant** 1035 *hrs./$13,810* • **Heating, Air Conditioning and Refrigeration Technology/Technician (ACH/ACR/ACHR/HRAC/HVAC/AC Technology)** 960 *hrs./$13,375* • **Medical Insurance Coding Specialist/Coder** 760 *hrs./$12,130* • **Pharmacy Technician/Assistant** 760 *hrs./$11,110* • **Truck and Bus Driver/Commercial Vehicle Operation** 480 *hrs./$9015*

STUDENT SERVICES Academic or career counseling, employment services for current students, placement services for program completers.

American Beauty Academy

2518 University Boulevard W, Wheaton, MD 20902-1911
http://americanbeautyacademy.org/

CONTACT Anita Perry-Strong, Vice President, Campus Operations
Telephone: 301-949-3000

GENERAL INFORMATION Private Institution. **Total program enrollment:** 214. **Application fee:** $100.

PROGRAM(S) OFFERED
• **Barbering/Barber** 1500 *hrs./$13,500* • **Cosmetology/Cosmetologist, General** 1500 *hrs./$15,300*

Americare School of Allied Health

11141 Georgia Avenue, #418, Wheaton, MD 20902
http://americareschool.com/

CONTACT Charles Finn, President
Telephone: 301-933-4660

GENERAL INFORMATION Private Institution. **Total program enrollment:** 51.

PROGRAM(S) OFFERED
• **Massage Therapy/Therapeutic Massage** 720 *hrs./$7200* • **Medical/Clinical Assistant** 900 *hrs./$9950* • **Nurse/Nursing Assistant/Aide and Patient Care Assistant** 120 *hrs./$1220*

STUDENT SERVICES Academic or career counseling, placement services for program completers.

Anne Arundel Community College

101 College Parkway, Arnold, MD 21012-1895
http://www.aacc.edu/

CONTACT Martha A. Smith, President
Telephone: 410-777-2222

GENERAL INFORMATION Public Institution. Founded 1961. **Accreditation:** Regional (MSA/CIHE); physical therapy assisting (APTA); radiologic technology: radiography (JRCERT). **Total program enrollment:** 5274.

PROGRAM(S) OFFERED
• **Accounting Technology/Technician and Bookkeeping** 13 *students enrolled* • **Allied Health and Medical Assisting Services, Other** 8 *students enrolled* • **Applied Horticulture/Horticultural Operations, General** 1 *student enrolled* • **Business Administration and Management, General** 83 *students enrolled* • **Business Administration, Management and Operations, Other** • **Child Care and Support Services Management** • **Clinical/Medical Laboratory Technician** 30 *students enrolled* • **Commercial and Advertising Art** 4 *students enrolled* • **Communications Technologies/Technicians and Support Services, Other** 6 *students enrolled* • **Computer Systems Networking and Telecommunications** 6 *students enrolled* • **Computer and Information Systems Security** • **Criminal Justice/Law Enforcement Administration** • **Criminal Justice/Police Science** 11 *students enrolled* • **Drafting and Design Technology/Technician, General** 2 *students enrolled* • **Education, Other** 2 *students enrolled* • **Electrical, Electronic and Communications Engineering Technology/Technician** 11 *students enrolled* • **Emergency Medical Technology/Technician (EMT Paramedic)** 7 *students enrolled* • **Entrepreneurship/Entrepreneurial Studies** • **Foodservice Systems Administration/Management** 7 *students enrolled* • **Health and Physical Education, General** • **Home Health Aide/Home Attendant** • **Hotel/Motel Administration/Management** 7 *students enrolled* • **Interior Design** 12 *students enrolled* • **Legal Assistant/Paralegal** 10 *students enrolled* • **Licensed Practical/Vocational Nurse Training (LPN, LVN, Cert, Dipl, AAS)** 7 *students enrolled* • **Management Information Systems and Services, Other** • **Management Information Systems, General** 9 *students enrolled* • **Medical Administrative/Executive Assistant and Medical Secretary** 21 *students enrolled* • **Nursing—Registered Nurse Training (RN, ASN, BSN, MSN)** • **Occupational Safety and Health Technology/Technician** 22 *students enrolled* • **Physician Assistant** 31 *students enrolled* • **Psychiatric/Mental Health Services Technician** 7 *students enrolled* • **Restaurant, Culinary, and Catering Management/Manager** 2 *students enrolled* • **Retailing and Retail Operations** • **Women's Studies** 7 *students enrolled*

STUDENT SERVICES Academic or career counseling, daycare for children of students, employment services for current students, placement services for program completers, remedial services.

Award Beauty School

26 East Antietam Street, Hagerstown, MD 21740

CONTACT James Bilney, President
Telephone: 301-459-2509

GENERAL INFORMATION Private Institution. Founded 1955. **Total program enrollment:** 53.

PROGRAM(S) OFFERED
● **Cosmetology/Cosmetologist, General** *900 hrs./$15,040*
STUDENT SERVICES Placement services for program completers.

Baltimore City Community College

2901 Liberty Heights Avenue, Baltimore, MD 21215-7893
http://www.bccc.state.md.us/

CONTACT Dr. Carolane Williams, President
Telephone: 410-462-8300

GENERAL INFORMATION Public Institution. Founded 1947. **Accreditation:** Regional (MSA/CIHE); dental hygiene (ADA); health information technology (AHIMA); physical therapy assisting (APTA); surgical technology (ARCST). **Total program enrollment: 2779. Application fee:** $10.

PROGRAM(S) OFFERED
● **Accounting Technology/Technician and Bookkeeping** *12 students enrolled* ● **Administrative Assistant and Secretarial Science, General** *4 students enrolled* ● **Banking and Financial Support Services** *1 student enrolled* ● **Building/Construction Finishing, Management, and Inspection, Other** ● **Business Administration, Management and Operations, Other** *2 students enrolled* ● **Child Care and Support Services Management** *4 students enrolled* ● **Computer Programming, Specific Applications** *2 students enrolled* ● **Corrections** *6 students enrolled* ● **Culinary Arts/Chef Training** *8 students enrolled* ● **Dietitian Assistant** ● **Drafting and Design Technology/Technician, General** *9 students enrolled* ● **Drama and Dramatics/Theatre Arts, General** ● **Education, General** *1 student enrolled* ● **Electrical, Electronic and Communications Engineering Technology/Technician** ● **Emergency Care Attendant (EMT Ambulance)** ● **Emergency Medical Technology/Technician (EMT Paramedic)** ● **Environmental Science** ● **Fashion/Apparel Design** *4 students enrolled* ● **Fire Protection and Safety Technology/Technician** *1 student enrolled* ● **Health Information/Medical Records Technology/Technician** *1 student enrolled* ● **Legal Assistant/Paralegal** *3 students enrolled* ● **Licensed Practical/Vocational Nurse Training (LPN, LVN, Cert, Dipl, AAS)** *15 students enrolled* ● **Machine Tool Technology/Machinist** ● **Management Information Systems, General** *1 student enrolled* ● **Mental and Social Health Services and Allied Professions, Other** *25 students enrolled* ● **Nursing—Registered Nurse Training (RN, ASN, BSN, MSN)** ● **Surgical Technology/Technologist**

STUDENT SERVICES Academic or career counseling, daycare for children of students, employment services for current students, placement services for program completers, remedial services.

Baltimore Hebrew University

5800 Park Heights Avenue, Baltimore, MD 21215-3996
http://www.bhu.edu/

CONTACT Ms. Erika Schon, Interim President
Telephone: 410-578-6900

GENERAL INFORMATION Private Institution. Founded 1919. **Accreditation:** Regional (MSA/CIHE). **Total program enrollment: 26. Application fee:** $50.

PROGRAM(S) OFFERED
● **Jewish/Judaic Studies**
STUDENT SERVICES Academic or career counseling.

Baltimore International College

Commerce Exchange, 17 Commerce Street, Baltimore, MD 21202-3230
http://www.bic.edu/

CONTACT Roger Chylinski, President
Telephone: 410-752-4710

GENERAL INFORMATION Private Institution. Founded 1972. **Accreditation:** Regional (MSA/CIHE). **Total program enrollment: 473. Application fee:** $50.

PROGRAM(S) OFFERED
● **Baking and Pastry Arts/Baker/Pastry Chef** ● **Culinary Arts/Chef Training** *11 students enrolled* ● **Hotel/Motel Administration/Management**

STUDENT SERVICES Academic or career counseling, employment services for current students, placement services for program completers, remedial services.

Baltimore School of Massage

6401 Dogwood Road, Baltimore, MD 21207
http://www.bsom.com/

CONTACT Stephen Lazarus, Chief Operations Officer
Telephone: 410-636-7929

GENERAL INFORMATION Private Institution. **Total program enrollment:** 312.

PROGRAM(S) OFFERED
● **Aesthetician/Esthetician and Skin Care Specialist** *49 hrs./$9605* ● **Asian Bodywork Therapy** *13 students enrolled* ● **Massage Therapy/Therapeutic Massage** *49 hrs./$12,000*

STUDENT SERVICES Academic or career counseling, employment services for current students, placement services for program completers.

Baltimore Studio of Hair Design

18 North Howard Street, Baltimore, MD 21201
http://www.baltimorestudio.net/

CONTACT Maxine Sisserman, Administrator
Telephone: 410-539-1935

GENERAL INFORMATION Private Institution. Founded 1973. **Total program enrollment:** 47.

PROGRAM(S) OFFERED
● **Cosmetology/Cosmetologist, General** *1500 hrs./$14,650* ● **Nail Technician/Specialist and Manicurist**

STUDENT SERVICES Academic or career counseling, employment services for current students, placement services for program completers.

Blades School of Hair Design

22576-316 MacArthur Boulevard, California, MD 20619

CONTACT Wanda A. Paduano, Director
Telephone: 301-862-9797

GENERAL INFORMATION Private Institution. **Total program enrollment:** 33.

PROGRAM(S) OFFERED
● **Cosmetology/Cosmetologist, General** *1500 hrs./$14,650*

STUDENT SERVICES Academic or career counseling, employment services for current students, placement services for program completers.

Capitol College

11301 Springfield Road, Laurel, MD 20708-9759
http://www.capitol-college.edu/

CONTACT Michael Wood, President
Telephone: 301-369-2800

GENERAL INFORMATION Private Institution. Founded 1964. **Accreditation:** Regional (MSA/CIHE); engineering technology (ABET/TAC). **Total program enrollment: 270. Application fee:** $25.

Capitol College (continued)

PROGRAM(S) OFFERED
• **Computer and Information Sciences, General** *2 students enrolled* • **Operations Management and Supervision** *2 students enrolled*

STUDENT SERVICES Academic or career counseling, employment services for current students, placement services for program completers, remedial services.

Carroll Community College

1601 Washington Road, Westminster, MD 21157
http://www.carrollcc.edu/

CONTACT Faye Pappalardo, President
Telephone: 410-386-8000

GENERAL INFORMATION Public Institution. Founded 1993. **Accreditation:** Regional (MSA/CIHE); physical therapy assisting (APTA). **Total program enrollment:** 1631.

PROGRAM(S) OFFERED
• **Accounting Technology/Technician and Bookkeeping** • **Administrative Assistant and Secretarial Science, General** *1 student enrolled* • **Architectural Drafting and Architectural CAD/CADD** • **Building/Construction Finishing, Management, and Inspection, Other** • **Child Care and Support Services Management** • **Commercial and Advertising Art** • **Computer Graphics** *1 student enrolled* • **Computer Systems Networking and Telecommunications** • **Criminal Justice/Police Science** • **Health Information/Medical Records Technology/Technician** • **Licensed Practical/Vocational Nurse Training (LPN, LVN, Cert, Dipl, AAS)** *25 students enrolled* • **Management Information Systems, General** • **Mental and Social Health Services and Allied Professions, Other** • **Quality Control Technology/Technician**

STUDENT SERVICES Academic or career counseling, daycare for children of students, employment services for current students, remedial services.

Cecil College

One Seahawk Drive, North East, MD 21901-1999
http://www.cecil.edu/

CONTACT W. Stephen Pannill, President
Telephone: 410-287-6060

GENERAL INFORMATION Public Institution. Founded 1968. **Accreditation:** Regional (MSA/CIHE). **Total program enrollment:** 810.

PROGRAM(S) OFFERED
• **Accounting Technology/Technician and Bookkeeping** *1 student enrolled* • **Aeronautics/Aviation/Aerospace Science and Technology, General** • **Animation, Interactive Technology, Video Graphics and Special Effects** • **Banking and Financial Support Services** • **Business Administration and Management, General** *5 students enrolled* • **Business Administration, Management and Operations, Other** • **Business/Corporate Communications** • **Commercial Photography** *26 students enrolled* • **Computer Installation and Repair Technology/Technician** • **Criminal Justice/Police Science** • **Curriculum and Instruction** *5 students enrolled* • **Electrical, Electronic and Communications Engineering Technology/Technician** • **Electromechanical Technology/Electromechanical Engineering Technology** • **Emergency Medical Technology/Technician (EMT Paramedic)** • **Graphic Design** *2 students enrolled* • **Horse Husbandry/Equine Science and Management** • **Industrial Electronics Technology/Technician** • **Licensed Practical/Vocational Nurse Training (LPN, LVN, Cert, Dipl, AAS)** *11 students enrolled* • **Management Information Systems, General** *4 students enrolled* • **Public Relations/Image Management** • **Robotics Technology/Technician** • **Transportation/Transportation Management** • **Water Quality and Wastewater Treatment Management and Recycling Technology/Technician** • **Web Page, Digital/Multimedia and Information Resources Design**

STUDENT SERVICES Academic or career counseling, employment services for current students, placement services for program completers, remedial services.

Chesapeake College

PO Box 8, Wye Mills, MD 21679-0008
http://www.chesapeake.edu/

CONTACT Barbara Viniar, President
Telephone: 410-822-5400

GENERAL INFORMATION Public Institution. Founded 1965. **Accreditation:** Regional (MSA/CIHE); physical therapy assisting (APTA); radiologic technology: radiography (JRCERT). **Total program enrollment:** 998.

PROGRAM(S) OFFERED
• **Accounting Technology/Technician and Bookkeeping** *1 student enrolled* • **Business Administration and Management, General** *1 student enrolled* • **Child Care and Support Services Management** • **Criminal Justice/Police Science** *5 students enrolled* • **Culinary Arts/Chef Training** *3 students enrolled* • **Data Processing and Data Processing Technology/Technician** • **Drafting/Design Engineering Technologies/Technicians, Other** *3 students enrolled* • **Education, General** • **Education, Other** • **Emergency Medical Technology/Technician (EMT Paramedic)** *7 students enrolled* • **Heating, Air Conditioning, Ventilation and Refrigeration Maintenance Technology/Technician (HAC, HACR, HVAC, HVACR)** • **Heavy/Industrial Equipment Maintenance Technologies, Other** • **Hospitality Administration/Management, Other** • **Legal Assistant/Paralegal** *2 students enrolled* • **Licensed Practical/Vocational Nurse Training (LPN, LVN, Cert, Dipl, AAS)** • **Manufacturing Technology/Technician** • **Massage Therapy/Therapeutic Massage** • **Surgical Technology/Technologist** *7 students enrolled*

STUDENT SERVICES Academic or career counseling, daycare for children of students, employment services for current students, placement services for program completers, remedial services.

College of Southern Maryland

8730 Mitchell Road, PO Box 910, La Plata, MD 20646-0910
http://www.csmd.edu/

CONTACT Dr. Bradley Gottfried, President
Telephone: 301-934-2251

GENERAL INFORMATION Public Institution. Founded 1958. **Accreditation:** Regional (MSA/CIHE); physical therapy assisting (APTA); practical nursing (NLN). **Total program enrollment:** 3302.

PROGRAM(S) OFFERED
• **Accounting Technology/Technician and Bookkeeping** *109 students enrolled* • **Administrative Assistant and Secretarial Science, General** *5 students enrolled* • **Allied Health Diagnostic, Intervention, and Treatment Professions, Other** • **Business Administration and Management, General** *9 students enrolled* • **CAD/CADD Drafting and/or Design Technology/Technician** *10 students enrolled* • **Child Care and Support Services Management** *4 students enrolled* • **Commercial and Advertising Art** *5 students enrolled* • **Communications Technologies/Technicians and Support Services, Other** • **Computer Programming/Programmer, General** *11 students enrolled* • **Criminal Justice/Law Enforcement Administration** *16 students enrolled* • **Drafting and Design Technology/Technician, General** • **Electrical, Electronic and Communications Engineering Technology/Technician** *1 student enrolled* • **Emergency Medical Technology/Technician (EMT Paramedic)** • **Engineering Technologies/Technicians, Other** *3 students enrolled* • **Environmental Engineering Technology/Environmental Technology** *1 student enrolled* • **Health Information/Medical Records Technology/Technician** *5 students enrolled* • **Health and Physical Education/Fitness, Other** • **Information Technology** *17 students enrolled* • **Licensed Practical/Vocational Nurse Training (LPN, LVN, Cert, Dipl, AAS)** *2 students enrolled* • **Manufacturing Technology/Technician** • **Medical Administrative/Executive Assistant and Medical Secretary** • **Mental and Social Health Services and Allied Professions, Other** *6 students enrolled* • **Pharmacy Technician/Assistant** • **Psychiatric/Mental Health Services Technician** *8 students enrolled* • **Truck and Bus Driver/Commercial Vehicle Operation**

STUDENT SERVICES Academic or career counseling, daycare for children of students, employment services for current students, placement services for program completers, remedial services.

Columbia Union College

7600 Flower Avenue, Takoma Park, MD 20912-7796
http://www.cuc.edu/

CONTACT Dr. Weymouth Spence, President
Telephone: 301-891-4000

GENERAL INFORMATION Private Institution. Founded 1904. **Accreditation:** Regional (MSA/CIHE). **Total program enrollment:** 648. **Application fee:** $25.

PROGRAM(S) OFFERED
• Licensed Practical/Vocational Nurse Training (LPN, LVN, Cert, Dipl, AAS)
• Office Management and Supervision

STUDENT SERVICES Academic or career counseling, employment services for current students, remedial services.

The Community College of Baltimore County

7201 Rossville Boulevard, Baltimore, MD 21228
http://www.ccbcmd.edu/

CONTACT Sandra L. Kurtinitis, President
Telephone: 410-682-6000

GENERAL INFORMATION Public Institution. Founded 1957. **Accreditation:** Regional (MSA/CIHE); funeral service (ABFSE); music (NASM); radiologic technology: radiation therapy technology (JRCERT); radiologic technology: radiography (JRCERT); theater (NAST). **Total program enrollment:** 7172. **Application fee:** $15.

PROGRAM(S) OFFERED
• Accounting Technology/Technician and Bookkeeping *17 students enrolled* • Administrative Assistant and Secretarial Science, General *2 students enrolled* • Aeronautics/Aviation/Aerospace Science and Technology, General *10 students enrolled* • Applied Horticulture/Horticultural Operations, General *4 students enrolled* • Architectural Drafting and Architectural CAD/CADD *34 students enrolled* • Automobile/Automotive Mechanics Technology/Technician *11 students enrolled* • Building/Construction Finishing, Management, and Inspection, Other *9 students enrolled* • Building/Construction Site Management/Manager *4 students enrolled* • Business Administration and Management, General *1 student enrolled* • Business Administration, Management and Operations, Other • Chemical Technology/Technician • Child Care Provider/Assistant • Child Care and Support Services Management *2 students enrolled* • Civil Engineering Technology/Technician *6 students enrolled* • Commercial and Advertising Art *18 students enrolled* • Computer Graphics • Computer Programming, Specific Applications *19 students enrolled* • Computer Systems Networking and Telecommunications *26 students enrolled* • Computer Technology/Computer Systems Technology • Criminal Justice/Police Science *120 students enrolled* • Drafting and Design Technology/Technician, General • Educational/Instructional Media Design • Emergency Medical Technology/Technician (EMT Paramedic) • Engineering Technology, General *14 students enrolled* • Engineering, General *1 student enrolled* • Environmental Engineering Technology/Environmental Technology *1 student enrolled* • Fire Protection and Safety Technology/Technician • Funeral Service and Mortuary Science, General • General Merchandising, Sales, and Related Marketing Operations, Other • Geography *1 student enrolled* • Graphic and Printing Equipment Operator, General Production • Health Information/Medical Records Technology/Technician • Health Professions and Related Clinical Sciences, Other • Health and Medical Administrative Services, Other *1 student enrolled* • Heating, Air Conditioning, Ventilation and Refrigeration Maintenance Technology/Technician (HAC, HACR, HVAC, HVACR) *1 student enrolled* • Heavy/Industrial Equipment Maintenance Technologies, Other *1 student enrolled* • Human Resources Management/Personnel Administration, General *3 students enrolled* • Hydraulics and Fluid Power Technology/Technician *1 student enrolled* • Industrial Production Technologies/Technicians, Other *1 student enrolled* • Labor and Industrial Relations • Legal Administrative Assistant/Secretary • Legal Assistant/Paralegal *7 students enrolled* • Licensed Practical/Vocational Nurse Training (LPN, LVN, Cert, Dipl, AAS) *28 students enrolled* • Management Information Systems, General *11 students enrolled* • Massage Therapy/Therapeutic Massage *2 students enrolled* • Medical Administrative/Executive Assistant and Medical Secretary *2 students enrolled* • Medical Radiologic Technology/Science—Radiation Therapist • Occupational Safety and Health Technology/Technician *3 students enrolled* • Parks, Recreation and Leisure Studies • Parks, Recreation, Leisure and Fitness Studies, Other *6 students enrolled* • Physician Assistant *26 students enrolled* • Psychiatric/Mental Health Services Technician *2 students enrolled* • Quality Control Technology/Technician • Radio and Television Broadcasting Technology/Technician • Real Estate • Science Technologies/

Technicians, Other *1 student enrolled* • Sign Language Interpretation and Translation *6 students enrolled* • Special Education and Teaching, General • Special Products Marketing Operations *1 student enrolled* • Substance Abuse/Addiction Counseling *4 students enrolled* • Surgical Technology/Technologist • Survey Technology/Surveying *13 students enrolled* • Visual and Performing Arts, Other *1 student enrolled*

STUDENT SERVICES Academic or career counseling, daycare for children of students, employment services for current students, placement services for program completers, remedial services.

Delmarva Beauty Academy

111 Milford Street, Salisbury, MD 21804-6952
http://delmarvabeautyacademy.com/

CONTACT Carol M. Evans, President
Telephone: 410-742-7929

GENERAL INFORMATION Private Institution. **Total program enrollment:** 68.

PROGRAM(S) OFFERED
• Cosmetology/Cosmetologist, General *1500 hrs./$14,526* • Nail Technician/Specialist and Manicurist *250 hrs./$2930*

STUDENT SERVICES Academic or career counseling, employment services for current students, placement services for program completers.

Empire Beauty School–Owings Mills

9616 Reisterstown Road, Owings Mills, MD 21117
http://www.empire.edu/

CONTACT Michael Bouman, President
Telephone: 800-223-3271

GENERAL INFORMATION Private Institution. **Total program enrollment:** 78. **Application fee:** $100.

PROGRAM(S) OFFERED
• Cosmetology/Cosmetologist, General *1530 hrs./$18,845* • Nail Technician/Specialist and Manicurist

STUDENT SERVICES Placement services for program completers.

Everest Institute

8757 Georgia Avenue, Silver Spring, MD 20910
http://www.everest.edu/

CONTACT Michael Trembley, President
Telephone: 301-495-4400

GENERAL INFORMATION Private Institution. **Total program enrollment:** 753.

PROGRAM(S) OFFERED
• Health Services/Allied Health/Health Sciences, General *720 hrs./$14,690*

STUDENT SERVICES Academic or career counseling, placement services for program completers.

The Fila Academy Inc

6320 F Ritchie Highway, Glen Burnie, MD 21061
http://www.FilaAcademy.com

CONTACT Larry V. Fila, Jr., Director
Telephone: 410-789-9516

GENERAL INFORMATION Private Institution. **Total program enrollment:** 54.

The Fila Academy Inc (continued)

PROGRAM(S) OFFERED
● **Aesthetician/Esthetician and Skin Care Specialist** *600 hrs./$6975*
● **Barbering/Barber** *1200 hrs./$16,150* ● **Nail Technician/Specialist and Manicurist** *250 hrs./$1550*

STUDENT SERVICES Employment services for current students, placement services for program completers.

Frederick Community College

7932 Opossumtown Pike, Frederick, MD 21702-2097
http://www.frederick.edu/

CONTACT Carol Eaton, President
Telephone: 301-846-2400

GENERAL INFORMATION Public Institution. Founded 1957. **Accreditation:** Regional (MSA/CIHE); surgical technology (ARCST). **Total program enrollment:** 2163.

PROGRAM(S) OFFERED
● **Accounting Technology/Technician and Bookkeeping** *11 students enrolled* ● **Architectural Drafting and Architectural CAD/CADD** ● **Banking and Financial Support Services** ● **Biology Technician/Biotechnology Laboratory Technician** ● **Building/Construction Finishing, Management, and Inspection, Other** *2 students enrolled* ● **Building/Construction Site Management/Manager** ● **Business Administration and Management, General** *1 student enrolled* ● **Business Administration, Management and Operations, Other** ● **Business Statistics** ● **Child Care and Support Services Management** *4 students enrolled* ● **Commercial and Advertising Art** *2 students enrolled* ● **Computer Software Technology/Technician** ● **Computer Technology/Computer Systems Technology** ● **Computer and Information Sciences, General** ● **Construction Trades, Other** ● **Corrections and Criminal Justice, Other** *2 students enrolled* ● **Culinary Arts/Chef Training** *1 student enrolled* ● **Drafting and Design Technology/Technician, General** ● **Early Childhood Education and Teaching** ● **Education/Teaching of Individuals with Hearing Impairments, Including Deafness** ● **Emergency Medical Technology/Technician (EMT Paramedic)** *2 students enrolled* ● **Hotel/Motel Administration/Management** *1 student enrolled* ● **Legal Assistant/Paralegal** *3 students enrolled* ● **Licensed Practical/Vocational Nurse Training (LPN, LVN, Cert, Dipl, AAS)** *21 students enrolled* ● **Management Information Systems and Services, Other** ● **Management Information Systems, General** *11 students enrolled* ● **Medical Administrative/Executive Assistant and Medical Secretary** *6 students enrolled* ● **Nuclear Medical Technology/Technologist** *3 students enrolled* ● **Public Administration** *4 students enrolled* ● **Radio and Television Broadcasting Technology/Technician** *1 student enrolled* ● **Substance Abuse/Addiction Counseling** ● **Surgical Technology/Technologist** *14 students enrolled*

STUDENT SERVICES Academic or career counseling, daycare for children of students, employment services for current students, placement services for program completers, remedial services.

Garrett College

687 Mosser Road, McHenry, MD 21541
http://www.garrettcollege.edu/

CONTACT Dr. Rebecca McBride Di Liddo, Acting President
Telephone: 301-387-3000

GENERAL INFORMATION Public Institution. Founded 1966. **Accreditation:** Regional (MSA/CIHE). **Total program enrollment:** 584.

PROGRAM(S) OFFERED
● **Business Administration and Management, General** *2 students enrolled* ● **Computer Technology/Computer Systems Technology** *5 students enrolled* ● **Corrections** *1 student enrolled* ● **Truck and Bus Driver/Commercial Vehicle Operation** *54 students enrolled* ● **Web Page, Digital/Multimedia and Information Resources Design** *1 student enrolled*

STUDENT SERVICES Academic or career counseling, employment services for current students, placement services for program completers, remedial services.

Hagerstown Community College

11400 Robinwood Drive, Hagerstown, MD 21742-6590
http://www.hagerstowncc.edu/

CONTACT Dr. Guy Altieri, President
Telephone: 301-766-4422

GENERAL INFORMATION Public Institution. Founded 1946. **Accreditation:** Regional (MSA/CIHE); radiologic technology: radiography (JRCERT). **Total program enrollment:** 1342.

PROGRAM(S) OFFERED
● **Administrative Assistant and Secretarial Science, General** ● **Allied Health Diagnostic, Intervention, and Treatment Professions, Other** *2 students enrolled* ● **Animation, Interactive Technology, Video Graphics and Special Effects** ● **Architectural Drafting and Architectural CAD/CADD** *3 students enrolled* ● **Biology Technician/Biotechnology Laboratory Technician** ● **Building/Property Maintenance and Management** ● **Business Administration and Management, General** *5 students enrolled* ● **Child Care and Support Services Management** ● **Commercial and Advertising Art** *2 students enrolled* ● **Computer Programming, Specific Applications** ● **Computer Programming, Vendor/Product Certification** *5 students enrolled* ● **Computer Programming/Programmer, General** ● **Corrections** ● **Criminal Justice/Police Science** ● **Data Processing and Data Processing Technology/Technician** ● **Education, General** *4 students enrolled* ● **Electromechanical Technology/Electromechanical Engineering Technology** ● **Emergency Medical Technology/Technician (EMT Paramedic)** ● **Executive Assistant/Executive Secretary** ● **General Office Occupations and Clerical Services** ● **Health and Physical Education, General** *2 students enrolled* ● **Industrial Technology/Technician** ● **Legal Assistant/Paralegal** *5 students enrolled* ● **Licensed Practical/Vocational Nurse Training (LPN, LVN, Cert, Dipl, AAS)** *22 students enrolled* ● **Management Information Systems, General** *28 students enrolled* ● **Marketing/Marketing Management, General** *3 students enrolled* ● **Mechanical Engineering/Mechanical Technology/Technician** ● **Medical Administrative/Executive Assistant and Medical Secretary** *6 students enrolled* ● **Medical Insurance Coding Specialist/Coder** *8 students enrolled* ● **Medical Radiologic Technology/Science—Radiation Therapist** *1 student enrolled* ● **Medical/Health Management and Clinical Assistant/Specialist** *2 students enrolled* ● **Nursing, Other** ● **Phlebotomy/Phlebotomist** *18 students enrolled* ● **Receptionist** *10 students enrolled* ● **Transportation/Transportation Management** ● **Truck and Bus Driver/Commercial Vehicle Operation** *112 students enrolled* ● **Web Page, Digital/Multimedia and Information Resources Design** *6 students enrolled*

STUDENT SERVICES Academic or career counseling, daycare for children of students, employment services for current students, placement services for program completers, remedial services.

Hair Academy–New Carrollton

8435 Old Annapolis Road, New Carrollton, MD 20784

CONTACT Carl F. Catlin, President
Telephone: 301-459-2509

GENERAL INFORMATION Private Institution. **Total program enrollment:** 110.

PROGRAM(S) OFFERED
● **Cosmetology/Cosmetologist, General** *900 hrs./$15,190*

STUDENT SERVICES Placement services for program completers.

Hair Expressions Academy

12450 Parklawn Drive, 2nd Floor, Rockville, MD 20852
http://www.hairex.com/

CONTACT Ed Ruiz, Owner/Director
Telephone: 301-984-8182

GENERAL INFORMATION Private Institution. **Total program enrollment:** 87. **Application fee:** $100.

PROGRAM(S) OFFERED
● **Cosmetology and Related Personal Grooming Arts, Other** *1500 hrs./$15,400*

Harford Community College

401 Thomas Run Road, Bel Air, MD 21015-1698
http://www.harford.edu/

CONTACT James F. Lacalle, President
Telephone: 410-836-4000

GENERAL INFORMATION Public Institution. Founded 1957. **Accreditation:** Regional (MSA/CIHE); histologic technology (NAACLS). **Total program enrollment:** 2751.

PROGRAM(S) OFFERED
• **Accounting Technology/Technician and Bookkeeping** *3 students enrolled* • **Business Administration and Management, General** *3 students enrolled* • **Commercial Photography** *2 students enrolled* • **Computer Programming, Specific Applications** *1 student enrolled* • **Design and Visual Communications, General** *1 student enrolled* • **Drafting and Design Technology/Technician, General** • **Elementary Education and Teaching** • **Interior Design** *1 student enrolled* • **Legal Assistant/Paralegal** *3 students enrolled* • **Licensed Practical/Vocational Nurse Training (LPN, LVN, Cert, Dipl, AAS)** *6 students enrolled* • **Medical/Clinical Assistant** *2 students enrolled* • **Political Science and Government, Other** • **Secondary Education and Teaching**

STUDENT SERVICES Academic or career counseling, daycare for children of students, employment services for current students, placement services for program completers, remedial services.

Howard Community College

10901 Little Patuxent Parkway, Columbia, MD 21044-3197
http://www.howardcc.edu/

CONTACT Kathleen Hetherington, President
Telephone: 410-772-4800

GENERAL INFORMATION Public Institution. Founded 1966. **Accreditation:** Regional (MSA/CIHE). **Total program enrollment:** 3046. **Application fee:** $25.

PROGRAM(S) OFFERED
• **Administrative Assistant and Secretarial Science, General** • **Allied Health Diagnostic, Intervention, and Treatment Professions, Other** • **Applied Horticulture/Horticultural Operations, General** • **Arts Management** • **Biomedical Technology/Technician** *2 students enrolled* • **Building/Construction Finishing, Management, and Inspection, Other** • **Business Administration and Management, General** *2 students enrolled* • **Business Administration, Management and Operations, Other** • **Cardiovascular Technology/Technologist** *6 students enrolled* • **Child Care and Support Services Management** • **Commercial Photography** • **Commercial and Advertising Art** *5 students enrolled* • **Communication Studies/Speech Communication and Rhetoric** • **Computer Systems Networking and Telecommunications** *1 student enrolled* • **Computer Technology/Computer Systems Technology** • **Drafting and Design Technology/Technician, General** *2 students enrolled* • **Electrical, Electronic and Communications Engineering Technology/Technician** • **Emergency Medical Technology/Technician (EMT Paramedic)** *6 students enrolled* • **Engineering Technologies/Technicians, Other** • **General Merchandising, Sales, and Related Marketing Operations, Other** • **Licensed Practical/Vocational Nurse Training (LPN, LVN, Cert, Dipl, AAS)** *20 students enrolled* • **Management Information Systems, General** • **Parks, Recreation, Leisure and Fitness Studies, Other** • **Psychiatric/Mental Health Services Technician** *2 students enrolled* • **Restaurant, Culinary, and Catering Management/Manager** *3 students enrolled*

STUDENT SERVICES Academic or career counseling, daycare for children of students, employment services for current students, remedial services.

International Beauty School 3

227 Archer Street, Bel Air, MD 21014

CONTACT Petros K. Alevras, Chief Executive Officer
Telephone: 410-838-0845 Ext. 10

GENERAL INFORMATION Private Institution. **Total program enrollment:** 13. **Application fee:** $25.

PROGRAM(S) OFFERED
• **Cosmetology/Cosmetologist, General** *1500 hrs./$11,435* • **Nail Technician/Specialist and Manicurist** *250 hrs./$2500*

STUDENT SERVICES Academic or career counseling, placement services for program completers.

International Beauty School 5

PO Box 1597, Cumberland, MD 21501-1597

CONTACT Ziad Fadel, President
Telephone: 301-777-3020

GENERAL INFORMATION Private Institution. **Total program enrollment:** 61.

PROGRAM(S) OFFERED
• **Cosmetology/Cosmetologist, General** *1500 hrs./$12,150*

STUDENT SERVICES Academic or career counseling, placement services for program completers.

Kaplan College–Hagerstown

18618 Crestwood Drive, Hagerstown, MD 21742-2797
http://www.kc-hagerstown.com

CONTACT W. Christopher Motz, President
Telephone: 301-739-2670 Ext. 0

GENERAL INFORMATION Private Institution. Founded 1938. **Accreditation:** Health information technology (AHIMA); state accredited or approved. **Total program enrollment:** 724.

PROGRAM(S) OFFERED
• **Accounting Technology/Technician and Bookkeeping** • **Business/Office Automation/Technology/Data Entry** • **Clinical/Medical Laboratory Science and Allied Professions, Other** • **Computer Technology/Computer Systems Technology** • **Dental Assisting/Assistant** *40 students enrolled* • **Health Information/Medical Records Technology/Technician** *14 students enrolled* • **Legal Administrative Assistant/Secretary** • **Medical Administrative/Executive Assistant and Medical Secretary** *31 students enrolled* • **Receptionist**

STUDENT SERVICES Academic or career counseling, employment services for current students, placement services for program completers, remedial services.

Lincoln Technical Institute

9325 Snowden River Parkway, Columbia, MD 21046
http://www.lincolnedu.com/

CONTACT Susan L. Sherwood, Executive Director
Telephone: 410-290-7100

GENERAL INFORMATION Private Institution. Founded 1946. **Total program enrollment:** 1227.

PROGRAM(S) OFFERED
• **Automobile/Automotive Mechanics Technology/Technician** *1560 hrs./$26,775* • **Culinary Arts/Chef Training** *1440 hrs./$27,992* • **Electrical/Electronics Equipment Installation and Repair, General** *1080 hrs./$18,228* • **Heating, Air Conditioning, Ventilation and Refrigeration Maintenance Technology/Technician (HAC, HACR, HVAC, HVACR)** *1200 hrs./$19,510*

STUDENT SERVICES Academic or career counseling, employment services for current students, placement services for program completers, remedial services.

Maple Springs Baptist Bible College and Seminary

4130 Belt Road, Capitol Heights, MD 20743
http://www.msbbcs.edu/

CONTACT Larry W. Jordan, President
Telephone: 301-736-3631

GENERAL INFORMATION Private Institution. Founded 1986. **Accreditation:** State accredited or approved. **Total program enrollment:** 12. **Application fee:** $40.

PROGRAM(S) OFFERED
• Bible/Biblical Studies *2 students enrolled*

STUDENT SERVICES Academic or career counseling.

Maryland Beauty Academy

152 Chartley Drive, Reisterstown, MD 21136
http://www.baltimorestudio.net/

CONTACT Jaime Davidov, Administrator
Telephone: 410-517-0442

GENERAL INFORMATION Private Institution. Founded 1971. **Total program enrollment:** 11.

PROGRAM(S) OFFERED
• Cosmetology/Cosmetologist, General *1500 hrs./$14,650*

STUDENT SERVICES Academic or career counseling, employment services for current students, placement services for program completers.

Maryland Beauty Academy of Essex

505 Eastern Boulevard, Essex, MD 21221
http://www.baltimorestudio.net/

CONTACT Justin Sisserman, Administrator
Telephone: 410-686-4477

GENERAL INFORMATION Private Institution. **Total program enrollment:** 20.

PROGRAM(S) OFFERED
• Cosmetology/Cosmetologist, General *1500 hrs./$14,650* • Nail Technician/Specialist and Manicurist *250 hrs./$1850*

STUDENT SERVICES Academic or career counseling, employment services for current students, placement services for program completers.

Maryland Institute College of Art

1300 Mount Royal Avenue, Baltimore, MD 21217
http://www.mica.edu/

CONTACT Fred Lazarus, IV, President
Telephone: 410-669-9200

GENERAL INFORMATION Private Institution. Founded 1826. **Accreditation:** Regional (MSA/CIHE); art and design (NASAD). **Total program enrollment:** 1763. **Application fee:** $50.

PROGRAM(S) OFFERED
• Art/Art Studies, General *2 students enrolled* • Commercial Photography *4 students enrolled* • Graphic Design *11 students enrolled* • Interior Design *16 students enrolled*

STUDENT SERVICES Academic or career counseling, employment services for current students, placement services for program completers, remedial services.

Medix School

700 York Road, Towson, MD 21204
http://www.medixschool.com/

CONTACT Sheila Kell, Director
Telephone: 410-337-5155

GENERAL INFORMATION Private Institution. **Total program enrollment:** 553. **Application fee:** $50.

PROGRAM(S) OFFERED
• Dental Assisting/Assistant *42 hrs./$13,850* • Massage Therapy/Therapeutic Massage *34 hrs./$10,000* • Medical Administrative/Executive Assistant and Medical Secretary *37 students enrolled* • Medical Office Assistant/Specialist *45 hrs./$10,650* • Medical/Clinical Assistant *45 hrs./$12,509*

STUDENT SERVICES Academic or career counseling, employment services for current students, placement services for program completers.

Medix School–West

6901 Security Boulevard, Suite 21, Baltimore, MD 21244
http://www.medixschool.edu

CONTACT Sidney Carey, Campus Director
Telephone: 410-907-8110 Ext. 241

GENERAL INFORMATION Private Institution. **Total program enrollment:** 580. **Application fee:** $50.

PROGRAM(S) OFFERED
• Cosmetology/Cosmetologist, General *19 students enrolled* • Health Services/Allied Health/Health Sciences, General *213 students enrolled*

STUDENT SERVICES Academic or career counseling, placement services for program completers.

Medix South

4351 Garden City Drive, Landover, MD 20785

CONTACT Mr. Don McMullen, School Director
Telephone: 301-459-3650

GENERAL INFORMATION Private Institution. **Total program enrollment:** 264.

PROGRAM(S) OFFERED
• Biology Technician/Biotechnology Laboratory Technician • Dental Assisting/Assistant • Medical Insurance Coding Specialist/Coder • Medical/Clinical Assistant

STUDENT SERVICES Academic or career counseling, employment services for current students, remedial services.

Montgomery Beauty School

8736 Arliss Street, Silver Spring, MD 20901

CONTACT James Bileny, President
Telephone: 301-459-2509

GENERAL INFORMATION Private Institution. **Total program enrollment:** 61.

PROGRAM(S) OFFERED
• Cosmetology/Cosmetologist, General *900 hrs./$15,190*

STUDENT SERVICES Placement services for program completers.

Montgomery College

900 Hungerford Drive, Rockville, MD 20850
http://www.montgomerycollege.edu/

CONTACT Dr. Brian K. Johnson, President
Telephone: 240-567-5000

GENERAL INFORMATION Public Institution. Founded 1946. **Accreditation:** Regional (MSA/CIHE); health information technology (AHIMA);

music (NASM); physical therapy assisting (APTA); surgical technology (ARCST). **Total program enrollment:** 9415. **Application fee:** $25.

PROGRAM(S) OFFERED
• **Accounting Technology/Technician and Bookkeeping** *29 students enrolled* • **Animation, Interactive Technology, Video Graphics and Special Effects** *1 student enrolled* • **Applied Horticulture/Horticultural Operations, General** *1 student enrolled* • **Architectural Drafting and Architectural CAD/CADD** *28 students enrolled* • **Area, Ethnic, Cultural, and Gender Studies, Other** • **Audiovisual Communications Technologies/Technicians, Other** *16 students enrolled* • **Automobile/Automotive Mechanics Technology/Technician** *42 students enrolled* • **Biology Technician/Biotechnology Laboratory Technician** *5 students enrolled* • **Building/Construction Finishing, Management, and Inspection, Other** *7 students enrolled* • **Business Administration and Management, General** *11 students enrolled* • **Child Care Provider/Assistant** *9 students enrolled* • **Commercial Photography** *6 students enrolled* • **Commercial and Advertising Art** *15 students enrolled* • **Computer Programming, Specific Applications** • **Computer Programming/Programmer, General** *3 students enrolled* • **Computer Systems Networking and Telecommunications** • **Computer Technology/Computer Systems Technology** *2 students enrolled* • **Computer and Information Systems Security** • **Data Entry/Microcomputer Applications, General** *1 student enrolled* • **Data Processing and Data Processing Technology/Technician** *9 students enrolled* • **Diagnostic Medical Sonography/Sonographer and Ultrasound Technician** *4 students enrolled* • **Fire Protection and Safety Technology/Technician** • **Geography** *4 students enrolled* • **Geography, Other** *6 students enrolled* • **Graphic and Printing Equipment Operator, General Production** *4 students enrolled* • **Health Information/Medical Records Technology/Technician** *13 students enrolled* • **Health and Physical Education/Fitness, Other** *3 students enrolled* • **Hotel/Motel Administration/Management** • **Human Resources Management/Personnel Administration, General** *1 student enrolled* • **Interior Design** *5 students enrolled* • **Legal Assistant/Paralegal** *19 students enrolled* • **Management Information Systems and Services, Other** *5 students enrolled* • **Parks, Recreation and Leisure Facilities Management** *5 students enrolled* • **Radio and Television Broadcasting Technology/Technician** *3 students enrolled* • **Restaurant, Culinary, and Catering Management/Manager** *3 students enrolled* • **Sign Language Interpretation and Translation** *1 student enrolled* • **Surgical Technology/Technologist** *4 students enrolled* • **Technical and Business Writing** *1 student enrolled*

STUDENT SERVICES Academic or career counseling, daycare for children of students, employment services for current students, placement services for program completers, remedial services.

New Creations Academy of Hair Design

3930 Bexley Place, Suitland, MD 20746

CONTACT Carla Robinson, Owner
Telephone: 301-899-9100

GENERAL INFORMATION Private Institution. **Total program enrollment:** 23. **Application fee:** $100.

PROGRAM(S) OFFERED
• **Cosmetology/Cosmetologist, General** *1500 hrs./$12,600*

North American Trade Schools

Route 40, Box 69, Grantsville, MD 21536
http://natradeschools.com/

CONTACT Matt Daly, Director
Telephone: 410-298-4844

GENERAL INFORMATION Private Institution. **Total program enrollment:** 486. **Application fee:** $25.

PROGRAM(S) OFFERED
• **Construction Trades, General** *1152 hrs./$12,864* • **Diesel Mechanics Technology/Technician** *1008 hrs./$11,442* • **Electrical and Power Transmission Installation/Installer, General** *31 students enrolled* • **Electrical/Electronics Equipment Installation and Repair, General** *1152 hrs./$12,333* • **Heating, Air Conditioning, Ventilation and Refrigeration Maintenance Technology/Technician (HAC, HACR, HVAC, HVACR)** *1152 hrs./$14,364* • **Truck and Bus Driver/Commercial Vehicle Operation** *320 hrs./$4800*

STUDENT SERVICES Employment services for current students, placement services for program completers.

Prince George's Community College

301 Largo Road, Largo, MD 20774-2199
http://www.pgcc.edu/

CONTACT Charlene M. Dukes, President
Telephone: 301-336-6000

GENERAL INFORMATION Public Institution. Founded 1958. **Accreditation:** Regional (MSA/CIHE); engineering technology (ABET/TAC); health information technology (AHIMA); nuclear medicine technology (JRC-NMT); radiologic technology: radiography (JRCERT). **Total program enrollment:** 3071. **Application fee:** $25.

PROGRAM(S) OFFERED
• **Accounting Technology/Technician and Bookkeeping** *6 students enrolled* • **Accounting and Related Services, Other** *1 student enrolled* • **Administrative Assistant and Secretarial Science, General** • **Building/Construction Finishing, Management, and Inspection, Other** *7 students enrolled* • **Building/Property Maintenance and Management** • **Business Administration and Management, General** *10 students enrolled* • **Child Care Provider/Assistant** *7 students enrolled* • **Commercial and Advertising Art** *6 students enrolled* • **Computer Installation and Repair Technology/Technician** *10 students enrolled* • **Computer Programming, Specific Applications** *2 students enrolled* • **Computer Programming, Vendor/Product Certification** • **Computer Systems Networking and Telecommunications** *8 students enrolled* • **Computer Technology/Computer Systems Technology** *13 students enrolled* • **Computer and Information Sciences and Support Services, Other** *2 students enrolled* • **Computer and Information Systems Security** • **Criminal Justice/Police Science** *1 student enrolled* • **Drafting and Design Technology/Technician, General** • **Electrical, Electronic and Communications Engineering Technology/Technician** *1 student enrolled* • **Emergency Medical Technology/Technician (EMT Paramedic)** *29 students enrolled* • **Engineering Technologies/Technicians, Other** • **Health Information/Medical Records Technology/Technician** *7 students enrolled* • **Hotel/Motel Administration/Management** • **Human Resources Management/Personnel Administration, General** *11 students enrolled* • **Legal Assistant/Paralegal** *5 students enrolled* • **Licensed Practical/Vocational Nurse Training (LPN, LVN, Cert, Dipl, AAS)** *7 students enrolled* • **Management Information Systems, General** *1 student enrolled* • **Marketing/Marketing Management, General** *1 student enrolled* • **Medical Office Management/Administration** • **Nuclear Medical Technology/Technologist** • **Public Administration** *1 student enrolled* • **Quality Control Technology/Technician** • **Special Education and Teaching, General** *10 students enrolled* • **Technical Theatre/Theatre Design and Technology** *2 students enrolled* • **Web Page, Digital/Multimedia and Information Resources Design**

STUDENT SERVICES Academic or career counseling, daycare for children of students, employment services for current students, placement services for program completers, remedial services.

Robert Paul Academy of Cosmetology Arts and Sciences

1811B York Road, Grand York Shopping Center, Timonium, MD 21093
http://www.robertpaulacademy.com/

CONTACT Daria Ferrara, Director
Telephone: 410-252-4244

GENERAL INFORMATION Private Institution. **Total program enrollment:** 34. **Application fee:** $100.

PROGRAM(S) OFFERED
• **Cosmetology and Related Personal Grooming Arts, Other** *10 students enrolled* • **Cosmetology/Cosmetologist, General** *1500 hrs./$15,750* • **Nail Technician/Specialist and Manicurist** *250 hrs./$2020*

STUDENT SERVICES Placement services for program completers.

Ross Medical Education Center–New Baltimore

51133 Birch Street, Suite 100, New Baltimore, MD 48047

CONTACT Paul Mitchell, President/CEO
Telephone: 586-716-3837

GENERAL INFORMATION Private Institution. **Total program enrollment:** 67. **Application fee:** $45.

PROGRAM(S) OFFERED
• Medical Insurance Specialist/Medical Biller *52 hrs./$13,555* • Medical/Clinical Assistant *45 hrs./$13,555*

STUDENT SERVICES Placement services for program completers.

Sanford-Brown Institute

8401 Corporate Drive, Suite 500, Landover, MD 20785
http://www.udseducation.com/

CONTACT Greta L. Bonaparte, President
Telephone: 301-683-2400

GENERAL INFORMATION Private Institution. **Total program enrollment:** 586. **Application fee:** $25.

PROGRAM(S) OFFERED
• Cardiovascular Technology/Technologist *1950 hrs./$32,975* • Diagnostic Medical Sonography/Sonographer and Ultrasound Technician *1860 hrs./$32,975* • Medical Insurance Coding Specialist/Coder *950 hrs./$12,903* • Medical/Clinical Assistant *900 hrs./$12,903*

STUDENT SERVICES Academic or career counseling, placement services for program completers.

TESST College of Technology

1520 South Caton Avenue, Baltimore, MD 21227-1063
http://www.tesst.com/

CONTACT Mark Millen, President
Telephone: 410-644-6400

GENERAL INFORMATION Private Institution. Founded 1956. **Accreditation:** State accredited or approved. **Total program enrollment:** 1066.

PROGRAM(S) OFFERED
• Computer Systems Networking and Telecommunications *43 hrs./$19,330* • Drafting and Design Technology/Technician, General *17 students enrolled* • Heating, Air Conditioning and Refrigeration Technology/Technician (ACH/ACR/ACHR/HRAC/HVAC/AC Technology) *46 hrs./$17,650* • Heating, Air Conditioning, Ventilation and Refrigeration Maintenance Technology/Technician (HAC, HACR, HVAC, HVACR) *37 hrs./$17,650* • Management Information Systems, General *34 students enrolled* • Medical/Clinical Assistant *45 hrs./$14,970* • Pharmacy Technician/Assistant *51 hrs./$14,200*

STUDENT SERVICES Employment services for current students, placement services for program completers, remedial services.

TESST College of Technology

4600 Powder Mill Road, Beltsville, MD 20705
http://www.tesst.com/

CONTACT Sandra Ugol, President
Telephone: 301-937-8448

GENERAL INFORMATION Private Institution. Founded 1967. **Accreditation:** State accredited or approved. **Total program enrollment:** 668.

PROGRAM(S) OFFERED
• Business/Office Automation/Technology/Data Entry *21 students enrolled* • Computer Systems Analysis/Analyst *14 students enrolled* • Computer Systems Networking and Telecommunications *90 hrs./$27,180* • Criminal Justice/Police Science *95 hrs./$28,170* • Data Entry/Microcomputer Applications,

General *43 hrs./$24,210* • Electrical, Electronic and Communications Engineering Technology/Technician *105 hrs./$29,910* • Electrician *71 hrs./$18,160* • Massage Therapy/Therapeutic Massage • Medical/Clinical Assistant *720 hrs./$14,350*

STUDENT SERVICES Academic or career counseling, employment services for current students, placement services for program completers.

TESST College of Technology

803 Glen Eagles Court, Towson, MD 21286-2201
http://www.tesst.com/

CONTACT Kevin Beaver, President
Telephone: 410-296-5350

GENERAL INFORMATION Private Institution. Founded 1992. **Accreditation:** State accredited or approved. **Total program enrollment:** 407.

PROGRAM(S) OFFERED
• Administrative Assistant and Secretarial Science, General • Business/Office Automation/Technology/Data Entry • Computer Systems Networking and Telecommunications *91 hrs./$26,910* • Computer and Information Sciences and Support Services, Other *54 hrs./$10,920* • Criminal Justice/Law Enforcement Administration *96 hrs./$27,010* • Electrical, Electronic and Communications Engineering Technology/Technician *106 hrs./$28,160* • Management Information Systems, General • Massage Therapy/Therapeutic Massage • Medical/Clinical Assistant *720 hrs./$14,970*

STUDENT SERVICES Academic or career counseling, employment services for current students, placement services for program completers.

University of Maryland, College Park

College Park, MD 20742
http://www.maryland.edu/

CONTACT Clayton Daniel Mote, Jr., President
Telephone: 301-405-1000

GENERAL INFORMATION Public Institution. Founded 1856. **Accreditation:** Regional (MSA/CIHE); audiology (ASHA); counseling (ACA); dietetics: postbaccalaureate internship (ADtA/CAADE); journalism and mass communications (ACEJMC); library and information science (ALA); music (NASM); public health: community health education (CEPH); speech-language pathology (ASHA); theater (NAST). **Total program enrollment:** 31317. **Application fee:** $55.

STUDENT SERVICES Academic or career counseling, daycare for children of students, employment services for current students, placement services for program completers, remedial services.

University of Phoenix–Maryland Campus

8830 Stanford Boulevard, Suite 100, Columbia, MD 21045-5424
http://www.phoenix.edu/

CONTACT William Pepicello, PhD, President
Telephone: 866-332-1333

GENERAL INFORMATION Private Institution. **Accreditation:** Regional (NCA). **Total program enrollment:** 812.

STUDENT SERVICES Academic or career counseling, remedial services.

Washington Bible College

6511 Princess Garden Parkway, Lanham, MD 20706-3599
http://www.bible.edu/

CONTACT Larry A. Mercer, President
Telephone: 301-552-1400

GENERAL INFORMATION Private Institution. Founded 1938. **Accreditation:** Regional (MSA/CIHE); state accredited or approved. **Total program enrollment:** 237. **Application fee:** $35.

PROGRAM(S) OFFERED
● Bible/Biblical Studies *2 students enrolled*

STUDENT SERVICES Academic or career counseling, remedial services.

Wor-Wic Community College

32000 Campus Drive, Salisbury, MD 21804
http://www.worwic.edu/

CONTACT Dr. Murray K. Hoy, President
Telephone: 410-334-2800

GENERAL INFORMATION Public Institution. Founded 1976. **Accreditation:** Regional (MSA/CIHE); radiologic technology: radiography (JRCERT). **Total program enrollment:** 1226.

PROGRAM(S) OFFERED
● Accounting Technology/Technician and Bookkeeping *2 students enrolled* ● Administrative Assistant and Secretarial Science, General *10 students enrolled* ● Architectural Drafting and Architectural CAD/CADD *4 students enrolled* ● Business Administration and Management, General ● Child Care and Support Services Management *1 student enrolled* ● Computer Systems Analysis/Analyst *4 students enrolled* ● Criminal Justice/Police Science *42 students enrolled* ● Electrical, Electronic and Communications Engineering Technology/Technician ● Emergency Medical Technology/Technician (EMT Paramedic) *9 students enrolled* ● Engineering Technologies/Technicians, Other ● Hospitality Administration/Management, General *8 students enrolled* ● Licensed Practical/Vocational Nurse Training (LPN, LVN, Cert, Dipl, AAS) *51 students enrolled* ● Substance Abuse/Addiction Counseling *1 student enrolled*

STUDENT SERVICES Academic or career counseling, daycare for children of students, employment services for current students, placement services for program completers, remedial services.

MASSACHUSETTS ———

Ailano School of Cosmetology

541 West Street, Brockton, MA 02401
http://www.ailanoschool.com/

CONTACT Karen F. Iolli, Administrator
Telephone: 508-583-5433

GENERAL INFORMATION Private Institution. **Total program enrollment:** 58. **Application fee:** $100.

PROGRAM(S) OFFERED
● Cosmetology/Cosmetologist, General *1000 hrs./$12,000* ● Nail Technician/Specialist and Manicurist *100 hrs./$1040*

STUDENT SERVICES Academic or career counseling, placement services for program completers.

American International College

1000 State Street, Springfield, MA 01109-3189
http://www.aic.edu/

CONTACT Vincent M. Maniaci, President
Telephone: 413-737-7000

GENERAL INFORMATION Private Institution. Founded 1885. **Accreditation:** Regional (NEASC/NEASCCIHE). **Total program enrollment:** 1751. **Application fee:** $25.

STUDENT SERVICES Academic or career counseling, employment services for current students, placement services for program completers, remedial services.

Assumption College

500 Salisbury Street, Worcester, MA 01609-1296
http://www.assumption.edu/

CONTACT Francesco C. Cesareo, President
Telephone: 508-767-7000

GENERAL INFORMATION Private Institution. Founded 1904. **Accreditation:** Regional (NEASC/NEASCCIHE). **Total program enrollment:** 2316. **Application fee:** $50.

PROGRAM(S) OFFERED
● Accounting *4 students enrolled* ● Business Administration and Management, General *3 students enrolled* ● Business/Corporate Communications ● Criminal Justice/Safety Studies *1 student enrolled* ● Graphic Design ● Health/Health Care Administration/Management ● Human Resources Management/Personnel Administration, General *8 students enrolled* ● Legal Assistant/Paralegal *4 students enrolled*

STUDENT SERVICES Academic or career counseling, employment services for current students, placement services for program completers.

Atlantic Union College

PO Box 1000, South Lancaster, MA 01561-1000
http://www.auc.edu/

CONTACT Norman Wendth, President
Telephone: 978-368-2000

GENERAL INFORMATION Private Institution. Founded 1882. **Accreditation:** Regional (NEASC/NEASCCIHE); music (NASM). **Total program enrollment:** 567. **Application fee:** $25.

PROGRAM(S) OFFERED
● Communication Studies/Speech Communication and Rhetoric ● Computer Science ● Computer and Information Sciences, General ● Culinary Arts/Chef Training *5 students enrolled* ● Legal Assistant/Paralegal

STUDENT SERVICES Academic or career counseling, employment services for current students, placement services for program completers, remedial services.

Bancroft School of Massage Therapy

333 Shrewsbury Street, Worcester, MA 01604
http://www.bancroftsmt.com/

CONTACT Steven Tankanow, President
Telephone: 508-757-7923

GENERAL INFORMATION Private Institution. Founded 1950. **Total program enrollment:** 80. **Application fee:** $50.

PROGRAM(S) OFFERED
● Massage Therapy/Therapeutic Massage *36 hrs./$14,575*

STUDENT SERVICES Academic or career counseling, employment services for current students, placement services for program completers.

Bay Path College

588 Longmeadow Street, Longmeadow, MA 01106-2292
http://www.baypath.edu/

CONTACT Carol A. Leary, President
Telephone: 413-565-1000

GENERAL INFORMATION Private Institution. Founded 1897. **Accreditation:** Regional (NEASC/NEASCCIHE). **Total program enrollment:** 1224. **Application fee:** $25.

PROGRAM(S) OFFERED
• Interior Design • Legal Assistant/Paralegal *7 students enrolled*

STUDENT SERVICES Academic or career counseling, employment services for current students, placement services for program completers, remedial services.

Bay State School of Technology

225 Turnpike Street, Route 138, Canton, MA 02021
http://www.baystatetech.com/

CONTACT Robert Mason, President
Telephone: 781-828-3434

GENERAL INFORMATION Private Institution. Founded 1982. **Total program enrollment:** 112. **Application fee:** $100.

PROGRAM(S) OFFERED
• Appliance Installation and Repair Technology/Technician *2 students enrolled* • Computer Installation and Repair Technology/Technician *36 hrs./$14,874* • Electrical/Electronics Equipment Installation and Repair, General *360 hrs./$5874* • Heating, Air Conditioning and Refrigeration Technology/Technician (ACH/ACR/ACHR/HRAC/HVAC/AC Technology) *24 hrs./$10,694* • Heating, Air Conditioning, Ventilation and Refrigeration Maintenance Technology/Technician (HAC, HACR, HVAC, HVACR) *14 students enrolled* • Industrial Electronics Technology/Technician *360 hrs./$5874* • Mechanic and Repair Technologies/Technicians, Other *360 hrs./$5874*

STUDENT SERVICES Academic or career counseling, employment services for current students, placement services for program completers.

Benjamin Franklin Institute of Technology

41 Berkeley Street, Boston, MA 02116-6296
http://www.bfit.edu/

CONTACT Stephen Lozen, Interim President
Telephone: 617-423-4630

GENERAL INFORMATION Private Institution. Founded 1908. **Accreditation:** Regional (NEASC/CVTCI); engineering technology (ABET/TAC). **Total program enrollment:** 416. **Application fee:** $25.

PROGRAM(S) OFFERED
• Automobile/Automotive Mechanics Technology/Technician *20 students enrolled* • Electrician *7 students enrolled* • Heating, Air Conditioning, Ventilation and Refrigeration Maintenance Technology/Technician (HAC, HACR, HVAC, HVACR) *8 students enrolled* • Marine Maintenance/Fitter and Ship Repair Technology/Technician *5 students enrolled* • Pharmacy Technician/Assistant *6 students enrolled*

STUDENT SERVICES Academic or career counseling, employment services for current students, placement services for program completers, remedial services.

Berkshire Community College

1350 West Street, Pittsfield, MA 01201-5786
http://www.berkshirecc.edu/

CONTACT Dr. Paul E. Raverta, President
Telephone: 413-499-4660

GENERAL INFORMATION Public Institution. Founded 1960. **Accreditation:** Regional (NEASC/NEASCCIHE); physical therapy assisting (APTA). **Total program enrollment:** 996. **Application fee:** $10.

PROGRAM(S) OFFERED
• Business Operations Support and Secretarial Services, Other *7 students enrolled* • Computer Programming/Programmer, General *1 student enrolled*

• Culinary Arts/Chef Training *4 students enrolled* • Early Childhood Education and Teaching *11 students enrolled* • Entrepreneurship/Entrepreneurial Studies • Health and Physical Education/Fitness, Other *4 students enrolled* • Industrial Technology/Technician • Licensed Practical/Vocational Nurse Training (LPN, LVN, Cert, Dipl, AAS) *27 students enrolled* • Massage Therapy/Therapeutic Massage *4 students enrolled* • Mental and Social Health Services and Allied Professions, Other *5 students enrolled* • Veterinary/Animal Health Technology/Technician and Veterinary Assistant *4 students enrolled*

STUDENT SERVICES Academic or career counseling, daycare for children of students, employment services for current students, placement services for program completers, remedial services.

Blaine! The Beauty Career Schools–Boston

530 Commonwealth Avenue, Boston, MA 02215
http://www.blainebeautyschools.com/

CONTACT Michael Bouman, President/COO
Telephone: 570-429-4321 Ext. 2414

GENERAL INFORMATION Private Institution. **Total program enrollment:** 121. **Application fee:** $100.

PROGRAM(S) OFFERED
• Cosmetology/Cosmetologist, General *1000 hrs./$11,750*

STUDENT SERVICES Academic or career counseling, placement services for program completers.

Blaine! The Beauty Career Schools–Framingham

624 Worcester Road, Framingham, MA 01701
http://www.blainebeautyschools.com/

CONTACT Michael Bouman, President/COO
Telephone: 570-429-4321 Ext. 2414

GENERAL INFORMATION Private Institution. **Total program enrollment:** 44. **Application fee:** $100.

PROGRAM(S) OFFERED
• Cosmetology/Cosmetologist, General *1000 hrs./$11,750* • Nail Technician/Specialist and Manicurist

STUDENT SERVICES Academic or career counseling, placement services for program completers.

Blaine! The Beauty Career Schools–Hyannis

18 Center Street, Hyannis, MA 02601
http://www.blainebeautyschools.com/

CONTACT Michael Bouman, President/COO
Telephone: 570-429-4321 Ext. 2414

GENERAL INFORMATION Private Institution. Founded 1984. **Total program enrollment:** 37. **Application fee:** $100.

PROGRAM(S) OFFERED
• Aesthetician/Esthetician and Skin Care Specialist *4 students enrolled* • Cosmetology/Cosmetologist, General *1550 hrs./$11,750*

STUDENT SERVICES Academic or career counseling, placement services for program completers.

Blaine! The Beauty Career Schools–Lowell

231 Central Street, Lowell, MA 01852
http://www.blainebeautyschools.com/

CONTACT Michael Bouman, President/COO
Telephone: 570-429-4321 Ext. 2414

GENERAL INFORMATION Private Institution. Founded 1985. **Total program enrollment:** 68. **Application fee:** $100.

PROGRAM(S) OFFERED
• **Aesthetician/Esthetician and Skin Care Specialist** *7 students enrolled*
• **Cosmetology/Cosmetologist, General** *1000 hrs./$11,750*

STUDENT SERVICES Academic or career counseling, placement services for program completers.

Blaine! The Beauty Career Schools–Malden

347 Pleasant Street, Malden, MA 02148
http://www.blainebeautyschools.com/

CONTACT Michael Bouman, President/COO
Telephone: 570-429-4321 Ext. 2414

GENERAL INFORMATION Private Institution. **Total program enrollment:** 89. **Application fee:** $100.

PROGRAM(S) OFFERED
• **Cosmetology/Cosmetologist, General** *1000 hrs./$11,750* • **Nail Technician/Specialist and Manicurist** *10 students enrolled*

STUDENT SERVICES Academic or career counseling, placement services for program completers.

Blaine! The Beauty Career Schools–Waltham

314 Moody Street, Waltham, MA 02154
http://www.blainebeautyschools.com/

CONTACT Michael Bouman, President/COO
Telephone: 570-429-4321 Ext. 2414

GENERAL INFORMATION Private Institution. **Total program enrollment:** 49. **Application fee:** $100.

PROGRAM(S) OFFERED
• **Aesthetician/Esthetician and Skin Care Specialist** *29 students enrolled*
• **Cosmetology/Cosmetologist, General** *1000 hrs./$11,750*

STUDENT SERVICES Academic or career counseling, placement services for program completers.

Blue Hills Regional Technical School

800 Randolph Street, Canton, MA 02021
http://www.bluehills.org/

CONTACT Joseph Ciccolo, Superintendent, Director
Telephone: 781-828-5800 Ext. 229

GENERAL INFORMATION Private Institution. **Total program enrollment:** 57. **Application fee:** $50.

PROGRAM(S) OFFERED
• **Licensed Practical/Vocational Nurse Training (LPN, LVN, Cert, Dipl, AAS)** *1147 hrs./$12,214*

STUDENT SERVICES Academic or career counseling, employment services for current students, placement services for program completers.

Boston Architectural College

320 Newbury Street, Boston, MA 02115-2795
http://www.the-bac.edu/

CONTACT Dr. Theodore C. Landsmark, President
Telephone: 617-262-5000

GENERAL INFORMATION Private Institution. Founded 1889. **Accreditation:** Regional (NEASC/NEASCCIHE); interior design: professional (CIDA). **Total program enrollment:** 1180. **Application fee:** $50.

STUDENT SERVICES Academic or career counseling, employment services for current students, placement services for program completers, remedial services.

Boston Baptist College

950 Metropolitan Avenue, Boston, MA 02136
http://www.boston.edu/

CONTACT David Melton, President
Telephone: 617-364-3510

GENERAL INFORMATION Private Institution. Founded 1976. **Accreditation:** State accredited or approved. **Total program enrollment:** 85. **Application fee:** $40.

PROGRAM(S) OFFERED
• **Bible/Biblical Studies** *3 students enrolled*

STUDENT SERVICES Academic or career counseling, employment services for current students, placement services for program completers, remedial services.

Branford Hall Career Institute–Springfield Campus

112 Industry Avenue, Springfield, MA 01104
http://www.branfordhall.com/

CONTACT Teri Firetto, School Director
Telephone: 413-781-2276

GENERAL INFORMATION Private Institution. **Total program enrollment:** 585. **Application fee:** $75.

PROGRAM(S) OFFERED
• **Culinary Arts/Chef Training** *68 hrs./$16,675* • **Health Information/Medical Records Technology/Technician** *41 hrs./$11,970* • **Heating, Air Conditioning and Refrigeration Technology/Technician (ACH/ACR/ACHR/HRAC/HVAC/AC Technology)** *54 hrs./$17,950* • **Heating, Air Conditioning, Ventilation and Refrigeration Maintenance Technology/Technician (HAC, HACR, HVAC, HVACR)** *43 hrs./$15,172* • **Massage Therapy/Therapeutic Massage** *48 hrs./$11,520* • **Medical/Clinical Assistant** *39 hrs./$12,770*

STUDENT SERVICES Academic or career counseling, placement services for program completers.

Bridgewater State College

Bridgewater, MA 02325-0001
http://www.bridgew.edu/

CONTACT Dana Mohler-Faria, President
Telephone: 508-531-1000

GENERAL INFORMATION Public Institution. Founded 1840. **Accreditation:** Regional (NEASC/NEASCCIHE); athletic training (JRCAT). **Total program enrollment:** 7506. **Application fee:** $25.

Bridgewater State College (continued)

PROGRAM(S) OFFERED
• Accounting • Business Administration and Management, General *1 student enrolled* • Educational/Instructional Media Design *1 student enrolled*

STUDENT SERVICES Academic or career counseling, daycare for children of students, employment services for current students, placement services for program completers, remedial services.

Bristol Community College

777 Elsbree Street, Fall River, MA 02720-7395
http://www.bristolcc.edu/

CONTACT John J. Sbrega, PhD, President
Telephone: 508-678-2811

GENERAL INFORMATION Public Institution. Founded 1965. **Accreditation:** Regional (NEASC/NEASCCIHE); dental hygiene (ADA); health information technology (AHIMA); medical laboratory technology (NAACLS). **Total program enrollment:** 3806. **Application fee:** $10.

PROGRAM(S) OFFERED
• Accounting Technology/Technician and Bookkeeping *1 student enrolled* • Aquaculture • Clinical/Medical Laboratory Science and Allied Professions, Other *15 students enrolled* • Commercial and Advertising Art *5 students enrolled* • Computer Engineering Technologies/Technicians, Other *5 students enrolled* • Computer Programming, Other *1 student enrolled* • Computer/Information Technology Services Administration and Management, Other *5 students enrolled* • Construction Engineering Technology/Technician *1 student enrolled* • Criminal Justice/Law Enforcement Administration *56 students enrolled* • Drafting and Design Technology/Technician, General *30 students enrolled* • Education, Other *2 students enrolled* • Entrepreneurial and Small Business Operations, Other *1 student enrolled* • Fashion Merchandising *1 student enrolled* • Fine Arts and Art Studies, Other *2 students enrolled* • Fire Protection and Safety Technology/Technician *1 student enrolled* • Fire Protection, Other *1 student enrolled* • Health and Medical Administrative Services, Other *14 students enrolled* • Industrial Technology/Technician *2 students enrolled* • Information Resources Management/CIO Training *5 students enrolled* • Information Technology *2 students enrolled* • International Business/Trade/Commerce *1 student enrolled* • Language Interpretation and Translation *3 students enrolled* • Legal Administrative Assistant/Secretary *2 students enrolled* • Management Information Systems and Services, Other *1 student enrolled* • Marketing, Other *2 students enrolled* • Massage Therapy/Therapeutic Massage *16 students enrolled* • Medical Office Management/Administration *4 students enrolled* • Medical Transcription/Transcriptionist *2 students enrolled* • Medical/Clinical Assistant *12 students enrolled* • Office Management and Supervision *1 student enrolled* • Parts, Warehousing, and Inventory Management Operations *2 students enrolled* • Personal and Culinary Services, Other *50 students enrolled* • Public Administration and Social Service Professions, Other *16 students enrolled* • Survey Technology/Surveying *6 students enrolled* • Teacher Assistant/Aide *1 student enrolled* • Tourism and Travel Services Management *2 students enrolled* • Web Page, Digital/Multimedia and Information Resources Design *2 students enrolled*

STUDENT SERVICES Academic or career counseling, daycare for children of students, employment services for current students, placement services for program completers, remedial services.

Bunker Hill Community College

250 New Rutherford Avenue, Boston, MA 02129-2925
http://www.bhcc.mass.edu/

CONTACT Mary L. Fifield, President
Telephone: 617-228-2000

GENERAL INFORMATION Public Institution. Founded 1973. **Accreditation:** Regional (NEASC/NEASCCIHE); diagnostic medical sonography (JRCEDMS); radiologic technology: radiography (JRCERT); surgical technology (ARCST). **Total program enrollment:** 3102. **Application fee:** $10.

PROGRAM(S) OFFERED
• Accounting Technology/Technician and Bookkeeping *9 students enrolled* • Accounting *1 student enrolled* • Clinical/Medical Laboratory Assistant *1 student enrolled* • Computer Programming, Specific Applications *2 students enrolled*

• Computer Systems Networking and Telecommunications *2 students enrolled* • Computer and Information Sciences and Support Services, Other *3 students enrolled* • Criminal Justice/Law Enforcement Administration *19 students enrolled* • Criminal Justice/Police Science *3 students enrolled* • Culinary Arts/Chef Training *2 students enrolled* • Early Childhood Education and Teaching *6 students enrolled* • Human Services, General *6 students enrolled* • International Business/Trade/Commerce *8 students enrolled* • Legal Assistant/Paralegal *17 students enrolled* • Medical Administrative/Executive Assistant and Medical Secretary *2 students enrolled* • Medical Insurance Coding Specialist/Coder *6 students enrolled* • Medical/Clinical Assistant *46 students enrolled* • Nurse/Nursing Assistant/Aide and Patient Care Assistant *17 students enrolled* • Phlebotomy/Phlebotomist *15 students enrolled* • Receptionist *1 student enrolled* • Surgical Technology/Technologist *22 students enrolled* • Tourism and Travel Services Management *5 students enrolled*

STUDENT SERVICES Academic or career counseling, daycare for children of students, employment services for current students, placement services for program completers, remedial services.

Cape Cod Community College

2240 Iyanough Road, West Barnstable, MA 02668-1599
http://www.capecod.mass.edu/

CONTACT Kathleen Schatzberg, President
Telephone: 508-362-2131

GENERAL INFORMATION Public Institution. Founded 1961. **Accreditation:** Regional (NEASC/NEASCCIHE); dental hygiene (ADA). **Total program enrollment:** 1712.

PROGRAM(S) OFFERED
• Applied Horticulture/Horticultural Operations, General *4 students enrolled* • Business Operations Support and Secretarial Services, Other • Clinical Nutrition/Nutritionist • Computer Technology/Computer Systems Technology • Construction Engineering Technology/Technician *2 students enrolled* • Corrections • Customer Service Management *15 students enrolled* • Diagnostic Medical Sonography/Sonographer and Ultrasound Technician *4 students enrolled* • Early Childhood Education and Teaching • Emergency Medical Technology/Technician (EMT Paramedic) *19 students enrolled* • Environmental Control Technologies/Technicians, Other *15 students enrolled* • Fire Protection and Safety Technology/Technician *1 student enrolled* • Hospitality Administration/Management, Other • Hotel/Motel Administration/Management *2 students enrolled* • Information Science/Studies *13 students enrolled* • Kindergarten/Preschool Education and Teaching *3 students enrolled* • Kinesiotherapy/Kinesiotherapist *12 students enrolled* • Legal Assistant/Paralegal *15 students enrolled* • Medical/Clinical Assistant • Natural Resources Management and Policy • Water Quality and Wastewater Treatment Management and Recycling Technology/Technician

STUDENT SERVICES Academic or career counseling, daycare for children of students, employment services for current students, placement services for program completers, remedial services.

Catherine Hinds Institute of Esthetics

300 Wildwood Avenue, Woburn, MA 01801
http://www.catherinehinds.edu/

CONTACT Kim St. Cyr, Executive School Director
Telephone: 781-935-3344 Ext. 254

GENERAL INFORMATION Private Institution. **Total program enrollment:** 143.

PROGRAM(S) OFFERED
• Aesthetician/Esthetician and Skin Care Specialist *300 hrs./$5392*

STUDENT SERVICES Academic or career counseling, placement services for program completers.

Central Mass School of Massage & Therapy

200 Main Street, Spencer, MA 01562
http://www.centralmassschool.com

CONTACT Gregory St. Jacques, Director
Telephone: 508-885-0306

GENERAL INFORMATION Private Institution. **Total program enrollment:** 10. **Application fee:** $50.

PROGRAM(S) OFFERED
• **Asian Bodywork Therapy** *603 hrs./$9829* • **Massage Therapy/Therapeutic Massage** *738 hrs./$13,020*

STUDENT SERVICES Placement services for program completers.

Cortiva Institute—Muscular Therapy Institute

103 Morse Street, Watertown, MA 02472
http://www.cortiva.com/locations/mti/

CONTACT Dianne Polseno, President
Telephone: 617-668-1000

GENERAL INFORMATION Private Institution. Founded 1974. **Application fee:** $100.

PROGRAM(S) OFFERED
• **Massage Therapy/Therapeutic Massage** *900 hrs./$14,195*

STUDENT SERVICES Academic or career counseling, placement services for program completers.

Dean College

99 Main Street, Franklin, MA 02038-1994
http://www.dean.edu/

CONTACT Dr. Paula M. Rooney, President
Telephone: 508-541-1900

GENERAL INFORMATION Private Institution. Founded 1865. **Accreditation:** Regional (NEASC/NEASCCIHE). **Total program enrollment:** 1030. **Application fee:** $35.

STUDENT SERVICES Academic or career counseling, employment services for current students, placement services for program completers, remedial services.

DiGrigoli School of Cosmetology

1578 Riverdale Street, West Springfield, MA 01089
http://www.digrigoli.com

CONTACT Paul J. DiGrigoli, President/CEO
Telephone: 413-827-0037

GENERAL INFORMATION Private Institution. **Total program enrollment:** 31. **Application fee:** $50.

PROGRAM(S) OFFERED
• **Cosmetology/Cosmetologist, General** *1000 hrs./$11,666*

STUDENT SERVICES Academic or career counseling, placement services for program completers.

Diman Regional Technical Institute

251 Stonehaven Road, Fall River, MA 02723
http://dimanregional.org/

CONTACT Rogerio Ramos, Superintendent Director
Telephone: 508-678-2891

GENERAL INFORMATION Public Institution. Founded 1959. **Total program enrollment:** 46. **Application fee:** $25.

PROGRAM(S) OFFERED
• **Licensed Practical/Vocational Nurse Training (LPN, LVN, Cert, Dipl, AAS)** *1106 hrs./$11,989*

STUDENT SERVICES Academic or career counseling, employment services for current students, placement services for program completers, remedial services.

Eastern Nazarene College

23 East Elm Avenue, Quincy, MA 02170-2999
http://www.enc.edu/

CONTACT Dr. Corlis McGee, President
Telephone: 617-745-3000

GENERAL INFORMATION Private Institution (Affiliated with Church of the Nazarene). Founded 1918. **Accreditation:** Regional (NEASC/NEASCCIHE). **Total program enrollment:** 938.

STUDENT SERVICES Academic or career counseling, daycare for children of students, employment services for current students, placement services for program completers, remedial services.

Electrology Institute of New England

1501 Main Street, Suite 50, Tewksbury, MA 01876
http://www.electrologyinstitute.com/

CONTACT Mary L. Evangelista, Director
Telephone: 978-851-4444

GENERAL INFORMATION Private Institution. **Total program enrollment:** 21. **Application fee:** $50.

PROGRAM(S) OFFERED
• **Aesthetician/Esthetician and Skin Care Specialist** *300 hrs./$4725*
• **Electrolysis/Electrology and Electrolysis Technician** *600 hrs./$7475*

STUDENT SERVICES Academic or career counseling, placement services for program completers.

Elizabeth Grady School of Esthetics

222 Boston Avenue, Medford, MA 02155-4248
http://elizabethgrady.com/

CONTACT Tracey Ford, Financial Aid Director
Telephone: 781-391-9380

GENERAL INFORMATION Private Institution. Founded 1979. **Total program enrollment:** 37.

PROGRAM(S) OFFERED
• **Aesthetician/Esthetician and Skin Care Specialist** *600 hrs./$8500* • **Massage Therapy/Therapeutic Massage** *750 hrs./$9525*

STUDENT SERVICES Placement services for program completers.

Elms College

291 Springfield Street, Chicopee, MA 01013-2839
http://www.elms.edu/

CONTACT Dr. Walter C. Breau, Interim President
Telephone: 413-594-2761

GENERAL INFORMATION Private Institution. Founded 1928. **Accreditation:** Regional (NEASC/NEASCCIHE). **Total program enrollment:** 787. **Application fee:** $30.

PROGRAM(S) OFFERED
● **Legal Assistant/Paralegal** 6 *students enrolled*

STUDENT SERVICES Academic or career counseling, employment services for current students, placement services for program completers.

Endicott College

376 Hale Street, Beverly, MA 01915-2096
http://www.endicott.edu/

CONTACT Richard E. Wylie, President
Telephone: 978-927-0585

GENERAL INFORMATION Private Institution. Founded 1939. **Accreditation:** Regional (NEASC/NEASCCIHE); athletic training (JRCAT); interior design: professional (CIDA). **Total program enrollment:** 2071. **Application fee:** $40.

STUDENT SERVICES Academic or career counseling, employment services for current students, placement services for program completers.

Everest Institute

1505 Commonwealth Avenue, #4, Brighton, MA 02135
http://www.everest.edu/

CONTACT Paul J. Flaherty, School President
Telephone: 617-783-9955

GENERAL INFORMATION Private Institution. Founded 1970. **Total program enrollment:** 680.

PROGRAM(S) OFFERED
● **Dental Assisting/Assistant** 720 hrs./$12,876 ● **Massage Therapy/Therapeutic Massage** 720 hrs./$13,020 ● **Medical Administrative/Executive Assistant and Medical Secretary** 50 *students enrolled* ● **Medical Office Assistant/Specialist** 720 hrs./$13,157 ● **Medical/Clinical Assistant** 720 hrs./$14,147

STUDENT SERVICES Academic or career counseling, placement services for program completers.

Everest Institute

70 Everett Avenue, Chelsea, MA 02150
http://www.everest.edu/

CONTACT Wade Charlton, President
Telephone: 617-889-5999

GENERAL INFORMATION Private Institution. **Total program enrollment:** 171.

PROGRAM(S) OFFERED
● **Health Services/Allied Health/Health Sciences, General** 720 hrs./$14,252 ● **Massage Therapy/Therapeutic Massage** 720 hrs./$13,020 ● **Medical Insurance Specialist/Medical Biller** 720 hrs./$12,154 ● **Pharmacy Technician/Assistant** 35 *students enrolled*

STUDENT SERVICES Academic or career counseling, placement services for program completers.

Fisher College

118 Beacon Street, Boston, MA 02116-1500
http://www.fisher.edu/

CONTACT Thomas M. McGovern, President
Telephone: 866-266-6007

GENERAL INFORMATION Private Institution. Founded 1903. **Accreditation:** Regional (NEASC/NEASCCIHE); health information technology (AHIMA). **Total program enrollment:** 875. **Application fee:** $50.

PROGRAM(S) OFFERED
● **Administrative Assistant and Secretarial Science, General** 4 *students enrolled* ● **Early Childhood Education and Teaching** 2 *students enrolled* ● **Legal Assistant/Paralegal** 2 *students enrolled* ● **Medical Insurance Coding Specialist/Coder** 16 *students enrolled* ● **Medical/Clinical Assistant** 5 *students enrolled*

STUDENT SERVICES Academic or career counseling, employment services for current students, placement services for program completers, remedial services.

Fitchburg State College

160 Pearl Street, Fitchburg, MA 01420-2697
http://www.fsc.edu/

CONTACT Robert V. Antonucci, President
Telephone: 978-345-2151

GENERAL INFORMATION Public Institution. Founded 1894. **Accreditation:** Regional (NEASC/NEASCCIHE); medical technology (NAACLS). **Total program enrollment:** 3608. **Application fee:** $10.

PROGRAM(S) OFFERED
● **Business Administration and Management, General** ● **Computer Programming/Programmer, General** ● **Computer and Information Sciences, General** ● **Plastics Engineering Technology/Technician** 2 *students enrolled* ● **Web Page, Digital/Multimedia and Information Resources Design** 1 *student enrolled*

STUDENT SERVICES Academic or career counseling, employment services for current students, placement services for program completers, remedial services.

Franklin W. Olin College of Engineering

Olin Way, Needham, MA 02492-1200
http://www.olin.edu/

CONTACT Dr. Richard K. Miller, President
Telephone: 781-292-2300

GENERAL INFORMATION Private Institution. Founded 2002. **Total program enrollment:** 308. **Application fee:** $70.

STUDENT SERVICES Academic or career counseling, employment services for current students, placement services for program completers.

Greenfield Community College

1 College Drive, Greenfield, MA 01301-9739
http://www.gcc.mass.edu/

CONTACT Robert Pura, President
Telephone: 413-775-1000

GENERAL INFORMATION Public Institution. Founded 1962. **Accreditation:** Regional (NEASC/NEASCCIHE). **Total program enrollment:** 873. **Application fee:** $10.

PROGRAM(S) OFFERED
● **Accounting Technology/Technician and Bookkeeping** 3 *students enrolled* ● **Administrative Assistant and Secretarial Science, General** ● **Community Health Services/Liaison/Counseling** 4 *students enrolled* ● **Data Entry/Microcomputer Applications, General** 3 *students enrolled* ● **Design and Visual**

Communications, General *2 students enrolled* • **Drafting and Design Technology/Technician, General** • **Emergency Medical Technology/Technician (EMT Paramedic)** *12 students enrolled* • **Licensed Practical/Vocational Nurse Training (LPN, LVN, Cert, Dipl, AAS)** *21 students enrolled* • **Management Information Systems, General** *1 student enrolled* • **Massage Therapy/Therapeutic Massage** *10 students enrolled* • **Natural Resources/Conservation, General** • **Parks, Recreation and Leisure Facilities Management** *16 students enrolled* • **Teacher Assistant/Aide** *1 student enrolled*

STUDENT SERVICES Academic or career counseling, employment services for current students, placement services for program completers, remedial services.

Hair in Motion Beauty Academy

73 Hamilton Street, Worcester, MA 01604

CONTACT Anthony Moossa, Director
Telephone: 508-756-6060

GENERAL INFORMATION Private Institution. **Total program enrollment:** 20. **Application fee:** $100.

PROGRAM(S) OFFERED
• **Cosmetology/Cosmetologist, General** *1000 hrs./$10,700* • **Nail Technician/Specialist and Manicurist** *7 students enrolled*

STUDENT SERVICES Placement services for program completers.

Hallmark Institute of Photography

241 Millers Falls Road, Turners Falls, MA 01376
http://www.hallmark.edu/

CONTACT George J. Rosa, III, President
Telephone: 413-863-2478

GENERAL INFORMATION Private Institution. Founded 1976. **Total program enrollment:** 213. **Application fee:** $25.

PROGRAM(S) OFFERED
• **Photography** *1400 hrs./$49,450*

STUDENT SERVICES Academic or career counseling, placement services for program completers.

Hebrew College

160 Herrick Road, Newton Centre, MA 02459
http://www.hebrewcollege.edu/

CONTACT Daniel Lehmann, President
Telephone: 617-559-8600

GENERAL INFORMATION Private Institution. Founded 1921. **Accreditation:** Regional (NEASC/NEASCCIHE). **Total program enrollment:** 79. **Application fee:** $50.

PROGRAM(S) OFFERED
• **Kindergarten/Preschool Education and Teaching**

STUDENT SERVICES Academic or career counseling.

Henri's School of Hair Design

276 Water Street, Fitchburg, MA 01420

CONTACT Mark S. Gauvin, Vice President
Telephone: 978-342-6061

GENERAL INFORMATION Private Institution. Founded 1962. **Total program enrollment:** 47. **Application fee:** $100.

PROGRAM(S) OFFERED
• **Cosmetology/Cosmetologist, General** *1000 hrs./$9825* • **Nail Technician/Specialist and Manicurist** *125 hrs./$1350*

STUDENT SERVICES Academic or career counseling, placement services for program completers.

Holyoke Community College

303 Homestead Avenue, Holyoke, MA 01040-1099
http://www.hcc.mass.edu/

CONTACT William F. Messner, President
Telephone: 413-552-2001

GENERAL INFORMATION Public Institution. Founded 1946. **Accreditation:** Regional (NEASC/NEASCCIHE); music (NASM); ophthalmic dispensing (COA); radiologic technology: radiography (JRCERT). **Total program enrollment:** 3558. **Application fee:** $10.

PROGRAM(S) OFFERED
• **Accounting Technology/Technician and Bookkeeping** *6 students enrolled* • **Administrative Assistant and Secretarial Science, General** *1 student enrolled* • **Child Care and Support Services Management** *3 students enrolled* • **Commercial and Advertising Art** *1 student enrolled* • **Communication Disorders Sciences and Services, Other** *1 student enrolled* • **Community Organization and Advocacy** *26 students enrolled* • **Computer Systems Networking and Telecommunications** *1 student enrolled* • **Computer and Information Sciences and Support Services, Other** *1 student enrolled* • **Computer and Information Systems Security** *2 students enrolled* • **Criminal Justice/Safety Studies** *14 students enrolled* • **Culinary Arts/Chef Training** *13 students enrolled* • **E-Commerce/Electronic Commerce** *1 student enrolled* • **Entrepreneurial and Small Business Operations, Other** *1 student enrolled* • **Film/Video and Photographic Arts, Other** *1 student enrolled* • **Forensic Science and Technology** *3 students enrolled* • **Health Information/Medical Records Technology/Technician** *7 students enrolled* • **Health and Physical Education, General** *8 students enrolled* • **Human Resources Management/Personnel Administration, General** *2 students enrolled* • **Human Services, General** *4 students enrolled* • **Licensed Practical/Vocational Nurse Training (LPN, LVN, Cert, Dipl, AAS)** *39 students enrolled* • **Medical/Clinical Assistant** *31 students enrolled* • **Music, General** *2 students enrolled* • **Ophthalmic and Optometric Support Services and Allied Professions, Other** *7 students enrolled* • **Pharmacy Technician/Assistant** *2 students enrolled* • **Physical Education Teaching and Coaching** *1 student enrolled* • **Retailing and Retail Operations** *1 student enrolled* • **Social Work** *3 students enrolled* • **Substance Abuse/Addiction Counseling** *2 students enrolled*

STUDENT SERVICES Academic or career counseling, daycare for children of students, employment services for current students, placement services for program completers, remedial services.

Jolie Hair and Beauty Academy

44 Sewall Street, Ludlow, MA 01056

CONTACT Bill Anjos, President
Telephone: 413-589-0747

GENERAL INFORMATION Private Institution. Founded 1991. **Total program enrollment:** 54. **Application fee:** $125.

PROGRAM(S) OFFERED
• **Aesthetician/Esthetician and Skin Care Specialist** *650 hrs./$9529* • **Cosmetology/Cosmetologist, General** *1000 hrs./$10,604* • **Nail Technician/Specialist and Manicurist** *150 hrs./$1124*

STUDENT SERVICES Academic or career counseling, placement services for program completers.

Kaplan Career Institute, Charlestown

570 Rutherford Avenue, Charlestown, MA 02129
http://charlestown.kaplancareerinstitute.com/pages/homepage.aspx

CONTACT Stephen Carter, Executive Director
Telephone: 617-580-4010

GENERAL INFORMATION Private Institution. Founded 1958. **Total program enrollment:** 594.

PROGRAM(S) OFFERED
• **Computer and Information Sciences and Support Services, Other** *720 hrs./$12,680* • **Electrical, Electronic and Communications Engineering**

Kaplan Career Institute, Charlestown (continued)

Technology/Technician *900 hrs./$14,700* ● **Heating, Air Conditioning, Ventilation and Refrigeration Maintenance Technology/Technician (HAC, HACR, HVAC, HVACR)** *1200 hrs./$19,225* ● **Medical/Clinical Assistant** *720 hrs./ $11,880*

STUDENT SERVICES Employment services for current students, placement services for program completers.

Kay-Harvey Hairdressing Academy

11 Central Street, West Springfield, MA 01089
http://labaronacademy.com/

CONTACT Lois Wroble, Chief Administration
Telephone: 413-732-7117

GENERAL INFORMATION Private Institution. **Total program enrollment:** 40.

PROGRAM(S) OFFERED
● **Cosmetology/Cosmetologist, General** *1000 hrs./$10,235* ● **Nail Technician/ Specialist and Manicurist** *100 hrs./$900*

STUDENT SERVICES Academic or career counseling, employment services for current students, placement services for program completers.

La Baron Hairdressing Academy

240 Liberty Street, Brockton, MA 02401
http://labaronacademy.com/

CONTACT Lois M. Wroble, Chief Administrator
Telephone: 508-583-1700

GENERAL INFORMATION Private Institution. Founded 1959. **Total program enrollment:** 46. **Application fee:** $100.

PROGRAM(S) OFFERED
● **Cosmetology/Cosmetologist, General** *1000 hrs./$11,087* ● **Nail Technician/ Specialist and Manicurist** *100 hrs./$1100*

STUDENT SERVICES Academic or career counseling, employment services for current students, placement services for program completers.

La Baron Hairdressing Academy

281 Union Street, New Bedford, MA 02740
http://labaronacademy.com/

CONTACT Lois Wroble, Chief Pres. Administrator
Telephone: 508-993-1309

GENERAL INFORMATION Private Institution. **Total program enrollment:** 34. **Application fee:** $100.

PROGRAM(S) OFFERED
● **Cosmetology/Cosmetologist, General** *1000 hrs./$10,388* ● **Nail Technician/ Specialist and Manicurist** *100 hrs./$1100*

STUDENT SERVICES Academic or career counseling, employment services for current students, placement services for program completers.

Labouré College

2120 Dorchester Avenue, Boston, MA 02124-5698
http://www.laboure.edu/

CONTACT Joseph W. McNabb, President
Telephone: 617-296-8300

GENERAL INFORMATION Private Institution. Founded 1971. **Accreditation:** Regional (NEASC/NEASCCIHE); electroneurodiagnostic technology (JRCEND); health information technology (AHIMA); radiologic technology: radiation therapy technology (JRCERT). **Total program enrollment:** 31. **Application fee:** $25.

PROGRAM(S) OFFERED
● **Electroneurodiagnostic/Electroencephalographic Technology/Technologist** *3 students enrolled* ● **Health Information/Medical Records Technology/Technician** *6 students enrolled*

STUDENT SERVICES Academic or career counseling, employment services for current students, placement services for program completers, remedial services.

Lincoln Technical Institute

375 Westgate-Drive, Brockton, MA 02301-1818
http://www.lincolnedu.com/

CONTACT David Carney, CEO
Telephone: 508-941-0730

GENERAL INFORMATION Private Institution. **Total program enrollment:** 169. **Application fee:** $50.

PROGRAM(S) OFFERED
● **Criminal Justice/Law Enforcement Administration** *900 hrs./$11,321* ● **Massage Therapy/Therapeutic Massage** *750 hrs./$12,434* ● **Medical Administrative/Executive Assistant and Medical Secretary** *1080 hrs./$16,315* ● **Medical/Clinical Assistant** *1080 hrs./$16,947*

STUDENT SERVICES Academic or career counseling, employment services for current students, placement services for program completers.

Lincoln Technical Institute

211 Plain Street, Lowell, MA 01852-5119
http://www.lincolnedu.com/

CONTACT David Carney, CEO
Telephone: 978-458-4800

GENERAL INFORMATION Private Institution. **Total program enrollment:** 338. **Application fee:** $50.

PROGRAM(S) OFFERED
● **Computer Systems Networking and Telecommunications** *38 students enrolled* ● **Criminal Justice/Law Enforcement Administration** *20 students enrolled* ● **Massage Therapy/Therapeutic Massage** *38 students enrolled* ● **Medical Insurance Coding Specialist/Coder** *41 students enrolled* ● **Medical/Clinical Assistant** *132 students enrolled* ● **Pharmacy Technician/Assistant** *6 students enrolled*

STUDENT SERVICES Academic or career counseling, employment services for current students, placement services for program completers.

Lincoln Technical Institute

5 Middlesex Avenue, Somerville, MA 02145-1102
http://www.lincolnedu.com/

CONTACT David Carney, CEO
Telephone: 617-776-3500

GENERAL INFORMATION Private Institution. **Total program enrollment:** 338. **Application fee:** $50.

PROGRAM(S) OFFERED
● **Computer Systems Networking and Telecommunications** *900 hrs./$13,980* ● **Computer and Information Systems Security** *1080 hrs./$16,930* ● **Criminal Justice/Law Enforcement Administration** *900 hrs./$11,321* ● **Massage Therapy/Therapeutic Massage** *750 hrs./$11,494* ● **Medical Administrative/ Executive Assistant and Medical Secretary** *1080 hrs./$16,315* ● **Medical Insurance Coding Specialist/Coder** *4 students enrolled* ● **Medical/Clinical Assistant** *1080 hrs./$15,929* ● **Pharmacy Technician/Assistant** *5 students enrolled*

STUDENT SERVICES Academic or career counseling, employment services for current students, placement services for program completers.

Lowell Academy Hairstyling Institute

136 Central Street, Lowell, MA 01852
http://www.lowellacademy.com/

CONTACT N. Akashian, Jr., President
Telephone: 978-453-3235

GENERAL INFORMATION Private Institution. Founded 1933. **Total program enrollment: 17. Application fee:** $50.

PROGRAM(S) OFFERED
• **Cosmetology/Cosmetologist, General** *1000 hrs./$12,433* • **Hair Styling/Stylist and Hair Design** *60 hrs./$900* • **Nail Technician/Specialist and Manicurist** *110 hrs./$1430*

STUDENT SERVICES Academic or career counseling, placement services for program completers.

Mansfield Beauty Schools

200 Parking Way, Quincy, MA 02169
http://www.mansfieldbeautyschools.com/

CONTACT Daniel Dorian, President
Telephone: 617-479-1090

GENERAL INFORMATION Private Institution. Founded 1909. **Total program enrollment: 39.**

PROGRAM(S) OFFERED
• **Cosmetology and Related Personal Grooming Arts, Other** *8 students enrolled* • **Cosmetology/Cosmetologist, General** *1000 hrs./$11,450* • **Nail Technician/Specialist and Manicurist** *100 hrs./$1550*

STUDENT SERVICES Academic or career counseling, placement services for program completers.

Mansfield Beauty Schools

266 Bridge Street, Springfield, MA 01103
http://www.mansfieldbeautyschools.com/

CONTACT Daniel Dorian, President
Telephone: 413-788-7575

GENERAL INFORMATION Private Institution. Founded 1909. **Total program enrollment: 31.**

PROGRAM(S) OFFERED
• **Cosmetology and Related Personal Grooming Arts, Other** *5 students enrolled* • **Cosmetology/Cosmetologist, General** *1000 hrs./$11,450* • **Nail Technician/Specialist and Manicurist** *100 hrs./$1550*

STUDENT SERVICES Academic or career counseling, placement services for program completers.

Marian Court College

35 Little's Point Road, Swampscott, MA 01907-2840
http://www.mariancourt.edu/

CONTACT Dr. Ghazi Darkazalli, President
Telephone: 781-595-6768

GENERAL INFORMATION Private Institution. Founded 1964. **Accreditation:** Regional (NEASC/NEASCCIHE). **Total program enrollment:** 180.

PROGRAM(S) OFFERED
• **Business Administration and Management, General** *3 students enrolled* • **Computer and Information Sciences and Support Services, Other** • **General Office Occupations and Clerical Services** • **Legal Assistant/Paralegal** *3 students enrolled*

STUDENT SERVICES Academic or career counseling, remedial services.

Massachusetts Bay Community College

50 Oakland Street, Wellesley Hills, MA 02481
http://www.massbay.edu/

CONTACT Carole M. Berotte Joseph, PhD, President
Telephone: 781-239-3000

GENERAL INFORMATION Public Institution. Founded 1961. **Accreditation:** Regional (NEASC/NEASCCIHE); physical therapy assisting (APTA); radiologic technology: radiography (JRCERT). **Total program enrollment:** 2034. **Application fee:** $20.

PROGRAM(S) OFFERED
• **Accounting Technology/Technician and Bookkeeping** *4 students enrolled* • **Allied Health and Medical Assisting Services, Other** *12 students enrolled* • **Automotive Engineering Technology/Technician** *5 students enrolled* • **Business, Management, Marketing, and Related Support Services, Other** *4 students enrolled* • **Child Care Provider/Assistant** *5 students enrolled* • **Computer and Information Sciences and Support Services, Other** • **Drafting and Design Technology/Technician, General** *2 students enrolled* • **Emergency Medical Technology/Technician (EMT Paramedic)** *52 students enrolled* • **Health Information/Medical Records Technology/Technician** *15 students enrolled* • **Health and Physical Education/Fitness, Other** *1 student enrolled* • **Hospitality Administration/Management, General** • **Interior Design** *5 students enrolled* • **Legal Assistant/Paralegal** *5 students enrolled* • **Licensed Practical/Vocational Nurse Training (LPN, LVN, Cert, Dipl, AAS)** *59 students enrolled* • **Medical Administrative/Executive Assistant and Medical Secretary** *1 student enrolled* • **Rehabilitation and Therapeutic Professions, Other** *8 students enrolled* • **Surgical Technology/Technologist** *32 students enrolled*

STUDENT SERVICES Academic or career counseling, employment services for current students, placement services for program completers, remedial services.

Massachusetts College of Art and Design

621 Huntington Avenue, Boston, MA 02115-5882
http://www.massart.edu/

CONTACT Katherine Sloan, President
Telephone: 617-879-7000

GENERAL INFORMATION Public Institution. Founded 1873. **Accreditation:** Regional (NEASC/NEASCCIHE); art and design (NASAD). **Total program enrollment:** 1614. **Application fee:** $65.

PROGRAM(S) OFFERED
• **Commercial and Advertising Art** *8 students enrolled* • **Fashion/Apparel Design** *7 students enrolled*

STUDENT SERVICES Academic or career counseling, employment services for current students, placement services for program completers, remedial services.

Massachusetts College of Liberal Arts

375 Church Street, North Adams, MA 01247-4100
http://www.mcla.edu/

CONTACT Mary K. Grant, President
Telephone: 413-662-5000

GENERAL INFORMATION Public Institution. Founded 1894. **Accreditation:** Regional (NEASC/NEASCCIHE). **Total program enrollment:** 1382. **Application fee:** $25.

STUDENT SERVICES Academic or career counseling, employment services for current students, placement services for program completers, remedial services.

Massachusetts College of Pharmacy and Health Sciences

179 Longwood Avenue, Boston, MA 02115-5896
http://www.mcphs.edu/

CONTACT Charles F. Monahan, Jr., President
Telephone: 617-732-2800

GENERAL INFORMATION Private Institution. Founded 1823. **Accreditation:** Regional (NEASC/NEASCCIHE); dental hygiene (ADA); nuclear medicine technology (JRCNMT). **Total program enrollment:** 3677. **Application fee:** $70.

PROGRAM(S) OFFERED
• Radiologic Technology/Science—Radiographer 11 *students enrolled*

STUDENT SERVICES Academic or career counseling, employment services for current students, placement services for program completers.

Massachusetts School of Barbering and Men's Hairstyling

152 Parkingway Street, Quincy, MA 02169-5058
http://massschoolofbarbering.com/

CONTACT Alan Conragan, Director
Telephone: 617-770-4444

GENERAL INFORMATION Private Institution. Founded 1947. **Total program enrollment:** 34.

PROGRAM(S) OFFERED
• Barbering/Barber 500 hrs./$4875

STUDENT SERVICES Academic or career counseling, placement services for program completers.

Massasoit Community College

1 Massasoit Boulevard, Brockton, MA 02302-3996
http://www.massasoit.mass.edu/

CONTACT Dr. Charles Wall, President
Telephone: 508-588-9100

GENERAL INFORMATION Public Institution. Founded 1966. **Accreditation:** Regional (NEASC/NEASCCIHE); dental assisting (ADA); radiologic technology: radiography (JRCERT). **Total program enrollment:** 3401.

PROGRAM(S) OFFERED
• Administrative Assistant and Secretarial Science, General • Allied Health Diagnostic, Intervention, and Treatment Professions, Other 14 *students enrolled* • Business/Office Automation/Technology/Data Entry 3 *students enrolled* • Computer Installation and Repair Technology/Technician 1 *student enrolled* • Computer and Information Sciences and Support Services, Other 1 *student enrolled* • Data Entry/Microcomputer Applications, General 2 *students enrolled* • Dental Assisting/Assistant 19 *students enrolled* • Diagnostic Medical Sonography/Sonographer and Ultrasound Technician 17 *students enrolled* • Fashion Merchandising 1 *student enrolled* • General Office Occupations and Clerical Services 1 *student enrolled* • Health Information/Medical Records Administration/Administrator 9 *students enrolled* • Human Development, Family Studies, and Related Services, Other • Medical Insurance Specialist/Medical Biller 21 *students enrolled* • Medical/Clinical Assistant 14 *students enrolled* • Phlebotomy/Phlebotomist 18 *students enrolled* • Photography • Psychiatric/Mental Health Services Technician 7 *students enrolled* • Radiologic Technology/Science—Radiographer 29 *students enrolled* • Security and Protective Services, Other • Substance Abuse/Addiction Counseling • Tourism and Travel Services Management 2 *students enrolled* • Web Page, Digital/Multimedia and Information Resources Design

STUDENT SERVICES Academic or career counseling, daycare for children of students, employment services for current students, placement services for program completers, remedial services.

Medical Professional Institute

388 Pleasant Street, 3rd Floor, Malden, MA 02148-8143
http://www.mpi.edu/

CONTACT Majid Pourshadi, PhD, President
Telephone: 781-397-6822

GENERAL INFORMATION Private Institution. **Total program enrollment:** 58. **Application fee:** $50.

PROGRAM(S) OFFERED
• Allied Health and Medical Assisting Services, Other 720 hrs./$9300 • Electrocardiograph Technology/Technician 50 hrs./$650 • Emergency Care Attendant (EMT Ambulance) • Emergency Medical Technology/Technician (EMT Paramedic) 608 hrs./$7500 • Health Professions and Related Clinical Sciences, Other 25 *students enrolled* • Licensed Practical/Vocational Nurse Training (LPN, LVN, Cert, Dipl, AAS) 1170 hrs./$18,320 • Medical Office Management/Administration 4 *students enrolled* • Medical/Clinical Assistant 16 *students enrolled* • Nurse/Nursing Assistant/Aide and Patient Care Assistant 97 hrs./$770 • Phlebotomy/Phlebotomist 330 hrs./$2000

STUDENT SERVICES Academic or career counseling, employment services for current students, placement services for program completers, remedial services.

Middlesex Community College

Springs Road, Bedford, MA 01730-1655
http://www.middlesex.mass.edu/

CONTACT Carole A. Cowan, President
Telephone: 978-656-3200

GENERAL INFORMATION Public Institution. Founded 1970. **Accreditation:** Regional (NEASC/NEASCCIHE); dental assisting (ADA); dental hygiene (ADA); dental laboratory technology (ADA); diagnostic medical sonography (JRCEDMS); medical assisting (AAMAE); radiologic technology: radiography (JRCERT). **Total program enrollment:** 3670.

PROGRAM(S) OFFERED
• Biology Technician/Biotechnology Laboratory Technician 17 *students enrolled* • Business Administration and Management, General 13 *students enrolled* • Commercial and Advertising Art 1 *student enrolled* • Computer and Information Sciences and Support Services, Other • Computer and Information Sciences, General 1 *student enrolled* • Criminal Justice/Safety Studies 5 *students enrolled* • Dental Assisting/Assistant 6 *students enrolled* • Diagnostic Medical Sonography/Sonographer and Ultrasound Technician 18 *students enrolled* • Electrical, Electronic and Communications Engineering Technology/Technician 10 *students enrolled* • Electrical/Electronics Drafting and Electrical/Electronics CAD/CADD 4 *students enrolled* • Energy Management and Systems Technology/Technician 10 *students enrolled* • Fine/Studio Arts, General • General Office Occupations and Clerical Services • Health Professions and Related Clinical Sciences, Other • Hotel/Motel Administration/Management 1 *student enrolled* • Kindergarten/Preschool Education and Teaching 6 *students enrolled* • Legal Assistant/Paralegal 2 *students enrolled* • Medical/Clinical Assistant 6 *students enrolled* • Psychiatric/Mental Health Services Technician 12 *students enrolled* • Sport and Fitness Administration/Management 2 *students enrolled* • Teacher Assistant/Aide 24 *students enrolled* • Web Page, Digital/Multimedia and Information Resources Design 3 *students enrolled*

STUDENT SERVICES Academic or career counseling, employment services for current students, placement services for program completers, remedial services.

Mildred Elley School

505 East Street, Pittsfield, MA 01201-5300
http://www.mildred-elley.edu/

CONTACT Faith A. Takes, President
Telephone: 413-499-8618 Ext. 221

GENERAL INFORMATION Private Institution. **Total program enrollment:** 146. **Application fee:** $25.

PROGRAM(S) OFFERED

• Accounting 5 *students enrolled* • Administrative Assistant and Secretarial Science, General 18 *students enrolled* • Criminal Justice/Law Enforcement Administration • Legal Assistant/Paralegal 1 *student enrolled* • Massage Therapy/Therapeutic Massage 14 *students enrolled* • Medical Office Assistant/Specialist • Medical/Clinical Assistant 32 *students enrolled* • Web Page, Digital/Multimedia and Information Resources Design 5 *students enrolled*

STUDENT SERVICES Academic or career counseling, employment services for current students, placement services for program completers, remedial services.

Millennium Training Institute

600 West Cummings Park, Suite 2550, Woburn, MA 01801

CONTACT Kevin O'Brien, Chief Executive Officer
Telephone: 781-933-8877

GENERAL INFORMATION Private Institution. **Total program enrollment:** 117. **Application fee:** $50.

PROGRAM(S) OFFERED

• Administrative Assistant and Secretarial Science, General 320 *hrs./$5547* • Business Operations Support and Secretarial Services, Other 360 *hrs./$6060* • Computer Installation and Repair Technology/Technician 1 *student enrolled* • Computer Systems Networking and Telecommunications 240 *hrs./$5945* • Medical Insurance Specialist/Medical Biller 400 *hrs./$5545* • Medical Office Management/Administration • Medical/Clinical Assistant 400 *hrs./$5545* • System Administration/Administrator 240 *hrs./$5745* • System, Networking, and LAN/WAN Management/Manager 2 *students enrolled*

STUDENT SERVICES Employment services for current students, placement services for program completers.

Mount Holyoke College

50 College Street, South Hadley, MA 01075
http://www.mtholyoke.edu/

CONTACT Joanne V. Creighton, President
Telephone: 413-538-2000

GENERAL INFORMATION Private Institution. Founded 1837. **Accreditation:** Regional (NEASC/NEASCCIHE). **Total program enrollment:** 2174. **Application fee:** $60.

PROGRAM(S) OFFERED

• American/United States Studies/Civilization 1 *student enrolled* • Art History, Criticism and Conservation 1 *student enrolled* • Asian Studies/Civilization 1 *student enrolled* • Fine/Studio Arts, General 1 *student enrolled* • Social Sciences, Other 1 *student enrolled*

STUDENT SERVICES Academic or career counseling, employment services for current students, placement services for program completers.

Mount Wachusett Community College

444 Green Street, Gardner, MA 01440-1000
http://www.mwcc.mass.edu/

CONTACT Daniel Asquino, President
Telephone: 978-632-6600

GENERAL INFORMATION Public Institution. Founded 1963. **Accreditation:** Regional (NEASC/NEASCCIHE); medical assisting (AAMAE); physical therapy assisting (APTA). **Total program enrollment:** 1913. **Application fee:** $10.

PROGRAM(S) OFFERED

• Accounting Technology/Technician and Bookkeeping 11 *students enrolled* • Alternative and Complementary Medical Support Services, Other 3 *students enrolled* • Athletic Training/Trainer 2 *students enrolled* • Automobile/Automotive Mechanics Technology/Technician 3 *students enrolled* • Business Administration and Management, General 8 *students enrolled* • Business Administration, Management and Operations, Other 10 *students enrolled* • Child Care Provider/Assistant 2 *students enrolled* • Computer Engineering Technologies/

Technicians, Other 1 *student enrolled* • Computer Graphics 2 *students enrolled* • Computer Systems Networking and Telecommunications 7 *students enrolled* • Computer and Information Sciences and Support Services, Other 2 *students enrolled* • Criminal Justice/Law Enforcement Administration 4 *students enrolled* • Entrepreneurship/Entrepreneurial Studies 2 *students enrolled* • Human Services, General 8 *students enrolled* • Legal Assistant/Paralegal 15 *students enrolled* • Licensed Practical/Vocational Nurse Training (LPN, LVN, Cert, Dipl, AAS) 86 *students enrolled* • Massage Therapy/Therapeutic Massage 8 *students enrolled* • Medical Administrative/Executive Assistant and Medical Secretary 16 *students enrolled* • Phlebotomy/Phlebotomist 1 *student enrolled* • Web Page, Digital/Multimedia and Information Resources Design 5 *students enrolled*

STUDENT SERVICES Academic or career counseling, daycare for children of students, employment services for current students, placement services for program completers, remedial services.

Newbury College

129 Fisher Avenue, Brookline, MA 02445
http://www.newbury.edu/

CONTACT Hannah McCarthy, President
Telephone: 617-730-7000

GENERAL INFORMATION Private Institution. Founded 1962. **Accreditation:** Regional (NEASC/NEASCCIHE); interior design: professional (CIDA). **Total program enrollment:** 866. **Application fee:** $50.

PROGRAM(S) OFFERED

• Accounting • Computer and Information Sciences, General • Culinary Arts/Chef Training 6 *students enrolled* • Hotel/Motel Administration/Management 1 *student enrolled* • Legal Assistant/Paralegal • Medical Office Assistant/Specialist 3 *students enrolled*

STUDENT SERVICES Academic or career counseling, employment services for current students, placement services for program completers, remedial services.

New England Hair Academy

492-500 Main Street, Malden, MA 02148-5105
http://www.newenglandhairacademy.com/

CONTACT Anthony Clemente, Director
Telephone: 781-324-6799

GENERAL INFORMATION Private Institution. Founded 1976. **Total program enrollment:** 120. **Application fee:** $50.

PROGRAM(S) OFFERED

• Barbering/Barber 1000 *hrs./$11,200* • Cosmetology/Cosmetologist, General 1000 *hrs./$11,440* • Nail Technician/Specialist and Manicurist 100 *hrs./$1300*

STUDENT SERVICES Academic or career counseling, employment services for current students, placement services for program completers.

Nichols College

PO Box 5000, Dudley, MA 01571-5000
http://www.nichols.edu/

CONTACT Debra M. Townsley, President
Telephone: 508-213-1560

GENERAL INFORMATION Private Institution. Founded 1815. **Accreditation:** Regional (NEASC/NEASCCIHE). **Total program enrollment:** 1132. **Application fee:** $25.

STUDENT SERVICES Academic or career counseling, employment services for current students, placement services for program completers, remedial services.

North Bennet Street School

39 North Bennet Street, Boston, MA 02113-1998
http://www.nbss.org/

CONTACT Miguel Gomez-Ibanez, Executive Director
Telephone: 617-227-0155 Ext. 100

GENERAL INFORMATION Private Institution. Founded 1885. **Total program enrollment:** 149.

PROGRAM(S) OFFERED
• **Carpentry/Carpenter** 2340 hrs./$33,552 • **Furniture Design and Manufacturing** 2340 hrs./$36,332 • **Locksmithing and Safe Repair** 7 students enrolled • **Musical Instrument Fabrication and Repair** 3900 hrs./$51,600 • **Precision Production, Other** 2340 hrs./$31,464 • **Watchmaking and Jewelrymaking** 2340 hrs./$30,618

STUDENT SERVICES Employment services for current students, placement services for program completers.

Northeastern University

360 Huntington Avenue, Boston, MA 02115-5096
http://www.northeastern.edu/

CONTACT Joseph E. Aoun, President
Telephone: 617-373-2000

GENERAL INFORMATION Private Institution. Founded 1898. **Accreditation:** Regional (NEASC/NEASCCIHE); athletic training (JRCAT); audiology (ASHA); computer science (ABET/CSAC); engineering technology (ABET/TAC); health information administration (AHIMA); medical technology (NAACLS); speech-language pathology (ASHA). **Total program enrollment:** 19957. **Application fee:** $75.

PROGRAM(S) OFFERED
• **Computer Engineering Technology/Technician** • **Electrical, Electronic and Communications Engineering Technology/Technician**

STUDENT SERVICES Academic or career counseling, employment services for current students, placement services for program completers, remedial services.

Northern Essex Community College

100 Elliott Street, Haverhill, MA 01830
http://www.necc.mass.edu/

CONTACT David F. Hartleb, President
Telephone: 978-556-3000

GENERAL INFORMATION Public Institution. Founded 1960. **Accreditation:** Regional (NEASC/NEASCCIHE); dental assisting (ADA); health information technology (AHIMA); radiologic technology: radiography (JRCERT); respiratory therapy technology (CoARC). **Total program enrollment:** 2606. **Application fee:** $25.

PROGRAM(S) OFFERED
• **Accounting Technology/Technician and Bookkeeping** 7 students enrolled • **Alternative and Complementary Medicine and Medical Systems, Other** 19 students enrolled • **Commercial and Advertising Art** 17 students enrolled • **Computer Programming/Programmer, General** 9 students enrolled • **Computer Systems Networking and Telecommunications** 1 student enrolled • **Computer and Information Sciences, General** 15 students enrolled • **Criminal Justice/Police Science** 33 students enrolled • **Critical Care Nursing** 3 students enrolled • **Dental Assisting/Assistant** 15 students enrolled • **Drafting/Design Engineering Technologies/Technicians, Other** 7 students enrolled • **Drama and Dance Teacher Education** 1 student enrolled • **Early Childhood Education and Teaching** • **Electrical and Electronic Engineering Technologies/Technicians, Other** 1 student enrolled • **Electromechanical and Instrumentation and Maintenance Technologies/Technicians, Other** 3 students enrolled • **Emergency Medical Technology/Technician (EMT Paramedic)** • **Health Information/Medical Records Technology/Technician** 1 student enrolled • **Health and Medical Administrative Services, Other** 13 students enrolled • **Hotel/Motel Administration/Management** 3 students enrolled • **Legal Assistant/Paralegal** 6 students enrolled • **Licensed Practical/Vocational Nurse Training (LPN, LVN, Cert, Dipl, AAS)** 19 students enrolled • **Logistics and Materials Management** 1

student enrolled • **Medical/Clinical Assistant** 21 students enrolled • **Phlebotomy/Phlebotomist** 1 student enrolled • **Psychiatric/Mental Health Services Technician** 3 students enrolled • **Respiratory Care Therapy/Therapist** • **Sign Language Interpretation and Translation** 11 students enrolled • **Substance Abuse/Addiction Counseling** 12 students enrolled

STUDENT SERVICES Academic or career counseling, daycare for children of students, employment services for current students, placement services for program completers, remedial services.

North Shore Community College

1 Ferncroft Road, Danvers, MA 01923-4093
http://www.northshore.edu/

CONTACT Dr. Wayne Burton, President
Telephone: 508-762-4000

GENERAL INFORMATION Public Institution. Founded 1965. **Accreditation:** Regional (NEASC/NEASCCIHE); physical therapy assisting (APTA); radiologic technology: radiography (JRCERT). **Total program enrollment:** 3120.

PROGRAM(S) OFFERED
• **Adult Development and Aging** 2 students enrolled • **Aesthetician/Esthetician and Skin Care Specialist** 15 students enrolled • **Agricultural and Domestic Animals Services, Other** 5 students enrolled • **Business/Office Automation/Technology/Data Entry** 1 student enrolled • **Child Care Provider/Assistant** 8 students enrolled • **Computer Programming/Programmer, General** 1 student enrolled • **Cosmetology/Cosmetologist, General** 34 students enrolled • **Criminal Justice/Safety Studies** 57 students enrolled • **Culinary Arts and Related Services, Other** 3 students enrolled • **Energy Management and Systems Technology/Technician** 19 students enrolled • **Fire Protection and Safety Technology/Technician** 23 students enrolled • **Floriculture/Floristry Operations and Management** • **Graphic Design** 5 students enrolled • **Health Professions and Related Clinical Sciences, Other** 13 students enrolled • **Legal Administrative Assistant/Secretary** 2 students enrolled • **Legal Assistant/Paralegal** 4 students enrolled • **Licensed Practical/Vocational Nurse Training (LPN, LVN, Cert, Dipl, AAS)** 41 students enrolled • **Mechanical Drafting and Mechanical Drafting CAD/CADD** 5 students enrolled • **Mechanical Engineering Related Technologies/Technicians, Other** 7 students enrolled • **Medical Administrative/Executive Assistant and Medical Secretary** 3 students enrolled • **Medical Insurance Coding Specialist/Coder** 5 students enrolled • **Medical/Clinical Assistant** 15 students enrolled • **Mental and Social Health Services and Allied Professions, Other** 10 students enrolled • **Psychiatric/Mental Health Services Technician** • **Substance Abuse/Addiction Counseling** 13 students enrolled • **Surgical Technology/Technologist** 16 students enrolled • **System, Networking, and LAN/WAN Management/Manager** 4 students enrolled • **Teacher Assistant/Aide** 13 students enrolled • **Web Page, Digital/Multimedia and Information Resources Design** 3 students enrolled

STUDENT SERVICES Academic or career counseling, employment services for current students, placement services for program completers, remedial services.

Quincy College

34 Coddington Street, Quincy, MA 02169-4522
http://www.quincycollege.edu/

CONTACT Sue Harris, President/CEO
Telephone: 800-698-1700

GENERAL INFORMATION Public Institution. Founded 1958. **Accreditation:** Regional (NEASC/NEASCCIHE); practical nursing (NLN). **Total program enrollment:** 1475. **Application fee:** $30.

PROGRAM(S) OFFERED
• **Early Childhood Education and Teaching** • **Kinesiology and Exercise Science** 1 student enrolled • **Legal Assistant/Paralegal** 4 students enrolled • **Licensed Practical/Vocational Nurse Training (LPN, LVN, Cert, Dipl, AAS)** 70 students enrolled • **Phlebotomy/Phlebotomist** 4 students enrolled • **Surgical Technology/Technologist** 7 students enrolled

STUDENT SERVICES Academic or career counseling, employment services for current students, placement services for program completers, remedial services.

Quinsigamond Community College

670 West Boylston Street, Worcester, MA 01606-2092
http://www.qcc.mass.edu/

CONTACT Gail Carberry, President
Telephone: 508-853-2300

GENERAL INFORMATION Public Institution. Founded 1963. **Accreditation:** Regional (NEASC/NEASCCIHE); dental assisting (ADA); dental hygiene (ADA); medical assisting (AAMAE); radiologic technology: radiography (JRCERT). **Total program enrollment:** 3436. **Application fee:** $20.

PROGRAM(S) OFFERED
• **Accounting** *1 student enrolled* • **Allied Health Diagnostic, Intervention, and Treatment Professions, Other** *1 student enrolled* • **Biomedical Technology/Technician** *8 students enrolled* • **Business Operations Support and Secretarial Services, Other** *2 students enrolled* • **Business, Management, Marketing, and Related Support Services, Other** *5 students enrolled* • **CAD/CADD Drafting and/or Design Technology/Technician** *1 student enrolled* • **Computer Engineering Technology/Technician** *1 student enrolled* • **Computer Systems Networking and Telecommunications** *2 students enrolled* • **Computer and Information Sciences and Support Services, Other** *2 students enrolled* • **Criminal Justice/Police Science** *8 students enrolled* • **Dental Assisting/Assistant** *6 students enrolled* • **Electrical, Electronic and Communications Engineering Technology/Technician** *3 students enrolled* • **Emergency Medical Technology/Technician (EMT Paramedic)** *4 students enrolled* • **Energy Management and Systems Technology/Technician** *14 students enrolled* • **Hotel/Motel Administration/Management** *4 students enrolled* • **Kindergarten/Preschool Education and Teaching** *2 students enrolled* • **Licensed Practical/Vocational Nurse Training (LPN, LVN, Cert, Dipl, AAS)** *65 students enrolled* • **Manufacturing Technology/Technician** *1 student enrolled* • **Mechanical Engineering Related Technologies/Technicians, Other** *2 students enrolled* • **Medical Administrative/Executive Assistant and Medical Secretary** *5 students enrolled* • **Medical/Clinical Assistant** *13 students enrolled* • **Occupational Safety and Health Technology/Technician** *1 student enrolled* • **Public Administration and Social Service Professions, Other** *10 students enrolled* • **Surgical Technology/Technologist** *7 students enrolled* • **Web Page, Digital/Multimedia and Information Resources Design** *6 students enrolled*

STUDENT SERVICES Academic or career counseling, daycare for children of students, employment services for current students, placement services for program completers, remedial services.

Rob Roy Academy–Fall River Campus

260 South Main Street, Fall River, MA 02721
http://www.rob-roy.com/

CONTACT Robert Lapierre, President
Telephone: 508-672-4751

GENERAL INFORMATION Private Institution. Founded 1933. **Total program enrollment:** 121. **Application fee:** $100.

PROGRAM(S) OFFERED
• **Aesthetician/Esthetician and Skin Care Specialist** *300 hrs./$3585* • **Barbering/Barber** *1000 hrs./$11,450* • **Cosmetology/Cosmetologist, General** *1000 hrs./$11,780*

STUDENT SERVICES Academic or career counseling, employment services for current students, placement services for program completers.

Rob Roy Academy–New Bedford Campus

1872 Acushnet Avenue, New Bedford, MA 02746-2114
http://www.rob-roy.com/

CONTACT Robert Lapierre, President
Telephone: 508-995-8711

GENERAL INFORMATION Private Institution. **Total program enrollment:** 35. **Application fee:** $100.

PROGRAM(S) OFFERED
• **Cosmetology/Cosmetologist, General** *1000 hrs./$11,785*

STUDENT SERVICES Academic or career counseling, placement services for program completers.

Rob Roy Academy–Taunton Campus

1 School Street, Taunton, MA 02780-5339
http://www.rob-roy.com/

CONTACT Robert La Pierre, President CEO
Telephone: 508-822-1405

GENERAL INFORMATION Private Institution. **Total program enrollment:** 67. **Application fee:** $100.

PROGRAM(S) OFFERED
• **Cosmetology/Cosmetologist, General** *1000 hrs./$11,785* • **Nail Technician/Specialist and Manicurist** *130 hrs./$1354*

STUDENT SERVICES Academic or career counseling, placement services for program completers.

Rob Roy Academy–Worcester Campus

150 Pleasant Street, Worcester, MA 01609
http://www.rob-roy.com/

CONTACT Robert D. Lapierre, President
Telephone: 508-799-2111

GENERAL INFORMATION Private Institution. Founded 1979. **Total program enrollment:** 205. **Application fee:** $100.

PROGRAM(S) OFFERED
• **Aesthetician/Esthetician and Skin Care Specialist** *600 hrs./$6300* • **Barbering/Barber** *1000 hrs./$11,450* • **Cosmetology and Related Personal Grooming Arts, Other** *26 students enrolled* • **Cosmetology/Cosmetologist, General** *1500 hrs./$14,650* • **Nail Technician/Specialist and Manicurist** *130 hrs./$1254*

STUDENT SERVICES Academic or career counseling, placement services for program completers.

Roxbury Community College

1234 Columbus Avenue, Roxbury Crossing, MA 02120-3400
http://www.rcc.mass.edu/

CONTACT Terrence Gomes, President
Telephone: 617-427-0060

GENERAL INFORMATION Public Institution. Founded 1973. **Accreditation:** Regional (NEASC/NEASCCIHE). **Total program enrollment:** 879. **Application fee:** $10.

PROGRAM(S) OFFERED
• **Administrative Assistant and Secretarial Science, General** *5 students enrolled* • **Business, Management, Marketing, and Related Support Services, Other** • **Business/Commerce, General** • **Business/Office Automation/Technology/Data Entry** • **Computer and Information Sciences and Support Services, Other** • **Criminal Justice/Safety Studies** *1 student enrolled* • **Health Services/Allied Health/Health Sciences, General** • **Licensed Practical/Vocational Nurse Training (LPN, LVN, Cert, Dipl, AAS)** *3 students enrolled* • **Mechanical Drafting and Mechanical Drafting CAD/CADD** • **Psychiatric/Mental Health Services Technician**

STUDENT SERVICES Academic or career counseling, employment services for current students, placement services for program completers, remedial services.

The Salter School

82 Hartwell Street, Fall River, MA 02720
http://www.salterschool.com/

CONTACT Mary Lynch, School Director
Telephone: 508-730-2740

GENERAL INFORMATION Private Institution. **Total program enrollment:** 340. **Application fee:** $25.

PROGRAM(S) OFFERED
• **Massage Therapy/Therapeutic Massage** *44 hrs./$11,950* • **Medical Insurance Coding Specialist/Coder** *40 hrs./$11,900* • **Medical/Clinical Assistant** *40 hrs./$12,875*

STUDENT SERVICES Academic or career counseling, placement services for program completers.

The Salter School

2 Florence Street, Malden, MA 02148
http://www.salterschool.com/

CONTACT Laurie O'Malley, School Director
Telephone: 781-324-5454

GENERAL INFORMATION Private Institution. **Total program enrollment:** 382. **Application fee:** $25.

PROGRAM(S) OFFERED
• **Legal Assistant/Paralegal** *46 hrs./$12,750* • **Massage Therapy/Therapeutic Massage** *47 hrs./$11,950* • **Medical Administrative/Executive Assistant and Medical Secretary** *42 hrs./$11,900* • **Medical/Clinical Assistant** *40 hrs./ $12,875*

STUDENT SERVICES Academic or career counseling, placement services for program completers.

The Salter School

515 Woburn Street, Tewksbury, MA 01876
http://www.salterschool.com/

CONTACT Joseph Lahoud, School Director
Telephone: 978-934-9300

GENERAL INFORMATION Private Institution. **Total program enrollment:** 243. **Application fee:** $25.

PROGRAM(S) OFFERED
• **Legal Assistant/Paralegal** *46 hrs./$12,750* • **Massage Therapy/Therapeutic Massage** *47 hrs./$11,950* • **Medical Administrative/Executive Assistant and Medical Secretary** *42 hrs./$11,900* • **Medical/Clinical Assistant** *43 hrs./ $12,875*

STUDENT SERVICES Academic or career counseling, placement services for program completers.

The Salter School

155 Ararat Street, Worcester, MA 01606
http://www.salterschool.com/

CONTACT Charlene Keefe, School Director
Telephone: 508-853-1074

GENERAL INFORMATION Private Institution. Founded 1937. **Total program enrollment:** 708. **Application fee:** $25.

PROGRAM(S) OFFERED
• **Accounting** *28 hrs./$10,375* • **Computer Engineering Technology/Technician** *2 students enrolled* • **Cooking and Related Culinary Arts, General** *29 hrs./ $13,770* • **Executive Assistant/Executive Secretary** *28 hrs./$11,125* • **Health and Medical Administrative Services, Other** • **Legal Administrative Assistant/ Secretary** *17 students enrolled* • **Massage Therapy/Therapeutic Massage** *29 hrs./$12,060* • **Medical Insurance Coding Specialist/Coder** *104 students enrolled* • **Medical Office Assistant/Specialist** *29 hrs./$11,595* • **Medical/ Clinical Assistant** *29 hrs./$14,125*

STUDENT SERVICES Academic or career counseling, placement services for program completers.

School of the Museum of Fine Arts, Boston

230 The Fenway, Boston, MA 02115
http://www.smfa.edu/

CONTACT Deborah H. Dluhy, Dean of the School and Deputy Director
Telephone: 617-267-6100

GENERAL INFORMATION Private Institution. Founded 1876. **Accreditation:** Art and design (NASAD). **Total program enrollment:** 660. **Application fee:** $60.

PROGRAM(S) OFFERED
• **Fine/Studio Arts, General** *5 students enrolled* • **Graphic Design** *7 students enrolled* • **Illustration** *1 student enrolled*

STUDENT SERVICES Academic or career counseling, employment services for current students, placement services for program completers, remedial services.

Shawsheen Valley Regional Vocational Technical School

100 Cook Street, Billerica, MA 01821-5499
http://www.shawsheen.tec.ma.us/

CONTACT Charles Lyons, Superintendent of Schools
Telephone: 978-667-2111

GENERAL INFORMATION Public Institution. **Total program enrollment:** 41. **Application fee:** $40.

PROGRAM(S) OFFERED
• **Licensed Practical/Vocational Nurse Training (LPN, LVN, Cert, Dipl, AAS)** *1080 hrs./$9175*

STUDENT SERVICES Academic or career counseling, employment services for current students, placement services for program completers, remedial services.

Southeastern Technical College

250 Foundry Street, South Easton, MA 02375
http://sersd.org/

CONTACT Luis Lopes, Superintendent
Telephone: 508-238-1860

GENERAL INFORMATION Public Institution. Founded 1967. **Accreditation:** State accredited or approved. **Total program enrollment:** 90. **Application fee:** $75.

PROGRAM(S) OFFERED
• **Allied Health and Medical Assisting Services, Other** *54 hrs./$5100* • **Business/Office Automation/Technology/Data Entry** *6 students enrolled* • **Dental Assisting/Assistant** *52 hrs./$5300* • **Executive Assistant/Executive Secretary** *30 hrs./$2750* • **Heating, Air Conditioning and Refrigeration Technology/Technician (ACH/ACR/ACHR/HRAC/HVAC/AC Technology)** *12 students enrolled* • **Heating, Air Conditioning, Ventilation and Refrigeration Maintenance Technology/Technician (HAC, HACR, HVAC, HVACR)** *40 hrs./ $5750* • **Licensed Practical/Vocational Nurse Training (LPN, LVN, Cert, Dipl, AAS)** *45 hrs./$8300* • **Massage Therapy/Therapeutic Massage** *650 hrs./$9470* • **Medical/Clinical Assistant** *20 students enrolled*

STUDENT SERVICES Academic or career counseling, employment services for current students, placement services for program completers, remedial services.

Spa Tech Institute–Ipswich

126 High Street, Ipswich, MA 01938
http://spatech.edu/

CONTACT Kris Stecker, Director of Operations
Telephone: 978-356-0980

GENERAL INFORMATION Private Institution. **Total program enrollment:** 52. **Application fee:** $50.

PROGRAM(S) OFFERED
• Aesthetician/Esthetician and Skin Care Specialist *300 hrs./$4400* • **Massage Therapy/Therapeutic Massage** *600 hrs./$11,750* • **Polarity Therapy** *660 hrs./ $12,525*

STUDENT SERVICES Academic or career counseling, placement services for program completers.

Spa Tech Institute–Plymouth

59 Industrial Park Road, Plymouth, MA 02360
http://www.spatech.edu/

CONTACT Kris Stecker, Director of Operations
Telephone: 508-747-3130

GENERAL INFORMATION Private Institution. **Total program enrollment:** 78. **Application fee:** $50.

PROGRAM(S) OFFERED
• Aesthetician/Esthetician and Skin Care Specialist *300 hrs./$4400* • **Massage Therapy/Therapeutic Massage** *600 hrs./$11,750*

STUDENT SERVICES Academic or career counseling, placement services for program completers.

Spa Tech Institute–Westboro

227 Turnpike Road, Suite 1, Westboro, MA 01581
http://www.spatech.edu/

CONTACT Kris Stecker, Director of Operations
Telephone: 508-836-8864 Ext. 31

GENERAL INFORMATION Private Institution. **Total program enrollment:** 54. **Application fee:** $50.

PROGRAM(S) OFFERED
• Aesthetician/Esthetician and Skin Care Specialist *300 hrs./$4400* • **Massage Therapy/Therapeutic Massage** *600 hrs./$11,750* • **Polarity Therapy** *660 hrs./ $12,525*

STUDENT SERVICES Academic or career counseling, placement services for program completers.

Springfield Technical Community College

1 Armory Square, Suite One, PO Box 9000, Springfield, MA 01102-9000
http://www.stcc.edu/

CONTACT Ira Rubenzahl, President
Telephone: 413-781-7822

GENERAL INFORMATION Public Institution. Founded 1967. **Accreditation:** Regional (NEASC/NEASCCIHE); dental assisting (ADA); dental hygiene (ADA); diagnostic medical sonography (JRCEDMS); medical assisting (AAMAE); medical laboratory technology (NAACLS); nuclear medicine technology (JRCNMT); physical therapy assisting (APTA); radiologic technology: radiography (JRCERT); surgical technology (ARCST). **Total program enrollment:** 2733. **Application fee:** $10.

PROGRAM(S) OFFERED
• **Architectural Drafting and Architectural CAD/CADD** *4 students enrolled* • **Building/Construction Finishing, Management, and Inspection, Other** *1 student enrolled* • **Clinical/Medical Laboratory Assistant** *3 students enrolled* • **Computer Software and Media Applications, Other** *2 students enrolled* • **Cosmetology/Cosmetologist, General** *25 students enrolled* • **Criminal Justice/ Police Science** *1 student enrolled* • **Data Entry/Microcomputer Applications, General** *3 students enrolled* • **Dental Assisting/Assistant** *11 students enrolled* • **Fire Science/Firefighting** *4 students enrolled* • **General Office Occupations and Clerical Services** *5 students enrolled* • **Geography** *1 student enrolled* • **Graphic and Printing Equipment Operator, General Production** *3 students enrolled* • **Health Aides/Attendants/Orderlies, Other** *1 student enrolled* • **Heating, Air Conditioning, Ventilation and Refrigeration Maintenance Technology/ Technician (HAC, HACR, HVAC, HVACR)** *22 students enrolled* • **Landscaping and Groundskeeping** *4 students enrolled* • **Massage Therapy/Therapeutic Massage** *2 students enrolled* • **Mechanical Drafting and Mechanical Drafting CAD/ CADD** *2 students enrolled* • **Mechanical Engineering/Mechanical Technology/ Technician** *3 students enrolled* • **Medical Insurance Coding Specialist/Coder** *11 students enrolled* • **Medical/Clinical Assistant** *18 students enrolled* • **Prepress/ Desktop Publishing and Digital Imaging Design** *4 students enrolled* • **Robotics Technology/Technician** *1 student enrolled* • **System Administration/ Administrator** *1 student enrolled* • **Web Page, Digital/Multimedia and Information Resources Design** *3 students enrolled*

STUDENT SERVICES Academic or career counseling, daycare for children of students, employment services for current students, placement services for program completers, remedial services.

Suffolk University

8 Ashburton Place, Boston, MA 02108-2770
http://www.suffolk.edu/

CONTACT David J. Sargent, President
Telephone: 617-573-8000

GENERAL INFORMATION Private Institution. Founded 1906. **Accreditation:** Regional (NEASC/NEASCCIHE); art and design (NASAD); interior design: professional (CIDA). **Total program enrollment:** 6796. **Application fee:** $50.

PROGRAM(S) OFFERED
• **Art/Art Studies, General** • **Business Administration and Management, General** • **Design and Applied Arts, Other** *1 student enrolled* • **Electrical/ Electronics Drafting and Electrical/Electronics CAD/CADD** *1 student enrolled* • **Financial Planning and Services** *3 students enrolled* • **Human Resources Management/Personnel Administration, General** *4 students enrolled* • **Legal Assistant/Paralegal** *17 students enrolled* • **Medical Radiologic Technology/ Science—Radiation Therapist** *1 student enrolled*

STUDENT SERVICES Academic or career counseling, employment services for current students, placement services for program completers, remedial services.

Sullivan and Cogliano Training Center

365 Westgate Drive, Brockton, MA 02301-1822
http://www.sctrain.com/

CONTACT Herb Cogliano, President
Telephone: 508-584-9909

GENERAL INFORMATION Private Institution. **Total program enrollment:** 584.

PROGRAM(S) OFFERED
• **Computer Installation and Repair Technology/Technician** *16 hrs./$6995* • **Computer Programming/Programmer, General** *19 hrs./$6995* • **Computer and Information Sciences and Support Services, Other** *16 hrs./$6495* • **Executive Assistant/Executive Secretary** *24 hrs./$9995* • **Information Science/ Studies** *16 hrs./$6995* • **Systems Engineering** *28 hrs./$6860* • **Web Page, Digital/Multimedia and Information Resources Design** *3 students enrolled*

STUDENT SERVICES Academic or career counseling, employment services for current students, placement services for program completers.

Universal Technical Institute

1 Upland Road, Building 200, Norwood, MA 02062
http://www.uticorp.com/

CONTACT Jorge Gutierrez, Campus President
Telephone: 781-948-2000

GENERAL INFORMATION Private Institution. **Total program enrollment:**
1177.

PROGRAM(S) OFFERED
● **Automobile/Automotive Mechanics Technology/Technician** *63 hrs./$24,250*
● **Diesel Mechanics Technology/Technician** *106 hrs./$33,200*

STUDENT SERVICES Academic or career counseling, employment
services for current students, placement services for program completers.

University of Massachusetts

250 Stuart Street, Boston, MA 02116-5435

CONTACT Jack M. Wilson, President
Telephone: 617-287-7000

GENERAL INFORMATION Public Institution. **Accreditation:** Regional
(NEASC/NEASCCIHE).

University of Massachusetts Amherst

Amherst, MA 01003
http://www.umass.edu/

CONTACT Robert C. Holub, Chancellor
Telephone: 413-545-0111

GENERAL INFORMATION Public Institution. Founded 1863. **Accreditation:**
Regional (NEASC/NEASCCIHE); audiology (ASHA); dietetics: postbaccalaureate internship (ADtA/CAADE); forestry (SAF); home
economics (AAFCS); music (NASM); speech-language pathology
(ASHA). **Total program enrollment:** 21055. **Application fee:** $40.

STUDENT SERVICES Academic or career counseling, daycare for children
of students, employment services for current students, placement services
for program completers, remedial services.

University of Massachusetts Boston

100 Morrissey Boulevard, Boston, MA 02125-3393
http://www.umb.edu/

CONTACT J. Keith Motley, Chancellor
Telephone: 617-287-5000

GENERAL INFORMATION Public Institution. Founded 1964. **Accreditation:**
Regional (NEASC/NEASCCIHE). **Total program enrollment:** 8303. **Application fee:** $40.

PROGRAM(S) OFFERED
● **Cartography** *4 students enrolled* ● **Communication Studies/Speech Communication and Rhetoric** *1 student enrolled* ● **Computer and Information Sciences, General** *1 student enrolled* ● **Geological and Earth Sciences/
Geosciences, Other** *1 student enrolled* ● **International Relations and Affairs** *17
students enrolled* ● **Legal Professions and Studies, Other** *2 students enrolled*
● **Substance Abuse/Addiction Counseling** *1 student enrolled*

STUDENT SERVICES Academic or career counseling, daycare for children
of students, employment services for current students, placement services
for program completers, remedial services.

Upper Cape Cod Regional Vocational-Technical School

220 Sandwich Road, Bourne, MA 02532
http://www.uppercapetech.com/

CONTACT Kevin C. Farr, Superintendent
Telephone: 508-759-7711 Ext. 285

GENERAL INFORMATION Public Institution. Founded 1966. **Total
program enrollment:** 67.

PROGRAM(S) OFFERED
● **Licensed Practical/Vocational Nurse Training (LPN, LVN, Cert, Dipl, AAS)**
65 students enrolled

STUDENT SERVICES Academic or career counseling, remedial services.

Urban College of Boston

178 Tremont Street, Boston, MA 02111
http://www.urbancollegeofboston.org/

CONTACT Linda E. Turner, PhD, President
Telephone: 617-348-6359

GENERAL INFORMATION Private Institution. Founded 1993. **Accreditation:** Regional (NEASC/NEASCCIHE). **Total program enrollment:** 14.
Application fee: $10.

PROGRAM(S) OFFERED
● **Early Childhood Education and Teaching** *29 students enrolled* ● **Human
Services, General** *4 students enrolled*

STUDENT SERVICES Academic or career counseling, employment
services for current students, placement services for program completers,
remedial services.

Wentworth Institute of Technology

550 Huntington Avenue, Boston, MA 02115-5998
http://www.wit.edu/

CONTACT Zorica Pantic, President
Telephone: 617-989-4590

GENERAL INFORMATION Private Institution. Founded 1904. **Accreditation:** Regional (NEASC/NEASCCIHE); engineering technology (ABET/
TAC); interior design: professional (CIDA). **Total program enrollment:**
3407. **Application fee:** $30.

PROGRAM(S) OFFERED
● **Communications Technologies/Technicians and Support Services, Other** *3
students enrolled* ● **Survey Technology/Surveying** ● **Web Page, Digital/
Multimedia and Information Resources Design**

STUDENT SERVICES Academic or career counseling, employment
services for current students, placement services for program completers,
remedial services.

Zion Bible College

320 S. Main Street, Haverhill, MA 01835
http://www.zbc.edu/

CONTACT Dr. Charles Crabtree, President
Telephone: 978-478-3400

GENERAL INFORMATION Private Institution (Affiliated with Assembly of
God Church). Founded 1924. **Accreditation:** State accredited or approved. **Total program enrollment:** 205. **Application fee:** $35.

PROGRAM(S) OFFERED
• Bible/Biblical Studies *11 students enrolled*

STUDENT SERVICES Academic or career counseling, employment services for current students, placement services for program completers, remedial services.

MICHIGAN ———————

Alpena Community College

666 Johnson Street, Alpena, MI 49707-1495
http://www.alpenacc.edu/

CONTACT Olin Joynton, President
Telephone: 989-356-9021

GENERAL INFORMATION Public Institution. Founded 1952. **Accreditation:** Regional (NCA); medical assisting (AAMAE). **Total program enrollment:** 1065.

PROGRAM(S) OFFERED
• Autobody/Collision and Repair Technology/Technician *12 students enrolled* • Automobile/Automotive Mechanics Technology/Technician *1 student enrolled* • Corrections and Criminal Justice, Other *14 students enrolled* • Electrician *9 students enrolled* • Entrepreneurship/Entrepreneurial Studies *1 student enrolled* • General Office Occupations and Clerical Services *3 students enrolled* • Licensed Practical/Vocational Nurse Training (LPN, LVN, Cert, Dipl, AAS) *26 students enrolled* • Lineworker *50 students enrolled* • Machine Tool Technology/Machinist *4 students enrolled* • Medical Transcription/Transcriptionist *2 students enrolled* • Tool and Die Technology/Technician *7 students enrolled* • Welding Technology/Welder *1 student enrolled*

STUDENT SERVICES Academic or career counseling, employment services for current students, placement services for program completers, remedial services.

Ann Arbor Institute of Massage Therapy

180 Jackson Plaza, #100, Ann Arbor, MI 48103
http://www.aaimt.edu/

CONTACT Jocelyn Granger, Director
Telephone: 734-677-4430

GENERAL INFORMATION Private Institution. **Total program enrollment:** 123. **Application fee:** $25.

PROGRAM(S) OFFERED
• Massage Therapy/Therapeutic Massage *750 hrs./$9790*

STUDENT SERVICES Placement services for program completers, remedial services.

The Art Institute of Michigan

28125 Cabot Drive, Suite 120, Novi, MI 48377
http://www.artinstitutes.edu/detroit/

CONTACT Gaby Chaalan-Bakr, Registrar
Telephone: 248-675-3800 Ext. 3820

GENERAL INFORMATION Private Institution. **Total program enrollment:** 188. **Application fee:** $50.

PROGRAM(S) OFFERED
• Baking and Pastry Arts/Baker/Pastry Chef

STUDENT SERVICES Academic or career counseling, employment services for current students.

Baker College Center for Graduate Studies

1116 West Bristol Road, Flint, MI 48507-9843
http://online.baker.edu/

CONTACT Mike Heberling, President
Telephone: 810-766-4021

GENERAL INFORMATION Private Institution. Founded 1911. **Accreditation:** Regional (NCA). **Total program enrollment:** 1883. **Application fee:** $20.

PROGRAM(S) OFFERED
• Web/Multimedia Management and Webmaster *7 students enrolled*

STUDENT SERVICES Academic or career counseling, employment services for current students, placement services for program completers.

Baker College Corporate Services

1050 W. Bristol Road, Flint, MI 48507-5508
http://www.baker.edu/

CONTACT Sandra K. Krug, PhD, Director
Telephone: 248-276-8260

GENERAL INFORMATION Private Institution. **Total program enrollment:** 27. **Application fee:** $20.

PROGRAM(S) OFFERED
• Entrepreneurship/Entrepreneurial Studies *1 student enrolled* • Industrial Technology/Technician • Medical Insurance Coding Specialist/Coder *3 students enrolled*

STUDENT SERVICES Academic or career counseling, employment services for current students, placement services for program completers.

Baker College of Allen Park

4500 Enterprise Drive, Allen Park, MI 48101
http://www.baker.edu/

CONTACT Aaron Maike, Campus President
Telephone: 313-425-3700

GENERAL INFORMATION Private Institution. Founded 2003. **Accreditation:** Regional (NCA). **Total program enrollment:** 1393. **Application fee:** $20.

PROGRAM(S) OFFERED
• Accounting Technology/Technician and Bookkeeping *1 student enrolled* • Child Development *1 student enrolled* • General Office Occupations and Clerical Services • Massage Therapy/Therapeutic Massage *9 students enrolled* • Medical Insurance Specialist/Medical Biller *7 students enrolled* • Medical/Clinical Assistant *1 student enrolled* • Web/Multimedia Management and Webmaster

STUDENT SERVICES Academic or career counseling, employment services for current students, placement services for program completers, remedial services.

Baker College of Auburn Hills

1500 University Drive, Auburn Hills, MI 48326-1586
http://www.baker.edu/

CONTACT Jeffrey M. Love, President
Telephone: 248-340-0600

GENERAL INFORMATION Private Institution. Founded 1911. **Accreditation:** Regional (NCA); medical assisting (AAMAE). **Total program enrollment:** 1895. **Application fee:** $20.

PROGRAM(S) OFFERED
• Accounting Technology/Technician and Bookkeeping *1 student enrolled* • Architectural Drafting and Architectural CAD/CADD • Computer Engineering Technology/Technician *2 students enrolled* • Corrections *2 students enrolled*

Baker College of Auburn Hills (continued)

• Electrocardiograph Technology/Technician • Entrepreneurship/ Entrepreneurial Studies *1 student enrolled* • General Office Occupations and Clerical Services *6 students enrolled* • Interior Design *10 students enrolled* • Licensed Practical/Vocational Nurse Training (LPN, LVN, Cert, Dipl, AAS) *11 students enrolled* • Massage Therapy/Therapeutic Massage *4 students enrolled* • Mechanical Drafting and Mechanical Drafting CAD/CADD *1 student enrolled* • Medical Insurance Coding Specialist/Coder *7 students enrolled* • Medical Insurance Specialist/Medical Biller *4 students enrolled* • Medical Reception/Receptionist • Medical/Clinical Assistant *5 students enrolled* • Pharmacy Technician/Assistant *6 students enrolled* • Phlebotomy/ Phlebotomist *19 students enrolled* • Web/Multimedia Management and Webmaster *1 student enrolled*

STUDENT SERVICES Academic or career counseling, employment services for current students, placement services for program completers, remedial services.

Baker College of Cadillac

9600 East 13th Street, Cadillac, MI 49601
http://www.baker.edu/

CONTACT Robert Vandellen, Campus President
Telephone: 231-876-3101

GENERAL INFORMATION Private Institution. Founded 1986. **Accreditation:** Regional (NCA); medical assisting (AAMAE); surgical technology (ARCST). **Total program enrollment:** 802. **Application fee:** $20.

PROGRAM(S) OFFERED

• Accounting Technology/Technician and Bookkeeping *3 students enrolled* • Architectural Drafting and Architectural CAD/CADD *1 student enrolled* • Automotive Engineering Technology/Technician *2 students enrolled* • Child Development *4 students enrolled* • Computer Engineering Technology/ Technician • Computer Systems Analysis/Analyst *1 student enrolled* • Computer Technology/Computer Systems Technology • Corrections *2 students enrolled* • Electrocardiograph Technology/Technician • Emergency Medical Technology/Technician (EMT Paramedic) *14 students enrolled* • General Office Occupations and Clerical Services *1 student enrolled* • Interior Design • Massage Therapy/Therapeutic Massage *10 students enrolled* • Mechanical Drafting and Mechanical Drafting CAD/CADD *1 student enrolled* • Medical Insurance Specialist/Medical Biller *1 student enrolled* • Medical Reception/Receptionist *1 student enrolled* • Medical Transcription/Transcriptionist • Medical/Clinical Assistant • Operations Management and Supervision • Phlebotomy/ Phlebotomist • Teacher Assistant/Aide • Truck and Bus Driver/Commercial Vehicle Operation *8 students enrolled* • Web/Multimedia Management and Webmaster *2 students enrolled*

STUDENT SERVICES Academic or career counseling, employment services for current students, placement services for program completers, remedial services.

Baker College of Clinton Township

34950 Little Mack Avenue, Clinton Township, MI 48035-4701
http://www.baker.edu/

CONTACT Donald R. Torline, President
Telephone: 586-791-6610

GENERAL INFORMATION Private Institution. Founded 1990. **Accreditation:** Regional (NCA); health information technology (AHIMA); medical assisting (AAMAE); surgical technology (ARCST). **Total program enrollment:** 3099. **Application fee:** $20.

PROGRAM(S) OFFERED

• Accounting Technology/Technician and Bookkeeping *2 students enrolled* • Automotive Engineering Technology/Technician *1 student enrolled* • Child Development *5 students enrolled* • Computer Engineering Technology/ Technician *1 student enrolled* • Computer Systems Analysis/Analyst *1 student enrolled* • Emergency Medical Technology/Technician (EMT Paramedic) *45 students enrolled* • Entrepreneurship/Entrepreneurial Studies • General Office Occupations and Clerical Services *5 students enrolled* • Interior Design *13 students enrolled* • Massage Therapy/Therapeutic Massage *16 students enrolled* • Medical Administrative/Executive Assistant and Medical Secretary • Medi-

cal Insurance Specialist/Medical Biller *8 students enrolled* • Medical Reception/Receptionist *2 students enrolled* • Medical/Clinical Assistant • Teacher Assistant/Aide • Web/Multimedia Management and Webmaster

STUDENT SERVICES Academic or career counseling, employment services for current students, placement services for program completers, remedial services.

Baker College of Flint

1050 West Bristol Road, Flint, MI 48507-5508
http://www.baker.edu/

CONTACT Julianne T. Princinsky, EdD, President
Telephone: 810-766-4000

GENERAL INFORMATION Private Institution. Founded 1911. **Accreditation:** Regional (NCA); health information technology (AHIMA); medical assisting (AAMAE); physical therapy assisting (APTA); surgical technology (ARCST). **Total program enrollment:** 3238. **Application fee:** $20.

PROGRAM(S) OFFERED

• Accounting Technology/Technician and Bookkeeping *4 students enrolled* • Architectural Drafting and Architectural CAD/CADD *1 student enrolled* • Automotive Engineering Technology/Technician *1 student enrolled* • Child Development *2 students enrolled* • Computer Engineering Technology/ Technician *1 student enrolled* • Computer Systems Analysis/Analyst • Computer Technology/Computer Systems Technology • Corrections *2 students enrolled* • General Office Occupations and Clerical Services *1 student enrolled* • Home Health Aide/Home Attendant • Industrial Technology/Technician *1 student enrolled* • Massage Therapy/Therapeutic Massage *11 students enrolled* • Mechanical Drafting and Mechanical Drafting CAD/CADD • Medical Insurance Coding Specialist/Coder • Medical Insurance Specialist/Medical Biller *14 students enrolled* • Medical Reception/Receptionist • Medical Transcription/ Transcriptionist *4 students enrolled* • Medical/Clinical Assistant *9 students enrolled* • Pharmacy Technician/Assistant *9 students enrolled* • Phlebotomy/ Phlebotomist *2 students enrolled* • Surgical Technology/Technologist *27 students enrolled* • Truck and Bus Driver/Commercial Vehicle Operation *8 students enrolled* • Web/Multimedia Management and Webmaster

STUDENT SERVICES Academic or career counseling, daycare for children of students, employment services for current students, placement services for program completers, remedial services.

Baker College of Jackson

2800 Springport Road, Jackson, MI 49202
http://www.baker.edu/

CONTACT Dr. Patricia Kaufman, Campus President
Telephone: 517-789-6123

GENERAL INFORMATION Private Institution. Founded 1994. **Accreditation:** Regional (NCA); health information technology (AHIMA); medical assisting (AAMAE); radiologic technology: radiation therapy technology (JRCERT); surgical technology (ARCST). **Total program enrollment:** 981. **Application fee:** $20.

PROGRAM(S) OFFERED

• Accounting Technology/Technician and Bookkeeping • Architectural Drafting and Architectural CAD/CADD • Child Development *2 students enrolled* • Computer Engineering Technology/Technician *1 student enrolled* • Corrections • Entrepreneurship/Entrepreneurial Studies • Massage Therapy/Therapeutic Massage *13 students enrolled* • Mechanical Drafting and Mechanical Drafting CAD/CADD • Medical Insurance Specialist/Medical Biller *3 students enrolled* • Medical Reception/Receptionist *2 students enrolled* • Opticianry/Ophthalmic Dispensing Optician • Phlebotomy/Phlebotomist *11 students enrolled* • Quality Control Technology/Technician *1 student enrolled* • Substance Abuse/Addiction Counseling • Surgical Technology/Technologist *17 students enrolled*

STUDENT SERVICES Academic or career counseling, employment services for current students, placement services for program completers, remedial services.

Baker College of Muskegon

1903 Marquette Avenue, Muskegon, MI 49442-3497
http://www.baker.edu/

CONTACT Rick E. Amidon, President
Telephone: 231-777-8800

GENERAL INFORMATION Private Institution. Founded 1888. **Accreditation:** Regional (NCA); health information technology (AHIMA); medical assisting (AAMAE); physical therapy assisting (APTA); surgical technology (ARCST). **Total program enrollment:** 3320. **Application fee:** $20.

PROGRAM(S) OFFERED
• **Accounting Technology/Technician and Bookkeeping** 3 *students enrolled* • **Baking and Pastry Arts/Baker/Pastry Chef** 9 *students enrolled* • **Child Development** 7 *students enrolled* • **Computer Engineering Technology/Technician** 2 *students enrolled* • **Computer Technology/Computer Systems Technology** 2 *students enrolled* • **Corrections** 3 *students enrolled* • **Emergency Medical Technology/Technician (EMT Paramedic)** 58 *students enrolled* • **Entrepreneurship/Entrepreneurial Studies** 4 *students enrolled* • **General Office Occupations and Clerical Services** 6 *students enrolled* • **Interior Design** 1 *student enrolled* • **Massage Therapy/Therapeutic Massage** 14 *students enrolled* • **Medical Insurance Specialist/Medical Biller** 7 *students enrolled* • **Medical Reception/Receptionist** 5 *students enrolled* • **Medical/Clinical Assistant** 6 *students enrolled* • **Pharmacy Technician/Assistant** 16 *students enrolled* • **Phlebotomy/Phlebotomist** 1 *student enrolled* • **Quality Control Technology/Technician** 2 *students enrolled* • **Surgical Technology/Technologist** 27 *students enrolled* • **Web/Multimedia Management and Webmaster**

STUDENT SERVICES Academic or career counseling, employment services for current students, placement services for program completers, remedial services.

Baker College of Owosso

1020 South Washington Street, Owosso, MI 48867-4400
http://www.baker.edu/

CONTACT Pete Karsten, President
Telephone: 989-729-3300

GENERAL INFORMATION Private Institution. Founded 1984. **Accreditation:** Regional (NCA); medical assisting (AAMAE); medical laboratory technology (NAACLS); medical technology (NAACLS); radiologic technology: radiography (JRCERT). **Total program enrollment:** 1877. **Application fee:** $20.

PROGRAM(S) OFFERED
• **Accounting Technology/Technician and Bookkeeping** 2 *students enrolled* • **Architectural Drafting and Architectural CAD/CADD** • **Automotive Engineering Technology/Technician** 1 *student enrolled* • **Child Development** 1 *student enrolled* • **Computer Engineering Technology/Technician** • **Computer Technology/Computer Systems Technology** 1 *student enrolled* • **Electrocardiograph Technology/Technician** • **General Office Occupations and Clerical Services** 2 *students enrolled* • **Heating, Air Conditioning and Refrigeration Technology/Technician (ACH/ACR/ACHR/HRAC/HVAC/AC Technology)** 4 *students enrolled* • **Home Health Aide/Home Attendant** • **Massage Therapy/Therapeutic Massage** 4 *students enrolled* • **Mechanical Drafting and Mechanical Drafting CAD/CADD** • **Medical Reception/Receptionist** 1 *student enrolled* • **Medical Transcription/Transcriptionist** • **Medical/Clinical Assistant** • **Pharmacy Technician/Assistant** 2 *students enrolled* • **Phlebotomy/Phlebotomist** 22 *students enrolled* • **Web/Multimedia Management and Webmaster**

STUDENT SERVICES Academic or career counseling, daycare for children of students, employment services for current students, placement services for program completers, remedial services.

Baker College of Port Huron

3403 Lapeer Road, Port Huron, MI 48060-2597
http://www.baker.edu/

CONTACT Connie Harrison, President
Telephone: 810-985-7000

GENERAL INFORMATION Private Institution. Founded 1990. **Accreditation:** Regional (NCA); dental hygiene (ADA); medical assisting

(AAMAE); surgical technology (ARCST). **Total program enrollment:** 1133. **Application fee:** $20.

PROGRAM(S) OFFERED
• **Accounting Technology/Technician and Bookkeeping** 1 *student enrolled* • **Child Development** 2 *students enrolled* • **Clinical/Medical Laboratory Technician** • **Computer Engineering Technology/Technician** 1 *student enrolled* • **Computer Technology/Computer Systems Technology** • **Corrections** 2 *students enrolled* • **Electrocardiograph Technology/Technician** 1 *student enrolled* • **General Office Occupations and Clerical Services** 1 *student enrolled* • **Management Information Systems, General** • **Massage Therapy/Therapeutic Massage** 7 *students enrolled* • **Medical Insurance Specialist/Medical Biller** 5 *students enrolled* • **Medical Reception/Receptionist** 1 *student enrolled* • **Medical Transcription/Transcriptionist** • **Medical/Clinical Assistant** 3 *students enrolled* • **Phlebotomy/Phlebotomist** • **Web/Multimedia Management and Webmaster** 1 *student enrolled*

STUDENT SERVICES Academic or career counseling, employment services for current students, placement services for program completers, remedial services.

Bay de Noc Community College

2001 North Lincoln Road, Escanaba, MI 49829-2511
http://www.baydenoc.cc.mi.us/

CONTACT Laura Coleman, President
Telephone: 906-786-5802

GENERAL INFORMATION Public Institution. Founded 1963. **Accreditation:** Regional (NCA). **Total program enrollment:** 1400. **Application fee:** $25.

PROGRAM(S) OFFERED
• **Accounting Technology/Technician and Bookkeeping** 7 *students enrolled* • **Accounting** • **Administrative Assistant and Secretarial Science, General** 4 *students enrolled* • **Autobody/Collision and Repair Technology/Technician** 1 *student enrolled* • **Automobile/Automotive Mechanics Technology/Technician** 1 *student enrolled* • **Baking and Pastry Arts/Baker/Pastry Chef** 1 *student enrolled* • **Banking and Financial Support Services** • **Carpentry/Carpenter** • **Clinical/Medical Laboratory Assistant** 4 *students enrolled* • **Corrections** 1 *student enrolled* • **Customer Service Support/Call Center/Teleservice Operation** 1 *student enrolled* • **Data Entry/Microcomputer Applications, General** 3 *students enrolled* • **Dental Assisting/Assistant** 2 *students enrolled* • **Entrepreneurial and Small Business Operations, Other** • **Entrepreneurship/Entrepreneurial Studies** 2 *students enrolled* • **Foodservice Systems Administration/Management** • **General Office Occupations and Clerical Services** 5 *students enrolled* • **Hotel/Motel Administration/Management** • **Licensed Practical/Vocational Nurse Training (LPN, LVN, Cert, Dipl, AAS)** 60 *students enrolled* • **Optometric Technician/Assistant** 1 *student enrolled* • **Pharmacy Technician/Assistant** • **Pipefitting/Pipefitter and Sprinkler Fitter** 1 *student enrolled* • **Retailing and Retail Operations** 1 *student enrolled* • **Small Engine Mechanics and Repair Technology/Technician** 1 *student enrolled* • **Teacher Assistant/Aide** 1 *student enrolled* • **Water Quality and Wastewater Treatment Management and Recycling Technology/Technician** 1 *student enrolled* • **Welding Technology/Welder** 10 *students enrolled*

STUDENT SERVICES Academic or career counseling, daycare for children of students, employment services for current students, placement services for program completers, remedial services.

Bay Mills Community College

12214 West Lakeshore Drive, Brimley, MI 49715
http://www.bmcc.edu/

CONTACT Michael C. Parish, President
Telephone: 906-248-3354

GENERAL INFORMATION Public Institution. Founded 1984. **Accreditation:** Regional (NCA). **Total program enrollment:** 234.

PROGRAM(S) OFFERED
• **American Indian/Native American Languages, Literatures, and Linguistics** • **Business/Commerce, General** • **Child Care and Support Services Management** • **Community Organization and Advocacy** • **Corrections** 10 *students enrolled* • **Foreign Language Teacher Education** • **Foreign Languages,**

Bay Mills Community College (continued)

Literatures, and Linguistics, Other • General Office Occupations and Clerical Services • Historic Preservation and Conservation • Medical Office Assistant/Specialist • Natural Resources/Conservation, General

STUDENT SERVICES Academic or career counseling, remedial services.

Bayshire Beauty Academy

917 Saginaw Street, Bay City, MI 48708

CONTACT James F. Goodrow, President
Telephone: 989-894-4923

GENERAL INFORMATION Private Institution. Founded 1936. **Total program enrollment:** 19.

PROGRAM(S) OFFERED
• Cosmetology, Barber/Styling, and Nail Instructor *600 hrs./$1700* • Cosmetology/Cosmetologist, General *1500 hrs./$6500* • Massage Therapy/Therapeutic Massage *600 hrs./$1700* • Nail Technician/Specialist and Manicurist *600 hrs./$1700*

STUDENT SERVICES Academic or career counseling, placement services for program completers.

Blue Water College of Cosmetology

1871 Gratiot Boulevard, Marysville, MI 48040

CONTACT Mark Van Kehrberg, Director/Owner
Telephone: 810-364-9595

GENERAL INFORMATION Private Institution. **Total program enrollment:** 34. **Application fee:** $50.

PROGRAM(S) OFFERED
• Cosmetology/Cosmetologist, General *500 hrs./$2765* • Nail Technician/Specialist and Manicurist *400 hrs./$2270*

STUDENT SERVICES Placement services for program completers.

Career Quest Learning Center

5000 Northwind Drive, Suite 120, East Lansing, MI 48823
http://www.cqlc.edu/

CONTACT Todd Brewer, School Director
Telephone: 517-318-3330

GENERAL INFORMATION Private Institution. **Total program enrollment:** 146.

PROGRAM(S) OFFERED
• Administrative Assistant and Secretarial Science, General *32 hrs./$11,900* • Allied Health and Medical Assisting Services, Other *13 students enrolled* • Business/Office Automation/Technology/Data Entry *16 students enrolled* • General Office Occupations and Clerical Services *23 hrs./$4995* • Health and Medical Administrative Services, Other *37 hrs./$11,900* • Medical Office Computer Specialist/Assistant *74 students enrolled* • Medical/Clinical Assistant *41 hrs./$13,900* • System Administration/Administrator *36 hrs./$11,900* • System, Networking, and LAN/WAN Management/Manager *18 students enrolled*

STUDENT SERVICES Academic or career counseling, employment services for current students, placement services for program completers.

Career Quest Learning Centers–Jackson

209 E. Washington Avenue, Suite 241, Jackson, MI 48901
http://www.cqlc.edu

CONTACT Todd Brewer, Director
Telephone: 517-990-9595

GENERAL INFORMATION Private Institution. **Total program enrollment:** 128.

PROGRAM(S) OFFERED
• Medical Office Assistant/Specialist • Medical Office Computer Specialist/Assistant • Medical/Clinical Assistant

STUDENT SERVICES Academic or career counseling, employment services for current students, placement services for program completers.

Carnegie Institute

550 Stephenson Highway, #100, Troy, MI 48083
http://www.carnegie-institute.edu/

CONTACT Linda M. Ingraham, Chief Operating Officer
Telephone: 248-589-1078

GENERAL INFORMATION Private Institution. Founded 1947. **Total program enrollment:** 172.

PROGRAM(S) OFFERED
• Allied Health Diagnostic, Intervention, and Treatment Professions, Other *15 students enrolled* • Electrocardiograph Technology/Technician *34 students enrolled* • Electroneurodiagnostic/Electroencephalographic Technology/Technologist *14 students enrolled* • Health and Medical Administrative Services, Other *10 students enrolled* • Medical Administrative/Executive Assistant and Medical Secretary *33 students enrolled* • Medical/Clinical Assistant *116 students enrolled* • Physical Therapist Assistant *8 students enrolled*

STUDENT SERVICES Academic or career counseling, employment services for current students, placement services for program completers.

Chic University of Cosmetology

1735 Four Mile, NE, Grand Rapids, MI 49525
http://www.chicuniversity.com/

CONTACT Michael Bouman, President/COO
Telephone: 570-429-4321 Ext. 2414

GENERAL INFORMATION Private Institution. **Total program enrollment:** 340. **Application fee:** $100.

PROGRAM(S) OFFERED
• Cosmetology, Barber/Styling, and Nail Instructor *600 hrs./$1760* • Cosmetology/Cosmetologist, General *1600 hrs./$10,850* • Education, Other *11 students enrolled*

STUDENT SERVICES Academic or career counseling, employment services for current students, placement services for program completers, remedial services.

Cleary University

3601 Plymouth Road, Ann Arbor, MI 48105-2659
http://www.cleary.edu/

CONTACT Thomas P. Sullivan, President/CEO
Telephone: 734-332-4477

GENERAL INFORMATION Private Institution. Founded 1883. **Accreditation:** Regional (NCA). **Total program enrollment:** 530. **Application fee:** $25.

STUDENT SERVICES Academic or career counseling, employment services for current students, placement services for program completers.

Cornerstone University

1001 East Beltline Avenue, NE, Grand Rapids, MI 49525-5897
http://www.cornerstone.edu/

CONTACT Joseph M. Stowell, President
Telephone: 616-949-5300

GENERAL INFORMATION Private Institution. Founded 1941. **Accreditation:** Regional (NCA); music (NASM). **Total program enrollment:** 1745. **Application fee:** $25.

PROGRAM(S) OFFERED
• **Theology/Theological Studies** *1 student enrolled*

STUDENT SERVICES Academic or career counseling, employment services for current students, placement services for program completers, remedial services.

Creative Hair School of Cosmetology

G-4439 Clio Road, Flint, MI 48504

CONTACT Corinthian Carouthers, II, Administrator
Telephone: 810-787-4247

GENERAL INFORMATION Private Institution. **Total program enrollment:** 23. **Application fee:** $100.

PROGRAM(S) OFFERED
• **Cosmetology and Related Personal Grooming Arts, Other** *1500 hrs./$10,500*
• **Cosmetology/Cosmetologist, General** *4 students enrolled*

STUDENT SERVICES Placement services for program completers.

Davenport University

415 East Fulton, Grand Rapids, MI 49503
http://www.davenport.edu/

CONTACT Randolph K. Flechsig, President
Telephone: 616-698-7111

GENERAL INFORMATION Private Institution. Founded 1866. **Accreditation:** Regional (NCA); medical assisting (AAMAE). **Total program enrollment:** 3147. **Application fee:** $25.

PROGRAM(S) OFFERED
• **Accounting Technology/Technician and Bookkeeping** *5 students enrolled*
• **Business Administration and Management, General** *13 students enrolled*
• **Computer and Information Sciences and Support Services, Other** • **Corrections** *4 students enrolled* • **Criminal Justice/Safety Studies** *2 students enrolled* • **Customer Service Support/Call Center/Teleservice Operation** • **Data Entry/Microcomputer Applications, General** • **Electrical, Electronic and Communications Engineering Technology/Technician** • **Health Information/Medical Records Technology/Technician** • **Human Resources Management/Personnel Administration, General** *1 student enrolled* • **Legal Assistant/Paralegal** • **Licensed Practical/Vocational Nurse Training (LPN, LVN, Cert, Dipl, AAS)** *109 students enrolled* • **Massage Therapy/Therapeutic Massage** *7 students enrolled* • **Medical Administrative/Executive Assistant and Medical Secretary** • **Medical Insurance Coding Specialist/Coder** *98 students enrolled* • **Medical Insurance Specialist/Medical Biller** *140 students enrolled* • **Medical Transcription/Transcriptionist** *18 students enrolled* • **Medical/Clinical Assistant** *41 students enrolled* • **Phlebotomy/Phlebotomist** *21 students enrolled* • **Prepress/Desktop Publishing and Digital Imaging Design** *1 student enrolled* • **Web/Multimedia Management and Webmaster** *2 students enrolled*

STUDENT SERVICES Academic or career counseling, employment services for current students, placement services for program completers, remedial services.

David Pressley Professional School of Cosmetology

1127 South Washington Street, Royal Oak, MI 48067
http://davidpressleyschool.com/

CONTACT Michelle Gutek, President
Telephone: 248-548-5090

GENERAL INFORMATION Private Institution. Founded 1959. **Total program enrollment:** 225.

PROGRAM(S) OFFERED
• **Aesthetician/Esthetician and Skin Care Specialist** *400 hrs./$3350*
• **Cosmetology, Barber/Styling, and Nail Instructor** *600 hrs./$2380*
• **Cosmetology/Cosmetologist, General** *1500 hrs./$10,100*

STUDENT SERVICES Academic or career counseling, employment services for current students, placement services for program completers.

Delta College

1961 Delta Road, University Center, MI 48710
http://www.delta.edu/

CONTACT Jean Goodnow, President
Telephone: 989-686-9000

GENERAL INFORMATION Public Institution. Founded 1961. **Accreditation:** Regional (NCA); dental assisting (ADA); dental hygiene (ADA); diagnostic medical sonography (JRCEDMS); engineering technology (ABET/TAC); physical therapy assisting (APTA); radiologic technology: radiography (JRCERT); surgical technology (ARCST). **Total program enrollment:** 4499. **Application fee:** $20.

PROGRAM(S) OFFERED
• **Accounting Technology/Technician and Bookkeeping** *28 students enrolled*
• **Administrative Assistant and Secretarial Science, General** *23 students enrolled* • **Automobile/Automotive Mechanics Technology/Technician** *2 students enrolled* • **Building/Construction Finishing, Management, and Inspection, Other** *2 students enrolled* • **Business Administration and Management, General** *3 students enrolled* • **Chemical Technology/Technician** *7 students enrolled* • **Child Care Provider/Assistant** *17 students enrolled* • **Computer Installation and Repair Technology/Technician** *15 students enrolled* • **Computer Software and Media Applications, Other** *3 students enrolled* • **Computer Systems Networking and Telecommunications** *11 students enrolled* • **Corrections** *28 students enrolled* • **Criminal Justice/Police Science** *15 students enrolled* • **Dental Assisting/Assistant** *9 students enrolled* • **Diagnostic Medical Sonography/Sonographer and Ultrasound Technician** *8 students enrolled* • **Drafting and Design Technology/Technician, General** *4 students enrolled* • **Environmental Engineering Technology/Environmental Technology** *3 students enrolled* • **Health Unit Coordinator/Ward Clerk** *47 students enrolled* • **Heating, Air Conditioning, Ventilation and Refrigeration Maintenance Technology/Technician (HAC, HACR, HVAC, HVACR)** *6 students enrolled* • **Interior Design** *2 students enrolled* • **Legal Assistant/Paralegal** *3 students enrolled* • **Licensed Practical/Vocational Nurse Training (LPN, LVN, Cert, Dipl, AAS)** *47 students enrolled* • **Medical Insurance Coding Specialist/Coder** *17 students enrolled* • **Medical Reception/Receptionist** *32 students enrolled* • **Medical Transcription/Transcriptionist** *4 students enrolled* • **Merchandising and Buying Operations** *4 students enrolled* • **Office Management and Supervision** *8 students enrolled* • **Pharmacy Technician/Assistant** *61 students enrolled* • **Phlebotomy/Phlebotomist** *27 students enrolled* • **Precision Metal Working, Other** *1 student enrolled* • **Precision Production, Other** *5 students enrolled* • **Retailing and Retail Operations** *1 student enrolled* • **Security and Loss Prevention Services** *4 students enrolled* • **Small Business Administration/Management** *7 students enrolled* • **Teacher Assistant/Aide** *1 student enrolled* • **Therapeutic Recreation/Recreational Therapy** *2 students enrolled* • **Web/Multimedia Management and Webmaster** *4 students enrolled* • **Welding Technology/Welder** *13 students enrolled*

STUDENT SERVICES Academic or career counseling, employment services for current students, placement services for program completers, remedial services.

Detroit Business Institute–Downriver

19100 Fort Street, Riverview, MI 48192
http://www.dbidownriver.com/

CONTACT Leon Gust, President
Telephone: 734-479-0660

GENERAL INFORMATION Private Institution. Founded 1976. **Total program enrollment:** 60. **Application fee:** $20.

PROGRAM(S) OFFERED
● Administrative Assistant and Secretarial Science, General *3 students enrolled* ● Business/Office Automation/Technology/Data Entry *1 student enrolled* ● Legal Administrative Assistant/Secretary *2 students enrolled* ● Medical Administrative/Executive Assistant and Medical Secretary *10 students enrolled* ● Medical/Clinical Assistant *34 students enrolled*

STUDENT SERVICES Academic or career counseling, employment services for current students, placement services for program completers, remedial services.

Detroit Business Institute–Southfield

23077 Greenfield Road, Suite LL28, Southfield, MI 48075
http://www.dbisouthfield.com/

CONTACT Leon D. Gust, President
Telephone: 248-552-6300

GENERAL INFORMATION Private Institution. Founded 1850. **Total program enrollment:** 188. **Application fee:** $20.

PROGRAM(S) OFFERED
● Administrative Assistant and Secretarial Science, General *44 hrs./$8110* ● Medical Insurance Specialist/Medical Biller *49 hrs./$8110* ● Medical/Clinical Assistant *50 hrs./$8260*

STUDENT SERVICES Academic or career counseling, employment services for current students, placement services for program completers.

Dorsey Business Schools

30821 Barrington, Madison Heights, MI 48071
http://www.dorsey.edu/

CONTACT Sharon McCaughrin, Director
Telephone: 248-588-9660

GENERAL INFORMATION Private Institution. Founded 1934. **Total program enrollment:** 147. **Application fee:** $25.

PROGRAM(S) OFFERED
● Accounting Technology/Technician and Bookkeeping *4 students enrolled* ● Administrative Assistant and Secretarial Science, General ● Computer Science *4 students enrolled* ● Executive Assistant/Executive Secretary *3 students enrolled* ● General Office Occupations and Clerical Services ● Legal Administrative Assistant/Secretary ● Legal Support Services, Other ● Medical Administrative/Executive Assistant and Medical Secretary ● Medical Insurance Specialist/Medical Biller *21 students enrolled* ● Medical Transcription/Transcriptionist *1 student enrolled* ● Medical/Clinical Assistant *16 students enrolled* ● Nurse/Nursing Assistant/Aide and Patient Care Assistant *32 students enrolled* ● Pharmacy Technician/Assistant *19 students enrolled*

STUDENT SERVICES Academic or career counseling, employment services for current students, placement services for program completers.

Dorsey Business Schools

31542 Gratiot, Roseville, MI 48066
http://www.dorsey.edu/

CONTACT Kim Peck, Director
Telephone: 586-296-3225

GENERAL INFORMATION Private Institution. **Total program enrollment:** 357. **Application fee:** $25.

PROGRAM(S) OFFERED
● Accounting and Related Services, Other ● Administrative Assistant and Secretarial Science, General *2 students enrolled* ● Computer Science *5 students enrolled* ● Executive Assistant/Executive Secretary *12 students enrolled* ● General Office Occupations and Clerical Services ● Legal Administrative Assistant/Secretary *7 students enrolled* ● Legal Support Services, Other ● Medical Insurance Specialist/Medical Biller *56 students enrolled* ● Medical Transcription/Transcriptionist *2 students enrolled* ● Medical/Clinical Assistant *23 students enrolled* ● Nurse/Nursing Assistant/Aide and Patient Care Assistant *109 students enrolled* ● Pharmacy Technician/Assistant *25 students enrolled*

STUDENT SERVICES Academic or career counseling, employment services for current students, placement services for program completers.

Dorsey Business Schools

15755 Northline Road, Southgate, MI 48195
http://www.dorsey.edu/

CONTACT Paul Goddard, Director
Telephone: 734-285-5400

GENERAL INFORMATION Private Institution. **Total program enrollment:** 152. **Application fee:** $25.

PROGRAM(S) OFFERED
● Accounting and Related Services, Other ● Administrative Assistant and Secretarial Science, General *1 student enrolled* ● Computer Science *8 students enrolled* ● Executive Assistant/Executive Secretary *9 students enrolled* ● Legal Administrative Assistant/Secretary *1 student enrolled* ● Legal Support Services, Other ● Medical Insurance Specialist/Medical Biller *28 students enrolled* ● Medical Transcription/Transcriptionist *2 students enrolled* ● Medical/Clinical Assistant *19 students enrolled* ● Nurse/Nursing Assistant/Aide and Patient Care Assistant *27 students enrolled* ● Pharmacy Technician/Assistant *10 students enrolled*

STUDENT SERVICES Academic or career counseling, employment services for current students, placement services for program completers.

Dorsey Business Schools

34841 Veterans Plaza, Wayne, MI 48184
http://www.dorsey.edu/

CONTACT Emily Moultry, Director
Telephone: 734-595-1540

GENERAL INFORMATION Private Institution. **Total program enrollment:** 167. **Application fee:** $25.

PROGRAM(S) OFFERED
● Computer Science *5 students enrolled* ● Medical Administrative/Executive Assistant and Medical Secretary ● Medical Insurance Specialist/Medical Biller *22 students enrolled* ● Medical Transcription/Transcriptionist *1 student enrolled* ● Medical/Clinical Assistant *13 students enrolled* ● Nurse/Nursing Assistant/Aide and Patient Care Assistant *27 students enrolled* ● Pharmacy Technician/Assistant *11 students enrolled* ● Retailing and Retail Operations *1 student enrolled*

STUDENT SERVICES Academic or career counseling, employment services for current students, placement services for program completers.

Douglas J. Educational Center

333 Albert Street, Suite 110, East Lansing, MI 48823
http://www.douglasj.com/

CONTACT Scott A. Weaver, President
Telephone: 517-333-9656

GENERAL INFORMATION Private Institution. Founded 1986. **Total program enrollment:** 371. **Application fee:** $100.

PROGRAM(S) OFFERED
- **Aesthetician/Esthetician and Skin Care Specialist** *600 hrs./$6100*
- **Cosmetology, Barber/Styling, and Nail Instructor** *300 hrs./$1800*
- **Cosmetology/Cosmetologist, General** *1500 hrs./$15,200*

STUDENT SERVICES Academic or career counseling, employment services for current students, placement services for program completers.

Ecumenical Theological Seminary

2930 Woodward Avenue, Detroit, MI 48201
http://www.etseminary.org/

CONTACT Dr. Marsha Foster Boyd, President
Telephone: 313-831-5200 Ext. 203

GENERAL INFORMATION Private Institution. **Total program enrollment:** 99. **Application fee:** $30.

PROGRAM(S) OFFERED
- **Theology/Theological Studies** *7 students enrolled*

STUDENT SERVICES Academic or career counseling.

Everest Institute

23400 Michigan Avenue, Suite 200, Dearborn, MI 48124
http://www.everest.edu/

CONTACT Joe Belliotti, School President
Telephone: 313-562-4228

GENERAL INFORMATION Private Institution. **Total program enrollment:** 534.

PROGRAM(S) OFFERED
- **Dental Assisting/Assistant** *720 hrs./$13,933* • **Health Information/Medical Records Administration/Administrator** *10 students enrolled* • **Health and Medical Administrative Services, Other** *14 students enrolled* • **Massage Therapy/Therapeutic Massage** *720 hrs./$13,199* • **Medical Administrative/Executive Assistant and Medical Secretary** *720 hrs./$13,106* • **Medical Insurance Specialist/Medical Biller** *720 hrs./$12,945* • **Medical/Clinical Assistant** *720 hrs./$14,341* • **Pharmacy Technician/Assistant** *100 students enrolled*

STUDENT SERVICES Academic or career counseling, employment services for current students, placement services for program completers.

Everest Institute

300 River Place Drive, Suite 2700, Detroit, MI 48207
http://www.everest.edu/

CONTACT Joseph Egelski, President
Telephone: 313-567-5350

GENERAL INFORMATION Private Institution. **Total program enrollment:** 933.

PROGRAM(S) OFFERED
- **Massage Therapy/Therapeutic Massage** *750 hrs./$13,190* • **Medical Administrative/Executive Assistant and Medical Secretary** *720 hrs./$12,974* • **Medical Insurance Specialist/Medical Biller** *560 hrs./$8800* • **Medical/Clinical Assistant** *720 hrs./$14,085* • **Pharmacy Technician/Assistant** *720 hrs./$13,475*

STUDENT SERVICES Academic or career counseling, employment services for current students, placement services for program completers.

Everest Institute

1750 Woodworth Street, NE, Grand Rapids, MI 49505
http://www.everest.edu/

CONTACT Ruth Stewart, College President
Telephone: 616-364-8464

GENERAL INFORMATION Private Institution. Founded 1972. **Total program enrollment:** 991.

PROGRAM(S) OFFERED
- **Allied Health and Medical Assisting Services, Other** *720 hrs./$13,454* • **Dental Assisting/Assistant** *720 hrs./$13,933* • **Licensed Practical/Vocational Nurse Training (LPN, LVN, Cert, Dipl, AAS)** *1425 hrs./$19,481* • **Massage Therapy/Therapeutic Massage** *720 hrs./$13,199* • **Medical Administrative/Executive Assistant and Medical Secretary** *720 hrs./$13,106* • **Medical Insurance Coding Specialist/Coder** *720 hrs./$12,945* • **Medical Insurance Specialist/Medical Biller** *48 students enrolled* • **Medical/Clinical Assistant** *253 students enrolled* • **Pharmacy Technician/Assistant**

STUDENT SERVICES Academic or career counseling, placement services for program completers.

Everest Institute

5349 West Main, Kalamazoo, MI 49009
http://www.everest.edu/

CONTACT Gloria Stender, President
Telephone: 269-381-9616

GENERAL INFORMATION Private Institution. Founded 1972. **Total program enrollment:** 306.

PROGRAM(S) OFFERED
- **Dental Assisting/Assistant** *720 hrs./$13,398* • **Health and Medical Administrative Services, Other** *720 hrs./$13,106* • **Massage Therapy/Therapeutic Massage** *750 hrs./$13,037* • **Medical Administrative/Executive Assistant and Medical Secretary** *72 students enrolled* • **Medical Insurance Specialist/Medical Biller** • **Medical/Clinical Assistant** *720 hrs./$14,541* • **Pharmacy Technician/Assistant** *720 hrs./$13,106*

STUDENT SERVICES Academic or career counseling, placement services for program completers.

Everest Institute

26555 Evergreen Road, #500, Southfield, MI 48076
http://www.everest.edu/

CONTACT Marchelle Weaver, School President
Telephone: 248-799-9933

GENERAL INFORMATION Private Institution. Founded 1935. **Total program enrollment:** 557.

PROGRAM(S) OFFERED
- **Computer Technology/Computer Systems Technology** *720 hrs./$13,725* • **Electrical and Electronic Engineering Technologies/Technicians, Other** *1440 hrs./$25,275* • **Massage Therapy/Therapeutic Massage** *720 hrs./$13,190* • **Medical Administrative/Executive Assistant and Medical Secretary** *158 students enrolled* • **Medical Insurance Specialist/Medical Biller** *720 hrs./$12,950* • **Medical Office Assistant/Specialist** *720 hrs./$12,974* • **Medical/Clinical Assistant** *720 hrs./$14,085*

STUDENT SERVICES Academic or career counseling, employment services for current students, placement services for program completers, remedial services.

Ferris State University

1201 South State Street, Big Rapids, MI 49307
http://www.ferris.edu/

CONTACT David L. Eisler, President
Telephone: 231-591-2000

GENERAL INFORMATION Public Institution. Founded 1884. **Accreditation:** Regional (NCA); art and design (NASAD); dental hygiene (ADA);

Ferris State University (continued)

engineering technology (ABET/TAC); health information administration (AHIMA); health information technology (AHIMA); medical laboratory technology (NAACLS); medical technology (NAACLS); nuclear medicine technology (JRCNMT); radiologic technology: radiography (JRCERT); recreation and parks (NRPA). **Total program enrollment:** 9872. **Application fee:** $30.

PROGRAM(S) OFFERED

• **Advertising** *1 student enrolled* • **Automobile/Automotive Mechanics Technology/Technician** *36 students enrolled* • **Automotive Engineering Technology/Technician** *3 students enrolled* • **Business Administration and Management, General** *17 students enrolled* • **Culinary Arts and Related Services, Other** *2 students enrolled* • **E-Commerce/Electronic Commerce** *8 students enrolled* • **Entrepreneurship/Entrepreneurial Studies** *3 students enrolled* • **Health Information/Medical Records Technology/Technician** *1 student enrolled* • **Hospitality and Recreation Marketing Operations** *1 student enrolled* • **Hotel/Motel Administration/Management** *2 students enrolled* • **Human Resources Management/Personnel Administration, General** *3 students enrolled* • **Industrial Electronics Technology/Technician** *4 students enrolled* • **International Business/Trade/Commerce** *3 students enrolled* • **Marketing Research** *1 student enrolled* • **Marketing/Marketing Management, General** *16 students enrolled* • **Medical Insurance Coding Specialist/Coder** *1 student enrolled* • **Medical Office Assistant/Specialist** *1 student enrolled* • **Office Management and Supervision** *28 students enrolled* • **Operations Management and Supervision** *9 students enrolled* • **Ornamental Horticulture** *4 students enrolled* • **Phlebotomy/Phlebotomist** *25 students enrolled* • **Public Relations/Image Management** *4 students enrolled* • **Quality Control Technology/Technician** *23 students enrolled* • **Real Estate** *2 students enrolled* • **Restaurant, Culinary, and Catering Management/Manager** *2 students enrolled* • **Selling Skills and Sales Operations** *20 students enrolled* • **Survey Technology/Surveying** *6 students enrolled* • **Technical and Business Writing** *2 students enrolled*

STUDENT SERVICES Academic or career counseling, daycare for children of students, employment services for current students, placement services for program completers, remedial services.

Fiser's College of Cosmetology

329-1/2 East Maumee, Adrian, MI 49221
http://www.adrianbeauty.edu/

CONTACT Pamela Fiser, President
Telephone: 517-263-0000

GENERAL INFORMATION Private Institution. **Total program enrollment:** 12. **Application fee:** $100.

PROGRAM(S) OFFERED

• **Aesthetician/Esthetician and Skin Care Specialist** *400 hrs./$3200* • **Cosmetology, Barber/Styling, and Nail Instructor** *750 hrs./$2750* • **Cosmetology/Cosmetologist, General** *1500 hrs./$8700* • **Nail Technician/Specialist and Manicurist** *400 hrs./$3200*

STUDENT SERVICES Academic or career counseling, employment services for current students, placement services for program completers.

Gallery College of Beauty

38132 S. Gratiot Avenue, Clinton Township, MI 48036

GENERAL INFORMATION Private Institution. **Total program enrollment:** 71.

PROGRAM(S) OFFERED

• **Cosmetology and Related Personal Grooming Arts, Other** *300 hrs./$2000* • **Cosmetology, Barber/Styling, and Nail Instructor** *300 hrs./$1575* • **Cosmetology/Cosmetologist, General** *1500 hrs./$8900*

STUDENT SERVICES Academic or career counseling, placement services for program completers.

Glen Oaks Community College

62249 Shimmel Road, Centreville, MI 49032-9719
http://www.glenoaks.edu/

CONTACT Gary Wheeler, President
Telephone: 269-467-9945 Ext. 0

GENERAL INFORMATION Public Institution. Founded 1965. **Accreditation:** Regional (NCA). **Total program enrollment:** 686.

PROGRAM(S) OFFERED

• **Accounting Technology/Technician and Bookkeeping** *6 students enrolled* • **Administrative Assistant and Secretarial Science, General** *4 students enrolled* • **Automobile/Automotive Mechanics Technology/Technician** *3 students enrolled* • **Child Care Provider/Assistant** *2 students enrolled* • **Computer Installation and Repair Technology/Technician** *1 student enrolled* • **Drafting and Design Technology/Technician, General** *8 students enrolled* • **Electrical, Electronic and Communications Engineering Technology/Technician** *4 students enrolled* • **Emergency Medical Technology/Technician (EMT Paramedic)** *1 student enrolled* • **Licensed Practical/Vocational Nurse Training (LPN, LVN, Cert, Dipl, AAS)** *32 students enrolled* • **Machine Tool Technology/Machinist** *5 students enrolled* • **Marketing/Marketing Management, General** *13 students enrolled* • **Mechanic and Repair Technologies/Technicians, Other** *1 student enrolled* • **Medical Administrative/Executive Assistant and Medical Secretary** *3 students enrolled* • **Medical Insurance Coding Specialist/Coder** *9 students enrolled* • **Medical Transcription/Transcriptionist** *4 students enrolled* • **Medical/Clinical Assistant** *4 students enrolled*

STUDENT SERVICES Academic or career counseling, daycare for children of students, employment services for current students, remedial services.

Gogebic Community College

E-4946 Jackson Road, Ironwood, MI 49938
http://www.gogebic.edu/

CONTACT James Lorenson, President
Telephone: 906-932-4231 Ext. 0

GENERAL INFORMATION Public Institution. Founded 1932. **Accreditation:** Regional (NCA); health information technology (AHIMA). **Total program enrollment:** 628. **Application fee:** $10.

PROGRAM(S) OFFERED

• **Accounting and Business/Management** • **Administrative Assistant and Secretarial Science, General** • **Automobile/Automotive Mechanics Technology/Technician** *7 students enrolled* • **Business/Commerce, General** • **Child Care Provider/Assistant** *1 student enrolled* • **Construction Trades, Other** *4 students enrolled* • **Corrections** • **Cosmetology/Cosmetologist, General** *7 students enrolled* • **Emergency Medical Technology/Technician (EMT Paramedic)** *4 students enrolled* • **Information Technology** • **Licensed Practical/Vocational Nurse Training (LPN, LVN, Cert, Dipl, AAS)** *65 students enrolled* • **Lineworker** *5 students enrolled* • **Medical Insurance Coding Specialist/Coder** *7 students enrolled* • **Medical Transcription/Transcriptionist** • **Physical Therapy/Therapist** • **Pre-Nursing Studies** • **Web/Multimedia Management and Webmaster** *1 student enrolled*

STUDENT SERVICES Academic or career counseling, employment services for current students, placement services for program completers, remedial services.

Grand Rapids Community College

143 Bostwick Avenue, NE, Grand Rapids, MI 49503-3201
http://www.grcc.edu/

CONTACT Anne E. Mulder, PhD, Interim President
Telephone: 616-234-4000

GENERAL INFORMATION Public Institution. Founded 1914. **Accreditation:** Regional (NCA); dental assisting (ADA); dental hygiene (ADA); music (NASM); practical nursing (NLN); radiologic technology: radiography (JRCERT). **Total program enrollment:** 6725. **Application fee:** $20.

PROGRAM(S) OFFERED

• **Adult Development and Aging** *3 students enrolled* • **Automobile/Automotive Mechanics Technology/Technician** *7 students enrolled* • **Baking and Pastry Arts/Baker/Pastry Chef** *23 students enrolled* • **Computer Programming/Programmer,**

General *1 student enrolled* • **Computer and Information Sciences and Support Services, Other** *2 students enrolled* • **Dental Assisting/Assistant** *12 students enrolled* • **Electrical/Electronics Maintenance and Repair Technology, Other** *2 students enrolled* • **Heating, Air Conditioning, Ventilation and Refrigeration Maintenance Technology/Technician (HAC, HACR, HVAC, HVACR)** *17 students enrolled* • **Industrial Mechanics and Maintenance Technology** *11 students enrolled* • **Licensed Practical/Vocational Nurse Training (LPN, LVN, Cert, Dipl, AAS)** *68 students enrolled* • **Machine Shop Technology/Assistant** *1 student enrolled* • **Mechanical Drafting and Mechanical Drafting CAD/CADD** *2 students enrolled* • **Mechanics and Repairers, General** *4 students enrolled* • **Medical Office Management/Administration** *1 student enrolled* • **Sales, Distribution and Marketing Operations, General** *1 student enrolled* • **Web/Multimedia Management and Webmaster** *2 students enrolled* • **Welding Technology/Welder** *4 students enrolled*

STUDENT SERVICES Academic or career counseling, daycare for children of students, employment services for current students, placement services for program completers, remedial services.

Great Lakes Academy of Hair Design

2950 Lapeer Road, Port Huron, MI 48060
http://www.glahd.com/

CONTACT Tina Black
Telephone: 801-302-8801 Ext. 1001

GENERAL INFORMATION Private Institution. **Total program enrollment:** 99. **Application fee:** $100.

PROGRAM(S) OFFERED
• **Cosmetology, Barber/Styling, and Nail Instructor** *500 hrs./$1600*
• **Cosmetology/Cosmetologist, General** *1500 hrs./$13,800*

STUDENT SERVICES Academic or career counseling, employment services for current students, placement services for program completers, remedial services.

Henry Ford Community College

5101 Evergreen Road, Dearborn, MI 48128-1495
http://www.hfcc.edu/

CONTACT Gail Mee, President
Telephone: 313-845-9600

GENERAL INFORMATION Public Institution. Founded 1938. **Accreditation:** Regional (NCA); health information technology (AHIMA); physical therapy assisting (APTA); surgical technology (ARCST). **Total program enrollment:** 5877. **Application fee:** $30.

PROGRAM(S) OFFERED
• **Accounting Technology/Technician and Bookkeeping** *2 students enrolled* • **Administrative Assistant and Secretarial Science, General** *8 students enrolled* • **Animation, Interactive Technology, Video Graphics and Special Effects** *3 students enrolled* • **Automobile/Automotive Mechanics Technology/Technician** *1 student enrolled* • **Baking and Pastry Arts/Baker/Pastry Chef** *5 students enrolled* • **CAD/CADD Drafting and/or Design Technology/Technician** *29 students enrolled* • **Child Care Provider/Assistant** *12 students enrolled* • **Commercial and Advertising Art** *3 students enrolled* • **Computer Software and Media Applications, Other** *8 students enrolled* • **Computer Systems Networking and Telecommunications** *4 students enrolled* • **Corrections** *6 students enrolled* • **Culinary Arts/Chef Training** *7 students enrolled* • **Customer Service Management** *6 students enrolled* • **Electrical, Electronic and Communications Engineering Technology/Technician** *4 students enrolled* • **Electromechanical and Instrumentation and Maintenance Technologies/Technicians, Other** *1 student enrolled* • **Energy Management and Systems Technology/Technician** *1 student enrolled* • **Food Service, Waiter/Waitress, and Dining Room Management/Manager** *1 student enrolled* • **Health and Physical Education/Fitness, Other** *1 student enrolled* • **Heating, Air Conditioning and Refrigeration Technology/Technician (ACH/ACR/ACHR/HRAC/HVAC/AC Technology)** *4 students enrolled* • **Hotel/Motel Administration/Management** *1 student enrolled* • **Illustration** *1 student enrolled* • **Industrial Mechanics and Maintenance Technology** *29 students enrolled* • **Industrial Production Technologies/Technicians, Other** *3 students enrolled* • **Logistics and Materials Management** *1 student enrolled* • **Manufacturing Technology/Technician** *4 students enrolled* • **Mechanic and Repair Technologies/Technicians, Other** *1 student enrolled* • **Medical Insurance Specialist/Medical Biller** *2 students enrolled* • **Medical Reception/Receptionist** *8 students enrolled* • **Medical/Clinical Assistant** *20 students enrolled* • **Nurse/**

Nursing Assistant/Aide and Patient Care Assistant *3 students enrolled* • **Office Management and Supervision** *25 students enrolled* • **Restaurant, Culinary, and Catering Management/Manager** *1 student enrolled* • **Web Page, Digital/Multimedia and Information Resources Design** *3 students enrolled*

STUDENT SERVICES Academic or career counseling, daycare for children of students, employment services for current students, placement services for program completers, remedial services.

Hillsdale Beauty College

64 Waldron Street, Hillsdale, MI 49242

CONTACT Gerald Kwiatkowski, Administrator
Telephone: 517-437-4670

GENERAL INFORMATION Private Institution. Founded 1932. **Total program enrollment:** 35.

PROGRAM(S) OFFERED
• **Cosmetology and Related Personal Grooming Arts, Other** • **Cosmetology/Cosmetologist, General** *20 students enrolled*

STUDENT SERVICES Academic or career counseling, employment services for current students, placement services for program completers.

Houghton Lake Institute of Cosmetology

5921 W. Houghton Lake Drive, Houghton Lake, MI 48629-9702

CONTACT Daniel W. Needham, Chief Executive Officer
Telephone: 989-422-4573

GENERAL INFORMATION Private Institution. **Total program enrollment:** 9.

PROGRAM(S) OFFERED
• **Cosmetology, Barber/Styling, and Nail Instructor** *600 hrs./$2460*
• **Cosmetology/Cosmetologist, General** *1600 hrs./$6884* • **Nail Technician/Specialist and Manicurist** *600 hrs./$2519*

STUDENT SERVICES Academic or career counseling, placement services for program completers.

In Session Arts of Cosmetology Beauty School

7212 Gratiot Road, Suite D, Saginaw, MI 48609
http://www.insessionschool.com/

CONTACT Roger Gomez, Owner
Telephone: 989-781-6282 Ext. 10

GENERAL INFORMATION Private Institution. **Total program enrollment:** 35.

PROGRAM(S) OFFERED
• **Cosmetology, Barber/Styling, and Nail Instructor** *900 hrs./$2800*
• **Cosmetology/Cosmetologist, General** *1500 hrs./$7000* • **Nail Technician/Specialist and Manicurist** *900 hrs./$2700*

Irene's Myomassology Institute

26061 Franklin Road, Southfield, MI 48034
http://www.imieducation.com/

CONTACT Kathleen Gauthier, Executive Director
Telephone: 248-350-1400

GENERAL INFORMATION Private Institution. **Total program enrollment:** 192. **Application fee:** $50.

PROGRAM(S) OFFERED
• **Massage Therapy/Therapeutic Massage** *625 hrs./$9872*

STUDENT SERVICES Placement services for program completers.

Jackson Community College

2111 Emmons Road, Jackson, MI 49201-8399
http://www.jccmi.edu/

CONTACT Daniel J. Phelan, PhD, President and CEO
Telephone: 517-787-0800

GENERAL INFORMATION Public Institution. Founded 1928. **Accreditation:** Regional (NCA); diagnostic medical sonography (JRCEDMS); medical assisting (AAMAE). **Total program enrollment:** 3090.

PROGRAM(S) OFFERED
• **Accounting and Finance** 17 *students enrolled* • **Administrative Assistant and Secretarial Science, General** 2 *students enrolled* • **Automobile/Automotive Mechanics Technology/Technician** 33 *students enrolled* • **Business Administration and Management, General** 15 *students enrolled* • **Computer Programming, Specific Applications** 1 *student enrolled* • **Computer Systems Networking and Telecommunications** 1 *student enrolled* • **Corrections** 34 *students enrolled* • **Criminal Justice/Police Science** 1 *student enrolled* • **Diagnostic Medical Sonography/Sonographer and Ultrasound Technician** 12 *students enrolled* • **Electrician** 1 *student enrolled* • **Emergency Medical Technology/Technician (EMT Paramedic)** 104 *students enrolled* • **Engineering, General** 1 *student enrolled* • **Fine/Studio Arts, General** 1 *student enrolled* • **Licensed Practical/Vocational Nurse Training (LPN, LVN, Cert, Dipl, AAS)** 42 *students enrolled* • **Marketing/Marketing Management, General** 3 *students enrolled* • **Medical Insurance Specialist/Medical Biller** 18 *students enrolled* • **Medical Transcription/Transcriptionist** 3 *students enrolled* • **Medical/Clinical Assistant** 14 *students enrolled* • **Photographic and Film/Video Technology/Technician and Assistant** 2 *students enrolled* • **Physical Sciences** 4 *students enrolled*

STUDENT SERVICES Academic or career counseling, daycare for children of students, employment services for current students, placement services for program completers, remedial services.

Kalamazoo Valley Community College

PO Box 4070, Kalamazoo, MI 49003-4070
http://www.kvcc.edu/

CONTACT Dr. Marilyn Schlack, President
Telephone: 269-488-4100

GENERAL INFORMATION Public Institution. Founded 1966. **Accreditation:** Regional (NCA); dental hygiene (ADA); medical assisting (AAMAE). **Total program enrollment:** 4667.

PROGRAM(S) OFFERED
• **Automobile/Automotive Mechanics Technology/Technician** 7 *students enrolled* • **Business Administration and Management, General** 2 *students enrolled* • **Business/Office Automation/Technology/Data Entry** 32 *students enrolled* • **CAD/CADD Drafting and/or Design Technology/Technician** 3 *students enrolled* • **Computer Systems Analysis/Analyst** 10 *students enrolled* • **Electrical, Electronic and Communications Engineering Technology/Technician** 4 *students enrolled* • **Emergency Medical Technology/Technician (EMT Paramedic)** 55 *students enrolled* • **Executive Assistant/Executive Secretary** 4 *students enrolled* • **Graphic Design** 1 *student enrolled* • **Heating, Air Conditioning and Refrigeration Technology/Technician (ACH/ACR/ACHR/HRAC/HVAC/AC Technology)** 2 *students enrolled* • **Legal Administrative Assistant/Secretary** 2 *students enrolled* • **Licensed Practical/Vocational Nurse Training (LPN, LVN, Cert, Dipl, AAS)** 47 *students enrolled* • **Mechanic and Repair Technologies/Technicians, Other** 13 *students enrolled* • **Mechanical Engineering/Mechanical Technology/Technician** 2 *students enrolled* • **Medical Insurance Coding Specialist/Coder** 14 *students enrolled* • **Medical Office Assistant/Specialist** 5 *students enrolled* • **Medical Transcription/Transcriptionist** 4 *students enrolled* • **Medical/Clinical Assistant** 13 *students enrolled* • **Sign Language Interpretation and Translation** 14 *students enrolled* • **Surgical Technology/Technologist** 7 *students enrolled* • **Welding Technology/Welder** 4 *students enrolled*

STUDENT SERVICES Academic or career counseling, daycare for children of students, employment services for current students, placement services for program completers, remedial services.

Kaplan Institute

3031 W. Grand Boulevard, Suite 236, Detroit, MI 48202
http://www.kaplaninstitute.com/

CONTACT Lisia Moore, Executive Director
Telephone: 313-456-8100

GENERAL INFORMATION Private Institution. **Total program enrollment:** 917.

PROGRAM(S) OFFERED
• **Computer and Information Sciences and Support Services, Other** *720 hrs./$12,610* • **Medical Office Assistant/Specialist** *720 hrs./$13,660* • **Medical/Clinical Assistant** *720 hrs./$14,470* • **Pharmacy Technician/Assistant** *720 hrs./$13,690*

STUDENT SERVICES Academic or career counseling, employment services for current students, placement services for program completers.

Kellogg Community College

450 North Avenue, Battle Creek, MI 49017-3397
http://www.kellogg.edu/

CONTACT G. Edward Haring, PhD, President
Telephone: 269-965-3931

GENERAL INFORMATION Public Institution. Founded 1956. **Accreditation:** Regional (NCA); dental hygiene (ADA); medical laboratory technology (NAACLS); physical therapy assisting (APTA); radiologic technology: radiography (JRCERT). **Total program enrollment:** 1852.

PROGRAM(S) OFFERED
• **Accounting Technology/Technician and Bookkeeping** 4 *students enrolled* • **Art/Art Studies, General** 1 *student enrolled* • **Business Administration and Management, General** 3 *students enrolled* • **Child Care and Support Services Management** 4 *students enrolled* • **Community Organization and Advocacy** 4 *students enrolled* • **Corrections** 25 *students enrolled* • **Data Entry/Microcomputer Applications, General** 3 *students enrolled* • **Electrician** 14 *students enrolled* • **Emergency Medical Technology/Technician (EMT Paramedic)** 22 *students enrolled* • **Executive Assistant/Executive Secretary** 8 *students enrolled* • **Graphic Design** 1 *student enrolled* • **Heating, Air Conditioning, Ventilation and Refrigeration Maintenance Technology/Technician (HAC, HACR, HVAC, HVACR)** 6 *students enrolled* • **Human Development, Family Studies, and Related Services, Other** 2 *students enrolled* • **Industrial Mechanics and Maintenance Technology** 2 *students enrolled* • **Instrumentation Technology/Technician** 1 *student enrolled* • **Legal Assistant/Paralegal** 2 *students enrolled* • **Licensed Practical/Vocational Nurse Training (LPN, LVN, Cert, Dipl, AAS)** 51 *students enrolled* • **Machine Tool Technology/Machinist** 1 *student enrolled* • **Mechanics and Repairers, General** 6 *students enrolled* • **Pipefitting/Pipefitter and Sprinkler Fitter** 1 *student enrolled* • **Robotics Technology/Technician** 5 *students enrolled* • **Web Page, Digital/Multimedia and Information Resources Design** 1 *student enrolled* • **Welding Technology/Welder** 5 *students enrolled*

STUDENT SERVICES Academic or career counseling, employment services for current students, placement services for program completers, remedial services.

Kettering University

1700 West Third Avenue, Flint, MI 48504-4898
http://www.kettering.edu/

CONTACT Stanley R. Liberty, President
Telephone: 800-955-4464

GENERAL INFORMATION Private Institution. Founded 1919. **Accreditation:** Regional (NCA). **Total program enrollment:** 1994. **Application fee:** $35.

STUDENT SERVICES Academic or career counseling, employment services for current students, placement services for program completers, remedial services.

Kirtland Community College

10775 North St. Helen Road, Roscommon, MI 48653-9699
http://www.kirtland.edu/

CONTACT Dr. Tom Quinn, President
Telephone: 989-275-5000

GENERAL INFORMATION Public Institution. Founded 1966. Accreditation: Regional (NCA); medical assisting (AAMAE). Total program enrollment: 710.

PROGRAM(S) OFFERED
• Business Administration and Management, General 2 students enrolled • Carpentry/Carpenter 5 students enrolled • Computer Systems Analysis/Analyst 2 students enrolled • Computer Systems Networking and Telecommunications 1 student enrolled • Corrections 1 student enrolled • Cosmetology/Cosmetologist, General 6 students enrolled • Drafting and Design Technology/Technician, General 3 students enrolled • Drafting/Design Engineering Technologies/Technicians, Other 1 student enrolled • Electrical, Electronic and Communications Engineering Technology/Technician 7 students enrolled • General Office Occupations and Clerical Services 3 students enrolled • Graphic Design 2 students enrolled • Heating, Air Conditioning, Ventilation and Refrigeration Maintenance Technology/Technician (HAC, HACR, HVAC, HVACR) 6 students enrolled • Hospitality Administration/Management, Other 1 student enrolled • Industrial Mechanics and Maintenance Technology 2 students enrolled • Licensed Practical/Vocational Nurse Training (LPN, LVN, Cert, Dipl, AAS) 92 students enrolled • Massage Therapy/Therapeutic Massage 7 students enrolled • Medical Insurance Specialist/Medical Biller 3 students enrolled • Medical Office Management/Administration 2 students enrolled • Medical Transcription/Transcriptionist 1 student enrolled • Small Engine Mechanics and Repair Technology/Technician 8 students enrolled • Word Processing 2 students enrolled

STUDENT SERVICES Academic or career counseling, daycare for children of students, employment services for current students, placement services for program completers, remedial services.

Kuyper College

3333 East Beltline, NE, Grand Rapids, MI 49525-9749
http://www.kuyper.edu/

CONTACT Nicholas V. Kroeze, President
Telephone: 616-222-3000

GENERAL INFORMATION Private Institution. Founded 1939. Accreditation: Regional (NCA); state accredited or approved. Total program enrollment: 267. Application fee: $25.

PROGRAM(S) OFFERED
• Bible/Biblical Studies 1 student enrolled • Teaching English as a Second or Foreign Language/ESL Language Instructor 2 students enrolled

STUDENT SERVICES Academic or career counseling, employment services for current students, placement services for program completers.

Lake Michigan College

2755 East Napier, Benton Harbor, MI 49022-1899
http://www.lmc.cc.mi.us/

CONTACT Randall Miller, EdD, President
Telephone: 269-927-3571

GENERAL INFORMATION Public Institution. Founded 1946. Accreditation: Regional (NCA); dental assisting (ADA); radiologic technology: radiography (JRCERT). Total program enrollment: 1261.

PROGRAM(S) OFFERED
• Appliance Installation and Repair Technology/Technician • Architectural Drafting and Architectural CAD/CADD • Business/Office Automation/Technology/Data Entry • CAD/CADD Drafting and/or Design Technology/Technician • Cardiovascular Technology/Technologist • Commercial and Advertising Art • Computer Programming/Programmer, General • Computer Systems Networking and Telecommunications • Dental Assisting/Assistant 5 students enrolled • Dental Hygiene/Hygienist • Early Childhood Education and Teaching 3 students enrolled • Emergency Medical Technology/Technician (EMT Paramedic) • Executive Assistant/Executive Secretary • Fire Science/

Firefighting • Hospitality Administration/Management, General 1 student enrolled • Industrial Mechanics and Maintenance Technology • Information Technology 1 student enrolled • Legal Administrative Assistant/Secretary • Licensed Practical/Vocational Nurse Training (LPN, LVN, Cert, Dipl, AAS) 15 students enrolled • Machine Tool Technology/Machinist • Management Information Systems, General • Marketing/Marketing Management, General • Medical Office Assistant/Specialist 2 students enrolled • Medical/Clinical Assistant • Plastics Engineering Technology/Technician • Precision Production, Other

STUDENT SERVICES Academic or career counseling, daycare for children of students, employment services for current students, placement services for program completers, remedial services.

Lake Superior State University

650 West Easterday Avenue, Sault Sainte Marie, MI 49783
http://www.lssu.edu/

CONTACT Dr. Rodney L. Lowman, President
Telephone: 906-632-6841

GENERAL INFORMATION Public Institution. Founded 1946. Accreditation: Regional (NCA); engineering technology (ABET/TAC). Total program enrollment: 2173. Application fee: $35.

PROGRAM(S) OFFERED
• Administrative Assistant and Secretarial Science, General • Emergency Medical Technology/Technician (EMT Paramedic) • Information Resources Management/CIO Training 1 student enrolled • Nursing—Registered Nurse Training (RN, ASN, BSN, MSN) 22 students enrolled

STUDENT SERVICES Academic or career counseling, daycare for children of students, employment services for current students, placement services for program completers, remedial services.

Lakewood School of Therapeutic Massage

1102 6th Street, Port Huron, MI 48060

GENERAL INFORMATION Private Institution. Application fee: $25.

PROGRAM(S) OFFERED
• Massage Therapy/Therapeutic Massage 600 hrs.

STUDENT SERVICES Placement services for program completers.

Lansing Community College

PO Box 40010, Lansing, MI 48901-7210
http://www.lcc.edu/

CONTACT Brent Knight, President
Telephone: 517-483-1957

GENERAL INFORMATION Public Institution. Founded 1957. Accreditation: Regional (NCA); dental hygiene (ADA); emergency medical services (JRCEMTP); histologic technology (NAACLS); radiologic technology: radiography (JRCERT). Total program enrollment: 6682.

PROGRAM(S) OFFERED
• Accounting Technology/Technician and Bookkeeping 3 students enrolled • Administrative Assistant and Secretarial Science, General 3 students enrolled • Adult Development and Aging 5 students enrolled • Aircraft Powerplant Technology/Technician 13 students enrolled • Airframe Mechanics and Aircraft Maintenance Technology/Technician 13 students enrolled • Architectural Technology/Technician 1 student enrolled • Autobody/Collision and Repair Technology/Technician 7 students enrolled • Automobile/Automotive Mechanics Technology/Technician 16 students enrolled • Aviation/Airway Management and Operations 11 students enrolled • Avionics Maintenance Technology/Technician 1 student enrolled • Banking and Financial Support Services 4 students enrolled • Business Administration and Management, General 12 students enrolled • CAD/CADD Drafting and/or Design Technology/Technician 2 students enrolled • Carpentry/Carpenter 2 students enrolled • Child Care Provider/Assistant 11 students enrolled • Cinematography and Film/Video Production 1 student enrolled • Civil Engineering Technology/Technician 6 students enrolled • Community Organization and Advocacy 31 students enrolled

Lansing Community College (continued)

- **Computer Programming, Specific Applications** 8 *students enrolled* • **Computer Systems Networking and Telecommunications** 1 *student enrolled* • **Computer Technology/Computer Systems Technology** 2 *students enrolled* • **Construction/Heavy Equipment/Earthmoving Equipment Operation** 19 *students enrolled* • **Corrections** 22 *students enrolled* • **Criminal Justice/Police Science** 29 *students enrolled* • **Customer Service Support/Call Center/Teleservice Operation** 5 *students enrolled* • **Data Modeling/Warehousing and Database Administration** 1 *student enrolled* • **Diagnostic Medical Sonography/Sonographer and Ultrasound Technician** 4 *students enrolled* • **E-Commerce/Electronic Commerce** 1 *student enrolled* • **Electrical and Power Transmission Installation/Installer, General** 4 *students enrolled* • **Electrician** 7 *students enrolled* • **Emergency Medical Technology/Technician (EMT Paramedic)** 48 *students enrolled* • **Energy Management and Systems Technology/Technician** 2 *students enrolled* • **Engine Machinist** 3 *students enrolled* • **Entrepreneurship/Entrepreneurial Studies** 2 *students enrolled* • **Fashion and Fabric Consultant** 2 *students enrolled* • **Fine/Studio Arts, General** 2 *students enrolled* • **Fire Science/Firefighting** 28 *students enrolled* • **Graphic Design** 2 *students enrolled* • **Health Unit Coordinator/Ward Clerk** 17 *students enrolled* • **Health and Medical Administrative Services, Other** 19 *students enrolled* • **Heating, Air Conditioning, Ventilation and Refrigeration Maintenance Technology/Technician (HAC, HACR, HVAC, HVACR)** 14 *students enrolled* • **Histologic Technician** 8 *students enrolled* • **Illustration** 2 *students enrolled* • **Interior Design** 7 *students enrolled* • **Juvenile Corrections** 1 *student enrolled* • **Labor and Industrial Relations** 1 *student enrolled* • **Legal Administrative Assistant/Secretary** 2 *students enrolled* • **Legal Assistant/Paralegal** 16 *students enrolled* • **Licensed Practical/Vocational Nurse Training (LPN, LVN, Cert, Dipl, AAS)** 140 *students enrolled* • **Massage Therapy/Therapeutic Massage** 23 *students enrolled* • **Mechanical Drafting and Mechanical Drafting CAD/CADD** 1 *student enrolled* • **Medical Administrative/Executive Assistant and Medical Secretary** 3 *students enrolled* • **Medical Insurance Specialist/Medical Biller** 28 *students enrolled* • **Medical Transcription/Transcriptionist** 8 *students enrolled* • **Nurse/Nursing Assistant/Aide and Patient Care Assistant** 151 *students enrolled* • **Office Management and Supervision** 6 *students enrolled* • **Pharmacy Technician/Assistant** 14 *students enrolled* • **Phlebotomy/Phlebotomist** 258 *students enrolled* • **Photography** 24 *students enrolled* • **Radio and Television Broadcasting Technology/Technician** 1 *student enrolled* • **Real Estate** 1 *student enrolled* • **Restaurant/Food Services Management** 1 *student enrolled* • **Sales, Distribution and Marketing Operations, General** 11 *students enrolled* • **Selling Skills and Sales Operations** 1 *student enrolled* • **Sign Language Interpretation and Translation** 19 *students enrolled* • **Teacher Assistant/Aide** 1 *student enrolled* • **Technical Theatre/Theatre Design and Technology** 2 *students enrolled* • **Tool and Die Technology/Technician** 1 *student enrolled* • **Tourism and Travel Services Management** 5 *students enrolled* • **Truck and Bus Driver/Commercial Vehicle Operation** 105 *students enrolled* • **Visual and Performing Arts, General** 7 *students enrolled* • **Welding Technology/Welder** 13 *students enrolled*

STUDENT SERVICES Academic or career counseling, employment services for current students, placement services for program completers, remedial services.

Lawrence Technological University

21000 West Ten Mile Road, Southfield, MI 48075-1058
http://www.ltu.edu/

CONTACT Lewis N. Walker, President & CEO
Telephone: 248-204-4000

GENERAL INFORMATION Private Institution. Founded 1932. **Accreditation:** Regional (NCA); art and design (NASAD); interior design: professional (CIDA). **Total program enrollment:** 1549. **Application fee:** $30.

PROGRAM(S) OFFERED
- **Communications Technology/Technician** 2 *students enrolled* • **Entrepreneurial and Small Business Operations, Other** 25 *students enrolled* • **Organizational Behavior Studies** 1 *student enrolled*

STUDENT SERVICES Academic or career counseling, employment services for current students, placement services for program completers, remedial services.

Lawton School

20755 Greenfield Road, #300, Southfield, MI 48075

CONTACT Andrew Burks, President
Telephone: 248-569-7787

GENERAL INFORMATION Private Institution. **Total program enrollment:** 111.

PROGRAM(S) OFFERED
- **Data Processing and Data Processing Technology/Technician** 10 *students enrolled* • **Entrepreneurial and Small Business Operations, Other** 700 *hrs./$9000* • **Legal Assistant/Paralegal** 760 *hrs./$9000* • **Medical/Clinical Assistant** 760 *hrs./$9450* • **Radio and Television Broadcasting Technology/Technician** 800 *hrs./$10,000* • **Radio and Television** 3 *students enrolled*

STUDENT SERVICES Academic or career counseling, employment services for current students, placement services for program completers.

Lawton School Warren Branch

13877 E. 8 Mile Road, Warren, MI 48089-3352

CONTACT Andrew Burks, President/CFO
Telephone: 586-777-7344

GENERAL INFORMATION Private Institution. **Total program enrollment:** 102.

PROGRAM(S) OFFERED
- **Entrepreneurial and Small Business Operations, Other** 49 *hrs./$9000* • **Legal Assistant/Paralegal** 61 *hrs./$9000* • **Medical/Clinical Assistant** 41 *hrs./$9450*

STUDENT SERVICES Academic or career counseling, employment services for current students, placement services for program completers, remedial services.

Macomb Community College

14500 East Twelve Mile Road, Warren, MI 48088-3896
http://www.macomb.edu/

CONTACT James Jacobs, President
Telephone: 586-445-7999

GENERAL INFORMATION Public Institution. Founded 1954. **Accreditation:** Regional (NCA); medical assisting (AAMAE); physical therapy assisting (APTA); surgical technology (ARCST). **Total program enrollment:** 9063.

PROGRAM(S) OFFERED
- **Accounting Technology/Technician and Bookkeeping** 5 *students enrolled* • **Accounting** 10 *students enrolled* • **Architectural Drafting and Architectural CAD/CADD** 14 *students enrolled* • **Automobile/Automotive Mechanics Technology/Technician** 43 *students enrolled* • **Business Administration and Management, General** 7 *students enrolled* • **Business/Commerce, General** 13 *students enrolled* • **Cabinetmaking and Millwork/Millwright** 5 *students enrolled* • **Commercial and Advertising Art** 10 *students enrolled* • **Computer Programming/Programmer, General** 6 *students enrolled* • **Criminal Justice/Police Science** 6 *students enrolled* • **Culinary Arts/Chef Training** 107 *students enrolled* • **Electrical, Electronic and Communications Engineering Technology/Technician** 8 *students enrolled* • **Electrical/Electronics Equipment Installation and Repair, General** 5 *students enrolled* • **Emergency Medical Technology/Technician (EMT Paramedic)** 10 *students enrolled* • **Fire Protection and Safety Technology/Technician** 7 *students enrolled* • **Fire Science/Firefighting** 1 *student enrolled* • **Heating, Air Conditioning and Refrigeration Technology/Technician (ACH/ACR/ACHR/HRAC/HVAC/AC Technology)** 51 *students enrolled* • **Industrial Electronics Technology/Technician** 4 *students enrolled* • **Industrial Mechanics and Maintenance Technology** 2 *students enrolled* • **Machine Tool Technology/Machinist** 1 *student enrolled* • **Manufacturing Technology/Technician** 9 *students enrolled* • **Marketing/Marketing Management, General** 1 *student enrolled* • **Mechanical Drafting and Mechanical Drafting CAD/CADD** 5 *students enrolled* • **Medical/Clinical Assistant** 62 *students enrolled* • **Plumbing Technology/Plumber** 16 *students enrolled* • **Quality Control Technology/Technician** 5 *students enrolled* • **Sheet Metal Technology/Sheetworking** 1 *student enrolled* • **Surgical Technology/Technologist** 12 *students enrolled* • **Survey Technology/**

Surveying *1 student enrolled* • **System, Networking, and LAN/WAN Management/Manager** *1 student enrolled* • **Tool and Die Technology/Technician** *19 students enrolled* • **Web/Multimedia Management and Webmaster** *18 students enrolled*

STUDENT SERVICES Academic or career counseling, employment services for current students, placement services for program completers, remedial services.

Madonna University

36600 Schoolcraft Road, Livonia, MI 48150-1173
http://www.madonna.edu/

CONTACT Sr. Rose Marie Kujawa, President
Telephone: 734-432-5300

GENERAL INFORMATION Private Institution. Founded 1947. **Accreditation:** Regional (NCA). **Total program enrollment:** 1721. **Application fee:** $25.

PROGRAM(S) OFFERED
• **Adult Development and Aging** • **Community Organization and Advocacy** • **E-Commerce/Electronic Commerce** • **Management Information Systems, General** • **Nursing, Other** • **Occupational Safety and Health Technology/Technician** • **Security and Protective Services, Other** *35 students enrolled* • **Selling Skills and Sales Operations** • **Sociology** • **Substance Abuse/Addiction Counseling** *11 students enrolled*

STUDENT SERVICES Academic or career counseling, employment services for current students, placement services for program completers, remedial services.

Marygrove College

8425 West McNichols Road, Detroit, MI 48221-2599
http://www.marygrove.edu/

CONTACT David Fike, President
Telephone: 313-927-1200

GENERAL INFORMATION Private Institution. Founded 1905. **Accreditation:** Regional (NCA); home economics (AAFCS); radiologic technology: radiography (JRCERT). **Total program enrollment:** 2443. **Application fee:** $25.

PROGRAM(S) OFFERED
• **Computer Graphics** • **Religious/Sacred Music** • **Youth Services/Administration**

STUDENT SERVICES Academic or career counseling, daycare for children of students, employment services for current students, placement services for program completers, remedial services.

Michigan Barber School, Inc.

8988-8990 Grand River Avenue, Detroit, MI 48204-2244

CONTACT Forrest F. Green, Jr., President/Director
Telephone: 313-894-2300

GENERAL INFORMATION Private Institution. Founded 1946. **Total program enrollment:** 231.

PROGRAM(S) OFFERED
• **Cosmetology, Barber/Styling, and Nail Instructor** *2000 hrs./$9160*

Michigan Career and Technical Institute

1611 West Pine Lake Road, Plainwell, MI 49080-9254
http://www.michigan.gov/

CONTACT F. Dennis Hart, Director
Telephone: 269-664-4461

GENERAL INFORMATION Public Institution. **Total program enrollment:** 233.

PROGRAM(S) OFFERED
• **Automobile/Automotive Mechanics Technology/Technician** *15 students enrolled* • **Business Operations Support and Secretarial Services, Other** *12 students enrolled* • **Business/Office Automation/Technology/Data Entry** *3 students enrolled* • **Cabinetmaking and Millwork/Millwright** *25 students enrolled* • **Computer Installation and Repair Technology/Technician** *10 students enrolled* • **Culinary Arts and Related Services, Other** *40 students enrolled* • **Graphic Communications, General** *17 students enrolled* • **Housing and Human Environments, Other** *44 students enrolled* • **Landscaping and Groundskeeping** *23 students enrolled* • **Machine Tool Technology/Machinist** *23 students enrolled* • **Nurse/Nursing Assistant/Aide and Patient Care Assistant** *67 students enrolled* • **Retailing and Retail Operations** *29 students enrolled*

STUDENT SERVICES Academic or career counseling, daycare for children of students, employment services for current students, placement services for program completers, remedial services.

Michigan College of Beauty

15233 South Dixie Highway, Monroe, MI 48161
http://michigancollegebeauty.com/

CONTACT Christine A. Dagenais, President
Telephone: 734-241-8877

GENERAL INFORMATION Private Institution. Founded 1972. **Total program enrollment:** 151.

PROGRAM(S) OFFERED
• **Aesthetician/Esthetician and Skin Care Specialist** *400 hrs./$3250* • **Cosmetology and Related Personal Grooming Arts, Other** *129 students enrolled* • **Cosmetology, Barber/Styling, and Nail Instructor** *600 hrs./$3100* • **Cosmetology/Cosmetologist, General** *900 hrs./$3600* • **Nail Technician/Specialist and Manicurist** *600 hrs./$3150*

STUDENT SERVICES Academic or career counseling, placement services for program completers.

Michigan College of Beauty

3498 Rochester Road, Troy, MI 48083

CONTACT David Dagenais, President
Telephone: 248-528-0303

GENERAL INFORMATION Private Institution. **Total program enrollment:** 189. **Application fee:** $100.

PROGRAM(S) OFFERED
• **Aesthetician/Esthetician and Skin Care Specialist** *600 hrs./$5550* • **Cosmetology, Barber/Styling, and Nail Instructor** *600 hrs./$5000* • **Cosmetology/Cosmetologist, General** *1500 hrs./$13,300* • **Nail Technician/Specialist and Manicurist** *600 hrs./$3550*

STUDENT SERVICES Academic or career counseling, placement services for program completers.

Michigan Institute of Aeronautics

Willow Run Airport East Side, 47884 D Street, Belleville, MI 48111
http://www.miat.edu/

CONTACT Charles A. Hawes, President
Telephone: 734-483-3758

GENERAL INFORMATION Private Institution. **Total program enrollment:** 720. **Application fee:** $25.

Michigan Institute of Aeronautics (continued)

PROGRAM(S) OFFERED
• **Aircraft Powerplant Technology/Technician** *5 students enrolled* • **Energy Management and Systems Technology/Technician** • **Industrial Technology/Technician** *45 students enrolled* • **Transportation and Materials Moving, Other** *9 students enrolled*

STUDENT SERVICES Employment services for current students, placement services for program completers, remedial services.

Michigan State University

East Lansing, MI 48824
http://www.msu.edu/

CONTACT Lou Anna K. Simon, President
Telephone: 517-355-1855

GENERAL INFORMATION Public Institution. Founded 1855. **Accreditation:** Regional (NCA); audiology (ASHA); dietetics: postbaccalaureate internship (ADtA/CAADE); forestry (SAF); home economics (AAFCS); interior design: professional (CIDA); journalism and mass communications (ACEJMC); medical technology (NAACLS); music (NASM); recreation and parks (NRPA); speech-language pathology (ASHA); state accredited or approved. **Total program enrollment:** 41016. **Application fee:** $35.

PROGRAM(S) OFFERED
• **Agricultural Business and Management, General** *4 students enrolled* • **Animal/Livestock Husbandry and Production** *3 students enrolled* • **Crop Production** *3 students enrolled* • **Dairy Science** *13 students enrolled* • **Electrician** *4 students enrolled* • **Horse Husbandry/Equine Science and Management** *8 students enrolled* • **Landscaping and Groundskeeping** *29 students enrolled* • **Plant Sciences, General** *3 students enrolled* • **Turf and Turfgrass Management** *24 students enrolled* • **Veterinary/Animal Health Technology/Technician and Veterinary Assistant** *10 students enrolled*

STUDENT SERVICES Academic or career counseling, daycare for children of students, employment services for current students, placement services for program completers, remedial services.

Michigan Technological University

1400 Townsend Drive, Houghton, MI 49931-1295
http://www.mtu.edu/

CONTACT Glenn Mroz, President
Telephone: 906-487-1885

GENERAL INFORMATION Public Institution. Founded 1885. **Accreditation:** Regional (NCA); engineering technology (ABET/TAC); engineering-related programs (ABET/RAC); forestry (SAF). **Total program enrollment:** 6227.

PROGRAM(S) OFFERED
• **Actuarial Science** *1 student enrolled* • **Cartography** • **Drafting and Design Technology/Technician, General** *27 students enrolled* • **Electrical, Electronics and Communications Engineering** • **Forest Management/Forest Resources Management** *2 students enrolled* • **French Language and Literature** • **German Language and Literature** • **International Business/Trade/Commerce** *2 students enrolled* • **Mining and Mineral Engineering** • **Organizational Communication, General** *2 students enrolled* • **Physical Education Teaching and Coaching** *13 students enrolled* • **Spanish Language and Literature** *4 students enrolled* • **Technical and Business Writing** *1 student enrolled*

STUDENT SERVICES Academic or career counseling, daycare for children of students, employment services for current students, placement services for program completers.

Mid Michigan Community College

1375 South Clare Avenue, Harrison, MI 48625-9447
http://www.midmich.edu/

CONTACT Carol Churchill, President
Telephone: 989-386-6622

GENERAL INFORMATION Public Institution. Founded 1965. **Accreditation:** Regional (NCA); radiologic technology: radiography (JRCERT). **Total program enrollment:** 2115.

PROGRAM(S) OFFERED
• **Automobile/Automotive Mechanics Technology/Technician** *6 students enrolled* • **Early Childhood Education and Teaching** *5 students enrolled* • **General Office Occupations and Clerical Services** *3 students enrolled* • **Heating, Air Conditioning, Ventilation and Refrigeration Maintenance Technology/Technician (HAC, HACR, HVAC, HVACR)** *22 students enrolled* • **Licensed Practical/Vocational Nurse Training (LPN, LVN, Cert, Dipl, AAS)** *75 students enrolled* • **Machine Shop Technology/Assistant** *2 students enrolled* • **Mechanical Drafting and Mechanical Drafting CAD/CADD** *4 students enrolled* • **Medical Insurance Coding Specialist/Coder** *8 students enrolled* • **Personal and Culinary Services, Other** *1 student enrolled* • **Pharmacy Technician/Assistant** *8 students enrolled* • **Welding Technology/Welder** *4 students enrolled*

STUDENT SERVICES Academic or career counseling, employment services for current students, placement services for program completers, remedial services.

M. J. Murphy Beauty College of Mount Pleasant

201 West Broadway, Mount Pleasant, MI 48858

CONTACT Brenda Brennan, Chief of Operations
Telephone: 989-772-2339

GENERAL INFORMATION Private Institution. **Total program enrollment:** 96.

PROGRAM(S) OFFERED
• **Cosmetology, Barber/Styling, and Nail Instructor** *500 hrs./$900* • **Cosmetology/Cosmetologist, General** *1500 hrs./$7200* • **Nail Technician/Specialist and Manicurist** *400 hrs./$2025*

STUDENT SERVICES Placement services for program completers.

Monroe County Community College

1555 South Raisinville Road, Monroe, MI 48161-9047
http://www.monroeccc.edu/

CONTACT David E. Nixon, President
Telephone: 734-242-7300

GENERAL INFORMATION Public Institution. Founded 1964. **Accreditation:** Regional (NCA); respiratory therapy technology (CoARC). **Total program enrollment:** 1823.

PROGRAM(S) OFFERED
• **Accounting Technology/Technician and Bookkeeping** *1 student enrolled* • **Administrative Assistant and Secretarial Science, General** *4 students enrolled* • **Automobile/Automotive Mechanics Technology/Technician** *2 students enrolled* • **Clinical/Medical Laboratory Assistant** *9 students enrolled* • **Computer Hardware Technology/Technician** *2 students enrolled* • **Electrocardiograph Technology/Technician** *8 students enrolled* • **Food Preparation/Professional Cooking/Kitchen Assistant** *14 students enrolled* • **Graphic Design** *1 student enrolled* • **Legal Administrative Assistant/Secretary** *1 student enrolled* • **Licensed Practical/Vocational Nurse Training (LPN, LVN, Cert, Dipl, AAS)** *8 students enrolled* • **Manufacturing Technology/Technician** *2 students enrolled* • **Mechanical Drafting and Mechanical Drafting CAD/CADD** *5 students enrolled* • **Quality Control Technology/Technician** *1 student enrolled* • **Web Page, Digital/Multimedia and Information Resources Design** *1 student enrolled* • **Welding Technology/Welder** *2 students enrolled*

STUDENT SERVICES Academic or career counseling, daycare for children of students, employment services for current students, placement services for program completers, remedial services.

Montcalm Community College

2800 College Drive, Sidney, MI 48885-9723
http://www.montcalm.edu/

CONTACT Donald C. Burns, President
Telephone: 989-328-2111

GENERAL INFORMATION Public Institution. Founded 1965. **Accreditation:** Regional (NCA). **Total program enrollment:** 850.

PROGRAM(S) OFFERED
- **Automobile/Automotive Mechanics Technology/Technician** *4 students enrolled*
- **Building/Property Maintenance and Management** *4 students enrolled*
- **Business/Office Automation/Technology/Data Entry** *1 student enrolled*
- **Computer Installation and Repair Technology/Technician** *3 students enrolled*
- **Corrections** *6 students enrolled* • **Drafting and Design Technology/Technician, General** *3 students enrolled* • **Entrepreneurship/Entrepreneurial Studies** *11 students enrolled* • **Industrial Technology/Technician** *19 students enrolled*
- **Information Resources Management/CIO Training** *36 students enrolled*
- **Licensed Practical/Vocational Nurse Training (LPN, LVN, Cert, Dipl, AAS)** *21 students enrolled* • **Machine Shop Technology/Assistant** *2 students enrolled*
- **Medical/Clinical Assistant** *14 students enrolled* • **Welding Technology/Welder** *11 students enrolled*

STUDENT SERVICES Academic or career counseling, employment services for current students, placement services for program completers, remedial services.

Mott Community College

1401 East Court Street, Flint, MI 48503-2089
http://www.mcc.edu/

CONTACT Dr. M. Richard Shaink, President
Telephone: 810-762-0200

GENERAL INFORMATION Public Institution. Founded 1923. **Accreditation:** Regional (NCA); dental assisting (ADA); dental hygiene (ADA); physical therapy assisting (APTA). **Total program enrollment:** 4326.

PROGRAM(S) OFFERED
- **Automobile/Automotive Mechanics Technology/Technician** *6 students enrolled*
- **Baking and Pastry Arts/Baker/Pastry Chef** *2 students enrolled* • **Business Administration and Management, General** *3 students enrolled* • **Computer Programming, Specific Applications** *1 student enrolled* • **Computer Programming/Programmer, General** *1 student enrolled* • **Computer and Information Sciences and Support Services, Other** *1 student enrolled*
- **Criminal Justice/Police Science** *6 students enrolled* • **Dental Assisting/Assistant** *6 students enrolled* • **Drafting and Design Technology/Technician, General** *4 students enrolled* • **Heating, Air Conditioning and Refrigeration Technology/Technician (ACH/ACR/ACHR/HRAC/HVAC/AC Technology)** *20 students enrolled* • **Licensed Practical/Vocational Nurse Training (LPN, LVN, Cert, Dipl, AAS)** *122 students enrolled* • **Marketing/Marketing Management, General** *7 students enrolled* • **Medical/Health Management and Clinical Assistant/Specialist** *6 students enrolled* • **Office Management and Supervision** *3 students enrolled* • **Quality Control Technology/Technician** *6 students enrolled*
- **Science Technologies/Technicians, Other** *5 students enrolled* • **System Administration/Administrator** *2 students enrolled*

STUDENT SERVICES Academic or career counseling, employment services for current students, placement services for program completers, remedial services.

Mr. Bela's School of Cosmetology

29475 John R. Street, Madison Heights, MI 48071

CONTACT Michael Deutsch, President
Telephone: 586-751-4000

GENERAL INFORMATION Private Institution. **Total program enrollment:** 59.

PROGRAM(S) OFFERED
- **Aesthetician/Esthetician and Skin Care Specialist** *600 hrs./$3875*
- **Cosmetology/Cosmetologist, General** *1500 hrs./$11,375* • **Nail Technician/Specialist and Manicurist** *8 students enrolled*

STUDENT SERVICES Academic or career counseling, employment services for current students, placement services for program completers.

Muskegon Community College

221 South Quarterline Road, Muskegon, MI 49442-1493
http://www.muskegoncc.edu/

CONTACT Diana R. Osborn, Interim President
Telephone: 231-773-9131

GENERAL INFORMATION Public Institution. Founded 1926. **Accreditation:** Regional (NCA); respiratory therapy technology (CoARC). **Total program enrollment:** 2022.

PROGRAM(S) OFFERED
- **Animation, Interactive Technology, Video Graphics and Special Effects** *1 student enrolled* • **Audiovisual Communications Technologies/Technicians, Other** • **Automobile/Automotive Mechanics Technology/Technician** • **Business/Office Automation/Technology/Data Entry** • **CAD/CADD Drafting and/or Design Technology/Technician** *2 students enrolled* • **Child Care Provider/Assistant**
- **Commercial and Advertising Art** • **Communications Technologies/Technicians and Support Services, Other** • **Computer Programming, Specific Applications** *1 student enrolled* • **Computer Systems Networking and Telecommunications** *2 students enrolled* • **Corrections** *4 students enrolled* • **Customer Service Management** *1 student enrolled* • **Data Entry/Microcomputer Applications, Other** *3 students enrolled* • **Early Childhood Education and Teaching** *3 students enrolled* • **Electrical, Electronic and Communications Engineering Technology/Technician** *2 students enrolled* • **Entrepreneurship/Entrepreneurial Studies** • **General Office Occupations and Clerical Services** *4 students enrolled* • **Geography, Other** • **Industrial Mechanics and Maintenance Technology** *1 student enrolled* • **Industrial Technology/Technician** *5 students enrolled* • **Legal Support Services, Other** • **Licensed Practical/Vocational Nurse Training (LPN, LVN, Cert, Dipl, AAS)** *82 students enrolled* • **Machine Shop Technology/Assistant** • **Machine Tool Technology/Machinist** *2 students enrolled*
- **Marketing/Marketing Management, General** • **Mechanic and Repair Technologies/Technicians, Other** • **Medical Office Assistant/Specialist** • **Medical Reception/Receptionist** *2 students enrolled* • **Medical Transcription/Transcriptionist** • **Prepress/Desktop Publishing and Digital Imaging Design** • **Quality Control Technology/Technician** *1 student enrolled* • **Retailing and Retail Operations** • **Teacher Assistant/Aide** • **Web Page, Digital/Multimedia and Information Resources Design** • **Welding Technology/Welder** *3 students enrolled* • **Word Processing**

STUDENT SERVICES Academic or career counseling, employment services for current students, placement services for program completers, remedial services.

North Central Michigan College

1515 Howard Street, Petoskey, MI 49770-8717
http://www.ncmich.edu/

CONTACT Dr. Cameron Brunet-Koch, President
Telephone: 231-348-6602

GENERAL INFORMATION Public Institution. Founded 1958. **Accreditation:** Regional (NCA). **Total program enrollment:** 1030.

PROGRAM(S) OFFERED
- **Accounting Technology/Technician and Bookkeeping** *4 students enrolled*
- **Advertising** • **Business Administration and Management, General** *3 students enrolled* • **Corrections** *3 students enrolled* • **Criminal Justice/Law Enforcement Administration** *1 student enrolled* • **Data Entry/Microcomputer Applications, General** • **Data Processing and Data Processing Technology/Technician**
- **Drafting and Design Technology/Technician, General** *1 student enrolled*
- **Early Childhood Education and Teaching** *1 student enrolled* • **Emergency Medical Technology/Technician (EMT Paramedic)** • **Entrepreneurship/Entrepreneurial Studies** • **General Office Occupations and Clerical Services**
- **Graphic Design** • **Hospitality Administration/Management, General**
- **Information Technology** • **Legal Assistant/Paralegal** • **Machine Tool Technology/Machinist** • **Marketing/Marketing Management, General** • **Medical Insurance Specialist/Medical Biller** *19 students enrolled* • **Medical Office Assistant/Specialist** *13 students enrolled* • **Medical Transcription/Transcriptionist** *2 students enrolled* • **Nurse/Nursing Assistant/Aide and Patient Care Assistant** *2 students enrolled* • **Phlebotomy/Phlebotomist**

STUDENT SERVICES Academic or career counseling, employment services for current students, placement services for program completers, remedial services.

Northern Michigan University

1401 Presque Isle Avenue, Marquette, MI 49855-5301
http://www.nmu.edu/

CONTACT Leslie E. Wong, President
Telephone: 906-227-1000

GENERAL INFORMATION Public Institution. Founded 1899. **Accreditation:** Regional (NCA); medical laboratory technology (NAACLS); medical technology (NAACLS); music (NASM); speech-language pathology (ASHA). **Total program enrollment:** 7873. **Application fee:** $30.

PROGRAM(S) OFFERED
● **Administrative Assistant and Secretarial Science, General** ● **Aircraft Power-plant Technology/Technician** *2 students enrolled* ● **Autobody/Collision and Repair Technology/Technician** *9 students enrolled* ● **Automobile/Automotive Mechanics Technology/Technician** *1 student enrolled* ● **Cartography** *1 student enrolled* ● **Clinical/Medical Laboratory Assistant** *6 students enrolled* ● **Computer Engineering Technology/Technician** *9 students enrolled* ● **Cosmetology/Cosmetologist, General** *14 students enrolled* ● **Heating, Air Conditioning, Ventilation and Refrigeration Maintenance Technology/Technician (HAC, HACR, HVAC, HVACR)** *4 students enrolled* ● **Licensed Practical/Vocational Nurse Training (LPN, LVN, Cert, Dipl, AAS)** *37 students enrolled* ● **Lineworker** *21 students enrolled* ● **Surgical Technology/Technologist** *17 students enrolled*

STUDENT SERVICES Academic or career counseling, employment services for current students, placement services for program completers, remedial services.

Northwestern Michigan College

1701 East Front Street, Traverse City, MI 49686-3061
http://www.nmc.edu/

CONTACT Timothy J. Nelson, President
Telephone: 231-995-1000

GENERAL INFORMATION Public Institution. Founded 1951. **Accreditation:** Regional (NCA); dental assisting (ADA). **Total program enrollment:** 2159. **Application fee:** $20.

PROGRAM(S) OFFERED
● **Automobile/Automotive Mechanics Technology/Technician** *1 student enrolled* ● **Child Development** *8 students enrolled* ● **Culinary Arts/Chef Training** *2 students enrolled* ● **Data Entry/Microcomputer Applications, General** *1 student enrolled* ● **Dental Assisting/Assistant** *8 students enrolled* ● **Engineering, General** *1 student enrolled* ● **Executive Assistant/Executive Secretary** *2 students enrolled* ● **Licensed Practical/Vocational Nurse Training (LPN, LVN, Cert, Dipl, AAS)** *7 students enrolled* ● **Machine Shop Technology/Assistant** *1 student enrolled*

STUDENT SERVICES Academic or career counseling, employment services for current students, placement services for program completers, remedial services.

Northwestern Technological Institute

24567 Northwestern Highway, Suite 200, Southfield, MI 48075
http://www.northwesterntech.org/

CONTACT Lorne P. Gauthier, School Director
Telephone: 248-358-4006

GENERAL INFORMATION Private Institution. **Total program enrollment:** 419.

PROGRAM(S) OFFERED
● **Heating, Air Conditioning and Refrigeration Technology/Technician (ACH/ACR/ACHR/HRAC/HVAC/AC Technology)** *90 hrs./$1460*

STUDENT SERVICES Academic or career counseling, placement services for program completers.

Nuvo College of Cosmetology

4236 Grand Haven Road, Norton Shores, MI 49441
http://www.nuvocollege.com/

GENERAL INFORMATION Private Institution. **Total program enrollment:** 41. **Application fee:** $100.

PROGRAM(S) OFFERED
● **Aesthetician/Esthetician and Skin Care Specialist** *400 hrs./$2315* ● **Cosmetology, Barber/Styling, and Nail Instructor** ● **Cosmetology/Cosmetologist, General** *600 hrs./$2615*

STUDENT SERVICES Academic or career counseling, employment services for current students, placement services for program completers.

Oakland Community College

2480 Opdyke Road, Bloomfield Hills, MI 48304-2266
http://www.oaklandcc.edu/

CONTACT Timothy Meyer, Chancellor
Telephone: 248-341-2000

GENERAL INFORMATION Public Institution. Founded 1964. **Accreditation:** Regional (NCA); dental hygiene (ADA); diagnostic medical sonography (JRCEDMS); medical assisting (AAMAE); radiologic technology: radiography (JRCERT). **Total program enrollment:** 8452.

PROGRAM(S) OFFERED
● **Accounting Technology/Technician and Bookkeeping** *5 students enrolled* ● **Adult Development and Aging** *3 students enrolled* ● **Autobody/Collision and Repair Technology/Technician** *8 students enrolled* ● **Automobile/Automotive Mechanics Technology/Technician** *5 students enrolled* ● **Baking and Pastry Arts/Baker/Pastry Chef** *12 students enrolled* ● **Business/Office Automation/Technology/Data Entry** *1 student enrolled* ● **Computer Programming/Programmer, General** *1 student enrolled* ● **Computer and Information Sciences and Support Services, Other** *1 student enrolled* ● **Computer and Information Systems Security** *5 students enrolled* ● **Computer/Information Technology Services Administration and Management, Other** *1 student enrolled* ● **Court Reporting/Court Reporter** *1 student enrolled* ● **Criminal Justice/Police Science** *1 student enrolled* ● **Criminalistics and Criminal Science** *1 student enrolled* ● **Data Modeling/Warehousing and Database Administration** *3 students enrolled* ● **Digital Communication and Media/Multimedia** *1 student enrolled* ● **Electrical, Electronic and Communications Engineering Technology/Technician** *1 student enrolled* ● **Emergency Medical Technology/Technician (EMT Paramedic)** *6 students enrolled* ● **Fire Science/Firefighting** *1 student enrolled* ● **Health/Health Care Administration/Management** *2 students enrolled* ● **Heating, Air Conditioning and Refrigeration Technology/Technician (ACH/ACR/ACHR/HRAC/HVAC/AC Technology)** *9 students enrolled* ● **Information Technology** *1 student enrolled* ● **Landscaping and Groundskeeping** *1 student enrolled* ● **Legal Assistant/Paralegal** *33 students enrolled* ● **Library Assistant/Technician** *2 students enrolled* ● **Licensed Practical/Vocational Nurse Training (LPN, LVN, Cert, Dipl, AAS)** *17 students enrolled* ● **Massage Therapy/Therapeutic Massage** *4 students enrolled* ● **Mechanical Drafting and Mechanical Drafting CAD/CADD** *8 students enrolled* ● **Medical Insurance Coding Specialist/Coder** *24 students enrolled* ● **Medical Office Assistant/Specialist** *7 students enrolled* ● **Medical Transcription/Transcriptionist** *1 student enrolled* ● **Medical/Clinical Assistant** *8 students enrolled* ● **Medical/Health Management and Clinical Assistant/Specialist** *6 students enrolled* ● **Optometric Technician/Assistant** *2 students enrolled* ● **Pharmacy Technician/Assistant** *3 students enrolled* ● **Phlebotomy/Phlebotomist** *17 students enrolled* ● **Photography** *5 students enrolled* ● **Robotics Technology/Technician** *1 student enrolled* ● **System, Networking, and LAN/WAN Management/Manager** *3 students enrolled* ● **Web/Multimedia Management and Webmaster** *1 student enrolled* ● **Welding Technology/Welder** *3 students enrolled*

STUDENT SERVICES Academic or career counseling, daycare for children of students, employment services for current students, placement services for program completers, remedial services.

P & A Schólars Beauty School

12001 Grandriver Avenue, Detroit, MI 48204

CONTACT Lakia Hairston, President
Telephone: 313-933-9393 Ext. 16

GENERAL INFORMATION Private Institution. **Total program enrollment:** 102.

PROGRAM(S) OFFERED

• **Aesthetician/Esthetician and Skin Care Specialist** • **Cosmetology, Barber/Styling, and Nail Instructor** *600 hrs./$3850* • **Cosmetology/Cosmetologist, General** *1500 hrs./$10,400* • **Nail Technician/Specialist and Manicurist** *600 hrs./$3850*

STUDENT SERVICES Academic or career counseling, placement services for program completers.

Port Huron Cosmetology College

5620 Dixie Highway, Waterford, MI 48329

CONTACT Susan Pantello, President, Director
Telephone: 248-623-9494

GENERAL INFORMATION Private Institution. **Total program enrollment:** 63. **Application fee:** $50.

PROGRAM(S) OFFERED

• **Aesthetician/Esthetician and Skin Care Specialist** *420 hrs./$3500* • **Cosmetology and Related Personal Grooming Arts, Other** *32 students enrolled* • **Cosmetology, Barber/Styling, and Nail Instructor** *600 hrs./$2300* • **Cosmetology/Cosmetologist, General** *1500 hrs./$14,475* • **Nail Technician/Specialist and Manicurist** *400 hrs./$2000* • **Trade and Industrial Teacher Education** *2 students enrolled*

Regency Beauty Institute–Detroit Southgate

15070 Dix-Toledo Road, Southgate, MI 48195

CONTACT J. Hayes Batson
Telephone: 734-759-0295

GENERAL INFORMATION Private Institution. **Total program enrollment:** 61. **Application fee:** $100.

PROGRAM(S) OFFERED

• **Cosmetology/Cosmetologist, General** *1500 hrs./$17,011*

STUDENT SERVICES Academic or career counseling, placement services for program completers.

Regency Beauty Institute–Flint

4205 Miller Road, Flint, MI 48507

CONTACT J. Hayes Batson
Telephone: 810-244-9720

GENERAL INFORMATION Private Institution. **Total program enrollment:** 33. **Application fee:** $100.

PROGRAM(S) OFFERED

• **Cosmetology/Cosmetologist, General** *1500 hrs./$17,011*

STUDENT SERVICES Academic or career counseling, placement services for program completers.

Regency Beauty Institute–Grand Rapids

3583 Alpine Avenue, Walker, MI 49544

CONTACT J. Hayes Batson
Telephone: 616-885-1430

GENERAL INFORMATION Private Institution. **Total program enrollment:** 48.

PROGRAM(S) OFFERED

• **Cosmetology/Cosmetologist, General** *1500 hrs./$17,011*

STUDENT SERVICES Academic or career counseling, placement services for program completers.

Ross Medical Education Center

4703 Washtenaw, Ann Arbor, MI 48108-1411
http://www.rossmedicaleducation.com/

CONTACT Paul Mitchell, President
Telephone: 734-434-7320 Ext. 2452

GENERAL INFORMATION Private Institution. **Total program enrollment:** 92. **Application fee:** $45.

PROGRAM(S) OFFERED

• **Medical Insurance Specialist/Medical Biller** *52 hrs./$13,555* • **Medical/Clinical Assistant** *45 hrs./$13,555*

STUDENT SERVICES Placement services for program completers.

Ross Medical Education Center

5757 Whitmore Lake Road, Suite 800, Brighton, MI 48116
http://www.rossmedicaleducation.com/

CONTACT Paul Mitchell, President
Telephone: 810-227-0160

GENERAL INFORMATION Private Institution. Founded 1983. **Total program enrollment:** 102. **Application fee:** $45.

PROGRAM(S) OFFERED

• **Dental Assisting/Assistant** *51 hrs./$13,555* • **Medical Insurance Specialist/Medical Biller** *52 hrs./$13,555* • **Medical/Clinical Assistant** *45 hrs./$13,555*

STUDENT SERVICES Placement services for program completers.

Ross Medical Education Center

1036 Gilbert Street, Flint, MI 48532
http://www.rossmedicaleducation.com/

CONTACT Paul Mitchell, President
Telephone: 810-733-7488

GENERAL INFORMATION Private Institution. **Total program enrollment:** 119. **Application fee:** $45.

PROGRAM(S) OFFERED

• **Dental Assisting/Assistant** *51 hrs./$13,555* • **Medical Insurance Specialist/Medical Biller** *52 hrs./$13,555* • **Medical/Clinical Assistant** *45 hrs./$13,555*

STUDENT SERVICES Placement services for program completers.

Ross Medical Education Center

2035 28th Street, SE, Grand Rapids, MI 49508
http://www.rossmedicaleducation.com/

CONTACT Paul Mitchell, President
Telephone: 616-243-3070 Ext. 2351

GENERAL INFORMATION Private Institution. **Total program enrollment:** 66. **Application fee:** $45.

PROGRAM(S) OFFERED

• **Medical Insurance Specialist/Medical Biller** *52 hrs./$13,555* • **Medical/Clinical Assistant** *45 hrs./$13,555*

STUDENT SERVICES Placement services for program completers.

Ross Medical Education Center

913 West Holmes, Suite 260, Lansing, MI 48910
http://www.rossmedicaleducation.com/

CONTACT Paul Mitchell, President
Telephone: 517-703-9044 Ext. 2500

GENERAL INFORMATION Private Institution. **Total program enrollment:** 68. **Application fee:** $45.

PROGRAM(S) OFFERED
• Medical Insurance Coding Specialist/Coder *7 students enrolled* • Medical Insurance Specialist/Medical Biller *52 hrs./$13,555* • Medical/Clinical Assistant *45 hrs./$13,555*

STUDENT SERVICES Placement services for program completers.

Ross Medical Education Center

3568 Pine Grove, Port Huron, MI 48060
http://www.rossmedicaleducation.com/

CONTACT Paul Mitchell, President
Telephone: 810-982-0454 Ext. 2553

GENERAL INFORMATION Private Institution. **Total program enrollment:** 50. **Application fee:** $45.

PROGRAM(S) OFFERED
• Medical/Clinical Assistant *45 hrs./$13,555*

STUDENT SERVICES Placement services for program completers.

Ross Medical Education Center

950 West Norton Avenue, Roosevelt Park, MI 49441
http://www.rossmedicaleducation.com/

CONTACT Paul Mitchell, President
Telephone: 231-739-1531 Ext. 2401

GENERAL INFORMATION Private Institution. **Total program enrollment:** 77. **Application fee:** $45.

PROGRAM(S) OFFERED
• Medical Insurance Specialist/Medical Biller *52 hrs./$13,555* • Medical/Clinical Assistant *45 hrs./$13,555*

STUDENT SERVICES Placement services for program completers.

Ross Medical Education Center

4054 Bay Road, Saginaw, MI 48603-1201
http://www.rossmedicaleducation.com/

CONTACT Paul Mitchell, President
Telephone: 989-791-5192

GENERAL INFORMATION Private Institution. Founded 1985. **Total program enrollment:** 121. **Application fee:** $45.

PROGRAM(S) OFFERED
• Dental Assisting/Assistant *51 hrs./$13,555* • Medical Insurance Specialist/Medical Biller *52 hrs./$13,555* • Medical/Clinical Assistant *45 hrs./$13,555*

STUDENT SERVICES Placement services for program completers.

Ross Medical Education Center

26417 Hoover Road, Warren, MI 48089-1190
http://www.rossmedicaleducation.com/

CONTACT Paul Mitchell, President
Telephone: 248-548-4389

GENERAL INFORMATION Private Institution. Founded 1978. **Total program enrollment:** 54. **Application fee:** $45.

PROGRAM(S) OFFERED
• Medical Insurance Specialist/Medical Biller *52 hrs./$13,555* • Medical/Clinical Assistant *45 hrs./$13,555*

STUDENT SERVICES Placement services for program completers.

Ross Medical Education Center

2495 Elizabeth Lake Road, Waterford, MI 48328
http://www.rossmedicaleducation.com/

CONTACT Paul Mitchell, President
Telephone: 313-794-6448

GENERAL INFORMATION Private Institution. Founded 1990. **Total program enrollment:** 32. **Application fee:** $45.

PROGRAM(S) OFFERED
• Medical/Clinical Assistant *45 hrs./$13,555*

STUDENT SERVICES Placement services for program completers.

Sacred Heart Major Seminary

2701 Chicago Boulevard, Detroit, MI 48206-1799
http://www.archdioceseofdetroit.org/shms/shms.htm

CONTACT Jeffrey Monforton, Rector/President
Telephone: 313-883-8512

GENERAL INFORMATION Private Institution. Founded 1919. **Accreditation:** Regional (NCA). **Total program enrollment:** 101. **Application fee:** $30.

PROGRAM(S) OFFERED
• Religious/Sacred Music • Theology/Theological Studies *30 students enrolled*

STUDENT SERVICES Academic or career counseling, remedial services.

St. Clair County Community College

323 Erie Street, PO Box 5015, Port Huron, MI 48061-5015
http://www.sc4.edu/

CONTACT Kirk Kramer, Interim President
Telephone: 810-984-3881

GENERAL INFORMATION Public Institution. Founded 1923. **Accreditation:** Regional (NCA). **Total program enrollment:** 1950.

PROGRAM(S) OFFERED
• Agricultural Business Technology *1 student enrolled* • Business/Commerce, General *5 students enrolled* • Data Processing and Data Processing Technology/Technician *1 student enrolled* • Electrical, Electronic and Communications Engineering Technology/Technician *15 students enrolled* • Fire Science/Firefighting *1 student enrolled* • General Office Occupations and Clerical Services *4 students enrolled* • Industrial Technology/Technician *1 student enrolled* • Licensed Practical/Vocational Nurse Training (LPN, LVN, Cert, Dipl, AAS) *76 students enrolled* • Marketing/Marketing Management, General *6 students enrolled* • Mechanical Drafting and Mechanical Drafting CAD/CADD *2 students enrolled* • Radio and Television Broadcasting Technology/Technician *4 students enrolled*

STUDENT SERVICES Academic or career counseling, daycare for children of students, employment services for current students, placement services for program completers, remedial services.

Schoolcraft College

18600 Haggerty Road, Livonia, MI 48152-2696
http://www.schoolcraft.edu/

CONTACT Dr. Conway A. Jeffress, President
Telephone: 734-462-4400

GENERAL INFORMATION Public Institution. Founded 1961. **Accreditation:** Regional (NCA); health information technology (AHIMA). **Total program enrollment:** 5283.

PROGRAM(S) OFFERED
• **Accounting Technology/Technician and Bookkeeping** *6 students enrolled* • **Administrative Assistant and Secretarial Science, General** *16 students enrolled* • **Baking and Pastry Arts/Baker/Pastry Chef** *30 students enrolled* • **Business/Commerce, General** *8 students enrolled* • **Child Care and Support Services Management** *2 students enrolled* • **Child Development** *6 students enrolled* • **Computer Graphics** *17 students enrolled* • **Computer Installation and Repair Technology/Technician** *3 students enrolled* • **Computer Programming/ Programmer, General** *6 students enrolled* • **Culinary Arts/Chef Training** *6 students enrolled* • **Drafting and Design Technology/Technician, General** *5 students enrolled* • **Education, General** *3 students enrolled* • **Electrical, Electronic and Communications Engineering Technology/Technician** *9 students enrolled* • **Emergency Medical Technology/Technician (EMT Paramedic)** *3 students enrolled* • **Environmental Engineering Technology/Environmental Technology** *1 student enrolled* • **Fire Science/Firefighting** *17 students enrolled* • **Health Information/Medical Records Technology/Technician** *14 students enrolled* • **Licensed Practical/Vocational Nurse Training (LPN, LVN, Cert, Dipl, AAS)** *16 students enrolled* • **Massage Therapy/Therapeutic Massage** *32 students enrolled* • **Medical Insurance Specialist/Medical Biller** *81 students enrolled* • **Medical Office Assistant/Specialist** *30 students enrolled* • **Medical Transcription/Transcriptionist** *13 students enrolled* • **Metallurgical Technology/ Technician** *1 student enrolled* • **Nurse/Nursing Assistant/Aide and Patient Care Assistant** *8 students enrolled* • **Phlebotomy/Phlebotomist** *57 students enrolled* • **Recording Arts Technology/Technician** *1 student enrolled* • **Restaurant, Culinary, and Catering Management/Manager** *1 student enrolled* • **Salon/ Beauty Salon Management/Manager** *5 students enrolled* • **Web Page, Digital/ Multimedia and Information Resources Design** *3 students enrolled* • **Welding Technology/Welder** *5 students enrolled*

STUDENT SERVICES Academic or career counseling, daycare for children of students, employment services for current students, placement services for program completers, remedial services.

School of Creative Hair Design

78 West Chicago Street, Coldwater, MI 49036

CONTACT Brian Jennette, Owner
Telephone: 517-279-2355

GENERAL INFORMATION Private Institution. **Total program enrollment:** 53. **Application fee:** $100.

PROGRAM(S) OFFERED
• **Cosmetology, Barber/Styling, and Nail Instructor** *500 hrs./$800*
• **Cosmetology/Cosmetologist, General** *1500 hrs./$9650* • **Trade and Industrial Teacher Education** *2 students enrolled*

STUDENT SERVICES Academic or career counseling, employment services for current students, placement services for program completers.

School of Designing Arts

3000 6th Avenue, Springfield, MI 49037-7995

CONTACT Terri L. Sill, Owner/Director
Telephone: 269-962-4400

GENERAL INFORMATION Private Institution. **Total program enrollment:** 43. **Application fee:** $50.

PROGRAM(S) OFFERED
• **Aesthetician/Esthetician and Skin Care Specialist** *400 hrs./$3965*
• **Cosmetology/Cosmetologist, General** *1500 hrs./$12,565*

Sharp's Academy of Hairstyling–Grand Blanc Campus

8166 Holly Road, Grand Blanc, MI 48499

CONTACT Patricia Sharp, President
Telephone: 810-695-6742

GENERAL INFORMATION Private Institution. Founded 1991. **Total program enrollment:** 4.

PROGRAM(S) OFFERED
• **Cosmetology, Barber/Styling, and Nail Instructor** • **Cosmetology/ Cosmetologist, General** *1500 hrs./$7710*

Southwestern Michigan College

58900 Cherry Grove Road, Dowagiac, MI 49047-9793
http://www.swmich.edu/

CONTACT Dayid M. Mathews, President
Telephone: 269-782-1000

GENERAL INFORMATION Public Institution. Founded 1964. **Accreditation:** Regional (NCA). **Total program enrollment:** 1146.

PROGRAM(S) OFFERED
• **Automobile/Automotive Mechanics Technology/Technician** *2 students enrolled* • **Computer and Information Sciences and Support Services, Other** *1 student enrolled* • **Electrical, Electronic and Communications Engineering Technology/ Technician** *1 student enrolled* • **Licensed Practical/Vocational Nurse Training (LPN, LVN, Cert, Dipl, AAS)** *15 students enrolled* • **Mechanic and Repair Technologies/Technicians, Other** *2 students enrolled* • **Medical Transcription/ Transcriptionist** *1 student enrolled* • **Medical/Clinical Assistant** *4 students enrolled* • **Welding Technology/Welder** *1 student enrolled*

STUDENT SERVICES Academic or career counseling, employment services for current students, remedial services.

Specs Howard School of Broadcast Arts

19900 West Nine Mile Road, Suite 115, Southfield, MI 48075-5273
http://specshoward.edu/

CONTACT Jonathan Liebman, President
Telephone: 248-358-9000

GENERAL INFORMATION Private Institution. Founded 1970. **Total program enrollment:** 652. **Application fee:** $50.

PROGRAM(S) OFFERED
• **Radio and Television Broadcasting Technology/Technician** *533 students enrolled* • **Radio and Television** *24 hrs./$11,595*

STUDENT SERVICES Academic or career counseling, employment services for current students, placement services for program completers.

Taylortown School of Beauty

23015 Ecorse Road, Taylor, MI 48180

CONTACT Cynthia Stramecky, President
Telephone: 313-291-2177

GENERAL INFORMATION Private Institution. Founded 1975. **Total program enrollment:** 12. **Application fee:** $50.

PROGRAM(S) OFFERED
• **Cosmetology/Cosmetologist, General** *1500 hrs./$9990* • **Nail Technician/ Specialist and Manicurist** *400 hrs./$1800*

STUDENT SERVICES Placement services for program completers.

Twin City Beauty College

2600 Lincoln Avenue, St. Joseph, MI 49085
http://www.tcbeautycollege.com/

CONTACT James Moored, Owner
Telephone: 616-748-0182

GENERAL INFORMATION Private Institution. Founded 1959. **Total program enrollment:** 16. **Application fee:** $200.

PROGRAM(S) OFFERED
• Cosmetology, Barber/Styling, and Nail Instructor *1000 hrs./$1615*
• Cosmetology/Cosmetologist, General *1500 hrs./$13,700*

STUDENT SERVICES Placement services for program completers.

University of Detroit Mercy

4001 West McNichols Road, Detroit, MI 48221
http://www.udmercy.edu/

CONTACT Fr. Gerard Stockhausen, SJ, PhD, President
Telephone: 313-993-1000

GENERAL INFORMATION Private Institution. Founded 1877. **Accreditation:** Regional (NCA); counseling (ACA); dental hygiene (ADA). **Total program enrollment:** 3887. **Application fee:** $25.

PROGRAM(S) OFFERED
• African-American/Black Studies *4 students enrolled* • Arabic Language and Literature • Christian Studies • French Language and Literature *1 student enrolled* • Italian Language and Literature *1 student enrolled* • Japanese Language and Literature *1 student enrolled* • Korean Language and Literature *1 student enrolled* • Latin Language and Literature • Legal Assistant/Paralegal • Portuguese Language and Literature • Pre-Law Studies *6 students enrolled* • Spanish Language and Literature *8 students enrolled* • Substance Abuse/Addiction Counseling *1 student enrolled* • Women's Studies *1 student enrolled*

STUDENT SERVICES Academic or career counseling, employment services for current students, placement services for program completers, remedial services.

University of Phoenix–Metro Detroit Campus

5480 Corporate Drive, Suite 240, Troy, MI 48098-2623
http://www.phoenix.edu/

CONTACT William Pepicello, PhD, President
Telephone: 800-834-2438

GENERAL INFORMATION Private Institution. **Accreditation:** Regional (NCA). **Total program enrollment:** 2669.

PROGRAM(S) OFFERED
• Human Resources Management/Personnel Administration, General *1 student enrolled*

STUDENT SERVICES Academic or career counseling, remedial services.

U.P. Academy of Hair Design

1619 Ludington Street, Escanaba, MI 49829

CONTACT Steven Cowan, Owner
Telephone: 801-302-8801 Ext. 1021

GENERAL INFORMATION Private Institution. **Total program enrollment:** 27. **Application fee:** $200.

PROGRAM(S) OFFERED
• Cosmetology, Barber/Styling, and Nail Instructor *500 hrs./$3450*
• Cosmetology/Cosmetologist, General *1500 hrs./$12,000* • Nail Technician/Specialist and Manicurist *400 hrs./$3000*

STUDENT SERVICES Academic or career counseling.

Virginia Farrell Beauty School

22925 Woodward Avenue, Ferndale, MI 48220
http://virginiafarrell.com/

CONTACT Pauline Drace, President
Telephone: 248-398-4647

GENERAL INFORMATION Private Institution. Founded 1966. **Total program enrollment:** 96. **Application fee:** $100.

PROGRAM(S) OFFERED
• Cosmetology, Barber/Styling, and Nail Instructor *600 hrs./$3500*
• Cosmetology/Cosmetologist, General *1500 hrs./$8328* • Nail Technician/Specialist and Manicurist *600 hrs./$3700*

STUDENT SERVICES Placement services for program completers.

Virginia Farrell Beauty School

33425 Five Mile Road, Livonia, MI 48154
http://virginiafarrell.com/

CONTACT Pauline Drace, President
Telephone: 734-427-3970

GENERAL INFORMATION Private Institution. Founded 1981. **Total program enrollment:** 66. **Application fee:** $100.

PROGRAM(S) OFFERED
• Cosmetology, Barber/Styling, and Nail Instructor *600 hrs./$3500*
• Cosmetology/Cosmetologist, General *1500 hrs./$8328*

STUDENT SERVICES Placement services for program completers.

Virginia Farrell Beauty School

23620 Harper Road, St. Clair Shores, MI 48080
http://virginiafarrell.com/

CONTACT Pauline Drace, President
Telephone: 586-775-6640

GENERAL INFORMATION Private Institution. **Total program enrollment:** 60. **Application fee:** $100.

PROGRAM(S) OFFERED
• Cosmetology, Barber/Styling, and Nail Instructor *600 hrs./$3500*
• Cosmetology/Cosmetologist, General *1500 hrs./$8328*

STUDENT SERVICES Placement services for program completers.

Virginia Farrell Beauty School

34580 Ford Road, Wayne, MI 48184
http://virginiafarrell.com/

CONTACT Pauline Drace, President
Telephone: 734-729-9220

GENERAL INFORMATION Private Institution. Founded 1971. **Total program enrollment:** 105. **Application fee:** $100.

PROGRAM(S) OFFERED
• Cosmetology, Barber/Styling, and Nail Instructor *600 hrs./$3500*
• Cosmetology/Cosmetologist, General *1500 hrs./$8328* • Nail Technician/Specialist and Manicurist *600 hrs./$3700*

STUDENT SERVICES Placement services for program completers.

Washtenaw Community College

4800 East Huron River Drive, PO Box D-1, Ann Arbor, MI 48106
http://www.wccnet.edu/

CONTACT Larry Whitworth, President
Telephone: 734-973-3543

GENERAL INFORMATION Public Institution. Founded 1965. **Accreditation:** Regional (NCA); dental assisting (ADA); radiologic technology: radiography (JRCERT). **Total program enrollment:** 4261.

PROGRAM(S) OFFERED
• **Accounting Technology/Technician and Bookkeeping** *31 students enrolled* • **Administrative Assistant and Secretarial Science, General** *29 students enrolled* • **Architectural Technology/Technician** *3 students enrolled* • **Autobody/Collision and Repair Technology/Technician** *5 students enrolled* • **Automobile/Automotive Mechanics Technology/Technician** *10 students enrolled* • **Baking and Pastry Arts/Baker/Pastry Chef** *11 students enrolled* • **Building/Construction Site Management/Manager** *2 students enrolled* • **CAD/CADD Drafting and/or Design Technology/Technician** *10 students enrolled* • **Cabinetmaking and Millwork/Millwright** *1 student enrolled* • **Child Care Provider/Assistant** *51 students enrolled* • **Computer Programming, Specific Applications** *5 students enrolled* • **Computer Programming/Programmer, General** *5 students enrolled* • **Computer Systems Networking and Telecommunications** *30 students enrolled* • **Computer Technology/Computer Systems Technology** *33 students enrolled* • **Computer and Information Systems Security** *17 students enrolled* • **Computer/Information Technology Services Administration and Management, Other** *2 students enrolled* • **Construction Trades, General** *15 students enrolled* • **Culinary Arts/Chef Training** *23 students enrolled* • **Data Entry/Microcomputer Applications, General** *12 students enrolled* • **Dental Assisting/Assistant** *28 students enrolled* • **Digital Communication and Media/Multimedia** *6 students enrolled* • **Drafting/Design Engineering Technologies/Technicians, Other** *6 students enrolled* • **Entrepreneurship/Entrepreneurial Studies** *3 students enrolled* • **Graphic Design** *15 students enrolled* • **Health Services/Allied Health/Health Sciences, General** *46 students enrolled* • **Heating, Air Conditioning, Ventilation and Refrigeration Maintenance Technology/Technician (HAC, HACR, HVAC, HVACR)** *31 students enrolled* • **Human Resources Management/Personnel Administration, General** *15 students enrolled* • **Hydraulics and Fluid Power Technology/Technician** *3 students enrolled* • **Industrial Electronics Technology/Technician** *14 students enrolled* • **Machine Tool Technology/Machinist** *2 students enrolled* • **Manufacturing Technology/Technician** *5 students enrolled* • **Medical Administrative/Executive Assistant and Medical Secretary** *23 students enrolled* • **Motorcycle Maintenance and Repair Technology/Technician** *6 students enrolled* • **Music, Other** *25 students enrolled* • **Nurse/Nursing Assistant/Aide and Patient Care Assistant** *421 students enrolled* • **Office Management and Supervision** *23 students enrolled* • **Pharmacy Technician/Assistant** *7 students enrolled* • **Photographic and Film/Video Technology/Technician and Assistant** *30 students enrolled* • **Precision Production, Other** *7 students enrolled* • **Restaurant/Food Services Management** *2 students enrolled* • **Robotics Technology/Technician** *5 students enrolled* • **Selling Skills and Sales Operations** *19 students enrolled* • **Technical and Business Writing** *2 students enrolled* • **Vehicle Maintenance and Repair Technologies, Other** *3 students enrolled* • **Web Page, Digital/Multimedia and Information Resources Design** *1 student enrolled* • **Welding Technology/Welder** *18 students enrolled*

STUDENT SERVICES Academic or career counseling, daycare for children of students, employment services for current students, placement services for program completers, remedial services.

Wayne County Community College District

801 West Fort Street, Detroit, MI 48226-3010
http://www.wcccd.edu/

CONTACT Curtis L. Ivery, Chancellor
Telephone: 313-496-2600

GENERAL INFORMATION Public Institution. Founded 1967. **Accreditation:** Regional (NCA); dental assisting (ADA); dental hygiene (ADA); respiratory therapy technology (CoARC); surgical technology (ARCST). **Total program enrollment:** 4832.

PROGRAM(S) OFFERED
• **Accounting Technology/Technician and Bookkeeping** *3 students enrolled* • **Adult Development and Aging** *1 student enrolled* • **Automobile/Automotive Mechanics Technology/Technician** *4 students enrolled* • **Building/Property Maintenance and Management** *2 students enrolled* • **Child Care and Support Services Management** *1 student enrolled* • **Computer and Information Sciences, General** *2 students enrolled* • **Dental Assisting/Assistant** *11 students enrolled* • **Dental Laboratory Technology/Technician** *9 students enrolled*

• **Electrical, Electronic and Communications Engineering Technology/Technician** *3 students enrolled* • **Emergency Medical Technology/Technician (EMT Paramedic)** *6 students enrolled* • **Foodservice Systems Administration/Management** *1 student enrolled* • **Heating, Air Conditioning, Ventilation and Refrigeration Maintenance Technology/Technician (HAC, HACR, HVAC, HVACR)** *10 students enrolled* • **Nursing—Registered Nurse Training (RN, ASN, BSN, MSN)** *1 student enrolled* • **Pharmacy Technician/Assistant** *12 students enrolled* • **Substance Abuse/Addiction Counseling** *9 students enrolled* • **Surgical Technology/Technologist** *2 students enrolled* • **Welding Technology/Welder** *1 student enrolled*

STUDENT SERVICES Academic or career counseling, daycare for children of students, employment services for current students, placement services for program completers, remedial services.

West Shore Community College

PO Box 277, 3000 North Stiles Road, Scottville, MI 49454-0277
http://www.westshore.edu/

CONTACT Charles T. Dillon, President
Telephone: 231-845-6211

GENERAL INFORMATION Public Institution. Founded 1967. **Accreditation:** Regional (NCA). **Total program enrollment:** 534. **Application fee:** $15.

PROGRAM(S) OFFERED
• **Administrative Assistant and Secretarial Science, General** *1 student enrolled* • **Business Administration, Management and Operations, Other** *3 students enrolled* • **Corrections** *3 students enrolled* • **Licensed Practical/Vocational Nurse Training (LPN, LVN, Cert, Dipl, AAS)** *18 students enrolled* • **Medical Insurance Coding Specialist/Coder** *1 student enrolled*

STUDENT SERVICES Academic or career counseling, employment services for current students, placement services for program completers, remedial services.

Wright Beauty Academy

492 Capital, SW, Battle Creek, MI 49015
http://www.wrightbeautyacademy.com/

CONTACT Jessica Gieske, Owner
Telephone: 269-964-4016

GENERAL INFORMATION Private Institution. **Total program enrollment:** 20. **Application fee:** $50.

PROGRAM(S) OFFERED
• **Cosmetology, Barber/Styling, and Nail Instructor** *500 hrs./$800* • **Cosmetology/Cosmetologist, General** *1500 hrs./$7600* • **Nail Technician/Specialist and Manicurist** *600 hrs./$2499*

STUDENT SERVICES Academic or career counseling, employment services for current students, placement services for program completers.

Wright Beauty Academy

6666 Lovers Lane, Portage, MI 49002
http://www.wrightbeautyacademy.com/

CONTACT Jes Gieske, Financial Aid Officer
Telephone: 269-321-8708

GENERAL INFORMATION Private Institution. **Total program enrollment:** 7. **Application fee:** $35.

PROGRAM(S) OFFERED
• **Cosmetology, Barber/Styling, and Nail Instructor** *600 hrs./$685* • **Cosmetology/Cosmetologist, General** *1500 hrs./$8500* • **Nail Technician/Specialist and Manicurist** *400 hrs./$2000*

STUDENT SERVICES Academic or career counseling, placement services for program completers.

MISSISSIPPI

Academy of Hair Design

2003B South Commerce, Grenada, MS 38901
http://www.academyofhair.com/

CONTACT Andrea Calton, Administrative Asst.
Telephone: 662-226-2464

GENERAL INFORMATION Private Institution. **Total program enrollment:** 17.

PROGRAM(S) OFFERED
• **Cosmetology, Barber/Styling, and Nail Instructor** *2000 hrs./$13,833*
• **Cosmetology/Cosmetologist, General** *1500 hrs./$10,600*

STUDENT SERVICES Placement services for program completers.

Academy of Hair Design

Cloverleaf Mall D-4, Hattiesburg, MS 39401
http://www.academyofhair.com/

CONTACT Andrea Calton, Administrative Assistant
Telephone: 601-583-1290

GENERAL INFORMATION Private Institution. **Total program enrollment:** 36.

PROGRAM(S) OFFERED
• **Cosmetology, Barber/Styling, and Nail Instructor** *750 hrs./$5250*
• **Cosmetology/Cosmetologist, General** *1500 hrs./$9200*

STUDENT SERVICES Placement services for program completers.

Academy of Hair Design

1815 Terry Road, Jackson, MS 39204
http://www.academyofhair.com/

CONTACT Andrea Calton, Administrative Asst.
Telephone: 601-372-9800

GENERAL INFORMATION Private Institution. **Total program enrollment:** 41.

PROGRAM(S) OFFERED
• **Barbering/Barber** *1500 hrs./$9000* • **Cosmetology, Barber/Styling, and Nail Instructor** *2000 hrs./$13,833* • **Cosmetology/Cosmetologist, General** *1500 hrs./$9200*

STUDENT SERVICES Placement services for program completers.

Academy of Hair Design

3167 Highway 80 East, Pearl, MS 39208
http://www.academyofhair.com/

CONTACT Andrea Calton, Administrative Asst.
Telephone: 601-939-4441

GENERAL INFORMATION Private Institution. **Total program enrollment:** 46.

PROGRAM(S) OFFERED
• **Cosmetology, Barber/Styling, and Nail Instructor** *2000 hrs./$13,833*
• **Cosmetology/Cosmetologist, General** *1500 hrs./$10,600*

Antonelli College

1500 North 31st Avenue, Hattiesburg, MS 39401
http://antonellicollege.edu/

CONTACT Mary Ann Davis, President
Telephone: 601-583-4100

GENERAL INFORMATION Private Institution. **Accreditation:** State accredited or approved. **Total program enrollment:** 337.

PROGRAM(S) OFFERED
• **Business/Office Automation/Technology/Data Entry** *3 students enrolled*
• **Medical Administrative/Executive Assistant and Medical Secretary** *2 students enrolled*

STUDENT SERVICES Academic or career counseling, employment services for current students, placement services for program completers.

Antonelli College

2323 Lakeland Drive, Jackson, MS 39232
http://www.antonellicollege.edu/

CONTACT Mary Ann Davis, President
Telephone: 601-362-9991

GENERAL INFORMATION Private Institution. **Accreditation:** State accredited or approved. **Total program enrollment:** 246. **Application fee:** $75.

PROGRAM(S) OFFERED
• **Business/Office Automation/Technology/Data Entry** • **Dental Assisting/Assistant** • **Medical/Clinical Assistant**

STUDENT SERVICES Academic or career counseling, employment services for current students, placement services for program completers.

Belhaven College

1500 Peachtree Street, Jackson, MS 39202-1789
http://www.belhaven.edu/

CONTACT Roger Parrott, President
Telephone: 601-968-5940

GENERAL INFORMATION Private Institution. Founded 1883. **Accreditation:** Regional (SACS/CC); art and design (NASAD); music (NASM). **Total program enrollment:** 2435. **Application fee:** $25.

PROGRAM(S) OFFERED
• **Accounting** • **Bible/Biblical Studies** • **Business Administration and Management, General** • **Computer Science** • **Dance, General** *2 students enrolled* • **Work and Family Studies**

STUDENT SERVICES Academic or career counseling, remedial services.

Blue Cliff College–Gulfport

942 Beach Drive, Gulfport, MS 39507-1354
http://bluecliffcollege.com/

CONTACT Ted Little, Director
Telephone: 228-896-9727 Ext. 0000

GENERAL INFORMATION Private Institution. **Total program enrollment:** 138.

PROGRAM(S) OFFERED
• **Allied Health and Medical Assisting Services, Other** *27 students enrolled* • **Cosmetology and Related Personal Grooming Arts, Other** • **Massage Therapy/Therapeutic Massage** *93 students enrolled*

STUDENT SERVICES Academic or career counseling, placement services for program completers.

Chris Beauty College

1265 Pass Road, Gulfport, MS 39501
http://www.chrisbeautycollege.com/

CONTACT Donald O. Simmons, President Owner
Telephone: 228-864-2920

GENERAL INFORMATION Private Institution. Founded 1961. **Total program enrollment: 91. Application fee:** $35.

PROGRAM(S) OFFERED
• **Barbering/Barber** • **Cosmetology, Barber/Styling, and Nail Instructor** *750 hrs./$2250* • **Cosmetology/Cosmetologist, General** *1500 hrs./$8500* • **Nail Technician/Specialist and Manicurist** *350 hrs./$1750*

STUDENT SERVICES Academic or career counseling, placement services for program completers.

Coahoma Community College

3240 Friars Point Road, Clarksdale, MS 38614-9799
http://www.ccc.cc.ms.us/

CONTACT Vivian M. Presley, President
Telephone: 662-627-2571

GENERAL INFORMATION Public Institution. Founded 1949. **Accreditation:** Regional (SACS/CC). **Total program enrollment: 2057.**

PROGRAM(S) OFFERED
• **Autobody/Collision and Repair Technology/Technician** *2 students enrolled* • **Barbering/Barber** *14 students enrolled* • **Carpentry/Carpenter** *2 students enrolled* • **Cosmetology/Cosmetologist, General** *5 students enrolled* • **Culinary Arts/Chef Training** *5 students enrolled* • **Heavy/Industrial Equipment Maintenance Technologies, Other** *1 student enrolled* • **Licensed Practical/Vocational Nurse Training (LPN, LVN, Cert, Dipl, AAS)** *22 students enrolled* • **Welding Technology/Welder** *12 students enrolled*

STUDENT SERVICES Academic or career counseling, employment services for current students, placement services for program completers, remedial services.

Copiah-Lincoln Community College

PO Box 649, Wesson, MS 39191-0649
http://www.colin.edu/

CONTACT Dr. Ronnie Nettles, President
Telephone: 601-643-8306

GENERAL INFORMATION Public Institution. Founded 1928. **Accreditation:** Regional (SACS/CC); medical laboratory technology (NAACLS); radiologic technology: radiography (JRCERT). **Total program enrollment: 2868.**

PROGRAM(S) OFFERED
• **Administrative Assistant and Secretarial Science, General** *4 students enrolled* • **Automobile/Automotive Mechanics Technology/Technician** *7 students enrolled* • **Computer Systems Networking and Telecommunications** • **Construction/Heavy Equipment/Earthmoving Equipment Operation** • **Cosmetology/Cosmetologist, General** *23 students enrolled* • **Diesel Mechanics Technology/Technician** *7 students enrolled* • **Heating, Air Conditioning, Ventilation and Refrigeration Maintenance Technology/Technician (HAC, HACR, HVAC, HVACR)** *10 students enrolled* • **Heavy Equipment Maintenance Technology/Technician** • **Licensed Practical/Vocational Nurse Training (LPN, LVN, Cert, Dipl, AAS)** *46 students enrolled* • **Machine Shop Technology/Assistant** *1 student enrolled* • **Management Information Systems, General** • **Nurse/Nursing Assistant/Aide and Patient Care Assistant** *18 students enrolled* • **Truck and Bus Driver/Commercial Vehicle Operation** *9 students enrolled* • **Welding Technology/Welder** *20 students enrolled*

STUDENT SERVICES Academic or career counseling, daycare for children of students, employment services for current students, placement services for program completers, remedial services.

Corinth Academy of Cosmetology

502 Cruise Street, Corinth, MS 38834

CONTACT Kathy Tollison, President
Telephone: 662-286-9200

GENERAL INFORMATION Private Institution. **Total program enrollment: 22. Application fee:** $100.

PROGRAM(S) OFFERED
• **Cosmetology, Barber/Styling, and Nail Instructor** *2000 hrs./$5080* • **Cosmetology/Cosmetologist, General** *1500 hrs./$4550* • **Nail Technician/Specialist and Manicurist** *350 hrs./$1250*

STUDENT SERVICES Academic or career counseling, placement services for program completers.

Creations College of Cosmetology

2419 West Main Street, PO Box 2635, Tupelo, MS 38803
http://www.creationscosmetology.com/

CONTACT Carolyn Kennedy Bowen, Owner
Telephone: 662-844-9264

GENERAL INFORMATION Private Institution. Founded 1984. **Total program enrollment: 51. Application fee:** $100.

PROGRAM(S) OFFERED
• **Cosmetology/Cosmetologist, General** *1500 hrs./$7200*

STUDENT SERVICES Academic or career counseling.

Day Spa Career College

3900 Bienville Boulevard, Ocean Spring, MS 39564

CONTACT Sandra Seymour, President, CEO
Telephone: 228-875-4809

GENERAL INFORMATION Private Institution. **Total program enrollment: 37.**

PROGRAM(S) OFFERED
• **Aesthetician/Esthetician and Skin Care Specialist** *6 students enrolled* • **Cosmetology and Related Personal Grooming Arts, Other** *1000 hrs./$5450* • **Cosmetology, Barber/Styling, and Nail Instructor** • **Cosmetology/Cosmetologist, General** *650 hrs./$7100* • **Nail Technician/Specialist and Manicurist** *1 student enrolled*

STUDENT SERVICES Academic or career counseling, placement services for program completers.

Delta Beauty College

697 Delta Plaza, Greenville, MS 38701

CONTACT Kenny O'Neal, President
Telephone: 662-332-0587

GENERAL INFORMATION Private Institution. **Total program enrollment: 43.**

PROGRAM(S) OFFERED
• **Cosmetology, Barber/Styling, and Nail Instructor** *1 student enrolled* • **Cosmetology/Cosmetologist, General** *2000 hrs./$7587*

STUDENT SERVICES Academic or career counseling, placement services for program completers.

Delta Technical College

1090 Main Street, Southaven, MS 38671
http://www.deltatechnicalcollege.com/

CONTACT Joan Hankins, Director of Education
Telephone: 662-280-1443

GENERAL INFORMATION Private Institution. **Total program enrollment:** 337.

PROGRAM(S) OFFERED
• **Aesthetician/Esthetician and Skin Care Specialist** *750 hrs./$6450* • **Heating, Air Conditioning, Ventilation and Refrigeration Maintenance Technology/Technician (HAC, HACR, HVAC, HVACR)** *720 hrs./$8975* • **Massage Therapy/Therapeutic Massage** *723 hrs./$8975* • **Medical/Clinical Assistant** *720 hrs./$9850*

STUDENT SERVICES Placement services for program completers.

East Central Community College

PO Box 129, Decatur, MS 39327-0129
http://www.eccc.cc.ms.us/

CONTACT Phil Sutphin, President
Telephone: 601-635-2111

GENERAL INFORMATION Public Institution. Founded 1928. **Accreditation:** Regional (SACS/CC); surgical technology (ARCST). **Total program enrollment:** 1915.

PROGRAM(S) OFFERED
• **Administrative Assistant and Secretarial Science, General** *2 students enrolled* • **Autobody/Collision and Repair Technology/Technician** *5 students enrolled* • **Automobile/Automotive Mechanics Technology/Technician** *2 students enrolled* • **Carpentry/Carpenter** *10 students enrolled* • **Cooking and Related Culinary Arts, General** *2 students enrolled* • **Cosmetology/Cosmetologist, General** *17 students enrolled* • **Electrician** *2 students enrolled* • **Heating, Air Conditioning, Ventilation and Refrigeration Maintenance Technology/Technician (HAC, HACR, HVAC, HVACR)** *3 students enrolled* • **Licensed Practical/Vocational Nurse Training (LPN, LVN, Cert, Dipl, AAS)** *19 students enrolled* • **Machine Tool Technology/Machinist** *4 students enrolled* • **Nurse/Nursing Assistant/Aide and Patient Care Assistant** *24 students enrolled* • **Surgical Technology/Technologist** *5 students enrolled* • **Welding Technology/Welder** *15 students enrolled*

STUDENT SERVICES Academic or career counseling, daycare for children of students, employment services for current students, placement services for program completers, remedial services.

East Mississippi Community College

PO Box 158, Scooba, MS 39358-0158
http://www.eastms.edu/

CONTACT Rick Young, President
Telephone: 662-476-5000

GENERAL INFORMATION Public Institution. Founded 1927. **Accreditation:** Regional (SACS/CC); funeral service (ABFSE). **Total program enrollment:** 2735.

PROGRAM(S) OFFERED
• **Administrative Assistant and Secretarial Science, General** *3 students enrolled* • **Automobile/Automotive Mechanics Technology/Technician** *5 students enrolled* • **Cosmetology/Cosmetologist, General** *18 students enrolled* • **Electrician** *15 students enrolled* • **Licensed Practical/Vocational Nurse Training (LPN, LVN, Cert, Dipl, AAS)** *29 students enrolled* • **Lineworker** *9 students enrolled* • **Machine Shop Technology/Assistant** *5 students enrolled* • **Management Information Systems, General** • **Nurse/Nursing Assistant/Aide and Patient Care Assistant** *21 students enrolled* • **Truck and Bus Driver/Commercial Vehicle Operation** *28 students enrolled* • **Welding Technology/Welder** *16 students enrolled*

STUDENT SERVICES Academic or career counseling, employment services for current students, placement services for program completers, remedial services.

Final Touch Beauty School

832 Highway 19 N, Suite 510, Meridian, MS 39307

CONTACT Sue Mitchell, Owner
Telephone: 601-485-7733

GENERAL INFORMATION Private Institution. **Total program enrollment:** 68. **Application fee:** $100.

PROGRAM(S) OFFERED
• **Cosmetology, Barber/Styling, and Nail Instructor** *750 hrs./$3900* • **Cosmetology/Cosmetologist, General** *1500 hrs./$7500* • **Nail Technician/Specialist and Manicurist** *350 hrs./$2100*

STUDENT SERVICES Academic or career counseling, placement services for program completers.

Foster's Cosmetology College

1813 Highway 15, N, Ripley, MS 38663

CONTACT Hazel L. Foster, Owner
Telephone: 662-837-9334

GENERAL INFORMATION Private Institution. Founded 1945. **Total program enrollment:** 15.

PROGRAM(S) OFFERED
• **Barbering/Barber** *1500 hrs./$7405* • **Cosmetology, Barber/Styling, and Nail Instructor** *600 hrs./$6400* • **Cosmetology/Cosmetologist, General** *1500 hrs./$7805*

STUDENT SERVICES Academic or career counseling, placement services for program completers.

Gibson Barber and Beauty College

120 East Main Street, West Point, MS 39773

CONTACT Evelyn Gibson, Administrator
Telephone: 662-494-5444

GENERAL INFORMATION Private Institution. Founded 1985. **Total program enrollment:** 43. **Application fee:** $100.

PROGRAM(S) OFFERED
• **Barbering/Barber** *1500 hrs./$7800* • **Cosmetology and Related Personal Grooming Arts, Other** *750 hrs./$2200* • **Cosmetology, Barber/Styling, and Nail Instructor** *600 hrs./$2200* • **Cosmetology/Cosmetologist, General** *1500 hrs./$7300* • **Nail Technician/Specialist and Manicurist**

STUDENT SERVICES Placement services for program completers.

Healing Touch School of Massage Therapy

4700 Hardy Street, Suite J-1, Hattiesburg, MS 39402
http://healingtouchms.com/

CONTACT Ibrahima Sidibe, Owner/Director/CFO
Telephone: 601-261-0111

GENERAL INFORMATION Private Institution. **Total program enrollment:** 12. **Application fee:** $25.

PROGRAM(S) OFFERED
• **Massage Therapy/Therapeutic Massage** *750 hrs./$10,500*

STUDENT SERVICES Academic or career counseling, placement services for program completers.

Hinds Community College

PO Box 1100, Raymond, MS 39154-1100
http://www.hindscc.edu/

CONTACT Dr. V. Clyde Muse, President
Telephone: 601-857-5261

GENERAL INFORMATION Public Institution. Founded 1917. **Accreditation:** Regional (SACS/CC); dental assisting (ADA); health information technology (AHIMA); medical assisting (AAMAE); medical laboratory technology (NAACLS); physical therapy assisting (APTA); radiologic technology: radiography (JRCERT); respiratory therapy technology (CoARC). **Total program enrollment:** 6609.

PROGRAM(S) OFFERED

• **Administrative Assistant and Secretarial Science, General** 12 students enrolled • **Agribusiness/Agricultural Business Operations** 3 students enrolled • **Apparel and Textile Manufacture** • **Apparel and Textile Marketing Management** 8 students enrolled • **Autobody/Collision and Repair Technology/Technician** 20 students enrolled • **Automobile/Automotive Mechanics Technology/Technician** 12 students enrolled • **Barbering/Barber** 15 students enrolled • **Carpentry/Carpenter** 12 students enrolled • **Cartography** 3 students enrolled • **Communications Systems Installation and Repair Technology** 1 student enrolled • **Computer Installation and Repair Technology/Technician** 1 student enrolled • **Cooking and Related Culinary Arts, General** 1 student enrolled • **Cosmetology/Cosmetologist, General** • **Dental Assisting/Assistant** 21 students enrolled • **Diagnostic Medical Sonography/Sonographer and Ultrasound Technician** • **Diesel Mechanics Technology/Technician** 7 students enrolled • **Drafting and Design Technology/Technician, General** • **Electrical, Electronic and Communications Engineering Technology/Technician** • **Electrician** 40 students enrolled • **Emergency Medical Technology/Technician (EMT Paramedic)** 2 students enrolled • **Engine Machinist** 1 student enrolled • **Graphic and Printing Equipment Operator, General Production** 4 students enrolled • **Heating, Air Conditioning, Ventilation and Refrigeration Maintenance Technology/Technician (HAC, HACR, HVAC, HVACR)** 10 students enrolled • **Heavy Equipment Maintenance Technology/Technician** • **Hospitality Administration/Management, General** • **Institutional Food Workers** 7 students enrolled • **Licensed Practical/Vocational Nurse Training (LPN, LVN, Cert, Dipl, AAS)** 98 students enrolled • **Machine Shop Technology/Assistant** • **Machine Tool Technology/Machinist** 1 student enrolled • **Mason/Masonry** 12 students enrolled • **Meat Cutting/Meat Cutter** 1 student enrolled • **Optometric Technician/Assistant** 1 student enrolled • **Plumbing Technology/Plumber** 2 students enrolled • **Surgical Technology/Technologist** 29 students enrolled • **Tourism and Travel Services Management** • **Vehicle and Vehicle Parts and Accessories Marketing Operations** 4 students enrolled • **Welding Technology/Welder** 29 students enrolled

STUDENT SERVICES Academic or career counseling, daycare for children of students, employment services for current students, placement services for program completers, remedial services.

Holmes Community College

PO Box 369, Goodman, MS 39079-0369
http://www.holmescc.edu/

CONTACT Dr. Glenn F. Boyce, President
Telephone: 662-472-2312

GENERAL INFORMATION Public Institution. Founded 1928. **Accreditation:** Regional (SACS/CC); emergency medical services (JRCEMTP); surgical technology (ARCST). **Total program enrollment:** 3838.

PROGRAM(S) OFFERED

• **Autobody/Collision and Repair Technology/Technician** 6 students enrolled • **Automobile/Automotive Mechanics Technology/Technician** • **Business/Office Automation/Technology/Data Entry** • **Cosmetology/Cosmetologist, General** 9 students enrolled • **Emergency Medical Technology/Technician (EMT Paramedic)** 7 students enrolled • **Heating, Air Conditioning, Ventilation and Refrigeration Maintenance Technology/Technician (HAC, HACR, HVAC, HVACR)** 9 students enrolled • **Licensed Practical/Vocational Nurse Training (LPN, LVN, Cert, Dipl, AAS)** 58 students enrolled • **Surgical Technology/Technologist** 9 students enrolled • **Welding Technology/Welder** 14 students enrolled

STUDENT SERVICES Academic or career counseling, placement services for program completers, remedial services.

ICS–The Wright Beauty College

2077 Highway 72, E, Corinth, MS 38834

CONTACT Linda Kay Richardson, Owner
Telephone: 662-287-0944

GENERAL INFORMATION Private Institution. Founded 1986. **Total program enrollment:** 34. **Application fee:** $100.

PROGRAM(S) OFFERED

• **Cosmetology, Barber/Styling, and Nail Instructor** 1 student enrolled • **Cosmetology/Cosmetologist, General** 1500 hrs./$6400 • **Nail Technician/Specialist and Manicurist** 9 students enrolled • **Trade and Industrial Teacher Education** 750 hrs./$3175

STUDENT SERVICES Academic or career counseling.

Itawamba Community College

602 West Hill Street, Fulton, MS 38843
http://www.icc.cc.ms.us/

CONTACT David C. Cole, PhD, President
Telephone: 601-862-8000

GENERAL INFORMATION Public Institution. Founded 1947. **Accreditation:** Regional (SACS/CC); health information technology (AHIMA); physical therapy assisting (APTA); radiologic technology: radiography (JRCERT); surgical technology (ARCST). **Total program enrollment:** 4805.

PROGRAM(S) OFFERED

• **Autobody/Collision and Repair Technology/Technician** 9 students enrolled • **Automobile/Automotive Mechanics Technology/Technician** 3 students enrolled • **Computer and Information Sciences, General** 1 student enrolled • **Licensed Practical/Vocational Nurse Training (LPN, LVN, Cert, Dipl, AAS)** 40 students enrolled • **Surgical Technology/Technologist** 5 students enrolled • **Truck and Bus Driver/Commercial Vehicle Operation** 26 students enrolled • **Welding Technology/Welder** 11 students enrolled

STUDENT SERVICES Academic or career counseling, daycare for children of students, employment services for current students, placement services for program completers, remedial services.

J & J Hair Design College

116 East Franklin Street, Carthage, MS 39051

CONTACT Ricky Jones, President Owner
Telephone: 601-267-3678

GENERAL INFORMATION Private Institution. **Total program enrollment:** 52. **Application fee:** $100.

PROGRAM(S) OFFERED

• **Barbering/Barber** 1500 hrs./$8450 • **Cosmetology and Related Personal Grooming Arts, Other** 80 hrs./$400 • **Cosmetology, Barber/Styling, and Nail Instructor** 1000 hrs./$5500 • **Hair Styling/Stylist and Hair Design** 2 students enrolled • **Personal and Culinary Services, Other** 1 student enrolled • **Salon/Beauty Salon Management/Manager** 80 hrs./$400

STUDENT SERVICES Academic or career counseling, placement services for program completers.

J & J Hair Design College

3905 Main Street, Moss Point, MS 39562

CONTACT Ricky Jones, President
Telephone: 228-864-4663

GENERAL INFORMATION Private Institution. **Total program enrollment:** 10. **Application fee:** $100.

PROGRAM(S) OFFERED

• **Barbering/Barber** 1500 hrs./$8300 • **Cosmetology, Barber/Styling, and Nail Instructor** 600 hrs./$3340

STUDENT SERVICES Academic or career counseling, placement services for program completers.

Jones County Junior College

900 South Court Street, Ellisville, MS 39437-3901
http://www.jcjc.edu/

CONTACT Jesse Smith, President
Telephone: 601-477-4000

GENERAL INFORMATION Public Institution. Founded 1928. **Accreditation:** Regional (SACS/CC); emergency medical services (JRCEMTP); radiologic technology: radiography (JRCERT). **Total program enrollment:** 3543.

PROGRAM(S) OFFERED
• **Administrative Assistant and Secretarial Science, General** 2 students enrolled • **Agricultural and Food Products Processing** 11 students enrolled • **Applied Horticulture/Horticultural Operations, General** 1 student enrolled • **Automobile/Automotive Mechanics Technology/Technician** 10 students enrolled • **Communications Systems Installation and Repair Technology** • **Cooking and Related Culinary Arts, General** 6 students enrolled • **Cosmetology/Cosmetologist, General** 19 students enrolled • **Diagnostic Medical Sonography/Sonographer and Ultrasound Technician** • **Electrician** 24 students enrolled • **Engine Machinist** 1 student enrolled • **Heating, Air Conditioning, Ventilation and Refrigeration Maintenance Technology/Technician (HAC, HACR, HVAC, HVACR)** 11 students enrolled • **Licensed Practical/Vocational Nurse Training (LPN, LVN, Cert, Dipl, AAS)** 58 students enrolled • **Machine Shop Technology/Assistant** 5 students enrolled • **Nurse/Nursing Assistant/Aide and Patient Care Assistant** 30 students enrolled • **Plastics Engineering Technology/Technician** • **Watchmaking and Jewelrymaking** 8 students enrolled • **Welding Technology/Welder** 17 students enrolled

STUDENT SERVICES Academic or career counseling, employment services for current students, placement services for program completers, remedial services.

Magnolia College of Cosmetology

4725 I-55, Jackson, MS 39206
http://www.magnoliacollegeofcosmetology.com/

CONTACT Marie Wells Butler, Owner President
Telephone: 601-362-6940

GENERAL INFORMATION Private Institution. Founded 1985. **Total program enrollment:** 178. **Application fee:** $100.

PROGRAM(S) OFFERED
• **Aesthetician/Esthetician and Skin Care Specialist** 600 hrs./$6100 • **Cosmetology, Barber/Styling, and Nail Instructor** 750 hrs./$5100 • **Cosmetology/Cosmetologist, General** 1500 hrs./$13,500 • **Nail Technician/Specialist and Manicurist** 350 hrs./$2550

STUDENT SERVICES Placement services for program completers.

Meridian Community College

910 Highway 19 North, Meridian, MS 39307
http://www.meridiancc.edu/

CONTACT Scott D. Elliott, President
Telephone: 601-483-8241 Ext. 668

GENERAL INFORMATION Public Institution. Founded 1937. **Accreditation:** Regional (SACS/CC); dental hygiene (ADA); health information technology (AHIMA); medical laboratory technology (NAACLS); physical therapy assisting (APTA); practical nursing (NLN); radiologic technology: radiography (JRCERT). **Total program enrollment:** 2651.

PROGRAM(S) OFFERED
• **Administrative Assistant and Secretarial Science, General** 9 students enrolled • **Carpentry/Carpenter** 18 students enrolled • **Cosmetology/Cosmetologist, General** 26 students enrolled • **Dental Assisting/Assistant** 6 students enrolled • **Industrial Mechanics and Maintenance Technology** 8 students enrolled • **Licensed Practical/Vocational Nurse Training (LPN, LVN, Cert, Dipl, AAS)** 32 students enrolled • **Machine Tool Technology/Machinist** 3 students enrolled

• **Nurse/Nursing Assistant/Aide and Patient Care Assistant** 38 students enrolled • **Surgical Technology/Technologist** 10 students enrolled • **Truck and Bus Driver/Commercial Vehicle Operation** 29 students enrolled

STUDENT SERVICES Academic or career counseling, employment services for current students, placement services for program completers, remedial services.

Mississippi College of Beauty Culture

732 Sawmill Road, Laurel, MS 39440

CONTACT Robert Hatfield, President
Telephone: 601-428-7043

GENERAL INFORMATION Private Institution. **Total program enrollment:** 89.

PROGRAM(S) OFFERED
• **Cosmetology, Barber/Styling, and Nail Instructor** • **Cosmetology/Cosmetologist, General** 1500 hrs./$9100

STUDENT SERVICES Placement services for program completers.

Mississippi Delta Community College

PO Box 668, Highway 3 and Cherry Street, Moorhead, MS 38761-0668
http://www.msdelta.edu/

CONTACT Dr. Larry G. Bailey, President
Telephone: 662-246-6322

GENERAL INFORMATION Public Institution. Founded 1926. **Accreditation:** Regional (SACS/CC); dental hygiene (ADA); medical laboratory technology (NAACLS); radiologic technology: radiography (JRCERT). **Total program enrollment:** 2431.

PROGRAM(S) OFFERED
• **Agricultural Mechanization, General** 2 students enrolled • **Agricultural Mechanization, Other** • **Automobile/Automotive Mechanics Technology/Technician** 3 students enrolled • **Construction/Heavy Equipment/Earthmoving Equipment Operation** 11 students enrolled • **Electrician** 12 students enrolled • **Engine Machinist** 8 students enrolled • **Heating, Air Conditioning, Ventilation and Refrigeration Maintenance Technology/Technician (HAC, HACR, HVAC, HVACR)** 11 students enrolled • **Licensed Practical/Vocational Nurse Training (LPN, LVN, Cert, Dipl, AAS)** 21 students enrolled • **Machine Shop Technology/Assistant** • **Mason/Masonry** 4 students enrolled • **Nuclear Medical Technology/Technologist** 3 students enrolled • **Sheet Metal Technology/Sheetworking** 5 students enrolled • **Welding Technology/Welder** 11 students enrolled

STUDENT SERVICES Academic or career counseling, employment services for current students, placement services for program completers, remedial services.

Mississippi Gulf Coast Community College

PO Box 609, Perkinston, MS 39573-0609
http://www.mgccc.edu/

CONTACT Willis Lott, President
Telephone: 601-928-5211

GENERAL INFORMATION Public Institution. Founded 1911. **Accreditation:** Regional (SACS/CC); emergency medical services (JRCEMTP); funeral service (ABFSE); medical laboratory technology (NAACLS); radiologic technology: radiography (JRCERT). **Total program enrollment:** 5770.

PROGRAM(S) OFFERED
• **Administrative Assistant and Secretarial Science, General** 12 students enrolled • **Aquaculture** • **Autobody/Collision and Repair Technology/Technician** 10 students enrolled • **Automobile/Automotive Mechanics Technology/Technician** 6 students enrolled • **Carpentry/Carpenter** • **Cosmetology/Cosmetologist, General** • **Drafting/Design Engineering Technologies/Technicians, Other** 1 student enrolled • **Electrician** 20 students enrolled • **Heating, Air Conditioning, Ventilation and Refrigeration Maintenance Technology/Technician (HAC, HACR, HVAC, HVACR)** 7 students enrolled • **Industrial**

Mechanics and Maintenance Technology *2 students enrolled* • Landscaping and Groundskeeping *11 students enrolled* • Licensed Practical/Vocational Nurse Training (LPN, LVN, Cert, Dipl, AAS) *89 students enrolled* • Machine Shop Technology/Assistant *13 students enrolled* • Marine Maintenance/Fitter and Ship Repair Technology/Technician *4 students enrolled* • Marine Transportation, Other • Plumbing Technology/Plumber *1 student enrolled* • Restaurant/Food Services Management *13 students enrolled* • Surgical Technology/Technologist *10 students enrolled* • Technical Teacher Education • Truck and Bus Driver/Commercial Vehicle Operation *6 students enrolled* • Welding Technology/Welder *9 students enrolled*

STUDENT SERVICES Academic or career counseling, daycare for children of students, employment services for current students, placement services for program completers, remedial services.

Mississippi State Board for Community and Junior Colleges

3825 Ridgewood Road, Jackson, MS 39211

CONTACT Eric Clark, Executive Director
Telephone: 601-432-6518

GENERAL INFORMATION Public Institution.

Northeast Mississippi Community College

101 Cunningham Boulevard, Booneville, MS 38829
http://www.nemcc.edu/

CONTACT Johnny Allen, President
Telephone: 662-728-7751

GENERAL INFORMATION Public Institution. Founded 1948. **Accreditation:** Regional (SACS/CC); dental hygiene (ADA); medical assisting (AAMAE); medical laboratory technology (NAACLS); radiologic technology: radiography (JRCERT). **Total program enrollment: 2685.**

PROGRAM(S) OFFERED
• Autobody/Collision and Repair Technology/Technician *11 students enrolled* • Automobile/Automotive Mechanics Technology/Technician *15 students enrolled* • Diesel Mechanics Technology/Technician *2 students enrolled* • Heating, Air Conditioning, Ventilation and Refrigeration Maintenance Technology/Technician (HAC, HACR, HVAC, HVACR) *2 students enrolled* • Licensed Practical/Vocational Nurse Training (LPN, LVN, Cert, Dipl, AAS) *61 students enrolled* • Machine Shop Technology/Assistant • Machine Tool Technology/Machinist *4 students enrolled*

STUDENT SERVICES Academic or career counseling, daycare for children of students, employment services for current students, placement services for program completers, remedial services.

Northwest Mississippi Community College

4975 Highway 51 North, Senatobia, MS 38668-1701
http://www.northwestms.edu/

CONTACT Gary Spears, President
Telephone: 662-562-3200

GENERAL INFORMATION Public Institution. Founded 1927. **Accreditation:** Regional (SACS/CC); funeral service (ABFSE). **Total program enrollment: 5435.**

PROGRAM(S) OFFERED
• Administrative Assistant and Secretarial Science, General *4 students enrolled* • Autobody/Collision and Repair Technology/Technician *9 students enrolled* • Automobile/Automotive Mechanics Technology/Technician • Cosmetology/Cosmetologist, General *39 students enrolled* • Emergency Medical Technology/Technician (EMT Paramedic) • Licensed Practical/Vocational Nurse Training (LPN, LVN, Cert, Dipl, AAS) *95 students enrolled* • Nurse/Nursing Assistant/

Aide and Patient Care Assistant *9 students enrolled* • Surgical Technology/Technologist *10 students enrolled* • Truck and Bus Driver/Commercial Vehicle Operation • Welding Technology/Welder *12 students enrolled*

STUDENT SERVICES Academic or career counseling, employment services for current students, placement services for program completers, remedial services.

Pearl River Community College

101 Highway 11 North, Poplarville, MS 39470
http://www.prcc.edu/

CONTACT William Lewis, President
Telephone: 601-403-1000

GENERAL INFORMATION Public Institution. Founded 1909. **Accreditation:** Regional (SACS/CC); dental assisting (ADA); dental hygiene (ADA); medical laboratory technology (NAACLS); physical therapy assisting (APTA); radiologic technology: radiography (JRCERT); surgical technology (ARCST). **Total program enrollment: 3718.**

PROGRAM(S) OFFERED
• Administrative Assistant and Secretarial Science, General *23 students enrolled* • Barbering/Barber *16 students enrolled* • Computer Programming, Specific Applications *11 students enrolled* • Cosmetology/Cosmetologist, General *17 students enrolled* • Dental Assisting/Assistant *12 students enrolled* • Licensed Practical/Vocational Nurse Training (LPN, LVN, Cert, Dipl, AAS) *60 students enrolled* • Respiratory Care Therapy/Therapist *20 students enrolled* • Surgical Technology/Technologist *20 students enrolled* • Welding Technology/Welder *54 students enrolled*

STUDENT SERVICES Academic or career counseling, employment services for current students, placement services for program completers, remedial services.

Southwest Mississippi Community College

College Drive, Summit, MS 39666
http://www.smcc.cc.ms.us/

CONTACT Oliver Young, President
Telephone: 601-276-2000

GENERAL INFORMATION Public Institution. Founded 1918. **Accreditation:** Regional (SACS/CC). **Total program enrollment: 1638.**

PROGRAM(S) OFFERED
• Administrative Assistant and Secretarial Science, General *1 student enrolled* • Automobile/Automotive Mechanics Technology/Technician *3 students enrolled* • Carpentry/Carpenter *6 students enrolled* • Computer Systems Networking and Telecommunications *1 student enrolled* • Cosmetology/Cosmetologist, General *25 students enrolled* • Heating, Air Conditioning, Ventilation and Refrigeration Maintenance Technology/Technician (HAC, HACR, HVAC, HVACR) *3 students enrolled* • Licensed Practical/Vocational Nurse Training (LPN, LVN, Cert, Dipl, AAS) *48 students enrolled* • Massage Therapy/Therapeutic Massage *5 students enrolled* • Nurse/Nursing Assistant/Aide and Patient Care Assistant *18 students enrolled* • Welding Technology/Welder *11 students enrolled*

STUDENT SERVICES Academic or career counseling, employment services for current students, placement services for program completers, remedial services.

Traxlers School of Hair

2845 Suncrest Drive, Jackson, MS 39212

CONTACT Thomas V. Traxlers, President
Telephone: 601-371-0226

GENERAL INFORMATION Private Institution. **Total program enrollment: 54.**

Traxlers School of Hair (continued)

PROGRAM(S) OFFERED
• **Barbering/Barber** *1500 hrs./$8110* • **Cosmetology, Barber/Styling, and Nail Instructor** *10 hrs./$5250*

STUDENT SERVICES Placement services for program completers.

University of Mississippi Medical Center

2500 North State Street, Jackson, MS 39216-4505
http://www.umc.edu/

CONTACT Daniel W. Jones, Vice Chancellor
Telephone: 601-984-1000

GENERAL INFORMATION Public Institution. Founded 1955. **Accreditation:** Regional (SACS/CC); cytotechnology (ASC); dental hygiene (ADA); health information administration (AHIMA); medical technology (NAACLS). **Total program enrollment:** 1960. **Application fee:** $25.

PROGRAM(S) OFFERED
• **Nuclear Medical Technology/Technologist** *7 students enrolled*

STUDENT SERVICES Academic or career counseling.

Virginia College at Jackson

5360 I-55 North, Jackson, MS 39211
http://www.vc.edu/

CONTACT David Podesta, Campus President
Telephone: 601-977-0960

GENERAL INFORMATION Private Institution. Founded 2000. **Accreditation:** State accredited or approved. **Total program enrollment:** 850.

PROGRAM(S) OFFERED
• **Administrative Assistant and Secretarial Science, General** *48 hrs./$14,496* • **Computer Systems Networking and Telecommunications** *14 students enrolled* • **Computer and Information Sciences and Support Services, Other** • **Cosmetology/Cosmetologist, General** *75 hrs./$15,525* • **Information Technology** *96 hrs./$30,816* • **Medical Insurance Coding Specialist/Coder** *60 hrs./$18,620* • **Medical Office Assistant/Specialist** *60 hrs./$18,620* • **Medical Office Management/Administration** *12 students enrolled* • **Medical/Clinical Assistant** *108 students enrolled* • **Pharmacy Technician/Assistant** *60 hrs./$18,620*

STUDENT SERVICES Academic or career counseling, employment services for current students, placement services for program completers.

Virginia College Gulf Coast at Biloxi

920 Cedar Lake Road, Biloxi, MS 39532
http://www.vc.edu/site/campus.cfm?campus=gulfcoast

CONTACT Donald J. Newton, Campus President
Telephone: 228-392-2994 Ext. 3109

GENERAL INFORMATION Private Institution. **Total program enrollment:** 321. **Application fee:** $100.

PROGRAM(S) OFFERED
• **Administrative Assistant and Secretarial Science, General** *3 students enrolled* • **Medical Insurance Coding Specialist/Coder** *18 students enrolled* • **Medical/Clinical Assistant** *15 students enrolled* • **Pharmacy Technician/Assistant** *1 student enrolled*

STUDENT SERVICES Academic or career counseling, employment services for current students, placement services for program completers, remedial services.

NEW HAMPSHIRE

Continental Academie of Hair Design

102 Derry Street, Hudson, NH 03051
http://continentalacademie.net/

CONTACT Sylvia Donah, Business Manager
Telephone: 603-889-1614

GENERAL INFORMATION Private Institution. Founded 1973. **Total program enrollment:** 58. **Application fee:** $50.

PROGRAM(S) OFFERED
• **Cosmetology/Cosmetologist, General** *1550 hrs./$14,600*

STUDENT SERVICES Academic or career counseling, placement services for program completers.

Continental Academie of Hair Design

311 Lincoln Street, Manchester, NH 03103
http://continentalacademie.net/

CONTACT Sylvia Donah, Treasurer-Business Manager
Telephone: 603-622-5851

GENERAL INFORMATION Private Institution. **Total program enrollment:** 28. **Application fee:** $50.

PROGRAM(S) OFFERED
• **Cosmetology/Cosmetologist, General** *1550 hrs./$14,600*

STUDENT SERVICES Academic or career counseling, placement services for program completers.

Daniel Webster College

20 University Drive, Nashua, NH 03063-1300
http://www.dwc.edu/

CONTACT Dr. Robert E. Myers, President
Telephone: 603-577-6000

GENERAL INFORMATION Private Institution. Founded 1965. **Accreditation:** Regional (NEASC/NEASCCIHE). **Total program enrollment:** 919. **Application fee:** $35.

PROGRAM(S) OFFERED
• **Computer Programming/Programmer, General** *2 students enrolled* • **Computer Systems Networking and Telecommunications** *3 students enrolled*

STUDENT SERVICES Academic or career counseling, employment services for current students, placement services for program completers, remedial services.

Empire Beauty School–Hooksett

1328 Hooksett Road, Hooksett, NH 03106
http://www.empirebeautyschools.com

CONTACT Norman Langlois, President
Telephone: 603-792-1400

GENERAL INFORMATION Private Institution. **Total program enrollment:** 148. **Application fee:** $50.

PROGRAM(S) OFFERED
• **Cosmetology/Cosmetologist, General** *1500 hrs./$17,000*

STUDENT SERVICES Placement services for program completers.

Empire Beauty School–Laconia

556 Main Street, Laconia, NH 03246
http://empirebeautyschools.com/

CONTACT Norman Langlois, Chief Executive Officer
Telephone: 603-524-8777

GENERAL INFORMATION Private Institution. **Total program enrollment:** 78. **Application fee:** $50.

PROGRAM(S) OFFERED
• **Aesthetician/Esthetician and Skin Care Specialist** *600 hrs./$8000*
• **Cosmetology/Cosmetologist, General** *1500 hrs./$17,000*

STUDENT SERVICES Placement services for program completers.

Empire Beauty School–Portsmouth

2545 Lafayette Road, Portsmouth, NH 03801
http://www.empirebeautyschools.com

CONTACT Norman Langlois, President
Telephone: 603-433-6664

GENERAL INFORMATION Private Institution. **Total program enrollment:** 82. **Application fee:** $50.

PROGRAM(S) OFFERED
• **Aesthetician/Esthetician and Skin Care Specialist** *600 hrs./$8000*
• **Cosmetology/Cosmetologist, General** *1500 hrs./$17,000*

STUDENT SERVICES Placement services for program completers.

Empire Beauty School–Somersworth

362 Route 108, Somersworth, NH 03878
http://empirebeautyschools.com/

CONTACT Norman Langlois, Chief Executive Office
Telephone: 603-692-1515

GENERAL INFORMATION Private Institution. **Total program enrollment:** 103. **Application fee:** $50.

PROGRAM(S) OFFERED
• **Barbering/Barber** *900 hrs./$8495* • **Cosmetology/Cosmetologist, General** *1500 hrs./$17,000*

STUDENT SERVICES Placement services for program completers.

Esthetics Institute at Concord Academy

20 South Main Street, Concord, NH 03301
http://www.estheticsinstitute.net/

CONTACT Judith C. Montore, President Owner
Telephone: 603-224-2211

GENERAL INFORMATION Private Institution. Founded 1981. **Total program enrollment:** 6. **Application fee:** $75.

PROGRAM(S) OFFERED
• **Aesthetician/Esthetician and Skin Care Specialist** *300 hrs./$4530*

Franklin Pierce University

40 University Drive, Rindge, NH 03461-0060
http://www.franklinpierce.edu/

CONTACT George J. Hagerty, President
Telephone: 603-899-4000

GENERAL INFORMATION Private Institution. Founded 1962. **Accreditation:** Regional (NEASC/NEASCCIHE). **Total program enrollment:** 1855.

STUDENT SERVICES Academic or career counseling, employment services for current students, placement services for program completers, remedial services.

Hesser College, Manchester

3 Sundial Avenue, Manchester, NH 03103-7245
http://www.manchester.hesser.edu/

CONTACT Dr. Harold Griffin, President
Telephone: 603-668-6660

GENERAL INFORMATION Private Institution. Founded 1900. **Accreditation:** Regional (NEASC/CVTCI); medical assisting (AAMAE); physical therapy assisting (APTA). **Total program enrollment:** 1868. **Application fee:** $20.

PROGRAM(S) OFFERED
• **Business/Office Automation/Technology/Data Entry** • **Data Entry/Microcomputer Applications, General** • **Education, Other** *14 students enrolled* • **Information Technology** • **Interior Design** • **Legal Assistant/Paralegal** • **Massage Therapy/Therapeutic Massage** *56 students enrolled* • **Medical Office Management/Administration** • **Medical/Clinical Assistant** *163 students enrolled*

STUDENT SERVICES Academic or career counseling, employment services for current students, placement services for program completers, remedial services.

Keene Beauty Academy

800 Park Avenue, Keene, NH 03431
http://www.keenebeautyacademy.com/

CONTACT Cara D. Calomb, Co-Owner
Telephone: 603-357-3736

GENERAL INFORMATION Private Institution. Founded 1964. **Total program enrollment:** 44. **Application fee:** $100.

PROGRAM(S) OFFERED
• **Cosmetology and Related Personal Grooming Arts, Other** *4 students enrolled*
• **Cosmetology/Cosmetologist, General** *1500 hrs./$14,875*

STUDENT SERVICES Placement services for program completers.

Lebanon College

1 Court Street, Suite 200, Lebanon, NH 03766
http://www.lebanoncollege.edu/

CONTACT Donald Wenz, President
Telephone: 603-448-2445 Ext. 101

GENERAL INFORMATION Private Institution. **Total program enrollment:** 57. **Application fee:** $40.

PROGRAM(S) OFFERED
• **Accounting** *1 student enrolled* • **Business Administration and Management, General** • **Commercial and Advertising Art** • **Computer Programming/Programmer, General** • **Computer and Information Sciences, General** • **Education, Other** • **Medical Illustration/Medical Illustrator** *1 student enrolled* • **Medical Insurance Coding Specialist/Coder** *3 students enrolled* • **Medical Office Assistant/Specialist** • **Medical Reception/Receptionist** • **Photography** *1 student enrolled* • **Security and Protective Services, Other** • **Teacher Assistant/Aide**

STUDENT SERVICES Academic or career counseling.

Manchester Community College

1066 Front Street, Manchester, NH 03102-8518
http://www.manchester.nhctc.edu/

CONTACT Darlene G. Miller, President
Telephone: 603-668-6706

GENERAL INFORMATION Public Institution. Founded 1945. **Accreditation:** Regional (NEASC/NEASCCIHE); medical assisting (AAMAE); surgical technology (ARCST). **Total program enrollment:** 755. **Application fee:** $10.

Manchester Community College (continued)

PROGRAM(S) OFFERED

• **Accounting** *3 students enrolled* • **Administrative Assistant and Secretarial Science, General** *1 student enrolled* • **Architectural Engineering Technology/Technician** *5 students enrolled* • **Business Administration and Management, General** *6 students enrolled* • **Carpentry/Carpenter** *1 student enrolled* • **Early Childhood Education and Teaching** *1 student enrolled* • **Graphic and Printing Equipment Operator, General Production** *1 student enrolled* • **Health and Physical Education/Fitness, Other** *1 student enrolled* • **Heating, Air Conditioning, Ventilation and Refrigeration Maintenance Technology/Technician (HAC, HACR, HVAC, HVACR)** *13 students enrolled* • **Medical Administrative/Executive Assistant and Medical Secretary** *2 students enrolled* • **Medical Insurance Coding Specialist/Coder** *4 students enrolled* • **Medical/Clinical Assistant** *4 students enrolled* • **Phlebotomy/Phlebotomist** *4 students enrolled* • **Welding Technology/Welder** *4 students enrolled*

STUDENT SERVICES Academic or career counseling, daycare for children of students, employment services for current students, placement services for program completers, remedial services.

McIntosh College

23 Cataract Avenue, Dover, NH 03820-3990
http://www.mcintoshcollege.edu/

CONTACT Richard E. Farmer, President
Telephone: 603-742-1234

GENERAL INFORMATION Private Institution. Founded 1896. **Accreditation:** Regional (NEASC/CVTCI). **Total program enrollment:** 182. **Application fee:** $50.

PROGRAM(S) OFFERED

• **Accounting** • **Commercial and Advertising Art** • **Computer and Information Sciences and Support Services, Other** • **Cooking and Related Culinary Arts, General** *16 students enrolled* • **Massage Therapy/Therapeutic Massage** *43 students enrolled* • **Medical Administrative/Executive Assistant and Medical Secretary** • **Medical/Clinical Assistant** • **Tourism and Travel Services Management**

STUDENT SERVICES Academic or career counseling, employment services for current students, placement services for program completers, remedial services.

Michael's School of Hair Design and Esthetics

533 Elm Street, Manchester, NH 03101

CONTACT Michael G. Kapos, Owner
Telephone: 603-668-4300

GENERAL INFORMATION Private Institution. Founded 1972. **Total program enrollment:** 143. **Application fee:** $150.

PROGRAM(S) OFFERED

• **Aesthetician/Esthetician and Skin Care Specialist** *600 hrs./$10,980* • **Barbering/Barber** *1500 hrs./$10,350* • **Cosmetology, Barber/Styling, and Nail Instructor** *1000 hrs./$6850* • **Cosmetology/Cosmetologist, General** *1500 hrs./$17,456* • **Nail Technician/Specialist and Manicurist** *300 hrs./$2450*

STUDENT SERVICES Academic or career counseling, employment services for current students, placement services for program completers.

New England School of Hair Design

12 Interchange Drive, West Lebanon, NH 03784
http://www.neschoolofhairdesign.com/

CONTACT Gary Trottier, President
Telephone: 603-298-5199

GENERAL INFORMATION Private Institution. Founded 1974. **Total program enrollment:** 40. **Application fee:** $100.

PROGRAM(S) OFFERED

• **Cosmetology, Barber/Styling, and Nail Instructor** *800 hrs./$7728* • **Cosmetology/Cosmetologist, General** *1500 hrs./$16,168* • **Nail Technician/Specialist and Manicurist** *300 hrs./$2898*

STUDENT SERVICES Academic or career counseling, placement services for program completers.

New Hampshire Community Technical College, Berlin/Laconia

2020 Riverside Drive, Berlin, NH 03570-3717
http://www.berlin.nhctc.edu/

CONTACT Katharine Eneguess, President
Telephone: 603-752-1113

GENERAL INFORMATION Public Institution. Founded 1966. **Accreditation:** Regional (NEASC/NEASCCIHE). **Total program enrollment:** 352. **Application fee:** $10.

PROGRAM(S) OFFERED

• **Automobile/Automotive Mechanics Technology/Technician** *6 students enrolled* • **Business Administration and Management, General** • **Business/Office Automation/Technology/Data Entry** *3 students enrolled* • **Cartography** *1 student enrolled* • **Computer and Information Sciences, General** • **Culinary Arts/Chef Training** *2 students enrolled* • **Diesel Mechanics Technology/Technician** *2 students enrolled* • **Early Childhood Education and Teaching** *4 students enrolled* • **Health Services/Allied Health/Health Sciences, General** *3 students enrolled* • **Human Services, General** *1 student enrolled* • **Medical Transcription/Transcriptionist** *1 student enrolled* • **Medical/Clinical Assistant** *8 students enrolled* • **Special Education and Teaching, General** *10 students enrolled* • **Technical Teacher Education** *2 students enrolled*

STUDENT SERVICES Academic or career counseling, daycare for children of students, employment services for current students, placement services for program completers, remedial services.

New Hampshire Community Technical College, Nashua/Claremont

505 Amherst Street, Nashua, NH 03063-1026
http://www.ncctc.edu/

CONTACT Steven Budd, President
Telephone: 603-542-7744

GENERAL INFORMATION Public Institution. Founded 1967. **Accreditation:** Regional (NEASC/NEASCCIHE); engineering technology (ABET/TAC); health information technology (AHIMA); medical laboratory technology (NAACLS). **Total program enrollment:** 232. **Application fee:** $10.

PROGRAM(S) OFFERED

• **Accounting Technology/Technician and Bookkeeping** *2 students enrolled* • **Administrative Assistant and Secretarial Science, General** *1 student enrolled* • **Computer Systems Networking and Telecommunications** *1 student enrolled* • **Early Childhood Education and Teaching** *5 students enrolled* • **Licensed Practical/Vocational Nurse Training (LPN, LVN, Cert, Dipl, AAS)** *23 students enrolled* • **Machine Shop Technology/Assistant** *1 student enrolled* • **Massage Therapy/Therapeutic Massage** *19 students enrolled* • **Medical Administrative/Executive Assistant and Medical Secretary** *6 students enrolled* • **Medical/Clinical Assistant** *8 students enrolled* • **Nurse/Nursing Assistant/Aide and Patient Care Assistant** *29 students enrolled* • **Phlebotomy/Phlebotomist** *10 students enrolled*

STUDENT SERVICES Academic or career counseling, employment services for current students, placement services for program completers, remedial services.

New Hampshire Community Technical College, Stratham

277 Portsmouth Avenue, Stratham, NH 03885
http://www.stratham.nhctc.edu/

CONTACT Wildolfo Arvelo, President
Telephone: 603-775-2215

GENERAL INFORMATION Public Institution. **Total program enrollment:** 575. **Application fee:** $10.

PROGRAM(S) OFFERED
• **Accounting** 1 student enrolled • **Animation, Interactive Technology, Video Graphics and Special Effects** 10 students enrolled • **Automobile/Automotive Mechanics Technology/Technician** 2 students enrolled • **Biology Technician/Biotechnology Laboratory Technician** 6 students enrolled • **Business Administration and Management, General** 4 students enrolled • **Computer Science** 2 students enrolled • **Computer Systems Networking and Telecommunications** • **Early Childhood Education and Teaching** 4 students enrolled • **Medical Insurance Coding Specialist/Coder** 6 students enrolled

STUDENT SERVICES Academic or career counseling, employment services for current students, remedial services.

New Hampshire Institute for Therapeutic Arts

153 Lowell Road, Hudson, NH 03051
http://www.nhita.com/

CONTACT Patrick Ian Cowan, PhD, Executive Director
Telephone: 603-882-3022

GENERAL INFORMATION Private Institution. **Total program enrollment:** 47. **Application fee:** $35.

PROGRAM(S) OFFERED
• **Massage Therapy/Therapeutic Massage** 24 hrs./$10,500

STUDENT SERVICES Academic or career counseling, placement services for program completers.

New Hampshire Technical Institute

11 Institute Drive, Concord, NH 03301-7412
http://www.nhti.edu/

CONTACT Lynn Kilchenstein, President
Telephone: 603-271-6484

GENERAL INFORMATION Public Institution. Founded 1964. **Accreditation:** Regional (NEASC/NEASCCIHE); dental assisting (ADA); dental hygiene (ADA); emergency medical services (JRCEMTP); engineering technology (ABET/TAC); radiologic technology: radiography (JRCERT). **Total program enrollment:** 1790. **Application fee:** $10.

PROGRAM(S) OFFERED
• **Accounting** 9 students enrolled • **Business Administration and Management, General** 5 students enrolled • **CAD/CADD Drafting and/or Design Technology/Technician** 3 students enrolled • **Dental Assisting/Assistant** 25 students enrolled • **Diagnostic Medical Sonography/Sonographer and Ultrasound Technician** 7 students enrolled • **Early Childhood Education and Teaching** 2 students enrolled • **Education, General** 1 student enrolled • **Electrical, Electronic and Communications Engineering Technology/Technician** • **Hospitality Administration/Management, General** 4 students enrolled • **Hotel/Motel Administration/Management** 2 students enrolled • **Human Resources Management/Personnel Administration, General** • **Human Services, General** • **Information Technology** 5 students enrolled • **Landscaping and Groundskeeping** 5 students enrolled • **Legal Assistant/Paralegal** 10 students enrolled • **Licensed Practical/Vocational Nurse Training (LPN, LVN, Cert, Dipl, AAS)** 14 students enrolled • **Medical Insurance Coding Specialist/Coder** 9 students enrolled • **Medical Radiologic Technology/Science—Radiation Therapist** 1 student enrolled • **Medical Transcription/Transcriptionist** • **Small Business Administration/**

Management 2 students enrolled • **Special Education and Teaching, General** 2 students enrolled • **Substance Abuse/Addiction Counseling** 1 student enrolled • **Tourism and Travel Services Management**

STUDENT SERVICES Academic or career counseling, daycare for children of students, employment services for current students, placement services for program completers, remedial services.

Portsmouth Beauty School of Hair Design

138 Congress Street, Portsmouth, NH 03801-4084
http://www.portsmouthbeautyschool.com/

CONTACT Nicole Nardello Lawton, President
Telephone: 603-436-7775

GENERAL INFORMATION Private Institution. Founded 1961. **Total program enrollment:** 41.

PROGRAM(S) OFFERED
• **Cosmetology/Cosmetologist, General** 23 students enrolled • **Hair Styling/Stylist and Hair Design** 1500 hrs./$14,000

STUDENT SERVICES Academic or career counseling, employment services for current students, placement services for program completers.

St. Joseph School of Practical Nursing

5 Woodward Avenue, Nashua, NH 03060
http://www.sjhacademiccenter.org/

CONTACT Peter Davis, President/CEO
Telephone: 603-594-2567

GENERAL INFORMATION Private Institution (Affiliated with Roman Catholic Church). Founded 1964. **Total program enrollment:** 49. **Application fee:** $35.

PROGRAM(S) OFFERED
• **Licensed Practical/Vocational Nurse Training (LPN, LVN, Cert, Dipl, AAS)** 48 students enrolled

STUDENT SERVICES Academic or career counseling, remedial services.

Seacoast Career Schools

Jefferson Mill Building, 670 North Commercial Street, Manchester, NH 03101
http://www.seacoastcareerschools.com/

CONTACT David Palmer, School Director
Telephone: 603-624-7222

GENERAL INFORMATION Private Institution. **Total program enrollment:** 204. **Application fee:** $100.

PROGRAM(S) OFFERED
• **Massage Therapy/Therapeutic Massage** 44 hrs./$11,920 • **Medical Insurance Coding Specialist/Coder** 40 hrs./$11,920 • **Medical/Clinical Assistant** 40 hrs./$13,120

STUDENT SERVICES Academic or career counseling, placement services for program completers.

Southern New Hampshire University

2500 North River Road, Manchester, NH 03106-1045
http://www.snhu.edu/

CONTACT Paul J. Leblanc, President
Telephone: 603-668-2211

GENERAL INFORMATION Private Institution. Founded 1932. **Accreditation:** Regional (NEASC/NEASCCIHE). **Total program enrollment:** 4303. **Application fee:** $40.

STUDENT SERVICES Academic or career counseling, employment services for current students, placement services for program completers, remedial services.

NEW JERSEY

Academy of Massage Therapy

401 S. Van Brunt Street, # 204, Englewood, NJ 07631
http://academyofmassage.com/

CONTACT Arilanna Sukhdeo, Business Office Manager
Telephone: 201-568-3220

GENERAL INFORMATION Private Institution. **Total program enrollment:** 138. **Application fee:** $50.

PROGRAM(S) OFFERED
• **Massage Therapy/Therapeutic Massage** *614 hrs./$8500*

STUDENT SERVICES Academic or career counseling, employment services for current students, placement services for program completers.

Adult and Continuing Education–Bergen County Technical Schools

200 Hackensack Avenue, Adult Education Building, Hackensack, NJ 07601-6637
http://www.bergen.org/

CONTACT Robert J. Aloia, Superintendent
Telephone: 201-343-6000 Ext. 2288

GENERAL INFORMATION Public Institution. **Total program enrollment:** 104.

PROGRAM(S) OFFERED
• **Administrative Assistant and Secretarial Science, General** • **Carpentry/Carpenter** *819 hrs./$6965* • **Construction Trades, General** *819 hrs./$6965* • **Electrician** *1200 hrs./$10,450* • **General Office Occupations and Clerical Services** *600 hrs./$4975* • **Heating, Air Conditioning, Ventilation and Refrigeration Maintenance Technology/Technician (HAC, HACR, HVAC, HVACR)** *1053 hrs./$8995* • **Plumbing Technology/Plumber** *819 hrs./$6965*

STUDENT SERVICES Academic or career counseling, employment services for current students, placement services for program completers, remedial services.

Artistic Academy of Hair Design

2121 Broadway, Fairlawn, NJ 07410
http://www.artisticacademy.com/

CONTACT Carmen de Pasquale, President
Telephone: 973-656-1401 Ext. 0

GENERAL INFORMATION Private Institution. **Total program enrollment:** 180.

PROGRAM(S) OFFERED
• **Aesthetician/Esthetician and Skin Care Specialist** *600 hrs./$7170* • **Cosmetology/Cosmetologist, General** *1200 hrs./$13,945* • **Make-Up Artist/Specialist** *34 students enrolled* • **Teacher Education and Professional Development, Specific Subject Areas, Other** *4 students enrolled*

STUDENT SERVICES Academic or career counseling, placement services for program completers.

Berdan Institute

265 State Route 46, Totowa, NJ 07512
http://berdaninstitute.com/

CONTACT Duncan Anderson, Chief Executive Officer
Telephone: 973-837-1818 Ext. 204

GENERAL INFORMATION Private Institution. **Total program enrollment:** 383. **Application fee:** $50.

PROGRAM(S) OFFERED
• **Biotechnology** *980 hrs./$14,900* • **Dental Assisting/Assistant** *910 hrs./$13,700* • **Health and Medical Administrative Services, Other** *40 students enrolled* • **Health/Health Care Administration/Management** *750 hrs./$11,000* • **Massage Therapy/Therapeutic Massage** *750 hrs./$11,000* • **Medical Administrative/Executive Assistant and Medical Secretary** *910 hrs./$13,700* • **Medical Office Management/Administration** *14 students enrolled* • **Medical/Clinical Assistant** *910 hrs./$14,200* • **Pharmacy Technician/Assistant** *18 students enrolled*

STUDENT SERVICES Academic or career counseling, employment services for current students, placement services for program completers.

Bergen Community College

400 Paramus Road, Paramus, NJ 07652-1595
http://www.bergen.edu/

CONTACT G. Jeremiah Ryan, President
Telephone: 201-447-7200

GENERAL INFORMATION Public Institution. Founded 1965. **Accreditation:** Regional (MSA/CIHE); dental hygiene (ADA); diagnostic medical sonography (JRCEDMS); medical assisting (AAMAE); medical laboratory technology (NAACLS); physical therapy assisting (APTA); radiologic technology: radiography (JRCERT). **Total program enrollment:** 8455.

PROGRAM(S) OFFERED
• **American/United States Studies/Civilization** *1 student enrolled* • **Applied Horticulture/Horticultural Operations, General** *1 student enrolled* • **Culinary Arts/Chef Training** *3 students enrolled* • **Drafting and Design Technology/Technician, General** *2 students enrolled* • **Entrepreneurship/Entrepreneurial Studies** *1 student enrolled* • **Hospitality Administration/Management, General** *3 students enrolled* • **Kinesiology and Exercise Science** *3 students enrolled* • **Management Information Systems and Services, Other** *3 students enrolled* • **Manufacturing Technology/Technician** *2 students enrolled* • **Medical Administrative/Executive Assistant and Medical Secretary** *3 students enrolled* • **Medical Radiologic Technology/Science—Radiation Therapist** *10 students enrolled* • **Music, Other** *1 student enrolled* • **Surgical Technology/Technologist** *22 students enrolled*

STUDENT SERVICES Academic or career counseling, daycare for children of students, employment services for current students, placement services for program completers, remedial services.

Berkeley College

44 Rifle Camp Road, West Paterson, NJ 07424-3353
http://www.berkeleycollege.edu/

CONTACT Dr. Dario Cortes, President
Telephone: 973-278-5400

GENERAL INFORMATION Private Institution. Founded 1931. **Accreditation:** Regional (MSA/CIHE). **Total program enrollment:** 2942. **Application fee:** $50.

PROGRAM(S) OFFERED
• **General Office Occupations and Clerical Services**

STUDENT SERVICES Academic or career counseling, daycare for children of students, employment services for current students, placement services for program completers, remedial services.

Bloomfield College

467 Franklin Street, Bloomfield, NJ 07003-9981
http://www.bloomfield.edu/

CONTACT Richard A. Levao, President
Telephone: 973-748-9000

GENERAL INFORMATION Private Institution (Affiliated with Presbyterian Church (U.S.A.)). Founded 1868. **Accreditation:** Regional (MSA/CIHE). **Total program enrollment:** 1584. **Application fee:** $40.

STUDENT SERVICES Academic or career counseling, employment services for current students, placement services for program completers, remedial services.

Brookdale Community College

765 Newman Springs Road, Lincroft, NJ 07738-1597
http://www.brookdalecc.edu/

CONTACT Peter F. Burnham, President
Telephone: 732-224-2345

GENERAL INFORMATION Public Institution. Founded 1967. **Accreditation:** Regional (MSA/CIHE); radiologic technology: radiography (JRCERT). **Total program enrollment:** 8386. **Application fee:** $25.

PROGRAM(S) OFFERED
• **Automobile/Automotive Mechanics Technology/Technician** 2 students enrolled • **Baking and Pastry Arts/Baker/Pastry Chef** 8 students enrolled • **Business Operations Support and Secretarial Services, Other** 3 students enrolled • **Computer and Information Sciences, General** 1 student enrolled • **Culinary Arts/Chef Training** 8 students enrolled • **Dental Assisting/Assistant** 2 students enrolled • **E-Commerce/Electronic Commerce** 1 student enrolled • **Mechanical Drafting and Mechanical Drafting CAD/CADD** 8 students enrolled • **Ornamental Horticulture** 3 students enrolled • **Prepress/Desktop Publishing and Digital Imaging Design** 3 students enrolled

STUDENT SERVICES Academic or career counseling, daycare for children of students, employment services for current students, placement services for program completers, remedial services.

Burlington County College

601 Pemberton Browns Mills Road, Pemberton, NJ 08068
http://www.bcc.edu/

CONTACT Robert C. Messina, Jr., President
Telephone: 609-894-9311

GENERAL INFORMATION Public Institution. Founded 1966. **Accreditation:** Regional (MSA/CIHE); engineering technology (ABET/TAC); health information technology (AHIMA). **Total program enrollment:** 4594. **Application fee:** $20.

PROGRAM(S) OFFERED
• **Criminal Justice/Police Science** 1 student enrolled • **Sign Language Interpretation and Translation** 1 student enrolled

STUDENT SERVICES Academic or career counseling, employment services for current students, placement services for program completers, remedial services.

Caldwell College

9 Ryerson Avenue, Caldwell, NJ 07006-6195
http://www.caldwell.edu/

CONTACT Sr. Patrice Werner, OP, President
Telephone: 973-618-3000

GENERAL INFORMATION Private Institution. Founded 1939. **Accreditation:** Regional (MSA/CIHE). **Total program enrollment:** 1299. **Application fee:** $40.

STUDENT SERVICES Academic or career counseling, employment services for current students, placement services for program completers, remedial services.

Camden County College

PO Box 200, Blackwood, NJ 08012-0200
http://www.camdencc.edu/

CONTACT Dr. Raymond A. Yannuzzi, President
Telephone: 856-227-7200

GENERAL INFORMATION Public Institution. Founded 1967. **Accreditation:** Regional (MSA/CIHE); dental assisting (ADA); dental hygiene (ADA); medical laboratory technology (NAACLS); ophthalmic dispensing (COA). **Total program enrollment:** 7799.

PROGRAM(S) OFFERED
• **Accounting and Related Services, Other** 2 students enrolled • **Administrative Assistant and Secretarial Science, General** 1 student enrolled • **Automobile/Automotive Mechanics Technology/Technician** 4 students enrolled • **Computer and Information Sciences and Support Services, Other** 1 student enrolled • **Computer and Information Sciences, General** 3 students enrolled • **Corrections and Criminal Justice, Other** 1 student enrolled • **Criminal Justice/Police Science** 46 students enrolled • **Dental Assisting/Assistant** 13 students enrolled • **Design and Applied Arts, Other** 1 student enrolled • **Drafting and Design Technology/Technician, General** 2 students enrolled • **Fire Science/Firefighting** 3 students enrolled • **Fire Services Administration** 2 students enrolled • **Forensic Science and Technology** 2 students enrolled • **Health Information/Medical Records Technology/Technician** 5 students enrolled • **Health and Physical Education, General** 12 students enrolled • **Hotel/Motel Administration/Management** 1 student enrolled • **Massage Therapy/Therapeutic Massage** 1 student enrolled • **Opticianry/Ophthalmic Dispensing Optician** 1 student enrolled • **Prepress/Desktop Publishing and Digital Imaging Design** 4 students enrolled • **Recording Arts Technology/Technician** 12 students enrolled • **Surgical Technology/Technologist** 11 students enrolled • **Teacher Assistant/Aide** 10 students enrolled • **Web Page, Digital/Multimedia and Information Resources Design** 3 students enrolled

STUDENT SERVICES Academic or career counseling, daycare for children of students, employment services for current students, placement services for program completers, remedial services.

Capri Institute of Hair Design

268 Brick Boulevard, Brick, NJ 08723
http://www.capriinstitute.com/

CONTACT Bridget Damiano, Director
Telephone: 800-232-2774

GENERAL INFORMATION Private Institution. Founded 1982. **Total program enrollment:** 162.

PROGRAM(S) OFFERED
• **Aesthetician/Esthetician and Skin Care Specialist** 600 hrs./$7350 • **Cosmetology/Cosmetologist, General** 1200 hrs./$12,510 • **Make-Up Artist/Specialist** 32 students enrolled • **Nail Technician/Specialist and Manicurist** 300 hrs./$2550

STUDENT SERVICES Academic or career counseling, employment services for current students, placement services for program completers, remedial services.

Capri Institute of Hair Design

1595 Main Avenue, Clifton, NJ 07011
http://www.capriinstitute.com/

CONTACT Bridget Damiano, Director
Telephone: 800-232-2774

GENERAL INFORMATION Private Institution. Founded 1962. **Total program enrollment:** 116.

PROGRAM(S) OFFERED
• **Aesthetician/Esthetician and Skin Care Specialist** 600 hrs./$7350 • **Cosmetology/Cosmetologist, General** 1200 hrs./$12,510 • **Nail Technician/Specialist and Manicurist** 300 hrs./$2550

STUDENT SERVICES Academic or career counseling, employment services for current students, placement services for program completers, remedial services.

Capri Institute of Hair Design

660 N. Michigan Avenue, Kenilworth, NJ 07033
http://www.capriinstitute.com/

CONTACT Bridget Damiano, Director
Telephone: 800-232-2774

GENERAL INFORMATION Private Institution. **Total program enrollment:** 79.

PROGRAM(S) OFFERED
• **Aesthetician/Esthetician and Skin Care Specialist** 600 hrs./$7350
• **Cosmetology/Cosmetologist, General** 1200 hrs./$12,510 • **Make-Up Artist/Specialist** 24 students enrolled • **Nail Technician/Specialist and Manicurist** 300 hrs./$2550

STUDENT SERVICES Academic or career counseling, employment services for current students, placement services for program completers, remedial services.

Capri Institute of Hair Design

615 Winter Avenue, Paramus, NJ 07652
http://www.capriinstitute.com/

CONTACT Bridget Damiano, Director
Telephone: 800-232-2774

GENERAL INFORMATION Private Institution. Founded 1980. **Total program enrollment:** 145.

PROGRAM(S) OFFERED
• **Aesthetician/Esthetician and Skin Care Specialist** 600 hrs./$7350
• **Cosmetology/Cosmetologist, General** 1200 hrs./$12,510 • **Make-Up Artist/Specialist** 27 students enrolled • **Nail Technician/Specialist and Manicurist** 300 hrs./$2550

STUDENT SERVICES Academic or career counseling, employment services for current students, placement services for program completers, remedial services.

Capri Institute of Hair Design

45 Sunset Street, Route 10 East, Succasunna, NJ 07876
http://www.capriinstitute.com/

CONTACT Bridget Damiano, Director
Telephone: 800-232-2774

GENERAL INFORMATION Private Institution. **Total program enrollment:** 45.

PROGRAM(S) OFFERED
• **Aesthetician/Esthetician and Skin Care Specialist** 600 hrs./$7350
• **Cosmetology and Related Personal Grooming Arts, Other** 5 students enrolled
• **Cosmetology/Cosmetologist, General** 1200 hrs./$12,510 • **Make-Up Artist/Specialist** 7 students enrolled • **Nail Technician/Specialist and Manicurist** 300 hrs./$2550

STUDENT SERVICES Academic or career counseling, employment services for current students, placement services for program completers, remedial services.

Central Career School

126 Corporate Boulevard, South Plainfield, NJ 07080
http://centralcareer.com/

CONTACT Timothy M. Rodgers, Director
Telephone: 908-412-8600

GENERAL INFORMATION Private Institution. **Total program enrollment:** 72.

PROGRAM(S) OFFERED
• **Computer and Information Sciences, General** 34 students enrolled • **Data Entry/Microcomputer Applications, General** 600 hrs./$4245 • **Dental Assisting/Assistant** 650 hrs./$6995 • **Health/Health Care Administration/Management** 600 hrs./$4245 • **Medical Administrative/Executive Assistant and Medical Secretary** 16 students enrolled

STUDENT SERVICES Academic or career counseling, employment services for current students, placement services for program completers, remedial services.

The Chubb Institute–Cherry Hill

2100 Route 38 & Mall Drive, Cherry Hill, NJ 08002
http://www.chubbinstitute.edu/

CONTACT Deanna West, Campus President
Telephone: 856-755-4800

GENERAL INFORMATION Private Institution. **Total program enrollment:** 583. **Application fee:** $50.

PROGRAM(S) OFFERED
• **Computer and Information Systems Security** 1200 hrs./$17,709 • **Massage Therapy/Therapeutic Massage** 820 hrs./$11,064 • **Medical Insurance Specialist/Medical Biller** 720 hrs./$10,985 • **Medical/Clinical Assistant** 746 hrs./$11,350 • **Web Page, Digital/Multimedia and Information Resources Design** 1200 hrs./$18,149

STUDENT SERVICES Placement services for program completers.

The Chubb Institute–Jersey City

40 Journal Square, 1st Floor, Jersey City, NJ 07306
http://www.chubbinstitute.com/

CONTACT Valeria Yancey, Campus President
Telephone: 201-876-3800

GENERAL INFORMATION Private Institution. **Total program enrollment:** 1009. **Application fee:** $50.

PROGRAM(S) OFFERED
• **Computer and Information Systems Security** 1200 hrs./$17,709 • **Massage Therapy/Therapeutic Massage** 820 hrs./$11,064 • **Medical Insurance Specialist/Medical Biller** 720 hrs./$10,985 • **Medical/Clinical Assistant** 746 hrs./$11,350 • **Web Page, Digital/Multimedia and Information Resources Design** 1200 hrs./$18,149

STUDENT SERVICES Placement services for program completers.

The Chubb Institute–North Brunswick

US Route 1, South, North Brunswick, NJ 08902
http://www.chubbinstitute.edu/

CONTACT Maria Veglia, Campus President
Telephone: 732-448-2600

GENERAL INFORMATION Private Institution. **Total program enrollment:** 680. **Application fee:** $50.

PROGRAM(S) OFFERED
• **Computer and Information Systems Security** 1200 hrs./$18,750 • **Massage Therapy/Therapeutic Massage** 51 students enrolled • **Mechanical Drafting and Mechanical Drafting CAD/CADD** 1200 hrs./$18,125 • **Medical Insurance Specialist/Medical Biller** 720 hrs./$10,985 • **Medical/Clinical Assistant** 746 hrs./$11,146 • **Surgical Technology/Technologist** 1340 hrs./$21,968 • **Web Page, Digital/Multimedia and Information Resources Design** 1200 hrs./$18,149

STUDENT SERVICES Placement services for program completers.

The Chubb Institute–Parsippany

8 Sylvan Way, Parsippany, NJ 07054
http://www.chubbinstitute.edu/

CONTACT Diane Gilles, Campus President
Telephone: 973-630-4900

GENERAL INFORMATION Private Institution. **Total program enrollment:** 501. **Application fee:** $50.

PROGRAM(S) OFFERED
• **Computer and Information Systems Security** *1200 hrs./$18,750* • **Massage Therapy/Therapeutic Massage** *820 hrs./$11,064* • **Mechanical Drafting and Mechanical Drafting CAD/CADD** *1200 hrs./$18,125* • **Medical Insurance Specialist/Medical Biller** *720 hrs./$10,985* • **Medical/Clinical Assistant** *746 hrs./$11,146* • **Web Page, Digital/Multimedia and Information Resources Design** *1200 hrs./$18,149*

STUDENT SERVICES Placement services for program completers.

College of Saint Elizabeth

2 Convent Road, Morristown, NJ 07960-6989
http://www.cse.edu/

CONTACT Sr. Francis Raftery, President
Telephone: 973-290-4000

GENERAL INFORMATION Private Institution. Founded 1899. **Accreditation:** Regional (MSA/CIHE); dietetics: postbaccalaureate internship (ADtA/CAADE); home economics (AAFCS). **Total program enrollment:** 889. **Application fee:** $35.

PROGRAM(S) OFFERED
• **Theological and Ministerial Studies, Other** *14 students enrolled* • **Youth Ministry** *2 students enrolled*

STUDENT SERVICES Academic or career counseling, employment services for current students, placement services for program completers, remedial services.

Concorde School of Hair Design

Route 35 and Sunset Avenue, Ocean Township, NJ 07712
http://www.naturalmotionmemberschools.com/

CONTACT Michael Bouman, President/COO
Telephone: 570-429-4321 Ext. 2414

GENERAL INFORMATION Private Institution. Founded 1981. **Total program enrollment:** 94. **Application fee:** $100.

PROGRAM(S) OFFERED
• **Aesthetician/Esthetician and Skin Care Specialist** *600 hrs./$5670*
• **Cosmetology/Cosmetologist, General** *1200 hrs./$12,590* • **Nail Technician/Specialist and Manicurist** *10 students enrolled*

STUDENT SERVICES Academic or career counseling, employment services for current students, placement services for program completers.

Concorde School of Hair Design–Bloomfield

9-15 Ward Street, Bloomfield, NJ 07003
http://naturalmotionmemberschools.com/

CONTACT Michael Bouman, President/COO
Telephone: 570-429-4321 Ext. 2414

GENERAL INFORMATION Private Institution. Founded 1989. **Total program enrollment:** 85. **Application fee:** $100.

PROGRAM(S) OFFERED
• **Cosmetology/Cosmetologist, General** *1200 hrs./$12,590*

STUDENT SERVICES Academic or career counseling, employment services for current students, placement services for program completers, remedial services.

Cooper Health System Center for Allied Health Education

1 Cooper Plaza, Camden, NJ 08103
http://www.cooperhealth.org/

CONTACT John P. Sheridan, President and Chief Executive
Telephone: 856-342-2000

GENERAL INFORMATION Private Institution. **Total program enrollment:** 45. **Application fee:** $35.

PROGRAM(S) OFFERED
• **Medical Radiologic Technology/Science—Radiation Therapist** *10 students enrolled*

STUDENT SERVICES Academic or career counseling, remedial services.

Cortiva Institute—Somerset School of Massage Therapy

180 Centennial Avenue, Piscataway, NJ 08854
http://www.cortiva.com/locations/ssmt/

CONTACT Michele Garbowski, Director
Telephone: 732-885-3400

GENERAL INFORMATION Private Institution. **Total program enrollment:** 78. **Application fee:** $100.

PROGRAM(S) OFFERED
• **Massage Therapy/Therapeutic Massage** *50 hrs./$9220*

STUDENT SERVICES Academic or career counseling, employment services for current students, placement services for program completers, remedial services.

County College of Morris

214 Center Grove Road, Randolph, NJ 07869-2086
http://www.ccm.edu/

CONTACT Edward Yaw, President
Telephone: 973-328-5000

GENERAL INFORMATION Public Institution. Founded 1966. **Accreditation:** Regional (MSA/CIHE); engineering technology (ABET/TAC); radiologic technology: radiography (JRCERT). **Total program enrollment:** 4760. **Application fee:** $30.

PROGRAM(S) OFFERED
• **CAD/CADD Drafting and/or Design Technology/Technician** *2 students enrolled*
• **Child Care Provider/Assistant** *2 students enrolled*

STUDENT SERVICES Academic or career counseling, daycare for children of students, employment services for current students, placement services for program completers, remedial services.

Cumberland County College

PO Box 1500, College Drive, Vineland, NJ 08362-1500
http://www.cccnj.edu/

CONTACT Kenneth L. Ender, President
Telephone: 856-691-8600

GENERAL INFORMATION Public Institution. Founded 1963. **Accreditation:** Regional (MSA/CIHE); radiologic technology: radiography (JRCERT). **Total program enrollment:** 2151. **Application fee:** $25.

PROGRAM(S) OFFERED
• **Accounting Technology/Technician and Bookkeeping** 3 *students enrolled* • **Administrative Assistant and Secretarial Science, General** 3 *students enrolled* • **Aquaculture** 2 *students enrolled* • **Business Administration and Management, General** 2 *students enrolled* • **Drafting and Design Technology/Technician, General** 2 *students enrolled* • **Engineering-Related Technologies, Other** 1 *student enrolled* • **Graphic and Printing Equipment Operator, General Production** 2 *students enrolled* • **Ornamental Horticulture** 2 *students enrolled*

STUDENT SERVICES Academic or career counseling, employment services for current students, placement services for program completers, remedial services.

Divers Academy International

2500 South Broadway, Camden, NJ 08104-2431
http://www.diversacademy.com/

CONTACT Tamara M. Brown, President/Director
Telephone: 856-404-6100 Ext. 17

GENERAL INFORMATION Private Institution. Founded 1975. **Total program enrollment:** 93. **Application fee:** $25.

PROGRAM(S) OFFERED
• **Diver, Professional and Instructor** 720 *hrs./$21,500*

STUDENT SERVICES Employment services for current students, placement services for program completers.

Dover Business College

East 81 Route 4, W, Paramus, NJ 07652
http://www.doverbusinesscollege.org/

CONTACT Timothy D. Luing, President
Telephone: 973-546-0123

GENERAL INFORMATION Private Institution. **Total program enrollment:** 511. **Application fee:** $25.

PROGRAM(S) OFFERED
• **Accounting and Business/Management** 10 *students enrolled* • **Accounting** 12 *students enrolled* • **Business Administration and Management, General** 35 *students enrolled* • **Data Entry/Microcomputer Applications, General** 18 *students enrolled* • **Executive Assistant/Executive Secretary** 3 *students enrolled* • **Licensed Practical/Vocational Nurse Training (LPN, LVN, Cert, Dipl, AAS)** 75 *students enrolled* • **Massage Therapy/Therapeutic Massage** 12 *students enrolled* • **Medical Insurance Coding Specialist/Coder** 19 *students enrolled* • **Medical/Clinical Assistant** 76 *students enrolled* • **Nurse/Nursing Assistant/Aide and Patient Care Assistant** 31 *students enrolled* • **Surgical Technology/Technologist** 29 *students enrolled* • **System Administration/Administrator** 16 *students enrolled*

STUDENT SERVICES Academic or career counseling, employment services for current students, placement services for program completers.

Drake College of Business

125 Broad Street, Elizabeth, NJ 07201
http://www.drakecollege.com/

CONTACT Ziad Fadel, CEO
Telephone: 908-352-5509

GENERAL INFORMATION Private Institution. **Total program enrollment:** 551.

PROGRAM(S) OFFERED
• **Allied Health and Medical Assisting Services, Other** 381 *students enrolled* • **Management Information Systems, General** 183 *students enrolled*

STUDENT SERVICES Academic or career counseling, placement services for program completers, remedial services.

Empire Beauty School–Cherry Hill

2100 State Highway #38, Cherry Hill, NJ 08002
http://www.empire.edu/

CONTACT Michael Bouman, President
Telephone: 570-429-4321 Ext. 2414

GENERAL INFORMATION Private Institution. **Total program enrollment:** 133. **Application fee:** $100.

PROGRAM(S) OFFERED
• **Cosmetology, Barber/Styling, and Nail Instructor** 600 *hrs./$6900* • **Cosmetology/Cosmetologist, General** 1200 *hrs./$15,050* • **Technical Teacher Education** 12 *students enrolled*

STUDENT SERVICES Placement services for program completers.

Empire Beauty School–Laurel Springs

1305 Blackwood-Clementon Road, Laurel Springs, NJ 08021-5602
http://www.empire.edu/

CONTACT Michael Bouman, President
Telephone: 800-223-3271

GENERAL INFORMATION Private Institution. **Total program enrollment:** 65. **Application fee:** $100.

PROGRAM(S) OFFERED
• **Cosmetology/Cosmetologist, General** 1200 *hrs./$15,050* • **Technical Teacher Education** 2 *students enrolled*

STUDENT SERVICES Placement services for program completers.

Empire Beauty School–Lawrenceville

1719 Brunswick Pike, Lawrenceville, NJ 08648
http://www.empire.edu/

CONTACT Michael Bouman, President
Telephone: 800-223-3271

GENERAL INFORMATION Private Institution. **Total program enrollment:** 121. **Application fee:** $100.

PROGRAM(S) OFFERED
• **Cosmetology/Cosmetologist, General** 1200 *hrs./$15,050* • **Technical Teacher Education** 2 *students enrolled*

STUDENT SERVICES Placement services for program completers.

Engine City Technical Institute

2365 Route 22 West, Union, NJ 07083
http://www.enginecitytech.com/

CONTACT James Rasmussen, School Director
Telephone: 800-305-3487 Ext. 276

GENERAL INFORMATION Private Institution. **Total program enrollment:** 182. **Application fee:** $100.

PROGRAM(S) OFFERED
• **Diesel Mechanics Technology/Technician** 220 *hrs./$3100*

STUDENT SERVICES Academic or career counseling, employment services for current students, placement services for program completers.

Essex County College

303 University Avenue, Newark, NJ 07102-1798
http://www.essex.edu/

CONTACT A. Zachary Yamba, President
Telephone: 973-877-3000

GENERAL INFORMATION Public Institution. Founded 1966. **Accreditation:** Regional (MSA/CIHE); ophthalmic dispensing (COA); physical therapy assisting (APTA); radiologic technology: radiography (JRCERT). **Total program enrollment: 6962. Application fee: $25.**

PROGRAM(S) OFFERED
● **Administrative Assistant and Secretarial Science, General** *2 students enrolled* ● **Art/Art Studies, General** *1 student enrolled* ● **Chemical Technology/Technician** *1 student enrolled* ● **Computer and Information Sciences and Support Services, Other** *2 students enrolled* ● **Data Processing and Data Processing Technology/Technician** *1 student enrolled* ● **Dental Assisting/Assistant** *1 student enrolled* ● **Drafting and Design Technology/Technician, General** *4 students enrolled* ● **Legal Assistant/Paralegal** *4 students enrolled* ● **Licensed Practical/Vocational Nurse Training (LPN, LVN, Cert, Dipl, AAS)** *33 students enrolled* ● **Massage Therapy/Therapeutic Massage** *5 students enrolled*

STUDENT SERVICES Academic or career counseling, daycare for children of students, employment services for current students, placement services for program completers, remedial services.

European Academy of Cosmetology

1126 Morris Avenue, Union, NJ 07083
http://www.naturalmotionmemberschool.com/

CONTACT Michael Bouman, President/COO
Telephone: 908-686-4422

GENERAL INFORMATION Private Institution. **Total program enrollment:** 67. **Application fee:** $100.

PROGRAM(S) OFFERED
● **Aesthetician/Esthetician and Skin Care Specialist** *9 students enrolled* ● **Cosmetology, Barber/Styling, and Nail Instructor** ● **Cosmetology/Cosmetologist, General** *1200 hrs./$12,590* ● **Nail Technician/Specialist and Manicurist**

STUDENT SERVICES Academic or career counseling, employment services for current students, placement services for program completers.

Everest College

5000 Hadley Road, South Plainfield, NJ 07080
http://www.everest.edu/

CONTACT Bob Johnson, President
Telephone: 908-222-9300

GENERAL INFORMATION Private Institution. **Total program enrollment:** 177.

PROGRAM(S) OFFERED
● **Allied Health and Medical Assisting Services, Other** *80 students enrolled* ● **Massage Therapy/Therapeutic Massage** *720 hrs./$12,527* ● **Medical Insurance Coding Specialist/Coder** *720 hrs./$12,543* ● **Medical Insurance Specialist/Medical Biller** *36 students enrolled* ● **Medical/Clinical Assistant** *720 hrs./$14,338* ● **Pharmacy Technician/Assistant** *720 hrs./$13,403*

STUDENT SERVICES Academic or career counseling, placement services for program completers, remedial services.

Fairleigh Dickinson University, Metropolitan Campus

1000 River Road, Teaneck, NJ 07666-1914
http://www.fdu.edu/

CONTACT J. Michael Adams, President
Telephone: 201-692-2000

GENERAL INFORMATION Private Institution. Founded 1942. **Accreditation:** Regional (MSA/CIHE); computer science (ABET/CSAC); engineering technology (ABET/TAC). **Total program enrollment:** 3228. **Application fee:** $40.

STUDENT SERVICES Academic or career counseling, employment services for current students, placement services for program completers, remedial services.

Felician College

262 South Main Street, Lodi, NJ 07644-2117
http://www.felician.edu/

CONTACT Theresa Martin, President
Telephone: 201-559-6000

GENERAL INFORMATION Private Institution. Founded 1942. **Accreditation:** Regional (MSA/CIHE); medical laboratory technology (NAACLS). **Total program enrollment:** 1356. **Application fee:** $30.

STUDENT SERVICES Academic or career counseling, daycare for children of students, employment services for current students, placement services for program completers, remedial services.

Fox Institute of Business–Clifton

346 Lexington Avenue, Clifton, NJ 07011

CONTACT Christopher Coutts, President
Telephone: 973-340-9500

GENERAL INFORMATION Private Institution. **Total program enrollment:** 105. **Application fee:** $25.

PROGRAM(S) OFFERED
● **Computer and Information Sciences and Support Services, Other** *625 hrs./$9800* ● **Diagnostic Medical Sonography/Sonographer and Ultrasound Technician** *60 hrs./$28,500* ● **Legal Administrative Assistant/Secretary** *35 hrs./$12,995* ● **Massage Therapy/Therapeutic Massage** *40 hrs./$12,995* ● **Medical/Clinical Assistant** *44 hrs./$15,995*

STUDENT SERVICES Academic or career counseling, placement services for program completers.

Gentle Healing School of Massage

1274 S. River Road, Cranbury, NJ 08512
http://www.gentlehealingschool.com

CONTACT Donda Sternberg, School Owner/Director
Telephone: 609-409-2700

GENERAL INFORMATION Private Institution. **Application fee:** $25.

PROGRAM(S) OFFERED
● **Massage Therapy/Therapeutic Massage** *600 hrs./$7475*

Georgian Court University

900 Lakewood Avenue, Lakewood, NJ 08701-2697
http://www.georgian.edu/

CONTACT Rosemary Jeffries Rsm, PhD, President
Telephone: 732-987-2200

GENERAL INFORMATION Private Institution. Founded 1908. **Accreditation:** Regional (MSA/CIHE). **Total program enrollment:** 1733. **Application fee:** $40.

PROGRAM(S) OFFERED
● **Health Professions and Related Clinical Sciences, Other** *1 student enrolled* ● **International Business/Trade/Commerce** *2 students enrolled*

STUDENT SERVICES Academic or career counseling, employment services for current students, placement services for program completers, remedial services.

Gloucester County College

1400 Tanyard Road, Sewell, NJ 08080
http://www.gccnj.edu/

CONTACT Russell A. Davis, President
Telephone: 856-468-5000

GENERAL INFORMATION Public Institution. Founded 1967. **Accreditation:** Regional (MSA/CIHE); diagnostic medical sonography (JRCEDMS);

Gloucester County College (continued)

nuclear medicine technology (JRCNMT); respiratory therapy technology (CoARC). **Total program enrollment:** 3435. **Application fee:** $20.

PROGRAM(S) OFFERED
● **Administrative Assistant and Secretarial Science, General** *2 students enrolled* ● **Computer Graphics** *2 students enrolled* ● **Data Modeling/Warehousing and Database Administration** *1 student enrolled* ● **Legal Assistant/Paralegal** *1 student enrolled*

STUDENT SERVICES Academic or career counseling, daycare for children of students, employment services for current students, placement services for program completers, remedial services.

Harris School of Business–Cherry Hill

654 Longwood Avenue, Cherry Hill, NJ 08002
http://www.harrisschool.com/

CONTACT Tim James, Director
Telephone: 856-662-5300

GENERAL INFORMATION Private Institution. **Total program enrollment:** 284. **Application fee:** $25.

PROGRAM(S) OFFERED
● **Accounting and Related Services, Other** *53 hrs./$8865* ● **Administrative Assistant and Secretarial Science, General** *25 students enrolled* ● **Business/Office Automation/Technology/Data Entry** *26 hrs./$4237* ● **Health and Medical Administrative Services, Other** *57 hrs./$9765* ● **Legal Administrative Assistant/Secretary** *59 hrs./$11,895* ● **Massage Therapy/Therapeutic Massage** *69 hrs./$11,945* ● **Medical Administrative/Executive Assistant and Medical Secretary** *42 students enrolled* ● **Medical/Clinical Assistant** *65 hrs./$12,695*

STUDENT SERVICES Academic or career counseling, placement services for program completers.

Harris School of Business–Hamilton

3620 Quakerbridge Road, Hamilton, NJ 08619

CONTACT April Lupinacci, Director
Telephone: 609-586-9104

GENERAL INFORMATION Private Institution. **Total program enrollment:** 284. **Application fee:** $75.

PROGRAM(S) OFFERED
● **Accounting and Related Services, Other** *53 hrs./$8865* ● **Health/Health Care Administration/Management** *57 hrs./$9765* ● **Legal Administrative Assistant/Secretary** *59 hrs./$11,895* ● **Massage Therapy/Therapeutic Massage** *69 hrs./$11,945* ● **Medical/Clinical Assistant** *65 hrs./$12,695*

STUDENT SERVICES Academic or career counseling, placement services for program completers.

Harris School of Business–Linwood

1201 New Road, Suite 226, Linwood, NJ 08221
http://www.harrisschool.edu/Campuses-Programs/Linwood/37/

CONTACT Linda Burke, School Director
Telephone: 609-927-4310

GENERAL INFORMATION Private Institution. **Total program enrollment:** 201. **Application fee:** $25.

PROGRAM(S) OFFERED
● **Accounting and Related Services, Other** *53 hrs./$8865* ● **Legal Administrative Assistant/Secretary** *59 hrs./$11,895* ● **Massage Therapy/Therapeutic Massage** *69 hrs./$11,945* ● **Medical/Clinical Assistant** *65 hrs./$12,695* ● **Pharmacy Technician/Assistant** *72 hrs./$11,920*

STUDENT SERVICES Academic or career counseling, placement services for program completers.

Healthcare Training Institute

1969 Morris Avenue, Union, NJ 07083
http://www.healthcaretraininginstitute.com/

CONTACT Bashir Mohammad, MD, Educational Director
Telephone: 908-851-7711

GENERAL INFORMATION Private Institution. **Total program enrollment:** 45. **Application fee:** $25.

PROGRAM(S) OFFERED
● **Allied Health and Medical Assisting Services, Other** *240 hrs./$1990* ● **Diagnostic Medical Sonography/Sonographer and Ultrasound Technician** *1000 hrs./$14,938* ● **Electrocardiograph Technology/Technician** ● **Medical Insurance Specialist/Medical Biller** *500 hrs./$5950* ● **Medical/Clinical Assistant** *800 hrs./$8900* ● **Nurse/Nursing Assistant/Aide and Patient Care Assistant** *90 hrs./$1149*

STUDENT SERVICES Academic or career counseling, placement services for program completers, remedial services.

HoHoKus Hackensack School of Business and Medical Sciences

66 Moore Street, Hackensack, NJ 07601
http://www.hohokushackensack.com/

CONTACT Thomas Eastwick, President
Telephone: 201-488-9400

GENERAL INFORMATION Private Institution. Founded 1969. **Total program enrollment:** 539. **Application fee:** $25.

PROGRAM(S) OFFERED
● **Accounting** *51 students enrolled* ● **Administrative Assistant and Secretarial Science, General** ● **Business/Office Automation/Technology/Data Entry** *67 students enrolled* ● **Executive Assistant/Executive Secretary** ● **Legal Administrative Assistant/Secretary** ● **Licensed Practical/Vocational Nurse Training (LPN, LVN, Cert, Dipl, AAS)** *157 students enrolled* ● **Medical Insurance Specialist/Medical Biller** *43 students enrolled* ● **Medical Office Assistant/Specialist** *75 students enrolled*

STUDENT SERVICES Academic or career counseling, employment services for current students, placement services for program completers.

HoHoKus RETS School of Business and Medical Technical Services

103 Park Avenue, Nutley, NJ 07110
http://www.hohokusrets.com/

CONTACT Thomas Eastwick, President
Telephone: 973-661-0600

GENERAL INFORMATION Private Institution. **Total program enrollment:** 453. **Application fee:** $25.

PROGRAM(S) OFFERED
● **Administrative Assistant and Secretarial Science, General** *20 students enrolled* ● **Computer Engineering Technology/Technician** *37 students enrolled* ● **Computer and Information Sciences, General** *44 students enrolled* ● **Diagnostic Medical Sonography/Sonographer and Ultrasound Technician** *42 students enrolled* ● **Electrical, Electronic and Communications Engineering Technology/Technician** *18 students enrolled* ● **Medical Insurance Coding Specialist/Coder** *34 students enrolled* ● **Medical/Clinical Assistant** *118 students enrolled*

STUDENT SERVICES Academic or career counseling, employment services for current students, placement services for program completers, remedial services.

HoHoKus School of Business and Medical Sciences

10 South Franklin Turnpike, Ramsey, NJ 07446
http://www.hohokus.com/

CONTACT Thomas Eastwick, President
Telephone: 201-327-8877

GENERAL INFORMATION Private Institution. **Total program enrollment:** 385. **Application fee:** $25.

PROGRAM(S) OFFERED
• **Administrative Assistant and Secretarial Science, General** • **Allied Health and Medical Assisting Services, Other** *50 students enrolled* • **Business Administration and Management, General** *3 students enrolled* • **Diagnostic Medical Sonography/Sonographer and Ultrasound Technician** *99 students enrolled* • **Licensed Practical/Vocational Nurse Training (LPN, LVN, Cert, Dipl, AAS)** *135 students enrolled* • **Medical Insurance Coding Specialist/Coder** *16 students enrolled* • **Surgical Technology/Technologist** *9 students enrolled*

STUDENT SERVICES Academic or career counseling, employment services for current students, placement services for program completers.

HoHoKus School of Trade and Technical Sciences

1118 Baltimore Avenue, Linden, NJ 07036-1899
http://www.eastwickcolleges.com/

CONTACT Thomas M. Eastwick, President
Telephone: 973-742-0009

GENERAL INFORMATION Private Institution. Founded 1954. **Total program enrollment:** 97. **Application fee:** $25.

PROGRAM(S) OFFERED
• **Building/Property Maintenance and Management** *45 hrs./$12,640* • **Plumbing Technology/Plumber** *45 hrs./$12,850* • **Welding Technology/Welder** *30 hrs./$8845*

STUDENT SERVICES Academic or career counseling, employment services for current students, placement services for program completers.

Holy Name Hospital School of Nursing

690 Teaneck Road, Teaneck, NJ 07666-4246
http://www.schoolofnursing.info

CONTACT Susan Andrews, Director
Telephone: 201-833-3008

GENERAL INFORMATION Private Institution (Affiliated with Roman Catholic Church). **Total program enrollment:** 116. **Application fee:** $35.

PROGRAM(S) OFFERED
• **Licensed Practical/Vocational Nurse Training (LPN, LVN, Cert, Dipl, AAS)** *27 students enrolled*

STUDENT SERVICES Academic or career counseling, daycare for children of students, employment services for current students, remedial services.

Hudson County Community College

25 Journal Square, Jersey City, NJ 07306
http://www.hccc.edu/

CONTACT Glen Gabert, PhD, President
Telephone: 201-714-7100

GENERAL INFORMATION Public Institution. Founded 1974. **Accreditation:** Regional (MSA/CIHE); engineering technology (ABET/TAC); health information technology (AHIMA); medical assisting (AAMAE). **Total program enrollment:** 4476. **Application fee:** $15.

PROGRAM(S) OFFERED
• **Baking and Pastry Arts/Baker/Pastry Chef** *3 students enrolled* • **Emergency Medical Technology/Technician (EMT Paramedic)** *1 student enrolled* • **Licensed Practical/Vocational Nurse Training (LPN, LVN, Cert, Dipl, AAS)** *8 students enrolled*

STUDENT SERVICES Academic or career counseling, employment services for current students, placement services for program completers, remedial services.

The Institute for Health Education

7 Spielman Road, Fairfield, NJ 07004
http://instituteforhealtheducation.com/

CONTACT Lalit Chabria, Owner
Telephone: 201-217-1113

GENERAL INFORMATION Private Institution. **Total program enrollment:** 91. **Application fee:** $25.

PROGRAM(S) OFFERED
• **Dental Assisting/Assistant** *900 hrs./$9500* • **Electrocardiograph Technology/Technician** *60 hrs./$549* • **Massage Therapy/Therapeutic Massage** *629 hrs./$6429* • **Medical Insurance Coding Specialist/Coder** *900 hrs./$8751* • **Medical/Clinical Assistant** *900 hrs./$8235* • **Phlebotomy/Phlebotomist** *80 hrs./$595*

STUDENT SERVICES Employment services for current students, placement services for program completers.

Institute for Therapeutic Massage

125 Wanaque Avenue, Pompton Lakes, NJ 07442
http://www.massageprogram.com/

CONTACT Valerie Donahue, Assistant Director
Telephone: 973-839-6131 Ext. 201

GENERAL INFORMATION Private Institution. **Total program enrollment:** 122. **Application fee:** $25.

PROGRAM(S) OFFERED
• **Asian Bodywork Therapy** • **Massage Therapy/Therapeutic Massage** *1138 hrs./$14,995* • **Somatic Bodywork** *8 students enrolled*

STUDENT SERVICES Academic or career counseling, placement services for program completers.

Keyskills Learning

50 Mt. Prospect Avenue, Clifton, NJ 07013
http://www.keyskillslearning.com/

CONTACT Richard Lore, President
Telephone: 973-778-8136

GENERAL INFORMATION Private Institution. **Total program enrollment:** 90.

PROGRAM(S) OFFERED
• **Accounting** *41 students enrolled* • **Administrative Assistant and Secretarial Science, General** *950 hrs./$11,995* • **Business/Commerce, General** *18 students enrolled* • **Business/Office Automation/Technology/Data Entry** *22 students enrolled* • **Executive Assistant/Executive Secretary** *953 hrs./$11,810* • **General Office Occupations and Clerical Services** *1 student enrolled* • **Medical Insurance Coding Specialist/Coder** *775 hrs./$10,065* • **Medical Insurance Specialist/Medical Biller** *7 students enrolled* • **Small Business Administration/Management** *1035 hrs./$13,730*

STUDENT SERVICES Academic or career counseling, employment services for current students, placement services for program completers, remedial services.

Lincoln Technical Institute

1697 Oak Tree Road, Edison, NJ 08820
http://www.lincolnedu.com/

CONTACT Lauraine Lehman, Director of Administrative Services
Telephone: 732-548-8798

GENERAL INFORMATION Private Institution. Founded 1967. **Total program enrollment:** 653. **Application fee:** $25.

PROGRAM(S) OFFERED
● **Computer Systems Networking and Telecommunications** *24 students enrolled* ● **Criminal Justice/Police Science** *57 students enrolled* ● **Massage Therapy/Therapeutic Massage** *55 students enrolled* ● **Medical Insurance Specialist/Medical Biller** *54 students enrolled* ● **Medical/Clinical Assistant** *154 students enrolled* ● **Pharmacy Technician/Assistant** *10 students enrolled*

STUDENT SERVICES Employment services for current students, placement services for program completers.

Lincoln Technical Institute

70 McKee Drive, Mahwah, NJ 07430
http://www.lincolnedu.com/

CONTACT Jason Honecker, Executive Director
Telephone: 201-529-1414

GENERAL INFORMATION Private Institution. **Total program enrollment:** 233. **Application fee:** $25.

PROGRAM(S) OFFERED
● **Automobile/Automotive Mechanics Technology/Technician** *1560 hrs./$25,090* ● **Electrical/Electronics Equipment Installation and Repair, General** *1080 hrs./$18,905* ● **Heating, Air Conditioning and Refrigeration Technology/Technician (ACH/ACR/ACHR/HRAC/HVAC/AC Technology)** *1360 hrs./$21,270*

STUDENT SERVICES Academic or career counseling, employment services for current students, placement services for program completers, remedial services.

Lincoln Technical Institute

523 Fellowship Road, Suite 625, Mount Laurel, NJ 08054-3414
http://www.lincolnedu.com/

CONTACT Gary Achilles, Executive Director
Telephone: 856-722-9333 Ext. 42201

GENERAL INFORMATION Private Institution. Founded 1989. **Total program enrollment:** 619. **Application fee:** $25.

PROGRAM(S) OFFERED
● **Computer Systems Networking and Telecommunications** *21 students enrolled* ● **Criminal Justice/Police Science** *23 students enrolled* ● **Information Technology** *2 students enrolled* ● **Licensed Practical/Vocational Nurse Training (LPN, LVN, Cert, Dipl, AAS)** *63 students enrolled* ● **Massage Therapy/Therapeutic Massage** *30 students enrolled* ● **Medical Administrative/Executive Assistant and Medical Secretary** *27 students enrolled* ● **Medical/Clinical Assistant** *135 students enrolled*

STUDENT SERVICES Academic or career counseling, employment services for current students, placement services for program completers, remedial services.

Lincoln Technical Institute

160 East Route 4, Paramus, NJ 07652
http://www.lincolnedu.com/

CONTACT Laurie Pringle, Exec Director
Telephone: 201-845-6868

GENERAL INFORMATION Private Institution. **Total program enrollment:** 842. **Application fee:** $25.

PROGRAM(S) OFFERED
● **Administrative Assistant and Secretarial Science, General** *14 students enrolled* ● **Computer Systems Networking and Telecommunications** *900 hrs./$15,650* ● **Criminal Justice/Police Science** *900 hrs./$13,840* ● **Licensed Practical/Vocational Nurse Training (LPN, LVN, Cert, Dipl, AAS)** *1500 hrs./$23,766* ● **Massage Therapy/Therapeutic Massage** *720 hrs./$11,880* ● **Medical Insurance Coding Specialist/Coder** *53 students enrolled* ● **Medical Insurance Specialist/Medical Biller** *900 hrs./$12,173* ● **Medical/Clinical Assistant** *900 hrs./$14,030* ● **Pharmacy Technician/Assistant** *11 students enrolled*

STUDENT SERVICES Employment services for current students, placement services for program completers.

Lincoln Technical Institute

2299 Vauxhall Road, Union, NJ 07083
http://www.lincolnedu.com/

CONTACT Kevin Kirkley, Executive Director
Telephone: 908-964-7800

GENERAL INFORMATION Private Institution. **Total program enrollment:** 1265. **Application fee:** $25.

PROGRAM(S) OFFERED
● **Automobile/Automotive Mechanics Technology/Technician** *62 hrs./$24,248* ● **Electrical, Electronic and Communications Engineering Technology/Technician** *52 hrs./$17,796* ● **Electrical/Electronics Equipment Installation and Repair, General** *194 students enrolled* ● **Heating, Air Conditioning and Refrigeration Technology/Technician (ACH/ACR/ACHR/HRAC/HVAC/AC Technology)** *72 hrs./$19,712* ● **Heating, Air Conditioning, Ventilation and Refrigeration Maintenance Technology/Technician (HAC, HACR, HVAC, HVACR)** *341 students enrolled*

STUDENT SERVICES Academic or career counseling, employment services for current students, placement services for program completers, remedial services.

Mercer County Community College

1200 Old Trenton Road, PO Box B, Trenton, NJ 08690-1004
http://www.mccc.edu/

CONTACT Dr. Patricia Donohue, President
Telephone: 609-570-4800

GENERAL INFORMATION Public Institution. Founded 1966. **Accreditation:** Regional (MSA/CIHE); funeral service (ABFSE); medical laboratory technology (NAACLS); physical therapy assisting (APTA); radiologic technology: radiography (JRCERT). **Total program enrollment:** 3805.

PROGRAM(S) OFFERED
● **Administrative Assistant and Secretarial Science, General** *2 students enrolled* ● **Architectural Engineering Technology/Technician** *2 students enrolled* ● **Business Administration, Management and Operations, Other** *1 student enrolled* ● **Data Entry/Microcomputer Applications, General** *1 student enrolled* ● **Drafting and Design Technology/Technician, General** *4 students enrolled* ● **Engineering Science** *1 student enrolled* ● **Entrepreneurship/Entrepreneurial Studies** *8 students enrolled* ● **Fire Protection and Safety Technology/Technician** *1 student enrolled* ● **Food Preparation/Professional Cooking/Kitchen Assistant** *1 student enrolled* ● **Funeral Service and Mortuary Science, General** *18 students enrolled* ● **Heating, Air Conditioning and Refrigeration Technology/Technician (ACH/ACR/ACHR/HRAC/HVAC/AC Technology)** *3 students enrolled* ● **Legal Assistant/Paralegal** *8 students enrolled* ● **Management Information Systems and Services, Other** *1 student enrolled* ● **Management Information Systems, General** *1 student enrolled* ● **Medical Administrative/Executive Assistant and Medical Secretary** *30 students enrolled* ● **Ornamental Horticulture** *2 students enrolled* ● **Restaurant, Culinary, and Catering Management/Manager** *1 student enrolled* ● **Retailing and Retail Operations** *1 student enrolled* ● **Substance Abuse/Addiction Counseling** *1 student enrolled* ● **Visual and Performing Arts, General** *2 students enrolled*

STUDENT SERVICES Academic or career counseling, employment services for current students, placement services for program completers, remedial services.

Metro Auto Electronics Training Institute

111 Market Street, Kenilworth, NJ 07033
metro-auto.com

CONTACT Donna Mulrain, Director of Finance
Telephone: 908-245-5335

GENERAL INFORMATION Private Institution. **Total program enrollment:** 21. **Application fee:** $25.

PROGRAM(S) OFFERED
• Automobile/Automotive Mechanics Technology/Technician *474 hrs./$8888*

STUDENT SERVICES Academic or career counseling, employment services for current students, placement services for program completers.

Micro Tech Training Center

251 Washington Avenue, Belleville, NJ 07109
http://microtechtrainingcenter.com/

CONTACT Bashir Mohsen, School President
Telephone: 973-751-9051

GENERAL INFORMATION Private Institution. **Total program enrollment:** 126. **Application fee:** $125.

PROGRAM(S) OFFERED
• Criminal Justice/Safety Studies *3 students enrolled* • Diagnostic Medical Sonography/Sonographer and Ultrasound Technician *2700 hrs./$29,875* • Massage Therapy/Therapeutic Massage *1000 hrs./$11,200* • Medical/Clinical Assistant *1000 hrs./$11,200* • Surgical Technology/Technologist *1200 hrs./$18,975*

STUDENT SERVICES Academic or career counseling, employment services for current students, placement services for program completers.

Micro Tech Training Center

3000 Kennedy Boulevard 3rd Floor, Jersey City, NJ 07306
http://www.microtechtrainingcenter.com/

CONTACT Bashir Mohsen, President/Owner
Telephone: 201-216-9901 Ext. 15

GENERAL INFORMATION Private Institution. **Total program enrollment:** 189. **Application fee:** $100.

PROGRAM(S) OFFERED
• Criminal Justice/Law Enforcement Administration *15 students enrolled* • Diagnostic Medical Sonography/Sonographer and Ultrasound Technician *2700 hrs./$29,125* • Massage Therapy/Therapeutic Massage *79 hrs./$11,200* • Medical/Clinical Assistant *66 hrs./$11,800* • Surgical Technology/Technologist *86 hrs./$18,975*

STUDENT SERVICES Academic or career counseling, employment services for current students, placement services for program completers.

Middlesex County College

2600 Woodbridge Avenue, PO Box 3050, Edison, NJ 08818-3050
http://www.middlesexcc.edu/

CONTACT Dr. Joann La Perla-Morales, President
Telephone: 732-548-6000

GENERAL INFORMATION Public Institution. Founded 1964. **Accreditation:** Regional (MSA/CIHE); dental hygiene (ADA); engineering technology (ABET/TAC); medical laboratory technology (NAACLS); radiologic technology: radiography (JRCERT). **Total program enrollment:** 6894. **Application fee:** $25.

PROGRAM(S) OFFERED
• Accounting Technology/Technician and Bookkeeping *8 students enrolled* • Computer Programming/Programmer, General *4 students enrolled* • Corrections *1 student enrolled* • Hotel/Motel Administration/Management *1 student*

enrolled • Legal Assistant/Paralegal *1 student enrolled* • Mechanical Engineering/Mechanical Technology/Technician *1 student enrolled* • Pharmacy Technician/Assistant *2 students enrolled* • Teacher Assistant/Aide *1 student enrolled*

STUDENT SERVICES Academic or career counseling, daycare for children of students, employment services for current students, placement services for program completers, remedial services.

Monmouth County Vocational School District

255 West End Avenue, Long Branch, NJ 07740
http://mcvsd.org/

CONTACT Brian D. McAndrew, Superintendent
Telephone: 732-431-7944

GENERAL INFORMATION Public Institution. Founded 1965. **Total program enrollment:** 144.

PROGRAM(S) OFFERED
• Automobile/Automotive Mechanics Technology/Technician *324 hrs./$1400* • Cosmetology and Related Personal Grooming Arts, Other *4 students enrolled* • Cosmetology/Cosmetologist, General *1000 hrs./$5500* • Licensed Practical/Vocational Nurse Training (LPN, LVN, Cert, Dipl, AAS) *1500 hrs./$7500* • Massage Therapy/Therapeutic Massage *600 hrs./$2200* • Nurse/Nursing Assistant/Aide and Patient Care Assistant *200 hrs./$750* • Water Quality and Wastewater Treatment Management and Recycling Technology/Technician *180 hrs./$550*

STUDENT SERVICES Academic or career counseling, employment services for current students, placement services for program completers, remedial services.

Monmouth University

400 Cedar Avenue, West Long Branch, NJ 07764-1898
http://www.monmouth.edu/

CONTACT Paul G. Gaffney, II, President
Telephone: 732-571-3400

GENERAL INFORMATION Private Institution. Founded 1933. **Accreditation:** Regional (MSA/CIHE). **Total program enrollment:** 4813. **Application fee:** $50.

PROGRAM(S) OFFERED
• African-American/Black Studies • Cartography • Computer and Information Sciences, General *73 students enrolled* • Spanish Language and Literature

STUDENT SERVICES Academic or career counseling, employment services for current students, placement services for program completers, remedial services.

Natural Motion Institute of Hair Design

2800 Kennedy Boulevard, Jersey City, NJ 07306
http://natural-motion.com/

CONTACT Michael Bouman, President/COO
Telephone: 201-659-0303

GENERAL INFORMATION Private Institution. Founded 1965. **Total program enrollment:** 60. **Application fee:** $100.

PROGRAM(S) OFFERED
• Cosmetology/Cosmetologist, General *1200 hrs./$12,590* • Nail Technician/Specialist and Manicurist

STUDENT SERVICES Academic or career counseling, employment services for current students, placement services for program completers, remedial services.

New Community Workforce Development Center

201 Bergen Street, Newark, NJ 07103

CONTACT Kathy Spivey, Chief of Staff
Telephone: 973-824-6484

GENERAL INFORMATION Private Institution. **Total program enrollment:** 295. **Application fee:** $25.

PROGRAM(S) OFFERED
• **Automobile/Automotive Mechanics Technology/Technician** *23 students enrolled* • **Automotive Engineering Technology/Technician** *1200 hrs./$5000* • **Building/Property Maintenance and Management** *7 students enrolled* • **Culinary Arts/Chef Training** *900 hrs./$5100* • **Licensed Practical/Vocational Nurse Training (LPN, LVN, Cert, Dipl, AAS)** *47 students enrolled* • **Nursing, Other** *1425 hrs./$13,431*

STUDENT SERVICES Academic or career counseling, employment services for current students, placement services for program completers, remedial services.

New Horizon Institute of Cosmetology

5518 Bergenline Avenue, West New York, NJ 07093

CONTACT Linda Karas, Associate Director
Telephone: 201-866-4000

GENERAL INFORMATION Private Institution. Founded 1979. **Total program enrollment:** 89. **Application fee:** $100.

PROGRAM(S) OFFERED
• **Barbering/Barber** • **Cosmetology/Cosmetologist, General** *1200 hrs./$12,900* • **Nail Technician/Specialist and Manicurist** *300 hrs./$3050* • **Teacher Education and Professional Development, Specific Subject Areas, Other**

STUDENT SERVICES Academic or career counseling, employment services for current students, placement services for program completers.

Ocean County College

College Drive, PO Box 2001, Toms River, NJ 08754-2001
http://www.ocean.edu/

CONTACT Dr. Jon H. Larson, President
Telephone: 732-255-0326

GENERAL INFORMATION Public Institution. Founded 1964. **Accreditation:** Regional (MSA/CIHE). **Total program enrollment:** 5593.

PROGRAM(S) OFFERED
• **Accounting** *2 students enrolled* • **Administrative Assistant and Secretarial Science, General** *4 students enrolled* • **CAD/CADD Drafting and/or Design Technology/Technician** *2 students enrolled* • **Commercial and Advertising Art** *1 student enrolled* • **Construction Engineering Technology/Technician** *1 student enrolled* • **Design and Applied Arts, Other** *2 students enrolled* • **Kinesiology and Exercise Science** *1 student enrolled* • **Legal Assistant/Paralegal** *7 students enrolled* • **Sign Language Interpretation and Translation** *18 students enrolled* • **Teacher Assistant/Aide** *1 student enrolled*

STUDENT SERVICES Academic or career counseling, daycare for children of students, employment services for current students, placement services for program completers, remedial services.

Ocean County Vocational Post Secondary Division

137 Bey Lea Road, Toms River, NJ 08753-2703
http://www.ocvts.org/

CONTACT William Hoey, Superintendent
Telephone: 732-473-3100

GENERAL INFORMATION Public Institution. **Total program enrollment:** 393. **Application fee:** $25.

PROGRAM(S) OFFERED
• **Applied Horticulture/Horticultural Operations, General** *3 students enrolled* • **Athletic Training/Trainer** *4 students enrolled* • **Autobody/Collision and Repair**

Technology/Technician *5 students enrolled* • **Automobile/Automotive Mechanics Technology/Technician** *900 hrs./$1500* • **Business/Office Automation/Technology/Data Entry** • **Cabinetmaking and Millwork/Millwright** *1 student enrolled* • **Carpentry/Carpenter** *4 students enrolled* • **Child Care and Support Services Management** *2 students enrolled* • **Commercial and Advertising Art** *900 hrs./$1500* • **Communications Technology/Technician** • **Corrections and Criminal Justice, Other** • **Cosmetology/Cosmetologist, General** *1000 hrs./$5000* • **Culinary Arts/Chef Training** *900 hrs./$2700* • **Dance, General** • **Dental Assisting/Assistant** *22 students enrolled* • **Diesel Mechanics Technology/Technician** *1 student enrolled* • **Drafting and Design Technology/Technician, General** *2 students enrolled* • **Electrical, Electronic and Communications Engineering Technology/Technician** *15 students enrolled* • **Electrician** *11 students enrolled* • **Fashion Merchandising** *1 student enrolled* • **Heating, Air Conditioning, Ventilation and Refrigeration Maintenance Technology/Technician (HAC, HACR, HVAC, HVACR)** *4 students enrolled* • **Licensed Practical/Vocational Nurse Training (LPN, LVN, Cert, Dipl, AAS)** *1379 hrs./$5250* • **Nurse/Nursing Assistant/Aide and Patient Care Assistant** *1 student enrolled* • **Vehicle Maintenance and Repair Technologies, Other** • **Welding Technology/Welder** *900 hrs./$1500*

STUDENT SERVICES Academic or career counseling, employment services for current students, placement services for program completers.

Omega Institute

7050 Route 38, E, Pennsauken, NJ 08109
http://www.omegacareers.com/

CONTACT Raymond J. Papin, School Director
Telephone: 856-663-4299

GENERAL INFORMATION Private Institution. Founded 1980. **Total program enrollment:** 133. **Application fee:** $25.

PROGRAM(S) OFFERED
• **Health Unit Coordinator/Ward Clerk** • **Massage Therapy/Therapeutic Massage** *750 hrs./$9100* • **Medical Insurance Specialist/Medical Biller** *900 hrs./$10,900* • **Medical Office Assistant/Specialist** *750 hrs./$9100* • **Medical/Clinical Assistant** *900 hrs./$11,735* • **Nurse/Nursing Assistant/Aide and Patient Care Assistant** *750 hrs./$9100* • **Pharmacy Technician/Assistant** *750 hrs./$9100*

STUDENT SERVICES Academic or career counseling, employment services for current students, placement services for program completers.

Parisian Beauty School

362 State Street, Hackensack, NJ 07601
http://www.parisianbeautyacademy.com/

CONTACT Harry Comp, Jr., President
Telephone: 201-487-2203 Ext. 10

GENERAL INFORMATION Private Institution. Founded 1949. **Total program enrollment:** 224.

PROGRAM(S) OFFERED
• **Aesthetician/Esthetician and Skin Care Specialist** *600 hrs./$7020* • **Cosmetology and Related Personal Grooming Arts, Other** *300 hrs./$2445* • **Cosmetology, Barber/Styling, and Nail Instructor** *3 students enrolled* • **Hair Styling/Stylist and Hair Design** *1200 hrs./$15,495* • **Nail Technician/Specialist and Manicurist** • **Trade and Industrial Teacher Education** *500 hrs./$2400*

STUDENT SERVICES Academic or career counseling, employment services for current students, placement services for program completers.

Passaic County Community College

One College Boulevard, Paterson, NJ 07505-1179
http://www.pccc.cc.nj.us/

CONTACT Steven M. Rose, EdD, President
Telephone: 973-684-6800

GENERAL INFORMATION Public Institution. Founded 1968. **Accreditation:** Regional (MSA/CIHE); health information technology (AHIMA); radiologic technology: radiography (JRCERT). **Total program enrollment:** 2327.

PROGRAM(S) OFFERED
• **Criminal Justice/Police Science** *7 students enrolled* • **Fire Protection and Safety Technology/Technician** *1 student enrolled* • **Medical Transcription/Transcriptionist** *6 students enrolled* • **Social Work** *9 students enrolled*

STUDENT SERVICES Academic or career counseling, daycare for children of students, employment services for current students, placement services for program completers, remedial services.

PB Cosmetology Education Center

110 Monmouth Street, Gloucester, NJ 08030
http://www.pbcosmetologyschool.com/

CONTACT Colleen M. Hogan, Director
Telephone: 856-456-4050

GENERAL INFORMATION Private Institution. Founded 1960. **Total program enrollment:** 175. **Application fee:** $25.

PROGRAM(S) OFFERED
• **Aesthetician/Esthetician and Skin Care Specialist** *600 hrs./$7000* • **Cosmetology and Related Personal Grooming Arts, Other** *4 students enrolled* • **Cosmetology/Cosmetologist, General** *1200 hrs./$16,300* • **Nail Technician/Specialist and Manicurist** *300 hrs./$2550* • **Teacher Education and Professional Development, Specific Levels and Methods, Other** *500 hrs./$4900*

STUDENT SERVICES Academic or career counseling, employment services for current students, placement services for program completers, remedial services.

PC Age Career Institute

Troy Office Center, 1259 Route 46 East, Building 4C, Parsippany, NJ 07054
http://www.pcage.com/

CONTACT Zafar Khizer, CEO/President
Telephone: 201-761-0144

GENERAL INFORMATION Private Institution. **Total program enrollment:** 28. **Application fee:** $100.

PROGRAM(S) OFFERED
• **Computer Systems Networking and Telecommunications** *960 hrs./$18,790*

STUDENT SERVICES Academic or career counseling, placement services for program completers.

PC Age Career Institute–Edison Campus

Durham Center, 2 Ethel Road, Suite 301, Edison, NJ 08817-2839
http://www.pcage.com/

CONTACT Zafar Khizer, CEO/President
Telephone: 732-287-3622 Ext. 13

GENERAL INFORMATION Private Institution. **Total program enrollment:** 10. **Application fee:** $100.

PROGRAM(S) OFFERED
• **Computer Systems Networking and Telecommunications** *960 hrs./$18,790*

STUDENT SERVICES Academic or career counseling, placement services for program completers.

PC Tech Learning Center

895 Bergen Avenue, Jersey City, NJ 07306
http://www.pctech2000.com/

CONTACT M. R. Somalingam, CEO/School Director
Telephone: 201-222-0038

GENERAL INFORMATION Private Institution. **Total program enrollment:** 93. **Application fee:** $25.

PROGRAM(S) OFFERED
• **Administrative Assistant and Secretarial Science, General** *360 hrs./$3800* • **Computer Systems Networking and Telecommunications** *25 hrs./$9865* • **Massage Therapy/Therapeutic Massage** *26 hrs./$8880* • **Medical Administrative/Executive Assistant and Medical Secretary** *360 hrs./$3500* • **Medical Insurance Coding Specialist/Coder** *13 students enrolled* • **Medical Office Management/Administration** *24 hrs./$7465* • **Medical/Clinical Assistant** *30 hrs./$7765*

STUDENT SERVICES Academic or career counseling, placement services for program completers.

Pennco Tech

99 Erial Road, PO Box 1427, Blackwood, NJ 08012-9961
http://www.penncotech.com/

CONTACT Robert Emme, School Director
Telephone: 856-232-0310

GENERAL INFORMATION Private Institution. **Total program enrollment:** 491. **Application fee:** $100.

PROGRAM(S) OFFERED
• **Autobody/Collision and Repair Technology/Technician** *11 students enrolled* • **Automobile/Automotive Mechanics Technology/Technician** *2100 hrs./$29,920* • **Diesel Mechanics Technology/Technician** *2100 hrs./$27,295* • **Drafting/Design Engineering Technologies/Technicians, Other** *4 students enrolled* • **Electrician** *900 hrs./$14,438* • **Heating, Air Conditioning, Ventilation and Refrigeration Maintenance Technology/Technician (HAC, HACR, HVAC, HVACR)** *960 hrs./$17,365* • **Marine Maintenance/Fitter and Ship Repair Technology/Technician** *16 students enrolled* • **Medical Administrative/Executive Assistant and Medical Secretary** *600 hrs./$6500* • **Pharmacy Technician/Assistant** *10 students enrolled*

STUDENT SERVICES Academic or career counseling, employment services for current students, placement services for program completers.

Performance Training

1012 Cox Cro Road, Toms River, NJ 08753
http://www.ptitraining.com/

CONTACT Charles P. Scholer, President, Owner
Telephone: 732-505-9119 Ext. 12

GENERAL INFORMATION Private Institution. **Total program enrollment:** 25.

PROGRAM(S) OFFERED
• **Administrative Assistant and Secretarial Science, General** *600 hrs./$6000* • **Executive Assistant/Executive Secretary** *13 students enrolled* • **General Office Occupations and Clerical Services** *740 hrs./$7825* • **Medical Insurance Coding Specialist/Coder** *480 hrs./$4800* • **Medical Office Assistant/Specialist** *740 hrs./$7400* • **Medical Reception/Receptionist** *540 hrs./$5400*

STUDENT SERVICES Placement services for program completers.

Prism Career Institute

150 Delsea Drive, Sewell, NJ 08080
http://prismcareerinstitute.com/

CONTACT David M. Hudiak, Special Assistant to Office of the President
Telephone: 609-407-7476

GENERAL INFORMATION Private Institution. **Total program enrollment:** 136. **Application fee:** $50.

PROGRAM(S) OFFERED
• **Accounting Technology/Technician and Bookkeeping** *660 hrs./$9776*
• **Administrative Assistant and Secretarial Science, General** *3 students enrolled* • **Business Administration and Management, General** *606 hrs./$9776*
• **Legal Administrative Assistant/Secretary** *900 hrs./$10,722* • **Medical Insurance Specialist/Medical Biller** *660 hrs./$9102* • **Medical Office Management/Administration** *666 hrs./$9776* • **Medical/Clinical Assistant** *900 hrs./$14,264*

STUDENT SERVICES Academic or career counseling, employment services for current students, placement services for program completers.

Prism Career Institute

Route 130 and Beverly-Rancocas Road, Suite 9, Willingboro, NJ 08046
http://prismcareerinstitute.com/

CONTACT David M. Hudiak, Special Assistant to Office of the President
Telephone: 856-317-0100 Ext. 127

GENERAL INFORMATION Private Institution. **Total program enrollment:** 180. **Application fee:** $100.

PROGRAM(S) OFFERED
• **Accounting Technology/Technician and Bookkeeping** *660 hrs./$9776*
• **Administrative Assistant and Secretarial Science, General** • **Legal Administrative Assistant/Secretary** *900 hrs./$10,722* • **Medical Insurance Specialist/Medical Biller** *660 hrs./$9102* • **Medical Office Management/Administration** *666 hrs./$9776* • **Medical/Clinical Assistant** *900 hrs./$13,404*
• **Pre-Nursing Studies** *1560 hrs./$18,812*

STUDENT SERVICES Academic or career counseling, employment services for current students, placement services for program completers.

Raritan Valley Community College

PO Box 3300, Somerville, NJ 08876-1265
http://www.raritanval.edu/

CONTACT Kathleen Crabill, President
Telephone: 908-526-1200

GENERAL INFORMATION Public Institution. Founded 1965. **Accreditation:** Regional (MSA/CIHE); ophthalmic dispensing (COA). **Total program enrollment:** 3399. **Application fee:** $25.

PROGRAM(S) OFFERED
• **Accounting and Related Services, Other** *8 students enrolled* • **Computer Programming, Vendor/Product Certification** *1 student enrolled* • **Computer Systems Networking and Telecommunications** *3 students enrolled* • **Computer and Information Sciences and Support Services, Other** *2 students enrolled* • **Corrections and Criminal Justice, Other** *2 students enrolled* • **Health Information/Medical Records Technology/Technician** *6 students enrolled* • **Health and Physical Education, General** *3 students enrolled* • **Hospitality Administration/Management, Other** *4 students enrolled* • **International Business/Trade/Commerce** *3 students enrolled* • **Kindergarten/Preschool Education and Teaching** *1 student enrolled* • **Legal Assistant/Paralegal** *19 students enrolled* • **Teaching Assistants/Aides, Other** *1 student enrolled* • **Web Page, Digital/Multimedia and Information Resources Design** *1 student enrolled*

STUDENT SERVICES Academic or career counseling, daycare for children of students, employment services for current students, remedial services.

Reignbow Beauty Academy

312 State Street, Perth Amboy, NJ 08861
http://www.reignbowbeautyacademy.com/

CONTACT Paul Ferrara, President
Telephone: 732-442-6007 Ext. 15

GENERAL INFORMATION Private Institution. Founded 1972. **Total program enrollment:** 120.

PROGRAM(S) OFFERED
• **Cosmetology, Barber/Styling, and Nail Instructor** *500 hrs./$1050*
• **Cosmetology/Cosmetologist, General** *1200 hrs./$16,940* • **Nail Technician/Specialist and Manicurist** *300 hrs./$3800*

STUDENT SERVICES Academic or career counseling, placement services for program completers.

Reignbow Hair Fashion Institute

121 Watchung Avenue, North Plainfield, NJ 07060
http://www.reignbowbeautyacademy.com/

CONTACT Paul Ferrara, Chief Executive Officer
Telephone: 908-754-4247 Ext. 16

GENERAL INFORMATION Private Institution. Founded 1981. **Total program enrollment:** 61.

PROGRAM(S) OFFERED
• **Cosmetology, Barber/Styling, and Nail Instructor** *500 hrs./$1050*
• **Cosmetology/Cosmetologist, General** *1200 hrs./$16,940* • **Nail Technician/Specialist and Manicurist** *300 hrs./$3800*

STUDENT SERVICES Academic or career counseling, placement services for program completers.

Rizzieri Aveda School for Beauty and Wellness

6001 W. Lincoln Drive, Marlton, NJ 08053
http://www.rizzieri.com/

CONTACT Katie Capone, Director of Recruiting and Financial Aid
Telephone: 856-988-8600

GENERAL INFORMATION Private Institution. **Total program enrollment:** 120. **Application fee:** $50.

PROGRAM(S) OFFERED
• **Aesthetician/Esthetician and Skin Care Specialist** *600 hrs./$7750*
• **Cosmetology/Cosmetologist, General** *1200 hrs./$17,650* • **Nail Technician/Specialist and Manicurist** *300 hrs./$4200*

STUDENT SERVICES Academic or career counseling, placement services for program completers, remedial services.

Roman Academy of Beauty Culture

431 Lafayette Avenue, Hawthorne, NJ 07506
http://romanacademy.com/

CONTACT Paul Scillia, Director
Telephone: 973-423-2223

GENERAL INFORMATION Private Institution. **Total program enrollment:** 55. **Application fee:** $100.

PROGRAM(S) OFFERED
• **Aesthetician/Esthetician and Skin Care Specialist** *600 hrs./$7100*
• **Cosmetology, Barber/Styling, and Nail Instructor** *500 hrs./$4350*
• **Cosmetology/Cosmetologist, General** *1200 hrs./$12,895*

STUDENT SERVICES Academic or career counseling, employment services for current students, placement services for program completers.

Saint Peter's College

2641 Kennedy Boulevard, Jersey City, NJ 07306-5997
http://www.spc.edu/

CONTACT Eugene Cornacchia, President
Telephone: 201-761-6000

GENERAL INFORMATION Private Institution. Founded 1872. **Accreditation:** Regional (MSA/CIHE). **Total program enrollment:** 2351.

STUDENT SERVICES Academic or career counseling, employment services for current students, placement services for program completers, remedial services.

Salem Community College

460 Hollywood Avenue, Carneys Point, NJ 08069-2799
http://www.salemcc.org/

CONTACT Peter B. Contini, President
Telephone: 856-299-2100

GENERAL INFORMATION Public Institution. Founded 1972. **Accreditation:** Regional (MSA/CIHE). **Total program enrollment:** 776. **Application fee:** $25.

PROGRAM(S) OFFERED
• **Administrative Assistant and Secretarial Science, General** 1 student enrolled • **Licensed Practical/Vocational Nurse Training (LPN, LVN, Cert, Dipl, AAS)** 39 students enrolled • **Teacher Assistant/Aide** 1 student enrolled

STUDENT SERVICES Academic or career counseling, employment services for current students, placement services for program completers, remedial services.

Sanford-Brown Institute

675 US Route 1, 2nd Floor, Iselin, NJ 08830
http://www.sb-nj.com/

CONTACT Dennis Mascali, School Director
Telephone: 732-623-5740

GENERAL INFORMATION Private Institution. Founded 1977. **Total program enrollment:** 344. **Application fee:** $35.

PROGRAM(S) OFFERED
• **Cardiovascular Technology/Technologist** 76 hrs./$34,880 • **Diagnostic Medical Sonography/Sonographer and Ultrasound Technician** 74 hrs./$34,845 • **Massage Therapy/Therapeutic Massage** 70 hrs./$11,900 • **Medical Insurance Coding Specialist/Coder** 45 hrs./$13,950 • **Medical/Clinical Assistant** 41 hrs./$13,950 • **Surgical Technology/Technologist** 69 hrs./$21,816

STUDENT SERVICES Academic or career counseling, employment services for current students, placement services for program completers.

Shore Beauty School

103 West Washington Avenue, Pleasantville, NJ 08232
http://www.shorebeautyschool.com/

CONTACT Kameron K. Rabenou, Director
Telephone: 609-645-3635

GENERAL INFORMATION Private Institution. Founded 1980. **Total program enrollment:** 78. **Application fee:** $25.

PROGRAM(S) OFFERED
• **Cosmetology, Barber/Styling, and Nail Instructor** 500 hrs./$4890 • **Cosmetology/Cosmetologist, General** 1200 hrs./$11,995 • **Nail Technician/Specialist and Manicurist** 300 hrs./$3150

STUDENT SERVICES Academic or career counseling, employment services for current students, placement services for program completers, remedial services.

Somerset Christian College

10 College Way, PO Box 9035, Zarephath, NJ 08890-9035
http://www.somerset.edu/

CONTACT David E. Schroeder, President
Telephone: 732-356-1595

GENERAL INFORMATION Private Institution. Founded 1908. **Accreditation:** State accredited or approved. **Total program enrollment:** 108. **Application fee:** $35.

STUDENT SERVICES Academic or career counseling, remedial services.

Somerset County Technical Institute

North Bridge Street and Vogt Drive, Bridgewater, NJ 08807-0350
http://www.scti.org/

CONTACT Michael Maddaluna, Superintendent
Telephone: 908-526-8900 Ext. 7353

GENERAL INFORMATION Public Institution. **Total program enrollment:** 158. **Application fee:** $25.

PROGRAM(S) OFFERED
• **Administrative Assistant and Secretarial Science, General** 2 students enrolled • **Computer Graphics** 12 students enrolled • **Computer and Information Sciences and Support Services, Other** 1 student enrolled • **Cosmetology/Cosmetologist, General** 29 students enrolled • **Dental Services and Allied Professions, Other** 13 students enrolled • **Drafting and Design Technology/Technician, General** 33 students enrolled • **Laser and Optical Technology/Technician** • **Licensed Practical/Vocational Nurse Training (LPN, LVN, Cert, Dipl, AAS)** 38 students enrolled • **Medical Insurance Specialist/Medical Biller** 4 students enrolled • **Medical Transcription/Transcriptionist** 5 students enrolled • **Medical/Clinical Assistant** 5 students enrolled • **Nurse/Nursing Assistant/Aide and Patient Care Assistant** 45 students enrolled • **Welding Technology/Welder** 10 students enrolled

STUDENT SERVICES Academic or career counseling, employment services for current students, placement services for program completers.

Star Technical Institute

Tano Mall, 1199 Amboy Avenue, Edison, NJ 08837
http://starinstitute.com/

CONTACT Audra Davis, Director
Telephone: 973-639-0789

GENERAL INFORMATION Private Institution. **Total program enrollment:** 74.

PROGRAM(S) OFFERED
• **Cardiovascular Technology/Technologist** 20 students enrolled • **Medical Administrative/Executive Assistant and Medical Secretary** 41 students enrolled • **Medical Insurance Specialist/Medical Biller** 16 students enrolled • **Medical/Health Management and Clinical Assistant/Specialist** 23 students enrolled • **Surgical Technology/Technologist** 950 hrs./$15,004

Star Technical Institute

43 South White Horse Pike, Stratford, NJ 08084
http://starinstitute.com/

CONTACT Corey Matthews, Director
Telephone: 609-435-7827

GENERAL INFORMATION Private Institution. **Total program enrollment:** 134. **Application fee:** $25.

PROGRAM(S) OFFERED
• **Cardiovascular Technology/Technologist** 40 hrs./$10,604 • **Medical Administrative/Executive Assistant and Medical Secretary** 37 hrs./$10,270 • **Medical Insurance Specialist/Medical Biller** 38 hrs./$10,667 • **Medical/**

Star Technical Institute (continued)

Health Management and Clinical Assistant/Specialist *35 hrs./$10,621* • **Pharmacy Technician/Assistant** *900 hrs./$13,162* • **Surgical Technology/ Technologist** *40 hrs./$14,764*

STUDENT SERVICES Placement services for program completers.

Steno Tech Career Institute

20 Just Road, Fairfield, NJ 07004-3413
http://www.stenotech.edu/

CONTACT Jean M. Melone, President
Telephone: 973-882-4875

GENERAL INFORMATION Private Institution. **Total program enrollment:** 39. **Application fee:** $25.

PROGRAM(S) OFFERED
• **Court Reporting/Court Reporter** *900 hrs./$7570* • **Medical Transcription/ Transcriptionist** *1800 hrs./$7380*

STUDENT SERVICES Academic or career counseling, employment services for current students, placement services for program completers, remedial services.

StenoTech Career Institute

262A Old New Brunswick Road, Piscataway, NJ 08854
http://www.stenotech.edu

CONTACT Jean Melone, President
Telephone: 732-562-1200

GENERAL INFORMATION Private Institution. **Total program enrollment:** 53. **Application fee:** $25.

PROGRAM(S) OFFERED
• **Court Reporting/Court Reporter** *900 hrs./$7570* • **Medical Transcription/ Transcriptionist** *1800 hrs./$7380*

STUDENT SERVICES Academic or career counseling, employment services for current students, placement services for program completers, remedial services.

Stuart School of Business Administration

2400 Belmar Boulevard, Wall, NJ 07719
http://www.stuartschool.com/

CONTACT Martin Klangasky, Executive Director
Telephone: 732-681-7200

GENERAL INFORMATION Private Institution. Founded 1961. **Total program enrollment:** 30. **Application fee:** $50.

PROGRAM(S) OFFERED
• **Administrative Assistant and Secretarial Science, General** *18 students enrolled* • **Medical Insurance Coding Specialist/Coder** *24 students enrolled* • **Medical/Clinical Assistant** *29 students enrolled*

STUDENT SERVICES Academic or career counseling, employment services for current students, placement services for program completers.

Sussex County Community College

1 College Hill, Newton, NJ 07860
http://www.sussex.edu/

CONTACT Dr. Constance Mierendorf, President
Telephone: 973-300-2100

GENERAL INFORMATION Public Institution. Founded 1981. **Accreditation:** Regional (MSA/CIHE). **Total program enrollment:** 2223. **Application fee:** $15.

PROGRAM(S) OFFERED
• **Automotive Engineering Technology/Technician** *1 student enrolled* • **Child Care Provider/Assistant** *3 students enrolled* • **Graphic Design** *1 student enrolled* • **Legal Assistant/Paralegal** *8 students enrolled*

STUDENT SERVICES Academic or career counseling, employment services for current students, placement services for program completers, remedial services.

Teterboro School of Aeronautics

Teterboro Airport, 80 Moonachie Avenue, Teterboro, NJ 07608-1083
http://www.teterboroschool.com/

CONTACT Donald Hulse, President
Telephone: 201-288-6300

GENERAL INFORMATION Private Institution. Founded 1947. **Total program enrollment:** 132. **Application fee:** $75.

PROGRAM(S) OFFERED
• **Aircraft Powerplant Technology/Technician** *1316 hrs./$13,893* • **Airframe Mechanics and Aircraft Maintenance Technology/Technician** *1316 hrs./ $13,893*

STUDENT SERVICES Academic or career counseling, employment services for current students, placement services for program completers.

Thomas Edison State College

101 West State Street, Trenton, NJ 08608-1176
http://www.tesc.edu/

CONTACT Dr. George A. Pruitt, President
Telephone: 609-984-1100

GENERAL INFORMATION Public Institution. Founded 1972. **Accreditation:** Regional (MSA/CIHE). **Application fee:** $75.

PROGRAM(S) OFFERED
• **Computer and Information Sciences, General** *1 student enrolled* • **Electrical, Electronic and Communications Engineering Technology/Technician** *1 student enrolled* • **Health and Physical Education/Fitness, Other** *1 student enrolled*

STUDENT SERVICES Academic or career counseling.

Union County College

1033 Springfield Avenue, Cranford, NJ 07016-1599
http://www.ucc.edu/

CONTACT Dr. Thomas H. Brown, President
Telephone: 908-709-7000

GENERAL INFORMATION Public Institution. Founded 1933. **Accreditation:** Regional (MSA/CIHE); physical therapy assisting (APTA); practical nursing (NLN). **Total program enrollment:** 5690. **Application fee:** $35.

PROGRAM(S) OFFERED
• **Administrative Assistant and Secretarial Science, General** *2 students enrolled* • **Computer Programming/Programmer, General** *1 student enrolled* • **Criminal Justice/Law Enforcement Administration** *2 students enrolled* • **Emergency Medical Technology/Technician (EMT Paramedic)** *29 students enrolled* • **Language Interpretation and Translation** *1 student enrolled* • **Licensed Practical/Vocational Nurse Training (LPN, LVN, Cert, Dipl, AAS)** *37 students enrolled* • **Sign Language Interpretation and Translation** *5 students enrolled* • **Web/Multimedia Management and Webmaster** *1 student enrolled*

STUDENT SERVICES Academic or career counseling, employment services for current students, placement services for program completers, remedial services.

University of Medicine and Dentistry of New Jersey

65 Bergen Street, PO Box 1709, Newark, NJ 07107-1709
http://www.umdnj.edu/

CONTACT William F. Owen, Jr., MD, President
Telephone: 973-972-4300

GENERAL INFORMATION Public Institution. Founded 1970. **Accreditation:** Regional (MSA/CIHE); cytotechnology (ASC); dental assisting (ADA); dental hygiene (ADA); dietetics: undergraduate, postbaccalaureate internship (ADtA/CAADE); medical laboratory technology (NAACLS); medical technology (NAACLS); respiratory therapy technology (CoARC). **Total program enrollment:** 4191. **Application fee:** $75.

PROGRAM(S) OFFERED
• **Cytotechnology/Cytotechnologist** *1 student enrolled* • **Dental Assisting/Assistant** *6 students enrolled* • **Diagnostic Medical Sonography/Sonographer and Ultrasound Technician** *3 students enrolled* • **Health Professions and Related Clinical Sciences, Other** *3 students enrolled* • **Nuclear Medical Technology/Technologist** *2 students enrolled*

STUDENT SERVICES Academic or career counseling, daycare for children of students, remedial services.

Warren County Community College

475 Route 57 West, Washington, NJ 07882-4343
http://www.warren.edu/

CONTACT Dr. William Austin, President
Telephone: 908-835-9222

GENERAL INFORMATION Public Institution. Founded 1981. **Accreditation:** Regional (MSA/CIHE). **Total program enrollment:** 810. **Application fee:** $25.

PROGRAM(S) OFFERED
• **Business Administration and Management, General** *1 student enrolled* • **Educational/Instructional Media Design** *2 students enrolled* • **Kindergarten/Preschool Education and Teaching** *1 student enrolled* • **Legal Assistant/Paralegal** *4 students enrolled*

STUDENT SERVICES Academic or career counseling, employment services for current students, placement services for program completers, remedial services.

NEW YORK

A.B.I. School of Barbering & Cosmetology of Tribeca

113 Chambers Street, New York, NY 10007
americanbarberinstitute.com

CONTACT Karen Tenesaca, Financial Aid Director
Telephone: 212-227-6353

GENERAL INFORMATION Private Institution. **Total program enrollment:** 84.

PROGRAM(S) OFFERED
• **Barbering/Barber** *660 hrs./$3425* • **Cosmetology/Cosmetologist, General** *1000 hrs./$4700* • **Nail Technician/Specialist and Manicurist** *250 hrs./$1100*

STUDENT SERVICES Academic or career counseling, employment services for current students, placement services for program completers.

Ace Computer Training Center

109-19 72nd Road, Suite # 4F, Forest Hills, NY 11375

CONTACT Amit Shorewala, President
Telephone: 718-575-3223

GENERAL INFORMATION Private Institution.

PROGRAM(S) OFFERED
• **Information Science/Studies** *900 hrs.*

STUDENT SERVICES Academic or career counseling, placement services for program completers.

Adirondack Beauty School

108 Dix Avenue, Glens Falls, NY 12801

CONTACT Mary L. Senecal, President
Telephone: 518-745-1646

GENERAL INFORMATION Private Institution. **Total program enrollment:** 29.

PROGRAM(S) OFFERED
• **Cosmetology/Cosmetologist, General** *1000 hrs./$9000*

STUDENT SERVICES Academic or career counseling, placement services for program completers.

Adirondack Community College

640 Bay Road, Queensbury, NY 12804
http://www.sunyacc.edu/

CONTACT Dr. Ronald C. Heacock, President
Telephone: 518-743-2200

GENERAL INFORMATION Public Institution. Founded 1960. **Accreditation:** Regional (MSA/CIHE); health information technology (AHIMA). **Total program enrollment:** 2059. **Application fee:** $40.

PROGRAM(S) OFFERED
• **Child Care and Support Services Management** *7 students enrolled* • **Drafting and Design Technology/Technician, General** *1 student enrolled* • **Teacher Assistant/Aide** *4 students enrolled* • **Tool and Die Technology/Technician** *2 students enrolled*

STUDENT SERVICES Academic or career counseling, daycare for children of students, employment services for current students, placement services for program completers, remedial services.

Adult Practical Nursing–Albany BOCES

1015 Watervliet Shaker Road, Albany, NY 12205
http://www.bocescareertech.org/

CONTACT Charles Dedrick, District Superintendent
Telephone: 518-862-4800

GENERAL INFORMATION Private Institution. **Total program enrollment:** 129. **Application fee:** $25.

PROGRAM(S) OFFERED
• **Licensed Practical/Vocational Nurse Training (LPN, LVN, Cert, Dipl, AAS)** *1100 hrs./$10,305*

STUDENT SERVICES Academic or career counseling, employment services for current students, placement services for program completers, remedial services.

The Ailey School

211 West 61st Street, 3rd Floor, New York, NY 10023
http://www.alvinailey.org/

CONTACT Sharon Luckman, Executive Director
Telephone: 212-405-9008

GENERAL INFORMATION Private Institution. **Total program enrollment:** 74. **Application fee:** $50.

PROGRAM(S) OFFERED
• **Dance, General**

STUDENT SERVICES Academic or career counseling, employment services for current students, placement services for program completers.

Albany College of Pharmacy and Health Sciences

106 New Scotland Avenue, Albany, NY 12208-3425
http://www.acphs.edu/

CONTACT James J. Gozzo, President
Telephone: 518-694-7200

GENERAL INFORMATION Private Institution. Founded 1881. **Accreditation:** Regional (MSA/CIHE); cytotechnology (ASC). **Total program enrollment:** 1515. **Application fee:** $75.

PROGRAM(S) OFFERED
• **Cytotechnology/Cytotechnologist** *14 students enrolled*

STUDENT SERVICES Academic or career counseling, employment services for current students, placement services for program completers.

Allen School–Brooklyn

188 Montague Street, Brooklyn, NY 11201
http://www.allenschool.edu/

CONTACT Robert Teich, President
Telephone: 718-243-1700

GENERAL INFORMATION Private Institution. **Total program enrollment:** 522. **Application fee:** $100.

PROGRAM(S) OFFERED
• **Allied Health and Medical Assisting Services, Other** *372 students enrolled*
• **Medical/Clinical Assistant** *900 hrs./$15,895*

STUDENT SERVICES Academic or career counseling, employment services for current students, placement services for program completers, remedial services.

Allen School–Jamaica

163-18 Jamaica Avenue, Jamaica, NY 11432
http://www.allenschool.edu/

CONTACT Robert Teich, President
Telephone: 718-291-2200

GENERAL INFORMATION Private Institution. **Total program enrollment:** 603. **Application fee:** $100.

PROGRAM(S) OFFERED
• **Allied Health and Medical Assisting Services, Other** *363 students enrolled*
• **Medical Insurance Coding Specialist/Coder** *900 hrs./$9024* • **Medical/Clinical Assistant** *900 hrs./$14,895*

STUDENT SERVICES Academic or career counseling, employment services for current students, placement services for program completers, remedial services.

American Barber Institute

252 West 29th Street, New York, NY 10001-5271
http://americanbarberinstitute.com/

CONTACT Feliks Maryanovskiy, Chief Administrator
Telephone: 212-290-2289

GENERAL INFORMATION Private Institution. **Total program enrollment:** 141.

PROGRAM(S) OFFERED
• **Barbering/Barber** *660 hrs./$3425* • **Cosmetology/Cosmetologist, General** *1000 hrs./$4700* • **Nail Technician/Specialist and Manicurist** *250 hrs./$1100*

STUDENT SERVICES Academic or career counseling, employment services for current students, placement services for program completers.

American Beauty School

2048-52 McGraw Avenue, Bronx, NY 10462
http://www.americanbeautyschool.com/

CONTACT Wendy Yang, Director
Telephone: 718-931-7400

GENERAL INFORMATION Private Institution. **Total program enrollment:** 75. **Application fee:** $100.

PROGRAM(S) OFFERED
• **Cosmetology/Cosmetologist, General** *1060 hrs./$7430*

STUDENT SERVICES Academic or career counseling, placement services for program completers.

Apex Technical School

635 Avenue Of The Americas, New York, NY 10011
http://www.apextechnical.com/

CONTACT William Z. Cann, Chairman
Telephone: 212-645-3300

GENERAL INFORMATION Private Institution. **Total program enrollment:** 980. **Application fee:** $100.

PROGRAM(S) OFFERED
• **Autobody/Collision and Repair Technology/Technician** *900 hrs./$15,477* • **Automobile/Automotive Mechanics Technology/Technician** *900 hrs./$15,544* • **Construction Trades, General** *900 hrs./$14,649* • **Electrician** *900 hrs./$15,073* • **Heating, Air Conditioning and Refrigeration Technology/Technician (ACH/ACR/ACHR/HRAC/HVAC/AC Technology)** *900 hrs./$15,783* • **Heating, Air Conditioning, Ventilation and Refrigeration Maintenance Technology/Technician (HAC, HACR, HVAC, HVACR)** *228 students enrolled* • **Welding Technology/Welder** *900 hrs./$16,592*

STUDENT SERVICES Academic or career counseling, employment services for current students, placement services for program completers, remedial services.

The Art Institute of New York City

75 Varick Street, 16th Floor, New York, NY 10013
http://www.artinstitutes.edu/newyork/

CONTACT Dr. David Warren, President
Telephone: 212-226-5500

GENERAL INFORMATION Private Institution. Founded 1980. **Accreditation:** State accredited or approved. **Total program enrollment:** 1115. **Application fee:** $50.

PROGRAM(S) OFFERED
• **Baking and Pastry Arts/Baker/Pastry Chef** *90 students enrolled* • **Culinary Arts/Chef Training** *126 students enrolled* • **Restaurant, Culinary, and Catering Management/Manager** *10 students enrolled*

STUDENT SERVICES Academic or career counseling, employment services for current students, placement services for program completers, remedial services.

ASA Institute, The College of Advanced Technology

151 Lawrence Street, 2nd Floor, Brooklyn, NY 11201
http://www.asa.edu/

CONTACT Alex Shchegol, President
Telephone: 718-522-9073

GENERAL INFORMATION Private Institution. Founded 1985. **Accreditation:** Medical assisting (AAMAE); state accredited or approved. **Total program enrollment:** 3463. **Application fee:** $25.

PROGRAM(S) OFFERED
• **Business Administration and Management, General** *4 students enrolled* • **Computer and Information Sciences and Support Services, Other** *6 students enrolled* • **Computer and Information Sciences, General** • **Legal Administrative Assistant/Secretary** *2 students enrolled* • **Medical/Clinical Assistant** *23 students enrolled*

STUDENT SERVICES Academic or career counseling, employment services for current students, placement services for program completers, remedial services.

Associated Beth Rivkah Schools

310 Crown Street, Brooklyn, NY 11225-3004

CONTACT Benzion Stock, Administrator
Telephone: 718-735-0400

GENERAL INFORMATION Private Institution. **Total program enrollment:** 75.

PROGRAM(S) OFFERED
• **Theological and Ministerial Studies, Other** *44 students enrolled*

STUDENT SERVICES Academic or career counseling, employment services for current students, placement services for program completers, remedial services.

Austin Beauty School

527 Central Avenue, Albany, NY 12206
http://www.austin.edu/

CONTACT Faith A. Takes, President and CEO
Telephone: 518-786-0855

GENERAL INFORMATION Private Institution. **Total program enrollment:** 265. **Application fee:** $100.

PROGRAM(S) OFFERED
• **Barbering/Barber** *600 hrs./$6100* • **Cosmetology/Cosmetologist, General** *103 hrs./$10,187* • **Nail Technician/Specialist and Manicurist** *250 hrs./$1700*

STUDENT SERVICES Academic or career counseling, employment services for current students, placement services for program completers.

Aveda Institute New York

233 Spring Street, New York, NY 10013
http://www.Aveda.com/

CONTACT Sarah Herold, Director
Telephone: 212-807-1492

GENERAL INFORMATION Private Institution. **Total program enrollment:** 166.

PROGRAM(S) OFFERED
• **Aesthetician/Esthetician and Skin Care Specialist** *600 hrs./$8020* • **Cosmetology/Cosmetologist, General** *8 hrs./$15,380*

STUDENT SERVICES Academic or career counseling, placement services for program completers, remedial services.

Beauty School of Middletown

9 Hyde Park Mall, Hyde Park, NY 12538
http://www.thebsm.com/

CONTACT Joanne Spano, Director
Telephone: 845-229-6541

GENERAL INFORMATION Private Institution. **Total program enrollment:** 17. **Application fee:** $100.

PROGRAM(S) OFFERED
• **Cosmetology and Related Personal Grooming Arts, Other** • **Cosmetology/Cosmetologist, General** *1000 hrs./$12,990* • **Nail Technician/Specialist and Manicurist** *250 hrs./$2850*

STUDENT SERVICES Placement services for program completers.

Beauty School of Middletown

225 Dolson Avenue, Middletown, NY 10940
http://www.thebsm.com/

CONTACT Robert J. Johnson, Director
Telephone: 845-343-2171

GENERAL INFORMATION Private Institution. Founded 1963. **Total program enrollment:** 42. **Application fee:** $100.

PROGRAM(S) OFFERED
• **Aesthetician/Esthetician and Skin Care Specialist** *600 hrs./$8500* • **Cosmetology and Related Personal Grooming Arts, Other** *12 students enrolled* • **Cosmetology/Cosmetologist, General** *1000 hrs./$12,990* • **Make-Up Artist/Specialist** *12 students enrolled* • **Nail Technician/Specialist and Manicurist** *250 hrs./$2850*

STUDENT SERVICES Placement services for program completers.

Berkeley College–New York City Campus

3 East 43rd Street, New York, NY 10017-4604
http://www.berkeleycollege.edu/

CONTACT Dr. Dario Cortes, President
Telephone: 212-986-4343

GENERAL INFORMATION Private Institution. Founded 1936. **Accreditation:** Regional (MSA/CIHE). **Total program enrollment:** 3408. **Application fee:** $50.

PROGRAM(S) OFFERED
• **Business/Office Automation/Technology/Data Entry** *2 students enrolled* • **General Office Occupations and Clerical Services**

STUDENT SERVICES Academic or career counseling, employment services for current students, placement services for program completers, remedial services.

Berk Trade and Business School

312 West 36th Street, 4th Floor, New York, NY 10018
http://www.berktradeschool.com/

CONTACT Marlin Fokusorgbor, School Director
Telephone: 718-729-0909

GENERAL INFORMATION Private Institution. **Total program enrollment:** 100.

PROGRAM(S) OFFERED
• Building/Property Maintenance and Management *600 hrs./$8000* • Electrical and Power Transmission Installation/Installer, General *600 hrs./$8300* • Plumbing Technology/Plumber *600 hrs./$8000*

STUDENT SERVICES Academic or career counseling, placement services for program completers, remedial services.

Borough of Manhattan Community College of the City University of New York

199 Chambers Street, New York, NY 10007-1097
http://www.bmcc.cuny.edu/

CONTACT Antonio Perez, President
Telephone: 212-220-8000

GENERAL INFORMATION Public Institution. Founded 1963. **Accreditation:** Regional (MSA/CIHE); emergency medical services (JRCEMTP); health information technology (AHIMA). **Total program enrollment:** 13690. **Application fee:** $65.

STUDENT SERVICES Academic or career counseling, daycare for children of students, employment services for current students, placement services for program completers, remedial services.

Bramson ORT College

69-30 Austin Street, Forest Hills, NY 11375-4239
http://www.bramsonort.edu/

CONTACT Ephraim Buhks, Director
Telephone: 718-261-5800

GENERAL INFORMATION Private Institution. Founded 1977. **Accreditation:** State program registration (RUSNY). **Total program enrollment:** 614. **Application fee:** $50.

PROGRAM(S) OFFERED
• Accounting Technology/Technician and Bookkeeping • Accounting *2 students enrolled* • Administrative Assistant and Secretarial Science, General • Business Administration and Management, General • Computer Programming/Programmer, General *2 students enrolled* • Electrical, Electronic and Communications Engineering Technology/Technician

STUDENT SERVICES Academic or career counseling, employment services for current students, placement services for program completers, remedial services.

Branford Hall Career Institute–Albany Campus

500 New Karner Road, Albany, NY 12205
http://www.branfordhall.com/

CONTACT Reggie Greene, School Director
Telephone: 518-456-4464

GENERAL INFORMATION Private Institution. **Total program enrollment:** 242. **Application fee:** $100.

PROGRAM(S) OFFERED
• Medical Insurance Coding Specialist/Coder *100 hrs./$7034* • Medical/Clinical Assistant *900 hrs./$11,484*
STUDENT SERVICES Academic or career counseling, placement services for program completers.

Branford Hall Career Institute–Bohemia Campus

3075 Veterans Memorial Highway, Ronkonkoma, NY 11779
http://www.branfordhall.com/

CONTACT David Goodwin, School Director
Telephone: 631-589-1222

GENERAL INFORMATION Private Institution. Founded 1997. **Total program enrollment:** 512. **Application fee:** $100.

PROGRAM(S) OFFERED
• Health and Medical Administrative Services, Other *960 hrs./$10,275* • Heating, Air Conditioning and Refrigeration Technology/Technician (ACH/ACR/ACHR/HRAC/HVAC/AC Technology) *1200 hrs./$16,400* • Medical/Clinical Assistant *960 hrs./$11,050*

STUDENT SERVICES Academic or career counseling, placement services for program completers.

Briarcliffe College

1055 Stewart Avenue, Bethpage, NY 11714
http://www.bcl.edu/

CONTACT Dr. George Santiago, Jr., President
Telephone: 516-918-3600

GENERAL INFORMATION Private Institution. Founded 1966. **Accreditation:** Regional (MSA/CIHE). **Total program enrollment:** 1145. **Application fee:** $35.

PROGRAM(S) OFFERED
• Accounting *3 students enrolled* • Computer Installation and Repair Technology/Technician • Computer Programming/Programmer, General *3 students enrolled*

STUDENT SERVICES Academic or career counseling, employment services for current students, placement services for program completers, remedial services.

Brittany Beauty School

210 East 188th Street, Bronx, NY 10458
http://www.BrittanyBeautySchool.com/

CONTACT Gary R. Ferrara, President/CEO
Telephone: 718-220-0400

GENERAL INFORMATION Private Institution. **Total program enrollment:** 134.

PROGRAM(S) OFFERED
• Cosmetology/Cosmetologist, General *1000 hrs./$12,700*
STUDENT SERVICES Placement services for program completers.

Brittany Beauty School

3272 Hempstead Turnpike, Levittown, NY 11756
http://www.brittanybeautyschool.com/

CONTACT Gary R. Ferrara, President/CEO
Telephone: 516-731-8300 Ext. 305

GENERAL INFORMATION Private Institution. Founded 1941. **Total program enrollment:** 105.

PROGRAM(S) OFFERED
• Cosmetology/Cosmetologist, General *1000 hrs./$12,700*
STUDENT SERVICES Placement services for program completers.

Bronx Community College of the City University of New York

University Avenue & West 181st Street, Bronx, NY 10453
http://www.bcc.cuny.edu/

CONTACT Carolyn G. Williams, President
Telephone: 718-289-5100

GENERAL INFORMATION Public Institution. Founded 1959. **Accreditation:** Regional (MSA/CIHE); engineering technology (ABET/TAC); nuclear medicine technology (JRCNMT); radiologic technology: radiography (JRCERT). **Total program enrollment:** 4936. **Application fee:** $65.

PROGRAM(S) OFFERED
• **Automobile/Automotive Mechanics Technology/Technician** 3 students enrolled • **Legal Assistant/Paralegal** 5 students enrolled • **Licensed Practical/Vocational Nurse Training (LPN, LVN, Cert, Dipl, AAS)** 6 students enrolled • **Teacher Assistant/Aide** 4 students enrolled • **Wildlife and Wildlands Science and Management** 2 students enrolled

STUDENT SERVICES Academic or career counseling, daycare for children of students, employment services for current students, placement services for program completers, remedial services.

Brooklyn College of the City University of New York

2900 Bedford Avenue, Brooklyn, NY 11210-2889
http://www.brooklyn.cuny.edu/

CONTACT Christoph M. Kimmich, President
Telephone: 718-951-5000

GENERAL INFORMATION Public Institution. Founded 1930. **Accreditation:** Regional (MSA/CIHE); audiology (ASHA); dietetics: postbaccalaureate internship (ADtA/CAADE); speech-language pathology (ASHA). **Total program enrollment:** 9711. **Application fee:** $65.

PROGRAM(S) OFFERED
• **Cinematography and Film/Video Production** 5 students enrolled

STUDENT SERVICES Academic or career counseling, daycare for children of students, employment services for current students, placement services for program completers.

Broome Community College

PO Box 1017, Binghamton, NY 13902-1017
http://www.sunybroome.edu/

CONTACT Dr. Daniel Hayes, Interim President
Telephone: 607-778-5000

GENERAL INFORMATION Public Institution. Founded 1946. **Accreditation:** Regional (MSA/CIHE); dental hygiene (ADA); engineering technology (ABET/TAC); health information technology (AHIMA); medical assisting (AAMAE); medical laboratory technology (NAACLS); physical therapy assisting (APTA); radiologic technology: radiography (JRCERT). **Total program enrollment:** 4234.

PROGRAM(S) OFFERED
• **Child Care and Support Services Management** 4 students enrolled • **Clinical/Medical Laboratory Science and Allied Professions, Other** 17 students enrolled • **Computer and Information Sciences and Support Services, Other** 2 students enrolled • **General Office Occupations and Clerical Services** 1 student enrolled • **Legal Assistant/Paralegal** 2 students enrolled • **Management Information Systems and Services, Other** 1 student enrolled • **Medical Transcription/Transcriptionist** 9 students enrolled • **Quality Control Technology/Technician** 1 student enrolled

STUDENT SERVICES Academic or career counseling, daycare for children of students, employment services for current students, placement services for program completers, remedial services.

Broome-Delaware-Tioga BOCES–Program in Practical Nursing

435 Glenwood Road, Binghamton, NY 13905
http://btboces.org/

CONTACT Allen Buyck, Superintendent
Telephone: 607-763-3465

GENERAL INFORMATION Public Institution. Founded 1953. **Total program enrollment:** 22. **Application fee:** $25.

PROGRAM(S) OFFERED
• **Licensed Practical/Vocational Nurse Training (LPN, LVN, Cert, Dipl, AAS)** 1200 hrs./$9068

STUDENT SERVICES Academic or career counseling, daycare for children of students, placement services for program completers, remedial services.

Bryant & Stratton College—Albany Campus

1259 Central Avenue, Albany, NY 12205-5230
http://www.bryantstratton.edu/

CONTACT Michael A. Gutierrez, Campus Director
Telephone: 518-437-1802

GENERAL INFORMATION Private Institution. Founded 1857. **Accreditation:** Regional (MSA/CIHE); state program registration (RUSNY); medical assisting (AAMAE). **Total program enrollment:** 468.

STUDENT SERVICES Academic or career counseling, employment services for current students, placement services for program completers, remedial services.

Bryant & Stratton College—Buffalo Campus

465 Main Street, Suite 400, Buffalo, NY 14203
http://www.bryantstratton.edu/

CONTACT Mr. Jeffrey P. Tredo, WNY Campus Director
Telephone: 716-884-9120

GENERAL INFORMATION Private Institution. Founded 1854. **Accreditation:** Regional (MSA/CIHE); state program registration (RUSNY); medical assisting (AAMAE). **Total program enrollment:** 473. **Application fee:** $35.

STUDENT SERVICES Academic or career counseling, employment services for current students, placement services for program completers, remedial services.

Bryant & Stratton College—Southtowns Campus

200 Redtail, Orchard Park, NY 14127
http://www.bryantstratton.edu/

CONTACT Mr. Paul Bahr, Campus Director
Telephone: 716-677-9500

GENERAL INFORMATION Private Institution. Founded 1989. **Accreditation:** Regional (MSA/CIHE); state program registration (RUSNY). **Total program enrollment:** 663. **Application fee:** $35.

STUDENT SERVICES Academic or career counseling, employment services for current students, placement services for program completers, remedial services.

Bryant & Stratton College—Syracuse Campus

953 James Street, Syracuse, NY 13203-2502
http://www.bryantstratton.edu/

CONTACT Michael Sattler, Campus Director
Telephone: 315-472-6603

GENERAL INFORMATION Private Institution. Founded 1854. **Accreditation:** Regional (MSA/CIHE); state program registration (RUSNY); medical assisting (AAMAE). **Total program enrollment:** 494.

STUDENT SERVICES Academic or career counseling, employment services for current students, placement services for program completers, remedial services.

Canisius College

2001 Main Street, Buffalo, NY 14208-1098
http://www.canisius.edu/

CONTACT Vincent M. Cooke, SJ, President
Telephone: 716-883-7000

GENERAL INFORMATION Private Institution. Founded 1870. **Accreditation:** Regional (MSA/CIHE); athletic training (JRCAT). **Total program enrollment:** 3984. **Application fee:** $40.

PROGRAM(S) OFFERED
• Women's Studies

STUDENT SERVICES Academic or career counseling, employment services for current students, placement services for program completers, remedial services.

Capri School of Hair Design

28 South Main Street, Spring Valley, NY 10977
http://caprinow.com/

CONTACT Anthony W. Fiore, Director
Telephone: 845-623-6339

GENERAL INFORMATION Private Institution. Founded 1963. **Total program enrollment:** 36. **Application fee:** $100.

PROGRAM(S) OFFERED
• Aesthetician/Esthetician and Skin Care Specialist 600 hrs./$8495
• Cosmetology/Cosmetologist, General 1000 hrs./$11,850 • Make-Up Artist/Specialist 18 students enrolled

STUDENT SERVICES Academic or career counseling, placement services for program completers.

Career Academy of New York

154 West 14th Street, New York, NY 10011

CONTACT Michael R. Iannacone, Chief Operating Officer
Telephone: 212-675-6655

GENERAL INFORMATION Private Institution. **Total program enrollment:** 251. **Application fee:** $100.

PROGRAM(S) OFFERED
• Clinical/Medical Laboratory Assistant 9 hrs./$9449 • Culinary Arts/Chef Training 9 hrs./$9745 • Food Preparation/Professional Cooking/Kitchen Assistant 86 students enrolled • Hotel/Motel Administration/Management 9 hrs./$11,635 • Medical/Clinical Assistant 21 students enrolled

STUDENT SERVICES Academic or career counseling, employment services for current students, placement services for program completers.

Career Institute of Health and Technology

340 Flatbush Avenue Ext-3rd Floor, Brooklyn, NY 11201
http://www.careerinstitute.edu/

CONTACT Kenneth G. Barrett, President
Telephone: 718-422-1212

GENERAL INFORMATION Private Institution. **Total program enrollment:** 322. **Application fee:** $50.

PROGRAM(S) OFFERED
• Electrician 780 hrs./$9850 • Health Information/Medical Records Technology/Technician 23 students enrolled • Medical/Clinical Assistant 900 hrs./$10,250

STUDENT SERVICES Academic or career counseling, employment services for current students, placement services for program completers, remedial services.

Career Institute of Health and Technology

200 Garden City Plaza, Garden City, NY 11530-3301
http://www.careerinstitute.edu/

CONTACT Kenneth G. Barrett, Executive Director
Telephone: 516-877-1225

GENERAL INFORMATION Private Institution. **Total program enrollment:** 319. **Application fee:** $50.

PROGRAM(S) OFFERED
• Automotive Engineering Technology/Technician 1200 hrs./$13,490
• Computer Engineering Technology/Technician 2 students enrolled • Electrician 780 hrs./$9850 • Health Information/Medical Records Technology/Technician 9 students enrolled • Medical/Clinical Assistant 900 hrs./$10,250

STUDENT SERVICES Academic or career counseling, employment services for current students, placement services for program completers.

Carsten Institute of New York

22 E. 17th Street, Second Floor, New York, NY 10003
http://carsteninstitute.com/

CONTACT Kirsten Wilms, Director
Telephone: 212-675-4884

GENERAL INFORMATION Private Institution. **Total program enrollment:** 44.

PROGRAM(S) OFFERED
• Aesthetician/Esthetician and Skin Care Specialist 600 hrs./$7500
• Cosmetology/Cosmetologist, General 1000 hrs./$12,700

STUDENT SERVICES Academic or career counseling, placement services for program completers.

Cattaraugus County BOCES–School of Practical Nursing

1825 Windfall Road, Olean, NY 14760
http://www.caboces.org/

CONTACT Robert Olczak, EdD, District Superintendent
Telephone: 716-376-8268

GENERAL INFORMATION Public Institution. Founded 1968.

PROGRAM(S) OFFERED
• Licensed Practical/Vocational Nurse Training (LPN, LVN, Cert, Dipl, AAS) 1300 hrs.

STUDENT SERVICES Academic or career counseling, employment services for current students, remedial services.

Cayuga County Community College

197 Franklin Street, Auburn, NY 13021-3099
http://www.cayuga-cc.edu/

CONTACT Dr. Daniel Larson, President
Telephone: 315-255-1743

GENERAL INFORMATION Public Institution. Founded 1953. **Accreditation:** Regional (MSA/CIHE). **Total program enrollment: 2007.**

PROGRAM(S) OFFERED
• **Business, Management, Marketing, and Related Support Services, Other** *3 students enrolled* • **Child Care and Support Services Management** *1 student enrolled* • **Computer and Information Sciences and Support Services, Other** *1 student enrolled* • **Electrical, Electronic and Communications Engineering Technology/Technician** *1 student enrolled*

STUDENT SERVICES Academic or career counseling, daycare for children of students, employment services for current students, placement services for program completers, remedial services.

Cayuga-Onondaga BOCES

5980 South Street Road, Auburn, NY 13021
http://www.cayboces.org/

CONTACT William S. Speck, District Superintendent
Telephone: 315-253-0361

GENERAL INFORMATION Public Institution. **Total program enrollment: 33. Application fee: $25.**

PROGRAM(S) OFFERED
• **Licensed Practical/Vocational Nurse Training (LPN, LVN, Cert, Dipl, AAS)** *32 students enrolled*

STUDENT SERVICES Academic or career counseling, remedial services.

Cazenovia College

22 Sullivan Street, Cazenovia, NY 13035-1084
http://www.cazenovia.edu/

CONTACT Mark J. Tierno, President
Telephone: 800-654-3210

GENERAL INFORMATION Private Institution. Founded 1824. **Accreditation:** Regional (MSA/CIHE). **Total program enrollment: 976. Application fee: $30.**

PROGRAM(S) OFFERED
• **Business Administration and Management, General**

STUDENT SERVICES Academic or career counseling, employment services for current students, placement services for program completers, remedial services.

Center for Natural Wellness School of Massage Therapy

3 Cerone Commercial Drive, Albany, NY 12205

GENERAL INFORMATION Private Institution. **Total program enrollment: 68. Application fee: $50.**

PROGRAM(S) OFFERED
• **Massage Therapy/Therapeutic Massage** *1020 hrs./$14,450*

STUDENT SERVICES Academic or career counseling, placement services for program completers, remedial services.

Charles Stuart School of Diamond Setting

1420 Kings Highway, 2nd Floor, Brooklyn, NY 11229
http://charlesstuartschool.com/

CONTACT Charles S. Wechsler, Director
Telephone: 718-339-2640

GENERAL INFORMATION Private Institution. Founded 1988. **Total program enrollment: 42. Application fee: $50.**

PROGRAM(S) OFFERED
• **Locksmithing and Safe Repair** *900 hrs./$10,950*

STUDENT SERVICES Academic or career counseling, placement services for program completers, remedial services.

Cheryl Fells School of Business

2541 Military Road, Niagara Falls, NY 14304

CONTACT Cheryl Fell, Director
Telephone: 716-297-2750

GENERAL INFORMATION Private Institution. **Total program enrollment: 31.**

PROGRAM(S) OFFERED
• **Accounting and Related Services, Other** *1500 hrs./$12,500* • **Accounting** • **Administrative Assistant and Secretarial Science, General** *1500 hrs./$12,500* • **Business/Office Automation/Technology/Data Entry** • **Health and Medical Administrative Services, Other** • **Legal Administrative Assistant/Secretary** *1500 hrs./$12,500* • **Legal Assistant/Paralegal** • **Medical Administrative/Executive Assistant and Medical Secretary** *8 students enrolled* • **Medical Office Management/Administration** *1500 hrs./$14,100* • **Medical Reception/Receptionist** *900 hrs./$7500*

STUDENT SERVICES Academic or career counseling, employment services for current students, placement services for program completers.

The Chubb Institute–New York

498 7th Avenue, 17th Floor, New York, NY 10018
http://www.chubbinstitute.edu/

CONTACT Gary E. Duchnowski, Campus President
Telephone: 212-659-2116

GENERAL INFORMATION Private Institution. **Total program enrollment: 859. Application fee: $50.**

PROGRAM(S) OFFERED
• **Computer and Information Systems Security** *1200 hrs./$17,760* • **Medical Insurance Specialist/Medical Biller** *860 hrs./$11,034* • **Medical Office Management/Administration** *41 students enrolled* • **Medical/Clinical Assistant** *816 hrs./$11,350* • **Web Page, Digital/Multimedia and Information Resources Design** *1200 hrs./$18,200*

STUDENT SERVICES Placement services for program completers.

City University of New York System

535 East 80th Street, New York, NY 10021-0767
http://www.cuny.edu/

CONTACT Dr. Matthew Goldstein, Chancellor
Telephone: 212-794-5500

GENERAL INFORMATION Public Institution.

Clinton Community College

136 Clinton Point Drive, Plattsburgh, NY 12901-9573
http://clintoncc.suny.edu/

CONTACT Dr. Fred Woodward, Interim President
Telephone: 518-562-4200

GENERAL INFORMATION Public Institution. Founded 1969. **Accreditation:** Regional (MSA/CIHE); medical laboratory technology (NAACLS). **Total program enrollment:** 1178.

PROGRAM(S) OFFERED
• **Administrative Assistant and Secretarial Science, General** *1 student enrolled* • **Child Care and Support Services Management** *1 student enrolled* • **Legal Administrative Assistant/Secretary** *1 student enrolled* • **Medical Office Management/Administration** *3 students enrolled* • **Substance Abuse/Addiction Counseling** *1 student enrolled*

STUDENT SERVICES Academic or career counseling, daycare for children of students, remedial services.

Clinton-Essex-Warren-Washington BOCES–Practical Nursing

PO Box 455, Plattsburgh, NY 12901
http://www.cves.org/

CONTACT Craig King, Superintendent
Telephone: 518-561-0100

GENERAL INFORMATION Public Institution. Founded 1971. **Total program enrollment:** 35.

PROGRAM(S) OFFERED
• **Licensed Practical/Vocational Nurse Training (LPN, LVN, Cert, Dipl, AAS)** *1200 hrs./$9772*

STUDENT SERVICES Academic or career counseling, daycare for children of students, employment services for current students, remedial services.

College of Staten Island of the City University of New York

2800 Victory Boulevard, Staten Island, NY 10314-6600
http://www.csi.cuny.edu/

CONTACT Tomas Morales, President
Telephone: 718-982-2000

GENERAL INFORMATION Public Institution. Founded 1955. **Accreditation:** Regional (MSA/CIHE); computer science (ABET/CSAC); engineering technology (ABET/TAC). **Total program enrollment:** 8681. **Application fee:** $65.

STUDENT SERVICES Academic or career counseling, daycare for children of students, employment services for current students, placement services for program completers, remedial services.

The College of Westchester

325 Central Avenue, PO Box 710, White Plains, NY 10602
http://www.cw.edu/

CONTACT Karen J. Smith, President
Telephone: 914-948-4442

GENERAL INFORMATION Private Institution. Founded 1915. **Accreditation:** Regional (MSA/CIHE). **Total program enrollment:** 1032. **Application fee:** $40.

PROGRAM(S) OFFERED
• **Accounting Technology/Technician and Bookkeeping** *2 students enrolled* • **Administrative Assistant and Secretarial Science, General** *9 students enrolled* • **Business Administration and Management, General** • **Computer**

Programming/Programmer, General • **Computer and Information Sciences and Support Services, Other** *3 students enrolled* • **Medical Office Management/Administration** *4 students enrolled*

STUDENT SERVICES Academic or career counseling, employment services for current students, placement services for program completers, remedial services.

Columbia-Greene Community College

4400 Route 23, Hudson, NY 12534-0327
http://www.sunycgcc.edu/

CONTACT James R. Campion, President
Telephone: 518-828-4181

GENERAL INFORMATION Public Institution. Founded 1969. **Accreditation:** Regional (MSA/CIHE). **Total program enrollment:** 997. **Application fee:** $40.

PROGRAM(S) OFFERED
• **Administrative Assistant and Secretarial Science, General** *1 student enrolled* • **Automobile/Automotive Mechanics Technology/Technician** *3 students enrolled* • **Computer and Information Sciences and Support Services, Other** *2 students enrolled* • **Information Science/Studies** *2 students enrolled* • **Medical Office Management/Administration** *4 students enrolled* • **Teacher Assistant/Aide** *21 students enrolled*

STUDENT SERVICES Academic or career counseling, daycare for children of students, employment services for current students, placement services for program completers, remedial services.

Continental School of Beauty Culture–Batavia

215 Main Street, Batavia, NY 14020
http://www.continentalschbeauty.com/

CONTACT Charles Shumway, President
Telephone: 585-344-0886

GENERAL INFORMATION Private Institution. Founded 1960. **Total program enrollment:** 30.

PROGRAM(S) OFFERED
• **Cosmetology/Cosmetologist, General** *1000 hrs./$10,460*

STUDENT SERVICES Placement services for program completers.

Continental School of Beauty Culture–Jefferson

633 Jefferson Road, Rochester, NY 14623
http://www.continentalschbeauty.com/

CONTACT Charles G. Shumway, President
Telephone: 585-272-8060

GENERAL INFORMATION Private Institution. Founded 1960. **Total program enrollment:** 200.

PROGRAM(S) OFFERED
• **Aesthetician/Esthetician and Skin Care Specialist** *600 hrs./$6700* • **Cosmetology and Related Personal Grooming Arts, Other** *75 hrs./$750* • **Cosmetology/Cosmetologist, General** *1000 hrs./$10,460* • **Nail Technician/Specialist and Manicurist** *250 hrs./$1887*

STUDENT SERVICES Placement services for program completers.

Continental School of Beauty Culture–Kenmore

326 Kenmore Avenue, Buffalo, NY 14223
http://www.continentalschbeauty.com/

CONTACT Charles Shumway, President
Telephone: 716-833-5016

GENERAL INFORMATION Private Institution. Founded 1960. **Total program enrollment:** 54.

PROGRAM(S) OFFERED
• **Aesthetician/Esthetician and Skin Care Specialist** *600 hrs./$6700*
• **Cosmetology/Cosmetologist, General** *1000 hrs./$10,460* • **Nail Technician/Specialist and Manicurist** *250 hrs./$1887*

STUDENT SERVICES Placement services for program completers.

Continental School of Beauty Culture–Olean

515 North Union Street, Olean, NY 14760
http://www.continentalschbeauty.com/

CONTACT Charles G. Shumway, President
Telephone: 716-372-5095

GENERAL INFORMATION Private Institution. Founded 1990. **Total program enrollment:** 44.

PROGRAM(S) OFFERED
• **Aesthetician/Esthetician and Skin Care Specialist** *600 hrs./$6700*
• **Cosmetology and Related Personal Grooming Arts, Other** *75 hrs./$750*
• **Cosmetology/Cosmetologist, General** *1000 hrs./$10,460* • **Nail Technician/Specialist and Manicurist** *250 hrs./$1888*

STUDENT SERVICES Placement services for program completers.

Continental School of Beauty Culture–West Seneca

1050 Union Road, West Seneca, NY 14224
http://www.continentalschbeauty.com/

CONTACT Charles Shumway, President
Telephone: 716-675-8205

GENERAL INFORMATION Private Institution. Founded 1960. **Total program enrollment:** 60.

PROGRAM(S) OFFERED
• **Aesthetician/Esthetician and Skin Care Specialist** *600 hrs./$6700*
• **Cosmetology/Cosmetologist, General** *1000 hrs./$10,460*

STUDENT SERVICES Placement services for program completers.

Cornell University

Ithaca, NY 14853-0001
http://www.cornell.edu/

CONTACT David Skorton, President
Telephone: 607-255-2000

GENERAL INFORMATION Private Institution. Founded 1865. **Accreditation:** Regional (MSA/CIHE); dietetics: postbaccalaureate internship (ADtA/CAADE); home economics (AAFCS); interior design: professional (CIDA). **Total program enrollment:** 20184. **Application fee:** $70.

PROGRAM(S) OFFERED
• **Labor and Industrial Relations** *37 students enrolled*

STUDENT SERVICES Academic or career counseling, employment services for current students, placement services for program completers.

Corning Community College

One Academic Drive, Corning, NY 14830-3297
http://www.corning-cc.edu/

CONTACT Dr. Floyd Amann, President
Telephone: 607-962-9011

GENERAL INFORMATION Public Institution. Founded 1956. **Accreditation:** Regional (MSA/CIHE). **Total program enrollment:** 2339. **Application fee:** $25.

PROGRAM(S) OFFERED
• **Accounting Technology/Technician and Bookkeeping** *1 student enrolled*
• **Automobile/Automotive Mechanics Technology/Technician** *3 students enrolled*
• **Child Care and Support Services Management** *3 students enrolled* • **Drafting and Design Technology/Technician, General** *2 students enrolled* • **Machine Shop Technology/Assistant** *3 students enrolled* • **Public Administration and Social Service Professions, Other** *4 students enrolled*

STUDENT SERVICES Academic or career counseling, employment services for current students, placement services for program completers, remedial services.

Culinary Academy of Long Island

141 Post Avenue, Westbury, NY 11590
http://culinaryacademy.edu/

CONTACT Michael Levitt, Director
Telephone: 516-364-4344

GENERAL INFORMATION Private Institution. **Total program enrollment:** 216. **Application fee:** $100.

PROGRAM(S) OFFERED
• **Baking and Pastry Arts/Baker/Pastry Chef** *600 hrs./$9110* • **Cooking and Related Culinary Arts, General** *600 hrs./$8385* • **Culinary Arts/Chef Training** *900 hrs./$16,400* • **Hospitality Administration/Management, General** *16 students enrolled* • **Hotel/Motel Administration/Management** *900 hrs./$11,380*

STUDENT SERVICES Academic or career counseling, employment services for current students, placement services for program completers.

The Culinary Institute of America

1946 Campus Drive, Hyde Park, NY 12538-1499
http://www.ciachef.edu/

CONTACT Dr. Tim Ryan, President
Telephone: 845-452-9600

GENERAL INFORMATION Private Institution. Founded 1946. **Accreditation:** Regional (MSA/CIHE); state accredited or approved. **Total program enrollment:** 2812. **Application fee:** $50.

PROGRAM(S) OFFERED
• **Culinary Arts and Related Services, Other** *81 students enrolled*

STUDENT SERVICES Academic or career counseling, employment services for current students, placement services for program completers, remedial services.

Daemen College

4380 Main Street, Amherst, NY 14226-3592
http://www.daemen.edu/

CONTACT Martin J. Anisman, President
Telephone: 716-839-3600

GENERAL INFORMATION Private Institution. Founded 1947. **Accreditation:** Regional (MSA/CIHE). **Total program enrollment:** 2045. **Application fee:** $25.

Daemen College (continued)

PROGRAM(S) OFFERED
● **Accounting** *34 students enrolled* ● **Human Resources Management/Personnel Administration, General** ● **Urban Studies/Affairs**

STUDENT SERVICES Academic or career counseling, employment services for current students, placement services for program completers, remedial services.

Davis College

400 Riverside Drive, Johnson City, NY 13790
http://www.davisny.edu/

CONTACT Dino Pedrone, President
Telephone: 607-729-1581

GENERAL INFORMATION Private Institution. Founded 1900. **Accreditation:** Regional (MSA/CIHE); state accredited or approved. **Total program enrollment:** 215. **Application fee:** $45.

PROGRAM(S) OFFERED
● **Bible/Biblical Studies** *1 student enrolled*

STUDENT SERVICES Academic or career counseling, employment services for current students, placement services for program completers, remedial services.

Delaware-Chenango-Madison-Otsego BOCES

6678 County Road 32, Norwich, NY 13815-3554

CONTACT Alan Pole, District Superintendent
Telephone: 607-335-1282

GENERAL INFORMATION Public Institution. **Total program enrollment:** 43. **Application fee:** $35.

PROGRAM(S) OFFERED
● **Licensed Practical/Vocational Nurse Training (LPN, LVN, Cert, Dipl, AAS)** *1239 hrs./$8614*

STUDENT SERVICES Academic or career counseling, daycare for children of students, employment services for current students, placement services for program completers, remedial services.

Dutchess BOCES–School of Practical Nursing

578 Salt Point Turnpike, Poughkeepsie, NY 12601-6599
http://www.dcboces.org/

CONTACT John C. Pennoyer, District Superintendent
Telephone: 845-486-8001

GENERAL INFORMATION Private Institution. **Total program enrollment:** 70. **Application fee:** $75.

PROGRAM(S) OFFERED
● **Licensed Practical/Vocational Nurse Training (LPN, LVN, Cert, Dipl, AAS)** *1100 hrs./$8675*

STUDENT SERVICES Academic or career counseling, placement services for program completers.

Dutchess Community College

53 Pendell Road, Poughkeepsie, NY 12601-1595
http://www.sunydutchess.edu/

CONTACT Dr. D. David Conklin, President
Telephone: 845-431-8000

GENERAL INFORMATION Public Institution. Founded 1957. **Accreditation:** Regional (MSA/CIHE); medical laboratory technology (NAACLS. **Total program enrollment:** 4456.

PROGRAM(S) OFFERED
● **Accounting Technology/Technician and Bookkeeping** *3 students enrolled*
● **Child Care and Support Services Management** *2 students enrolled* ● **Clinical/**

Medical Laboratory Science and Allied Professions, Other *9 students enrolled*
● **Computer Programming/Programmer, General** *1 student enrolled* ● **Drafting and Design Technology/Technician, General** *2 students enrolled* ● **Heating, Air Conditioning and Refrigeration Technology/Technician (ACH/ACR/ACHR/HRAC/HVAC/AC Technology)** *1 student enrolled* ● **Legal Assistant/Paralegal** *7 students enrolled* ● **Music Performance, General** *1 student enrolled* ● **Substance Abuse/Addiction Counseling** *5 students enrolled* ● **Teacher Assistant/Aide** *34 students enrolled*

STUDENT SERVICES Academic or career counseling, daycare for children of students, employment services for current students, placement services for program completers, remedial services.

Eastern-Suffolk School of Practical Nursing BOCES

201 Sunrise Highway, Patchogue, NY 11772

CONTACT Gary D. Bixhorn, Chief Operating Officer
Telephone: 631-582-2387

GENERAL INFORMATION Public Institution. **Total program enrollment:** 212. **Application fee:** $125.

PROGRAM(S) OFFERED
● **Licensed Practical/Vocational Nurse Training (LPN, LVN, Cert, Dipl, AAS)** *1260 hrs./$11,475*

STUDENT SERVICES Academic or career counseling, remedial services.

Elite Academy of Beauty Arts

426 Kings Highway, Brooklyn, NY 11223
http://www.beautysalonschool.com/

CONTACT Lina Sapronova, Director
Telephone: 718-998-8182

GENERAL INFORMATION Private Institution. **Total program enrollment:** 150. **Application fee:** $100.

PROGRAM(S) OFFERED
● **Aesthetician/Esthetician and Skin Care Specialist** *600 hrs./$6000*
● **Cosmetology and Related Personal Grooming Arts, Other** *75 hrs./$800*
● **Cosmetology/Cosmetologist, General** *1200 hrs./$10,700* ● **Hair Styling/Stylist and Hair Design** *180 hrs./$2000* ● **Nail Technician/Specialist and Manicurist** *250 hrs./$1500*

STUDENT SERVICES Academic or career counseling, placement services for program completers.

Elmira Business Institute

303 North Main Street, Elmira, NY 14901
http://www.ebi-college.com/

CONTACT Brad C. Phillips, President
Telephone: 607-733-7177

GENERAL INFORMATION Private Institution. Founded 1858. **Accreditation:** State accredited or approved. **Total program enrollment:** 316.

PROGRAM(S) OFFERED
● **Accounting** *5 students enrolled* ● **Administrative Assistant and Secretarial Science, General** *6 students enrolled* ● **Legal Administrative Assistant/Secretary** *4 students enrolled* ● **Medical Administrative/Executive Assistant and Medical Secretary** *22 students enrolled* ● **Medical Insurance Coding Specialist/Coder** *13 students enrolled* ● **Medical/Clinical Assistant** *11 students enrolled*

STUDENT SERVICES Academic or career counseling, employment services for current students, placement services for program completers, remedial services.

Elmira College

One Park Place, Elmira, NY 14901
http://www.elmira.edu/

CONTACT Thomas K. Meier, President
Telephone: 607-735-1800

GENERAL INFORMATION Private Institution. Founded 1855. **Accreditation:** Regional (MSA/CIHE). **Total program enrollment:** 1185. **Application fee:** $50.

PROGRAM(S) OFFERED
• Parks, Recreation and Leisure Studies

STUDENT SERVICES Academic or career counseling, employment services for current students, placement services for program completers, remedial services.

Empire Beauty School

38-15 Broadway, Astoria, NY 11103
http://www.empire.edu/

CONTACT Michael Bouman, President
Telephone: 800-223-3271

GENERAL INFORMATION Private Institution. **Total program enrollment:** 122. **Application fee:** $100.

PROGRAM(S) OFFERED
• Cosmetology/Cosmetologist, General 1000 hrs./$12,750

STUDENT SERVICES Placement services for program completers.

Empire Beauty School

22 West 34th Street, New York, NY 10001
http://www.empire.edu/

CONTACT Michael Bouman, President
Telephone: 800-223-3271

GENERAL INFORMATION Private Institution. **Total program enrollment:** 288. **Application fee:** $100.

PROGRAM(S) OFFERED
• Cosmetology/Cosmetologist, General 1000 hrs./$12,750

STUDENT SERVICES Placement services for program completers.

Empire Beauty School–Bensonhurst

2384 86th Street, Bensonhurst, NY 11214
http://www.empire.edu/

CONTACT Michael Bouman, President
Telephone: 800-223-3271

GENERAL INFORMATION Private Institution. **Total program enrollment:** 110. **Application fee:** $100.

PROGRAM(S) OFFERED
• Cosmetology/Cosmetologist, General 1000 hrs./$12,750

STUDENT SERVICES Placement services for program completers.

Erie #1 BOCES–Practical Nursing Program

355 Harlem Road, West Seneca, NY 14224
http://e1b.org/

CONTACT Patricia Riegle, Supervisor
Telephone: 716-822-3333

GENERAL INFORMATION Public Institution. **Total program enrollment:** 152. **Application fee:** $100.

PROGRAM(S) OFFERED
• Cosmetology/Cosmetologist, General 1000 hrs./$5500 • Licensed Practical/Vocational Nurse Training (LPN, LVN, Cert, Dipl, AAS) 1100 hrs./$8150 • Nursing, Other 128 students enrolled

STUDENT SERVICES Academic or career counseling, employment services for current students, placement services for program completers, remedial services.

Erie #2 Chautauqua-Cattaraugus BOCES

8685 Erie Road, Angola, NY 14006
http://www.e2ccb.org/

CONTACT Robert Guiffreda, District Superintendent
Telephone: 716-549-4454 Ext. 4060

GENERAL INFORMATION Public Institution. Founded 1987. **Total program enrollment:** 149. **Application fee:** $15.

PROGRAM(S) OFFERED
• Licensed Practical/Vocational Nurse Training (LPN, LVN, Cert, Dipl, AAS) 1158 hrs./$8550

STUDENT SERVICES Academic or career counseling, employment services for current students, placement services for program completers, remedial services.

Erie Community College

121 Ellicott Street, Buffalo, NY 14203-2698
http://www.ecc.edu/

CONTACT Mr. Jack Quinn, President
Telephone: 716-842-2770

GENERAL INFORMATION Public Institution. Founded 1971. **Accreditation:** Regional (MSA/CIHE); engineering technology (ABET/TAC); medical assisting (AAMAE); ophthalmic dispensing (COA); radiologic technology: radiation therapy technology (JRCERT). **Total program enrollment:** 9229. **Application fee:** $25.

PROGRAM(S) OFFERED
• Baking and Pastry Arts/Baker/Pastry Chef 4 students enrolled • Building/Construction Finishing, Management, and Inspection, Other 2 students enrolled • Community Organization and Advocacy 28 students enrolled • Computer and Information Sciences and Support Services, Other 1 student enrolled • Computer and Information Systems Security 3 students enrolled • Court Reporting/Court Reporter 1 student enrolled • Criminal Justice/Police Science 4 students enrolled • Dental Assisting/Assistant 11 students enrolled • Electrical/Electronics Equipment Installation and Repair, General 16 students enrolled • Emergency Medical Technology/Technician (EMT Paramedic) 19 students enrolled • Entrepreneurship/Entrepreneurial Studies 4 students enrolled • General Office Occupations and Clerical Services 3 students enrolled • Geography 2 students enrolled • Heating, Air Conditioning, Ventilation and Refrigeration Maintenance Technology/Technician (HAC, HACR, HVAC, HVACR) 5 students enrolled • Medical Office Management/Administration 8 students enrolled • Teacher Assistant/Aide 7 students enrolled • Web Page, Digital/Multimedia and Information Resources Design 10 students enrolled • Web/Multimedia Management and Webmaster 2 students enrolled

STUDENT SERVICES Academic or career counseling, daycare for children of students, employment services for current students, placement services for program completers, remedial services.

Eugenio María de Hostos Community College of the City University of New York

500 Grand Concourse, Bronx, NY 10451
http://www.hostos.cuny.edu/

CONTACT Dolores M. Fernandez, President
Telephone: 718-518-4444

GENERAL INFORMATION Public Institution. Founded 1968. **Accreditation:** Regional (MSA/CIHE); dental hygiene (ADA); radiologic technology: radiography (JRCERT). **Total program enrollment:** 2979. **Application fee:** $65.

PROGRAM(S) OFFERED
• Licensed Practical/Vocational Nurse Training (LPN, LVN, Cert, Dipl, AAS) *47 students enrolled*

STUDENT SERVICES Academic or career counseling, daycare for children of students, employment services for current students, placement services for program completers, remedial services.

Everest Institute

1630 Portland Avenue, Rochester, NY 14621
http://www.everest.edu/campus/rochester

CONTACT Carl A. Silvio, President
Telephone: 585-266-0430

GENERAL INFORMATION Private Institution. Founded 1863. **Accreditation:** State accredited or approved. **Total program enrollment:** 218.

PROGRAM(S) OFFERED
• Accounting Technology/Technician and Bookkeeping • Administrative Assistant and Secretarial Science, General • Business Administration and Management, General • Data Processing and Data Processing Technology/Technician

STUDENT SERVICES Employment services for current students, placement services for program completers.

Excelsior College

7 Columbia Circle, Albany, NY 12203-5159
http://www.excelsior.edu/

CONTACT John F. Ebersole, President
Telephone: 518-464-8500

GENERAL INFORMATION Private Institution. Founded 1970. **Accreditation:** Regional (MSA/CIHE); engineering technology (ABET/TAC). **Application fee:** $75.

PROGRAM(S) OFFERED
• Criminal Justice/Police Science *109 students enrolled* • Nursing—Registered Nurse Training (RN, ASN, BSN, MSN)

STUDENT SERVICES Academic or career counseling, placement services for program completers.

Farmingdale State College

2350 Broadhollow Road, Farmingdale, NY 11735
http://www.farmingdale.edu/

CONTACT Dr. Hubert Keen, President
Telephone: 516-420-2000

GENERAL INFORMATION Public Institution. Founded 1912. **Accreditation:** Regional (MSA/CIHE); dental hygiene (ADA); engineering technology (ABET/TAC); medical laboratory technology (NAACLS). **Total program enrollment:** 4878. **Application fee:** $40.

PROGRAM(S) OFFERED
• Accounting Technology/Technician and Bookkeeping *1 student enrolled*
• Electrical, Electronic and Communications Engineering Technology/Technician *2 students enrolled* • Health Professions and Related Clinical Sciences, Other *4 students enrolled* • Licensed Practical/Vocational Nurse Training (LPN, LVN, Cert, Dipl, AAS) *30 students enrolled* • Ornamental Horticulture *2 students enrolled*

STUDENT SERVICES Academic or career counseling, daycare for children of students, employment services for current students, placement services for program completers, remedial services.

Fashion Institute of Technology

Seventh Avenue at 27th Street, New York, NY 10001-5992
http://www.fitnyc.edu/

CONTACT Joyce F. Brown, President
Telephone: 212-217-7999

GENERAL INFORMATION Public Institution. Founded 1944. **Accreditation:** Regional (MSA/CIHE); art and design (NASAD); interior design: professional (CIDA). **Total program enrollment:** 7055. **Application fee:** $40.

PROGRAM(S) OFFERED
• Fashion/Apparel Design *13 students enrolled*

STUDENT SERVICES Academic or career counseling, employment services for current students, placement services for program completers, remedial services.

Finger Lakes Community College

4355 Lakeshore Drive, Canandaigua, NY 14424-8395
http://www.flcc.edu/

CONTACT Barbara G. Risser, President
Telephone: 585-394-3500

GENERAL INFORMATION Public Institution. Founded 1965. **Accreditation:** Regional (MSA/CIHE). **Total program enrollment:** 3121.

PROGRAM(S) OFFERED
• Computer Programming/Programmer, General *1 student enrolled* • Computer and Information Sciences and Support Services, Other *3 students enrolled* • Criminal Justice/Safety Studies *11 students enrolled* • Ornamental Horticulture *2 students enrolled* • Parks, Recreation and Leisure Studies *8 students enrolled* • Taxidermy/Taxidermist *1 student enrolled* • Teacher Assistant/Aide *1 student enrolled*

STUDENT SERVICES Academic or career counseling, daycare for children of students, employment services for current students, placement services for program completers, remedial services.

Fiorello H. LaGuardia Community College of the City University of New York

31-10 Thomson Avenue, Long Island City, NY 11101-3071
http://www.lagcc.cuny.edu/

CONTACT Gail O. Mellow, President
Telephone: 718-482-7200

GENERAL INFORMATION Public Institution. Founded 1970. **Accreditation:** Regional (MSA/CIHE); physical therapy assisting (APTA). **Total program enrollment:** 8550. **Application fee:** $65.

PROGRAM(S) OFFERED
• Administrative Assistant and Secretarial Science, General *1 student enrolled*
• Licensed Practical/Vocational Nurse Training (LPN, LVN, Cert, Dipl, AAS) *110 students enrolled* • Photographic and Film/Video Technology/Technician and Assistant *1 student enrolled*

STUDENT SERVICES Academic or career counseling, daycare for children of students, employment services for current students, placement services for program completers, remedial services.

Franklin Career Institute

91 North Franklin Street, Hempstead, NY 11550
http://www.franklincareer.edu/

CONTACT Randy Rock, President
Telephone: 516-481-4444

GENERAL INFORMATION Private Institution. **Total program enrollment:** 817. **Application fee:** $100.

PROGRAM(S) OFFERED
• **Medical/Clinical Assistant** *1500 hrs./$19,605* • **Teaching English as a Second or Foreign Language/ESL Language Instructor**

STUDENT SERVICES Academic or career counseling, employment services for current students, placement services for program completers, remedial services.

French Culinary Institute

462 Broadway, New York, NY 10013
http://www.frenchculinary.com/

CONTACT Gary M. Apito, President
Telephone: 212-219-8890

GENERAL INFORMATION Private Institution. Founded 1984. **Total program enrollment:** 122. **Application fee:** $100.

PROGRAM(S) OFFERED
• **Baking and Pastry Arts/Baker/Pastry Chef** *240 hrs./$8900* • **Culinary Arts/Chef Training** *6 hrs./$40,850* • **Personal and Culinary Services, Other** *32 students enrolled*

STUDENT SERVICES Academic or career counseling, employment services for current students, placement services for program completers.

Fulton-Montgomery Community College

2805 State Highway 67, Johnstown, NY 12095-3790
http://www.fmcc.suny.edu/

CONTACT Dr. Dustin Swanger, President
Telephone: 518-762-4651

GENERAL INFORMATION Public Institution. Founded 1964. **Accreditation:** Regional (MSA/CIHE). **Total program enrollment:** 1552.

PROGRAM(S) OFFERED
• **Automobile/Automotive Mechanics Technology/Technician** *4 students enrolled* • **Child Care and Support Services Management** *3 students enrolled* • **Community Organization and Advocacy** *1 student enrolled* • **Computer Engineering Technology/Technician** *1 student enrolled* • **General Office Occupations and Clerical Services** *1 student enrolled* • **Journalism, Other** *4 students enrolled* • **Medical Administrative/Executive Assistant and Medical Secretary** *4 students enrolled* • **Medical Office Management/Administration** *6 students enrolled* • **Science Technologies/Technicians, Other** *1 student enrolled* • **Teacher Assistant/Aide** *4 students enrolled*

STUDENT SERVICES Academic or career counseling, daycare for children of students, employment services for current students, placement services for program completers, remedial services.

Gemological Institute of America

580 5th Avenue, Room 300, New York, NY 10036-4794
http://www.gia.edu/

CONTACT Donna Baker, President
Telephone: 212-944-5900 Ext. 3063

GENERAL INFORMATION Private Institution. **Total program enrollment:** 72. **Application fee:** $75.

PROGRAM(S) OFFERED
• **Metal and Jewelry Arts** *270 hrs./$4965*
STUDENT SERVICES Academic or career counseling, placement services for program completers.

Genesee Community College

1 College Road, Batavia, NY 14020-9704
http://www.genesee.edu/

CONTACT Stuart Steiner, President
Telephone: 585-343-0055

GENERAL INFORMATION Public Institution. Founded 1966. **Accreditation:** Regional (MSA/CIHE); physical therapy assisting (APTA). **Total program enrollment:** 3124.

PROGRAM(S) OFFERED
• **Accounting Technology/Technician and Bookkeeping** • **Administrative Assistant and Secretarial Science, General** • **Adult Development and Aging** *7 students enrolled* • **Business Administration and Management, General** *4 students enrolled* • **Child Care and Support Services Management** *16 students enrolled* • **Community Organization and Advocacy** • **Computer Technology/Computer Systems Technology** *3 students enrolled* • **Computer and Information Sciences and Support Services, Other** • **Computer/Information Technology Services Administration and Management, Other** • **Criminal Justice/Law Enforcement Administration** *1 student enrolled* • **Drafting and Design Technology/Technician, General** • **Health Professions and Related Clinical Sciences, Other** *7 students enrolled* • **Medical Administrative/Executive Assistant and Medical Secretary** *4 students enrolled* • **Music, Other** *1 student enrolled* • **Public Administration and Social Service Professions, Other** *1 student enrolled* • **Selling Skills and Sales Operations** • **Teacher Assistant/Aide** *3 students enrolled* • **Tourism Promotion Operations** • **Web/Multimedia Management and Webmaster** *1 student enrolled*

STUDENT SERVICES Academic or career counseling, daycare for children of students, employment services for current students, placement services for program completers, remedial services.

Genesee Valley BOCES

Adult Education Office, 8250 State Street Road, Batavia, NY 14020
http://www.gvboces.org/

CONTACT Michael A. Glover, District Superintendent of School
Telephone: 585-344-7788

GENERAL INFORMATION Private Institution. **Total program enrollment:** 196. **Application fee:** $50.

PROGRAM(S) OFFERED
• **Licensed Practical/Vocational Nurse Training (LPN, LVN, Cert, Dipl, AAS)** *1200 hrs./$8250*

STUDENT SERVICES Academic or career counseling, employment services for current students, placement services for program completers, remedial services.

Global Business Institute

1931 Mott Avenue, Far Rockaway, NY 11691

CONTACT Michael J. Hatten, President
Telephone: 718-327-2220

GENERAL INFORMATION Private Institution. Founded 1992. **Total program enrollment:** 162.

PROGRAM(S) OFFERED
• **Administrative Assistant and Secretarial Science, General** *50 students enrolled*

STUDENT SERVICES Academic or career counseling, employment services for current students, placement services for program completers, remedial services.

Global Business Institute

209 West 125th Street, New York, NY 10027

CONTACT Michael J. Hatten, President
Telephone: 212-663-1500

GENERAL INFORMATION Private Institution. **Total program enrollment:** 436.

PROGRAM(S) OFFERED
• **Administrative Assistant and Secretarial Science, General** *81 students enrolled*

STUDENT SERVICES Academic or career counseling, employment services for current students, placement services for program completers, remedial services.

Globe Institute of Technology

500 7th Avenue, New York, NY 10018
http://www.globe.edu/

CONTACT Martin Oliner, President
Telephone: 212-624-1613 Ext. 1613

GENERAL INFORMATION Private Institution. **Accreditation:** Regional (MSA/CIHE); state program registration (RUSNY); state accredited or approved. **Total program enrollment:** 223. **Application fee:** $50.

PROGRAM(S) OFFERED
• **Banking and Financial Support Services** *3 students enrolled* • **Business Administration and Management, General** *2 students enrolled* • **Business, Management, Marketing, and Related Support Services, Other** *1 student enrolled* • **Computer Programming/Programmer, General** *4 students enrolled*

STUDENT SERVICES Academic or career counseling, employment services for current students, placement services for program completers, remedial services.

Graduate School and University Center of the City University of New York

365 Fifth Avenue, New York, NY 10016-4039
http://www.gc.cuny.edu/

CONTACT William P. Kelly, President
Telephone: 212-817-7000

GENERAL INFORMATION Public Institution. Founded 1961. **Accreditation:** Regional (MSA/CIHE). **Total program enrollment:** 4467. **Application fee:** $65.

PROGRAM(S) OFFERED
• **Business/Commerce, General** *5 students enrolled* • **Business/Corporate Communications** *4 students enrolled* • **Education, General** *15 students enrolled* • **Finance, General** *3 students enrolled* • **Labor Studies** *6 students enrolled* • **Organizational Behavior Studies** *9 students enrolled* • **Public Administration** *14 students enrolled*

STUDENT SERVICES Academic or career counseling, daycare for children of students, employment services for current students, placement services for program completers.

Hair Design Institute at Fifth Avenue

6711 5th Avenue, Brooklyn, NY 11220
http://hairdesigninstitute.com/

CONTACT Anthony W. Civitano, President
Telephone: 718-745-1000 Ext. 101

GENERAL INFORMATION Private Institution. **Total program enrollment:** 66.

PROGRAM(S) OFFERED
• **Cosmetology/Cosmetologist, General** *1000 hrs./$9960*

STUDENT SERVICES Academic or career counseling, placement services for program completers.

Harlem School of Technology

215 W. 125th Street, New York, NY 10027-4426

CONTACT Ben Walker, Owner/Director
Telephone: 212-932-2849

GENERAL INFORMATION Private Institution. **Application fee:** $100.

PROGRAM(S) OFFERED
• **Heating, Air Conditioning and Refrigeration Technology/Technician (ACH/ACR/ACHR/HRAC/HVAC/AC Technology)** *900 hrs./$11,350* • **Heating, Air Conditioning, Ventilation and Refrigeration Maintenance Technology/Technician (HAC, HACR, HVAC, HVACR)** *360 hrs./$3060* • **Plumbing Technology/Plumber** *900 hrs./$11,700*

STUDENT SERVICES Academic or career counseling, placement services for program completers.

Herkimer County BOCES–Practical Nursing Program

352 Gros Boulevard, Herkimer, NY 13350
http://www.herkimer-boces.org/

CONTACT S. Simpson, District Superintendent
Telephone: 315-895-2210

GENERAL INFORMATION Private Institution. **Total program enrollment:** 32. **Application fee:** $20.

PROGRAM(S) OFFERED
• **Licensed Practical/Vocational Nurse Training (LPN, LVN, Cert, Dipl, AAS)** *1180 hrs./$8970*

STUDENT SERVICES Academic or career counseling, remedial services.

Herkimer County Community College

Reservoir Road, Herkimer, NY 13350
http://www.herkimer.edu/

CONTACT Ann Marie Murray, President
Telephone: 315-866-0300

GENERAL INFORMATION Public Institution. Founded 1966. **Accreditation:** Regional (MSA/CIHE); physical therapy assisting (APTA). **Total program enrollment:** 2319.

PROGRAM(S) OFFERED
• **Corrections** *1 student enrolled* • **Entrepreneurship/Entrepreneurial Studies** *1 student enrolled* • **Teacher Assistant/Aide** *16 students enrolled*

STUDENT SERVICES Academic or career counseling, daycare for children of students, employment services for current students, placement services for program completers, remedial services.

Hudson Valley Community College

80 Vandenburgh Avenue, Troy, NY 12180-6096
http://www.hvcc.edu/

CONTACT Andrew J. Matonak, President
Telephone: 518-629-4822

GENERAL INFORMATION Public Institution. Founded 1953. **Accreditation:** Regional (MSA/CIHE); dental hygiene (ADA); emergency medical services (JRCEMTP); engineering technology (ABET/TAC); funeral service (ABFSE); radiologic technology: radiography (JRCERT). **Total program enrollment: 7222. Application fee:** $30.

PROGRAM(S) OFFERED
• **Cardiovascular Technology/Technologist** *7 students enrolled* • **Computer Programming/Programmer, General** *1 student enrolled* • **Construction Engineering Technology/Technician** *7 students enrolled* • **Dental Assisting/Assistant** *13 students enrolled* • **Diagnostic Medical Sonography/Sonographer and Ultrasound Technician** *23 students enrolled* • **Drafting and Design Technology/Technician, General** *4 students enrolled* • **Emergency Medical Technology/Technician (EMT Paramedic)** *33 students enrolled* • **Information Science/Studies** *5 students enrolled* • **Medical Administrative/Executive Assistant and Medical Secretary** *1 student enrolled* • **Medical Radiologic Technology/Science—Radiation Therapist** *5 students enrolled* • **Teacher Assistant/Aide** *30 students enrolled*

STUDENT SERVICES Academic or career counseling, daycare for children of students, employment services for current students, placement services for program completers, remedial services.

Hudson Valley School of Advanced Aesthetic Skin Care

256 Main Street, New Paltz, NY 12561
http://www.HVSAesthetics.com/

CONTACT Maria Ferguson, Director
Telephone: 845-255-0013

GENERAL INFORMATION Private Institution. **Total program enrollment:** 38. **Application fee:** $100.

PROGRAM(S) OFFERED
• **Aesthetician/Esthetician and Skin Care Specialist** *600 hrs./$12,365*

STUDENT SERVICES Academic or career counseling, employment services for current students.

Hudson Valley School of Massage Therapy

85 South Street, Highland, NY 12528-2418
http://www.hvsmassagetherapy.com

CONTACT Maria Ferguson, Director
Telephone: 845-691-2547

GENERAL INFORMATION Private Institution. **Total program enrollment:** 41. **Application fee:** $100.

PROGRAM(S) OFFERED
• **Massage Therapy/Therapeutic Massage** *1040 hrs./$16,055*

STUDENT SERVICES Academic or career counseling, employment services for current students.

Hunter Business School

3601 Hempstead Turnpike, Levittown, NY 11756
http://hunterbusinessschool.com/

CONTACT Jay Fund, President
Telephone: 516-796-1000

GENERAL INFORMATION Private Institution. **Total program enrollment:** 410. **Application fee:** $50.

PROGRAM(S) OFFERED
• **Accounting** *61 students enrolled* • **Allied Health and Medical Assisting Services, Other** *900 hrs./$11,035* • **Business Operations Support and Secretarial Services, Other** *600 hrs./$12,197* • **Computer Technology/Computer Systems Technology** *900 hrs./$11,245* • **Data Processing and Data**

Processing Technology/Technician *50 students enrolled* • **Executive Assistant/Executive Secretary** *300 hrs./$4500* • **Medical Administrative/Executive Assistant and Medical Secretary** *900 hrs./$10,770* • **Medical/Clinical Assistant** *185 students enrolled*

STUDENT SERVICES Academic or career counseling, employment services for current students, placement services for program completers.

Institute of Allied Medical Professions

91-31 Queens Boulevard, Suite 407, Elmhurst, NY 11373
http://www.iamp.edu

CONTACT Thomas Haggerty, President
Telephone: 718-779-7738

GENERAL INFORMATION Private Institution. **Total program enrollment:** 201. **Application fee:** $90.

PROGRAM(S) OFFERED
• **Diagnostic Medical Sonography/Sonographer and Ultrasound Technician** *1687 hrs./$25,000*

STUDENT SERVICES Academic or career counseling, placement services for program completers.

Institute of Audio Research

64 University Place, New York, NY 10003
http://audioschool.com/

CONTACT Barry Puritz, President
Telephone: 212-677-7580

GENERAL INFORMATION Private Institution. **Total program enrollment:** 494. **Application fee:** $100.

PROGRAM(S) OFFERED
• **Communications Technologies/Technicians and Support Services, Other** *415 students enrolled* • **Communications Technology/Technician** *900 hrs./$14,825*

STUDENT SERVICES Academic or career counseling, placement services for program completers.

Iona College

715 North Avenue, New Rochelle, NY 10801-1890
http://www.iona.edu/

CONTACT Br. James A. Liguori, CFC, President
Telephone: 914-633-2000

GENERAL INFORMATION Private Institution (Affiliated with Roman Catholic Church). Founded 1940. **Accreditation:** Regional (MSA/CIHE); journalism and mass communications (ACEJMC). **Total program enrollment:** 3565. **Application fee:** $50.

STUDENT SERVICES Academic or career counseling, employment services for current students, placement services for program completers.

Isabella G. Hart School of Practical Nursing

1425 Portland Avenue, Rochester, NY 14621
http://www.viahealth.org/

CONTACT Nina Morris, Director
Telephone: 585-922-1474

GENERAL INFORMATION Private Institution. Founded 1963. **Total program enrollment:** 39. **Application fee:** $50.

PROGRAM(S) OFFERED
• **Licensed Practical/Vocational Nurse Training (LPN, LVN, Cert, Dipl, AAS)** *1200 hrs./$9795*

STUDENT SERVICES Academic or career counseling, remedial services.

Island Drafting and Technical Institute

128 Broadway, Amityville, NY 11787
http://www.idti.edu/

CONTACT James Di Liberto, President
Telephone: 631-691-8733

GENERAL INFORMATION Private Institution. Founded 1957. **Accreditation:** State accredited or approved. **Total program enrollment:** 131. **Application fee:** $25.

PROGRAM(S) OFFERED
• Computer Engineering Technology/Technician • Drafting and Design Technology/Technician, General • Drafting/Design Engineering Technologies/Technicians, Other *1 student enrolled* • Electrical, Electronic and Communications Engineering Technology/Technician

STUDENT SERVICES Academic or career counseling, employment services for current students, placement services for program completers.

Ithaca College

953 Danby Road, Ithaca, NY 14850-7020
http://www.ithaca.edu/

CONTACT Dr. Thomas Rochon, President
Telephone: 607-274-3011

GENERAL INFORMATION Private Institution. Founded 1892. **Accreditation:** Regional (MSA/CIHE); athletic training (JRCAT); music (NASM); recreation and parks (NRPA); speech-language pathology (ASHA); theater (NAST). **Total program enrollment:** 6323. **Application fee:** $60.

PROGRAM(S) OFFERED
• Business Administration and Management, General *1 student enrolled*
• International Business/Trade/Commerce *1 student enrolled*

STUDENT SERVICES Academic or career counseling, employment services for current students, placement services for program completers.

Jamestown Business College

7 Fairmount Avenue, Box 429, Jamestown, NY 14702-0429
http://www.jbcny.org/

CONTACT Tyler Swanson, President
Telephone: 716-664-5100

GENERAL INFORMATION Private Institution. Founded 1886. **Accreditation:** Regional (MSA/CIHE). **Total program enrollment:** 257. **Application fee:** $25.

PROGRAM(S) OFFERED
• Administrative Assistant and Secretarial Science, General *1 student enrolled*

STUDENT SERVICES Academic or career counseling, employment services for current students, placement services for program completers.

Jamestown Community College

525 Falconer Street, Jamestown, NY 14701-1999
http://www.sunyjcc.edu/

CONTACT Gregory T. Decinque, President
Telephone: 716-338-1000

GENERAL INFORMATION Public Institution. Founded 1950. **Accreditation:** Regional (MSA/CIHE). **Total program enrollment:** 2453.

PROGRAM(S) OFFERED
• Administrative Assistant and Secretarial Science, General *1 student enrolled* • Audiovisual Communications Technologies/Technicians, Other *1 student enrolled* • Child Care and Support Services Management *7 students enrolled* • Corrections *2 students enrolled* • Drafting and Design Technology/Technician,

General *2 students enrolled* • Health Information/Medical Records Technology/Technician *1 student enrolled* • Industrial Production Technologies/Technicians, Other *5 students enrolled* • Information Science/Studies *1 student enrolled*

STUDENT SERVICES Academic or career counseling, employment services for current students, placement services for program completers, remedial services.

Jefferson Community College

1220 Coffeen Street, Watertown, NY 13601
http://www.sunyjefferson.edu/

CONTACT Carole A. McCoy, President
Telephone: 315-786-2200

GENERAL INFORMATION Public Institution. Founded 1961. **Accreditation:** Regional (MSA/CIHE). **Total program enrollment:** 1756.

PROGRAM(S) OFFERED
• Accounting Technology/Technician and Bookkeeping *4 students enrolled*
• Criminal Justice/Law Enforcement Administration *1 student enrolled*
• Emergency Medical Technology/Technician (EMT Paramedic) *2 students enrolled* • Teacher Assistant/Aide *6 students enrolled*

STUDENT SERVICES Academic or career counseling, daycare for children of students, employment services for current students, placement services for program completers, remedial services.

Jefferson-Lewis BOCES–Program of Practical Nursing

20104 New York State Route 3, Watertown, NY 13601
http://www.boces.com/

CONTACT Jack J. Boak, District Superintendent
Telephone: 315-779-7200 Ext. 7230

GENERAL INFORMATION Private Institution. **Total program enrollment:** 52.

PROGRAM(S) OFFERED
• Licensed Practical/Vocational Nurse Training (LPN, LVN, Cert, Dipl, AAS) *45 students enrolled*

STUDENT SERVICES Placement services for program completers, remedial services.

John Jay College of Criminal Justice of the City University of New York

899 Tenth Avenue, New York, NY 10019-1093
http://www.jjay.cuny.edu/

CONTACT Jeremy Travis, President
Telephone: 212-237-8000

GENERAL INFORMATION Public Institution. Founded 1964. **Accreditation:** Regional (MSA/CIHE). **Total program enrollment:** 10007. **Application fee:** $65.

STUDENT SERVICES Academic or career counseling, daycare for children of students, employment services for current students, placement services for program completers, remedial services.

Kingsborough Community College of the City University of New York

2001 Oriental Blvd, Manhattan Beach, Brooklyn, NY 11235
http://www.kbcc.cuny.edu/

CONTACT Regina S. Peruggi, President
Telephone: 718-265-5343

GENERAL INFORMATION Public Institution. Founded 1963. **Accreditation:** Regional (MSA/CIHE); physical therapy assisting (APTA). **Total program enrollment:** 8704. **Application fee:** $65.

PROGRAM(S) OFFERED
• **Marine Maintenance/Fitter and Ship Repair Technology/Technician** *2 students enrolled* • **Substance Abuse/Addiction Counseling** *5 students enrolled*

STUDENT SERVICES Academic or career counseling, daycare for children of students, employment services for current students, placement services for program completers, remedial services.

Leon Studio 1 School of Hair Design & Career Training Center

5221 Main Street, Williamsville, NY 14221
http://www.leonstudioone.com/

CONTACT Mark Custard, Administration Director
Telephone: 716-631-3878 Ext. 1

GENERAL INFORMATION Private Institution. **Total program enrollment:** 113.

PROGRAM(S) OFFERED
• **Aesthetician/Esthetician and Skin Care Specialist** *600 hrs./$4500*
• **Cosmetology/Cosmetologist, General** *1000 hrs./$10,600*

STUDENT SERVICES Academic or career counseling, employment services for current students, placement services for program completers.

Lia Schorr Institute of Cosmetic Skin Care Training

686 Lexington Avenue 4th Fl, New York, NY 10022-2614
http://www.liaschorrinstitute.com/

CONTACT Lia Schorr, Owner
Telephone: 212-486-9541

GENERAL INFORMATION Private Institution. **Total program enrollment:** 10.

PROGRAM(S) OFFERED
• **Aesthetician/Esthetician and Skin Care Specialist** *600 hrs./$6500*

STUDENT SERVICES Academic or career counseling, placement services for program completers.

Lincoln Technical Institute

15-30 Petracca Place, Whitestone, NY 11357
http://www.lincolnedu.com/

CONTACT Sean McAlmont, President/COO
Telephone: 718-640-9800

GENERAL INFORMATION Private Institution. **Total program enrollment:** 552. **Application fee:** $100.

PROGRAM(S) OFFERED
• **Automobile/Automotive Mechanics Technology/Technician** *1560 hrs./$26,500*

STUDENT SERVICES Academic or career counseling, employment services for current students, placement services for program completers.

Long Island Beauty School

544 Route 111, Hauppauge, NY 11788

CONTACT Salvatore D. Pappacoda, President
Telephone: 631-724-0440

GENERAL INFORMATION Private Institution. Founded 1967. **Total program enrollment:** 72. **Application fee:** $100.

PROGRAM(S) OFFERED
• **Cosmetology/Cosmetologist, General** *1000 hrs./$10,500*

STUDENT SERVICES Placement services for program completers.

Long Island Beauty School

173A Fulton Avenue, Hempstead, NY 11550
http://www.longislandbeautyschool.com/

CONTACT Frank S. Pappacoda, Jr., President
Telephone: 516-483-6259

GENERAL INFORMATION Private Institution. Founded 1941. **Total program enrollment:** 93. **Application fee:** $100.

PROGRAM(S) OFFERED
• **Cosmetology/Cosmetologist, General** *1000 hrs./$10,500*

STUDENT SERVICES Academic or career counseling, placement services for program completers.

Long Island Business Institute

6500 Jericho Turnpike, Commack, NY 11725
http://www.libi.edu/commack/index.html

CONTACT Ms. Monica Foote, President
Telephone: 718-939-5100

GENERAL INFORMATION Private Institution. Founded 1968. **Accreditation:** State accredited or approved. **Total program enrollment:** 371. **Application fee:** $50.

PROGRAM(S) OFFERED
• **General Office Occupations and Clerical Services** *5 students enrolled* • **Medical Insurance Coding Specialist/Coder** *19 students enrolled*

STUDENT SERVICES Academic or career counseling, placement services for program completers, remedial services.

Long Island University–University Center

700 Northern Boulevard, Brookville, NY 11548
http://liu.edu/

CONTACT Dr. David J. Steinberg, President
Telephone: 516-299-1926

GENERAL INFORMATION Private Institution.

Madison-Oneida BOCES–Continuing Education

4937 Spring Road, Verona, NY 13478-0168
http://www.moboces.org/adulted.html/

CONTACT Jacklin G. Starks, District Superintendent
Telephone: 315-361-5800

GENERAL INFORMATION Public Institution. **Total program enrollment:** 100.

Madison-Oneida BOCES–Continuing Education (continued)

PROGRAM(S) OFFERED
● **Licensed Practical/Vocational Nurse Training (LPN, LVN, Cert, Dipl, AAS)** *1263 hrs./$8836*

STUDENT SERVICES Academic or career counseling, employment services for current students, placement services for program completers, remedial services.'

Mandl School

254 West 54th Street, 9th Floor, New York, NY 10019
http://www.mandlschool.com/

CONTACT Melvyn Weiner, President
Telephone: 212-247-3434

GENERAL INFORMATION Private Institution. **Total program enrollment:** 536. **Application fee:** $25.

PROGRAM(S) OFFERED
● **Dental Assisting/Assistant** *900 hrs./$9595* ● **Medical/Clinical Assistant** *60 hrs./$10,800* ● **Surgical Technology/Technologist** *1200 hrs./$21,100*

STUDENT SERVICES Academic or career counseling, placement services for program completers, remedial services.

Manhattan School of Computer Technology

42 Broadway—22nd Floor, New York, NY 10004
http://www.manhattanschool.com/

CONTACT Alevtina Bogatova, Director
Telephone: 212-349-9768 Ext. 101

GENERAL INFORMATION Private Institution. **Total program enrollment:** 116.

PROGRAM(S) OFFERED
● **Accounting Technology/Technician and Bookkeeping** *1500 hrs./$18,234* ● **Accounting** ● **Medical Office Assistant/Specialist** *1500 hrs./$18,334* ● **Teaching English as a Second or Foreign Language/ESL Language Instructor** *600 hrs./$3104*

STUDENT SERVICES Academic or career counseling, placement services for program completers.

Maria College

700 New Scotland Avenue, Albany, NY 12208-1798
http://www.mariacollege.edu/

CONTACT Laureen Fitzgerald, President
Telephone: 518-438-3111

GENERAL INFORMATION Private Institution. Founded 1958. **Accreditation:** Regional (MSA/CIHE). **Total program enrollment:** 215. **Application fee:** $35.

PROGRAM(S) OFFERED
● **Business, Management, Marketing, and Related Support Services, Other** *4 students enrolled* ● **Health Professions and Related Clinical Sciences, Other** *14 students enrolled* ● **Licensed Practical/Vocational Nurse Training (LPN, LVN, Cert, Dipl, AAS)** *25 students enrolled* ● **Teaching Assistants/Aides, Other** *1 student enrolled*

STUDENT SERVICES Academic or career counseling, employment services for current students, placement services for program completers, remedial services.

Marion S. Whelan School of Nursing of Geneva General Hospital

196-198 North Street, Geneva, NY 14456

CONTACT Victoria Record, Director
Telephone: 315-787-4005

GENERAL INFORMATION Private Institution. Founded 1956. **Total program enrollment:** 40. **Application fee:** $35.

PROGRAM(S) OFFERED
● **Licensed Practical/Vocational Nurse Training (LPN, LVN, Cert, Dipl, AAS)** *27 students enrolled*

STUDENT SERVICES Academic or career counseling, daycare for children of students, employment services for current students, placement services for program completers.

Marist College

3399 North Road, Poughkeepsie, NY 12601-1387
http://www.marist.edu/

CONTACT Dennis J. Murray, President
Telephone: 845-575-3000

GENERAL INFORMATION Private Institution. Founded 1929. **Accreditation:** Regional (MSA/CIHE); medical technology (NAACLS). **Total program enrollment:** 4687. **Application fee:** $50.

PROGRAM(S) OFFERED
● **Fine/Studio Arts, General** *27 students enrolled* ● **Information Science/Studies** *1 student enrolled*

STUDENT SERVICES Academic or career counseling, employment services for current students, placement services for program completers, remedial services.

MarJon School of Beauty Culture

3153 Eggert Road, Tonawanda, NY 14150
http://marjonbeautyschool.com/

CONTACT Gracine Phelps Lewis, President
Telephone: 716-836-6240

GENERAL INFORMATION Private Institution. Founded 1972. **Total program enrollment:** 37. **Application fee:** $100.

PROGRAM(S) OFFERED
● **Cosmetology/Cosmetologist, General** *1000 hrs./$8652*

STUDENT SERVICES Academic or career counseling, employment services for current students, placement services for program completers, remedial services.

Marymount Manhattan College

221 East 71st Street, New York, NY 10021-4597
http://www.mmm.edu/

CONTACT Judson R. Shaver, President
Telephone: 212-517-0400

GENERAL INFORMATION Private Institution. Founded 1936. **Accreditation:** Regional (MSA/CIHE). **Total program enrollment:** 1689. **Application fee:** $60.

STUDENT SERVICES Academic or career counseling, employment services for current students, placement services for program completers, remedial services.

Medaille College

18 Agassiz Circle, Buffalo, NY 14214-2695
http://www.medaille.edu/

CONTACT Richard T. Jurasek, PhD, President
Telephone: 716-880-2000

GENERAL INFORMATION Private Institution. Founded 1875. **Accreditation:** Regional (MSA/CIHE). **Total program enrollment:** 2759. **Application fee:** $25.

PROGRAM(S) OFFERED
• Intermedia/Multimedia • Security and Protective Services, Other

STUDENT SERVICES Academic or career counseling, employment services for current students, placement services for program completers, remedial services.

Medgar Evers College of the City University of New York

1650 Bedford Street, Brooklyn, NY 11225-2298
http://www.mec.cuny.edu/

CONTACT Edison O. Jackson, President
Telephone: 718-270-4900

GENERAL INFORMATION Public Institution. Founded 1969. **Accreditation:** Regional (MSA/CIHE). **Total program enrollment:** 3705. **Application fee:** $65.

PROGRAM(S) OFFERED
• Licensed Practical/Vocational Nurse Training (LPN, LVN, Cert, Dipl, AAS) *23 students enrolled*

STUDENT SERVICES Academic or career counseling, daycare for children of students, employment services for current students, placement services for program completers, remedial services.

Mercy College

555 Broadway, Dobbs Ferry, NY 10522-1189
http://www.mercy.edu/

CONTACT Kimberly R. Cline, President
Telephone: 800-637-2969

GENERAL INFORMATION Private Institution. Founded 1951. **Accreditation:** Regional (MSA/CIHE); acupuncture and Oriental Medicine (ACAOM); physical therapy assisting (APTA); speech-language pathology (ASHA). **Total program enrollment:** 4816. **Application fee:** $37.

PROGRAM(S) OFFERED
• Accounting Technology/Technician and Bookkeeping *1 student enrolled*
• Business/Commerce, General • Community Organization and Advocacy
• Computer/Information Technology Services Administration and Management, Other *1 student enrolled* • Health Professions and Related Clinical Sciences, Other • Public Administration and Social Service Professions, Other *2 students enrolled*

STUDENT SERVICES Academic or career counseling, employment services for current students, placement services for program completers, remedial services.

Merkaz Bnos-Business School

54 Avenue O, Brooklyn, NY 11204
http://www.mbs-career.org/

CONTACT Chaim A. Waldman, Director
Telephone: 718-234-4000

GENERAL INFORMATION Private Institution. **Total program enrollment:** 124.

PROGRAM(S) OFFERED
• Computer and Information Sciences and Support Services, Other *1440 hrs./ $17,300* • Medical Office Management/Administration *1440 hrs./$17,300*

STUDENT SERVICES Academic or career counseling, placement services for program completers.

Metropolitan Learning Institute

104-70 Queens Boulevard, Suite 307, Forest Hills, NY 11375
http://www.gettraining.org/

CONTACT Boris Davidoff, PhD, President/Director
Telephone: 718-897-0482

GENERAL INFORMATION Private Institution. **Total program enrollment:** 425.

PROGRAM(S) OFFERED
• Accounting Technology/Technician and Bookkeeping *1500 hrs./$15,400*
• Business/Office Automation/Technology/Data Entry *1500 hrs./$15,905*
• Legal Administrative Assistant/Secretary *1500 hrs./$15,400* • Legal Support Services, Other • Licensed Practical/Vocational Nurse Training (LPN, LVN, Cert, Dipl, AAS) *1440 hrs./$18,775* • Medical Office Computer Specialist/ Assistant *1500 hrs./$15,400*

STUDENT SERVICES Academic or career counseling, employment services for current students, placement services for program completers, remedial services.

Micropower Career Institute

243 W. 30th Street, New York, NY 10001

GENERAL INFORMATION Private Institution. **Total program enrollment:** 39. **Application fee:** $100.

PROGRAM(S) OFFERED
• Computer Hardware Technology/Technician *960 hrs./$9500* • Computer Systems Networking and Telecommunications *20 students enrolled*

STUDENT SERVICES Academic or career counseling, employment services for current students, placement services for program completers.

Midway Paris Beauty School

54-40 Myrtle Avenue, Ridgewood, NY 11385
http://www.nacas.org/midway-paris/

CONTACT Robert Schoenbrun, Director
Telephone: 718-418-2790

GENERAL INFORMATION Private Institution. Founded 1967. **Total program enrollment:** 62. **Application fee:** $100.

PROGRAM(S) OFFERED
• Cosmetology/Cosmetologist, General *1000 hrs./$10,900*

STUDENT SERVICES Academic or career counseling, employment services for current students, placement services for program completers.

Mildred Elley School

855 Central Avenue, Albany, NY 12206
http://www.mildred-elley.edu/

CONTACT Faith Ann Takes, President
Telephone: 518-786-0855

GENERAL INFORMATION Private Institution. Founded 1917. **Accreditation:** State accredited or approved. **Total program enrollment:** 510. **Application fee:** $25.

Mildred Elley School (continued)

PROGRAM(S) OFFERED
● **Accounting** ● **Administrative Assistant and Secretarial Science, General** *5 students enrolled* ● **Animation, Interactive Technology, Video Graphics and Special Effects** ● **Computer Software and Media Applications, Other** *4 students enrolled* ● **Information Technology** *1 student enrolled* ● **Legal Assistant/Paralegal** *2 students enrolled* ● **Licensed Practical/Vocational Nurse Training (LPN, LVN, Cert, Dipl, AAS)** ● **Massage Therapy/Therapeutic Massage** *37 students enrolled* ● **Medical Office Assistant/Specialist** *8 students enrolled* ● **Medical/Clinical Assistant** *7 students enrolled* ● **Tourism and Travel Services Management** ● **Web Page, Digital/Multimedia and Information Resources Design** *6 students enrolled*

STUDENT SERVICES Academic or career counseling, employment services for current students, placement services for program completers, remedial services.

Modern Welding School

1842 State Street, Schenectady, NY 12304
http://www.modernwelding.com/

CONTACT Timothy Fuller, Director
Telephone: 518-374-1216

GENERAL INFORMATION Private Institution. Founded 1936. **Total program enrollment: 77. Application fee:** $100.

PROGRAM(S) OFFERED
● **Welding Technology/Welder** *107 hrs./$1365*

STUDENT SERVICES Academic or career counseling, employment services for current students, placement services for program completers, remedial services.

Mohawk Valley Community College

1101 Sherman Drive, Utica, NY 13501-5394
http://www.mvcc.edu/

CONTACT Dr. Randall VanWagoner, President
Telephone: 315-792-5400

GENERAL INFORMATION Public Institution. Founded 1946. **Accreditation:** Regional (MSA/CIHE); engineering technology (ABET/TAC); health information technology (AHIMA); respiratory therapy technology (CoARC). **Total program enrollment:** 3880.

PROGRAM(S) OFFERED
● **Accounting Technology/Technician and Bookkeeping** *1 student enrolled* ● **Airframe Mechanics and Aircraft Maintenance Technology/Technician** *32 students enrolled* ● **Allied Health and Medical Assisting Services, Other** *3 students enrolled* ● **Architectural Drafting and Architectural CAD/CADD** *1 student enrolled* ● **Business and Personal/Financial Services Marketing Operations** *1 student enrolled* ● **Carpentry/Carpenter** *3 students enrolled* ● **Clinical/Medical Laboratory Science and Allied Professions, Other** *2 students enrolled* ● **Computer and Information Sciences and Support Services, Other** *1 student enrolled* ● **Electrical and Power Transmission Installation/Installer, General** *1 student enrolled* ● **Entrepreneurship/Entrepreneurial Studies** *2 students enrolled* ● **Forensic Science and Technology** *1 student enrolled* ● **General Office Occupations and Clerical Services** *4 students enrolled* ● **Industrial Production Technologies/Technicians, Other** *6 students enrolled* ● **Machine Shop Technology/Assistant** *14 students enrolled* ● **Medical/Clinical Assistant** *1 student enrolled* ● **Photographic and Film/Video Technology/Technician and Assistant** *2 students enrolled* ● **Physical Education Teaching and Coaching** *1 student enrolled* ● **Tourism and Travel Services Management** *3 students enrolled*

STUDENT SERVICES Academic or career counseling, daycare for children of students, employment services for current students, placement services for program completers, remedial services.

Monroe 2–Orleans BOCES Center for Workforce Development

3545 Buffalo Road, Rochester, NY 14624
http://www.cwdadulteducation.org

CONTACT Mary Ellen Spennacchio-Wagner, Director
Telephone: 585-349-9100

GENERAL INFORMATION Public Institution. **Total program enrollment:** 75.

PROGRAM(S) OFFERED
● **Administrative Assistant and Secretarial Science, General** *600 hrs./$5900* ● **Building/Property Maintenance and Management** *450 hrs./$4725* ● **Computer Software Technology/Technician** *350 hrs./$4500* ● **Dental Assisting/Assistant** *600 hrs./$4900* ● **Heating, Air Conditioning and Refrigeration Technology/Technician (ACH/ACR/ACHR/HRAC/HVAC/AC Technology)** *450 hrs./$4725* ● **Medical Office Assistant/Specialist** *600 hrs./$5900*

STUDENT SERVICES Academic or career counseling, employment services for current students, placement services for program completers, remedial services.

Monroe College

Monroe College Way, Bronx, NY 10468-5407
http://www.monroecoll.edu/

CONTACT Stephen J. Jerome, President
Telephone: 718-933-6700

GENERAL INFORMATION Private Institution. Founded 1933. **Accreditation:** Regional (MSA/CIHE); health information technology (AHIMA). **Total program enrollment:** 3835. **Application fee:** $35.

PROGRAM(S) OFFERED
● **Licensed Practical/Vocational Nurse Training (LPN, LVN, Cert, Dipl, AAS)** *18 students enrolled*

STUDENT SERVICES Academic or career counseling, employment services for current students, placement services for program completers, remedial services.

Monroe College

434 Main Street, New Rochelle, NY 10801-6410
http://www.monroecollege.edu/

CONTACT Marc Jerome, Executive Vice President
Telephone: 914-632-5400

GENERAL INFORMATION Private Institution. Founded 1983. **Total program enrollment:** 1896. **Application fee:** $35.

STUDENT SERVICES Academic or career counseling, employment services for current students, placement services for program completers, remedial services.

Monroe Community College

1000 East Henrietta Road, Rochester, NY 14623-5780
http://www.monroecc.edu/

CONTACT Lawrence Tyree, Interim President
Telephone: 585-292-2000

GENERAL INFORMATION Public Institution. Founded 1961. **Accreditation:** Regional (MSA/CIHE); dental assisting (ADA); dental hygiene (ADA); emergency medical services (JRCEMTP); engineering technology (ABET/TAC); health information technology (AHIMA); radiologic technology: radiography (JRCERT). **Total program enrollment:** 11058. **Application fee:** $20.

PROGRAM(S) OFFERED

• **Administrative Assistant and Secretarial Science, General** *2 students enrolled* • **Automobile/Automotive Mechanics Technology/Technician** *4 students enrolled* • **Child Care and Support Services Management** *2 students enrolled* • **Communications Systems Installation and Repair Technology** *2 students enrolled* • **Community Organization and Advocacy** *54 students enrolled* • **Court Reporting/Court Reporter** *3 students enrolled* • **Criminal Justice/Police Science** *72 students enrolled* • **Dental Assisting/Assistant** *16 students enrolled* • **Emergency Medical Technology/Technician (EMT Paramedic)** *2 students enrolled* • **Entrepreneurship/Entrepreneurial Studies** *1 student enrolled* • **Foods, Nutrition, and Related Services, Other** *5 students enrolled* • **General Office Occupations and Clerical Services** *1 student enrolled* • **Heating, Air Conditioning, Ventilation and Refrigeration Maintenance Technology/Technician (HAC, HACR, HVAC, HVACR)** *11 students enrolled* • **Hotel/Motel Administration/Management** *1 student enrolled* • **Institutional Food Workers** *2 students enrolled* • **Legal Assistant/Paralegal** *14 students enrolled* • **Medical Administrative/Executive Assistant and Medical Secretary** *24 students enrolled* • **Tool and Die Technology/Technician** *12 students enrolled* • **Tourism and Travel Services Marketing Operations** *3 students enrolled*

STUDENT SERVICES Academic or career counseling, daycare for children of students, employment services for current students, placement services for program completers, remedial services.

Mount Saint Mary College

330 Powell Avenue, Newburgh, NY 12550-3494
http://www.msmc.edu/

CONTACT Fr. Kevin Mackin, President
Telephone: 845-561-0800

GENERAL INFORMATION Private Institution. Founded 1960. **Accreditation:** Regional (MSA/CIHE). **Total program enrollment:** 1872. **Application fee:** $40.

PROGRAM(S) OFFERED
• **Accounting Technology/Technician and Bookkeeping** *1 student enrolled* • **Business Administration and Management, General** • **Communication Studies/Speech Communication and Rhetoric** • **Data Processing and Data Processing Technology/Technician**

STUDENT SERVICES Academic or career counseling, employment services for current students, placement services for program completers, remedial services.

Nassau Community College

1 Education Drive, Garden City, NY 11530-6793
http://www.ncc.edu/

CONTACT Sean Fanelli, President
Telephone: 516-572-7501

GENERAL INFORMATION Public Institution. Founded 1959. **Accreditation:** Regional (MSA/CIHE); engineering technology (ABET/TAC); funeral service (ABFSE); music (NASM); physical therapy assisting (APTA); radiologic technology: radiation therapy technology (JRCERT); radiologic technology: radiography (JRCERT); surgical technology (ARCST). **Total program enrollment:** 14702. **Application fee:** $40.

PROGRAM(S) OFFERED
• **Accounting Technology/Technician and Bookkeeping** *1 student enrolled* • **Administrative Assistant and Secretarial Science, General** *2 students enrolled* • **Business Administration and Management, General** *2 students enrolled* • **Communications Technologies/Technicians and Support Services, Other** *10 students enrolled* • **Construction Trades, Other** *5 students enrolled* • **Culinary Arts and Related Services, Other** *1 student enrolled* • **Dietitian Assistant** *6 students enrolled* • **Legal Assistant/Paralegal** *54 students enrolled* • **Medical Administrative/Executive Assistant and Medical Secretary** *4 students enrolled*

STUDENT SERVICES Academic or career counseling, daycare for children of students, employment services for current students, placement services for program completers, remedial services.

National Tractor Trailer School–Buffalo Campus

175 Katherine Street, Buffalo, NY 14210-2007
http://www.ntts.edu/

CONTACT Lisa M. Tucker, Director
Telephone: 716-849-6887

GENERAL INFORMATION Private Institution. Founded 1971. **Total program enrollment:** 87. **Application fee:** $25.

PROGRAM(S) OFFERED
• **Truck and Bus Driver/Commercial Vehicle Operation** *90 hrs./$2485*

STUDENT SERVICES Placement services for program completers.

National Tractor Trailer School, Inc.

PO Box 208, Liverpool, NY 13088-0208
http://www.ntts.edu/

CONTACT Harry Kowalchyk, President
Telephone: 315-451-2430

GENERAL INFORMATION Private Institution. Founded 1971. **Total program enrollment:** 76. **Application fee:** $25.

PROGRAM(S) OFFERED
• **Truck and Bus Driver/Commercial Vehicle Operation** *90 hrs./$2485*

STUDENT SERVICES Placement services for program completers.

New Age Training

500 8th Avenue, 12th Floor, New York, NY 10018-6504
http://www.newagetraining.com

GENERAL INFORMATION Private Institution. **Total program enrollment:** 93. **Application fee:** $25.

PROGRAM(S) OFFERED
• **Receptionist** *47 students enrolled*

STUDENT SERVICES Academic or career counseling, employment services for current students, placement services for program completers.

New School of Radio and Television

50 Colvin Avenue, Albany, NY 12206
http://nsrt.org/

CONTACT Thomas Brownlie, Director
Telephone: 518-438-7682 Ext. 6

GENERAL INFORMATION Private Institution. Founded 1973. **Total program enrollment:** 56. **Application fee:** $75.

PROGRAM(S) OFFERED
• **Broadcast Journalism** *630 hrs./$9450* • **Radio and Television Broadcasting Technology/Technician** *630 hrs./$9450* • **Radio and Television** *630 hrs./$9650*

STUDENT SERVICES Academic or career counseling, placement services for program completers, remedial services.

New York Automotive and Diesel Institute

178-18 Liberty Avenue, Jamaica, NY 11433
http://www.newyorkadi.com/

CONTACT Michael J. Hatten, CEO
Telephone: 718-658-0006

GENERAL INFORMATION Private Institution. **Total program enrollment:** 337. **Application fee:** $50.

New York Automotive and Diesel Institute (continued)

PROGRAM(S) OFFERED
- **Autobody/Collision and Repair Technology/Technician** *1440 hrs./$19,920*
- **Automobile/Automotive Mechanics Technology/Technician** *900 hrs./$12,450*
- **Medium/Heavy Vehicle and Truck Technology/Technician** *900 hrs./$12,450*

STUDENT SERVICES Employment services for current students, placement services for program completers.

New York Career Institute

11 Park Place- 4th Floor, New York, NY 10007
http://www.nyci.com/

CONTACT Ivan Londa, CEO
Telephone: 212-962-0002

GENERAL INFORMATION Private Institution. Founded 1942. **Accreditation:** State program registration (RUSNY). **Total program enrollment:** 480. **Application fee:** $50.

PROGRAM(S) OFFERED
- **Court Reporting/Court Reporter** *58 students enrolled* • **Legal Assistant/Paralegal** *12 students enrolled* • **Medical Office Management/Administration** *4 students enrolled*

STUDENT SERVICES Academic or career counseling, employment services for current students, placement services for program completers, remedial services.

New York City College of Technology of the City University of New York

300 Jay Street, Brooklyn, NY 11201-2983
http://www.citytech.cuny.edu/

CONTACT Russell K. Hotzler, President
Telephone: 718-260-5500

GENERAL INFORMATION Public Institution. Founded 1946. **Accreditation:** Regional (MSA/CIHE); dental hygiene (ADA); dental laboratory technology (ADA); engineering technology (ABET/TAC); ophthalmic laboratory technology (COA); radiologic technology: radiography (JRCERT). **Total program enrollment:** 8293. **Application fee:** $65.

PROGRAM(S) OFFERED
- **Construction Engineering Technology/Technician** *1 student enrolled* • **Heating, Air Conditioning and Refrigeration Technology/Technician (ACH/ACR/ACHR/HRAC/HVAC/AC Technology)** *10 students enrolled*

STUDENT SERVICES Academic or career counseling, daycare for children of students, employment services for current students, placement services for program completers, remedial services.

New York Institute of Business Technology

401 Park Avenue, S, New York, NY 10016
http://www.nyibt.org/

CONTACT Leith E. Yetman, President
Telephone: 212-725-9400

GENERAL INFORMATION Private Institution. **Total program enrollment:** 476. **Application fee:** $100.

PROGRAM(S) OFFERED
- **Accounting** *33 students enrolled* • **Administrative Assistant and Secretarial Science, General** *10 students enrolled* • **Computer/Information Technology Services Administration and Management, Other** *49 students enrolled* • **Medical/Clinical Assistant** *21 students enrolled*

STUDENT SERVICES Academic or career counseling, placement services for program completers.

New York Institute of Massage

4701 Transit Road, Box 645, Buffalo, NY 14231
http://www.nyinstituteofmassage.com/

CONTACT Diane Dinsmore, Director
Telephone: 716-633-0355

GENERAL INFORMATION Private Institution. Founded 1994. **Total program enrollment:** 83. **Application fee:** $25.

PROGRAM(S) OFFERED
- **Massage Therapy/Therapeutic Massage** *1104 hrs./$13,025*

STUDENT SERVICES Academic or career counseling, placement services for program completers.

New York International Beauty School

210 West 50 Street, New York, NY 10019
http://www.nyibs.com/

CONTACT John Saffa, Vice President
Telephone: 212-868-7171

GENERAL INFORMATION Private Institution. **Total program enrollment:** 213. **Application fee:** $100.

PROGRAM(S) OFFERED
- **Cosmetology/Cosmetologist, General** *1000 hrs./$11,696*

STUDENT SERVICES Placement services for program completers.

New York Paralegal School

299 Broadway 2nd Fl, New York, NY 10007

CONTACT Mr. William Jenkins, Director
Telephone: 212-349-8800

GENERAL INFORMATION Private Institution.

PROGRAM(S) OFFERED
- **Legal Assistant/Paralegal** *911 hrs./$9895*

STUDENT SERVICES Academic or career counseling, employment services for current students, placement services for program completers.

New York School for Medical/Dental Assistants

116-16 Queens Boulevard, Forest Hills, NY 11375-2330
http://nysmda.com/

CONTACT Douglas Jordan Clinton Arnabo, Co Presidents
Telephone: 718-793-2330

GENERAL INFORMATION Private Institution. Founded 1967. **Total program enrollment:** 380. **Application fee:** $100.

PROGRAM(S) OFFERED
- **Dental Assisting/Assistant** *900 hrs./$9500* • **Medical/Clinical Assistant** *900 hrs./$9700*

STUDENT SERVICES Placement services for program completers, remedial services.

New York School of Interior Design

170 East 70th Street, New York, NY 10021-5110
http://www.nysid.edu/

CONTACT Dr. Christopher Cyphers, President
Telephone: 212-472-1500

GENERAL INFORMATION Private Institution. Founded 1916. **Accreditation:** Art and design (NASAD); interior design: professional (CIDA). **Total program enrollment:** 206. **Application fee:** $50.

PROGRAM(S) OFFERED
• **Interior Design** *15 students enrolled*

STUDENT SERVICES Academic or career counseling, employment services for current students, placement services for program completers, remedial services.

New York University

70 Washington Square South, New York, NY 10012-1019
http://www.nyu.edu/

CONTACT John E. Sexton, President
Telephone: 212-998-1212

GENERAL INFORMATION Private Institution. Founded 1831. **Accreditation:** Regional (MSA/CIHE); dental hygiene (ADA); diagnostic medical sonography (JRCEDMS); dietetics: postbaccalaureate internship (ADtA/CAADE); journalism and mass communications (ACEJMC); physical therapy assisting (APTA); public health: community health education (CEPH); speech-language pathology (ASHA). **Total program enrollment:** 32237. **Application fee:** $65.

PROGRAM(S) OFFERED
• **Banking and Financial Support Services** *13 students enrolled* • **Business Administration and Management, General** • **Business, Management, Marketing, and Related Support Services, Other** *64 students enrolled* • **Dental Assisting/Assistant** • **Visual and Performing Arts, General** *1 student enrolled*

STUDENT SERVICES Academic or career counseling, employment services for current students, placement services for program completers.

Niagara County Community College

3111 Saunders Settlement Road, Sanborn, NY 14132-9460
http://www.niagaracc.suny.edu/

CONTACT James P. Klyczek, President
Telephone: 716-614-6222

GENERAL INFORMATION Public Institution. Founded 1962. **Accreditation:** Regional (MSA/CIHE); electroneurodiagnostic technology (JRCEND); medical assisting (AAMAE); physical therapy assisting (APTA); radiologic technology: radiography (JRCERT); surgical technology (ARCST). **Total program enrollment:** 3941.

PROGRAM(S) OFFERED
• **Accounting Technology/Technician and Bookkeeping** *2 students enrolled* • **Administrative Assistant and Secretarial Science, General** *2 students enrolled* • **Applied Horticulture/Horticultural Operations, General** *7 students enrolled* • **Baking and Pastry Arts/Baker/Pastry Chef** *7 students enrolled* • **Business, Management, Marketing, and Related Support Services, Other** *4 students enrolled* • **Computer and Information Sciences and Support Services, Other** *5 students enrolled* • **Drafting and Design Technology/Technician, General** *2 students enrolled* • **Licensed Practical/Vocational Nurse Training (LPN, LVN, Cert, Dipl, AAS)** *40 students enrolled* • **Public Administration and Social Service Professions, Other** *1 student enrolled* • **Substance Abuse/Addiction Counseling** *14 students enrolled* • **Teacher Assistant/Aide** *41 students enrolled*

STUDENT SERVICES Academic or career counseling, daycare for children of students, employment services for current students, placement services for program completers, remedial services.

North Country Community College

23 Santanoni Avenue, PO Box 89, Saranac Lake, NY 12983-0089
http://www.nccc.edu/

CONTACT Fredrick Smith, Interim President
Telephone: 518-891-2915

GENERAL INFORMATION Public Institution. Founded 1967. **Accreditation:** Regional (MSA/CIHE); radiologic technology: radiography (JRCERT). **Total program enrollment:** 963.

PROGRAM(S) OFFERED
• **Administrative Assistant and Secretarial Science, General** *2 students enrolled* • **Community Organization and Advocacy** *6 students enrolled* • **Computer and Information Sciences and Support Services, Other** *1 student enrolled* • **Licensed Practical/Vocational Nurse Training (LPN, LVN, Cert, Dipl, AAS)** *70 students enrolled*

STUDENT SERVICES Academic or career counseling, employment services for current students, remedial services.

Northern Westchester School of Hairdressing

19 Bank Street, Peekskill, NY 10566

CONTACT C. F. Fragomeni, Financial Aid Director
Telephone: 914-739-8400 Ext. 10

GENERAL INFORMATION Private Institution. Founded 1983. **Total program enrollment:** 30.

PROGRAM(S) OFFERED
• **Cosmetology/Cosmetologist, General** *1000 hrs./$10,975*

STUDENT SERVICES Academic or career counseling, employment services for current students, placement services for program completers.

Olean Business Institute

301 North Union Street, Olean, NY 14760-2691
http://www.obi.edu/

CONTACT Jennifer Madison, President/Owner
Telephone: 716-372-7978

GENERAL INFORMATION Private Institution. Founded 1961. **Accreditation:** State accredited or approved. **Total program enrollment:** 60. **Application fee:** $25.

PROGRAM(S) OFFERED
• **Accounting and Related Services, Other** *1 student enrolled* • **Administrative Assistant and Secretarial Science, General** *2 students enrolled* • **Computer and Information Sciences and Support Services, Other** • **Legal Assistant/Paralegal** • **Medical/Clinical Assistant** *4 students enrolled*

STUDENT SERVICES Academic or career counseling, employment services for current students, placement services for program completers.

Onondaga Community College

4585 West Seneca Turnpike, Syracuse, NY 13215-4585
http://www.sunyocc.edu/

CONTACT Dr. Debbie Sydow, President
Telephone: 315-498-2622

GENERAL INFORMATION Public Institution. Founded 1962. **Accreditation:** Regional (MSA/CIHE); dental hygiene (ADA); engineering technology (ABET/TAC); health information technology (AHIMA); physical therapy assisting (APTA); respiratory therapy technology (CoARC). **Total program enrollment:** 6010.

Onondaga Community College (continued)

PROGRAM(S) OFFERED
• **Child Care and Support Services Management** *13 students enrolled*
• **Computer and Information Sciences and Support Services, Other** *3 students enrolled* • **Security and Protective Services, Other** *44 students enrolled* • **Surgical Technology/Technologist** *15 students enrolled*

STUDENT SERVICES Academic or career counseling, daycare for children of students, employment services for current students, placement services for program completers, remedial services.

Onondaga-Courtland-Madison BOCES

4500 Crown Road, Liverpool, NY 13090
http://ocmboces.org/

CONTACT Dr. Jessica Cohen, District Superintendent
Telephone: 315-453-4455

GENERAL INFORMATION Public Institution. **Total program enrollment:** 749.

PROGRAM(S) OFFERED
• **Aesthetician/Esthetician and Skin Care Specialist** • **Automobile/Automotive Mechanics Technology/Technician** • **CAD/CADD Drafting and/or Design Technology/Technician** *15 students enrolled* • **Construction Trades, General** *9 students enrolled* • **Cosmetology/Cosmetologist, General** *1078 hrs./$7400* • **Dental Assisting/Assistant** *682 hrs./$6100* • **General Office Occupations and Clerical Services** *51 students enrolled* • **Heating, Air Conditioning, Ventilation and Refrigeration Maintenance Technology/Technician (HAC, HACR, HVAC, HVACR)** *715 hrs./$6100* • **Licensed Practical/Vocational Nurse Training (LPN, LVN, Cert, Dipl, AAS)** *1278 hrs./$7400* • **Medical Office Assistant/Specialist** *65 students enrolled* • **Medical/Clinical Assistant** *780 hrs./$6100* • **Pharmacy Technician/Assistant** • **Welding Technology/Welder** *812 hrs./$6300*

STUDENT SERVICES Academic or career counseling, employment services for current students, placement services for program completers, remedial services.

Orange County Community College

115 South Street, Middletown, NY 10940-6437
http://www.orange.cc.ny.us/

CONTACT William Richards, President
Telephone: 845-344-6222

GENERAL INFORMATION Public Institution. Founded 1950. **Accreditation:** Regional (MSA/CIHE); dental hygiene (ADA); medical laboratory technology (NAACLS); physical therapy assisting (APTA). **Total program enrollment:** 3653. **Application fee:** $30.

PROGRAM(S) OFFERED
• **Administrative Assistant and Secretarial Science, General** *1 student enrolled* • **Child Care and Support Services Management** *1 student enrolled* • **Teacher Assistant/Aide** *10 students enrolled*

STUDENT SERVICES Academic or career counseling, daycare for children of students, employment services for current students, placement services for program completers, remedial services.

Orange-Ulster BOCES School of Practical Nursing

53 Gibson Road, Goshen, NY 10924
http://www.ouboces.org/

CONTACT Terry Olivo, Chief Operating Officer
Telephone: 845-291-0100

GENERAL INFORMATION Public Institution. **Total program enrollment:** 40.

PROGRAM(S) OFFERED
• **Licensed Practical/Vocational Nurse Training (LPN, LVN, Cert, Dipl, AAS)** *1104 hrs./$10,042*

STUDENT SERVICES Academic or career counseling, remedial services.

Orleans Niagara BOCES—Practical Nursing Program

3181 Saunders Settlement Road, Sanborn, NY 14132
http://www.ONBOCES.org

CONTACT Dr. Clark Godshall, Superintendent
Telephone: 800-836-7510 Ext. 3006

GENERAL INFORMATION Public Institution. **Total program enrollment:** 39.

PROGRAM(S) OFFERED
• **Licensed Practical/Vocational Nurse Training (LPN, LVN, Cert, Dipl, AAS)** • **Nurse/Nursing Assistant/Aide and Patient Care Assistant** *1500 hrs./$10,580*

STUDENT SERVICES Academic or career counseling, daycare for children of students, employment services for current students, placement services for program completers, remedial services.

Orlo School of Hair Design and Cosmetology

232 North Allen Street, Albany, NY 12206
http://www.theorloschool.com/

CONTACT Richard Caputo, President
Telephone: 518-459-7832 Ext. 101

GENERAL INFORMATION Private Institution. Founded 1984. **Total program enrollment:** 110. **Application fee:** $100.

PROGRAM(S) OFFERED
• **Cosmetology/Cosmetologist, General** *1000 hrs./$9900*

STUDENT SERVICES Academic or career counseling, placement services for program completers, remedial services.

Oswego County BOCES

Country Route 64, Mexico, NY 13114
http://www.oswegoboces.org/

CONTACT Dr. Joseph P. Camerino, District Superintendent
Telephone: 315-963-4251

GENERAL INFORMATION Public Institution. Founded 1964. **Total program enrollment:** 46. **Application fee:** $50.

PROGRAM(S) OFFERED
• **Dental Assisting/Assistant** *690 hrs./$4995* • **Licensed Practical/Vocational Nurse Training (LPN, LVN, Cert, Dipl, AAS)** *1176 hrs./$7500*

STUDENT SERVICES Academic or career counseling, placement services for program completers, remedial services.

Otsego Area School of Practical Nursing

400 Main Street, Oneonta, NY 13820

CONTACT Dr. Geoffrey Davis, Interim District Superintendent
Telephone: 607-431-2562

GENERAL INFORMATION Public Institution. **Total program enrollment:** 46. **Application fee:** $35.

PROGRAM(S) OFFERED
• Licensed Practical/Vocational Nurse Training (LPN, LVN, Cert, Dipl, AAS) *1204 hrs./$9008*

STUDENT SERVICES Academic or career counseling, remedial services.

Pace University

One Pace Plaza, New York, NY 10038
http://www.pace.edu/

CONTACT Stephen J. Friedman, President
Telephone: 212-346-1200

GENERAL INFORMATION Private Institution. Founded 1906. **Accreditation:** Regional (MSA/CIHE); computer science (ABET/CSAC). **Total program enrollment:** 7647. **Application fee:** $45.

PROGRAM(S) OFFERED
• Accounting • Banking and Financial Support Services • Business Administration and Management, General • Business/Commerce, General • Business/Office Automation/Technology/Data Entry • Commercial and Advertising Art • Communication, Journalism and Related Programs, Other • Computer Programming/Programmer, General • Computer Science • Computer Systems Networking and Telecommunications *4 students enrolled* • Computer and Information Sciences and Support Services, Other • Computer and Information Sciences, General • Data Entry/Microcomputer Applications, General *14 students enrolled* • Data Processing and Data Processing Technology/Technician • Human Resources Management and Services, Other • Information Technology • Interior Design • International Marketing • Italian Language and Literature • Latin American Studies *1 student enrolled* • Political Science and Government, General • Telecommunications Technology/Technician *10 students enrolled*

STUDENT SERVICES Academic or career counseling, employment services for current students, placement services for program completers, remedial services.

Paul Smith's College

PO Box 265, Paul Smiths, NY 12970-0265
http://www.paulsmiths.edu/

CONTACT John W. Mills, President
Telephone: 518-327-6000

GENERAL INFORMATION Private Institution. Founded 1937. **Accreditation:** Regional (MSA/CIHE); engineering technology (ABET/TAC). **Total program enrollment:** 913. **Application fee:** $30.

PROGRAM(S) OFFERED
• Baking and Pastry Arts/Baker/Pastry Chef *5 students enrolled* • Engineering-Related Technologies, Other *26 students enrolled*

STUDENT SERVICES Academic or career counseling, employment services for current students, placement services for program completers, remedial services.

Phillips Hairstyling Institute

709 East Genesee Street, Syracuse, NY 13210
http://phillipshairinstitute.com/

CONTACT Steven C. Phillips, President
Telephone: 315-422-9656 Ext. 13

GENERAL INFORMATION Private Institution. **Total program enrollment:** 92.

PROGRAM(S) OFFERED
• Cosmetology/Cosmetologist, General *1000 hrs./$7973* • Nail Technician/Specialist and Manicurist *250 hrs./$1750*

STUDENT SERVICES Placement services for program completers.

Plaza College

7409 37th Avenue, Jackson Heights, NY 11372-6300
http://www.plazacollege.edu/

CONTACT Charles Callahan, President
Telephone: 718-779-1430

GENERAL INFORMATION Private Institution. Founded 1916. **Accreditation:** Regional (MSA/CIHE). **Total program enrollment:** 724. **Application fee:** $100.

PROGRAM(S) OFFERED
• Accounting Technology/Technician and Bookkeeping *22 students enrolled* • Administrative Assistant and Secretarial Science, General

STUDENT SERVICES Academic or career counseling, employment services for current students, placement services for program completers, remedial services.

Professional Business Institute

125 Canal Street, New York, NY 10002-5049
http://www.pbcny.edu/

CONTACT Leon Y. Lee, President
Telephone: 212-226-7300

GENERAL INFORMATION Private Institution. **Total program enrollment:** 697. **Application fee:** $100.

PROGRAM(S) OFFERED
• Accounting and Related Services, Other *1 student enrolled* • Business Operations Support and Secretarial Services, Other *1 student enrolled* • Business, Management, Marketing, and Related Support Services, Other

STUDENT SERVICES Academic or career counseling, employment services for current students, placement services for program completers, remedial services.

Purchase College, State University of New York

735 Anderson Hill Road, Purchase, NY 10577-1400
http://www.purchase.edu/

CONTACT Thomas Schwarz, President
Telephone: 914-251-6000

GENERAL INFORMATION Public Institution. Founded 1967. **Accreditation:** Regional (MSA/CIHE); art and design (NASAD); music (NASM). **Total program enrollment:** 3788. **Application fee:** $40.

STUDENT SERVICES Academic or career counseling, daycare for children of students, employment services for current students, placement services for program completers, remedial services.

Putnam-Westchester BOCES

200 BOCES Drive, Yorktown Heights, NY 10598-4399
http://www.pnwboces.org/

CONTACT Dr. James T. Langlois, District Superintendent
Telephone: 914-245-2700

GENERAL INFORMATION Public Institution. **Total program enrollment:** 22. **Application fee:** $100.

PROGRAM(S) OFFERED
• Licensed Practical/Vocational Nurse Training (LPN, LVN, Cert, Dipl, AAS) *1200 hrs./$10,400*

STUDENT SERVICES Academic or career counseling, employment services for current students, placement services for program completers, remedial services.

Queensborough Community College of the City University of New York

222-05 56th Avenue, Bayside, NY 11364
http://www.qcc.cuny.edu/

CONTACT Eduardo Marti, President
Telephone: 718-631-6262

GENERAL INFORMATION Public Institution. Founded 1958. **Accreditation:** Regional (MSA/CIHE); engineering technology (ABET/TAC). **Total program enrollment:** 7410. **Application fee:** $65.

PROGRAM(S) OFFERED
• Administrative Assistant and Secretarial Science, General *2 students enrolled*
• Computer Installation and Repair Technology/Technician *1 student enrolled*
• Data Processing and Data Processing Technology/Technician *3 students enrolled* • Medical Office Management/Administration *6 students enrolled*
• Medical/Clinical Assistant *18 students enrolled* • Photography *2 students enrolled* • Teacher Assistant/Aide *5 students enrolled*

STUDENT SERVICES Academic or career counseling, daycare for children of students, employment services for current students, placement services for program completers, remedial services.

Rensselaer BOCES School of Practical Nursing

35 Colleen Road, Troy, NY 12180
http://www.questar.org/

CONTACT David Leavitt, Director of Career, Technical and Alternative Education
Telephone: 518-266-9033

GENERAL INFORMATION Public Institution. **Total program enrollment:** 67. **Application fee:** $100.

PROGRAM(S) OFFERED
• Licensed Practical/Vocational Nurse Training (LPN, LVN, Cert, Dipl, AAS) *1200 hrs./$9670*

STUDENT SERVICES Academic or career counseling, placement services for program completers.

Ridley-Lowell Business and Technical Institute

116 Front Street, Binghamton, NY 13905
http://www.ridley.edu/

CONTACT David Lounsbury, Director
Telephone: 607-724-2941

GENERAL INFORMATION Private Institution. Founded 1850. **Total program enrollment:** 111. **Application fee:** $50.

PROGRAM(S) OFFERED
• Accounting *1230 hrs./$12,800* • Administrative Assistant and Secretarial Science, General • Corrections and Criminal Justice, Other *900 hrs./$9600*
• Information Technology *12 students enrolled* • Legal Administrative Assistant/Secretary *2 students enrolled* • Medical Administrative/Executive Assistant and Medical Secretary *720 hrs./$7500* • Medical Insurance Coding Specialist/Coder *5 students enrolled* • Medical Transcription/Transcriptionist *1 student enrolled* • Medical/Clinical Assistant *1260 hrs./$12,800* • Word Processing *1 student enrolled*

STUDENT SERVICES Academic or career counseling, employment services for current students, placement services for program completers.

Ridley-Lowell School of Business

26 S. Hamilton Street, Poughkeepsie, NY 12601
http://www.ridley.edu/

CONTACT W. T. Weymouth, President
Telephone: 845-471-0330

GENERAL INFORMATION Private Institution. **Total program enrollment:** 215. **Application fee:** $100.

PROGRAM(S) OFFERED
• Accounting *1230 hrs./$13,200* • Business/Office Automation/Technology/Data Entry • Computer and Information Sciences and Support Services, Other
• Criminalistics and Criminal Science *6 students enrolled* • Executive Assistant/Executive Secretary • General Office Occupations and Clerical Services • Information Technology *960 hrs./$10,930* • Legal Administrative Assistant/Secretary *1 student enrolled* • Medical Administrative/Executive Assistant and Medical Secretary *930 hrs./$9750* • Medical Insurance Coding Specialist/Coder *690 hrs./$8025* • Medical/Clinical Assistant *1260 hrs./$13,200*

STUDENT SERVICES Academic or career counseling, employment services for current students, placement services for program completers, remedial services.

Rochester Institute of Technology

One Lomb Memorial Drive, Rochester, NY 14623-5603
http://www.rit.edu/

CONTACT William W. Destler, President
Telephone: 585-475-2411

GENERAL INFORMATION Private Institution. Founded 1829. **Accreditation:** Regional (MSA/CIHE); art and design (NASAD); computer science (ABET/CSAC); diagnostic medical sonography (JRCEDMS); engineering technology (ABET/TAC); interior design: professional (CIDA); nuclear medicine technology (JRCNMT). **Total program enrollment:** 12648. **Application fee:** $50.

PROGRAM(S) OFFERED
• Accounting Technology/Technician and Bookkeeping • Administrative Assistant and Secretarial Science, General • American Sign Language (ASL)
• Architectural Drafting and Architectural CAD/CADD • Athletic Training/Trainer *3 students enrolled* • Business Administration and Management, General *118 students enrolled* • Business, Management, Marketing, and Related Support Services, Other *3 students enrolled* • Business/Commerce, General • CAD/CADD Drafting and/or Design Technology/Technician • Commercial and Advertising Art *8 students enrolled* • Communication, Journalism and Related Programs, Other • Communications Technologies/Technicians and Support Services, Other • Communications Technology/Technician
• Community Organization and Advocacy *1 student enrolled* • Computer Programming/Programmer, General • Data Processing and Data Processing Technology/Technician • Diagnostic Medical Sonography/Sonographer and Ultrasound Technician *1 student enrolled* • Drafting and Design Technology/Technician, General • Ecology • Electromechanical Technology/Electromechanical Engineering Technology *4 students enrolled* • Engineering Technologies/Technicians, Other • Engineering/Industrial Management *1 student enrolled* • Environmental Engineering Technology/Environmental Technology *4 students enrolled* • Graphic Communications, Other • Graphic and Printing Equipment Operator, General Production • Health Professions and Related Clinical Sciences, Other • Health Services Administration *2 students enrolled* • Hospital and Health Care Facilities Administration/Management • Industrial Technology/Technician *1 student enrolled* • International Business/Trade/Commerce • Kinesiology and Exercise Science
• Management Information Systems and Services, Other • Management Information Systems, General • Manufacturing Technology/Technician
• Mechanical Drafting and Mechanical Drafting CAD/CADD • Mechanical Engineering/Mechanical Technology/Technician • Nuclear Medical Technology/Technologist • Occupational Safety and Health Technology/Technician • Photographic and Film/Video Technology/Technician and Assistant *1 student enrolled* • Public Administration and Social Service Professions, Other *4 students enrolled* • Radio and Television Broadcasting Technology/Technician *13 students enrolled* • Robotics Technology/Technician
• Science Technologies/Technicians, Other • Telecommunications Technology/Technician • Visual and Performing Arts, General *5 students enrolled*

STUDENT SERVICES Academic or career counseling, daycare for children of students, employment services for current students, placement services for program completers.

Rockland Community College

145 College Road, Suffern, NY 10901-3699
http://www.sunyrockland.edu/

CONTACT Dr. Cliff L. Wood, President
Telephone: 845-574-4000

GENERAL INFORMATION Public Institution. Founded 1959. **Accreditation:** Regional (MSA/CIHE); health information technology (AHIMA). **Total program enrollment:** 4315. **Application fee:** $30.

PROGRAM(S) OFFERED
• **Child Care and Support Services Management** 7 *students enrolled* • **Drafting and Design Technology/Technician, General** 2 *students enrolled* • **Legal Assistant/Paralegal** 11 *students enrolled* • **Therapeutic Recreation/Recreational Therapy** 3 *students enrolled*

STUDENT SERVICES Academic or career counseling, daycare for children of students, employment services for current students, placement services for program completers, remedial services.

Rockland County BOCES Practical Nursing

65 Parrott Road, West Nyack, NY 10994
http://www.rocklandboces.org/

CONTACT William Renella, Chief Operating Officer
Telephone: 845-627-4770

GENERAL INFORMATION Public Institution. **Total program enrollment:** 53. **Application fee:** $100.

PROGRAM(S) OFFERED
• **Licensed Practical/Vocational Nurse Training (LPN, LVN, Cert, Dipl, AAS)** 1080 *hrs./*$8690

STUDENT SERVICES Academic or career counseling, employment services for current students, placement services for program completers, remedial services.

Sage College of Albany

140 New Scotland Avenue, Albany, NY 12208-3425
http://www.sage.edu/sca/index.php

CONTACT Dr. Susan Scrimshaw, President
Telephone: 518-292-1717

GENERAL INFORMATION Private Institution. Founded 1957. **Accreditation:** Regional (MSA/CIHE); art and design (NASAD). **Total program enrollment:** 877. **Application fee:** $30.

PROGRAM(S) OFFERED
• **Legal Studies, General** 2 *students enrolled*

STUDENT SERVICES Academic or career counseling, employment services for current students, placement services for program completers, remedial services.

Sage Colleges System Office

45 Ferry Street, Troy, NY 12180
http://www.sage.edu

CONTACT Dr. Susan Scrimshaw, President
Telephone: 518-244-2214

GENERAL INFORMATION Private Institution.

St. John's University

8000 Utopia Parkway, Queens, NY 11439
http://www.stjohns.edu/

CONTACT Rev. Donald J. Harrington, CM, President
Telephone: 718-990-6161

GENERAL INFORMATION Private Institution (Affiliated with Roman Catholic Church). Founded 1870. **Accreditation:** Regional (MSA/CIHE);

audiology (ASHA); counseling (ACA); library and information science (ALA); speech-language pathology (ASHA). **Total program enrollment:** 14025. **Application fee:** $30.

PROGRAM(S) OFFERED
• **Computer and Information Sciences, General** • **Insurance** 3 *students enrolled* • **Legal Studies, General** 3 *students enrolled* • **Sport and Fitness Administration/Management**

STUDENT SERVICES Academic or career counseling, employment services for current students, placement services for program completers, remedial services.

St. Joseph's College, Long Island Campus

155 West Roe Boulevard, Patchogue, NY 11772-2399
http://www.sjcny.edu/

CONTACT Elizabeth A. Hill, CSJ, MA, JD, President
Telephone: 631-447-3200

GENERAL INFORMATION Private Institution. Founded 1916. **Accreditation:** Regional (MSA/CIHE). **Total program enrollment:** 2928. **Application fee:** $25.

PROGRAM(S) OFFERED
• **Adult Development and Aging** • **Business Administration and Management, General** 44 *students enrolled* • **Business, Management, Marketing, and Related Support Services, Other** • **Community Organization and Advocacy** 5 *students enrolled* • **Computer/Information Technology Services Administration and Management, Other** 1 *student enrolled* • **Criminal Justice/Police Science** • **Health Professions and Related Clinical Sciences, Other** 4 *students enrolled* • **Human Resources Management/Personnel Administration, General** 1 *student enrolled*

STUDENT SERVICES Academic or career counseling, employment services for current students, remedial services.

St. Joseph's College, New York

245 Clinton Avenue, Brooklyn, NY 11205-3688
http://www.sjcny.edu/

CONTACT Elizabeth A. Hill, CSJ, MA, JD, President
Telephone: 718-636-6800

GENERAL INFORMATION Private Institution. Founded 1916. **Accreditation:** Regional (MSA/CIHE). **Total program enrollment:** 727. **Application fee:** $25.

PROGRAM(S) OFFERED
• **Adult Development and Aging** • **Business Administration and Management, General** • **Business, Management, Marketing, and Related Support Services, Other** 12 *students enrolled* • **Community Organization and Advocacy** 22 *students enrolled* • **Computer/Information Technology Services Administration and Management, Other** 1 *student enrolled* • **Health Professions and Related Clinical Sciences, Other** 5 *students enrolled* • **Medical/Clinical Assistant** • **Parks, Recreation and Leisure Facilities Management** 1 *student enrolled* • **Parks, Recreation and Leisure Studies**

STUDENT SERVICES Academic or career counseling, employment services for current students, remedial services.

St. Joseph's Medical Center School of Radiography

127 S. Broadway, Yonkers, NY 10701

CONTACT John Ohnmacht, Financial Aid Officer
Telephone: 914-751-0391

GENERAL INFORMATION Private Institution. **Total program enrollment:** 31. **Application fee:** $50.

St. Joseph's Medical Center School of Radiography (continued)
PROGRAM(S) OFFERED
• Health/Medical Physics *900 hrs./$10,000*
STUDENT SERVICES Academic or career counseling.

St. Lawrence-Lewis County BOCES Nursing Program

7227 State Highway 56, Norwood, NY 13668
http://www.sllboces.org/

CONTACT Jack J. Boak, Jr., Interim District Superintendent
Telephone: 315-353-6693 Ext. 20415

GENERAL INFORMATION Public Institution. **Total program enrollment:** 32.

PROGRAM(S) OFFERED
• Licensed Practical/Vocational Nurse Training (LPN, LVN, Cert, Dipl, AAS) *1200 hrs./$8188*
STUDENT SERVICES Academic or career counseling, remedial services.

Samaritan Hospital School of Nursing

2215 Burdett Avenue, Troy, NY 12180
http://www.nehealth.com/

CONTACT Teresa Smith, Director
Telephone: 518-271-3285

GENERAL INFORMATION Private Institution. **Total program enrollment:** 42.

PROGRAM(S) OFFERED
• Licensed Practical/Vocational Nurse Training (LPN, LVN, Cert, Dipl, AAS) *13 students enrolled*
STUDENT SERVICES Academic or career counseling, daycare for children of students, employment services for current students, placement services for program completers, remedial services.

Sanford-Brown Institute

711 Stewart Avenue, 2nd Floor, Garden City, NY 11530
http://www.sblongisland.com/

CONTACT James Swift, School President
Telephone: 516-247-2900

GENERAL INFORMATION Private Institution. **Total program enrollment:** 848. **Application fee:** $25.

PROGRAM(S) OFFERED
• Cardiovascular Technology/Technologist *1950 hrs./$33,175* • Diagnostic Medical Sonography/Sonographer and Ultrasound Technician *1950 hrs./ $33,175* • Medical Insurance Coding Specialist/Coder *900 hrs./$12,925* • Medical Insurance Specialist/Medical Biller *38 students enrolled* • Medical/ Clinical Assistant *900 hrs./$12,900* • Pharmacy Technician/Assistant *720 hrs./ $10,000*
STUDENT SERVICES Academic or career counseling, employment services for current students, placement services for program completers.

Sanford-Brown Institute

120 East 16th Street, 2nd Floor, New York, NY 10003
http://www.sbnewyork.com/

CONTACT Diane Engelhardt, School President
Telephone: 646-313-4519

GENERAL INFORMATION Private Institution. **Total program enrollment:** 1653. **Application fee:** $25.

PROGRAM(S) OFFERED
• Cardiovascular Technology/Technologist *1950 hrs./$33,175* • Diagnostic Medical Sonography/Sonographer and Ultrasound Technician *1950 hrs./*

$33,175 • Medical Insurance Specialist/Medical Biller *900 hrs./$12,925* • Medical/Clinical Assistant *900 hrs./$13,153* • Pharmacy Technician/ Assistant *720 hrs./$10,000*
STUDENT SERVICES Academic or career counseling, placement services for program completers.

Sanford-Brown Institute

333 Westchester Avenue, White Plains, NY 10604
http://www.sbwhiteplains.com/

CONTACT Winn Sanderson, School President
Telephone: 914-874-2500

GENERAL INFORMATION Private Institution. **Total program enrollment:** 594. **Application fee:** $25.

PROGRAM(S) OFFERED
• Cardiovascular Technology/Technologist *1950 hrs./$33,175* • Diagnostic Medical Sonography/Sonographer and Ultrasound Technician *1950 hrs./ $33,175* • Medical Insurance Coding Specialist/Coder *900 hrs./$12,925* • Medical Insurance Specialist/Medical Biller *32 students enrolled* • Medical/ Clinical Assistant *900 hrs./$12,925* • Pharmacy Technician/Assistant *1 student enrolled*
STUDENT SERVICES Academic or career counseling, employment services for current students, placement services for program completers.

Schenectady County Community College

78 Washington Avenue, Schenectady, NY 12305-2294
http://www.sunysccc.edu/

CONTACT Gabriel J. Basil, President
Telephone: 518-381-1200

GENERAL INFORMATION Public Institution. **Founded** 1969. **Accreditation:** Regional (MSA/CIHE); music (NASM). **Total program enrollment:** 2228.

PROGRAM(S) OFFERED
• Child Care and Support Services Management *1 student enrolled* • Computer Programming/Programmer, General *2 students enrolled* • Computer and Information Sciences and Support Services, Other *2 students enrolled* • Criminal Justice/Law Enforcement Administration *1 student enrolled* • Culinary Arts/Chef Training *1 student enrolled* • Health Professions and Related Clinical Sciences, Other *20 students enrolled* • Music, General *12 students enrolled* • Teacher Assistant/Aide *8 students enrolled* • Tourism Promotion Operations *2 students enrolled*
STUDENT SERVICES Academic or career counseling, daycare for children of students, employment services for current students, placement services for program completers, remedial services.

Schuyler-Chemung-Tioga Practical Nursing Program

459 Philo Road, Elmira, NY 14903
http://www.gstboces.org/

CONTACT Anthony Micha, District Superintendent
Telephone: 607-962-3175 Ext. 2261

GENERAL INFORMATION Public Institution. **Total program enrollment:** 79. **Application fee:** $20.

PROGRAM(S) OFFERED
• Licensed Practical/Vocational Nurse Training (LPN, LVN, Cert, Dipl, AAS) *145 students enrolled* • Nursing, Other *1200 hrs./$7910*
STUDENT SERVICES Remedial services.

Seminar L'moros Bais Yaakov

4409 15th Avenue, Brooklyn, NY 11219

CONTACT Israel J. Kaplan, Dean of Administration
Telephone: 718-851-2900

GENERAL INFORMATION Private Institution. **Total program enrollment:** 236.

PROGRAM(S) OFFERED
• **Teacher Education and Professional Development, Specific Subject Areas, Other** *383 students enrolled*

STUDENT SERVICES Academic or career counseling, employment services for current students, placement services for program completers.

Shear Ego International School of Hair Design

525 Titus Avenue, Rochester, NY 14617

CONTACT Eugene P. Cardamone, Director/CEO
Telephone: 585-342-0070 Ext. 0

GENERAL INFORMATION Private Institution. Founded 1987. **Total program enrollment: 98. Application fee:** $100.

PROGRAM(S) OFFERED
• **Aesthetician/Esthetician and Skin Care Specialist** *600 hrs./$6867*
• **Barbering/Barber** *600 hrs./$7742* • **Cosmetology/Cosmetologist, General** *1000 hrs./$12,774* • **Nail Technician/Specialist and Manicurist** *250 hrs./$2000*

STUDENT SERVICES Placement services for program completers.

Siena College

515 Loudon Road, Loudonville, NY 12211-1462
http://www.siena.edu/

CONTACT Fr. Kevin Mullen, OFM, President
Telephone: 518-783-2300

GENERAL INFORMATION Private Institution. Founded 1937. **Accreditation:** Regional (MSA/CIHE). **Total program enrollment: 3110. Application fee:** $50.

PROGRAM(S) OFFERED
• **Accounting** *2 students enrolled* • **Secondary Education and Teaching** *1 student enrolled*

STUDENT SERVICES Academic or career counseling, employment services for current students, placement services for program completers.

Southern Westchester BOCES

310 East Boston Post Road, Mamaroneck, NY 10543
http://www.swbocesadulted.org/

CONTACT Harry Kaplan, Supervisor
Telephone: 914-592-0849

GENERAL INFORMATION Public Institution. **Total program enrollment:** 89. **Application fee:** $75.

PROGRAM(S) OFFERED
• **Licensed Practical/Vocational Nurse Training (LPN, LVN, Cert, Dipl, AAS)** *1080 hrs./$8950*

STUDENT SERVICES Academic or career counseling, placement services for program completers, remedial services.

Spanish-American Institute

215 West 43rd Street, New York, NY 10036-3913
http://www.sai2000.org/

CONTACT Dante V. Ferrano, President
Telephone: 212-840-7111

GENERAL INFORMATION Private Institution. **Application fee:** $100.

PROGRAM(S) OFFERED
• **Accounting and Related Services, Other** • **Accounting** *1600 hrs./$9700*
• **Business Administration and Management, General** *1 student enrolled*
• **Business/Office Automation/Technology/Data Entry** *1600 hrs./$10,900*

STUDENT SERVICES Academic or career counseling, placement services for program completers, remedial services.

State University of New York College at Old Westbury

PO Box 210, Old Westbury, NY 11568-0210
http://www.oldwestbury.edu/

CONTACT Dr. Calvin O. Butts, III, President
Telephone: 516-876-3000

GENERAL INFORMATION Public Institution. Founded 1965. **Accreditation:** Regional (MSA/CIHE). **Total program enrollment: 2907. Application fee:** $40.

STUDENT SERVICES Academic or career counseling, daycare for children of students, employment services for current students, placement services for program completers, remedial services.

State University of New York College of Agriculture and Technology at Morrisville

PO Box 901, Morrisville, NY 13408-0901
http://www.morrisville.edu/

CONTACT Raymond W. Cross, President
Telephone: 315-684-6000

GENERAL INFORMATION Public Institution. Founded 1908. **Accreditation:** Regional (MSA/CIHE); engineering technology (ABET/TAC). **Total program enrollment: 2866. Application fee:** $40.

STUDENT SERVICES Academic or career counseling, daycare for children of students, employment services for current students, placement services for program completers, remedial services.

State University of New York College of Technology at Alfred

10 Upper College Drive, Alfred, NY 14802
http://www.alfredstate.edu/

CONTACT John M. Anderson, President
Telephone: 800-425-3733

GENERAL INFORMATION Public Institution. Founded 1908. **Accreditation:** Regional (MSA/CIHE); engineering technology (ABET/TAC); health information technology (AHIMA). **Total program enrollment: 2947. Application fee:** $40.

PROGRAM(S) OFFERED
• **Entrepreneurial and Small Business Operations, Other** *1 student enrolled*
• **Health Information/Medical Records Technology/Technician** *4 students enrolled* • **Heavy/Industrial Equipment Maintenance Technologies, Other** *1*

State University of New York College of Technology at Alfred (continued)
student enrolled • **Industrial Production Technologies/Technicians, Other** 2 *students enrolled* • **Machine Shop Technology/Assistant** 1 *student enrolled* • **Vehicle Maintenance and Repair Technologies, Other** 1 *student enrolled*

STUDENT SERVICES Academic or career counseling, employment services for current students, placement services for program completers, remedial services.

State University of New York College of Technology at Canton

Cornell Drive, Canton, NY 13617
http://www.canton.edu/

CONTACT Joseph L. Kennedy, President
Telephone: 315-386-7011

GENERAL INFORMATION Public Institution. Founded 1906. **Accreditation:** Regional (MSA/CIHE); engineering technology (ABET/TAC); funeral service (ABFSE); physical therapy assisting (APTA). **Total program enrollment:** 2301. **Application fee:** $40.

PROGRAM(S) OFFERED
• **Administrative Assistant and Secretarial Science, General** 2 *students enrolled* • **Automobile/Automotive Mechanics Technology/Technician** 1 *student enrolled* • **Construction Trades, Other** 6 *students enrolled* • **Electrical and Power Transmission Installation/Installer, General** 8 *students enrolled* • **Health Professions and Related Clinical Sciences, Other** 29 *students enrolled* • **Heating, Air Conditioning and Refrigeration Technology/Technician (ACH/ACR/ACHR/HRAC/HVAC/AC Technology)** 4 *students enrolled* • **Heating, Air Conditioning, Ventilation and Refrigeration Maintenance Technology/Technician (HAC, HACR, HVAC, HVACR)** 8 *students enrolled* • **Mechanical Drafting and Mechanical Drafting CAD/CADD** 1 *student enrolled* • **Security and Loss Prevention Services** 1 *student enrolled* • **Vehicle Maintenance and Repair Technologies, Other** 18 *students enrolled*

STUDENT SERVICES Academic or career counseling, employment services for current students, placement services for program completers, remedial services.

State University of New York College of Technology at Delhi

Main Street, Delhi, NY 13753
http://www.delhi.edu/

CONTACT Candace Vancko, President
Telephone: 607-746-4000

GENERAL INFORMATION Public Institution. Founded 1913. **Accreditation:** Regional (MSA/CIHE). **Total program enrollment:** 2494. **Application fee:** $40.

PROGRAM(S) OFFERED
• **Carpentry/Carpenter** 2 *students enrolled* • **Electrical and Power Transmission Installation/Installer, General** 6 *students enrolled* • **Heating, Air Conditioning, Ventilation and Refrigeration Maintenance Technology/Technician (HAC, HACR, HVAC, HVACR)** 2 *students enrolled* • **Industrial Production Technologies/Technicians, Other** 1 *student enrolled* • **Licensed Practical/Vocational Nurse Training (LPN, LVN, Cert, Dipl, AAS)** 1 *student enrolled* • **Mechanical Drafting and Mechanical Drafting CAD/CADD** 10 *students enrolled* • **Pipefitting/Pipefitter and Sprinkler Fitter** 4 *students enrolled*

STUDENT SERVICES Academic or career counseling, daycare for children of students, employment services for current students, placement services for program completers, remedial services.

State University of New York System

State University Plaza, Albany, NY 12246
http://www.suny.edu/

CONTACT Dr. John B. Clark, Interim Chancellor
Telephone: 518-443-5355

GENERAL INFORMATION Public Institution.

Stony Brook University, State University of New York

Nicolls Road, Stony Brook, NY 11794
http://www.sunysb.edu/

CONTACT Shirley Strum Kenny, President
Telephone: 631-632-6000

GENERAL INFORMATION Public Institution. Founded 1957. **Accreditation:** Regional (MSA/CIHE); cytotechnology (ASC); dietetics: post-baccalaureate internship (ADtA/CAADE); medical technology (NAA-CLS). **Total program enrollment:** 19296. **Application fee:** $40.

STUDENT SERVICES Academic or career counseling, daycare for children of students, employment services for current students, placement services for program completers, remedial services.

Studio Jewelers

32 East 31 Street, New York, NY 10016-4112
http://www.studiojewelersltd.com/

CONTACT Robert Streppone, Director
Telephone: 212-686-1944

GENERAL INFORMATION Private Institution. **Total program enrollment:** 14.

PROGRAM(S) OFFERED
• **Metal and Jewelry Arts** 36 *hrs./$600*

STUDENT SERVICES Placement services for program completers.

Suburban Technical School

175 Fulton Avenue, Hempstead, NY 11550
http://suburbantech.com/

CONTACT Paul Pari, Director
Telephone: 516-481-6660

GENERAL INFORMATION Private Institution. **Total program enrollment:** 248. **Application fee:** $20.

PROGRAM(S) OFFERED
• **Medical/Clinical Assistant** 960 *hrs./$11,150*

STUDENT SERVICES Academic or career counseling, placement services for program completers.

Suffolk County Community College

533 College Road, Selden, NY 11784-2899
http://www.sunysuffolk.edu/

CONTACT Dr. Shirley Robinson Pippins, President
Telephone: 631-451-4110

GENERAL INFORMATION Public Institution. Founded 1959. **Accreditation:** Regional (MSA/CIHE); health information technology (AHIMA); medical assisting (AAMAE); physical therapy assisting (APTA). **Total program enrollment:** 12659. **Application fee:** $35.

PROGRAM(S) OFFERED
• **Accounting Technology/Technician and Bookkeeping** 8 *students enrolled* • **Administrative Assistant and Secretarial Science, General** 2 *students enrolled* • **Criminal Justice/Law Enforcement Administration** 1 *student enrolled* • **Drafting and Design Technology/Technician, General** 12 *students enrolled* • **Entrepreneurship/Entrepreneurial Studies** 5 *students enrolled* • **Fire Science/**

Firefighting *1 student enrolled* • **Information Science/Studies** *6 students enrolled* • **Legal Assistant/Paralegal** *23 students enrolled* • **Technical Theatre/Theatre Design and Technology** *4 students enrolled*

STUDENT SERVICES Academic or career counseling, daycare for children of students, employment services for current students, placement services for program completers, remedial services.

Sullivan County Board of Cooperative Education Services

52 Ferndale Loomis Road, Liberty, NY 12754
http://scboces.org/

CONTACT Martin Handler, District Superintendent
Telephone: 845-295-4136

GENERAL INFORMATION Public Institution. **Total program enrollment:** 34. **Application fee:** $30.

PROGRAM(S) OFFERED
• **Licensed Practical/Vocational Nurse Training (LPN, LVN, Cert, Dipl, AAS)** *1188 hrs./$8200*

STUDENT SERVICES Academic or career counseling, remedial services.

Sullivan County Community College

112 College Road, Loch Sheldrake, NY 12759
http://www.sullivan.suny.edu/

CONTACT Dr. Mamie Howard Golladay, President
Telephone: 845-434-5750

GENERAL INFORMATION Public Institution. Founded 1962. **Accreditation:** Regional (MSA/CIHE). **Total program enrollment:** 1056.

PROGRAM(S) OFFERED
• **Accounting Technology/Technician and Bookkeeping** *1 student enrolled* • **Computer/Information Technology Services Administration and Management, Other** *1 student enrolled* • **Electrician** *1 student enrolled*

STUDENT SERVICES Academic or career counseling, daycare for children of students, employment services for current students, placement services for program completers, remedial services.

Syracuse Central Technical High School Licensed Practical Nursing Program

258 E. Adams Street, Syracuse, NY 13202
http://cccam.scsd.us/ct/

CONTACT Kathy Lent, Director of Adult Programs
Telephone: 315-435-4150

GENERAL INFORMATION Public Institution. **Total program enrollment:** 55.

PROGRAM(S) OFFERED
• **Licensed Practical/Vocational Nurse Training (LPN, LVN, Cert, Dipl, AAS)** *1210 hrs./$8595*

STUDENT SERVICES Academic or career counseling, employment services for current students, placement services for program completers, remedial services.

Syracuse University

Syracuse, NY 13244
http://www.syracuse.edu/

CONTACT Nancy Cantor, Chancellor and President
Telephone: 315-443-1870

GENERAL INFORMATION Private Institution. Founded 1870. **Accreditation:** Regional (MSA/CIHE); art and design (NASAD); audiology

(ASHA); computer science (ABET/CSAC); counseling (ACA); dietetics: undergraduate, postbaccalaureate internship (ADtA/CAADE); interior design: professional (CIDA); journalism and mass communications (ACEJMC); library and information science (ALA); music (NASM); speech-language pathology (ASHA). **Total program enrollment:** 16822. **Application fee:** $70.

PROGRAM(S) OFFERED
• **Business Administration and Management, General** *3 students enrolled* • **Computer/Information Technology Services Administration and Management, Other** *2 students enrolled* • **Social Sciences, General** *4 students enrolled*

STUDENT SERVICES Academic or career counseling, daycare for children of students, employment services for current students, placement services for program completers.

TCI–The College of Technology

320 West 31st Street, New York, NY 10001-2705
http://www.tciedu.com/

CONTACT Dr. James Melville, President
Telephone: 212-594-4000

GENERAL INFORMATION Private Institution. Founded 1909. **Accreditation:** Regional (MSA/CIHE); state program registration (RUSNY); engineering technology (ABET/TAC). **Total program enrollment:** 3805.

PROGRAM(S) OFFERED
• **Business/Office Automation/Technology/Data Entry** • **Construction Engineering Technology/Technician** *2 students enrolled* • **Electrical, Electronic and Communications Engineering Technology/Technician** • **Heating, Air Conditioning and Refrigeration Technology/Technician (ACH/ACR/ACHR/HRAC/HVAC/AC Technology)** *5 students enrolled*

STUDENT SERVICES Academic or career counseling, employment services for current students, placement services for program completers, remedial services.

Tompkins Cortland Community College

170 North Street, PO Box 139, Dryden, NY 13053-0139
http://www.TC3.edu/

CONTACT Carl E. Haynes, President
Telephone: 607-844-8211

GENERAL INFORMATION Public Institution. Founded 1968. **Accreditation:** Regional (MSA/CIHE). **Total program enrollment:** 2487. **Application fee:** $15.

PROGRAM(S) OFFERED
• **Accounting Technology/Technician and Bookkeeping** *1 student enrolled* • **Entrepreneurship/Entrepreneurial Studies** *1 student enrolled*

STUDENT SERVICES Academic or career counseling, daycare for children of students, employment services for current students, placement services for program completers, remedial services.

Touro College

27-33 West 23rd Street, New York, NY 10010
http://www.touro.edu/

CONTACT Bernard Lander, President
Telephone: 212-463-0400

GENERAL INFORMATION Private Institution. Founded 1971. **Accreditation:** Regional (MSA/CIHE); physical therapy assisting (APTA); speech-language pathology (ASHA). **Total program enrollment:** 9701. **Application fee:** $50.

Touro College (continued)

PROGRAM(S) OFFERED
• **Bilingual and Multilingual Education** *33 students enrolled* • **Digital Communication and Media/Multimedia** *45 students enrolled* • **Education, Other** *4 students enrolled* • **Health Information/Medical Records Administration/Administrator** *1 student enrolled* • **Higher Education/Higher Education Administration** *7 students enrolled*

STUDENT SERVICES Academic or career counseling, employment services for current students, placement services for program completers, remedial services.

Trocaire College

360 Choate Avenue, Buffalo, NY 14220-2094
http://www.trocaire.edu/

CONTACT Paul B. Hurley, Jr., PhD, President
Telephone: 716-826-1200

GENERAL INFORMATION Private Institution. Founded 1958. **Accreditation:** Regional (MSA/CIHE); health information technology (AHIMA); medical assisting (AAMAE); radiologic technology: radiography (JRCERT); surgical technology (ARCST). **Total program enrollment:** 604. **Application fee:** $25.

PROGRAM(S) OFFERED
• **Business/Office Automation/Technology/Data Entry** • **Computer Systems Networking and Telecommunications** *1 student enrolled* • **Diagnostic Medical Sonography/Sonographer and Ultrasound Technician** *10 students enrolled* • **Hospitality Administration/Management, General** *1 student enrolled* • **Licensed Practical/Vocational Nurse Training (LPN, LVN, Cert, Dipl, AAS)** *37 students enrolled* • **Massage Therapy/Therapeutic Massage** *2 students enrolled* • **Medical Insurance Coding Specialist/Coder** • **Medical Office Assistant/Specialist** • **Medical Transcription/Transcriptionist** *1 student enrolled*

STUDENT SERVICES Academic or career counseling, employment services for current students, placement services for program completers, remedial services.

Ulster County BOCES–School of Practical Nursing

PO Box 601, Port Ewen, NY 12466

CONTACT Martin Ruglis, Chief Executive Officer
Telephone: 845-331-6680

GENERAL INFORMATION Public Institution. Founded 1979. **Total program enrollment:** 77. **Application fee:** $100.

PROGRAM(S) OFFERED
• **Licensed Practical/Vocational Nurse Training (LPN, LVN, Cert, Dipl, AAS)** *1200 hrs./$9070*

STUDENT SERVICES Academic or career counseling, daycare for children of students, placement services for program completers, remedial services.

Ulster County Community College

Cottekill Road, Stone Ridge, NY 12484
http://www.sunyulster.edu/

CONTACT Dr. Donald C. Katt, President
Telephone: 845-687-5000

GENERAL INFORMATION Public Institution. Founded 1961. **Accreditation:** Regional (MSA/CIHE). **Total program enrollment:** 1623.

PROGRAM(S) OFFERED
• **Animal Sciences, General** *7 students enrolled* • **Business, Management, Marketing, and Related Support Services, Other** *1 student enrolled* • **Computer and Information Sciences and Support Services, Other** *14 students enrolled*

• **Criminal Justice/Police Science** *23 students enrolled* • **Emergency Medical Technology/Technician (EMT Paramedic)** *14 students enrolled* • **Sign Language Interpretation and Translation** *1 student enrolled*

STUDENT SERVICES Academic or career counseling, daycare for children of students, employment services for current students, placement services for program completers, remedial services.

University at Buffalo, the State University of New York

Capen Hall, Buffalo, NY 14260
http://www.buffalo.edu/

CONTACT John B. Simpson, President
Telephone: 716-645-2000

GENERAL INFORMATION Public Institution. Founded 1846. **Accreditation:** Regional (MSA/CIHE); art and design (NASAD); audiology (ASHA); dietetics: postbaccalaureate internship (ADtA/CAADE); library and information science (ALA); medical technology (NAACLS); nuclear medicine technology (JRCNMT); speech-language pathology (ASHA). **Total program enrollment:** 23808. **Application fee:** $40.

PROGRAM(S) OFFERED
• **Journalism** *1 student enrolled*

STUDENT SERVICES Academic or career counseling, daycare for children of students, employment services for current students, placement services for program completers, remedial services.

USA Beauty School International

87 Walker Street, 1st Floor, New York, NY 10013
http://www.usabeautyschool.com

CONTACT Pam Yuen, Director
Telephone: 212-431-0505

GENERAL INFORMATION Private Institution. **Total program enrollment:** 122. **Application fee:** $20.

PROGRAM(S) OFFERED
• **Aesthetician/Esthetician and Skin Care Specialist** *600 hrs./$4800* • **Barbering/Barber** • **Cosmetology/Cosmetologist, General** *150 hrs./$1480* • **Nail Technician/Specialist and Manicurist** *250 hrs./$1380*

STUDENT SERVICES Academic or career counseling, placement services for program completers.

Utica College

1600 Burrstone Road, Utica, NY 13502-4892
http://www.utica.edu/

CONTACT Todd S. Hutton, President
Telephone: 315-792-3111

GENERAL INFORMATION Private Institution. Founded 1946. **Accreditation:** Regional (MSA/CIHE). **Total program enrollment:** 2208. **Application fee:** $40.

PROGRAM(S) OFFERED
• **Health Services/Allied Health/Health Sciences, General**

STUDENT SERVICES Academic or career counseling, employment services for current students, placement services for program completers, remedial services.

Utica School of Commerce

201 Bleecker Street, Utica, NY 13501-2280
http://www.uscny.edu/

CONTACT Philip Williams, President
Telephone: 315-733-2307

GENERAL INFORMATION Private Institution. Founded 1896. **Accreditation:** State program registration (RUSNY). **Total program enrollment:** 300.

PROGRAM(S) OFFERED
● **Accounting Technology/Technician and Bookkeeping** 2 *students enrolled* ● **Administrative Assistant and Secretarial Science, General** 10 *students enrolled* ● **Data Entry/Microcomputer Applications, General** ● **Data Processing and Data Processing Technology/Technician** 1 *student enrolled*

STUDENT SERVICES Academic or career counseling, employment services for current students, placement services for program completers, remedial services.

Vaughn College of Aeronautics and Technology

8601 23rd Avenue, Flushing, NY 11369-1037
http://www.vaughn.edu/

CONTACT John C. Fitzpatrick, President
Telephone: 718-429-6600

GENERAL INFORMATION Private Institution. Founded 1932. **Accreditation:** Regional (MSA/CIHE); engineering technology (ABET/TAC). **Total program enrollment:** 825. **Application fee:** $40.

PROGRAM(S) OFFERED
● **Airframe Mechanics and Aircraft Maintenance Technology/Technician**

STUDENT SERVICES Academic or career counseling, employment services for current students, placement services for program completers, remedial services.

VEEB Nassau County–School of Practical Nursing

899A Jerusalem Avenue, Uniondale, NY 11553

CONTACT Allan Havranek, Director of Financial Aid
Telephone: 516-572-1704

GENERAL INFORMATION Public Institution. Founded 1963. **Total program enrollment:** 198. **Application fee:** $150.

PROGRAM(S) OFFERED
● **Licensed Practical/Vocational Nurse Training (LPN, LVN, Cert, Dipl, AAS)** 200 *students enrolled*

STUDENT SERVICES Academic or career counseling, employment services for current students.

Washington-Saratoga-Warren-Hamilton-Essex BOCES

Henning Road, Saratoga Springs, NY 12866

CONTACT John Stoothoff, District Superintendent
Telephone: 518-581-3670

GENERAL INFORMATION Private Institution. **Total program enrollment:** 31.

PROGRAM(S) OFFERED
● **Licensed Practical/Vocational Nurse Training (LPN, LVN, Cert, Dipl, AAS)** 1200 *hrs./$9093*

STUDENT SERVICES Academic or career counseling, daycare for children of students, remedial services.

Wayne-Finger Lakes BOCES School of Practical Nursing

131 Drumlin Court, Newark, NY 14513-1863
http://www.wflboces.org/

CONTACT Joseph Marinelli, Superintendent
Telephone: 315-332-7400

GENERAL INFORMATION Public Institution. **Total program enrollment:** 184. **Application fee:** $50.

PROGRAM(S) OFFERED
● **Licensed Practical/Vocational Nurse Training (LPN, LVN, Cert, Dipl, AAS)** 1125 *hrs./$13,350*

STUDENT SERVICES Academic or career counseling, placement services for program completers, remedial services.

Westchester Community College

75 Grasslands Road, Valhalla, NY 10595-1698
http://www.sunywcc.edu/

CONTACT Dr. Joseph N. Hankin, President
Telephone: 914-606-6600

GENERAL INFORMATION Public Institution. Founded 1946. **Accreditation:** Regional (MSA/CIHE); radiologic technology: radiography (JRCERT). **Total program enrollment:** 6600. **Application fee:** $25.

PROGRAM(S) OFFERED
● **Accounting Technology/Technician and Bookkeeping** 3 *students enrolled* ● **Administrative Assistant and Secretarial Science, General** 4 *students enrolled* ● **Child Care and Support Services Management** 6 *students enrolled* ● **Commercial and Advertising Art** 1 *student enrolled* ● **Community Organization and Advocacy** 2 *students enrolled* ● **Computer and Information Sciences and Support Services, Other** 8 *students enrolled* ● **Design and Applied Arts, Other** 4 *students enrolled* ● **Drafting and Design Technology/Technician, General** 14 *students enrolled* ● **Emergency Medical Technology/Technician (EMT Paramedic)** 1 *student enrolled* ● **Legal Assistant/Paralegal** 20 *students enrolled* ● **Licensed Practical/Vocational Nurse Training (LPN, LVN, Cert, Dipl, AAS)** 37 *students enrolled* ● **Medical Administrative/Executive Assistant and Medical Secretary** 12 *students enrolled* ● **Small Business Administration/Management** 1 *student enrolled* ● **Substance Abuse/Addiction Counseling** 5 *students enrolled* ● **Teacher Assistant/Aide** 4 *students enrolled*

STUDENT SERVICES Academic or career counseling, daycare for children of students, employment services for current students, placement services for program completers, remedial services.

Westchester School of Beauty Culture

6 Gramatan Avenue, Mount Vernon, NY 10550

CONTACT Jessica Salamone, Director
Telephone: 914-699-2344

GENERAL INFORMATION Private Institution. Founded 1961. **Total program enrollment:** 38.

PROGRAM(S) OFFERED
● **Aesthetician/Esthetician and Skin Care Specialist** 600 *hrs./$5546* ● **Cosmetology and Related Personal Grooming Arts, Other** ● **Cosmetology/Cosmetologist, General** 1040 *hrs./$8500* ● **Nail Technician/Specialist and Manicurist** 250 *hrs./$1495*

STUDENT SERVICES Academic or career counseling, placement services for program completers.

Western Suffolk BOCES

152 Laurel Hill Road, Northport, NY 11768-3499
http://www.wilsontech.org/

CONTACT Debra Montaruli, Principal-Adult Education
Telephone: 631-667-6000 Ext. 320

GENERAL INFORMATION Public Institution. **Total program enrollment:** 183. **Application fee:** $25.

PROGRAM(S) OFFERED
• Aesthetician/Esthetician and Skin Care Specialist *600 hrs./$5249* • Airframe Mechanics and Aircraft Maintenance Technology/Technician *1910 hrs./ $18,396* • Cosmetology/Cosmetologist, General *1000 hrs./$6715* • Diagnostic Medical Sonography/Sonographer and Ultrasound Technician *2733 hrs./ $26,699* • Licensed Practical/Vocational Nurse Training (LPN, LVN, Cert, Dipl, AAS) *1245 hrs./$15,499* • Surgical Technology/Technologist *1200 hrs./ $13,500*

STUDENT SERVICES Academic or career counseling, daycare for children of students, employment services for current students, placement services for program completers, remedial services.

Willsey Institute

120 Stuyvesant Place, Staten Island, NY 10301

CONTACT Linda Chapilliquen, President
Telephone: 718-442-5706

GENERAL INFORMATION Private Institution. **Total program enrollment:** 29. **Application fee:** $50.

PROGRAM(S) OFFERED
• Dental Assisting/Assistant *900 hrs./$7700* • Medical/Clinical Assistant *900 hrs./$7820* • Nurse/Nursing Assistant/Aide and Patient Care Assistant *10 students enrolled*

STUDENT SERVICES Academic or career counseling, placement services for program completers, remedial services.

Wood Tobe–Coburn School

8 East 40th Street, New York, NY 10016
http://www.woodtobecoburn.edu/

CONTACT Sandi Gruninger, President
Telephone: 212-686-9040

GENERAL INFORMATION Private Institution. Founded 1879. **Accreditation:** State program registration (RUSNY). **Total program enrollment:** 305. **Application fee:** $50.

PROGRAM(S) OFFERED
• Accounting Technology/Technician and Bookkeeping • Administrative Assistant and Secretarial Science, General • Allied Health and Medical Assisting Services, Other *28 students enrolled* • Computer Programming/ Programmer, General • Graphic Design *1 student enrolled* • Tourism and Travel Services Management

STUDENT SERVICES Academic or career counseling, placement services for program completers.

NORTH CAROLINA

Alamance Community College

PO Box 8000, Graham, NC 27253-8000
http://www.alamancecc.edu/

CONTACT Martin Nadelman, President
Telephone: 336-578-2002

GENERAL INFORMATION Public Institution. Founded 1959. **Accreditation:** Regional (SACS/CC); dental assisting (ADA); medical laboratory technology (NAACLS). **Total program enrollment:** 1908.

PROGRAM(S) OFFERED
• Accounting *47 students enrolled* • Applied Horticulture/Horticultural Operations, General *2 students enrolled* • Automobile/Automotive Mechanics

Technology/Technician *1 student enrolled* • Biology Technician/Biotechnology Laboratory Technician *7 students enrolled* • Business Administration and Management, General *7 students enrolled* • Cabinetmaking and Millwork/Millwright *9 students enrolled* • Carpentry/Carpenter • Commercial and Advertising Art • Computer Programming, Specific Applications *2 students enrolled* • Computer Systems Networking and Telecommunications *1 student enrolled* • Cosmetology/Cosmetologist, General *26 students enrolled* • Culinary Arts/ Chef Training *3 students enrolled* • Dental Assisting/Assistant *21 students enrolled* • Early Childhood Education and Teaching *17 students enrolled* • Electrical, Electronic and Communications Engineering Technology/ Technician • Electromechanical and Instrumentation and Maintenance Technologies/Technicians, Other *1 student enrolled* • Fire Protection and Safety Technology/Technician *1 student enrolled* • Heating, Air Conditioning, Ventilation and Refrigeration Maintenance Technology/Technician (HAC, HACR, HVAC, HVACR) *2 students enrolled* • Human Resources Management/ Personnel Administration, General *2 students enrolled* • Information Science/ Studies *4 students enrolled* • Information Technology *2 students enrolled* • Language Interpretation and Translation *15 students enrolled* • Legal Administrative Assistant/Secretary • Marketing/Marketing Management, General • Mechanical Drafting and Mechanical Drafting CAD/CADD *7 students enrolled* • Medical Office Management/Administration *94 students enrolled* • Nurse/Nursing Assistant/Aide and Patient Care Assistant *3 students enrolled* • Office Management and Supervision *14 students enrolled* • Operations Management and Supervision • Phlebotomy/Phlebotomist *12 students enrolled* • Real Estate • Welding Technology/Welder *4 students enrolled*

STUDENT SERVICES Academic or career counseling, daycare for children of students, employment services for current students, placement services for program completers, remedial services.

The Art Institute of Charlotte

2110 Water Ridge Parkway, Charlotte, NC 28217
http://www.artinstitutes.edu/charlotte/

CONTACT Brad Janis, President
Telephone: 704-357-8020

GENERAL INFORMATION Private Institution. Founded 1973. **Accreditation:** State accredited or approved. **Total program enrollment:** 776. **Application fee:** $50.

PROGRAM(S) OFFERED
• Culinary Arts/Chef Training *6 students enrolled* • Graphic Design *11 students enrolled* • Interior Design *16 students enrolled* • Web Page, Digital/Multimedia and Information Resources Design *4 students enrolled*

STUDENT SERVICES Academic or career counseling, employment services for current students, placement services for program completers, remedial services.

Asheboro Beauty School of Randolph

736 S. Fayetteville Street, Asheboro, NC 27203

CONTACT Barbara Alston, President
Telephone: 336-629-9639

GENERAL INFORMATION Private Institution. **Total program enrollment:** 25. **Application fee:** $25.

PROGRAM(S) OFFERED
• Cosmetology, Barber/Styling, and Nail Instructor *800 hrs./$1800* • Cosmetology/Cosmetologist, General *1500 hrs./$7475* • Nail Technician/ Specialist and Manicurist *300 hrs./$1400*

STUDENT SERVICES Academic or career counseling, placement services for program completers.

Asheville-Buncombe Technical Community College

340 Victoria Road, Asheville, NC 28801-4897
http://www.abtech.edu/

CONTACT Dr. Betty Young, President
Telephone: 828-254-1921

GENERAL INFORMATION Public Institution. Founded 1959. **Accreditation:** Regional (SACS/CC); dental assisting (ADA); dental hygiene (ADA);

medical laboratory technology (NAACLS); radiologic technology: radiography (JRCERT). **Total program enrollment:** 2390.

PROGRAM(S) OFFERED

• **Accounting** 2 *students enrolled* • **Automobile/Automotive Mechanics Technology/Technician** 6 *students enrolled* • **Baking and Pastry Arts/Baker/ Pastry Chef** • **Business Administration and Management, General** 1 *student enrolled* • **CAD/CADD Drafting and/or Design Technology/Technician** 10 *students enrolled* • **Carpentry/Carpenter** 2 *students enrolled* • **Child Development** 2 *students enrolled* • **Computer Engineering Technology/Technician** 2 *students enrolled* • **Computer Systems Networking and Telecommunications** 1 *student enrolled* • **Criminal Justice/Police Science** 47 *students enrolled* • **Dental Assisting/Assistant** 21 *students enrolled* • **Diesel Mechanics Technology/ Technician** 4 *students enrolled* • **Early Childhood Education and Teaching** 5 *students enrolled* • **Electrician** 6 *students enrolled* • **Fire Protection and Safety Technology/Technician** 2 *students enrolled* • **Foodservice Systems Administration/Management** 25 *students enrolled* • **Heating, Air Conditioning, Ventilation and Refrigeration Maintenance Technology/Technician (HAC, HACR, HVAC, HVACR)** 5 *students enrolled* • **Information Science/Studies** 2 *students enrolled* • **Information Technology** 7 *students enrolled* • **Licensed Practical/Vocational Nurse Training (LPN, LVN, Cert, Dipl, AAS)** 36 *students enrolled* • **Machine Shop Technology/Assistant** • **Marketing/Marketing Management, General** • **Medical Office Management/Administration** 6 *students enrolled* • **Medical Transcription/Transcriptionist** 9 *students enrolled* • **Office Management and Supervision** • **Phlebotomy/Phlebotomist** 21 *students enrolled* • **Real Estate** • **Surgical Technology/Technologist** 10 *students enrolled* • **Survey Technology/Surveying** 2 *students enrolled* • **Welding Technology/Welder** 12 *students enrolled*

STUDENT SERVICES Academic or career counseling, daycare for children of students, employment services for current students, placement services for program completers, remedial services.

Beaufort County Community College

PO Box 1069, Washington, NC 27889-1069
http://www.beaufortccc.edu/

CONTACT Dr. David McLawhorn, President
Telephone: 252-946-6194

GENERAL INFORMATION Public Institution. Founded 1967. **Accreditation:** Regional (SACS/CC); medical laboratory technology (NAACLS). **Total program enrollment:** 652.

PROGRAM(S) OFFERED

• **Accounting Technology/Technician and Bookkeeping** 1 *student enrolled* • **Accounting** • **Aesthetician/Esthetician and Skin Care Specialist** 6 *students enrolled* • **Applied Horticulture/Horticultural Operations, General** 9 *students enrolled* • **Automobile/Automotive Mechanics Technology/Technician** • **Business Administration and Management, General** • **Computer Systems Networking and Telecommunications** 3 *students enrolled* • **Cosmetology and Related Personal Grooming Arts, Other** 3 *students enrolled* • **Cosmetology/ Cosmetologist, General** 6 *students enrolled* • **Criminal Justice/Police Science** 11 *students enrolled* • **Diesel Mechanics Technology/Technician** 1 *student enrolled* • **Early Childhood Education and Teaching** 10 *students enrolled* • **Electrical, Electronic and Communications Engineering Technology/ Technician** • **Electrician** • **Executive Assistant/Executive Secretary** 5 *students enrolled* • **Language Interpretation and Translation** 2 *students enrolled* • **Licensed Practical/Vocational Nurse Training (LPN, LVN, Cert, Dipl, AAS)** 13 *students enrolled* • **Mechanical Drafting and Mechanical Drafting CAD/CADD** • **Mechanical Engineering/Mechanical Technology/Technician** 8 *students enrolled* • **Medical Office Management/Administration** 3 *students enrolled* • **Office Management and Supervision** • **System, Networking, and LAN/WAN Management/Manager** 2 *students enrolled* • **Welding Technology/Welder** 18 *students enrolled*

STUDENT SERVICES Academic or career counseling, employment services for current students, placement services for program completers, remedial services.

Bladen Community College

PO Box 266, Dublin, NC 28332-0266
http://www.bladen.cc.nc.us/

CONTACT Dr. William Findt, President
Telephone: 910-879-5500

GENERAL INFORMATION Public Institution. Founded 1967. **Accreditation:** Regional (SACS/CC). **Total program enrollment:** 527.

PROGRAM(S) OFFERED

• **Business Administration and Management, General** 13 *students enrolled* • **Carpentry/Carpenter** • **Cosmetology, Barber/Styling, and Nail Instructor** • **Cosmetology/Cosmetologist, General** 1 *student enrolled* • **Criminal Justice/ Law Enforcement Administration** • **Early Childhood Education and Teaching** 9 *students enrolled* • **Electrician** 7 *students enrolled* • **Electromechanical and Instrumentation and Maintenance Technologies/Technicians, Other** 3 *students enrolled* • **Engineering Technologies/Technicians, Other** • **Information Technology** 1 *student enrolled* • **Licensed Practical/Vocational Nurse Training (LPN, LVN, Cert, Dipl, AAS)** 9 *students enrolled* • **Nurse/Nursing Assistant/Aide and Patient Care Assistant** • **Office Management and Supervision** 7 *students enrolled* • **Welding Technology/Welder** 2 *students enrolled*

STUDENT SERVICES Academic or career counseling, employment services for current students, placement services for program completers, remedial services.

Blue Ridge Community College

180 West Campus Drive, Flat Rock, NC 28731-4728
http://www.blueridge.edu/

CONTACT Molly A. Parkhill, President
Telephone: 828-694-1700

GENERAL INFORMATION Public Institution. Founded 1969. **Accreditation:** Regional (SACS/CC). **Total program enrollment:** 592.

PROGRAM(S) OFFERED

• **Applied Horticulture/Horticultural Operations, General** • **Autobody/Collision and Repair Technology/Technician** 1 *student enrolled* • **Automobile/Automotive Mechanics Technology/Technician** • **Building/Construction Finishing, Management, and Inspection, Other** • **Building/Property Maintenance and Management** • **Business Administration and Management, General** 9 *students enrolled* • **Carpentry/Carpenter** 1 *student enrolled* • **Child Care and Support Services Management** • **Computer Programming, Specific Applications** • **Computer Programming/Programmer, General** • **Computer and Information Sciences and Support Services, Other** • **Cosmetology, Barber/Styling, and Nail Instructor** • **Cosmetology/Cosmetologist, General** 24 *students enrolled* • **Early Childhood Education and Teaching** • **Electrical, Electronic and Communications Engineering Technology/Technician** 1 *student enrolled* • **Electrician** • **Electromechanical Technology/Electromechanical Engineering Technology** • **Environmental Science** • **Executive Assistant/Executive Secretary** 6 *students enrolled* • **Health Unit Coordinator/Ward Clerk** • **Heating, Air Conditioning, Ventilation and Refrigeration Maintenance Technology/ Technician (HAC, HACR, HVAC, HVACR)** 2 *students enrolled* • **Heavy/Industrial Equipment Maintenance Technologies, Other** • **Information Science/Studies** • **Information Technology** • **Machine Shop Technology/Assistant** • **Make-Up Artist/Specialist** • **Mechanic and Repair Technologies/Technicians, Other** • **Mechanical Engineering Related Technologies/Technicians, Other** • **Mechanical Engineering/Mechanical Technology/Technician** • **Nail Technician/Specialist and Manicurist** • **Plumbing Technology/Plumber** 4 *students enrolled* • **Plumbing and Related Water Supply Services, Other** • **Real Estate** • **Sign Language Interpretation and Translation** • **Special Education and Teaching, General** 1 *student enrolled* • **Surgical Technology/Technologist** • **System, Networking, and LAN/WAN Management/Manager** • **Tourism Promotion Operations** • **Tourism and Travel Services Marketing Operations** • **Water Quality and Wastewater Treatment Management and Recycling Technology/Technician** 1 *student enrolled* • **Welding Technology/Welder** 2 *students enrolled*

STUDENT SERVICES Academic or career counseling, daycare for children of students, employment services for current students, placement services for program completers, remedial services.

Brookstone College of Business

8307 University Executive Park, Charlotte, NC 28262
http://www.brookstone.edu/

CONTACT Kevin Williams, Director
Telephone: 704-547-8600

GENERAL INFORMATION Private Institution. Founded 1939. **Total program enrollment:** 146. **Application fee:** $25.

PROGRAM(S) OFFERED
• Accounting Technology/Technician and Bookkeeping *42 hrs./$8400*
• Administrative Assistant and Secretarial Science, General *56 hrs./$10,800*
• Computer Technology/Computer Systems Technology • Medical Administrative/Executive Assistant and Medical Secretary *62 hrs./$12,000*
• Medical/Clinical Assistant *78 hrs./$17,812* • Pharmacy Technician/Assistant *62 hrs./$11,700*

STUDENT SERVICES Academic or career counseling, employment services for current students, placement services for program completers.

Brookstone College of Business

7815 National Service Road, Greensboro, NC 27409
http://www.brookstone.edu/

CONTACT F. Jack Henderson, III, President
Telephone: 336-668-2627

GENERAL INFORMATION Private Institution. **Total program enrollment:** 84. **Application fee:** $25.

PROGRAM(S) OFFERED
• Accounting Technology/Technician and Bookkeeping *54 hrs./$10,800* • Accounting and Related Services, Other *6 students enrolled* • Accounting
• Administrative Assistant and Secretarial Science, General *42 hrs./$8400*
• Allied Health and Medical Assisting Services, Other *20 students enrolled*
• Computer Installation and Repair Technology/Technician *2 students enrolled*
• Executive Assistant/Executive Secretary *4 students enrolled* • Medical Administrative/Executive Assistant and Medical Secretary *62 hrs./$12,000*
• Medical/Clinical Assistant *78 hrs./$17,812* • Pharmacy Technician/Assistant *62 hrs./$11,700*

STUDENT SERVICES Academic or career counseling, employment services for current students, placement services for program completers.

Brunswick Community College

50 College Road, PO Box 30, Supply, NC 28462-0030
http://www.brunswickcc.edu/

CONTACT Stephen G. Greiner, President
Telephone: 910-755-7300

GENERAL INFORMATION Public Institution. Founded 1979. **Accreditation:** Regional (SACS/CC); health information technology (AHIMA). **Total program enrollment:** 642.

PROGRAM(S) OFFERED
• Aesthetician/Esthetician and Skin Care Specialist *2 students enrolled* • Applied Horticulture/Horticultural Operations, General • Aquaculture *1 student enrolled* • Business Administration and Management, General *13 students enrolled* • Child Care and Support Services Management *32 students enrolled*
• Child Development *11 students enrolled* • Clinical/Medical Laboratory Science and Allied Professions, Other *11 students enrolled* • Computer Systems Networking and Telecommunications • Cosmetology and Related Personal Grooming Arts, Other • Cosmetology/Cosmetologist, General *10 students enrolled* • Criminal Justice/Police Science *13 students enrolled* • Executive Assistant/Executive Secretary *2 students enrolled* • Health Information/Medical Records Technology/Technician *3 students enrolled* • Licensed Practical/Vocational Nurse Training (LPN, LVN, Cert, Dipl, AAS) *17 students enrolled*
• Management Information Systems and Services, Other • Nail Technician/Specialist and Manicurist • Nurse/Nursing Assistant/Aide and Patient Care Assistant • Special Education and Teaching, General *6 students enrolled*
• Teacher Assistant/Aide *6 students enrolled* • Turf and Turfgrass Management *6 students enrolled* • Welding Technology/Welder *5 students enrolled*

STUDENT SERVICES Academic or career counseling, employment services for current students, placement services for program completers, remedial services.

Cabarrus College of Health Sciences

401 Medical Park Drive, Concord, NC 28025
http://www.cabarruscollege.edu/

CONTACT Dianne O. Snyder, Chancellor
Telephone: 704-403-1555

GENERAL INFORMATION Private Institution. Founded 1942. **Accreditation:** Regional (SACS/CC); surgical technology (ARCST). **Total program enrollment:** 226. **Application fee:** $35.

PROGRAM(S) OFFERED
• Health and Medical Administrative Services, Other *4 students enrolled*
• Health/Medical Physics *17 students enrolled* • Medical/Clinical Assistant *11 students enrolled* • Nurse/Nursing Assistant/Aide and Patient Care Assistant *244 students enrolled* • Phlebotomy/Phlebotomist *39 students enrolled* • Surgical Technology/Technologist *5 students enrolled*

STUDENT SERVICES Academic or career counseling, daycare for children of students, employment services for current students, placement services for program completers.

Caldwell Community College and Technical Institute

2855 Hickory Boulevard, Hudson, NC 28638-2397
http://www.cccti.edu/

CONTACT Kenneth A. Boham, President
Telephone: 828-726-2200

GENERAL INFORMATION Public Institution. Founded 1964. **Accreditation:** Regional (SACS/CC); diagnostic medical sonography (JRCEDMS); nuclear medicine technology (JRCNMT); radiologic technology: radiography (JRCERT). **Total program enrollment:** 1392.

PROGRAM(S) OFFERED
• Accounting *1 student enrolled* • Airline/Commercial/Professional Pilot and Flight Crew *2 students enrolled* • Allied Health Diagnostic, Intervention, and Treatment Professions, Other *1 student enrolled* • Autobody/Collision and Repair Technology/Technician *13 students enrolled* • Automobile/Automotive Mechanics Technology/Technician *8 students enrolled* • Business Administration and Management, General *12 students enrolled* • Child Care and Support Services Management *19 students enrolled* • Computer Programming, Specific Applications *15 students enrolled* • Computer Systems Networking and Telecommunications *2 students enrolled* • Cosmetology/Cosmetologist, General *4 students enrolled* • Criminal Justice/Police Science *19 students enrolled*
• Electrical, Electronic and Communications Engineering Technology/Technician • Electrician *5 students enrolled* • Executive Assistant/Executive Secretary *23 students enrolled* • Fire Protection, Other *5 students enrolled* • Information Science/Studies *1 student enrolled* • Information Technology *15 students enrolled* • Landscaping and Groundskeeping • Legal Assistant/Paralegal *29 students enrolled* • Machine Shop Technology/Assistant
• Mechanical Engineering/Mechanical Technology/Technician *22 students enrolled* • Medical Office Management/Administration *11 students enrolled*
• Nurse/Nursing Assistant/Aide and Patient Care Assistant *1 student enrolled*
• Ophthalmic Technician/Technologist *10 students enrolled* • Truck and Bus Driver/Commercial Vehicle Operation *52 students enrolled*

STUDENT SERVICES Academic or career counseling, employment services for current students, placement services for program completers, remedial services.

Cape Fear Community College

411 North Front Street, Wilmington, NC 28401-3993
http://www.cfcc.edu/

CONTACT Eric B. McKeithan, President
Telephone: 910-362-7000

GENERAL INFORMATION Public Institution. Founded 1959. **Accreditation:** Regional (SACS/CC); dental assisting (ADA); dental hygiene (ADA). **Total program enrollment:** 3693.

PROGRAM(S) OFFERED
• **Accounting Technology/Technician and Bookkeeping** 3 *students enrolled* • **Aesthetician/Esthetician and Skin Care Specialist** 16 *students enrolled* • **Autobody/Collision and Repair Technology/Technician** 3 *students enrolled* • **Automobile/Automotive Mechanics Technology/Technician** • **Business Administration and Management, General** 10 *students enrolled* • **Carpentry/Carpenter** 26 *students enrolled* • **Cinematography and Film/Video Production** 3 *students enrolled* • **Clinical/Medical Laboratory Science and Allied Professions, Other** 23 *students enrolled* • **Computer Engineering Technology/Technician** 8 *students enrolled* • **Cosmetology and Related Personal Grooming Arts, Other** 1 *student enrolled* • **Cosmetology, Barber/Styling, and Nail Instructor** • **Cosmetology/Cosmetologist, General** 43 *students enrolled* • **Criminal Justice/Police Science** 86 *students enrolled* • **Culinary Arts/Chef Training** • **Dental Assisting/Assistant** 12 *students enrolled* • **Diesel Mechanics Technology/Technician** 27 *students enrolled* • **Early Childhood Education and Teaching** 1 *student enrolled* • **Electrical, Electronic and Communications Engineering Technology/Technician** 3 *students enrolled* • **Electrician** 16 *students enrolled* • **Electromechanical and Instrumentation and Maintenance Technologies/Technicians, Other** 1 *student enrolled* • **Executive Assistant/Executive Secretary** • **Facial Treatment Specialist/Facialist** • **Heating, Air Conditioning, Ventilation and Refrigeration Maintenance Technology/Technician (HAC, HACR, HVAC, HVACR)** 5 *students enrolled* • **Hotel/Motel Administration/Management** 3 *students enrolled* • **Information Technology** • **Instrumentation Technology/Technician** 1 *student enrolled* • **Landscaping and Groundskeeping** 17 *students enrolled* • **Language Interpretation and Translation** 2 *students enrolled* • **Legal Assistant/Paralegal** 1 *student enrolled* • **Licensed Practical/Vocational Nurse Training (LPN, LVN, Cert, Dipl, AAS)** 14 *students enrolled* • **Machine Shop Technology/Assistant** • **Marine Maintenance/Fitter and Ship Repair Technology/Technician** • **Mechanical Engineering/Mechanical Technology/Technician** 19 *students enrolled* • **Medical Transcription/Transcriptionist** 8 *students enrolled* • **Pharmacy Technician/Assistant** 1 *student enrolled* • **Truck and Bus Driver/Commercial Vehicle Operation** 80 *students enrolled* • **Welding Technology/Welder** 4 *students enrolled*

STUDENT SERVICES Academic or career counseling, employment services for current students, placement services for program completers, remedial services.

Carolina Academy of Cosmetic Art & Science
284 E. Garrison Boulevard, Gastonia, NC 28054
http://www.carolinaacademy.com/
CONTACT Steve Pollak, Owner
Telephone: 704-864-8723
GENERAL INFORMATION Private Institution. **Total program enrollment:** 83. **Application fee:** $100.
PROGRAM(S) OFFERED
• **Aesthetician/Esthetician and Skin Care Specialist** 600 *hrs./$6750* • **Cosmetology, Barber/Styling, and Nail Instructor** 800 *hrs./$8000* • **Cosmetology/Cosmetologist, General** 1500 *hrs./$16,900* • **Nail Technician/Specialist and Manicurist**

Carolina Beauty College
1201 Stafford Street, Suite B2, Monroe, NC 28110
CONTACT Debra Perry, Director
Telephone: 704-226-8830
GENERAL INFORMATION Private Institution. **Total program enrollment:** 15.
PROGRAM(S) OFFERED
• **Cosmetology/Cosmetologist, General** 1500 *hrs./$15,075*
STUDENT SERVICES Placement services for program completers.

Carolina Beauty College–Charlotte
North Park Mall, 5430-O North Tryon Street, Charlotte, NC 28213
http://carolinabeautycollege.com/
CONTACT M. Scott Fields, President
Telephone: 704-597-5503
GENERAL INFORMATION Private Institution. Founded 1950. **Total program enrollment:** 69.
PROGRAM(S) OFFERED
• **Cosmetology/Cosmetologist, General** 1500 *hrs./$14,325*
STUDENT SERVICES Academic or career counseling, placement services for program completers.

Carolina Beauty College–Durham Campus
5106 North Roxboro Road, Durham, NC 27704
http://carolinabeautycollege.com/
CONTACT M. Scott Fields, President
Telephone: 919-477-4014
GENERAL INFORMATION Private Institution. **Total program enrollment:** 54.
PROGRAM(S) OFFERED
• **Cosmetology and Related Personal Grooming Arts, Other** • **Cosmetology/Cosmetologist, General** 1500 *hrs./$14,325*
STUDENT SERVICES Academic or career counseling, placement services for program completers.

Carolina Beauty College–Greensboro Campus
2001 East Wendover Avenue, Greensboro, NC 27405
http://carolinabeautycollege.com/
CONTACT M. Scott Fields, President
Telephone: 336-272-2966
GENERAL INFORMATION Private Institution. Founded 1969. **Total program enrollment:** 69.
PROGRAM(S) OFFERED
• **Cosmetology/Cosmetologist, General** 1500 *hrs./$14,325*
STUDENT SERVICES Academic or career counseling, placement services for program completers.

Carolina Beauty College–Winston-Salem Campus
7736 North Pointe Boulevard, Winston-Salem, NC 27106
http://carolinabeautycollege.com/
CONTACT M. Scott Fields, President
Telephone: 336-759-7969
GENERAL INFORMATION Private Institution. Founded 1960. **Total program enrollment:** 65.
PROGRAM(S) OFFERED
• **Cosmetology/Cosmetologist, General** 1500 *hrs./$14,325*
STUDENT SERVICES Academic or career counseling, placement services for program completers.

Carolina School of Broadcasting
7003 Wallace Road, Suite 100, Charlotte, NC 28212
http://www.csb-radio-tv.com
CONTACT Alyson M. Young, Director
Telephone: 704-395-9272
GENERAL INFORMATION Private Institution. Founded 1957. **Total program enrollment:** 52. **Application fee:** $150.
PROGRAM(S) OFFERED
• **Radio, Television, and Digital Communication, Other** 777 *hrs./$14,650*
STUDENT SERVICES Placement services for program completers.

Carolinas College of Health Sciences

PO Box 32861, 1200 Blythe Boulevard, Charlotte, NC 28232-2861
http://www.carolinascollege.edu/

CONTACT V. Ellen Sheppard, President
Telephone: 704-355-5043

GENERAL INFORMATION Private Institution. Founded 1990. **Accreditation:** Regional (SACS/CC); medical technology (NAACLS). **Total program enrollment:** 134. **Application fee:** $50.

PROGRAM(S) OFFERED
• **Clinical Laboratory Science/Medical Technology/Technologist** *1643 hrs./$5940* • **Emergency Medical Technology/Technician (EMT Paramedic)** *14 students enrolled* • **Nurse/Nursing Assistant/Aide and Patient Care Assistant** *127 hrs./$510* • **Nursing—Registered Nurse Training (RN, ASN, BSN, MSN)** *1799 hrs./$12,799* • **Pre-Nursing Studies** *25 hrs./$5556* • **Radiologic Technology/Science—Radiographer** *24 hrs./$7935* • **Surgical Technology/Technologist** *40 hrs./$8920*

STUDENT SERVICES Academic or career counseling, placement services for program completers.

Carteret Community College

3505 Arendell Street, Morehead City, NC 28557-2989
http://www.carteret.edu/

CONTACT Kerry Youngblood, President
Telephone: 252-222-6000

GENERAL INFORMATION Public Institution. Founded 1963. **Accreditation:** Regional (SACS/CC); radiologic technology: radiography (JRCERT). **Total program enrollment:** 654.

PROGRAM(S) OFFERED
• **Aesthetician/Esthetician and Skin Care Specialist** *6 students enrolled* • **Applied Horticulture/Horticultural Operations, General** *6 students enrolled* • **Aquaculture** • **Cosmetology, Barber/Styling, and Nail Instructor** • **Cosmetology/Cosmetologist, General** *9 students enrolled* • **Criminal Justice/Police Science** *21 students enrolled* • **Criminal Justice/Safety Studies** *2 students enrolled* • **Culinary Arts/Chef Training** *6 students enrolled* • **Diagnostic Medical Sonography/Sonographer and Ultrasound Technician** *3 students enrolled* • **Diesel Mechanics Technology/Technician** *6 students enrolled* • **Early Childhood Education and Teaching** *2 students enrolled* • **Elementary Education and Teaching** • **Hotel/Motel Administration/Management** *3 students enrolled* • **Information Technology** • **Licensed Practical/Vocational Nurse Training (LPN, LVN, Cert, Dipl, AAS)** *9 students enrolled* • **Massage Therapy/Therapeutic Massage** *11 students enrolled* • **Medical/Clinical Assistant** *8 students enrolled* • **Nail Technician/Specialist and Manicurist** • **Office Management and Supervision** *1 student enrolled* • **Photographic and Film/Video Technology/Technician and Assistant** *13 students enrolled*

STUDENT SERVICES Academic or career counseling, employment services for current students, placement services for program completers, remedial services.

Catawba Valley Community College

2550 Highway 70 SE, Hickory, NC 28602-9699
http://www.cvcc.cc.nc.us/

CONTACT Dr. Garrett Hinshaw, President
Telephone: 828-327-7000

GENERAL INFORMATION Public Institution. Founded 1960. **Accreditation:** Regional (SACS/CC); dental hygiene (ADA); emergency medical services (JRCEMTP); health information technology (AHIMA). **Total program enrollment:** 1711.

PROGRAM(S) OFFERED
• **Accounting Technology/Technician and Bookkeeping** *1 student enrolled* • **Applied Horticulture/Horticultural Operations, General** *2 students enrolled* • **Automobile/Automotive Mechanics Technology/Technician** *1 student enrolled* • **Banking and Financial Support Services** • **Business Administration and Management, General** *5 students enrolled* • **Cosmetology/Cosmetologist, General** *1 student enrolled* • **Criminal Justice/Police Science** *20 students enrolled* • **Criminal Justice/Safety Studies** *1 student enrolled* • **Customer**

Service Support/Call Center/Teleservice Operation *2 students enrolled* • **E-Commerce/Electronic Commerce** *2 students enrolled* • **Early Childhood Education and Teaching** *4 students enrolled* • **Electrician** *5 students enrolled* • **Furniture Design and Manufacturing** *30 students enrolled* • **Health Information/Medical Records Technology/Technician** *1 student enrolled* • **Health Services/Allied Health/Health Sciences, General** • **Heating, Air Conditioning, Ventilation and Refrigeration Maintenance Technology/Technician (HAC, HACR, HVAC, HVACR)** *18 students enrolled* • **Information Science/Studies** *1 student enrolled* • **Machine Shop Technology/Assistant** • **Medical Office Management/Administration** *11 students enrolled* • **Medical Transcription/Transcriptionist** *12 students enrolled* • **Office Management and Supervision** *2 students enrolled* • **Surgical Technology/Technologist** *10 students enrolled* • **Truck and Bus Driver/Commercial Vehicle Operation** *76 students enrolled* • **Upholstery/Upholsterer** *26 students enrolled* • **Welding Technology/Welder** *1 student enrolled*

STUDENT SERVICES Academic or career counseling, daycare for children of students, employment services for current students, placement services for program completers, remedial services.

Center for Employment Training–Research Triangle Park

4022 Stirrup Creek Drive, Suite 325, Research Triangle Park, NC 27703-9000
http://www.cet2000.org/

CONTACT Tyrone Everett, Director/Regional Director
Telephone: 408-287-7924

GENERAL INFORMATION Private Institution. Founded 1995. **Total program enrollment:** 110.

PROGRAM(S) OFFERED
• **Administrative Assistant and Secretarial Science, General** *1 student enrolled* • **Building/Property Maintenance and Management** *630 hrs./$7083* • **Business/Office Automation/Technology/Data Entry** *900 hrs./$8864* • **Health and Medical Administrative Services, Other** *330 hrs./$5106* • **Medical Administrative/Executive Assistant and Medical Secretary** *720 hrs./$7676* • **Medical Insurance Coding Specialist/Coder** *24 students enrolled* • **Medical Insurance Specialist/Medical Biller** *630 hrs./$7083* • **Medical Office Assistant/Specialist** *12 students enrolled*

STUDENT SERVICES Academic or career counseling, employment services for current students, placement services for program completers, remedial services.

Central Carolina Community College

1105 Kelly Drive, Sanford, NC 27330-9000
http://www.cccc.edu/

CONTACT Dr. T. Eston Marchant, President
Telephone: 919-775-5401

GENERAL INFORMATION Public Institution. Founded 1962. **Accreditation:** Regional (SACS/CC). **Total program enrollment:** 1515.

PROGRAM(S) OFFERED
• **Accounting** *14 students enrolled* • **Aesthetician/Esthetician and Skin Care Specialist** *36 students enrolled* • **Agricultural Business and Management, General** • **Autobody/Collision and Repair Technology/Technician** • **Automobile/Automotive Mechanics Technology/Technician** *34 students enrolled* • **Barbering/Barber** *9 students enrolled* • **Business Administration and Management, General** • **Carpentry/Carpenter** *7 students enrolled* • **Child Development** *38 students enrolled* • **Computer Programming/Programmer, General** *1 student enrolled* • **Computer Systems Networking and Telecommunications** *23 students enrolled* • **Cosmetology, Barber/Styling, and Nail Instructor** *6 students enrolled* • **Cosmetology/Cosmetologist, General** *32 students enrolled* • **Criminal Justice/Police Science** *34 students enrolled* • **Dental Assisting/Assistant** *9 students enrolled* • **Early Childhood Education and Teaching** *33 students enrolled* • **Electrical, Electronic and Communications Engineering Technology/Technician** *8 students enrolled* • **Electrical/Electronics Maintenance and Repair Technology, Other** *26 students enrolled* • **Electrician** *14 students enrolled* • **Electromechanical and Instrumentation and Maintenance Technologies/Technicians, Other** *7 students enrolled* • **Foodservice Systems Administration/Management** *49 students enrolled* • **Human Resources Management/Personnel Administration, General** *3 students enrolled*

• **Information Technology** 25 students enrolled • **Journalism** 5 students enrolled • **Legal Assistant/Paralegal** 1 student enrolled • **Library Assistant/Technician** 30 students enrolled • **Licensed Practical/Vocational Nurse Training (LPN, LVN, Cert, Dipl, AAS)** 39 students enrolled • **Machine Shop Technology/Assistant** 5 students enrolled • **Manufacturing Technology/Technician** 6 students enrolled • **Marketing/Marketing Management, General** 1 student enrolled • **Mason/Masonry** 14 students enrolled • **Mechanical Engineering/Mechanical Technology/Technician** 16 students enrolled • **Medical Office Management/Administration** 5 students enrolled • **Medical/Clinical Assistant** 8 students enrolled • **Motorcycle Maintenance and Repair Technology/Technician** 8 students enrolled • **Office Management and Supervision** 54 students enrolled • **Operations Management and Supervision** 5 students enrolled • **Radio and Television Broadcasting Technology/Technician** 5 students enrolled • **Sculpture** 3 students enrolled • **Small Engine Mechanics and Repair Technology/Technician** 30 students enrolled • **Welding Technology/Welder** 13 students enrolled

STUDENT SERVICES Academic or career counseling, employment services for current students, remedial services.

Central Piedmont Community College

PO Box 35009, Charlotte, NC 28235-5009
http://www.cpcc.edu/

CONTACT Anthony Zeiss, President
Telephone: 704-330-2722

GENERAL INFORMATION Public Institution. Founded 1963. **Accreditation:** Regional (SACS/CC); dental assisting (ADA); dental hygiene (ADA); engineering technology (ABET/TAC); health information technology (AHIMA); medical assisting (AAMAE); medical laboratory technology (NAACLS); physical therapy assisting (APTA). **Total program enrollment:** 6987.

PROGRAM(S) OFFERED
• **Accounting Technology/Technician and Bookkeeping** • **Accounting** 1 student enrolled • **Administrative Assistant and Secretarial Science, General** • **Applied Horticulture/Horticultural Operations, General** 2 students enrolled • **Architectural Engineering Technology/Technician** 11 students enrolled • **Autobody/Collision and Repair Technology/Technician** 20 students enrolled • **Automobile/Automotive Mechanics Technology/Technician** • **Building/Property Maintenance and Management** 15 students enrolled • **Business Administration and Management, General** 27 students enrolled • **Business/Office Automation/Technology/Data Entry** • **Child Development** 27 students enrolled • **Civil Engineering Technology/Technician** 2 students enrolled • **Civil Engineering, Other** • **Commercial and Advertising Art** 2 students enrolled • **Computer Engineering Technologies/Technicians, Other** • **Computer Engineering Technology/Technician** 2 students enrolled • **Computer Programming/Programmer, General** 3 students enrolled • **Computer Systems Networking and Telecommunications** 8 students enrolled • **Computer and Information Sciences, General** • **Criminal Justice/Police Science** • **Culinary Arts/Chef Training** 7 students enrolled • **Cytotechnology/Cytotechnologist** • **Data Modeling/Warehousing and Database Administration** 4 students enrolled • **Data Processing and Data Processing Technology/Technician** 32 students enrolled • **Dental Assisting/Assistant** • **Diesel Mechanics Technology/Technician** 2 students enrolled • **Early Childhood Education and Teaching** 44 students enrolled • **Electrical, Electronic and Communications Engineering Technology/Technician** 2 students enrolled • **Electrical, Electronics and Communications Engineering** • **Electrician** 31 students enrolled • **Engineering/Industrial Management** • **Executive Assistant/Executive Secretary** • **Graphic Communications, General** 1 student enrolled • **Graphic Design** 5 students enrolled • **Graphic and Printing Equipment Operator, General Production** • **Health Information/Medical Records Technology/Technician** • **Health Professions and Related Clinical Sciences, Other** 39 students enrolled • **Heating, Air Conditioning, Ventilation and Refrigeration Maintenance Technology/Technician (HAC, HACR, HVAC, HVACR)** 61 students enrolled • **Hospitality Administration/Management, General** • **Hotel/Motel Administration/Management** 4 students enrolled • **Human Resources Management/Personnel Administration, General** 5 students enrolled • **Information Science/Studies** 2 students enrolled • **Information Technology** • **Interior Design** 2 students enrolled • **International Business/Trade/Commerce** 1 student enrolled • **Legal Administrative Assistant/Secretary** • **Legal Assistant/Paralegal** 18 students enrolled • **Machine Shop Technology/Assistant** 2 students enrolled • **Marketing/Marketing Management, General** 4 students enrolled • **Mechanical Drafting and Mechanical Drafting CAD/CADD** • **Medical/Clinical Assistant** 2 students enrolled • **Office Management and Supervision** 3 students enrolled • **Parks, Recreation and Leisure Facilities Management** • **Psychiatric/Mental Health Services Technician** • **Rehabilitation and Therapeutic Professions, Other** • **Retailing and Retail Operations** • **Sign Language Interpretation and Translation** 2 students enrolled • **Social Work** • **Substance Abuse/Addiction Counseling** 18 students enrolled • **Survey**

Technology/Surveying • **System, Networking, and LAN/WAN Management/Manager** • **Teacher Assistant/Aide** • **Tourism and Travel Services Management** • **Turf and Turfgrass Management** • **Vehicle Maintenance and Repair Technologies, Other** • **Web/Multimedia Management and Webmaster** • **Welding Technology/Welder** 7 students enrolled

STUDENT SERVICES Academic or career counseling, employment services for current students, placement services for program completers, remedial services.

Cleveland Community College

137 South Post Road, Shelby, NC 28152
http://www.clevelandcommunitycollege.edu/

CONTACT L. Steve Thornburg, President
Telephone: 704-484-4000

GENERAL INFORMATION Public Institution. Founded 1965. **Accreditation:** Regional (SACS/CC); radiologic technology: radiography (JRCERT). **Total program enrollment:** 1117.

PROGRAM(S) OFFERED
• **Aesthetician/Esthetician and Skin Care Specialist** 3 students enrolled • **Autobody/Collision and Repair Technology/Technician** 6 students enrolled • **Building/Property Maintenance and Management** 2 students enrolled • **Business Administration and Management, General** 3 students enrolled • **Carpentry/Carpenter** • **Child Care Provider/Assistant** • **Child Development** • **Clinical/Medical Laboratory Science and Allied Professions, Other** • **Computer Systems Networking and Telecommunications** • **Cosmetology and Related Personal Grooming Arts, Other** • **Cosmetology, Barber/Styling, and Nail Instructor** • **Cosmetology/Cosmetologist, General** 14 students enrolled • **Criminal Justice/Police Science** 26 students enrolled • **Early Childhood Education and Teaching** 52 students enrolled • **Electrical, Electronic and Communications Engineering Technology/Technician** 6 students enrolled • **Electrician** 5 students enrolled • **Electromechanical Technology/Electromechanical Engineering Technology** • **Electromechanical and Instrumentation and Maintenance Technologies/Technicians, Other** 2 students enrolled • **Executive Assistant/Executive Secretary** • **Heating, Air Conditioning, Ventilation and Refrigeration Maintenance Technology/Technician (HAC, HACR, HVAC, HVACR)** 2 students enrolled • **Information Technology** 17 students enrolled • **Licensed Practical/Vocational Nurse Training (LPN, LVN, Cert, Dipl, AAS)** 6 students enrolled • **Machine Shop Technology/Assistant** 1 student enrolled • **Marketing/Marketing Management, General** 1 student enrolled • **Mechanical Drafting and Mechanical Drafting CAD/CADD** 10 students enrolled • **Mechanical Engineering/Mechanical Technology/Technician** • **Medical Administrative/Executive Assistant and Medical Secretary** • **Medical Office Management/Administration** 24 students enrolled • **Medical Transcription/Transcriptionist** 5 students enrolled • **Nail Technician/Specialist and Manicurist** • **Office Management and Supervision** 15 students enrolled • **Operations Management and Supervision** • **Phlebotomy/Phlebotomist** 10 students enrolled • **Plumbing Technology/Plumber** 2 students enrolled • **Radio and Television Broadcasting Technology/Technician** • **Retailing and Retail Operations** • **Surgical Technology/Technologist** 5 students enrolled • **Teacher Assistant/Aide** • **Welding Technology/Welder** 19 students enrolled

STUDENT SERVICES Academic or career counseling, employment services for current students, remedial services.

Coastal Carolina Community College

444 Western Boulevard, Jacksonville, NC 28546-6899
http://www.coastalcarolina.edu/

CONTACT Ronald K. Lingle, President
Telephone: 910-455-1221

GENERAL INFORMATION Public Institution. Founded 1964. **Accreditation:** Regional (SACS/CC); dental assisting (ADA); dental hygiene (ADA); medical laboratory technology (NAACLS); surgical technology (ARCST). **Total program enrollment:** 1542.

PROGRAM(S) OFFERED
• **Accounting** 2 students enrolled • **Architectural Engineering Technology/Technician** 21 students enrolled • **Autobody/Collision and Repair Technology/Technician** 16 students enrolled • **Automobile/Automotive Mechanics Technology/Technician** 34 students enrolled • **Business Administration and Management, General** 1 student enrolled • **Child Development** 11 students enrolled • **Cosmetology, Barber/Styling, and Nail Instructor** • **Cosmetology/**

Coastal Carolina Community College (continued)

Cosmetologist, General 29 *students enrolled* • **Criminal Justice/Police Science** 34 *students enrolled* • **Dental Assisting/Assistant** 21 *students enrolled* • **Diesel Mechanics Technology/Technician** 5 *students enrolled* • **Early Childhood Education and Teaching** 13 *students enrolled* • **Electrical/Electronics Maintenance and Repair Technology, Other** 8 *students enrolled* • **Electrician** 16 *students enrolled* • **Fire Protection and Safety Technology/Technician** 47 *students enrolled* • **Heating, Air Conditioning, Ventilation and Refrigeration Maintenance Technology/Technician (HAC, HACR, HVAC, HVACR)** 19 *students enrolled* • **Information Technology** • **Licensed Practical/Vocational Nurse Training (LPN, LVN, Cert, Dipl, AAS)** 14 *students enrolled* • **Medical Office Management/Administration** 5 *students enrolled* • **Nail Technician/Specialist and Manicurist** 6 *students enrolled* • **Nurse/Nursing Assistant/Aide and Patient Care Assistant** 27 *students enrolled* • **Surgical Technology/Technologist** 8 *students enrolled* • **System, Networking, and LAN/WAN Management/Manager** • **Welding Technology/Welder** 27 *students enrolled*

STUDENT SERVICES Academic or career counseling, employment services for current students, placement services for program completers, remedial services.

College of The Albemarle

PO Box 2327, Elizabeth City, NC 27906-2327
http://www.albemarle.edu/

CONTACT Lynne M. Bunch, President
Telephone: 252-335-0821

GENERAL INFORMATION Public Institution. Founded 1960. **Accreditation:** Regional (SACS/CC). **Total program enrollment:** 848.

PROGRAM(S) OFFERED
• **Architectural Engineering Technology/Technician** 2 *students enrolled* • **Building/Construction Finishing, Management, and Inspection, Other** 7 *students enrolled* • **Computer Engineering Technology/Technician** 4 *students enrolled* • **Computer Technology/Computer Systems Technology** 4 *students enrolled* • **Cosmetology/Cosmetologist, General** 21 *students enrolled* • **Crafts/Craft Design, Folk Art and Artisanry** 1 *student enrolled* • **Criminal Justice/Police Science** 24 *students enrolled* • **Culinary Arts/Chef Training** 11 *students enrolled* • **Early Childhood Education and Teaching** 23 *students enrolled* • **Electrician** 14 *students enrolled* • **Foodservice Systems Administration/Management** 32 *students enrolled* • **Heating, Air Conditioning, Ventilation and Refrigeration Maintenance Technology/Technician (HAC, HACR, HVAC, HVACR)** 19 *students enrolled* • **Information Science/Studies** 2 *students enrolled* • **Information Technology** 2 *students enrolled* • **Licensed Practical/Vocational Nurse Training (LPN, LVN, Cert, Dipl, AAS)** 17 *students enrolled* • **Machine Shop Technology/Assistant** 6 *students enrolled* • **Medical Office Management/Administration** 4 *students enrolled* • **Medical/Clinical Assistant** 9 *students enrolled* • **Nail Technician/Specialist and Manicurist** 3 *students enrolled* • **Office Management and Supervision** 7 *students enrolled* • **Phlebotomy/Phlebotomist** 11 *students enrolled* • **Surgical Technology/Technologist** 8 *students enrolled* • **Watchmaking and Jewelrymaking**

STUDENT SERVICES Academic or career counseling, employment services for current students, placement services for program completers, remedial services.

Cosmetology Institute of Beauty Arts and Sciences

807 Corporation Parkway, Winston-Salem, NC 27127

CONTACT Victoria Srour, President
Telephone: 336-773-1472

GENERAL INFORMATION Private Institution. Founded 1988. **Total program enrollment:** 120.

PROGRAM(S) OFFERED
• **Aesthetician/Esthetician and Skin Care Specialist** 600 *hrs.*/$6000 • **Cosmetology, Barber/Styling, and Nail Instructor** 800 *hrs.*/$5500 • **Cosmetology/Cosmetologist, General** 1500 *hrs.*/$14,600 • **Nail Technician/Specialist and Manicurist** 300 *hrs.*/$3500

STUDENT SERVICES Academic or career counseling.

Craven Community College

800 College Court, New Bern, NC 28562-4984
http://www.craven.cc.nc.us/

CONTACT Catherine Chew, President
Telephone: 252-638-7200

GENERAL INFORMATION Public Institution. Founded 1965. **Accreditation:** Regional (SACS/CC). **Total program enrollment:** 1052.

PROGRAM(S) OFFERED
• **Accounting** • **Autobody/Collision and Repair Technology/Technician** 1 *student enrolled* • **Banking and Financial Support Services** 1 *student enrolled* • **Child Development** 12 *students enrolled* • **Computer Programming/Programmer, General** • **Computer Systems Networking and Telecommunications** 6 *students enrolled* • **Cosmetology/Cosmetologist, General** 10 *students enrolled* • **Criminal Justice/Police Science** 21 *students enrolled* • **Criminal Justice/Safety Studies** 5 *students enrolled* • **Early Childhood Education and Teaching** 6 *students enrolled* • **Electrical, Electronic and Communications Engineering Technology/Technician** • **Heating, Air Conditioning, Ventilation and Refrigeration Maintenance Technology/Technician (HAC, HACR, HVAC, HVACR)** • **Information Technology** 1 *student enrolled* • **Licensed Practical/Vocational Nurse Training (LPN, LVN, Cert, Dipl, AAS)** 12 *students enrolled* • **Machine Shop Technology/Assistant** 1 *student enrolled* • **Mechanical Engineering/Mechanical Technology/Technician** 1 *student enrolled* • **Medical Office Management/Administration** 49 *students enrolled* • **Medical/Clinical Assistant** 3 *students enrolled* • **Office Management and Supervision** • **Operations Management and Supervision** 1 *student enrolled* • **Welding Technology/Welder** 7 *students enrolled*

STUDENT SERVICES Academic or career counseling, employment services for current students, remedial services.

Davidson County Community College

PO Box 1287, Lexington, NC 27293-1287
http://www.davidsonccc.edu/

CONTACT Mary E. Rittling, President
Telephone: 336-249-8186

GENERAL INFORMATION Public Institution. Founded 1958. **Accreditation:** Regional (SACS/CC); engineering technology (ABET/TAC); health information technology (AHIMA); medical laboratory technology (NAACLS). **Total program enrollment:** 1132.

PROGRAM(S) OFFERED
• **Accounting** 12 *students enrolled* • **Aesthetician/Esthetician and Skin Care Specialist** 31 *students enrolled* • **Automobile/Automotive Mechanics Technology/Technician** 3 *students enrolled* • **Business Administration and Management, General** 10 *students enrolled* • **Child Development** 11 *students enrolled* • **Computer Programming/Programmer, General** 5 *students enrolled* • **Computer Systems Networking and Telecommunications** 35 *students enrolled* • **Cosmetology/Cosmetologist, General** 10 *students enrolled* • **Criminal Justice/Police Science** 55 *students enrolled* • **Criminal Justice/Safety Studies** 17 *students enrolled* • **Early Childhood Education and Teaching** 52 *students enrolled* • **Electrical, Electronic and Communications Engineering Technology/Technician** • **Electrician** 3 *students enrolled* • **Electromechanical and Instrumentation and Maintenance Technologies/Technicians, Other** 6 *students enrolled* • **Emergency Medical Technology/Technician (EMT Paramedic)** • **Heating, Air Conditioning, Ventilation and Refrigeration Maintenance Technology/Technician (HAC, HACR, HVAC, HVACR)** 33 *students enrolled* • **Human Resources Management/Personnel Administration, General** 4 *students enrolled* • **Information Technology** 45 *students enrolled* • **Legal Assistant/Paralegal** 4 *students enrolled* • **Machine Shop Technology/Assistant** • **Massage Therapy/Therapeutic Massage** 6 *students enrolled* • **Medical/Clinical Assistant** 5 *students enrolled* • **Motorcycle Maintenance and Repair Technology/Technician** 4 *students enrolled* • **Nail Technician/Specialist and Manicurist** • **Pharmacy Technician/Assistant** 15 *students enrolled* • **Phlebotomy/Phlebotomist** 21 *students enrolled* • **Plastics Engineering Technology/Technician** 5 *students enrolled* • **Truck and Bus Driver/Commercial Vehicle Operation** 86 *students enrolled* • **Welding Technology/Welder** 9 *students enrolled*

STUDENT SERVICES Academic or career counseling, employment services for current students, placement services for program completers, remedial services.

Durham Beauty Academy

4600 Durham Chapel Hill Boulevard, Durham, NC 27707

CONTACT Hengel Mark Richardson, President
Telephone: 919-493-9557

GENERAL INFORMATION Private Institution. **Total program enrollment:** 94. **Application fee:** $50.

PROGRAM(S) OFFERED
• Cosmetology/Cosmetologist, General *1500 hrs./$14,350*

STUDENT SERVICES Academic or career counseling, placement services for program completers.

Durham Technical Community College

1637 Lawson Street, Durham, NC 27703-5023
http://www.durhamtech.edu/

CONTACT William G. Ingram, President
Telephone: 919-536-7201 Ext. 1015

GENERAL INFORMATION Public Institution. Founded 1961. **Accreditation:** Regional (SACS/CC); dental laboratory technology (ADA); ophthalmic dispensing (COA). **Total program enrollment:** 1115.

PROGRAM(S) OFFERED
• Allied Health Diagnostic, Intervention, and Treatment Professions, Other *18 students enrolled* • Architectural Engineering Technology/Technician • Automobile/Automotive Mechanics Technology/Technician *1 student enrolled* • Clinical/Medical Laboratory Science and Allied Professions, Other • Computer Programming/Programmer, General *4 students enrolled* • Computer Systems Networking and Telecommunications *1 student enrolled* • Criminal Justice/Police Science *23 students enrolled* • Dental Laboratory Technology/Technician *3 students enrolled* • Early Childhood Education and Teaching *24 students enrolled* • Electrical, Electronic and Communications Engineering Technology/Technician *3 students enrolled* • Electrician *4 students enrolled* • Electromechanical and Instrumentation and Maintenance Technologies/Technicians, Other *7 students enrolled* • Elementary Education and Teaching • Fire Protection and Safety Technology/Technician *3 students enrolled* • Health Information/Medical Records Technology/Technician *5 students enrolled* • Information Science/Studies *1 student enrolled* • Information Technology • Language Interpretation and Translation • Legal Assistant/Paralegal *7 students enrolled* • Licensed Practical/Vocational Nurse Training (LPN, LVN, Cert, Dipl, AAS) *6 students enrolled* • Machine Shop Technology/Assistant *2 students enrolled* • Management Information Systems, General *2 students enrolled* • Occupational Safety and Health Technology/Technician • Office Management and Supervision *1 student enrolled* • Operations Management and Supervision *1 student enrolled* • Opticianry/Ophthalmic Dispensing Optician • Optometric Technician/Assistant *6 students enrolled* • Pharmacy Technician/Assistant *8 students enrolled* • Phlebotomy/Phlebotomist • Spanish Language and Literature *17 students enrolled* • Surgical Technology/Technologist *10 students enrolled* • System, Networking, and LAN/WAN Management/Manager • Teacher Assistant/Aide

STUDENT SERVICES Academic or career counseling, employment services for current students, placement services for program completers, remedial services.

Edgecombe Community College

2009 West Wilson Street, Tarboro, NC 27886-9399
http://www.edgecombe.edu/

CONTACT Deborah L. Lamm, President
Telephone: 252-823-5166

GENERAL INFORMATION Public Institution. Founded 1968. **Accreditation:** Regional (SACS/CC); health information technology (AHIMA); radiologic technology: radiography (JRCERT). **Total program enrollment:** 642.

PROGRAM(S) OFFERED
• Accounting Technology/Technician and Bookkeeping • Allied Health Diagnostic, Intervention, and Treatment Professions, Other *18 students enrolled* • Autobody/Collision and Repair Technology/Technician *12 students enrolled* • Automobile/Automotive Mechanics Technology/Technician *6 students enrolled* • Building/Property Maintenance and Management *3 students enrolled*

• Business Administration and Management, General *1 student enrolled*
• Child Care and Support Services Management *1 student enrolled*
• Cosmetology/Cosmetologist, General *6 students enrolled* • Electrical, Electronic and Communications Engineering Technology/Technician *5 students enrolled* • Health Information/Medical Records Technology/Technician *12 students enrolled* • Licensed Practical/Vocational Nurse Training (LPN, LVN, Cert, Dipl, AAS) *23 students enrolled* • Mechanical Engineering/Mechanical Technology/Technician *3 students enrolled* • Medical Transcription/Transcriptionist *1 student enrolled* • Motorcycle Maintenance and Repair Technology/Technician • Nail Technician/Specialist and Manicurist *7 students enrolled* • Surgical Technology/Technologist *7 students enrolled*

STUDENT SERVICES Academic or career counseling, employment services for current students, placement services for program completers, remedial services.

Empire Beauty School

10075 Weddington Road Extension, Concord, NC 28027
http://www.empire.edu/

CONTACT Michael Bouman, President
Telephone: 704-979-3500

GENERAL INFORMATION Private Institution. **Total program enrollment:** 112. **Application fee:** $100.

PROGRAM(S) OFFERED
• Cosmetology, Barber/Styling, and Nail Instructor *3 students enrolled*
• Cosmetology/Cosmetologist, General *1530 hrs./$18,845*

STUDENT SERVICES Placement services for program completers.

Empire Beauty School–Matthews

11032 East Independence Boulevard, Matthews, NC 28105
http://www.empire.edu/

CONTACT Michael Bouman, President
Telephone: 800-223-3271

GENERAL INFORMATION Private Institution. **Total program enrollment:** 87. **Application fee:** $100.

PROGRAM(S) OFFERED
• Cosmetology/Cosmetologist, General *1530 hrs./$18,845* • Technical Teacher Education *2 students enrolled*

STUDENT SERVICES Placement services for program completers.

Fayetteville Beauty College

3442 Bragg Boulevard, PO Box 35758, Fayetteville, NC 28303

CONTACT Daniel Koceja, President
Telephone: 910-487-0227

GENERAL INFORMATION Private Institution. Founded 1931. **Total program enrollment:** 44. **Application fee:** $100.

PROGRAM(S) OFFERED
• Cosmetology, Barber/Styling, and Nail Instructor *822 hrs./$4400*
• Cosmetology/Cosmetologist, General *1500 hrs./$7800*

STUDENT SERVICES Academic or career counseling, employment services for current students, placement services for program completers, remedial services.

Fayetteville Technical Community College

PO Box 35236, Fayetteville, NC 28303-0236
http://www.faytechcc.edu/

CONTACT Dr. J. Larry Keen, President
Telephone: 910-678-8400

GENERAL INFORMATION Public Institution. Founded 1961. **Accreditation:** Regional (SACS/CC); dental assisting (ADA); dental hygiene (ADA);

Fayetteville Technical Community College (continued)

engineering technology (ABET/TAC); funeral service (ABFSE); physical therapy assisting (APTA); radiologic technology: radiography (JRCERT). **Total program enrollment: 3320.**

PROGRAM(S) OFFERED
- **Architectural Engineering Technology/Technician** *19 students enrolled* - **Autobody/Collision and Repair Technology/Technician** *6 students enrolled* - **Automobile/Automotive Mechanics Technology/Technician** *11 students enrolled* - **Business Administration and Management, General** *31 students enrolled* - **Business Operations Support and Secretarial Services, Other** - **Cabinetmaking and Millwork/Millwright** *2 students enrolled* - **Computer Programming/Programmer, General** *15 students enrolled* - **Computer Software and Media Applications, Other** - **Computer Systems Networking and Telecommunications** *15 students enrolled* - **Computer and Information Sciences and Support Services, Other** - **Computer and Information Systems Security** - **Cosmetology/Cosmetologist, General** *19 students enrolled* - **Criminal Justice/Police Science** - **Culinary Arts/Chef Training** *2 students enrolled* - **Dental Assisting/Assistant** *28 students enrolled* - **Early Childhood Education and Teaching** *78 students enrolled* - **Electrician** *5 students enrolled* - **Electromechanical Technology/Electromechanical Engineering Technology** - **Emergency Medical Technology/Technician (EMT Paramedic)** *1 student enrolled* - **Executive Assistant/Executive Secretary** *10 students enrolled* - **Forensic Science and Technology** *4 students enrolled* - **Funeral Service and Mortuary Science, General** *50 students enrolled* - **Heating, Air Conditioning, Ventilation and Refrigeration Maintenance Technology/Technician (HAC, HACR, HVAC, HVACR)** *7 students enrolled* - **Information Science/Studies** *3 students enrolled* - **Information Technology** - **Legal Assistant/Paralegal** *2 students enrolled* - **Licensed Practical/Vocational Nurse Training (LPN, LVN, Cert, Dipl, AAS)** *57 students enrolled* - **Marketing/Marketing Management, General** *2 students enrolled* - **Mason/Masonry** - **Mechanical Engineering/Mechanical Technology/Technician** - **Medical Office Computer Specialist/Assistant** *26 students enrolled* - **Medical Office Management/Administration** - **Nuclear Medical Technology/Technologist** *3 students enrolled* - **Nurse/Nursing Assistant/Aide and Patient Care Assistant** - **Operations Management and Supervision** *29 students enrolled* - **Pharmacy Technician/Assistant** *17 students enrolled* - **Phlebotomy/Phlebotomist** *39 students enrolled* - **Plumbing Technology/Plumber** *9 students enrolled* - **Social Sciences, Other** - **Surgical Technology/Technologist** *11 students enrolled* - **Welding Technology/Welder** *5 students enrolled*

STUDENT SERVICES Academic or career counseling, daycare for children of students, employment services for current students, placement services for program completers, remedial services.

Forsyth Technical Community College

2100 Silas Creek Parkway, Winston-Salem, NC 27103-5197
http://www.forsythtech.edu/

CONTACT Dr. Gary Green, President
Telephone: 336-723-0371

GENERAL INFORMATION Public Institution. Founded 1964. **Accreditation:** Regional (SACS/CC); dental assisting (ADA); dental hygiene (ADA); diagnostic medical sonography (JRCEDMS); engineering technology (ABET/TAC); medical assisting (AAMAE); nuclear medicine technology (JRCNMT); radiologic technology: radiation therapy technology (JRCERT); radiologic technology: radiography (JRCERT). **Total program enrollment: 3253.**

PROGRAM(S) OFFERED
- **Accounting** *2 students enrolled* - **Allied Health Diagnostic, Intervention, and Treatment Professions, Other** *25 students enrolled* - **Applied Horticulture/Horticultural Operations, General** *5 students enrolled* - **Architectural Engineering Technology/Technician** *7 students enrolled* - **Autobody/Collision and Repair Technology/Technician** *27 students enrolled* - **Automobile/Automotive Mechanics Technology/Technician** - **Business Administration and Management, General** *6 students enrolled* - **Carpentry/Carpenter** *2 students enrolled* - **Computer Hardware Technology/Technician** - **Computer Programming, Specific Applications** *1 student enrolled* - **Computer Systems Networking and Telecommunications** *1 student enrolled* - **Computer and Information Sciences, General** - **Criminal Justice/Safety Studies** - **Dental Assisting/Assistant** *12 students enrolled* - **Diagnostic Medical Sonography/Sonographer and Ultrasound Technician** - **Diesel Mechanics Technology/Technician** *5 students enrolled* - **Early Childhood Education and Teaching** *51 students enrolled* - **Electrical, Electronic and Communications Engineering Technology/Technician** *2 students enrolled* - **Electrician** *1 student enrolled* - **Electromechanical and Instrumentation and Maintenance Technologies/Technicians, Other** *6*

students enrolled - **Graphic Design** - **Health Professions and Related Clinical Sciences, Other** *15 students enrolled* - **Heating, Air Conditioning, Ventilation and Refrigeration Maintenance Technology/Technician (HAC, HACR, HVAC, HVACR)** *12 students enrolled* - **Information Science/Studies** *2 students enrolled* - **Information Technology** *1 student enrolled* - **International Business/Trade/Commerce** *1 student enrolled* - **Legal Assistant/Paralegal** *9 students enrolled* - **Licensed Practical/Vocational Nurse Training (LPN, LVN, Cert, Dipl, AAS)** *40 students enrolled* - **Logistics and Materials Management** *3 students enrolled* - **Machine Shop Technology/Assistant** *4 students enrolled* - **Massage Therapy/Therapeutic Massage** *10 students enrolled* - **Mechanical Engineering/Mechanical Technology/Technician** - **Medical Office Management/Administration** *33 students enrolled* - **Medical Transcription/Transcriptionist** *9 students enrolled* - **Office Management and Supervision** *4 students enrolled* - **Plumbing Technology/Plumber** *6 students enrolled* - **Real Estate** - **Vehicle Maintenance and Repair Technologies, Other** *1 student enrolled* - **Welding Technology/Welder** *12 students enrolled*

STUDENT SERVICES Academic or career counseling, employment services for current students, placement services for program completers, remedial services.

Gaston College

201 Highway 321 South, Dallas, NC 28034-1499
http://www.gaston.edu/

CONTACT Patricia Skinner, President
Telephone: 704-922-6200

GENERAL INFORMATION Public Institution. Founded 1963. **Accreditation:** Regional (SACS/CC); engineering technology (ABET/TAC); medical assisting (AAMAE). **Total program enrollment: 2117.**

PROGRAM(S) OFFERED
- **Accounting Technology/Technician and Bookkeeping** - **Accounting** *27 students enrolled* - **Architectural Engineering Technology/Technician** - **Automobile/Automotive Mechanics Technology/Technician** *2 students enrolled* - **Civil Engineering Technology/Technician** - **Computer Programming/Programmer, General** *2 students enrolled* - **Computer Systems Networking and Telecommunications** *6 students enrolled* - **Cosmetology/Cosmetologist, General** - **Criminal Justice/Police Science** *40 students enrolled* - **Dietitian Assistant** - **Early Childhood Education and Teaching** *4 students enrolled* - **Electrical, Electronic and Communications Engineering Technology/Technician** *1 student enrolled* - **Electrician** *3 students enrolled* - **Electromechanical and Instrumentation and Maintenance Technologies/Technicians, Other** *1 student enrolled* - **Engineering/Industrial Management** - **Executive Assistant/Executive Secretary** - **Heating, Air Conditioning, Ventilation and Refrigeration Maintenance Technology/Technician (HAC, HACR, HVAC, HVACR)** *45 students enrolled* - **Industrial Electronics Technology/Technician** - **Industrial Mechanics and Maintenance Technology** - **Information Science/Studies** *4 students enrolled* - **Information Technology** *2 students enrolled* - **Legal Administrative Assistant/Secretary** *3 students enrolled* - **Legal Assistant/Paralegal** - **Licensed Practical/Vocational Nurse Training (LPN, LVN, Cert, Dipl, AAS)** *35 students enrolled* - **Logistics and Materials Management** *16 students enrolled* - **Machine Shop Technology/Assistant** *9 students enrolled* - **Massage Therapy/Therapeutic Massage** *14 students enrolled* - **Mechanical Engineering/Mechanical Technology/Technician** *8 students enrolled* - **Medical Office Management/Administration** *28 students enrolled* - **Medical Transcription/Transcriptionist** *3 students enrolled* - **Nurse/Nursing Assistant/Aide and Patient Care Assistant** *2 students enrolled* - **Office Management and Supervision** *5 students enrolled* - **Phlebotomy/Phlebotomist** - **Radio and Television Broadcasting Technology/Technician** *1 student enrolled* - **Welding Technology/Welder** *3 students enrolled*

STUDENT SERVICES Academic or career counseling, daycare for children of students, employment services for current students, placement services for program completers, remedial services.

Greensboro College

815 West Market Street, Greensboro, NC 27401-1875
http://www.greensborocollege.edu/

CONTACT Craven E. Williams, President
Telephone: 336-272-7102

GENERAL INFORMATION Private Institution. Founded 1838. **Accreditation:** Regional (SACS/CC); music (NASM). **Total program enrollment:** 975. **Application fee:** $35.

STUDENT SERVICES Academic or career counseling, employment services for current students, placement services for program completers, remedial services.

Guilford College

5800 West Friendly Avenue, Greensboro, NC 27410-4173
http://www.guilford.edu/

CONTACT Kent John Chabotar, President
Telephone: 336-316-2000

GENERAL INFORMATION Private Institution (Affiliated with Society of Friends). Founded 1837. **Accreditation:** Regional (SACS/CC). **Total program enrollment:** 2217. **Application fee:** $25.

PROGRAM(S) OFFERED
● **Accounting** 2 students enrolled ● **Biology/Biological Sciences, General** 1 student enrolled ● **Communication Studies/Speech Communication and Rhetoric** 2 students enrolled ● **Communication, Journalism and Related Programs, Other** 1 student enrolled

STUDENT SERVICES Academic or career counseling, employment services for current students, placement services for program completers, remedial services.

Guilford Technical Community College

PO Box 309, Jamestown, NC 27282-0309
http://www.gtcc.edu/

CONTACT Don Cameron, President
Telephone: 336-334-4822

GENERAL INFORMATION Public Institution. Founded 1958. **Accreditation:** Regional (SACS/CC); dental assisting (ADA); dental hygiene (ADA); medical assisting (AAMAE); physical therapy assisting (APTA). **Total program enrollment:** 6079.

PROGRAM(S) OFFERED
● **Accounting Technology/Technician and Bookkeeping** 7 students enrolled ● **Airline/Commercial/Professional Pilot and Flight Crew** ● **Architectural Engineering Technology/Technician** 3 students enrolled ● **Autobody/Collision and Repair Technology/Technician** 24 students enrolled ● **Automobile/ Automotive Mechanics Technology/Technician** 9 students enrolled ● **Avionics Maintenance Technology/Technician** 3 students enrolled ● **Building/Property Maintenance and Management** 2 students enrolled ● **Business Administration and Management, General** 7 students enrolled ● **Carpentry/Carpenter** 11 students enrolled ● **Chemical Technology/Technician** 1 student enrolled ● **Civil Engineering Technology/Technician** 1 student enrolled ● **Commercial and Advertising Art** 23 students enrolled ● **Computer Systems Networking and Telecommunications** 4 students enrolled ● **Cosmetology/Cosmetologist, General** 20 students enrolled ● **Criminal Justice/Police Science** 30 students enrolled ● **Culinary Arts/Chef Training** 5 students enrolled ● **Dental Assisting/Assistant** 22 students enrolled ● **Early Childhood Education and Teaching** 57 students enrolled ● **Education, General** ● **Education, Other** ● **Electrical, Electronic and Communications Engineering Technology/Technician** ● **Electrician** 7 students enrolled ● **Electromechanical Technology/Electromechanical Engineering Technology** ● **Health Unit Coordinator/Ward Clerk** 11 students enrolled ● **Heating, Air Conditioning, Ventilation and Refrigeration Maintenance Technology/ Technician (HAC, HACR, HVAC, HVACR)** 5 students enrolled ● **Human Resources Management/Personnel Administration, General** 6 students enrolled ● **Industrial Production Technologies/Technicians, Other** ● **Information Science/Studies** 3 students enrolled ● **Information Technology** 13 students enrolled ● **Legal Assistant/Paralegal** 10 students enrolled ● **Licensed Practical/ Vocational Nurse Training (LPN, LVN, Cert, Dipl, AAS)** 16 students enrolled ● **Machine Shop Technology/Assistant** 8 students enrolled ● **Mechanical Engineering/Mechanical Technology/Technician** 2 students enrolled ● **Medical Office Management/Administration** 54 students enrolled ● **Medical Transcription/Transcriptionist** 11 students enrolled ● **Office Management and Supervision** 8 students enrolled ● **Pharmacy Technician/Assistant** 30 students enrolled ● **Plumbing Technology/Plumber** 1 student enrolled ● **Psychiatric/Mental Health Services Technician** ● **Substance Abuse/Addiction Counseling** 2 students enrolled ● **Surgical Technology/Technologist** 26 students enrolled ● **Survey Technology/Surveying** 3 students enrolled ● **System, Networking, and LAN/WAN Management/Manager** 2 students enrolled ● **Telecommunications Technology/Technician** ● **Upholstery/Upholsterer** 1 student enrolled ● **Vehicle Maintenance and Repair Technologies, Other** 4 students enrolled ● **Welding Technology/Welder** 10 students enrolled

STUDENT SERVICES Academic or career counseling, daycare for children of students, employment services for current students, placement services for program completers, remedial services.

Hairstyling Institute of Charlotte

209-B South Kings Drive, Charlotte, NC 28204-2621

CONTACT C. Melissaris, President
Telephone: 704-334-5511

GENERAL INFORMATION Private Institution. Founded 1975. **Total program enrollment:** 63. **Application fee:** $100.

PROGRAM(S) OFFERED
● **Barbering/Barber** 1500 hrs./$10,050 ● **Cosmetology/Cosmetologist, General** 1500 hrs./$15,500

STUDENT SERVICES Academic or career counseling, placement services for program completers.

Halifax Community College

PO Drawer 809, Weldon, NC 27890-0809
http://www.hcc.cc.nc.us/

CONTACT Dr. Ervin Griffin, President
Telephone: 252-536-7242

GENERAL INFORMATION Public Institution. Founded 1967. **Accreditation:** Regional (SACS/CC); dental hygiene (ADA); medical laboratory technology (NAACLS). **Total program enrollment:** 793.

PROGRAM(S) OFFERED
● **Automobile/Automotive Mechanics Technology/Technician** 38 students enrolled ● **Building/Property Maintenance and Management** 22 students enrolled ● **Business Administration and Management, General** 1 student enrolled ● **Commercial and Advertising Art** 13 students enrolled ● **Computer Systems Networking and Telecommunications** ● **Cosmetology/Cosmetologist, General** 9 students enrolled ● **Criminal Justice/Police Science** 21 students enrolled ● **E-Commerce/Electronic Commerce** ● **Electrical, Electronic and Communications Engineering Technology/Technician** ● **Electrician** 26 students enrolled ● **Electromechanical and Instrumentation and Maintenance Technologies/ Technicians, Other** 1 student enrolled ● **Elementary Education and Teaching** ● **Foodservice Systems Administration/Management** 29 students enrolled ● **Greenhouse Operations and Management** 10 students enrolled ● **Information Technology** ● **Interior Design** 3 students enrolled ● **Licensed Practical/ Vocational Nurse Training (LPN, LVN, Cert, Dipl, AAS)** 8 students enrolled ● **Mason/Masonry** 23 students enrolled ● **Medical Office Management/ Administration** 9 students enrolled ● **Office Management and Supervision** 2 students enrolled ● **Phlebotomy/Phlebotomist** 7 students enrolled ● **Plumbing Technology/Plumber** 24 students enrolled ● **Small Engine Mechanics and Repair Technology/Technician** 22 students enrolled ● **Welding Technology/ Welder** 1 student enrolled ● **Wood Science and Wood Products/Pulp and Paper Technology** 2 students enrolled

STUDENT SERVICES Academic or career counseling, daycare for children of students, employment services for current students, placement services for program completers, remedial services.

Haywood Community College

185 Freedlander Drive, Clyde, NC 28721-9453
http://www.haywood.edu/

CONTACT Dr. Rose Johnson, President
Telephone: 828-627-2821

GENERAL INFORMATION Public Institution. Founded 1964. **Accreditation:** Regional (SACS/CC); medical assisting (AAMAE). **Total program enrollment:** 605.

PROGRAM(S) OFFERED
● **Applied Horticulture/Horticultural Operations, General** ● **Autobody/Collision and Repair Technology/Technician** 11 students enrolled ● **Automobile/ Automotive Mechanics Technology/Technician** 12 students enrolled ● **Building/ Construction Finishing, Management, and Inspection, Other** 2 students enrolled ● **Business Administration and Management, General** ● **Child Care and Support Services Management** 29 students enrolled ● **Cinematography and Film/Video Production** 2 students enrolled ● **Civil Engineering, Other** 5 students enrolled ● **Computer Systems Analysis/Analyst** 1 student enrolled ● **Computer Systems Networking and Telecommunications** 10 students enrolled ● **Cosmetology and Related Personal Grooming Arts, Other** 8 students enrolled

Haywood Community College (continued)

• **Cosmetology/Cosmetologist, General** 9 *students enrolled* • **Electrical, Electronic and Communications Engineering Technology/Technician** 1 *student enrolled* • **Electrician** 6 *students enrolled* • **Electromechanical Technology/ Electromechanical Engineering Technology** • **Engineering Technologies/ Technicians, Other** • **Executive Assistant/Executive Secretary** • **Machine Shop Technology/Assistant** 7 *students enrolled* • **Make-Up Artist/Specialist** • **Mechanical Engineering/Mechanical Technology/Technician** 3 *students enrolled* • **Medical/Clinical Assistant** 4 *students enrolled* • **Precision Production, Other** 4 *students enrolled* • **Watchmaking and Jewelrymaking** 2 *students enrolled* • **Welding Technology/Welder** 1 *student enrolled* • **Wood Science and Wood Products/Pulp and Paper Technology** 11 *students enrolled*

STUDENT SERVICES Academic or career counseling, daycare for children of students, employment services for current students, placement services for program completers, remedial services.

Hood Theological Seminary

1810 Lutheran Synod Drive, Salisbury, NC 28144
http://www.hoodseminary.edu/

CONTACT Albert J.D. Aymer, President
Telephone: 704-636-7611

GENERAL INFORMATION Private Institution. Founded 1879. **Total program enrollment:** 182. **Application fee:** $30.

PROGRAM(S) OFFERED
• **Theology and Religious Vocations, Other** 5 *students enrolled*
STUDENT SERVICES Remedial services.

Isothermal Community College

PO Box 804, Spindale, NC 28160-0804
http://www.isothermal.edu/

CONTACT Myra B. Johnson, President
Telephone: 828-286-3636 Ext. 239

GENERAL INFORMATION Public Institution. Founded 1965. **Accreditation:** Regional (SACS/CC). **Total program enrollment:** 1027.

PROGRAM(S) OFFERED
• **Aesthetician/Esthetician and Skin Care Specialist** • **Autobody/Collision and Repair Technology/Technician** 5 *students enrolled* • **Building/Construction Finishing, Management, and Inspection, Other** • **Business Administration and Management, General** 2 *students enrolled* • **Child Development** 8 *students enrolled* • **Computer Engineering Technology/Technician** • **Computer Systems Networking and Telecommunications** • **Cosmetology, Barber/Styling, and Nail Instructor** • **Cosmetology/Cosmetologist, General** • **Criminal Justice/Police Science** 2 *students enrolled* • **Criminal Justice/Safety Studies** 2 *students enrolled* • **Customer Service Support/Call Center/Teleservice Operation** • **Early Childhood Education and Teaching** 7 *students enrolled* • **Education, Other** • **Electrician** 9 *students enrolled* • **Information Technology** • **Insurance** • **Licensed Practical/Vocational Nurse Training (LPN, LVN, Cert, Dipl, AAS)** • **Machine Shop Technology/Assistant** 1 *student enrolled* • **Mechanical Drafting and Mechanical Drafting CAD/CADD** 3 *students enrolled* • **Medical Office Management/Administration** 7 *students enrolled* • **Nail Technician/Specialist and Manicurist** 1 *student enrolled* • **Office Management and Supervision** 20 *students enrolled* • **Operations Management and Supervision** • **Plastics Engineering Technology/Technician** • **Radio and Television Broadcasting Technology/Technician** • **Real Estate** • **Surgical Technology/Technologist** 5 *students enrolled* • **Welding Technology/Welder** 9 *students enrolled*

STUDENT SERVICES Academic or career counseling, remedial services.

James Sprunt Community College

PO Box 398, Kenansville, NC 28349-0398
http://www.jamessprunt.com/

CONTACT Lawrence L. Rouse, President
Telephone: 910-296-2400

GENERAL INFORMATION Public Institution. Founded 1964. **Accreditation:** Regional (SACS/CC); medical assisting (AAMAE). **Total program enrollment:** 469.

PROGRAM(S) OFFERED
• **Accounting** 7 *students enrolled* • **Agriculture, Agriculture Operations and Related Sciences, Other** 6 *students enrolled* • **Animal/Livestock Husbandry and**

Production • **Automobile/Automotive Mechanics Technology/Technician** 8 *students enrolled* • **Child Development** 35 *students enrolled* • **Clinical/Medical Laboratory Science and Allied Professions, Other** • **Commercial and Advertising Art** • **Cosmetology, Barber/Styling, and Nail Instructor** 1 *student enrolled* • **Cosmetology/Cosmetologist, General** 1 *student enrolled* • **Criminal Justice/Police Science** 12 *students enrolled* • **Early Childhood Education and Teaching** 32 *students enrolled* • **Electrician** 6 *students enrolled* • **Foodservice Systems Administration/Management** 12 *students enrolled* • **Information Technology** 4 *students enrolled* • **Licensed Practical/Vocational Nurse Training (LPN, LVN, Cert, Dipl, AAS)** 8 *students enrolled* • **Mason/Masonry** 17 *students enrolled* • **Office Management and Supervision** 4 *students enrolled* • **Welding Technology/Welder** 2 *students enrolled*

STUDENT SERVICES Academic or career counseling, employment services for current students, placement services for program completers, remedial services.

Johnston Community College

PO Box 2350, Smithfield, NC 27577-2350
http://www.johnston.cc.nc.us/

CONTACT Donald L. Reichard, President
Telephone: 919-934-3051

GENERAL INFORMATION Public Institution. Founded 1969. **Accreditation:** Regional (SACS/CC); radiologic technology: radiography (JRCERT). **Total program enrollment:** 1949.

PROGRAM(S) OFFERED
• **Accounting** 3 *students enrolled* • **Aesthetician/Esthetician and Skin Care Specialist** 9 *students enrolled* • **Allied Health Diagnostic, Intervention, and Treatment Professions, Other** 1 *student enrolled* • **Applied Horticulture/ Horticultural Operations, General** 43 *students enrolled* • **Business Administration and Management, General** 4 *students enrolled* • **Cardiovascular Technology/Technologist** 7 *students enrolled* • **Commercial and Advertising Art** 6 *students enrolled* • **Computer Programming/Programmer, General** 1 *student enrolled* • **Cosmetology, Barber/Styling, and Nail Instructor** 1 *student enrolled* • **Cosmetology/Cosmetologist, General** 18 *students enrolled* • **Criminal Justice/ Police Science** 28 *students enrolled* • **Diagnostic Medical Sonography/ Sonographer and Ultrasound Technician** 2 *students enrolled* • **Diesel Mechanics Technology/Technician** • **Early Childhood Education and Teaching** 7 *students enrolled* • **Electrical/Electronics Maintenance and Repair Technology, Other** 25 *students enrolled* • **Electrician** 50 *students enrolled* • **Foodservice Systems Administration/Management** 48 *students enrolled* • **Greenhouse Operations and Management** • **Heating, Air Conditioning, Ventilation and Refrigeration Maintenance Technology/Technician (HAC, HACR, HVAC, HVACR)** 1 *student enrolled* • **Landscaping and Groundskeeping** 2 *students enrolled* • **Legal Assistant/Paralegal** 3 *students enrolled* • **Machine Shop Technology/Assistant** 1 *student enrolled* • **Mason/Masonry** 34 *students enrolled* • **Massage Therapy/Therapeutic Massage** 9 *students enrolled* • **Medical Office Management/Administration** 8 *students enrolled* • **Medical/Clinical Assistant** 23 *students enrolled* • **Nail Technician/Specialist and Manicurist** 16 *students enrolled* • **Nuclear Medical Technology/Technologist** 7 *students enrolled* • **Office Management and Supervision** 44 *students enrolled* • **Phlebotomy/Phlebotomist** 1 *student enrolled* • **Plumbing Technology/Plumber** 32 *students enrolled* • **System, Networking, and LAN/WAN Management/Manager** • **Truck and Bus Driver/Commercial Vehicle Operation** 199 *students enrolled* • **Welding Technology/Welder** 1 *student enrolled*

STUDENT SERVICES Academic or career counseling, daycare for children of students, employment services for current students, placement services for program completers, remedial services.

John Wesley College

2314 North Centennial Street, High Point, NC 27265-3197
http://www.johnwesley.edu/

CONTACT Joel T. Key, Interim President
Telephone: 336-889-2262

GENERAL INFORMATION Private Institution. Founded 1932. **Accreditation:** State accredited or approved. **Total program enrollment:** 59. **Application fee:** $35.

STUDENT SERVICES Academic or career counseling, remedial services.

King's College

322 Lamar Avenue, Charlotte, NC 28204-2436
http://www.kingscollegecharlotte.edu/

CONTACT Barbara Rockecharlie, Director/Chief Academic Officer
Telephone: 704-372-0266

GENERAL INFORMATION Private Institution. Founded 1901. **Accreditation:** State accredited or approved. **Total program enrollment:** 588. **Application fee:** $50.

PROGRAM(S) OFFERED
• **Accounting** *1 student enrolled* • **Administrative Assistant and Secretarial Science, General** *14 students enrolled* • **Allied Health and Medical Assisting Services, Other** *102 students enrolled* • **Computer Programming, Specific Applications** *4 students enrolled* • **Graphic Design** *4 students enrolled* • **Legal Administrative Assistant/Secretary** *1 student enrolled* • **Tourism and Travel Services Management** *3 students enrolled*

STUDENT SERVICES Placement services for program completers.

Lenoir Community College

PO Box 188, Kinston, NC 28502-0188
http://www.lenoircc.edu/

CONTACT Brantley Briley, President
Telephone: 252-527-6223

GENERAL INFORMATION Public Institution. Founded 1960. **Accreditation:** Regional (SACS/CC); medical assisting (AAMAE). **Total program enrollment:** 1215.

PROGRAM(S) OFFERED
• **Accounting Technology/Technician and Bookkeeping** • **Accounting** *4 students enrolled* • **Airline/Commercial/Professional Pilot and Flight Crew** • **Applied Horticulture/Horticultural Operations, General** *71 students enrolled* • **Automobile/Automotive Mechanics Technology/Technician** • **Business Administration and Management, General** • **Child Care and Support Services Management** • **Clinical/Medical Laboratory Science and Allied Professions, Other** • **Clinical/Medical Social Work** *1 student enrolled* • **Computer Engineering Technology/Technician** *2 students enrolled* • **Computer Systems Analysis/Analyst** • **Computer Systems Networking and Telecommunications** *4 students enrolled* • **Cosmetology/Cosmetologist, General** *29 students enrolled* • **Court Reporting/Court Reporter** *1 student enrolled* • **Criminal Justice/Police Science** • **Culinary Arts/Chef Training** *26 students enrolled* • **E-Commerce/Electronic Commerce** *4 students enrolled* • **Early Childhood Education and Teaching** *3 students enrolled* • **Education, Other** • **Electrical, Electronic and Communications Engineering Technology/Technician** • **Electromechanical Technology/Electromechanical Engineering Technology** • **Executive Assistant/Executive Secretary** • **Graphic Design** *1 student enrolled* • **Graphic and Printing Equipment Operator, General Production** • **Industrial Electronics Technology/Technician** *18 students enrolled* • **Industrial Production Technologies/Technicians, Other** • **Information Technology** *3 students enrolled* • **Licensed Practical/Vocational Nurse Training (LPN, LVN, Cert, Dipl, AAS)** • **Logistics and Materials Management** *4 students enrolled* • **Machine Shop Technology/Assistant** • **Management Information Systems, General** • **Massage Therapy/Therapeutic Massage** *7 students enrolled* • **Mechanical Engineering/Mechanical Technology/Technician** • **Medical Office Management/Administration** *28 students enrolled* • **Office Management and Supervision** *6 students enrolled* • **Operations Management and Supervision** *7 students enrolled* • **Radiologic Technology/Science—Radiographer** • **Social Work** • **Surgical Technology/Technologist** *13 students enrolled* • **System, Networking, and LAN/WAN Management/Manager** • **Water Quality and Wastewater Treatment Management and Recycling Technology/Technician** *15 students enrolled* • **Welding Technology/Welder** *1 student enrolled*

STUDENT SERVICES Academic or career counseling, employment services for current students, placement services for program completers, remedial services.

Leon's Beauty School

1410 West Lee Street, Greensboro, NC 27403
http://leonsbeautyschool.com/

CONTACT Parker Washburn, President
Telephone: 336-274-4601

GENERAL INFORMATION Private Institution. Founded 1963. **Total program enrollment:** 88.

PROGRAM(S) OFFERED
• **Aesthetician/Esthetician and Skin Care Specialist** *650 hrs./$2050* • **Cosmetology, Barber/Styling, and Nail Instructor** *320 hrs./$1050* • **Cosmetology/Cosmetologist, General** *900 hrs./$6700* • **Electrolysis/Electrology and Electrolysis Technician** *35 students enrolled* • **Nail Technician/Specialist and Manicurist** *300 hrs./$1000*

STUDENT SERVICES Academic or career counseling, employment services for current students, placement services for program completers.

Martin Community College

1161 Kehukee Park Road, Williamston, NC 27892
http://www.martin.cc.nc.us/

CONTACT Dr. Ann R. Britt, President
Telephone: 252-792-1521

GENERAL INFORMATION Public Institution. Founded 1968. **Accreditation:** Regional (SACS/CC); dental assisting (ADA); medical assisting (AAMAE); physical therapy assisting (APTA). **Total program enrollment:** 215.

PROGRAM(S) OFFERED
• **Accounting** • **Aesthetician/Esthetician and Skin Care Specialist** • **Automobile/Automotive Mechanics Technology/Technician** *1 student enrolled* • **Business Administration and Management, General** • **Cosmetology, Barber/Styling, and Nail Instructor** • **Cosmetology/Cosmetologist, General** • **Dental Assisting/Assistant** *11 students enrolled* • **E-Commerce/Electronic Commerce** • **Early Childhood Education and Teaching** • **Electrician** • **Electromechanical and Instrumentation and Maintenance Technologies/Technicians, Other** • **Elementary Education and Teaching** • **Equestrian/Equine Studies** *2 students enrolled* • **Heating, Air Conditioning, Ventilation and Refrigeration Maintenance Technology/Technician (HAC, HACR, HVAC, HVACR)** *1 student enrolled* • **Information Science/Studies** • **Information Technology** • **Medical Office Management/Administration** • **Medical/Clinical Assistant** *2 students enrolled* • **Nail Technician/Specialist and Manicurist** *3 students enrolled* • **Office Management and Supervision**

STUDENT SERVICES Academic or career counseling, employment services for current students, remedial services.

Mayland Community College

PO Box 547, Spruce Pine, NC 28777-0547
http://www.mayland.edu/

CONTACT Dr. Suzanne Y. Owens, President
Telephone: 828-765-7351

GENERAL INFORMATION Public Institution. Founded 1971. **Accreditation:** Regional (SACS/CC). **Total program enrollment:** 540.

PROGRAM(S) OFFERED
• **Accounting Technology/Technician and Bookkeeping** • **Applied Horticulture/Horticultural Operations, General** *87 students enrolled* • **Autobody/Collision and Repair Technology/Technician** *5 students enrolled* • **Business Administration and Management, General** • **Cabinetmaking and Millwork/Millwright** *48 students enrolled* • **Child Care and Support Services Management** *10 students enrolled* • **Computer Engineering Technology/Technician** *83 students enrolled* • **Cosmetology/Cosmetologist, General** *12 students enrolled* • **Criminal Justice/Police Science** *11 students enrolled* • **Electrical, Electronic and Communications Engineering Technology/Technician** • **Electrician** *1 student enrolled* • **Electromechanical Technology/Electromechanical Engineering Technology** *16 students enrolled* • **Executive Assistant/Executive Secretary** *3 students enrolled* • **Heating, Air Conditioning, Ventilation and Refrigeration Maintenance Technology/Technician (HAC, HACR, HVAC, HVACR)** • **Industrial Electronics Technology/Technician** • **Licensed Practical/Vocational Nurse**

Mayland Community College (continued)

Training (LPN, LVN, Cert, Dipl, AAS) *16 students enrolled* ● Management Information Systems, General *83 students enrolled* ● Mason/Masonry *91 students enrolled* ● Medical Administrative/Executive Assistant and Medical Secretary ● Medical/Clinical Assistant *13 students enrolled* ● Welding Technology/Welder *42 students enrolled*

STUDENT SERVICES Academic or career counseling, daycare for children of students, employment services for current students, placement services for program completers, remedial services.

McDowell Technical Community College

Route 1, Box 170, Marion, NC 28752-9724
http://www.mcdowelltech.cc.nc.us/

CONTACT Dr. Bryan Wilson, President
Telephone: 828-652-6021

GENERAL INFORMATION Public Institution. Founded 1964. **Accreditation:** Regional (SACS/CC). **Total program enrollment:** 397.

PROGRAM(S) OFFERED
● Accounting ● Aesthetician/Esthetician and Skin Care Specialist *2 students enrolled* ● Applied Horticulture/Horticultural Operations, General *1 student enrolled* ● Autobody/Collision and Repair Technology/Technician *1 student enrolled* ● Automobile/Automotive Mechanics Technology/Technician *1 student enrolled* ● Cabinetmaking and Millwork/Millwright *4 students enrolled* ● Carpentry/Carpenter *2 students enrolled* ● Commercial and Advertising Art ● Cosmetology, Barber/Styling, and Nail Instructor *1 student enrolled* ● Cosmetology/Cosmetologist, General *5 students enrolled* ● Criminal Justice/Police Science *12 students enrolled* ● Early Childhood Education and Teaching *3 students enrolled* ● Electrician ● Electromechanical and Instrumentation and Maintenance Technologies/Technicians, Other ● Health Information/Medical Records Technology/Technician *5 students enrolled* ● Heating, Air Conditioning, Ventilation and Refrigeration Maintenance Technology/Technician (HAC, HACR, HVAC, HVACR) *12 students enrolled* ● Information Technology *6 students enrolled* ● Licensed Practical/Vocational Nurse Training (LPN, LVN, Cert, Dipl, AAS) *36 students enrolled* ● Machine Shop Technology/Assistant *2 students enrolled* ● Nail Technician/Specialist and Manicurist ● Nurse/Nursing Assistant/Aide and Patient Care Assistant ● Office Management and Supervision ● Operations Management and Supervision ● Real Estate ● Surgical Technology/Technologist *6 students enrolled* ● Welding Technology/Welder *1 student enrolled*

STUDENT SERVICES Academic or career counseling, daycare for children of students, employment services for current students, placement services for program completers, remedial services.

Medical Arts Massage School

2321 Blue Ridge Road, Raleigh, NC 27603
http://www.massageandestheticsschool.com/

CONTACT Michael Davis, President
Telephone: 919-872-6386 Ext. 300

GENERAL INFORMATION Private Institution. **Total program enrollment:** 75. **Application fee:** $100.

PROGRAM(S) OFFERED
● Allied Health and Medical Assisting Services, Other *60 hrs./$11,008* ● Massage Therapy/Therapeutic Massage *56 hrs./$11,898* ● Medical/Clinical Assistant

STUDENT SERVICES Placement services for program completers.

Miller-Motte Technical College

2205 Walnut Street, Cary, NC 27511
http://www.miller-motte.com/

CONTACT Joseph A. Kennedy, Chief Executive
Telephone: 919-532-7171

GENERAL INFORMATION Private Institution. **Total program enrollment:** 298. **Application fee:** $35.

PROGRAM(S) OFFERED
● Cosmetology/Cosmetologist, General *62 students enrolled* ● Medical Office Assistant/Specialist *5 students enrolled*

STUDENT SERVICES Academic or career counseling, employment services for current students, placement services for program completers, remedial services.

Miller-Motte Technical College

606 South College Road, Wilmington, NC 28403
http://www.miller-motte.com/

CONTACT David Tipps, School Director
Telephone: 910-392-4660

GENERAL INFORMATION Private Institution. Founded 1989. **Accreditation:** Medical assisting (AAMAE); surgical technology (ARCST); state accredited or approved. **Total program enrollment:** 410. **Application fee:** $35.

PROGRAM(S) OFFERED
● Accounting Technology/Technician and Bookkeeping *1 student enrolled* ● Computer Systems Networking and Telecommunications *8 students enrolled* ● Cosmetology, Barber/Styling, and Nail Instructor *4 students enrolled* ● Cosmetology/Cosmetologist, General *11 students enrolled* ● Data Entry/Microcomputer Applications, General *17 students enrolled* ● Massage Therapy/Therapeutic Massage *24 students enrolled* ● Medical Office Assistant/Specialist *1 student enrolled* ● Surgical Technology/Technologist *3 students enrolled*

STUDENT SERVICES Academic or career counseling, employment services for current students, placement services for program completers, remedial services.

Mitchell Community College

500 West Broad, Statesville, NC 28677-5293
http://www.mitchell.cc.nc.us/

CONTACT Douglas Eason, President
Telephone: 704-878-3200

GENERAL INFORMATION Public Institution. Founded 1852. **Accreditation:** Regional (SACS/CC); medical assisting (AAMAE). **Total program enrollment:** 1270.

PROGRAM(S) OFFERED
● Accounting *3 students enrolled* ● Aesthetician/Esthetician and Skin Care Specialist *2 students enrolled* ● Business Administration and Management, General *6 students enrolled* ● Child Care and Support Services Management *26 students enrolled* ● Clinical/Medical Laboratory Science and Allied Professions, Other ● Computer Programming, Specific Applications ● Computer Systems Analysis/Analyst *1 student enrolled* ● Cosmetology and Related Personal Grooming Arts, Other *1 student enrolled* ● Cosmetology, Barber/Styling, and Nail Instructor ● Cosmetology/Cosmetologist, General *9 students enrolled* ● Criminal Justice/Police Science *27 students enrolled* ● Early Childhood Education and Teaching ● Electrical, Electronic and Communications Engineering Technology/Technician *7 students enrolled* ● Electrician *2 students enrolled* ● Electromechanical Technology/Electromechanical Engineering Technology ● Electromechanical and Instrumentation and Maintenance Technologies/Technicians, Other ● Engineering Technologies/Technicians, Other ● Engineering/Industrial Management ● Executive Assistant/Executive Secretary *3 students enrolled* ● Heating, Air Conditioning, Ventilation and Refrigeration Maintenance Technology/Technician (HAC, HACR, HVAC, HVACR) *15 students enrolled* ● Information Science/Studies ● Kindergarten/Preschool Education and Teaching ● Machine Shop Technology/Assistant ● Manufacturing Technology/Technician ● Mechanical Drafting and Mechanical Drafting CAD/CADD ● Mechanical Engineering/Mechanical Technology/Technician *6 students enrolled* ● Medical Transcription/Transcriptionist *1 student enrolled* ● Medical/Clinical Assistant *7 students enrolled* ● Nail Technician/Specialist and Manicurist ● Office Management and Supervision

STUDENT SERVICES Academic or career counseling, employment services for current students, placement services for program completers, remedial services.

Mitchell's Hairstyling Academy

1021 North Spence Avenue, Goldsboro, NC 27534
http://www.mitchells.edu/

CONTACT Ray Mitchell, President
Telephone: 919-778-8200

GENERAL INFORMATION Private Institution. Founded 1988. **Total program enrollment:** 6. **Application fee:** $50.

PROGRAM(S) OFFERED
• Cosmetology/Cosmetologist, General 1500 hrs./$6900

STUDENT SERVICES Placement services for program completers.

Mitchell's Hairstyling Academy

426 Arlington Boulevard, Greenville, NC 27858
http://www.mitchells.edu/

CONTACT B. Mitchell, President
Telephone: 252-756-3050

GENERAL INFORMATION Private Institution. Founded 1968. **Total program enrollment:** 6. **Application fee:** $50.

PROGRAM(S) OFFERED
• Cosmetology/Cosmetologist, General 1500 hrs./$6900

Mitchell's Hairstyling Academy

1235 Buck Jones Road, Raleigh, NC 27606
http://www.mitchells.edu/

CONTACT Ray Mitchell, President
Telephone: 919-469-5807

GENERAL INFORMATION Private Institution. Founded 1985. **Total program enrollment:** 91. **Application fee:** $50.

PROGRAM(S) OFFERED
• Cosmetology/Cosmetologist, General 1500 hrs./$9900

Mitchell's Hairstyling Academy

2620 Forest Hills Road, Suite A, Wilson, NC 27893
http://www.mitchells.edu/

CONTACT Ray Mitchell, President
Telephone: 252-243-3158

GENERAL INFORMATION Private Institution. Founded 1968. **Total program enrollment:** 3. **Application fee:** $50.

PROGRAM(S) OFFERED
• Cosmetology/Cosmetologist, General 1500 hrs./$6900

Montgomery Community College

1011 Page Street, Troy, NC 27371
http://www.montgomery.edu/

CONTACT Mary P. Kirk, President
Telephone: 910-576-6222 Ext. 600

GENERAL INFORMATION Public Institution. Founded 1967. **Accreditation:** Regional (SACS/CC); medical assisting (AAMAE). **Total program enrollment:** 337.

PROGRAM(S) OFFERED
• Autobody/Collision and Repair Technology/Technician 7 students enrolled
• Business Administration and Management, General 22 students enrolled
• Computer Systems Networking and Telecommunications 1 student enrolled
• Crafts/Craft Design, Folk Art and Artisanry 3 students enrolled • Criminal Justice/Police Science 13 students enrolled • Culinary Arts/Chef Training 12

students enrolled • Dental Assisting/Assistant 10 students enrolled • Early Childhood Education and Teaching 8 students enrolled • Electrician 1 student enrolled • Foodservice Systems Administration/Management 8 students enrolled • Gunsmithing/Gunsmith 1 student enrolled • Health Professions and Related Clinical Sciences, Other 1 student enrolled • Information Technology 4 students enrolled • Licensed Practical/Vocational Nurse Training (LPN, LVN, Cert, Dipl, AAS) 26 students enrolled • Office Management and Supervision 12 students enrolled • Taxidermy/Taxidermist 20 students enrolled

STUDENT SERVICES Academic or career counseling, daycare for children of students, employment services for current students, remedial services.

Montgomery's Hairstyling Academy

222 Tallywood Shopping Center, Fayetteville, NC 28303

CONTACT Loretta Montgomery, President
Telephone: 910-485-6310

GENERAL INFORMATION Private Institution. Founded 1988. **Total program enrollment:** 102. **Application fee:** $100.

PROGRAM(S) OFFERED
• Cosmetology, Barber/Styling, and Nail Instructor 900 hrs./$2650
• Cosmetology/Cosmetologist, General 51 students enrolled • Nail Technician/Specialist and Manicurist 300 hrs./$1150

Mr. David's School of Hair Design

4348 Market Street, North 17 Shopping Center, Wilmington, NC 28403
http://hometown.aol.com/ssassabear/index.html/

CONTACT Ashley Wallace, Vice President
Telephone: 910-763-4418

GENERAL INFORMATION Private Institution. Founded 1969. **Total program enrollment:** 78. **Application fee:** $25.

PROGRAM(S) OFFERED
• Cosmetology and Related Personal Grooming Arts, Other 800 hrs./$4720
• Cosmetology, Barber/Styling, and Nail Instructor • Cosmetology/Cosmetologist, General 1500 hrs./$7250 • Nail Technician/Specialist and Manicurist

STUDENT SERVICES Academic or career counseling, employment services for current students, placement services for program completers, remedial services.

NASCAR Technical Institute

220 Byers Creek Road, Mooresville, NC 28117
http://www.uticorp.com/

CONTACT James Bartholomew, Campus President
Telephone: 704-658-1950

GENERAL INFORMATION Private Institution. **Total program enrollment:** 1528.

PROGRAM(S) OFFERED
• Automobile/Automotive Mechanics Technology/Technician 74 hrs./$27,250

STUDENT SERVICES Academic or career counseling, employment services for current students, placement services for program completers.

Nash Community College

522 North Old Carriage Road, Rocky Mount, NC 27804
http://www.nash.cc.nc.us/

CONTACT William S. Carver, II, President
Telephone: 252-443-4011

GENERAL INFORMATION Public Institution. Founded 1967. **Accreditation:** Regional (SACS/CC); physical therapy assisting (APTA). **Total program enrollment:** 829.

PROGRAM(S) OFFERED
● **Accounting** *1 student enrolled* ● **Cosmetology, Barber/Styling, and Nail Instructor** ● **Cosmetology/Cosmetologist, General** *2 students enrolled* ● **Early Childhood Education and Teaching** *16 students enrolled* ● **Electrical, Electronic and Communications Engineering Technology/Technician** ● **Electrician** *1 student enrolled* ● **Elementary Education and Teaching** *3 students enrolled* ● **Hospitality Administration/Management, General** *2 students enrolled* ● **Industrial Technology/Technician** ● **Information Technology** ● **Legal Administrative Assistant/Secretary** ● **Licensed Practical/Vocational Nurse Training (LPN, LVN, Cert, Dipl, AAS)** ● **Lineworker** *1 student enrolled* ● **Machine Shop Technology/Assistant** *3 students enrolled* ● **Medical Insurance Coding Specialist/Coder** *15 students enrolled* ● **Medical Office Management/Administration** *7 students enrolled* ● **Office Management and Supervision** *3 students enrolled* ● **Phlebotomy/Phlebotomist** *21 students enrolled* ● **Restaurant, Culinary, and Catering Management/Manager** ● **Special Education and Teaching, General** *3 students enrolled* ● **System, Networking, and LAN/WAN Management/Manager** ● **Web/Multimedia Management and Webmaster** ● **Welding Technology/Welder** *2 students enrolled*

STUDENT SERVICES Academic or career counseling, daycare for children of students, employment services for current students, placement services for program completers, remedial services.

New Life Theological Seminary

PO Box 790106, Charlotte, NC 28206-7901
http://www.nlts.org/

CONTACT Dr. Eddie G. Grigg, President
Telephone: 704-334-6882

GENERAL INFORMATION Private Institution. Founded 1996. **Accreditation:** State accredited or approved. **Total program enrollment:** 52. **Application fee:** $40.

PROGRAM(S) OFFERED
● **Pre-Theology/Pre-Ministerial Studies**

STUDENT SERVICES Academic or career counseling, employment services for current students.

Pamlico Community College

PO Box 185, Grantsboro, NC 28529-0185
http://www.pamlico.cc.nc.us/

CONTACT F. Marion Altman, Jr., President
Telephone: 252-249-1851

GENERAL INFORMATION Public Institution. Founded 1963. **Accreditation:** Regional (SACS/CC); medical assisting (AAMAE). **Total program enrollment:** 231.

PROGRAM(S) OFFERED
● **Accounting Technology/Technician and Bookkeeping** ● **Applied Horticulture/Horticultural Operations, General** *24 students enrolled* ● **Business Administration and Management, General** *1 student enrolled* ● **Carpentry/Carpenter** *27 students enrolled* ● **Corrections and Criminal Justice, Other** *20 students enrolled* ● **Cosmetology/Cosmetologist, General** ● **Early Childhood Education and Teaching** *1 student enrolled* ● **Electrician** *19 students enrolled* ● **Environmental Engineering Technology/Environmental Technology** *2 students enrolled* ● **Executive Assistant/Executive Secretary** ● **Information Science/Studies** *26 students enrolled* ● **Mason/Masonry** *22 students enrolled* ● **Medical/Clinical Assistant** *9 students enrolled*

STUDENT SERVICES Academic or career counseling, employment services for current students, placement services for program completers, remedial services.

Piedmont Baptist College and Graduate School

420 South Broad Street, Winston-Salem, NC 27101-5197
http://www.pbc.edu/

CONTACT Charles W. Petitt, President
Telephone: 336-725-8344 Ext. 7955

GENERAL INFORMATION Private Institution. Founded 1947. **Accreditation:** State accredited or approved. **Total program enrollment:** 206. **Application fee:** $50.

PROGRAM(S) OFFERED
● **Bible/Biblical Studies** *1 student enrolled*

STUDENT SERVICES Academic or career counseling, employment services for current students, placement services for program completers, remedial services.

Piedmont Community College

PO Box 1197, Roxboro, NC 27573-1197
http://www.piedmont.cc.nc.us/

CONTACT H. James Owen, President
Telephone: 336-599-1181 Ext. 221

GENERAL INFORMATION Public Institution. Founded 1970. **Accreditation:** Regional (SACS/CC). **Total program enrollment:** 1113.

PROGRAM(S) OFFERED
● **Accounting** *1 student enrolled* ● **Applied Horticulture/Horticultural Operations, General** *9 students enrolled* ● **Building/Property Maintenance and Management** *23 students enrolled* ● **Business Administration and Management, General** *28 students enrolled* ● **Carpentry/Carpenter** *60 students enrolled* ● **Child Care and Support Services Management** *5 students enrolled* ● **Child Development** *9 students enrolled* ● **Computer Programming, Specific Applications** ● **Computer Systems Networking and Telecommunications** ● **Computer and Information Systems Security** ● **Cosmetology/Cosmetologist, General** *2 students enrolled* ● **Criminal Justice/Safety Studies** ● **E-Commerce/Electronic Commerce** ● **Electrician** *46 students enrolled* ● **Electromechanical and Instrumentation and Maintenance Technologies/Technicians, Other** *14 students enrolled* ● **Foodservice Systems Administration/Management** *32 students enrolled* ● **Gunsmithing/Gunsmith** *9 students enrolled* ● **Heating, Air Conditioning, Ventilation and Refrigeration Maintenance Technology/Technician (HAC, HACR, HVAC, HVACR)** *16 students enrolled* ● **Information Technology** *1 student enrolled* ● **Mechanical Engineering/Mechanical Technology/Technician** ● **Medical Office Management/Administration** *3 students enrolled* ● **Nurse/Nursing Assistant/Aide and Patient Care Assistant** *12 students enrolled* ● **Office Management and Supervision** *22 students enrolled* ● **Phlebotomy/Phlebotomist** *29 students enrolled* ● **Pre-Nursing Studies** ● **Web Page, Digital/Multimedia and Information Resources Design** ● **Welding Technology/Welder** *17 students enrolled*

STUDENT SERVICES Academic or career counseling, daycare for children of students, employment services for current students, placement services for program completers, remedial services.

Pinnacle Institute of Cosmetology

113 Water Street, Statesville, NC 28677
http://pinnacleinst.com/

CONTACT Don Anderson, President
Telephone: 704-235-0185

GENERAL INFORMATION Private Institution. Founded 1985. **Total program enrollment:** 44.

PROGRAM(S) OFFERED
● **Cosmetology, Barber/Styling, and Nail Instructor** *800 hrs./$6650*
● **Cosmetology/Cosmetologist, General** *1500 hrs./$15,400* ● **Nail Technician/Specialist and Manicurist** *300 hrs./$4050*

STUDENT SERVICES Academic or career counseling, placement services for program completers.

Pitt Community College

Highway 11 South, PO Drawer 7007, Greenville, NC 27835-7007
http://www.pittcc.edu/

CONTACT G. Dennis Massey, President
Telephone: 252-493-7200

GENERAL INFORMATION Public Institution. Founded 1961. **Accreditation:** Regional (SACS/CC); diagnostic medical sonography (JRCEDMS); health information technology (AHIMA); medical assisting (AAMAE); radiologic technology: radiography (JRCERT). **Total program enrollment:** 3822.

PROGRAM(S) OFFERED
● **Accounting** 2 students enrolled ● **Allied Health Diagnostic, Intervention, and Treatment Professions, Other** 22 students enrolled ● **Architectural Engineering Technology/Technician** 1 student enrolled ● **Automobile/Automotive Mechanics Technology/Technician** ● **Building/Construction Finishing, Management, and Inspection, Other** 1 student enrolled ● **Business Administration and Management, General** ● **Cardiovascular Technology/Technologist** ● **Computer Programming/Programmer, General** 9 students enrolled ● **Computer Systems Networking and Telecommunications** ● **Cosmetology/Cosmetologist, General** 3 students enrolled ● **Criminal Justice/Police Science** 33 students enrolled ● **Early Childhood Education and Teaching** 12 students enrolled ● **Electrical, Electronic and Communications Engineering Technology/Technician** 7 students enrolled ● **Electrical/Electronics Maintenance and Repair Technology, Other** ● **Electrician** 1 student enrolled ● **Electromechanical and Instrumentation and Maintenance Technologies/Technicians, Other** 3 students enrolled ● **Greenhouse Operations and Management** 7 students enrolled ● **Health Information/Medical Records Technology/Technician** 5 students enrolled ● **Health Professions and Related Clinical Sciences, Other** ● **Health Services/Allied Health/Health Sciences, General** 1 student enrolled ● **Health Unit Coordinator/Ward Clerk** 28 students enrolled ● **Heating, Air Conditioning, Ventilation and Refrigeration Maintenance Technology/Technician (HAC, HACR, HVAC, HVACR)** ● **Human Resources Management/Personnel Administration, General** ● **Information Science/Studies** ● **Information Technology** 2 students enrolled ● **Machine Shop Technology/Assistant** ● **Marketing/Marketing Management, General** ● **Mason/Masonry** 2 students enrolled ● **Mechanical Engineering/Mechanical Technology/Technician** ● **Medical Office Management/Administration** 16 students enrolled ● **Medical Radiologic Technology/Science—Radiation Therapist** 21 students enrolled ● **Medical/Clinical Assistant** 15 students enrolled ● **Nuclear Medical Technology/Technologist** 13 students enrolled ● **Office Management and Supervision** 3 students enrolled ● **Radiologic Technology/Science—Radiographer** 9 students enrolled ● **Real Estate** ● **Substance Abuse/Addiction Counseling** 6 students enrolled ● **System, Networking, and LAN/WAN Management/Manager** ● **Welding Technology/Welder** 40 students enrolled

STUDENT SERVICES Academic or career counseling, daycare for children of students, employment services for current students, placement services for program completers, remedial services.

Randolph Community College

PO Box 1009, Asheboro, NC 27204-1009
http://www.randolph.edu/

CONTACT Dr. Robert S. Shackleford, Jr., President
Telephone: 336-633-0200

GENERAL INFORMATION Public Institution. Founded 1962. **Accreditation:** Regional (SACS/CC). **Total program enrollment:** 791.

PROGRAM(S) OFFERED
● **Autobody/Collision and Repair Technology/Technician** 1 student enrolled ● **Automobile/Automotive Mechanics Technology/Technician** ● **Criminal Justice/Police Science** 21 students enrolled ● **Criminal Justice/Safety Studies** 1 student enrolled ● **Early Childhood Education and Teaching** 8 students enrolled ● **Electrician** 1 student enrolled ● **Entrepreneurship/Entrepreneurial Studies** ● **Health/Health Care Administration/Management** ● **Industrial Mechanics and Maintenance Technology** ● **Interior Design** 3 students enrolled ● **Machine Shop Technology/Assistant** 1 student enrolled ● **Office Management and Supervision** 1 student enrolled

STUDENT SERVICES Academic or career counseling, employment services for current students, placement services for program completers, remedial services.

Regency Beauty Institute–Charlotte

9101 Kings Parade Boulevard, Charlotte, NC 28273

CONTACT J. Hayes Batson
Telephone: 704-936-1591

GENERAL INFORMATION Private Institution. **Total program enrollment:** 42. **Application fee:** $100.

PROGRAM(S) OFFERED
● **Cosmetology/Cosmetologist, General** 1500 hrs./$16,011

STUDENT SERVICES Academic or career counseling, placement services for program completers.

Richmond Community College

PO Box 1189, Hamlet, NC 28345-1189
http://www.richmondcc.edu/

CONTACT Dr. Sharon Morrissey, President
Telephone: 910-410-1700

GENERAL INFORMATION Public Institution. Founded 1964. **Accreditation:** Regional (SACS/CC). **Total program enrollment:** 796.

PROGRAM(S) OFFERED
● **Business Administration and Management, General** 6 students enrolled ● **Child Development** 2 students enrolled ● **Criminal Justice/Safety Studies** 1 student enrolled ● **Early Childhood Education and Teaching** 8 students enrolled ● **Education, General** ● **Electrician** ● **Electromechanical and Instrumentation and Maintenance Technologies/Technicians, Other** 2 students enrolled ● **Foodservice Systems Administration/Management** 20 students enrolled ● **Information Science/Studies** ● **Licensed Practical/Vocational Nurse Training (LPN, LVN, Cert, Dipl, AAS)** 17 students enrolled ● **Machine Shop Technology/Assistant** 4 students enrolled ● **Mechanical Engineering/Mechanical Technology/Technician** 4 students enrolled ● **Nurse/Nursing Assistant/Aide and Patient Care Assistant** 9 students enrolled ● **Office Management and Supervision** 2 students enrolled

STUDENT SERVICES Academic or career counseling, employment services for current students, placement services for program completers, remedial services.

Roanoke Bible College

715 North Poindexter Street, Elizabeth City, NC 27909-4054
http://www.roanokebible.edu/

CONTACT D. Clay Perkins, President
Telephone: 252-334-2000

GENERAL INFORMATION Private Institution. Founded 1948. **Accreditation:** Regional (SACS/CC); state accredited or approved. **Total program enrollment:** 125. **Application fee:** $50.

PROGRAM(S) OFFERED
● **Bible/Biblical Studies** 1 student enrolled ● **Teaching English as a Second or Foreign Language/ESL Language Instructor**

STUDENT SERVICES Academic or career counseling, employment services for current students, placement services for program completers, remedial services.

Roanoke-Chowan Community College

109 Community College Road, Ahoskie, NC 27910
http://www.roanokechowan.edu/

CONTACT Dr. Ralph G. Soney, President
Telephone: 252-862-1200

GENERAL INFORMATION Public Institution. Founded 1967. **Accreditation:** Regional (SACS/CC). **Total program enrollment:** 295.

Roanoke-Chowan Community College (continued)

PROGRAM(S) OFFERED
• Accounting Technology/Technician and Bookkeeping • Accounting *19 students enrolled* • Architectural Engineering Technology/Technician • Barbering/Barber *1 student enrolled* • Building/Construction Finishing, Management, and Inspection, Other *16 students enrolled* • Business Administration and Management, General *36 students enrolled* • Cosmetology and Related Personal Grooming Arts, Other • Cosmetology/Cosmetologist, General *3 students enrolled* • Electromechanical Technology/Electromechanical Engineering Technology • Electromechanical and Instrumentation and Maintenance Technologies/Technicians, Other *4 students enrolled* • Health Information/Medical Records Technology/Technician • Health Professions and Related Clinical Sciences, Other • Heating, Air Conditioning, Ventilation and Refrigeration Maintenance Technology/Technician (HAC, HACR, HVAC, HVACR) *23 students enrolled* • Nail Technician/Specialist and Manicurist *2 students enrolled* • Nursing—Registered Nurse Training (RN, ASN, BSN, MSN) *17 students enrolled* • Plumbing Technology/Plumber *19 students enrolled* • Psychiatric/Mental Health Services Technician • Welding Technology/Welder *4 students enrolled*

STUDENT SERVICES Academic or career counseling, placement services for program completers, remedial services.

Robeson Community College

PO Box 1420, 5160 Fayetteville Road, Lumberton, NC 28359-1420
http://www.robeson.cc.nc.us/

CONTACT Dr. Charles V. Chrestman, President
Telephone: 910-272-3700

GENERAL INFORMATION Public Institution. Founded 1965. **Accreditation:** Regional (SACS/CC). **Total program enrollment:** 1072.

PROGRAM(S) OFFERED
• Carpentry/Carpenter *33 students enrolled* • Cosmetology/Cosmetologist, General *7 students enrolled* • Criminal Justice/Police Science *39 students enrolled* • Electrician *10 students enrolled* • Electromechanical and Instrumentation and Maintenance Technologies/Technicians, Other *1 student enrolled* • Heating, Air Conditioning, Ventilation and Refrigeration Maintenance Technology/Technician (HAC, HACR, HVAC, HVACR) *58 students enrolled* • Nurse/Nursing Assistant/Aide and Patient Care Assistant *24 students enrolled* • Surgical Technology/Technologist *6 students enrolled*

STUDENT SERVICES Academic or career counseling, employment services for current students, placement services for program completers, remedial services.

Rockingham Community College

PO Box 38, Wentworth, NC 27375-0038
http://www.rcc.cc.nc.us/

CONTACT Robert C. Keys, President
Telephone: 336-342-4261

GENERAL INFORMATION Public Institution. Founded 1964. **Accreditation:** Regional (SACS/CC). **Total program enrollment:** 916.

PROGRAM(S) OFFERED
• Applied Horticulture/Horticulture Operations, General *1 student enrolled* • Business Administration and Management, General *1 student enrolled* • Clinical/Medical Laboratory Science and Allied Professions, Other *9 students enrolled* • Computer Systems Networking and Telecommunications • Cosmetology/Cosmetologist, General *11 students enrolled* • Criminal Justice/Police Science *25 students enrolled* • Early Childhood Education and Teaching *5 students enrolled* • Electrical and Electronic Engineering Technologies/Technicians, Other *1 student enrolled* • Electrical, Electronic and Communications Engineering Technology/Technician • Executive Assistant/Executive Secretary *3 students enrolled* • Heating, Air Conditioning, Ventilation and Refrigeration Maintenance Technology/Technician (HAC, HACR, HVAC, HVACR) *3 students enrolled* • Heavy/Industrial Equipment Maintenance Technologies, Other *10 students enrolled* • Human Resources Management/Personnel Administration, General • Information Technology • Licensed Practical/Vocational Nurse Training (LPN, LVN, Cert, Dipl, AAS) *28 students enrolled* • Machine Shop Technology/Assistant *11 students enrolled* • Medical

• Office Management/Administration *6 students enrolled* • Surgical Technology/Technologist *11 students enrolled* • Tool and Die Technology/Technician *4 students enrolled* • Woodworking, General

STUDENT SERVICES Academic or career counseling, daycare for children of students, employment services for current students, placement services for program completers, remedial services.

Rowan-Cabarrus Community College

PO Box 1595, Salisbury, NC 28145-1595
http://www.rowancabarrus.edu/

CONTACT Dr. Carol Spalding, President
Telephone: 704-216-3602

GENERAL INFORMATION Public Institution. Founded 1963. **Accreditation:** Regional (SACS/CC); dental assisting (ADA); radiologic technology: radiography (JRCERT). **Total program enrollment:** 1751.

PROGRAM(S) OFFERED
• Accounting • Aesthetician/Esthetician and Skin Care Specialist *21 students enrolled* • Automobile/Automotive Mechanics Technology/Technician • Building/Property Maintenance and Management • Business Administration and Management, General *6 students enrolled* • Business Administration, Management and Operations, Other *4 students enrolled* • Child Development • Computer Programming/Programmer, General • Computer Systems Networking and Telecommunications *12 students enrolled* • Cosmetology, Barber/Styling, and Nail Instructor *1 student enrolled* • Cosmetology/Cosmetologist, General *9 students enrolled* • Criminal Justice/Police Science *48 students enrolled* • Criminal Justice/Safety Studies • Dental Assisting/Assistant *17 students enrolled* • Early Childhood Education and Teaching *7 students enrolled* • Electrician *2 students enrolled* • Elementary Education and Teaching *4 students enrolled* • Heating, Air Conditioning, Ventilation and Refrigeration Maintenance Technology/Technician (HAC, HACR, HVAC, HVACR) *59 students enrolled* • Industrial Electronics Technology/Technician *17 students enrolled* • Information Science/Studies *6 students enrolled* • Information Technology *3 students enrolled* • Licensed Practical/Vocational Nurse Training (LPN, LVN, Cert, Dipl, AAS) *22 students enrolled* • Machine Shop Technology/Assistant *4 students enrolled* • Marketing/Marketing Management, General *6 students enrolled* • Mechanical Drafting and Mechanical Drafting CAD/CADD *6 students enrolled* • Medical Office Management/Administration *8 students enrolled* • Nail Technician/Specialist and Manicurist *13 students enrolled* • Office Management and Supervision *4 students enrolled* • System, Networking, and LAN/WAN Management/Manager • Welding Technology/Welder *38 students enrolled*

STUDENT SERVICES Academic or career counseling, daycare for children of students, employment services for current students, placement services for program completers, remedial services.

Sampson Community College

PO Box 318, 1801 Sunset Avenue, Highway 24 West, Clinton, NC 28329-0318
http://www.sampsoncc.edu/

CONTACT William Aiken, President
Telephone: 910-592-8081 Ext. 2017

GENERAL INFORMATION Public Institution. Founded 1965. **Accreditation:** Regional (SACS/CC). **Total program enrollment:** 504.

PROGRAM(S) OFFERED
• Accounting *8 students enrolled* • Animal/Livestock Husbandry and Production *18 students enrolled* • Applied Horticulture/Horticulture Operations, General • Building/Construction Finishing, Management, and Inspection, Other *23 students enrolled* • Business Administration and Management, General *10 students enrolled* • Computer and Information Systems Security *3 students enrolled* • Cosmetology, Barber/Styling, and Nail Instructor • Cosmetology/Cosmetologist, General *11 students enrolled* • Criminal Justice/Police Science *8 students enrolled* • Criminal Justice/Safety Studies • Early Childhood Education and Teaching *110 students enrolled* • Electromechanical and Instrumentation and Maintenance Technologies/Technicians, Other • Elementary Education and Teaching • Heating, Air Conditioning, Ventilation and Refrigeration Maintenance Technology/Technician (HAC, HACR, HVAC, HVACR) *10 students enrolled* • Information Technology • Licensed Practical/Vocational Nurse Training (LPN, LVN, Cert, Dipl, AAS) *19 students enrolled* • Nail Technician/

Specialist and Manicurist • Office Management and Supervision *10 students enrolled* • System, Networking, and LAN/WAN Management/Manager *1 student enrolled* • Welding Technology/Welder *11 students enrolled*

STUDENT SERVICES Academic or career counseling, employment services for current students, placement services for program completers, remedial services.

Sandhills Community College

3395 Airport Road, Pinehurst, NC 28374-8299
http://www.sandhills.edu/

CONTACT John Dempsey, President
Telephone: 910-692-6185

GENERAL INFORMATION Public Institution. Founded 1963. **Accreditation:** Regional (SACS/CC); medical laboratory technology (NAACLS); radiologic technology: radiography (JRCERT). **Total program enrollment:** 1849.

PROGRAM(S) OFFERED
• Aesthetician/Esthetician and Skin Care Specialist *15 students enrolled* • Autobody/Collision and Repair Technology/Technician *2 students enrolled* • Automobile/Automotive Mechanics Technology/Technician *1 student enrolled* • Business Administration and Management, General *14 students enrolled* • Computer Engineering Technology/Technician *3 students enrolled* • Cosmetology and Related Personal Grooming Arts, Other • Cosmetology, Barber/Styling, and Nail Instructor *1 student enrolled* • Cosmetology/Cosmetologist, General *6 students enrolled* • Culinary Arts/Chef Training *1 student enrolled* • Early Childhood Education and Teaching *35 students enrolled* • Electromechanical and Instrumentation and Maintenance Technologies/Technicians, Other • Information Science/Studies *1 student enrolled* • Information Technology • Licensed Practical/Vocational Nurse Training (LPN, LVN, Cert, Dipl, AAS) *25 students enrolled* • Management Information Systems and Services, Other • Massage Therapy/Therapeutic Massage *12 students enrolled* • Medical Office Management/Administration *2 students enrolled* • Surgical Technology/Technologist *11 students enrolled*

STUDENT SERVICES Academic or career counseling, employment services for current students, placement services for program completers, remedial services.

School of Communication Arts

3000 Wakefield Crossing Drive, Raleigh, NC 27614
http://www.higherdigital.com/

CONTACT Debra A. Hooper, Vice President
Telephone: 919-488-8500

GENERAL INFORMATION Private Institution. Founded 1992. **Accreditation:** State accredited or approved. **Total program enrollment:** 373. **Application fee:** $25.

PROGRAM(S) OFFERED
• Animation, Interactive Technology, Video Graphics and Special Effects *12 students enrolled* • Audiovisual Communications Technologies/Technicians, Other *25 students enrolled* • Cinematography and Film/Video Production *10 students enrolled* • Web Page, Digital/Multimedia and Information Resources Design *10 students enrolled*

STUDENT SERVICES Academic or career counseling, employment services for current students, placement services for program completers.

South College–Asheville

1567 Patton Avenue, Asheville, NC 28806
http://www.southcollegenc.com/

CONTACT Robert A. Davis, Executive Director
Telephone: 828-277-5521

GENERAL INFORMATION Private Institution. Founded 1905. **Accreditation:** State accredited or approved. **Total program enrollment:** 144. **Application fee:** $50.

PROGRAM(S) OFFERED
• Computer and Information Sciences, General • Medical Transcription/Transcriptionist *3 students enrolled* • Surgical Technology/Technologist *8 students enrolled*

STUDENT SERVICES Academic or career counseling, employment services for current students, placement services for program completers.

Southeastern Community College

PO Box 151, Whiteville, NC 28472-0151
http://www.sccnc.edu/

CONTACT Kathy Matlock, President
Telephone: 910-642-7141 Ext. 270

GENERAL INFORMATION Public Institution. Founded 1964. **Accreditation:** Regional (SACS/CC); medical laboratory technology (NAACLS). **Total program enrollment:** 778.

PROGRAM(S) OFFERED
• Aesthetician/Esthetician and Skin Care Specialist • Banking and Financial Support Services *5 students enrolled* • Business Administration and Management, General *20 students enrolled* • Cosmetology/Cosmetologist, General *1 student enrolled* • Criminal Justice/Police Science *8 students enrolled* • Customer Service Support/Call Center/Teleservice Operation *4 students enrolled* • E-Commerce/Electronic Commerce • Early Childhood Education and Teaching • Electrician *2 students enrolled* • Electromechanical and Instrumentation and Maintenance Technologies/Technicians, Other • Forestry Technology/Technician *2 students enrolled* • Heating, Air Conditioning, Ventilation and Refrigeration Maintenance Technology/Technician (HAC, HACR, HVAC, HVACR) *2 students enrolled* • Information Technology *5 students enrolled* • Licensed Practical/Vocational Nurse Training (LPN, LVN, Cert, Dipl, AAS) • Mason/Masonry *23 students enrolled* • Massage Therapy/Therapeutic Massage • Nail Technician/Specialist and Manicurist • Office Management and Supervision *2 students enrolled* • Pharmacy Technician/Assistant *4 students enrolled* • Phlebotomy/Phlebotomist *20 students enrolled* • Plumbing Technology/Plumber *29 students enrolled* • Special Education and Teaching, General • System, Networking, and LAN/WAN Management/Manager • Welding Technology/Welder

STUDENT SERVICES Academic or career counseling, daycare for children of students, employment services for current students, placement services for program completers, remedial services.

Southeastern School of Neuromuscular Therapy–Charlotte

4 Woodlawn Green, Suite 200, Charlotte, NC 28217
http://www.southeasternmassageschools.com

CONTACT Kimberly Williams, Vice President
Telephone: 704-527-4979

GENERAL INFORMATION Private Institution. **Total program enrollment:** 207. **Application fee:** $100.

PROGRAM(S) OFFERED
• Massage Therapy/Therapeutic Massage *500 hrs./$10,356*

STUDENT SERVICES Academic or career counseling, employment services for current students, placement services for program completers, remedial services.

South Piedmont Community College

PO Box 126, Polkton, NC 28135-0126
http://www.spcc.edu/

CONTACT Dr. John McKay, President
Telephone: 704-272-5300

GENERAL INFORMATION Public Institution. Founded 1962. **Accreditation:** Regional (SACS/CC); health information technology (AHIMA); medical assisting (AAMAE). **Total program enrollment:** 688.

South Piedmont Community College (continued)

PROGRAM(S) OFFERED
● Accounting Technology/Technician and Bookkeeping 5 *students enrolled*
● Autobody/Collision and Repair Technology/Technician 3 *students enrolled*
● Business Administration and Management, General 21 *students enrolled*
● Child Development 5 *students enrolled* ● Commercial and Advertising Art 26 *students enrolled* ● Computer Programming, Specific Applications ● Criminal Justice/Police Science 29 *students enrolled* ● Criminal Justice/Safety Studies
● Early Childhood Education and Teaching 2 *students enrolled* ● Electrician 5 *students enrolled* ● Electromechanical Technology/Electromechanical Engineering Technology ● Executive Assistant/Executive Secretary 4 *students enrolled* ● Food Preparation/Professional Cooking/Kitchen Assistant 12 *students enrolled* ● Heating, Air Conditioning, Ventilation and Refrigeration Maintenance Technology/Technician (HAC, HACR, HVAC, HVACR) 1 *student enrolled* ● Legal Assistant/Paralegal ● Licensed Practical/Vocational Nurse Training (LPN, LVN, Cert, Dipl, AAS) 16 *students enrolled* ● Management Information Systems, General ● Massage Therapy/Therapeutic Massage 14 *students enrolled* ● Mechanical Engineering/Mechanical Technology/Technician 14 *students enrolled* ● Medical Administrative/Executive Assistant and Medical Secretary 16 *students enrolled* ● Medical/Clinical Assistant 15 *students enrolled* ● Social Work 1 *student enrolled* ● Surgical Technology/Technologist 10 *students enrolled* ● Teacher Assistant/Aide

STUDENT SERVICES Academic or career counseling, remedial services.

Southwestern Community College

447 College Drive, Sylva, NC 28779
http://www.southwesterncc.edu/

CONTACT Cecil L. Groves, President
Telephone: 828-586-4091

GENERAL INFORMATION Public Institution. Founded 1964. **Accreditation:** Regional (SACS/CC); electroneurodiagnostic technology (JRCEND); health information technology (AHIMA); medical laboratory technology (NAACLS); physical therapy assisting (APTA); radiologic technology: radiography (JRCERT). **Total program enrollment:** 841.

PROGRAM(S) OFFERED
● Accounting 1 *student enrolled* ● Automobile/Automotive Mechanics Technology/Technician 1 *student enrolled* ● Business Administration and Management, General 2 *students enrolled* ● Carpentry/Carpenter ● Child Development 15 *students enrolled* ● Computer Systems Networking and Telecommunications 1 *student enrolled* ● Cosmetology/Cosmetologist, General 18 *students enrolled* ● Culinary Arts/Chef Training ● Diagnostic Medical Sonography/Sonographer and Ultrasound Technician 5 *students enrolled* ● Early Childhood Education and Teaching 3 *students enrolled* ● Education, Other 1 *student enrolled* ● Electrician 3 *students enrolled* ● Elementary Education and Teaching 2 *students enrolled* ● Executive Assistant/Executive Secretary 3 *students enrolled* ● Forensic Science and Technology ● Health Information/Medical Records Technology/Technician ● Heating, Air Conditioning, Ventilation and Refrigeration Maintenance Technology/Technician (HAC, HACR, HVAC, HVACR) ● Hotel/Motel Administration/Management 2 *students enrolled* ● Information Technology 1 *student enrolled* ● Licensed Practical/Vocational Nurse Training (LPN, LVN, Cert, Dipl, AAS) 9 *students enrolled* ● Massage Therapy/Therapeutic Massage 14 *students enrolled* ● Medical Transcription/Transcriptionist 4 *students enrolled* ● Nail Technician/Specialist and Manicurist ● Parks, Recreation and Leisure Studies 1 *student enrolled* ● Phlebotomy/Phlebotomist 2 *students enrolled* ● Real Estate ● Substance Abuse/Addiction Counseling 2 *students enrolled* ● Web/Multimedia Management and Webmaster 2 *students enrolled* ● Welding Technology/Welder 6 *students enrolled*

STUDENT SERVICES Academic or career counseling, employment services for current students, placement services for program completers, remedial services.

Stanly Community College

141 College Drive, Albemarle, NC 28001-7458
http://www.stanly.edu/

CONTACT Michael R. Taylor, President
Telephone: 704-982-0121

GENERAL INFORMATION Public Institution. Founded 1971. **Accreditation:** Regional (SACS/CC); medical assisting (AAMAE). **Total program enrollment:** 505.

PROGRAM(S) OFFERED
● Accounting 1 *student enrolled* ● Aesthetician/Esthetician and Skin Care Specialist 6 *students enrolled* ● Business Administration and Management, General 15 *students enrolled* ● Cardiovascular Technology/Technologist 2 *students enrolled* ● Commercial and Advertising Art 1 *student enrolled* ● Computer Engineering Technology/Technician 18 *students enrolled* ● Computer and Information Systems Security 1 *student enrolled* ● Cosmetology/Cosmetologist, General 38 *students enrolled* ● Criminal Justice/Police Science 22 *students enrolled* ● Criminal Justice/Safety Studies 3 *students enrolled* ● Early Childhood Education and Teaching 15 *students enrolled* ● Electrical, Electronic and Communications Engineering Technology/Technician 2 *students enrolled* ● Electrician 25 *students enrolled* ● Health Professions and Related Clinical Sciences, Other 21 *students enrolled* ● Heating, Air Conditioning, Ventilation and Refrigeration Maintenance Technology/Technician (HAC, HACR, HVAC, HVACR) 46 *students enrolled* ● Information Technology 20 *students enrolled* ● Medical/Clinical Assistant 18 *students enrolled* ● Nursing—Registered Nurse Training (RN, ASN, BSN, MSN) 8 *students enrolled* ● Special Education and Teaching, General 2 *students enrolled*

STUDENT SERVICES Academic or career counseling, employment services for current students, placement services for program completers, remedial services.

Surry Community College

630 South Main Street, PO Box 304, Dobson, NC 27017-8432
http://www.surry.cc.nc.us/

CONTACT Dr. Deborah Friedman, President
Telephone: 336-386-8121 Ext. 3264

GENERAL INFORMATION Public Institution. Founded 1965. **Accreditation:** Regional (SACS/CC). **Total program enrollment:** 1513.

PROGRAM(S) OFFERED
● Accounting 2 *students enrolled* ● Agriculture, Agriculture Operations and Related Sciences, Other ● Animal/Livestock Husbandry and Production ● Applied Horticulture/Horticultural Operations, General ● Autobody/Collision and Repair Technology/Technician 2 *students enrolled* ● Automobile/Automotive Mechanics Technology/Technician 3 *students enrolled* ● Business Administration and Management, General 1 *student enrolled* ● Carpentry/Carpenter ● Child Development 7 *students enrolled* ● Computer Programming/Programmer, General ● Cosmetology/Cosmetologist, General ● Early Childhood Education and Teaching 9 *students enrolled* ● Electrician ● Electromechanical and Instrumentation and Maintenance Technologies/Technicians, Other ● Elementary Education and Teaching 2 *students enrolled* ● Heating, Air Conditioning, Ventilation and Refrigeration Maintenance Technology/Technician (HAC, HACR, HVAC, HVACR) ● Information Science/Studies 2 *students enrolled* ● Information Technology ● Language Interpretation and Translation 1 *student enrolled* ● Licensed Practical/Vocational Nurse Training (LPN, LVN, Cert, Dipl, AAS) 20 *students enrolled* ● Machine Shop Technology/Assistant 1 *student enrolled* ● Mechanical Drafting and Mechanical Drafting CAD/CADD ● Medical Office Management/Administration ● Office Management and Supervision ● Real Estate ● System, Networking, and LAN/WAN Management/Manager ● Welding Technology/Welder

STUDENT SERVICES Academic or career counseling, employment services for current students, placement services for program completers, remedial services.

Tri-County Community College

4600 East US 64, Murphy, NC 28906-7919
http://www.tricountycc.edu/

CONTACT Donna Tipton-Rogers, President
Telephone: 828-837-6810

GENERAL INFORMATION Public Institution. Founded 1964. **Accreditation:** Regional (SACS/CC). **Total program enrollment:** 391.

PROGRAM(S) OFFERED
● Accounting Technology/Technician and Bookkeeping ● Automobile/Automotive Mechanics Technology/Technician ● Business Administration and Management, General 1 *student enrolled* ● Cosmetology/Cosmetologist, General ● Electrician 1 *student enrolled* ● Executive Assistant/Executive Secretary ● Heating, Air Conditioning, Ventilation and Refrigeration

Maintenance Technology/Technician (HAC, HACR, HVAC, HVACR) 1 student enrolled • Special Education and Teaching, General 3 students enrolled • Teacher Assistant/Aide • Welding Technology/Welder 1 student enrolled

STUDENT SERVICES Academic or career counseling, daycare for children of students, employment services for current students, placement services for program completers, remedial services.

The University of North Carolina

910 Raleigh Road, PO Box 2688, Chapel Hill, NC 27515-2688
http://www.ga.unc.edu/

CONTACT Erskine Bowles, President
Telephone: 919-962-1000

GENERAL INFORMATION Public Institution.

The University of North Carolina at Chapel Hill

Chapel Hill, NC 27599
http://www.unc.edu/

CONTACT Holden Thorp, Chancellor
Telephone: 919-962-2211

GENERAL INFORMATION Public Institution. Founded 1789. **Accreditation:** Regional (SACS/CC); athletic training (JRCAT); audiology (ASHA); counseling (ACA); dental assisting (ADA); dental hygiene (ADA); engineering-related programs (ABET/RAC); journalism and mass communications (ACEJMC); library and information science (ALA); medical technology (NAACLS); radiologic technology: radiation therapy technology (JRCERT); radiologic technology: radiography (JRCERT); recreation and parks (NRPA); speech-language pathology (ASHA). **Total program enrollment:** 23788. **Application fee:** $70.

PROGRAM(S) OFFERED
• Cytotechnology/Cytotechnologist 3 students enrolled • Dental Assisting/Assistant • Dental Hygiene/Hygienist 16 students enrolled • Medical Radiologic Technology/Science—Radiation Therapist • Nuclear Medical Technology/Technologist

STUDENT SERVICES Academic or career counseling, employment services for current students, placement services for program completers.

Vance-Granville Community College

PO Box 917, Henderson, NC 27536-0917
http://www.vgcc.cc.nc.us/

CONTACT Randy Parker, President
Telephone: 252-492-2061

GENERAL INFORMATION Public Institution. Founded 1969. **Accreditation:** Regional (SACS/CC); radiologic technology: radiography (JRCERT). **Total program enrollment:** 1148.

PROGRAM(S) OFFERED
• Automobile/Automotive Mechanics Technology/Technician 9 students enrolled • Business Administration and Management, General 17 students enrolled • Carpentry/Carpenter 3 students enrolled • Child Care and Support Services Management 8 students enrolled • Computer and Information Sciences, General 21 students enrolled • Cosmetology and Related Personal Grooming Arts, Other • Cosmetology/Cosmetologist, General 9 students enrolled • Criminal Justice/Police Science 9 students enrolled • Electrician 13 students enrolled • Electromechanical Technology/Electromechanical Engineering Technology 4 students enrolled • Executive Assistant/Executive Secretary 37 students enrolled • Heating, Air Conditioning, Ventilation and Refrigeration Maintenance Technology/Technician (HAC, HACR, HVAC, HVACR) 1 student enrolled • Licensed Practical/Vocational Nurse Training (LPN, LVN, Cert, Dipl,

AAS) 32 students enrolled • Medical/Clinical Assistant 17 students enrolled • Pharmacy Technician/Assistant 13 students enrolled • Teacher Assistant/Aide 1 student enrolled • Welding Technology/Welder 8 students enrolled

STUDENT SERVICES Academic or career counseling, daycare for children of students, employment services for current students, placement services for program completers, remedial services.

Wake Technical Community College

9101 Fayetteville Road, Raleigh, NC 27603-5696
http://www.waketech.edu/

CONTACT Stephen C. Scott, President
Telephone: 919-866-5500

GENERAL INFORMATION Public Institution. Founded 1958. **Accreditation:** Regional (SACS/CC); dental assisting (ADA); dental hygiene (ADA); engineering technology (ABET/TAC); medical laboratory technology (NAACLS); radiologic technology: radiography (JRCERT). **Total program enrollment:** 3936.

PROGRAM(S) OFFERED
• Accounting 8 students enrolled • Allied Health Diagnostic, Intervention, and Treatment Professions, Other • Architectural Engineering Technology/Technician 13 students enrolled • Automobile/Automotive Mechanics Technology/Technician 1 student enrolled • Building/Property Maintenance and Management 9 students enrolled • Business Administration and Management, General 11 students enrolled • Civil Engineering Technology/Technician • Commercial and Advertising Art 14 students enrolled • Computer Engineering Technology/Technician • Computer Programming/Programmer, General • Computer Systems Networking and Telecommunications 7 students enrolled • Computer and Information Sciences and Support Services, Other • Computer and Information Sciences, Other • Criminal Justice/Police Science 42 students enrolled • Culinary Arts/Chef Training 5 students enrolled • Data Modeling/Warehousing and Database Administration 3 students enrolled • Dental Assisting/Assistant 11 students enrolled • Diesel Mechanics Technology/Technician 3 students enrolled • E-Commerce/Electronic Commerce 4 students enrolled • Early Childhood Education and Teaching 140 students enrolled • Electrical, Electronic and Communications Engineering Technology/Technician 2 students enrolled • Electrical/Electronics Maintenance and Repair Technology, Other • Electrician 1 student enrolled • Electromechanical and Instrumentation and Maintenance Technologies/Technicians, Other • Foodservice Systems Administration/Management 2 students enrolled • Heating, Air Conditioning, Ventilation and Refrigeration Maintenance Technology/Technician (HAC, HACR, HVAC, HVACR) 3 students enrolled • Hotel/Motel Administration/Management 1 student enrolled • Human Resources Management/Personnel Administration, General 12 students enrolled • Industrial Electronics Technology/Technician • Information Science/Studies 15 students enrolled • Information Technology 18 students enrolled • Legal Administrative Assistant/Secretary • Machine Shop Technology/Assistant • Management Information Systems, General • Massage Therapy/Therapeutic Massage 8 students enrolled • Mechanical Drafting and Mechanical Drafting CAD/CADD • Mechanical Engineering/Mechanical Technology/Technician 1 student enrolled • Medical Office Management/Administration 25 students enrolled • Medical/Clinical Assistant 17 students enrolled • Office Management and Supervision 18 students enrolled • Pharmacy Technician/Assistant 1 student enrolled • Phlebotomy/Phlebotomist 18 students enrolled • Plastics Engineering Technology/Technician 2 students enrolled • Plumbing Technology/Plumber • Robotics Technology/Technician • Special Education and Teaching, General • Substance Abuse/Addiction Counseling 2 students enrolled • Surgical Technology/Technologist 8 students enrolled • Survey Technology/Surveying 1 student enrolled • Telecommunications Technology/Technician 1 student enrolled • Tool and Die Technology/Technician • Welding Technology/Welder 7 students enrolled

STUDENT SERVICES Academic or career counseling, employment services for current students, placement services for program completers, remedial services.

Wayne Community College

PO Box 8002, Goldsboro, NC 27533-8002
http://www.waynecc.edu/

CONTACT Dr. Kay H. Albertson, President
Telephone: 919-735-5151

GENERAL INFORMATION Public Institution. Founded 1957. **Accreditation:** Regional (SACS/CC); dental assisting (ADA); dental hygiene (ADA); medical assisting (AAMAE). **Total program enrollment:** 1548.

PROGRAM(S) OFFERED
● **Agribusiness/Agricultural Business Operations** ● **Animal/Livestock Husbandry and Production** 1 student enrolled ● **Autobody/Collision and Repair Technology/Technician** 3 students enrolled ● **Avionics Maintenance Technology/Technician** 11 students enrolled ● **Business Administration and Management, General** ● **Child Development** 3 students enrolled ● **Computer Systems Networking and Telecommunications** 1 student enrolled ● **Cosmetology/Cosmetologist, General** 3 students enrolled ● **Criminal Justice/Police Science** 18 students enrolled ● **Dental Assisting/Assistant** 14 students enrolled ● **Early Childhood Education and Teaching** 7 students enrolled ● **Electromechanical and Instrumentation and Maintenance Technologies/Technicians, Other** 2 students enrolled ● **Executive Assistant/Executive Secretary** ● **Fire Protection, Other** 5 students enrolled ● **Heating, Air Conditioning, Ventilation and Refrigeration Maintenance Technology/Technician (HAC, HACR, HVAC, HVACR)** 6 students enrolled ● **Information Science/Studies** 1 student enrolled ● **Information Technology** 1 student enrolled ● **Licensed Practical/Vocational Nurse Training (LPN, LVN, Cert, Dipl, AAS)** 12 students enrolled ● **Machine Shop Technology/Assistant** ● **Medical Office Management/Administration** 15 students enrolled ● **Medical Transcription/Transcriptionist** 2 students enrolled ● **Phlebotomy/Phlebotomist** 13 students enrolled ● **Welding Technology/Welder** 2 students enrolled

STUDENT SERVICES Academic or career counseling, daycare for children of students, employment services for current students, placement services for program completers, remedial services.

Western Piedmont Community College

1001 Burkemont Avenue, Morganton, NC 28655-4511
http://www.wpcc.edu/

CONTACT Jim Burnett, President
Telephone: 828-438-6141

GENERAL INFORMATION Public Institution. Founded 1964. **Accreditation:** Regional (SACS/CC); dental assisting (ADA); medical assisting (AAMAE); medical laboratory technology (NAACLS). **Total program enrollment:** 1153.

PROGRAM(S) OFFERED
● **Accounting Technology/Technician and Bookkeeping** 4 students enrolled ● **Applied Horticulture/Horticultural Operations, General** 6 students enrolled ● **Building/Construction Finishing, Management, and Inspection, Other** 14 students enrolled ● **Business Administration and Management, General** 41 students enrolled ● **Child Care and Support Services Management** 8 students enrolled ● **Civil Engineering Technology/Technician** ● **Computer Systems Analysis/Analyst** 11 students enrolled ● **Computer Technology/Computer Systems Technology** 2 students enrolled ● **Criminal Justice/Police Science** 80 students enrolled ● **Dental Assisting/Assistant** 15 students enrolled ● **Environmental Science** 1 student enrolled ● **Executive Assistant/Executive Secretary** 9 students enrolled ● **Interior Design** 4 students enrolled ● **Legal Assistant/Paralegal** 1 student enrolled ● **Machine Shop Technology/Assistant** ● **Mechanical Engineering/Mechanical Technology/Technician** ● **Medical Administrative/Executive Assistant and Medical Secretary** 3 students enrolled ● **Medical/Clinical Assistant** 20 students enrolled ● **Operations Management and Supervision** 1 student enrolled ● **Substance Abuse/Addiction Counseling** ● **Upholstery/Upholsterer** 4 students enrolled ● **Welding Technology/Welder**

STUDENT SERVICES Academic or career counseling, employment services for current students, placement services for program completers, remedial services.

Wilkes Community College

1328 Collegiate Drive, PO Box 120, Wilkesboro, NC 28697
http://www.wilkescc.edu/

CONTACT Gordon Burns, President
Telephone: 336-838-6100

GENERAL INFORMATION Public Institution. Founded 1965. **Accreditation:** Regional (SACS/CC); dental assisting (ADA). **Total program enrollment:** 1082.

PROGRAM(S) OFFERED
● **Accounting** 6 students enrolled ● **Applied Horticulture/Horticultural Operations, General** 1 student enrolled ● **Architectural Engineering Technology/Technician** ● **Autobody/Collision and Repair Technology/Technician** 6 students enrolled ● **Automobile/Automotive Mechanics Technology/Technician** 9 students enrolled ● **Building/Construction Finishing, Management, and Inspection, Other** ● **Business Administration and Management, General** 2 students enrolled ● **Computer Programming/Programmer, General** 1 student enrolled ● **Computer Systems Networking and Telecommunications** ● **Criminal Justice/Police Science** 33 students enrolled ● **Criminal Justice/Safety Studies** ● **Culinary Arts/Chef Training** 3 students enrolled ● **Dental Assisting/Assistant** 15 students enrolled ● **Diesel Mechanics Technology/Technician** ● **Early Childhood Education and Teaching** ● **Electrical, Electronic and Communications Engineering Technology/Technician** ● **Electromechanical and Instrumentation and Maintenance Technologies/Technicians, Other** 10 students enrolled ● **Elementary Education and Teaching** ● **Health Professions and Related Clinical Sciences, Other** ● **Information Science/Studies** ● **Information Technology** 1 student enrolled ● **Marketing/Marketing Management, General** 2 students enrolled ● **Medical/Clinical Assistant** 1 student enrolled ● **Office Management and Supervision** 1 student enrolled ● **Radio and Television Broadcasting Technology/Technician** ● **System, Networking, and LAN/WAN Management/Manager** 6 students enrolled ● **Welding Technology/Welder** 2 students enrolled

STUDENT SERVICES Academic or career counseling, daycare for children of students, employment services for current students, placement services for program completers, remedial services.

Wilson Community College

902 Herring Avenue, PO Box 4305, Wilson, NC 27893-3310
http://www.wilsoncc.edu/

CONTACT Rusty Stephens, President
Telephone: 252-291-1195

GENERAL INFORMATION Public Institution. Founded 1958. **Accreditation:** Regional (SACS/CC). **Total program enrollment:** 761.

PROGRAM(S) OFFERED
● **Allied Health Diagnostic, Intervention, and Treatment Professions, Other** 1 student enrolled ● **Automobile/Automotive Mechanics Technology/Technician** 3 students enrolled ● **Business Administration and Management, General** 1 student enrolled ● **Cosmetology/Cosmetologist, General** 1 student enrolled ● **Criminal Justice/Police Science** 23 students enrolled ● **Diesel Mechanics Technology/Technician** 1 student enrolled ● **Early Childhood Education and Teaching** 74 students enrolled ● **Electrician** 3 students enrolled ● **Elementary Education and Teaching** 10 students enrolled ● **Executive Assistant/Executive Secretary** 2 students enrolled ● **Fire Protection and Safety Technology/Technician** 1 student enrolled ● **Heating, Air Conditioning, Ventilation and Refrigeration Maintenance Technology/Technician (HAC, HACR, HVAC, HVACR)** 9 students enrolled ● **Heavy Equipment Maintenance Technology/Technician** 3 students enrolled ● **Information Technology** 4 students enrolled ● **Licensed Practical/Vocational Nurse Training (LPN, LVN, Cert, Dipl, AAS)** 22 students enrolled ● **Mechanical Engineering/Mechanical Technology/Technician** 5 students enrolled ● **Renal/Dialysis Technologist/Technician** 8 students enrolled ● **Sign Language Interpretation and Translation** 1 student enrolled ● **Surgical Technology/Technologist** 8 students enrolled ● **Vehicle Maintenance and Repair Technologies, Other** 2 students enrolled ● **Welding Technology/Welder** 2 students enrolled

STUDENT SERVICES Academic or career counseling, employment services for current students, placement services for program completers, remedial services.

Winston-Salem Barber School

1531 Silas Creek Parkway, Winston-Salem, NC 27127-3757

CONTACT Joseph A. Long, President
Telephone: 336-724-1459

GENERAL INFORMATION Private Institution. Founded 1935. **Total program enrollment:** 33. **Application fee:** $20.

PROGRAM(S) OFFERED
● **Barbering/Barber** *1528 hrs./$6520*

STUDENT SERVICES Academic or career counseling, placement services for program completers, remedial services.

OHIO

Academy of Court Reporting

2930 West Market Street, Akron, OH 44333
http://www.acr.edu/

CONTACT J. P. Schippert, Director
Telephone: 330-867-4030

GENERAL INFORMATION Private Institution. **Total program enrollment:** 71. **Application fee:** $25.

PROGRAM(S) OFFERED
● **Legal Administrative Assistant/Secretary** *1 student enrolled*

STUDENT SERVICES Academic or career counseling, placement services for program completers.

Academy of Court Reporting

2044 Euclid Avenue, Cleveland, OH 44115
http://www.acr.edu/

CONTACT Lynn M. Mizanin, CRI/CPE, Campus Director
Telephone: 216-861-3222

GENERAL INFORMATION Private Institution. Founded 1970. **Accreditation:** State accredited or approved. **Total program enrollment:** 95. **Application fee:** $100.

STUDENT SERVICES Academic or career counseling, employment services for current students, placement services for program completers, remedial services.

Academy of Court Reporting

630 East Broad Street, Columbus, OH 43215
http://www.acr.edu/

CONTACT Joanie Krein, Director
Telephone: 614-221-7770

GENERAL INFORMATION Private Institution. **Total program enrollment:** 148. **Application fee:** $25.

PROGRAM(S) OFFERED
● **Legal Administrative Assistant/Secretary** *3 students enrolled*

STUDENT SERVICES Academic or career counseling, employment services for current students, placement services for program completers.

Adult and Community Education–Hudson

100 Arcadia Avenue, Columbus, OH 43202
http://www.columbus.k12.oh.us/north_ed/index

CONTACT Dr. Gene Harris, Superintendent
Telephone: 614-365-6000 Ext. 244

GENERAL INFORMATION Public Institution. Founded 1953. **Total program enrollment:** 108.

PROGRAM(S) OFFERED
● **Automobile/Automotive Mechanics Technology/Technician** *900 hrs./$6075*
● **Boilermaking/Boilermaker** *128 hrs./$900* ● **Business/Office Automation/Technology/Data Entry** *720 hrs./$4575* ● **Data Processing and Data Processing Technology/Technician** *5 students enrolled* ● **Heating, Air Conditioning and Refrigeration Technology/Technician (ACH/ACR/ACHR/HRAC/HVAC/AC Technology)** *900 hrs./$7375* ● **Heating, Air Conditioning, Ventilation and Refrigeration Maintenance Technology/Technician (HAC, HACR, HVAC, HVACR)** *10 students enrolled* ● **Licensed Practical/Vocational Nurse Training (LPN, LVN, Cert, Dipl, AAS)** *1440 hrs./$11,875* ● **Nurse/Nursing Assistant/Aide and Patient Care Assistant** *86 hrs./$600*

STUDENT SERVICES Academic or career counseling, employment services for current students, remedial services.

Adult Center for Education

400 Richards Road, Zanesville, OH 43701
http://www.mid-east.k12.oh.us/

CONTACT William Bussey, Superintendent
Telephone: 740-455-3111

GENERAL INFORMATION Private Institution. **Total program enrollment:** 146. **Application fee:** $25.

PROGRAM(S) OFFERED
● **Automobile/Automotive Mechanics Technology/Technician** *3 students enrolled* ● **Building/Property Maintenance and Management** *12 students enrolled* ● **Business Operations Support and Secretarial Services, Other** *600 hrs./$4920* ● **Criminal Justice/Law Enforcement Administration** *600 hrs./$4325* ● **Emergency Medical Technology/Technician (EMT Paramedic)** *800 hrs./$4290* ● **Fire Science/Firefighting** *13 students enrolled* ● **Heating, Air Conditioning, Ventilation and Refrigeration Maintenance Technology/Technician (HAC, HACR, HVAC, HVACR)** *600 hrs./$4750* ● **Licensed Practical/Vocational Nurse Training (LPN, LVN, Cert, Dipl, AAS)** *1248 hrs./$8150* ● **Medical Office Computer Specialist/Assistant** *600 hrs./$3900* ● **Medical Reception/Receptionist** *22 students enrolled* ● **Nurse/Nursing Assistant/Aide and Patient Care Assistant** *236 students enrolled*

STUDENT SERVICES Academic or career counseling, daycare for children of students, placement services for program completers, remedial services.

Akron Adult Vocational Services

147 Park Street, Akron, OH 44308
http://akronschools.com/

CONTACT Minnie Carter-Page, Coordinator
Telephone: 330-761-1385

GENERAL INFORMATION Private Institution.

PROGRAM(S) OFFERED
● **Accounting Technology/Technician and Bookkeeping** *910 hrs./$6370* ● **Accounting** *24 students enrolled* ● **Administrative Assistant and Secretarial Science, General** ● **Automobile/Automotive Mechanics Technology/Technician** *987 hrs./$6909* ● **Business Administration and Management, General** *10 students enrolled* ● **Computer and Information Sciences and Support Services, Other** *13 students enrolled* ● **Construction Trades, Other** *7 students enrolled* ● **Emergency Medical Technology/Technician (EMT Paramedic)** *180 hrs./$980* ● **General Office Occupations and Clerical Services** *910 hrs./$6370* ● **Industrial Mechanics and Maintenance Technology** *16 students enrolled* ● **Machine Shop Technology/Assistant** ● **Mason/Masonry** *9 students enrolled* ● **Mechanic and Repair Technologies/Technicians, Other** ● **Nurse/Nursing**

Akron Adult Vocational Services (continued)

Assistant/Aide and Patient Care Assistant 716 hrs./$6038 • **Plumbing Technology/Plumber** 8 students enrolled • **Tool and Die Technology/Technician** 5 students enrolled • **Welding Technology/Welder** 81 hrs./$730

STUDENT SERVICES Academic or career counseling, employment services for current students, remedial services.

Akron Institute

1625 Portage Trail, Cuyahoga Falls, OH 44223
http://www.akroninstitute.com/

CONTACT David L. LaRue, Campus President
Telephone: 330-724-1600

GENERAL INFORMATION Private Institution. Founded 1970. **Total program enrollment:** 614.

PROGRAM(S) OFFERED
• **Computer and Information Sciences, General** 6 students enrolled • **Dental Assisting/Assistant** 28 students enrolled • **General Office Occupations and Clerical Services** 13 students enrolled • **Medical Administrative/Executive Assistant and Medical Secretary** 63 students enrolled • **Medical/Clinical Assistant** 62 students enrolled

STUDENT SERVICES Academic or career counseling, employment services for current students, placement services for program completers, remedial services.

Akron School of Practical Nursing

619 Sumner Street, Akron, OH 44311

CONTACT Anna Maria Glorioso, Director
Telephone: 330-761-3255

GENERAL INFORMATION Public Institution. Founded 1951. **Total program enrollment:** 56. **Application fee:** $35.

PROGRAM(S) OFFERED
• **Licensed Practical/Vocational Nurse Training (LPN, LVN, Cert, Dipl, AAS)** 1200 hrs./$9850

STUDENT SERVICES Academic or career counseling, placement services for program completers, remedial services.

American Institute of Alternative Medicine

6685 Doubletree Avenue, Columbus, OH 43229
http://www.aiam.edu/

CONTACT Linda Fleming-Willis, Director of Administration
Telephone: 614-825-6255

GENERAL INFORMATION Private Institution. **Total program enrollment:** 62. **Application fee:** $75.

PROGRAM(S) OFFERED
• **Massage Therapy/Therapeutic Massage** 28 students enrolled • **Traditional Chinese/Asian Medicine and Chinese Herbology** 1 student enrolled

STUDENT SERVICES Academic or career counseling, placement services for program completers, remedial services.

American School of Technology

2100 Morse Road, Columbus, OH 43229-6665
http://www.ast.edu/

CONTACT Timothy Campagna, President/CEO
Telephone: 614-436-4820

GENERAL INFORMATION Private Institution. **Total program enrollment:** 161.

PROGRAM(S) OFFERED
• **Heating, Air Conditioning, Ventilation and Refrigeration Maintenance Technology/Technician (HAC, HACR, HVAC, HVACR)** 24 hrs./$9120 • **Medical Insurance Coding Specialist/Coder** 480 hrs./$6080 • **Medical Office Assistant/Specialist** 72 students enrolled • **Medical/Clinical Assistant** 28 hrs./$11,615

STUDENT SERVICES Employment services for current students, placement services for program completers.

Antonelli College

124 East Seventh Street, Cincinnati, OH 45202-2592
http://www.antonellicollege.edu/

CONTACT Mary Ann Davis, President
Telephone: 513-241-4338

GENERAL INFORMATION Private Institution. Founded 1947. **Accreditation:** State accredited or approved. **Total program enrollment:** 201. **Application fee:** $100.

PROGRAM(S) OFFERED
• **Interior Design** 1 student enrolled

STUDENT SERVICES Academic or career counseling, employment services for current students, placement services for program completers, remedial services.

Apollo School of Practical Nursing

3325 Shawnee Road, Lima, OH 45806-1497
http://www.apollocareercenter.com/

CONTACT J. Chris Pfister, Superintendent
Telephone: 419-998-3000

GENERAL INFORMATION Public Institution. Founded 1976. **Total program enrollment:** 260. **Application fee:** $30.

PROGRAM(S) OFFERED
• **Allied Health and Medical Assisting Services, Other** 10 students enrolled • **Building/Property Maintenance and Management** 7 students enrolled • **Child Care and Support Services Management** 6 students enrolled • **Construction Trades, General** 1 student enrolled • **Criminal Justice/Police Science** 11 students enrolled • **General Office Occupations and Clerical Services** 3 students enrolled • **Industrial Mechanics and Maintenance Technology** 900 hrs./$10,990 • **Licensed Practical/Vocational Nurse Training (LPN, LVN, Cert, Dipl, AAS)** 1376 hrs./$9200 • **Manufacturing Engineering** 8 students enrolled • **Manufacturing Technology/Technician** 900 hrs./$10,990 • **Nurse/Nursing Assistant/Aide and Patient Care Assistant** 76 hrs./$650 • **Surgical Technology/Technologist** 1100 hrs./$8700 • **System, Networking, and LAN/WAN Management/Manager** • **Truck and Bus Driver/Commercial Vehicle Operation** 240 hrs./$4800

STUDENT SERVICES Academic or career counseling, employment services for current students, placement services for program completers, remedial services.

Ashland University

401 College Avenue, Ashland, OH 44805-3702
http://www.exploreashland.com/

CONTACT Dr. Fred Finks, President
Telephone: 419-289-4142

GENERAL INFORMATION Private Institution (Affiliated with Brethren Church). Founded 1878. **Accreditation:** Regional (NCA); home economics (AAFCS); music (NASM). **Total program enrollment:** 3829.

PROGRAM(S) OFFERED
• **Business Administration and Management, General** 36 students enrolled • **Business/Commerce, General** 93 students enrolled • **General Office Occupations and Clerical Services** 15 students enrolled • **Hospitality Administration/**

Management, General *17 students enrolled* ● **Office Management and Supervision** *16 students enrolled* ● **Religion/Religious Studies** ● **Retailing and Retail Operations** *20 students enrolled* ● **Theology/Theological Studies** *21 students enrolled*

STUDENT SERVICES Academic or career counseling, employment services for current students, placement services for program completers.

Ashtabula County Joint Vocational School

1565 State Route 167, Jefferson, OH 44047
http://www.acjvs.org/

CONTACT Jerome R. Brockway, Superintendent
Telephone: 440-576-6015

GENERAL INFORMATION Public Institution. Founded 1969. **Total program enrollment:** 103. **Application fee:** $25.

PROGRAM(S) OFFERED
● **Automobile/Automotive Mechanics Technology/Technician** *990 hrs./$5400* ● **Business Operations Support and Secretarial Services, Other** *600 hrs./$3900* ● **Cosmetology/Cosmetologist, General** *1500 hrs./$7850* ● **Electrician** *300 hrs./$2875* ● **Heating, Air Conditioning, Ventilation and Refrigeration Maintenance Technology/Technician (HAC, HACR, HVAC, HVACR)** *600 hrs./$5890* ● **Machine Tool Technology/Machinist** *5 students enrolled* ● **Nursing, Other** *1500 hrs./$9010* ● **Welding Technology/Welder** *7 students enrolled*

STUDENT SERVICES Placement services for program completers, remedial services.

ATS Institute of Technology

230 Alpha Park, Highland Heights, OH 44143
http://www.atsinstitute.com/

CONTACT Yelena Bykov, School Director
Telephone: 440-449-1700

GENERAL INFORMATION Private Institution. **Accreditation:** State accredited or approved. **Total program enrollment:** 383. **Application fee:** $30.

PROGRAM(S) OFFERED
● **Nursing, Other** *113 students enrolled*

STUDENT SERVICES Academic or career counseling, employment services for current students, placement services for program completers, remedial services.

Auburn Career Center

8140 Auburn Road, Painesville, OH 44077
http://www.auburncc.org/

CONTACT G. Thomas Schultz, Superintendent
Telephone: 800-544-9750 Ext. 8017

GENERAL INFORMATION Public Institution. Founded 1965. **Total program enrollment:** 209. **Application fee:** $100.

PROGRAM(S) OFFERED
● **Automobile/Automotive Mechanics Technology/Technician** *600 hrs./$3550* ● **Building/Construction Finishing, Management, and Inspection, Other** *600 hrs./$3442* ● **Building/Property Maintenance and Management** *19 students enrolled* ● **Construction Trades, Other** *7 students enrolled* ● **Culinary Arts/Chef Training** *625 hrs./$4987* ● **Electrical/Electronics Equipment Installation and Repair, General** *17 students enrolled* ● **Emergency Medical Technology/Technician (EMT Paramedic)** *10 students enrolled* ● **Fire Science/Firefighting** *25 students enrolled* ● **Heating, Air Conditioning, Ventilation and Refrigeration Maintenance Technology/Technician (HAC, HACR, HVAC, HVACR)** *600 hrs./$4013* ● **Industrial Mechanics and Maintenance Technology** ● **Licensed**

Practical/Vocational Nurse Training (LPN, LVN, Cert, Dipl, AAS) *1200 hrs./$10,800* ● **Machine Tool Technology/Machinist** *8 students enrolled* ● **Welding Technology/Welder** *420 hrs./$3400*

STUDENT SERVICES Academic or career counseling, employment services for current students, placement services for program completers, remedial services.

Aveda Fredric's Institute

3654 Edwards Road, Cincinnati, OH 45208

GENERAL INFORMATION Private Institution. **Total program enrollment:** 188. **Application fee:** $50.

PROGRAM(S) OFFERED
● **Aesthetician/Esthetician and Skin Care Specialist** *750 hrs./$7250* ● **Cosmetology/Cosmetologist, General** *1500 hrs./$15,950* ● **Nail Technician/Specialist and Manicurist** *300 hrs./$3265* ● **Salon/Beauty Salon Management/Manager** *300 hrs./$1095*

Baldwin-Wallace College

275 Eastland Road, Berea, OH 44017-2088
http://www.bw.edu/

CONTACT Richard W. Durst, President
Telephone: 440-826-2900

GENERAL INFORMATION Private Institution. Founded 1845. **Accreditation:** Regional (NCA); music (NASM). **Total program enrollment:** 3464. **Application fee:** $25.

PROGRAM(S) OFFERED
● **Accounting** *1 student enrolled* ● **Communication Studies/Speech Communication and Rhetoric** *1 student enrolled* ● **Computer Software and Media Applications, Other** *1 student enrolled* ● **Computer Systems Networking and Telecommunications** ● **Human Resources Management/Personnel Administration, General** *18 students enrolled*

STUDENT SERVICES Academic or career counseling, employment services for current students, remedial services.

Belmont Technical College

120 Fox Shannon Place, St. Clairsville, OH 43950-9735
http://www.btc.edu/

CONTACT Joseph E. Bukowski, President
Telephone: 740-695-9500

GENERAL INFORMATION Public Institution. Founded 1971. **Accreditation:** Regional (NCA); medical assisting (AAMAE). **Total program enrollment:** 1215.

PROGRAM(S) OFFERED
● **Accounting Technology/Technician and Bookkeeping** *4 students enrolled* ● **Administrative Assistant and Secretarial Science, General** *1 student enrolled* ● **Computer Programming/Programmer, General** *2 students enrolled* ● **Heating, Air Conditioning and Refrigeration Technology/Technician (ACH/ACR/ACHR/HRAC/HVAC/AC Technology)** *3 students enrolled* ● **Licensed Practical/Vocational Nurse Training (LPN, LVN, Cert, Dipl, AAS)** *58 students enrolled* ● **Medical Insurance Coding Specialist/Coder** *17 students enrolled* ● **Medical Transcription/Transcriptionist** *9 students enrolled* ● **Medical/Clinical Assistant** *1 student enrolled* ● **Welding Technology/Welder** *2 students enrolled*

STUDENT SERVICES Academic or career counseling, daycare for children of students, employment services for current students, placement services for program completers, remedial services.

Bohecker College–Cincinnati

11499 Chester Road, Suite 200, Cincinnati, OH 45246

CONTACT David Rose, Campus Director
Telephone: 513-771-2795

GENERAL INFORMATION Private Institution. **Total program enrollment:** 468. **Application fee:** $100.

PROGRAM(S) OFFERED
• **Allied Health and Medical Assisting Services, Other** • **Medical Insurance Specialist/Medical Biller** 22 students enrolled • **Medical Office Assistant/Specialist** 29 students enrolled

STUDENT SERVICES Academic or career counseling, employment services for current students, placement services for program completers, remedial services.

Bohecker College–Columbus

4151 Executive Parkway, Suite 240, Westerville, OH 43081
http://www.boheckercollege.edu

CONTACT Martin Ehrenberg, School President
Telephone: 614-882-2551

GENERAL INFORMATION Private Institution. **Total program enrollment:** 1020. **Application fee:** $100.

PROGRAM(S) OFFERED
• **Allied Health and Medical Assisting Services, Other** 100 students enrolled
• **Medical Insurance Specialist/Medical Biller** 27 students enrolled

STUDENT SERVICES Academic or career counseling, employment services for current students, placement services for program completers.

Bohecker College–Ravenna

653 Enterprise Parkway, Ravenna, OH 44266
http://www.boheckercollege.edu/

CONTACT Trudy Diehl, Financial Aid Director
Telephone: 330-297-7319 Ext. 1110

GENERAL INFORMATION Private Institution. **Accreditation:** State accredited or approved. **Total program enrollment:** 469. **Application fee:** $60.

PROGRAM(S) OFFERED
• **Computer Software and Media Applications, Other** • **Heating, Air Conditioning and Refrigeration Technology/Technician (ACH/ACR/ACHR/HRAC/HVAC/AC Technology)** 39 students enrolled • **Licensed Practical/Vocational Nurse Training (LPN, LVN, Cert, Dipl, AAS)** 46 students enrolled • **Medical Insurance Coding Specialist/Coder** 14 students enrolled

STUDENT SERVICES Academic or career counseling, employment services for current students, placement services for program completers.

Bowling Green State University–Firelands College

One University Drive, Huron, OH 44839-9791
http://www.firelands.bgsu.edu/

CONTACT James M. Smith, Interim Dean
Telephone: 419-433-5560

GENERAL INFORMATION Public Institution. Founded 1968. **Accreditation:** Regional (NCA); health information technology (AHIMA). **Total program enrollment:** 1190. **Application fee:** $40.

PROGRAM(S) OFFERED
• **Accounting and Related Services, Other** 2 students enrolled • **Business Administration and Management, General** 2 students enrolled • **Business/Office Automation/Technology/Data Entry** 2 students enrolled

STUDENT SERVICES Academic or career counseling, employment services for current students, placement services for program completers, remedial services.

Bradford School

2469 Stelzer Road, Columbus, OH 43219
http://www.bradfordschoolcolumbus.edu/

CONTACT Dennis Bartels, President
Telephone: 614-416-6200

GENERAL INFORMATION Private Institution. Founded 1911. **Accreditation:** State accredited or approved. **Total program enrollment:** 575. **Application fee:** $50.

PROGRAM(S) OFFERED
• **Accounting Technology/Technician and Bookkeeping** • **Administrative Assistant and Secretarial Science, General** • **Computer Programming/Programmer, General** 3 students enrolled • **Graphic Design** 25 students enrolled • **Legal Administrative Assistant/Secretary** 1 student enrolled • **Medical/Clinical Assistant** 20 students enrolled • **Tourism and Travel Services Management** 1 student enrolled

STUDENT SERVICES Academic or career counseling, placement services for program completers.

Brown Aveda Institute

8816 Mentor Avenue, Mentor, OH 44060
http://www.brownaveda.com/

CONTACT Edward Brown, Chief Financial Officer
Telephone: 440-255-9494 Ext. 212

GENERAL INFORMATION Private Institution. **Total program enrollment:** 118. **Application fee:** $50.

PROGRAM(S) OFFERED
• **Aesthetician/Esthetician and Skin Care Specialist** 600 hrs./$8000
• **Cosmetology/Cosmetologist, General** 1500 hrs./$13,500 • **Salon/Beauty Salon Management/Manager** 750 hrs./$9600

STUDENT SERVICES Academic or career counseling, placement services for program completers.

Brown Aveda Institute

19336 Detroit Road, Rocky River, OH 44116
http://www.brownaveda.com

CONTACT Edward Brown, Chief Financial Officer
Telephone: 440-255-9494 Ext. 212

GENERAL INFORMATION Private Institution. **Total program enrollment:** 117. **Application fee:** $50.

PROGRAM(S) OFFERED
• **Aesthetician/Esthetician and Skin Care Specialist** 600 hrs./$8000
• **Cosmetology/Cosmetologist, General** 1500 hrs./$13,500 • **Salon/Beauty Salon Management/Manager** 750 hrs./$9600

STUDENT SERVICES Academic or career counseling, placement services for program completers.

Brown Mackie College–Akron

755 White Pond Drive, Suite 101, Akron, OH 44320
http://www.brownmackie.edu/Akron/

CONTACT Rick Reikob, President
Telephone: 330-869-3600 Ext. 51

GENERAL INFORMATION Private Institution. Founded 1968. **Accreditation:** Medical assisting (AAMAE); state accredited or approved. **Total program enrollment:** 852.

PROGRAM(S) OFFERED
● Accounting ● Business Administration and Management, General ● Business/Office Automation/Technology/Data Entry ● Computer Programming/Programmer, General ● Criminal Justice/Law Enforcement Administration ● Legal Assistant/Paralegal 1 student enrolled ● Medical/Clinical Assistant 1 student enrolled ● Nurse/Nursing Assistant/Aide and Patient Care Assistant 89 students enrolled

STUDENT SERVICES Academic or career counseling, employment services for current students, placement services for program completers, remedial services.

Brown Mackie College–Cincinnati

1011 Glendale-Milford Road, Cincinnati, OH 45215
http://www.brownmackie.edu/Cincinnati/

CONTACT Robin Krout, Campus President
Telephone: 513-771-2424

GENERAL INFORMATION Private Institution. Founded 1927. **Accreditation:** Medical assisting (AAMAE); state accredited or approved. **Total program enrollment:** 1621.

PROGRAM(S) OFFERED
● Accounting Technology/Technician and Bookkeeping ● Business/Commerce, General 1 student enrolled ● CAD/CADD Drafting and/or Design Technology/Technician ● Cinematography and Film/Video Production 2 students enrolled ● Computer Programming, Other ● Computer Systems Networking and Telecommunications 1 student enrolled ● Computer and Information Sciences and Support Services, Other ● Criminal Justice/Law Enforcement Administration 1 student enrolled ● Legal Assistant/Paralegal 1 student enrolled ● Medical/Clinical Assistant 2 students enrolled ● Nursing, Other 179 students enrolled

STUDENT SERVICES Academic or career counseling, employment services for current students, placement services for program completers, remedial services.

Brown Mackie College–Findlay

1700 Fostoria Avenue, Suite 100, Findlay, OH 45840
http://www.brownmackie.edu/Findlay/

CONTACT Wayne Korpics, President
Telephone: 419-423-2211

GENERAL INFORMATION Private Institution. Founded 1929. **Accreditation:** State accredited or approved. **Total program enrollment:** 790.

PROGRAM(S) OFFERED
● Business Administration and Management, General ● Criminal Justice/Law Enforcement Administration ● Legal Assistant/Paralegal ● Licensed Practical/Vocational Nurse Training (LPN, LVN, Cert, Dipl, AAS) 133 students enrolled ● Medical Transcription/Transcriptionist 6 students enrolled ● Medical/Clinical Assistant 2 students enrolled ● Office Management and Supervision

STUDENT SERVICES Academic or career counseling, employment services for current students, placement services for program completers, remedial services.

Brown Mackie College–North Canton

4300 Munson Street NW, Canton, OH 44718-3674
http://www.brownmackie.edu/NorthCanton/

CONTACT Peter J. Perkowski, Campus President
Telephone: 330-494-1214

GENERAL INFORMATION Private Institution. Founded 1929. **Accreditation:** State accredited or approved. **Total program enrollment:** 1293.

PROGRAM(S) OFFERED
● Accounting and Related Services, Other 1 student enrolled ● Business Administration and Management, General 1 student enrolled ● Criminal Justice/Safety Studies ● Drafting and Design Technology/Technician, General ● Legal Assistant/Paralegal ● Medical/Clinical Assistant 8 students enrolled ● Nurse/Nursing Assistant/Aide and Patient Care Assistant 65 students enrolled

STUDENT SERVICES Academic or career counseling, employment services for current students, placement services for program completers, remedial services.

Buckeye Hills Career Center

PO Box 157, Rio Grande, OH 45674
http://bhcc.k12.oh.us/

CONTACT D. Kent Lewis, Superintendent
Telephone: 740-245-5334

GENERAL INFORMATION Public Institution. Founded 1975. **Total program enrollment:** 151. **Application fee:** $25.

PROGRAM(S) OFFERED
● Building/Property Maintenance and Management 600 hrs./$3200 ● Corrections and Criminal Justice, Other 12 students enrolled ● Criminal Justice/Police Science 600 hrs./$3300 ● Fire Science/Firefighting ● Health Professions and Related Clinical Sciences, Other ● Heavy/Industrial Equipment Maintenance Technologies, Other 12 students enrolled ● Industrial Mechanics and Maintenance Technology 600 hrs./$3500 ● Licensed Practical/Vocational Nurse Training (LPN, LVN, Cert, Dipl, AAS) 1382 hrs./$7030 ● Medical Administrative/Executive Assistant and Medical Secretary 18 students enrolled ● Nurse/Nursing Assistant/Aide and Patient Care Assistant 48 students enrolled ● Pharmacy Technician/Assistant 600 hrs./$2800 ● Surgical Technology/Technologist 1265 hrs./$4600

STUDENT SERVICES Academic or career counseling, employment services for current students, placement services for program completers, remedial services.

Buckeye Joint Vocational School

545 University Drive NE, New Philadelphia, OH 44663-9450
http://www.buckeyecareercenter.org/

CONTACT Paul Hickman, Superintendent
Telephone: 330-308-5720

GENERAL INFORMATION Public Institution. **Total program enrollment:** 120. **Application fee:** $30.

PROGRAM(S) OFFERED
● Allied Health and Medical Assisting Services, Other 900 hrs./$4500 ● Autobody/Collision and Repair Technology/Technician ● Automobile/Automotive Mechanics Technology/Technician 900 hrs./$4500 ● Cosmetology/Cosmetologist, General ● Criminal Justice/Police Science 11 students enrolled ● Electrical, Electronic and Communications Engineering Technology/Technician ● General Office Occupations and Clerical Services 9 students enrolled ● Legal Administrative Assistant/Secretary 900 hrs./$4500 ● Licensed Practical/Vocational Nurse Training (LPN, LVN, Cert, Dipl, AAS) 1200 hrs./$10,225 ● Lineworker 750 hrs./$3750 ● Medical Office Assistant/Specialist 900 hrs./$4500 ● Medical/Clinical Assistant 15 students enrolled

STUDENT SERVICES Academic or career counseling, employment services for current students, placement services for program completers, remedial services.

Butler Technology and Career Development Schools–D. Russel Lee Career-Technology Center

3603 Hamilton-Middletown Road, Hamilton, OH 45011
http://www.butlertech.org/

CONTACT Robert D. Sommers, CEO
Telephone: 513-645-8205

GENERAL INFORMATION Public Institution. Founded 1975. **Total program enrollment:** 422. **Application fee:** $25.

PROGRAM(S) OFFERED
• **Allied Health and Medical Assisting Services, Other** 6 *students enrolled* • **Business Operations Support and Secretarial Services, Other** 16 *students enrolled* • **Corrections and Criminal Justice, Other** 70 *students enrolled* • **Criminal Justice/Law Enforcement Administration** 630 *hrs./$4687* • **Data Processing and Data Processing Technology/Technician** 4 *students enrolled* • **Emergency Medical Technology/Technician (EMT Paramedic)** 800 *hrs./$4120* • **Fire Protection, Other** 626 *hrs./$5066* • **Heating, Air Conditioning, Ventilation and Refrigeration Maintenance Technology/Technician (HAC, HACR, HVAC, HVACR)** 600 *hrs./$5443* • **Industrial Mechanics and Maintenance Technology** 10 *students enrolled* • **Licensed Practical/Vocational Nurse Training (LPN, LVN, Cert, Dipl, AAS)** 1400 *hrs./$11,449* • **Welding Technology/Welder** 600 *hrs./$6575*

STUDENT SERVICES Academic or career counseling, remedial services.

Carnegie Career College

1292 Waterloo Road, Suffield, OH 44260
http://carnegieinstitute.net/

GENERAL INFORMATION Private Institution. **Total program enrollment:** 114.

PROGRAM(S) OFFERED
• **Forensic Science and Technology** 75 *hrs./$12,000* • **Massage Therapy/Therapeutic Massage** 750 *hrs./$11,120* • **Medical/Clinical Assistant** 910 *hrs./$6900* • **Substance Abuse/Addiction Counseling** 69 *hrs./$10,960*

STUDENT SERVICES Academic or career counseling, employment services for current students, placement services for program completers, remedial services.

Carousel Beauty College

125 East Second Street, Dayton, OH 45402
http://carouselbeauty.com/

CONTACT Don Yearwood, President
Telephone: 937-223-3572 Ext. 221

GENERAL INFORMATION Private Institution. **Total program enrollment:** 31.

PROGRAM(S) OFFERED
• **Cosmetology/Cosmetologist, General** 1500 *hrs./$9625* • **Nail Technician/Specialist and Manicurist** 200 *hrs./$1300*

STUDENT SERVICES Academic or career counseling, placement services for program completers.

Carousel Beauty College

3120 Woodman Drive, Kettering, OH 45420
http://carouselbeauty.com/

CONTACT Don F. Yearwood, Jr., President
Telephone: 937-223-3572 Ext. 221

GENERAL INFORMATION Private Institution. **Total program enrollment:** 35.

PROGRAM(S) OFFERED
• **Cosmetology/Cosmetologist, General** 1500 *hrs./$11,125* • **Nail Technician/Specialist and Manicurist** 200 *hrs./$1300*

STUDENT SERVICES Placement services for program completers.

Carousel Beauty College

633 South Breil Boulevard, Middletown, OH 45044

CONTACT Don Yearwood, President
Telephone: 937-223-3572 Ext. 221

GENERAL INFORMATION Private Institution. Founded 1959. **Total program enrollment:** 29.

PROGRAM(S) OFFERED
• **Cosmetology/Cosmetologist, General** 1500 *hrs./$11,125* • **Nail Technician/Specialist and Manicurist** 200 *hrs./$1300*

STUDENT SERVICES Placement services for program completers.

Carousel Beauty College

1475 Upper Valley Pike, Springfield, OH 45504
http://carouselbeauty.com/

CONTACT Don F. Yearwood, Jr., President
Telephone: 937-223-3572 Ext. 221

GENERAL INFORMATION Private Institution. **Total program enrollment:** 25.

PROGRAM(S) OFFERED
• **Cosmetology/Cosmetologist, General** 1500 *hrs./$11,125* • **Nail Technician/Specialist and Manicurist** 200 *hrs./$1300*

STUDENT SERVICES Placement services for program completers.

Carousel of Miami Valley Beauty College

7809 Waynetowne Boulevard, Huber Heights, OH 45424
http://carouselbeauty.com/

CONTACT Don Yearwood, President
Telephone: 937-223-3572 Ext. 221

GENERAL INFORMATION Private Institution. **Total program enrollment:** 40.

PROGRAM(S) OFFERED
• **Cosmetology/Cosmetologist, General** 1500 *hrs./$11,125* • **Nail Technician/Specialist and Manicurist** 200 *hrs./$1300*

STUDENT SERVICES Academic or career counseling, placement services for program completers.

Casal Aveda Institute

6000 Mahoning Avenue, Austintown Plaza, Austintown, OH 44515

CONTACT Deborah Bayless, Director
Telephone: 330-792-6504 Ext. 103

GENERAL INFORMATION Private Institution. Founded 1990. **Total program enrollment:** 171. **Application fee:** $30.

PROGRAM(S) OFFERED
• **Aesthetician/Esthetician and Skin Care Specialist** 600 *hrs./$6150* • **Cosmetology and Related Personal Grooming Arts, Other** 14 *students enrolled* • **Cosmetology/Cosmetologist, General** 1800 *hrs./$13,628* • **Nail Technician/Specialist and Manicurist** 300 *hrs./$1900* • **Technical Teacher Education** 1000 *hrs./$5950*

STUDENT SERVICES Academic or career counseling, placement services for program completers.

Cedarville University

251 North Main Street, Cedarville, OH 45314-0601
http://www.cedarville.edu/

CONTACT Dr. Bill Brown, President
Telephone: 937-766-2211

GENERAL INFORMATION Private Institution. Founded 1887. **Accreditation:** Regional (NCA). **Total program enrollment:** 2871. **Application fee:** $30.

PROGRAM(S) OFFERED
• Bible/Biblical Studies

STUDENT SERVICES Academic or career counseling, employment services for current students, placement services for program completers.

Central Ohio Technical College

1179 University Drive, Newark, OH 43055-1767
http://www.cotc.edu/

CONTACT Bonnie L. Coe, PhD, President
Telephone: 740-366-1351

GENERAL INFORMATION Public Institution. Founded 1971. **Accreditation:** Regional (NCA); diagnostic medical sonography (JRCEDMS); radiologic technology: radiography (JRCERT); surgical technology (ARCST). **Total program enrollment:** 1777. **Application fee:** $20.

PROGRAM(S) OFFERED
• Licensed Practical/Vocational Nurse Training (LPN, LVN, Cert, Dipl, AAS) *57 students enrolled* • Surgical Technology/Technologist *28 students enrolled*

STUDENT SERVICES Academic or career counseling, daycare for children of students, employment services for current students, placement services for program completers, remedial services.

Central School of Practical Nursing

4600 Carnegie Avenue, Cleveland, OH 44103
http://www.cspnohio.org/

CONTACT Alberta Plocica, Executive Director
Telephone: 216-391-8434

GENERAL INFORMATION Private Institution. **Total program enrollment:** 86.

PROGRAM(S) OFFERED
• Licensed Practical/Vocational Nurse Training (LPN, LVN, Cert, Dipl, AAS) *1240 hrs./$9975*

STUDENT SERVICES Academic or career counseling.

Chancellor University

3921 Chester Avenue, Cleveland, OH 44114-4624
http://www.myers.edu/

CONTACT Mr. George Kidd, President
Telephone: 216-391-6937

GENERAL INFORMATION Private Institution. Founded 1848. **Accreditation:** Regional (NCA). **Total program enrollment:** 220. **Application fee:** $100.

PROGRAM(S) OFFERED
• Accounting • Business Administration, Management and Operations, Other • Criminal Justice/Law Enforcement Administration • Financial Planning and Services • Health/Health Care Administration/Management • Human Resources Management/Personnel Administration, General • Legal Assistant/Paralegal *3 students enrolled* • Marketing/Marketing Management, General *1 student enrolled* • Public Administration

STUDENT SERVICES Academic or career counseling, employment services for current students, placement services for program completers, remedial services.

Choffin Career Center

200 East Wood Street, Youngstown, OH 44503
http://www.choffincareers.com/

CONTACT Denise Vaclav-Danko, Administrative Specialist
Telephone: 330-744-8710

GENERAL INFORMATION Public Institution. Founded 1973. **Total program enrollment:** 96. **Application fee:** $25.

PROGRAM(S) OFFERED
• Clinical/Medical Laboratory Assistant • Construction Trades, General • Dental Assisting/Assistant *25 students enrolled* • Dental Hygiene/Hygienist • Licensed Practical/Vocational Nurse Training (LPN, LVN, Cert, Dipl, AAS) *18 students enrolled* • Nurse/Nursing Assistant/Aide and Patient Care Assistant *24 students enrolled* • Pharmacy Technician/Assistant • Phlebotomy/Phlebotomist *35 students enrolled* • Precision Metal Working, Other • Surgical Technology/Technologist *13 students enrolled* • Welding Technology/Welder

STUDENT SERVICES Academic or career counseling, placement services for program completers, remedial services.

Cincinnati State Technical and Community College

3520 Central Parkway, Cincinnati, OH 45223-2690
http://www.cincinnatistate.edu/

CONTACT John Henderson, EdD, Interim President
Telephone: 513-569-1500

GENERAL INFORMATION Public Institution. Founded 1966. **Accreditation:** Regional (NCA); engineering technology (ABET/TAC); health information technology (AHIMA); medical assisting (AAMAE); medical laboratory technology (NAACLS); surgical technology (ARCST). **Total program enrollment:** 3332.

PROGRAM(S) OFFERED
• Accounting *7 students enrolled* • Athletic Training/Trainer *2 students enrolled* • Automotive Engineering Technology/Technician • Avionics Maintenance Technology/Technician *5 students enrolled* • Baking and Pastry Arts/Baker/Pastry Chef *7 students enrolled* • Business Administration and Management, General *1 student enrolled* • Business Operations Support and Secretarial Services, Other *4 students enrolled* • Business/Office Automation/Technology/Data Entry *2 students enrolled* • Child Care Provider/Assistant *4 students enrolled* • Child Care and Support Services Management *2 students enrolled* • Civil Engineering Technology/Technician • Communications Technologies/Technicians and Support Services, Other • Computer Installation and Repair Technology/Technician *4 students enrolled* • Culinary Arts/Chef Training *17 students enrolled* • Diagnostic Medical Sonography/Sonographer and Ultrasound Technician • Dietetic Technician (DTR) *1 student enrolled* • Dietetics/Dietitians • Electrical and Electronic Engineering Technologies/Technicians, Other *7 students enrolled* • Emergency Medical Technology/Technician (EMT Paramedic) *7 students enrolled* • Environmental Engineering Technology/Environmental Technology • Health Information/Medical Records Technology/Technician *1 student enrolled* • Health Unit Coordinator/Ward Clerk *15 students enrolled* • Human Resources Management/Personnel Administration, General • Human Services, General *13 students enrolled* • Instrumentation Technology/Technician *7 students enrolled* • Landscaping and Groundskeeping *4 students enrolled* • Legal Assistant/Paralegal *8 students enrolled* • Manufacturing Technology/Technician *5 students enrolled* • Mechanical Engineering/Mechanical Technology/Technician *4 students enrolled* • Medical Insurance Coding Specialist/Coder *3 students enrolled* • Medical/Clinical Assistant *21 students enrolled* • Parks, Recreation, Leisure and Fitness Studies, Other *1 student enrolled* • Platemaker/Imager *3 students enrolled* • Prepress/Desktop Publishing and Digital Imaging Design • Quality Control and Safety Technologies/Technicians, Other *9 students enrolled* • Sales, Distribution and Marketing Operations, General *5 students enrolled* • Sign Language Interpreta-

Cincinnati State Technical and Community College (continued)

tion and Translation *9 students enrolled* • **Survey Technology/Surveying** *1 student enrolled* • **Turf and Turfgrass Management** *1 student enrolled* • **Web Page, Digital/Multimedia and Information Resources Design**

STUDENT SERVICES Academic or career counseling, daycare for children of students, employment services for current students, placement services for program completers, remedial services.

Clark State Community College

570 East Leffel Lane, PO Box 570, Springfield, OH 45501-0570
http://www.clarkstate.edu/

CONTACT Karen E. Rafinski, PhD, President
Telephone: 937-325-0691

GENERAL INFORMATION Public Institution. Founded 1962. **Accreditation:** Regional (NCA); medical laboratory technology (NAACLS); physical therapy assisting (APTA). **Total program enrollment:** 1351. **Application fee:** $15.

PROGRAM(S) OFFERED
• **Accounting Technology/Technician and Bookkeeping** *6 students enrolled* • **Business Administration and Management, General** *4 students enrolled* • **Business Operations Support and Secretarial Services, Other** *1 student enrolled* • **CAD/CADD Drafting and/or Design Technology/Technician** • **Computer Systems Networking and Telecommunications** • **Drafting and Design Technology/Technician, General** • **Early Childhood Education and Teaching** • **Electrical and Electronic Engineering Technologies/Technicians, Other** • **Emergency Medical Technology/Technician (EMT Paramedic)** • **Industrial Technology/Technician** • **Information Science/Studies** • **Licensed Practical/Vocational Nurse Training (LPN, LVN, Cert, Dipl, AAS)** *34 students enrolled* • **Manufacturing Technology/Technician** • **Photography** *1 student enrolled*

STUDENT SERVICES Academic or career counseling, employment services for current students, placement services for program completers, remedial services.

Cleveland Institute of Dental-Medical Assistants

1836 Euclid Avenue, Room 401, Cleveland, OH 44115-2285
http://www.cidma.com/

CONTACT Beverly A. Davis, President
Telephone: 216-241-2930

GENERAL INFORMATION Private Institution. Founded 1968. **Total program enrollment:** 140.

PROGRAM(S) OFFERED
• **Dental Assisting/Assistant** *900 hrs./$9050* • **Health Information/Medical Records Administration/Administrator** *31 students enrolled* • **Medical Administrative/Executive Assistant and Medical Secretary** *900 hrs./$9050* • **Medical/Clinical Assistant** *900 hrs./$9750* • **Pharmacy Technician/Assistant** *900 hrs./$9050*

STUDENT SERVICES Placement services for program completers.

Cleveland Institute of Dental-Medical Assistants

5564 Mayfield Road, Lyndhurst, OH 44124
http://www.cidma.com/

CONTACT Beverly A. Davis, President
Telephone: 216-241-2930

GENERAL INFORMATION Private Institution. Founded 1987. **Total program enrollment:** 81.

PROGRAM(S) OFFERED
• **Health Information/Medical Records Administration/Administrator** *28 students enrolled* • **Medical Administrative/Executive Assistant and Medical Secretary** *900 hrs./$9050* • **Medical/Clinical Assistant** *900 hrs./$9750* • **Pharmacy Technician/Assistant** *900 hrs./$9050*

STUDENT SERVICES Placement services for program completers.

Cleveland Institute of Dental-Medical Assistants

5733 Hopkins Road, Mentor, OH 44060
http://www.cidma.com/

CONTACT Beverly A. Davis, President
Telephone: 216-241-2930

GENERAL INFORMATION Private Institution. Founded 1969. **Total program enrollment:** 159.

PROGRAM(S) OFFERED
• **Dental Assisting/Assistant** *900 hrs./$9050* • **Health Information/Medical Records Administration/Administrator** *54 students enrolled* • **Medical Administrative/Executive Assistant and Medical Secretary** *900 hrs./$9050* • **Medical/Clinical Assistant** *900 hrs./$9750* • **Pharmacy Technician/Assistant** *900 hrs./$9050*

STUDENT SERVICES Placement services for program completers.

Cleveland Institute of Electronics

1776 East Seventeenth Street, Cleveland, OH 44114-3636
http://www.cie-wc.edu/

CONTACT John R. Drinko, President
Telephone: 216-781-9400

GENERAL INFORMATION Private Institution. Founded 1934. **Accreditation:** State accredited or approved.

PROGRAM(S) OFFERED
• **Communications Technology/Technician** *19 students enrolled* • **Computer Programming, Vendor/Product Certification** *705 hrs./$1295* • **Computer Programming/Programmer, General** *4 students enrolled* • **Computer Systems Networking and Telecommunications** *18 students enrolled* • **Computer/Information Technology Services Administration and Management, Other** *96 hrs./$15,080* • **Data Processing and Data Processing Technology/Technician** *4 students enrolled* • **Electrical, Electronic and Communications Engineering Technology/Technician** *106 hrs.* • **Electrical, Electronics and Communications Engineering** *1 student enrolled* • **Engineering Technologies/Technicians, Other** *1780 hrs./$2295* • **Engineering Technology, General** *3 students enrolled* • **Industrial Engineering** *1518 hrs./$1795* • **Information Technology** *14 students enrolled* • **Radio and Television Broadcasting Technology/Technician** *1478 hrs./$1795*

Cleveland Municipal School District Adult and Continuing Education

4600 Detroit Avenue, Cleveland, OH 44102
http://www.cmsdnet.net/

CONTACT Dr. Eugene Sanders, Chief Executive Officer
Telephone: 216-634-2157

GENERAL INFORMATION Public Institution. **Total program enrollment:** 106.

PROGRAM(S) OFFERED
• **Business/Office Automation/Technology/Data Entry** *900 hrs./$4731* • **Carpentry/Carpenter** *900 hrs./$4731* • **Child Care Provider/Assistant** *900 hrs./$4731* • **Electrician** *900 hrs./$4731* • **Machine Tool Technology/Machinist** *900 hrs./$4731* • **Welding Technology/Welder** *900 hrs./$4731*

STUDENT SERVICES Academic or career counseling, placement services for program completers, remedial services.

College of Mount St. Joseph

5701 Delhi Road, Cincinnati, OH 45233-1670
http://www.msj.edu/

CONTACT Tony Aretz, PhD, President
Telephone: 513-244-4200

GENERAL INFORMATION Private Institution. Founded 1920. **Accreditation:** Regional (NCA); music (NASM). **Total program enrollment:** 1453. **Application fee:** $25.

PROGRAM(S) OFFERED
• **Legal Assistant/Paralegal** 3 students enrolled • **Religion/Religious Studies, Other** 1 student enrolled

STUDENT SERVICES Academic or career counseling, daycare for children of students, employment services for current students, placement services for program completers, remedial services.

Columbiana County Vocation School

9364 Street Route 45, Lisbon, OH 44432
http://www.ccctc.k12.oh.us/

CONTACT Edna Anderson, Superintendent
Telephone: 330-424-9561 Ext. 174

GENERAL INFORMATION Private Institution. **Total program enrollment:** 138.

PROGRAM(S) OFFERED
• **Business Operations Support and Secretarial Services, Other** 8 students enrolled • **Child Care Provider/Assistant** 8 students enrolled • **Emergency Medical Technology/Technician (EMT Paramedic)** 38 students enrolled • **Fire Protection, Other** 18 students enrolled • **Fire Science/Firefighting** 13 students enrolled • **Machine Tool Technology/Machinist** • **Medical Office Management/Administration** 46 students enrolled • **Medical/Clinical Assistant** 43 students enrolled • **Nurse/Nursing Assistant/Aide and Patient Care Assistant** 96 students enrolled • **Occupational Safety and Health Technology/Technician** 52 students enrolled • **Welding Technology/Welder** 50 students enrolled • **Work and Family Studies** 370 students enrolled

STUDENT SERVICES Academic or career counseling, employment services for current students, placement services for program completers, remedial services.

Columbus State Community College

Box 1609, Columbus, OH 43216-1609
http://www.cscc.edu/

CONTACT M. Valeriana Moeller, President
Telephone: 614-287-5353

GENERAL INFORMATION Public Institution. Founded 1963. **Accreditation:** Regional (NCA); dental hygiene (ADA); emergency medical services (JRCEMTP); engineering technology (ABET/TAC); health information technology (AHIMA); histologic technology (NAACLS); medical assisting (AAMAE); medical laboratory technology (NAACLS); radiologic technology: radiography (JRCERT); surgical technology (ARCST). **Total program enrollment:** 10742. **Application fee:** $50.

PROGRAM(S) OFFERED
• **Accounting Technology/Technician and Bookkeeping** 16 students enrolled • **Administrative Assistant and Secretarial Science, General** • **Aeronautical/Aerospace Engineering Technology/Technician** • **Airframe Powerplant Technology/Technician** 19 students enrolled • **Airframe Mechanics and Aircraft Maintenance Technology/Technician** • **Architectural Engineering Technology/Technician** 4 students enrolled • **Automotive Engineering Technology/Technician** 68 students enrolled • **Baking and Pastry Arts/Baker/Pastry Chef** 3 students enrolled • **Boilermaking/Boilermaker** 2 students enrolled • **Child Care and Support Services Management** • **Civil Engineering Technology/Technician** • **Clinical/Medical Laboratory Science and Allied Professions, Other** 5 students enrolled • **Computer Programming/Programmer, General** • **Computer and Information Sciences and Support Services, Other** • **Construction Engineering Technology/Technician** 25 students enrolled • **Dental Laboratory Technology/Technician** 11 students enrolled • **Electrical and Electronic**

Engineering Technologies/Technicians, Other 14 students enrolled • **Emergency Medical Technology/Technician (EMT Paramedic)** • **Engineering Technologies/Technicians, Other** 18 students enrolled • **Family and Community Services** 1 student enrolled • **Graphic and Printing Equipment Operator, General Production** 6 students enrolled • **Health and Physical Education/Fitness, Other** 49 students enrolled • **Health/Health Care Administration/Management** 7 students enrolled • **Heating, Air Conditioning and Refrigeration Technology/Technician (ACH/ACR/ACHR/HRAC/HVAC/AC Technology)** 13 students enrolled • **Hospitality Administration/Management, General** • **Human Resources Management and Services, Other** 18 students enrolled • **Industrial Production Technologies/Technicians, Other** 3 students enrolled • **Legal Assistant/Paralegal** 13 students enrolled • **Licensed Practical/Vocational Nurse Training (LPN, LVN, Cert, Dipl, AAS)** 34 students enrolled • **Logistics and Materials Management** • **Medical Insurance Coding Specialist/Coder** 9 students enrolled • **Medical Transcription/Transcriptionist** • **Medical/Clinical Assistant** 8 students enrolled • **Mental and Social Health Services and Allied Professions, Other** 1 student enrolled • **Non-Profit/Public/Organizational Management** 8 students enrolled • **Occupational Safety and Health Technology/Technician** 2 students enrolled • **Photography** • **Physical Therapist Assistant** 2 students enrolled • **Purchasing, Procurement/Acquisitions and Contracts Management** • **Selling Skills and Sales Operations** 18 students enrolled • **Sign Language Interpretation and Translation** 40 students enrolled • **Substance Abuse/Addiction Counseling** 2 students enrolled • **Surgical Technology/Technologist** 18 students enrolled • **Survey Technology/Surveying** • **Water Quality and Wastewater Treatment Management and Recycling Technology/Technician** • **Word Processing** 14 students enrolled

STUDENT SERVICES Academic or career counseling, daycare for children of students, employment services for current students, placement services for program completers, remedial services.

Community Services Division–Alliance City

200 Glamorgan, Alliance, OH 44601
http://www.alliancelink.com/users/acc/

CONTACT Peter Basile, Superintendent
Telephone: 330-821-2102

GENERAL INFORMATION Private Institution. **Total program enrollment:** 46. **Application fee:** $30.

PROGRAM(S) OFFERED
• **Accounting Technology/Technician and Bookkeeping** • **Allied Health and Medical Assisting Services, Other** 900 hrs./$4600 • **Automobile/Automotive Mechanics Technology/Technician** • **Business Operations Support and Secretarial Services, Other** • **Computer and Information Sciences and Support Services, Other** 1 student enrolled • **Cosmetology/Cosmetologist, General** 1500 hrs./$7300 • **Licensed Practical/Vocational Nurse Training (LPN, LVN, Cert, Dipl, AAS)** 1422 hrs./$4188 • **Machine Tool Technology/Machinist** • **Medical Administrative/Executive Assistant and Medical Secretary** 900 hrs./$4600 • **Medical Transcription/Transcriptionist** 900 hrs./$4600 • **Welding Technology/Welder** 648 hrs./$3500

STUDENT SERVICES Academic or career counseling, placement services for program completers, remedial services.

Creative Images–a Certified Matrix Design Academy

568 Miamisburg-Centerville Road, Dayton, OH 45459
http://www.cosmetologyexcellence.com/

CONTACT Nicholas E. Schindler, President
Telephone: 937-433-1944

GENERAL INFORMATION Private Institution. **Total program enrollment:** 98. **Application fee:** $50.

PROGRAM(S) OFFERED
• **Aesthetician/Esthetician and Skin Care Specialist** 750 hrs./$7080 • **Cosmetology and Related Personal Grooming Arts, Other** 6 students enrolled • **Cosmetology, Barber/Styling, and Nail Instructor** 1800 hrs./$17,435 • **Cosmetology/Cosmetologist, General** 1500 hrs./$13,650 • **Nail Technician/Specialist and Manicurist** 24 students enrolled

STUDENT SERVICES Placement services for program completers.

Creative Images College of Beauty

1076 Kauffman Avenue, Fairborn, OH 45324
http://www.cosmetologyexcellence.com/

CONTACT Nicholas E. Schindler, President
Telephone: 937-454-1200

GENERAL INFORMATION Private Institution. **Total program enrollment:** 100. **Application fee:** $50.

PROGRAM(S) OFFERED
- **Aesthetician/Esthetician and Skin Care Specialist** *750 hrs./$6930*
- **Cosmetology and Related Personal Grooming Arts, Other** *3 students enrolled*
- **Cosmetology, Barber/Styling, and Nail Instructor** *1800 hrs./$17,285*
- **Cosmetology/Cosmetologist, General** *1500 hrs./$13,500* • **Nail Technician/ Specialist and Manicurist** *20 students enrolled*

STUDENT SERVICES Placement services for program completers.

Cuyahoga Community College

700 Carnegie Avenue, Cleveland, OH 44115-2878
http://www.tri-c.edu/

CONTACT Jerry Sue Thornton, President
Telephone: 800-954-8742

GENERAL INFORMATION Public Institution. Founded 1963. **Accreditation:** Regional (NCA); dental hygiene (ADA); diagnostic medical sonography (JRCEDMS); health information technology (AHIMA); nuclear medicine technology (JRCNMT); physical therapy assisting (APTA); radiologic technology: radiography (JRCERT); surgical technology (ARCST). **Total program enrollment:** 9533.

PROGRAM(S) OFFERED
- **Administrative Assistant and Secretarial Science, General** *15 students enrolled* • **Allied Health Diagnostic, Intervention, and Treatment Professions, Other** *9 students enrolled* • **Automotive Engineering Technology/Technician** *4 students enrolled* • **Banking and Financial Support Services** *2 students enrolled* • **Commercial and Advertising Art** *6 students enrolled* • **Culinary Arts/Chef Training** *5 students enrolled* • **Dental Assisting/Assistant** *5 students enrolled* • **Dietetics/Dietitians** *2 students enrolled* • **Early Childhood Education and Teaching** *6 students enrolled* • **Emergency Medical Technology/Technician (EMT Paramedic)** *2 students enrolled* • **Engineering Technologies/Technicians, Other** *8 students enrolled* • **Environmental Health** *1 student enrolled* • **Health Information/Medical Records Technology/Technician** *6 students enrolled* • **Hotel/Motel Administration/Management** *1 student enrolled* • **Industrial Technology/Technician** *1 student enrolled* • **Legal Assistant/Paralegal** *30 students enrolled* • **Legal Professions and Studies, Other** *6 students enrolled* • **Licensed Practical/Vocational Nurse Training (LPN, LVN, Cert, Dipl, AAS)** *61 students enrolled* • **Massage Therapy/Therapeutic Massage** *9 students enrolled* • **Medical Insurance Coding Specialist/Coder** *6 students enrolled* • **Medical/Clinical Assistant** *20 students enrolled* • **Pharmacy Technician/ Assistant** *10 students enrolled* • **Phlebotomy/Phlebotomist** *22 students enrolled* • **Plant Sciences, General** *1 student enrolled* • **Public Administration** *1 student enrolled* • **Restaurant/Food Services Management** *2 students enrolled*

STUDENT SERVICES Academic or career counseling, daycare for children of students, employment services for current students, placement services for program completers, remedial services.

Davis College

4747 Monroe Street, Toledo, OH 43623-4307
http://daviscollege.edu/

CONTACT Diane Brunner, President
Telephone: 419-473-2700

GENERAL INFORMATION Private Institution. Founded 1858. **Accreditation:** Regional (NCA); medical assisting (AAMAE). **Total program enrollment:** 205. **Application fee:** $30.

PROGRAM(S) OFFERED
- **Accounting Technology/Technician and Bookkeeping** *1 student enrolled*
- **Human Resources Management/Personnel Administration, General** *2*

students enrolled • **Medical Insurance Coding Specialist/Coder** *4 students enrolled* • **Prepress/Desktop Publishing and Digital Imaging Design** *1 student enrolled*

STUDENT SERVICES Academic or career counseling, placement services for program completers.

Daymar College

1410 Industrial Drive, Chillicothe, OH 45601
http://www.daymarcollege.edu/

CONTACT Bill Ward, Executive Director
Telephone: 740-774-6300

GENERAL INFORMATION Private Institution. Founded 1976. **Accreditation:** State accredited or approved. **Total program enrollment:** 44. **Application fee:** $125.

PROGRAM(S) OFFERED
- **Accounting and Related Services, Other** • **Computer Software and Media Applications, Other** • **Customer Service Support/Call Center/Teleservice Operation**

STUDENT SERVICES Academic or career counseling, placement services for program completers.

Dayton Barber College

28 W. Fifth Street, Dayton, OH 45402
http://www.daytonbarbercollege.com/

CONTACT Todd Lemaster, President
Telephone: 937-222-9101

GENERAL INFORMATION Private Institution. **Total program enrollment:** 72.

PROGRAM(S) OFFERED
- **Barbering/Barber** *1800 hrs./$9675*

STUDENT SERVICES Academic or career counseling, employment services for current students, placement services for program completers.

Dayton School of Medical Massage

4457 Far Hills Avenue, Dayton, OH 45429
http://www.massageschools.com

CONTACT William Tahy, Director
Telephone: 937-294-6994

GENERAL INFORMATION Private Institution. **Total program enrollment:** 322. **Application fee:** $35.

PROGRAM(S) OFFERED
- **Massage Therapy/Therapeutic Massage** *312 students enrolled*

STUDENT SERVICES Placement services for program completers.

Delaware JVS District

4565 Columbus Pike, Delaware, OH 43015
http://www.delawareareaacc.org/

CONTACT Mary Beth Freeman, Superintendent
Telephone: 740-548-0708 Ext. 3206

GENERAL INFORMATION Public Institution. Founded 1973. **Total program enrollment:** 87. **Application fee:** $100.

PROGRAM(S) OFFERED
- **Child Care Provider/Assistant** *3 students enrolled* • **Computer Systems Analysis/Analyst** *576 hrs./$1670* • **Criminal Justice/Police Science** *589 hrs./ $2850* • **Dental Assisting/Assistant** • **Emergency Medical Technology/ Technician (EMT Paramedic)** *130 hrs./$715* • **Fire Protection, Other** *259 hrs./*

$2115 • **Fire Science/Firefighting** 23 *students enrolled* • **Medical Insurance Coding Specialist/Coder** 308 *hrs./*$3170 • **Nurse/Nursing Assistant/Aide and Patient Care Assistant** 76 *hrs./*$450

STUDENT SERVICES Academic or career counseling, employment services for current students, remedial services.

Eastern Gateway Community College

4000 Sunset Boulevard, Steubenville, OH 43952-3598
http://www.easterngatewaycc.com/

CONTACT Laura M. Meeks, President
Telephone: 740-264-5591

GENERAL INFORMATION Public Institution. Founded 1966. **Accreditation:** Regional (NCA); dental assisting (ADA); medical assisting (AAMAE); medical laboratory technology (NAACLS); radiologic technology: radiography (JRCERT). **Total program enrollment:** 948. **Application fee:** $20.

PROGRAM(S) OFFERED
• **Business/Office Automation/Technology/Data Entry** 3 *students enrolled* • **Clinical/Medical Laboratory Technician** 17 *students enrolled* • **Computer and Information Sciences, General** 3 *students enrolled* • **Criminal Justice/Police Science** 1 *student enrolled* • **Dental Assisting/Assistant** 23 *students enrolled* • **Emergency Medical Technology/Technician (EMT Paramedic)** 3 *students enrolled* • **Executive Assistant/Executive Secretary** 2 *students enrolled* • **Licensed Practical/Vocational Nurse Training (LPN, LVN, Cert, Dipl, AAS)** 29 *students enrolled* • **Medical Insurance Coding Specialist/Coder** 12 *students enrolled* • **Medical Transcription/Transcriptionist** 1 *student enrolled* • **Medical/Clinical Assistant** 9 *students enrolled* • **Real Estate** 5 *students enrolled* • **Welding Technology/Welder** 1 *student enrolled*

STUDENT SERVICES Academic or career counseling, daycare for children of students, employment services for current students, placement services for program completers, remedial services.

Eastern Hills Academy of Hair Design

7681 Beechmont Avenue, Cincinnati, OH 45230
http://www.schoolsofcosmetology.com/

CONTACT Carlo Hornsby, President
Telephone: 513-231-8621

GENERAL INFORMATION Private Institution. **Total program enrollment:** 40. **Application fee:** $100.

PROGRAM(S) OFFERED
• **Aesthetician/Esthetician and Skin Care Specialist** 750 *hrs./*$8990 • **Cosmetology and Related Personal Grooming Arts, Other** 1050 *hrs./*$8990 • **Cosmetology/Cosmetologist, General** 1800 *hrs./*$14,990 • **Nail Technician/Specialist and Manicurist** 300 *hrs./*$2990

STUDENT SERVICES Academic or career counseling, employment services for current students, placement services for program completers.

Eastland Career Center

4300 Amalgamated Place, Groveport, OH 43112

CONTACT Dr. Mark Weedy, Superintendent
Telephone: 614-836-4541

GENERAL INFORMATION Private Institution. **Total program enrollment:** 268.

PROGRAM(S) OFFERED
• **Criminal Justice/Police Science** 600 *hrs./*$3824 • **Dental Assisting/Assistant** 900 *hrs./*$5885 • **Emergency Medical Technology/Technician (EMT Paramedic)** 840 *hrs./*$4042 • **Heating, Air Conditioning and Refrigeration Technology/Technician (ACH/ACR/ACHR/HRAC/HVAC/AC Technology)** 12 *students enrolled* • **Heating, Air Conditioning, Ventilation and Refrigeration Maintenance**

Technology/Technician (HAC, HACR, HVAC, HVACR) 1150 *hrs./*$7693 • **Medical Office Assistant/Specialist** 21 *students enrolled* • **Medical Office Computer Specialist/Assistant** 600 *hrs./*$4812 • **Medical/Clinical Assistant** 900 *hrs./*$7980

STUDENT SERVICES Academic or career counseling, employment services for current students, placement services for program completers, remedial services.

Edison State Community College

1973 Edison Drive, Piqua, OH 45356-9253
http://www.edisonohio.edu/

CONTACT Kenneth Yowell, President
Telephone: 937-778-8600

GENERAL INFORMATION Public Institution. Founded 1973. **Accreditation:** Regional (NCA). **Total program enrollment:** 1168. **Application fee:** $20.

PROGRAM(S) OFFERED
• **Accounting** 2 *students enrolled* • **Administrative Assistant and Secretarial Science, General** 1 *student enrolled* • **Business/Commerce, General** 2 *students enrolled* • **Computer Hardware Technology/Technician** 1 *student enrolled* • **Computer Programming/Programmer, General** 1 *student enrolled* • **Computer Systems Networking and Telecommunications** 5 *students enrolled* • **Computer and Information Sciences and Support Services, Other** 2 *students enrolled* • **Computer and Information Sciences, General** 1 *student enrolled* • **Customer Service Management** 1 *student enrolled* • **Health and Medical Administrative Services, Other** 3 *students enrolled* • **Human Resources Management/Personnel Administration, General** 2 *students enrolled* • **Legal Assistant/Paralegal** 1 *student enrolled* • **Marketing/Marketing Management, General** 1 *student enrolled* • **Medical Administrative/Executive Assistant and Medical Secretary** 6 *students enrolled* • **Medical/Clinical Assistant** 45 *students enrolled* • **Phlebotomy/Phlebotomist** 11 *students enrolled* • **Prepress/Desktop Publishing and Digital Imaging Design** 1 *student enrolled* • **Quality Control Technology/Technician** 1 *student enrolled* • **Real Estate** 6 *students enrolled*

STUDENT SERVICES Academic or career counseling, daycare for children of students, employment services for current students, placement services for program completers, remedial services.

Ehove Career Center

316 West Mason Road, Milan, OH 44846
http://www.ehove.net/

CONTACT Sharon Mastroianni, Superintendent
Telephone: 419-499-4663 Ext. 280

GENERAL INFORMATION Private Institution. **Total program enrollment:** 286. **Application fee:** $35.

PROGRAM(S) OFFERED
• **Administrative Assistant and Secretarial Science, General** 7 *students enrolled* • **Cosmetology/Cosmetologist, General** 4 *students enrolled* • **Criminal Justice/Police Science** 12 *students enrolled* • **Emergency Medical Technology/Technician (EMT Paramedic)** 744 *hrs./*$5500 • **Licensed Practical/Vocational Nurse Training (LPN, LVN, Cert, Dipl, AAS)** 1260 *hrs./*$8150 • **Marine Maintenance/Fitter and Ship Repair Technology/Technician** 6 *students enrolled* • **Massage Therapy/Therapeutic Massage** 816 *hrs./*$8000 • **Medical Insurance Coding Specialist/Coder** 4 *students enrolled* • **Medical/Clinical Assistant** 900 *hrs./*$5000 • **Phlebotomy/Phlebotomist** 600 *hrs./*$3600 • **Surgical Technology/Technologist** 1211 *hrs./*$6600

STUDENT SERVICES Academic or career counseling, daycare for children of students, employment services for current students, placement services for program completers, remedial services.

ETI Technical College of Niles

2076 Youngstown-Warren Road, Niles, OH 44446-4398
http://www.eti-college.com/

CONTACT Renee Zuzolo, Director
Telephone: 330-652-9919

GENERAL INFORMATION Private Institution. Founded 1989. **Accreditation:** State accredited or approved. **Total program enrollment:** 163. **Application fee:** $50.

PROGRAM(S) OFFERED
• **Administrative Assistant and Secretarial Science, General** 1 *student enrolled* • **Electrical, Electronic and Communications Engineering Technology/**

ETI Technical College of Niles (continued)

Technician *1 student enrolled* ● **Heating, Air Conditioning, Ventilation and Refrigeration Maintenance Technology/Technician (HAC, HACR, HVAC, HVACR)** *18 students enrolled* ● **Medical/Clinical Assistant**

STUDENT SERVICES Academic or career counseling, employment services for current students, placement services for program completers.

Euclidian Beauty School

22741 Shore Center Drive, Euclid, OH 44123

CONTACT William Church, Director
Telephone: 440-391-5040

GENERAL INFORMATION Private Institution. **Total program enrollment:** 67. **Application fee:** $100.

PROGRAM(S) OFFERED
● **Cosmetology/Cosmetologist, General** *1500 hrs./$13,775* ● **Hair Styling/ Stylist and Hair Design** *2 students enrolled* ● **Nail Technician/Specialist and Manicurist** *17 students enrolled* ● **Salon/Beauty Salon Management/Manager** *10 students enrolled*

STUDENT SERVICES Academic or career counseling, placement services for program completers.

Everest Institute

2545 Bailey Road, Cuyahoga Falls, OH 44221
http://www.everest.edu/

CONTACT Carson Burke, Director
Telephone: 330-923-9959 Ext. 1200

GENERAL INFORMATION Private Institution. **Accreditation:** State accredited or approved. **Total program enrollment:** 496. **Application fee:** $55.

PROGRAM(S) OFFERED
● **Dental Assisting/Assistant** ● **General Office Occupations and Clerical Services** ● **Medical Insurance Coding Specialist/Coder** *9 students enrolled*

STUDENT SERVICES Academic or career counseling, placement services for program completers.

Everest Institute

825 Tech Center Drive, Gahanna, OH 43230-6653
http://www.everest.edu/

CONTACT William DeFusco, President
Telephone: 614-322-3414

GENERAL INFORMATION Private Institution. **Total program enrollment:** 834.

PROGRAM(S) OFFERED
● **Accounting** *750 hrs./$12,715* ● **Massage Therapy/Therapeutic Massage** *750 hrs./$13,875* ● **Medical Administrative/Executive Assistant and Medical Secretary** *47 students enrolled* ● **Medical Insurance Coding Specialist/Coder** *720 hrs./$12,955* ● **Medical/Clinical Assistant** *721 hrs./$11,750*

STUDENT SERVICES Academic or career counseling, placement services for program completers.

Fairview Beauty Academy

22610 Lorain Road, Fairview Park, OH 44126

CONTACT Beverly Dudek, Financial Aid Consultant
Telephone: 216-734-5555

GENERAL INFORMATION Private Institution. **Total program enrollment:** 28. **Application fee:** $100.

PROGRAM(S) OFFERED
● **Cosmetology/Cosmetologist, General** *1500 hrs./$6900* ● **Nail Technician/ Specialist and Manicurist** *300 hrs./$1175* ● **Salon/Beauty Salon Management/ Manager** *1800 hrs./$7200*

STUDENT SERVICES Academic or career counseling, placement services for program completers.

Gallipolis Career College

1176 Jackson Pike, Suite 312, Gallipolis, OH 45631
http://www.gallipoliscareercollege.com/

CONTACT Robert L. Shirey, President
Telephone: 740-446-4367

GENERAL INFORMATION Private Institution. Founded 1962. **Accreditation:** State accredited or approved. **Total program enrollment:** 140. **Application fee:** $50.

PROGRAM(S) OFFERED
● **Accounting** ● **Administrative Assistant and Secretarial Science, General** *2 students enrolled* ● **Computer Software and Media Applications, Other** *2 students enrolled* ● **Medical Administrative/Executive Assistant and Medical Secretary** *1 student enrolled*

STUDENT SERVICES Academic or career counseling, employment services for current students, placement services for program completers, remedial services.

Gerber's Akron Beauty School

33 Shiawassee Avenue, Fairlawn, OH 44333
http://akronbeautyschool.com/

CONTACT Joseph Mako, President
Telephone: 330-867-6200

GENERAL INFORMATION Private Institution. Founded 1947. **Total program enrollment:** 34.

PROGRAM(S) OFFERED
● **Aesthetician/Esthetician and Skin Care Specialist** *750 hrs./$3665* ● **Cosmetology and Related Personal Grooming Arts, Other** *24 students enrolled* ● **Cosmetology/Cosmetologist, General** *1500 hrs./$7507* ● **Nail Technician/Specialist and Manicurist** *200 hrs./$1355*

STUDENT SERVICES Employment services for current students.

Grant Joint Vocational School

718 West Plane Street, Bethel, OH 45106
http://www.grantcareer.com/

CONTACT Jean Grider, Adult Director
Telephone: 513-734-6222

GENERAL INFORMATION Public Institution. **Total program enrollment:** 20. **Application fee:** $40.

PROGRAM(S) OFFERED
● **Medical Administrative/Executive Assistant and Medical Secretary** *18 students enrolled*

STUDENT SERVICES Placement services for program completers.

Hamrick Truck Driving School

1156 Medina Road, Medina, OH 44256-9615
http://hamrickschool.com/

CONTACT Denver Hamrick, President
Telephone: 330-239-2229 Ext. 248

GENERAL INFORMATION Private Institution. Founded 1979. **Total program enrollment:** 109.

PROGRAM(S) OFFERED

• **Massage Therapy/Therapeutic Massage** 63 hrs./$10,771 • **Truck and Bus Driver/Commercial Vehicle Operation** 404 hrs./$7945

STUDENT SERVICES Placement services for program completers.

Hannah E. Mullins School of Practical Nursing

Salem Senior High School, 1200 East Sixth Street, Salem, OH 44460
http://www.salem.k12.oh.us/mullins/mullins.html/

CONTACT Louis Ramunno, Superintendent
Telephone: 330-332-8940

GENERAL INFORMATION Public Institution. Founded 1957. **Total program enrollment:** 60. **Application fee:** $50.

PROGRAM(S) OFFERED

• **Licensed Practical/Vocational Nurse Training (LPN, LVN, Cert, Dipl, AAS)** 32 hrs./$9550

STUDENT SERVICES Academic or career counseling.

Healing Arts Institute

340 Three Meadows Drive, Perrysburg, OH 43551
http://www.haiohio.com/

CONTACT Amanda Tebbe, Financial Aid Administrator
Telephone: 419-874-4496

GENERAL INFORMATION Private Institution. **Application fee:** $50.

PROGRAM(S) OFFERED

• **Massage Therapy/Therapeutic Massage** 750 hrs.

STUDENT SERVICES Placement services for program completers.

Hobart Institute of Welding Technology

400 Trade Square, E, Troy, OH 45373
http://www.welding.org/

CONTACT Brenda K. Scott, Director of Compliance & Student Service
Telephone: 937-332-5000

GENERAL INFORMATION Private Institution. Founded 1930. **Total program enrollment:** 245. **Application fee:** $75.

PROGRAM(S) OFFERED

• **Welding Technology/Welder** 735 hrs./$8070

STUDENT SERVICES Placement services for program completers.

Hocking College

3301 Hocking Parkway, Nelsonville, OH 45764-9588
http://www.hocking.edu/

CONTACT John Light, President
Telephone: 740-753-3591

GENERAL INFORMATION Public Institution. Founded 1968. **Accreditation:** Regional (NCA); engineering technology (ABET/TAC); health information technology (AHIMA); medical assisting (AAMAE); physical therapy assisting (APTA); practical nursing (NLN). **Total program enrollment:** 3567. **Application fee:** $15.

PROGRAM(S) OFFERED

• **Accounting Technology/Technician and Bookkeeping** 34 students enrolled • **Accounting** 166 students enrolled • **Administrative Assistant and Secretarial Science, General** 12 students enrolled • **Allied Health Diagnostic, Intervention, and Treatment Professions, Other** 3 students enrolled • **Aquaculture** 15 students enrolled • **Archeology** 20 students enrolled • **Bartending/Bartender** 11 students enrolled • **Business Operations Support and Secretarial Services, Other** 1 student enrolled • **Business, Management, Marketing, and Related Support Services, Other** 1 student enrolled • **Business/Commerce, General** 207 students enrolled • **Computer Engineering Technology/Technician** 12 students enrolled • **Computer and Information Sciences and Support Services, Other** 44 students enrolled • **Crafts/Craft Design, Folk Art and Artisanry** 23 students enrolled • **Culinary Arts and Related Services, Other** 37 students enrolled • **Dietetics/Dietitians** 13 students enrolled • **Drafting and Design Technology/Technician, General** 32 students enrolled • **Electrical, Electronic and Communications Engineering Technology/Technician** 1 student enrolled • **Electrocardiograph Technology/Technician** 36 students enrolled • **Electromechanical and Instrumentation and Maintenance Technologies/Technicians, Other** 8 students enrolled • **Engineering Technologies/Technicians, Other** 10 students enrolled • **Entrepreneurial and Small Business Operations, Other** 61 students enrolled • **Equestrian/Equine Studies** 55 students enrolled • **Food Preparation/Professional Cooking/Kitchen Assistant** 78 students enrolled • **Forestry, Other** 11 students enrolled • **General Merchandising, Sales, and Related Marketing Operations, Other** 28 students enrolled • **General Office Occupations and Clerical Services** 11 students enrolled • **Geography** 14 students enrolled • **Health Information/Medical Records Administration/Administrator** 1 student enrolled • **Health Professions and Related Clinical Sciences, Other** 20 students enrolled • **Health and Medical Administrative Services, Other** 5 students enrolled • **Heating, Air Conditioning and Refrigeration Technology/Technician (ACH/ACR/ACHR/HRAC/HVAC/AC Technology)** 3 students enrolled • **Hospitality Administration/Management, Other** 63 students enrolled • **Hotel/Motel Administration/Management** 31 students enrolled • **Human Resources Management/Personnel Administration, General** 23 students enrolled • **International Business/Trade/Commerce** 1 student enrolled • **Legal Administrative Assistant/Secretary** 2 students enrolled • **Licensed Practical/Vocational Nurse Training (LPN, LVN, Cert, Dipl, AAS)** 170 students enrolled • **Medical Transcription/Transcriptionist** 2 students enrolled • **Music Management and Merchandising** 19 students enrolled • **Natural Resources Management/Development** 821 students enrolled • **Parks, Recreation and Leisure Studies** 56 students enrolled • **Petroleum Technology/Technician** 16 students enrolled • **Purchasing, Procurement/Acquisitions and Contracts Management** 50 students enrolled • **Radio and Television** 21 students enrolled • **Real Estate** 25 students enrolled • **Receptionist** 6 students enrolled • **Taxation** 37 students enrolled • **Technical Theatre/Theatre Design and Technology** 4 students enrolled • **Vehicle and Vehicle Parts and Accessories Marketing Operations** 48 students enrolled • **Wildlife and Wildlands Science and Management** 30 students enrolled

STUDENT SERVICES Academic or career counseling, daycare for children of students, employment services for current students, placement services for program completers, remedial services.

Hondros College

4140 Executive Parkway, Westerville, OH 43081-3855
http://www.hondroscollege.com/

CONTACT Linda Schwan Hondros, President
Telephone: 888-466-3767

GENERAL INFORMATION Private Institution. Founded 1981. **Accreditation:** State accredited or approved. **Total program enrollment:** 422. **Application fee:** $25.

PROGRAM(S) OFFERED

• **Licensed Practical/Vocational Nurse Training (LPN, LVN, Cert, Dipl, AAS)** 74 students enrolled

STUDENT SERVICES Academic or career counseling, employment services for current students, placement services for program completers.

Inner State Beauty School

5150 Mayfield Road, Lyndhurst, OH 44124
http://www.innerstatebeautyschool.com/

CONTACT Judson DiVincenzo, Director
Telephone: 440-461-1000

GENERAL INFORMATION Private Institution. **Total program enrollment:** 152.

PROGRAM(S) OFFERED

• **Aesthetician/Esthetician and Skin Care Specialist** $4375 • **Cosmetology/Cosmetologist, General** 1800 hrs./$10,340 • **Nail Technician/Specialist and Manicurist** $1482

STUDENT SERVICES Academic or career counseling, placement services for program completers.

Institute of Medical and Dental Technology

375 Glensprings Drive, Suite 201, Cincinnati, OH 45246
http://imdtcareers.com/

CONTACT Paul Mitchell, President
Telephone: 513-851-8500

GENERAL INFORMATION Private Institution. Founded 1977. **Total program enrollment:** 37. **Application fee:** $100.

PROGRAM(S) OFFERED
● **Dental Assisting/Assistant** 27 hrs./$7080 ● **Medical/Clinical Assistant** 29 hrs./$7320

STUDENT SERVICES Placement services for program completers.

International Academy of Hair Design

8419 Colerain Avenue, Cincinnati, OH 45239
http://www.mybeautycareer.com/

CONTACT Cassandra Mooar, Vice President
Telephone: 513-741-4777

GENERAL INFORMATION Private Institution. Founded 1983. **Total program enrollment:** 84. **Application fee:** $50.

PROGRAM(S) OFFERED
● **Aesthetician/Esthetician and Skin Care Specialist** 750 hrs./$6700 ● **Cosmetology and Related Personal Grooming Arts, Other** ● **Cosmetology/Cosmetologist, General** 1500 hrs./$13,900 ● **Nail Technician/Specialist and Manicurist** 300 hrs./$2580

STUDENT SERVICES Placement services for program completers.

International College of Broadcasting

6 South Smithville Road, Dayton, OH 45431-1833
http://www.icbcollege.com/

CONTACT Michael A. Lemaster, President
Telephone: 937-258-8251 Ext. 200

GENERAL INFORMATION Private Institution. Founded 1968. **Accreditation:** State accredited or approved. **Total program enrollment:** 123. **Application fee:** $100.

PROGRAM(S) OFFERED
● **Music, Other** 88 students enrolled ● **Radio and Television** 88 students enrolled

STUDENT SERVICES Academic or career counseling, employment services for current students, placement services for program completers.

James A. Rhodes State College

4240 Campus Drive, Lima, OH 45804-3597
http://www.rhodesstate.edu/

CONTACT Debra L. McCurdy, President
Telephone: 419-221-1112

GENERAL INFORMATION Public Institution. Founded 1971. **Accreditation:** Regional (NCA); dental hygiene (ADA); engineering technology (ABET/TAC); medical assisting (AAMAE); physical therapy assisting (APTA); radiologic technology: radiography (JRCERT). **Total program enrollment:** 1974. **Application fee:** $25.

PROGRAM(S) OFFERED
● **Accounting Technology/Technician and Bookkeeping** 5 students enrolled ● **Administrative Assistant and Secretarial Science, General** 5 students enrolled ● **Business, Management, Marketing, and Related Support Services, Other** 8 students enrolled ● **Civil Engineering Technology/Technician** 3 students enrolled ● **Computer Programming, Specific Applications** 7 students enrolled ● **Computer Technology/Computer Systems Technology** 1 student enrolled ● **Emergency Medical Technology/Technician (EMT Paramedic)** 14 students enrolled ● **Environmental Control Technologies/Technicians, Other** 14 students

enrolled ● **Finance and Financial Management Services, Other** 22 students enrolled ● **Industrial Technology/Technician** 4 students enrolled ● **Legal Assistant/Paralegal** ● **Licensed Practical/Vocational Nurse Training (LPN, LVN, Cert, Dipl, AAS)** 25 students enrolled ● **Marketing/Marketing Management, General** ● **Mechanical Engineering/Mechanical Technology/Technician** 11 students enrolled ● **Medical/Clinical Assistant** 9 students enrolled ● **Quality Control Technology/Technician** 2 students enrolled ● **Respiratory Care Therapy/Therapist** 17 students enrolled ● **Robotics Technology/Technician** 3 students enrolled ● **Social Work** 9 students enrolled

STUDENT SERVICES Academic or career counseling, daycare for children of students, employment services for current students, placement services for program completers, remedial services.

Kent State University

PO Box 5190, Kent, OH 44242-0001
http://www.kent.edu/

CONTACT Dr. Lester Lefton, President
Telephone: 330-672-3000

GENERAL INFORMATION Public Institution. Founded 1910. **Accreditation:** Regional (NCA); art and design (NASAD); audiology (ASHA); counseling (ACA); dance (NASD); dietetics: postbaccalaureate internship (ADtA/CAADE); interior design: professional (CIDA); journalism and mass communications (ACEJMC); library and information science (ALA); music (NASM); recreation and parks (NRPA); speech-language pathology (ASHA); theater (NAST). **Total program enrollment:** 18388. **Application fee:** $30.

PROGRAM(S) OFFERED
● **Airline/Commercial/Professional Pilot and Flight Crew** 1 student enrolled ● **Business, Management, Marketing, and Related Support Services, Other** 2 students enrolled ● **Business/Commerce, General** 2 students enrolled ● **Computer Systems Analysis/Analyst** 3 students enrolled ● **Computer and Information Systems Security** 6 students enrolled ● **Drama and Dramatics/Theatre Arts, General** 1 student enrolled ● **Industrial Production Technologies/Technicians, Other** 1 student enrolled ● **International Business/Trade/Commerce** 21 students enrolled ● **Teaching English as a Second or Foreign Language/ESL Language Instructor** 25 students enrolled

STUDENT SERVICES Academic or career counseling, employment services for current students, placement services for program completers, remedial services.

Kent State University, Ashtabula Campus

3300 Lake Road West, Ashtabula, OH 44004-2299
http://www.ashtabula.kent.edu/

CONTACT Dr. Susan Stocker, Dean
Telephone: 440-964-3322

GENERAL INFORMATION Public Institution. Founded 1958. **Accreditation:** Regional (NCA); physical therapy assisting (APTA). **Total program enrollment:** 854. **Application fee:** $30.

PROGRAM(S) OFFERED
● **Foods, Nutrition, and Wellness Studies, General** 1 student enrolled

STUDENT SERVICES Academic or career counseling, employment services for current students, placement services for program completers, remedial services.

Kent State University, East Liverpool Campus

400 East 4th Street, East Liverpool, OH 43920-3497
http://www.kenteliv.kent.edu/

CONTACT Dr. Jeffrey Nolte, Dean
Telephone: 330-382-7400

GENERAL INFORMATION Public Institution. Founded 1967. **Accreditation:** Regional (NCA); physical therapy assisting (APTA). **Total program enrollment:** 481. **Application fee:** $30.

STUDENT SERVICES Academic or career counseling, employment services for current students, placement services for program completers, remedial services.

Kent State University, Salem Campus

2491 State Route 45 South, Salem, OH 44460-9412
http://www.salem.kent.edu/

CONTACT Dr. Jeffrey Nolte, Dean
Telephone: 330-332-0361

GENERAL INFORMATION Public Institution. Founded 1966. **Accreditation:** Regional (NCA); nuclear medicine technology (JRCNMT); radiologic technology: radiography (JRCERT). **Total program enrollment:** 871. **Application fee:** $30.

PROGRAM(S) OFFERED
• Business/Commerce, General *1 student enrolled*

STUDENT SERVICES Academic or career counseling, employment services for current students, placement services for program completers, remedial services.

Kent State University, Trumbull Campus

4314 Mahoning Avenue, NW, Warren, OH 44483-1998
http://www.trumbull.kent.edu/

CONTACT Dr. Wanda Thomas, Dean
Telephone: 330-847-0571

GENERAL INFORMATION Public Institution. Founded 1954. **Accreditation:** Regional (NCA). **Total program enrollment:** 1221. **Application fee:** $30.

PROGRAM(S) OFFERED
• Business/Commerce, General *3 students enrolled* • Computer Programming, Specific Applications *1 student enrolled* • Computer Systems Analysis/Analyst *1 student enrolled* • Computer Systems Networking and Telecommunications *1 student enrolled* • Computer and Information Systems Security *1 student enrolled*

STUDENT SERVICES Academic or career counseling, employment services for current students, placement services for program completers, remedial services.

Kent State University, Tuscarawas Campus

330 University Drive, NE, New Philadelphia, OH 44663-9403
http://www.tusc.kent.edu/

CONTACT Dr. Gregg Andrews, Dean
Telephone: 330-339-3391

GENERAL INFORMATION Public Institution. Founded 1962. **Accreditation:** Regional (NCA); engineering technology (ABET/TAC). **Total program enrollment:** 1173. **Application fee:** $30.

PROGRAM(S) OFFERED
• Business/Commerce, General *7 students enrolled* • Computer and Information Systems Security *7 students enrolled* • Human Development, Family Studies, and Related Services, Other *7 students enrolled*

STUDENT SERVICES Academic or career counseling, employment services for current students, placement services for program completers, remedial services.

Kettering College of Medical Arts

3737 Southern Boulevard, Kettering, OH 45429-1299
http://www.kcma.edu/

CONTACT Charles Scriven, President
Telephone: 937-395-8601

GENERAL INFORMATION Private Institution. Founded 1967. **Accreditation:** Regional (NCA); diagnostic medical sonography (JRCEDMS); radiologic technology: radiography (JRCERT). **Total program enrollment:** 429. **Application fee:** $25.

PROGRAM(S) OFFERED
• Radiologic Technology/Science—Radiographer *11 students enrolled*

STUDENT SERVICES Academic or career counseling, employment services for current students, placement services for program completers, remedial services.

Knox County Career Center

306 Martinsburg Road, Mount Vernon, OH 43050
http://www.kccc.k12.oh.us/

CONTACT Kenneth Boeshart, Supervisor
Telephone: 740-393-2933

GENERAL INFORMATION Public Institution. Founded 1969. **Total program enrollment:** 246. **Application fee:** $50.

PROGRAM(S) OFFERED
• Business Operations Support and Secretarial Services, Other *16 students enrolled* • Computer and Information Sciences, General *900 hrs./$9053* • Cosmetology/Cosmetologist, General *1500 hrs./$12,296* • Health Information/Medical Records Administration/Administrator *4 students enrolled* • Licensed Practical/Vocational Nurse Training (LPN, LVN, Cert, Dipl, AAS) *1270 hrs./$11,790* • Massage Therapy/Therapeutic Massage *800 hrs./$7801* • Medical Administrative/Executive Assistant and Medical Secretary *900 hrs./$7175* • Medical Insurance Specialist/Medical Biller *900 hrs./$7062* • Medical/Clinical Assistant *10 students enrolled*

STUDENT SERVICES Academic or career counseling, daycare for children of students, employment services for current students, placement services for program completers, remedial services.

Lakeland Community College

7700 Clocktower Drive, Kirtland, OH 44094-5198
http://www.lakeland.cc.oh.us/

CONTACT Morris W. Beverage, Jr., President
Telephone: 440-525-7000

GENERAL INFORMATION Public Institution. Founded 1967. **Accreditation:** Regional (NCA); dental hygiene (ADA); engineering technology (ABET/TAC); medical laboratory technology (NAACLS); ophthalmic medical technology (JCAHPO); radiologic technology: radiography (JRCERT); surgical technology (ARCST). **Total program enrollment:** 3895. **Application fee:** $15.

PROGRAM(S) OFFERED
• Accounting *6 students enrolled* • Administrative Assistant and Secretarial Science, General *3 students enrolled* • Allied Health Diagnostic, Intervention, and Treatment Professions, Other *7 students enrolled* • Architectural Drafting and Architectural CAD/CADD *1 student enrolled* • Biology Technician/Biotechnology Laboratory Technician • Business Administration and Management, General *12 students enrolled* • Chemical Technology/Technician *2 students enrolled* • Clinical/Medical Laboratory Technician *10 students enrolled* • Computer Engineering Technology/Technician • Computer Programming, Specific Applications *7 students enrolled* • Computer Systems Networking and Telecommunications *5 students enrolled* • Construction Engineering Technology/Technician *1 student enrolled* • Corrections • Criminal Justice/Police Science *2 students enrolled* • Design and Applied Arts, Other *5 students enrolled* • Design and Visual Communications, General • Electrical, Electronic and Communications Engineering Technology/Technician *2 students enrolled* • Emergency Medical Technology/Technician (EMT Paramedic) *2 students enrolled* • Entrepreneurship/Entrepreneurial Studies *2 students enrolled* • Fire Science/Firefighting *1 student enrolled* • Health and Medical Administrative Services, Other • Home Health Aide/Home Attendant *5 students enrolled* • Hospitality Administration/Management, General *1 student enrolled* • Industrial Technology/Technician • Intermedia/Multimedia • Legal Assistant/Paralegal *10 students enrolled* • Marketing/Marketing Management, General *2 students enrolled* • Mechanical Drafting and Mechanical Drafting CAD/CADD *16 students enrolled* • Medical Administrative/Executive Assistant and Medical Secretary *37 students enrolled* • Medical Radiologic Technology/Science—Radiation Therapist *1 student enrolled* • Medical Transcription/Transcriptionist *4 students enrolled* • Medical/Clinical Assistant *5 students enrolled* • Operations

Lakeland Community College (continued)

Management and Supervision • Quality Control Technology/Technician • Security and Protective Services, Other *2 students enrolled* **• Social Work** *1 student enrolled* **• Survey Technology/Surveying • Tourism and Travel Services Management**

STUDENT SERVICES Academic or career counseling, daycare for children of students, employment services for current students, placement services for program completers, remedial services.

Licking County Joint Vocational School–Newark

150 Price Road, Newark, OH 43055
http://www.c-tec.edu/

CONTACT Kelly Wallace, Adult Director
Telephone: 614-364-2333

GENERAL INFORMATION Private Institution. Founded 1978. **Total program enrollment:** 91.

PROGRAM(S) OFFERED
• **Administrative Assistant and Secretarial Science, General** *8 students enrolled* • **Autobody/Collision and Repair Technology/Technician** *11 students enrolled* • **Computer and Information Sciences and Support Services, Other** *6 students enrolled* • **Cosmetology/Cosmetologist, General** *1530 hrs./$8997* • **Electrical and Power Transmission Installation/Installer, General** *900 hrs./$6699* • **Electrician** *11 students enrolled* • **Emergency Medical Technology/Technician (EMT Paramedic)** *66 students enrolled* • **Fire Science/Firefighting** *62 students enrolled* • **General Office Occupations and Clerical Services** *800 hrs./$4604* • **Health Aides/Attendants/Orderlies, Other** *3 students enrolled* • **Heating, Air Conditioning and Refrigeration Technology/Technician (ACH/ACR/ACHR/HRAC/HVAC/AC Technology)** *810 hrs./$5147* • **Heating, Air Conditioning, Ventilation and Refrigeration Maintenance Technology/Technician (HAC, HACR, HVAC, HVACR)** *6 students enrolled* • **Heavy Equipment Maintenance Technology/Technician** *7 students enrolled* • **Industrial Mechanics and Maintenance Technology** *810 hrs./$5112* • **Machine Tool Technology/Machinist** *5 students enrolled* • **Medical Insurance Coding Specialist/Coder** *19 students enrolled* • **Medical Office Computer Specialist/Assistant** *11 students enrolled* • **Medical/Clinical Assistant** *40 students enrolled* • **Nurse/Nursing Assistant/Aide and Patient Care Assistant** *315 students enrolled* • **Ornamental Horticulture** *6 students enrolled* • **Phlebotomy/Phlebotomist** *5 students enrolled* • **Plumbing Technology/Plumber** *8 students enrolled* • **System, Networking, and LAN/WAN Management/Manager** *8 students enrolled*

STUDENT SERVICES Academic or career counseling, employment services for current students, placement services for program completers, remedial services.

Lorain County Community College

1005 Abbe Road, North, Elyria, OH 44035
http://www.lorainccc.edu/

CONTACT Dr. Roy Church, President
Telephone: 440-366-5222

GENERAL INFORMATION Public Institution. Founded 1963. **Accreditation:** Regional (NCA); dental hygiene (ADA); diagnostic medical sonography (JRCEDMS); medical assisting (AAMAE); medical laboratory technology (NAACLS); physical therapy assisting (APTA); practical nursing (NLN); radiologic technology: radiography (JRCERT); surgical technology (ARCST). **Total program enrollment:** 4805.

PROGRAM(S) OFFERED
• **Athletic Training/Trainer** *1 student enrolled* • **Computer Engineering Technology/Technician • Criminal Justice/Police Science** *4 students enrolled* • **Drafting and Design Technology/Technician, General** *4 students enrolled* • **Early Childhood Education and Teaching • Electrical, Electronic and Communications Engineering Technology/Technician** *3 students enrolled* • **Electrical, Electronics and Communications Engineering** *8 students enrolled* • **Electrolysis/Electrology and Electrolysis Technician • Entrepreneurship/Entrepreneurial Studies** *3 students enrolled* • **General Office Occupations and Clerical Services** *9 students enrolled* • **Information Technology** *3 students enrolled* • **Licensed Practical/Vocational Nurse Training (LPN, LVN, Cert, Dipl, AAS)** *68 students enrolled* • **Manufacturing Technology/Technician • Mechanical**

Engineering/Mechanical Technology/Technician *2 students enrolled* • **Medical Administrative/Executive Assistant and Medical Secretary • Medical/Clinical Assistant** *10 students enrolled* • **Public Administration** *2 students enrolled* • **Quality Control Technology/Technician** *1 student enrolled*

STUDENT SERVICES Academic or career counseling, daycare for children of students, employment services for current students, placement services for program completers, remedial services.

Lorain County JVS Adult Career Center

15181 Route 58, S, Oberlin, OH 44074
http://www.loraincounty.com/jvsadult/

CONTACT William Aubuchon, Superintendent
Telephone: 440-774-1051

GENERAL INFORMATION Public Institution. Founded 1975. **Total program enrollment:** 89.

PROGRAM(S) OFFERED
• **Administrative Assistant and Secretarial Science, General** *953 hrs./$5750* • **Automobile/Automotive Mechanics Technology/Technician** *600 hrs./$4595* • **Business Administration, Management and Operations, Other** *13 students enrolled* • **Construction Engineering Technology/Technician** *600 hrs./$4995* • **Construction Trades, Other** *10 students enrolled* • **Cosmetology/Cosmetologist, General** *1500 hrs./$8020* • **Machine Tool Technology/Machinist** *600 hrs./$4595* • **Mechanic and Repair Technologies/Technicians, Other** *15 students enrolled* • **Medical/Clinical Assistant** *956 hrs./$7690* • **Precision Metal Working, Other** *7 students enrolled*

STUDENT SERVICES Academic or career counseling, placement services for program completers, remedial services.

Lourdes College

6832 Convent Boulevard, Sylvania, OH 43560-2898
http://www.lourdes.edu/

CONTACT Robert C. Helmer, PhD, President
Telephone: 419-885-3211

GENERAL INFORMATION Private Institution. Founded 1958. **Accreditation:** Regional (NCA). **Total program enrollment:** 1171. **Application fee:** $25.

PROGRAM(S) OFFERED
• **Religion/Religious Studies**

STUDENT SERVICES Academic or career counseling, employment services for current students, placement services for program completers, remedial services.

Madison Local Schools–Madison Adult Education

600 Esley Lane, Mansfield, OH 44905
http://www.madison-richland.k12.oh.us/adulted/

CONTACT Sonja Pluck, Adult Director
Telephone: 419-589-6363

GENERAL INFORMATION Public Institution. Founded 1975. **Total program enrollment:** 114.

PROGRAM(S) OFFERED
• **Administrative Assistant and Secretarial Science, General** *12 students enrolled* • **Automobile/Automotive Mechanics Technology/Technician** *3 students enrolled* • **Cosmetology/Cosmetologist, General** *1500 hrs./$10,277* • **Dental Assisting/Assistant** *140 hrs./$840* • **Medical/Clinical Assistant** *720 hrs./$4320*

• Nurse/Nursing Assistant/Aide and Patient Care Assistant *100 hrs./$600*
• Phlebotomy/Phlebotomist *244 hrs./$1464* • Precision Metal Working, Other *375 hrs./$2250* • Welding Technology/Welder *5 students enrolled*

STUDENT SERVICES Academic or career counseling, employment services for current students, placement services for program completers, remedial services.

Mahoning County Joint Vocational School District

7300 North Palmyra Road, Canfield, OH 44406
http://www.mahoningctc.com/

CONTACT Roan M. Craig, PhD, Superintendent
Telephone: 330-729-4100 Ext. 1901

GENERAL INFORMATION Private Institution. **Total program enrollment:** 13. **Application fee:** $25.

PROGRAM(S) OFFERED
• Administrative Assistant and Secretarial Science, General • Clinical/Medical Laboratory Assistant *249 hrs./$3100* • Cosmetology/Cosmetologist, General *5 students enrolled* • Fire Science/Firefighting *120 hrs./$680* • Health Unit Coordinator/Ward Clerk *6 students enrolled* • Machine Shop Technology/Assistant • Medical Insurance Coding Specialist/Coder *242 hrs./$2975* • Medical Office Assistant/Specialist • Medical/Clinical Assistant *960 hrs./$6960* • Phlebotomy/Phlebotomist *166 hrs./$1374* • Welding Technology/Welder *4 students enrolled*

STUDENT SERVICES Academic or career counseling, employment services for current students, placement services for program completers, remedial services.

Marion Technical College

1467 Mount Vernon Avenue, Marion, OH 43302-5694
http://www.mtc.edu/

CONTACT J. Bryson, President
Telephone: 740-389-4636 Ext. 229

GENERAL INFORMATION Public Institution. Founded 1971. **Accreditation:** Regional (NCA); medical laboratory technology (NAACLS); physical therapy assisting (APTA); radiologic technology: radiography (JRCERT). **Total program enrollment:** 1032. **Application fee:** $20.

PROGRAM(S) OFFERED
• Architectural Engineering Technology/Technician *1 student enrolled* • Business Administration and Management, General *92 students enrolled* • Clinical/Medical Laboratory Science and Allied Professions, Other *13 students enrolled* • Computer Programming, Specific Applications *6 students enrolled* • Computer Systems Networking and Telecommunications *3 students enrolled* • Criminal Justice/Police Science *4 students enrolled* • Criminal Justice/Safety Studies *9 students enrolled* • Electrical and Electronic Engineering Technologies/Technicians, Other • Electrical, Electronic and Communications Engineering Technology/Technician *1 student enrolled* • Health Unit Coordinator/Ward Clerk *10 students enrolled* • Industrial Production Technologies/Technicians, Other • Mechanical Engineering/Mechanical Technology/Technician • Medical Administrative/Executive Assistant and Medical Secretary • Medical Transcription/Transcriptionist • Medical/Clinical Assistant *5 students enrolled* • Nursing, Other *117 students enrolled* • Quality Control Technology/Technician *1 student enrolled*

STUDENT SERVICES Academic or career counseling, employment services for current students, placement services for program completers, remedial services.

Medina County Career Center

1101 West Liberty Street, Medina, OH 44256
http://mccc-jvsd.org/

CONTACT Michael S. Larson, Superintendent
Telephone: 330-725-8461

GENERAL INFORMATION Private Institution. **Total program enrollment:** 75. **Application fee:** $50.

PROGRAM(S) OFFERED
• Cosmetology/Cosmetologist, General *1500 hrs./$7280* • Criminal Justice/Law Enforcement Administration *600 hrs./$3850* • Criminal Justice/Police

Science *11 students enrolled* • Dental Assisting/Assistant *600 hrs./$2779* • Heating, Air Conditioning, Ventilation and Refrigeration Maintenance Technology/Technician (HAC, HACR, HVAC, HVACR) *600 hrs./$4444* • Medical Insurance Coding Specialist/Coder • Medical Insurance Specialist/Medical Biller *900 hrs./$4254* • Medical/Clinical Assistant *910 hrs./$4395*

STUDENT SERVICES Academic or career counseling, daycare for children of students, placement services for program completers, remedial services.

Miami-Jacobs Career College

630 Main Street, Cincinnati, OH 45202
http://www.acr.edu

CONTACT Mary Percell, Director
Telephone: 513-723-0551

GENERAL INFORMATION Private Institution. **Total program enrollment:** 85. **Application fee:** $100.

STUDENT SERVICES Academic or career counseling, placement services for program completers, remedial services.

Miami-Jacobs Career College–Troy

865 W. Market Street, Troy, OH 45373
http://www.miamijacobs.edu

CONTACT Darlene Waite, President
Telephone: 937-332-8580 Ext. 302

GENERAL INFORMATION Private Institution. **Total program enrollment:** 399. **Application fee:** $20.

PROGRAM(S) OFFERED
• Aesthetician/Esthetician and Skin Care Specialist *19 students enrolled* • Licensed Practical/Vocational Nurse Training (LPN, LVN, Cert, Dipl, AAS) *177 students enrolled* • Nail Technician/Specialist and Manicurist

STUDENT SERVICES Academic or career counseling, placement services for program completers, remedial services.

Miami–Jacobs College

PO Box 1433, Dayton, OH 45401-1433
http://www.miamijacobs.edu/

CONTACT Darlene R. Waite, President
Telephone: 937-461-5174 Ext. 120

GENERAL INFORMATION Private Institution. Founded 1860. **Accreditation:** Medical assisting (AAMAE); state accredited or approved. **Total program enrollment:** 605. **Application fee:** $20.

PROGRAM(S) OFFERED
• Licensed Practical/Vocational Nurse Training (LPN, LVN, Cert, Dipl, AAS) *37 students enrolled*

STUDENT SERVICES Academic or career counseling, employment services for current students, placement services for program completers.

Miami-Jacobs–Springboro, Ohio Campus

875 West Central Avenue, Springboro, OH 45066
http://www.miamijacobs.edu/indexSpringboroSignIn.htm

CONTACT Joseph Kennedy, Chief Executive
Telephone: 937-746-1830

GENERAL INFORMATION Private Institution. **Total program enrollment:** 343. **Application fee:** $20.

Miami-Jacobs–Springboro, Ohio Campus (continued)

PROGRAM(S) OFFERED
• **Aesthetician/Esthetician and Skin Care Specialist** 5 *students enrolled* • **Dental Assisting/Assistant** • **Facial Treatment Specialist/Facialist** 5 *students enrolled* • **Licensed Practical/Vocational Nurse Training (LPN, LVN, Cert, Dipl, AAS)** 9 *students enrolled* • **Nail Technician/Specialist and Manicurist** 3 *students enrolled*

STUDENT SERVICES Academic or career counseling, employment services for current students, placement services for program completers.

Miami University

Oxford, OH 45056
http://www.muohio.edu/

CONTACT David Hodge, President
Telephone: 513-529-1809

GENERAL INFORMATION Public Institution. Founded 1809. **Accreditation:** Regional (NCA); art and design (NASAD); athletic training (JRCAT); audiology (ASHA); engineering technology (ABET/TAC); interior design: professional (CIDA); music (NASM); speech-language pathology (ASHA); theater (NAST). **Total program enrollment:** 15532. **Application fee:** $45.

PROGRAM(S) OFFERED
• **Accounting Technology/Technician and Bookkeeping** 2 *students enrolled* • **Administrative Assistant and Secretarial Science, General** 1 *student enrolled* • **Computer Technology/Computer Systems Technology** 1 *student enrolled* • **Geography** 5 *students enrolled* • **Office Management and Supervision** 2 *students enrolled*

STUDENT SERVICES Academic or career counseling, daycare for children of students, employment services for current students, placement services for program completers.

Miami University Hamilton

1601 Peck Boulevard, Hamilton, OH 45011-3399
http://www.ham.muohio.edu/

CONTACT Daniel E. Hall, Executive Director
Telephone: 513-785-3000

GENERAL INFORMATION Public Institution. Founded 1968. **Accreditation:** Regional (NCA). **Total program enrollment:** 2025. **Application fee:** $20.

STUDENT SERVICES Academic or career counseling, daycare for children of students, employment services for current students, placement services for program completers, remedial services.

Miami University–Middletown Campus

4200 East University Boulevard, Middletown, OH 45042-3497
http://www.mid.muohio.edu/

CONTACT Kelly Cowan, Executive Director
Telephone: 513-727-3200

GENERAL INFORMATION Public Institution. Founded 1966. **Accreditation:** Regional (NCA). **Total program enrollment:** 1229. **Application fee:** $20.

STUDENT SERVICES Academic or career counseling, daycare for children of students, employment services for current students, placement services for program completers, remedial services.

Moler Hollywood Beauty College

26 East 6th Street, Cincinnati, OH 45202

CONTACT Patty Marquet, Owner
Telephone: 513-621-5262

GENERAL INFORMATION Private Institution. **Total program enrollment:** 41. **Application fee:** $100.

PROGRAM(S) OFFERED
• **Cosmetology, Barber/Styling, and Nail Instructor** 300 *hrs./$2250* • **Cosmetology/Cosmetologist, General** 1800 *hrs./$13,500*

STUDENT SERVICES Placement services for program completers.

Moler Pickens Beauty College

6625G Dixie Highway, Fairfield, OH 45014

CONTACT Patty Marquet, Chief Executive Officer
Telephone: 513-874-5116

GENERAL INFORMATION Private Institution. **Total program enrollment:** 41. **Application fee:** $100.

PROGRAM(S) OFFERED
• **Cosmetology/Cosmetologist, General** 36 *students enrolled*

STUDENT SERVICES Placement services for program completers.

Moore University of Hair Design

6011 Montgomery Road, Cincinnati, OH 45213

CONTACT Marvin Gentry, President
Telephone: 513-531-3100

GENERAL INFORMATION Private Institution. **Total program enrollment:** 16. **Application fee:** $100.

PROGRAM(S) OFFERED
• **Cosmetology, Barber/Styling, and Nail Instructor** 1500 *hrs./$7900* • **Cosmetology/Cosmetologist, General** • **Nail Technician/Specialist and Manicurist** 200 *hrs./$1560* • **Salon/Beauty Salon Management/Manager** 1800 *hrs./$9880*

STUDENT SERVICES Academic or career counseling, placement services for program completers.

National Beauty College

4642 Cleveland Avenue, NW, Canton, OH 44709
http://www.nationalbc.com/

CONTACT Marlene Alfman, Director CEO
Telephone: 330-499-5596

GENERAL INFORMATION Private Institution. Founded 1955. **Total program enrollment:** 114.

PROGRAM(S) OFFERED
• **Aesthetician/Esthetician and Skin Care Specialist** 600 *hrs./$4900* • **Cosmetology/Cosmetologist, General** 1799 *hrs./$12,775* • **Nail Technician/Specialist and Manicurist** 430 *hrs./$2795* • **Salon/Beauty Salon Management/Manager** 300 *hrs./$1100*

STUDENT SERVICES Placement services for program completers.

National Institute of Massotherapy

2110 Copley Road, Akron, OH 44320
http://www.nim.edu/

CONTACT D. Bilich, Director
Telephone: 330-867-1996

GENERAL INFORMATION Private Institution. Founded 1991. **Total program enrollment:** 60. **Application fee:** $75.

PROGRAM(S) OFFERED
• **Massage Therapy/Therapeutic Massage** *65 hrs./$11,204*

STUDENT SERVICES Placement services for program completers.

Nationwide Beauty Academy

5300 Westpointe Plaza, Columbus, OH 43228

CONTACT Bobby Lott, Vice President
Telephone: 614-252-5252 Ext. 12

GENERAL INFORMATION Private Institution. **Total program enrollment:** 101.

PROGRAM(S) OFFERED
• **Cosmetology/Cosmetologist, General** *1500 hrs./$14,000* • **Nail Technician/Specialist and Manicurist**

STUDENT SERVICES Academic or career counseling, placement services for program completers.

NewLife Academy of Information Technology

114 W. Fifth Street, East Liverpool, OH 43920
http://www.newlife.edu

CONTACT Sandra A. Grace, Director of Operations
Telephone: 330-386-0445

GENERAL INFORMATION Private Institution. **Total program enrollment:** 6.

PROGRAM(S) OFFERED
• **Computer Programming/Programmer, General** *1000 hrs./$15,500*
• **Computer and Information Sciences and Support Services, Other** *731 hrs./$11,250*

STUDENT SERVICES Academic or career counseling, employment services for current students, placement services for program completers.

North Central State College

2441 Kenwood Circle, PO Box 698, Mansfield, OH 44901-0698
http://www.ncstatecollege.edu/

CONTACT Donald L. Plotts, Interim President
Telephone: 419-755-4800

GENERAL INFORMATION Public Institution. Founded 1961. **Accreditation:** Regional (NCA); physical therapy assisting (APTA); radiologic technology: radiography (JRCERT). **Total program enrollment:** 1132.

PROGRAM(S) OFFERED
• **Accounting** *8 students enrolled* • **Administrative Assistant and Secretarial Science, General** • **Business Administration and Management, General** • **Business/Commerce, General** *4 students enrolled* • **Child Development** • **Computer Science** • **Drafting and Design Technology/Technician, General** *2 students enrolled* • **Electromechanical Technology/Electromechanical Engineering Technology** • **Health Aide** *12 students enrolled* • **Heating, Air Conditioning and Refrigeration Technology/Technician (ACH/ACR/ACHR/HRAC/HVAC/AC Technology)** *1 student enrolled* • **Human Resources Management/Personnel Administration, General** • **Industrial Production Technologies/Technicians, Other** • **International Business/Trade/Commerce** • **Licensed Practical/Vocational Nurse Training (LPN, LVN, Cert, Dipl, AAS)** *61 students enrolled* • **Psychiatric/Mental Health Services Technician** *17 students enrolled* • **Purchasing, Procurement/Acquisitions and Contracts Management** • **Sales,**

Distribution and Marketing Operations, General • **Taxation** • **Teacher Assistant/Aide** • **Teaching Assistants/Aides, Other** • **Tool and Die Technology/Technician** • **Web Page, Digital/Multimedia and Information Resources Design** *1 student enrolled*

STUDENT SERVICES Academic or career counseling, daycare for children of students, employment services for current students, placement services for program completers, remedial services.

Northcoast Medical Training Academy

1832 State Route 59, Kent, OH 44240
northcoastmedicalacademy.com

CONTACT Timothy J. Runge, Campus Director
Telephone: 330-678-6600 Ext. 224

GENERAL INFORMATION Private Institution. **Total program enrollment:** 230. **Application fee:** $50.

PROGRAM(S) OFFERED
• **Massage Therapy/Therapeutic Massage** *18 students enrolled* • **Medical Staff Services Technology/Technician** *10 students enrolled* • **Medical/Clinical Assistant** *58 students enrolled* • **Nurse/Nursing Assistant/Aide and Patient Care Assistant** *46 students enrolled* • **Veterinary/Animal Health Technology/Technician and Veterinary Assistant** *37 students enrolled*

STUDENT SERVICES Placement services for program completers.

Northern Institute of Cosmetology

667-669 Broadway, Lorain, OH 44052

CONTACT Daniel Sechel, Director
Telephone: 440-244-4282

GENERAL INFORMATION Private Institution. Founded 1949. **Total program enrollment:** 29.

PROGRAM(S) OFFERED
• **Cosmetology/Cosmetologist, General** *1500 hrs./$6295*

STUDENT SERVICES Academic or career counseling, placement services for program completers.

Northwest State Community College

22-600 State Route 34, Archbold, OH 43502-9542
http://www.northweststate.edu/

CONTACT Thomas Stuckey, President
Telephone: 419-267-5511

GENERAL INFORMATION Public Institution. Founded 1968. **Accreditation:** Regional (NCA); engineering technology (ABET/TAC). **Total program enrollment:** 828. **Application fee:** $20.

PROGRAM(S) OFFERED
• **Accounting** • **Computer Engineering Technology/Technician** *1 student enrolled* • **Data Processing and Data Processing Technology/Technician** • **Electrical, Electronic and Communications Engineering Technology/Technician** *5 students enrolled* • **Emergency Medical Technology/Technician (EMT Paramedic)** *1 student enrolled* • **General Office Occupations and Clerical Services** *5 students enrolled* • **Heating, Air Conditioning and Refrigeration Technology/Technician (ACH/ACR/ACHR/HRAC/HVAC/AC Technology)** *1 student enrolled* • **Licensed Practical/Vocational Nurse Training (LPN, LVN, Cert, Dipl, AAS)** *76 students enrolled* • **Machine Tool Technology/Machinist** *2 students enrolled* • **Mechanical Engineering Related Technologies/Technicians, Other** • **Mechanical Engineering/Mechanical Technology/Technician** *4 students enrolled* • **Plastics Engineering Technology/Technician** *3 students enrolled* • **Precision Metal Working, Other** *2 students enrolled* • **Real Estate** *3 students enrolled* • **Tool and Die Technology/Technician** *1 student enrolled*

STUDENT SERVICES Academic or career counseling, daycare for children of students, employment services for current students, placement services for program completers, remedial services.

O. C. Collins Career Center

11627 State Route 243, Chesapeake, OH 45619
http://www.collins-cc.k12.oh.us/

CONTACT Stephen K. Dodgion, Superintendent
Telephone: 740-867-6641 Ext. 202

GENERAL INFORMATION Private Institution. **Total program enrollment:** 503. **Application fee:** $10.

PROGRAM(S) OFFERED
• **Autobody/Collision and Repair Technology/Technician** 9 *students enrolled* • **Automobile/Automotive Mechanics Technology/Technician** 4 *students enrolled* • **Boilermaking/Boilermaker** 11 *students enrolled* • **Communications Technologies/Technicians and Support Services, Other** • **Computer Technology/Computer Systems Technology** • **Cosmetology/Cosmetologist, General** 1 *student enrolled* • **Criminal Justice/Police Science** 20 *students enrolled* • **Diagnostic Medical Sonography/Sonographer and Ultrasound Technician** 2200 *hrs./$7000* • **Electrician** 2 *students enrolled* • **Electrocardiograph Technology/Technician** • **Emergency Medical Technology/Technician (EMT Paramedic)** 23 *students enrolled* • **Fire Science/Firefighting** 11 *students enrolled* • **Heating, Air Conditioning, Ventilation and Refrigeration Maintenance Technology/Technician (HAC, HACR, HVAC, HVACR)** 4 *students enrolled* • **Heavy/Industrial Equipment Maintenance Technologies, Other** 4 *students enrolled* • **Licensed Practical/Vocational Nurse Training (LPN, LVN, Cert, Dipl, AAS)** 1500 *hrs./$7950* • **Massage Therapy/Therapeutic Massage** • **Medical Insurance Coding Specialist/Coder** 20 *students enrolled* • **Nurse/Nursing Assistant/Aide and Patient Care Assistant** 31 *students enrolled* • **Pharmacy Technician/Assistant** 5 *students enrolled* • **Radiologic Technology/Science—Radiographer** 2200 *hrs./$7000* • **Renal/Dialysis Technologist/Technician** 600 *hrs./$3000* • **Respiratory Care Therapy/Therapist** 2200 *hrs./$5750* • **Surgical Technology/Technologist** 1000 *hrs./$4800* • **Welding Technology/Welder** 22 *students enrolled*

STUDENT SERVICES Academic or career counseling, employment services for current students, placement services for program completers, remedial services.

Ohio Business College

1907 North Ridge Road, Lorain, OH 44055
http://www.ohiobusinesscollege.com/

CONTACT Rosanne Catella, Vice President/Director
Telephone: 440-934-3101

GENERAL INFORMATION Private Institution. Founded 1903. **Accreditation:** State accredited or approved. **Total program enrollment:** 296. **Application fee:** $25.

PROGRAM(S) OFFERED
• **Accounting** • **Administrative Assistant and Secretarial Science, General** 2 *students enrolled* • **Computer Software and Media Applications, Other** 2 *students enrolled* • **Computer Technology/Computer Systems Technology** 1 *student enrolled* • **Medical Administrative/Executive Assistant and Medical Secretary** 2 *students enrolled*

STUDENT SERVICES Academic or career counseling, employment services for current students, placement services for program completers, remedial services.

Ohio Business College

5202 Timber Commons Drive, Sandusky, OH 44870
http://www.ohiobusinesscollege.com/

CONTACT Theresa M. Fisher, School Director
Telephone: 419-627-8345

GENERAL INFORMATION Private Institution. Founded 1982. **Accreditation:** State accredited or approved. **Total program enrollment:** 243. **Application fee:** $25.

PROGRAM(S) OFFERED
• **Accounting** • **Administrative Assistant and Secretarial Science, General** 4 *students enrolled* • **Computer Software and Media Applications, Other** • **Computer Technology/Computer Systems Technology** • **Medical Administrative/Executive Assistant and Medical Secretary** 7 *students enrolled*

STUDENT SERVICES Employment services for current students, placement services for program completers, remedial services.

Ohio Center for Broadcasting

4790 Red Bank Expressway, Suite 102, Cincinnati, OH 45227
http://www.beonair.com/

CONTACT Robert Mills, President
Telephone: 513-271-6060

GENERAL INFORMATION Private Institution. **Total program enrollment:** 24. **Application fee:** $125.

PROGRAM(S) OFFERED
• **Radio and Television** 36 *hrs./$12,585*

STUDENT SERVICES Academic or career counseling, employment services for current students, placement services for program completers, remedial services.

Ohio Center for Broadcasting

5330 East Main Street, Columbus, OH 43213
beonair.com

CONTACT Robert Mills, President
Telephone: 614-245-0555

GENERAL INFORMATION Private Institution. **Total program enrollment:** 130.

PROGRAM(S) OFFERED
• **Radio and Television**

STUDENT SERVICES Academic or career counseling, employment services for current students, placement services for program completers, remedial services.

Ohio Center for Broadcasting

9000 Sweet Valley Drive, Valley View, OH 44125
http://www.beonair.com/

CONTACT Robert Mills, President
Telephone: 216-447-9117

GENERAL INFORMATION Private Institution. Founded 1986. **Total program enrollment:** 215. **Application fee:** $125.

PROGRAM(S) OFFERED
• **Radio and Television** 36 *hrs./$15,141*

STUDENT SERVICES Academic or career counseling, employment services for current students, placement services for program completers, remedial services.

Ohio College of Massotherapy

225 Heritage Woods Drive, Akron, OH 44321
http://www.ocm.edu/

CONTACT Jeffrey S. Morrow, President
Telephone: 330-665-1084

GENERAL INFORMATION Private Institution. Founded 1973. **Accreditation:** State accredited or approved. **Total program enrollment:** 176. **Application fee:** $25.

PROGRAM(S) OFFERED
• **Massage Therapy/Therapeutic Massage** 16 *students enrolled*

STUDENT SERVICES Academic or career counseling, employment services for current students, placement services for program completers.

Ohio Hi Point Joint Vocational School District

2280 Street, Route 540, Bellefontaine, OH 43311-9594
http://www.ohp.k12.oh.us/

CONTACT Kimberly S. Davis, Superintendent
Telephone: 937-599-3010 Ext. 1398

GENERAL INFORMATION Private Institution. **Total program enrollment:** 102. **Application fee:** $20.

PROGRAM(S) OFFERED
• **Administrative Assistant and Secretarial Science, General** • **Health Information/Medical Records Administration/Administrator** *6 students enrolled* • **Heating, Air Conditioning, Ventilation and Refrigeration Maintenance Technology/Technician (HAC, HACR, HVAC, HVACR)** • **Industrial Mechanics and Maintenance Technology** *4 students enrolled* • **Licensed Practical/Vocational Nurse Training (LPN, LVN, Cert, Dipl, AAS)** *21 students enrolled*

STUDENT SERVICES Academic or career counseling, daycare for children of students, employment services for current students, placement services for program completers, remedial services.

Ohio Institute of Health Careers

1900 East Grandville Road, Building A, Suite 210, Columbus, OH 43229
http://ohioinstituteofhealthcareers.com/

CONTACT Melissa Warner, President
Telephone: 614-891-5030

GENERAL INFORMATION Private Institution. **Total program enrollment:** 329. **Application fee:** $33.

PROGRAM(S) OFFERED
• **Dental Assisting/Assistant** *804 hrs./$11,038* • **Health and Medical Administrative Services, Other** *19 students enrolled* • **Massage Therapy/Therapeutic Massage** *840 hrs./$12,163* • **Medical Administrative/Executive Assistant and Medical Secretary** *876 hrs./$11,627* • **Medical/Clinical Assistant** *900 hrs./$12,994*

STUDENT SERVICES Placement services for program completers.

Ohio Institute of Health Careers

631 Griswold Road, Elyria, OH 44035
http://ohioinstituteofhealthcareers.com/

CONTACT Melissa Warner, President
Telephone: 440-934-3101

GENERAL INFORMATION Private Institution. **Total program enrollment:** 43. **Application fee:** $25.

PROGRAM(S) OFFERED
• **Allied Health and Medical Assisting Services, Other** *59 students enrolled* • **Dental Assisting/Assistant** *28 students enrolled* • **Massage Therapy/Therapeutic Massage** *24 students enrolled* • **Medical Administrative/Executive Assistant and Medical Secretary** *35 students enrolled*

STUDENT SERVICES Academic or career counseling, employment services for current students, placement services for program completers.

Ohio Institute of Photography and Technology

2029 Edgefield Road, Dayton, OH 45439-1917
http://www.oipt.com/

CONTACT Derek Koebel, President
Telephone: 937-294-6155

GENERAL INFORMATION Private Institution. Founded 1971. **Accreditation:** State accredited or approved. **Total program enrollment:** 547. **Application fee:** $20.

PROGRAM(S) OFFERED
• **Medical/Clinical Assistant** *93 students enrolled* • **Pharmacy Technician/Assistant** *127 students enrolled*

STUDENT SERVICES Academic or career counseling, employment services for current students, placement services for program completers.

Ohio State Beauty Academy

57 Town Square, Lima, OH 45801
http://www.ohiostatebeauty.com/

CONTACT Greg Stolly, President
Telephone: 419-229-7896

GENERAL INFORMATION Private Institution. Founded 1965. **Total program enrollment:** 167. **Application fee:** $100.

PROGRAM(S) OFFERED
• **Cosmetology/Cosmetologist, General** *1500 hrs./$9950* • **Nail Technician/Specialist and Manicurist** *200 hrs./$1925* • **Salon/Beauty Salon Management/Manager** *300 hrs./$1775*

STUDENT SERVICES Academic or career counseling, placement services for program completers.

The Ohio State University Agricultural Technical Institute

1328 Dover Road, Wooster, OH 44691
http://www.ati.ohio-state.edu/

CONTACT Stephen Nameth, Director
Telephone: 330-264-3911

GENERAL INFORMATION Public Institution. Founded 1971. **Accreditation:** Regional (NCA). **Total program enrollment:** 672. **Application fee:** $40.

PROGRAM(S) OFFERED
• **Agricultural Power Machinery Operation** *6 students enrolled* • **Turf and Turfgrass Management** *1 student enrolled*

STUDENT SERVICES Academic or career counseling, daycare for children of students, employment services for current students, placement services for program completers, remedial services.

Ohio Technical College

1374 East 51st Street, Cleveland, OH 44103
http://www.ohiotechnicalcollege.com/

CONTACT Marc L. Brenner, Chief Executive Officer
Telephone: 216-881-1700

GENERAL INFORMATION Private Institution. Founded 1969. **Accreditation:** State accredited or approved. **Total program enrollment:** 966. **Application fee:** $100.

PROGRAM(S) OFFERED
• **Autobody/Collision and Repair Technology/Technician** *1800 hrs./$26,280* • **Automobile/Automotive Mechanics Technology/Technician** *1800 hrs./$26,280* • **Electrical/Electronics Equipment Installation and Repair, General** *17 students enrolled* • **Mechanic and Repair Technologies/Technicians, Other** *1800 hrs./$26,280* • **Motorcycle Maintenance and Repair Technology/Technician** *1200 hrs./$18,400* • **Truck and Bus Driver/Commercial Vehicle Operation** *120 hrs./$2700* • **Vehicle Maintenance and Repair Technologies, Other** *1800 hrs./$26,280*

STUDENT SERVICES Academic or career counseling, employment services for current students, placement services for program completers.

Ohio University

Athens, OH 45701-2979
http://www.ohio.edu/

CONTACT Dr. Roderick J. McDavis, President
Telephone: 740-593-1000

GENERAL INFORMATION Public Institution. Founded 1804. **Accreditation:** Regional (NCA); athletic training (JRCAT); audiology (ASHA); computer science (ABET/CSAC); counseling (ACA); dance (NASD); engineering-related programs (ABET/RAC); home economics (AAFCS); interior design: professional (CIDA); journalism and mass communications (ACEJMC); music (NASM); recreation and parks (NRPA); speech-language pathology (ASHA); theater (NAST). **Total program enrollment:** 19176. **Application fee:** $45.

PROGRAM(S) OFFERED
• **African Studies** 3 students enrolled • **Chemical Engineering** 2 students enrolled • **East Asian Studies** 8 students enrolled • **European Studies/Civilization** 9 students enrolled • **Financial Planning and Services** 5 students enrolled • **Latin American Studies** 7 students enrolled • **Marketing/Marketing Management, General** 77 students enrolled • **Political Science and Government, General** 15 students enrolled

STUDENT SERVICES Academic or career counseling, employment services for current students, placement services for program completers, remedial services.

Oregon Career Center

5721 Seaman Street, Oregon, OH 43616
http://www.oregon.k12.oh.us/pages/adulted.html

CONTACT Michael Zalar, Superintendent
Telephone: 419-697-3450

GENERAL INFORMATION Public Institution. **Total program enrollment:** 23.

PROGRAM(S) OFFERED
• **Culinary Arts/Chef Training** 670 hrs./$3350 • **Emergency Medical Technology/Technician (EMT Paramedic)** 130 hrs./$550 • **Medical Office Management/Administration** 695 hrs./$3929

STUDENT SERVICES Academic or career counseling, remedial services.

Owens Community College

PO Box 10000, Toledo, OH 43699-1947
http://www.owens.edu/

CONTACT Dr. Christa Adams, President
Telephone: 567-661-7000

GENERAL INFORMATION Public Institution. Founded 1966. **Accreditation:** Regional (NCA); dental hygiene (ADA); diagnostic medical sonography (JRCEDMS); engineering technology (ABET/TAC); physical therapy assisting (APTA); radiologic technology: radiography (JRCERT); surgical technology (ARCST). **Total program enrollment:** 6867.

PROGRAM(S) OFFERED
• **Accounting Technology/Technician and Bookkeeping** 14 students enrolled • **Accounting** 19 students enrolled • **Administrative Assistant and Secretarial Science, General** 1 student enrolled • **Architectural Drafting and Architectural CAD/CADD** 5 students enrolled • **Architectural Engineering Technology/Technician** 6 students enrolled • **Autobody/Collision and Repair Technology/Technician** 2 students enrolled • **Automotive Engineering Technology/Technician** 17 students enrolled • **Business Operations Support and Secretarial Services, Other** 6 students enrolled • **CAD/CADD Drafting and/or Design Technology/Technician** 2 students enrolled • **Commercial Photography** 2 students enrolled • **Commercial and Advertising Art** 8 students enrolled • **Computer Engineering Technology/Technician** 1 student enrolled • **Computer Programming, Specific Applications** 7 students enrolled • **Computer Systems Networking and Telecommunications** 1 student enrolled • **Construction Engineering Technology/Technician** 4 students enrolled • **Electrical, Electronic and Communications Engineering Technology/Technician** 11 students enrolled • **Environmental Engineering Technology/Environmental Technology** 1 student

enrolled • **Executive Assistant/Executive Secretary** 14 students enrolled • **Health Information/Medical Records Technology/Technician** 24 students enrolled • **Heating, Air Conditioning and Refrigeration Technology/Technician (ACH/ACR/ACHR/HRAC/HVAC/AC Technology)** 6 students enrolled • **Industrial Technology/Technician** 1 student enrolled • **Interior Design** 1 student enrolled • **Licensed Practical/Vocational Nurse Training (LPN, LVN, Cert, Dipl, AAS)** 86 students enrolled • **Massage Therapy/Therapeutic Massage** 11 students enrolled • **Medical Administrative/Executive Assistant and Medical Secretary** 7 students enrolled • **Medical Insurance Specialist/Medical Biller** 4 students enrolled • **Medical Transcription/Transcriptionist** 6 students enrolled • **Music Management and Merchandising** 2 students enrolled • **Occupational Safety and Health Technology/Technician** 3 students enrolled • **Operations Management and Supervision** 57 students enrolled • **Quality Control Technology/Technician** 12 students enrolled • **Radiologic Technology/Science—Radiographer** 4 students enrolled • **Real Estate** 4 students enrolled • **Restaurant/Food Services Management** 3 students enrolled • **Sales, Distribution and Marketing Operations, General** 19 students enrolled • **Surgical Technology/Technologist** 4 students enrolled • **Survey Technology/Surveying** 4 students enrolled • **Teacher Education and Professional Development, Specific Levels and Methods, Other** 13 students enrolled • **Tool and Die Technology/Technician** 5 students enrolled • **Welding Technology/Welder** 43 students enrolled

STUDENT SERVICES Academic or career counseling, daycare for children of students, employment services for current students, placement services for program completers, remedial services.

Paramount Beauty Academy

1745 11th Street, Portsmouth, OH 45662

CONTACT Joyce C. Goddard, President
Telephone: 740-353-2436

GENERAL INFORMATION Private Institution. **Total program enrollment:** 55. **Application fee:** $50.

PROGRAM(S) OFFERED
• **Aesthetician/Esthetician and Skin Care Specialist** 750 hrs./$7591 • **Cosmetology and Related Personal Grooming Arts, Other** • **Cosmetology/Cosmetologist, General** 1800 hrs./$12,846 • **Nail Technician/Specialist and Manicurist** 300 hrs./$2450 • **Salon/Beauty Salon Management/Manager** 300 hrs./$2420

STUDENT SERVICES Academic or career counseling, placement services for program completers.

Penta County Joint Vocational School

30095 Oregon Road, Perrysburg, OH 43551-4594
http://www.pentanet.k12.oh.us/

CONTACT Fred Susor, Superintendent
Telephone: 419-661-6555 Ext. 6181

GENERAL INFORMATION Public Institution. **Total program enrollment:** 67. **Application fee:** $30.

PROGRAM(S) OFFERED
• **Autobody/Collision and Repair Technology/Technician** 600 hrs./$4095 • **Automobile/Automotive Mechanics Technology/Technician** 735 hrs./$4095 • **Building/Property Maintenance and Management** 882 hrs./$4910 • **Data Entry/Microcomputer Applications, General** 4 students enrolled • **Heating, Air Conditioning, Ventilation and Refrigeration Maintenance Technology/Technician (HAC, HACR, HVAC, HVACR)** 882 hrs./$4910 • **Machine Shop Technology/Assistant** • **Medical Office Management/Administration** 735 hrs./$4095 • **Welding Technology/Welder** 735 hrs./$4095

STUDENT SERVICES Academic or career counseling, employment services for current students, placement services for program completers, remedial services.

Pickaway Ross Joint Vocational School District

895 Crouse Chapel Road, Chillicothe, OH 45601-9010
http://www.pickawayross.com/

CONTACT Brett Smith, Superintendent
Telephone: 740-642-1200 Ext. 288

GENERAL INFORMATION Private Institution. **Total program enrollment:** 308. **Application fee:** $50.

PROGRAM(S) OFFERED
• **Automobile/Automotive Mechanics Technology/Technician** *3 students enrolled* • **Emergency Medical Technology/Technician (EMT Paramedic)** *4 students enrolled* • **General Office Occupations and Clerical Services** *7 students enrolled* • **Heating, Air Conditioning, Ventilation and Refrigeration Maintenance Technology/Technician (HAC, HACR, HVAC, HVACR)** *5 students enrolled* • **Heavy/Industrial Equipment Maintenance Technologies, Other** *3 students enrolled* • **Licensed Practical/Vocational Nurse Training (LPN, LVN, Cert, Dipl, AAS)** *60 students enrolled* • **Management Information Systems, General** • **Medical Office Management/Administration** • **Medical/Clinical Assistant** *9 students enrolled* • **Nurse/Nursing Assistant/Aide and Patient Care Assistant** *9 students enrolled*

STUDENT SERVICES Academic or career counseling, employment services for current students, placement services for program completers, remedial services.

Pioneer Career and Technology Center: A Vocational School District

27 Ryan Road, Shelby, OH 44875
http://www.pctc.k12.oh.us/

CONTACT Glenna Cannon, Superintendent
Telephone: 419-347-7744 Ext. 1313

GENERAL INFORMATION Private Institution. **Total program enrollment:** 51.

PROGRAM(S) OFFERED
• **Business Administration and Management, General** *600 hrs./$3750* • **General Office Occupations and Clerical Services** *95 hrs./$594* • **Legal Administrative Assistant/Secretary** *600 hrs./$3750* • **Medical Transcription/Transcriptionist** *600 hrs./$4882* • **Nurse/Nursing Assistant/Aide and Patient Care Assistant** *80 hrs./$550* • **Welding Technology/Welder** *600 hrs./$3750*

STUDENT SERVICES Academic or career counseling, employment services for current students, placement services for program completers, remedial services.

Polaris Career Center

7285 Old Oak Boulevard, Middleburg Heights, OH 44130-3375
http://www.polaris.edu/

CONTACT Robert G. Timmons, Superintendent
Telephone: 440-891-7600

GENERAL INFORMATION Public Institution. **Total program enrollment:** 127.

PROGRAM(S) OFFERED
• **Automobile/Automotive Mechanics Technology/Technician** *23 students enrolled* • **Cosmetology and Related Personal Grooming Arts, Other** *8 students enrolled* • **Criminal Justice/Law Enforcement Administration** *28 students enrolled* • **Dental Assisting/Assistant** *11 students enrolled* • **Heating, Air Conditioning, Ventilation and Refrigeration Maintenance Technology/Technician (HAC, HACR, HVAC, HVACR)** *32 students enrolled* • **Machine Tool Technology/Machinist** *5 students enrolled* • **Medical/Clinical Assistant** *18 students enrolled* • **Welding Technology/Welder** *8 students enrolled*

STUDENT SERVICES Academic or career counseling, placement services for program completers, remedial services.

Portage Lakes Career Center

4401 Shriver Road, Green, OH 44232-0248
http://www.portagelakescareercenter.org/

CONTACT James Brown, Superintendent
Telephone: 330-896-8200

GENERAL INFORMATION Public Institution. **Total program enrollment:** 64. **Application fee:** $100.

PROGRAM(S) OFFERED
• **Automobile/Automotive Mechanics Technology/Technician** *600 hrs./$5400* • **Computer Technology/Computer Systems Technology** *600 hrs./$5000* • **Cosmetology/Cosmetologist, General** *1500 hrs./$6000* • **Heating, Air Conditioning, Ventilation and Refrigeration Maintenance Technology/Technician (HAC, HACR, HVAC, HVACR)** *600 hrs./$6000* • **Licensed Practical/Vocational Nurse Training (LPN, LVN, Cert, Dipl, AAS)** *26 students enrolled* • **Medical Insurance Coding Specialist/Coder** *720 hrs./$6000* • **Medical/Clinical Assistant** *900 hrs./$6800*

STUDENT SERVICES Academic or career counseling, employment services for current students, placement services for program completers, remedial services.

Practical Nurse Program of Canton City Schools

1253 Third Street, SE, Canton, OH 44707-4798
http://www.ccsdistrict.org/

CONTACT Michele D. Evans-Gardell, PhD, Superintendent
Telephone: 330-453-3271

GENERAL INFORMATION Public Institution. Founded 1967. **Total program enrollment:** 68. **Application fee:** $30.

PROGRAM(S) OFFERED
• **Licensed Practical/Vocational Nurse Training (LPN, LVN, Cert, Dipl, AAS)** *1302 hrs./$7990*

STUDENT SERVICES Remedial services.

Professional Skills Institute

20 Arco Drive, Toledo, OH 43607
http://www.proskills.com/

CONTACT Daniel A. Finch, Executive Director
Telephone: 419-720-6670

GENERAL INFORMATION Private Institution. Founded 1984. **Accreditation:** Physical therapy assisting (APTA); state accredited or approved. **Total program enrollment:** 360. **Application fee:** $25.

PROGRAM(S) OFFERED
• **Health Information/Medical Records Technology/Technician** *3 students enrolled* • **Licensed Practical/Vocational Nurse Training (LPN, LVN, Cert, Dipl, AAS)** *120 students enrolled* • **Medical Insurance Coding Specialist/Coder** *13 students enrolled* • **Medical Transcription/Transcriptionist** *1 student enrolled* • **Medical/Clinical Assistant** *20 students enrolled*

STUDENT SERVICES Academic or career counseling, placement services for program completers, remedial services.

Raphael's School of Beauty Culture

1324 Youngstown Warren Road, Niles, OH 44446
http://www.raphaelsbeautyschool.com/

CONTACT Ralph P. Delserone, III, President
Telephone: 330-652-1559

GENERAL INFORMATION Private Institution. **Total program enrollment:** 26.

Raphael's School of Beauty Culture (continued)

PROGRAM(S) OFFERED
● **Aesthetician/Esthetician and Skin Care Specialist** *750 hrs./$6975* ● **Business, Management, Marketing, and Related Support Services, Other**
● **Cosmetology, Barber/Styling, and Nail Instructor** *1000 hrs./$4400*
● **Cosmetology/Cosmetologist, General** *1800 hrs./$13,800* ● **Massage Therapy/Therapeutic Massage** *750 hrs./$8725* ● **Nail Technician/Specialist and Manicurist** *300 hrs./$2350* ● **Salon/Beauty Salon Management/Manager** *300 hrs./$2300*

STUDENT SERVICES Placement services for program completers.

Raphael's School of Beauty Culture

330 East State Street, Salem, OH 44460
http://www.raphaelsbeautyschool.com/

CONTACT Ralph P. Delserone, III, President
Telephone: 330-823-3884

GENERAL INFORMATION Private Institution. **Total program enrollment:** 11.

PROGRAM(S) OFFERED
● **Aesthetician/Esthetician and Skin Care Specialist** *750 hrs./$6975*
● **Cosmetology and Related Personal Grooming Arts, Other** *1050 hrs./$8375*
● **Cosmetology, Barber/Styling, and Nail Instructor** *1000 hrs./$4400*
● **Cosmetology/Cosmetologist, General** *1800 hrs./$13,800* ● **Nail Technician/Specialist and Manicurist** *300 hrs./$2350* ● **Salon/Beauty Salon Management/Manager** *300 hrs./$2300*

STUDENT SERVICES Placement services for program completers.

Raphael's School of Beauty Culture

3035 Belmont Avenue, Youngstown, OH 44505
http://www.raphaelsbeautyschool.com/

CONTACT Ralph P. Delserone, III, President
Telephone: 330-782-3395

GENERAL INFORMATION Private Institution. **Total program enrollment:** 11.

PROGRAM(S) OFFERED
● **Aesthetician/Esthetician and Skin Care Specialist** *750 hrs./$6975*
● **Cosmetology and Related Personal Grooming Arts, Other** *1050 hrs./$8375*
● **Cosmetology, Barber/Styling, and Nail Instructor** *1000 hrs./$4400*
● **Cosmetology/Cosmetologist, General** *1800 hrs./$13,800* ● **Nail Technician/Specialist and Manicurist** *300 hrs./$2350* ● **Salon/Beauty Salon Management/Manager** *300 hrs./$2300*

STUDENT SERVICES Placement services for program completers.

Regency Beauty Institute–Akron

1912 Buchholzer Boulevard, Akron, OH 44310

CONTACT J. Hayes Batson
Telephone: 330-633-3715

GENERAL INFORMATION Private Institution. **Total program enrollment:** 76. **Application fee:** $100.

PROGRAM(S) OFFERED
● **Cosmetology/Cosmetologist, General** *1500 hrs./$16,011*

STUDENT SERVICES Academic or career counseling, placement services for program completers.

Regency Beauty Institute–Cincinnati

4450 Eastgate Boulevard, Space #5, Cincinnati, OH 45246

GENERAL INFORMATION Private Institution. **Total program enrollment:** 48. **Application fee:** $100.

PROGRAM(S) OFFERED
● **Cosmetology/Cosmetologist, General** *1500 hrs./$16,011*

STUDENT SERVICES Academic or career counseling, placement services for program completers.

Regency Beauty Institute–Columbus

155 Graceland Boulevard, Columbus, OH 43214

CONTACT J. Hayes Batson
Telephone: 614-468-0495

GENERAL INFORMATION Private Institution. **Total program enrollment:** 9. **Application fee:** $100.

PROGRAM(S) OFFERED
● **Cosmetology/Cosmetologist, General** *1500 hrs./$16,011*

STUDENT SERVICES Academic or career counseling, placement services for program completers.

Regency Beauty Institute–Dayton

2040 Miamisburg-Centerville Road, Dayton, OH 45459

CONTACT J. Hayes Batson
Telephone: 937-558-0569

GENERAL INFORMATION Private Institution. **Total program enrollment:** 20. **Application fee:** $100.

PROGRAM(S) OFFERED
● **Cosmetology/Cosmetologist, General** *1500 hrs./$16,011*

STUDENT SERVICES Academic or career counseling, placement services for program completers.

Regency Beauty Institute–North Olmsted

26508 Lorain Road, North Olmsted, OH 44070

CONTACT J. Hayes Batson
Telephone: 440-249-5274

GENERAL INFORMATION Private Institution. **Total program enrollment:** 14. **Application fee:** $100.

PROGRAM(S) OFFERED
● **Cosmetology/Cosmetologist, General** *1500 hrs./$16,011*

STUDENT SERVICES Academic or career counseling, placement services for program completers.

Regency Beauty Institute–Springdale

11489 Princeton Pike, Springdale, OH 45246

GENERAL INFORMATION Private Institution. **Total program enrollment:** 49. **Application fee:** $100.

PROGRAM(S) OFFERED
● **Cosmetology/Cosmetologist, General** *1500 hrs./$16,011*

STUDENT SERVICES Academic or career counseling, placement services for program completers.

Remington College–Cleveland Campus

14445 Broadway Avenue, Cleveland, OH 44125
http://www.remingtoncollege.edu/

CONTACT Charles Dull, President
Telephone: 216-475-7520

GENERAL INFORMATION Private Institution. **Accreditation:** State accredited or approved. **Total program enrollment:** 541. **Application fee:** $50.

PROGRAM(S) OFFERED
• Electrical, Electronic and Communications Engineering Technology/Technician • Medical Insurance Coding Specialist/Coder 82 *students enrolled* • Medical/Clinical Assistant 152 *students enrolled* • Pharmacy Technician/Assistant 32 *students enrolled*

STUDENT SERVICES Academic or career counseling, employment services for current students, placement services for program completers.

Remington College–Cleveland West Campus

26350 Brookpark Road, North Olmstead, OH 44070
http://www.remingtoncollege.edu/

CONTACT Gary A. Azotea, Campus President
Telephone: 440-777-2560

GENERAL INFORMATION Private Institution. Founded 2003. **Total program enrollment:** 426. **Application fee:** $50.

PROGRAM(S) OFFERED
• Dental Assisting/Assistant 45 *students enrolled* • Medical Insurance Coding Specialist/Coder 63 *students enrolled* • Medical/Clinical Assistant 136 *students enrolled* • Pharmacy Technician/Assistant 28 *students enrolled*

STUDENT SERVICES Academic or career counseling, employment services for current students, placement services for program completers.

RETS Tech Center

555 East Alex Bell Road, Centerville, OH 45459
http://www.retstechcenter.com/

CONTACT Richard Rucker, PhD, Director
Telephone: 937-433-3410

GENERAL INFORMATION Private Institution. Founded 1953. **Accreditation:** Medical assisting (AAMAE); state accredited or approved. **Total program enrollment:** 1073. **Application fee:** $100.

PROGRAM(S) OFFERED
• Heating, Air Conditioning and Refrigeration Technology/Technician (ACH/ACR/ACHR/HRAC/HVAC/AC Technology) 121 *students enrolled* • Medical Insurance Coding Specialist/Coder 32 *students enrolled* • Nursing, Other 342 *students enrolled* • Tourism and Travel Services Marketing Operations 5 *students enrolled*

STUDENT SERVICES Employment services for current students, placement services for program completers, remedial services.

Rosedale Bible College

2270 Rosedale Road, Irwin, OH 43029-9501
http://www.rosedalebible.org/

CONTACT Christopher Jones, Dean of Students
Telephone: 740-857-1311

GENERAL INFORMATION Private Institution. Founded 1952. **Accreditation:** State accredited or approved. **Total program enrollment:** 55. **Application fee:** $50.

PROGRAM(S) OFFERED
• Bible/Biblical Studies 18 *students enrolled*

STUDENT SERVICES Academic or career counseling, employment services for current students.

Ross Medical Education Center–Sylvania

5834 Monroe Street, Suite F-J, Sylvania, OH 43560

CONTACT Paul Mitchell, President/CEO
Telephone: 419-882-3203

GENERAL INFORMATION Private Institution. **Total program enrollment:** 60. **Application fee:** $45.

PROGRAM(S) OFFERED
• Medical Insurance Specialist/Medical Biller 51 *hrs./$13,555* • Medical/Clinical Assistant 45 *hrs./$13,555*

STUDENT SERVICES Placement services for program completers.

Sandusky Adult Education

2130 Hayes Avenue, Sandusky, OH 44870
http://www.sanduskycareercenter.org/

CONTACT Nancy Zechman, Director
Telephone: 419-625-9294

GENERAL INFORMATION Public Institution. **Total program enrollment:** 88. **Application fee:** $40.

PROGRAM(S) OFFERED
• Business Administration, Management and Operations, Other 640 *hrs./$4509* • Cosmetology/Cosmetologist, General 1500 *hrs./$8920* • Criminal Justice/Police Science 640 *hrs./$4400* • Licensed Practical/Vocational Nurse Training (LPN, LVN, Cert, Dipl, AAS) 1210 *hrs./$9065* • Medical Office Management/Administration 720 *hrs./$4750* • Medical/Clinical Assistant 900 *hrs./$6107* • Nurse/Nursing Assistant/Aide and Patient Care Assistant 61 *students enrolled*

STUDENT SERVICES Academic or career counseling, employment services for current students, remedial services.

Sanford-Brown Institute

17535 Rosbough Drive, Suite 100, Middleburg Heights, OH 44130
http://www.sbcleveland.com/

CONTACT Christine Smith, President
Telephone: 440-202-3232

GENERAL INFORMATION Private Institution. **Total program enrollment:** 1028. **Application fee:** $25.

PROGRAM(S) OFFERED
• Cardiovascular Technology/Technologist 1860 *hrs./$34,140* • Criminal Justice/Safety Studies 6 *students enrolled* • Diagnostic Medical Sonography/Sonographer and Ultrasound Technician 1860 *hrs./$34,140* • Health and Medical Administrative Services, Other 114 *students enrolled* • Massage Therapy/Therapeutic Massage 960 *hrs./$14,865* • Medical Insurance Coding Specialist/Coder 900 *hrs./$13,865* • Medical/Clinical Assistant 900 *hrs./$14,165* • Pharmacy Technician/Assistant 900 *hrs./$11,820*

STUDENT SERVICES Academic or career counseling, employment services for current students, placement services for program completers.

School of Nursing at Cuyahoga Valley Career Center

6726 Ridge Road, Parma, OH 44129
http://www.cvcc.k12.oh.us/

CONTACT Myrna George, Coordinator
Telephone: 440-746-8200

GENERAL INFORMATION Public Institution. Founded 1963. **Total program enrollment:** 66. **Application fee:** $45.

PROGRAM(S) OFFERED
● **Licensed Practical/Vocational Nurse Training (LPN, LVN, Cert, Dipl, AAS)** *1200 hrs./$11,000*

STUDENT SERVICES Academic or career counseling, placement services for program completers, remedial services.

Scioto County Joint Vocational School District

PO Box 766, Lucasville, OH 45648
http://www.scjvs.com/

CONTACT Stan Jennings, Superintendent
Telephone: 740-259-5526

GENERAL INFORMATION Private Institution. **Total program enrollment:** 198.

PROGRAM(S) OFFERED
● **Construction Trades, General** *1200 hrs./$7954* ● **Criminal Justice/Police Science** *20 students enrolled* ● **Dental Assisting/Assistant** *900 hrs./$4835* ● **Electrician** *1200 hrs./$6591* ● **Executive Assistant/Executive Secretary** *23 students enrolled* ● **General Office Occupations and Clerical Services** *10 students enrolled* ● **Health Services/Allied Health/Health Sciences, General** *8 students enrolled* ● **Heavy/Industrial Equipment Maintenance Technologies, Other** *12 students enrolled* ● **Industrial Mechanics and Maintenance Technology** *1200 hrs./$7293* ● **Licensed Practical/Vocational Nurse Training (LPN, LVN, Cert, Dipl, AAS)** *1350 hrs./$10,804* ● **Medical Office Computer Specialist/Assistant** *900 hrs./$4747* ● **Surgical Technology/Technologist** *10 students enrolled*

STUDENT SERVICES Academic or career counseling, employment services for current students, placement services for program completers, remedial services.

Shawnee State University

940 Second Street, Portsmouth, OH 45662-4344
http://www.shawnee.edu/

CONTACT Dr. Rita Rice Morris, President
Telephone: 740-354-3205

GENERAL INFORMATION Public Institution. Founded 1986. **Accreditation:** Regional (NCA); dental hygiene (ADA); medical laboratory technology (NAACLS); medical technology (NAACLS); physical therapy assisting (APTA); radiologic technology: radiography (JRCERT). **Total program enrollment:** 3282.

PROGRAM(S) OFFERED
● **Computer Engineering Technology/Technician** ● **Drafting and Design Technology/Technician, General** *1 student enrolled* ● **Ecology** ● **Plastics Engineering Technology/Technician** ● **Sign Language Interpretation and Translation**

STUDENT SERVICES Academic or career counseling, daycare for children of students, employment services for current students, placement services for program completers, remedial services.

Sinclair Community College

444 West Third Street, Dayton, OH 45402-1460
http://www.sinclair.edu/

CONTACT Dr. Steven Lee Johnson, President
Telephone: 937-512-3000

GENERAL INFORMATION Public Institution. Founded 1887. **Accreditation:** Regional (NCA); art and design (NASAD); dental hygiene (ADA); engineering technology (ABET/TAC); health information technology (AHIMA); medical assisting (AAMAE); music (NASM); physical therapy assisting (APTA); radiologic technology: radiography (JRCERT); surgical technology (ARCST). **Total program enrollment:** 8188. **Application fee:** $20.

PROGRAM(S) OFFERED
● **Accounting Technology/Technician and Bookkeeping** *3 students enrolled* ● **Aeronautics/Aviation/Aerospace Science and Technology, General** *5 students enrolled* ● **Aircraft Powerplant Technology/Technician** *4 students enrolled* ● **Airframe Mechanics and Aircraft Maintenance Technology/Technician** *3 students enrolled* ● **Arts Management** ● **Automotive Engineering Technology/Technician** *17 students enrolled* ● **Avionics Maintenance Technology/Technician** *2 students enrolled* ● **Banking and Financial Support Services** *3 students enrolled* ● **Business Administration and Management, General** *34 students enrolled* ● **Business Operations Support and Secretarial Services, Other** *5 students enrolled* ● **Business/Office Automation/Technology/Data Entry** *2 students enrolled* ● **Civil Engineering Technology/Technician** *6 students enrolled* ● **Communication Studies/Speech Communication and Rhetoric** *2 students enrolled* ● **Computer and Information Sciences and Support Services, Other** *91 students enrolled* ● **Computer and Information Sciences, General** *3 students enrolled* ● **Computer and Information Systems Security** *2 students enrolled* ● **Construction Engineering Technology/Technician** *24 students enrolled* ● **Cytotechnology/Cytotechnologist** *4 students enrolled* ● **Dance, General** *2 students enrolled* ● **Dental Hygiene/Hygienist** *61 students enrolled* ● **Dietetics/Dietitians** *27 students enrolled* ● **Drafting and Design Technology/Technician, General** ● **Drawing** *4 students enrolled* ● **Early Childhood Education and Teaching** *3 students enrolled* ● **Electrical, Electronic and Communications Engineering Technology/Technician** *34 students enrolled* ● **Electrocardiograph Technology/Technician** *54 students enrolled* ● **Electromechanical Technology/Electromechanical Engineering Technology** *2 students enrolled* ● **Emergency Medical Technology/Technician (EMT Paramedic)** *401 students enrolled* ● **Family and Community Services** *2 students enrolled* ● **Fire Protection and Safety Technology/Technician** *60 students enrolled* ● **General Office Occupations and Clerical Services** *33 students enrolled* ● **Health Information/Medical Records Technology/Technician** *81 students enrolled* ● **Heating, Air Conditioning and Refrigeration Technology/Technician (ACH/ACR/ACHR/HRAC/HVAC/AC Technology)** *13 students enrolled* ● **Hematology Technology/Technician** ● **Human Resources Management/Personnel Administration, General** *35 students enrolled* ● **Industrial Production Technologies/Technicians, Other** *18 students enrolled* ● **Instrumentation Technology/Technician** ● **Intermedia/Multimedia** *26 students enrolled* ● **Kindergarten/Preschool Education and Teaching** *41 students enrolled* ● **Management Information Systems and Services, Other** *7 students enrolled* ● **Manufacturing Technology/Technician** *3 students enrolled* ● **Mechanical Engineering/Mechanical Technology/Technician** *1 student enrolled* ● **Medical Administrative/Executive Assistant and Medical Secretary** *14 students enrolled* ● **Medical Office Management/Administration** *1 student enrolled* ● **Medical Transcription/Transcriptionist** *5 students enrolled* ● **Music, General** *1 student enrolled* ● **Pharmacy Technician/Assistant** *28 students enrolled* ● **Phlebotomy/Phlebotomist** *60 students enrolled* ● **Photographic and Film/Video Technology/Technician and Assistant** *11 students enrolled* ● **Physical Education Teaching and Coaching** *11 students enrolled* ● **Prepress/Desktop Publishing and Digital Imaging Design** *6 students enrolled* ● **Printing Press Operator** ● **Printmaking** *201 students enrolled* ● **Quality Control Technology/Technician** *1 student enrolled* ● **Real Estate** *281 students enrolled* ● **Restaurant/Food Services Management** *37 students enrolled* ● **Sculpture** *1 student enrolled* ● **Sign Language Interpretation and Translation** *44 students enrolled* ● **Substance Abuse/Addiction Counseling** *2 students enrolled* ● **Survey Technology/Surveying** *4 students enrolled* ● **Tool and Die Technology/Technician** *4 students enrolled*

STUDENT SERVICES Academic or career counseling, daycare for children of students, employment services for current students, placement services for program completers, remedial services.

Southern State Community College

100 Hobart Drive, Hillsboro, OH 45133-9487
http://www.sscc.edu/

CONTACT Sherry A. Stout, President
Telephone: 937-393-3431

GENERAL INFORMATION Public Institution. Founded 1975. **Accreditation:** Regional (NCA); medical assisting (AAMAE). **Total program enrollment:** 1136.

PROGRAM(S) OFFERED
● **Business/Office Automation/Technology/Data Entry** *3 students enrolled*
● **Criminal Justice/Police Science** *15 students enrolled* ● **Emergency Medical Technology/Technician (EMT Paramedic)** *3 students enrolled* ● **General Office Occupations and Clerical Services** *4 students enrolled* ● **Horticultural Science** *2 students enrolled* ● **Licensed Practical/Vocational Nurse Training (LPN, LVN, Cert, Dipl, AAS)** *22 students enrolled* ● **Medical Transcription/Transcriptionist** *10 students enrolled* ● **Pharmacy Technician/Assistant** *1 student enrolled*
● **Phlebotomy/Phlebotomist** *10 students enrolled*

STUDENT SERVICES Academic or career counseling, daycare for children of students, employment services for current students, placement services for program completers, remedial services.

Southwestern College of Business

149 Northland Boulevard, Cincinnati, OH 45246-1122
http://www.swcollege.net/

CONTACT David Caldwell, Executive Director
Telephone: 513-874-0432

GENERAL INFORMATION Private Institution. Founded 1972. **Accreditation:** State accredited or approved. **Total program enrollment:** 826. **Application fee:** $100.

PROGRAM(S) OFFERED
● **Accounting** ● **Clinical/Medical Laboratory Technician** *35 students enrolled*
● **Computer and Information Sciences, General** *3 students enrolled* ● **Health Information/Medical Records Administration/Administrator** *113 students enrolled* ● **Massage Therapy/Therapeutic Massage** ● **Medical/Clinical Assistant** *66 students enrolled*

STUDENT SERVICES Academic or career counseling, employment services for current students, placement services for program completers, remedial services.

Southwestern College of Business

632 Vine Street, Suite 200, Cincinnati, OH 45202-4304
http://www.swcollege.net/

CONTACT Mark Mann
Telephone: 513-421-3212

GENERAL INFORMATION Private Institution. Founded 1972. **Accreditation:** State accredited or approved. **Total program enrollment:** 446. **Application fee:** $100.

PROGRAM(S) OFFERED
● **Allied Health and Medical Assisting Services, Other** *11 students enrolled*
● **Computer/Information Technology Services Administration and Management, Other** ● **Medical Insurance Coding Specialist/Coder** *14 students enrolled* ● **Phlebotomy/Phlebotomist** *12 students enrolled*

STUDENT SERVICES Academic or career counseling, employment services for current students, placement services for program completers.

Southwestern College of Business

111 West First Street, Dayton, OH 45402-3003
http://www.swcollege.net/

CONTACT James A. Smolinski, Director
Telephone: 937-224-0061

GENERAL INFORMATION Private Institution. Founded 1972. **Accreditation:** State accredited or approved. **Total program enrollment:** 689.

PROGRAM(S) OFFERED
● **Accounting and Related Services, Other** ● **Clinical/Medical Laboratory Assistant** *20 students enrolled* ● **Information Science/Studies** ● **Massage Therapy/Therapeutic Massage** ● **Medical Administrative/Executive Assistant and Medical Secretary** *25 students enrolled* ● **Medical/Clinical Assistant** *22 students enrolled*

STUDENT SERVICES Academic or career counseling, employment services for current students, placement services for program completers.

Southwestern College of Business

201 East Second Street, Franklin, OH 45005
http://www.swcollege.net/

CONTACT Ronald L. Mills, Jr., Executive Director
Telephone: 937-746-6633

GENERAL INFORMATION Private Institution. Founded 1981. **Accreditation:** State accredited or approved. **Total program enrollment:** 273.

PROGRAM(S) OFFERED
● **Computer and Information Sciences, General** ● **Medical Insurance Specialist/Medical Biller** *21 students enrolled* ● **Medical/Clinical Assistant** *42 students enrolled* ● **Phlebotomy/Phlebotomist** *14 students enrolled*

STUDENT SERVICES Academic or career counseling, employment services for current students, placement services for program completers, remedial services.

The Spa School

5050 N. High, Columbus, OH 43214
http://www.beauty-schools.com/

CONTACT Bobby Lott, Vice President
Telephone: 614-252-5252 Ext. 12

GENERAL INFORMATION Private Institution. **Total program enrollment:** 95.

PROGRAM(S) OFFERED
● **Aesthetician/Esthetician and Skin Care Specialist** *750 hrs./$8750*
● **Cosmetology and Related Personal Grooming Arts, Other** ● **Cosmetology/Cosmetologist, General** *1800 hrs./$14,400* ● **Nail Technician/Specialist and Manicurist** *300 hrs./$3800*

Stark State College of Technology

6200 Frank Avenue, NW, North Canton, OH 44720-7299
http://www.starkstate.edu/

CONTACT John O'Donnell, President
Telephone: 330-494-6170

GENERAL INFORMATION Public Institution. Founded 1970. **Accreditation:** Regional (NCA); dental hygiene (ADA); engineering technology (ABET/TAC); health information technology (AHIMA); medical assisting (AAMAE); medical laboratory technology (NAACLS); physical therapy assisting (APTA). **Total program enrollment:** 2987. **Application fee:** $65.

PROGRAM(S) OFFERED
● **Accounting Technology/Technician and Bookkeeping** *20 students enrolled*
● **Administrative Assistant and Secretarial Science, General** *6 students enrolled* ● **Fire Protection and Safety Technology/Technician** *11 students*

Stark State College of Technology (continued)

enrolled • **Health Information/Medical Records Technology/Technician** *25 students enrolled* • **Health Professions and Related Clinical Sciences, Other** *9 students enrolled* • **Heating, Air Conditioning and Refrigeration Technology/ Technician (ACH/ACR/ACHR/HRAC/HVAC/AC Technology)** *16 students enrolled* • **Industrial Technology/Technician** *1 student enrolled* • **Rehabilitation and Therapeutic Professions, Other** *35 students enrolled*

STUDENT SERVICES Academic or career counseling, employment services for current students, placement services for program completers, remedial services.

Stautzenberger College

1796 Indian Wood Circle, Maumee, OH 43537
http://www.stautzen.com/

CONTACT George A. Simon, President
Telephone: 419-866-0261

GENERAL INFORMATION Private Institution. **Accreditation:** Medical assisting (AAMAE); state accredited or approved. **Total program enrollment:** 574. **Application fee:** $25.

PROGRAM(S) OFFERED
• **Business/Office Automation/Technology/Data Entry** *1 student enrolled*
• **Computer Systems Networking and Telecommunications** *2 students enrolled*
• **Massage Therapy/Therapeutic Massage** *9 students enrolled* • **Medical Insurance Coding Specialist/Coder** *9 students enrolled* • **Medical Office Assistant/ Specialist** *2 students enrolled* • **Medical Transcription/Transcriptionist** *2 students enrolled* • **Medical/Clinical Assistant** *38 students enrolled*

STUDENT SERVICES Academic or career counseling, employment services for current students, placement services for program completers.

TCTC Adult Training Center

528 Educational Highway, Warren, OH 44483
http://www.tctcadulttraining.org/

CONTACT Wayne McClain, Superintendent
Telephone: 330-847-0503 Ext. 1600

GENERAL INFORMATION Public Institution. **Total program enrollment:** 220.

PROGRAM(S) OFFERED
• **Administrative Assistant and Secretarial Science, General** *$4200*
• **Automobile/Automotive Mechanics Technology/Technician** *$7365* • **Building/ Property Maintenance and Management** *8 students enrolled* • **Construction Trades, General** *$4150* • **Licensed Practical/Vocational Nurse Training (LPN, LVN, Cert, Dipl, AAS)** *1160 hrs./$9977* • **Medical Office Computer Specialist/ Assistant** *$4637* • **Medical/Clinical Assistant** *$6780* • **Pharmacy Technician/ Assistant** *5 students enrolled*

STUDENT SERVICES Academic or career counseling, placement services for program completers, remedial services.

TDDS

1688 North Pricetown Road, Diamond, OH 44412-9608
http://www.tdds.edu/

CONTACT Richard A. Rathburn, Jr., President, School Director
Telephone: 330-538-2216

GENERAL INFORMATION Private Institution. Founded 1973. **Total program enrollment:** 237.

PROGRAM(S) OFFERED
• **Diesel Mechanics Technology/Technician** *1500 hrs./$15,095* • **Transportation and Materials Moving, Other** *270 hrs./$5645* • **Truck and Bus Driver/ Commercial Vehicle Operation** *262 students enrolled*

STUDENT SERVICES Academic or career counseling, employment services for current students, placement services for program completers, remedial services.

Technology Education College

2745 Winchester Pike, Columbus, OH 43232
http://www.teceducation.com/

CONTACT James Vaas, Executive Director
Telephone: 614-456-4600

GENERAL INFORMATION Private Institution. **Accreditation:** State accredited or approved. **Total program enrollment:** 478.

PROGRAM(S) OFFERED
• **Data Processing and Data Processing Technology/Technician** *35 students enrolled* • **Medical/Clinical Assistant** *170 students enrolled* • **Pharmacy Technician/Assistant**

STUDENT SERVICES Academic or career counseling, employment services for current students, placement services for program completers.

TechSkills—Columbus

2400 Corporate Exchange Drive, Suite 270, Columbus, OH 43231

CONTACT Jason Mahoney, Chief Financial Officer
Telephone: 614-891-3200

GENERAL INFORMATION Private Institution.

PROGRAM(S) OFFERED
• **Accounting Technology/Technician and Bookkeeping** • **Business Administration and Management, General** *2 students enrolled* • **Business/Office Automation/Technology/Data Entry** *6 students enrolled* • **Computer Engineering, General** *1 student enrolled* • **Computer Programming, Vendor/Product Certification** *4 students enrolled* • **Computer Software Engineering** • **Computer Systems Networking and Telecommunications** *60 hrs./$1425* • **Computer and Information Sciences and Support Services, Other** *150 hrs./$1890* • **Computer and Information Systems Security** *1 student enrolled* • **Computer/Information Technology Services Administration and Management, Other** *24 students enrolled* • **Data Modeling/Warehousing and Database Administration** *3 students enrolled* • **Health Information/Medical Records Administration/Administrator** *12 students enrolled* • **Information Technology** *360 hrs.* • **Medical Insurance Coding Specialist/Coder** • **Medical Insurance Specialist/Medical Biller** *3 students enrolled* • **Medical Office Management/Administration** *360 hrs./$4700* • **Medical Transcription/Transcriptionist** *8 students enrolled* • **Pharmacy Technician/Assistant** *3 students enrolled* • **System Administration/Administrator** *555 hrs./$7850* • **System, Networking, and LAN/WAN Management/Manager** *90 hrs./$1430* • **Web Page, Digital/Multimedia and Information Resources Design** *4 students enrolled*

STUDENT SERVICES Academic or career counseling, placement services for program completers.

Terra State Community College

2830 Napoleon Road, Fremont, OH 43420-9670
http://www.terra.edu/

CONTACT Dr. Marsha Bordner, President
Telephone: 419-334-8400

GENERAL INFORMATION Public Institution. Founded 1968. **Accreditation:** Regional (NCA). **Total program enrollment:** 985.

PROGRAM(S) OFFERED
• **Accounting** • **Allied Health and Medical Assisting Services, Other** • **Automotive Engineering Technology/Technician** *7 students enrolled* • **Business Administration and Management, General** *3 students enrolled* • **Commercial and Advertising Art** • **Computer Programming/Programmer, General** *1 student enrolled* • **Electrical, Electronic and Communications Engineering Technology/ Technician** *1 student enrolled* • **Entrepreneurship/Entrepreneurial Studies** • **Executive Assistant/Executive Secretary** *6 students enrolled* • **Fine Arts and Art Studies, Other** • **General Office Occupations and Clerical Services** • **Health Information/Medical Records Technology/Technician** • **Health and Medical Administrative Services, Other** *3 students enrolled* • **Heating, Air Conditioning and Refrigeration Technology/Technician (ACH/ACR/ACHR/HRAC/ HVAC/AC Technology)** *10 students enrolled* • **Marketing/Marketing Management, General** *1 student enrolled* • **Mechanical Engineering Related Technologies/Technicians, Other** *4 students enrolled* • **Medical Administrative/ Executive Assistant and Medical Secretary** • **Operations Management and Supervision** *1 student enrolled* • **Plastics Engineering Technology/Technician**

• Quality Control Technology/Technician • Robotics Technology/Technician • Social Work *3 students enrolled* • Tool and Die Technology/Technician • Welding Technology/Welder *2 students enrolled*

STUDENT SERVICES Academic or career counseling, daycare for children of students, employment services for current students, placement services for program completers, remedial services.

Tiffin Academy of Hair Design

104 East Market Street, Tiffin, OH 44883
http://tiffinacademy.com/

CONTACT Therese E. Vogel, President
Telephone: 419-447-3117

GENERAL INFORMATION Private Institution. Founded 1962. **Total program enrollment:** 62. **Application fee:** $100.

PROGRAM(S) OFFERED
• Nail Technician/Specialist and Manicurist *4 students enrolled*

STUDENT SERVICES Academic or career counseling.

Toledo Academy of Beauty Culture–South

1554 South Byrne Road, Glenbyrne Center, Toledo, OH 43614

CONTACT Leonard H. Rosenberg, President
Telephone: 419-381-7218

GENERAL INFORMATION Private Institution. Founded 1982. **Total program enrollment:** 34.

PROGRAM(S) OFFERED
• Cosmetology/Cosmetologist, General *300 hrs./$1894*

STUDENT SERVICES Academic or career counseling, placement services for program completers.

Toledo School of Practical Nursing

1602 Washington Street, Whitney Building, Toledo, OH 43624
http://www.tps.org/

CONTACT Joan Reasonover, Director, Adult Education
Telephone: 419-671-8700

GENERAL INFORMATION Public Institution. Founded 1949. **Total program enrollment:** 410. **Application fee:** $50.

PROGRAM(S) OFFERED
• Administrative Assistant and Secretarial Science, General • Barbering/Barber *5 students enrolled* • Construction Trades, General *1 student enrolled* • Corrections and Criminal Justice, Other *7 students enrolled* • Licensed Practical/Vocational Nurse Training (LPN, LVN, Cert, Dipl, AAS) *77 students enrolled* • Medical Insurance Coding Specialist/Coder • Nurse/Nursing Assistant/Aide and Patient Care Assistant *118 students enrolled*

STUDENT SERVICES Academic or career counseling, employment services for current students, placement services for program completers, remedial services.

Total Technical Institute

8700 Brook Park Road, Brooklyn, OH 44129
http://www.ttinst.com/

CONTACT Jodi Donnelly, Executive Director
Telephone: 216-485-0900

GENERAL INFORMATION Private Institution. **Total program enrollment:** 482.

PROGRAM(S) OFFERED
• Electrical/Electronics Maintenance and Repair Technology, Other *94 students enrolled* • Machine Tool Technology/Machinist *127 students enrolled* • Medical Office Assistant/Specialist *56 students enrolled* • Medical/Clinical Assistant *99 students enrolled* • Pharmacy Technician/Assistant *16 students enrolled*

STUDENT SERVICES Academic or career counseling, employment services for current students, placement services for program completers, remedial services.

Tri-County Vocational School Adult Career Center

15676 State Rte. 691, Nelsonville, OH 45764
http://tricountyhightech.com/

CONTACT William Wittman, Superintendent
Telephone: 740-753-5464

GENERAL INFORMATION Public Institution. **Total program enrollment:** 61.

PROGRAM(S) OFFERED
• Administrative Assistant and Secretarial Science, General *2 students enrolled* • Cosmetology, Barber/Styling, and Nail Instructor *6 students enrolled* • Cosmetology/Cosmetologist, General *1500 hrs./$6500* • Medical Administrative/Executive Assistant and Medical Secretary *903 hrs./$3900* • Medical/Clinical Assistant *1204 hrs./$6225* • Welding Technology/Welder *903 hrs./$3900*

STUDENT SERVICES Academic or career counseling, daycare for children of students, employment services for current students, placement services for program completers, remedial services.

Tri-Rivers Career Center

2222 Marion Mount Gilead Road, Marion, OH 43302
http://tririvers.com/

CONTACT Richard George, Adult Director
Telephone: 740-389-4681 Ext. 700

GENERAL INFORMATION Private Institution. **Total program enrollment:** 136. **Application fee:** $95.

PROGRAM(S) OFFERED
• Emergency Medical Technology/Technician (EMT Paramedic) *800 hrs./$4295* • Health Aide *12 students enrolled* • Industrial Mechanics and Maintenance Technology *600 hrs./$6779* • Licensed Practical/Vocational Nurse Training (LPN, LVN, Cert, Dipl, AAS) *1387 hrs./$8315* • Massage Therapy/Therapeutic Massage *800 hrs./$7720* • Nurse/Nursing Assistant/Aide and Patient Care Assistant *624 hrs./$5568* • Nursing—Registered Nurse Training (RN, ASN, BSN, MSN) *1400 hrs./$8085*

STUDENT SERVICES Academic or career counseling, daycare for children of students, employment services for current students, placement services for program completers, remedial services.

Tri-State Bible College

506 Margaret Street, PO Box 445, South Point, OH 45680-8402
http://www.tsbc.edu/

CONTACT Clifford L. Marquardt, President
Telephone: 740-377-2520

GENERAL INFORMATION Private Institution. Founded 1970. **Accreditation:** State accredited or approved. **Total program enrollment:** 9. **Application fee:** $25.

PROGRAM(S) OFFERED
• Theology and Religious Vocations, Other *2 students enrolled*

STUDENT SERVICES Academic or career counseling, employment services for current students, placement services for program completers.

Tri-State College of Massotherapy

9159 Market Street, Suite 26, North Lima, OH 44452
http://www.tristatemasso.com/

CONTACT Diane Alexander, Vice President/Director
Telephone: 330-629-9998

GENERAL INFORMATION Private Institution. **Total program enrollment:** 8. **Application fee:** $50.

PROGRAM(S) OFFERED
• **Massage Therapy/Therapeutic Massage** 11 *students enrolled*

STUDENT SERVICES Placement services for program completers.

Trumbull Business College

3200 Ridge Road, Warren, OH 44484
http://www.tbc-trumbullbusiness.com/

CONTACT Dennis R. Griffith, Director/President
Telephone: 330-369-3200

GENERAL INFORMATION Private Institution. Founded 1972. **Accreditation:** State accredited or approved. **Total program enrollment:** 268. **Application fee:** $75.

PROGRAM(S) OFFERED
• **Accounting** • **Administrative Assistant and Secretarial Science, General** • **Data Processing and Data Processing Technology/Technician** • **Legal Administrative Assistant/Secretary** • **Medical Office Assistant/Specialist**

STUDENT SERVICES Academic or career counseling, employment services for current students, placement services for program completers, remedial services.

The University of Akron

302 Buchtel Common, Akron, OH 44325
http://www.uakron.edu/

CONTACT Luis M. Proenza, President
Telephone: 330-972-7111

GENERAL INFORMATION Public Institution. Founded 1870. **Accreditation:** Regional (NCA); art and design (NASAD); audiology (ASHA); counseling (ACA); cytotechnology (ASC); dance (NASD); engineering technology (ABET/TAC); home economics (AAFCS); interior design: professional (CIDA); medical assisting (AAMAE); music (NASM); speech-language pathology (ASHA); surgical technology (ARCST). **Total program enrollment:** 17444. **Application fee:** $30.

PROGRAM(S) OFFERED
• **Accounting Technology/Technician and Bookkeeping** 1 *student enrolled* • **Administrative Assistant and Secretarial Science, General** 1 *student enrolled* • **African Studies** • **Archeology** • **Athletic Training/Trainer** • **Biology/Biological Sciences, General** 10 *students enrolled* • **Business Administration and Management, General** 1 *student enrolled* • **Cartography** 3 *students enrolled* • **Chemical Engineering** 4 *students enrolled* • **Community Organization and Advocacy** • **Computer Science** 1 *student enrolled* • **Computer Systems Analysis/Analyst** • **Computer Systems Networking and Telecommunications** • **Computer and Information Sciences and Support Services, Other** 3 *students enrolled* • **Construction Engineering Technology/Technician** 1 *student enrolled* • **Criminal Justice/Police Science** 1 *student enrolled* • **Culinary Arts/Chef Training** • **Data Modeling/Warehousing and Database Administration** • **Development Economics and International Development** • **Drafting and Design Technology/Technician, General** • **Early Childhood Education and Teaching** 2 *students enrolled* • **Education, Other** • **Electrical, Electronic and Communications Engineering Technology/Technician** 1 *student enrolled* • **Entrepreneurship/Entrepreneurial Studies** • **Executive Assistant/Executive Secretary** • **Family Systems** 13 *students enrolled* • **Financial Planning and Services** • **Fire Protection and Safety Technology/Technician** • **Fire Protection, Other** • **Forensic Science and Technology** • **French Language and Literature** • **General Office Occupations and Clerical Services** • **Health and Physical Education/Fitness, Other** • **Hospitality Administration/Management, General** 3 *students enrolled* • **Hotel/Motel Administration/Management** • **International Business/Trade/Commerce** • **International Relations and Affairs** 4 *students enrolled* • **Legal**

Assistant/Paralegal • **Linguistics** • **Logistics and Materials Management** • **Marketing/Marketing Management, General** 1 *student enrolled* • **Mechanical Engineering** • **Medical Office Management/Administration** 1 *student enrolled* • **Office Management and Supervision** 1 *student enrolled* • **Organizational Communication, General** 1 *student enrolled* • **Physical Education Teaching and Coaching** • **Piano and Organ** 5 *students enrolled* • **Political Science and Government, Other** 7 *students enrolled* • **Polymer/Plastics Engineering** • **Pre-Law Studies** 1 *student enrolled* • **Public Administration and Social Service Professions, Other** 1 *student enrolled* • **Quality Control Technology/Technician** • **Real Estate** • **Restaurant/Food Services Management** • **Retailing and Retail Operations** • **Russian Language and Literature** • **Selling Skills and Sales Operations** • **Sign Language Interpretation and Translation** • **Small Business Administration/Management** • **Social Work** • **Social Work, Other** • **Sociology** • **Spanish Language and Literature** • **Sport and Fitness Administration/Management** • **Substance Abuse/Addiction Counseling** 2 *students enrolled* • **Surgical Technology/Technologist** • **Survey Technology/Surveying** 2 *students enrolled* • **Teaching English as a Second or Foreign Language/ESL Language Instructor** 1 *student enrolled* • **Technical Teacher Education** • **Therapeutic Recreation/Recreational Therapy** • **Tourism and Travel Services Management** • **Web Page, Digital/Multimedia and Information Resources Design** • **Women's Studies**

STUDENT SERVICES Academic or career counseling, daycare for children of students, employment services for current students, placement services for program completers, remedial services.

The University of Akron–Wayne College

1901 Smucker Road, Orrville, OH 44667-9192
http://www.wayne.uakron.edu/

CONTACT John P. Kristofco, Dean
Telephone: 800-221-8308

GENERAL INFORMATION Public Institution. Founded 1972. **Accreditation:** Regional (NCA). **Total program enrollment:** 916. **Application fee:** $30.

PROGRAM(S) OFFERED
• **Administrative Assistant and Secretarial Science, General** • **Computer Systems Networking and Telecommunications** • **Education, Other** • **Environmental Health** • **Medical Office Management/Administration** 8 *students enrolled* • **Medical Transcription/Transcriptionist** 5 *students enrolled* • **Organizational Communication, General** 1 *student enrolled* • **Social Work** 9 *students enrolled* • **Social Work, Other**

STUDENT SERVICES Academic or career counseling, employment services for current students, placement services for program completers, remedial services.

University of Cincinnati

2624 Clifton Avenue, Cincinnati, OH 45221
http://www.uc.edu/

CONTACT Nancy L. Zimpher, President
Telephone: 513-556-6000

GENERAL INFORMATION Public Institution. Founded 1819. **Accreditation:** Regional (NCA); art and design (NASAD); athletic training (JRCAT); audiology (ASHA); counseling (ACA); dance (NASD); dietetics: post-baccalaureate internship (ADtA/CAADE); engineering technology (ABET/TAC); engineering-related programs (ABET/RAC); interior design: professional (CIDA); medical technology (NAACLS); music (NASM); nuclear medicine technology (JRCNMT); physical therapy assisting (APTA); speech-language pathology (ASHA); theater (NAST). **Total program enrollment:** 22493. **Application fee:** $40.

PROGRAM(S) OFFERED
• **Arabic Language and Literature** 1 *student enrolled* • **Asian Studies/Civilization** 24 *students enrolled* • **Business, Management, Marketing, and Related Support Services, Other** 1 *student enrolled* • **Clinical Laboratory Science/Medical Technology/Technologist** 7 *students enrolled* • **Computer and Information Sciences, General** 1 *student enrolled* • **Dietetics/Dietitians** 6 *students enrolled* • **Education/Teaching of Individuals with Hearing Impairments, Including Deafness** 7 *students enrolled* • **Horticultural Science** 3 *students enrolled* • **Human Development, Family Studies, and Related Services, Other** 3 *students enrolled* • **Journalism** 5 *students enrolled* • **Legal Assistant/Paralegal** 2 *students enrolled* • **Marriage and Family Therapy/**

Counseling *2 students enrolled* • **Political Science and Government, General** *19 students enrolled* • **Public Relations/Image Management** *9 students enrolled* • **Social Sciences, General** *8 students enrolled* • **Spanish Language and Literature** *4 students enrolled* • **Turf and Turfgrass Management** *1 student enrolled*

STUDENT SERVICES Academic or career counseling, daycare for children of students, employment services for current students, placement services for program completers, remedial services.

University of Cincinnati Clermont College

4200 Clermont College Drive, Batavia, OH 45103-1785
http://www.clc.uc.edu/

CONTACT David Devier, Dean
Telephone: 513-732-5200

GENERAL INFORMATION Public Institution. Founded 1972. **Accreditation:** Regional (NCA). **Total program enrollment: 2032. Application fee:** $40.

PROGRAM(S) OFFERED
• **Business Administration and Management, General** *3 students enrolled* • **Computer Technology/Computer Systems Technology** *1 student enrolled* • **Computer Typography and Composition Equipment Operator** *3 students enrolled* • **Computer and Information Sciences, General** *3 students enrolled* • **Criminal Justice/Safety Studies** *2 students enrolled* • **Emergency Medical Technology/Technician (EMT Paramedic)** *17 students enrolled* • **Finance and Financial Management Services, Other** *1 student enrolled* • **Marketing/Marketing Management, General** *3 students enrolled* • **Medical Administrative/Executive Assistant and Medical Secretary** *2 students enrolled* • **Medical/Clinical Assistant** *4 students enrolled* • **Office Management and Supervision** *1 student enrolled* • **Quality Control and Safety Technologies/Technicians, Other** *1 student enrolled* • **Rehabilitation and Therapeutic Professions, Other** *1 student enrolled* • **Surgical Technology/Technologist** *3 students enrolled*

STUDENT SERVICES Academic or career counseling, employment services for current students, placement services for program completers, remedial services.

University of Cincinnati Raymond Walters College

9555 Plainfield Road, Cincinnati, OH 45236-1007
http://www.rwc.uc.edu/

CONTACT Dolores Straker, Dean
Telephone: 513-745-5600

GENERAL INFORMATION Public Institution. Founded 1967. **Accreditation:** Regional (NCA); dental hygiene (ADA); radiologic technology: radiation therapy technology (JRCERT); radiologic technology: radiography (JRCERT). **Total program enrollment: 2275. Application fee:** $40.

PROGRAM(S) OFFERED
• **Computer Programming/Programmer, General** *3 students enrolled* • **Design and Applied Arts, Other** *3 students enrolled* • **Emergency Medical Technology/Technician (EMT Paramedic)** *29 students enrolled* • **Ethnic, Cultural Minority, and Gender Studies, Other** *3 students enrolled* • **Medical Administrative/Executive Assistant and Medical Secretary** *1 student enrolled* • **Medical Transcription/Transcriptionist** *2 students enrolled* • **Radio and Television Broadcasting Technology/Technician** *2 students enrolled* • **Women's Studies** *1 student enrolled*

STUDENT SERVICES Academic or career counseling, daycare for children of students, employment services for current students, placement services for program completers, remedial services.

University of Northwestern Ohio

1441 North Cable Road, Lima, OH 45805-1498
http://www.unoh.edu/

CONTACT Jeffrey Jarvis, President
Telephone: 419-998-3140

GENERAL INFORMATION Private Institution. Founded 1920. **Accreditation:** Regional (NCA); medical assisting (AAMAE). **Total program enrollment: 3145. Application fee:** $50.

PROGRAM(S) OFFERED
• **Agricultural Business and Management, General** • **Agricultural Mechanics and Equipment/Machine Technology** *34 students enrolled* • **Automobile/**

Automotive Mechanics Technology/Technician *199 students enrolled* • **Computer and Information Sciences and Support Services, Other** • **Diesel Mechanics Technology/Technician** *33 students enrolled* • **Executive Assistant/Executive Secretary** • **General Office Occupations and Clerical Services** • **Heating, Air Conditioning, Ventilation and Refrigeration Maintenance Technology/Technician (HAC, HACR, HVAC, HVACR)** *19 students enrolled* • **Legal Assistant/Paralegal** *4 students enrolled* • **Mechanic and Repair Technologies/Technicians, Other** • **Medical Insurance Coding Specialist/Coder** *1 student enrolled* • **Medical Transcription/Transcriptionist** • **Tourism Promotion Operations**

STUDENT SERVICES Academic or career counseling, employment services for current students, placement services for program completers, remedial services.

University of Rio Grande

218 North College Avenue, Rio Grande, OH 45674
http://www.rio.edu/

CONTACT Greg Sojka, President
Telephone: 740-245-7206

GENERAL INFORMATION Private Institution. Founded 1876. **Accreditation:** Regional (NCA); medical laboratory technology (NAACLS). **Total program enrollment: 1498. Application fee:** $25.

PROGRAM(S) OFFERED
• **Administrative Assistant and Secretarial Science, General** *2 students enrolled* • **Business/Office Automation/Technology/Data Entry** • **Pre-Pharmacy Studies** *1 student enrolled* • **Welding Technology/Welder**

STUDENT SERVICES Academic or career counseling, daycare for children of students, employment services for current students, placement services for program completers, remedial services.

The University of Toledo

2801 West Bancroft, Toledo, OH 43606-3390
http://www.utoledo.edu/

CONTACT Lloyd A. Jacobs, MD, President
Telephone: 419-530-4636

GENERAL INFORMATION Public Institution. Founded 1872. **Accreditation:** Regional (NCA); athletic training (JRCAT); cardiovascular technology (JRCECT); computer science (ABET/CSAC); counseling (ACA); engineering technology (ABET/TAC); medical assisting (AAMAE); music (NASM); recreation and parks (NRPA); respiratory therapy technology (CoARC); speech-language pathology (ASHA). **Total program enrollment: 17331. Application fee:** $40.

PROGRAM(S) OFFERED
• **Child Care and Support Services Management** • **Civil Engineering Technology/Technician** • **Electrocardiograph Technology/Technician** • **Emergency Medical Technology/Technician (EMT Paramedic)** • **Family Resource Management Studies, General** • **General Office Occupations and Clerical Services** • **Geography** • **Health Information/Medical Records Administration/Administrator** *6 students enrolled* • **Health and Medical Administrative Services, Other** • **Health/Health Care Administration/Management** • **Legal Assistant/Paralegal** *8 students enrolled* • **Legal Professions and Studies, Other** • **Mechanical Engineering/Mechanical Technology/Technician** • **Medical Administrative/Executive Assistant and Medical Secretary** • **Occupational Therapy/Therapist** *20 students enrolled* • **Public Administration and Social Service Professions, Other** • **Public Administration**

STUDENT SERVICES Academic or career counseling, daycare for children of students, employment services for current students, placement services for program completers, remedial services.

Upper Valley JVS

8811 Career Drive, Piqua, OH 45356
http://www.uvjvs.org/

CONTACT Dr. Nancy Luce, Superintendent
Telephone: 937-778-1980

GENERAL INFORMATION Public Institution. Founded 1975. **Total program enrollment:** 93. **Application fee:** $35.

PROGRAM(S) OFFERED
• **Accounting Technology/Technician and Bookkeeping** *1 student enrolled* • **Administrative Assistant and Secretarial Science, General** *900 hrs./$7230* • **Heating, Air Conditioning, Ventilation and Refrigeration Maintenance Technology/Technician (HAC, HACR, HVAC, HVACR)** *3 students enrolled* • **Industrial Electronics Technology/Technician** *7 students enrolled* • **Industrial Mechanics and Maintenance Technology** *800 hrs./$10,570* • **Licensed Practical/Vocational Nurse Training (LPN, LVN, Cert, Dipl, AAS)** *1356 hrs./ $14,719* • **Machine Tool Technology/Machinist** *640 hrs./$8456* • **Mechanics and Repairers, General** *9 students enrolled* • **Medical Administrative/Executive Assistant and Medical Secretary** *1 student enrolled* • **Word Processing** *2 students enrolled*

STUDENT SERVICES Academic or career counseling, employment services for current students, placement services for program completers, remedial services.

Urbana University

579 College Way, Urbana, OH 43078-2091
http://www.urbana.edu/

CONTACT Stephen B. Jones, President
Telephone: 937-484-1301

GENERAL INFORMATION Private Institution (Affiliated with Church of the New Jerusalem). Founded 1850. **Accreditation:** Regional (NCA). **Total program enrollment:** 861. **Application fee:** $25.

PROGRAM(S) OFFERED
• **Accounting**

STUDENT SERVICES Academic or career counseling, employment services for current students, placement services for program completers, remedial services.

Ursuline College

2550 Lander Road, Pepper Pike, OH 44124-4398
http://www.ursuline.edu/

CONTACT Diana Stano, OSU, PhD, President
Telephone: 440-449-4200

GENERAL INFORMATION Private Institution. Founded 1871. **Accreditation:** Regional (NCA). **Total program enrollment:** 783. **Application fee:** $25.

STUDENT SERVICES Academic or career counseling, remedial services.

Vanguard Career Center

1306 Cedar Street, Fremont, OH 43420
http://www.vscc.k12.oh.us/

CONTACT Gregory A. Edinger, Superintendent
Telephone: 419-334-6901

GENERAL INFORMATION Public Institution. **Total program enrollment:** 19.

PROGRAM(S) OFFERED
• **Building/Property Maintenance and Management** *600 hrs./$2530* • **Computer Installation and Repair Technology/Technician** *900 hrs./$3495* • **Emergency Medical Technology/Technician (EMT Paramedic)** *720 hrs./$6280* • **General Office Occupations and Clerical Services** *720 hrs./$3180* • **Health Professions and Related Clinical Sciences, Other** *900 hrs./$5499*

STUDENT SERVICES Remedial services.

Vantage Vocational School

818 North Franklin Street, Van Wert, OH 45891

CONTACT Ms. Staci Kaufman, Superintendent
Telephone: 419-238-5411 Ext. 110

GENERAL INFORMATION Public Institution. Founded 1976. **Total program enrollment:** 58.

PROGRAM(S) OFFERED
• **Criminal Justice/Police Science** *622 hrs./$2075* • **Medical Office Assistant/ Specialist** *1000 hrs./$3679* • **Medical Office Computer Specialist/Assistant** *900 hrs./$4499* • **Nurse/Nursing Assistant/Aide and Patient Care Assistant** *85 hrs./$501* • **Phlebotomy/Phlebotomist** *900 hrs./$3579* • **Truck and Bus Driver/ Commercial Vehicle Operation** *240 hrs./$3825*

STUDENT SERVICES Academic or career counseling, employment services for current students, placement services for program completers, remedial services.

Vatterott College

5025 East Royalton Road, Broadview Heights, OH 44147
http://www.vatterott-college.edu/

CONTACT Kate Spies, Director
Telephone: 440-526-1660

GENERAL INFORMATION Private Institution. **Accreditation:** State accredited or approved. **Total program enrollment:** 202.

PROGRAM(S) OFFERED
• **Building/Property Maintenance and Management** *9 students enrolled* • **Electrician** *23 students enrolled* • **Heating, Air Conditioning, Ventilation and Refrigeration Maintenance Technology/Technician (HAC, HACR, HVAC, HVACR)** *33 students enrolled* • **Information Technology** *3 students enrolled*

STUDENT SERVICES Academic or career counseling, employment services for current students, placement services for program completers.

Vogue Beauty Academy

13238 Cedar Road, Cleveland Heights, OH 44118

CONTACT Harold G. Underwood, FAA
Telephone: 216-320-1444

GENERAL INFORMATION Private Institution. **Total program enrollment:** 84. **Application fee:** $50.

PROGRAM(S) OFFERED
• **Cosmetology and Related Personal Grooming Arts, Other** *50 students enrolled* • **Cosmetology/Cosmetologist, General** *1000 hrs./$6330*

STUDENT SERVICES Employment services for current students, placement services for program completers.

Warren County Career Center

3525 N. Street Rte. 48, Lebanon, OH 45036-1099
http://www.wccareercenter.com/

CONTACT Margaret Hess, Superintendent
Telephone: 513-932-8145 Ext. 5270

GENERAL INFORMATION Public Institution. **Total program enrollment:** 147. **Application fee:** $45.

PROGRAM(S) OFFERED
• **Allied Health and Medical Assisting Services, Other** *900 hrs./$6895* • **Construction/Heavy Equipment/Earthmoving Equipment Operation** *450 hrs./*

$5040 • **Cosmetology/Cosmetologist, General** 26 *students enrolled* • **Electrical and Power Transmission Installation/Installer, General** 900 *hrs./$9950* • **Emergency Medical Technology/Technician (EMT Paramedic)** 80 *students enrolled* • **Fire Protection and Safety Technology/Technician** 49 *students enrolled* • **Hair Styling/Stylist and Hair Design** 1500 *hrs./$8045* • **Heating, Air Conditioning, Ventilation and Refrigeration Maintenance Technology/ Technician (HAC, HACR, HVAC, HVACR)** • **Heavy Equipment Maintenance Technology/Technician** 55 *students enrolled* • **Information Technology** 59 *students enrolled* • **Medical Insurance Coding Specialist/Coder** 720 *hrs./$5725* • **Nurse/Nursing Assistant/Aide and Patient Care Assistant** 208 *students enrolled* • **Welding Technology/Welder** 600 *hrs./$7045*

STUDENT SERVICES Academic or career counseling, placement services for program completers, remedial services.

Washington County Career Center Adult Education

Rte. 2, Marietta, OH 45750
http://www.mycareerschool.com/

CONTACT Dewayne Poling, Director-Adult Technical Training
Telephone: 740-373-6283

GENERAL INFORMATION Public Institution. **Total program enrollment:** 197.

PROGRAM(S) OFFERED
• **Carpentry/Carpenter** 720 *hrs./$6000* • **Construction Trades, Other** 14 *students enrolled* • **Electrician** 720 *hrs./$7000* • **Heating, Air Conditioning, Ventilation and Refrigeration Maintenance Technology/Technician (HAC, HACR, HVAC, HVACR)** 720 *hrs./$10,010* • **Industrial Mechanics and Maintenance Technology** 720 *hrs./$7000* • **Industrial Production Technologies/Technicians, Other** 6 *students enrolled* • **Instrumentation Technology/Technician** 12 *students enrolled* • **Medical Administrative/Executive Assistant and Medical Secretary** 42 *students enrolled* • **Medical/Clinical Assistant** 900 *hrs./$5000* • **Welding Technology/Welder** 720 *hrs./$7000*

STUDENT SERVICES Academic or career counseling, employment services for current students, placement services for program completers, remedial services.

Washington State Community College

710 Colegate Drive, Marietta, OH 45750-9225
http://www.wscc.edu/

CONTACT Charlotte Hatfield, President
Telephone: 740-374-8716

GENERAL INFORMATION Public Institution. Founded 1971. **Accreditation:** Regional (NCA); medical laboratory technology (NAACLS); physical therapy assisting (APTA). **Total program enrollment:** 872.

PROGRAM(S) OFFERED
• **Licensed Practical/Vocational Nurse Training (LPN, LVN, Cert, Dipl, AAS)** 48 *students enrolled*

STUDENT SERVICES Academic or career counseling, daycare for children of students, remedial services.

Western Hills School of Beauty and Hair Design

6490 Glenway, Cincinnati, OH 45211
http://www.schoolsofcosmetology.com/

CONTACT Carlo Hornsby, President
Telephone: 513-574-3818

GENERAL INFORMATION Private Institution. **Total program enrollment:** 118. **Application fee:** $50.

PROGRAM(S) OFFERED
• **Aesthetician/Esthetician and Skin Care Specialist** 750 *hrs./$8890* • **Cosmetology and Related Personal Grooming Arts, Other** 1050 *hrs./$9890* • **Cosmetology/Cosmetologist, General** 1800 *hrs./$15,890* • **Nail Technician/ Specialist and Manicurist** 300 *hrs./$3400*

STUDENT SERVICES Employment services for current students, placement services for program completers.

W. Howard Nicol School of Practical Nursing

4401 Shriver Road, PO Box 248, Green, OH 44232-0248
http://plcc.k12.oh.us/

CONTACT James Brown, Superintendent
Telephone: 330-896-8105

GENERAL INFORMATION Public Institution. Founded 1966. **Total program enrollment:** 35. **Application fee:** $50.

PROGRAM(S) OFFERED
• **Licensed Practical/Vocational Nurse Training (LPN, LVN, Cert, Dipl, AAS)** 1300 *hrs./$10,500*

STUDENT SERVICES Academic or career counseling, employment services for current students, placement services for program completers, remedial services.

Willoughby-Eastlake School of Practical Nursing

25 Public Square, Willoughby, OH 44094
http://www.willoughby-eastlake.k12.oh.us/tech/nursingweb/

CONTACT Keith Miller, Superintendent
Telephone: 440-946-7085

GENERAL INFORMATION Private Institution. **Total program enrollment:** 76. **Application fee:** $25.

PROGRAM(S) OFFERED
• **Nursing, Other** 52 *students enrolled*

STUDENT SERVICES Academic or career counseling, employment services for current students, remedial services.

Xavier University

3800 Victory Parkway, Cincinnati, OH 45207
http://www.xu.edu/

CONTACT Michael J. Graham, SJ, President
Telephone: 513-745-3000

GENERAL INFORMATION Private Institution. Founded 1831. **Accreditation:** Regional (NCA); athletic training (JRCAT); radiologic technology: radiography (JRCERT). **Total program enrollment:** 4202. **Application fee:** $35.

PROGRAM(S) OFFERED
• **Business, Management, Marketing, and Related Support Services, Other**

STUDENT SERVICES Academic or career counseling, employment services for current students, placement services for program completers, remedial services.

Youngstown State University

One University Plaza, Youngstown, OH 44555-0001
http://www.ysu.edu/

CONTACT David C. Sweet, President
Telephone: 877-468-6978

GENERAL INFORMATION Public Institution. Founded 1908. **Accreditation:** Regional (NCA); art and design (NASAD); counseling (ACA); dental

Youngstown State University (continued)

hygiene (ADA); emergency medical services (JRCEMTP); engineering technology (ABET/TAC); histologic technology (NAACLS); home economics (AAFCS); medical assisting (AAMAE); medical laboratory technology (NAACLS); music (NASM); theater (NAST). **Total program enrollment:** 10255. **Application fee:** $30.

PROGRAM(S) OFFERED
• Biology/Biological Sciences, General *3 students enrolled* • Business Administration and Management, General *1 student enrolled* • Entrepreneurship/Entrepreneurial Studies *3 students enrolled* • Fine Arts and Art Studies, Other *2 students enrolled* • Geography *7 students enrolled* • Non-Profit/Public/Organizational Management *3 students enrolled*

STUDENT SERVICES Academic or career counseling, daycare for children of students, employment services for current students, placement services for program completers, remedial services.

Zane State College

1555 Newark Road, Zanesville, OH 43701-2626
http://www.zanestate.edu/

CONTACT Paul Brown, President
Telephone: 740-454-2501

GENERAL INFORMATION Public Institution. Founded 1969. **Accreditation:** Regional (NCA); engineering technology (ABET/TAC); medical assisting (AAMAE); medical laboratory technology (NAACLS); physical therapy assisting (APTA); radiologic technology: radiography (JRCERT). **Total program enrollment:** 1279. **Application fee:** $25.

PROGRAM(S) OFFERED
• Accounting • Business Administration and Management, General *31 students enrolled* • Data Processing and Data Processing Technology/Technician *37 students enrolled* • Gene/Genetic Therapy • Marketing/Marketing Management, General • Medical Transcription/Transcriptionist • Medical/Clinical Assistant *1 student enrolled*

STUDENT SERVICES Academic or career counseling, employment services for current students, placement services for program completers, remedial services.

PENNSYLVANIA ———

Academy of Court Reporting Inc

235 4th Avenue, Pittsburgh, PA 15222
http://www.acr.edu

CONTACT Anna Bartolini, Campus Director
Telephone: 412-535-0560

GENERAL INFORMATION Private Institution. **Total program enrollment:** 120. **Application fee:** $100.

PROGRAM(S) OFFERED
• Legal Assistant/Paralegal • Security and Loss Prevention Services *1 student enrolled*

STUDENT SERVICES Academic or career counseling, employment services for current students, placement services for program completers.

Academy of Creative Hair Design

252 West Side Mall Office Complex, Kingston, PA 18704

CONTACT Joan Welgus, Co-Owner
Telephone: 570-825-8363

GENERAL INFORMATION Private Institution. **Total program enrollment:** 50. **Application fee:** $100.

PROGRAM(S) OFFERED
• Cosmetology, Barber/Styling, and Nail Instructor *500 hrs./$5000* • Cosmetology/Cosmetologist, General *1250 hrs./$15,375* • Nail Technician/Specialist and Manicurist *200 hrs./$1800*

Academy of Hair Design

5 East Third Street, Bloomsburg, PA 17815

CONTACT Joan Welgus, President
Telephone: 570-459-5501

GENERAL INFORMATION Private Institution. Founded 1976. **Total program enrollment:** 78. **Application fee:** $100.

PROGRAM(S) OFFERED
• Aesthetician/Esthetician and Skin Care Specialist *125 hrs./$3600* • Cosmetology and Related Personal Grooming Arts, Other *125 hrs./$15,375* • Cosmetology, Barber/Styling, and Nail Instructor *270 hrs./$6000* • Cosmetology/Cosmetologist, General *7 students enrolled* • Nail Technician/Specialist and Manicurist *125 hrs./$2700*

STUDENT SERVICES Placement services for program completers.

Allentown School of Cosmetology

1921 Union Boulevard, Allentown, PA 18103-1629

CONTACT Truc Do, President
Telephone: 610-437-4626

GENERAL INFORMATION Private Institution. Founded 1952. **Total program enrollment:** 102. **Application fee:** $100.

PROGRAM(S) OFFERED
• Aesthetician/Esthetician and Skin Care Specialist *300 hrs./$4200* • Cosmetology, Barber/Styling, and Nail Instructor *500 hrs./$5000* • Cosmetology/Cosmetologist, General *125 hrs./$17,550* • Nail Technician/Specialist and Manicurist *200 hrs./$3000*

STUDENT SERVICES Academic or career counseling, placement services for program completers.

Allied Medical and Technical Institute

166 Slocum Street, Forty Fort, PA 18704-2936
http://www.alliedteched.edu/forty_fort.htm

CONTACT Ruth L. Brumagin, Director
Telephone: 570-288-8400

GENERAL INFORMATION Private Institution. Founded 1984. **Accreditation:** State accredited or approved. **Total program enrollment:** 417. **Application fee:** $50.

PROGRAM(S) OFFERED
• Clinical/Medical Laboratory Assistant *59 students enrolled* • Construction Trades, General *25 students enrolled* • Construction Trades, Other *960 hrs./$15,775* • Massage Therapy/Therapeutic Massage *730 hrs./$11,440* • Medical Transcription/Transcriptionist *730 hrs./$10,945* • Medical/Clinical Assistant *730 hrs./$10,945* • Pharmacy Technician/Assistant *25 students enrolled* • Phlebotomy/Phlebotomist *730 hrs./$10,945*

STUDENT SERVICES Placement services for program completers.

Allied Medical and Technical Institute

517 Ash Street, Scranton, PA 18509-2903
http://www.alliedteched.edu/

CONTACT Duncan Anderson, President/CEO
Telephone: 570-558-1818

GENERAL INFORMATION Private Institution. **Total program enrollment:** 202. **Application fee:** $50.

PROGRAM(S) OFFERED
• Clinical/Medical Laboratory Assistant *20 students enrolled* • Clinical/Medical Laboratory Science and Allied Professions, Other *730 hrs./$11,712* • Dental Assisting/Assistant *1100 hrs./$16,410* • Dental Laboratory Technology/Technician *1500 hrs./$22,121* • Health Professions and Related Clinical Sciences, Other *27 students enrolled* • Medical Administrative/Executive Assistant and Medical Secretary *12 students enrolled* • Medical Transcription/Transcriptionist *730 hrs./$11,989* • Medical/Clinical Assistant *1500 hrs./$23,471* • Web Page, Digital/Multimedia and Information Resources Design *1500 hrs./$22,151*

STUDENT SERVICES Academic or career counseling, employment services for current students, placement services for program completers.

All-State Career School

501 Seminole Street, Lester, PA 19029-1825
http://www.allstatecareer.com/

CONTACT Duncan Anderson, President
Telephone: 610-521-1818 Ext. 226

GENERAL INFORMATION Private Institution. Founded 1984. **Total program enrollment:** 245.

PROGRAM(S) OFFERED
• Dental Assisting/Assistant *48 hrs./$15,680* • Emergency Medical Technology/Technician (EMT Paramedic) *77 hrs./$23,200* • Heating, Air Conditioning and Refrigeration Technology/Technician (ACH/ACR/ACHR/HRAC/HVAC/AC Technology) *50 hrs./$13,080* • Medical Insurance Specialist/Medical Biller *37 hrs./$11,575* • Medical/Clinical Assistant *37 hrs./$11,575* • Truck and Bus Driver/Commercial Vehicle Operation *23 hrs./$9231*

STUDENT SERVICES Academic or career counseling, employment services for current students, placement services for program completers.

All-State Career School

97 Second Street, North Versailles, PA 15137
http://www.allstatecareer.com/

CONTACT Duncan Anderson, President
Telephone: 412-823-1818

GENERAL INFORMATION Private Institution.

PROGRAM(S) OFFERED
• Truck and Bus Driver/Commercial Vehicle Operation *62 hrs./$2365*

STUDENT SERVICES Academic or career counseling, employment services for current students, placement services for program completers, remedial services.

Altoona Beauty School of Hair Design and Cosmetology

1100 Sixth Avenue, Altoona, PA 16602
http://www.altoonabeautyschool.com/

CONTACT Linzi J. Biesinger, Owner
Telephone: 814-942-3141

GENERAL INFORMATION Private Institution. Founded 1956. **Total program enrollment:** 45. **Application fee:** $50.

PROGRAM(S) OFFERED
• Aesthetician/Esthetician and Skin Care Specialist *450 hrs./$3160* • Cosmetology, Barber/Styling, and Nail Instructor *3 students enrolled* • Cosmetology/Cosmetologist, General *1250 hrs./$9038* • Electrolysis/Electrology and Electrolysis Technician *2 students enrolled* • Nail Technician/Specialist and Manicurist *300 hrs./$2140* • Trade and Industrial Teacher Education *600 hrs./$4180*

STUDENT SERVICES Academic or career counseling, placement services for program completers.

Antonelli Medical and Professional Institute

1700 Industrial Highway, Pottstown, PA 19464-9250

CONTACT G. Michael Orthaus, Director
Telephone: 610-323-7270

GENERAL INFORMATION Private Institution. Founded 1986. **Total program enrollment:** 58.

PROGRAM(S) OFFERED
• Medical Administrative/Executive Assistant and Medical Secretary *725 hrs./$6275* • Medical/Clinical Assistant *975 hrs./$9675* • Nurse/Nursing Assistant/Aide and Patient Care Assistant *100 hrs./$750*

STUDENT SERVICES Academic or career counseling, employment services for current students, placement services for program completers, remedial services.

The Art Institute of Philadelphia

1622 Chestnut Street, Philadelphia, PA 19103-5198
http://www.artinstitutes.edu/philadelphia/

CONTACT Dr. William Larkin, President
Telephone: 800-275-2474

GENERAL INFORMATION Private Institution. Founded 1966. **Accreditation:** State accredited or approved. **Total program enrollment:** 2426. **Application fee:** $50.

PROGRAM(S) OFFERED
• Baking and Pastry Arts/Baker/Pastry Chef *38 students enrolled* • Culinary Arts/Chef Training *22 students enrolled*

STUDENT SERVICES Academic or career counseling, employment services for current students, placement services for program completers, remedial services.

The Art Institute of Pittsburgh

420 Boulevard of the Allies, Pittsburgh, PA 15219
http://www.artinstitutes.edu/pittsburgh/

CONTACT George L. Pry, President
Telephone: 412-291-6200

GENERAL INFORMATION Private Institution. Founded 1921. **Accreditation:** Regional (MSA/CIHE); state accredited or approved. **Total program enrollment:** 2402. **Application fee:** $50.

PROGRAM(S) OFFERED
• Commercial and Advertising Art *13 students enrolled* • Culinary Arts/Chef Training *8 students enrolled* • Interior Design *12 students enrolled* • Web Page, Digital/Multimedia and Information Resources Design *7 students enrolled*

STUDENT SERVICES Academic or career counseling, employment services for current students, placement services for program completers, remedial services.

The Art Institute of York–Pennsylvania

1409 Williams Road, York, PA 17402-9012
http://www.artinstitutes.edu/york/

CONTACT Tim Howard, President
Telephone: 717-755-2300

GENERAL INFORMATION Private Institution. Founded 1952. **Accreditation:** Regional (MSA/CIHE); state accredited or approved. **Total program enrollment:** 436. **Application fee:** $50.

STUDENT SERVICES Academic or career counseling, employment services for current students, placement services for program completers, remedial services.

Automotive Training Center

114 Pickering Way, Exton, PA 19341
http://www.autotraining.edu/

CONTACT Steven C. Hiscox, President
Telephone: 610-363-6716

GENERAL INFORMATION Private Institution. Founded 1917. **Total program enrollment:** 200. **Application fee:** $150.

PROGRAM(S) OFFERED
• Autobody/Collision and Repair Technology/Technician *1344 hrs./$20,800*
• Automobile/Automotive Mechanics Technology/Technician *1344 hrs./$20,800*
• Diesel Mechanics Technology/Technician *2400 hrs./$38,275*

STUDENT SERVICES Academic or career counseling, employment services for current students, placement services for program completers.

Automotive Training Center

900 Johnsville Boulevard, Warminster, PA 18974
http://www.autotraining.com/campuslocations.htm#warminster

CONTACT Steven C. Hiscox, President
Telephone: 215-259-1900

GENERAL INFORMATION Private Institution. **Total program enrollment:** 274. **Application fee:** $150.

PROGRAM(S) OFFERED
• Autobody/Collision and Repair Technology/Technician *1344 hrs./$20,800*
• Automobile/Automotive Mechanics Technology/Technician *1344 hrs./$20,800*
• Diesel Mechanics Technology/Technician *2400 hrs./$38,275*

STUDENT SERVICES Academic or career counseling, employment services for current students, placement services for program completers.

Baptist Bible College of Pennsylvania

538 Venard Road, Clarks Summit, PA 18411-1297
http://www.bbc.edu/

CONTACT James E. Jeffery, President
Telephone: 570-586-2400

GENERAL INFORMATION Private Institution. Founded 1932. **Accreditation:** Regional (MSA/CIHE); state accredited or approved. **Total program enrollment:** 703. **Application fee:** $30.

PROGRAM(S) OFFERED
• Bible/Biblical Studies *3 students enrolled*

STUDENT SERVICES Academic or career counseling, employment services for current students, placement services for program completers, remedial services.

Beaver Falls Beauty Academy

720 13th Street, Beaver Falls, PA 15010

CONTACT Gerald G. Camp, Owner
Telephone: 724-724-0708

GENERAL INFORMATION Private Institution. Founded 1993. **Total program enrollment:** 37.

PROGRAM(S) OFFERED
• Cosmetology, Barber/Styling, and Nail Instructor *625 hrs./$4600*
• Cosmetology/Cosmetologist, General *1250 hrs./$12,400* • Nail Technician/Specialist and Manicurist *200 hrs./$2200*

STUDENT SERVICES Academic or career counseling, employment services for current students, placement services for program completers.

Berks Technical Institute

2205 Ridgewood Road, Wyomissing, PA 19610-1168
http://www.berkstech.com/

CONTACT Pat Latham, Registrar
Telephone: 610-372-1722

GENERAL INFORMATION Private Institution. Founded 1977. **Accreditation:** Medical assisting (AAMAE); state accredited or approved. **Total program enrollment:** 485. **Application fee:** $50.

PROGRAM(S) OFFERED
• Administrative Assistant and Secretarial Science, General *1 student enrolled*
• Massage Therapy/Therapeutic Massage *51 students enrolled* • Medical/Clinical Assistant

STUDENT SERVICES Academic or career counseling, employment services for current students, placement services for program completers, remedial services.

Bidwell Training Center

1815 Metropolitan Street, Pittsburgh, PA 15233-2234
http://www.bidwell-training.org/

CONTACT Wm E. Strickland, Jr., President/Chief Executive Officer
Telephone: 412-323-4000

GENERAL INFORMATION Private Institution. Founded 1968. **Accreditation:** State accredited or approved. **Total program enrollment:** 175.

PROGRAM(S) OFFERED
• Applied Horticulture/Horticultural Operations, General *940 hrs./$7800*
• Chemical Technology/Technician *1500 hrs./$7360* • Computer and Information Sciences and Support Services, Other *20 students enrolled* • Culinary Arts/Chef Training *1428 hrs./$9420* • Health Information/Medical Records Technology/Technician *900 hrs./$7700* • Health Unit Coordinator/Ward Clerk *18 students enrolled* • Medical Administrative/Executive Assistant and Medical Secretary • Medical Office Management/Administration *1220 hrs./$7700* • Medical Transcription/Transcriptionist • Pharmacy Technician/Assistant *1140 hrs./$7550*

STUDENT SERVICES Academic or career counseling, placement services for program completers, remedial services.

Bloomsburg University of Pennsylvania

400 East Second Street, Bloomsburg, PA 17815-1301
http://www.bloomu.edu/

CONTACT Jessica S. Kozloff, President
Telephone: 570-389-4000

GENERAL INFORMATION Public Institution. Founded 1839. **Accreditation:** Regional (MSA/CIHE); audiology (ASHA); speech-language pathology (ASHA). **Total program enrollment:** 7852. **Application fee:** $30.

STUDENT SERVICES Academic or career counseling, daycare for children of students, employment services for current students, placement services for program completers, remedial services.

Bradford School

125 West Station Square Drive, Suite 129, Pittsburgh, PA 15219
http://www.bradfordpittsburgh.edu/

CONTACT Vincent S. Graziano, President
Telephone: 412-391-6710

GENERAL INFORMATION Private Institution. Founded 1968. **Accreditation:** State accredited or approved. **Total program enrollment:** 348. **Application fee:** $50.

PROGRAM(S) OFFERED
• **Accounting** 3 *students enrolled* • **Administrative Assistant and Secretarial Science, General** • **Commercial and Advertising Art** 2 *students enrolled* • **Computer and Information Sciences and Support Services, Other** 2 *students enrolled* • **Dental Assisting/Assistant** • **Hospitality and Recreation Marketing Operations** 1 *student enrolled* • **Legal Assistant/Paralegal** 5 *students enrolled* • **Medical/Clinical Assistant** 8 *students enrolled* • **Retailing and Retail Operations** 2 *students enrolled*

STUDENT SERVICES Employment services for current students, placement services for program completers.

Bucks County Community College

275 Swamp Road, Newtown, PA 18940-1525
http://www.bucks.edu/

CONTACT James J. Linksz, President
Telephone: 215-968-8000

GENERAL INFORMATION Public Institution. Founded 1964. **Accreditation:** Regional (MSA/CIHE); art and design (NASAD); medical assisting (AAMAE); music (NASM). **Total program enrollment:** 4767. **Application fee:** $30.

PROGRAM(S) OFFERED
• **Accounting Technology/Technician and Bookkeeping** 6 *students enrolled* • **Animation, Interactive Technology, Video Graphics and Special Effects** 1 *student enrolled* • **Business Administration and Management, General** 1 *student enrolled* • **Business/Office Automation/Technology/Data Entry** 3 *students enrolled* • **Computer Programming/Programmer, General** • **Computer Systems Networking and Telecommunications** • **Computer Technology/Computer Systems Technology** 2 *students enrolled* • **Computer and Information Sciences, General** • **Corrections** 1 *student enrolled* • **Criminal Justice/Law Enforcement Administration** 1 *student enrolled* • **Culinary Arts and Related Services, Other** 2 *students enrolled* • **E-Commerce/Electronic Commerce** • **Education, General** 2 *students enrolled* • **Electrical, Electronic and Communications Engineering Technology/Technician** • **Entrepreneurship/Entrepreneurial Studies** 1 *student enrolled* • **Fire Protection and Safety Technology/Technician** 3 *students enrolled* • **General Office Occupations and Clerical Services** 4 *students enrolled* • **Historic Preservation and Conservation** 6 *students enrolled* • **Hotel/Motel Administration/Management** • **Journalism, Other** • **Kindergarten/Preschool Education and Teaching** • **Legal Administrative Assistant/Secretary** • **Legal Assistant/Paralegal** 6 *students enrolled* • **Mathematics, General** • **Medical Insurance Coding Specialist/Coder** 3 *students enrolled* • **Medical Office Assistant/Specialist** 3 *students enrolled* • **Medical Transcription/Transcriptionist** 3 *students enrolled* • **Medical/Clinical Assistant** 13 *students enrolled* • **Nursing—Registered Nurse Training (RN, ASN, BSN, MSN)** 5 *students enrolled* • **Office Management and Supervision** 1 *student enrolled* • **Phlebotomy/Phlebotomist** 24 *students enrolled* • **Photographic and Film/Video Technology/Technician and Assistant** 1 *student enrolled* • **Prepress/Desktop Publishing and Digital Imaging Design** 1 *student enrolled* • **Radio and Television Broadcasting Technology/Technician** • **Sales, Distribution and Marketing Operations, General** • **System Administration/Administrator** • **Tourism and Travel Services Management** 1 *student enrolled* • **Web Page, Digital/Multimedia and Information Resources Design** 3 *students enrolled* • **Women's Studies** 1 *student enrolled*

STUDENT SERVICES Academic or career counseling, daycare for children of students, employment services for current students, placement services for program completers, remedial services.

Bucks County School of Beauty Culture

1761 Bustleton Pike, Feasterville, PA 19647
http://www.bcsbc.com/

CONTACT Stephen Wallin, Chief Operating Officer
Telephone: 215-322-0666

GENERAL INFORMATION Private Institution. Founded 1974. **Total program enrollment:** 51.

PROGRAM(S) OFFERED
• **Aesthetician/Esthetician and Skin Care Specialist** 480 *hrs./$5950* • **Cosmetology and Related Personal Grooming Arts, Other** 22 *students enrolled* • **Cosmetology/Cosmetologist, General** 1500 *hrs./$14,250* • **Electrolysis/Electrology and Electrolysis Technician** 480 *hrs./$5950* • **Nail Technician/Specialist and Manicurist** 480 *hrs./$5950* • **Personal and Culinary Services, Other** 1 *student enrolled*

STUDENT SERVICES Academic or career counseling, placement services for program completers.

Butler Beauty School

233 South Main Street, Butler, PA 16001

CONTACT Gerald Camp, Owner
Telephone: 724-287-0708

GENERAL INFORMATION Private Institution. Founded 1939. **Total program enrollment:** 71.

PROGRAM(S) OFFERED
• **Cosmetology, Barber/Styling, and Nail Instructor** 625 *hrs./$4600* • **Cosmetology/Cosmetologist, General** 1250 *hrs./$12,400* • **Nail Technician/Specialist and Manicurist** 200 *hrs./$2200*

STUDENT SERVICES Academic or career counseling, employment services for current students, placement services for program completers.

Butler County Community College

College Drive, PO Box 1203, Butler, PA 16003-1203
http://www.bc3.edu/

CONTACT Nicholas Neupauer, President
Telephone: 724-287-8711

GENERAL INFORMATION Public Institution. Founded 1965. **Accreditation:** Regional (MSA/CIHE); physical therapy assisting (APTA). **Total program enrollment:** 1992. **Application fee:** $25.

PROGRAM(S) OFFERED
• **Accounting Technology/Technician and Bookkeeping** 1 *student enrolled* • **Business Administration and Management, General** • **Business/Commerce, General** • **Corrections** • **Data Entry/Microcomputer Applications, Other** • **Entrepreneurship/Entrepreneurial Studies** • **Fire Science/Firefighting** 1 *student enrolled* • **Foodservice Systems Administration/Management** 1 *student enrolled* • **General Office Occupations and Clerical Services** • **Human Resources Management/Personnel Administration, General** 2 *students enrolled* • **Machine Shop Technology/Assistant** • **Marketing, Other** 1 *student enrolled* • **Massage Therapy/Therapeutic Massage** 10 *students enrolled* • **Medical Insurance Coding Specialist/Coder** 14 *students enrolled* • **Medical Office Assistant/Specialist** 3 *students enrolled* • **Operations Management and Supervision** 1 *student enrolled*

STUDENT SERVICES Academic or career counseling, daycare for children of students, employment services for current students, placement services for program completers, remedial services.

Cabrini College

610 King of Prussia Road, Radnor, PA 19087-3698
http://www.cabrini.edu/

CONTACT Marie George, President
Telephone: 610-902-8100

GENERAL INFORMATION Private Institution. Founded 1957. **Accreditation:** Regional (MSA/CIHE). **Total program enrollment:** 1808. **Application fee:** $35.

STUDENT SERVICES Academic or career counseling, employment services for current students, placement services for program completers, remedial services.

Cambria-Rowe Business College

422 South 13th Street, Indiana, PA 15701
http://www.crbc.net/

CONTACT Jeff Allen, Director
Telephone: 724-463-0222

GENERAL INFORMATION Private Institution. Founded 1959. **Accreditation:** State accredited or approved. **Total program enrollment:** 106. **Application fee:** $15.

PROGRAM(S) OFFERED
• Accounting • Administrative Assistant and Secretarial Science, General • Medical Office Assistant/Specialist *2 students enrolled*

STUDENT SERVICES Academic or career counseling, employment services for current students, placement services for program completers.

Cambria-Rowe Business College

221 Central Avenue, Johnstown, PA 15902-2494
http://www.crbc.net/

CONTACT Jeffrey Allen, Director
Telephone: 814-536-5168

GENERAL INFORMATION Private Institution. Founded 1891. **Accreditation:** State accredited or approved. **Total program enrollment:** 188. **Application fee:** $15.

PROGRAM(S) OFFERED
• Accounting *1 student enrolled* • Administrative Assistant and Secretarial Science, General *1 student enrolled* • Medical Administrative/Executive Assistant and Medical Secretary *1 student enrolled*

STUDENT SERVICES Academic or career counseling, employment services for current students, placement services for program completers.

Career Development & Employment

100 N. Wilkes Barre Boulevard, Suite 203, Wilkes Barre, PA 18702

CONTACT Nick Cohen, President, CEO
Telephone: 570-823-3891

GENERAL INFORMATION Private Institution. **Total program enrollment:** 48.

PROGRAM(S) OFFERED
• Administrative Assistant and Secretarial Science, General *300 hrs./$4100* • Business Operations Support and Secretarial Services, Other *780 hrs./$11,125* • Health and Medical Administrative Services, Other *940 hrs./$11,369*

STUDENT SERVICES Academic or career counseling, placement services for program completers.

Career Technology Center of Lackawanna County

3201 Rockwell Avenue, Scranton, PA 18508
http://www.ctc.tec.pa.us

CONTACT Vincent P. Nallo, Director Vocational Education
Telephone: 570-346-8728

GENERAL INFORMATION Public Institution. **Total program enrollment:** 35. **Application fee:** $30.

PROGRAM(S) OFFERED
• Licensed Practical/Vocational Nurse Training (LPN, LVN, Cert, Dipl, AAS) *33 students enrolled*

STUDENT SERVICES Academic or career counseling, placement services for program completers, remedial services.

Career Training Academy

4314 Old William Penn Highway, Suite 103, Monroeville, PA 15146
http://www.careerta.edu/

CONTACT Michael Joyce, Director
Telephone: 412-372-3900

GENERAL INFORMATION Private Institution. Founded 1986. **Accreditation:** Medical assisting (AAMAE); state accredited or approved. **Total program enrollment:** 23. **Application fee:** $30.

PROGRAM(S) OFFERED
• Massage Therapy/Therapeutic Massage *1622 hrs./$20,713* • Medical Insurance Coding Specialist/Coder *1500 hrs./$16,882* • Medical Insurance Specialist/Medical Biller *900 hrs./$8003* • Medical/Clinical Assistant *1500 hrs./$17,878*

STUDENT SERVICES Academic or career counseling, employment services for current students, placement services for program completers, remedial services.

Career Training Academy

950 Fifth Avenue, New Kensington, PA 15068-6301
http://www.careerta.com/

CONTACT John M. Reddy, Owner Director
Telephone: 724-337-1000

GENERAL INFORMATION Private Institution. Founded 1986. **Accreditation:** Medical assisting (AAMAE); state accredited or approved. **Total program enrollment:** 72. **Application fee:** $30.

PROGRAM(S) OFFERED
• Allied Health and Medical Assisting Services, Other • Dental Assisting/Assistant *900 hrs./$8487* • Massage Therapy/Therapeutic Massage *1532 hrs./$8457* • Medical Administrative/Executive Assistant and Medical Secretary • Medical Insurance Coding Specialist/Coder *1500 hrs./$16,882* • Medical Insurance Specialist/Medical Biller *900 hrs./$8003* • Medical/Clinical Assistant *1500 hrs./$17,878*

STUDENT SERVICES Academic or career counseling, daycare for children of students, employment services for current students, placement services for program completers, remedial services.

Career Training Academy

1500 Northway Mall, Suite 200, Pittsburgh, PA 15237
http://www.careerta.edu/

CONTACT Carla Ryba, Director
Telephone: 412-367-4000

GENERAL INFORMATION Private Institution. **Accreditation:** State accredited or approved. **Total program enrollment:** 64. **Application fee:** $30.

PROGRAM(S) OFFERED

• **Allied Health and Medical Assisting Services, Other** *900 hrs./$8424*
• **Health Professions and Related Clinical Sciences, Other** *9 students enrolled*
• **Massage Therapy/Therapeutic Massage** *1622 hrs./$20,710* • **Medical Insurance Coding Specialist/Coder** *1500 hrs./$16,882* • **Medical Insurance Specialist/Medical Biller** *900 hrs./$8003* • **Medical/Clinical Assistant** *8 students enrolled*

STUDENT SERVICES Academic or career counseling, employment services for current students, placement services for program completers, remedial services.

Cedar Crest College

100 College Drive, Allentown, PA 18104-6196
http://www.cedarcrest.edu/

CONTACT Carmen Twillie Ambar, President
Telephone: 610-606-4666 Ext. 3329

GENERAL INFORMATION Private Institution (Affiliated with United Church of Christ). Founded 1867. **Accreditation:** Regional (MSA/CIHE); nuclear medicine technology (JRCNMT). **Total program enrollment:** 987. **Application fee:** $30.

PROGRAM(S) OFFERED

• **Health/Health Care Administration/Management** *1 student enrolled* • **Teacher Assistant/Aide**

STUDENT SERVICES Academic or career counseling, employment services for current students, placement services for program completers, remedial services.

Center for Arts and Technology–Brandywine Campus

1635 East Lincoln Highway, Coatesville, PA 19320
http://www.cciu.org/Departments/CustomEd/pnp2/pnphome/

CONTACT Joseph O'Brien, Executive Director
Telephone: 610-384-6214

GENERAL INFORMATION Private Institution. **Total program enrollment:** 103. **Application fee:** $50.

PROGRAM(S) OFFERED

• **Licensed Practical/Vocational Nurse Training (LPN, LVN, Cert, Dipl, AAS)** *1635 hrs./$16,246*

STUDENT SERVICES Academic or career counseling, employment services for current students, placement services for program completers, remedial services.

Central Pennsylvania College

College Hill & Valley Roads, Summerdale, PA 17093-0309
http://www.centralpenn.edu/

CONTACT Todd Milano, President
Telephone: 800-759-2727

GENERAL INFORMATION Private Institution. Founded 1881. **Accreditation:** Regional (MSA/CIHE); medical assisting (AAMAE); physical therapy assisting (APTA). **Total program enrollment:** 614.

PROGRAM(S) OFFERED

• **Computer Science** • **Criminalistics and Criminal Science** *13 students enrolled* • **Health Information/Medical Records Technology/Technician** • **Human Resources Management/Personnel Administration, General** *11 students enrolled* • **Optometric Technician/Assistant**

STUDENT SERVICES Academic or career counseling, daycare for children of students, employment services for current students, placement services for program completers, remedial services.

Central Pennsylvania Institute of Science and Technology

540 North Harrison Road, Pleasant Gap, PA 16823
http://www.cpi.tec.pa.us

CONTACT Gregory Michelone, Executive Director
Telephone: 814-359-2793

GENERAL INFORMATION Public Institution. Founded 1958. **Total program enrollment:** 74. **Application fee:** $45.

PROGRAM(S) OFFERED

• **Allied Health and Medical Assisting Services, Other** *1172 hrs./$7845* • **Construction/Heavy Equipment/Earthmoving Equipment Operation** *608 hrs./$8885* • **Heating, Air Conditioning and Refrigeration Technology/Technician (ACH/ACR/ACHR/HRAC/HVAC/AC Technology)** *900 hrs./$5989* • **Heating, Air Conditioning, Ventilation and Refrigeration Maintenance Technology/Technician (HAC, HACR, HVAC, HVACR)** *15 students enrolled* • **Licensed Practical/Vocational Nurse Training (LPN, LVN, Cert, Dipl, AAS)** *1560 hrs./$9895* • **Nurse/Nursing Assistant/Aide and Patient Care Assistant** *38 students enrolled* • **Truck and Bus Driver/Commercial Vehicle Operation** *320 hrs./$5295* • **Welding Technology/Welder** *900 hrs./$7160*

STUDENT SERVICES Academic or career counseling, employment services for current students, placement services for program completers, remedial services.

Central Susquehanna LPN Career Center

1145 North Fourth Street, Sunbury, PA 17801
http://www.csiu.org/lpn

CONTACT Carol Barbarich, Director
Telephone: 570-988-6760

GENERAL INFORMATION Public Institution. Founded 1967. **Total program enrollment:** 56. **Application fee:** $60.

PROGRAM(S) OFFERED

• **Licensed Practical/Vocational Nurse Training (LPN, LVN, Cert, Dipl, AAS)** *1547 hrs./$14,311* • **Nursing, Other** *56 students enrolled*

STUDENT SERVICES Academic or career counseling, placement services for program completers, remedial services.

Chambersburg Beauty School

171 Cedar Avenue, Chambersburg, PA 17201

CONTACT James R. Bilney, President
Telephone: 717-267-0075

GENERAL INFORMATION Private Institution. **Total program enrollment:** 65.

PROGRAM(S) OFFERED

• **Cosmetology, Barber/Styling, and Nail Instructor** *900 hrs./$14,440* • **Cosmetology/Cosmetologist, General** *500 hrs./$5750*

STUDENT SERVICES Placement services for program completers.

Chestnut Hill College

9601 Germantown Avenue, Philadelphia, PA 19118-2693
http://www.chc.edu/

CONTACT Carol Jean Vale, SSJ, PhD, President
Telephone: 215-248-7000

GENERAL INFORMATION Private Institution. Founded 1924. **Accreditation:** Regional (MSA/CIHE). **Total program enrollment:** 1230. **Application fee:** $35.

STUDENT SERVICES Academic or career counseling, employment services for current students, placement services for program completers, remedial services.

CHI Institute, Broomall Campus

1991 Sproul Road, Suite 42, Broomall, PA 19008
http://www.chitraining.com/

CONTACT Dale Wintemberg, Campus President
Telephone: 610-353-7630

GENERAL INFORMATION Private Institution. Founded 1958. **Accreditation:** State accredited or approved. **Total program enrollment:** 697. **Application fee:** $20.

PROGRAM(S) OFFERED
• **Computer Technology/Computer Systems Technology** *12 students enrolled* • **Dental Assisting/Assistant** *53 students enrolled* • **Electrician** *99 students enrolled* • **Heating, Air Conditioning, Ventilation and Refrigeration Maintenance Technology/Technician (HAC, HACR, HVAC, HVACR)** *78 students enrolled* • **Pharmacy Technician/Assistant** *42 students enrolled* • **Phlebotomy/Phlebotomist** *110 students enrolled* • **Surgical Technology/Technologist** *53 students enrolled*

STUDENT SERVICES Academic or career counseling, employment services for current students, placement services for program completers, remedial services.

CHI Institute, Franklin Mills Campus

125 Franklin Mills Boulevard, Philadelphia, PA 19154
http://www.chitraining.com/

CONTACT Eric Heller, President
Telephone: 215-612-6600

GENERAL INFORMATION Private Institution. Founded 1981. **Accreditation:** State accredited or approved. **Total program enrollment:** 864.

PROGRAM(S) OFFERED
• **Computer Engineering Technology/Technician** *132 hrs./$31,780* • **Computer Programming/Programmer, General** • **Computer Systems Analysis/Analyst** *9 students enrolled* • **Criminal Justice/Law Enforcement Administration** *139 hrs./$29,530* • **Electrician** *72 hrs./$18,500* • **Medical Office Assistant/Specialist** *50 hrs./$13,730* • **Medical/Clinical Assistant** *64 hrs./$15,390* • **Pharmacy Technician/Assistant** *20 students enrolled* • **Respiratory Therapy Technician/Assistant** *131 hrs./$42,300*

STUDENT SERVICES Academic or career counseling, employment services for current students, placement services for program completers.

The Chubb Institute–Springfield

965 Baltimore Pike, Springfield, PA 19064-3957

CONTACT Dana Marra, Campus President
Telephone: 610-338-2300

GENERAL INFORMATION Private Institution. **Total program enrollment:** 595. **Application fee:** $50.

PROGRAM(S) OFFERED
• **Computer and Information Systems Security** *1200 hrs./$17,709* • **Massage Therapy/Therapeutic Massage** *820 hrs./$10,964* • **Medical Insurance Specialist/Medical Biller** *720 hrs./$10,985* • **Medical/Clinical Assistant** *746 hrs./$11,350* • **Web Page, Digital/Multimedia and Information Resources Design** *1200 hrs./$18,149*

STUDENT SERVICES Placement services for program completers.

Clarion County Career Center Practical Nursing Program

447 Career Road, Shippenville, PA 16254-8975
http://www.ccccntr.org/

CONTACT Larry Bornak, Chief School Administrator
Telephone: 814-226-5857 Ext. 100

GENERAL INFORMATION Public Institution. **Total program enrollment:** 48. **Application fee:** $30.

PROGRAM(S) OFFERED
• **Licensed Practical/Vocational Nurse Training (LPN, LVN, Cert, Dipl, AAS)** *1580 hrs./$12,125*

STUDENT SERVICES Academic or career counseling, employment services for current students, placement services for program completers, remedial services.

Clearfield County Career and Technology Center

RR 1 Box 5, Clearfield, PA 16830
http://www.ccctc.org/

CONTACT Lois Richards, Director
Telephone: 814-765-4047

GENERAL INFORMATION Public Institution. **Total program enrollment:** 61. **Application fee:** $35.

PROGRAM(S) OFFERED
• **Licensed Practical/Vocational Nurse Training (LPN, LVN, Cert, Dipl, AAS)** *1500 hrs./$12,500*

STUDENT SERVICES Academic or career counseling, placement services for program completers, remedial services.

Commonwealth Technical Institute

727 Goucher Street, Johnstown, PA 15905-3092
http://www.hgac.org/

CONTACT Donald Rullman, Director
Telephone: 814-255-8200

GENERAL INFORMATION Public Institution. **Accreditation:** State accredited or approved. **Total program enrollment:** 217.

PROGRAM(S) OFFERED
• **Automobile/Automotive Mechanics Technology/Technician** *5 students enrolled* • **Building/Home/Construction Inspection/Inspector** *14 students enrolled* • **Building/Property Maintenance and Management** *8 students enrolled* • **Construction Trades, General** *14 students enrolled* • **Consumer Merchandising/Retailing Management** *1 student enrolled* • **Culinary Arts and Related Services, Other** *28 students enrolled* • **Dental Assisting/Assistant** *2 students enrolled* • **Logistics and Materials Management** *14 students enrolled* • **Nurse/Nursing Assistant/Aide and Patient Care Assistant** *11 students enrolled* • **Printing Press Operator** *6 students enrolled* • **Retailing and Retail Operations** *6 students enrolled* • **Sales, Distribution and Marketing Operations, General** *1 student enrolled* • **Small Engine Mechanics and Repair Technology/Technician** *7 students enrolled* • **Watchmaking and Jewelrymaking** *3 students enrolled*

STUDENT SERVICES Academic or career counseling, remedial services.

Community College of Allegheny County

800 Allegheny Avenue, Pittsburgh, PA 15233-1894
http://www.ccac.edu/

CONTACT Alex Johnson, PhD, President
Telephone: 412-323-2323

GENERAL INFORMATION Public Institution. Founded 1966. **Accreditation:** Regional (MSA/CIHE); diagnostic medical sonography (JRCEDMS); health information technology (AHIMA); medical assisting (AAMAE);

medical laboratory technology (NAACLS); nuclear medicine technology (JRCNMT); physical therapy assisting (APTA); radiologic technology: radiation therapy technology (JRCERT); radiologic technology: radiography (JRCERT); surgical technology (ARCST). **Total program enrollment:** 7675.

PROGRAM(S) OFFERED

• **Accounting Technology/Technician and Bookkeeping** 13 *students enrolled* • **American Sign Language (ASL)** 3 *students enrolled* • **Area Studies, Other** 2 *students enrolled* • **Automobile/Automotive Mechanics Technology/Technician** 3 *students enrolled* • **Business Administration and Management, General** 16 *students enrolled* • **Business/Office Automation/Technology/Data Entry** 1 *student enrolled* • **CAD/CADD Drafting and/or Design Technology/Technician** 2 *students enrolled* • **Carpentry/Carpenter** 149 *students enrolled* • **Child Care Provider/Assistant** 16 *students enrolled* • **Child Care and Support Services Management** 9 *students enrolled* • **Child Development** 17 *students enrolled* • **Computer Programming/Programmer, General** 3 *students enrolled* • **Computer Software Technology/Technician** 2 *students enrolled* • **Computer Technology/Computer Systems Technology** 4 *students enrolled* • **Computer and Information Sciences and Support Services, Other** 1 *student enrolled* • **Court Reporting/Court Reporter** 4 *students enrolled* • **Diagnostic Medical Sonography/Sonographer and Ultrasound Technician** 2 *students enrolled* • **Dietetics and Clinical Nutrition Services, Other** 7 *students enrolled* • **Dietitian Assistant** 2 *students enrolled* • **E-Commerce/Electronic Commerce** 1 *student enrolled* • **Floriculture/Floristry Operations and Management** 1 *student enrolled* • **Graphic Design** 2 *students enrolled* • **Health and Medical Administrative Services, Other** 1 *student enrolled* • **Heating, Air Conditioning, Ventilation and Refrigeration Maintenance Technology/Technician (HAC, HACR, HVAC, HVACR)** 9 *students enrolled* • **Hotel/Motel Administration/Management** 2 *students enrolled* • **Human Resources Management/Personnel Administration, General** 3 *students enrolled* • **Industrial Electronics Technology/Technician** 1 *student enrolled* • **Industrial Mechanics and Maintenance Technology** 1 *student enrolled* • **Ironworking/Ironworker** 1 *student enrolled* • **Landscaping and Groundskeeping** 1 *student enrolled* • **Legal Assistant/Paralegal** 21 *students enrolled* • **Massage Therapy/Therapeutic Massage** 6 *students enrolled* • **Medical Insurance Coding Specialist/Coder** 16 *students enrolled* • **Medical Radiologic Technology/Science—Radiation Therapist** 10 *students enrolled* • **Medical Transcription/Transcriptionist** 1 *student enrolled* • **Medical/Clinical Assistant** 15 *students enrolled* • **Nuclear Medical Technology/Technologist** 10 *students enrolled* • **Pharmacy Technician/Assistant** 1 *student enrolled* • **Phlebotomy/Phlebotomist** 33 *students enrolled* • **Radiologic Technology/Science—Radiographer** 14 *students enrolled* • **Sheet Metal Technology/Sheetworking** 20 *students enrolled* • **Social Work** 4 *students enrolled* • **Social Work, Other** 3 *students enrolled* • **Substance Abuse/Addiction Counseling** 12 *students enrolled* • **Surgical Technology/Technologist** 6 *students enrolled* • **System Administration/Administrator** 12 *students enrolled* • **Teacher Assistant/Aide** 2 *students enrolled* • **Technical Theatre/Theatre Design and Technology** 2 *students enrolled* • **Therapeutic Recreation/Recreational Therapy** 1 *student enrolled* • **Web Page, Digital/Multimedia and Information Resources Design** 5 *students enrolled* • **Welding Technology/Welder** 15 *students enrolled*

STUDENT SERVICES Academic or career counseling, daycare for children of students, employment services for current students, placement services for program completers, remedial services.

Community College of Beaver County

One Campus Drive, Monaca, PA 15061-2588
http://www.ccbc.edu/

CONTACT Joe D. Forrester, President
Telephone: 724-775-8561

GENERAL INFORMATION Public Institution. Founded 1966. **Accreditation:** Regional (MSA/CIHE). **Total program enrollment:** 1242.

PROGRAM(S) OFFERED

• **Accounting Technology/Technician and Bookkeeping** 3 *students enrolled* • **Administrative Assistant and Secretarial Science, General** 2 *students enrolled* • **Air Traffic Controller** • **Architectural Drafting and Architectural CAD/CADD** • **Cosmetology/Cosmetologist, General** • **Criminal Justice/Police Science** • **Culinary Arts/Chef Training** 5 *students enrolled* • **Customer Service Support/Call Center/Teleservice Operation** • **Diesel Mechanics Technology/Technician** • **E-Commerce/Electronic Commerce** • **Environmental Engineering Technology/Environmental Technology** • **Health Aide** 3 *students enrolled* • **Health and Medical Administrative Services, Other** 11 *students enrolled* • **Landscaping and Groundskeeping** • **Licensed Practical/Vocational Nurse Training (LPN, LVN, Cert, Dipl, AAS)** 5 *students enrolled* • **Medical Administrative/Executive Assistant and Medical Secretary** • **Pharmacy**

Technician/Assistant 10 *students enrolled* • **Retailing and Retail Operations** • **Teacher Assistant/Aide** • **Web Page, Digital/Multimedia and Information Resources Design** 6 *students enrolled* • **Yoga Teacher Training/Yoga Therapy** 1 *student enrolled*

STUDENT SERVICES Academic or career counseling, daycare for children of students, employment services for current students, placement services for program completers, remedial services.

Community College of Philadelphia

1700 Spring Garden Street, Philadelphia, PA 19130-3991
http://www.ccp.edu/

CONTACT Stephen M. Curtis, President
Telephone: 215-751-8000

GENERAL INFORMATION Public Institution. Founded 1964. **Accreditation:** Regional (MSA/CIHE); dental assisting (ADA); dental hygiene (ADA); health information technology (AHIMA); medical assisting (AAMAE); medical laboratory technology (NAACLS); radiologic technology: radiography (JRCERT). **Total program enrollment:** 5641. **Application fee:** $20.

PROGRAM(S) OFFERED

• **Business Administration and Management, General** 5 *students enrolled* • **CAD/CADD Drafting and/or Design Technology/Technician** • **Computer and Information Sciences, Other** • **Corrections and Criminal Justice, Other** 61 *students enrolled* • **Fashion Merchandising** • **Fire Protection and Safety Technology/Technician** • **Human Services, General** 174 *students enrolled* • **Sales, Distribution and Marketing Operations, General** 4 *students enrolled* • **Social Work, Other** 10 *students enrolled* • **Substance Abuse/Addiction Counseling** 68 *students enrolled*

STUDENT SERVICES Academic or career counseling, daycare for children of students, employment services for current students, placement services for program completers, remedial services.

Computer Learning Network

2900 Fairway Drive, Altoona, PA 16602
http://www.cln.edu/

CONTACT Darius Markham, President
Telephone: 814-944-5643 Ext. 5612

GENERAL INFORMATION Private Institution. **Total program enrollment:** 285. **Application fee:** $100.

PROGRAM(S) OFFERED

• **Accounting and Business/Management** 43 *hrs./$10,800* • **Administrative Assistant and Secretarial Science, General** 62 *hrs./$10,600* • **Computer Systems Networking and Telecommunications** 9 *students enrolled* • **Computer and Information Sciences and Support Services, Other** 5 *students enrolled* • **Criminal Justice/Safety Studies** 59 *hrs./$12,860* • **Legal Administrative Assistant/Secretary** 1 *student enrolled* • **Massage Therapy/Therapeutic Massage** 7 *students enrolled* • **Medical Office Management/Administration** 62 *hrs./$11,100* • **Medical/Clinical Assistant** 63 *hrs./$13,450* • **Medical/Health Management and Clinical Assistant/Specialist** 5 *students enrolled* • **Pharmacy Technician/Assistant** 59 *hrs./$11,700*

STUDENT SERVICES Academic or career counseling, employment services for current students, placement services for program completers, remedial services.

Computer Learning Network

1110 Fernwood Avenue, Camp Hill, PA 17011-6996
http://www.clntraining.net/

CONTACT Carla Horn, President
Telephone: 717-761-1481

GENERAL INFORMATION Private Institution. Founded 1982. **Total program enrollment:** 277. **Application fee:** $50.

Computer Learning Network (continued)

PROGRAM(S) OFFERED
• **Allied Health and Medical Assisting Services, Other** *60 hrs./$13,340*
• **Computer and Information Sciences and Support Services, Other** *80 hrs./ $14,972* • **Corrections and Criminal Justice, Other** *2 students enrolled* • **Legal Assistant/Paralegal** *42 hrs./$11,376* • **Massage Therapy/Therapeutic Massage** *64 hrs./$13,640* • **Medical/Clinical Assistant** *59 hrs./$13,340* • **Pharmacy Technician/Assistant** *63 hrs./$13,640*

STUDENT SERVICES Academic or career counseling, employment services for current students, placement services for program completers, remedial services.

Conemaugh Valley Memorial Hospital

1086 Franklin Street, Johnstown, PA 15905-4398
http://www.conemaugh.org/
template_article.aspx?menu_id=90&id=1546

CONTACT Louise Pugliese, Director, School of Nursing & Allied Health
Telephone: 814-534-9118

GENERAL INFORMATION Private Institution. **Total program enrollment:** 194. **Application fee:** $30.

PROGRAM(S) OFFERED
• **Clinical Laboratory Science/Medical Technology/Technologist** *1620 hrs./ $6825* • **Histologic Technology/Histotechnologist** *1595 hrs./$6525* • **Nursing—Registered Nurse Training (RN, ASN, BSN, MSN)** *1997 hrs./$21,595* • **Radiologic Technology/Science—Radiographer** *3290 hrs./$11,189*

STUDENT SERVICES Academic or career counseling, placement services for program completers, remedial services.

Consolidated School of Business

2124 Ambassador Circle, Lancaster, PA 17603
http://www.csb.edu/

CONTACT Robert L. Safran, Jr., President
Telephone: 717-394-6211

GENERAL INFORMATION Private Institution. Founded 1986. **Accreditation:** State accredited or approved. **Total program enrollment:** 133. **Application fee:** $25.

PROGRAM(S) OFFERED
• **Accounting** *83 hrs./$23,700* • **Administrative Assistant and Secretarial Science, General** *2 students enrolled* • **Business Administration and Management, General** *83 hrs./$23,700* • **Computer Software and Media Applications, Other** *81 hrs./$23,700* • **Legal Administrative Assistant/Secretary** • **Legal Assistant/ Paralegal** *81 hrs./$23,700* • **Medical Administrative/Executive Assistant and Medical Secretary** *81 hrs./$26,450* • **Medical Office Assistant/Specialist** *41 hrs./$11,850*

STUDENT SERVICES Academic or career counseling, employment services for current students, placement services for program completers.

Consolidated School of Business

1605 Clugston Road, York, PA 17404
http://www.csb.edu/

CONTACT Robert Safran, Jr., President
Telephone: 717-764-9550

GENERAL INFORMATION Private Institution. Founded 1981. **Accreditation:** State accredited or approved. **Total program enrollment:** 125. **Application fee:** $25.

PROGRAM(S) OFFERED
• **Accounting** *83 hrs./$23,700* • **Administrative Assistant and Secretarial Science, General** *1 student enrolled* • **Business Administration and Management, General** *83 hrs./$23,700* • **Computer Software and Media Applications, Other**

81 hrs./$23,700 • **Legal Administrative Assistant/Secretary** • **Legal Assistant/ Paralegal** *81 hrs./$23,700* • **Medical Administrative/Executive Assistant and Medical Secretary** *81 hrs./$26,450* • **Medical Office Assistant/Specialist** *41 hrs./$1250*

STUDENT SERVICES Academic or career counseling, employment services for current students, placement services for program completers.

Cortiva Institute—Pennsylvania School of Muscle Therapy

1173 Egypt Road, Oaks, PA 19456
http://www.cortiva.com/locations/psmt/

CONTACT Jeffrey Mann, President
Telephone: 610-666-9060

GENERAL INFORMATION Private Institution. **Total program enrollment:** 40. **Application fee:** $100.

PROGRAM(S) OFFERED
• **Massage Therapy/Therapeutic Massage** *47 hrs./$9700*

STUDENT SERVICES Academic or career counseling, employment services for current students, placement services for program completers.

Crawford County Career and Technical School–Practical Nursing Program

860 Thurston Road, Meadville, PA 16335
http://www.ccvts.org/

CONTACT Neal Donovan, Vocational Director
Telephone: 814-724-6028

GENERAL INFORMATION Public Institution. Founded 1968. **Total program enrollment:** 28. **Application fee:** $50.

PROGRAM(S) OFFERED
• **Licensed Practical/Vocational Nurse Training (LPN, LVN, Cert, Dipl, AAS)** *32 students enrolled*

STUDENT SERVICES Academic or career counseling, placement services for program completers, remedial services.

DCI Career Institute

366 Route 18, Beaver Valley Mall, Monaca, PA 15061
http://www.dci.edu/

CONTACT Peggy L. Tiderman, Executive Director
Telephone: 724-728-0260

GENERAL INFORMATION Private Institution. Founded 1985. **Total program enrollment:** 73.

PROGRAM(S) OFFERED
• **Allied Health and Medical Assisting Services, Other** *73 students enrolled* • **Computer Technology/Computer Systems Technology** *7 students enrolled* • **Computer and Information Sciences and Support Services, Other** *18 students enrolled* • **Data Entry/Microcomputer Applications, Other** *24 hrs./$9545* • **Massage Therapy/Therapeutic Massage** *24 hrs./$9545* • **Medical/Clinical Assistant** *24 hrs./$10,595* • **System, Networking, and LAN/WAN Management/ Manager** *24 hrs./$9545*

STUDENT SERVICES Academic or career counseling, employment services for current students, placement services for program completers, remedial services.

Dean Institute of Technology

1501 West Liberty Avenue, Pittsburgh, PA 15226-1103
http://home.earthlink.net/~deantech/

CONTACT James Dean, President Director
Telephone: 412-531-4433

GENERAL INFORMATION Private Institution. Founded 1947. **Accreditation:** State accredited or approved. **Total program enrollment:** 80. **Application fee:** $50.

PROGRAM(S) OFFERED
● **Building/Property Maintenance and Management** 14 students enrolled ● **Welding Technology/Welder** 19 students enrolled

STUDENT SERVICES Academic or career counseling, employment services for current students, placement services for program completers.

Delaware County Community College

901 South Media Line Road, Media, PA 19063-1094
http://www.dccc.edu/

CONTACT Jerome S. Parker, President
Telephone: 610-359-5000

GENERAL INFORMATION Public Institution. Founded 1967. **Accreditation:** Regional (MSA/CIHE); medical assisting (AAMAE); surgical technology (ARCST). **Total program enrollment:** 4782. **Application fee:** $25.

PROGRAM(S) OFFERED
● **Accounting Technology/Technician and Bookkeeping** 8 students enrolled ● **Administrative Assistant and Secretarial Science, General** ● **Automobile/Automotive Mechanics Technology/Technician** 6 students enrolled ● **Building/Construction Site Management/Manager** 1 student enrolled ● **Building/Property Maintenance and Management** ● **CAD/CADD Drafting and/or Design Technology/Technician** 1 student enrolled ● **Carpentry/Carpenter** 8 students enrolled ● **Chemical Technology/Technician** ● **Criminal Justice/Police Science** 97 students enrolled ● **Data Entry/Microcomputer Applications, General** ● **E-Commerce/Electronic Commerce** 1 student enrolled ● **Electrician** 29 students enrolled ● **Emergency Medical Technology/Technician (EMT Paramedic)** ● **Entrepreneurship/Entrepreneurial Studies** ● **General Office Occupations and Clerical Services** ● **Health Unit Coordinator/Ward Clerk** 18 students enrolled ● **Health Unit Manager/Ward Supervisor** 2 students enrolled ● **Heating, Air Conditioning, Ventilation and Refrigeration Maintenance Technology/Technician (HAC, HACR, HVAC, HVACR)** 23 students enrolled ● **Human Resources Management/Personnel Administration, General** 10 students enrolled ● **Industrial Mechanics and Maintenance Technology** ● **Legal Assistant/Paralegal** 6 students enrolled ● **Machine Shop Technology/Assistant** ● **Machine Tool Technology/Machinist** 1 student enrolled ● **Mechanical Engineering/Mechanical Technology/Technician** 9 students enrolled ● **Medical Insurance Coding Specialist/Coder** ● **Medical Transcription/Transcriptionist** ● **Medical/Clinical Assistant** 8 students enrolled ● **Nurse/Nursing Assistant/Aide and Patient Care Assistant** 3 students enrolled ● **Perioperative/Operating Room and Surgical Nurse/Nursing** 38 students enrolled ● **Photography** 1 student enrolled ● **Plumbing Technology/Plumber** ● **Robotics Technology/Technician** ● **Science Technologies/Technicians, Other** ● **Surgical Technology/Technologist** ● **Web Page, Digital/Multimedia and Information Resources Design** 1 student enrolled ● **Web/Multimedia Management and Webmaster** 2 students enrolled

STUDENT SERVICES Academic or career counseling, employment services for current students, placement services for program completers, remedial services.

Delaware County Technical School

Delmar Drive and Henderson Boulevard, Folcroft, PA 19032-1998
http://www.dciu.org/923201311081063/site/default.asp

CONTACT Barry R. Ersek, EdD, Interim Executive Director
Telephone: 610-583-2934

GENERAL INFORMATION Private Institution. **Total program enrollment:** 81. **Application fee:** $60.

PROGRAM(S) OFFERED
● **Licensed Practical/Vocational Nurse Training (LPN, LVN, Cert, Dipl, AAS)** 1500 hrs./$13,379

STUDENT SERVICES Academic or career counseling, employment services for current students, remedial services.

Delaware Valley Academy of Medical and Dental Assistants

3330 Grant Avenue, Philadelphia, PA 19114

CONTACT Glenn Goldsmith, Director
Telephone: 215-676-1200

GENERAL INFORMATION Private Institution. **Total program enrollment:** 112. **Application fee:** $150.

PROGRAM(S) OFFERED
● **Dental Assisting/Assistant** 32 students enrolled ● **Medical/Health Management and Clinical Assistant/Specialist** 80 students enrolled

STUDENT SERVICES Academic or career counseling, placement services for program completers, remedial services.

Delaware Valley College

700 East Butler Avenue, Doylestown, PA 18901-2697
http://www.delval.edu/

CONTACT Dr. Joseph Brosnan, President
Telephone: 215-345-1500

GENERAL INFORMATION Private Institution. Founded 1896. **Accreditation:** Regional (MSA/CIHE). **Total program enrollment:** 1739. **Application fee:** $35.

PROGRAM(S) OFFERED
● **Computer Programming/Programmer, General** ● **Special Products Marketing Operations**

STUDENT SERVICES Academic or career counseling, employment services for current students, placement services for program completers, remedial services.

Douglas Education Center

130 Seventh Street, Monessen, PA 15062
http://www.douglas-school.com/

CONTACT Jeffrey D. Imbrescia, President
Telephone: 724-684-3684

GENERAL INFORMATION Private Institution. Founded 1904. **Accreditation:** State accredited or approved. **Total program enrollment:** 290. **Application fee:** $50.

PROGRAM(S) OFFERED
● **Business Operations Support and Secretarial Services, Other** ● **Business, Management, Marketing, and Related Support Services, Other** ● **Cosmetology, Barber/Styling, and Nail Instructor** 6 students enrolled ● **Cosmetology/Cosmetologist, General** 23 students enrolled ● **Executive Assistant/Executive Secretary** 3 students enrolled ● **Health Information/Medical Records Technology/Technician** 3 students enrolled ● **Medical Transcription/Transcriptionist** 2 students enrolled

STUDENT SERVICES Academic or career counseling, employment services for current students, placement services for program completers, remedial services.

DPT Business School

9122 Blue Grass Road, Philadelphia, PA 19114-3202
http://www.dptschool.com/

CONTACT Kishore Ramanjulu, Chief Operating Officer
Telephone: 215-673-2275

GENERAL INFORMATION Private Institution. Founded 1987. **Total program enrollment:** 512. **Application fee:** $75.

PROGRAM(S) OFFERED
• Accounting Technology/Technician and Bookkeeping *39 hrs./$11,000*
• Business/Office Automation/Technology/Data Entry *17 students enrolled*
• Massage Therapy/Therapeutic Massage *37 hrs./$10,500* • Medical Administrative/Executive Assistant and Medical Secretary *39 hrs./$11,000*
• Medical Office Management/Administration *36 hrs./$10,500* • Medical/Clinical Assistant • Pharmacy Technician/Assistant *33 hrs./$11,000* • Teaching English as a Second or Foreign Language/ESL Language Instructor *38 hrs./$4800*

STUDENT SERVICES Academic or career counseling, placement services for program completers.

Drexel University

3141 Chestnut Street, Philadelphia, PA 19104-2875
http://www.drexel.edu/

CONTACT Constantine N. Papadakis, PhD, President
Telephone: 215-895-2000

GENERAL INFORMATION Private Institution. Founded 1891. **Accreditation:** Regional (MSA/CIHE); art and design (NASAD); computer science (ABET/CSAC); interior design: professional (CIDA); library and information science (ALA). **Total program enrollment:** 14749. **Application fee:** $75.

PROGRAM(S) OFFERED
• Alternative and Complementary Medicine and Medical Systems, Other *16 students enrolled* • Environmental Science *7 students enrolled* • Health Services/Allied Health/Health Sciences, General *5 students enrolled* • Medical Insurance Coding Specialist/Coder *1 student enrolled*

STUDENT SERVICES Academic or career counseling, employment services for current students, placement services for program completers, remedial services.

DuBois Business College

1 Beaver Drive, DuBois, PA 15801-2401
http://www.dbcollege.com/

CONTACT Jackie Diehl Syktich, President
Telephone: 814-371-6920

GENERAL INFORMATION Private Institution. Founded 1885. **Accreditation:** State accredited or approved. **Total program enrollment:** 190. **Application fee:** $25.

PROGRAM(S) OFFERED
• Administrative Assistant and Secretarial Science, General *2 students enrolled*
• Business, Management, Marketing, and Related Support Services, Other
• Computer Systems Networking and Telecommunications

STUDENT SERVICES Academic or career counseling, employment services for current students, placement services for program completers, remedial services.

DuBois Business College

Huntingdon County Campus, 1001 Moore Street, Huntingdon, PA 16652
http://www.dbcollege.com/

CONTACT Jackie Diehl Syktich, President/CEO
Telephone: 814-371-6920

GENERAL INFORMATION Private Institution. **Total program enrollment:** 36. **Application fee:** $25.

PROGRAM(S) OFFERED
• Administrative Assistant and Secretarial Science, General • Business, Management, Marketing, and Related Support Services, Other • Computer Systems Networking and Telecommunications

STUDENT SERVICES Academic or career counseling, employment services for current students, placement services for program completers, remedial services.

DuBois Business College

701 East Third Street, Oil City, PA 16301
http://www.dbcollege.com/

CONTACT Jackie Diehl Syktich, President/CEO
Telephone: 814-371-6920

GENERAL INFORMATION Private Institution. **Total program enrollment:** 50. **Application fee:** $25.

PROGRAM(S) OFFERED
• Administrative Assistant and Secretarial Science, General *1 student enrolled*
• Business, Management, Marketing, and Related Support Services, Other
• Computer Systems Networking and Telecommunications

STUDENT SERVICES Academic or career counseling, employment services for current students, placement services for program completers, remedial services.

Eastern Center for Arts and Technology

3075 Terwood Road, Willow Grove, PA 19090
http://www.eastech.org/

CONTACT Joseph Colaneri, Director
Telephone: 215-784-4819

GENERAL INFORMATION Public Institution. Founded 1966. **Total program enrollment:** 100. **Application fee:** $75.

PROGRAM(S) OFFERED
• Licensed Practical/Vocational Nurse Training (LPN, LVN, Cert, Dipl, AAS) *1530 hrs./$12,000*

Elizabethtown College

1 Alpha Drive, Elizabethtown, PA 17022-2298
http://www.etown.edu/

CONTACT Theodore E. Long, President
Telephone: 717-361-1000

GENERAL INFORMATION Private Institution (Affiliated with Church of the Brethren). Founded 1899. **Accreditation:** Regional (MSA/CIHE); music (NASM). **Total program enrollment:** 1895. **Application fee:** $30.

PROGRAM(S) OFFERED
• Accounting *3 students enrolled* • Business Administration, Management and Operations, Other • Information Science/Studies • Social Work

STUDENT SERVICES Academic or career counseling, employment services for current students, remedial services.

Empire Beauty School

4768 McKnight Road, Pittsburgh, PA 15237
http://www.empire.edu/

CONTACT Michael Bouman, President
Telephone: 412-367-1765

GENERAL INFORMATION Private Institution. **Total program enrollment:** 61. **Application fee:** $100.

PROGRAM(S) OFFERED
• **Cosmetology, Barber/Styling, and Nail Instructor** *5 students enrolled*
• **Cosmetology/Cosmetologist, General** *1260 hrs./$15,740* • **Nail Technician/Specialist and Manicurist** *2 students enrolled*

STUDENT SERVICES Placement services for program completers.

Empire Beauty School–Center City Philadelphia

1522 Chestnut Street, Philadelphia, PA 19102-2701
http://www.empire.edu/

CONTACT Michael Bouman, President
Telephone: 800-223-3271

GENERAL INFORMATION Private Institution. **Total program enrollment:** 278. **Application fee:** $100.

PROGRAM(S) OFFERED
• **Cosmetology, Barber/Styling, and Nail Instructor** *600 hrs./$6900*
• **Cosmetology/Cosmetologist, General** *1260 hrs./$15,740* • **Technical Teacher Education** *8 students enrolled*

STUDENT SERVICES Placement services for program completers.

Empire Beauty School–Exton

313 West Market Street, West Chester, PA 15382
http://www.empire.edu/

CONTACT Michael Bouman, President
Telephone: 800-223-3271

GENERAL INFORMATION Private Institution. **Total program enrollment:** 85. **Application fee:** $100.

PROGRAM(S) OFFERED
• **Cosmetology/Cosmetologist, General** *1260 hrs./$15,740* • **Nail Technician/Specialist and Manicurist** *6 students enrolled* • **Technical Teacher Education** *5 students enrolled*

STUDENT SERVICES Placement services for program completers.

Empire Beauty School–Hanover

Clearview Shopping Center, Carlisle Street, Hanover, PA 17331
http://www.empire.edu/

CONTACT Michael Bouman, President
Telephone: 800-223-3271

GENERAL INFORMATION Private Institution. **Total program enrollment:** 47. **Application fee:** $100.

PROGRAM(S) OFFERED
• **Cosmetology, Barber/Styling, and Nail Instructor** *600 hrs./$6900*
• **Cosmetology/Cosmetologist, General** *1260 hrs./$15,740* • **Nail Technician/Specialist and Manicurist** *210 hrs./$2415* • **Technical Teacher Education** *1 student enrolled*

STUDENT SERVICES Placement services for program completers.

Empire Beauty School–Harrisburg

3941 Jonestown Road, Harrisburg, PA 17109
http://www.empire.edu/

CONTACT Michael Bouman, President
Telephone: 800-223-3271

GENERAL INFORMATION Private Institution. Founded 1929. **Total program enrollment:** 100. **Application fee:** $100.

PROGRAM(S) OFFERED
• **Cosmetology, Barber/Styling, and Nail Instructor** *600 hrs./$6900*
• **Cosmetology/Cosmetologist, General** *1260 hrs./$15,740* • **Nail Technician/Specialist and Manicurist** *210 hrs./$2415* • **Technical Teacher Education** *1 student enrolled*

STUDENT SERVICES Placement services for program completers.

Empire Beauty School–Lancaster

1801 Columbia Avenue, Wheatland Shopping Center, Lancaster, PA 17603
http://www.empire.edu/

CONTACT Michael Bouman, President
Telephone: 800-223-3271

GENERAL INFORMATION Private Institution. Founded 1929. **Total program enrollment:** 60. **Application fee:** $100.

PROGRAM(S) OFFERED
• **Cosmetology/Cosmetologist, General** *1260 hrs./$15,740* • **Technical Teacher Education** *5 students enrolled*

STUDENT SERVICES Placement services for program completers.

Empire Beauty School–Lebanon

1776 Quentin Road, Cedar Crest Square, Lebanon, PA 17042
http://www.empire.edu/

CONTACT Michael Bouman, President
Telephone: 800-223-3271

GENERAL INFORMATION Private Institution. **Total program enrollment:** 37. **Application fee:** $100.

PROGRAM(S) OFFERED
• **Cosmetology/Cosmetologist, General** *1260 hrs./$15,740* • **Nail Technician/Specialist and Manicurist** *2 students enrolled* • **Technical Teacher Education** *1 student enrolled*

STUDENT SERVICES Placement services for program completers.

Empire Beauty School–Monroeville

320 Mall Boulevard, Monroeville, PA 15146-2229
http://www.empire.edu/

CONTACT Michael Bouman, President
Telephone: 800-223-3271

GENERAL INFORMATION Private Institution. **Total program enrollment:** 88. **Application fee:** $100.

PROGRAM(S) OFFERED
• **Cosmetology, Barber/Styling, and Nail Instructor** *600 hrs./$6900*
• **Cosmetology/Cosmetologist, General** *1260 hrs./$15,740* • **Nail Technician/Specialist and Manicurist** *3 students enrolled* • **Technical Teacher Education** *4 students enrolled*

STUDENT SERVICES Placement services for program completers.

Empire Beauty School–Moosic

3370 Birney Avenue, Moosic, PA 18507
http://www.empire.edu/

CONTACT Michael Bouman, President
Telephone: 800-223-3271

GENERAL INFORMATION Private Institution. **Total program enrollment:** 142. **Application fee:** $100.

PROGRAM(S) OFFERED
• **Cosmetology, Barber/Styling, and Nail Instructor** 600 hrs./$6900
• **Cosmetology/Cosmetologist, General** 1260 hrs./$15,740 • **Nail Technician/Specialist and Manicurist** 210 hrs./$2415 • **Technical Teacher Education** 10 students enrolled

STUDENT SERVICES Placement services for program completers.

Empire Beauty School–Pottsville

324 N. Centre Street, Pottsville, PA 17901
http://www.empire.edu/

CONTACT Michael Bouman, President
Telephone: 800-223-3271

GENERAL INFORMATION Private Institution. **Total program enrollment:** 34. **Application fee:** $100.

PROGRAM(S) OFFERED
• **Cosmetology, Barber/Styling, and Nail Instructor** 600 hrs./$6900
• **Cosmetology/Cosmetologist, General** 1260 hrs./$15,740 • **Nail Technician/Specialist and Manicurist** 2 students enrolled • **Technical Teacher Education** 4 students enrolled

STUDENT SERVICES Placement services for program completers.

Empire Beauty School–Reading

2302 North 5th Street, Reading, PA 19605
http://www.empire.edu/

CONTACT Michael Bouman, President
Telephone: 800-223-3271

GENERAL INFORMATION Private Institution. Founded 1929. **Total program enrollment:** 86. **Application fee:** $100.

PROGRAM(S) OFFERED
• **Cosmetology, Barber/Styling, and Nail Instructor** 600 hrs./$6900
• **Cosmetology/Cosmetologist, General** 1260 hrs./$15,740 • **Nail Technician/Specialist and Manicurist** 210 hrs./$2415 • **Technical Teacher Education** 5 students enrolled

STUDENT SERVICES Placement services for program completers.

Empire Beauty School–Shamokin Dam

Orchard Hills Plaza, U.S. Rte. 11 & 15, Shamokin Dam, PA 17876
http://www.empire.edu/

CONTACT Michael Bouman, President
Telephone: 800-223-3271

GENERAL INFORMATION Private Institution. **Total program enrollment:** 48. **Application fee:** $100.

PROGRAM(S) OFFERED
• **Cosmetology, Barber/Styling, and Nail Instructor** 600 hrs./$6900
• **Cosmetology/Cosmetologist, General** 1260 hrs./$15,740 • **Nail Technician/Specialist and Manicurist** 2 students enrolled • **Technical Teacher Education** 7 students enrolled

STUDENT SERVICES Placement services for program completers.

Empire Beauty School–State College

208 West Hamilton Street, State College, PA 16801
http://www.empire.edu/

CONTACT Michael Bouman, President
Telephone: 800-223-3271

GENERAL INFORMATION Private Institution. Founded 1929. **Total program enrollment:** 19. **Application fee:** $100.

PROGRAM(S) OFFERED
• **Cosmetology/Cosmetologist, General** 1260 hrs./$15,740 • **Nail Technician/Specialist and Manicurist** 2 students enrolled • **Technical Teacher Education** 1 student enrolled

STUDENT SERVICES Placement services for program completers.

Empire Beauty School–Warminster

435 York Road, Warminster, PA 18974
http://www.empire.edu/

CONTACT Michael Bouman, President
Telephone: 800-223-3271

GENERAL INFORMATION Private Institution. Founded 1929. **Total program enrollment:** 39. **Application fee:** $100.

PROGRAM(S) OFFERED
• **Cosmetology/Cosmetologist, General** 1260 hrs./$15,740 • **Nail Technician/Specialist and Manicurist** 1 student enrolled • **Technical Teacher Education** 3 students enrolled

STUDENT SERVICES Placement services for program completers.

Empire Beauty School–West Mifflin

2393 Mountainview Drive, West Mifflin, PA 15122
http://www.empire.edu/

CONTACT Michael Bouman, President
Telephone: 800-223-3271

GENERAL INFORMATION Private Institution. **Total program enrollment:** 76. **Application fee:** $100.

PROGRAM(S) OFFERED
• **Cosmetology/Cosmetologist, General** 1260 hrs./$15,740 • **Nail Technician/Specialist and Manicurist** 3 students enrolled • **Technical Teacher Education** 4 students enrolled

STUDENT SERVICES Placement services for program completers.

Empire Beauty School–Whitehall

1634 MacArthur Road, Whitehall, PA 18052
http://www.empire.edu/

CONTACT Michael Bouman, President
Telephone: 800-223-3271

GENERAL INFORMATION Private Institution. Founded 1929. **Total program enrollment:** 99. **Application fee:** $100.

PROGRAM(S) OFFERED
• **Cosmetology, Barber/Styling, and Nail Instructor** 600 hrs./$6900
• **Cosmetology/Cosmetologist, General** 1260 hrs./$15,740 • **Nail Technician/Specialist and Manicurist** 210 hrs./$2415 • **Technical Teacher Education** 4 students enrolled

STUDENT SERVICES Placement services for program completers.

Empire Beauty School–Williamsport

1808 East Third Street, Williamsport, PA 17701
http://www.empire.edu/

CONTACT Michael Bouman, President
Telephone: 800-223-3271

GENERAL INFORMATION Private Institution. Founded 1929. **Total program enrollment:** 52. **Application fee:** $100.

PROGRAM(S) OFFERED
• **Cosmetology/Cosmetologist, General** *1260 hrs./$15,740* • **Nail Technician/ Specialist and Manicurist** • **Technical Teacher Education** *4 students enrolled*

STUDENT SERVICES Placement services for program completers.

Empire Beauty School–York

1101G South Edgar Street, York, PA 17403
http://www.empire.edu/

CONTACT Michael Bouman, President
Telephone: 800-223-3271

GENERAL INFORMATION Private Institution. Founded 1929. **Total program enrollment:** 119. **Application fee:** $100.

PROGRAM(S) OFFERED.
• **Cosmetology/Cosmetologist, General** *1260 hrs./$15,740* • **Nail Technician/ Specialist and Manicurist** *7 students enrolled* • **Technical Teacher Education** *1 student enrolled*

STUDENT SERVICES Placement services for program completers.

Erie Business Center, Main

246 West Ninth Street, Erie, PA 16501-1392
http://www.eriebc.edu/

CONTACT Sam McCaughtry, Chief Executive Officer
Telephone: 814-456-7504

GENERAL INFORMATION Private Institution. Founded 1884. **Accreditation:** State accredited or approved. **Total program enrollment:** 184. **Application fee:** $25.

PROGRAM(S) OFFERED
• **Executive Assistant/Executive Secretary** *1 student enrolled* • **Health Information/Medical Records Technology/Technician** *7 students enrolled* • **Hotel/Motel Administration/Management** *7 students enrolled* • **Medical Office Management/Administration** *5 students enrolled* • **Nurse/Nursing Assistant/Aide and Patient Care Assistant** *35 students enrolled* • **Physical Therapist Assistant** *9 students enrolled*

STUDENT SERVICES Academic or career counseling, employment services for current students, placement services for program completers.

Erie Business Center, South

170 Cascade Galleria, New Castle, PA 16101-3950
http://www.eriebc.edu/

CONTACT Samuel Mc Caughtry, Chief Executive Officer
Telephone: 724-658-9066

GENERAL INFORMATION Private Institution. Founded 1894. **Accreditation:** State accredited or approved. **Total program enrollment:** 44. **Application fee:** $25.

PROGRAM(S) OFFERED
• **Data Processing and Data Processing Technology/Technician** • **Health Information/Medical Records Technology/Technician** *7 students enrolled*

STUDENT SERVICES Academic or career counseling, placement services for program completers.

Everest Institute

100 Forbes Avenue, Suite 1200, Pittsburgh, PA 15222
http://www.everest.edu/

CONTACT James P. Callahan, School President
Telephone: 412-261-4520

GENERAL INFORMATION Private Institution. Founded 1840. **Accreditation:** State accredited or approved. **Total program enrollment:** 590.

PROGRAM(S) OFFERED
• **Business Operations Support and Secretarial Services, Other** *5 students enrolled* • **Health Information/Medical Records Administration/Administrator** *53 students enrolled* • **Medical/Clinical Assistant** *44 students enrolled* • **Nurse/ Nursing Assistant/Aide and Patient Care Assistant** *37 students enrolled* • **Pharmacy Technician/Assistant** *29 students enrolled*

STUDENT SERVICES Academic or career counseling, employment services for current students, placement services for program completers.

Fayette County Area Vocational-Technical School-Practical Nursing Program

175 Georges Fairchance Road, Uniontown, PA 15401
http://fayettevo-tech.org/

CONTACT Edward Jeffreys, Director of Vocational Education
Telephone: 724-437-2721

GENERAL INFORMATION Public Institution. Founded 1967. **Total program enrollment:** 96. **Application fee:** $20.

PROGRAM(S) OFFERED
• **Licensed Practical/Vocational Nurse Training (LPN, LVN, Cert, Dipl, AAS)** *1554 hrs./$8518*

STUDENT SERVICES Academic or career counseling, employment services for current students, placement services for program completers.

Franklin County Career and Technology Center

2463 Loop Road, Chambersburg, PA 17201
http://www.franklinctc.com/

CONTACT Janyce L. Collier, Administrator
Telephone: 717-263-5667

GENERAL INFORMATION Public Institution. Founded 1958. **Total program enrollment:** 61. **Application fee:** $25.

PROGRAM(S) OFFERED
• **Licensed Practical/Vocational Nurse Training (LPN, LVN, Cert, Dipl, AAS)** *1610 hrs./$10,100*

STUDENT SERVICES Daycare for children of students.

Gannon University

University Square, Erie, PA 16541-0001
http://www.gannon.edu/

CONTACT Dr. Antoine Garibaldi, President
Telephone: 814-871-7000

GENERAL INFORMATION Private Institution. Founded 1925. **Accreditation:** Regional (MSA/CIHE); radiologic technology: radiography (JRCERT). **Total program enrollment:** 2868. **Application fee:** $25.

PROGRAM(S) OFFERED
• **Business/Commerce, General** • **Criminalistics and Criminal Science** • **Data Entry/Microcomputer Applications, General** • **Human Resources Management/ Personnel Administration, General** *2 students enrolled* • **Insurance** *1 student*

Gannon University (continued)

enrolled • **Juvenile Corrections** • **Legal Assistant/Paralegal** • **Public Administration and Social Service Professions, Other** • **Social Work, Other** *1 student enrolled* • **Web/Multimedia Management and Webmaster**

STUDENT SERVICES Academic or career counseling, employment services for current students, placement services for program completers, remedial services.

Greater Altoona Career and Technology Center

1500 Fourth Avenue, Altoona, PA 16602-3695
http://www.gactc.com/

CONTACT Dr. Lanny Ross, Executive Director
Telephone: 814-946-8450 Ext. 1256

GENERAL INFORMATION Public Institution. Founded 1970. **Total program enrollment:** 172. **Application fee:** $40.

PROGRAM(S) OFFERED
• **Administrative Assistant and Secretarial Science, General** *2 students enrolled* • **Autobody/Collision and Repair Technology/Technician** *2 students enrolled* • **Automobile/Automotive Mechanics Technology/Technician** *1 student enrolled* • **Baking and Pastry Arts/Baker/Pastry Chef** *1 student enrolled* • **Cabinetmaking and Millwork/Millwright** • **Carpentry/Carpenter** • **Clinical/Medical Laboratory Science and Allied Professions, Other** *13 students enrolled* • **Computer Technology/Computer Systems Technology** • **Computer and Information Sciences and Support Services, Other** • **Culinary Arts/Chef Training** • **Dental Assisting/Assistant** • **Drafting and Design Technology/Technician, General** *1 student enrolled* • **Electrician** *6 students enrolled* • **Electromechanical Technology/Electromechanical Engineering Technology** • **Graphic Design** • **Graphic and Printing Equipment Operator, General Production** • **Heating, Air Conditioning, Ventilation and Refrigeration Maintenance Technology/Technician (HAC, HACR, HVAC, HVACR)** *990 hrs./$6400* • **Institutional Food Workers** • **Interior Design** *1 student enrolled* • **Licensed Practical/Vocational Nurse Training (LPN, LVN, Cert, Dipl, AAS)** *1564 hrs./$10,200* • **Machine Tool Technology/Machinist** *1 student enrolled* • **Mason/Masonry** • **Medical Administrative/Executive Assistant and Medical Secretary** *3 students enrolled* • **Medical Insurance Coding Specialist/Coder** *8 students enrolled* • **Medical Office Assistant/Specialist** *1395 hrs./$8200* • **Medical/Clinical Assistant** *10 students enrolled* • **Natural Resources/Conservation, General** *1 student enrolled* • **Nurse/Nursing Assistant/Aide and Patient Care Assistant** *240 hrs./$744* • **Parts, Warehousing, and Inventory Management Operations** • **Phlebotomy/Phlebotomist** *240 hrs./$1259* • **Plumbing Technology/Plumber** • **Sales, Distribution and Marketing Operations, General** • **Small Engine Mechanics and Repair Technology/Technician** *1 student enrolled* • **Truck and Bus Driver/Commercial Vehicle Operation** *13 students enrolled* • **Web Page, Digital/Multimedia and Information Resources Design** • **Welding Technology/Welder** *900 hrs./$4500*

STUDENT SERVICES Academic or career counseling, placement services for program completers, remedial services.

Great Lakes Institute of Technology

5100 Peach Street, Erie, PA 16509
http://www.glit.edu/

CONTACT Raymond A. Piccirillo, Executive Director
Telephone: 814-864-6666

GENERAL INFORMATION Private Institution. Founded 1965. **Total program enrollment:** 523. **Application fee:** $25.

PROGRAM(S) OFFERED
• **Cosmetology/Cosmetologist, General** *1250 hrs./$13,480* • **Dental Assisting/Assistant** *24 students enrolled* • **Diagnostic Medical Sonography/Sonographer and Ultrasound Technician** *2270 hrs./$26,154* • **Massage Therapy/Therapeutic Massage** *1115 hrs./$11,695* • **Medical Administrative/Executive Assistant and Medical Secretary** *8 students enrolled* • **Medical/Clinical Assistant** *1060 hrs./$10,792* • **Nail Technician/Specialist and Manicurist** *6 students enrolled* • **Pharmacy Technician/Assistant** *29 students enrolled* • **Surgical Technology/**

Technologist *1340 hrs./$13,620* • **Trade and Industrial Teacher Education** *15 students enrolled* • **Veterinary/Animal Health Technology/Technician and Veterinary Assistant** *1060 hrs./$10,815*

STUDENT SERVICES Academic or career counseling, employment services for current students, placement services for program completers.

Greene County Career and Technology Center

60 Zimmerman Drive, Waynesburg, PA 15370-8281
http://www.grvt.org/

CONTACT Janice Quailey, Director
Telephone: 724-627-3106 Ext. 201

GENERAL INFORMATION Public Institution. **Total program enrollment:** 30.

PROGRAM(S) OFFERED
• **Licensed Practical/Vocational Nurse Training (LPN, LVN, Cert, Dipl, AAS)** *1610 hrs./$9614*

STUDENT SERVICES Academic or career counseling, daycare for children of students, placement services for program completers.

Gwynedd-Mercy College

Sumneytown Pike, PO Box 901, Gwynedd Valley, PA 19437-0901
http://www.gmc.edu/

CONTACT Dr. Kathleen Owens, PhD, President
Telephone: 215-646-7300

GENERAL INFORMATION Private Institution. Founded 1948. **Accreditation:** Regional (MSA/CIHE); cardiovascular technology (JRCECT); health information administration (AHIMA); health information technology (AHIMA); radiologic technology: radiation therapy technology (JRCERT); respiratory therapy technology (CoARC). **Total program enrollment:** 1577. **Application fee:** $25.

STUDENT SERVICES Academic or career counseling, employment services for current students, remedial services.

Hanover Public School District–Practical Nursing Program

403 Moul Avenue, Hanover, PA 17331
http://www.hpsd.k12.pa.us/?q=node/2193

CONTACT Dr. Jill Dillon, Superintendent of Schools
Telephone: 717-637-2111

GENERAL INFORMATION Public Institution. **Total program enrollment:** 45. **Application fee:** $35.

PROGRAM(S) OFFERED
• **Licensed Practical/Vocational Nurse Training (LPN, LVN, Cert, Dipl, AAS)** *1560 hrs./$7850*

STUDENT SERVICES Academic or career counseling.

Harcum College

750 Montgomery Avenue, Bryn Mawr, PA 19010-3476
http://www.harcum.edu/

CONTACT JonJay DeTemple, PhD, President
Telephone: 610-525-4100

GENERAL INFORMATION Private Institution. Founded 1915. **Accreditation:** Regional (MSA/CIHE); dental assisting (ADA); dental hygiene

(ADA); medical laboratory technology (NAACLS); physical therapy assisting (APTA). **Total program enrollment:** 600. **Application fee:** $40.

PROGRAM(S) OFFERED
● **Dental Assisting/Assistant** *2 students enrolled*

STUDENT SERVICES Academic or career counseling, daycare for children of students, employment services for current students, placement services for program completers, remedial services.

Harrisburg Area Community College

1 HACC Drive, Harrisburg, PA 17110-2999
http://www.hacc.edu/

CONTACT Edna V. Baehre, President
Telephone: 717-780-2300

GENERAL INFORMATION Public Institution. Founded 1964. **Accreditation:** Regional (MSA/CIHE); dental assisting (ADA); dental hygiene (ADA); emergency medical services (JRCEMTP); medical laboratory technology (NAACLS). **Total program enrollment:** 3981. **Application fee:** $35.

PROGRAM(S) OFFERED
● **Accounting Technology/Technician and Bookkeeping** *2 students enrolled* ● **Administrative Assistant and Secretarial Science, General** *2 students enrolled* ● **Adult Development and Aging** *3 students enrolled* ● **Agribusiness/Agricultural Business Operations** ● **Architectural Engineering Technology/Technician** ● **Auctioneering** *13 students enrolled* ● **Automobile/Automotive Mechanics Technology/Technician** *6 students enrolled* ● **Baking and Pastry Arts/Baker/Pastry Chef** *2 students enrolled* ● **Building/Construction Finishing, Management, and Inspection, Other** ● **Building/Construction Site Management/Manager** ● **Building/Home/Construction Inspection/Inspector** *2 students enrolled* ● **Business Administration and Management, General** ● **Business/Commerce, General** ● **CAD/CADD Drafting and/or Design Technology/Technician** *1 student enrolled* ● **Cabinetmaking and Millwork/Millwright** *2 students enrolled* ● **Cardiovascular Technology/Technologist** *4 students enrolled* ● **Child Care Provider/Assistant** *2 students enrolled* ● **Civil Engineering Technology/Technician** ● **Computer Installation and Repair Technology/Technician** *1 student enrolled* ● **Computer Systems Networking and Telecommunications** ● **Computer and Information Sciences and Support Services, Other** ● **Computer and Information Sciences, General** ● **Construction Engineering Technology/Technician** ● **Construction Trades, General** ● **Corrections** *1 student enrolled* ● **Criminal Justice/Police Science** *2 students enrolled* ● **Culinary Arts/Chef Training** ● **Data Entry/Microcomputer Applications, General** *4 students enrolled* ● **Dental Assisting/Assistant** *17 students enrolled* ● **Diagnostic Medical Sonography/Sonographer and Ultrasound Technician** ● **Dietitian Assistant** *3 students enrolled* ● **Electrician** *4 students enrolled* ● **Engineering Technologies/Technicians, Other** *1 student enrolled* ● **Engineering-Related Technologies, Other** ● **Fine Arts and Art Studies, Other** *1 student enrolled* ● **Foodservice Systems Administration/Management** *1 student enrolled* ● **Graphic Design** ● **Heating, Air Conditioning, Ventilation and Refrigeration Maintenance Technology/Technician (HAC, HACR, HVAC, HVACR)** *6 students enrolled* ● **Human Services, General** *2 students enrolled* ● **Industrial Mechanics and Maintenance Technology** ● **Information Technology** *3 students enrolled* ● **Legal Assistant/Paralegal** *12 students enrolled* ● **Licensed Practical/Vocational Nurse Training (LPN, LVN, Cert, Dipl, AAS)** *86 students enrolled* ● **Mechanical Engineering/Mechanical Technology/Technician** ● **Medical/Clinical Assistant** *3 students enrolled* ● **Music Management and Merchandising** ● **Music, General** *3 students enrolled* ● **Phlebotomy/Phlebotomist** *50 students enrolled* ● **Photography** *2 students enrolled* ● **Precision Metal Working, Other** ● **Real Estate** ● **Recording Arts Technology/Technician** *7 students enrolled* ● **Restaurant, Culinary, and Catering Management/Manager** *5 students enrolled* ● **Sales, Distribution and Marketing Operations, General** *3 students enrolled* ● **Securities Services Administration/Management** ● **Selling Skills and Sales Operations** ● **Small Business Administration/Management** ● **Surgical Technology/Technologist** *1 student enrolled* ● **Tourism and Travel Services Management** ● **Web Page, Digital/Multimedia and Information Resources Design** *1 student enrolled* ● **Welding Technology/Welder** *1 student enrolled*

STUDENT SERVICES Academic or career counseling, daycare for children of students, employment services for current students, placement services for program completers, remedial services.

Harrisburg Area Community College–Gettysburg

705 Old Harrisburg Road, Suite 2, Gettysburg, PA 17325
http://www.hacc.edu/gettysburg

CONTACT Edna V. Baehre, President
Telephone: 717-337-3855

GENERAL INFORMATION Private Institution. **Total program enrollment:** 539. **Application fee:** $35.

STUDENT SERVICES Academic or career counseling, employment services for current students, placement services for program completers, remedial services.

Harrisburg Area Community College–Lancaster

1641 Old Philadelphia Pike, Lancaster, PA 17602
http://www.hacc.edu/

CONTACT Edna V. Baehre, President
Telephone: 717-293-5000

GENERAL INFORMATION Public Institution. **Total program enrollment:** 1714. **Application fee:** $35.

STUDENT SERVICES Academic or career counseling, daycare for children of students, employment services for current students, placement services for program completers, remedial services.

Harrisburg Area Community College–Lebanon

735 Cumberland Street, Lebanon, PA 17042
http://www.hacc.edu/

CONTACT Edna V. Baehre, President
Telephone: 717-270-4222

GENERAL INFORMATION Public Institution. **Total program enrollment:** 420. **Application fee:** $35.

STUDENT SERVICES Academic or career counseling, daycare for children of students, employment services for current students, placement services for program completers, remedial services.

Harrisburg Area Community College York Center

2010 Pennsylvania Avenue, York, PA 17404
http://www.hacc.edu/

CONTACT Dr. Edna V. Baehre, President
Telephone: 717-718-0328

GENERAL INFORMATION Public Institution. **Total program enrollment:** 844. **Application fee:** $35.

STUDENT SERVICES Academic or career counseling, employment services for current students, placement services for program completers, remedial services.

Harrisburg University of Science and Technology

304 Market Street, Harrisburg, PA 17101
http://www.harrisburgu.net/

CONTACT Dr. Melvyn Schiavelli, President
Telephone: 717-901-5152

GENERAL INFORMATION Private Institution. Founded 2005. **Total program enrollment:** 135.

PROGRAM(S) OFFERED
● **Computer and Information Sciences, General** ● **Computer and Information Systems Security** ● **Forensic Science and Technology** ● **Geological and Earth Sciences/Geosciences, Other**

STUDENT SERVICES Academic or career counseling, employment services for current students, placement services for program completers, remedial services.

Hazleton Area Career Center Practical Nursing Program

1451 West 23rd Street, Hazleton, PA 18201

CONTACT Samuel Marolo, Acting Superintendent of Schools
Telephone: 570-459-3221 Ext. 82407

GENERAL INFORMATION Public Institution. Founded 1970. **Total program enrollment:** 46. **Application fee:** $30.

PROGRAM(S) OFFERED
● **Licensed Practical/Vocational Nurse Training (LPN, LVN, Cert, Dipl, AAS)** *1540 hrs./$10,136*

STUDENT SERVICES Academic or career counseling, remedial services.

Huntingdon County Career and Technology

Vo-Tech Drive, Mill Creek, PA 07060
http://www.hcctc.org/

CONTACT Steven Walk, Acting Director
Telephone: 814-643-0951

GENERAL INFORMATION Public Institution. **Total program enrollment:** 42. **Application fee:** $25.

PROGRAM(S) OFFERED
● **Allied Health and Medical Assisting Services, Other** *1760 hrs./$8320*
● **Electrical and Power Transmission Installers, Other** *1760 hrs./$8320* ● **Heating, Air Conditioning, Ventilation and Refrigeration Maintenance Technology/Technician (HAC, HACR, HVAC, HVACR)** *1760 hrs./$8320* ● **Institutional Food Workers** *1760 hrs./$8320* ● **Licensed Practical/Vocational Nurse Training (LPN, LVN, Cert, Dipl, AAS)** *1563 hrs./$10,557* ● **Pipefitting/Pipefitter and Sprinkler Fitter** *1760 hrs./$8320*

Indiana University of Pennsylvania

Indiana, PA 15705-1087
http://www.iup.edu/

CONTACT Dr. Tony Atwater, President
Telephone: 724-357-2100

GENERAL INFORMATION Public Institution. Founded 1875. **Accreditation:** Regional (MSA/CIHE); athletic training (JRCAT); dietetics: post-baccalaureate internship (ADtA/CAADE); engineering-related programs (ABET/RAC); home economics (AAFCS); music (NASM); speech-language pathology (ASHA); theater (NAST). **Total program enrollment:** 12077. **Application fee:** $35.

PROGRAM(S) OFFERED
● **Culinary Arts and Related Services, Other** *11 students enrolled* ● **Culinary Arts/Chef Training** *84 students enrolled*

STUDENT SERVICES Academic or career counseling, daycare for children of students, employment services for current students, placement services for program completers, remedial services.

Jean Madeline Education Center

315a Bainbridge Street, Philadelphia, PA 19147
http://jeanmadeline.com/

CONTACT Samuel W. Lehman, President
Telephone: 215-238-9998

GENERAL INFORMATION Private Institution. **Total program enrollment:** 285.

PROGRAM(S) OFFERED
● **Aesthetician/Esthetician and Skin Care Specialist** *300 hrs./$3810*
● **Cosmetology and Related Personal Grooming Arts, Other** ● **Cosmetology, Barber/Styling, and Nail Instructor** *500 hrs./$7040* ● **Cosmetology/Cosmetologist, General** *1250 hrs./$17,675*

STUDENT SERVICES Academic or career counseling, employment services for current students, placement services for program completers.

Jefferson County-DuBois Area Vocational Technology–Practical Nursing

100 Jeff Tech Drive, Reynoldsville, PA 15851
http://www.jefftech.tec.pa.us/jefftech/site/default.asp

CONTACT Marsha Welsh, Director
Telephone: 814-653-8420

GENERAL INFORMATION Public Institution. Founded 1968. **Total program enrollment:** 36.

PROGRAM(S) OFFERED
● **Licensed Practical/Vocational Nurse Training (LPN, LVN, Cert, Dipl, AAS)** *35 students enrolled*

STUDENT SERVICES Remedial services.

JNA Institute of Culinary Arts

1212 South Broad Street, Philadelphia, PA 19146
http://www.culinaryarts.com/

CONTACT Joseph Digironimo, Director
Telephone: 215-468-8800

GENERAL INFORMATION Private Institution. Founded 1988. **Accreditation:** State accredited or approved. **Total program enrollment:** 64.

PROGRAM(S) OFFERED
● **Food Preparation/Professional Cooking/Kitchen Assistant** *3 students enrolled* ● **Hospitality Administration/Management, General** ● **Restaurant/Food Services Management**

STUDENT SERVICES Academic or career counseling, employment services for current students, placement services for program completers, remedial services.

Kaplan Career Institute–Harrisburg

5650 Derry Street, Harrisburg, PA 17111-3518
http://www.kci-Harrisburg.com/

CONTACT Sherry Rosenberg, Executive Director
Telephone: 717-564-4112

GENERAL INFORMATION Private Institution. Founded 1918. **Accreditation:** State accredited or approved. **Total program enrollment:** 537.

PROGRAM(S) OFFERED
• Business Administration and Management, General *121 hrs./$27,850*
• Computer Systems Networking and Telecommunications *24 students enrolled*
• Corrections and Criminal Justice, Other *121 hrs./$24,040* • Digital Communication and Media/Multimedia *120 hrs./$36,070* • Health Information/Medical Records Technology/Technician *59 hrs./$12,850* • Medical/Clinical Assistant *730 hrs./$14,210* • System, Networking, and LAN/WAN Management/Manager *108 hrs./$32,290*

STUDENT SERVICES Academic or career counseling, employment services for current students, placement services for program completers.

Kaplan Career Institute–ICM Campus

10 Wood Street, Pittsburgh, PA 15222-1977
http://www.icmschool.com/

CONTACT Thomas Rocks, Jr., Director of Education
Telephone: 412-261-2647

GENERAL INFORMATION Private Institution. Founded 1963. **Accreditation:** State accredited or approved. **Total program enrollment:** 653.

PROGRAM(S) OFFERED
• Computer Engineering Technology/Technician *3 students enrolled* • Computer Software and Media Applications, Other *4 students enrolled* • Medical/Clinical Assistant *68 students enrolled* • System Administration/Administrator • Web/Multimedia Management and Webmaster *13 students enrolled*

STUDENT SERVICES Academic or career counseling, employment services for current students, placement services for program completers, remedial services.

Keystone College

One College Green, La Plume, PA 18440
http://www.keystone.edu/

CONTACT Edward G. Boehm, Jr., President
Telephone: 570-945-8000

GENERAL INFORMATION Private Institution. Founded 1868. **Accreditation:** Regional (MSA/CIHE). **Total program enrollment:** 1299. **Application fee:** $30.

PROGRAM(S) OFFERED
• Computer and Information Sciences and Support Services, Other
• Computer/Information Technology Services Administration and Management, Other • Culinary Arts and Related Services, Other *1 student enrolled*
• Human Resources Management and Services, Other *3 students enrolled*
• Legal Assistant/Paralegal • Restaurant, Culinary, and Catering Management/Manager • Teacher Education and Professional Development, Specific Levels and Methods, Other

STUDENT SERVICES Academic or career counseling, daycare for children of students, employment services for current students, placement services for program completers, remedial services.

Keystone Technical Institute

2301 Academy Drive, Harrisburg, PA 17112
http://www.acadcampus.com/

CONTACT David W. Snyder, President
Telephone: 717-545-4747

GENERAL INFORMATION Private Institution. Founded 1980. **Accreditation:** State accredited or approved. **Total program enrollment:** 186. **Application fee:** $20.

PROGRAM(S) OFFERED
• Child Care Provider/Assistant *69 hrs./$21,719* • Culinary Arts/Chef Training *65 hrs./$26,820* • Dental Assisting/Assistant *70 hrs./$23,240* • Legal Assistant/Paralegal *74 hrs./$22,067* • Massage Therapy/Therapeutic Massage *70 hrs./$23,166* • Medical Office Management/Administration • Medical/Clinical Assistant *69 hrs./$24,570* • Web/Multimedia Management and Webmaster

STUDENT SERVICES Academic or career counseling, employment services for current students, placement services for program completers, remedial services.

King's College

133 North River Street, Wilkes-Barre, PA 18711-0801
http://www.kings.edu/

CONTACT President
Telephone: 570-208-5900

GENERAL INFORMATION Private Institution. Founded 1946. **Accreditation:** Regional (MSA/CIHE); athletic training (JRCAT). **Total program enrollment:** 2062. **Application fee:** $30.

PROGRAM(S) OFFERED
• Education, Other *6 students enrolled* • Family and Consumer Sciences/Human Sciences, Other • Human Resources Management/Personnel Administration, General

STUDENT SERVICES Academic or career counseling, employment services for current students, placement services for program completers, remedial services.

Kittanning Beauty School of Cosmetology Arts

120 Market Street, Kittanning, PA 16201

CONTACT Gerald Camp, Owner
Telephone: 724-287-0708

GENERAL INFORMATION Private Institution. Founded 1981. **Total program enrollment:** 21.

PROGRAM(S) OFFERED
• Cosmetology, Barber/Styling, and Nail Instructor *625 hrs./$4600*
• Cosmetology/Cosmetologist, General *1250 hrs./$12,400* • Nail Technician/Specialist and Manicurist *200 hrs./$2200*

STUDENT SERVICES Academic or career counseling, employment services for current students, placement services for program completers.

Lackawanna College

501 Vine Street, Scranton, PA 18509
http://www.lackawanna.edu/

CONTACT Ray Angeli, President
Telephone: 570-961-7810

GENERAL INFORMATION Private Institution. Founded 1894. **Accreditation:** Regional (MSA/CIHE). **Total program enrollment:** 1046. **Application fee:** $30.

Lackawanna College (continued)

PROGRAM(S) OFFERED
• Computer Software and Media Applications, Other • Criminal Justice/Police Science *76 students enrolled* • Emergency Medical Technology/Technician (EMT Paramedic) *7 students enrolled*

STUDENT SERVICES Academic or career counseling, employment services for current students, placement services for program completers, remedial services.

Lancaster Bible College

901 Eden Road, PO Box 83403, Lancaster, PA 17608-3403
http://www.lbc.edu/

CONTACT Peter W. Teague, President
Telephone: 717-569-7071

GENERAL INFORMATION Private Institution. Founded 1933. **Accreditation:** Regional (MSA/CIHE); state accredited or approved. **Total program enrollment:** 562. **Application fee:** $25.

PROGRAM(S) OFFERED
• Bible/Biblical Studies *9 students enrolled*

STUDENT SERVICES Academic or career counseling, employment services for current students, placement services for program completers, remedial services.

Lancaster County Career and Technology Center

1730 Hans Herr Drive, Willow Street, PA 17584
http://www.lcctc.org/

CONTACT Dr. Michael K. Curley, Executive Director
Telephone: 717-464-7050

GENERAL INFORMATION Public Institution. **Total program enrollment:** 335. **Application fee:** $35.

PROGRAM(S) OFFERED
• Administrative Assistant and Secretarial Science, General *2 students enrolled* • Applied Horticulture/Horticultural Operations, General *2 students enrolled* • Architectural Drafting and Architectural CAD/CADD *1 student enrolled* • Autobody/Collision and Repair Technology/Technician *1 student enrolled* • Automobile/Automotive Mechanics Technology/Technician *3 students enrolled* • Baking and Pastry Arts/Baker/Pastry Chef *2 students enrolled* • Cabinetmaking and Millwork/Millwright *1 student enrolled* • Carpentry/Carpenter *3 students enrolled* • Child Care and Support Services Management • Commercial Photography *1 student enrolled* • Commercial and Advertising Art • Computer Technology/Computer Systems Technology • Cosmetology/Cosmetologist, General *7 students enrolled* • Criminal Justice/Police Science • Dental Assisting/Assistant *16 students enrolled* • Dental Clinical Sciences, General (MS, PhD) *1080 hrs./$5995* • Diesel Mechanics Technology/Technician • Drafting and Design Technology/Technician, General • Electrical and Power Transmission Installers, General *2 students enrolled* • Electrician *1080 hrs./$5995* • Fire Protection, Other • Graphic Communications, Other *2 students enrolled* • Health Information/Medical Records Technology/Technician *15 students enrolled* • Heating, Air Conditioning, Ventilation and Refrigeration Maintenance Technology/Technician (HAC, HACR, HVAC, HVACR) *1080 hrs./$5995* • Heavy Equipment Maintenance Technology/Technician *2 students enrolled* • Industrial Mechanics and Maintenance Technology • Licensed Practical/Vocational Nurse Training (LPN, LVN, Cert, Dipl, AAS) *1575 hrs./$10,369* • Machine Tool Technology/Machinist *2 students enrolled* • Mason/Masonry • Medical/Clinical Assistant *1080 hrs./$5995* • Painting/Painter and Wall Coverer • Pipefitting/Pipefitter and Sprinkler Fitter *1 student enrolled* • Security and Protective Services, Other • Sheet Metal Technology/Sheetworking • Small Engine Mechanics and Repair Technology/Technician • Tourism and Travel Services Marketing Operations • Veterinary/Animal Health Technology/Technician and Veterinary Assistant *1080 hrs./$5995* • Web Page, Digital/Multimedia and Information Resources Design • Welding Technology/Welder *1 student enrolled*

STUDENT SERVICES Academic or career counseling, employment services for current students, placement services for program completers, remedial services.

Lancaster General College of Nursing & Health Sciences

410 North Lime Street, Lancaster, PA 17602
http://www.lancastergeneralcollege.edu/content/

CONTACT Dr. Mary Grace Simcox, President
Telephone: 717-544-4912

GENERAL INFORMATION Private Institution. Founded 1903. **Total program enrollment:** 346. **Application fee:** $60.

PROGRAM(S) OFFERED
• Cardiovascular Technology/Technologist *3 students enrolled* • Clinical/Medical Laboratory Technician *4 students enrolled* • Diagnostic Medical Sonography/Sonographer and Ultrasound Technician *1 student enrolled* • Nuclear Medical Technology/Technologist *21 students enrolled* • Surgical Technology/Technologist *1 student enrolled*

STUDENT SERVICES Academic or career counseling, employment services for current students, remedial services.

Lancaster School of Cosmetology

50 Ranck Avenue, Lancaster, PA 17602
http://lancasterschoolofcosmetology.com/

CONTACT Deborah A. Dunn, CEO
Telephone: 717-299-0200

GENERAL INFORMATION Private Institution. Founded 1979. **Total program enrollment:** 38. **Application fee:** $100.

PROGRAM(S) OFFERED
• Aesthetician/Esthetician and Skin Care Specialist *300 hrs./$4300* • Cosmetology and Related Personal Grooming Arts, Other • Cosmetology/Cosmetologist, General *1250 hrs./$11,100* • Make-Up Artist/Specialist *55 students enrolled* • Massage Therapy/Therapeutic Massage *600 hrs./$6600* • Nail Technician/Specialist and Manicurist *300 hrs./$3100* • Technical Teacher Education *600 hrs./$4270*

STUDENT SERVICES Academic or career counseling, employment services for current students, placement services for program completers.

Lansdale School of Business

201 Church Road, North Wales, PA 19454-4148
http://www.lsbonline.com/

CONTACT Marlon Keller, President
Telephone: 215-699-5700

GENERAL INFORMATION Private Institution. Founded 1918. **Accreditation:** State accredited or approved. **Total program enrollment:** 197. **Application fee:** $30.

PROGRAM(S) OFFERED
• Accounting *5 students enrolled* • Business/Office Automation/Technology/Data Entry *3 students enrolled* • Computer Graphics *2 students enrolled* • Computer Hardware Technology/Technician *4 students enrolled* • Computer Software and Media Applications, Other *6 students enrolled* • Corrections and Criminal Justice, Other *2 students enrolled* • Medical Office Assistant/Specialist *16 students enrolled* • Pharmacy Technician/Assistant • Web Page, Digital/Multimedia and Information Resources Design

STUDENT SERVICES Academic or career counseling, employment services for current students, placement services for program completers.

Lansdale School of Cosmetology

215 West Main Street, Lansdale, PA 19446
http://lansdalebeauty.com/

CONTACT Robbin J. Voltz, President Administrator
Telephone: 215-362-2322

GENERAL INFORMATION Private Institution. Founded 1990. **Total program enrollment:** 38.

PROGRAM(S) OFFERED
• **Aesthetician/Esthetician and Skin Care Specialist** *300 hrs./$4295*
• **Cosmetology, Barber/Styling, and Nail Instructor** *500 hrs./$4625*
• **Cosmetology/Cosmetologist, General** *1250 hrs./$12,646* • **Nail Technician/Specialist and Manicurist**

STUDENT SERVICES Academic or career counseling, employment services for current students, placement services for program completers, remedial services.

La Roche College

9000 Babcock Boulevard, Pittsburgh, PA 15237-5898
http://www.laroche.edu/

CONTACT Candace Introcaso, President
Telephone: 412-367-9300

GENERAL INFORMATION Private Institution (Affiliated with Roman Catholic Church). Founded 1963. **Accreditation:** Regional (MSA/CIHE); art and design (NASAD); interior design: professional (CIDA). **Total program enrollment:** 1127. **Application fee:** $50.

PROGRAM(S) OFFERED
• **Business Administration and Management, General** *1 student enrolled*
• **Nursing, Other** *5 students enrolled* • **Special Education and Teaching, General** *1 student enrolled*

STUDENT SERVICES Academic or career counseling, employment services for current students, placement services for program completers, remedial services.

La Salle University

1900 West Olney Avenue, Philadelphia, PA 19141-1199
http://www.lasalle.edu/

CONTACT Michael McGinniss, President
Telephone: 215-951-1000

GENERAL INFORMATION Private Institution. Founded 1863. **Accreditation:** Regional (MSA/CIHE); speech-language pathology (ASHA). **Total program enrollment:** 3552. **Application fee:** $35.

PROGRAM(S) OFFERED
• **Public Health Education and Promotion** *1 student enrolled*

STUDENT SERVICES Academic or career counseling, daycare for children of students, employment services for current students, placement services for program completers, remedial services.

Laurel Business Institute

11-15 Penn Street, Uniontown, PA 15401
http://www.laurel.edu/

CONTACT Nancy Decker, President
Telephone: 724-439-4900

GENERAL INFORMATION Private Institution. Founded 1985. **Accreditation:** Medical assisting (AAMAE); state accredited or approved. **Total program enrollment:** 306. **Application fee:** $55.

PROGRAM(S) OFFERED
• **Administrative Assistant and Secretarial Science, General** • **Cosmetology, Barber/Styling, and Nail Instructor** *3 students enrolled* • **Facial Treatment Specialist/Facialist** *5 students enrolled* • **Hair Styling/Stylist and Hair Design** *11 students enrolled* • **Legal Administrative Assistant/Secretary** • **Massage Therapy/Therapeutic Massage** *3 students enrolled* • **Medical Administrative/Executive Assistant and Medical Secretary** • **Nail Technician/Specialist and Manicurist** • **Pharmacy Technician/Assistant**

STUDENT SERVICES Academic or career counseling, employment services for current students, placement services for program completers.

Laurel Technical Institute

335 Boyd Drive, Sharon, PA 16146
http://www.laurel.edu/lti/

CONTACT Edward Petrunak, Director
Telephone: 724-983-0700

GENERAL INFORMATION Private Institution. Founded 1926. **Accreditation:** State accredited or approved. **Total program enrollment:** 149. **Application fee:** $55.

PROGRAM(S) OFFERED
• **Accounting** • **Business/Office Automation/Technology/Data Entry** • **Child Care and Support Services Management** • **Data Entry/Microcomputer Applications, General** • **Information Science/Studies** • **Medical Transcription/Transcriptionist**

STUDENT SERVICES Academic or career counseling, employment services for current students, placement services for program completers.

Lawrence County Career &Technical Practical Nursing Program

750 Phelps Way, New Castle, PA 16101-5099
http://www.lcvt.tec.pa.us

CONTACT Andrew Tommelleo, Director
Telephone: 724-658-3583 Ext. 7112

GENERAL INFORMATION Public Institution. **Total program enrollment:** 50. **Application fee:** $25.

PROGRAM(S) OFFERED
• **Licensed Practical/Vocational Nurse Training (LPN, LVN, Cert, Dipl, AAS)** *1500 hrs./$10,325*

STUDENT SERVICES Placement services for program completers, remedial services.

Lebanon County Area Vocational Technical School

833 Metro Drive, Lebanon, PA 17042
http://www.lcctc.k12.pa.us/

CONTACT George Custer, Administrative Director
Telephone: 717-273-4401

GENERAL INFORMATION Private Institution. **Total program enrollment:** 52. **Application fee:** $20.

PROGRAM(S) OFFERED
• **Allied Health and Medical Assisting Services, Other** • **Autobody/Collision and Repair Technology/Technician** • **Automobile/Automotive Mechanics Technology/Technician** • **Baking and Pastry Arts/Baker/Pastry Chef** *2 students enrolled* • **Business Operations Support and Secretarial Services, Other** *2 students enrolled* • **Carpentry/Carpenter** • **Child Care Provider/Assistant** • **Cinematography and Film/Video Production** • **Commercial and Advertising Art** • **Cooking and Related Culinary Arts, General** • **Cosmetology/Cosmetologist, General** *1 student enrolled* • **Criminal Justice/Police Science** • **Diesel Mechanics Technology/Technician** • **Drafting and Design Technology/Technician, General** • **Electrical and Power Transmission Installers, Other** • **Electrical, Electronic and Communications Engineering Technology/**

Lebanon County Area Vocational Technical School (continued)

Technician • **Health Professions and Related Clinical Sciences, Other** • **Industrial Technology/Technician** • **Management Information Systems, General** • **Nursing, Other** *49 students enrolled* • **Plumbing and Related Water Supply Services, Other** • **Welding Technology/Welder**

STUDENT SERVICES Academic or career counseling, employment services for current students, placement services for program completers, remedial services.

Lebanon Valley College

101 North College Avenue, Annville, PA 17003-1400
http://www.lvc.edu/

CONTACT Stephen C. MacDonald, President
Telephone: 717-867-6100

GENERAL INFORMATION Private Institution. Founded 1866. **Accreditation:** Regional (MSA/CIHE); music (NASM). **Total program enrollment:** 1648. **Application fee:** $30.

PROGRAM(S) OFFERED
• **Accounting** • **Business Administration and Management, General**

STUDENT SERVICES Academic or career counseling, employment services for current students, placement services for program completers.

Lehigh Carbon Community College

4525 Education Park Drive, Schnecksville, PA 18078-2598
http://www.lccc.edu/

CONTACT Donald W. Snyder, President
Telephone: 610-799-2121

GENERAL INFORMATION Public Institution. Founded 1967. **Accreditation:** Regional (MSA/CIHE); health information technology (AHIMA); medical assisting (AAMAE); physical therapy assisting (APTA). **Total program enrollment:** 2881. **Application fee:** $30.

PROGRAM(S) OFFERED
• **Accounting Technology/Technician and Bookkeeping** *5 students enrolled* • **Accounting** • **Administrative Assistant and Secretarial Science, General** • **Animation, Interactive Technology, Video Graphics and Special Effects** • **Art/Art Studies, General** *1 student enrolled* • **Business Administration and Management, General** *7 students enrolled* • **Computer Programming/Programmer, General** • **Computer Systems Analysis/Analyst** • **Computer Systems Networking and Telecommunications** *1 student enrolled* • **Computer Technology/Computer Systems Technology** • **Construction Engineering Technology/Technician** *1 student enrolled* • **Corrections and Criminal Justice, Other** *2 students enrolled* • **Corrections** *2 students enrolled* • **Culinary Arts and Related Services, Other** *1 student enrolled* • **Drafting and Design Technology/Technician, General** *2 students enrolled* • **Early Childhood Education and Teaching** *16 students enrolled* • **Education, General** *7 students enrolled* • **Electrician** *1 student enrolled* • **Heating, Air Conditioning, Ventilation and Refrigeration Maintenance Technology/Technician (HAC, HACR, HVAC, HVACR)** *6 students enrolled* • **Human Resources Management/Personnel Administration, General** • **Industrial Electronics Technology/Technician** • **Information Science/Studies** • **Legal Assistant/Paralegal** *3 students enrolled* • **Licensed Practical/Vocational Nurse Training (LPN, LVN, Cert, Dipl, AAS)** *31 students enrolled* • **Logistics and Materials Management** • **Manufacturing Technology/Technician** *1 student enrolled* • **Medical Insurance Coding Specialist/Coder** *22 students enrolled* • **Medical Insurance Specialist/Medical Biller** *10 students enrolled* • **Medical Transcription/Transcriptionist** *7 students enrolled* • **Montessori Teacher Education** • **Public Administration and Social Service Professions, Other** *1 student enrolled* • **Teacher Assistant/Aide** • **Teaching English or French as a Second or Foreign Language, Other** • **Tool and Die Technology/Technician** • **Tourism and Travel Services Management** *1 student enrolled* • **Web Page, Digital/Multimedia and Information Resources Design**

STUDENT SERVICES Academic or career counseling, daycare for children of students, employment services for current students, placement services for program completers, remedial services.

Lenape Area Vocational Tech School, Practical Nursing Program

83 Glade Drive, Kittanning, PA 16201
http://www.lenape.k12.pa.us

CONTACT Dawn Kocher-Taylor, Administrative Director
Telephone: 724-545-7311

GENERAL INFORMATION Public Institution. **Total program enrollment:** 44.

PROGRAM(S) OFFERED
• **Licensed Practical/Vocational Nurse Training (LPN, LVN, Cert, Dipl, AAS)** *1554 hrs./$10,917*

STUDENT SERVICES Academic or career counseling, remedial services.

Levittown Beauty Academy

4257 Newportville Road, Levittown, PA 19056
http://www.levittownbeautyacademy.com/

CONTACT Joseph Devenuto, Director
Telephone: 215-943-0298

GENERAL INFORMATION Private Institution. Founded 1964. **Total program enrollment:** 52.

PROGRAM(S) OFFERED
• **Cosmetology and Related Personal Grooming Arts, Other** *200 hrs./$2000* • **Cosmetology, Barber/Styling, and Nail Instructor** *500 hrs./$4000* • **Cosmetology/Cosmetologist, General** *1250 hrs./$13,000* • **Technical Teacher Education** *3 students enrolled*

STUDENT SERVICES Academic or career counseling, employment services for current students, placement services for program completers, remedial services.

Lincoln Technical Institute

5151 Tilghman Street, Allentown, PA 18104-3298
http://www.lincolnedu.com/

CONTACT Lisa Kuntz, Executive Director
Telephone: 610-398-5300

GENERAL INFORMATION Private Institution. Founded 1949. **Accreditation:** State accredited or approved. **Total program enrollment:** 691. **Application fee:** $25.

PROGRAM(S) OFFERED
• **Allied Health and Medical Assisting Services, Other** *1530 hrs./$23,550* • **Computer Systems Networking and Telecommunications** *1530 hrs./$26,920* • **Drafting and Design Technology/Technician, General** *2100 hrs./$25,730* • **Electrical and Electronic Engineering Technologies/Technicians, Other** *1600 hrs./$27,150* • **Medical Insurance Coding Specialist/Coder** *55 students enrolled* • **Medical Insurance Specialist/Medical Biller** *720 hrs./$12,920* • **Medical/Clinical Assistant** *164 students enrolled* • **Pharmacy Technician/Assistant** *40 students enrolled*

STUDENT SERVICES Academic or career counseling, employment services for current students, placement services for program completers, remedial services.

Lincoln Technical Institute

2180 Hornig Road, Building A, Philadelphia, PA 19116-4202
http://www.lincolnedu.com/

CONTACT Edward Isselmann, Exec Director
Telephone: 215-969-0869

GENERAL INFORMATION Private Institution. **Total program enrollment:** 143.

PROGRAM(S) OFFERED
- **Allied Health and Medical Assisting Services, Other** *900 hrs./$14,161*
- **Criminal Justice/Law Enforcement Administration** *1530 hrs./$22,876*
- **Health Information/Medical Records Administration/Administrator** *3 students enrolled* • **Massage Therapy/Therapeutic Massage** *720 hrs./$11,644* • **Medical Insurance Coding Specialist/Coder** *720 hrs./$12,844* • **Medical/Clinical Assistant** *73 students enrolled* • **Pharmacy Technician/Assistant** *720 hrs./$11,984*
- **System Administration/Administrator** *23 students enrolled*

STUDENT SERVICES Placement services for program completers.

Lincoln Technical Institute

3600 Market Street, Philadelphia, PA 19104-2641
http://www.lincolnedu.com/

CONTACT Ed Stranix, Exec Director
Telephone: 215-382-1553

GENERAL INFORMATION Private Institution. **Total program enrollment:** 506. **Application fee:** $50.

PROGRAM(S) OFFERED
- **Administrative Assistant and Secretarial Science, General** *720 hrs./$12,302*
- **Computer and Information Sciences and Support Services, Other** *720 hrs./$13,234* • **Medical/Clinical Assistant** *900 hrs./$14,289* • **Pharmacy Technician/Assistant** *720 hrs./$12,111*

STUDENT SERVICES Academic or career counseling, employment services for current students, placement services for program completers.

Lincoln Technical Institute

9191 Torresdale Avenue, Philadelphia, PA 19136-1595
http://www.lincolnedu.com/

CONTACT Mark Bohen, Director
Telephone: 215-335-0800

GENERAL INFORMATION Private Institution. Founded 1946. **Accreditation:** State accredited or approved. **Total program enrollment:** 397. **Application fee:** $25.

PROGRAM(S) OFFERED
- **Automobile/Automotive Mechanics Technology/Technician** *103 students enrolled* • **Diesel Mechanics Technology/Technician**

STUDENT SERVICES Academic or career counseling, employment services for current students, placement services for program completers, remedial services.

L. T. International Beauty School

1238 Spring Garden Street, Philadelphia, PA 19123

CONTACT Michael Trinh, Chief Financial Officer
Telephone: 215-922-4478

GENERAL INFORMATION Private Institution. **Total program enrollment:** 56. **Application fee:** $100.

PROGRAM(S) OFFERED
- **Cosmetology/Cosmetologist, General** *1250 hrs./$12,000*

STUDENT SERVICES Academic or career counseling, employment services for current students, placement services for program completers.

Luzerne County Community College

1333 South Prospect Street, Nanticoke, PA 18634-9804
http://www.luzerne.edu/

CONTACT Mr. Thomas P. Leary, President
Telephone: 570-740-0200

GENERAL INFORMATION Public Institution. Founded 1966. **Accreditation:** Regional (MSA/CIHE); dental assisting (ADA); dental hygiene (ADA); surgical technology (ARCST). **Total program enrollment:** 3272. **Application fee:** $40.

PROGRAM(S) OFFERED
- **Accounting Technology/Technician and Bookkeeping** • **Administrative Assistant and Secretarial Science, General** *1 student enrolled* • **Applied Horticulture/Horticultural Operations, General** • **Architectural Drafting and Architectural CAD/CADD** *1 student enrolled* • **Baking and Pastry Arts/Baker/Pastry Chef** *1 student enrolled* • **Building/Property Maintenance and Management** *2 students enrolled* • **Business/Commerce, General** *4 students enrolled* • **CAD/CADD Drafting and/or Design Technology/Technician** • **Commercial and Advertising Art** • **Communications Systems Installation and Repair Technology** • **Computer Programming, Specific Applications** • **Computer Systems Networking and Telecommunications** *2 students enrolled* • **Computer Technology/Computer Systems Technology** • **Computer Typography and Composition Equipment Operator** • **Computer and Information Systems Security** • **Dental Assisting/Assistant** *24 students enrolled* • **Electrical, Electronic and Communications Engineering Technology/Technician** • **Electrician** • **Emergency Medical Technology/Technician (EMT Paramedic)** • **Fire Protection and Safety Technology/Technician** • **Food Preparation/Professional Cooking/Kitchen Assistant** • **General Office Occupations and Clerical Services** • **Graphic Design** *4 students enrolled* • **Health and Medical Administrative Services, Other** • **Hospitality Administration/Management, Other** • **Illustration** *1 student enrolled* • **Logistics and Materials Management** • **Machine Shop Technology/Assistant** *1 student enrolled* • **Machine Tool Technology/Machinist** • **Perioperative/Operating Room and Surgical Nurse/Nursing** • **Personal and Culinary Services, Other** • **Plumbing Technology/Plumber** *1 student enrolled* • **Recording Arts Technology/Technician** *3 students enrolled* • **Restaurant, Culinary, and Catering Management/Manager** *1 student enrolled* • **Security and Protective Services, Other** • **Small Business Administration/Management** • **Tourism Promotion Operations** • **Web Page, Digital/Multimedia and Information Resources Design**

STUDENT SERVICES Academic or career counseling, placement services for program completers, remedial services.

Magnolia School

50 East Butler Pike, Ambler, PA 19002
http://www.themagnoliaschool.com/

CONTACT Truc Do, Chief Executive Officer
Telephone: 215-643-5994

GENERAL INFORMATION Private Institution. **Total program enrollment:** 81. **Application fee:** $100.

PROGRAM(S) OFFERED
- **Aesthetician/Esthetician and Skin Care Specialist** *300 hrs./$3850*
- **Cosmetology/Cosmetologist, General** *1250 hrs./$15,400* • **Nail Technician/Specialist and Manicurist** *200 hrs./$2700* • **Teacher Education and Professional Development, Specific Levels and Methods, Other** *500 hrs./$4800*
- **Teacher Education and Professional Development, Specific Subject Areas, Other** *1 student enrolled*

STUDENT SERVICES Academic or career counseling, employment services for current students, placement services for program completers, remedial services.

Manor College

700 Fox Chase Road, Jenkintown, PA 19046
http://www.manor.edu/

CONTACT Sr. Mary Cecilia Jurasinski, OSBM, President
Telephone: 215-885-2360

GENERAL INFORMATION Private Institution. Founded 1947. **Accreditation:** Regional (MSA/CIHE); dental assisting (ADA); dental hygiene (ADA). **Total program enrollment:** 458. **Application fee:** $25.

PROGRAM(S) OFFERED
● **Legal Assistant/Paralegal** 5 *students enrolled* ● **Religious Education** 1 *student enrolled*

STUDENT SERVICES Academic or career counseling, employment services for current students, remedial services.

Marywood University

2300 Adams Avenue, Scranton, PA 18509-1598
http://www.marywood.edu/

CONTACT Sr. Anne Munley, President
Telephone: 570-348-6211

GENERAL INFORMATION Private Institution. Founded 1915. **Accreditation:** Regional (MSA/CIHE); art and design (NASAD); counseling (ACA); dietetics: undergraduate, postbaccalaureate internship (ADtA/CAADE); home economics (AAFCS); music (NASM); speech-language pathology (ASHA). **Total program enrollment:** 2488. **Application fee:** $35.

PROGRAM(S) OFFERED
● **Art History, Criticism and Conservation** ● **Business/Commerce, General** ● **Communication, Journalism and Related Programs, Other** ● **Computer and Information Sciences and Support Services, Other** ● **Design and Visual Communications, General** ● **Fashion Merchandising** ● **Fine/Studio Arts, General** ● **Hospitality Administration/Management, General**

STUDENT SERVICES Academic or career counseling, daycare for children of students, employment services for current students, placement services for program completers, remedial services.

McCann School of Business & Technology

2650 Woodglen Road, Pottsville, PA 17901
http://www.mccannschool.com/

CONTACT Linda Walinsky, President
Telephone: 570-622-7622

GENERAL INFORMATION Private Institution. Founded 1897. **Accreditation:** State accredited or approved. **Total program enrollment:** 1277. **Application fee:** $40.

PROGRAM(S) OFFERED
● **Accounting Technology/Technician and Bookkeeping** 2 *students enrolled* ● **Computer and Information Sciences, General** ● **Cosmetology and Related Personal Grooming Arts, Other** ● **Cosmetology/Cosmetologist, General** 3 *students enrolled* ● **Data Entry/Microcomputer Applications, General** 1 *student enrolled* ● **General Office Occupations and Clerical Services** 1 *student enrolled* ● **Massage Therapy/Therapeutic Massage** 9 *students enrolled* ● **Medical Office Assistant/Specialist** 4 *students enrolled* ● **Medical/Clinical Assistant** 2 *students enrolled*

STUDENT SERVICES Academic or career counseling, placement services for program completers, remedial services.

Mercer County Career Center

776 Greenville Road, Mercer, PA 16137
http://www.mctec.net/

CONTACT Rachel Martin, Administrative Director
Telephone: 724-662-3000

GENERAL INFORMATION Private Institution. **Total program enrollment:** 24. **Application fee:** $25.

PROGRAM(S) OFFERED
● **Licensed Practical/Vocational Nurse Training (LPN, LVN, Cert, Dipl, AAS)** *1500 hrs./$9000*

STUDENT SERVICES Academic or career counseling, employment services for current students, placement services for program completers, remedial services.

Mercyhurst College

501 East 38th Street, Erie, PA 16546
http://www.mercyhurst.edu/

CONTACT Thomas J. Gamble, PhD, President
Telephone: 814-824-2000

GENERAL INFORMATION Private Institution. Founded 1926. **Accreditation:** Regional (MSA/CIHE); athletic training (JRCAT); home economics (AAFCS); music (NASM); physical therapy assisting (APTA). **Total program enrollment:** 3656. **Application fee:** $30.

PROGRAM(S) OFFERED
● **Computer Technology/Computer Systems Technology** ● **Criminal Justice/Safety Studies** 36 *students enrolled* ● **Culinary Arts/Chef Training** ● **Licensed Practical/Vocational Nurse Training (LPN, LVN, Cert, Dipl, AAS)** 44 *students enrolled* ● **Medical Insurance Coding Specialist/Coder** 1 *student enrolled* ● **Medical Office Assistant/Specialist** 1 *student enrolled* ● **Medical Transcription/Transcriptionist** 2 *students enrolled* ● **Religious Education**

STUDENT SERVICES Academic or career counseling, employment services for current students, placement services for program completers, remedial services.

Mifflin Juniata Career and Technology Center

700 Pitt Street, Lewistown, PA 17044
http://www.mjctc.org/

CONTACT Kevin J. O'Donnell, Administrative Director
Telephone: 717-248-3933

GENERAL INFORMATION Public Institution. **Total program enrollment:** 43. **Application fee:** $25.

PROGRAM(S) OFFERED
● **Licensed Practical/Vocational Nurse Training (LPN, LVN, Cert, Dipl, AAS)** 36 *students enrolled*

STUDENT SERVICES Academic or career counseling.

Misericordia University

301 Lake Street, Dallas, PA 18612-1098
http://www.misericordia.edu/

CONTACT Michael A. MacDowell, President
Telephone: 570-674-6400

GENERAL INFORMATION Private Institution. Founded 1924. **Accreditation:** Regional (MSA/CIHE); radiologic technology: radiography (JRCERT); speech-language pathology (ASHA). **Total program enrollment:** 1568. **Application fee:** $25.

STUDENT SERVICES Academic or career counseling, employment services for current students, placement services for program completers, remedial services.

Montgomery County Community College

340 DeKalb Pike, Blue Bell, PA 19422-0796
http://www.mc3.edu/

CONTACT Dr. Karen Stout, President
Telephone: 215-641-6300

GENERAL INFORMATION Public Institution. Founded 1964. **Accreditation:** Regional (MSA/CIHE); dental hygiene (ADA); medical laboratory technology (NAACLS). **Total program enrollment:** 4505. **Application fee:** $25.

PROGRAM(S) OFFERED
• Accounting Technology/Technician and Bookkeeping 6 *students enrolled* • Accounting 2 *students enrolled* • Administrative Assistant and Secretarial Science, General 5 *students enrolled* • Automotive Engineering Technology/Technician 1 *student enrolled* • Business Administration and Management, General 5 *students enrolled* • Child Care Provider/Assistant 3 *students enrolled* • Computer Systems Networking and Telecommunications 1 *student enrolled* • Management Information Systems and Services, Other 3 *students enrolled* • Management Information Systems, General 1 *student enrolled* • Medical/Clinical Assistant 13 *students enrolled* • Psychiatric/Mental Health Services Technician 10 *students enrolled* • Retailing and Retail Operations 1 *student enrolled* • Sales, Distribution and Marketing Operations, General 1 *student enrolled* • Security and Loss Prevention Services 1 *student enrolled* • Substance Abuse/Addiction Counseling 3 *students enrolled* • Surgical Technology/Technologist 2 *students enrolled*

STUDENT SERVICES Academic or career counseling, daycare for children of students, employment services for current students, placement services for program completers, remedial services.

Montgomery County Community College–West Campus

101 College Dr, Pottstown, PA 19464
http://www.mc3.edu/

CONTACT Dr. Karen A. Stout, President
Telephone: 610-718-1800

GENERAL INFORMATION Public Institution. **Total program enrollment:** 1079. **Application fee:** $25.

STUDENT SERVICES Academic or career counseling, employment services for current students, placement services for program completers, remedial services.

Mount Aloysius College

7373 Admiral Peary Highway, Cresson, PA 16630-1999
http://www.mtaloy.edu/

CONTACT Mary Ann Dillon, President
Telephone: 814-886-4131

GENERAL INFORMATION Private Institution. Founded 1939. **Accreditation:** Regional (MSA/CIHE); medical assisting (AAMAE); physical therapy assisting (APTA); surgical technology (ARCST). **Total program enrollment:** 1175. **Application fee:** $30.

PROGRAM(S) OFFERED
• Criminal Justice/Law Enforcement Administration 1 *student enrolled*

STUDENT SERVICES Academic or career counseling, daycare for children of students, employment services for current students, placement services for program completers, remedial services.

Muhlenberg College

2400 Chew Street, Allentown, PA 18104-5586
http://www.muhlenberg.edu/

CONTACT Dr. Peyton R. Helm, President
Telephone: 484-664-3100

GENERAL INFORMATION Private Institution (Affiliated with Lutheran Church). Founded 1848. **Accreditation:** Regional (MSA/CIHE). **Total program enrollment:** 2318. **Application fee:** $50.

PROGRAM(S) OFFERED
• Accounting 6 *students enrolled* • Business Administration and Management, General 4 *students enrolled* • Economics, General 1 *student enrolled* • German Studies 1 *student enrolled* • Health/Health Care Administration/Management 1 *student enrolled* • Human Resources Management/Personnel Administration, General

STUDENT SERVICES Academic or career counseling, employment services for current students, placement services for program completers.

National Massage Therapy Institute

10050 Roosevelt Boulevard, Philadelphia, PA 19116
http://www.studymassage.com/

CONTACT Steven Kemler, CEO
Telephone: 800-264-9845

GENERAL INFORMATION Private Institution. **Total program enrollment:** 684. **Application fee:** $50.

PROGRAM(S) OFFERED
• Massage Therapy/Therapeutic Massage 30 *hrs./$11,225*

STUDENT SERVICES Placement services for program completers.

NAWCC School of Horology

514 Poplar Street, Columbia, PA 17512-2130
http://www.nawcc.org/school/

CONTACT James O. Michaels, School Director
Telephone: 717-684-8261 Ext. 218

GENERAL INFORMATION Private Institution. **Total program enrollment:** 13.

PROGRAM(S) OFFERED
• Watchmaking and Jewelrymaking 770 *hrs./$12,505*

STUDENT SERVICES Academic or career counseling.

Neumann University

One Neumann Drive, Aston, PA 19014-1298
http://www.neumann.edu/

CONTACT Rosalie M. Mirenda, President
Telephone: 610-459-0905

GENERAL INFORMATION Private Institution. Founded 1965. **Accreditation:** Regional (MSA/CIHE); medical technology (NAACLS). **Total program enrollment:** 2147. **Application fee:** $35.

STUDENT SERVICES Academic or career counseling, daycare for children of students, employment services for current students, placement services for program completers, remedial services.

New Castle School of Beauty Culture

314 East Washington Street, New Castle, PA 16101

CONTACT Gerald Camp, Owner
Telephone: 724-287-0708

GENERAL INFORMATION Private Institution. **Total program enrollment:**
37.

PROGRAM(S) OFFERED
• **Cosmetology, Barber/Styling, and Nail Instructor** 625 hrs./$4600
• **Cosmetology/Cosmetologist, General** 1250 hrs./$12,400 • **Nail Technician/
Specialist and Manicurist** 200 hrs./$2200

STUDENT SERVICES Academic or career counseling, employment
services for current students, placement services for program completers.

New Castle School of Trades

New Castle Youngstown Road, Route 422 RD1, Pulaski, PA
16143-9721
http://www.ncstrades.com/

CONTACT Jim Buttermore, Director
Telephone: 724-964-8811

GENERAL INFORMATION Private Institution. Founded 1945. **Accreditation:** State accredited or approved. **Total program enrollment:** 573. **Application fee:** $25.

PROGRAM(S) OFFERED
• **Automobile/Automotive Mechanics Technology/Technician** 1500 hrs./$17,560
• **Building/Property Maintenance and Management** • **Construction/Heavy
Equipment/Earthmoving Equipment Operation** 792 hrs./$13,505 • **Electrical/
Electronics Equipment Installation and Repair, General** • **Electrical/
Electronics Maintenance and Repair Technology, Other** 1500 hrs./$18,436
• **Heating, Air Conditioning, Ventilation and Refrigeration Maintenance
Technology/Technician (HAC, HACR, HVAC, HVACR)** 1500 hrs./$15,595
• **Industrial Mechanics and Maintenance Technology** 7 students enrolled
• **Machine Shop Technology/Assistant** 7 students enrolled • **Machine Tool
Technology/Machinist** 1500 hrs./$15,595 • **Truck and Bus Driver/Commercial
Vehicle Operation** 38 students enrolled • **Welding Technology/Welder** 1000 hrs./
$11,600

STUDENT SERVICES Academic or career counseling, employment
services for current students, placement services for program completers.

Newport Business Institute

945 Greensburg Road, Lower Burrell, PA 15068-3929
http://www.nbi.edu/

CONTACT Raymond Wroblewski, Director
Telephone: 724-339-0455 Ext. 17

GENERAL INFORMATION Private Institution. Founded 1895. **Accreditation:** State accredited or approved. **Total program enrollment:** 66. **Application fee:** $25.

PROGRAM(S) OFFERED
• **Accounting** 1 student enrolled • **Administrative Assistant and Secretarial Science, General** 1 student enrolled • **Computer and Information Sciences and
Support Services, Other** • **General Office Occupations and Clerical Services**
• **Medical Administrative/Executive Assistant and Medical Secretary** 12
students enrolled • **Medical/Clinical Assistant** • **Tourism Promotion Operations**
1 student enrolled

STUDENT SERVICES Academic or career counseling, employment
services for current students, placement services for program completers.

Newport Business Institute

941 West Third Street, Williamsport, PA 17701-5855
http://www.nbi.edu/

CONTACT Mary O. Weaver, Director
Telephone: 570-326-2869

GENERAL INFORMATION Private Institution. Founded 1955. **Accreditation:** State accredited or approved. **Total program enrollment:** 69. **Application fee:** $25.

PROGRAM(S) OFFERED
• **Accounting** • **Administrative Assistant and Secretarial Science, General**
STUDENT SERVICES Placement services for program completers.

Northampton County Area Community College

3835 Green Pond Road, Bethlehem, PA 18020-7599
http://www.northampton.edu/

CONTACT Arthur Scott, President
Telephone: 610-861-5300

GENERAL INFORMATION Public Institution. Founded 1967. **Accreditation:** Regional (MSA/CIHE); dental hygiene (ADA); funeral service
(ABFSE); practical nursing (NLN); radiologic technology: radiography
(JRCERT). **Total program enrollment:** 4742. **Application fee:** $25.

PROGRAM(S) OFFERED
• **Accounting Technology/Technician and Bookkeeping** 3 students enrolled
• **Automobile/Automotive Mechanics Technology/Technician** 4 students enrolled
• **Child Care Provider/Assistant** 44 students enrolled • **Child Care and Support
Services Management** 31 students enrolled • **Computer Installation and Repair
Technology/Technician** 1 student enrolled • **Computer Programming/
Programmer, General** 1 student enrolled • **Culinary Arts/Chef Training** 22
students enrolled • **Diagnostic Medical Sonography/Sonographer and Ultra-
sound Technician** 2 students enrolled • **Dietetic Technician (DTR)** 1 student
enrolled • **Emergency Medical Technology/Technician (EMT Paramedic)** 30
students enrolled • **Entrepreneurship/Entrepreneurial Studies** 7 students enrolled
• **Fire Services Administration** 1 student enrolled • **General Office Occupations
and Clerical Services** 14 students enrolled • **Heating, Air Conditioning, Ventilation and Refrigeration Maintenance Technology/Technician (HAC, HACR,
HVAC, HVACR)** 4 students enrolled • **Industrial Electronics Technology/
Technician** 4 students enrolled • **Library Assistant/Technician** 14 students
enrolled • **Licensed Practical/Vocational Nurse Training (LPN, LVN, Cert, Dipl,
AAS)** 47 students enrolled • **Medical Administrative/Executive Assistant and
Medical Secretary** 11 students enrolled • **Medical Insurance Coding Specialist/
Coder** 48 students enrolled • **Medical Transcription/Transcriptionist** 4 students
enrolled • **Real Estate** 1 student enrolled • **Substance Abuse/Addiction Counsel-
ing** 8 students enrolled • **Teacher Assistant/Aide** 1 student enrolled • **Web Page,
Digital/Multimedia and Information Resources Design** 7 students enrolled
• **Welding Technology/Welder** 4 students enrolled

STUDENT SERVICES Academic or career counseling, daycare for children
of students, employment services for current students, placement services
for program completers, remedial services.

Northern Tier Career Center–Practical Nursing Program

RR 1, Box 157A, Towanda, PA 18848-9731
http://ntccschool.org/

CONTACT Donald Butler, Chief School Administrator
Telephone: 570-265-8113

GENERAL INFORMATION Public Institution. Founded 1983. **Total
program enrollment:** 32. **Application fee:** $25.

PROGRAM(S) OFFERED
• **Licensed Practical/Vocational Nurse Training (LPN, LVN, Cert, Dipl, AAS)**
30 students enrolled

STUDENT SERVICES Academic or career counseling, placement services
for program completers.

Northwest Regional Technology Institute

3104 State Street, Erie, PA 16508
http://www.nwrti.com/

CONTACT Khalil Rabat, President and School Director
Telephone: 814-455-4446

GENERAL INFORMATION Private Institution. **Total program enrollment:** 41. **Application fee:** $25.

PROGRAM(S) OFFERED
• **Accounting and Computer Science** *900 hrs./$10,215* • **Business Operations Support and Secretarial Services, Other** *670 hrs./$6732* • **Data Entry/Microcomputer Applications, General** *600 hrs./$6060* • **Medical Office Assistant/Specialist** *1090 hrs./$12,199* • **Medical Office Management/Administration** *1820 hrs./$18,222*

STUDENT SERVICES Academic or career counseling, employment services for current students, placement services for program completers.

Oakbridge Academy of Arts

1250 Greensburg Road, Lower Burrell, PA 15068
http://www.akvalley.com/oakbridge/

CONTACT J. Bryant Mullen, President
Telephone: 724-335-5336

GENERAL INFORMATION Private Institution. Founded 1972. **Accreditation:** State accredited or approved. **Total program enrollment:** 50. **Application fee:** $25.

STUDENT SERVICES Employment services for current students, placement services for program completers.

Ohio Valley General Hospital

25 Heckel Road, McKees Rocks, PA 15136-1694
http://www.ohiovalleyhospital.org/asp/schoolofnur.asp

CONTACT William F. Provenzano, President
Telephone: 412-777-6204

GENERAL INFORMATION Private Institution. **Total program enrollment:** 36. **Application fee:** $50.

PROGRAM(S) OFFERED
• **Nursing—Registered Nurse Training (RN, ASN, BSN, MSN)** *26 students enrolled*

STUDENT SERVICES Academic or career counseling, employment services for current students.

Orleans Technical Institute

1330 Rhawn Street, Philadelphia, PA 19111
http://www.jevs.org/schools_svs.asp

CONTACT Jayne Siniari, Executive Director
Telephone: 215-728-4400

GENERAL INFORMATION Private Institution. **Total program enrollment:** 465.

PROGRAM(S) OFFERED
• **Building/Property Maintenance and Management** *30 hrs./$9350* • **Carpentry/Carpenter** *33 hrs./$8825* • **Court Reporting/Court Reporter** *139 hrs./$33,225* • **Electrician** *33 hrs./$8825* • **Heating, Air Conditioning, Ventilation and Refrigeration Maintenance Technology/Technician (HAC, HACR, HVAC, HVACR)** *31 hrs./$8825* • **Human Services, General** *27 students enrolled* • **Plumbing Technology/Plumber** *33 hrs./$8825*

STUDENT SERVICES Academic or career counseling, employment services for current students, placement services for program completers, remedial services.

Pace Institute

606 Court Street, Reading, PA 19601
http://www.paceinstitute.com/

CONTACT Rhoda E. Dersh, President
Telephone: 610-375-1212

GENERAL INFORMATION Private Institution. Founded 1977. **Accreditation:** State accredited or approved. **Total program enrollment:** 274. **Application fee:** $10.

PROGRAM(S) OFFERED
• **Accounting Technology/Technician and Bookkeeping** *1 student enrolled* • **Business/Office Automation/Technology/Data Entry** • **Computer Programming/Programmer, General** • **Data Entry/Microcomputer Applications, General** *10 students enrolled* • **Electrical, Electronics and Communications Engineering** • **Legal Administrative Assistant/Secretary** *2 students enrolled* • **Medical Administrative/Executive Assistant and Medical Secretary** *3 students enrolled*

STUDENT SERVICES Academic or career counseling, employment services for current students, placement services for program completers, remedial services.

Peirce College

1420 Pine Street, Philadelphia, PA 19102-4699
http://www.peirce.edu/

CONTACT Arthur J. Lendo, President and CEO
Telephone: 888-467-3472

GENERAL INFORMATION Private Institution. Founded 1865. **Accreditation:** Regional (MSA/CIHE). **Total program enrollment:** 793. **Application fee:** $50.

PROGRAM(S) OFFERED
• **Computer Programming, Vendor/Product Certification** • **Computer and Information Systems Security** *2 students enrolled* • **Legal Assistant/Paralegal** *15 students enrolled* • **Pre-Law Studies** • **System Administration/Administrator** *1 student enrolled*

STUDENT SERVICES Academic or career counseling, employment services for current students.

Penn Commercial Business and Technical School

242 Oak Spring Road, Washington, PA 15301
http://www.penncommercial.net/

CONTACT Robert S. Bazant, Director
Telephone: 724-222-5330

GENERAL INFORMATION Private Institution. Founded 1929. **Accreditation:** Medical assisting (AAMAE); state accredited or approved. **Total program enrollment:** 403. **Application fee:** $25.

PROGRAM(S) OFFERED
• **Accounting** • **Business/Office Automation/Technology/Data Entry** • **Construction Trades, General** *25 students enrolled* • **Massage Therapy/Therapeutic Massage** *17 students enrolled* • **Medical Insurance Coding Specialist/Coder** *19 students enrolled* • **Medical Transcription/Transcriptionist** *3 students enrolled* • **Phlebotomy/Phlebotomist** *12 students enrolled*

STUDENT SERVICES Academic or career counseling, daycare for children of students, employment services for current students, placement services for program completers, remedial services.

Pennco Tech

3815 Otter Street, Bristol, PA 19007-3696
http://www.penncotech.com/

CONTACT Michael Hobyak, President
Telephone: 215-785-0111

GENERAL INFORMATION Private Institution. Founded 1961. **Accreditation:** State accredited or approved. **Total program enrollment:** 276. **Application fee:** $100.

PROGRAM(S) OFFERED
● **Autobody/Collision and Repair Technology/Technician** *1200 hrs./$18,516* ● **Automobile/Automotive Mechanics Technology/Technician** *2100 hrs./$31,220* ● **Child Care Provider/Assistant** *7 students enrolled* ● **Computer Installation and Repair Technology/Technician** *10 students enrolled* ● **Electrical/Electronics Maintenance and Repair Technology, Other** *900 hrs./$14,438* ● **Heating, Air Conditioning and Refrigeration Technology/Technician (ACH/ACR/ACHR/HRAC/HVAC/AC Technology)** *960 hrs./$17,365* ● **Medical Administrative/Executive Assistant and Medical Secretary** *29 students enrolled* ● **Pharmacy Technician/Assistant** *6 students enrolled* ● **Plumbing Technology/Plumber** *7 students enrolled* ● **Vehicle Maintenance and Repair Technologies, Other** *1200 hrs./$19,935*

STUDENT SERVICES Academic or career counseling, daycare for children of students, employment services for current students, placement services for program completers.

Penn State Altoona

3000 Ivyside Park, Altoona, PA 16601-3760
http://www.aa.psu.edu/

CONTACT Lori J. Bechtel-Wherry, Chancellor
Telephone: 814-949-5000

GENERAL INFORMATION Public Institution. Founded 1939. **Accreditation:** Regional (MSA/CIHE); engineering technology (ABET/TAC). **Total program enrollment:** 3778. **Application fee:** $50.

PROGRAM(S) OFFERED
● **Computer and Information Systems Security** *1 student enrolled* ● **Criminal Justice/Law Enforcement Administration** *4 students enrolled* ● **Engineering, General** *25 students enrolled* ● **Substance Abuse/Addiction Counseling** *24 students enrolled*

STUDENT SERVICES Academic or career counseling, employment services for current students, placement services for program completers, remedial services.

Penn State Beaver

100 University Drive, Monaca, PA 15061
http://www.br.psu.edu/

CONTACT Gary B. Keefer, Chancellor
Telephone: 724-773-3800

GENERAL INFORMATION Public Institution. Founded 1964. **Accreditation:** Regional (MSA/CIHE); engineering technology (ABET/TAC). **Total program enrollment:** 696. **Application fee:** $50.

STUDENT SERVICES Academic or career counseling, employment services for current students, placement services for program completers, remedial services.

Penn State Berks

Tulpehocken Road, PO Box 7009, Reading, PA 19610-6009
http://www.bk.psu.edu/

CONTACT Susan Phillips Speece, Chancellor
Telephone: 610-396-6000

GENERAL INFORMATION Public Institution. Founded 1924. **Accreditation:** Regional (MSA/CIHE); engineering technology (ABET/TAC). **Total program enrollment:** 2455. **Application fee:** $50.

STUDENT SERVICES Academic or career counseling, employment services for current students, placement services for program completers, remedial services.

Penn State Brandywine

25 Yearsley Mill Road, Media, PA 19063-5596
http://www.de.psu.edu/

CONTACT Sophia T. Wisniewska, Chancellor
Telephone: 610-892-1200

GENERAL INFORMATION Public Institution. Founded 1966. **Accreditation:** Regional (MSA/CIHE). **Total program enrollment:** 1420. **Application fee:** $50.

PROGRAM(S) OFFERED
● **Business Administration and Management, General** *1 student enrolled*

STUDENT SERVICES Academic or career counseling, employment services for current students, placement services for program completers, remedial services.

Penn State DuBois

College Place, DuBois, PA 15801-3199
http://www.ds.psu.edu/

CONTACT Anita D. McDonald, Chancellor
Telephone: 814-375-4700

GENERAL INFORMATION Public Institution. Founded 1935. **Accreditation:** Regional (MSA/CIHE); engineering technology (ABET/TAC); physical therapy assisting (APTA). **Total program enrollment:** 708. **Application fee:** $50.

STUDENT SERVICES Academic or career counseling, employment services for current students, placement services for program completers.

Penn State Erie, The Behrend College

5091 Station Road, Erie, PA 16563-0001
http://www.pserie.psu.edu/

CONTACT John D. Burke, Chancellor
Telephone: 814-898-6000

GENERAL INFORMATION Public Institution. Founded 1948. **Accreditation:** Regional (MSA/CIHE); engineering technology (ABET/TAC). **Total program enrollment:** 4008. **Application fee:** $50.

PROGRAM(S) OFFERED
● **Criminalistics and Criminal Science** *3 students enrolled* ● **E-Commerce/Electronic Commerce** *53 students enrolled* ● **Financial Planning and Services** *3 students enrolled* ● **Mechanical Engineering Related Technologies/Technicians, Other** *5 students enrolled*

STUDENT SERVICES Academic or career counseling, daycare for children of students, employment services for current students, placement services for program completers, remedial services.

Penn State Harrisburg

777 West Harrisburg Pike, Middletown, PA 17057-4898
http://www.hbg.psu.edu/

CONTACT Madlyn L. Hanes, Chancellor
Telephone: 717-948-6452

GENERAL INFORMATION Public Institution. Founded 1966. **Accreditation:** Regional (MSA/CIHE); engineering technology (ABET/TAC). **Total program enrollment:** 2280. **Application fee:** $50.

STUDENT SERVICES Academic or career counseling, daycare for children of students, employment services for current students, placement services for program completers.

Penn State New Kensington

3550 7th Street Road, RT 780, New Kensington, PA 15068-1798
http://www.nk.psu.edu/

CONTACT Larry R. Pollock, Chancellor
Telephone: 724-334-5466

GENERAL INFORMATION Public Institution. Founded 1958. **Accreditation:** Regional (MSA/CIHE); engineering technology (ABET/TAC); medical laboratory technology (NAACLS); radiologic technology: radiography (JRCERT). **Total program enrollment:** 624. **Application fee:** $50.

PROGRAM(S) OFFERED
• **Nursing, Other** 1 student enrolled

STUDENT SERVICES Academic or career counseling, employment services for current students, placement services for program completers.

Penn State Shenango

147 Shenango Avenue, Sharon, PA 16146-1537
http://www.shenango.psu.edu/

CONTACT Fredric M. Leeds, Chancellor
Telephone: 724-983-2803

GENERAL INFORMATION Public Institution. Founded 1965. **Accreditation:** Regional (MSA/CIHE); engineering technology (ABET/TAC); physical therapy assisting (APTA). **Total program enrollment:** 505. **Application fee:** $50.

PROGRAM(S) OFFERED
• **Adult Development and Aging** 1 student enrolled • **Business Administration and Management, General** 3 students enrolled • **Business Administration, Management and Operations, Other** 1 student enrolled • **Computer Systems Networking and Telecommunications** 1 student enrolled • **Ethnic, Cultural Minority, and Gender Studies, Other** 4 students enrolled • **Human Development and Family Studies, General** 1 student enrolled • **Retailing and Retail Operations** 2 students enrolled • **Small Business Administration/Management** 1 student enrolled

STUDENT SERVICES Academic or career counseling, employment services for current students, placement services for program completers, remedial services.

Penn State University Park

201 Old Main, University Park, PA 16802-1503
http://www.psu.edu/

CONTACT Dr. Graham B. Spanier, President
Telephone: 814-865-4700

GENERAL INFORMATION Public Institution. Founded 1855. **Accreditation:** Regional (MSA/CIHE); art and design (NASAD); athletic training (JRCAT); counseling (ACA); dietetics: postbaccalaureate internship (ADtA/CAADE); forestry (SAF); journalism and mass communications (ACEJMC); music (NASM); speech-language pathology (ASHA); theater (NAST). **Total program enrollment:** 42211. **Application fee:** $50.

PROGRAM(S) OFFERED
• **Aerospace, Aeronautical and Astronautical Engineering** 1 student enrolled • **African Studies** 7 students enrolled • **African-American/Black Studies** 18 students enrolled • **Agricultural Mechanics and Equipment/Machine Technology** 3 students enrolled • **Business Administration and Management, General** 1 student enrolled • **Chemical Engineering** 1 student enrolled • **Chinese Language and Literature** 24 students enrolled • **Civil Engineering, General** 13 students enrolled • **Comparative Literature** 5 students enrolled • **Computer and Information Sciences, General** 2 students enrolled • **Engineering Mechanics** 78 students enrolled • **Engineering, General** 10 students enrolled • **Engineering, Other** 2 students enrolled • **Human Resources Management and Services, Other** 1 student enrolled • **Information Technology** 44 students enrolled • **Japanese Language and Literature** 21 students enrolled • **Labor and Industrial Relations** 1 student enrolled • **Landscaping and Groundskeeping** 20 students enrolled • **Latin American Studies** 4 students enrolled • **Near and Middle Eastern Studies** 14 students enrolled • **Oceanography, Chemical and Physical** 4 students enrolled • **Organizational Communication, General** 2

students enrolled • **Science, Technology and Society** 7 students enrolled • **Spanish Language and Literature** 228 students enrolled • **Technical and Business Writing** 10 students enrolled • **Women's Studies** 48 students enrolled

STUDENT SERVICES Academic or career counseling, daycare for children of students, employment services for current students, placement services for program completers, remedial services.

Pennsylvania Academy of Cosmetology and Sciences

2445 Bedford Street, Johnstown, PA 15904
http://www.pacas.com/

CONTACT Daniel J. Leaser, President
Telephone: 814-269-3444

GENERAL INFORMATION Private Institution. Founded 1962. **Total program enrollment:** 42.

PROGRAM(S) OFFERED
• **Cosmetology, Barber/Styling, and Nail Instructor** 600 hrs./$4300
• **Cosmetology/Cosmetologist, General** 1250 hrs./$12,950

STUDENT SERVICES Placement services for program completers.

Pennsylvania Academy of Cosmetology Arts and Sciences

19 North Brady Street, DuBois, PA 15801
http://www.pacas.com/

CONTACT Daniel J. Leaser, President
Telephone: 814-371-4151

GENERAL INFORMATION Private Institution. Founded 1964. **Total program enrollment:** 53.

PROGRAM(S) OFFERED
• **Cosmetology, Barber/Styling, and Nail Instructor** 600 hrs./$4300
• **Cosmetology/Cosmetologist, General** 1250 hrs./$12,950

STUDENT SERVICES Placement services for program completers.

Pennsylvania College of Art & Design

204 North Prince Street, PO Box 59, Lancaster, PA 17608-0059
http://www.pcad.edu/

CONTACT Mary Colleen Heil, President
Telephone: 717-396-7833

GENERAL INFORMATION Private Institution. Founded 1982. **Accreditation:** Art and design (NASAD). **Total program enrollment:** 277. **Application fee:** $40.

STUDENT SERVICES Academic or career counseling, employment services for current students, remedial services.

Pennsylvania College of Technology

One College Avenue, Williamsport, PA 17701-5778
http://www.pct.edu/

CONTACT Davie Jane Gilmour, President
Telephone: 570-326-3761

GENERAL INFORMATION Public Institution. Founded 1965. **Accreditation:** Regional (MSA/CIHE); dental hygiene (ADA); emergency medical services (JRCEMTP); engineering technology (ABET/TAC); radiologic technology: radiography (JRCERT). **Total program enrollment:** 5575. **Application fee:** $50.

Pennsylvania College of Technology (continued)

PROGRAM(S) OFFERED

• **Mason/Masonry** *1 student enrolled* • **Medical Insurance Coding Specialist/Coder** *3 students enrolled* • **Plumbing Technology/Plumber** *8 students enrolled*

STUDENT SERVICES Academic or career counseling, daycare for children of students, employment services for current students, placement services for program completers, remedial services.

Pennsylvania Highlands Community College

101 Community College Way, Johnstown, PA 15904
http://www.pennhighlands.edu/

CONTACT Dr. Walter Asonevich, President
Telephone: 814-262-6400

GENERAL INFORMATION Public Institution. Founded 1994. **Accreditation:** Regional (MSA/CIHE). **Total program enrollment:** 680. **Application fee:** $20.

PROGRAM(S) OFFERED

• **Building/Home/Construction Inspection/Inspector** *17 students enrolled* • **Child Care and Support Services Management** *3 students enrolled* • **Computer and Information Systems Security** • **Court Reporting/Court Reporter** • **Data Entry/Microcomputer Applications, General** *2 students enrolled* • **Dietetics and Clinical Nutrition Services, Other** *1 student enrolled* • **General Office Occupations and Clerical Services** *29 students enrolled* • **Health and Medical Administrative Services, Other** *7 students enrolled* • **Human Services, General** • **Legal Support Services, Other** *1 student enrolled* • **Manufacturing Technology/Technician** • **Medical Insurance Coding Specialist/Coder** *7 students enrolled* • **Pharmacy Technician/Assistant** *6 students enrolled*

STUDENT SERVICES Academic or career counseling, employment services for current students, remedial services.

Pennsylvania Institute of Taxidermy, Inc.

118 Industrial Park Road, Ebensberg, PA 15931
http://www.studytaxidermy.com/

CONTACT Dan Bantley, President
Telephone: 814-472-4510

GENERAL INFORMATION Private Institution. Founded 1983. **Total program enrollment:** 9.

PROGRAM(S) OFFERED

• **Precision Production, Other** *17 students enrolled*

Pennsylvania Institute of Technology

800 Manchester Avenue, Media, PA 19063-4098
http://www.pit.edu/

CONTACT John C. Strayer, President
Telephone: 610-565-7900

GENERAL INFORMATION Private Institution. Founded 1953. **Accreditation:** Regional (MSA/CIHE). **Total program enrollment:** 807. **Application fee:** $25.

PROGRAM(S) OFFERED

• **Allied Health and Medical Assisting Services, Other** *161 students enrolled* • **Engineering Technology, General** *3 students enrolled* • **Medical Office Management/Administration** *31 students enrolled* • **Nurse/Nursing Assistant/Aide and Patient Care Assistant** *39 students enrolled* • **Pharmacy Technician/Assistant** *56 students enrolled*

STUDENT SERVICES Academic or career counseling, employment services for current students, placement services for program completers, remedial services.

Pennsylvania Myotherapy Institute

668 Rte. 194 North, Abbottstown, PA 17301
http://www.pamyotherapyinstitute.com/

CONTACT Wilhelmina Blank, President
Telephone: 717-259-7000

GENERAL INFORMATION Private Institution. **Total program enrollment:** 13. **Application fee:** $50.

PROGRAM(S) OFFERED

• **Massage Therapy/Therapeutic Massage** *3 students enrolled*

STUDENT SERVICES Academic or career counseling, employment services for current students, placement services for program completers.

Pennsylvania School of Business

406 West Hamilton Street, Allentown, PA 18101
http://www.pennschoolofbusiness.edu/

CONTACT Michael O'Brien, Executive Director
Telephone: 610-841-3333

GENERAL INFORMATION Private Institution. Founded 1978. **Accreditation:** State accredited or approved. **Total program enrollment:** 229.

PROGRAM(S) OFFERED

• **Administrative Assistant and Secretarial Science, General** • **Business Administration and Management, General** *13 students enrolled* • **Computer and Information Sciences, General** *13 students enrolled* • **Medical Office Management/Administration** *12 students enrolled*

STUDENT SERVICES Academic or career counseling, employment services for current students, placement services for program completers.

Pennsylvania State System of Higher Education

2986 North Second Street, Harrisburg, PA 17110
http://www.sshechan.edu/

CONTACT Dr. John C. Cavanaugh, Chancellor
Telephone: 717-720-4000

GENERAL INFORMATION Public Institution.

Philadelphia Biblical University

200 Manor Avenue, Langhorne, PA 19047-2990
http://www.pbu.edu/

CONTACT Dr. Todd J. Williams, President
Telephone: 215-752-5800

GENERAL INFORMATION Private Institution. Founded 1913. **Accreditation:** Regional (MSA/CIHE); state accredited or approved; music (NASM). **Total program enrollment:** 992. **Application fee:** $25.

PROGRAM(S) OFFERED

• **Religion/Religious Studies** *22 students enrolled*

STUDENT SERVICES Academic or career counseling, employment services for current students, placement services for program completers, remedial services.

Pittsburgh Institute of Aeronautics

PO Box 10897, Pittsburgh, PA 15236-0897
http://www.pia.edu/

CONTACT John Graham, III, President
Telephone: 412-346-2100

GENERAL INFORMATION Private Institution. Founded 1929. **Accreditation:** State accredited or approved. **Total program enrollment:** 280. **Application fee:** $150.

PROGRAM(S) OFFERED
● Truck and Bus Driver/Commercial Vehicle Operation *382 students enrolled*

STUDENT SERVICES Academic or career counseling, employment services for current students, placement services for program completers, remedial services.

Pittsburgh Institute of Mortuary Science, Incorporated

5808 Baum Boulevard, Pittsburgh, PA 15206-3706
http://www.pims.edu/

CONTACT Eugene C. Ogrodnik, President & CEO
Telephone: 412-362-8500

GENERAL INFORMATION Private Institution. Founded 1939. **Accreditation:** Funeral service (ABFSE). **Total program enrollment:** 97. **Application fee:** $40.

PROGRAM(S) OFFERED
● Funeral Direction/Service *60 hrs./$14,780* ● Funeral Service and Mortuary Science, General *60 hrs./$15,646* ● Funeral Service and Mortuary Science, Other *96 hrs./$20,928*

STUDENT SERVICES Academic or career counseling, employment services for current students, placement services for program completers, remedial services.

Pittsburgh Technical Institute

1111 McKee Road, Oakdale, PA 15071
http://www.pti.edu/

CONTACT Greg Defeo, President
Telephone: 412-809-5100

GENERAL INFORMATION Private Institution. Founded 1946. **Accreditation:** Regional (MSA/CIHE). **Total program enrollment:** 2073.

PROGRAM(S) OFFERED
● Accounting Technology/Technician and Bookkeeping ● Computer and Information Systems Security ● Data Modeling/Warehousing and Database Administration ● Electrical/Electronics Equipment Installation and Repair, General ● Massage Therapy/Therapeutic Massage *24 students enrolled* ● Medical Insurance Coding Specialist/Coder *19 students enrolled* ● Medical/Health Management and Clinical Assistant/Specialist ● System Administration/Administrator *22 students enrolled*

STUDENT SERVICES Academic or career counseling, employment services for current students, placement services for program completers, remedial services.

The PJA School

7900 West Chester Pike, Upper Darby, PA 19082-1926
http://www.pjaschool.com/

CONTACT David M. Hudiak, Special Assistant to Office of the President
Telephone: 610-789-6700

GENERAL INFORMATION Private Institution. Founded 1981. **Accreditation:** State accredited or approved. **Total program enrollment:** 325.

PROGRAM(S) OFFERED
● Accounting Technology/Technician and Bookkeeping *6 students enrolled* ● Computer/Information Technology Services Administration and Management, Other *1 student enrolled* ● Legal Administrative Assistant/Secretary *8 students enrolled* ● Legal Assistant/Paralegal *21 students enrolled*

STUDENT SERVICES Academic or career counseling, employment services for current students, placement services for program completers, remedial services.

Point Park University

201 Wood Street, Pittsburgh, PA 15222-1984
http://www.pointpark.edu/

CONTACT Paul Hennigan, President
Telephone: 412-391-4100

GENERAL INFORMATION Private Institution. Founded 1960. **Accreditation:** Regional (MSA/CIHE); dance (NASD); engineering technology (ABET/TAC). **Total program enrollment:** 2717. **Application fee:** $40.

PROGRAM(S) OFFERED
● Accounting ● Business Administration and Management, General ● Early Childhood Education and Teaching ● Information Technology

STUDENT SERVICES Academic or career counseling, daycare for children of students, employment services for current students, placement services for program completers, remedial services.

Precision Manufacturing Institute

764 Bessemer Street, Suite 105, Meadville, PA 16335
http://www.pmionline.edu/

CONTACT Jerry E. Knight, Executive Director
Telephone: 814-333-2415

GENERAL INFORMATION Private Institution. **Total program enrollment:** 38.

PROGRAM(S) OFFERED
● Computer and Information Sciences, General *6 students enrolled* ● Electromechanical Technology/Electromechanical Engineering Technology *7 students enrolled* ● General Office Occupations and Clerical Services *556 hrs./$6395* ● Industrial Mechanics and Maintenance Technology *959 hrs./$15,840* ● Machine Tool Technology/Machinist *1328 hrs./$21,910* ● Plastics Engineering Technology/Technician *1 student enrolled* ● Precision Production Trades, General *823 hrs./$13,580* ● Precision Production, Other *17 students enrolled* ● Quality Control Technology/Technician *1 student enrolled* ● Robotics Technology/Technician *967 hrs./$16,055* ● Tool and Die Technology/Technician *4 students enrolled* ● Welding Technology/Welder *8 students enrolled*

STUDENT SERVICES Academic or career counseling, placement services for program completers.

Prism Career Institute

8040 Roosevelt Boulevard, Philadelphia, PA 19152
http://www.prismcareerinstitute.com/

CONTACT David M. Hudiak, Special Assistant to Office of the President
Telephone: 215-331-4600

GENERAL INFORMATION Private Institution. **Total program enrollment:** 288. **Application fee:** $100.

PROGRAM(S) OFFERED
● Accounting Technology/Technician and Bookkeeping *660 hrs./$9776* ● Administrative Assistant and Secretarial Science, General *8 students enrolled* ● Legal Administrative Assistant/Secretary *900 hrs./$10,722* ● Legal

Prism Career Institute (continued)

Assistant/Paralegal • **Medical Insurance Specialist/Medical Biller** *660 hrs./$9102* • **Medical Office Management/Administration** *666 hrs./$9776* • **Medical/Clinical Assistant** *900 hrs./$13,404* • **Pre-Nursing Studies** *1560 hrs./$18,812*

STUDENT SERVICES Academic or career counseling, employment services for current students, placement services for program completers.

Pruonto's Hair Design Institute

705 12th Street, Altoona, PA 16602
http://www.pruontos.com/

CONTACT Kimberly Jo Hofer, President
Telephone: 814-944-4494

GENERAL INFORMATION Private Institution. Founded 1960. **Total program enrollment:** 16.

PROGRAM(S) OFFERED
• **Cosmetology and Related Personal Grooming Arts, Other** *200 hrs./$1850*
• **Cosmetology, Barber/Styling, and Nail Instructor** *500 hrs./$3950*
• **Cosmetology/Cosmetologist, General** *1250 hrs./$8900* • **Nail Technician/Specialist and Manicurist** *5 students enrolled*

STUDENT SERVICES Academic or career counseling, placement services for program completers.

Quaker City Institute of Aviation

9800 Ashton Road, Philadelphia, PA 19114

CONTACT Kyle Berry, School Director
Telephone: 215-676-7700

GENERAL INFORMATION Private Institution. Founded 1946. **Total program enrollment:** 275. **Application fee:** $25.

PROGRAM(S) OFFERED
• **Aircraft Powerplant Technology/Technician** *65 hrs./$20,800* • **Airframe Mechanics and Aircraft Maintenance Technology/Technician** *65 hrs./$20,800*

STUDENT SERVICES Academic or career counseling, placement services for program completers.

Reading Area Community College

PO Box 1706, Reading, PA 19603-1706
http://www.racc.edu/

CONTACT Anna Weitz, President
Telephone: 610-372-4721

GENERAL INFORMATION Public Institution. Founded 1971. **Accreditation:** Regional (MSA/CIHE); medical laboratory technology (NAACLS); respiratory therapy technology (CoARC). **Total program enrollment:** 1836.

PROGRAM(S) OFFERED
• **Accounting Technology/Technician and Bookkeeping** *9 students enrolled* • **Administrative Assistant and Secretarial Science, General** • **Business Administration and Management, General** *2 students enrolled* • **Child Care Provider/Assistant** • **Child Care and Support Services Management** • **Computer Programming/Programmer, General** • **Computer Systems Networking and Telecommunications** • **Computer Technology/Computer Systems Technology** • **Food Preparation/Professional Cooking/Kitchen Assistant** • **General Office Occupations and Clerical Services** • **Heating, Air Conditioning, Ventilation and Refrigeration Maintenance Technology/Technician (HAC, HACR, HVAC, HVACR)** *2 students enrolled* • **Human Resources Management/Personnel Administration, General** • **Legal Administrative Assistant/Secretary** • **Licensed Practical/Vocational Nurse Training (LPN, LVN, Cert, Dipl, AAS)** *42 students enrolled* • **Machine Shop Technology/Assistant** • **Medical Administrative/Executive Assistant and Medical Secretary** • **Medical Transcription/Transcriptionist** *6 students enrolled*

• **Respiratory Care Therapy/Therapist** • **Retailing and Retail Operations** • **Science Technologies/Technicians, Other** *1 student enrolled* • **Small Business Administration/Management** • **Web Page, Digital/Multimedia and Information Resources Design**

STUDENT SERVICES Academic or career counseling, daycare for children of students, employment services for current students, placement services for program completers, remedial services.

Robert Morris University

6001 University Boulevard, Moon Township, PA 15108-1189
http://www.rmu.edu/

CONTACT Gregory G. Dell'Omo, President
Telephone: 412-762-0097

GENERAL INFORMATION Private Institution. Founded 1921. **Accreditation:** Regional (MSA/CIHE); computer science (ABET/CSAC); radiologic technology: radiography (JRCERT). **Total program enrollment:** 3119. **Application fee:** $30.

PROGRAM(S) OFFERED
• **Accounting** *9 students enrolled* • **Business Administration and Management, General** • **Communication Studies/Speech Communication and Rhetoric** • **Health/Health Care Administration/Management** • **Management Information Systems, General** • **Marketing/Marketing Management, General** *1 student enrolled*

STUDENT SERVICES Academic or career counseling, employment services for current students, placement services for program completers, remedial services.

Rosedale Technical Institute

215 Beecham Drive, Suite 2, Pittsburgh, PA 15205-9791
http://www.rosedaletech.org/

CONTACT Dennis Wilke, President
Telephone: 412-521-6200

GENERAL INFORMATION Private Institution. Founded 1949. **Accreditation:** State accredited or approved. **Total program enrollment:** 216. **Application fee:** $20.

PROGRAM(S) OFFERED
• **Automobile/Automotive Mechanics Technology/Technician** *4 students enrolled*

STUDENT SERVICES Academic or career counseling, employment services for current students, placement services for program completers, remedial services.

St. Charles Borromeo Seminary, Overbrook

100 East Wynnewood Road, Wynnewood, PA 19096
http://www.scs.edu/

CONTACT Rev. Msgr. Joseph G. Prior, Rector President
Telephone: 610-667-3394

GENERAL INFORMATION Private Institution. Founded 1832. **Accreditation:** Regional (MSA/CIHE). **Total program enrollment:** 148.

PROGRAM(S) OFFERED
• **Theological and Ministerial Studies, Other** *9 students enrolled*

STUDENT SERVICES Academic or career counseling.

Saint Joseph's University

5600 City Avenue, Philadelphia, PA 19131-1395
http://www.sju.edu/

CONTACT Timothy R. Lannon, SJ, President
Telephone: 610-660-1000

GENERAL INFORMATION Private Institution. Founded 1851. **Accreditation:** Regional (MSA/CIHE). **Total program enrollment:** 4989. **Application fee:** $60.

STUDENT SERVICES Academic or career counseling, employment services for current students, remedial services.

Saint Vincent College

300 Fraser Purchase Road, Latrobe, PA 15650-2690
http://www.stvincent.edu/

CONTACT H. James Towey, President
Telephone: 724-539-9761

GENERAL INFORMATION Private Institution. Founded 1846. **Accreditation:** Regional (MSA/CIHE). **Total program enrollment:** 1795. **Application fee:** $25.

PROGRAM(S) OFFERED
• **Business Administration and Management, General** • **Substance Abuse/Addiction Counseling** *6 students enrolled*

STUDENT SERVICES Academic or career counseling, employment services for current students, placement services for program completers, remedial services.

Sanford-Brown Institute

3600 Horizon Boulevard, Suite GL1, Trevose, PA 19053
http://www.sbphilly.com/

CONTACT Matt Diacont, President
Telephone: 215-436-6900

GENERAL INFORMATION Private Institution. **Total program enrollment:** 1142. **Application fee:** $25.

PROGRAM(S) OFFERED
• **Cardiovascular Technology/Technologist** *2195 hrs./$36,400* • **Dental Assisting/Assistant** *1200 hrs./$13,800* • **Diagnostic Medical Sonography/Sonographer and Ultrasound Technician** *1860 hrs./$36,400* • **Massage Therapy/Therapeutic Massage** *8 students enrolled* • **Medical Insurance Coding Specialist/Coder** *900 hrs./$13,950* • **Medical/Clinical Assistant** *900 hrs./$14,100*

STUDENT SERVICES Employment services for current students, placement services for program completers.

Sanford-Brown Institute–Monroeville

Penn Center East, 777 Penn Center Boulevard, Building 7, Pittsburgh, PA 15235
http://www.monroeville.sanfordbrown.edu/

CONTACT R. Thomas Contrella, President
Telephone: 412-373-6400

GENERAL INFORMATION Private Institution. Founded 1980. **Accreditation:** State accredited or approved. **Total program enrollment:** 556. **Application fee:** $25.

PROGRAM(S) OFFERED
• **Dental Assisting/Assistant** *900 hrs./$10,262* • **Massage Therapy/Therapeutic Massage** *54 students enrolled* • **Medical/Clinical Assistant** *49 hrs./$13,832* • **Pharmacy Technician/Assistant** *76 hrs./$24,235* • **Respiratory Care Therapy/Therapist** *100 hrs./$36,860* • **Surgical Technology/Technologist** *67 hrs./$23,730*

STUDENT SERVICES Academic or career counseling, employment services for current students, placement services for program completers, remedial services.

Sanford-Brown Institute–Pittsburgh

421 Seventh Avenue, Pittsburgh, PA 15219-1907
http://www.sanfordbrown.edu/

CONTACT Patti Yakshe, President
Telephone: 412-281-2600

GENERAL INFORMATION Private Institution. Founded 1980. **Accreditation:** Diagnostic medical sonography (JRCEDMS); radiologic technology: radiography (JRCERT); state accredited or approved. **Total program enrollment:** 835. **Application fee:** $25.

PROGRAM(S) OFFERED
• **Anesthesiologist Assistant** *66 hrs./$23,510* • **Criminal Justice/Law Enforcement Administration** *4 students enrolled* • **Diagnostic Medical Sonography/Sonographer and Ultrasound Technician** *99 hrs./$36,860* • **Massage Therapy/Therapeutic Massage** *900 hrs./$8530* • **Medical Administrative/Executive Assistant and Medical Secretary** *2 students enrolled* • **Medical Radiologic Technology/Science—Radiation Therapist** *107 hrs./$36,910* • **Medical/Clinical Assistant** *70 hrs./$18,313* • **Veterinary/Animal Health Technology/Technician and Veterinary Assistant** *88 hrs./$22,920*

STUDENT SERVICES Academic or career counseling, employment services for current students, placement services for program completers.

Schuylkill Technology Center–North Campus

101 Technology Drive, Frackville, PA 17931
http://www.iu29.org/STCenters/AdultPrograms/Programs/NorthCampus/Nursing.asp

CONTACT Dr. Diane Niederriter, Executive Director, Elect
Telephone: 570-874-1034 Ext. 4880

GENERAL INFORMATION Public Institution. **Total program enrollment:** 129. **Application fee:** $25.

PROGRAM(S) OFFERED
• **Autobody/Collision and Repair Technology/Technician** • **Automobile/Automotive Mechanics Technology/Technician** • **Carpentry/Carpenter** • **Child Care Provider/Assistant** • **Computer Engineering Technology/Technician** • **Computer Programming/Programmer, General** • **Construction/Heavy Equipment/Earthmoving Equipment Operation** *400 hrs./$7687* • **Cosmetology, Barber/Styling, and Nail Instructor** • **Cosmetology/Cosmetologist, General** *3 students enrolled* • **Dental Assisting/Assistant** • **Drafting and Design Technology/Technician, General** • **Electrical, Electronic and Communications Engineering Technology/Technician** • **Electrician** • **Electromechanical Technology/Electromechanical Engineering Technology** *1080 hrs./$6804* • **Entrepreneurship/Entrepreneurial Studies** • **Ground Transportation, Other** *800 hrs./$12,699* • **Heavy/Industrial Equipment Maintenance Technologies, Other** *6 students enrolled* • **Institutional Food Workers** *1 student enrolled* • **Licensed Practical/Vocational Nurse Training (LPN, LVN, Cert, Dipl, AAS)** *1545 hrs./$12,015* • **Machine Tool Technology/Machinist** • **Management Information Systems, General** • **Mason/Masonry** • **Medical/Clinical Assistant** • **Mining Technology/Technician** • **Nail Technician/Specialist and Manicurist** • **Nurse/Nursing Assistant/Aide and Patient Care Assistant** *140 hrs./$1100* • **Nursing, Other** • **Ornamental Horticulture** • **Plumbing Technology/Plumber** *1 student enrolled* • **Sign Language Interpretation and Translation** • **Small Engine Mechanics and Repair Technology/Technician** • **Truck and Bus Driver/Commercial Vehicle Operation** *400 hrs./$5473* • **Welding Technology/Welder**

STUDENT SERVICES Academic or career counseling, daycare for children of students, placement services for program completers, remedial services.

Sharon Regional Health System School of Nursing

740 E. State Street, Sharon, PA 16146
http://www.sharonregional.com/

CONTACT John Zidansek, President
Telephone: 724-983-3988

GENERAL INFORMATION Private Institution. **Total program enrollment:** 21. **Application fee:** $25.

Sharon Regional Health System School of Nursing (continued)

PROGRAM(S) OFFERED
● **Nursing—Registered Nurse Training (RN, ASN, BSN, MSN)** *70 hrs.*

STUDENT SERVICES Academic or career counseling, employment services for current students, placement services for program completers.

Slippery Rock University of Pennsylvania

1 Morrow Way, Slippery Rock, PA 16057-1383
http://www.sru.edu/

CONTACT Robert M. Smith, President
Telephone: 724-738-9000

GENERAL INFORMATION Public Institution. Founded 1889. **Accreditation:** Regional (MSA/CIHE); athletic training (JRCAT); counseling (ACA); dance (NASD); music (NASM); recreation and parks (NRPA). **Total program enrollment:** 7525. **Application fee:** $30.

PROGRAM(S) OFFERED
● **Business Administration and Management, General** *5 students enrolled*
● **Social Work** *1 student enrolled*

STUDENT SERVICES Academic or career counseling, daycare for children of students, employment services for current students, placement services for program completers, remedial services.

South Hills Beauty Academy

3269 West Liberty Avenue, Pittsburgh, PA 15216

CONTACT Mary Pernatozzi, Owner Director
Telephone: 412-561-3381

GENERAL INFORMATION Private Institution. **Total program enrollment:** 34. **Application fee:** $65.

PROGRAM(S) OFFERED
● **Aesthetician/Esthetician and Skin Care Specialist** *325 hrs./$2925*
● **Cosmetology and Related Personal Grooming Arts, Other** *500 hrs./$5000*
● **Cosmetology, Barber/Styling, and Nail Instructor** *12 students enrolled*
● **Cosmetology/Cosmetologist, General** *350 hrs./$2700* ● **Massage Therapy/Therapeutic Massage** *900 hrs./$8000* ● **Nail Technician/Specialist and Manicurist** *21 students enrolled*

STUDENT SERVICES Placement services for program completers.

South Hills School of Business & Technology

480 Waupelani Drive, State College, PA 16801-4516
http://www.southhills.edu/

CONTACT Mark Maggs, Director
Telephone: 814-234-7755

GENERAL INFORMATION Private Institution. Founded 1970. **Accreditation:** Health information technology (AHIMA); state accredited or approved. **Total program enrollment:** 583. **Application fee:** $25.

PROGRAM(S) OFFERED
● **Accounting Technology/Technician and Bookkeeping** *1 student enrolled*
● **Administrative Assistant and Secretarial Science, General** *1 student enrolled*
● **Computer/Information Technology Services Administration and Management, Other** ● **General Office Occupations and Clerical Services** *1 student enrolled* ● **Retailing and Retail Operations**

STUDENT SERVICES Academic or career counseling, employment services for current students, placement services for program completers.

Star Technical Institute

9121 Roosevelt Boulevard, Philadelphia, PA 19114
http://starinstitute.com/

CONTACT Barbara McKarens, Director
Telephone: 215-969-5877

GENERAL INFORMATION Private Institution. **Total program enrollment:** 97.

PROGRAM(S) OFFERED
● **Cardiovascular Technology/Technologist** *30 students enrolled* ● **Emergency Medical Technology/Technician (EMT Paramedic)** *1520 hrs./$23,204* ● **Health/Medical Claims Examiner** *20 students enrolled* ● **Hematology Technology/Technician** *31 students enrolled* ● **Medical Administrative/Executive Assistant and Medical Secretary** *54 students enrolled* ● **Medical/Health Management and Clinical Assistant/Specialist** *60 students enrolled* ● **Surgical Technology/Technologist** *48 students enrolled*

Star Technical Institute

1570 Garrett Road, Upper Darby, PA 19082
http://starinstitute.com/

CONTACT Tim James, Acting Director
Telephone: 610-626-2700

GENERAL INFORMATION Private Institution. **Application fee:** $25.

PROGRAM(S) OFFERED
● **Cardiovascular Technology/Technologist** *14 students enrolled* ● **Medical Administrative/Executive Assistant and Medical Secretary** *11 students enrolled* ● **Medical Office Computer Specialist/Assistant** *22 students enrolled* ● **Medical/Health Management and Clinical Assistant/Specialist** *16 students enrolled* ● **Surgical Technology/Technologist** *40 hrs./$14,232*

STUDENT SERVICES Placement services for program completers.

Stroudsburg School of Cosmetology

100 North Eighth Street, Stroudsburg, PA 18360-1720
http://www.asc-ssc.com/

CONTACT Truc Do, President
Telephone: 570-421-3387

GENERAL INFORMATION Private Institution. Founded 1960. **Total program enrollment:** 20. **Application fee:** $25.

PROGRAM(S) OFFERED
● **Cosmetology, Barber/Styling, and Nail Instructor** *500 hrs./$4700*
● **Cosmetology/Cosmetologist, General** *125 hrs./$15,400* ● **Nail Technician/Specialist and Manicurist** *200 hrs./$2450*

STUDENT SERVICES Academic or career counseling, placement services for program completers.

Temple University

1801 North Broad Street, Philadelphia, PA 19122-6096
http://www.temple.edu/

CONTACT Ann Weaver Hart, President
Telephone: 215-204-7000

GENERAL INFORMATION Public Institution. Founded 1884. **Accreditation:** Regional (MSA/CIHE); art and design (NASAD); athletic training (JRCAT); dance (NASD); engineering technology (ABET/TAC); health information administration (AHIMA); journalism and mass communications (ACEJMC); music (NASM); public health: community health education (CEPH); recreation and parks (NRPA); speech-language pathology (ASHA); theater (NAST). **Total program enrollment:** 28899. **Application fee:** $50.

PROGRAM(S) OFFERED
• **Applied Horticulture/Horticultural Operations, General** *1 student enrolled*
• **Arabic Language and Literature** *1 student enrolled* • **Jewish/Judaic Studies** *2 students enrolled*

STUDENT SERVICES Academic or career counseling, employment services for current students, placement services for program completers, remedial services.

Thaddeus Stevens College of Technology

750 East King Street, Lancaster, PA 17602-3198
http://www.stevenscollege.edu/

CONTACT William E. Griscom, President
Telephone: 717-299-7730

GENERAL INFORMATION Public Institution. Founded 1905. **Accreditation:** Regional (MSA/CIHE). **Total program enrollment:** 789. **Application fee:** $25.

PROGRAM(S) OFFERED
• **Electrician** *14 students enrolled*

STUDENT SERVICES Academic or career counseling, employment services for current students, placement services for program completers, remedial services.

Thompson Institute

3440 Market Street, 2nd Floor, Philadelphia, PA 19104
http://www.thompson.edu/

CONTACT Jeremiah Staropoli, Interim President
Telephone: 215-594-4000 Ext. 4054

GENERAL INFORMATION Private Institution. **Total program enrollment:** 1106.

PROGRAM(S) OFFERED
• **Dental Assisting/Assistant** *53 hrs./$12,830* • **Electrician** *71 hrs./$13,050*
• **Medical Office Management/Administration** *47 hrs./$12,870* • **Medical/Clinical Assistant** *740 hrs./$14,470*

STUDENT SERVICES Academic or career counseling, employment services for current students, placement services for program completers, remedial services.

Triangle Tech, Inc.–Bethlehem

Lehigh Valley Industrial Park IV, 31 S. Commerce Way, Bethlehem, PA 18017
http://www.triangle-tech.edu/

CONTACT Michael Biechy, Director
Telephone: 610-691-1300

GENERAL INFORMATION Private Institution. **Total program enrollment:** 105.

PROGRAM(S) OFFERED
• **Electrician** *7 students enrolled*

STUDENT SERVICES Academic or career counseling, employment services for current students, placement services for program completers, remedial services.

Triangle Tech, Inc.–DuBois School

PO Box 551, DuBois, PA 15801-0551
http://www.triangle-tech.edu/

CONTACT Stephanie A. Craig, Director
Telephone: 814-371-2090

GENERAL INFORMATION Private Institution. Founded 1944. **Accreditation:** State accredited or approved. **Total program enrollment:** 236.

PROGRAM(S) OFFERED
• **Electrician**

STUDENT SERVICES Academic or career counseling, employment services for current students, placement services for program completers, remedial services.

Triangle Tech, Inc.–Erie School

2000 Liberty Street, Erie, PA 16502-2594
http://www.triangle-tech.com/

CONTACT David A. McMutrie, Director
Telephone: 814-453-6016

GENERAL INFORMATION Private Institution. Founded 1976. **Accreditation:** State accredited or approved. **Total program enrollment:** 147.

PROGRAM(S) OFFERED
• **Electrician** *4 students enrolled*

STUDENT SERVICES Academic or career counseling, employment services for current students, placement services for program completers, remedial services.

Triangle Tech, Inc.–Greensburg School

222 East Pittsburgh Street, Suite A, Greensburg, PA 15601-3304
http://www.triangle-tech.com/

CONTACT Teresa L. Trathowen, Director
Telephone: 724-832-1050

GENERAL INFORMATION Private Institution. Founded 1944. **Accreditation:** State accredited or approved. **Total program enrollment:** 222.

PROGRAM(S) OFFERED
• **Electrician** *6 students enrolled* • **Heating, Air Conditioning, Ventilation and Refrigeration Maintenance Technology/Technician (HAC, HACR, HVAC, HVACR)** *5 students enrolled*

STUDENT SERVICES Academic or career counseling, employment services for current students, placement services for program completers, remedial services.

Triangle Tech, Inc.–Pittsburgh School

1940 Perrysville Avenue, Pittsburgh, PA 15214-3897
http://www.triangle-tech.edu/

CONTACT Deborah Hepburn, Senior Director
Telephone: 412-359-1000 Ext. 7198

GENERAL INFORMATION Private Institution. Founded 1944. **Accreditation:** State accredited or approved. **Total program enrollment:** 265.

PROGRAM(S) OFFERED
• **Electrician** *6 students enrolled* • **Heating, Air Conditioning, Ventilation and Refrigeration Maintenance Technology/Technician (HAC, HACR, HVAC, HVACR)** *7 students enrolled*

STUDENT SERVICES Academic or career counseling, employment services for current students, placement services for program completers, remedial services.

Triangle Tech, Inc.–Sunbury School

RR #1, Box 51, Sunbury, PA 17801
http://www.triangle-tech.com/

CONTACT Joseph Drumm, Director
Telephone: 570-988-0700

GENERAL INFORMATION Private Institution. **Accreditation:** State accredited or approved. **Total program enrollment:** 111.

PROGRAM(S) OFFERED
• Electrician

STUDENT SERVICES Academic or career counseling, employment services for current students, placement services for program completers, remedial services.

Tri-State Business Institute

5757 West 26th Street, Erie, PA 16506
http://www.tsbi.org/

CONTACT Guy M. Euliano, President
Telephone: 814-838-7673

GENERAL INFORMATION Private Institution. **Accreditation:** State accredited or approved. **Total program enrollment:** 1070. **Application fee:** $50.

PROGRAM(S) OFFERED
• Computer Programming/Programmer, General • Computer Science • Computer and Information Sciences and Support Services, Other • Computer and Information Sciences, General *7 students enrolled* • Medical/Clinical Assistant *7 students enrolled* • Welding Technology/Welder *74 students enrolled*

STUDENT SERVICES Academic or career counseling, employment services for current students, placement services for program completers, remedial services.

Universal Technical Institute

750 Pennsylvania Avenue, Exton, PA 19341
http://www.uticorp.com/

CONTACT Kenneth Lewandowski, Campus President
Telephone: 610-458-5595

GENERAL INFORMATION Private Institution. **Total program enrollment:** 1462.

PROGRAM(S) OFFERED
• Automobile/Automotive Mechanics Technology/Technician *73 hrs./$26,700* • Diesel Mechanics Technology/Technician *102 students enrolled*

University of Pennsylvania

3451 Walnut Street, Philadelphia, PA 19104
http://www.upenn.edu/

CONTACT Amy Gutmann, President
Telephone: 215-898-5000

GENERAL INFORMATION Private Institution. Founded 1740. **Accreditation:** Regional (MSA/CIHE). **Total program enrollment:** 20128. **Application fee:** $75.

STUDENT SERVICES Academic or career counseling, daycare for children of students, employment services for current students, placement services for program completers.

University of Phoenix–Philadelphia Campus

170 South Warner Road, Suite 200, Wayne, PA 19087-2121
http://www.phoenix.edu/

CONTACT William Pepicello, PhD, President
Telephone: 610-989-0880

GENERAL INFORMATION Private Institution. Founded 1999. **Accreditation:** Regional (NCA). **Total program enrollment:** 911.

STUDENT SERVICES Academic or career counseling, remedial services.

University of Phoenix–Pittsburgh Campus

Penn Center West Six, Suite 100, Pittsburgh, PA 15276
http://www.phoenix.edu/

CONTACT William Pepicello, PhD, President
Telephone: 412-747-9000

GENERAL INFORMATION Private Institution. Founded 2001. **Accreditation:** Regional (NCA). **Total program enrollment:** 81.

STUDENT SERVICES Academic or career counseling, remedial services.

University of Pittsburgh

4200 Fifth Avenue, Pittsburgh, PA 15260
http://www.pitt.edu/

CONTACT Mark A. Nordenberg, Chancellor
Telephone: 412-624-4141

GENERAL INFORMATION Public Institution. Founded 1787. **Accreditation:** Regional (MSA/CIHE); athletic training (JRCAT); audiology (ASHA); counseling (ACA); dental hygiene (ADA); dietetics: undergraduate, postbaccalaureate internship (ADtA/CAADE); emergency medical services (JRCEMTP); health information administration (AHIMA); library and information science (ALA); speech-language pathology (ASHA); theater (NAST). **Total program enrollment:** 23181. **Application fee:** $45.

PROGRAM(S) OFFERED
• Accounting *16 students enrolled* • African Studies *14 students enrolled* • Area Studies, Other *33 students enrolled* • Asian Studies/Civilization *38 students enrolled* • Civil Engineering, General *2 students enrolled* • Computer and Information Sciences and Support Services, Other *2 students enrolled* • Dental Hygiene/Hygienist *1 student enrolled* • Engineering, General *1 student enrolled* • Engineering, Other *3 students enrolled* • European Studies/Civilization *7 students enrolled* • Film/Cinema Studies *13 students enrolled* • Geography *7 students enrolled* • German Language and Literature *9 students enrolled* • Health Professions and Related Clinical Sciences, Other *9 students enrolled* • Historic Preservation and Conservation *10 students enrolled* • International Business/Trade/Commerce *46 students enrolled* • Jewish/Judaic Studies *8 students enrolled* • Kinesiotherapy/Kinesiotherapist *30 students enrolled* • Latin American Studies *39 students enrolled* • Linguistics *23 students enrolled* • Mass Communication/Media Studies *37 students enrolled* • Nuclear Engineering *11 students enrolled* • Organizational Behavior Studies *17 students enrolled* • Public Administration *10 students enrolled* • Rehabilitation and Therapeutic Professions, Other *15 students enrolled* • Russian Studies *25 students enrolled* • Western European Studies *43 students enrolled* • Women's Studies *20 students enrolled*

STUDENT SERVICES Academic or career counseling, daycare for children of students, employment services for current students, placement services for program completers, remedial services.

University of Pittsburgh at Bradford

300 Campus Drive, Bradford, PA 16701-2812
http://www.upb.pitt.edu/

CONTACT Livingston Alexander, President
Telephone: 814-362-7500

GENERAL INFORMATION Public Institution. Founded 1963. **Accreditation:** Regional (MSA/CIHE). **Total program enrollment:** 1322. **Application fee:** $45.

STUDENT SERVICES Academic or career counseling, employment services for current students, placement services for program completers, remedial services.

University of Pittsburgh at Greensburg

1150 Mount Pleasant Road, Greensburg, PA 15601-5860
http://www.upg.pitt.edu/

CONTACT Sharon P. Smith, President
Telephone: 412-837-7040

GENERAL INFORMATION Public Institution. Founded 1963. **Accreditation:** Regional (MSA/CIHE). **Total program enrollment:** 1678. **Application fee:** $45.

PROGRAM(S) OFFERED
● **Latin American Studies** *2 students enrolled*

STUDENT SERVICES Academic or career counseling, placement services for program completers, remedial services.

University of Pittsburgh at Johnstown

450 Schoolhouse Road, Johnstown, PA 15904-2990
http://www.upj.pitt.edu/

CONTACT Jem M. Spectar, President
Telephone: 814-269-7000

GENERAL INFORMATION Public Institution. Founded 1927. **Accreditation:** Regional (MSA/CIHE); engineering technology (ABET/TAC). **Total program enrollment:** 2887. **Application fee:** $45.

PROGRAM(S) OFFERED
● **Area, Ethnic, Cultural, and Gender Studies, Other** *7 students enrolled*

STUDENT SERVICES Academic or career counseling, employment services for current students, placement services for program completers, remedial services.

University of Pittsburgh at Titusville

PO Box 287, Titusville, PA 16354
http://www.upt.pitt.edu/

CONTACT William A. Shields, President
Telephone: 814-827-4400

GENERAL INFORMATION Public Institution. Founded 1963. **Accreditation:** Regional (MSA/CIHE); physical therapy assisting (APTA). **Total program enrollment:** 428. **Application fee:** $45.

STUDENT SERVICES Academic or career counseling, employment services for current students, placement services for program completers, remedial services.

The University of Scranton

800 Linden Street, Scranton, PA 18510
http://www.scranton.edu/

CONTACT Scott R. Pilarz, SJ, President
Telephone: 570-941-7400

GENERAL INFORMATION Private Institution. Founded 1888. **Accreditation:** Regional (MSA/CIHE); computer science (ABET/CSAC); counseling (ACA). **Total program enrollment:** 4655. **Application fee:** $40.

PROGRAM(S) OFFERED
● Accounting ● Adult Development and Aging ● Business Administration and Management, General ● Business Administration, Management and Operations, Other ● Human Resources Management/Personnel Administration, General ● Information Science/Studies

STUDENT SERVICES Academic or career counseling, employment services for current students, placement services for program completers, remedial services.

The University of the Arts

320 South Broad Street, Philadelphia, PA 19102-4944
http://www.uarts.edu/

CONTACT Sean T. Buffington, President
Telephone: 215-717-6000

GENERAL INFORMATION Private Institution. Founded 1870. **Accreditation:** Regional (MSA/CIHE); art and design (NASAD); music (NASM). **Total program enrollment:** 2299. **Application fee:** $60.

STUDENT SERVICES Academic or career counseling, employment services for current students, placement services for program completers, remedial services.

Valley Forge Christian College

1401 Charlestown Road, Phoenixville, PA 19460
http://www.vfcc.edu/

CONTACT Don Meyer, PhD, President
Telephone: 610-935-0450

GENERAL INFORMATION Private Institution. Founded 1938. **Accreditation:** Regional (MSA/CIHE). **Total program enrollment:** 816. **Application fee:** $25.

PROGRAM(S) OFFERED
● **Bible/Biblical Studies** *1 student enrolled*

STUDENT SERVICES Academic or career counseling, employment services for current students, placement services for program completers, remedial services.

Venango County Area Vocational Technical School

1 Vo-Tech Drive, Oil City, PA 16301
http://www.vtc1.org/

CONTACT Robert Garrity, Director
Telephone: 814-677-3097 Ext. 207

GENERAL INFORMATION Private Institution. **Total program enrollment:** 32.

PROGRAM(S) OFFERED
● **Licensed Practical/Vocational Nurse Training (LPN, LVN, Cert, Dipl, AAS)** *1500 hrs./$10,909*

STUDENT SERVICES Academic or career counseling, placement services for program completers.

Venus Beauty School

1033 Chester Pike, Sharon Hill, PA 19079
http://www.venusbeautyacademy.com/

CONTACT Richard M. Falcone, President
Telephone: 610-586-2500

GENERAL INFORMATION Private Institution. Founded 1960. **Total program enrollment:** 77. **Application fee:** $50.

PROGRAM(S) OFFERED
● **Aesthetician/Esthetician and Skin Care Specialist** *350 hrs./$4360*
● **Cosmetology, Barber/Styling, and Nail Instructor** *600 hrs./$5570*
● **Cosmetology/Cosmetologist, General** *1250 hrs./$17,045* ● **Electrolysis/Electrology and Electrolysis Technician** *300 hrs./$3730* ● **Nail Technician/Specialist and Manicurist** *200 hrs./$2660*

STUDENT SERVICES Academic or career counseling, employment services for current students, placement services for program completers.

Welder Training and Testing Institute

1144 North Graham Street, Allentown, PA 18103-1263

CONTACT Robert Wiswesser, President
Telephone: 610-437-9720

GENERAL INFORMATION Private Institution. Founded 1922. **Total program enrollment:** 45.

PROGRAM(S) OFFERED
• Welding Technology/Welder *60 hrs./$1020*

STUDENT SERVICES Placement services for program completers.

Western Area Career and Technology Center

688 Western Avenue, Canonsburg, PA 15317
http://www.wactc.net/

CONTACT Dr. Joseph Iannetti, Director Vocational Education
Telephone: 724-746-2890 Ext. 118

GENERAL INFORMATION Public Institution. Founded 1971. **Total program enrollment:** 41. **Application fee:** $20.

PROGRAM(S) OFFERED
• Licensed Practical/Vocational Nurse Training (LPN, LVN, Cert, Dipl, AAS) *1582 hrs./$10,047*

STUDENT SERVICES Academic or career counseling, daycare for children of students.

Westmoreland County Community College

145 Pavilion Lane, Youngwood, PA 15697-1898
http://www.wccc.edu/

CONTACT Steven Ender, President
Telephone: 724-925-4000

GENERAL INFORMATION Public Institution. Founded 1970. **Accreditation:** Regional (MSA/CIHE); dental assisting (ADA); dental hygiene (ADA). **Total program enrollment:** 3064. **Application fee:** $10.

PROGRAM(S) OFFERED
• Accounting Technology/Technician and Bookkeeping *3 students enrolled* • Administrative Assistant and Secretarial Science, General *1 student enrolled* • Baking and Pastry Arts/Baker/Pastry Chef *2 students enrolled* • Banking and Financial Support Services *1 student enrolled* • Business Administration and Management, General *7 students enrolled* • Child Care Provider/Assistant *9 students enrolled* • Commercial and Advertising Art • Computer Graphics • Computer Installation and Repair Technology/Technician *3 students enrolled* • Computer Programming, Specific Applications • Computer Systems Networking and Telecommunications *1 student enrolled* • Computer and Information Systems Security *3 students enrolled* • Corrections *2 students enrolled* • Culinary Arts and Related Services, Other *6 students enrolled* • Culinary Arts/Chef Training *2 students enrolled* • Data Entry/Microcomputer Applications, General *2 students enrolled* • Data Modeling/Warehousing and Database Administration • Data Processing and Data Processing Technology/Technician *1 student enrolled* • Dental Assisting/Assistant *10 students enrolled* • Fire Protection and Safety Technology/Technician • Food Service, Waiter/Waitress, and Dining Room Management/Manager *1 student enrolled* • Graphic Design • Heating, Air Conditioning, Ventilation and Refrigeration Maintenance Technology/Technician (HAC, HACR, HVAC, HVACR) *14 students enrolled* • Hotel/Motel Administration/Management *1 student enrolled* • Human Resources Management/Personnel Administration, General *5 students enrolled* • Legal Assistant/Paralegal *1 student enrolled* • Licensed Practical/Vocational Nurse Training (LPN, LVN, Cert, Dipl, AAS) *8 students enrolled* • Machine Shop Technology/Assistant *2 students enrolled* • Machine Tool Technology/Machinist • Marketing/Marketing Management, General *3 students enrolled* • Medical Insurance Coding Specialist/Coder *38 students enrolled* • Medical Office Assistant/Specialist *14 students enrolled* • Medical Transcription/Transcriptionist *18 students enrolled* • Medical/Clinical Assistant *13 students enrolled* • Photographic and Film/Video Technology/Technician and Assistant *3 students enrolled* • Radio and Television Broadcasting Technology/Technician *3 students enrolled* • Real Estate *1 student enrolled* • Small Business

Administration/Management • Surgical Technology/Technologist *4 students enrolled* • Web Page, Digital/Multimedia and Information Resources Design *1 student enrolled* • Welding Technology/Welder *1 student enrolled*

STUDENT SERVICES Academic or career counseling, daycare for children of students, employment services for current students, placement services for program completers, remedial services.

West Virginia Career Institute

Mount Braddock Road, Mount Braddock, PA 15465
http://www.wvjcchas.net/

CONTACT Patricia A. Callen, Executive Director
Telephone: 724-437-4600

GENERAL INFORMATION Private Institution. **Total program enrollment:** 102. **Application fee:** $25.

PROGRAM(S) OFFERED
• Accounting Technology/Technician and Bookkeeping *3 students enrolled* • Medical Administrative/Executive Assistant and Medical Secretary *7 students enrolled*

STUDENT SERVICES Academic or career counseling, employment services for current students, placement services for program completers.

Widener University

One University Place, Chester, PA 19013-5792
http://www.widener.edu/

CONTACT James T. Harris, III, President
Telephone: 610-499-4000

GENERAL INFORMATION Private Institution. Founded 1821. **Accreditation:** Regional (MSA/CIHE). **Total program enrollment:** 3251. **Application fee:** $35.

STUDENT SERVICES Academic or career counseling, employment services for current students, placement services for program completers, remedial services.

WyoTech

500 Innovation Drive, Blairsville, PA 15717
http://www.wyotech.com/

CONTACT Steve Whitson, President
Telephone: 800-822-8253

GENERAL INFORMATION Private Institution. Founded 2002. **Accreditation:** State accredited or approved. **Total program enrollment:** 1313. **Application fee:** $100.

PROGRAM(S) OFFERED
• Autobody/Collision and Repair Technology/Technician *1501 hrs./$25,000* • Automobile/Automotive Mechanics Technology/Technician *1501 hrs./$25,700* • Diesel Mechanics Technology/Technician *1501 hrs./$25,700*

STUDENT SERVICES Academic or career counseling, employment services for current students, placement services for program completers.

York County School of Technology–Practical Nursing Program

2179 South Queen Street, York, PA 17402
http://www.ycstech.org/

CONTACT James A. Kraft, Administrative Director
Telephone: 717-741-0820 Ext. 4306

GENERAL INFORMATION Public Institution. Founded 1963. **Total program enrollment:** 60.

PROGRAM(S) OFFERED

• **Nursing, Other** 40 *students enrolled* • **Truck and Bus Driver/Commercial Vehicle Operation** 56 *students enrolled*

STUDENT SERVICES Academic or career counseling, remedial services.

Yorktowne Business Institute

West Seventh Avenue, York, PA 17404
http://www.ybi.edu/

CONTACT James P. Murphy, President
Telephone: 717-846-5000

GENERAL INFORMATION Private Institution. Founded 1976. **Accreditation:** State accredited or approved. **Total program enrollment:** 182. **Application fee:** $55.

PROGRAM(S) OFFERED

• **Baking and Pastry Arts/Baker/Pastry Chef** 5 *students enrolled* • **Health Information/Medical Records Administration/Administrator** 15 *students enrolled*

STUDENT SERVICES Academic or career counseling, employment services for current students, placement services for program completers.

YTI Career Institute–York

1405 Williams Road, York, PA 17402-9017
http://www.yti.edu/

CONTACT Timothy Foster, Chairman & CEO
Telephone: 717-757-1100

GENERAL INFORMATION Private Institution. Founded 1967. **Accreditation:** State accredited or approved. **Total program enrollment:** 1472. **Application fee:** $50.

PROGRAM(S) OFFERED

• **Architectural Drafting and Architectural CAD/CADD** 100 *hrs./$34,650* • **Baking and Pastry Arts/Baker/Pastry Chef** 32 *students enrolled* • **Computer and Information Sciences and Support Services, Other** 109 *hrs./$39,970* • **Culinary Arts/Chef Training** 101 *hrs./$42,510* • **Dental Assisting/Assistant** 22 *students enrolled* • **Electrical, Electronic and Communications Engineering Technology/Technician** 7 *students enrolled* • **Heating, Air Conditioning and Refrigeration Technology/Technician (ACH/ACR/ACHR/HRAC/HVAC/AC Technology)** 54 *hrs./$16,640* • **Management Information Systems, General** 17 *students enrolled* • **Manufacturing Technology/Technician** 1 *student enrolled* • **Medical Insurance Coding Specialist/Coder** 43 *students enrolled* • **Medical Office Assistant/Specialist** 14 *students enrolled* • **Medical/Clinical Assistant** 111 *hrs./$28,560* • **Motorcycle Maintenance and Repair Technology/Technician** 40 *hrs./$20,550* • **Tourism and Travel Services Marketing Operations** 31 *students enrolled*

STUDENT SERVICES Academic or career counseling, employment services for current students, placement services for program completers, remedial services.

PUERTO RICO ⸺

Academia Serrant

Concordia 8180 Esq. Aurora, Ponce, PR 00717-1568
http://www.serrant.com/

CONTACT Helen Serrant, Executive Director/President
Telephone: 787-259-4900

GENERAL INFORMATION Private Institution. **Total program enrollment:** 259. **Application fee:** $25.

PROGRAM(S) OFFERED

• **Administrative Assistant and Secretarial Science, General** 1350 *hrs./$8117* • **Apparel and Textile Manufacture** 1200 *hrs./$6908* • **Baking and Pastry Arts/Baker/Pastry Chef** 29 *students enrolled* • **Culinary Arts/Chef Training** 900 *hrs./$5631* • **Fashion/Apparel Design** 1350 *hrs./$9665* • **Floriculture/Floristry Operations and Management** 900 *hrs./$5331* • **Machine Tool Technology/Machinist** 81 *students enrolled* • **Photography** 8 *students enrolled* • **Securities Services Administration/Management** 1200 *hrs./$7008* • **Security and Protective Services, Other** 21 *students enrolled*

STUDENT SERVICES Academic or career counseling, employment services for current students, placement services for program completers, remedial services.

Advanced Tech College

Barbosa Street, #24, Bayamón, PR 00961

CONTACT Jesus Sanchez Olmo, President
Telephone: 787-787-6841

GENERAL INFORMATION Private Institution. **Total program enrollment:** 67. **Application fee:** $25.

PROGRAM(S) OFFERED

• **Accounting and Computer Science** 1000 *hrs./$3887* • **Data Entry/Microcomputer Applications, General** 1000 *hrs./$3887* • **Data Processing and Data Processing Technology/Technician** 1 *student enrolled* • **Health Information/Medical Records Administration/Administrator** 1000 *hrs./$4037* • **Medical Administrative/Executive Assistant and Medical Secretary** 12 *students enrolled*

STUDENT SERVICES Placement services for program completers.

Aguadilla Technical College

Barrio Caimital Alto Careterra 433, Aguadilla, PR 00603

CONTACT Carmen Ocasio, Owner
Telephone: 787-891-6966

GENERAL INFORMATION Private Institution. **Total program enrollment:** 49. **Application fee:** $35.

PROGRAM(S) OFFERED

• **Electrician** 1000 *hrs./$5880* • **Plumbing Technology/Plumber** 1000 *hrs./$5730*

STUDENT SERVICES Academic or career counseling, placement services for program completers.

American Educational College

PO Box 62, Bayamón, PR 00960

CONTACT J. E. Gonzalez Pinto, President
Telephone: 787-798-1199

GENERAL INFORMATION Private Institution. Founded 1981. **Total program enrollment:** 610. **Application fee:** $25.

PROGRAM(S) OFFERED

• **Accounting and Related Services, Other** • **Administrative Assistant and Secretarial Science, General** 2 *students enrolled* • **Barbering/Barber** 37 *students enrolled* • **Computer Installation and Repair Technology/Technician** 22 *students enrolled* • **Computer Programming/Programmer, General** 12 *students enrolled* • **Cosmetology and Related Personal Grooming Arts, Other** 12 *students enrolled* • **Cosmetology/Cosmetologist, General** 59 *students enrolled* • **Hotel/Motel Administration/Management** 6 *students enrolled* • **Legal Administrative Assistant/Secretary** • **Medical Administrative/Executive Assistant and Medical Secretary** 65 *students enrolled* • **Nail Technician/Specialist and Manicurist** 2 *students enrolled* • **Pre-Law Studies** 5 *students enrolled*

STUDENT SERVICES Academic or career counseling, placement services for program completers.

Antilles School of Technical Careers

Calle Domenech #107, Apartado 1536, Hato Rey, PR 00919

CONTACT Alex A. de Jorge, President
Telephone: 787-268-2244

GENERAL INFORMATION Private Institution. Founded 1970. **Total program enrollment: 324. Application fee:** $50.

PROGRAM(S) OFFERED
• **Aesthetician/Esthetician and Skin Care Specialist** 48 hrs./$7500 • **Dental Assisting/Assistant** • **Funeral Service and Mortuary Science, General** 77 hrs./$11,200 • **Licensed Practical/Vocational Nurse Training (LPN, LVN, Cert, Dipl, AAS)** 62 hrs./$11,132 • **Massage Therapy/Therapeutic Massage** 53 hrs./$8355 • **Pharmacy Technician/Assistant** 58 hrs./$11,482 • **Surgical Technology/Technologist** 44 hrs./$8355

STUDENT SERVICES Academic or career counseling, employment services for current students, placement services for program completers, remedial services.

ASPIRA de Puerto Rico

Road 8887, Km 11.9 San Anton Ward, Carolina, PR 00987
pr.aspira.org

CONTACT Adalexis Rios-Orlandi, Executive Director
Telephone: 787-641-1985 Ext. 222

GENERAL INFORMATION Private Institution. **Application fee:** $50.

PROGRAM(S) OFFERED
• **Computer Installation and Repair Technology/Technician** 80 hrs./$1500 • **Data Entry/Microcomputer Applications, Other** 96 hrs./$579 • **System, Networking, and LAN/WAN Management/Manager** 300 hrs.

STUDENT SERVICES Placement services for program completers.

Atenas College

Paseo De La Atenas #101 Altos, Manati, PR 00674

CONTACT Maria L. Hernandez, Executive Director
Telephone: 787-884-3838

GENERAL INFORMATION Private Institution. **Total program enrollment:** 1470.

PROGRAM(S) OFFERED
• **Cardiovascular Technology/Technologist** 38 students enrolled • **Clinical/Medical Laboratory Technician** • **Emergency Medical Technology/Technician (EMT Paramedic)** 14 students enrolled • **Executive Assistant/Executive Secretary** • **Health Information/Medical Records Technology/Technician** • **Licensed Practical/Vocational Nurse Training (LPN, LVN, Cert, Dipl, AAS)** 102 students enrolled • **Medical Administrative/Executive Assistant and Medical Secretary** 92 students enrolled • **Medical Radiologic Technology/Science—Radiation Therapist** 92 students enrolled • **Pharmacy Technician/Assistant** 126 students enrolled • **Respiratory Care Therapy/Therapist** 26 students enrolled • **Surgical Technology/Technologist** 65 students enrolled

STUDENT SERVICES Academic or career counseling, placement services for program completers.

Automeca Technical College

PO Box 427, Aguadilla, PR 00605-0427
http://www.automeca.com/

CONTACT Luis Acosta, President
Telephone: 787-882-2828

GENERAL INFORMATION Private Institution. **Total program enrollment:** 259. **Application fee:** $35.

PROGRAM(S) OFFERED
• **Automobile/Automotive Mechanics Technology/Technician** 92 students enrolled • **Diesel Mechanics Technology/Technician** 16 students enrolled • **Electromechanical Technology/Electromechanical Engineering Technology**
58 students enrolled • **Heating, Air Conditioning, Ventilation and Refrigeration Maintenance Technology/Technician (HAC, HACR, HVAC, HVACR)** • **Mechanic and Repair Technologies/Technicians, Other** 22 students enrolled • **Small Engine Mechanics and Repair Technology/Technician** • **Vehicle Maintenance and Repair Technologies, Other** 5 students enrolled

STUDENT SERVICES Academic or career counseling, employment services for current students, placement services for program completers.

Automeca Technical College

PO Box 8569, Bayamón, PR 00960
http://www.automeca.com/

CONTACT Luis Acosta, President
Telephone: 787-779-6161

GENERAL INFORMATION Private Institution. Founded 1982. **Total program enrollment: 479. Application fee:** $35.

PROGRAM(S) OFFERED
• **Automobile/Automotive Mechanics Technology/Technician** 153 students enrolled • **Diesel Mechanics Technology/Technician** 32 students enrolled • **Electromechanical Technology/Electromechanical Engineering Technology** 56 students enrolled • **Heating, Air Conditioning, Ventilation and Refrigeration Maintenance Technology/Technician (HAC, HACR, HVAC, HVACR)** 32 students enrolled • **Mechanic and Repair Technologies/Technicians, Other** 75 students enrolled • **Small Engine Mechanics and Repair Technology/Technician** 35 students enrolled • **Vehicle Maintenance and Repair Technologies, Other** 12 students enrolled

STUDENT SERVICES Academic or career counseling, employment services for current students, placement services for program completers.

Automeca Technical College

Munoz Rivera 69, Caguas, PR 00625
http://www.automeca.com/

CONTACT Luis Acosta, President
Telephone: 787-746-3468

GENERAL INFORMATION Private Institution. **Total program enrollment:** 299. **Application fee:** $35.

PROGRAM(S) OFFERED
• **Automobile/Automotive Mechanics Technology/Technician** 86 students enrolled • **Diesel Mechanics Technology/Technician** 24 students enrolled • **Electromechanical Technology/Electromechanical Engineering Technology** 24 students enrolled • **Heating, Air Conditioning, Ventilation and Refrigeration Maintenance Technology/Technician (HAC, HACR, HVAC, HVACR)** 14 students enrolled • **Mechanic and Repair Technologies/Technicians, Other** 24 students enrolled • **Small Engine Mechanics and Repair Technology/Technician** 8 students enrolled • **Vehicle Maintenance and Repair Technologies, Other**

STUDENT SERVICES Academic or career counseling, employment services for current students, placement services for program completers.

Automeca Technical College

Calle Villa 452, Ponce, PR 00731
http://www.automeca.com/

CONTACT Luis Acosta, President
Telephone: 787-840-7880

GENERAL INFORMATION Private Institution. **Total program enrollment:** 327. **Application fee:** $35.

PROGRAM(S) OFFERED
• **Automobile/Automotive Mechanics Technology/Technician** 127 students enrolled • **Diesel Mechanics Technology/Technician** 35 students enrolled • **Electromechanical Technology/Electromechanical Engineering Technology** 23 students enrolled • **Heating, Air Conditioning, Ventilation and Refrigeration Maintenance Technology/Technician (HAC, HACR, HVAC, HVACR)** • **Mechanic**

and Repair Technologies/Technicians, Other 67 *students enrolled* • **Small Engine Mechanics and Repair Technology/Technician** 12 *students enrolled* • **Vehicle Maintenance and Repair Technologies, Other** 6 *students enrolled*

STUDENT SERVICES Academic or career counseling, employment services for current students, placement services for program completers.

Bayamón Central University

Avenida Zaya Verde, La Milagrosa Barrio Hato Tejas, Bayamón, PR 00960-1725
http://www.ucb.edu.pr/

CONTACT Prof. Nilda Nadal Carreras, President
Telephone: 787-786-3030 Ext. 2100

GENERAL INFORMATION Private Institution. Founded 1970. **Accreditation:** Regional (MSA/CIHE). **Total program enrollment:** 1545. **Application fee:** $15.

STUDENT SERVICES Academic or career counseling, daycare for children of students, employment services for current students, remedial services.

Bayamón Community College

P.M.B. #103, PO Box 607079, Bayamón, PR 00960
http://www.bccpr.org/

CONTACT Tanus Saad, President
Telephone: 787-780-4242

GENERAL INFORMATION Private Institution. **Total program enrollment:** 265.

PROGRAM(S) OFFERED
• **Accounting Technology/Technician and Bookkeeping** 17 *students enrolled* • **Administrative Assistant and Secretarial Science, General** 31 *students enrolled* • **Medical Office Computer Specialist/Assistant** 50 *students enrolled*

STUDENT SERVICES Academic or career counseling, placement services for program completers.

Caguas Institute of Mechanical Technology

PO Box 6118, Caguas, PR 00726
http://mechtechcollege.com/

CONTACT Edwin Colon, President
Telephone: 787-744-1060 Ext. 1000

GENERAL INFORMATION Private Institution. Founded 1984. **Total program enrollment:** 2295. **Application fee:** $40.

PROGRAM(S) OFFERED
• **Automobile/Automotive Mechanics Technology/Technician** 671 *students enrolled* • **Diesel Mechanics Technology/Technician** 69 *students enrolled* • **Electrical, Electronic and Communications Engineering Technology/Technician** • **Electrician** 83 *students enrolled* • **Electromechanical Technology/Electromechanical Engineering Technology** 204 *students enrolled* • **Electromechanical and Instrumentation and Maintenance Technologies/Technicians, Other** • **Heating, Air Conditioning and Refrigeration Technology/Technician (ACH/ACR/ACHR/HRAC/HVAC/AC Technology)** 39 *students enrolled* • **Machine Tool Technology/Machinist** • **Precision Systems Maintenance and Repair Technologies, Other** 59 *students enrolled* • **Tool and Die Technology/Technician** 108 *students enrolled*

STUDENT SERVICES Academic or career counseling, employment services for current students, placement services for program completers, remedial services.

Cambridge Technical Institute

Calle Carazo #67, Guaynabo, PR 00969

CONTACT Juan C. Vargas, President & CEO
Telephone: 787-263-0453

GENERAL INFORMATION Private Institution. **Total program enrollment:** 109. **Application fee:** $30.

PROGRAM(S) OFFERED
• **Medical Administrative/Executive Assistant and Medical Secretary** 600 *hrs./* $2600 • **Medical/Clinical Assistant** 7 *students enrolled*

STUDENT SERVICES Placement services for program completers.

Caribbean Forensic and Technical College

Paseo De Diego Street #5 3rd Fl, Río Piedras, PR 00926
http://www.cafotech.com/

CONTACT Ismael Mercado, President & CEO
Telephone: 787-759-6995

GENERAL INFORMATION Private Institution. **Total program enrollment:** 217. **Application fee:** $25.

PROGRAM(S) OFFERED
• **Criminal Justice/Police Science** 23 *students enrolled* • **Criminalistics and Criminal Science** 52 *students enrolled* • **Forensic Science and Technology** 15 *students enrolled*

STUDENT SERVICES Academic or career counseling, placement services for program completers, remedial services.

Caribbean University

Box 493, Bayamón, PR 00960-0493
http://www.caribbean.edu/

CONTACT Dr. Ana E. Cucurella-Adorno, President
Telephone: 787-780-0070

GENERAL INFORMATION Private Institution. Founded 1969. **Accreditation:** Regional (MSA/CIHE). **Total program enrollment:** 1295. **Application fee:** $25.

PROGRAM(S) OFFERED
• **Barbering/Barber** 5 *students enrolled* • **Cosmetology/Cosmetologist, General** 9 *students enrolled*

STUDENT SERVICES Academic or career counseling, employment services for current students, placement services for program completers, remedial services.

Carib Technological Institute

Carretera #2, Km 14.4 Barrio Hato Tejas, Bayamón, PR 00960

CONTACT Luis Lafontaine
Telephone: 787-798-9595

GENERAL INFORMATION Private Institution. **Total program enrollment:** 42. **Application fee:** $25.

PROGRAM(S) OFFERED
• **Electrical/Electronics Drafting and Electrical/Electronics CAD/CADD** 1200 *hrs./* $7200 • **Electrician** 25 *students enrolled* • **Heating, Air Conditioning and Refrigeration Technology/Technician (ACH/ACR/ACHR/HRAC/HVAC/AC Technology)** 900 *hrs./* $5510

STUDENT SERVICES Academic or career counseling, placement services for program completers.

Centro de Estudios Multidisciplinarios

25 Degetau Street, Bayamón, PR 00961
http://www.cempr.edu

CONTACT Raul I. Medina, Branch Director
Telephone: 787-780-8900

GENERAL INFORMATION Private Institution. **Total program enrollment:** 438. **Application fee:** $30.

PROGRAM(S) OFFERED
● **Emergency Medical Technology/Technician (EMT Paramedic)** 59 *students enrolled* ● **Licensed Practical/Vocational Nurse Training (LPN, LVN, Cert, Dipl, AAS)** 49 *students enrolled* ● **Medical Insurance Specialist/Medical Biller** 8 *students enrolled* ● **Respiratory Care Therapy/Therapist** 32 *students enrolled*

STUDENT SERVICES Academic or career counseling, placement services for program completers.

Centro de Estudios Multidisciplinarios

6. Drive Vidal Street, Humacao, PR 00791
http://www.cempr.edu/

CONTACT Audberto Cordero, Branch Director
Telephone: 787-850-8333

GENERAL INFORMATION Private Institution. **Total program enrollment:** 572. **Application fee:** $30.

PROGRAM(S) OFFERED
● **Emergency Medical Technology/Technician (EMT Paramedic)** 41 *students enrolled* ● **Licensed Practical/Vocational Nurse Training (LPN, LVN, Cert, Dipl, AAS)** 9 *students enrolled* ● **Medical Insurance Specialist/Medical Biller** 3 *students enrolled* ● **Respiratory Care Therapy/Therapist** 11 *students enrolled*

STUDENT SERVICES Academic or career counseling, placement services for program completers.

Centro de Estudios Multidisciplinarios

Calle 13 #1206, Ext. San Agustin, San Juan, PR 00926
http://www.cempr.edu/

CONTACT Laura Delgado, Branch Director
Telephone: 787-765-4210 Ext. 105

GENERAL INFORMATION Private Institution. Founded 1980. **Accreditation:** State accredited or approved. **Total program enrollment:** 918. **Application fee:** $30.

PROGRAM(S) OFFERED
● **Emergency Medical Technology/Technician (EMT Paramedic)** 59 *students enrolled* ● **Licensed Practical/Vocational Nurse Training (LPN, LVN, Cert, Dipl, AAS)** 54 *students enrolled* ● **Medical Insurance Specialist/Medical Biller** 51 *students enrolled*

STUDENT SERVICES Academic or career counseling, placement services for program completers.

Century College

Calle Progresso #125, Aguadilla, PR 00603
http://www.centurycollegepr.com/

CONTACT Anna Sanfilippo, President
Telephone: 787-882-5086

GENERAL INFORMATION Private Institution. **Total program enrollment:** 95. **Application fee:** $25.

PROGRAM(S) OFFERED
● **Computer/Information Technology Services Administration and Management, Other** 11 *students enrolled* ● **Cosmetology/Cosmetologist, General** 31 *students enrolled* ● **Office Management and Supervision** 6 *students enrolled* ● **Respiratory Care Therapy/Therapist** 4 *students enrolled* ● **Security and Protective Services, Other** 42 *students enrolled*

STUDENT SERVICES Placement services for program completers.

Charlie's Guard-Detective Bureau and Academy

Road 107, Km 3.1, Bo. Borinquen, Aguadilla, PR 00603
http://www.charliesacademy.edu/

CONTACT Mr. Leocadio Nieves, President
Telephone: 787-882-7222

GENERAL INFORMATION Private Institution. **Total program enrollment:** 193. **Application fee:** $25.

PROGRAM(S) OFFERED
● **Cosmetology and Related Personal Grooming Arts, Other** ● **Cosmetology, Barber/Styling, and Nail Instructor** ● **Cosmetology/Cosmetologist, General** 18 *students enrolled* ● **Criminal Justice/Police Science** 22 *students enrolled* ● **Medical Office Management/Administration** 7 *students enrolled* ● **Security and Protective Services, Other** 21 *students enrolled*

STUDENT SERVICES Academic or career counseling, placement services for program completers.

Colegio de Las Ciencias Arte y Television

Escorial Lote 15 Urb. Industrial Mario Julia, Caparra Heights, PR 00922-0774
http://ccat.edu/

CONTACT Margarita Gonzalez, Administrative Director
Telephone: 787-779-2500

GENERAL INFORMATION Private Institution. **Total program enrollment:** 193. **Application fee:** $25.

PROGRAM(S) OFFERED
● **Animation, Interactive Technology, Video Graphics and Special Effects** 8 *students enrolled* ● **Film/Video and Photographic Arts, Other** 16 *students enrolled* ● **Radio, Television, and Digital Communication, Other** 10 *students enrolled* ● **Recording Arts Technology/Technician** 89 *students enrolled* ● **Tourism Promotion Operations**

STUDENT SERVICES Academic or career counseling, placement services for program completers, remedial services.

Colegio Mayor de Tecnologia–Arroyo

Calle Morse 151, Arroyo, PR 00714-2615
http://www.cmtarroyo.com/

CONTACT Mancio Vicente, President
Telephone: 787-839-5266 Ext. 22

GENERAL INFORMATION Private Institution. **Total program enrollment:** 240. **Application fee:** $25.

PROGRAM(S) OFFERED
● **Automobile/Automotive Mechanics Technology/Technician** 1795 *hrs.*/$8900 ● **Computer Installation and Repair Technology/Technician** 11 *students enrolled* ● **Computer and Information Sciences and Support Services, Other** 6 *students enrolled* ● **Dental Assisting/Assistant** 1795 *hrs.*/$10,980 ● **Electrician** 1720 *hrs.*/$10,465 ● **Electromechanical Technology/Electromechanical Engineering Technology** 14 *students enrolled* ● **Emergency Medical Technology/Technician (EMT Paramedic)** 1690 *hrs.*/$10,235 ● **Foods, Nutrition, and Wellness Studies, General** 10 *students enrolled* ● **General Office Occupations and Clerical Services** 2 *students enrolled* ● **Health Information/Medical Records Administration/Administrator** 28 *students enrolled* ● **Legal Administrative Assistant/Secretary** 6 *students enrolled* ● **Licensed Practical/Vocational Nurse**

Training (LPN, LVN, Cert, Dipl, AAS) *1795 hrs./$11,210* ● **Massage Therapy/Therapeutic Massage** *7 students enrolled* ● **Security and Protective Services, Other** *5 students enrolled* ● **Welding Technology/Welder** *1665 hrs./$10,120*

STUDENT SERVICES Academic or career counseling, employment services for current students, placement services for program completers.

Colegio Pentecostal Mizpa

Bo Caimito Road 199, Apartado 20966, Río Piedras, PR 00928-0966

CONTACT Daniel Cruz, President
Telephone: 787-720-4476

GENERAL INFORMATION Private Institution (Affiliated with Pentecostal Church). Founded 1937. **Accreditation:** State accredited or approved. **Total program enrollment:** 91. **Application fee:** $40.

PROGRAM(S) OFFERED
● **Theology and Religious Vocations, Other**

STUDENT SERVICES Academic or career counseling, remedial services.

Colegio Tecnico de Electricidad Galloza

Carr 4416, Km 2.5 Interior, Aguada, PR 00602

GENERAL INFORMATION Private Institution. **Total program enrollment:** 76. **Application fee:** $25.

PROGRAM(S) OFFERED
● **Barbering/Barber** *1020 hrs./$5890* ● **Cosmetology/Cosmetologist, General** *1020 hrs./$5890* ● **Electrician** *1020 hrs./$6337* ● **Heating, Air Conditioning and Refrigeration Technology/Technician (ACH/ACR/ACHR/HRAC/HVAC/AC Technology)** *1020 hrs./$5890* ● **Plumbing Technology/Plumber** *1020 hrs./$5890*

STUDENT SERVICES Academic or career counseling, placement services for program completers.

Colegio Tecnologico y Comercial de Puerto Rico

Calle Paz 165 Altos, Box 960, Aguada, PR 00602

CONTACT Roberto Davila, President
Telephone: 787-868-2688

GENERAL INFORMATION Private Institution. **Total program enrollment:** 152. **Application fee:** $25.

PROGRAM(S) OFFERED
● **Management Information Systems and Services, Other** *1000 hrs./$5996* ● **Medical Office Management/Administration** *1000 hrs./$5996* ● **Pharmacy Technician/Assistant** *1240 hrs./$7863*

STUDENT SERVICES Academic or career counseling, placement services for program completers, remedial services.

Colegio Universitario de San Juan

180 Jose R Oliver Street, Tres Monjitas Industrial Park, San Juan, PR 00918
http://www.cunisanjuan.edu/

CONTACT Deborah Drahus-Capo, Acting Chancellor
Telephone: 787-250-7111 Ext. 2227

GENERAL INFORMATION Public Institution. Founded 1971. **Accreditation:** Regional (MSA/CIHE). **Total program enrollment:** 1242. **Application fee:** $15.

PROGRAM(S) OFFERED
● **Business Operations Support and Secretarial Services, Other**

STUDENT SERVICES Academic or career counseling, employment services for current students, placement services for program completers, remedial services.

Columbia College

PO Box 8517, Caguas, PR 00726
http://www.columbiaco.edu/

CONTACT Ana R. Burgos, Executive Director
Telephone: 787-743-4041 Ext. 240

GENERAL INFORMATION Private Institution. Founded 1966. **Accreditation:** Regional (MSA/CIHE); state accredited or approved. **Total program enrollment:** 510. **Application fee:** $50.

PROGRAM(S) OFFERED
● **Communications Technology/Technician** *24 students enrolled* ● **Massage Therapy/Therapeutic Massage** *23 students enrolled* ● **Securities Services Administration/Management** *9 students enrolled*

STUDENT SERVICES Academic or career counseling, daycare for children of students, employment services for current students, placement services for program completers.

Columbia College

Box 3062, Yauco, PR 00698
http://www.columbiaco.edu/

CONTACT Rosario Padilla, Executive Director
Telephone: 787-856-0845

GENERAL INFORMATION Private Institution. Founded 1976. **Accreditation:** State accredited or approved. **Total program enrollment:** 348. **Application fee:** $50.

PROGRAM(S) OFFERED
● **Business Operations Support and Secretarial Services, Other** *5 students enrolled* ● **Communications Technology/Technician** *11 students enrolled* ● **Computer Programming, Other** *4 students enrolled* ● **Pharmacy Technician/Assistant** *24 students enrolled*

STUDENT SERVICES Academic or career counseling, employment services for current students, placement services for program completers.

D'mart Institute

Carr 156 Km 17.1 Bo Honduras, Suite 202, Centro Comercial, Barranquitas, PR 00794
http://www.dmartpr.com/

CONTACT Juan C. Vargas, Administrator/President
Telephone: 787-263-0453

GENERAL INFORMATION Private Institution. **Total program enrollment:** 1746. **Application fee:** $25.

PROGRAM(S) OFFERED
● **Aesthetician/Esthetician and Skin Care Specialist** *14 students enrolled* ● **Barbering/Barber** *45 students enrolled* ● **Cosmetology and Related Personal Grooming Arts, Other** *13 students enrolled* ● **Cosmetology/Cosmetologist, General** *158 students enrolled* ● **Data Processing and Data Processing Technology/Technician** *41 students enrolled* ● **Drafting and Design Technology/Technician, General** *26 students enrolled* ● **Electrician** *72 students enrolled* ● **Fashion Modeling** ● **Floriculture/Floristry Operations and Management** *8 students enrolled* ● **Hair Styling/Stylist and Hair Design** *323 students enrolled* ● **Heating, Air Conditioning, Ventilation and Refrigeration Maintenance Technology/Technician (HAC, HACR, HVAC, HVACR)** *32 students enrolled* ● **Information Technology** *32 students enrolled* ● **Legal Administrative Assistant/Secretary** *41 students enrolled* ● **Massage Therapy/Therapeutic Massage** *58 students enrolled* ● **Medical Insurance Specialist/Medical Biller** *54 students*

D'mart Institute (continued)

enrolled • **Nail Technician/Specialist and Manicurist** *187 students enrolled* • **Permanent Cosmetics/Makeup and Tattooing** *9 students enrolled* • **Special Products Marketing Operations** • **Teaching English or French as a Second or Foreign Language, Other**

STUDENT SERVICES Academic or career counseling, employment services for current students, placement services for program completers.

Educational Technical College–Bayamón

5 Degetau Street, Corner Betances, Bayamón, PR 00961-6208
http://webmail.mbenitez@edutecpr.com/

CONTACT Miriam Benitez, President
Telephone: 787-780-8234

GENERAL INFORMATION Private Institution. Founded 1983. **Total program enrollment:** 385. **Application fee:** $25.

PROGRAM(S) OFFERED
• **Apparel and Textile Manufacture** *12 students enrolled* • **Business/Commerce, General** *29 students enrolled* • **Child Care Provider/Assistant** *21 students enrolled* • **Computer Installation and Repair Technology/Technician** *49 hrs./$4975* • **Cosmetology/Cosmetologist, General** *57 hrs./$4975* • **Electrician** *49 hrs./$4975* • **Emergency Medical Technology/Technician (EMT Paramedic)** *56 hrs./$4795* • **Orthoptics/Orthoptist** *56 hrs./$4975* • **Respiratory Therapy Technician/Assistant** *70 hrs./$6338*

STUDENT SERVICES Academic or career counseling, employment services for current students, placement services for program completers.

Educational Technical College–Recinto de Coama

Calle Ramón Power, #5, Coama, PR 00769

CONTACT Miriam Benites, President
Telephone: 787-825-0370

GENERAL INFORMATION Private Institution. **Total program enrollment:** 318. **Application fee:** $25.

PROGRAM(S) OFFERED
• **Apparel and Textile Manufacture** *8 students enrolled* • **Business/Commerce, General** *46 students enrolled* • **Child Care Provider/Assistant** *46 hrs./$4975* • **Computer Installation and Repair Technology/Technician** *56 hrs./$4975* • **Cosmetology/Cosmetologist, General** *57 hrs./$4975* • **Electrician** *49 hrs./$4975* • **Orthoptics/Orthoptist** *56 hrs./$4975* • **Respiratory Therapy Technician/Assistant** *70 hrs./$6338*

STUDENT SERVICES Academic or career counseling, employment services for current students, placement services for program completers.

Educational Technical College–Recinto de San Sebastian

Calle Hosto, #20, San Sebastian, PR 00769

CONTACT Miriam Benites, President
Telephone: 787-825-0370

GENERAL INFORMATION Private Institution. **Total program enrollment:** 302. **Application fee:** $25.

PROGRAM(S) OFFERED
• **Apparel and Textile Manufacture** • **Business/Commerce, General** *49 students enrolled* • **Computer Installation and Repair Technology/Technician** *51 hrs./$4975* • **Cosmetology/Cosmetologist, General** *57 hrs./$4975* • **Electrician** *49 hrs./$4975* • **Emergency Medical Technology/Technician (EMT Paramedic)** *56 hrs./$4975* • **Medical Administrative/Executive Assistant and Medical Secretary** *51 hrs./$4975* • **Respiratory Care Therapy/Therapist** *9 students enrolled* • **Respiratory Therapy Technician/Assistant** *70 hrs./$6338*

STUDENT SERVICES Academic or career counseling, employment services for current students, placement services for program completers.

Emma's Beauty Academy

Bo Amuelas Sector Guanabanos Carr 149 Km 5.7, Juana Diaz, PR 00794

CONTACT Jose H. Cuevas, President
Telephone: 787-837-0303

GENERAL INFORMATION Private Institution. **Total program enrollment:** 436. **Application fee:** $25.

PROGRAM(S) OFFERED
• **Aesthetician/Esthetician and Skin Care Specialist** *36 hrs./$7442* • **Barbering/Barber** *36 hrs./$7442* • **Cosmetology/Cosmetologist, General** *48 hrs./$10,830* • **Hair Styling/Stylist and Hair Design** *36 hrs./$7442* • **Make-Up Artist/Specialist** *24 hrs./$4982* • **Nail Technician/Specialist and Manicurist** *30 hrs./$5117*

STUDENT SERVICES Academic or career counseling, employment services for current students, placement services for program completers.

Emma's Beauty Academy

Calle Munoz Rivera 9 Oeste, Mayagüez, PR 00680
http://www.emmasbeautyacademy.com/

CONTACT Carlos Ramos Camara, Vice President
Telephone: 787-833-0980

GENERAL INFORMATION Private Institution. **Total program enrollment:** 466. **Application fee:** $25.

PROGRAM(S) OFFERED
• **Aesthetician/Esthetician and Skin Care Specialist** *36 hrs./$7780* • **Barbering/Barber** *36 hrs./$7774* • **Cosmetology/Cosmetologist, General** *42 hrs./$9595* • **Hair Styling/Stylist and Hair Design** *900 hrs./$5004* • **Make-Up Artist/Specialist** *600 hrs./$3314*

STUDENT SERVICES Academic or career counseling, placement services for program completers, remedial services.

Escuela de Peritos Electricitas de Isabel

PO Box 457, Avenue Aguadilla 242, Isabel, PR 00662

CONTACT Juan Santiago, Presidente
Telephone: 787-830-4267

GENERAL INFORMATION Private Institution. **Total program enrollment:** 101. **Application fee:** $25.

PROGRAM(S) OFFERED
• **Electrician** *1020 hrs./$7063* • **Heating, Air Conditioning and Refrigeration Technology/Technician (ACH/ACR/ACHR/HRAC/HVAC/AC Technology)** *1000 hrs./$5863*

STUDENT SERVICES Placement services for program completers, remedial services.

Escuela Hotelera de San Juan in Puerto Rico

Calle Guayama 229, Hato Rey, PR 00917
http://www.escuelahotelera.com/

CONTACT Mrs. Sylvia Cestero León, President
Telephone: 787-759-7599 Ext. 206

GENERAL INFORMATION Private Institution. **Total program enrollment:** 290. **Application fee:** $100.

PROGRAM(S) OFFERED
• **Baking and Pastry Arts/Baker/Pastry Chef** *53 students enrolled* • **Culinary Arts and Related Services, Other** *287 students enrolled*

STUDENT SERVICES Employment services for current students, placement services for program completers.

Escuela Tecnica de Electricidad

Villa Street 190, Ponce, PR 00731
http://www.etepr.edu/

CONTACT Jose A. Santiago, Executive Director
Telephone: 787-843-7100

GENERAL INFORMATION Private Institution. **Total program enrollment:** 420. **Application fee:** $50.

PROGRAM(S) OFFERED
• **Electrical and Electronic Engineering Technologies/Technicians, Other** *305 students enrolled* • **Heating, Air Conditioning and Refrigeration Technology/ Technician (ACH/ACR/ACHR/HRAC/HVAC/AC Technology)** *39 students enrolled* • **Heavy/Industrial Equipment Maintenance Technologies, Other** *6 students enrolled*

STUDENT SERVICES Employment services for current students, placement services for program completers.

Globelle Technical Institute

114 Calle Marginal Monte Carlo, Vega Baja, PR 00693-4218

CONTACT Gloria E. Cruz Lugo, Administrator
Telephone: 787-858-0236

GENERAL INFORMATION Private Institution. **Total program enrollment:** 94.

PROGRAM(S) OFFERED
• **Computer and Information Sciences, General** *21 students enrolled* • **Cosmetology/Cosmetologist, General** *6 students enrolled* • **Food Preparation/ Professional Cooking/Kitchen Assistant** *17 students enrolled*

STUDENT SERVICES Academic or career counseling, employment services for current students, placement services for program completers.

Hispanic American College

Avenue Campo Rico Go 9 & Go 10 Country Club, Carolina, PR 00982

CONTACT Richard Thompson Parker, President
Telephone: 787-258-4758

GENERAL INFORMATION Private Institution. **Total program enrollment:** 270. **Application fee:** $30.

PROGRAM(S) OFFERED
• **Aesthetician/Esthetician and Skin Care Specialist** *36 hrs./$7946* • **Barbering/ Barber** *36 hrs./$8546* • **Computer Programming, Other** *36 hrs./$7946* • **Cosmetology/Cosmetologist, General** *36 hrs./$7946* • **Hair Styling/Stylist and Hair Design** *24 hrs./$5204* • **Nail Technician/Specialist and Manicurist** *32 students enrolled* • **Photography** *36 hrs./$7946*

STUDENT SERVICES Academic or career counseling, employment services for current students, placement services for program completers.

Huertas Junior College

PO Box 8429, Caguas, PR 00726
http://www.huertas.edu/

CONTACT Edwin Ramos Rivera, Esq., President
Telephone: 787-746-1400 Ext. 1007

GENERAL INFORMATION Private Institution. Founded 1945. **Accreditation:** Regional (MSA/CIHE); state accredited or approved; health information technology (AHIMA). **Total program enrollment:** 1468. **Application fee:** $25.

PROGRAM(S) OFFERED
• **Computer Installation and Repair Technology/Technician** *44 students enrolled* • **Computer and Information Sciences and Support Services, Other** • **Dental Services and Allied Professions, Other** *15 students enrolled* • **Electrical, Electronic and Communications Engineering Technology/Technician** *47*

students enrolled • **General Office Occupations and Clerical Services** *15 students enrolled* • **Health and Physical Education/Fitness, Other** *48 students enrolled* • **Heating, Air Conditioning and Refrigeration Technology/Technician (ACH/ACR/ACHR/HRAC/HVAC/AC Technology)** *38 students enrolled* • **Legal Assistant/Paralegal** *15 students enrolled* • **Manufacturing Technology/ Technician** *10 students enrolled* • **Massage Therapy/Therapeutic Massage** *42 students enrolled*

STUDENT SERVICES Academic or career counseling, daycare for children of students, employment services for current students, placement services for program completers.

Humacao Community College

PO Box 9139, Humacao, PR 00792

CONTACT Jorge E. Mojica Rodriguez, President
Telephone: 787-852-1430

GENERAL INFORMATION Private Institution. **Accreditation:** State accredited or approved. **Total program enrollment:** 581. **Application fee:** $15.

PROGRAM(S) OFFERED
• **Electrical, Electronics and Communications Engineering** *2 students enrolled* • **Executive Assistant/Executive Secretary** *1 student enrolled* • **Heating, Air Conditioning and Refrigeration Technology/Technician (ACH/ACR/ACHR/HRAC/ HVAC/AC Technology)** *11 students enrolled* • **Medical Administrative/Executive Assistant and Medical Secretary** *8 students enrolled*

STUDENT SERVICES Academic or career counseling, employment services for current students, placement services for program completers, remedial services.

ICPR Junior College–Arecibo Campus

Apartado 140067, Arecibo, PR 00614
http://www.icprjc.edu/

CONTACT Ivette Charriez, Director
Telephone: 787-878-6000

GENERAL INFORMATION Private Institution. **Total program enrollment:** 410. **Application fee:** $25.

PROGRAM(S) OFFERED
• **Child Care Provider/Assistant** *34 students enrolled* • **Computer Technology/ Computer Systems Technology** • **Cooking and Related Culinary Arts, General** *32 students enrolled* • **Hotel/Motel Administration/Management** • **Massage Therapy/Therapeutic Massage** *8 students enrolled* • **Medical Administrative/ Executive Assistant and Medical Secretary** *18 students enrolled* • **Security and Protective Services, Other** *9 students enrolled* • **Web Page, Digital/Multimedia and Information Resources Design** *8 students enrolled*

STUDENT SERVICES Academic or career counseling, employment services for current students, placement services for program completers.

ICPR Junior College–Mayagüez Campus

Apartado 1108, Mayagüez, PR 00681
http://www.icprjc.edu/

CONTACT Luz Milagros Ortiz, Director
Telephone: 787-832-6000

GENERAL INFORMATION Private Institution. **Total program enrollment:** 445. **Application fee:** $25.

PROGRAM(S) OFFERED
• **Child Care Provider/Assistant** *28 students enrolled* • **Computer Technology/ Computer Systems Technology** *18 students enrolled* • **Cooking and Related Culinary Arts, General** *17 students enrolled* • **Massage Therapy/Therapeutic Massage** *3 students enrolled* • **Medical Administrative/Executive Assistant and**

ICPR Junior College–Mayagüez Campus (continued)

Medical Secretary *7 students enrolled* • **Security and Protective Services, Other** *6 students enrolled* • **Tourism Promotion Operations** *5 students enrolled* • **Web Page, Digital/Multimedia and Information Resources Design** *2 students enrolled*

STUDENT SERVICES Academic or career counseling, employment services for current students, placement services for program completers.

Industrial Technical College

No 16 Carreras Street, Humacao, PR 00791

CONTACT Jorge Davila, President
Telephone: 787-852-8806

GENERAL INFORMATION Private Institution. **Total program enrollment:** 210. **Application fee:** $25.

PROGRAM(S) OFFERED
• **Apparel and Textile Manufacture** *15 students enrolled* • **Automobile/Automotive Mechanics Technology/Technician** *21 students enrolled* • **Electrician** *6 students enrolled* • **Heating, Air Conditioning and Refrigeration Technology/Technician (ACH/ACR/ACHR/HRAC/HVAC/AC Technology)** *5 students enrolled* • **Industrial Mechanics and Maintenance Technology** *25 students enrolled*

STUDENT SERVICES Employment services for current students, placement services for program completers.

Institute of Beauty Careers

Avenue Llorens Torres, Suite 199, PO Box 809, Arecibo, PR 00613

CONTACT Magaly Gonzalez, Fiscal Officer
Telephone: 787-878-2880

GENERAL INFORMATION Private Institution. Founded 1969. **Total program enrollment:** 555. **Application fee:** $25.

PROGRAM(S) OFFERED
• **Aesthetician/Esthetician and Skin Care Specialist** *33 hrs./$6995* • **Barbering/Barber** *33 hrs./$6995* • **Cosmetology and Related Personal Grooming Arts, Other** *30 hrs./$6600* • **Cosmetology/Cosmetologist, General** *33 hrs./$7295* • **Hair Styling/Stylist and Hair Design** *30 hrs./$6600* • **Massage Therapy/Therapeutic Massage** *33 hrs./$6995*

STUDENT SERVICES Academic or career counseling, employment services for current students, placement services for program completers.

Institute of Beauty Occupations and Technology

500 Calle Concepcion Vera, Moca, PR 00676

CONTACT Ivette Acevedo Soto, Chief Executive Officer
Telephone: 787-818-0355

GENERAL INFORMATION Private Institution. **Total program enrollment:** 31. **Application fee:** $30.

PROGRAM(S) OFFERED
• **Barbering/Barber** *42 hrs./$9355* • **Cosmetology/Cosmetologist, General** *42 hrs./$9955*

STUDENT SERVICES Placement services for program completers, remedial services.

Instituto Chaviano de Mayagüez

Calle Ramos Antonini 116, Este, Mayagüez, PR 00608-5045

CONTACT Jaime Torres Paulino, Executive Director
Telephone: 787-833-2474

GENERAL INFORMATION Private Institution. Founded 1976. **Total program enrollment:** 56. **Application fee:** $25.

PROGRAM(S) OFFERED
• **Apparel and Textile Manufacture** *15 students enrolled* • **Apparel and Textile Marketing Management** • **Apparel and Textiles, General** *3 students enrolled*

• **Cosmetology, Barber/Styling, and Nail Instructor** • **Cosmetology/Cosmetologist, General** • **Medical Administrative/Executive Assistant and Medical Secretary** *10 students enrolled* • **Special Products Marketing Operations** *27 students enrolled* • **Upholstery/Upholsterer** *21 students enrolled*

STUDENT SERVICES Academic or career counseling, employment services for current students, placement services for program completers.

Instituto Comercial de Puerto Rico Junior College

558 Munoz Rivera Avenue, PO Box 190304, San Juan, PR 00919-0304
http://www.icprjc.edu/

CONTACT Olga Rivera, President/CEO
Telephone: 787-753-6000

GENERAL INFORMATION Private Institution. Founded 1946. **Accreditation:** Regional (MSA/CIHE). **Total program enrollment:** 436. **Application fee:** $25.

PROGRAM(S) OFFERED
• **Child Care and Support Services Management** *18 students enrolled* • **Cooking and Related Culinary Arts, General** *23 students enrolled* • **Massage Therapy/Therapeutic Massage** *4 students enrolled* • **Medical Administrative/Executive Assistant and Medical Secretary** *6 students enrolled* • **Security and Protective Services, Other** *5 students enrolled* • **Web Page, Digital/Multimedia and Information Resources Design** *4 students enrolled*

STUDENT SERVICES Academic or career counseling, employment services for current students, placement services for program completers.

Instituto de Banca y Comercio–Aprendes Practicanco

Avenue Munoz Rivera 996, Río Piedras, PR 00925
http://www.ibanca.net/

CONTACT Guillermo Nigaglioni, CEO
Telephone: 787-982-3000

GENERAL INFORMATION Private Institution. Founded 1975. **Total program enrollment:** 10910. **Application fee:** $25.

PROGRAM(S) OFFERED
• **Administrative Assistant and Secretarial Science, General** *54 hrs./$8105* • **Baking and Pastry Arts/Baker/Pastry Chef** *102 students enrolled* • **Banking and Financial Support Services** *54 hrs./$8105* • **Barbering/Barber** *426 students enrolled* • **Bartending/Bartender** *7 students enrolled* • **Computer Systems Networking and Telecommunications** *301 students enrolled* • **Computer Technology/Computer Systems Technology** *176 students enrolled* • **Cosmetology/Cosmetologist, General** *54 hrs./$8480* • **Culinary Arts/Chef Training** *54 hrs./$8180* • **Dental Assisting/Assistant** *14 students enrolled* • **Drafting and Design Technology/Technician, General** *200 students enrolled* • **Electrical and Electronic Engineering Technologies/Technicians, Other** *54 hrs./$8130* • **Emergency Medical Technology/Technician (EMT Paramedic)** *381 students enrolled* • **Hair Styling/Stylist and Hair Design** *22 students enrolled* • **Heating, Air Conditioning and Refrigeration Technology/Technician (ACH/ACR/ACHR/HRAC/HVAC/AC Technology)** *229 students enrolled* • **Licensed Practical/Vocational Nurse Training (LPN, LVN, Cert, Dipl, AAS)** *54 hrs./$8080* • **Massage Therapy/Therapeutic Massage** *19 students enrolled* • **Medical Administrative/Executive Assistant and Medical Secretary** *615 students enrolled* • **Nail Technician/Specialist and Manicurist** *362 students enrolled* • **Plumbing Technology/Plumber** *149 students enrolled* • **Respiratory Care Therapy/Therapist** *134 students enrolled* • **Surgical Technology/Technologist** *161 students enrolled* • **Tourism Promotion Operations** *189 students enrolled*

STUDENT SERVICES Academic or career counseling, employment services for current students, placement services for program completers, remedial services.

Instituto de Educacion Tecnica Ocupacional La Reine

Calle Mercedes Moreno, #9, Aguadilla, PR 00603

CONTACT Carmen Ocasio, Chief Executive
Telephone: 787-819-0222

GENERAL INFORMATION Private Institution. **Total program enrollment:** 185. **Application fee:** $35.

PROGRAM(S) OFFERED
• **Aesthetician/Esthetician and Skin Care Specialist** *900 hrs./$5180*
• **Barbering/Barber** *48 hrs./$7600* • **Cosmetology/Cosmetologist, General** *48 hrs./$7664* • **Culinary Arts/Chef Training** *48 hrs./$7600* • **Hair Styling/Stylist and Hair Design** *48 hrs./$7625*

STUDENT SERVICES Academic or career counseling, placement services for program completers.

Instituto de Educacion Tecnica Ocupacional La Reine

Avenida Colon A 8, Manati, PR 00674-0000

CONTACT Carmen Ocasio, Director
Telephone: 787-854-1119

GENERAL INFORMATION Private Institution. **Total program enrollment:** 391. **Application fee:** $35.

PROGRAM(S) OFFERED
• **Aesthetician/Esthetician and Skin Care Specialist** *1100 hrs./$6275*
• **Barbering/Barber** *48 hrs./$7600* • **Cosmetology/Cosmetologist, General** *48 hrs./$7664* • **Culinary Arts/Chef Training** *48 hrs./$7600* • **Hair Styling/Stylist and Hair Design** *48 hrs./$7625* • **Plumbing Technology/Plumber** *52 hrs./$7625*

STUDENT SERVICES Academic or career counseling, placement services for program completers.

Instituto Educativo Premier

Calle Isabel #15, Ponce, PR 00731

CONTACT Nancy Valedon, On Site Director
Telephone: 787-840-0919

GENERAL INFORMATION Private Institution. **Total program enrollment:** 26. **Application fee:** $100.

PROGRAM(S) OFFERED
• **Accounting and Computer Science** *44 hrs./$5425* • **Computer Installation and Repair Technology/Technician** *46 hrs./$6229* • **Word Processing** *1200 hrs./$6200*

STUDENT SERVICES Placement services for program completers.

Instituto Merlix

Box 6241, Station One, Calle Betances 24, Bayamón, PR 00961-9998

CONTACT Felix M. Vargas, Executive Director
Telephone: 787-786-7035 Ext. 26

GENERAL INFORMATION Private Institution. **Total program enrollment:** 116. **Application fee:** $25.

PROGRAM(S) OFFERED
• **Apparel and Textiles, Other** *900 hrs./$5950* • **Banking and Financial Support Services** *5 students enrolled* • **Cosmetology/Cosmetologist, General** *1200 hrs./ $6800* • **Data Processing and Data Processing Technology/Technician** *900 hrs./$5950* • **Floriculture/Floristry Operations and Management** *900 hrs./ $5950* • **Medical Insurance Specialist/Medical Biller** *900 hrs./$5950* • **Nail Technician/Specialist and Manicurist** *600 hrs./$4495*

STUDENT SERVICES Academic or career counseling, employment services for current students, placement services for program completers.

Instituto Pre-Vocacional E Indust de Puerto Rico

Calle Eugenio Maria De Hostos Esq, Puro Girau #175, Arecibo, PR 00612

CONTACT Nilsa Lopez, Executive Director
Telephone: 787-879-3300

GENERAL INFORMATION Private Institution. **Total program enrollment:** 109. **Application fee:** $15.

PROGRAM(S) OFFERED
• **Administrative Assistant and Secretarial Science, General** • **Drafting and Design Technology/Technician, General** *11 students enrolled* • **Electrician** *21 students enrolled* • **Executive Assistant/Executive Secretary** *5 students enrolled* • **Heating, Air Conditioning and Refrigeration Technology/Technician (ACH/ACR/ACHR/HRAC/HVAC/AC Technology)** *16 students enrolled* • **Respiratory Care Therapy/Therapist** *16 students enrolled*

STUDENT SERVICES Academic or career counseling, daycare for children of students, employment services for current students, placement services for program completers, remedial services.

Instituto Vocacional Aurea E. Mendez

14 Intendente Ramirez Street, Caguas, PR 00725-0000
http://www.ivaempr.com/

CONTACT Luis A. Herrera Mendez, President
Telephone: 787-743-5327 Ext. 24

GENERAL INFORMATION Private Institution. **Total program enrollment:** 186. **Application fee:** $50.

PROGRAM(S) OFFERED
• **Baking and Pastry Arts/Baker/Pastry Chef** *36 hrs./$7740* • **Bartending/Bartender** *24 hrs./$4800* • **Culinary Arts/Chef Training** *36 hrs./$8290*

STUDENT SERVICES Academic or career counseling, employment services for current students, placement services for program completers.

Instituto Vocational y Commercial EDIC

Calle 8, Equina 5 Urb., Box 9120, Caguas, PR 00726
http://www.ediccollege.com/

CONTACT Jose A. Cartagena, Director
Telephone: 787-744-8519

GENERAL INFORMATION Private Institution. **Total program enrollment:** 618. **Application fee:** $25.

PROGRAM(S) OFFERED
• **Cardiovascular Technology/Technologist** *78 students enrolled* • **Emergency Medical Technology/Technician (EMT Paramedic)** *22 students enrolled* • **Kindergarten/Preschool Education and Teaching** *40 students enrolled* • **Licensed Practical/Vocational Nurse Training (LPN, LVN, Cert, Dipl, AAS)** *53 students enrolled* • **Medical Administrative/Executive Assistant and Medical Secretary** *57 students enrolled* • **Respiratory Therapy Technician/Assistant** *16 students enrolled* • **Surgical Technology/Technologist** *79 students enrolled*

STUDENT SERVICES Academic or career counseling, employment services for current students, placement services for program completers, remedial services.

Inter American University of Puerto Rico, Aguadilla Campus

Call Box 20000, Aguadilla, PR 00605
http://www.aguadilla.inter.edu/

CONTACT Dr. Elie A. Agesilas, Chancellor
Telephone: 787-891-0925 Ext. 2100

GENERAL INFORMATION Private Institution. Founded 1957. **Accreditation:** Regional (MSA/CIHE). **Total program enrollment:** 3750.

PROGRAM(S) OFFERED
• **Baking and Pastry Arts/Baker/Pastry Chef** *5 students enrolled* • **CAD/CADD Drafting and/or Design Technology/Technician** *14 students enrolled* • **Child**

Inter American University of Puerto Rico, Aguadilla Campus (continued)

Care Provider/Assistant ● Computer and Information Sciences, Other *19 students enrolled* ● Foodservice Systems Administration/Management *23 students enrolled* ● Medical Insurance Specialist/Medical Biller *11 students enrolled* ● Pharmacy Technician/Assistant *8 students enrolled*

STUDENT SERVICES Academic or career counseling, employment services for current students, placement services for program completers, remedial services.

Inter American University of Puerto Rico, Arecibo Campus

PO Box 4050, Arecibo, PR 00614-4050
http://www.arecibo.inter.edu/

CONTACT Dr. Rafael Ramirez-Rivera, Chancellor
Telephone: 787-878-5475 Ext. 2268

GENERAL INFORMATION Private Institution. Founded 1957. Accreditation: Regional (MSA/CIHE). Total program enrollment: 3769.

PROGRAM(S) OFFERED
● Clinical/Medical Laboratory Science and Allied Professions, Other *8 students enrolled*

STUDENT SERVICES Academic or career counseling, employment services for current students, placement services for program completers, remedial services.

Inter American University of Puerto Rico, Barranquitas Campus

PO Box 517, Barranquitas, PR 00794
http://www.br.inter.edu/

CONTACT Dr. Irene Fernandez, Chancellor
Telephone: 787-857-3600 Ext. 2011

GENERAL INFORMATION Private Institution. Founded 1957. Accreditation: Regional (MSA/CIHE). Total program enrollment: 1864.

PROGRAM(S) OFFERED
● Photographic and Film/Video Technology/Technician and Assistant

STUDENT SERVICES Academic or career counseling, employment services for current students, placement services for program completers, remedial services.

Inter American University of Puerto Rico, Bayamón Campus

500 Road 830, Bayamón, PR 00957
http://www.bc.inter.edu/

CONTACT Prof. Juan F. Martinez, Chancellor
Telephone: 787-279-1912

GENERAL INFORMATION Private Institution. Founded 1912. Accreditation: Regional (MSA/CIHE). Total program enrollment: 4533.

PROGRAM(S) OFFERED
● Accounting Technology/Technician and Bookkeeping *3 students enrolled* ● Business Operations Support and Secretarial Services, Other *1 student enrolled* ● Child Care Provider/Assistant *3 students enrolled* ● Computer and Information Sciences, Other *6 students enrolled* ● Foodservice Systems Administration/Management *10 students enrolled* ● Hospital and Health Care Facilities Administration/Management ● Medical Insurance Specialist/Medical Biller *3 students enrolled* ● Photographic and Film/Video Technology/Technician and Assistant *3 students enrolled* ● Small Business Administration/

Management *3 students enrolled* ● Specialized Merchandising, Sales, and Marketing Operations, Other *4 students enrolled* ● Web Page, Digital/Multimedia and Information Resources Design *2 students enrolled*

STUDENT SERVICES Academic or career counseling, daycare for children of students, employment services for current students, placement services for program completers.

Inter American University of Puerto Rico, Fajardo Campus

Call Box 70003, Fajardo, PR 00738-7003
http://www.fajardo.inter.edu/

CONTACT Dr. Ismael Suarez, Chancellor
Telephone: 787-863-2390

GENERAL INFORMATION Private Institution. Founded 1965. Accreditation: Regional (MSA/CIHE). Total program enrollment: 1787.

STUDENT SERVICES Academic or career counseling, employment services for current students, placement services for program completers, remedial services.

Inter American University of Puerto Rico, Guayama Campus

Call Box 10004, Guayama, PR 00785
http://www.guayama.inter.edu/

CONTACT Prof. Carlos E. Colon-Ramos, Chancellor
Telephone: 787-864-2222

GENERAL INFORMATION Private Institution. Founded 1958. Accreditation: Regional (MSA/CIHE). Total program enrollment: 1782.

PROGRAM(S) OFFERED
● Medical Insurance Specialist/Medical Biller *8 students enrolled* ● Pharmacy Technician/Assistant *10 students enrolled*

STUDENT SERVICES Academic or career counseling, employment services for current students, placement services for program completers, remedial services.

Inter American University of Puerto Rico, Metropolitan Campus

PO Box 191293, San Juan, PR 00919-1293
http://metro.inter.edu/

CONTACT Prof. Marilina Wayland, Chancellor
Telephone: 787-250-1912

GENERAL INFORMATION Private Institution. Founded 1960. Accreditation: Regional (MSA/CIHE); medical technology (NAACLS). Total program enrollment: 7758.

PROGRAM(S) OFFERED
● Child Care Provider/Assistant *11 students enrolled* ● Computer Systems Networking and Telecommunications *1 student enrolled* ● Computer and Information Sciences, Other *9 students enrolled* ● Emergency Medical Technology/Technician (EMT Paramedic) *4 students enrolled* ● Medical Insurance Specialist/Medical Biller ● Small Business Administration/Management *4 students enrolled*

STUDENT SERVICES Academic or career counseling, daycare for children of students, employment services for current students, remedial services.

Inter American University of Puerto Rico, Ponce Campus

104 Industrial Park Turpò RD 1, Mercedita, PR 00715-1602
http://www.ponce.inter.edu/

CONTACT Dra. Vilma Colon, Chancellor
Telephone: 787-284-1912

GENERAL INFORMATION Private Institution. Founded 1962. **Accreditation:** Regional (MSA/CIHE). **Total program enrollment:** 4872.

PROGRAM(S) OFFERED
● **Child Care Provider/Assistant** 3 *students enrolled* ● **Computer Installation and Repair Technology/Technician** 8 *students enrolled* ● **Foodservice Systems Administration/Management** 9 *students enrolled* ● **Medical Insurance Specialist/Medical Biller** 4 *students enrolled* ● **Pharmacy Technician/Assistant** 20 *students enrolled*

STUDENT SERVICES Academic or career counseling, daycare for children of students, employment services for current students, remedial services.

Inter American University of Puerto Rico, San Germán Campus

PO Box 5100, San Germán, PR 00683-5008
http://www.sg.inter.edu/

CONTACT Prof. Agnes Mojica, Chancellor
Telephone: 787-264-1912

GENERAL INFORMATION Private Institution. Founded 1912. **Accreditation:** Regional (MSA/CIHE); health information technology (AHIMA); medical technology (NAACLS). **Total program enrollment:** 4638.

PROGRAM(S) OFFERED
● **CAD/CADD Drafting and/or Design Technology/Technician** 6 *students enrolled* ● **Computer and Information Sciences, Other** 7 *students enrolled* ● **Electrical, Electronic and Communications Engineering Technology/Technician** 18 *students enrolled* ● **Hotel/Motel Administration/Management** 2 *students enrolled* ● **Medical Insurance Specialist/Medical Biller** 9 *students enrolled* ● **Pharmacy Technician/Assistant** 22 *students enrolled* ● **Respiratory Therapy Technician/Assistant** 7 *students enrolled*

STUDENT SERVICES Academic or career counseling, daycare for children of students, employment services for current students, placement services for program completers, remedial services.

Inter American University of Puerto Rico System

GPO Box 363255, San Juan, PR 00936-3255
http://www.inter.edu/

CONTACT Lic. Manuel J. Fernos, President
Telephone: 787-766-1912

GENERAL INFORMATION Private Institution.

International Technical College

104 Loaiza Cordero Street, San Juan, PR 00918
http://intecpr.com/

CONTACT Liza Y. Hernandez-Cortiella, President
Telephone: 787-767-8389

GENERAL INFORMATION Private Institution. **Total program enrollment:** 136. **Application fee:** $20.

PROGRAM(S) OFFERED
● **Accounting** 1 *student enrolled* ● **Administrative Assistant and Secretarial Science, General** 8 *students enrolled* ● **Computer Installation and Repair Technology/Technician** 47 *hrs./$8035* ● **Computer Systems Networking and Telecommunications** 48 *hrs./$8035* ● **Electrical/Electronics Equipment Instal-**lation and Repair, General 46 *hrs./$8035* ● **Electrical/Electronics Maintenance and Repair Technology, Other** 50 *hrs./$8335* ● **Health Information/Medical Records Technology/Technician** 53 *hrs./$8035* ● **Medical Insurance Specialist/ Medical Biller** 55 *hrs./$3058*

STUDENT SERVICES Academic or career counseling, employment services for current students, placement services for program completers.

John Dewey College

Industrial Park Corujo 2446 Road #2, Bayamón, PR 00959
http://www.johndeweycollegepr.com/

CONTACT lLuis Santiago, Director
Telephone: 787-778-1200

GENERAL INFORMATION Private Institution. **Total program enrollment:** 1156. **Application fee:** $15.

PROGRAM(S) OFFERED
● **Administrative Assistant and Secretarial Science, General** 34 *students enrolled* ● **Automobile/Automotive Mechanics Technology/Technician** 36 *students enrolled* ● **Barbering/Barber** 19 *students enrolled* ● **Child Care Provider/ Assistant** 56 *students enrolled* ● **Computer Software and Media Applications, Other** ● **Computer Technology/Computer Systems Technology** 34 *students enrolled* ● **Cosmetology/Cosmetologist, General** 20 *students enrolled* ● **Data Entry/Microcomputer Applications, General** ● **Electrician** 31 *students enrolled* ● **Heating, Air Conditioning and Refrigeration Technology/Technician (ACH/ ACR/ACHR/HRAC/HVAC/AC Technology)** 28 *students enrolled* ● **Medical Administrative/Executive Assistant and Medical Secretary** 45 *students enrolled* ● **Nurse/Nursing Assistant/Aide and Patient Care Assistant** 32 *students enrolled* ● **Plumbing Technology/Plumber** ● **Receptionist**

STUDENT SERVICES Academic or career counseling, placement services for program completers, remedial services.

John Dewey College

427 Barbosa Ave., Hato Rey, PR 00910-9538
http://www.johndeweycollegepr.com/

CONTACT Carlos A. Quiones Alfonso, President
Telephone: 787-753-0039

GENERAL INFORMATION Private Institution. **Total program enrollment:** 1069. **Application fee:** $15.

PROGRAM(S) OFFERED
● **Administrative Assistant and Secretarial Science, General** 53 *students enrolled* ● **Barbering/Barber** 15 *students enrolled* ● **Child Care Provider/Assistant** 88 *students enrolled* ● **Computer Technology/Computer Systems Technology** 28 *students enrolled* ● **Cosmetology/Cosmetologist, General** 66 *students enrolled* ● **Data Entry/Microcomputer Applications, General** ● **Electrical, Electronic and Communications Engineering Technology/Technician** 33 *students enrolled* ● **Heating, Air Conditioning and Refrigeration Technology/Technician (ACH/ ACR/ACHR/HRAC/HVAC/AC Technology)** 32 *students enrolled* ● **Medical Reception/Receptionist** 53 *students enrolled* ● **Plumbing Technology/Plumber** 5 *students enrolled* ● **Receptionist**

STUDENT SERVICES Academic or career counseling, employment services for current students, placement services for program completers, remedial services.

John Dewey College

Bo. Palmas, Road 3, Km. 129.7, Arroyo, PR 00910

CONTACT Hector Dávila, Branch Director
Telephone: 787-271-1515

GENERAL INFORMATION Private Institution. **Total program enrollment:** 270. **Application fee:** $15.

PROGRAM(S) OFFERED
● **Administrative Assistant and Secretarial Science, General** 13 *students enrolled* ● **Barbering/Barber** 6 *students enrolled* ● **Child Care Provider/Assistant** 24 *students enrolled* ● **Computer Technology/Computer Systems Technology** 7 *students enrolled* ● **Cosmetology/Cosmetologist, General** 10 *students enrolled*

John Dewey College (continued)

• **Electrician** *19 students enrolled* • **Family Practice Nurse/Nurse Practitioner** *20 students enrolled* • **Heating, Air Conditioning and Refrigeration Technology/Technician (ACH/ACR/ACHR/HRAC/HVAC/AC Technology)** *18 students enrolled* • **Medical Administrative/Executive Assistant and Medical Secretary** *19 students enrolled* • **Plumbing Technology/Plumber** *4 students enrolled* • **Receptionist**

STUDENT SERVICES Academic or career counseling, employment services for current students, placement services for program completers, remedial services.

John Dewey College

Boad 3 Compound 11, Lot 7, Carolina Industrial Park, Carolina, PR 00986

http://www.johndeweycollegepr.com/

CONTACT Luis A. Santiago, President
Telephone: 787-753-1515

GENERAL INFORMATION Private Institution. **Total program enrollment:** 876. **Application fee:** $15.

PROGRAM(S) OFFERED
• **Administrative Assistant and Secretarial Science, General** *29 students enrolled* • **Automobile/Automotive Mechanics Technology/Technician** *62 students enrolled* • **Child Care Provider/Assistant** *93 students enrolled* • **Computer Software and Media Applications, Other** • **Computer Systems Analysis/Analyst** • **Computer Technology/Computer Systems Technology** *63 students enrolled* • **Cosmetology, Barber/Styling, and Nail Instructor** *7 students enrolled* • **Cosmetology/Cosmetologist, General** *34 students enrolled* • **Data Entry/Microcomputer Applications, General** • **Electrician** *36 students enrolled* • **Heating, Air Conditioning and Refrigeration Technology/Technician (ACH/ACR/ACHR/HRAC/HVAC/AC Technology)** *50 students enrolled* • **Medical Administrative/Executive Assistant and Medical Secretary** *58 students enrolled* • **Plumbing Technology/Plumber** *11 students enrolled* • **Receptionist**

STUDENT SERVICES Academic or career counseling, employment services for current students, placement services for program completers, remedial services.

John Dewey College

267 Valero Street, Fajardo, PR 00910

CONTACT Rosalind Martínez, Branch Director
Telephone: 787-860-1212

GENERAL INFORMATION Private Institution. **Total program enrollment:** 342. **Application fee:** $15.

PROGRAM(S) OFFERED
• **Administrative Assistant and Secretarial Science, General** *13 students enrolled* • **Automobile/Automotive Mechanics Technology/Technician** *61 students enrolled* • **Barbering/Barber** *5 students enrolled* • **Child Care Provider/Assistant** *33 students enrolled* • **Computer Technology/Computer Systems Technology** *13 students enrolled* • **Cosmetology/Cosmetologist, General** *22 students enrolled* • **Electrician** *6 students enrolled* • **Heating, Air Conditioning and Refrigeration Technology/Technician (ACH/ACR/ACHR/HRAC/HVAC/AC Technology)** *3 students enrolled* • **Medical Administrative/Executive Assistant and Medical Secretary** *21 students enrolled* • **Plumbing Technology/Plumber** *4 students enrolled* • **Receptionist**

STUDENT SERVICES Academic or career counseling, employment services for current students, placement services for program completers, remedial services.

John Dewey College

Bo. Lomas, Road 149, Km. 67.02, Juana Diaz, PR 00910

CONTACT Aracelis Melendez, Branch Director
Telephone: 787-260-1023 Ext. 0

GENERAL INFORMATION Private Institution. **Total program enrollment:** 542. **Application fee:** $15.

PROGRAM(S) OFFERED
• **Administrative Assistant and Secretarial Science, General** *7 students enrolled* • **Barbering/Barber** *18 students enrolled* • **Child Care Provider/Assistant** *16 students enrolled* • **Computer Software and Media Applications, Other** *20 students enrolled* • **Cosmetology/Cosmetologist, General** *20 students enrolled* • **Data Entry/Microcomputer Applications, General** • **Electrician** *47 students enrolled* • **Heating, Air Conditioning and Refrigeration Technology/Technician (ACH/ACR/ACHR/HRAC/HVAC/AC Technology)** *27 students enrolled* • **Medical Administrative/Executive Assistant and Medical Secretary** *47 students enrolled*

STUDENT SERVICES Academic or career counseling, placement services for program completers, remedial services.

Leston College

Calle Dr. Veve, #52, Bayamón, PR 00961

CONTACT Angel A. Garcia Caban, President
Telephone: 787-787-9661

GENERAL INFORMATION Private Institution. **Total program enrollment:** 116. **Application fee:** $25.

PROGRAM(S) OFFERED
• **Barbering/Barber** *1000 hrs./$6068* • **Cosmetology/Cosmetologist, General** *1000 hrs./$6233* • **Nail Technician/Specialist and Manicurist** *600 hrs./$3671*

STUDENT SERVICES Placement services for program completers.

Liceo de Arte y Disenos

47 Acosta Street, PO Box 1889, Caguas, PR 00626-1889

CONTACT Betty Caban, Presidente
Telephone: 787-743-7447 Ext. 29

GENERAL INFORMATION Private Institution. Founded 1985. **Total program enrollment:** 410. **Application fee:** $50.

PROGRAM(S) OFFERED
• **Apparel and Textile Manufacture** *42 students enrolled* • **Apparel and Textiles, Other** *6 students enrolled* • **Barbering/Barber** *151 students enrolled* • **Child Care and Support Services Management** *156 students enrolled* • **Computer Programming/Programmer, General** • **Cosmetology/Cosmetologist, General** *284 students enrolled* • **Medical Administrative/Executive Assistant and Medical Secretary** *147 students enrolled* • **Special Products Marketing Operations** *62 students enrolled*

STUDENT SERVICES Academic or career counseling, placement services for program completers, remedial services.

Liceo de Arte y Tecnologia

405 Ponce de Leon Avenue, Hato Rey, PR 00919-2346

http://www.liceopr.com/

CONTACT Carlos Manzanal, President
Telephone: 787-999-2473 Ext. 2246

GENERAL INFORMATION Private Institution. **Total program enrollment:** 1517. **Application fee:** $25.

PROGRAM(S) OFFERED
• **Administrative Assistant and Secretarial Science, General** *9 students enrolled* • **Automobile/Automotive Mechanics Technology/Technician** *107 students enrolled* • **CAD/CADD Drafting and/or Design Technology/Technician** *154 students enrolled* • **Electrician** *103 students enrolled* • **Heating, Air Conditioning, Ventilation and Refrigeration Maintenance Technology/Technician (HAC, HACR, HVAC, HVACR)** *85 students enrolled* • **Vehicle Maintenance and Repair Technologies, Other**

STUDENT SERVICES Placement services for program completers, remedial services.

Maison D'esthetique Academy

Ponce De Leon 904, Stop 14, San Juan, PR 00907

CONTACT Carlos R. Montano, President
Telephone: 787-723-4672

GENERAL INFORMATION Private Institution. **Total program enrollment:** 219. **Application fee:** $25.

PROGRAM(S) OFFERED
• **Aesthetician/Esthetician and Skin Care Specialist** 30 hrs./$5825 • **Barbering/Barber** 33 hrs./$6410 • **Cosmetology/Cosmetologist, General** 40 hrs./$7800 • **Facial Treatment Specialist/Facialist** 30 hrs./$5825 • **Massage Therapy/Therapeutic Massage** 33 hrs./$6560

STUDENT SERVICES Academic or career counseling, employment services for current students, placement services for program completers, remedial services.

MBTI Business Training Institute

1256 Ponce de Leon Avenue, Santurce, PR 00907-3917
http://www.mbtipr.com/

CONTACT Barbara Alonso, President
Telephone: 787-723-9403

GENERAL INFORMATION Private Institution. **Total program enrollment:** 520. **Application fee:** $25.

PROGRAM(S) OFFERED
• **Accounting Technology/Technician and Bookkeeping** 54 hrs./$8105 • **Accounting** 6 students enrolled • **Administrative Assistant and Secretarial Science, General** 54 hrs./$8130 • **Banking and Financial Support Services** 54 hrs./$8130 • **Business Administration and Management, General** 54 hrs./$8105 • **Computer Hardware Technology/Technician** 48 students enrolled • **Data Entry/Microcomputer Applications, General** 20 students enrolled • **Legal Administrative Assistant/Secretary** 24 students enrolled • **Medical Administrative/Executive Assistant and Medical Secretary** 54 hrs./$8280 • **Teaching English as a Second or Foreign Language/ESL Language Instructor** 60 students enrolled • **Tourism and Travel Services Management** 54 hrs./$8130

STUDENT SERVICES Academic or career counseling, employment services for current students, placement services for program completers, remedial services.

Modern Hairstyling Institute

Road 174, Building 11, #15, Santa Rosa, Bayamón, PR 00959

CONTACT Israel Berrios, President
Telephone: 787-778-0300

GENERAL INFORMATION Private Institution. Founded 1957. **Total program enrollment:** 139. **Application fee:** $18.

PROGRAM(S) OFFERED
• **Barbering/Barber** 1000 hrs./$6600 • **Cosmetology and Related Personal Grooming Arts, Other** 600 hrs./$4600 • **Cosmetology/Cosmetologist, General** 900 hrs./$6600 • **Nail Technician/Specialist and Manicurist** 600 hrs./$4600

STUDENT SERVICES Academic or career counseling, employment services for current students, placement services for program completers.

Modern Hairstyling Institute

3 De Diego Street, Carolina, PR 00630
http://www.modernhairstylinginstitute.com/

CONTACT Israel N. Berrios, President
Telephone: 787-816-2991

GENERAL INFORMATION Private Institution. Founded 1957. **Total program enrollment:** 48. **Application fee:** $18.

PROGRAM(S) OFFERED
• **Barbering/Barber** 1000 hrs./$6600 • **Cosmetology and Related Personal Grooming Arts, Other** 600 hrs./$4600 • **Cosmetology/Cosmetologist, General** 900 hrs./$6600 • **Nail Technician/Specialist and Manicurist** 600 hrs./$4600

STUDENT SERVICES Academic or career counseling, employment services for current students, placement services for program completers.

Modern Hairstyling Institute

Ave. Fernandez Juncos #60, Carolina, PR 00980
http://www.modernhairstylinginstitute.com/

CONTACT Israel N. Berrios, President
Telephone: 787-778-0300

GENERAL INFORMATION Private Institution. **Total program enrollment:** 159. **Application fee:** $18.

PROGRAM(S) OFFERED
• **Barbering/Barber** 1000 hrs./$6600 • **Cosmetology and Related Personal Grooming Arts, Other** 600 hrs./$4600 • **Cosmetology/Cosmetologist, General** 900 hrs./$6600 • **Massage Therapy/Therapeutic Massage** 1 student enrolled • **Nail Technician/Specialist and Manicurist** 600 hrs./$4600

STUDENT SERVICES Academic or career counseling, employment services for current students, placement services for program completers.

Monteclaro Escuela de Hoteleria y Artes Culinarias

Carr. 955 Km. 4.8 Barrio Palmer, Rio Grande, PR 00721-0000
http://www.monteclaro.edu/

CONTACT Ana T. Garcia, Administrative Director
Telephone: 787-888-1135

GENERAL INFORMATION Private Institution. **Total program enrollment:** 4. **Application fee:** $15.

PROGRAM(S) OFFERED
• **Hospitality Administration/Management, General** 6 students enrolled • **Hospitality Administration/Management, Other** 720 hrs./$5733

STUDENT SERVICES Academic or career counseling, employment services for current students, placement services for program completers.

MyrAngel Beauty Institute

Calle Munoz Rivera, #57 Sur, San Lorenzo, PR 00754

CONTACT Carlos R. Badillo, President
Telephone: 787-736-0435

GENERAL INFORMATION Private Institution. **Total program enrollment:** 122. **Application fee:** $25.

PROGRAM(S) OFFERED
• **Barbering/Barber** 34 hrs./$6895 • **Cosmetology and Related Personal Grooming Arts, Other** 30 hrs./$6095 • **Cosmetology/Cosmetologist, General** 34 hrs./$7195

STUDENT SERVICES Academic or career counseling, employment services for current students, placement services for program completers.

Nova College de Puerto Rico

Box 55016, Station 1, Bayamón, PR 00960

CONTACT Ismael Reyes, CEO
Telephone: 787-740-5030

GENERAL INFORMATION Private Institution. **Total program enrollment:** 232. **Application fee:** $25.

Nova College de Puerto Rico (continued)

PROGRAM(S) OFFERED
● **Administrative Assistant and Secretarial Science, General** *48 hrs./$10,702*
● **Banking and Financial Support Services** *24 hrs./$5656* ● **Commercial and Advertising Art** *24 hrs./$5351* ● **Data Entry/Microcomputer Applications, General** *24 hrs./$5351* ● **Medical Office Assistant/Specialist** *24 hrs./$5351*
● **Pharmacy Technician/Assistant** *71 hrs./$13,307*

STUDENT SERVICES Academic or career counseling, employment services for current students, placement services for program completers.

Ponce Paramedical College

L-15 Acacia Street Villa Flores Urbanizacion, Ponce, PR 00731
http://www.popac.edu/

CONTACT María de los A. Pagán Negrón, Operations Director
Telephone: 787-848-1589

GENERAL INFORMATION Private Institution. Founded 1983. **Total program enrollment: 2605. Application fee:** $25.

PROGRAM(S) OFFERED
● **Athletic Training/Trainer** *11 students enrolled* ● **Cardiovascular Technology/Technologist** *41 students enrolled* ● **Child Care Provider/Assistant** *56 students enrolled* ● **Computer Installation and Repair Technology/Technician** *11 students enrolled* ● **Culinary Arts/Chef Training** *68 students enrolled* ● **Dental Assisting/Assistant** *42 hrs./$9750* ● **Emergency Medical Technology/Technician (EMT Paramedic)** *42 hrs./$9750* ● **Health Professions and Related Clinical Sciences, Other** *9 students enrolled* ● **Health and Medical Administrative Services, Other** *73 students enrolled* ● **Legal Assistant/Paralegal** *14 students enrolled* ● **Licensed Practical/Vocational Nurse Training (LPN, LVN, Cert, Dipl, AAS)** ● **Massage Therapy/Therapeutic Massage** *42 hrs./$9750* ● **Medical Administrative/Executive Assistant and Medical Secretary** *52 students enrolled* ● **Mortuary Science and Embalming/Embalmer** *6 students enrolled* ● **Pharmacy Technician/Assistant** *54 hrs./$11,700* ● **Respiratory Care Therapy/Therapist** *48 hrs./$10,750* ● **Surgical Technology/Technologist** *48 hrs./$10,750*

STUDENT SERVICES Academic or career counseling, placement services for program completers.

Pontifical Catholic University of Puerto Rico–Arecibo

PO Box 144045, Arecibo, PR 00614-4045
http://arecibo.pucpr.edu/

CONTACT Dr. Jose Arnaldo Torres, Rector
Telephone: 787-881-1212 Ext. 6000

GENERAL INFORMATION Private Institution (Affiliated with Roman Catholic Church). **Total program enrollment: 462. Application fee:** $15.

PROGRAM(S) OFFERED
● **Computer and Information Sciences, General** *4 students enrolled*
● **Kindergarten/Preschool Education and Teaching** *4 students enrolled*

STUDENT SERVICES Academic or career counseling, remedial services.

Professional Electric School

3 Ramos Velez Street, Manati, PR 00674
http://pespr.com/

CONTACT Paulino Delgado Negron, Director
Telephone: 787-854-4776

GENERAL INFORMATION Private Institution. Founded 1987. **Total program enrollment: 92. Application fee:** $25.

PROGRAM(S) OFFERED
● **Electrician** *1000 hrs./$7100* ● **Heating, Air Conditioning and Refrigeration Technology/Technician (ACH/ACR/ACHR/HRAC/HVAC/AC Technology)** *900 hrs./$5400*

STUDENT SERVICES Placement services for program completers.

Professional Technical Institution

Calle Comerio Final 20.5 La Aldea, Bayamón, PR 00959
http://www.estudiapti.com/

CONTACT Francisco Lafontaine, President
Telephone: 787-740-6810

GENERAL INFORMATION Private Institution. **Total program enrollment: 491. Application fee:** $100.

PROGRAM(S) OFFERED
● **Computer Installation and Repair Technology/Technician** *900 hrs./$7290*
● **Computer Technology/Computer Systems Technology** *33 students enrolled*
● **Electrician** *900 hrs./$7290* ● **Heating, Air Conditioning and Refrigeration Technology/Technician (ACH/ACR/ACHR/HRAC/HVAC/AC Technology)** *1200 hrs./$7290* ● **Security System Installation, Repair, and Inspection Technology/Technician** *900 hrs./$7990*

STUDENT SERVICES Placement services for program completers.

Puerto Rico Barber College

#7 Garrido Morales Street, Fajardo, PR 00738

CONTACT Yolanda Rivera, President
Telephone: 787-863-2970

GENERAL INFORMATION Private Institution. **Total program enrollment: 77. Application fee:** $10.

PROGRAM(S) OFFERED
● **Barbering/Barber** *1200 hrs./$7676* ● **Cosmetology/Cosmetologist, General** *1200 hrs./$7446* ● **Nail Technician/Specialist and Manicurist** *600 hrs./$3190*

STUDENT SERVICES Academic or career counseling, placement services for program completers.

Puerto Rico Technical Junior College

703 Ponce De Leon Avenue, Hato Rey, San Juan, PR 00917

CONTACT Hector M. Collazo, President
Telephone: 787-754-3431

GENERAL INFORMATION Private Institution. **Accreditation:** State accredited or approved. **Total program enrollment: 62. Application fee:** $25.

PROGRAM(S) OFFERED
● **Funeral Service and Mortuary Science, General** *1095 hrs./$7190* ● **Ophthalmic Laboratory Technology/Technician** *1350 hrs./$6474*

STUDENT SERVICES Academic or career counseling, employment services for current students, placement services for program completers, remedial services.

Quality Technical and Beauty College

Calle Degetau, #19, Bayamón, PR 00961

CONTACT Jesus Ivan Melendez, Proprietor Administer
Telephone: 787-740-7490

GENERAL INFORMATION Private Institution. Founded 1984. **Total program enrollment: 45. Application fee:** $25.

PROGRAM(S) OFFERED
● **Barbering/Barber** *18 students enrolled* ● **Cosmetology and Related Personal Grooming Arts, Other** ● **Cosmetology/Cosmetologist, General** *25 students enrolled*

Rogies School of Beauty Culture

Avenue Ponce De Leon 1315, Santurce, PR 00910

CONTACT Elba I. Santiago, Director
Telephone: 787-722-2293

GENERAL INFORMATION Private Institution. **Total program enrollment:** 148. **Application fee:** $25.

PROGRAM(S) OFFERED
• **Aesthetician/Esthetician and Skin Care Specialist** 36 hrs./$5350 • **Barbering/Barber** 54 hrs./$6425 • **Cosmetology, Barber/Styling, and Nail Instructor** 36 hrs./$5350 • **Cosmetology/Cosmetologist, General** 54 hrs./$7075 • **Nail Technician/Specialist and Manicurist** 36 hrs./$5350

STUDENT SERVICES Academic or career counseling, placement services for program completers, remedial services.

Ryder School for Practical Nursing

355 Font Martelo, Humacao, PR 00791

CONTACT Jose R. Feliciano, Executive Director
Telephone: 787-656-0711 Ext. 4715

GENERAL INFORMATION Private Institution. Founded 1956. **Total program enrollment:** 23.

PROGRAM(S) OFFERED
• **Licensed Practical/Vocational Nurse Training (LPN, LVN, Cert, Dipl, AAS)** 1689 hrs./$8301

Serbias School of Beauty Culture

61 Palmer Street, Guayama, PR 00654
http://www.serbiastechnicalcollege.com/

CONTACT Juanita Serbia, Chief Executive Officer
Telephone: 787-864-7254

GENERAL INFORMATION Private Institution. **Total program enrollment:** 243. **Application fee:** $25.

PROGRAM(S) OFFERED
• **Aesthetician/Esthetician and Skin Care Specialist** 900 hrs./$5356 • **Barbering/Barber** 1000 hrs./$5900 • **Cosmetology/Cosmetologist, General** 1200 hrs./$6891 • **Electrical and Electronic Engineering Technologies/Technicians, Other** 1000 hrs./$5925 • **Hair Styling/Stylist and Hair Design** 900 hrs./$5373 • **Nail Technician/Specialist and Manicurist** 600 hrs./$2695

STUDENT SERVICES Academic or career counseling, employment services for current students, placement services for program completers.

Sistema Universitario Ana G. Mendez Central Office

Río Piedras, PR 00929

CONTACT Jose F. Mendez, President
Telephone: 787-751-0178

GENERAL INFORMATION Private Institution.

Trinity College of Puerto Rico

Hostos Avenue, 834, Ponce, PR 00716-1111
http://www.csifpr.org/trinitycollege/

CONTACT Maria I. Colon Colon, Executive Director
Telephone: 787-842-0000 Ext. 226

GENERAL INFORMATION Private Institution. Founded 1988. **Total program enrollment:** 205. **Application fee:** $30.

PROGRAM(S) OFFERED
• **Accounting Technology/Technician and Bookkeeping** 3 students enrolled • **Administrative Assistant and Secretarial Science, General** • **Computer Systems Networking and Telecommunications** 4 students enrolled • **Computer and Information Sciences and Support Services, Other** 9 students enrolled • **Health Aides/Attendants/Orderlies, Other** 19 students enrolled • **Health Information/Medical Records Technology/Technician** 13 students enrolled • **Licensed Practical/Vocational Nurse Training (LPN, LVN, Cert, Dipl, AAS)** 28 students enrolled • **Teacher Assistant/Aide** 6 students enrolled

STUDENT SERVICES Academic or career counseling, placement services for program completers, remedial services.

Universal Career Counseling Centers

Avenue Fernandez Juncos 1902, Santurce, PR 00907

CONTACT Richard D'costa Ofrey, CEO & President
Telephone: 787-728-7299

GENERAL INFORMATION Private Institution. **Total program enrollment:** 654. **Application fee:** $25.

PROGRAM(S) OFFERED
• **Baking and Pastry Arts/Baker/Pastry Chef** 54 students enrolled • **Business Administration and Management, General** 54 students enrolled • **Business/Office Automation/Technology/Data Entry** 85 students enrolled • **Computer Installation and Repair Technology/Technician** 56 students enrolled • **Culinary Arts/Chef Training** 150 students enrolled • **General Merchandising, Sales, and Related Marketing Operations, Other** • **Information Science/Studies** 16 students enrolled • **Medical Administrative/Executive Assistant and Medical Secretary** 44 students enrolled • **Tourism and Travel Services Marketing Operations** 36 students enrolled

STUDENT SERVICES Academic or career counseling, placement services for program completers, remedial services.

Universal Technology College of Puerto Rico

Calle Comercio #111, Aguadilla, PR 00605
http://www.unitecpr.edu/

CONTACT Luis Lopez Vale, President
Telephone: 787-882-2065

GENERAL INFORMATION Private Institution. Founded 1987. **Total program enrollment:** 1721. **Application fee:** $20.

PROGRAM(S) OFFERED
• **Accounting and Related Services, Other** • **Apparel and Textiles, Other** 33 students enrolled • **Business Operations Support and Secretarial Services, Other** 73 hrs./$10,261 • **Drafting/Design Engineering Technologies/Technicians, Other** 1275 hrs./$5890 • **Electrical, Electronic and Communications Engineering Technology/Technician** 66 students enrolled • **Electrician** 100 students enrolled • **Emergency Medical Technology/Technician (EMT Paramedic)** 1215 hrs./$5890 • **Fashion/Apparel Design** 22 students enrolled • **Heating, Air Conditioning, Ventilation and Refrigeration Maintenance Technology/Technician (HAC, HACR, HVAC, HVACR)** 64 students enrolled • **Interior Design** 24 students enrolled • **Licensed Practical/Vocational Nurse Training (LPN, LVN, Cert, Dipl, AAS)** 50 students enrolled • **Medical Administrative/Executive Assistant and Medical Secretary** 124 students enrolled • **Nursing—Registered Nurse Training (RN, ASN, BSN, MSN)** 74 hrs./$18,684 • **Respiratory Care Therapy/Therapist** 1200 hrs./$5890

STUDENT SERVICES Daycare for children of students, employment services for current students, placement services for program completers.

Universidad del Este

PO Box 2010, Carolina, PR 00983
http://www.suagm.edu/une/

CONTACT Alberto Maldonado, Chancellor
Telephone: 787-257-7373

GENERAL INFORMATION Private Institution. Founded 1949. **Accreditation:** Regional (MSA/CIHE); health information technology (AHIMA). **Total program enrollment:** 8747. **Application fee:** $15.

Universidad del Este (continued)

PROGRAM(S) OFFERED
• **Architectural Drafting and Architectural CAD/CADD** 8 *students enrolled* • **Baking and Pastry Arts/Baker/Pastry Chef** 1 *student enrolled* • **Banking and Financial Support Services** 6 *students enrolled* • **Bartending/Bartender** 3 *students enrolled* • **Computer Software and Media Applications, Other** 12 *students enrolled* • **Computer Systems Networking and Telecommunications** 3 *students enrolled* • **Computer and Information Sciences and Support Services, Other** • **Criminal Justice/Police Science** • **Culinary Arts/Chef Training** 7 *students enrolled* • **Diagnostic Medical Sonography/Sonographer and Ultrasound Technician** 1 *student enrolled* • **Facilities Planning and Management** • **Medical Administrative/Executive Assistant and Medical Secretary** 60 *students enrolled* • **Medical Office Assistant/Specialist** 7 *students enrolled* • **Parks, Recreation and Leisure Facilities Management** • **Receptionist** • **Sales, Distribution and Marketing Operations, General** 5 *students enrolled* • **Teacher Assistant/Aide** 83 *students enrolled* • **Tourism and Travel Services Management** 4 *students enrolled*

STUDENT SERVICES Academic or career counseling, daycare for children of students, employment services for current students, placement services for program completers, remedial services.

Universidad del Turabo

PO Box 3030, Gurabo, PR 00778-3030
http://www.suagm.edu/ut/

CONTACT Dennis Alicea, Chancellor
Telephone: 787-743-7979 Ext. 4000

GENERAL INFORMATION Private Institution. Founded 1972. **Accreditation:** Regional (MSA/CIHE). **Total program enrollment:** 11805. **Application fee:** $15.

PROGRAM(S) OFFERED
• **Architectural Drafting and Architectural CAD/CADD** 24 *students enrolled* • **Computer Engineering Technologies/Technicians, Other** 8 *students enrolled* • **Legal Assistant/Paralegal** 10 *students enrolled* • **Medical Administrative/Executive Assistant and Medical Secretary** 10 *students enrolled* • **Teacher Assistant/Aide** 47 *students enrolled* • **Tourism and Travel Services Management** 8 *students enrolled*

STUDENT SERVICES Academic or career counseling, employment services for current students, placement services for program completers.

Universidad Metropolitana

Apartado 21150, San Juan, PR 00928-1150
http://www.suagm.edu/umet/

CONTACT Federico Matheu, Chancellor
Telephone: 787-766-1717

GENERAL INFORMATION Private Institution. Founded 1980. **Accreditation:** Regional (MSA/CIHE). **Total program enrollment:** 8895. **Application fee:** $15.

PROGRAM(S) OFFERED
• **Banking and Financial Support Services** 2 *students enrolled* • **Business/Office Automation/Technology/Data Entry** • **Computer Programming/Programmer, General** 31 *students enrolled* • **Criminal Justice/Law Enforcement Administration** • **Criminal Justice/Safety Studies** 33 *students enrolled* • **Drafting and Design Technology/Technician, General** 20 *students enrolled* • **Environmental Control Technologies/Technicians, Other** 1 *student enrolled* • **Health/Medical Claims Examiner** 26 *students enrolled* • **Insurance** 6 *students enrolled* • **Legal Assistant/Paralegal** 2 *students enrolled* • **Medical Administrative/Executive Assistant and Medical Secretary** • **Sales, Distribution and Marketing Operations, General** • **Sport and Fitness Administration/Management** • **Teacher Assistant/Aide** 72 *students enrolled*

STUDENT SERVICES Academic or career counseling, employment services for current students, placement services for program completers.

University of Puerto Rico at Bayamón

170 Carretera 174 Parque Industrial Minillas, Bayamón, PR 00959
http://www.uprb.edu/

CONTACT Irma Schmidt Sotero, Chancellor
Telephone: 787-993-0000 Ext. 3050

GENERAL INFORMATION Public Institution. Founded 1971. **Accreditation:** Regional (MSA/CIHE). **Total program enrollment:** 4187. **Application fee:** $15.

STUDENT SERVICES Academic or career counseling, employment services for current students, placement services for program completers, remedial services.

RHODE ISLAND

Arthur Angelo School of Cosmetology and Hair Design

151 Broadway, Providence, RI 02903
http://www.arthurangelo.com/

CONTACT Michael Bouman, President/COO
Telephone: 570-429-4321 Ext. 2414

GENERAL INFORMATION Private Institution. Founded 1959. **Total program enrollment:** 93. **Application fee:** $100.

PROGRAM(S) OFFERED
• **Aesthetician/Esthetician and Skin Care Specialist** 900 *hrs./*$10,150 • **Cosmetology/Cosmetologist, General** 1500 *hrs./*$12,980 • **Facial Treatment Specialist/Facialist** 22 *students enrolled* • **Massage Therapy/Therapeutic Massage** • **Nail Technician/Specialist and Manicurist** • **Trade and Industrial Teacher Education**

STUDENT SERVICES Academic or career counseling, placement services for program completers, remedial services.

Community College of Rhode Island

400 East Avenue, Warwick, RI 02886-1807
http://www.ccri.edu/

CONTACT Raymond M. DiPasquale, President
Telephone: 401-825-1000

GENERAL INFORMATION Public Institution. Founded 1964. **Accreditation:** Regional (NEASC/NEASCCIHE); dental assisting (ADA); dental hygiene (ADA); medical laboratory technology (NAACLS); physical therapy assisting (APTA); practical nursing (NLN); radiologic technology: radiography (JRCERT). **Total program enrollment:** 6519. **Application fee:** $20.

PROGRAM(S) OFFERED
• **Accounting** 15 *students enrolled* • **Administrative Assistant and Secretarial Science, General** • **Adult Development and Aging** • **Business Administration and Management, General** 2 *students enrolled* • **Chemical Technology/Technician** • **Child Care Provider/Assistant** • **Computer Hardware Technology/Technician** 2 *students enrolled* • **Computer Programming, Specific Applications** 3 *students enrolled* • **Computer Systems Networking and Telecommunications** 2 *students enrolled* • **Computer Technology/Computer Systems Technology** • **Computer and Information Sciences, General** • **Dental Assisting/Assistant** 18 *students enrolled* • **Diagnostic Medical Sonography/Sonographer and Ultrasound Technician** • **Early Childhood Education and Teaching** 1 *student enrolled* • **Electrical, Electronic and Communications Engineering Technology/Technician** • **Entrepreneurship/Entrepreneurial Studies** 3 *students enrolled* • **General Office Occupations and Clerical Services** 6 *students enrolled* • **Health and Medical Administrative Services, Other** 7 *students enrolled* • **Industrial Production Technologies/Technicians, Other** • **Instrumentation**

Technology/Technician • Legal Administrative Assistant/Secretary • Legal Support Services, Other • Licensed Practical/Vocational Nurse Training (LPN, LVN, Cert, Dipl, AAS) 48 students enrolled • Manufacturing Engineering • Manufacturing Technology/Technician • Marketing/Marketing Management, General 1 student enrolled • Mechanical Engineering/Mechanical Technology/Technician • Medical Insurance Specialist/Medical Biller 9 students enrolled • Medical Transcription/Transcriptionist 1 student enrolled • Phlebotomy/Phlebotomist 22 students enrolled • Public Health, Other • Radiologic Technology/Science—Radiographer 3 students enrolled • Renal/Dialysis Technologist/Technician 2 students enrolled • Retailing and Retail Operations • Telecommunications Technology/Technician • Tourism Promotion Operations 5 students enrolled • Word Processing

STUDENT SERVICES Academic or career counseling, daycare for children of students, employment services for current students, placement services for program completers, remedial services.

The International Yacht Restoration School

449 Thames Street, Newport, RI 02840
http://www.iyrs.org

CONTACT Lydia Bergeron, General Manager, VP Finance
Telephone: 401-848-5777

GENERAL INFORMATION Private Institution. Founded 1993. **Total program enrollment:** 46.

PROGRAM(S) OFFERED
• Marine Maintenance/Fitter and Ship Repair Technology/Technician 1225 hrs./$14,950

STUDENT SERVICES Academic or career counseling, placement services for program completers.

Johnson & Wales University

8 Abbott Park Place, Providence, RI 02903-3703
http://www.jwu.edu/

CONTACT Dr. John J. Bowen, University President
Telephone: 401-598-1000

GENERAL INFORMATION Private Institution. Founded 1914. **Accreditation:** Regional (NEASC/NEASCCIHE). **Total program enrollment:** 9449.

PROGRAM(S) OFFERED
• CAD/CADD Drafting and/or Design Technology/Technician 4 students enrolled • Culinary Arts/Chef Training 4 students enrolled • Legal Assistant/Paralegal 3 students enrolled

STUDENT SERVICES Academic or career counseling, employment services for current students, placement services for program completers, remedial services.

Lincoln Technical Institute

622 George Washington Highway, At the Lincoln Mall, Lincoln, RI 02865-4211
http://www.lincolnedu.com/

CONTACT David Carney, CEO
Telephone: 401-334-2430

GENERAL INFORMATION Private Institution. **Total program enrollment:** 1051. **Application fee:** $100.

PROGRAM(S) OFFERED
• Computer and Information Sciences, General • Cosmetology/Cosmetologist, General • Criminal Justice/Law Enforcement Administration • Dental Assisting/Assistant 1200 hrs./$15,430 • Electrical/Electronics Maintenance and Repair Technology, Other 1080 hrs./$15,960 • Massage Therapy/Therapeutic Massage 720 hrs./$12,750 • Medical Insurance Coding

Specialist/Coder 900 hrs./$13,925 • Medical Insurance Specialist/Medical Biller 152 students enrolled • Medical/Clinical Assistant 900 hrs./$13,925 • Pharmacy Technician/Assistant 41 students enrolled

STUDENT SERVICES Academic or career counseling, employment services for current students, placement services for program completers.

Motoring Technical Training Institute

54 Water Street, East Providence, RI 02914
http://www.mtti.edu/

CONTACT Edward R. Ring, President
Telephone: 401-434-4840

GENERAL INFORMATION Private Institution. Founded 1985. **Total program enrollment:** 159. **Application fee:** $50.

PROGRAM(S) OFFERED
• Automobile/Automotive Mechanics Technology/Technician 720 hrs./$11,600 • Building/Property Maintenance and Management 780 hrs./$11,300 • Business/Commerce, General 10 students enrolled • Communications Systems Installation and Repair Technology 16 students enrolled • Computer Installation and Repair Technology/Technician 858 hrs./$12,800 • Marine Maintenance/Fitter and Ship Repair Technology/Technician 8 students enrolled • Medical Office Management/Administration 858 hrs./$12,600 • Medical/Clinical Assistant 858 hrs./$12,600 • Medical/Health Management and Clinical Assistant/Specialist 30 students enrolled • Motorcycle Maintenance and Repair Technology/Technician 858 hrs./$13,450

STUDENT SERVICES Academic or career counseling, employment services for current students, placement services for program completers, remedial services.

New England Institute of Technology

2500 Post Road, Warwick, RI 02886-2244
http://www.neit.edu/

CONTACT Richard Gouse, President
Telephone: 401-467-7744

GENERAL INFORMATION Private Institution. Founded 1940. **Accreditation:** Regional (NEASC/NEASCCIHE); engineering technology (ABET/TAC); surgical technology (ARCST). **Total program enrollment:** 2734. **Application fee:** $25.

PROGRAM(S) OFFERED
• Autobody/Collision and Repair Technology/Technician 1 student enrolled • Automobile/Automotive Mechanics Technology/Technician • Construction Engineering Technology/Technician • Heating, Air Conditioning and Refrigeration Technology/Technician (ACH/ACR/ACHR/HRAC/HVAC/AC Technology) 2 students enrolled • Plumbing Technology/Plumber 2 students enrolled

STUDENT SERVICES Academic or career counseling, employment services for current students, placement services for program completers, remedial services.

New England Tractor Trailer Training School of Rhode Island

10 Dunnell Lane, Pawtucket, RI 02860-5801
http://www.nettts.com/

CONTACT Christopher Whelpley, PhD, DSE, Director
Telephone: 401-725-1220

GENERAL INFORMATION Private Institution. Founded 1985. **Total program enrollment:** 375. **Application fee:** $100.

PROGRAM(S) OFFERED
• Truck and Bus Driver/Commercial Vehicle Operation 80 hrs./$2895

STUDENT SERVICES Placement services for program completers.

Newport School of Hairdressing–Main Campus

226 Main Street, Pawtucket, RI 02860

CONTACT Michael Berger, Owner/Director
Telephone: 401-725-6882

GENERAL INFORMATION Private Institution. **Application fee:** $100.

PROGRAM(S) OFFERED
• **Cosmetology and Related Personal Grooming Arts, Other** *1 student enrolled*
• **Cosmetology, Barber/Styling, and Nail Instructor** *300 hrs./$1100*
• **Cosmetology/Cosmetologist, General** *1500 hrs.*

STUDENT SERVICES Academic or career counseling.

Paul Mitchell the School—Rhode Island

379 Atwood Avenue, Cranston, RI 02920
http://www.paulmitchelltheschool.com/

CONTACT Michael Galvin, Owner
Telephone: 801-302-8801 Ext. 1021

GENERAL INFORMATION Private Institution. **Total program enrollment:** 206. **Application fee:** $100.

PROGRAM(S) OFFERED
• **Aesthetician/Esthetician and Skin Care Specialist** *600 hrs./$8075*
• **Cosmetology, Barber/Styling, and Nail Instructor** *300 hrs./$1825*
• **Cosmetology/Cosmetologist, General** *1500 hrs./$19,400* • **Nail Technician/Specialist and Manicurist** *300 hrs./$3250*

STUDENT SERVICES Academic or career counseling, placement services for program completers, remedial services.

Providence College

549 River Avenue, Providence, RI 02918
http://www.providence.edu/

CONTACT Rev. Brian J. Shanley, OP, President
Telephone: 401-865-1000

GENERAL INFORMATION Private Institution. Founded 1917. **Accreditation:** Regional (NEASC/NEASCCIHE). **Total program enrollment:** 4026. **Application fee:** $55.

PROGRAM(S) OFFERED
• **Business Administration and Management, General** *1 student enrolled*
• **Business Administration, Management and Operations, Other** *95 students enrolled* • **Community Organization and Advocacy** • **Hospital and Health Care Facilities Administration/Management** • **Organizational Communication, General** • **Public Administration** • **Secondary Education and Teaching** *36 students enrolled*

STUDENT SERVICES Academic or career counseling, employment services for current students, placement services for program completers.

Rhode Island College

600 Mount Pleasant Avenue, Providence, RI 02908-1991
http://www.ric.edu/

CONTACT Nancy Carriuolo, President
Telephone: 401-456-8000

GENERAL INFORMATION Public Institution. Founded 1854. **Accreditation:** Regional (NEASC/NEASCCIHE); art and design (NASAD); music (NASM). **Total program enrollment:** 5777. **Application fee:** $50.

PROGRAM(S) OFFERED
• **Non-Profit/Public/Organizational Management** *2 students enrolled* • **Social Work, Other** *1 student enrolled*

STUDENT SERVICES Academic or career counseling, daycare for children of students, employment services for current students, placement services for program completers, remedial services.

Roger Williams University

1 Old Ferry Road, Bristol, RI 02809
http://www.rwu.edu/

CONTACT Roy J. Nirschel, PhD, President
Telephone: 401-253-1040

GENERAL INFORMATION Private Institution. Founded 1956. **Accreditation:** Regional (NEASC/NEASCCIHE). **Total program enrollment:** 3849. **Application fee:** $50.

PROGRAM(S) OFFERED
• **Environmental Health** *1 student enrolled*

STUDENT SERVICES Academic or career counseling, employment services for current students, placement services for program completers.

Sawyer School

101 Main Street, Pawtucket, RI 02860
http://www.sawyerschool.org/

CONTACT Carol Paradise, President
Telephone: 401-272-8400

GENERAL INFORMATION Private Institution. **Total program enrollment:** 800. **Application fee:** $100.

PROGRAM(S) OFFERED
• **Hospitality Administration/Management, General** *54 hrs./$19,300* • **Management Information Systems and Services, Other** *54 hrs./$19,300* • **Management Information Systems, General** *48 hrs./$19,200* • **Medical Administrative/Executive Assistant and Medical Secretary** *36 hrs./$16,300* • **Medical/Clinical Assistant** *54 hrs./$19,300* • **Tourism and Travel Services Marketing Operations**

STUDENT SERVICES Academic or career counseling, employment services for current students, placement services for program completers, remedial services.

Warwick Academy of Beauty Culture

1800 Post Road, Warwick, RI 02886

CONTACT Michael Bouman, President/COO
Telephone: 401-826-2022

GENERAL INFORMATION Private Institution. Founded 1967. **Total program enrollment:** 95. **Application fee:** $100.

PROGRAM(S) OFFERED
• **Aesthetician/Esthetician and Skin Care Specialist** *700 hrs./$6800*
• **Cosmetology/Cosmetologist, General** *1500 hrs./$13,250*

STUDENT SERVICES Academic or career counseling, placement services for program completers.

SOUTH CAROLINA ———

Academy of Cosmetology

5060 Dorchester Road, North Charleston, SC 29418
http://www.realpages.com/academy/

CONTACT Sewell Gelberd, President
Telephone: 843-552-3241

GENERAL INFORMATION Private Institution. Founded 1990. **Total program enrollment:** 182. **Application fee:** $50.

PROGRAM(S) OFFERED
- **Aesthetician/Esthetician and Skin Care Specialist** *300 hrs./$5350*
- **Cosmetology and Related Personal Grooming Arts, Other** *1 student enrolled*
- **Cosmetology, Barber/Styling, and Nail Instructor** *700 hrs./$2450*
- **Cosmetology/Cosmetologist, General** *1500 hrs./$12,450* • **Make-Up Artist/Specialist** *2 students enrolled* • **Nail Technician/Specialist and Manicurist** *600 hrs./$3310*

STUDENT SERVICES Placement services for program completers.

Academy of Hair Technology

3715 East North Street, Suite F, Greenville, SC 29615
http://www.hairchamps.com/

CONTACT James W. King, Jr., President
Telephone: 864-322-0300

GENERAL INFORMATION Private Institution. Founded 1984. **Total program enrollment:** 135. **Application fee:** $100.

PROGRAM(S) OFFERED
- **Aesthetician/Esthetician and Skin Care Specialist** *10 students enrolled*
- **Cosmetology and Related Personal Grooming Arts, Other** *600 hrs./$6000*
- **Cosmetology, Barber/Styling, and Nail Instructor** *300 hrs./$1800*
- **Cosmetology/Cosmetologist, General** *1500 hrs./$10,850* • **Nail Technician/Specialist and Manicurist** *12 students enrolled*

STUDENT SERVICES Academic or career counseling, employment services for current students, placement services for program completers.

Aiken Technical College

PO Drawer 696, Aiken, SC 29802-0696
http://www.aik.tec.sc.us/

CONTACT Susan A. Winsor, President
Telephone: 803-593-9231

GENERAL INFORMATION Public Institution. Founded 1972. **Accreditation:** Regional (SACS/CC); dental assisting (ADA); engineering technology (ABET/TAC). **Total program enrollment:** 1357.

PROGRAM(S) OFFERED
- **Accounting Technology/Technician and Bookkeeping** *8 students enrolled*
- **Administrative Assistant and Secretarial Science, General** *4 students enrolled* • **Automobile/Automotive Mechanics Technology/Technician** *19 students enrolled* • **Business Administration and Management, General** *14 students enrolled* • **Child Care Provider/Assistant** *11 students enrolled* • **Criminal Justice/Safety Studies** *1 student enrolled* • **Data Processing and Data Processing Technology/Technician** *48 students enrolled* • **Dental Assisting/Assistant** *7 students enrolled* • **Dental Hygiene/Hygienist** *7 students enrolled* • **Electrical, Electronic and Communications Engineering Technology/Technician** *3 students enrolled* • **General Office Occupations and Clerical Services** *2 students enrolled* • **Health Information/Medical Records Technology/Technician** *8 students enrolled* • **Health Professions and Related Clinical Sciences, Other** *58 students enrolled* • **Heating, Air Conditioning, Ventilation and Refrigeration Maintenance Technology/Technician (HAC, HACR, HVAC, HVACR)** *27 students enrolled* • **Industrial Electronics Technology/Technician** *16 students enrolled* • **Industrial Mechanics and Maintenance Technology** *1 student enrolled* • **Legal Assistant/Paralegal** *11 students enrolled* • **Licensed Practical/Vocational Nurse Training (LPN, LVN, Cert, Dipl, AAS)** *24 students enrolled* • **Machine Tool Technology/Machinist** *2 students enrolled* • **Mechanical Drafting and Mechanical Drafting CAD/CADD** *4 students enrolled* • **Medical/Clinical Assistant** *9*

students enrolled • **Nuclear/Nuclear Power Technology/Technician** *1 student enrolled* • **Nursing—Registered Nurse Training (RN, ASN, BSN, MSN)** *4 students enrolled* • **Pharmacy Technician/Assistant** *2 students enrolled* • **Sales, Distribution and Marketing Operations, General** *5 students enrolled* • **Social Work** *35 students enrolled* • **Surgical Technology/Technologist** *12 students enrolled* • **Welding Technology/Welder** *33 students enrolled*

STUDENT SERVICES Academic or career counseling, employment services for current students, placement services for program completers, remedial services.

The Art Institute of Charleston

The Carroll Building, 24 North Market Street, Charleston, SC 29401
http://www.artinstitutes.edu/charleston/

CONTACT Rick Jerue, President
Telephone: 843-727-3500

GENERAL INFORMATION Private Institution. Founded 2007. **Total program enrollment:** 436. **Application fee:** $50.

PROGRAM(S) OFFERED
- **Cinematography and Film/Video Production** • **Culinary Arts/Chef Training**

STUDENT SERVICES Employment services for current students, remedial services.

Beta Tech

7500 Two Notch Road, Columbia, SC 29223
http://www.betatech.edu/

CONTACT Barry Hill, Director
Telephone: 803-754-7544

GENERAL INFORMATION Private Institution. **Total program enrollment:** 157. **Application fee:** $25.

PROGRAM(S) OFFERED
- **Administrative Assistant and Secretarial Science, General** *36 hrs./$11,880*
- **Computer Systems Networking and Telecommunications** *36 hrs./$11,880*
- **Criminal Justice/Law Enforcement Administration** *93 hrs./$27,900*
- **Medical/Clinical Assistant** *41 hrs./$14,706*

STUDENT SERVICES Academic or career counseling, placement services for program completers.

Beta Tech

8088 Rivers Avenue, North Charleston, SC 29406-9235
http://www.betatech.edu/

CONTACT David Riggs, School Director
Telephone: 843-569-0889

GENERAL INFORMATION Private Institution. **Total program enrollment:** 182. **Application fee:** $25.

PROGRAM(S) OFFERED
- **Computer Installation and Repair Technology/Technician** *720 hrs./$11,880*
- **Computer Systems Networking and Telecommunications** *16 students enrolled*
- **Computer and Information Sciences, General** *12 students enrolled* • **Data Entry/Microcomputer Applications, General** *720 hrs./$11,880* • **Legal Assistant/Paralegal** *720 hrs./$11,988* • **Medical/Clinical Assistant** *850 hrs./$14,370*

STUDENT SERVICES Academic or career counseling, employment services for current students, placement services for program completers, remedial services.

Bob Jones University

1700 Wade Hampton Boulevard, Greenville, SC 29614
http://www.bju.edu/

CONTACT David Fisher, Provost
Telephone: 864-242-5100

GENERAL INFORMATION Private Institution. Founded 1927. **Total program enrollment:** 3837. **Application fee:** $45.

PROGRAM(S) OFFERED
• General Office Occupations and Clerical Services 2 *students enrolled*

STUDENT SERVICES Academic or career counseling, employment services for current students, placement services for program completers, remedial services.

Central Carolina Technical College

506 North Guignard Drive, Sumter, SC 29150-2499
http://www.cctech.edu/

CONTACT Blon Tim Hardee, EdD, President
Telephone: 803-778-1961

GENERAL INFORMATION Public Institution. Founded 1963. **Accreditation:** Regional (SACS/CC); engineering technology (ABET/TAC). **Total program enrollment:** 1046.

PROGRAM(S) OFFERED
• Accounting 7 *students enrolled* • Administrative Assistant and Secretarial Science, General 11 *students enrolled* • Automobile/Automotive Mechanics Technology/Technician 4 *students enrolled* • Child Care Provider/Assistant 12 *students enrolled* • Data Processing and Data Processing Technology/Technician 22 *students enrolled* • Electrical/Electronics Equipment Installation and Repair, General 2 *students enrolled* • General Office Occupations and Clerical Services 10 *students enrolled* • Heating, Air Conditioning, Ventilation and Refrigeration Maintenance Technology/Technician (HAC, HACR, HVAC, HVACR) 1 *student enrolled* • Industrial Mechanics and Maintenance Technology 28 *students enrolled* • Licensed Practical/Vocational Nurse Training (LPN, LVN, Cert, Dipl, AAS) 20 *students enrolled* • Machine Tool Technology/Machinist 4 *students enrolled* • Mechanical Drafting and Mechanical Drafting CAD/CADD 1 *student enrolled* • Medical/Clinical Assistant 13 *students enrolled* • Nursing—Registered Nurse Training (RN, ASN, BSN, MSN) 85 *students enrolled* • Pharmacy Technician/Assistant 5 *students enrolled* • Physical Therapist Assistant 4 *students enrolled* • Surgical Technology/Technologist 13 *students enrolled* • Welding Technology/Welder 7 *students enrolled*

STUDENT SERVICES Academic or career counseling, placement services for program completers, remedial services.

Charleston Cosmetology Institute

8484 Dorchester Road, Charleston, SC 29420
http://www.charlestoncosmetology.com/

CONTACT Jerry Poer, Owner
Telephone: 843-552-3670

GENERAL INFORMATION Private Institution. Founded 1984. **Total program enrollment:** 111. **Application fee:** $100.

PROGRAM(S) OFFERED
• Aesthetician/Esthetician and Skin Care Specialist 600 *hrs./$8450*
• Cosmetology, Barber/Styling, and Nail Instructor 750 *hrs./$4550*
• Cosmetology/Cosmetologist, General 1500 *hrs./$14,500* • Nail Technician/Specialist and Manicurist 600 *hrs./$4550*

STUDENT SERVICES Academic or career counseling, placement services for program completers.

Charleston School of Massage

778 Folly Road, Charleston, SC 29412
http://charlestonmassage.com/

CONTACT Mark Hendler, PhD, President
Telephone: 843-762-7727

GENERAL INFORMATION Private Institution. **Total program enrollment:** 18. **Application fee:** $100.

PROGRAM(S) OFFERED
• Massage Therapy/Therapeutic Massage 26 *hrs./$7225*

STUDENT SERVICES Academic or career counseling, placement services for program completers.

Charzanne Beauty College

1549 Highway 72, E, Greenwood, SC 29649

CONTACT Cille C. Bishop, President
Telephone: 864-223-7321

GENERAL INFORMATION Private Institution. **Total program enrollment:** 61. **Application fee:** $100.

PROGRAM(S) OFFERED
• Cosmetology/Cosmetologist, General 1500 *hrs./$9000*

STUDENT SERVICES Academic or career counseling, placement services for program completers.

Columbia International University

PO Box 3122, Columbia, SC 29230-3122
http://www.ciu.edu/

CONTACT William H. Jones, President
Telephone: 803-754-4100

GENERAL INFORMATION Private Institution. Founded 1923. **Accreditation:** Regional (SACS/CC); state accredited or approved. **Total program enrollment:** 650. **Application fee:** $45.

PROGRAM(S) OFFERED
• Bible/Biblical Studies 1 *student enrolled*

STUDENT SERVICES Academic or career counseling, employment services for current students, placement services for program completers, remedial services.

Denmark Technical College

Solomon Blatt Boulevard, Box 327, Denmark, SC 29042-0327
http://www.denmarktech.edu/

CONTACT Dr. John K. Waddell, President
Telephone: 803-793-5100

GENERAL INFORMATION Public Institution. Founded 1948. **Accreditation:** Regional (SACS/CC); engineering technology (ABET/TAC). **Total program enrollment:** 960. **Application fee:** $10.

PROGRAM(S) OFFERED
• Accounting 5 *students enrolled* • Barbering/Barber 18 *students enrolled* • Business/Office Automation/Technology/Data Entry 8 *students enrolled* • Child Care Provider/Assistant 6 *students enrolled* • Construction Engineering Technology/Technician 15 *students enrolled* • Cosmetology/Cosmetologist, General 13 *students enrolled* • Criminal Justice/Safety Studies 1 *student enrolled* • Culinary Arts/Chef Training 14 *students enrolled* • General Office Occupations and Clerical Services 6 *students enrolled* • Industrial Electronics Technology/Technician 8 *students enrolled* • Pharmacy Technician/Assistant 10 *students enrolled* • Welding Technology/Welder 15 *students enrolled*

STUDENT SERVICES Academic or career counseling, placement services for program completers, remedial services.

Erskine College

2 Washington Street, PO Box 338, Due West, SC 29639
http://www.erskine.edu/

CONTACT Dr. Randy Ruble, President
Telephone: 864-379-2131

GENERAL INFORMATION Private Institution (Affiliated with Associate Reformed Presbyterian Church). Founded 1839. **Accreditation:** Regional (SACS/CC). **Total program enrollment:** 664. **Application fee:** $25.

PROGRAM(S) OFFERED
• Bible/Biblical Studies *1 student enrolled*

STUDENT SERVICES Academic or career counseling, employment services for current students, placement services for program completers.

Florence-Darlington Technical College

2715 West Lucas Street, PO Box 100548, Florence, SC 29501-0548
http://www.fdtc.edu/

CONTACT Charles W. Gould, President
Telephone: 843-661-8324

GENERAL INFORMATION Public Institution. Founded 1963. **Accreditation:** Regional (SACS/CC); dental assisting (ADA); dental hygiene (ADA); engineering technology (ABET/TAC); health information technology (AHIMA); medical laboratory technology (NAACLS); radiologic technology: radiography (JRCERT). **Total program enrollment:** 2446.

PROGRAM(S) OFFERED
• Autobody/Collision and Repair Technology/Technician *13 students enrolled* • Automobile/Automotive Mechanics Technology/Technician *5 students enrolled* • Child Care Provider/Assistant *11 students enrolled* • Cosmetology/Cosmetologist, General *15 students enrolled* • Dental Assisting/Assistant *10 students enrolled* • Electrical, Electronic and Communications Engineering Technology/Technician *6 students enrolled* • Electroneurodiagnostic/Electroencephalographic Technology/Technologist *2 students enrolled* • General Office Occupations and Clerical Services *2 students enrolled* • Health Information/Medical Records Technology/Technician *4 students enrolled* • Health Professions and Related Clinical Sciences, Other *18 students enrolled* • Heating, Air Conditioning, Ventilation and Refrigeration Maintenance Technology/Technician (HAC, HACR, HVAC, HVACR) *11 students enrolled* • International Business/Trade/Commerce *1 student enrolled* • Licensed Practical/Vocational Nurse Training (LPN, LVN, Cert, Dipl, AAS) *94 students enrolled* • Machine Tool Technology/Machinist *7 students enrolled* • Mechanical Drafting and Mechanical Drafting CAD/CADD *3 students enrolled* • Medical Transcription/Transcriptionist *2 students enrolled* • Medical/Clinical Assistant *16 students enrolled* • Nail Technician/Specialist and Manicurist *4 students enrolled* • Nursing—Registered Nurse Training (RN, ASN, BSN, MSN) *3 students enrolled* • Physical Therapist Assistant *1 student enrolled* • Surgical Technology/Technologist *20 students enrolled* • Welding Technology/Welder *21 students enrolled*

STUDENT SERVICES Academic or career counseling, daycare for children of students, employment services for current students, placement services for program completers, remedial services.

Forrest Junior College

601 East River Street, Anderson, SC 29624
http://www.forrestcollege.com/

CONTACT Rodney Kruse, President
Telephone: 864-225-7653 Ext. 201

GENERAL INFORMATION Private Institution. Founded 1946. **Accreditation:** State accredited or approved. **Total program enrollment:** 79. **Application fee:** $50.

PROGRAM(S) OFFERED
• Accounting and Related Services, Other • Administrative Assistant and Secretarial Science, General • Computer Installation and Repair Technology/Technician • Computer Systems Networking and Telecommunications • Corrections and Criminal Justice, Other • Criminal Justice/Law Enforcement

Administration • Medical Office Management/Administration *3 students enrolled* • Medical/Clinical Assistant *1 student enrolled* • Nurse/Nursing Assistant/Aide and Patient Care Assistant • Phlebotomy/Phlebotomist *6 students enrolled*

STUDENT SERVICES Academic or career counseling, daycare for children of students, employment services for current students, placement services for program completers, remedial services.

Greenville Technical College

PO Box 5616, Greenville, SC 29606-5616
http://www.greenvilletech.com/

CONTACT Keith Miller, PhD, President
Telephone: 864-250-8111

GENERAL INFORMATION Public Institution. Founded 1962. **Accreditation:** Regional (SACS/CC); dental assisting (ADA); dental hygiene (ADA); emergency medical services (JRCEMTP); engineering technology (ABET/TAC); health information technology (AHIMA); medical laboratory technology (NAACLS); physical therapy assisting (APTA); radiologic technology: radiography (JRCERT). **Total program enrollment:** 6271. **Application fee:** $35.

PROGRAM(S) OFFERED
• Accounting Technology/Technician and Bookkeeping *2 students enrolled* • Accounting *13 students enrolled* • Administrative Assistant and Secretarial Science, General *17 students enrolled* • Allied Health Diagnostic, Intervention, and Treatment Professions, Other *21 students enrolled* • Autobody/Collision and Repair Technology/Technician *25 students enrolled* • Automobile/Automotive Mechanics Technology/Technician *263 students enrolled* • Business Administration and Management, General *113 students enrolled* • Carpentry/Carpenter *2 students enrolled* • Cartography *30 students enrolled* • Child Care Provider/Assistant *32 students enrolled* • Civil Engineering Technology/Technician *8 students enrolled* • Commercial and Advertising Art *6 students enrolled* • Computer Programming/Programmer, General *6 students enrolled* • Computer and Information Sciences and Support Services, Other *27 students enrolled* • Construction Engineering Technology/Technician *13 students enrolled* • Cosmetology/Cosmetologist, General *36 students enrolled* • Criminal Justice/Safety Studies *41 students enrolled* • Data Processing and Data Processing Technology/Technician *60 students enrolled* • Dental Assisting/Assistant *4 students enrolled* • Diagnostic Medical Sonography/Sonographer and Ultrasound Technician *11 students enrolled* • Diesel Mechanics Technology/Technician *10 students enrolled* • Electrician *6 students enrolled* • Fire Science/Firefighting *9 students enrolled* • Heating, Air Conditioning, Ventilation and Refrigeration Maintenance Technology/Technician (HAC, HACR, HVAC, HVACR) *75 students enrolled* • Industrial Mechanics and Maintenance Technology *18 students enrolled* • Institutional Food Workers *11 students enrolled* • Legal Assistant/Paralegal *2 students enrolled* • Licensed Practical/Vocational Nurse Training (LPN, LVN, Cert, Dipl, AAS) *123 students enrolled* • Machine Tool Technology/Machinist *2 students enrolled* • Mason/Masonry *3 students enrolled* • Massage Therapy/Therapeutic Massage *10 students enrolled* • Mechanic and Repair Technologies/Technicians, Other *16 students enrolled* • Mechanical Drafting and Mechanical Drafting CAD/CADD *13 students enrolled* • Medical Administrative/Executive Assistant and Medical Secretary *6 students enrolled* • Medical Radiologic Technology/Science—Radiation Therapist *33 students enrolled* • Nursing—Registered Nurse Training (RN, ASN, BSN, MSN) *171 students enrolled* • Pharmacy Technician/Assistant *12 students enrolled* • Physical Therapist Assistant *65 students enrolled* • Precision Production, Other *16 students enrolled* • Sales, Distribution and Marketing Operations, General *24 students enrolled* • Social Work *32 students enrolled* • Surgical Technology/Technologist *25 students enrolled* • Truck and Bus Driver/Commercial Vehicle Operation *89 students enrolled* • Veterinary/Animal Health Technology/Technician and Veterinary Assistant *51 students enrolled* • Welding Technology/Welder *36 students enrolled*

STUDENT SERVICES Academic or career counseling, daycare for children of students, employment services for current students, placement services for program completers, remedial services.

Harley's Beauty and Barber Career Institute

1527 Lyon Street, Columbia, SC 29204
http://www.hbbci.com/

CONTACT Douglas Harley, Owner
Telephone: 803-254-0050

GENERAL INFORMATION Private Institution. **Total program enrollment:** 8. **Application fee:** $50.

PROGRAM(S) OFFERED
• **Barbering/Barber** *1500 hrs./$13,700* • **Cosmetology, Barber/Styling, and Nail Instructor** *1500 hrs./$13,200*

Horry-Georgetown Technical College

2050 Highway 501, PO Box 261966, Conway, SC 29528-6066
http://www.hgtc.edu/

CONTACT H. Neyle Wilson, President
Telephone: 843-347-3186

GENERAL INFORMATION Public Institution. Founded 1966. **Accreditation:** Regional (SACS/CC); dental assisting (ADA); engineering technology (ABET/TAC); radiologic technology: radiography (JRCERT). **Total program enrollment:** 2330. **Application fee:** $25.

PROGRAM(S) OFFERED
• **Administrative Assistant and Secretarial Science, General** *3 students enrolled* • **Business/Commerce, General** *9 students enrolled* • **Child Care Provider/Assistant** *19 students enrolled* • **Computer and Information Sciences and Support Services, Other** *1 student enrolled* • **Cosmetology/Cosmetologist, General** *40 students enrolled* • **Data Processing and Data Processing Technology/Technician** *7 students enrolled* • **Dental Assisting/Assistant** *12 students enrolled* • **Diagnostic Medical Sonography/Sonographer and Ultrasound Technician** *5 students enrolled* • **Entrepreneurship/Entrepreneurial Studies** *16 students enrolled* • **Forestry, General** *4 students enrolled* • **General Office Occupations and Clerical Services** *13 students enrolled* • **Health Information/Medical Records Technology/Technician** *4 students enrolled* • **Heating, Air Conditioning, Ventilation and Refrigeration Maintenance Technology/Technician (HAC, HACR, HVAC, HVACR)** *19 students enrolled* • **Licensed Practical/Vocational Nurse Training (LPN, LVN, Cert, Dipl, AAS)** *31 students enrolled* • **Medical Radiologic Technology/Science—Radiation Therapist** *15 students enrolled* • **Medical/Clinical Assistant** *3 students enrolled* • **Nuclear Medical Technology/Technologist** *7 students enrolled* • **Nursing—Registered Nurse Training (RN, ASN, BSN, MSN)** *8 students enrolled* • **Pharmacy Technician/Assistant** *4 students enrolled* • **Physical Therapist Assistant** *17 students enrolled* • **Surgical Technology/Technologist** *14 students enrolled* • **Turf and Turfgrass Management** *7 students enrolled* • **Welding Technology/Welder** *1 student enrolled*

STUDENT SERVICES Academic or career counseling, daycare for children of students, employment services for current students, placement services for program completers, remedial services.

Institute of Cosmetic Arts

7474 Garners Ferry Road, Columbia, SC 29209
http://instituteofcosmeticarts.com/

CONTACT Darlene Roy, Director of Financial Planning
Telephone: 803-776-9100

GENERAL INFORMATION Private Institution. **Total program enrollment:** 75. **Application fee:** $50.

PROGRAM(S) OFFERED
• **Cosmetology/Cosmetologist, General** *1500 hrs./$14,150*

STUDENT SERVICES Placement services for program completers.

Institute of Cosmetic Arts

1515 John B White Sr. Boulevard, Spartanburg, SC 29301
http://instituteofcosmeticarts.com/

CONTACT Darlene Roy, Director of Financial Planning
Telephone: 864-587-6000

GENERAL INFORMATION Private Institution. **Total program enrollment:** 147. **Application fee:** $50.

PROGRAM(S) OFFERED
• **Aesthetician/Esthetician and Skin Care Specialist** *16 students enrolled* • **Cosmetology/Cosmetologist, General** *1500 hrs./$17,650* • **Nail Technician/Specialist and Manicurist** *600 hrs./$4150*

STUDENT SERVICES Placement services for program completers.

Kenneth Shuler's School of Cosmetology and Hair Design

449 Street Andrews Road, Columbia, SC 29210
http://www.kennethshuler.com/

CONTACT Darlene Roy, Director of Financial Planning
Telephone: 803-772-6042

GENERAL INFORMATION Private Institution. Founded 1968. **Total program enrollment:** 141. **Application fee:** $50.

PROGRAM(S) OFFERED
• **Cosmetology/Cosmetologist, General** *1500 hrs./$17,650* • **Nail Technician/Specialist and Manicurist** *600 hrs./$4150*

STUDENT SERVICES Placement services for program completers.

Kenneth Shuler's School of Cosmetology and Hair Design

736 Martintown Road, E, North Augusta, SC 29841
http://www.kennethshuler.com/

CONTACT Darlene Roy, Director of Financial Planning
Telephone: 803-278-1200

GENERAL INFORMATION Private Institution. **Total program enrollment:** 112. **Application fee:** $50.

PROGRAM(S) OFFERED
• **Cosmetology, Barber/Styling, and Nail Instructor** *2 students enrolled* • **Cosmetology/Cosmetologist, General** *1500 hrs./$17,650* • **Nail Technician/Specialist and Manicurist** *600 hrs./$4150*

STUDENT SERVICES Placement services for program completers.

Lacy Cosmetology School

3084 Whiskey Road, Aiken, SC 29803
http://www.lacyschools.com/

CONTACT Jay Lacy, Chief Administrator
Telephone: 803-648-6181

GENERAL INFORMATION Private Institution. **Total program enrollment:** 33. **Application fee:** $100.

PROGRAM(S) OFFERED
• **Aesthetician/Esthetician and Skin Care Specialist** *600 hrs./$4995* • **Cosmetology, Barber/Styling, and Nail Instructor** *750 hrs./$5400* • **Cosmetology/Cosmetologist, General** *1500 hrs./$13,700* • **Facial Treatment Specialist/Facialist** • **Nail Technician/Specialist and Manicurist** *600 hrs./$4995*

STUDENT SERVICES Academic or career counseling, placement services for program completers.

Lacy Cosmetology School

98 Davenport Street, Goose Creek, SC 29445
http://www.lacyschools.com

CONTACT Jay Lacy, CEO
Telephone: 843-572-8705

GENERAL INFORMATION Private Institution. **Total program enrollment:** 17. **Application fee:** $100.

PROGRAM(S) OFFERED
• **Aesthetician/Esthetician and Skin Care Specialist** 600 hrs./$4995
• **Cosmetology, Barber/Styling, and Nail Instructor** 750 hrs./$5400
• **Cosmetology/Cosmetologist, General** 1500 hrs./$17,765 • **Nail Technician/Specialist and Manicurist** 600 hrs./$4995

STUDENT SERVICES Placement services for program completers.

Lacy Cosmetology School

2361 Augusta Highway, Lexington, SC 29073
http://www.lacyschools.com

CONTACT Jay Lacy, CEO
Telephone: 803-951-2236

GENERAL INFORMATION Private Institution. **Total program enrollment:** 35. **Application fee:** $100.

PROGRAM(S) OFFERED
• **Aesthetician/Esthetician and Skin Care Specialist** 600 hrs./$4995
• **Cosmetology, Barber/Styling, and Nail Instructor** 750 hrs./$5400
• **Cosmetology/Cosmetologist, General** 1500 hrs./$15,765 • **Nail Technician/Specialist and Manicurist** 600 hrs./$4995

STUDENT SERVICES Placement services for program completers.

Lander University

320 Stanley Avenue, Greenwood, SC 29649-2099
http://www.lander.edu/

CONTACT Dr. Daniel W. Ball, President
Telephone: 864-388-8000

GENERAL INFORMATION Public Institution. Founded 1872. **Accreditation:** Regional (SACS/CC); art and design (NASAD); music (NASM); theater (NAST). **Total program enrollment:** 2294. **Application fee:** $35.

PROGRAM(S) OFFERED
• **Business Administration and Management, General** 1 student enrolled
STUDENT SERVICES Academic or career counseling, employment services for current students, placement services for program completers, remedial services.

LeGrand Institute of Cosmetology

2418 Broad Street, Camden, SC 29020
http://www.legrandinstitute.com/

CONTACT Debra R. Legrand, CEO
Telephone: 803-425-8449

GENERAL INFORMATION Private Institution. **Total program enrollment:** 35. **Application fee:** $50.

PROGRAM(S) OFFERED
• **Cosmetology/Cosmetologist, General** 1500 hrs./$9500

Midlands Technical College

PO Box 2408, Columbia, SC 29202-2408
http://www.midlandstech.edu/

CONTACT Dr. Marshall White, Jr., President
Telephone: 803-738-8324

GENERAL INFORMATION Public Institution. Founded 1974. **Accreditation:** Regional (SACS/CC); dental assisting (ADA); dental hygiene (ADA);

engineering technology (ABET/TAC); health information technology (AHIMA); medical laboratory technology (NAACLS); physical therapy assisting (APTA); practical nursing (NLN); radiologic technology: radiography (JRCERT); respiratory therapy technology (CoARC). **Total program enrollment:** 5168.

PROGRAM(S) OFFERED
• **Administrative Assistant and Secretarial Science, General** 12 students enrolled • **Automobile/Automotive Mechanics Technology/Technician** 142 students enrolled • **Business/Commerce, General** 4 students enrolled • **Chemical Technology/Technician** 3 students enrolled • **Child Care Provider/Assistant** 15 students enrolled • **Clinical/Medical Laboratory Technician** 2 students enrolled • **Computer Systems Networking and Telecommunications** 15 students enrolled • **Computer and Information Sciences and Support Services, Other** 32 students enrolled • **Court Reporting/Court Reporter** 2 students enrolled • **Data Processing and Data Processing Technology/Technician** 15 students enrolled • **Dental Assisting/Assistant** 18 students enrolled • **Dental Hygiene/Hygienist** 12 students enrolled • **Electrical, Electronic and Communications Engineering Technology/Technician** 9 students enrolled • **Electrician** 24 students enrolled • **Graphic and Printing Equipment Operator, General Production** 2 students enrolled • **Health Information/Medical Records Technology/Technician** 33 students enrolled • **Heating, Air Conditioning, Ventilation and Refrigeration Maintenance Technology/Technician (HAC, HACR, HVAC, HVACR)** 1 student enrolled • **Industrial Electronics Technology/Technician** 9 students enrolled • **Legal Assistant/Paralegal** 37 students enrolled • **Licensed Practical/Vocational Nurse Training (LPN, LVN, Cert, Dipl, AAS)** 56 students enrolled • **Machine Tool Technology/Machinist** 18 students enrolled • **Mechanical Drafting and Mechanical Drafting CAD/CADD** 2 students enrolled • **Medical Administrative/Executive Assistant and Medical Secretary** 6 students enrolled • **Medical Radiologic Technology/Science—Radiation Therapist** 8 students enrolled • **Nuclear Medical Technology/Technologist** 13 students enrolled • **Nurse/Nursing Assistant/Aide and Patient Care Assistant** 16 students enrolled • **Nursing—Registered Nurse Training (RN, ASN, BSN, MSN)** 233 students enrolled • **Pharmacy Technician/Assistant** 10 students enrolled • **Physical Therapist Assistant** 5 students enrolled • **Respiratory Care Therapy/Therapist** 7 students enrolled • **Surgical Technology/Technologist** 17 students enrolled • **Welding Technology/Welder** 2 students enrolled

STUDENT SERVICES Academic or career counseling, employment services for current students, placement services for program completers, remedial services.

Miller-Motte Technical College

8085 Rivers Avenue, Suite E, Charleston, SC 29418
http://www.miller-motte.com/

CONTACT Elaine Cue
Telephone: 843-574-0101

GENERAL INFORMATION Private Institution. Founded 2000. **Accreditation:** State accredited or approved. **Total program enrollment:** 483. **Application fee:** $35.

PROGRAM(S) OFFERED
• **Cosmetology/Cosmetologist, General** 47 students enrolled • **Massage Therapy/Therapeutic Massage** 1 student enrolled • **Surgical Technology/Technologist** 17 students enrolled

STUDENT SERVICES Academic or career counseling, employment services for current students, placement services for program completers, remedial services.

Northeastern Technical College

PO Drawer 1007, Cheraw, SC 29520-1007
http://www.netc.edu/

CONTACT Ron Bartley, President
Telephone: 843-921-6900

GENERAL INFORMATION Public Institution. Founded 1967. **Accreditation:** Regional (SACS/CC). **Total program enrollment:** 441. **Application fee:** $25.

Northeastern Technical College (continued)

PROGRAM(S) OFFERED

• Accounting Technology/Technician and Bookkeeping *3 students enrolled* • Administrative Assistant and Secretarial Science, General *16 students enrolled* • Architectural Drafting and Architectural CAD/CADD *1 student enrolled* • Business Administration and Management, General *2 students enrolled* • Child Care Provider/Assistant *17 students enrolled* • Criminal Justice/Safety Studies *7 students enrolled* • Data Processing and Data Processing Technology/Technician *1 student enrolled* • Electrical and Electronic Engineering Technologies/Technicians, Other *16 students enrolled* • Electrician *7 students enrolled* • General Office Occupations and Clerical Services *11 students enrolled* • Industrial Electronics Technology/Technician *6 students enrolled* • Licensed Practical/Vocational Nurse Training (LPN, LVN, Cert, Dipl, AAS) *9 students enrolled* • Machine Shop Technology/Assistant *2 students enrolled* • Machine Tool Technology/Machinist *1 student enrolled* • Mechanical Drafting and Mechanical Drafting CAD/CADD *7 students enrolled* • Nursing—Registered Nurse Training (RN, ASN, BSN, MSN) *13 students enrolled* • Precision Production, Other *1 student enrolled* • Welding Technology/Welder *2 students enrolled*

STUDENT SERVICES Academic or career counseling, employment services for current students, placement services for program completers, remedial services.

Orangeburg-Calhoun Technical College

3250 St Matthews Road, NE, Orangeburg, SC 29118-8299
http://www.octech.edu/

CONTACT Anne Smoak Crook, PhD, President
Telephone: 803-536-0311

GENERAL INFORMATION Public Institution. Founded 1968. **Accreditation:** Regional (SACS/CC); engineering technology (ABET/TAC); medical laboratory technology (NAACLS); radiologic technology: radiography (JRCERT). **Total program enrollment:** 1292. **Application fee:** $15.

PROGRAM(S) OFFERED

• Accounting *2 students enrolled* • Administrative Assistant and Secretarial Science, General *16 students enrolled* • Allied Health Diagnostic, Intervention, and Treatment Professions, Other *5 students enrolled* • Automobile/Automotive Mechanics Technology/Technician *35 students enrolled* • Child Care Provider/Assistant *10 students enrolled* • Clinical/Medical Laboratory Assistant *11 students enrolled* • Computer and Information Sciences and Support Services, Other *13 students enrolled* • Criminal Justice/Safety Studies *5 students enrolled* • Data Processing and Data Processing Technology/Technician *11 students enrolled* • Dental Hygiene/Hygienist *4 students enrolled* • Diesel Mechanics Technology/Technician *3 students enrolled* • General Office Occupations and Clerical Services *10 students enrolled* • Industrial Mechanics and Maintenance Technology *4 students enrolled* • Licensed Practical/Vocational Nurse Training (LPN, LVN, Cert, Dipl, AAS) *6 students enrolled* • Mechanical Drafting and Mechanical Drafting CAD/CADD *2 students enrolled* • Medical Radiologic Technology/Science—Radiation Therapist *5 students enrolled* • Nurse/Nursing Assistant/Aide and Patient Care Assistant *21 students enrolled* • Physical Therapist Assistant *2 students enrolled* • Welding Technology/Welder *4 students enrolled*

STUDENT SERVICES Academic or career counseling, employment services for current students, placement services for program completers, remedial services.

Piedmont Technical College

620 North Emerald Road, PO Box 1467, Greenwood, SC 29648-1467
http://www.ptc.edu/

CONTACT Ray Brooks, President
Telephone: 864-941-8324

GENERAL INFORMATION Public Institution. Founded 1966. **Accreditation:** Regional (SACS/CC); engineering technology (ABET/TAC); funeral service (ABFSE); radiologic technology: radiography (JRCERT). **Total program enrollment:** 2179.

PROGRAM(S) OFFERED

• Accounting *13 students enrolled* • Administrative Assistant and Secretarial Science, General *29 students enrolled* • Business Administration and Management, General *11 students enrolled* • Business/Commerce, General *15*

• Child Care Provider/Assistant *10 students enrolled* • Child Care and Support Services Management *7 students enrolled* • Clinical/Medical Laboratory Technician *1 student enrolled* • Commercial and Advertising Art *20 students enrolled* • Computer Programming/Programmer, General *1 student enrolled* • Construction Engineering Technology/Technician *72 students enrolled* • Data Processing and Data Processing Technology/Technician *38 students enrolled* • Electrical/Electronics Equipment Installation and Repair, General *4 students enrolled* • Emergency Medical Technology/Technician (EMT Paramedic) *1 student enrolled* • Engineering Technology, General *3 students enrolled* • General Office Occupations and Clerical Services *54 students enrolled* • Gunsmithing/Gunsmith *8 students enrolled* • Health Professions and Related Clinical Sciences, Other *35 students enrolled* • Heating, Air Conditioning, Ventilation and Refrigeration Maintenance Technology/Technician (HAC, HACR, HVAC, HVACR) *22 students enrolled* • Licensed Practical/Vocational Nurse Training (LPN, LVN, Cert, Dipl, AAS) *14 students enrolled* • Machine Shop Technology/Assistant *7 students enrolled* • Machine Tool Technology/Machinist *12 students enrolled* • Medical/Clinical Assistant *14 students enrolled* • Nursing—Registered Nurse Training (RN, ASN, BSN, MSN) *12 students enrolled* • Occupational Therapist Assistant *3 students enrolled* • Pharmacy Technician/Assistant *24 students enrolled* • Physical Therapist Assistant *5 students enrolled* • Social Work *14 students enrolled* • Surgical Technology/Technologist *14 students enrolled* • Welding Technology/Welder *3 students enrolled*

STUDENT SERVICES Academic or career counseling, employment services for current students, placement services for program completers, remedial services.

Plaza School of Beauty

946 Oakland Avenue, Rock Hill, SC 29730

CONTACT Orri J. Putnam, Owner
Telephone: 803-328-5166

GENERAL INFORMATION Private Institution. **Total program enrollment:** 8. **Application fee:** $100.

PROGRAM(S) OFFERED

• Cosmetology/Cosmetologist, General *18 students enrolled* • Salon/Beauty Salon Management/Manager *1500 hrs./$9900*

STUDENT SERVICES Academic or career counseling, employment services for current students, placement services for program completers, remedial services.

Southeastern School of Neuromuscular & Massage Therapy

1420 Colonial Life Boulevard, Suite 80, Columbia, SC 29210
http://www.southeasternmassageschools.com/

CONTACT Lindsay Ott, Vice President
Telephone: 803-798-8800

GENERAL INFORMATION Private Institution. **Total program enrollment:** 101. **Application fee:** $100.

PROGRAM(S) OFFERED

• Massage Therapy/Therapeutic Massage *25 hrs./$10,356*

STUDENT SERVICES Academic or career counseling, employment services for current students, placement services for program completers, remedial services.

Southeastern School of Neuromuscular & Massage Therapy–Charleston

4600 Goer Drive, Suite 105, North Charleston, SC 29406
http://southeasternmassageschools.com/

CONTACT Ronda S. Villa, Vice President
Telephone: 843-747-1279

GENERAL INFORMATION Private Institution. **Total program enrollment:** 6. **Application fee:** $100.

PROGRAM(S) OFFERED
• **Massage Therapy/Therapeutic Massage** *25 hrs./$10,356*

STUDENT SERVICES Academic or career counseling, employment services for current students, placement services for program completers, remedial services.

Spartanburg Community College

Business I-85 & New Cut Road, PO Box 4386, Spartanburg, SC 29305-4386
http://www.stcsc.edu/

CONTACT Dan Terhune, President
Telephone: 864-592-4600

GENERAL INFORMATION Public Institution. Founded 1961. **Accreditation:** Regional (SACS/CC); dental assisting (ADA); engineering technology (ABET/TAC); medical laboratory technology (NAACLS); radiologic technology: radiography (JRCERT). **Total program enrollment:** 2503.

PROGRAM(S) OFFERED
• **Accounting** *4 students enrolled* • **Administrative Assistant and Secretarial Science, General** *7 students enrolled* • **Architectural Drafting and Architectural CAD/CADD** *6 students enrolled* • **Child Care Provider/Assistant** *3 students enrolled* • **Clinical/Medical Laboratory Assistant** *18 students enrolled* • **Commercial and Advertising Art** *1 student enrolled* • **Culinary Arts/Chef Training** *2 students enrolled* • **Data Processing and Data Processing Technology/Technician** *5 students enrolled* • **Dental Assisting/Assistant** *10 students enrolled* • **Electrical and Electronic Engineering Technologies/Technicians, Other** *2 students enrolled* • **Hazardous Materials Information Systems Technology/Technician** *16 students enrolled* • **Health Professions and Related Clinical Sciences, Other** *14 students enrolled* • **Heating, Air Conditioning, Ventilation and Refrigeration Maintenance Technology/Technician (HAC, HACR, HVAC, HVACR)** *10 students enrolled* • **Industrial Mechanics and Maintenance Technology** *12 students enrolled* • **Landscaping and Groundskeeping** *2 students enrolled* • **Mechanical Drafting and Mechanical Drafting CAD/CADD** *3 students enrolled* • **Medical Administrative/Executive Assistant and Medical Secretary** *5 students enrolled* • **Medical/Clinical Assistant** *14 students enrolled* • **Pharmacy Technician/Assistant** *23 students enrolled* • **Physical Therapist Assistant** *9 students enrolled* • **Sign Language Interpretation and Translation** *3 students enrolled* • **Surgical Technology/Technologist** *1 student enrolled* • **Welding Technology/Welder** *9 students enrolled*

STUDENT SERVICES Academic or career counseling, employment services for current students, placement services for program completers, remedial services.

Strand College of Hair Design

423 79th Avenue, N, Myrtle Beach, SC 29572
http://strandcollege.com/

CONTACT Nancy Poole, President
Telephone: 843-467-2397

GENERAL INFORMATION Private Institution. **Total program enrollment:** 62. **Application fee:** $50.

PROGRAM(S) OFFERED
• **Aesthetician/Esthetician and Skin Care Specialist** *450 hrs./$6000*
• **Cosmetology, Barber/Styling, and Nail Instructor** *750 hrs./$5700*
• **Cosmetology/Cosmetologist, General** *1500 hrs./$12,700* • **Nail Technician/Specialist and Manicurist** *300 hrs./$4200*

STUDENT SERVICES Academic or career counseling, placement services for program completers.

Styletrends Barber and Hairstyling Academy

239 Hampton Street, Rock Hill, SC 29730

CONTACT Charlene McCleod
Telephone: 803-328-0807

GENERAL INFORMATION Private Institution. **Total program enrollment:** 31.

PROGRAM(S) OFFERED
• **Barbering/Barber** *1500 hrs./$10,400*

STUDENT SERVICES Placement services for program completers.

Sumter Beauty College

921 Carolina Avenue, Sumter, SC 29150
http://www.sumterbeautycollege.com/

CONTACT Faye H. Smith, Owner
Telephone: 803-773-7311

GENERAL INFORMATION Private Institution. Founded 1961. **Total program enrollment:** 44. **Application fee:** $100.

PROGRAM(S) OFFERED
• **Cosmetology and Related Personal Grooming Arts, Other** • **Cosmetology/Cosmetologist, General** *1500 hrs./$9125*

STUDENT SERVICES Academic or career counseling, placement services for program completers.

Technical College of the Lowcountry

921 Ribaut Road, PO Box 1288, Beaufort, SC 29901-1288
http://www.tclonline.org/

CONTACT Dr. Tom Leitzel, President
Telephone: 800-768-8252

GENERAL INFORMATION Public Institution. Founded 1972. **Accreditation:** Regional (SACS/CC). **Total program enrollment:** 684. **Application fee:** $25.

PROGRAM(S) OFFERED
• **Accounting** *3 students enrolled* • **Administrative Assistant and Secretarial Science, General** *1 student enrolled* • **Business Administration and Management, General** *1 student enrolled* • **Business/Commerce, General** *4 students enrolled* • **Child Care Provider/Assistant** *4 students enrolled* • **Construction Engineering Technology/Technician** *1 student enrolled* • **Cosmetology/Cosmetologist, General** *12 students enrolled* • **Electrical and Electronic Engineering Technologies/Technicians, Other** *19 students enrolled* • **General Office Occupations and Clerical Services** *1 student enrolled* • **Heating, Air Conditioning, Ventilation and Refrigeration Maintenance Technology/Technician (HAC, HACR, HVAC, HVACR)** *30 students enrolled* • **Industrial Electronics Technology/Technician** *14 students enrolled* • **Legal Administrative Assistant/Secretary** *1 student enrolled* • **Legal Assistant/Paralegal** *3 students enrolled* • **Licensed Practical/Vocational Nurse Training (LPN, LVN, Cert, Dipl, AAS)** *13 students enrolled* • **Mechanical Drafting and Mechanical Drafting CAD/CADD** *12 students enrolled* • **Medical Administrative/Executive Assistant and Medical Secretary** *2 students enrolled* • **Pharmacy Technician/Assistant** *1 student enrolled* • **Physical Therapist Assistant** *11 students enrolled* • **Surgical Technology/Technologist** *11 students enrolled*

STUDENT SERVICES Academic or career counseling, employment services for current students, placement services for program completers, remedial services.

Tri-County Technical College

PO Box 587, 7900 Highway 76, Pendleton, SC 29670-0587
http://www.tctc.edu/

CONTACT Ronnie L. Booth, President
Telephone: 864-646-1500

GENERAL INFORMATION Public Institution. Founded 1962. **Accreditation:** Regional (SACS/CC); dental assisting (ADA); engineering technology (ABET/TAC); medical laboratory technology (NAACLS). **Total program enrollment:** 3316. **Application fee:** $20.

PROGRAM(S) OFFERED
• **Accounting** *6 students enrolled* • **Administrative Assistant and Secretarial Science, General** *55 students enrolled* • **Business/Commerce, General** *10 students enrolled* • **Child Care Provider/Assistant** *32 students enrolled* • **Criminal Justice/Safety Studies** *5 students enrolled* • **Data Processing and Data**

Tri-County Technical College (continued)

Processing Technology/Technician *13 students enrolled* ● Dental Assisting/Assistant *13 students enrolled* ● Electrical and Electronic Engineering Technologies/Technicians, Other *2 students enrolled* ● General Office Occupations and Clerical Services *5 students enrolled* ● Industrial Mechanics and Maintenance Technology *17 students enrolled* ● Industrial Production Technologies/Technicians, Other *5 students enrolled* ● Licensed Practical/Vocational Nurse Training (LPN, LVN, Cert, Dipl, AAS) *34 students enrolled* ● Machine Tool Technology/Machinist *1 student enrolled* ● Manufacturing Technology/Technician *1 student enrolled* ● Medical/Clinical Assistant *19 students enrolled* ● Nursing—Registered Nurse Training (RN, ASN, BSN, MSN) *4 students enrolled* ● Quality Control Technology/Technician *2 students enrolled* ● Radio and Television Broadcasting Technology/Technician *6 students enrolled* ● Sales, Distribution and Marketing Operations, General *27 students enrolled* ● Surgical Technology/Technologist *22 students enrolled* ● Welding Technology/Welder *22 students enrolled*

STUDENT SERVICES Academic or career counseling, employment services for current students, placement services for program completers, remedial services.

Trident Technical College

PO Box 118067, Charleston, SC 29423-8067
http://www.tridenttech.edu/

CONTACT Mary Thornley, President
Telephone: 843-574-6111

GENERAL INFORMATION Public Institution. Founded 1964. **Accreditation:** Regional (SACS/CC); dental assisting (ADA); dental hygiene (ADA); engineering technology (ABET/TAC); medical laboratory technology (NAACLS); physical therapy assisting (APTA); radiologic technology: radiography (JRCERT). **Total program enrollment: 5544. Application fee: $25.**

PROGRAM(S) OFFERED
● Accounting *40 students enrolled* ● Administrative Assistant and Secretarial Science, General *2 students enrolled* ● Aircraft Powerplant Technology/Technician *17 students enrolled* ● Airframe Mechanics and Aircraft Maintenance Technology/Technician *8 students enrolled* ● Applied Horticulture/Horticultural Operations, General *1 student enrolled* ● Automobile/Automotive Mechanics Technology/Technician *8 students enrolled* ● Banking and Financial Support Services *2 students enrolled* ● Business/Commerce, General *2 students enrolled* ● Business/Office Automation/Technology/Data Entry *32 students enrolled* ● Child Care Provider/Assistant *9 students enrolled* ● Child Care and Support Services Management *2 students enrolled* ● Civil Engineering Technology/Technician *5 students enrolled* ● Commercial and Advertising Art *14 students enrolled* ● Computer Programming/Programmer, General *2 students enrolled* ● Computer and Information Sciences and Support Services, Other *10 students enrolled* ● Construction Engineering Technology/Technician *10 students enrolled* ● Cosmetology/Cosmetologist, General *51 students enrolled* ● Criminal Justice/Safety Studies *20 students enrolled* ● Culinary Arts/Chef Training *11 students enrolled* ● Data Processing and Data Processing Technology/Technician *10 students enrolled* ● Dental Assisting/Assistant *11 students enrolled* ● Electrical and Electronic Engineering Technologies/Technicians, Other *5 students enrolled* ● Electrical, Electronic and Communications Engineering Technology/Technician *1 student enrolled* ● Entrepreneurship/Entrepreneurial Studies *1 student enrolled* ● Environmental Control Technologies/Technicians, Other *3 students enrolled* ● Health Information/Medical Records Technology/Technician *10 students enrolled* ● Heating, Air Conditioning, Ventilation and Refrigeration Maintenance Technology/Technician (HAC, HACR, HVAC, HVACR) *10 students enrolled* ● Hotel/Motel Administration/Management *21 students enrolled* ● Legal Assistant/Paralegal *15 students enrolled* ● Licensed Practical/Vocational Nurse Training (LPN, LVN, Cert, Dipl, AAS) *13 students enrolled* ● Machine Shop Technology/Assistant *1 student enrolled* ● Mechanical Drafting and Mechanical Drafting CAD/CADD *20 students enrolled* ● Medical Transcription/Transcriptionist *4 students enrolled* ● Medical/Clinical Assistant *15 students enrolled* ● Nursing—Registered Nurse Training (RN, ASN, BSN, MSN) *127 students enrolled* ● Pharmacy Technician/Assistant *6 students enrolled* ● Physical Therapist Assistant *18 students enrolled* ● Radio and Television Broadcasting Technology/Technician *6 students enrolled* ● Respiratory Care Therapy/Therapist *6 students enrolled* ● Sales, Distribution and Marketing Operations, General *1 student enrolled* ● Social Work *62 students enrolled* ● Survey Technology/Surveying *3 students enrolled* ● Turf and Turfgrass Management *1 student enrolled* ● Welding Technology/Welder *10 students enrolled*

STUDENT SERVICES Academic or career counseling, employment services for current students, placement services for program completers, remedial services.

University of South Carolina Upstate

800 University Way, Spartanburg, SC 29303-4999
http://www.uscupstate.edu/

CONTACT John C. Stockwell, Chancellor
Telephone: 864-503-5000

GENERAL INFORMATION Public Institution. Founded 1967. **Accreditation:** Regional (SACS/CC); computer science (ABET/CSAC). **Total program enrollment: 4152. Application fee: $40.**

PROGRAM(S) OFFERED
● Teaching English as a Second or Foreign Language/ESL Language Instructor

STUDENT SERVICES Academic or career counseling, daycare for children of students, employment services for current students, placement services for program completers, remedial services.

Virginia College–Greenville

78 Global Drive, Suite 200, Greenville, SC 29607
vc.edu

CONTACT Paul Wright, Campus President
Telephone: 864-679-4900

GENERAL INFORMATION Private Institution. **Total program enrollment: 209. Application fee: $100.**

STUDENT SERVICES Academic or career counseling, placement services for program completers, remedial services.

Williamsburg Technical College

601 Martin Luther King, Jr Avenue, Kingstree, SC 29556-4197
http://www.wiltech.edu/

CONTACT Dr. Cleve H. Cox, President
Telephone: 843-355-4110

GENERAL INFORMATION Public Institution. Founded 1969. **Accreditation:** Regional (SACS/CC). **Total program enrollment: 271. Application fee: $10.**

PROGRAM(S) OFFERED
● Administrative Assistant and Secretarial Science, General *2 students enrolled* ● Automobile/Automotive Mechanics Technology/Technician *5 students enrolled* ● Child Care Provider/Assistant *1 student enrolled* ● Cosmetology/Cosmetologist, General *6 students enrolled* ● Data Processing and Data Processing Technology/Technician *3 students enrolled* ● Heating, Air Conditioning, Ventilation and Refrigeration Maintenance Technology/Technician (HAC, HACR, HVAC, HVACR) *1 student enrolled* ● Licensed Practical/Vocational Nurse Training (LPN, LVN, Cert, Dipl, AAS) *7 students enrolled* ● Medical Administrative/Executive Assistant and Medical Secretary *8 students enrolled* ● Social Work *2 students enrolled* ● Welding Technology/Welder *9 students enrolled*

STUDENT SERVICES Academic or career counseling, employment services for current students, placement services for program completers, remedial services.

Winthrop University

701 Oakland Avenue, Rock Hill, SC 29733
http://www.winthrop.edu/

CONTACT Anthony Digiorgio, President
Telephone: 803-323-2211

GENERAL INFORMATION Public Institution. Founded 1886. **Accreditation:** Regional (SACS/CC); art and design (NASAD); computer science (ABET/CSAC); counseling (ACA); dance (NASD); dietetics: postbaccalaureate internship (ADtA/CAADE); interior design: professional (CIDA); journalism and mass communications (ACEJMC); music (NASM); theater (NAST). **Total program enrollment: 4894. Application fee: $40.**

STUDENT SERVICES Academic or career counseling, employment services for current students, placement services for program completers.

W. L. Bonner College

4430 Argent Court, Columbia, SC 29203

CONTACT William L. Bonner, President
Telephone: 803-754-3950

GENERAL INFORMATION Private Institution (Affiliated with Pentecostal Holiness Church). **Total program enrollment: 26. Application fee: $30.**

PROGRAM(S) OFFERED
• **Bible/Biblical Studies** 3 students enrolled • **Missions/Missionary Studies and Missiology** • **Theological and Ministerial Studies, Other** 6 students enrolled • **Theology and Religious Vocations, Other** 5 students enrolled • **Youth Ministry**

STUDENT SERVICES Academic or career counseling, remedial services.

York Technical College

452 South Anderson Road, Rock Hill, SC 29730-3395
http://www.yorktech.com/

CONTACT Greg Rutherford, President
Telephone: 803-327-8000

GENERAL INFORMATION Public Institution. Founded 1961. **Accreditation:** Regional (SACS/CC); dental assisting (ADA); dental hygiene (ADA); engineering technology (ABET/TAC); medical laboratory technology (NAACLS); radiologic technology: radiography (JRCERT). **Total program enrollment: 2374.**

PROGRAM(S) OFFERED
• **Accounting** 13 students enrolled • **Administrative Assistant and Secretarial Science, General** 50 students enrolled • **Automobile/Automotive Mechanics Technology/Technician** 8 students enrolled • **Building/Home/Construction Inspection/Inspector** 10 students enrolled • **Business Administration and Management, General** 8 students enrolled • **Carpentry/Carpenter** 6 students enrolled • **Child Care Provider/Assistant** 2 students enrolled • **Commercial and Advertising Art** 2 students enrolled • **Computer and Information Sciences and Support Services, Other** 1 student enrolled • **Construction Engineering Technology/Technician** 2 students enrolled • **Criminal Justice/Safety Studies** 2 students enrolled • **Data Processing and Data Processing Technology/Technician** 16 students enrolled • **Dental Assisting/Assistant** 16 students enrolled • **Electrical and Electronic Engineering Technologies/Technicians, Other** 22 students enrolled • **Electrical, Electronic and Communications Engineering Technology/Technician** 3 students enrolled • **General Office Occupations and Clerical Services** 7 students enrolled • **Heating, Air Conditioning, Ventilation and Refrigeration Maintenance Technology/Technician (HAC, HACR, HVAC, HVACR)** 11 students enrolled • **Industrial Electronics Technology/Technician** 1 student enrolled • **Industrial Mechanics and Maintenance Technology** 1 student enrolled • **Legal Administrative Assistant/Secretary** 2 students enrolled • **Licensed Practical/Vocational Nurse Training (LPN, LVN, Cert, Dipl, AAS)** 32 students enrolled • **Machine Tool Technology/Machinist** 14 students enrolled • **Mechanical Drafting and Mechanical Drafting CAD/CADD** 3 students enrolled • **Medical Administrative/Executive Assistant and Medical Secretary** 15 students enrolled • **Medical/Clinical Assistant** 67 students enrolled • **Nursing—Registered Nurse Training (RN, ASN, BSN, MSN)** 2 students enrolled • **Radio and Television Broadcasting Technology/Technician** 10 students enrolled • **Surgical Technology/Technologist** 3 students enrolled • **Water Quality and Wastewater Treatment Management and Recycling Technology/Technician** 3 students enrolled • **Welding Technology/Welder** 10 students enrolled

STUDENT SERVICES Academic or career counseling, employment services for current students, placement services for program completers, remedial services.

TENNESSEE

American Baptist College of American Baptist Theological Seminary

1800 Baptist World Center Drive, Nashville, TN 37207
http://www.abcnash.edu/

CONTACT Forrest E. Harris, Sr., President
Telephone: 615-256-1463

GENERAL INFORMATION Private Institution. Founded 1924. **Accreditation:** State accredited or approved. **Total program enrollment: 78. Application fee: $20.**

Aquinas College

4210 Harding Road, Nashville, TN 37205-2005
http://www.aquinascollege.edu/

CONTACT Sr. Mary Peter, OP, President
Telephone: 615-297-7545

GENERAL INFORMATION Private Institution. Founded 1961. **Accreditation:** Regional (SACS/CC). **Total program enrollment: 330. Application fee: $25.**

STUDENT SERVICES Academic or career counseling, remedial services.

Arnold's Beauty School

1179 South Second Street, Milan, TN 38358

CONTACT Norma Arnold, Director
Telephone: 731-686-7351

GENERAL INFORMATION Private Institution. Founded 1941. **Total program enrollment: 56.**

PROGRAM(S) OFFERED
• **Cosmetology/Cosmetologist, General** 1500 hrs./$10,975

STUDENT SERVICES Academic or career counseling, employment services for current students, placement services for program completers.

The Art Institute of Tennessee–Nashville

100 CNA Drive, Nashville, TN 37214
http://www.artinstitutes.edu/nashville/

CONTACT Carol Menck, President
Telephone: 615-874-1067

GENERAL INFORMATION Private Institution. Founded 2006. **Total program enrollment: 393. Application fee: $50.**

PROGRAM(S) OFFERED
• **Culinary Arts/Chef Training** 8 students enrolled

STUDENT SERVICES Academic or career counseling, employment services for current students, placement services for program completers, remedial services.

Baptist College of Health Sciences

1003 Monroe Avenue, Memphis, TN 38104
http://www.bchs.edu/

CONTACT Bettysue McGarvey, DSN, President
Telephone: 901-572-2468

GENERAL INFORMATION Private Institution. Founded 1994. **Accreditation:** Regional (SACS/CC); diagnostic medical sonography (JRCEDMS);

Baptist College of Health Sciences (continued)
nuclear medicine technology (JRCNMT). **Total program enrollment:** 561. **Application fee:** $25.

STUDENT SERVICES Academic or career counseling, employment services for current students.

Buchanan Beauty College

925 Sevier Street, Shelbyville, TN 37160

CONTACT Diana Buchanan, Director
Telephone: 931-684-4080

GENERAL INFORMATION Private Institution. **Total program enrollment:** 21. **Application fee:** $50.

PROGRAM(S) OFFERED
• **Aesthetician/Esthetician and Skin Care Specialist** *750 hrs./$4550*
• **Cosmetology and Related Personal Grooming Arts, Other** *300 hrs./$1650*
• **Cosmetology, Barber/Styling, and Nail Instructor** *300 hrs./$1800*
• **Cosmetology/Cosmetologist, General** *1500 hrs./$9725* • **Nail Technician/Specialist and Manicurist** *600 hrs./$3550*

STUDENT SERVICES Academic or career counseling.

Career Beauty College

110 Waterloo Street, Lawrenceburg, TN 38464

CONTACT Karen Risner
Telephone: 931-766-9900

GENERAL INFORMATION Private Institution. **Total program enrollment:** 27. **Application fee:** $100.

PROGRAM(S) OFFERED
• **Cosmetology, Barber/Styling, and Nail Instructor** *100 hrs./$1750*
• **Cosmetology/Cosmetologist, General** *1500 hrs./$7000* • **Nail Technician/Specialist and Manicurist** *100 hrs./$2800*

Chattanooga College–Medical, Dental and Technical Careers

3805 Brainerd Road, Chattanooga, TN 37411-3798
http://www.ecpconline.com/

CONTACT William G. Faour, Director
Telephone: 423-624-0077

GENERAL INFORMATION Private Institution. **Accreditation:** State accredited or approved. **Total program enrollment:** 189. **Application fee:** $75.

PROGRAM(S) OFFERED
• **Data Processing and Data Processing Technology/Technician** *5 students enrolled* • **Health Information/Medical Records Technology/Technician** *51 students enrolled*

STUDENT SERVICES Academic or career counseling, employment services for current students, placement services for program completers.

Chattanooga State Technical Community College

4501 Amnicola Highway, Chattanooga, TN 37406-1097
http://www.chattanoogastate.edu/

CONTACT James Catanzaro, President
Telephone: 423-697-4400

GENERAL INFORMATION Public Institution. Founded 1965. **Accreditation:** Regional (SACS/CC); dental assisting (ADA); dental hygiene (ADA); engineering technology (ABET/TAC); health information technology

(AHIMA); physical therapy assisting (APTA). **Total program enrollment:** 3875. **Application fee:** $15.

PROGRAM(S) OFFERED
• **Administrative Assistant and Secretarial Science, General** • **Business/Office Automation/Technology/Data Entry** *13 students enrolled* • **Diagnostic Medical Sonography/Sonographer and Ultrasound Technician** *14 students enrolled* • **Drafting and Design Technology/Technician, General** *3 students enrolled* • **Engineering Technology, General** • **Management Information Systems, General** *2 students enrolled* • **Medical Radiologic Technology/Science—Radiation Therapist** *15 students enrolled* • **Nuclear Medical Technology/Technologist** *36 students enrolled* • **Pharmacy Technician/Assistant** *21 students enrolled*

STUDENT SERVICES Academic or career counseling, daycare for children of students, employment services for current students, placement services for program completers, remedial services.

Cleveland State Community College

PO Box 3570, Cleveland, TN 37320-3570
http://www.clevelandstatecc.edu/

CONTACT Carl Hite, President
Telephone: 423-472-7141

GENERAL INFORMATION Public Institution. Founded 1967. **Accreditation:** Regional (SACS/CC); medical assisting (AAMAE). **Total program enrollment:** 1646. **Application fee:** $10.

PROGRAM(S) OFFERED
• **Administrative Assistant and Secretarial Science, General** *21 students enrolled* • **Criminal Justice/Police Science** *6 students enrolled* • **Emergency Medical Technology/Technician (EMT Paramedic)** *2 students enrolled*

STUDENT SERVICES Academic or career counseling, employment services for current students, placement services for program completers, remedial services.

Columbia State Community College

PO Box 1315, Columbia, TN 38402-1315
http://www.columbiastate.edu/

CONTACT Janet F. Smith, President
Telephone: 931-540-2722

GENERAL INFORMATION Public Institution. Founded 1966. **Accreditation:** Regional (SACS/CC); emergency medical services (JRCEMTP); radiologic technology: radiography (JRCERT). **Total program enrollment:** 2342. **Application fee:** $10.

PROGRAM(S) OFFERED
• **Business Administration and Management, General** *17 students enrolled* • **Child Development** *10 students enrolled* • **Criminal Justice/Police Science** • **Emergency Medical Technology/Technician (EMT Paramedic)** *3 students enrolled* • **Music, Other** *1 student enrolled*

STUDENT SERVICES Academic or career counseling, employment services for current students, remedial services.

Concorde Career College

5100 Poplar Avenue, Suite 132, Memphis, TN 38137
http://www.concordecareercolleges.com/

CONTACT Tommy Stewart, Campus President
Telephone: 901-761-9494

GENERAL INFORMATION Private Institution. Founded 1969. **Accreditation:** State accredited or approved. **Total program enrollment:** 1147.

PROGRAM(S) OFFERED
• **Dental Assisting/Assistant** *800 hrs./$12,201* • **Home Health Aide/Home Attendant** *124 students enrolled* • **Massage Therapy/Therapeutic Massage** *37 students enrolled* • **Medical Office Management/Administration** *108 students*

enrolled • **Medical/Clinical Assistant** *720 hrs./$12,923* • **Nurse/Nursing Assistant/Aide and Patient Care Assistant** *488 hrs./$5235* • **Office Management and Supervision** *720 hrs./$11,471* • **Pharmacy Technician/Assistant** *47 students enrolled* • **Respiratory Care Therapy/Therapist** *1605 hrs./$23,013* • **Respiratory Therapy Technician/Assistant** *29 students enrolled* • **Surgical Technology/Technologist** *1220 hrs./$21,268*

STUDENT SERVICES Academic or career counseling, employment services for current students, placement services for program completers, remedial services.

Crichton College

255 North Highland Street, Memphis, TN 38111
http://www.crichton.edu/

CONTACT Larry Lloyd, President
Telephone: 901-320-9700

GENERAL INFORMATION Private Institution. Founded 1941. **Accreditation:** Regional (SACS/CC). **Total program enrollment:** 762. **Application fee:** $25.

PROGRAM(S) OFFERED
• Bible/Biblical Studies

STUDENT SERVICES Academic or career counseling, employment services for current students, remedial services.

Draughons Junior College

1860 Wilma Rudolph Boulevard, Clarksville, TN 37040
http://www.draughons.edu/

CONTACT Amye Melton, Campus Director
Telephone: 931-552-7600

GENERAL INFORMATION Private Institution. Founded 1987. **Accreditation:** State accredited or approved. **Total program enrollment:** 369.

PROGRAM(S) OFFERED
• Accounting Technology/Technician and Bookkeeping • Accounting • Business Administration, Management and Operations, Other • Computer and Information Sciences, General • Criminal Justice/Law Enforcement Administration • Dental Assisting/Assistant • Health Information/Medical Records Administration/Administrator • Medical Insurance Coding Specialist/Coder • Medical/Clinical Assistant *5 students enrolled* • Pharmacy, Pharmaceutical Sciences, and Administration, Other

STUDENT SERVICES Academic or career counseling, employment services for current students, placement services for program completers, remedial services.

Draughons Junior College

1237 Commerce Park, Murfreesboro, TN 37130
http://www.draughons.edu/

CONTACT Mark A. Gabis, President
Telephone: 615-217-9347

GENERAL INFORMATION Private Institution. **Total program enrollment:** 370.

PROGRAM(S) OFFERED
• Accounting *1 student enrolled* • Business Administration and Management, General *1 student enrolled* • Corrections and Criminal Justice, Other • Dental Assisting/Assistant • Health Information/Medical Records Administration/Administrator *1 student enrolled* • Medical/Clinical Assistant *4 students enrolled* • Pharmacy Technician/Assistant

STUDENT SERVICES Academic or career counseling, employment services for current students, placement services for program completers.

Draughons Junior College

340 Plus Park Boulevard, Nashville, TN 37217
http://www.draughons.edu/

CONTACT Mark A. Gabis, President
Telephone: 615-361-7555

GENERAL INFORMATION Private Institution. Founded 1884. **Accreditation:** State accredited or approved. **Total program enrollment:** 266.

PROGRAM(S) OFFERED
• Accounting • Business Administration, Management and Operations, Other *1 student enrolled* • Criminal Justice/Safety Studies • Dental Assisting/Assistant • E-Commerce/Electronic Commerce *1 student enrolled* • Health Information/Medical Records Technology/Technician • Massage Therapy/Therapeutic Massage • Medical Office Management/Administration • Medical/Clinical Assistant • Pharmacy Technician/Assistant

STUDENT SERVICES Academic or career counseling, employment services for current students, placement services for program completers, remedial services.

Dudley Nwani–The School

3532 W. Hamilton Road, Nashville, TN 37218
http://1wcu.org/

CONTACT Uchendi Nwani, CEO
Telephone: 615-496-3977

GENERAL INFORMATION Private Institution. **Total program enrollment:** 126. **Application fee:** $100.

PROGRAM(S) OFFERED
• Barbering/Barber *38 students enrolled* • Cosmetology, Barber/Styling, and Nail Instructor *1500 hrs./$12,900*

STUDENT SERVICES Placement services for program completers.

Dyersburg State Community College

1510 Lake Road, Dyersburg, TN 38024
http://www.dscc.edu/

CONTACT Karen Bowyer, President
Telephone: 731-286-3200

GENERAL INFORMATION Public Institution. Founded 1969. **Accreditation:** Regional (SACS/CC). **Total program enrollment:** 1298. **Application fee:** $10.

PROGRAM(S) OFFERED
• Child Development *2 students enrolled* • Health Information/Medical Records Technology/Technician *4 students enrolled* • Medical Transcription/Transcriptionist *3 students enrolled*

STUDENT SERVICES Academic or career counseling, employment services for current students, placement services for program completers, remedial services.

Elite College of Cosmetology

459 N. Main Street, Lexington, TN 38351

CONTACT Melda Mills, Owner
Telephone: 731-968-5400

GENERAL INFORMATION Private Institution. **Total program enrollment:** 47.

PROGRAM(S) OFFERED
• Cosmetology and Related Personal Grooming Arts, Other *1500 hrs./$11,775* • Nail Technician/Specialist and Manicurist *600 hrs./$4450*

STUDENT SERVICES Placement services for program completers.

Fayettville Beauty School

Southwest Public Square, PO Box 135, Fayetteville, TN 37334-0135
http://www.fayettevillebeautyschool.com/

CONTACT Rufus Hereford, Owner
Telephone: 931-433-1305

GENERAL INFORMATION Private Institution. Founded 1957. **Total program enrollment:** 9. **Application fee:** $100.

PROGRAM(S) OFFERED
• **Aesthetician/Esthetician and Skin Care Specialist** *750 hrs./$4665*
• **Cosmetology, Barber/Styling, and Nail Instructor** *450 hrs./$2799*
• **Cosmetology/Cosmetologist, General** *1500 hrs./$10,245* • **Nail Technician/Specialist and Manicurist** *750 hrs./$4665*

STUDENT SERVICES Academic or career counseling, placement services for program completers.

Franklin Academy

303 Keith Street Village Center, Cleveland, TN 37311
http://www.franklinacademy.edu/

CONTACT Patty Patterson, Executive Director
Telephone: 423-476-3742

GENERAL INFORMATION Private Institution. **Total program enrollment:** 30. **Application fee:** $25.

PROGRAM(S) OFFERED
• **Aesthetician/Esthetician and Skin Care Specialist** *$3850* • **Cosmetology/Cosmetologist, General** *12 hrs./$8195* • **Nail Technician/Specialist and Manicurist** *$3100*

STUDENT SERVICES Academic or career counseling, placement services for program completers.

High-Tech Institute

5865 Shelby Oaks Circle, Suite 100, Memphis, TN 38134
http://www.high-techinstitute.com/

CONTACT Catherine McClarin, Campus President
Telephone: 901-432-3800

GENERAL INFORMATION Private Institution. Founded 2003. **Accreditation:** State accredited or approved. **Total program enrollment:** 1014. **Application fee:** $50.

PROGRAM(S) OFFERED
• **Massage Therapy/Therapeutic Massage** *820 hrs./$10,612* • **Medical Insurance Specialist/Medical Biller** *720 hrs./$10,831* • **Medical Radiologic Technology/Science—Radiation Therapist** *810 hrs./$12,834* • **Medical/Clinical Assistant** *1236 hrs./$21,350* • **Pharmacy Technician/Assistant** *720 hrs./$10,991* • **Surgical Technology/Technologist** *1 student enrolled*

STUDENT SERVICES Placement services for program completers.

High-Tech Institute

560 Royal Parkway, Nashville, TN 37214
http://www.high-techinstitute.com/

CONTACT Michelle Bonocore, Operations Manager
Telephone: 615-232-3700

GENERAL INFORMATION Private Institution. Founded 1999. **Accreditation:** State accredited or approved. **Total program enrollment:** 605. **Application fee:** $50.

PROGRAM(S) OFFERED
• **Dental Assisting/Assistant** *720 hrs./$10,585* • **Massage Therapy/Therapeutic Massage** *820 hrs./$11,250* • **Medical Insurance Specialist/Medical Biller** *720 hrs./$10,831* • **Medical Radiologic Technology/Science—Radiation Therapist** *810 hrs./$12,834* • **Medical/Clinical Assistant** *1236 hrs./$21,350* • **Radiologic Technology/Science—Radiographer** *9 students enrolled* • **Surgical Technology/Technologist**

STUDENT SERVICES Placement services for program completers.

Institute of Hair Design

205 Enterprise Drive, Adamsville, TN 38310
http://ihd4me.com/

CONTACT Cherry Johnson, Director
Telephone: 731-632-9533

GENERAL INFORMATION Private Institution. **Total program enrollment:** 53. **Application fee:** $100.

PROGRAM(S) OFFERED
• **Cosmetology/Cosmetologist, General** *1500 hrs./$11,950*

STUDENT SERVICES Placement services for program completers.

Jackson State Community College

2046 North Parkway, Jackson, TN 38301-3797
http://www.jscc.edu/

CONTACT Dr. Bruce Blanding, President
Telephone: 731-424-3520

GENERAL INFORMATION Public Institution. Founded 1967. **Accreditation:** Regional (SACS/CC); emergency medical services (JRCEMTP); medical laboratory technology (NAACLS); physical therapy assisting (APTA); radiologic technology: radiography (JRCERT). **Total program enrollment:** 2151. **Application fee:** $10.

PROGRAM(S) OFFERED
• **Applied Horticulture/Horticultural Operations, General** • **Emergency Medical Technology/Technician (EMT Paramedic)** *12 students enrolled* • **Human Development, Family Studies, and Related Services, Other** *3 students enrolled* • **Manufacturing Technology/Technician**

STUDENT SERVICES Academic or career counseling, employment services for current students, placement services for program completers, remedial services.

Jenny Lea Academy of Cosmetology and Aesthetics

222 E. Unaka Avenue, Johnson City, TN 37601

CONTACT Virginia Lewis, CEO
Telephone: 423-926-9095

GENERAL INFORMATION Private Institution. **Total program enrollment:** 87. **Application fee:** $100.

PROGRAM(S) OFFERED
• **Aesthetician/Esthetician and Skin Care Specialist** *750 hrs./$7095*
• **Cosmetology, Barber/Styling, and Nail Instructor** *300 hrs./$2500*
• **Cosmetology/Cosmetologist, General** *1500 hrs./$10,295* • **Nail Technician/Specialist and Manicurist** *650 hrs./$6095*

STUDENT SERVICES Academic or career counseling.

John A. Gupton College

1616 Church Street, Nashville, TN 37203-2920
http://www.guptoncollege.edu/

CONTACT B. Steven Spann, President
Telephone: 615-327-3927

GENERAL INFORMATION Private Institution. Founded 1946. **Accreditation:** Regional (SACS/CC); funeral service (ABFSE). **Total program enrollment:** 64. **Application fee:** $20.

PROGRAM(S) OFFERED
● **Funeral Service and Mortuary Science, General** *11 students enrolled*

STUDENT SERVICES Academic or career counseling.

Jon Nave University of Unisex Cosmetology

5128 Charlotte Avenue, Nashville, TN 37209
http://www.creativedesignsba.com/

CONTACT Dale Jones, Owner
Telephone: 801-302-8801 Ext. 1021

GENERAL INFORMATION Private Institution. **Total program enrollment:** 253. **Application fee:** $100.

PROGRAM(S) OFFERED
● **Aesthetician/Esthetician and Skin Care Specialist** *750 hrs./$7800*
● **Cosmetology, Barber/Styling, and Nail Instructor** *300 hrs./$2200*
● **Cosmetology/Cosmetologist, General** *1500 hrs./$15,900*

STUDENT SERVICES Academic or career counseling, employment services for current students, placement services for program completers.

Kaplan Career Institute–Nashville Campus

750 Envious Lane, Nashville, TN 37217
http://www.kci-nashville.com

CONTACT Adam Butler, Executive Director
Telephone: 615-279-8300

GENERAL INFORMATION Private Institution. Founded 1981. **Accreditation:** State accredited or approved. **Total program enrollment:** 669.

PROGRAM(S) OFFERED
● **Criminal Justice/Law Enforcement Administration** *96 hrs./$29,500* ● **Dental Assisting/Assistant** *55 hrs./$13,100* ● **Legal Assistant/Paralegal** *44 hrs./$13,000* ● **Massage Therapy/Therapeutic Massage** ● **Medical Office Assistant/Specialist** *33 students enrolled* ● **Medical Office Management/Administration** *50 hrs./$14,950* ● **Medical/Clinical Assistant** *720 hrs./$14,330*

STUDENT SERVICES Academic or career counseling, employment services for current students, placement services for program completers.

Last Minute Cuts School of Barbering and Cosmetology

2195 S. Third Street, Memphis, TN 38109
http://www.lastminutecuts.com/

CONTACT Quannah Harris, Director of Administrations
Telephone: 901-774-9699

GENERAL INFORMATION Private Institution.

PROGRAM(S) OFFERED
● **Barbering/Barber** *1500 hrs./$11,752* ● **Cosmetology, Barber/Styling, and Nail Instructor** *1 student enrolled* ● **Cosmetology/Cosmetologist, General** *1 student enrolled* ● **Hair Styling/Stylist and Hair Design** ● **Nail Technician/Specialist and Manicurist**

McCollum and Ross–the Hair School

1433 Hollywood, Jackson, TN 38301
http://leadersinbeautyed.com/

CONTACT Ruby Klyce, Executive Director
Telephone: 901-323-6100

GENERAL INFORMATION Private Institution. **Total program enrollment:** 58.

PROGRAM(S) OFFERED
● **Cosmetology/Cosmetologist, General** *1500 hrs./$14,325*

STUDENT SERVICES Placement services for program completers.

MedVance Institute

1025 Highway 111, Cookeville, TN 38501
http://www.medvance.edu/

CONTACT John Hopkins, CEO
Telephone: 931-526-3660

GENERAL INFORMATION Private Institution. Founded 1970. **Accreditation:** Medical laboratory technology (NAACLS); state accredited or approved. **Total program enrollment:** 377. **Application fee:** $25.

PROGRAM(S) OFFERED
● **Clinical/Medical Laboratory Technician** *99 hrs./$23,995* ● **Health Information/Medical Records Technology/Technician** *67 hrs./$12,995* ● **Medical Office Assistant/Specialist** *23 students enrolled* ● **Medical Radiologic Technology/Science—Radiation Therapist** *130 hrs./$31,895* ● **Medical/Clinical Assistant** *49 hrs./$9995* ● **Pharmacy Technician/Assistant** *49 hrs./$10,000* ● **Surgical Technology/Technologist** *98 hrs./$19,995*

STUDENT SERVICES Employment services for current students, placement services for program completers.

MedVance Institute–Nashville

2400 Parman Place, Suite 3, Nashville, TN 37203
http://www.medvance.edu

CONTACT John Hopkins, CEO
Telephone: 615-320-5917

GENERAL INFORMATION Private Institution. **Total program enrollment:** 404. **Application fee:** $25.

PROGRAM(S) OFFERED
● **Biomedical Technology/Technician** *120 hrs./$25,500* ● **Health Information/Medical Records Technology/Technician** *67 hrs./$13,500* ● **Health Professions and Related Clinical Sciences, Other** *36 hrs./$9900* ● **Medical Radiologic Technology/Science—Radiation Therapist** *130 hrs./$34,500* ● **Medical/Clinical Assistant** *49 hrs./$12,500* ● **Pharmacy Technician/Assistant** *16 students enrolled* ● **Surgical Technology/Technologist** *98 hrs./$21,500*

STUDENT SERVICES Employment services for current students, placement services for program completers.

Memphis Institute of Barbering

1309 Jackson Avenue, Memphis, TN 38107

GENERAL INFORMATION Private Institution. **Total program enrollment:** 61. **Application fee:** $100.

PROGRAM(S) OFFERED
● **Barbering/Barber** *1500 hrs./$9525*

Middle Tennessee School of Cosmetology

868 East Tenth Street, Cookeville, TN 38501
http://www.midtncosmo.com/

CONTACT Richard Bundy, President
Telephone: 931-526-4515

GENERAL INFORMATION Private Institution. Founded 1950. **Total program enrollment:** 106. **Application fee:** $100.

PROGRAM(S) OFFERED
• **Aesthetician/Esthetician and Skin Care Specialist** *900 hrs./$8955*
• **Cosmetology, Barber/Styling, and Nail Instructor** *300 hrs./$1905*
• **Cosmetology/Cosmetologist, General** *1500 hrs./$11,795* • **Nail Technician/Specialist and Manicurist** *600 hrs./$5370*

STUDENT SERVICES Academic or career counseling, placement services for program completers.

Miller-Motte Technical College

6020 Shallowford Road, Suite 100, Chattanooga, TN 37421
http://www.miller-motte.com/

CONTACT Alan Sussna, President
Telephone: 423-510-9675 Ext. 200

GENERAL INFORMATION Private Institution. **Total program enrollment:** 436. **Application fee:** $50.

PROGRAM(S) OFFERED
• **Cosmetology and Related Personal Grooming Arts, Other** *34 students enrolled* • **Cosmetology/Cosmetologist, General** *7 students enrolled* • **Data Entry/Microcomputer Applications, Other** *1 student enrolled* • **Dental Assisting/Assistant** • **Health Professions and Related Clinical Sciences, Other** *8 students enrolled* • **Massage Therapy/Therapeutic Massage** *31 students enrolled*

STUDENT SERVICES Academic or career counseling, employment services for current students, placement services for program completers, remedial services.

Miller-Motte Technical College

1820 Business Park Drive, Clarksville, TN 37040
http://www.miller-motte.com/

CONTACT Gina Castleberry, Director
Telephone: 931-553-0071

GENERAL INFORMATION Private Institution. Founded 1916. **Accreditation:** Medical assisting (AAMAE); state accredited or approved. **Total program enrollment:** 405.

PROGRAM(S) OFFERED
• **Aesthetician/Esthetician and Skin Care Specialist** *20 students enrolled* • **Computer and Information Sciences and Support Services, Other** • **Cosmetology and Related Personal Grooming Arts, Other** *10 students enrolled* • **Massage Therapy/Therapeutic Massage** *11 students enrolled* • **Medical Office Assistant/Specialist** *4 students enrolled* • **Phlebotomy/Phlebotomist** *3 students enrolled*

STUDENT SERVICES Academic or career counseling, employment services for current students, placement services for program completers, remedial services.

Miller-Motte Technical College

801 Space Park North, Goodlettsville, TN 37072
http://www.miller-motte.com/

CONTACT Kevin Suhr, Campus Administrator
Telephone: 615-859-8090

GENERAL INFORMATION Private Institution. **Total program enrollment:** 179. **Application fee:** $35.

PROGRAM(S) OFFERED
• **Electrician** *24 students enrolled* • **Heating, Air Conditioning and Refrigeration Technology/Technician (ACH/ACR/ACHR/HRAC/HVAC/AC Technology)** *39 students enrolled* • **Welding Technology/Welder** *10 students enrolled*

STUDENT SERVICES Academic or career counseling, employment services for current students, placement services for program completers.

Motlow State Community College

PO Box 8500, Lynchburg, TN 37352-8500
http://www.mscc.cc.tn.us/

CONTACT MaryLou Apple, President
Telephone: 931-393-1500

GENERAL INFORMATION Public Institution. Founded 1969. **Accreditation:** Regional (SACS/CC). **Total program enrollment:** 2322. **Application fee:** $10.

STUDENT SERVICES Academic or career counseling, employment services for current students, placement services for program completers, remedial services.

Mr. Wayne's School of Unisex Hair Design

170 South Willow Avenue, Cookeville, TN 38501
http://www.misterwaynes.com/

CONTACT Charles W. Fletcher, Owner
Telephone: 931-526-1478

GENERAL INFORMATION Private Institution. **Total program enrollment:** 18.

PROGRAM(S) OFFERED
• **Barbering/Barber** *1500 hrs./$10,000*

STUDENT SERVICES Academic or career counseling, placement services for program completers.

Nashville Auto Diesel College

1524 Gallatin Road, Nashville, TN 37206-3298
http://www.nadcedu.com/

CONTACT Lisa Bacon, President
Telephone: 800-228-6232

GENERAL INFORMATION Private Institution. Founded 1919. **Accreditation:** State accredited or approved. **Total program enrollment:** 2380. **Application fee:** $100.

PROGRAM(S) OFFERED
• **Alternative Fuel Vehicle Technology/Technician** *156 students enrolled* • **Autobody/Collision and Repair Technology/Technician** *66 hrs./$23,500* • **Automobile/Automotive Mechanics Technology/Technician** *89 hrs./$28,300* • **Diesel Mechanics Technology/Technician** *79 hrs./$27,200* • **Engine Machinist** *17 students enrolled* • **Heavy Equipment Maintenance Technology/Technician** *7 students enrolled* • **Mechanic and Repair Technologies/Technicians, Other** *100 students enrolled* • **Medium/Heavy Vehicle and Truck Technology/Technician** *6 students enrolled* • **Vehicle Maintenance and Repair Technologies, Other** *80 hrs./$29,800*

STUDENT SERVICES Academic or career counseling, employment services for current students, placement services for program completers.

Nashville College of Medical Careers

1556 Crestview Drive, Madison, TN 37115
http://www.nashvillecollege.com/

CONTACT A. Malek, President
Telephone: 615-868-2963

GENERAL INFORMATION Private Institution. **Total program enrollment:** 239. **Application fee:** $10.

PROGRAM(S) OFFERED
• **Medical Administrative/Executive Assistant and Medical Secretary** 44 *students enrolled* • **Medical Insurance Coding Specialist/Coder** *36 hrs./$11,500* • **Medical Office Assistant/Specialist** *36 hrs./$11,500* • **Medical/Clinical Assistant** *36 hrs./$12,000*

STUDENT SERVICES Academic or career counseling, placement services for program completers.

Nashville State Technical Community College

120 White Bridge Road, Nashville, TN 37209-4515
http://www.nscc.edu/

CONTACT George H. Van Allen, President
Telephone: 615-353-3333

GENERAL INFORMATION Public Institution. Founded 1970. **Accreditation:** Regional (SACS/CC); engineering technology (ABET/TAC). **Total program enrollment:** 2660. **Application fee:** $5.

PROGRAM(S) OFFERED
• **Child Development** *36 students enrolled* • **Culinary Arts/Chef Training** • **Drafting and Design Technology/Technician, General** *9 students enrolled* • **Electrician** *6 students enrolled* • **Entrepreneurship/Entrepreneurial Studies** *1 student enrolled* • **Landscaping and Groundskeeping** *7 students enrolled* • **Machine Tool Technology/Machinist** • **Music, Other** *22 students enrolled* • **Photography** *6 students enrolled* • **Robotics Technology/Technician** • **Surgical Technology/Technologist** *33 students enrolled* • **Technical and Business Writing** *1 student enrolled* • **Web Page, Digital/Multimedia and Information Resources Design** *2 students enrolled*

STUDENT SERVICES Academic or career counseling, employment services for current students, placement services for program completers, remedial services.

National College

5042 Linbar Drive, Suite 200, Nashville, TN 37211
http://www.national-college.edu/

CONTACT Frank Longaker, President
Telephone: 615-333-3344

GENERAL INFORMATION Private Institution. Founded 1915. **Accreditation:** Medical assisting (AAMAE); state accredited or approved. **Total program enrollment:** 1021. **Application fee:** $30.

PROGRAM(S) OFFERED
• **Accounting Technology/Technician and Bookkeeping** *3 students enrolled* • **Business Administration and Management, General** • **Business/Commerce, General** *7 students enrolled* • **Computer and Information Sciences and Support Services, Other** *1 student enrolled* • **Data Entry/Microcomputer Applications, General** *2 students enrolled* • **Health and Medical Administrative Services, Other** *24 students enrolled* • **Hospitality Administration/Management, General** • **Information Technology** • **Medical Office Assistant/Specialist** • **Medical Transcription/Transcriptionist** • **Pharmacy Technician/Assistant** *14 students enrolled*

STUDENT SERVICES Academic or career counseling, employment services for current students, placement services for program completers, remedial services.

Nave Cosmetology Academy

112 E. James Campbell Boulevard, Columbia, TN 38401

CONTACT Joyce Meadows, Owner
Telephone: 931-388-7717

GENERAL INFORMATION Private Institution. **Total program enrollment:** 143.

PROGRAM(S) OFFERED
• **Aesthetician/Esthetician and Skin Care Specialist** *750 hrs./$8000* • **Cosmetology/Cosmetologist, General** *1500 hrs./$12,800* • **Nail Technician/Specialist and Manicurist** *600 hrs./$4850*

STUDENT SERVICES Academic or career counseling, employment services for current students, placement services for program completers.

New Concepts School of Cosmetology

1412 South Lee Highway, Cleveland, TN 37311

CONTACT Linda Luster, Owner
Telephone: 423-478-3231

GENERAL INFORMATION Private Institution. **Total program enrollment:** 16. **Application fee:** $50.

PROGRAM(S) OFFERED
• **Aesthetician/Esthetician and Skin Care Specialist** *5 students enrolled* • **Cosmetology, Barber/Styling, and Nail Instructor** • **Cosmetology/Cosmetologist, General** *1500 hrs./$8400* • **Nail Technician/Specialist and Manicurist** *1 student enrolled*

STUDENT SERVICES Placement services for program completers.

New Directions Hair Academy

7106 Moores Lane, Brentwood, TN 37027
http://leadersinbeautyed.com/

CONTACT Ruby Klyce, Executive Director
Telephone: 901-323-6100

GENERAL INFORMATION Private Institution. **Total program enrollment:** 69.

PROGRAM(S) OFFERED
• **Aesthetician/Esthetician and Skin Care Specialist** *750 hrs./$8350* • **Cosmetology/Cosmetologist, General** *1500 hrs./$15,175* • **Nail Technician/Specialist and Manicurist** *600 hrs./$6770*

STUDENT SERVICES Placement services for program completers.

New Directions Hair Academy

568 Colonial Road, Memphis, TN 38111
http://leadersinbeautyed.com/

CONTACT Ruby Klyce, Executive Director
Telephone: 901-323-6100

GENERAL INFORMATION Private Institution. **Total program enrollment:** 96.

PROGRAM(S) OFFERED
• **Aesthetician/Esthetician and Skin Care Specialist** *750 hrs./$8350* • **Cosmetology and Related Personal Grooming Arts, Other** *62 students enrolled* • **Cosmetology, Barber/Styling, and Nail Instructor** *1500 hrs./$15,175* • **Cosmetology/Cosmetologist, General** *68 students enrolled* • **Nail Technician/Specialist and Manicurist** *600 hrs./$6770*

STUDENT SERVICES Placement services for program completers.

New Wave Hair Academy

3641 Brainerd Road, Chattanooga, TN 37411
http://leadersinbeautyed.com/

CONTACT Ruby Klyce, Executive Director
Telephone: 901-323-2100

GENERAL INFORMATION Private Institution. **Total program enrollment:** 116.

PROGRAM(S) OFFERED
• **Cosmetology/Cosmetologist, General** *1500 hrs./$14,325*

STUDENT SERVICES Placement services for program completers.

New Wave Hair Academy

804 South Highland, Memphis, TN 38111
http://leadersinbeautyed.com/

CONTACT Ruby Klyce, Executive Director
Telephone: 901-323-2100

GENERAL INFORMATION Private Institution. **Total program enrollment:** 150.

PROGRAM(S) OFFERED
• **Cosmetology/Cosmetologist, General** *1500 hrs./$14,325*

STUDENT SERVICES Placement services for program completers.

North Central Institute

168 Jack Miller Boulevard, Clarksville, TN 37042
http://www.nci.edu/

CONTACT John D. McCurdy, CEO
Telephone: 931-431-9700

GENERAL INFORMATION Private Institution. Founded 1988. **Accreditation:** State accredited or approved. **Total program enrollment:** 46. **Application fee:** $35.

PROGRAM(S) OFFERED
• **Aircraft Powerplant Technology/Technician** *88 hrs./$1577* • **Airframe Mechanics and Aircraft Maintenance Technology/Technician** *1960 hrs./$14,590* • **Avionics Maintenance Technology/Technician** *62 hrs./$5042*

STUDENT SERVICES Academic or career counseling, employment services for current students, placement services for program completers.

Northeast State Technical Community College

PO Box 246, Blountville, TN 37617-0246
http://www.northeaststate.edu/

CONTACT William W. Locke, President
Telephone: 423-323-3191

GENERAL INFORMATION Public Institution. Founded 1966. **Accreditation:** Regional (SACS/CC); dental assisting (ADA); dental laboratory technology (ADA); medical assisting (AAMAE); medical laboratory technology (NAACLS). **Total program enrollment:** 2927. **Application fee:** $10.

PROGRAM(S) OFFERED
• **Accounting Technology/Technician and Bookkeeping** *17 students enrolled* • **Administrative Assistant and Secretarial Science, General** *2 students enrolled* • **Automobile/Automotive Mechanics Technology/Technician** *15 students enrolled* • **Chemical Technology/Technician** *8 students enrolled* • **Child Development** *8 students enrolled* • **Computer Programming, Vendor/Product Certification** • **Computer Systems Networking and Telecommunications** *2 students enrolled* • **Dental Assisting/Assistant** *11 students enrolled* • **Electrician** *20 students enrolled* • **Emergency Medical Technology/Technician (EMT**

Paramedic) *9 students enrolled* • **Heating, Air Conditioning, Ventilation and Refrigeration Maintenance Technology/Technician (HAC, HACR, HVAC, HVACR)** *18 students enrolled* • **Industrial Mechanics and Maintenance Technology** *9 students enrolled* • **Machine Shop Technology/Assistant** *8 students enrolled* • **Mechanical Drafting and Mechanical Drafting CAD/CADD** *8 students enrolled* • **Surgical Technology/Technologist** • **System, Networking, and LAN/WAN Management/Manager** • **Welding Technology/Welder** *8 students enrolled*

STUDENT SERVICES Academic or career counseling, employment services for current students, placement services for program completers, remedial services.

Pellissippi State Technical Community College

PO Box 22990, Knoxville, TN 37933-0990
http://www.pstcc.edu/

CONTACT Dr. Allen G. Edwards, President
Telephone: 865-694-6400

GENERAL INFORMATION Public Institution. Founded 1974. **Accreditation:** Regional (SACS/CC); engineering technology (ABET/TAC). **Total program enrollment:** 4570. **Application fee:** $10.

STUDENT SERVICES Academic or career counseling, employment services for current students, placement services for program completers, remedial services.

Plaza Beauty School

4682 Spottswood Avenue, Memphis, TN 38117
http://www.plazabeautyschool.com/

CONTACT Joan E. Sparks, Vice President
Telephone: 901-761-4445

GENERAL INFORMATION Private Institution. **Total program enrollment:** 89. **Application fee:** $100.

PROGRAM(S) OFFERED
• **Cosmetology/Cosmetologist, General** *1500 hrs./$12,550*

STUDENT SERVICES Academic or career counseling, placement services for program completers.

Queen City College

1594 Fort Campbell Boulevard, Clarksville, TN 37042
http://www.queencitycollege.com/

CONTACT Laura E. Payne, Chief Administrator
Telephone: 931-645-2361

GENERAL INFORMATION Private Institution. Founded 1984. **Total program enrollment:** 141. **Application fee:** $100.

PROGRAM(S) OFFERED
• **Aesthetician/Esthetician and Skin Care Specialist** *750 hrs./$4013* • **Barbering/Barber** *1500 hrs./$6136* • **Cosmetology, Barber/Styling, and Nail Instructor** • **Cosmetology/Cosmetologist, General** *1500 hrs./$7201* • **Hair Styling/Stylist and Hair Design** • **Nail Technician/Specialist and Manicurist** *600 hrs./$2454*

STUDENT SERVICES Placement services for program completers.

Regency Beauty Institute–Nashville

5383 Mt View Road, Antioch, TN 37013

CONTACT J. Hayes Batson
Telephone: 615-916-2001

GENERAL INFORMATION Private Institution. **Total program enrollment:** 42. **Application fee:** $100.

PROGRAM(S) OFFERED
• **Cosmetology/Cosmetologist, General** *1500 hrs./$16,011*

STUDENT SERVICES Academic or career counseling, placement services for program completers.

Remington College–Memphis Campus

2731 Nonconnah Boulevard, Memphis, TN 38132-2131
http://www.remingtoncollege.edu/

CONTACT Lori May, Campus President
Telephone: 901-345-1000

GENERAL INFORMATION Private Institution. **Accreditation:** State accredited or approved. **Total program enrollment:** 922. **Application fee:** $50.

PROGRAM(S) OFFERED
• **Medical Insurance Coding Specialist/Coder** *111 students enrolled* • **Medical/Clinical Assistant** *203 students enrolled* • **Pharmacy Technician/Assistant** *70 students enrolled*

STUDENT SERVICES Academic or career counseling, employment services for current students, placement services for program completers.

Remington College–Nashville Campus

441 Donelson Pike, Suite 150, Nashville, TN 37214
http://www.remingtoncollege.edu/

CONTACT Larry Collins, Campus President
Telephone: 615-889-5520

GENERAL INFORMATION Private Institution. Founded 2003. **Total program enrollment:** 408. **Application fee:** $50.

PROGRAM(S) OFFERED
• **Cosmetology/Cosmetologist, General** • **Dental Assisting/Assistant** *87 students enrolled* • **Medical Insurance Coding Specialist/Coder** *13 students enrolled* • **Medical/Clinical Assistant** *158 students enrolled*

STUDENT SERVICES Academic or career counseling, employment services for current students, placement services for program completers.

Reuben-Allen College

120 Center Park Drive, Knoxville, TN 37922
http://www.rosstheboss.com/

CONTACT Ross Badgett, Director
Telephone: 865-966-0400

GENERAL INFORMATION Private Institution. **Total program enrollment:** 49. **Application fee:** $100.

PROGRAM(S) OFFERED
• **Cosmetology/Cosmetologist, General** *1500 hrs./$10,650*

STUDENT SERVICES Academic or career counseling, placement services for program completers.

Roane State Community College

276 Patton Lane, Harriman, TN 37748-5011
http://www.roanestate.edu/

CONTACT Gary Goff, President
Telephone: 865-354-3000

GENERAL INFORMATION Public Institution. Founded 1971. **Accreditation:** Regional (SACS/CC); dental hygiene (ADA); health information technology (AHIMA); ophthalmic dispensing (COA); physical therapy assisting (APTA); radiologic technology: radiography (JRCERT). **Total program enrollment:** 2977. **Application fee:** $10.

PROGRAM(S) OFFERED
• **Administrative Assistant and Secretarial Science, General** *1 student enrolled* • **Allied Health Diagnostic, Intervention, and Treatment Professions, Other** *10 students enrolled* • **Cartography** *7 students enrolled* • **Clinical/Medical Laboratory Science and Allied Professions, Other** *13 students enrolled* • **Computer and Information Sciences and Support Services, Other** • **Criminal Justice/Police Science** *1 student enrolled* • **Emergency Medical Technology/Technician (EMT Paramedic)** *19 students enrolled* • **Massage Therapy/Therapeutic Massage** *15 students enrolled* • **Medical Transcription/Transcriptionist** *9 students enrolled* • **Pharmacy Technician/Assistant** *8 students enrolled* • **Security and Protective Services, Other** *3 students enrolled*

STUDENT SERVICES Academic or career counseling, employment services for current students, placement services for program completers, remedial services.

SAE Institute of Technology

7 Music Circle N, Nashville, TN 37203
http://www.sae-nashville.com/

CONTACT Prema Thiagarajah, Director
Telephone: 615-244-5848

GENERAL INFORMATION Private Institution. **Total program enrollment:** 168. **Application fee:** $100.

PROGRAM(S) OFFERED
• **Recording Arts Technology/Technician** *900 hrs./$18,900*

STUDENT SERVICES Academic or career counseling, placement services for program completers.

Shear Academy

780 West Avenue, Crossville, TN 38555

CONTACT James Everitt, Owner
Telephone: 931-456-5391

GENERAL INFORMATION Private Institution. **Total program enrollment:** 21. **Application fee:** $25.

PROGRAM(S) OFFERED
• **Barbering/Barber** *1500 hrs./$8500* • **Cosmetology, Barber/Styling, and Nail Instructor** *450 hrs./$2000*

STUDENT SERVICES Placement services for program completers.

South College

720 North Fifth Avenue, Knoxville, TN 37917
http://www.southcollegetn.edu/

CONTACT Stephen A. South, President
Telephone: 865-251-1800

GENERAL INFORMATION Private Institution. Founded 1882. **Accreditation:** Regional (SACS/CC); medical assisting (AAMAE); physical therapy assisting (APTA). **Total program enrollment:** 825. **Application fee:** $50.

South College (continued)

PROGRAM(S) OFFERED
● **Administrative Assistant and Secretarial Science, General** *1 student enrolled*
● **Medical Insurance Coding Specialist/Coder** *4 students enrolled* ● **Nuclear Medical Technology/Technologist** *5 students enrolled*

STUDENT SERVICES Academic or career counseling, employment services for current students, placement services for program completers.

Southern Adventist University

PO Box 370, Collegedale, TN 37315-0370
http://www.southern.edu/

CONTACT Gordon Bietz, President
Telephone: 423-236-2000

GENERAL INFORMATION Private Institution. Founded 1892. **Accreditation:** Regional (SACS/CC); music (NASM). **Total program enrollment:** 2211. **Application fee:** $25.

STUDENT SERVICES Academic or career counseling, employment services for current students, placement services for program completers, remedial services.

Southern Institute of Cosmetology

3099 S. Perkin, Memphis, TN 38118-3239

CONTACT Nancy Ryall, President
Telephone: 901-363-3553

GENERAL INFORMATION Private Institution. **Total program enrollment:** 64. **Application fee:** $100.

PROGRAM(S) OFFERED
● **Cosmetology/Cosmetologist, General** *1500 hrs./$9400* ● **Nail Technician/ Specialist and Manicurist** *600 hrs./$2400*

STUDENT SERVICES Academic or career counseling, placement services for program completers.

Southwest Tennessee Community College

PO Box 780, Memphis, TN 38101-0780
http://www.southwest.tn.edu/

CONTACT Nathan L. Essex, President
Telephone: 901-333-5000

GENERAL INFORMATION Public Institution. Founded 2000. **Accreditation:** Regional (SACS/CC); engineering technology (ABET/TAC); medical laboratory technology (NAACLS); physical therapy assisting (APTA); radiologic technology: radiography (JRCERT). **Total program enrollment:** 5298. **Application fee:** $10.

PROGRAM(S) OFFERED
● **Accounting Technology/Technician and Bookkeeping** *19 students enrolled*
● **Architectural Engineering Technology/Technician** *9 students enrolled* ● **Blood Bank Technology Specialist** *25 students enrolled* ● **Business, Management, Marketing, and Related Support Services, Other** *28 students enrolled*
● **Business/Commerce, General** *1 student enrolled* ● **Child Care and Support Services Management** ● **Child Development** *5 students enrolled* ● **Computer Engineering Technology/Technician** *18 students enrolled* ● **Computer Programming, Specific Applications** *28 students enrolled* ● **Construction Trades, Other**
● **Criminal Justice/Police Science** *1 student enrolled* ● **Electrical, Electronic and Communications Engineering Technology/Technician** *22 students enrolled*
● **Electrician** *4 students enrolled* ● **Emergency Medical Technology/Technician (EMT Paramedic)** *142 students enrolled* ● **Foodservice Systems Administration/ Management** *7 students enrolled* ● **Health and Medical Administrative Services, Other** ● **Human Development, Family Studies, and Related Services, Other** *9 students enrolled* ● **Industrial Technology/Technician**
● **Landscaping and Groundskeeping** *4 students enrolled* ● **Manufacturing Technology/Technician** ● **Mechanic and Repair Technologies/Technicians, Other** *18 students enrolled* ● **Pharmacy Technician/Assistant** *9 students enrolled*

● **Quality Control Technology/Technician** *11 students enrolled* ● **Security and Protective Services, Other** *3 students enrolled* ● **Substance Abuse/Addiction Counseling** *18 students enrolled* ● **Turf and Turfgrass Management**

STUDENT SERVICES Academic or career counseling, daycare for children of students, employment services for current students, placement services for program completers, remedial services.

State University and Community College System of Tennessee

1415 Murfreesboro Road, Suite 350, Nashville, TN 37217-2829

CONTACT Dr. Charles W. Manning, Chancellor
Telephone: 615-366-4400

GENERAL INFORMATION Public Institution.

Stylemasters Beauty Academy

223 North Cumberland, Lebanon, TN 37087
http://www.stylemasters.net/

CONTACT Richard J. Bundy, President
Telephone: 615-248-1927

GENERAL INFORMATION Private Institution. **Total program enrollment:** 315. **Application fee:** $100.

PROGRAM(S) OFFERED
● **Cosmetology, Barber/Styling, and Nail Instructor** *300 hrs./$1905*
● **Cosmetology/Cosmetologist, General** *1500 hrs./$11,795* ● **Nail Technician/ Specialist and Manicurist** *600 hrs./$5370*

STUDENT SERVICES Academic or career counseling, employment services for current students, placement services for program completers.

Styles and Profiles Beauty College

119 South Second Street, Selmer, TN 38375

CONTACT Phoebe M. Prather, Owner
Telephone: 731-645-9728

GENERAL INFORMATION Private Institution. **Total program enrollment:** 28. **Application fee:** $75.

PROGRAM(S) OFFERED
● **Cosmetology, Barber/Styling, and Nail Instructor** *300 hrs./$2297*
● **Cosmetology/Cosmetologist, General** *1500 hrs./$6949* ● **Nail Technician/ Specialist and Manicurist** *600 hrs./$4499*

STUDENT SERVICES Academic or career counseling, employment services for current students.

Tennessee Academy of Cosmetology

7020 East Shelby Drive, Suite 104, Memphis, TN 38125

CONTACT William Oxley, President
Telephone: 901-757-4166

GENERAL INFORMATION Private Institution. **Total program enrollment:** 48. **Application fee:** $100.

PROGRAM(S) OFFERED
● **Aesthetician/Esthetician and Skin Care Specialist** *750 hrs./$5828*
● **Cosmetology and Related Personal Grooming Arts, Other** *600 hrs./$4368*
● **Cosmetology/Cosmetologist, General** *1500 hrs./$11,920* ● **Make-Up Artist/ Specialist** *142 students enrolled*

STUDENT SERVICES Academic or career counseling, placement services for program completers.

Tennessee Academy of Cosmetology

7041 Stage Road, Suite 101, Memphis, TN 38133

CONTACT William Oxley, President
Telephone: 901-382-9085

GENERAL INFORMATION Private Institution. Founded 1984. **Total program enrollment:** 56. **Application fee:** $100.

PROGRAM(S) OFFERED
• **Aesthetician/Esthetician and Skin Care Specialist** *750 hrs./$5460*
• **Cosmetology and Related Personal Grooming Arts, Other** *600 hrs./$4368*
• **Cosmetology/Cosmetologist, General** *1500 hrs./$11,920*

STUDENT SERVICES Academic or career counseling, placement services for program completers.

Tennessee School of Beauty

4704 Western Avenue, Knoxville, TN 37921
http://www.tennesseeschoolofbeauty.com/

CONTACT Adam J. Brown, President
Telephone: 865-588-7878

GENERAL INFORMATION Private Institution. Founded 1930. **Total program enrollment:** 290. **Application fee:** $100.

PROGRAM(S) OFFERED
• **Aesthetician/Esthetician and Skin Care Specialist** *750 hrs./$7495*
• **Cosmetology, Barber/Styling, and Nail Instructor** *300 hrs./$3995*
• **Cosmetology/Cosmetologist, General** *1500 hrs./$9995* • **Nail Technician/Specialist and Manicurist** *600 hrs./$2645*

STUDENT SERVICES Academic or career counseling, placement services for program completers.

Tennessee Technology Center at Athens

1635 Vo-Tech Drive, Athens, TN 37303
http://www.athens.tec.tn.us/

CONTACT Stewart Smith, Director
Telephone: 423-744-2814

GENERAL INFORMATION Public Institution. Founded 1965. **Total program enrollment:** 161.

PROGRAM(S) OFFERED
• **Autobody/Collision and Repair Technology/Technician** *2160 hrs./$3810*
• **Automobile/Automotive Mechanics Technology/Technician** *2160 hrs./$3810*
• **Business Operations Support and Secretarial Services, Other** *1296 hrs./$2286* • **Electrical/Electronics Equipment Installation and Repair, General** *10 students enrolled* • **Electrician** *1728 hrs./$3048* • **Industrial Electronics Technology/Technician** *7 students enrolled* • **Industrial Mechanics and Maintenance Technology** *11 students enrolled* • **Licensed Practical/Vocational Nurse Training (LPN, LVN, Cert, Dipl, AAS)** *1296 hrs./$4586* • **Machine Tool Technology/Machinist** • **Pharmacy Technician/Assistant** • **Welding Technology/Welder** *1296 hrs./$2286*

STUDENT SERVICES Academic or career counseling, employment services for current students, placement services for program completers, remedial services.

Tennessee Technology Center at Covington

PO Box 249, Covington, TN 38019
http://www.covington.tec.tn.us/

CONTACT William N. Ray, Director
Telephone: 901-475-2526

GENERAL INFORMATION Public Institution. **Total program enrollment:** 134.

PROGRAM(S) OFFERED
• **Administrative Assistant and Secretarial Science, General** *1296 hrs./$2286*
• **Computer and Information Sciences, General** *2160 hrs./$3810* • **Heating, Air Conditioning, Ventilation and Refrigeration Maintenance Technology/Technician (HAC, HACR, HVAC, HVACR)** *2160 hrs./$3810* • **Heavy/Industrial Equipment Maintenance Technologies, Other** *14 students enrolled* • **Industrial Mechanics and Maintenance Technology** *1728 hrs./$3048* • **Licensed Practical/Vocational Nurse Training (LPN, LVN, Cert, Dipl, AAS)** *1296 hrs./$5105* • **Machine Tool Technology/Machinist** *1944 hrs./$3674*

STUDENT SERVICES Academic or career counseling, employment services for current students, placement services for program completers, remedial services.

Tennessee Technology Center at Crossville

910 Miller Avenue, Crossville, TN 38555
http://www.crossville.tec.tn.us/

CONTACT Donald Sadler, Director
Telephone: 931-484-7502

GENERAL INFORMATION Public Institution. Founded 1967. **Total program enrollment:** 259.

PROGRAM(S) OFFERED
• **Autobody/Collision and Repair Technology/Technician** *863 hrs./$3810*
• **Automobile/Automotive Mechanics Technology/Technician** *2160 hrs./$5194*
• **Automotive Engineering Technology/Technician** • **Business Operations Support and Secretarial Services, Other** *14 students enrolled* • **Business/Office Automation/Technology/Data Entry** *1296 hrs./$2286* • **Construction Trades, Other** *1 student enrolled* • **Drafting and Design Technology/Technician, General** *2 students enrolled* • **Heating, Air Conditioning, Ventilation and Refrigeration Maintenance Technology/Technician (HAC, HACR, HVAC, HVACR)** *1 student enrolled* • **Industrial Electronics Technology/Technician** *400 hrs./$3048* • **Industrial Mechanics and Maintenance Technology** *915 hrs./$3048* • **Licensed Practical/Vocational Nurse Training (LPN, LVN, Cert, Dipl, AAS)** *1164 hrs./$2586* • **Machine Shop Technology/Assistant** • **Mason/Masonry** *3 students enrolled* • **Surgical Technology/Technologist** *4 students enrolled* • **Welding Technology/Welder** *3 students enrolled*

STUDENT SERVICES Academic or career counseling, daycare for children of students, employment services for current students, placement services for program completers, remedial services.

Tennessee Technology Center at Crump

Highway 64, West, Crump, TN 38327
http://www.crumpttc.edu/

CONTACT Dan Spears, Director
Telephone: 731-632-3393 Ext. 221

GENERAL INFORMATION Public Institution. Founded 1965. **Total program enrollment:** 225.

PROGRAM(S) OFFERED
• **Autobody/Collision and Repair Technology/Technician** *2160 hrs./$3406*
• **Business Operations Support and Secretarial Services, Other** *16 students enrolled* • **Business/Office Automation/Technology/Data Entry** *2160 hrs./$2286* • **Commercial and Advertising Art** *6 students enrolled* • **Drafting and Design Technology/Technician, General** *2160 hrs./$2286* • **Electrical and Power Transmission Installation/Installer, General** *1728 hrs./$2286* • **Electrical/Electronics Equipment Installation and Repair, General** *16 students enrolled* • **Heating, Air Conditioning, Ventilation and Refrigeration Maintenance Technology/Technician (HAC, HACR, HVAC, HVACR)** *15 students enrolled* • **Industrial Electronics Technology/Technician** *1944 hrs./$2286* • **Industrial Mechanics and Maintenance Technology** *15 students enrolled* • **Licensed Practical/Vocational Nurse Training (LPN, LVN, Cert, Dipl, AAS)** *20 students enrolled* • **Machine Shop Technology/Assistant** *1944 hrs./$2286* • **Truck and Bus Driver/Commercial Vehicle Operation** *25 students enrolled*

STUDENT SERVICES Academic or career counseling, employment services for current students, placement services for program completers, remedial services.

Tennessee Technology Center at Dickson

740 Highway 46, Dickson, TN 37055
http://www.dickson.tec.tn.us/

CONTACT Warner Taylor, Interim Director
Telephone: 615-441-6220

GENERAL INFORMATION Public Institution. Founded 1965. **Total program enrollment:** 374.

PROGRAM(S) OFFERED
• **Automobile/Automotive Mechanics Technology/Technician** *2160 hrs./$3810* • **Business Operations Support and Secretarial Services, Other** *1296 hrs./ $2286* • **Computer Installation and Repair Technology/Technician** *2160 hrs./ $3810* • **Cosmetology/Cosmetologist, General** *1500 hrs./$3048* • **Dental Assisting/Assistant** *15 students enrolled* • **Heating, Air Conditioning, Ventilation and Refrigeration Maintenance Technology/Technician (HAC, HACR, HVAC, HVACR)** *6 students enrolled* • **Heavy Equipment Maintenance Technology/Technician** *5 students enrolled* • **Industrial Mechanics and Maintenance Technology** *2592 hrs./$4572* • **Licensed Practical/Vocational Nurse Training (LPN, LVN, Cert, Dipl, AAS)** *1296 hrs./$4147* • **Machine Shop Technology/Assistant** *1 student enrolled* • **Mechanical Drafting and Mechanical Drafting CAD/CADD** • **Surgical Technology/Technologist** *11 students enrolled*

STUDENT SERVICES Academic or career counseling, employment services for current students, placement services for program completers, remedial services.

Tennessee Technology Center at Elizabethton

425 Highway 91, PO Box 789, Elizabethton, TN 37644
http://www.elizabethton.tec.tn.us/

CONTACT Jerry Patton, Director
Telephone: 423-543-0070

GENERAL INFORMATION Public Institution. Founded 1965. **Total program enrollment:** 446.

PROGRAM(S) OFFERED
• **Automobile/Automotive Mechanics Technology/Technician** *2160 hrs./$3880* • **Business Operations Support and Secretarial Services, Other** *1296 hrs./ $2286* • **Business/Office Automation/Technology/Data Entry** *2160 hrs./$3880* • **Dietetics/Dietitians** *34 students enrolled* • **Electrical/Electronics Equipment Installation and Repair, General** *1728 hrs./$3048* • **Health Aides/Attendants/ Orderlies, Other** *116 students enrolled* • **Heating, Air Conditioning, Ventilation and Refrigeration Maintenance Technology/Technician (HAC, HACR, HVAC, HVACR)** • **Industrial Mechanics and Maintenance Technology** *20 students enrolled* • **Licensed Practical/Vocational Nurse Training (LPN, LVN, Cert, Dipl, AAS)** *1296 hrs./$5076* • **Welding Technology/Welder** *1296 hrs./$2286*

STUDENT SERVICES Academic or career counseling, employment services for current students, placement services for program completers, remedial services.

Tennessee Technology Center at Harriman

1745 Harriman Highway, Harriman, TN 37748-1109
http://www.ttcharriman.edu/

CONTACT Mark Powers, Director
Telephone: 865-882-6703

GENERAL INFORMATION Public Institution. Founded 1970. **Total program enrollment:** 170.

PROGRAM(S) OFFERED
• **Automobile/Automotive Mechanics Technology/Technician** *2160 hrs./$2286* • **Business Operations Support and Secretarial Services, Other** *1296 hrs./ $2286* • **Cosmetology/Cosmetologist, General** *1500 hrs./$2286* • **Diesel Mechanics Technology/Technician** *2160 hrs./$2286* • **Industrial Mechanics and Maintenance Technology** *1728 hrs./$2286* • **Information Technology** *4 students enrolled* • **Licensed Practical/Vocational Nurse Training (LPN, LVN, Cert, Dipl, AAS)** *1296 hrs./$4869* • **Machine Shop Technology/Assistant** *7 students enrolled*

STUDENT SERVICES Academic or career counseling, employment services for current students, placement services for program completers, remedial services.

Tennessee Technology Center at Hartsville

716 McMurry Boulevard, Hartsville, TN 37074
http://hartsville.tec.tn.us/

CONTACT Mae W. Banks, Director
Telephone: 615-374-2147

GENERAL INFORMATION Public Institution. Founded 1965. **Total program enrollment:** 282.

PROGRAM(S) OFFERED
• **Automobile/Automotive Mechanics Technology/Technician** *2160 hrs./$3810* • **Business Operations Support and Secretarial Services, Other** *1296 hrs./ $2286* • **Business/Office Automation/Technology/Data Entry** *2160 hrs./$3810* • **Drafting and Design Technology/Technician, General** *2160 hrs./$3810* • **Licensed Practical/Vocational Nurse Training (LPN, LVN, Cert, Dipl, AAS)** *1296 hrs./$3486* • **Machine Shop Technology/Assistant** *1944 hrs./$3810* • **Welding Technology/Welder** *9 students enrolled*

STUDENT SERVICES Academic or career counseling, employment services for current students, placement services for program completers, remedial services.

Tennessee Technology Center at Hohenwald

813 West Main Street, Hohenwald, TN 38462-2201
http://www.hohenwald.tec.tn.us/

CONTACT Rick C. Brewer, Director
Telephone: 931-796-5351 Ext. 124

GENERAL INFORMATION Public Institution. Founded 1967. **Total program enrollment:** 330.

PROGRAM(S) OFFERED
• **Automobile/Automotive Mechanics Technology/Technician** *2160 hrs./$3810* • **Business Operations Support and Secretarial Services, Other** *1296 hrs./ $2286* • **Business/Office Automation/Technology/Data Entry** *2160 hrs./$3810* • **Cosmetology/Cosmetologist, General** *1500 hrs./$2645* • **Drafting and Design Technology/Technician, General** *2 students enrolled* • **Early Childhood Education and Teaching** *3 students enrolled* • **Heavy/Industrial Equipment Maintenance Technologies, Other** • **Industrial Electronics Technology/ Technician** • **Industrial Mechanics and Maintenance Technology** *1728 hrs./ $3048* • **Licensed Practical/Vocational Nurse Training (LPN, LVN, Cert, Dipl, AAS)** *1296 hrs./$4946* • **Machine Shop Technology/Assistant** *2 students enrolled* • **Surgical Technology/Technologist** *12 students enrolled*

STUDENT SERVICES Academic or career counseling, daycare for children of students, employment services for current students, placement services for program completers, remedial services.

Tennessee Technology Center at Jacksboro

Elkins Road, Jacksboro, TN 37757
http://www.jacksboro.tec.tn.us/

CONTACT David R. Browder, Director
Telephone: 423-566-9629 Ext. 100

GENERAL INFORMATION Public Institution. Founded 1967. **Total program enrollment:** 165.

PROGRAM(S) OFFERED
• **Administrative Assistant and Secretarial Science, General** *22 students enrolled* • **Automobile/Automotive Mechanics Technology/Technician** *2160 hrs./ $3810* • **Business/Office Automation/Technology/Data Entry** *1296 hrs./$2247* • **Computer Installation and Repair Technology/Technician** *11 students enrolled* • **Computer Technology/Computer Systems Technology** *2160 hrs./$3810* • **Drafting and Design Technology/Technician, General** *5 students enrolled* • **Electrical/Electronics Equipment Installation and Repair, General** *9 students enrolled* • **Electrical/Electronics Maintenance and Repair Technology, Other** *1728 hrs./$3048* • **Licensed Practical/Vocational Nurse Training (LPN, LVN, Cert, Dipl, AAS)** *1296 hrs./$4786* • **Machine Tool Technology/Machinist** • **Welding Technology/Welder** *1296 hrs./$2247*

STUDENT SERVICES Academic or career counseling, employment services for current students, placement services for program completers, remedial services.

Tennessee Technology Center at Jackson

2468 Westover Road, Jackson, TN 38301
http://www.jackson.tec.tn.us/

CONTACT Dr. Don Williams, Director
Telephone: 731-424-0691

GENERAL INFORMATION Public Institution. Founded 1965. **Total program enrollment:** 446.

PROGRAM(S) OFFERED
● **Autobody/Collision and Repair Technology/Technician** *13 students enrolled*
● **Automobile/Automotive Mechanics Technology/Technician** *2150 hrs./$3180*
● **Business Operations Support and Secretarial Services, Other** *1296 hrs./$2286* ● **Computer Systems Analysis/Analyst** *1718 hrs./$3048* ● **Drafting and Design Technology/Technician, General** *4 students enrolled* ● **Electrical/Electronics Equipment Installation and Repair, General** *5 students enrolled*
● **Electrician** *1 student enrolled* ● **Heating, Air Conditioning, Ventilation and Refrigeration Maintenance Technology/Technician (HAC, HACR, HVAC, HVACR)** *1 student enrolled* ● **Industrial Mechanics and Maintenance Technology** *11 students enrolled* ● **Licensed Practical/Vocational Nurse Training (LPN, LVN, Cert, Dipl, AAS)** *1296 hrs./$4686* ● **Machine Shop Technology/Assistant** *2 students enrolled* ● **Machine Tool Technology/Machinist** *2150 hrs./$3810* ● **Pharmacy Technician/Assistant** *11 students enrolled* ● **Surgical Technology/Technologist** *14 students enrolled* ● **Tool and Die Technology/Technician** *1 student enrolled* ● **Welding Technology/Welder** *1296 hrs./$2286*

STUDENT SERVICES Academic or career counseling, employment services for current students, placement services for program completers, remedial services.

Tennessee Technology Center at Knoxville

1100 Liberty Street, Knoxville, TN 37919
http://www.knoxville.tec.tn.us/

CONTACT Jeff Davis, Director
Telephone: 865-546-5567

GENERAL INFORMATION Public Institution. Founded 1968. **Total program enrollment:** 313.

PROGRAM(S) OFFERED
● **Autobody/Collision and Repair Technology/Technician** *10 students enrolled*
● **Automobile/Automotive Mechanics Technology/Technician** *9 students enrolled*
● **Business Operations Support and Secretarial Services, Other** *1296 hrs./$2286* ● **Cosmetology/Cosmetologist, General** *1500 hrs./$2912* ● **Dental Assisting/Assistant** *1296 hrs./$2286* ● **Diesel Mechanics Technology/Technician** ● **Drafting and Design Technology/Technician, General** *9 students enrolled* ● **Electrician** *10 students enrolled* ● **Heating, Air Conditioning, Ventilation and Refrigeration Maintenance Technology/Technician (HAC, HACR, HVAC, HVACR)** *1 student enrolled* ● **Heavy/Industrial Equipment Maintenance Technologies, Other** *11 students enrolled* ● **Industrial Electronics Technology/Technician** *1 student enrolled* ● **Licensed Practical/Vocational Nurse Training (LPN, LVN, Cert, Dipl, AAS)** *1296 hrs./$3808* ● **Machine Shop Technology/Assistant** ● **Medical Administrative/Executive Assistant and Medical Secretary** *632 hrs./$1388* ● **Medical/Clinical Assistant** *18 students enrolled* ● **Surgical Technology/Technologist** *1498 hrs./$3048* ● **Truck and Bus Driver/Commercial Vehicle Operation** *29 students enrolled* ● **Welding Technology/Welder**

STUDENT SERVICES Academic or career counseling, employment services for current students, placement services for program completers, remedial services.

Tennessee Technology Center at Livingston

740 Airport Road, PO Box 219, Livingston, TN 38570
http://www.livingston.tec.tn.us/

CONTACT Ralph Robbins, Director
Telephone: 931-823-5525 Ext. 0

GENERAL INFORMATION Public Institution. Founded 1966. **Total program enrollment:** 289.

PROGRAM(S) OFFERED
● **Autobody/Collision and Repair Technology/Technician** *5 students enrolled*
● **Automobile/Automotive Mechanics Technology/Technician** *2592 hrs./$4572*
● **Business Operations Support and Secretarial Services, Other** *1296 hrs./$2586* ● **Business, Management, Marketing, and Related Support Services, Other** ● **Business/Office Automation/Technology/Data Entry** *1728 hrs./$3048* ● **Construction Trades, Other** *11 students enrolled* ● **Cosmetology/Cosmetologist, General** *1500 hrs./$2912* ● **Electrical/Electronics Equipment Installation and Repair, General** *1 student enrolled* ● **Industrial Mechanics and Maintenance Technology** *2160 hrs./$3810* ● **Licensed Practical/Vocational Nurse Training (LPN, LVN, Cert, Dipl, AAS)** *1296 hrs./$4760* ● **Machine Shop Technology/Assistant** ● **Pharmacy Technician/Assistant**

STUDENT SERVICES Academic or career counseling, employment services for current students, placement services for program completers, remedial services.

Tennessee Technology Center at McKenzie

16940 Highland Drive, McKenzie, TN 38201
http://www.mckenzie.tec.tn.us/

CONTACT Elizabeth Check, Director
Telephone: 731-352-5364

GENERAL INFORMATION Public Institution. Founded 1964. **Total program enrollment:** 247.

PROGRAM(S) OFFERED
● **Automobile/Automotive Mechanics Technology/Technician** *2160 hrs./$3810*
● **Business Operations Support and Secretarial Services, Other** *1296 hrs./$3894* ● **Business/Office Automation/Technology/Data Entry** *2160 hrs./$3810*
● **Drafting and Design Technology/Technician, General** ● **Electrical/Electronics Equipment Installation and Repair, General** *4 students enrolled* ● **Industrial Electronics Technology/Technician** *1728 hrs./$3048* ● **Licensed Practical/Vocational Nurse Training (LPN, LVN, Cert, Dipl, AAS)** *1296 hrs./$2586*
● **Welding Technology/Welder** *1296 hrs./$2286*

STUDENT SERVICES Academic or career counseling, employment services for current students, placement services for program completers, remedial services.

Tennessee Technology Center at McMinnville

241 Vo Tech Drive, McMinnville, TN 37110
http://www.mcminnville.tec.tn.us/

CONTACT Marvin Lusk, Interim Director
Telephone: 931-473-5587

GENERAL INFORMATION Public Institution. **Total program enrollment:** 192.

PROGRAM(S) OFFERED
● **Administrative Assistant and Secretarial Science, General** *5 students enrolled*
● **Automobile/Automotive Mechanics Technology/Technician** *2160 hrs./$3810*
● **Business Operations Support and Secretarial Services, Other** *1296 hrs./$2286* ● **Business/Office Automation/Technology/Data Entry** *2160 hrs./$3810*
● **Industrial Electronics Technology/Technician** ● **Industrial Mechanics and Maintenance Technology** *1728 hrs./$3048* ● **Licensed Practical/Vocational Nurse Training (LPN, LVN, Cert, Dipl, AAS)** *1296 hrs./$5029* ● **Machine Shop Technology/Assistant** *1944 hrs./$3810* ● **Medical/Clinical Assistant** *14 students enrolled* ● **Surgical Technology/Technologist** *13 students enrolled*

STUDENT SERVICES Academic or career counseling, employment services for current students, placement services for program completers, remedial services.

Tennessee Technology Center at Memphis

550 Alabama Avenue, Memphis, TN 38105-3799
http://www.memphis.tec.tn.us/

CONTACT Lana Pierce, Director
Telephone: 901-543-6100

GENERAL INFORMATION Public Institution. Founded 1963. **Total program enrollment:** 696.

PROGRAM(S) OFFERED
● **Aircraft Powerplant Technology/Technician** *1918 hrs./$5296* ● **Autobody/Collision and Repair Technology/Technician** *7 students enrolled* ● **Automobile/**

Tennessee Technology Center at Memphis (continued)

Automotive Mechanics Technology/Technician 4 *students enrolled* • **Avionics Maintenance Technology/Technician** • **Barbering/Barber** *1500 hrs./$2974* • **Business Operations Support and Secretarial Services, Other** *1296 hrs./$2286* • **Business/Office Automation/Technology/Data Entry** 3 *students enrolled* • **Commercial and Advertising Art** 19 *students enrolled* • **Construction Trades, Other** 12 *students enrolled* • **Cosmetology/Cosmetologist, General** *1500 hrs./$2974* • **Dental Assisting/Assistant** 24 *students enrolled* • **Dental Laboratory Technology/Technician** 13 *students enrolled* • **Diesel Mechanics Technology/Technician** 11 *students enrolled* • **Drafting and Design Technology/Technician, General** 4 *students enrolled* • **Graphic and Printing Equipment Operator, General Production** 1 *student enrolled* • **Heating, Air Conditioning, Ventilation and Refrigeration Maintenance Technology/Technician (HAC, HACR, HVAC, HVACR)** 8 *students enrolled* • **Industrial Electronics Technology/Technician** 20 *students enrolled* • **Industrial Mechanics and Maintenance Technology** 3 *students enrolled* • **Licensed Practical/Vocational Nurse Training (LPN, LVN, Cert, Dipl, AAS)** *1296 hrs./$2386* • **Machine Shop Technology/Assistant** 11 *students enrolled* • **Mason/Masonry** 5 *students enrolled* • **Nurse/Nursing Assistant/Aide and Patient Care Assistant** 22 *students enrolled* • **Pharmacy Technician/Assistant** 14 *students enrolled* • **Surgical Technology/Technologist** *1296 hrs./$2286* • **Truck and Bus Driver/Commercial Vehicle Operation** 77 *students enrolled* • **Welding Technology/Welder** 15 *students enrolled*

STUDENT SERVICES Academic or career counseling, employment services for current students, placement services for program completers, remedial services.

Tennessee Technology Center at Morristown

821 West Louise Avenue, Morristown, TN 37813
http://www.morristown.tec.tn.us/

CONTACT B. Lynn Elkins, Director
Telephone: 423-586-5771

GENERAL INFORMATION Public Institution. Founded 1966. **Total program enrollment:** 443.

PROGRAM(S) OFFERED
• **Administrative Assistant and Secretarial Science, General** *1296 hrs./$2286* • **Aircraft Powerplant Technology/Technician** • **Autobody/Collision and Repair Technology/Technician** *2160 hrs./$3810* • **Automobile/Automotive Mechanics Technology/Technician** • **Business Operations Support and Secretarial Services, Other** 35 *students enrolled* • **Business/Office Automation/Technology/Data Entry** 3 *students enrolled* • **Computer Installation and Repair Technology/Technician** *2160 hrs./$3810* • **Drafting and Design Technology/Technician, General** 2 *students enrolled* • **Electrician** *1728 hrs./$3048* • **Graphic and Printing Equipment Operator, General Production** 2 *students enrolled* • **Heating, Air Conditioning, Ventilation and Refrigeration Maintenance Technology/Technician (HAC, HACR, HVAC, HVACR)** • **Industrial Mechanics and Maintenance Technology** *1728 hrs./$3048* • **Licensed Practical/Vocational Nurse Training (LPN, LVN, Cert, Dipl, AAS)** *1296 hrs./$4133* • **Machine Shop Technology/Assistant** 8 *students enrolled* • **Mason/Masonry** • **Truck and Bus Driver/Commercial Vehicle Operation** 41 *students enrolled* • **Welding Technology/Welder** 6 *students enrolled*

STUDENT SERVICES Academic or career counseling, employment services for current students, placement services for program completers, remedial services.

Tennessee Technology Center at Murfreesboro

1303 Old Fort Parkway, Murfreesboro, TN 37129-3312
http://www.ttcmurfreesboro.edu/

CONTACT Carol Puryear, Director
Telephone: 615-898-8010

GENERAL INFORMATION Public Institution. Founded 1969. **Total program enrollment:** 243.

PROGRAM(S) OFFERED
• **Automobile/Automotive Mechanics Technology/Technician** *2160 hrs./$3525* • **Business Operations Support and Secretarial Services, Other** 4 *students enrolled* • **Business/Office Automation/Technology/Data Entry** *2160 hrs./$3810* • **Clinical/Medical Laboratory Science and Allied Professions, Other** 30 *students enrolled* • **Dental Assisting/Assistant** 11 *students enrolled* • **Drafting and**

Design Technology/Technician, General *1728 hrs./$3048* • **Heating, Air Conditioning, Ventilation and Refrigeration Maintenance Technology/Technician (HAC, HACR, HVAC, HVACR)** *1728 hrs./$3048* • **Industrial Mechanics and Maintenance Technology** *1728 hrs./$3048* • **Licensed Practical/Vocational Nurse Training (LPN, LVN, Cert, Dipl, AAS)** 43 *students enrolled* • **Machine Shop Technology/Assistant** *1944 hrs./$3810* • **Pharmacy Technician/Assistant** 9 *students enrolled* • **Surgical Technology/Technologist** 12 *students enrolled*

STUDENT SERVICES Academic or career counseling, employment services for current students, placement services for program completers, remedial services.

Tennessee Technology Center at Nashville

100 White Bridge Road, Nashville, TN 37209
http://www.nashville.tec.tn.us/

CONTACT Johnny W. Williams, EdD, Director
Telephone: 615-425-5500 Ext. 5500

GENERAL INFORMATION Public Institution. Founded 1967. **Total program enrollment:** 536.

PROGRAM(S) OFFERED
• **Aesthetician/Esthetician and Skin Care Specialist** *864 hrs./$1524* • **Aircraft Powerplant Technology/Technician** *1918 hrs./$3674* • **Autobody/Collision and Repair Technology/Technician** 1 *student enrolled* • **Automobile/Automotive Mechanics Technology/Technician** *2160 hrs./$3810* • **Business/Office Automation/Technology/Data Entry** 8 *students enrolled* • **Child Care and Support Services Management** • **Clinical/Medical Laboratory Science and Allied Professions, Other** 33 *students enrolled* • **Cosmetology/Cosmetologist, General** *1500 hrs./$2912* • **Dental Laboratory Technology/Technician** 4 *students enrolled* • **Drafting and Design Technology/Technician, General** 7 *students enrolled* • **Electrical and Power Transmission Installation/Installer, General** 3 *students enrolled* • **Electrical/Electronics Equipment Installation and Repair, General** 5 *students enrolled* • **Heating, Air Conditioning, Ventilation and Refrigeration Maintenance Technology/Technician (HAC, HACR, HVAC, HVACR)** *2160 hrs./$3810* • **Licensed Practical/Vocational Nurse Training (LPN, LVN, Cert, Dipl, AAS)** *1296 hrs./$4985* • **Machine Shop Technology/Assistant** 9 *students enrolled* • **Management Information Systems, General** 4 *students enrolled* • **Medical Insurance Specialist/Medical Biller** 5 *students enrolled* • **Pharmacy Technician/Assistant** 14 *students enrolled* • **Truck and Bus Driver/Commercial Vehicle Operation** 47 *students enrolled* • **Welding Technology/Welder** 6 *students enrolled*

STUDENT SERVICES Academic or career counseling, employment services for current students, placement services for program completers, remedial services.

Tennessee Technology Center at Newbern

340 Washington Street, Newbern, TN 38059
http://www.newbern.tec.tn.us/

CONTACT Brian Collins, Director
Telephone: 731-627-2511

GENERAL INFORMATION Public Institution. **Total program enrollment:** 149.

PROGRAM(S) OFFERED
• **Automobile/Automotive Mechanics Technology/Technician** *2160 hrs./$3430* • **Business Operations Support and Secretarial Services, Other** *1296 hrs./$2058* • **Drafting and Design Technology/Technician, General** 2 *students enrolled* • **Electrical/Electronics Equipment Installation and Repair, General** 1 *student enrolled* • **Heating, Air Conditioning, Ventilation and Refrigeration Maintenance Technology/Technician (HAC, HACR, HVAC, HVACR)** *2160 hrs./$3430* • **Industrial Mechanics and Maintenance Technology** *2160 hrs./$5100* • **Licensed Practical/Vocational Nurse Training (LPN, LVN, Cert, Dipl, AAS)** *1296 hrs./$2358* • **Machine Shop Technology/Assistant** *1944 hrs./$2744*

STUDENT SERVICES Academic or career counseling, employment services for current students, placement services for program completers, remedial services.

Tennessee Technology Center at Oneida/Huntsville

355 Scott High Drive, Huntsville, TN 37756
http://www.huntsville.tec.tn.us/

CONTACT Dwight E. Murphy, Director
Telephone: 423-663-4900

GENERAL INFORMATION Public Institution. Founded 1967. **Total program enrollment:** 79.

PROGRAM(S) OFFERED
- **Autobody/Collision and Repair Technology/Technician** *2160 hrs./$3810*
- **Automobile/Automotive Mechanics Technology/Technician** *2160 hrs./$3810*
- **Business Operations Support and Secretarial Services, Other** *1296 hrs./$2586* • **Business/Office Automation/Technology/Data Entry** *1 student enrolled*
- **Cosmetology/Cosmetologist, General** *1500 hrs./$3048* • **Drafting and Design Technology/Technician, General** • **Industrial Electronics Technology/Technician** • **Licensed Practical/Vocational Nurse Training (LPN, LVN, Cert, Dipl, AAS)** *1296 hrs./$3717* • **Machine Shop Technology/Assistant** *1 student enrolled* • **Welding Technology/Welder** *1296 hrs./$2286*

STUDENT SERVICES Academic or career counseling, employment services for current students, placement services for program completers, remedial services.

Tennessee Technology Center at Paris

312 South Wilson Street, Paris, TN 38242
http://www.paris.tec.tn.us/

CONTACT Brad White, Director
Telephone: 731-644-7365

GENERAL INFORMATION Public Institution. Founded 1971. **Total program enrollment:** 235.

PROGRAM(S) OFFERED
- **Autobody/Collision and Repair Technology/Technician** *2160 hrs./$3810*
- **Business Operations Support and Secretarial Services, Other** *1296 hrs./$2286* • **Business/Office Automation/Technology/Data Entry** *2160 hrs./$4765*
- **Child Care and Support Services Management** *10 students enrolled*
- **Cosmetology/Cosmetologist, General** *2 students enrolled* • **Industrial Mechanics and Maintenance Technology** *1728 hrs./$3048* • **Licensed Practical/Vocational Nurse Training (LPN, LVN, Cert, Dipl, AAS)** *1296 hrs./$2586* • **Machine Shop Technology/Assistant** *12 students enrolled* • **Machine Tool Technology/Machinist** *1944 hrs./$3429* • **Motorcycle Maintenance and Repair Technology/Technician** *3 students enrolled* • **Robotics Technology/Technician** *5 students enrolled* • **Surgical Technology/Technologist** *9 students enrolled*

STUDENT SERVICES Academic or career counseling, employment services for current students, placement services for program completers, remedial services.

Tennessee Technology Center at Pulaski

1233 East College Street, Pulaski, TN 38478
http://www.pulaski.tec.tn.us/files/special%20industry%20training.html/

CONTACT James Dixon, Director
Telephone: 931-424-4014

GENERAL INFORMATION Public Institution. **Total program enrollment:** 81.

PROGRAM(S) OFFERED
- **Business, Management, Marketing, and Related Support Services, Other** *1296 hrs./$4506* • **Computer Technology/Computer Systems Technology** *3 students enrolled* • **Computer and Information Sciences and Support Services, Other** *2160 hrs./$3810* • **Electrical and Electronic Engineering Technologies/Technicians, Other** *1728 hrs./$3048* • **Heating, Air Conditioning and Refrigeration Technology/Technician (ACH/ACR/ACHR/HRAC/HVAC/AC Technology)** *2160 hrs./$3810* • **Heavy/Industrial Equipment Maintenance Technologies, Other** *1728 hrs./$3048* • **Licensed Practical/Vocational Nurse Training (LPN, LVN, Cert, Dipl, AAS)** *1296 hrs./$2586* • **Machine Tool Technology/Machinist** *2 students enrolled* • **Plastics Engineering Technology/Technician** *5 students enrolled* • **Welding Technology/Welder** *5 students enrolled*

STUDENT SERVICES Academic or career counseling, employment services for current students, placement services for program completers, remedial services.

Tennessee Technology Center at Ripley

127 Industrial Drive, Ripley, TN 38063

CONTACT Brian Collins, Director
Telephone: 731-635-3368

GENERAL INFORMATION Public Institution. **Total program enrollment:** 142.

PROGRAM(S) OFFERED
- **Allied Health and Medical Assisting Services, Other** *864 hrs./$1524* • **Business Operations Support and Secretarial Services, Other** *1296 hrs./$2286* • **Computer Systems Analysis/Analyst** *2 students enrolled* • **Data Processing and Data Processing Technology/Technician** *2160 hrs./$3810* • **Drafting and Design Technology/Technician, General** • **Electrician** *1728 hrs./$3048* • **Licensed Practical/Vocational Nurse Training (LPN, LVN, Cert, Dipl, AAS)** *1296 hrs./$5425* • **Nursing, Other** *13 students enrolled* • **Truck and Bus Driver/Commercial Vehicle Operation** *216 hrs./$926*

STUDENT SERVICES Academic or career counseling, employment services for current students, placement services for program completers, remedial services.

Tennessee Technology Center at Shelbyville

1405 Madison Street, Shelbyville, TN 37160
http://www.shelbyville.tec.tn.us/

CONTACT Ivan Jones, Director
Telephone: 931-685-5013

GENERAL INFORMATION Public Institution. Founded 1964. **Total program enrollment:** 311.

PROGRAM(S) OFFERED
- **Autobody/Collision and Repair Technology/Technician** *2160 hrs./$3810*
- **Automobile/Automotive Mechanics Technology/Technician** *8 students enrolled* • **Business Operations Support and Secretarial Services, Other** *1296 hrs./$2286* • **Computer and Information Sciences, General** *2160 hrs./$3810* • **Drafting and Design Technology/Technician, General** *7 students enrolled* • **Electrical/Electronics Equipment Installation and Repair, General** *1728 hrs./$3048* • **Heating, Air Conditioning, Ventilation and Refrigeration Maintenance Technology/Technician (HAC, HACR, HVAC, HVACR)** *6 students enrolled* • **Industrial Mechanics and Maintenance Technology** *2160 hrs./$3810* • **Licensed Practical/Vocational Nurse Training (LPN, LVN, Cert, Dipl, AAS)** *1296 hrs./$3596* • **Machine Shop Technology/Assistant** *6 students enrolled* • **Nurse/Nursing Assistant/Aide and Patient Care Assistant** *11 students enrolled* • **Truck and Bus Driver/Commercial Vehicle Operation** *25 students enrolled* • **Welding Technology/Welder** *10 students enrolled*

STUDENT SERVICES Academic or career counseling, employment services for current students, placement services for program completers, remedial services.

Tennessee Technology Center at Whiteville

PO Box 489, Whiteville, TN 38075
http://www.whiteville.tec.tn.us/

CONTACT Jeff Sisk, Director
Telephone: 731-254-8521

GENERAL INFORMATION Public Institution. **Total program enrollment:** 156.

Tennessee Technology Center at Whiteville (continued)

PROGRAM(S) OFFERED
• Automobile/Automotive Mechanics Technology/Technician *2160 hrs./$3810*
• Business Administration, Management and Operations, Other *1296 hrs./ $2286* • Business Operations Support and Secretarial Services, Other *18 students enrolled* • Business/Office Automation/Technology/Data Entry *2160 hrs./$3810* • Drafting and Design Technology/Technician, General • Electrician • Heating, Air Conditioning, Ventilation and Refrigeration Maintenance Technology/Technician (HAC, HACR, HVAC, HVACR) *9 students enrolled* • Industrial Electronics Technology/Technician *11 students enrolled* • Industrial Mechanics and Maintenance Technology *1 student enrolled* • Licensed Practical/Vocational Nurse Training (LPN, LVN, Cert, Dipl, AAS) *1296 hrs./ $4158* • Machine Tool Technology/Machinist *1944 hrs./$3810* • Nurse/Nursing Assistant/Aide and Patient Care Assistant • Welding Technology/Welder *1296 hrs./$2286*

STUDENT SERVICES Academic or career counseling, employment services for current students, placement services for program completers, remedial services.

Union University

1050 Union University Drive, Jackson, TN 38305-3697
http://www.uu.edu/

CONTACT David S. Dockery, President
Telephone: 731-668-1818

GENERAL INFORMATION Private Institution. Founded 1823. **Accreditation:** Regional (SACS/CC); art and design (NASAD); music (NASM). **Total program enrollment:** 2681. **Application fee:** $35.

PROGRAM(S) OFFERED
• Christian Studies

STUDENT SERVICES Academic or career counseling, employment services for current students, placement services for program completers.

Vatterott College

2655 Dividend Drive, Memphis, TN 38132
http://www.vatterott-college.edu/

CONTACT Theresa Rice, Director
Telephone: 901-761-5730

GENERAL INFORMATION Private Institution. Founded 2004. **Accreditation:** State accredited or approved. **Total program enrollment:** 478.

PROGRAM(S) OFFERED
• Cosmetology/Cosmetologist, General *10 students enrolled* • Electrician *18 students enrolled* • Heating, Air Conditioning, Ventilation and Refrigeration Maintenance Technology/Technician (HAC, HACR, HVAC, HVACR) *75 students enrolled* • Information Technology *18 students enrolled* • Medical Office Assistant/Specialist *7 students enrolled*

STUDENT SERVICES Academic or career counseling, employment services for current students, placement services for program completers.

Virginia College School of Business and Health at Chattanooga

721 Eastgate Loop Road, Chattanooga, TN 37411
http://www.vc.edu/site/campus.cfm?campus=chattanooga

CONTACT Don Newton, Campus Director
Telephone: 423-893-2000

GENERAL INFORMATION Private Institution. **Total program enrollment:** 413. **Application fee:** $100.

PROGRAM(S) OFFERED
• Administrative Assistant and Secretarial Science, General *4 students enrolled*
• Medical Insurance Coding Specialist/Coder *6 students enrolled* • Medical/ Clinical Assistant *7 students enrolled* • Pharmacy Technician/Assistant

STUDENT SERVICES Academic or career counseling, placement services for program completers, remedial services.

Visible School—Music and Worships Arts College

9817 Huff and Puff Road, Lakeland, TN 38002
http://www.visibleschool.com

CONTACT Ken Steorts, President
Telephone: 901-381-3939

GENERAL INFORMATION Private Institution. **Total program enrollment:** 90. **Application fee:** $40.

PROGRAM(S) OFFERED
• Digital Communication and Media/Multimedia • Music Management and Merchandising • Music Performance, General *3 students enrolled* • Theology/ Theological Studies

STUDENT SERVICES Academic or career counseling, employment services for current students, placement services for program completers, remedial services.

Volunteer Beauty Academy

1057-A Vendall Road, Dyersburg, TN 38024

CONTACT Dorothy H. Chitwood, President
Telephone: 731-285-1542

GENERAL INFORMATION Private Institution. **Total program enrollment:** 62. **Application fee:** $100.

PROGRAM(S) OFFERED
• Cosmetology/Cosmetologist, General *1500 hrs./$10,950*

STUDENT SERVICES Academic or career counseling, placement services for program completers.

Volunteer Beauty Academy

1791B Gallatin Pike, N, Madison, TN 37115
http://www.volunteerbeauty.com/

CONTACT Dorothy H. Chitwood, President
Telephone: 615-865-4477

GENERAL INFORMATION Private Institution. **Total program enrollment:** 66. **Application fee:** $100.

PROGRAM(S) OFFERED
• Aesthetician/Esthetician and Skin Care Specialist *750 hrs./$6850*
• Cosmetology and Related Personal Grooming Arts, Other *5 students enrolled*
• Cosmetology/Cosmetologist, General *1500 hrs./$10,950* • Nail Technician/ Specialist and Manicurist *600 hrs./$4000*

STUDENT SERVICES Academic or career counseling, placement services for program completers.

Volunteer Beauty Academy

5666 Nolensville Road, Nashville, TN 37211
http://www.volunteerbeauty.com/

CONTACT Dorothy H. Chitwood, President
Telephone: 615-298-4600

GENERAL INFORMATION Private Institution. Founded 1985. **Total program enrollment:** 26. **Application fee:** $100.

PROGRAM(S) OFFERED

• **Cosmetology/Cosmetologist, General** *750 hrs./$2900*

STUDENT SERVICES Academic or career counseling, placement services for program completers.

Volunteer Beauty Academy–System Office

5668 Nolensville Road, Nashville, TN 37211

CONTACT Dorothy Chitwood, President
Telephone: 615-860-4996

GENERAL INFORMATION Private Institution.

Volunteer State Community College

1480 Nashville Pike, Gallatin, TN 37066-3188
http://www.volstate.edu/

CONTACT Dr. Warren Nichols, President
Telephone: 615-452-8600

GENERAL INFORMATION Public Institution. Founded 1970. **Accreditation:** Regional (SACS/CC); dental assisting (ADA); emergency medical services (JRCEMTP); health information technology (AHIMA); physical therapy assisting (APTA); radiologic technology: radiography (JRCERT); respiratory therapy technology (CoARC). **Total program enrollment:** 3530. **Application fee:** $10.

PROGRAM(S) OFFERED

• **Administrative Assistant and Secretarial Science, General** *6 students enrolled* • **Clinical/Medical Laboratory Science and Allied Professions, Other** *16 students enrolled* • **Dental Assisting/Assistant** *23 students enrolled* • **Diagnostic Medical Sonography/Sonographer and Ultrasound Technician** *11 students enrolled* • **Emergency Medical Technology/Technician (EMT Paramedic)** *157 students enrolled* • **Fire Science/Firefighting** *10 students enrolled* • **Logistics and Materials Management** *7 students enrolled*

STUDENT SERVICES Academic or career counseling, employment services for current students, placement services for program completers, remedial services.

Walters State Community College

500 South Davy Crockett Parkway, Morristown, TN 37813-6899
http://www.ws.edu/

CONTACT Wade B. McCamey, President
Telephone: 423-585-2600

GENERAL INFORMATION Public Institution. Founded 1970. **Accreditation:** Regional (SACS/CC); physical therapy assisting (APTA); respiratory therapy technology (CoARC). **Total program enrollment:** 3241. **Application fee:** $10.

PROGRAM(S) OFFERED

• **Child Development** *4 students enrolled* • **Criminal Justice/Police Science** *148 students enrolled* • **Culinary Arts/Chef Training** *5 students enrolled* • **Emergency Medical Technology/Technician (EMT Paramedic)** *51 students enrolled* • **Health Information/Medical Records Technology/Technician** *19 students enrolled* • **Industrial Mechanics and Maintenance Technology** • **Management Information Systems and Services, Other** • **Medical Insurance Coding Specialist/Coder** *10 students enrolled* • **Medical Transcription/Transcriptionist** *9 students enrolled* • **Pharmacy Technician/Assistant** *14 students enrolled* • **Quality Control Technology/Technician** *1 student enrolled* • **Web Page, Digital/Multimedia and Information Resources Design**

STUDENT SERVICES Academic or career counseling, employment services for current students, placement services for program completers, remedial services.

Watkins College of Art, Design, & Film

2298 MetroCenter Boulevard, Nashville, TN 37228
http://www.watkins.edu/

CONTACT Ellen L. Meyer, President
Telephone: 615-383-4848

GENERAL INFORMATION Private Institution. Founded 1885. **Accreditation:** Art and design (NASAD); interior design: professional (CIDA). **Total program enrollment:** 254. **Application fee:** $50.

PROGRAM(S) OFFERED

• **Cinematography and Film/Video Production** *1 student enrolled* • **Graphic Design**

STUDENT SERVICES Academic or career counseling, employment services for current students.

West Tennessee Business College

1186 Highway 45 Bypass, Jackson, TN 38343
http://www.wtbc.com/

CONTACT Charlotte V. Burch, President
Telephone: 731-668-7240

GENERAL INFORMATION Private Institution. Founded 1888. **Total program enrollment:** 376. **Application fee:** $50.

PROGRAM(S) OFFERED

• **Administrative Assistant and Secretarial Science, General** *37 hrs./$11,470* • **Aesthetician/Esthetician and Skin Care Specialist** *750 hrs./$8275* • **Cosmetology/Cosmetologist, General** *1500 hrs./$11,275* • **General Office Occupations and Clerical Services** *1 student enrolled* • **Make-Up Artist/Specialist** *23 students enrolled* • **Medical Administrative/Executive Assistant and Medical Secretary** *43 students enrolled* • **Medical Insurance Coding Specialist/Coder** *34 hrs./$11,300* • **Medical Office Assistant/Specialist** *34 hrs./$10,540* • **Medical/Clinical Assistant** *37 hrs./$11,470* • **Nail Technician/Specialist and Manicurist** *12 students enrolled*

STUDENT SERVICES Employment services for current students, placement services for program completers.

William R. Moore School of Technology

1200 Poplar Avenue, Memphis, TN 38104
http://www.williamrmoore.org/

CONTACT Don R. Smith, Director/Chief Administrative Officer
Telephone: 901-726-1977

GENERAL INFORMATION Private Institution. Founded 1939. **Total program enrollment:** 33.

PROGRAM(S) OFFERED

• **Computer Installation and Repair Technology/Technician** *3 students enrolled* • **Welding Technology/Welder** *9 students enrolled*

STUDENT SERVICES Academic or career counseling, placement services for program completers.

VERMONT

Burlington College

95 North Avenue, Burlington, VT 05401-2998
http://www.burlington.edu/

CONTACT Jane O'Meara Sanders, President
Telephone: 802-862-9616

GENERAL INFORMATION Private Institution. Founded 1972. **Accreditation:** Regional (NEASC/NEASCCIHE). **Total program enrollment:** 108. **Application fee:** $50.

PROGRAM(S) OFFERED

• **Cinematography and Film/Video Production** *3 students enrolled* • **Film/Cinema Studies** • **Journalism, Other** • **Legal Assistant/Paralegal** *3 students enrolled* • **Playwriting and Screenwriting**

STUDENT SERVICES Academic or career counseling, employment services for current students.

Burlington Technical Center

52 Institute Road, Burlington, VT 05401-2721
http://burlingtontech.org/

CONTACT Mark Aliquo, Director
Telephone: 802-864-8436

GENERAL INFORMATION Public Institution. **Total program enrollment:** 7.

PROGRAM(S) OFFERED
• **Aircraft Powerplant Technology/Technician** *750 hrs./$8300* • **Airframe Mechanics and Aircraft Maintenance Technology/Technician** *750 hrs./$10,136*

STUDENT SERVICES Academic or career counseling, employment services for current students, placement services for program completers, remedial services.

Champlain College

PO Box 670, Burlington, VT 05402-0670
http://www.champlain.edu/

CONTACT David/Finney, President
Telephone: 802-860-2700

GENERAL INFORMATION Private Institution. Founded 1878. **Accreditation:** Regional (NEASC/NEASCCIHE); radiologic technology: radiography (JRCERT). **Total program enrollment:** 2095. **Application fee:** $50.

PROGRAM(S) OFFERED
• **Accounting** *17 students enrolled* • **Business Administration and Management, General** • **Business/Commerce, General** *1 student enrolled* • **Computer Programming/Programmer, General** *5 students enrolled* • **Computer Software and Media Applications, Other** *17 students enrolled* • **Computer Systems Networking and Telecommunications** *8 students enrolled* • **Computer and Information Sciences and Support Services, Other** *21 students enrolled* • **Human Resources Management/Personnel Administration, General** *8 students enrolled* • **Intermedia/Multimedia** *4 students enrolled* • **International Finance** • **Legal Assistant/Paralegal** *5 students enrolled* • **Management Information Systems and Services, Other** *3 students enrolled* • **System Administration/Administrator** *8 students enrolled*

STUDENT SERVICES Academic or career counseling, employment services for current students, placement services for program completers.

Community College of Vermont

PO Box 120, Waterbury, VT 05676-0120
http://www.ccv.edu/

CONTACT Timothy Donovan, President
Telephone: 802-241-3535

GENERAL INFORMATION Public Institution. Founded 1970. **Accreditation:** Regional (NEASC/NEASCCIHE). **Total program enrollment:** 1094.

PROGRAM(S) OFFERED
• **Child Care Provider/Assistant** *4 students enrolled* • **Clinical Laboratory Science/Medical Technology/Technologist** *3 students enrolled* • **Computer/Information Technology Services Administration and Management, Other** *1 student enrolled* • **Health Services/Allied Health/Health Sciences, General** *5 students enrolled* • **Massage Therapy/Therapeutic Massage** *10 students enrolled* • **Medical Office Assistant/Specialist** *3 students enrolled* • **Medical/Clinical Assistant** *9 students enrolled* • **Substance Abuse/Addiction Counseling** *4 students enrolled* • **Teacher Assistant/Aide** *1 student enrolled*

STUDENT SERVICES Academic or career counseling, remedial services.

Green Mountain College

One College Circle, Poultney, VT 05764-1199
http://www.greenmtn.edu/

CONTACT Paul Fonteyn, President
Telephone: 802-287-8000

GENERAL INFORMATION Private Institution. Founded 1834. **Accreditation:** Regional (NEASC/NEASCCIHE); recreation and parks (NRPA). **Total program enrollment:** 840. **Application fee:** $30.

PROGRAM(S) OFFERED
• **Resort Management**

STUDENT SERVICES Academic or career counseling, employment services for current students, placement services for program completers, remedial services.

Johnson State College

337 College Hill, Johnson, VT 05656-9405
http://www.johnsonstatecollege.edu/

CONTACT Barbara Murphy, President
Telephone: 802-635-2356

GENERAL INFORMATION Public Institution. Founded 1828. **Accreditation:** Regional (NEASC/NEASCCIHE). **Total program enrollment:** 1130. **Application fee:** $37.

PROGRAM(S) OFFERED
• **Education, General** *1 student enrolled* • **Small Business Administration/Management**

STUDENT SERVICES Academic or career counseling, daycare for children of students, employment services for current students, placement services for program completers, remedial services.

Marlboro College Graduate Center

28 Vernon Street, Suite 120, Brattleboro, VT 05301
http://gradcenter.marlboro.edu/

CONTACT Ellen McCulloch-Lovell, President
Telephone: 802-258-9200

GENERAL INFORMATION Private Institution. **Total program enrollment:** 24.

PROGRAM(S) OFFERED
• **E-Commerce/Electronic Commerce** • **Information Resources Management/CIO Training**

New England Culinary Institute

56 College Street, Montpelier, VT 05602-9720
http://www.neci.edu/

CONTACT Francis Voigt, Chief Executive Officer
Telephone: 802-223-6324

GENERAL INFORMATION Private Institution. Founded 1980. **Accreditation:** State accredited or approved. **Total program enrollment:** 516. **Application fee:** $50.

PROGRAM(S) OFFERED
• **Baking and Pastry Arts/Baker/Pastry Chef** *1191 hrs./$6236* • **Culinary Arts/Chef Training** *90 hrs./$26,031* • **Food Preparation/Professional Cooking/Kitchen Assistant** *148 hrs./$78,501* • **Restaurant/Food Services Management** *68 hrs./$27,551*

STUDENT SERVICES Academic or career counseling, employment services for current students, placement services for program completers, remedial services.

New England Culinary Institute at Essex

48½ Park Street, Essex Junction, VT 05452
http://www.neci.edu/

CONTACT Francis Voigt, Chief Executive Officer
Telephone: 802-223-6324

GENERAL INFORMATION Private Institution. Founded 1989. **Accreditation:** State accredited or approved. **Total program enrollment:** 152. **Application fee:** $50.

PROGRAM(S) OFFERED
● **Cooking and Related Culinary Arts, General** *1352 hrs./$6236* ● **Culinary Arts/Chef Training** *90 hrs./$26,031* ● **Food Preparation/Professional Cooking/ Kitchen Assistant** *148 hrs./$78,501* ● **Restaurant/Food Services Management** *77 hrs./$36,066*

STUDENT SERVICES Academic or career counseling, employment services for current students, placement services for program completers, remedial services.

O'Brien's Training Center

1475 Shelburne Road, South Burlington, VT 05403

CONTACT Anne Orr, School Director
Telephone: 802-658-9591

GENERAL INFORMATION Private Institution. **Total program enrollment:** 11. **Application fee:** $50.

PROGRAM(S) OFFERED
● **Cosmetology/Cosmetologist, General** *1500 hrs./$14,600*

Vermont College of Cosmetology

187 Pearl Street, Burlington, VT 05401
http://www.vtcollegeofcosmo.com/

CONTACT Rita Jutras, Director
Telephone: 802-879-4811

GENERAL INFORMATION Private Institution. Founded 1964. **Total program enrollment:** 78. **Application fee:** $200.

PROGRAM(S) OFFERED
● **Aesthetician/Esthetician and Skin Care Specialist** *600 hrs./$6200* ● **Cosmetology and Related Personal Grooming Arts, Other** *20 students enrolled* ● **Cosmetology/Cosmetologist, General** *1500 hrs./$16,050* ● **Nail Technician/Specialist and Manicurist** *400 hrs./$4190*

STUDENT SERVICES Academic or career counseling, placement services for program completers.

Vermont State Colleges System

PO Box 359, Waterbury, VT 05676-0359

CONTACT Robert G. Clarke, Chancellor
Telephone: 802-241-2520

GENERAL INFORMATION Public Institution.

Vermont Technical College

PO Box 500, Randolph Center, VT 05061-0500
http://www.vtc.edu/

CONTACT Ty J. Handy, President
Telephone: 802-728-1000

GENERAL INFORMATION Public Institution. Founded 1866. **Accreditation:** Regional (NEASC/NEASCCIHE); engineering technology (ABET/ TAC). **Total program enrollment:** 1175. **Application fee:** $37.

PROGRAM(S) OFFERED
● **Licensed Practical/Vocational Nurse Training (LPN, LVN, Cert, Dipl, AAS)**
138 students enrolled

STUDENT SERVICES Academic or career counseling, employment services for current students, placement services for program completers, remedial services.

Woodbury College

660 Elm Street, Montpelier, VT 05602
http://www.woodbury-college.edu/

CONTACT Lawrence Mandell, President
Telephone: 802-229-0516 Ext. 241

GENERAL INFORMATION Private Institution. Founded 1975. **Accreditation:** Regional (NEASC/NEASCCIHE). **Total program enrollment:** 28. **Application fee:** $30.

PROGRAM(S) OFFERED
● **Community Organization and Advocacy** *2 students enrolled* ● **Legal Assistant/ Paralegal** *11 students enrolled*

STUDENT SERVICES Academic or career counseling, remedial services.

VIRGINIA

ACT College

1100 Wilson Boulevard, Arlington, VA 22209
http://www.healthtraining.com/

CONTACT Jeffrey S. Moore, President/CEO
Telephone: 703-527-6660

GENERAL INFORMATION Private Institution. Founded 1983. **Total program enrollment:** 482. **Application fee:** $50.

PROGRAM(S) OFFERED
● **Dental Assisting/Assistant** *58 hrs./$12,980* ● **Health and Medical Administrative Services, Other** *30 hrs./$5600* ● **Medical Insurance Specialist/ Medical Biller** *7 students enrolled* ● **Medical Office Assistant/Specialist** *41 hrs./ $8446* ● **Medical Radiologic Technology/Science—Radiation Therapist** *77 hrs./$28,413* ● **Medical/Clinical Assistant** *62 hrs./$12,958* ● **Pharmacy Technician/Assistant** *73 hrs./$10,950* ● **Pharmacy, Pharmaceutical Sciences, and Administration, Other** *19 students enrolled*

STUDENT SERVICES Academic or career counseling, employment services for current students, placement services for program completers, remedial services.

Advanced Technology Institute

5700 Southern Boulevard, Virginia Beach, VA 23462
http://www.auto.edu/

CONTACT Mark Dreyfus, President
Telephone: 757-490-1241

GENERAL INFORMATION Private Institution. **Total program enrollment:** 586. **Application fee:** $100.

Advanced Technology Institute (continued)

PROGRAM(S) OFFERED
● **Automobile/Automotive Mechanics Technology/Technician** *91 students enrolled* ● **Diesel Mechanics Technology/Technician** *23 students enrolled* ● **Heating, Air Conditioning, Ventilation and Refrigeration Maintenance Technology/Technician (HAC, HACR, HVAC, HVACR)** *33 students enrolled* ● **Truck and Bus Driver/Commercial Vehicle Operation** *165 students enrolled*

STUDENT SERVICES Academic or career counseling, employment services for current students, placement services for program completers, remedial services.

Ana Visage Academy

10130-B Colvin Run Road, Great Falls, VA 22066

GENERAL INFORMATION Private Institution. **Total program enrollment:** 15. **Application fee:** $100.

PROGRAM(S) OFFERED
● **Aesthetician/Esthetician and Skin Care Specialist** *600 hrs./$7950*
● **Cosmetology and Related Personal Grooming Arts, Other** *1500 hrs./$15,450*
● **Electrolysis/Electrology and Electrolysis Technician** *600 hrs./$6450* ● **Massage Therapy/Therapeutic Massage** *600 hrs./$8950*

STUDENT SERVICES Academic or career counseling, employment services for current students, placement services for program completers.

The Art Institute of Washington

1820 North Fort Meyer Drive, Ground Floor, Arlington, VA 22209
http://www.artinstitutes.edu/arlington/

CONTACT George Sebolt, President
Telephone: 703-358-9550

GENERAL INFORMATION Private Institution. Founded 2000. **Accreditation:** Regional (SACS/CC). **Total program enrollment:** 1487. **Application fee:** $50.

PROGRAM(S) OFFERED
● **Baking and Pastry Arts/Baker/Pastry Chef** *2 students enrolled* ● **Culinary Arts/Chef Training** *13 students enrolled*

STUDENT SERVICES Academic or career counseling, employment services for current students, placement services for program completers, remedial services.

Aviation Institute of Maintenance–Manassas

9821 Godwin Drive, Manassas, VA 20110
http://www.aviationmaintenance.edu/aviation-washington-dc.asp

CONTACT Keith Zobel, School Director
Telephone: 703-257-5515

GENERAL INFORMATION Private Institution. **Total program enrollment:** 140. **Application fee:** $25.

PROGRAM(S) OFFERED
● **Airframe Mechanics and Aircraft Maintenance Technology/Technician** *130 hrs./$52,860* ● **Avionics Maintenance Technology/Technician** *32 hrs./$9936*

STUDENT SERVICES Academic or career counseling, placement services for program completers.

Bar Palma Beauty Careers Academy

3535 D Franklin Road, SW, Roanoke, VA 24014
http://atihollywood.com/

CONTACT Barbara L. Hensley, President
Telephone: 540-343-0153

GENERAL INFORMATION Private Institution. Founded 1957. **Total program enrollment:** 54. **Application fee:** $125.

PROGRAM(S) OFFERED
● **Cosmetology/Cosmetologist, General** *1500 hrs./$12,000*

STUDENT SERVICES Academic or career counseling, placement services for program completers.

Beta Tech

7914 Midlothian Turnpike, Richmond, VA 23235
http://www.betatech.edu/

CONTACT Zoe Thompson, School Director
Telephone: 804-330-0111

GENERAL INFORMATION Private Institution. Founded 1992. **Total program enrollment:** 197. **Application fee:** $25.

PROGRAM(S) OFFERED
● **Allied Health and Medical Assisting Services, Other** *91 hrs./$29,003*
● **Computer/Information Technology Services Administration and Management, Other** *91 hrs./$27,300* ● **Legal Assistant/Paralegal** *90 hrs./$27,000*
● **Massage Therapy/Therapeutic Massage** *100 hrs./$30,000* ● **Nursing, Other** *72 hrs./$28,800*

STUDENT SERVICES Academic or career counseling, placement services for program completers.

Beta Tech

7914 Midlothian Turnpike, Richmond, VA 23235-5230
http://www.betatech.edu/

CONTACT Antoinette S. Bennett, Director
Telephone: 804-672-2300 Ext. 121

GENERAL INFORMATION Private Institution. **Total program enrollment:** 89. **Application fee:** $25.

PROGRAM(S) OFFERED
● **Allied Health and Medical Assisting Services, Other** *91 hrs./$22,625* ● **Business Administration and Management, General** *90 hrs./$22,500* ● **Corrections and Criminal Justice, Other** *93 hrs./$27,900* ● **Licensed Practical/Vocational Nurse Training (LPN, LVN, Cert, Dipl, AAS)** *72 hrs./$23,400*

STUDENT SERVICES Academic or career counseling, placement services for program completers.

Blue Ridge Community College

PO Box 80, Weyers Cave, VA 24486-0080
http://www.brcc.edu/

CONTACT James R. Perkins, President
Telephone: 540-234-9261

GENERAL INFORMATION Public Institution. Founded 1967. **Accreditation:** Regional (SACS/CC). **Total program enrollment:** 1715.

PROGRAM(S) OFFERED
● **Aircraft Powerplant Technology/Technician** ● **Airframe Mechanics and Aircraft Maintenance Technology/Technician** ● **Allied Health Diagnostic, Intervention, and Treatment Professions, Other** *1 student enrolled*
● **Automobile/Automotive Mechanics Technology/Technician** *5 students enrolled*
● **Business Administration, Management and Operations, Other** *1 student enrolled* ● **Business Operations Support and Secretarial Services, Other**
● **CAD/CADD Drafting and/or Design Technology/Technician** ● **Criminal**

Justice/Law Enforcement Administration *1 student enrolled* ● **Mental and Social Health Services and Allied Professions, Other** *50 students enrolled* ● **Visual and Performing Arts, Other** *2 students enrolled*

STUDENT SERVICES Academic or career counseling, employment services for current students, placement services for program completers, remedial services.

Bryant & Stratton College—Richmond Campus

8141 Hull Street Road, Richmond, VA 23235-6411
http://www.bryantstratton.edu/

CONTACT Beth Murphy, Campus Director
Telephone: 804-745-2444

GENERAL INFORMATION Private Institution. Founded 1952. **Accreditation:** Regional (MSA/CIHE). **Total program enrollment:** 283. **Application fee:** $35.

PROGRAM(S) OFFERED
● **Legal Assistant/Paralegal**

STUDENT SERVICES Academic or career counseling, daycare for children of students, employment services for current students, placement services for program completers, remedial services.

Career Training Solutions

4343 Plank Road, Suite 115, Fredericksburg, VA 22407
http://www.careertrainingsolutions.com/

CONTACT A. Christine Carroll, President
Telephone: 540-373-2200

GENERAL INFORMATION Private Institution. **Total program enrollment:** 215. **Application fee:** $100.

PROGRAM(S) OFFERED
● **Aesthetician/Esthetician and Skin Care Specialist** *32 hrs./$9700* ● **Allied Health and Medical Assisting Services, Other** *36 hrs./$11,150* ● **Licensed Practical/Vocational Nurse Training (LPN, LVN, Cert, Dipl, AAS)** *70 hrs./ $22,100* ● **Massage Therapy/Therapeutic Massage** *35 hrs./$11,225* ● **Medical Insurance Coding Specialist/Coder** *43 students enrolled* ● **Medical Insurance Specialist/Medical Biller** *27 hrs./$6850* ● **Medical/Clinical Assistant** *54 students enrolled* ● **Nursing—Registered Nurse Training (RN, ASN, BSN, MSN)** *93 hrs./$29,500*

STUDENT SERVICES Academic or career counseling, placement services for program completers.

Center for Employment Training–Alexandria

2762 Duke Street, Alexandria, VA 22301

CONTACT Amy Bell, Director
Telephone: 408-287-7924

GENERAL INFORMATION Private Institution. **Total program enrollment:** 33.

PROGRAM(S) OFFERED
● **Administrative Assistant and Secretarial Science, General** *900 hrs./$8864* ● **Building/Property Maintenance and Management** *900 hrs./$8864* ● **Business/ Office Automation/Technology/Data Entry** *6 students enrolled* ● **Construction Trades, Other** *12 students enrolled* ● **Health and Medical Administrative Services, Other** *19 students enrolled* ● **Heating, Air Conditioning, Ventilation and Refrigeration Maintenance Technology/Technician (HAC, HACR, HVAC, HVACR)** *630 hrs./$7083* ● **Medical Administrative/Executive Assistant and Medical Secretary** *720 hrs./$7676*

STUDENT SERVICES Academic or career counseling, employment services for current students, placement services for program completers, remedial services.

Central School of Practical Nursing

1330 North Military Highway, Norfolk, VA 23502

CONTACT Linda K. Cockrell, Program Leader, Health and Medical Sciences
Telephone: 757-892-3300

GENERAL INFORMATION Public Institution. Founded 1968. **Total program enrollment:** 9. **Application fee:** $45.

PROGRAM(S) OFFERED
● **Nursing, Other** *1440 hrs.*

STUDENT SERVICES Academic or career counseling.

Central Virginia Community College

3506 Wards Road, Lynchburg, VA 24502-2498
http://www.cvcc.vccs.edu/

CONTACT Darrel Staat, President
Telephone: 434-832-7600

GENERAL INFORMATION Public Institution. Founded 1966. **Accreditation:** Regional (SACS/CC); medical laboratory technology (NAACLS); radiologic technology: radiography (JRCERT). **Total program enrollment:** 1315.

PROGRAM(S) OFFERED
● **Accounting and Related Services, Other** *2 students enrolled* ● **Business Operations Support and Secretarial Services, Other** *6 students enrolled* ● **Child Care Provider/Assistant** *4 students enrolled* ● **Electrician** *3 students enrolled* ● **Legal Assistant/Paralegal** *1 student enrolled* ● **Mental and Social Health Services and Allied Professions, Other** *87 students enrolled* ● **Precision Metal Working, Other** *5 students enrolled*

STUDENT SERVICES Academic or career counseling, employment services for current students, remedial services.

Centura College

6295 Edsall Road, Suite 250, Alexandria, VA 22312

CONTACT Carol Miller, School Director
Telephone: 703-778-4444

GENERAL INFORMATION Private Institution. **Total program enrollment:** 24. **Application fee:** $25.

PROGRAM(S) OFFERED
● **Allied Health and Medical Assisting Services, Other** *41 hrs./$13,365* ● **Massage Therapy/Therapeutic Massage** *36 hrs./$13,352*

STUDENT SERVICES Academic or career counseling, employment services for current students, placement services for program completers.

Culpeper Cosmetology Training Center

311 S East Street, #120, Culpeper, VA 22701-1055

CONTACT Sue Hansohn, Director
Telephone: 540-727-8003

GENERAL INFORMATION Public Institution. **Total program enrollment:** 13. **Application fee:** $50.

PROGRAM(S) OFFERED
● **Cosmetology/Cosmetologist, General** *1500 hrs./$8600*

STUDENT SERVICES Academic or career counseling, employment services for current students, placement services for program completers.

Dabney S. Lancaster Community College

100 Dabney Drive, PO Box 1000, Clifton Forge, VA 24422
http://www.dl.vccs.edu/

CONTACT Richard R. Teaff, President
Telephone: 540-863-2815

GENERAL INFORMATION Public Institution. Founded 1964. **Accreditation:** Regional (SACS/CC). **Total program enrollment:** 477.

PROGRAM(S) OFFERED
• Allied Health Diagnostic, Intervention, and Treatment Professions, Other *3 students enrolled* • Applied Horticulture/Horticultural Operations, General • Banking and Financial Support Services • Business Administration, Management and Operations, Other *5 students enrolled* • Business Operations Support and Secretarial Services, Other *8 students enrolled* • Cooking and Related Culinary Arts, General *8 students enrolled* • Corrections • Criminal Justice/Law Enforcement Administration *9 students enrolled* • Electrical, Electronic and Communications Engineering Technology/Technician • Forensic Science and Technology *2 students enrolled* • Hospitality Administration/Management, General *2 students enrolled* • Industrial Production Technologies/Technicians, Other *2 students enrolled* • Licensed Practical/Vocational Nurse Training (LPN, LVN, Cert, Dipl, AAS) *23 students enrolled* • Massage Therapy/Therapeutic Massage *1 student enrolled* • Mental and Social Health Services and Allied Professions, Other *56 students enrolled* • Technical and Business Writing *7 students enrolled* • Welding Technology/Welder *10 students enrolled*

STUDENT SERVICES Academic or career counseling, employment services for current students, placement services for program completers, remedial services.

Danville Community College

1008 South Main Street, Danville, VA 24541-4088
http://www.dcc.vccs.edu/

CONTACT B. Carlyle Ramsey, President
Telephone: 434-797-2222

GENERAL INFORMATION Public Institution. Founded 1967. **Accreditation:** Regional (SACS/CC). **Total program enrollment:** 1286.

PROGRAM(S) OFFERED
• Allied Health Diagnostic, Intervention, and Treatment Professions, Other *68 students enrolled* • Autobody/Collision and Repair Technology/Technician *9 students enrolled* • Automobile/Automotive Mechanics Technology/Technician *13 students enrolled* • Business Operations Support and Secretarial Services, Other *18 students enrolled* • CAD/CADD Drafting and/or Design Technology/Technician • Child Care Provider/Assistant *4 students enrolled* • Corrections *3 students enrolled* • Criminal Justice/Law Enforcement Administration *1 student enrolled* • Electrical, Electronic and Communications Engineering Technology/Technician *23 students enrolled* • Electrical/Electronics Maintenance and Repair Technology, Other *5 students enrolled* • Electrician *26 students enrolled* • Engineering Technologies/Technicians, Other *1 student enrolled* • Graphic Communications, General *9 students enrolled* • Heating, Air Conditioning, Ventilation and Refrigeration Maintenance Technology/Technician (HAC, HACR, HVAC, HVACR) *7 students enrolled* • Industrial Electronics Technology/Technician *19 students enrolled* • Industrial Production Technologies/Technicians, Other *9 students enrolled* • Licensed Practical/Vocational Nurse Training (LPN, LVN, Cert, Dipl, AAS) *13 students enrolled* • Mechanical Engineering Related Technologies/Technicians, Other *1 student enrolled* • Mental and Social Health Services and Allied Professions, Other *251 students enrolled* • Precision Metal Working, Other *15 students enrolled* • Security and Loss Prevention Services

STUDENT SERVICES Academic or career counseling, daycare for children of students, employment services for current students, placement services for program completers, remedial services.

Dominion School of Hair Design

1755 George Washington Memorial Highway, Gloucester Point, VA 23062
http://www.dominionschoolofhairdesign.com

CONTACT Lynn Murray, School Owner/Director
Telephone: 804-684-9150

GENERAL INFORMATION Private Institution. **Total program enrollment:** 17. **Application fee:** $50.

PROGRAM(S) OFFERED
• Cosmetology and Related Personal Grooming Arts, Other *115 hrs./$1350*
• Cosmetology, Barber/Styling, and Nail Instructor *500 hrs./$2150*
• Cosmetology/Cosmetologist, General *1500 hrs./$10,736*

STUDENT SERVICES Academic or career counseling, employment services for current students, placement services for program completers, remedial services.

Eastern Shore Community College

29300 Lankford Highway, Melfa, VA 23410-3000
http://www.es.cc.va.us/

CONTACT Cheryl Thompson-Stacy, President
Telephone: 757-789-1789

GENERAL INFORMATION Public Institution. Founded 1971. **Accreditation:** Regional (SACS/CC). **Total program enrollment:** 281.

PROGRAM(S) OFFERED
• Automobile/Automotive Mechanics Technology/Technician • Business Operations Support and Secretarial Services, Other *2 students enrolled* • CAD/CADD Drafting and/or Design Technology/Technician *2 students enrolled* • Computer and Information Sciences, General • Electrical, Electronic and Communications Engineering Technology/Technician • Licensed Practical/Vocational Nurse Training (LPN, LVN, Cert, Dipl, AAS) *22 students enrolled* • Medical/Clinical Assistant *6 students enrolled* • Mental and Social Health Services and Allied Professions, Other *39 students enrolled* • Welding Technology/Welder

STUDENT SERVICES Academic or career counseling, employment services for current students, placement services for program completers, remedial services.

Eastern Virginia Medical School

Box 1980, Norfolk, VA 23501-1980
http://www.evms.edu/

CONTACT Gerald J. Pepe, PhD, Dean/Provost
Telephone: 757-446-8422

GENERAL INFORMATION Private Institution. Founded 1964. **Accreditation:** Regional (SACS/CC); ophthalmic medical technology (JCAHPO). **Total program enrollment:** 733. **Application fee:** $60.

PROGRAM(S) OFFERED
• Surgical Technology/Technologist *9 students enrolled*

STUDENT SERVICES Academic or career counseling, employment services for current students, placement services for program completers, remedial services.

ECPI College of Technology

5555 Greenwich Road, Virginia Beach, VA 23462
http://www.ecpi.edu/

CONTACT Mark Dreyfus, President
Telephone: 757-671-7171

GENERAL INFORMATION Private Institution. Founded 1966. **Accreditation:** Regional (SACS/CC). **Total program enrollment:** 7991. **Application fee:** $100.

PROGRAM(S) OFFERED
• **Business Administration and Management, General** *9 students enrolled*
• **Computer Hardware Technology/Technician** *3 students enrolled* • **Computer Systems Networking and Telecommunications** *12 students enrolled* • **Computer Technology/Computer Systems Technology** *24 students enrolled* • **Culinary Arts/Chef Training** *1 student enrolled* • **Health Services/Allied Health/Health Sciences, General** *38 students enrolled* • **Health/Health Care Administration/Management** *45 students enrolled* • **Licensed Practical/Vocational Nurse Training (LPN, LVN, Cert, Dipl, AAS)** *405 students enrolled* • **Medical/Clinical Assistant** *191 students enrolled*

STUDENT SERVICES Academic or career counseling, employment services for current students, placement services for program completers, remedial services.

ECPI Technical College

800 Moorefield Park Drive, Richmond, VA 23236
http://www.ecpitech.edu/

CONTACT Mark Dreyfus, President
Telephone: 804-330-5533

GENERAL INFORMATION Private Institution. Founded 1966. **Accreditation:** State accredited or approved. **Total program enrollment:** 605. **Application fee:** $100.

PROGRAM(S) OFFERED
• **Computer Technology/Computer Systems Technology** *1 student enrolled*
• **Health/Health Care Administration/Management** *1 student enrolled*

STUDENT SERVICES Academic or career counseling, employment services for current students, placement services for program completers, remedial services.

ECPI Technical College

5234 Airport Road, Roanoke, VA 24012
http://www.ecpi.net/

CONTACT Mark Dreyfus, President
Telephone: 540-563-8080

GENERAL INFORMATION Private Institution. Founded 1966. **Accreditation:** State accredited or approved. **Total program enrollment:** 374. **Application fee:** $100.

PROGRAM(S) OFFERED
• **Licensed Practical/Vocational Nurse Training (LPN, LVN, Cert, Dipl, AAS)** *99 students enrolled*

STUDENT SERVICES Academic or career counseling, employment services for current students, placement services for program completers, remedial services.

Empire Beauty School–Midlothian

10807 Hull Street Road, Midlothian, VA 23112
http://www.empire.edu/

CONTACT McHael Bouman, President
Telephone: 800-223-3271

GENERAL INFORMATION Private Institution. **Total program enrollment:** 62. **Application fee:** $100.

PROGRAM(S) OFFERED
• **Cosmetology/Cosmetologist, General** *1530 hrs./$18,845* • **Nail Technician/Specialist and Manicurist** *2 students enrolled*

STUDENT SERVICES Placement services for program completers.

Empire Beauty School–Richmond

9049 West Broad Street, #3, Richmond, VA 23294
http://www.empire.edu

CONTACT Michael Bouman, President
Telephone: 804-270-2095

GENERAL INFORMATION Private Institution. **Total program enrollment:** 92. **Application fee:** $100.

PROGRAM(S) OFFERED
• **Cosmetology/Cosmetologist, General** *1530 hrs./$18,845* • **Nail Technician/Specialist and Manicurist** *1 student enrolled*

STUDENT SERVICES Placement services for program completers.

Everest College

801 North Quincy Street, Suite 501, Arlington, VA 22203
http://www.everest.edu/

CONTACT Stephen Goddard, President
Telephone: 703-248-8887

GENERAL INFORMATION Private Institution. Founded 2001. **Accreditation:** State accredited or approved. **Total program enrollment:** 599.

PROGRAM(S) OFFERED
• **Allied Health and Medical Assisting Services, Other** *118 students enrolled*
• **Security and Protective Services, Other** *42 students enrolled*

STUDENT SERVICES Academic or career counseling, employment services for current students, placement services for program completers.

Everest College

1430 Spring Hill Road, Suite 200, McLean, VA 22102-3000
http://www.everest.edu/

CONTACT Danielle Rodriguez, Director of Finance
Telephone: 703-288-3131

GENERAL INFORMATION Private Institution. **Total program enrollment:** 90.

PROGRAM(S) OFFERED
• **Allied Health and Medical Assisting Services, Other** *720 hrs./$14,690*
• **Business Administration and Management, General** *96 hrs./$31,392*
• **Criminal Justice/Law Enforcement Administration** *96 hrs./$31,392* • **Massage Therapy/Therapeutic Massage** *750 hrs./$12,825* • **Medical Insurance Coding Specialist/Coder** *560 hrs./$10,290* • **Medical Insurance Specialist/Medical Biller** *54 students enrolled* • **Medical Office Assistant/Specialist** *6 students enrolled* • **Medical/Clinical Assistant** *38 students enrolled*

STUDENT SERVICES Academic or career counseling, employment services for current students, placement services for program completers.

Everest College

803 Diligence Drive, Newport News, VA 23606
http://www.everest.edu/

CONTACT Lisa Barbato, School President
Telephone: 757-873-1111

GENERAL INFORMATION Private Institution. **Total program enrollment:** 136.

PROGRAM(S) OFFERED
• **Accounting and Business/Management** *720 hrs./$11,797* • **Corrections and Criminal Justice, Other** *96 hrs./$27,000* • **Health and Medical Administrative Services, Other** *720 hrs./$14,695* • **Massage Therapy/Therapeutic Massage**

Everest College (continued)

750 hrs./$15,911 ● **Medical Insurance Coding Specialist/Coder** 720 hrs./
$13,849 ● **Medical/Clinical Assistant** 720 hrs./$15,803 ● **Security and Protective Services, Other** 12 students enrolled

STUDENT SERVICES Academic or career counseling, employment services for current students, placement services for program completers.

Everest Institute

825 Greenbrier Circle, Chesapeake, VA 23320-2637
http://www.everest.edu/

CONTACT Tonya Pearson, Regional Director of Finance
Telephone: 757-361-3900

GENERAL INFORMATION Private Institution. **Total program enrollment:** 895.

PROGRAM(S) OFFERED
● **Accounting and Business/Management** 720 hrs./$11,797 ● **Computer Software and Media Applications, Other** ● **Dental Assisting/Assistant** 720 hrs./$15,248 ● **Health and Medical Administrative Services, Other** 720 hrs./$14,733 ● **Massage Therapy/Therapeutic Massage** 750 hrs./$15,911 ● **Medical Insurance Coding Specialist/Coder** 720 hrs./$13,849 ● **Medical Office Assistant/Specialist** 48 students enrolled ● **Medical/Clinical Assistant** 720 hrs./$15,833 ● **Security and Protective Services, Other** 10 students enrolled

STUDENT SERVICES Academic or career counseling, employment services for current students, placement services for program completers, remedial services.

Ferrum College

PO Box 1000, Ferrum, VA 24088-9001
http://www.ferrum.edu/

CONTACT Jennifer L. Braaten, President
Telephone: 540-365-2121

GENERAL INFORMATION Private Institution. Founded 1913. **Accreditation:** Regional (SACS/CC); recreation and parks (NRPA). **Total program enrollment:** 1373. **Application fee:** $25.

PROGRAM(S) OFFERED
● **Electrocardiograph Technology/Technician** ● **Medical Insurance Coding Specialist/Coder** ● **Pharmacy Technician/Assistant**

STUDENT SERVICES Academic or career counseling, employment services for current students, placement services for program completers, remedial services.

Germanna Community College

2130 Germanna Highway, Locust Grove, VA 22508-2102
http://www.gcc.vccs.edu/

CONTACT David A. Sam, President
Telephone: 540-423-9030

GENERAL INFORMATION Public Institution. Founded 1970. **Accreditation:** Regional (SACS/CC). **Total program enrollment:** 1967.

PROGRAM(S) OFFERED
● **Accounting and Related Services, Other** ● **Child Care Provider/Assistant** 5 students enrolled ● **Criminal Justice/Law Enforcement Administration** 11 students enrolled ● **Design and Visual Communications, General** 1 student enrolled ● **Electrical, Electronic and Communications Engineering Technology/Technician** ● **Fire Science/Firefighting** ● **Licensed Practical/Vocational Nurse Training (LPN, LVN, Cert, Dipl, AAS)** 4 students enrolled ● **Mental and Social Health Services and Allied Professions, Other** 178 students enrolled ● **Visual and Performing Arts, Other** 2 students enrolled

STUDENT SERVICES Academic or career counseling, employment services for current students, remedial services.

Graham Webb International Academy of Hair

2625 Wilson Boulevard, Arlington, VA 22201
http://www.grahamwebbacademyonline.com/

CONTACT Christine Gordon, President
Telephone: 800-869-9322 Ext. 100

GENERAL INFORMATION Private Institution. Founded 1987. **Total program enrollment:** 190. **Application fee:** $100.

PROGRAM(S) OFFERED
● **Aesthetician/Esthetician and Skin Care Specialist** 100 hrs./$8600
● **Cosmetology/Cosmetologist, General** 1500 hrs./$15,200

STUDENT SERVICES Academic or career counseling, employment services for current students, placement services for program completers.

Henrico County-Saint Mary's Hospital School of Practical Nursing

201 East Nine Mile Road, Highland Springs, VA 23075

CONTACT Fred Morton, Superintendent
Telephone: 804-652-3823

GENERAL INFORMATION Private Institution. Founded 1965. **Total program enrollment:** 60.

PROGRAM(S) OFFERED
● **Licensed Practical/Vocational Nurse Training (LPN, LVN, Cert, Dipl, AAS)** 30 students enrolled

STUDENT SERVICES Academic or career counseling, daycare for children of students, employment services for current students, remedial services.

Heritage Institute

8255 Shopper's Square, Manassas, VA 20111
http://www.heritage-education.com/

CONTACT Tess Anderson, School Director
Telephone: 703-334-2501

GENERAL INFORMATION Private Institution. **Total program enrollment:** 369.

PROGRAM(S) OFFERED
● **Allied Health and Medical Assisting Services, Other** 94 hrs./$21,523
● **Cosmetology/Cosmetologist, General** 1500 hrs./$20,500 ● **Health and Physical Education/Fitness, Other** 94 hrs./$19,353 ● **Massage Therapy/Therapeutic Massage** 95 hrs./$19,594

STUDENT SERVICES Academic or career counseling, employment services for current students, placement services for program completers.

Jefferson College of Health Sciences

PO Box 13186, Roanoke, VA 24031-3186
http://www.jchs.edu/

CONTACT Dr. Carol M. Seavor, President
Telephone: 888-985-8483

GENERAL INFORMATION Private Institution. Founded 1982. **Accreditation:** Regional (SACS/CC); emergency medical services (JRCEMTP); physical therapy assisting (APTA). **Total program enrollment:** 702. **Application fee:** $35.

PROGRAM(S) OFFERED
● **Clinical/Medical Laboratory Science and Allied Professions, Other**

STUDENT SERVICES Academic or career counseling, remedial services.

John Tyler Community College

13101 Jefferson Davis Highway, Chester, VA 23831-5316
http://www.jtcc.edu/

CONTACT Marshall W. Smith, President
Telephone: 804-796-4000

GENERAL INFORMATION Public Institution. Founded 1967. **Accreditation:** Regional (SACS/CC); funeral service (ABFSE). **Total program enrollment:** 2076.

PROGRAM(S) OFFERED
● Biology Technician/Biotechnology Laboratory Technician ● Child Care Provider/Assistant 4 *students enrolled* ● Construction Trades, General 8 *students enrolled* ● Criminal Justice/Law Enforcement Administration ● Mental and Social Health Services and Allied Professions, Other 218 *students enrolled* ● Precision Metal Working, Other 4 *students enrolled* ● Teacher Assistant/Aide 1 *student enrolled* ● Visual and Performing Arts, Other 6 *students enrolled* ● Welding Technology/Welder 1 *student enrolled*

STUDENT SERVICES Academic or career counseling, employment services for current students, remedial services.

J. Sargeant Reynolds Community College

PO Box 85622, Richmond, VA 23285-5622
http://www.reynolds.edu/

CONTACT Dr. Gary Rhodes, President
Telephone: 804-371-3000

GENERAL INFORMATION Public Institution. Founded 1972. **Accreditation:** Regional (SACS/CC); dental assisting (ADA); dental laboratory technology (ADA); medical laboratory technology (NAACLS); ophthalmic dispensing (COA); respiratory therapy technology (CoARC). **Total program enrollment:** 3383.

PROGRAM(S) OFFERED
● Accounting and Related Services, Other 7 *students enrolled* ● Audiovisual Communications Technologies/Technicians, Other ● Automobile/Automotive Mechanics Technology/Technician 1 *student enrolled* ● Biology Technician/Biotechnology Laboratory Technician ● Business Administration, Management and Operations, Other 3 *students enrolled* ● Business Operations Support and Secretarial Services, Other 6 *students enrolled* ● Child Care Provider/Assistant 7 *students enrolled* ● Dental Assisting/Assistant 13 *students enrolled* ● Diesel Mechanics Technology/Technician 4 *students enrolled* ● Electrical, Electronic and Communications Engineering Technology/Technician ● Fire Science/Firefighting 20 *students enrolled* ● Licensed Practical/Vocational Nurse Training (LPN, LVN, Cert, Dipl, AAS) 33 *students enrolled* ● Mental and Social Health Services and Allied Professions, Other 206 *students enrolled*

STUDENT SERVICES Academic or career counseling, employment services for current students, placement services for program completers, remedial services.

Legends Institute

Forest Plaza West Shopping Center, Old Forest Road, Lynchburg, VA 24501
http://www.legendsinstitute.com/

CONTACT James Looney, President
Telephone: 434-385-7722

GENERAL INFORMATION Private Institution. Founded 1960. **Total program enrollment:** 33. **Application fee:** $100.

PROGRAM(S) OFFERED
● Cosmetology/Cosmetologist, General 1500 *hrs./$13,795*

STUDENT SERVICES Academic or career counseling.

Lord Fairfax Community College

173 Skirmisher Lane, Middletown, VA 22645
http://www.lfcc.edu/

CONTACT John Capps, Interim President
Telephone: 540-868-7000

GENERAL INFORMATION Public Institution. Founded 1969. **Accreditation:** Regional (SACS/CC). **Total program enrollment:** 1764.

PROGRAM(S) OFFERED
● Applied Horticulture/Horticultural Operations, General ● Business Administration, Management and Operations, Other ● Business Operations Support and Secretarial Services, Other 4 *students enrolled* ● CAD/CADD Drafting and/or Design Technology/Technician ● Health and Medical Administrative Services, Other 7 *students enrolled* ● Legal Assistant/Paralegal 6 *students enrolled* ● Licensed Practical/Vocational Nurse Training (LPN, LVN, Cert, Dipl, AAS) 51 *students enrolled* ● Mental and Social Health Services and Allied Professions, Other 84 *students enrolled* ● Surgical Technology/Technologist ● Technical and Business Writing ● Visual and Performing Arts, Other 1 *student enrolled*

STUDENT SERVICES Academic or career counseling, employment services for current students, placement services for program completers, remedial services.

Lynchburg General Hospital School of Nursing

1901 Tate Springs Road, Lynchburg, VA 24501
http://www.centrahealth.com/

CONTACT Debra Patterson, Dean, Schools of Nursing
Telephone: 434-200-3070

GENERAL INFORMATION Private Institution. **Total program enrollment:** 130. **Application fee:** $20.

PROGRAM(S) OFFERED
● Licensed Practical/Vocational Nurse Training (LPN, LVN, Cert, Dipl, AAS) 18 *students enrolled*

STUDENT SERVICES Academic or career counseling.

Marymount University

2807 North Glebe Road, Arlington, VA 22207-4299
http://www.marymount.edu/

CONTACT Dr. James E. Bundschuh, President
Telephone: 703-522-5600

GENERAL INFORMATION Private Institution (Affiliated with Roman Catholic Church). Founded 1950. **Accreditation:** Regional (SACS/CC); counseling (ACA); interior design: professional (CIDA). **Total program enrollment:** 2368. **Application fee:** $40.

PROGRAM(S) OFFERED
● Accounting 1 *student enrolled* ● Finance, General ● Forensic Science and Technology 4 *students enrolled* ● Legal Assistant/Paralegal 4 *students enrolled*

STUDENT SERVICES Academic or career counseling, employment services for current students, remedial services.

Medical Careers Institute

1001 Omni Boulevard, Suite 200, Newport News, VA 23606
http://www.medical.edu/

CONTACT Mark Dreyfus, President
Telephone: 804-521-0400

GENERAL INFORMATION Private Institution. Founded 1978. **Accreditation:** State accredited or approved. **Total program enrollment:** 319. **Application fee:** $100.

Medical Careers Institute (continued)

PROGRAM(S) OFFERED
• Licensed Practical/Vocational Nurse Training (LPN, LVN, Cert, Dipl, AAS)
157 students enrolled

STUDENT SERVICES Academic or career counseling, employment services for current students, placement services for program completers, remedial services.

Miller-Motte Technical College

1912 Memorial Avenue, Lynchburg, VA 24501
http://www.miller-motte.com/

CONTACT Ned Snyder, Director
Telephone: 434-239-5222

GENERAL INFORMATION Private Institution. Founded 1929. **Accreditation:** Medical assisting (AAMAE). **Total program enrollment:** 167. **Application fee:** $35.

PROGRAM(S) OFFERED
• Administrative Assistant and Secretarial Science, General • Aesthetician/Esthetician and Skin Care Specialist *13 students enrolled* • Massage Therapy/Therapeutic Massage *19 students enrolled* • Medical Office Assistant/Specialist *8 students enrolled* • Pharmacy Technician/Assistant • Phlebotomy/Phlebotomist *1 student enrolled*

STUDENT SERVICES Academic or career counseling, employment services for current students, placement services for program completers, remedial services.

Mountain Empire Community College

PO Drawer 700, Big Stone Gap, VA 24219-0700
http://www.me.vccs.edu/

CONTACT Terrance Suarez, President
Telephone: 276-523-2400

GENERAL INFORMATION Public Institution. Founded 1972. **Accreditation:** Regional (SACS/CC). **Total program enrollment:** 1260.

PROGRAM(S) OFFERED
• Accounting and Related Services, Other *6 students enrolled* • Business Operations Support and Secretarial Services, Other *34 students enrolled* • Criminal Justice/Law Enforcement Administration *4 students enrolled* • Health and Medical Administrative Services, Other *11 students enrolled* • Heating, Air Conditioning, Ventilation and Refrigeration Maintenance Technology/Technician (HAC, HACR, HVAC, HVACR) *6 students enrolled* • Industrial Production Technologies/Technicians, Other *1 student enrolled* • Legal Assistant/Paralegal *9 students enrolled* • Licensed Practical/Vocational Nurse Training (LPN, LVN, Cert, Dipl, AAS) *31 students enrolled* • Mental and Social Health Services and Allied Professions, Other *177 students enrolled* • Mining Technology/Technician • Respiratory Care Therapy/Therapist • Welding Technology/Welder *2 students enrolled*

STUDENT SERVICES Academic or career counseling, employment services for current students, remedial services.

National College

1813 East Main Street, Salem, VA 24153
http://www.national-college.edu/

CONTACT Frank Longaker, President
Telephone: 540-986-1800

GENERAL INFORMATION Private Institution. Founded 1886. **Accreditation:** Medical assisting (AAMAE); state accredited or approved. **Total program enrollment:** 2882. **Application fee:** $30.

PROGRAM(S) OFFERED
• Accounting Technology/Technician and Bookkeeping *1 student enrolled* • Business Administration and Management, General *1 student enrolled* • Business/Commerce, General *23 students enrolled* • Computer and Informa-

tion Sciences and Support Services, Other *24 students enrolled* • Data Entry/Microcomputer Applications, General • Emergency Medical Technology/Technician (EMT Paramedic) *5 students enrolled* • Executive Assistant/Executive Secretary *10 students enrolled* • Health and Medical Administrative Services, Other *93 students enrolled* • Hospitality Administration/Management, General *6 students enrolled* • Information Technology *1 student enrolled* • Medical Office Assistant/Specialist *15 students enrolled* • Medical Transcription/Transcriptionist *38 students enrolled* • Pharmacy Technician/Assistant *107 students enrolled* • Phlebotomy/Phlebotomist

STUDENT SERVICES Academic or career counseling, employment services for current students, placement services for program completers, remedial services.

New River Community College

PO Box 1127, Dublin, VA 24084-1127
http://www.nr.cc.va.us/

CONTACT Jack M. Lewis, President
Telephone: 540-674-3600

GENERAL INFORMATION Public Institution. Founded 1969. **Accreditation:** Regional (SACS/CC). **Total program enrollment:** 1749.

PROGRAM(S) OFFERED
• Accounting and Related Services, Other *2 students enrolled* • Automobile/Automotive Mechanics Technology/Technician *9 students enrolled* • Business Operations Support and Secretarial Services, Other *3 students enrolled* • Child Care Provider/Assistant • Computer Software and Media Applications, Other • Industrial Production Technologies/Technicians, Other *6 students enrolled* • Licensed Practical/Vocational Nurse Training (LPN, LVN, Cert, Dipl, AAS) *12 students enrolled* • Mental and Social Health Services and Allied Professions, Other *76 students enrolled* • Precision Metal Working, Other • Welding Technology/Welder *4 students enrolled*

STUDENT SERVICES Academic or career counseling, daycare for children of students, employment services for current students, placement services for program completers, remedial services.

Northern Virginia Community College

4001 Wakefield Chapel Road, Annandale, VA 22003-3796
http://www.nvcc.edu/

CONTACT Robert G. Templin, Jr., President
Telephone: 703-323-3000

GENERAL INFORMATION Public Institution. Founded 1965. **Accreditation:** Regional (SACS/CC); dental hygiene (ADA); emergency medical services (JRCEMTP); health information technology (AHIMA); medical laboratory technology (NAACLS); physical therapy assisting (APTA). **Total program enrollment:** 14966.

PROGRAM(S) OFFERED
• Accounting and Related Services, Other *8 students enrolled* • Allied Health and Medical Assisting Services, Other • Architectural Drafting and Architectural CAD/CADD *12 students enrolled* • Audiovisual Communications Technologies/Technicians, Other *5 students enrolled* • Automobile/Automotive Mechanics Technology/Technician *10 students enrolled* • Business Administration, Management and Operations, Other *3 students enrolled* • Business Operations Support and Secretarial Services, Other • CAD/CADD Drafting and/or Design Technology/Technician • Child Care Provider/Assistant *2 students enrolled* • Civil Engineering Technology/Technician • Construction Trades, General • Cooking and Related Culinary Arts, General *5 students enrolled* • Criminal Justice/Law Enforcement Administration *25 students enrolled* • Design and Visual Communications, General *2 students enrolled* • Electrical, Electronic and Communications Engineering Technology/Technician • Heating, Air Conditioning, Ventilation and Refrigeration Maintenance Technology/Technician (HAC, HACR, HVAC, HVACR) *5 students enrolled* • Hospitality Administration/Management, General *21 students enrolled* • Mechanical Engineering Related Technologies/Technicians, Other *1 student enrolled* • Mental and Social Health Services and Allied Professions, Other *225 students enrolled* • Public Administration *1 student enrolled* • Real Estate *1 student enrolled* • Substance Abuse/Addiction Counseling *1 student enrolled* • Surgical Technology/Technologist • Technical and Business Writing *1*

student enrolled • **Tourism and Travel Services Management** *2 students enrolled* • **Web Page, Digital/Multimedia and Information Resources Design** *4 students enrolled* • **Welding Technology/Welder**

STUDENT SERVICES Academic or career counseling, employment services for current students, remedial services.

Patrick Henry Community College

PO Box 5311, Martinsville, VA 24115-5311
http://www.ph.vccs.edu/

CONTACT Max Wingett, President
Telephone: 276-656-0311

GENERAL INFORMATION Public Institution. Founded 1962. **Accreditation:** Regional (SACS/CC). **Total program enrollment:** 1293.

PROGRAM(S) OFFERED
• **Accounting and Related Services, Other** • **Allied Health Diagnostic, Intervention, and Treatment Professions, Other** *5 students enrolled* • **Automobile/Automotive Mechanics Technology/Technician** *3 students enrolled* • **Business Administration, Management and Operations, Other** *8 students enrolled* • **Business Operations Support and Secretarial Services, Other** *10 students enrolled* • **CAD/CADD Drafting and/or Design Technology/Technician** *1 student enrolled* • **Child Care Provider/Assistant** *8 students enrolled* • **Design and Visual Communications, General** • **Emergency Medical Technology/Technician (EMT Paramedic)** • **Heating, Air Conditioning, Ventilation and Refrigeration Maintenance Technology/Technician (HAC, HACR, HVAC, HVACR)** *3 students enrolled* • **Industrial Production Technologies/Technicians, Other** • **Legal Assistant/Paralegal** • **Licensed Practical/Vocational Nurse Training (LPN, LVN, Cert, Dipl, AAS)** *20 students enrolled* • **Massage Therapy/Therapeutic Massage** *7 students enrolled* • **Mental and Social Health Services and Allied Professions, Other** *97 students enrolled* • **Precision Metal Working, Other** • **Welding Technology/Welder** *3 students enrolled*

STUDENT SERVICES Academic or career counseling, employment services for current students, placement services for program completers, remedial services.

Paul D. Camp Community College

PO Box 737, 100 North College Drive, Franklin, VA 23851-0737
http://www.pc.vccs.edu/

CONTACT Donald Boyce, President
Telephone: 757-569-6700

GENERAL INFORMATION Public Institution. Founded 1971. **Accreditation:** Regional (SACS/CC). **Total program enrollment:** 404.

PROGRAM(S) OFFERED
• **Business Operations Support and Secretarial Services, Other** *6 students enrolled* • **CAD/CADD Drafting and/or Design Technology/Technician** • **Child Care Provider/Assistant** *5 students enrolled* • **Electrician** *1 student enrolled* • **Industrial Production Technologies/Technicians, Other** • **Mental and Social Health Services and Allied Professions, Other** *31 students enrolled* • **Welding Technology/Welder**

STUDENT SERVICES Academic or career counseling, remedial services.

Piedmont Virginia Community College

501 College Drive, Charlottesville, VA 22902-7589
http://www.pvcc.edu/

CONTACT Frank Friedman, President
Telephone: 434-977-3900

GENERAL INFORMATION Public Institution. Founded 1972. **Accreditation:** Regional (SACS/CC). **Total program enrollment:** 1151.

PROGRAM(S) OFFERED
• **Business Operations Support and Secretarial Services, Other** *2 students enrolled* • **Criminal Justice/Law Enforcement Administration** • **Health and Medical Administrative Services, Other** • **Licensed Practical/Vocational Nurse**

Training **(LPN, LVN, Cert, Dipl, AAS)** • **Mental and Social Health Services and Allied Professions, Other** *36 students enrolled* • **Surgical Technology/Technologist** *15 students enrolled*

STUDENT SERVICES Academic or career counseling, employment services for current students, placement services for program completers, remedial services.

Potomac College

1029 Herndon Parkway, Herndon, VA 20170
http://www.potomac.edu/

CONTACT Florence Tate, President
Telephone: 703-709-5875

GENERAL INFORMATION Private Institution. **Total program enrollment:** 90. **Application fee:** $15.

PROGRAM(S) OFFERED
• **Business Administration and Management, General** • **Computer and Information Systems Security**

STUDENT SERVICES Academic or career counseling.

Rappahannock Community College

12745 College Drive, Glenns, VA 23149-2616
http://www.rcc.vccs.edu/

CONTACT Elizabeth H. Crowther, President
Telephone: 804-758-6700

GENERAL INFORMATION Public Institution. Founded 1970. **Accreditation:** Regional (SACS/CC). **Total program enrollment:** 702.

PROGRAM(S) OFFERED
• **Accounting and Related Services, Other** *4 students enrolled* • **Business Operations Support and Secretarial Services, Other** *4 students enrolled* • **Criminal Justice/Law Enforcement Administration** *1 student enrolled* • **Industrial Production Technologies/Technicians, Other** • **Licensed Practical/Vocational Nurse Training (LPN, LVN, Cert, Dipl, AAS)** *19 students enrolled* • **Mental and Social Health Services and Allied Professions, Other** *34 students enrolled*

STUDENT SERVICES Academic or career counseling, employment services for current students, placement services for program completers, remedial services.

Richmond School of Health and Technology

1601 Willow Lawn Drive, Suite 320, Richmond, VA 23230

CONTACT Carolyn Lake, CEO
Telephone: 804-288-1000

GENERAL INFORMATION Private Institution. **Total program enrollment:** 440. **Application fee:** $75.

PROGRAM(S) OFFERED
• **Licensed Practical/Vocational Nurse Training (LPN, LVN, Cert, Dipl, AAS)** *1500 hrs./$18,000* • **Medical Insurance Coding Specialist/Coder** *36 hrs./$11,016* • **Medical/Clinical Assistant** *62 hrs./$18,972* • **Pharmacy Technician/Assistant** *33 hrs./$10,098* • **Radiologic Technology/Science—Radiographer** *68 hrs./$28,152* • **Surgical Technology/Technologist** *76 hrs./$23,256*

STUDENT SERVICES Academic or career counseling, employment services for current students, placement services for program completers, remedial services.

Riverside School of Health Careers

316 Main Street, Newport News, VA 23601
http://www.riverside-online.com/rshc

CONTACT Tracee Carmean, Vice President
Telephone: 757-240-2200

GENERAL INFORMATION Private Institution. **Total program enrollment:**
282. **Application fee:** $30.

PROGRAM(S) OFFERED
• **Licensed Practical/Vocational Nurse Training (LPN, LVN, Cert, Dipl, AAS)**
54 hrs./$8700 • **Nursing—Registered Nurse Training (RN, ASN, BSN, MSN)**
75 hrs./$9692 • **Radiologic Technology/Science—Radiographer** *78 hrs./$8250*

STUDENT SERVICES Academic or career counseling, placement services
for program completers, remedial services.

Rudy & Kelly Academy of Hair and Nails

5606-8 Princess Anne Road, Virginia Beach, VA 23462
http://www.rudyandkelly.com/

CONTACT Rudolph R. Russo, President
Telephone: 757-473-0994

GENERAL INFORMATION Private Institution. **Total program enrollment:**
131. **Application fee:** $100.

PROGRAM(S) OFFERED
• **Cosmetology/Cosmetologist, General** *1500 hrs./$14,575*

STUDENT SERVICES Placement services for program completers.

Sentara Norfolk General Hospital School of Health Professions

600 Gresham Drive, Jenkins Hall, Norfolk, VA 23507
http://www.sentara.com/healthprofessions/

CONTACT Shelly Cohen, Director
Telephone: 757-388-2900

GENERAL INFORMATION Private Institution. **Total program enrollment:**
379. **Application fee:** $50.

PROGRAM(S) OFFERED
• **Cardiovascular Technology/Technologist** *60 hrs./$12,200* • **Licensed
Practical/Vocational Nurse Training (LPN, LVN, Cert, Dipl, AAS)** *31 students
enrolled* • **Nursing—Registered Nurse Training (RN, ASN, BSN, MSN)** *58 hrs./
$14,123* • **Surgical Technology/Technologist** *41 hrs./$8484*

STUDENT SERVICES Academic or career counseling, employment
services for current students, placement services for program completers,
remedial services.

Shenandoah University

1460 University Drive, Winchester, VA 22601-5195
http://www.su.edu/

CONTACT Tracy Fitzsimmons, PhD, President
Telephone: 540-665-4500

GENERAL INFORMATION Private Institution. Founded 1875. **Accreditation:** Regional (SACS/CC); music (NASM). **Total program enrollment:**
2340. **Application fee:** $30.

PROGRAM(S) OFFERED
• **Elementary Education and Teaching** • **Health/Health Care Administration/
Management** *4 students enrolled* • **Language Interpretation and Translation** *3
students enrolled* • **Music Therapy/Therapist** • **Music, Other** *1 student enrolled*
• **Pre-Theology/Pre-Ministerial Studies** • **Secondary Education and Teaching**
• **Teaching English as a Second or Foreign Language/ESL Language Instructor** *4 students enrolled*

STUDENT SERVICES Academic or career counseling, employment
services for current students, placement services for program completers,
remedial services.

Southeast Culinary & Hospitality College

100 Piedmont Avenue, Bristol, VA 24201
southeastculinary.edu

CONTACT Richard K. Erskine, President
Telephone: 276-591-5699

GENERAL INFORMATION Private Institution. **Total program enrollment:**
34.

PROGRAM(S) OFFERED
• **Culinary Arts/Chef Training** *2 students enrolled*

STUDENT SERVICES Academic or career counseling, employment
services for current students, placement services for program completers.

Southside Regional Medical Center

801 South Adams Street, Petersburg, VA 23803
http://www.srmconline.com/

CONTACT David J. Fikse, CEO
Telephone: 804-765-5800

GENERAL INFORMATION Private Institution. **Total program enrollment:**
167. **Application fee:** $70.

PROGRAM(S) OFFERED
• **Nursing—Registered Nurse Training (RN, ASN, BSN, MSN)**

STUDENT SERVICES Academic or career counseling, employment
services for current students, placement services for program completers.

Southside Virginia Community College

109 Campus Drive, Alberta, VA 23821-9719
http://www.sv.vccs.edu/

CONTACT John J. Cavan, President
Telephone: 888-220-7822

GENERAL INFORMATION Public Institution. Founded 1970. **Accreditation:**
Regional (SACS/CC). **Total program enrollment:** 1649.

PROGRAM(S) OFFERED
• **Allied Health Diagnostic, Intervention, and Treatment Professions, Other** *2
students enrolled* • **Automobile/Automotive Mechanics Technology/Technician** *3
students enrolled* • **Business Administration, Management and Operations,
Other** *1 student enrolled* • **Business Operations Support and Secretarial
Services, Other** *3 students enrolled* • **CAD/CADD Drafting and/or Design
Technology/Technician** • **Computer and Information Sciences, General** *7
students enrolled* • **Criminal Justice/Law Enforcement Administration** *4 students
enrolled* • **Diesel Mechanics Technology/Technician** *1 student enrolled* • **Electrical, Electronic and Communications Engineering Technology/Technician**
• **Electrician** *7 students enrolled* • **Fire Science/Firefighting** *1 student enrolled*
• **Ground Transportation, Other** • **Heating, Air Conditioning, Ventilation and
Refrigeration Maintenance Technology/Technician (HAC, HACR, HVAC,
HVACR)** *6 students enrolled* • **Industrial Production Technologies/Technicians,
Other** *4 students enrolled* • **Licensed Practical/Vocational Nurse Training (LPN,
LVN, Cert, Dipl, AAS)** *64 students enrolled* • **Mental and Social Health
Services and Allied Professions, Other** *2 students enrolled* • **Motorcycle
Maintenance and Repair Technology/Technician**

STUDENT SERVICES Academic or career counseling, employment
services for current students, placement services for program completers,
remedial services.

Southwest Virginia Community College

PO Box SVCC, Richlands, VA 24641-1101
http://www.sw.edu/

CONTACT J. Mark Estepp, President
Telephone: 276-964-2555

GENERAL INFORMATION Public Institution. Founded 1968. **Accreditation:**
Regional (SACS/CC); radiologic technology: radiography (JRCERT).
Total program enrollment: 1344.

PROGRAM(S) OFFERED
• **Accounting and Related Services, Other** *2 students enrolled* • **Allied Health
Diagnostic, Intervention, and Treatment Professions, Other** *18 students*

enrolled • **Audiovisual Communications Technologies/Technicians, Other** 2 students enrolled • **Banking and Financial Support Services** 1 student enrolled • **Business Operations Support and Secretarial Services, Other** • **CAD/CADD Drafting and/or Design Technology/Technician** • **Child Care Provider/Assistant** 8 students enrolled • **Criminal Justice/Law Enforcement Administration** 6 students enrolled • **Diagnostic Medical Sonography/Sonographer and Ultrasound Technician** • **Diesel Mechanics Technology/Technician** 4 students enrolled • **Electrical, Electronic and Communications Engineering Technology/Technician** • **Electrical/Electronics Maintenance and Repair Technology, Other** • **Heating, Air Conditioning, Ventilation and Refrigeration Maintenance Technology/Technician (HAC, HACR, HVAC, HVACR)** 1 student enrolled • **Hospitality Administration/Management, General** • **Journalism, Other** • **Legal Assistant/Paralegal** 1 student enrolled • **Licensed Practical/Vocational Nurse Training (LPN, LVN, Cert, Dipl, AAS)** 14 students enrolled • **Mental and Social Health Services and Allied Professions, Other** 248 students enrolled • **Occupational Therapist Assistant** 12 students enrolled • **Photography** 1 student enrolled • **Precision Metal Working, Other** 2 students enrolled • **Visual and Performing Arts, Other** • **Welding Technology/Welder** 1 student enrolled

STUDENT SERVICES Academic or career counseling, employment services for current students, placement services for program completers, remedial services.

Springfield Beauty Academy

4223 Annandale Road, Annandale, VA 22003

CONTACT Anthony N. Katsakis, Executive Officer
Telephone: 703-256-5662

GENERAL INFORMATION Private Institution. Founded 1974. **Total program enrollment:** 83. **Application fee:** $50.

PROGRAM(S) OFFERED
• **Cosmetology/Cosmetologist, General** 1500 hrs./$11,495

STUDENT SERVICES Academic or career counseling, placement services for program completers.

Staunton School of Cosmetology

128 East Beverly Street, PO Box 2385, Staunton, VA 24401

CONTACT Bonnie G. Traylor-Bender, Director
Telephone: 540-885-0808

GENERAL INFORMATION Private Institution. Founded 1956. **Total program enrollment:** 29. **Application fee:** $100.

PROGRAM(S) OFFERED
• **Cosmetology/Cosmetologist, General** 1500 hrs./$13,400

STUDENT SERVICES Academic or career counseling, placement services for program completers.

Stratford University

7777 Leesburg Pike, Suite 100 South, Falls Church, VA 22043
http://www.stratford.edu/

CONTACT Dr. Richard R. Shurtz, II, President
Telephone: 800-444-0804

GENERAL INFORMATION Private Institution. Founded 1976. **Accreditation:** State accredited or approved. **Total program enrollment:** 808. **Application fee:** $50.

PROGRAM(S) OFFERED
• **Culinary Arts/Chef Training** 2 students enrolled

STUDENT SERVICES Academic or career counseling, employment services for current students, placement services for program completers.

Suffolk Beauty School

860 Portsmouth Boulevard, Suffolk, VA 23434-3020

CONTACT Sandra Richardson, Owner
Telephone: 757-934-0656

GENERAL INFORMATION Private Institution. **Total program enrollment:** 47. **Application fee:** $50.

PROGRAM(S) OFFERED
• **Cosmetology/Cosmetologist, General** 1500 hrs./$13,000

STUDENT SERVICES Academic or career counseling, placement services for program completers.

Suffolk Public Schools–Sentara Obici Hospital School of Practical Nursing

2800 Godwin Boulevard, Suffolk, VA 23434
http://www.sentara.com/obicilpnschool

CONTACT Michael W. Mounie, Director of Finance
Telephone: 757-934-4826

GENERAL INFORMATION Public Institution. **Total program enrollment:** 12. **Application fee:** $30.

PROGRAM(S) OFFERED
• **Licensed Practical/Vocational Nurse Training (LPN, LVN, Cert, Dipl, AAS)** 17 students enrolled

TAP This Valley Works CET

108 N. Jefferson Street, Suite 303, Roanoke, VA 24016
http://taproanoke.org/

CONTACT Annette Lewis, Director
Telephone: 540-767-6220

GENERAL INFORMATION Private Institution. **Total program enrollment:** 8. **Application fee:** $25.

PROGRAM(S) OFFERED
• **Business/Office Automation/Technology/Data Entry** 810 hrs./$6500

STUDENT SERVICES Academic or career counseling, employment services for current students, placement services for program completers, remedial services.

Thomas Nelson Community College

PO Box 9407, Hampton, VA 23670-0407
http://www.tncc.edu/

CONTACT Dr. Charles Taylor, President
Telephone: 757-825-2700

GENERAL INFORMATION Public Institution. Founded 1968. **Accreditation:** Regional (SACS/CC); medical laboratory technology (NAACLS). **Total program enrollment:** 3063.

PROGRAM(S) OFFERED
• **Automobile/Automotive Mechanics Technology/Technician** 5 students enrolled • **CAD/CADD Drafting and/or Design Technology/Technician** 16 students enrolled • **Child Care Provider/Assistant** 5 students enrolled • **Clinical/Medical Laboratory Technician** 72 students enrolled • **Design and Visual Communications, General** 2 students enrolled • **Heating, Air Conditioning, Ventilation and Refrigeration Maintenance Technology/Technician (HAC, HACR, HVAC, HVACR)** 2 students enrolled • **Industrial Production Technologies/Technicians, Other** 1 student enrolled • **Legal Assistant/Paralegal** 8 students enrolled • **Mental and Social Health Services and Allied Professions, Other** 361 students enrolled • **Public Administration**

STUDENT SERVICES Academic or career counseling, employment services for current students, placement services for program completers, remedial services.

Tidewater Community College

121 College Place, Norfolk, VA 23510
http://www.tcc.edu/

CONTACT Deborah M. Dicroce, President
Telephone: 757-822-1122

GENERAL INFORMATION Public Institution. Founded 1968. **Accreditation:** Regional (SACS/CC); emergency medical services (JRCEMTP); health information technology (AHIMA); radiologic technology: radiography (JRCERT). **Total program enrollment:** 9863.

PROGRAM(S) OFFERED
• **Accounting and Related Services, Other** 5 *students enrolled* • **Allied Health Diagnostic, Intervention, and Treatment Professions, Other** 2 *students enrolled* • **Applied Horticulture/Horticultural Operations, General** • **Automobile/ Automotive Mechanics Technology/Technician** • **Business Operations Support and Secretarial Services, Other** 4 *students enrolled* • **Business/Commerce, General** • **CAD/CADD Drafting and/or Design Technology/Technician** 5 *students enrolled* • **Child Care Provider/Assistant** 18 *students enrolled* • **Computer and Information Sciences, General** 1 *student enrolled* • **Diagnostic Medical Sonography/Sonographer and Ultrasound Technician** • **Electrical, Electronic and Communications Engineering Technology/Technician** • **Electrician** 5 *students enrolled* • **Engineering Technology, General** 13 *students enrolled* • **Ground Transportation, Other** • **Heating, Air Conditioning, Ventilation and Refrigeration Maintenance Technology/Technician (HAC, HACR, HVAC, HVACR)** 11 *students enrolled* • **Legal Assistant/Paralegal** 2 *students enrolled* • **Medical/Clinical Assistant** 12 *students enrolled* • **Mental and Social Health Services and Allied Professions, Other** 184 *students enrolled* • **Occupational Therapist Assistant** 1 *student enrolled* • **Precision Metal Working, Other** 1 *student enrolled* • **Visual and Performing Arts, Other** • **Welding Technology/ Welder** 4 *students enrolled*

STUDENT SERVICES Academic or career counseling, employment services for current students, placement services for program completers, remedial services.

Tidewater Tech

932 Ventures Way, Chesapeake, VA 23320
http://www.tidetech.com/

CONTACT Yvonna Santos, Director
Telephone: 757-549-2121

GENERAL INFORMATION Private Institution. Founded 1982. **Total program enrollment:** 158. **Application fee:** $25.

PROGRAM(S) OFFERED
• **Business Administration and Management, General** 90 *hrs./$27,000* • **Computer and Information Sciences, General** 91 *hrs./$27,300* • **Legal Assistant/Paralegal** 90 *hrs./$27,000* • **Massage Therapy/Therapeutic Massage** 60 *hrs./$18,000* • **Medical/Health Management and Clinical Assistant/ Specialist** 91 *hrs./$28,965*

STUDENT SERVICES Academic or career counseling, placement services for program completers.

Tidewater Tech

7020 North Military Highway, Norfolk, VA 23518
http://www.tidetech.com/

CONTACT Gerald Yagen, Owner
Telephone: 757-853-2121

GENERAL INFORMATION Private Institution. **Total program enrollment:** 202. **Application fee:** $25.

PROGRAM(S) OFFERED
• **Dental Assisting/Assistant** 43 *hrs./$14,190* • **Licensed Practical/Vocational Nurse Training (LPN, LVN, Cert, Dipl, AAS)** 72 *hrs./$30,600* • **Medical/Health Management and Clinical Assistant/Specialist** 91 *hrs./$27,150*

STUDENT SERVICES Academic or career counseling, placement services for program completers.

Tidewater Tech

2697 Dean Drive, Suite 100, Virginia Beach, VA 23452
http://www.tidetech.com/

CONTACT Beth Hall, Director
Telephone: 757-340-2121

GENERAL INFORMATION Private Institution. Founded 1969. **Accreditation:** State accredited or approved. **Total program enrollment:** 1277. **Application fee:** $25.

PROGRAM(S) OFFERED
• **Business Administration and Management, General** 93 *hrs./$27,900* • **Computer and Information Systems Security** 92 *hrs./$27,600* • **Corrections and Criminal Justice, Other** 90 *hrs./$27,000* • **Legal Assistant/Paralegal** 90 *hrs./$27,000* • **Massage Therapy/Therapeutic Massage** 100 *hrs./$30,000* • **Medical/Clinical Assistant** 91 *hrs./$25,435*

STUDENT SERVICES Academic or career counseling, employment services for current students, placement services for program completers, remedial services.

Tidewater Tech-Trades

922 West 21st Street, Norfolk, VA 23517-1516
http://www.tidewatertech.edu/

CONTACT Greg Smith, School Director
Telephone: 757-858-8324

GENERAL INFORMATION Public Institution. Founded 1963. **Total program enrollment:** 114. **Application fee:** $25.

PROGRAM(S) OFFERED
• **Automobile/Automotive Mechanics Technology/Technician** 3 *students enrolled* • **Automotive Engineering Technology/Technician** 79 *hrs./$19,900* • **Heating, Air Conditioning and Refrigeration Technology/Technician (ACH/ACR/ACHR/ HRAC/HVAC/AC Technology)** 86 *hrs./$19,900* • **Heating, Air Conditioning, Ventilation and Refrigeration Maintenance Technology/Technician (HAC, HACR, HVAC, HVACR)** 8 *students enrolled* • **Welding Technology/Welder** 48 *hrs./$12,275*

STUDENT SERVICES Academic or career counseling, employment services for current students, placement services for program completers.

University of Mary Washington

1301 College Avenue, Fredericksburg, VA 22401-5358
http://www.umw.edu/

CONTACT Judy G. Hample, President
Telephone: 540-654-1000

GENERAL INFORMATION Public Institution. Founded 1908. **Accreditation:** Regional (SACS/CC); music (NASM). **Total program enrollment:** 3749. **Application fee:** $50.

PROGRAM(S) OFFERED
• **Business Administration, Management and Operations, Other** 1 *student enrolled*

STUDENT SERVICES Academic or career counseling, employment services for current students, placement services for program completers.

University of Richmond

28 Westhampton Way, University of Richmond, VA 23173
http://www.richmond.edu/

CONTACT Edward L. Ayers, President
Telephone: 804-289-8000

GENERAL INFORMATION Private Institution. Founded 1830. **Accreditation:** Regional (SACS/CC); music (NASM). **Total program enrollment:** 3473. **Application fee:** $50.

PROGRAM(S) OFFERED
• **Human Resources Management/Personnel Administration, General** • **Human Services, General** *1 student enrolled* • **Information Science/Studies** *4 students enrolled* • **Legal Assistant/Paralegal** *11 students enrolled* • **Organizational Behavior Studies**

STUDENT SERVICES Academic or career counseling, employment services for current students, placement services for program completers.

Virginia Beach City Public School of Practical Nursing

2925 North Landing Road, Virginia Beach, VA 23456-2499
http://www.techcenter.vbschools.com/

CONTACT James Merrill, Superintendent
Telephone: 757-648-6050 Ext. 0

GENERAL INFORMATION Public Institution. Founded 1972. **Total program enrollment:** 16.

PROGRAM(S) OFFERED
• **Licensed Practical/Vocational Nurse Training (LPN, LVN, Cert, Dipl, AAS)** *1494 hrs.*

STUDENT SERVICES Academic or career counseling, remedial services.

Virginia Career Institute

1001 Boulders Parkway, Suite 305, Richmond, VA 23225
http://www.vstsuccess.com/

CONTACT Katharine Walton, School Director
Telephone: 804-323-1020

GENERAL INFORMATION Private Institution. **Total program enrollment:** 196. **Application fee:** $75.

PROGRAM(S) OFFERED
• **Allied Health and Medical Assisting Services, Other** *720 hrs./$11,340* • **Clinical/Medical Laboratory Assistant** *34 students enrolled* • **Massage Therapy/Therapeutic Massage** *720 hrs./$11,825* • **Medical Office Assistant/Specialist** *720 hrs./$11,340* • **Surgical Technology/Technologist** *1440 hrs./$21,800*

STUDENT SERVICES Placement services for program completers.

Virginia Career Institute

100 Constitution Drive, Suite 101, Virginia Beach, VA 23462
http://www.vstsuccess.com/

CONTACT Cynthia Solari, Campus Director
Telephone: 757-499-5447

GENERAL INFORMATION Private Institution. **Total program enrollment:** 307. **Application fee:** $75.

PROGRAM(S) OFFERED
• **Court Reporting/Court Reporter** *1890 hrs./$24,180* • **Legal Support Services, Other** *1020 hrs./$24,180* • **Licensed Practical/Vocational Nurse Training (LPN, LVN, Cert, Dipl, AAS)** *1440 hrs./$24,145* • **Massage Therapy/Therapeutic Massage** *720 hrs./$11,340* • **Medical Office Assistant/Specialist** *34 students enrolled* • **Medical Office Management/Administration** *720 hrs./$11,340* • **Medical/Clinical Assistant** *720 hrs./$11,340*

STUDENT SERVICES Placement services for program completers.

Virginia Highlands Community College

PO Box 828, 100 VHCC Drive Abingdon, Abingdon, VA 24210
http://www.vhcc.edu/

CONTACT F. David Wilkin, President
Telephone: 276-739-2400

GENERAL INFORMATION Public Institution. Founded 1967. **Accreditation:** Regional (SACS/CC); radiologic technology: radiography (JRCERT). **Total program enrollment:** 975.

PROGRAM(S) OFFERED
• **Accounting and Related Services, Other** *2 students enrolled* • **Allied Health Diagnostic, Intervention, and Treatment Professions, Other** *4 students enrolled* • **Business Administration, Management and Operations, Other** *4 students enrolled* • **Business Operations Support and Secretarial Services, Other** • **CAD/CADD Drafting and/or Design Technology/Technician** • **Child Care Provider/Assistant** *1 student enrolled* • **Computer and Information Sciences, General** *3 students enrolled* • **Corrections** *3 students enrolled* • **Electrician** *17 students enrolled* • **Health Information/Medical Records Technology/Technician** *2 students enrolled* • **Heating, Air Conditioning, Ventilation and Refrigeration Maintenance Technology/Technician (HAC, HACR, HVAC, HVACR)** *4 students enrolled* • **Hospitality Administration/Management, General** • **Industrial Electronics Technology/Technician** • **Mental and Social Health Services and Allied Professions, Other** *147 students enrolled* • **Precision Metal Working, Other** *6 students enrolled* • **Web Page, Digital/Multimedia and Information Resources Design** *3 students enrolled*

STUDENT SERVICES Academic or career counseling, employment services for current students, placement services for program completers, remedial services.

Virginia School of Hair Design

101 West Queens Way, Hampton, VA 23669

CONTACT Donald Allhouse, Executive Director
Telephone: 757-722-0211

GENERAL INFORMATION Private Institution. Founded 1959. **Total program enrollment:** 42. **Application fee:** $100.

PROGRAM(S) OFFERED
• **Barbering/Barber** *1500 hrs./$7780* • **Cosmetology, Barber/Styling, and Nail Instructor** *600 hrs./$2239* • **Cosmetology/Cosmetologist, General** *1500 hrs./$8272* • **Nail Technician/Specialist and Manicurist** *150 hrs./$656*

STUDENT SERVICES Academic or career counseling, employment services for current students, placement services for program completers.

Virginia School of Massage

2008 Morton Drive, Charlottesville, VA 22903
http://www.vasom.com/

CONTACT Stephen Lazarus, Chief Operations Officer
Telephone: 434-293-4031

GENERAL INFORMATION Private Institution. Founded 1989. **Total program enrollment:** 140.

PROGRAM(S) OFFERED
• **Aesthetician/Esthetician and Skin Care Specialist** *45 hrs./$9146* • **Massage Therapy/Therapeutic Massage** *49 hrs./$10,414*

STUDENT SERVICES Academic or career counseling, employment services for current students, placement services for program completers.

Virginia University of Lynchburg

2058 Garfield Avenue, Lynchburg, VA 24501-6417
http://www.vul.edu/

CONTACT Ralph Reavis, President
Telephone: 434-528-5276 Ext. 126

GENERAL INFORMATION Private Institution. Founded 1886. **Accreditation:** State accredited or approved. **Total program enrollment:** 137. **Application fee:** $25.

PROGRAM(S) OFFERED
• **Religion/Religious Studies** *10 students enrolled*

STUDENT SERVICES Academic or career counseling, employment services for current students, placement services for program completers, remedial services.

Virginia Western Community College

PO Box 14007, Roanoke, VA 24038
http://www.virginiawestern.edu/

CONTACT Robert Sandel, President
Telephone: 540-857-7311

GENERAL INFORMATION Public Institution. Founded 1966. **Accreditation:** Regional (SACS/CC); dental hygiene (ADA); radiologic technology: radiography (JRCERT). **Total program enrollment:** 2291.

PROGRAM(S) OFFERED
• **Architectural Drafting and Architectural CAD/CADD** • **Audiovisual Communications Technologies/Technicians, Other** • **Business Operations Support and Secretarial Services, Other** *5 students enrolled* • **Child Care Provider/Assistant** • **Health and Medical Administrative Services, Other** *2 students enrolled* • **Heating, Air Conditioning, Ventilation and Refrigeration Maintenance Technology/Technician (HAC, HACR, HVAC, HVACR)** *4 students enrolled* • **Interior Design** *3 students enrolled* • **Licensed Practical/Vocational Nurse Training (LPN, LVN, Cert, Dipl, AAS)** *25 students enrolled* • **Medical Radiologic Technology/Science—Radiation Therapist** *8 students enrolled* • **Mental and Social Health Services and Allied Professions, Other** *96 students enrolled* • **Surveying Engineering** • **Welding Technology/Welder** *1 student enrolled*

STUDENT SERVICES Academic or career counseling, employment services for current students, placement services for program completers, remedial services.

Wards Corner Beauty Academy

216 East Little Creek Road, Norfolk, VA 23505

CONTACT Mark Richardson, President
Telephone: 757-583-3300

GENERAL INFORMATION Private Institution. **Total program enrollment:** 116. **Application fee:** $50.

PROGRAM(S) OFFERED
• **Cosmetology/Cosmetologist, General** *1500 hrs./$14,350*

STUDENT SERVICES Academic or career counseling, placement services for program completers.

Wards Corner Beauty Academy–Virginia Beach

103 S. Witchduck Road, Virginia Beach, VA 23462

CONTACT Mark Richardson, CEO
Telephone: 757-473-5555

GENERAL INFORMATION Private Institution. **Total program enrollment:** 78. **Application fee:** $50.

PROGRAM(S) OFFERED
• **Cosmetology/Cosmetologist, General** *1500 hrs./$14,350*

STUDENT SERVICES Academic or career counseling, placement services for program completers.

Washington County Adult Skill Center

848 Thompson Drive, Abingdon, VA 24210
http://wcsc.wcs.k12.va.us/

CONTACT Darrell Blankenship, Administrator
Telephone: 276-676-1948

GENERAL INFORMATION Public Institution. **Total program enrollment:** 98.

PROGRAM(S) OFFERED
• **Administrative Assistant and Secretarial Science, General** *14 students enrolled* • **Allied Health and Medical Assisting Services, Other** *900 hrs./$4872* • **Business/Office Automation/Technology/Data Entry** *900 hrs./$4575* • **Dental Assisting/Assistant** *900 hrs./$5090* • **Diesel Mechanics Technology/Technician** *925 hrs./$4608* • **Machine Tool Technology/Machinist** *900 hrs./$4575* • **Welding Technology/Welder** *900 hrs./$5046*

STUDENT SERVICES Academic or career counseling, employment services for current students, placement services for program completers, remedial services.

Woodrow Wilson Rehabilitation Center

Route 250, Fishersville, VA 22939-1500
http://wwrc.virginia.gov/

CONTACT Richard L. Sizemore, Director
Telephone: 540-332-7265

GENERAL INFORMATION Public Institution. **Total program enrollment:** 237.

PROGRAM(S) OFFERED
• **Automobile/Automotive Mechanics Technology/Technician** *13 students enrolled* • **Carpentry/Carpenter** *900 hrs./$10,730* • **Data Entry/Microcomputer Applications, General** *1400 hrs./$16,576* • **Food Preparation/Professional Cooking/Kitchen Assistant** *875 hrs./$10,360* • **Information Technology** *10 students enrolled* • **Mechanical Drafting and Mechanical Drafting CAD/CADD** *4 students enrolled* • **Nurse/Nursing Assistant/Aide and Patient Care Assistant** *730 hrs./$8732* • **Receptionist** *1140 hrs./$13,468* • **Sales, Distribution and Marketing Operations, General** *750 hrs./$9155*

STUDENT SERVICES Academic or career counseling, employment services for current students, placement services for program completers, remedial services.

Wytheville Community College

1000 East Main Street, Wytheville, VA 24382-3308
http://www.wcc.vccs.edu/

CONTACT Charlie White, President
Telephone: 276-223-4700

GENERAL INFORMATION Public Institution. Founded 1967. **Accreditation:** Regional (SACS/CC); dental assisting (ADA); dental hygiene (ADA); medical laboratory technology (NAACLS); physical therapy assisting (APTA). **Total program enrollment:** 1100.

PROGRAM(S) OFFERED
• **Business Operations Support and Secretarial Services, Other** *16 students enrolled* • **CAD/CADD Drafting and/or Design Technology/Technician** • **Construction Trades, General** *2 students enrolled* • **Corrections** *7 students enrolled* • **Criminal Justice/Law Enforcement Administration** *17 students enrolled* • **Dental Assisting/Assistant** • **Health and Medical Administrative**

Services, Other • Licensed Practical/Vocational Nurse Training (LPN, LVN, Cert, Dipl, AAS) *54 students enrolled* • Mental and Social Health Services and Allied Professions, Other *132 students enrolled* • Precision Metal Working, Other *18 students enrolled*

STUDENT SERVICES Academic or career counseling, employment services for current students, remedial services.

WEST VIRGINIA ——————

Academy of Careers and Technology

390 Stanaford Road, Beckley, WV 25801
http://wvact.net/

CONTACT Nelson Spencer, Acting Director
Telephone: 304-256-4615 Ext. 302

GENERAL INFORMATION Private Institution. **Total program enrollment:** 45. **Application fee:** $60.

PROGRAM(S) OFFERED
• Automobile/Automotive Mechanics Technology/Technician *4 students enrolled* • Clinical/Medical Laboratory Assistant *34 students enrolled* • Computer and Information Sciences, General *8 students enrolled* • Construction Trades, Other *2 students enrolled* • Dental Assisting/Assistant *2 students enrolled* • Diesel Mechanics Technology/Technician • Drafting and Design Technology/Technician, General *4 students enrolled* • Electrician *1080 hrs./$3605* • Graphic and Printing Equipment Operator, General Production • Heating, Air Conditioning, Ventilation and Refrigeration Maintenance Technology/Technician (HAC, HACR, HVAC, HVACR) • Licensed Practical/Vocational Nurse Training (LPN, LVN, Cert, Dipl, AAS) *1313 hrs./$5000* • Mason/Masonry • Medical Office Assistant/Specialist *900 hrs./$2935* • Medical/Clinical Assistant *10 students enrolled* • Pharmacy Technician/Assistant *600 hrs./$2110* • Phlebotomy/Phlebotomist *170 hrs./$785* • Welding Technology/Welder *648 hrs./$2414*

STUDENT SERVICES Academic or career counseling, employment services for current students, placement services for program completers, remedial services.

Alderson-Broaddus College

1 College Hill Drive, Philippi, WV 26416
http://www.ab.edu/

CONTACT J. Michael Clyburn, President
Telephone: 304-457-1700

GENERAL INFORMATION Private Institution (Affiliated with American Baptist Churches in the U.S.A.). Founded 1871. **Accreditation:** Regional (NCA). **Total program enrollment:** 677. **Application fee:** $25.

PROGRAM(S) OFFERED
• Business/Commerce, General • Computer and Information Sciences, General

STUDENT SERVICES Academic or career counseling, remedial services.

American Public University System

111 West Congress Street, Charles Town, WV 25414
http://www.apus.edu/

CONTACT Wallace E. Boston, President and Chief Executive
Telephone: 877-468-6268

GENERAL INFORMATION Private Institution. Founded 1991. **Accreditation:** State accredited or approved. **Total program enrollment:** 2683.

PROGRAM(S) OFFERED
• Aeronautics/Aviation/Aerospace Science and Technology, General • Asian Studies/Civilization *1 student enrolled* • Business Administration and Management, General • Child Care Provider/Assistant • Computer and Information Sciences and Support Services, Other • Computer and Information Sciences, Other *6 students enrolled* • Computer and Information Systems Security *4 students enrolled* • Corrections Administration *1 student enrolled* • Corrections and Criminal Justice, Other *4 students enrolled* • Criminal Justice/Law Enforcement Administration • Educational/Instructional Media Design *1 student enrolled* • European Studies/Civilization • Fire Protection, Other *45 students enrolled* • Fire Science/Firefighting *4 students enrolled* • Fire Services Administration • Forensic Science and Technology • Hazardous Materials Information Systems Technology/Technician *2 students enrolled* • Hazardous Materials Management and Waste Technology/Technician • Human Resources Management/Personnel Administration, General *5 students enrolled* • Intercultural/Multicultural and Diversity Studies *1 student enrolled* • International Relations and Affairs *1 student enrolled* • Legal Assistant/Paralegal *1 student enrolled* • Logistics and Materials Management *2 students enrolled* • Military Technologies *3 students enrolled* • Public Administration *1 student enrolled* • Real Estate *1 student enrolled* • Securities Services Administration/Management *2 students enrolled* • Security and Protective Services, Other • Social Sciences, Other • Web/Multimedia Management and Webmaster *1 student enrolled* • Work and Family Studies *1 student enrolled*

STUDENT SERVICES Academic or career counseling, employment services for current students, remedial services.

Appalachian Bible College

PO Box ABC, Bradley, WV 25818
http://www.abc.edu/

CONTACT Daniel Anderson, President
Telephone: 304-877-6428

GENERAL INFORMATION Private Institution. Founded 1950. **Accreditation:** Regional (NCA); state accredited or approved. **Total program enrollment:** 208. **Application fee:** $20.

PROGRAM(S) OFFERED
• Bible/Biblical Studies *6 students enrolled*

STUDENT SERVICES Academic or career counseling, employment services for current students, placement services for program completers, remedial services.

Beckley Beauty Academy

109 South Fayette Street, Beckley, WV 25801

CONTACT Roberta J. Saunders, Chief Executive Officer
Telephone: 304-253-8326

GENERAL INFORMATION Private Institution. Founded 1976. **Total program enrollment:** 44.

PROGRAM(S) OFFERED
• Cosmetology/Cosmetologist, General *2000 hrs./$9130* • Nail Technician/Specialist and Manicurist *400 hrs./$1300*

STUDENT SERVICES Academic or career counseling, placement services for program completers.

Ben Franklin Career Center

500 28th Street, Dunbar, WV 25064
http://dtodd@access.k12.wv.us/

CONTACT John Baird, Principal
Telephone: 304-766-0369

GENERAL INFORMATION Public Institution. Founded 1971. **Total program enrollment:** 150. **Application fee:** $25.

Ben Franklin Career Center (continued)

PROGRAM(S) OFFERED
• **Automobile/Automotive Mechanics Technology/Technician** *1 student enrolled* • **CAD/CADD Drafting and/or Design Technology/Technician** *5 students enrolled* • **Computer Installation and Repair Technology/Technician** *11 students enrolled* • **Computer Systems Networking and Telecommunications** *3 students enrolled* • **Computer and Information Sciences, Other** *8 students enrolled* • **Construction Trades, General** *1 student enrolled* • **Diesel Mechanics Technology/Technician** *6 students enrolled* • **Early Childhood Education and Teaching** *2 students enrolled* • **Electrical/Electronics Equipment Installation and Repair, General** *23 students enrolled* • **Graphic Communications, General** • **Health Aide** *6 students enrolled* • **Heating, Air Conditioning, Ventilation and Refrigeration Maintenance Technology/Technician (HAC, HACR, HVAC, HVACR)** *10 students enrolled* • **Heavy Equipment Maintenance Technology/Technician** *10 students enrolled* • **Machine Shop Technology/Assistant** *1 student enrolled* • **Medical Office Assistant/Specialist** *8 students enrolled* • **Web Page, Digital/Multimedia and Information Resources Design** *2 students enrolled* • **Welding Technology/Welder** *9 students enrolled*

STUDENT SERVICES Academic or career counseling, employment services for current students, placement services for program completers, remedial services.

Blue Ridge Community and Technical College

400 West Stephen Street, Martinsburg, WV 25401
http://www.blueridgectc.edu/

CONTACT Dr. Peter G. Checkovich, President
Telephone: 304-260-4380

GENERAL INFORMATION Public Institution. Founded 1974. **Total program enrollment:** 720. **Application fee:** $25.

PROGRAM(S) OFFERED
• **Business/Office Automation/Technology/Data Entry** *35 students enrolled* • **Criminal Justice/Safety Studies** *9 students enrolled* • **Emergency Medical Technology/Technician (EMT Paramedic)** *5 students enrolled* • **Fire Protection and Safety Technology/Technician** • **Heavy/Industrial Equipment Maintenance Technologies, Other** *6 students enrolled* • **Information Science/Studies** *3 students enrolled* • **Legal Assistant/Paralegal** *5 students enrolled* • **Occupational Safety and Health Technology/Technician**

STUDENT SERVICES Academic or career counseling, employment services for current students, placement services for program completers, remedial services.

B. M. Spurr School of Practical Nursing

800 Wheeling Avenue, Glen Dale, WV 26038
http://www.reynoldsmemorial.com/programs.php?id=12

CONTACT John Sicurella, Executive Director
Telephone: 304-843-3255

GENERAL INFORMATION Private Institution. Founded 1951. **Total program enrollment:** 21. **Application fee:** $20.

PROGRAM(S) OFFERED
• **Licensed Practical/Vocational Nurse Training (LPN, LVN, Cert, Dipl, AAS)** *1501 hrs./$2800*

STUDENT SERVICES Academic or career counseling, placement services for program completers, remedial services.

Cabell County Vocational Technical Center

1035 Norway Avenue, Huntington, WV 25705
http://boe.cabe.k12.wv.us/ctc/

CONTACT Brenda Tanner, Director/Principal
Telephone: 304-528-5106

GENERAL INFORMATION Public Institution. Founded 1940. **Total program enrollment:** 86.

PROGRAM(S) OFFERED
• **Autobody/Collision and Repair Technology/Technician** *4 students enrolled* • **Automobile/Automotive Mechanics Technology/Technician** *4 students enrolled* • **Business/Office Automation/Technology/Data Entry** *10 students enrolled* • **Computer Installation and Repair Technology/Technician** • **Computer Systems Networking and Telecommunications** *1 student enrolled* • **Construction Trades, General** *5 students enrolled* • **Electrical/Electronics Maintenance and Repair Technology, Other** *6 students enrolled* • **Graphic Design** • **Heating, Air Conditioning and Refrigeration Technology/Technician (ACH/ACR/ACHR/HRAC/HVAC/AC Technology)** *6 students enrolled* • **Interior Design** • **Licensed Practical/Vocational Nurse Training (LPN, LVN, Cert, Dipl, AAS)** *25 students enrolled* • **Machine Shop Technology/Assistant** *2 students enrolled* • **Welding Technology/Welder** *4 students enrolled*

STUDENT SERVICES Academic or career counseling, employment services for current students, placement services for program completers, remedial services.

Carver Career Center

4799 Midland Drive, Charleston, WV 25306-6397
http://kcs.kana.k12.wv.us/carver/

CONTACT James Casdorph, Principal
Telephone: 304-348-1965

GENERAL INFORMATION Private Institution. **Total program enrollment:** 185. **Application fee:** $20.

PROGRAM(S) OFFERED
• **Agricultural Business and Management, General** • **Autobody/Collision and Repair Technology/Technician** *4 students enrolled* • **Automobile/Automotive Mechanics Technology/Technician** • **Building/Construction Finishing, Management, and Inspection, Other** • **Cosmetology/Cosmetologist, General** *2000 hrs./$4702* • **Dental Assisting/Assistant** *7 students enrolled* • **Drafting and Design Technology/Technician, General** • **Electrical and Power Transmission Installation/Installer, General** *1250 hrs./$2091* • **Emergency Care Attendant (EMT Ambulance)** *1 student enrolled* • **Health Services/Allied Health/Health Sciences, General** • **Heating, Air Conditioning and Refrigeration Technology/Technician (ACH/ACR/ACHR/HRAC/HVAC/AC Technology)** *1250 hrs./$2752* • **Medical Transcription/Transcriptionist** *15 students enrolled* • **Nail Technician/Specialist and Manicurist** *3 students enrolled* • **Pharmacy Technician/Assistant** *10 students enrolled* • **Plumbing Technology/Plumber** *7 students enrolled* • **Respiratory Care Therapy/Therapist** *2051 hrs./$5488* • **Surgical Technology/Technologist** *1250 hrs./$2469* • **Veterinary/Animal Health Technology/Technician and Veterinary Assistant** *1399 hrs./$6256* • **Welding Technology/Welder** • **Word Processing** *2 students enrolled*

STUDENT SERVICES Academic or career counseling, employment services for current students, placement services for program completers, remedial services.

Charleston School of Beauty Culture

210 Capitol Street, Charleston, WV 25301

CONTACT Jack Donta, President
Telephone: 304-346-9603

GENERAL INFORMATION Private Institution. Founded 1957. **Total program enrollment:** 80.

PROGRAM(S) OFFERED
• **Barbering/Barber** *300 hrs./$1600* • **Cosmetology/Cosmetologist, General** *2000 hrs./$9800* • **Nail Technician/Specialist and Manicurist** *600 hrs./$3100*

STUDENT SERVICES Academic or career counseling, placement services for program completers.

Clarksburg Beauty Academy

120 South 3rd Street, Clarksburg, WV 26301

CONTACT Angela Policano, Director
Telephone: 304-624-6475

GENERAL INFORMATION Private Institution. **Total program enrollment:** 95.

PROGRAM(S) OFFERED
● Cosmetology, Barber/Styling, and Nail Instructor *500 hrs./$2450*
● Cosmetology/Cosmetologist, General *2000 hrs./$11,900* ● Massage Therapy/
Therapeutic Massage *600 hrs./$6700* ● Nail Technician/Specialist and
Manicurist *400 hrs./$2700*

STUDENT SERVICES Academic or career counseling, placement services
for program completers.

Community & Technical College at West Virginia University Institute of Technology

405 Fayette Pike, Montgomery, WV 25136
http://ctc.wvutech.edu/

CONTACT Beverly Jo Harris, President
Telephone: 304-442-3071

GENERAL INFORMATION Public Institution. **Total program enrollment:**
482.

PROGRAM(S) OFFERED
● Administrative Assistant and Secretarial Science, General *18 students
enrolled* ● Business/Commerce, General *2 students enrolled* ● Printing Press
Operator

STUDENT SERVICES Academic or career counseling, daycare for children
of students, employment services for current students, placement services
for program completers, remedial services.

Eastern West Virginia Community and Technical College

HC 65 Box 402, Moorefield, WV 26836
http://www.eastern.wvnet.edu/

CONTACT Mr. Robert Sisk, Interim President
Telephone: 304-434-8000

GENERAL INFORMATION Public Institution. Founded 1999. **Accreditation:**
Regional (NCA). **Total program enrollment:** 99.

PROGRAM(S) OFFERED
● Heavy/Industrial Equipment Maintenance Technologies, Other *1 student
enrolled* ● Science Technologies/Technicians, Other

STUDENT SERVICES Academic or career counseling, placement services
for program completers, remedial services.

Everest Institute

5514 Big Tyler Road, Cross Lanes, WV 25313-1390
http://www.everest.edu/

CONTACT Aimee Switzer, School President
Telephone: 304-776-6290

GENERAL INFORMATION Private Institution. Founded 1938. **Accreditation:** State accredited or approved. **Total program enrollment:** 487.

PROGRAM(S) OFFERED
● Electrical, Electronic and Communications Engineering Technology/
Technician *124 hrs./$25,620* ● Health and Medical Administrative Services,
Other *32 students enrolled* ● Massage Therapy/Therapeutic Massage *750 hrs./
$12,590* ● Medical Insurance Specialist/Medical Biller *720 hrs./$12,590*
● Medical Office Management/Administration *720 hrs./$12,730* ● Medical/
Clinical Assistant *720 hrs./$13,963* ● Pharmacy Technician/Assistant

STUDENT SERVICES Academic or career counseling, employment
services for current students, placement services for program completers,
remedial services.

Fred W. Eberle Technical Center

Route 5, Box 2, Buckhannon, WV 26201
http://fetc.upsh.tec.wv.us

CONTACT Michael Cutright, Director
Telephone: 304-472-1259

GENERAL INFORMATION Public Institution. Founded 1979. **Total
program enrollment:** 51.

PROGRAM(S) OFFERED
● Allied Health and Medical Assisting Services, Other ● Autobody/Collision
and Repair Technology/Technician *1 student enrolled* ● Automobile/Automotive
Mechanics Technology/Technician ● Computer Installation and Repair
Technology/Technician *1080 hrs./$2500* ● Computer and Information Sciences
and Support Services, Other *3 students enrolled* ● Construction Engineering
Technology/Technician *1 student enrolled* ● Diesel Mechanics Technology/
Technician *1080 hrs./$2500* ● Electrician *1080 hrs./$2800* ● Forestry, General
1 student enrolled ● Licensed Practical/Vocational Nurse Training (LPN, LVN,
Cert, Dipl, AAS) *1350 hrs./$3650* ● Mason/Masonry *1080 hrs./$2500* ● Truck
and Bus Driver/Commercial Vehicle Operation *33 students enrolled* ● Welding
Technology/Welder *1080 hrs./$2500*

STUDENT SERVICES Academic or career counseling, placement services
for program completers, remedial services.

Garnet Career Center

422 Dickinson Street, Charleston, WV 25301
http://kcs.kana.k12.wv.us/garnet/

CONTACT James Vickers, Principal
Telephone: 304-348-6195

GENERAL INFORMATION Private Institution. **Total program enrollment:**
105. **Application fee:** $15.

PROGRAM(S) OFFERED
● Accounting Technology/Technician and Bookkeeping *1350 hrs./$2495*
● Automobile/Automotive Mechanics Technology/Technician *1284 hrs./$2746*
● Business Operations Support and Secretarial Services, Other *1350 hrs./
$2495* ● Licensed Practical/Vocational Nurse Training (LPN, LVN, Cert, Dipl,
AAS) *1350 hrs./$4198* ● Medical Administrative/Executive Assistant and Medi-
cal Secretary *1350 hrs./$2495*

STUDENT SERVICES Academic or career counseling, employment
services for current students, remedial services.

Glenville State College

200 High Street, Glenville, WV 26351-1200
http://www.glenville.edu/

CONTACT Peter B. Barr, President
Telephone: 304-462-7361

GENERAL INFORMATION Public Institution. Founded 1872. **Accreditation:**
Regional (NCA). **Total program enrollment:** 1123. **Application fee:** $10.

STUDENT SERVICES Academic or career counseling, employment
services for current students, placement services for program completers,
remedial services.

HRDE-Stanley Technical Institute–Clarksburg

120 South Linden Avenue, Clarksburg, WV 26301-2270

CONTACT Kenneth M. Perdue, President
Telephone: 304-296-8223 Ext. 26

GENERAL INFORMATION Private Institution. Founded 1981. **Total
program enrollment:** 12.

HRDE-Stanley Technical Institute–Clarksburg (continued)

PROGRAM(S) OFFERED
• Computer and Information Sciences, General *720 hrs./$7150* • Construction Engineering Technology/Technician *980 hrs./$9732*

STUDENT SERVICES Academic or career counseling, employment services for current students, placement services for program completers, remedial services.

HRDE-Stanley Technical Institute–Hinton

320½ 2nd Street, Hinton, WV 25951

CONTACT Kenneth M. Perdue, President
Telephone: 304-296-8223 Ext. 26

GENERAL INFORMATION Private Institution. **Total program enrollment:** 8.

PROGRAM(S) OFFERED
• Computer and Information Sciences, General *720 hrs./$7150* • Data Processing and Data Processing Technology/Technician *10 students enrolled*

STUDENT SERVICES Academic or career counseling, employment services for current students, placement services for program completers, remedial services.

HRDE-Stanley Technical Institute–Parkersburg

800 Camden Avenue, Parkersburg, WV 26101

CONTACT Kenneth M. Perdue, President
Telephone: 304-296-8223 Ext. 10

GENERAL INFORMATION Private Institution. **Total program enrollment:** 6.

PROGRAM(S) OFFERED
• Computer and Information Sciences, General *475 hrs./$4717*

STUDENT SERVICES Academic or career counseling, employment services for current students, placement services for program completers, remedial services.

Human Resource Development and Training

1644 Mileground, Morgantown, WV 26505
http://www.stanleytechnical.com

CONTACT Kenneth M. Perdue, President
Telephone: 304-296-8223 Ext. 10

GENERAL INFORMATION Private Institution.

Huntington Junior College

900 Fifth Avenue, Huntington, WV 25701-2004
http://www.huntingtonjuniorcollege.com/

CONTACT Carolyn Smith, CEO
Telephone: 304-697-7550

GENERAL INFORMATION Private Institution. Founded 1936. **Accreditation:** Regional (NCA); medical assisting (AAMAE). **Total program enrollment:** 770.

PROGRAM(S) OFFERED
• Administrative Assistant and Secretarial Science, General *3 students enrolled*
• Allied Health and Medical Assisting Services, Other *1 student enrolled*
• Dental Assisting/Assistant *1 student enrolled*

STUDENT SERVICES Academic or career counseling, employment services for current students, placement services for program completers, remedial services.

Huntington School of Beauty Culture–Main Campus

5185 Route 60, East Hills Mall, Huntington, WV 25705-2030

CONTACT Catherine Belvin, President
Telephone: 304-736-6289

GENERAL INFORMATION Private Institution. **Total program enrollment:** 133.

PROGRAM(S) OFFERED
• Aesthetician/Esthetician and Skin Care Specialist *600 hrs./$4500*
• Cosmetology/Cosmetologist, General *500 hrs./$1500* • Nail Technician/Specialist and Manicurist *400 hrs./$1700*

STUDENT SERVICES Academic or career counseling, placement services for program completers, remedial services.

International Beauty School

329 South Queen Street, Martinsburg, WV 25401

CONTACT Jorgina Andrawos, Director
Telephone: 304-263-4929

GENERAL INFORMATION Private Institution. Founded 1938. **Total program enrollment:** 66. **Application fee:** $100.

PROGRAM(S) OFFERED
• Aesthetician/Esthetician and Skin Care Specialist *600 hrs./$7000*
• Cosmetology/Cosmetologist, General *2000 hrs./$15,500* • Nail Technician/Specialist and Manicurist *400 hrs./$4000*

STUDENT SERVICES Academic or career counseling, placement services for program completers.

James Rumsey Technical Institute

Route 6, Box 268, Martinsburg, WV 25403-0259
http://www.jamesrumsey.com/

CONTACT Vicki Jenkins, Director
Telephone: 304-754-7925

GENERAL INFORMATION Public Institution. Founded 1967. **Total program enrollment:** 138. **Application fee:** $50.

PROGRAM(S) OFFERED
• Automobile/Automotive Mechanics Technology/Technician *1200 hrs./$2609*
• Culinary Arts/Chef Training *1200 hrs./$2424* • Electrician *5 students enrolled*
• Electromechanical Technology/Electromechanical Engineering Technology *1200 hrs./$2429* • Heating, Air Conditioning and Refrigeration Technology/Technician (ACH/ACR/ACHR/HRAC/HVAC/AC Technology) *1200 hrs./$2544*
• Licensed Practical/Vocational Nurse Training (LPN, LVN, Cert, Dipl, AAS) *1360 hrs./$5088* • Management Information Systems and Services, Other *4 students enrolled* • Surgical Technology/Technologist *1200 hrs./$6456* • Truck and Bus Driver/Commercial Vehicle Operation *14 students enrolled*

STUDENT SERVICES Academic or career counseling, daycare for children of students, employment services for current students, placement services for program completers, remedial services.

John D. Rockefeller, IV Career Center– School of Practical Nursing

95 Rockyside Road, New Cumberland, WV 26047
http://jdrcc.hanc.tec.wv.us

CONTACT George R. Danford, Director
Telephone: 304-564-3337

GENERAL INFORMATION Public Institution. **Total program enrollment:** 14. **Application fee:** $25.

PROGRAM(S) OFFERED
● **Licensed Practical/Vocational Nurse Training (LPN, LVN, Cert, Dipl, AAS)** *14 students enrolled*

STUDENT SERVICES Academic or career counseling, employment services for current students, placement services for program completers.

Logan-Mingo School of Practical Nursing

Three Mile Curve, Box 1747, Logan, WV 25601

CONTACT Ernest Amburgey, Jr., Director
Telephone: 304-752-4687 Ext. 413

GENERAL INFORMATION Public Institution. Founded 1977. **Total program enrollment:** 28.

PROGRAM(S) OFFERED
● **Autobody/Collision and Repair Technology/Technician** *1080 hrs./$1450*
● **Automobile/Automotive Mechanics Technology/Technician** *1080 hrs./$1450*
● **Carpentry/Carpenter** ● **Computer Systems Analysis/Analyst** ● **Computer and Information Sciences and Support Services, Other** ● **Electrician** *1080 hrs./ $1450* ● **Environmental Science** ● **Food Preparation/Professional Cooking/ Kitchen Assistant** ● **Graphic Communications, General** ● **Heating, Air Conditioning, Ventilation and Refrigeration Maintenance Technology/ Technician (HAC, HACR, HVAC, HVACR)** *1 student enrolled* ● **Heavy/Industrial Equipment Maintenance Technologies, Other** *1080 hrs./$1450* ● **Licensed Practical/Vocational Nurse Training (LPN, LVN, Cert, Dipl, AAS)** *1350 hrs./ $4725* ● **Machine Tool Technology/Machinist** ● **Welding Technology/Welder** *1080 hrs./$1900*

STUDENT SERVICES Academic or career counseling, placement services for program completers, remedial services.

Marshall Community and Technical College

One John Marshall Drive, Huntington, WV 25755
http://www.mctc.edu/

CONTACT Dr. Keith J. Cotroneo, President
Telephone: 304-696-6282

GENERAL INFORMATION Public Institution. **Accreditation:** Medical assisting (AAMAE). **Total program enrollment:** 1400. **Application fee:** $15.

PROGRAM(S) OFFERED
● **Criminal Justice/Police Science** *36 students enrolled* ● **Data Processing and Data Processing Technology/Technician** *17 students enrolled* ● **Health Services/ Allied Health/Health Sciences, General** *1 student enrolled* ● **Library Assistant/ Technician** *2 students enrolled*

STUDENT SERVICES Academic or career counseling, daycare for children of students, employment services for current students, placement services for program completers, remedial services.

Meredith Manor International Equestrian Center

Rte. 1 Box 66, Waverly, WV 26184
http://www.meredithmanor.com/

CONTACT Ronald W. Meredith, President
Telephone: 304-679-3128

GENERAL INFORMATION Private Institution. **Total program enrollment:** 95.

PROGRAM(S) OFFERED
● **Equestrian/Equine Studies**

STUDENT SERVICES Academic or career counseling, placement services for program completers.

Monongalia County Technical Education Center

1000 Mississippi Street, Morgantown, WV 26505
http://boe.mono.k12.wv.us/mtec/

CONTACT John A. George, Principal/Director
Telephone: 304-291-9240 Ext. 223

GENERAL INFORMATION Private Institution. **Total program enrollment:** 93. **Application fee:** $50.

PROGRAM(S) OFFERED
● **Autobody/Collision and Repair Technology/Technician** *1 student enrolled*
● **Automobile/Automotive Mechanics Technology/Technician** ● **Child Care Provider/Assistant** ● **Computer Technology/Computer Systems Technology** *1 student enrolled* ● **Culinary Arts/Chef Training** *2 students enrolled* ● **Dental Assisting/Assistant** *3 students enrolled* ● **Electromechanical Technology/ Electromechanical Engineering Technology** *8 students enrolled* ● **Health Information/Medical Records Administration/Administrator** *5 students enrolled* ● **Heating, Air Conditioning, Ventilation and Refrigeration Maintenance Technology/Technician (HAC, HACR, HVAC, HVACR)** *4 students enrolled* ● **Landscaping and Groundskeeping** *3 students enrolled* ● **Licensed Practical/ Vocational Nurse Training (LPN, LVN, Cert, Dipl, AAS)** *13 students enrolled* ● **Medical/Clinical Assistant** *12 students enrolled* ● **Pharmacy Technician/ Assistant** *8 students enrolled* ● **Surgical Technology/Technologist** *8 students enrolled* ● **Welding Technology/Welder** *2 students enrolled*

STUDENT SERVICES Academic or career counseling, employment services for current students, placement services for program completers, remedial services.

Morgantown Beauty College

276 Walnut Street, Morgantown, WV 26505
http://morgantownbeautycollege.com/

CONTACT Michael Sodomick, President
Telephone: 304-292-8475 Ext. 0

GENERAL INFORMATION Private Institution. Founded 1946. **Total program enrollment:** 49. **Application fee:** $50.

PROGRAM(S) OFFERED
● **Aesthetician/Esthetician and Skin Care Specialist** *600 hrs./$6352*
● **Barbering/Barber** ● **Cosmetology, Barber/Styling, and Nail Instructor** *250 hrs./$750* ● **Cosmetology/Cosmetologist, General** *500 hrs./$1400* ● **Massage Therapy/Therapeutic Massage** *600 hrs./$6670* ● **Nail Technician/Specialist and Manicurist** *400 hrs./$2320* ● **Personal and Culinary Services, Other** *2 students enrolled* ● **Teacher Education and Professional Development, Specific Levels and Methods, Other**

STUDENT SERVICES Placement services for program completers.

Mountaineer Beauty College

700 Sixth Avenue, PO Box 547, St. Albans, WV 25177
http://www.webmbc.com/

CONTACT Toni E. Madia, President
Telephone: 304-727-9999

GENERAL INFORMATION Private Institution. Founded 1991. **Total program enrollment:** 26. **Application fee:** $100.

PROGRAM(S) OFFERED
● **Cosmetology/Cosmetologist, General** *2000 hrs./$9360* ● **Nail Technician/ Specialist and Manicurist** *400 hrs./$1900*

STUDENT SERVICES Academic or career counseling, placement services for program completers.

Mountain State College

1508 Spring Street, Parkersburg, WV 26101-3993
http://www.mountainstate.org/

CONTACT Judith Sutton, Director
Telephone: 304-485-5487

GENERAL INFORMATION Private Institution. Founded 1888. **Accreditation:** State accredited or approved. **Total program enrollment:** 85. **Application fee:** $115.

PROGRAM(S) OFFERED
• Accounting • Administrative Assistant and Secretarial Science, General • Legal Administrative Assistant/Secretary

STUDENT SERVICES Academic or career counseling, employment services for current students, placement services for program completers, remedial services.

Mountain State School of Massage

601 50th Street, Charleston, WV 25304
http://www.mtnstmassage.com/

CONTACT Robert Rogers, Executive Director
Telephone: 304-926-8822

GENERAL INFORMATION Private Institution. **Total program enrollment:** 52. **Application fee:** $50.

PROGRAM(S) OFFERED
• Massage Therapy/Therapeutic Massage 733 hrs./$11,479

STUDENT SERVICES Academic or career counseling, placement services for program completers.

Mountain State University

Box 9003, Beckley, WV 25802-9003
http://www.mountainstate.edu/

CONTACT Charles H. Polk, President
Telephone: 304-253-7351

GENERAL INFORMATION Private Institution. Founded 1933. **Accreditation:** Regional (NCA); medical assisting (AAMAE); physical therapy assisting (APTA). **Total program enrollment:** 3893. **Application fee:** $25.

PROGRAM(S) OFFERED
• Administrative Assistant and Secretarial Science, General • Baking and Pastry Arts/Baker/Pastry Chef • Cooking and Related Culinary Arts, General • Culinary Arts/Chef Training • Diagnostic Medical Sonography/Sonographer and Ultrasound Technician • Health Information/Medical Records Technology/Technician • Medical Insurance Coding Specialist/Coder • Phlebotomy/Phlebotomist 6 students enrolled

STUDENT SERVICES Academic or career counseling, employment services for current students, placement services for program completers, remedial services.

New River Community and Technical College

167 Dye Drive, Beckley, WV 25801
http://www.newriver.edu/

CONTACT Dr. Ted Spring, President
Telephone: 304-929-5472

GENERAL INFORMATION Public Institution. Founded 2003. **Total program enrollment:** 1175.

PROGRAM(S) OFFERED
• Administrative Assistant and Secretarial Science, General 3 students enrolled • Science Technologies/Technicians, Other 37 students enrolled

STUDENT SERVICES Academic or career counseling, remedial services.

Opportunities Industrialization Center–North Central West Virginia

120 Jackson Street, Fairmont, WV 26554
http://www.oicwv.org/

CONTACT Philip Keith, Executive Director
Telephone: 304-366-8142

GENERAL INFORMATION Private Institution. **Total program enrollment:** 66.

PROGRAM(S) OFFERED
• Administrative Assistant and Secretarial Science, General • Clinical/Medical Laboratory Assistant • Dental Assisting/Assistant 600 hrs./$6367 • Electrocardiograph Technology/Technician 3 students enrolled • General Office Occupations and Clerical Services • Home Health Aide/Home Attendant • Medical Administrative/Executive Assistant and Medical Secretary • Medical Insurance Coding Specialist/Coder 600 hrs./$6203 • Medical Office Management/Administration • Medical Transcription/Transcriptionist 600 hrs./$6322 • Medical/Clinical Assistant 900 hrs./$10,920 • Nurse/Nursing Assistant/Aide and Patient Care Assistant 11 students enrolled • Pharmacy Technician/Assistant 600 hrs./$6388 • Phlebotomy/Phlebotomist 300 hrs./$2873

STUDENT SERVICES Academic or career counseling, employment services for current students, placement services for program completers, remedial services.

Pierpont Community & Technical College of Fairmont State University

1201 Locust Avenue, Fairmont, WV 26554
http://www.fairmontstate.edu/

CONTACT Blair Montgomery, President
Telephone: 304-367-4692

GENERAL INFORMATION Public Institution. Founded 1974. **Accreditation:** Regional (NCA); health information technology (AHIMA); medical laboratory technology (NAACLS); physical therapy assisting (APTA). **Total program enrollment:** 1575.

PROGRAM(S) OFFERED
• Clinical/Medical Laboratory Science and Allied Professions, Other 9 students enrolled • Hospitality and Recreation Marketing Operations • Nurse/Nursing Assistant/Aide and Patient Care Assistant 94 students enrolled • Sign Language Interpretation and Translation 5 students enrolled • Teacher Assistant/Aide 5 students enrolled

STUDENT SERVICES Academic or career counseling, employment services for current students, placement services for program completers, remedial services.

Potomac State College of West Virginia University

101 Fort Avenue, Keyser, WV 26726-2698
http://www.potomacstatecollege.edu/

CONTACT Kerry S. Odell, Provost
Telephone: 304-788-6820

GENERAL INFORMATION Public Institution. Founded 1901. **Accreditation:** Regional (NCA). **Total program enrollment:** 1096.

PROGRAM(S) OFFERED
• Criminal Justice/Safety Studies 8 students enrolled

STUDENT SERVICES Academic or career counseling, daycare for children of students, employment services for current students, placement services for program completers, remedial services.

Putnam Career and Technology Center School of Practical Nursing

PO Box 640, Eleanor, WV 25070-0640
http://putnam.schoolspan.com/pctc/

CONTACT Robert Manley, Principal
Telephone: 304-586-3494 Ext. 204

GENERAL INFORMATION Public Institution. **Total program enrollment:** 58. **Application fee:** $30.

PROGRAM(S) OFFERED
• **Architectural Drafting and Architectural CAD/CADD** • **Autobody/Collision and Repair Technology/Technician** 2 students enrolled • **Automobile/Automotive Mechanics Technology/Technician** 8 students enrolled • **Building/Home/ Construction Inspection/Inspector** 3 students enrolled • **Computer Installation and Repair Technology/Technician** 5 students enrolled • **Computer Systems Networking and Telecommunications** 2 students enrolled • **Cooking and Related Culinary Arts, General** 1 student enrolled • **Dental Assisting/Assistant** 2 students enrolled • **Dental Laboratory Technology/Technician** 3 students enrolled • **E-Commerce/Electronic Commerce** • **Electrician** 2 students enrolled • **Graphic Design** 1 student enrolled • **Health Aide** • **Heating, Air Conditioning, Ventilation and Refrigeration Maintenance Technology/Technician (HAC, HACR, HVAC, HVACR)** 2 students enrolled • **Licensed Practical/Vocational Nurse Training (LPN, LVN, Cert, Dipl, AAS)** 9 students enrolled • **Mason/ Masonry** • **Mechanical Drafting and Mechanical Drafting CAD/CADD** • **Plumbing Technology/Plumber** • **Small Engine Mechanics and Repair Technology/ Technician** 2 students enrolled • **Welding Technology/Welder** 1 student enrolled

STUDENT SERVICES Academic or career counseling, employment services for current students, placement services for program completers, remedial services.

Scott College of Cosmetology

1502 Market Street, Wheeling, WV 26003

CONTACT Joe Mamone, Director
Telephone: 304-232-7798

GENERAL INFORMATION Private Institution. **Total program enrollment:** 46. **Application fee:** $50.

PROGRAM(S) OFFERED
• **Cosmetology/Cosmetologist, General** 2000 hrs./$14,780 • **Nail Technician/ Specialist and Manicurist** 400 hrs./$1870

STUDENT SERVICES Academic or career counseling, placement services for program completers.

Southern West Virginia Community and Technical College

Dempsey Branch Road, PO Box 2900, Mount Gay, WV 25637-2900
http://southernwv.edu/

CONTACT Joanne Tomblin, President
Telephone: 304-896-7420

GENERAL INFORMATION Public Institution. Founded 1971. **Accreditation:** Regional (NCA); medical laboratory technology (NAACLS); radiologic technology: radiography (JRCERT); surgical technology (ARCST). **Total program enrollment:** 1343.

PROGRAM(S) OFFERED
• **Criminal Justice/Safety Studies** 11 students enrolled • **Electrical, Electronic and Communications Engineering Technology/Technician** 6 students enrolled • **Executive Assistant/Executive Secretary** 4 students enrolled • **Health Professions and Related Clinical Sciences, Other** 10 students enrolled • **Information Science/Studies** 3 students enrolled • **Science Technologies/Technicians, Other** 4 students enrolled

STUDENT SERVICES Academic or career counseling, employment services for current students, placement services for program completers, remedial services.

Valley College of Technology

330 Harper Park Drive, Beckley, WV 25801
http://www.vct.edu/

CONTACT Beth Gardner, Executive Director
Telephone: 304-252-9547

GENERAL INFORMATION Private Institution. Founded 1983. **Total program enrollment:** 62.

PROGRAM(S) OFFERED
• **Administrative Assistant and Secretarial Science, General** 10 students enrolled

STUDENT SERVICES Employment services for current students, placement services for program completers.

Valley College of Technology

287 Aikens Center, Martinsburg, WV 25401
http://www.vct.edu/

CONTACT Anne M. Ganse, Executive Director
Telephone: 304-263-0979

GENERAL INFORMATION Private Institution. Founded 1983. **Accreditation:** State accredited or approved. **Total program enrollment:** 88.

PROGRAM(S) OFFERED
• **Business Operations Support and Secretarial Services, Other** 36 students enrolled

STUDENT SERVICES Academic or career counseling, employment services for current students, placement services for program completers.

Valley College of Technology

616 Harrison Street, Princeton, WV 24740
http://www.vct.edu/

CONTACT Sonya Davis, Vice President
Telephone: 304-425-2323

GENERAL INFORMATION Private Institution. Founded 1983. **Total program enrollment:** 32.

PROGRAM(S) OFFERED
• **Administrative Assistant and Secretarial Science, General** 20 students enrolled

STUDENT SERVICES Employment services for current students, placement services for program completers.

West Virginia Business College

116 Pennsylvania Avenue, Nutter Fort, WV 26301
http://www.wvbc.edu/

CONTACT Karen D. Shaw, Director
Telephone: 304-232-0361

GENERAL INFORMATION Private Institution. **Accreditation:** State accredited or approved. **Total program enrollment:** 64. **Application fee:** $50.

PROGRAM(S) OFFERED
• **Accounting** 7 students enrolled • **Business Administration and Management, General** 17 students enrolled • **Computer Programming/Programmer, General** 2 students enrolled • **Executive Assistant/Executive Secretary** 1 student enrolled • **Legal Administrative Assistant/Secretary** 4 students enrolled • **Medical Administrative/Executive Assistant and Medical Secretary** 16 students enrolled

STUDENT SERVICES Academic or career counseling, employment services for current students, placement services for program completers, remedial services.

West Virginia Junior College

176 Thompson Drive, Bridgeport, WV 26330
http://www.wvjc.com/

CONTACT Sharron Stevens, Exec Director
Telephone: 304-842-4007

GENERAL INFORMATION Private Institution. Founded 1922. **Accreditation:** State accredited or approved. **Total program enrollment:** 173.

PROGRAM(S) OFFERED
• Computer Technology/Computer Systems Technology • Medical Administrative/Executive Assistant and Medical Secretary • Medical/Clinical Assistant

STUDENT SERVICES Academic or career counseling, employment services for current students, placement services for program completers.

West Virginia Junior College

1000 Virginia Street East, Charleston, WV 25301-2817
http://www.wvjc.com/

CONTACT Sharron Stephens, Director
Telephone: 304-345-2820

GENERAL INFORMATION Private Institution. Founded 1892. **Accreditation:** State accredited or approved. **Total program enrollment:** 182.

PROGRAM(S) OFFERED
• Computer Technology/Computer Systems Technology • Legal Administrative Assistant/Secretary • Medical Office Assistant/Specialist • Medical/Clinical Assistant • Word Processing

STUDENT SERVICES Academic or career counseling, employment services for current students, placement services for program completers.

West Virginia Junior College

148 Willey Street, Morgantown, WV 26505-5521
http://www.wvjc.com/

CONTACT Patricia Callen, Director
Telephone: 304-296-8282

GENERAL INFORMATION Private Institution. Founded 1922. **Accreditation:** State accredited or approved. **Total program enrollment:** 150. **Application fee:** $25.

PROGRAM(S) OFFERED
• Data Entry/Microcomputer Applications, General 4 students enrolled • Legal Administrative Assistant/Secretary 2 students enrolled • Medical Administrative/Executive Assistant and Medical Secretary 3 students enrolled

STUDENT SERVICES Academic or career counseling, employment services for current students, placement services for program completers.

West Virginia Northern Community College

1704 Market Street, Wheeling, WV 26003-3699
http://www.wvncc.edu/

CONTACT Dr. Martin J. Olshinsky, President
Telephone: 304-233-5900

GENERAL INFORMATION Public Institution. Founded 1972. **Accreditation:** Regional (NCA); health information technology (AHIMA); medical laboratory technology (NAACLS); surgical technology (ARCST). **Total program enrollment:** 1367.

PROGRAM(S) OFFERED
• Administrative Assistant and Secretarial Science, General 3 students enrolled • Appliance Installation and Repair Technology/Technician 7 students enrolled • Business/Commerce, General 5 students enrolled • Business/Office Automation/Technology/Data Entry 7 students enrolled • Entrepreneurship/Entrepreneurial Studies 3 students enrolled • Food Preparation/Professional

Cooking/Kitchen Assistant 1 student enrolled • Health Professions and Related Clinical Sciences, Other 5 students enrolled • Heavy/Industrial Equipment Maintenance Technologies, Other 7 students enrolled • Medical/Clinical Assistant 20 students enrolled • Surgical Technology/Technologist 26 students enrolled

STUDENT SERVICES Academic or career counseling, employment services for current students, placement services for program completers, remedial services.

West Virginia State Community and Technical College

Thomas W. Cole, Jr., Complex, PO Box 1000, Institute, WV 25112
http://www.wvsctc.edu/

CONTACT Dr. Joseph Badgley, President
Telephone: 304-766-3118

GENERAL INFORMATION Public Institution. **Accreditation:** Nuclear medicine technology (JRCNMT). **Total program enrollment:** 1101.

PROGRAM(S) OFFERED
• Accounting Technology/Technician and Bookkeeping • Advertising • Banking and Financial Support Services • Emergency Medical Technology/Technician (EMT Paramedic) • Legal Administrative Assistant/Secretary 1 student enrolled • Psychiatric/Mental Health Services Technician 7 students enrolled • Science Technologies/Technicians, Other 1 student enrolled • Selling Skills and Sales Operations 2 students enrolled • Teacher Assistant/Aide 1 student enrolled

STUDENT SERVICES Academic or career counseling, daycare for children of students, employment services for current students, placement services for program completers, remedial services.

West Virginia University at Parkersburg

300 Campus Drive, Parkersburg, WV 26104-8647
http://www.wvup.edu/

CONTACT Marie Foster Gnage, President
Telephone: 304-424-8000

GENERAL INFORMATION Public Institution. Founded 1961. **Accreditation:** Regional (NCA). **Total program enrollment:** 2230.

PROGRAM(S) OFFERED
• Engineering Technologies/Technicians, Other 5 students enrolled • Executive Assistant/Executive Secretary 1 student enrolled • Information Science/Studies 9 students enrolled • Machine Shop Technology/Assistant 6 students enrolled • Science Technologies/Technicians, Other 3 students enrolled • Surgical Technology/Technologist 15 students enrolled • Teacher Assistant/Aide 4 students enrolled • Welding Technology/Welder 4 students enrolled

STUDENT SERVICES Academic or career counseling, daycare for children of students, employment services for current students, placement services for program completers, remedial services.

West Virginia University Hospital–School of Radiology Technology

Medical Center Drive, PO Box 8062, Morgantown, WV 26506-8062
http://www.wvuhradtech.com/

CONTACT Bruce McClymmonds, President
Telephone: 304-598-4251

GENERAL INFORMATION Private Institution. **Total program enrollment:** 52.

PROGRAM(S) OFFERED
• Diagnostic Medical Sonography/Sonographer and Ultrasound Technician 2400 hrs./$3000 • Dietetics/Dietitians 1400 hrs./$2000 • Medical Radiologic Technology/Science—Radiation Therapist 1780 hrs./$2000 • Nuclear Medical Technology/Technologist 1780 hrs./$2000 • Radiologic Technology/Science—Radiographer 3600 hrs./$5300

STUDENT SERVICES Academic or career counseling, employment services for current students, placement services for program completers.

Wood County Vocational School of Practical Nursing

1515 Blizzard Drive, Parkersburg, WV 26101-6424

CONTACT Tina Hawley, Coordinator
Telephone: 304-424-8305

GENERAL INFORMATION Public Institution. Founded 1968. **Total program enrollment:** 29. **Application fee:** $10.

PROGRAM(S) OFFERED
• Licensed Practical/Vocational Nurse Training (LPN, LVN, Cert, Dipl, AAS) *1430 hrs./$3181*

STUDENT SERVICES Daycare for children of students.

WISCONSIN ——————

Academy of Cosmetology

2310 W. Court Street, Janesville, WI 53548

GENERAL INFORMATION Private Institution. **Total program enrollment:** 51. **Application fee:** $10.

PROGRAM(S) OFFERED
• Aesthetician/Esthetician and Skin Care Specialist *450 hrs./$4661*
• Cosmetology, Barber/Styling, and Nail Instructor *150 hrs./$1220*
• Cosmetology/Cosmetologist, General *1800 hrs./$16,121* • Nail Technician/Specialist and Manicurist *300 hrs./$2508*

STUDENT SERVICES Academic or career counseling, employment services for current students, placement services for program completers.

Advanced Institute of Hair Design

5655 South 27 Street, Milwaukee, WI 53221

CONTACT Penny Rushing, Chief Executive Officer
Telephone: 414-525-1700

GENERAL INFORMATION Private Institution. **Total program enrollment:** 150. **Application fee:** $35.

PROGRAM(S) OFFERED
• Aesthetician/Esthetician and Skin Care Specialist *600 hrs./$4274*
• Cosmetology/Cosmetologist, General *1800 hrs./$16,357*

STUDENT SERVICES Academic or career counseling, placement services for program completers.

Blackhawk Technical College

PO Box 5009, Janesville, WI 53547-5009
http://www.blackhawk.edu/

CONTACT Eric Larson, President
Telephone: 608-758-6900

GENERAL INFORMATION Public Institution. Founded 1968. **Accreditation:** Regional (NCA); dental assisting (ADA); dental hygiene (ADA); physical therapy assisting (APTA); radiologic technology: radiography (JRCERT). **Total program enrollment:** 1319. **Application fee:** $30.

PROGRAM(S) OFFERED
• Carpentry/Carpenter • Computer Installation and Repair Technology/Technician *7 students enrolled* • Computer and Information Systems Security *7 students enrolled* • Criminal Justice/Police Science *40 students enrolled* • Dental Assisting/Assistant *10 students enrolled* • Electrician *12 students enrolled* • Emergency Medical Technology/Technician (EMT Paramedic) *90 students*

enrolled • Farm/Farm and Ranch Management *7 students enrolled* • Industrial Mechanics and Maintenance Technology *5 students enrolled* • Landscaping and Groundskeeping *4 students enrolled* • Licensed Practical/Vocational Nurse Training (LPN, LVN, Cert, Dipl, AAS) • Lineworker *17 students enrolled* • Medical Insurance Coding Specialist/Coder *5 students enrolled* • Medical/Clinical Assistant *19 students enrolled* • Nurse/Nursing Assistant/Aide and Patient Care Assistant *221 students enrolled* • Plumbing Technology/Plumber *6 students enrolled* • Welding Technology/Welder *12 students enrolled*

STUDENT SERVICES Academic or career counseling, daycare for children of students, employment services for current students, placement services for program completers, remedial services.

Blue Sky School of Professional Massage and Therapeutic Bodywork

220 Oak Street, Grafton, WI 53024
http://www.BlueSkyMassage.com/

CONTACT Karen N. Lewis, Dean
Telephone: 262-692-9500

GENERAL INFORMATION Private Institution. **Total program enrollment:** 99. **Application fee:** $50.

PROGRAM(S) OFFERED
• Massage Therapy/Therapeutic Massage *27 hrs./$10,075*

Carthage College

2001 Alford Park Drive, Kenosha, WI 53140
http://www.carthage.edu/

CONTACT F. Gregory Campbell, President
Telephone: 262-551-8500

GENERAL INFORMATION Private Institution (Affiliated with Evangelical Lutheran Church in America). Founded 1847. **Accreditation:** Regional (NCA); music (NASM). **Total program enrollment:** 2374. **Application fee:** $35.

PROGRAM(S) OFFERED
• Legal Assistant/Paralegal *45 students enrolled*

STUDENT SERVICES Academic or career counseling, employment services for current students, placement services for program completers.

Chippewa Valley Technical College

620 West Clairemont Avenue, Eau Claire, WI 54701-6162
http://www.cvtc.edu/

CONTACT Bruce Barker, President
Telephone: 715-833-6200

GENERAL INFORMATION Public Institution. Founded 1912. **Accreditation:** Regional (NCA); diagnostic medical sonography (JRCEDMS); health information technology (AHIMA); medical laboratory technology (NAACLS); radiologic technology: radiography (JRCERT). **Total program enrollment:** 2868. **Application fee:** $30.

PROGRAM(S) OFFERED
• Allied Health Diagnostic, Intervention, and Treatment Professions, Other • Allied Health and Medical Assisting Services, Other *6 students enrolled* • Autobody/Collision and Repair Technology/Technician *19 students enrolled* • Automobile/Automotive Mechanics Technology/Technician *18 students enrolled* • Building/Construction Finishing, Management, and Inspection, Other *27 students enrolled* • Child Care Provider/Assistant *14 students enrolled* • Criminal Justice/Police Science *91 students enrolled* • Dental Assisting/Assistant *26 students enrolled* • Electrical, Electronic and Communications Engineering Technology/Technician • Electrician *13 students enrolled* • Emergency Medical Technology/Technician (EMT Paramedic) • Farm/Farm and Ranch Management • General Office Occupations and Clerical Services *13 students enrolled* • Hair Styling/Stylist and Hair Design *13 students enrolled* • Heating, Air Conditioning, Ventilation and Refrigeration Maintenance

Chippewa Valley Technical College (continued)

Technology/Technician (HAC, HACR, HVAC, HVACR) *13 students enrolled* • **Housing and Human Environments, Other** *48 students enrolled* • **Industrial Electronics Technology/Technician** • **Industrial Mechanics and Maintenance Technology** *11 students enrolled* • **Licensed Practical/Vocational Nurse Training (LPN, LVN, Cert, Dipl, AAS)** *90 students enrolled* • **Lineworker** *33 students enrolled* • **Massage Therapy/Therapeutic Massage** *19 students enrolled* • **Medical/Clinical Assistant** *45 students enrolled* • **Nurse/Nursing Assistant/Aide and Patient Care Assistant** • **Pharmacy Technician/Assistant** *13 students enrolled* • **Pipefitting/Pipefitter and Sprinkler Fitter** *1 student enrolled* • **Plumbing Technology/Plumber** *5 students enrolled* • **Renal/Dialysis Technologist/Technician** *12 students enrolled* • **Sheet Metal Technology/Sheetworking** *3 students enrolled* • **Small Engine Mechanics and Repair Technology/Technician** *19 students enrolled* • **Surgical Technology/Technologist** *12 students enrolled* • **Truck and Bus Driver/Commercial Vehicle Operation** *89 students enrolled* • **Welding Technology/Welder** *25 students enrolled*

STUDENT SERVICES Academic or career counseling, employment services for current students, placement services for program completers, remedial services.

College of Menominee Nation

PO Box 1179, Keshena, WI 54135
http://www.menominee.edu/

CONTACT Verna Fowler, President
Telephone: 715-799-5600

GENERAL INFORMATION Private Institution. Founded 1993. **Accreditation:** Regional (NCA). **Total program enrollment:** 268.

PROGRAM(S) OFFERED
• **Carpentry/Carpenter** • **Criminal Justice/Police Science** *1 student enrolled*

STUDENT SERVICES Academic or career counseling, remedial services.

Concordia University Wisconsin

12800 North Lake Shore Drive, Mequon, WI 53097-2402
http://www.cuw.edu/

CONTACT Patrick Ferry, President
Telephone: 262-243-5700

GENERAL INFORMATION Private Institution (Affiliated with Lutheran Church–Missouri Synod). Founded 1881. **Accreditation:** Regional (NCA). **Total program enrollment:** 3899. **Application fee:** $35.

PROGRAM(S) OFFERED
• **Allied Health and Medical Assisting Services, Other** *12 students enrolled* • **Theology and Religious Vocations, Other** *7 students enrolled*

STUDENT SERVICES Academic or career counseling, employment services for current students, placement services for program completers.

Empire Beauty School–Milwaukee

5655 South 27th Street, Milwaukee, WI 53221
http://www.empire.edu

CONTACT Michael Bouman, President/COO
Telephone: 920-684-3028

GENERAL INFORMATION Private Institution. **Total program enrollment:** 107. **Application fee:** $100.

PROGRAM(S) OFFERED
• **Cosmetology/Cosmetologist, General** *1800 hrs./$14,930*

STUDENT SERVICES Academic or career counseling.

Four Seasons Salon & Day Spa

128 W. 8th Street, Monroe, WI 53566

CONTACT Kristin Allison, President
Telephone: 608-329-7004

GENERAL INFORMATION Private Institution. **Total program enrollment:** 19.

PROGRAM(S) OFFERED
• **Cosmetology, Barber/Styling, and Nail Instructor** *150 hrs./$1500* • **Cosmetology/Cosmetologist, General** *1800 hrs./$9800* • **Nail Technician/Specialist and Manicurist** *300 hrs./$2650* • **Salon/Beauty Salon Management/Manager** *150 hrs./$1500*

STUDENT SERVICES Academic or career counseling, employment services for current students, placement services for program completers.

Fox Valley Technical College

1825 North Bluemound, PO Box 2277, Appleton, WI 54912-2277
http://www.fvtc.edu/

CONTACT Dr. Susan May, President
Telephone: 920-735-5600

GENERAL INFORMATION Public Institution. Founded 1967. **Accreditation:** Regional (NCA); dental assisting (ADA). **Total program enrollment:** 2571. **Application fee:** $30.

PROGRAM(S) OFFERED
• **Accounting Technology/Technician and Bookkeeping** *13 students enrolled* • **Agricultural Production Operations, General** *7 students enrolled* • **Applied Horticulture/Horticultural Business Services, Other** *15 students enrolled* • **Autobody/Collision and Repair Technology/Technician** *1 student enrolled* • **Automobile/Automotive Mechanics Technology/Technician** *4 students enrolled* • **Cabinetmaking and Millwork/Millwright** *11 students enrolled* • **Carpentry/Carpenter** *24 students enrolled* • **Criminal Justice/Police Science** *81 students enrolled* • **Dental Assisting/Assistant** *39 students enrolled* • **Electrician** *14 students enrolled* • **Emergency Medical Technology/Technician (EMT Paramedic)** *50 students enrolled* • **Food Preparation/Professional Cooking/Kitchen Assistant** *1 student enrolled* • **General Office Occupations and Clerical Services** *44 students enrolled* • **Heavy Equipment Maintenance Technology/Technician** *7 students enrolled* • **Hydraulics and Fluid Power Technology/Technician** *1 student enrolled* • **Licensed Practical/Vocational Nurse Training (LPN, LVN, Cert, Dipl, AAS)** *50 students enrolled* • **Machine Shop Technology/Assistant** *8 students enrolled* • **Medical Insurance Coding Specialist/Coder** *39 students enrolled* • **Medical Transcription/Transcriptionist** *16 students enrolled* • **Medical/Clinical Assistant** *14 students enrolled* • **Nurse/Nursing Assistant/Aide and Patient Care Assistant** *461 students enrolled* • **Printing Press Operator** *16 students enrolled* • **Small Engine Mechanics and Repair Technology/Technician** *7 students enrolled* • **Truck and Bus Driver/Commercial Vehicle Operation** *145 students enrolled* • **Vehicle Maintenance and Repair Technologies, Other** *9 students enrolled* • **Welding Technology/Welder** *3 students enrolled*

STUDENT SERVICES Academic or career counseling, daycare for children of students, employment services for current students, placement services for program completers, remedial services.

Gateway Technical College

3520 30th Avenue, Kenosha, WI 53144-1690
http://www.gtc.edu/

CONTACT Bryan Albrecht, President
Telephone: 262-564-2200

GENERAL INFORMATION Public Institution. Founded 1911. **Accreditation:** Regional (NCA); dental assisting (ADA); health information technology (AHIMA); physical therapy assisting (APTA); surgical technology (ARCST). **Total program enrollment:** 1824. **Application fee:** $30.

PROGRAM(S) OFFERED
• **Automobile/Automotive Mechanics Technology/Technician** *3 students enrolled* • **Building/Property Maintenance and Management** *5 students enrolled* • **Carpentry/Carpenter** • **Dental Assisting/Assistant** *9 students enrolled* • **Electrician** *8 students enrolled* • **Emergency Medical Technology/Technician (EMT Paramedic)** *169 students enrolled* • **General Office Occupations and Clerical**

Services *8 students enrolled* • Hair Styling/Stylist and Hair Design *48 students enrolled* • Health Unit Coordinator/Ward Clerk *23 students enrolled* • Industrial Electronics Technology/Technician • Industrial Mechanics and Maintenance Technology • Licensed Practical/Vocational Nurse Training (LPN, LVN, Cert, Dipl, AAS) *127 students enrolled* • Machine Tool Technology/Machinist • Mason/Masonry *1 student enrolled* • Mechanical Drafting and Mechanical Drafting CAD/CADD *1 student enrolled* • Medical Transcription/Transcriptionist *2 students enrolled* • Medical/Clinical Assistant *45 students enrolled* • Metal Building Assembly/Assembler *6 students enrolled* • Nurse/Nursing Assistant/Aide and Patient Care Assistant *689 students enrolled* • Nursing, Other *11 students enrolled* • Painting/Painter and Wall Coverer *1 student enrolled* • Pipefitting/Pipefitter and Sprinkler Fitter • Plumbing Technology/Plumber *12 students enrolled* • Welding Technology/Welder *9 students enrolled*

STUDENT SERVICES Academic or career counseling, daycare for children of students, employment services for current students, placement services for program completers, remedial services.

Gill-Tech Academy of Hair Design

423 West College Avenue, Appleton, WI 54911
http://www.gill-tech.com/

CONTACT Sheryl Bruemmer-Fisk, President
Telephone: 920-739-8684

GENERAL INFORMATION Private Institution. Founded 1984. **Total program enrollment: 94. Application fee:** $100.

PROGRAM(S) OFFERED
• Aesthetician/Esthetician and Skin Care Specialist *8 students enrolled* • Cosmetology/Cosmetologist, General *1800 hrs./$13,150* • Facial Treatment Specialist/Facialist *450 hrs./$4800* • Nail Technician/Specialist and Manicurist *300 hrs./$2350*

STUDENT SERVICES Academic or career counseling, placement services for program completers.

Herzing College

5218 East Terrace Drive, Madison, WI 53718
http://www.herzing.edu/madison

CONTACT Donald G. Madelung, President
Telephone: 800-582-1227

GENERAL INFORMATION Private Institution. Founded 1948. **Accreditation:** Regional (NCA); state accredited or approved. **Total program enrollment: 754. Application fee:** $25.

PROGRAM(S) OFFERED
• Medical Insurance Coding Specialist/Coder *160 students enrolled* • Medical Office Management/Administration *38 students enrolled* • Nursing—Registered Nurse Training (RN, ASN, BSN, MSN) *36 students enrolled* • Web Page, Digital/Multimedia and Information Resources Design

STUDENT SERVICES Academic or career counseling, employment services for current students, placement services for program completers, remedial services.

High-Tech Institute–Milwaukee

440 S. Executive Drive, Suite 200, Brookfield, WI 53005
http://www.hightechinstitute.edu/

CONTACT Jeff Engh, Operations Manager
Telephone: 262-373-7000

GENERAL INFORMATION Private Institution. Founded 2006. **Total program enrollment: 519. Application fee:** $50.

PROGRAM(S) OFFERED
• Massage Therapy/Therapeutic Massage *820 hrs./$11,383* • Medical Insurance Specialist/Medical Biller *1210 hrs./$23,336* • Medical/Clinical Assistant *746 hrs./$11,361* • Surgical Technology/Technologist *1620 hrs./$27,850*

STUDENT SERVICES Placement services for program completers.

The Institute of Beauty and Wellness

342 North Water Street, Milwaukee, WI 53202

CONTACT Susan Haise, Owner
Telephone: 414-227-2889

GENERAL INFORMATION Private Institution. **Total program enrollment: 94. Application fee:** $50.

PROGRAM(S) OFFERED
• Aesthetician/Esthetician and Skin Care Specialist *450 hrs./$3723* • Cosmetology/Cosmetologist, General *1800 hrs./$18,450* • Facial Treatment Specialist/Facialist *59 students enrolled* • Massage Therapy/Therapeutic Massage *600 hrs./$6681* • Nail Technician/Specialist and Manicurist *300 hrs./$1663*

STUDENT SERVICES Academic or career counseling, employment services for current students, placement services for program completers, remedial services.

Kaplan College–Milwaukee

111 W. Pleasant Street, Suite 101, Milwaukee, WI 53212

CONTACT Michael O'Herron, Executive Director
Telephone: 414-225-4600

GENERAL INFORMATION Private Institution. **Total program enrollment: 678.**

PROGRAM(S) OFFERED
• Computer Systems Analysis/Analyst *720 hrs./$12,420* • Dental Assisting/Assistant *900 hrs./$14,060* • Medical Office Assistant/Specialist *720 hrs./$13,060* • Medical/Clinical Assistant *720 hrs./$14,480* • Pharmacy Technician/Assistant *720 hrs./$13,750*

STUDENT SERVICES Academic or career counseling, employment services for current students, placement services for program completers, remedial services.

Lac Courte Oreilles Ojibwa Community College

13466 West Trepania Road, Hayward, WI 54843-2181
http://www.lco.edu/

CONTACT Danielle Hornett, President
Telephone: 715-634-4790 Ext. 100

GENERAL INFORMATION Public Institution. Founded 1982. **Accreditation:** Regional (NCA); medical assisting (AAMAE). **Total program enrollment: 317. Application fee:** $10.

PROGRAM(S) OFFERED
• Carpentry/Carpenter *1 student enrolled* • Child Care Provider/Assistant • Computer and Information Sciences, General *2 students enrolled* • Data Processing and Data Processing Technology/Technician • Hospitality and Recreation Marketing Operations *1 student enrolled* • Medical Transcription/Transcriptionist • Solar Energy Technology/Technician *2 students enrolled*

STUDENT SERVICES Academic or career counseling, remedial services.

Lakeshore Technical College

1290 North Avenue, Cleveland, WI 53015-1414
http://www.gotoltc.com/

CONTACT Michael Lanser, President
Telephone: 920-693-1000

GENERAL INFORMATION Public Institution. Founded 1967. **Accreditation:** Regional (NCA); dental hygiene (ADA); radiologic technology: radiography (JRCERT). **Total program enrollment: 858. Application fee:** $30.

Lakeshore Technical College (continued)

PROGRAM(S) OFFERED
• Autobody/Collision and Repair Technology/Technician 9 *students enrolled* • Automobile/Automotive Mechanics Technology/Technician 11 *students enrolled* • Carpentry/Carpenter 6 *students enrolled* • Child Care Provider/Assistant 6 *students enrolled* • Dairy Husbandry and Production 11 *students enrolled* • Dental Assisting/Assistant 16 *students enrolled* • Emergency Medical Technology/Technician (EMT Paramedic) 49 *students enrolled* • Farm/Farm and Ranch Management 10 *students enrolled* • General Office Occupations and Clerical Services 5 *students enrolled* • Health Unit Coordinator/Ward Clerk 22 *students enrolled* • Industrial Electronics Technology/Technician 8 *students enrolled* • Industrial Mechanics and Maintenance Technology 9 *students enrolled* • Licensed Practical/Vocational Nurse Training (LPN, LVN, Cert, Dipl, AAS) 63 *students enrolled* • Machine Shop Technology/Assistant 12 *students enrolled* • Machine Tool Technology/Machinist 11 *students enrolled* • Mason/Masonry 2 *students enrolled* • Medical Transcription/Transcriptionist 2 *students enrolled* • Medical/Clinical Assistant 18 *students enrolled* • Metal Building Assembly/Assembler 4 *students enrolled* • Nurse/Nursing Assistant/Aide and Patient Care Assistant 299 *students enrolled* • Nursing, Other 4 *students enrolled* • Pharmacy Technician/Assistant 8 *students enrolled* • Plumbing Technology/Plumber 2 *students enrolled* • Sheet Metal Technology/Sheetworking 1 *student enrolled* • Surgical Technology/Technologist 4 *students enrolled* • Tool and Die Technology/Technician 3 *students enrolled* • Welding Technology/Welder 13 *students enrolled*

STUDENT SERVICES Academic or career counseling, daycare for children of students, employment services for current students, placement services for program completers, remedial services.

Lakeside School of Massage Therapy

6101 Odana Road, Madison, WI 53719
http://www.lakeside.edu/

CONTACT Carole Ostendorf, CEO
Telephone: 414-372-4345

GENERAL INFORMATION Private Institution. Founded 1983. **Total program enrollment:** 45. **Application fee:** $25.

PROGRAM(S) OFFERED
• Massage Therapy/Therapeutic Massage 41 *hrs./$9794*

STUDENT SERVICES Academic or career counseling, placement services for program completers.

Madison Area Technical College

3550 Anderson Street, Madison, WI 53704-2599
http://www.matcmadison.edu/matc/

CONTACT Bettsey Barhorst, President
Telephone: 608-246-6100

GENERAL INFORMATION Public Institution. Founded 1911. **Accreditation:** Regional (NCA); dental hygiene (ADA); medical laboratory technology (NAACLS); optometric technology (AOA); radiologic technology: radiography (JRCERT). **Total program enrollment:** 5274. **Application fee:** $35.

PROGRAM(S) OFFERED
• Accounting Technology/Technician and Bookkeeping 18 *students enrolled* • Allied Health Diagnostic, Intervention, and Treatment Professions, Other 7 *students enrolled* • Applied Horticulture/Horticultural Operations, General 25 *students enrolled* • Autobody/Collision and Repair Technology/Technician 6 *students enrolled* • Baking and Pastry Arts/Baker/Pastry Chef 10 *students enrolled* • Building/Property Maintenance and Management 9 *students enrolled* • Carpentry/Carpenter 26 *students enrolled* • Computer and Information Sciences and Support Services, Other 9 *students enrolled* • Cosmetology and Related Personal Grooming Arts, Other 32 *students enrolled* • Criminal Justice/Police Science 86 *students enrolled* • Data Processing and Data Processing Technology/Technician 7 *students enrolled* • Dental Assisting/Assistant 24 *students enrolled* • Emergency Medical Technology/Technician (EMT Paramedic) 264 *students enrolled* • Fire Science/Firefighting 31 *students enrolled* • Graphic and Printing Equipment Operator, General Production 3 *students enrolled* • Housing and Human Environments, Other 23 *students enrolled* • Licensed Practical/Vocational Nurse Training (LPN, LVN, Cert, Dipl, AAS) 1096 *students enrolled* • Massage Therapy/Therapeutic Massage 19

• Medical Insurance Coding Specialist/Coder 13 *students enrolled* • Medical Transcription/Transcriptionist 25 *students enrolled* • Medical/Clinical Assistant 32 *students enrolled* • Nurse/Nursing Assistant/Aide and Patient Care Assistant 2 *students enrolled* • Optometric Technician/Assistant 9 *students enrolled* • Small Business Administration/Management 19 *students enrolled* • Small Engine Mechanics and Repair Technology/Technician 20 *students enrolled* • Surgical Technology/Technologist 15 *students enrolled* • Web Page, Digital/Multimedia and Information Resources Design 4 *students enrolled* • Welding Technology/Welder 16 *students enrolled*

STUDENT SERVICES Academic or career counseling, daycare for children of students, employment services for current students, placement services for program completers, remedial services.

Martin's School of Hair Design

2310 West College Avenue, Appleton, WI 54914
http://www.mcofc.com/

CONTACT Michael Bouman, President/COO
Telephone: 920-684-3028

GENERAL INFORMATION Private Institution. Founded 1992. **Total program enrollment:** 54. **Application fee:** $100.

PROGRAM(S) OFFERED
• Aesthetician/Esthetician and Skin Care Specialist 600 *hrs./$5700* • Cosmetology, Barber/Styling, and Nail Instructor 5 *students enrolled* • Cosmetology/Cosmetologist, General 1800 *hrs./$14,930* • Nail Technician/Specialist and Manicurist 2 *students enrolled*

STUDENT SERVICES Academic or career counseling.

Martin's School of Hair Design

2575 West Mason Street, Green Bay, WI 54304
http://www.mcofc.com/

CONTACT Michael Bouman, President/COO
Telephone: 920-684-3028

GENERAL INFORMATION Private Institution. Founded 1988. **Total program enrollment:** 102. **Application fee:** $100.

PROGRAM(S) OFFERED
• Aesthetician/Esthetician and Skin Care Specialist 600 *hrs./$5700* • Cosmetology, Barber/Styling, and Nail Instructor 2 *students enrolled* • Cosmetology/Cosmetologist, General 1800 *hrs./$14,930* • Massage Therapy/Therapeutic Massage 40 *students enrolled* • Nail Technician/Specialist and Manicurist 8 *students enrolled*

STUDENT SERVICES Academic or career counseling.

Martin's School of Hair Design

1034 South 18th Street, Manitowoc, WI 54220
http://www.mcofc.com/

CONTACT Michael Bouman, President/COO
Telephone: 920-684-3028

GENERAL INFORMATION Private Institution. Founded 1983. **Total program enrollment:** 99. **Application fee:** $100.

PROGRAM(S) OFFERED
• Aesthetician/Esthetician and Skin Care Specialist 41 *students enrolled* • Cosmetology, Barber/Styling, and Nail Instructor 11 *students enrolled* • Cosmetology/Cosmetologist, General 1800 *hrs./$14,930* • Nail Technician/Specialist and Manicurist 3 *students enrolled*

STUDENT SERVICES Academic or career counseling.

Martin's School of Hair Design

620 West Murdock Avenue, Oshkosh, WI 54901
http://www.mcofc.com/

CONTACT Michael Bouman, President/COO
Telephone: 920-684-3028

GENERAL INFORMATION Private Institution. Founded 1981. **Total program enrollment:** 57. **Application fee:** $100.

PROGRAM(S) OFFERED
• Cosmetology, Barber/Styling, and Nail Instructor *1 student enrolled*
• Cosmetology/Cosmetologist, General *1800 hrs./$14,930* • Nail Technician/Specialist and Manicurist

STUDENT SERVICES Academic or career counseling.

Mid-State Technical College

500 32nd Street North, Wisconsin Rapids, WI 54494-5599
http://www.mstc.edu/

CONTACT John Clark, President
Telephone: 715-422-5500

GENERAL INFORMATION Public Institution. Founded 1917. **Accreditation:** Regional (NCA). **Total program enrollment:** 1245. **Application fee:** $30.

PROGRAM(S) OFFERED
• Agricultural Production Operations, General *5 students enrolled* • Allied Health and Medical Assisting Services, Other *8 students enrolled* • Banking and Financial Support Services *2 students enrolled* • Business/Office Automation/Technology/Data Entry *8 students enrolled* • Carpentry/Carpenter *3 students enrolled* • Construction/Heavy Equipment/Earthmoving Equipment Operation *7 students enrolled* • Criminal Justice/Police Science *25 students enrolled* • Electrician *5 students enrolled* • Emergency Medical Technology/Technician (EMT Paramedic) *30 students enrolled* • Hair Styling/Stylist and Hair Design *21 students enrolled* • Health Unit Coordinator/Ward Clerk *12 students enrolled* • Industrial Mechanics and Maintenance Technology *1 student enrolled* • Ironworking/Ironworker *2 students enrolled* • Licensed Practical/Vocational Nurse Training (LPN, LVN, Cert, Dipl, AAS) *8 students enrolled* • Mason/Masonry *1 student enrolled* • Medical Transcription/Transcriptionist *8 students enrolled* • Medical/Clinical Assistant *35 students enrolled* • Metal Building Assembly/Assembler *2 students enrolled* • Nurse/Nursing Assistant/Aide and Patient Care Assistant *293 students enrolled* • Phlebotomy/Phlebotomist *20 students enrolled* • Pipefitting/Pipefitter and Sprinkler Fitter *4 students enrolled* • Plumbing Technology/Plumber *4 students enrolled* • Precision Systems Maintenance and Repair Technologies, Other *5 students enrolled* • Surgical Technology/Technologist *8 students enrolled* • Welding Technology/Welder *10 students enrolled*

STUDENT SERVICES Academic or career counseling, employment services for current students, placement services for program completers, remedial services.

Milwaukee Area Technical College

700 West State Street, Milwaukee, WI 53233-1443
http://www.matc.edu/

CONTACT Darnell E. Cole, President
Telephone: 414-297-6370

GENERAL INFORMATION Public Institution. Founded 1912. **Accreditation:** Regional (NCA); cardiovascular technology (JRCECT); dental hygiene (ADA); funeral service (ABFSE); medical laboratory technology (NAA-CLS); ophthalmic dispensing (COA); physical therapy assisting (APTA); practical nursing (NLN); radiologic technology: radiography (JRCERT); surgical technology (ARCST). **Total program enrollment:** 6042. **Application fee:** $30.

PROGRAM(S) OFFERED
• Accounting Technology/Technician and Bookkeeping *8 students enrolled*
• Aircraft Powerplant Technology/Technician *2 students enrolled* • Airframe Mechanics and Aircraft Maintenance Technology/Technician *3 students enrolled*
• Allied Health Diagnostic, Intervention, and Treatment Professions, Other
• Appliance Installation and Repair Technology/Technician *7 students enrolled*
• Autobody/Collision and Repair Technology/Technician *19 students enrolled*
• Automobile/Automotive Mechanics Technology/Technician *28 students enrolled* • Baking and Pastry Arts/Baker/Pastry Chef • Building/Construction Finishing, Management, and Inspection, Other • Cabinetmaking and Millwork/Millwright • Carpentry/Carpenter *28 students enrolled* • Child Care and Support Services Management • Communications Systems Installation and Repair Technology • Concrete Finishing/Concrete Finisher • Cosmetology and Related Personal Grooming Arts, Other • Culinary Arts/Chef Training *8 students enrolled* • Dental Assisting/Assistant *33 students enrolled* • Dental Laboratory Technology/Technician *14 students enrolled* • Diesel Mechanics Technology/Technician *10 students enrolled* • Drywall Installation/Drywaller • Electrical and Power Transmission Installation/Installer, General *1 student enrolled* • Electrician • Emergency Medical Technology/Technician (EMT Paramedic) *95 students enrolled* • Engineering Technologies/Technicians, Other • Foods, Nutrition, and Related Services, Other • Foodservice Systems Administration/Management • General Office Occupations and Clerical Services *6 students enrolled* • Glazier • Graphic Communications, Other • Graphic and Printing Equipment Operator, General Production *2 students enrolled* • Hair Styling/Stylist and Hair Design *38 students enrolled* • Health Unit Coordinator/Ward Clerk *21 students enrolled* • Heating, Air Conditioning, Ventilation and Refrigeration Maintenance Technology/Technician (HAC, HACR, HVAC, HVACR) *29 students enrolled* • Heavy Equipment Maintenance Technology/Technician • Human Development, Family Studies, and Related Services, Other • Industrial Electronics Technology/Technician *7 students enrolled* • Industrial Mechanics and Maintenance Technology • Language Interpretation and Translation *1 student enrolled* • Licensed Practical/Vocational Nurse Training (LPN, LVN, Cert, Dipl, AAS) *139 students enrolled* • Lineworker *13 students enrolled* • Machine Shop Technology/Assistant *14 students enrolled* • Machine Tool Technology/Machinist • Mason/Masonry *1 student enrolled* • Mechanic and Repair Technologies/Technicians, Other *10 students enrolled* • Mechanical Drafting and Mechanical Drafting CAD/CADD *1 student enrolled* • Medical Insurance Coding Specialist/Coder *17 students enrolled* • Medical/Clinical Assistant *15 students enrolled* • Metal Building Assembly/Assembler • Nurse/Nursing Assistant/Aide and Patient Care Assistant *264 students enrolled* • Opticianry/Ophthalmic Dispensing Optician *2 students enrolled* • Optometric Technician/Assistant • Painting/Painter and Wall Coverer *14 students enrolled* • Personal and Culinary Services, Other *1 student enrolled* • Pharmacy Technician/Assistant • Phlebotomy/Phlebotomist *32 students enrolled* • Pipefitting/Pipefitter and Sprinkler Fitter *10 students enrolled* • Plumbing and Related Water Supply Services, Other *7 students enrolled* • Renal/Dialysis Technologist/Technician *11 students enrolled* • Roofer • Small Business Administration/Management *9 students enrolled* • Tool and Die Technology/Technician *1 student enrolled* • Tourism and Travel Services Management *2 students enrolled* • Welding Technology/Welder *25 students enrolled*

STUDENT SERVICES Academic or career counseling, daycare for children of students, employment services for current students, placement services for program completers, remedial services.

Milwaukee Career College

3077 N. Mayfair Road, Suite 300, Milwaukee, WI 53222
http://www.mkecc.edu

CONTACT Jack Takahashi, President
Telephone: 414-257-2939

GENERAL INFORMATION Private Institution. **Total program enrollment:** 136. **Application fee:** $20.

PROGRAM(S) OFFERED
• Computer Installation and Repair Technology/Technician *650 hrs./$4800*
• Computer Systems Networking and Telecommunications *140 hrs./$1730*
• Customer Service Support/Call Center/Teleservice Operation *320 hrs./$2550*
• Medical Insurance Coding Specialist/Coder *720 hrs./$10,800* • Medical/Clinical Assistant *720 hrs./$11,747* • Pharmacy Technician/Assistant *720 hrs./$10,800*

STUDENT SERVICES Academic or career counseling, employment services for current students, placement services for program completers.

Moraine Park Technical College

235 North National Avenue, PO Box 1940, Fond du Lac, WI
54936-1940
http://www.morainepark.edu/

CONTACT Dr. Gayle Hytrek, President
Telephone: 920-922-8611

GENERAL INFORMATION Public Institution. Founded 1967. **Accreditation:**
Regional (NCA); health information technology (AHIMA); practical
nursing (NLN). **Total program enrollment:** 1287. **Application fee:** $30.

PROGRAM(S) OFFERED
• Accounting Technology/Technician and Bookkeeping 5 students enrolled • Applied Horticulture/Horticultural Business Services, Other • Autobody/Collision and Repair Technology/Technician • Automobile/Automotive Mechanics Technology/Technician • Blood Bank Technology Specialist • Building/Property Maintenance and Management 75 students enrolled • Business Operations Support and Secretarial Services, Other • Business and Personal/Financial Services Marketing Operations • Cabinetmaking and Millwork/Millwright 14 students enrolled • Child Care and Support Services Management 1 student enrolled • Chiropractic Assistant/Technician • Computer Engineering, Other • Computer Systems Networking and Telecommunications • Computer and Information Sciences and Support Services, Other • Construction Trades, Other • Cosmetology/Cosmetologist, General 9 students enrolled • Data Entry/Microcomputer Applications, Other • Dental Laboratory Technology/Technician 6 students enrolled • Electrical and Power Transmission Installation/Installer, General 31 students enrolled • Emergency Medical Technology/Technician (EMT Paramedic) • Environmental Control Technologies/Technicians, Other • Food Preparation/Professional Cooking/Kitchen Assistant 1 student enrolled • General Merchandising, Sales, and Related Marketing Operations, Other • General Office Occupations and Clerical Services 7 students enrolled • Health Information/Medical Records Technology/Technician • Health and Medical Administrative Services, Other • Heating, Air Conditioning and Refrigeration Technology/Technician (ACH/ACR/ACHR/HRAC/HVAC/AC Technology) 14 students enrolled • Heating, Air Conditioning, Ventilation and Refrigeration Maintenance Technology/Technician (HAC, HACR, HVAC, HVACR) • Human Development, Family Studies, and Related Services, Other • Human Resources Management/Personnel Administration, General • Institutional Food Workers • Landscaping and Groundskeeping • Legal Administrative Assistant/Secretary • Licensed Practical/Vocational Nurse Training (LPN, LVN, Cert, Dipl, AAS) 69 students enrolled • Lineworker 14 students enrolled • Machine Shop Technology/Assistant • Machine Tool Technology/Machinist 12 students enrolled • Management Information Systems and Services, Other • Management Sciences and Quantitative Methods, Other • Marine Maintenance/Fitter and Ship Repair Technology/Technician 5 students enrolled • Marketing, Other • Mason/Masonry 31 students enrolled • Mechanical Drafting and Mechanical Drafting CAD/CADD 7 students enrolled • Medical Office Assistant/Specialist 16 students enrolled • Medical Office Computer Specialist/Assistant 30 students enrolled • Medical Transcription/Transcriptionist 11 students enrolled • Medication Aide 10 students enrolled • Nail Technician/Specialist and Manicurist • Nurse/Nursing Assistant/Aide and Patient Care Assistant 242 students enrolled • Quality Control and Safety Technologies/Technicians, Other • Salon/Beauty Salon Management/Manager • Technical and Business Writing • Vehicle Maintenance and Repair Technologies, Other • Water Quality and Wastewater Treatment Management and Recycling Technology/Technician • Web Page, Digital/Multimedia and Information Resources Design 5 students enrolled • Web/Multimedia Management and Webmaster • Welding Technology/Welder 36 students enrolled

STUDENT SERVICES Academic or career counseling, employment
services for current students, placement services for program completers,
remedial services.

Nicolet Area Technical College

Box 518, Rhinelander, WI 54501-0518
http://www.nicoletcollege.edu/

CONTACT Adrian Lorbetske, President
Telephone: 715-365-4410

GENERAL INFORMATION Public Institution. Founded 1968. **Accreditation:**
Regional (NCA). **Total program enrollment:** 555. **Application fee:** $30.

PROGRAM(S) OFFERED
• Accounting and Related Services, Other 8 students enrolled • Automobile/Automotive Mechanics Technology/Technician 6 students enrolled • Business Administration and Management, General 7 students enrolled • Business

Administration, Management and Operations, Other • Child Care and Support Services Management 28 students enrolled • Emergency Medical Technology/Technician (EMT Paramedic) 72 students enrolled • Food Preparation/Professional Cooking/Kitchen Assistant 11 students enrolled • General Office Occupations and Clerical Services 8 students enrolled • Hair Styling/Stylist and Hair Design 6 students enrolled • Information Technology 1 student enrolled • Licensed Practical/Vocational Nurse Training (LPN, LVN, Cert, Dipl, AAS) 25 students enrolled • Marketing/Marketing Management, General 2 students enrolled • Medical/Clinical Assistant 15 students enrolled • Nurse/Nursing Assistant/Aide and Patient Care Assistant 117 students enrolled • Nursing, Other 5 students enrolled • Receptionist 9 students enrolled • Small Engine Mechanics and Repair Technology/Technician 1 student enrolled • Welding Technology/Welder 9 students enrolled

STUDENT SERVICES Academic or career counseling, daycare for children
of students, employment services for current students, placement services
for program completers, remedial services.

Northcentral Technical College

1000 West Campus Drive, Wausau, WI 54401-1899
http://www.ntc.edu/

CONTACT Dr. Lori Weyers, President
Telephone: 715-675-3331

GENERAL INFORMATION Public Institution. Founded 1912. **Accreditation:**
Regional (NCA); dental hygiene (ADA); radiologic technology:
radiography (JRCERT). **Total program enrollment:** 1401. **Application fee:**
$30.

PROGRAM(S) OFFERED
• Accounting Technology/Technician and Bookkeeping • Accounting 14 students enrolled • Agricultural Mechanics and Equipment/Machine Technology 1 student enrolled • Autobody/Collision and Repair Technology/Technician 6 students enrolled • Automobile/Automotive Mechanics Technology/Technician 7 students enrolled • Building/Construction Finishing, Management, and Inspection, Other 20 students enrolled • Criminal Justice/Police Science 18 students enrolled • Data Entry/Microcomputer Applications, General 1 student enrolled • Emergency Medical Technology/Technician (EMT Paramedic) 113 students enrolled • General Office Occupations and Clerical Services 9 students enrolled • Heating, Air Conditioning, Ventilation and Refrigeration Maintenance Technology/Technician (HAC, HACR, HVAC, HVACR) 2 students enrolled • Licensed Practical/Vocational Nurse Training (LPN, LVN, Cert, Dipl, AAS) 105 students enrolled • Machine Shop Technology/Assistant 17 students enrolled • Medical Insurance Coding Specialist/Coder 23 students enrolled • Medical Transcription/Transcriptionist 9 students enrolled • Medical/Clinical Assistant 19 students enrolled • Nurse/Nursing Assistant/Aide and Patient Care Assistant 391 students enrolled • Surgical Technology/Technologist 13 students enrolled • Welding Technology/Welder 31 students enrolled

STUDENT SERVICES Academic or career counseling, daycare for children
of students, employment services for current students, placement services
for program completers, remedial services.

Northeast Wisconsin Technical College

2740 W Mason Street, PO Box 19042, Green Bay, WI 54307-9042
http://www.nwtc.edu/

CONTACT H. Jeffery Rafn, President
Telephone: 920-498-5400

GENERAL INFORMATION Public Institution. Founded 1913. **Accreditation:**
Regional (NCA); dental assisting (ADA); dental hygiene (ADA);
engineering technology (ABET/TAC); health information administration
(AHIMA); health information technology (AHIMA); medical laboratory technology (NAACLS); physical therapy assisting (APTA). **Total
program enrollment:** 2664. **Application fee:** $30.

PROGRAM(S) OFFERED
• Building/Construction Finishing, Management, and Inspection, Other 8 students enrolled • Computer and Information Sciences and Support Services, Other 2 students enrolled • Criminal Justice/Police Science 26 students enrolled • Dental Assisting/Assistant 17 students enrolled • Electrician 15 students enrolled • Emergency Medical Technology/Technician (EMT Paramedic) 112 students enrolled • Farm/Farm and Ranch Management 14 students enrolled • General Office Occupations and Clerical Services 23 students enrolled

- Graphic and Printing Equipment Operator, General Production 7 *students enrolled* • Industrial Mechanics and Maintenance Technology 6 *students enrolled* • Licensed Practical/Vocational Nurse Training (LPN, LVN, Cert, Dipl, AAS) 171 *students enrolled* • Lineworker 33 *students enrolled* • Machine Shop Technology/Assistant 36 *students enrolled* • Mechanic and Repair Technologies/Technicians, Other • Medical/Clinical Assistant 33 *students enrolled* • Nurse/Nursing Assistant/Aide and Patient Care Assistant 691 *students enrolled* • Nursing, Other 12 *students enrolled* • Surgical Technology/Technologist 43 *students enrolled* • Watchmaking and Jewelrymaking 9 *students enrolled* • Welding Technology/Welder 54 *students enrolled*

STUDENT SERVICES Academic or career counseling, employment services for current students, placement services for program completers, remedial services.

Ottawa University–Milwaukee

245 South Executive Drive, Suite 110, Brookfield, WI 53005
http://www.ottawa.edu/

CONTACT Robin Ware, Campus Executive Officer
Telephone: 262-879-0200

GENERAL INFORMATION Private Institution (Affiliated with American Baptist Churches in the U.S.A.). **Total program enrollment: 14.** **Application fee:** $50.

STUDENT SERVICES Academic or career counseling.

Philadelphia Biblical University–Wisconsin Wilderness Campus

HC 60, Box 60, Cable, WI 54821
http://www.pbu.edu/programs/wwc/

CONTACT Mark Jalovick, Director
Telephone: 715-798-3525

GENERAL INFORMATION Private Institution. **Total program enrollment: 32.** **Application fee:** $25.

PROGRAM(S) OFFERED
- Bible/Biblical Studies 34 *students enrolled*

STUDENT SERVICES Academic or career counseling, employment services for current students.

Professional Hair Design Academy

3408 Mall Drive, Eau Claire, WI 54701-7633
http://www.phdacademy.com/

CONTACT William Rauckman, Chief Executive Officer
Telephone: 715-835-2345

GENERAL INFORMATION Private Institution. **Total program enrollment: 69.**

PROGRAM(S) OFFERED
- Cosmetology and Related Personal Grooming Arts, Other 288 *hrs./*$1900
- Cosmetology, Barber/Styling, and Nail Instructor 150 *hrs./*$800
- Cosmetology/Cosmetologist, General 1800 *hrs./*$11,091 • Massage Therapy/Therapeutic Massage 630 *hrs./*$6300 • Nail Technician/Specialist and Manicurist 300 *hrs./*$1700

STUDENT SERVICES Academic or career counseling, employment services for current students, placement services for program completers.

Rasmussen College Green Bay

940 South Taylor Street, Suite 100, Green Bay, WI 54303
http://www.rasmussen.edu/

CONTACT Scott Borley, Campus Director
Telephone: 920-593-8400

GENERAL INFORMATION Private Institution. **Total program enrollment: 254.** **Application fee:** $60.

PROGRAM(S) OFFERED
- Child Care and Support Services Management • Massage Therapy/Therapeutic Massage • Medical Insurance Coding Specialist/Coder • Medical Transcription/Transcriptionist

STUDENT SERVICES Academic or career counseling, employment services for current students, placement services for program completers, remedial services.

Regency Beauty Institute–Greenfield

7995 West Layton Avenue, Greenfield, WI 53220

GENERAL INFORMATION Private Institution. **Total program enrollment: 54.** **Application fee:** $100.

PROGRAM(S) OFFERED
- Cosmetology/Cosmetologist, General 1799 *hrs./*$16,011

STUDENT SERVICES Academic or career counseling, placement services for program completers.

Regency Beauty Institute–Madison

2358 East Springs Drive, Madison, WI 53704
http://www.regencybeauty.com

CONTACT J. Hayes Batson, President
Telephone: 608-819-0469

GENERAL INFORMATION Private Institution. **Total program enrollment: 90.** **Application fee:** $100.

PROGRAM(S) OFFERED
- Cosmetology/Cosmetologist, General 1799 *hrs./*$16,011

STUDENT SERVICES Academic or career counseling, placement services for program completers.

St. Luke's Medical Center–School of Diagnostic Medical Sonography

2900 West Oklahoma Avenue, Milwaukee, WI 53215
http://www.aurorahealthcare.org/

CONTACT Laura Sorenson, Program Director
Telephone: 414-747-4360

GENERAL INFORMATION Private Institution. **Total program enrollment: 9.** **Application fee:** $25.

PROGRAM(S) OFFERED
- Diagnostic Medical Sonography/Sonographer and Ultrasound Technician 7 *students enrolled*

The Salon Professional Academy

3355 W. College Avenue, Appleton, WI 54915

CONTACT Josif Wittnik, President
Telephone: 920-968-0433

GENERAL INFORMATION Private Institution. **Total program enrollment: 86.**

The Salon Professional Academy (continued)

PROGRAM(S) OFFERED
- **Aesthetician/Esthetician and Skin Care Specialist** *450 hrs./$4990*
- **Cosmetology and Related Personal Grooming Arts, Other** *1800 hrs./$13,000*
- **Cosmetology/Cosmetologist, General** *43 students enrolled* ● **Nail Technician/ Specialist and Manicurist** *300 hrs./$2890*

Sanford-Brown College

6737 West Washington Street, Suite 2355, West Allis, WI 53214
http://www.sanford-brown.edu/

CONTACT Steve Guell, Chief Administrator
Telephone: 414-771-2200

GENERAL INFORMATION Private Institution. **Total program enrollment:** 748. **Application fee:** $35.

PROGRAM(S) OFFERED
- **Medical Insurance Coding Specialist/Coder** *105 students enrolled* ● **Medical/ Clinical Assistant** *198 students enrolled*

STUDENT SERVICES Academic or career counseling, employment services for current students, placement services for program completers.

Southwest Wisconsin Technical College

1800 Bronson Boulevard, Fennimore, WI 53809-9778
http://www.swtc.edu/

CONTACT Karen R. Knox, President
Telephone: 608-822-3262

GENERAL INFORMATION Public Institution. Founded 1967. **Accreditation:** Regional (NCA). **Total program enrollment:** 811. **Application fee:** $30.

PROGRAM(S) OFFERED
- **Accounting Technology/Technician and Bookkeeping** *9 students enrolled*
- **Aesthetician/Esthetician and Skin Care Specialist** *8 students enrolled*
- **Autobody/Collision and Repair Technology/Technician** *17 students enrolled*
- **Business/Office Automation/Technology/Data Entry** *7 students enrolled*
- **Carpentry/Carpenter** *8 students enrolled* ● **Child Care Provider/Assistant** *6 students enrolled* ● **Criminal Justice/Police Science** *20 students enrolled* ● **Dairy Husbandry and Production** *8 students enrolled* ● **Dental Assisting/Assistant** *16 students enrolled* ● **Electrician** *3 students enrolled* ● **Engine Machinist** *11 students enrolled* ● **Farm/Farm and Ranch Management** *23 students enrolled* ● **General Office Occupations and Clerical Services** *16 students enrolled* ● **Hair Styling/ Stylist and Hair Design** *22 students enrolled* ● **Industrial Electronics Technology/Technician** *7 students enrolled* ● **Industrial Mechanics and Maintenance Technology** *1 student enrolled* ● **Licensed Practical/Vocational Nurse Training (LPN, LVN, Cert, Dipl, AAS)** *51 students enrolled* ● **Machine Shop Technology/Assistant** *9 students enrolled* ● **Mason/Masonry** *12 students enrolled* ● **Medical Insurance Coding Specialist/Coder** *41 students enrolled* ● **Medical Transcription/Transcriptionist** *12 students enrolled* ● **Medical/Clinical Assistant** *30 students enrolled* ● **Nurse/Nursing Assistant/Aide and Patient Care Assistant** *235 students enrolled* ● **Plumbing Technology/Plumber** *5 students enrolled* ● **Welding Technology/Welder** *23 students enrolled*

STUDENT SERVICES Academic or career counseling, daycare for children of students, employment services for current students, placement services for program completers, remedial services.

State College of Beauty Culture

527½ Washington Street, Wausau, WI 54403
http://www.statecollegeofbeauty.com/

CONTACT Andrea L. Burns, President
Telephone: 715-845-2888

GENERAL INFORMATION Private Institution. Founded 1967. **Total program enrollment:** 58. **Application fee:** $100.

PROGRAM(S) OFFERED
- **Aesthetician/Esthetician and Skin Care Specialist** *600 hrs./$6200*
- **Cosmetology/Cosmetologist, General** *1800 hrs./$11,500* ● **Nail Technician/ Specialist and Manicurist** *300 hrs./$3000*

STUDENT SERVICES Academic or career counseling, employment services for current students, placement services for program completers.

University of Phoenix–Wisconsin Campus

20075 Watertower Boulevard, Brookfield, WI 53045-6608
http://www.phoenix.edu/

CONTACT William Pepicello, PhD, President
Telephone: 262-785-0608

GENERAL INFORMATION Private Institution. Founded 2001. **Accreditation:** Regional (NCA). **Total program enrollment:** 476.

STUDENT SERVICES Academic or career counseling, remedial services.

University of Wisconsin–La Crosse

1725 State Street, La Crosse, WI 54601-3742
http://www.uwlax.edu/

CONTACT Joe Gow, Chancellor
Telephone: 608-785-8000

GENERAL INFORMATION Public Institution. Founded 1909. **Accreditation:** Regional (NCA); athletic training (JRCAT); medical technology (NAACLS); music (NASM); public health: community health education (CEPH); radiologic technology: radiation therapy technology (JRCERT); recreation and parks (NRPA). **Total program enrollment:** 8676. **Application fee:** $44.

STUDENT SERVICES Academic or career counseling, daycare for children of students, employment services for current students, placement services for program completers, remedial services.

University of Wisconsin–Parkside

900 Wood Road, Box 2000, Kenosha, WI 53141-2000
http://www.uwp.edu/

CONTACT Lane Earns, Interim Chancellor
Telephone: 262-595-2573

GENERAL INFORMATION Public Institution. Founded 1968. **Accreditation:** Regional (NCA). **Total program enrollment:** 3696. **Application fee:** $44.

STUDENT SERVICES Academic or career counseling, daycare for children of students, employment services for current students, placement services for program completers, remedial services.

University of Wisconsin–Stout

Menomonie, WI 54751
http://www.uwstout.edu/

CONTACT Charles Sorensen, Chancellor
Telephone: 715-232-1431

GENERAL INFORMATION Public Institution. Founded 1891. **Accreditation:** Regional (NCA); art and design (NASAD); dietetics: postbaccalaureate internship (ADtA/CAADE); interior design: professional (CIDA). **Total program enrollment:** 7141. **Application fee:** $44.

STUDENT SERVICES Academic or career counseling, daycare for children of students, employment services for current students, placement services for program completers, remedial services.

University of Wisconsin–Superior

Belknap and Catlin, PO Box 2000, Superior, WI 54880-4500
http://www.uwsuper.edu/

CONTACT Julius E. Erlenbach, Chancellor
Telephone: 715-394-8101

GENERAL INFORMATION Public Institution. Founded 1893. **Accreditation:** Regional (NCA); counseling (ACA); music (NASM). **Total program enrollment:** 2035. **Application fee:** $44.

STUDENT SERVICES Academic or career counseling, daycare for children of students, employment services for current students, placement services for program completers, remedial services.

University of Wisconsin System

1220 Linden Dr, 1720 Van Hise Hall, Madison, WI 53706-1559
http://www.uwsa.edu/

CONTACT Kevin Reilly, President
Telephone: 608-262-1234

GENERAL INFORMATION Public Institution. **Accreditation:** Regional (NCA).

Waukesha County Technical College

800 Main Street, Pewaukee, WI 53072-4601
http://www.wctc.edu/

CONTACT Barbara Prindiville, PhD, President
Telephone: 262-691-5566

GENERAL INFORMATION Public Institution. Founded 1923. **Accreditation:** Regional (NCA); dental hygiene (ADA); surgical technology (ARCST). **Total program enrollment:** 2128. **Application fee:** $30.

PROGRAM(S) OFFERED
• Allied Health and Medical Assisting Services, Other 6 students enrolled • Autobody/Collision and Repair Technology/Technician • Automobile/Automotive Mechanics Technology/Technician 10 students enrolled • Building/Property Maintenance and Management 12 students enrolled • CAD/CADD Drafting and/or Design Technology/Technician 5 students enrolled • Carpentry/Carpenter 20 students enrolled • Computer Programming/Programmer, General • Computer Software and Media Applications, Other 2 students enrolled • Computer Technology/Computer Systems Technology • Concrete Finishing/Concrete Finisher 1 student enrolled • Criminal Justice/Police Science 46 students enrolled • Data Processing and Data Processing Technology/Technician 1 student enrolled • Dental Assisting/Assistant 17 students enrolled • Electrician • Emergency Medical Technology/Technician (EMT Paramedic) 156 students enrolled • Fire Science/Firefighting 1 student enrolled • Food Preparation/Professional Cooking/Kitchen Assistant 2 students enrolled • General Office Occupations and Clerical Services 5 students enrolled • Graphic and Printing Equipment Operator, General Production 1 student enrolled • Hair Styling/Stylist and Hair Design 27 students enrolled • Health Unit Coordinator/Ward Clerk 13 students enrolled • Heating, Air Conditioning, Ventilation and Refrigeration Maintenance Technology/Technician (HAC, HACR, HVAC, HVACR) • Industrial Electronics Technology/Technician 1 student enrolled • Industrial Mechanics and Maintenance Technology 13 students enrolled • Information Technology 10 students enrolled • Language Interpretation and Translation 11 students enrolled • Licensed Practical/Vocational Nurse Training (LPN, LVN, Cert, Dipl, AAS) 72 students enrolled • Machine Shop Technology/Assistant 1 student enrolled • Machine Tool Technology/Machinist 4 students enrolled • Manufacturing Technology/Technician 4 students enrolled • Mason/Masonry 1 student enrolled • Medical Insurance Coding Specialist/Coder 30 students enrolled • Medical Transcription/Transcriptionist 7 students enrolled • Medical/Clinical Assistant 30 students enrolled • Nurse/Nursing Assistant/Aide and Patient Care Assistant 331 students enrolled • Operations Management and Supervision 9 students enrolled • Phlebotomy/Phlebotomist 16 students enrolled • Plumbing Technology/Plumber • Precision Production, Other 9 students enrolled • Tool and Die Technology/Technician 13 students enrolled • Truck and Bus Driver/Commercial Vehicle Operation 26 students enrolled • Welding Technology/Welder 19 students enrolled

STUDENT SERVICES Academic or career counseling, daycare for children of students, employment services for current students, placement services for program completers, remedial services.

Western Technical College

304 6th Street North, PO Box C-908, La Crosse, WI 54602-0908
http://www.westerntc.edu/

CONTACT J. Lee Rasch, EdD, President, District Director
Telephone: 608-785-9200

GENERAL INFORMATION Public Institution. Founded 1911. **Accreditation:** Regional (NCA); dental assisting (ADA); electroneurodiagnostic technology (JRCEND); health information technology (AHIMA); medical laboratory technology (NAACLS); physical therapy assisting (APTA); radiologic technology: radiography (JRCERT). **Total program enrollment:** 1837. **Application fee:** $30.

PROGRAM(S) OFFERED
• Accounting Technology/Technician and Bookkeeping 2 students enrolled • Building/Construction Finishing, Management, and Inspection, Other 15 students enrolled • Computer and Information Sciences and Support Services, Other 3 students enrolled • Criminal Justice/Law Enforcement Administration 13 students enrolled • Dental Assisting/Assistant 15 students enrolled • Emergency Medical Technology/Technician (EMT Paramedic) 49 students enrolled • Farm/Farm and Ranch Management • Food Preparation/Professional Cooking/Kitchen Assistant 5 students enrolled • General Office Occupations and Clerical Services 11 students enrolled • Health Information/Medical Records Technology/Technician 12 students enrolled • Heating, Air Conditioning, Ventilation and Refrigeration Maintenance Technology/Technician (HAC, HACR, HVAC, HVACR) 11 students enrolled • Industrial Mechanics and Maintenance Technology 12 students enrolled • Licensed Practical/Vocational Nurse Training (LPN, LVN, Cert, Dipl, AAS) 59 students enrolled • Machine Shop Technology/Assistant 4 students enrolled • Massage Therapy/Therapeutic Massage 16 students enrolled • Medical Staff Services Technology/Technician 11 students enrolled • Medical/Clinical Assistant 37 students enrolled • Nurse/Nursing Assistant/Aide and Patient Care Assistant 446 students enrolled • Surgical Technology/Technologist 16 students enrolled • Teacher Assistant/Aide • Welding Technology/Welder 24 students enrolled

STUDENT SERVICES Academic or career counseling, daycare for children of students, employment services for current students, placement services for program completers, remedial services.

Wisconsin Indianhead Technical College

505 Pine Ridge Drive, Shell Lake, WI 54871
http://www.witc.edu/

CONTACT Bob Meyer, President
Telephone: 715-468-2815

GENERAL INFORMATION Public Institution. Founded 1912. **Accreditation:** Regional (NCA). **Total program enrollment:** 1556. **Application fee:** $30.

PROGRAM(S) OFFERED
• Accounting Technology/Technician and Bookkeeping 23 students enrolled • Aesthetician/Esthetician and Skin Care Specialist 15 students enrolled • Autobody/Collision and Repair Technology/Technician 10 students enrolled • Automobile/Automotive Mechanics Technology/Technician 21 students enrolled • Building/Construction Finishing, Management, and Inspection, Other 2 students enrolled • Business/Office Automation/Technology/Data Entry 27 students enrolled • Communications Systems Installation and Repair Technology 6 students enrolled • Computer Installation and Repair Technology/Technician 2 students enrolled • Dairy Husbandry and Production 9 students enrolled • Emergency Medical Technology/Technician (EMT Paramedic) 155 students enrolled • Farm/Farm and Ranch Management 10 students enrolled • Hair Styling/Stylist and Hair Design 4 students enrolled • Industrial Mechanics and Maintenance Technology 2 students enrolled • Licensed Practical/Vocational Nurse Training (LPN, LVN, Cert, Dipl, AAS) 64 students enrolled • Machine Shop Technology/Assistant 4 students enrolled • Mason/Masonry 2 students enrolled • Massage Therapy/Therapeutic Massage 44 students enrolled • Medical/Clinical Assistant 49 students enrolled • Nurse/Nursing Assistant/Aide and Patient Care Assistant 829 students enrolled • Plumbing Technology/Plumber 9 students enrolled • Small Engine Mechanics and Repair Technology/Technician 14 students enrolled • Welding Technology/Welder 45 students enrolled

STUDENT SERVICES Academic or career counseling, employment services for current students, placement services for program completers, remedial services.

Appendixes

State Offices of Apprenticeship Contacts

Alabama

Gregory Collins
State Director
USDOL/ETA/OA
Medical Forum Building
Room 648
950 22nd Street North
Birmingham, AL 35203
205-731-1308
E-mail: collins.gregory@dol.gov

Alaska

John Hakala
State Director
USDOL/ETA/OA
605 West 4th Avenue, Room G-30
Anchorage, AK 99501
907-271-5035
E-mail: hakala.john@dol.gov

Arizona

Colleen Henry
Acting State Director
USDOL/ETA/OA
230 North 1st Avenue, Suite 510
Phoenix, AZ 85025
602-514-7007
E-mail: henry.colleen@dol.gov

Arkansas

Donald E. Reese
State Director
USDOL/ETA/OA
Federal Building, Room 3507
700 West Capitol Street
Little Rock, AR 72201-3204
501-324-5415
E-mail: reese.donald@dol.gov

California

Rick Davis
State Director
USDOL/ETA/OA
2800 Cottage Way
Room W-1836
Sacramento, CA 95825-1846
916-978-4618
E-mail: davis.richard@dol.gov

Colorado

Charles J. Noon (John)
State Director
USDOL/ETA/OA
U.S. Custom House
721 19th Street, Room 465
Denver, CO 80202-2517
303-844-6362
E-mail: noon.charles@dol.gov

Florida

Nora Carlton
Acting State Director
USDOL/ETA/OA
400 West Bay Street, Suite 934
Jacksonville, FL 32202-4446
904-359-9252
Fax: 904-359-9251
E-mail: carlton.nora@dol.gov

Georgia

Anita Reyes
State Director
USDOL/ETA/OA
61 Forsyth Street, SW
Room 6T80
Atlanta, GA 30303
404-302-5897

Hawaii

Alfred Valles
State Director
USDOL/ETA/OA
300 Ala Moana Boulevard
Room 5-117
Honolulu, HI 96850
808-541-2519
E-mail: valles.alfred@dol.gov

Idaho

William Kolber
State Director
USDOL/ETA/OA
1150 North Curtis Road, Suite 204
Boise, ID 83706-1234
208-321-2972
E-mail: kolber.william@dol.gov

Illinois

David Wyatt
State Director
USDOL/ETA/OA
230 South Dearborn Street
Room 656
Chicago, IL 60604
312-596-5508
E-mail: wyatt.david@dol.gov

Indiana

John Delgado
State Director
USDOL/ETA/OA
Federal Building and
U.S. Courthouse
46 East Ohio Street, Room 528
Indianapolis, IN 46204
317-226-7001
E-mail: delgado.john@dol.gov

Iowa

Greer Sisson
State Director
USDOL/ETA/OA
210 Walnut Street, Room 715
Des Moines, IA 50309
515-284-4690
E-mail: sisson.greer@dol.gov

Kansas

Neil Perry
Acting State Director
USDOL/ETA/OA
444 Southeast Quincy Street
Room 247
Topeka, KS 66683-3571
785-295-2624
E-mail: perry.neil@dol.gov

Kentucky

John Delgado
Acting State Director
USDOL/ETA/OA
Federal Building, Room 168
600 Martin Luther King Place
Louisville, KY 40202
502-582-5223
E-mail: delgado.john@dol.gov

Massachusetts

Jill Houser
Acting State Director
USDOL/ETA/OA
JFK Federal Building
Room E-370
Boston, MA 02203
617-788-0177
E-mail: houser.jill@dol.gov

Maryland

Robert Laudeman
State Director
USDOL/ETA/OA
Federal Building, Room 430-B
31 Hopkins Plaza
Baltimore, MD 21201
410-962-2676
E-mail: laudeman.robert@dol.gov

Michigan

Glenn Bivins
State Director
USDOL/ETA/OAELS-BAT
315 West Allegan, Room 209
Lansing, MI 48933
517-377-1746
E-mail: bivins.glenn@dol.gov

Minnesota

David Wyatt
Acting State Director
USDOL/ETA/OA
316 North Robert Street
Room 144
St. Paul, MN 55101
312-596-5508
E-mail: wyatt.david@dol.gov

Mississippi

Fred Westcott
State Director
USDOL/ETA/OA
Federal Building, Suite 515
100 West Capitol Street
Jackson, MS 39269
601-965-4346
E-mail: westcott.fred@dol.gov

Missouri

Neil Perry
State Director
USDOL/ETA/OA
1222 Spruce Street, Room 9.102E
Robert A. Young Federal Building
St. Louis, MO 63103
314-539-2522
E-mail: perry.neil@dol.gov

Nebraska

Tim Carson
State Director
USDOL/ETA/OA
Suite C-49
111 South 18th Plaza
Omaha, NE 68102-1322
402-221-3281
E-mail: carson.timothy@dol.gov

Nevada

Colleen Henry
State Director
USDOL/ETA/OA
600 South Las Vegas Boulevard,
Suite 520
Las Vegas, NV 89101
702-388-6771
E-mail: henry.colleen@dol.gov

New Hampshire

Charles Vaughan
State Director
USDOL/ETA/OA
55 Pleasant Street
Concord, NH 03301
603-225-1444
E-mail: vaughan.charles@dol.gov

New Jersey

Joann A. Tomenchok
State Director
USDOL/ETA/OA
Metro Star Plaza, Suite 201A
190 Middlesex Essex Turnpike
Iselin, NJ 08830
732-750-9191
E-mail: tomenchok.joann@dol.gov

New Mexico

Dennis Goodson
Acting State Director
USDOL/ETA/OA
500 4th Street NW, Suite 401
Albuquerque, NM 87102
505-248-6530
E-mail: goodson.dennis@dol.gov

New York

Charles Vaughan
Acting State Director
USDOL/ETA/OA
55 Pleasant Street
Concord, NH 03301
603-225-1444
E-mail: vaughan.charles@dol.gov

North Dakota

Barry Dutton
State Director
USDOL/ETA/OA
304 Broadway
Room 332
Bismarck, ND 58501-5900
701-250-4700
E-mail: dutton.barry@dol.gov

Ohio

John Delgado
Acting State Director
USDOL/ETA/OA
200 North High Street, Room 605
Columbus, OH 43215
614-469-7375
E-mail: delgado.john@dol.gov

Oklahoma

Cynthia McLain
State Director
USDOL/ETA/OA
215 Dean A. McGee Avenue
Suite 346
Oklahoma City, OK 73102
405-231-4338
E-mail: mclain.cynthia@dol.gov

Pennsylvania

Thomas Bydlon
State Director
USDOL/ETA/OA
Federal Building
228 Walnut Street, Room 356
Harrisburg, PA 17108
717-221-3496
E-mail: bydlon.thomas@dol.gov

Rhode Island

Howard Carney
State Director
USDOL/ETA/OA
Federal Building
100 Hartford Avenue
Providence, RI 02909
401-528-5198
E-mail: carney.howard@dol.gov

South Carolina

Ronald Johnson
State Director
USDOL/ETA/OATELS-BAT
Strom Thurmond Federal Building
1835 Assembly Street, Room 838
Columbia, SC 29201
803-765-5547
E-mail: johnson.ronald@dol.gov

South Dakota

Barry Dutton
Acting State Director
USDOL/ETA/OA
4804 South Minnesota, Room 103
Sioux Falls, SD 57108
701-250-4700
E-mail: dutton.barry@dol.gov

Tennessee

Nathaniel Brown
State Director
USDOL/ETA/OA
Airport Executive Plaza
1321 Murfreesboro Road
Suite 541
Nashville, TN 37210
615-781-5318
E-mail: brown.nat@dol.gov

Texas

Dennis Goodson
State Director
USDOL/ETA/OA
300 East 8th Street
Suite 914
Austin, TX 78701
512-916-5435
E-mail: goodson.dennis@dol.gov

Utah

Juan Pelaez-Gary
State Director
USDOL/ETA/OA
125 South State Street, Room 2412
Salt Lake City, UT 84138
801-524-5450
E-mail: pelaez-gary.juan@dol.gov

Virginia

James Walker
State Director
USDOL/ETA/OA
400 North 8th Street
Federal Building, Suite 404
Richmond, VA 23219-23240
804-771-2488
E-mail: walker.james@dol.gov

Washington

Anne Wetmore
State Director
USDOL/ETA/OA
1111 Third Avenue, Suite 850
Seattle, WA 98101-3212
206-553-0076
E-mail: wetmore.anne@dol.gov

West Virginia

Kenneth Milnes
State Director
USDOL/ETA/OA
405 Capitol Street, Suite 409
Charleston, WV 25301
304-347-5794
E-mail: milnes.kenneth@dol.gov

Wisconsin

David Wyatt
Acting State Director
USDOL/ETA/OA
Suite 104
740 Regent Street
Madison, WI 53715-1233
608-441-5377
E-mail: wyatt.david@dol.gov

Wyoming

Michael Ann Broad
State Director
USDOL/ETA/OA
American National Bank Building
1912 Capitol Avenue, Room 508
Cheyenne, WY 82001-3661
307-772-2448
E-mail: broad.michael@dol.gov

Accrediting Organizations

The following accrediting bodies are recognized by the U.S. Department of Education or the Council for Higher Education Accreditation (CHEA).

General Accreditation—Regional

General accreditation applies to an institution as a whole and is not limited to institutions or programs in a particular field of specialization.

Regional accreditation denotes accreditation of an institution as a whole by one of the six regional associations of schools and colleges, each of which covers a specified portion of the United States and its territories as indicated in the following listings.

Middle States

Delaware, the District of Columbia, Maryland, New Jersey, New York, Pennsylvania, Puerto Rico, and the Virgin Islands

Middle States Association of Colleges and Schools, Middle States Commission on Higher Education

Elizabeth H. Sibolski, Acting President
3624 Market Street, 2nd Floor Annex
Philadelphia, PA 19104
Phone: 267-284-5000
Fax: 215-662-5950
E-mail: info@msche.org
Web site: www.msche.org

**New York State Board of Regents,
New York State Education Department**

89 Washington Avenue
Room 110EB
Albany, NY 12234
Robert M. Bennett, Chancellor
Phone: 518-474-5889
Web site: www.regents.nysed.gov

New England

Connecticut, Maine, Massachusetts, New Hampshire, Rhode Island, and Vermont

New England Association of Schools and Colleges, Commission on Institutions of Higher Education (NEASC-CIHE)

Barbara E. Brittingham, President/Director of the Commission
209 Burlington Road
Bedford, MA 01730

Phone: 781-271-0022
Fax: 781-271-0950
E-mail: CIHE@neasc.org
Web site: www.neasc.org

Colleges and institutions that offer programs leading to the associate degree but do not offer programs leading to a degree in liberal arts or general studies are covered by:

New England Association of Schools and Colleges, Commission on Technical and Career Institutions

Paul Bento, Director of the Commission
209 Burlington Road, Suite 201
Bedford, MA 01730-1433
Phone: 781-541-5416
E-mail: pbento@neasc.org
Web site: www.ctci.neasc.org

North Central

Arizona, Arkansas, Colorado, Illinois, Indiana, Iowa, Kansas, Michigan, Minnesota, Missouri, Nebraska, New Mexico, North Dakota, Ohio, Oklahoma, South Dakota, West Virginia, Wisconsin, and Wyoming

North Central Association of Colleges and Schools, The Higher Learning Commission (NCA-HLC)

Sylvia Manning, President
30 North LaSalle Street, Suite 2400
Chicago, IL 60602
Phone: 312-263-0456
Fax: 312-263-7462
E-mail: info@hlcommission.org
Web site: www.ncahigherlearningcommission.org

Northwest

Alaska, Idaho, Montana, Nevada, Oregon, Utah, and Washington

Northwest Commission on Colleges and Universities (NWCCU)

Sandra E. Elman, President
8060 165th Avenue, NE, Suite 100
Redmond, WA 98052
Dr. Sandra E. Elman, President
Phone: 425-558-4224
Fax: 425-376-0596
E-mail: selman@nwccu.org
Web site: www.nwccu.org

Southern

Alabama, Florida, Georgia, Kentucky, Louisiana, Mississippi, North Carolina, South Carolina, Tennessee, Texas, and Virginia

Southern Association of Colleges and Schools (SACS), Commission on Colleges

Belle S. Wheelan, President
1866 Southern Lane
Decatur, GA 30033
Phone: 404-679-4500
Fax: 404-679-4558
E-mail: bwheelan@sacscoc.org
Web site: www.sacscoc.org

Western

California, Hawaii, the Territories of Guam and American Samoa, the Commonwealth of the Northern Mariana Islands, the Republic of Palau, the Federated States of Micronesia, and the Republic of the Marshall Islands.

Institutions that offer one or more educational programs of at least one academic year in length at the postsecondary level are covered by:

Western Associaton of Schools and Colleges, Accrediting Commission for Community and Junior Colleges (WASC-ACCJC)

Barbara A. Beno, President
10 Commercial Boulevard, Suite 204
Novato, CA 94949
Phone: 415-506-0234
Fax: 415-506-0238
E-mail: accjc@accjc.org
Web site: www.accjc.org

Institutions that offer one or more educational programs of at least one academic year in length beyond the first two years of college are covered by:

Western Association of Schools and Colleges, Accrediting Commission for Senior Colleges and Universities (WASC-ACSCU)

Ralph A. Wolff, President and Executive Director
985 Atlantic Avenue, Suite 100
Alameda, CA 94501
Phone: 510-748-9001
Fax: 510-748-9797
E-mail: wascsr@wascsenior.org
Web site: www.wascweb.org

Specialized Accreditation

Specialized accreditation applies to an institution or program limited to a particular field of academic or professional specialization or to a particular type of instruction. The following listings for the categories of specialized accreditation are organized alphabetically by field of specialization.

Acupuncture and Oriental Medicine

Accreditation Commission for Acupuncture and Oriental Medicine

Dort S. Bigg, Executive Director
Maryland Trade Center #3
7501 Greenway Center Drive, Suite 760
Greenbelt, MD 20770
Phone: 301-313-0855
Fax: 301-313-0912
E-mail: coordinator@acaom.org
Web site: www.acaom.org

Allied Health

Accrediting Bureau of Health Education Schools

Carol Moneymaker, Executive Director
7777 Leesburg Pike, Suite 314N
Falls Church, VA 22043
Phone: 703-917-9503
Fax: 703-917-4109
E-mail: info@abhes.org
Web site: www.abhes.org

Commission on Accreditation of Allied Health Education Programs (CAAHEP)

Kathleen Megivern, Executive Director
1361 Park Street
Clearwater, FL 33756
Phone: 727-210-2350
Fax: 727-210-2354
E-mail: mail@caahep.org
Web site: www.caahep.org

Art and Design

Art and design institutions and units within institutions offering degree and nondegree programs in art, design, and art/design-related disciplines.

National Association of Schools of Art and Design (NASAD), Commission on Accreditation

Samuel Hope, Executive Director
Karen P. Moynahan, Associate Director
11250 Roger Bacon Drive, Suite 21
Reston, VA 20190-5243
Phone: 703-437-0700
Fax: 703-437-6312
E-mail: info@arts-accredit.org
Web site: www.arts-accredit.org

Athletic Training

Athletic Training Programs for the athletic trainer.

Commission on Accreditation of Allied Health Education Programs (CAAHEP)—see Allied Health

In conjunction with:

Joint Review Committee on Educational Programs in Athletic Training

5142 South Andes Street
Centennial, CO 80015
Phone: 303-627-6229
Fax: 303-632-5915

Audiology—see Speech-Language Pathology and Audiology

Bible College Education

Association for Biblical Higher Education (ABHE), Commission on Accreditation

Ralph Enlow, Executive Director
5575 South Semoran Boulevard
Orlando, FL 32822
Phone: 407-207-0808
Fax: 407-207-0840
E-mail: info@abhe.org
Web site: www.abhe.org

Business

Business private postsecondary institutions that are predominantly organized to train students for business careers, including business schools (one- or two-year noncollegiate postsecondary programs), junior colleges (associate degrees), and senior colleges (baccalaureate and master's degrees).

Accrediting Council for Independent Colleges and Schools (ACICS)

Albert Grey, Executive Director and CEO
750 First Street, NE, Suite 980
Washington, DC 20002
Phone: 202-336-6780
Fax: 202-842-2593
E-mail: info@acics.org
Web site: www.acics.org

Christian Education

**Transnational Association of Christian Colleges and Schools (TRACS),
Accreditation Commission**

Russell Guy Fitzgerald, Executive Director
15935 Forest Road
P.O. Box 328
Forest, VA 24551

Phone: 434-525-9539
Fax: 434-525-9538
E-mail: info@tracs.org
Web site: www.tracs.org

Computer Science

Accrediting Board for Engineering and Technology, Inc. (ABET)

Michael Milligan, Executive Director
111 Market Place, Suite 1050
Baltimore, MD 21202
Phone: 410-347-7700
Fax: 410-625-2238
E-mail: info@abet.org
Web site: www.abet.org

Construction

American Council for Construction Education (ACCE)

Michael Holland, Executive Vice President
1717 North Loop
1604 East, Suite 320
San Antonio, TX 78232
Phone: 210-495-6161
Fax: 210-495-6168
E-mail: acce@acce-hq.org
Web site: www.acce-hq.org

Counseling

Council for Accreditation of Counseling and Related Educational Programs (CACREP)

Carol L. Bobby, Executive Director
1000 North Fairfax Street, Suite 510
Alexandria, VA 22314
Phone: 703-535-5990
Fax: 703-739-6209
E-mail: cacrep@cacrep.org
Web site: www.cacrep.org

Cytopathology

Commission on Accreditation of Allied Health Education Programs—see Allied Health

In conjunction with:

American Society of Cytopathology

Elizabeth Jenkins, Executive Director
100 West 10th Street, Suite 605
Wilmington, DE 19801
Phone: 302-543-6583
Fax: 302-543-6597
E-mail: asc@cytopathology.org
Web site: www.cytopathology.org

Dance

National Association of Schools of Dance (NASD), Commission on Accreditation

Samuel Hope, Executive Director
Karen P. Moynahan, Associate Director
11250 Roger Bacon Drive, Suite 21
Reston, VA 20190
Phone: 703-437-0700
Fax: 703-437-6312
E-mail: shope@arts-accredit.org
Web site: www.arts-accredit.org

Dentistry

Programs leading to the first professional (D.D.S. or D.M.D.) degree and advanced programs in general dentistry and dental specialties. Dental Auxiliary Technologies: dental assisting, dental hygiene, and dental laboratory technology education programs.

American Dental Association

211 East Chicago Avenue
Chicago, IL 60611
Phone: 312-440-2500
Web site: www.ada.org

Diagnostic Medical Sonography

Commission on Accreditation of Allied Health Education Programs—see Allied Health

In conjunction with:

Joint Review Committee on Education in Diagnostic Medical Sonography

2025 Woodlane Drive
St. Paul, MN 55125-2998
Phone: 651-731-1582
Fax: 651-731-0410
E-mail: jrc-dms@jcahpo.org
Web site: www.jrcdms.org

Dietics

American Dietetic Association, Commission on Accreditation for Dietetics Education (CADE-ADA)

Ulric K. Chung, Senior Director
120 South Riverside Plaza, Suite 2000
Chicago, IL 60606
Phone: 800-877-1600 Ext. 5400 (toll-free)
Fax: 312-899-4817
E-mail: uchung@eatright.org
Web site: www.eatright.org/cade

Distance Learning

Distance Education and Training Council (DETC), Accrediting Commission

Michael P. Cambert, Executive Director
1601 18th Street, NW, Suite 2
Washington, DC 20009
Phone: 202-234-5100
Fax: 202-332-1386
E-mail: detc@detc.org
Web site: www.detc.org

Emergency Medical Services

Commission on Accreditation of Allied Health Education Programs—see Allied Health

In conjunction with:

Joint Review Committee on Educational Programs for the EMT-Paramedic

7108-C South Alton Way, Suite 150
Englewood, CO 80112-2106
Phone: 303-694-6191
Fax: 303-741-3655
Web site: www.caahep.org

Engineering and Engineering Technology

ABET, Inc.

111 Market Place, Suite 1050
Baltimore, MD 21202
Phone: 410-347-7700
Fax: 410-625-2238
Web site: www.abet.org

Environmental Health Science

National Environmental Health Association

720 South Colorado Boulevard, Suite 1000-N
Denver, CO 80246
Phone: 303-756-9090
Fax: 303-691-9490
E-mail: staff@neha.org
Web site: www.neha.org

Society of American Foresters

Terence Clark, Associate Director of
    Science & Education
5400 Grosvenor Lane
Bethesda, MD 20814
Phone: 301-897-8720 Ext. 123
Fax: 301-897-3690
E-mail: clarkt@safnet.org
Web site: www.safnet.org

Funeral Service and Mortuary Science

American Board of Funeral Service Education (ABFSE),
Committee on Accreditation
3414 Ashland Avenue, Suite G
St. Joseph, MO 64506
Phone: 816-233-3747
Fax: 816-233-3793
E-mail: exdir@abfse.org
Web site: www.abfse.org

Health Information Administration and Technology

American Health Information Management Association (AHIMA)
Linda Kloss, Chief Executive Officer
233 North Michigan Avenue, 21st Floor
Chicago, IL 60601-5809
Phone: 312-233-1100
Fax: 312-233-1090
E-mail: info@ahima.org
Web site: www.ahima.org

Histologic Technology

American Association of Family & Consumer Sciences, Council for Accreditation
Karen Tucker Thomas, Director of Credentialing and
   Professional Development
400 North Columbus Street, Suite 202
Alexandria, VA 22314
Phone: 703-706-4600 or 800-424-8080 (toll-free)
Fax: 703-706-4663
E-mail: accreditation@aafcs.org
Web site: www.aafcs.org

National Accrediting Agency for Clinical Laboratory Sciences (NAACLS)
Dianne M. Cearlock, Chief Executive Officer
5600 North River Road, Suite 720
Rosemont, IL 60018
Phone: 773-714-8880
Fax: 773-714-8886
E-mail: dcearlock@naacls.org
Web site: www.naacls.org

Interior Design

Council for Interior Design Accreditation (CIDA)
Holly Mattson, Executive Director
206 Grandville Avenue, Suite 350
Grand Rapids, MI 49503
Phone: 616-458-0400
Fax: 616-458-0460
E-mail: info@accredit-id.org
Web site: www.accredit-id.org

Liberal Studies

American Academy for Liberal Education
1050 17th Street, NW, Suite 400
Washington, DC 20036
Phone: 202-452-8611
Fax: 202-452-8620
E-mail: aaleinfo@aale.org
Web site: www.aale.org

Library Science

American Library Association (ALA),
Committee on Accreditation (CoA)
Karen O'Brien, Director, Office for Accreditation
50 East Huron Street
Chicago, IL 60611
Phone: 800-545-2433 Ext. 2432 (toll-free)
Fax: 312-280-2433
E-mail: kobrien@ala.org
Web site: www.ala.org/accreditation/

Medical Assisting

Accrediting Bureau of Health Education Schools (ABHES)
Carol Moneymaker, Executive Director
7777 Leesburg Pike, Suite 314 N.
Falls Church, VA 22043
Phone: 703-917-9503
Fax: 703-907-4109
E-mail: info@abhes.org
Web site: www.abhes.org

Commission on Accreditation of Allied Health Education Programs
In conjunction with:
American Association of Medical Assistants
20 North Wacker Drive, Suite 1575
Chicago, IL 60606
Phone: 312-899-1500
Fax: 312-899-1259
Web site: www.aama-ntl.org

Medical/Clinical Laboratory Technology

National Accrediting Agency for Clinical Laboratory Sciences (NAACLS)
Dianne M. Cearlock, Chief Executive Officer
5600 North River Road, Suite 720
Rosemont, IL 60018
Phone: 773-714-8880
Fax: 773-714-8886
E-mail: dcearlock@naacls.org
Web site: www.naacls.org

Music

National Association of Schools of Music (NASM), Commission on Accreditation

Samuel Hope, Executive Director
11250 Roger Bacon Drive, Suite 21
Reston, VA 20190
Phone: 703-437-0700
Fax: 703-437-6312
E-mail: info@arts-accredit.org
Web site: www.arts-accredit.org

Nuclear Medicine Technology

Joint Review Committee on Educational Programs in Nuclear Medicine Technology (JRCNMT)

Jan M. Winn, Executive Director
2000 West Danforth Road, Suite 130, #203
Edmond, OK 73003
Phone: 405-285-0546
Fax: 405-285-0546
E-mail: jrcnmt@coxinent.net
Web site: www.jrcnmt.org

Nursing

American College of Nurse-Midwives

8403 Colesville Road, Suite 1550
Silver Spring, MD 20910
Phone: 240-485-1800
Fax: 240-485-1818
Web site: www.midwife.org

Occupational Education

Council on Occupational Education

41 Perimeter Center East, NE, Suite 640
Atlanta, GA 30346
Phone: 404-396-3898
Fax: 404-396-3790
Web site: www.council.org

Occupational Therapy

Commission on Accreditation of Allied Health Education Programs—see Allied Health

In conjunction with:

American Occupational Therapy Association, Inc.

4720 Montgomery Lane, P.O. Box 31220
Bethesda, MD 20824-1220
Phone: 301-652-2682
Fax: 301-652-7711
Web site: www.aota.org

Ophthalmic Dispensing and Laboratory Technology

Commission on Opticianry Accreditation

Ellen Stoner, Director of Accreditation
P.O. Box 142
Florence, IN 47020
Phone: 703-468-0566
Fax: 888-306-9036
E-mail: ellen@coaccreditation.com
Web site: www.coaccreditation.com

Ophthalmic Medical Technology

Commission on Accreditation of Allied Health Education Programs—see Allied Health

In conjunction with:

Joint Commission on Allied Health Personnel in Ophthalmology® (JCAHPO)

2025 Woodland Drive
St. Paul, MN 55125-2998
Phone: 651-731-2944 or 800-284-3937 (toll-free)
Fax: 651-731-0410
E-mail: jcahpo@jcahpo.org
Web site: www.jcahpo.org

Optometry and Optometric Technology

American Optometric Association (ADA), Accreditation Council on Optometric Education (ACOE)

Joyce L. Urbek, Administrative Director
243 North Lindbergh Boulevard
St. Louis, MO 63141
Phone: 314-991-4100 Ext. 246
Fax: 314-991-4101
E-mail: acoe@aoa.org
Web site: www.theacoe.org

Physical Therapy

American Physical Therapy Association

1111 North Fairfax Street
Alexandria, VA 22314-1488
Phone: 703-684-2782
Fax: 703-684-7343
Web site: www.apta.org

Physician and Surgeon's Assistant Practice

Commission on Accreditation of Allied Health Education Programs—see Allied Health

In conjunction with:

Accreditation Review Commission on Education for the Physician Assistant, Inc. (ARC-PA)

John E. McCarty, Executive Director
12000 Findley Road, Suite 240
Duluth, GA 30097
Phone: 770-476-1224
Fax: 770-476-1738
E-mail: arc-pa@arc-pa.org
Web site: http://www.arc-pa.org

Council on Education for Public Health

800 Eye Street, NW, Suite 202
Washington, DC 20001-3710
Phone: 202-789-1050
Fax: 202-789-1895
Web site: www.ceph.org

Radiologic Technology

Joint Review Committee on Education Programs in Radiologic Technology

Leslie Winter, Chief Executive Officer
20 North Wacker Drive, Suite 2850
Chicago, IL 60606
Phone: 312-704-5300
Fax: 312-704-5304
E-mail: mail@jrcert.org
Web site: www.jrcert.org

Recreation

Council on Rehabilitation Education (CORE), Commission on Standards and Accreditation

Marvin D. Kuehn, Executive Director
300 North Martingdale Road, Suite 460
Schaumburg, IL 60173
Phone: 847-944-1345
Fax: 847-944-1324
E-mail: mkuehn@emporia.edu
Web site: www.core-rehab.org

National Recreation & Park Association, Council on Accreditation (NRPA/COA)

James O'Connor, Accreditation Manager
22377 Belmont Ridge Road
Ashburn, VA 20148
Phone: 703-858-2150
Fax: 703-858-0794
E-mail: jthorner@nrpa.org
Web site: www.councilonaccreditation.org

Respiratory Therapy

Commission on Accreditation of Allied Health Education Programs—see Allied Health

In conjunction with:

Committee on Accreditation for Respiratory Care

1248 Harwood Road
Bedford, TX 76021-4244
Phone: 817-283-2835
Fax: 817-354-8519
Web site: www.coarc.com

Speech-Language Pathology and Audiology

American Speech-Language-Hearing Association (ASHA),
Council on Academic Accreditation in Audiology and Speech-Language Pathology

Patrima Tice, Director of Accreditation
2700 Research Boulevard
Rockville, MD 20852
Phone: 301-296-5796
Fax: 301-296-8750
E-mail: ptice@asha.org
Web site:
    www.asha.org/about/credentialing/accreditation

Surgical Technology

Commission on Accreditation of Allied Health Education Programs—see Allied Health

In conjunction with:

Accreditation Review Committee on Education in Surgical Technology and Surgical Assisting (ARC/STSA)

Keith Orloff, Executive Director
6 West Dry Creek Circle, Suite 110
Littleton, CO 80120
Phone: 303-694-9262
Fax: 303-741-3655
Web site: www.arcst.org

Technology Fields

Accrediting Commission of Career Schools and Colleges (ACCSC)

Michale S. McComis, Executive Director
2101 Wilson Boulevard, Suite 302
Arlington, VA 22201
Phone: 703-247-4212
Fax: 703-247-4533
E-mail: mccomis@accsc.org
Web site: www.accsc.org

Theater and Theater-Related Disciplines

National Association of Schools of Theatre (NAST)

Samuel Hope, Executive Director
11250 Roger Bacon Drive, Suite 21
Reston, VA 20190-5248
Phone: 703-437-0700
Fax: 703-437-6312
E-mail: info@arts-accredit.org
Web site: http://nast.arts-accredit.org

Indexes

Career Training Programs

ACCOUNTING

Alabama
Virginia College at Birmingham (Birmingham), 48

Connecticut
Goodwin College (East Hartford), 53
Ridley-Lowell Business and Technical Institute (New London), 56

Delaware
Delaware Technical & Community College, Stanton/Wilmington Campus (Newark), 59
Delaware Technical & Community College, Terry Campus (Dover), 60

District of Columbia
Strayer University (Washington), 62

Florida
Atlantic Vocational-Technical Center (Coconut Creek), 66
Bradford Union Area Vocational Technical Center (Starke), 67
Charlotte Vocational-Technical Center (Port Charlotte), 69
George Stone Area Vocational-Technical Center (Pensacola), 79
Lake Technical Center (Eustis), 83
Lee County High Tech Center North (Cape Coral), 83
Lee County Vocational High Tech Center–Central (Fort Myers), 84
Lively Technical Center (Tallahassee), 84
Manatee Technical Institute (Bradenton), 85
Pinellas Technical Education Center–Clearwater (Clearwater), 91
Radford M. Locklin Technical Center (Milton), 92
Rasmussen College Ocala (Ocala), 93
Rasmussen College Pasco County (Holiday), 93
Ridge Technical Center (Winter Haven), 93
Robert Morgan Vocational-Technical Center (Miami), 94
Sarasota County Technical Institute (Sarasota), 96
Technical Career Institute (Miami Springs), 99
Traviss Technical Center (Lakeland), 99

Georgia
Gwinnett College (Lilburn), 113

Illinois
Brown Mackie College–Moline (Moline), 125
Carl Sandburg College (Galesburg), 127
City Colleges of Chicago, Harold Washington College (Chicago), 127
City Colleges of Chicago, Harry S. Truman College (Chicago), 128
City Colleges of Chicago, Olive-Harvey College (Chicago), 128
City Colleges of Chicago, Richard J. Daley College (Chicago), 128
City Colleges of Chicago, Wilbur Wright College (Chicago), 129
College of Lake County (Grayslake), 129
East-West University (Chicago), 132
Harper College (Palatine), 135
Heartland Community College (Normal), 136
Highland Community College (Freeport), 136
John Wood Community College (Quincy), 139

Joliet Junior College (Joliet), 139
Kaskaskia College (Centralia), 139
Lake Land College (Mattoon), 140
Lewis and Clark Community College (Godfrey), 141
McHenry County College (Crystal Lake), 142
Parkland College (Champaign), 145
Saint Xavier University (Chicago), 150
Sauk Valley Community College (Dixon), 150
Sparks College (Shelbyville), 152
Taylor Business Institute (Chicago), 152
Waubonsee Community College (Sugar Grove), 154
Zarem/Golde ORT Technical Institute (Chicago), 154

Indiana
Brown Mackie College–Fort Wayne (Fort Wayne), 155
Brown Mackie College–Merrillville (Merrillville), 156
Brown Mackie College–Michigan City (Michigan City), 156
Calumet College of Saint Joseph (Whiting), 156
Harrison College (Anderson), 158
Harrison College (Fort Wayne), 158
Harrison College (Indianapolis), 158
Harrison College (Lafayette), 159
Harrison College (Muncie), 159
Harrison College (Terre Haute), 159
Indiana Business College–Elkhart (Elkhart), 159
International Business College (Indianapolis), 161
Kaplan College–Merrillville Campus (Merrillville), 164
Purdue University (West Lafayette), 166

Kentucky
Brown Mackie College–Hopkinsville (Hopkinsville), 170
Draughons Junior College (Bowling Green), 172
Thomas More College (Crestview Hills), 179
Western Kentucky University (Bowling Green), 180

Maine
Andover College (South Portland), 180

Massachusetts
Assumption College (Worcester), 193
Bridgewater State College (Bridgewater), 195
Bunker Hill Community College (Boston), 196
Mildred Elley School (Pittsfield), 202
Newbury College (Brookline), 203
Quinsigamond Community College (Worcester), 205
The Salter School (Worcester), 206

Michigan
Bay de Noc Community College (Escanaba), 211
Macomb Community College (Warren), 220

Mississippi
Belhaven College (Jackson), 230

New Hampshire
Lebanon College (Lebanon), 237
Manchester Community College (Manchester), 237
McIntosh College (Dover), 238
New Hampshire Community Technical College, Stratham (Stratham), 239

New Hampshire Technical Institute (Concord), 239

New Jersey
Dover Business College (Paramus), 244
HoHoKus Hackensack School of Business and Medical Sciences (Hackensack), 246
Keyskills Learning (Clifton), 247
Ocean County College (Toms River), 250

New York
Bramson ORT College (Forest Hills), 258
Briarcliffe College (Bethpage), 258
Cheryl Fells School of Business (Niagara Falls), 261
Daemen College (Amherst), 263
Elmira Business Institute (Elmira), 264
Hunter Business School (Levittown), 269
Manhattan School of Computer Technology (New York), 272
Mildred Elley School (Albany), 273
New York Institute of Business Technology (New York), 276
Pace University (New York), 279
Ridley-Lowell Business and Technical Institute (Binghamton), 280
Ridley-Lowell School of Business (Poughkeepsie), 280
Siena College (Loudonville), 283
Spanish-American Institute (New York), 283

North Carolina
Alamance Community College (Graham), 288
Asheville-Buncombe Technical Community College (Asheville), 288
Beaufort County Community College (Washington), 289
Brookstone College of Business (Greensboro), 290
Caldwell Community College and Technical Institute (Hudson), 290
Central Carolina Community College (Sanford), 292
Central Piedmont Community College (Charlotte), 293
Coastal Carolina Community College (Jacksonville), 293
Craven Community College (New Bern), 294
Davidson County Community College (Lexington), 294
Forsyth Technical Community College (Winston-Salem), 296
Gaston College (Dallas), 296
Guilford College (Greensboro), 297
James Sprunt Community College (Kenansville), 298
Johnston Community College (Smithfield), 298
King's College (Charlotte), 299
Lenoir Community College (Kinston), 299
Martin Community College (Williamston), 299
McDowell Technical Community College (Marion), 300
Mitchell Community College (Statesville), 300
Nash Community College (Rocky Mount), 302
Piedmont Community College (Roxboro), 302
Pitt Community College (Greenville), 303
Roanoke-Chowan Community College (Ahoskie), 303
Rowan-Cabarrus Community College (Salisbury), 304

Sampson Community College (Clinton), 304
Southwestern Community College (Sylva), 306
Stanly Community College (Albemarle), 306
Surry Community College (Dobson), 306
Wake Technical Community College (Raleigh), 307
Wilkes Community College (Wilkesboro), 308

Ohio
Akron Adult Vocational Services (Akron), 309
Baldwin-Wallace College (Berea), 311
Brown Mackie College–Akron (Akron), 313
Chancellor University (Cleveland), 315
Cincinnati State Technical and Community College (Cincinnati), 315
Edison State Community College (Piqua), 319
Everest Institute (Gahanna), 320
Gallipolis Career College (Gallipolis), 320
Hocking College (Nelsonville), 321
Lakeland Community College (Kirtland), 323
North Central State College (Mansfield), 327
Northwest State Community College (Archbold), 327
Ohio Business College (Lorain), 328
Ohio Business College (Sandusky), 328
Owens Community College (Toledo), 330
Southwestern College of Business (Cincinnati), 335
Terra State Community College (Fremont), 336
Trumbull Business College (Warren), 338
Urbana University (Urbana), 340
Zane State College (Zanesville), 342

Pennsylvania
Bradford School (Pittsburgh), 345
Cambria-Rowe Business College (Indiana), 346
Cambria-Rowe Business College (Johnstown), 346
Consolidated School of Business (Lancaster), 350
Consolidated School of Business (York), 350
Elizabethtown College (Elizabethtown), 352
Lansdale School of Business (North Wales), 360
Laurel Technical Institute (Sharon), 361
Lebanon Valley College (Annville), 362
Lehigh Carbon Community College (Schnecksville), 362
Montgomery County Community College (Blue Bell), 365
Muhlenberg College (Allentown), 365
Newport Business Institute (Lower Burrell), 366
Newport Business Institute (Williamsport), 366
Penn Commercial Business and Technical School (Washington), 367
Point Park University (Pittsburgh), 371
Robert Morris University (Moon Township), 372
University of Pittsburgh (Pittsburgh), 376
The University of Scranton (Scranton), 377

Puerto Rico
International Technical College (San Juan), 389
MBTI Business Training Institute (Santurce), 391

Rhode Island
Community College of Rhode Island (Warwick), 394

South Carolina
Central Carolina Technical College (Sumter), 398
Denmark Technical College (Denmark), 398
Greenville Technical College (Greenville), 399
Orangeburg-Calhoun Technical College (Orangeburg), 402
Piedmont Technical College (Greenwood), 402
Spartanburg Community College (Spartanburg), 403
Technical College of the Lowcountry (Beaufort), 403
Tri-County Technical College (Pendleton), 403

Trident Technical College (Charleston), 404
York Technical College (Rock Hill), 405
Tennessee
Draughons Junior College (Clarksville), 407
Draughons Junior College (Murfreesboro), 407
Draughons Junior College (Nashville), 407
Vermont
Champlain College (Burlington), 422
Virginia
Marymount University (Arlington), 429
West Virginia
Mountain State College (Parkersburg), 442
West Virginia Business College (Nutter Fort), 443
Wisconsin
Northcentral Technical College (Wausau), 450

ACCOUNTING AND BUSINESS/ MANAGEMENT

Illinois
Elgin Community College (Elgin), 132
Kaskaskia College (Centralia), 139
Sanford-Brown College (Collinsville), 150
South Suburban College (South Holland), 151
Indiana
Vincennes University (Vincennes), 168
Michigan
Gogebic Community College (Ironwood), 216
New Jersey
Dover Business College (Paramus), 244
Pennsylvania
Computer Learning Network (Altoona), 349
Virginia
Everest College (Newport News), 427
Everest Institute (Chesapeake), 428

ACCOUNTING AND COMPUTER SCIENCE

Pennsylvania
Northwest Regional Technology Institute (Erie), 367
Puerto Rico
Advanced Tech College (Bayamón), 379
Instituto Educativo Premier (Ponce), 387

ACCOUNTING AND FINANCE

Michigan
Jackson Community College (Jackson), 218

ACCOUNTING AND RELATED SERVICES, OTHER

Alabama
Virginia College at Mobile (Mobile), 48
Connecticut
Ridley-Lowell Business and Technical Institute (New London), 56
Florida
Brevard Community College (Cocoa), 67
Broward Community College (Fort Lauderdale), 68
Central Florida Community College (Ocala), 69
Daytona State College (Daytona Beach), 72
Edison State College (Fort Myers), 72
Gulf Coast Community College (Panama City), 79
Hillsborough Community College (Tampa), 81
Indian River State College (Fort Pierce), 81
Lake City Community College (Lake City), 83
Lake-Sumter Community College (Leesburg), 83
Miami Dade College (Miami), 87
Northwest Florida State College (Niceville), 89
Palm Beach Community College (Lake Worth), 90
Pensacola Junior College (Pensacola), 91

St. Johns River Community College (Palatka), 94
St. Petersburg College (St. Petersburg), 94
Santa Fe Community College (Gainesville), 95
Seminole Community College (Sanford), 96
South Florida Community College (Avon Park), 97
State College of Florida Manatee-Sarasota (Bradenton), 98
Valencia Community College (Orlando), 101
Virginia College at Pensacola (Pensacola), 102
Winter Park Tech (Winter Park), 102
Georgia
Interactive College of Technology (College Park), 115
Illinois
BIR Training Center (Chicago), 125
Everest College (North Aurora), 134
Everest College (Skokie), 134
Roosevelt University (Chicago), 149
Sparks College (Shelbyville), 152
Indiana
Ivy Tech Community College–Bloomington (Bloomington), 161
Ivy Tech Community College–North Central (South Bend), 162
Ivy Tech Community College–Northeast (Fort Wayne), 163
Ivy Tech Community College–Southwest (Evansville), 163
Ivy Tech Community College–Whitewater (Richmond), 164
Kentucky
Interactive Learning Systems (Florence), 174
Maryland
Prince George's Community College (Largo), 191
Michigan
Dorsey Business Schools (Roseville), 214
Dorsey Business Schools (Southgate), 214
New Jersey
Camden County College (Blackwood), 241
Harris School of Business–Cherry Hill (Cherry Hill), 246
Harris School of Business–Hamilton (Hamilton), 246
Harris School of Business–Linwood (Linwood), 246
Raritan Valley Community College (Somerville), 252
New York
Cheryl Fells School of Business (Niagara Falls), 261
Olean Business Institute (Olean), 277
Professional Business Institute (New York), 279
Spanish-American Institute (New York), 283
North Carolina
Brookstone College of Business (Greensboro), 290
Ohio
Bowling Green State University–Firelands College (Huron), 312
Brown Mackie College–North Canton (Canton), 313
Daymar College (Chillicothe), 318
Southwestern College of Business (Dayton), 335
Puerto Rico
American Educational College (Bayamón), 379
Universal Technology College of Puerto Rico (Aguadilla), 393
South Carolina
Forrest Junior College (Anderson), 399
Virginia
Central Virginia Community College (Lynchburg), 425

Germanna Community College (Locust Grove), 428

J. Sargeant Reynolds Community College (Richmond), 429

Mountain Empire Community College (Big Stone Gap), 430

New River Community College (Dublin), 430

Northern Virginia Community College (Annandale), 430

Patrick Henry Community College (Martinsville), 431

Rappahannock Community College (Glenns), 431

Southwest Virginia Community College (Richlands), 432

Tidewater Community College (Norfolk), 434

Virginia Highlands Community College (Abingdon), 435

Wisconsin

Nicolet Area Technical College (Rhinelander), 450

ACCOUNTING TECHNOLOGY/TECHNICIAN AND BOOKKEEPING

Alabama

Bishop State Community College (Mobile), 41

Gadsden State Community College (Gadsden), 42

H. Councill Trenholm State Technical College (Montgomery), 43

Jefferson Davis Community College (Brewton), 44

Jefferson State Community College (Birmingham), 44

J. F. Drake State Technical College (Huntsville), 44

Lawson State Community College (Birmingham), 44

Lurleen B. Wallace Community College (Andalusia), 45

Northwest-Shoals Community College (Muscle Shoals), 45

Snead State Community College (Boaz), 46

Virginia College at Huntsville (Huntsville), 48

Connecticut

Asnuntuck Community College (Enfield), 49

Capital Community College (Hartford), 51 .

Housatonic Community College (Bridgeport), 53

Manchester Community College (Manchester), 54

Middlesex Community College (Middletown), 54

Naugatuck Valley Community College (Waterbury), 54

Norwalk Community College (Norwalk), 55

Quinebaug Valley Community College (Danielson), 56

Ridley-Lowell Business and Technical Institute (New London), 56

Three Rivers Community College (Norwich), 57

Tunxis Community College (Farmington), 57

Delaware

Delaware Technical & Community College, Jack F. Owens Campus (Georgetown), 59

Delaware Technical & Community College, Stanton/Wilmington Campus (Newark), 59

Delaware Technical & Community College, Terry Campus (Dover), 60

Florida

Brevard Community College (Cocoa), 67

Florida Community College at Jacksonville (Jacksonville), 77

James Lorenzo Walker Vocational-Technical Center (Naples), 82

Miami Dade College (Miami), 87

Miami-Dade County Public Schools (Miami), 87

Miami Lakes Technical Education Center (Miami), 87

Northwest Florida State College (Niceville), 89

Orlando Technical Center (Orlando), 90

Palm Beach Community College (Lake Worth), 90

St. Johns River Community College (Palatka), 94

St. Petersburg College (St. Petersburg), 94

Sarasota County Technical Institute (Sarasota), 96

Seminole Community College (Sanford), 96

Sheridan Vocational-Technical Center (Hollywood), 96

Technical Career Institute (Miami Springs), 99

Tom P. Haney Technical Center (Panama City), 99

Georgia

Albany Technical College (Albany), 103

Altamaha Technical College (Jesup), 104

Appalachian Technical College (Jasper), 104

Athens Technical College (Athens), 105

Atlanta Technical College (Atlanta), 105

Augusta Technical College (Augusta), 106

Bainbridge College (Bainbridge), 106

Brown Mackie College–Atlanta (Atlanta), 107

Central Georgia Technical College (Macon), 107

Chattahoochee Technical College (Marietta), 107

Columbus Technical College (Columbus), 108

Coosa Valley Technical College (Rome), 109

Darton College (Albany), 109

DeKalb Technical College (Clarkston), 109

East Central Technical College (Fitzgerald), 110

Flint River Technical College (Thomaston), 111

Griffin Technical College (Griffin), 113

Gwinnett Technical College (Lawrenceville), 113

Heart of Georgia Technical College (Dublin), 114

Interactive College of Technology (Chamblee), 114

Interactive College of Technology (Gainesville), 115

Lanier Technical College (Oakwood), 115

Middle Georgia Technical College (Warner Robbins), 117

Moultrie Technical College (Moultrie), 117

North Georgia Technical College (Clarkesville), 118

North Metro Technical College (Acworth), 118

Northwestern Technical College (Rock Spring), 118

Ogeechee Technical College (Statesboro), 119

Okefenokee Technical College (Waycross), 119

Sandersville Technical College (Sandersville), 120

Savannah River College (Augusta), 121

Savannah Technical College (Savannah), 121

Southeastern Technical College (Vidalia), 121

South Georgia Technical College (Americus), 122

Southwest Georgia Technical College (Thomasville), 122

Swainsboro Technical College (Swainsboro), 123

Valdosta Technical College (Valdosta), 123

West Central Technical College (Waco), 124

West Georgia Technical College (LaGrange), 124

Illinois

Black Hawk College (Moline), 125

College of DuPage (Glen Ellyn), 129

College of Lake County (Grayslake), 129

Danville Area Community College (Danville), 131

Fox College (Bedford Park), 134

Harper College (Palatine), 135

Highland Community College (Freeport), 136

Illinois Central College (East Peoria), 136

Illinois Valley Community College (Oglesby), 138

John A. Logan College (Carterville), 138

Kankakee Community College (Kankakee), 139

Lewis and Clark Community College (Godfrey), 141

McHenry County College (Crystal Lake), 142

Moraine Valley Community College (Palos Hills), 143

Northwestern Business College–Southwestern Campus (Bridgeview), 144

Northwestern College (Chicago), 144

Northwestern University (Evanston), 145

Oakton Community College (Des Plaines), 145

Prairie State College (Chicago Heights), 146

Richland Community College (Decatur), 148

Robert Morris University (Chicago), 149

Rock Valley College (Rockford), 149

St. Augustine College (Chicago), 150

Southeastern Illinois College (Harrisburg), 151

South Suburban College (South Holland), 151

Triton College (River Grove), 153

Waubonsee Community College (Sugar Grove), 154

Zarem/Golde ORT Technical Institute (Chicago), 154

Indiana

International Business College (Fort Wayne), 161

Ivy Tech Community College–Bloomington (Bloomington), 161

Ivy Tech Community College–Central Indiana (Indianapolis), 161

Ivy Tech Community College–Columbus (Columbus), 162

Ivy Tech Community College–East Central (Muncie), 162

Ivy Tech Community College–Kokomo (Kokomo), 162

Ivy Tech Community College–Lafayette (Lafayette), 162

Ivy Tech Community College–North Central (South Bend), 162

Ivy Tech Community College–Northeast (Fort Wayne), 163

Ivy Tech Community College–Northwest (Gary), 163

Ivy Tech Community College–Southeast (Madison), 163

Ivy Tech Community College–Southern Indiana (Sellersburg), 163

Ivy Tech Community College–Southwest (Evansville), 163

Ivy Tech Community College–Wabash Valley (Terre Haute), 164

Ivy Tech Community College–Whitewater (Richmond), 164

TechSkills—Indianapolis (Indianapolis), 167

Kentucky

Jefferson Community and Technical College (Louisville), 175

National College (Lexington), 176

Somerset Community College (Somerset), 178

Spencerian College (Louisville), 179

West Kentucky Community and Technical College (Paducah), 180

Maryland

Allegany College of Maryland (Cumberland), 184

Anne Arundel Community College (Arnold), 184

ACTUARIAL SCIENCE

Michigan

Michigan Technological University (Houghton), 222

ADMINISTRATIVE ASSISTANT AND SECRETARIAL SCIENCE, GENERAL

Alabama

Alabama Southern Community College (Monroeville), 41
Bevill State Community College (Sumiton), 41
Bishop State Community College (Mobile), 41
Central Alabama Community College (Alexander City), 42
Chattahoochee Valley Community College (Phenix City), 42
Enterprise-Ozark Community College (Enterprise), 42
Gadsden State Community College (Gadsden), 42
George Corley Wallace State Community College (Selma), 43
George C. Wallace Community College (Dothan), 43
H. Councill Trenholm State Technical College (Montgomery), 43
Jefferson Davis Community College (Brewton), 44
Jefferson State Community College (Birmingham), 44
J. F. Drake State Technical College (Huntsville), 44
Lawson State Community College (Birmingham), 44
Lurleen B. Wallace Community College (Andalusia), 45
Northwest-Shoals Community College (Muscle Shoals), 45
Reid State Technical College (Evergreen), 46
Shelton State Community College (Tuscaloosa), 46
Snead State Community College (Boaz), 46
Southern Union State Community College (Wadley), 47
Virginia College at Birmingham (Birmingham), 48
Virginia College at Huntsville (Huntsville), 48
Virginia College at Mobile (Mobile), 48

Connecticut

Asnuntuck Community College (Enfield), 49
Butler Business School (Bridgeport), 51
Capital Community College (Hartford), 51
Gateway Community College (New Haven), 52
Housatonic Community College (Bridgeport), 53
Manchester Community College (Manchester), 54
Middlesex Community College (Middletown), 54
Naugatuck Valley Community College (Waterbury), 54
Northwestern Connecticut Community College (Winsted), 55
Norwalk Community College (Norwalk), 55
Quinebaug Valley Community College (Danielson), 56
Ridley-Lowell Business and Technical Institute (New London), 56
Stone Academy (Hamden), 57
Stone Academy (Waterbury), 57
Three Rivers Community College (Norwich), 57
Tunxis Community College (Farmington), 57

Delaware

Delaware Technical & Community College, Jack F. Owens Campus (Georgetown), 59

Delaware Technical & Community College, Stanton/Wilmington Campus (Newark), 59
Delaware Technical & Community College, Terry Campus (Dover), 60

Florida

Atlantic Vocational-Technical Center (Coconut Creek), 66
Bradford Union Area Vocational Technical Center (Starke), 67
Brevard Community College (Cocoa), 67
Charlotte Vocational-Technical Center (Port Charlotte), 69
College of Business and Technology–Flagler Campus (Miami), 70
College of Business and Technology–Hialeah Campus (Hialeah), 70
College of Business and Technology (Miami), 70
First Coast Technical Institute (St. Augustine), 75
Florida Career Institute (Lakeland), 76
Galiano Career Academy (Altamonte Sprints), 79
George Stone Area Vocational-Technical Center (Pensacola), 79
Henry W. Brewster Technical Center (Tampa), 80
James Lorenzo Walker Vocational-Technical Center (Naples), 82
Jones College (Jacksonville), 82
Lake Technical Center (Eustis), 83
Lee County High Tech Center North (Cape Coral), 83
Lee County Vocational High Tech Center–Central (Fort Myers), 84
Manatee Technical Institute (Bradenton), 85
Marion County Community Technical and Adult Education Center (Ocala), 85
Miami Lakes Technical Education Center (Miami), 87
Okaloosa Applied Technology Center (Ft. Walton Beach), 89
Orlando Technical Center (Orlando), 90
Radford M. Locklin Technical Center (Milton), 92
Ridge Technical Center (Winter Haven), 93
Robert Morgan Vocational-Technical Center (Miami), 94
Sarasota County Technical Institute (Sarasota), 96
Sheridan Vocational-Technical Center (Hollywood), 96
Southern Technical Institute (Winter Park), 97
Tom P. Haney Technical Center (Panama City), 99
Traviss Technical Center (Lakeland), 99
Washington-Holmes Technical Center (Chipley), 102
Westside Tech (Winter Garden), 102
Winter Park Tech (Winter Park), 102
Withlacoochee Technical Institute (Inverness), 103

Georgia

Advanced Career Training (Atlanta), 103
Albany Technical College (Albany), 103
Altamaha Technical College (Jesup), 104
Appalachian Technical College (Jasper), 104
Athens Technical College (Athens), 105
Atlanta Technical College (Atlanta), 105
Augusta Technical College (Augusta), 106
Bainbridge College (Bainbridge), 106
Central Georgia Technical College (Macon), 107
Chattahoochee Technical College (Marietta), 107
College of Coastal Georgia (Brunswick), 108
Columbus Technical College (Columbus), 108
Coosa Valley Technical College (Rome), 109
Darton College (Albany), 109

DeKalb Technical College (Clarkston), 109
East Central Technical College (Fitzgerald), 110
Flint River Technical College (Thomaston), 111
Griffin Technical College (Griffin), 113
Gwinnett College (Lilburn), 113
Gwinnett Technical College (Lawrenceville), 113
Heart of Georgia Technical College (Dublin), 114
Interactive College of Technology (Chamblee), 114
Interactive College of Technology (College Park), 115
Interactive College of Technology (Gainesville), 115
Iverson Business School (Atlanta), 115
Lanier Technical College (Oakwood), 115
Middle Georgia Technical College (Warner Robbins), 117
Moultrie Technical College (Moultrie), 117
North Georgia Technical College (Clarkesville), 118
North Metro Technical College (Acworth), 118
Northwestern Technical College (Rock Spring), 118
Ogeechee Technical College (Statesboro), 119
Okefenokee Technical College (Waycross), 119
Sandersville Technical College (Sandersville), 120
Savannah River College (Augusta), 121
Savannah Technical College (Savannah), 121
Southeastern Technical College (Vidalia), 121
South Georgia Technical College (Americus), 122
Southwest Georgia Technical College (Thomasville), 122
Swainsboro Technical College (Swainsboro), 123
Valdosta Technical College (Valdosta), 123
West Central Technical College (Waco), 124
West Georgia Technical College (LaGrange), 124

Illinois

Carl Sandburg College (Galesburg), 127
Center for Employment Training–Chicago (Chicago), 127
College of DuPage (Glen Ellyn), 129
College of Lake County (Grayslake), 129
Danville Area Community College (Danville), 131
Elgin Community College (Elgin), 132
Fox College (Bedford Park), 134
Heartland Community College (Normal), 136
Illinois Central College (East Peoria), 136
Illinois Eastern Community Colleges, Frontier Community College (Fairfield), 137
Illinois Eastern Community Colleges, Lincoln Trail College (Robinson), 137
Illinois Eastern Community Colleges, Wabash Valley College (Mount Carmel), 137
John A. Logan College (Carterville), 138
John Wood Community College (Quincy), 139
Kaskaskia College (Centralia), 139
Kishwaukee College (Malta), 140
Lake Land College (Mattoon), 140
Lewis and Clark Community College (Godfrey), 141
McHenry County College (Crystal Lake), 142
Moraine Valley Community College (Palos Hills), 143
Morton College (Cicero), 143
Northwestern Business College–Southwestern Campus (Bridgeview), 144
Parkland College (Champaign), 145
Prairie State College (Chicago Heights), 146
Richland Community College (Decatur), 148
Robert Morris University (Chicago), 149
Rockford Business College (Rockford), 149

Rock Valley College (Rockford), 149
St. Augustine College (Chicago), 150
South Suburban College (South Holland), 151
Southwestern Illinois College (Belleville), 151
Spanish Coalition for Jobs, Inc. (Chicago), 152
Sparks College (Shelbyville), 152
Spoon River College (Canton), 152
Triton College (River Grove), 153

Indiana
College of Court Reporting (Hobart), 156
Harrison College (Anderson), 158
Harrison College (Fort Wayne), 158
Harrison College (Lafayette), 159
Harrison College (Muncie), 159
Harrison College (Terre Haute), 159
Indiana Business College–Elkhart (Elkhart), 159
International Business College (Fort Wayne), 161
International Business College (Indianapolis), 161

Kentucky
Interactive Learning Systems (Florence), 174

Maine
Andover College (South Portland), 180
Beal College (Bangor), 180
Central Maine Community College (Auburn), 181
Eastern Maine Community College (Bangor), 181

Maryland
Allegany College of Maryland (Cumberland), 184
Baltimore City Community College (Baltimore), 185
Carroll Community College (Westminster), 186
College of Southern Maryland (La Plata), 186
The Community College of Baltimore County (Baltimore), 187
Hagerstown Community College (Hagerstown), 188
Howard Community College (Columbia), 189
Prince George's Community College (Largo), 191
TESST College of Technology (Towson), 192
Wor-Wic Community College (Salisbury), 193

Massachusetts
Fisher College (Boston), 198
Greenfield Community College (Greenfield), 198
Holyoke Community College (Holyoke), 199
Massasoit Community College (Brockton), 202
Mildred Elley School (Pittsfield), 202
Millennium Training Institute (Woburn), 203
Roxbury Community College (Roxbury Crossing), 205

Michigan
Bay de Noc Community College (Escanaba), 211
Career Quest Learning Center (East Lansing), 212
Delta College (University Center), 213
Detroit Business Institute–Downriver (Riverview), 214
Detroit Business Institute–Southfield (Southfield), 214
Dorsey Business Schools (Madison Heights), 214
Dorsey Business Schools (Roseville), 214
Dorsey Business Schools (Southgate), 214
Glen Oaks Community College (Centreville), 216
Gogebic Community College (Ironwood), 216
Henry Ford Community College (Dearborn), 217
Jackson Community College (Jackson), 218
Lake Superior State University (Sault Sainte Marie), 219

Lansing Community College (Lansing), 219
Monroe County Community College (Monroe), 222
Northern Michigan University (Marquette), 224
Schoolcraft College (Livonia), 227
Washtenaw Community College (Ann Arbor), 229
West Shore Community College (Scottville), 229

Mississippi
Copiah-Lincoln Community College (Wesson), 231
East Central Community College (Decatur), 232
East Mississippi Community College (Scooba), 232
Hinds Community College (Raymond), 232
Jones County Junior College (Ellisville), 234
Meridian Community College (Meridian), 234
Mississippi Gulf Coast Community College (Perkinston), 234
Northwest Mississippi Community College (Senatobia), 235
Pearl River Community College (Poplarville), 235
Southwest Mississippi Community College (Summit), 235
Virginia College at Jackson (Jackson), 236
Virginia College Gulf Coast at Biloxi (Biloxi), 236

New Hampshire
Manchester Community College (Manchester), 237
New Hampshire Community Technical College, Nashua/Claremont (Nashua), 238

New Jersey
Adult and Continuing Education–Bergen County Technical Schools (Hackensack), 240
Camden County College (Blackwood), 241
Cumberland County College (Vineland), 244
Essex County College (Newark), 244
Gloucester County College (Sewell), 245
Harris School of Business–Cherry Hill (Cherry Hill), 246
HoHoKus Hackensack School of Business and Medical Sciences (Hackensack), 246
HoHoKus RETS School of Business and Medical Technical Services (Nutley), 246
HoHoKus School of Business and Medical Sciences (Ramsey), 247
Keyskills Learning (Clifton), 247
Lincoln Technical Institute (Paramus), 248
Mercer County Community College (Trenton), 248
Ocean County College (Toms River), 250
PC Tech Learning Center (Jersey City), 251
Performance Training (Toms River), 251
Prism Career Institute (Sewell), 252
Prism Career Institute (Willingboro), 252
Salem Community College (Carneys Point), 253
Somerset County Technical Institute (Bridgewater), 253
Stuart School of Business Administration (Wall), 254
Union County College (Cranford), 254

New York
Bramson ORT College (Forest Hills), 258
Cheryl Fells School of Business (Niagara Falls), 261
Clinton Community College (Plattsburgh), 262
The College of Westchester (White Plains), 262
Columbia-Greene Community College (Hudson), 262
Elmira Business Institute (Elmira), 264
Everest Institute (Rochester), 266

Fiorello H. LaGuardia Community College of the City University of New York (Long Island City), 266
Genesee Community College (Batavia), 267
Global Business Institute (Far Rockaway), 267
Global Business Institute (New York), 268
Jamestown Business College (Jamestown), 270
Jamestown Community College (Jamestown), 270
Mildred Elley School (Albany), 273
Monroe 2–Orleans BOCES Center for Workforce Development (Rochester), 274
Monroe Community College (Rochester), 274
Nassau Community College (Garden City), 275
New York Institute of Business Technology (New York), 276
Niagara County Community College (Sanborn), 277
North Country Community College (Saranac Lake), 277
Olean Business Institute (Olean), 277
Orange County Community College (Middletown), 278
Plaza College (Jackson Heights), 279
Queensborough Community College of the City University of New York (Bayside), 280
Ridley-Lowell Business and Technical Institute (Binghamton), 280
Rochester Institute of Technology (Rochester), 280
State University of New York College of Technology at Canton (Canton), 284
Suffolk County Community College (Selden), 284
Utica School of Commerce (Utica), 287
Westchester Community College (Valhalla), 287
Wood Tobe–Coburn School (New York), 288

North Carolina
Brookstone College of Business (Charlotte), 290
Brookstone College of Business (Greensboro), 290
Center for Employment Training–Research Triangle Park (Research Triangle Park), 292
Central Piedmont Community College (Charlotte), 293
King's College (Charlotte), 299

Ohio
Akron Adult Vocational Services (Akron), 309
Belmont Technical College (St. Clairsville), 311
Bradford School (Columbus), 312
Columbus State Community College (Columbus), 317
Cuyahoga Community College (Cleveland), 318
Edison State Community College (Piqua), 319
Ehove Career Center (Milan), 319
ETI Technical College of Niles (Niles), 319
Gallipolis Career College (Gallipolis), 320
Hocking College (Nelsonville), 321
James A. Rhodes State College (Lima), 322
Lakeland Community College (Kirtland), 323
Licking County Joint Vocational School–Newark (Newark), 324
Lorain County JVS Adult Career Center (Oberlin), 324
Madison Local Schools–Madison Adult Education (Mansfield), 324
Mahoning County Joint Vocational School District (Canfield), 325
Miami University (Oxford), 326
North Central State College (Mansfield), 327
Ohio Business College (Lorain), 328
Ohio Business College (Sandusky), 328
Ohio Hi Point Joint Vocational School District (Bellefontaine), 329
Owens Community College (Toledo), 330
Stark State College of Technology (North Canton), 335

TCTC Adult Training Center (Warren), 336
Toledo School of Practical Nursing (Toledo), 337
Tri-County Vocational School Adult Career Center (Nelsonville), 337
Trumbull Business College (Warren), 338
The University of Akron (Akron), 338
The University of Akron–Wayne College (Orrville), 338
University of Rio Grande (Rio Grande), 339
Upper Valley JVS (Piqua), 340

Pennsylvania
Berks Technical Institute (Wyomissing), 344
Bradford School (Pittsburgh), 345
Cambria-Rowe Business College (Indiana), 346
Cambria-Rowe Business College (Johnstown), 346
Career Development & Employment (Wilkes Barre), 346
Community College of Beaver County (Monaca), 349
Computer Learning Network (Altoona), 349
Consolidated School of Business (Lancaster), 350
Consolidated School of Business (York), 350
Delaware County Community College (Media), 351
DuBois Business College (DuBois), 352
DuBois Business College (Huntingdon), 352
DuBois Business College (Oil City), 352
Greater Altoona Career and Technology Center (Altoona), 356
Harrisburg Area Community College (Harrisburg), 357
Lancaster County Career and Technology Center (Willow Street), 360
Laurel Business Institute (Uniontown), 361
Lehigh Carbon Community College (Schnecksville), 362
Lincoln Technical Institute (Philadelphia), 363
Luzerne County Community College (Nanticoke), 363
Montgomery County Community College (Blue Bell), 365
Newport Business Institute (Lower Burrell), 366
Newport Business Institute (Williamsport), 366
Pennsylvania School of Business (Allentown), 370
Prism Career Institute (Philadelphia), 371
Reading Area Community College (Reading), 372
South Hills School of Business & Technology (State College), 374
Westmoreland County Community College (Youngwood), 378

Puerto Rico
Academia Serrant (Ponce), 379
American Educational College (Bayamón), 379
Bayamón Community College (Bayamón), 381
Instituto de Banca y Comercio–Aprendes Practicanco (Río Piedras), 386
Instituto Pre-Vocacional E Indust de Puerto Rico (Arecibo), 387
International Technical College (San Juan), 389
John Dewey College, 389, 390
Liceo de Arte y Tecnologia (Hato Rey), 390
MBTI Business Training Institute (Santurce), 391
Nova College de Puerto Rico (Bayamón), 391
Trinity College of Puerto Rico (Ponce), 393

Rhode Island
Community College of Rhode Island (Warwick), 394

South Carolina
Aiken Technical College (Aiken), 397
Beta Tech (Columbia), 397

Central Carolina Technical College (Sumter), 398
Forrest Junior College (Anderson), 399
Greenville Technical College (Greenville), 399
Horry-Georgetown Technical College (Conway), 400
Midlands Technical College (Columbia), 401
Northeastern Technical College (Cheraw), 401
Orangeburg-Calhoun Technical College (Orangeburg), 402
Piedmont Technical College (Greenwood), 402
Spartanburg Community College (Spartanburg), 403
Technical College of the Lowcountry (Beaufort), 403
Tri-County Technical College (Pendleton), 403
Trident Technical College (Charleston), 404
Williamsburg Technical College (Kingstree), 404
York Technical College (Rock Hill), 405

Tennessee
Chattanooga State Technical Community College (Chattanooga), 406
Cleveland State Community College (Cleveland), 406
Northeast State Technical Community College (Blountville), 412
Roane State Community College (Harriman), 413
South College (Knoxville), 413
Tennessee Technology Center at Covington (Covington), 415
Tennessee Technology Center at Jacksboro (Jacksboro), 416
Tennessee Technology Center at McMinnville (McMinnville), 417
Tennessee Technology Center at Morristown (Morristown), 418
Virginia College School of Business and Health at Chattanooga (Chattanooga), 420
Volunteer State Community College (Gallatin), 421
West Tennessee Business College (Jackson), 421

Virginia
Center for Employment Training–Alexandria (Alexandria), 425
Miller-Motte Technical College (Lynchburg), 430
Washington County Adult Skill Center (Abingdon), 436

West Virginia
Community & Technical College at West Virginia University Institute of Technology (Montgomery), 439
Huntington Junior College (Huntington), 440
Mountain State College (Parkersburg), 442
Mountain State University (Beckley), 442
New River Community and Technical College (Beckley), 442
Opportunities Industrialization Center–North Central West Virginia (Fairmont), 442
Valley College of Technology (Beckley), 443
Valley College of Technology (Princeton), 443
West Virginia Northern Community College (Wheeling), 444

ADULT DEVELOPMENT AND AGING

Alabama
Shelton State Community College (Tuscaloosa), 46

Georgia
Albany Technical College (Albany), 103
Okefenokee Technical College (Waycross), 119
Southwest Georgia Technical College (Thomasville), 122

Massachusetts
North Shore Community College (Danvers), 204

Michigan
Grand Rapids Community College (Grand Rapids), 216
Lansing Community College (Lansing), 219
Madonna University (Livonia), 221
Oakland Community College (Bloomfield Hills), 224
Wayne County Community College District (Detroit), 229

New York
Genesee Community College (Batavia), 267
St. Joseph's College, Long Island Campus (Patchogue), 281
St. Joseph's College, New York (Brooklyn), 281

Pennsylvania
Harrisburg Area Community College (Harrisburg), 357
Penn State Shenango (Sharon), 369
The University of Scranton (Scranton), 377

Rhode Island
Community College of Rhode Island (Warwick), 394

ADULT HEALTH NURSE/NURSING

Florida
Saber (Miami), 94

ADVERTISING

Connecticut
Three Rivers Community College (Norwich), 57

Georgia
The Art Institute of Atlanta (Atlanta), 105

Michigan
Ferris State University (Big Rapids), 215
North Central Michigan College (Petoskey), 223

West Virginia
West Virginia State Community and Technical College (Institute), 444

AERONAUTICAL/AEROSPACE ENGINEERING TECHNOLOGY/TECHNICIAN

Ohio
Columbus State Community College (Columbus), 317

AERONAUTICS/AVIATION/AEROSPACE SCIENCE AND TECHNOLOGY, GENERAL

Connecticut
Naugatuck Valley Community College (Waterbury), 54

Georgia
Middle Georgia College (Cochran), 117

Maryland
Cecil College (North East), 186
The Community College of Baltimore County (Baltimore), 187

Ohio
Sinclair Community College (Dayton), 334

West Virginia
American Public University System (Charles Town), 437

AEROSPACE, AERONAUTICAL AND ASTRONAUTICAL ENGINEERING

Pennsylvania
Penn State University Park (University Park), 369

AESTHETICIAN/ESTHETICIAN AND SKIN CARE SPECIALIST

Connecticut

Academy Di Capelli—School of Cosmetology (Wallingford), 48
Albert School (Niantic), 49
Brio Academy of Cosmetology–East Hartford (East Hartford), 50
Brio Academy of Cosmetology–Fairfield (Fairfield), 50
Brio Academy of Cosmetology–Meriden (Meriden), 50
Brio Academy of Cosmetology–New Haven (New Haven), 50
Brio Academy of Cosmetology–Torrington (Torrington), 50
Brio Academy of Cosmetology–Willimantic (Willimantic), 51

Delaware

Academy of Massage and Bodywork (Bear), 58
Dawn Training Centre (Wilmington), 58
Delaware Learning Institute of Cosmetology (Dagsboro), 59

Florida

Academy of Career Training (Kissimmee), 63
Academy of Healing Arts, Massage, and Facial Skin Care (Lake Worth), 63
Academy of Professional Careers (Winter Park), 63
Artistic Nails and Beauty Academy (Tampa), 65
ASM Beauty World Academy (Hollywood), 65
The Beauty Institute (West Palm Beach), 66
Beauty Schools of America (Hialeah), 66
Beauty Schools of America (Miami), 66
Benes International School of Beauty (New Port Richey), 67
Bradenton Beauty Academy (Bradenton), 67
Central Florida College (Winter Park), 68
Daytona College (Ormond Beach), 72
Edutech Centers (Clearwater), 72
Fashion Focus Hair Academy (Sarasota), 74
Florida College of Natural Health (Bradenton), 76
Florida College of Natural Health (Maitland), 76
Florida College of Natural Health (Miami), 76
Florida College of Natural Health (Pompano Beach), 76
Gulf Coast College (Tampa), 79
Heritage Institute (Fort Myers), 80
Heritage Institute (Jacksonville), 80
Hi-Tech School of Cosmetology (Miami), 81
International Academy (South Daytona), 81
Keiser Career College–Greenacres (Greenacres), 82
Manhattan Beauty School (Tampa), 85
New Concept Massage and Beauty School (Miami), 88
North Florida Cosmetology Institute (Tallahassee), 88
North Florida Institute (Orange Park), 89
Paul Mitchell the School—Orlando (Casselberry), 91
Robert Morgan Vocational-Technical Center (Miami), 94
Sunstate Academy of Hair Design (Sarasota), 98
Ultimate Medical Academy (Clearwater), 100
Universal Massage and Beauty Institute (Sweetwater), 100
Westside Tech (Winter Garden), 102

Georgia

Appalachian Technical College (Jasper), 104
Atlanta School of Massage (Atlanta), 105
Central Georgia Technical College (Macon), 107
The Esani Institute (Roswell), 111
Flint River Technical College (Thomaston), 111

Georgia Career Institute (Conyers), 112
Griffin Technical College (Griffin), 113
International School of Skin and Nailcare (Atlanta), 115
Lanier Technical College (Oakwood), 115
Moultrie Technical College (Moultrie), 117
North Georgia Technical College (Clarkesville), 118
Ogeechee Technical College (Statesboro), 119
Rivertown School of Beauty (Columbus), 120
Valdosta Technical College (Valdosta), 123
West Georgia Technical College (LaGrange), 124

Illinois

Hair Professional Career College (De Kalb), 134
Hair Professionals Academy of Cosmetology (Elgin), 135
Hair Professionals Academy of Cosmetology (Wheaton), 135
Hair Professionals Career College (Palos Hills), 135
La' James College of Hairstyling (East Moline), 140
Ms. Robert's Academy of Beauty Culture–Villa Park (Villa Park), 144
Mr. John's School of Cosmetology (Decatur), 144
Pivot Point Beauty School (Chicago), 146
Pivot Point International Cosmetology Research Center (Elk Grove Villiage), 146
Rosel School of Cosmetology (Chicago), 149
Trend Setter's College of Cosmetology (Bradley), 152
University of Spa & Cosmetology Arts (Springfield), 153

Indiana

Creative Hairstyling Academy (Highland), 156
A Cut Above Beauty College (Indianapolis), 155
Don Roberts School of Hair Design (Munster), 157
Hair Fashions by Kaye Beauty College (Noblesville), 158
Honors Beauty College, Inc. (Indianapolis), 159
Ideal Beauty Academy (Jeffersonville), 159
Lafayette Beauty Academy (Lafayette), 165
Masters of Cosmetology College (Fort Wayne), 165
Ravenscroft Beauty College (Fort Wayne), 166
Rudae's School of Beauty Culture (Kokomo), 167

Kentucky

Bluegrass Community and Technical College (Lexington), 170
Collins School of Cosmetology (Middlesboro), 171
The Hair Design School (Florence), 173
The Hair Design School (Louisville), 173, 174
The Hair Design School (Radcliff), 174
Lexington Beauty College (Lexington), 175
West Kentucky Community and Technical College (Paducah), 180

Maine

Pierre's School of Beauty Culture (Portland), 182
Spa Tech Institute–Westbrook (Westbrook), 183

Maryland

Aesthetics Institute of Cosmetology (Gaithersburg), 183
Baltimore School of Massage (Baltimore), 185
The Fila Academy Inc (Glen Burnie), 187

Massachusetts

Blaine! The Beauty Career Schools–Hyannis (Hyannis), 194
Blaine! The Beauty Career Schools–Lowell (Lowell), 195

Blaine! The Beauty Career Schools–Waltham (Waltham), 195
Catherine Hinds Institute of Esthetics (Woburn), 196
Electrology Institute of New England (Tewksbury), 197
Elizabeth Grady School of Esthetics (Medford), 197
Jolie Hair and Beauty Academy (Ludlow), 199
North Shore Community College (Danvers), 204
Rob Roy Academy–Fall River Campus (Fall River), 205
Rob Roy Academy–Worcester Campus (Worcester), 205
Spa Tech Institute–Ipswich (Ipswich), 207
Spa Tech Institute–Plymouth (Plymouth), 207
Spa Tech Institute–Westboro (Westboro), 207

Michigan

David Pressley Professional School of Cosmetology (Royal Oak), 213
Douglas J. Educational Center (East Lansing), 214
Fiser's College of Cosmetology (Adrian), 216
Michigan College of Beauty (Monroe), 221
Michigan College of Beauty (Troy), 221
Mr. Bela's School of Cosmetology (Madison Heights), 223
Nuvo College of Cosmetology (Norton Shores), 224
P & A Scholars Beauty School (Detroit), 224
Port Huron Cosmetology College (Waterford), 225
School of Designing Arts (Springfield), 227

Mississippi

Day Spa Career College (Ocean Spring), 231
Delta Technical College (Southaven), 232
Magnolia College of Cosmetology (Jackson), 234

New Hampshire

Empire Beauty School–Laconia (Laconia), 237
Empire Beauty School–Portsmouth (Portsmouth), 237
Esthetics Institute at Concord Academy (Concord), 237
Michael's School of Hair Design and Esthetics (Manchester), 238

New Jersey

Artistic Academy of Hair Design (Fairlawn), 240
Capri Institute of Hair Design (Brick), 241
Capri Institute of Hair Design (Clifton), 241
Capri Institute of Hair Design (Kenilworth), 242
Capri Institute of Hair Design (Paramus), 242
Capri Institute of Hair Design (Succasunna), 242
Concorde School of Hair Design (Ocean Township), 243
European Academy of Cosmetology (Union), 245
Parisian Beauty School (Hackensack), 250
PB Cosmetology Education Center (Gloucester), 251
Rizzieri Aveda School for Beauty and Wellness (Marlton), 252
Roman Academy of Beauty Culture (Hawthorne), 252

New York

Aveda Institute New York (New York), 257
Beauty School of Middletown (Middletown), 257
Capri School of Hair Design (Spring Valley), 260
Carsten Institute of New York (New York), 260
Continental School of Beauty Culture–Jefferson (Rochester), 262

AFRICAN AMERICAN/BLACK STUDIES

AFRICAN STUDIES

AGRIBUSINESS/AGRICULTURAL BUSINESS OPERATIONS

AGRICULTURAL AND DOMESTIC ANIMALS SERVICES, OTHER

Massachusetts
North Shore Community College (Danvers), 204

AGRICULTURAL AND FOOD PRODUCTS PROCESSING

Mississippi
Jones County Junior College (Ellisville), 234

AGRICULTURAL BUSINESS AND MANAGEMENT, GENERAL

Alabama
Jefferson State Community College (Birmingham), 44

Illinois
Lake Land College (Mattoon), 140

Indiana
Vincennes University (Vincennes), 168

Michigan
Michigan State University (East Lansing), 222

North Carolina
Central Carolina Community College (Sanford), 292

Ohio
University of Northwestern Ohio (Lima), 339

West Virginia
Carver Career Center (Charleston), 438

AGRICULTURAL BUSINESS TECHNOLOGY

Georgia
Moultrie Technical College (Moultrie), 117

Illinois
Illinois Eastern Community Colleges, Wabash Valley College (Mount Carmel), 137

Michigan
St. Clair County Community College (Port Huron), 226

AGRICULTURAL/FARM SUPPLIES RETAILING AND WHOLESALING

Florida
Okaloosa Applied Technology Center (Ft. Walton Beach), 89

AGRICULTURAL MECHANICS AND EQUIPMENT/MACHINE TECHNOLOGY

Illinois
Danville Area Community College (Danville), 131

Ohio
University of Northwestern Ohio (Lima), 339

Pennsylvania
Penn State University Park (University Park), 369

Wisconsin
Northcentral Technical College (Wausau), 450

AGRICULTURAL MECHANIZATION, GENERAL

Georgia
Ogeechee Technical College (Statesboro), 119

Illinois
Black Hawk College (Moline), 125
Rend Lake College (Ina), 148

Mississippi
Mississippi Delta Community College (Moorhead), 234

AGRICULTURAL MECHANIZATION, OTHER

Florida
Lake City Community College (Lake City), 83

Mississippi
Mississippi Delta Community College (Moorhead), 234

AGRICULTURAL POWER MACHINERY OPERATION

Illinois
Kishwaukee College (Malta), 140
Lake Land College (Mattoon), 140
Parkland College (Champaign), 145

Ohio
The Ohio State University Agricultural Technical Institute (Wooster), 329

AGRICULTURAL PRODUCTION OPERATIONS, GENERAL

Alabama
Wallace State Community College (Hanceville), 48

Delaware
Delaware Technical & Community College, Jack F. Owens Campus (Georgetown), 59

Kentucky
Henderson Community College (Henderson), 174
Hopkinsville Community College (Hopkinsville), 174
Owensboro Community and Technical College (Owensboro), 177

Wisconsin
Fox Valley Technical College (Appleton), 446
Mid-State Technical College (Wisconsin Rapids), 449

AGRICULTURE, AGRICULTURE OPERATIONS AND RELATED SCIENCES, OTHER

Delaware
Delaware Technical & Community College, Jack F. Owens Campus (Georgetown), 59

North Carolina
James Sprunt Community College (Kenansville), 298
Surry Community College (Dobson), 306

AIRCRAFT POWERPLANT TECHNOLOGY/ TECHNICIAN

Alabama
Enterprise-Ozark Community College (Enterprise), 42
George C. Wallace Community College (Dothan), 43

Florida
Broward Community College (Fort Lauderdale), 68
Florida Community College at Jacksonville (Jacksonville), 77
George T. Baker Aviation School (Miami), 79
James Lorenzo Walker Vocational-Technical Center (Naples), 82

Georgia
Middle Georgia College (Cochran), 117
Savannah Technical College (Savannah), 121

Kentucky
Jefferson Community and Technical College (Louisville), 175
Somerset Community College (Somerset), 178

Michigan
Lansing Community College (Lansing), 219
Michigan Institute of Aeronautics (Belleville), 221
Northern Michigan University (Marquette), 224

New Jersey
Teterboro School of Aeronautics (Teterboro), 254

Ohio
Columbus State Community College (Columbus), 317
Sinclair Community College (Dayton), 334

Pennsylvania
Quaker City Institute of Aviation (Philadelphia), 372

South Carolina
Trident Technical College (Charleston), 404

Tennessee
North Central Institute (Clarksville), 412
Tennessee Technology Center at Memphis (Memphis), 417
Tennessee Technology Center at Morristown (Morristown), 418
Tennessee Technology Center at Nashville (Nashville), 418

Vermont
Burlington Technical Center (Burlington), 422

Virginia
Blue Ridge Community College (Weyers Cave), 424

Wisconsin
Milwaukee Area Technical College (Milwaukee), 449

AIRFRAME MECHANICS AND AIRCRAFT MAINTENANCE TECHNOLOGY/TECHNICIAN

Alabama
Enterprise-Ozark Community College (Enterprise), 42
George C. Wallace Community College (Dothan), 43

Florida
Broward Community College (Fort Lauderdale), 68
Florida Community College at Jacksonville (Jacksonville), 77
George T. Baker Aviation School (Miami), 79
James Lorenzo Walker Vocational-Technical Center (Naples), 82
National Aviation Academy (Clearwater), 88

Georgia
Central Georgia Technical College (Macon), 107
Middle Georgia College (Cochran), 117
Middle Georgia Technical College (Warner Robbins), 117
Savannah Technical College (Savannah), 121
South Georgia Technical College (Americus), 122

Illinois
Lewis University (Romeoville), 141
Rock Valley College (Rockford), 149

Indiana
Aviation Institute of Maintenance–Indianapolis (Indianapolis), 155

Michigan
Lansing Community College (Lansing), 219

New Jersey
Teterboro School of Aeronautics (Teterboro), 254

New York
Mohawk Valley Community College (Utica), 274
Vaughn College of Aeronautics and Technology (Flushing), 287
Western Suffolk BOCES (Northport), 288

Ohio
Columbus State Community College (Columbus), 317
Sinclair Community College (Dayton), 334

Pennsylvania
Quaker City Institute of Aviation
(Philadelphia), 372

South Carolina
Trident Technical College (Charleston), 404

Tennessee
North Central Institute (Clarksville), 412

Vermont
Burlington Technical Center (Burlington), 422

Virginia
Aviation Institute of Maintenance–Manassas
(Manassas), 424
Blue Ridge Community College (Weyers Cave),
424

Wisconsin
Milwaukee Area Technical College
(Milwaukee), 449

AIRLINE/COMMERCIAL/PROFESSIONAL PILOT AND FLIGHT CREW

Florida
Ari Ben Aviator (Fort Pierce), 65

Illinois
Kishwaukee College (Malta), 140
Southwestern Illinois College (Belleville), 151

North Carolina
Caldwell Community College and Technical
Institute (Hudson), 290
Guilford Technical Community College
(Jamestown), 297
Lenoir Community College (Kinston), 299

Ohio
Kent State University (Kent), 322

AIR TRAFFIC CONTROLLER

Pennsylvania
Community College of Beaver County
(Monaca), 349

ALLIED HEALTH AND MEDICAL ASSISTING SERVICES, OTHER

Connecticut
Capital Community College (Hartford), 51
Connecticut School of Electronics (Branford),
52
Gateway Community College (New Haven), 52
Goodwin College (East Hartford), 53
Housatonic Community College (Bridgeport),
53
Manchester Community College (Manchester),
54
Middlesex Community College (Middletown),
54
Naugatuck Valley Community College
(Waterbury), 54
Northwestern Connecticut Community College
(Winsted), 55
Quinebaug Valley Community College
(Danielson), 56
Three Rivers Community College (Norwich),
57

Delaware
Delaware Technical & Community College,
Jack F. Owens Campus (Georgetown), 59
Delaware Technical & Community College,
Terry Campus (Dover), 60

District of Columbia
Technical Learning Centers (Washington), 62

Florida
Americare School of Nursing (Fern Park), 64
Americare School of Nursing (St. Petersburg),
64
ATI Career Training Center (Fort Lauderdale),
65

Central Florida College (Saint Petersburg), 68
Central Florida College (Winter Park), 68
Concorde Career Institute (Tampa), 71
Everest Institute (Fort Lauderdale), 72
Florida Career College (Miami), 76
Heritage Institute (Fort Myers), 80
Heritage Institute (Jacksonville), 80
Lake Technical Center (Eustis), 83
Manatee Technical Institute (Bradenton), 85
Marion County Community Technical and
Adult Education Center (Ocala), 85
McFatter Technical Center (Davie), 86
Robert Morgan Vocational-Technical Center
(Miami), 94
Sanford-Brown Institute (Tampa), 95
Sheridan Vocational-Technical Center
(Hollywood), 96
Southern Technical Institute (Winter Park), 97
Sunstate Academy of Hair Design (Sarasota), 98
Westside Tech (Winter Garden), 102

Georgia
Bauder College (Atlanta), 106
Brown Mackie College–Atlanta (Atlanta), 107
Everest Institute (Marietta), 111

Illinois
Coyne American Institute Incorporated
(Chicago), 131
Everest College (Merrionette Park), 134
First Institute of Travel (Crystal Lake), 134
Fox College (Bedford Park), 134
Illinois School of Health Careers (Chicago), 138

Indiana
Everest College (Merrillville), 157

Kentucky
Spencerian College–Lexington (Lexington),
179

Maryland
All-State Career School (Baltimore), 184
Anne Arundel Community College (Arnold),
184

Massachusetts
Massachusetts Bay Community College
(Wellesley Hills), 201
Medical Professional Institute (Malden), 202
Southeastern Technical College (South Easton),
206

Michigan
Career Quest Learning Center (East Lansing),
212
Everest Institute (Grand Rapids), 215

Mississippi
Blue Cliff College–Gulfport (Gulfport), 230

New Jersey
Drake College of Business (Elizabeth), 244
Everest College (South Plainfield), 245
Healthcare Training Institute (Union), 246
HoHoKus School of Business and Medical
Sciences (Ramsey), 247

New York
Allen School–Brooklyn (Brooklyn), 256
Allen School–Jamaica (Jamaica), 256
Hunter Business School (Levittown), 269
Mohawk Valley Community College (Utica),
274
Wood Tobe–Coburn School (New York), 288

North Carolina
Brookstone College of Business (Greensboro),
290
King's College (Charlotte), 299
Medical Arts Massage School (Raleigh), 300

Ohio
Apollo School of Practical Nursing (Lima), 310
Bohecker College–Cincinnati (Cincinnati), 312
Bohecker College–Columbus (Westerville), 312

Buckeye Joint Vocational School (New
Philadelphia), 313
Butler Technology and Career Development
Schools–D. Russel Lee Career-Technology
Center (Hamilton), 314
Community Services Division–Alliance City
(Alliance), 317
Ohio Institute of Health Careers (Elyria), 329
Southwestern College of Business (Cincinnati),
335
Terra State Community College (Fremont), 336
Warren County Career Center (Lebanon), 340

Pennsylvania
Career Training Academy (New Kensington),
346
Career Training Academy (Pittsburgh), 346
Central Pennsylvania Institute of Science and
Technology (Pleasant Gap), 347
Computer Learning Network (Camp Hill), 349
DCI Career Institute (Monaca), 350
Huntingdon County Career and Technology
(Mill Creek), 358
Lebanon County Area Vocational Technical
School (Lebanon), 361
Lincoln Technical Institute (Allentown), 362
Lincoln Technical Institute (Philadelphia), 362
Pennsylvania Institute of Technology (Media),
370

Tennessee
Tennessee Technology Center at Ripley
(Ripley), 419

Virginia
Beta Tech (Richmond), 424
Career Training Solutions (Fredericksburg), 425
Centura College (Alexandria), 425
Everest College (Arlington), 427
Everest College (McLean), 427
Heritage Institute (Manassas), 428
Northern Virginia Community College
(Annandale), 430
Virginia Career Institute (Richmond), 435
Washington County Adult Skill Center
(Abingdon), 436

West Virginia
Fred W. Eberle Technical Center
(Buckhannon), 439
Huntington Junior College (Huntington), 440

Wisconsin
Chippewa Valley Technical College (Eau
Claire), 445
Concordia University Wisconsin (Mequon), 446
Mid-State Technical College (Wisconsin
Rapids), 449
Waukesha County Technical College
(Pewaukee), 453

ALLIED HEALTH DIAGNOSTIC, INTERVENTION, AND TREATMENT PROFESSIONS, OTHER

Alabama
Calhoun Community College (Decatur), 41
Wallace State Community College
(Hanceville), 48

Connecticut
Gateway Community College (New Haven), 52

Florida
Comp-Med Vocational Careers Corporation
(Hialeah), 70

Georgia
Grady Health System (Atlanta), 113

Kentucky
Gateway Community and Technical College
(Covington), 173

Maryland
College of Southern Maryland (La Plata), 186

Hagerstown Community College (Hagerstown), 188

Howard Community College (Columbia), 189

Massachusetts
Massasoit Community College (Brockton), 202
Quinsigamond Community College (Worcester), 205

Michigan
Carnegie Institute (Troy), 212

North Carolina
Caldwell Community College and Technical Institute (Hudson), 290
Durham Technical Community College (Durham), 295
Edgecombe Community College (Tarboro), 295
Forsyth Technical Community College (Winston-Salem), 296
Johnston Community College (Smithfield), 298
Pitt Community College (Greenville), 303
Wake Technical Community College (Raleigh), 307
Wilson Community College (Wilson), 308

Ohio
Cuyahoga Community College (Cleveland), 318
Hocking College (Nelsonville), 321
Lakeland Community College (Kirtland), 323

South Carolina
Greenville Technical College (Greenville), 399
Orangeburg-Calhoun Technical College (Orangeburg), 402

Tennessee
Roane State Community College (Harriman), 413

Virginia
Blue Ridge Community College (Weyers Cave), 424
Dabney S. Lancaster Community College (Clifton Forge), 426
Danville Community College (Danville), 426
Patrick Henry Community College (Martinsville), 431
Southside Virginia Community College (Alberta), 432
Southwest Virginia Community College (Richlands), 432
Tidewater Community College (Norfolk), 434
Virginia Highlands Community College (Abingdon), 435

Wisconsin
Chippewa Valley Technical College (Eau Claire), 445
Madison Area Technical College (Madison), 448
Milwaukee Area Technical College (Milwaukee), 449

ALTERNATIVE AND COMPLEMENTARY MEDICAL SUPPORT SERVICES, OTHER

Massachusetts
Mount Wachusett Community College (Gardner), 203

ALTERNATIVE AND COMPLEMENTARY MEDICINE AND MEDICAL SYSTEMS, OTHER

Massachusetts
Northern Essex Community College (Haverhill), 204

Pennsylvania
Drexel University (Philadelphia), 352

ALTERNATIVE FUEL VEHICLE TECHNOLOGY/ TECHNICIAN

Tennessee
Nashville Auto Diesel College (Nashville), 410

AMERICAN INDIAN/NATIVE AMERICAN LANGUAGES, LITERATURES, AND LINGUISTICS

Michigan
Bay Mills Community College (Brimley), 211

AMERICAN SIGN LANGUAGE (ASL)

Delaware
Delaware Technical & Community College, Stanton/Wilmington Campus (Newark), 59

New York
Rochester Institute of Technology (Rochester), 280

Pennsylvania
Community College of Allegheny County (Pittsburgh), 348

AMERICAN SIGN LANGUAGE, OTHER

Delaware
Delaware Technical & Community College, Stanton/Wilmington Campus (Newark), 59

AMERICAN/UNITED STATES STUDIES/ CIVILIZATION

Connecticut
Central Connecticut State University (New Britain), 51

District of Columbia
American University (Washington), 61

Massachusetts
Mount Holyoke College (South Hadley), 203

New Jersey
Bergen Community College (Paramus), 240

ANESTHESIOLOGIST ASSISTANT

Pennsylvania
Sanford-Brown Institute–Pittsburgh (Pittsburgh), 373

ANIMAL/LIVESTOCK HUSBANDRY AND PRODUCTION

Georgia
Abraham Baldwin Agricultural College (Tifton), 103

Illinois
Black Hawk College (Moline), 125
John Wood Community College (Quincy), 139

Michigan
Michigan State University (East Lansing), 222

North Carolina
James Sprunt Community College (Kenansville), 298
Sampson Community College (Clinton), 304
Surry Community College (Dobson), 306
Wayne Community College (Goldsboro), 308

ANIMAL SCIENCES, GENERAL

New York
Ulster County Community College (Stone Ridge), 286

ANIMAL SCIENCES, OTHER

Florida
Okaloosa Applied Technology Center (Ft. Walton Beach), 89

ANIMAL TRAINING

Illinois
Lake Land College (Mattoon), 140

ANIMATION, INTERACTIVE TECHNOLOGY, VIDEO GRAPHICS AND SPECIAL EFFECTS

District of Columbia
Corcoran College of Art and Design (Washington), 61

Florida
Orlando Technical Center (Orlando), 90

Georgia
Central Georgia Technical College (Macon), 107
Gwinnett Technical College (Lawrenceville), 113
North Metro Technical College (Acworth), 118
Sandersville Technical College (Sandersville), 120
West Georgia Technical College (LaGrange), 124

Illinois
City Colleges of Chicago, Harold Washington College (Chicago), 127
City Colleges of Chicago, Kennedy-King College (Chicago), 128
McHenry County College (Crystal Lake), 142
Moraine Valley Community College (Palos Hills), 143
Waubonsee Community College (Sugar Grove), 154

Maryland
Cecil College (North East), 186
Hagerstown Community College (Hagerstown), 188
Montgomery College (Rockville), 190

Michigan
Henry Ford Community College (Dearborn), 217
Muskegon Community College (Muskegon), 223

New Hampshire
New Hampshire Community Technical College, Stratham (Stratham), 239

New York
Mildred Elley School (Albany), 273

North Carolina
School of Communication Arts (Raleigh), 305

Pennsylvania
Bucks County Community College (Newtown), 345
Lehigh Carbon Community College (Schnecksville), 362

Puerto Rico
Colegio de Las Ciencias Arte y Television (Caparra Heights), 382

ANTHROPOLOGY

Indiana
Indiana University–Purdue University Fort Wayne (Fort Wayne), 160

APPAREL AND ACCESSORIES MARKETING OPERATIONS

Georgia
Gwinnett Technical College (Lawrenceville), 113

APPAREL AND TEXTILE MANUFACTURE

Alabama
Bishop State Community College (Mobile), 41
H. Councill Trenholm State Technical College (Montgomery), 43
Lawson State Community College (Birmingham), 44

Mississippi
Hinds Community College (Raymond), 232

Puerto Rico
Academia Serrant (Ponce), 379
Educational Technical College–Bayamón (Bayamón), 384
Educational Technical College–Recinto de Coama (Coama), 384
Educational Technical College–Recinto de San Sebastian (San Sebastian), 384
Industrial Technical College (Humacao), 386
Instituto Chaviano de Mayagüez (Mayagüez), 386
Liceo de Arte y Disenos (Caguas), 390

APPAREL AND TEXTILE MARKETING MANAGEMENT
Mississippi
Hinds Community College (Raymond), 232
Puerto Rico
Instituto Chaviano de Mayagüez (Mayagüez), 386

APPAREL AND TEXTILES, GENERAL
Puerto Rico
Instituto Chaviano de Mayagüez (Mayagüez), 386

APPAREL AND TEXTILES, OTHER
Florida
Orlando Technical Center (Orlando), 90
Puerto Rico
Instituto Merlix (Bayamón), 387
Liceo de Arte y Disenos (Caguas), 390
Universal Technology College of Puerto Rico (Aguadilla), 393

APPLIANCE INSTALLATION AND REPAIR TECHNOLOGY/TECHNICIAN
Florida
Manatee Technical Institute (Bradenton), 85
Miami Lakes Technical Education Center (Miami), 87
Robert Morgan Vocational-Technical Center (Miami), 94
Georgia
Columbus Technical College (Columbus), 108
Illinois
City Colleges of Chicago, Harry S. Truman College (Chicago), 128
Massachusetts
Bay State School of Technology (Canton), 194
Michigan
Lake Michigan College (Benton Harbor), 219
West Virginia
West Virginia Northern Community College (Wheeling), 444
Wisconsin
Milwaukee Area Technical College (Milwaukee), 449

APPLIED HORTICULTURE/HORTICULTURAL BUSINESS SERVICES, OTHER
Florida
First Coast Technical Institute (St. Augustine), 75
Wisconsin
Fox Valley Technical College (Appleton), 446
Moraine Park Technical College (Fond du Lac), 450

APPLIED HORTICULTURE/HORTICULTURAL OPERATIONS, GENERAL
Alabama
Calhoun Community College (Decatur), 41

Jefferson Davis Community College (Brewton), 44
Delaware
Delaware Technical & Community College, Jack F. Owens Campus (Georgetown), 59
Georgia
Albany Technical College (Albany), 103
Augusta Technical College (Augusta), 106
Chattahoochee Technical College (Marietta), 107
Columbus Technical College (Columbus), 108
Coosa Valley Technical College (Rome), 109
Griffin Technical College (Griffin), 113
Gwinnett Technical College (Lawrenceville), 113
Heart of Georgia Technical College (Dublin), 114
Moultrie Technical College (Moultrie), 117
North Georgia Technical College (Clarkesville), 118
North Metro Technical College (Acworth), 118
Ogeechee Technical College (Statesboro), 119
Okefenokee Technical College (Waycross), 119
South Georgia Technical College (Americus), 122
Valdosta Technical College (Valdosta), 123
Illinois
College of DuPage (Glen Ellyn), 129
Harper College (Palatine), 135
Illinois Central College (East Peoria), 136
Illinois Eastern Community Colleges, Lincoln Trail College (Robinson), 137
Illinois Valley Community College (Oglesby), 138
John Wood Community College (Quincy), 139
Lake Land College (Mattoon), 140
McHenry County College (Crystal Lake), 142
Rend Lake College (Ina), 148
Richland Community College (Decatur), 148
Southeastern Illinois College (Harrisburg), 151
Southwestern Illinois College (Belleville), 151
Spoon River College (Canton), 152
Triton College (River Grove), 153
Kentucky
Bluegrass Community and Technical College (Lexington), 170
Jefferson Community and Technical College (Louisville), 175
Maysville Community and Technical College (Maysville), 176
West Kentucky Community and Technical College (Paducah), 180
Maryland
Anne Arundel Community College (Arnold), 184
The Community College of Baltimore County (Baltimore), 187
Howard Community College (Columbia), 189
Montgomery College (Rockville), 190
Massachusetts
Cape Cod Community College (West Barnstable), 196
Mississippi
Jones County Junior College (Ellisville), 234
New Jersey
Bergen Community College (Paramus), 240
Ocean County Vocational Post Secondary Division (Toms River), 250
New York
Niagara County Community College (Sanborn), 277
North Carolina
Alamance Community College (Graham), 288
Beaufort County Community College (Washington), 289

Blue Ridge Community College (Flat Rock), 289
Brunswick Community College (Supply), 290
Carteret Community College (Morehead City), 292
Catawba Valley Community College (Hickory), 292
Central Piedmont Community College (Charlotte), 293
Forsyth Technical Community College (Winston-Salem), 296
Haywood Community College (Clyde), 297
Johnston Community College (Smithfield), 298
Lenoir Community College (Kinston), 299
Mayland Community College (Spruce Pine), 299
McDowell Technical Community College (Marion), 300
Pamlico Community College (Grantsboro), 302
Piedmont Community College (Roxboro), 302
Rockingham Community College (Wentworth), 304
Sampson Community College (Clinton), 304
Surry Community College (Dobson), 306
Western Piedmont Community College (Morganton), 308
Wilkes Community College (Wilkesboro), 308
Pennsylvania
Bidwell Training Center (Pittsburgh), 344
Lancaster County Career and Technology Center (Willow Street), 360
Luzerne County Community College (Nanticoke), 363
Temple University (Philadelphia), 374
South Carolina
Trident Technical College (Charleston), 404
Tennessee
Jackson State Community College (Jackson), 408
Virginia
Dabney S. Lancaster Community College (Clifton Forge), 426
Lord Fairfax Community College (Middletown), 429
Tidewater Community College (Norfolk), 434
Wisconsin
Madison Area Technical College (Madison), 448

APPLIED MATHEMATICS
District of Columbia
American University (Washington), 61

AQUACULTURE
Alabama
Gadsden State Community College (Gadsden), 42
Florida
Hillsborough Community College (Tampa), 81
Indian River State College (Fort Pierce), 81
Massachusetts
Bristol Community College (Fall River), 196
Mississippi
Mississippi Gulf Coast Community College (Perkinston), 234
New Jersey
Cumberland County College (Vineland), 244
North Carolina
Brunswick Community College (Supply), 290
Carteret Community College (Morehead City), 292
Ohio
Hocking College (Nelsonville), 321

ARABIC LANGUAGE AND LITERATURE

Michigan
University of Detroit Mercy (Detroit), 228

Ohio
University of Cincinnati (Cincinnati), 338

Pennsylvania
Temple University (Philadelphia), 374

ARCHEOLOGY

Connecticut
Norwalk Community College (Norwalk), 55

Ohio
Hocking College (Nelsonville), 321
The University of Akron (Akron), 338

ARCHITECTURAL DRAFTING AND ARCHITECTURAL CAD/CADD

Connecticut
Connecticut School of Electronics (Branford), 52
Naugatuck Valley Community College (Waterbury), 54
Porter and Chester Institute (Stratford), 56
Three Rivers Community College (Norwich), 57

Florida
Atlantic Vocational-Technical Center (Coconut Creek), 66
George Stone Area Vocational-Technical Center (Pensacola), 79
Lake Technical Center (Eustis), 83
Lincoln College of Technology (West Palm Beach), 84
Lively Technical Center (Tallahassee), 84
McFatter Technical Center (Davie), 86
Miami Lakes Technical Education Center (Miami), 87
Pinellas Technical Education Center–St. Petersburg (St. Petersburg), 92
Robert Morgan Vocational-Technical Center (Miami), 94
Sheridan Vocational-Technical Center (Hollywood), 96
Tom P. Haney Technical Center (Panama City), 99
Washington-Holmes Technical Center (Chipley), 102

Georgia
Atlanta Technical College (Atlanta), 105
Chattahoochee Technical College (Marietta), 107
Coosa Valley Technical College (Rome), 109
DeKalb Technical College (Clarkston), 109
Lanier Technical College (Oakwood), 115
Middle Georgia Technical College (Warner Robbins), 117
Northwestern Technical College (Rock Spring), 118
Ogeechee Technical College (Statesboro), 119
Southwest Georgia Technical College (Thomasville), 122
West Central Technical College (Waco), 124
West Georgia Technical College (LaGrange), 124

Illinois
City Colleges of Chicago, Harold Washington College (Chicago), 127
City Colleges of Chicago, Wilbur Wright College (Chicago), 129
College of DuPage (Glen Ellyn), 129
College of Lake County (Grayslake), 129
Harper College (Palatine), 135
Illinois Central College (East Peoria), 136
Illinois Valley Community College (Oglesby), 138

Kankakee Community College (Kankakee), 139
Kaskaskia College (Centralia), 139
Lincoln Land Community College (Springfield), 141
Oakton Community College (Des Plaines), 145
Rend Lake College (Ina), 148
Rock Valley College (Rockford), 149
Triton College (River Grove), 153

Maryland
Carroll Community College (Westminster), 186
The Community College of Baltimore County (Baltimore), 187
Frederick Community College (Frederick), 188
Hagerstown Community College (Hagerstown), 188
Montgomery College (Rockville), 190
Wor-Wic Community College (Salisbury), 193

Massachusetts
Springfield Technical Community College (Springfield), 207

Michigan
Baker College of Auburn Hills (Auburn Hills), 209
Baker College of Cadillac (Cadillac), 210
Baker College of Flint (Flint), 210
Baker College of Jackson (Jackson), 210
Baker College of Owosso (Owosso), 211
Lake Michigan College (Benton Harbor), 219
Macomb Community College (Warren), 220

New York
Mohawk Valley Community College (Utica), 274
Rochester Institute of Technology (Rochester), 280

Ohio
Lakeland Community College (Kirtland), 323
Owens Community College (Toledo), 330

Pennsylvania
Community College of Beaver County (Monaca), 349
Lancaster County Career and Technology Center (Willow Street), 360
Luzerne County Community College (Nanticoke), 363
YTI Career Institute–York (York), 379

Puerto Rico
Universidad del Este (Carolina), 393
Universidad del Turabo (Gurabo), 394

South Carolina
Northeastern Technical College (Cheraw), 401
Spartanburg Community College (Spartanburg), 403

Virginia
Northern Virginia Community College (Annandale), 430
Virginia Western Community College (Roanoke), 436

West Virginia
Putnam Career and Technology Center School of Practical Nursing (Eleanor), 443

ARCHITECTURAL ENGINEERING TECHNOLOGY/TECHNICIAN

Connecticut
Norwalk Community College (Norwalk), 55

Delaware
Delaware Technical & Community College, Jack F. Owens Campus (Georgetown), 59

Florida
Brevard Community College (Cocoa), 67
Broward Community College (Fort Lauderdale), 68
Daytona State College (Daytona Beach), 72

Florida Community College at Jacksonville (Jacksonville), 77
Hillsborough Community College (Tampa), 81
Miami Dade College (Miami), 87
Northwest Florida State College (Niceville), 89
Palm Beach Community College (Lake Worth), 90
Pensacola Junior College (Pensacola), 91
St. Johns River Community College (Palatka), 94
St. Petersburg College (St. Petersburg), 94
Valencia Community College (Orlando), 101

Indiana
Purdue University (West Lafayette), 166
Purdue University Calumet (Hammond), 166

New Hampshire
Manchester Community College (Manchester), 237

New Jersey
Mercer County Community College (Trenton), 248

North Carolina
Central Piedmont Community College (Charlotte), 293
Coastal Carolina Community College (Jacksonville), 293
College of The Albemarle (Elizabeth City), 294
Durham Technical Community College (Durham), 295
Fayetteville Technical Community College (Fayetteville), 295
Forsyth Technical Community College (Winston-Salem), 296
Gaston College (Dallas), 296
Guilford Technical Community College (Jamestown), 297
Pitt Community College (Greenville), 303
Roanoke-Chowan Community College (Ahoskie), 303
Wake Technical Community College (Raleigh), 307
Wilkes Community College (Wilkesboro), 308

Ohio
Columbus State Community College (Columbus), 317
Marion Technical College (Marion), 325
Owens Community College (Toledo), 330

Pennsylvania
Harrisburg Area Community College (Harrisburg), 357

Tennessee
Southwest Tennessee Community College (Memphis), 414

ARCHITECTURAL TECHNOLOGY/TECHNICIAN

Michigan
Lansing Community College (Lansing), 219
Washtenaw Community College (Ann Arbor), 229

ARCHITECTURE AND RELATED SERVICES, OTHER

Florida
James Lorenzo Walker Vocational-Technical Center (Naples), 82

AREA, ETHNIC, CULTURAL, AND GENDER STUDIES, OTHER

Maryland
Montgomery College (Rockville), 190

Pennsylvania
University of Pittsburgh at Johnstown (Johnstown), 377

AREA STUDIES, OTHER

Pennsylvania
Community College of Allegheny County (Pittsburgh), 348
University of Pittsburgh (Pittsburgh), 376

ART/ART STUDIES, GENERAL

Connecticut
Naugatuck Valley Community College (Waterbury), 54
Northwestern Connecticut Community College (Winsted), 55
Quinebaug Valley Community College (Danielson), 56

Georgia
Darton College (Albany), 109

Maryland
Maryland Institute College of Art (Baltimore), 190

Massachusetts
Suffolk University (Boston), 207

Michigan
Kellogg Community College (Battle Creek), 218

New Jersey
Essex County College (Newark), 244

Pennsylvania
Lehigh Carbon Community College (Schnecksville), 362

ART HISTORY, CRITICISM AND CONSERVATION

Massachusetts
Mount Holyoke College (South Hadley), 203

Pennsylvania
Marywood University (Scranton), 364

ARTS MANAGEMENT

Illinois
Columbia College Chicago (Chicago), 130

Maryland
Howard Community College (Columbia), 189

Ohio
Sinclair Community College (Dayton), 334

ASIAN BODYWORK THERAPY

Maryland
Baltimore School of Massage (Baltimore), 185

Massachusetts
Central Mass School of Massage & Therapy (Spencer), 197

New Jersey
Institute for Therapeutic Massage (Pompton Lakes), 247

ASIAN STUDIES/CIVILIZATION

Massachusetts
Mount Holyoke College (South Hadley), 203

Ohio
University of Cincinnati (Cincinnati), 338

Pennsylvania
University of Pittsburgh (Pittsburgh), 376

West Virginia
American Public University System (Charles Town), 437

ATHLETIC TRAINING/TRAINER

Alabama
Virginia College at Birmingham (Birmingham), 48

Georgia
West Georgia Technical College (LaGrange), 124

Massachusetts
Mount Wachusett Community College (Gardner), 203

New Jersey
Ocean County Vocational Post Secondary Division (Toms River), 250

New York
Rochester Institute of Technology (Rochester), 280

Ohio
Cincinnati State Technical and Community College (Cincinnati), 315
Lorain County Community College (Elyria), 324
The University of Akron (Akron), 338

Puerto Rico
Ponce Paramedical College (Ponce), 392

AUCTIONEERING

Pennsylvania
Harrisburg Area Community College (Harrisburg), 357

AUDIOVISUAL COMMUNICATIONS TECHNOLOGIES/TECHNICIANS, OTHER

Maryland
Montgomery College (Rockville), 190

Michigan
Muskegon Community College (Muskegon), 223

New York
Jamestown Community College (Jamestown), 270

North Carolina
School of Communication Arts (Raleigh), 305

Virginia
J. Sargeant Reynolds Community College (Richmond), 429
Northern Virginia Community College (Annandale), 430
Southwest Virginia Community College (Richlands), 432
Virginia Western Community College (Roanoke), 436

AUTOBODY/COLLISION AND REPAIR TECHNOLOGY/TECHNICIAN

Alabama
Bevill State Community College (Sumiton), 41
Bishop State Community College (Mobile), 41
Calhoun Community College (Decatur), 41
Gadsden State Community College (Gadsden), 42
George Corley Wallace State Community College (Selma), 43
George C. Wallace Community College (Dothan), 43
H. Councill Trenholm State Technical College (Montgomery), 43
Jefferson Davis Community College (Brewton), 44
Lawson State Community College (Birmingham), 44
Northwest-Shoals Community College (Muscle Shoals), 45
Reid State Technical College (Evergreen), 46
Shelton State Community College (Tuscaloosa), 46
Southern Union State Community College (Wadley), 47
Wallace State Community College (Hanceville), 48

Connecticut
Baran Institute of Technology (Windsor), 49

Florida
Atlantic Vocational-Technical Center (Coconut Creek), 66
Central Florida Community College (Ocala), 69
Daytona State College (Daytona Beach), 72
Florida Community College at Jacksonville (Jacksonville), 77
George Stone Area Vocational-Technical Center (Pensacola), 79
Hillsborough Community College (Tampa), 81
Indian River State College (Fort Pierce), 81
Lake Technical Center (Eustis), 83
Lee County Vocational High Tech Center–Central (Fort Myers), 84
Miami Lakes Technical Education Center (Miami), 87
Mid-Florida Tech (Orlando), 87
Palm Beach Community College (Lake Worth), 90
Pinellas Technical Education Center–St. Petersburg (St. Petersburg), 92
Robert Morgan Vocational-Technical Center (Miami), 94
Sarasota County Technical Institute (Sarasota), 96
Sheridan Vocational-Technical Center (Hollywood), 96
South Florida Community College (Avon Park), 97
Suwannee-Hamilton Area Vocational, Technical, and Adult Education Center (Live Oak), 98
Tom P. Haney Technical Center (Panama City), 99
Traviss Technical Center (Lakeland), 99
Washington-Holmes Technical Center (Chipley), 102
Withlacoochee Technical Institute (Inverness), 103

Georgia
Albany Technical College (Albany), 103
Appalachian Technical College (Jasper), 104
Athens Technical College (Athens), 105
Atlanta Technical College (Atlanta), 105
Central Georgia Technical College (Macon), 107
College of Coastal Georgia (Brunswick), 108
Columbus Technical College (Columbus), 108
Coosa Valley Technical College (Rome), 109
Griffin Technical College (Griffin), 113
Heart of Georgia Technical College (Dublin), 114
Lanier Technical College (Oakwood), 115
Moultrie Technical College (Moultrie), 117
North Georgia Technical College (Clarkesville), 118
Okefenokee Technical College (Waycross), 119
Savannah Technical College (Savannah), 121
South Georgia Technical College (Americus), 122
Valdosta Technical College (Valdosta), 123

Illinois
City Colleges of Chicago, Kennedy-King College (Chicago), 128
College of Lake County (Grayslake), 129
Highland Community College (Freeport), 136
John A. Logan College (Carterville), 138
Kaskaskia College (Centralia), 139
Kishwaukee College (Malta), 140
Lake Land College (Mattoon), 140
Lincoln Land Community College (Springfield), 141
Parkland College (Champaign), 145
Southeastern Illinois College (Harrisburg), 151
Southwestern Illinois College (Belleville), 151
Waubonsee Community College (Sugar Grove), 154

Indiana

Lincoln Technical Institute (Indianapolis), 165
Vincennes University (Vincennes), 168

Kentucky

Big Sandy Community and Technical College
(Prestonsburg), 170
Bluegrass Community and Technical College
(Lexington), 170
Bowling Green Technical College (Bowling
Green), 170
Gateway Community and Technical College
(Covington), 173
Hazard Community and Technical College
(Hazard), 174
Jefferson Community and Technical College
(Louisville), 175
Owensboro Community and Technical College
(Owensboro), 177
Somerset Community College (Somerset), 178
Southeast Kentucky Community and Technical
College (Cumberland), 178
West Kentucky Community and Technical
College (Paducah), 180

Maine

Northern Maine Community College (Presque
Isle), 182

Michigan

Alpena Community College (Alpena), 209
Bay de Noc Community College (Escanaba),
211
Lansing Community College (Lansing), 219
Northern Michigan University (Marquette), 224
Oakland Community College (Bloomfield
Hills), 224
Washtenaw Community College (Ann Arbor),
229

Mississippi

Coahoma Community College (Clarksdale), 231
East Central Community College (Decatur),
232
Hinds Community College (Raymond), 232
Holmes Community College (Goodman), 233
Itawamba Community College (Fulton), 233
Mississippi Gulf Coast Community College
(Perkinston), 234
Northeast Mississippi Community College
(Booneville), 235
Northwest Mississippi Community College
(Senatobia), 235

New Jersey

Ocean County Vocational Post Secondary
Division (Toms River), 250
Pennco Tech (Blackwood), 251

New York

Apex Technical School (New York), 256
New York Automotive and Diesel Institute
(Jamaica), 275

North Carolina

Blue Ridge Community College (Flat Rock),
289
Caldwell Community College and Technical
Institute (Hudson), 290
Cape Fear Community College (Wilmington),
290
Central Carolina Community College
(Sanford), 292
Central Piedmont Community College
(Charlotte), 293
Cleveland Community College (Shelby), 293
Coastal Carolina Community College
(Jacksonville), 293
Craven Community College (New Bern), 294
Edgecombe Community College (Tarboro), 295
Fayetteville Technical Community College
(Fayetteville), 295

Forsyth Technical Community College
(Winston-Salem), 296
Guilford Technical Community College
(Jamestown), 297
Haywood Community College (Clyde), 297
Isothermal Community College (Spindale), 298
Mayland Community College (Spruce Pine),
299
McDowell Technical Community College
(Marion), 300
Montgomery Community College (Troy), 301
Randolph Community College (Asheboro), 303
Sandhills Community College (Pinehurst), 305
South Piedmont Community College (Polkton),
305
Surry Community College (Dobson), 306
Wayne Community College (Goldsboro), 308
Wilkes Community College (Wilkesboro), 308

Ohio

Buckeye Joint Vocational School (New
Philadelphia), 313
Licking County Joint Vocational School–
Newark (Newark), 324
O. C. Collins Career Center (Chesapeake), 328
Ohio Technical College (Cleveland), 329
Owens Community College (Toledo), 330
Penta County Joint Vocational School
(Perrysburg), 330

Pennsylvania

Automotive Training Center (Exton), 344
Automotive Training Center (Warminster), 344
Greater Altoona Career and Technology Center
(Altoona), 356
Lancaster County Career and Technology
Center (Willow Street), 360
Lebanon County Area Vocational Technical
School (Lebanon), 361
Pennco Tech (Bristol), 368
Schuylkill Technology Center–North Campus
(Frackville), 373
WyoTech (Blairsville), 378

Rhode Island

New England Institute of Technology
(Warwick), 395

South Carolina

Florence-Darlington Technical College
(Florence), 399
Greenville Technical College (Greenville), 399

Tennessee

Nashville Auto Diesel College (Nashville), 410
Tennessee Technology Center at Athens
(Athens), 415
Tennessee Technology Center at Crossville
(Crossville), 415
Tennessee Technology Center at Crump
(Crump), 415
Tennessee Technology Center at Jackson
(Jackson), 417
Tennessee Technology Center at Knoxville
(Knoxville), 417
Tennessee Technology Center at Livingston
(Livingston), 417
Tennessee Technology Center at Memphis
(Memphis), 417
Tennessee Technology Center at Morristown
(Morristown), 418
Tennessee Technology Center at Nashville
(Nashville), 418
Tennessee Technology Center at Oneida/
Huntsville (Huntsville), 419
Tennessee Technology Center at Paris (Paris),
419
Tennessee Technology Center at Shelbyville
(Shelbyville), 419

Virginia

Danville Community College (Danville), 426

West Virginia

Cabell County Vocational Technical Center
(Huntington), 438
Carver Career Center (Charleston), 438
Fred W. Eberle Technical Center
(Buckhannon), 439
Logan-Mingo School of Practical Nursing
(Logan), 441
Monongalia County Technical Education
Center (Morgantown), 441
Putnam Career and Technology Center School
of Practical Nursing (Eleanor), 443

Wisconsin

Chippewa Valley Technical College (Eau
Claire), 445
Fox Valley Technical College (Appleton), 446
Lakeshore Technical College (Cleveland), 447
Madison Area Technical College (Madison),
448
Milwaukee Area Technical College
(Milwaukee), 449
Moraine Park Technical College (Fond du Lac),
450
Northcentral Technical College (Wausau), 450
Southwest Wisconsin Technical College
(Fennimore), 452
Waukesha County Technical College
(Pewaukee), 453
Wisconsin Indianhead Technical College (Shell
Lake), 453

AUTOMOBILE/AUTOMOTIVE MECHANICS TECHNOLOGY/TECHNICIAN

Alabama

Bevill State Community College (Sumiton), 41
Calhoun Community College (Decatur), 41
Central Alabama Community College
(Alexander City), 42
Gadsden State Community College (Gadsden),
42
Jefferson Davis Community College (Brewton),
44
J. F. Drake State Technical College (Huntsville),
44
Lawson State Community College
(Birmingham), 44
Lurleen B. Wallace Community College
(Andalusia), 45
Northwest-Shoals Community College (Muscle
Shoals), 45
Shelton State Community College (Tuscaloosa),
46
Southern Union State Community College
(Wadley), 47
Wallace State Community College
(Hanceville), 48

Connecticut

Baran Institute of Technology (Windsor), 49
Connecticut School of Electronics (Branford),
52
Lincoln Technical Institute (New Britain), 54
Naugatuck Valley Community College
(Waterbury), 54
Porter and Chester Institute (Stratford), 56

Delaware

Delaware Technical & Community College,
Jack F. Owens Campus (Georgetown), 59
Delaware Technical & Community College,
Stanton/Wilmington Campus (Newark), 59

Florida

American Advanced Technicians Institute
(Hialeah), 64
ATI Career Training Center (Oakland Park), 65
Atlantic Vocational-Technical Center (Coconut
Creek), 66
First Coast Technical Institute (St. Augustine),
75

George Stone Area Vocational-Technical Center (Pensacola), 79

Henry W. Brewster Technical Center (Tampa), 80

James Lorenzo Walker Vocational-Technical Center (Naples), 82

Lee County Vocational High Tech Center–Central (Fort Myers), 84

Lincoln College of Technology (West Palm Beach), 84

Lindsey Hopkins Technical Education Center (Miami), 84

Lively Technical Center (Tallahassee), 84

Manatee Technical Institute (Bradenton), 85

McFatter Technical Center (Davie), 86

Miami Lakes Technical Education Center (Miami), 87

Mid-Florida Tech (Orlando), 87

Motorcycle and Marine Mechanics Institute–Division of Universal Technical Institute (Orlando), 88

Okaloosa Applied Technology Center (Ft. Walton Beach), 89

Pinellas Technical Education Center–Clearwater (Clearwater), 91

Robert Morgan Vocational-Technical Center (Miami), 94

Sheridan Vocational-Technical Center (Hollywood), 96

Suwannee-Hamilton Area Vocational, Technical, and Adult Education Center (Live Oak), 98

Taylor Technical Institute (Perry), 99

Tom P. Haney Technical Center (Panama City), 99

Traviss Technical Center (Lakeland), 99

Withlacoochee Technical Institute (Inverness), 103

Georgia

Albany Technical College (Albany), 103

Altamaha Technical College (Jesup), 104

Appalachian Technical College (Jasper), 104

Athens Technical College (Athens), 105

Atlanta Technical College (Atlanta), 105

Augusta Technical College (Augusta), 106

Central Georgia Technical College (Macon), 107

Chattahoochee Technical College (Marietta), 107

College of Coastal Georgia (Brunswick), 108

Columbus Technical College (Columbus), 108

Coosa Valley Technical College (Rome), 109

Dalton State College (Dalton), 109

DeKalb Technical College (Clarkston), 109

East Central Technical College (Fitzgerald), 110

Flint River Technical College (Thomaston), 111

Griffin Technical College (Griffin), 113

Gwinnett Technical College (Lawrenceville), 113

Heart of Georgia Technical College (Dublin), 114

Lanier Technical College (Oakwood), 115

Middle Georgia Technical College (Warner Robbins), 117

Moultrie Technical College (Moultrie), 117

North Georgia Technical College (Clarkesville), 118

North Metro Technical College (Acworth), 118

Northwestern Technical College (Rock Spring), 118

Ogeechee Technical College (Statesboro), 119

Okefenokee Technical College (Waycross), 119

Savannah Technical College (Savannah), 121

South Georgia Technical College (Americus), 122

Southwest Georgia Technical College (Thomasville), 122

Swainsboro Technical College (Swainsboro), 123

Valdosta Technical College (Valdosta), 123

West Central Technical College (Waco), 124

West Georgia Technical College (LaGrange), 124

Illinois

Black Hawk College (Moline), 125

Carl Sandburg College (Galesburg), 127

City Colleges of Chicago, Harry S. Truman College (Chicago), 128

City Colleges of Chicago, Kennedy-King College (Chicago), 128

College of DuPage (Glen Ellyn), 129

College of Lake County (Grayslake), 129

Elgin Community College (Elgin), 132

Illinois Central College (East Peoria), 136

Illinois Eastern Community Colleges, Frontier Community College (Fairfield), 137

Illinois Eastern Community Colleges, Olney Central College (Olney), 137

Illinois Valley Community College (Oglesby), 138

John A. Logan College (Carterville), 138

Joliet Junior College (Joliet), 139

Kankakee Community College (Kankakee), 139

Kaskaskia College (Centralia), 139

Kishwaukee College (Malta), 140

Lake Land College (Mattoon), 140

Lewis and Clark Community College (Godfrey), 141

Lincoln Land Community College (Springfield), 141

Lincoln Technical Institute (Norridge), 142

McHenry County College (Crystal Lake), 142

Moraine Valley Community College (Palos Hills), 143

Morton College (Cicero), 143

Oakton Community College (Des Plaines), 145

Parkland College (Champaign), 145

Prairie State College (Chicago Heights), 146

Rend Lake College (Ina), 148

Richland Community College (Decatur), 148

Rock Valley College (Rockford), 149

Shawnee Community College (Ullin), 150

Southeastern Illinois College (Harrisburg), 151

Spoon River College (Canton), 152

Triton College (River Grove), 153

Universal Technical Institute (Glendale Heights), 153

Indiana

Ivy Tech Community College–Central Indiana (Indianapolis), 161

Ivy Tech Community College–East Central (Muncie), 162

Ivy Tech Community College–Kokomo (Kokomo), 162

Ivy Tech Community College–Lafayette (Lafayette), 162

Ivy Tech Community College–North Central (South Bend), 162

Ivy Tech Community College–Northeast (Fort Wayne), 163

Ivy Tech Community College–Northwest (Gary), 163

Ivy Tech Community College–Southern Indiana (Sellersburg), 163

Ivy Tech Community College–Southwest (Evansville), 163

Ivy Tech Community College–Wabash Valley (Terre Haute), 164

Ivy Tech Community College–Whitewater (Richmond), 164

Lincoln Technical Institute (Indianapolis), 165

Kentucky

Ashland Community and Technical College (Ashland), 169

Big Sandy Community and Technical College (Prestonsburg), 170

Bluegrass Community and Technical College (Lexington), 170

Bowling Green Technical College (Bowling Green), 170

Elizabethtown Community and Technical College (Elizabethtown), 172

Gateway Community and Technical College (Covington), 173

Hazard Community and Technical College (Hazard), 174

Jefferson Community and Technical College (Louisville), 175

Maysville Community and Technical College (Maysville), 176

Owensboro Community and Technical College (Owensboro), 177

Somerset Community College (Somerset), 178

Southeast Kentucky Community and Technical College (Cumberland), 178

Maine

Eastern Maine Community College (Bangor), 181

Northern Maine Community College (Presque Isle), 182

Washington County Community College (Calais), 183

Maryland

Allegany College of Maryland (Cumberland), 184

The Community College of Baltimore County (Baltimore), 187

Lincoln Technical Institute (Columbia), 189

Montgomery College (Rockville), 190

Massachusetts

Benjamin Franklin Institute of Technology (Boston), 194

Mount Wachusett Community College (Gardner), 203

Universal Technical Institute (Norwood), 208

Michigan

Alpena Community College (Alpena), 209

Bay de Noc Community College (Escanaba), 211

Delta College (University Center), 213

Ferris State University (Big Rapids), 215

Glen Oaks Community College (Centreville), 216

Gogebic Community College (Ironwood), 216

Grand Rapids Community College (Grand Rapids), 216

Henry Ford Community College (Dearborn), 217

Jackson Community College (Jackson), 218

Kalamazoo Valley Community College (Kalamazoo), 218

Lansing Community College (Lansing), 219

Macomb Community College (Warren), 220

Michigan Career and Technical Institute (Plainwell), 221

Mid Michigan Community College (Harrison), 222

Monroe County Community College (Monroe), 222

Montcalm Community College (Sidney), 223

Mott Community College (Flint), 223

Muskegon Community College (Muskegon), 223

Northern Michigan University (Marquette), 224

Northwestern Michigan College (Traverse City), 224

Oakland Community College (Bloomfield Hills), 224

Southwestern Michigan College (Dowagiac), 227

Washtenaw Community College (Ann Arbor), 229

Wayne County Community College District (Detroit), 229

Mississippi

Copiah-Lincoln Community College (Wesson), 231

East Central Community College (Decatur), 232

East Mississippi Community College (Scooba), 232

Hinds Community College (Raymond), 232

Holmes Community College (Goodman), 233

Itawamba Community College (Fulton), 233

Jones County Junior College (Ellisville), 234

Mississippi Delta Community College (Moorhead), 234

Mississippi Gulf Coast Community College (Perkinston), 234

Northeast Mississippi Community College (Booneville), 235

Northwest Mississippi Community College (Senatobia), 235

Southwest Mississippi Community College (Summit), 235

New Hampshire

New Hampshire Community Technical College, Berlin/Laconia (Berlin), 238

New Hampshire Community Technical College, Stratham (Stratham), 239

New Jersey

Brookdale Community College (Lincroft), 241

Camden County College (Blackwood), 241

Lincoln Technical Institute (Mahwah), 248

Lincoln Technical Institute (Union), 248

Metro Auto Electronics Training Institute (Kenilworth), 249

Monmouth County Vocational School District (Long Branch), 249

New Community Workforce Development Center (Newark), 250

Ocean County Vocational Post Secondary Division (Toms River), 250

Pennco Tech (Blackwood), 251

New York

Apex Technical School (New York), 256

Bronx Community College of the City University of New York (Bronx), 259

Columbia-Greene Community College (Hudson), 262

Corning Community College (Corning), 263

Fulton-Montgomery Community College (Johnstown), 267

Lincoln Technical Institute (Whitestone), 271

Monroe Community College (Rochester), 274

New York Automotive and Diesel Institute (Jamaica), 275

Onondaga-Courtland-Madison BOCES (Liverpool), 278

State University of New York College of Technology at Canton (Canton), 284

North Carolina

Alamance Community College (Graham), 288

Asheville-Buncombe Technical Community College (Asheville), 288

Beaufort County Community College (Washington), 289

Blue Ridge Community College (Flat Rock), 289

Caldwell Community College and Technical Institute (Hudson), 290

Cape Fear Community College (Wilmington), 290

Catawba Valley Community College (Hickory), 292

Central Carolina Community College (Sanford), 292

Central Piedmont Community College (Charlotte), 293

Coastal Carolina Community College (Jacksonville), 293

Davidson County Community College (Lexington), 294

Durham Technical Community College (Durham), 295

Edgecombe Community College (Tarboro), 295

Fayetteville Technical Community College (Fayetteville), 295

Forsyth Technical Community College (Winston-Salem), 296

Gaston College (Dallas), 296

Guilford Technical Community College (Jamestown), 297

Halifax Community College (Weldon), 297

Haywood Community College (Clyde), 297

James Sprunt Community College (Kenansville), 298

Lenoir Community College (Kinston), 299

Martin Community College (Williamston), 299

McDowell Technical Community College (Marion), 300

NASCAR Technical Institute (Mooresville), 301

Pitt Community College (Greenville), 303

Randolph Community College (Asheboro), 303

Rowan-Cabarrus Community College (Salisbury), 304

Sandhills Community College (Pinehurst), 305

Southwestern Community College (Sylva), 306

Surry Community College (Dobson), 306

Tri-County Community College (Murphy), 306

Vance-Granville Community College (Henderson), 307

Wake Technical Community College (Raleigh), 307

Wilkes Community College (Wilkesboro), 308

Wilson Community College (Wilson), 308

Ohio

Adult and Community Education–Hudson (Columbus), 309

Adult Center for Education (Zanesville), 309

Akron Adult Vocational Services (Akron), 309

Ashtabula County Joint Vocational School (Jefferson), 311

Auburn Career Center (Painesville), 311

Buckeye Joint Vocational School (New Philadelphia), 313

Community Services Division–Alliance City (Alliance), 317

Lorain County JVS Adult Career Center (Oberlin), 324

Madison Local Schools–Madison Adult Education (Mansfield), 324

O. C. Collins Career Center (Chesapeake), 328

Ohio Technical College (Cleveland), 329

Penta County Joint Vocational School (Perrysburg), 330

Pickaway Ross Joint Vocational School District (Chillicothe), 331

Polaris Career Center (Middleburg Heights), 331

Portage Lakes Career Center (Green), 331

TCTC Adult Training Center (Warren), 336

University of Northwestern Ohio (Lima), 339

Pennsylvania

Automotive Training Center (Exton), 344

Automotive Training Center (Warminster), 344

Commonwealth Technical Institute (Johnstown), 348

Community College of Allegheny County (Pittsburgh), 348

Delaware County Community College (Media), 351

Greater Altoona Career and Technology Center (Altoona), 356

Harrisburg Area Community College (Harrisburg), 357

Lancaster County Career and Technology Center (Willow Street), 360

Lebanon County Area Vocational Technical School (Lebanon), 361

Lincoln Technical Institute (Philadelphia), 363

New Castle School of Trades (Pulaski), 366

Northampton County Area Community College (Bethlehem), 366

Pennco Tech (Bristol), 368

Rosedale Technical Institute (Pittsburgh), 372

Schuylkill Technology Center–North Campus (Frackville), 373

Universal Technical Institute (Exton), 376

WyoTech (Blairsville), 378

Puerto Rico

Automeca Technical College (Aguadilla), 380

Automeca Technical College (Bayamón), 380

Automeca Technical College (Caguas), 380

Automeca Technical College (Ponce), 380

Caguas Institute of Mechanical Technology (Caguas), 381

Colegio Mayor de Tecnologia–Arroyo (Arroyo), 382

Industrial Technical College (Humacao), 386

John Dewey College, 389, 390

Liceo de Arte y Tecnologia (Hato Rey), 390

Rhode Island

Motoring Technical Training Institute (East Providence), 395

New England Institute of Technology (Warwick), 395

South Carolina

Aiken Technical College (Aiken), 397

Central Carolina Technical College (Sumter), 398

Florence-Darlington Technical College (Florence), 399

Greenville Technical College (Greenville), 399

Midlands Technical College (Columbia), 401

Orangeburg-Calhoun Technical College (Orangeburg), 402

Trident Technical College (Charleston), 404

Williamsburg Technical College (Kingstree), 404

York Technical College (Rock Hill), 405

Tennessee

Nashville Auto Diesel College (Nashville), 410

Northeast State Technical Community College (Blountville), 412

Tennessee Technology Center at Athens (Athens), 415

Tennessee Technology Center at Crossville (Crossville), 415

Tennessee Technology Center at Dickson (Dickson), 416

Tennessee Technology Center at Elizabethton (Elizabethton), 416

Tennessee Technology Center at Harriman (Harriman), 416

Tennessee Technology Center at Hartsville (Hartsville), 416

Tennessee Technology Center at Hohenwald (Hohenwald), 416

Tennessee Technology Center at Jacksboro (Jacksboro), 416

Tennessee Technology Center at Jackson (Jackson), 417

Tennessee Technology Center at Knoxville (Knoxville), 417

Tennessee Technology Center at Livingston (Livingston), 417

Tennessee Technology Center at McKenzie (McKenzie), 417

Tennessee Technology Center at McMinnville (McMinnville), 417

Tennessee Technology Center at Memphis (Memphis), 417

Tennessee Technology Center at Morristown (Morristown), 418

Tennessee Technology Center at Murfreesboro (Murfreesboro), 418

Tennessee Technology Center at Nashville (Nashville), 418

Tennessee Technology Center at Newbern (Newbern), 418

Tennessee Technology Center at Oneida/ Huntsville (Huntsville), 419

Tennessee Technology Center at Shelbyville (Shelbyville), 419

Tennessee Technology Center at Whiteville (Whiteville), 419

Virginia

Advanced Technology Institute (Virginia Beach), 423

Blue Ridge Community College (Weyers Cave), 424

Danville Community College (Danville), 426

Eastern Shore Community College (Melfa), 426

J. Sargeant Reynolds Community College (Richmond), 429

New River Community College (Dublin), 430

Northern Virginia Community College (Annandale), 430

Patrick Henry Community College (Martinsville), 431

Southside Virginia Community College (Alberta), 432

Thomas Nelson Community College (Hampton), 433

Tidewater Community College (Norfolk), 434

Tidewater Tech-Trades (Norfolk), 434

Woodrow Wilson Rehabilitation Center (Fishersville), 436

West Virginia

Academy of Careers and Technology (Beckley), 437

Ben Franklin Career Center (Dunbar), 437

Cabell County Vocational Technical Center (Huntington), 438

Carver Career Center (Charleston), 438

Fred W. Eberle Technical Center (Buckhannon), 439

Garnet Career Center (Charleston), 439

James Rumsey Technical Institute (Martinsburg), 440

Logan-Mingo School of Practical Nursing (Logan), 441

Monongalia County Technical Education Center (Morgantown), 441

Putnam Career and Technology Center School of Practical Nursing (Eleanor), 443

Wisconsin

Chippewa Valley Technical College (Eau Claire), 445

Fox Valley Technical College (Appleton), 446

Gateway Technical College (Kenosha), 446

Lakeshore Technical College (Cleveland), 447

Milwaukee Area Technical College (Milwaukee), 449

Moraine Park Technical College (Fond du Lac), 450

Nicolet Area Technical College (Rhinelander), 450

Northcentral Technical College (Wausau), 450

Waukesha County Technical College (Pewaukee), 453

Wisconsin Indianhead Technical College (Shell Lake), 453

AUTOMOTIVE ENGINEERING TECHNOLOGY/ TECHNICIAN

Alabama

George C. Wallace Community College (Dothan), 43

H. Councill Trenholm State Technical College (Montgomery), 43

Connecticut

Gateway Community College (New Haven), 52

Delaware

Delaware Technical & Community College, Jack F. Owens Campus (Georgetown), 59

Florida

ATI Career Training Center (Miami), 65

David G. Erwin Technical Center (Tampa), 71

Massachusetts

Massachusetts Bay Community College (Wellesley Hills), 201

Michigan

Baker College of Cadillac (Cadillac), 210

Baker College of Clinton Township (Clinton Township), 210

Baker College of Flint (Flint), 210

Baker College of Owosso (Owosso), 211

Ferris State University (Big Rapids), 215

New Jersey

New Community Workforce Development Center (Newark), 250

Sussex County Community College (Newton), 254

New York

Career Institute of Health and Technology (Garden City), 260

Ohio

Cincinnati State Technical and Community College (Cincinnati), 315

Columbus State Community College (Columbus), 317

Cuyahoga Community College (Cleveland), 318

Owens Community College (Toledo), 330

Sinclair Community College (Dayton), 334

Terra State Community College (Fremont), 336

Pennsylvania

Montgomery County Community College (Blue Bell), 365

Tennessee

Tennessee Technology Center at Crossville (Crossville), 415

Virginia

Tidewater Tech-Trades (Norfolk), 434

AVIATION/AIRWAY MANAGEMENT AND OPERATIONS

Florida

Miami Dade College (Miami), 87

Michigan

Lansing Community College (Lansing), 219

AVIONICS MAINTENANCE TECHNOLOGY/ TECHNICIAN

Alabama

Enterprise-Ozark Community College (Enterprise), 42

Florida

National Aviation Academy (Clearwater), 88

Georgia

Middle Georgia College (Cochran), 117

South Georgia Technical College (Americus), 122

Indiana

Aviation Institute of Maintenance–Indianapolis (Indianapolis), 155

Vincennes University (Vincennes), 168

Michigan

Lansing Community College (Lansing), 219

North Carolina

Guilford Technical Community College (Jamestown), 297

Wayne Community College (Goldsboro), 308

Ohio

Cincinnati State Technical and Community College (Cincinnati), 315

Sinclair Community College (Dayton), 334

Tennessee

North Central Institute (Clarksville), 412

Tennessee Technology Center at Memphis (Memphis), 417

Virginia

Aviation Institute of Maintenance–Manassas (Manassas), 424

BAKING AND PASTRY ARTS/BAKER/PASTRY CHEF

Connecticut

Connecticut Culinary Institute–Hartford (Hartford), 52

Connecticut Culinary Institute–Suffield (Suffield), 52

Manchester Community College (Manchester), 54

Florida

Lincoln College of Technology (West Palm Beach), 84

Orlando Culinary Academy (Orlando), 89

Valencia Community College (Orlando), 101

Georgia

Le Cordon Bleu College of Culinary Arts, Atlanta (Tucker), 116

North Georgia Technical College (Clarkesville), 118

Illinois

City Colleges of Chicago, Kennedy-King College (Chicago), 128

College of DuPage (Glen Ellyn), 129

Elgin Community College (Elgin), 132

Harper College (Palatine), 135

The Illinois Institute of Art–Chicago (Chicago), 138

Lincoln Land Community College (Springfield), 141

Triton College (River Grove), 153

Indiana

The Art Institute of Indianapolis (Indianapolis), 155

Kentucky

Sullivan University (Louisville), 179

Maryland

Baltimore International College (Baltimore), 185

Michigan

The Art Institute of Michigan (Novi), 209

Baker College of Muskegon (Muskegon), 211

Bay de Noc Community College (Escanaba), 211

Grand Rapids Community College (Grand Rapids), 216

Henry Ford Community College (Dearborn), 217

Mott Community College (Flint), 223

BANKING AND FINANCIAL SUPPORT SERVICES

BARBERING/BARBER

New Hampshire
New Hampshire Community Technical College, Stratham (Stratham), 239

North Carolina
Alamance Community College (Graham), 288

Ohio
Lakeland Community College (Kirtland), 323

Virginia
John Tyler Community College (Chester), 429
J. Sargeant Reynolds Community College (Richmond), 429

BIOMEDICAL/MEDICAL ENGINEERING

Florida
Advance Science Institute (Hialeah), 64

BIOMEDICAL TECHNOLOGY/TECHNICIAN

Florida
Broward Community College (Fort Lauderdale), 68

Illinois
South Suburban College (South Holland), 151

Maryland
Howard Community College (Columbia), 189

Massachusetts
Quinsigamond Community College (Worcester), 205

Tennessee
MedVance Institute–Nashville (Nashville), 409

BIOTECHNOLOGY

New Jersey
Berdan Institute (Totowa), 240

BLOOD BANK TECHNOLOGY SPECIALIST

Florida
Brevard Community College (Cocoa), 67
Indian River State College (Fort Pierce), 81
Lake City Community College (Lake City), 83
Miami Dade College (Miami), 87
Pasco-Hernando Community College (New Port Richey), 90
Pensacola Junior College (Pensacola), 91
St. Johns River Community College (Palatka), 94
Seminole Community College (Sanford), 96
Suwannee-Hamilton Area Vocational, Technical, and Adult Education Center (Live Oak), 98
Technical Career Institute (Miami Springs), 99

Kentucky
Southwestern College of Business (Florence), 178
Spencerian College (Louisville), 179

Tennessee
Southwest Tennessee Community College (Memphis), 414

Wisconsin
Moraine Park Technical College (Fond du Lac), 450

BOILERMAKING/BOILERMAKER

Ohio
Adult and Community Education–Hudson (Columbus), 309
Columbus State Community College (Columbus), 317
O. C. Collins Career Center (Chesapeake), 328

BROADCAST JOURNALISM

New York
New School of Radio and Television (Albany), 275

BUILDING/CONSTRUCTION FINISHING, MANAGEMENT, AND INSPECTION, OTHER

Alabama
H. Councill Trenholm State Technical College (Montgomery), 43
Lawson State Community College (Birmingham), 44

Florida
Pinellas Technical Education Center–St. Petersburg (St. Petersburg), 92

Maryland
Baltimore City Community College (Baltimore), 185
Carroll Community College (Westminster), 186
The Community College of Baltimore County (Baltimore), 187
Frederick Community College (Frederick), 188
Howard Community College (Columbia), 189
Montgomery College (Rockville), 190
Prince George's Community College (Largo), 191

Massachusetts
Springfield Technical Community College (Springfield), 207

Michigan
Delta College (University Center), 213

New York
Erie Community College (Buffalo), 265

North Carolina
Blue Ridge Community College (Flat Rock), 289
College of The Albemarle (Elizabeth City), 294
Haywood Community College (Clyde), 297
Isothermal Community College (Spindale), 298
Pitt Community College (Greenville), 303
Roanoke-Chowan Community College (Ahoskie), 303
Sampson Community College (Clinton), 304
Western Piedmont Community College (Morganton), 308
Wilkes Community College (Wilkesboro), 308

Ohio
Auburn Career Center (Painesville), 311

Pennsylvania
Harrisburg Area Community College (Harrisburg), 357

West Virginia
Carver Career Center (Charleston), 438

Wisconsin
Chippewa Valley Technical College (Eau Claire), 445
Milwaukee Area Technical College (Milwaukee), 449
Northcentral Technical College (Wausau), 450
Northeast Wisconsin Technical College (Green Bay), 450
Western Technical College (La Crosse), 453
Wisconsin Indianhead Technical College (Shell Lake), 453

BUILDING/CONSTRUCTION SITE MANAGEMENT/MANAGER

Maryland
The Community College of Baltimore County (Baltimore), 187
Frederick Community College (Frederick), 188

Michigan
Washtenaw Community College (Ann Arbor), 229

Pennsylvania
Delaware County Community College (Media), 351
Harrisburg Area Community College (Harrisburg), 357

BUILDING/HOME/CONSTRUCTION INSPECTION/INSPECTOR

Florida
Radford M. Locklin Technical Center (Milton), 92

Georgia
Gwinnett Technical College (Lawrenceville), 113

Illinois
City Colleges of Chicago, Kennedy-King College (Chicago), 128
Harper College (Palatine), 135
McHenry County College (Crystal Lake), 142

Pennsylvania
Commonwealth Technical Institute (Johnstown), 348
Harrisburg Area Community College (Harrisburg), 357
Pennsylvania Highlands Community College (Johnstown), 370

South Carolina
York Technical College (Rock Hill), 405

West Virginia
Putnam Career and Technology Center School of Practical Nursing (Eleanor), 443

BUILDING/PROPERTY MAINTENANCE AND MANAGEMENT

Florida
David G. Erwin Technical Center (Tampa), 71
Daytona State College (Daytona Beach), 72
Pinellas Technical Education Center–Clearwater (Clearwater), 91
South Florida Community College (Avon Park), 97
Traviss Technical Center (Lakeland), 99
Westside Tech (Winter Garden), 102

Georgia
East Central Technical College (Fitzgerald), 110
Okefenokee Technical College (Waycross), 119

Illinois
Center for Employment Training–Chicago (Chicago), 127
College of DuPage (Glen Ellyn), 129
Harper College (Palatine), 135
Lake Land College (Mattoon), 140
Lincoln Land Community College (Springfield), 141
Parkland College (Champaign), 145
Waubonsee Community College (Sugar Grove), 154

Indiana
Vincennes University (Vincennes), 168

Kentucky
Employment Solutions (Lexington), 172

Maryland
Hagerstown Community College (Hagerstown), 188
Prince George's Community College (Largo), 191

Michigan
Montcalm Community College (Sidney), 223
Wayne County Community College District (Detroit), 229

New Jersey
HoHoKus School of Trade and Technical Sciences (Linden), 247
New Community Workforce Development Center (Newark), 250

New York
Berk Trade and Business School (New York), 258

Building/Property Maintenance and Management

Monroe 2–Orleans BOCES Center for
Workforce Development (Rochester), 274

North Carolina
Blue Ridge Community College (Flat Rock),
289
Center for Employment Training–Research
Triangle Park (Research Triangle Park), 292
Central Piedmont Community College
(Charlotte), 293
Cleveland Community College (Shelby), 293
Edgecombe Community College (Tarboro), 295
Guilford Technical Community College
(Jamestown), 297
Halifax Community College (Weldon), 297
Piedmont Community College (Roxboro), 302
Rowan-Cabarrus Community College
(Salisbury), 304
Wake Technical Community College (Raleigh),
307

Ohio
Adult Center for Education (Zanesville), 309
Apollo School of Practical Nursing (Lima), 310
Auburn Career Center (Painesville), 311
Buckeye Hills Career Center (Rio Grande), 313
Penta County Joint Vocational School
(Perrysburg), 330
TCTC Adult Training Center (Warren), 336
Vanguard Career Center (Fremont), 340
Vatterott College (Broadview Heights), 340

Pennsylvania
Commonwealth Technical Institute
(Johnstown), 348
Dean Institute of Technology (Pittsburgh), 351
Delaware County Community College (Media),
351
Luzerne County Community College
(Nanticoke), 363
New Castle School of Trades (Pulaski), 366
Orleans Technical Institute (Philadelphia), 367

Rhode Island
Motoring Technical Training Institute (East
Providence), 395

Virginia
Center for Employment Training–Alexandria
(Alexandria), 425

Wisconsin
Gateway Technical College (Kenosha), 446
Madison Area Technical College (Madison),
448
Moraine Park Technical College (Fond du Lac),
450
Waukesha County Technical College
(Pewaukee), 453

BUSINESS ADMINISTRATION AND MANAGEMENT, GENERAL

Alabama
Calhoun Community College (Decatur), 41
Enterprise-Ozark Community College
(Enterprise), 42
Northwest-Shoals Community College (Muscle
Shoals), 45

Connecticut
Goodwin College (East Hartford), 53
University of Bridgeport (Bridgeport), 58

Delaware
Delaware Technical & Community College,
Jack F. Owens Campus (Georgetown), 59
Delaware Technical & Community College,
Stanton/Wilmington Campus (Newark), 59
Delaware Technical & Community College,
Terry Campus (Dover), 60

District of Columbia
Potomac College (Washington), 62
Strayer University (Washington), 62

Florida
Broward Community College (Fort Lauderdale),
68
Central Florida Community College (Ocala), 69
College of Business and Technology–Flagler
Campus (Miami), 70
College of Business and Technology–Hialeah
Campus (Hialeah), 70
College of Business and Technology (Miami), 70
Everest Institute (Hialeah), 72
Everest Institute (Miami), 73
Florida Community College at Jacksonville
(Jacksonville), 77
Florida Education Institute (Miami), 77
Florida Technical College (Jacksonville), 78
Florida Technical College (Orlando), 78
Hillsborough Community College (Tampa), 81
Lee County High Tech Center North (Cape
Coral), 83
Lee County Vocational High Tech Center–
Central (Fort Myers), 84
Miami Dade College (Miami), 87
Palm Beach Community College (Lake Worth),
90
Pasco-Hernando Community College (New Port
Richey), 90
St. Johns River Community College (Palatka),
94
St. Petersburg College (St. Petersburg), 94
Santa Fe Community College (Gainesville), 95
Seminole Community College (Sanford), 96
Southern Technical Institute (Winter Park), 97
Technical Career Institute (Miami Springs), 99
Tom P. Haney Technical Center (Panama City),
99
University of Phoenix–West Florida Campus
(Temple Terrace), 101
Valencia Community College (Orlando), 101

Georgia
Bauder College (Atlanta), 106
College of Coastal Georgia (Brunswick), 108
Gwinnett College (Lilburn), 113
Macon State College (Macon), 116
South Georgia College (Douglas), 122

Illinois
Brown Mackie College–Moline (Moline), 125
Carl Sandburg College (Galesburg), 127
City Colleges of Chicago, Harold Washington
College (Chicago), 127
City Colleges of Chicago, Harry S. Truman
College (Chicago), 128
City Colleges of Chicago, Richard J. Daley
College (Chicago), 128
City Colleges of Chicago, Wilbur Wright
College (Chicago), 129
College of DuPage (Glen Ellyn), 129
Danville Area Community College (Danville),
131
East-West University (Chicago), 132
Harper College (Palatine), 135
Illinois Central College (East Peoria), 136
Illinois Eastern Community Colleges, Lincoln
Trail College (Robinson), 137
John Wood Community College (Quincy), 139
Kankakee Community College (Kankakee), 139
Lake Land College (Mattoon), 140
Lewis and Clark Community College (Godfrey),
141
Lincoln Land Community College (Springfield),
141
MacCormac College (Chicago), 142
McHenry County College (Crystal Lake), 142
Northwestern Business College–Southwestern
Campus (Bridgeview), 144
Northwestern College (Chicago), 144
Oakton Community College (Des Plaines), 145
Quincy University (Quincy), 147

Richland Community College (Decatur), 148
Robert Morris University (Chicago), 149
Rockford Business College (Rockford), 149
Sanford-Brown College (Collinsville), 150
Sauk Valley Community College (Dixon), 150
Southeastern Illinois College (Harrisburg), 151
Southwestern Illinois College (Belleville), 151
Spoon River College (Canton), 152
Triton College (River Grove), 153
Waubonsee Community College (Sugar Grove),
154

Indiana
Ancilla College (Donaldson), 155
Brown Mackie College–Merrillville
(Merrillville), 156
Calumet College of Saint Joseph (Whiting), 156
Goshen College (Goshen), 157
Ivy Tech Community College–Bloomington
(Bloomington), 161
Ivy Tech Community College–Columbus
(Columbus), 162
Ivy Tech Community College–East Central
(Muncie), 162
Ivy Tech Community College–Kokomo
(Kokomo), 162
Ivy Tech Community College–North Central
(South Bend), 162
Ivy Tech Community College–Northeast (Fort
Wayne), 163
Ivy Tech Community College–Northwest
(Gary), 163
Ivy Tech Community College–Southeast
(Madison), 163
Ivy Tech Community College–Southern Indiana
(Sellersburg), 163
Ivy Tech Community College–Southwest
(Evansville), 163
Purdue University (West Lafayette), 166
TechSkills—Indianapolis (Indianapolis), 167
Vincennes University (Vincennes), 168

Kentucky
Ashland Community and Technical College
(Ashland), 169
Big Sandy Community and Technical College
(Prestonsburg), 170
Brown Mackie College–Hopkinsville
(Hopkinsville), 170
Daymar College (Paducah), 172
Elizabethtown Community and Technical
College (Elizabethtown), 172
Gateway Community and Technical College
(Covington), 173
Hazard Community and Technical College
(Hazard), 174
Hopkinsville Community College
(Hopkinsville), 174
Jefferson Community and Technical College
(Louisville), 175
Madisonville Community College
(Madisonville), 176
Maysville Community and Technical College
(Maysville), 176
National College (Lexington), 176
Owensboro Community and Technical College
(Owensboro), 177
Somerset Community College (Somerset), 178
Southeast Kentucky Community and Technical
College (Cumberland), 178
Sullivan University (Louisville), 179
West Kentucky Community and Technical
College (Paducah), 180

Maine
Central Maine Community College (Auburn),
181
Southern Maine Community College (South
Portland), 182

Maryland

Allegany College of Maryland (Cumberland), 184

Anne Arundel Community College (Arnold), 184

Cecil College (North East), 186

Chesapeake College (Wye Mills), 186

College of Southern Maryland (La Plata), 186

The Community College of Baltimore County (Baltimore), 187

Frederick Community College (Frederick), 188

Garrett College (McHenry), 188

Hagerstown Community College (Hagerstown), 188

Harford Community College (Bel Air), 189

Howard Community College (Columbia), 189

Montgomery College (Rockville), 190

Prince George's Community College (Largo), 191

Wor-Wic Community College (Salisbury), 193

Massachusetts

Assumption College (Worcester), 193

Bridgewater State College (Bridgewater), 195

Fitchburg State College (Fitchburg), 198

Marian Court College (Swampscott), 201

Middlesex Community College (Bedford), 202

Mount Wachusett Community College (Gardner), 203

Suffolk University (Boston), 207

Michigan

Davenport University (Grand Rapids), 213

Delta College (University Center), 213

Ferris State University (Big Rapids), 215

Jackson Community College (Jackson), 218

Kalamazoo Valley Community College (Kalamazoo), 218

Kellogg Community College (Battle Creek), 218

Kirtland Community College (Roscommon), 219

Lansing Community College (Lansing), 219

Macomb Community College (Warren), 220

Mott Community College (Flint), 223

North Central Michigan College (Petoskey), 223

Mississippi

Belhaven College (Jackson), 230

New Hampshire

Lebanon College (Lebanon), 237

Manchester Community College (Manchester), 237

New Hampshire Community Technical College, Berlin/Laconia (Berlin), 238

New Hampshire Community Technical College, Stratham (Stratham), 239

New Hampshire Technical Institute (Concord), 239

New Jersey

Cumberland County College (Vineland), 244

Dover Business College (Paramus), 244

HoHoKus School of Business and Medical Sciences (Ramsey), 247

Prism Career Institute (Sewell), 252

Warren County Community College (Washington), 255

New York

ASA Institute, The College of Advanced Technology (Brooklyn), 257

Bramson ORT College (Forest Hills), 258

Cazenovia College (Cazenovia), 261

The College of Westchester (White Plains), 262

Everest Institute (Rochester), 266

Genesee Community College (Batavia), 267

Globe Institute of Technology (New York), 268

Ithaca College (Ithaca), 270

Mount Saint Mary College (Newburgh), 275

Nassau Community College (Garden City), 275

New York University (New York), 277

Pace University (New York), 279

Rochester Institute of Technology (Rochester), 280

St. Joseph's College, Long Island Campus (Patchogue), 281

St. Joseph's College, New York (Brooklyn), 281

Spanish-American Institute (New York), 283

Syracuse University (Syracuse), 285

North Carolina

Alamance Community College (Graham), 288

Asheville-Buncombe Technical Community College (Asheville), 288

Beaufort County Community College (Washington), 289

Bladen Community College (Dublin), 289

Blue Ridge Community College (Flat Rock), 289

Brunswick Community College (Supply), 290

Caldwell Community College and Technical Institute (Hudson), 290

Cape Fear Community College (Wilmington), 290

Catawba Valley Community College (Hickory), 292

Central Carolina Community College (Sanford), 292

Central Piedmont Community College (Charlotte), 293

Cleveland Community College (Shelby), 293

Coastal Carolina Community College (Jacksonville), 293

Davidson County Community College (Lexington), 294

Edgecombe Community College (Tarboro), 295

Fayetteville Technical Community College (Fayetteville), 295

Forsyth Technical Community College (Winston-Salem), 296

Guilford Technical Community College (Jamestown), 297

Halifax Community College (Weldon), 297

Haywood Community College (Clyde), 297

Isothermal Community College (Spindale), 298

Johnston Community College (Smithfield), 298

Lenoir Community College (Kinston), 299

Martin Community College (Williamston), 299

Mayland Community College (Spruce Pine), 299

Mitchell Community College (Statesville), 300

Montgomery Community College (Troy), 301

Pamlico Community College (Grantsboro), 302

Piedmont Community College (Roxboro), 302

Pitt Community College (Greenville), 303

Richmond Community College (Hamlet), 303

Roanoke-Chowan Community College (Ahoskie), 303

Rockingham Community College (Wentworth), 304

Rowan-Cabarrus Community College (Salisbury), 304

Sampson Community College (Clinton), 304

Sandhills Community College (Pinehurst), 305

Southeastern Community College (Whiteville), 305

South Piedmont Community College (Polkton), 305

Southwestern Community College (Sylva), 306

Stanly Community College (Albemarle), 306

Surry Community College (Dobson), 306

Tri-County Community College (Murphy), 306

Vance-Granville Community College (Henderson), 307

Wake Technical Community College (Raleigh), 307

Wayne Community College (Goldsboro), 308

Western Piedmont Community College (Morganton), 308

Wilkes Community College (Wilkesboro), 308

Wilson Community College (Wilson), 308

Ohio

Akron Adult Vocational Services (Akron), 309

Ashland University (Ashland), 310

Bowling Green State University–Firelands College (Huron), 312

Brown Mackie College–Akron (Akron), 313

Brown Mackie College–Findlay (Findlay), 313

Brown Mackie College–North Canton (Canton), 313

Cincinnati State Technical and Community College (Cincinnati), 315

Clark State Community College (Springfield), 316

Lakeland Community College (Kirtland), 323

Marion Technical College (Marion), 325

North Central State College (Mansfield), 327

Pioneer Career and Technology Center: A Vocational School District (Shelby), 331

Sinclair Community College (Dayton), 334

TechSkills—Columbus (Columbus), 336

Terra State Community College (Fremont), 336

The University of Akron (Akron), 338

University of Cincinnati Clermont College (Batavia), 339

Youngstown State University (Youngstown), 341

Zane State College (Zanesville), 342

Pennsylvania

Bucks County Community College (Newtown), 345

Butler County Community College (Butler), 345

Community College of Allegheny County (Pittsburgh), 348

Community College of Philadelphia (Philadelphia), 349

Consolidated School of Business (Lancaster), 350

Consolidated School of Business (York), 350

Harrisburg Area Community College (Harrisburg), 357

Kaplan Career Institute–Harrisburg (Harrisburg), 359

La Roche College (Pittsburgh), 361

Lebanon Valley College (Annville), 362

Lehigh Carbon Community College (Schnecksville), 362

Montgomery County Community College (Blue Bell), 365

Muhlenberg College (Allentown), 365

Penn State Brandywine (Media), 368

Penn State Shenango (Sharon), 369

Penn State University Park (University Park), 369

Pennsylvania School of Business (Allentown), 370

Point Park University (Pittsburgh), 371

Reading Area Community College (Reading), 372

Robert Morris University (Moon Township), 372

Saint Vincent College (Latrobe), 373

Slippery Rock University of Pennsylvania (Slippery Rock), 374

The University of Scranton (Scranton), 377

Westmoreland County Community College (Youngwood), 378

Puerto Rico

MBTI Business Training Institute (Santurce), 391

Universal Career Counseling Centers (Santurce), 393

Rhode Island

Community College of Rhode Island (Warwick), 394

Providence College (Providence), 396

South Carolina

Aiken Technical College (Aiken), 397
Greenville Technical College (Greenville), 399
Lander University (Greenwood), 401
Northeastern Technical College (Cheraw), 401
Piedmont Technical College (Greenwood), 402
Technical College of the Lowcountry (Beaufort), 403
York Technical College (Rock Hill), 405

Tennessee

Columbia State Community College (Columbia), 406
Draughons Junior College (Murfreesboro), 407
National College (Nashville), 411

Vermont

Champlain College (Burlington), 422

Virginia

Beta Tech (Richmond), 424
ECPI College of Technology (Virginia Beach), 426
Everest College (McLean), 427
National College (Salem), 430
Potomac College (Herndon), 431
Tidewater Tech (Chesapeake), 434
Tidewater Tech (Virginia Beach), 434

West Virginia

American Public University System (Charles Town), 437
West Virginia Business College (Nutter Fort), 443

Wisconsin

Nicolet Area Technical College (Rhinelander), 450

BUSINESS ADMINISTRATION, MANAGEMENT AND OPERATIONS, OTHER

Georgia

Bainbridge College (Bainbridge), 106
Heart of Georgia Technical College (Dublin), 114
North Georgia Technical College (Clarkesville), 118
Southwest Georgia Technical College (Thomasville), 122

Illinois

Northwestern University (Evanston), 145

Indiana

Kaplan College–Northwest Indianapolis Campus (Indianapolis), 165

Maryland

Anne Arundel Community College (Arnold), 184
Baltimore City Community College (Baltimore), 185
Cecil College (North East), 186
The Community College of Baltimore County (Baltimore), 187
Frederick Community College (Frederick), 188
Howard Community College (Columbia), 189

Massachusetts

Mount Wachusett Community College (Gardner), 203

Michigan

West Shore Community College (Scottville), 229

New Jersey

Mercer County Community College (Trenton), 248

North Carolina

Rowan-Cabarrus Community College (Salisbury), 304

Ohio

Chancellor University (Cleveland), 315

Lorain County JVS Adult Career Center (Oberlin), 324
Sandusky Adult Education (Sandusky), 333

Pennsylvania

Elizabethtown College (Elizabethtown), 352
Penn State Shenango (Sharon), 369
The University of Scranton (Scranton), 377

Rhode Island

Providence College (Providence), 396

Tennessee

Draughons Junior College (Clarksville), 407
Draughons Junior College (Nashville), 407
Tennessee Technology Center at Whiteville (Whiteville), 419

Virginia

Blue Ridge Community College (Weyers Cave), 424
Dabney S. Lancaster Community College (Clifton Forge), 426
J. Sargeant Reynolds Community College (Richmond), 429
Lord Fairfax Community College (Middletown), 429
Northern Virginia Community College (Annandale), 430
Patrick Henry Community College (Martinsville), 431
Southside Virginia Community College (Alberta), 432
University of Mary Washington (Fredericksburg), 434
Virginia Highlands Community College (Abingdon), 435

Wisconsin

Nicolet Area Technical College (Rhinelander), 450

BUSINESS AND PERSONAL/FINANCIAL SERVICES MARKETING OPERATIONS

Alabama

Central Alabama Community College (Alexander City), 42
Jefferson Davis Community College (Brewton), 44

Florida

Florida Community College at Jacksonville (Jacksonville), 77
Palm Beach Community College (Lake Worth), 90

New York

Mohawk Valley Community College (Utica), 274

Wisconsin

Moraine Park Technical College (Fond du Lac), 450

BUSINESS/COMMERCE, GENERAL

Alabama

Central Alabama Community College (Alexander City), 42
Jefferson Davis Community College (Brewton), 44
Jefferson State Community College (Birmingham), 44
Lawson State Community College (Birmingham), 44
Southern Union State Community College (Wadley), 47

Connecticut

Goodwin College (East Hartford), 53

Delaware

Delaware Technical & Community College, Jack F. Owens Campus (Georgetown), 59
Delaware Technical & Community College, Stanton/Wilmington Campus (Newark), 59

Delaware Technical & Community College, Terry Campus (Dover), 60

Florida

ATI Career Training Center (Oakland Park), 65
David G. Erwin Technical Center (Tampa), 71
Sheridan Vocational-Technical Center (Hollywood), 96

Georgia

Brown Mackie College–Atlanta (Atlanta), 107
Darton College (Albany), 109
Macon State College (Macon), 116
Savannah River College (Augusta), 121

Illinois

John A. Logan College (Carterville), 138
Kendall College (Chicago), 140
Moraine Valley Community College (Palos Hills), 143
Northwestern University (Evanston), 145
Rock Valley College (Rockford), 149
Saint Xavier University (Chicago), 150

Indiana

Ancilla College (Donaldson), 155
Brown Mackie College–Fort Wayne (Fort Wayne), 155
Brown Mackie College–Michigan City (Michigan City), 156
Brown Mackie College–South Bend (South Bend), 156
Indiana University Bloomington (Bloomington), 160
Indiana University–Purdue University Fort Wayne (Fort Wayne), 160
Indiana University–Purdue University Indianapolis (Indianapolis), 160

Kentucky

National College (Lexington), 176

Maine

Beal College (Bangor), 180

Massachusetts

Roxbury Community College (Roxbury Crossing), 205

Michigan

Bay Mills Community College (Brimley), 211
Gogebic Community College (Ironwood), 216
Macomb Community College (Warren), 220
St. Clair County Community College (Port Huron), 226
Schoolcraft College (Livonia), 227

New Jersey

Keyskills Learning (Clifton), 247

New York

Graduate School and University Center of the City University of New York (New York), 268
Mercy College (Dobbs Ferry), 273
Pace University (New York), 279
Rochester Institute of Technology (Rochester), 280

Ohio

Ashland University (Ashland), 310
Brown Mackie College–Cincinnati (Cincinnati), 313
Edison State Community College (Piqua), 319
Hocking College (Nelsonville), 321
Kent State University (Kent), 322
Kent State University, Salem Campus (Salem), 323
Kent State University, Trumbull Campus (Warren), 323
Kent State University, Tuscarawas Campus (New Philadelphia), 323
North Central State College (Mansfield), 327

Pennsylvania

Butler County Community College (Butler), 345
Gannon University (Erie), 355

Harrisburg Area Community College (Harrisburg), 357
Luzerne County Community College (Nanticoke), 363
Marywood University (Scranton), 364

Puerto Rico
Educational Technical College–Bayamón (Bayamón), 384
Educational Technical College–Recinto de Coama (Coama), 384
Educational Technical College–Recinto de San Sebastian (San Sebastian), 384

Rhode Island
Motoring Technical Training Institute (East Providence), 395

South Carolina
Horry-Georgetown Technical College (Conway), 400
Midlands Technical College (Columbia), 401
Piedmont Technical College (Greenwood), 402
Technical College of the Lowcountry (Beaufort), 403
Tri-County Technical College (Pendleton), 403
Trident Technical College (Charleston), 404

Tennessee
National College (Nashville), 411
Southwest Tennessee Community College (Memphis), 414

Vermont
Champlain College (Burlington), 422

Virginia
National College (Salem), 430
Tidewater Community College (Norfolk), 434

West Virginia
Alderson-Broaddus College (Philippi), 437
Community & Technical College at West Virginia University Institute of Technology (Montgomery), 439
West Virginia Northern Community College (Wheeling), 444

BUSINESS/CORPORATE COMMUNICATIONS

Maryland
Cecil College (North East), 186

Massachusetts
Assumption College (Worcester), 193

New York
Graduate School and University Center of the City University of New York (New York), 268

BUSINESS, MANAGEMENT, MARKETING, AND RELATED SUPPORT SERVICES, OTHER

Connecticut
Asnuntuck Community College (Enfield), 49
Capital Community College (Hartford), 51
Gateway Community College (New Haven), 52
Manchester Community College (Manchester), 54
Middlesex Community College (Middletown), 54
Naugatuck Valley Community College (Waterbury), 54
Northwestern Connecticut Community College (Winsted), 55
Quinebaug Valley Community College (Danielson), 56
Three Rivers Community College (Norwich), 57
Tunxis Community College (Farmington), 57

Florida
Brevard Community College (Cocoa), 67
Broward Community College (Fort Lauderdale), 68
Central Florida Community College (Ocala), 69

Florida Community College at Jacksonville (Jacksonville), 77
Miami Dade College (Miami), 87
Sheridan Vocational-Technical Center (Hollywood), 96

Kentucky
Spencerian College (Louisville), 179

Massachusetts
Massachusetts Bay Community College (Wellesley Hills), 201
Quinsigamond Community College (Worcester), 205
Roxbury Community College (Roxbury Crossing), 205

New York
Cayuga County Community College (Auburn), 261
Globe Institute of Technology (New York), 268
Maria College (Albany), 272
New York University (New York), 277
Niagara County Community College (Sanborn), 277
Professional Business Institute (New York), 279
Rochester Institute of Technology (Rochester), 280
St. Joseph's College, Long Island Campus (Patchogue), 281
St. Joseph's College, New York (Brooklyn), 281
Ulster County Community College (Stone Ridge), 286

Ohio
Hocking College (Nelsonville), 321
James A. Rhodes State College (Lima), 322
Kent State University (Kent), 322
Raphael's School of Beauty Culture (Niles), 331
University of Cincinnati (Cincinnati), 338
Xavier University (Cincinnati), 341

Pennsylvania
Douglas Education Center (Monessen), 351
DuBois Business College (DuBois), 352
DuBois Business College (Huntingdon), 352
DuBois Business College (Oil City), 352

Tennessee
Southwest Tennessee Community College (Memphis), 414
Tennessee Technology Center at Livingston (Livingston), 417
Tennessee Technology Center at Pulaski (Pulaski), 419

BUSINESS/MANAGERIAL ECONOMICS

Connecticut
Albertus Magnus College (New Haven), 49

BUSINESS/OFFICE AUTOMATION/ TECHNOLOGY/DATA ENTRY

Connecticut
Ridley-Lowell Business and Technical Institute (New London), 56

Delaware
Delaware Technical & Community College, Jack F. Owens Campus (Georgetown), 59
Delaware Technical & Community College, Terry Campus (Dover), 60

Florida
Advanced Technical Centers (Miami), 64
Technical Career Institute (Miami Springs), 99

Georgia
Advanced Career Training (Atlanta), 103
Bainbridge College (Bainbridge), 106
Brown College of Court Reporting and Medical Transcription (Atlanta), 107
Dalton State College (Dalton), 109

Illinois
City Colleges of Chicago, Richard J. Daley College (Chicago), 128
City Colleges of Chicago, Wilbur Wright College (Chicago), 129
College of Lake County (Grayslake), 129
Computer Systems Institute (Skokie), 130
Elgin Community College (Elgin), 132
Gem City College (Quincy), 134
Heartland Community College (Normal), 136
Illinois Central College (East Peoria), 136
Illinois Eastern Community Colleges, Lincoln Trail College (Robinson), 137
Illinois Valley Community College (Oglesby), 138
John A. Logan College (Carterville), 138
Kankakee Community College (Kankakee), 139
Kaskaskia College (Centralia), 139
Lake Land College (Mattoon), 140
Lewis and Clark Community College (Godfrey), 141
Lincoln Land Community College (Springfield), 141
MacCormac College (Chicago), 142
McHenry County College (Crystal Lake), 142
Moraine Valley Community College (Palos Hills), 143
Morton College (Cicero), 143
Parkland College (Champaign), 145
Pyramid Career Institute (Chicago), 147
Rend Lake College (Ina), 148
Richland Community College (Decatur), 148
Rock Valley College (Rockford), 149
Sauk Valley Community College (Dixon), 150
Southeastern Illinois College (Harrisburg), 151
Southwestern Illinois College (Belleville), 151
Sparks College (Shelbyville), 152
Spoon River College (Canton), 152

Indiana
Brown Mackie College–Indianapolis (Indianapolis), 156
TechSkills—Indianapolis (Indianapolis), 167
Vincennes University (Vincennes), 168

Kentucky
Daymar College (Louisville), 171
Daymar College (Paducah), 172
Spencerian College (Louisville), 179

Maryland
Kaplan College–Hagerstown (Hagerstown), 189
TESST College of Technology (Beltsville), 192
TESST College of Technology (Towson), 192

Massachusetts
Massasoit Community College (Brockton), 202
North Shore Community College (Danvers), 204
Roxbury Community College (Roxbury Crossing), 205
Southeastern Technical College (South Easton), 206

Michigan
Career Quest Learning Center (East Lansing), 212
Detroit Business Institute–Downriver (Riverview), 214
Kalamazoo Valley Community College (Kalamazoo), 218
Lake Michigan College (Benton Harbor), 219
Michigan Career and Technical Institute (Plainwell), 221
Montcalm Community College (Sidney), 223
Muskegon Community College (Muskegon), 223
Oakland Community College (Bloomfield Hills), 224

Mississippi
Antonelli College (Hattiesburg), 230
Antonelli College (Jackson), 230

BUSINESS STATISTICS

CABINETMAKING AND MILLWORK/ MILLWRIGHT

CAD/CADD DRAFTING AND/OR DESIGN TECHNOLOGY/TECHNICIAN

CAD/CADD Drafting and/or Design Technology/Technician

CANADIAN STUDIES

CARDIOVASCULAR TECHNOLOGY/ TECHNOLOGIST

CARPENTRY/CARPENTER

Michigan
Bay de Noc Community College (Escanaba), 211
Kirtland Community College (Roscommon), 219
Lansing Community College (Lansing), 219

Mississippi
Coahoma Community College (Clarksdale), 231
East Central Community College (Decatur), 232
Hinds Community College (Raymond), 232
Meridian Community College (Meridian), 234
Mississippi Gulf Coast Community College (Perkinston), 234
Southwest Mississippi Community College (Summit), 235

New Hampshire
Manchester Community College (Manchester), 237

New Jersey
Adult and Continuing Education–Bergen County Technical Schools (Hackensack), 240
Ocean County Vocational Post Secondary Division (Toms River), 250

New York
Mohawk Valley Community College (Utica), 274
State University of New York College of Technology at Delhi (Delhi), 284

North Carolina
Alamance Community College (Graham), 288
Asheville-Buncombe Technical Community College (Asheville), 288
Bladen Community College (Dublin), 289
Blue Ridge Community College (Flat Rock), 289
Cape Fear Community College (Wilmington), 290
Central Carolina Community College (Sanford), 292
Cleveland Community College (Shelby), 293
Forsyth Technical Community College (Winston-Salem), 296
Guilford Technical Community College (Jamestown), 297
McDowell Technical Community College (Marion), 300
Pamlico Community College (Grantsboro), 302
Piedmont Community College (Roxboro), 302
Robeson Community College (Lumberton), 304
Southwestern Community College (Sylva), 306
Surry Community College (Dobson), 306
Vance-Granville Community College (Henderson), 307

Ohio
Cleveland Municipal School District Adult and Continuing Education (Cleveland), 316
Washington County Career Center Adult Education (Marietta), 341

Pennsylvania
Community College of Allegheny County (Pittsburgh), 348
Delaware County Community College (Media), 351
Greater Altoona Career and Technology Center (Altoona), 356
Lancaster County Career and Technology Center (Willow Street), 360
Lebanon County Area Vocational Technical School (Lebanon), 361
Orleans Technical Institute (Philadelphia), 367
Schuylkill Technology Center–North Campus (Frackville), 373

South Carolina
Greenville Technical College (Greenville), 399
York Technical College (Rock Hill), 405

Virginia
Woodrow Wilson Rehabilitation Center (Fishersville), 436

West Virginia
Logan-Mingo School of Practical Nursing (Logan), 441

Wisconsin
Blackhawk Technical College (Janesville), 445
College of Menominee Nation (Keshena), 446
Fox Valley Technical College (Appleton), 446
Gateway Technical College (Kenosha), 446
Lac Courte Oreilles Ojibwa Community College (Hayward), 447
Lakeshore Technical College (Cleveland), 447
Madison Area Technical College (Madison), 448
Mid-State Technical College (Wisconsin Rapids), 449
Milwaukee Area Technical College (Milwaukee), 449
Southwest Wisconsin Technical College (Fennimore), 452
Waukesha County Technical College (Pewaukee), 453

CARTOGRAPHY

Alabama
Enterprise-Ozark Community College (Enterprise), 42
Lawson State Community College (Birmingham), 44

Georgia
East Central Technical College (Fitzgerald), 110

Illinois
DePaul University (Chicago), 131

Kentucky
Bluegrass Community and Technical College (Lexington), 170
Western Kentucky University (Bowling Green), 180

Massachusetts
University of Massachusetts Boston (Boston), 208

Michigan
Michigan Technological University (Houghton), 222
Northern Michigan University (Marquette), 224

Mississippi
Hinds Community College (Raymond), 232

New Hampshire
New Hampshire Community Technical College, Berlin/Laconia (Berlin), 238

New Jersey
Monmouth University (West Long Branch), 249

Ohio
The University of Akron (Akron), 338

South Carolina
Greenville Technical College (Greenville), 399

Tennessee
Roane State Community College (Harriman), 413

CHEMICAL ENGINEERING

Ohio
Ohio University (Athens), 330
The University of Akron (Akron), 338

Pennsylvania
Penn State University Park (University Park), 369

CHEMICAL TECHNOLOGY/TECHNICIAN

Alabama
Jefferson Davis Community College (Brewton), 44

Northwest-Shoals Community College (Muscle Shoals), 45

Florida
Brevard Community College (Cocoa), 67
St. Johns River Community College (Palatka), 94

Georgia
Athens Technical College (Athens), 105
Augusta Technical College (Augusta), 106

Maryland
The Community College of Baltimore County (Baltimore), 187

Michigan
Delta College (University Center), 213

New Jersey
Essex County College (Newark), 244

North Carolina
Guilford Technical Community College (Jamestown), 297

Ohio
Lakeland Community College (Kirtland), 323

Pennsylvania
Bidwell Training Center (Pittsburgh), 344
Delaware County Community College (Media), 351

Rhode Island
Community College of Rhode Island (Warwick), 394

South Carolina
Midlands Technical College (Columbia), 401

Tennessee
Northeast State Technical Community College (Blountville), 412

CHILD-CARE AND SUPPORT SERVICES MANAGEMENT

Alabama
Bevill State Community College (Sumiton), 41
Bishop State Community College (Mobile), 41
Calhoun Community College (Decatur), 41
Central Alabama Community College (Alexander City), 42
Chattahoochee Valley Community College (Phenix City), 42
Enterprise-Ozark Community College (Enterprise), 42
Gadsden State Community College (Gadsden), 42
George C. Wallace Community College (Dothan), 43
H. Councill Trenholm State Technical College (Montgomery), 43
James H. Faulkner State Community College (Bay Minette), 44
Jefferson State Community College (Birmingham), 44
Lawson State Community College (Birmingham), 44
Lurleen B. Wallace Community College (Andalusia), 45
Northeast Alabama Community College (Rainsville), 45
Northwest-Shoals Community College (Muscle Shoals), 45
Reid State Technical College (Evergreen), 46
Shelton State Community College (Tuscaloosa), 46
Snead State Community College (Boaz), 46
Southern Union State Community College (Wadley), 47
Wallace State Community College (Hanceville), 48

Child-Care and Support Services Management

Connecticut
Asnuntuck Community College (Enfield), 49
Briarwood College (Southington), 50
Capital Community College (Hartford), 51
Gateway Community College (New Haven), 52
Housatonic Community College (Bridgeport), 53
Middlesex Community College (Middletown), 54
Naugatuck Valley Community College (Waterbury), 54
Northwestern Connecticut Community College (Winsted), 55
Norwalk Community College (Norwalk), 55
Post University (Waterbury), 56
Quinebaug Valley Community College (Danielson), 56
Three Rivers Community College (Norwich), 57
Tunxis Community College (Farmington), 57

Florida
Florida Community College at Jacksonville (Jacksonville), 77
Lively Technical Center (Tallahassee), 84
Manatee Technical Institute (Bradenton), 85
Miami Lakes Technical Education Center (Miami), 87
Orlando Technical Center (Orlando), 90
Palm Beach Community College (Lake Worth), 90
Sarasota County Technical Institute (Sarasota), 96
Seminole Community College (Sanford), 96
Suwannee-Hamilton Area Vocational, Technical, and Adult Education Center (Live Oak), 98
Tom P. Haney Technical Center (Panama City), 99

Georgia
Albany Technical College (Albany), 103
Athens Technical College (Athens), 105
Atlanta Technical College (Atlanta), 105
Bainbridge College (Bainbridge), 106
Central Georgia Technical College (Macon), 107
Chattahoochee Technical College (Marietta), 107
Coosa Valley Technical College (Rome), 109
Dalton State College (Dalton), 109
DeKalb Technical College (Clarkston), 109
Flint River Technical College (Thomaston), 111
Griffin Technical College (Griffin), 113
Heart of Georgia Technical College (Dublin), 114
Lanier Technical College (Oakwood), 115
Ogeechee Technical College (Statesboro), 119
Sandersville Technical College (Sandersville), 120
Valdosta Technical College (Valdosta), 123

Illinois
College of DuPage (Glen Ellyn), 129

Indiana
Purdue University Calumet (Hammond), 166

Maine
Andover College (South Portland), 180

Maryland
Anne Arundel Community College (Arnold), 184
Baltimore City Community College (Baltimore), 185
Carroll Community College (Westminster), 186
Chesapeake College (Wye Mills), 186
College of Southern Maryland (La Plata), 186
The Community College of Baltimore County (Baltimore), 187
Frederick Community College (Frederick), 188

Hagerstown Community College (Hagerstown), 188
Howard Community College (Columbia), 189
Wor-Wic Community College (Salisbury), 193

Massachusetts
Holyoke Community College (Holyoke), 199

Michigan
Bay Mills Community College (Brimley), 211
Kellogg Community College (Battle Creek), 218
Schoolcraft College (Livonia), 227
Wayne County Community College District (Detroit), 229

New Jersey
Ocean County Vocational Post Secondary Division (Toms River), 250

New York
Adirondack Community College (Queensbury), 255
Broome Community College (Binghamton), 259
Cayuga County Community College (Auburn), 261
Clinton Community College (Plattsburgh), 262
Corning Community College (Corning), 263
Dutchess Community College (Poughkeepsie), 264
Fulton-Montgomery Community College (Johnstown), 267
Genesee Community College (Batavia), 267
Jamestown Community College (Jamestown), 270
Monroe Community College (Rochester), 274
Onondaga Community College (Syracuse), 277
Orange County Community College (Middletown), 278
Rockland Community College (Suffern), 281
Schenectady County Community College (Schenectady), 282
Westchester Community College (Valhalla), 287

North Carolina
Blue Ridge Community College (Flat Rock), 289
Brunswick Community College (Supply), 290
Caldwell Community College and Technical Institute (Hudson), 290
Edgecombe Community College (Tarboro), 295
Haywood Community College (Clyde), 297
Lenoir Community College (Kinston), 299
Mayland Community College (Spruce Pine), 299
Mitchell Community College (Statesville), 300
Piedmont Community College (Roxboro), 302
Vance-Granville Community College (Henderson), 307
Western Piedmont Community College (Morganton), 308

Ohio
Apollo School of Practical Nursing (Lima), 310
Cincinnati State Technical and Community College (Cincinnati), 315
Columbus State Community College (Columbus), 317
The University of Toledo (Toledo), 339

Pennsylvania
Community College of Allegheny County (Pittsburgh), 348
Lancaster County Career and Technology Center (Willow Street), 360
Laurel Technical Institute (Sharon), 361
Northampton County Area Community College (Bethlehem), 366
Pennsylvania Highlands Community College (Johnstown), 370
Reading Area Community College (Reading), 372

Puerto Rico
Instituto Comercial de Puerto Rico Junior College (San Juan), 386
Liceo de Arte y Disenos (Caguas), 390

South Carolina
Piedmont Technical College (Greenwood), 402
Trident Technical College (Charleston), 404

Tennessee
Southwest Tennessee Community College (Memphis), 414
Tennessee Technology Center at Nashville (Nashville), 418
Tennessee Technology Center at Paris (Paris), 419

Wisconsin
Milwaukee Area Technical College (Milwaukee), 449
Moraine Park Technical College (Fond du Lac), 450
Nicolet Area Technical College (Rhinelander), 450
Rasmussen College Green Bay (Green Bay), 451

CHILD-CARE PROVIDER/ASSISTANT

Connecticut
Goodwin College (East Hartford), 53
Manchester Community College (Manchester), 54
Post University (Waterbury), 56

Florida
Bradford Union Area Vocational Technical Center (Starke), 67
Brevard Community College (Cocoa), 67
Central Florida Community College (Ocala), 69
Charlotte Vocational-Technical Center (Port Charlotte), 69
Chipola College (Marianna), 69
Coral Ridge Nurses Assistant Training School (Ft. Lauderdale), 71
First Coast Technical Institute (St. Augustine), 75
Florida Community College at Jacksonville (Jacksonville), 77
Gulf Coast Community College (Panama City), 79
Henry W. Brewster Technical Center (Tampa), 80
Hillsborough Community College (Tampa), 81
Indian River State College (Fort Pierce), 81
James Lorenzo Walker Vocational-Technical Center (Naples), 82
Lake Technical Center (Eustis), 83
Lee County Vocational High Tech Center–Central (Fort Myers), 84
Miami-Dade County Public Schools (Miami), 87
Miami Lakes Technical Education Center (Miami), 87
North Florida Community College (Madison), 88
Northwest Florida State College (Niceville), 89
Orlando Technical Center (Orlando), 90
Palm Beach Community College (Lake Worth), 90
Pensacola Junior College (Pensacola), 91
Pinellas Technical Education Center–St. Petersburg (St. Petersburg), 92
Radford M. Locklin Technical Center (Milton), 92
St. Johns River Community College (Palatka), 94
Santa Fe Community College (Gainesville), 95
Seminole Community College (Sanford), 96
State College of Florida Manatee-Sarasota (Bradenton), 98

Suwannee-Hamilton Area Vocational, Technical, and Adult Education Center (Live Oak), 98

Georgia
Albany Technical College (Albany), 103
Central Georgia Technical College (Macon), 107
Chattahoochee Technical College (Marietta), 107
Columbus Technical College (Columbus), 108
Coosa Valley Technical College (Rome), 109
DeKalb Technical College (Clarkston), 109
Flint River Technical College (Thomaston), 111
Griffin Technical College (Griffin), 113
Gwinnett Technical College (Lawrenceville), 113
Heart of Georgia Technical College (Dublin), 114
Lanier Technical College (Oakwood), 115
Middle Georgia Technical College (Warner Robbins), 117
Moultrie Technical College (Moultrie), 117
North Metro Technical College (Acworth), 118
Northwestern Technical College (Rock Spring), 118
Ogeechee Technical College (Statesboro), 119
Sandersville Technical College (Sandersville), 120
Savannah Technical College (Savannah), 121
Swainsboro Technical College (Swainsboro), 123
Valdosta Technical College (Valdosta), 123
West Central Technical College (Waco), 124
West Georgia Technical College (LaGrange), 124

Illinois
Black Hawk College (Moline), 125
City Colleges of Chicago, Harold Washington College (Chicago), 127
City Colleges of Chicago, Harry S. Truman College (Chicago), 128
City Colleges of Chicago, Kennedy-King College (Chicago), 128
City Colleges of Chicago, Malcolm X College (Chicago), 128
City Colleges of Chicago, Olive-Harvey College (Chicago), 128
City Colleges of Chicago, Richard J. Daley College (Chicago), 128
College of DuPage (Glen Ellyn), 129
College of Lake County (Grayslake), 129
Elgin Community College (Elgin), 132
Harper College (Palatine), 135
Heartland Community College (Normal), 136
Highland Community College (Freeport), 136
Illinois Central College (East Peoria), 136
Illinois Valley Community College (Oglesby), 138
John A. Logan College (Carterville), 138
Joliet Junior College (Joliet), 139
Kankakee Community College (Kankakee), 139
Lake Land College (Mattoon), 140
Lewis and Clark Community College (Godfrey), 141
McHenry County College (Crystal Lake), 142
Morton College (Cicero), 143
Oakton Community College (Des Plaines), 145
Parkland College (Champaign), 145
Prairie State College (Chicago Heights), 146
Rend Lake College (Ina), 148
Richland Community College (Decatur), 148
Rock Valley College (Rockford), 149
Sauk Valley Community College (Dixon), 150
Southeastern Illinois College (Harrisburg), 151
South Suburban College (South Holland), 151
Southwestern Illinois College (Belleville), 151
Triton College (River Grove), 153

Waubonsee Community College (Sugar Grove), 154

Indiana
Vincennes University (Vincennes), 168

Kentucky
Ashland Community and Technical College (Ashland), 169
Bluegrass Community and Technical College (Lexington), 170
Elizabethtown Community and Technical College (Elizabethtown), 172
Gateway Community and Technical College (Covington), 173
Hazard Community and Technical College (Hazard), 174
Henderson Community College (Henderson), 174
Hopkinsville Community College (Hopkinsville), 174
Jefferson Community and Technical College (Louisville), 175
Madisonville Community College (Madisonville), 176
Maysville Community and Technical College (Maysville), 176
Owensboro Community and Technical College (Owensboro), 177
St. Catharine College (St. Catharine), 178
Somerset Community College (Somerset), 178
Sullivan University (Louisville), 179
West Kentucky Community and Technical College (Paducah), 180

Maryland
The Community College of Baltimore County (Baltimore), 187
Montgomery College (Rockville), 190
Prince George's Community College (Largo), 191

Massachusetts
Massachusetts Bay Community College (Wellesley Hills), 201
Mount Wachusett Community College (Gardner), 203
North Shore Community College (Danvers), 204

Michigan
Delta College (University Center), 213
Glen Oaks Community College (Centreville), 216
Gogebic Community College (Ironwood), 216
Henry Ford Community College (Dearborn), 217
Lansing Community College (Lansing), 219
Muskegon Community College (Muskegon), 223
Washtenaw Community College (Ann Arbor), 229

New Jersey
County College of Morris (Randolph), 243
Sussex County Community College (Newton), 254

North Carolina
Cleveland Community College (Shelby), 293

Ohio
Cincinnati State Technical and Community College (Cincinnati), 315
Cleveland Municipal School District Adult and Continuing Education (Cleveland), 316
Columbiana County Vocation School (Lisbon), 317
Delaware JVS District (Delaware), 318

Pennsylvania
Community College of Allegheny County (Pittsburgh), 348
Harrisburg Area Community College (Harrisburg), 357

Keystone Technical Institute (Harrisburg), 359
Lebanon County Area Vocational Technical School (Lebanon), 361
Montgomery County Community College (Blue Bell), 365
Northampton County Area Community College (Bethlehem), 366
Pennco Tech (Bristol), 368
Reading Area Community College (Reading), 372
Schuylkill Technology Center–North Campus (Frackville), 373
Westmoreland County Community College (Youngwood), 378

Puerto Rico
Educational Technical College–Bayamón (Bayamón), 384
Educational Technical College–Recinto de Coama (Coama), 384
ICPR Junior College–Arecibo Campus (Arecibo), 385
ICPR Junior College–Mayagüez Campus (Mayagüez), 385
Inter American University of Puerto Rico, Aguadilla Campus (Aguadilla), 387
Inter American University of Puerto Rico, Bayamón Campus (Bayamón), 388
Inter American University of Puerto Rico, Metropolitan Campus (San Juan), 388
Inter American University of Puerto Rico, Ponce Campus (Mercedita), 389
John Dewey College, 389, 390
Ponce Paramedical College (Ponce), 392

Rhode Island
Community College of Rhode Island (Warwick), 394

South Carolina
Aiken Technical College (Aiken), 397
Central Carolina Technical College (Sumter), 398
Denmark Technical College (Denmark), 398
Florence-Darlington Technical College (Florence), 399
Greenville Technical College (Greenville), 399
Horry-Georgetown Technical College (Conway), 400
Midlands Technical College (Columbia), 401
Northeastern Technical College (Cheraw), 401
Orangeburg-Calhoun Technical College (Orangeburg), 402
Piedmont Technical College (Greenwood), 402
Spartanburg Community College (Spartanburg), 403
Technical College of the Lowcountry (Beaufort), 403
Tri-County Technical College (Pendleton), 403
Trident Technical College (Charleston), 404
Williamsburg Technical College (Kingstree), 404
York Technical College (Rock Hill), 405

Vermont
Community College of Vermont (Waterbury), 422

Virginia
Central Virginia Community College (Lynchburg), 425
Danville Community College (Danville), 426
Germanna Community College (Locust Grove), 428
John Tyler Community College (Chester), 429
J. Sargeant Reynolds Community College (Richmond), 429
New River Community College (Dublin), 430
Northern Virginia Community College (Annandale), 430
Patrick Henry Community College (Martinsville), 431

Paul D. Camp Community College (Franklin), 431

Southwest Virginia Community College (Richlands), 432

Thomas Nelson Community College (Hampton), 433

Tidewater Community College (Norfolk), 434

Virginia Highlands Community College (Abingdon), 435

Virginia Western Community College (Roanoke), 436

West Virginia

American Public University System (Charles Town), 437

Monongalia County Technical Education Center (Morgantown), 441

Wisconsin

Chippewa Valley Technical College (Eau Claire), 445

Lac Courte Oreilles Ojibwa Community College (Hayward), 447

Lakeshore Technical College (Cleveland), 447

Southwest Wisconsin Technical College (Fennimore), 452

CHILD DEVELOPMENT

Connecticut

Norwalk Community College (Norwalk), 55

Delaware

Delaware Technical & Community College, Jack F. Owens Campus (Georgetown), 59

Delaware Technical & Community College, Stanton/Wilmington Campus (Newark), 59

Maine

Central Maine Community College (Auburn), 181

Northern Maine Community College (Presque Isle), 182

Washington County Community College (Calais), 183

York County Community College (Wells), 183

Michigan

Baker College of Allen Park (Allen Park), 209

Baker College of Cadillac (Cadillac), 210

Baker College of Clinton Township (Clinton Township), 210

Baker College of Flint (Flint), 210

Baker College of Jackson (Jackson), 210

Baker College of Muskegon (Muskegon), 211

Baker College of Owosso (Owosso), 211

Baker College of Port Huron (Port Huron), 211

Northwestern Michigan College (Traverse City), 224

Schoolcraft College (Livonia), 227

North Carolina

Asheville-Buncombe Technical Community College (Asheville), 288

Brunswick Community College (Supply), 290

Central Carolina Community College (Sanford), 292

Central Piedmont Community College (Charlotte), 293

Cleveland Community College (Shelby), 293

Coastal Carolina Community College (Jacksonville), 293

Craven Community College (New Bern), 294

Davidson County Community College (Lexington), 294

Isothermal Community College (Spindale), 298

James Sprunt Community College (Kenansville), 298

Piedmont Community College (Roxboro), 302

Richmond Community College (Hamlet), 303

Rowan-Cabarrus Community College (Salisbury), 304

South Piedmont Community College (Polkton), 305

Southwestern Community College (Sylva), 306

Surry Community College (Dobson), 306

Wayne Community College (Goldsboro), 308

Ohio

North Central State College (Mansfield), 327

Pennsylvania

Community College of Allegheny County (Pittsburgh), 348

Tennessee

Columbia State Community College (Columbia), 406

Dyersburg State Community College (Dyersburg), 407

Nashville State Technical Community College (Nashville), 411

Northeast State Technical Community College (Blountville), 412

Southwest Tennessee Community College (Memphis), 414

Walters State Community College (Morristown), 421

CHINESE LANGUAGE AND LITERATURE

Pennsylvania

Penn State University Park (University Park), 369

CHIROPRACTIC ASSISTANT/TECHNICIAN

Illinois

National University of Health Sciences (Lombard), 144

Wisconsin

Moraine Park Technical College (Fond du Lac), 450

CHRISTIAN STUDIES

Maine

Saint Joseph's College of Maine (Standish), 182

Michigan

University of Detroit Mercy (Detroit), 228

Tennessee

Union University (Jackson), 420

CINEMATOGRAPHY AND FILM/VIDEO PRODUCTION

Florida

Brevard Community College (Cocoa), 67

Broward Community College (Fort Lauderdale), 68

Florida Community College at Jacksonville (Jacksonville), 77

Gulf Coast Community College (Panama City), 79

Hillsborough Community College (Tampa), 81

Northwest Florida State College (Niceville), 89

Palm Beach Community College (Lake Worth), 90

St. Petersburg College (St. Petersburg), 94

Valencia Community College (Orlando), 101

Illinois

Columbia College Chicago (Chicago), 130

Kentucky

Bluegrass Community and Technical College (Lexington), 170

Michigan

Lansing Community College (Lansing), 219

New York

Brooklyn College of the City University of New York (Brooklyn), 259

North Carolina

Cape Fear Community College (Wilmington), 290

Haywood Community College (Clyde), 297

School of Communication Arts (Raleigh), 305

Ohio

Brown Mackie College–Cincinnati (Cincinnati), 313

Pennsylvania

Lebanon County Area Vocational Technical School (Lebanon), 361

South Carolina

The Art Institute of Charleston (Charleston), 397

Tennessee

Watkins College of Art, Design, & Film (Nashville), 421

Vermont

Burlington College (Burlington), 421

CIVIL DRAFTING AND CIVIL ENGINEERING CAD/CADD

Florida

Sheridan Vocational-Technical Center (Hollywood), 96

Tom P. Haney Technical Center (Panama City), 99

CIVIL ENGINEERING, GENERAL

Pennsylvania

Penn State University Park (University Park), 369

University of Pittsburgh (Pittsburgh), 376

CIVIL ENGINEERING, OTHER

North Carolina

Central Piedmont Community College (Charlotte), 293

Haywood Community College (Clyde), 297

CIVIL ENGINEERING TECHNOLOGY/ TECHNICIAN

Alabama

Gadsden State Community College (Gadsden), 42

Florida

Henry W. Brewster Technical Center (Tampa), 80

Georgia

Altamaha Technical College (Jesup), 104

Augusta Technical College (Augusta), 106

Coosa Valley Technical College (Rome), 109

Flint River Technical College (Thomaston), 111

Moultrie Technical College (Moultrie), 117

Swainsboro Technical College (Swainsboro), 123

Indiana

Purdue University Calumet (Hammond), 166

Maryland

The Community College of Baltimore County (Baltimore), 187

Michigan

Lansing Community College (Lansing), 219

North Carolina

Central Piedmont Community College (Charlotte), 293

Gaston College (Dallas), 296

Guilford Technical Community College (Jamestown), 297

Wake Technical Community College (Raleigh), 307

Western Piedmont Community College (Morganton), 308

Ohio

Cincinnati State Technical and Community College (Cincinnati), 315

Columbus State Community College
(Columbus), 317
James A. Rhodes State College (Lima), 322
Sinclair Community College (Dayton), 334
The University of Toledo (Toledo), 339

Pennsylvania
Harrisburg Area Community College
(Harrisburg), 357

South Carolina
Greenville Technical College (Greenville), 399
Trident Technical College (Charleston), 404

Virginia
Northern Virginia Community College
(Annandale), 430

CLINICAL LABORATORY SCIENCE/MEDICAL TECHNOLOGY/TECHNOLOGIST

Florida
ATI Career Training Center (Miami), 65

Illinois
St. Johns Hospital School of Clinical Lab
Science (Springfield), 150

North Carolina
Carolinas College of Health Sciences
(Charlotte), 292

Ohio
University of Cincinnati (Cincinnati), 338

Pennsylvania
Conemaugh Valley Memorial Hospital
(Johnstown), 350

Vermont
Community College of Vermont (Waterbury),
422

CLINICAL/MEDICAL LABORATORY ASSISTANT

Florida
Orlando Technical Center (Orlando), 90
Ultimate Medical Academy (Clearwater), 100
Ultimate Medical Academy–Tampa (Tampa),
100

Indiana
Kaplan College–Merrillville Campus
(Merrillville), 164

Kentucky
Spencerian College (Louisville), 179

Massachusetts
Bunker Hill Community College (Boston), 196
Springfield Technical Community College
(Springfield), 207

Michigan
Bay de Noc Community College (Escanaba),
211
Monroe County Community College (Monroe),
222
Northern Michigan University (Marquette), 224

New York
Career Academy of New York (New York), 260

Ohio
Choffin Career Center (Youngstown), 315
Mahoning County Joint Vocational School
District (Canfield), 325
Southwestern College of Business (Dayton), 335

Pennsylvania
Allied Medical and Technical Institute (Forty
Fort), 342
Allied Medical and Technical Institute
(Scranton), 343

South Carolina
Orangeburg-Calhoun Technical College
(Orangeburg), 402
Spartanburg Community College (Spartanburg),
403

Virginia
Virginia Career Institute (Richmond), 435

West Virginia
Academy of Careers and Technology (Beckley),
437
Opportunities Industrialization Center–North
Central West Virginia (Fairmont), 442

CLINICAL/MEDICAL LABORATORY SCIENCE AND ALLIED PROFESSIONS, OTHER

Kentucky
ATA Career Education (Louisville), 169

Maryland
Allegany College of Maryland (Cumberland),
184
Kaplan College–Hagerstown (Hagerstown), 189

Massachusetts
Bristol Community College (Fall River), 196

New York
Broome Community College (Binghamton), 259
Dutchess Community College (Poughkeepsie),
264
Mohawk Valley Community College (Utica),
274

North Carolina
Brunswick Community College (Supply), 290
Cape Fear Community College (Wilmington),
290
Cleveland Community College (Shelby), 293
Durham Technical Community College
(Durham), 295
James Sprunt Community College
(Kenansville), 298
Lenoir Community College (Kinston), 299
Mitchell Community College (Statesville), 300
Rockingham Community College (Wentworth),
304

Ohio
Columbus State Community College
(Columbus), 317
Marion Technical College (Marion), 325

Pennsylvania
Allied Medical and Technical Institute
(Scranton), 343
Greater Altoona Career and Technology Center
(Altoona), 356

Puerto Rico
Inter American University of Puerto Rico,
Arecibo Campus (Arecibo), 388

Tennessee
Roane State Community College (Harriman),
413
Tennessee Technology Center at Murfreesboro
(Murfreesboro), 418
Tennessee Technology Center at Nashville
(Nashville), 418
Volunteer State Community College (Gallatin),
421

Virginia
Jefferson College of Health Sciences (Roanoke),
428

West Virginia
Pierpont Community & Technical College of
Fairmont State University (Fairmont), 442

CLINICAL/MEDICAL LABORATORY TECHNICIAN

District of Columbia
The George Washington University
(Washington), 61

Florida
David G. Erwin Technical Center (Tampa), 71
Marion County Community Technical and
Adult Education Center (Ocala), 85

Sheridan Vocational-Technical Center
(Hollywood), 96

Illinois
Elgin Community College (Elgin), 132

Kentucky
Bluegrass Community and Technical College
(Lexington), 170
Henderson Community College (Henderson),
174
Jefferson Community and Technical College
(Louisville), 175
Madisonville Community College
(Madisonville), 176
Somerset Community College (Somerset), 178
Southeast Kentucky Community and Technical
College (Cumberland), 178
Spencerian College–Lexington (Lexington),
179
West Kentucky Community and Technical
College (Paducah), 180

Maryland
Anne Arundel Community College (Arnold),
184

Michigan
Baker College of Port Huron (Port Huron), 211

Ohio
Eastern Gateway Community College
(Steubenville), 319
Lakeland Community College (Kirtland), 323
Southwestern College of Business (Cincinnati),
335

Pennsylvania
Lancaster General College of Nursing & Health
Sciences (Lancaster), 360

Puerto Rico
Atenas College (Manati), 380

South Carolina
Midlands Technical College (Columbia), 401
Piedmont Technical College (Greenwood), 402

Tennessee
MedVance Institute (Cookeville), 409

Virginia
Thomas Nelson Community College
(Hampton), 433

CLINICAL/MEDICAL SOCIAL WORK

Florida
Coral Ridge Nurses Assistant Training School
(Ft. Lauderdale), 71

North Carolina
Lenoir Community College (Kinston), 299

CLINICAL NUTRITION/NUTRITIONIST

Massachusetts
Cape Cod Community College (West
Barnstable), 196

COMMERCIAL AND ADVERTISING ART

Alabama
James H. Faulkner State Community College
(Bay Minette), 44
Lawson State Community College
(Birmingham), 44
Shelton State Community College (Tuscaloosa),
46

Connecticut
Asnuntuck Community College (Enfield), 49
Housatonic Community College (Bridgeport),
53
Manchester Community College (Manchester),
54
Northwestern Connecticut Community College
(Winsted), 55
Norwalk Community College (Norwalk), 55

Paier College of Art, Inc. (Hamden), 55
Three Rivers Community College (Norwich), 57
Tunxis Community College (Farmington), 57

Florida
The Art Institute of Fort Lauderdale (Fort Lauderdale), 65
Brevard Community College (Cocoa), 67
Broward Community College (Fort Lauderdale), 68
First Coast Technical Institute (St. Augustine), 75
Florida Community College at Jacksonville (Jacksonville), 77
Lake City Community College (Lake City), 83
Lake Technical Center (Eustis), 83
Lee County High Tech Center North (Cape Coral), 83
Lindsey Hopkins Technical Education Center (Miami), 84
Lively Technical Center (Tallahassee), 84
Miami Dade College (Miami), 87
Northwest Florida State College (Niceville), 89
Palm Beach Community College (Lake Worth), 90
Pinellas Technical Education Center–Clearwater (Clearwater), 91
St. Petersburg College (St. Petersburg), 94
Santa Fe Community College (Gainesville), 95
Seminole Community College (Sanford), 96
Valencia Community College (Orlando), 101
Westside Tech (Winter Garden), 102

Georgia
Albany Technical College (Albany), 103
Atlanta Technical College (Atlanta), 105
North Metro Technical College (Acworth), 118
Southeastern Technical College (Vidalia), 121

Illinois
College of DuPage (Glen Ellyn), 129
Robert Morris University (Chicago), 149

Indiana
International Business College (Fort Wayne), 161
International Business College (Indianapolis), 161

Maryland
Anne Arundel Community College (Arnold), 184
Carroll Community College (Westminster), 186
College of Southern Maryland (La Plata), 186
The Community College of Baltimore County (Baltimore), 187
Frederick Community College (Frederick), 188
Hagerstown Community College (Hagerstown), 188
Howard Community College (Columbia), 189
Montgomery College (Rockville), 190
Prince George's Community College (Largo), 191

Massachusetts
Bristol Community College (Fall River), 196
Holyoke Community College (Holyoke), 199
Massachusetts College of Art and Design (Boston), 201
Middlesex Community College (Bedford), 202
Northern Essex Community College (Haverhill), 204

Michigan
Henry Ford Community College (Dearborn), 217
Lake Michigan College (Benton Harbor), 219
Macomb Community College (Warren), 220
Muskegon Community College (Muskegon), 223

New Hampshire
Lebanon College (Lebanon), 237
McIntosh College (Dover), 238

New Jersey
Ocean County College (Toms River), 250
Ocean County Vocational Post Secondary Division (Toms River), 250

New York
Pace University (New York), 279
Rochester Institute of Technology (Rochester), 280
Westchester Community College (Valhalla), 287

North Carolina
Alamance Community College (Graham), 288
Central Piedmont Community College (Charlotte), 293
Guilford Technical Community College (Jamestown), 297
Halifax Community College (Weldon), 297
James Sprunt Community College (Kenansville), 298
Johnston Community College (Smithfield), 298
McDowell Technical Community College (Marion), 300
South Piedmont Community College (Polkton), 305
Stanly Community College (Albemarle), 306
Wake Technical Community College (Raleigh), 307

Ohio
Cuyahoga Community College (Cleveland), 318
Owens Community College (Toledo), 330
Terra State Community College (Fremont), 336

Pennsylvania
The Art Institute of Pittsburgh (Pittsburgh), 343
Bradford School (Pittsburgh), 345
Lancaster County Career and Technology Center (Willow Street), 360
Lebanon County Area Vocational Technical School (Lebanon), 361
Luzerne County Community College (Nanticoke), 363
Westmoreland County Community College (Youngwood), 378

Puerto Rico
Nova College de Puerto Rico (Bayamón), 391

South Carolina
Greenville Technical College (Greenville), 399
Piedmont Technical College (Greenwood), 402
Spartanburg Community College (Spartanburg), 403
Trident Technical College (Charleston), 404
York Technical College (Rock Hill), 405

Tennessee
Tennessee Technology Center at Crump (Crump), 415
Tennessee Technology Center at Memphis (Memphis), 417

COMMERCIAL PHOTOGRAPHY
Florida
The Art Institute of Fort Lauderdale (Fort Lauderdale), 65
Lively Technical Center (Tallahassee), 84
McFatter Technical Center (Davie), 86
Mid-Florida Tech (Orlando), 87

Georgia
Gwinnett Technical College (Lawrenceville), 113
North Georgia Technical College (Clarkesville), 118

Illinois
College of DuPage (Glen Ellyn), 129
Oakton Community College (Des Plaines), 145

Prairie State College (Chicago Heights), 146
Waubonsee Community College (Sugar Grove), 154

Maryland
Cecil College (North East), 186
Harford Community College (Bel Air), 189
Howard Community College (Columbia), 189
Maryland Institute College of Art (Baltimore), 190
Montgomery College (Rockville), 190

Ohio
Owens Community College (Toledo), 330

Pennsylvania
Lancaster County Career and Technology Center (Willow Street), 360

COMMUNICATION AND MEDIA STUDIES, OTHER
Florida
Manatee Technical Institute (Bradenton), 85
Illinois
Northwestern University (Evanston), 145

COMMUNICATION DISORDERS SCIENCES AND SERVICES, OTHER
Massachusetts
Holyoke Community College (Holyoke), 199

COMMUNICATION, JOURNALISM AND RELATED PROGRAMS, OTHER
Connecticut
Capital Community College (Hartford), 51
Florida
Palm Beach Community College (Lake Worth), 90
Tallahassee Community College (Tallahassee), 98
New York
Pace University (New York), 279
Rochester Institute of Technology (Rochester), 280
North Carolina
Guilford College (Greensboro), 297
Pennsylvania
Marywood University (Scranton), 364

COMMUNICATIONS SYSTEMS INSTALLATION AND REPAIR TECHNOLOGY
Georgia
DeKalb Technical College (Clarkston), 109
East Central Technical College (Fitzgerald), 110
Griffin Technical College (Griffin), 113
Heart of Georgia Technical College (Dublin), 114
Lanier Technical College (Oakwood), 115
Moultrie Technical College (Moultrie), 117
North Metro Technical College (Acworth), 118
Southeastern Technical College (Vidalia), 121
South Georgia Technical College (Americus), 122
Valdosta Technical College (Valdosta), 123
Illinois
Coyne American Institute Incorporated (Chicago), 131
Illinois Eastern Community Colleges, Lincoln Trail College (Robinson), 137
Lake Land College (Mattoon), 140
Sauk Valley Community College (Dixon), 150
Mississippi
Hinds Community College (Raymond), 232
Jones County Junior College (Ellisville), 234
New York
Monroe Community College (Rochester), 274

Pennsylvania
Luzerne County Community College
(Nanticoke), 363

Rhode Island
Motoring Technical Training Institute (East
Providence), 395

Wisconsin
Milwaukee Area Technical College
(Milwaukee), 449
Wisconsin Indianhead Technical College (Shell
Lake), 453

COMMUNICATIONS TECHNOLOGIES/ TECHNICIANS AND SUPPORT SERVICES, OTHER

Connecticut
Naugatuck Valley Community College
(Waterbury), 54

Florida
Winter Park Tech (Winter Park), 102

Maryland
Anne Arundel Community College (Arnold),
184
College of Southern Maryland (La Plata), 186

Massachusetts
Wentworth Institute of Technology (Boston),
208

Michigan
Muskegon Community College (Muskegon),
223

New York
Institute of Audio Research (New York), 269
Nassau Community College (Garden City), 275
Rochester Institute of Technology (Rochester),
280

Ohio
Cincinnati State Technical and Community
College (Cincinnati), 315
O. C. Collins Career Center (Chesapeake), 328

COMMUNICATIONS TECHNOLOGY/ TECHNICIAN

Florida
Sheridan Vocational-Technical Center
(Hollywood), 96

Kentucky
Big Sandy Community and Technical College
(Prestonsburg), 170
Bowling Green Technical College (Bowling
Green), 170
Gateway Community and Technical College
(Covington), 173
Jefferson Community and Technical College
(Louisville), 175
Somerset Community College (Somerset), 178
West Kentucky Community and Technical
College (Paducah), 180

Michigan
Lawrence Technological University
(Southfield), 220

New Jersey
Ocean County Vocational Post Secondary
Division (Toms River), 250

New York
Institute of Audio Research (New York), 269
Rochester Institute of Technology (Rochester),
280

Ohio
Cleveland Institute of Electronics (Cleveland),
316

Puerto Rico
Columbia College (Caguas), 383
Columbia College (Yauco), 383

COMMUNICATION STUDIES/SPEECH COMMUNICATION AND RHETORIC

Connecticut
Tunxis Community College (Farmington), 57

Indiana
Purdue University North Central (Westville),
166

Maryland
Howard Community College (Columbia), 189

Massachusetts
Atlantic Union College (South Lancaster), 193
University of Massachusetts Boston (Boston),
208

New York
Mount Saint Mary College (Newburgh), 275

North Carolina
Guilford College (Greensboro), 297

Ohio
Baldwin-Wallace College (Berea), 311
Sinclair Community College (Dayton), 334

Pennsylvania
Robert Morris University (Moon Township),
372

COMMUNITY HEALTH SERVICES/LIAISON/ COUNSELING

Florida
Central Florida Community College (Ocala), 69
Hillsborough Community College (Tampa), 81

Massachusetts
Greenfield Community College (Greenfield),
198

COMMUNITY ORGANIZATION AND ADVOCACY

Connecticut
Manchester Community College (Manchester),
54

Massachusetts
Holyoke Community College (Holyoke), 199

Michigan
Bay Mills Community College (Brimley), 211
Kellogg Community College (Battle Creek), 218
Lansing Community College (Lansing), 219
Madonna University (Livonia), 221

New York
Erie Community College (Buffalo), 265
Fulton-Montgomery Community College
(Johnstown), 267
Genesee Community College (Batavia), 267
Mercy College (Dobbs Ferry), 273
Monroe Community College (Rochester), 274
North Country Community College (Saranac
Lake), 277
Rochester Institute of Technology (Rochester),
280
St. Joseph's College, Long Island Campus
(Patchogue), 281
St. Joseph's College, New York (Brooklyn), 281
Westchester Community College (Valhalla),
287

Ohio
The University of Akron (Akron), 338

Rhode Island
Providence College (Providence), 396

Vermont
Woodbury College (Montpelier), 423

COMPARATIVE LITERATURE

Pennsylvania
Penn State University Park (University Park),
369

COMPUTER AND INFORMATION SCIENCES AND SUPPORT SERVICES, OTHER

Connecticut
Capital Community College (Hartford), 51
Fox Institute of Business (Hartford), 52
Norwalk Community College (Norwalk), 55

Delaware
Star Technical Institute (Dover), 60

Florida
George Stone Area Vocational-Technical
Center (Pensacola), 79
Lee County Vocational High Tech Center–
Central (Fort Myers), 84
Management Resources Institute (Miami), 85
Saber (Miami), 94
Sarasota County Technical Institute (Sarasota),
96
Southern Technical Institute (Winter Park), 97

Georgia
Interactive College of Technology (Chamblee),
114
Javelin Technical Training Center (Atlanta),
115
Macon State College (Macon), 116
Omnitech Institute (Decatur), 119

Illinois
Northwestern Business College–Southwestern
Campus (Bridgeview), 144
Northwestern College (Chicago), 144
Northwestern University (Evanston), 145
Rockford Business College (Rockford), 149

Indiana
Brown Mackie College–Fort Wayne (Fort
Wayne), 155
Brown Mackie College–Michigan City
(Michigan City), 156
Brown Mackie College–South Bend (South
Bend), 156
Indiana University–Purdue University
Indianapolis (Indianapolis), 160
Purdue University Calumet (Hammond), 166
TechSkills—Indianapolis (Indianapolis), 167
Vincennes University (Vincennes), 168

Kentucky
National College (Lexington), 176
Sullivan University (Louisville), 179

Maryland
Prince George's Community College (Largo),
191
TESST College of Technology (Towson), 192

Massachusetts
Bunker Hill Community College (Boston), 196
Holyoke Community College (Holyoke), 199
Kaplan Career Institute, Charlestown
(Charlestown), 199
Marian Court College (Swampscott), 201
Massachusetts Bay Community College
(Wellesley Hills), 201
Massasoit Community College (Brockton), 202
Middlesex Community College (Bedford), 202
Mount Wachusett Community College
(Gardner), 203
Quinsigamond Community College
(Worcester), 205
Roxbury Community College (Roxbury
Crossing), 205
Sullivan and Cogliano Training Center
(Brockton), 207

Michigan
Davenport University (Grand Rapids), 213
Grand Rapids Community College (Grand
Rapids), 216
Kaplan Institute (Detroit), 218
Mott Community College (Flint), 223

Oakland Community College (Bloomfield Hills), 224
Southwestern Michigan College (Dowagiac), 227

Mississippi
Virginia College at Jackson (Jackson), 236

New Hampshire
McIntosh College (Dover), 238

New Jersey
Camden County College (Blackwood), 241
Essex County College (Newark), 244
Fox Institute of Business–Clifton (Clifton), 245
Raritan Valley Community College (Somerville), 252
Somerset County Technical Institute (Bridgewater), 253

New York
ASA Institute, The College of Advanced Technology (Brooklyn), 257
Broome Community College (Binghamton), 259
Cayuga County Community College (Auburn), 261
The College of Westchester (White Plains), 262
Columbia-Greene Community College (Hudson), 262
Erie Community College (Buffalo), 265
Finger Lakes Community College (Canandaigua), 266
Genesee Community College (Batavia), 267
Merkaz Bnos-Business School (Brooklyn), 273
Mohawk Valley Community College (Utica), 274
Niagara County Community College (Sanborn), 277
North Country Community College (Saranac Lake), 277
Olean Business Institute (Olean), 277
Onondaga Community College (Syracuse), 277
Pace University (New York), 279
Ridley-Lowell School of Business (Poughkeepsie), 280
Schenectady County Community College (Schenectady), 282
Ulster County Community College (Stone Ridge), 286
Westchester Community College (Valhalla), 287

North Carolina
Blue Ridge Community College (Flat Rock), 289
Fayetteville Technical Community College (Fayetteville), 295
Wake Technical Community College (Raleigh), 307

Ohio
Akron Adult Vocational Services (Akron), 309
Brown Mackie College–Cincinnati (Cincinnati), 313
Columbus State Community College (Columbus), 317
Community Services Division–Alliance City (Alliance), 317
Edison State Community College (Piqua), 319
Hocking College (Nelsonville), 321
Licking County Joint Vocational School–Newark (Newark), 324
NewLife Academy of Information Technology (East Liverpool), 327
Sinclair Community College (Dayton), 334
TechSkills—Columbus (Columbus), 336
The University of Akron (Akron), 338
University of Northwestern Ohio (Lima), 339

Pennsylvania
Bidwell Training Center (Pittsburgh), 344
Bradford School (Pittsburgh), 345

Community College of Allegheny County (Pittsburgh), 348
Computer Learning Network (Altoona), 349
Computer Learning Network (Camp Hill), 349
DCI Career Institute (Monaca), 350
Greater Altoona Career and Technology Center (Altoona), 356
Harrisburg Area Community College (Harrisburg), 357
Keystone College (La Plume), 359
Lincoln Technical Institute (Philadelphia), 363
Marywood University (Scranton), 364
Newport Business Institute (Lower Burrell), 366
Tri-State Business Institute (Erie), 376
University of Pittsburgh (Pittsburgh), 376
YTI Career Institute–York (York), 379

Puerto Rico
Colegio Mayor de Tecnologia–Arroyo (Arroyo), 382
Huertas Junior College (Caguas), 385
Trinity College of Puerto Rico (Ponce), 393
Universidad del Este (Carolina), 393

South Carolina
Greenville Technical College (Greenville), 399
Horry-Georgetown Technical College (Conway), 400
Midlands Technical College (Columbia), 401
Orangeburg-Calhoun Technical College (Orangeburg), 402
Trident Technical College (Charleston), 404
York Technical College (Rock Hill), 405

Tennessee
Miller-Motte Technical College (Clarksville), 410
National College (Nashville), 411
Roane State Community College (Harriman), 413
Tennessee Technology Center at Pulaski (Pulaski), 419

Vermont
Champlain College (Burlington), 422

Virginia
National College (Salem), 430

West Virginia
American Public University System (Charles Town), 437
Fred W. Eberle Technical Center (Buckhannon), 439
Logan-Mingo School of Practical Nursing (Logan), 441

Wisconsin
Madison Area Technical College (Madison), 448
Moraine Park Technical College (Fond du Lac), 450
Northeast Wisconsin Technical College (Green Bay), 450
Western Technical College (La Crosse), 453

COMPUTER AND INFORMATION SCIENCES, GENERAL

Alabama
Bevill State Community College (Sumiton), 41
Calhoun Community College (Decatur), 41
Central Alabama Community College (Alexander City), 42
Enterprise-Ozark Community College (Enterprise), 42
Gadsden State Community College (Gadsden), 42
George Corley Wallace State Community College (Selma), 43
George C. Wallace Community College (Dothan), 43
H. Councill Trenholm State Technical College (Montgomery), 43

James H. Faulkner State Community College (Bay Minette), 44
Jefferson State Community College (Birmingham), 44
J. F. Drake State Technical College (Huntsville), 44
Lawson State Community College (Birmingham), 44
Lurleen B. Wallace Community College (Andalusia), 45
Northwest-Shoals Community College (Muscle Shoals), 45
Reid State Technical College (Evergreen), 46
Shelton State Community College (Tuscaloosa), 46
Southern Union State Community College (Wadley), 47
Spring Hill College (Mobile), 47

Connecticut
Goodwin College (East Hartford), 53
Manchester Community College (Manchester), 54
Naugatuck Valley Community College (Waterbury), 54

Delaware
Delaware Technical & Community College, Jack F. Owens Campus (Georgetown), 59

District of Columbia
Technical Learning Centers (Washington), 62

Florida
Bradford Union Area Vocational Technical Center (Starke), 67
Comp-Med Vocational Careers Corporation (Hialeah), 70
New Professions Technical Institute (Miami), 88

Georgia
Interactive College of Technology (Chamblee), 114
Interactive College of Technology (College Park), 115
Interactive College of Technology (Gainesville), 115
Omnitech Institute (Decatur), 119
Savannah River College (Augusta), 121

Illinois
East-West University (Chicago), 132
St. Augustine College (Chicago), 150

Indiana
Indiana University–Purdue University Fort Wayne (Fort Wayne), 160
Indiana University–Purdue University Indianapolis (Indianapolis), 160
International Business College (Fort Wayne), 161
International Business College (Indianapolis), 161
Ivy Tech Community College–Columbus (Columbus), 162
Ivy Tech Community College–East Central (Muncie), 162
Ivy Tech Community College–Kokomo (Kokomo), 162
Ivy Tech Community College–North Central (South Bend), 162
Ivy Tech Community College–Northeast (Fort Wayne), 163
Ivy Tech Community College–Northwest (Gary), 163
Ivy Tech Community College–Whitewater (Richmond), 164
Vincennes University (Vincennes), 168

Kentucky
Ashland Community and Technical College (Ashland), 169
Big Sandy Community and Technical College (Prestonsburg), 170

COMPUTER AND INFORMATION SCIENCES, OTHER

COMPUTER AND INFORMATION SYSTEMS SECURITY

Computer and Information Systems Security

New York
The Chubb Institute–New York (New York), 261

Erie Community College (Buffalo), 265

North Carolina
Fayetteville Technical Community College (Fayetteville), 295

Piedmont Community College (Roxboro), 302

Sampson Community College (Clinton), 304

Stanly Community College (Albemarle), 306

Ohio
Kent State University (Kent), 322

Kent State University, Trumbull Campus (Warren), 323

Kent State University, Tuscarawas Campus (New Philadelphia), 323

Sinclair Community College (Dayton), 334

TechSkills—Columbus (Columbus), 336

Pennsylvania
The Chubb Institute–Springfield (Springfield), 348

Harrisburg University of Science and Technology (Harrisburg), 358

Luzerne County Community College (Nanticoke), 363

Peirce College (Philadelphia), 367

Penn State Altoona (Altoona), 368

Pennsylvania Highlands Community College (Johnstown), 370

Pittsburgh Technical Institute (Oakdale), 371

Westmoreland County Community College (Youngwood), 378

Virginia
Potomac College (Herndon), 431

Tidewater Tech (Virginia Beach), 434

West Virginia
American Public University System (Charles Town), 437

Wisconsin
Blackhawk Technical College (Janesville), 445

COMPUTER ENGINEERING, GENERAL

Connecticut
Goodwin College (East Hartford), 53

Florida
Florida Career College (Miami), 76

Southern Technical Institute (Winter Park), 97

Georgia
Omnitech Institute (Decatur), 119

Indiana
TechSkills—Indianapolis (Indianapolis), 167

Ohio
TechSkills—Columbus (Columbus), 336

COMPUTER ENGINEERING, OTHER

Wisconsin
Moraine Park Technical College (Fond du Lac), 450

COMPUTER ENGINEERING TECHNOLOGIES/ TECHNICIANS, OTHER

Massachusetts
Bristol Community College (Fall River), 196

Mount Wachusett Community College (Gardner), 203

North Carolina
Central Piedmont Community College (Charlotte), 293

Puerto Rico
Universidad del Turabo (Gurabo), 394

COMPUTER ENGINEERING TECHNOLOGY/ TECHNICIAN

Connecticut
Capital Community College (Hartford), 51

Gateway Community College (New Haven), 52

Naugatuck Valley Community College (Waterbury), 54

Three Rivers Community College (Norwich), 57

Delaware
Delaware Technical & Community College, Stanton/Wilmington Campus (Newark), 59

Delaware Technical & Community College, Terry Campus (Dover), 60

Florida
Florida Career Institute (Lakeland), 76

James Lorenzo Walker Vocational-Technical Center (Naples), 82

Southwest Florida College (Fort Myers), 97

Taylor Technical Institute (Perry), 99

Washington-Holmes Technical Center (Chipley), 102

Georgia
Advanced Career Training (Atlanta), 103

Dalton State College (Dalton), 109

DeKalb Technical College (Clarkston), 109

Omnitech Institute (Decatur), 119

Illinois
John A. Logan College (Carterville), 138

Lincoln Land Community College (Springfield), 141

Moraine Valley Community College (Palos Hills), 143

Rend Lake College (Ina), 148

Kentucky
Daymar College (Paducah), 172

Massachusetts
Northeastern University (Boston), 204

Quinsigamond Community College (Worcester), 205

The Salter School (Worcester), 206

Michigan
Baker College of Auburn Hills (Auburn Hills), 209

Baker College of Cadillac (Cadillac), 210

Baker College of Clinton Township (Clinton Township), 210

Baker College of Flint (Flint), 210

Baker College of Jackson (Jackson), 210

Baker College of Muskegon (Muskegon), 211

Baker College of Owosso (Owosso), 211

Baker College of Port Huron (Port Huron), 211

Northern Michigan University (Marquette), 224

New Jersey
HoHoKus RETS School of Business and Medical Technical Services (Nutley), 246

New York
Career Institute of Health and Technology (Garden City), 260

Fulton-Montgomery Community College (Johnstown), 267

Island Drafting and Technical Institute (Amityville), 270

North Carolina
Asheville-Buncombe Technical Community College (Asheville), 288

Cape Fear Community College (Wilmington), 290

Central Piedmont Community College (Charlotte), 293

College of The Albemarle (Elizabeth City), 294

Isothermal Community College (Spindale), 298

Lenoir Community College (Kinston), 299

Mayland Community College (Spruce Pine), 299

Sandhills Community College (Pinehurst), 305

Stanly Community College (Albemarle), 306

Wake Technical Community College (Raleigh), 307

Ohio
Hocking College (Nelsonville), 321

Lakeland Community College (Kirtland), 323

Lorain County Community College (Elyria), 324

Northwest State Community College (Archbold), 327

Owens Community College (Toledo), 330

Shawnee State University (Portsmouth), 334

Pennsylvania
CHI Institute, Franklin Mills Campus (Philadelphia), 348

Kaplan Career Institute–ICM Campus (Pittsburgh), 359

Schuylkill Technology Center–North Campus (Frackville), 373

Tennessee
Southwest Tennessee Community College (Memphis), 414

COMPUTER GRAPHICS

Florida
Miami-Dade County Public Schools (Miami), 87

South Florida Institute of Technology (Miami), 97

Illinois
Parkland College (Champaign), 145

Maryland
Carroll Community College (Westminster), 186

The Community College of Baltimore County (Baltimore), 187

Massachusetts
Mount Wachusett Community College (Gardner), 203

Michigan
Marygrove College (Detroit), 221

Schoolcraft College (Livonia), 227

New Jersey
Gloucester County College (Sewell), 245

Somerset County Technical Institute (Bridgewater), 253

Pennsylvania
Lansdale School of Business (North Wales), 360

Westmoreland County Community College (Youngwood), 378

COMPUTER HARDWARE TECHNOLOGY/ TECHNICIAN

Delaware
Delaware Technical & Community College, Terry Campus (Dover), 60

Florida
Florida Career College (Miami), 76

Michigan
Monroe County Community College (Monroe), 222

New York
Micropower Career Institute (New York), 273

North Carolina
Forsyth Technical Community College (Winston-Salem), 296

Ohio
Edison State Community College (Piqua), 319

Pennsylvania
Lansdale School of Business (North Wales), 360

Puerto Rico
MBTI Business Training Institute (Santurce), 391

Rhode Island
Community College of Rhode Island (Warwick), 394

Virginia
ECPI College of Technology (Virginia Beach), 426

COMPUTER/INFORMATION TECHNOLOGY SERVICES ADMINISTRATION AND MANAGEMENT, OTHER

Florida
Brevard Community College (Cocoa), 67
Broward Community College (Fort Lauderdale), 68
Charlotte Vocational-Technical Center (Port Charlotte), 69
Daytona State College (Daytona Beach), 72
Edison State College (Fort Myers), 72
Florida Community College at Jacksonville (Jacksonville), 77
Hillsborough Community College (Tampa), 81
Miami Dade College (Miami), 87
New Professions Technical Institute (Miami), 88
Northwest Florida State College (Niceville), 89
Palm Beach Community College (Lake Worth), 90
Pasco-Hernando Community College (New Port Richey), 90
St. Johns River Community College (Palatka), 94
St. Petersburg College (St. Petersburg), 94
Santa Fe Community College (Gainesville), 95
South Florida Community College (Avon Park), 97
Valencia Community College (Orlando), 101

Indiana
Ivy Tech Community College–Bloomington (Bloomington), 161
Ivy Tech Community College–Lafayette (Lafayette), 162
Ivy Tech Community College–North Central (South Bend), 162
TechSkills—Indianapolis (Indianapolis), 167

Massachusetts
Bristol Community College (Fall River), 196

Michigan
Oakland Community College (Bloomfield Hills), 224
Washtenaw Community College (Ann Arbor), 229

New York
Genesee Community College (Batavia), 267
Mercy College (Dobbs Ferry), 273
New York Institute of Business Technology (New York), 276
St. Joseph's College, Long Island Campus (Patchogue), 281
St. Joseph's College, New York (Brooklyn), 281
Sullivan County Community College (Loch Sheldrake), 285
Syracuse University (Syracuse), 285

Ohio
Cleveland Institute of Electronics (Cleveland), 316
Southwestern College of Business (Cincinnati), 335
TechSkills—Columbus (Columbus), 336

Pennsylvania
Keystone College (La Plume), 359
The PJA School (Upper Darby), 371
South Hills School of Business & Technology (State College), 374

Puerto Rico
Century College (Aguadilla), 382

Vermont
Community College of Vermont (Waterbury), 422

Virginia
Beta Tech (Richmond), 424

COMPUTER INSTALLATION AND REPAIR TECHNOLOGY/TECHNICIAN

Connecticut
Fox Institute of Business (Hartford), 52
Gateway Community College (New Haven), 52

Florida
Atlantic Vocational-Technical Center (Coconut Creek), 66
Bradford Union Area Vocational Technical Center (Starke), 67
Chipola College (Marianna), 69
Daytona State College (Daytona Beach), 72
FastTrain of Clearwater (Clearwater), 74
FastTrain of Ft. Lauderdale (Ft. Lauderdale), 74
FastTrain of Jacksonville (Jacksonville), 75
FastTrain of Kendall (Miami), 75
FastTrain of Miami (Miami), 75
FastTrain of Pembroke Pines (Pembroke Pines), 75
FastTrain of Tampa (Tampa), 75
Florida Community College at Jacksonville (Jacksonville), 77
Lake Technical Center (Eustis), 83
Lee County High Tech Center North (Cape Coral), 83
Miami Lakes Technical Education Center (Miami), 87
Mid-Florida Tech (Orlando), 87
Okaloosa Applied Technology Center (Ft. Walton Beach), 89
Pinellas Technical Education Center–Clearwater (Clearwater), 91
Robert Morgan Vocational-Technical Center (Miami), 94
Sarasota County Technical Institute (Sarasota), 96
Sheridan Vocational-Technical Center (Hollywood), 96
South Florida Community College (Avon Park), 97
Technical Career Institute (Miami Springs), 99
Tom P. Haney Technical Center (Panama City), 99

Georgia
Albany Technical College (Albany), 103
Appalachian Technical College (Jasper), 104
Atlanta Technical College (Atlanta), 105
Augusta Technical College (Augusta), 106
Bainbridge College (Bainbridge), 106
Central Georgia Technical College (Macon), 107
Chattahoochee Technical College (Marietta), 107
Columbus Technical College (Columbus), 108
Coosa Valley Technical College (Rome), 109
DeKalb Technical College (Clarkston), 109
Griffin Technical College (Griffin), 113
Gwinnett Technical College (Lawrenceville), 113
Heart of Georgia Technical College (Dublin), 114
Lanier Technical College (Oakwood), 115
Middle Georgia Technical College (Warner Robbins), 117
Moultrie Technical College (Moultrie), 117
North Georgia Technical College (Clarkesville), 118
North Metro Technical College (Acworth), 118
Northwestern Technical College (Rock Spring), 118
Ogeechee Technical College (Statesboro), 119

Okefenokee Technical College (Waycross), 119
Sandersville Technical College (Sandersville), 120
Savannah Technical College (Savannah), 121
Southeastern Technical College (Vidalia), 121
South Georgia Technical College (Americus), 122
Southwest Georgia Technical College (Thomasville), 122
Swainsboro Technical College (Swainsboro), 123
West Central Technical College (Waco), 124
West Georgia Technical College (LaGrange), 124

Illinois
City Colleges of Chicago, Richard J. Daley College (Chicago), 128
City Colleges of Chicago, Wilbur Wright College (Chicago), 129
College of DuPage (Glen Ellyn), 129
College of Lake County (Grayslake), 129
Elgin Community College (Elgin), 132
Highland Community College (Freeport), 136
Illinois Eastern Community Colleges, Lincoln Trail College (Robinson), 137
Joliet Junior College (Joliet), 139
Kankakee Community College (Kankakee), 139
Kishwaukee College (Malta), 140
Lewis and Clark Community College (Godfrey), 141
Morton College (Cicero), 143
Prairie State College (Chicago Heights), 146
Sauk Valley Community College (Dixon), 150
Southwestern Illinois College (Belleville), 151
Spoon River College (Canton), 152
Triton College (River Grove), 153

Kentucky
Spencerian College–Lexington (Lexington), 179

Maine
Eastern Maine Community College (Bangor), 181
Northern Maine Community College (Presque Isle), 182
Washington County Community College (Calais), 183

Maryland
Cecil College (North East), 186
Prince George's Community College (Largo), 191

Massachusetts
Bay State School of Technology (Canton), 194
Massasoit Community College (Brockton), 202
Millennium Training Institute (Woburn), 203
Sullivan and Cogliano Training Center (Brockton), 207

Michigan
Delta College (University Center), 213
Glen Oaks Community College (Centreville), 216
Michigan Career and Technical Institute (Plainwell), 221
Montcalm Community College (Sidney), 223
Schoolcraft College (Livonia), 227

Mississippi
Hinds Community College (Raymond), 232

New York
Briarcliffe College (Bethpage), 258
Queensborough Community College of the City University of New York (Bayside), 280

North Carolina
Brookstone College of Business (Greensboro), 290

Ohio
Cincinnati State Technical and Community College (Cincinnati), 315

Vanguard Career Center (Fremont), 340

Pennsylvania
Harrisburg Area Community College (Harrisburg), 357
Northampton County Area Community College (Bethlehem), 366
Pennco Tech (Bristol), 368
Westmoreland County Community College (Youngwood), 378

Puerto Rico
American Educational College (Bayamón), 379
ASPIRA de Puerto Rico (Carolina), 380
Colegio Mayor de Tecnologia–Arroyo (Arroyo), 382
Educational Technical College–Bayamón (Bayamón), 384
Educational Technical College–Recinto de Coama (Coama), 384
Educational Technical College–Recinto de San Sebastian (San Sebastian), 384
Huertas Junior College (Caguas), 385
Instituto Educativo Premier (Ponce), 387
Inter American University of Puerto Rico, Ponce Campus (Mercedita), 389
International Technical College (San Juan), 389
Ponce Paramedical College (Ponce), 392
Professional Technical Institution (Bayamón), 392
Universal Career Counseling Centers (Santurce), 393

Rhode Island
Motoring Technical Training Institute (East Providence), 395

South Carolina
Beta Tech (North Charleston), 397
Forrest Junior College (Anderson), 399

Tennessee
Tennessee Technology Center at Dickson (Dickson), 416
Tennessee Technology Center at Jacksboro (Jacksboro), 416
Tennessee Technology Center at Morristown (Morristown), 418
William R. Moore School of Technology (Memphis), 421

West Virginia
Ben Franklin Career Center (Dunbar), 437
Cabell County Vocational Technical Center (Huntington), 438
Fred W. Eberle Technical Center (Buckhannon), 439
Putnam Career and Technology Center School of Practical Nursing (Eleanor), 443

Wisconsin
Blackhawk Technical College (Janesville), 445
Milwaukee Career College (Milwaukee), 449
Wisconsin Indianhead Technical College (Shell Lake), 453

COMPUTER PROGRAMMING, OTHER

Florida
Winter Park Tech (Winter Park), 102

Indiana
Ivy Tech Community College–Bloomington (Bloomington), 161
Ivy Tech Community College–Lafayette (Lafayette), 162

Massachusetts
Bristol Community College (Fall River), 196

Ohio
Brown Mackie College–Cincinnati (Cincinnati), 313

Puerto Rico
Columbia College (Yauco), 383
Hispanic American College (Carolina), 385

COMPUTER PROGRAMMING/ PROGRAMMER, GENERAL

Connecticut
Goodwin College (East Hartford), 53
Manchester Community College (Manchester), 54
Norwalk Community College (Norwalk), 55
University of New Haven (West Haven), 58

Delaware
Delaware Technical & Community College, Jack F. Owens Campus (Georgetown), 59
Delaware Technical & Community College, Stanton/Wilmington Campus (Newark), 59

Florida
Florida Technical College (Jacksonville), 78
Florida Technical College (Orlando), 78
McFatter Technical Center (Davie), 86
Miami Lakes Technical Education Center (Miami), 87

Georgia
East Central Technical College (Fitzgerald), 110
Interactive College of Technology (College Park), 115
Interactive College of Technology (Gainesville), 115
Omnitech Institute (Decatur), 119
South Georgia Technical College (Americus), 122

Illinois
Danville Area Community College (Danville), 131
Harper College (Palatine), 135
Lincoln Land Community College (Springfield), 141
Morton College (Cicero), 143
Parkland College (Champaign), 145
Sauk Valley Community College (Dixon), 150
South Suburban College (South Holland), 151

Kentucky
Brown Mackie College–Hopkinsville (Hopkinsville), 170
Interactive Learning Systems (Florence), 174

Maryland
College of Southern Maryland (La Plata), 186
Hagerstown Community College (Hagerstown), 188
Montgomery College (Rockville), 190

Massachusetts
Berkshire Community College (Pittsfield), 194
Fitchburg State College (Fitchburg), 198
Northern Essex Community College (Haverhill), 204
North Shore Community College (Danvers), 204
Sullivan and Cogliano Training Center (Brockton), 207

Michigan
Grand Rapids Community College (Grand Rapids), 216
Lake Michigan College (Benton Harbor), 219
Macomb Community College (Warren), 220
Mott Community College (Flint), 223
Oakland Community College (Bloomfield Hills), 224
Schoolcraft College (Livonia), 227
Washtenaw Community College (Ann Arbor), 229

New Hampshire
Daniel Webster College (Nashua), 236
Lebanon College (Lebanon), 237

New Jersey
Middlesex County College (Edison), 249
Union County College (Cranford), 254

New York
Bramson ORT College (Forest Hills), 258
Briarcliffe College (Bethpage), 258
The College of Westchester (White Plains), 262
Dutchess Community College (Poughkeepsie), 264
Finger Lakes Community College (Canandaigua), 266
Globe Institute of Technology (New York), 268
Hudson Valley Community College (Troy), 268
Pace University (New York), 279
Rochester Institute of Technology (Rochester), 280
Schenectady County Community College (Schenectady), 282
Wood Tobe–Coburn School (New York), 288

North Carolina
Blue Ridge Community College (Flat Rock), 289
Central Carolina Community College (Sanford), 292
Central Piedmont Community College (Charlotte), 293
Craven Community College (New Bern), 294
Davidson County Community College (Lexington), 294
Durham Technical Community College (Durham), 295
Fayetteville Technical Community College (Fayetteville), 295
Gaston College (Dallas), 296
Johnston Community College (Smithfield), 298
Pitt Community College (Greenville), 303
Rowan-Cabarrus Community College (Salisbury), 304
Surry Community College (Dobson), 306
Wake Technical Community College (Raleigh), 307
Wilkes Community College (Wilkesboro), 308

Ohio
Belmont Technical College (St. Clairsville), 311
Bradford School (Columbus), 312
Brown Mackie College–Akron (Akron), 313
Cleveland Institute of Electronics (Cleveland), 316
Columbus State Community College (Columbus), 317
Edison State Community College (Piqua), 319
NewLife Academy of Information Technology (East Liverpool), 327
Terra State Community College (Fremont), 336
University of Cincinnati Raymond Walters College (Cincinnati), 339

Pennsylvania
Bucks County Community College (Newtown), 345
CHI Institute, Franklin Mills Campus (Philadelphia), 348
Community College of Allegheny County (Pittsburgh), 348
Delaware Valley College (Doylestown), 351
Lehigh Carbon Community College (Schnecksville), 362
Northampton County Area Community College (Bethlehem), 366
Pace Institute (Reading), 367
Reading Area Community College (Reading), 372
Schuylkill Technology Center–North Campus (Frackville), 373
Tri-State Business Institute (Erie), 376

Puerto Rico
American Educational College (Bayamón), 379
Liceo de Arte y Disenos (Caguas), 390
Universidad Metropolitana (San Juan), 394

South Carolina
Greenville Technical College (Greenville), 399
Piedmont Technical College (Greenwood), 402
Trident Technical College (Charleston), 404

Vermont
Champlain College (Burlington), 422

West Virginia
West Virginia Business College (Nutter Fort), 443

Wisconsin
Waukesha County Technical College (Pewaukee), 453

COMPUTER PROGRAMMING, SPECIFIC APPLICATIONS

Connecticut
Capital Community College (Hartford), 51
Naugatuck Valley Community College (Waterbury), 54
Northwestern Connecticut Community College (Winsted), 55

Florida
Atlantic Vocational-Technical Center (Coconut Creek), 66
Broward Community College (Fort Lauderdale), 68
Florida Community College at Jacksonville (Jacksonville), 77
Hillsborough Community College (Tampa), 81
Lake Technical Center (Eustis), 83
Lively Technical Center (Tallahassee), 84
Miami Dade College (Miami), 87
Northwest Florida State College (Niceville), 89
Palm Beach Community College (Lake Worth), 90
Pasco-Hernando Community College (New Port Richey), 90
St. Johns River Community College (Palatka), 94
St. Petersburg College (St. Petersburg), 94
State College of Florida Manatee-Sarasota (Bradenton), 98
Valencia Community College (Orlando), 101
Washington-Holmes Technical Center (Chipley), 102

Georgia
Athens Technical College (Athens), 105
Chattahoochee Technical College (Marietta), 107
Coosa Valley Technical College (Rome), 109
DeKalb Technical College (Clarkston), 109
East Central Technical College (Fitzgerald), 110
Gwinnett Technical College (Lawrenceville), 113
Middle Georgia Technical College (Warner Robbins), 117

Illinois
College of DuPage (Glen Ellyn), 129
College of Lake County (Grayslake), 129
Lewis and Clark Community College (Godfrey), 141
Moraine Valley Community College (Palos Hills), 143
Northwestern College (Chicago), 144
Parkland College (Champaign), 145
Rock Valley College (Rockford), 149
Southwestern Illinois College (Belleville), 151

Maryland
Baltimore City Community College (Baltimore), 185
The Community College of Baltimore County (Baltimore), 187
Hagerstown Community College (Hagerstown), 188
Harford Community College (Bel Air), 189
Montgomery College (Rockville), 190

Prince George's Community College (Largo), 191

Massachusetts
Bunker Hill Community College (Boston), 196

Michigan
Jackson Community College (Jackson), 218
Lansing Community College (Lansing), 219
Mott Community College (Flint), 223
Muskegon Community College (Muskegon), 223
Washtenaw Community College (Ann Arbor), 229

Mississippi
Pearl River Community College (Poplarville), 235

North Carolina
Alamance Community College (Graham), 288
Blue Ridge Community College (Flat Rock), 289
Caldwell Community College and Technical Institute (Hudson), 290
Forsyth Technical Community College (Winston-Salem), 296
King's College (Charlotte), 299
Mitchell Community College (Statesville), 300
Piedmont Community College (Roxboro), 302
South Piedmont Community College (Polkton), 305

Ohio
James A. Rhodes State College (Lima), 322
Kent State University, Trumbull Campus (Warren), 323
Lakeland Community College (Kirtland), 323
Marion Technical College (Marion), 325
Owens Community College (Toledo), 330

Pennsylvania
Luzerne County Community College (Nanticoke), 363
Westmoreland County Community College (Youngwood), 378

Rhode Island
Community College of Rhode Island (Warwick), 394

Tennessee
Southwest Tennessee Community College (Memphis), 414

COMPUTER PROGRAMMING, VENDOR/PRODUCT CERTIFICATION

Georgia
Javelin Technical Training Center (Atlanta), 115

Illinois
Morton College (Cicero), 143
Oakton Community College (Des Plaines), 145
Richland Community College (Decatur), 148

Indiana
TechSkills—Indianapolis (Indianapolis), 167

Maryland
Hagerstown Community College (Hagerstown), 188
Prince George's Community College (Largo), 191

New Jersey
Raritan Valley Community College (Somerville), 252

Ohio
Cleveland Institute of Electronics (Cleveland), 316
TechSkills—Columbus (Columbus), 336

Pennsylvania
Peirce College (Philadelphia), 367

Tennessee
Northeast State Technical Community College (Blountville), 412

COMPUTER SCIENCE

Florida
Atlantic Vocational-Technical Center (Coconut Creek), 66
Sheridan Vocational-Technical Center (Hollywood), 96

Illinois
Dominican University (River Forest), 131

Kentucky
Draughons Junior College (Bowling Green), 172

Massachusetts
Atlantic Union College (South Lancaster), 193

Michigan
Dorsey Business Schools (Madison Heights), 214
Dorsey Business Schools (Roseville), 214
Dorsey Business Schools (Southgate), 214
Dorsey Business Schools (Wayne), 214

Mississippi
Belhaven College (Jackson), 230

New Hampshire
New Hampshire Community Technical College, Stratham (Stratham), 239

New York
Pace University (New York), 279

Ohio
North Central State College (Mansfield), 327
The University of Akron (Akron), 338

Pennsylvania
Central Pennsylvania College (Summerdale), 347
Tri-State Business Institute (Erie), 376

COMPUTER SOFTWARE AND MEDIA APPLICATIONS, OTHER

District of Columbia
Technical Learning Centers (Washington), 62

Florida
Florida National College (Hialeah), 78

Illinois
Midstate College (Peoria), 143
Rockford Business College (Rockford), 149

Kentucky
Brown Mackie College–Hopkinsville (Hopkinsville), 170

Massachusetts
Springfield Technical Community College (Springfield), 207

Michigan
Delta College (University Center), 213
Henry Ford Community College (Dearborn), 217

New York
Mildred Elley School (Albany), 273

North Carolina
Fayetteville Technical Community College (Fayetteville), 295

Ohio
Baldwin-Wallace College (Berea), 311
Bohecker College–Ravenna (Ravenna), 312
Daymar College (Chillicothe), 318
Gallipolis Career College (Gallipolis), 320
Ohio Business College (Lorain), 328
Ohio Business College (Sandusky), 328

Pennsylvania
Consolidated School of Business (Lancaster), 350
Consolidated School of Business (York), 350

Kaplan Career Institute–ICM Campus
(Pittsburgh), 359
Lackawanna College (Scranton), 359
Lansdale School of Business (North Wales), 360
Puerto Rico
John Dewey College, 389, 390
Universidad del Este (Carolina), 393
Vermont
Champlain College (Burlington), 422
Virginia
Everest Institute (Chesapeake), 428
New River Community College (Dublin), 430
Wisconsin
Waukesha County Technical College
(Pewaukee), 453

COMPUTER SOFTWARE ENGINEERING
Indiana
TechSkills—Indianapolis (Indianapolis), 167
Ohio
TechSkills—Columbus (Columbus), 336

COMPUTER SOFTWARE TECHNOLOGY/
TECHNICIAN
Delaware
Delaware Technical & Community College,
Jack F. Owens Campus (Georgetown), 59
Delaware Technical & Community College,
Terry Campus (Dover), 60
Illinois
Brown Mackie College–Moline (Moline), 125
Oakton Community College (Des Plaines), 145
Indiana
Brown Mackie College–Merrillville
(Merrillville), 156
Maryland
Frederick Community College (Frederick), 188
New York
Monroe 2–Orleans BOCES Center for
Workforce Development (Rochester), 274
Pennsylvania
Community College of Allegheny County
(Pittsburgh), 348

COMPUTER SYSTEMS ANALYSIS/ANALYST
Florida
Brevard Community College (Cocoa), 67
Broward Community College (Fort Lauderdale),
68
Central Florida Community College (Ocala), 69
Daytona State College (Daytona Beach), 72
Florida Community College at Jacksonville
(Jacksonville), 77
Hillsborough Community College (Tampa), 81
Lake-Sumter Community College (Leesburg),
83
Lively Technical Center (Tallahassee), 84
Miami Dade College (Miami), 87
Northwest Florida State College (Niceville), 89
Polk Community College (Winter Haven), 92
St. Petersburg College (St. Petersburg), 94
Santa Fe Community College (Gainesville), 95
Seminole Community College (Sanford), 96
Valencia Community College (Orlando), 101
Indiana
Goshen College (Goshen), 157
Maryland
TESST College of Technology (Beltsville), 192
Wor-Wic Community College (Salisbury), 193
Michigan
Baker College of Cadillac (Cadillac), 210
Baker College of Clinton Township (Clinton
Township), 210
Baker College of Flint (Flint), 210

Kalamazoo Valley Community College
(Kalamazoo), 218
Kirtland Community College (Roscommon),
219
North Carolina
Haywood Community College (Clyde), 297
Lenoir Community College (Kinston), 299
Mitchell Community College (Statesville), 300
Western Piedmont Community College
(Morganton), 308
Ohio
Delaware JVS District (Delaware), 318
Kent State University (Kent), 322
Kent State University, Trumbull Campus
(Warren), 323
The University of Akron (Akron), 338
Pennsylvania
CHI Institute, Franklin Mills Campus
(Philadelphia), 348
Lehigh Carbon Community College
(Schnecksville), 362
Puerto Rico
John Dewey College, 390
Tennessee
Tennessee Technology Center at Jackson
(Jackson), 417
Tennessee Technology Center at Ripley
(Ripley), 419
West Virginia
Logan-Mingo School of Practical Nursing
(Logan), 441
Wisconsin
Kaplan College–Milwaukee (Milwaukee), 447

COMPUTER SYSTEMS NETWORKING AND
TELECOMMUNICATIONS
Alabama
Virginia College at Birmingham (Birmingham),
48
Virginia College at Huntsville (Huntsville), 48
Connecticut
Branford Hall Career Institute–Branford
Campus (Branford), 49
Branford Hall Career Institute–Southington
Campus (Southington), 49
Quinebaug Valley Community College
(Danielson), 56
Ridley-Lowell Business and Technical Institute
(New London), 56
Delaware
Delaware Technical & Community College,
Terry Campus (Dover), 60
Florida
Advanced Technical Centers (Miami), 64
ATI Career Training Center (Fort Lauderdale),
65
Florida National College (Hialeah), 78
Florida Technical College (Jacksonville), 78
Florida Technical College (Orlando), 78
George Stone Area Vocational-Technical
Center (Pensacola), 79
Lee County High Tech Center North (Cape
Coral), 83
Lincoln College of Technology (West Palm
Beach), 84
Lively Technical Center (Tallahassee), 84
Manatee Technical Institute (Bradenton), 85
Polytechnic Institute of America (Orlando), 92
Radford M. Locklin Technical Center (Milton),
92
Ridge Technical Center (Winter Haven), 93
Sheridan Vocational-Technical Center
(Hollywood), 96
Traviss Technical Center (Lakeland), 99

Washington-Holmes Technical Center
(Chipley), 102
Georgia
Albany Technical College (Albany), 103
Atlanta Technical College (Atlanta), 105
Augusta Technical College (Augusta), 106
Central Georgia Technical College (Macon),
107
Chattahoochee Technical College (Marietta),
107
Clayton State University (Morrow), 108
Columbus Technical College (Columbus), 108
Coosa Valley Technical College (Rome), 109
DeKalb Technical College (Clarkston), 109
East Central Technical College (Fitzgerald), 110
Flint River Technical College (Thomaston), 111
Griffin Technical College (Griffin), 113
Gwinnett Technical College (Lawrenceville),
113
Heart of Georgia Technical College (Dublin),
114
Iverson Business School (Atlanta), 115
Lanier Technical College (Oakwood), 115
Middle Georgia Technical College (Warner
Robbins), 117
New Horizons Computer Learning Centers
(Atlanta), 117
North Georgia Technical College (Clarkesville),
118
North Metro Technical College (Acworth), 118
Northwestern Technical College (Rock Spring),
118
Ogeechee Technical College (Statesboro), 119
Okefenokee Technical College (Waycross), 119
Sandersville Technical College (Sandersville),
120
Savannah Technical College (Savannah), 121
South Georgia Technical College (Americus),
122
Southwest Georgia Technical College
(Thomasville), 122
Swainsboro Technical College (Swainsboro),
123
West Georgia Technical College (LaGrange),
124
Illinois
Black Hawk College (Moline), 125
CALC Institute of Technology (Alton), 126
City Colleges of Chicago, Harry S. Truman
College (Chicago), 128
City Colleges of Chicago, Richard J. Daley
College (Chicago), 128
College of Lake County (Grayslake), 129
The College of Office Technology (Chicago),
130
Harper College (Palatine), 135
Illinois Central College (East Peoria), 136
Illinois Valley Community College (Oglesby),
138
Joliet Junior College (Joliet), 139
Kaskaskia College (Centralia), 139
Kishwaukee College (Malta), 140
Lewis and Clark Community College (Godfrey),
141
McHenry County College (Crystal Lake), 142
Midstate College (Peoria), 143
Moraine Valley Community College (Palos
Hills), 143
Morton College (Cicero), 143
Oakton Community College (Des Plaines), 145
Parkland College (Champaign), 145
Prairie State College (Chicago Heights), 146
Rend Lake College (Ina), 148
Richland Community College (Decatur), 148
Robert Morris University (Chicago), 149
Rock Valley College (Rockford), 149
Sauk Valley Community College (Dixon), 150
South Suburban College (South Holland), 151

COMPUTER TECHNOLOGY/COMPUTER SYSTEMS TECHNOLOGY

College of Business and Technology–Hialeah Campus (Hialeah), 70
College of Business and Technology (Miami), 70
Daytona State College (Daytona Beach), 72
Florida Community College at Jacksonville (Jacksonville), 77
Florida Education Center (Lauderhill), 77
Henry W. Brewster Technical Center (Tampa), 80
Hillsborough Community College (Tampa), 81
James Lorenzo Walker Vocational-Technical Center (Naples), 82
Lindsey Hopkins Technical Education Center (Miami), 84
Manatee Technical Institute (Bradenton), 85
Miami Dade College (Miami), 87
Northwest Florida State College (Niceville), 89
Palm Beach Community College (Lake Worth), 90
Pinellas Technical Education Center–Clearwater (Clearwater), 91
Polk Community College (Winter Haven), 92
Radford M. Locklin Technical Center (Milton), 92
Saber (Miami), 94
St. Johns River Community College (Palatka), 94
St. Petersburg College (St. Petersburg), 94
Santa Fe Community College (Gainesville), 95
Seminole Community College (Sanford), 96
Total International Career Institute (Hialeah), 99
Valencia Community College (Orlando), 101
Westside Tech (Winter Garden), 102
Winter Park Tech (Winter Park), 102
Withlacoochee Technical Institute (Inverness), 103

Georgia
Advanced Career Training (Atlanta), 103

Illinois
College of DuPage (Glen Ellyn), 129
Heartland Community College (Normal), 136
Illinois Valley Community College (Oglesby), 138
Lake Land College (Mattoon), 140
Lincoln Land Community College (Springfield), 141
McHenry County College (Crystal Lake), 142
Morton College (Cicero), 143
Oakton Community College (Des Plaines), 145
Triton College (River Grove), 153
Waubonsee Community College (Sugar Grove), 154

Indiana
Harrison College (Indianapolis), 158
Harrison College (Muncie), 159

Kentucky
Bowling Green Technical College (Bowling Green), 170

Maryland
Allegany College of Maryland (Cumberland), 184
The Community College of Baltimore County (Baltimore), 187
Frederick Community College (Frederick), 188
Garrett College (McHenry), 188
Howard Community College (Columbia), 189
Kaplan College–Hagerstown (Hagerstown), 189
Montgomery College (Rockville), 190
Prince George's Community College (Largo), 191

Massachusetts
Cape Cod Community College (West Barnstable), 196

Michigan
Baker College of Cadillac (Cadillac), 210
Baker College of Flint (Flint), 210

Baker College of Muskegon (Muskegon), 211
Baker College of Owosso (Owosso), 211
Baker College of Port Huron (Port Huron), 211
Everest Institute (Southfield), 215
Lansing Community College (Lansing), 219
Washtenaw Community College (Ann Arbor), 229

New York
Genesee Community College (Batavia), 267
Hunter Business School (Levittown), 269

North Carolina
Brookstone College of Business (Charlotte), 290
College of The Albemarle (Elizabeth City), 294
Western Piedmont Community College (Morganton), 308

Ohio
James A. Rhodes State College (Lima), 322
Miami University (Oxford), 326
O. C. Collins Career Center (Chesapeake), 328
Ohio Business College (Lorain), 328
Ohio Business College (Sandusky), 328
Portage Lakes Career Center (Green), 331
University of Cincinnati Clermont College (Batavia), 339

Pennsylvania
Bucks County Community College (Newtown), 345
CHI Institute, Broomall Campus (Broomall), 348
Community College of Allegheny County (Pittsburgh), 348
DCI Career Institute (Monaca), 350
Greater Altoona Career and Technology Center (Altoona), 356
Lancaster County Career and Technology Center (Willow Street), 360
Lehigh Carbon Community College (Schnecksville), 362
Luzerne County Community College (Nanticoke), 363
Mercyhurst College (Erie), 364
Reading Area Community College (Reading), 372

Puerto Rico
ICPR Junior College–Arecibo Campus (Arecibo), 385
ICPR Junior College–Mayagüez Campus (Mayagüez), 385
Instituto de Banca y Comercio–Aprendes Practicanco (Río Piedras), 386
John Dewey College, 389, 390
Professional Technical Institution (Bayamón), 392

Rhode Island
Community College of Rhode Island (Warwick), 394

Tennessee
Tennessee Technology Center at Jacksboro (Jacksboro), 416
Tennessee Technology Center at Pulaski (Pulaski), 419

Virginia
ECPI College of Technology (Virginia Beach), 426
ECPI Technical College (Richmond), 427

West Virginia
Monongalia County Technical Education Center (Morgantown), 441
West Virginia Junior College (Bridgeport), 444
West Virginia Junior College (Charleston), 444

Wisconsin
Waukesha County Technical College (Pewaukee), 453

COMPUTER TYPOGRAPHY AND COMPOSITION EQUIPMENT OPERATOR

Ohio
University of Cincinnati Clermont College (Batavia), 339

Pennsylvania
Luzerne County Community College (Nanticoke), 363

CONCRETE FINISHING/CONCRETE FINISHER

Illinois
Southwestern Illinois College (Belleville), 151

Wisconsin
Milwaukee Area Technical College (Milwaukee), 449
Waukesha County Technical College (Pewaukee), 453

CONSTRUCTION ENGINEERING TECHNOLOGY/TECHNICIAN

Alabama
Jefferson State Community College (Birmingham), 44

Delaware
Delaware Technical & Community College, Jack F. Owens Campus (Georgetown), 59

Florida
Palm Beach Community College (Lake Worth), 90
Pensacola Junior College (Pensacola), 91
Seminole Community College (Sanford), 96
Suwannee-Hamilton Area Vocational, Technical, and Adult Education Center (Live Oak), 98
Valencia Community College (Orlando), 101

Illinois
College of Lake County (Grayslake), 129
Danville Area Community College (Danville), 131
Kankakee Community College (Kankakee), 139

Maine
Central Maine Community College (Auburn), 181
Eastern Maine Community College (Bangor), 181

Massachusetts
Bristol Community College (Fall River), 196
Cape Cod Community College (West Barnstable), 196

New Jersey
Ocean County College (Toms River), 250

New York
Hudson Valley Community College (Troy), 268
New York City College of Technology of the City University of New York (Brooklyn), 276
TCI–The College of Technology (New York), 285

Ohio
Columbus State Community College (Columbus), 317
Lakeland Community College (Kirtland), 323
Lorain County JVS Adult Career Center (Oberlin), 324
Owens Community College (Toledo), 330
Sinclair Community College (Dayton), 334
The University of Akron (Akron), 338

Pennsylvania
Harrisburg Area Community College (Harrisburg), 357
Lehigh Carbon Community College (Schnecksville), 362

Rhode Island
New England Institute of Technology (Warwick), 395

South Carolina
Denmark Technical College (Denmark), 398
Greenville Technical College (Greenville), 399
Piedmont Technical College (Greenwood), 402
Technical College of the Lowcountry (Beaufort), 403
Trident Technical College (Charleston), 404
York Technical College (Rock Hill), 405

West Virginia
Fred W. Eberle Technical Center (Buckhannon), 439
HRDE-Stanley Technical Institute–Clarksburg (Clarksburg), 439

CONSTRUCTION/HEAVY EQUIPMENT/ EARTHMOVING EQUIPMENT OPERATION

Alabama
Jefferson Davis Community College (Brewton), 44
Shelton State Community College (Tuscaloosa), 46

Florida
Mid-Florida Tech (Orlando), 87
Washington-Holmes Technical Center (Chipley), 102

Illinois
Joliet Junior College (Joliet), 139

Kentucky
Hazard Community and Technical College (Hazard), 174
Southeast Kentucky Community and Technical College (Cumberland), 178

Maine
Southern Maine Community College (South Portland), 182
Washington County Community College (Calais), 183

Michigan
Lansing Community College (Lansing), 219

Mississippi
Copiah-Lincoln Community College (Wesson), 231
Mississippi Delta Community College (Moorhead), 234

Ohio
Warren County Career Center (Lebanon), 340

Pennsylvania
Central Pennsylvania Institute of Science and Technology (Pleasant Gap), 347
New Castle School of Trades (Pulaski), 366
Schuylkill Technology Center–North Campus (Frackville), 373

Wisconsin
Mid-State Technical College (Wisconsin Rapids), 449

CONSTRUCTION MANAGEMENT

Connecticut
Three Rivers Community College (Norwich), 57

Delaware
Delaware Technical & Community College, Terry Campus (Dover), 60

Georgia
Central Georgia Technical College (Macon), 107
Coosa Valley Technical College (Rome), 109
Griffin Technical College (Griffin), 113
Gwinnett Technical College (Lawrenceville), 113
Southern Polytechnic State University (Marietta), 122

Illinois
Oakton Community College (Des Plaines), 145
Rock Valley College (Rockford), 149
South Suburban College (South Holland), 151
Triton College (River Grove), 153

CONSTRUCTION TRADES, GENERAL

Delaware
Delaware Technical & Community College, Stanton/Wilmington Campus (Newark), 59

Florida
Manatee Technical Institute (Bradenton), 85

Illinois
Illinois Central College (East Peoria), 136
Joliet Junior College (Joliet), 139
Kaskaskia College (Centralia), 139
Lake Land College (Mattoon), 140
Parkland College (Champaign), 145
Rend Lake College (Ina), 148
Richland Community College (Decatur), 148
Rock Valley College (Rockford), 149
Southeastern Illinois College (Harrisburg), 151
South Suburban College (South Holland), 151
Southwestern Illinois College (Belleville), 151
Spoon River College (Canton), 152

Indiana
Vincennes University (Vincennes), 168

Maryland
North American Trade Schools (Grantsville), 191

Michigan
Washtenaw Community College (Ann Arbor), 229

New Jersey
Adult and Continuing Education–Bergen County Technical Schools (Hackensack), 240

New York
Apex Technical School (New York), 256
Onondaga-Courtland-Madison BOCES (Liverpool), 278

Ohio
Apollo School of Practical Nursing (Lima), 310
Choffin Career Center (Youngstown), 315
Scioto County Joint Vocational School District (Lucasville), 334
TCTC Adult Training Center (Warren), 336
Toledo School of Practical Nursing (Toledo), 337

Pennsylvania
Allied Medical and Technical Institute (Forty Fort), 342
Commonwealth Technical Institute (Johnstown), 348
Harrisburg Area Community College (Harrisburg), 357
Penn Commercial Business and Technical School (Washington), 367

Virginia
John Tyler Community College (Chester), 429
Northern Virginia Community College (Annandale), 430
Wytheville Community College (Wytheville), 436

West Virginia
Ben Franklin Career Center (Dunbar), 437
Cabell County Vocational Technical Center (Huntington), 438

CONSTRUCTION TRADES, OTHER

Florida
James Lorenzo Walker Vocational-Technical Center (Naples), 82
Miami Lakes Technical Education Center (Miami), 87
Mid-Florida Tech (Orlando), 87

Illinois
Lincoln Technical Institute (Norridge), 142

Indiana
Ivy Tech Community College–East Central (Muncie), 162
Ivy Tech Community College–Kokomo (Kokomo), 162
Ivy Tech Community College–Northeast (Fort Wayne), 163
Ivy Tech Community College–Northwest (Gary), 163
Ivy Tech Community College–Whitewater (Richmond), 164

Maine
York County Community College (Wells), 183

Maryland
Allegany College of Maryland (Cumberland), 184
Frederick Community College (Frederick), 188

Michigan
Gogebic Community College (Ironwood), 216

New York
Nassau Community College (Garden City), 275
State University of New York College of Technology at Canton (Canton), 284

Ohio
Akron Adult Vocational Services (Akron), 309
Auburn Career Center (Painesville), 311
Lorain County JVS Adult Career Center (Oberlin), 324
Washington County Career Center Adult Education (Marietta), 341

Pennsylvania
Allied Medical and Technical Institute (Forty Fort), 342

Tennessee
Southwest Tennessee Community College (Memphis), 414
Tennessee Technology Center at Crossville (Crossville), 415
Tennessee Technology Center at Livingston (Livingston), 417
Tennessee Technology Center at Memphis (Memphis), 417

Virginia
Center for Employment Training–Alexandria (Alexandria), 425

West Virginia
Academy of Careers and Technology (Beckley), 437

Wisconsin
Moraine Park Technical College (Fond du Lac), 450

CONSUMER MERCHANDISING/RETAILING MANAGEMENT

Pennsylvania
Commonwealth Technical Institute (Johnstown), 348

COOKING AND RELATED CULINARY ARTS, GENERAL

Alabama
Virginia College at Birmingham (Birmingham), 48

Florida
Marion County Community Technical and Adult Education Center (Ocala), 85
Radford M. Locklin Technical Center (Milton), 92
Robert Morgan Vocational-Technical Center (Miami), 94

Illinois
St. Augustine College (Chicago), 150

Kentucky
Employment Solutions (Lexington), 172

Massachusetts
The Salter School (Worcester), 206

Mississippi
East Central Community College (Decatur), 232
Hinds Community College (Raymond), 232
Jones County Junior College (Ellisville), 234

New Hampshire
McIntosh College (Dover), 238

New York
Culinary Academy of Long Island (Westbury), 263

Pennsylvania
Lebanon County Area Vocational Technical School (Lebanon), 361

Puerto Rico
ICPR Junior College–Arecibo Campus (Arecibo), 385
ICPR Junior College–Mayagüez Campus (Mayagüez), 385
Instituto Comercial de Puerto Rico Junior College (San Juan), 386

Vermont
New England Culinary Institute at Essex (Essex Junction), 423

Virginia
Dabney S. Lancaster Community College (Clifton Forge), 426
Northern Virginia Community College (Annandale), 430

West Virginia
Mountain State University (Beckley), 442
Putnam Career and Technology Center School of Practical Nursing (Eleanor), 443

CORRECTIONS

Florida
Brevard Community College (Cocoa), 67
Broward Community College (Fort Lauderdale), 68
Central Florida Community College (Ocala), 69
Chipola College (Marianna), 69
Daytona State College (Daytona Beach), 72
Florida Community College at Jacksonville (Jacksonville), 77
Florida Keys Community College (Key West), 78
George Stone Area Vocational-Technical Center (Pensacola), 79
Gulf Coast Community College (Panama City), 79
Hillsborough Community College (Tampa), 81
Indian River State College (Fort Pierce), 81
Lake City Community College (Lake City), 83
Lake Technical Center (Eustis), 83
Miami Dade College (Miami), 87
North Florida Community College (Madison), 88
Northwest Florida State College (Niceville), 89
Palm Beach Community College (Lake Worth), 90
Pasco-Hernando Community College (New Port Richey), 90
Polk Community College (Winter Haven), 92
St. Johns River Community College (Palatka), 94
St. Petersburg College (St. Petersburg), 94
Santa Fe Community College (Gainesville), 95
Sarasota County Technical Institute (Sarasota), 96
South Florida Community College (Avon Park), 97

Tallahassee Community College (Tallahassee), 98
Valencia Community College (Orlando), 101
Washington-Holmes Technical Center (Chipley), 102
Withlacoochee Technical Institute (Inverness), 103

Illinois
Heartland Community College (Normal), 136
Richland Community College (Decatur), 148
Southeastern Illinois College (Harrisburg), 151

Maryland
Baltimore City Community College (Baltimore), 185
Garrett College (McHenry), 188
Hagerstown Community College (Hagerstown), 188

Massachusetts
Cape Cod Community College (West Barnstable), 196

Michigan
Baker College of Auburn Hills (Auburn Hills), 209
Baker College of Cadillac (Cadillac), 210
Baker College of Flint (Flint), 210
Baker College of Jackson (Jackson), 210
Baker College of Muskegon (Muskegon), 211
Baker College of Port Huron (Port Huron), 211
Bay de Noc Community College (Escanaba), 211
Bay Mills Community College (Brimley), 211
Davenport University (Grand Rapids), 213
Delta College (University Center), 213
Gogebic Community College (Ironwood), 216
Henry Ford Community College (Dearborn), 217
Jackson Community College (Jackson), 218
Kellogg Community College (Battle Creek), 218
Kirtland Community College (Roscommon), 219
Lansing Community College (Lansing), 219
Montcalm Community College (Sidney), 223
Muskegon Community College (Muskegon), 223
North Central Michigan College (Petoskey), 223
West Shore Community College (Scottville), 229

New Jersey
Middlesex County College (Edison), 249

New York
Herkimer County Community College (Herkimer), 268
Jamestown Community College (Jamestown), 270

Ohio
Lakeland Community College (Kirtland), 323

Pennsylvania
Bucks County Community College (Newtown), 345
Butler County Community College (Butler), 345
Harrisburg Area Community College (Harrisburg), 357
Lehigh Carbon Community College (Schnecksville), 362
Westmoreland County Community College (Youngwood), 378

Virginia
Dabney S. Lancaster Community College (Clifton Forge), 426
Danville Community College (Danville), 426
Virginia Highlands Community College (Abingdon), 435
Wytheville Community College (Wytheville), 436

CORRECTIONS ADMINISTRATION

West Virginia
American Public University System (Charles Town), 437

CORRECTIONS AND CRIMINAL JUSTICE, OTHER

Connecticut
Asnuntuck Community College (Enfield), 49
University of New Haven (West Haven), 58

Florida
Lake Technical Center (Eustis), 83
Washington-Holmes Technical Center (Chipley), 102
Withlacoochee Technical Institute (Inverness), 103

Illinois
Elgin Community College (Elgin), 132
Saint Xavier University (Chicago), 150

Indiana
Brown Mackie College–Fort Wayne (Fort Wayne), 155
Brown Mackie College–Merrillville (Merrillville), 156
Brown Mackie College–Michigan City (Michigan City), 156
Brown Mackie College–South Bend (South Bend), 156

Maryland
Frederick Community College (Frederick), 188

Michigan
Alpena Community College (Alpena), 209

New Jersey
Camden County College (Blackwood), 241
Ocean County Vocational Post Secondary Division (Toms River), 250
Raritan Valley Community College (Somerville), 252

New York
Ridley-Lowell Business and Technical Institute (Binghamton), 280

North Carolina
Pamlico Community College (Grantsboro), 302

Ohio
Buckeye Hills Career Center (Rio Grande), 313
Butler Technology and Career Development Schools–D. Russel Lee Career-Technology Center (Hamilton), 314
Toledo School of Practical Nursing (Toledo), 337

Pennsylvania
Community College of Philadelphia (Philadelphia), 349
Computer Learning Network (Camp Hill), 349
Kaplan Career Institute–Harrisburg (Harrisburg), 359
Lansdale School of Business (North Wales), 360
Lehigh Carbon Community College (Schnecksville), 362

South Carolina
Forrest Junior College (Anderson), 399

Tennessee
Draughons Junior College (Murfreesboro), 407

Virginia
Beta Tech (Richmond), 424
Everest College (Newport News), 427
Tidewater Tech (Virginia Beach), 434

West Virginia
American Public University System (Charles Town), 437

COSMETOLOGY AND RELATED PERSONAL GROOMING ARTS, OTHER

Alabama
Bevill State Community College (Sumiton), 41
Calhoun Community College (Decatur), 41
George Corley Wallace State Community College (Selma), 43
H. Councill Trenholm State Technical College (Montgomery), 43
Northwest-Shoals Community College (Muscle Shoals), 45
Reid State Technical College (Evergreen), 46
Shelton State Community College (Tuscaloosa), 46

Florida
Academy of Cosmetology (Merritt Island), 63
Academy of Cosmetology (Palm Bay), 63
Academy of Professional Careers (Winter Park), 63
Artistic Nails and Beauty Academy (Tampa), 65
ASM Beauty World Academy (Hollywood), 65
Atlantic Vocational-Technical Center (Coconut Creek), 66
The Beauty Institute (West Palm Beach), 66
Benes International School of Beauty (New Port Richey), 67
Bradenton Beauty Academy (Bradenton), 67
Charlotte Vocational-Technical Center (Port Charlotte), 69
Florida Academy of Health & Beauty (Wilton Manor), 75
James Lorenzo Walker Vocational-Technical Center (Naples), 82
La Belle Beauty Academy (Miami), 83
La Belle Beauty School (Hialeah), 83
Manhattan Beauty School (Tampa), 85
New Concept Massage and Beauty School (Miami), 88
North Florida Cosmetology Institute (Tallahassee), 88
Nouvelle Institute (Miami), 89
Praxis Institute (Miami), 92
Sarasota County Technical Institute (Sarasota), 96
Sheridan Vocational-Technical Center (Hollywood), 96
Sunstate Academy of Hair Design (Fort Myers), 98
Sunstate Academy of Hair Design (Sarasota), 98
Taylor Technical Institute (Perry), 99
Traviss Technical Center (Lakeland), 99
Universal Massage and Beauty Institute (Sweetwater), 100

Georgia
American Professional Institute (Macon), 104
International City Beauty College (Warner Robins), 115
Rivertown School of Beauty (Columbus), 120
Roffler Moler Hairstyling College (Marietta), 120

Illinois
Ms. Robert's Academy of Beauty Culture–Villa Park (Villa Park), 144
Mr. John's School of Cosmetology & Nails (Jacksonville), 144
Mr. John's School of Cosmetology (Decatur), 144
Professionals Choice Hair Design Academy (Joliet), 146
Rosel School of Cosmetology (Chicago), 149

Indiana
Hair Arts Academy (Bloomington), 157
Hair Fashions by Kaye Beauty College (Indianapolis), 157
Hair Fashions by Kaye Beauty College (Noblesville), 158

J. Michael Harrold Beauty Academy (Terre Haute), 164
Masters of Cosmetology College (Fort Wayne), 165
PJ's College of Cosmetology (Clarksville), 166

Kentucky
Barrett and Company School of Hair Design (Nicholasville), 169
Pat Wilson's Beauty College (Henderson), 177
PJ's College of Cosmetology (Bowling Green), 177
PJ's College of Cosmetology (Glasgow), 177

Maryland
Hair Expressions Academy (Rockville), 188
Robert Paul Academy of Cosmetology Arts and Sciences (Timonium), 191

Massachusetts
Mansfield Beauty Schools (Quincy), 201
Mansfield Beauty Schools (Springfield), 201
Rob Roy Academy–Worcester Campus (Worcester), 205

Michigan
Creative Hair School of Cosmetology (Flint), 213
Gallery College of Beauty (Clinton Township), 216
Hillsdale Beauty College (Hillsdale), 217
Michigan College of Beauty (Monroe), 221
Port Huron Cosmetology College (Waterford), 225

Mississippi
Blue Cliff College–Gulfport (Gulfport), 230
Day Spa Career College (Ocean Spring), 231
Gibson Barber and Beauty College (West Point), 232
J & J Hair Design College (Carthage), 233

New Hampshire
Keene Beauty Academy (Keene), 237

New Jersey
Capri Institute of Hair Design (Succasunna), 242
Monmouth County Vocational School District (Long Branch), 249
Parisian Beauty School (Hackensack), 250
PB Cosmetology Education Center (Gloucester), 251

New York
Beauty School of Middletown (Hyde Park), 257
Beauty School of Middletown (Middletown), 257
Continental School of Beauty Culture–Jefferson (Rochester), 262
Continental School of Beauty Culture–Olean (Olean), 263
Elite Academy of Beauty Arts (Brooklyn), 264
Westchester School of Beauty Culture (Mount Vernon), 287

North Carolina
Beaufort County Community College (Washington), 289
Brunswick Community College (Supply), 290
Cape Fear Community College (Wilmington), 290
Carolina Beauty College–Durham Campus (Durham), 291
Cleveland Community College (Shelby), 293
Haywood Community College (Clyde), 297
Mr. David's School of Hair Design (Wilmington), 301
Mitchell Community College (Statesville), 300
Roanoke-Chowan Community College (Ahoskie), 303
Sandhills Community College (Pinehurst), 305
Vance-Granville Community College (Henderson), 307

Ohio
Casal Aveda Institute (Austintown), 314
Creative Images–a Certified Matrix Design Academy (Dayton), 317
Creative Images College of Beauty (Fairborn), 318
Eastern Hills Academy of Hair Design (Cincinnati), 319
Gerber's Akron Beauty School (Fairlawn), 320
International Academy of Hair Design (Cincinnati), 322
Paramount Beauty Academy (Portsmouth), 330
Polaris Career Center (Middleburg Heights), 331
Raphael's School of Beauty Culture (Salem), 332
Raphael's School of Beauty Culture (Youngstown), 332
The Spa School (Columbus), 335
Vogue Beauty Academy (Cleveland Heights), 340
Western Hills School of Beauty and Hair Design (Cincinnati), 341

Pennsylvania
Academy of Hair Design (Bloomsburg), 342
Bucks County School of Beauty Culture (Feasterville), 345
Jean Madeline Education Center (Philadelphia), 358
Lancaster School of Cosmetology (Lancaster), 360
Levittown Beauty Academy (Levittown), 362
McCann School of Business & Technology (Pottsville), 364
Pruonto's Hair Design Institute (Altoona), 372
South Hills Beauty Academy (Pittsburgh), 374

Puerto Rico
American Educational College (Bayamón), 379
Charlie's Guard-Detective Bureau and Academy (Aguadilla), 382
D'mart Institute (Barranquitas), 383
Institute of Beauty Careers (Arecibo), 386
Modern Hairstyling Institute (Bayamón), 391
Modern Hairstyling Institute (Carolina), 391
MyrAngel Beauty Institute (San Lorenzo), 391
Quality Technical and Beauty College (Bayamón), 392

Rhode Island
Newport School of Hairdressing–Main Campus (Pawtucket), 396

South Carolina
Academy of Cosmetology (North Charleston), 397
Academy of Hair Technology (Greenville), 397
Sumter Beauty College (Sumter), 403

Tennessee
Buchanan Beauty College (Shelbyville), 406
Elite College of Cosmetology (Lexington), 407
Miller-Motte Technical College (Chattanooga), 410
Miller-Motte Technical College (Clarksville), 410
New Directions Hair Academy (Memphis), 411
Tennessee Academy of Cosmetology (Memphis), 414, 415
Volunteer Beauty Academy (Madison), 420

Vermont
Vermont College of Cosmetology (Burlington), 423

Virginia
Ana Visage Academy (Great Falls), 424
Dominion School of Hair Design (Gloucester Point), 426

Wisconsin
Madison Area Technical College (Madison), 448

Milwaukee Area Technical College (Milwaukee), 449
Professional Hair Design Academy (Eau Claire), 451
The Salon Professional Academy (Appleton), 451

COSMETOLOGY, BARBER/STYLING, AND NAIL INSTRUCTOR

Alabama
Mimi's Beauty Academy of Cosmetology (Huntsville), 45

Connecticut
Academy Di Capelli—School of Cosmetology (Wallingford), 48
The Leon Institute of Hair Design (Bridgeport), 53

Delaware
Delaware Learning Institute of Cosmetology (Dagsboro), 59
Schilling-Douglas School of Hair Design (Newark), 60

District of Columbia
Bennett Beauty Institute (Washington), 61
Dudley Beauty College (Washington), 61

Florida
Academy of Cosmetology (Merritt Island), 63
Academy of Professional Careers (Winter Park), 63
ASM Beauty World Academy (Hollywood), 65
Bradenton Beauty Academy (Bradenton), 67
Florida Academy of Health & Beauty (Wilton Manor), 75
La Belle Beauty Academy (Miami), 83
La Belle Beauty School (Hialeah), 83
Lindsey Hopkins Technical Education Center (Miami), 84
Shear Excellence International Hair Academy (Tampa), 96
Sheridan Vocational-Technical Center (Hollywood), 96
Sunstate Academy of Hair Design (Clearwater), 98
Sunstate Academy of Hair Design (Fort Myers), 98
Trendsetters School of Beauty & Barbering (Jacksonville), 100

Georgia
Beauty College of America (Forest Park), 106
Central Georgia Technical College (Macon), 107
Cobb Beauty College (Kennesaw), 108
Empire Beauty School–Kennesaw (Kennesaw), 110
The Esani Institute (Roswell), 111
The Esani Institution (Forest Park), 111
Georgia Career Institute (Conyers), 112
International School of Skin and Nailcare (Atlanta), 115
Michael's School of Beauty (Macon), 116
Middle Georgia Technical College (Warner Robbins), 117
Rivertown School of Beauty (Columbus), 120
Roffler Moler Hairstyling College (Marietta), 120
Southeastern Beauty School (Columbus), 121
Vogue Beauty School (Hiram), 123

Illinois
Alvareitas College of Cosmetology (Belleville), 124
Alvareita's College of Cosmetology (Edwardsville), 124
Alvareita's College of Cosmetology (Godfrey), 124
American Career College (Berwyn), 125
Bell Mar Beauty College (Cicero), 125

Cain's Barber College (Chicago), 125
Cameo Beauty Academy (Oak Lawn), 126
Capri Garfield Ridge School of Beauty Culture (Chicago), 127
Capri Oak Forest School of Beauty Culture (Oak Forest), 127
Carl Sandburg College (Galesburg), 127
Concept College of Cosmetology (Danville), 130
Concept College of Cosmetology (Urbana), 130
CSI The Cosmetology and Spa Institute (McHenry), 131
Educators of Beauty (La Salle), 132
Educators of Beauty (Rockford), 132
Educators of Beauty (Sterling), 132
Empire Beauty School–Arlington Heights (Arlington Heights), 133
Empire Beauty School–Lisle (Lisle), 133
Hairmasters Institute of Cosmetology (Bloomington), 134
Hair Professional Career College (De Kalb), 134
Hair Professionals Academy of Cosmetology (Elgin), 135
Hair Professionals Academy of Cosmetology (Wheaton), 135
Hair Professionals Career College (Palos Hills), 135
Hair Professionals School of Cosmetology (Oswego), 135
La' James College of Hairstyling (East Moline), 140
Lake Land College (Mattoon), 140
MacDaniel's Beauty School (Chicago), 142
Mr. John's School of Cosmetology & Nails (Jacksonville), 144
Mr. John's School of Cosmetology (Decatur), 144
Niles School of Cosmetology (Niles), 144
Professionals Choice Hair Design Academy (Joliet), 146
Rend Lake College (Ina), 148
Rosel School of Cosmetology (Chicago), 149
Trend Setter's College of Cosmetology (Bradley), 152
Tri-County Beauty Academy (Litchfield), 153

Indiana
Creative Hairstyling Academy (Highland), 156
David Demuth Institute of Cosmetology (Richmond), 157
Don Roberts Beauty School (Valparaiso), 157
Don Roberts School of Hair Design (Munster), 157
Hair Fashions by Kaye Beauty College (Noblesville), 158
Honors Beauty College, Inc. (Indianapolis), 159
Knox Beauty College (Knox), 165
Lafayette Beauty Academy (Lafayette), 165
Masters of Cosmetology College (Fort Wayne), 165
Merrillville Beauty College (Merrillville), 165
PJ's College of Cosmetology (Clarksville), 166
PJ's College of Cosmetology (Richmond), 166
Ruade's School of Beauty Culture (Ft. Wayne), 167
Rudae's School of Beauty Culture (Kokomo), 167
Success Schools LLC (Merrillville), 167
Vincennes Beauty College (Vincennes), 168
West Michigan College of Barbering and Beauty (Kalamazoo), 169

Kentucky
Barrett and Company School of Hair Design (Nicholasville), 169
Bellefonte Academy of Beauty (Russell), 169
Collins School of Cosmetology (Middlesboro), 171
Ezell's Beauty School (Murray), 173
The Hair Design School (Florence), 173

The Hair Design School (Louisville), 173, 174
The Hair Design School (Radcliff), 174
Head's West Kentucky Beauty School (Madisonville), 174
J & M Academy of Cosmetology (Frankfort), 175
Jenny Lea Academy of Cosmetology (Harlan), 175
Jenny Lea Academy of Cosmetology (Whitesburg), 175
Kaufman's Beauty School (Lexington), 175
Lexington Beauty College (Lexington), 175
Nu-Tek Academy of Beauty (Mount Sterling), 177
Pat Wilson's Beauty College (Henderson), 177
PJ's College of Cosmetology (Bowling Green), 177
PJ's College of Cosmetology (Glasgow), 177
Regency School of Hair Design (Prestonburg), 177
Southeast School of Cosmetology (Manchester), 178
Trend Setter's Academy (Louisville), 179
Trend Setter's Academy of Beauty Culture (Elizabethtown), 179

Maine
Mr. Bernard's School of Hair Fashion (Lewiston), 182
Pierre's School of Beauty Culture (Portland), 182

Michigan
Bayshire Beauty Academy (Bay City), 212
Chic University of Cosmetology (Grand Rapids), 212
David Pressley Professional School of Cosmetology (Royal Oak), 213
Douglas J. Educational Center (East Lansing), 214
Fiser's College of Cosmetology (Adrian), 216
Gallery College of Beauty (Clinton Township), 216
Great Lakes Academy of Hair Design (Port Huron), 217
Houghton Lake Institute of Cosmetology (Houghton Lake), 217
In Session Arts of Cosmetology Beauty School (Saginaw), 217
Michigan Barber School, Inc. (Detroit), 221
Michigan College of Beauty (Monroe), 221
Michigan College of Beauty (Troy), 221
M. J. Murphy Beauty College of Mount Pleasant (Mount Pleasant), 222
Nuvo College of Cosmetology (Norton Shores), 224
P & A Scholars Beauty School (Detroit), 224
Port Huron Cosmetology College (Waterford), 225
School of Creative Hair Design (Coldwater), 227
Sharp's Academy of Hairstyling–Grand Blanc Campus (Grand Blanc), 227
Twin City Beauty College (St. Joseph), 228
U.P. Academy of Hair Design (Escanaba), 228
Virginia Farrell Beauty School (Ferndale), 228
Virginia Farrell Beauty School (Livonia), 228
Virginia Farrell Beauty School (St. Clair Shores), 228
Virginia Farrell Beauty School (Wayne), 228
Wright Beauty Academy (Battle Creek), 229
Wright Beauty Academy (Portage), 229

Mississippi
Academy of Hair Design (Grenada), 230
Academy of Hair Design (Hattiesburg), 230
Academy of Hair Design (Jackson), 230
Academy of Hair Design (Pearl), 230
Chris Beauty College (Gulfport), 231
Corinth Academy of Cosmetology (Corinth), 231

Day Spa Career College (Ocean Spring), 231
Delta Beauty College (Greenville), 231
Final Touch Beauty School (Meridian), 232
Foster's Cosmetology College (Ripley), 232
Gibson Barber and Beauty College (West Point), 232
ICS–The Wright Beauty College (Corinth), 233
J & J Hair Design College (Carthage), 233
J & J Hair Design College (Moss Point), 233
Magnolia College of Cosmetology (Jackson), 234
Mississippi College of Beauty Culture (Laurel), 234
Traxlers School of Hair (Jackson), 235

New Hampshire
Michael's School of Hair Design and Esthetics (Manchester), 238
New England School of Hair Design (West Lebanon), 238

New Jersey
Empire Beauty School–Cherry Hill (Cherry Hill), 244
European Academy of Cosmetology (Union), 245
Parisian Beauty School (Hackensack), 250
Reignbow Beauty Academy (Perth Amboy), 252
Reignbow Hair Fashion Institute (North Plainfield), 252
Roman Academy of Beauty Culture (Hawthorne), 252
Shore Beauty School (Pleasantville), 253

North Carolina
Asheboro Beauty School of Randolph (Asheboro), 288
Bladen Community College (Dublin), 289
Blue Ridge Community College (Flat Rock), 289
Cape Fear Community College (Wilmington), 290
Carolina Academy of Cosmetic Art & Science (Gastonia), 291
Carteret Community College (Morehead City), 292
Central Carolina Community College (Sanford), 292
Cleveland Community College (Shelby), 293
Coastal Carolina Community College (Jacksonville), 293
Cosmetology Institute of Beauty Arts and Sciences (Winston-Salem), 294
Empire Beauty School (Concord), 295
Fayetteville Beauty College (Fayetteville), 295
Isothermal Community College (Spindale), 298
James Sprunt Community College (Kenansville), 298
Johnston Community College (Smithfield), 298
Leon's Beauty School (Greensboro), 299
Martin Community College (Williamston), 299
McDowell Technical Community College (Marion), 300
Miller-Motte Technical College (Wilmington), 300
Mr. David's School of Hair Design (Wilmington), 301
Mitchell Community College (Statesville), 300
Montgomery's Hairstyling Academy (Fayetteville), 301
Nash Community College (Rocky Mount), 302
Pinnacle Institute of Cosmetology (Statesville), 302
Rowan-Cabarrus Community College (Salisbury), 304
Sampson Community College (Clinton), 304
Sandhills Community College (Pinehurst), 305

Ohio
Creative Images–a Certified Matrix Design Academy (Dayton), 317

Creative Images College of Beauty (Fairborn), 318
Moler Hollywood Beauty College (Cincinnati), 326
Moore University of Hair Design (Cincinnati), 326
Raphael's School of Beauty Culture (Niles), 331
Raphael's School of Beauty Culture (Salem), 332
Raphael's School of Beauty Culture (Youngstown), 332
Tri-County Vocational School Adult Career Center (Nelsonville), 337

Pennsylvania
Academy of Creative Hair Design (Kingston), 342
Academy of Hair Design (Bloomsburg), 342
Allentown School of Cosmetology (Allentown), 342
Altoona Beauty School of Hair Design and Cosmetology (Altoona), 343
Beaver Falls Beauty Academy (Beaver Falls), 344
Butler Beauty School (Butler), 345
Chambersburg Beauty School (Chambersburg), 347
Douglas Education Center (Monessen), 351
Empire Beauty School–Center City Philadelphia (Philadelphia), 353
Empire Beauty School–Hanover (Hanover), 353
Empire Beauty School–Harrisburg (Harrisburg), 353
Empire Beauty School–Monroeville (Monroeville), 353
Empire Beauty School–Moosic (Moosic), 354
Empire Beauty School (Pittsburgh), 353
Empire Beauty School–Pottsville (Pottsville), 354
Empire Beauty School–Reading (Reading), 354
Empire Beauty School–Shamokin Dam (Shamokin Dam), 354
Empire Beauty School–Whitehall (Whitehall), 354
Jean Madeline Education Center (Philadelphia), 358
Kittanning Beauty School of Cosmetology Arts (Kittanning), 359
Lansdale School of Cosmetology (Lansdale), 361
Laurel Business Institute (Uniontown), 361
Levittown Beauty Academy (Levittown), 362
New Castle School of Beauty Culture (New Castle), 366
Pennsylvania Academy of Cosmetology and Sciences (Johnstown), 369
Pennsylvania Academy of Cosmetology Arts and Sciences (DuBois), 369
Pruonto's Hair Design Institute (Altoona), 372
Schuylkill Technology Center–North Campus (Frackville), 373
South Hills Beauty Academy (Pittsburgh), 374
Stroudsburg School of Cosmetology (Stroudsburg), 374
Venus Beauty School (Sharon Hill), 377

Puerto Rico
Charlie's Guard-Detective Bureau and Academy (Aguadilla), 382
Instituto Chaviano de Mayagüez (Mayagüez), 386
John Dewey College, 390
Rogies School of Beauty Culture (Santurce), 393

Rhode Island
Newport School of Hairdressing–Main Campus (Pawtucket), 396
Paul Mitchell the School—Rhode Island (Cranston), 396

South Carolina
Academy of Cosmetology (North Charleston), 397
Academy of Hair Technology (Greenville), 397
Charleston Cosmetology Institute (Charleston), 398
Harley's Beauty and Barber Career Institute (Columbia), 400
Kenneth Shuler's School of Cosmetology and Hair Design (North Augusta), 400
Lacy Cosmetology School (Aiken), 400
Lacy Cosmetology School (Goose Creek), 401
Lacy Cosmetology School (Lexington), 401
Strand College of Hair Design (Myrtle Beach), 403

Tennessee
Buchanan Beauty College (Shelbyville), 406
Career Beauty College (Lawrenceburg), 406
Dudley Nwani–The School (Nashville), 407
Fayettville Beauty School (Fayetteville), 408
Jenny Lea Academy of Cosmetology and Aesthetics (Johnson City), 408
Jon Nave University of Unisex Cosmetology (Nashville), 409
Last Minute Cuts School of Barbering and Cosmetology (Memphis), 409
Middle Tennessee School of Cosmetology (Cookeville), 410
New Concepts School of Cosmetology (Cleveland), 411
New Directions Hair Academy (Memphis), 411
Queen City College (Clarksville), 412
Shear Academy (Crossville), 413
Stylemasters Beauty Academy (Lebanon), 414
Styles and Profiles Beauty College (Selmer), 414
Tennessee School of Beauty (Knoxville), 415

Virginia
Dominion School of Hair Design (Gloucester Point), 426
Virginia School of Hair Design (Hampton), 435

West Virginia
Clarksburg Beauty Academy (Clarksburg), 438
Morgantown Beauty College (Morgantown), 441

Wisconsin
Academy of Cosmetology (Janesville), 445
Four Seasons Salon & Day Spa (Monroe), 446
Martin's School of Hair Design (Appleton), 448
Martin's School of Hair Design (Green Bay), 448
Martin's School of Hair Design (Manitowoc), 448
Martin's School of Hair Design (Oshkosh), 449
Professional Hair Design Academy (Eau Claire), 451

COSMETOLOGY/COSMETOLOGIST, GENERAL

Alabama
Alabama Southern Community College (Monroeville), 41
Bevill State Community College (Sumiton), 41
Bishop State Community College (Mobile), 41
Calhoun Community College (Decatur), 41
Capps College (Mobile), 42
Central Alabama Community College (Alexander City), 42
Gadsden State Community College (Gadsden), 42
George Corley Wallace State Community College (Selma), 43
George C. Wallace Community College (Dothan), 43
H. Councill Trenholm State Technical College (Montgomery), 43
J. F. Drake State Technical College (Huntsville), 44

Cosmetology/Cosmetologist, General

Lawson State Community College (Birmingham), 44
Lurleen B. Wallace Community College (Andalusia), 45
Mimi's Beauty Academy of Cosmetology (Huntsville), 45
Northeast Alabama Community College (Rainsville), 45
Northwest-Shoals Community College (Muscle Shoals), 45
Reid State Technical College (Evergreen), 46
Shelton State Community College (Tuscaloosa), 46
Snead State Community College (Boaz), 46
Southeastern School of Cosmetology (Midfield), 47
Southern Union State Community College (Wadley), 47
Virginia College at Huntsville (Huntsville), 48
Wallace State Community College (Hanceville), 48

Connecticut

Academy Di Capelli—School of Cosmetology (Wallingford), 48
Albert School (Niantic), 49
Branford Academy of Hair & Cosmetology (Branford), 49
Brio Academy of Cosmetology–East Hartford (East Hartford), 50
Brio Academy of Cosmetology–Fairfield (Fairfield), 50
Brio Academy of Cosmetology–Meriden (Meriden), 50
Brio Academy of Cosmetology–New Haven (New Haven), 50
Brio Academy of Cosmetology–Torrington (Torrington), 50
Brio Academy of Cosmetology–Willimantic (Willimantic), 51
Northhaven Academy (North Haven), 55
Paul Mitchell the School—Danbury (Danbury), 56
Renasci Academy of Hair (Stratford), 56

Delaware

Delaware Learning Institute of Cosmetology (Dagsboro), 59
Schilling-Douglas School of Hair Design (Newark), 60

District of Columbia

Bennett Beauty Institute (Washington), 61
Dudley Beauty College (Washington), 61

Florida

Academy of Career Training (Kissimmee), 63
Academy of Cosmetology (Merritt Island), 63
Academy of Cosmetology (Palm Bay), 63
Academy of Healing Arts, Massage, and Facial Skin Care (Lake Worth), 63
Academy of Professional Careers (Winter Park), 63
American Institute of Beauty (Largo), 64
American Institute (Pompano Beach), 64
Artistic Nails and Beauty Academy (Tampa), 65
ASM Beauty World Academy (Hollywood), 65
Atlantic Vocational-Technical Center (Coconut Creek), 66
Aveda Institute–Saint Petersburg (Saint Petersburg), 66
Aveda Institute–Tallahassee (Tallahassee), 66
The Beauty Institute (West Palm Beach), 66
Beauty Schools of America (Hialeah), 66
Beauty Schools of America (Miami), 66
Beauty Schools of America (North Miami Beach), 67
Benes International School of Beauty (New Port Richey), 67
Bradenton Beauty Academy (Bradenton), 67

Bradford Union Area Vocational Technical Center (Starke), 67
Brevard Community College (Cocoa), 67
Central Florida College (Saint Petersburg), 68
Central Florida Community College (Ocala), 69
Charlotte Vocational-Technical Center (Port Charlotte), 69
Chipola College (Marianna), 69
David G. Erwin Technical Center (Tampa), 71
Daytona State College (Daytona Beach), 72
Fashion Focus Hair Academy (Sarasota), 74
First Coast Technical Institute (St. Augustine), 75
Florida Academy of Health & Beauty (Wilton Manor), 75
Florida Community College at Jacksonville (Jacksonville), 77
Fort Pierce Beauty Academy (Fort Pierce), 78
George Stone Area Vocational-Technical Center (Pensacola), 79
Hi-Tech School of Cosmetology (Miami), 81
Indian River State College (Fort Pierce), 81
International Academy (South Daytona), 81
Jacksonville Beauty Institute (Jacksonville), 82
James Lorenzo Walker Vocational-Technical Center (Naples), 82
La Belle Beauty Academy (Miami), 83
La Belle Beauty School (Hialeah), 83
Lake City Community College (Lake City), 83
Lake Technical Center (Eustis), 83
Lee County Vocational High Tech Center–Central (Fort Myers), 84
Lincoln College of Technology (West Palm Beach), 84
Lindsey Hopkins Technical Education Center (Miami), 84
Lively Technical Center (Tallahassee), 84
Loraine's Academy. (St. Petersburg), 85
Manatee Technical Institute (Bradenton), 85
Manhattan Beauty School (Tampa), 85
Marion County Community Technical and Adult Education Center (Ocala), 85
Miami-Dade County Public Schools (Miami), 87
Miami Lakes Technical Education Center (Miami), 87
New Concept Massage and Beauty School (Miami), 88
North Florida Cosmetology Institute (Tallahassee), 88
North Florida Institute–Jacksonville (Jacksonville), 89
Nouvelle Institute (Miami), 89
Okaloosa Applied Technology Center (Ft. Walton Beach), 89
Palm Beach Academy of Health & Beauty (Lake Park), 90
Palm Beach Community College (Lake Worth), 90
Pasco-Hernando Community College (New Port Richey), 90
Paul Mitchell the School—Orlando (Casselberry), 91
Paul Mitchell the School—Tampa (Tampa), 91
Pensacola Junior College (Pensacola), 91
Pinellas Technical Education Center–Clearwater (Clearwater), 91
Praxis Institute (Miami), 92
Ridge Technical Center (Winter Haven), 93
Riverside Hairstyling Academy (Jacksonville), 94
Robert Morgan Vocational-Technical Center (Miami), 94
Sarasota County Technical Institute (Sarasota), 96
Sheridan Vocational-Technical Center (Hollywood), 96

South Florida Community College (Avon Park), 97
Sunstate Academy of Hair Design (Clearwater), 98
Sunstate Academy of Hair Design (Fort Myers), 98
Sunstate Academy of Hair Design (Sarasota), 98
Superior Career Institute (Lauderdale Lakes), 98
Suwannee-Hamilton Area Vocational, Technical, and Adult Education Center (Live Oak), 98
Taylor Technical Institute (Perry), 99
Tom P. Haney Technical Center (Panama City), 99
Traviss Technical Center (Lakeland), 99
Trendsetters School of Beauty & Barbering (Jacksonville), 100
Universal Massage and Beauty Institute (Sweetwater), 100
Washington-Holmes Technical Center (Chipley), 102
Westside Tech (Winter Garden), 102
Withlacoochee Technical Institute (Inverness), 103

Georgia

Albany Technical College (Albany), 103
Altamaha Technical College (Jesup), 104
American Professional Institute (Macon), 104
Appalachian Technical College (Jasper), 104
Athens Technical College (Athens), 105
Atlanta Technical College (Atlanta), 105
Augusta Technical College (Augusta), 106
Beauty College of America (Forest Park), 106
Central Georgia Technical College (Macon), 107
Chattahoochee Technical College (Marietta), 107
Cobb Beauty College (Kennesaw), 108
Columbus Technical College (Columbus), 108
Coosa Valley Technical College (Rome), 109
DeKalb Technical College (Clarkston), 109
East Central Technical College (Fitzgerald), 110
Empire Beauty School–Dunwoody (Dunwoody), 110
Empire Beauty School–Kennesaw (Kennesaw), 110
Empire Beauty School–Lawrenceville (Lawrenceville), 110
The Esani Institute (Roswell), 111
The Esani Institution (Forest Park), 111
Fayette Beauty Academy (Fayetteville), 111
Flint River Technical College (Thomaston), 111
Georgia Career Institute (Conyers), 112
Georgia Institute of Cosmetology (Athens), 112
Griffin Technical College (Griffin), 113
Gwinnett Technical College (Lawrenceville), 113
International City Beauty College (Warner Robins), 115
Lanier Technical College (Oakwood), 115
Michael's School of Beauty (Macon), 116
Middle Georgia Technical College (Warner Robbins), 117
Moultrie Technical College (Moultrie), 117
North Georgia Technical College (Clarkesville), 118
North Metro Technical College (Acworth), 118
Northwestern Technical College (Rock Spring), 118
Ogeechee Technical College (Statesboro), 119
Okefenokee Technical College (Waycross), 119
Powder Springs Beauty College (Powder Springs), 119
Pro Way Hair School (Stone Mountain), 120
Rivertown School of Beauty (Columbus), 120

Blaine! The Beauty Career Schools–Boston (Boston), 194

Blaine! The Beauty Career Schools–Framingham (Framingham), 194

Blaine! The Beauty Career Schools–Hyannis (Hyannis), 194

Blaine! The Beauty Career Schools–Lowell (Lowell), 195

Blaine! The Beauty Career Schools–Malden (Malden), 195

Blaine! The Beauty Career Schools–Waltham (Waltham), 195

DiGrigoli School of Cosmetology (West Springfield), 197

Hair in Motion Beauty Academy (Worcester), 199

Henri's School of Hair Design (Fitchburg), 199

Jolie Hair and Beauty Academy (Ludlow), 199

Kay-Harvey Hairdressing Academy (West Springfield), 200

La Baron Hairdressing Academy (Brockton), 200

La Baron Hairdressing Academy (New Bedford), 200

Lowell Academy Hairstyling Institute (Lowell), 201

Mansfield Beauty Schools (Quincy), 201

Mansfield Beauty Schools (Springfield), 201

New England Hair Academy (Malden), 203

North Shore Community College (Danvers), 204

Rob Roy Academy–Fall River Campus (Fall River), 205

Rob Roy Academy–New Bedford Campus (New Bedford), 205

Rob Roy Academy–Taunton Campus (Taunton), 205

Rob Roy Academy–Worcester Campus (Worcester), 205

Springfield Technical Community College (Springfield), 207

Michigan

Bayshire Beauty Academy (Bay City), 212

Blue Water College of Cosmetology (Marysville), 212

Chic University of Cosmetology (Grand Rapids), 212

Creative Hair School of Cosmetology (Flint), 213

David Pressley Professional School of Cosmetology (Royal Oak), 213

Douglas J. Educational Center (East Lansing), 214

Fiser's College of Cosmetology (Adrian), 216

Gallery College of Beauty (Clinton Township), 216

Gogebic Community College (Ironwood), 216

Great Lakes Academy of Hair Design (Port Huron), 217

Hillsdale Beauty College (Hillsdale), 217

Houghton Lake Institute of Cosmetology (Houghton Lake), 217

In Session Arts of Cosmetology Beauty School (Saginaw), 217

Kirtland Community College (Roscommon), 219

Michigan College of Beauty (Monroe), 221

Michigan College of Beauty (Troy), 221

Mr. Bela's School of Cosmetology (Madison Heights), 223

M. J. Murphy Beauty College of Mount Pleasant (Mount Pleasant), 222

Northern Michigan University (Marquette), 224

Nuvo College of Cosmetology (Norton Shores), 224

P & A Scholars Beauty School (Detroit), 224

Port Huron Cosmetology College (Waterford), 225

Regency Beauty Institute–Detroit Southgate (Southgate), 225

Regency Beauty Institute–Flint (Flint), 225

Regency Beauty Institute–Grand Rapids (Walker), 225

School of Creative Hair Design (Coldwater), 227

School of Designing Arts (Springfield), 227

Sharp's Academy of Hairstyling–Grand Blanc Campus (Grand Blanc), 227

Taylortown School of Beauty (Taylor), 227

Twin City Beauty College (St. Joseph), 228

U.P. Academy of Hair Design (Escanaba), 228

Virginia Farrell Beauty School (Ferndale), 228

Virginia Farrell Beauty School (Livonia), 228

Virginia Farrell Beauty School (St. Clair Shores), 228

Virginia Farrell Beauty School (Wayne), 228

Wright Beauty Academy (Battle Creek), 229

Wright Beauty Academy (Portage), 229

Mississippi

Academy of Hair Design (Grenada), 230

Academy of Hair Design (Hattiesburg), 230

Academy of Hair Design (Jackson), 230

Academy of Hair Design (Pearl), 230

Chris Beauty College (Gulfport), 231

Coahoma Community College (Clarksdale), 231

Copiah-Lincoln Community College (Wesson), 231

Corinth Academy of Cosmetology (Corinth), 231

Creations College of Cosmetology (Tupelo), 231

Day Spa Career College (Ocean Spring), 231

Delta Beauty College (Greenville), 231

East Central Community College (Decatur), 232

East Mississippi Community College (Scooba), 232

Final Touch Beauty School (Meridian), 232

Foster's Cosmetology College (Ripley), 232

Gibson Barber and Beauty College (West Point), 232

Hinds Community College (Raymond), 232

Holmes Community College (Goodman), 233

ICS–The Wright Beauty College (Corinth), 233

Jones County Junior College (Ellisville), 234

Magnolia College of Cosmetology (Jackson), 234

Meridian Community College (Meridian), 234

Mississippi College of Beauty Culture (Laurel), 234

Mississippi Gulf Coast Community College (Perkinston), 234

Northwest Mississippi Community College (Senatobia), 235

Pearl River Community College (Poplarville), 235

Southwest Mississippi Community College (Summit), 235

Virginia College at Jackson (Jackson), 236

New Hampshire

Continental Academie of Hair Design (Hudson), 236

Continental Academie of Hair Design (Manchester), 236

Empire Beauty School–Hooksett (Hooksett), 236

Empire Beauty School–Laconia (Laconia), 237

Empire Beauty School–Portsmouth (Portsmouth), 237

Empire Beauty School–Somersworth (Somersworth), 237

Keene Beauty Academy (Keene), 237

Michael's School of Hair Design and Esthetics (Manchester), 238

New England School of Hair Design (West Lebanon), 238

Portsmouth Beauty School of Hair Design (Portsmouth), 239

New Jersey

Artistic Academy of Hair Design (Fairlawn), 240

Capri Institute of Hair Design (Brick), 241

Capri Institute of Hair Design (Clifton), 241

Capri Institute of Hair Design (Kenilworth), 242

Capri Institute of Hair Design (Paramus), 242

Capri Institute of Hair Design (Succasunna), 242

Concorde School of Hair Design–Bloomfield (Bloomfield), 243

Concorde School of Hair Design (Ocean Township), 243

Empire Beauty School–Cherry Hill (Cherry Hill), 244

Empire Beauty School–Laurel Springs (Laurel Springs), 244

Empire Beauty School–Lawrenceville (Lawrenceville), 244

European Academy of Cosmetology (Union), 245

Monmouth County Vocational School District (Long Branch), 249

Natural Motion Institute of Hair Design (Jersey City), 249

New Horizon Institute of Cosmetology (West New York), 250

Ocean County Vocational Post Secondary Division (Toms River), 250

PB Cosmetology Education Center (Gloucester), 251

Reignbow Beauty Academy (Perth Amboy), 252

Reignbow Hair Fashion Institute (North Plainfield), 252

Rizzieri Aveda School for Beauty and Wellness (Marlton), 252

Roman Academy of Beauty Culture (Hawthorne), 252

Shore Beauty School (Pleasantville), 253

Somerset County Technical Institute (Bridgewater), 253

New York

A.B.I. School of Barbering & Cosmetology of Tribeca (New York), 255

Adirondack Beauty School (Glens Falls), 255

American Barber Institute (New York), 256

American Beauty School (Bronx), 256

Austin Beauty School (Albany), 257

Aveda Institute New York (New York), 257

Beauty School of Middletown (Hyde Park), 257

Beauty School of Middletown (Middletown), 257

Brittany Beauty School (Bronx), 258

Brittany Beauty School (Levittown), 258

Capri School of Hair Design (Spring Valley), 260

Carsten Institute of New York (New York), 260

Continental School of Beauty Culture–Batavia (Batavia), 262

Continental School of Beauty Culture–Jefferson (Rochester), 262

Continental School of Beauty Culture–Kenmore (Buffalo), 263

Continental School of Beauty Culture–Olean (Olean), 263

Continental School of Beauty Culture–West Seneca (West Seneca), 263

Elite Academy of Beauty Arts (Brooklyn), 264

Empire Beauty School (Astoria), 265

Empire Beauty School–Bensonhurst (Bensonhurst), 265

Empire Beauty School (New York), 265

Erie #1 BOCES–Practical Nursing Program (West Seneca), 265

Hair Design Institute at Fifth Avenue (Brooklyn), 268

Leon Studio 1 School of Hair Design & Career Training Center (Williamsville), 271

Long Island Beauty School (Hauppauge), 271

Long Island Beauty School (Hempstead), 271

MarJon School of Beauty Culture (Tonawanda), 272

Midway Paris Beauty School (Ridgewood), 273

New York International Beauty School (New York), 276

Northern Westchester School of Hairdressing (Peekskill), 277

Onondaga-Courtland-Madison BOCES (Liverpool), 278

Orlo School of Hair Design and Cosmetology (Albany), 278

Phillips Hairstyling Institute (Syracuse), 279

Shear Ego International School of Hair Design (Rochester), 283

USA Beauty School International (New York), 286

Westchester School of Beauty Culture (Mount Vernon), 287

Western Suffolk BOCES (Northport), 288

North Carolina

Alamance Community College (Graham), 288

Asheboro Beauty School of Randolph (Asheboro), 288

Beaufort County Community College (Washington), 289

Bladen Community College (Dublin), 289

Blue Ridge Community College (Flat Rock), 289

Brunswick Community College (Supply), 290

Caldwell Community College and Technical Institute (Hudson), 290

Cape Fear Community College (Wilmington), 290

Carolina Academy of Cosmetic Art & Science (Gastonia), 291

Carolina Beauty College–Charlotte (Charlotte), 291

Carolina Beauty College–Durham Campus (Durham), 291

Carolina Beauty College–Greensboro Campus (Greensboro), 291

Carolina Beauty College (Monroe), 291

Carolina Beauty College–Winston-Salem Campus (Winston-Salem), 291

Carteret Community College (Morehead City), 292

Catawba Valley Community College (Hickory), 292

Central Carolina Community College (Sanford), 292

Cleveland Community College (Shelby), 293

Coastal Carolina Community College (Jacksonville), 293

College of The Albemarle (Elizabeth City), 294

Cosmetology Institute of Beauty Arts and Sciences (Winston-Salem), 294

Craven Community College (New Bern), 294

Davidson County Community College (Lexington), 294

Durham Beauty Academy (Durham), 295

Edgecombe Community College (Tarboro), 295

Empire Beauty School (Concord), 295

Empire Beauty School–Matthews (Matthews), 295

Fayetteville Beauty College (Fayetteville), 295

Fayetteville Technical Community College (Fayetteville), 295

Gaston College (Dallas), 296

Guilford Technical Community College (Jamestown), 297

Hairstyling Institute of Charlotte (Charlotte), 297

Halifax Community College (Weldon), 297

Haywood Community College (Clyde), 297

Isothermal Community College (Spindale), 298

James Sprunt Community College (Kenansville), 298

Johnston Community College (Smithfield), 298

Lenoir Community College (Kinston), 299

Leon's Beauty School (Greensboro), 299

Martin Community College (Williamston), 299

Mayland Community College (Spruce Pine), 299

McDowell Technical Community College (Marion), 300

Miller-Motte Technical College (Cary), 300

Miller-Motte Technical College (Wilmington), 300

Mr. David's School of Hair Design (Wilmington), 301

Mitchell Community College (Statesville), 300

Mitchell's Hairstyling Academy (Goldsboro), 301

Mitchell's Hairstyling Academy (Greenville), 301

Mitchell's Hairstyling Academy (Raleigh), 301

Mitchell's Hairstyling Academy (Wilson), 301

Montgomery's Hairstyling Academy (Fayetteville), 301

Nash Community College (Rocky Mount), 302

Pamlico Community College (Grantsboro), 302

Piedmont Community College (Roxboro), 302

Pinnacle Institute of Cosmetology (Statesville), 302

Pitt Community College (Greenville), 303

Regency Beauty Institute–Charlotte (Charlotte), 303

Roanoke-Chowan Community College (Ahoskie), 303

Robeson Community College (Lumberton), 304

Rockingham Community College (Wentworth), 304

Rowan-Cabarrus Community College (Salisbury), 304

Sampson Community College (Clinton), 304

Sandhills Community College (Pinehurst), 305

Southeastern Community College (Whiteville), 305

Southwestern Community College (Sylva), 306

Stanly Community College (Albemarle), 306

Surry Community College (Dobson), 306

Tri-County Community College (Murphy), 306

Vance-Granville Community College (Henderson), 307

Wayne Community College (Goldsboro), 308

Wilson Community College (Wilson), 308

Ohio

Ashtabula County Joint Vocational School (Jefferson), 311

Aveda Fredric's Institute (Cincinnati), 311

Brown Aveda Institute (Mentor), 312

Brown Aveda Institute (Rocky River), 312

Buckeye Joint Vocational School (New Philadelphia), 313

Carousel Beauty College (Dayton), 314

Carousel Beauty College (Kettering), 314

Carousel Beauty College (Middletown), 314

Carousel Beauty College (Springfield), 314

Carousel of Miami Valley Beauty College (Huber Heights), 314

Casal Aveda Institute (Austintown), 314

Community Services Division–Alliance City (Alliance), 317

Creative Images–a Certified Matrix Design Academy (Dayton), 317

Creative Images College of Beauty (Fairborn), 318

Eastern Hills Academy of Hair Design (Cincinnati), 319

Ehove Career Center (Milan), 319

Euclidian Beauty School (Euclid), 320

Fairview Beauty Academy (Fairview Park), 320

Gerber's Akron Beauty School (Fairlawn), 320

Inner State Beauty School (Lyndhurst), 321

International Academy of Hair Design (Cincinnati), 322

Knox County Career Center (Mount Vernon), 323

Licking County Joint Vocational School–Newark (Newark), 324

Lorain County JVS Adult Career Center (Oberlin), 324

Madison Local Schools–Madison Adult Education (Mansfield), 324

Mahoning County Joint Vocational School District (Canfield), 325

Medina County Career Center (Medina), 325

Moler Hollywood Beauty College (Cincinnati), 326

Moler Pickens Beauty College (Fairfield), 326

Moore University of Hair Design (Cincinnati), 326

National Beauty College (Canton), 326

Nationwide Beauty Academy (Columbus), 327

Northern Institute of Cosmetology (Lorain), 327

O. C. Collins Career Center (Chesapeake), 328

Ohio State Beauty Academy (Lima), 329

Paramount Beauty Academy (Portsmouth), 330

Portage Lakes Career Center (Green), 331

Raphael's School of Beauty Culture (Niles), 331

Raphael's School of Beauty Culture (Salem), 332

Raphael's School of Beauty Culture (Youngstown), 332

Regency Beauty Institute–Akron (Akron), 332

Regency Beauty Institute–Cincinnati (Cincinnati), 332

Regency Beauty Institute–Columbus (Columbus), 332

Regency Beauty Institute–Dayton (Dayton), 332

Regency Beauty Institute–North Olmsted (North Olmsted), 332

Regency Beauty Institute–Springdale (Springdale), 332

Sandusky Adult Education (Sandusky), 333

The Spa School (Columbus), 335

Toledo Academy of Beauty Culture–South (Toledo), 337

Tri-County Vocational School Adult Career Center (Nelsonville), 337

Vogue Beauty Academy (Cleveland Heights), 340

Warren County Career Center (Lebanon), 340

Western Hills School of Beauty and Hair Design (Cincinnati), 341

Pennsylvania

Academy of Creative Hair Design (Kingston), 342

Academy of Hair Design (Bloomsburg), 342

Allentown School of Cosmetology (Allentown), 342

Altoona Beauty School of Hair Design and Cosmetology (Altoona), 343

Beaver Falls Beauty Academy (Beaver Falls), 344

Bucks County School of Beauty Culture (Feasterville), 345

Butler Beauty School (Butler), 345

Chambersburg Beauty School (Chambersburg), 347

Community College of Beaver County (Monaca), 349

Douglas Education Center (Monessen), 351

Empire Beauty School–Center City Philadelphia (Philadelphia), 353

Legends Institute (Lynchburg), 429
Rudy & Kelly Academy of Hair and Nails (Virginia Beach), 432
Springfield Beauty Academy (Annandale), 433
Staunton School of Cosmetology (Staunton), 433
Suffolk Beauty School (Suffolk), 433
Virginia School of Hair Design (Hampton), 435
Wards Corner Beauty Academy (Norfolk), 436
Wards Corner Beauty Academy–Virginia Beach (Virginia Beach), 436

West Virginia
Beckley Beauty Academy (Beckley), 437
Carver Career Center (Charleston), 438
Charleston School of Beauty Culture (Charleston), 438
Clarksburg Beauty Academy (Clarksburg), 438
Huntington School of Beauty Culture–Main Campus (Huntington), 440
International Beauty School (Martinsburg), 440
Morgantown Beauty College (Morgantown), 441
Mountaineer Beauty College (St. Albans), 441
Scott College of Cosmetology (Wheeling), 443

Wisconsin
Academy of Cosmetology (Janesville), 445
Advanced Institute of Hair Design (Milwaukee), 445
Empire Beauty School–Milwaukee (Milwaukee), 446
Four Seasons Salon & Day Spa (Monroe), 446
Gill-Tech Academy of Hair Design (Appleton), 447
The Institute of Beauty and Wellness (Milwaukee), 447
Martin's School of Hair Design (Appleton), 448
Martin's School of Hair Design (Green Bay), 448
Martin's School of Hair Design (Manitowoc), 448
Martin's School of Hair Design (Oshkosh), 449
Moraine Park Technical College (Fond du Lac), 450
Professional Hair Design Academy (Eau Claire), 451
Regency Beauty Institute–Greenfield (Greenfield), 451
Regency Beauty Institute–Madison (Madison), 451
The Salon Professional Academy (Appleton), 451
State College of Beauty Culture (Wausau), 452

COUNSELOR EDUCATION/SCHOOL COUNSELING AND GUIDANCE SERVICES
Georgia
Darton College (Albany), 109

COURT REPORTING/COURT REPORTER
Alabama
Gadsden State Community College (Gadsden), 42

Florida
Sheridan Vocational-Technical Center (Hollywood), 96

Illinois
South Suburban College (South Holland), 151
Sparks College (Shelbyville), 152

Michigan
Oakland Community College (Bloomfield Hills), 224

New Jersey
Steno Tech Career Institute (Fairfield), 254
StenoTech Career Institute (Piscataway), 254

New York
Erie Community College (Buffalo), 265
Monroe Community College (Rochester), 274
New York Career Institute (New York), 276

North Carolina
Lenoir Community College (Kinston), 299

Pennsylvania
Community College of Allegheny County (Pittsburgh), 348
Orleans Technical Institute (Philadelphia), 367
Pennsylvania Highlands Community College (Johnstown), 370

South Carolina
Midlands Technical College (Columbia), 401

Virginia
Virginia Career Institute (Virginia Beach), 435

CRAFTS/CRAFT DESIGN, FOLK ART AND ARTISANRY
Kentucky
Hazard Community and Technical College (Hazard), 174

North Carolina
College of The Albemarle (Elizabeth City), 294
Montgomery Community College (Troy), 301

Ohio
Hocking College (Nelsonville), 321

CRIMINALISTICS AND CRIMINAL SCIENCE
Illinois
City Colleges of Chicago, Wilbur Wright College (Chicago), 129

Michigan
Oakland Community College (Bloomfield Hills), 224

New York
Ridley-Lowell School of Business (Poughkeepsie), 280

Pennsylvania
Central Pennsylvania College (Summerdale), 347
Gannon University (Erie), 355
Penn State Erie, The Behrend College (Erie), 368

Puerto Rico
Caribbean Forensic and Technical College (Río Piedras), 381

CRIMINAL JUSTICE/LAW ENFORCEMENT ADMINISTRATION
Alabama
Virginia College at Mobile (Mobile), 48

Delaware
Delaware Technical & Community College, Terry Campus (Dover), 60

Florida
Everest Institute (Hialeah), 72
Everest Institute (Miami), 73
Florida Technical College (Orlando), 78
George Stone Area Vocational-Technical Center (Pensacola), 79
Lake Technical Center (Eustis), 83
Manatee Technical Institute (Bradenton), 85
Sarasota County Technical Institute (Sarasota), 96
Virginia College at Pensacola (Pensacola), 102
Withlacoochee Technical Institute (Inverness), 103

Georgia
Brown Mackie College–Atlanta (Atlanta), 107

Illinois
Kaskaskia College (Centralia), 139
Southwestern Illinois College (Belleville), 151

Taylor Business Institute (Chicago), 152
Triton College (River Grove), 153

Indiana
Calumet College of Saint Joseph (Whiting), 156

Kentucky
Brown Mackie College–Hopkinsville (Hopkinsville), 170
University of Louisville (Louisville), 180

Maine
Beal College (Bangor), 180

Maryland
Anne Arundel Community College (Arnold), 184
College of Southern Maryland (La Plata), 186
TESST College of Technology (Towson), 192

Massachusetts
Bristol Community College (Fall River), 196
Bunker Hill Community College (Boston), 196
Lincoln Technical Institute (Brockton), 200
Lincoln Technical Institute (Lowell), 200
Lincoln Technical Institute (Somerville), 200
Mildred Elley School (Pittsfield), 202
Mount Wachusett Community College (Gardner), 203

Michigan
North Central Michigan College (Petoskey), 223

New Jersey
Micro Tech Training Center (Jersey City), 249
Union County College (Cranford), 254

New York
Genesee Community College (Batavia), 267
Jefferson Community College (Watertown), 270
Schenectady County Community College (Schenectady), 282
Suffolk County Community College (Selden), 284

North Carolina
Bladen Community College (Dublin), 289

Ohio
Adult Center for Education (Zanesville), 309
Brown Mackie College–Akron (Akron), 313
Brown Mackie College–Cincinnati (Cincinnati), 313
Brown Mackie College–Findlay (Findlay), 313
Butler Technology and Career Development Schools–D. Russel Lee Career-Technology Center (Hamilton), 314
Chancellor University (Cleveland), 315
Medina County Career Center (Medina), 325
Polaris Career Center (Middleburg Heights), 331

Pennsylvania
Bucks County Community College (Newtown), 345
CHI Institute, Franklin Mills Campus (Philadelphia), 348
Lincoln Technical Institute (Philadelphia), 362
Mount Aloysius College (Cresson), 365
Penn State Altoona (Altoona), 368
Sanford-Brown Institute–Pittsburgh (Pittsburgh), 373

Puerto Rico
Universidad Metropolitana (San Juan), 394

Rhode Island
Lincoln Technical Institute (Lincoln), 395

South Carolina
Beta Tech (Columbia), 397
Forrest Junior College (Anderson), 399

Tennessee
Draughons Junior College (Clarksville), 407
Kaplan Career Institute–Nashville Campus (Nashville), 409

Virginia

Blue Ridge Community College (Weyers Cave), 424

Dabney S. Lancaster Community College (Clifton Forge), 426

Danville Community College (Danville), 426

Everest College (McLean), 427

Germanna Community College (Locust Grove), 428

John Tyler Community College (Chester), 429

Mountain Empire Community College (Big Stone Gap), 430

Northern Virginia Community College (Annandale), 430

Piedmont Virginia Community College (Charlottesville), 431

Rappahannock Community College (Glenns), 431

Southside Virginia Community College (Alberta), 432

Southwest Virginia Community College (Richlands), 432

Wytheville Community College (Wytheville), 436

West Virginia

American Public University System (Charles Town), 437

Wisconsin

Western Technical College (La Crosse), 453

CRIMINAL JUSTICE/POLICE SCIENCE

Alabama

Calhoun Community College (Decatur), 41

Central Alabama Community College (Alexander City), 42

Chattahoochee Valley Community College (Phenix City), 42

Enterprise-Ozark Community College (Enterprise), 42

George Corley Wallace State Community College (Selma), 43

Jefferson State Community College (Birmingham), 44

Connecticut

Asnuntuck Community College (Enfield), 49

Capital Community College (Hartford), 51

Gateway Community College (New Haven), 52

Goodwin College (East Hartford), 53

Housatonic Community College (Bridgeport), 53

Manchester Community College (Manchester), 54

Middlesex Community College (Middletown), 54

Naugatuck Valley Community College (Waterbury), 54

Three Rivers Community College (Norwich), 57

Tunxis Community College (Farmington), 57

University of New Haven (West Haven), 58

District of Columbia

The George Washington University (Washington), 61

Florida

Brevard Community College (Cocoa), 67

Broward Community College (Fort Lauderdale), 68

Central Florida Community College (Ocala), 69

Chipola College (Marianna), 69

Daytona State College (Daytona Beach), 72

Florida Community College at Jacksonville (Jacksonville), 77

Florida Keys Community College (Key West), 78

George Stone Area Vocational-Technical Center (Pensacola), 79

Gulf Coast Community College (Panama City), 79

Hillsborough Community College (Tampa), 81

Indian River State College (Fort Pierce), 81

James Lorenzo Walker Vocational-Technical Center (Naples), 82

Lake City Community College (Lake City), 83

Lake Technical Center (Eustis), 83

Miami Dade College (Miami), 87

North Florida Community College (Madison), 88

Northwest Florida State College (Niceville), 89

Palm Beach Community College (Lake Worth), 90

Pasco-Hernando Community College (New Port Richey), 90

Polk Community College (Winter Haven), 92

St. Johns River Community College (Palatka), 94

St. Petersburg College (St. Petersburg), 94

Santa Fe Community College (Gainesville), 95

Sarasota County Technical Institute (Sarasota), 96

Seminole Community College (Sanford), 96

South Florida Community College (Avon Park), 97

Tallahassee Community College (Tallahassee), 98

Valencia Community College (Orlando), 101

Withlacoochee Technical Institute (Inverness), 103

Georgia

Armstrong Atlantic State University (Savannah), 104

Central Georgia Technical College (Macon), 107

College of Coastal Georgia (Brunswick), 108

DeKalb Technical College (Clarkston), 109

East Central Technical College (Fitzgerald), 110

Macon State College (Macon), 116

Northwestern Technical College (Rock Spring), 118

Ogeechee Technical College (Statesboro), 119

Illinois

Black Hawk College (Moline), 125

Carl Sandburg College (Galesburg), 127

City Colleges of Chicago, Richard J. Daley College (Chicago), 128

College of DuPage (Glen Ellyn), 129

College of Lake County (Grayslake), 129

Harper College (Palatine), 135

Illinois Valley Community College (Oglesby), 138

John A. Logan College (Carterville), 138

Joliet Junior College (Joliet), 139

Kankakee Community College (Kankakee), 139

Lewis and Clark Community College (Godfrey), 141

Lincoln Land Community College (Springfield), 141

Oakton Community College (Des Plaines), 145

Prairie State College (Chicago Heights), 146

Rend Lake College (Ina), 148

Richland Community College (Decatur), 148

Shawnee Community College (Ullin), 150

Southeastern Illinois College (Harrisburg), 151

South Suburban College (South Holland), 151

Southwestern Illinois College (Belleville), 151

Waubonsee Community College (Sugar Grove), 154

Indiana

Vincennes University (Vincennes), 168

Maryland

Allegany College of Maryland (Cumberland), 184

Anne Arundel Community College (Arnold), 184

Carroll Community College (Westminster), 186

Cecil College (North East), 186

Chesapeake College (Wye Mills), 186

The Community College of Baltimore County (Baltimore), 187

Hagerstown Community College (Hagerstown), 188

Prince George's Community College (Largo), 191

TESST College of Technology (Beltsville), 192

Wor-Wic Community College (Salisbury), 193

Massachusetts

Bunker Hill Community College (Boston), 196

Northern Essex Community College (Haverhill), 204

Quinsigamond Community College (Worcester), 205

Springfield Technical Community College (Springfield), 207

Michigan

Delta College (University Center), 213

Jackson Community College (Jackson), 218

Lansing Community College (Lansing), 219

Macomb Community College (Warren), 220

Mott Community College (Flint), 223

Oakland Community College (Bloomfield Hills), 224

New Jersey

Burlington County College (Pemberton), 241

Camden County College (Blackwood), 241

Lincoln Technical Institute (Edison), 248

Lincoln Technical Institute (Mount Laurel), 248

Lincoln Technical Institute (Paramus), 248

Passaic County Community College (Paterson), 251

New York

Erie Community College (Buffalo), 265

Excelsior College (Albany), 266

Monroe Community College (Rochester), 274

St. Joseph's College, Long Island Campus (Patchogue), 281

Ulster County Community College (Stone Ridge), 286

North Carolina

Asheville-Buncombe Technical Community College (Asheville), 288

Beaufort County Community College (Washington), 289

Brunswick Community College (Supply), 290

Caldwell Community College and Technical Institute (Hudson), 290

Cape Fear Community College (Wilmington), 290

Carteret Community College (Morehead City), 292

Catawba Valley Community College (Hickory), 292

Central Carolina Community College (Sanford), 292

Central Piedmont Community College (Charlotte), 293

Cleveland Community College (Shelby), 293

Coastal Carolina Community College (Jacksonville), 293

College of The Albemarle (Elizabeth City), 294

Craven Community College (New Bern), 294

Davidson County Community College (Lexington), 294

Durham Technical Community College (Durham), 295

Fayetteville Technical Community College (Fayetteville), 295

Gaston College (Dallas), 296

Guilford Technical Community College (Jamestown), 297

Halifax Community College (Weldon), 297

Isothermal Community College (Spindale), 298

James Sprunt Community College (Kenansville), 298
Johnston Community College (Smithfield), 298
Lenoir Community College (Kinston), 299
Mayland Community College (Spruce Pine), 299
McDowell Technical Community College (Marion), 300
Mitchell Community College (Statesville), 300
Montgomery Community College (Troy), 301
Pitt Community College (Greenville), 303
Randolph Community College (Asheboro), 303
Robeson Community College (Lumberton), 304
Rockingham Community College (Wentworth), 304
Rowan-Cabarrus Community College (Salisbury), 304
Sampson Community College (Clinton), 304
Southeastern Community College (Whiteville), 305
South Piedmont Community College (Polkton), 305
Stanly Community College (Albemarle), 306
Vance-Granville Community College (Henderson), 307
Wake Technical Community College (Raleigh), 307
Wayne Community College (Goldsboro), 308
Western Piedmont Community College (Morganton), 308
Wilkes Community College (Wilkesboro), 308
Wilson Community College (Wilson), 308

Ohio
Apollo School of Practical Nursing (Lima), 310
Buckeye Hills Career Center (Rio Grande), 313
Buckeye Joint Vocational School (New Philadelphia), 313
Delaware JVS District (Delaware), 318
Eastern Gateway Community College (Steubenville), 319
Eastland Career Center (Groveport), 319
Ehove Career Center (Milan), 319
Lakeland Community College (Kirtland), 323
Lorain County Community College (Elyria), 324
Marion Technical College (Marion), 325
Medina County Career Center (Medina), 325
O. C. Collins Career Center (Chesapeake), 328
Sandusky Adult Education (Sandusky), 333
Scioto County Joint Vocational School District (Lucasville), 334
Southern State Community College (Hillsboro), 335
The University of Akron (Akron), 338
Vantage Vocational School (Van Wert), 340

Pennsylvania
Community College of Beaver County (Monaca), 349
Delaware County Community College (Media), 351
Harrisburg Area Community College (Harrisburg), 357
Lackawanna College (Scranton), 359
Lancaster County Career and Technology Center (Willow Street), 360
Lebanon County Area Vocational Technical School (Lebanon), 361

Puerto Rico
Caribbean Forensic and Technical College (Río Piedras), 381
Charlie's Guard-Detective Bureau and Academy (Aguadilla), 382
Universidad del Este (Carolina), 393

Tennessee
Cleveland State Community College (Cleveland), 406

Columbia State Community College (Columbia), 406
Roane State Community College (Harriman), 413
Southwest Tennessee Community College (Memphis), 414
Walters State Community College (Morristown), 421

West Virginia
Marshall Community and Technical College (Huntington), 441

Wisconsin
Blackhawk Technical College (Janesville), 445
Chippewa Valley Technical College (Eau Claire), 445
College of Menominee Nation (Keshena), 446
Fox Valley Technical College (Appleton), 446
Madison Area Technical College (Madison), 448
Mid-State Technical College (Wisconsin Rapids), 449
Northcentral Technical College (Wausau), 450
Northeast Wisconsin Technical College (Green Bay), 450
Southwest Wisconsin Technical College (Fennimore), 452
Waukesha County Technical College (Pewaukee), 453

CRIMINAL JUSTICE/SAFETY STUDIES

Florida
North Florida Institute (Orange Park), 89
St. Thomas University (Miami Gardens), 95

Georgia
Albany Technical College (Albany), 103
Altamaha Technical College (Jesup), 104
Appalachian Technical College (Jasper), 104
Athens Technical College (Athens), 105
Augusta Technical College (Augusta), 106
Bainbridge College (Bainbridge), 106
Bauder College (Atlanta), 106
Central Georgia Technical College (Macon), 107
Chattahoochee Technical College (Marietta), 107
Columbus State University (Columbus), 108
Coosa Valley Technical College (Rome), 109
DeKalb Technical College (Clarkston), 109
East Central Technical College (Fitzgerald), 110
Flint River Technical College (Thomaston), 111
Griffin Technical College (Griffin), 113
Heart of Georgia Technical College (Dublin), 114
Lanier Technical College (Oakwood), 115
Middle Georgia Technical College (Warner Robbins), 117
Moultrie Technical College (Moultrie), 117
New Horizons Computer Learning Centers (Atlanta), 117
North Georgia Technical College (Clarkesville), 118
Northwestern Technical College (Rock Spring), 118
Okefenokee Technical College (Waycross), 119
Savannah Technical College (Savannah), 121
Southeastern Technical College (Vidalia), 121
South Georgia Technical College (Americus), 122
Southwest Georgia Technical College (Thomasville), 122
Swainsboro Technical College (Swainsboro), 123
Valdosta Technical College (Valdosta), 123
West Central Technical College (Waco), 124
West Georgia Technical College (LaGrange), 124

Illinois
City Colleges of Chicago, Harold Washington College (Chicago), 127
City Colleges of Chicago, Kennedy-King College (Chicago), 127
City Colleges of Chicago, Olive-Harvey College (Chicago), 128
City Colleges of Chicago, Richard J. Daley College (Chicago), 128
City Colleges of Chicago, Wilbur Wright College (Chicago), 129

Maine
Saint Joseph's College of Maine (Standish), 182

Massachusetts
Assumption College (Worcester), 193
Holyoke Community College (Holyoke), 199
Middlesex Community College (Bedford), 202
North Shore Community College (Danvers), 204
Roxbury Community College (Roxbury Crossing), 205

Michigan
Davenport University (Grand Rapids), 213

New Jersey
Micro Tech Training Center (Belleville), 249

New York
Finger Lakes Community College (Canandaigua), 266

North Carolina
Carteret Community College (Morehead City), 292
Catawba Valley Community College (Hickory), 292
Craven Community College (New Bern), 294
Davidson County Community College (Lexington), 294
Forsyth Technical Community College (Winston-Salem), 296
Isothermal Community College (Spindale), 298
Piedmont Community College (Roxboro), 302
Randolph Community College (Asheboro), 303
Richmond Community College (Hamlet), 303
Rowan-Cabarrus Community College (Salisbury), 304
Sampson Community College (Clinton), 304
South Piedmont Community College (Polkton), 305
Stanly Community College (Albemarle), 306
Wilkes Community College (Wilkesboro), 308

Ohio
Brown Mackie College–North Canton (Canton), 313
Marion Technical College (Marion), 325
Sanford-Brown Institute (Middleburg Heights), 333
University of Cincinnati Clermont College (Batavia), 339

Pennsylvania
Computer Learning Network (Altoona), 349
Mercyhurst College (Erie), 364

Puerto Rico
Universidad Metropolitana (San Juan), 394

South Carolina
Aiken Technical College (Aiken), 397
Denmark Technical College (Denmark), 398
Greenville Technical College (Greenville), 399
Northeastern Technical College (Cheraw), 401
Orangeburg-Calhoun Technical College (Orangeburg), 402
Tri-County Technical College (Pendleton), 403
Trident Technical College (Charleston), 404
York Technical College (Rock Hill), 405

Tennessee
Draughons Junior College (Nashville), 407

West Virginia
Blue Ridge Community and Technical College (Martinsburg), 438
Potomac State College of West Virginia University (Keyser), 442
Southern West Virginia Community and Technical College (Mount Gay), 443

CRITICAL CARE NURSING

Massachusetts
Northern Essex Community College (Haverhill), 204

CROP PRODUCTION

Illinois
Lake Land College (Mattoon), 140

Michigan
Michigan State University (East Lansing), 222

CULINARY ARTS AND RELATED SERVICES, OTHER

Connecticut
Norwalk Community College (Norwalk), 55
University of New Haven (West Haven), 58

Florida
Charlotte Vocational-Technical Center (Port Charlotte), 69
David G. Erwin Technical Center (Tampa), 71
Lee County Vocational High Tech Center–Central (Fort Myers), 84
Lindsey Hopkins Technical Education Center (Miami), 84
McFatter Technical Center (Davie), 86
Traviss Technical Center (Lakeland), 99
Washington-Holmes Technical Center (Chipley), 102

Maine
Washington County Community College (Calais), 183

Massachusetts
North Shore Community College (Danvers), 204

Michigan
Ferris State University (Big Rapids), 215
Michigan Career and Technical Institute (Plainwell), 221

New York
The Culinary Institute of America (Hyde Park), 263
Nassau Community College (Garden City), 275

Ohio
Hocking College (Nelsonville), 321

Pennsylvania
Bucks County Community College (Newtown), 345
Commonwealth Technical Institute (Johnstown), 348
Indiana University of Pennsylvania (Indiana), 358
Keystone College (La Plume), 359
Lehigh Carbon Community College (Schnecksville), 362
Westmoreland County Community College (Youngwood), 378

Puerto Rico
Escuela Hotelera de San Juan in Puerto Rico (Hato Rey), 384

CULINARY ARTS/CHEF TRAINING

Alabama
H. Councill Trenholm State Technical College (Montgomery), 43

Connecticut
Connecticut Culinary Institute–Hartford (Hartford), 52
Connecticut Culinary Institute–Suffield (Suffield), 52
Lincoln Technical Institute (Cromwell), 54
Lincoln Technical Institute (Shelton), 54

Florida
The Art Institute of Fort Lauderdale (Fort Lauderdale), 65
Atlantic Vocational-Technical Center (Coconut Creek), 66
First Coast Technical Institute (St. Augustine), 75
George Stone Area Vocational-Technical Center (Pensacola), 79
James Lorenzo Walker Vocational-Technical Center (Naples), 82
Lake Technical Center (Eustis), 83
Lee County High Tech Center North (Cape Coral), 83
Lincoln College of Technology (West Palm Beach), 84
Manatee Technical Institute (Bradenton), 85
Miami Lakes Technical Education Center (Miami), 87
Mid-Florida Tech (Orlando), 87
Orlando Culinary Academy (Orlando), 89
Pinellas Technical Education Center–Clearwater (Clearwater), 91
Sarasota County Technical Institute (Sarasota), 96
Sheridan Vocational-Technical Center (Hollywood), 96
Suwannee-Hamilton Area Vocational, Technical, and Adult Education Center (Live Oak), 98
Valencia Community College (Orlando), 101
Withlacoochee Technical Institute (Inverness), 103

Georgia
The Art Institute of Atlanta (Atlanta), 105
College of Coastal Georgia (Brunswick), 108
Le Cordon Bleu College of Culinary Arts, Atlanta (Tucker), 116

Illinois
City Colleges of Chicago, Kennedy-King College (Chicago), 128
College of DuPage (Glen Ellyn), 129
College of Lake County (Grayslake), 129
The Cooking and Hospitality Institute of Chicago (Chicago), 131
Danville Area Community College (Danville), 131
Elgin Community College (Elgin), 132
Harper College (Palatine), 135
Illinois Central College (East Peoria), 136
John Wood Community College (Quincy), 139
Kaskaskia College (Centralia), 139
Kendall College (Chicago), 140
Rend Lake College (Ina), 148
Southwestern Illinois College (Belleville), 151
Triton College (River Grove), 153

Indiana
Vincennes University (Vincennes), 168

Kentucky
Ashland Community and Technical College (Ashland), 169
Bowling Green Technical College (Bowling Green), 170
Elizabethtown Community and Technical College (Elizabethtown), 172
Jefferson Community and Technical College (Louisville), 175
Owensboro Community and Technical College (Owensboro), 177
Sullivan University (Louisville), 179

West Kentucky Community and Technical College (Paducah), 180

Maine
Central Maine Community College (Auburn), 181
Eastern Maine Community College (Bangor), 181
York County Community College (Wells), 183

Maryland
Baltimore City Community College (Baltimore), 185
Baltimore International College (Baltimore), 185
Chesapeake College (Wye Mills), 186
Frederick Community College (Frederick), 188
Lincoln Technical Institute (Columbia), 189

Massachusetts
Atlantic Union College (South Lancaster), 193
Berkshire Community College (Pittsfield), 194
Branford Hall Career Institute–Springfield Campus (Springfield), 195
Bunker Hill Community College (Boston), 196
Holyoke Community College (Holyoke), 199
Newbury College (Brookline), 203

Michigan
Henry Ford Community College (Dearborn), 217
Macomb Community College (Warren), 220
Northwestern Michigan College (Traverse City), 224
Schoolcraft College (Livonia), 227
Washtenaw Community College (Ann Arbor), 229

Mississippi
Coahoma Community College (Clarksdale), 231

New Hampshire
New Hampshire Community Technical College, Berlin/Laconia (Berlin), 238

New Jersey
Bergen Community College (Paramus), 240
Brookdale Community College (Lincroft), 241
New Community Workforce Development Center (Newark), 250
Ocean County Vocational Post Secondary Division (Toms River), 250

New York
The Art Institute of New York City (New York), 256
Career Academy of New York (New York), 260
Culinary Academy of Long Island (Westbury), 263
French Culinary Institute (New York), 267
Schenectady County Community College (Schenectady), 282

North Carolina
Alamance Community College (Graham), 288
The Art Institute of Charlotte (Charlotte), 288
Cape Fear Community College (Wilmington), 290
Carteret Community College (Morehead City), 292
Central Piedmont Community College (Charlotte), 293
College of The Albemarle (Elizabeth City), 294
Fayetteville Technical Community College (Fayetteville), 295
Guilford Technical Community College (Jamestown), 297
Lenoir Community College (Kinston), 299
Montgomery Community College (Troy), 301
Sandhills Community College (Pinehurst), 305
Southwestern Community College (Sylva), 306
Wake Technical Community College (Raleigh), 307
Wilkes Community College (Wilkesboro), 308

Ohio
Auburn Career Center (Painesville), 311
Cincinnati State Technical and Community
College (Cincinnati), 315
Cuyahoga Community College (Cleveland), 318
Oregon Career Center (Oregon), 330
The University of Akron (Akron), 338

Pennsylvania
The Art Institute of Philadelphia
(Philadelphia), 343
The Art Institute of Pittsburgh (Pittsburgh), 343
Bidwell Training Center (Pittsburgh), 344
Community College of Beaver County
(Monaca), 349
Greater Altoona Career and Technology Center
(Altoona), 356
Harrisburg Area Community College
(Harrisburg), 357
Indiana University of Pennsylvania (Indiana),
358
Keystone Technical Institute (Harrisburg), 359
Mercyhurst College (Erie), 364
Northampton County Area Community College
(Bethlehem), 366
Westmoreland County Community College
(Youngwood), 378
YTI Career Institute–York (York), 379

Puerto Rico
Academia Serrant (Ponce), 379
Instituto de Banca y Comercio–Aprendes
Practicanco (Río Piedras), 386
Instituto de Educacion Tecnica Ocupacional La
Reine (Aguadilla), 387
Instituto de Educacion Tecnica Ocupacional La
Reine (Manati), 387
Instituto Vocacional Aurea E. Mendez (Caguas),
387
Ponce Paramedical College (Ponce), 392
Universal Career Counseling Centers
(Santurce), 393
Universidad del Este (Carolina), 393

Rhode Island
Johnson & Wales University (Providence), 395

South Carolina
The Art Institute of Charleston (Charleston),
397
Denmark Technical College (Denmark), 398
Spartanburg Community College (Spartanburg),
403
Trident Technical College (Charleston), 404

Tennessee
The Art Institute of Tennessee–Nashville
(Nashville), 405
Nashville State Technical Community College
(Nashville), 411
Walters State Community College
(Morristown), 421

Vermont
New England Culinary Institute at Essex (Essex
Junction), 423
New England Culinary Institute (Montpelier),
422

Virginia
The Art Institute of Washington (Arlington),
424
ECPI College of Technology (Virginia Beach),
426
Southeast Culinary & Hospitality College
(Bristol), 432
Stratford University (Falls Church), 433

West Virginia
James Rumsey Technical Institute
(Martinsburg), 440
Monongalia County Technical Education
Center (Morgantown), 441
Mountain State University (Beckley), 442

Wisconsin
Milwaukee Area Technical College
(Milwaukee), 449

CURRICULUM AND INSTRUCTION

Maryland
Cecil College (North East), 186

CUSTOMER SERVICE MANAGEMENT

Illinois
Spanish Coalition for Jobs, Inc. (Chicago), 152

Massachusetts
Cape Cod Community College (West
Barnstable), 196

Michigan
Henry Ford Community College (Dearborn),
217
Muskegon Community College (Muskegon),
223

Ohio
Edison State Community College (Piqua), 319

CUSTOMER SERVICE SUPPORT/CALL CENTER/TELESERVICE OPERATION

Connecticut
Goodwin College (East Hartford), 53

Florida
Advanced Technical Centers (Miami), 64
Management Resources Institute (Miami), 85
Ridge Technical Center (Winter Haven), 93
Sarasota County Technical Institute (Sarasota),
96

Georgia
Albany Technical College (Albany), 103
Altamaha Technical College (Jesup), 104
Augusta Technical College (Augusta), 106
Bainbridge College (Bainbridge), 106
Central Georgia Technical College (Macon),
107
Chattahoochee Technical College (Marietta),
107
Columbus Technical College (Columbus), 108
Coosa Valley Technical College (Rome), 109
DeKalb Technical College (Clarkston), 109
Flint River Technical College (Thomaston), 111
Heart of Georgia Technical College (Dublin),
114
Middle Georgia Technical College (Warner
Robbins), 117
North Georgia Technical College (Clarkesville),
118
Okefenokee Technical College (Waycross), 119
Southwest Georgia Technical College
(Thomasville), 122
Valdosta Technical College (Valdosta), 123
West Georgia Technical College (LaGrange),
124

Michigan
Bay de Noc Community College (Escanaba),
211
Davenport University (Grand Rapids), 213
Lansing Community College (Lansing), 219

North Carolina
Catawba Valley Community College (Hickory),
292
Isothermal Community College (Spindale), 298
Southeastern Community College (Whiteville),
305

Ohio
Daymar College (Chillicothe), 318

Pennsylvania
Community College of Beaver County
(Monaca), 349

Wisconsin
Milwaukee Career College (Milwaukee), 449

CYTOTECHNOLOGY/CYTOTECHNOLOGIST

New Jersey
University of Medicine and Dentistry of New
Jersey (Newark), 255

New York
Albany College of Pharmacy and Health
Sciences (Albany), 256

North Carolina
Central Piedmont Community College
(Charlotte), 293
The University of North Carolina at Chapel
Hill (Chapel Hill), 307

Ohio
Sinclair Community College (Dayton), 334

DAIRY HUSBANDRY AND PRODUCTION

Wisconsin
Lakeshore Technical College (Cleveland), 447
Southwest Wisconsin Technical College
(Fennimore), 452
Wisconsin Indianhead Technical College (Shell
Lake), 453

DAIRY SCIENCE

Michigan
Michigan State University (East Lansing), 222

DANCE, GENERAL

Mississippi
Belhaven College (Jackson), 230

New Jersey
Ocean County Vocational Post Secondary
Division (Toms River), 250

New York
The Ailey School (New York), 256

Ohio
Sinclair Community College (Dayton), 334

DANCE, OTHER

Indiana
Vincennes University (Vincennes), 168

DATA ENTRY/MICROCOMPUTER APPLICATIONS, GENERAL

Connecticut
Norwalk Community College (Norwalk), 55

District of Columbia
Career Blazers Learning Center (Washington),
61

Florida
Florida Career College (Miami), 76
Florida National College (Hialeah), 78
Management Resources Institute (Miami), 85
Miami-Dade County Public Schools (Miami),
87

Georgia
Albany Technical College (Albany), 103
Altamaha Technical College (Jesup), 104
Appalachian Technical College (Jasper), 104
Atlanta Technical College (Atlanta), 105
Augusta Technical College (Augusta), 106
Central Georgia Technical College (Macon),
107
Chattahoochee Technical College (Marietta),
107
Coosa Valley Technical College (Rome), 109
DeKalb Technical College (Clarkston), 109
East Central Technical College (Fitzgerald), 110
Flint River Technical College (Thomaston), 111
Griffin Technical College (Griffin), 113
Gwinnett College (Lilburn), 113
Heart of Georgia Technical College (Dublin),
114
Lanier Technical College (Oakwood), 115

Moultrie Technical College (Moultrie), 117
North Georgia Technical College (Clarkesville), 118
North Metro Technical College (Acworth), 118
Northwestern Technical College (Rock Spring), 118
Ogeechee Technical College (Statesboro), 119
Okefenokee Technical College (Waycross), 119
Southeastern Technical College (Vidalia), 121
South Georgia Technical College (Americus), 122
Swainsboro Technical College (Swainsboro), 123
Valdosta Technical College (Valdosta), 123
West Central Technical College (Waco), 124
West Georgia Technical College (LaGrange), 124

Illinois
College of DuPage (Glen Ellyn), 129
The College of Office Technology (Chicago), 130
Hebrew Theological College (Skokie), 136
Illinois Central College (East Peoria), 136
Kankakee Community College (Kankakee), 139
Waubonsee Community College (Sugar Grove), 154

Maryland
Montgomery College (Rockville), 190
TESST College of Technology (Beltsville), 192

Massachusetts
Greenfield Community College (Greenfield), 198
Massasoit Community College (Brockton), 202
Springfield Technical Community College (Springfield), 207

Michigan
Bay de Noc Community College (Escanaba), 211
Davenport University (Grand Rapids), 213
Kellogg Community College (Battle Creek), 218
North Central Michigan College (Petoskey), 223
Northwestern Michigan College (Traverse City), 224
Washtenaw Community College (Ann Arbor), 229

New Hampshire
Hesser College, Manchester (Manchester), 237

New Jersey
Central Career School (South Plainfield), 242
Dover Business College (Paramus), 244
Mercer County Community College (Trenton), 248

New York
Pace University (New York), 279
Utica School of Commerce (Utica), 287

North Carolina
Miller-Motte Technical College (Wilmington), 300

Ohio
Penta County Joint Vocational School (Perrysburg), 330

Pennsylvania
Delaware County Community College (Media), 351
Gannon University (Erie), 355
Harrisburg Area Community College (Harrisburg), 357
Laurel Technical Institute (Sharon), 361
McCann School of Business & Technology (Pottsville), 364
Northwest Regional Technology Institute (Erie), 367
Pace Institute (Reading), 367

Pennsylvania Highlands Community College (Johnstown), 370
Westmoreland County Community College (Youngwood), 378

Puerto Rico
Advanced Tech College (Bayamón), 379
John Dewey College, 389, 390
MBTI Business Training Institute (Santurce), 391
Nova College de Puerto Rico (Bayamón), 391

South Carolina
Beta Tech (North Charleston), 397

Tennessee
National College (Nashville), 411

Virginia
National College (Salem), 430
Woodrow Wilson Rehabilitation Center (Fishersville), 436

West Virginia
West Virginia Junior College (Morgantown), 444

Wisconsin
Northcentral Technical College (Wausau), 450

DATA ENTRY/MICROCOMPUTER APPLICATIONS, OTHER

Florida
Advanced Technical Centers (Miami), 64
South Florida Institute of Technology (Miami), 97

Illinois
The College of Office Technology (Chicago), 130

Michigan
Muskegon Community College (Muskegon), 223

Pennsylvania
Butler County Community College (Butler), 345
DCI Career Institute (Monaca), 350

Puerto Rico
ASPIRA de Puerto Rico (Carolina), 380

Tennessee
Miller-Motte Technical College (Chattanooga), 410

Wisconsin
Moraine Park Technical College (Fond du Lac), 450

DATA MODELING/WAREHOUSING AND DATABASE ADMINISTRATION

Georgia
Atlanta Technical College (Atlanta), 105
Middle Georgia Technical College (Warner Robbins), 117

Illinois
Oakton Community College (Des Plaines), 145
Parkland College (Champaign), 145
Triton College (River Grove), 153

Indiana
TechSkills—Indianapolis (Indianapolis), 167

Michigan
Lansing Community College (Lansing), 219
Oakland Community College (Bloomfield Hills), 224

New Jersey
Gloucester County College (Sewell), 245

North Carolina
Central Piedmont Community College (Charlotte), 293
Wake Technical Community College (Raleigh), 307

Ohio
TechSkills—Columbus (Columbus), 336
The University of Akron (Akron), 338

Pennsylvania
Pittsburgh Technical Institute (Oakdale), 371
Westmoreland County Community College (Youngwood), 378

DATA PROCESSING AND DATA PROCESSING TECHNOLOGY/TECHNICIAN

Connecticut
Quinebaug Valley Community College (Danielson), 56

Florida
Mid-Florida Tech (Orlando), 87
Pinellas Technical Education Center–Clearwater (Clearwater), 91

Georgia
Albany Technical College (Albany), 103
Bainbridge College (Bainbridge), 106
Coosa Valley Technical College (Rome), 109
Griffin Technical College (Griffin), 113
Gwinnett Technical College (Lawrenceville), 113
Lanier Technical College (Oakwood), 115
Middle Georgia Technical College (Warner Robbins), 117
Northwestern Technical College (Rock Spring), 118
Sandersville Technical College (Sandersville), 120
Savannah Technical College (Savannah), 121
South Georgia Technical College (Americus), 122
Swainsboro Technical College (Swainsboro), 123
Valdosta Technical College (Valdosta), 123
West Central Technical College (Waco), 124

Illinois
The College of Office Technology (Chicago), 130
Joliet Junior College (Joliet), 139
Oakton Community College (Des Plaines), 145
Prairie State College (Chicago Heights), 146
Vatterott College (Quincy), 154

Indiana
Kaplan College–Hammond Campus (Hammond), 164
Kaplan College–Merrillville Campus (Merrillville), 164
Vincennes University (Vincennes), 168

Kentucky
Bluegrass Community and Technical College (Lexington), 170

Maryland
Chesapeake College (Wye Mills), 186
Hagerstown Community College (Hagerstown), 188
Montgomery College (Rockville), 190

Michigan
Lawton School (Southfield), 220
North Central Michigan College (Petoskey), 223
St. Clair County Community College (Port Huron), 226

New Jersey
Essex County College (Newark), 244

New York
Everest Institute (Rochester), 266
Hunter Business School (Levittown), 269
Mount Saint Mary College (Newburgh), 275
Pace University (New York), 279
Queensborough Community College of the City University of New York (Bayside), 280

Rochester Institute of Technology (Rochester), 280

Utica School of Commerce (Utica), 287

North Carolina

Central Piedmont Community College (Charlotte), 293

Ohio

Adult and Community Education–Hudson (Columbus), 309

Butler Technology and Career Development Schools–D. Russel Lee Career-Technology Center (Hamilton), 314

Cleveland Institute of Electronics (Cleveland), 316

Northwest State Community College (Archbold), 327

Technology Education College (Columbus), 336

Trumbull Business College (Warren), 338

Zane State College (Zanesville), 342

Pennsylvania

Erie Business Center, South (New Castle), 355

Westmoreland County Community College (Youngwood), 378

Puerto Rico

Advanced Tech College (Bayamón), 379

D'mart Institute (Barranquitas), 383

Instituto Merlix (Bayamón), 387

South Carolina

Aiken Technical College (Aiken), 397

Central Carolina Technical College (Sumter), 398

Greenville Technical College (Greenville), 399

Horry-Georgetown Technical College (Conway), 400

Midlands Technical College (Columbia), 401

Northeastern Technical College (Cheraw), 401

Orangeburg-Calhoun Technical College (Orangeburg), 402

Piedmont Technical College (Greenwood), 402

Spartanburg Community College (Spartanburg), 403

Tri-County Technical College (Pendleton), 403

Trident Technical College (Charleston), 404

Williamsburg Technical College (Kingstree), 404

York Technical College (Rock Hill), 405

Tennessee

Chattanooga College–Medical, Dental and Technical Careers (Chattanooga), 406

Tennessee Technology Center at Ripley (Ripley), 419

West Virginia

HRDE-Stanley Technical Institute–Hinton (Hinton), 440

Marshall Community and Technical College (Huntington), 441

Wisconsin

Lac Courte Oreilles Ojibwa Community College (Hayward), 447

Madison Area Technical College (Madison), 448

Waukesha County Technical College (Pewaukee), 453

DENTAL ASSISTING/ASSISTANT

Alabama

Calhoun Community College (Decatur), 41

Capps College (Mobile), 42

H. Councill Trenholm State Technical College (Montgomery), 43

James H. Faulkner State Community College (Bay Minette), 44

Lawson State Community College (Birmingham), 44

The University of Alabama at Birmingham (Birmingham), 47

Wallace State Community College (Hanceville), 48

Connecticut

Briarwood College (Southington), 50

Connecticut School of Electronics (Branford), 52

Porter and Chester Institute (Stratford), 56

Tunxis Community College (Farmington), 57

Delaware

Dawn Training Centre (Wilmington), 58

Florida

Americare School of Nursing (Fern Park), 64

Americare School of Nursing (St. Petersburg), 64

Angley College (Deland), 64

Atlantic Vocational-Technical Center (Coconut Creek), 66

Brevard Community College (Cocoa), 67

Broward Community College (Fort Lauderdale), 68

Central Florida Community College (Ocala), 69

Central Florida Institute (Palm Harbor), 69

Charlotte Vocational-Technical Center (Port Charlotte), 69

Comp-Med Vocational Careers Corporation (Hialeah), 70

Concorde Career Institute (Jacksonville), 70

Concorde Career Institute (Lauderdale Lake), 70

Concorde Career Institute (Tampa), 71

David G. Erwin Technical Center (Tampa), 71

Daytona State College (Daytona Beach), 72

Edison State College (Fort Myers), 72

First Coast Technical Institute (St. Augustine), 75

Florida Community College at Jacksonville (Jacksonville), 77

Florida Education Center (Lauderhill), 77

Florida National College (Hialeah), 78

Gulf Coast Community College (Panama City), 79

High-Tech Institute (Orlando), 80

Hillsborough Community College (Tampa), 81

Indian River State College (Fort Pierce), 81

James Lorenzo Walker Vocational-Technical Center (Naples), 82

Lincoln College of Technology (West Palm Beach), 84

Lindsey Hopkins Technical Education Center (Miami), 84

Manatee Technical Institute (Bradenton), 85

Northwest Florida State College (Niceville), 89

Orlando Technical Center (Orlando), 90

Palm Beach Community College (Lake Worth), 90

Pasco-Hernando Community College (New Port Richey), 90

Pensacola Junior College (Pensacola), 91

Pinellas Technical Education Center–St. Petersburg (St. Petersburg), 92

Robert Morgan Vocational-Technical Center (Miami), 94

Sanford-Brown Institute (Fort Lauderdale), 95

Sanford-Brown Institute (Tampa), 95

Santa Fe Community College (Gainesville), 95

School of Health Careers (Lauderdale Lakes), 96

South Florida Community College (Avon Park), 97

Superior Career Institute (Lauderdale Lakes), 98

Tallahassee Community College (Tallahassee), 98

Traviss Technical Center (Lakeland), 99

Georgia

Advanced Career Training (Atlanta), 103

Albany Technical College (Albany), 103

Athens Technical College (Athens), 105

Atlanta Technical College (Atlanta), 105

Augusta Technical College (Augusta), 106

Columbus Technical College (Columbus), 108

Coosa Valley Technical College (Rome), 109

Everest Institute (Jonesboro), 111

Everest Institute (Norcross), 111

Griffin Technical College (Griffin), 113

Gwinnett Technical College (Lawrenceville), 113

Lanier Technical College (Oakwood), 115

Medix School (Smyrna), 116

Middle Georgia Technical College (Warner Robbins), 117

Ogeechee Technical College (Statesboro), 119

Savannah Technical College (Savannah), 121

Swainsboro Technical College (Swainsboro), 123

Valdosta Technical College (Valdosta), 123

West Central Technical College (Waco), 124

Illinois

City Colleges of Chicago, Wilbur Wright College (Chicago), 129

Elgin Community College (Elgin), 132

Everest College (Burr Ridge), 133

Everest College (Chicago), 133

Illinois School of Health Careers (Chicago), 138

Illinois School of Health Careers–O'Hare Campus (Chicago), 138

Illinois Valley Community College (Oglesby), 138

John A. Logan College (Carterville), 138

Kaskaskia College (Centralia), 139

Lewis and Clark Community College (Godfrey), 141

Midwest Technical Institute (Lincoln), 143

Indiana

Everest College (Merrillville), 157

Indiana University Northwest (Gary), 160

Indiana University–Purdue University Fort Wayne (Fort Wayne), 160

Indiana University–Purdue University Indianapolis (Indianapolis), 160

Indiana University South Bend (South Bend), 161

Ivy Tech Community College–Columbus (Columbus), 162

Ivy Tech Community College–East Central (Muncie), 162

Ivy Tech Community College–Kokomo (Kokomo), 162

Ivy Tech Community College–Lafayette (Lafayette), 162

Kaplan College–Northwest Indianapolis Campus (Indianapolis), 165

University of Southern Indiana (Evansville), 168

Kentucky

ATA Career Education (Louisville), 169

Maine

University of Maine at Augusta (Augusta), 183

Maryland

All-State Career School (Baltimore), 184

Kaplan College–Hagerstown (Hagerstown), 189

Medix School (Towson), 190

Medix South (Landover), 190

Massachusetts

Everest Institute (Brighton), 198

Massasoit Community College (Brockton), 202

Middlesex Community College (Bedford), 202

Northern Essex Community College (Haverhill), 204

Quinsigamond Community College (Worcester), 205

Southeastern Technical College (South Easton), 206

Springfield Technical Community College (Springfield), 207

Michigan

Bay de Noc Community College (Escanaba), 211

Delta College (University Center), 213

Everest Institute (Dearborn), 215

Everest Institute (Grand Rapids), 215

Everest Institute (Kalamazoo), 215

Grand Rapids Community College (Grand Rapids), 216

Lake Michigan College (Benton Harbor), 219

Mott Community College (Flint), 223

Northwestern Michigan College (Traverse City), 224

Ross Medical Education Center (Brighton), 225

Ross Medical Education Center (Flint), 225

Ross Medical Education Center (Saginaw), 226

Washtenaw Community College (Ann Arbor), 229

Wayne County Community College District (Detroit), 229

Mississippi

Antonelli College (Jackson), 230

Hinds Community College (Raymond), 232

Meridian Community College (Meridian), 234

Pearl River Community College (Poplarville), 235

New Hampshire

New Hampshire Technical Institute (Concord), 239

New Jersey

Berdan Institute (Totowa), 240

Brookdale Community College (Lincroft), 241

Camden County College (Blackwood), 241

Central Career School (South Plainfield), 242

Essex County College (Newark), 244

The Institute for Health Education (Fairfield), 247

Ocean County Vocational Post Secondary Division (Toms River), 250

University of Medicine and Dentistry of New Jersey (Newark), 255

New York

Erie Community College (Buffalo), 265

Hudson Valley Community College (Troy), 268

Mandl School (New York), 272

Monroe 2–Orleans BOCES Center for Workforce Development (Rochester), 274

Monroe Community College (Rochester), 274

New York School for Medical/Dental Assistants (Forest Hills), 276

New York University (New York), 277

Onondaga-Courtland-Madison BOCES (Liverpool), 278

Oswego County BOCES (Mexico), 278

Willsey Institute (Staten Island), 288

North Carolina

Alamance Community College (Graham), 288

Asheville-Buncombe Technical Community College (Asheville), 288

Cape Fear Community College (Wilmington), 290

Central Carolina Community College (Sanford), 292

Central Piedmont Community College (Charlotte), 293

Coastal Carolina Community College (Jacksonville), 293

Fayetteville Technical Community College (Fayetteville), 295

Forsyth Technical Community College (Winston-Salem), 296

Guilford Technical Community College (Jamestown), 297

Martin Community College (Williamston), 299

Montgomery Community College (Troy), 301

Rowan-Cabarrus Community College (Salisbury), 304

The University of North Carolina at Chapel Hill (Chapel Hill), 307

Wake Technical Community College (Raleigh), 307

Wayne Community College (Goldsboro), 308

Western Piedmont Community College (Morganton), 308

Wilkes Community College (Wilkesboro), 308

Ohio

Akron Institute (Cuyahoga Falls), 310

Choffin Career Center (Youngstown), 315

Cleveland Institute of Dental-Medical Assistants (Cleveland), 316

Cleveland Institute of Dental-Medical Assistants (Mentor), 316

Cuyahoga Community College (Cleveland), 318

Delaware JVS District (Delaware), 318

Eastern Gateway Community College (Steubenville), 319

Eastland Career Center (Groveport), 319

Everest Institute (Cuyahoga Falls), 320

Institute of Medical and Dental Technology (Cincinnati), 322

Madison Local Schools–Madison Adult Education (Mansfield), 324

Medina County Career Center (Medina), 325

Miami-Jacobs–Springboro, Ohio Campus (Springboro), 325

Ohio Institute of Health Careers (Columbus), 329

Ohio Institute of Health Careers (Elyria), 329

Polaris Career Center (Middleburg Heights), 331

Remington College–Cleveland West Campus (North Olmstead), 333

Scioto County Joint Vocational School District (Lucasville), 334

Pennsylvania

Allied Medical and Technical Institute (Scranton), 343

All-State Career School (Lester), 343

Bradford School (Pittsburgh), 345

Career Training Academy (New Kensington), 346

CHI Institute, Broomall Campus (Broomall), 348

Commonwealth Technical Institute (Johnstown), 348

Delaware Valley Academy of Medical and Dental Assistants (Philadelphia), 351

Greater Altoona Career and Technology Center (Altoona), 356

Great Lakes Institute of Technology (Erie), 356

Harcum College (Bryn Mawr), 356

Harrisburg Area Community College (Harrisburg), 357

Keystone Technical Institute (Harrisburg), 359

Lancaster County Career and Technology Center (Willow Street), 360

Luzerne County Community College (Nanticoke), 363

Sanford-Brown Institute–Monroeville (Pittsburgh), 373

Sanford-Brown Institute (Trevose), 373

Schuylkill Technology Center–North Campus (Frackville), 373

Thompson Institute (Philadelphia), 375

Westmoreland County Community College (Youngwood), 378

YTI Career Institute–York (York), 379

Puerto Rico

Antilles School of Technical Careers (Hato Rey), 380

Colegio Mayor de Tecnologia–Arroyo (Arroyo), 382

Instituto de Banca y Comercio–Aprendes Practicanco (Río Piedras), 386

Ponce Paramedical College (Ponce), 392

Rhode Island

Community College of Rhode Island (Warwick), 394

Lincoln Technical Institute (Lincoln), 395

South Carolina

Aiken Technical College (Aiken), 397

Florence-Darlington Technical College (Florence), 399

Greenville Technical College (Greenville), 399

Horry-Georgetown Technical College (Conway), 400

Midlands Technical College (Columbia), 401

Spartanburg Community College (Spartanburg), 403

Tri-County Technical College (Pendleton), 403

Trident Technical College (Charleston), 404

York Technical College (Rock Hill), 405

Tennessee

Concorde Career College (Memphis), 406

Draughons Junior College (Clarksville), 407

Draughons Junior College (Murfreesboro), 407

Draughons Junior College (Nashville), 407

High-Tech Institute (Nashville), 408

Kaplan Career Institute–Nashville Campus (Nashville), 409

Miller-Motte Technical College (Chattanooga), 410

Northeast State Technical Community College (Blountville), 412

Remington College–Nashville Campus (Nashville), 413

Tennessee Technology Center at Dickson (Dickson), 416

Tennessee Technology Center at Knoxville (Knoxville), 417

Tennessee Technology Center at Memphis (Memphis), 417

Tennessee Technology Center at Murfreesboro (Murfreesboro), 418

Volunteer State Community College (Gallatin), 421

Virginia

ACT College (Arlington), 423

Everest Institute (Chesapeake), 428

J. Sargeant Reynolds Community College (Richmond), 429

Tidewater Tech (Norfolk), 434

Washington County Adult Skill Center (Abingdon), 436

Wytheville Community College (Wytheville), 436

West Virginia

Academy of Careers and Technology (Beckley), 437

Carver Career Center (Charleston), 438

Huntington Junior College (Huntington), 440

Monongalia County Technical Education Center (Morgantown), 441

Opportunities Industrialization Center–North Central West Virginia (Fairmont), 442

Putnam Career and Technology Center School of Practical Nursing (Eleanor), 443

Wisconsin

Blackhawk Technical College (Janesville), 445

Chippewa Valley Technical College (Eau Claire), 445

Fox Valley Technical College (Appleton), 446

Gateway Technical College (Kenosha), 446

Kaplan College–Milwaukee (Milwaukee), 447

Lakeshore Technical College (Cleveland), 447

Madison Area Technical College (Madison), 448

Milwaukee Area Technical College (Milwaukee), 449

Northeast Wisconsin Technical College (Green Bay), 450

Southwest Wisconsin Technical College (Fennimore), 452

Waukesha County Technical College (Pewaukee), 453

Western Technical College (La Crosse), 453

DENTAL CLINICAL SCIENCES, GENERAL (MS, PHD)

Pennsylvania

Lancaster County Career and Technology Center (Willow Street), 360

DENTAL HYGIENE/HYGIENIST

Indiana

Vincennes University (Vincennes), 168

Kentucky

Bluegrass Community and Technical College (Lexington), 170

West Kentucky Community and Technical College (Paducah), 180

Michigan

Lake Michigan College (Benton Harbor), 219

North Carolina

The University of North Carolina at Chapel Hill (Chapel Hill), 307

Ohio

Choffin Career Center (Youngstown), 315

Sinclair Community College (Dayton), 334

Pennsylvania

University of Pittsburgh (Pittsburgh), 376

South Carolina

Aiken Technical College (Aiken), 397

Midlands Technical College (Columbia), 401

Orangeburg-Calhoun Technical College (Orangeburg), 402

DENTAL LABORATORY TECHNOLOGY/ TECHNICIAN

Florida

Florida National College (Hialeah), 78

McFatter Technical Center (Davie), 86

Georgia

Gwinnett Technical College (Lawrenceville), 113

Kentucky

Bluegrass Community and Technical College (Lexington), 170

Michigan

Wayne County Community College District (Detroit), 229

North Carolina

Durham Technical Community College (Durham), 295

Ohio

Columbus State Community College (Columbus), 317

Pennsylvania

Allied Medical and Technical Institute (Scranton), 343

Tennessee

Tennessee Technology Center at Memphis (Memphis), 417

Tennessee Technology Center at Nashville (Nashville), 418

West Virginia

Putnam Career and Technology Center School of Practical Nursing (Eleanor), 443

Wisconsin

Milwaukee Area Technical College (Milwaukee), 449

Moraine Park Technical College (Fond du Lac), 450

DENTAL SERVICES AND ALLIED PROFESSIONS, OTHER

Florida

Florida National College (Hialeah), 78

New Jersey

Somerset County Technical Institute (Bridgewater), 253

Puerto Rico

Huertas Junior College (Caguas), 385

DESIGN AND APPLIED ARTS, OTHER

Massachusetts

Suffolk University (Boston), 207

New Jersey

Camden County College (Blackwood), 241

Ocean County College (Toms River), 250

New York

Westchester Community College (Valhalla), 287

Ohio

Lakeland Community College (Kirtland), 323

University of Cincinnati Raymond Walters College (Cincinnati), 339

DESIGN AND VISUAL COMMUNICATIONS, GENERAL

Alabama

Chattahoochee Valley Community College (Phenix City), 42

Florida

Tom P. Haney Technical Center (Panama City), 99

Illinois

Sauk Valley Community College (Dixon), 150

Triton College (River Grove), 153

Maryland

Harford Community College (Bel Air), 189

Massachusetts

Greenfield Community College (Greenfield), 198

Ohio

Lakeland Community College (Kirtland), 323

Pennsylvania

Marywood University (Scranton), 364

Virginia

Germanna Community College (Locust Grove), 428

Northern Virginia Community College (Annandale), 430

Patrick Henry Community College (Martinsville), 431

Thomas Nelson Community College (Hampton), 433

DEVELOPMENT ECONOMICS AND INTERNATIONAL DEVELOPMENT

Ohio

The University of Akron (Akron), 338

DIAGNOSTIC MEDICAL SONOGRAPHY/ SONOGRAPHER AND ULTRASOUND TECHNICIAN

Connecticut

Fox Institute of Business (Hartford), 52

Gateway Community College (New Haven), 52

Delaware

Delaware Technical & Community College, Stanton/Wilmington Campus (Newark), 59

District of Columbia

The George Washington University (Washington), 61

Florida

Broward Community College (Fort Lauderdale), 68

Central Florida Institute (Palm Harbor), 69

Dade Medical College (Hialeah), 71

Dade Medical Institute (Miami), 71

Everest Institute (Hialeah), 72

Florida Hospital College of Health Sciences (Orlando), 77

Gulf Coast Community College (Panama City), 79

Palm Beach Community College (Lake Worth), 90

Professional Training Centers (Miami), 92

Sanford-Brown Institute (Fort Lauderdale), 95

Sanford-Brown Institute (Jacksonville), 95

Sanford-Brown Institute (Tampa), 95

Santa Fe Community College (Gainesville), 95

School of Health Careers (Lauderdale Lakes), 96

Tallahassee Community College (Tallahassee), 98

Georgia

Grady Health System (Atlanta), 113

Sanford-Brown Institute (Atlanta), 120

Illinois

Carl Sandburg College (Galesburg), 127

College of DuPage (Glen Ellyn), 129

College of Lake County (Grayslake), 129

John A. Logan College (Carterville), 138

Kaskaskia College (Centralia), 139

South Suburban College (South Holland), 151

Triton College (River Grove), 153

Kentucky

Bowling Green Technical College (Bowling Green), 170

Maryland

Montgomery College (Rockville), 190

Sanford-Brown Institute (Landover), 192

Massachusetts

Cape Cod Community College (West Barnstable), 196

Massasoit Community College (Brockton), 202

Middlesex Community College (Bedford), 202

Michigan

Delta College (University Center), 213

Jackson Community College (Jackson), 218

Lansing Community College (Lansing), 219

Mississippi

Hinds Community College (Raymond), 232

Jones County Junior College (Ellisville), 234

New Hampshire

New Hampshire Technical Institute (Concord), 239

New Jersey

Fox Institute of Business–Clifton (Clifton), 245

Healthcare Training Institute (Union), 246

HoHoKus RETS School of Business and Medical Technical Services (Nutley), 246

HoHoKus School of Business and Medical Sciences (Ramsey), 247

Micro Tech Training Center (Belleville), 249

Micro Tech Training Center (Jersey City), 249

Sanford-Brown Institute (Iselin), 253

University of Medicine and Dentistry of New Jersey (Newark), 255

New York

Hudson Valley Community College (Troy), 268

Institute of Allied Medical Professions (Elmhurst), 269

Rochester Institute of Technology (Rochester), 280

Sanford-Brown Institute (Garden City), 282

Sanford-Brown Institute (New York), 282

Sanford-Brown Institute (White Plains), 282

Trocaire College (Buffalo), 286

Western Suffolk BOCES (Northport), 288

North Carolina

Carteret Community College (Morehead City), 292

Forsyth Technical Community College (Winston-Salem), 296

Johnston Community College (Smithfield), 298

Southwestern Community College (Sylva), 306

Ohio

Cincinnati State Technical and Community College (Cincinnati), 315

O. C. Collins Career Center (Chesapeake), 328

Sanford-Brown Institute (Middleburg Heights), 333

Pennsylvania

Community College of Allegheny County (Pittsburgh), 348

Great Lakes Institute of Technology (Erie), 356

Harrisburg Area Community College (Harrisburg), 357

Lancaster General College of Nursing & Health Sciences (Lancaster), 360

Northampton County Area Community College (Bethlehem), 366

Sanford-Brown Institute–Pittsburgh (Pittsburgh), 373

Sanford-Brown Institute (Trevose), 373

Puerto Rico

Universidad del Este (Carolina), 393

Rhode Island

Community College of Rhode Island (Warwick), 394

South Carolina

Greenville Technical College (Greenville), 399

Horry-Georgetown Technical College (Conway), 400

Tennessee

Chattanooga State Technical Community College (Chattanooga), 406

Volunteer State Community College (Gallatin), 421

Virginia

Southwest Virginia Community College (Richlands), 432

Tidewater Community College (Norfolk), 434

West Virginia

Mountain State University (Beckley), 442

West Virginia University Hospital–School of Radiology Technology (Morgantown), 444

Wisconsin

St. Luke's Medical Center–School of Diagnostic Medical Sonography (Milwaukee), 451

DIESEL MECHANICS TECHNOLOGY/ TECHNICIAN

Alabama

Bevill State Community College (Sumiton), 41

Bishop State Community College (Mobile), 41

Gadsden State Community College (Gadsden), 42

H. Councill Trenholm State Technical College (Montgomery), 43

Lawson State Community College (Birmingham), 44

Lurleen B. Wallace Community College (Andalusia), 45

Shelton State Community College (Tuscaloosa), 46

Wallace State Community College (Hanceville), 48

Connecticut

Baran Institute of Technology (Windsor), 49

Florida

Bradford Union Area Vocational Technical Center (Starke), 67

Florida Community College at Jacksonville (Jacksonville), 77

Miami Lakes Technical Education Center (Miami), 87

Mid-Florida Tech (Orlando), 87

Palm Beach Community College (Lake Worth), 90

Pinellas Technical Education Center– Clearwater (Clearwater), 91

Ridge Technical Center (Winter Haven), 93

Robert Morgan Vocational-Technical Center (Miami), 94

Traviss Technical Center (Lakeland), 99

Georgia

Atlanta Technical College (Atlanta), 105

Illinois

Carl Sandburg College (Galesburg), 127

Rend Lake College (Ina), 148

Southeastern Illinois College (Harrisburg), 151

Universal Technical Institute (Glendale Heights), 153

Indiana

Lincoln Technical Institute (Indianapolis), 165

Kentucky

Ashland Community and Technical College (Ashland), 169

Big Sandy Community and Technical College (Prestonsburg), 170

Elizabethtown Community and Technical College (Elizabethtown), 172

Hazard Community and Technical College (Hazard), 174

Maysville Community and Technical College (Maysville), 176

Owensboro Community and Technical College (Owensboro), 177

Somerset Community College (Somerset), 178

Southeast Kentucky Community and Technical College (Cumberland), 178

West Kentucky Community and Technical College (Paducah), 180

Maine

Washington County Community College (Calais), 183

Maryland

North American Trade Schools (Grantsville), 191

Massachusetts

Universal Technical Institute (Norwood), 208

Mississippi

Copiah-Lincoln Community College (Wesson), 231

Hinds Community College (Raymond), 232

Northeast Mississippi Community College (Booneville), 235

New Hampshire

New Hampshire Community Technical College, Berlin/Laconia (Berlin), 238

New Jersey

Engine City Technical Institute (Union), 244

Ocean County Vocational Post Secondary Division (Toms River), 250

Pennco Tech (Blackwood), 251

North Carolina

Asheville-Buncombe Technical Community College (Asheville), 288

Beaufort County Community College (Washington), 289

Cape Fear Community College (Wilmington), 290

Carteret Community College (Morehead City), 292

Central Piedmont Community College (Charlotte), 293

Coastal Carolina Community College (Jacksonville), 293

Forsyth Technical Community College (Winston-Salem), 296

Johnston Community College (Smithfield), 298

Wake Technical Community College (Raleigh), 307

Wilkes Community College (Wilkesboro), 308

Wilson Community College (Wilson), 308

Ohio

TDDS (Diamond), 336

University of Northwestern Ohio (Lima), 339

Pennsylvania

Automotive Training Center (Exton), 344

Automotive Training Center (Warminster), 344

Community College of Beaver County (Monaca), 349

Lancaster County Career and Technology Center (Willow Street), 360

Lebanon County Area Vocational Technical School (Lebanon), 361

Lincoln Technical Institute (Philadelphia), 363

Universal Technical Institute (Exton), 376

WyoTech (Blairsville), 378

Puerto Rico

Automeca Technical College (Aguadilla), 380

Automeca Technical College (Bayamón), 380

Automeca Technical College (Caguas), 380

Automeca Technical College (Ponce), 380

Caguas Institute of Mechanical Technology (Caguas), 381

South Carolina

Greenville Technical College (Greenville), 399

Orangeburg-Calhoun Technical College (Orangeburg), 402

Tennessee

Nashville Auto Diesel College (Nashville), 410

Tennessee Technology Center at Harriman (Harriman), 416

Tennessee Technology Center at Knoxville (Knoxville), 417

Tennessee Technology Center at Memphis (Memphis), 417

Virginia

Advanced Technology Institute (Virginia Beach), 423

J. Sargeant Reynolds Community College (Richmond), 429

Southside Virginia Community College (Alberta), 432

Southwest Virginia Community College (Richlands), 432

Washington County Adult Skill Center (Abingdon), 436

West Virginia

Academy of Careers and Technology (Beckley), 437

Ben Franklin Career Center (Dunbar), 437

Fred W. Eberle Technical Center (Buckhannon), 439

Wisconsin

Milwaukee Area Technical College (Milwaukee), 449

DIETETICS AND CLINICAL NUTRITION SERVICES, OTHER

Florida

Lindsey Hopkins Technical Education Center (Miami), 84

Maine

Southern Maine Community College (South Portland), 182

Pennsylvania
Community College of Allegheny County (Pittsburgh), 348
Pennsylvania Highlands Community College (Johnstown), 370

DIETETICS/DIETITIANS
Illinois
Dominican University (River Forest), 131
Ohio
Cincinnati State Technical and Community College (Cincinnati), 315
Cuyahoga Community College (Cleveland), 318
Hocking College (Nelsonville), 321
Sinclair Community College (Dayton), 334
University of Cincinnati (Cincinnati), 338
Tennessee
Tennessee Technology Center at Elizabethton (Elizabethton), 416
West Virginia
West Virginia University Hospital–School of Radiology Technology (Morgantown), 444

DIETETIC TECHNICIAN (DTR)
Illinois
Harper College (Palatine), 135
Ohio
Cincinnati State Technical and Community College (Cincinnati), 315
Pennsylvania
Northampton County Area Community College (Bethlehem), 366

DIETITIAN ASSISTANT
Connecticut
Gateway Community College (New Haven), 52
Florida
Florida Community College at Jacksonville (Jacksonville), 77
Indian River State College (Fort Pierce), 81
Sarasota County Technical Institute (Sarasota), 96
Illinois
Lincoln Land Community College (Springfield), 141
Maryland
Baltimore City Community College (Baltimore), 185
New York
Nassau Community College (Garden City), 275
North Carolina
Gaston College (Dallas), 296
Pennsylvania
Community College of Allegheny County (Pittsburgh), 348
Harrisburg Area Community College (Harrisburg), 357

DIGITAL COMMUNICATION AND MEDIA/ MULTIMEDIA
Florida
Atlantic Vocational-Technical Center (Coconut Creek), 66
Lee County High Tech Center North (Cape Coral), 83
McFatter Technical Center (Davie), 86
Mid-Florida Tech (Orlando), 87
Orlando Technical Center (Orlando), 90
Sheridan Vocational-Technical Center (Hollywood), 96
Illinois
East-West University (Chicago), 132

Michigan
Oakland Community College (Bloomfield Hills), 224
Washtenaw Community College (Ann Arbor), 229
New York
Touro College (New York), 285
Pennsylvania
Kaplan Career Institute–Harrisburg (Harrisburg), 359
Tennessee
Visible School—Music and Worships Arts College (Lakeland), 420

DIVER, PROFESSIONAL AND INSTRUCTOR
Florida
Commercial Diving Academy (Jacksonville), 70
New Jersey
Divers Academy International (Camden), 244

DOG/PET/ANIMAL GROOMING
Florida
Florida Institute of Animal Arts (Winter Park), 77
Illinois
Lake Land College (Mattoon), 140

DRAFTING AND DESIGN TECHNOLOGY/ TECHNICIAN, GENERAL
Alabama
Bevill State Community College (Sumiton), 41
Bishop State Community College (Mobile), 41
Calhoun Community College (Decatur), 41
Central Alabama Community College (Alexander City), 42
Gadsden State Community College (Gadsden), 42
George Corley Wallace State Community College (Selma), 43
George C. Wallace Community College (Dothan), 43
H. Councill Trenholm State Technical College (Montgomery), 43
Jefferson Davis Community College (Brewton), 44
J. F. Drake State Technical College (Huntsville), 44
Lawson State Community College (Birmingham), 44
Lurleen B. Wallace Community College (Andalusia), 45
Northeast Alabama Community College (Rainsville), 45
Northwest-Shoals Community College (Muscle Shoals), 45
Shelton State Community College (Tuscaloosa), 46
Southern Union State Community College (Wadley), 47
Wallace State Community College (Hanceville), 48
Florida
Brevard Community College (Cocoa), 67
David G. Erwin Technical Center (Tampa), 71
Daytona State College (Daytona Beach), 72
Florida Community College at Jacksonville (Jacksonville), 77
Florida Technical College (Jacksonville), 78
Florida Technical College (Orlando), 78
Gulf Coast Community College (Panama City), 79
Hillsborough Community College (Tampa), 81
Miami Dade College (Miami), 87
Northwest Florida State College (Niceville), 89
Pasco-Hernando Community College (New Port Richey), 90

Pensacola Junior College (Pensacola), 91
St. Petersburg College (St. Petersburg), 94
Seminole Community College (Sanford), 96
Valencia Community College (Orlando), 101
Georgia
Albany Technical College (Albany), 103
Appalachian Technical College (Jasper), 104
Athens Technical College (Athens), 105
Atlanta Technical College (Atlanta), 105
Bainbridge College (Bainbridge), 106
Central Georgia Technical College (Macon), 107
Chattahoochee Technical College (Marietta), 107
Clayton State University (Morrow), 108
College of Coastal Georgia (Brunswick), 108
Columbus Technical College (Columbus), 108
Coosa Valley Technical College (Rome), 109
Dalton State College (Dalton), 109
DeKalb Technical College (Clarkston), 109
Gwinnett Technical College (Lawrenceville), 113
Lanier Technical College (Oakwood), 115
Middle Georgia Technical College (Warner Robbins), 117
Moultrie Technical College (Moultrie), 117
Northwestern Technical College (Rock Spring), 118
Ogeechee Technical College (Statesboro), 119
Okefenokee Technical College (Waycross), 119
Savannah Technical College (Savannah), 121
South Georgia Technical College (Americus), 122
Southwest Georgia Technical College (Thomasville), 122
Swainsboro Technical College (Swainsboro), 123
Valdosta Technical College (Valdosta), 123
West Georgia Technical College (LaGrange), 124
Illinois
Heartland Community College (Normal), 136
Kankakee Community College (Kankakee), 139
Robert Morris University (Chicago), 149
Sauk Valley Community College (Dixon), 150
Zarem/Golde ORT Technical Institute (Chicago), 154
Indiana
Ivy Tech Community College–Central Indiana (Indianapolis), 161
Ivy Tech Community College–Lafayette (Lafayette), 162
Ivy Tech Community College–North Central (South Bend), 162
Ivy Tech Community College–Northeast (Fort Wayne), 163
Ivy Tech Community College–Northwest (Gary), 163
Ivy Tech Community College–Southern Indiana (Sellersburg), 163
Kentucky
Ashland Community and Technical College (Ashland), 169
Big Sandy Community and Technical College (Prestonsburg), 170
Bluegrass Community and Technical College (Lexington), 170
Bowling Green Technical College (Bowling Green), 170
Elizabethtown Community and Technical College (Elizabethtown), 172
Hazard Community and Technical College (Hazard), 174
Hopkinsville Community College (Hopkinsville), 174
Owensboro Community and Technical College (Owensboro), 177

Somerset Community College (Somerset), 178
Southeast Kentucky Community and Technical College (Cumberland), 178
Spencerian College–Lexington (Lexington), 179
Sullivan College of Technology and Design (Louisville), 179
West Kentucky Community and Technical College (Paducah), 180

Maine
Kennebec Valley Community College (Fairfield), 181
Northern Maine Community College (Presque Isle), 182

Maryland
Anne Arundel Community College (Arnold), 184
Baltimore City Community College (Baltimore), 185
College of Southern Maryland (La Plata), 186
The Community College of Baltimore County (Baltimore), 187
Frederick Community College (Frederick), 188
Harford Community College (Bel Air), 189
Howard Community College (Columbia), 189
Prince George's Community College (Largo), 191
TESST College of Technology (Baltimore), 192

Massachusetts
Bristol Community College (Fall River), 196
Greenfield Community College (Greenfield), 198
Massachusetts Bay Community College (Wellesley Hills), 201

Michigan
Delta College (University Center), 213
Glen Oaks Community College (Centreville), 216
Kirtland Community College (Roscommon), 219
Michigan Technological University (Houghton), 222
Montcalm Community College (Sidney), 223
Mott Community College (Flint), 223
North Central Michigan College (Petoskey), 223
Schoolcraft College (Livonia), 227

Mississippi
Hinds Community College (Raymond), 232

New Jersey
Bergen Community College (Paramus), 240
Camden County College (Blackwood), 241
Cumberland County College (Vineland), 244
Essex County College (Newark), 244
Mercer County Community College (Trenton), 248
Ocean County Vocational Post Secondary Division (Toms River), 250
Somerset County Technical Institute (Bridgewater), 253

New York
Adirondack Community College (Queensbury), 255
Corning Community College (Corning), 263
Dutchess Community College (Poughkeepsie), 264
Genesee Community College (Batavia), 267
Hudson Valley Community College (Troy), 268
Island Drafting and Technical Institute (Amityville), 270
Jamestown Community College (Jamestown), 270
Niagara County Community College (Sanborn), 277
Rochester Institute of Technology (Rochester), 280

Rockland Community College (Suffern), 281
Suffolk County Community College (Selden), 284
Westchester Community College (Valhalla), 287

Ohio
Brown Mackie College–North Canton (Canton), 313
Clark State Community College (Springfield), 316
Hocking College (Nelsonville), 321
Lorain County Community College (Elyria), 324
North Central State College (Mansfield), 327
Shawnee State University (Portsmouth), 334
Sinclair Community College (Dayton), 334
The University of Akron (Akron), 338

Pennsylvania
Greater Altoona Career and Technology Center (Altoona), 356
Lancaster County Career and Technology Center (Willow Street), 360
Lebanon County Area Vocational Technical School (Lebanon), 361
Lehigh Carbon Community College (Schnecksville), 362
Lincoln Technical Institute (Allentown), 362
Schuylkill Technology Center–North Campus (Frackville), 373

Puerto Rico
D'mart Institute (Barranquitas), 383
Instituto de Banca y Comercio–Aprendes Practicanco (Río Piedras), 386
Instituto Pre-Vocacional E Indust de Puerto Rico (Arecibo), 387
Universidad Metropolitana (San Juan), 394

Tennessee
Chattanooga State Technical Community College (Chattanooga), 406
Nashville State Technical Community College (Nashville), 411
Tennessee Technology Center at Crossville (Crossville), 415
Tennessee Technology Center at Crump (Crump), 415
Tennessee Technology Center at Hartsville (Hartsville), 416
Tennessee Technology Center at Hohenwald (Hohenwald), 416
Tennessee Technology Center at Jacksboro (Jacksboro), 416
Tennessee Technology Center at Jackson (Jackson), 417
Tennessee Technology Center at Knoxville (Knoxville), 417
Tennessee Technology Center at McKenzie (McKenzie), 417
Tennessee Technology Center at Memphis (Memphis), 417
Tennessee Technology Center at Morristown (Morristown), 418
Tennessee Technology Center at Murfreesboro (Murfreesboro), 418
Tennessee Technology Center at Nashville (Nashville), 418
Tennessee Technology Center at Newbern (Newbern), 418
Tennessee Technology Center at Oneida/ Huntsville (Huntsville), 419
Tennessee Technology Center at Ripley (Ripley), 419
Tennessee Technology Center at Shelbyville (Shelbyville), 419
Tennessee Technology Center at Whiteville (Whiteville), 419

West Virginia
Academy of Careers and Technology (Beckley), 437
Carver Career Center (Charleston), 438

DRAFTING/DESIGN ENGINEERING TECHNOLOGIES/TECHNICIANS, OTHER

Connecticut
Connecticut School of Electronics (Branford), 52

Delaware
Delaware Technical & Community College, Jack F. Owens Campus (Georgetown), 59
Delaware Technical & Community College, Stanton/Wilmington Campus (Newark), 59

Florida
Lee County High Tech Center North (Cape Coral), 83
Sheridan Vocational-Technical Center (Hollywood), 96

Maryland
Chesapeake College (Wye Mills), 186

Massachusetts
Northern Essex Community College (Haverhill), 204

Michigan
Kirtland Community College (Roscommon), 219
Washtenaw Community College (Ann Arbor), 229

Mississippi
Mississippi Gulf Coast Community College (Perkinston), 234

New Jersey
Pennco Tech (Blackwood), 251

New York
Island Drafting and Technical Institute (Amityville), 270

Puerto Rico
Universal Technology College of Puerto Rico (Aguadilla), 393

DRAMA AND DANCE TEACHER EDUCATION

Massachusetts
Northern Essex Community College (Haverhill), 204

DRAMA AND DRAMATICS/THEATRE ARTS, GENERAL

Maryland
Baltimore City Community College (Baltimore), 185

Ohio
Kent State University (Kent), 322

DRAMATIC/THEATRE ARTS AND STAGECRAFT, OTHER

District of Columbia
National Conservatory of Dramatic Arts (Washington), 62

DRAWING

District of Columbia
Corcoran College of Art and Design (Washington), 61

Ohio
Sinclair Community College (Dayton), 334

DRYWALL INSTALLATION/DRYWALLER

Wisconsin
Milwaukee Area Technical College (Milwaukee), 449

EARLY CHILDHOOD EDUCATION AND TEACHING

Delaware
Delaware Technical & Community College, Jack F. Owens Campus (Georgetown), 59
Delaware Technical & Community College, Stanton/Wilmington Campus (Newark), 59
Delaware Technical & Community College, Terry Campus (Dover), 60

Florida
Henry W. Brewster Technical Center (Tampa), 80
Lindsey Hopkins Technical Education Center (Miami), 84
Manatee Technical Institute (Bradenton), 85
Robert Morgan Vocational-Technical Center (Miami), 94
Sarasota County Technical Institute (Sarasota), 96
Sheridan Vocational-Technical Center (Hollywood), 96
Tom P. Haney Technical Center (Panama City), 99
Withlacoochee Technical Institute (Inverness), 103

Georgia
Albany Technical College (Albany), 103
Altamaha Technical College (Jesup), 104
Appalachian Technical College (Jasper), 104
Athens Technical College (Athens), 105
Atlanta Technical College (Atlanta), 105
Augusta Technical College (Augusta), 106
Central Georgia Technical College (Macon), 107
Chattahoochee Technical College (Marietta), 107
Columbus Technical College (Columbus), 108
Coosa Valley Technical College (Rome), 109
DeKalb Technical College (Clarkston), 109
East Central Technical College (Fitzgerald), 110
Flint River Technical College (Thomaston), 111
Griffin Technical College (Griffin), 113
Gwinnett Technical College (Lawrenceville), 113
Heart of Georgia Technical College (Dublin), 114
Lanier Technical College (Oakwood), 115
Middle Georgia Technical College (Warner Robbins), 117
Moultrie Technical College (Moultrie), 117
North Georgia Technical College (Clarkesville), 118
North Metro Technical College (Acworth), 118
Northwestern Technical College (Rock Spring), 118
Ogeechee Technical College (Statesboro), 119
Okefenokee Technical College (Waycross), 119
Sandersville Technical College (Sandersville), 120
Savannah Technical College (Savannah), 121
Southeastern Technical College (Vidalia), 121
South Georgia Technical College (Americus), 122
Southwest Georgia Technical College (Thomasville), 122
Swainsboro Technical College (Swainsboro), 123
Valdosta Technical College (Valdosta), 123
West Central Technical College (Waco), 124
West Georgia Technical College (LaGrange), 124

Illinois
College of Lake County (Grayslake), 129
St. Augustine College (Chicago), 150
Shawnee Community College (Ullin), 150

Indiana
Ancilla College (Donaldson), 155
Ivy Tech Community College–Bloomington (Bloomington), 161
Ivy Tech Community College–Columbus (Columbus), 162
Ivy Tech Community College–East Central (Muncie), 162
Ivy Tech Community College–Kokomo (Kokomo), 162
Ivy Tech Community College–North Central (South Bend), 162
Ivy Tech Community College–Northeast (Fort Wayne), 163
Ivy Tech Community College–Northwest (Gary), 163
Ivy Tech Community College–Southern Indiana (Sellersburg), 163
Ivy Tech Community College–Southwest (Evansville), 163
Ivy Tech Community College–Wabash Valley (Terre Haute), 164

Maine
Beal College (Bangor), 180
Eastern Maine Community College (Bangor), 181

Maryland
Frederick Community College (Frederick), 188

Massachusetts
Berkshire Community College (Pittsfield), 194
Bunker Hill Community College (Boston), 196
Cape Cod Community College (West Barnstable), 196
Fisher College (Boston), 198
Northern Essex Community College (Haverhill), 204
Quincy College (Quincy), 204
Urban College of Boston (Boston), 208

Michigan
Lake Michigan College (Benton Harbor), 219
Mid Michigan Community College (Harrison), 222
Muskegon Community College (Muskegon), 223
North Central Michigan College (Petoskey), 223

New Hampshire
Manchester Community College (Manchester), 237
New Hampshire Community Technical College, Berlin/Laconia (Berlin), 238
New Hampshire Community Technical College, Nashua/Claremont (Nashua), 238
New Hampshire Community Technical College, Stratham (Stratham), 239
New Hampshire Technical Institute (Concord), 239

North Carolina
Alamance Community College (Graham), 288
Asheville-Buncombe Technical Community College (Asheville), 288
Beaufort County Community College (Washington), 289
Bladen Community College (Dublin), 289
Blue Ridge Community College (Flat Rock), 289
Cape Fear Community College (Wilmington), 290
Carteret Community College (Morehead City), 292
Catawba Valley Community College (Hickory), 292
Central Carolina Community College (Sanford), 292
Central Piedmont Community College (Charlotte), 293
Cleveland Community College (Shelby), 293
Coastal Carolina Community College (Jacksonville), 293
College of The Albemarle (Elizabeth City), 294
Craven Community College (New Bern), 294
Davidson County Community College (Lexington), 294
Durham Technical Community College (Durham), 295
Fayetteville Technical Community College (Fayetteville), 295
Forsyth Technical Community College (Winston-Salem), 296
Gaston College (Dallas), 296
Guilford Technical Community College (Jamestown), 297
Isothermal Community College (Spindale), 298
James Sprunt Community College (Kenansville), 298
Johnston Community College (Smithfield), 298
Lenoir Community College (Kinston), 299
Martin Community College (Williamston), 299
McDowell Technical Community College (Marion), 300
Mitchell Community College (Statesville), 300
Montgomery Community College (Troy), 301
Nash Community College (Rocky Mount), 302
Pamlico Community College (Grantsboro), 302
Pitt Community College (Greenville), 303
Randolph Community College (Asheboro), 303
Richmond Community College (Hamlet), 303
Rockingham Community College (Wentworth), 304
Rowan-Cabarrus Community College (Salisbury), 304
Sampson Community College (Clinton), 304
Sandhills Community College (Pinehurst), 305
Southeastern Community College (Whiteville), 305
South Piedmont Community College (Polkton), 305
Southwestern Community College (Sylva), 306
Stanly Community College (Albemarle), 306
Surry Community College (Dobson), 306
Wake Technical Community College (Raleigh), 307
Wayne Community College (Goldsboro), 308
Wilkes Community College (Wilkesboro), 308
Wilson Community College (Wilson), 308

Ohio
Clark State Community College (Springfield), 316
Cuyahoga Community College (Cleveland), 318
Lorain County Community College (Elyria), 324
Sinclair Community College (Dayton), 334
The University of Akron (Akron), 338

Pennsylvania
Lehigh Carbon Community College (Schnecksville), 362
Point Park University (Pittsburgh), 371

Rhode Island
Community College of Rhode Island (Warwick), 394

Tennessee
Tennessee Technology Center at Hohenwald (Hohenwald), 416

West Virginia
Ben Franklin Career Center (Dunbar), 437

EAST ASIAN STUDIES

Ohio
Ohio University (Athens), 330

ECOLOGY

New York
Rochester Institute of Technology (Rochester), 280

Ecology

Ohio
Shawnee State University (Portsmouth), 334

E-COMMERCE/ELECTRONIC COMMERCE

Florida
Miami Lakes Technical Education Center (Miami), 87
Pinellas Technical Education Center–Clearwater (Clearwater), 91

Georgia
South Georgia Technical College (Americus), 122

Illinois
Danville Area Community College (Danville), 131
Illinois Central College (East Peoria), 136
Moraine Valley Community College (Palos Hills), 143
Prairie State College (Chicago Heights), 146

Kentucky
Draughons Junior College (Bowling Green), 172

Massachusetts
Holyoke Community College (Holyoke), 199

Michigan
Ferris State University (Big Rapids), 215
Lansing Community College (Lansing), 219
Madonna University (Livonia), 221

New Jersey
Brookdale Community College (Lincroft), 241

North Carolina
Catawba Valley Community College (Hickory), 292
Halifax Community College (Weldon), 297
Lenoir Community College (Kinston), 299
Martin Community College (Williamston), 299
Piedmont Community College (Roxboro), 302
Southeastern Community College (Whiteville), 305
Wake Technical Community College (Raleigh), 307

Pennsylvania
Bucks County Community College (Newtown), 345
Community College of Allegheny County (Pittsburgh), 348
Community College of Beaver County (Monaca), 349
Delaware County Community College (Media), 351
Penn State Erie, The Behrend College (Erie), 368

Tennessee
Draughons Junior College (Nashville), 407

Vermont
Marlboro College Graduate Center (Brattleboro), 422

West Virginia
Putnam Career and Technology Center School of Practical Nursing (Eleanor), 443

ECONOMICS, GENERAL

Pennsylvania
Muhlenberg College (Allentown), 365

EDUCATIONAL ADMINISTRATION AND SUPERVISION, OTHER

Delaware
Delaware Technical & Community College, Jack F. Owens Campus (Georgetown), 59
Delaware Technical & Community College, Terry Campus (Dover), 60

EDUCATIONAL/INSTRUCTIONAL MEDIA DESIGN

Connecticut
Middlesex Community College (Middletown), 54
Northwestern Connecticut Community College (Winsted), 55

Georgia
Southwest Georgia Technical College (Thomasville), 122

Maryland
The Community College of Baltimore County (Baltimore), 187

Massachusetts
Bridgewater State College (Bridgewater), 195

New Jersey
Warren County Community College (Washington), 255

West Virginia
American Public University System (Charles Town), 437

EDUCATION, GENERAL

Georgia
Abraham Baldwin Agricultural College (Tifton), 103

Maryland
Baltimore City Community College (Baltimore), 185
Chesapeake College (Wye Mills), 186
Hagerstown Community College (Hagerstown), 188

Michigan
Schoolcraft College (Livonia), 227

New Hampshire
New Hampshire Technical Institute (Concord), 239

New York
Graduate School and University Center of the City University of New York (New York), 268

North Carolina
Guilford Technical Community College (Jamestown), 297
Richmond Community College (Hamlet), 303

Pennsylvania
Bucks County Community College (Newtown), 345
Lehigh Carbon Community College (Schnecksville), 362

Vermont
Johnson State College (Johnson), 422

EDUCATION, OTHER

Connecticut
Saint Joseph College (West Hartford), 57

Delaware
Delaware Technical & Community College, Jack F. Owens Campus (Georgetown), 59
Delaware Technical & Community College, Stanton/Wilmington Campus (Newark), 59
Delaware Technical & Community College, Terry Campus (Dover), 60

Illinois
Niles School of Cosmetology (Niles), 144

Indiana
Ravenscroft Beauty College (Fort Wayne), 166

Maryland
Anne Arundel Community College (Arnold), 184
Chesapeake College (Wye Mills), 186

Massachusetts
Bristol Community College (Fall River), 196

Michigan
Chic University of Cosmetology (Grand Rapids), 212

New Hampshire
Hesser College, Manchester (Manchester), 237
Lebanon College (Lebanon), 237

New York
Touro College (New York), 285

North Carolina
Guilford Technical Community College (Jamestown), 297
Isothermal Community College (Spindale), 298
Lenoir Community College (Kinston), 299
Southwestern Community College (Sylva), 306

Ohio
The University of Akron (Akron), 338
The University of Akron–Wayne College (Orrville), 338

Pennsylvania
King's College (Wilkes-Barre), 359

EDUCATION/TEACHING OF INDIVIDUALS WITH HEARING IMPAIRMENTS, INCLUDING DEAFNESS

Florida
Miami Dade College (Miami), 87

Maryland
Frederick Community College (Frederick), 188

Ohio
University of Cincinnati (Cincinnati), 338

ELECTRICAL AND ELECTRONIC ENGINEERING TECHNOLOGIES/TECHNICIANS, OTHER

Connecticut
Northwestern Connecticut Community College (Winsted), 55

Delaware
Delaware Technical & Community College, Jack F. Owens Campus (Georgetown), 59
Delaware Technical & Community College, Stanton/Wilmington Campus (Newark), 59

Florida
Brevard Community College (Cocoa), 67
Manatee Technical Institute (Bradenton), 85
Miami Lakes Technical Education Center (Miami), 87

Kentucky
Daymar College (Paducah), 172

Massachusetts
Northern Essex Community College (Haverhill), 204

Michigan
Everest Institute (Southfield), 215

North Carolina
Rockingham Community College (Wentworth), 304

Ohio
Cincinnati State Technical and Community College (Cincinnati), 315
Clark State Community College (Springfield), 316
Columbus State Community College (Columbus), 317
Marion Technical College (Marion), 325

Pennsylvania
Lincoln Technical Institute (Allentown), 362

Puerto Rico
Escuela Tecnica de Electricidad (Ponce), 385
Instituto de Banca y Comercio–Aprendes Practicanco (Río Piedras), 386
Serbias School of Beauty Culture (Guayama), 393

South Carolina
Northeastern Technical College (Cheraw), 401
Spartanburg Community College (Spartanburg), 403
Technical College of the Lowcountry (Beaufort), 403
Tri-County Technical College (Pendleton), 403
Trident Technical College (Charleston), 404
York Technical College (Rock Hill), 405

Tennessee
Tennessee Technology Center at Pulaski (Pulaski), 419

ELECTRICAL AND POWER TRANSMISSION INSTALLATION/INSTALLER, GENERAL

Connecticut
Lincoln Technical Institute (Hamden), 54

Florida
Lindsey Hopkins Technical Education Center (Miami), 84
Manatee Technical Institute (Bradenton), 85

Illinois
Illinois Eastern Community Colleges, Frontier Community College (Fairfield), 137
Richland Community College (Decatur), 148

Maryland
North American Trade Schools (Grantsville), 191

Michigan
Lansing Community College (Lansing), 219

New York
Berk Trade and Business School (New York), 258
Mohawk Valley Community College (Utica), 274
State University of New York College of Technology at Canton (Canton), 284
State University of New York College of Technology at Delhi (Delhi), 284

Ohio
Licking County Joint Vocational School–Newark (Newark), 324
Warren County Career Center (Lebanon), 340

Tennessee
Tennessee Technology Center at Crump (Crump), 415
Tennessee Technology Center at Nashville (Nashville), 418

West Virginia
Carver Career Center (Charleston), 438

Wisconsin
Milwaukee Area Technical College (Milwaukee), 449
Moraine Park Technical College (Fond du Lac), 450

ELECTRICAL AND POWER TRANSMISSION INSTALLERS, OTHER

Connecticut
Lincoln Technical Institute (New Britain), 54
Lincoln Technical Institute (Shelton), 54

Pennsylvania
Huntingdon County Career and Technology (Mill Creek), 358
Lancaster County Career and Technology Center (Willow Street), 360
Lebanon County Area Vocational Technical School (Lebanon), 361

ELECTRICAL, ELECTRONIC AND COMMUNICATIONS ENGINEERING TECHNOLOGY/TECHNICIAN

Alabama
Bishop State Community College (Mobile), 41
Calhoun Community College (Decatur), 41

Gadsden State Community College (Gadsden), 42
Lawson State Community College (Birmingham), 44

Delaware
Delaware Technical & Community College, Jack F. Owens Campus (Georgetown), 59
Delaware Technical & Community College, Stanton/Wilmington Campus (Newark), 59
Delaware Technical & Community College, Terry Campus (Dover), 60

Florida
Charlotte Vocational-Technical Center (Port Charlotte), 69
Daytona State College (Daytona Beach), 72
Florida Career Institute (Lakeland), 76
Florida Community College at Jacksonville (Jacksonville), 77
Hillsborough Community College (Tampa), 81
Indian River State College (Fort Pierce), 81
Lake-Sumter Community College (Leesburg), 83
Lindsey Hopkins Technical Education Center (Miami), 84
Lively Technical Center (Tallahassee), 84
Manatee Technical Institute (Bradenton), 85
Mid-Florida Tech (Orlando), 87
Okaloosa Applied Technology Center (Ft. Walton Beach), 89
Palm Beach Community College (Lake Worth), 90
Pensacola Junior College (Pensacola), 91
Pinellas Technical Education Center–Clearwater (Clearwater), 91
Remington College–Tampa Campus (Tampa), 93
St. Petersburg College (St. Petersburg), 94
Seminole Community College (Sanford), 96
Sheridan Vocational-Technical Center (Hollywood), 96
South Florida Community College (Avon Park), 97
Tom P. Haney Technical Center (Panama City), 99
Valencia Community College (Orlando), 101

Georgia
Swainsboro Technical College (Swainsboro), 123

Illinois
College of Lake County (Grayslake), 129
East-West University (Chicago), 132
Heartland Community College (Normal), 136
Illinois Central College (East Peoria), 136
John A. Logan College (Carterville), 138
Kaskaskia College (Centralia), 139
Kishwaukee College (Malta), 140
Lincoln Land Community College (Springfield), 141
Moraine Valley Community College (Palos Hills), 143
Rend Lake College (Ina), 148
South Suburban College (South Holland), 151
Southwestern Illinois College (Belleville), 151
Spoon River College (Canton), 152
Taylor Business Institute (Chicago), 152
Waubonsee Community College (Sugar Grove), 154

Indiana
Indiana University–Purdue University Fort Wayne (Fort Wayne), 160
Purdue University (West Lafayette), 166
Purdue University Calumet (Hammond), 166
Vincennes University (Vincennes), 168

Kentucky
Daymar College (Paducah), 172

Maryland
Anne Arundel Community College (Arnold), 184
Baltimore City Community College (Baltimore), 185
Cecil College (North East), 186
College of Southern Maryland (La Plata), 186
Howard Community College (Columbia), 189
Prince George's Community College (Largo), 191
TESST College of Technology (Beltsville), 192
TESST College of Technology (Towson), 192
Wor-Wic Community College (Salisbury), 193

Massachusetts
Kaplan Career Institute, Charlestown (Charlestown), 199
Middlesex Community College (Bedford), 202
Northeastern University (Boston), 204
Quinsigamond Community College (Worcester), 205

Michigan
Davenport University (Grand Rapids), 213
Glen Oaks Community College (Centreville), 216
Henry Ford Community College (Dearborn), 217
Kalamazoo Valley Community College (Kalamazoo), 218
Kirtland Community College (Roscommon), 219
Macomb Community College (Warren), 220
Muskegon Community College (Muskegon), 223
Oakland Community College (Bloomfield Hills), 224
St. Clair County Community College (Port Huron), 226
Schoolcraft College (Livonia), 227
Southwestern Michigan College (Dowagiac), 227
Wayne County Community College District (Detroit), 229

Mississippi
Hinds Community College (Raymond), 232

New Hampshire
New Hampshire Technical Institute (Concord), 239

New Jersey
HoHoKus RETS School of Business and Medical Technical Services (Nutley), 246
Lincoln Technical Institute (Union), 248
Ocean County Vocational Post Secondary Division (Toms River), 250
Thomas Edison State College (Trenton), 254

New York
Bramson ORT College (Forest Hills), 258
Cayuga County Community College (Auburn), 261
Farmingdale State College (Farmingdale), 266
Island Drafting and Technical Institute (Amityville), 270
TCI–The College of Technology (New York), 285

North Carolina
Alamance Community College (Graham), 288
Beaufort County Community College (Washington), 289
Blue Ridge Community College (Flat Rock), 289
Caldwell Community College and Technical Institute (Hudson), 290
Cape Fear Community College (Wilmington), 290
Central Carolina Community College (Sanford), 292

Central Piedmont Community College (Charlotte), 293
Cleveland Community College (Shelby), 293
Craven Community College (New Bern), 294
Davidson County Community College (Lexington), 294
Durham Technical Community College (Durham), 295
Edgecombe Community College (Tarboro), 295
Forsyth Technical Community College (Winston-Salem), 296
Gaston College (Dallas), 296
Guilford Technical Community College (Jamestown), 297
Halifax Community College (Weldon), 297
Haywood Community College (Clyde), 297
Lenoir Community College (Kinston), 299
Mayland Community College (Spruce Pine), 299
Mitchell Community College (Statesville), 300
Nash Community College (Rocky Mount), 302
Pitt Community College (Greenville), 303
Rockingham Community College (Wentworth), 304
Stanly Community College (Albemarle), 306
Wake Technical Community College (Raleigh), 307
Wilkes Community College (Wilkesboro), 308

Ohio
Buckeye Joint Vocational School (New Philadelphia), 313
Cleveland Institute of Electronics (Cleveland), 316
ETI Technical College of Niles (Niles), 319
Hocking College (Nelsonville), 321
Lakeland Community College (Kirtland), 323
Lorain County Community College (Elyria), 324
Marion Technical College (Marion), 325
Northwest State Community College (Archbold), 327
Owens Community College (Toledo), 330
Remington College–Cleveland Campus (Cleveland), 333
Sinclair Community College (Dayton), 334
Terra State Community College (Fremont), 336
The University of Akron (Akron), 338

Pennsylvania
Bucks County Community College (Newtown), 345
Lebanon County Area Vocational Technical School (Lebanon), 361
Luzerne County Community College (Nanticoke), 363
Schuylkill Technology Center–North Campus (Frackville), 373
YTI Career Institute–York (York), 379

Puerto Rico
Caguas Institute of Mechanical Technology (Caguas), 381
Huertas Junior College (Caguas), 385
Inter American University of Puerto Rico, San Germán Campus (San Germán), 389
John Dewey College, 389
Universal Technology College of Puerto Rico (Aguadilla), 393

Rhode Island
Community College of Rhode Island (Warwick), 394

South Carolina
Aiken Technical College (Aiken), 397
Florence-Darlington Technical College (Florence), 399
Midlands Technical College (Columbia), 401
Trident Technical College (Charleston), 404
York Technical College (Rock Hill), 405

Tennessee
Southwest Tennessee Community College (Memphis), 414

Virginia
Dabney S. Lancaster Community College (Clifton Forge), 426
Danville Community College (Danville), 426
Eastern Shore Community College (Melfa), 426
Germanna Community College (Locust Grove), 428
J. Sargeant Reynolds Community College (Richmond), 429
Northern Virginia Community College (Annandale), 430
Southside Virginia Community College (Alberta), 432
Southwest Virginia Community College (Richlands), 432
Tidewater Community College (Norfolk), 434

West Virginia
Everest Institute (Cross Lanes), 439
Southern West Virginia Community and Technical College (Mount Gay), 443

Wisconsin
Chippewa Valley Technical College (Eau Claire), 445

ELECTRICAL, ELECTRONICS AND COMMUNICATIONS ENGINEERING

Kentucky
Brown Mackie College–Louisville (Louisville), 171

Michigan
Michigan Technological University (Houghton), 222

North Carolina
Central Piedmont Community College (Charlotte), 293

Ohio
Cleveland Institute of Electronics (Cleveland), 316
Lorain County Community College (Elyria), 324

Pennsylvania
Pace Institute (Reading), 367

Puerto Rico
Humacao Community College (Humacao), 385

ELECTRICAL/ELECTRONICS DRAFTING AND ELECTRICAL/ELECTRONICS CAD/CADD

Florida
Sheridan Vocational-Technical Center (Hollywood), 96

Illinois
Kaskaskia College (Centralia), 139

Massachusetts
Middlesex Community College (Bedford), 202
Suffolk University (Boston), 207

Puerto Rico
Carib Technological Institute (Bayamón), 381

ELECTRICAL/ELECTRONICS EQUIPMENT INSTALLATION AND REPAIR, GENERAL

Alabama
Jefferson Davis Community College (Brewton), 44

Connecticut
Baran Institute of Technology (Windsor), 49
Connecticut School of Electronics (Branford), 52
Industrial Management Training Institute (Waterbury), 53

Florida
David G. Erwin Technical Center (Tampa), 71
Lee County High Tech Center North (Cape Coral), 83
Okaloosa Applied Technology Center (Ft. Walton Beach), 89
South Florida Institute of Technology (Miami), 97

Georgia
Albany Technical College (Albany), 103
Altamaha Technical College (Jesup), 104
Appalachian Technical College (Jasper), 104
Athens Technical College (Athens), 105
Central Georgia Technical College (Macon), 107
Dalton State College (Dalton), 109
DeKalb Technical College (Clarkston), 109
Flint River Technical College (Thomaston), 111
Heart of Georgia Technical College (Dublin), 114
Lanier Technical College (Oakwood), 115
Middle Georgia Technical College (Warner Robbins), 117
Moultrie Technical College (Moultrie), 117
North Metro Technical College (Acworth), 118
Northwestern Technical College (Rock Spring), 118
Okefenokee Technical College (Waycross), 119
Southeastern Technical College (Vidalia), 121
South Georgia Technical College (Americus), 122
Southwest Georgia Technical College (Thomasville), 122
West Georgia Technical College (LaGrange), 124

Illinois
Harper College (Palatine), 135

Indiana
Brown Mackie College–South Bend (South Bend), 156
Lincoln Technical Institute (Indianapolis), 165

Maryland
Lincoln Technical Institute (Columbia), 189
North American Trade Schools (Grantsville), 191

Massachusetts
Bay State School of Technology (Canton), 194

Michigan
Macomb Community College (Warren), 220

New Jersey
Lincoln Technical Institute (Mahwah), 248
Lincoln Technical Institute (Union), 248

New York
Erie Community College (Buffalo), 265

Ohio
Auburn Career Center (Painesville), 311
Ohio Technical College (Cleveland), 329

Pennsylvania
New Castle School of Trades (Pulaski), 366
Pittsburgh Technical Institute (Oakdale), 371

Puerto Rico
International Technical College (San Juan), 389

South Carolina
Central Carolina Technical College (Sumter), 398
Piedmont Technical College (Greenwood), 402

Tennessee
Tennessee Technology Center at Athens (Athens), 415
Tennessee Technology Center at Crump (Crump), 415
Tennessee Technology Center at Elizabethton (Elizabethton), 416

Tennessee Technology Center at Jacksboro (Jacksboro), 416

Tennessee Technology Center at Jackson (Jackson), 417

Tennessee Technology Center at Livingston (Livingston), 417

Tennessee Technology Center at McKenzie (McKenzie), 417

Tennessee Technology Center at Nashville (Nashville), 418

Tennessee Technology Center at Newbern (Newbern), 418

Tennessee Technology Center at Shelbyville (Shelbyville), 419

West Virginia

Ben Franklin Career Center (Dunbar), 437

ELECTRICAL/ELECTRONICS MAINTENANCE AND REPAIR TECHNOLOGY, OTHER

Connecticut

Porter and Chester Institute (Stratford), 56

Florida

Brevard Community College (Cocoa), 67

College of Business and Technology–Flagler Campus (Miami), 70

College of Business and Technology (Miami), 70

Lee County Vocational High Tech Center–Central (Fort Myers), 84

Southern Technical Institute (Winter Park), 97

Georgia

Central Georgia Technical College (Macon), 107

New Horizons Computer Learning Centers (Atlanta), 117

Indiana

Lincoln Technical Institute (Indianapolis), 165

Michigan

Grand Rapids Community College (Grand Rapids), 216

North Carolina

Central Carolina Community College (Sanford), 292

Coastal Carolina Community College (Jacksonville), 293

Johnston Community College (Smithfield), 298

Pitt Community College (Greenville), 303

Wake Technical Community College (Raleigh), 307

Ohio

Total Technical Institute (Brooklyn), 337

Pennsylvania

New Castle School of Trades (Pulaski), 366

Pennco Tech (Bristol), 368

Puerto Rico

International Technical College (San Juan), 389

Rhode Island

Lincoln Technical Institute (Lincoln), 395

Tennessee

Tennessee Technology Center at Jacksboro (Jacksboro), 416

Virginia

Danville Community College (Danville), 426

Southwest Virginia Community College (Richlands), 432

West Virginia

Cabell County Vocational Technical Center (Huntington), 438

ELECTRICIAN

Alabama

Bevill State Community College (Sumiton), 41

Bishop State Community College (Mobile), 41

Calhoun Community College (Decatur), 41

George Corley Wallace State Community College (Selma), 43

George C. Wallace Community College (Dothan), 43

H. Councill Trenholm State Technical College (Montgomery), 43

Jefferson Davis Community College (Brewton), 44

J. F. Drake State Technical College (Huntsville), 44

Lawson State Community College (Birmingham), 44

Northwest-Shoals Community College (Muscle Shoals), 45

Shelton State Community College (Tuscaloosa), 46

Connecticut

Baran Institute of Technology (Windsor), 49

Industrial Management Training Institute (Waterbury), 53

Lincoln Technical Institute (Hamden), 54

Lincoln Technical Institute (New Britain), 54

Lincoln Technical Institute (Shelton), 54

Porter and Chester Institute (Stratford), 56

Florida

Atlantic Vocational-Technical Center (Coconut Creek), 66

David G. Erwin Technical Center (Tampa), 71

Florida Community College at Jacksonville (Jacksonville), 77

George Stone Area Vocational-Technical Center (Pensacola), 79

Lee County Vocational High Tech Center–Central (Fort Myers), 84

Lindsey Hopkins Technical Education Center (Miami), 84

Lively Technical Center (Tallahassee), 84

Manatee Technical Institute (Bradenton), 85

Mid-Florida Tech (Orlando), 87

Okaloosa Applied Technology Center (Ft. Walton Beach), 89

Palm Beach Community College (Lake Worth), 90

Pensacola Junior College (Pensacola), 91

Pinellas Technical Education Center–Clearwater (Clearwater), 91

Pinellas Technical Education Center–St. Petersburg (St. Petersburg), 92

Radford M. Locklin Technical Center (Milton), 92

Ridge Technical Center (Winter Haven), 93

Tom P. Haney Technical Center (Panama City), 99

Traviss Technical Center (Lakeland), 99

Washington-Holmes Technical Center (Chipley), 102

Westside Tech (Winter Garden), 102

Withlacoochee Technical Institute (Inverness), 103

Georgia

Albany Technical College (Albany), 103

Altamaha Technical College (Jesup), 104

Athens Technical College (Athens), 105

Atlanta Technical College (Atlanta), 105

Augusta Technical College (Augusta), 106

Bainbridge College (Bainbridge), 106

Central Georgia Technical College (Macon), 107

Chattahoochee Technical College (Marietta), 107

Coosa Valley Technical College (Rome), 109

East Central Technical College (Fitzgerald), 110

Flint River Technical College (Thomaston), 111

Griffin Technical College (Griffin), 113

Heart of Georgia Technical College (Dublin), 114

Lanier Technical College (Oakwood), 115

Moultrie Technical College (Moultrie), 117

North Georgia Technical College (Clarkesville), 118

Ogeechee Technical College (Statesboro), 119

Okefenokee Technical College (Waycross), 119

Sandersville Technical College (Sandersville), 120

Savannah Technical College (Savannah), 121

Southeastern Technical College (Vidalia), 121

South Georgia Technical College (Americus), 122

Southwest Georgia Technical College (Thomasville), 122

Swainsboro Technical College (Swainsboro), 123

Valdosta Technical College (Valdosta), 123

West Central Technical College (Waco), 124

Illinois

Coyne American Institute Incorporated (Chicago), 131

Illinois Valley Community College (Oglesby), 138

John Wood Community College (Quincy), 139

Joliet Junior College (Joliet), 139

Kishwaukee College (Malta), 140

Lewis and Clark Community College (Godfrey), 141

Prairie State College (Chicago Heights), 146

Southwestern Illinois College (Belleville), 151

Triton College (River Grove), 153

Vatterott College (Quincy), 154

Waubonsee Community College (Sugar Grove), 154

Indiana

Ivy Tech Community College–East Central (Muncie), 162

Ivy Tech Community College–Lafayette (Lafayette), 162

Ivy Tech Community College–Northeast (Fort Wayne), 163

Ivy Tech Community College–Northwest (Gary), 163

Kentucky

Ashland Community and Technical College (Ashland), 169

Big Sandy Community and Technical College (Prestonsburg), 170

Bluegrass Community and Technical College (Lexington), 170

Bowling Green Technical College (Bowling Green), 170

Elizabethtown Community and Technical College (Elizabethtown), 172

Gateway Community and Technical College (Covington), 173

Hazard Community and Technical College (Hazard), 174

Hopkinsville Community College (Hopkinsville), 174

Jefferson Community and Technical College (Louisville), 175

Madisonville Community College (Madisonville), 176

Maysville Community and Technical College (Maysville), 176

Owensboro Community and Technical College (Owensboro), 177

Somerset Community College (Somerset), 178

Southeast Kentucky Community and Technical College (Cumberland), 178

West Kentucky Community and Technical College (Paducah), 180

Maine

Eastern Maine Community College (Bangor), 181

Kennebec Valley Community College (Fairfield), 181

Putnam Career and Technology Center School of Practical Nursing (Eleanor), 443

Wisconsin
Blackhawk Technical College (Janesville), 445
Chippewa Valley Technical College (Eau Claire), 445
Fox Valley Technical College (Appleton), 446
Gateway Technical College (Kenosha), 446
Mid-State Technical College (Wisconsin Rapids), 449
Milwaukee Area Technical College (Milwaukee), 449
Northeast Wisconsin Technical College (Green Bay), 450
Southwest Wisconsin Technical College (Fennimore), 452
Waukesha County Technical College (Pewaukee), 453

ELECTROCARDIOGRAPH TECHNOLOGY/ TECHNICIAN

Florida
Atlantic Vocational-Technical Center (Coconut Creek), 66
David G. Erwin Technical Center (Tampa), 71
Health Opportunity Technical Center (Miami Gardens), 80
Lively Technical Center (Tallahassee), 84
Winter Park Tech (Winter Park), 102

Georgia
Griffin Technical College (Griffin), 113

Illinois
College of DuPage (Glen Ellyn), 129
Joliet Junior College (Joliet), 139

Massachusetts
Medical Professional Institute (Malden), 202

Michigan
Baker College of Auburn Hills (Auburn Hills), 209
Baker College of Cadillac (Cadillac), 210
Baker College of Owosso (Owosso), 211
Baker College of Port Huron (Port Huron), 211
Carnegie Institute (Troy), 212
Monroe County Community College (Monroe), 222

New Jersey
Healthcare Training Institute (Union), 246
The Institute for Health Education (Fairfield), 247

Ohio
Hocking College (Nelsonville), 321
O. C. Collins Career Center (Chesapeake), 328
Sinclair Community College (Dayton), 334
The University of Toledo (Toledo), 339

Virginia
Ferrum College (Ferrum), 428

West Virginia
Opportunities Industrialization Center–North Central West Virginia (Fairmont), 442

ELECTROLYSIS/ELECTROLOGY AND ELECTROLYSIS TECHNICIAN

Indiana
Lafayette Beauty Academy (Lafayette), 165

Massachusetts
Electrology Institute of New England (Tewksbury), 197

North Carolina
Leon's Beauty School (Greensboro), 299

Ohio
Lorain County Community College (Elyria), 324

Pennsylvania
Altoona Beauty School of Hair Design and Cosmetology (Altoona), 343
Bucks County School of Beauty Culture (Feasterville), 345
Venus Beauty School (Sharon Hill), 377

Virginia
Ana Visage Academy (Great Falls), 424

ELECTROMECHANICAL AND INSTRUMENTATION AND MAINTENANCE TECHNOLOGIES/TECHNICIANS, OTHER

Florida
Pinellas Technical Education Center–St. Petersburg (St. Petersburg), 92

Kentucky
Bowling Green Technical College (Bowling Green), 170

Massachusetts
Northern Essex Community College (Haverhill), 204

Michigan
Henry Ford Community College (Dearborn), 217

North Carolina
Alamance Community College (Graham), 288
Bladen Community College (Dublin), 289
Cape Fear Community College (Wilmington), 290
Central Carolina Community College (Sanford), 292
Cleveland Community College (Shelby), 293
Davidson County Community College (Lexington), 294
Durham Technical Community College (Durham), 295
Forsyth Technical Community College (Winston-Salem), 296
Gaston College (Dallas), 296
Halifax Community College (Weldon), 297
Martin Community College (Williamston), 299
McDowell Technical Community College (Marion), 300
Mitchell Community College (Statesville), 300
Piedmont Community College (Roxboro), 302
Pitt Community College (Greenville), 303
Richmond Community College (Hamlet), 303
Roanoke-Chowan Community College (Ahoskie), 303
Robeson Community College (Lumberton), 304
Sampson Community College (Clinton), 304
Sandhills Community College (Pinehurst), 305
Southeastern Community College (Whiteville), 305
Surry Community College (Dobson), 306
Wake Technical Community College (Raleigh), 307
Wayne Community College (Goldsboro), 308
Wilkes Community College (Wilkesboro), 308

Ohio
Hocking College (Nelsonville), 321

Puerto Rico
Caguas Institute of Mechanical Technology (Caguas), 381

ELECTROMECHANICAL TECHNOLOGY/ ELECTROMECHANICAL ENGINEERING TECHNOLOGY

Florida
Brevard Community College (Cocoa), 67

Illinois
Black Hawk College (Moline), 125

Kentucky
Jefferson Community and Technical College (Louisville), 175

Maysville Community and Technical College (Maysville), 176

Maine
Central Maine Community College (Auburn), 181

Maryland
Cecil College (North East), 186
Hagerstown Community College (Hagerstown), 188

New York
Rochester Institute of Technology (Rochester), 280

North Carolina
Blue Ridge Community College (Flat Rock), 289
Cleveland Community College (Shelby), 293
Fayetteville Technical Community College (Fayetteville), 295
Guilford Technical Community College (Jamestown), 297
Haywood Community College (Clyde), 297
Lenoir Community College (Kinston), 299
Mayland Community College (Spruce Pine), 299
Mitchell Community College (Statesville), 300
Roanoke-Chowan Community College (Ahoskie), 303
South Piedmont Community College (Polkton), 305
Vance-Granville Community College (Henderson), 307

Ohio
North Central State College (Mansfield), 327
Sinclair Community College (Dayton), 334

Pennsylvania
Greater Altoona Career and Technology Center (Altoona), 356
Precision Manufacturing Institute (Meadville), 371
Schuylkill Technology Center–North Campus (Frackville), 373

Puerto Rico
Automeca Technical College (Aguadilla), 380
Automeca Technical College (Bayamón), 380
Automeca Technical College (Caguas), 380
Automeca Technical College (Ponce), 380
Caguas Institute of Mechanical Technology (Caguas), 381
Colegio Mayor de Tecnologia–Arroyo (Arroyo), 382

West Virginia
James Rumsey Technical Institute (Martinsburg), 440
Monongalia County Technical Education Center (Morgantown), 441

ELECTRONEURODIAGNOSTIC/ ELECTROENCEPHALOGRAPHIC TECHNOLOGY/TECHNOLOGIST

Florida
Central Florida Institute (Palm Harbor), 69

Georgia
Central Georgia Technical College (Macon), 107
Griffin Technical College (Griffin), 113

Illinois
Northwestern Business College–Southwestern Campus (Bridgeview), 144
Northwestern College (Chicago), 144

Massachusetts
Labouré College (Boston), 200

Michigan
Carnegie Institute (Troy), 212

South Carolina

Florence-Darlington Technical College
(Florence), 399

ELEMENTARY EDUCATION AND TEACHING

Delaware

Delaware Technical & Community College,
Stanton/Wilmington Campus (Newark), 59

Maryland

Harford Community College (Bel Air), 189

North Carolina

Carteret Community College (Morehead City),
292
Durham Technical Community College
(Durham), 295
Halifax Community College (Weldon), 297
Martin Community College (Williamston), 299
Nash Community College (Rocky Mount), 302
Rowan-Cabarrus Community College
(Salisbury), 304
Sampson Community College (Clinton), 304
Southwestern Community College (Sylva), 306
Surry Community College (Dobson), 306
Wilkes Community College (Wilkesboro), 308
Wilson Community College (Wilson), 308

Virginia

Shenandoah University (Winchester), 432

EMERGENCY CARE ATTENDANT (EMT AMBULANCE)

Delaware

Delaware Technical & Community College,
Terry Campus (Dover), 60

Florida

Health Opportunity Technical Center (Miami
Gardens), 80
Manatee Technical Institute (Bradenton), 85

Illinois

City Colleges of Chicago, Malcolm X College
(Chicago), 128
Harper College (Palatine), 135
Illinois Central College (East Peoria), 136
Illinois Eastern Community Colleges, Frontier
Community College (Fairfield), 137
Illinois Eastern Community Colleges, Olney
Central College (Olney), 137
Illinois Eastern Community Colleges, Wabash
Valley College (Mount Carmel), 137
Kankakee Community College (Kankakee), 139
Kishwaukee College (Malta), 140
Lincoln Land Community College (Springfield),
141
McHenry County College (Crystal Lake), 142
Parkland College (Champaign), 145
Prairie State College (Chicago Heights), 146
Sauk Valley Community College (Dixon), 150
South Suburban College (South Holland), 151
Waubonsee Community College (Sugar Grove),
154

Maryland

Baltimore City Community College
(Baltimore), 185

Massachusetts

Medical Professional Institute (Malden), 202

West Virginia

Carver Career Center (Charleston), 438

EMERGENCY MEDICAL TECHNOLOGY/ TECHNICIAN (EMT PARAMEDIC)

Alabama

Bevill State Community College (Sumiton), 41
Calhoun Community College (Decatur), 41

Central Alabama Community College
(Alexander City), 42
Chattahoochee Valley Community College
(Phenix City), 42
Enterprise-Ozark Community College
(Enterprise), 42
Gadsden State Community College (Gadsden),
42
George C. Wallace Community College
(Dothan), 43
H. Councill Trenholm State Technical College
(Montgomery), 43
James H. Faulkner State Community College
(Bay Minette), 44
Jefferson Davis Community College (Brewton),
44
Jefferson State Community College
(Birmingham), 44
Lawson State Community College
(Birmingham), 44
Lurleen B. Wallace Community College
(Andalusia), 45
Northeast Alabama Community College
(Rainsville), 45
Northwest-Shoals Community College (Muscle
Shoals), 45
Shelton State Community College (Tuscaloosa),
46
Southern Union State Community College
(Wadley), 47
University of South Alabama (Mobile), 47
Wallace State Community College
(Hanceville), 48

Connecticut

Capital Community College (Hartford), 51
Goodwin College (East Hartford), 53
Norwalk Community College (Norwalk), 55

Delaware

Delaware Technical & Community College,
Stanton/Wilmington Campus (Newark), 59
Delaware Technical & Community College,
Terry Campus (Dover), 60

Florida

Brevard Community College (Cocoa), 67
Broward Community College (Fort Lauderdale),
68
Central Florida Community College (Ocala), 69
Chipola College (Marianna), 69
Commercial Diving Academy (Jacksonville), 70
Daytona State College (Daytona Beach), 72
Edison State College (Fort Myers), 72
First Coast Technical Institute (St. Augustine),
75
Florida Career Institute (Lakeland), 76
Florida Community College at Jacksonville
(Jacksonville), 77
Florida Keys Community College (Key West),
78
Gulf Coast Community College (Panama City),
79
Hillsborough Community College (Tampa), 81
Indian River State College (Fort Pierce), 81
Keiser Career College–Greenacres (Greenacres),
82
Lake City Community College (Lake City), 83
Lake Technical Center (Eustis), 83
Manatee Technical Institute (Bradenton), 85
McFatter Technical Center (Davie), 86
Miami Dade College (Miami), 87
Mid-Florida Tech (Orlando), 87
North Florida Community College (Madison),
88
Northwest Florida State College (Niceville), 89
Palm Beach Community College (Lake Worth),
90

Pasco-Hernando Community College (New Port
Richey), 90
Pensacola Junior College (Pensacola), 91
Polk Community College (Winter Haven), 92
St. Petersburg College (St. Petersburg), 94
Santa Fe Community College (Gainesville), 95
Sarasota County Technical Institute (Sarasota),
96
Seminole Community College (Sanford), 96
South Florida Community College (Avon Park),
97
Tallahassee Community College (Tallahassee),
98
Taylor Technical Institute (Perry), 99
Valencia Community College (Orlando), 101

Georgia

Albany Technical College (Albany), 103
Altamaha Technical College (Jesup), 104
Appalachian Technical College (Jasper), 104
Athens Technical College (Athens), 105
Atlanta Technical College (Atlanta), 105
Augusta Technical College (Augusta), 106
Bainbridge College (Bainbridge), 106
Central Georgia Technical College (Macon),
107
Chattahoochee Technical College (Marietta),
107
College of Coastal Georgia (Brunswick), 108
Coosa Valley Technical College (Rome), 109
Darton College (Albany), 109
DeKalb Technical College (Clarkston), 109
Griffin Technical College (Griffin), 113
Gwinnett Technical College (Lawrenceville),
113
Lanier Technical College (Oakwood), 115
Medix School (Smyrna), 116
Moultrie Technical College (Moultrie), 117
North Georgia Technical College (Clarkesville),
118
North Metro Technical College (Acworth), 118
Ogeechee Technical College (Statesboro), 119
Okefenokee Technical College (Waycross), 119
Savannah Technical College (Savannah), 121
Southeastern Technical College (Vidalia), 121
Southwest Georgia Technical College
(Thomasville), 122
Swainsboro Technical College (Swainsboro),
123
Valdosta Technical College (Valdosta), 123
West Central Technical College (Waco), 124

Illinois

Black Hawk College (Moline), 125
City Colleges of Chicago, Olive-Harvey College
(Chicago), 128
City Colleges of Chicago, Richard J. Daley
College (Chicago), 128
City Colleges of Chicago, Wilbur Wright
College (Chicago), 129
College of DuPage (Glen Ellyn), 129
College of Lake County (Grayslake), 129
Elgin Community College (Elgin), 132
Harper College (Palatine), 135
Lewis and Clark Community College (Godfrey),
141
Lincoln Land Community College (Springfield),
141
Moraine Valley Community College (Palos
Hills), 143
Oakton Community College (Des Plaines), 145
Parkland College (Champaign), 145
Prairie State College (Chicago Heights), 146
Richland Community College (Decatur), 148
Sauk Valley Community College (Dixon), 150
South Suburban College (South Holland), 151
Trinity College of Nursing and Health Sciences
(Rock Island), 153

Triton College (River Grove), 153

Indiana
Vincennes University (Vincennes), 168

Kentucky
Elizabethtown Community and Technical
College (Elizabethtown), 172
Jefferson Community and Technical College
(Louisville), 175
Owensboro Community and Technical College
(Owensboro), 177
West Kentucky Community and Technical
College (Paducah), 180

Maine
Eastern Maine Community College (Bangor),
181
Kennebec Valley Community College
(Fairfield), 181
Northern Maine Community College (Presque
Isle), 182

Maryland
Anne Arundel Community College (Arnold),
184
Baltimore City Community College
(Baltimore), 185
Cecil College (North East), 186
Chesapeake College (Wye Mills), 186
College of Southern Maryland (La Plata), 186
The Community College of Baltimore County
(Baltimore), 187
Frederick Community College (Frederick), 188
Hagerstown Community College (Hagerstown),
188
Howard Community College (Columbia), 189
Prince George's Community College (Largo),
191
Wor-Wic Community College (Salisbury), 193

Massachusetts
Cape Cod Community College (West
Barnstable), 196
Greenfield Community College (Greenfield),
198
Massachusetts Bay Community College
(Wellesley Hills), 201
Medical Professional Institute (Malden), 202
Northern Essex Community College
(Haverhill), 204
Quinsigamond Community College
(Worcester), 205

Michigan
Baker College of Cadillac (Cadillac), 210
Baker College of Clinton Township (Clinton
Township), 210
Baker College of Muskegon (Muskegon), 211
Glen Oaks Community College (Centreville),
216
Gogebic Community College (Ironwood), 216
Jackson Community College (Jackson), 218
Kalamazoo Valley Community College
(Kalamazoo), 218
Kellogg Community College (Battle Creek), 218
Lake Michigan College (Benton Harbor), 219
Lake Superior State University (Sault Sainte
Marie), 219
Lansing Community College (Lansing), 219
Macomb Community College (Warren), 220
North Central Michigan College (Petoskey),
223
Oakland Community College (Bloomfield
Hills), 224
Schoolcraft College (Livonia), 227
Wayne County Community College District
(Detroit), 229

Mississippi
Hinds Community College (Raymond), 232
Holmes Community College (Goodman), 233

Northwest Mississippi Community College
(Senatobia), 235

New Jersey
Hudson County Community College (Jersey
City), 247
Union County College (Cranford), 254

New York
Erie Community College (Buffalo), 265
Hudson Valley Community College (Troy), 268
Jefferson Community College (Watertown), 270
Monroe Community College (Rochester), 274
Ulster County Community College (Stone
Ridge), 286
Westchester Community College (Valhalla),
287

North Carolina
Carolinas College of Health Sciences
(Charlotte), 292
Davidson County Community College
(Lexington), 294
Fayetteville Technical Community College
(Fayetteville), 295

Ohio
Adult Center for Education (Zanesville), 309
Akron Adult Vocational Services (Akron), 309
Auburn Career Center (Painesville), 311
Butler Technology and Career Development
Schools–D. Russel Lee Career-Technology
Center (Hamilton), 314
Cincinnati State Technical and Community
College (Cincinnati), 315
Clark State Community College (Springfield),
316
Columbiana County Vocation School (Lisbon),
317
Columbus State Community College
(Columbus), 317
Cuyahoga Community College (Cleveland), 318
Delaware JVS District (Delaware), 318
Eastern Gateway Community College
(Steubenville), 319
Eastland Career Center (Groveport), 319
Ehove Career Center (Milan), 319
James A. Rhodes State College (Lima), 322
Lakeland Community College (Kirtland), 323
Licking County Joint Vocational School–
Newark (Newark), 324
Northwest State Community College
(Archbold), 327
O. C. Collins Career Center (Chesapeake), 328
Oregon Career Center (Oregon), 330
Pickaway Ross Joint Vocational School District
(Chillicothe), 331
Sinclair Community College (Dayton), 334
Southern State Community College (Hillsboro),
335
Tri-Rivers Career Center (Marion), 337
University of Cincinnati Clermont College
(Batavia), 339
University of Cincinnati Raymond Walters
College (Cincinnati), 339
The University of Toledo (Toledo), 339
Vanguard Career Center (Fremont), 340
Warren County Career Center (Lebanon), 340

Pennsylvania
All-State Career School (Lester), 343
Delaware County Community College (Media),
351
Lackawanna College (Scranton), 359
Luzerne County Community College
(Nanticoke), 363
Northampton County Area Community College
(Bethlehem), 366
Star Technical Institute (Philadelphia), 374

Puerto Rico
Atenas College (Manati), 380

Centro de Estudios Multidisciplinarios
(Bayamón), 382
Centro de Estudios Multidisciplinarios
(Humacao), 382
Centro de Estudios Multidisciplinarios (San
Juan), 382
Colegio Mayor de Tecnologia–Arroyo (Arroyo),
382
Educational Technical College–Bayamón
(Bayamón), 384
Educational Technical College–Recinto de San
Sebastian (San Sebastian), 384
Instituto de Banca y Comercio–Aprendes
Practicanco (Río Piedras), 386
Instituto Vocational y Commercial EDIC
(Caguas), 387
Inter American University of Puerto Rico,
Metropolitan Campus (San Juan), 388
Ponce Paramedical College (Ponce), 392
Universal Technology College of Puerto Rico
(Aguadilla), 393

South Carolina
Piedmont Technical College (Greenwood), 402

Tennessee
Cleveland State Community College
(Cleveland), 406
Columbia State Community College
(Columbia), 406
Jackson State Community College (Jackson),
408
Northeast State Technical Community College
(Blountville), 412
Roane State Community College (Harriman),
413
Southwest Tennessee Community College
(Memphis), 414
Volunteer State Community College (Gallatin),
421
Walters State Community College
(Morristown), 421

Virginia
National College (Salem), 430
Patrick Henry Community College
(Martinsville), 431

West Virginia
Blue Ridge Community and Technical College
(Martinsburg), 438
West Virginia State Community and Technical
College (Institute), 444

Wisconsin
Blackhawk Technical College (Janesville), 445
Chippewa Valley Technical College (Eau
Claire), 445
Fox Valley Technical College (Appleton), 446
Gateway Technical College (Kenosha), 446
Lakeshore Technical College (Cleveland), 447
Madison Area Technical College (Madison),
448
Mid-State Technical College (Wisconsin
Rapids), 449
Milwaukee Area Technical College
(Milwaukee), 449
Moraine Park Technical College (Fond du Lac),
450
Nicolet Area Technical College (Rhinelander),
450
Northcentral Technical College (Wausau), 450
Northeast Wisconsin Technical College (Green
Bay), 450
Waukesha County Technical College
(Pewaukee), 453
Western Technical College (La Crosse), 453
Wisconsin Indianhead Technical College (Shell
Lake), 453

ENERGY MANAGEMENT AND SYSTEMS TECHNOLOGY/TECHNICIAN

Alabama
Northwest-Shoals Community College (Muscle Shoals), 45

Illinois
City Colleges of Chicago, Wilbur Wright College (Chicago), 129

Kentucky
Maysville Community and Technical College (Maysville), 176

Massachusetts
Middlesex Community College (Bedford), 202
North Shore Community College (Danvers), 204
Quinsigamond Community College (Worcester), 205

Michigan
Henry Ford Community College (Dearborn), 217
Lansing Community College (Lansing), 219
Michigan Institute of Aeronautics (Belleville), 221

ENGINEERING, GENERAL

Maryland
The Community College of Baltimore County (Baltimore), 187

Michigan
Jackson Community College (Jackson), 218
Northwestern Michigan College (Traverse City), 224

Pennsylvania
Penn State Altoona (Altoona), 368
Penn State University Park (University Park), 369
University of Pittsburgh (Pittsburgh), 376

ENGINEERING/INDUSTRIAL MANAGEMENT

New York
Rochester Institute of Technology (Rochester), 280

North Carolina
Central Piedmont Community College (Charlotte), 293
Gaston College (Dallas), 296
Mitchell Community College (Statesville), 300

ENGINEERING MECHANICS

Pennsylvania
Penn State University Park (University Park), 369

ENGINEERING, OTHER

Pennsylvania
Penn State University Park (University Park), 369
University of Pittsburgh (Pittsburgh), 376

ENGINEERING-RELATED TECHNOLOGIES, OTHER

Connecticut
Naugatuck Valley Community College (Waterbury), 54

New Jersey
Cumberland County College (Vineland), 244

New York
Paul Smith's College (Paul Smiths), 279

Pennsylvania
Harrisburg Area Community College (Harrisburg), 357

ENGINEERING SCIENCE

New Jersey
Mercer County Community College (Trenton), 248

ENGINEERING TECHNOLOGIES/ TECHNICIANS, OTHER

Connecticut
Naugatuck Valley Community College (Waterbury), 54

Delaware
Delaware Technical & Community College, Jack F. Owens Campus (Georgetown), 59

Florida
ATI Career Training Center (Miami), 65

Maryland
College of Southern Maryland (La Plata), 186
Howard Community College (Columbia), 189
Prince George's Community College (Largo), 191
Wor-Wic Community College (Salisbury), 193

New York
Rochester Institute of Technology (Rochester), 280

North Carolina
Bladen Community College (Dublin), 289
Haywood Community College (Clyde), 297
Mitchell Community College (Statesville), 300

Ohio
Cleveland Institute of Electronics (Cleveland), 316
Columbus State Community College (Columbus), 317
Cuyahoga Community College (Cleveland), 318
Hocking College (Nelsonville), 321

Pennsylvania
Harrisburg Area Community College (Harrisburg), 357

Virginia
Danville Community College (Danville), 426

West Virginia
West Virginia University at Parkersburg (Parkersburg), 444

Wisconsin
Milwaukee Area Technical College (Milwaukee), 449

ENGINEERING TECHNOLOGY, GENERAL

Alabama
Jefferson State Community College (Birmingham), 44

Connecticut
Asnuntuck Community College (Enfield), 49
Capital Community College (Hartford), 51
Gateway Community College (New Haven), 52
Housatonic Community College (Bridgeport), 53
Manchester Community College (Manchester), 54
Middlesex Community College (Middletown), 54
Naugatuck Valley Community College (Waterbury), 54
Northwestern Connecticut Community College (Winsted), 55
Quinebaug Valley Community College (Danielson), 56
Three Rivers Community College (Norwich), 57
Tunxis Community College (Farmington), 57

Kentucky
Big Sandy Community and Technical College (Prestonsburg), 170
Bluegrass Community and Technical College (Lexington), 170
Bowling Green Technical College (Bowling Green), 170
Elizabethtown Community and Technical College (Elizabethtown), 172
Henderson Community College (Henderson), 174
Hopkinsville Community College (Hopkinsville), 174
Jefferson Community and Technical College (Louisville), 175
Madisonville Community College (Madisonville), 176
Maysville Community and Technical College (Maysville), 176
Owensboro Community and Technical College (Owensboro), 177
Somerset Community College (Somerset), 178
Southeast Kentucky Community and Technical College (Cumberland), 178
West Kentucky Community and Technical College (Paducah), 180

Maryland
The Community College of Baltimore County (Baltimore), 187

Ohio
Cleveland Institute of Electronics (Cleveland), 316

Pennsylvania
Pennsylvania Institute of Technology (Media), 370

South Carolina
Piedmont Technical College (Greenwood), 402

Tennessee
Chattanooga State Technical Community College (Chattanooga), 406

Virginia
Tidewater Community College (Norfolk), 434

ENGINE MACHINIST

Michigan
Lansing Community College (Lansing), 219

Mississippi
Hinds Community College (Raymond), 232
Jones County Junior College (Ellisville), 234
Mississippi Delta Community College (Moorhead), 234

Tennessee
Nashville Auto Diesel College (Nashville), 410

Wisconsin
Southwest Wisconsin Technical College (Fennimore), 452

ENGLISH LANGUAGE AND LITERATURE, GENERAL

District of Columbia
Sanz School (Washington), 62

Illinois
BIR Training Center (Chicago), 125
Zarem/Golde ORT Technical Institute (Chicago), 154

ENTREPRENEURIAL AND SMALL BUSINESS OPERATIONS, OTHER

Massachusetts
Bristol Community College (Fall River), 196
Holyoke Community College (Holyoke), 199

Michigan
Bay de Noc Community College (Escanaba), 211
Lawrence Technological University (Southfield), 220
Lawton School (Southfield), 220

Environmental Science

Maryland
Baltimore City Community College
(Baltimore), 185

North Carolina
Blue Ridge Community College (Flat Rock),
289
Western Piedmont Community College
(Morganton), 308

Pennsylvania
Drexel University (Philadelphia), 352

West Virginia
Logan-Mingo School of Practical Nursing
(Logan), 441

EQUESTRIAN/EQUINE STUDIES

Connecticut
Post University (Waterbury), 56

Florida
Central Florida Community College (Ocala), 69

Kentucky
Bluegrass Community and Technical College
(Lexington), 170

North Carolina
Martin Community College (Williamston), 299

Ohio
Hocking College (Nelsonville), 321

West Virginia
Meredith Manor International Equestrian
Center (Waverly), 441

ETHNIC, CULTURAL MINORITY, AND GENDER STUDIES, OTHER

Ohio
University of Cincinnati Raymond Walters
College (Cincinnati), 339

Pennsylvania
Penn State Shenango (Sharon), 369

EUROPEAN STUDIES/CIVILIZATION

Ohio
Ohio University (Athens), 330

Pennsylvania
University of Pittsburgh (Pittsburgh), 376

West Virginia
American Public University System (Charles
Town), 437

EXECUTIVE ASSISTANT/EXECUTIVE SECRETARY

Connecticut
Briarwood College (Southington), 50

Florida
Brevard Community College (Cocoa), 67
Broward Community College (Fort Lauderdale),
68
Central Florida Community College (Ocala), 69
Daytona State College (Daytona Beach), 72
Florida Community College at Jacksonville
(Jacksonville), 77
Gulf Coast Community College (Panama City),
79
Hillsborough Community College (Tampa), 81
Indian River State College (Fort Pierce), 81
Lake City Community College (Lake City), 83
Lake-Sumter Community College (Leesburg),
83
Miami Dade College (Miami), 87
North Florida Community College (Madison),
88
Northwest Florida State College (Niceville), 89
Palm Beach Community College (Lake Worth),
90
Pasco-Hernando Community College (New Port
Richey), 90

Pensacola Junior College (Pensacola), 91
Polk Community College (Winter Haven), 92
St. Johns River Community College (Palatka),
94
St. Petersburg College (St. Petersburg), 94
Santa Fe Community College (Gainesville), 95
Seminole Community College (Sanford), 96
South Florida Community College (Avon Park),
97
State College of Florida Manatee-Sarasota
(Bradenton), 98
Tallahassee Community College (Tallahassee),
98
Valencia Community College (Orlando), 101

Illinois
Elgin Community College (Elgin), 132
Moraine Valley Community College (Palos
Hills), 143
Oakton Community College (Des Plaines), 145
South Suburban College (South Holland), 151
Waubonsee Community College (Sugar Grove),
154
Zarem/Golde ORT Technical Institute
(Chicago), 154

Indiana
Ivy Tech Community College–Bloomington
(Bloomington), 161
Ivy Tech Community College–Central Indiana
(Indianapolis), 161
Ivy Tech Community College–Columbus
(Columbus), 162
Ivy Tech Community College–East Central
(Muncie), 162
Ivy Tech Community College–Kokomo
(Kokomo), 162
Ivy Tech Community College–Lafayette
(Lafayette), 162
Ivy Tech Community College–North Central
(South Bend), 162
Ivy Tech Community College–Northeast (Fort
Wayne), 163
Ivy Tech Community College–Southeast
(Madison), 163
Ivy Tech Community College–Southwest
(Evansville), 163
Ivy Tech Community College–Wabash Valley
(Terre Haute), 164
Ivy Tech Community College–Whitewater
(Richmond), 164

Kentucky
Ashland Community and Technical College
(Ashland), 169
Big Sandy Community and Technical College
(Prestonsburg), 170
Bluegrass Community and Technical College
(Lexington), 170
Bowling Green Technical College (Bowling
Green), 170
Elizabethtown Community and Technical
College (Elizabethtown), 172
Gateway Community and Technical College
(Covington), 173
Hazard Community and Technical College
(Hazard), 174
Hopkinsville Community College
(Hopkinsville), 174
Jefferson Community and Technical College
(Louisville), 175
Maysville Community and Technical College
(Maysville), 176
National College (Lexington), 176
Owensboro Community and Technical College
(Owensboro), 177
Somerset Community College (Somerset), 178
Southeast Kentucky Community and Technical
College (Cumberland), 178
Spencerian College (Louisville), 179

Sullivan University (Louisville), 179
West Kentucky Community and Technical
College (Paducah), 180

Maine
Kennebec Valley Community College
(Fairfield), 181

Maryland
Hagerstown Community College (Hagerstown),
188

Massachusetts
The Salter School (Worcester), 206
Southeastern Technical College (South Easton),
206
Sullivan and Cogliano Training Center
(Brockton), 207

Michigan
Dorsey Business Schools (Madison Heights),
214
Dorsey Business Schools (Roseville), 214
Dorsey Business Schools (Southgate), 214
Kalamazoo Valley Community College
(Kalamazoo), 218
Kellogg Community College (Battle Creek), 218
Lake Michigan College (Benton Harbor), 219
Northwestern Michigan College (Traverse
City), 224

New Jersey
Dover Business College (Paramus), 244
HoHoKus Hackensack School of Business and
Medical Sciences (Hackensack), 246
Keyskills Learning (Clifton), 247
Performance Training (Toms River), 251

New York
Hunter Business School (Levittown), 269
Ridley-Lowell School of Business
(Poughkeepsie), 280

North Carolina
Beaufort County Community College
(Washington), 289
Blue Ridge Community College (Flat Rock),
289
Brookstone College of Business (Greensboro),
290
Brunswick Community College (Supply), 290
Caldwell Community College and Technical
Institute (Hudson), 290
Cape Fear Community College (Wilmington),
290
Central Piedmont Community College
(Charlotte), 293
Cleveland Community College (Shelby), 293
Fayetteville Technical Community College
(Fayetteville), 295
Gaston College (Dallas), 296
Haywood Community College (Clyde), 297
Lenoir Community College (Kinston), 299
Mayland Community College (Spruce Pine),
299
Mitchell Community College (Statesville), 300
Pamlico Community College (Grantsboro), 302
Rockingham Community College (Wentworth),
304
South Piedmont Community College (Polkton),
305
Southwestern Community College (Sylva), 306
Tri-County Community College (Murphy), 306
Vance-Granville Community College
(Henderson), 307
Wayne Community College (Goldsboro), 308
Western Piedmont Community College
(Morganton), 308
Wilson Community College (Wilson), 308

Ohio
Eastern Gateway Community College
(Steubenville), 319
Owens Community College (Toledo), 330

FINANCE AND FINANCIAL MANAGEMENT SERVICES, OTHER

Illinois
BIR Training Center (Chicago), 125

Ohio
James A. Rhodes State College (Lima), 322
University of Cincinnati Clermont College (Batavia), 339

FINANCE, GENERAL

Connecticut
Post University (Waterbury), 56

Florida
Florida Community College at Jacksonville (Jacksonville), 77
Miami Dade College (Miami), 87

Illinois
Joliet Junior College (Joliet), 139
Northwestern University (Evanston), 145

New York
Graduate School and University Center of the City University of New York (New York), 268

Virginia
Marymount University (Arlington), 429

FINANCIAL PLANNING AND SERVICES

Kentucky
Western Kentucky University (Bowling Green), 180

Massachusetts
Suffolk University (Boston), 207

Ohio
Chancellor University (Cleveland), 315
Ohio University (Athens), 330
The University of Akron (Akron), 338

Pennsylvania
Penn State Erie, The Behrend College (Erie), 368

FINE ARTS AND ART STUDIES, OTHER

Alabama
Jefferson Davis Community College (Brewton), 44

Massachusetts
Bristol Community College (Fall River), 196

Ohio
Terra State Community College (Fremont), 336
Youngstown State University (Youngstown), 341

Pennsylvania
Harrisburg Area Community College (Harrisburg), 357

FINE/STUDIO ARTS, GENERAL

Connecticut
Capital Community College (Hartford), 51
Naugatuck Valley Community College (Waterbury), 54

Massachusetts
Middlesex Community College (Bedford), 202
Mount Holyoke College (South Hadley), 203
School of the Museum of Fine Arts, Boston (Boston), 206

Michigan
Jackson Community College (Jackson), 218
Lansing Community College (Lansing), 219

New York
Marist College (Poughkeepsie), 272

Pennsylvania
Marywood University (Scranton), 364

FIRE PROTECTION AND SAFETY TECHNOLOGY/TECHNICIAN

Connecticut
University of New Haven (West Haven), 58

Delaware
Delaware Technical & Community College, Stanton/Wilmington Campus (Newark), 59

Florida
Palm Beach Community College (Lake Worth), 90
State College of Florida Manatee-Sarasota (Bradenton), 98

Illinois
College of DuPage (Glen Ellyn), 129
Lincoln Land Community College (Springfield), 141
Rock Valley College (Rockford), 149

Maryland
Baltimore City Community College (Baltimore), 185
The Community College of Baltimore County (Baltimore), 187
Montgomery College (Rockville), 190

Massachusetts
Bristol Community College (Fall River), 196
Cape Cod Community College (West Barnstable), 196
North Shore Community College (Danvers), 204

Michigan
Macomb Community College (Warren), 220

New Jersey
Mercer County Community College (Trenton), 248
Passaic County Community College (Paterson), 251

North Carolina
Alamance Community College (Graham), 288
Asheville-Buncombe Technical Community College (Asheville), 288
Coastal Carolina Community College (Jacksonville), 293
Durham Technical Community College (Durham), 295
Wilson Community College (Wilson), 308

Ohio
Sinclair Community College (Dayton), 334
Stark State College of Technology (North Canton), 335
The University of Akron (Akron), 338
Warren County Career Center (Lebanon), 340

Pennsylvania
Bucks County Community College (Newtown), 345
Community College of Philadelphia (Philadelphia), 349
Luzerne County Community College (Nanticoke), 363
Westmoreland County Community College (Youngwood), 378

West Virginia
Blue Ridge Community and Technical College (Martinsburg), 438

FIRE PROTECTION, OTHER

Connecticut
University of New Haven (West Haven), 58

Florida
Palm Beach Community College (Lake Worth), 90

Massachusetts
Bristol Community College (Fall River), 196

North Carolina
Caldwell Community College and Technical Institute (Hudson), 290
Wayne Community College (Goldsboro), 308

Ohio
Butler Technology and Career Development Schools–D. Russel Lee Career-Technology Center (Hamilton), 314
Columbiana County Vocation School (Lisbon), 317
Delaware JVS District (Delaware), 318
The University of Akron (Akron), 338

Pennsylvania
Lancaster County Career and Technology Center (Willow Street), 360

West Virginia
American Public University System (Charles Town), 437

FIRE SCIENCE/FIREFIGHTING

Florida
Brevard Community College (Cocoa), 67
Chipola College (Marianna), 69
Daytona State College (Daytona Beach), 72
First Coast Technical Institute (St. Augustine), 75
Florida Community College at Jacksonville (Jacksonville), 77
Gulf Coast Community College (Panama City), 79
Hillsborough Community College (Tampa), 81
Indian River State College (Fort Pierce), 81
James Lorenzo Walker Vocational-Technical Center (Naples), 82
Lake Technical Center (Eustis), 83
Manatee Technical Institute (Bradenton), 85
Marion County Community Technical and Adult Education Center (Ocala), 85
McFatter Technical Center (Davie), 86
Miami Dade College (Miami), 87
Mid-Florida Tech (Orlando), 87
Palm Beach Community College (Lake Worth), 90
Pensacola Junior College (Pensacola), 91
Pinellas Technical Education Center–St. Petersburg (St. Petersburg), 92
Ridge Technical Center (Winter Haven), 93
St. Petersburg College (St. Petersburg), 94
Sarasota County Technical Institute (Sarasota), 96
Seminole Community College (Sanford), 96
Tallahassee Community College (Tallahassee), 98
Washington-Holmes Technical Center (Chipley), 102

Georgia
Albany Technical College (Albany), 103
Atlanta Technical College (Atlanta), 105
Augusta Technical College (Augusta), 106
Coosa Valley Technical College (Rome), 109
Griffin Technical College (Griffin), 113
Lanier Technical College (Oakwood), 115
Moultrie Technical College (Moultrie), 117
North Georgia Technical College (Clarkesville), 118
Valdosta Technical College (Valdosta), 123
West Georgia Technical College (LaGrange), 124

Illinois
Elgin Community College (Elgin), 132
Illinois Eastern Community Colleges, Frontier Community College (Fairfield), 137
Joliet Junior College (Joliet), 139
Lewis and Clark Community College (Godfrey), 141

Lincoln Land Community College (Springfield), 141

McHenry County College (Crystal Lake), 142

Oakton Community College (Des Plaines), 145

Prairie State College (Chicago Heights), 146

Richland Community College (Decatur), 148

Rock Valley College (Rockford), 149

Southwestern Illinois College (Belleville), 151

Triton College (River Grove), 153

Waubonsee Community College (Sugar Grove), 154

Indiana
Vincennes University (Vincennes), 168

Kentucky
Bluegrass Community and Technical College (Lexington), 170

Elizabethtown Community and Technical College (Elizabethtown), 172

Hazard Community and Technical College (Hazard), 174

West Kentucky Community and Technical College (Paducah), 180

Maine
Southern Maine Community College (South Portland), 182

Massachusetts
Springfield Technical Community College (Springfield), 207

Michigan
Lake Michigan College (Benton Harbor), 219

Lansing Community College (Lansing), 219

Macomb Community College (Warren), 220

Oakland Community College (Bloomfield Hills), 224

St. Clair County Community College (Port Huron), 226

Schoolcraft College (Livonia), 227

New Jersey
Camden County College (Blackwood), 241

New York
Suffolk County Community College (Selden), 284

Ohio
Adult Center for Education (Zanesville), 309

Auburn Career Center (Painesville), 311

Buckeye Hills Career Center (Rio Grande), 313

Columbiana County Vocation School (Lisbon), 317

Delaware JVS District (Delaware), 318

Lakeland Community College (Kirtland), 323

Licking County Joint Vocational School–Newark (Newark), 324

Mahoning County Joint Vocational School District (Canfield), 325

O. C. Collins Career Center (Chesapeake), 328

Pennsylvania
Butler County Community College (Butler), 345

South Carolina
Greenville Technical College (Greenville), 399

Tennessee
Volunteer State Community College (Gallatin), 421

Virginia
Germanna Community College (Locust Grove), 428

J. Sargeant Reynolds Community College (Richmond), 429

Southside Virginia Community College (Alberta), 432

West Virginia
American Public University System (Charles Town), 437

Wisconsin
Madison Area Technical College (Madison), 448

Waukesha County Technical College (Pewaukee), 453

FIRE SERVICES ADMINISTRATION

Alabama
Calhoun Community College (Decatur), 41

Central Alabama Community College (Alexander City), 42

Chattahoochee Valley Community College (Phenix City), 42

Jefferson Davis Community College (Brewton), 44

Jefferson State Community College (Birmingham), 44

Lawson State Community College (Birmingham), 44

Northwest-Shoals Community College (Muscle Shoals), 45

Shelton State Community College (Tuscaloosa), 46

Southern Union State Community College (Wadley), 47

Connecticut
Capital Community College (Hartford), 51

Florida
First Coast Technical Institute (St. Augustine), 75

Mid-Florida Tech (Orlando), 87

Palm Beach Community College (Lake Worth), 90

Illinois
Joliet Junior College (Joliet), 139

Lewis and Clark Community College (Godfrey), 141

Lincoln Land Community College (Springfield), 141

McHenry County College (Crystal Lake), 142

Richland Community College (Decatur), 148

Rock Valley College (Rockford), 149

Southwestern Illinois College (Belleville), 151

Waubonsee Community College (Sugar Grove), 154

New Jersey
Camden County College (Blackwood), 241

Pennsylvania
Northampton County Area Community College (Bethlehem), 366

West Virginia
American Public University System (Charles Town), 437

FLORICULTURE/FLORISTRY OPERATIONS AND MANAGEMENT

Georgia
Albany Technical College (Albany), 103

Gwinnett Technical College (Lawrenceville), 113

Moultrie Technical College (Moultrie), 117

Illinois
Harper College (Palatine), 135

Joliet Junior College (Joliet), 139

Kishwaukee College (Malta), 140

McHenry County College (Crystal Lake), 142

Parkland College (Champaign), 145

Southwestern Illinois College (Belleville), 151

Massachusetts
North Shore Community College (Danvers), 204

Pennsylvania
Community College of Allegheny County (Pittsburgh), 348

Puerto Rico
Academia Serrant (Ponce), 379

D'mart Institute (Barranquitas), 383

Instituto Merlix (Bayamón), 387

FOOD PREPARATION/PROFESSIONAL COOKING/KITCHEN ASSISTANT

Florida
Lindsey Hopkins Technical Education Center (Miami), 84

Georgia
Albany Technical College (Albany), 103

Altamaha Technical College (Jesup), 104

Athens Technical College (Athens), 105

Atlanta Technical College (Atlanta), 105

Augusta Technical College (Augusta), 106

Central Georgia Technical College (Macon), 107

Chattahoochee Technical College (Marietta), 107

Gwinnett Technical College (Lawrenceville), 113

Heart of Georgia Technical College (Dublin), 114

Middle Georgia Technical College (Warner Robbins), 117

Ogeechee Technical College (Statesboro), 119

Okefenokee Technical College (Waycross), 119

Savannah Technical College (Savannah), 121

South Georgia Technical College (Americus), 122

Valdosta Technical College (Valdosta), 123

West Central Technical College (Waco), 124

West Georgia Technical College (LaGrange), 124

Illinois
Elgin Community College (Elgin), 132

The Illinois Institute of Art–Chicago (Chicago), 138

Joliet Junior College (Joliet), 139

Kaskaskia College (Centralia), 139

Southwestern Illinois College (Belleville), 151

Spoon River College (Canton), 152

Indiana
Vincennes University (Vincennes), 168

Michigan
Monroe County Community College (Monroe), 222

New Jersey
Mercer County Community College (Trenton), 248

New York
Career Academy of New York (New York), 260

North Carolina
South Piedmont Community College (Polkton), 305

Ohio
Hocking College (Nelsonville), 321

Pennsylvania
JNA Institute of Culinary Arts (Philadelphia), 358

Luzerne County Community College (Nanticoke), 363

Reading Area Community College (Reading), 372

Puerto Rico
Globelle Technical Institute (Vega Baja), 385

Vermont
New England Culinary Institute at Essex (Essex Junction), 423

New England Culinary Institute (Montpelier), 422

Virginia
Woodrow Wilson Rehabilitation Center (Fishersville), 436

West Virginia
Logan-Mingo School of Practical Nursing (Logan), 441
West Virginia Northern Community College (Wheeling), 444

Wisconsin
Fox Valley Technical College (Appleton), 446
Moraine Park Technical College (Fond du Lac), 450
Nicolet Area Technical College (Rhinelander), 450
Waukesha County Technical College (Pewaukee), 453
Western Technical College (La Crosse), 453

FOODSERVICE SYSTEMS ADMINISTRATION/MANAGEMENT

Alabama
Bishop State Community College (Mobile), 41
Jefferson Davis Community College (Brewton), 44
Lawson State Community College (Birmingham), 44
Shelton State Community College (Tuscaloosa), 46
Wallace State Community College (Hanceville), 48

Connecticut
Gateway Community College (New Haven), 52
Manchester Community College (Manchester), 54
Naugatuck Valley Community College (Waterbury), 54

Florida
Brevard Community College (Cocoa), 67
Florida Community College at Jacksonville (Jacksonville), 77
South Florida Community College (Avon Park), 97

Illinois
City Colleges of Chicago, Harold Washington College (Chicago), 127

Maryland
Anne Arundel Community College (Arnold), 184

Michigan
Bay de Noc Community College (Escanaba), 211
Wayne County Community College District (Detroit), 229

North Carolina
Asheville-Buncombe Technical Community College (Asheville), 288
Central Carolina Community College (Sanford), 292
College of The Albemarle (Elizabeth City), 294
Halifax Community College (Weldon), 297
James Sprunt Community College (Kenansville), 298
Johnston Community College (Smithfield), 298
Montgomery Community College (Troy), 301
Piedmont Community College (Roxboro), 302
Richmond Community College (Hamlet), 303
Wake Technical Community College (Raleigh), 307

Pennsylvania
Butler County Community College (Butler), 345
Harrisburg Area Community College (Harrisburg), 357

Puerto Rico
Inter American University of Puerto Rico, Aguadilla Campus (Aguadilla), 387
Inter American University of Puerto Rico, Bayamón Campus (Bayamón), 388
Inter American University of Puerto Rico, Ponce Campus (Mercedita), 389

Tennessee
Southwest Tennessee Community College (Memphis), 414

Wisconsin
Milwaukee Area Technical College (Milwaukee), 449

FOOD SERVICE, WAITER/WAITRESS, AND DINING ROOM MANAGEMENT/MANAGER

Florida
Ridge Technical Center (Winter Haven), 93

Illinois
College of Lake County (Grayslake), 129
Harper College (Palatine), 135
Illinois Central College (East Peoria), 136
Illinois Eastern Community Colleges, Lincoln Trail College (Robinson), 137
Illinois Valley Community College (Oglesby), 138
Kaskaskia College (Centralia), 139
Lake Land College (Mattoon), 140
Rend Lake College (Ina), 148
Richland Community College (Decatur), 148
Southeastern Illinois College (Harrisburg), 151

Michigan
Henry Ford Community College (Dearborn), 217

Pennsylvania
Westmoreland County Community College (Youngwood), 378

FOODS, NUTRITION, AND RELATED SERVICES, OTHER

Florida
Lively Technical Center (Tallahassee), 84

New York
Monroe Community College (Rochester), 274

Wisconsin
Milwaukee Area Technical College (Milwaukee), 449

FOODS, NUTRITION, AND WELLNESS STUDIES, GENERAL

Ohio
Kent State University, Ashtabula Campus (Ashtabula), 322

Puerto Rico
Colegio Mayor de Tecnologia–Arroyo (Arroyo), 382

FOREIGN LANGUAGES, LITERATURES, AND LINGUISTICS, OTHER

Indiana
Indiana State University (Terre Haute), 159

Michigan
Bay Mills Community College (Brimley), 211

FOREIGN LANGUAGE TEACHER EDUCATION

Michigan
Bay Mills Community College (Brimley), 211

FORENSIC SCIENCE AND TECHNOLOGY

Connecticut
University of New Haven (West Haven), 58

Florida
Gulf Coast Community College (Panama City), 79

Hillsborough Community College (Tampa), 81
Palm Beach Community College (Lake Worth), 90
St. Petersburg College (St. Petersburg), 94
Santa Fe Community College (Gainesville), 95
Tallahassee Community College (Tallahassee), 98

Illinois
Illinois Central College (East Peoria), 136
Illinois Valley Community College (Oglesby), 138

Massachusetts
Holyoke Community College (Holyoke), 199

New Jersey
Camden County College (Blackwood), 241

New York
Mohawk Valley Community College (Utica), 274

North Carolina
Fayetteville Technical Community College (Fayetteville), 295
Southwestern Community College (Sylva), 306

Ohio
Carnegie Career College (Suffield), 314
The University of Akron (Akron), 338

Pennsylvania
Harrisburg University of Science and Technology (Harrisburg), 358

Puerto Rico
Caribbean Forensic and Technical College (Río Piedras), 381

Virginia
Dabney S. Lancaster Community College (Clifton Forge), 426
Marymount University (Arlington), 429

West Virginia
American Public University System (Charles Town), 437

FOREST MANAGEMENT/FOREST RESOURCES MANAGEMENT

Florida
Lake City Community College (Lake City), 83

Michigan
Michigan Technological University (Houghton), 222

FORESTRY, GENERAL

South Carolina
Horry-Georgetown Technical College (Conway), 400

West Virginia
Fred W. Eberle Technical Center (Buckhannon), 439

FORESTRY, OTHER

Ohio
Hocking College (Nelsonville), 321

FORESTRY TECHNOLOGY/TECHNICIAN

Alabama
Lurleen B. Wallace Community College (Andalusia), 45

Georgia
Bainbridge College (Bainbridge), 106
Lanier Technical College (Oakwood), 115
Okefenokee Technical College (Waycross), 119
Swainsboro Technical College (Swainsboro), 123

Illinois
College of Lake County (Grayslake), 129
Harper College (Palatine), 135

Maine
Kennebec Valley Community College
(Fairfield), 181

Maryland
Allegany College of Maryland (Cumberland),
184

North Carolina
Southeastern Community College (Whiteville),
305

FRENCH LANGUAGE AND LITERATURE

Michigan
Michigan Technological University
(Houghton), 222
University of Detroit Mercy (Detroit), 228

Ohio
The University of Akron (Akron), 338

FUNERAL DIRECTION/SERVICE

Pennsylvania
Pittsburgh Institute of Mortuary Science,
Incorporated (Pittsburgh), 371

FUNERAL SERVICE AND MORTUARY SCIENCE, GENERAL

Alabama
Jefferson State Community College
(Birmingham), 44

Illinois
Worsham College of Mortuary Science
(Wheeling), 154

Maryland
The Community College of Baltimore County
(Baltimore), 187

New Jersey
Mercer County Community College (Trenton),
248

North Carolina
Fayetteville Technical Community College
(Fayetteville), 295

Pennsylvania
Pittsburgh Institute of Mortuary Science,
Incorporated (Pittsburgh), 371

Puerto Rico
Antilles School of Technical Careers (Hato
Rey), 380
Puerto Rico Technical Junior College (San
Juan), 392

Tennessee
John A. Gupton College (Nashville), 409

FUNERAL SERVICE AND MORTUARY SCIENCE, OTHER

Pennsylvania
Pittsburgh Institute of Mortuary Science,
Incorporated (Pittsburgh), 371

FURNITURE DESIGN AND MANUFACTURING

Alabama
Gadsden State Community College (Gadsden),
42

Indiana
Vincennes University (Vincennes), 168

Massachusetts
North Bennet Street School (Boston), 204

North Carolina
Catawba Valley Community College (Hickory),
292

GENE/GENETIC THERAPY

Ohio
Zane State College (Zanesville), 342

GENERAL MERCHANDISING, SALES, AND RELATED MARKETING OPERATIONS, OTHER

Connecticut
Manchester Community College (Manchester),
54
Middlesex Community College (Middletown),
54
Naugatuck Valley Community College
(Waterbury), 54
Three Rivers Community College (Norwich),
57
Tunxis Community College (Farmington), 57

Florida
Indian River State College (Fort Pierce), 81
Lake City Community College (Lake City), 83
Northwest Florida State College (Niceville), 89

Indiana
Vincennes University (Vincennes), 168

Maryland
The Community College of Baltimore County
(Baltimore), 187
Howard Community College (Columbia), 189

Ohio
Hocking College (Nelsonville), 321

Puerto Rico
Universal Career Counseling Centers
(Santurce), 393

Wisconsin
Moraine Park Technical College (Fond du Lac),
450

GENERAL OFFICE OCCUPATIONS AND CLERICAL SERVICES

Alabama
Central Alabama Community College
(Alexander City), 42
Gadsden State Community College (Gadsden),
42

Connecticut
Three Rivers Community College (Norwich),
57

Florida
Lee County High Tech Center North (Cape
Coral), 83
Management Resources Institute (Miami), 85

Georgia
Atlanta Technical College (Atlanta), 105
Augusta Technical College (Augusta), 106
Clayton State University (Morrow), 108
Columbus Technical College (Columbus), 108
Coosa Valley Technical College (Rome), 109
Dalton State College (Dalton), 109
Gwinnett Technical College (Lawrenceville),
113
Iverson Business School (Atlanta), 115
Javelin Technical Training Center (Atlanta),
115
Lanier Technical College (Oakwood), 115
Middle Georgia Technical College (Warner
Robbins), 117
Moultrie Technical College (Moultrie), 117
Northwestern Technical College (Rock Spring),
118
Ogeechee Technical College (Statesboro), 119
Okefenokee Technical College (Waycross), 119
Sandersville Technical College (Sandersville),
120
Southeastern Technical College (Vidalia), 121
Southwest Georgia Technical College
(Thomasville), 122
West Central Technical College (Waco), 124
West Georgia Technical College (LaGrange),
124

Illinois
Elgin Community College (Elgin), 132
Harper College (Palatine), 135
Highland Community College (Freeport), 136
Illinois Central College (East Peoria), 136
Illinois Valley Community College (Oglesby),
138
John A. Logan College (Carterville), 138
Kaskaskia College (Centralia), 139
Kishwaukee College (Malta), 140
Lake Land College (Mattoon), 140
Lewis and Clark Community College (Godfrey),
141
Lincoln Land Community College (Springfield),
141
Midstate College (Peoria), 143
Morton College (Cicero), 143
Sauk Valley Community College (Dixon), 150
Southeastern Illinois College (Harrisburg), 151
Waubonsee Community College (Sugar Grove),
154

Indiana
Harrison College (Fort Wayne), 158
Vincennes University (Vincennes), 168

Kentucky
Daymar College (Paducah), 172
Employment Solutions (Lexington), 172

Maine
Northern Maine Community College (Presque
Isle), 182

Maryland
Hagerstown Community College (Hagerstown),
188

Massachusetts
Marian Court College (Swampscott), 201
Massasoit Community College (Brockton), 202
Middlesex Community College (Bedford), 202
Springfield Technical Community College
(Springfield), 207

Michigan
Alpena Community College (Alpena), 209
Baker College of Allen Park (Allen Park), 209
Baker College of Auburn Hills (Auburn Hills),
209
Baker College of Cadillac (Cadillac), 210
Baker College of Clinton Township (Clinton
Township), 210
Baker College of Flint (Flint), 210
Baker College of Muskegon (Muskegon), 211
Baker College of Owosso (Owosso), 211
Baker College of Port Huron (Port Huron), 211
Bay de Noc Community College (Escanaba),
211
Bay Mills Community College (Brimley), 211
Career Quest Learning Center (East Lansing),
212
Dorsey Business Schools (Madison Heights),
214
Dorsey Business Schools (Roseville), 214
Kirtland Community College (Roscommon),
219
Mid Michigan Community College (Harrison),
222
Muskegon Community College (Muskegon),
223
North Central Michigan College (Petoskey),
223
St. Clair County Community College (Port
Huron), 226

New Jersey
Adult and Continuing Education–Bergen
County Technical Schools (Hackensack), 240
Berkeley College (West Paterson), 240
Keyskills Learning (Clifton), 247
Performance Training (Toms River), 251

New York

Berkeley College–New York City Campus (New York), 257

Broome Community College (Binghamton), 259

Erie Community College (Buffalo), 265

Fulton-Montgomery Community College (Johnstown), 267

Long Island Business Institute (Commack), 271

Mohawk Valley Community College (Utica), 274

Monroe Community College (Rochester), 274

Onondaga-Courtland-Madison BOCES (Liverpool), 278

Ridley-Lowell School of Business (Poughkeepsie), 280

Ohio

Akron Adult Vocational Services (Akron), 309

Akron Institute (Cuyahoga Falls), 310

Apollo School of Practical Nursing (Lima), 310

Ashland University (Ashland), 310

Buckeye Joint Vocational School (New Philadelphia), 313

Everest Institute (Cuyahoga Falls), 320

Hocking College (Nelsonville), 321

Licking County Joint Vocational School–Newark (Newark), 324

Lorain County Community College (Elyria), 324

Northwest State Community College (Archbold), 327

Pickaway Ross Joint Vocational School District (Chillicothe), 331

Pioneer Career and Technology Center: A Vocational School District (Shelby), 331

Scioto County Joint Vocational School District (Lucasville), 334

Sinclair Community College (Dayton), 334

Southern State Community College (Hillsboro), 335

Terra State Community College (Fremont), 336

The University of Akron (Akron), 338

University of Northwestern Ohio (Lima), 339

The University of Toledo (Toledo), 339

Vanguard Career Center (Fremont), 340

Pennsylvania

Bucks County Community College (Newtown), 345

Butler County Community College (Butler), 345

Delaware County Community College (Media), 351

Luzerne County Community College (Nanticoke), 363

McCann School of Business & Technology (Pottsville), 364

Newport Business Institute (Lower Burrell), 366

Northampton County Area Community College (Bethlehem), 366

Pennsylvania Highlands Community College (Johnstown), 370

Precision Manufacturing Institute (Meadville), 371

Reading Area Community College (Reading), 372

South Hills School of Business & Technology (State College), 374

Puerto Rico

Colegio Mayor de Tecnología–Arroyo (Arroyo), 382

Huertas Junior College (Caguas), 385

Rhode Island

Community College of Rhode Island (Warwick), 394

South Carolina

Aiken Technical College (Aiken), 397

Bob Jones University (Greenville), 398

Central Carolina Technical College (Sumter), 398

Denmark Technical College (Denmark), 398

Florence-Darlington Technical College (Florence), 399

Horry-Georgetown Technical College (Conway), 400

Northeastern Technical College (Cheraw), 401

Orangeburg-Calhoun Technical College (Orangeburg), 402

Piedmont Technical College (Greenwood), 402

Technical College of the Lowcountry (Beaufort), 403

Tri-County Technical College (Pendleton), 403

York Technical College (Rock Hill), 405

Tennessee

West Tennessee Business College (Jackson), 421

West Virginia

Opportunities Industrialization Center–North Central West Virginia (Fairmont), 442

Wisconsin

Chippewa Valley Technical College (Eau Claire), 445

Fox Valley Technical College (Appleton), 446

Gateway Technical College (Kenosha), 446

Lakeshore Technical College (Cleveland), 447

Milwaukee Area Technical College (Milwaukee), 449

Moraine Park Technical College (Fond du Lac), 450

Nicolet Area Technical College (Rhinelander), 450

Northcentral Technical College (Wausau), 450

Northeast Wisconsin Technical College (Green Bay), 450

Southwest Wisconsin Technical College (Fennimore), 452

Waukesha County Technical College (Pewaukee), 453

Western Technical College (La Crosse), 453

GEOGRAPHY

Georgia

Gainesville State College (Gainesville), 112

Illinois

Roosevelt University (Chicago), 149

Indiana

Indiana State University (Terre Haute), 159

Maryland

The Community College of Baltimore County (Baltimore), 187

Montgomery College (Rockville), 190

Massachusetts

Springfield Technical Community College (Springfield), 207

New York

Erie Community College (Buffalo), 265

Ohio

Hocking College (Nelsonville), 321

Miami University (Oxford), 326

The University of Toledo (Toledo), 339

Youngstown State University (Youngstown), 341

Pennsylvania

University of Pittsburgh (Pittsburgh), 376

GEOGRAPHY, OTHER

Illinois

Illinois Central College (East Peoria), 136

Maryland

Montgomery College (Rockville), 190

Michigan

Muskegon Community College (Muskegon), 223

GEOLOGICAL AND EARTH SCIENCES/GEOSCIENCES, OTHER

Massachusetts

University of Massachusetts Boston (Boston), 208

Pennsylvania

Harrisburg University of Science and Technology (Harrisburg), 358

GERMAN LANGUAGE AND LITERATURE

Michigan

Michigan Technological University (Houghton), 222

Pennsylvania

University of Pittsburgh (Pittsburgh), 376

GERMAN STUDIES

Pennsylvania

Muhlenberg College (Allentown), 365

GLAZIER

Florida

Mid-Florida Tech (Orlando), 87

Illinois

Parkland College (Champaign), 145

Wisconsin

Milwaukee Area Technical College (Milwaukee), 449

GRAPHIC AND PRINTING EQUIPMENT OPERATOR, GENERAL PRODUCTION

Alabama

Lawson State Community College (Birmingham), 44

Connecticut

Gateway Community College (New Haven), 52

Florida

First Coast Technical Institute (St. Augustine), 75

McFatter Technical Center (Davie), 86

Georgia

Albany Technical College (Albany), 103

Augusta Technical College (Augusta), 106

DeKalb Technical College (Clarkston), 109

Flint River Technical College (Thomaston), 111

Griffin Technical College (Griffin), 113

Lanier Technical College (Oakwood), 115

Valdosta Technical College (Valdosta), 123

West Georgia Technical College (LaGrange), 124

Illinois

Harper College (Palatine), 135

Kaskaskia College (Centralia), 139

Lake Land College (Mattoon), 140

Rock Valley College (Rockford), 149

Maine

Central Maine Community College (Auburn), 181

Maryland

The Community College of Baltimore County (Baltimore), 187

Montgomery College (Rockville), 190

Massachusetts

Springfield Technical Community College (Springfield), 207

Mississippi

Hinds Community College (Raymond), 232

New Hampshire

Manchester Community College (Manchester), 237

New Jersey

Cumberland County College (Vineland), 244

New York
Rochester Institute of Technology (Rochester), 280

North Carolina
Central Piedmont Community College (Charlotte), 293
Lenoir Community College (Kinston), 299

Ohio
Columbus State Community College (Columbus), 317

Pennsylvania
Greater Altoona Career and Technology Center (Altoona), 356

South Carolina
Midlands Technical College (Columbia), 401

Tennessee
Tennessee Technology Center at Memphis (Memphis), 417
Tennessee Technology Center at Morristown (Morristown), 418

West Virginia
Academy of Careers and Technology (Beckley), 437

Wisconsin
Madison Area Technical College (Madison), 448
Milwaukee Area Technical College (Milwaukee), 449
Northeast Wisconsin Technical College (Green Bay), 450
Waukesha County Technical College (Pewaukee), 453

GRAPHIC COMMUNICATIONS, GENERAL

Illinois
City Colleges of Chicago, Kennedy-King College (Chicago), 128

Michigan
Michigan Career and Technical Institute (Plainwell), 221

North Carolina
Central Piedmont Community College (Charlotte), 293

Virginia
Danville Community College (Danville), 426

West Virginia
Ben Franklin Career Center (Dunbar), 437
Logan-Mingo School of Practical Nursing (Logan), 441

GRAPHIC COMMUNICATIONS, OTHER

Alabama
Bishop State Community College (Mobile), 41
H. Councill Trenholm State Technical College (Montgomery), 43
J. F. Drake State Technical College (Huntsville), 44

New York
Rochester Institute of Technology (Rochester), 280

Pennsylvania
Lancaster County Career and Technology Center (Willow Street), 360

Wisconsin
Milwaukee Area Technical College (Milwaukee), 449

GRAPHIC DESIGN

Delaware
Delaware College of Art and Design (Wilmington), 59

District of Columbia
Corcoran College of Art and Design (Washington), 61

Florida
Miami Lakes Technical Education Center (Miami), 87
Robert Morgan Vocational-Technical Center (Miami), 94

Georgia
The Art Institute of Atlanta (Atlanta), 105
Savannah College of Art and Design (Savannah), 120

Illinois
Columbia College Chicago (Chicago), 130
Highland Community College (Freeport), 136
The Illinois Institute of Art–Schaumburg (Schaumburg), 138
Illinois Valley Community College (Oglesby), 138
Lewis and Clark Community College (Godfrey), 141
Rend Lake College (Ina), 148
Richland Community College (Decatur), 148
Spoon River College (Canton), 152
Waubonsee Community College (Sugar Grove), 154

Indiana
The Art Institute of Indianapolis (Indianapolis), 155

Kentucky
Daymar College (Louisville), 171

Maryland
Cecil College (North East), 186
Maryland Institute College of Art (Baltimore), 190

Massachusetts
Assumption College (Worcester), 193
North Shore Community College (Danvers), 204
School of the Museum of Fine Arts, Boston (Boston), 206

Michigan
Kalamazoo Valley Community College (Kalamazoo), 218
Kellogg Community College (Battle Creek), 218
Kirtland Community College (Roscommon), 219
Lansing Community College (Lansing), 219
Monroe County Community College (Monroe), 222
North Central Michigan College (Petoskey), 223
Washtenaw Community College (Ann Arbor), 229

New Jersey
Sussex County Community College (Newton), 254

New York
Wood Tobe–Coburn School (New York), 288

North Carolina
The Art Institute of Charlotte (Charlotte), 288
Central Piedmont Community College (Charlotte), 293
Forsyth Technical Community College (Winston-Salem), 296
King's College (Charlotte), 299
Lenoir Community College (Kinston), 299

Ohio
Bradford School (Columbus), 312

Pennsylvania
Community College of Allegheny County (Pittsburgh), 348
Greater Altoona Career and Technology Center (Altoona), 356

Harrisburg Area Community College (Harrisburg), 357
Luzerne County Community College (Nanticoke), 363
Westmoreland County Community College (Youngwood), 378

Tennessee
Watkins College of Art, Design, & Film (Nashville), 421

West Virginia
Cabell County Vocational Technical Center (Huntington), 438
Putnam Career and Technology Center School of Practical Nursing (Eleanor), 443

GREENHOUSE OPERATIONS AND MANAGEMENT

Georgia
Gwinnett Technical College (Lawrenceville), 113

Illinois
Kishwaukee College (Malta), 140
McHenry County College (Crystal Lake), 142
Richland Community College (Decatur), 148

North Carolina
Halifax Community College (Weldon), 297
Johnston Community College (Smithfield), 298
Pitt Community College (Greenville), 303

GROUND TRANSPORTATION, OTHER

Florida
Ridge Technical Center (Winter Haven), 93

Illinois
City Colleges of Chicago, Olive-Harvey College (Chicago), 128

Pennsylvania
Schuylkill Technology Center–North Campus (Frackville), 373

Virginia
Southside Virginia Community College (Alberta), 432
Tidewater Community College (Norfolk), 434

GUNSMITHING/GUNSMITH

Alabama
Jefferson Davis Community College (Brewton), 44

North Carolina
Montgomery Community College (Troy), 301
Piedmont Community College (Roxboro), 302

South Carolina
Piedmont Technical College (Greenwood), 402

HAIR STYLING/STYLIST AND HAIR DESIGN

Florida
American Institute of Beauty (Largo), 64
North Florida Institute–Jacksonville (Jacksonville), 89

Georgia
Beauty College of America (Forest Park), 106

Illinois
Alvareitas College of Cosmetology (Belleville), 124
Alvareita's College of Cosmetology (Edwardsville), 124
Alvareita's College of Cosmetology (Godfrey), 124

Indiana
Creative Hairstyling Academy (Highland), 156

Kentucky
PJ's College of Cosmetology (Glasgow), 177

Massachusetts
Lowell Academy Hairstyling Institute (Lowell), 201

Mississippi
J & J Hair Design College (Carthage), 233

New Hampshire
Portsmouth Beauty School of Hair Design (Portsmouth), 239

New Jersey
Parisian Beauty School (Hackensack), 250

New York
Elite Academy of Beauty Arts (Brooklyn), 264

Ohio
Euclidian Beauty School (Euclid), 320
Warren County Career Center (Lebanon), 340

Pennsylvania
Laurel Business Institute (Uniontown), 361

Puerto Rico
D'mart Institute (Barranquitas), 383
Emma's Beauty Academy (Juana Diaz), 384
Emma's Beauty Academy (Mayagüez), 384
Hispanic American College (Carolina), 385
Institute of Beauty Careers (Arecibo), 386
Instituto de Banca y Comercio–Aprendes Practicanco (Río Piedras), 386
Instituto de Educacion Tecnica Ocupacional La Reine (Aguadilla), 387
Instituto de Educacion Tecnica Ocupacional La Reine (Manati), 387
Serbias School of Beauty Culture (Guayama), 393

Tennessee
Last Minute Cuts School of Barbering and Cosmetology (Memphis), 409
Queen City College (Clarksville), 412

Wisconsin
Chippewa Valley Technical College (Eau Claire), 445
Gateway Technical College (Kenosha), 446
Mid-State Technical College (Wisconsin Rapids), 449
Milwaukee Area Technical College (Milwaukee), 449
Nicolet Area Technical College (Rhinelander), 450
Southwest Wisconsin Technical College (Fennimore), 452
Waukesha County Technical College (Pewaukee), 453
Wisconsin Indianhead Technical College (Shell Lake), 453

HAZARDOUS MATERIALS INFORMATION SYSTEMS TECHNOLOGY/TECHNICIAN

South Carolina
Spartanburg Community College (Spartanburg), 403

West Virginia
American Public University System (Charles Town), 437

HAZARDOUS MATERIALS MANAGEMENT AND WASTE TECHNOLOGY/TECHNICIAN

West Virginia
American Public University System (Charles Town), 437

HEALTH AIDE

Florida
Concorde Career Institute (Jacksonville), 70
Henry W. Brewster Technical Center (Tampa), 80

Ohio
North Central State College (Mansfield), 327
Tri-Rivers Career Center (Marion), 337

Pennsylvania
Community College of Beaver County (Monaca), 349

West Virginia
Ben Franklin Career Center (Dunbar), 437
Putnam Career and Technology Center School of Practical Nursing (Eleanor), 443

HEALTH AIDES/ATTENDANTS/ORDERLIES, OTHER

Florida
First Coast Technical Institute (St. Augustine), 75
Henry W. Brewster Technical Center (Tampa), 80
Lindsey Hopkins Technical Education Center (Miami), 84
Ultimate Medical Academy (Clearwater), 100
Ultimate Medical Academy–Tampa (Tampa), 100

Massachusetts
Springfield Technical Community College (Springfield), 207

Ohio
Licking County Joint Vocational School–Newark (Newark), 324

Puerto Rico
Trinity College of Puerto Rico (Ponce), 393

Tennessee
Tennessee Technology Center at Elizabethton (Elizabethton), 416

HEALTH AND MEDICAL ADMINISTRATIVE SERVICES, OTHER

Delaware
Dawn Training Centre (Wilmington), 58

Florida
ATI Career Training Center (Fort Lauderdale), 65
Central Florida College (Saint Petersburg), 68
Concorde Career Institute (Jacksonville), 70
Concorde Career Institute (Lauderdale Lake), 70
Concorde Career Institute (Tampa), 71
David G. Erwin Technical Center (Tampa), 71
Florida National College (Hialeah), 78
Indian River State College (Fort Pierce), 81
Lee County High Tech Center North (Cape Coral), 83
North Florida Institute (Orange Park), 89
Pensacola School of Massage Therapy & Health Careers (Pensacola), 91
Sheridan Vocational-Technical Center (Hollywood), 96

Georgia
Everest Institute (Marietta), 111

Kentucky
National College (Lexington), 176
Southwestern College of Business (Florence), 178

Maryland
The Community College of Baltimore County (Baltimore), 187

Massachusetts
Bristol Community College (Fall River), 196
Northern Essex Community College (Haverhill), 204
The Salter School (Worcester), 206

Michigan
Career Quest Learning Center (East Lansing), 212

Carnegie Institute (Troy), 212
Everest Institute (Dearborn), 215
Everest Institute (Kalamazoo), 215
Lansing Community College (Lansing), 219

New Jersey
Berdan Institute (Totowa), 240
Harris School of Business–Cherry Hill (Cherry Hill), 246

New York
Branford Hall Career Institute–Bohemia Campus (Ronkonkoma), 258
Cheryl Fells School of Business (Niagara Falls), 261

North Carolina
Cabarrus College of Health Sciences (Concord), 290
Center for Employment Training–Research Triangle Park (Research Triangle Park), 292

Ohio
Edison State Community College (Piqua), 319
Hocking College (Nelsonville), 321
Lakeland Community College (Kirtland), 323
Ohio Institute of Health Careers (Columbus), 329
Sanford-Brown Institute (Middleburg Heights), 333
Terra State Community College (Fremont), 336
The University of Toledo (Toledo), 339

Pennsylvania
Career Development & Employment (Wilkes Barre), 346
Community College of Allegheny County (Pittsburgh), 348
Community College of Beaver County (Monaca), 349
Luzerne County Community College (Nanticoke), 363
Pennsylvania Highlands Community College (Johnstown), 370

Puerto Rico
Ponce Paramedical College (Ponce), 392

Rhode Island
Community College of Rhode Island (Warwick), 394

Tennessee
National College (Nashville), 411
Southwest Tennessee Community College (Memphis), 414

Virginia
ACT College (Arlington), 423
Center for Employment Training–Alexandria (Alexandria), 425
Everest College (Newport News), 427
Everest Institute (Chesapeake), 428
Lord Fairfax Community College (Middletown), 429
Mountain Empire Community College (Big Stone Gap), 430
National College (Salem), 430
Piedmont Virginia Community College (Charlottesville), 431
Virginia Western Community College (Roanoke), 436
Wytheville Community College (Wytheville), 436

West Virginia
Everest Institute (Cross Lanes), 439

Wisconsin
Moraine Park Technical College (Fond du Lac), 450

HEALTH AND PHYSICAL EDUCATION/ FITNESS, OTHER

Alabama
Shelton State Community College (Tuscaloosa), 46

Florida
ATI Career Training Center (Fort Lauderdale), 65
Heritage Institute (Fort Myers), 80
Lincoln College of Technology (West Palm Beach), 84

Georgia
Gainesville State College (Gainesville), 112

Maryland
College of Southern Maryland (La Plata), 186
Montgomery College (Rockville), 190

Massachusetts
Berkshire Community College (Pittsfield), 194
Massachusetts Bay Community College (Wellesley Hills), 201

Michigan
Henry Ford Community College (Dearborn), 217

New Hampshire
Manchester Community College (Manchester), 237

New Jersey
Thomas Edison State College (Trenton), 254

Ohio
Columbus State Community College (Columbus), 317
The University of Akron (Akron), 338

Puerto Rico
Huertas Junior College (Caguas), 385

Virginia
Heritage Institute (Manassas), 428

HEALTH AND PHYSICAL EDUCATION, GENERAL

Illinois
McHenry County College (Crystal Lake), 142
Prairie State College (Chicago Heights), 146

Maryland
Anne Arundel Community College (Arnold), 184
Hagerstown Community College (Hagerstown), 188

Massachusetts
Holyoke Community College (Holyoke), 199

New Jersey
Camden County College (Blackwood), 241
Raritan Valley Community College (Somerville), 252

HEALTH/HEALTH-CARE ADMINISTRATION/ MANAGEMENT

Illinois
Roosevelt University (Chicago), 149

Maine
Saint Joseph's College of Maine (Standish), 182
Seacoast Career Schools (Sanford), 182

Massachusetts
Assumption College (Worcester), 193

Michigan
Oakland Community College (Bloomfield Hills), 224

New Jersey
Berdan Institute (Totowa), 240
Central Career School (South Plainfield), 242
Harris School of Business–Hamilton (Hamilton), 246

North Carolina
Randolph Community College (Asheboro), 303

Ohio
Chancellor University (Cleveland), 315
Columbus State Community College (Columbus), 317

The University of Toledo (Toledo), 339

Pennsylvania
Cedar Crest College (Allentown), 347
Muhlenberg College (Allentown), 365
Robert Morris University (Moon Township), 372

Virginia
ECPI College of Technology (Virginia Beach), 426
ECPI Technical College (Richmond), 427
Shenandoah University (Winchester), 432

HEALTH INFORMATION/MEDICAL RECORDS ADMINISTRATION/ADMINISTRATOR

Florida
Concorde Career Institute (Jacksonville), 70
Concorde Career Institute (Lauderdale Lake), 70
Concorde Career Institute (Tampa), 71
Medical Career Institute of South Florida (West Palm Beach), 86
New Professions Technical Institute (Miami), 88
Southwest Florida College (Fort Myers), 97

Georgia
Medical College of Georgia (Augusta), 116
Omnitech Institute (Decatur), 119

Illinois
Everest College (Skokie), 134

Indiana
TechSkills—Indianapolis (Indianapolis), 167

Maine
Eastern Maine Community College (Bangor), 181

Massachusetts
Massasoit Community College (Brockton), 202

Michigan
Everest Institute (Dearborn), 215

New York
Touro College (New York), 285

Ohio
Cleveland Institute of Dental-Medical Assistants (Cleveland), 316
Cleveland Institute of Dental-Medical Assistants (Lyndhurst), 316
Cleveland Institute of Dental-Medical Assistants (Mentor), 316
Hocking College (Nelsonville), 321
Knox County Career Center (Mount Vernon), 323
Ohio Hi Point Joint Vocational School District (Bellefontaine), 329
Southwestern College of Business (Cincinnati), 335
TechSkills—Columbus (Columbus), 336
The University of Toledo (Toledo), 339

Pennsylvania
Everest Institute (Pittsburgh), 355
Lincoln Technical Institute (Philadelphia), 362
Yorktowne Business Institute (York), 379

Puerto Rico
Advanced Tech College (Bayamón), 379
Colegio Mayor de Tecnologia–Arroyo (Arroyo), 382

Tennessee
Draughons Junior College (Clarksville), 407
Draughons Junior College (Murfreesboro), 407

West Virginia
Monongalia County Technical Education Center (Morgantown), 441

HEALTH INFORMATION/MEDICAL RECORDS TECHNOLOGY/TECHNICIAN

Alabama
Bishop State Community College (Mobile), 41

Enterprise-Ozark Community College (Enterprise), 42
Wallace State Community College (Hanceville), 48

Connecticut
Briarwood College (Southington), 50
Quinebaug Valley Community College (Danielson), 56

Delaware
Deep Muscle Therapy School (Wilmington), 58

District of Columbia
Sanz School (Washington), 62

Florida
Brevard Community College (Cocoa), 67
Central Florida College (Winter Park), 68
Central Florida Community College (Ocala), 69
Coral Ridge Nurses Assistant Training School (Ft. Lauderdale), 71
Daytona State College (Daytona Beach), 72
Florida Community College at Jacksonville (Jacksonville), 77
Hillsborough Community College (Tampa), 81
Indian River State College (Fort Pierce), 81
Lake City Community College (Lake City), 83
Lake-Sumter Community College (Leesburg), 83
MedVance Institute (Atlantis), 86
MedVance Institute (Fort Lauderdale), 86
MedVance Institute (Miami), 86
MedVance Institute (Stuart), 86
Miami Dade College (Miami), 87
Northwest Florida State College (Niceville), 89
Palm Beach Community College (Lake Worth), 90
Pasco-Hernando Community College (New Port Richey), 90
Pensacola Junior College (Pensacola), 91
Polk Community College (Winter Haven), 92
St. Johns River Community College (Palatka), 94
St. Petersburg College (St. Petersburg), 94
Santa Fe Community College (Gainesville), 95
Seminole Community College (Sanford), 96
Superior Career Institute (Lauderdale Lakes), 98
Tallahassee Community College (Tallahassee), 98
Valencia Community College (Orlando), 101

Georgia
Atlanta Technical College (Atlanta), 105
Brown College of Court Reporting and Medical Transcription (Atlanta), 107
Darton College (Albany), 109
Heart of Georgia Technical College (Dublin), 114
Ogeechee Technical College (Statesboro), 119

Illinois
BIR Training Center (Chicago), 125
Morton College (Cicero), 143
Northwestern Business College–Southwestern Campus (Bridgeview), 144
Northwestern College (Chicago), 144
Spoon River College (Canton), 152
Triton College (River Grove), 153

Indiana
Vincennes University (Vincennes), 168

Kentucky
Daymar College (Louisville), 171
Draughons Junior College (Bowling Green), 172
Gateway Community and Technical College (Covington), 173
Spencerian College (Louisville), 179

Maine
Beal College (Bangor), 180
Kennebec Valley Community College (Fairfield), 181

Maryland

Allegany College of Maryland (Cumberland), 184

Baltimore City Community College (Baltimore), 185

Carroll Community College (Westminster), 186

College of Southern Maryland (La Plata), 186

The Community College of Baltimore County (Baltimore), 187

Kaplan College–Hagerstown (Hagerstown), 189

Montgomery College (Rockville), 190

Prince George's Community College (Largo), 191

Massachusetts

Branford Hall Career Institute–Springfield Campus (Springfield), 195

Holyoke Community College (Holyoke), 199

Labouré College (Boston), 200

Massachusetts Bay Community College (Wellesley Hills), 201

Northern Essex Community College (Haverhill), 204

Michigan

Davenport University (Grand Rapids), 213

Ferris State University (Big Rapids), 215

Schoolcraft College (Livonia), 227

New Jersey

Camden County College (Blackwood), 241

Raritan Valley Community College (Somerville), 252

New York

Career Institute of Health and Technology (Brooklyn), 260

Career Institute of Health and Technology (Garden City), 260

Jamestown Community College (Jamestown), 270

State University of New York College of Technology at Alfred (Alfred), 283

North Carolina

Brunswick Community College (Supply), 290

Catawba Valley Community College (Hickory), 292

Central Piedmont Community College (Charlotte), 293

Durham Technical Community College (Durham), 295

Edgecombe Community College (Tarboro), 295

McDowell Technical Community College (Marion), 300

Pitt Community College (Greenville), 303

Roanoke-Chowan Community College (Ahoskie), 303

Southwestern Community College (Sylva), 306

Ohio

Cincinnati State Technical and Community College (Cincinnati), 315

Cuyahoga Community College (Cleveland), 318

Owens Community College (Toledo), 330

Professional Skills Institute (Toledo), 331

Sinclair Community College (Dayton), 334

Stark State College of Technology (North Canton), 335

Terra State Community College (Fremont), 336

Pennsylvania

Bidwell Training Center (Pittsburgh), 344

Central Pennsylvania College (Summerdale), 347

Douglas Education Center (Monessen), 351

Erie Business Center, Main (Erie), 355

Erie Business Center, South (New Castle), 355

Kaplan Career Institute–Harrisburg (Harrisburg), 359

Lancaster County Career and Technology Center (Willow Street), 360

Puerto Rico

Atenas College (Manati), 380

International Technical College (San Juan), 389

Trinity College of Puerto Rico (Ponce), 393

South Carolina

Aiken Technical College (Aiken), 397

Florence-Darlington Technical College (Florence), 399

Horry-Georgetown Technical College (Conway), 400

Midlands Technical College (Columbia), 401

Trident Technical College (Charleston), 404

Tennessee

Chattanooga College–Medical, Dental and Technical Careers (Chattanooga), 406

Draughons Junior College (Nashville), 407

Dyersburg State Community College (Dyersburg), 407

MedVance Institute (Cookeville), 409

MedVance Institute–Nashville (Nashville), 409

Walters State Community College (Morristown), 421

Virginia

Virginia Highlands Community College (Abingdon), 435

West Virginia

Mountain State University (Beckley), 442

Wisconsin

Moraine Park Technical College (Fond du Lac), 450

Western Technical College (La Crosse), 453

HEALTH/MEDICAL CLAIMS EXAMINER

Pennsylvania

Star Technical Institute (Philadelphia), 374

Puerto Rico

Universidad Metropolitana (San Juan), 394

HEALTH/MEDICAL PHYSICS

Kentucky

West Kentucky Community and Technical College (Paducah), 180

New York

St. Joseph's Medical Center School of Radiography (Yonkers), 281

North Carolina

Cabarrus College of Health Sciences (Concord), 290

HEALTH/MEDICAL PREPARATORY PROGRAMS, OTHER

Illinois

Northwestern University (Evanston), 145

HEALTH PROFESSIONS AND RELATED CLINICAL SCIENCES, OTHER

Delaware

Delaware Technical & Community College, Stanton/Wilmington Campus (Newark), 59

Florida

Bradford Union Area Vocational Technical Center (Starke), 67

Comp-Med Vocational Careers Corporation (Hialeah), 70

MedVance Institute (Fort Lauderdale), 86

Ultimate Medical Academy–Tampa (Tampa), 100

Georgia

Medix School (Smyrna), 116

Illinois

Southeastern Illinois College (Harrisburg), 151

Maine

Washington County Community College (Calais), 183

Maryland

Allegany College of Maryland (Cumberland), 184

The Community College of Baltimore County (Baltimore), 187

Massachusetts

Medical Professional Institute (Malden), 202

Middlesex Community College (Bedford), 202

North Shore Community College (Danvers), 204

New Jersey

Georgian Court University (Lakewood), 245

University of Medicine and Dentistry of New Jersey (Newark), 255

New York

Farmingdale State College (Farmingdale), 266

Genesee Community College (Batavia), 267

Maria College (Albany), 272

Mercy College (Dobbs Ferry), 273

Rochester Institute of Technology (Rochester), 280

St. Joseph's College, Long Island Campus (Patchogue), 281

St. Joseph's College, New York (Brooklyn), 281

Schenectady County Community College (Schenectady), 282

State University of New York College of Technology at Canton (Canton), 284

North Carolina

Central Piedmont Community College (Charlotte), 293

Forsyth Technical Community College (Winston-Salem), 296

Montgomery Community College (Troy), 301

Pitt Community College (Greenville), 303

Roanoke-Chowan Community College (Ahoskie), 303

Stanly Community College (Albemarle), 306

Wilkes Community College (Wilkesboro), 308

Ohio

Buckeye Hills Career Center (Rio Grande), 313

Hocking College (Nelsonville), 321

Stark State College of Technology (North Canton), 335

Vanguard Career Center (Fremont), 340

Pennsylvania

Allied Medical and Technical Institute (Scranton), 343

Career Training Academy (Pittsburgh), 346

Lebanon County Area Vocational Technical School (Lebanon), 361

University of Pittsburgh (Pittsburgh), 376

Puerto Rico

Ponce Paramedical College (Ponce), 392

South Carolina

Aiken Technical College (Aiken), 397

Florence-Darlington Technical College (Florence), 399

Piedmont Technical College (Greenwood), 402

Spartanburg Community College (Spartanburg), 403

Tennessee

MedVance Institute–Nashville (Nashville), 409

Miller-Motte Technical College (Chattanooga), 410

West Virginia

Southern West Virginia Community and Technical College (Mount Gay), 443

West Virginia Northern Community College (Wheeling), 444

HEALTH SERVICES ADMINISTRATION

New York

Rochester Institute of Technology (Rochester), 280

HEALTH SERVICES/ALLIED HEALTH/HEALTH SCIENCES, GENERAL

Connecticut
Asnuntuck Community College (Enfield), 49

Florida
Atlantic Vocational-Technical Center (Coconut Creek), 66
Cambridge Institute of Allied Health (Longwood), 68
Sunstate Academy of Hair Design (Sarasota), 98

Illinois
Lincoln Technical Institute (Norridge), 142

Kentucky
Brown Mackie College–Northern Kentucky (Fort Mitchell), 171

Maine
Kennebec Valley Community College (Fairfield), 181

Maryland
Everest Institute (Silver Spring), 187
Medix School–West (Baltimore), 190

Massachusetts
Everest Institute (Chelsea), 198
Roxbury Community College (Roxbury Crossing), 205

Michigan
Washtenaw Community College (Ann Arbor), 229

New Hampshire
New Hampshire Community Technical College, Berlin/Laconia (Berlin), 238

New York
Utica College (Utica), 286

North Carolina
Catawba Valley Community College (Hickory), 292
Pitt Community College (Greenville), 303

Ohio
Scioto County Joint Vocational School District (Lucasville), 334

Pennsylvania
Drexel University (Philadelphia), 352

Vermont
Community College of Vermont (Waterbury), 422

Virginia
ECPI College of Technology (Virginia Beach), 426

West Virginia
Carver Career Center (Charleston), 438
Marshall Community and Technical College (Huntington), 441

HEALTH UNIT COORDINATOR/WARD CLERK

Florida
Atlantic Vocational-Technical Center (Coconut Creek), 66
Concorde Career Institute (Tampa), 71
Coral Ridge Nurses Assistant Training School (Ft. Lauderdale), 71
Henry W. Brewster Technical Center (Tampa), 80
Orlando Technical Center (Orlando), 90
Pasco-Hernando Community College (New Port Richey), 90
Pensacola Junior College (Pensacola), 91
Sheridan Vocational-Technical Center (Hollywood), 96
Traviss Technical Center (Lakeland), 99

Georgia
Southwest Georgia Technical College (Thomasville), 122

Illinois
Southwestern Illinois College (Belleville), 151

Kentucky
Bowling Green Technical College (Bowling Green), 170
Gateway Community and Technical College (Covington), 173
Jefferson Community and Technical College (Louisville), 175
Spencerian College (Louisville), 179

Michigan
Delta College (University Center), 213
Lansing Community College (Lansing), 219

New Jersey
Omega Institute (Pennsauken), 250

North Carolina
Blue Ridge Community College (Flat Rock), 289
Guilford Technical Community College (Jamestown), 297
Pitt Community College (Greenville), 303

Ohio
Cincinnati State Technical and Community College (Cincinnati), 315
Mahoning County Joint Vocational School District (Canfield), 325
Marion Technical College (Marion), 325

Pennsylvania
Bidwell Training Center (Pittsburgh), 344
Delaware County Community College (Media), 351

Wisconsin
Gateway Technical College (Kenosha), 446
Lakeshore Technical College (Cleveland), 447
Mid-State Technical College (Wisconsin Rapids), 449
Milwaukee Area Technical College (Milwaukee), 449
Waukesha County Technical College (Pewaukee), 453

HEALTH UNIT MANAGER/WARD SUPERVISOR

Pennsylvania
Delaware County Community College (Media), 351

HEATING, AIR CONDITIONING AND REFRIGERATION TECHNOLOGY/TECHNICIAN (ACH/ACR/ACHR/HRAC/HVAC/AC TECHNOLOGY)

Alabama
Bevill State Community College (Sumiton), 41
Bishop State Community College (Mobile), 41
Calhoun Community College (Decatur), 41
Gadsden State Community College (Gadsden), 42
George C. Wallace Community College (Dothan), 43
H. Councill Trenholm State Technical College (Montgomery), 43
Jefferson Davis Community College (Brewton), 44
Lawson State Community College (Birmingham), 44
Lurleen B. Wallace Community College (Andalusia), 45
Northwest-Shoals Community College (Muscle Shoals), 45
Shelton State Community College (Tuscaloosa), 46

Connecticut
Industrial Management Training Institute (Waterbury), 53

Delaware
Delaware Technical & Community College, Jack F. Owens Campus (Georgetown), 59

Florida
ATI Career Training Center (Miami), 65
ATI Career Training Center (Oakland Park), 65
College of Business and Technology–Flagler Campus (Miami), 70
College of Business and Technology–Hialeah Campus (Hialeah), 70
College of Business and Technology (Miami), 70
David G. Erwin Technical Center (Tampa), 71
Florida Community College at Jacksonville (Jacksonville), 77
Indian River State College (Fort Pierce), 81
Miami Lakes Technical Education Center (Miami), 87
Robert Morgan Vocational-Technical Center (Miami), 94
Sheridan Vocational-Technical Center (Hollywood), 96
South Florida Institute of Technology (Miami), 97
Tom P. Haney Technical Center (Panama City), 99
Withlacoochee Technical Institute (Inverness), 103

Georgia
Interactive College of Technology (Chamblee), 114
Medix School (Smyrna), 116

Illinois
Environmental Technical Institute–Blue Island Campus (Blue Island), 133
Environmental Technical Institute (Itasca), 133

Maine
Southern Maine Community College (South Portland), 182

Maryland
All-State Career School (Baltimore), 184
TESST College of Technology (Baltimore), 192

Massachusetts
Bay State School of Technology (Canton), 194
Branford Hall Career Institute–Springfield Campus (Springfield), 195
Southeastern Technical College (South Easton), 206

Michigan
Baker College of Owosso (Owosso), 211
Henry Ford Community College (Dearborn), 217
Kalamazoo Valley Community College (Kalamazoo), 218
Macomb Community College (Warren), 220
Mott Community College (Flint), 223
Northwestern Technological Institute (Southfield), 224
Oakland Community College (Bloomfield Hills), 224

New Jersey
Lincoln Technical Institute (Mahwah), 248
Lincoln Technical Institute (Union), 248
Mercer County Community College (Trenton), 248

New York
Apex Technical School (New York), 256
Branford Hall Career Institute–Bohemia Campus (Ronkonkoma), 258
Dutchess Community College (Poughkeepsie), 264
Harlem School of Technology (New York), 268
Monroe 2–Orleans BOCES Center for Workforce Development (Rochester), 274
New York City College of Technology of the City University of New York (Brooklyn), 276

HEATING, AIR CONDITIONING, VENTILATION AND REFRIGERATION MAINTENANCE TECHNOLOGY/TECHNICIAN (HAC, HACR, HVAC, HVACR)

Kentucky

Ashland Community and Technical College (Ashland), 169

Big Sandy Community and Technical College (Prestonsburg), 170

Bluegrass Community and Technical College (Lexington), 170

Bowling Green Technical College (Bowling Green), 170

Gateway Community and Technical College (Covington), 173

Hazard Community and Technical College (Hazard), 174

Jefferson Community and Technical College (Louisville), 175

Madisonville Community College (Madisonville), 176

Maysville Community and Technical College (Maysville), 176

Owensboro Community and Technical College (Owensboro), 177

Somerset Community College (Somerset), 178

Southeast Kentucky Community and Technical College (Cumberland), 178

West Kentucky Community and Technical College (Paducah), 180

Maine

Northern Maine Community College (Presque Isle), 182

Washington County Community College (Calais), 183

Maryland

Chesapeake College (Wye Mills), 186

The Community College of Baltimore County (Baltimore), 187

Lincoln Technical Institute (Columbia), 189

North American Trade Schools (Grantsville), 191

TESST College of Technology (Baltimore), 192

Massachusetts

Bay State School of Technology (Canton), 194

Benjamin Franklin Institute of Technology (Boston), 194

Branford Hall Career Institute–Springfield Campus (Springfield), 195

Kaplan Career Institute, Charlestown (Charlestown), 199

Southeastern Technical College (South Easton), 206

Springfield Technical Community College (Springfield), 207

Michigan

Delta College (University Center), 213

Grand Rapids Community College (Grand Rapids), 216

Kellogg Community College (Battle Creek), 218

Kirtland Community College (Roscommon), 219

Lansing Community College (Lansing), 219

Mid Michigan Community College (Harrison), 222

Northern Michigan University (Marquette), 224

Washtenaw Community College (Ann Arbor), 229

Wayne County Community College District (Detroit), 229

Mississippi

Copiah-Lincoln Community College (Wesson), 231

Delta Technical College (Southaven), 232

East Central Community College (Decatur), 232

Hinds Community College (Raymond), 232

Holmes Community College (Goodman), 233

Jones County Junior College (Ellisville), 234

Mississippi Delta Community College (Moorhead), 234

Mississippi Gulf Coast Community College (Perkinston), 234

Northeast Mississippi Community College (Booneville), 235

Southwest Mississippi Community College (Summit), 235

New Hampshire

Manchester Community College (Manchester), 237

New Jersey

Adult and Continuing Education–Bergen County Technical Schools (Hackensack), 240

Lincoln Technical Institute (Union), 248

Ocean County Vocational Post Secondary Division (Toms River), 250

Pennco Tech (Blackwood), 251

New York

Apex Technical School (New York), 256

Erie Community College (Buffalo), 265

Harlem School of Technology (New York), 268

Monroe Community College (Rochester), 274

Onondaga-Courtland-Madison BOCES (Liverpool), 278

State University of New York College of Technology at Canton (Canton), 284

State University of New York College of Technology at Delhi (Delhi), 284

North Carolina

Alamance Community College (Graham), 288

Asheville-Buncombe Technical Community College (Asheville), 288

Blue Ridge Community College (Flat Rock), 289

Cape Fear Community College (Wilmington), 290

Catawba Valley Community College (Hickory), 292

Central Piedmont Community College (Charlotte), 293

Cleveland Community College (Shelby), 293

Coastal Carolina Community College (Jacksonville), 293

College of The Albemarle (Elizabeth City), 294

Craven Community College (New Bern), 294

Davidson County Community College (Lexington), 294

Fayetteville Technical Community College (Fayetteville), 295

Forsyth Technical Community College (Winston-Salem), 296

Gaston College (Dallas), 296

Guilford Technical Community College (Jamestown), 297

Johnston Community College (Smithfield), 298

Martin Community College (Williamston), 299

Mayland Community College (Spruce Pine), 299

McDowell Technical Community College (Marion), 300

Mitchell Community College (Statesville), 300

Piedmont Community College (Roxboro), 302

Pitt Community College (Greenville), 303

Roanoke-Chowan Community College (Ahoskie), 303

Robeson Community College (Lumberton), 304

Rockingham Community College (Wentworth), 304

Rowan-Cabarrus Community College (Salisbury), 304

Sampson Community College (Clinton), 304

Southeastern Community College (Whiteville), 305

South Piedmont Community College (Polkton), 305

Southwestern Community College (Sylva), 306

Stanly Community College (Albemarle), 306

Surry Community College (Dobson), 306

Tri-County Community College (Murphy), 306

Vance-Granville Community College (Henderson), 307

Wake Technical Community College (Raleigh), 307

Wayne Community College (Goldsboro), 308

Wilson Community College (Wilson), 308

Ohio

Adult and Community Education–Hudson (Columbus), 309

Adult Center for Education (Zanesville), 309

American School of Technology (Columbus), 310

Ashtabula County Joint Vocational School (Jefferson), 311

Auburn Career Center (Painesville), 311

Butler Technology and Career Development Schools–D. Russel Lee Career-Technology Center (Hamilton), 314

Eastland Career Center (Groveport), 319

ETI Technical College of Niles (Niles), 319

Licking County Joint Vocational School–Newark (Newark), 324

Medina County Career Center (Medina), 325

O. C. Collins Career Center (Chesapeake), 328

Ohio Hi Point Joint Vocational School District (Bellefontaine), 329

Penta County Joint Vocational School (Perrysburg), 330

Pickaway Ross Joint Vocational School District (Chillicothe), 331

Polaris Career Center (Middleburg Heights), 331

Portage Lakes Career Center (Green), 331

University of Northwestern Ohio (Lima), 339

Upper Valley JVS (Piqua), 340

Vatterott College (Broadview Heights), 340

Warren County Career Center (Lebanon), 340

Washington County Career Center Adult Education (Marietta), 341

Pennsylvania

Central Pennsylvania Institute of Science and Technology (Pleasant Gap), 347

CHI Institute, Broomall Campus (Broomall), 348

Community College of Allegheny County (Pittsburgh), 348

Delaware County Community College (Media), 351

Greater Altoona Career and Technology Center (Altoona), 356

Harrisburg Area Community College (Harrisburg), 357

Huntingdon County Career and Technology (Mill Creek), 358

Lancaster County Career and Technology Center (Willow Street), 360

Lehigh Carbon Community College (Schnecksville), 362

New Castle School of Trades (Pulaski), 366

Northampton County Area Community College (Bethlehem), 366

Orleans Technical Institute (Philadelphia), 367

Reading Area Community College (Reading), 372

Triangle Tech, Inc.–Greensburg School (Greensburg), 375

Triangle Tech, Inc.–Pittsburgh School (Pittsburgh), 375

Westmoreland County Community College (Youngwood), 378

Puerto Rico

Automeca Technical College (Aguadilla), 380

Automeca Technical College (Bayamón), 380

Automeca Technical College (Caguas), 380

Automeca Technical College (Ponce), 380

D'mart Institute (Barranquitas), 383

Liceo de Arte y Tecnologia (Hato Rey), 390
Universal Technology College of Puerto Rico
(Aguadilla), 393
South Carolina
Aiken Technical College (Aiken), 397
Central Carolina Technical College (Sumter),
398
Florence-Darlington Technical College
(Florence), 399
Greenville Technical College (Greenville), 399
Horry-Georgetown Technical College
(Conway), 400
Midlands Technical College (Columbia), 401
Piedmont Technical College (Greenwood), 402
Spartanburg Community College (Spartanburg),
403
Technical College of the Lowcountry
(Beaufort), 403
Trident Technical College (Charleston), 404
Williamsburg Technical College (Kingstree),
404
York Technical College (Rock Hill), 405
Tennessee
Northeast State Technical Community College
(Blountville), 412
Tennessee Technology Center at Covington
(Covington), 415
Tennessee Technology Center at Crossville
(Crossville), 415
Tennessee Technology Center at Crump
(Crump), 415
Tennessee Technology Center at Dickson
(Dickson), 416
Tennessee Technology Center at Elizabethton
(Elizabethton), 416
Tennessee Technology Center at Jackson
(Jackson), 417
Tennessee Technology Center at Knoxville
(Knoxville), 417
Tennessee Technology Center at Memphis
(Memphis), 417
Tennessee Technology Center at Morristown
(Morristown), 418
Tennessee Technology Center at Murfreesboro
(Murfreesboro), 418
Tennessee Technology Center at Nashville
(Nashville), 418
Tennessee Technology Center at Newbern
(Newbern), 418
Tennessee Technology Center at Shelbyville
(Shelbyville), 419
Tennessee Technology Center at Whiteville
(Whiteville), 419
Vatterott College (Memphis), 420
Virginia
Advanced Technology Institute (Virginia
Beach), 423
Center for Employment Training–Alexandria
(Alexandria), 425
Danville Community College (Danville), 426
Mountain Empire Community College (Big
Stone Gap), 430
Northern Virginia Community College
(Annandale), 430
Patrick Henry Community College
(Martinsville), 431
Southside Virginia Community College
(Alberta), 432
Southwest Virginia Community College
(Richlands), 432
Thomas Nelson Community College
(Hampton), 433
Tidewater Community College (Norfolk), 434
Tidewater Tech-Trades (Norfolk), 434
Virginia Highlands Community College
(Abingdon), 435
Virginia Western Community College
(Roanoke), 436

West Virginia
Academy of Careers and Technology (Beckley),
437
Ben Franklin Career Center (Dunbar), 437
Logan-Mingo School of Practical Nursing
(Logan), 441
Monongalia County Technical Education
Center (Morgantown), 441
Putnam Career and Technology Center School
of Practical Nursing (Eleanor), 443
Wisconsin
Chippewa Valley Technical College (Eau
Claire), 445
Milwaukee Area Technical College
(Milwaukee), 449
Moraine Park Technical College (Fond du Lac),
450
Northcentral Technical College (Wausau), 450
Waukesha County Technical College
(Pewaukee), 453
Western Technical College (La Crosse), 453

HEAVY EQUIPMENT MAINTENANCE TECHNOLOGY/TECHNICIAN

Florida
Miami Lakes Technical Education Center
(Miami), 87
Washington-Holmes Technical Center
(Chipley), 102
Georgia
Albany Technical College (Albany), 103
Altamaha Technical College (Jesup), 104
Gwinnett Technical College (Lawrenceville),
113
North Georgia Technical College (Clarkesville),
118
Okefenokee Technical College (Waycross), 119
West Central Technical College (Waco), 124
Illinois
Joliet Junior College (Joliet), 139
Maine
Washington County Community College
(Calais), 183
Mississippi
Copiah-Lincoln Community College (Wesson),
231
Hinds Community College (Raymond), 232
North Carolina
Wilson Community College (Wilson), 308
Ohio
Licking County Joint Vocational School–
Newark (Newark), 324
Warren County Career Center (Lebanon), 340
Pennsylvania
Lancaster County Career and Technology
Center (Willow Street), 360
Tennessee
Nashville Auto Diesel College (Nashville), 410
Tennessee Technology Center at Dickson
(Dickson), 416
West Virginia
Ben Franklin Career Center (Dunbar), 437
Wisconsin
Fox Valley Technical College (Appleton), 446
Milwaukee Area Technical College
(Milwaukee), 449

HEAVY/INDUSTRIAL EQUIPMENT MAINTENANCE TECHNOLOGIES, OTHER

Florida
McFatter Technical Center (Davie), 86
Maryland
Chesapeake College (Wye Mills), 186

The Community College of Baltimore County
(Baltimore), 187
Mississippi
Coahoma Community College (Clarksdale), 231
New York
State University of New York College of
Technology at Alfred (Alfred), 283
North Carolina
Blue Ridge Community College (Flat Rock),
289
Rockingham Community College (Wentworth),
304
Ohio
Buckeye Hills Career Center (Rio Grande), 313
O. C. Collins Career Center (Chesapeake), 328
Pickaway Ross Joint Vocational School District
(Chillicothe), 331
Scioto County Joint Vocational School District
(Lucasville), 334
Pennsylvania
Schuylkill Technology Center–North Campus
(Frackville), 373
Puerto Rico
Escuela Tecnica de Electricidad (Ponce), 385
Tennessee
Tennessee Technology Center at Covington
(Covington), 415
Tennessee Technology Center at Hohenwald
(Hohenwald), 416
Tennessee Technology Center at Knoxville
(Knoxville), 417
Tennessee Technology Center at Pulaski
(Pulaski), 419
West Virginia
Blue Ridge Community and Technical College
(Martinsburg), 438
Eastern West Virginia Community and
Technical College (Moorefield), 439
Logan-Mingo School of Practical Nursing
(Logan), 441
West Virginia Northern Community College
(Wheeling), 444

HEMATOLOGY TECHNOLOGY/TECHNICIAN

Ohio
Sinclair Community College (Dayton), 334
Pennsylvania
Star Technical Institute (Philadelphia), 374

HIGHER EDUCATION/HIGHER EDUCATION ADMINISTRATION

New York
Touro College (New York), 285

HISTOLOGIC TECHNICIAN

Connecticut
Goodwin College (East Hartford), 53
Georgia
Darton College (Albany), 109
Indiana
Indiana University–Purdue University
Indianapolis (Indianapolis), 160
Michigan
Lansing Community College (Lansing), 219

HISTOLOGIC TECHNOLOGY/ HISTOTECHNOLOGIST

Delaware
Delaware Technical & Community College,
Stanton/Wilmington Campus (Newark), 59
Pennsylvania
Conemaugh Valley Memorial Hospital
(Johnstown), 350

HISTORIC PRESERVATION AND CONSERVATION

Michigan
Bay Mills Community College (Brimley), 211

Pennsylvania
Bucks County Community College (Newtown), 345
University of Pittsburgh (Pittsburgh), 376

HOME FURNISHINGS AND EQUIPMENT INSTALLERS

Alabama
H. Councill Trenholm State Technical College (Montgomery), 43

Florida
Washington-Holmes Technical Center (Chipley), 102
Winter Park Tech (Winter Park), 102

HOME HEALTH AIDE/HOME ATTENDANT

Alabama
Jefferson Davis Community College (Brewton), 44
Southern Union State Community College (Wadley), 47

Florida
Concorde Career Institute (Jacksonville), 70
Lindsey Hopkins Technical Education Center (Miami), 84
Orlando Technical Center (Orlando), 90
Seminole Community College (Sanford), 96
Superior Career Institute (Lauderdale Lakes), 98
Taylor College (Belleview), 99

Georgia
Athens Technical College (Athens), 105
Central Georgia Technical College (Macon), 107
East Central Technical College (Fitzgerald), 110
Griffin Technical College (Griffin), 113

Illinois
College of DuPage (Glen Ellyn), 129

Maryland
Allegany College of Maryland (Cumberland), 184
Anne Arundel Community College (Arnold), 184

Michigan
Baker College of Flint (Flint), 210
Baker College of Owosso (Owosso), 211

Ohio
Lakeland Community College (Kirtland), 323

Tennessee
Concorde Career College (Memphis), 406

West Virginia
Opportunities Industrialization Center–North Central West Virginia (Fairmont), 442

HORSE HUSBANDRY/EQUINE SCIENCE AND MANAGEMENT

Illinois
Parkland College (Champaign), 145

Maryland
Cecil College (North East), 186

Michigan
Michigan State University (East Lansing), 222

HORTICULTURAL SCIENCE

Connecticut
Naugatuck Valley Community College (Waterbury), 54

Ohio
Southern State Community College (Hillsboro), 335

University of Cincinnati (Cincinnati), 338

HOSPITAL AND HEALTH-CARE FACILITIES ADMINISTRATION/MANAGEMENT

Florida
Broward Community College (Fort Lauderdale), 68
St. Johns River Community College (Palatka), 94
St. Petersburg College (St. Petersburg), 94

Illinois
City Colleges of Chicago, Wilbur Wright College (Chicago), 129
College of DuPage (Glen Ellyn), 129

New York
Rochester Institute of Technology (Rochester), 280

Puerto Rico
Inter American University of Puerto Rico, Bayamón Campus (Bayamón), 388

Rhode Island
Providence College (Providence), 396

HOSPITALITY ADMINISTRATION/ MANAGEMENT, GENERAL

Alabama
James H. Faulkner State Community College (Bay Minette), 44
Jefferson State Community College (Birmingham), 44

Connecticut
Butler Business School (Bridgeport), 51
Three Rivers Community College (Norwich), 57
University of New Haven (West Haven), 58

Florida
Orlando Culinary Academy (Orlando), 89

Georgia
Albany Technical College (Albany), 103
Athens Technical College (Athens), 105
Central Georgia Technical College (Macon), 107
Columbus Technical College (Columbus), 108
DeKalb Technical College (Clarkston), 109
Gwinnett Technical College (Lawrenceville), 113
Ogeechee Technical College (Statesboro), 119
Savannah Technical College (Savannah), 121

Illinois
Elgin Community College (Elgin), 132
Joliet Junior College (Joliet), 139
Moraine Valley Community College (Palos Hills), 143
Northwestern Business College–Southwestern Campus (Bridgeview), 144
Northwestern College (Chicago), 144
Roosevelt University (Chicago), 149

Maryland
Allegany College of Maryland (Cumberland), 184
Wor-Wic Community College (Salisbury), 193

Massachusetts
Massachusetts Bay Community College (Wellesley Hills), 201

Michigan
Lake Michigan College (Benton Harbor), 219
North Central Michigan College (Petoskey), 223

Mississippi
Hinds Community College (Raymond), 232

New Hampshire
New Hampshire Technical Institute (Concord), 239

New Jersey
Bergen Community College (Paramus), 240

New York
Culinary Academy of Long Island (Westbury), 263
Trocaire College (Buffalo), 286

North Carolina
Central Piedmont Community College (Charlotte), 293
Nash Community College (Rocky Mount), 302

Ohio
Ashland University (Ashland), 310
Columbus State Community College (Columbus), 317
Lakeland Community College (Kirtland), 323
The University of Akron (Akron), 338

Pennsylvania
JNA Institute of Culinary Arts (Philadelphia), 358
Marywood University (Scranton), 364

Puerto Rico
Monteclaro Escuela de Hoteleria y Artes Culinarias (Rio Grande), 391

Rhode Island
Sawyer School (Pawtucket), 396

Tennessee
National College (Nashville), 411

Virginia
Dabney S. Lancaster Community College (Clifton Forge), 426
National College (Salem), 430
Northern Virginia Community College (Annandale), 430
Southwest Virginia Community College (Richlands), 432
Virginia Highlands Community College (Abingdon), 435

HOSPITALITY ADMINISTRATION/ MANAGEMENT, OTHER

Florida
Galiano Career Academy (Altamonte Sprints), 79
Mid-Florida Tech (Orlando), 87

Indiana
Indiana University–Purdue University Indianapolis (Indianapolis), 160
Ivy Tech Community College–Northeast (Fort Wayne), 163
Ivy Tech Community College–Northwest (Gary), 163
Purdue University Calumet (Hammond), 166

Maryland
Chesapeake College (Wye Mills), 186

Massachusetts
Cape Cod Community College (West Barnstable), 196

Michigan
Kirtland Community College (Roscommon), 219

New Jersey
Raritan Valley Community College (Somerville), 252

Ohio
Hocking College (Nelsonville), 321

Pennsylvania
Luzerne County Community College (Nanticoke), 363

Puerto Rico
Monteclaro Escuela de Hoteleria y Artes Culinarias (Rio Grande), 391

HOSPITALITY AND RECREATION MARKETING OPERATIONS

Michigan
Ferris State University (Big Rapids), 215

Pennsylvania
Bradford School (Pittsburgh), 345

West Virginia
Pierpont Community & Technical College of Fairmont State University (Fairmont), 442

Wisconsin
Lac Courte Oreilles Ojibwa Community College (Hayward), 447

HOTEL/MOTEL ADMINISTRATION/ MANAGEMENT

Connecticut
Gateway Community College (New Haven), 52
International College of Hospitality Management (Suffield), 53
Three Rivers Community College (Norwich), 57

Delaware
Delaware Technical & Community College, Stanton/Wilmington Campus (Newark), 59

Florida
Broward Community College (Fort Lauderdale), 68
Florida Community College at Jacksonville (Jacksonville), 77
Henry W. Brewster Technical Center (Tampa), 80
Miami Dade College (Miami), 87
St. Petersburg College (St. Petersburg), 94
Valencia Community College (Orlando), 101

Illinois
College of DuPage (Glen Ellyn), 129
Elgin Community College (Elgin), 132
Harper College (Palatine), 135
Lincoln Land Community College (Springfield), 141
Parkland College (Champaign), 145
Triton College (River Grove), 153

Indiana
Purdue University Calumet (Hammond), 166

Maryland
Anne Arundel Community College (Arnold), 184
Baltimore International College (Baltimore), 185
Frederick Community College (Frederick), 188
Montgomery College (Rockville), 190
Prince George's Community College (Largo), 191

Massachusetts
Cape Cod Community College (West Barnstable), 196
Middlesex Community College (Bedford), 202
Newbury College (Brookline), 203
Northern Essex Community College (Haverhill), 204
Quinsigamond Community College (Worcester), 205

Michigan
Bay de Noc Community College (Escanaba), 211
Ferris State University (Big Rapids), 215
Henry Ford Community College (Dearborn), 217

New Hampshire
New Hampshire Technical Institute (Concord), 239

New Jersey
Camden County College (Blackwood), 241
Middlesex County College (Edison), 249

New York
Career Academy of New York (New York), 260
Culinary Academy of Long Island (Westbury), 263
Monroe Community College (Rochester), 274

North Carolina
Cape Fear Community College (Wilmington), 290
Carteret Community College (Morehead City), 292
Central Piedmont Community College (Charlotte), 293
Southwestern Community College (Sylva), 306
Wake Technical Community College (Raleigh), 307

Ohio
Cuyahoga Community College (Cleveland), 318
Hocking College (Nelsonville), 321
The University of Akron (Akron), 338

Pennsylvania
Bucks County Community College (Newtown), 345
Community College of Allegheny County (Pittsburgh), 348
Erie Business Center, Main (Erie), 355
Westmoreland County Community College (Youngwood), 378

Puerto Rico
American Educational College (Bayamón), 379
ICPR Junior College–Arecibo Campus (Arecibo), 385
Inter American University of Puerto Rico, San Germán Campus (San Germán), 389

South Carolina
Trident Technical College (Charleston), 404

HOUSING AND HUMAN ENVIRONMENTS, OTHER

Florida
Indian River State College (Fort Pierce), 81
South Florida Community College (Avon Park), 97

Illinois
Illinois Central College (East Peoria), 136
Illinois Eastern Community Colleges, Lincoln Trail College (Robinson), 137
Illinois Valley Community College (Oglesby), 138
Kaskaskia College (Centralia), 139
Lake Land College (Mattoon), 140
Rend Lake College (Ina), 148
Richland Community College (Decatur), 148
Southeastern Illinois College (Harrisburg), 151

Michigan
Michigan Career and Technical Institute (Plainwell), 221

Wisconsin
Chippewa Valley Technical College (Eau Claire), 445
Madison Area Technical College (Madison), 448

HUMAN DEVELOPMENT AND FAMILY STUDIES, GENERAL

Florida
Indian River State College (Fort Pierce), 81

Pennsylvania
Penn State Shenango (Sharon), 369

HUMAN DEVELOPMENT, FAMILY STUDIES, AND RELATED SERVICES, OTHER

Connecticut
Post University (Waterbury), 56

Massachusetts
Massasoit Community College (Brockton), 202

Michigan
Kellogg Community College (Battle Creek), 218

Ohio
Kent State University, Tuscarawas Campus (New Philadelphia), 323
University of Cincinnati (Cincinnati), 338

Tennessee
Jackson State Community College (Jackson), 408
Southwest Tennessee Community College (Memphis), 414

Wisconsin
Milwaukee Area Technical College (Milwaukee), 449
Moraine Park Technical College (Fond du Lac), 450

HUMAN RESOURCES DEVELOPMENT

Illinois
Roosevelt University (Chicago), 149

HUMAN RESOURCES MANAGEMENT AND SERVICES, OTHER

New York
Pace University (New York), 279

Ohio
Columbus State Community College (Columbus), 317

Pennsylvania
Keystone College (La Plume), 359
Penn State University Park (University Park), 369

HUMAN RESOURCES MANAGEMENT/ PERSONNEL ADMINISTRATION, GENERAL

Alabama
Virginia College at Mobile (Mobile), 48

Connecticut
Post University (Waterbury), 56

Florida
Virginia College at Pensacola (Pensacola), 102

Georgia
DeKalb Technical College (Clarkston), 109
Griffin Technical College (Griffin), 113
Gwinnett Technical College (Lawrenceville), 113
Northwestern Technical College (Rock Spring), 118
Ogeechee Technical College (Statesboro), 119
Valdosta Technical College (Valdosta), 123

Illinois
Harper College (Palatine), 135
Joliet Junior College (Joliet), 139
Lewis and Clark Community College (Godfrey), 141
Moraine Valley Community College (Palos Hills), 143
Oakton Community College (Des Plaines), 145
Triton College (River Grove), 153

Indiana
Vincennes University (Vincennes), 168

Maryland
The Community College of Baltimore County (Baltimore), 187
Montgomery College (Rockville), 190
Prince George's Community College (Largo), 191

Massachusetts
Assumption College (Worcester), 193
Holyoke Community College (Holyoke), 199
Suffolk University (Boston), 207

HUMAN SERVICES, GENERAL

HYDRAULICS AND FLUID POWER TECHNOLOGY/TECHNICIAN

ILLUSTRATION

INDUSTRIAL DESIGN

INDUSTRIAL ELECTRONICS TECHNOLOGY/ TECHNICIAN

Industrial Electronics Technology/Technician

Lehigh Carbon Community College
(Schnecksville), 362
Northampton County Area Community College
(Bethlehem), 366

South Carolina
Aiken Technical College (Aiken), 397
Denmark Technical College (Denmark), 398
Midlands Technical College (Columbia), 401
Northeastern Technical College (Cheraw), 401
Technical College of the Lowcountry
(Beaufort), 403
York Technical College (Rock Hill), 405

Tennessee
Tennessee Technology Center at Athens
(Athens), 415
Tennessee Technology Center at Crossville
(Crossville), 415
Tennessee Technology Center at Crump
(Crump), 415
Tennessee Technology Center at Hohenwald
(Hohenwald), 416
Tennessee Technology Center at Knoxville
(Knoxville), 417
Tennessee Technology Center at McKenzie
(McKenzie), 417
Tennessee Technology Center at McMinnville
(McMinnville), 417
Tennessee Technology Center at Memphis
(Memphis), 417
Tennessee Technology Center at Oneida/
Huntsville (Huntsville), 419
Tennessee Technology Center at Whiteville
(Whiteville), 419

Virginia
Danville Community College (Danville), 426
Virginia Highlands Community College
(Abingdon), 435

Wisconsin
Chippewa Valley Technical College (Eau
Claire), 445
Gateway Technical College (Kenosha), 446
Lakeshore Technical College (Cleveland), 447
Milwaukee Area Technical College
(Milwaukee), 449
Southwest Wisconsin Technical College
(Fennimore), 452
Waukesha County Technical College
(Pewaukee), 453

INDUSTRIAL ENGINEERING

Ohio
Cleveland Institute of Electronics (Cleveland),
316

INDUSTRIAL MECHANICS AND MAINTENANCE TECHNOLOGY

Alabama
Gadsden State Community College (Gadsden),
42
George C. Wallace Community College
(Dothan), 43
H. Councill Trenholm State Technical College
(Montgomery), 43
J. F. Drake State Technical College (Huntsville),
44
Lawson State Community College
(Birmingham), 44
Shelton State Community College (Tuscaloosa),
46
Southern Union State Community College
(Wadley), 47

Florida
Henry W. Brewster Technical Center (Tampa),
80
Manatee Technical Institute (Bradenton), 85

Pinellas Technical Education Center–
Clearwater (Clearwater), 91
Pinellas Technical Education Center–St.
Petersburg (St. Petersburg), 92
Taylor Technical Institute (Perry), 99

Georgia
Albany Technical College (Albany), 103
Altamaha Technical College (Jesup), 104
Athens Technical College (Athens), 105
Augusta Technical College (Augusta), 106
Bainbridge College (Bainbridge), 106
Central Georgia Technical College (Macon),
107
College of Coastal Georgia (Brunswick), 108
Columbus Technical College (Columbus), 108
Coosa Valley Technical College (Rome), 109
DeKalb Technical College (Clarkston), 109
East Central Technical College (Fitzgerald), 110
Flint River Technical College (Thomaston), 111
Griffin Technical College (Griffin), 113
Heart of Georgia Technical College (Dublin),
114
Lanier Technical College (Oakwood), 115
Middle Georgia Technical College (Warner
Robbins), 117
Moultrie Technical College (Moultrie), 117
North Georgia Technical College (Clarkesville),
118
North Metro Technical College (Acworth), 118
Northwestern Technical College (Rock Spring),
118
Ogeechee Technical College (Statesboro), 119
Okefenokee Technical College (Waycross), 119
Sandersville Technical College (Sandersville),
120
Savannah Technical College (Savannah), 121
South Georgia Technical College (Americus),
122
Valdosta Technical College (Valdosta), 123
West Georgia Technical College (LaGrange),
124

Illinois
City Colleges of Chicago, Richard J. Daley
College (Chicago), 128
City Colleges of Chicago, Wilbur Wright
College (Chicago), 129
College of Lake County (Grayslake), 129
Elgin Community College (Elgin), 132
Highland Community College (Freeport), 136
Illinois Central College (East Peoria), 136
Illinois Eastern Community Colleges, Olney
Central College (Olney), 137
Illinois Valley Community College (Oglesby),
138
Kankakee Community College (Kankakee), 139
Kaskaskia College (Centralia), 139
Prairie State College (Chicago Heights), 146
Rend Lake College (Ina), 148
Richland Community College (Decatur), 148
Waubonsee Community College (Sugar Grove),
154

Kentucky
Ashland Community and Technical College
(Ashland), 169
Big Sandy Community and Technical College
(Prestonsburg), 170
Bluegrass Community and Technical College
(Lexington), 170
Bowling Green Technical College (Bowling
Green), 170
Elizabethtown Community and Technical
College (Elizabethtown), 172
Gateway Community and Technical College
(Covington), 173
Hazard Community and Technical College
(Hazard), 174
Henderson Community College (Henderson),
174

Hopkinsville Community College
(Hopkinsville), 174
Jefferson Community and Technical College
(Louisville), 175
Madisonville Community College
(Madisonville), 176
Maysville Community and Technical College
(Maysville), 176
Owensboro Community and Technical College
(Owensboro), 177
Somerset Community College (Somerset), 178
West Kentucky Community and Technical
College (Paducah), 180

Michigan
Grand Rapids Community College (Grand
Rapids), 216
Henry Ford Community College (Dearborn),
217
Kellogg Community College (Battle Creek), 218
Kirtland Community College (Roscommon),
219
Lake Michigan College (Benton Harbor), 219
Macomb Community College (Warren), 220
Muskegon Community College (Muskegon),
223

Mississippi
Meridian Community College (Meridian), 234
Mississippi Gulf Coast Community College
(Perkinston), 234

North Carolina
Gaston College (Dallas), 296
Randolph Community College (Asheboro), 303

Ohio
Akron Adult Vocational Services (Akron), 309
Apollo School of Practical Nursing (Lima), 310
Auburn Career Center (Painesville), 311
Buckeye Hills Career Center (Rio Grande), 313
Butler Technology and Career Development
Schools–D. Russel Lee Career-Technology
Center (Hamilton), 314
Licking County Joint Vocational School–
Newark (Newark), 324
Ohio Hi Point Joint Vocational School District
(Bellefontaine), 329
Scioto County Joint Vocational School District
(Lucasville), 334
Tri-Rivers Career Center (Marion), 337
Upper Valley JVS (Piqua), 340
Washington County Career Center Adult
Education (Marietta), 341

Pennsylvania
Community College of Allegheny County
(Pittsburgh), 348
Delaware County Community College (Media),
351
Harrisburg Area Community College
(Harrisburg), 357
Lancaster County Career and Technology
Center (Willow Street), 360
New Castle School of Trades (Pulaski), 366
Precision Manufacturing Institute (Meadville),
371

Puerto Rico
Industrial Technical College (Humacao), 386

South Carolina
Aiken Technical College (Aiken), 397
Central Carolina Technical College (Sumter),
398
Greenville Technical College (Greenville), 399
Orangeburg-Calhoun Technical College
(Orangeburg), 402
Spartanburg Community College (Spartanburg),
403
Tri-County Technical College (Pendleton), 403
York Technical College (Rock Hill), 405

Tennessee

Northeast State Technical Community College (Blountville), 412

Tennessee Technology Center at Athens (Athens), 415

Tennessee Technology Center at Covington (Covington), 415

Tennessee Technology Center at Crossville (Crossville), 415

Tennessee Technology Center at Crump (Crump), 415

Tennessee Technology Center at Dickson (Dickson), 416

Tennessee Technology Center at Elizabethton (Elizabethton), 416

Tennessee Technology Center at Harriman (Harriman), 416

Tennessee Technology Center at Hohenwald (Hohenwald), 416

Tennessee Technology Center at Jackson (Jackson), 417

Tennessee Technology Center at Livingston (Livingston), 417

Tennessee Technology Center at McMinnville (McMinnville), 417

Tennessee Technology Center at Memphis (Memphis), 417

Tennessee Technology Center at Morristown (Morristown), 418

Tennessee Technology Center at Murfreesboro (Murfreesboro), 418

Tennessee Technology Center at Newbern (Newbern), 418

Tennessee Technology Center at Paris (Paris), 419

Tennessee Technology Center at Shelbyville (Shelbyville), 419

Tennessee Technology Center at Whiteville (Whiteville), 419

Walters State Community College (Morristown), 421

Wisconsin

Blackhawk Technical College (Janesville), 445

Chippewa Valley Technical College (Eau Claire), 445

Gateway Technical College (Kenosha), 446

Lakeshore Technical College (Cleveland), 447

Mid-State Technical College (Wisconsin Rapids), 449

Milwaukee Area Technical College (Milwaukee), 449

Northeast Wisconsin Technical College (Green Bay), 450

Southwest Wisconsin Technical College (Fennimore), 452

Waukesha County Technical College (Pewaukee), 453

Western Technical College (La Crosse), 453

Wisconsin Indianhead Technical College (Shell Lake), 453

INDUSTRIAL PRODUCTION TECHNOLOGIES/ TECHNICIANS, OTHER

Connecticut

Capital Community College (Hartford), 51

Gateway Community College (New Haven), 52

Delaware

Delaware Technical & Community College, Stanton/Wilmington Campus (Newark), 59

Florida

St. Petersburg College (St. Petersburg), 94

Georgia

Southern Polytechnic State University (Marietta), 122

Indiana

Ivy Tech Community College–Bloomington (Bloomington), 161

Ivy Tech Community College–Central Indiana (Indianapolis), 161

Ivy Tech Community College–Columbus (Columbus), 162

Ivy Tech Community College–East Central (Muncie), 162

Ivy Tech Community College–Kokomo (Kokomo), 162

Ivy Tech Community College–Lafayette (Lafayette), 162

Ivy Tech Community College–North Central (South Bend), 162

Ivy Tech Community College–Northeast (Fort Wayne), 163

Ivy Tech Community College–Northwest (Gary), 163

Ivy Tech Community College–Southeast (Madison), 163

Ivy Tech Community College–Southern Indiana (Sellersburg), 163

Ivy Tech Community College–Southwest (Evansville), 163

Ivy Tech Community College–Wabash Valley (Terre Haute), 164

Maryland

The Community College of Baltimore County (Baltimore), 187

Michigan

Henry Ford Community College (Dearborn), 217

New York

Jamestown Community College (Jamestown), 270

Mohawk Valley Community College (Utica), 274

State University of New York College of Technology at Alfred (Alfred), 283

State University of New York College of Technology at Delhi (Delhi), 284

North Carolina

Guilford Technical Community College (Jamestown), 297

Lenoir Community College (Kinston), 299

Ohio

Columbus State Community College (Columbus), 317

Kent State University (Kent), 322

Marion Technical College (Marion), 325

North Central State College (Mansfield), 327

Sinclair Community College (Dayton), 334

Washington County Career Center Adult Education (Marietta), 341

Rhode Island

Community College of Rhode Island (Warwick), 394

South Carolina

Tri-County Technical College (Pendleton), 403

Virginia

Dabney S. Lancaster Community College (Clifton Forge), 426

Danville Community College (Danville), 426

Mountain Empire Community College (Big Stone Gap), 430

New River Community College (Dublin), 430

Patrick Henry Community College (Martinsville), 431

Paul D. Camp Community College (Franklin), 431

Rappahannock Community College (Glenns), 431

Southside Virginia Community College (Alberta), 432

Thomas Nelson Community College (Hampton), 433

INDUSTRIAL RADIOLOGIC TECHNOLOGY/ TECHNICIAN

Alabama

Northwest-Shoals Community College (Muscle Shoals), 45

INDUSTRIAL TECHNOLOGY/TECHNICIAN

Alabama

Alabama Southern Community College (Monroeville), 41

Connecticut

Asnuntuck Community College (Enfield), 49

Florida

Manatee Technical Institute (Bradenton), 85

Illinois

Highland Community College (Freeport), 136

Illinois Eastern Community Colleges, Wabash Valley College (Mount Carmel), 137

Rock Valley College (Rockford), 149

Indiana

Purdue University Calumet (Hammond), 166

Maryland

Hagerstown Community College (Hagerstown), 188

Massachusetts

Berkshire Community College (Pittsfield), 194

Bristol Community College (Fall River), 196

Michigan

Baker College Corporate Services (Flint), 209

Baker College of Flint (Flint), 210

Michigan Institute of Aeronautics (Belleville), 221

Montcalm Community College (Sidney), 223

Muskegon Community College (Muskegon), 223

St. Clair County Community College (Port Huron), 226

New York

Rochester Institute of Technology (Rochester), 280

North Carolina

Nash Community College (Rocky Mount), 302

Ohio

Clark State Community College (Springfield), 316

Cuyahoga Community College (Cleveland), 318

James A. Rhodes State College (Lima), 322

Lakeland Community College (Kirtland), 323

Owens Community College (Toledo), 330

Stark State College of Technology (North Canton), 335

Pennsylvania

Lebanon County Area Vocational Technical School (Lebanon), 361

Tennessee

Southwest Tennessee Community College (Memphis), 414

INFORMATION RESOURCES MANAGEMENT/ CIO TRAINING

Massachusetts

Bristol Community College (Fall River), 196

Michigan

Lake Superior State University (Sault Sainte Marie), 219

Montcalm Community College (Sidney), 223

Vermont

Marlboro College Graduate Center (Brattleboro), 422

INFORMATION SCIENCE/STUDIES

Connecticut

Gateway Community College (New Haven), 52

INFORMATION TECHNOLOGY

South Georgia Technical College (Americus), 122

Valdosta Technical College (Valdosta), 123

West Georgia Technical College (LaGrange), 124

Illinois

College of DuPage (Glen Ellyn), 129

College of Lake County (Grayslake), 129

Harper College (Palatine), 135

Lincoln Land Community College (Springfield), 141

McHenry County College (Crystal Lake), 142

Triton College (River Grove), 153

Massachusetts

Springfield Technical Community College (Springfield), 207

Michigan

Michigan Career and Technical Institute (Plainwell), 221

Michigan State University (East Lansing), 222

Oakland Community College (Bloomfield Hills), 224

Mississippi

Mississippi Gulf Coast Community College (Perkinston), 234

New Hampshire

New Hampshire Technical Institute (Concord), 239

North Carolina

Caldwell Community College and Technical Institute (Hudson), 290

Cape Fear Community College (Wilmington), 290

Johnston Community College (Smithfield), 298

Ohio

Cincinnati State Technical and Community College (Cincinnati), 315

Pennsylvania

Community College of Allegheny County (Pittsburgh), 348

Community College of Beaver County (Monaca), 349

Penn State University Park (University Park), 369

South Carolina

Spartanburg Community College (Spartanburg), 403

Tennessee

Nashville State Technical Community College (Nashville), 411

Southwest Tennessee Community College (Memphis), 414

West Virginia

Monongalia County Technical Education Center (Morgantown), 441

Wisconsin

Blackhawk Technical College (Janesville), 445

Moraine Park Technical College (Fond du Lac), 450

LANGUAGE INTERPRETATION AND TRANSLATION

District of Columbia

American University (Washington), 61

Massachusetts

Bristol Community College (Fall River), 196

New Jersey

Union County College (Cranford), 254

North Carolina

Alamance Community College (Graham), 288

Beaufort County Community College (Washington), 289

Cape Fear Community College (Wilmington), 290

Durham Technical Community College (Durham), 295

Surry Community College (Dobson), 306

Virginia

Shenandoah University (Winchester), 432

Wisconsin

Milwaukee Area Technical College (Milwaukee), 449

Waukesha County Technical College (Pewaukee), 453

LASER AND OPTICAL TECHNOLOGY/TECHNICIAN

Delaware

Delaware Technical & Community College, Stanton/Wilmington Campus (Newark), 59

New Jersey

Somerset County Technical Institute (Bridgewater), 253

LATIN AMERICAN STUDIES

New York

Pace University (New York), 279

Ohio

Ohio University (Athens), 330

Pennsylvania

Penn State University Park (University Park), 369

University of Pittsburgh at Greensburg (Greensburg), 377

University of Pittsburgh (Pittsburgh), 376

LATIN LANGUAGE AND LITERATURE

Michigan

University of Detroit Mercy (Detroit), 228

LEGAL ADMINISTRATIVE ASSISTANT/SECRETARY

Connecticut

Briarwood College (Southington), 50

Fox Institute of Business (Hartford), 52

Norwalk Community College (Norwalk), 55

Delaware

Delaware Technical & Community College, Jack F. Owens Campus (Georgetown), 59

Florida

Henry W. Brewster Technical Center (Tampa), 80

James Lorenzo Walker Vocational-Technical Center (Naples), 82

Lake Technical Center (Eustis), 83

Lee County High Tech Center North (Cape Coral), 83

Lively Technical Center (Tallahassee), 84

Miami Dade College (Miami), 87

North Florida Community College (Madison), 88

Okaloosa Applied Technology Center (Ft. Walton Beach), 89

Sarasota County Technical Institute (Sarasota), 96

Sheridan Vocational-Technical Center (Hollywood), 96

Tom P. Haney Technical Center (Panama City), 99

Traviss Technical Center (Lakeland), 99

Winter Park Tech (Winter Park), 102

Georgia

Augusta Technical College (Augusta), 106

Central Georgia Technical College (Macon), 107

DeKalb Technical College (Clarkston), 109

Gwinnett College (Lilburn), 113

Illinois

Black Hawk College (Moline), 125

Harper College (Palatine), 135

John A. Logan College (Carterville), 138

Kaskaskia College (Centralia), 139

Lewis and Clark Community College (Godfrey), 141

Lincoln Land Community College (Springfield), 141

MacCormac College (Chicago), 142

Moraine Valley Community College (Palos Hills), 143

Richland Community College (Decatur), 148

Robert Morris University (Chicago), 149

Rockford Business College (Rockford), 149

Sparks College (Shelbyville), 152

Indiana

International Business College (Fort Wayne), 161

International Business College (Indianapolis), 161

Maryland

The Community College of Baltimore County (Baltimore), 187

Kaplan College–Hagerstown (Hagerstown), 189

Massachusetts

Bristol Community College (Fall River), 196

North Shore Community College (Danvers), 204

The Salter School (Worcester), 206

Michigan

Detroit Business Institute–Downriver (Riverview), 214

Dorsey Business Schools (Madison Heights), 214

Dorsey Business Schools (Roseville), 214

Dorsey Business Schools (Southgate), 214

Kalamazoo Valley Community College (Kalamazoo), 218

Lake Michigan College (Benton Harbor), 219

Lansing Community College (Lansing), 219

Monroe County Community College (Monroe), 222

New Jersey

Fox Institute of Business–Clifton (Clifton), 245

Harris School of Business–Cherry Hill (Cherry Hill), 246

Harris School of Business–Hamilton (Hamilton), 246

Harris School of Business–Linwood (Linwood), 246

HoHoKus Hackensack School of Business and Medical Sciences (Hackensack), 246

Prism Career Institute (Sewell), 252

Prism Career Institute (Willingboro), 252

New York

ASA Institute, The College of Advanced Technology (Brooklyn), 257

Cheryl Fells School of Business (Niagara Falls), 261

Clinton Community College (Plattsburgh), 262

Elmira Business Institute (Elmira), 264

Metropolitan Learning Institute (Forest Hills), 273

Ridley-Lowell Business and Technical Institute (Binghamton), 280

Ridley-Lowell School of Business (Poughkeepsie), 280

North Carolina

Alamance Community College (Graham), 288

Central Piedmont Community College (Charlotte), 293

Gaston College (Dallas), 296

King's College (Charlotte), 299

Nash Community College (Rocky Mount), 302

Wake Technical Community College (Raleigh), 307

Ohio

Academy of Court Reporting (Akron), 309
Academy of Court Reporting (Columbus), 309
Bradford School (Columbus), 312
Buckeye Joint Vocational School (New Philadelphia), 313
Hocking College (Nelsonville), 321
Pioneer Career and Technology Center: A Vocational School District (Shelby), 331
Trumbull Business College (Warren), 338

Pennsylvania

Bucks County Community College (Newtown), 345
Computer Learning Network (Altoona), 349
Consolidated School of Business (Lancaster), 350
Consolidated School of Business (York), 350
Laurel Business Institute (Uniontown), 361
Pace Institute (Reading), 367
The PJA School (Upper Darby), 371
Prism Career Institute (Philadelphia), 371
Reading Area Community College (Reading), 372

Puerto Rico

American Educational College (Bayamón), 379
Colegio Mayor de Tecnologia–Arroyo (Arroyo), 382
D'mart Institute (Barranquitas), 383
MBTI Business Training Institute (Santurce), 391

Rhode Island

Community College of Rhode Island (Warwick), 394

South Carolina

Technical College of the Lowcountry (Beaufort), 403
York Technical College (Rock Hill), 405

West Virginia

Mountain State College (Parkersburg), 442
West Virginia Business College (Nutter Fort), 443
West Virginia Junior College (Charleston), 444
West Virginia Junior College (Morgantown), 444
West Virginia State Community and Technical College (Institute), 444

Wisconsin

Moraine Park Technical College (Fond du Lac), 450

LEGAL ASSISTANT/PARALEGAL

Alabama

Bevill State Community College (Sumiton), 41
Enterprise-Ozark Community College (Enterprise), 42
Samford University (Birmingham), 46
Shelton State Community College (Tuscaloosa), 46
Virginia College at Mobile (Mobile), 48

Connecticut

Branford Hall Career Institute–Branford Campus (Branford), 49
Branford Hall Career Institute–Southington Campus (Southington), 49
Branford Hall Career Institute–Windsor Campus (Windsor), 50
Manchester Community College (Manchester), 54
Naugatuck Valley Community College (Waterbury), 54
Norwalk Community College (Norwalk), 55
Post University (Waterbury), 56
Sacred Heart University (Fairfield), 56
University of Hartford (West Hartford), 58

University of New Haven (West Haven), 58

Delaware

Dawn Training Centre (Wilmington), 58
Wesley College (Dover), 60

Florida

Hillsborough Community College (Tampa), 81
Polytechnic Institute of America (Orlando), 92
Rasmussen College Fort Myers (Fort Myers), 93
State College of Florida Manatee-Sarasota (Bradenton), 98
Virginia College at Pensacola (Pensacola), 102

Georgia

Appalachian Technical College (Jasper), 104
Atlanta Technical College (Atlanta), 105
Brown Mackie College–Atlanta (Atlanta), 107
Clayton State University (Morrow), 108
Darton College (Albany), 109
DeKalb Technical College (Clarkston), 109
Gainesville State College (Gainesville), 112
Gwinnett College (Lilburn), 113
Iverson Business School (Atlanta), 115
Middle Georgia Technical College (Warner Robbins), 117

Illinois

Brown Mackie College–Moline (Moline), 125
College of Lake County (Grayslake), 129
Elgin Community College (Elgin), 132
Harper College (Palatine), 135
Illinois Central College (East Peoria), 136
Kankakee Community College (Kankakee), 139
Lewis and Clark Community College (Godfrey), 141
MacCormac College (Chicago), 142
Northwestern Business College–Southwestern Campus (Bridgeview), 144
Northwestern College (Chicago), 144
Robert Morris University (Chicago), 149
South Suburban College (South Holland), 151

Indiana

Brown Mackie College–Fort Wayne (Fort Wayne), 155
Brown Mackie College–Merrillville (Merrillville), 156
Brown Mackie College–Michigan City (Michigan City), 156
Brown Mackie College–South Bend (South Bend), 156
Calumet College of Saint Joseph (Whiting), 156

Kentucky

Beckfield College (Florence), 169
Brown Mackie College–Hopkinsville (Hopkinsville), 170

Maine

Andover College (South Portland), 180
Husson University (Bangor), 181

Maryland

Anne Arundel Community College (Arnold), 184
Baltimore City Community College (Baltimore), 185
Chesapeake College (Wye Mills), 186
The Community College of Baltimore County (Baltimore), 187
Frederick Community College (Frederick), 188
Hagerstown Community College (Hagerstown), 188
Harford Community College (Bel Air), 189
Montgomery College (Rockville), 190
Prince George's Community College (Largo), 191

Massachusetts

Assumption College (Worcester), 193
Atlantic Union College (South Lancaster), 193
Bay Path College (Longmeadow), 194
Bunker Hill Community College (Boston), 196

Cape Cod Community College (West Barnstable), 196
Elms College (Chicopee), 198
Fisher College (Boston), 198
Marian Court College (Swampscott), 201
Massachusetts Bay Community College (Wellesley Hills), 201
Middlesex Community College (Bedford), 202
Mildred Elley School (Pittsfield), 202
Mount Wachusett Community College (Gardner), 203
Newbury College (Brookline), 203
Northern Essex Community College (Haverhill), 204
North Shore Community College (Danvers), 204
Quincy College (Quincy), 204
The Salter School (Malden), 206
The Salter School (Tewksbury), 206
Suffolk University (Boston), 207

Michigan

Davenport University (Grand Rapids), 213
Delta College (University Center), 213
Kellogg Community College (Battle Creek), 218
Lansing Community College (Lansing), 219
Lawton School (Southfield), 220
Lawton School Warren Branch (Warren), 220
North Central Michigan College (Petoskey), 223
Oakland Community College (Bloomfield Hills), 224
University of Detroit Mercy (Detroit), 228

New Hampshire

Hesser College, Manchester (Manchester), 237
New Hampshire Technical Institute (Concord), 239

New Jersey

Essex County College (Newark), 244
Gloucester County College (Sewell), 245
Mercer County Community College (Trenton), 248
Middlesex County College (Edison), 249
Ocean County College (Toms River), 250
Raritan Valley Community College (Somerville), 252
Sussex County Community College (Newton), 254
Warren County Community College (Washington), 255

New York

Bronx Community College of the City University of New York (Bronx), 259
Broome Community College (Binghamton), 259
Cheryl Fells School of Business (Niagara Falls), 261
Dutchess Community College (Poughkeepsie), 264
Mildred Elley School (Albany), 273
Monroe Community College (Rochester), 274
Nassau Community College (Garden City), 275
New York Career Institute (New York), 276
New York Paralegal School (New York), 276
Olean Business Institute (Olean), 277
Rockland Community College (Suffern), 281
Suffolk County Community College (Selden), 284
Westchester Community College (Valhalla), 287

North Carolina

Caldwell Community College and Technical Institute (Hudson), 290
Cape Fear Community College (Wilmington), 290
Central Carolina Community College (Sanford), 292
Central Piedmont Community College (Charlotte), 293

Davidson County Community College (Lexington), 294
Durham Technical Community College (Durham), 295
Fayetteville Technical Community College (Fayetteville), 295
Forsyth Technical Community College (Winston-Salem), 296
Gaston College (Dallas), 296
Guilford Technical Community College (Jamestown), 297
Johnston Community College (Smithfield), 298
South Piedmont Community College (Polkton), 305
Western Piedmont Community College (Morganton), 308

Ohio
Brown Mackie College–Akron (Akron), 313
Brown Mackie College–Cincinnati (Cincinnati), 313
Brown Mackie College–Findlay (Findlay), 313
Brown Mackie College–North Canton (Canton), 313
Chancellor University (Cleveland), 315
Cincinnati State Technical and Community College (Cincinnati), 315
College of Mount St. Joseph (Cincinnati), 317
Columbus State Community College (Columbus), 317
Cuyahoga Community College (Cleveland), 318
Edison State Community College (Piqua), 319
James A. Rhodes State College (Lima), 322
Lakeland Community College (Kirtland), 323
The University of Akron (Akron), 338
University of Cincinnati (Cincinnati), 338
University of Northwestern Ohio (Lima), 339
The University of Toledo (Toledo), 339

Pennsylvania
Academy of Court Reporting Inc (Pittsburgh), 342
Bradford School (Pittsburgh), 345
Bucks County Community College (Newtown), 345
Community College of Allegheny County (Pittsburgh), 348
Computer Learning Network (Camp Hill), 349
Consolidated School of Business (Lancaster), 350
Consolidated School of Business (York), 350
Delaware County Community College (Media), 351
Gannon University (Erie), 355
Harrisburg Area Community College (Harrisburg), 357
Keystone College (La Plume), 359
Keystone Technical Institute (Harrisburg), 359
Lehigh Carbon Community College (Schnecksville), 362
Manor College (Jenkintown), 364
Peirce College (Philadelphia), 367
The PJA School (Upper Darby), 371
Prism Career Institute (Philadelphia), 371
Westmoreland County Community College (Youngwood), 378

Puerto Rico
Huertas Junior College (Caguas), 385
Ponce Paramedical College (Ponce), 392
Universidad del Turabo (Gurabo), 394
Universidad Metropolitana (San Juan), 394

Rhode Island
Johnson & Wales University (Providence), 395

South Carolina
Aiken Technical College (Aiken), 397
Beta Tech (North Charleston), 397
Greenville Technical College (Greenville), 399
Midlands Technical College (Columbia), 401

Technical College of the Lowcountry (Beaufort), 403
Trident Technical College (Charleston), 404

Tennessee
Kaplan Career Institute–Nashville Campus (Nashville), 409

Vermont
Burlington College (Burlington), 421
Champlain College (Burlington), 422
Woodbury College (Montpelier), 423

Virginia
Beta Tech (Richmond), 424
Bryant & Stratton College—Richmond Campus (Richmond), 425
Central Virginia Community College (Lynchburg), 425
Lord Fairfax Community College (Middletown), 429
Marymount University (Arlington), 429
Mountain Empire Community College (Big Stone Gap), 430
Patrick Henry Community College (Martinsville), 431
Southwest Virginia Community College (Richlands), 432
Thomas Nelson Community College (Hampton), 433
Tidewater Community College (Norfolk), 434
Tidewater Tech (Chesapeake), 434
Tidewater Tech (Virginia Beach), 434
University of Richmond (University of Richmond), 434

West Virginia
American Public University System (Charles Town), 437
Blue Ridge Community and Technical College (Martinsburg), 438

Wisconsin
Carthage College (Kenosha), 445

LEGAL PROFESSIONS AND STUDIES, OTHER
Florida
Florida National College (Hialeah), 78
Kentucky
Sullivan University (Louisville), 179
Massachusetts
University of Massachusetts Boston (Boston), 208
Ohio
Cuyahoga Community College (Cleveland), 318
The University of Toledo (Toledo), 339

LEGAL STUDIES, GENERAL
New York
Sage College of Albany (Albany), 281
St. John's University (Queens), 281

LEGAL SUPPORT SERVICES, OTHER
Alabama
Prince Institute of Professional Studies (Montgomery), 45
Connecticut
Post University (Waterbury), 56
Florida
Atlantic Vocational-Technical Center (Coconut Creek), 66
Illinois
MacCormac College (Chicago), 142
Michigan
Dorsey Business Schools (Madison Heights), 214
Dorsey Business Schools (Roseville), 214
Dorsey Business Schools (Southgate), 214

Muskegon Community College (Muskegon), 223

New York
Metropolitan Learning Institute (Forest Hills), 273

Pennsylvania
Pennsylvania Highlands Community College (Johnstown), 370

Rhode Island
Community College of Rhode Island (Warwick), 394

Virginia
Virginia Career Institute (Virginia Beach), 435

LIBRARY ASSISTANT/TECHNICIAN
Connecticut
Three Rivers Community College (Norwich), 57

Illinois
City Colleges of Chicago, Wilbur Wright College (Chicago), 129
College of DuPage (Glen Ellyn), 129
College of Lake County (Grayslake), 129
Joliet Junior College (Joliet), 139
Lewis and Clark Community College (Godfrey), 141

Michigan
Oakland Community College (Bloomfield Hills), 224

North Carolina
Central Carolina Community College (Sanford), 292

Pennsylvania
Northampton County Area Community College (Bethlehem), 366

West Virginia
Marshall Community and Technical College (Huntington), 441

LICENSED PRACTICAL/VOCATIONAL NURSE TRAINING (LPN, LVN, CERT, DIPL, AAS)
Alabama
Alabama Southern Community College (Monroeville), 41
Bevill State Community College (Sumiton), 41
Bishop State Community College (Mobile), 41
Calhoun Community College (Decatur), 41
Central Alabama Community College (Alexander City), 42
Chattahoochee Valley Community College (Phenix City), 42
Gadsden State Community College (Gadsden), 42
George Corley Wallace State Community College (Selma), 43
George C. Wallace Community College (Dothan), 43
H. Councill Trenholm State Technical College (Montgomery), 43
James H. Faulkner State Community College (Bay Minette), 44
Jefferson State Community College (Birmingham), 44
J. F. Drake State Technical College (Huntsville), 44
Lawson State Community College (Birmingham), 44
Lurleen B. Wallace Community College (Andalusia), 45
Northeast Alabama Community College (Rainsville), 45
Northwest-Shoals Community College (Muscle Shoals), 45
Reid State Technical College (Evergreen), 46

Shelton State Community College (Tuscaloosa), 46

Snead State Community College (Boaz), 46

Southern Union State Community College (Wadley), 47

Wallace State Community College (Hanceville), 48

Connecticut

Lincoln Technical Institute (Hamden), 54

Lincoln Technical Institute (New Britain), 54

Lincoln Technical Institute (Shelton), 54

Porter and Chester Institute (Stratford), 56

Stone Academy (East Hartford), 57

Stone Academy (Hamden), 57

Delaware

Delaware Technical & Community College, Jack F. Owens Campus (Georgetown), 59

Delaware Technical & Community College, Terry Campus (Dover), 60

Florida

Academy for Practical Nursing & Health Occupations (West Palm Beach), 63

Americare School of Nursing (Fern Park), 64

Atlantic Vocational-Technical Center (Coconut Creek), 66

Bradford Union Area Vocational Technical Center (Starke), 67

Brevard Community College (Cocoa), 67

Central Florida Community College (Ocala), 69

Charlotte Vocational-Technical Center (Port Charlotte), 69

Concorde Career Institute (Jacksonville), 70

Coral Ridge Nurses Assistant Training School (Ft. Lauderdale), 71

David G. Erwin Technical Center (Tampa), 71

Daytona State College (Daytona Beach), 72

First Coast Technical Institute (St. Augustine), 75

Florida Community College at Jacksonville (Jacksonville), 77

Florida National College (Hialeah), 78

Galen Health Institute–Tampa Bay (St. Petersburg), 79

Gulf Coast Community College (Panama City), 79

Health Opportunity Technical Center (Miami Gardens), 80

Henry W. Brewster Technical Center (Tampa), 80

Indian River State College (Fort Pierce), 81

James Lorenzo Walker Vocational-Technical Center (Naples), 82

Keiser Career College–Greenacres (Greenacres), 82

Lake City Community College (Lake City), 83

Lake Technical Center (Eustis), 83

Lee County High Tech Center North (Cape Coral), 83

Lee County Vocational High Tech Center–Central (Fort Myers), 84

Lindsey Hopkins Technical Education Center (Miami), 84

Lively Technical Center (Tallahassee), 84

Manatee Technical Institute (Bradenton), 85

MedVance Institute (Atlantis), 86

MedVance Institute (Miami), 86

MedVance Institute (Stuart), 86

Mercy Hospital School of Practical Nursing (Miami), 87

Miami Dade College (Miami), 87

Miami Lakes Technical Education Center (Miami), 87

North Florida Community College (Madison), 88

Okaloosa Applied Technology Center (Ft. Walton Beach), 89

Orlando Technical Center (Orlando), 90

Palm Beach Community College (Lake Worth), 90

Pasco-Hernando Community College (New Port Richey), 90

Pensacola Junior College (Pensacola), 91

Pinellas Technical Education Center–Clearwater (Clearwater), 91

Pinellas Technical Education Center–St. Petersburg (St. Petersburg), 92

Rasmussen College Pasco County (Holiday), 93

Ridge Technical Center (Winter Haven), 93

Robert Morgan Vocational-Technical Center (Miami), 94

Santa Fe Community College (Gainesville), 95

Sarasota County Technical Institute (Sarasota), 96

Seminole Community College (Sanford), 96

Sheridan Vocational-Technical Center (Hollywood), 96

South Florida Community College (Avon Park), 97

Suwannee-Hamilton Area Vocational, Technical, and Adult Education Center (Live Oak), 98

Tom P. Haney Technical Center (Panama City), 99

Traviss Technical Center (Lakeland), 99

Virginia College at Pensacola (Pensacola), 102

Washington-Holmes Technical Center (Chipley), 102

Withlacoochee Technical Institute (Inverness), 103

Georgia

Bainbridge College (Bainbridge), 106

College of Coastal Georgia (Brunswick), 108

Dalton State College (Dalton), 109

Illinois

Beck Area Career Center–Red Bud (Red Bud), 125

Black Hawk College (Moline), 125

Capital Area School of Practical Nursing (Springfield), 127

Carl Sandburg College (Galesburg), 127

City Colleges of Chicago, Wilbur Wright College (Chicago), 129

Elgin Community College (Elgin), 132

Harper College (Palatine), 135

Heartland Community College (Normal), 136

Highland Community College (Freeport), 136

Illinois Central College (East Peoria), 136

Illinois Eastern Community Colleges, Olney Central College (Olney), 137

Illinois Valley Community College (Oglesby), 138

John A. Logan College (Carterville), 138

John Wood Community College (Quincy), 139

Joliet Junior College (Joliet), 139

Kankakee Community College (Kankakee), 139

Kaskaskia College (Centralia), 139

Kishwaukee College (Malta), 140

Lake Land College (Mattoon), 140

Lincoln Land Community College (Springfield), 141

Morton College (Cicero), 143

Parkland College (Champaign), 145

Rend Lake College (Ina), 148

Richland Community College (Decatur), 148

Rock Valley College (Rockford), 149

Sauk Valley Community College (Dixon), 150

Shawnee Community College (Ullin), 150

Southeastern Illinois College (Harrisburg), 151

South Suburban College (South Holland), 151

Spoon River College (Canton), 152

Triton College (River Grove), 153

Indiana

Everest College (Merrillville), 157

Ivy Tech Community College–Bloomington (Bloomington), 161

Ivy Tech Community College–Central Indiana (Indianapolis), 161

Ivy Tech Community College–Columbus (Columbus), 162

Ivy Tech Community College–East Central (Muncie), 162

Ivy Tech Community College–Kokomo (Kokomo), 162

Ivy Tech Community College–Lafayette (Lafayette), 162

Ivy Tech Community College–North Central (South Bend), 162

Ivy Tech Community College–Northeast (Fort Wayne), 163

Ivy Tech Community College–Northwest (Gary), 163

Ivy Tech Community College–Southeast (Madison), 163

Ivy Tech Community College–Southern Indiana (Sellersburg), 163

Ivy Tech Community College–Southwest (Evansville), 163

Ivy Tech Community College–Wabash Valley (Terre Haute), 164

Ivy Tech Community College–Whitewater (Richmond), 164

J. Everett Light Career Center (Indianapolis), 164

Marion Community Schools Tucker Area Vocational Tech Center (Marion), 165

Vincennes University (Vincennes), 168

Kentucky

Ashland Community and Technical College (Ashland), 169

Big Sandy Community and Technical College (Prestonsburg), 170

Bluegrass Community and Technical College (Lexington), 170

Bowling Green Technical College (Bowling Green), 170

Elizabethtown Community and Technical College (Elizabethtown), 172

Galen Health Institutes (Louisville), 173

Gateway Community and Technical College (Covington), 173

Hazard Community and Technical College (Hazard), 174

Hopkinsville Community College (Hopkinsville), 174

Jefferson Community and Technical College (Louisville), 175

Madisonville Community College (Madisonville), 176

Maysville Community and Technical College (Maysville), 176

Owensboro Community and Technical College (Owensboro), 177

Somerset Community College (Somerset), 178

Southeast Kentucky Community and Technical College (Cumberland), 178

Spencerian College (Louisville), 179

West Kentucky Community and Technical College (Paducah), 180

Maine

Central Maine Community College (Auburn), 181

Kennebec Valley Community College (Fairfield), 181

Maryland

Allegany College of Maryland (Cumberland), 184

Anne Arundel Community College (Arnold), 184

Baltimore City Community College (Baltimore), 185

Carroll Community College (Westminster), 186

Cecil College (North East), 186

LOGISTICS AND MATERIALS MANAGEMENT

Connecticut
University of New Haven (West Haven), 58

Georgia
Albany Technical College (Albany), 103
Atlanta Technical College (Atlanta), 105
Central Georgia Technical College (Macon), 107
Columbus Technical College (Columbus), 108
Ogeechee Technical College (Statesboro), 119
Sandersville Technical College (Sandersville), 120
Savannah Technical College (Savannah), 121

Illinois
Illinois Central College (East Peoria), 136
Waubonsee Community College (Sugar Grove), 154

Massachusetts
Northern Essex Community College (Haverhill), 204

Michigan
Henry Ford Community College (Dearborn), 217

North Carolina
Forsyth Technical Community College (Winston-Salem), 296
Gaston College (Dallas), 296
Lenoir Community College (Kinston), 299

Ohio
Columbus State Community College (Columbus), 317
The University of Akron (Akron), 338

Pennsylvania
Commonwealth Technical Institute (Johnstown), 348
Lehigh Carbon Community College (Schnecksville), 362
Luzerne County Community College (Nanticoke), 363

Tennessee
Volunteer State Community College (Gallatin), 421

West Virginia
American Public University System (Charles Town), 437

MACHINE SHOP TECHNOLOGY/ASSISTANT

Alabama
Central Alabama Community College (Alexander City), 42
Northwest-Shoals Community College (Muscle Shoals), 45
Southern Union State Community College (Wadley), 47

Florida
Lively Technical Center (Tallahassee), 84
Manatee Technical Institute (Bradenton), 85
Mid-Florida Tech (Orlando), 87
Palm Beach Community College (Lake Worth), 90

Georgia
Altamaha Technical College (Jesup), 104
Appalachian Technical College (Jasper), 104
Athens Technical College (Athens), 105
Augusta Technical College (Augusta), 106
College of Coastal Georgia (Brunswick), 108
Columbus Technical College (Columbus), 108
Coosa Valley Technical College (Rome), 109
DeKalb Technical College (Clarkston), 109
Flint River Technical College (Thomaston), 111
Griffin Technical College (Griffin), 113
Gwinnett Technical College (Lawrenceville), 113

Heart of Georgia Technical College (Dublin), 114
Lanier Technical College (Oakwood), 115
Middle Georgia Technical College (Warner Robbins), 117
North Georgia Technical College (Clarkesville), 118
Northwestern Technical College (Rock Spring), 118
Savannah Technical College (Savannah), 121
South Georgia Technical College (Americus), 122
Southwest Georgia Technical College (Thomasville), 122
Valdosta Technical College (Valdosta), 123
West Central Technical College (Waco), 124
West Georgia Technical College (LaGrange), 124

Illinois
Illinois Eastern Community Colleges, Wabash Valley College (Mount Carmel), 137
John A. Logan College (Carterville), 138

Kentucky
Ashland Community and Technical College (Ashland), 169
Bluegrass Community and Technical College (Lexington), 170
Bowling Green Technical College (Bowling Green), 170
Elizabethtown Community and Technical College (Elizabethtown), 172
Gateway Community and Technical College (Covington), 173
Hopkinsville Community College (Hopkinsville), 174
Jefferson Community and Technical College (Louisville), 175
Madisonville Community College (Madisonville), 176
Maysville Community and Technical College (Maysville), 176
Owensboro Community and Technical College (Owensboro), 177
Somerset Community College (Somerset), 178
Southeast Kentucky Community and Technical College (Cumberland), 178
West Kentucky Community and Technical College (Paducah), 180

Michigan
Grand Rapids Community College (Grand Rapids), 216
Mid Michigan Community College (Harrison), 222
Montcalm Community College (Sidney), 223
Muskegon Community College (Muskegon), 223
Northwestern Michigan College (Traverse City), 224

Mississippi
Copiah-Lincoln Community College (Wesson), 231
East Mississippi Community College (Scooba), 232
Hinds Community College (Raymond), 232
Jones County Junior College (Ellisville), 234
Mississippi Delta Community College (Moorhead), 234
Mississippi Gulf Coast Community College (Perkinston), 234
Northeast Mississippi Community College (Booneville), 235

New Hampshire
New Hampshire Community Technical College, Nashua/Claremont (Nashua), 238

New York
Corning Community College (Corning), 263

Mohawk Valley Community College (Utica), 274
State University of New York College of Technology at Alfred (Alfred), 283

North Carolina
Asheville-Buncombe Technical Community College (Asheville), 288
Blue Ridge Community College (Flat Rock), 289
Caldwell Community College and Technical Institute (Hudson), 290
Cape Fear Community College (Wilmington), 290
Catawba Valley Community College (Hickory), 292
Central Carolina Community College (Sanford), 292
Central Piedmont Community College (Charlotte), 293
Cleveland Community College (Shelby), 293
College of The Albemarle (Elizabeth City), 294
Craven Community College (New Bern), 294
Davidson County Community College (Lexington), 294
Durham Technical Community College (Durham), 295
Forsyth Technical Community College (Winston-Salem), 296
Gaston College (Dallas), 296
Guilford Technical Community College (Jamestown), 297
Haywood Community College (Clyde), 297
Isothermal Community College (Spindale), 298
Johnston Community College (Smithfield), 298
Lenoir Community College (Kinston), 299
McDowell Technical Community College (Marion), 300
Mitchell Community College (Statesville), 300
Nash Community College (Rocky Mount), 302
Pitt Community College (Greenville), 303
Randolph Community College (Asheboro), 303
Richmond Community College (Hamlet), 303
Rockingham Community College (Wentworth), 304
Rowan-Cabarrus Community College (Salisbury), 304
Surry Community College (Dobson), 306
Wake Technical Community College (Raleigh), 307
Wayne Community College (Goldsboro), 308
Western Piedmont Community College (Morganton), 308

Ohio
Akron Adult Vocational Services (Akron), 309
Mahoning County Joint Vocational School District (Canfield), 325
Penta County Joint Vocational School (Perrysburg), 330

Pennsylvania
Butler County Community College (Butler), 345
Delaware County Community College (Media), 351
Luzerne County Community College (Nanticoke), 363
New Castle School of Trades (Pulaski), 366
Reading Area Community College (Reading), 372
Westmoreland County Community College (Youngwood), 378

South Carolina
Northeastern Technical College (Cheraw), 401
Piedmont Technical College (Greenwood), 402
Trident Technical College (Charleston), 404

Tennessee
Northeast State Technical Community College (Blountville), 412

Tennessee Technology Center at Crossville (Crossville), 415

Tennessee Technology Center at Crump (Crump), 415

Tennessee Technology Center at Dickson (Dickson), 416

Tennessee Technology Center at Harriman (Harriman), 416

Tennessee Technology Center at Hartsville (Hartsville), 416

Tennessee Technology Center at Hohenwald (Hohenwald), 416

Tennessee Technology Center at Jackson (Jackson), 417

Tennessee Technology Center at Knoxville (Knoxville), 417

Tennessee Technology Center at Livingston (Livingston), 417

Tennessee Technology Center at McMinnville (McMinnville), 417

Tennessee Technology Center at Memphis (Memphis), 417

Tennessee Technology Center at Morristown (Morristown), 418

Tennessee Technology Center at Murfreesboro (Murfreesboro), 418

Tennessee Technology Center at Nashville (Nashville), 418

Tennessee Technology Center at Newbern (Newbern), 418

Tennessee Technology Center at Oneida/ Huntsville (Huntsville), 419

Tennessee Technology Center at Paris (Paris), 419

Tennessee Technology Center at Shelbyville (Shelbyville), 419

West Virginia
Ben Franklin Career Center (Dunbar), 437

Cabell County Vocational Technical Center (Huntington), 438

West Virginia University at Parkersburg (Parkersburg), 444

Wisconsin
Fox Valley Technical College (Appleton), 446

Lakeshore Technical College (Cleveland), 447

Milwaukee Area Technical College (Milwaukee), 449

Moraine Park Technical College (Fond du Lac), 450

Northcentral Technical College (Wausau), 450

Northeast Wisconsin Technical College (Green Bay), 450

Southwest Wisconsin Technical College (Fennimore), 452

Waukesha County Technical College (Pewaukee), 453

Western Technical College (La Crosse), 453

Wisconsin Indianhead Technical College (Shell Lake), 453

MACHINE TOOL TECHNOLOGY/MACHINIST

Alabama
H. Councill Trenholm State Technical College (Montgomery), 43

Florida
Atlantic Vocational-Technical Center (Coconut Creek), 66

Pinellas Technical Education Center– Clearwater (Clearwater), 91

Illinois
Black Hawk College (Moline), 125

City Colleges of Chicago, Richard J. Daley College (Chicago), 128

College of Lake County (Grayslake), 129

Danville Area Community College (Danville), 131

Elgin Community College (Elgin), 132

Illinois Valley Community College (Oglesby), 138

Lewis and Clark Community College (Godfrey), 141

Prairie State College (Chicago Heights), 146

Sauk Valley Community College (Dixon), 150

Southwestern Illinois College (Belleville), 151

Indiana
Ivy Tech Community College–North Central (South Bend), 162

Maine
Central Maine Community College (Auburn), 181

Kennebec Valley Community College (Fairfield), 181

Northern Maine Community College (Presque Isle), 182

Southern Maine Community College (South Portland), 182

Maryland
Baltimore City Community College (Baltimore), 185

Michigan
Alpena Community College (Alpena), 209

Glen Oaks Community College (Centreville), 216

Kellogg Community College (Battle Creek), 218

Lake Michigan College (Benton Harbor), 219

Macomb Community College (Warren), 220

Michigan Career and Technical Institute (Plainwell), 221

Muskegon Community College (Muskegon), 223

North Central Michigan College (Petoskey), 223

Washtenaw Community College (Ann Arbor), 229

Mississippi
East Central Community College (Decatur), 232

Hinds Community College (Raymond), 232

Meridian Community College (Meridian), 234

Northeast Mississippi Community College (Booneville), 235

Ohio
Ashtabula County Joint Vocational School (Jefferson), 311

Auburn Career Center (Painesville), 311

Cleveland Municipal School District Adult and Continuing Education (Cleveland), 316

Columbiana County Vocation School (Lisbon), 317

Community Services Division–Alliance City (Alliance), 317

Licking County Joint Vocational School– Newark (Newark), 324

Lorain County JVS Adult Career Center (Oberlin), 324

Northwest State Community College (Archbold), 327

Polaris Career Center (Middleburg Heights), 331

Total Technical Institute (Brooklyn), 337

Upper Valley JVS (Piqua), 340

Pennsylvania
Delaware County Community College (Media), 351

Greater Altoona Career and Technology Center (Altoona), 356

Lancaster County Career and Technology Center (Willow Street), 360

Luzerne County Community College (Nanticoke), 363

New Castle School of Trades (Pulaski), 366

Precision Manufacturing Institute (Meadville), 371

Schuylkill Technology Center–North Campus (Frackville), 373

Westmoreland County Community College (Youngwood), 378

Puerto Rico
Academia Serrant (Ponce), 379

Caguas Institute of Mechanical Technology (Caguas), 381

South Carolina
Aiken Technical College (Aiken), 397

Central Carolina Technical College (Sumter), 398

Florence-Darlington Technical College (Florence), 399

Greenville Technical College (Greenville), 399

Midlands Technical College (Columbia), 401

Northeastern Technical College (Cheraw), 401

Piedmont Technical College (Greenwood), 402

Tri-County Technical College (Pendleton), 403

York Technical College (Rock Hill), 405

Tennessee
Nashville State Technical Community College (Nashville), 411

Tennessee Technology Center at Athens (Athens), 415

Tennessee Technology Center at Covington (Covington), 415

Tennessee Technology Center at Jacksboro (Jacksboro), 416

Tennessee Technology Center at Jackson (Jackson), 417

Tennessee Technology Center at Paris (Paris), 419

Tennessee Technology Center at Pulaski (Pulaski), 419

Tennessee Technology Center at Whiteville (Whiteville), 419

Virginia
Washington County Adult Skill Center (Abingdon), 436

West Virginia
Logan-Mingo School of Practical Nursing (Logan), 441

Wisconsin
Gateway Technical College (Kenosha), 446

Lakeshore Technical College (Cleveland), 447

Milwaukee Area Technical College (Milwaukee), 449

Moraine Park Technical College (Fond du Lac), 450

Waukesha County Technical College (Pewaukee), 453

MAKE-UP ARTIST/SPECIALIST

Florida
Beauty Schools of America (Hialeah), 66

Beauty Schools of America (Miami), 66

La Belle Beauty Academy (Miami), 83

La Belle Beauty School (Hialeah), 83

Washington-Holmes Technical Center (Chipley), 102

Illinois
Mr. John's School of Cosmetology (Decatur), 144

Indiana
Hair Arts Academy (Bloomington), 157

Hair Fashions by Kaye Beauty College (Indianapolis), 157

Hair Fashions by Kaye Beauty College (Noblesville), 158

Maryland
Aesthetics Institute of Cosmetology (Gaithersburg), 183

New Jersey

Artistic Academy of Hair Design (Fairlawn), 240

Capri Institute of Hair Design (Brick), 241

Capri Institute of Hair Design (Kenilworth), 242

Capri Institute of Hair Design (Paramus), 242

Capri Institute of Hair Design (Succasunna), 242

New York

Beauty School of Middletown (Middletown), 257

Capri School of Hair Design (Spring Valley), 260

North Carolina

Blue Ridge Community College (Flat Rock), 289

Haywood Community College (Clyde), 297

Pennsylvania

Lancaster School of Cosmetology (Lancaster), 360

Puerto Rico

Emma's Beauty Academy (Juana Diaz), 384

Emma's Beauty Academy (Mayagüez), 384

South Carolina

Academy of Cosmetology (North Charleston), 397

Tennessee

Tennessee Academy of Cosmetology (Memphis), 414

West Tennessee Business College (Jackson), 421

MANAGEMENT INFORMATION SYSTEMS AND SERVICES, OTHER

Connecticut

Butler Business School (Bridgeport), 51

Florida

Brevard Community College (Cocoa), 67

Broward Community College (Fort Lauderdale), 68

Daytona State College (Daytona Beach), 72

Florida Community College at Jacksonville (Jacksonville), 77

Hillsborough Community College (Tampa), 81

James Lorenzo Walker Vocational-Technical Center (Naples), 82

Lake City Community College (Lake City), 83

Miami Dade College (Miami), 87

Orlando Technical Center (Orlando), 90

Palm Beach Community College (Lake Worth), 90

Pasco-Hernando Community College (New Port Richey), 90

Pensacola Junior College (Pensacola), 91

St. Johns River Community College (Palatka), 94

St. Petersburg College (St. Petersburg), 94

Tallahassee Community College (Tallahassee), 98

Georgia

Interactive College of Technology (Chamblee), 114

Indiana

Purdue University North Central (Westville), 166

Maine

Washington County Community College (Calais), 183

Maryland

Anne Arundel Community College (Arnold), 184

Frederick Community College (Frederick), 188

Montgomery College (Rockville), 190

Massachusetts

Bristol Community College (Fall River), 196

New Jersey

Bergen Community College (Paramus), 240

Mercer County Community College (Trenton), 248

New York

Broome Community College (Binghamton), 259

Rochester Institute of Technology (Rochester), 280

North Carolina

Brunswick Community College (Supply), 290

Sandhills Community College (Pinehurst), 305

Ohio

Sinclair Community College (Dayton), 334

Pennsylvania

Montgomery County Community College (Blue Bell), 365

Puerto Rico

Colegio Tecnologico y Comercial de Puerto Rico (Aguada), 383

Rhode Island

Sawyer School (Pawtucket), 396

Tennessee

Walters State Community College (Morristown), 421

Vermont

Champlain College (Burlington), 422

West Virginia

James Rumsey Technical Institute (Martinsburg), 440

Wisconsin

Moraine Park Technical College (Fond du Lac), 450

MANAGEMENT INFORMATION SYSTEMS, GENERAL

Connecticut

Albertus Magnus College (New Haven), 49

Asnuntuck Community College (Enfield), 49

Butler Business School (Bridgeport), 51

Capital Community College (Hartford), 51

Gateway Community College (New Haven), 52

Housatonic Community College (Bridgeport), 53

Manchester Community College (Manchester), 54

Middlesex Community College (Middletown), 54

Norwalk Community College (Norwalk), 55

Post University (Waterbury), 56

Tunxis Community College (Farmington), 57

Florida

Brevard Community College (Cocoa), 67

Daytona State College (Daytona Beach), 72

Edison State College (Fort Myers), 72

FastTrain of Clearwater (Clearwater), 74

FastTrain of Ft. Lauderdale (Ft. Lauderdale), 74

FastTrain of Jacksonville (Jacksonville), 75

FastTrain of Kendall (Miami), 75

FastTrain of Miami (Miami), 75

FastTrain of Pembroke Pines (Pembroke Pines), 75

FastTrain of Tampa (Tampa), 75

Florida Community College at Jacksonville (Jacksonville), 77

Florida Keys Community College (Key West), 78

Gulf Coast Community College (Panama City), 79

Hillsborough Community College (Tampa), 81

Indian River State College (Fort Pierce), 81

Lake-Sumter Community College (Leesburg), 83

Lee County High Tech Center North (Cape Coral), 83

Miami Dade College (Miami), 87

Northwest Florida State College (Niceville), 89

Palm Beach Community College (Lake Worth), 90

Pasco-Hernando Community College (New Port Richey), 90

Pensacola Junior College (Pensacola), 91

Polk Community College (Winter Haven), 92

St. Johns River Community College (Palatka), 94

St. Petersburg College (St. Petersburg), 94

Seminole Community College (Sanford), 96

South Florida Community College (Avon Park), 97

State College of Florida Manatee-Sarasota (Bradenton), 98

Tallahassee Community College (Tallahassee), 98

Valencia Community College (Orlando), 101

Georgia

Darton College (Albany), 109

Illinois

Northwestern College (Chicago), 144

Robert Morris University (Chicago), 149

Sauk Valley Community College (Dixon), 150

Maine

Andover College (South Portland), 180

Kennebec Valley Community College (Fairfield), 181

Maryland

Allegany College of Maryland (Cumberland), 184

Anne Arundel Community College (Arnold), 184

Baltimore City Community College (Baltimore), 185

Carroll Community College (Westminster), 186

Cecil College (North East), 186

The Community College of Baltimore County (Baltimore), 187

Frederick Community College (Frederick), 188

Hagerstown Community College (Hagerstown), 188

Howard Community College (Columbia), 189

Prince George's Community College (Largo), 191

TESST College of Technology (Baltimore), 192

TESST College of Technology (Towson), 192

Massachusetts

Greenfield Community College (Greenfield), 198

Michigan

Baker College of Port Huron (Port Huron), 211

Lake Michigan College (Benton Harbor), 219

Madonna University (Livonia), 221

Mississippi

Copiah-Lincoln Community College (Wesson), 231

East Mississippi Community College (Scooba), 232

New Jersey

Drake College of Business (Elizabeth), 244

Mercer County Community College (Trenton), 248

New York

Rochester Institute of Technology (Rochester), 280

North Carolina

Durham Technical Community College (Durham), 295

Lenoir Community College (Kinston), 299

Mayland Community College (Spruce Pine), 299

South Piedmont Community College (Polkton), 305

Wake Technical Community College (Raleigh), 307

Ohio
Pickaway Ross Joint Vocational School District (Chillicothe), 331

Pennsylvania
Lebanon County Area Vocational Technical School (Lebanon), 361
Montgomery County Community College (Blue Bell), 365
Robert Morris University (Moon Township), 372
Schuylkill Technology Center–North Campus (Frackville), 373
YTI Career Institute–York (York), 379

Rhode Island
Sawyer School (Pawtucket), 396

Tennessee
Chattanooga State Technical Community College (Chattanooga), 406
Tennessee Technology Center at Nashville (Nashville), 418

MANAGEMENT SCIENCES AND QUANTITATIVE METHODS, OTHER

Wisconsin
Moraine Park Technical College (Fond du Lac), 450

MANUFACTURING ENGINEERING

Ohio
Apollo School of Practical Nursing (Lima), 310

Rhode Island
Community College of Rhode Island (Warwick), 394

MANUFACTURING TECHNOLOGY/ TECHNICIAN

Alabama
Central Alabama Community College (Alexander City), 42
Jefferson State Community College (Birmingham), 44
Wallace State Community College (Hanceville), 48

Connecticut
Naugatuck Valley Community College (Waterbury), 54

Delaware
Delaware Technical & Community College, Stanton/Wilmington Campus (Newark), 59

Georgia
Coosa Valley Technical College (Rome), 109
West Georgia Technical College (LaGrange), 124

Illinois
Black Hawk College (Moline), 125
College of Lake County (Grayslake), 129
Elgin Community College (Elgin), 132
Heartland Community College (Normal), 136
Highland Community College (Freeport), 136
Illinois Valley Community College (Oglesby), 138
Joliet Junior College (Joliet), 139
Oakton Community College (Des Plaines), 145
Richland Community College (Decatur), 148

Maryland
Chesapeake College (Wye Mills), 186
College of Southern Maryland (La Plata), 186

Massachusetts
Quinsigamond Community College (Worcester), 205

Michigan
Henry Ford Community College (Dearborn), 217
Macomb Community College (Warren), 220
Monroe County Community College (Monroe), 222
Washtenaw Community College (Ann Arbor), 229

New Jersey
Bergen Community College (Paramus), 240

New York
Rochester Institute of Technology (Rochester), 280

North Carolina
Central Carolina Community College (Sanford), 292
Mitchell Community College (Statesville), 300

Ohio
Apollo School of Practical Nursing (Lima), 310
Cincinnati State Technical and Community College (Cincinnati), 315
Clark State Community College (Springfield), 316
Lorain County Community College (Elyria), 324
Sinclair Community College (Dayton), 334

Pennsylvania
Lehigh Carbon Community College (Schnecksville), 362
Pennsylvania Highlands Community College (Johnstown), 370
YTI Career Institute–York (York), 379

Puerto Rico
Huertas Junior College (Caguas), 385

Rhode Island
Community College of Rhode Island (Warwick), 394

South Carolina
Tri-County Technical College (Pendleton), 403

Tennessee
Jackson State Community College (Jackson), 408
Southwest Tennessee Community College (Memphis), 414

Wisconsin
Waukesha County Technical College (Pewaukee), 453

MARINE MAINTENANCE/FITTER AND SHIP REPAIR TECHNOLOGY/TECHNICIAN

Florida
George Stone Area Vocational-Technical Center (Pensacola), 79
Lee County Vocational High Tech Center–Central (Fort Myers), 84
Manatee Technical Institute (Bradenton), 85
McFatter Technical Center (Davie), 86
Miami Lakes Technical Education Center (Miami), 87
Okaloosa Applied Technology Center (Ft. Walton Beach), 89
Pinellas Technical Education Center–Clearwater (Clearwater), 91
Sarasota County Technical Institute (Sarasota), 96
Tom P. Haney Technical Center (Panama City), 99
Withlacoochee Technical Institute (Inverness), 103
Wyotech–Daytona (Daytona Beach), 103

Georgia
Central Georgia Technical College (Macon), 107
North Georgia Technical College (Clarkesville), 118

Maine
Husson University (Bangor), 181
Washington County Community College (Calais), 183

Massachusetts
Benjamin Franklin Institute of Technology (Boston), 194

Mississippi
Mississippi Gulf Coast Community College (Perkinston), 234

New Jersey
Pennco Tech (Blackwood), 251

New York
Kingsborough Community College of the City University of New York (Brooklyn), 271

North Carolina
Cape Fear Community College (Wilmington), 290

Ohio
Ehove Career Center (Milan), 319

Rhode Island
The International Yacht Restoration School (Newport), 395
Motoring Technical Training Institute (East Providence), 395

Wisconsin
Moraine Park Technical College (Fond du Lac), 450

MARINE TRANSPORTATION, OTHER

Florida
Commercial Diving Academy (Jacksonville), 70

Mississippi
Mississippi Gulf Coast Community College (Perkinston), 234

MARKETING/MARKETING MANAGEMENT, GENERAL

Connecticut
Tunxis Community College (Farmington), 57

Delaware
Delaware Technical & Community College, Jack F. Owens Campus (Georgetown), 59
Delaware Technical & Community College, Stanton/Wilmington Campus (Newark), 59
Delaware Technical & Community College, Terry Campus (Dover), 60

Florida
Brevard Community College (Cocoa), 67
Broward Community College (Fort Lauderdale), 68
Indian River State College (Fort Pierce), 81
Miami Dade College (Miami), 87
Northwest Florida State College (Niceville), 89
Palm Beach Community College (Lake Worth), 90
Pasco-Hernando Community College (New Port Richey), 90
St. Johns River Community College (Palatka), 94
Sheridan Vocational-Technical Center (Hollywood), 96
State College of Florida Manatee-Sarasota (Bradenton), 98

Georgia
Abraham Baldwin Agricultural College (Tifton), 103
Bainbridge College (Bainbridge), 106
Darton College (Albany), 109

Illinois
City Colleges of Chicago, Harold Washington College (Chicago), 127
City Colleges of Chicago, Olive-Harvey College (Chicago), 128

City Colleges of Chicago, Richard J. Daley
College (Chicago), 128
City Colleges of Chicago, Wilbur Wright
College (Chicago), 129
Columbia College Chicago (Chicago), 130
Elgin Community College (Elgin), 132
Richland Community College (Decatur), 148

Maine
Saint Joseph's College of Maine (Standish), 182

Maryland
Hagerstown Community College (Hagerstown),
188
Prince George's Community College (Largo),
191

Michigan
Ferris State University (Big Rapids), 215
Glen Oaks Community College (Centreville),
216
Jackson Community College (Jackson), 218
Lake Michigan College (Benton Harbor), 219
Macomb Community College (Warren), 220
Mott Community College (Flint), 223
Muskegon Community College (Muskegon),
223
North Central Michigan College (Petoskey),
223
St. Clair County Community College (Port
Huron), 226

North Carolina
Alamance Community College (Graham), 288
Asheville-Buncombe Technical Community
College (Asheville), 288
Central Carolina Community College
(Sanford), 292
Central Piedmont Community College
(Charlotte), 293
Cleveland Community College (Shelby), 293
Fayetteville Technical Community College
(Fayetteville), 295
Pitt Community College (Greenville), 303
Rowan-Cabarrus Community College
(Salisbury), 304
Wilkes Community College (Wilkesboro), 308

Ohio
Chancellor University (Cleveland), 315
Edison State Community College (Piqua), 319
James A. Rhodes State College (Lima), 322
Lakeland Community College (Kirtland), 323
Ohio University (Athens), 330
Terra State Community College (Fremont), 336
The University of Akron (Akron), 338
University of Cincinnati Clermont College
(Batavia), 339
Zane State College (Zanesville), 342

Pennsylvania
Robert Morris University (Moon Township),
372
Westmoreland County Community College
(Youngwood), 378

Rhode Island
Community College of Rhode Island
(Warwick), 394

Wisconsin
Nicolet Area Technical College (Rhinelander),
450

MARKETING, OTHER

Georgia
Darton College (Albany), 109

Massachusetts
Bristol Community College (Fall River), 196

Pennsylvania
Butler County Community College (Butler),
345

Wisconsin
Moraine Park Technical College (Fond du Lac),
450

MARKETING RESEARCH

Michigan
Ferris State University (Big Rapids), 215

MARRIAGE AND FAMILY THERAPY/ COUNSELING

Ohio
University of Cincinnati (Cincinnati), 338

MASON/MASONRY

Alabama
Bishop State Community College (Mobile), 41
Calhoun Community College (Decatur), 41
Gadsden State Community College (Gadsden),
42
George Corley Wallace State Community
College (Selma), 43
George C. Wallace Community College
(Dothan), 43
Jefferson Davis Community College (Brewton),
44
Lawson State Community College
(Birmingham), 44

Florida
Chipola College (Marianna), 69
James Lorenzo Walker Vocational-Technical
Center (Naples), 82
Lindsey Hopkins Technical Education Center
(Miami), 84
Manatee Technical Institute (Bradenton), 85
Mid-Florida Tech (Orlando), 87
Pinellas Technical Education Center–St.
Petersburg (St. Petersburg), 92
Radford M. Locklin Technical Center (Milton),
92
Suwannee-Hamilton Area Vocational,
Technical, and Adult Education Center (Live
Oak), 98
Tallahassee Community College (Tallahassee),
98

Georgia
Altamaha Technical College (Jesup), 104
Central Georgia Technical College (Macon),
107

Illinois
City Colleges of Chicago, Kennedy-King
College (Chicago), 128
Southwestern Illinois College (Belleville), 151

Indiana
Ivy Tech Community College–North Central
(South Bend), 162
Ivy Tech Community College–Northeast (Fort
Wayne), 163
Ivy Tech Community College–Southwest
(Evansville), 163
Ivy Tech Community College–Wabash Valley
(Terre Haute), 164

Kentucky
Big Sandy Community and Technical College
(Prestonsburg), 170
Bluegrass Community and Technical College
(Lexington), 170
Employment Solutions (Lexington), 172
Jefferson Community and Technical College
(Louisville), 175
Madisonville Community College
(Madisonville), 176
Maysville Community and Technical College
(Maysville), 176

Maine
Southern Maine Community College (South
Portland), 182

Mississippi
Hinds Community College (Raymond), 232
Mississippi Delta Community College
(Moorhead), 234

North Carolina
Central Carolina Community College
(Sanford), 292
Fayetteville Technical Community College
(Fayetteville), 295
Halifax Community College (Weldon), 297
James Sprunt Community College
(Kenansville), 298
Johnston Community College (Smithfield), 298
Mayland Community College (Spruce Pine),
299
Pamlico Community College (Grantsboro), 302
Pitt Community College (Greenville), 303
Southeastern Community College (Whiteville),
305

Ohio
Akron Adult Vocational Services (Akron), 309

Pennsylvania
Greater Altoona Career and Technology Center
(Altoona), 356
Lancaster County Career and Technology
Center (Willow Street), 360
Pennsylvania College of Technology
(Williamsport), 369
Schuylkill Technology Center–North Campus
(Frackville), 373

South Carolina
Greenville Technical College (Greenville), 399

Tennessee
Tennessee Technology Center at Crossville
(Crossville), 415
Tennessee Technology Center at Memphis
(Memphis), 417
Tennessee Technology Center at Morristown
(Morristown), 418

West Virginia
Academy of Careers and Technology (Beckley),
437
Fred W. Eberle Technical Center
(Buckhannon), 439
Putnam Career and Technology Center School
of Practical Nursing (Eleanor), 443

Wisconsin
Gateway Technical College (Kenosha), 446
Lakeshore Technical College (Cleveland), 447
Mid-State Technical College (Wisconsin
Rapids), 449
Milwaukee Area Technical College
(Milwaukee), 449
Moraine Park Technical College (Fond du Lac),
450
Southwest Wisconsin Technical College
(Fennimore), 452
Waukesha County Technical College
(Pewaukee), 453
Wisconsin Indianhead Technical College (Shell
Lake), 453

MASSAGE THERAPY/THERAPEUTIC MASSAGE

Alabama
Calhoun Community College (Decatur), 41
Capps College (Mobile), 42
Gadsden State Community College (Gadsden),
42
H. Councill Trenholm State Technical College
(Montgomery), 43
Lurleen B. Wallace Community College
(Andalusia), 45
Southern Union State Community College
(Wadley), 47

Connecticut

Branford Hall Career Institute–Branford Campus (Branford), 49
Branford Hall Career Institute–Southington Campus (Southington), 49
Branford Hall Career Institute–Windsor Campus (Windsor), 50
Connecticut Center for Massage Therapy–Groton (Groton), 51
Connecticut Center for Massage Therapy–Newington (Newington), 51
Connecticut Center for Massage Therapy–Westport (Westport), 52
Fox Institute of Business (Hartford), 52
Ridley-Lowell Business and Technical Institute (New London), 56

Delaware

Academy of Massage and Bodywork (Bear), 58
Dawn Training Centre (Wilmington), 58
Deep Muscle Therapy School (Wilmington), 58
Delaware Learning Institute of Cosmetology (Dagsboro), 59

Florida

Academy of Career Training (Kissimmee), 63
Academy of Cosmetology (Merritt Island), 63
Academy of Cosmetology (Palm Bay), 63
Academy of Healing Arts, Massage, and Facial Skin Care (Lake Worth), 63
Academy of Professional Careers (Winter Park), 63
Acupuncture and Massage College (Miami), 63
American Institute (Pompano Beach), 64
Angley College (Deland), 64
Atlantic Vocational-Technical Center (Coconut Creek), 66
Aveda Institute–Saint Petersburg (Saint Petersburg), 66
Beauty Schools of America (Hialeah), 66
Benes International School of Beauty (New Port Richey), 67
Broward Community College (Fort Lauderdale), 68
Concorde Career Institute (Jacksonville), 70
Cortiva Institute—Humanities Center (Pinellas Park), 71
Dade Medical College (Hialeah), 71
Dade Medical Institute (Miami), 71
David G. Erwin Technical Center (Tampa), 71
Daytona College (Ormond Beach), 72
Daytona State College (Daytona Beach), 72
Edutech Centers (Clearwater), 72
Everest Institute (Fort Lauderdale), 72
Everest Institute (Hialeah), 72
Everest Institute (Miami), 73
Everest University (Clearwater), 73
Everest University (Lakeland), 73
Everest University (Orange Park), 73
Everest University (Orlando), 73, 74
Everest University (Pompano Beach), 74
Everest University (Tampa), 74
First Coast Technical Institute (St. Augustine), 75
Florida Career College (Miami), 76
Florida Career Institute (Lakeland), 76
Florida College of Natural Health (Bradenton), 76
Florida College of Natural Health (Maitland), 76
Florida College of Natural Health (Miami), 76
Florida College of Natural Health (Pompano Beach), 76
Florida Community College at Jacksonville (Jacksonville), 77
Florida Education Institute (Miami), 77
Florida School of Massage (Gainesville), 78
Heritage Institute (Fort Myers), 80
Heritage Institute (Jacksonville), 80

Herzing College (Winter Park), 80
High-Tech Institute (Orlando), 80
International Academy (South Daytona), 81
James Lorenzo Walker Vocational-Technical Center (Naples), 82
Keiser Career College–Greenacres (Greenacres), 82
Lake Technical Center (Eustis), 83
Lee County Vocational High Tech Center–Central (Fort Myers), 84
Loraine's Academy. (St. Petersburg), 85
Manatee Technical Institute (Bradenton), 85
Marion County Community Technical and Adult Education Center (Ocala), 85
Medical Career Institute of South Florida (West Palm Beach), 86
MedVance Institute (Atlantis), 86
MedVance Institute (Fort Lauderdale), 86
MedVance Institute (Stuart), 86
Miami Dade College (Miami), 87
New Concept Massage and Beauty School (Miami), 88
Palm Beach Academy of Health & Beauty (Lake Park), 90
Palm Beach Community College (Lake Worth), 90
Pensacola Junior College (Pensacola), 91
Pensacola School of Massage Therapy & Health Careers (Pensacola), 91
Polytechnic Institute of America (Orlando), 92
Praxis Institute (Miami), 92
Ridge Technical Center (Winter Haven), 93
Sanford-Brown Institute (Fort Lauderdale), 95
Sanford-Brown Institute (Jacksonville), 95
Sanford-Brown Institute (Tampa), 95
Sarasota School of Massage (Sarasota), 96
Sheridan Vocational-Technical Center (Hollywood), 96
Southeastern School of Neuromuscular & Massage Therapy–Jacksonville (Jacksonville), 97
Southwest Florida College (Fort Myers), 97
Sunstate Academy of Hair Design (Clearwater), 98
Sunstate Academy of Hair Design (Sarasota), 98
Superior Career Institute (Lauderdale Lakes), 98
Technical Career Institute (Miami Springs), 99
Tom P. Haney Technical Center (Panama City), 99
Traviss Technical Center (Lakeland), 99
Universal Massage and Beauty Institute (Sweetwater), 100
Westside Tech (Winter Garden), 102
Withlacoochee Technical Institute (Inverness), 103

Georgia

Academy of Somatic Healing Arts (Atlanta), 103
Advanced Career Training (Atlanta), 103
American Professional Institute (Macon), 104
Atlanta School of Massage (Atlanta), 105
Augusta School of Massage (Evans), 106
Coosa Valley Technical College (Rome), 109
Everest Institute (Atlanta), 111
Everest Institute (Jonesboro), 111
Everest Institute (Marietta), 111
Everest Institute (Norcross), 111
Georgia Career Institute (Conyers), 112
Gwinnett College (Lilburn), 113
Hi-Tech Institute – Atlanta (Marietta), 114
International School of Skin and Nailcare (Atlanta), 115
Moultrie Technical College (Moultrie), 117
New Horizons Computer Learning Centers (Atlanta), 117
North Georgia Technical College (Clarkesville), 118

Rising Spirit Institute of Natural Health (Atlanta), 120
Sanford-Brown Institute (Atlanta), 120
Savannah School of Massage Therapy (Savannah), 121

Illinois

Alvareita's College of Cosmetology (Godfrey), 124
Black Hawk College (Moline), 125
Carl Sandburg College (Galesburg), 127
College of DuPage (Glen Ellyn), 129
Cortiva Institute—Chicago School of Massage Therapy (Chicago), 131
European Massage Therapy School (Skokie), 133
Everest College (Burr Ridge), 133
Everest College (Chicago), 133
Everest College (Merrionette Park), 134
Everest College (North Aurora), 134
Everest College (Skokie), 134
First Institute of Travel (Crystal Lake), 134
Illinois Central College (East Peoria), 136
Illinois Eastern Community Colleges, Olney Central College (Olney), 137
Illinois Valley Community College (Oglesby), 138
John A. Logan College (Carterville), 138
Kaskaskia College (Centralia), 139
Kishwaukee College (Malta), 140
La' James College of Hairstyling (East Moline), 140
Lake Land College (Mattoon), 140
Lewis and Clark Community College (Godfrey), 141
Midwest Institute of Massage Therapy (Belleville), 143
Midwest Technical Institute (Lincoln), 143
Moraine Valley Community College (Palos Hills), 143
Morton College (Cicero), 143
National University of Health Sciences (Lombard), 144
Northwestern Business College–Southwestern Campus (Bridgeview), 144
Northwestern College (Chicago), 144
Pacific College of Oriental Medicine-Chicago (Chicago), 145
Parkland College (Champaign), 145
Rasmussen College Aurora (Aurora), 147
Rasmussen College Rockford, Illinois (Rockford), 147
Rend Lake College (Ina), 148
Rockford Business College (Rockford), 149
Sanford-Brown College (Collinsville), 150
Shawnee Community College (Ullin), 150
SOLEX Medical Academy (Wheeling), 151
Soma Institute–The National School of Clinical Massage Therapy (Chicago), 151
Southeastern Illinois College (Harrisburg), 151
South Suburban College (South Holland), 151
Southwestern Illinois College (Belleville), 151
University of Spa & Cosmetology Arts (Springfield), 153
Waubonsee Community College (Sugar Grove), 154

Indiana

Alexandria School of Scientific Therapeutics (Alexandria), 155
Everest College (Merrillville), 157
Harrison College (Indianapolis), 158
Ivy Tech Community College–Northeast (Fort Wayne), 163
Kaplan College–Merrillville Campus (Merrillville), 164
Kaplan College–Northwest Indianapolis Campus (Indianapolis), 165
MedTech College (Indianapolis), 165

Great Lakes Institute of Technology (Erie), 356
Keystone Technical Institute (Harrisburg), 359
Lancaster School of Cosmetology (Lancaster), 360
Laurel Business Institute (Uniontown), 361
Lincoln Technical Institute (Philadelphia), 362
McCann School of Business & Technology (Pottsville), 364
National Massage Therapy Institute (Philadelphia), 365
Penn Commercial Business and Technical School (Washington), 367
Pennsylvania Myotherapy Institute (Abbottstown), 370
Pittsburgh Technical Institute (Oakdale), 371
Sanford-Brown Institute–Monroeville (Pittsburgh), 373
Sanford-Brown Institute–Pittsburgh (Pittsburgh), 373
Sanford-Brown Institute (Trevose), 373
South Hills Beauty Academy (Pittsburgh), 374

Puerto Rico
Antilles School of Technical Careers (Hato Rey), 380
Colegio Mayor de Tecnologia–Arroyo (Arroyo), 382
Columbia College (Caguas), 383
D'mart Institute (Barranquitas), 383
Huertas Junior College (Caguas), 385
ICPR Junior College–Arecibo Campus (Arecibo), 385
ICPR Junior College–Mayagüez Campus (Mayagüez), 385
Institute of Beauty Careers (Arecibo), 386
Instituto Comercial de Puerto Rico Junior College (San Juan), 386
Instituto de Banca y Comercio–Aprendes Practicanco (Río Piedras), 386
Maison D'esthetique Academy (San Juan), 391
Modern Hairstyling Institute (Carolina), 391
Ponce Paramedical College (Ponce), 392

Rhode Island
Arthur Angelo School of Cosmetology and Hair Design (Providence), 394
Lincoln Technical Institute (Lincoln), 395

South Carolina
Charleston School of Massage (Charleston), 398
Greenville Technical College (Greenville), 399
Miller-Motte Technical College (Charleston), 401
Southeastern School of Neuromuscular & Massage Therapy–Charleston (North Charleston), 402
Southeastern School of Neuromuscular & Massage Therapy (Columbia), 402

Tennessee
Concorde Career College (Memphis), 406
Draughons Junior College (Nashville), 407
High-Tech Institute (Memphis), 408
High-Tech Institute (Nashville), 408
Kaplan Career Institute–Nashville Campus (Nashville), 409
Miller-Motte Technical College (Chattanooga), 410
Miller-Motte Technical College (Clarksville), 410
Roane State Community College (Harriman), 413

Vermont
Community College of Vermont (Waterbury), 422

Virginia
Ana Visage Academy (Great Falls), 424
Beta Tech (Richmond), 424
Career Training Solutions (Fredericksburg), 425
Centura College (Alexandria), 425

Dabney S. Lancaster Community College (Clifton Forge), 426
Everest College (McLean), 427
Everest College (Newport News), 427
Everest Institute (Chesapeake), 428
Heritage Institute (Manassas), 428
Miller-Motte Technical College (Lynchburg), 430
Patrick Henry Community College (Martinsville), 431
Tidewater Tech (Chesapeake), 434
Tidewater Tech (Virginia Beach), 434
Virginia Career Institute (Richmond), 435
Virginia Career Institute (Virginia Beach), 435
Virginia School of Massage (Charlottesville), 435

West Virginia
Clarksburg Beauty Academy (Clarksburg), 438
Everest Institute (Cross Lanes), 439
Morgantown Beauty College (Morgantown), 441
Mountain State School of Massage (Charleston), 442

Wisconsin
Blue Sky School of Professional Massage and Therapeutic Bodywork (Grafton), 445
Chippewa Valley Technical College (Eau Claire), 445
High-Tech Institute–Milwaukee (Brookfield), 447
The Institute of Beauty and Wellness (Milwaukee), 447
Lakeside School of Massage Therapy (Madison), 448
Madison Area Technical College (Madison), 448
Martin's School of Hair Design (Green Bay), 448
Professional Hair Design Academy (Eau Claire), 451
Rasmussen College Green Bay (Green Bay), 451
Western Technical College (La Crosse), 453
Wisconsin Indianhead Technical College (Shell Lake), 453

MASS COMMUNICATION/MEDIA STUDIES
Connecticut
University of New Haven (West Haven), 58

Pennsylvania
University of Pittsburgh (Pittsburgh), 376

MATERIALS ENGINEERING
Maine
Landing School of Boat Building and Design (Kennebunkport), 181

MATHEMATICS AND STATISTICS, OTHER
Delaware
Delaware Technical & Community College, Stanton/Wilmington Campus (Newark), 59

MATHEMATICS, GENERAL
Delaware
Delaware Technical & Community College, Stanton/Wilmington Campus (Newark), 59

Pennsylvania
Bucks County Community College (Newtown), 345

MEAT CUTTING/MEAT CUTTER
Mississippi
Hinds Community College (Raymond), 232

MECHANICAL DRAFTING AND MECHANICAL DRAFTING CAD/CADD
Connecticut
Gateway Community College (New Haven), 52
Manchester Community College (Manchester), 54
Naugatuck Valley Community College (Waterbury), 54
Northwestern Connecticut Community College (Winsted), 55
Porter and Chester Institute (Stratford), 56

Florida
Lake Technical Center (Eustis), 83
McFatter Technical Center (Davie), 86
Sheridan Vocational-Technical Center (Hollywood), 96
Tom P. Haney Technical Center (Panama City), 99
Traviss Technical Center (Lakeland), 99

Georgia
Chattahoochee Technical College (Marietta), 107
Coosa Valley Technical College (Rome), 109
DeKalb Technical College (Clarkston), 109
Middle Georgia Technical College (Warner Robbins), 117

Illinois
City Colleges of Chicago, Harry S. Truman College (Chicago), 128
City Colleges of Chicago, Wilbur Wright College (Chicago), 129
Kankakee Community College (Kankakee), 139
Kaskaskia College (Centralia), 139
Kishwaukee College (Malta), 140
Moraine Valley Community College (Palos Hills), 143
Morton College (Cicero), 143
Richland Community College (Decatur), 148
Southwestern Illinois College (Belleville), 151

Indiana
Purdue University Calumet (Hammond), 166

Massachusetts
North Shore Community College (Danvers), 204
Roxbury Community College (Roxbury Crossing), 205
Springfield Technical Community College (Springfield), 207

Michigan
Baker College of Auburn Hills (Auburn Hills), 209
Baker College of Cadillac (Cadillac), 210
Baker College of Flint (Flint), 210
Baker College of Jackson (Jackson), 210
Baker College of Owosso (Owosso), 211
Grand Rapids Community College (Grand Rapids), 216
Lansing Community College (Lansing), 219
Macomb Community College (Warren), 220
Mid Michigan Community College (Harrison), 222
Monroe County Community College (Monroe), 222
Oakland Community College (Bloomfield Hills), 224
St. Clair County Community College (Port Huron), 226

New Jersey
Brookdale Community College (Lincroft), 241
The Chubb Institute–North Brunswick (North Brunswick), 242
The Chubb Institute–Parsippany (Parsippany), 243

New York
Rochester Institute of Technology (Rochester), 280

State University of New York College of Technology at Canton (Canton), 284
State University of New York College of Technology at Delhi (Delhi), 284

North Carolina
Alamance Community College (Graham), 288
Beaufort County Community College (Washington), 289
Central Piedmont Community College (Charlotte), 293
Cleveland Community College (Shelby), 293
Isothermal Community College (Spindale), 298
Mitchell Community College (Statesville), 300
Rowan-Cabarrus Community College (Salisbury), 304
Surry Community College (Dobson), 306
Wake Technical Community College (Raleigh), 307

Ohio
Lakeland Community College (Kirtland), 323

South Carolina
Aiken Technical College (Aiken), 397
Central Carolina Technical College (Sumter), 398
Florence-Darlington Technical College (Florence), 399
Greenville Technical College (Greenville), 399
Midlands Technical College (Columbia), 401
Northeastern Technical College (Cheraw), 401
Orangeburg-Calhoun Technical College (Orangeburg), 402
Spartanburg Community College (Spartanburg), 403
Technical College of the Lowcountry (Beaufort), 403
Trident Technical College (Charleston), 404
York Technical College (Rock Hill), 405

Tennessee
Northeast State Technical Community College (Blountville), 412
Tennessee Technology Center at Dickson (Dickson), 416

Virginia
Woodrow Wilson Rehabilitation Center (Fishersville), 436

West Virginia
Putnam Career and Technology Center School of Practical Nursing (Eleanor), 443

Wisconsin
Gateway Technical College (Kenosha), 446
Milwaukee Area Technical College (Milwaukee), 449
Moraine Park Technical College (Fond du Lac), 450

MECHANICAL ENGINEERING
Ohio
The University of Akron (Akron), 338

MECHANICAL ENGINEERING/MECHANICAL TECHNOLOGY/TECHNICIAN
Connecticut
Capital Community College (Hartford), 51
Delaware
Delaware Technical & Community College, Stanton/Wilmington Campus (Newark), 59
Florida
Pensacola Junior College (Pensacola), 91
Illinois
Joliet Junior College (Joliet), 139
McHenry County College (Crystal Lake), 142
Oakton Community College (Des Plaines), 145
Maine
Central Maine Community College (Auburn), 181

Maryland
Hagerstown Community College (Hagerstown), 188
Massachusetts
Springfield Technical Community College (Springfield), 207
Michigan
Kalamazoo Valley Community College (Kalamazoo), 218
New Jersey
Middlesex County College (Edison), 249
New York
Rochester Institute of Technology (Rochester), 280
North Carolina
Beaufort County Community College (Washington), 289
Blue Ridge Community College (Flat Rock), 289
Caldwell Community College and Technical Institute (Hudson), 290
Cape Fear Community College (Wilmington), 290
Central Carolina Community College (Sanford), 292
Cleveland Community College (Shelby), 293
Craven Community College (New Bern), 294
Edgecombe Community College (Tarboro), 295
Fayetteville Technical Community College (Fayetteville), 295
Forsyth Technical Community College (Winston-Salem), 296
Gaston College (Dallas), 296
Guilford Technical Community College (Jamestown), 297
Haywood Community College (Clyde), 297
Lenoir Community College (Kinston), 299
Mitchell Community College (Statesville), 300
Piedmont Community College (Roxboro), 302
Pitt Community College (Greenville), 303
Richmond Community College (Hamlet), 303
South Piedmont Community College (Polkton), 305
Wake Technical Community College (Raleigh), 307
Western Piedmont Community College (Morganton), 308
Wilson Community College (Wilson), 308
Ohio
Cincinnati State Technical and Community College (Cincinnati), 315
James A. Rhodes State College (Lima), 322
Lorain County Community College (Elyria), 324
Marion Technical College (Marion), 325
Northwest State Community College (Archbold), 327
Sinclair Community College (Dayton), 334
The University of Toledo (Toledo), 339
Pennsylvania
Delaware County Community College (Media), 351
Harrisburg Area Community College (Harrisburg), 357
Rhode Island
Community College of Rhode Island (Warwick), 394

MECHANICAL ENGINEERING RELATED TECHNOLOGIES/TECHNICIANS, OTHER
Delaware
Delaware Technical & Community College, Stanton/Wilmington Campus (Newark), 59

Florida
Florida Keys Community College (Key West), 78
Illinois
BIR Training Center (Chicago), 125
Massachusetts
North Shore Community College (Danvers), 204
Quinsigamond Community College (Worcester), 205
North Carolina
Blue Ridge Community College (Flat Rock), 289
Ohio
Northwest State Community College (Archbold), 327
Terra State Community College (Fremont), 336
Pennsylvania
Penn State Erie, The Behrend College (Erie), 368
Virginia
Danville Community College (Danville), 426
Northern Virginia Community College (Annandale), 430

MECHANIC AND REPAIR TECHNOLOGIES/ TECHNICIANS, OTHER
Alabama
James H. Faulkner State Community College (Bay Minette), 44
Florida
James Lorenzo Walker Vocational-Technical Center (Naples), 82
Lake Technical Center (Eustis), 83
Motorcycle and Marine Mechanics Institute–Division of Universal Technical Institute (Orlando), 88
Illinois
Triton College (River Grove), 153
Maine
Washington County Community College (Calais), 183
Massachusetts
Bay State School of Technology (Canton), 194
Michigan
Glen Oaks Community College (Centreville), 216
Henry Ford Community College (Dearborn), 217
Kalamazoo Valley Community College (Kalamazoo), 218
Muskegon Community College (Muskegon), 223
Southwestern Michigan College (Dowagiac), 227
North Carolina
Blue Ridge Community College (Flat Rock), 289
Ohio
Akron Adult Vocational Services (Akron), 309
Lorain County JVS Adult Career Center (Oberlin), 324
Ohio Technical College (Cleveland), 329
University of Northwestern Ohio (Lima), 339
Puerto Rico
Automeca Technical College (Aguadilla), 380
Automeca Technical College (Bayamón), 380
Automeca Technical College (Caguas), 380
Automeca Technical College (Ponce), 380
South Carolina
Greenville Technical College (Greenville), 399
Tennessee
Nashville Auto Diesel College (Nashville), 410

North Carolina

Brookstone College of Business (Charlotte), 290
Brookstone College of Business (Greensboro), 290
Center for Employment Training–Research Triangle Park (Research Triangle Park), 292
Cleveland Community College (Shelby), 293
Mayland Community College (Spruce Pine), 299
South Piedmont Community College (Polkton), 305
Western Piedmont Community College (Morganton), 308

Ohio

Akron Institute (Cuyahoga Falls), 310
Buckeye Hills Career Center (Rio Grande), 313
Cleveland Institute of Dental-Medical Assistants (Cleveland), 316
Cleveland Institute of Dental-Medical Assistants (Lyndhurst), 316
Cleveland Institute of Dental-Medical Assistants (Mentor), 316
Community Services Division–Alliance City (Alliance), 317
Edison State Community College (Piqua), 319
Everest Institute (Gahanna), 320
Gallipolis Career College (Gallipolis), 320
Grant Joint Vocational School (Bethel), 320
Knox County Career Center (Mount Vernon), 323
Lakeland Community College (Kirtland), 323
Lorain County Community College (Elyria), 324
Marion Technical College (Marion), 325
Ohio Business College (Lorain), 328
Ohio Business College (Sandusky), 328
Ohio Institute of Health Careers (Columbus), 329
Ohio Institute of Health Careers (Elyria), 329
Owens Community College (Toledo), 330
Sinclair Community College (Dayton), 334
Southwestern College of Business (Dayton), 335
Terra State Community College (Fremont), 336
Tri-County Vocational School Adult Career Center (Nelsonville), 337
University of Cincinnati Clermont College (Batavia), 339
University of Cincinnati Raymond Walters College (Cincinnati), 339
The University of Toledo (Toledo), 339
Upper Valley JVS (Piqua), 340
Washington County Career Center Adult Education (Marietta), 341

Pennsylvania

Allied Medical and Technical Institute (Scranton), 343
Antonelli Medical and Professional Institute (Pottstown), 343
Bidwell Training Center (Pittsburgh), 344
Cambria-Rowe Business College (Johnstown), 346
Career Training Academy (New Kensington), 346
Community College of Beaver County (Monaca), 349
Consolidated School of Business (Lancaster), 350
Consolidated School of Business (York), 350
DPT Business School (Philadelphia), 352
Greater Altoona Career and Technology Center (Altoona), 356
Great Lakes Institute of Technology (Erie), 356
Laurel Business Institute (Uniontown), 361
Newport Business Institute (Lower Burrell), 366
Northampton County Area Community College (Bethlehem), 366
Pace Institute (Reading), 367
Pennco Tech (Bristol), 368

Reading Area Community College (Reading), 372
Sanford-Brown Institute–Pittsburgh (Pittsburgh), 373
Star Technical Institute (Philadelphia), 374
Star Technical Institute (Upper Darby), 374
West Virginia Career Institute (Mount Braddock), 378

Puerto Rico

Advanced Tech College (Bayamón), 379
American Educational College (Bayamón), 379
Atenas College (Manati), 380
Cambridge Technical Institute (Guaynabo), 381
Educational Technical College–Recinto de San Sebastian (San Sebastian), 384
Humacao Community College (Humacao), 385
ICPR Junior College–Arecibo Campus (Arecibo), 385
ICPR Junior College–Mayagüez Campus (Mayagüez), 385
Instituto Chaviano de Mayagüez (Mayagüez), 386
Instituto Comercial de Puerto Rico Junior College (San Juan), 386
Instituto de Banca y Comercio–Aprendes Practicanco (Río Piedras), 386
Instituto Vocational y Commercial EDIC (Caguas), 387
John Dewey College, 389, 390
Liceo de Arte y Disenos (Caguas), 390
MBTI Business Training Institute (Santurce), 391
Ponce Paramedical College (Ponce), 392
Universal Career Counseling Centers (Santurce), 393
Universal Technology College of Puerto Rico (Aguadilla), 393
Universidad del Este (Carolina), 393
Universidad del Turabo (Gurabo), 394
Universidad Metropolitana (San Juan), 394

Rhode Island

Sawyer School (Pawtucket), 396

South Carolina

Greenville Technical College (Greenville), 399
Midlands Technical College (Columbia), 401
Spartanburg Community College (Spartanburg), 403
Technical College of the Lowcountry (Beaufort), 403
Williamsburg Technical College (Kingstree), 404
York Technical College (Rock Hill), 405

Tennessee

Nashville College of Medical Careers (Madison), 411
Tennessee Technology Center at Knoxville (Knoxville), 417
West Tennessee Business College (Jackson), 421

Virginia

Center for Employment Training–Alexandria (Alexandria), 425

West Virginia

Garnet Career Center (Charleston), 439
Opportunities Industrialization Center–North Central West Virginia (Fairmont), 442
West Virginia Business College (Nutter Fort), 443
West Virginia Junior College (Bridgeport), 444
West Virginia Junior College (Morgantown), 444

MEDICAL/CLINICAL ASSISTANT

Alabama

Capps College (Foley), 42
Capps College (Mobile), 42

Chattahoochee Valley Community College (Phenix City), 42
George C. Wallace Community College (Dothan), 43
H. Councill Trenholm State Technical College (Montgomery), 43
Herzing College (Birmingham), 43
Northeast Alabama Community College (Rainsville), 45
Remington College–Mobile Campus (Mobile), 46
Virginia College at Huntsville (Huntsville), 48
Virginia College at Mobile (Mobile), 48

Connecticut

Branford Hall Career Institute–Branford Campus (Branford), 49
Branford Hall Career Institute–Southington Campus (Southington), 49
Branford Hall Career Institute–Windsor Campus (Windsor), 50
Briarwood College (Southington), 50
Butler Business School (Bridgeport), 51
Capital Community College (Hartford), 51
Fox Institute of Business (Hartford), 52
Goodwin College (East Hartford), 53
Lincoln Technical Institute (Hamden), 54
Lincoln Technical Institute (New Britain), 54
Lincoln Technical Institute (Shelton), 54
Northwestern Connecticut Community College (Winsted), 55
Porter and Chester Institute (Stratford), 56
Quinebaug Valley Community College (Danielson), 56
Ridley-Lowell Business and Technical Institute (New London), 56
Stone Academy (Hamden), 57
Stone Academy (Waterbury), 57

Delaware

Dawn Training Centre (Wilmington), 58
Deep Muscle Therapy School (Wilmington), 58
Delaware Technical & Community College, Jack F. Owens Campus (Georgetown), 59
Delaware Technical & Community College, Stanton/Wilmington Campus (Newark), 59

District of Columbia

Sanz School (Washington), 62

Florida

Americare School of Nursing (Fern Park), 64
Americare School of Nursing (St. Petersburg), 64
Angley College (Deland), 64
Brevard Community College (Cocoa), 67
Broward Community College (Fort Lauderdale), 68
Brown Mackie College–Miami (Miami), 68
Cambridge Institute of Allied Health (Longwood), 68
Central Florida College (Saint Petersburg), 68
Central Florida College (Winter Park), 68
Central Florida Institute (Palm Harbor), 69
College of Business and Technology–Flagler Campus (Miami), 70
College of Business and Technology–Hialeah Campus (Hialeah), 70
College of Business and Technology (Miami), 70
Comp-Med Vocational Careers Corporation (Hialeah), 70
Concorde Career Institute (Jacksonville), 70
Concorde Career Institute (Lauderdale Lake), 70
Concorde Career Institute (Tampa), 71
Dade Medical College (Hialeah), 71
Dade Medical Institute (Miami), 71
David G. Erwin Technical Center (Tampa), 71
Daytona State College (Daytona Beach), 72
Edutech Centers (Clearwater), 72
Everest Institute (Fort Lauderdale), 72

Everest Institute (Hialeah), 72
Everest Institute (Miami), 73
Everest University (Lakeland), 73
Everest University (Orange Park), 73
Everest University (Orlando), 73
Everest University (Pompano Beach), 74
FastTrain of Clearwater (Clearwater), 74
FastTrain of Ft. Lauderdale (Ft. Lauderdale), 74
FastTrain of Jacksonville (Jacksonville), 75
FastTrain of Kendall (Miami), 75
FastTrain of Miami (Miami), 75
FastTrain of Pembroke Pines (Pembroke Pines), 75
FastTrain of Tampa (Tampa), 75
First Coast Technical Institute (St. Augustine), 75
Florida Career Institute (Lakeland), 76
Florida Community College at Jacksonville (Jacksonville), 77
Florida Education Center (Lauderhill), 77
Florida Education Institute (Miami), 77
Florida National College (Hialeah), 78
Florida Technical College (Jacksonville), 78
Florida Technical College (Orlando), 78
Galiano Career Academy (Altamonte Sprints), 79
Gulf Coast College (Tampa), 79
High-Tech Institute (Orlando), 80
Indian River State College (Fort Pierce), 81
James Lorenzo Walker Vocational-Technical Center (Naples), 82
Jones College (Jacksonville), 82
Keiser Career College–Greenacres (Greenacres), 82
Lee County High Tech Center North (Cape Coral), 83
Lincoln College of Technology (West Palm Beach), 84
Lively Technical Center (Tallahassee), 84
Medical Career Institute of South Florida (West Palm Beach), 86
MedVance Institute (Atlantis), 86
MedVance Institute (Fort Lauderdale), 86
MedVance Institute (Miami), 86
MedVance Institute (Stuart), 86
Miami Dade College (Miami), 87
Miami Lakes Technical Education Center (Miami), 87
North Florida Institute (Orange Park), 89
Palm Beach Community College (Lake Worth), 90
Pensacola Junior College (Pensacola), 91
Pensacola School of Massage Therapy & Health Careers (Pensacola), 91
Pinellas Technical Education Center–St. Petersburg (St. Petersburg), 92
Polytechnic Institute of America (Orlando), 92
Professional Training Centers (Miami), 92
Rasmussen College Fort Myers (Fort Myers), 93
Rasmussen College Ocala (Ocala), 93
Rasmussen College Pasco County (Holiday), 93
Remington College–Largo Campus (Largo), 93
Remington College–Tampa Campus (Tampa), 93
Sanford-Brown Institute (Fort Lauderdale), 95
Sanford-Brown Institute (Jacksonville), 95
Sanford-Brown Institute (Tampa), 95
School of Health Careers (Lauderdale Lakes), 96
Seminole Community College (Sanford), 96
South Florida Institute of Technology (Miami), 97
Southwest Florida College (Fort Myers), 97
Superior Career Institute (Lauderdale Lakes), 98
Technical Career Institute (Miami Springs), 99
Virginia College at Pensacola (Pensacola), 102

Winter Park Tech (Winter Park), 102

Georgia
Advanced Career Training (Atlanta), 103
Albany Technical College (Albany), 103
American Professional Institute (Macon), 104
Appalachian Technical College (Jasper), 104
Athens Technical College (Athens), 105
Atlanta Technical College (Atlanta), 105
Augusta Technical College (Augusta), 106
Bainbridge College (Bainbridge), 106
Central Georgia Technical College (Macon), 107
Chattahoochee Technical College (Marietta), 107
Clayton State University (Morrow), 108
Columbus Technical College (Columbus), 108
Coosa Valley Technical College (Rome), 109
Dalton State College (Dalton), 109
DeKalb Technical College (Clarkston), 109
East Central Technical College (Fitzgerald), 110
Everest Institute (Atlanta), 111
Everest Institute (Jonesboro), 111
Everest Institute (Marietta), 111
Everest Institute (Norcross), 111
Flint River Technical College (Thomaston), 111
Griffin Technical College (Griffin), 113
Gwinnett College (Lilburn), 113
Gwinnett Technical College (Lawrenceville), 113
Heart of Georgia Technical College (Dublin), 114
Hi-Tech Institute – Atlanta (Marietta), 114
Iverson Business School (Atlanta), 115
Lanier Technical College (Oakwood), 115
Medix School (Smyrna), 116
Middle Georgia Technical College (Warner Robbins), 117
Moultrie Technical College (Moultrie), 117
New Horizons Computer Learning Centers (Atlanta), 117
North Georgia Technical College (Clarkesville), 118
North Metro Technical College (Acworth), 118
Northwestern Technical College (Rock Spring), 118
Ogeechee Technical College (Statesboro), 119
Okefenokee Technical College (Waycross), 119
Rising Spirit Institute of Natural Health (Atlanta), 120
Sandersville Technical College (Sandersville), 120
Sanford-Brown Institute (Atlanta), 120
Savannah River College (Augusta), 121
Savannah Technical College (Savannah), 121
Southeastern Technical College (Vidalia), 121
South Georgia Technical College (Americus), 122
Swainsboro Technical College (Swainsboro), 123
Valdosta Technical College (Valdosta), 123
West Central Technical College (Waco), 124
West Georgia Technical College (LaGrange), 124

Illinois
Brown Mackie College–Moline (Moline), 125
CALC Institute of Technology (Alton), 126
Carl Sandburg College (Galesburg), 127
Center for Employment Training–Chicago (Chicago), 127
College of Lake County (Grayslake), 129
The College of Office Technology (Chicago), 130
Coyne American Institute Incorporated (Chicago), 131
Everest College (Burr Ridge), 133

Everest College (Chicago), 133
Everest College (North Aurora), 134
Everest College (Skokie), 134
Harper College (Palatine), 135
Illinois Eastern Community Colleges, Lincoln Trail College (Robinson), 137
Illinois School of Health Careers (Chicago), 138
Illinois School of Health Careers–O'Hare Campus (Chicago), 138
John A. Logan College (Carterville), 138
Lincoln Technical Institute (Norridge), 142
Midwest Technical Institute (Lincoln), 143
Moraine Valley Community College (Palos Hills), 143
Northwestern Business College–Southwestern Campus (Bridgeview), 144
Northwestern College (Chicago), 144
Parkland College (Champaign), 145
Robert Morris University (Chicago), 149
Rockford Business College (Rockford), 149
Sanford-Brown College (Collinsville), 150
South Suburban College (South Holland), 151
Southwestern Illinois College (Belleville), 151
Spanish Coalition for Jobs, Inc. (Chicago), 152
Waubonsee Community College (Sugar Grove), 154
Zarem/Golde ORT Technical Institute (Chicago), 154

Indiana
Brown Mackie College–Fort Wayne (Fort Wayne), 155
Brown Mackie College–Indianapolis (Indianapolis), 156
Brown Mackie College–Merrillville (Merrillville), 156
Brown Mackie College–Michigan City (Michigan City), 156
Brown Mackie College–South Bend (South Bend), 156
Everest College (Merrillville), 157
International Business College (Fort Wayne), 161
International Business College (Indianapolis), 161
Ivy Tech Community College–Central Indiana (Indianapolis), 161
Ivy Tech Community College–Columbus (Columbus), 162
Ivy Tech Community College–East Central (Muncie), 162
Ivy Tech Community College–Kokomo (Kokomo), 162
Ivy Tech Community College–Lafayette (Lafayette), 162
Ivy Tech Community College–North Central (South Bend), 162
Ivy Tech Community College–Northeast (Fort Wayne), 163
Ivy Tech Community College–Northwest (Gary), 163
Ivy Tech Community College–Southeast (Madison), 163
Ivy Tech Community College–Southern Indiana (Sellersburg), 163
Ivy Tech Community College–Southwest (Evansville), 163
Ivy Tech Community College–Wabash Valley (Terre Haute), 164
Ivy Tech Community College–Whitewater (Richmond), 164
Kaplan College–Hammond Campus (Hammond), 164
Kaplan College–Merrillville Campus (Merrillville), 164

Kaplan College–Northwest Indianapolis
   Campus (Indianapolis), 165
MedTech College (Indianapolis), 165

Kentucky
Bluegrass Community and Technical College
   (Lexington), 170
Brighton Center's Center for Employment
   Training (Newport), 170
Brown Mackie College–Hopkinsville
   (Hopkinsville), 170
Brown Mackie College–Louisville (Louisville),
   171
Daymar College (Paducah), 172
Draughons Junior College (Bowling Green), 172
Gateway Community and Technical College
   (Covington), 173
Henderson Community College (Henderson),
   174
Jefferson Community and Technical College
   (Louisville), 175
Maysville Community and Technical College
   (Maysville), 176
Somerset Community College (Somerset), 178
Southeast Kentucky Community and Technical
   College (Cumberland), 178
Southwestern College of Business (Florence),
   178
Spencerian College–Lexington (Lexington),
   179
Spencerian College (Louisville), 179
West Kentucky Community and Technical
   College (Paducah), 180

Maine
Andover College (South Portland), 180
Beal College (Bangor), 180
Intercoast Career Institute (South Portland),
   181
Seacoast Career Schools (Sanford), 182
Southern Maine Community College (South
   Portland), 182

Maryland
Americare School of Allied Health (Wheaton),
   184
Harford Community College (Bel Air), 189
Medix School (Towson), 190
Medix South (Landover), 190
Ross Medical Education Center–New Baltimore
   (New Baltimore), 192
Sanford-Brown Institute (Landover), 192
TESST College of Technology (Baltimore), 192
TESST College of Technology (Beltsville), 192
TESST College of Technology (Towson), 192

Massachusetts
Branford Hall Career Institute–Springfield
   Campus (Springfield), 195
Bristol Community College (Fall River), 196
Bunker Hill Community College (Boston), 196
Cape Cod Community College (West
   Barnstable), 196
Everest Institute (Brighton), 198
Fisher College (Boston), 198
Holyoke Community College (Holyoke), 199
Kaplan Career Institute, Charlestown
   (Charlestown), 199
Lincoln Technical Institute (Brockton), 200
Lincoln Technical Institute (Lowell), 200
Lincoln Technical Institute (Somerville), 200
Massasoit Community College (Brockton), 202
Medical Professional Institute (Malden), 202
Middlesex Community College (Bedford), 202
Mildred Elley School (Pittsfield), 202
Millennium Training Institute (Woburn), 203
Northern Essex Community College
   (Haverhill), 204
North Shore Community College (Danvers),
   204

Quinsigamond Community College
   (Worcester), 205
The Salter School (Fall River), 206
The Salter School (Malden), 206
The Salter School (Tewksbury), 206
The Salter School (Worcester), 206
Southeastern Technical College (South Easton),
   206
Springfield Technical Community College
   (Springfield), 207

Michigan
Baker College of Allen Park (Allen Park), 209
Baker College of Auburn Hills (Auburn Hills),
   209
Baker College of Cadillac (Cadillac), 210
Baker College of Clinton Township (Clinton
   Township), 210
Baker College of Flint (Flint), 210
Baker College of Muskegon (Muskegon), 211
Baker College of Owosso (Owosso), 211
Baker College of Port Huron (Port Huron), 211
Career Quest Learning Center (East Lansing),
   212
Career Quest Learning Centers–Jackson
   (Jackson), 212
Carnegie Institute (Troy), 212
Davenport University (Grand Rapids), 213
Detroit Business Institute–Downriver
   (Riverview), 214
Detroit Business Institute–Southfield
   (Southfield), 214
Dorsey Business Schools (Madison Heights),
   214
Dorsey Business Schools (Roseville), 214
Dorsey Business Schools (Southgate), 214
Dorsey Business Schools (Wayne), 214
Everest Institute (Dearborn), 215
Everest Institute (Detroit), 215
Everest Institute (Grand Rapids), 215
Everest Institute (Kalamazoo), 215
Everest Institute (Southfield), 215
Glen Oaks Community College (Centreville),
   216
Henry Ford Community College (Dearborn),
   217
Jackson Community College (Jackson), 218
Kalamazoo Valley Community College
   (Kalamazoo), 218
Kaplan Institute (Detroit), 218
Lake Michigan College (Benton Harbor), 219
Lawton School (Southfield), 220
Lawton School Warren Branch (Warren), 220
Macomb Community College (Warren), 220
Montcalm Community College (Sidney), 223
Oakland Community College (Bloomfield
   Hills), 224
Ross Medical Education Center (Ann Arbor),
   225
Ross Medical Education Center (Brighton), 225
Ross Medical Education Center (Flint), 225
Ross Medical Education Center (Grand Rapids),
   225
Ross Medical Education Center (Lansing), 226
Ross Medical Education Center (Port Huron),
   226
Ross Medical Education Center (Roosevelt
   Park), 226
Ross Medical Education Center (Saginaw), 226
Ross Medical Education Center (Warren), 226
Ross Medical Education Center (Waterford),
   226
Southwestern Michigan College (Dowagiac),
   227

Mississippi
Antonelli College (Jackson), 230
Delta Technical College (Southaven), 232
Virginia College at Jackson (Jackson), 236

Virginia College Gulf Coast at Biloxi (Biloxi),
   236

New Hampshire
Hesser College, Manchester (Manchester), 237
Manchester Community College (Manchester),
   237
McIntosh College (Dover), 238
New Hampshire Community Technical College,
   Berlin/Laconia (Berlin), 238
New Hampshire Community Technical College,
   Nashua/Claremont (Nashua), 238
Seacoast Career Schools (Manchester), 239

New Jersey
Berdan Institute (Totowa), 240
The Chubb Institute–Cherry Hill (Cherry Hill),
   242
The Chubb Institute–Jersey City (Jersey City),
   242
The Chubb Institute–North Brunswick (North
   Brunswick), 242
The Chubb Institute–Parsippany (Parsippany),
   243
Dover Business College (Paramus), 244
Everest College (South Plainfield), 245
Fox Institute of Business–Clifton (Clifton), 245
Harris School of Business–Cherry Hill (Cherry
   Hill), 246
Harris School of Business–Hamilton
   (Hamilton), 246
Harris School of Business–Linwood (Linwood),
   246
Healthcare Training Institute (Union), 246
HoHoKus RETS School of Business and
   Medical Technical Services (Nutley), 246
The Institute for Health Education (Fairfield),
   247
Lincoln Technical Institute (Edison), 248
Lincoln Technical Institute (Mount Laurel), 248
Lincoln Technical Institute (Paramus), 248
Micro Tech Training Center (Belleville), 249
Micro Tech Training Center (Jersey City), 249
Omega Institute (Pennsauken), 250
PC Tech Learning Center (Jersey City), 251
Prism Career Institute (Sewell), 252
Prism Career Institute (Willingboro), 252
Sanford-Brown Institute (Iselin), 253
Somerset County Technical Institute
   (Bridgewater), 253
Stuart School of Business Administration
   (Wall), 254

New York
Allen School–Brooklyn (Brooklyn), 256
Allen School–Jamaica (Jamaica), 256
ASA Institute, The College of Advanced
   Technology (Brooklyn), 257
Branford Hall Career Institute–Albany Campus
   (Albany), 258
Branford Hall Career Institute–Bohemia
   Campus (Ronkonkoma), 258
Career Academy of New York (New York), 260
Career Institute of Health and Technology
   (Brooklyn), 260
Career Institute of Health and Technology
   (Garden City), 260
The Chubb Institute–New York (New York),
   261
Elmira Business Institute (Elmira), 264
Franklin Career Institute (Hempstead), 267
Hunter Business School (Levittown), 269
Mandl School (New York), 272
Mildred Elley School (Albany), 273
Mohawk Valley Community College (Utica),
   274
New York Institute of Business Technology
   (New York), 276
New York School for Medical/Dental Assistants
   (Forest Hills), 276

Kaplan Career Institute–Nashville Campus
(Nashville), 409
MedVance Institute (Cookeville), 409
MedVance Institute–Nashville (Nashville), 409
Nashville College of Medical Careers
(Madison), 411
Remington College–Memphis Campus
(Memphis), 413
Remington College–Nashville Campus
(Nashville), 413
Tennessee Technology Center at Knoxville
(Knoxville), 417
Tennessee Technology Center at McMinnville
(McMinnville), 417
Virginia College School of Business and Health
at Chattanooga (Chattanooga), 420
West Tennessee Business College (Jackson), 421

Vermont
Community College of Vermont (Waterbury),
422

Virginia
ACT College (Arlington), 423
Career Training Solutions (Fredericksburg), 425
Eastern Shore Community College (Melfa), 426
ECPI College of Technology (Virginia Beach),
426
Everest College (McLean), 427
Everest College (Newport News), 427
Everest Institute (Chesapeake), 428
Richmond School of Health and Technology
(Richmond), 431
Tidewater Community College (Norfolk), 434
Tidewater Tech (Virginia Beach), 434
Virginia Career Institute (Virginia Beach), 435

West Virginia
Academy of Careers and Technology (Beckley),
437
Everest Institute (Cross Lanes), 439
Monongalia County Technical Education
Center (Morgantown), 441
Opportunities Industrialization Center–North
Central West Virginia (Fairmont), 442
West Virginia Junior College (Bridgeport), 444
West Virginia Junior College (Charleston), 444
West Virginia Northern Community College
(Wheeling), 444

Wisconsin
Blackhawk Technical College (Janesville), 445
Chippewa Valley Technical College (Eau
Claire), 445
Fox Valley Technical College (Appleton), 446
Gateway Technical College (Kenosha), 446
High-Tech Institute–Milwaukee (Brookfield),
447
Kaplan College–Milwaukee (Milwaukee), 447
Lakeshore Technical College (Cleveland), 447
Madison Area Technical College (Madison),
448
Mid-State Technical College (Wisconsin
Rapids), 449
Milwaukee Area Technical College
(Milwaukee), 449
Milwaukee Career College (Milwaukee), 449
Nicolet Area Technical College (Rhinelander),
450
Northcentral Technical College (Wausau), 450
Northeast Wisconsin Technical College (Green
Bay), 450
Sanford-Brown College (West Allis), 452
Southwest Wisconsin Technical College
(Fennimore), 452
Waukesha County Technical College
(Pewaukee), 453
Western Technical College (La Crosse), 453
Wisconsin Indianhead Technical College (Shell
Lake), 453

MEDICAL/HEALTH MANAGEMENT AND CLINICAL ASSISTANT/SPECIALIST

Delaware
Star Technical Institute (Dover), 60

Florida
Herzing College (Winter Park), 80

Georgia
Central Georgia Technical College (Macon),
107
Ogeechee Technical College (Statesboro), 119
Okefenokee Technical College (Waycross), 119
Southeastern Technical College (Vidalia), 121

Maryland
Hagerstown Community College (Hagerstown),
188

Michigan
Mott Community College (Flint), 223
Oakland Community College (Bloomfield
Hills), 224

New Jersey
Star Technical Institute (Edison), 253
Star Technical Institute (Stratford), 253

Pennsylvania
Computer Learning Network (Altoona), 349
Delaware Valley Academy of Medical and
Dental Assistants (Philadelphia), 351
Pittsburgh Technical Institute (Oakdale), 371
Star Technical Institute (Philadelphia), 374
Star Technical Institute (Upper Darby), 374

Rhode Island
Motoring Technical Training Institute (East
Providence), 395

Virginia
Tidewater Tech (Chesapeake), 434
Tidewater Tech (Norfolk), 434

MEDICAL ILLUSTRATION/MEDICAL ILLUSTRATOR

New Hampshire
Lebanon College (Lebanon), 237

MEDICAL INSURANCE CODING SPECIALIST/ CODER

Alabama
Remington College–Mobile Campus (Mobile),
46
Virginia College at Huntsville (Huntsville), 48
Virginia College at Mobile (Mobile), 48

Connecticut
Goodwin College (East Hartford), 53
Ridley-Lowell Business and Technical Institute
(New London), 56

Delaware
Delaware Technical & Community College,
Stanton/Wilmington Campus (Newark), 59
Delaware Technical & Community College,
Terry Campus (Dover), 60

Florida
Americare School of Nursing (Fern Park), 64
Americare School of Nursing (St. Petersburg),
64
Atlantic Vocational-Technical Center (Coconut
Creek), 66
Career Institute of Florida (Saint Petersburg), 68
College of Business and Technology–Flagler
Campus (Miami), 70
College of Business and Technology–Hialeah
Campus (Hialeah), 70
College of Business and Technology (Miami), 70
Edutech Centers (Clearwater), 72
Everest Institute (Fort Lauderdale), 72
Everest Institute (Hialeah), 72
Everest Institute (Miami), 73
Everest University (Pompano Beach), 74

FastTrain of Clearwater (Clearwater), 74
FastTrain of Ft. Lauderdale (Ft. Lauderdale), 74
FastTrain of Jacksonville (Jacksonville), 75
FastTrain of Kendall (Miami), 75
FastTrain of Miami (Miami), 75
FastTrain of Pembroke Pines (Pembroke Pines),
75
FastTrain of Tampa (Tampa), 75
Florida Career College (Miami), 76
Florida Career Institute (Lakeland), 76
Florida Education Institute (Miami), 77
Herzing College (Winter Park), 80
Jones College (Jacksonville), 82
Keiser Career College–Greenacres (Greenacres),
82
Lincoln College of Technology (West Palm
Beach), 84
Management Resources Institute (Miami), 85
Manatee Technical Institute (Bradenton), 85
Professional Training Centers (Miami), 92
Rasmussen College Fort Myers (Fort Myers), 93
Rasmussen College Ocala (Ocala), 93
Remington College–Largo Campus (Largo), 93
Remington College–Tampa Campus (Tampa),
93
Sanford-Brown Institute (Fort Lauderdale), 95
Sanford-Brown Institute (Jacksonville), 95
Sanford-Brown Institute (Tampa), 95
School of Health Careers (Lauderdale Lakes), 96
Superior Career Institute (Lauderdale Lakes), 98
Ultimate Medical Academy (Clearwater), 100
Ultimate Medical Academy–Tampa (Tampa),
100
Virginia College at Pensacola (Pensacola), 102
Winter Park Tech (Winter Park), 102

Georgia
Albany Technical College (Albany), 103
Altamaha Technical College (Jesup), 104
American Professional Institute (Macon), 104
Atlanta Technical College (Atlanta), 105
Augusta Technical College (Augusta), 106
Central Georgia Technical College (Macon),
107
Columbus Technical College (Columbus), 108
Coosa Valley Technical College (Rome), 109
Everest Institute (Atlanta), 111
Everest Institute (Norcross), 111
Flint River Technical College (Thomaston), 111
Griffin Technical College (Griffin), 113
Heart of Georgia Technical College (Dublin),
114
Herzing College (Atlanta), 114
Iverson Business School (Atlanta), 115
Javelin Technical Training Center (Atlanta),
115
Lanier Technical College (Oakwood), 115
Moultrie Technical College (Moultrie), 117
New Horizons Computer Learning Centers
(Atlanta), 117
North Georgia Technical College (Clarkesville),
118
North Metro Technical College (Acworth), 118
Northwestern Technical College (Rock Spring),
118
Ogeechee Technical College (Statesboro), 119
Omnitech Institute (Decatur), 119
Sanford-Brown Institute (Atlanta), 120
Savannah River College (Augusta), 121
South Georgia Technical College (Americus),
122
Southwest Georgia Technical College
(Thomasville), 122
Valdosta Technical College (Valdosta), 123
West Georgia Technical College (LaGrange),
124

Illinois
Black Hawk College (Moline), 125

City Colleges of Chicago, Kennedy-King College (Chicago), 128

City Colleges of Chicago, Olive-Harvey College (Chicago), 128

City Colleges of Chicago, Richard J. Daley College (Chicago), 128

City Colleges of Chicago, Wilbur Wright College (Chicago), 129

College of DuPage (Glen Ellyn), 129

College of Lake County (Grayslake), 129

Everest College (Burr Ridge), 133

Everest College (Merrionette Park), 134

Everest College (North Aurora), 134

Harper College (Palatine), 135

Highland Community College (Freeport), 136

Illinois Central College (East Peoria), 136

Joliet Junior College (Joliet), 139

Kankakee Community College (Kankakee), 139

Kishwaukee College (Malta), 140

Lincoln Land Community College (Springfield), 141

Midstate College (Peoria), 143

Midwest Technical Institute (Lincoln), 143

Moraine Valley Community College (Palos Hills), 143

Northwestern Business College–Southwestern Campus (Bridgeview), 144

Oakton Community College (Des Plaines), 145

Rasmussen College Aurora (Aurora), 147

Rasmussen College Rockford, Illinois (Rockford), 147

Richland Community College (Decatur), 148

Rock Valley College (Rockford), 149

Sanford-Brown College (Collinsville), 150

Shawnee Community College (Ullin), 150

Southeastern Illinois College (Harrisburg), 151

South Suburban College (South Holland), 151

Southwestern Illinois College (Belleville), 151

Spoon River College (Canton), 152

Westwood College–Chicago River Oaks (Calumet City), 154

Indiana

Brown Mackie College–Fort Wayne (Fort Wayne), 155

Everest College (Merrillville), 157

Harrison College (Anderson), 158

Harrison College (Fort Wayne), 158

Harrison College (Indianapolis), 158

Harrison College (Muncie), 159

MedTech College (Indianapolis), 165

TechSkills—Indianapolis (Indianapolis), 167

Vincennes University (Vincennes), 168

Kentucky

ATA Career Education (Louisville), 169

Brown Mackie College–Hopkinsville (Hopkinsville), 170

Daymar College (Louisville), 171

Daymar College (Newport), 171

Interactive Learning Systems (Florence), 174

Spencerian College–Lexington (Lexington), 179

Maine

Beal College (Bangor), 180

Central Maine Community College (Auburn), 181

Northern Maine Community College (Presque Isle), 182

Maryland

All-State Career School (Baltimore), 184

Hagerstown Community College (Hagerstown), 188

Medix South (Landover), 190

Sanford-Brown Institute (Landover), 192

Massachusetts

Bunker Hill Community College (Boston), 196

Fisher College (Boston), 198

Lincoln Technical Institute (Lowell), 200

Lincoln Technical Institute (Somerville), 200

North Shore Community College (Danvers), 204

The Salter School (Fall River), 206

The Salter School (Worcester), 206

Springfield Technical Community College (Springfield), 207

Michigan

Baker College Corporate Services (Flint), 209

Baker College of Auburn Hills (Auburn Hills), 209

Baker College of Flint (Flint), 210

Davenport University (Grand Rapids), 213

Delta College (University Center), 213

Everest Institute (Grand Rapids), 215

Ferris State University (Big Rapids), 215

Glen Oaks Community College (Centreville), 216

Gogebic Community College (Ironwood), 216

Kalamazoo Valley Community College (Kalamazoo), 218

Mid Michigan Community College (Harrison), 222

Oakland Community College (Bloomfield Hills), 224

Ross Medical Education Center (Lansing), 226

West Shore Community College (Scottville), 229

Mississippi

Virginia College at Jackson (Jackson), 236

Virginia College Gulf Coast at Biloxi (Biloxi), 236

New Hampshire

Lebanon College (Lebanon), 237

Manchester Community College (Manchester), 237

New Hampshire Community Technical College, Stratham (Stratham), 239

New Hampshire Technical Institute (Concord), 239

Seacoast Career Schools (Manchester), 239

New Jersey

Dover Business College (Paramus), 244

Everest College (South Plainfield), 245

HoHoKus RETS School of Business and Medical Technical Services (Nutley), 246

HoHoKus School of Business and Medical Sciences (Ramsey), 247

The Institute for Health Education (Fairfield), 247

Keyskills Learning (Clifton), 247

Lincoln Technical Institute (Paramus), 248

PC Tech Learning Center (Jersey City), 251

Performance Training (Toms River), 251

Sanford-Brown Institute (Iselin), 253

Stuart School of Business Administration (Wall), 254

New York

Allen School–Jamaica (Jamaica), 256

Branford Hall Career Institute–Albany Campus (Albany), 258

Elmira Business Institute (Elmira), 264

Long Island Business Institute (Commack), 271

Ridley-Lowell Business and Technical Institute (Binghamton), 280

Ridley-Lowell School of Business (Poughkeepsie), 280

Sanford-Brown Institute (Garden City), 282

Sanford-Brown Institute (White Plains), 282

Trocaire College (Buffalo), 286

North Carolina

Center for Employment Training–Research Triangle Park (Research Triangle Park), 292

Nash Community College (Rocky Mount), 302

Ohio

American School of Technology (Columbus), 310

Belmont Technical College (St. Clairsville), 311

Bohecker College–Ravenna (Ravenna), 312

Cincinnati State Technical and Community College (Cincinnati), 315

Columbus State Community College (Columbus), 317

Cuyahoga Community College (Cleveland), 318

Davis College (Toledo), 318

Delaware JVS District (Delaware), 318

Eastern Gateway Community College (Steubenville), 319

Ehove Career Center (Milan), 319

Everest Institute (Cuyahoga Falls), 320

Everest Institute (Gahanna), 320

Licking County Joint Vocational School–Newark (Newark), 324

Mahoning County Joint Vocational School District (Canfield), 325

Medina County Career Center (Medina), 325

O. C. Collins Career Center (Chesapeake), 328

Portage Lakes Career Center (Green), 331

Professional Skills Institute (Toledo), 331

Remington College–Cleveland Campus (Cleveland), 333

Remington College–Cleveland West Campus (North Olmsted), 333

RETS Tech Center (Centerville), 333

Sanford-Brown Institute (Middleburg Heights), 333

Southwestern College of Business (Cincinnati), 335

Stautzenberger College (Maumee), 336

TechSkills—Columbus (Columbus), 336

Toledo School of Practical Nursing (Toledo), 337

University of Northwestern Ohio (Lima), 339

Warren County Career Center (Lebanon), 340

Pennsylvania

Bucks County Community College (Newtown), 345

Butler County Community College (Butler), 345

Career Training Academy (Monroeville), 346

Career Training Academy (New Kensington), 346

Career Training Academy (Pittsburgh), 346

Community College of Allegheny County (Pittsburgh), 348

Delaware County Community College (Media), 351

Drexel University (Philadelphia), 352

Greater Altoona Career and Technology Center (Altoona), 356

Lehigh Carbon Community College (Schnecksville), 362

Lincoln Technical Institute (Allentown), 362

Lincoln Technical Institute (Philadelphia), 362

Mercyhurst College (Erie), 364

Northampton County Area Community College (Bethlehem), 366

Penn Commercial Business and Technical School (Washington), 367

Pennsylvania College of Technology (Williamsport), 369

Pennsylvania Highlands Community College (Johnstown), 370

Pittsburgh Technical Institute (Oakdale), 371

Sanford-Brown Institute (Trevose), 373

Westmoreland County Community College (Youngwood), 378

YTI Career Institute–York (York), 379

Rhode Island

Lincoln Technical Institute (Lincoln), 395

Tennessee

Draughons Junior College (Clarksville), 407

Nashville College of Medical Careers (Madison), 411

Remington College–Memphis Campus (Memphis), 413
Remington College–Nashville Campus (Nashville), 413
South College (Knoxville), 413
Virginia College School of Business and Health at Chattanooga (Chattanooga), 420
Walters State Community College (Morristown), 421
West Tennessee Business College (Jackson), 421

Virginia
Career Training Solutions (Fredericksburg), 425
Everest College (McLean), 427
Everest College (Newport News), 427
Everest Institute (Chesapeake), 428
Ferrum College (Ferrum), 428
Richmond School of Health and Technology (Richmond), 431

West Virginia
Mountain State University (Beckley), 442
Opportunities Industrialization Center–North Central West Virginia (Fairmont), 442

Wisconsin
Blackhawk Technical College (Janesville), 445
Fox Valley Technical College (Appleton), 446
Herzing College (Madison), 447
Madison Area Technical College (Madison), 448
Milwaukee Area Technical College (Milwaukee), 449
Milwaukee Career College (Milwaukee), 449
Northcentral Technical College (Wausau), 450
Rasmussen College Green Bay (Green Bay), 451
Sanford-Brown College (West Allis), 452
Southwest Wisconsin Technical College (Fennimore), 452
Waukesha County Technical College (Pewaukee), 453

MEDICAL INSURANCE SPECIALIST/MEDICAL BILLER

Alabama
Herzing College (Birmingham), 43
Virginia College at Birmingham (Birmingham), 48

Connecticut
Branford Hall Career Institute–Branford Campus (Branford), 49
Branford Hall Career Institute–Southington Campus (Southington), 49
Branford Hall Career Institute–Windsor Campus (Windsor), 50
Fox Institute of Business (Hartford), 52
Ridley-Lowell Business and Technical Institute (New London), 56

Delaware
Dawn Training Centre (Wilmington), 58
Star Technical Institute (Dover), 60

District of Columbia
Career Blazers Learning Center (Washington), 61
Sanz School (Washington), 62

Florida
Central Florida College (Saint Petersburg), 68
Central Florida College (Winter Park), 68
Coral Ridge Nurses Assistant Training School (Ft. Lauderdale), 71
Everest University (Jacksonville), 73
Florida Technical College (Orlando), 78
High-Tech Institute (Orlando), 80
Lindsey Hopkins Technical Education Center (Miami), 84
Marion County Community Technical and Adult Education Center (Ocala), 85
Saber (Miami), 94
Sanford-Brown Institute (Jacksonville), 95

Sarasota County Technical Institute (Sarasota), 96
Sheridan Vocational-Technical Center (Hollywood), 96

Georgia
Advanced Career Training (Atlanta), 103
Atlanta Technical College (Atlanta), 105
Everest Institute (Jonesboro), 111
Griffin Technical College (Griffin), 113
Hi-Tech Institute – Atlanta (Marietta), 114
Laurus Technical Institute (Atlanta), 116
Middle Georgia Technical College (Warner Robbins), 117
Savannah Technical College (Savannah), 121
West Central Technical College (Waco), 124

Illinois
Black Hawk College (Moline), 125
College of Lake County (Grayslake), 129
Computer Systems Institute (Skokie), 130
Coyne American Institute Incorporated (Chicago), 131
East-West University (Chicago), 132
Everest College (Chicago), 133
Everest College (Skokie), 134
Lewis and Clark Community College (Godfrey), 141
Oakton Community College (Des Plaines), 145
Taylor Business Institute (Chicago), 152

Indiana
Kaplan College–Merrillville Campus (Merrillville), 164
TechSkills—Indianapolis (Indianapolis), 167

Kentucky
Daymar College (Owensboro), 171
Daymar College (Paducah), 172

Maryland
Ross Medical Education Center–New Baltimore (New Baltimore), 192

Massachusetts
Everest Institute (Chelsea), 198
Massasoit Community College (Brockton), 202
Millennium Training Institute (Woburn), 203

Michigan
Baker College of Allen Park (Allen Park), 209
Baker College of Auburn Hills (Auburn Hills), 209
Baker College of Cadillac (Cadillac), 210
Baker College of Clinton Township (Clinton Township), 210
Baker College of Flint (Flint), 210
Baker College of Jackson (Jackson), 210
Baker College of Muskegon (Muskegon), 211
Baker College of Port Huron (Port Huron), 211
Davenport University (Grand Rapids), 213
Detroit Business Institute–Southfield (Southfield), 214
Dorsey Business Schools (Madison Heights), 214
Dorsey Business Schools (Roseville), 214
Dorsey Business Schools (Southgate), 214
Dorsey Business Schools (Wayne), 214
Everest Institute (Dearborn), 215
Everest Institute (Detroit), 215
Everest Institute (Grand Rapids), 215
Everest Institute (Kalamazoo), 215
Everest Institute (Southfield), 215
Henry Ford Community College (Dearborn), 217
Jackson Community College (Jackson), 218
Kirtland Community College (Roscommon), 219
Lansing Community College (Lansing), 219
North Central Michigan College (Petoskey), 223
Ross Medical Education Center (Ann Arbor), 225

Ross Medical Education Center (Brighton), 225
Ross Medical Education Center (Flint), 225
Ross Medical Education Center (Grand Rapids), 225
Ross Medical Education Center (Lansing), 226
Ross Medical Education Center (Roosevelt Park), 226
Ross Medical Education Center (Saginaw), 226
Ross Medical Education Center (Warren), 226
Schoolcraft College (Livonia), 227

New Jersey
The Chubb Institute–Cherry Hill (Cherry Hill), 242
The Chubb Institute–Jersey City (Jersey City), 242
The Chubb Institute–North Brunswick (North Brunswick), 242
The Chubb Institute–Parsippany (Parsippany), 243
Everest College (South Plainfield), 245
Healthcare Training Institute (Union), 246
HoHoKus Hackensack School of Business and Medical Sciences (Hackensack), 246
Keyskills Learning (Clifton), 247
Lincoln Technical Institute (Edison), 248
Lincoln Technical Institute (Paramus), 248
Omega Institute (Pennsauken), 250
Prism Career Institute (Sewell), 252
Prism Career Institute (Willingboro), 252
Somerset County Technical Institute (Bridgewater), 253
Star Technical Institute (Edison), 253
Star Technical Institute (Stratford), 253

New York
The Chubb Institute–New York (New York), 261
Sanford-Brown Institute (Garden City), 282
Sanford-Brown Institute (New York), 282
Sanford-Brown Institute (White Plains), 282

North Carolina
Center for Employment Training–Research Triangle Park (Research Triangle Park), 292

Ohio
Bohecker College–Cincinnati (Cincinnati), 312
Bohecker College–Columbus (Westerville), 312
Knox County Career Center (Mount Vernon), 323
Medina County Career Center (Medina), 325
Owens Community College (Toledo), 330
Ross Medical Education Center–Sylvania (Sylvania), 333
Southwestern College of Business (Franklin), 335
TechSkills—Columbus (Columbus), 336

Pennsylvania
All-State Career School (Lester), 343
Career Training Academy (Monroeville), 346
Career Training Academy (New Kensington), 346
Career Training Academy (Pittsburgh), 346
The Chubb Institute–Springfield (Springfield), 348
Lehigh Carbon Community College (Schnecksville), 362
Lincoln Technical Institute (Allentown), 362
Prism Career Institute (Philadelphia), 371

Puerto Rico
Centro de Estudios Multidisciplinarios (Bayamón), 382
Centro de Estudios Multidisciplinarios (Humacao), 382
Centro de Estudios Multidisciplinarios (San Juan), 382
D'mart Institute (Barranquitas), 383
Instituto Merlix (Bayamón), 387
Inter American University of Puerto Rico, Aguadilla Campus (Aguadilla), 387

Inter American University of Puerto Rico, Bayamón Campus (Bayamón), 388

Inter American University of Puerto Rico, Guayama Campus (Guayama), 388

Inter American University of Puerto Rico, Metropolitan Campus (San Juan), 388

Inter American University of Puerto Rico, Ponce Campus (Mercedita), 389

Inter American University of Puerto Rico, San Germán Campus (San Germán), 389

International Technical College (San Juan), 389

Rhode Island

Community College of Rhode Island (Warwick), 394

Lincoln Technical Institute (Lincoln), 395

Tennessee

High-Tech Institute (Memphis), 408

High-Tech Institute (Nashville), 408

Tennessee Technology Center at Nashville (Nashville), 418

Virginia

ACT College (Arlington), 423

Career Training Solutions (Fredericksburg), 425

Everest College (McLean), 427

West Virginia

Everest Institute (Cross Lanes), 439

Wisconsin

High-Tech Institute–Milwaukee (Brookfield), 447

MEDICAL OFFICE ASSISTANT/SPECIALIST

Alabama

Capps College (Foley), 42

Capps College (Mobile), 42

Virginia College at Birmingham (Birmingham), 48

Connecticut

Goodwin College (East Hartford), 53

St. Vincent's College (Bridgeport), 57

Stone Academy (Hamden), 57

District of Columbia

Sanz School (Washington), 62

Florida

Advance Science Institute (Hialeah), 64

Career Institute of Florida (Saint Petersburg), 68

Central Florida College (Winter Park), 68

Florida Education Center (Lauderhill), 77

Galiano Career Academy (Altamonte Sprints), 79

New Professions Technical Institute (Miami), 88

Georgia

Appalachian Technical College (Jasper), 104

Columbus Technical College (Columbus), 108

Everest Institute (Marietta), 111

Everest Institute (Norcross), 111

Gwinnett College (Lilburn), 113

Gwinnett Technical College (Lawrenceville), 113

Javelin Technical Training Center (Atlanta), 115

Lanier Technical College (Oakwood), 115

Laurus Technical Institute (Atlanta), 116

Middle Georgia Technical College (Warner Robbins), 117

North Georgia Technical College (Clarkesville), 118

Savannah Technical College (Savannah), 121

South Georgia Technical College (Americus), 122

Swainsboro Technical College (Swainsboro), 123

West Central Technical College (Waco), 124

Illinois

BIR Training Center (Chicago), 125

CALC Institute of Technology (Alton), 126

The College of Office Technology (Chicago), 130

Everest College (Burr Ridge), 133

Everest College (Chicago), 133

Everest College (Merrionette Park), 134

First Institute of Travel (Crystal Lake), 134

Illinois Central College (East Peoria), 136

Kankakee Community College (Kankakee), 139

McHenry County College (Crystal Lake), 142

Oakton Community College (Des Plaines), 145

Richland Community College (Decatur), 148

The Vanderschmidt School (Schiller Park), 153

Vatterott College (Quincy), 154

Indiana

Harrison College (Anderson), 158

Harrison College (Fort Wayne), 158

Harrison College (Indianapolis), 158

Harrison College (Lafayette), 159

Harrison College (Muncie), 159

Harrison College (Terre Haute), 159

Indiana Business College–Elkhart (Elkhart), 159

Vincennes University (Vincennes), 168

Kentucky

Beckfield College (Florence), 169

Daymar College (Louisville), 171

Daymar College (Newport), 171

Daymar College (Owensboro), 171

National College (Lexington), 176

Maryland

Medix School (Towson), 190

Massachusetts

Everest Institute (Brighton), 198

Mildred Elley School (Pittsfield), 202

Newbury College (Brookline), 203

The Salter School (Worcester), 206

Michigan

Bay Mills Community College (Brimley), 211

Career Quest Learning Centers–Jackson (Jackson), 212

Everest Institute (Southfield), 215

Ferris State University (Big Rapids), 215

Kalamazoo Valley Community College (Kalamazoo), 218

Kaplan Institute (Detroit), 218

Lake Michigan College (Benton Harbor), 219

Muskegon Community College (Muskegon), 223

North Central Michigan College (Petoskey), 223

Oakland Community College (Bloomfield Hills), 224

Schoolcraft College (Livonia), 227

Mississippi

Virginia College at Jackson (Jackson), 236

New Hampshire

Lebanon College (Lebanon), 237

New Jersey

HoHoKus Hackensack School of Business and Medical Sciences (Hackensack), 246

Omega Institute (Pennsauken), 250

Performance Training (Toms River), 251

New York

Manhattan School of Computer Technology (New York), 272

Mildred Elley School (Albany), 273

Monroe 2–Orleans BOCES Center for Workforce Development (Rochester), 274

Onondaga-Courtland-Madison BOCES (Liverpool), 278

Trocaire College (Buffalo), 286

North Carolina

Center for Employment Training–Research Triangle Park (Research Triangle Park), 292

Miller-Motte Technical College (Cary), 300

Miller-Motte Technical College (Wilmington), 300

Ohio

American School of Technology (Columbus), 310

Bohecker College–Cincinnati (Cincinnati), 312

Buckeye Joint Vocational School (New Philadelphia), 313

Eastland Career Center (Groveport), 319

Mahoning County Joint Vocational School District (Canfield), 325

Stautzenberger College (Maumee), 336

Total Technical Institute (Brooklyn), 337

Trumbull Business College (Warren), 338

Vantage Vocational School (Van Wert), 340

Pennsylvania

Bucks County Community College (Newtown), 345

Butler County Community College (Butler), 345

Cambria-Rowe Business College (Indiana), 346

CHI Institute, Franklin Mills Campus (Philadelphia), 348

Consolidated School of Business (Lancaster), 350

Consolidated School of Business (York), 350

Greater Altoona Career and Technology Center (Altoona), 356

Lansdale School of Business (North Wales), 360

McCann School of Business & Technology (Pottsville), 364

Mercyhurst College (Erie), 364

Northwest Regional Technology Institute (Erie), 367

Westmoreland County Community College (Youngwood), 378

YTI Career Institute–York (York), 379

Puerto Rico

Nova College de Puerto Rico (Bayamón), 391

Universidad del Este (Carolina), 393

Tennessee

Kaplan Career Institute–Nashville Campus (Nashville), 409

MedVance Institute (Cookeville), 409

Miller-Motte Technical College (Clarksville), 410

Nashville College of Medical Careers (Madison), 411

National College (Nashville), 411

Vatterott College (Memphis), 420

West Tennessee Business College (Jackson), 421

Vermont

Community College of Vermont (Waterbury), 422

Virginia

ACT College (Arlington), 423

Everest College (McLean), 427

Everest Institute (Chesapeake), 428

Miller-Motte Technical College (Lynchburg), 430

National College (Salem), 430

Virginia Career Institute (Richmond), 435

Virginia Career Institute (Virginia Beach), 435

West Virginia

Academy of Careers and Technology (Beckley), 437

Ben Franklin Career Center (Dunbar), 437

West Virginia Junior College (Charleston), 444

Wisconsin

Kaplan College–Milwaukee (Milwaukee), 447

Moraine Park Technical College (Fond du Lac), 450

MEDICAL OFFICE COMPUTER SPECIALIST/ASSISTANT

MEDICAL OFFICE MANAGEMENT/ADMINISTRATION

MEDICAL RADIOLOGIC TECHNOLOGY/SCIENCE—RADIATION THERAPIST

Valencia Community College (Orlando), 101

Georgia
Dalton State College (Dalton), 109

Illinois
College of DuPage (Glen Ellyn), 129
South Suburban College (South Holland), 151

Kentucky
Madisonville Community College
(Madisonville), 176
Southeast Kentucky Community and Technical
College (Cumberland), 178
Spencerian College (Louisville), 179
West Kentucky Community and Technical
College (Paducah), 180

Maryland
The Community College of Baltimore County
(Baltimore), 187
Hagerstown Community College (Hagerstown),
188

Massachusetts
Suffolk University (Boston), 207

New Hampshire
New Hampshire Technical Institute (Concord),
239

New Jersey
Bergen Community College (Paramus), 240
Cooper Health System Center for Allied Health
Education (Camden), 243

New York
Hudson Valley Community College (Troy), 268

North Carolina
Pitt Community College (Greenville), 303
The University of North Carolina at Chapel
Hill (Chapel Hill), 307

Ohio
Lakeland Community College (Kirtland), 323

Pennsylvania
Community College of Allegheny County
(Pittsburgh), 348
Sanford-Brown Institute–Pittsburgh
(Pittsburgh), 373

Puerto Rico
Atenas College (Manati), 380

South Carolina
Greenville Technical College (Greenville), 399
Horry-Georgetown Technical College
(Conway), 400
Midlands Technical College (Columbia), 401
Orangeburg-Calhoun Technical College
(Orangeburg), 402

Tennessee
Chattanooga State Technical Community
College (Chattanooga), 406
High-Tech Institute (Memphis), 408
High-Tech Institute (Nashville), 408
MedVance Institute (Cookeville), 409
MedVance Institute–Nashville (Nashville), 409

Virginia
ACT College (Arlington), 423
Virginia Western Community College
(Roanoke), 436

West Virginia
West Virginia University Hospital–School of
Radiology Technology (Morgantown), 444

MEDICAL RECEPTION/RECEPTIONIST
Georgia
Central Georgia Technical College (Macon),
107
Columbus Technical College (Columbus), 108
Coosa Valley Technical College (Rome), 109
East Central Technical College (Fitzgerald), 110
Flint River Technical College (Thomaston), 111

Gwinnett Technical College (Lawrenceville),
113
Lanier Technical College (Oakwood), 115
Laurus Technical Institute (Atlanta), 116
Moultrie Technical College (Moultrie), 117
North Georgia Technical College (Clarkesville),
118
North Metro Technical College (Acworth), 118
Northwestern Technical College (Rock Spring),
118
Ogeechee Technical College (Statesboro), 119
West Central Technical College (Waco), 124
West Georgia Technical College (LaGrange),
124

Indiana
Everest College (Merrillville), 157

Kentucky
ATA Career Education (Louisville), 169

Michigan
Baker College of Auburn Hills (Auburn Hills),
209
Baker College of Cadillac (Cadillac), 210
Baker College of Clinton Township (Clinton
Township), 210
Baker College of Flint (Flint), 210
Baker College of Jackson (Jackson), 210
Baker College of Muskegon (Muskegon), 211
Baker College of Owosso (Owosso), 211
Baker College of Port Huron (Port Huron), 211
Delta College (University Center), 213
Henry Ford Community College (Dearborn),
217
Muskegon Community College (Muskegon),
223

New Hampshire
Lebanon College (Lebanon), 237

New Jersey
Performance Training (Toms River), 251

New York
Cheryl Fells School of Business (Niagara Falls),
261

Ohio
Adult Center for Education (Zanesville), 309

Puerto Rico
John Dewey College, 389

MEDICAL STAFF SERVICES TECHNOLOGY/ TECHNICIAN
Illinois
City Colleges of Chicago, Richard J. Daley
College (Chicago), 128
The Vanderschmidt School (Schiller Park), 153
Westwood College–Chicago River Oaks
(Calumet City), 154

Ohio
Northcoast Medical Training Academy (Kent),
327

Wisconsin
Western Technical College (La Crosse), 453

MEDICAL TRANSCRIPTION/ TRANSCRIPTIONIST
Alabama
Bishop State Community College (Mobile), 41
Snead State Community College (Boaz), 46
Southern Union State Community College
(Wadley), 47
Wallace State Community College
(Hanceville), 48

Connecticut
Briarwood College (Southington), 50

Delaware
Dawn Training Centre (Wilmington), 58

Delaware Technical & Community College,
Jack F. Owens Campus (Georgetown), 59
Delaware Technical & Community College,
Stanton/Wilmington Campus (Newark), 59

Florida
Career Institute of Florida (Saint Petersburg), 68
Lively Technical Center (Tallahassee), 84
Sheridan Vocational-Technical Center
(Hollywood), 96
Winter Park Tech (Winter Park), 102

Georgia
Albany Technical College (Albany), 103
Altamaha Technical College (Jesup), 104
Atlanta Technical College (Atlanta), 105
Augusta Technical College (Augusta), 106
Brown College of Court Reporting and Medical
Transcription (Atlanta), 107
Central Georgia Technical College (Macon),
107
Coosa Valley Technical College (Rome), 109
Flint River Technical College (Thomaston), 111
Griffin Technical College (Griffin), 113
Gwinnett Technical College (Lawrenceville),
113
Iverson Business School (Atlanta), 115
Lanier Technical College (Oakwood), 115
Middle Georgia Technical College (Warner
Robbins), 117
Moultrie Technical College (Moultrie), 117
North Metro Technical College (Acworth), 118
Northwestern Technical College (Rock Spring),
118
Okefenokee Technical College (Waycross), 119
Savannah Technical College (Savannah), 121
Southwest Georgia Technical College
(Thomasville), 122
Valdosta Technical College (Valdosta), 123
West Central Technical College (Waco), 124
West Georgia Technical College (LaGrange),
124

Illinois
Black Hawk College (Moline), 125
College of DuPage (Glen Ellyn), 129
College of Lake County (Grayslake), 129
Harper College (Palatine), 135
Highland Community College (Freeport), 136
Illinois Central College (East Peoria), 136
Illinois Eastern Community Colleges, Lincoln
Trail College (Robinson), 137
Illinois Eastern Community Colleges, Olney
Central College (Olney), 137
John A. Logan College (Carterville), 138
Joliet Junior College (Joliet), 139
Kaskaskia College (Centralia), 139
Kishwaukee College (Malta), 140
Lake Land College (Mattoon), 140
Lewis and Clark Community College (Godfrey),
141
Lincoln Land Community College (Springfield),
141
MacCormac College (Chicago), 142
Midstate College (Peoria), 143
Moraine Valley Community College (Palos
Hills), 143
Oakton Community College (Des Plaines), 145
Parkland College (Champaign), 145
Rasmussen College Aurora (Aurora), 147
Rasmussen College Rockford, Illinois
(Rockford), 147
Rend Lake College (Ina), 148
Richland Community College (Decatur), 148
Rockford Business College (Rockford), 149
Rock Valley College (Rockford), 149
Shawnee Community College (Ullin), 150
Southeastern Illinois College (Harrisburg), 151
Southwestern Illinois College (Belleville), 151
Sparks College (Shelbyville), 152

Virginia
Blue Ridge Community College (Weyers Cave), 424
Central Virginia Community College (Lynchburg), 425
Dabney S. Lancaster Community College (Clifton Forge), 426
Danville Community College (Danville), 426
Eastern Shore Community College (Melfa), 426
Germanna Community College (Locust Grove), 428
John Tyler Community College (Chester), 429
J. Sargeant Reynolds Community College (Richmond), 429
Lord Fairfax Community College (Middletown), 429
Mountain Empire Community College (Big Stone Gap), 430
New River Community College (Dublin), 430
Northern Virginia Community College (Annandale), 430
Patrick Henry Community College (Martinsville), 431
Paul D. Camp Community College (Franklin), 431
Piedmont Virginia Community College (Charlottesville), 431
Rappahannock Community College (Glenns), 431
Southside Virginia Community College (Alberta), 432
Southwest Virginia Community College (Richlands), 432
Thomas Nelson Community College (Hampton), 433
Tidewater Community College (Norfolk), 434
Virginia Highlands Community College (Abingdon), 435
Virginia Western Community College (Roanoke), 436
Wytheville Community College (Wytheville), 436

MENTAL HEALTH COUNSELING/COUNSELOR
Illinois
City Colleges of Chicago, Kennedy-King College (Chicago), 128

MERCHANDISING AND BUYING OPERATIONS
Michigan
Delta College (University Center), 213

METAL AND JEWELRY ARTS
District of Columbia
Corcoran College of Art and Design (Washington), 61
Florida
Pinellas Technical Education Center–St. Petersburg (St. Petersburg), 92
New York
Gemological Institute of America (New York), 267
Studio Jewelers (New York), 284

METAL BUILDING ASSEMBLY/ASSEMBLER
Wisconsin
Gateway Technical College (Kenosha), 446
Lakeshore Technical College (Cleveland), 447
Mid-State Technical College (Wisconsin Rapids), 449
Milwaukee Area Technical College (Milwaukee), 449

METALLURGICAL TECHNOLOGY/TECHNICIAN
Michigan
Schoolcraft College (Livonia), 227

MILITARY TECHNOLOGIES
West Virginia
American Public University System (Charles Town), 437

MINING AND MINERAL ENGINEERING
Michigan
Michigan Technological University (Houghton), 222

MINING TECHNOLOGY/TECHNICIAN
Illinois
Illinois Eastern Community Colleges, Wabash Valley College (Mount Carmel), 137
Kentucky
Madisonville Community College (Madisonville), 176
Southeast Kentucky Community and Technical College (Cumberland), 178
Pennsylvania
Schuylkill Technology Center–North Campus (Frackville), 373
Virginia
Mountain Empire Community College (Big Stone Gap), 430

MISSIONS/MISSIONARY STUDIES AND MISSIOLOGY
South Carolina
W. L. Bonner College (Columbia), 405

MONTESSORI TEACHER EDUCATION
Pennsylvania
Lehigh Carbon Community College (Schnecksville), 362

MORTUARY SCIENCE AND EMBALMING/ EMBALMER
Puerto Rico
Ponce Paramedical College (Ponce), 392

MOTORCYCLE MAINTENANCE AND REPAIR TECHNOLOGY/TECHNICIAN
Connecticut
Baran Institute of Technology (Windsor), 49
Florida
Motorcycle and Marine Mechanics Institute– Division of Universal Technical Institute (Orlando), 88
Wyotech–Daytona (Daytona Beach), 103
Georgia
Chattahoochee Technical College (Marietta), 107
DeKalb Technical College (Clarkston), 109
North Georgia Technical College (Clarkesville), 118
Michigan
Washtenaw Community College (Ann Arbor), 229
North Carolina
Central Carolina Community College (Sanford), 292
Davidson County Community College (Lexington), 294
Edgecombe Community College (Tarboro), 295
Ohio
Ohio Technical College (Cleveland), 329
Pennsylvania
YTI Career Institute–York (York), 379
Rhode Island
Motoring Technical Training Institute (East Providence), 395

Tennessee
Tennessee Technology Center at Paris (Paris), 419
Virginia
Southside Virginia Community College (Alberta), 432

MUSICAL INSTRUMENT FABRICATION AND REPAIR
Massachusetts
North Bennet Street School (Boston), 204

MUSIC, GENERAL
Georgia
Atlanta Institute of Music (Norcross), 105
Omnitech Institute (Decatur), 119
Illinois
City Colleges of Chicago, Harold Washington College (Chicago), 127
Southwestern Illinois College (Belleville), 151
Massachusetts
Holyoke Community College (Holyoke), 199
New York
Schenectady County Community College (Schenectady), 282
Ohio
Sinclair Community College (Dayton), 334
Pennsylvania
Harrisburg Area Community College (Harrisburg), 357

MUSIC HISTORY, LITERATURE, AND THEORY
Alabama
Calhoun Community College (Decatur), 41

MUSIC MANAGEMENT AND MERCHANDISING
Ohio
Hocking College (Nelsonville), 321
Owens Community College (Toledo), 330
Pennsylvania
Harrisburg Area Community College (Harrisburg), 357
Tennessee
Visible School—Music and Worships Arts College (Lakeland), 420

MUSIC, OTHER
Florida
Northwest Florida State College (Niceville), 89
Valencia Community College (Orlando), 101
Georgia
Omnitech Institute (Decatur), 119
Michigan
Washtenaw Community College (Ann Arbor), 229
New Jersey
Bergen Community College (Paramus), 240
New York
Genesee Community College (Batavia), 267
Ohio
International College of Broadcasting (Dayton), 322
Tennessee
Columbia State Community College (Columbia), 406
Nashville State Technical Community College (Nashville), 411
Virginia
Shenandoah University (Winchester), 432

MUSIC PEDAGOGY

Illinois
Roosevelt University (Chicago), 149

MUSIC PERFORMANCE, GENERAL

Georgia
Atlanta Institute of Music (Norcross), 105

New York
Dutchess Community College (Poughkeepsie), 264

Tennessee
Visible School—Music and Worships Arts College (Lakeland), 420

MUSIC TEACHER EDUCATION

Illinois
DePaul University (Chicago), 131

MUSIC THERAPY/THERAPIST

Virginia
Shenandoah University (Winchester), 432

NAIL TECHNICIAN/SPECIALIST AND MANICURIST

Alabama
Calhoun Community College (Decatur), 41
Mimi's Beauty Academy of Cosmetology (Huntsville), 45
Shelton State Community College (Tuscaloosa), 46

Delaware
Delaware Learning Institute of Cosmetology (Dagsboro), 59
Schilling-Douglas School of Hair Design (Newark), 60

District of Columbia
Dudley Beauty College (Washington), 61

Florida
Academy of Career Training (Kissimmee), 63
Academy of Cosmetology (Merritt Island), 63
Academy of Cosmetology (Palm Bay), 63
Academy of Healing Arts, Massage, and Facial Skin Care (Lake Worth), 63
Academy of Professional Careers (Winter Park), 63
Artistic Nails and Beauty Academy (Tampa), 65
ASM Beauty World Academy (Hollywood), 65
The Beauty Institute (West Palm Beach), 66
Beauty Schools of America (Hialeah), 66
Beauty Schools of America (Miami), 66
Benes International School of Beauty (New Port Richey), 67
Bradenton Beauty Academy (Bradenton), 67
Daytona State College (Daytona Beach), 72
Fashion Focus Hair Academy (Sarasota), 74
Florida Community College at Jacksonville (Jacksonville), 77
Indian River State College (Fort Pierce), 81
International Academy (South Daytona), 81
La Belle Beauty Academy (Miami), 83
La Belle Beauty School (Hialeah), 83
Lake City Community College (Lake City), 83
Lake Technical Center (Eustis), 83
Lee County High Tech Center North (Cape Coral), 83
Lindsey Hopkins Technical Education Center (Miami), 84
Lively Technical Center (Tallahassee), 84
Loraine's Academy. (St. Petersburg), 85
Manatee Technical Institute (Bradenton), 85
Manhattan Beauty School (Tampa), 85
Miami-Dade County Public Schools (Miami), 87
New Concept Massage and Beauty School (Miami), 88

North Florida Cosmetology Institute (Tallahassee), 88
North Florida Institute–Jacksonville (Jacksonville), 89
Okaloosa Applied Technology Center (Ft. Walton Beach), 89
Palm Beach Community College (Lake Worth), 90
Pensacola Junior College (Pensacola), 91
Ridge Technical Center (Winter Haven), 93
Robert Morgan Vocational-Technical Center (Miami), 94
Sarasota County Technical Institute (Sarasota), 96
Shear Excellence International Hair Academy (Tampa), 96
Sunstate Academy of Hair Design (Clearwater), 98
Sunstate Academy of Hair Design (Fort Myers), 98
Sunstate Academy of Hair Design (Sarasota), 98
Superior Career Institute (Lauderdale Lakes), 98
Universal Massage and Beauty Institute (Sweetwater), 100
Westside Tech (Winter Garden), 102
Winter Park Tech (Winter Park), 102
Withlacoochee Technical Institute (Inverness), 103

Georgia
Athens Technical College (Athens), 105
Augusta Technical College (Augusta), 106
Beauty College of America (Forest Park), 106
Central Georgia Technical College (Macon), 107
East Central Technical College (Fitzgerald), 110
Flint River Technical College (Thomaston), 111
Georgia Career Institute (Conyers), 112
Griffin Technical College (Griffin), 113
International School of Skin and Nailcare (Atlanta), 115
Moultrie Technical College (Moultrie), 117
North Georgia Technical College (Clarkesville), 118
Northwestern Technical College (Rock Spring), 118
Rivertown School of Beauty (Columbus), 120
South Georgia Technical College (Americus), 122
Valdosta Technical College (Valdosta), 123
Vogue Beauty School (Hiram), 123

Illinois
American Career College (Berwyn), 125
Educators of Beauty (La Salle), 132
Educators of Beauty (Rockford), 132
Educators of Beauty (Sterling), 132
Empire Beauty School–Arlington Heights (Arlington Heights), 133
Empire Beauty School–Hanover Park (Hanover Park), 133
Empire Beauty School–Lisle (Lisle), 133
Hair Professional Career College (De Kalb), 134
Hair Professionals Academy of Cosmetology (Elgin), 135
Hair Professionals Career College (Palos Hills), 135
Highland Community College (Freeport), 136
La' James College of Hairstyling (East Moline), 140
Lake Land College (Mattoon), 140
MacDaniel's Beauty School (Chicago), 142
Mr. John's School of Cosmetology & Nails (Jacksonville), 144
Mr. John's School of Cosmetology (Decatur), 144
Pivot Point Beauty School (Chicago), 146
Rosel School of Cosmetology (Chicago), 149
Trend Setter's College of Cosmetology (Bradley), 152

University of Spa & Cosmetology Arts (Springfield), 153

Indiana
Creative Hairstyling Academy (Highland), 156
A Cut Above Beauty College (Indianapolis), 155
David Demuth Institute of Cosmetology (Richmond), 157
Don Roberts Beauty School (Valparaiso), 157
Don Roberts School of Hair Design (Munster), 157
Honors Beauty College, Inc. (Indianapolis), 159
Ideal Beauty Academy (Jeffersonville), 159
Lafayette Beauty Academy (Lafayette), 165
Masters of Cosmetology College (Fort Wayne), 165
Merrillville Beauty College (Merrillville), 165
PJ's College of Cosmetology (Clarksville), 166
PJ's College of Cosmetology (Richmond), 166
Ravenscroft Beauty College (Fort Wayne), 166
Ruade's School of Beauty Culture (Ft. Wayne), 167
Rudae's School of Beauty Culture (Kokomo), 167

Kentucky
Barrett and Company School of Hair Design (Nicholasville), 169
Bellefonte Academy of Beauty (Russell), 169
Collins School of Cosmetology (Middlesboro), 171
Ezell's Beauty School (Murray), 173
The Hair Design School (Florence), 173
The Hair Design School (Louisville), 173, 174
The Hair Design School (Radcliff), 174
Head's West Kentucky Beauty School (Madisonville), 174
J & M Academy of Cosmetology (Frankfort), 175
Jenny Lea Academy of Cosmetology (Harlan), 175
Kaufman's Beauty School (Lexington), 175
Lexington Beauty College (Lexington), 175
Nu-Tek Academy of Beauty (Mount Sterling), 177
Pat Wilson's Beauty College (Henderson), 177
PJ's College of Cosmetology (Bowling Green), 177
PJ's College of Cosmetology (Glasgow), 177
Regency School of Hair Design (Prestonburg), 177
Trend Setter's Academy (Louisville), 179
Trend Setter's Academy of Beauty Culture (Elizabethtown), 179

Maryland
Aaron's Academy of Beauty (Waldorf), 183
Aesthetics Institute of Cosmetology (Gaithersburg), 183
Baltimore Studio of Hair Design (Baltimore), 185
Delmarva Beauty Academy (Salisbury), 187
Empire Beauty School–Owings Mills (Owings Mills), 187
The Fila Academy Inc (Glen Burnie), 187
International Beauty School 3 (Bel Air), 189
Maryland Beauty Academy of Essex (Essex), 190
Robert Paul Academy of Cosmetology Arts and Sciences (Timonium), 191

Massachusetts
Ailano School of Cosmetology (Brockton), 193
Blaine! The Beauty Career Schools–Framingham (Framingham), 194
Blaine! The Beauty Career Schools–Malden (Malden), 195
Hair in Motion Beauty Academy (Worcester), 199
Henri's School of Hair Design (Fitchburg), 199
Jolie Hair and Beauty Academy (Ludlow), 199

NATURAL RESOURCES/CONSERVATION, GENERAL

NATURAL RESOURCES MANAGEMENT AND POLICY

NATURAL RESOURCES MANAGEMENT/DEVELOPMENT

NAVAL ARCHITECTURE AND MARINE ENGINEERING

NEAR AND MIDDLE EASTERN STUDIES

NONPROFIT/PUBLIC/ORGANIZATIONAL MANAGEMENT

NUCLEAR ENGINEERING

NUCLEAR MEDICAL TECHNOLOGY/TECHNOLOGIST

NUCLEAR/NUCLEAR POWER TECHNOLOGY/TECHNICIAN

NURSE/NURSING ASSISTANT/AIDE AND PATIENT CARE ASSISTANT

Rock Valley College (Rockford), 149
Sauk Valley Community College (Dixon), 150
Shawnee Community College (Ullin), 150
South Suburban College (South Holland), 151
Southwestern Illinois College (Belleville), 151
Triton College (River Grove), 153
Waubonsee Community College (Sugar Grove), 154

Indiana
Brown Mackie College–Fort Wayne (Fort Wayne), 155
Everest College (Merrillville), 157

Kentucky
Maysville Community and Technical College (Maysville), 176
West Kentucky Community and Technical College (Paducah), 180

Maine
Intercoast Career Institute (South Portland), 181

Maryland
Allegany College of Maryland (Cumberland), 184
Americare School of Allied Health (Wheaton), 184

Massachusetts
Bunker Hill Community College (Boston), 196
Medical Professional Institute (Malden), 202

Michigan
Dorsey Business Schools (Madison Heights), 214
Dorsey Business Schools (Roseville), 214
Dorsey Business Schools (Southgate), 214
Dorsey Business Schools (Wayne), 214
Henry Ford Community College (Dearborn), 217
Lansing Community College (Lansing), 219
Michigan Career and Technical Institute (Plainwell), 221
North Central Michigan College (Petoskey), 223
Schoolcraft College (Livonia), 227
Washtenaw Community College (Ann Arbor), 229

Mississippi
Copiah-Lincoln Community College (Wesson), 231
East Central Community College (Decatur), 232
East Mississippi Community College (Scooba), 232
Jones County Junior College (Ellisville), 234
Meridian Community College (Meridian), 234
Northwest Mississippi Community College (Senatobia), 235
Southwest Mississippi Community College (Summit), 235

New Hampshire
New Hampshire Community Technical College, Nashua/Claremont (Nashua), 238

New Jersey
Dover Business College (Paramus), 244
Healthcare Training Institute (Union), 246
Monmouth County Vocational School District (Long Branch), 249
Ocean County Vocational Post Secondary Division (Toms River), 250
Omega Institute (Pennsauken), 250
Somerset County Technical Institute (Bridgewater), 253

New York
Orleans Niagara BOCES—Practical Nursing Program (Sanborn), 278
Willsey Institute (Staten Island), 288

North Carolina
Alamance Community College (Graham), 288
Bladen Community College (Dublin), 289
Brunswick Community College (Supply), 290
Cabarrus College of Health Sciences (Concord), 290
Caldwell Community College and Technical Institute (Hudson), 290
Carolinas College of Health Sciences (Charlotte), 292
Coastal Carolina Community College (Jacksonville), 293
Fayetteville Technical Community College (Fayetteville), 295
Gaston College (Dallas), 296
McDowell Technical Community College (Marion), 300
Piedmont Community College (Roxboro), 302
Richmond Community College (Hamlet), 303
Robeson Community College (Lumberton), 304

Ohio
Adult and Community Education–Hudson (Columbus), 309
Adult Center for Education (Zanesville), 309
Akron Adult Vocational Services (Akron), 309
Apollo School of Practical Nursing (Lima), 310
Brown Mackie College–Akron (Akron), 313
Brown Mackie College–North Canton (Canton), 313
Buckeye Hills Career Center (Rio Grande), 313
Choffin Career Center (Youngstown), 315
Columbiana County Vocation School (Lisbon), 317
Delaware JVS District (Delaware), 318
Licking County Joint Vocational School–Newark (Newark), 324
Madison Local Schools–Madison Adult Education (Mansfield), 324
Northcoast Medical Training Academy (Kent), 327
O. C. Collins Career Center (Chesapeake), 328
Pickaway Ross Joint Vocational School District (Chillicothe), 331
Pioneer Career and Technology Center: A Vocational School District (Shelby), 331
Sandusky Adult Education (Sandusky), 333
Toledo School of Practical Nursing (Toledo), 337
Tri-Rivers Career Center (Marion), 337
Vantage Vocational School (Van Wert), 340
Warren County Career Center (Lebanon), 340

Pennsylvania
Antonelli Medical and Professional Institute (Pottstown), 343
Central Pennsylvania Institute of Science and Technology (Pleasant Gap), 347
Commonwealth Technical Institute (Johnstown), 348
Delaware County Community College (Media), 351
Erie Business Center, Main (Erie), 355
Everest Institute (Pittsburgh), 355
Greater Altoona Career and Technology Center (Altoona), 356
Pennsylvania Institute of Technology (Media), 370
Schuylkill Technology Center–North Campus (Frackville), 373

Puerto Rico
John Dewey College, 389

South Carolina
Forrest Junior College (Anderson), 399
Midlands Technical College (Columbia), 401
Orangeburg-Calhoun Technical College (Orangeburg), 402

Tennessee
Concorde Career College (Memphis), 406

Tennessee Technology Center at Memphis (Memphis), 417
Tennessee Technology Center at Shelbyville (Shelbyville), 419
Tennessee Technology Center at Whiteville (Whiteville), 419

Virginia
Woodrow Wilson Rehabilitation Center (Fishersville), 436

West Virginia
Opportunities Industrialization Center–North Central West Virginia (Fairmont), 442
Pierpont Community & Technical College of Fairmont State University (Fairmont), 442

Wisconsin
Blackhawk Technical College (Janesville), 445
Chippewa Valley Technical College (Eau Claire), 445
Fox Valley Technical College (Appleton), 446
Gateway Technical College (Kenosha), 446
Lakeshore Technical College (Cleveland), 447
Madison Area Technical College (Madison), 448
Mid-State Technical College (Wisconsin Rapids), 449
Milwaukee Area Technical College (Milwaukee), 449
Moraine Park Technical College (Fond du Lac), 450
Nicolet Area Technical College (Rhinelander), 450
Northcentral Technical College (Wausau), 450
Northeast Wisconsin Technical College (Green Bay), 450
Southwest Wisconsin Technical College (Fennimore), 452
Waukesha County Technical College (Pewaukee), 453
Western Technical College (La Crosse), 453
Wisconsin Indianhead Technical College (Shell Lake), 453

NURSING—REGISTERED NURSE TRAINING (RN, ASN, BSN, MSN)

Connecticut
Bridgeport Hospital School of Nursing (Bridgeport), 50
Capital Community College (Hartford), 51

Delaware
Delaware Technical & Community College, Jack F. Owens Campus (Georgetown), 59
Delaware Technical & Community College, Terry Campus (Dover), 60

Florida
Broward Community College (Fort Lauderdale), 68
Florida Community College at Jacksonville (Jacksonville), 77
Galen Health Institute–Tampa Bay (St. Petersburg), 79
Hillsborough Community College (Tampa), 81
Indian River State College (Fort Pierce), 81
Palm Beach Community College (Lake Worth), 90
Saber (Miami), 94
St. Petersburg College (St. Petersburg), 94

Illinois
Oakton Community College (Des Plaines), 145
Rend Lake College (Ina), 148

Indiana
Purdue University Calumet (Hammond), 166

Kentucky
Galen Health Institutes (Louisville), 173
Spalding University (Louisville), 178

Maryland
Anne Arundel Community College (Arnold), 184
Baltimore City Community College (Baltimore), 185

Michigan
Lake Superior State University (Sault Sainte Marie), 219
Wayne County Community College District (Detroit), 229

New York
Excelsior College (Albany), 266

North Carolina
Carolinas College of Health Sciences (Charlotte), 292
Roanoke-Chowan Community College (Ahoskie), 303
Stanly Community College (Albemarle), 306

Ohio
Tri-Rivers Career Center (Marion), 337

Pennsylvania
Bucks County Community College (Newtown), 345
Conemaugh Valley Memorial Hospital (Johnstown), 350
Ohio Valley General Hospital (McKees Rocks), 367
Sharon Regional Health System School of Nursing (Sharon), 373

Puerto Rico
Universal Technology College of Puerto Rico (Aguadilla), 393

South Carolina
Aiken Technical College (Aiken), 397
Central Carolina Technical College (Sumter), 398
Florence-Darlington Technical College (Florence), 399
Greenville Technical College (Greenville), 399
Horry-Georgetown Technical College (Conway), 400
Midlands Technical College (Columbia), 401
Northeastern Technical College (Cheraw), 401
Piedmont Technical College (Greenwood), 402
Tri-County Technical College (Pendleton), 403
Trident Technical College (Charleston), 404
York Technical College (Rock Hill), 405

Virginia
Career Training Solutions (Fredericksburg), 425
Riverside School of Health Careers (Newport News), 432
Sentara Norfolk General Hospital School of Health Professions (Norfolk), 432
Southside Regional Medical Center (Petersburg), 432

Wisconsin
Herzing College (Madison), 447

NURSING, OTHER

Alabama
Herzing College (Birmingham), 43

Florida
Atlantic Vocational-Technical Center (Coconut Creek), 66
Bradford Union Area Vocational Technical Center (Starke), 67
Brevard Community College (Cocoa), 67
College of Business and Technology–Flagler Campus (Miami), 70
College of Business and Technology–Hialeah Campus (Hialeah), 70
College of Business and Technology (Miami), 70
Comp-Med Vocational Careers Corporation (Hialeah), 70
Daytona State College (Daytona Beach), 72

Florida Community College at Jacksonville (Jacksonville), 77
Gulf Coast College (Tampa), 79
Indian River State College (Fort Pierce), 81
Lake City Community College (Lake City), 83
Lee County High Tech Center North (Cape Coral), 83
Management Resources Institute (Miami), 85
Manatee Technical Institute (Bradenton), 85
MedVance Institute (Atlantis), 86
MedVance Institute (Miami), 86
MedVance Institute (Stuart), 86
North Florida Community College (Madison), 88
North Florida Institute (Orange Park), 89
Orlando Technical Center (Orlando), 90
Palm Beach Community College (Lake Worth), 90
Pensacola Junior College (Pensacola), 91
Polytechnic Institute of America (Orlando), 92
Ridge Technical Center (Winter Haven), 93
Saber (Miami), 94
St. Johns River Community College (Palatka), 94
Santa Fe Community College (Gainesville), 95
Seminole Community College (Sanford), 96
Sheridan Vocational-Technical Center (Hollywood), 96
South Florida Community College (Avon Park), 97
Taylor College (Belleview), 99

Indiana
Brown Mackie College–Merrillville (Merrillville), 156
Brown Mackie College–South Bend (South Bend), 156

Kentucky
ATA Career Education (Louisville), 169
Brown Mackie College–Northern Kentucky (Fort Mitchell), 171

Maryland
Hagerstown Community College (Hagerstown), 188

Michigan
Madonna University (Livonia), 221

New Jersey
New Community Workforce Development Center (Newark), 250

New York
Erie #1 BOCES–Practical Nursing Program (West Seneca), 265
Schuyler-Chemung-Tioga Practical Nursing Program (Elmira), 282

Ohio
Ashtabula County Joint Vocational School (Jefferson), 311
ATS Institute of Technology (Highland Heights), 311
Brown Mackie College–Cincinnati (Cincinnati), 313
Marion Technical College (Marion), 325
RETS Tech Center (Centerville), 333
Willoughby-Eastlake School of Practical Nursing (Willoughby), 341

Pennsylvania
Central Susquehanna LPN Career Center (Sunbury), 347
La Roche College (Pittsburgh), 361
Lebanon County Area Vocational Technical School (Lebanon), 361
Penn State New Kensington (New Kensington), 369
Schuylkill Technology Center–North Campus (Frackville), 373
York County School of Technology–Practical Nursing Program (York), 378

Tennessee
Tennessee Technology Center at Ripley (Ripley), 419

Virginia
Beta Tech (Richmond), 424
Central School of Practical Nursing (Norfolk), 425

Wisconsin
Gateway Technical College (Kenosha), 446
Lakeshore Technical College (Cleveland), 447
Nicolet Area Technical College (Rhinelander), 450
Northeast Wisconsin Technical College (Green Bay), 450

OCCUPATIONAL HEALTH AND INDUSTRIAL HYGIENE

Connecticut
University of New Haven (West Haven), 58

OCCUPATIONAL SAFETY AND HEALTH TECHNOLOGY/TECHNICIAN

Connecticut
University of New Haven (West Haven), 58

Delaware
Delaware Technical & Community College, Stanton/Wilmington Campus (Newark), 59

Florida
Northwest Florida State College (Niceville), 89

Indiana
Indiana University Bloomington (Bloomington), 160
Ivy Tech Community College–Kokomo (Kokomo), 162

Maine
Central Maine Community College (Auburn), 181

Maryland
Allegany College of Maryland (Cumberland), 184
Anne Arundel Community College (Arnold), 184
The Community College of Baltimore County (Baltimore), 187

Massachusetts
Quinsigamond Community College (Worcester), 205

Michigan
Madonna University (Livonia), 221

New York
Rochester Institute of Technology (Rochester), 280

North Carolina
Durham Technical Community College (Durham), 295

Ohio
Columbiana County Vocation School (Lisbon), 317
Columbus State Community College (Columbus), 317
Owens Community College (Toledo), 330

West Virginia
Blue Ridge Community and Technical College (Martinsburg), 438

OCCUPATIONAL THERAPIST ASSISTANT

South Carolina
Piedmont Technical College (Greenwood), 402

Virginia
Southwest Virginia Community College (Richlands), 432
Tidewater Community College (Norfolk), 434

OCCUPATIONAL THERAPY/THERAPIST

Ohio
The University of Toledo (Toledo), 339

OCEANOGRAPHY, CHEMICAL AND PHYSICAL

Pennsylvania
Penn State University Park (University Park), 369

OFFICE MANAGEMENT AND SUPERVISION

Connecticut
Stone Academy (Hamden), 57

Delaware
Delaware Technical & Community College, Jack F. Owens Campus (Georgetown), 59
Delaware Technical & Community College, Stanton/Wilmington Campus (Newark), 59
Delaware Technical & Community College, Terry Campus (Dover), 60

Florida
Broward Community College (Fort Lauderdale), 68
Florida Community College at Jacksonville (Jacksonville), 77
Galiano Career Academy (Altamonte Sprints), 79
Indian River State College (Fort Pierce), 81
Lively Technical Center (Tallahassee), 84
Management Resources Institute (Miami), 85
Miami Dade College (Miami), 87
North Florida Community College (Madison), 88
Northwest Florida State College (Niceville), 89
Palm Beach Community College (Lake Worth), 90
South Florida Community College (Avon Park), 97
Suwannee-Hamilton Area Vocational, Technical, and Adult Education Center (Live Oak), 98

Illinois
College of Lake County (Grayslake), 129
Danville Area Community College (Danville), 131
Elgin Community College (Elgin), 132
Kaskaskia College (Centralia), 139
Lincoln College (Lincoln), 141
Sanford-Brown College (Collinsville), 150
Sauk Valley Community College (Dixon), 150
South Suburban College (South Holland), 151

Kentucky
Daymar College (Owensboro), 171

Maryland
Columbia Union College (Takoma Park), 187

Massachusetts
Bristol Community College (Fall River), 196

Michigan
Delta College (University Center), 213
Ferris State University (Big Rapids), 215
Henry Ford Community College (Dearborn), 217
Lansing Community College (Lansing), 219
Mott Community College (Flint), 223
Washtenaw Community College (Ann Arbor), 229

North Carolina
Alamance Community College (Graham), 288
Asheville-Buncombe Technical Community College (Asheville), 288
Beaufort County Community College (Washington), 289
Bladen Community College (Dublin), 289
Carteret Community College (Morehead City), 292

Catawba Valley Community College (Hickory), 292
Central Carolina Community College (Sanford), 292
Central Piedmont Community College (Charlotte), 293
Cleveland Community College (Shelby), 293
College of The Albemarle (Elizabeth City), 294
Craven Community College (New Bern), 294
Durham Technical Community College (Durham), 295
Forsyth Technical Community College (Winston-Salem), 296
Gaston College (Dallas), 296
Guilford Technical Community College (Jamestown), 297
Halifax Community College (Weldon), 297
Isothermal Community College (Spindale), 298
James Sprunt Community College (Kenansville), 298
Johnston Community College (Smithfield), 298
Lenoir Community College (Kinston), 299
Martin Community College (Williamston), 299
McDowell Technical Community College (Marion), 300
Mitchell Community College (Statesville), 300
Montgomery Community College (Troy), 301
Nash Community College (Rocky Mount), 302
Piedmont Community College (Roxboro), 302
Pitt Community College (Greenville), 303
Randolph Community College (Asheboro), 303
Richmond Community College (Hamlet), 303
Rowan-Cabarrus Community College (Salisbury), 304
Sampson Community College (Clinton), 304
Southeastern Community College (Whiteville), 305
Surry Community College (Dobson), 306
Wake Technical Community College (Raleigh), 307
Wilkes Community College (Wilkesboro), 308

Ohio
Ashland University (Ashland), 310
Brown Mackie College–Findlay (Findlay), 313
Miami University (Oxford), 326
The University of Akron (Akron), 338
University of Cincinnati Clermont College (Batavia), 339

Pennsylvania
Bucks County Community College (Newtown), 345

Puerto Rico
Century College (Aguadilla), 382

Tennessee
Concorde Career College (Memphis), 406

OPERATIONS MANAGEMENT AND SUPERVISION

Connecticut
Naugatuck Valley Community College (Waterbury), 54

Georgia
Albany Technical College (Albany), 103
Appalachian Technical College (Jasper), 104
Athens Technical College (Athens), 105
Augusta Technical College (Augusta), 106
Central Georgia Technical College (Macon), 107
Chattahoochee Technical College (Marietta), 107
Columbus Technical College (Columbus), 108
Coosa Valley Technical College (Rome), 109
DeKalb Technical College (Clarkston), 109
Flint River Technical College (Thomaston), 111
Griffin Technical College (Griffin), 113

Gwinnett Technical College (Lawrenceville), 113
Lanier Technical College (Oakwood), 115
Macon State College (Macon), 116
Moultrie Technical College (Moultrie), 117
North Georgia Technical College (Clarkesville), 118
North Metro Technical College (Acworth), 118
Northwestern Technical College (Rock Spring), 118
Savannah Technical College (Savannah), 121
Southeastern Technical College (Vidalia), 121
South Georgia Technical College (Americus), 122
Southwest Georgia Technical College (Thomasville), 122
Valdosta Technical College (Valdosta), 123
West Georgia Technical College (LaGrange), 124

Illinois
Joliet Junior College (Joliet), 139
McHenry County College (Crystal Lake), 142
Oakton Community College (Des Plaines), 145
Prairie State College (Chicago Heights), 146

Indiana
Indiana University–Purdue University Fort Wayne (Fort Wayne), 160
Indiana University–Purdue University Indianapolis (Indianapolis), 160
Purdue University (West Lafayette), 166
Purdue University Calumet (Hammond), 166
Purdue University North Central (Westville), 166

Maryland
Capitol College (Laurel), 185

Michigan
Baker College of Cadillac (Cadillac), 210
Ferris State University (Big Rapids), 215

North Carolina
Alamance Community College (Graham), 288
Central Carolina Community College (Sanford), 292
Cleveland Community College (Shelby), 293
Craven Community College (New Bern), 294
Durham Technical Community College (Durham), 295
Fayetteville Technical Community College (Fayetteville), 295
Isothermal Community College (Spindale), 298
Lenoir Community College (Kinston), 299
McDowell Technical Community College (Marion), 300
Western Piedmont Community College (Morganton), 308

Ohio
Lakeland Community College (Kirtland), 323
Owens Community College (Toledo), 330
Terra State Community College (Fremont), 336

Pennsylvania
Butler County Community College (Butler), 345

Wisconsin
Waukesha County Technical College (Pewaukee), 453

OPHTHALMIC AND OPTOMETRIC SUPPORT SERVICES AND ALLIED PROFESSIONS, OTHER

Florida
Manatee Technical Institute (Bradenton), 85

Massachusetts
Holyoke Community College (Holyoke), 199

OPHTHALMIC LABORATORY TECHNOLOGY/ TECHNICIAN

Puerto Rico
Puerto Rico Technical Junior College (San Juan), 392

OPHTHALMIC TECHNICIAN/TECHNOLOGIST

District of Columbia
Georgetown University (Washington), 61

North Carolina
Caldwell Community College and Technical Institute (Hudson), 290

OPTICIANRY/OPHTHALMIC DISPENSING OPTICIAN

Alabama
George C. Wallace Community College (Dothan), 43

Florida
Hillsborough Community College (Tampa), 81
St. Petersburg College (St. Petersburg), 94

Georgia
DeKalb Technical College (Clarkston), 109
Ogeechee Technical College (Statesboro), 119
Valdosta Technical College (Valdosta), 123

Michigan
Baker College of Jackson (Jackson), 210

New Jersey
Camden County College (Blackwood), 241

North Carolina
Durham Technical Community College (Durham), 295

Wisconsin
Milwaukee Area Technical College (Milwaukee), 449

OPTOMETRIC TECHNICIAN/ASSISTANT

Florida
McFatter Technical Center (Davie), 86
Traviss Technical Center (Lakeland), 99

Michigan
Bay de Noc Community College (Escanaba), 211
Oakland Community College (Bloomfield Hills), 224

Mississippi
Hinds Community College (Raymond), 232

North Carolina
Durham Technical Community College (Durham), 295

Pennsylvania
Central Pennsylvania College (Summerdale), 347

Wisconsin
Madison Area Technical College (Madison), 448
Milwaukee Area Technical College (Milwaukee), 449

ORGANIZATIONAL BEHAVIOR STUDIES

Florida
Management Resources Institute (Miami), 85

Illinois
Roosevelt University (Chicago), 149

Michigan
Lawrence Technological University (Southfield), 220

New York
Graduate School and University Center of the City University of New York (New York), 268

Pennsylvania
University of Pittsburgh (Pittsburgh), 376

Virginia
University of Richmond (University of Richmond), 434

ORGANIZATIONAL COMMUNICATION, GENERAL

Michigan
Michigan Technological University (Houghton), 222

Ohio
The University of Akron (Akron), 338
The University of Akron–Wayne College (Orrville), 338

Pennsylvania
Penn State University Park (University Park), 369

Rhode Island
Providence College (Providence), 396

ORNAMENTAL HORTICULTURE

Alabama
H. Councill Trenholm State Technical College (Montgomery), 43
Lawson State Community College (Birmingham), 44

Illinois
College of DuPage (Glen Ellyn), 129

Michigan
Ferris State University (Big Rapids), 215

New Jersey
Brookdale Community College (Lincroft), 241
Cumberland County College (Vineland), 244
Mercer County Community College (Trenton), 248

New York
Farmingdale State College (Farmingdale), 266
Finger Lakes Community College (Canandaigua), 266

Ohio
Licking County Joint Vocational School– Newark (Newark), 324

Pennsylvania
Schuylkill Technology Center–North Campus (Frackville), 373

ORTHOPTICS/ORTHOPTIST

Puerto Rico
Educational Technical College–Bayamón (Bayamón), 384
Educational Technical College–Recinto de Coama (Coama), 384

PAINTING

Connecticut
Paier College of Art, Inc. (Hamden), 55

PAINTING/PAINTER AND WALL COVERER

Florida
Mid-Florida Tech (Orlando), 87

Illinois
City Colleges of Chicago, Kennedy-King College (Chicago), 128
Southwestern Illinois College (Belleville), 151

Indiana
Ivy Tech Community College–Southwest (Evansville), 163

Pennsylvania
Lancaster County Career and Technology Center (Willow Street), 360

Wisconsin
Gateway Technical College (Kenosha), 446
Milwaukee Area Technical College (Milwaukee), 449

PARKS, RECREATION AND LEISURE FACILITIES MANAGEMENT

Alabama
James H. Faulkner State Community College (Bay Minette), 44

Georgia
Gwinnett Technical College (Lawrenceville), 113

Maryland
Montgomery College (Rockville), 190

Massachusetts
Greenfield Community College (Greenfield), 198

New York
St. Joseph's College, New York (Brooklyn), 281

North Carolina
Central Piedmont Community College (Charlotte), 293

Puerto Rico
Universidad del Este (Carolina), 393

PARKS, RECREATION AND LEISURE STUDIES

Connecticut
Norwalk Community College (Norwalk), 55

Georgia
North Metro Technical College (Acworth), 118

Maine
Washington County Community College (Calais), 183

Maryland
The Community College of Baltimore County (Baltimore), 187

New York
Elmira College (Elmira), 265
Finger Lakes Community College (Canandaigua), 266
St. Joseph's College, New York (Brooklyn), 281

North Carolina
Southwestern Community College (Sylva), 306

Ohio
Hocking College (Nelsonville), 321

PARKS, RECREATION, LEISURE AND FITNESS STUDIES, OTHER

Maryland
The Community College of Baltimore County (Baltimore), 187
Howard Community College (Columbia), 189

Ohio
Cincinnati State Technical and Community College (Cincinnati), 315

PARTS, WAREHOUSING, AND INVENTORY MANAGEMENT OPERATIONS

Illinois
Harper College (Palatine), 135
Illinois Valley Community College (Oglesby), 138
Lake Land College (Mattoon), 140
Southwestern Illinois College (Belleville), 151

Massachusetts
Bristol Community College (Fall River), 196

Pennsylvania
Greater Altoona Career and Technology Center (Altoona), 356

PASTORAL STUDIES/COUNSELING

Illinois
Dominican University (River Forest), 131

Indiana
Saint Joseph's College (Rensselaer), 167

PERIOPERATIVE/OPERATING ROOM AND SURGICAL NURSE/NURSING

Kentucky
Spalding University (Louisville), 178

PERIOPERATIVE/OPERATING ROOM AND SURGICAL NURSE/NURSING

Illinois
Oakton Community College (Des Plaines), 145

Pennsylvania
Delaware County Community College (Media), 351
Luzerne County Community College (Nanticoke), 363

PERMANENT COSMETICS/MAKEUP AND TATTOOING

Florida
North Florida Cosmetology Institute (Tallahassee), 88
Superior Career Institute (Lauderdale Lakes), 98

Maryland
Aesthetics Institute of Cosmetology (Gaithersburg), 183

Puerto Rico
D'mart Institute (Barranquitas), 383

PERSONAL AND CULINARY SERVICES, OTHER

Florida
Academy of Healing Arts, Massage, and Facial Skin Care (Lake Worth), 63
New Concept Massage and Beauty School (Miami), 88

Massachusetts
Bristol Community College (Fall River), 196

Michigan
Mid Michigan Community College (Harrison), 222

Mississippi
J & J Hair Design College (Carthage), 233

New York
French Culinary Institute (New York), 267

Pennsylvania
Bucks County School of Beauty Culture (Feasterville), 345
Luzerne County Community College (Nanticoke), 363

West Virginia
Morgantown Beauty College (Morgantown), 441

Wisconsin
Milwaukee Area Technical College (Milwaukee), 449

PETROLEUM TECHNOLOGY/TECHNICIAN

Ohio
Hocking College (Nelsonville), 321

PHARMACY, PHARMACEUTICAL SCIENCES, AND ADMINISTRATION, OTHER

Tennessee
Draughons Junior College (Clarksville), 407

Virginia
ACT College (Arlington), 423

PHARMACY TECHNICIAN/ASSISTANT

Alabama
Capps College (Foley), 42
Capps College (Mobile), 42
Remington College–Mobile Campus (Mobile), 46
Virginia College at Birmingham (Birmingham), 48
Virginia College at Huntsville (Huntsville), 48

Virginia College at Mobile (Mobile), 48
Wallace State Community College (Hanceville), 48

Connecticut
Briarwood College (Southington), 50

Delaware
Dawn Training Centre (Wilmington), 58
Star Technical Institute (Dover), 60

Florida
Americare School of Nursing (Fern Park), 64
Atlantic Vocational-Technical Center (Coconut Creek), 66
Central Florida College (Winter Park), 68
Concorde Career Institute (Lauderdale Lake), 70
Concorde Career Institute (Tampa), 71
Coral Ridge Nurses Assistant Training School (Ft. Lauderdale), 71
Everest Institute (Fort Lauderdale), 72
Everest Institute (Hialeah), 72
Everest Institute (Miami), 73
Everest University (Clearwater), 73
Everest University (Lakeland), 73
Everest University (Pompano Beach), 74
Florida Community College at Jacksonville (Jacksonville), 77
Florida Education Center (Lauderhill), 77
Florida Education Institute (Miami), 77
Galiano Career Academy (Altamonte Sprints), 79
Health Opportunity Technical Center (Miami Gardens), 80
Henry W. Brewster Technical Center (Tampa), 80
Heritage Institute (Fort Myers), 80
Heritage Institute (Jacksonville), 80
High-Tech Institute (Orlando), 80
Indian River State College (Fort Pierce), 81
Keiser Career College–Greenacres (Greenacres), 82
Lake City Community College (Lake City), 83
McFatter Technical Center (Davie), 86
MedVance Institute (Atlantis), 86
MedVance Institute (Fort Lauderdale), 86
Miami Dade College (Miami), 87
North Florida Institute (Orange Park), 89
Pinellas Technical Education Center–St. Petersburg (St. Petersburg), 92
Professional Training Centers (Miami), 92
Remington College–Largo Campus (Largo), 93
Remington College–Tampa Campus (Tampa), 93
Ridge Technical Center (Winter Haven), 93
Sanford-Brown Institute (Fort Lauderdale), 95
Sanford-Brown Institute (Jacksonville), 95
Sanford-Brown Institute (Tampa), 95
Technical Career Institute (Miami Springs), 99
Virginia College at Pensacola (Pensacola), 102
Westside Tech (Winter Garden), 102
Winter Park Tech (Winter Park), 102

Georgia
Albany Technical College (Albany), 103
American Professional Institute (Macon), 104
Atlanta Technical College (Atlanta), 105
Augusta Technical College (Augusta), 106
Central Georgia Technical College (Macon), 107
Columbus Technical College (Columbus), 108
East Central Technical College (Fitzgerald), 110
Everest Institute (Jonesboro), 111
Griffin Technical College (Griffin), 113
Heart of Georgia Technical College (Dublin), 114
Hi-Tech Institute – Atlanta (Marietta), 114
Iverson Business School (Atlanta), 115
Lanier Technical College (Oakwood), 115
Medix School (Smyrna), 116

North Georgia Technical College (Clarkesville), 118
Northwestern Technical College (Rock Spring), 118
Ogeechee Technical College (Statesboro), 119
Southeastern Technical College (Vidalia), 121
Southwest Georgia Technical College (Thomasville), 122
Valdosta Technical College (Valdosta), 123

Illinois
City Colleges of Chicago, Harry S. Truman College (Chicago), 128
City Colleges of Chicago, Malcolm X College (Chicago), 128
City Colleges of Chicago, Olive-Harvey College (Chicago), 128
City Colleges of Chicago, Richard J. Daley College (Chicago), 128
City Colleges of Chicago, Wilbur Wright College (Chicago), 129
College of DuPage (Glen Ellyn), 129
Coyne American Institute Incorporated (Chicago), 131
Everest College (Chicago), 133
Everest College (Merrionette Park), 134
Everest College (Skokie), 134
Illinois Eastern Community Colleges, Lincoln Trail College (Robinson), 137
Midwest Technical Institute (Lincoln), 143
Northwestern Business College–Southwestern Campus (Bridgeview), 144
Northwestern College (Chicago), 144
Oakton Community College (Des Plaines), 145
Richland Community College (Decatur), 148
Rockford Business College (Rockford), 149
South Suburban College (South Holland), 151

Indiana
TechSkills—Indianapolis (Indianapolis), 167
Vincennes University (Vincennes), 168

Kentucky
Ashland Community and Technical College (Ashland), 169
Daymar College (Paducah), 172
National College (Lexington), 176
St. Catharine College (St. Catharine), 178
West Kentucky Community and Technical College (Paducah), 180

Maine
Intercoast Career Institute (South Portland), 181

Maryland
Allegany College of Maryland (Cumberland), 184
All-State Career School (Baltimore), 184
College of Southern Maryland (La Plata), 186
TESST College of Technology (Baltimore), 192

Massachusetts
Benjamin Franklin Institute of Technology (Boston), 194
Everest Institute (Chelsea), 198
Holyoke Community College (Holyoke), 199
Lincoln Technical Institute (Lowell), 200
Lincoln Technical Institute (Somerville), 200

Michigan
Baker College of Auburn Hills (Auburn Hills), 209
Baker College of Flint (Flint), 210
Baker College of Muskegon (Muskegon), 211
Baker College of Owosso (Owosso), 211
Bay de Noc Community College (Escanaba), 211
Delta College (University Center), 213
Dorsey Business Schools (Madison Heights), 214
Dorsey Business Schools (Roseville), 214
Dorsey Business Schools (Southgate), 214

PHOTOGRAPHIC AND FILM/VIDEO TECHNOLOGY/TECHNICIAN AND ASSISTANT

Ohio
Northwest State Community College
(Archbold), 327
Shawnee State University (Portsmouth), 334
Terra State Community College (Fremont), 336

Pennsylvania
Precision Manufacturing Institute (Meadville),
371

Tennessee
Tennessee Technology Center at Pulaski
(Pulaski), 419

PLATEMAKER/IMAGER

Illinois
City Colleges of Chicago, Kennedy-King
College (Chicago), 128
College of DuPage (Glen Ellyn), 129
Triton College (River Grove), 153

Ohio
Cincinnati State Technical and Community
College (Cincinnati), 315

PLAYWRITING AND SCREENWRITING

Vermont
Burlington College (Burlington), 421

PLUMBING AND RELATED WATER SUPPLY SERVICES, OTHER

North Carolina
Blue Ridge Community College (Flat Rock),
289

Pennsylvania
Lebanon County Area Vocational Technical
School (Lebanon), 361

Wisconsin
Milwaukee Area Technical College
(Milwaukee), 449

PLUMBING TECHNOLOGY/PLUMBER

Alabama
Bishop State Community College (Mobile), 41
George C. Wallace Community College
(Dothan), 43
Lawson State Community College
(Birmingham), 44

Connecticut
Industrial Management Training Institute
(Waterbury), 53

Florida
David G. Erwin Technical Center (Tampa), 71
Florida Community College at Jacksonville
(Jacksonville), 77
Gulf Coast Community College (Panama City),
79
Lee County Vocational High Tech Center–
Central (Fort Myers), 84
Manatee Technical Institute (Bradenton), 85
Mid-Florida Tech (Orlando), 87
Okaloosa Applied Technology Center (Ft.
Walton Beach), 89
Pensacola Junior College (Pensacola), 91
Pinellas Technical Education Center–St.
Petersburg (St. Petersburg), 92
Radford M. Locklin Technical Center (Milton),
92
St. Petersburg College (St. Petersburg), 94
South Florida Institute of Technology (Miami),
97

Georgia
Altamaha Technical College (Jesup), 104
Atlanta Technical College (Atlanta), 105
Central Georgia Technical College (Macon),
107
Lanier Technical College (Oakwood), 115

Middle Georgia Technical College (Warner
Robbins), 117
Moultrie Technical College (Moultrie), 117
Sandersville Technical College (Sandersville),
120
South Georgia Technical College (Americus),
122

Kentucky
Elizabethtown Community and Technical
College (Elizabethtown), 172
Jefferson Community and Technical College
(Louisville), 175
Maysville Community and Technical College
(Maysville), 176

Maine
Southern Maine Community College (South
Portland), 182
Washington County Community College
(Calais), 183

Michigan
Macomb Community College (Warren), 220

Mississippi
Hinds Community College (Raymond), 232
Mississippi Gulf Coast Community College
(Perkinston), 234

New Jersey
Adult and Continuing Education–Bergen
County Technical Schools (Hackensack), 240
HoHoKus School of Trade and Technical
Sciences (Linden), 247

New York
Berk Trade and Business School (New York),
258
Harlem School of Technology (New York), 268

North Carolina
Blue Ridge Community College (Flat Rock),
289
Cleveland Community College (Shelby), 293
Fayetteville Technical Community College
(Fayetteville), 295
Forsyth Technical Community College
(Winston-Salem), 296
Guilford Technical Community College
(Jamestown), 297
Halifax Community College (Weldon), 297
Johnston Community College (Smithfield), 298
Roanoke-Chowan Community College
(Ahoskie), 303
Southeastern Community College (Whiteville),
305
Wake Technical Community College (Raleigh),
307

Ohio
Akron Adult Vocational Services (Akron), 309
Licking County Joint Vocational School–
Newark (Newark), 324

Pennsylvania
Delaware County Community College (Media),
351
Greater Altoona Career and Technology Center
(Altoona), 356
Luzerne County Community College
(Nanticoke), 363
Orleans Technical Institute (Philadelphia), 367
Pennco Tech (Bristol), 368
Pennsylvania College of Technology
(Williamsport), 369
Schuylkill Technology Center–North Campus
(Frackville), 373

Puerto Rico
Aguadilla Technical College (Aguadilla), 379
Colegio Tecnico de Electricidad Galloza
(Aguada), 383
Instituto de Banca y Comercio–Aprendes
Practicanco (Río Piedras), 386

Instituto de Educacion Tecnica Ocupacional La
Reine (Manati), 387
John Dewey College, 389, 390

Rhode Island
New England Institute of Technology
(Warwick), 395

West Virginia
Carver Career Center (Charleston), 438
Putnam Career and Technology Center School
of Practical Nursing (Eleanor), 443

Wisconsin
Blackhawk Technical College (Janesville), 445
Chippewa Valley Technical College (Eau
Claire), 445
Gateway Technical College (Kenosha), 446
Lakeshore Technical College (Cleveland), 447
Mid-State Technical College (Wisconsin
Rapids), 449
Southwest Wisconsin Technical College
(Fennimore), 452
Waukesha County Technical College
(Pewaukee), 453
Wisconsin Indianhead Technical College (Shell
Lake), 453

POLARITY THERAPY

Maine
Spa Tech Institute–Westbrook (Westbrook), 183

Massachusetts
Spa Tech Institute–Ipswich (Ipswich), 207
Spa Tech Institute–Westboro (Westboro), 207

POLITICAL SCIENCE AND GOVERNMENT, GENERAL

District of Columbia
American University (Washington), 61

Indiana
Indiana University–Purdue University Fort
Wayne (Fort Wayne), 160

New York
Pace University (New York), 279

Ohio
Ohio University (Athens), 330
University of Cincinnati (Cincinnati), 338

POLITICAL SCIENCE AND GOVERNMENT, OTHER

Connecticut
University of New Haven (West Haven), 58

District of Columbia
American University (Washington), 61

Maryland
Harford Community College (Bel Air), 189

Ohio
The University of Akron (Akron), 338

POLYMER/PLASTICS ENGINEERING

Ohio
The University of Akron (Akron), 338

PORTUGUESE LANGUAGE AND LITERATURE

Michigan
University of Detroit Mercy (Detroit), 228

POULTRY SCIENCE

Delaware
Delaware Technical & Community College,
Jack F. Owens Campus (Georgetown), 59

PRECISION METAL WORKING, OTHER

Alabama
Central Alabama Community College
(Alexander City), 42

Shelton State Community College (Tuscaloosa), 46

Wallace State Community College (Hanceville), 48

Florida
Manatee Technical Institute (Bradenton), 85
Mid-Florida Tech (Orlando), 87
Taylor Technical Institute (Perry), 99

Indiana
Vincennes University (Vincennes), 168

Michigan
Delta College (University Center), 213

Ohio
Choffin Career Center (Youngstown), 315
Lorain County JVS Adult Career Center (Oberlin), 324
Madison Local Schools–Madison Adult Education (Mansfield), 324
Northwest State Community College (Archbold), 327

Pennsylvania
Harrisburg Area Community College (Harrisburg), 357

Virginia
Central Virginia Community College (Lynchburg), 425
Danville Community College (Danville), 426
John Tyler Community College (Chester), 429
New River Community College (Dublin), 430
Patrick Henry Community College (Martinsville), 431
Southwest Virginia Community College (Richlands), 432
Tidewater Community College (Norfolk), 434
Virginia Highlands Community College (Abingdon), 435
Wytheville Community College (Wytheville), 436

PRECISION PRODUCTION, OTHER

Massachusetts
North Bennet Street School (Boston), 204

Michigan
Delta College (University Center), 213
Lake Michigan College (Benton Harbor), 219
Washtenaw Community College (Ann Arbor), 229

North Carolina
Haywood Community College (Clyde), 297

Pennsylvania
Pennsylvania Institute of Taxidermy, Inc. (Ebensberg), 370
Precision Manufacturing Institute (Meadville), 371

South Carolina
Greenville Technical College (Greenville), 399
Northeastern Technical College (Cheraw), 401

Wisconsin
Waukesha County Technical College (Pewaukee), 453

PRECISION PRODUCTION TRADES, GENERAL

Pennsylvania
Precision Manufacturing Institute (Meadville), 371

PRECISION SYSTEMS MAINTENANCE AND REPAIR TECHNOLOGIES, OTHER

Puerto Rico
Caguas Institute of Mechanical Technology (Caguas), 381

Wisconsin
Mid-State Technical College (Wisconsin Rapids), 449

PRE-LAW STUDIES

Michigan
University of Detroit Mercy (Detroit), 228

Ohio
The University of Akron (Akron), 338

Pennsylvania
Peirce College (Philadelphia), 367

Puerto Rico
American Educational College (Bayamón), 379

PRENURSING STUDIES

Florida
Saber (Miami), 94

Michigan
Gogebic Community College (Ironwood), 216

New Jersey
Prism Career Institute (Willingboro), 252

North Carolina
Carolinas College of Health Sciences (Charlotte), 292
Piedmont Community College (Roxboro), 302

Pennsylvania
Prism Career Institute (Philadelphia), 371

PRE-PHARMACY STUDIES

Ohio
University of Rio Grande (Rio Grande), 339

PREPRESS/DESKTOP PUBLISHING AND DIGITAL IMAGING DESIGN

District of Columbia
Corcoran College of Art and Design (Washington), 61

Florida
Sarasota County Technical Institute (Sarasota), 96
Sheridan Vocational-Technical Center (Hollywood), 96
Winter Park Tech (Winter Park), 102

Georgia
DeKalb Technical College (Clarkston), 109
Lanier Technical College (Oakwood), 115
Valdosta Technical College (Valdosta), 123

Illinois
College of DuPage (Glen Ellyn), 129
Elgin Community College (Elgin), 132
Illinois Central College (East Peoria), 136
Joliet Junior College (Joliet), 139
Lake Land College (Mattoon), 140
Lewis and Clark Community College (Godfrey), 141
Prairie State College (Chicago Heights), 146
Richland Community College (Decatur), 148
Sauk Valley Community College (Dixon), 150
Southeastern Illinois College (Harrisburg), 151
Southwestern Illinois College (Belleville), 151
Zarem/Golde ORT Technical Institute (Chicago), 154

Massachusetts
Springfield Technical Community College (Springfield), 207

Michigan
Davenport University (Grand Rapids), 213
Muskegon Community College (Muskegon), 223

New Jersey
Brookdale Community College (Lincroft), 241
Camden County College (Blackwood), 241

Ohio
Cincinnati State Technical and Community College (Cincinnati), 315
Davis College (Toledo), 318
Edison State Community College (Piqua), 319
Sinclair Community College (Dayton), 334

Pennsylvania
Bucks County Community College (Newtown), 345

PRE-THEOLOGY/PRE-MINISTERIAL STUDIES

Georgia
Toccoa Falls College (Toccoa Falls), 123

North Carolina
New Life Theological Seminary (Charlotte), 302

Virginia
Shenandoah University (Winchester), 432

PRINTING PRESS OPERATOR

Ohio
Sinclair Community College (Dayton), 334

Pennsylvania
Commonwealth Technical Institute (Johnstown), 348

West Virginia
Community & Technical College at West Virginia University Institute of Technology (Montgomery), 439

Wisconsin
Fox Valley Technical College (Appleton), 446

PRINTMAKING

Connecticut
Capital Community College (Hartford), 51

District of Columbia
Corcoran College of Art and Design (Washington), 61

Ohio
Sinclair Community College (Dayton), 334

PSYCHIATRIC/MENTAL HEALTH NURSE/ NURSING

Florida
Manatee Technical Institute (Bradenton), 85

Illinois
Saint Xavier University (Chicago), 150

PSYCHIATRIC/MENTAL HEALTH SERVICES TECHNICIAN

Connecticut
Asnuntuck Community College (Enfield), 49
Capital Community College (Hartford), 51
Gateway Community College (New Haven), 52
Housatonic Community College (Bridgeport), 53
Manchester Community College (Manchester), 54
Middlesex Community College (Middletown), 54
Naugatuck Valley Community College (Waterbury), 54
Northwestern Connecticut Community College (Winsted), 55
Norwalk Community College (Norwalk), 55
Quinebaug Valley Community College (Danielson), 56
Three Rivers Community College (Norwich), 57
Tunxis Community College (Farmington), 57

Delaware
Delaware Technical & Community College, Jack F. Owens Campus (Georgetown), 59

Ohio

Edison State Community College (Piqua), 319
James A. Rhodes State College (Lima), 322
Lakeland Community College (Kirtland), 323
Lorain County Community College (Elyria), 324
Marion Technical College (Marion), 325
Owens Community College (Toledo), 330
Sinclair Community College (Dayton), 334
Terra State Community College (Fremont), 336
The University of Akron (Akron), 338

Pennsylvania

Precision Manufacturing Institute (Meadville), 371

South Carolina

Tri-County Technical College (Pendleton), 403

Tennessee

Southwest Tennessee Community College (Memphis), 414
Walters State Community College (Morristown), 421

RADIATION PROTECTION/HEALTH PHYSICS TECHNICIAN

Florida

Advance Science Institute (Hialeah), 64

RADIO AND TELEVISION

Connecticut

Manchester Community College (Manchester), 54

Florida

Lively Technical Center (Tallahassee), 84

Illinois

Columbia College Chicago (Chicago), 130
Illinois Center for Broadcasting (Lombard), 136
Lake Land College (Mattoon), 140
Lewis and Clark Community College (Godfrey), 141
Rock Valley College (Rockford), 149

Michigan

Lawton School (Southfield), 220
Specs Howard School of Broadcast Arts (Southfield), 227

New York

New School of Radio and Television (Albany), 275

Ohio

Hocking College (Nelsonville), 321
International College of Broadcasting (Dayton), 322
Ohio Center for Broadcasting (Cincinnati), 328
Ohio Center for Broadcasting (Columbus), 328
Ohio Center for Broadcasting (Valley View), 328

RADIO AND TELEVISION BROADCASTING TECHNOLOGY/TECHNICIAN

Alabama

H. Councill Trenholm State Technical College (Montgomery), 43
Jefferson State Community College (Birmingham), 44
Lawson State Community College (Birmingham), 44

Connecticut

Asnuntuck Community College (Enfield), 49
Middlesex Community College (Middletown), 54

Florida

Manatee Technical Institute (Bradenton), 85
McFatter Technical Center (Davie), 86
Miami Dade College (Miami), 87

Miami Lakes Technical Education Center (Miami), 87
Orlando Technical Center (Orlando), 90
Pinellas Technical Education Center–St. Petersburg (St. Petersburg), 92

Georgia

Augusta Technical College (Augusta), 106
Chattahoochee Technical College (Marietta), 107

Illinois

Waubonsee Community College (Sugar Grove), 154

Kentucky

National College (Lexington), 176

Maryland

The Community College of Baltimore County (Baltimore), 187
Frederick Community College (Frederick), 188
Montgomery College (Rockville), 190

Michigan

Lansing Community College (Lansing), 219
Lawton School (Southfield), 220
St. Clair County Community College (Port Huron), 226
Specs Howard School of Broadcast Arts (Southfield), 227

New York

New School of Radio and Television (Albany), 275
Rochester Institute of Technology (Rochester), 280

North Carolina

Central Carolina Community College (Sanford), 292
Cleveland Community College (Shelby), 293
Gaston College (Dallas), 296
Isothermal Community College (Spindale), 298
Wilkes Community College (Wilkesboro), 308

Ohio

Cleveland Institute of Electronics (Cleveland), 316
University of Cincinnati Raymond Walters College (Cincinnati), 339

Pennsylvania

Bucks County Community College (Newtown), 345
Westmoreland County Community College (Youngwood), 378

South Carolina

Tri-County Technical College (Pendleton), 403
Trident Technical College (Charleston), 404
York Technical College (Rock Hill), 405

RADIOLOGIC TECHNOLOGY/SCIENCE— RADIOGRAPHER

Delaware

Delaware Technical & Community College, Stanton/Wilmington Campus (Newark), 59

Florida

Americare School of Nursing (Fern Park), 64
Cambridge Institute of Allied Health (Longwood), 68
Dade Medical College (Hialeah), 71
Dade Medical Institute (Miami), 71
Florida Hospital College of Health Sciences (Orlando), 77
Professional Training Centers (Miami), 92
Ultimate Medical Academy (Clearwater), 100
Ultimate Medical Academy–Tampa (Tampa), 100

Georgia

Central Georgia Technical College (Macon), 107
Coosa Valley Technical College (Rome), 109

Gwinnett Technical College (Lawrenceville), 113
Ogeechee Technical College (Statesboro), 119
West Georgia Technical College (LaGrange), 124

Illinois

Carl Sandburg College (Galesburg), 127

Kentucky

Jefferson Community and Technical College (Louisville), 175
Spencerian College–Lexington (Lexington), 179

Massachusetts

Massachusetts College of Pharmacy and Health Sciences (Boston), 202
Massasoit Community College (Brockton), 202

North Carolina

Carolinas College of Health Sciences (Charlotte), 292
Lenoir Community College (Kinston), 299
Pitt Community College (Greenville), 303

Ohio

Kettering College of Medical Arts (Kettering), 323
O. C. Collins Career Center (Chesapeake), 328
Owens Community College (Toledo), 330

Pennsylvania

Community College of Allegheny County (Pittsburgh), 348
Conemaugh Valley Memorial Hospital (Johnstown), 350

Rhode Island

Community College of Rhode Island (Warwick), 394

Tennessee

High-Tech Institute (Nashville), 408

Virginia

Richmond School of Health and Technology (Richmond), 431
Riverside School of Health Careers (Newport News), 432

West Virginia

West Virginia University Hospital–School of Radiology Technology (Morgantown), 444

RADIO, TELEVISION, AND DIGITAL COMMUNICATION, OTHER

North Carolina

Carolina School of Broadcasting (Charlotte), 291

Puerto Rico

Colegio de Las Ciencias Arte y Television (Caparra Heights), 382

REAL ESTATE

Alabama

James H. Faulkner State Community College (Bay Minette), 44
Jefferson Davis Community College (Brewton), 44

Connecticut

Manchester Community College (Manchester), 54

Florida

Florida Community College at Jacksonville (Jacksonville), 77
Lively Technical Center (Tallahassee), 84
Miami Dade College (Miami), 87
Mid-Florida Tech (Orlando), 87
Orlando Technical Center (Orlando), 90
Palm Beach Community College (Lake Worth), 90
Sheridan Vocational-Technical Center (Hollywood), 96

RESPIRATORY THERAPY TECHNICIAN/ ASSISTANT

RESTAURANT, CULINARY, AND CATERING MANAGEMENT/MANAGER

RESTAURANT/FOOD SERVICES MANAGEMENT

RETAILING AND RETAIL OPERATIONS

ROBOTICS TECHNOLOGY/TECHNICIAN

Robotics Technology/Technician

New York
Rochester Institute of Technology (Rochester), 280

North Carolina
Wake Technical Community College (Raleigh), 307

Ohio
James A. Rhodes State College (Lima), 322
Terra State Community College (Fremont), 336

Pennsylvania
Delaware County Community College (Media), 351
Precision Manufacturing Institute (Meadville), 371

Tennessee
Nashville State Technical Community College (Nashville), 411
Tennessee Technology Center at Paris (Paris), 419

ROOFER

Wisconsin
Milwaukee Area Technical College (Milwaukee), 449

RUSSIAN LANGUAGE AND LITERATURE

Ohio
The University of Akron (Akron), 338

RUSSIAN STUDIES

Pennsylvania
University of Pittsburgh (Pittsburgh), 376

SALES, DISTRIBUTION AND MARKETING OPERATIONS, GENERAL

Connecticut
Gateway Community College (New Haven), 52

Florida
Washington-Holmes Technical Center (Chipley), 102

Georgia
Albany Technical College (Albany), 103
Altamaha Technical College (Jesup), 104
Athens Technical College (Athens), 105
Atlanta Technical College (Atlanta), 105
Augusta Technical College (Augusta), 106
Central Georgia Technical College (Macon), 107
Chattahoochee Technical College (Marietta), 107
Clayton State University (Morrow), 108
Coosa Valley Technical College (Rome), 109
DeKalb Technical College (Clarkston), 109
East Central Technical College (Fitzgerald), 110
Gwinnett Technical College (Lawrenceville), 113
Lanier Technical College (Oakwood), 115
Middle Georgia Technical College (Warner Robbins), 117
Moultrie Technical College (Moultrie), 117
North Metro Technical College (Acworth), 118
Ogeechee Technical College (Statesboro), 119
Okefenokee Technical College (Waycross), 119
Savannah Technical College (Savannah), 121
Southeastern Technical College (Vidalia), 121
South Georgia Technical College (Americus), 122
Valdosta Technical College (Valdosta), 123
West Central Technical College (Waco), 124

Illinois
College of DuPage (Glen Ellyn), 129
Harper College (Palatine), 135
Oakton Community College (Des Plaines), 145
Southwestern Illinois College (Belleville), 151

Michigan
Grand Rapids Community College (Grand Rapids), 216
Lansing Community College (Lansing), 219

Ohio
Cincinnati State Technical and Community College (Cincinnati), 315
North Central State College (Mansfield), 327
Owens Community College (Toledo), 330

Pennsylvania
Bucks County Community College (Newtown), 345
Commonwealth Technical Institute (Johnstown), 348
Community College of Philadelphia (Philadelphia), 349
Greater Altoona Career and Technology Center (Altoona), 356
Harrisburg Area Community College (Harrisburg), 357
Montgomery County Community College (Blue Bell), 365

Puerto Rico
Universidad del Este (Carolina), 393
Universidad Metropolitana (San Juan), 394

South Carolina
Aiken Technical College (Aiken), 397
Greenville Technical College (Greenville), 399
Tri-County Technical College (Pendleton), 403
Trident Technical College (Charleston), 404

Virginia
Woodrow Wilson Rehabilitation Center (Fishersville), 436

SALON/BEAUTY SALON MANAGEMENT/MANAGER

District of Columbia
Bennett Beauty Institute (Washington), 61
Dudley Beauty College (Washington), 61

Illinois
Vee's School of Beauty Culture (East St. Louis), 154

Michigan
Schoolcraft College (Livonia), 227

Mississippi
J & J Hair Design College (Carthage), 233

Ohio
Aveda Fredric's Institute (Cincinnati), 311
Brown Aveda Institute (Mentor), 312
Brown Aveda Institute (Rocky River), 312
Euclidian Beauty School (Euclid), 320
Fairview Beauty Academy (Fairview Park), 320
Moore University of Hair Design (Cincinnati), 326
National Beauty College (Canton), 326
Ohio State Beauty Academy (Lima), 329
Paramount Beauty Academy (Portsmouth), 330
Raphael's School of Beauty Culture (Niles), 331
Raphael's School of Beauty Culture (Salem), 332
Raphael's School of Beauty Culture (Youngstown), 332

South Carolina
Plaza School of Beauty (Rock Hill), 402

Wisconsin
Four Seasons Salon & Day Spa (Monroe), 446
Moraine Park Technical College (Fond du Lac), 450

SCIENCE TECHNOLOGIES/TECHNICIANS, OTHER

Alabama
Calhoun Community College (Decatur), 41

Delaware
Delaware Technical & Community College, Stanton/Wilmington Campus (Newark), 59

Maryland
The Community College of Baltimore County (Baltimore), 187

Michigan
Mott Community College (Flint), 223

New York
Fulton-Montgomery Community College (Johnstown), 267
Rochester Institute of Technology (Rochester), 280

Pennsylvania
Delaware County Community College (Media), 351
Reading Area Community College (Reading), 372

West Virginia
Eastern West Virginia Community and Technical College (Moorefield), 439
New River Community and Technical College (Beckley), 442
Southern West Virginia Community and Technical College (Mount Gay), 443
West Virginia State Community and Technical College (Institute), 444
West Virginia University at Parkersburg (Parkersburg), 444

SCIENCE, TECHNOLOGY AND SOCIETY

Pennsylvania
Penn State University Park (University Park), 369

SCULPTURE

District of Columbia
Corcoran College of Art and Design (Washington), 61

North Carolina
Central Carolina Community College (Sanford), 292

Ohio
Sinclair Community College (Dayton), 334

SECONDARY EDUCATION AND TEACHING

Maryland
Harford Community College (Bel Air), 189

New York
Siena College (Loudonville), 283

Rhode Island
Providence College (Providence), 396

Virginia
Shenandoah University (Winchester), 432

SECURITIES SERVICES ADMINISTRATION/MANAGEMENT

Illinois
College of Lake County (Grayslake), 129

Kentucky
Bluegrass Community and Technical College (Lexington), 170

Pennsylvania
Harrisburg Area Community College (Harrisburg), 357

Puerto Rico
Academia Serrant (Ponce), 379
Columbia College (Caguas), 383

West Virginia
American Public University System (Charles Town), 437

Pennsylvania
Community College of Allegheny County
(Pittsburgh), 348
Community College of Philadelphia
(Philadelphia), 349
Gannon University (Erie), 355

Rhode Island
Rhode Island College (Providence), 396

SOCIOLOGY

Connecticut
University of Hartford (West Hartford), 58

Michigan
Madonna University (Livonia), 221

Ohio
The University of Akron (Akron), 338

SOLAR ENERGY TECHNOLOGY/TECHNICIAN

Wisconsin
Lac Courte Oreilles Ojibwa Community College
(Hayward), 447

SOMATIC BODYWORK

New Jersey
Institute for Therapeutic Massage (Pompton
Lakes), 247

SPANISH LANGUAGE AND LITERATURE

Michigan
Michigan Technological University
(Houghton), 222
University of Detroit Mercy (Detroit), 228

New Jersey
Monmouth University (West Long Branch), 249

North Carolina
Durham Technical Community College
(Durham), 295

Ohio
The University of Akron (Akron), 338
University of Cincinnati (Cincinnati), 338

Pennsylvania
Penn State University Park (University Park),
369

SPECIAL EDUCATION AND TEACHING, GENERAL

Connecticut
Gateway Community College (New Haven), 52

Florida
Loraine's Academy. (St. Petersburg), 85

Maryland
The Community College of Baltimore County
(Baltimore), 187
Prince George's Community College (Largo),
191

New Hampshire
New Hampshire Community Technical College,
Berlin/Laconia (Berlin), 238
New Hampshire Technical Institute (Concord),
239

North Carolina
Blue Ridge Community College (Flat Rock),
289
Brunswick Community College (Supply), 290
Nash Community College (Rocky Mount), 302
Southeastern Community College (Whiteville),
305
Stanly Community College (Albemarle), 306
Tri-County Community College (Murphy), 306
Wake Technical Community College (Raleigh),
307

Pennsylvania
La Roche College (Pittsburgh), 361

SPECIALIZED MERCHANDISING, SALES, AND MARKETING OPERATIONS, OTHER

Puerto Rico
Inter American University of Puerto Rico,
Bayamón Campus (Bayamón), 388

SPECIAL PRODUCTS MARKETING OPERATIONS

Florida
David G. Erwin Technical Center (Tampa), 71
Westside Tech (Winter Garden), 102

Maryland
The Community College of Baltimore County
(Baltimore), 187

Pennsylvania
Delaware Valley College (Doylestown), 351

Puerto Rico
D'mart Institute (Barranquitas), 383
Instituto Chaviano de Mayagüez (Mayagüez),
386
Liceo de Arte y Disenos (Caguas), 390

SPORT AND FITNESS ADMINISTRATION/ MANAGEMENT

Connecticut
Northwestern Connecticut Community College
(Winsted), 55

Georgia
Gwinnett Technical College (Lawrenceville),
113

Massachusetts
Middlesex Community College (Bedford), 202

New York
St. John's University (Queens), 281

Ohio
The University of Akron (Akron), 338

Puerto Rico
Universidad Metropolitana (San Juan), 394

SUBSTANCE ABUSE/ADDICTION COUNSELING

Connecticut
Gateway Community College (New Haven), 52
Manchester Community College (Manchester),
54

Delaware
Delaware Technical & Community College,
Stanton/Wilmington Campus (Newark), 59
Delaware Technical & Community College,
Terry Campus (Dover), 60

Illinois
City Colleges of Chicago, Harold Washington
College (Chicago), 127
City Colleges of Chicago, Kennedy-King
College (Chicago), 128
City Colleges of Chicago, Wilbur Wright
College (Chicago), 129
College of DuPage (Glen Ellyn), 129
College of Lake County (Grayslake), 129
Elgin Community College (Elgin), 132
Illinois Central College (East Peoria), 136
Illinois Valley Community College (Oglesby),
138
Moraine Valley Community College (Palos
Hills), 143
Oakton Community College (Des Plaines), 145
Rock Valley College (Rockford), 149
St. Augustine College (Chicago), 150
Shawnee Community College (Ullin), 150
Southeastern Illinois College (Harrisburg), 151
South Suburban College (South Holland), 151
Triton College (River Grove), 153
Waubonsee Community College (Sugar Grove),
154

Indiana
Vincennes University (Vincennes), 168

Maine
Intercoast Career Institute (South Portland),
181

Maryland
The Community College of Baltimore County
(Baltimore), 187
Frederick Community College (Frederick), 188
Wor-Wic Community College (Salisbury), 193

Massachusetts
Holyoke Community College (Holyoke), 199
Massasoit Community College (Brockton), 202
Northern Essex Community College
(Haverhill), 204
North Shore Community College (Danvers),
204
University of Massachusetts Boston (Boston),
208

Michigan
Baker College of Jackson (Jackson), 210
Madonna University (Livonia), 221
University of Detroit Mercy (Detroit), 228
Wayne County Community College District
(Detroit), 229

New Hampshire
New Hampshire Technical Institute (Concord),
239

New Jersey
Mercer County Community College (Trenton),
248

New York
Clinton Community College (Plattsburgh), 262
Dutchess Community College (Poughkeepsie),
264
Kingsborough Community College of the City
University of New York (Brooklyn), 271
Niagara County Community College (Sanborn),
277
Westchester Community College (Valhalla),
287

North Carolina
Central Piedmont Community College
(Charlotte), 293
Guilford Technical Community College
(Jamestown), 297
Pitt Community College (Greenville), 303
Southwestern Community College (Sylva), 306
Wake Technical Community College (Raleigh),
307
Western Piedmont Community College
(Morganton), 308

Ohio
Carnegie Career College (Suffield), 314
Columbus State Community College
(Columbus), 317
Sinclair Community College (Dayton), 334
The University of Akron (Akron), 338

Pennsylvania
Community College of Allegheny County
(Pittsburgh), 348
Community College of Philadelphia
(Philadelphia), 349
Montgomery County Community College (Blue
Bell), 365
Northampton County Area Community College
(Bethlehem), 366
Penn State Altoona (Altoona), 368
Saint Vincent College (Latrobe), 373

Tennessee
Southwest Tennessee Community College
(Memphis), 414

Vermont
Community College of Vermont (Waterbury),
422

Virginia

Northern Virginia Community College (Annandale), 430

SURGICAL TECHNOLOGY/TECHNOLOGIST

Alabama

Bevill State Community College (Sumiton), 41
Calhoun Community College (Decatur), 41
Gadsden State Community College (Gadsden), 42
James H. Faulkner State Community College (Bay Minette), 44
Lurleen B. Wallace Community College (Andalusia), 45
Southern Union State Community College (Wadley), 47
Virginia College at Mobile (Mobile), 48

Connecticut

Bridgeport Hospital School of Nursing (Bridgeport), 50

Delaware

Star Technical Institute (Dover), 60

Florida

Americare School of Nursing (Fern Park), 64
Americare School of Nursing (St. Petersburg), 64
Brevard Community College (Cocoa), 67
Central Florida Community College (Ocala), 69
Central Florida Institute (Palm Harbor), 69
Concorde Career Institute (Jacksonville), 70
Concorde Career Institute (Lauderdale Lake), 70
Concorde Career Institute (Tampa), 71
David G. Erwin Technical Center (Tampa), 71
Daytona State College (Daytona Beach), 72
Everest Institute (Hialeah), 72
Everest Institute (Miami), 73
Florida Community College at Jacksonville (Jacksonville), 77
Gulf Coast Community College (Panama City), 79
High-Tech Institute (Orlando), 80
Indian River State College (Fort Pierce), 81
James Lorenzo Walker Vocational-Technical Center (Naples), 82
Lee County High Tech Center North (Cape Coral), 83
Lindsey Hopkins Technical Education Center (Miami), 84
Manatee Technical Institute (Bradenton), 85
MedVance Institute (Atlantis), 86
MedVance Institute (Fort Lauderdale), 86
North Florida Institute (Orange Park), 89
Northwest Florida State College (Niceville), 89
Orlando Technical Center (Orlando), 90
Palm Beach Community College (Lake Worth), 90
Pensacola Junior College (Pensacola), 91
Pinellas Technical Education Center–St. Petersburg (St. Petersburg), 92
Sanford-Brown Institute (Fort Lauderdale), 95
Sanford-Brown Institute (Jacksonville), 95
Sanford-Brown Institute (Tampa), 95
Santa Fe Community College (Gainesville), 95
Sarasota County Technical Institute (Sarasota), 96
Sheridan Vocational-Technical Center (Hollywood), 96
Traviss Technical Center (Lakeland), 99
Virginia College at Pensacola (Pensacola), 102

Georgia

Albany Technical College (Albany), 103
American Professional Institute (Macon), 104
Athens Technical College (Athens), 105
Augusta Technical College (Augusta), 106
Central Georgia Technical College (Macon), 107

Chattahoochee Technical College (Marietta), 107
College of Coastal Georgia (Brunswick), 108
Columbus Technical College (Columbus), 108
Coosa Valley Technical College (Rome), 109
DeKalb Technical College (Clarkston), 109
Everest Institute (Marietta), 111
Flint River Technical College (Thomaston), 111
Griffin Technical College (Griffin), 113
Gwinnett Technical College (Lawrenceville), 113
Hi-Tech Institute – Atlanta (Marietta), 114
Iverson Business School (Atlanta), 115
Lanier Technical College (Oakwood), 115
Middle Georgia Technical College (Warner Robbins), 117
Moultrie Technical College (Moultrie), 117
Northwestern Technical College (Rock Spring), 118
Ogeechee Technical College (Statesboro), 119
Okefenokee Technical College (Waycross), 119
Savannah Technical College (Savannah), 121
Southeastern Technical College (Vidalia), 121
Southwest Georgia Technical College (Thomasville), 122
Valdosta Technical College (Valdosta), 123
West Central Technical College (Waco), 124

Illinois

City Colleges of Chicago, Malcolm X College (Chicago), 128
College of DuPage (Glen Ellyn), 129
College of Lake County (Grayslake), 129
Elgin Community College (Elgin), 132
Illinois Central College (East Peoria), 136
John A. Logan College (Carterville), 138
John Wood Community College (Quincy), 139
Prairie State College (Chicago Heights), 146
Rend Lake College (Ina), 148
Richland Community College (Decatur), 148
Rock Valley College (Rockford), 149
Shawnee Community College (Ullin), 150
Southeastern Illinois College (Harrisburg), 151
Trinity College of Nursing and Health Sciences (Rock Island), 153
Triton College (River Grove), 153
Waubonsee Community College (Sugar Grove), 154

Indiana

Everest College (Merrillville), 157
Vincennes University (Vincennes), 168

Kentucky

Ashland Community and Technical College (Ashland), 169
Bluegrass Community and Technical College (Lexington), 170
Bowling Green Technical College (Bowling Green), 170
Jefferson Community and Technical College (Louisville), 175
Madisonville Community College (Madisonville), 176
Maysville Community and Technical College (Maysville), 176
Owensboro Community and Technical College (Owensboro), 177
Southeast Kentucky Community and Technical College (Cumberland), 178
Spencerian College (Louisville), 179
West Kentucky Community and Technical College (Paducah), 180

Maryland

Baltimore City Community College (Baltimore), 185
Chesapeake College (Wye Mills), 186
The Community College of Baltimore County (Baltimore), 187
Frederick Community College (Frederick), 188

Montgomery College (Rockville), 190

Massachusetts

Bunker Hill Community College (Boston), 196
Massachusetts Bay Community College (Wellesley Hills), 201
North Shore Community College (Danvers), 204
Quincy College (Quincy), 204
Quinsigamond Community College (Worcester), 205

Michigan

Baker College of Flint (Flint), 210
Baker College of Jackson (Jackson), 210
Baker College of Muskegon (Muskegon), 211
Kalamazoo Valley Community College (Kalamazoo), 218
Macomb Community College (Warren), 220
Northern Michigan University (Marquette), 224
Wayne County Community College District (Detroit), 229

Mississippi

East Central Community College (Decatur), 232
Hinds Community College (Raymond), 232
Holmes Community College (Goodman), 233
Itawamba Community College (Fulton), 233
Meridian Community College (Meridian), 234
Mississippi Gulf Coast Community College (Perkinston), 234
Northwest Mississippi Community College (Senatobia), 235
Pearl River Community College (Poplarville), 235

New Jersey

Bergen Community College (Paramus), 240
Camden County College (Blackwood), 241
The Chubb Institute–North Brunswick (North Brunswick), 242
Dover Business College (Paramus), 244
HoHoKus School of Business and Medical Sciences (Ramsey), 247
Micro Tech Training Center (Belleville), 249
Micro Tech Training Center (Jersey City), 249
Sanford-Brown Institute (Iselin), 253
Star Technical Institute (Edison), 253
Star Technical Institute (Stratford), 253

New York

Mandl School (New York), 272
Onondaga Community College (Syracuse), 277
Western Suffolk BOCES (Northport), 288

North Carolina

Asheville-Buncombe Technical Community College (Asheville), 288
Blue Ridge Community College (Flat Rock), 289
Cabarrus College of Health Sciences (Concord), 290
Carolinas College of Health Sciences (Charlotte), 292
Catawba Valley Community College (Hickory), 292
Cleveland Community College (Shelby), 293
Coastal Carolina Community College (Jacksonville), 293
College of The Albemarle (Elizabeth City), 294
Durham Technical Community College (Durham), 295
Edgecombe Community College (Tarboro), 295
Fayetteville Technical Community College (Fayetteville), 295
Guilford Technical Community College (Jamestown), 297
Isothermal Community College (Spindale), 298
Lenoir Community College (Kinston), 299
McDowell Technical Community College (Marion), 300

Miller-Motte Technical College (Wilmington), 300

Robeson Community College (Lumberton), 304

Rockingham Community College (Wentworth), 304

Sandhills Community College (Pinehurst), 305

South College–Asheville (Asheville), 305

South Piedmont Community College (Polkton), 305

Wake Technical Community College (Raleigh), 307

Wilson Community College (Wilson), 308

Ohio

Apollo School of Practical Nursing (Lima), 310

Buckeye Hills Career Center (Rio Grande), 313

Central Ohio Technical College (Newark), 315

Choffin Career Center (Youngstown), 315

Columbus State Community College (Columbus), 317

Ehove Career Center (Milan), 319

O. C. Collins Career Center (Chesapeake), 328

Owens Community College (Toledo), 330

Scioto County Joint Vocational School District (Lucasville), 334

The University of Akron (Akron), 338

University of Cincinnati Clermont College (Batavia), 339

Pennsylvania

CHI Institute, Broomall Campus (Broomall), 348

Community College of Allegheny County (Pittsburgh), 348

Delaware County Community College (Media), 351

Great Lakes Institute of Technology (Erie), 356

Harrisburg Area Community College (Harrisburg), 357

Lancaster General College of Nursing & Health Sciences (Lancaster), 360

Montgomery County Community College (Blue Bell), 365

Sanford-Brown Institute–Monroeville (Pittsburgh), 373

Star Technical Institute (Philadelphia), 374

Star Technical Institute (Upper Darby), 374

Westmoreland County Community College (Youngwood), 378

Puerto Rico

Antilles School of Technical Careers (Hato Rey), 380

Atenas College (Manati), 380

Instituto de Banca y Comercio–Aprendes Practicanco (Río Piedras), 386

Instituto Vocational y Commercial EDIC (Caguas), 387

Ponce Paramedical College (Ponce), 392

South Carolina

Aiken Technical College (Aiken), 397

Central Carolina Technical College (Sumter), 398

Florence-Darlington Technical College (Florence), 399

Greenville Technical College (Greenville), 399

Horry-Georgetown Technical College (Conway), 400

Midlands Technical College (Columbia), 401

Miller-Motte Technical College (Charleston), 401

Piedmont Technical College (Greenwood), 402

Spartanburg Community College (Spartanburg), 403

Technical College of the Lowcountry (Beaufort), 403

Tri-County Technical College (Pendleton), 403

York Technical College (Rock Hill), 405

Tennessee

Concorde Career College (Memphis), 406

High-Tech Institute (Memphis), 408

High-Tech Institute (Nashville), 408

MedVance Institute (Cookeville), 409

MedVance Institute–Nashville (Nashville), 409

Nashville State Technical Community College (Nashville), 411

Northeast State Technical Community College (Blountville), 412

Tennessee Technology Center at Crossville (Crossville), 415

Tennessee Technology Center at Dickson (Dickson), 416

Tennessee Technology Center at Hohenwald (Hohenwald), 416

Tennessee Technology Center at Jackson (Jackson), 417

Tennessee Technology Center at Knoxville (Knoxville), 417

Tennessee Technology Center at McMinnville (McMinnville), 417

Tennessee Technology Center at Memphis (Memphis), 417

Tennessee Technology Center at Murfreesboro (Murfreesboro), 418

Tennessee Technology Center at Paris (Paris), 419

Virginia

Eastern Virginia Medical School (Norfolk), 426

Lord Fairfax Community College (Middletown), 429

Northern Virginia Community College (Annandale), 430

Piedmont Virginia Community College (Charlottesville), 431

Richmond School of Health and Technology (Richmond), 431

Sentara Norfolk General Hospital School of Health Professions (Norfolk), 432

Virginia Career Institute (Richmond), 435

West Virginia

Carver Career Center (Charleston), 438

James Rumsey Technical Institute (Martinsburg), 440

Monongalia County Technical Education Center (Morgantown), 441

West Virginia Northern Community College (Wheeling), 444

West Virginia University at Parkersburg (Parkersburg), 444

Wisconsin

Chippewa Valley Technical College (Eau Claire), 445

High-Tech Institute–Milwaukee (Brookfield), 447

Lakeshore Technical College (Cleveland), 447

Madison Area Technical College (Madison), 448

Mid-State Technical College (Wisconsin Rapids), 449

Northcentral Technical College (Wausau), 450

Northeast Wisconsin Technical College (Green Bay), 450

Western Technical College (La Crosse), 453

SURVEYING ENGINEERING

Virginia

Virginia Western Community College (Roanoke), 436

SURVEY TECHNOLOGY/SURVEYING

Delaware

Delaware Technical & Community College, Jack F. Owens Campus (Georgetown), 59

Florida

Chipola College (Marianna), 69

Georgia

Middle Georgia College (Cochran), 117

Okefenokee Technical College (Waycross), 119

Southern Polytechnic State University (Marietta), 122

Illinois

Waubonsee Community College (Sugar Grove), 154

Kentucky

Big Sandy Community and Technical College (Prestonsburg), 170

Hazard Community and Technical College (Hazard), 174

Maryland

The Community College of Baltimore County (Baltimore), 187

Massachusetts

Bristol Community College (Fall River), 196

Wentworth Institute of Technology (Boston), 208

Michigan

Ferris State University (Big Rapids), 215

Macomb Community College (Warren), 220

North Carolina

Asheville-Buncombe Technical Community College (Asheville), 288

Central Piedmont Community College (Charlotte), 293

Guilford Technical Community College (Jamestown), 297

Wake Technical Community College (Raleigh), 307

Ohio

Cincinnati State Technical and Community College (Cincinnati), 315

Columbus State Community College (Columbus), 317

Lakeland Community College (Kirtland), 323

Owens Community College (Toledo), 330

Sinclair Community College (Dayton), 334

The University of Akron (Akron), 338

South Carolina

Trident Technical College (Charleston), 404

SYSTEM ADMINISTRATION/ADMINISTRATOR

Florida

Career Institute of Florida (Saint Petersburg), 68

Westside Tech (Winter Garden), 102

Winter Park Tech (Winter Park), 102

Illinois

College of Lake County (Grayslake), 129

Heartland Community College (Normal), 136

Kaskaskia College (Centralia), 139

Lewis and Clark Community College (Godfrey), 141

Lincoln Land Community College (Springfield), 141

Moraine Valley Community College (Palos Hills), 143

Oakton Community College (Des Plaines), 145

Parkland College (Champaign), 145

Richland Community College (Decatur), 148

Sauk Valley Community College (Dixon), 150

Triton College (River Grove), 153

Waubonsee Community College (Sugar Grove), 154

Indiana

Ivy Tech Community College–Bloomington (Bloomington), 161

Ivy Tech Community College–Lafayette (Lafayette), 162

Ivy Tech Community College–Whitewater (Richmond), 164

TechSkills—Indianapolis (Indianapolis), 167

Florida
Galiano Career Academy (Altamonte Sprints), 79

Georgia
Gwinnett Technical College (Lawrenceville), 113

Illinois
Illinois Central College (East Peoria), 136
Moraine Valley Community College (Palos Hills), 143
Northwestern Business College–Southwestern Campus (Bridgeview), 144
Waubonsee Community College (Sugar Grove), 154

Indiana
International Business College (Indianapolis), 161

Maine
Andover College (South Portland), 180

Maryland
Allegany College of Maryland (Cumberland), 184

Massachusetts
Bristol Community College (Fall River), 196
Bunker Hill Community College (Boston), 196
Massasoit Community College (Brockton), 202

Michigan
Lansing Community College (Lansing), 219

Mississippi
Hinds Community College (Raymond), 232

New Hampshire
McIntosh College (Dover), 238
New Hampshire Technical Institute (Concord), 239

New York
Mildred Elley School (Albany), 273
Mohawk Valley Community College (Utica), 274
Wood Tobe–Coburn School (New York), 288

North Carolina
Central Piedmont Community College (Charlotte), 293
King's College (Charlotte), 299

Ohio
Bradford School (Columbus), 312
Lakeland Community College (Kirtland), 323
The University of Akron (Akron), 338

Pennsylvania
Bucks County Community College (Newtown), 345
Harrisburg Area Community College (Harrisburg), 357
Lehigh Carbon Community College (Schnecksville), 362

Puerto Rico
MBTI Business Training Institute (Santurce), 391
Universidad del Este (Carolina), 393
Universidad del Turabo (Gurabo), 394

Virginia
Northern Virginia Community College (Annandale), 430

Wisconsin
Milwaukee Area Technical College (Milwaukee), 449

TOURISM AND TRAVEL SERVICES MARKETING OPERATIONS

Florida
Advanced Technical Centers (Miami), 64
Galiano Career Academy (Altamonte Sprints), 79
Manatee Technical Institute (Bradenton), 85

Miami Dade College (Miami), 87
Mid-Florida Tech (Orlando), 87

Illinois
College of DuPage (Glen Ellyn), 129
Lincoln College (Lincoln), 141
MacCormac College (Chicago), 142
Pyramid Career Institute (Chicago), 147

Kentucky
Sullivan University (Louisville), 179

New York
Monroe Community College (Rochester), 274

North Carolina
Blue Ridge Community College (Flat Rock), 289

Ohio
RETS Tech Center (Centerville), 333

Pennsylvania
Lancaster County Career and Technology Center (Willow Street), 360
YTI Career Institute–York (York), 379

Puerto Rico
Universal Career Counseling Centers (Santurce), 393

Rhode Island
Sawyer School (Pawtucket), 396

TOURISM PROMOTION OPERATIONS

Connecticut
Three Rivers Community College (Norwich), 57

Indiana
International Business College (Fort Wayne), 161

New York
Genesee Community College (Batavia), 267
Schenectady County Community College (Schenectady), 282

North Carolina
Blue Ridge Community College (Flat Rock), 289

Ohio
University of Northwestern Ohio (Lima), 339

Pennsylvania
Luzerne County Community College (Nanticoke), 363
Newport Business Institute (Lower Burrell), 366

Puerto Rico
Colegio de Las Ciencias Arte y Television (Caparra Heights), 382
ICPR Junior College–Mayagüez Campus (Mayagüez), 385
Instituto de Banca y Comercio–Aprendes Practicanco (Río Piedras), 386

Rhode Island
Community College of Rhode Island (Warwick), 394

TRADE AND INDUSTRIAL TEACHER EDUCATION

Florida
Universal Massage and Beauty Institute (Sweetwater), 100

Illinois
Cameo Beauty Academy (Oak Lawn), 126

Kentucky
Head's West Kentucky Beauty School (Madisonville), 174

Michigan
Port Huron Cosmetology College (Waterford), 225
School of Creative Hair Design (Coldwater), 227

Mississippi
ICS–The Wright Beauty College (Corinth), 233

New Jersey
Parisian Beauty School (Hackensack), 250

Pennsylvania
Altoona Beauty School of Hair Design and Cosmetology (Altoona), 343
Great Lakes Institute of Technology (Erie), 356

Rhode Island
Arthur Angelo School of Cosmetology and Hair Design (Providence), 394

TRADITIONAL CHINESE/ASIAN MEDICINE AND CHINESE HERBOLOGY

Ohio
American Institute of Alternative Medicine (Columbus), 310

TRANSPORTATION AND MATERIALS MOVING, OTHER

Florida
New Professions Technical Institute (Miami), 88
Washington-Holmes Technical Center (Chipley), 102

Michigan
Michigan Institute of Aeronautics (Belleville), 221

Ohio
TDDS (Diamond), 336

TRANSPORTATION/TRANSPORTATION MANAGEMENT

Maryland
Cecil College (North East), 186
Hagerstown Community College (Hagerstown), 188

TRUCK AND BUS DRIVER/COMMERCIAL VEHICLE OPERATION

Alabama
Bevill State Community College (Sumiton), 41
Bishop State Community College (Mobile), 41
Calhoun Community College (Decatur), 41
H. Councill Trenholm State Technical College (Montgomery), 43
Reid State Technical College (Evergreen), 46

Connecticut
Baran Institute of Technology (Windsor), 49
New England Tractor Trailer Training of Connecticut (Somers), 55

Delaware
Delaware Technical & Community College, Jack F. Owens Campus (Georgetown), 59

Florida
Bradford Union Area Vocational Technical Center (Starke), 67
Central Florida Community College (Ocala), 69
Florida Community College at Jacksonville (Jacksonville), 77
Gulf Coast Community College (Panama City), 79
Indian River State College (Fort Pierce), 81
Lake City Community College (Lake City), 83
McFatter Technical Center (Davie), 86
Miami Lakes Technical Education Center (Miami), 87
Mid-Florida Tech (Orlando), 87
Palm Beach Community College (Lake Worth), 90
Pinellas Technical Education Center–Clearwater (Clearwater), 91
Pinellas Technical Education Center–St. Petersburg (St. Petersburg), 92
Ridge Technical Center (Winter Haven), 93

South Florida Community College (Avon Park), 97

Washington-Holmes Technical Center (Chipley), 102

Georgia

Albany Technical College (Albany), 103

Altamaha Technical College (Jesup), 104

Athens Technical College (Athens), 105

Bainbridge College (Bainbridge), 106

Coosa Valley Technical College (Rome), 109

DeKalb Technical College (Clarkston), 109

East Central Technical College (Fitzgerald), 110

Flint River Technical College (Thomaston), 111

Griffin Technical College (Griffin), 113

Heart of Georgia Technical College (Dublin), 114

Middle Georgia Technical College (Warner Robbins), 117

Moultrie Technical College (Moultrie), 117

North Georgia Technical College (Clarkesville), 118

North Metro Technical College (Acworth), 118

Northwestern Technical College (Rock Spring), 118

Ogeechee Technical College (Statesboro), 119

Okefenokee Technical College (Waycross), 119

Sandersville Technical College (Sandersville), 120

Savannah Technical College (Savannah), 121

Southeastern Technical College (Vidalia), 121

South Georgia Technical College (Americus), 122

Valdosta Technical College (Valdosta), 123

West Central Technical College (Waco), 124

West Georgia Technical College (LaGrange), 124

Illinois

City Colleges of Chicago, Harold Washington College (Chicago), 127

Danville Area Community College (Danville), 131

Elgin Community College (Elgin), 132

Illinois Eastern Community Colleges, Frontier Community College (Fairfield), 137

Illinois Eastern Community Colleges, Wabash Valley College (Mount Carmel), 137

Illinois Valley Community College (Oglesby), 138

John Wood Community College (Quincy), 139

Kaskaskia College (Centralia), 139

Lincoln Land Community College (Springfield), 141

Parkland College (Champaign), 145

Sauk Valley Community College (Dixon), 150

Shawnee Community College (Ullin), 150

Spoon River College (Canton), 152

Indiana

Vincennes University (Vincennes), 168

Kentucky

West Kentucky Community and Technical College (Paducah), 180

Maryland

All-State Career School (Baltimore), 184

College of Southern Maryland (La Plata), 186

Garrett College (McHenry), 188

Hagerstown Community College (Hagerstown), 188

North American Trade Schools (Grantsville), 191

Michigan

Baker College of Cadillac (Cadillac), 210

Baker College of Flint (Flint), 210

Lansing Community College (Lansing), 219

Mississippi

Copiah-Lincoln Community College (Wesson), 231

East Mississippi Community College (Scooba), 232

Itawamba Community College (Fulton), 233

Meridian Community College (Meridian), 234

Mississippi Gulf Coast Community College (Perkinston), 234

Northwest Mississippi Community College (Senatobia), 235

New York

National Tractor Trailer School–Buffalo Campus (Buffalo), 275

National Tractor Trailer School, Inc. (Liverpool), 275

North Carolina

Caldwell Community College and Technical Institute (Hudson), 290

Cape Fear Community College (Wilmington), 290

Catawba Valley Community College (Hickory), 292

Davidson County Community College (Lexington), 294

Johnston Community College (Smithfield), 298

Ohio

Apollo School of Practical Nursing (Lima), 310

Hamrick Truck Driving School (Medina), 320

Ohio Technical College (Cleveland), 329

TDDS (Diamond), 336

Vantage Vocational School (Van Wert), 340

Pennsylvania

All-State Career School (Lester), 343

All-State Career School (North Versailles), 343

Central Pennsylvania Institute of Science and Technology (Pleasant Gap), 347

Greater Altoona Career and Technology Center (Altoona), 356

New Castle School of Trades (Pulaski), 366

Pittsburgh Institute of Aeronautics (Pittsburgh), 371

Schuylkill Technology Center–North Campus (Frackville), 373

York County School of Technology–Practical Nursing Program (York), 378

Rhode Island

New England Tractor Trailer Training School of Rhode Island (Pawtucket), 395

South Carolina

Greenville Technical College (Greenville), 399

Tennessee

Tennessee Technology Center at Crump (Crump), 415

Tennessee Technology Center at Knoxville (Knoxville), 417

Tennessee Technology Center at Memphis (Memphis), 417

Tennessee Technology Center at Morristown (Morristown), 418

Tennessee Technology Center at Nashville (Nashville), 418

Tennessee Technology Center at Ripley (Ripley), 419

Tennessee Technology Center at Shelbyville (Shelbyville), 419

Virginia

Advanced Technology Institute (Virginia Beach), 423

West Virginia

Fred W. Eberle Technical Center (Buckhannon), 439

James Rumsey Technical Institute (Martinsburg), 440

Wisconsin

Chippewa Valley Technical College (Eau Claire), 445

Fox Valley Technical College (Appleton), 446

Waukesha County Technical College (Pewaukee), 453

TURF AND TURFGRASS MANAGEMENT

Delaware

Delaware Technical & Community College, Jack F. Owens Campus (Georgetown), 59

Delaware Technical & Community College, Stanton/Wilmington Campus (Newark), 59

Florida

First Coast Technical Institute (St. Augustine), 75

Washington-Holmes Technical Center (Chipley), 102

Georgia

Augusta Technical College (Augusta), 106

Lanier Technical College (Oakwood), 115

Moultrie Technical College (Moultrie), 117

North Georgia Technical College (Clarkesville), 118

Ogeechee Technical College (Statesboro), 119

South Georgia Technical College (Americus), 122

Illinois

Harper College (Palatine), 135

Illinois Eastern Community Colleges, Wabash Valley College (Mount Carmel), 137

Rend Lake College (Ina), 148

Richland Community College (Decatur), 148

Michigan

Michigan State University (East Lansing), 222

North Carolina

Brunswick Community College (Supply), 290

Central Piedmont Community College (Charlotte), 293

Ohio

Cincinnati State Technical and Community College (Cincinnati), 315

The Ohio State University Agricultural Technical Institute (Wooster), 329

University of Cincinnati (Cincinnati), 338

South Carolina

Horry-Georgetown Technical College (Conway), 400

Trident Technical College (Charleston), 404

Tennessee

Southwest Tennessee Community College (Memphis), 414

UPHOLSTERY/UPHOLSTERER

Alabama

Calhoun Community College (Decatur), 41

Jefferson Davis Community College (Brewton), 44

Lurleen B. Wallace Community College (Andalusia), 45

Southern Union State Community College (Wadley), 47

Wallace State Community College (Hanceville), 48

Kentucky

Jefferson Community and Technical College (Louisville), 175

North Carolina

Catawba Valley Community College (Hickory), 292

Guilford Technical Community College (Jamestown), 297

Western Piedmont Community College (Morganton), 308

Puerto Rico

Instituto Chaviano de Mayagüez (Mayagüez), 386

URBAN STUDIES/AFFAIRS

New York
Daemen College (Amherst), 263

VEHICLE AND VEHICLE PARTS AND ACCESSORIES MARKETING OPERATIONS

Florida
Florida Community College at Jacksonville (Jacksonville), 77
Mid-Florida Tech (Orlando), 87
Mississippi
Hinds Community College (Raymond), 232
Ohio
Hocking College (Nelsonville), 321

VEHICLE MAINTENANCE AND REPAIR TECHNOLOGIES, OTHER

Delaware
Delaware Technical & Community College, Jack F. Owens Campus (Georgetown), 59
Florida
Robert Morgan Vocational-Technical Center (Miami), 94
Maine
Landing School of Boat Building and Design (Kennebunkport), 181
Northern Maine Community College (Presque Isle), 182
Michigan
Washtenaw Community College (Ann Arbor), 229
New Jersey
Ocean County Vocational Post Secondary Division (Toms River), 250
New York
State University of New York College of Technology at Alfred (Alfred), 283
State University of New York College of Technology at Canton (Canton), 284
North Carolina
Central Piedmont Community College (Charlotte), 293
Forsyth Technical Community College (Winston-Salem), 296
Guilford Technical Community College (Jamestown), 297
Wilson Community College (Wilson), 308
Ohio
Ohio Technical College (Cleveland), 329
Pennsylvania
Pennco Tech (Bristol), 368
Puerto Rico
Automeca Technical College (Aguadilla), 380
Automeca Technical College (Bayamón), 380
Automeca Technical College (Caguas), 380
Automeca Technical College (Ponce), 380
Liceo de Arte y Tecnologia (Hato Rey), 390
Tennessee
Nashville Auto Diesel College (Nashville), 410
Wisconsin
Fox Valley Technical College (Appleton), 446
Moraine Park Technical College (Fond du Lac), 450

VETERINARY/ANIMAL HEALTH TECHNOLOGY/TECHNICIAN AND VETERINARY ASSISTANT

Florida
Florida Institute of Animal Arts (Winter Park), 77
Marion County Community Technical and Adult Education Center (Ocala), 85
St. Petersburg College (St. Petersburg), 94

Westside Tech (Winter Garden), 102
Georgia
Gwinnett Technical College (Lawrenceville), 113
Massachusetts
Berkshire Community College (Pittsfield), 194
Michigan
Michigan State University (East Lansing), 222
Ohio
Northcoast Medical Training Academy (Kent), 327
Pennsylvania
Great Lakes Institute of Technology (Erie), 356
Lancaster County Career and Technology Center (Willow Street), 360
Sanford-Brown Institute–Pittsburgh (Pittsburgh), 373
South Carolina
Greenville Technical College (Greenville), 399
West Virginia
Carver Career Center (Charleston), 438

VISUAL AND PERFORMING ARTS, GENERAL

Michigan
Lansing Community College (Lansing), 219
New Jersey
Mercer County Community College (Trenton), 248
New York
New York University (New York), 277
Rochester Institute of Technology (Rochester), 280

VISUAL AND PERFORMING ARTS, OTHER

Connecticut
Tunxis Community College (Farmington), 57
Florida
Florida Community College at Jacksonville (Jacksonville), 77
Valencia Community College (Orlando), 101
Maryland
The Community College of Baltimore County (Baltimore), 187
Virginia
Blue Ridge Community College (Weyers Cave), 424
Germanna Community College (Locust Grove), 428
John Tyler Community College (Chester), 429
Lord Fairfax Community College (Middletown), 429
Southwest Virginia Community College (Richlands), 432
Tidewater Community College (Norfolk), 434

WATCHMAKING AND JEWELRYMAKING

Alabama
Bishop State Community College (Mobile), 41
Florida
Winter Park Tech (Winter Park), 102
Illinois
Gem City College (Quincy), 134
Massachusetts
North Bennet Street School (Boston), 204
Mississippi
Jones County Junior College (Ellisville), 234
North Carolina
College of The Albemarle (Elizabeth City), 294
Haywood Community College (Clyde), 297
Pennsylvania
Commonwealth Technical Institute (Johnstown), 348
NAWCC School of Horology (Columbia), 365

Wisconsin
Northeast Wisconsin Technical College (Green Bay), 450

WATER QUALITY AND WASTEWATER TREATMENT MANAGEMENT AND RECYCLING TECHNOLOGY/TECHNICIAN

Alabama
Northwest-Shoals Community College (Muscle Shoals), 45
Florida
Lake City Community College (Lake City), 83
Georgia
North Georgia Technical College (Clarkesville), 118
Maryland
Cecil College (North East), 186
Massachusetts
Cape Cod Community College (West Barnstable), 196
Michigan
Bay de Noc Community College (Escanaba), 211
New Jersey
Monmouth County Vocational School District (Long Branch), 249
North Carolina
Blue Ridge Community College (Flat Rock), 289
Lenoir Community College (Kinston), 299
Ohio
Columbus State Community College (Columbus), 317
South Carolina
York Technical College (Rock Hill), 405
Wisconsin
Moraine Park Technical College (Fond du Lac), 450

WEB/MULTIMEDIA MANAGEMENT AND WEBMASTER

Florida
Lee County Vocational High Tech Center–Central (Fort Myers), 84
Miami-Dade County Public Schools (Miami), 87
Illinois
Oakton Community College (Des Plaines), 145
Parkland College (Champaign), 145
Prairie State College (Chicago Heights), 146
Indiana
Ivy Tech Community College–Bloomington (Bloomington), 161
Ivy Tech Community College–Lafayette (Lafayette), 162
Ivy Tech Community College–Whitewater (Richmond), 164
Michigan
Baker College Center for Graduate Studies (Flint), 209
Baker College of Allen Park (Allen Park), 209
Baker College of Auburn Hills (Auburn Hills), 209
Baker College of Cadillac (Cadillac), 210
Baker College of Clinton Township (Clinton Township), 210
Baker College of Flint (Flint), 210
Baker College of Muskegon (Muskegon), 211
Baker College of Owosso (Owosso), 211
Baker College of Port Huron (Port Huron), 211
Davenport University (Grand Rapids), 213
Delta College (University Center), 213
Gogebic Community College (Ironwood), 216

Grand Rapids Community College (Grand Rapids), 216
Macomb Community College (Warren), 220
Oakland Community College (Bloomfield Hills), 224

New Jersey
Union County College (Cranford), 254

New York
Erie Community College (Buffalo), 265
Genesee Community College (Batavia), 267

North Carolina
Central Piedmont Community College (Charlotte), 293
Nash Community College (Rocky Mount), 302
Southwestern Community College (Sylva), 306

Pennsylvania
Delaware County Community College (Media), 351
Gannon University (Erie), 355
Kaplan Career Institute–ICM Campus (Pittsburgh), 359
Keystone Technical Institute (Harrisburg), 359

West Virginia
American Public University System (Charles Town), 437

Wisconsin
Moraine Park Technical College (Fond du Lac), 450

WEB PAGE, DIGITAL/MULTIMEDIA AND INFORMATION RESOURCES DESIGN

Connecticut
Gateway Community College (New Haven), 52

Delaware
Delaware College of Art and Design (Wilmington), 59

District of Columbia
Corcoran College of Art and Design (Washington), 61

Florida
Atlantic Vocational-Technical Center (Coconut Creek), 66
College of Business and Technology–Flagler Campus (Miami), 70
College of Business and Technology–Hialeah Campus (Hialeah), 70
College of Business and Technology (Miami), 70
Florida Career College (Miami), 76
George Stone Area Vocational-Technical Center (Pensacola), 79
Lee County High Tech Center North (Cape Coral), 83
Lee County Vocational High Tech Center–Central (Fort Myers), 84
Lively Technical Center (Tallahassee), 84
Manatee Technical Institute (Bradenton), 85
Miami-Dade County Public Schools (Miami), 87
Orlando Technical Center (Orlando), 90
Pinellas Technical Education Center–Clearwater (Clearwater), 91
Radford M. Locklin Technical Center (Milton), 92
Robert Morgan Vocational-Technical Center (Miami), 94
Sarasota County Technical Institute (Sarasota), 96
Sheridan Vocational-Technical Center (Hollywood), 96
Winter Park Tech (Winter Park), 102

Georgia
Albany Technical College (Albany), 103
Athens Technical College (Athens), 105
Augusta Technical College (Augusta), 106

Central Georgia Technical College (Macon), 107
Chattahoochee Technical College (Marietta), 107
Columbus Technical College (Columbus), 108
Coosa Valley Technical College (Rome), 109
East Central Technical College (Fitzgerald), 110
Flint River Technical College (Thomaston), 111
Georgia Southwestern State University (Americus), 112
Gwinnett Technical College (Lawrenceville), 113
Lanier Technical College (Oakwood), 115
Middle Georgia Technical College (Warner Robbins), 117
Moultrie Technical College (Moultrie), 117
North Georgia Technical College (Clarkesville), 118
North Metro Technical College (Acworth), 118
Northwestern Technical College (Rock Spring), 118
Okefenokee Technical College (Waycross), 119
Sandersville Technical College (Sandersville), 120
Savannah Technical College (Savannah), 121
Southeastern Technical College (Vidalia), 121
Southwest Georgia Technical College (Thomasville), 122
Valdosta Technical College (Valdosta), 123
West Central Technical College (Waco), 124

Illinois
City Colleges of Chicago, Harry S. Truman College (Chicago), 128
City Colleges of Chicago, Kennedy-King College (Chicago), 128
College of DuPage (Glen Ellyn), 129
College of Lake County (Grayslake), 129
Columbia College Chicago (Chicago), 130
Elgin Community College (Elgin), 132
Harper College (Palatine), 135
Illinois Central College (East Peoria), 136
Illinois Eastern Community Colleges, Olney Central College (Olney), 137
Illinois Eastern Community Colleges, Wabash Valley College (Mount Carmel), 137
The Illinois Institute of Art–Schaumburg (Schaumburg), 138
Lewis and Clark Community College (Godfrey), 141
Lincoln Land Community College (Springfield), 141
Midstate College (Peoria), 143
Moraine Valley Community College (Palos Hills), 143
Oakton Community College (Des Plaines), 145
Parkland College (Champaign), 145
Prairie State College (Chicago Heights), 146
Richland Community College (Decatur), 148
Rockford Business College (Rockford), 149
Southwestern Illinois College (Belleville), 151
Spoon River College (Canton), 152
Triton College (River Grove), 153
Waubonsee Community College (Sugar Grove), 154

Indiana
Kaplan College–Merrillville Campus (Merrillville), 164
TechSkills—Indianapolis (Indianapolis), 167
Vincennes University (Vincennes), 168

Maryland
Cecil College (North East), 186
Garrett College (McHenry), 188
Hagerstown Community College (Hagerstown), 188
Prince George's Community College (Largo), 191

Massachusetts
Bristol Community College (Fall River), 196
Fitchburg State College (Fitchburg), 198
Massasoit Community College (Brockton), 202
Middlesex Community College (Bedford), 202
Mildred Elley School (Pittsfield), 202
Mount Wachusett Community College (Gardner), 203
North Shore Community College (Danvers), 204
Quinsigamond Community College (Worcester), 205
Springfield Technical Community College (Springfield), 207
Sullivan and Cogliano Training Center (Brockton), 207
Wentworth Institute of Technology (Boston), 208

Michigan
Henry Ford Community College (Dearborn), 217
Kellogg Community College (Battle Creek), 218
Monroe County Community College (Monroe), 222
Muskegon Community College (Muskegon), 223
Schoolcraft College (Livonia), 227
Washtenaw Community College (Ann Arbor), 229

New Jersey
Camden County College (Blackwood), 241
The Chubb Institute–Cherry Hill (Cherry Hill), 242
The Chubb Institute–Jersey City (Jersey City), 242
The Chubb Institute–North Brunswick (North Brunswick), 242
The Chubb Institute–Parsippany (Parsippany), 243
Raritan Valley Community College (Somerville), 252

New York
The Chubb Institute–New York (New York), 261
Erie Community College (Buffalo), 265
Mildred Elley School (Albany), 273

North Carolina
The Art Institute of Charlotte (Charlotte), 288
Piedmont Community College (Roxboro), 302
School of Communication Arts (Raleigh), 305

Ohio
Cincinnati State Technical and Community College (Cincinnati), 315
North Central State College (Mansfield), 327
TechSkills—Columbus (Columbus), 336
The University of Akron (Akron), 338

Pennsylvania
Allied Medical and Technical Institute (Scranton), 343
The Art Institute of Pittsburgh (Pittsburgh), 343
Bucks County Community College (Newtown), 345
The Chubb Institute–Springfield (Springfield), 348
Community College of Allegheny County (Pittsburgh), 348
Community College of Beaver County (Monaca), 349
Delaware County Community College (Media), 351
Greater Altoona Career and Technology Center (Altoona), 356
Harrisburg Area Community College (Harrisburg), 357
Lancaster County Career and Technology Center (Willow Street), 360

WELDING TECHNOLOGY/WELDER

Owensboro Community and Technical College (Owensboro), 177
Somerset Community College (Somerset), 178
Southeast Kentucky Community and Technical College (Cumberland), 178
West Kentucky Community and Technical College (Paducah), 180

Maine
Eastern Maine Community College (Bangor), 181
Southern Maine Community College (South Portland), 182
Washington County Community College (Calais), 183

Michigan
Alpena Community College (Alpena), 209
Bay de Noc Community College (Escanaba), 211
Delta College (University Center), 213
Grand Rapids Community College (Grand Rapids), 216
Kalamazoo Valley Community College (Kalamazoo), 218
Kellogg Community College (Battle Creek), 218
Lansing Community College (Lansing), 219
Mid Michigan Community College (Harrison), 222
Monroe County Community College (Monroe), 222
Montcalm Community College (Sidney), 223
Muskegon Community College (Muskegon), 223
Oakland Community College (Bloomfield Hills), 224
Schoolcraft College (Livonia), 227
Southwestern Michigan College (Dowagiac), 227
Washtenaw Community College (Ann Arbor), 229
Wayne County Community College District (Detroit), 229

Mississippi
Coahoma Community College (Clarksdale), 231
Copiah-Lincoln Community College (Wesson), 231
East Central Community College (Decatur), 232
East Mississippi Community College (Scooba), 232
Hinds Community College (Raymond), 232
Holmes Community College (Goodman), 233
Itawamba Community College (Fulton), 233
Jones County Junior College (Ellisville), 234
Mississippi Delta Community College (Moorhead), 234
Mississippi Gulf Coast Community College (Perkinston), 234
Northwest Mississippi Community College (Senatobia), 235
Pearl River Community College (Poplarville), 235
Southwest Mississippi Community College (Summit), 235

New Hampshire
Manchester Community College (Manchester), 237

New Jersey
HoHoKus School of Trade and Technical Sciences (Linden), 247
Ocean County Vocational Post Secondary Division (Toms River), 250
Somerset County Technical Institute (Bridgewater), 253

New York
Apex Technical School (New York), 256
Modern Welding School (Schenectady), 274

Onondaga-Courtland-Madison BOCES (Liverpool), 278

North Carolina
Alamance Community College (Graham), 288
Asheville-Buncombe Technical Community College (Asheville), 288
Beaufort County Community College (Washington), 289
Bladen Community College (Dublin), 289
Blue Ridge Community College (Flat Rock), 289
Brunswick Community College (Supply), 290
Cape Fear Community College (Wilmington), 290
Catawba Valley Community College (Hickory), 292
Central Carolina Community College (Sanford), 292
Central Piedmont Community College (Charlotte), 293
Cleveland Community College (Shelby), 293
Coastal Carolina Community College (Jacksonville), 293
Craven Community College (New Bern), 294
Davidson County Community College (Lexington), 294
Fayetteville Technical Community College (Fayetteville), 295
Forsyth Technical Community College (Winston-Salem), 296
Gaston College (Dallas), 296
Guilford Technical Community College (Jamestown), 297
Halifax Community College (Weldon), 297
Haywood Community College (Clyde), 297
Isothermal Community College (Spindale), 298
James Sprunt Community College (Kenansville), 298
Johnston Community College (Smithfield), 298
Lenoir Community College (Kinston), 299
Mayland Community College (Spruce Pine), 299
McDowell Technical Community College (Marion), 300
Nash Community College (Rocky Mount), 302
Piedmont Community College (Roxboro), 302
Pitt Community College (Greenville), 303
Roanoke-Chowan Community College (Ahoskie), 303
Rowan-Cabarrus Community College (Salisbury), 304
Sampson Community College (Clinton), 304
Southeastern Community College (Whiteville), 305
Southwestern Community College (Sylva), 306
Surry Community College (Dobson), 306
Tri-County Community College (Murphy), 306
Vance-Granville Community College (Henderson), 307
Wake Technical Community College (Raleigh), 307
Wayne Community College (Goldsboro), 308
Western Piedmont Community College (Morganton), 308
Wilkes Community College (Wilkesboro), 308
Wilson Community College (Wilson), 308

Ohio
Akron Adult Vocational Services (Akron), 309
Ashtabula County Joint Vocational School (Jefferson), 311
Auburn Career Center (Painesville), 311
Belmont Technical College (St. Clairsville), 311
Butler Technology and Career Development Schools–D. Russel Lee Career-Technology Center (Hamilton), 314
Choffin Career Center (Youngstown), 315
Cleveland Municipal School District Adult and Continuing Education (Cleveland), 316

Columbiana County Vocation School (Lisbon), 317
Community Services Division–Alliance City (Alliance), 317
Eastern Gateway Community College (Steubenville), 319
Hobart Institute of Welding Technology (Troy), 321
Madison Local Schools–Madison Adult Education (Mansfield), 324
Mahoning County Joint Vocational School District (Canfield), 325
O. C. Collins Career Center (Chesapeake), 328
Owens Community College (Toledo), 330
Penta County Joint Vocational School (Perrysburg), 330
Pioneer Career and Technology Center: A Vocational School District (Shelby), 331
Polaris Career Center (Middleburg Heights), 331
Terra State Community College (Fremont), 336
Tri-County Vocational School Adult Career Center (Nelsonville), 337
University of Rio Grande (Rio Grande), 339
Warren County Career Center (Lebanon), 340
Washington County Career Center Adult Education (Marietta), 341

Pennsylvania
Central Pennsylvania Institute of Science and Technology (Pleasant Gap), 347
Community College of Allegheny County (Pittsburgh), 348
Dean Institute of Technology (Pittsburgh), 351
Greater Altoona Career and Technology Center (Altoona), 356
Harrisburg Area Community College (Harrisburg), 357
Lancaster County Career and Technology Center (Willow Street), 360
Lebanon County Area Vocational Technical School (Lebanon), 361
New Castle School of Trades (Pulaski), 366
Northampton County Area Community College (Bethlehem), 366
Precision Manufacturing Institute (Meadville), 371
Schuylkill Technology Center–North Campus (Frackville), 373
Tri-State Business Institute (Erie), 376
Welder Training and Testing Institute (Allentown), 378
Westmoreland County Community College (Youngwood), 378

Puerto Rico
Colegio Mayor de Tecnologia–Arroyo (Arroyo), 382

South Carolina
Aiken Technical College (Aiken), 397
Central Carolina Technical College (Sumter), 398
Denmark Technical College (Denmark), 398
Florence-Darlington Technical College (Florence), 399
Greenville Technical College (Greenville), 399
Horry-Georgetown Technical College (Conway), 400
Midlands Technical College (Columbia), 401
Northeastern Technical College (Cheraw), 401
Orangeburg-Calhoun Technical College (Orangeburg), 402
Piedmont Technical College (Greenwood), 402
Spartanburg Community College (Spartanburg), 403
Tri-County Technical College (Pendleton), 403
Trident Technical College (Charleston), 404
Williamsburg Technical College (Kingstree), 404

Yoga Teacher Training/Yoga Therapy

Pennsylvania
Community College of Beaver County
(Monaca), 349

YOUTH MINISTRY
New Jersey
College of Saint Elizabeth (Morristown), 243
South Carolina
W. L. Bonner College (Columbia), 405

YOUTH SERVICES/ADMINISTRATION
Connecticut
Goodwin College (East Hartford), 53
Michigan
Marygrove College (Detroit), 221

Alphabetical Listing of Vo-Tech Schools

Peterson's Vocational and Technical Schools East
www.petersons.com
637

Alphabetical Listing of Vo-Tech Schools

NOTES

NOTES

Peterson's
Book Satisfaction Survey

Give Us Your Feedback

Thank you for choosing Peterson's as your source for personalized solutions for your education and career achievement. Please take a few minutes to answer the following questions. Your answers will go a long way in helping us to produce the most user-friendly and comprehensive resources to meet your individual needs.

When completed, please tear out this page and mail it to us at:

Publishing Department
Peterson's, a Nelnet company
2000 Lenox Drive
Lawrenceville, NJ 08648

You can also complete this survey online at **www.petersons.com/booksurvey.**

1. **What is the ISBN of the book you have purchased? (The ISBN can be found on the book's back cover in the lower right-hand corner.)** _____

2. **Where did you purchase this book?**
   - ❑ Retailer, such as Barnes & Noble
   - ❑ Online reseller, such as Amazon.com
   - ❑ Petersons.com
   - ❑ Other (please specify) _____

3. **If you purchased this book on Petersons.com, please rate the following aspects of your online purchasing experience on a scale of 4 to 1 (4 = Excellent and 1 = Poor).**

	4	3	2	1
Comprehensiveness of Peterson's Online Bookstore page	❑	❑	❑	❑
Overall online customer experience	❑	❑	❑	❑

4. **Which category best describes you?**
   - ❑ High school student
   - ❑ Parent of high school student
   - ❑ College student
   - ❑ Graduate/professional student
   - ❑ Returning adult student
   - ❑ Teacher
   - ❑ Counselor
   - ❑ Working professional/military
   - ❑ Other (please specify) _____

5. **Rate your overall satisfaction with this book.**

Extremely Satisfied	Satisfied	Not Satisfied
❑	❑	❑

6. **Rate each of the following aspects of this book on a scale of 4 to 1 (4 = Excellent and 1 = Poor).**

	4	3	2	1
Comprehensiveness of the information	❑	❑	❑	❑
Accuracy of the information	❑	❑	❑	❑
Usability	❑	❑	❑	❑
Cover design	❑	❑	❑	❑
Book layout	❑	❑	❑	❑
Special features (e.g., CD, flashcards, charts, etc.)	❑	❑	❑	❑
Value for the money	❑	❑	❑	❑

7. **This book was recommended by:**
   - ❑ Guidance counselor
   - ❑ Parent/guardian
   - ❑ Family member/relative
   - ❑ Friend
   - ❑ Teacher
   - ❑ Not recommended by anyone—I found the book on my own
   - ❑ Other (please specify) _____

8. **Would you recommend this book to others?**

   Yes   Not Sure   No

   ❑   ❑   ❑

9. **Please provide any additional comments.**

   _____

   _____

   _____

   _____

Remember, you can tear out this page and mail it to us at:

> Publishing Department
> Peterson's, a Nelnet company
> 2000 Lenox Drive
> Lawrenceville, NJ 08648

or you can complete the survey online at **www.petersons.com/booksurvey.**

Your feedback is important to us at Peterson's, and we thank you for your time!

If you would like us to keep in touch with you about new products and services, please include your e-mail address here: _____